THE EDUCATION
OF POOR
AND MINORITY
CHILDREN

THE EDUCATION OF POOR AND MINORITY CHILDREN

A World Bibliography

Volume 1

Compiled by Meyer Weinberg

GREENWOOD PRESS
WESTPORT, CONNECTICUT • LONDON, ENGLAND

Library of Congress Cataloging in Publication Data

Weinberg, Meyer, 1920-
    The education of poor and minority children.

    Includes index.
        1. Educational equalization—United States—Bib-
liography.   2. Minorities—Education—United States—
Bibliography.   3. Educational equalization—Bibliography.
4. Socially handicapped—Education—Bibliography.
I. Title.
Z5814.E68W44   [LC214.2]   370.19'34'0973   80-29441
ISBN 0-313-21996-6 (lib. bdg.) (set)
ISBN 0-313-23023-4 (lib. bdg.) (vol. 1)
ISBN 0-313-23024-2 (lib. bdg.) (vol. 2)

Library of Congress Catalog Card Number: 80-29441
ISBN: 0-313-21996-6 (set)
ISBN: 0-313-23023-4 (vol. 1)
ISBN: 0-313-23024-2 (vol. 2)

First published in 1981

Greenwood Press
A division of Congressional Information Service, Inc.
88 Post Road West, Westport, Connecticut 06881

Printed in the United States of America

10 9 8 7 6 5 4 3 2 1

To
Monroe Nathan Work,
Pioneer bibliographer

CONTENTS

XII / CONTENTS

ACKNOWLEDGMENTS

Gathering references for this work took over a decade and was the task of the compiler alone. After that, however, he was fortunate to have the help of a corps of coworkers who, after nearly two more years, succeeded in completing the job. Typists were Patricia Milne, Judith Stark, Judith Rose, and Betty Craker.

Compiling and proofreading the index were the principal assignments of Ken Nolan who was ably aided by Ernest Borden, Kevin Fachetti, Andrew Goldstein, Donna Savage, Patricia Titterington, and Dan Weinberg.

Elaine Grennan coordinated the work of the above-named persons and Kevin Grennan helped in numerous ways.

Monroe Nathan Work, to whom the present work is dedicated, pioneered when it took immense inner conviction and security merely to ''save references'' on the world's black people. The pre–World War I volumes of *The Negro Year Book* are evidences of his contribution. His masterpiece, *A Bibliography of the Negro in Africa and America* (New York: Wilson, 1928), is a jewel that continues to inform and inspire other workers, including the present compiler.

INTRODUCTION

This bibliography is an introduction to the literature on the education of poor and minority children. It contains some forty thousand entries, nearly one-fourth of which deal with countries and areas outside the United States. The references are drawn from a broad range of sources covering the social sciences, law, history, education, and several other disciplines. A special effort has been made to include references from publications sponsored by minority groups and written by minority authors.

The subject matter of this work is schooling as it is affected by the social, economic, and political forces revolving around it. The school itself, including internal organization, curriculum, and educational outcomes, is covered in considerable detail. Matters such as economic equality and inequality, racism and antiracism, class structure, ethnic organization, and other influential factors bearing on education are also covered in depth.

Over the past decade, the literature on education has expanded greatly, in some directions more than in others. Academic research in the form of doctoral dissertations is far more plentiful now than earlier. This is true not only for narrow studies on education but also for studies on the historical aspects of the subject. More doctoral research today includes consideration of the social and political features of the subject under investigation. Research on the life and history of minority peoples has begun to yield rich dividends. This is most evident in studies on blacks, but Chicano researchers, mostly young, have completed a number of meaningful works about Mexican-American life. Asian-American researchers are also working with great energy. Education, however, remains generally understudied.

Surprisingly little has changed in the established centers of educational research, be they universities or government facilities. Too much of this research remains oriented toward managerial concerns of institutions. Too little of it raises questions of distributive justice or educational goals. Psychological and sociological research in education continues to employ very largely a microfocus on schooling, concerned with individual students and individual mobility. The pages of such research reports are surprisingly bare of social context. They are excessively ''safe.''

A new, refreshing source of empirical material consists of investigative journalistic reports, involving events and processes of individual cities, school systems, and even single schools. As the standards of investigative journalism have risen, various individual journalists have cultivated a knowledge of their subject that often exceeds that of academic specialists. In many instances, newspapers are the sole source of information about a topic of importance.

Minority views on education can be found but they must be sought out. They are located in biographies, autobiographies, personal correspondence, letters and articles in the black press—itself a disappearing institution—and in legal proceedings. Official school documents generally contain little of the minority community's views. Government documents are a rich source of such information, but are usually overlooked. Testimony by minority persons touching on education can be found in published transcripts contained in printed records of hearings. These have been used abundantly in the present volumes.

Black scholarship in education is almost unknown territory. Contemporary writers on the subject, both black and white, are not generally aware of its existence. Graduate school training in research virtually never requires study of black journals in education and the social sciences. Over the years, this inattention has come to be misrepresented as the absence of black and other minority research in various fields. The present work may be viewed, in part, as an effort to retrieve many valuable contributions that have been overlooked.

Conventional scholarship also tends to undervalue the role of the parents of poor and minority children. The present work lists many references that contradict such a portrayal. A long campaign for educational equality has been waged by organized parents, who thus disprove the stereotype of passive parents. Boycotts, lawsuits, and legislative lobbying are only some forms of civic action utilized by poor and minority parents. Many references to such action can be found in these volumes.

This bibliography aims, however, at more than recording work already done. It aspires to stimulate work that is yet to be done. Conventional research and writing in education all too often proceed in an abstract manner, far removed from the realities of systematic exclusion and group deprivation that have marked the education of poor and minority children. These realities are amply documented herein through citation to numerous items. It is hoped that increased knowledge of such materials will help shape a more accurate scholarship.

Inclusion of materials dealing with the United States and other countries is meant to underscore both similarities and differences between the two. Clearly, the materials on other countries are highly selective. An effort has been made, however, to touch on the major dimensions of the subject. This has been easier in some cases than others. References, for example, to British and Canadian materials are perhaps more ample than existing guides in either Britain or Canada. On the other hand, coverage for some African countries is quite slim.

Many processes affecting the education of poor and minority children in other countries resemble those in the United States. The heritage and contemporary shape of racism are preeminent. Slavery and other forms of unfree labor deeply influenced the development of many countries' educational institutions. Economic inequality and cultural exclusion are common features of the world educational scene. Also instructive in the study of education are remedial measures. Some undertaken elsewhere seem to be patterned after parallels in the United States. Others are quite novel. A few go far beyond innovative devices and involve fundamental social change. A comparative approach to these and other aspects of education can underscore commonalities as well as differences, and suggest fresh approaches to the study of education and the implementation of equitable practices in education.

THE EDUCATION
OF POOR
AND MINORITY
CHILDREN

1.
HISTORY

Persons and Events

"A Blow at Negro Education." *Current Literature* 36(Ja-Je, 1904):491-492.

"A Statement Adopted by a Group of Southern Negro Educators, Hot Springs, Arkansas. October 27, 1954." *Quarterly Review of Higher Education Among Negroes* 22(O, 1954): 151-153.

Abbott, Martin. "Voices of Freedom: The Response of Southern Freedmen to Liberty." *Phylon* 34(D, 1973):398-405.

Allmendinger, David F., Jr. "Indigent Students and Their Institutions, 1800-1860." Doctoral dissertation, U. of Wisconsin, 1968.

An Autobiography of Mrs. Amanda Smith, the Colored Evangelist. Chicago: Meyer and Bros., 1893.

Anderson, James D. "Education for Servitude: The Social Purposes of Schooling in the Black South, 1870-1930." Doctoral dissertation, U. of Illinois, 1973.

Angus, David Lee. "The Dropout Problem: An Interpretive History." Doctoral dissertation, Ohio State U., 1966.

Anscomb, Francis C. "The Contributions of the Quakers to the Reconstruction of the Southern States." Doctoral dissertation, U. of North Carolina, 1926.

Appel, John J. "American Negro and Immigrant Experience: Similarities and Differences." *American Quarterly*. Spring, 1966.

Aptheker, Herbert (ed.). *The Correspondence of W. E. B. Du Bois*. Vol. I: *Selections 1877-1934*. Amherst, MA: U. of Mass. Press, 1973.

_____(ed.). *The Education of Black People. Ten Critiques 1906-1960 by W. E. B. Du Bois*. Amherst, MA: U. of Mass. Press, 1973.

Armstrong, Warren B. "Union Chaplains and the Education of the Freedmen." *Journal of Negro History* 52(Ap, 1967):104-115.

Ashmore, Harry S. *The Negro and the Schools*. Chapel Hill: U. of North Carolina Press, 1954.

Austin, Frank Eugene. *The History of Segregation*. Winter Park, Florida: Rollins Press, 1956.

Axelrod, Bernard. "Historical Studies of Emigration from the United States." *International Migration Review* 6(Spring, 1972):32-49.

Ayers, Leonard. *Laggards in Our Schools*. New York: n.p., 1909.

Bahney, Robert S. "Generals and Negroes: Education of Negroes by the Union Army, 1861-65." Doctoral dissertation, U. of Michigan, 1965. Univ. Microfilms Order No. 66-5035.

Bailey, Thomas Brantley. "Historical Interpretation of the Reconstruction Era in United States History as Reflected in Southern State Required Secondary School Level Textbooks of State Histories." Doctoral dissertation, U. of New Mexico, 1967.

Baldwin, Charles Henry. "A Trend Analysis of Black Americans' Political and Racial Attitudes." Doctoral dissertation, U. of North Carolina, 1977. Univ. Microfilm Order No. 780 7456 [1952-1972].

Baldwin, James. *Autobiographical Notes*. New York: A. A. Knopf, 1953.

Bartley, Numan V. *The Rise of Massive Resistance. Race and Politics in the South During the 1950's*. Baton Rouge, LA: Louisiana State Univ. Press, 1969.

Beam, Lura. _He Called Them by Lightning:_ _A_ _Teacher's Odessey in the Negro South._ 1908-1909. Indianapolis: Bobbs-Merrill, 1967.

Bedini, Silvio A. _The Life of Benjamin_ _Banneker._ New York: Scribners, 1972.

Beeson, Marvin Foster. _Die Organisation der_ _Negererziehung in den Vereinigten Staaten_ _von Amerika seit 1860._ Leipzig: n.p., 1915.

Bellisfield, Gwen. "Changes in White Attitudes Toward Integration, 1963-1968." Master's thesis, New York U., 1971.

_____. "White Attitudes Toward Racial Integration and the Urban Riots of the 1960's." _Public Opinion Quarterly_ 36(Winter, 1972-1973).

Bender, Eugene I. "Reflections on Negro-Jewish Relationships: The Historical Dimension." _Phylon._ Spring, 1969.

Bennett, Lerone, Jr. "Benjamin Elijah Mays: The Last of the Great Schoolmasters." _Ebony_ 33(D, 1977):72-80.

Berlin, Ira. _Slaves Without Masters._ _The Free_ _Negro in the Antebellum South._ New York: Pantheon, 1974.

_____. "The Structure of the Free Negro Caste in the Antebellum United States." _Journal of_ _Social History_ 9(Spring, 1976):297-318.

Berry, Mary F. _Military Necessity and Civil_ _Rights Policy:_ _Black Citizenship and the_ _Constitution, 1861-1868._ Port Washington, NY: Kennikat Press, 1977.

Berwanger, Eugene H. _The Frontier Against_ _Slavery:_ _Western Anti-Negro Prejudices and_ _the Slavery Extension Controversy._ Urbana, IL: U. of Illinois Press, 1967.

Billingsley, Andrew, and Greene, Marilyn Cynthia. "Family Life Among the Free Black Population in the 18th Century." _Journal of Social and_ _Behavioral Sciences_ 20(Spring, 1974):1-18.

Binder, Frederick M. _The Color Problem in Early_ _National America._ The Hague: Mouton, 1968.

Bland, R. W. "The Collective Struggle for Negro Rights: 1915-1940." _North Carolina Central_ _Law Review_ 2(Spring, 1970).

Blassingame, John W. _Frederick Douglass:_ _The_ _Clarion Voice._ Washington, DC: Government Printing Office, 1976.

_____. "The Union Army as an Educational Institution for Negroes, 1862-1865." _Journal_ _of Negro Education._ Spring, 1965.

Blaustein, Albert P., and Zangrando, Robert L. (eds.). _Civil Rights and the American Negro:_ _A Documentary History._ New York: Trident, 1968.

Blose, David T. _Statistics of Education of the_ _Negro Race, 1925-1926._ U.S. Office of Education Bulletin No. 19. Washington, DC: Government Printing Office, 1928.

Blose, David T., and Caliver, Ambrose. _Statistics of the Education of Negroes, 1935-_ _1936._ Office of Education Bulletin No. 13. Washington, DC: Government Printing Office, 1938.

_____ and _____. _Statistics of the Education_ _of Negroes (A Decade of Progress)._ 2 parts. U.S. Office of Education Circular No. 215. Washington, DC: Government Printing Office, 1943.

Bogin, Ruth. "Sarah Parker Remond: Black Abolitionist from Salem." _Essex Institute_ _Historical Collections_ 110(Ap, 1974):120-150.

Bonar, Francis E. "The Civil Rights Act of 1875." Master's thesis, Ohio State U., 1940.

Bond, Horace Mann. _Black American Scholars:_ _A_ _Study of Their Beginnings._ Detroit: Balamys Publishing, 1972.

_____. _The Education of the Negro in the_ _American Social Order._ New York: Octagon Books, 1966.

_____. "Howe and Isaacs in the Bush." _Negro_ _History Bulletin_ 25(D, 1961).

_____. "The Negro." In _The Dictionary of_ _American History._ New York: Scribner and Sons, 1961.

_____. "The Negro in the Armed Forces of the United States Prior to World War I." _Journal_ _of Negro Education_ 12(Summer, 1943):268-287.

_____. "The Negro Scholar and Professional in America." In _The American Negro Reference_ _Book._ Edited by John P. Davis. Englewood Cliffs, NJ: Prentice-Hall, 1966.

_____. "The Role of the History of Education in Understanding the Struggle for Equalizing Educational Opportunity." _History of Educa-_ _tion Journal_ 1(Spring, 1950):101-107.

_____. "Social and Economic Forces in Reconstruction." _Journal of Negro History_ 23(Jl, 1938):290-348.

Bontemps, Arna, and Conroy, Jack. _Anyplace But_ _Here._ New York: Hill and Wang, 1966.

Boskin, Joseph. "Sambo, the National Jester in the Popular Culture." In _The Great Fear._ _Race in the Mind of America,_ pp. 165-185. Edited by Gary B. Nash and Richard Weiss. New York: Holt, Rinehart & Winston, 1970.

Bowles, Samuel, and Gintis, Herbert. "Capitalism and Education in the United States." _Socialist_ _Revolution_ 5(1975):101-138.

Bozewan, Herman H. "Attitudes of Selected Racial Leadership Organizations Towards Educational Policies and Practices for Negroes During the Twentieth Century." Doctoral dissertation, U. of Michigan, n.d.

Bracey, John, Jr., Meier, August, and Rudwick, Elliott (eds.). The Rise of the Ghetto. Belmont, CA: n.p., 1971.

Brauer, Carl M. John F. Kennedy and the Second Reconstruction. New York: Columbia U. Press, 1977.

_____. "The Kennedy Administration and Civil Rights." Doctoral dissertation, Howard U., 1973.

Brawley, Benjamin G. The Negro Genius. New York: Dodd, Mead and Co., 1937.

Breitman, George. The Last Year of Malcolm X: The Evolution of a Revolution. New York: Merit Publishers, 1967.

Bremner, Robert H. and others (eds.). Children and Youth in America. A Documentary History, Vol. II: 1866-1932. In 2 parts. Cambridge, MA: Harvard U. Press, 1971.

Brent, Linda. Incidents in the Life of a Slave Girl. Boston: Privately published, 1861.

Broderick, Francis L., and Meier, August (eds.). Negro Protest Thought in the Twentieth Century. Indianapolis: Bobbs-Merrill, 1966.

Brooks, Gwendolyn. Report From Part One. Detroit, MI: Broadside Press, 1973.

Brown, Hallie Quinn (ed.). Homespun Heroines and Other Women of Distinction. Xenia, OH: Aldine, 1926.

Browne, Rose Butler, and English, James W. Love My Children: An Autobiography. 2nd ed. Elgin, IL: David C. Cook Publishing Co., 1974.

Bruns, Roger A. "Anthony Benezet and the Natural Rights of the Negro." Pennsylvania Magazine of History and Biography, Ja, 1972.

_____. "Anthony Benezet's Assertions of Negro Equality." Journal of Negro History 56(Jl, 1971):230-238.

Bryce-Laporte, Roy Simon. "The American Slave Plantation and Our Heritage of Communal Deprivation." American Behavioral Scientist, Mr-Ap, 1969.

_____. "The Slave Plantation: Background to Present Conditions of Urban Blacks." In Race, Change, and Urban Society, pp. 257-284. Edited by Peter Orleans and William Russell Ellis, Jr. Beverly Hills, CA: Sage, 1971.

Buchanan, A Russell. Black Americans in World War II. Santa Barbara, CA: Clio Press, 1977.

Bullock, Henry Allen. A History of Negro Education in the South from 1619 to the Present. Cambridge, MA: Harvard U. Press, 1967.

Burlingame, Martin. "The NAACP and Equal Educational Opportunities for Negroes, 1909-1954." Doctoral dissertation, U. of Chicago, 1969.

Burran, James A. III. "Racial Violence in the South During World War II." Doctoral dissertation, U. of Tennessee, 1977.

Butchart, Ronald E. "Educating for Freedom: Northern Whites and the Origins of Black Education in the South." Doctoral dissertation, State U. of New York at Binghamton, 1976.

Calam, John. Parsons and Pedagogues: The S.P.G. Adventure in American Education. New York: Columbia U. Press, 1971.

Caldwell, Arthur Bunyan (ed.). History of the American Negro and His Institutions. 7 vols. Atlanta: n.p., 1917-1923.

Campbell, Angus, and Hatchell, Shirley. "Racial Attitude Trends: 1964-1974." Integ_raffeducation 14(Ja-F, 1976).

Campbell, Will D. Brother to a Dragonfly. New York: Seabury, 1977.

Carlisle, Rodney P. The Roots of Black Nationalism. Port Washington, NY: Kennikat, 1975.

Carstens, H. "Horace Greeley on Segregation." Negro Educational Review, Ja, 1956.

Carter, L. Edward. "Rise and Fall of the Invisible Empire Knights of the Ku Klux Klan." Great Plains Journal 16(Spring, 1977):83-106.

Caulfield, Mina Davis. "Slavery and the Origins of Black Culture: Elkins Revisited." In Melvin D. Gillespie (comp.), Afro-American Culture. Patrick Air Force Base, FL: Defense Race Relations Institute, 1974.

Cayton, Horace R. Long Old Road. New York: Trident, 1965.

Chancellor, W. E. "The Education of Colored Persons in America." School Journal 80 (1913).

Chapman, Robert C. "...And in God's House." Newsletter. International Afro-American Museum, Fall, 1966.

Charlop, Simone. "The Origin and Nature of Black Nationalism in the United States Before 1830." Doctoral dissertation, New School for Social Research, 1975. Univ. Microfilms Order No. 75-25446.

Cheek, William F. III. "Forgotten Prophet: The Life of John Mercer Langston." Doctoral dissertation, U. of Virginia, 1961. Univ. Microfilm No. 61-4534.

_____. John Mercer Langston: Black Protest Leader and Abolitionist." Civil War History 16(Je, 1970):101-120.

Clark, Septima. Echo in My Soul. New York: Dutton, 1962.

Clark, Thomas D., and Kirwan, Albert D. The South Since Appomattox: A Century of Regional Change. New York: Oxford Univ. Press, 1967.

Clarke, John H. "The Fight to Reclaim African History." Negro Digest, F, 1970. [African Studies Association.]

_____. "The Meaning of Black History." Jewish Currents, My, 1969.

Clift, Virgil A. "Educating the American Negro." In The American Negro Reference Book. Edited by John P. Davis. Englewood Cliffs, NJ: Prentice-Hall, 1966.

_____. "The History of Racial Segregation in American Education." School and Society 88 (My 7, 1960):220-229.

Cochrane, William G. "Freedom Without Equality: A Study of Northern Opinion of the Negro Issue, 1861-1870." Doctoral dissertation, U. of Minnesota, 1957. Univ. Microfilm Order No. 239-28.

Cohen, David K., and Lazerson, Marvin. "Education and the Corporate Order." Socialist Revolution 2(Mr-Ap, 1972):47-72.

Cohen, David K. and others. "Schooling in Capitalist America." History of Education Quarterly 17(Summer, 1977):111-168.

Cohen, Robert Carl. Black Crusader: A Biography of Robert Franklyn Williams. Secaucus, NJ: Lyle Stuart, 1973.

Cohen, Sol. "The Industrial Education Movement, 1906-1917." American Quarterly 20(Spring, 1968):95-110.

Cohen, William. "Negro Involuntary Servitude in the South, 1865-1940: A Preliminary Analysis." Journal of Southern History 42(F, 1976):31-60.

Conrad, Earl. The Invention of the Negro. New York: Hill and Wang, 1966.

Coppin, Fannie Jackson. Reminiscences of School Life, and Hints on Teaching. Philadelphia: African Methodist Episcopal Book Concern, 1913.

Crofts, Daniel W. "The Black Response to the Blair Educational Bill." Journal of Southern History 37(F, 1971):41-65.

_____. "The Blair Bill and The Elections Bill: The Congressional Aftermath to Reconstruction." Doctoral dissertation, Yale U., 1968.

Crosby, Jerry O. "Two Hundred Years of Educational Development Through Self-Help, Self-Reliance, and Self-Determination." Negro Educational Review 27(Jl-O, 1976):207-226.

Council of Chief State School Officers. Education in the States: Historical Development and Outlook. Washington, DC: National Education Association, 1969.

Curry, Richard O. (ed.). Radicalism, Racism, and Party Realignment: The Border States During Reconstruction. Baltimore, MD: Johns Hopkins Press, 1969.

Curtin, Philip D. The Atlantic Slave Trade: A Census. Madison, WI: U. of Wisconsin Press, 1969.

Dabney, Charles W. Universal Education in the South. 2 vols. Chapel Hill, NC: U. of North Carolina Press, 1936.

Dalfiume, Richard M. Desegregation of the U.S. Armed Forces. Fighting in Two Fronts, 1939-1953. Columbia, MO: U. of Missouri Press, 1971.

Dann, Martin E. (ed.). The Black Press, 1827-1890. The Quest for National Identity. New York: Putnam's, 1971.

Dauterive, Verna B. "Historical Legal Development of Integration in Public Schools." Educational Horizons, Winter, 1966-1967.

D'Elia, Donald J. "Dr. Benjamin Rush and the Negro." Journal of the History of Ideas 30 (Jl-S, 1969):413-422.

DeGraaf, Lawrence B. "Recognition, Racism, and Reflections on the Writing of Western Black History." Pacific Historical Review 44(F, 1975):22-51.

Demarco, Joseph P. "The Concept of Race in the Social Thought of W. E. B. Du Bois." Philosophical Forum 3(Winter, 1971-1972).

Dennis, Rutledge M. "Du Bois and the Role of the Educated Elite." Journal of Negro Education 46(Fall, 1977):388-402.

Dickerman, G. S. History of Negro Education. U.S. Bureau of Educational Bulletin No. 38. Washington, DC: Government Printing Office, 1916.

[Digest of replies from 200 black leaders in 1886 on conditions of blacks in the South] Independent, Ja 6, 13, 20, 27; F 3, 17, 1887. Editorial comments: F 3, 24, 1887.

Diggins, John P. "Slavery, Race, and Equality: Jefferson and the Pathos of the Enlightenment." American Quarterly 28(Summer, 1976): 206-228.

Donovan, Marjorie Elizabeth. "And Let Who Must Believe: High School Education and White-Collar Work in Nineteenth Century America." Doctoral dissertation, U. of California, Davis, 1977. Univ. Microfilm Order No. 780-3607.

Doughty, James Jefferson. "A Historical Analysis of Black Education--Focusing on the Contemporary Independent Black School Movement." Doctoral dissertatation, Ohio State U., 1973.

Douglass, Frederick. "Equality in Schools, 1872." Integrated Education, Ap-My, 1965.

The Frederick Douglass Years. A Cultural History Exhibition. Washington, DC: Smithsonian Institution Press, 1970.

Drake, Richard B. "The American Missionary Association and the Southern Negro, 1861-1888." Doctoral dissertation, Emory U., 1957.

Drake, St. Clair. The American Dream and the Negro: 100 Years of Freedom. Chicago: Roosevelt U. Press, 1964.

_____. "The Black Experience in Black Historical Perspective." In Black Experience. Edited by Carlene Young. San Rafael, CA: Leswing Communications, 1972.

_____. "In the Mirror of Black Scholarship: W. Allison Davis and Deep South." In Education and Black Struggle: Notes from the Colonized World. Edited by Institute of the Black World. Cambridge, MA: Harvard Educational Review, 1974.

Drinan, Robert F., S.J. "Reflections on the First Decade of the Freedom Movement (1955-1965)." Vital Speeches, Ag 1, 1965.

Driske, Carol, and Toppin, Edgar A. The Unfinished March: The Negro in the United States. Reconstruction to World War I. Garden City, NY: Doubleday, 1967.

Drotning, Philip T. A Guide to Negro History in America. Garden City, NY: Doubleday, 1968.

Duberman, Martin. "The Northern Response to Slavery." In The Anti-Slavery Abolitionists. Edited by Martin Duberman. Princeton: Princeton U. Press, 1965.

DuBois, W. E. B. "Africa and the American Negro Intelligentsia." Presence Africaine, D, 1954-Ja, 1955.

_____. "A Portrait of Carter G. Woodson." Masses and Mainstream, Je, 1950.

_____. The Autobiography of W. E. B. DuBois. New York: International Publishers, 1968.

_____. "History of Segregation Philosophy." Crisis, Mr, 1934.

_____. "200 Years of Segregated Schools." In Jewish Life Anthology. Edited by Louis Harap. New York: Jewish Life Magazine, 1955.

"W. E. B. DuBois' Confrontation with White Liberalism During the Progressive Era: A Phylon Document." Phylon 35(S, 1974):241-258.

Dyer, Thomas G. "An Early Black Textbook: Floyd's Flowers or Duty and Beauty for Colored Children." Phylon 37(Winter, 1976):359-361. [Written by Silas X. Floyd, 1905.]

Eblin, Jack E. "Growth of the Black Population in ante bellum America, 1820-1860." Population Studies, J1, 1972.

Edelman, Marian Wright. "Southern School De-Segregation, 1954-1973: A Judicial-Political Overview." Annals 407(My, 1973):32-42.

Education of Negroes in Ante-bellum America. A Guide to an Exhibition in the William L. Clements Library. Ann Arbor, MI: The Library, 1969.

Edwards, Adolph. Marcus Garvey, 1887-1940. London: New Beacon Publications, 1967.

Elazar, Daniel J. "Urban Problems and the Federal Government: A Historical Inquiry." Political Science Quarterly, D, 1967.

Elliot, Jeffrey M. "The Civil Rights Movement Re-examined." Negro History Bulletin 39(S/O, 1976):606-610.

Ellis, Ann W. "The Commission on Interracial Cooperation, 1919-1944: Activities and Results." Doctoral dissertation, Georgia State U, 1975.

Ellison, Curtis W., and Metcalf, E. W. (eds.). William Wells Brown and Martin R. Delaney: A Reference Guide. Boston: G. K. Hall, 1978.

Elmore, Inez K. The Story of a Great Pioneer in Black Education, Bennie Carl Elmore, 1909-1973. Hicksville, NY: Exposition Press, 1975.

Emerson, Rupert, and Kilson, Martin. "The American Dilemma in a Changing World: The Rise of Africa and the Negro American." Daedalus, Fall, 1965.

Enck, Henry S. "Black Self-Help in the Progressive Era: The 'Northern Campaigns' of Smaller Southern Black Industrial Schools, 1900-1915." Journal of Negro History 41(Ja, 1976):73-87.

_____. "The Burden Borne: Northern White Philanthropy and Southern Black Industrial Education, 1900-1915." Doctoral dissertation, U. of Cincinnati, 1970.

Engerman, Stanley L. "Black Fertility and Family Structure in the U.S., 1880-1940." Journal of Family History 2(Summer, 1977): 117-138.

Escott, Paul D. Slavery Remembered. A Record of Twentieth-Century Slave Narratives. Chapel Hill: U. of North Carolina Press, 1979.

Evers, Mrs. Medgar, with Peters, William. For Us, the Living. New York: Doubleday, 1967.

Ezeani, Eboh. "Economic Conditions of Freed Black Slaves in the United States, 1870-1920." Review of Black Political Economy 8 (1977):104-118.

Falkner, R. P. "Some Further Considerations Upon the Retardation of the Pupils of Five School Systems." Psychological Clinic, My 15, 1908.

Farley, Reynolds. "The Urbanization of Negroes in the United States." Journal of Social History, Spring, 1968.

Ferriss, Abbott L. Indicators of Trends in American Education. New York: Russell Sage Foundation, 1969.

Finkle, Lee. "The Conservative Aims of Militant Rhetoric: Black Protest during World War II." Journal of American History 60(D, 1973):692-713.

_____. "Forum for Protest: The Black Protest During World War II." Doctoral dissertation, New York U., 1971.

_____. "Quotas or Integration: The NAACP versus the Pittsburgh Courier and the Committee on Participation of Negroes." Journalism Quarterly 52(Spring, 1975):76-84. [Blacks in the armed forces, 1838 and after.]

Fishel, Leslie H., Jr. "The Negro in the New Deal Era." Wisconsin Magazine of History, Winter, 1964-1965.

_____. "The North and the Negro, 1865-1900: A Study in Race Discrimination." Doctoral dissertation, Harvard U., 1954.

Fishel, Leslie, and Quarles, Benjamin (eds.). The Negro American: A Documentary Story. Glenview, IL: Scott, Foresman, 1967.

Fisher, William H. (comp.). Free At Last: A Bibliography of Martin Luther King, Jr. Metuchen, NJ: Scarecrow Press, 1978.

Fishlow, Albert. "The American Common School Revival: Fact or Fallacy?" In Industrialization in Two Systems: Essays in Honor of Alexander Gerschenkron. Edited by Henry Rosovsky. New York: Wiley, 1966.

_____. "Levels of Nineteenth-Century American Investment in Education." Journal of Economic History, D, 1966.

Fitzgerald, Bertram A. (ed.). "The Saga of Toussaint L'Overture and the Birth of Haiti." Golden Legacy Illustrated History Magazine. New York: Fitzgerald Publishing Co.

Fleming, Donald, and Bailyn, Bernard (eds.). "Dislocation and Emigration. The Demographic Background of American Immigration." Perspectives in American History 7(1973).

Fleming, Harold C. "The Federal Executive and Civil Rights, 1961-1965." Daedalus, Fall, 1965.

Fleming, John E. The Lengthening Shadow of Slavery. Washington, DC: Howard U. Press, 1976.

Florin, John W. "The Diffusion of the Decision to Integrate: Southern Schools Desegregate, 1954-1964." Southeastern Geographer 11 (1971):139-144.

Flusche, Michael. "On the Color Line: Charles Waddell Chesnutt." North Carolina History 53 (Winter, 1976):1-24.

Fogel, Robert William, and Engerman, Stanley L. Time on the Cross. The Economics of American Negro Slavery. 2 vols. Boston: Little, Brown, 1974.

Foner, Philip S. American Socialism and Black Americans: From the Age of Jackson to World War II. Westport, CT: Greenwood, 1977.

_____ (ed.). W. E. B. DuBois Speaks. Speeches and Addresses [1890-1963]. 2 vols. New York: Pathfinder Press, 1970.

_____ (ed.). Paul Robeson Speaks. Writings, Speeches, Interviews, 1918-1974. New York: Brunner/Mazel, 1978.

Foner, Philip S., and Lewis, Ronald L. (eds.). The Black Worker. A Documentary History from Colonial Times to the Present. Vol. I. From Colonial Times to 1869. Philadelphia: Temple U. Press, 1978.

Forbes, Jack D. Afro-Americans in the Far West: A Handbook for Educators. Far West Laboratory for Educational Research and Development. Washington, DC: Government Printing Office, 1970.

Forman, James. The Making of Black Revolutionaries: A Personal Account. New York: Macmillan, 1972.

Forrest, Leon. "Professor and Pioneer." Muhammad Speaks, Je 26, 1970. [Prof. Allison Davis]

Franklin, John Hope. "A Little Learning." In The Militant South, 1800-1861. Cambridge: Harvard U. Press, 1956.

_____. "The Dignity of Man: Perspectives for Tomorrow." Social Education, My, 1964.

_____. "The Enforcement of the Civil Rights Act of 1875." *Prologue* 6(Winter, 1974).

_____. *From Slavery to Freedom.* 3rd edition. New York: Random House, 1967.

_____. "The Historians and Public Policy." *History Teacher* 11(My, 1978):371-391.

_____. "History of Racial Segregation in the United States. *Annals*, Mr, 1956.

_____. "Jim Crow Goes to School: The Genesis of Legal Separation in Southern Schools." *South Atlantic Quarterly*, Spring, 1959.

_____. "The Two Worlds of Race: A Historical View." *Daedalus*, Fall, 1965.

Franklin, John Hope, and Starr, Isidore (eds.). *The Negro in Twentieth-Century America: A Reader in the Struggle for Civil Rights.* New York: Random House, 1967.

Franklin, Vincent P. "Education for Colonization: Attempts to Educate Free Blacks in the United States for Emigration to Africa, 1823-1833." *Journal of Negro Educators* 43 (Winter, 1974):91-103.

Franklin, Vincent P., and Anderson, James D. (eds.). *New Perspectives on Black Educational History.* Boston: G. K. Hall, 1978.

Fraser, Walter J., Jr. "John Eaton, Jr., Radical Republican, Champion of the Negro and Federal Aid to Southern Education." *Tennessee Historical Quarterly*, Fall, 1966.

Frazier, Thomas R. (ed.). *The Underside of American History.* New York: Harcourt Brace Jovanovich, 1971.

Frederickson, George M. *The Black Image in the White Mind. The Debate on Afro-American Character and Destiny, 1817-1914.* New York: Harper and Row, 1971.

Freelain, Norman. "Black Scholar: John Hope Franklin." 2 parts. *Muhammad Speaks*, S 19 and 26, 1969.

Freeman, M. H. "The Educational Wants of the Free Colored People, 1859." *Integrated Education* 10(Ja-F, 1972):30-34. Reprinted from *Anglo-African Magazine*, 1859.

Fries, Sylvia D. "The Slavery Issue in Northern School Readers, Geographies and Histories 1850-1875." *Journal of Popular Culture* 4 (Winter, 1971):718-731.

From Servitude to Service: Being the Old South Lectures on the History and Work of Southern Institutions for the Education of the Negro. Boston: American Unitarian Association, 1905.

Galloway, Gladys G. "The Education of the Negro during Reconstruction." Master's thesis, Howard U., 1930.

Gardner, Booker T. "The Educational Contribution of Booker T. Washington." *Journal of Negro Education* 44(Fall, 1975):502-518.

Garrison, W. P., and Garrison, F. J. *William Lloyd Garrison, 1805-1879. The Story of His Life.* 4 vols. New York: Century, 1885-1889.

Garrow, David J. *Protest at Selma: Martin Luther King, Jr. and the Voting Rights Act of 1965.* New Haven, CT: Yale U. Press, 1978.

Gatlin, Douglas S. "Party Identification, States, and Race in the South: 1952-1972." *Public Opinion Quarterly* 39(Spring, 1975):39-51.

Gavins, Raymond. "Gordon Blaine Hancock: Southern Black Leader in a Time of Crisis, 1920-1954." Doctoral dissertation, U. of Virginia, 1970.

_____. "Gordon Hancock: An Appraisal." *New South* 25(Fall, 1970):36-43.

_____. *The Perils and Prospects of Southern Black Leadership. Gordon Blaine Hancock, 1884-1970.* Durham, NC: Duke U Press, 1977.

Gayle, Addison, Jr. *Wayward Child.* Garden City, NY: Doubleday, 1977.

Genovese, Eugene D. "Black Plantation Preachers in the Slave South." *Louisiana Studies* 11 (Fall, 1972).

_____. *In Red and Black: Marxian Explorations in Southern and Afro-American History.* New York: Pantheon, 1971.

_____. "The Influence of the Black Power Movement on Historical Scholarship: Reflections of a White Historian." *Daedalus* 99(1970):473-494.

_____. "Rebelliousness and Docility in the Negro Slave: A Critique of the Elkins Thesis." *Civil War History*, December, 1967.

_____. *Roll, Jordan, Roll. The World The Slaves Made.* New York: Pantheon, 1974.

_____. "The Slave States of North America." In *Neither Slave Nor Free. The Freedmen of African Descent in the Slave Societies of the New World*, pp. 258-277. Edited by David W. Cohen and Jack P. Greene. Baltimore, MD: Johns Hopkins U. Press, 1972.

_____ (ed.). *The Slave Economies. Vol. I: Historical and Theoretical Perspectives.* New York: Wiley, 1973.

George, Carol V. R. *Segregated Sabbaths. Richard Allen and the Rise of Independent Black Churches, 1760-1840.* New York: Oxford U. Press, 1973.

Gershenberg, Irving. "Southern Values and Public Education: A Revision." *History of Education Quarterly* 10(Winter, 1971):413-422.

Gerteis, Louis S. From Contraband to Freedman: Federal Policy toward Southern Blacks, 1861-1865. Westport, CT: Greenwood, 1973.

Gibbs, Mifflin W. Shadow and Light. New York: n.p., 1968. Reprint.

Gibson, William Marvin. "The Social Element in Negro Education, 1865-1935." Doctoral dissertation, Clark U, 1936.

Gilliam, Dorothy Butler. Paul Robeson: All-American. Washington, DC: New Republic, 1976.

Gilpin, Patrick J. "Charles S. Johnson: An Intellectual Biography." Doctoral dissertation, Vanderbilt U., 1973.

_____. "Charles S. Johnson: Scholar and Educator." Negro History Bulletin 39(Mr, 1976):544-548.

Ginzberg, Eli, and Eichner, Alfred. The Troublesome Presence: American Democracy and the Negro. New York: Free Press of Glencoe, 1964.

Goldman, Robert M. "'A Free Ballot and a Fair Count': The Department of Justice and the Enforcement of Voting Rights in the South, 1877-1893." Doctoral dissertation, U. of Michigan, 1976.

Goldstein, Leslie Friedman. "Racial Loyalty in America: The Example of Frederick Douglass." Western Political Quarterly 28(S, 1975):463-476.

Gonzalez, Gilbert G. "The Relationship Between Monopoly Capitalism and Progressive Education." Insurgent Sociologist 7(Fall, 1977).

Goodenow, Ronald K. "Paradox in Progressive Educational Reform: The South and the Education of Blacks in the Depression Years." Phylon 39(Spring, 1978):49-65.

_____. "The Progressive Education Movement and Blacks in the Depression Years: An Exploratory Study." Doctoral dissertation, U. of California, Berkeley, 1973.

_____. "The Progressive Educator, Race and Ethnicity in the Depression Years: An Overview." History of Education Quarterly 15 (Winter, 1975).

Gordon, D. M. "Class Struggle and the Stages of American Urban Development." In The Rise of the Sunbelt Cities. Edited by David C. Perry and Alfred J. Watkins. Beverly Hills, CA: Sage, 1977.

Gower, Calvin W. "The Struggle of Blacks for Leadership Positions in the Civilian Conservation Corps: 1933-1942." Journal of Negro History 41(Ap, 1976):123-135.

Graham, Patricia Albjerg. Community and Class in American Education, 1865-1918. New York: Wiley, 1974.

Graham, Thomas. "Harriet Beecher Stowe and the Question of Race." New England Quarterly 46(D, 1973).

Grant, Donald L. The Anti-lynching Reform Movement: 1883-1932. San Francisco: R and E Associates, 1977.

Green, Constance M. The Rise of Urban America. New York: Harper & Row, 1965.

Greene, Lorenzo Johnston. The Negro in Colonial New England, 1620-1776. Port Washington, NY: Kennikat Press, 1966.

Greenfield, Thomas A. "Race and Passive Voice at Monticello." Integrateducation 15(Mr-Ap, 1977).

Greer, Colin. The Great School Legend. A Revisionist Interpretation of American Public Education. New York: Basic Books, 1972.

_____. "An Historical Note: Problems of the Negro Child in the North, 1900-1912." Urban Review, Jl, 1966.

_____. "Immigrants, Negroes, and the Public Schools." Urban Review, Ja, 1969.

Grimsted, David. "Rioting in Its Jacksonian Setting." American Historical Review 77 (Ap, 1972):361-397.

Grob, Gerald N. "Class, Ethnicity, and Race in American Mental Hospitals, 1830-75." J. Hist. Medicine Allied Sci. 28(Jl, 1973):207-229.

Grotberg, Edith (ed.). 200 Years of Children. Washington, DC: Office of Human Development, U.S. Department of Health, Education, and Welfare, 1976.

Groves, Paul A., and Shaw, Edward K. "The Evolution of Black Residential Areas in Late Nineteenth Century Cities." Journal of Historical Geography 1(Ap, 1975):169-192.

Hall, Gwendolyn Midlo. "Africans in the Americas." Negro Digest, F, 1969.

_____. "The Myth of Benevolent Spanish Slave Law." Negro Digest, F, 1970.

Halperin, Morton H. and others. "The FBI's Vendetta against Martin Luther King, Jr." In The Lawless State. The Crimes of the U.S. Intelligence Agencies, pp. 61-89. New York: Penguin, 1976.

Halseth, James A., and Glasrud, Bruce A. (eds.). The Northwest Mosaic: Minority Conflicts in Pacific Northwest History. Boulder, CO: Pruett Publishing Co., 1977.

Hamilton, Virginia. _Paul Robeson. The Life and Times of a Free Man_. New York: Harper & Row, 1974.

Handlin, Oscar, and Handlin, Mary F. "The New History and the Ethnic Factor in American Life." _Perspectives in American History_ 4(1970).

Hansberry, Lorraine. "The Scars of the Ghetto." _Monthly Review_, F, 1965.

Hansberry, William Leo. _A Survey of Native Documentary Sources Available for the Study of Ancient Ethiopian History_. Washington, DC: n.p., 1931.

Harding, Vincent. "Beyond Chaos. Black History and the Search for the New Land." In _Amistad 1_. Edited by John S. Williams and Charles F. Harris. New York: Vintage Books, 1970.

_____. "The Black Wedge in America: Struggle, Crisis and Hope, 1955-1985." _Black Scholar_ 7(D, 1975):28-46.

_____. "W. E. B. DuBois and the Black Messianic Vision." _Freedomways_, Winter, 1969.

Harlan, Louis R. "Booker T. Washington in Biographical Perspective." _American Historical Review_ 75(O, 1970):1581-1599.

_____. _Booker T. Washington: The Making of a Black Leader, 1856-1901_. New York: Oxford U. Press, 1972.

_____. _Separate and Unequal. Public School Campaigns and Racism in the Southern Seaboard States. 1901-1915_. Chapel Hill: U. of North Carolina Press, 1958.

_____. "The Southern Education Board and the Race Issue in Public Education." _Journal of Southern History_ 23(My, 1957).

Harper, Richard C. "The Course of the Melting Pot Idea to 1910." Doctoral dissertation, Columbia U., 1968. Univ. Microfilm Order No. 68-2424.

Harris, Grace E. "The Life and Work of E. Franklin Frazier." Doctoral dissertation, U. of Virginia, 1975. Univ. Microfilm Order No. 75-26,010.

Harris, Robert L., Jr. "Daniel Murray and _The Encyclopedia of the Colored Race_." _Phylon_ 13(F, 1976):270-282.

Hart, J. F. "The Changing Distribution of the American Negro." _Annals of the Association of American Geographers_ 50(S, 1960):242-266.

Harvey, James C. _Black Civil Rights During the Johnson Administration_. Jackson, MS: Univ. and College Press of Mississippi, 1973.

Hawkins, Homer C. "Trends in Black Migration from 1863 to 1960." _Phylon_ 34(Je, 1973): 140-152.

Haws, Robert (ed.). _The Age of Segregation: Race Relations in the South, 1890-1945: Essays_. Jackson, MS: University Press of Mississippi, 1978.

Haynes, Arthur Vertrease. _Scars of Segregation. An Autobiography_. New York: Vantage Press, 1974.

Haywood, Harry. _Black Bolshevik: An Autobiography of an Afro-American Communist_. Chicago: Liberator Press, 1978.

Heath, G. Louis (ed.). _The History and Literature of the Black Panther Party_. Metuchen, NJ: Scarecrow Press, 1976.

Hedgeman, Anna Arnold. _The Gift of Chaos_. New York: Oxford U. Press, 1977.

_____. _The Trumpet Sounds: A Memoir of Negro Leadership_. New York: Holt, Rinehart and Winston, 1964.

Hellriegel, Don, and Short, Larry. "Equal Employment Opportunity in the Federal Government: A Comparative Analysis." _Public Administration Review_ 32(N-D, 1972):851-858.

Hemesath, Caroline. _From Slave to Priest_. Franciscan Herald Press, 1974. [Fr. Augustine Tolton, b. 185]

Hemi, Florette. _Black Migration. Movement North 1900-1920_. Garden City, NY: Anchor, 1975.

Higgs, Robert. _Competition and Coercion. Blacks in the American Economy 1865-1914_. New York: Cambridge U. Press, 1977.

_____. "Participation of Blacks and Immigrants in the American Merchant Clans, 1890-1910: Demographic Relations." _Explorations in Economic History_ 13(1976):153-164.

Hileman, Gregor. "The Iron-Willed Black School Master and His Granite Academy." _Middlebury College News Letter_ 48(Spring, 1974):6-14. [Alexander L. Twilight]

Hindus, Michael S. "Black Justice Under White Law: Criminal Prosecution of Blacks in Antebellum South Carolina." _Journal of American History_ 63(D, 1976):575-599.

Hines, Linda O. "White Mythology and Black Duality: George W. Carver's Response to Racism and the Radical Left." _Journal of Negro History_ 62(Ap, 1977):134-146.

Historical Highlights in the Education of Black Americans. Washington, DC: National Education Association, 1969.

Holt, Rackham. Mary McLeod Bethune: A Biography. Garden City, NY: Doubleday, 1964.

Hornick, Nancy Clocum. "Anthony Benezet: Eighteenth Century Social Critic, Educator and Abolitionist." Doctoral dissertation, U. of Maryland, 1974.

Horowitz, Donald L. "Color Differentiation in the American Systems of Slavery." Journal of Interdisciplinary History 3(Winter, 1973).

Hosmer, John, and Fineman, Joseph. "Black Congressmen in Reconstruction Historiography." Phylon 39(Summer, 1978):97-107.

Hudson, Hosea. Black Worker in the Deep South. New York: International, 1972. [Autobiography]

Hutchison, Peyton Smith. "Marginal Man with a Marginal Mission: A Study of the Administrative Strategies of Ambrose Caliver, Black Administrator of Negro and Adult Education, the United States Office of Education, 1930-1962." Doctoral dissertation, Michigan State U., 1975. Univ. Microfilm Order No. 76-05575.

Jackson, Kenneth T. The Ku Klux Klan in the City, 1915-1930. New York: Oxford U. Press, 1967.

Jacobs, Donald M. (ed.). Antebellum Black Newspapers. Westport, CT: Greenwood, 1976. [Catalogue items in four newspapers, 1827-1841]

Jacobs, Paul, and Landau, Saul, with Pell, Eve (eds.). To Serve the Devil. 2 vols. New York: Random House, 1971. [America's racial history]

Jacoby, Susan. "'We Did Overcome.'" New York Times Magazine, Ap 10, 1977. [College students in civil rights movement during the 1960's]

Johnson, Charles. "The Army, the Negro and the Civilian Conservation Corps: 1933-1942." Military Affairs 36(O, 1972):82-88.

Johnson, F. M., Jr. "School Desegreation Problems in the South: An Historical Perspective." Minnesota Law Review 54(Je, 1970).

Jones, Faustine, C. "Black Americans and the City: A Historical Survey." Journal of Negro Education 42(Summer, 1973):261-282.

Jones, Johnny L. "Assessing the Academic Achievement of Negro Children." The Clearing House, O, 1964.

Jones, Leon. "Desegregation and Social Reform Since 1954." Journal of Negro Education 43 (Spring, 1974):155-171.

Jones, Rhett S. "Blacks in Colonial America." Black World 21(F, 1972):12-30. [Historiography of the topic, 1858-1969]

Jones, Thomas Jesse. Negro Education. U.S. Dept. of Interior, Bureau of Educational Bulletin 1716, No. 38. Washington, DC: Government Printing Office, 1917.

_____. "Negro Education." Vol. I. In U.S. Commissioner of Education, Annual Report, 1914, pp. 417-424. Washington, DC: GPO, 1915.

_____. "Recent Movements in Negro Education." Vol. I. In U.S. Commissioner of Education, Annual Report, 1912, pp. 243-56. Washington, DC: GPO, 1913.

_____. Recent Progress in Negro Education. U.S. Office of Education Bulletin No. 27. Washington, DC: GPO, 1919.

Juhnke, William E. "Benjamin Franklin's View of the Negro and Slavery." Pennsylvania History 41(O, 1974).

Kaczorowski, Robert J. "The Naturalization of Civil Rights: Constitutional Theory and Practice in a Racist Society, 1866-1875." Doctoral dissertation, U. of Minnesota, 1971.

Kantrowitz, Nathan. "The Index of Dissimilarity: A Measurement of Residential Segregation for Historical Analysis." Historical Methods Newsletter 7(S, 1974).

Kates, Don B., Jr. "Abolition, Deportation, Integration: Attitudes Toward Slavery in the Early Republic." Journal of Negro History, Ja, 1968.

Katz, Michael B. (ed.). School Reform. Past and Present. Boston: Little, Brown, 1971.

Katz, William Loren (ed.). Eyewitness: The Negro in American History. New York: Pitman, 1967.

Katznelson, Ira. Black Men, White Cities: Race, Politics and Migration in the United States, 1900-1930, and Britain, 1948-1968. New York: Oxford U. Press, 1973.

Keesing's Research Report. Race Relations in the USA, 1954-68. New York: Scribner's, 1970.

Kelley, Florence. "The Denial of Education." World Tomorrow 5(Mr, 1922).

Kellogg, C. Flint. The N.A.A.C.P. Vol. I, 1909-1920. Baltimore: Johns Hopkins Press, 1967.

Kellogg, Peter J. "Northern Liberals and Black America: A History of White Attitudes, 1936-1952." Doctoral dissertation, Northwestern U., 1971.

Kennedy, Flo. Color Me Flo: My Hard Life and Good Times. Englewood Cliffs, NJ: Prentice-Hall, 1976.

Kilson, Marion D. DeB. "Afro-American Social Structure, 1790-1970." In The African Diaspora. Edited by Martin L. Kilson and Robert J. Rotberg. Cambridge: Harvard U. Press, 1976.

Kincaid, Larry. "Two Steps Forward, One Step Back. Racial Attitudes during the Civil War and Reconstruction." In The Great Fear. Race in the Mind of America, pp. 45-70. Edited by Gary B. Nash and Richard Wein. New York: Holt, Rinehart & Winston, 1970.

Kirby, Jack Temple. Darkness at the Dawning. Race and Reform in the Progressive South. Philadelphia: Lippincott, 1972.

Knox, Ellis O. "A Historical Sketch of Secondary Education for Negroes." Journal of Negro Education, Jl, 1940.

Kogut, Alvin. "The Settlements and Ethnicity: 1890-1914." Social Work 17(My, 1972):22-31.

Komisar, Lucy. Down and Out in the USA: A History of Social Welfare. New York: Watts, 1977.

Kotz, Nick, and Kotz, Mary Lynn. A Passion for Equality. George A. Wiley and the Movement. New York: Norton, 1977.

Kousser, J. Morgan. The Shaping of Southern Politics: Suffrage Restriction and the Establishment of the One-Party South, 1880-1910. New Haven, CT: Yale U. Press, 1974.

Kraditor, Aileen S. Means and Ends in American Abolitionism: Garrison and His Critics on Strategy and Tactics, 1834-1850. New York: Pantheon, 1969.

Krueger, Thomas A. And Promises to Keep: The Southern Conference for Human Welfare, 1938-1948. Nashville, TN: Vanderbilt U. Press, 1967.

Kruman, Mark W. "Quotas for Blacks: The Public Works Administration and the Black Construction Worker." Labor History 16(Winter, 1975).

Kuritz, Hyman. "Education and the Poor in 18th Century America." Educational Forum 35(Mr, 1971):367-374.

Lacy, Dan. The White Use of Blacks in America. New York: Atheneum, 1972.

Lal, Barbara Ballis. "Robert E. Park on Race, Ethnicity, and Urbanization: A Study of the Chicago School of American Sociology, 1914-1936." Doctoral dissertation, U. of California, Berkeley, 1975. Univ. Microfilm Order No. 76-15,268.

Lampard, Eric E. " The Dimensions of Urban History: A Footnote to the 'Urban Crisis.'" Pacific Historical Review, Ag, 1970.

Landes, William M., and Solmon, Lewis C. "Compulsory Schooling Legislation: An Economic Analysis of Law and Social Change in the Nineteenth Century." Journal of Economic History 32(Mr, 1972):54-91.

Lane, David A., Jr. "An Army Project in the Duty-Time General Education of Negro Troops in Europe, 1947-1951." Journal of Negro Education, Spring, 1964.

Lang, Jane, and Scheiber, Harry N. "The Wilson Administration and the Wartime Mobilization of Black Americans, 1917-1918." Labor History, Summer, 1969.

Lang, William Louis. "Black Bootstraps: The Abolitionist Educators' Ideology and the Education of the Northern Free Negro, 1828-1860." Doctoral dissertation, U. of Delaware, 1974. Univ. Microfilm Order No. 74-27,858.

Lawson, James (ed.). How to Solve the Race Problem: The Proceedings of the Washington Conference on the Race Problem in the United States. Washington, DC: n.p., 1904.

Lawson, Steven F. Black Ballots. Voting Rights in the South, 1944-1969. New York: Columbia U. Press, 1976.

_____. "Give Us the Ballot: The Expansion of Black Voting Rights in the South, 1944-1969." Doctoral dissertation, Columbia U., 1974. Univ. Microfilm Order No. 7804371.

Lazerson, Marvin. "Social Reform and Early Childhood Education: Some Historical Perspectives." Urban Education 5(1970):84-102.

Leab, Daniel J. "The Gamut from A to B: The Image of the Black in Pre-1915 Movies." Political Science Quarterly 88(Mr, 1973):53-70.

Lee, Ulysses. United States Army in World War II. The Employment of Negro Troops. Washington, DC: GPO, 1966.

Lemons, J. Stanley. "Black Stereotypes as Reflected in Popular Culture, 1880-1920." American Quarterly (Spring, 1977):102-116.

Lester, Julius (ed.). The Seventh Son: The Thought and Writings of W. E. B. DuBois. 2 vols. New York: Random House, 1971.

Levy, Eugene. James Weldon Johnson: Black Leader, Black Voice. Chicago: U. of Chicago Press, 1973.

Lewis, Anthony and others. Portrait of a Decade: The Second American Revolution. New York: Random House, 1964.

Litwack, Leon F. "The Abolitionist Dilemma:
The Antislavery Movement and the Northern
Negro.: New England Quarterly 34(Mr, 1961):
50-73.

Logan, Rayford W. "Educational Segregation in
the North." Journal of Negro Education,
Ja, 1933.

_____. The Betrayal of the Negro. New York:
Collier, 1965.

Logue, Cal M. "Rhetorical Ridicule of Reconstruction Blacks." Quarterly Journal of
Speech 62(D, 1976):400-409.

[Lowitt], Suzanne Carson. "Samuel Chapman
Armstrong: Missionary to the South."
Doctoral dissertation, Johns Hopkins U.,
1952.

Lynd, Staughton (ed.). Nonviolence in America:
A Documentary History. Indianapolis: Bobbs-
Merrill, 1966.

_____. "Rethinking Slavery and Reconstruction."
Journal of Negro History, Jl, 1965.

McClean, Vernon E. "Trends in Afro-American
Social Thought: 1954-1970 (An Interpretation of the Black Revolution)." Doctoral
dissertation, Columbia U., 1978. Univ.
Microfilm Order No. 7821820.

McCoy, Donald R., and Ruetten, Richard T.
Quest and Response: Minority Rights and
the Truman Administration. Lawrence, KS:
U. of Kansas Press, 1973.

McFeely, William S. Yankee Stepfather. General
O. O. Howard and the Freedmen. New Haven,
CT: Yale U. Press, 1968.

McGee, Leo. A Study of the Types of Adult
Education Existing in America for the Black
Man 1860-1880. ERIC ED 097 255, Je, 1973.

_____. "Early Black Education." Liberator 11
(Mr, 1971:4-7). [Pre-Civil War]

MacGregor, Morris J., and Nalty, Bernard C.
(eds.). Blacks in the United States Armed
Forces: Basic Documents. Vol. I: A Time
of Slavery. Wilmington, DE: Scholarly
Resources, 1977.

McKelvey, Blake. The Emergence of Metropolitan
America, 1915-1966. New Brunswick, NJ:
Rutgers U. Press, 1968.

_____. "The Metropolis and the Historian."
Niagara Frontier, Autumn, 1965.

McKinney, Theophilus E., Jr. "United States
Transportation Segregation 1865-1954."
Quarterly Review of Higher Education Among
Negroes 22(Jl, 1954):101-148.

McLaughlin, Tom L. "Grass-Roots Attitudes
Toward Black Rights in Twelve Nonslaveholding
States, 1846-1869." Mid-America 56(Jl, 1974).

MacLeod, Duncan. "Racial Attitudes in Revolutionary and Early National America." Doctoral
dissertation, Cambridge U., 1969.

McManus, Edgar J. Black Bondage in the North.
Syracuse, NY: Syracuse U. Press, 1973.

McMillen, Neil R. The Citizens' Council. Organized Resistance to the Second Reconstruction, 1954-64. Urbana, IL: U. of Illinois
Press, 1971.

McNeil, Genna Rae. "Charles Hamilton Houston
(1895-1950) and the Struggle for Civil
Rights." Doctoral dissertation, U. of
Chicago, 1975.

McPherson, James M. The Abolitionist Legacy
From Reconstruction to the NAACP. Princeton,
NJ: Princeton U. Press, 1975.

_____. "Abolitionists and the Civil Rights
Act of 1875." Journal of American History
52(1965):493-510.

Magdol, Edward. A Right to the Land: Essays on
Freedmen's Community. Westport, CT:
Greenwood, 1977.

_____. "Local Black Leaders in the South: An
Essay toward the Reconstruction of Reconstruction History." Societas 4(Spring, 1974):
81-110.

Mandle, Jay R. "The Plantation States as a
Sub-Region of the Post-Bellum South."
Journal of Economic History 34(S, 1974):
732-738.

_____. "The Re-establishment of the Plantation
Economy in the South, 1865-1910." Review of
Black Political Economy 3(1973):68-88.

_____. The Roots of Black Poverty. The
Southern Plantation Economy After the Civil
War. Durham, NC: Duke U. Press, 1978.

Marshall, J. F. B. "Does It Pay to Educate the
Negro?" Boston Evening Transcript, Mr 2,
1886.

Martin, Tony. Race First: The Ideological
Struggle of Marcus Garvey and the Universal
Negro Improvement Association. Westport, CT:
Greenwood Press, 1975.

Maskin, Melvin R. "Black Education and the New
Deal: The Urban Experience." Doctoral
dissertation, New York U., 1973.

Matthews, Ethel Mae. "'Things Have Happened
I Never . . . Thought Would Happen.' A
Conversation . . ." New South 28(Summer,
1973):48-56.

Matthews, Fred H. "Robert Park, Congo Reform and Tuskegee: The Molding of a Race Relations Expert, 1905-1913." Canadian Journal of History 8(Mr, 1973).

Matthews, John Michael. "The Dilemma of Negro Leadership in the New South: The Case of the Negro Young People's Congress of 1902." South Atlantic Quarterly 73(Winter, 1974).

Mays, Benjamin E. Born to Rebel: An Autobiography. New York: Scribner, 1971,

Meeker, Edward. "Freedom, Economic Opportunity, and Fertility: Black Americans, 1860-1910." Economic Inquiry 15(Jl, 1977).

_____. "Mortality Trends of Southern Blacks, 1850-1910: Some Preliminary Findings." Explorations in Economic History 13(Ja, 1976):13-42.

Meeker, Edward, and Kau, James. "Racial Discrimination and Occupational Attainment at the Turn of the Century." Explorations in Economic History 14(Jl, 1977):250-276.

Meier, August. Negro Thought in America, 1880-1915. Ann Arbor: U. of Michigan Press, 1963.

_____. From Plantation to Ghetto: An Interpretive History of American Negroes. New York: Hill and Wang, 1966.

_____. "Negro Boycotts of Jim Crow Schools in the North, 1897-1925." Integrated Education, Ag-S, 1967.

_____. "The Racial and Educational Philosophy Of Kelly Miller: 1895-1915." Journal of Negro Education (Winter, 1960):121-127.

Meier, August, and Rudwick, Elliott. Along the Color Line. Urbana, IL: U. of Illinois Press, 1977.

_____ and _____. CORE: A Study in the Civil Rights Movement 1942-1968. New York: Oxford U. Press, 1973.

_____ and _____. "How CORE Began." Social Science Quarterly, Mr, 1969.

_____ and _____. "The Rise of Segregation in the Federal Bureaucracy, 1900-1930." Phylon, Summer, 1967.

Meltzer, Milton, and Meier, August. Time of Trial, Time of Hope: The Negro in America, 1919-1941. Garden City, NY: Doubleday, 1966.

Merton, Thomas. "An Anti-Poem. Plessy vs. Ferguson: Theme and Variations." Commonweal, F 7, 1969.

Meyer, Howard N. Colonel of the Black Regiment. The Life of Thomas Wentworth Higginson. New York: Norton, 1967.

_____. Let Us Have Peace: The Life of Ulysses S. Grant. New York: Collier, 1966.

Miller, Elinor, and Geneovese, Eugene D. (eds.). Plantation, Town, and County. Essays on the Local History of American Slave Society. Urbana, IL: U. of Illinois Press, 1973.

Miller, Floyd J. The Search for a Black Nationality. Black Colonization and Emigration, 1787-1863. Urbana, IL: U. of Illinois Press, 1975.

Miller, J. F. "The Effects of Emancipation Upon the Mental and Physical Qualifications of the Negro of the South. North Carolina Medical Journal 38(1896):285-294.

Miller, Kelly. An Estimate of Carter G. Woodson and His Work in Connection with the Association for the Study of Negro Life and History, Inc. Washington, DC: The Association for the Study of Negro Life and History, 1926.

_____. "Education of the Negro in the North." In The Everlasting Stain. Washington, DC: Associated Publishers, 1924.

_____. Forty Years of Negro Education. New York: n.p., 1908.

Miller, Mignon. "The American Negro Academy: An Intellectual Movement During the Era of Negro Disenfranchisement, 1897-1924." Master's thesis, Howard U., 1966.

"Mixed Schools." National Teachers' Monthly 3 (Jl, 1877):275-276.

Mohr, James C. (ed.). Radical Republicans in the North. State Politics during Reconstruction. Baltimore: Johns Hopkins U. Press, 1976.

Moore, Faye Emily. "Disparate Patterns of Minority Education, 1865-1917." Doctoral dissertation, Northern Illinois U., 1976. Univ. Microfilm Order No. 77-3806. [European immigrants, blacks, American Indians]

Moore, Jesse T., Jr. "The Urban League and the Black Revolution, 1941-1961: Its Philosoph-and Policies." Doctoral dissertation, Pennsylvania State U., 1971.

Moore, R. Laurence. "Flawed Fraternity--American Socialist Response to the Negro, 1901-1912." Historian 32(N, 1969):1-18.

Moore, Richard B. The Name "Negro." Its Origin and Evil Use. New York: Afroamerican Publishers, 1960.

Morris, Robert C. "Reading, 'Riting, and Reconstruction: Freedmen's Education in the South, 1865-1870." Doctoral dissertation, U. of Chicago.

Morris, Thomas D. _Free Men All. The Personal Liberty Laws of the North, 1780-1861._ Baltimore, MD: Johns Hopkins U. Press, 1974.

Morrill, Richard L., and Donaldson, O. Fred. "Geographical Perspectives on the History of Black America." _Economic Geography_ 48 (Ja, 1972):1-23.

Moses, Wilson Jeremiah. "Assimilationist Black Nationalism, 1890-1925." _Social Studies_ 68 (N-D, 1977):259-263.

_____. "Black Bourgeois Nationalism at the Turn of the Century: Some Problems for Scholars." In _Identity and Awareness in the Minority Experience_, pp. 253-269. Edited by George E. Carter and Bruce Mouser. Selected Proceedings of the 1st and 2nd Annual Conferences on Minority Studies. Lacrosse, WI: U. of Wisconsin, 1975.

_____. _The Golden Age of Black Nationalism, 1850-1925._ Hamden, CT: Anchor Books, 1978.

Mowry, George E. _The Urban Nation: 1920-1960._ New York: Hill and Wang, 1965.

Moynihan, Kenneth James. "History as a Weapon for Social Advancement: Group History as Told by Jewish, Irish, and Black Americans." Doctoral dissertation, Clark U., 1973.

Muse, Benjamin. _Ten Years of Prelude. The Story of Integration Since the Supreme Court's 1954 Decision._ New York: Viking, 1964.

"Myth of Reverse Race Discrimination: An Historical Perspective." _Cleveland State Law Review_ 23(Spring, 1974):319-336.

N.A.A.C.P. _Thirty Years of Lynching in the United States._ New York: Negro Universities Press, 1969 (orig. 1919).

Nadiri, M. I. "Estimates of the Costs of Schooling in 1880 and 1890." _Explorations in Environmental History._ Supplement 7(1970).

Neary, John. _Julian Bond. Black Rebel. A Biography._ New York: Morrow, 1971.

Neverdon, Cynthia A. C. "The Articulation and Implementation of Educational Goals for Blac Blacks in the South, 1895-1925." Doctoral dissertation, Howard U, 1974. Univ. Microfilm Order No. 75-2185.

Newby, I. A. (ed.). "Historians and Negroes." _Journal of Negro History_, Ja, 1969.

Newman, Dorothy K. "The Negro's Journey to the City." Part II. _Monthly Labor Review_, Je, 1965.

Nielson, Arthur C. III. "The Second Ku Klux Klan: 1915-1928. The Life History of a Social Movement." Senior honors thesis, Harvard U., 1968.

Nielson, David Gordon. "Black Ethos: The Northern Urban Negro, 1890-1930." Doctoral dissertation, State U. of New York, Binghamton, 1972. Univ. Microfilms Order No. 72-24062.

_____. _Black Ethos: Northern Urban Negro Life and Thought, 1890-1930._ Westport, CT: Greenwood Press, 1977.

Nieman, Donald G. "To Set the Law in Motion: The Freedmen's Bureau and the Legal Rights of Blacks, 1865-1868." Vols. I and II. Doctoral dissertation, Rice U., 1975. Univ. Microfilms Order No. 75-22051.

Noble, Stuart G. "Education of the Negro." In _Twenty-Five Years of American Education_, pp. 405-429. Edited by J. L. Kandel. Freeport, NY: Books for Libraries, Inc. reprinted 1966 (orig. 1924).

Nolen, Claude. _The Negro's Image in the South._ Lexington, KY: U. of Kentucky Press, 1967.

Novak, Daniel A. _The Wheel of Servitude: Black Forced Labor After Slavery._ Lexington: U. of Kentucky Press, 1978.

Ofari, Earl. _"Let Your Motto be Resistance": The Life and Thought of Henry Highland Garnet._ Boston: Beacon Press, 1972.

Olsen, Otto H. (ed.). _The Thin Disguise: Turning Point in Negro History. Plessy vs. Ferguson: A Documentary Presentation (1864-1896)._ New York: Humanities Press, 1968.

Osofsky, Gilbert (ed.). _The Burden of Race: A Documentary History of Negro-White Relations in America._ New York: Harper & Row, 1967.

_____. "The Enduring Ghetto." _Journal of American History_, S, 1968.

Osur, Alan Michael. "Negroes in the Army Air Forces During World War II: The Problem of Race Relations." Doctoral dissertation, U. of Denver, 1974. Univ. Microfilms Order No. 75-2209.

Oubre, Claude F. _Forty Acres and a Mule: The Freedmen's Bureau and Black Land Ownership._ Baton Rouge: Louisiana State U. Press, 1978.

Owen, Ross C. "Leisure-time Activities of the American Negro Prior to the Civil War." Master's thesis, U. of Michigan, 1938.

Oxley, Howard W. "The Civilian Conservation Corps and the Education of the Negro." _Journal of Negro Education_ 8(J1, 1938):375-382.

Palmer, R. Roderick. "Colonial Statutes and Present-Day Obstacles Restricting Negro Education." _Journal of Negro Education_ 26 (Fall, 1957):525-529.

Parker, Marjorie H. "The Educational Activities of the Freedman's Bureau." Doctoral dissertation, U. of Chicago, 1952.

Parks, Robert J. "The Development of Segregation in U.S. Army Hospitals, 1940-1942." Military Affairs 37(D, 1973).

Parmet, Robert D. "Schools for the Freedmen." Negro History Bulletin 34(O, 1971):128-132.

Parris, Guichard, and Brooks, Lester. Blacks in the City: A History of the Urban League. Boston: Little, Brown, 1971.

Patterson, Orlando. "Toward a Future that Has No Past: Reflections on the Fate of Blacks in the Americas." Public Interest 27(Spring, 1972):25-62.

Patterson, William L. The Man Who Cried Genocide: An Autobiography. New York: International Publishers, 1971.

Paynter, Julie. "An End to Innocence." Journal, Ja, 1969. Published by Division of Higher Education, United Church of Christ.

Pease, William H., and Pease, Jane H. "Antislavery Ambivalence: Immediatism, Expedience, Race." American Quarterly 17 (Winter 1965):682-695.

_____ and _____. "Black Power--The Debate in 1840." Phylon, Spring, 1968.

_____ and _____. They Who Would Be Free: Blacks' Search for Freedom, 1830-61. New York: Atheneum, 1975.

Peniston, Gregory S. "The Slave Builder-Artisan." Western Journal of Black Studies 2(Winter 1978):284-295.

Pennington, Edgar L. "The Reverend Francis LeJau's Work Among Indians and Negro Slaves." Journal of Southern History 1 (1935):442-458.

_____. Thomas Bray's Associates and Their Work Among the Negroes. Worcester, MA: n.p., 1939.

Perdue, Robert E. Black Laborers and Black Professionals in Early America, 1750-1830. New York: Vantage Press, 1975.

Perlman, Daniel. "Stirring Up the White Conscience: The Life of George Edmund Haynes." Doctoral dissertation, New York U., 1972.

Peskin, Allan (ed.). North Into Freedom: The Autobiography of John Malvin, Free Negro, 1795-1800. Cleveland: Press of Western Reserve U., 1966.

Pessen, Edward. "The Equalitarian Myth and the American Social Reality: Wealth, Mobility, and Equality in the 'Era of the Common Man.'" American Historical Review 76 (O, 1971):989-1034.

_____. "Equality and Opportunity in America, 1800-1940." Wilson Quarterly 1(Autumn, 1977): 136-142.

_____. Riches, Clan, and Power Before the Civil War. Lexington, MA: Heath, 1973.

Peterson, Robert W. Only the Ball Was White. Englewood Cliffs, NJ: Prentice-Hall, 1970. [Negro baseball, 1898-1946.]

Pickens, William. Bursting Bonds. Boston: Jordan and Moore Press, 1929.

Picott, J. Rupert. A Quarter Century of the Black Experience in Elementary and Secondary Education, 1950-1975. Washington, DC: Associated Publishers, 1977.

_____. "A Quarter Century of the Black Experience in Elementary and Secondary Education, 1950-1974." Negro Educational Review 27(Ja, 1976):45-71.

Pole, J. R. The Pursuit of Equality in American History. Berkeley, CA: U. of California Press, 1978.

Polos, Nicholas C. "Black Anti-Semitism in Twentieth-Century America: Historical Myth or Reality? American Jewish Archives 7 (Ap, 1975):8-31.

Porter, Dorothy B. "Maria Louise Baldwin." Journal of Negro Education, Winter, 1952.

_____. "The Organized Educational Activities of Negro Literary Societies, 1828-1846." Journal of Negro History 5(O, 1936):555-576.

_____. "Sarah Parker Remond, Abolitionist and Physician." Journal of Negro History 20 (Jl, 1935):287-293.

_____(ed.). "Societies for Educational Improvement, 1808-1836." In Early Negro Writing, 1760-1837, pp. 79-166. Boston: Beacon, 1971.

Powell, Adam Clayton, Jr. Adam. New York: Dial, 1971. [Autobiography]

_____. Marching Blacks. 2nd ed. New York: Dial, 1973.

Prather, H. Leon, Sr. "The Origin of the Slater Philanthropy in Negro Education 1882-1913." Journal of Social and Behavioral Sciences 15 (Spring, 1970):32-40.

Prunty, Merle C., and Aiken, Charles S. "The Demise of the Piedmont Cotton Region." Annals of the Association of American Geographers 62(Je, 1972):283-306.

Rabinowitz, Howard Neil. "The Conflict Between Blacks and the Police in the Urban South, 1865-1900." Historian 39(N, 1976):62-76.

_____. "From Exclusion to Segregation: Health and Welfare Services for Southern Blacks, 1865-1890." Social Service Review 48(S, 1974).

_____. "From Exclusion to Segregation: Southern Race Relations, 1865-1890." Journal of American History 63(S, 1976):325-350.

_____. "Half a Loaf: The Shift from White to Black Teachers in the Negro Schools of the Urban South, 1865-1890." Journal of Southern History 40(N, 1974).

_____. "Search for Social Control: Race Relations in the Urban South, 1865-1890." 2 vols. Doctoral dissertation, U. of Chicago, 1973.

Raines, Howell. My Soul Is Rested. Movement Days in the Deep South. New York: Putnam, 1977. [1955-1968]

Ravitch, Diane. "On the History of Minority Group Education in the United States." Teachers College Record 78(D, 1976):213-228.

Rawick, George P. From Sundown to Sunup, the Working of the Black Community. Vol. I of The American Slave: A Composite Autobiography. Westport, CT: Greenwood Press, 1972.

Reddix, Jacob L. A Voice Crying in the Wilderness: The Memoirs of Jacob L. Reddix. N.p.: n.p., n.d.

Reid, Ira De A. The Negro Immigrant...1899-1937. New York: Columbia U. Press, 1939.

Reps, John W. The Making of Urban America: A History of City Planning in the United States. Princeton: Princeton U. Press, n.d.

Robbins, Richard. "Shadow of Macon County: The Life and Work of Charles S. Johnson." Journal of Social and Behavioral Sciences 18(Fall-Winter, 1971-1972):21-26.

Roberts, Edward B. "The Administration of the Peabody Education Fund from 1880 to 1905." Doctoral dissertation, George Peabody College for Teachers, 1936.

Roberts, Herbert C. "The Sentiment of Congress toward the Education of Negroes from 1860-1890." Master's thesis, Fisk U., 1933.

Robeson, Paul. Here I Stand. New York: Othello Associates, 1958.

Robinson, Dorothy R. The Bell Rings at Four: A Black Teacher's Chronicle of Change. Austin, TX: Madrona Press, 1978.

Roche, John P. The Quest for the Dream. New York: Macmillan, 1963.

Rollins, Bryant. "The Clarks." Essence 7(Je, 1976). [Kenneth B. Clark's family]

Romagnolo, D. J. Paternalism and Ruling Class Ideology in the Ante-Bellum South: A Critique of the Social Function of Paternalism as Presented in the Analysis of Eugene D. Genovese. Irvine, CA: Program in Comparative Culture, U. of California, Irvine, My, 1976.

Rosen, Bruce. "Abolition and Colonization, the Years of Conflict: 1829-1834." Phylon 33 (Summer, 1972):177-192.

Rosenbaum, Judy Jolley. "Black Education in Three Northern Cities in the Early Twentieth Century." Doctoral dissertation, U. of Illinois, 1974. Microfilms Order No. 75-11,741.

Ross, B. Joyce. J. E. Spingarn and the Rise of the NAACP. New York: Atheneum, 1972.

Ross, J. Michael. "Resistance to Racial Change in the Urban North: 1962-1968." Doctoral dissertation, Harvard U, 1973.

Rubin, Barry. "Marxism and Education--Radical Thought and Educational Theory in the 1930's." Science & Society 36(Summer, 1972):171-201.

Salmond, John A. "The Civilian Conservation Corps and the Negro." Journal of American History, Je, 1965.

Sanford, Delacy Wendell, Jr. "Congressional Investigation of Black Communism, 1919-1967." Doctoral dissertation, State U. of New York at Stony Brook, 1973.

Sarratt, Reed. The Ordeal of Desegregation. New York: Harper & Row, 1966.

Savage, W. Sherman. "Education," In Blacks in the West, chapter 8. Westport, CT: Greenwood Press, 1976.

Sawyer, R. McLaran. "The National Education Association and Negro Education, 1865-1884." Journal of Negro Education 39(Fall, 1970):341-345.

Schappes, Morris U. "Spirit of 1776. Bicentennial of the American Revolution." Jewish Currents (F, 1972):14-19, 29-32. [Ethnic factors in early American history]

Schlesinger, Arthur. "Nationalism and History." Journal of Negro History, Ja, 1969.

Schlossman, Steven L. "The 'Culture of Poverty' in Ante-Bellum Social Thought." Science & Society 38(Summer, 1975):150-166.

Schor, Joel S. "The Anti-Slavery and Civil Rights Role of Henry Highland Garnet, 1840-1865." Doctoral dissertation, Howard U., 1973. Univ. Microfilms Order No. 75-2188.

_____. Henry Highland Garnet: A Voice of Black Radicalism in the Nineteenth Century. Westport, CT: Greenwood Press, 1977.

Scott, Osborne. "Pre- and Post-Emancipation Schools." Urban Review 9(Winter, 1976): 234-241.

Schuyler, George S. Black and Conservative: Autobiography. New Rochelle, NY: Arlington House, 1966.

Schwartz, Sandra K., and Schwartz, David C. "Convergence and Divergence in Political Orientations between Blacks and Whites: 1960-1973." Journal of Social Issues 32 (1976):153-168.

Seale, Bobby. A Lonely Rage: The Autobiography of Bobby Seale. New York: Times Books, 1977.

Segal, Geraldine R. "A Sketch of the Life of Charles H. Houston." Master's thesis, U. of Pennsylvania, 1963.

Sitkoff, Harvard. A New Deal for Blacks. The Emergence of Civil Rights as a National Issue: The Depression Decade. New York: Oxford U. Press, 1978.

_____. The Civil Rights Movement in the 20th Century. New York: Praeger, 1974.

_____. "The Coming of Age of Civil Rights, 1932-1954, Part I: The New Deal Era." Doctoral dissertation, Columbia U., 1975.

_____. "Racial Militancy and Interracial Violence in the Second World War." Journal of American History 58(D, 1971).

Sizer, Theodore. Secondary Education at the Turn of the Century. New Haven: Yale U. Press, 1964.

Slater, Jack. "1954 Revisited." Ebony 29 (My, 1974):116-127.

Small, Sandra E. "The Yankee Schoolmarm in Southern Freedmen's Schools, 1861-1871: The Career of a Stereotype." Doctoral dissertation, Washington State U., 1976.

Smith, Donald J. C. "Thaddeus Stevens and the Politics of Educational Reform, 1825-1868." Doctoral dissertation, Rutgers--The State U., 1968. Univ. Microfilms Order No. 69-9300.

Smith, Linda Brown. "25 Years Ago She Opened Door to Desegregation." Boston Globe, My 16, 1979.

Smith, James M. "The 'Separate But Equal' Doctrine: An Abolitionist Discusses Racial Segregation and Education Policy During the Civil War." Journal of Negro History 41 (1956):138-147.

Smith, Richard Kent. "The Economics of Education and Discrimination in the U.S. South: 1870-1910." Doctoral dissertation, U. of Wisconsin, 1973. Univ. Microfilms Order No. 74-10,269.

Smith, T. Lynn. "The Redistribution of the Negro Population of the United States, 1910-1960." Journal of Negro History, Jl, 1966.

Sobel, Lester (ed.). Civil Rights, 1960-66. New York: Facts on File, 1967.

Sochen, June. The Unbridgeable Gap: Blacks and Their Quest for the American Dream, 1900-1930. Chicago: Rand McNally, 1972.

Solmon, Lewis C. "Estimates of the Costs of Schooling in 1880 and 1890." Explorations in Economic History, Supplement 7(1970), 531-581.

_____. "Opportunity Costs and Models of Schooling in the Nineteenth Century." Southern Economic Journal 37(Jl, 1970):66-83.

Soltow, Lee. "Economic Inequality in the United States in the Period from 1790 to 1860." Journal of Economic History 31(D, 1971):822-839.

Soltow, Lee, and Stevens, Edward. "Economic Aspects of School Participation in Mid-Nineteenth Century United States." Journal of Interdisciplinary History 8(Autumn, 1977): 221-243.

Sosna, Morton., In Search of the Silent South. Southern Liberals and the Race Issue. New York: Columbia U. Press, 1977.

Southern, David W. The Malignant Heritage: Yankee Progressives and the Negro Question, 1901-1914. Chicago: Loyola U. Press, 1968.

Spain, Rufus B. At Ease in Zion: Social Attitudes of Southern Baptists, 1865-1900. Nashville, TN: Vanderbilt U. Press, 1967.

Spear, Allan. "The Origins of the Urban Ghetto, 1870-1915." In Key Issues in the Afro-American Experience, Vol. II, pp. 153-166. Edited by Nathan I. Huggins, Martin Kilson and Daniel M. Fox. New York: n.p., 1971.

Spellman, Cecil L. Rough Steps on My Stairway: The Life History of a Negro Educator. New York: Exposition, 1953.

Spiegel, Sydney. "The Hidden History of Educational Administration in the U.S." Changing Education 5(Fall, 1973):6-13.

Spivey, Donald. Schooling for the New Slavery: Black Industrial Education, 1868-1915. Westport, CT: Greenwood Press, 1978.

Spring, Joel H. "Education and the Rise of the Corporate State. Socialist Revolution 2 (Mr-Ap, 1972):73-101.

Stampp, Kenneth M. "Rebels and Sambos: The Search for the Negro's Personality in Slavery." Journal of Southern History 37 (Ag, 1971):367-392.

Star, Jack. "Above All, A Scholar." Change 9 (F, 1977):27-33. [John Hope Franklin.]

Steffgen, Kent H. The Bondage of the Free: A Critical Examination of the Misnamed "Civil Rights" Cause from the Civil War through the Cold War. Berkeley, CA: Vanguard Books, 1966.

Stevens, Walter J. Chip on My Shoulder. Boston: Meador, 1946.

Stoper, Emily. "The Student Nonviolent Coordinating Committee: Rise and Fall of a Redemptive Organization." Journal of Black Studies 8(S, 1977):13-34.

Stowe, Harriet Beecher. "The Education of the Freedmen." North American Review 128(1879): 605-615.

Stuckert, Robert P. "Race Mixture: The African Ancestry of White Americans." In Physical Anthropology and Archaelogy: Selected Readings. Edited by Peter Hammond. New York: Macmillan, 1964.

Stuckey, Sterling. "'I Want to Be African': Paul Robeson and the Ends of Nationalist Theory and Practice." Massachusetts Review 17(Spring, 1975):81-138.

_____. "I Want to Be African": Paul Robeson and the Ends of Nationalist Theory and Practice, 1919-1945. Los Angeles: Afro-American Studies Center, U. of California, 1976.

_____. "The Spell of Africa: The Development of Black Nationalist Theory, 1829-1945." Doctoral dissertation, Northwestern U., 1973.

_____ (ed.) The Ideological Origins of Black Nationalism. Boston: Beacon Press, 1972.

Swint, Henry L. (ed.). Dear Ones at Home. Letters from Contraband Camps. Nashville, TN: Vanderbilt U. Press, 1966.

Synnestvedt, Sig. The White Response to Black Emancipation. Second-Class Citizenship in the United States Since Reconstruction. New York: Macmillan, 1972.

Taggart, John H. Free Military School for Applicants for Command of Colored Troops. Philadelphia: King and Baird, 1864.

Takaki, Ronald. "The Black Child-Savage in Ante-Bellum America." In The Great Fear. Race in the Mind of America. Edited by Gary B. Nash and Richard Weiss. New York: Holt, Rinehart & Winston, 1970.

Tarry, Ellen. The Third Door: The Autobiography of an American Negro Woman. New York: McKay, 1955.

Taylor, Arnold H. Travail and Triumph: Black Life and Culture in the South Since the Civil War. Westport, CT: Greenwood Press, 1977.

Taylor, Hoy. "An Interpretation of the Early Administration of the Peabody Fund." Doctor's thesis, George Peabody College for Teachers, 1933.

Taylor, William R. "The Patrician-South and the Common Schools." Harvard Educational Review, Fall, 1966.

Terjen, Kitty. "Kenneth B. Clark: The Fighter Turns 60." Southern Voices 1(O-N, 1974): 25-32.

Terrell, Mary Church. A Colored Woman in a White World. Washington, DC: Ransdell, 1940.

Thernstrom, Stephan. "Urbanization, Migration and Social Mobility in Late-Nineteenth Century America." In Towards a New Past. Edited by Barton Bernstein. New York: Pantheon, 1968.

Thernstrom, Stephan, and Sennett, Richard (eds.). Nineteenth-Century Cities: Essays in the New Urban History. New Haven: Yale U. Press, 1969.

Thompson, Charles H. "75 Years of Negro Education." Crisis, Jl, 1938.

Thornbrough, Emma L. "Negro Slavery in the North: Its Legal and Constitutional Aspects." Doctoral dissertation, U. of Michigan, 1946.

Thorpe, Earle T. "Negro Historiography in the United States." Doctoral dissertation, Ohio State U., 1954.

Tillery, Tyrone. "The Inevitability of the Douglass-Garrison Conflict." Phylon 37(Je, 1976):137-149.

Tindall, George Brown. The Emergence of the New South, 1913-1945. Baton Rouge, LA: Louisiana State U. Press, 1967.

Trelease, Allen W. White Terror. The Ku Klux The Ku Klux Klan Conspiracy and Southern Reconstruction. New York: Harper & Row, 1971.

Tuinman, Jaap and others. "Reading Achievement in the United States: Then and Now." Journal of Reading 19(Mr, 1976):455-463. [Fifty years ago]

Tyack, David B. "Growing Up Black: Perspectives on the History of Education in Northern Ghettoes." History of Education Quarterly 9 (1969):287-297.

_____. The One Best System. A History of American Urban Education. Cambridge, MA: Harvard U. Press, 1974.

United States Bureau of Education. Education in the Various States. Education of the Colored Race. Slater Fund and Education of the Negro. Washington, DC: GPO, 1896.

U.S. Bureau of Education. "Education of the Colored Race." In Report of 1902, pp. 2063-2095. Washington, DC: GPO, 1902.

_____. "Schools for the Colored Race." In Report of 1903, pp. 2253-2285. Washington, DC: GPO, 1904.

_____. "Schools for the Colored Race." In Annual Report, 1904, II, pp. 2175-2207. Washington, DC: GPO, 1906.

_____. "Schools for the Colored Race." In Annual Report of 1905, pp. 1293-1327. Washington, DC: GPO, 1907.

_____. "Schools for the Colored Race." In Annual Report, 1906, II, pp. 1149-1173. Washington, DC: GPO, 1908.

_____. "Schools for the Colored Race." In Annual Report, 1907, II, pp. 1127-1139. Washington, DC: GPO, 1908.

_____. "Schools for the Colored Race." In Annual Report, 1908, II, pp. 941-955. Washington, DC: GPO, 1908.

_____. "Schools for the Colored Race." In Annual Report, 1909, II, pp. 1213-1227. Washington, DC: GPO, 1909.

_____. "Schools for the Colored Race." In Annual Report, 1910, II, pp. 1259-1275. Washington, DC: GPO, 1910.

_____. "Statistics of Schools for Negroes." In Annual Report, 1911, II, pp. 1287-1305. Washington, DC: GPO, 1911.

_____. "Statistics of Schools for Negroes." In Annual Report, 1912, II, pp. 575-593. Washington, DC: GPO, 1913.

_____. "Statistics of Schools for Negroes." In Annual Report, 1913, II, pp. 607-621. Washington, DC: GPO, 1914.

_____. "Statistics of Schools for Negroes." In Annual Report, 1914, II, pp. 491-503. Washington, DC: GPO, 1915.

_____. "Statistics of Schools for Negroes." In Annual Report, 1916, II, pp. 585-600. Washington, DC: GPO, 1917.

_____. "Statistics of Schools for Negroes." In Annual Report, 1917, II, pp. 611-624. Washington, DC: GPO, 1917.

United States Commissioner of Education. "Education of the Colored Race." In Report of 1895-1896, pp. 2081-2115. Washington, DC: GPO, 1897.

_____. "Education of the Colored Race." In Report of 1897-1898, pp. 2479-2507. Washington, DC: GPO, 1899.

_____. "Education of the Colored Race." In Report of 1898-1899, pp. 2201-2225. Washington, DC: GPO, 1900.

_____. "Education of the Colored Race." In Report of 1899-1900, pp. 2501-2531. Washington, DC: GPO, 1901.

_____. "Education of the Colored Race." In Report of 1900-1901, pp. 2299-2331. Washington, DC: GPO, 1902.

_____. "The Future of the Colored Race." In Report of 1898-1899, pp. 1227-1248. Washington, DC: GPO, 1900.

U.S. Commission on Civil Rights. Freedom to the Free, 1963. Washington, DC: GPO, 1963.

U.S. Congress, 90th, 2nd Session, House of Representatives, Report No. 1679. Providing for the Establishment of a Commission on Negro History and Culture, Jl 1, 1968.

U.S. Congress, 90th, 2nd Session, House of Representatives, Committee on Education and Labor, Select Subcommittee on Labor. To Establish a National Commission on Negro History and Culture. Hearing. Washington, DC: GPO, 1968.

U.S. Congress, 90th, 2nd Session, Senate, Committee on Labor and Public Welfare, Special Subcommittee on Arts and Humanities. Commission on Negro History and Culture-- Hearings. Washington, DC: GPO, 1968.

U.S. Congress, 91st, 1st Session, House of Representatives, Committee on Education and Labor, Select Subcommittee on Education. Establishment of a Commission on Afro-American History and Culture. Hearing. Washington, DC: GPO, 1969.

U.S. Congress, 91st, 1st Session, Senate, Committee on Interior and Insular Affairs, Subcommittee on Parks and Recreation. Frederick Douglass Home. Hearing. Washington, DC: GPO, 1969.

U.S. Industrial Commission. Reports of the Industrial Commission on Immigration Including Testimony, With Review and Digest, and Special Reports on Education Including Testimony With Review and Digest. Washington, DC: GPO, 1901.

Uya, Okon E. "The Culture of Slavery: Black Experience Through a White Filter." Afro-American Studies 1(Ja, 1971):203-209.

Vaughn, William P. "Partners in Segregation: Barnas Sears and the Peabody Fund." Civil War History, S, 1964.

_____. Schools for All. The Blacks and Public Education in the South, 1865-1877. Lexington, KY: The U. Press of Kentucky, 1974.

_____. "The Sectional Conflict in Southern Public Education: 1865-1876." Doctoral dissertation, Ohio State U., 1961. Univ. Microfilm Order No. 61-5130.

_____. "Separate and Unequal: The Civil Rights Act of 1875 and Defeat of the School Integration Clause." Southwestern Social Science Quarterly 48(1967):146-154.

Voegeli, V. Jacque. Free but Not Equal: The Midwest and the Negro During the Civil War. Chicago: U. of Chicago Press, 1967.

Wade, Richard C. "The City in History--Some American Perspectives." In Urban Life and Form. Edited by Werner Z. Hirsch. New York: Holt, Rinehart and Winston, 1963.

_____. "Historical Analogies and Public Policy: One Black and Immigrant Experience in Urban America." In Essays on Urban America. Edited by Margaret F. Morris and Elliott West. Austin, TX: U. of Texas Press, 1975.

_____. "The Inner City in a Mobile Society." Urban Education, Summer, 1964.

Wallace, Les. "Charles Lenox Remond: The Lost Prince of Abolitionism." Negro History Bulletin 40(My-Je, 1977):696-701.

Warner, Sam Bass. The Urban Wilderness: A History of the American City. New York: Harper & Row, 1972.

Warner, Stafford Allen. Yardley Warner: The Freedman's Friend. Abington, England: n.p., 1957. [Quaker leader, active in freedmen's schools in North Carolina and Tennessee]

Waskow, Arthur I. From Race Riot to Sit-in, 1919 and the 1960's: A Study in the Connections Between Conflict and Violence. Garden City, NY: Doubleday, 1966.

Webber, Thomas L. Deep Like the Rivers: Education in the Slave Quarter Community, 1831-1865. New York: Norton, 1978.

Weinberg, Meyer. A Chance to Learn: A History of Race and Education in the United States. New York: Cambridge U. Press, 1977.

_____. "A Historical Framework for Multi-cultural Education." In Teaching in a Multicultural Society. Edited by Dolores E. Cross and others. New York: Free Press, 1977.

_____. "A Historical Framework for Multi-cultural Education." In Black/Brown/White Relations. Edited by Charles V. Willie. New Brunswick, NJ: Transaction, 1977.

_____. "A Yearning for Learning: Blacks and Jews Through History. Integrated Education, My-Je, 1969, pp. 20-29.

_____. "School Desegregation and Planned Deprivation." Integrateducation 13(My-Je, 1975):112-15.

_____. "School Integration in American History." Integrated Education, D, 1963-Ja, 1964.

Weiss, Nancy J. The National Urban League, 1910-1940. New York: Oxford U. Press, 1974.

_____. "The Negro and the New Freedom: Fighting Wilsonian Segregation." Political Science Quarterly 84(Mr, 1969):61-79.

Wesley, Charles H. "Background and Achievement for Negro-Americans." Crisis, Mr, 1960.

_____. "The Education of Black Americans." Ebony 30(Ag, 1975):143-147.

_____. History of Sigma Pi Phi, First of the Negro-American Greek Letter Fraternities. Washington, DC: Association for the Study of Negro Life and History, 1954.

_____. "Jonathan Davis and the Rise of Black Fraternal Organizations. Crisis 84(Mr, 1977): 112-113, 116-118.

_____. Neglected History: Essays in Negro History by a College President. Wilberforce, OH: Central State College Press, 1965.

West, Earle H. "The Life and Educational Contributions of Barnas Sears." Doctoral dissertation, George Peabody College for Teachers, 1961. Univ. Microfilm Order No. 61-5832.

_____. "Peabody Education Fund and Negro Education, 1867-1880." History of Education Quarterly, Summer, 1966.

White, Arthur O. "Black Parents for Desegregation in the 19th Century." Integrated Education 10(N-D, 1972):37-47.

White, Dana L. White. "Education in the Turn-of-the-Century City: the Search for Control." Urban Education, Jl, 1969.

White, William Bruce. "The Military and the Melting Pot: The American Army and Minority Groups, 1865-1924." Doctoral dissertation, U. of Wisconsin, 1968.

Wilhoit, Francis M. The Politics of Massive Resistance. New York: Braziller, 1974.

Wilkerson, Doxey A. "The Ghetto School Struggles in Historical Perspective." Science & Society, Spring, 1969.

Wilkie, Jane Riblett. "The Black Urban Population of the Pre-Civil War South." Phylon 37 (S, 1976):250-262.

_____. "The United States Population by Race and Urban-Rural Residence 1790-1860: Reference Tables." Demography 13(F, 1976): 139-148.

_____. "Urbanization and De-urbanization of the Black Population Before the Civil War." Demography 13(Ag, 1976).

Wilkins, Roger. "The Sound of One Hand Clapping." New York Times Magazine, My 12, 1974. [Twenty years after the Brown decision]

Williams, Anderson C. "The Origins of SNCC and the Civil Rights Movement: A Reappraisal." Journal of Social and Behavioral Sciences 19 (Summer-Fall, 1972):46-50.

Williams, George Washington. History of the Negro Race in America from 1619 to 1880: Negroes as Slaves, as Soldiers, and as Citizens, together with a Preliminary Consideration of the Unity of the Human Family, an Historical Sketch of Africa and an account of the Negro Governments of Sierra Leone and Liberia. New York, London: G. P. Putnam's Sons, 1882.

Williams, John A. "Race, War, and Politics: A Dissenting Look at American History." Negro Digest, Ag., 1967.

Williams, William Taylor "The Yankee School Ma'am in Negro Education." Southern Workman 44(F, 1915).

Williamson, Joel (ed.). The Origins of Segregation. Boston: Heath, 1968.

Wilson, Joseph T. "The Phalanx at School." The Black Phalanx: A History of the Negro Soldiers of the United States in the Wars of 1775-1812, 1861-1865. Hartford, CT: American Publishing Co., 1890.

Wilson, W. J. "Class Conflict and Jim Crow Segregation in the Postbellum South." Pacific Sociological Review 19(0, 1976): 431-446. [1865-1900]

Wise, Harvey. "Negro Education and the Progressive Movement." Journal of Negro History, Jl, 1964.

_____. "A Historian Looks at School Segregation." Western Reserve Law Review, Ap, 1965.

Wise, Stephen S. "Abolition and Fifty Years After." Crisis, F, 1913.

Wood, Forrest B. Wood. Black Scare. The Racist Response to Emancipation and Reconstruction. Berkeley: U. of California Press, 1968.

Woodard, Frederick. "W. E. B. DuBois: The Native Impulse: Notes Toward an Ideological Biography, 1868-1897." Doctoral dissertation, U. of Iowa, 1976.

Woodson, Carter G. "The Education of the Negro," The African Background Outlined or Handbook for the Study of the Negro. Washington, DC: The Association for the Study of Negro Life and History, 1936.

_____. Education of the Negro Prior to 1861: A History of the Education of the Colored People of the United States from the Beginning of Slavery to the Civil War. New York: G. P. Putnam's Sons, 1915.

Woodward, C. Vann. American Counterpoint: Slavery and Racism in the North-South Dialogue. Boston: Little, Brown, 1971.

_____. "Clio With Soul." Journal of American History, Je, 1969.

_____. "Flight from History. The Heritage of the Negro." Nation, S 20, 1965.

_____. "The Hidden Sources of Negro History." Saturday Review, Ja 18, 1969.

_____. "Seeds of Failure in Radical [Republican] Race Policy." Proceedings of the American Philosophical Society, F 18, 1966.

_____. The Strange Career of Jim Crow. 2nd ed. New York: Oxford U. Press, 1965.

Wortham, Jacob. "Benjamin Mays At 81." Black Enterprise 7(My, 1977):27-29.

Wright, Charles H. Robeson: Labor's Forgotten Champion. Detroit: Balamys, 1976.

Wright, Richard D., Jr. 87 Years Behind the Black Curtain. Philadelphia: The Rare Book Company, 1965.

Wright, Stephen J. "A Study of Certain Attitudes Toward the Education of Negroes Since 1865." Doctoral dissertation, New York U., 1943.

Wright, W. D. "The Thought and Leadership of Kelly Miller." Phylon 39(Summer, 1978):180-192.

Wye, Christopher G. "The New Deal and the Negro Community: Toward a Broader Conceptualization." Journal of American History 59(D, 1972):621-639.

Wynn, Neil A. The Afro-American and the Second World War. London: Paul Elek, 1976.

Young, Alfred. "The Educational Philosophy of Booker T. Washington. A Perspective for Black Liberation." Phylon 37(S, 1976):224-235.

Zashin, Elliot. "The Progress of Black Americans in Civil Rights: The Past Two Decades Assessed." Daedalus (Winter, 1978):239-262.

Zilversmit, Arthur. The First Emancipation. The Abolition of Negro Slavery in the North. Chicago: U. of Chicago Press, 1967.

Study and Teaching

Bailey, Thomas A. "The Mythmakers of American History." Journal of American History, Je, 1968.

Barton J. J., and Moorer, F. "Report on Oral History at the Martin Luther King, Jr. Memorial Center." Journal of Library History 7(Ja, 1972):61-63.

Gergen, Kenneth J. "Social Psychology as History." Journal of Personality and Social Psychology. Psychology 26(My, 193):309-320.

Harding, Vincent. "The Afro-American Past and the American Present." Motive, Ap, 1968.

Heitzmann, William Ray. "An Individual Pro-grammed Instructional Experience in Afro-American History." Social Studies Journal 4 (Winter, 1975):24-28.

Jones, Stuart M. "The Schlesingers On Black History." Phylon 33(Summer, 1972):104-111.

Kreamer, Ralph S. "Minority History No Longer Forgotten." Pennsylvania Education 2(Mr-Ap, 1970):19-23.

Krug, Mark. M. "For a Fair Deal in the Teaching of Reconstruction." Social Education, Ja, 1965.

McHugh, Raymond, and Rayner, Guy H., Jr. Land of the Free and Its Critics. Burlingame, CA: Publication Supply, California Teachers Association, O, 1967.

Monro, John. "Connecting American Historio-graphy--and Other Inequities." In The Campus and the Racial Crisis. Edited by David C. Nichols and Olive Mills. Washing-ton, DC: American Council on Education, 1970.

Moore, John Robert, and Fink, William B. "State History Textbook: Essays in Ethnocentrism." Journal of the Lancaster County Historical Society, Easter, 1968.

New York City Board of Education. The Negro in America: The End of a Myth. Manual for In-Service Teleivision Course. New York: Board of Education, S, 1964.

Payne, Robert Glen. "The Effects of Teaching the Concept Lesson, 'The Underground Railroad in Michigan,' to Black and White Fourth Grade Students." Doctoral dissertation, U. of Michigan, 1970.

Pearson, Floyd H. "A Content Analysis of the Treatment of Black People and Race Relations in United States History Textbooks." Doctoral dissertation, U. of Minnesota, 1976.

Reddick, L. D. "What Now Do We Learn of Race and Minorities People?" Journal of Negro Education, Summer, 1965.

Slavery Guide. ERIC ED 053 052, 1971.

"The Slavery Issue in Northern School Book Readers, Geographies & Histories, 1850-1878." Internationale/Jahrbuch Geschichte-und Geographieunterricht 13(1970-1971).

Stampp, Kenneth M., Jordan, Winthrop, D., Levine, Lawrence W., Middlekauff, Robert L., Sellers, Charles G., and Stocking, George W., Jr. "The Negro in American History Textbooks." Integrated Education, O-N, 1964.

Witt, William T. Racist Myths About Africa and Africans. Detroit: People Against Racism, F 1-Mr 1, 1968.

_____. Racist Myths About the Civil War. Detroit: People Against Racism, F 1-Mr 1, 1968.

_____. Racist Myths About the Era of Recon-struction. Detroit: People Against Racism, F 1-Mr 1, 1968.

_____. Racist Myths About the Period of Reunion and Reaction. Detroit: People Against Racism, F 1-Mr 1, 1968.

_____. Myths About the Peculiar Institution. Detroit: People Against Racism, F 1-Mr 1, 1968.

Bibliographies

Afro and Mexican-Americana, 1969. A Bibliography. Fresno, CA: The Library, Fresno State College, 1969.

Aptheker, Herbert (comp.). Annotated Biblio-graphy of the Published Writings of W. E. B. DuBois. Milwood, NY: Kraus-Thomson Organi-zation Limited, 1973.

_____. Writings of W. E. B. DuBois on Education." In The Education of Black People. Ten Critiques 1906-1960, pp. 159-167. Edited by Herbert Aptheker. Amherst, MA: U. of Massachusetts Press, 1973.

Bakewell, Dennis C. (comp.). The Black Experi-ence in the United States. Northridge, CA: San Frernando Valley College Foundation, 1970.

Bell, Barbara L. (comp.). Black Biographical Sources: An Annotated Bibliography. New Haven, CT: Yale U. Library, 1970.

Bethune, Lebert (comp.). Selected Bibliography on the Black Experience. New York: ERIC Clearinghouse on the Urban Disadvantaged, Teachers College, Columbia U., 1969.

A Bibliography of Books and Educational Media Related to Negro Culture. Miami, FL: Dade County Board of Public Instruction, 27 pp., Ap, 1969. Available from Textbook Dept., Board of Public Instruction, 2210 S.W. 3rd St., Miami, FL 33135, ERIC ED 046 829.

Black and Afro-American Art: Sources for Visual Materials. Albany, NY: Division of Humanities and Arts, NY Education Department, 22 pp., 1970. ERIC ED 048 312.

The Black Record. Commercial recordings on Afro-American topics, 1971. St. Louis, MO: Audio-Visual Department, Washington U. Libraries.

Brickman, William W. (comp.). Guide to Research in Educational History. New York: New York U. Bookstore, 1949.

Bridgford, Clay. Teaching About Minorities: An Annotated Bibliography on Blacks, Chicanos, and Indians. Boulder, CO: ERIC Clearinghouse for Social Studies/Social Science Education; Social Science Education Consortium, 18 pp., Ap, 1971. ERIC ED 049 970.

A Brief Listing of Bibliographies, Periodicals, and Curriculum Guides on Negro Literature and History. Ann Arbor, MI: Foreign Language Innovative Curricula Studies, 10 pp., F, 1969. ERIC ED 030 655. For a microfilm copy, send 25 cents to EDRS, The National Cash Register Company, Box 2206, Rockville, MD 20852.

Brignano, Russell C. (comp.). "Autobiographical Books by Black Americans: A Bibliography of Works Written Since the Civil War." Negro American Literature Forum 7(Winter, 1973): 148-156.

Brown, Carol (comp.). Afro-American History. Bloomington: Indiana U. Libraries and Focus: Black America, Summer, 1969.

Buffalo Public Schools. The Cultural and Historical Contributions of American Minorities: A Bibliography. Buffalo Public Schools, 1967.

Bureau of Naval Personnel, General Military Training & Support Division, Library Services Branch (comp.). Black Heritage: The American Experience. A Selected, Annotated Bibliography. Washington, DC: GPO, 1972.

Cederholm, Theresa D. (comp.). Afro-American Artists: A Bio-Bibliographical Directory. Boston: Boston Public Library, 1973.

Center for the Study of Instruction. A Selected Guide to Curriculum Literature: An Annotated Bibliography. Washington, DC: National Education Association, 1970.

Chung, Inso (comp.). Black Bibliography. Hayward, CA: Hayward State College, 1969.

Cohen, Hening (comp.). Articles in American Studies, 1954-1968. 2 vols. Ann Arbor, MI: Pieran Press, 1972.

Collins, L. M. Books by Black Americans. Nashville, TN: Fisk U., 1970, 56 pp. ERIC ED 051 856.

Committee on Treatment of Minorities in Library Books and Other Instructional Materials. "Multiethnic Media: Selected Bibliographies." School Libraries 19(Winter, 1970):49-57. Supplement, 19(Summer, 1970):44-47.

Cook, P. A. W. (comp.). "A Guide to the Literature on Negro Education." Teachers College Record 34(1933):671-677.

Cooper, Edna. "Bibliography of Robert E. Park." Phylon 6(1945):372-382.

Cordasco, Francesco, and Brickman, W. W. A Bibliography of American Educational History: An Annotated and Classified Guide. New York: AMS Press, 1975.

De'Ath, Colin and others. Black Education in the United States and Its Relevance to International Development Education. Black Education and Black Society in the United States: A Bibliography for Development Educators. Pittsburgh, PA: U. of Pittsburgh, School of Education, 56 pp., Ja, 1969. ERIC ED 048 047.

Davison, Ruth, and Legler, April (comps.). Government Publications on the Negro in America, 1948-1968. Bloomington: Indiana U. Libraries and Focus: Black America, Summer, 1969.

Edwards, Helen H. (comp.). A List of References for the History of Agriculture in the Southern United States, 1865-1900. Davis, CA: Agricultural History Center, U. of California, Mr, 1971.

Fediuk, Simon (comp.). Bibliography on Education. New York: New York State Division of Human Rights, Jl 1, 1970.

Fraser, Stewart E., with Reeves, Dorothy, and Peterson, Allan (comps.). British Commentary on American Education: A Select and Annotated Bibliography: The Nineteenth and Twentieth Centuries. London: Institute of Education, 1970.

Gersman, Elinor Mondale (comp.). "A Bibliography for Historians of Education." History of Education Quarterly 12(Spring, 1972):81-88.

Godbey, Gordon C. "The Negro & Adult Education: Some References from Selected Literature." Adult Leadership 18(Ap, 1970):309-310.

Haberbosch, John F. and others. <u>Annotated Bibliography: Afro-American, Hispano and Amerind; with Audio-Visual Materials List</u>. Denver, CO: Colorado State Department of Education, Division of Elementary and Secondary Education, 201 E. Colfax Street, Denver, CO 80203 (free upon request), 48 pp., Ap, 1969. ERIC ED 023 635. For a microfiche copy, send 25 cents to EDRS, The National Cash Register Company, Box 2206, Rockville, MD 20852.

Havelock Ronald G., Huber, Janet C., and Zimmerman, Shaindel (comps.). <u>Major Works on Change in Education. An Annotated Bibliography</u>. Ann Arbor, MI: Institute for Social Research, U. of Michigan, 1969.

Herman, Henrietta (ed.). <u>The American Negro: His History and His Contribution in Our Culture: A Bibliography Prepared for the Elementary Schools As a Part of the ESEA Title III Project</u>. Yonkers, NY: Yonkers City School District, 45 pp., Je, 1969. ERIC ED 041 086.

Hoerder, Dirk (comp.). <u>Protest, Direct Action, Repression: Dissent in American Society from Colonial Times to the Present</u>. Munich, Germany: Verlag Dokumentation, 1977.

Holt, Glen E. (comp.). "The Urban Negro American in the Twentieth Century: A Survey of Resources." In <u>Social and Economic Information for Urban Planning</u>, II, pp. 295-312. Edited by Doris B. Holleb. Chicago: Center for Urban Studies, U. of Chicago, 1969.

Houston, H. R. (comp.). "Contributions of the American Negro to American Culture: A Selected Checklist." <u>Bulletin of Bibliography</u> 26(J1, 1969):71-79.

Hudson, Ralph M. (comp.). "Afro-American Art: A Bibliography." <u>Art Education</u> 23(Je, 1970):20-23.

<u>Index to Selected Periodicals Received in the Hallie Q. Brown Library</u>. Decennial Cumulation 1950-1959. Edited by Charlotte W. Lytle. Boston: G. K. Hall & Co., 1961.

Jayarilleke, Raja. <u>Human Relations in the Classroom. An Annotated Bibliography: Supplement I. ERIC-IRCD Urban Disadvantaged Series, Number 28, June, 1972</u>. New York: Columbia U.; ERIC Clearinghouse on the Urban Disadvantaged, 102 pp., Je, 1972. ERIC ED 064 417.

Jenkins, Betty, Kent, Lorna, and Perry, Jeanne (comps.). <u>Kenneth B. Clark, A Bibliography</u>. New York: Metroplitan Applied Research Center, 1970.

Johnson, Charles S. and others. <u>Statistical Atlas of Southern Counties</u>. Chapel Hill, NC: The U. of North Carolina Press, 1941. [Bibliography, pp. 301-355, on Southern education]

Kaiser, Ernest. "In Defense of the People's Black and White History and Culture." <u>Freedomways</u> 10(Third Quarter, 1970):198-225.

_____. In Defense of the People's Black and White History and Culture. New York: <u>Freedomways</u>, 1971.

Kelley, Don Quinn. "The Political Economy of Booker T. Washington: A Bibliographic Essay." <u>Journal of Negro Education</u> 46(Fall, 1977): 403-418.

<u>Martin Luther King, Jr.: A Selected Reading List of Significant Books and Periodical Articles</u>. Afro-American Bibliographic Researcher, 3344 Lucas Hunt Road, Normandy, MO, F, 1971.

Knezo, Genevieve Johanna (comp.). <u>Social Service Policies: An Annotated List of Recent Literature</u>, July 8, 1971. In U.S. Congress, 92nd, 1st Session, Senate Committee on Labor and Public Welfare, Special Subcommittee on Evaluation and Planning of Social Programs, <u>Full Opportunity and National Goals and Priorities Act. Hearing</u>, pp. 113-190. Washington, DC: GPO, 1971.

Knox, Ellis O. (comp.). "Masters' Theses and Doctoral Dissertations [on Negro Education]." <u>Journal of Negro Education</u> 21(Winter, 1952): 61-88.

Lester, Julius. "The Black Experience." <u>New York Times Book Review</u>, Part II, F 15, 1970.

Lillard, Richard G. (comp.). <u>American Life in Autobiography</u>. Stanford, CA: Stanford U. Press, 1956.

Long Beach State College Library. <u>Black Bibliography. A Selected List of Books on Africa, Africans, and Afro-Americans</u>. Long Beach, CA: Long Beach State College, 1969.

McCabe, Jane A. (comp.). <u>Education and the Afro-American</u>. Bloomington: Indiana U. Libraries and Focus: Black America, Summer, 1969.

McPherson, James M., Holland, Laurence B., Banner, James M., Jr., Weiss, Nancy J., and Bell, Michael D. (comps.). <u>Blacks in America. Bibliographical Essays</u>. Garden City, NY: Doubleday, 1971.

Michigan Department of Education. <u>Adult Basic Education</u>. A Bibliography of Materials. Lansing, MI: State Department of Education, 1969.

Michigan Department of Education. <u>The Heritage of the Negro in America</u>. A Bibliography. Revised edition. Lansing, MI: Department of Education, 1970.

Molenda, Michael. <u>Annotated Bibliography on the Educational Implications of Cable Television (CATV)</u>. Greensboro, NC: School of Education, North Carolina U., 29 pp., Ja, 1972. ERIC ED 059 607.

Moore, Mary Jo (comp.). A Preliminary Bibliography of American English Dialects. Washington, DC: Center for Applied Linguistics, 61 pp, N, 1969. ERIC ED 033 327. For a microfiche copy, send 50 cents to EDRS, The National Cash Register Company, Box 2206, Rockville, MD 20852.

Morain, Genelle. "Teaching for Cross-Cultural Understanding: An Annotated Bibliography." Foreign Language Annals 5(O, 1971):82-83.

"Multi-Ethnic Media: Selected Bibliographies." School Libraries 19(Winter, 1970):49-57.

"Multi-Ethnic Media: Selected Bibliographies (Supplement II)." School Libraries 20 (Summer, 1971):42-48.

"Multi-Ethnic Media: Selected Bibliographies (Supplement III)." School Libraries 21 (Summer, 1972):47-54.

Navarro, Joseph P. (comp.). "Carey McWilliams and Ethnic Relations." Journal of Mexican American History 2(Fall, 1971):20-21. [Bibliography]

The Negro Freedom Movement: Past and Present. An Annotated Bibliography. Detroit, MI: Wayne County Intermediate School District, 107 pp., My, 1967. ERIC ED 030 681. For a microfiche copy, send 50 cents to EDRS, The National Cash Register Company, Box 2206, Rockville, MD 20852.

Parker, John W. (comp.). "A Bibliography of the Published Writings of Benjamin G. Brawley." North Carolina Historical Review 34(Ap, 1957):165-178.

Partington, Paul G. (comp.). W. E. B. DuBois. A Bibliography of His Published Writings. The Author, 7320 South Gretna Avenue, Whittier, CA 90606.

Psencik, Leroy F. (comp.). "Teaching Black History in Secondary Schools: A Bibliography." History Teacher 6(My, 1973).

Rancier, Gordon J., and Brooke, W. Michael. An Annotated Bibliography of Adult Basic Education. Ottawa (Ontario): Canadian Dept. of Regional Economic Expansion, 280 pp., Ag, 1970. Available from Queen's Printer, Ottawa, Canada. ERIC ED 050 328.

Reardon, William R., and Pawley, Thomas D. (eds.). The Black Teacher and the Dramatic Arts: A Dialogue, Bibliography, and Anthology. Westport, CT: Negro Universities Press, 1970.

Ross, Frank S., and Kennedy, Louise V. (comps.). A Bibliography of Negro Migration. New York: Columbia U. Press, 1935.

Rugh, Patricia A., and Scardamalia, Marlene L. Learning Problems of the Migrant Child. Annotated Bibliography. Lewisburg, PA: Bucknell U., 15 pp., Ag, 1967. ERIC ED 036 380.

San Fernando Valley State College. Black Brown Bibliography. Northridge, CA: Library, The College, 1968.

Seig, Vera (comp.). The Negro Problem: A Bibliography. Madison, WI: Wisconsin Free Library Commission, 1908.

Shumway, Gary L. (comp.). Oral History in the United States. A Directory. New York: Oral History Association, 1971.

Sjolund, James, and Burton, Warren (comps.). Music of Minority Groups. Part I: The American Negro: A Selected Bibliography of Materials Including Children's books, Reference Books, Collections and Anthologies, Recordings, Films and Filmstrips. Olympia, WA: Washington State Office of Public Instruction, 11 pp., 1969. ERIC ED 042 842.

Slonaker, John (comp.). The U.S. Army and the Negro. A Military History Research Collection Bibliography. Carlisle Barracks, PA: U.S. Army Military History Research Collection, Ja, 1971.

Smith, Donna M., and Fitch, Judith Pruess. Team Teaching Bibliography. Minneapolis, MN: Upper Midwest Regional Educational Lab, Inc., 103 pp., 1969. ERIC ED 035 098.

Smith, Dwight L. (comp.). Afro-American History. A Bibliography. Santa Barbara, CA: ABC-CLIO, 1974.

Smith, Edwin H., and Bradtmueller (comps.). A Selected Annotated Bibliography of Instructional Literacy Materials for Adult Basic Education. Tallahassee, FL: State Department of Education, 1968.

Smith, Jessie Carney. "Developing Collections of Black Literature." Black World 20 (Je, 1971):18-29.

Smith, Suzanne M. An Annotated Bibliography of Small Town Research. Madison, WI: Department of Sociology, U. of Wisconsin, 142 pp., 1970. ERIC ED 042 562.

Spaights, Ernest, and Hudson, Audrey C. "Educational Opoortunity: A Review of the Literature." Education 92(S-O, 1971):4-13.

Sullivan, Margaret (comp.). A Bibliography of Lillian Smith and Paula Snelling with an Index to South Today. Memphis, TN: John Willard Brister Library, Memphis State U., 1971.

Tarone, Elaine. A Selected Annotated Bibliography on Social Dialects, for Teachers of Speech and English. Seattle, WA: U. of Washington, 41 pp., 1970. ERIC ED 043 853.

Thompson, Bryan, and Vance, Mary (eds.).
Ethnic Groups in Urban Areas; Community
Formation and Growth: A Selected Biblio-
graphy. Council of Planning Libraries
Exchange Bibliography Series, Number 202.
Monticello, IL: Council of Planning
Librarians, 18 pp., Jl, 1971. ERIC ED
060 148.

Tirotta, Richard (comp.). No Crystal Stair.
A Bibliography of Black Literature (10th
edition of The Negro in the United States.)
New York: New York Public Library,
1971.

Tomkins, Dorothy Campbell (comp.). Poverty in
the United States During the [Nineteen]
Sixties. A Bibliography. Berkeley, CA:
Institute of Governmental Studies, U. of
California, Berkeley, 1970.

Tri-College Consortium. The Negro in American
History: A Selective Bibliography. Atlanta,
GA: United Board for College Development,
159 Forrest Avenue, N.E., Suite 514, 1970.

U.S. Air Forces in Europe, Reference Library.
The Black American. AD-739 402.
Springfield, VA: National Technical In-
formation Service, O 1, 1971. [Bibliography]

U.S. Bureau of Education. Analytical Index to
Barnard's American Journal of Education.
Washington, DC: GPO, 1892. [1855-1881]

U.S. Department of Health, Education, and
Welfare, Social Security Administration.
Poverty Studies in the Sixties. A Selected
Annotated Bibliography. Washington, DC:
GPO, Ap, 1970.

Vail Memorial Library. Catalog of the Special
Negro and African Collection. 2 vols.
Lincoln University, PA: Vail Memorial
Library, Lincoln U, 1970.

Wakstein, Allen M. (comp.). A Bibliography of
Urban History. Monticello, IL: Council of
Planning Librarians, 1975.

Walters, Mary Dawson (comp.). Afro-Americana:
A Comprehensive Bibligrophy of Resource
Materials in the Ohio State University
Libraries By or About Black Americans.
Columbus, OH: Ohio State U. Libraries, 1969.

Walton, Hanes, Jr. (comp.). The Study and
Analysis of Black Politics: A Bibliography.
Metuchen, NJ: Scarecrow Press, n.d.

Waserman, Manfred J. (comp.). Bibliography on
Oral History. New York: Oral History
Association, 1971.

Williams, Daniel T. (comp.). Eight Negro
Bibliographies. New York: Kraus Reprint
Co., 1970.

Williams, F., and Naremore, R. C. (comps.).
Language and Poverty: An Annotated
Bibliography. Madison, WI: Institute for
Research in Poverty, 1967.

Worster, Stanley R., and Heathman, James
(comps.). Rural Education and Small Schools,
A Selected Bibliography. University Park,
NM: New Mexico State U., N 19, 1969. ERIC
Clearinghouse on Rural Education and Small
Schools. ERIC ED 033 257. For a
microfiche copy, send 75 cents to EDRS, The
National Cash Register Company, Box 2206,
Rockville, MD 20852.

Young, Beverly S., and Garde, Linda Vande
(comps.). A Bibliography of High-Interest-
Low Vocabulary Books. Iowa City, IA:
Division of Extension and University Services, U. of Iowa, 1967.

2.
CHILDREN

Biological Factors

Abraham, Sidney, Lowenstein, Frank W., and O'Connell, Daniel E. Preliminary Findings of the First Health and Nutrition Examination Survey, United States, 1971-1972: Anthropometric and Clinical Findings. Washington, DC: GPO, Ap, 1975.

Abraham, Sidney, Lowenstein, Frank W., and Joynson, Clifford L. Preliminary Findings of the First Health and Nutrition Examination Survey, United States, 1971-1972: Dietary Intake and Biochemical Findings. Washington, DC: GPO, 1974.

Adler, Sol. The Health and Education of the Economically Deprived Child. St. Louis, MO: Warren H. Green, Inc., 1968.

Allen, R. L., and Michel, David L. "The Negro and Learning to Swim: The Buoyancy Problem Related to Reported Biological Differences." Journal of Negro Education, Fall, 1969.

Altes, Jane, and Bittner, Marguerite. Birth Weight, Early Childhood, and School Achievement, Je, 1974. ERIC ED 095 237.

Anand, J. K. "The Smells of Prejudice." New Society, Jl 11, 1968. [The biology of human smells]

Askins, Billy E. and others. Effect of the Responsive Environment Early Education Program for Low Birth Weight Children of Preschool Age, Ap, 1977. ERIC ED 138 352.

Barnard, Kathryn E., and Douglas, Helen Bee (eds.). Child Health Assessment. Part I: A Literature Review. Washington, DC: GPO, D, 1974.

Barr, G. D. and others. "Height and Weight of 7,500 Children of Three Skin Colors." American Journal of Diseases of Children 124(D, 1972):866-872.

Beasley, Daniel S., and Beasley, Daun C. "Auditory Reassembly Abilities of Black and White First- and Third-Grade Children." Journal of Speech and Hearing Research 16 (Je, 1973):213-221.

Bejar, J., and Regmovic, V. Final Report: The Secondary Analysis of the Cali Intervention Project. Evanston, IL: Division of Methodology and Evaluation Research, Northwestern U., 1977.

Birch, Herbert G. "Health and the Education of Socially Disadvantaged Children." Developmental Medicine and Child Neurology 10(1968): 580-599.

_____. "Malnutrition, Learning, and Intelligence." American Journal of Public Health 62(Jl, 1972):773-784.

Birch, Herbert G., and Gussow, Joan D. Disadvantaged Children. Health, Nutrition, and School Failure. New York: Harcourt Brace Jovanovich, Inc., and Grune & Stratton, 1970.

Birch, Herbert G. and others. "Relation of Kwashiorkor in Early Childhood and Intelligence at School Age." Pediatric Research 5 (Spring, 1971):579-585.

Black, Bill. "Hungry Children Come First." Integrated Education 58(Jl-Ag, 1972):55-57. [Testimony of May 26, 1971, before the U.S. Senate Select Committee on Nutrition and Human Needs]

Bowe, Frank G., Jr. "Educational, Psychological, and Occupational Aspects of the Nonwhite Deaf Population." Journal of Rehabilitation of the Deaf 5(Ja, 1972):33-39.

_____. "Non-white Deaf Persons: Educational, Psychological, and Occupational Considerations: A Review of the Literature." American Annals of the Deaf 116(Je, 1971): 357-361.

Brazier, Mary A. B. (ed.). Growth and Development of the Brain: Nutritional, Genetic and Environmental Factors. New York: Raven Press, 1975

Brown, Kenneth and others. "Prevalence of Anemia Among Pre-adolescent and Young Adolescent Urban Black Americans." Journal of Pediatrics 81(O, 1972):714-718.

Brown, Roy E. "Decreased Brain Weight in Malnutrition and Its Implications." East African Medical Journal (N, 1965):584-595.

_____. Starving Children: The Tyranny of Hunger. New York: Springer, 1977. [Nigeria, Bangladesh, and Mississippi]

Brown, Roy E., and Halpern, Florence. "The Variable Pattern of Mental Development of Rural Black Children. Results and Interpretations of Results of Studies on Mississippi Children Aged One Week to Three Years by the Gesell Developmental Scales." Clinical Pediatrics 10(1971):404-409.

Bulatao-Jayme, J., et al. Implications of Malnutrition in Preschool Children. Manila, Philippines: Food and Nutrition Research Center, 1972.

Cabak, V., and Nejdanvic, R. "Effect of Undernutrition in Early Life on Physical and Mental Development." Archives of Disease in Childhood 40(1965):532-534.

Castile, Anne S., and Jerrick, Stephen J. "School Health in America: A Summary Report of a Survey of State School Health Programs." Journal of School Health 46(Ap, 1976):216-221.

Chase, Helen C. "Infant Mortality and Weight at Birth: 1960 United States Birth Cohort." American Journal of Public Health 59(1969): 1618-1628. [Black-white differentials]

_____. Trends in Low Birth Weight Ratios. United States and Each State. 1950-68. Washington, DC: GPO, Jl, 1973.

_____ (ed.). "A Study of Risks, Medical Care, and Infant Mortality." American Journal of Public Health 63, Supplement(S, 1973):1-56. [Blacks and Puerto Ricans in New York City]

Chase, Harold P., and Martin, H. P. "Undernutrition and Child Development." New England Journal of Medicine 282(Ap 23, 1970):933-939.

Christmas, June Jackson. "How Our Health System Fails Minorities." Civil Rights Digest 10(Fall, 1977):3-11.

Comptroller General of the U.S. The Summer Feeding Program for Children: Reforms Begun, Many More Urgently Needed. Washington, DC: General Accounting Office, Mr 31, 1978.

Cook, Judith and others. "A Survey of the Nutritional Status of School Children: Relation Between Nutrient Intake and Socio-Economic Factors." British Journal of Preventive and Social Medicine 27(My, 1973): 91-99.

Coursin, David Baird. "Nutrition and Brain Development in Infants." Merrill-Palmer Quarterly 18(Ap, 1972):177-202.

Craig, Patricia A., and McEarphron, Norman B. Studies of Handicapped Students. Vol I: Whom Do Teachers Identify as Handicapped? Menlo Park, CA: Stanford Research Institute, 1976.

Cravioto, J., and DeLicardie, E. R. "The Long-Term Consequences of Protein-Calorie Malnutrition." Nutrition Review 29(My, 1971): 107-111.

_____ and _____. "Nutrition and Behavior and Learning." World Review of Nutrition and Dietetics 16(1973):80-96.

Cravioto, Joaquin, Hambraeus, Lief, and Vahilquist, Bo (eds.). Early Malnutrition and Mental Development. Stockholm: Almquist & Wilssell, 1974.

Damon, A. "Race, Ethnic Group and Disease." Social Biology 16(1969):69-80.

Davenport, Yolande B. "Depressive Illness: Problems of Diagnosis in Children and Blacks." Integrateducation 13(S-O, 1975): 19-23.

Davis, Karen, and Schoen, Cathy. Health and the War on Poverty: A Ten-Year Appraisal. Washington, DC: Brookings Institution, 1978.

Dennis, Ruth E. "Social Stress and Mortality Among Nonwhite Males." Phylon 38(S, 1977): 315-328.

Dorman, M. F., and Geffren, Donna S. "Hemispheric Specialization for Speech Perception in Six-Year-Old Black and White Children from Low and Middle Socioeconomic Classes." Cortex 10(Je, 1974):171-176.

Drillien, Cecil Mary. "School Disposal and Performance for Children of Different Birthweights Born 1953-1960." Archives of Diseases of Children 44(1969). [Birthweight and I.Q.]

Ellis, C. Edward. "Growth, Intelligence, and School Performance in Children with Cystic Fibrosis Who Have Had an Episode of Malnutrition During Infancy." Journal of Pediatrics 87(O, 1975):565-568.

Epstein, E. H., and Weisbrod, B. A. "Parasitic Diseases and Academic Performance of Schoolchildren." Social and Economic Studies 23 (D, 1974).

Evans, T. N. "Prenatal Nutrition and Later Education." Integrated Education 10(Je-Ag, 1972).

Evans, Therman, E. "On the Health of Black Americans." Ebony 32(Mr, 1977):112.

Eyer, Joseph, and Stirling, Peter. "Stress-Related Mortality and Social Organization." Review of Radical Political Economics 9 (Spring, 1977):1-44.

Falkner, Frank (ed.). Key Issues in Infant Mortality. Washington, DC: Government Printing Office, 1970.

Finnerty, Frank A., and others. "Hypertension in the Inner City." Circulation 47(Ja, 1973):73-75.

Fomon, Samuel J., and Anderson, Thomas A. (eds.). Practices of Low-Income Families in Feeding Infants and Small Children with Particular Attention to Cultural Subgroups. Washington, DC: GPO, 1972.

Ford, Nelson, and DBS Corporation. "Racial Ethnic Background Findings." In Analysis of 1973 Participation of Handicapped Children in Local Education Programs, pp. 18-26, S 15, 1975. Arlington, VA: DBS Corporation.

Frisch, Rose E. "Does Malnutrition Cause Permanent Mental Retardation in Human Beings?" Psychiatr. Neurol. Neurochir. 74(N-D, 1971): 463-479.

_____. "Present Status of the Supposition that Malnutrition Causes Permanent Mental Retardation." American Journal of Clinical Nutrition 23(1970):189-195.

Gallaudet College. Ethnic Background in Relation to Other Characteristics of Hearing Impaired Students in the United States. ERIC ED 132 785, Ag, 1975.

Goggin, James E. and others. "Observations of Postnatal Developmental Activity in Infants with Fetal Malnutrition." Journal of Genetic Pscyhology 132(Je, 1978):247-253.

Gortmaker, Steven L. Poverty, Race, and Infant Mortality in the United States. ERIC ED 145 032, Mr, 1977.

Greene, Lawrence S. (ed.). Malnutrition, Behavior, and Social Organization. New York: Academic Press, 1977.

Gussow, Joan Dye. "Bodies, Brains and Poverty: Poor Children and the Schools." IRCD Bulletin 6(S, 1970):3-4,9-12.

Harburg, E. and others. "Socio-ecological Stress, Suppressed Hostility, Skin Color, and Black-White Male Blood Pressure: Detroit." Psychosomatic Medicine 35(1973):276-296.

Haughton, James G. "Trends in Morbidity and Mortality in the Negro American." Integrated Education, Je-Jl, 1967.

Hawrylewicz, E. J., and Chow, Bacon E. (eds.). The Relationship of Perinatal Nutrition to Brain Development. Nutrition Reports International 4(N, 1971).

Henderson, Maureen, and Cowan, Linda. Morbidity and Mortality in American Blacks. ERIC ED 126 222, O, 1974.

Henderson, Norman B. and others. Contributions of Selected Perinatal Variables to Seven-Year Psychological and Achievement Test Scores, Ap, 1971. ERIC ED 054 216.

Hercules, John J. and others (eds.). Proceedings of the First National Symposium on Sickle Cell Disease. Bethesda, MD: National Institutes of Health, 1974.

Hertzig, Margaret E. and others. "Intellectual Levels of School Children Severely Malnourished During the First Two Years of Life." Pediatrics 49(Je, 1972):814-824.

"Highlights from the Ten-State Nutrition Survey." Nutrition Today 7(Jl-Ag, 1972):4-11.

Honesty, Eva T. "The Handicapped-Negro Child." Journal of Negro Education 1(Jl, 1932):304-324.

"Hungry Children Lag in Learning." Opportunity 1(My, 1971):10-13.

"Hypertension is Different in Blacks." Journal of the American Medical Association 216(Je 7, 1975):1634-1635.

Ireland, Charles S. "The Health Woes of Blacks." Reader's Digest, Je, 1976.

Isaac, Blanche K. "Perceptual-Motor Development of First Graders as Related to Class, Race, Intelligence, Visual Discrimination, and Motivation." Journal of School Psychology 11 (Mr, 1973):47-56.

Jensema, Carl. The Relationship Between Academic Achievement and the Demographic Characteristic of Hearing Impaired Children and Youth, S, 1975. ERIC ED 131 121.

Jernison, Harry. Evolution of the Brain and Intelligence. New York: Academic Press, 1973.

Jewett-Baranski, Grace, and Allen, Fred H. "Serving the Deaf: Black and White." Community 34(Summer, 1975):9-14.

Kallen, David J. Nutrition, Development and Social Behavior. Proceedings of the Conference on the Assessment of Tests of Behavior from Studies of Nutrition in the Western Hemisphere. Washington, DC: GPO, 1973.

Keil, Julian Eugene. "Hypertension: Effects of Social Class and Racial Admixture in a Negro Community of Charleston, South Carolina." Doctoral dissertation, U. of North Carolina, 1975. Univ. Microfilm Order No. 76-20092.

Kelly, James E., and Scanlon, James V. Decayed, Missing, and Filled Teeth Among Children. United States. Washington, DC: GPO, Ag, 1971.

Kernodle, Ruth. "Appetite and Hunger Among Southern Negro Children." Master's thesis, Alabama Polytechnic Institute, 1929.

Kiple, Kenneth F., and Kiple, Virginia H. "Slave Child Mortality: Some Nutritional Answers to a Perennial Puzzle." Journal of Social History 10(Mr, 1977):284-309.

Knobloch, H., and Pasamanick, B. "Prospective Studies on the Epidemiology of Reproductive Casuality: Methods, Findings, and Some Implications." Merrill-Palmer Quarterly, Ja, 1966.

Knox, J. H. Mason. "Morbidity and Mortality in the Negro Infant." Transactions of the American Pediatric Society 36(1924).

Kornegay, Francis A. Minorities and Malnutrition. ERIC ED 129 937, D, 1975.

Ladson, Melvin. "Media and the Affective Domain of Minority Deaf Children." American Annals of the Deaf 117(O, 1972):482-484.

Latham, Michael C. "Protein-Calorie Malnutrition in Children and its Relation to Psychological Development and Behavior." Psychological Review 54(J1, 1974):541-565.

Latham, Michael C., and Cobos, F. "The Effects of Malnutrition on Intellectual Development and Learning." American Journal of Public Health 61(J1, 1971):1307-1324.

Leveson, Irving, Ullman, Doris, and Wassall, Gregory. The Effects of Improved Health on Productivity Through Education. Santa Monica, CA: Rand, 1968.

Levine, Seymour. Neuroendocrine Factors in Mother and Infant. Bethesda, MD: National Institute of Child Health and Human Development, 1968.

Lewis, Andrew H. "A Comparison of Body Buoyancy of Black and White Males and Females Between the Ages of Nine and Fourteen." Master's thesis, U. of Tennessee, 1974.

Lloyd-Still, John D. and others. "Intellectual Development After Severe Malnutrition in Infancy." Pediatrics 54(S, 1974):306-311.

_____ (ed.). Malnutrition and Intellectual Development. Littleton, MA: Publishing Sciences Group, 1976.

Lowe, Charles, and Alexander, Duane. "Health Care of Poor Children." In Children and Decent People. Edited by Alvin Schorr. New York: Basic Books, 1974.

McCandless, Boyd R. and others. "Perceived Opportunity, Delinquency, Race and Body Build Along Deliquent Youth." Journal of Consulting and Clinical Psychology 38 (Ap, 1972):281-287.

McClure, John W. "Two Views of Black and White Swimmers." Integrated Education(My-Je, 1972):40-43.

MacIsaac, David S. "Learning and Behavioral Functioning of Low Income, Black Preschoolers with Asymptomatic Lead Poisoning." Doctoral dissertation, Fordham U., 1976. Univ. Microfilm Order No. 76-25,778.

Malina, Robert M. "Skinfolds in American Negro and White Children." Journal of the American Dietetic Association 59(J1, 1971):34-40.

Malina, Robert M., Hamill, Peter, and Lemeshaw, Stanley. Body Dimensions and Proportions, White and Negro Children 6-11 Years. United States. Washington, DC: GPO, D, 1974.

Malnutrition, Learning, and Behaviour. Cambridge, MA: M.I.T. Press, 1969.

Martin, H.P. "Nutrition: Its Relationship to Children's Physical, Mental, and Emotional Development." American Journal of Clinical Nutrition 28(J1, 1973):766-775.

Mayer, Jean. "The Nutritional Status of American Negroes." Nutrition Reviews 23(Je, 1965): 161-164.

Mazur, Allan, and Robertson, Leon S. Biology and Social Behavior. New York: Free Press, 1972.

Monckeberg, F. and others. "Malnutrition and Mental Development." American Journal of Clinical Nutrition 25(Ag, 1972):766-772.

Montagu, Ashley. "Sociogenic Brain Damage." American Anthropologist 74(O, 1972):1045-1061.

Naeye, Richard L., and Blanc, William A. "Relation of Poverty and Race to Antenatal Infection." New England Journal of Medicine 283(1970):555-559.

Naeye, Richard L., Blanc, William A., and Paul, Cheryl. "Effects of Maternal Malnutrition on the Human Fetus." Pediatrics, O, 1973.

Naeye, Richard L., Diener, M. M., and Dellinger, W. S. "Urban Poverty: Effects on Prenatal Nutrition." Science 166(1969):1026.

National Institute of Child Health and Human Development. Child Health and Human Development: Research Program. Washington, DC: GPO, 1972.

Nutrition and Intellectual Growth in Children. Washington, DC: Association for Childhood Education International, 1969.

Paige, David M., Bayless, Theodore M., and Graham, George G. "Milk Programs: Helpful or Harmful to Negro Children?" American Journal of Public Health 62(1972).

Paige, David M., and Graham, George G. "School Milk Programs and Negro Children: A Nutritional Dilemma." Journal of School Health 44(Ja, 1974):8-10.

Paige, David M. and others. "Nutritional Supplementation of Disadvantaged Elementary-School Children." Pediatrics 58(N, 1976): 697-703.

Paige, J. C. "Health Programs for the Disadvantaged: Implications for School Health." Journal of School Health 40(Mr, 1970):123-126.

Pan American Health Organization and World Health Organization. Seminar on Malnutrition in Early Life and Subsequent Mental Development. Mona, Jamaica, Ja 10-14, 1972. PAHO Scientific Publication No. 251, 1972.

Pasamanick, Benjamin. "Comment on 'The Epidemiological Distribution of CNS Dysfunction.'" Journal of Social Issues 27(1971):129-137. [On racism and scientific research on disturbances of the central nervous system]

Penchaszadeh, V. and others. "Growth and Development in an 'Inner City' Population: An Assessment of Possible Biological and Environmental Influences, II. The Effect of Certain Maternal Characteristics on Birth Weight, Gestational Age and Intra-Uterine Growth." Johns Hopkins Medical Journal 131 (Jl, 1972):11-23.

Perino, Joseph, and Eruhart, Claire B. "The Relation of Subclinical Lead Level to Cognitive and Sensorimotor Impairment in Black Preschoolers." Journal of Learning Disabilities 7(D, 1974):616-620 .

Perkins, Stanley A. "Malnutrition: A Selected Review of its Effects on the Learning and Behavior of Children." International Journal of Early Childhood 5(1973):173-180.

_____. "Malnutrition and Mental Development." Exceptional Children 43(Ja, 1977):214-219.

Pettigrew, Ann Hallman, and Pettigrew, Thomas F. "Race, Disease and Desegregation: A New Look." Phylon, Winter, 1973.

Piaget, Jean. Biology and Knowledge. An Essay on the Relations between Organic Regulations and Cognitive Processes. Chicago: U. of Chicago Press, 1971.

Pierre, Thelma. "The Relationship Between Hypertension and Psycho-Social Functioning in Young Black Men." Journal of Afro-American Issues 4(Summer, 1976):408-419.

Platt, B. S. "Early Malnutrition and Later Intelligence." Developmental Medicine and Child Neurology 10(1968):233.

_____. Nutrition and Psycho-Social Deprivation. Bethesda, MD: National Institute of Child Health and Human Development, 1968.

Prescott, James W., Read, Merrill S., and Coursin, David B. (eds.). Brain Function and Malnutrition: Neuropsychological Methods of Assessment. New York: Wiley, 1975.

Ramey, Craig T., and Smith, Barbara J. "Assessing the Intellectual Consequences of Early Intervention with High-Risk Infants." American Journal of Mental Deficiency 81(Ja, 1977):318-324.

Read, Merrill S. "Malnutrition and Mental Development," pp. 2671-2682 in U.S. Congress, 91st, 1st session, Senate, Select Committee on Nutrition and Human Needs, Nutrition and Human Needs . . . Hearings, Part 8. Washington, DC: GPO, 1969.

_____. Malnutrition, Learning, and Behavior. Bethesda, MD: Center for Research for Mothers and Children, U.S. Department of Health, Education, and Welfare, 1976.

"The Relationship of Nutrition to Brain Development and Behavior." Nutrition Today 9 (Jl-Ag, 1974):12-13,16-17.

Ricciuti, Henry N. Malnutrition, Learning, and Intellectual Development: Research and Remediation. ERIC ED 039 017, S, 1969.

Richardson, Stephen A., and Emerson, P. "Race and Physical Handicap in Children's Preference for Other Children: A Replication in a Southern City." Human Relations 23(1970): 31-36.

Richardson, Stephen A. and others. "School Performance of Children Who Were Severely Malnourished in Infancy." American Journal of Mental Deficiency 77(Mr, 1973):623-632.

Rippey, Robert. "Are You There? Can You Hear Me?" Integrated Education: Race and Schools 8(S-O, 1969):3-9.

Roberts, Jean. Eye Examination Findings Among Youths Aged 12-17 Years. United States. Washington, DC: GPO, N, 1975.

_____. Hearing Sensitivity and Related Medical Findings Among Youths Aged 12-17 Years. United States. Washington, DC: GPO, N, 1975.

Roberts, Jean, and Maurer, Kurt. Blood Pressure Levels of Persons 6-74 Years: United States, 1971-1974. Hyattsville, MD: National Center for Health Statistics, 1977.

_____ and _____. Blood Pressure of Youths 12-17 Years, United States. Washington, DC: GPO, 1977.

Robinson, John S. Special Milk Program Evaluation and National School Lunch Program Survey. Washington, DC: Food and Nutrition Service, U.S. Department of Agriculture, 1978.

Roche, A.F., Roberts, Jean, and Hamill, Peter. Skeletal Maturity of Children 6-11 Years: Racial, Area, and Socio-economic Differentials, United States. Rockville, MD: National Center for Health Statistics, 1975.

Rosenwaike, I. "The Influence of Socioeconomic Status on the Incidence of Low Birth Weight." HSMHA Reports 86(J1, 1971):641-649.

Rubin, Barbara A. "Black Skin." Journal of School Health 47(Je, 1977):365-367.

Rushing, William David. "Relationship of Malnutrition and Mental Functioning." Doctoral dissertation, Southern Illinois U., 1975. Univ. Microfilm Order No. 76-26,962.

Salvatore, Santo. The Ability of Elementary and Secondary School Children to Sense On-coming Car Velocity. Injury Control Research Laboratory, H.E.W. Washington, DC: GPO, 1972. [DHEW Pub. No. (HSM) 72-10015]

Sandstead, Harold M. and others. "Nutritional Deficiencies in Disadvantaged Preschool Children." American Journal of Diseases of Children 121(Je, 1971):455-463.

Seham, Max. Blacks and American Medical Care. Minneapolis: U. of Minnesota Press, 1973.

Scheinfeld, Sandra J. P. "Malnutrition and Poverty in the United States: A Chicago Case Study." Doctoral dissertation, U. of Chicago, 1976.

Schmeck, Harold M., Jr. "Brain Harm in U.S. Laid to Food Lack." New York Times, N 2, 1975.

Scott, R. B., Ferguson, A. D., Jenkins, M. E., and Cutter, F. F. "Growth and Development of Negro Infants." Pediatrics 16(1955):24-29.

Selham, Max. "Poverty, Illness, and the Negro Child." Pediatrics 46(Ag, 1970):305-311.

Shiloh, Ailon, and Selevan, Ida Cohen. Ethnic Groups of America. Their Morbidity, Mortality and Behavior Disorders. Vol II: The Blacks. Springfield, IL: Charles C. Thomas, 1974.

Shnoeur, Elie A. The Malnourished Mind. Garden City, NY: Doubleday, 1974.

Shnoeur, Elie A., and Shnoeur, Joan B. "Malnutrition and Learning." Prospects 7(1977): 3-13.

Smart, K. F. (ed.). Malnutrition and Endemic Diseases: Their Effects on Education in the Developing Countries. Hamburg: Unesco Institute for Education, 1972.

Soewondo, S. and others. "The Effect of Nutritional Status on Some Aspects of Intelligence." Paediatr. Indones. 11(S-O, 1971): 28-36.

Southern Regional Council. Hungry Children. Atlanta, GA: Southern Regional Council, 1967.

Stein, Zena and others. "Nutrition and Mental Performance." Science 178(N, 1972):708-713. [Netherlands]

Stoch, M. B., and Smythe, P. M. "The Effect of Undernutrition During Infancy on Subsequent Brain Growth and Intellectual Development." South African Medical Journal 41(1967):1027.

Stott, D. H. "Children in the Womb: The Effects of Stress." New Society 40(My 19, 1977):329-331.

Swartz, Hillary, and Leitch, Cynthia J. "Differences in Mean Adolescent Blood Pressure by Age, Sex, Ethnic Origin, Obesity, and Familial Tendency." Journal of School Health 45(F, 1975):76-82.

Terris, Milton. "Desegregating Health Statistics." American Journal of Public Health 63(Je, 1973):477-480.

Thompson, Harriet L. "Malnutrition as a Possible Contributing Factor to Learning Disabilities." Journal of Learning Disabilities 4 (Je-J1, 1971):312-315.

Tjossen, T. (ed.). Intervention Strategies for High-Risk Infants and Young Children. Baltimore: University Park Press, 1976.

Tizard, Jack. "Can the Brain Catch Up?" World Health, F-Mr, 1974, pp. 10-15. [Malnutrition]

Torchia, Marion M. "Tuberculosis among American Negroes: Medical Research on a Racial Disease, 1830-1950." J. Hist. Medicine Allied Sci. 32(J1, 1977):252-279.

U.S. Congress, 90th, 1st Session, Senate, Committee on Labor and Public Welfare, Subcommittee on Labor and Public Welfare. Hunger and Malnutrition in America. Hearings. Washington, DC: GPO, 1967.

U.S. Congress, 90th, 2nd Session, House of Representatives, Committee on Agriculture. Hunger Study. Washington, DC: GPO, Je 11, 1968.

U.S. Congress, 90th, 2nd Session, House of Representatives, Committee on Agriculture. Hunger Study Supplement. Washington, DC: GPO, Ag 17, 1968.

U.S. Congress, 90th, 2nd Session, House of Representatives, Committee on Education and Labor. Malnutrition and Federal Food Service Programs. Hearings . . . Part 1. Washington, DC: GPO, 1968.

U.S. Congress, 90th, 2nd Session, Senate, Committee on Government Operations, Subcommittee on Government Research. Human Resources Development. Hearings . . . Deprivation and Personality--A New Challenge to Human Resources Development. 2 parts. Washington, DC: GPO, 1968.

U.S. Congress, 90th, 2nd Session and 91st, 1st Session, Senate, Select Committee on Nutrition and Human Needs. Hearings, 2 parts. Washington, DC: GPO, 1969.

U.S. Congress, 90th, 2nd Session, Senate, Committee on Labor and Public Welfare, Subcommittee on Employment, Manpower, and Poverty. Hunger and Malnutrition in the United States . . . Hearings . . . My-Je, 1968. Washington, DC: GPO, 1968.

U.S. Congress, 92nd, 1st Session, Senate, Committee on Agriculture and Forestry, Subcommittee on Agricultural Research and General Legislation. Child Nutrition Programs. Hearing . . . Washington, DC: GPO, 1971.

U.S. Congress, 92nd, 1st Session, Senate, Select Committee on Nutrition and Human Needs. Nutrition and Human Needs--1971. Hearings . . . Part 4--P.L. 91-248--Implementation, 1970. Amendments to the National School Lunch Act. Washington, DC: GPO, 1971.

U.S. Congress, 92nd, 1st Session, Senate, Select Committee on Nutrition and Human Needs. Nutrition and Human Needs--1971. Hearings . . . Part 9--Universal School Lunch Program. Washington, DC: GPO, 1971.

U.S. Congress 92nd, 2nd Session, Senate, Committee on Agriculture and Forestry, Subcommittee on Agricultural Research and General Legislation. Extension of Child Nutrition Programs. Hearing . . . Washington, DC: GPO, 1972.

U.S. Congress, 92nd, 2nd Session, Senate, Select Committee on Nutrition and Human Needs. Studies of Human Need. Washington, DC: GPO, 1972.

U.S. Congress, 92nd, 2nd Session, Senate, Select Committee on Nutrition and Human Needs. Nutrition and Human Needs--1972. Hearings . . . Part 1--School Breakfast Program Survey. Washington, DC: GPO, 1972.

U.S. Congress, 93rd, 1st Session, Senate, Select Committee on Nutrition and Human Needs. Hunger--1973. Washington, DC: GPO, 1973.

U.S. Congress, 93rd, 2nd Session, Senate, Select Committee on Nutrition and Human Needs. To Save the Children. Nutritional Intervention Through Supplemental Feeding. Washington, DC: GPO, 1974.

U.S. Congress, 95th, 1st Session, House of Representatives, Committee on Agriculture. Commission on Domestic and International Hunger and Malnutrition. Washington, DC: GPO, 1977.

U.S. Congress, 95th, 1st Session, House of Representatives, Committee on Interstate and Foreign Commerce, Subcommittee on Health and the Environment. Child Health Assessment Act: Hearings . . . Washington, DC: GPO, 1977.

U.S. Congress, 95th, 2nd Session, House of Representatives, Committee on Education and Labor. Child Nutrition Amendments of 1978: Report . . . Washington, DC: GPO, 1978.

U.S. Department of H.E.W. The Health of Children--1970. Washington, DC: GPO, 1970.

U.S. Department of Health, Education, and Welfare, Public Health Service. Body Weight, Stature, and Sitting Height: White and Negro Youths 12-17 Years, United States. Washington, DC: GPO, Ag, 1973.

U.S. Department of Health, Education, and Welfare. Health. United States. 1975. Washington, DC: GPO, 1976.

U.S. Department of Health, Education, and Welfare. The Nation's Youth. A Chart Book. Children's Bureau Pub. No. 460. Washington, DC: GPO, 1969.

U.S. Department of Health, Education, and Welfare, Public Health Service, National Institute of Child Health and Human Development. Perspectives on Human Deprivation: Biological, Psychological, and Sociological. Washington, DC: GPO, 1968.

U.S. National Institute of Health. If You're Black, Here Are Some Facts You Should Know About High Blood Pressure. Bethesda, MD: National Institute of Health, 1978.

U.S. Office of Health Resources Opportunity. *Health of the Disadvantaged.* Hyattsville, MD: Office of Health Resources Opportunity, 1977.

U.S. Public Health Service. *Differentials in Health Characteristics by Color. United States, July 1965-June, 1967.* Washington, DC: GPO, O, 1969.

U.S. Public Health Service. *An Assessment of the Occlusion of the Teeth of Children. 6-11 Years. United States.* Washington, DC: GPO, N, 1973.

U.S. Public Health Service. *Children and Youth. Selected Health Characteristics. United States--1958 and 1968.* Washington, DC: GPO, F, 1971.

U.S. Public Health Service. *Eye Examination Findings Among Children. United States.* Washington, DC: GPO, Je, 1972.

U.S. Public Health Service. *Health Characteristics of Low-Income Persons.* Washington, DC: GPO, Ju, 1972.

U.S. Public Health Service. *Hearing and Related Medical Findings Among Children: Race, Area, and Socioeconomic Differentials, United States.* Washington, DC: GPO, O, 1972. [Data, 1963-1965]

U.S. Public Health Service. *Hearing Levels of Children by Demographic and Socioeconomic Characteristics.* Washington, DC: GPO, F, 1972.

U.S. Public Health Service. *Height and Weight of Children: Socioeconomic Status. United States.* Washington, DC: GPO, O, 1972.

U.S. Public Health Service. *Infant Mortality Rates: Socioeconomic Factors. United States.* Washington, DC: GPO, Mr, 1972. 1964-1966 data.

U.S. Public Health Service. *Minority Health Chart Book.* Washington, DC: H.E.W., 1974.

U.S. Public Health Service. *Skeletal Maturity of Children 6-11 Years: Racial, Geographic Area, and Socioeconomic Differentials. United States.* Washington, DC: GPO, O, 1975.

Ventura, Stephanie J. *Selected Vital and Health Statistics in Poverty and Nonpoverty Areas of 19 Large Cities. United States, 1969-71.* Washington, DC: GPO, N, 1975. [Race as control variable]

Vogt, Dorothee K. *Health Attitudes and Behavior of Youths 12-17 Years: Demographic and Socioeconomic Factors, United States.* Washington, DC: GPO, O, 1975.

Vore, David A. "Prenatal Nutrition and Postnatal Intellectual Development." *Merrill Palmer Quarterly* 19(O, 1973):252-260.

Walker, A. R., Richardson, B. D., and Walker, F. "Nutrition and Intelligence." *South African Medical Journal* 44(Je 20, 1970):717-718.

Walter, John P. "Nutritional Determinants of Urban Deprived Youth: An Economic and Cross-Cultural Analysis of the U.S., Colombia, and Peru." *Comparative Urban Research* 4(1977): 61-74.

Wan, Thomas T. H., and Tarver, James D. "Socioeconomic Status, Migration, and Morbidity." *Social Biology* 19(Mr, 1972):51-59.

Warren, N. "Malnutrition and Mental Development." *Psychological Bulletin* 80(1973): 314-328.

Welsing, Frances Cress. "The 'Conspiracy' to Make Blacks Inferior." *Ebony* 29(S, 1974): 84-94.

Werner, E., Simonian, K., Bierman, J. M., and French, F. E. "Cumulative Effect of Perinatal Complications and Deprived Environment on Physical, Intellectual, and Social Development of Preschool Children." *Pediatrics* 39(1967):490-505.

Wiener, S., and Milton, T. "Demographic Correlates of Low Birth Weight." *Am. J. Epidemiol.* 91(Mr, 1970):260-272.

Wiener, S. and others. "Correlates of Low Birth Weight: Psychological Status at Six to Seven Years of Age." *Pediatrics* 35(Mr, 1965):434-444.

Willerman, Lee. "Biosocial Influence on Human Development." *American Journal of Orthopsychiatry* 42(Ap, 1972):452-462.

Williams, Richard Allen (ed.). *Textbook of Black-Related Diseases.* New York: McGraw-Hill, 1975.

Winick, Myron. *Malnutrition and Brain Development.* New York: Oxford U. Press, 1976.

_____. "Nutrition and Mental Development." *Med. Clin. North Am.* 54(N, 1970):1413-1429.

Tests and Measurements

Abraham, Theodore. "The Influence of Examiner Race on First-Grade and Kindergarten Subjects' Peabody Picture Vocabulary Test Scores." *Journal of Educational Measurement* 6(Winter, 1969):241-246.

Ace, M. E. "Psychological Testing: Unfair Discrimination?" *Industrial Relations* 10(O, 1971).

Adkins, Dorothy C., Payne, Frank D., and Ballif, Bonnie L. "Motivation Factor Scores and Response Set Scores for Ten Ethnic-Cultural Groups of Preschool Children." American Educational Research Journal 9(Fall, 1972):557-572. [Oahu, Hawaii]

Afram Associates, Inc. Black Experience Test. New York: Afram Associates, Inc., 1970.

Abbott, William L., and Gunn, Harry E. "Bender-Gestalt Performance by Culturally Disadvantaged First Graders." Perceptual and Motor Skills 33(Ag, 1971):247-250.

Alcorn, Charles L., and Miholson, Charles L. "Validity of the Slosson Drawing Coordination Test with Adolescents of Below-Average Ability." Perceptual and Motor Skills 34(F, 1972):261-262.

Ames, Louise B., and August, J. "Rorschach Responses of Negro and White Five to Ten Year Olds." Journal of Genetic Psychology 109 (1966):297-309.

Ammon, Paul R., and Sue, Mary. "Effects of Training Black Preschool Children in Vocabulary Versus Sentence Construction." Journal of Educational Psychology 62(O, 1971):421-426.

Anastasi, Anne, and Cordova, Fernando A. "Some Effects of Bilingualism upon the Intelligence Test Performance of Puerto Rican Children in New York City." Journal of Educational Psychology, Ja, 1953.

Angoff, William A., and Ford, Susan F. "Item-Race Interaction on a Test of Scholastic Aptitude." Journal of Educational Measurement 10(Summer, 1973):95-106.

Ansell, Edgar M. "An Assessment of Vocational Maturity of Lower-Class Caucasions, Lower-Class Negroes and Middle-Class Caucasions in Grades Eight through Twelve." Doctoral dissertation, State U. of New York at Buffalo, 1970.

Anthony, John J. "A Comparison of Wechsler Preschool and Primary Scale of Intelligence and Stanford Binet Intelligence Scale Scores for Disadvantaged Preschool Children." Psychology in the Schools 10(, 1973):297-299.

Arnold, Karen South, and Reed, Lauren. "The Grammatic Closure Subtest of the ITPA: A Comparative Study of Black and White Children." Journal of Speech and Hearing Disorders 41(N, 1976):477-485.

Asbury, Charles A. "An Essay on the Proper Relation Between Testing and School Desegregation: A Non-Technical Opinion." Journal of Negro Education 47(Winter, 1978):69-71.

_____. "The Methodology Used in the Jencks Report: A Critique." Journal of Negro Education 42(Fall, 1973):530-536.

Babad, Elisha Y. and others. "Bias in Scoring the WISC Subtests." Journal of Consulting and Clinical Psychology 43(Ap, 1975).

Baca, Leonard, and Cervantes, Hermes. "The Assessment of Minority Students: Are Adaptive Behavior Scales the Answer?" Psychology in the Schools 15(Jl, 1978):366-370.

Backman, Margaret E. "Patterns of Mental Abilities: Ethnic, Socioeconomic and Sex Differences." American Educational Research Journal 9(Winter, 1972):1-12.

_____. "Relationships of Ethnicity, Socioeconomic Status, and Sex to Patterns of Mental Abilities." Doctoral dissertation, Columbia University, 1970.

Baldwin, Alexinia Young. "Tests Can Underpredict: A Case Study." Phi Delta Kappan, Ap, 1977. [24 black children]

Barabasz, Arreed F. and others. "Focal-Point Dependency in Inversion Perception Among Negro, Urban Caucasian and Rural Caucasian Children." Perceptual and Motor Skills 31 (Ag, 1970):136-138.

Barabasz, Arreed F. "Galvanic Skin Response and Test Anxiety Among Negroes and Caucasians." Child Study Journal 1(Fall, 1970):33-35.

_____. "Group Desensitization of Test Anxiety in Elementary School." Journal of Psychology 83(Mr, 1973):295-301.

Baratz, "Effect of Race of Experimenter, Instructions, and Comparison Population Upon Level of Reported Anxiety in Negro Subjects." Journal of Personality and Social Psychology, O, 1967.

Barclay, Allan G., and Cusumano, D. R. "Testing Masculinity in Boys Without Fathers." Transaction, D, 1967.

Barnebey, Norma S. "The Effect of the Race of Examiner on the Test Performance of Negro and White Children." Proceedings of the 81st Annual Convention of the American Psychological Association 8(1973):649-650.

_____. "The Study of the Effect of the Race of Examiner on the Test Performance of Negro and White Children." Doctoral dissertation, Ohio State U., 1972.

Barnes, Edward J. "IQ Testing and Minority School Children: Imperatives for Change." Journal of Non-White Concerns 2(O, 1973):4-19.

Baron, Reuben M. "The SRS Model as a Predictor of Negro Responsiveness to Reinforcement." Journal of Social Issues 26(Spring, 1970):61-81.

Baron, Reuben M., and Ganz, Richard L. "Effects of Locus of Control and Type of Feedback on the Task Performance of Lower-Class Black Children." Journal of Personality and Social Psychology 21(Ja, 1972):124-130.

Barritt, Loren S. A Comparison of the Auditory Memory Performance of Negro and White Children from Different Socio-Economic Backgrounds. ERIC ED 029 350, F 1, 1969.

Bartlett, Donald P. and others. "Raven Progressive Matrices: An Item and Set Analysis of Subjects Grouped by Race, Sex, and Social Class." Journal of Consulting and Clinical Psychology 38(F, 1972).

Baughman, E. Earl, and Dahlstrom, W. Grant. "Racial Differences on the Minnesota Multiphasic Personality Inventory." In Black Psyche: The Modal Personality Patterns of Black Americans. Edited by S.S. Guterman. Berkeley, CA: Glendessary, 1972.

Bayley, Nancy. "Comparisons of Mental and Motor Test Scores for Ages 1-15 Months by Sex, Birth Order, Race, Geographical Location, and Education of Parents." Child Development 36(1965):379-411.

Beckham, Albert Sidney. "A Study of Race Attitudes in Negro Children of Adolescent Age." Journal of Abnormal and Social Psychology 29(Ap-Je, 1934):18-29.

Beckwith, James P., Jr. "Constitutional Requirements for Standardized Ability Tests Used in Education." Vanderbilt Law Review 26 (My, 1973):789-821.

Bennett, George K. and others. "Response to Robert Williams." Counseling Psychologist 2 (Fall, 1970):88-96. [On charges of racism in testing]

Bernauer, Edmund, and Chui, Edward. "Anthropometric and Physical Fitness Characteristics of Four Ethnic Groups of High School Boys." Educational Perspectives 12(O, 1973):15-18.

Bert, Deborah L. "Race of Examiner Effects on the Racial Attitude Responses of Preschool Children." Master's thesis, Wake Forest U., 1972.

Bikson, Tora K. Standardized Testing and the Status of Children's Intellectual Rights. Santa Monica, CA: Rand Corporation, F, 1977.

_____. "The Status of Children's Intellectual Rights." Journal of Social Issues 34, No. 2 (1978):69-86.

Birns, Beverly, and Golden, Mark. "Prediction of Intellectual Performance at 3 Years from Infant Tests and Personality Measures." Merrill Palmer Quarterly 18(Ja, 1972):52-53.

Bonner, Mary W. "A Comparative Study of the Performance of Negro Seniors of Oklahoma City High School on the Wechsler Adult Intelligence Scale and the Peabody Picture Vocabulary Test." Diss. Abstr. Intl. 1969, 30 (3-A) 921.

Bosma, Boyd. "The NEW Testing Moratorium." Journal of School Psychology 11(1972):304-306.

Bowles, Frank L. "Sub-Test Score Changes Over Twenty Months on the Wechsler Intelligence Scale for Children for White and Negro Special Education Students." Diss. Abstr. Intl. 1969, 30 (1-A) 54-5.

Bradley, Robert H. and others. "Home Environment, Social Status, and Mental Performance." Journal of Educational Psychology 69(D, 1977):697-701.

Breland, Hunter M. An Investigation of Cross-Cultural Stability in Mental Test Items. ERIC ED 093 916, Ap, 1974.

Bridgeman, Brent, and Buthram, Joan. "Race Differences on Nonverbal Analogy Test Performance as a Function of Verbal Strategy Training." Journal of Educational Psychology 67(Ag, 1975):586-590.

Brooks, J. R. "Achievement Test for Indian Children (ATIC) Progress Report." Northian 13(Spring, 1978):20-27.

Bryen, Diane N. "Speech-Sound Discrimination Ability on Linguistically Unbiased Tests." Exceptional Children 42(Ja, 1976):195-201.

Bucky, Steven F. "The Interaction Between Negro and White Preschool Children and Negro and White Experimenters and Its Effect on Tests on Motor Impulse Control, Reflectivity, Creativity and Curiosity." Diss. Abstr. Intl. 31, 9-B (Mr, 1971) 5616-17.

Budoff, Milton, and Corman, Louise. The Effectiveness of a Group Training Procedure on the Raven Learning Potential Measure with Children from Diverse Racial and Socioeconomic Backgrounds. ERIC ED 086 923, 1973.

Burnes, Kay. "Clinical Assumptions About WISC Subtest Score and Test Behavior Relationships." Journal of Consulting and Clinical Psychology 36(Ap, 1971):299.

_____. "Patterns of WISC Scores for Children of Two Socioeconomic Classes and Races." Child Development 41(Je, 1970):493-499.

Callicut, Laurie T. "The Construction and Evaluation of Parallel Tests of Reading in English and Spanish." Doctoral dissertation, U. of Texas, 1942.

Cameron, Colin (comp.). Discrimination in Testing. Bibliography. Revised, Ap, 1973. ERIC ED 086 736.

Campbell, Joel T. "Tests Are Valid for Minority Groups Too." Public Personnel Management 2 (Ja, 1973):70-73.

Cantor, Gordon N. "Effects of Familiarization on Children's Ratings of Pictures of Whites and Blacks." Child Development 43(D, 1972): 1219-1229.

Carver, Ronald P. "The Coleman Report: Using Inappropriately Designed Achievement Tests." American Educational Research Journal 12 (Winter, 1975):77-86.

_____. "Designing an Aural Aptitude Test for Negroes: An Experiment that Failed." College Board Review, Winter, 1968-69.

Cerbus, George, and Oziel, L. Jerome. "Correlation of the Bender-Gestalt and WISC for Negro Children." Perceptual and Motor Skills 32(F, 1971):276.

Chissom, Brad S., and Thomas, Jerry R. "Relationship Between Perceptual-Motor and Academic Measures for Disadvantaged Pre-School Children." Perceptual and Motor Skills 36 (F, 1973):152-154.

Chovan, William L., and Hathaway, Mildred L. "The Performance of Two Culturally Divergent Groups of Children on a Culture-Free Test." Journal of School Psychology 8(1970):66.

Cicirelli, Victor G. and others. "Performance of Disadvantaged Primary Grade Children on the Revised Illinois Test of Psycholinguistic Abilities." Psychology in the Schools 8(Jl, 1971):240-246.

Clasby, Miriam, Webster, Maureen, and White, Naomi. Laws, Tests and Schooling. Changing Contexts for Educational Decision-Making. Syracuse, NY: Syracuse U. Research Corporation, O, 1973.

Cleary, T. Anne. Test Bias: Validity of the Scholastic Aptitude Test for Negro and White Students in Integrated Colleges. Princeton, NJ: Educational Testing Service, 1966.

Cleary, T. Anne, and Hilton, Thomas L. An Investigation of Item Bias. ERIC ED 211 269.

Cleary, T. Anne and others. "Educational Uses of Tests with Disadvantaged Students." American Psychologist 30(Ja, 1975):15-41.

Coffman, William E. "Developing Tests for the Culturally Different." School and Society, N 13, 1965.

Cohen, Rosalie. "The Influence of Conceptual Rule-Sets on Measures of Learning Ability." In Race and Intelligence, pp. 41-57. Edited by C. Loring Brace, George R. Gamble, and James T. Bond. Washington, DC: American Anthropological Association, 1971.

Colarusso, Ronald and others. "Use of the Peabody Picture Vocabulary Test and the Slosson Intelligence Test with Urban Black Kindergarten Children." Journal of Special Education 11(Winter, 1977):427-433.

Cole, Spurgeon, and Hunter, Mildred. "Pattern Analysis of WISC Scores Achieved by Culturally Disadvantaged Children." Psychological Reports 29(Ag, 1971):191-194.

"Competency Testing: Potential for Discrimination." Clearinghouse Review, S, 1977.

Condie, J. Spencer, and Christiansen, James W. "An Indirect Technique for the Measurement of Changes in Black Identity." Phylon 38 (Mr, 1977):46-54.

Cook, Keith E. Differences between Self-Concepts of Disadvantaged and Non-Disadvantaged High School Students Within Certain Types of Rural and Urban Communities. Final Report. ERIC ED 037 797, S, 1969.

Cooper, James G. The Effects of Ethnicity Upon School Achievement. ERIC ED 157 675, 1977. [New Mexico]

Cornwell, Henry G. Comparison of Changes in Self-Image of Black and White Students Kindergarten Through High School. Final Report. ERIC ED 051 308, N, 1970.

Cosby, Arthur G., and Picou, J. Steven. "Structural Models and Occupational Aspirations: Black-White Variations Among Deep-South Adolescents." Journal of Vocational Behavior 3(Ja, 1973):1-14.

Costello, Joan, and Faizunisa, Ali. "Reliability and Validity of Peabody Picture Vocabulary Test Scores of Disadvantaged Preschool Children." Psychological Reports 28(Je, 1971): 755-760.

Cowles, Milly, and Daniel, Kathryn Barchard. Psycholinguistic Behaviors of Black, Disadvantaged Rural Children. ERIC ED 039 037, Mr 5, 1970.

Cox, Roy, "Traditional Examination in a Changing Society." Universities Quarterly 27(Spring, 1973):200-216.

Currier, Joseph R. "Relationship of Race-Image of Negro Males to Figure-Ground Perception in a Black-White Perceptual Field." Doctoral dissertation, U. of Maryland, 1971.

Darlington, Richard B. "Another Look at 'Cultural Farmers.'" Journal of Educational Measurement 8(Summer, 1971):71-82.

Datta, Lois-ellin. Changes in Observed Social Interactions Among Children of Same and Other Ethnic Groups in Ethnically Heterogeneous Preschool Programs. ERIC ED 077 569, 1972.

Datta, Lois-ellin and others. Sex and Scholastic Aptitude as Variables in Teachers' Ratings of the Adjustment and Classroom Behavior of Negro and other Seventh Grade Students. ERIC ED 028 206, 1966.

Davis, Frederick B. The Measurement of Mental Capability Through Evoked-Potential Recordings. Greenwich, CT: Education Records Bureau, 1971.

Dawkins, Arthur, and Snyder, Robert. "Disadvantaged Junior High School Students Compared with Norms of Seashore Measures." Journal of Research in Music Education 20(Winter, 1972):438-444.

Dean, Raymond S. "Analysis of the PIAT with Anglo and Mexican-American Children." Journal of School Psychology 15(Winter, 1977): 329-333. [Peabody Individual Achievement Test]

_____. "Reliability of the WISC-R with Mexican-American Children." Journal of School Psychology 15(F, 1977):267-268.

Denmark, Florence L. and others. Communication Patterns in Integrated Classrooms and Pre-integration Subject Variables as they Affect the Academic Achievement and Self-concept of Previously Segregated Children. ERIC ED 016 721, Ag, 1967.

Dershowitz, Zecharia, and Frankel, Yaakov. "Jewish Culture and the WISC and WAIS Test Patterns." Journal of Consulting and Clinical Psychology 43(Ap, 1975):126-134.

Diamond, James J. and others. "Are Inner City Children Test-Wise?" Journal of Educational Measurement 14(Spring, 1977):39-46.

Dickerson, Ann Elizabeth. "Social-Class Differences in the Performance of Black Preschoolers on Tests of Information Identification." Doctoral dissertation, U. of Illinois, 1975. Univ. Microfilm Order No. 76-06747.

Diener, Robert, and Maroney, Robert J. "Relationship Between Quick Test and WAIS for Black Male Adolescent Underachievers." Psychological Reports 34(Je, 1974):1232-1234.

Divas, Chris. "The Effect of Motion Pictures Portraying Black Models on the Self-Concept of Black Elementary School Children." Diss. Abstr. Intl. 31, 6A (D, 1970) 2609-2610.

Dinsmore, Grant C. "Developmental Bender Gestalt Performance as a Function of Educational Setting and Sex of Young Negro Schoolchildren." Doctoral dissertation, U. of Pennsylvania, 1972.

Dinucci, James M., and Shows, David A. "A Comparison of the Motor Performance of Black and Caucasian Girls Age 6-8." Research Quarterly 48(D, 1977):680-684.

Dodd, William E. "Background and Situational Factors Related to Anxiety in Negro Test Performance." Doctoral dissertation, New York U., 1972.

Doke, Larry A. Stimulus Generalization Across Individuals Along Dimensions of Sex and Race: Some Findings with Children from an All-Negro Neighborhood. Progress Report. ERIC ED 042 297, Ag, 1969.

Doll, Paddy A. and others. "Experimenter Effect on Sex-Role Preference Among Black and White Lower-Class Male Children." Psychological Reports 29(D, 1971):1295-1301.

Doucette, John, and St. Pierre, Robert. Anchor Test Study: School, Classroom, and Pupil Correlates of Fifth-Grade Reading Achievement. ERIC ED 141 418, 1977.

Dreger, R., and Miller, K. "Comparative Psychological Studies of Negroes and Whites in the United States." Psychological Bulletin, 1960, 361-402.

_____ and _____. "Comparative Psychological Studies of Negroes and Whites in the United States, 1959-1965." Psychological Bulletin, Monograph Supplement, S, 1968.

Drew, Clifford J. "Criterion-Referenced and Norm-Referenced Assessment of Minority Group Children." Journal of School Psychology 11 (1973):323-329.

Droege, Robert G. Alternatives to a Moratorium on Testing. ERIC ED 053 199, Ap, 1971.

Dube, Gary B., and Rudolph, Jeffrey A. "Performance of the Black Head Start Children on the Vane Kindergarten Test and the Stanford-Binet as Related to Age and Sex Variables." Journal of Clinical Psychology 34(Ap, 1978): 431-437.

Dubin, Jerry A. "Effects of Practice and Speed on Negro and White Mental Ability Test Performances. Diss. Abstr. Intl. 1969, 30 (1-B) 367-8.

Dugas, Edmond A. The Influence of Observers of the Same Race and a Racially Mixed Audience on Level of Aspiration and Gross Motor Performance of College Males. 31, 9-A (Mr, 1971) 4516.

Dunn, Charleta J., and Payne, Bill F. The Effects of Group Guidance Upon the Self-Esteem, Interpersonal Relationships, and Educational Achievement of the Culturally Different Child. Houston, TX: College of Education, U. of Houston, S, 1969. [East Texas]

Duprey, Harold J., and Gruvaeus, Gunnar. The Construction and Utility of Three Indexes of Intellectual Achievement. Hyattsville, MD: National Center for Health Statistics, S, 1977.

Dyer, Patricia J. "Effects of Test Conditions on Negro White Differences in Test Scores." Doctoral dissertation, Columbia U., 1970.

Eagle, Norman, and Harris, Anna S. "Interaction of Race and Test on Reading Performance Scores." Journal of Educational Measurement Fall, 1969.

Educational Change: Implications for Measurement. Proceedings of the 1971 Invitational Conference on Testing Problems. Princeton, NJ: Educational Testing Service, 1972.

Educational Measurement and the Law. Princeton, NJ: Educational Testing Service, 1978.

Edwards, C. D. "Semantic Generalization of an Operant Conditional Response to Positive and Negative Evaluative Words in Preschool Children." Master's thesis, Wake Forest U., 1968.

Edwards, C. D., and Williams, John E. "Generalization Between Evaluative Words Associated with Racial Figures in Preschool Children." Journal of Experimental Research in Personality 4(1970):144-155.

Eichorn, Dorothy H. Effects of Biological and Psychosocial Deprivation on Physical Growth and Motor Development. Bethesda, MD: National Institute of Child Health and Human Development, 1968.

Elder, Glen H., Jr. Age Groups, Status Transitions, and Socialization. Bethesda, MD: National Institute of Child Health and Human Development, 1968.

Elenbogen, Elaine M., and Thompson, Glen Robbins. "A Comparison of Social Class Effects in Two Tests of Auditory Discrimination." Journal of Learning Disabilities 5 (Ap, 1972):209-212.

Entwisle, Doris R., and Greenberger, Ellen. A Survey of Cognitive Style in Maryland Ninth Graders. II. Test Anxiety. Baltimore, MD: Center for Social Organization of Schools, Johns Hopkins U., My, 1970.

Eppes, John W. "The Effect of Varying the Race of the Experimenter on the Level of Aspiration of Externally Controlled Inner City School Children." Diss. Abstr. Int'l. 1970 (Ag) Vol. 31 (2-13) 912.

Epps, Edgar G. "Situational Effects in Testing." In The Testing of Black Students: A Symposium. Edited by L.P. Miller. Englewood Cliffs, NJ: Prentice-Hall, 1974.

Estrada, Elette S. "Production Deficiency of Nonverbal Mediators in Young Rural Black Children." Diss. Abstr. Int'l. Vol. 31 (9-A) (Mr, 2972) 4543.

Farley, Frank H., and Dowling, Phyllis M. "Aesthetic Preference in Adolescents as a Function of Race and Visual Complexity." Studies in Art Education 13 (Winter, 1972): 23-26.

Featherstone, Joseph. "Learning and Testing." New Republic, D 15, 1973.

Feldman, David H., and Markwalder, Winston. "Systematic Scoring of Ranked Distractors for the Assessment of Piagetian Reasoning Levels." Educational and Psychological Measurement 31(Summer, 1971):347-362.

Felen, Barbara K. Information Processed by Negro and Caucasian Children Engaged in Problem-Solving Tasks. ERIC ED 061 101, Ap, 1972.

Fishbein, Ronald L. The Fairness of Test Items for Statistically Equated Groups. ERIC ED 139 820, Ap, 1977.

Fishman, Jacob and others. "Guidelines for Testing Minority Group Children." Journal of Social Issues, Ap, 1964.

Fishman, Joshua A. "Minority-Group Testing." College Board Review 80(Summer, 1971):32-33. [A letter]

Fitzgibbon, Thomas J. (ed.). Evaluation in the Inner City. Report of an Invitational Conference on Measurement in Education. New York: Harcourt, Brace and World, 1970.

Flaugher, Ronald L. "The New Definitions of Test Fairness in Selection: Developments and Implications." Educational Researcher 3 (0, 1974):13-16.

_____. Project Access Research Report No. 2: Patterns of Test Performance by High School Students of Four Ethnic Identities. ERIC ED 055 102, My, 1971.

_____. Testing Practices, Minority Groups, and Higher Education: A Review and Discussion of the Research. ERIC ED 063 324, Je, 1970.

Flowers, C. E. "Effects of an Arbitrary Accelerated Group Placement on the Tested Academic Achievement of Educationally Disadvantaged Students." Doctoral dissertation, Teachers College, Columbia U., 1966.

Flynn, John T., and Anderson, Barbara E. "The Effect of Test Administration Procedures on Achievement Test Performance." Journal of Negro Education 45(Winter, 1976):37-45.

Foley, J. W., Jr. "Effects of Racial and Color Labels on Semantic Differential Ratings of Negroes and Caucasians." Master's thesis, Wake Forest U., 1968.

Fowles, Barbara R., and Kimple, James A. "Language Tests and the 'Disadvantaged' Reader." Reading World 11(Mr, 1972):183-195.

Gaertner, Samuel, and Bickman, Leonard. "Effects of Race on the Elicitation of Helping Behavior: The Wrong Number Technique." Journal of Personality and Social Psychology 20(N, 1971):218-222.

Gallagher, Buell G. (ed.). NAACP Report on Minority Testing. New York: NAACP Special Contribution Fund, 1976.

Gay, Geneva, and Abrahams, Roger D. "Does the Pot Melt, Boil, or Brew? Black Children and White Assessment Procedures." Journal of School Psychology 11(1973):330-340.

Geffner, D. S., and Hochberg, J. "Ear Laterality Performance of Children From Low and Middle Socioeconomic Levels on a Verbal Dichotic Listening Task." Cortex 7(Je, 1971):193-203.

Geiger, Edwin L., and Epps, Edgar G. Effects of Social Class Integration of Preschool Negro Children on Test Performance and Self-Concept. Final Report. ERIC ED 050 831, Je, 1970.

Gillooly, William B., and Thomas, C. L. The Effects of Familiarization on the Verbal Intelligence Test Performance of Socially Disadvantaged Youth. New Brunswick, NJ: Rutgers, U., Je, 1970.

Ginther, Joan R., and Begle, E. G. The Effect of Pretraining Chicano Students on Parallel Test Items Before Administration of a Mathematics Predictor Test. ERIC ED 142 407, Ag, 1975.

Goffeney, Barbara and others. "Negro-White, Male-Female Eight-Month Developmental Scores Compared With Seven-Year WISC and Bender Test Scores." Child Development 42(Je, 1971):595-604.

Gonzalez, Carlos M. "Effects of Ethnic Background, Socioeconomic Status, Education, General Mental Ability, English Proficiency, and Age on Aptitude Test Scores." Doctoral dissertation, New Mexico State U., 1977. Univ. Microfilm Order No. 7817139.

Goolsby, Thomas M., Jr., and Frary, Robert B. "Validity of the Metropolitan Readiness Test for White and Negro Students in a Southern City." Educational and Psychological Measurement 30(Summer, 1970):443-450. [Gulf-port, Mississippi]

Gottesman, Ruth L. "Auditory Discrimination in Negro Dialect-Speaking Children." Journal of Learning Disabilities 5(F, 1972):94-101.

Gould, Lawrence J., and Klein, Edward B. "Performance of Black and White Adolescents on Intellectual and Attitudinal Measures as a Function of Race of Tester." Journal of Consulting and Clinical Psychology 37(1971):195-200.

Green, Donald Ross. Racial and Ethnic Bias in Achievement Tests and What To Do About It. Monterey, CA: CTB/McGraw-Hill, 1973.

_____. Racial and Ethnic Bias in Test Construction. Final Report. ERIC ED 056 090, S 24, 1971.

_____. "What Does It Mean to Say a Test Is Biased?" Education and Urban Society 8(N, 1975):33-52.

Green, Richard B., and Rohwer, William D., Jr. "SES Differences on Learning and Ability Tests in Black Children." American Educational Research Journal 8(N, 1971):601-609.

Greenberger, Ellen, Campbell, Paul, Sorensen, Aage B., and O'Connor, Jeanne. Toward the Measurement of Psychosocial Maturity. Center for the Social Organization of Schools, Johns Hopkins U., Report No. 110, Jl, 1971.

Griffiths, Anita. Tests as a Form of Rejection of Minority Group Children. ERIC ED 055 289, 1971.

Grimmett, Sadie. The Influence of Ethnicity and Age on Solving Twenty Questions. Nashville, TN: Demonstration and Research Center for Early Education, George Peabody College, 1970.

Guilford, Joan S. Development of a Values Inventory for Grades 1 Through 3 in Five Ethnic Groups. Progress Report. ERIC ED 043 083, Jl 15, 1970.

Guilford, Joan S. and others. Development of a Values Inventory for Grades 1 Through 3 in Five Ethnic Groups. Final Report. ERIC ED 050 178, Ja, 1971.

Guinn, Nancy, Tupes, Ernest C., and Alley, William E. Demographic Differences in Aptitude Test Performance. Lackland Air Force Base, TX: Personnel Research Division, Air Force Human Resources Laboratory, Air Force Systems Command, My, 1970.

Gunnings, Thomas S. "Response to Critics of Robert L. Williams." Counseling Psychologist 2(1971):73-77.

Guthrie, George M. and others. A Culture-Fair Information Test of Intelligence. ERIC ED 054 212, Ag, 1970.

Gynther, Malcolm D. and others. "False Positive Galore: The Application of Standard MMPI Criteria to a Rural, Isolated, Negro Sample." Journal of Clinical Psychology 27(Ap, 1971):234-237.

Hall, Joseph C., and Chansky, Norman M. "Relationships Between Selected Ability and Achievement Tests in an Economically Disadvantaged Negro Sample." Psychological Reports 28(Je, 1971):741-742.

Hammill, Donald, and Wiederholt, J. Lee. "Appropriateness of the Metropolitan Tests in an Economically Deprived, Urban Neighborhood." Psychology in the Schools 8(Ja, 1971):49-50.

Haney, Joanne H., and Hooper, Frank H. "A Developmental Comparison of Social Class and Verbal Ability Influences on Piagetian Tasks." Journal of Genetic Psychology 122(Je, 1973): 235-245.

Hankins, Norman and others. "Correlations Between WISC-R Subtests and Verbal, Performance, and Full Scale IQ Scores for Minority Group Children." Psychology in the Schools 15(Ap, 1978):154-159.

Harris, Albert J., and Lovinger, Robert J. "Longitudinal Measures of the Intelligence of Disadvantaged Negro Adolescents." School Review, Mr, 1968.

Harrison, Murelle G., Messe, Lawrence S., and Stollak, Gary E. "Effects of Racial Composition and Group Size on Interactional Patterns in Preschool Children." Proceedings of the Annual Convention of the APA 6, PA (1971):325-326.

Harrison, Murelle G. and others. The Effects of Racial Composition and Group Size on Interaction Patterns in Preschool Children. ERIC ED 059 495, 1970.

Hawkes, Thomas, and Koff, Robert H. "Difference in Anxiety of Private and Inner City Public Elementary School Children." Psychology in the Schools 7(Jl, 1970):250-259.

Hawkes, Thomas Howell, and Furst, Norma Fields. Racial-Socioeconomic Situation, Achievement, I.Q., and Teacher Ratings of Behavior as Factors Relating to Anxiety in Upper Elementary School Children: A Follow-Up Study. ERIC ED 040 254, Mr, 1970.

Helfand, Abe, and Feifer, Irwin. Problems of the Disadvantaged in Test-Taking. PB-199 431. Springfield, VA: National Technical Information Service, 1971.

Hendrick, Clyde and others. "Race versus Belief as Determinants of Attraction: A Search for a Fair Test." Journal of Personality and Social Psychology 17(Mr, 1971):250-258.

Hitchcock, Dale C., and Oliver, Lincoln I. Intellectual Development and School Achievement of Youths 12-17 Years: Demographic and Socioeconomic Factors. Washington, DC: GPO, 1976.

Hoepfner, Ralph. The Validity of Tests of Social Intelligence. Los Angeles: Center for the Study of Evaluation, U. of California, 1973.

Hogan, Thomas P. "Prediction of Within-School System Variance in Test Scores from Within-Community Variance in Socioeconomic Status." Journal of Educational Measurement 9(Summer, 1972):155-158.

Holowinsky, Ivan Z, and Pascale, Pietro J. "Performance on Selected WISC Subtests of Subjects Referred for Psychological Evaluation Because of Educational Difficulties." Journal of Special Education 6(Fall,1972): 231-235.

Humphreys, Doyd G. and others. "Causes of Racial and Socioeconomic Differences in Cognitive Tests." Journal of Research in Personality 11(Je, 1977):191-208.

Hutchinson, June O'Shields. "Reading Tests and Nonstandard Language." Reading Teacher 25 (F, 1972):30-37. [Metropolitan Reading Tests]

Jacobs, John F., and DeGraaf, Carl A. "Expectancy and Race: Their Influences on Intelligence Test Scores." Exceptional Children 40(0, 1973):108-109.

Jantz, Richard K. "The Effects of Sex, Race, IQ and SES on the Reading Scores of Sixth Graders for Both Levels and Gains in Performance." Psychology in the Schools 11(Ja, 1974):90-94.

Jensen, Arthur R. "An Examination of Culture Bias in the Wonderlic Personnel Test." Intelligence 1(1977):51-64.

_____. "An Unfounded Conclusion in M.W. Smith's Analysis of Culture Bias in the Stanford-Binet Intelligence Scale." Journal of Genetic Psychology 130(Mr, 1977):113-115. [See Reply by Smith, pp. 117-120.]

_____. "The Effect of Race of Examiner on the Mental Test Scores of White and Black Pupils." Journal of Educational Measurement 11(Spring, 1974):1-14.

_____. "How Biased Are Culture-Loaded Tests?" Genetic Psychology Monographs 90(1974):185-244.

_____. "Test Bias and Construct Validity." Phi Delta Kappan 58(D, 1976):340-346.

Jernigan, A.J. "Judging Whether Patient is White or Black by His Draw-A-Person Test." Journal of Projective Techniques and Personality Assessment 34(D, 1970):503-506.

Johnson, Dale L., and Johnson, Carmen A. "Comparison of Four Intelligence Tests Used With Culturally Disadvantaged Children." Psychological Reports 28(F, 1971):209-210.

Johnson, Geraldine F. "Metropolitan Tests: Inappropriate for ESEA Pupils." Integrated Education (N-D, 1971):22-26.

Jones, Randall L., and Spolsky, Bernard (eds.). Testing Language Proficiency. Arlington, VA: Center for Applied Linguistics, 1975.

Karier, Clarence J. "Testing for Order and
Control in the Corporate Liberal State."
Educational Theory 22(Spring, 1972):154-180.

Kassinove, Howard and others. "Cross Validation
of the Environmental Participation Index in a
Group of Economically Deprived High School
Students." Journal of Clinical Psychology
26(Jl, 1970):373-376.

Katz, Irwin, Henchy, Thomas, and Allen, Harvey.
"Effects of Race of Tester, Approval-Disap-
proval, and Need on Negro Children's Learning." Journal of Personality and Social
Psychology, Ja, 1968.

Katz, Irwin, Roberts, S. Oliver, and Robinson,
James S. "Effects of Task Difficulty, Race
of Administrator, and Instructions of Digit
Symbol Performance of Negroes," Journal of
Personality and Social Psychology, Jl, 1965.

Katz, Irwin and other. "Race of Evaluator,
Race of Norm, and Expectancy as Determinants
of Black Performance." Journal of Experimental Social Psychology 8(Ja, 1972):1-15.

Kaufman, Alan S. "Comparison of the Performance
of Matched Groups of Black Children and White
Children on the Wechsler Preschool and Primary Scale of Intelligence." Journal of
Consulting and Clinical Psychology 41(O,
1973):186-191.

_____. "Comparison of WPPSI IQ's Obtained by
Matched Groups of Black and White Children."
Proceedings of the Annual Convention of the
American Psychological Association 7(1972):
Part 1, 39-40.

Kaufman, Alan S., and Kaufman, Nodeen L. "Black-
White Differences at Ages 2½-8½ on the
McCarthy Scales of Children's Abilities."
Journal of School Psychology 11(F, 1973):196-
206.

Kendrick, S. A. "College Board Scores and Cultural Bias." College Board Review, Winter,
1964-1965.

Kennedy, Wallace A., and Vega, Manuel. "Negro
Children's Performance on a Discrimination
Task as a Function of Examiner Race and Ver-
bal Incentive." Journal of Personality and
Social Psychology, D, 1965.

Keough, Barbara K., and Barkett, Catherine J.
"Children's Rights in Assessment and School
Placement." Journal of Social Issues 34, No.
2(1978):87-100.

Kevles, Daniel. "Testing the Army's Intelligence: Psychology and the Military in World
War I." Journal of American History 55(1968):
565-581.

Khan, S. B. "The Relative Magnitude of Speed
and Power in SCAT." Journal of Educational
Measurement 5(1968):327-329.

King, Mary L. "The Effectiveness of Social Reinforcement on a Motor Performance of Negro
Preschool Children as a Function of Socio-
economic Level." Doctoral dissertation, U.
of Mississippi, 1970.

King, William L., and Seegmiller, Bonnie.
"Performance of 14- to 22-Month-Old Black,
Firstborn Male Infants on Two Tests of Cog-
nitive Development: The Bayley Scales and
the Infant Psychological Development Scales."
Developmental Psychology 8(My, 1973):317-326.

Kirk, Samuel A. "Ethnic Differences in Psycholinguistic Differences." Exceptional Children 39(O, 1972):112-118.

Klein, Isobel P. "The Effect of Junior High
School Students' Race and Perceived Locus
of Control on Achievement and on Reactions
to Different Test Instructions." Diss.
Abstr. Int'l 32(6-B) D, 1971, 3640.

Koslin, Sandra Cohen, Awarel, Marianne, and
Ames, Nancy. "The Effect of Race on Peer
Evaluation and Preference in Primary Grade
Children: An Exploratory Study." Journal
of Negro Education 39(Fall, 1970):346-350.

Kuznik, Anthony. "Qualifications and Background
of Administrators of College Placement Tests."
Journal of Non-White Concerns 1(Jl, 1973):
192-198. [Test-giving]

Kyle, George T. "A Possible Reason Why Negroes
Make Low Scores on Mental Tests." Quarterly
Review of Higher Education Among Negroes 3
(Ap, 1935):102-105.

Lally, John R. "A Study of the Scores of Trained
and Untrained Twelve Month Old Environmentally
Deprived Infants on the Griffiths Mental Development Scale." Diss. Abstr. Int'l. 1969,
30(2-A):587.

Lambert, Nadine M. "The Present Status of the
Culture Fair Testing Movement." Psychology
in the Schools, Jl, 1964.

Larsen, Mary J., and Allen, Jerry C. "Effects
of Certain Subject Variables on Stanford-
Binet Item Performance of Five-Year-Old
Children." Psychological Reports 26(Je,
1970):975-984.

Lessing, Elise E., and Harrod, Alan R. "Comparative Predictive Validity of the IPAT
Jr.-Sr. High School Personality Questionnaire
for White and Black Subsamples." Proceedings
of the Annual Convention of the APA 6, PA11
(1971):245-246.

Leventhal, Donald S., and Stedman, Donald J.
"A Factor Analytic Study of the Illinois
Test of Psycholinguistic Abilities." Journal
of Clinical Psychology 26(O, 1970):473-477.

Linn, Robert L. "Fair Test Use in Selection."
Review of Educational Research 43(Spring,
1973):139-161.

Long, Howard H. "Test Results of Third-Grade Negro Children Selected on the Basis of Socio-economic Status." Journal of Negro Education 4(Ap, 1935):192-212.

Long, Peggie A., and Anthony, John J. "The Measurement of Mental Retardation by a Culture-Specific Test." Psychology in the Schools 11(Jl, 1974):310-312.

Lovins, Richard. "The Influence of Differential Testing Environments on Achievement in Culturally Deprived Negro Youth." Doctoral dissertation, U. of Connecticut, 1972.

Lowe, James D., and Karnes, Frances A. "A Comparison of Scores on the WISC-R and Lorge-Thorndike Intelligence Test for Disadvantaged Black Elementary School Children." Southern Journal of Educational Research 10(Summer, 1976):152-154.

Lubera, Eugene T. "The Effects of the Race and the Sex of Test Interviewer on the Responses of Intermediate Grade American Children on the Measurement of Interest in School Work." Diss. Abstr. Int'l. 1970, 30(7-A):2765-6.

McClelland, David C. "Testing for Competence Rather Than for 'Intelligence.'" In The New Assault on Equality. IQ and Social Stratification, pp. 163-197. Edited by Alan Gartner, Colin Greer, and Frank Reissman. New York: Perennial Library, 1974.

McClung, Merle. "Competency Testing: Potential for Discrimination." Clearinghouse Review 11(S, 1977):439-448.

MacDonald, Randolph and others. "Socioeconomic Status as Related to Two Levels of Conceptual Attainment." Journal of Genetic Psychology 125(D, 1974):195-200.

MacGinitie, Walter H. "Testing Reading Achievement in Urban Schools." Reading Teacher 27 (O, 1973):13-21.

McPhail, Irving P. "A Psycholinguistic Approach to Training Urban High School Students in Test-Taking Strategies." Journal of Negro Education 47(Spring, 1978):168-176.

Magoon, Jon, and Cox, Richard C. "An Evaluation of the Screening Test of Academic Readiness." Educational and Psychological Measurement 29 (1969):941-950.

Maier, Milton H. Effects of General Ability, Education, and Racial Group on Aptitude Test Performance. AD-738 985 Springfield, VA: National Technical Information Service, My, 1971.

Marion, Tovah S. "An Adaptation of the Tasks of Emotional Development (T.E.D.) Test for Black Lower Class Children and Its Relationship to Academic Achievement." Diss. Abstr. Int'l. 31, 5-B(N, 1970):2997.

Mecham, Merlin J. "Performance of Certain Minority Children on the Utah Test of Language Development." Language, Speech, and Hearing Services in Schools 9(Ap, 1978):98-102.

Mensing, Patricia M., and Traxler, Anthony J. "Social Class Differences in Free Recall of Categorized and Uncategorized Lists in Black Children." Journal of Educational Psychology 65(D, 1973):378-382. [I.Q.]

Mercer, Jane R., and Smith, Joyce M. "Subtest Estimates of the WISC Full Scale IQ's for Children." Vital Health Statistics, Series 2, No. 47, Mr, 1972.

Messick, Samuel, and Anderson, Scarvia. Educational Testing, Individual Development, and Social Responsibility. ERIC ED 047 003, N, 1970.

Meyers, Edna O. The Revised WISC: Does It Serve Inner City Children? ERIC ED 132 173, Mr, 1976.

Michael, William B. and others. "The Relationship of Average Scores on Intelligence and Reading Tests to Percentages of Minority Group Students in Elementary Schools and High Schools in a Large Metropolitan Area." Educational and Psychological Measurement 31 (Summer, 1971):539-540.

Miller, Kent S., and Dreger, Ralph Mason (eds.). Comparative Studies of Blacks and Whites in the United States. New York: Seminar Press, 1973.

Miller, Wesley. "Educator Finds Reading Score Decline Stems from Demographic Changes." New York Teacher, O 7, 1973.

Mills, Roger, and Bryan, Miriam M. Testing ... Grouping: The New Segregation in Southern Schools? Atlanta: Southern Regional Council, 1976.

Mitchell, Blythe C. "Predictive Validity of the Metropolitan Readiness Tests and the Murphy-Durrell Reading Readiness Analysis for White and for Negro Pupils." Educational and Psychological Measurement 27(1967):1047-1054.

Moore, Alexander M. "Testing the Inner-City Negro Child." ISSQ, Spring, 1964. [Indiana Council of the Social Studies, Ball State Teachers College, Muncie, Indiana]

Moore, Clifford L., and Retish, Paul M. "Effect of the Examiner's Race on Black Children's Wechsler Preschool and Primary Scale of Intelligence IQ." Developmental Psychology 10 (S, 1974):672-676.

Moses, E. G., Zirkel, Perry A., and Greene, John F. "Measuring the Self-Concept of Minority Group Pupils." Journal of Negro Education 42(Winter, 1973):93-98.

Mowsesian, Richard, and Holley, Steven I. Reliability and Validity of the CMI by Sex, Ethnicity and Time. ERIC ED 137 339, Ap, 1977. [Career Maturity Inventory]

Mueser, Anne Marie. "Effects of Different Reinforcers and Operant Level on Reading Task Behavior of Black Kindergarteners." Doctoral dissertation, Yeshiva U., 1971.

Mungester, R. J. "An Empirical Examination of Three Models of Item Bias." Doctoral dissertation, Florida State U., 1977.

Murray, Michael E. Differences Between WISC and WAIS Scores in Delinquent Boys." Journal of Experimental Education 42(Winter, 1973):68-72.

National Assessment of Educational Progress. "Comparative Performance of Blacks." In National Assessment Report 9. Citizenship. 1969-1970 Assessment: Group Results for Parental Education, Color, Size and Type of Community, pp. 46-75. Washington, DC: GPO, My, 1972.

Newell, Reginald. "Psychological Testing and Collective Bargaining." American Federationist, F, 1968.

Oakland, Thomas. "Assessing Minority Group Children: Challenge for School Psychologists." Journal of School Psychology 11 (1973):294-303.

_____. "The Effects of Test-Wiseness Materials on Standardized Test Performance of Preschool Disadvantaged Children." Journal of School Psychology 10(D, 1972):355-360.

_____. Psychological and Educational Assessment of Minority Children. New York: Brunner/Mazel, 1977.

Oakland, Thomas, and Emmer, Edmund. "Effects of Knowledge in Criterion Groups on Actual and Expected Test Performance of Negro and Mexican-American Eighth Graders." Journal of Consulting and Clinical Psychology 40 (F, 1973):155-159.

Oakland, Thomas, King, John D., White, Linda A., and Eckman, Robert. "A Comparison of Performance on the WPPSI, WISC, and SB with Preschool Children: Companion Studies." Journal of School Psychology 9(1971):144-149.

O'Keefe, Rip. "Influences of Age, Sex, and Ethnic Origin on Goodenough-Harris Drawing Test Performances by Disadvantaged Preschool Children." Perceptual and Motor Skills 33 (D, 1971):708-710.

Palermo, David. "Racial Comparisons and Additional Normative Data on the Children's Manifest Anxiety Scale." Child Development 30 (Mr, 1959):53-57.

Pandey, R. F. "The SCAT and Race." Psychological Reports 28(Ap, 1971):459-462.

Parella, Victoria Morrow. "A Study of the Validity of Language Usage as an Indicator of Ethnic Identification." Master's thesis, Texas A & M, 1971. ERIC ED 051 943.

Pascale, Pietro J., and Jakubovic, Shaena. The Impossible Dream: A Culture Free Test. ERIC ED 054 217, 1971.

Pasewark, Richard A. and others. "Relationship of the Wechsler Pre-School and Primary Scale of Intelligence and the Stanford-Binet (L-M) in Lower-Class Children." Journal of School Psychology 9(1971):43-50.

Pelosi, John W. "A Study of the Effects of Examiner Race, Sex, and Style on Test Responses on Negro Examiners." Doctoral dissertation, Syracuse U., 1968.

Perlman, Daniel, and Oskamp, Stuart. The Effects of Picture Content and Exposure Frequency on Evaluations of Negroes and Whites. ERIC ED 044 744, S, 1970.

Phillips, Beeman N. (ed.). Assessing Minority Group Children: A Special Issue of Journal of School Psychology. New York: Behavioral Publications, 1973.

Pike, Lewis W., and Mahoney, Margaret H. Cross-Ethnic Cross Validation of Aptitude Batteries. ERIC ED 034 260, 1969.

Ratusnik, David L., and Koenings-Snecht, Roy A. "Biracial Testing: The Question of Clinicians' Influence on Children's Test Performance." Language, Speech and Hearing Services in Schools 8(Ja, 1977):5-14.

Reichert, Conrad A. The Effects of Race on Test Taking. ERIC ED 093 988, Ap, 1974.

Resnick, Robert J., and Entin, Alan D. "Is An Abbreviated Form of the WISC Valid for Afro-American Children?" Journal of Consulting and Clinical Psychology 36(F, 1971):97-99.

Richmond, Bert O., and Long, Marvin. "WISC-R and PPVT Scores for Black and White Mentally Retarded Children." Journal of School Psychology 15(F, 1977):261-263.

Ringle, Ken. "Overcoming Cultural Bias." Washington Post, Mr 19, 1978.

Roberts, Launey Franklin, Jr. "An Assessment of Selected Culture-Free Intelligence Tests and the Culturally Different Child." Negro Educational Review 21(O, 1970).

Roberts, S. O., and Oppenheim, Don B. The Effect of Special Instruction upon Test Performance of High School Students in Tennessee. ERIC ED 053 158, Ju, 1966.

Roberts, S. O., Dickerson, Ann E., and Horton, Carrell P. "Longitudinal Performance of Negro American Children at Five and Ten Years on the Stanford-Binet." _American Psychologist_ 20(1965):524.

Roca, Pablo. _Problems of Adapting Intelligence Scales from One Culture to Another._ San Juan, Puerto Rico: Department of Education Press, 1955.

Rosenbaum, Edward. "Effects of Race of Observer, Examiner, and Model on Imitation of a School-life Task." Doctoral dissertation, U. of Wisconsin, 1971.

Rudner, L. M. "An Evaluation of Select Approaches for Biased Item Identification." Doctoral dissertation, Catholic U. of America, 1977.

St. John, Nancy H. _Measuring the Social Class Background of School Children._ Cambridge, MA: Harvard Graduate School of Education, 1969.

Samuda, Ronald J. "From Ethnocentricism to a Multi-Cultural Perspective in Educational Testing." _Journal of Afro-American Issues_ 3(Winter, 1975).

_____. _Psychological Testing of American Minorities: Issues and Consequences._ New York: Dodd, Mead, 1975.

Sandler, Louise and others. _Developmental Test Performance and Behavioral Styles of Disadvantaged Nursery School Children._ ERIC ED 053 183, My, 1971.

_____ and others. "Developmental Test Performance of Disadvantaged Children." _Exceptional Children_ 39(N, 1972):201-208. Pre-School.

Sattler, J. "Racial 'Experimenter Effects' in Experimentation, Testing, Interviewing, and Psychotherapy." _Psychological Bulletin_ 73 (1970):136-160.

Saunders, Mauderie H., and Teska, Percy T. "An Analysis of Cultural Differences on Certain Projective Techniques." _Journal of Negro Education_ 39(1970):109-115.

Schmidt, Frank L., and Hunter, John E. "Racial and Ethnic Bias in Psychological Tests. Divergent Implications of Two Definitions of Test Bias." _American Psychologist_ 29(Ja, 1974):1-8.

Schwarz, Robert H., and Flanagan, Patrick J. "Evaluation of Examiner Bias in Intelligence Testing." _American Journal of Mental Deficiency_ 76(S, 1971):262-265.

Seiler, Joseph. "Preparing the Disadvantaged for Tests." _Vocational Guidance Quarterly_ 19(Mr, 1971):201-206.

Sewell, Trevor E. "A Comparison of the WPPSI and Stanford-Binet Intelligence Scale (1972) Among Lower SES Black Children." _Psychology in the Schools_ 14(Ap, 1977):158-160.

Sewell, Trevor E., and Severson, Roger A. "Intelligence and Achievement in First-Grade Black Children." _Journal of Consulting and Clinical Psychology_ 43(F, 1975).

_____ and _____. "Learning Ability and Intelligence as Cognitive Predictors of Achievement in First-Grade Black Children." _Journal of Educational Psychology_ 66(D, 1974):948-955.

Silverstein, A. B. "Factor Structure of the Wechsler Intelligence Scale for Children from Three Ethnic Groups." _Journal of Educational Psychology_ 65(D, 1973):408-410.

Snyder, Robert T. and others. "A Cross-Cultural Item-Analysis of Bender-Gestalt Protocols Administered to Ghetto and Suburban Children." _Perceptual and Motor Skills_ 33 (D, 1971):791-796.

Solkoff, Norman. "Race of Examiner and Performance on the Wechsler Intelligence Scale for Children: A Replication." _Perceptual and Motor Skills_ 39(D, 1974):1036-1066.

Spencer, Thelma L. _Ethnic Minorities and National Standardized Testing._ ERIC ED 141 467, 1975.

Stablein, J. E., Willey, D. S., and Thomson, C. W. "An Evaluation of the Davis-Eeels Test Using Spanish and Anglo-American Children." _Journal of Educational Sociology_ 35(1961): 73-79.

Stabler, John R., and Johnson, Edward E. _The Measurement of Children's Self-Concepts as Related to Racial Membership_, 1970. ERIC ED 041 065.

Sternlof, R. ., Parker, H. J., and McCoy, J. F. "Relationships Between the Goodenough DAM Test and the Columbia Mental Maturity Test for Negro and White Headstart Children." _Perceptual and Motor Skills_, 0, 1968.

Strickland, Bonnie R. "Delay of Gratification as a Function of Race of the Experimenter." _Journal of Personality and Social Psychology_ 22(Ap, 1972):108-112.

Sullivan, John A. _Measured Mental Ability, Service School Achievement and Performance._ Springfield, VA: National Technical Information Service, Jl, 1970. [Armed Forces Qualification Test]

Swerdlik, Mark E. "Comparison of WISC amd WISC-R Scores of Referred Black, White and Latino Children." _Journal of School Psychology_ 16 (Summer, 1978):110-124.

Teahan, John E. Some Effects of Audio-Visual Techniques on Aspirational Level and Ethnocentric Shift. Final Report, S, 1967. ERIC ED 013 862.

Theiner, Eric C. "Current Approaches to Symbolization: The Kahn Test of Symbol Arrangement." International Journal of Symbology 1 (Ag, 1969): 52-58.

Thelen, Mark and others. "Model's Race and S's Race in Imitation of Cognitive and Motor Tasks." Psychological Reports 33(0, 1973): 485-576.

Thomas, Alexander, Hertzig, Margaret E., Dryman, Irving, and Fernandez, Paulina. "Examiner Effect in IQ Testing of Puerto Rican Working-Class Children." American Journal of Orthopsychiatry 41 0, 1971):809-821.

Thompson, Bruce and others. "Correspondence Across Three Ethnic Groups of Constructs Measured by the Iowa Test of Basic Skills." Psychology in the Schools 15(Jl, 1978):347-349.

Thorndike, Robert L. "Concepts of Culture-Fairness." Journal of Educational Measurement 8 (Summer, 1971):63-70.

Tittle, Carol Kehr. "Fairness in Educational Achievement Testing." Education and Urban Society 8(N, 1975):86-103.

Torrance, E. Paul. "Are the Torrance Tests of Creative Thinking Biased Against or in Favor of 'Disadvantaged Groups?'" Gifted Child Quarterly 15(Summer, 1971):75-80.

Tractenberg, Paul L., and Jacoby, Elaine. "Pupil Testing: A Legal View." Phi Delta Kappan 59(D, 1977):249-254.

Tulkin, S. R., and Konner, M. J. "Alternative Conceptions of Intellectual Functioning." Human Development 16(1973):33-52.

Tulkin, S. R., and Newbrough, J. R. "Social Class, Race, and Sex Differences on the Raven (1956) Standard Progressive Matrices," Journal of Consulting and Clinical Psychology, Ag, 1968.

Tuma, June M. and others. "Comparability of the WISC and the WISC-R in Normal Children of Divergent Socioeconomic Backgrounds." Psychology in the Schools 15(Jl, 1978): 339-346.

Tyler, Ralph W., and Wolf, Richard M. (eds.). Crucial Issues in Testing. Berkeley, CA: McCutchan, 1974.

Vance, Hubert B., and Gaynor, Patricia E. "A Note on Cultural Difference as Reflected in the Wechsler Intelligence Scale for Children. Journal of Genetic Psychology 129 (S, 1976):171-172.

Vandermyn, Gaye. National Assessment Achievements. Findings, Interpretations and Uses. Denver, CO: Education Commission of the States, June, 1974.

Vane, Julia R. "Intelligence and Achievement Test Results of K Age Children in England, Ireland, and the U.S." Journal of Clinical Psychology 29(Ap, 1973):191-193.

Vega, Manuel, and Powell, Arnold. "The Effects of Practice on Bender Gestalt Performance of Culturally Disadvantaged Children." Florida Journal of Educational Research 12 (Ja, 1970):45-49.

Verducci, Frank. "Racial Ethnic Comparisons on Selected Motor Performance Tests." Research Quarterly 45(0, 1974):324-328.

Vernon, P. E. "Environmental Handicaps and Intellectual Development: Parts I and II," British Journal of Educational Pyschology, F, 1965, Je, 1965.

Veroff, Joseph, McClelland, Lou, and Marquis, Kent. Measuring Intelligence and Achievement Motivation in Surveys. Ann Arbor, MI: Institute for Social Research, U. of Michigan, 1971.

Vroegh, Karen, and Handrich, Millicent. "The Validity of the Howard Maze Test as a Measure of Stimulus-Seeking in Preschool Children." Educational & Psychological Measurement 29 (1969):495-502.

Wargo, Michael (ed.). Minority Group Testing. New York: McGraw-Hill, 1977.

Wargo, Michael, and Green, D. Ross (eds.). Achievement Testing of Disadvantaged and Minority Students for Education Program Evaluation. New York: McGraw-Hill, 1978.

Wasik, John L., and Wasik, Barbara H. "Use of the WPPSI and the WISC with Culturally Deprived Children." Measurement and Evaluation in Guidelines 5(Ap, 1972):280-285.

Weber, George. Uses and Abuses of Standardized Testing in the Schools. Washington, DC: Council for Basic Education, My, 1974.

Wei, Tom T. D. and others. "Piaget's Concept of Classification: A Comparative Study of Socially Disadvantaged and Middle-Class Young Children." Child Development 42(S, 1971):

Williams, John E. and others. "The Measurement of Children's Racial Attitudes in the Early School Years." Child Development 46 (Je, 1975):494-500.

Weisgerber, Robert A., and Coles, Gary J. Evaluating the Potential of Films for Improving Self-Image in Minority Group Children. Final Report, D, 1971. ERIC ED 061 726.

Weisgerber, Robert A., and Danoff, Malcolm N. Evaluating the Potential of Films for Improving Self-Image in Minority Group Children. Interim Technical Report: Phase I, D 31, 1969. ERIC ED 044 026.

Wilcox, Roger. "Music Ability Among Negro Grade School Pupils, Or I Got Rhythm?" Perceptual and Motor Skills 29(1969):167-168.

Willard, Louisa S. "A Comparison of Culture Fair Test Scores with Group and Individual Intelligence Test Scores of Disadvantaged Negro Children." Journal of Learning Disabilities 1(0, 1968):584-589.

Williams, Barbara I., and Gilliard, June. "One More Time: NAEP and Blacks." Social Education 38(My, 1974): 422-424. [National Assessment of Educational Progress]

Williams, E. Belvin. Testing of the Disadvantaged: New Opportunities, S, 1971. ERIC ED 054 282.

Williams, John E. Preschool Racial Attitude Measure II (PRAM II), General Information and Manual of Directions, 1971. ERIC ED 055. 660.

_____. Preschool Racial Attitude Measure II (PRAM II): Technical Report #1: 1970-71 Standardization Study, 1971. ERIC ED 056 772.

Williams, John E., and Roberson, J. K. "A Method for Assessing Racial Attitudes in Pre-School Children." Educational and Psychological Measurement 27(1967):671-89.

Williams, Robert L. "Abuses and Minuses in Testing Black Children." Counseling Psychologist 2(1971):62-73.

_____. "The BITCH-100: A Culture Specific Test." Journal of Afro-American Issues 3 (Winter, 1975):103-116.

_____. "Black Students and the Zero Sum Game." Washington Post, S 30, 1974. [Printed in column by William Raspberry.]

_____. "Moderator Variables as Bias in Testing Black Children." Journal of Afro-American Issues 3(Winter, 1975).

Williams, Robert L. and others. Psychological Tests and Minorities. Washington, DC: GPO, 1977.

Wirtz, Lyndall R. Performance on Raven's Progressive Matrices of Elementary School Negro Children Involved in an Algebra Program, Jl, 1971. ERIC ED 054 218.

Wise, James H. "Self-Reports by Negro and White Adolescents to the Draw-A-Person," Perceptual and Motor Skills, F, 1969.

Wright, Brenda Johnson, and Isenstein, Vivian R. Psychological Tests and Minorities, 1977. ERIC ED 150 773.

Yater, Allan C. and others. "A Comparative Study of WPPSI and WISC Performances of Disadvantaged Children." Journal of Clinical Psychology 31 (Ja, 1975):78-80.

Yawkey, Thomas D., and Jantz, Richard K. "Differential Effects of Intelligence, Race, SES, & Sex Variables on Peformance and Gains in Performance Based Upon Standardized Arithmetic Achievement Tests of 11 and 12 Year Old Subjects." Southern Journal of Educational Research 9(Summer, 1975):123-141.

Zigler, Edward and others. "Motivational Factors in the Performance of Economically Disadvantaged Children on the Peabody Picture Vocabulary Test." Child Development 44 (Je, 1973):249-303.

Zirkel, Perry A. "Spanish-speaking Students and Standardized Tests." Urban Review, 1972: 32-40.

Zirkel, Perry A., and Greene, John F. Cultural Attitude Scale Technical Report. Austin, TX: Learning Concepts, Ap, 1974.

The I.Q. Issue

"A Public Debate on Education, Race, I.Q., Intelligence." CSSRS Bulletin (Cambridge Society for Social Responsibility in Science). Special issue, Jl 18, 1970. [Write: CSSRS, 91, High Street, Little Wilbraham, Cambridgeshire, England.]

Aaron, Leroy. "The Shocking Assertions of Dr. Shockley." Chicago Sun-Times, Mr 26, 1972. [Story from Washington Post]

Adams, Phillip. "False Gods of a New Religion." Australian Journal of Mental Retardation 4 (D, 1977):13-15.

Adler, Manfred. "Intelligence Testing of the Culturally Disadvantaged: Some Pitfalls." Journal of Negro Education, Fall, 1968.

Agassi, Joseph. "The Twisting of the IQ Test." Philosophical Forum 3(Winter, 1971-1972).

Alland, Alexander, Jr. Human Diversity. New York: Columbia U. Press, 1971.

Allen, Garland E. "Genetics, Eugenics, and Class Struggle." Genetics 79(Je, 1975):29-45.

Allen, William G. The American Prejudice Against Color. New York: Arno Press, 1969, reprint.

Alper, Thelma G., and Boring, Edwin G. "Intelligence-Test Scores of Northern and Southern White and Negro Recruits in 1918." Journal of Abnormal and Social Psychology 39(1944):471-474.

50 / CHILDREN

Anastasi, Anne. Common Fallacies About Heredity, Environment, and Human Behavior, My, 1973. American College Testing Program, Box 168, Iowa City, IA 52210.

Anastasi, Anne, and D'Angelo, Rita Y. "A Comparison of Negro and White Pre-School Children in Language Development and Goodenough Draw-A-Man I.Q." Journal of Genetic Psychology, D, 1952.

Anastiow, Nicholas. "Educational Relevance and Jensen's Conclusions." Phi Delta Kappan, S, 1969.

Anderson, E. N., Jr. "The Social Factors Have Been Ignored." Harvard Educational Review, Summer, 1969. [In re: Arthur R. Jensen]

Armstrong, Roy A. "Test Bias from the Non-Anglo Viewpoint: A Critical Evaluation of Intelligence Test Items by Members of Three Cultural Minorities." Doctoral dissertation, U. of Arizona, 1972.

Arnott, Hilary. "Race & Intelligence." Race Today 5(S, 1973):272-273.

Aronowitz, Stanley. "The Trap of Environmentalism." In The New Assault on Equality. IQ and Social Stratification, pp. 198-205. Edited by Alan Gartner, Colin Greer, and Frank Riessman. New York: Perennial Library, 1974.

Arp, Halton. "Heritability of Intelligence." Science 182(1973):115.

Bagley, Christopher. "On the Intellectual Equality of Races." In Race and Education Across Cultures. Edited by G. K. Verma and Christopher Bagley. Stamford, CT: Greylock Publishers, 1975.

Baker, John R. Race. London: Oxford U. Press, 1974.

Bane, Mary Jo, and Jencks, Christopher. "Five Myths About Your IQ." Harper's Magazine, F, 1973.

Banton, Michael. The Idea of Race. London: Tavistock, 1977.

Baptiste, Hansom Prentice, Jr. "A Black Educator's View: The Pseudo-Sacrosanct Role of Intelligence in Education." Notre Dame Journal of Education I(Summer, 1970):122-127.

Barry, John W., and Annis, Robert C. "Ecology, Culture, and Psychological Differentiation." International Journal of Psychology 9(1974): 173-193. [Canadian Indians, hunters and gatherers].

Bart, William M., and Kaustubh, Lele. Defusing the Intelligence x Race Debate: Comparison of Intelligence Test Item Hierarchies for Two Races, Ap, 1977. ERIC ED 138 627.

Bauernfeind, Robert H. "The Four Major Fallacies of Group IQ Testing." School Counselor 18(Ja, 1971):156-163.

Beckham, Albert Sidney. "A Study of the Intelligence of Colored Adolescents of Different Economic and Social Status in Typical Metropolitan Areas." Doctoral dissertation, New York U., 1930.

_____. "A Study of the Intelligence of Colored Adolescents of Different Socio-economic Status in Typical Metropolitan Areas." Journal of Social Psychology 4(F, 1933):70-91. [New York, City, Washington, D.C., and Baltimore]

Beeghley, Leonard, and Butler, Edgar W. "The Consequences of Intelligence Testing in the Public Schools Before and After Desegregation." Social Problems 21(Je, 1974):740-754.

Benda, Clemens E. "Herrnstein Revisited." Harvard Crimson, N 20, 1973.

Bereiter, Carl. "The Future of Individual Differences." Harvard Educational Review, Spring, 1969. [Critique of Arthur R. Jensen]

_____. "The IQ Differences and Social Policy." In Education, Inequality, and National Policy, pp. 137-146. Edited by Nelson F. Ashline, Thomas R. Pezzullo, and Charles I. Morris. Lexington, MA: Lexington Books, 1976.

Berg, Norman L., and Berg, Sandra D. "Comparison of Verbal Intelligence of Young Children from Low to Middle Socioeconomic Status." Psychological Reports 28(Ap, 1971):559-562.

Berger, Brigitte. "A New Interpretation of the I.Q. Controversy." Public Interest 50 (Winter, 1978):29-44.

Bermingham, Patrick J. "Are Ideas in Three Dimensions Beyond You?" Times Higher Education Supplement, N 5, 1976. [Racial factors in spatial & mechanical reasoning]

Bernstein, Marilyn, and Guaquinta, Joseph. "Misunderstanding Compensatory Education." Harvard Educational Review, Summer, 1969. [In re: Arthur R. Jensen]

Berry, J. W. "Radical Cultural Relativism and the Concept of Intelligence." In Culture and Cognition: Readings in Cross-Cultural Psychology. Edited by J. W. Berry. London: Methuen, 1975.

Berube, Maurice R. "Professor Jensen and Race and Intelligence." Community (N.Y.), Summer, 1969.

Bett, Bryan. "Jensen, Race, and Genes." Times Higher Education Supplement, Mr 10, 1972.

Biasco, Frank. "An Obituary: The Death of Mr. I.Q." Integrated Education 12(Ja-Ap, 1974): 28.

Bickham, Stephen. "The Educational Implications of Arthur Jensen's Research." Intellect 103 (D, 1974):161-164.

Bickley, Richard. "Race, Class, and the IQ Controversy." RT (Rough Times) 2(F, 1972).

Biesheuvel, S. "An Examination of Jensen's Theory Concerning Educability, Heritability and Population Differences." Psychologia Africana 14(1972):87-94. [Reprinted in Montague (ed.), 1975; see below.]

_____. "Psychological Tests and Their Application to Non- European Peoples." In D. R. Price-Williams, Cross-Cultural Studies. Harmondsworth, England: Penguin, 1969.

Biggs, J. B. "Genetics and Education: Alternative to Jensenism." Educational Researcher 7(Ap, 1978):11-17.

Birch, Herbert G. "Intelligence, Ethnic Origin, and Integration." In Proceedings of the Third Annual Invitational Conference on Urban Education, 1964. New York: Graduate School of Education, Yeshiva U., n.d.

Block, N. J., and Dworkin, Gerald. "IQ: Heritability and Inequality." Part 1 Philosophy and Public Affairs (Summer, 1974): 331-409.

_____ and _____. The IQ Controversy: Critical Readings. New York: Pantheon, 1975.

Bloom, Benjamin S. "The Jensen Article" (letter). Harvard Educational Review, Spring, 1969. [Critique of Arthur R. Jensen]

Blum, Jeffrey M. Pseudoscience and Mental Ability. New York: Monthly Review Press, 1978.

Boas, Franz. "The Anthropological Position of the Negro." Van Norden Magazine 2(Ap, 1907): 40-47.

_____. "Fallacies of Racial Inferiority." Current History, F, 1927.

_____. "Heredity and Environment." Jewish Social Studies 1(1939):5-14.

Bodmer, W. F., and Cavalli-Sforza, L. L. Genetics, Evolution, and Man. San Francisco: Freeman, 1976.

_____, and _____. "Intelligence and Race." Scientific American 223(O, 1970):19-29.

Bodmer, W. F. and others. "Jensenism." The Listener, Ja 4, 1973.

Boeth, Richard. "The Great IQ Controversy." Newsweek, D 17, 1973.

Bohannan, Paul. "Heritability of Intelligence." Science 182(1973):115.

Bond, Horace Mann. "Intelligence Tests & Propaganda." Crisis 28(Je, 1924):61-64.

_____. "What the Army 'Intelligence Tests' Measured." Opportunity, Jl, 1924.

Boone, James A. "Racial Differences in Standard I.Q. = Cultural Bias." Negro Educational Review 28(Jl-O, 1977):183-188.

Boone, James A., and Adesso, Vincent J. "Racial Differences on a Black Intelligence Test." Journal of Negro Education 43 (Fall, 1974): 429-436.

Born to Be Unemployed. U.A.G. Critique of Richard Herrnstein's "I.Q.", 1971. University Action Group, 60 Fairmont Street, Cambridge, MA 02139.

Bosworth, Stanley. "How Useful Is IQ?" (letter). New York Review of Books, My 2, 1974. [Headmaster, Saint Ann's Episcopal School, Brooklyn Heights, NY]

Bousfield, Mandelle Brown. "A Study of the Intelligence and School Achievement of Negro Children." Master's thesis, U. of Chicago, 1931 [Chicago].

Bowles, Samuel, and Gintis, Herbert. "IQ in the United States Class Structure." In The New Assault on Equality. I.Q. and Social Stratification. Edited by Alan Gartner, Colin Greer, and Frank Riessman. New York: Perennial Library, 1974.

_____ and _____. "The IQ Ideology." This Magazine Is About Schools 6 (Winter, 1972-1973):47-62.

Brace, C. Loring, Gamble, George R., and Bond, James T. (eds.). Race and Intelligence. Washington, DC: American Anthropological Association, 1971.

Brazziel, William F. "A Letter from the South." Harvard Educational Review, Spring, 1969. [Critique of Arthur R. Jensen]

Breland, Hunter and others. The Cross-Cultural Stability of Mental Test Items. An Investigation of Response Patterns for Ten Socio-Cultural Groups, F, 1974. ERIC ED 137 370.

Bridgeman, Brent, and Buttram, Joan. "Reply to Humphreys and to Jensen." Journal of Educational Psychology 68(Ap, 1976):132.

Brigham, Carl C. A Study of American Intelligence. Princeton, NJ: Princeton U. Press, 1923.

Bristow, Anthony T. "Furor Over Shockley Grows." Race Relations Reporter 4(D 3, 1973).

Brim, Orville G., Jr. et al. American Beliefs and Attitudes About Intelligence. New York: Russell Sage Foundation, 1969.

Broman, Sarah H., Nichols, Paul L., and
Kennedy, Wallace A. Preschool IQ: Prenatal
and Early Developmental Correlates. Hills-
dale, NJ: Lawrence Erlbaum Associates,
1975.

Brown, Roy L. "Who's Being 'Reasonable' Now?"
Harvard Educational Review, Summer, 1969.
[In re: Arthur R. Jensen]

Brown, William W., and Reynolds, Morgan O.
"A Model of IQ, Occupation, and Earnings."
American Economic Review 65(D, 1975):1002-
1007.

Bruce, Myrtle. "Factors Affecting Intelligence
Test Performance of Whites and Negroes in the
Rural South." Archives of Psychology 36
(1940).

Bruner, Jerome. "Advocate Eysenck versus
Scientist Eysenck--and the Compleat Environmentalist." Times Educational Supplement, N 16, 1973.

Buck, Carol and others. "Variables Associated
with Social Class Differences in the Intelligence of Young Children." Multivariate
Behavioral Research 8(Ap, 1972):213-226.

Bumstead, Horace. "The Freedmen's Children at
School." Andover Review 4(D, 1885):550-551.

_____. "Handicaps of the Negro Race." New York
Evening Post, Ap 25, 1908.

Burt, Cyril. "Inheritance of General Intelligence." American Psychologist 27(Mr, 1972):
175-190.

_____. "The Inheritance of Mental Ability."
American Psychologist 13(1958):1-15.

_____. "Intelligence and Heredity." New
Scientist 1(1969):226-228.

Buss, Allan R. "Regression, Heritability, and
Race Differences in IQ." Developmental
Psychology 11(Ja, 1975).

Caldwell, Mark B., and Knight, David. "The
Effect of Negro and White Examiners on Negro
Intelligence Test Performance." Journal of
Negro Education 39(1970):177-179.

Cameron, Howard K. "Cultural Myopia." Measurement & Evaluation in Guidance 3(1970):10-17.
[In re: Arthur R. Jensen]

Campbell, J. T. Ethnic Groups, Intelligence
Testing, and the Abilities to Learn.
Princeton, NJ: Educational Testing Service,
1965.

Canady, H. G. "The American Caste System and the
Question of Negro Intelligence." Journal of
Educational Psychology 33(1942):161-172.

Cancro, Robert (ed.). Intelligence. Genetic
and Environmental Influences. New York:
Grune and Stratton, 1971.

Cardey, R. M. "Cultural Integration and
Intelligence Test Performance." Master's
thesis, U. of Saskatchewan (Regina), 1973.

Carlson, Elliott. "Measurements of I.Q. Draw
Mounting Fire from Minority Groups." Wall
Street Journal, Je 12, 1969.

Carroll, Imogene V. "A Comparison of the
Intelligence Quotients of Sixth-Grade
Children of Negro & Caucasian Educators &
Non-Educators." Diss. Abstr. Intl. 31 (7A),
Ja, 1971, 3161.

Cartwright, Walter J., and Burtis, Thomas R.
"Race and Intelligence: Changing Opinions
in Social Science." Social Science Quarterly
49(1968):603-618.

"The Case for Zero Heritability." Science for
the People 6(Mr, 1974):23-25.

Cassel, Russell N. "Group Intelligence Test
I.P. Paradox." College Student Journal 5
(S-O, 1971):31-33.

Chapin, John. "A Commentary on Jensen."
Research Journal (U. of Md.) 1(Jl, 1970):37-
39.

Chase, Allan. The Legacy of Malthus: The Social
Costs of the New Scientific Racism. New York:
Knopf, 1977.

Chase, Clinton I., and Pugh, Richard C. Social
Class and Performance on an Intelligence Test,
1970. ERIC ED 038 678.

_____ and _____. "Social Class and Performance on an Intelligence Test." Journal of
Educational Measurement 8(F, 1971):197-202.

Child, L. Maria. "Intellect of Negroes." In
An Appeal in Favor of That Class of Americans
Called Africans. New York: John S. Taylor,
1836.

Chomsky, Noam. "The Fallacy of Richard
Herrnstein's IQ." Social Policy 3(My-Je,
1972):19-25.

_____. "IQ Tests: Building Blocks for the New
Class System." Ramparts 11(Jl, 1972):24-30.
[In re: Richard Herrnstein]

Clark, Kenneth B. "Some Factors Influencing a
Group of Negroes in Their Estimation of the
Intelligence and Personality-wholesomeness
of Negro Subjects." Journal of Psychology 19,
75-78.

Clark, Raymond M. "The Effect of Schooling Upon
Intelligence Quotients of Negro Children."
Doctoral dissertation, Cleveland, OH:
Western Reserve U., 1933. [Cleveland and
Detroit]

Clarke, A. M., and Clarke, A. D. B. "Genetic-
Environmental Interactions in Cognitive De-
velopment." In Mental Deficiency: The
Changing Outlook. Edited by Clarke and
Clarke. 3rd ed. London: Methuen, 1974.

Cohen, David K. "Does IQ Matter?" Commentary 53(Ap, 1972):51-59.

Cole, Michael. "Culture, Cognition, and IQ Testing." National Elementary Principal 54 (Mr-Ap, 1975):49-52.

Cooley, C. H. "Genius, Fame and the Comparison of Races." Annals 10(1897):317-358.

Corman, Louise, and Budoff, Milton. "Factor Structures of Spanish-Speaking and Non-Spanish-Speaking Children on Raven's Progressive Matrices." Educational and Psychological Measurement 34(Winter, 1974): 977-981.

_____ and _____. IQ & Learning Potential Measurements of General Intelligence: A Comparison of Relationships, S, 1973. ERIC ED 086 921.

Cottle, Thomas J. "The Edge of the I.Q. Storm." Saturday Review 55(Ap 15, 1972):50-53.

Cravens, Hamilton. "American Scientists and the Heredity-Environment Controversy." Doctoral dissertation, U. of Iowa, 1969.

_____. Triumph of Evolution. American Scientists and the Heredity-Environment Controversy 1900-1941. Philadelphia: U. of Pennsylvania Press, 1978.

Cronbach, L. J. "Five Decades of Public Controversy Over Mental Testing." American Psychologist 30(1975):1-14.

_____. "Heredity, Environment, and Educational Policy." Harvard Educational Review, Spring, 1969. [Critique of Arthur R. Jensen]

Cronbach, L. J., and Drenth, P. J. D. Mental Tests and Cultural Adaptation. The Hague, Netherlands: Mouton, 1972.

Crow, James F. "Genetic Theories and Influences: Comments on the Value of Diversity." Harvard Educational Review, Spring, 1969. [Critique of Arthur R. Jensen]

D'Angelo, R. and others. "IQ's of Negro Head Start Children on the Vane Kindergarten Test." Journal of Clinical Psychology 27 (Ja, 1971):82-85.

Daniels, Norman. "IQ, Intelligence and Educability." Philosophical Forum, 1975.

_____. "The Smart White Man's Burden." Harper's 247(O, 1973):24-40.

Davey, A. G. "Teachers, Race, and Intelligence." Race 15(O, 1973):195-211.

Davis, Allison, and Eels, Kenneth W. (eds.) Intelligence and Cultural Differences. Chicago: U. of Chicago Press, 1959.

Davis, Bernard D., and Flaherty, Patricia (eds.). Human Diversity: Its Causes and Social Significance. Cambridge, MA: Ballinger, 1975.

De Francesco, Domenic. "The Intelligence of the Second Generation of Italians." Master's thesis, Rochester, NY: U. of Rochester, 1930.

De Lacey, Philip R. "Classificatory Ability & Verbal Intelligence Among High-Contact Aboriginal & Low-Socioeconomic White Australian Children." Journal of Cross-Cultural Psychology 2(D, 1971):393-396.

Deutsch, Karl W., and Edsall, Thomas. "The Meritocracy Scare." Society 9(S-O, 1972): 71-79. [In re: Richard Herrnstein]

Deutsch, Martin. "Happenings on the Way Back to the Forum." Harvard Educational Review, Summer, 1969. [In re: Arthur R. Jensen]

Deutsch, Martin, and Deutsch, Cynthia P. "Intelligence, Heredity, and Environment: The Critical Appraisal of an Outmoded Controversy." New York University Education Quarterly 5(Winter, 1974):4-12.

Dobzhansky, Theodosius. "Differences Are Not Deficits." Psychology Today 7(D, 1973): 97-101.

_____. Genetic Diversity and Human Equality. New York: Basic Books, 1973.

_____. "Race Equality." In The Biological and Social Meaning of Race. Edited by R. H. Osborne. San Francisco: Freeman, 1971.

Dockrell, W. B. (ed.). On Intelligence: The Toronto Symposium, 1969. New York: Barnes, 1971.

Douglass, Harlan Paul. Christian Reconstruction in the South. Boston: n.p., 1909.

DuBois, W. E. B. Review of Mayo, The Mental Capacity of the American Negro. Journal of Philosophy 11(S 24, 1914):557-558.

_____. "Vardaman." Voice of the Negro 3 (Mr, 1906):189-194.

Dyer, Frederick N. "The Prenatal Environment Is More Than Genetic." Harvard Educational Review, Summer, 1969. [In re: Arthur R. Jensen]

Ebling, F. J. (ed.). Racial Variation in Man. New York: Wiley, 1975.

Eckland, Bruce K. "Genetics and Sociology: A Reconsideration." American Sociological Review, Ap, 1967.

54 / CHILDREN

Edmonds, Ronald and others. "A Black Response to Christopher Jencks's Inequality and Certain Other Issues." Harvard Educational Review 43 (F, 1973):76-91.

Edson, Lee. "Jensenism, n. The Theory that I.Q. is Largely Determined by the Genes." New York Times Magazine, Ag 31, 1969.

Ehrman, Lee, Omenn, Gilbert S., and Caspari, Ernest W. (eds.). Genetics, Environment, and Behavior: Implications for Educational Policy. New York: Academic Press, 1972.

Eisenberg, Leon. "The Social Development of Intelligence." In Progress in Mental Health, pp. 167-177. Edited by Hugh Freeman. New York: Grune & Stratton, 1969.

Elkind, David. "Piagetian and Psychometric Conceptions of Intelligence." Harvard Educational Review, Spring, 1969. [Critique of Arthur R. Jensen]

Ellwood, Marcia Sue. "Black Intelligence: Familiarity as a Factor in Intelligence Test Performance." Doctoral dissertation, U. of Southern California, 1974. Univ. Microfilm Order No. 74-23581.

Epps, Edgar G. "Race, Intelligence, and Learning: Some Consequences of the Misuse of Test Results." Phylon 34(Je, 1973): 153-159.

_____. "Racism, Science, and the I.Q." Integrated Education 11(Ja-F, 1973):35-44.

"Equal Protection and Intelligence Classifications." Stanford Law Review 26(F, 1974): 647-672.

Evans, Ross A. "Psychology's White Face." In The New Assault on Equality. IQ and Social Stratification, pp. 102-113. Edited by Alan Gastner, Colin Greer, and Frank Riessman. New York: Perennial Library, 1974.

Eysenck, H. J. "A Better Understanding of I.Q. and the Myths Surrounding It." Times Education Supplement, My 18, 1973

_____. "The Case of Sir Cyril Burt. On Fraud and Presjudice in a Scientific Community." Encounter (Ja, 1977).

_____. "The Dangers in a New Orthodoxy." New Humanist (England), Jl, 1973.

_____. "I.Q., Social Class, & Educational Policy." Change 5(S, 1973):38-42.

_____. The Inequality of Man. London: Temple Smith, 1973.

_____. "Nurture" (letter). New Society, Ja 24, 1974.

_____. "Race, Intelligence and Education." New Society 17(Je 17, 1971):1045-1047.

_____. "The Triumph of the Average." New Society, O 25, 1973.

Farber, Bernard. "Social Class and Intelligence." Social Forces, D, 1965.

Fehr, F. S. "Critique of Hereditarian Accounts of 'Intelligence' and Contrary Findings: A Reply to [Arthur R.] Jensen." Harvard Educational Review, Summer, 1969.

Feldman, Carol Fleisher, Lee, Benjamin, McLean, James Dickson, Pilleiner, David B., and Murray, James R. The Development of Adaptive Intelligence. San Francisco: Jossey-Bass, 1974. [Eskimo children]

Feldman, M. W., and Lewontin, Richard C. "The Heritability Hang-Up." Science 190 (1975):1163-1168.

Felton, Gary S. "Changes in I.Q. Scores of Black Low Achievers in a Process-Oriented Learning Program." College Student Journal 7(Ja, 1973):83-86.

Fields, Cheryl. "Heredity and Environment, But Not Race, Found to Influence Intelligence." Chronicle of Higher Education, S 12, 1977. [Research of Sandra Scarr]

Fincher, Jack. "Arthur Jensen. In the Eye of the I.Q. Storm." Human Behavior 1(Mr-Ap, 1972):16-23.

Fischbach, Thomas J., and Walberg, Herbert J. "Weighted and Unweighted Means for Estimation: A Note on the Humphreys-Dachler and Jensen Papers." Journal of Educational Psychology 62(F, 1971):79-80.

Fjellman, Janet. "The Myth of Primitive Mentality." Doctoral dissertation, Stanford U., 1971.

Flew, Anthony. "Reason, Racism and Obscurantism." New Humanist (England), Jl, 1973.

Footlick, Jerrold. "Jensen for the Defense." Newsweek, Mr 19, 1973.

Fox, Robin. "Chinese Have Bigger Brains Than Whites--Are They Superior?" New York Times Magazine, Je 30, 1968.

France, Kenneth. "Effects of 'White' and of 'Black' Examiner Voices on I.Q. Scores of Children." Developmental Psychology 8(Ja, 1973.

Frederickson, Lowry C. "Measured Intelligence: Species Specific? Perhaps; Race Specific? Perhaps Not." Journal of Genetic Psychology 130(Mr, 1977):95-104.

Freeman, Frank N. "The Interpretation of Test Results with Special Reference to Race Comparisons." Journal of Negro Education 3(Jl, 1934):519-522.

Freeman, Frank N., Holzinger, K. J., and Mitchell, B. C. "The Influence of Environment on the Intelligence, School Achievement, and Conduct of Foster Children." In National Society for the Study of Education, Twenty-Seventh Yearbook: Nature and Nurture, Part I, Their Influence on Intelligence, pp. 103-217. Bloomington, IL: The Society, 1928.

Freeman, Roger A. "In Praise of [A. R.] Jensen." Harvard Educational Review, Summer, 1969.

Fried, M. "The Need to End the Pseudoscientific Investigation of Race." In Science and the Concept of Race. Edited by M. Mead, T. Dobzhansky, E. Tolach, and R. Light. New York: Columbia U. Press, 1968.

Friedenberg, Edgar Z. "The New Assault on Equality: A Symposium." Social Policy 3 (Mr-Ap, 1973):55-61.

Friedrichs, Robert W. "The Impact of Social Factors Upon Scientific Judgment: The 'Jensen Thesis' as Appraised by Members of the American Psychological Association." Journal of Negro Education 42(Fall, 1973):429-438.

Furby, Lita. "Implications of Within-Group Heritabilities for Sources of Between-Group Differences: IQ and Racial Differences." Developmental Psychology 9(Jl, 1973):28-37.

Furth, H. G. "Piaget, IQ & the Nature-Nurture Controversy." Human Development 16(1973): 61-73.

Gage, N. L. "The Causes of Race Differences in I.Q." Phi Delta Kappan (Mr, 1972):422-427.

_____. "I.Q. Heritability, Race Differences, and Educational Research." Phi Delta Kappan 53(Ja, 1972):208-312.

Garcia, John. "I.Q.: The Conspiracy." Psychology Today, S, 1972.

Garn, Stanley M. "Race, Behavior, and Intelligence." In Human Races, pp. 111-116. 2nd ed. Springfield, IL: Charles C. Thomas, 1965.

Garnett, Henry E. "A Note on the Intelligence Scores of Negroes and Whites in 1918." Journal of Abnormal and Social Psychology 40 (1949):344-346.

_____. "'Facts' and 'Interpretations' Regarding Race Differences." Science 101(1945):404-405.

_____. IQ and Racial Differences, 1973. Howard Allen, Box 76, Cape Canaveral, FL 32920.

_____. "I.Q. and School Achievement of Negro and White Children of Comparable Age and School Status." Western Destiny, Ja, 1965.

_____. "Klineberg's Chapter on Race and Psychology." Mankind Quarterly 1(1960):15-22.

Garth, T. R. "Intelligence and Achievement of Southern Negro Children." School and Society 32(S 27, 1930):431-435.

Gartner, Alan, and Riessman, Frank. The Lingering Infatuation With I.Q., 1974. Social Policy, 184 Fifth Avenue, NY, NY, 10010.

Gartner, Alan, Greer, Colin, and Reissman, Frank (eds.). The New Assault on Equality. IQ and Social Stratification. New York: Perennial Library, 1974.

Gay, Cleveland J. "Academic Achievement and Intelligence among Negro Eighth Grade Students as a Function of Self Concept." Doctoral dissertation, North Texas State U., 1966. Univ. Microfilms Order No. 66-6409.

"Genetic Differences in Intelligence." Intellect 105(Ja, 1977):214-215.

"Geneticists Reluctant to Take Sides over Jensen." Times Higher Education Supplement, S 21, 1973.

Gerken, Kathryn Clark. "Performance of Mexican American Children on Intelligence Tests." Exceptional Children 44(Mr, 1978):438-443.

Gillie, Oliver. "Did Sir Cyril Burt Fake His Research on Heritability of Intelligence?" Phi Delta Kappan 58(F, 1977):469-471. [Reprinted from the London Times, O 27, 1976.]

_____. "Sir Cyril Burt and the Great IQ Fraud." New Statesman, N 24, 1978.

_____. Who Do You Think You Are? London: Hart-Davis, MacGibbon, 1976.

Ginsburg, Benson E. "Developmental Genetics of Behavioral Capacities: The Nature-Nurture Problem Re-Evaluated." Merrill-Palmer Quarterly of Behavior and Development 17(Ap, 1971):187-202.

Ginsburg, Benson, and Laughlin, W. S. "The Multiple Bases of Human Adaptability and Achievement: A Species Point of View." Eugenics Quarterly, S, 1966.

Goldberger, Arthur S. "Jensen on Burks and on Jensen's Method for Twins." Educational Psychologist 12(1976):64-82.

_____. Mysteries of the Meritocracy. Madison: Institute for Research on Poverty, U of Wisconsin, O, 1974.

_____. On Jensen's Method for Twins. Madison: Institute for Research on Poverty, U of Wisconsin, Mr, 1976.

_____. Professor Jensen, Meet Miss Burks. Madison: Institute for Research on Poverty, U of Wisconsin, D, 1974.

_____. Statistical Inference in the Great IQ Debate. Madison: Institute for Research on Poverty, U of Wisconsin, S, 1975.

Goldberger, Arthur S., and Lewontin, Richard C. Jensen's Twin Fantasy. Madison: Institute for Research on Poverty, U of Wisconsin, Mr, 1976.

Golden, Mark, and Bridger, Wagner. "A Refutation of Jensen's Position on Intelligence, Race, Social Class, and Heredity." Mental Hygiene, O, 1969.

Goldsby, Richard A. "Human Races: Their Reality and Significance." Science Teacher 40 (Ja, 1973):14-18.

_____. Race and Races. 2nd ed. New York: Macmillan, 1977.

Gottesman, Irving I. "Biology, Social Structure, and Equality." In U.S. Congress, 92nd, 2nd Session, Senate, Select Committee on Equal Educational Opportunity, Environment, Intelligence, and Scholastic Achievement. A Completion of Testimony . . ., pp. 40-54. Washington, DC: GPO, Je, 1972.

Gould, Stephen Jay. "Racist Arguments and I.Q." Natural History 83(My, 1974):24-29.

Grant, Thomas E., and Renzulli, Joseph S. "Identifying Achievement Potential in Minority Group Students." Exceptional Children 41 (Ja, 1975):255-259.

Green, Philip. "IQ and the Future of Equality." Dissent 23(Fall, 1976):398-414.

_____. "The Pseudoscience of Arthur Jensen." Dissent 23(Summer, 1976):284-297.

_____. "Race and IQ: Fallacy of Heritability." Dissent 23(Spring, 1976):181-196.

Green, Robert Lee. "The Awesome Danger of Intelligence Tests." Ebony 29(Ag, 1974):68-72.

Green, Robert Lee, Griffore, Robert J., and Simmons, Cassandra. "A Restatement of the IQ/Culture Issue." Phi Delta Kappan 57(Je, 1976):674-676.

Green, Russel F. "On the Correlation between I.Q. and Amount of 'White' Blood." Proceedings of the Annual Convention of the American Psychological Association 7(1972), part I, 285-286.

Gregg, James E. "The Comparison of Races." Southern Workman 54(Ja, 1925):70-75.

Grimmett, Sadie A. "Black and White Children's Free Recall of Unorganized and Organized Lists: Jensen's Level I and Level II." Journal of Negro Education 44(Winter, 1975): 24-33.

_____. "The Similarities in Performance Patterns of Black and White Children: Jensen's Racial Difference Theory Questioned." Journal of Afro-American Issues 4 (Winter 1976):109-120.

Guinagh, Barry J. "An Experimental Study of Basic Learning Ability and Intelligence in Low Socio-economic Populations." Doctoral dissertation, Michigan State U., 1969.

_____. "An Experimental Study of Basic Learning Ability and Intelligence in Low Socio-economic-Status Children." Child Development 42(Mr, 1971):27-36.

Haertel, Geneva D. "A Construct Validation of Jensen's Level I and Level II Intelligence Using a Sample of Fifth Grade Children." Doctoral dissertation, Kent State U., 1975. Univ. Microfilm Order No. 76-4929.

Haggard, Ernest S. "Social Status and Intelligence." Genetic Psychology Monographs 49 (1954):141-186.

Haller, John S., Jr. Outcasts from Evolution. Scientific Attitudes of Racial Inferiority, 1859-1900. Urbana, IL: U. of Illinois Press, 1971.

Halsey, A. H. (ed.). Heredity and Environment. London: Methuen, 1977.

Hammerton, Max. "Race, Morals and Research." Listener, Ja 28, 1971. [Reprinted in Community 2(Ap, 1971):17-20] [In re: Arthur R. Jensen]

Harris, Chester W., and McArthur, David L. "Another View of the Relation of Environment to Mental Abilities." Journal of Educational Psychology 66(1974):457-459.

Harris, Dale B, and Pinder, Glenn D. The Goodenough-Harris Drawing Test as a Measure of Intellectual Maturity of Youths 12-17 Years. United States. Washington, DC: GPO, My, 1974.

Hart, Albert B. "Is the Southern Negro Deteriorating?" Boston Evening Transcript, Mr 18, 1905.

Hart, Leslie A. "This 'Science' Has Nothing to Do With Schools." Harvard Educational Review, Summer, 1969. [In re: Arthur R. Jensen]

Hartmann, Walter. "Potential Is Not Measured by Performance." Harvard Educational Review, Summer, 1969. [In re: Arthur R. Jensen]

Harwood, Jonathan. "The Race and Intelligence Controversy: A Sociological Approach. I: Professional Factors." Social Studies of Science 6 (Autumn, 1976).

_____. "The Race-Intelligence Controversy: A Sociological Approach: II--External Factors." Social Studies of Science 7(F, 1977).

Häyrynen, Yrjö-Paavo. "Some Remarks on the Educability of People on the Basis of Torsten Husen's Report." Acta Sociologica 16(1973): 324-331.

Heber, Rick, and Garber, Howard. "An Experiment in the Prevention of Cultural-Familial Mental Retardation." In U.S. Congress, 92nd, 2nd Session, Senate Select Committee on Equal Educational Opportunity, Environment, Intelligence, and Scholastic Achievement. A Compilation of Testimony..., pp. 478-493. Washington, DC: GPO, Je, 1972.

Henderson, Norman B. and others. "Will the IQ Test Bank Decrease the Effectiveness of Reading Prediction?" Journal of Educational Psychology 65(D, 1973):345-355.

Hennessy, James J., and Merrifield, Philip R. "A Comparison of the Factor Structures of Mental Abilities in Four Ethnic Groups." Journal of Educational Psychology 68(D, 1976):754-759.

Hennessey, Peter. "Herrnstein Thesis Attacks Environmental Theories." Times Higher Education Supplement, My 5, 1972.

Henton, Comradge L., and Johnson, Edward E. Relationship Between Self Concepts of Negro Elementary School Children and their Academic Achievements, Intelligence, and Manifest Anxiety. Baton Rouge, LA: Southern U., 1964.

Hendrick, Clyde, Stikes, C. Scully, Murray, Edward J., and Puthoff, Carol. "Race vs. Belief as Determinants of Attraction in a Group Interaction Context." Memory & Cognition 1(Ja, 1973):41-46.

"Heritability: A Scientific Snow Job." Science for the People 6(Mr, 1974):21-22.

Herrnstein, Richard J. "Comments on Professor Layzer's 'Science or Superstition.'" Cognition 1(1972):419-421.

_____. "The Ersatz Controversy." Harvard Crimson, N 27, 1973. [On I.Q.]

_____. "I.Q." Atlantic 228(S, 1971):43-64.

_____. "I.Q.: Measurement of Race and Class?" Society 10(My-Je, 1973):5-6. [See, also, reply by Deutsch & Edsoll.]

_____. "On Challenging an Orthodoxy." Commentary 55(Ap, 1973):52-62.

Hertzig, Margaret E., and Birch, Herbert G. "Longitudinal Course of Measured Intelligence in Preschool Children of Different Social and Ethnic Backgrounds." American Journal of Orthopsychiatry 41(Ap, 1971):416-426.

Hilliard, Asa G. III. Alternatives to IQ Testing: An Approach to the Identification of Gifted "Minority" Children, Je 30, 1976. ERIC ED 147 009.

_____. "The Intellectual Strengths of Black Children and Adolescents: A Challenge to Pseudoscience." Journal of Non-White Concerns in Personnel and Guidance 2(Jl, 1974):178-188.

Hines, Brainard W. Analysis of Intelligence Scores. Charleston, WV: Appalachian Educational Lab, F, 1971. ERIC ED 052 866.

Hirsch, Jerry. "Behavior-Genetic Analysis and Its Biosocial Consequences." Seminars in Psychiatry 2(F, 1970):89-105. [In re: Arthur R. Jensen]

_____. "Jensenism: The Bankruptcy of 'Science' Without Scholarship." Educational Theory 25 (Winter, 1975).

Hogben, Lancelot. [Letter on the irrelevance of skull capacity for intellectual functioning] Journal of the Royal African Society 33(O, 1934):36-39.

Holden, Constance. "R. J. Herrnstein: The Perils of Expounding Meritocracy." Science 181(Jl 6, 1973):36-39.

Hudson, Liam. "Intelligence, Race, and the Selection of Data." Race 12(Ja, 1971):283-292. [On Arthur R. Jensen]

Hughson, Arthur. "The Case for Intelligence Testing." Phi Delta Kappa, N, 1964. [See Yourman, below.]

Humphreys, Lloyd G. Strategy Training Has No Significant Effect on Race Differences in Non-Verbal Reasoning." Journal of Educational Psychology 68(Ap, 1976):128-129. [See Bridgman and Buttram.]

Humphreys, Lloyd G., and Dachler, Hans Peter. "Jensen's Theory of Intelligence." Journal of Educational Psychology 60(1969):19-26.

_____ and _____. "Jensen's Theory of Intelligence: A Rebuttal." Journal of Educational Psychology 60(1969):432-433.

Hunt, J. McVicker. "Black Genes--White Environment." Trans-action, Je, 1969.

Huntley, R. M. C. "Heritability of Intelligence." In Genetic and Environmental Factors in Human Ability, pp. 201-218. Edited by J. E. Meade and A. S. Parker. New York: Plenum Press, 1966.

Hurst, John. "Some Further Thoughts re: Resolution on Scientific Freedom Regarding Human Behavior and Heredity." New School of Education Journal 2 and 3(1973):93-97. [In re: research on racial and genetic factors in intelligence]

"Innate Intelligence: Another Genetic Avatar." Psychological Record 20(1970):123-130.

"Intelligence and Race." New Republic, Ap 5, 1969. [Critique of A.R. Jensen]

"I.Q. and Environment." Race Today, My, 1969.

"IQ, Lysenkoism and Liberal Orthodoxy." Commentary (Ju, 1973):4-14.

"IQ Scores: Money Isn't Everything." Science News 113(Ja, 1978):58.

Ireland, Thomas R. "The Relevance of Race Research." Ethics 84(Ja, 1974):140-145.

"Is Intelligence Racial?" Newsweek, My 10, 1971. [On William Shockley and Arthur Jensen]

Isaacs, Charles. "Free Speech for William Shockley?" Chronicle of Higher Education, D 3, 1973.

Jacoby, Russell. "A Falling Rate of Intelligence?" Telos 27(Spring, 1976):141-146.

Jastak, Joseph F. "Intelligence Is More Than Measurement." Harvard Educational Review, Summer, 1969. In re: Arthur R. Jensen

Jayakar, S.D. "Racial Differences in Man: A Population Geneticist's View." International Social Science Journal 26(1974).

Jencks, Christopher. "Intelligence and Race." New Republic, S 13, 1969.

_____ and Brown, M. "Genes and Social Stratification." In Kinometrics: The Determinants of Economic Success Within and Between Families. Edited by P. Taubman. North Holland: Elsevier, 1977.

Jensen, Arthur R. An Examination of Culture Bias in the Wonderlic Personnel Test. ERIC ED 086 726, 1973.

_____. "Can We and Should We Study Race Differences?" In Race and Intelligence, pp. 10-31. Edited by C. Loring Brace, George R. Gamble, and James T. Bond. Washington, DC: American Anthropological Association, 1971.

_____. Can We and Should We Study Race Difference? ERIC ED 041 059, 1970.

_____. "The Cause of Twin Differences in I.Q." Phi Delta Kappan (Mr, 1972):420-421.

_____. Cumulative Deficit: A Testable Hypothesis? ERIC ED 090 337, Je, 1973.

_____. "Did Sir Cyril Burt Fake His Research on Heritability of Intelligence?" Phi Delta Kappan 58(F, 1977):471, 492. [Reprinted from the London Times]

_____. "The Differences Are Real." Psychology Today 7(D, 1973):80-86.

_____. Do Schools Cheat Minority Children? ERIC ED 046 976, 1970.

_____. "Do Schools Cheat Minority Children?" Educational Research 14(1971):3-28.

_____. Educational Differences. London: Methuen, 1973.

_____. "The Effect of Race of Examiner on the Mental Test Scores of White and Black Pupils." Journal of Educational Measurement 11(1974): 1-14.

_____. "Environmentalist Rationalization Versus Environmental Research." In U.S. Congress, 92nd, 2nd Session, Senate, Select Committee on Equal Educational Opportunity, Environment, Intelligence, and Scholastic Achievement. A Compilation of Testimony..., pp. 271-431. Washington, DC: GPO, Je, 1972.

_____. "Equality and Diversity in Education." In Education, Inequality, and National Policy, pp. 125-136. Edited by Nelson F. Ashline, Thomas R. Pezzullo, and Charles I. Morris. Lexington, MA: Lexington Books, 1976.

_____. Genetics and Education. London, Methuen, 1972.

_____. "The Heritability of Intelligence." Engineering and Science, Ap, 1970.

_____. "Hierarchical Theories of Mental Ability." In On Intelligence, pp. 119-190. Edited by B. Docksell. Toronto, Canada: Ontario Institute for Studies in Education, 1970.

_____. "How Much Can We Boost I.Q. and Scholastic Achievement?" Harvard Educational Review, Winter, 1969.

_____. "The IQ Controversy: A Reply to Layzer." Cognition 1(1972):427-452.

_____. Improving the Assessment of Intelligence. ERIC ED 062 483, Ap 28, 1972.

_____. "Intelligence, Learning Ability, and Socio-Economic Status." Journal of Special Education, Winter-Spring, 1969.

_____. "Interaction of Level I and Level II Abilities with Race and Socioeconomic Status." Journal of Educational Psychology 66(F, 1974): 99-111.

_____. "I.Q.'s of Identical Twins Reared Apart." Behavioral Genetics (1970):133-146.

_____. "Jensen on Hirsch on 'jensenism.'" Educational Researcher 1(Je, 1972):15-16.

_____. "Jensen's Theory of Intelligence: A Reply." Journal of Educational Psychology 60(1969):427-431.

_____. "Kinship Correlations Reported by Sir Cyril Burt." Behavior Genetics 4(Mr, 1974): 1-28.

_____. "Let's Understand Skodak and Skeels, Finally." Educational Psychologist 10(1973): 30-35.

_____. "Level I and Level II Abilities in Three Ethnic Groups." American Educational Research Journal 10(Fall, 1973):263-276.

_____. "The Meaning of Heritability in the Behavioral Sciences." Educational Psychologist 11(1975):171-183.

_____. "On 'Jensenism': A Reply to Critics." In Educational Yearbook 1973-74, pp. 276-298. New York: Macmillan, 1973.

_____. "Patterns of Mental Ability and Socioeconomic Status." Proceedings of the National Academy of Sciences 60(1968):1330-1337.

_____. "Personality and Scholastic Achievement in Three Ethnic Groups." British Journal of Educational Psychology 43(Je, 1973): Part 2, 115-125.

_____. "Race and Intelligence: The Case for Genetics." Times Educational Supplement, S 20, 1974.

_____. "Race and Mental Ability." In Racial Variation in Man. Edited by J.F. Ebling. New York: Academic Press, 1975.

_____. "Race and the Genetics of Intelligence: A Reply to Lewontin." Bulletin of Atomic Scientists, My, 1970.

_____. "Race Differences, Strategy Training, and Improper Inference." Journal of Educational Psychology 68(Ap, 1976):130-131. [See Bridgeman and Buttram]

_____. "Race Put-Down." New Society 19(F 24, 1972):408-410. Review discussion of Richardson, Spears, and Richards (eds.), Race, Culture, and Intelligence, 1972.

_____. "Reducing the Heredity-Environment Uncertainty: A Reply." Harvard Educational Review, Summer, 1969.

_____. "The Role of Verbal Mediation in Mental Development." Journal of Genetic Psychology 118(Mr, 1971):39-70.

_____. The Role of Verbal Mediation in Mental Development. Bethesda, MD: National Institute of Child Health and Human Development, 1968.

_____. "Sir Cyril Burt in Perspective." American Psychologist 33(My, 1978):499-503. [See Michael McAskie, below]

_____. "Social Class, Race, and Genetics: Implications for Education." American Educational Research Journal, Ja, 1968.

_____. "Statement...Before the General Subcommittee on Education, House Education and Labor Committee." Congressional Record, Jl 1, 1970. H6324-H6326.

_____. [Statement and Testimony] in U.S. Congress, 91st, 2nd Session, House of Representatives, Committee on Education and Labor, General Subcommittee on Education. Emergency School Aid Act of 1970. Hearing... Washington, DC: GPO, 1970.

_____. "Statement..." In U.S. Congress, 92nd, 2nd Session, Senate, Select Committee on Equal Educational Opportunity, Environment, Intelligence, and Scholastic Achievement. A Completion of Testimony..., pp. 55-68. Washington, DC: GPO, Je, 1972.

_____. "A Theoretical Note on Sex Linkage and Race Differences in Spatial Visualization Ability." Behavior Genetics 5(1975):151-163.

_____. "Twin Differences and Race Differences in I.Q.: A Reply to Buagen and Jahoda." Bulletin of the British Psychological Society 24(1971):195-198.

_____. "Another Look at Culture-Fair Tests." Western Regional Conference on Testing Problems, Proceedings for 1968. Berkeley, CA: Educational Testing Service, 1968.

Jensen, Arthur R., and Figueroa, Richard A. "Forward and Backward Digit Span Interaction With Race and IQ: Predictions from Jensen's Theory." Journal of Educational Psychology 67(D, 1975):882-893.

Jensen, Arthur R., and Frederiksen, Janet. "Free Recall of Categorized and Uncategorized Lists: A Test of the Jensen Hypothesis." Journal of Educational Psychology 65(D, 1973): 304-312.

Jensen, Arthur R., and Rohwer, William D., Jr. An Experimental Analysis of Learning Abilities in Culturally Disadvantaged Children. Final Report. ERIC ED 043 690, Jl, 1970.

"Jensen Intercepted." New Society, Ag 10, 1972.

Jerrison, Harry J. "Evolution of the Brain and Intelligence." Current Anthropology 16(S, 1975):403-426. [Symposium on Jensen's book]

Jinks, J. L., and Eaves, L. J. "IQ and Inequality." Nature 248(Mr 22, 1974):287-289.

Johnson, Charles S. "Mental Measurements of Negro Groups." Opportunity 1(F, 1923):21-25.

Johnson, Charles S., and Bond, Horace M. "The Investigation of Racial Differences Prior to 1910." Journal of Negro Education 3(Jl, 1934):328-339.

Johnson, Douglas F. "Race and I.Q.--Why Computer Tests Are Best." Times Education Supplement, D 8, 1972. [Experiment in Rochester, NY]

Johnson, Douglas F., and Michal, William J. "Performance of Blacks and Whites in Computerized Versus Manual Testing Environments." American Psychologist 28(Ag, 1973). [I.Q.]

Johnson, Oliver. "Brain Knows No Color." Advance, S 16, 1880. [Reprinted in Women's Journal, S 25, 1880]

Johnson, Francis E., Pollitzer, William S., and Giles, Eugene. Culture and Genetics. Washington, DC: American Anthropological Association, 1972.

Jones, Faustine C. "The Inequality Controversy." Journal of Negro Education 42(Fall, 1973): 537-549.

Jordan, Winthrop D. "A Sense of Success: Heredity, Intelligence, and Race in American History and Culture." In Anthropology and the Public Interest. Edited by Peggy R. Sanday. New York: Academic Press, 1976.

Jorgensen, Carl C. "I.Q. Tests and Their Educational Supporters." Journal of Social Issues 29(1973):33-40.

_____. "Racism in Mental Testing: The Use of IQ Tests to Mislabel Black Children." In Explorations in Psychology, pp. 194-215. Edited by Albert A. Harrison. Monterey, CA: Brooks/Cole, 1974.

Joseph, Andre. Intelligence, IQ, and Race: When, How and Why They Become Associated. San Francisco: R & E Research Associates, 1977.

Kadane, Joseph B. and others. An Econometric Model for Estimating IQ Scores and Environmental Influences on the Pattern of IQ Scores Over Time, 1973. ERIC ED 097 403. [Pittsburgh]

_____. "Models of Environmental Effects on the Development of IQ." Journal of Educational Statistics 1(Autumn, 1976):181-231.

Kagan, Jerome. "The I.Q. Puzzle: What Are We Measuring?" Inequality in Education 14(Jl, 1973):5-13.

_____. "Inadequate Evidence and Illogical Conclusions." Harvard Educational Review, Spring, 1969. [Critique of Arthur R. Jensen]

_____. "What Is Intelligence?" In The New Assault on Equality. IQ and Social Stratification, pp. 114-130. Edited by Alan Gartner, Colin Greer and Frank Riessman. New York: Perennial Library, 1974.

Kajaku, Jon. "The IQ Debate. If Shockley is Right, Should Whites Be Sterilized?" Bridge 4 (F, 1976):31-33. [In re: Asian Americans]

Kamin, Leon. "The Hole in Heredity." New Society, D 2, 1976.

_____. "IQ Tests As Instruments of Oppression-- From Immigration Quotas to Welfare." South Today 4(Jl, 1973).

_____. "The Misuse of IQ Testing." Change 5 (O, 1973):40-43. [Interview by John Egerton]

_____. "The Politics of IQ." National Elementary Principal 54(Mr-Ap, 1975):15-22.

_____. The Science and Politics of I.Q. New York: Wiley, 1974.

_____. "The Science and Politics of I.Q." Social Research 41(Autumn, 1974). [1905-1930]

Kamin, Leon and others. "Kamin on Thompson's Review of Herrnstein." Contemporary Psychology 19(1974):788-790.

Kaplan, Bernice. "Environment and Human Plasticity." American Anthropologist 56(1954): 780-800.

Katz, Phyllis. Modification of Children's Racial Attitudes, 1976. ERIC ED 135 882.

_____ (ed.). Towards the Elimination of Racism. Elmsford, NY: Pergamon Press, 1976.

Kaye, Kenneth. "I.Q.: A Conceptual Deterrent to Revolution in Education." Elementary School Journal 74(O, 1973):9-23.

Kaylani, Abdallah H. Investigating the Relationship Between Measures of Learning and Measures of Intelligence in Racial and Socio-economic Groups. Diss. Abstr. Int'l., 1970, 30 (9-B) 4362.

Kee, Daniel W. "Learning Efficiency in Four Ethnic Groups." Integrated Education 10 (N-D, 1972):29-32.

Kee, Daniel W., and Rohwer, William D., Jr. "Noun-Pair Learning in Four Ethnic Groups: Conditions of Presentation and Response." Journal of Educational Psychology 65(O, 1973): 226-232.

Keller, Susanne. "Tests machen dumm. Warum man 'Intelligenz' nicht messen kann." Neues Forum 261(S, 1975).

Kennedy, Wallace A. A Follow-Up Normative Study of Negro Intelligence and Achievement. Monographs of the Society for Research in Child Development 126, Vol. 34, 1969.

_____. "Native Differences in Intelligence?" University Bookman, Winter, 1969.

Kessler, Jane W. "Environmental Components of Measured Intelligence." School Review, Winter, 1965.

Kilgore, William J., and Sullivan, Barbara. "Academic Values and the Jensen-Shockley Controversy." Journal of General Education 27(F, 1975):177-197.

Kinnie, Ernest J., and Sternlof, Richard E. "The Influence of Nonintellective Factors on the IQ Scores of Middle- and Lower-Class Children." Child Development 42(D, 1971): 1989-1995.

Klein, Robert E. and others. "Cognitive Test Performance and Indigenous Conceptions of Intelligence." Journal of Pyschology 93(Jl, 1976):273-280.

Kleinfeld, J. S. "Intellectual Strengths in Culturally Different Groups: An Eskimo Illustration." Review of Educational Research 43(Summer, 1973):341-359.

Klineberg, Otto. Negro Intelligence and Selective Migration. New York: Columbia U. Press, 1935.

Knobloch, H., and Pasamanick, B. "Environmental Factors Affecting Human Development, Before and After Birth." Pediatrics, Ag, 1960.

Knobloch, H. "The Relationship of Race and Socioeconomic Status to the Development of Motor Behavior Patterns in Infancy." Social Aspects of Psychiatry, D, 1958, Psychiatric Research Report No. 10, American Psychiatric Association.

Krasner, William, and Mercer, Jane R. Labeling the Children. Washington, DC: GPO, 1977.

Kresbeck, Janet D., and Nicolosi, Lucille. "A Comparison of Black & White Children's Scores on the Peabody Picture Vocabulary Test." Language, Speech & Hearing Services in Schools 4(Ja, 1973):37-40.

Kuttner, Robert E. (ed.). Race and Modern Science. New York: Social Science Press, 1967.

Labov, William. "Academic Ignorance and Black Intelligence." Atlantic Monthly 229(Je, 1972):59-67.

Laishley, Jennie. "Some Perspectives on Race and Intelligence." New Community 2(Spring, 1973):187-193.

Lawler, James. "IQ: Biological Fact or Methodological Construct?" Science and Society 41(Summer, 1977):208-218.

_____. IQ, Heritability and Racism. New York: International, 1978.

Lawrence, Daniel. "The Continuing Debate on Heredity and Environment." Patterns of Prejudice 11(My-Je, 1977):5-9.

_____. "Race, Intelligence and Culture." Patterns of Prejudice 9(Mr-Ap, 1975):21-25.

Lawson, M. J., and Jarman, R. F. "A Note on Jensen's Theory of Level 1 Ability and Recent Research on Human Memory." British Journal of Educational Psychology 47(F, 1977):91-94.

Layzer, David. "A Rejoinder to Professor Herrnstein's Comments." Cognition 1(1972): 423-426.

_____. "Heritability Analyses of IQ Scores: Science or Numerology?" Science 183(1974): 1259-1266. [See discussion in 188(Je 13, 1975)1125-1130]

_____. "Is There Any Real Evidence That IQ Scores Are Heritable?" Scientific American (Jl, 1975):126-128.

_____. "Jensen's Reply: The Sounds of Silence." Cognition 1(1972):453-473.

_____. "Science or Superstition: A Physical Scientist Looks at the IQ Controversy." Cognition (Winter, 1973).

Leach, Edmund. "The Jensen Race Row." The Listener, Je 28, 1973.

Lederberg, Joshua. "Racial Alienation and Intelligence." Harvard Educational Review, Summer, 1969. [In re: Arthur R. Jensen]

Lee, Dorothy. "Freeing Capacity to Learn." In Papers and Reports from the Fourth ASCD Research Institute. Edited by Alexander Frazier. Washington, DC: Association for Supervision & Curriculum Development, 1960.

"The Legal Implication of Cultural Bias in the Intelligence Testing of Disadvantaged School Children." Georgetown Law Journal 61(Mr, 1973).

Leifer, Anna. "Mosaics of Disadvantaged Negro and White Preschoolers." Journal of Genetic Psychology 121(S, 1972):59-63.

Levidow, Les. "A Marxist Critique of the IQ Debate." Radical Science Journal 6-7(1978).

Lewontin, Richard C. "The Apportionment of Human Diversity." In Evolutionary Biology, VI, pp. 381-398. Edited by T. Dobzhansky, M. K. Hecht, and W. C. Steele. New York: Appleton-Century-Crofts, 1972.

_____. "Further Remarks on Race and the Genetics of Intelligence." Bulletin of Atomic Scientists, My, 1970.

_____. "Herrnstein's Sleight-of-Hand." Harvard Crimson, D 11, 1973.

_____. "Race and Intelligence." Bulletin of Atomic Scientists 26(1970):2-8.

Lieberman, Leonard. "The Debate Over Race: A Study in the Sociology of Knowledge." Phylon, Summer, 1968.

Light, Richard J. "Intelligence and Genes." Humanist 32(Ja-F, 1972):12-13.

Light, Richard J., and Smith, Paul V. "Social Allocation Models of Intelligence." Harvard Educational Reviews, Summer, 1969. [In re: Arthur R. Jensen]

_____ and _____. "Statistical Issues in Social Allocation Models of Intelligence: A Review and a Response." Review of Educational Research 41(0, 1971):351-367. [Reply to Shockley]

Lindsey, Richard A. "Negro Intelligence and Educational Theory." Clearing House 45(0, 1970):67-71.

Little, William B., Kenny, Charles T., and Middleton, Morris C. "Differences in Intelligence Among Low Socioeconomic Class Negro Children as a Function of Sex, Age, Educational Level of Parents, and Home Stability." Journal of Genetic Psychology 123(D, 1973):241-250.

Liungman, Carl G. What is I.Q.? Heredity and Environment.

Lodge, Henry Cabot. "The Distribution of Ability in the United States." Century Magazine 42(1891):687-694.

Loeb, Jacques. "Heredity and Racial Inferiority." Crisis 8(Je, 1914):83-84.

_____. "Science and Race." Crisis 9(D, 1914): 92-93.

Loehlin, John C., Vandenberg, Steven G., and Osborne, R. Travis. "Blood-Group Genes and Negro-White Ability Differences." Behavior Genetics 3(S, 1973):263-270.

Loehlin, John C. and others. Race Differences in Intelligence. San Francisco: Freeman, 1975.

Long, Richard A. "The Shockley Archipelago." Nation 218(Ap 13, 1974):452.

Luneman, Alan. "The Correlational Validity of IQ as a Function of Ethnicity & Desegregation." Journal of School Psychology 12 (Winter, 1974):263-268.

Lyons, Charles H. "To Wash an Aethiop White": British Ideas About Black African Educability: 1530-1960. New York: Teachers College Press, 1975.

McAskie, Michael. "Carelessness or Fraud in Sir Cyril Burt's Kinship Data? A Critique of Jensen's Analysis." American Psychologist 33(My, 1978):496-498. [See reply by Jensen in same issue of journal]

McAskie, Michael, and Clarke, Ann M. "Parent-Offspring Resemblances in Intelligence: Theories and Evidence." British Journal of Psychology 67(1976):243-273.

McClearn, Gerald E. Contributions of Genetics to Biological and Behavioral Development and the Influence of Various Deprivations. Bethesda, MD: National Institute of Child Health and Human Development, 1968.

McCullough, James L. A Study of the Predictive Efficiency of the California Short-Form Test of Mental Maturity, Level 2, for Negro and White Subjects. Diss. Abstr. Int'l., 1969, 30 (6-A) 2260.

McGonigle, Brendan, and McPhilemy, Sean. "Genesis of an Irish Myth." Times Higher Education Supplement, S 13, 1974. [In re: views of H. J. Eysenck on the intelligence of Irishmen]

_____, and _____. "Dispelling the Mist Around an Irish Myth." Times Higher Education Supplement, O 25, 1974. [In re: H. J. Eysenck's theories of the I.Q. of Irishmen]

McGurk, Francis C. J. "On White and Negro Test Performance and Socioeconomic Factors." Journal of Abnormal and Social Psychology 48 (1953):448-450.

McPherson, James M. "History and Biology." In The Abolitionist Legacy From Reconstruction to the NAACP, Chapter 18. Princeton, NJ: Princeton U. Press, 1975.

McQueen, Robert, and Church, Browning. "The Intelligence and Educational Achievement of a Matched Sample of White and Negro Students." School and Society, S 24, 1960.

Mackintosh, Nicholas. "But They Do Measure Something." Times Educational Supplement, Ap 22, 1977.

Maddox, John. "Why the Tricky Issue of Racial Differences Should Not be Sidestepped." Times Educational Supplement, N 3, 1978.

Makins, Virginia. "Interview with Arthur Jensen." Times Educational Supplement, S 3, 1971.

Manning, Winton H. "The Measurement of Intellectual Capacity and Performance." Journal of Negro Education, Summer, 1968.

Marjoribanks, Kevin. "Another View of the Relation of Environment to Mental Abilities: A Reply." Journal of Educational Psychology 66(1974):460-463.

_____. "Ethnic and Environmental Influences on Levels and Profiles of Mental Abilities." Doctoral dissertation, U. of Toronto, 1972.

Marks, Russell. "Providing for Individual Differences: A History of the Intelligence Testing Movement in North America." Interchange 7(1976-1977):3-16.

_____. "Testers, Trackers and Trustees: The Ideology of the Intelligence Testing Movement in America 1900-1954." Doctoral dissertation, U. of Illinois, 1972.

Markwood, Evelyn Herwitz. In Search of Self-Evident Truths: A Review of Background Literature on School Desegregation, My, 1977. ERIC ED 148 909.

Marsh, Alan. "Race, Heredity and I.Q." New Community 1(O, 1971):71-74.

Martin, Charles A. "'There's More than One Way to Skin a Cat' (The Issue of Heredity and Anti-Egalitarian Research)." Journal of Negro Education 42(Fall, 1973):559-569.

Mason, Philip. "Race, Intelligence and Professor Jensen." Race Today, Jl, 1969.

Mayeske, George W. On the Explanation of Racial-Ethnic Group Differences in Achievement Test Scores, S, 1971. ERIC ED 057 114.

Mazrui, Ali S. "Science and Black Marginality." In World Culture and the Black Experience, pp. 38-81. Seattle, WA: U. of Washington Press, 1974.

Mead, Margaret. "The Methodology of Racial Testing: Its Significance for Sociology." American Journal of Sociology 31(Mr, 1926):657-667.

Medewar, P. B. "Unnatural Science." New York Review of Books 24(F 3, 1977). [IQ & Race]

Meehl, Paul. "Law and the Fireside Inductions: Some Reflections of a Clinical Psychologist." Journal of Social Issues 27(1971):65-100 [Deals with socioeconomic influences on mental tests]

"Men and Mice at Edinburgh: Reports from the Genetics Congress. The Geneticists' Manifesto." Journal of Heredity 30(1939):371-373.

Mensing, Patricia M., and Traxler, Anthony J. "Social Class Differences in Free Recall of Categorized and Uncategorized Lists in Black Children." Journal of Educational Psychology 65(D, 1973):378-382. [In re: Jensen's Level I and Level II intelligence]

Mercer, Jane R. Labeling the Mentally Retarded. Berkeley, CA: U. of California Press, 1973.

_____. "Sociocultural Factors in the Educational Evaluation of Black and Chicano Children." In U.S. Congress, 92nd, 2nd session, Senate, Select Committee on Equal Educational Opportunity, Environmental, Intelligence, and Scholastic Achievement. A Compilation of Testimony..., pp. 438-449. Washington, DC: GPO, Je, 1972.

_____. "Statement..." In U.S. Congress, 92nd, 2nd session, Senate, Select Committee on Equal Educational Opportunity, Environment, Intelligence, and Scholastic Achievement. A Compilation of Testimony..., pp. 433-437. Washington, DC: GPO, Je, 1972.

Meyer, William J., and Egeland, Byron. Changes in Stanford-Binet IQ: Performance vs. Competence, 1968. ERIC ED 056 745.

Meyer, William J., and Goldstein, David. Performance Characteristics of Middle-Class and Lower-Class Preschool Children on the Stanford-Binet, 1960 Revision, 1969. ERIC ED 044 429.

Milgram, Norman A. "IQ Constancy in Disadvantaged Negro Children." Psychological Reports 29(Ag, 1971):319-326.

Miller, Brian P. "I.Q. Tests and Minority Groups." Training and Development Journal 25(O, 1971):26-27.

Miller, Henry. "The Shockley Affair." New Community 2(Summer, 1973):300-301. [Reprinted from The Listener]

Miller, Max D. "Patterns of Relationships of Fluid and Crystallized Mental Abilities to Achievement in Different Ethnic Group.s" Doctoral dissertation, U. of Houston, 1972.

Mirsky, Alfred. "Genetics and Human Affairs." Scientific American (O, 1964).

"Mixture of Races and Mental Character." Daily Democratic Statesman (Austin, TX), Ja 9, 1876, p. 1.

Money, John, and Nurcombe, Barry. "Ability Tests and Cultural Heritage: The Draw-A-Person and Bender Tests in Aboriginal Australia." Journal of Learning Disabilities 7(My, 1974):298-303.

Montagu, Ashley (ed.). Race and IQ. New York: Oxford U. Press, 1975.

Moore, Clifford L., and Retish, Paul M. "Effect of the Examiner's Race on Black Children's Wechsler Preschool and Primary Scale of Intelligence IQ." Developmental Psychology 10(S, 1974):672-676.

Moran, P. A. P. "A Note on Heritability and the Correlation Between Relatives." Annals of Human Genetics 37(1973).

"More About I.Q." Atlantic 228(D, 1971):101-110. [In re: R. J. Herrnstein]

Morgan, Harry. "Myth and Reality of I.Q. Scores." Black Scholar 4(My-Je, 1973):28-31.

Morris, F. The Jensen Hypothesis: Social Science Research or Social Science Racism? Los Angeles, CA: Center of Afro-American Studies, U. of California, 1971.

Moyer, F. L. "A Study of the Effects of Classification by Intelligence Tests." In The Twenty-Third Yearbook of the National Society of the Study of Education. Edited by G. M. Whipple. Bloomington, IL: Public School Publishing, 1924.

Moynihan, Daniel P. "Jensen Not 'Must Reading' in the Nixon Cabinet." Journal of Social Issues 26(Spring, 1970):191-192 (letter).

Munford, W. B., and Smith, C. E. "Racial Comparisons and Intelligence Testing." Journal of the Royal African Society 37(1938):46-57.

Munsinger, Harry. "The Adopted Child's IQ: A Critical Review." Psychological Bulletin (S, 1975):623-659.

Murray, W. I. "The I.Q. and Social Class in the Negro Caste." Southwestern Journal of Anthropology 4(1949):187-201.

Narrol, Harvey, and Bachor, Dan G. "An Introduction to Feuerstein's Approach to Assessing and Developing Cognitive Potential." Interchange 6(1975):2-16.

National Academy of Sciences Ad Hoc Committee on Genetic Factors in Human Performance. "Recommendations With Respect to Human Genetics." Proceedings of the National Academy of Sciences, U.S.A. 69(1972):1-3.

Neary, John. "A Scientist's Variations on a Disturbing Racial Theme." Life, Je 12, 1970. [About Arthur Jensen]

Nelson, James D. "A Black Neuropsychiatrist Responds." Harvard Educational Review, Summer, 1969. [In re: Arthur R. Jensen]

New York Scientists' Committee for Public Information. "A Statement from SCPI." Harvard Educational Review, Summer, 1969. [In re: Arthur R. Jensen]

Nichols, Paul L. "The Effects of Heredity and Environment on Intelligence Test Performance in 4 and 7 Year Old White and Negro Sibling Pairs." Doctoral dissertation, U. of Minnesota, 1970. Univ. Microfilms Order No. 71-18,874.

Nichols, Paul L., and Anderson, V. Elving. "Intellectual Performance, Race, and Socioeconomic Status." Social Biology 20(D, 1973):367-374.

Nichols, Paul L., and Broman, Sarah H. "Familial Resemblance in Infant Mental Development." Developmental Psychology 10 (1974):442-446.

Nichols, Robert C., and Loehlin, John C. Heredity, Environment and Personality: A Study of 850 Sets of Twins. Austin: U. of Texas Press, 1976.

Nisbett, John, and Coard, Bernard. "Race, Intelligence and Education." Times Educational Supplement, Je 18, 1971.

Northrop, James. Affective Education to Facilitate Integration. Gainesville, FL: P. K. Yonge Laboratory School, n.d.

Nwafor, Azinna. "History and the Intelligence of the Disinherited." Review of Radical Political Economics 7(Fall, 1975):43-54.

Ogbu, John U. Social Structure and Cognitive Behavior: A Critique of the Heredity-Environment Hypothesis and an Alternative Interpretation of Black-White Differences in IQ, Mr, 1974. ERIC ED 097 401.

"Opportunity Lost." New Society, Jl 23, 1970. [Account of debate on race and intelligence involving Prof. Arthur R. Jensen]

Orn, D. E., and Das, J. P. "I.Q., Socioeconomic Status, and Short-Term Memory." Journal of Educational Psychology 63(Ag, 1972):327-333.

Osborne, R. Travis. "Fertility Ratio: Its Relationship to Mental Ability, School Achievement, and Race." Journal of Psychology 84 (My, 1973):159-164.

_____. "Racial Differences in Mental Growth and School Achievement." In Race and Modern Science, pp. 383-406. Edited by Robert E. Kuttner. New York: Social Science Press, 1967.

Osborne, R. Travis, and Gregor, A. J. Racial Differences in Heritability Estimates for Tests of Spatial Ability, F, 1968. ERIC ED 017 012.

_____ and _____. "Racial Differences in Heritability Estimates for Tests of Spatial Ability." Perceptual and Motor Skills, D, 1968.

Osborne, R. Travis, and Miele, Frank. "Racial Differences in Environmental Influences on Numerical Ability as Determined by Heritability Estimates." Perceptual and Motor Skills, Ap, 1969.

Osborne, R. Travis, and Suddick, D. E. "Blood Type Gene Frequency and Mental Ability." Psychological Reports 29(D, 1971):1243-1249.

Padilla, Amado M., and Garza, Blas M. "IQ Tests: A Case of Cultural Myopia." National Elementary Principal 54(Mr-Ap, 1975):53-58.

Page, Ellis B. "Miracle in Milwaukee: Raising the IQ." Educational Researcher 1(O, 1972):8-1 8-16. [Critique of "Milwaukee Project" study study by Rick Heber and others]

Panda, Kailash, C., and Lynch, William W. "Effects of Race and Sex on Attribution of Intellectual Achievement: Responsibility for Success and Failure Situations Among Educable Mentally Retarded Children." Indian Journal of Mental Retardation 7(J1, 1974):72-80.

Patin, Henry A. "Intelligence and Education." School Review, Winter, 1965.

Perney, Lawrence R. and others. "Black Intelligence--A Re-Evaluation." Journal of Negro Education 46(Fall, 1977):450-455. [East Cleveland, Ohio]

Peterson, Joseph. "Basic Considerations in Methodology in Race Testing." Journal of Negro Education 3(J1, 1934):403-410.

Pettigrew, Thomas F. "Blacks on Campus. IQ's and Uncle Toms." Commonweal 99(O 5, 1973). [Book reviews in re: race and intelligence]

Pezzulo, Thomas R., Thorsen, Eric E., and Madaus, George F. "The Heritability of Jensen's Level I and II and Divergent Thinking." American Educational Research Journal 9(Fall, 1972):539-546.

Phye, Gary D., and Zimmerman, Bonnie B. Effects of Organization and Instruction on Free and Cued Recall in Lower Socioeconomic Status Fourth Graders, Ap, 1976. ERIC ED 121 890.

Piel, Gerard. "The New Hereditarians." Nation 220(Ap 19, 1975):455-459.

Piersel, Wayne C. and others. "A Further Examination of Motivational Influences on Disadvantaged Minority Group Children's Intelligence Test Performance." Child Development 48(S, 1977):1142-1145.

Plomin, Robert. "Critique of Scarr and Weinberg's IQ Adoption Study: Putting the Problem in Perspective." Intelligence 2(Ja-Mr, 1978):74-79.

Pocock, C. "Race and Culture." Biology and Human Affairs 37(Fall, 1971):33-38.

Price, James D. "Analysis of Changes in Intelligence Test Scores of Mexican-American Youth Assigned to Special Classes in Relation to Jensen's Two-Level Theory of Mental Abilities." Diss. Abstr. Int'l. 32 (6-A), D, 1971, 3125-3126.

Pringle, J. W. S. (ed.). Biology and the Human Sciences. London: Oxford U. Press, 1972.

"Professor Rips I.Q. Tests of Black Youths as 'Inaccurate and Unfair.'" Muhammad Speaks, Ap 18, 1969. [Robert Coles' critique of A. R. Jensen's analysis of racial differentils in I.Q. scores]

Progressive Labor Party. Racism, Intelligence, and the Working Class. Progressive Labor Party, Box 1336, Boston, MA 02104.

Provine, William B. "Geneticists and the Biology of Race Crossing." Science 182 (N, 1973):790-796.

Purvin, George. "Intro to Herrnstein." In The New Assault on Equality. IQ and Social Stratification, pp. 131-162. Edited by Alan Gartner, Colin Greer, and Frank Riessman. New York: Perennial Library, 1974.

Quay, Lorene C. "Language Dialect, Age, and Intelligence-Test Performance in Disadvantaged Black Children." Child Development 45(Je, 1974):463-468.

_____. "Negro Dialect and Binet Performance in Severely Disadvantaged Black Four-Year-Olds." Child Development 43(Mr, 1972):245-250.

_____. "Reinforcement and Binet Performance in Disadvantaged Children." Journal of Educational Psychology 67(F, 1975):132-135.

Rankin, Jeremiah E. "The Aesthetic Capacity of the Afro-American." Our Day 13(J1-Ag, 1894).

Ratusink, David L., and Koeingsknecht, Roy A. "Normative Study of the Goodenough Drawing Test and the Columbia Mental Maturity Scale in a Metropolitan Setting." Perceptual and Motor Skills 40(Je, 1975):835-838.

Reed, T. Edward. "Caucasian Genes in American Negroes." Science 165(1969):762-768.

Reid, Inez Smith. "Science, Politics and Race." Signs 1(1976).

Reinhold, Robert. "A Limit on Scholarship?" New York Times, D 9, 1973. [In re: William B. Shockley]

Reiss, Elizabeth W. "The Influence of Race and Social Class Upon the Measurement of Intelligence, Cognitive Style, and Direct Learning Ability." Doctoral dissertation, Ohio State U., 1972.

Rice, Berkeley. "The High Cost of Thinking the Unthinkable." Psychology Today 7(D, 1973): 89-93. [Race and I.Q.]

Richards, Martin. "Putting Jensenism In Its Proper Place." Times Higher Education Supplement, J1 20, 1973.

Richardson, Ken, and Houghton, Vic. "Race and IQ." New Humanist, S, 1973.

Richardson, Ken, Spears, David, and Richards, Martin (eds.). Race, Culture and Intelligence. Harmondsworth, Middlesex, England: Penguin, 1972.

Rivers, Larry W. "The Stability of Differential Patterns of Mental Abilities in Children from Different Ethnic Groups." Diss. Abstr. Int'l. 32 (2-B), Ag, 1971, 1194.

Roach, Robert E., and Rosecrans, C. J. "Intelligence Test Performance of Black Children with High Frequency Hearing Loss." Journal of Auditory Research 11(Ap, 1971): 136-139.

Roberts, Jean. Family Background, Early Development, and Intelligence of Children 6-11 Years. Washington, DC: GPO, Ag, 1974.

Rohwer, William D., Jr., Ammon, Mary S., Suzuki, Nancy, and Levin, Joel R. "Population Differences and Learning Proficiency." Journal of Educational Psychology 62(F, 1971):1-14.

Rose, Hilary, and Rose, Steven. "The IQ Myth." Race and Class 20(Summer, 1978):63-74.

Rose, Steven. "Jensen Debate: Science and Pseudo-Science." Times Higher Education Supplement, Mr 10, 1972.

Rose, Steven, Hambley, John, and Haywood, Jeff. "Science, Racism and Ideology." In Socialist Register, pp. 235-260, 1973.

Rose, Steven, and Richardson, Ken. Race, Education and Intelligence. London: National Union of Teachers, 1978.

Rosen, S. R. "Personality and Negro-White Intelligence." Journal of Abnormal and Social Psychology 61(1960):148-150.

Rowan, Carl T. "Cheers! Blacks Are Not Inferior After All." Chicago Daily News, F 28, 1976.

Rubin-Rabson, Grace. "Behavioral Science Versus Intelligence." Wall Street Journal, Jl 1, 1969.

_____. "Nature-Nurture and the Intelligence Issue." Phylon 35(Mr, 1974):16-21.

Rustin, Bayard. "Being Frank About People, Places, & Problems." Chicago Defender, N 1, 1969. [On race and intelligence]

_____. "Free Speech for Shockley." New America, D 30, 1973.

_____. "The Irrelevant Doctrines of William Shockley." New York Teacher, J 20, 1974.

Samuel, William and others. "Motivation, Race, Social Class, and IQ." Journal of Educational Psychology 68(Je, 1976):273-285.

Samelson, Franz. "On the Science and Politics of the IQ. Social Research 42(Autumn, 1975). [See "Reply to Samelson" by Leon Kamin, same issue]

Sanday, Peggy R. "An Alternative Interpretation of the Relationship Between Heredity, Race, Environment, and IQ." Phi Delta Kappan 54 (D, 1972):250-254.

_____. "On the Causes of IQ Differences Between Groups and Implications for Social Policy." Human Organization 31(1972).

Sanua, Victor D. A Critique of Jensen's Article: How Much Can We Boost IQ and Scholastic Achievement?, Ap 17, 1970. Available from Victor D. Sanua, Associate Professor, City College, CUNY K-8, New York, NY 10031.

Sarason, Seymour B. "The Unfortunate Fate of Alfred Binet and School Psychology." Teachers College Record 77(My, 1976):579-592.

Sattler, Jerome M., and Kuncik, Thomas M. "Ethnicity, Socioeconomic Status, and Pattern of WISC Scores as Variables that Affect Psychologists' Estimates of 'Effective Intelligence.'" Journal of Clinical Psychology 32(Ap, 1976):362-366.

Scarr, Sandra. Genetic Effects on Human Behavior: Recent Family Studies, 1977. ERIC ED 146 249.

_____. "Race, Social Class, and IQ." Science 174(D, 1971):1285-1295.

_____. "Unknowns in the IQ Equation." Science 174(1971):1223-1228.

Scarr, Sandra, Pakstis, A. J., Katz, S. H., and Barker, W. B. "Absence of a Relationship between Degree of White Ancestry and Intellectual Skills within a Black Population." Human Genetics (Spring, 1977):1-18

Scarr, Sandra, and Weinberg, R. A. "IQ Test Performance of Black Children Adopted by White Families." American Psychologist 31 (1976):726-739.

_____ and _____. "Intellectual Similarities Within Families of Both Adopted and Biological Children." Intelligence (1977).

_____ and _____. "Nature and Nurture Strike (Out) Again." Intelligence (1977).

_____ and _____. "When Black Children Grow Up in White Houses." Psychology Today 9 (D, 1975):80-82.

Schaie, K. Warner and others (eds.). Developmental Human Behavior Genetics: Nature-Nurture Redefined. Lexington, MA: Lexington Books, 1975.

Schiff, Michel and others. "Intellectual Status of Working-Class Children Adopted Early into Upper-Middle-Class Families." Science 200 (Je, 1978):1503-1504.

Schoenfeld, William N. "Notes on a Bit of Psychological Nonsense: 'Race Differences in Intelligence.'" Psychological Record 24 (1974):17-32.

Schroth, Marvin L. "The Use of IQ as a Measure of Learning Rate with Minority Children." Journal of Genetic Psychology 128(Mr, 1976): 101-108.

Schuyler, George S. "The Negro and Nordic Civilization." Messenger 7(My, 1925):201-208.

Schwartz, Edward M., and Elonen, Anna S. "IQ and the Myth of Stability: A 16-Year Longitudinal Study of Variations in Intelligence Test Performance." Journal of Clinical Psychology 31(O, 1975):687-694.

Schwartz, M., and Schwartz, J. "Evidence Against a Genetical Component to Performance on IQ Tests." Nature 248(1974):84-85.

Schwebel, Milton. "Correcting an Interpretation." Harvard Educational Review, Summer, 1969. [In re: Arthur R. Jensen]

Scriven, Michael. "The Values of the Academy (Moral Issues for American Education and Educational Research Arising from the Jensen Case)." Review of Educational Research 40 (O, 1970):541-549.

Scrofani, Philip J. and others. "Conceptual Ability in Black and White Children of Different Social Classes: An Experimental Test of Jensen's Hypothesis." American Journal of Orthopsychiatry 43(Jl, 1973).

Senna, Carl (ed.). The Fallacy of I.Q. New York: The Third Press, 1973.

Shapiro, Peter. "Richard Herrnstein: A Target Speaks About His Attackers." Harvard Crimson, Ap 17, 1972.

Sherwood, John J., and Nataupsky, Mark. "Predicting the Conclusions of Negro-White Intelligence Research from Biographical Characteristics of the Investigation." Journal of Personality and Social Psychology Ja, 1968.

Shockley, William. "'Cooperative Correlation' Hypothesis for Racial Differences in Earning Power." Proceedings of the National Academy of Sciences 66(1970):245.

_____. "Dysgenics, Geneticity, Raceology: A Challenge to the Intellectual Responsibility of Educators." Phi Delta Kappan 53(Ja, 1972):297-307.

_____. "Geneticity Is 80% for White Identical Twins' I.Q.'s." Phi Delta Kappan (Mr, 1972):415-419.

_____. "Hardy-Weinberg Law Generalized to Estimate Hybrid Variance for Negro Populations and Reduce Racial Aspects of the Environment-Heredity Uncertainty." Proceedings of the National Academy of Sciences 68(1971):1390A.

_____. "Human-Quality Problems and Research Taboos." New Concepts and Directions in Research. Greenwich, CT: Educational Records Bureau, 1969.

_____. "Models, Mathematics, and the Moral Obligation to Diagnose the Origin of Negro IQ Deficits." Review of Educational Research 41(O, 1971):369-377.

_____. "Negro IQ Deficit: Failure of a 'Malicious Coincidence" Model Warrants New Research Proposals." Review of Educational Research 41(Je, 1971):227-248.

_____. "New Methodology to Reduce the Environment-Heredity Uncertainty About Dysgenics." Proceedings of the National Academy of Sciences 67(1970):10A-11A.

_____. "Offset Analysis Description of Racial Differences." Proceedings of the National Academy of Sciences 64(1969):1432.

_____. [Statement] in U.S. Congress, 91st, 2nd Session, House of Representatives, Committee on Education and Labor, General Subcommittee on Education. Emergency School Aid Act of 1970. Hearings... Washington, DC: GPO, 1970.

Shuey, Audrey M. The Testing of Negro Intelligence, 2nd ed. New York: Social Science Press, 1966.

Simon, Brian. Intelligence, Psychology, and Education. London: Lawrence & Wishart, 1971.

_____. "Intelligence, Race, Class, and Education." Marxism Today (N, 1970):237-263.

Singer, Dorothy. "The Influence of Intelligence on an Interracial Classroom on Social Attitudes." In The Urban R's. Edited by Robert A. Dentler and others. New York: Praeger, 1967.

Smith, Annie Mabelle. "A Critique of Some Negro Intelligence Test Results." Master's thesis, U. of Southern California, 1928.

Smith, Margot Wiesinger. "Alfred Binet's Remarkable Question: A Cross-National & Cross-Temporal Analysis of the Cultural Biases Built Into the Stanford-Binet Intelligence Scale and Other Binet Tests." Genetic Psychology Monographs 89(1974):307-334.

Smith, Paul M., Jr. "Perhaps We Should Be Suspicious." Harvard Educational Review, Summer, 1969. [In re: Arthur R. Jensen]

Smith, Stanley H. "Race, Intelligence and Learning." Journal of Social and Behavioral Sciences 17(Summer, 1971):14-21.

Society for the Psychological Study of Social Issues. "The SPSSI Statement." Harvard Educational Review, Summer, 1969. [In re: Arthur R. Jensen]

Sowell, Thomas. "The Great IQ Controversy." Change 5(My, 1972).

_____. "New Light on Black I.Q." New York Times Magazine, Mr 27, 1977.

68 / CHILDREN

_____. User's Guide for Ethnic Minorities IQ Data File. Washington, DC: Urban Institute, Mr, 1977.

Spivak, Jonathan. "Race and IQ: Hard to Test, or to Ignore." Wall Street Journal, Ja 5, 1970.

Spring, Joel H. "Psychologists and the First World War: The Meaning of Intelligence in the Alpha and Beta Tests." History of Education Quarterly 12(Spring, 1972):3-15.

Spuhler, J. N. (ed.). Behavioral Consequences of Genetic Differences in Man. Viking Fund Publications in Anthropology, 1967.

Spuhler, J. N., and Lindzey, G. "Racial Differences in Behavior." In Behavior-Genetic Analysis. Edited by J. Hirsch. New York: McGraw-Hill, 1967.

Stafford, R. E. "Hereditary and Environmental Components of Quantitative Reasoning." Review of Educational Research 42(Spring, 1972):183-201.

Standards for Educational and Psychological Tests. Washington, DC: American Psychological Association, 1974.

Starkman, Stanley and others. "The Relationship Among Measures of Cognitive Development Learning Proficiency, Academic Achievement, and IQ for Seventh Grade, Low Economic Status Black Males." Journal of Experimental Education 45(Winter, 1976):52-56.

Stein, Zena, and Susser, Mervyn. "Mutability of Intelligence and Epidemiology of Mild Mental Retardation." Review of Educational Research 40(F, 1970):29-67.

Stinchombe, Arthur L. "Environment: The Cumulation of Events." Harvard Educational Review, Summer, 1969. [In re: Arthur R. Jensen]

Stone, Vernon W. "The Interaction Component Is Critical." Harvard Educational Review, Summer, 1969. [In re: Arthur R. Jensen]

Stranch, A. Barry. "An Investigation into the Sex x Race x Ability Interaction." Doctoral dissertation, Pennsylvania State U., 1975. Univ. Microfilms Order No. 76-17,228. [In re: hypothesis by A. R. Jensen]

Sullivan, Allen R. "Counter Balance Intelligence Testing." Black Academy Review 2(Winter, 1971):5-16.

Tate, Douglas Tyrone. "A Study of the Relationship of Socioeconomic Status & Intelligence and Achievement Scores of White & Negro Group." Doctoral dissertation, Oklahoma State U., 1967. DA 4882-A.

Taubman, Paul. "Earnings, Education, Genetics, and Environment." Journal of Human Resources 11(F, 1976):447-461.

Taylor, Howard F. "IQ Heritability: A Checklist of Methodological Fallacies." Journal of Afro-American Issues 4(Winter, 1976):35-49.

Taylor, Lorne J., and Shanes, Graham R. "Level I and Level II Intelligence in Iniut and White Children from Similar Environments." Journal of Cross-Cultural Psychology 7(Je, 1976):157-168.

Thoday, J. M. "Limitations to Genetic Comparison of Populations." Journal of Biosocial Science Supplement 1(1969):3-14. [In re: Heritability of I.Q.]

Thomas, William Isaac. "Race Psychology: Standpoint and Questionnaire with Particular Reference to the Immigrant and the Negro." American Journal of Sociology 17(My, 1912):725-775.

Thompson, W. O. "The Negro. The Racial Inferiority Argument in the Light of Science and History." Voice of the Negro 3(N, 1906):507-513.

Thorndike, Robert L. "Mr. Binet's Test 70 Years Later." Educational Researcher 4(My, 1975):3-7.

Throne, John M. "Is the Proportion of Genetic to Total Variance in Intelligence Empirically Determined? Socially Useful? Individually Relevant?" Educational Technology 15(F, 1975):9-13.

Tizard, Barbara. "In Defense of Nurture." New Society, Ja 10, 1974.

Tizard, Jack. "Race and IQ: The Limits of Probability." New Community 4(Autumn, 1975):371-375. [Reprinted from New Behaviour]

Tobias, Phillip V. "Brain-Size, Grey Matter and Race--Fact or Fiction?" American Journal of Physical Anthropology 32(1970):3-25.

Topoff, Howard. "Genes, Intelligence and Race." In The Four Horsemen. New York: Behavioral Publications, 1974.

Trotman, Frances Keith. "Race, IQ, and the Middle Class." Journal of Educational Psychology 69(Je, 1977):266-273.

Trout, Jean, Packwood, Gene, and Wilson, Barry J. "Ertl's Neural Efficiency Analyzer: Still Promising--But What?" Phi Delta Kappan 57 (Mr, 1976):448-451.

Tuddenham, Reed D. "The Nature & Measurement of Intelligence." In Psychology in the Making, pp. 469-525. Edited by L. Postman, 1962.

Tufano, Louis Gerald. "The Effect of Effort and Performance Reinforcement on WISC-R IQ Scores of Black and White EMR Boys." Doctoral dissertation, U. of Georgia, 1975. Univ. Microfilms Order No. 76 06455.

Urbach, P. "Progress and Degeneration in the IQ Debate." British Journal of the Philosophy of Science, Summer, 1974.

U.S. Congress, 92nd, 2nd session, Senate, Select Committee on Equal Educational Opportunity. Environment, Intelligence, and Scholastic Achievement. A Compilation of Testimony... Washington, D.C.: GPO, Je, 1972.

Vallejo, Carlos John. "A Comparative Analysis of Intelligence and Achievement Involving Mexican American and Anglo American Students in Selected Nebraska Elementary Schools." Doctoral dissertation, U. of Nebraska, 1976. Univ. Microfilm Order No. 77-896.

Vance, Hubert "B," and Engin, Ann. "Analysis of Cognitive Abilities of Black Children's Performance on WISC-R." Journal of Clinical Psychology 34(Ap, 1978):452-456.

Vandenberg, Steven G. "Human Behavior Genetics: Present Status and Suggestions for Future Research." Merrill-Palmer Quarterly, Ja, 1969.

_____. "What Do We Know Today About the Inheritance of Intelligence and How Do We Know It?" In Intelligence: Genetic and Environmental Influences, pp. 182-218. Edited by R. Canero. New York: Grune and Stratton, 1971.

Van Den Haag, Ernest. "[Arthur R.] Jensen's Article Is a Good Beginning." Harvard Educational Review, Summer, 1969.

Veroff, Joseph and others. Measuring Intelligence and Achievement Motivation in Surveys, O, 1971. ERIC ED 146 177-146 179.

Vasgird, Dan. "Oh God, Oh Galton, Mr. Herrnstein!" Crisis 82(N, 1975):341-347.

Vernon, Philip E. "Genes, G, and Jensen." Contemporary Psychology 15(Mr, 1970):161-163. [In re: Arthur R. Jensen]

_____. "Heredity and Environment in the Growth and Decline of Intelligence." Journal of Educational Thought 9(Ag, 1975):83-92.

_____. "Intelligence Across Cultures." In Race and Education Across Cultures. Edited by G. K. Verma and Christopher Bagley. Stamford, CT: Greylock Publishers, 1976.

_____. Intelligence and Cultural Environment. London: Methuen, 1969.

_____. "Vernon on Jensen." New Society, D 14, 1972.

Vernon, Philip E., Dill, John R., Gottesman, Irving I., Biederman, Irving, and Clark, Kenneth E. "Testing Negro Intelligence. Comments on Eysenck." Humanist (Ja-F, 1970): 34-37.

Vernon, Philip E., and Mitchell, Margaret C. "Social-Class Differences in Associative Learning. Journal of Special Education 8 (Winter, 1974):297-311.

Voyat, Gilbert. "I.Q.: God-Given or Man-Made?" Saturday Review, My 17, 1969.

Wade, Nicholas. "IQ and Heredity: Suspicion of Fraud Beclouds Classic Experiment." Science 194(N, 1976):916-919. [In re: Cyril Burt]

Wallace, Bruce. "Genetics and the Great IQ Controversy." American Biology Teacher 37 (Ja, 1975):12-18, 50.

Walsh, John F., and D'Angelo, Rita. "IQ's of Puerto Rican Head Start Children on the Vane Kindergarten Test." Journal of School Psychology 9(1971):173-176.

Warner, Charles Dudley. [On supposed intellectual incapacity of blacks] Journal of Social Science 38(1901):1-14.

Watson, Peter. "How Race Affects IQ." New Society, Jl 16, 1970.

_____. "Stability of IQ of Immigrant and Non-Immigrant Slow-Learning Pupils." British Journal of Educational Psychology 43(F, 1973): 80-82.

_____. "Unimportance of I.Q." Times Education Supplement, Jl 20, 1973.

_____ (ed.). Psychology and Race. Penguin, 1973.

Weinberg, Meyer. "Race and Intelligence in America." In Minority Students: A Research Appraisal, pp. 37-54. Washington, DC: GPO, 1977.

Welsing, Frances, and Shockley, William. "The Great Debate." Muhammad Speaks, F 22, 1974.

Wenkert, Bob. "An Open Letter." New School of Education Journal 2 and 3(1973):86-92. [In re: research on racial and genetic factors in intelligence]

Wesley, Charles H. "Negro Inferiority in American Thought." Journal of Negro History, O, 1940.

West, Gerald. Intelligence Tests and the Black Child. Pacifica Tape Library, 2217 Shattuck Avenue, Berkeley, CA 94704.

Whimbey, Arthur, and Barberena, Celia J. A Cognitive-Skills Approach to the Disciplines: Intelligence Beyond Arthur Jensen, D, 1977. ERIC ED 148 793.

White, Sheldon H. "Social Implications of IQ." National Elementary Principal 54(Mr-Ap, 1975): 4-14.

Whiteman, Martin. "Intelligence and Learning." Merrill-Palmer Quarterly, Jl, 1964.

Willerman, L., Naylor, A. F., and
Myrianthopoulos, N. C. "Intellectual Develop-
ment of Children from Interracial Matings:
Performance in Infancy and at 4 Years."
Behavior Genetics 4(1974):83-90.

Williams, George W. "The Negro Intellect." In
History of the Negro Race in America From
1619 to 1880, I. New York: G. P. Putnam's
Sons, 1883.

Williams, Robert L. "On Black Intelligence."
Journal of Black Studies 4(S, 1973):29-39.

Williams, Robert L. "Moderator Variables as
Bias in Testing Black Children." Journal of
Afro- American Issues 3(Winter, 1975):77-90.

_____. "On Black Intelligence." Journal of
Non-White Concerns in Personnel and Guidance
1(0, 1972):9-14.

_____. "On Black Intelligence." Washington
University Magazine 41(Spring, 1971).

Wiseman, S. "Environmental and Innate Factors
and Educational Attainment." In J. E. Meade
and A. S. Parkes, Genetic and Environmental
Factors in Human Ability. Edinburgh: Oliver
and Boyd, 1966.

_____ (ed). Intelligence and Ability. Penguin,
1967.

Witty, Paul A., and Lehman, Harvey C. "Racial
Differences: The Dogma of Superiority."
Journal of Social Psychology 1(Ag, 1930):
394-418.

Woodworth, R. S. "Comparative Psychology of
Races." Psychological Bulletin, 1916.

X (Clark), Cedric. "The Shockley-Jensen Thesis:
A Contextual Appraisal." Black Scholar 6
(Jl-Ag, 1975):3-11.

67X, Charles. "The Shockley Smokescreen."
Muhammad Speaks, Ja 4, 1974.

Yates, Louise G. "Comparative Intelligence of
Negro and White Children from a Rural-
Southern Culture." Ph.D. dissertation, U. of
North Carolina, 1967.

Yawkey, Thomas D., and Jantz, Richard K. "Differential Effects of Intelligence, Race, SES,
and Sex Variables on Arithmetic Achievement
Test Performance." Journal of Instructional
Psychology 1(Spring, 1974).

Yerkes, Robert Means. Psychological Examining
in the United States Army. Memoirs National
Academy of Sciences, V.XV, 890 pp. Washington,
DC: GPO, 1921.

Yourman, Julius. "The Case Against Group I.Q.
Testing." Phi Delta Kappan, N, 1964. [See
Hughson, above.]

Zach, Lillian. "The IQ Debate." Today's Education (S, 1972):40-43, 65-68.

_____. "The IQ Test: Does It Make Black
Children Unequal?" School Review 78
(F, 1970):249-258.

Zigler, E., and Butterfield, E. C. "Motivational
Aspects of Changes in I.Q. Test Performance
of Culturally Deprived Nursery School
Children." Child Development 39(1968):1-14.

Desegregation Effects

Aberdeen, F. D. "Adjustment to Desegregation:
A Description of Some Differences Among
Negro Elementary Pupils." Doctoral disser-
tation, U. of Michigan, 1969.

Acland, Henry. Secondary Analysis of the
Emergency School Assistance Program, D, 1975.
ERIC ED 124 672.

Allen, Howard Webster. "A Study of Black and
White Students' Perceptions Toward their
Participation in the Student Activity Program
in Selected Recently Desegregated Senior High
Schools in Virginia." Doctoral dissertation,
U. of Virginia, 1973. Univ. Microfilm Order
No. 73-31113.

Allen, Irving M. and others. "Psychological
Stress of Young Black Children and Result of
School Desegregation." Journal of the
American Academy of Child Psychiatry 16
(Autumn, 1977):739-747. [Boston]

Anderson, David Ross. "The Effects of First
Year Desegregation on the Year-End Grade
Average-Dropout Rate, and Discipline Problems
of a Group of Eleventh-Grade Black Pupils."
Doctoral dissertation, U. of Florida, 1973.
Univ. Microfilm Order No. 74-09572.

Archibald, David K. Report on Change in Academic
Achievement for a Sample of Elementary School
Children: Progress Report on METCO.
Roxbury, MA: METCO, 1967.

Armor, David J. "The Evidence on Busing." The
Public Interest 28(Summer, 1972):90-126.

_____. "Has Busing Succeeded?" New Society,
Ja 18, 1973.

_____. "The Double Double Standard: A Reply."
Public Interest 30(Winter, 1973):119-131.

Armstrong, C. P., and Gregor, A. James. "Integrated Schools and Negro Character Development: Some Considerations of the Possible
Effects." Psychiatry, F, 1964. [See
article on Holland, below]

Arnez, Nancy Levi. "Desegregation of Public
Schools: A Discriminatory Process." Journal
of Afro-American Issues 4(Winter, 1976):274-
281.

_____. "Implementation of Desegregation as a
Discriminatory Process." Journal of Negro
Education 47(Winter 1978):28-45.

Aronson, Elliot with others. "Busing and Racial Tension. The Jigsaw Route to Learning and Liking." Psychology Today 8 (F, 1975):43-50. [Austin]

Arulanandam, Saleth J. "School Busing: Solution or Evasion. A Critical Analysis of the Literature from 1960 to 1972." Master's thesis, Loyola U., Chicago, 1972.

Ayling, Richard. "The Relationships Between Black and White Students in a Large High School." Doctoral dissertation, Michigan State U., 1972.

Baird, John Lawrence. "An Exploration of Alienation of Secondary School Students Participating in Planned Desegregation." Doctoral dissertation, Oklahoma State U., 1969. Univ. Microfilm Order No. 70-21,341.

Baker, Eugene A., and Owen, David R. "Negro-White Personality Differences in Integrated Classrooms." Proceedings of the 77th Annual Convention of the American Psychological Association, 1969, 4 (Pt. 2):539-540.

Ballinger, Cornelia. "A Two-Year Study of the Desegregation of the Bowling Green, Warren County, Kentucky Public Elementary Schools During 1964-66." Master's thesis, Jackson State College, 1968.

Baltzell, Dora Catherine. "A Longitudinal Analysis of Reading and Arithmetic Achievement and Court-Ordered Desegregation (with 'Forced' Busing) in a Large Urban School District in the South." Doctoral dissertation, U. of Florida, 1976. [Jacksonville, Florida]

Barkham, Carl S. and others. "Implementation of a Simulation of Change Model for Elementary Students." Journal of Non-White Concerns in Personnel & Guidance 2(Ja, 1974):71-78. [Prince George's County, MD]

Barnett, Betty. "The Effects of School Integration Experiences on the Academic Achievement of Negro Students." Master's thesis, Humboldt State College, 1971.

Bartel, Helmut W., Bartel, Nettie R., and Grill, J. Jeffrey. "A Sociometric View of Some Integrated Open Classrooms." Journal of Social Issues 29(1973):159-173.

Bazeli, Frank P. "Dilemmas of Pupil Evaluation in the Desegregated High School." High School Journal 58(Ap, 1975):295-300.

_____. "Integrating the Desegregated School." NASSP Bulletin 60(F, 1976):80-84.

Bennett, John E. "The Effects of Integration on Achievement in a Large Elementary School." Florida Journal of Educational Research 16 (1974):12-15.

Berkowitz, Morris I. Studies of School Desegregation and Achievement: A Summary. Pittsburgh: Commission on Human Relations, 1967.

Bilodeau, W. "Status and Interracial Relationships in the Integrated Classroom." Doctoral dissertation, U. of Chicago, 1972.

Binderman, Murray. Factors in School Integration Decisions of Negro Mothers. Final Report, D 15, 1968. ERIC ED 026 441.

Blake, Elias, Jr. "A Comparison of Intraracial and Interracial Levels of Aspiration." Ph.D. dissertation, U. of Illinois, 1960.

Blanchard, Yvonne L. "A Study to Examine Learner Efficiency and Institutional Effectiveness as Measured by Perceived Self-Concept and Locus of Control of Black Students in Segregated v. Desegregated Schools." Doctoral dissertation, U. of Massachusetts, 1978. Univ. Microfilms Order No. 7810686.

Blodgett, Michael William. "Student Violence Status Maximization and Anonymity as Factors Subject to Staff Control in Potentially Explosive Desegregating Public Schools." Doctoral dissertation, U. of Michigan, 1975. Univ. Microfilms Order No. 75-21,037.

Bosco, James, and Robin, Stanley. "White Flight from Court-Ordered Busing?" Urban Education 9(Ap, 1974):87-98. [Pontiac and Kalamazoo, Michigan]

Bradley, Gladyce H. "Friendships among Students in Desegregated Schools." Journal of Negro Education, Winter, 1964.

Bradley, Laurence A., and Bradley, Gifford W. "The Academic Achievement of Black Students in Desegregated Schools: A Critical Review." Review of Educational Research 47(Summer, 1977):399-449.

Bregner, Jeffrey Lee. "The Relationship of Administrative Practices and Procedures to the Integration of Desegregated Secondary Schools." Doctoral dissertation, 1974. Univ. Microfilms Order No. 75-4148.

Brooks, Bernice D. "A Study of Ninety-Five Children Traveling by Bus to a K-5 School as Part of the Open Environment Program in a Large Urban School System." Doctoral dissertation, Columbia U., 1970.

Brookshire, William K., and Ernst, Nora S. Group Composition in a Voluntarily Integrated School, 1977. ERIC ED 146 313.

Brown, Barry S., and Albee, George W. "The Effect of Integrated Hospital Experiences on Racial Attitudes--A Discordant Note." Social Problems, Winter, 1966.

Brozovich, Richard William. "Group Norms in Sixth Grade Classrooms of Contrasting Socio-Economic Status and Differing Racial Composition." Doctoral dissertation, George Peabody College, 1966. Univ. Microfilms Order No. 66-12238.

Bryant, Bunyan I., Chesler, Mark A., and Crowfoot, James E. "Barometers of Conflict." Educational Leadership 33(O, 1975):17-20.

Bullock, Charles S. III. "The Coming of School Desegregation: A Before and After Study of Black and White Student Perceptions." Social Science Quarterly 54(Je, 1973): 132-138.

_____. "Interracial Contact and Student Prejudice. The Impact of Southern School Desegregation." Youth and Society 7(Mr, 1976):271-310.

_____. School Desegregation, Inter-Racial Contact and Prejudice. Washington, DC: National Institute of Education, Jl 30, 1976. [Georgia]

Bullock, Charles S. III, and Rodgers, Harrell R. "Coercion and Southern School Desegregation: Implications for the North." School Review 83(Ag, 1975):645-662.

Bureau of Social Science Research, Inc. Racial Integration and the Social Adjustment of Public School Children. Washington, DC: BSSR Study No. 528, F, 1956.

Burden, Carol A. Consulting Techniques in Racially Integrated Elementary Schools, Ap, 1972. ERIC ED 062 485.

Bush, Patricia L. and others. "Effects of Schools' Racial Composition on the Self-Concept of Black and White Students." Journal of Educational Research 67(O, 1973): 57-63.

Byalick, Robert L. "Expressed Preference and Observed Use of Positive Reinforcement in Bi-racial Classrooms." Doctoral dissertation, U. of Georgia, 1972.

Calhoun, Lillian S. Desegregation Works: A Primer for Parents and Teachers. Chicago: Integrated Education Associates, 1968.

Campbell, Bruce A. "The Impact of School De-segregation: An Investigation of Three Mediating Variables." Youth and Society 9 (S, 1977):79-111. [Atlanta]

Campbell, Robert. A Summary of Studies on the Effects of Integration on Academic Achieve-ment. San Francisco, CA: San Francisco Unified School District, Mr, 1972.

Carithers, Martha W. "School Desegregation and Racial Cleavage 1954-1970: A Review of the Literature." Journal of Social Issues 26 (Autumn, 1970):25-47.

Carrigan, Patricia. School Desegregation via Compulsory Pupil Transfer: Early Effects on Elementary School Children. Ann Arbor, MI: Ann Arbor Public Schools, 1969. ERIC ED 036 597.

Carrigan, Patricia, and Aberdeen, David. Some Early Effects of Compulsory Desegrega-tion on Elementary School Children, Mr 2, 1970. ERIC ED 038 658.

Carter, Donald E. "A Preliminary Study of School Attitudes of the Disadvantaged Student as the Result of a Busing Program." Child Study Journal 1(Fall, 1970):20-24.

Carter, Donald E., Spero, June, Benson, Forrest W., and De Tine, Susan. "A Study of Peer Acceptance and Related Variables in an In-tegrated Junior High School." Proceedings of the 81st Annual Convention of the American Psychological Association 8(1973):645-646.

Carter, Donald E. and others. School Integra-tion: An Attempt to Predict Peer Acceptance, Ap, 1974. ERIC ED 096 364.

_____ and others. "Peer Acceptance and School-Related Variables in an Integrated Junior High School." Journal of Educational Psychology 67(Ap, 1975):267-273.

Cassell, Joan. A Fieldwork Manual for Studying Desegregated Schools. Washington, DC: National Institute of Education, S, 1978.

Cheffers, John T. F. and others. Achieving Racial Integration Through Movement Oriented Programs, 1976. ERIC ED 123 215.

Chesler, Mark A. Desegregation and Integration Within the School. Ann Arbor, MI: Community Resources Limited, Jl, 1971.

_____. "What Happened After You Desegregated the White Schools?" New South, Winter, 1967.

Chesler, Mark A., Guskin, Judith, and Erenberg, Phyllis. Planning Educational Change, Vol. II. Human Resources in School Desegregation. Washington, DC: GPO, 1969.

Chesler, Mark A. and others. Desegregation/ Integration: Planning for School Change. A Training Program for Intergroup Educators. Washington, DC: National Education Asso-ciation, 1974.

Christison, Milton, and Sida, Donald. Shedding More Light and Less Heat on the Results of School Integration: The Georgia Experience, 1976. ERIC ED 142 599.

Clark, Kenneth B. and others. "Desegregation: Its Implications for Orthopsychiatry." American Journal of Orthopsychiatry 26(1956): 445-470.

Clark, Todd. "Integration: The First Year": A Role-Playing Simulation on School Inte-gration, O, 1970. ERIC ED 050 215.

Clement, Dorothy C. and others. Moving Closer: An Ethnography of a Southern Desegregated School. Washington, DC: National Institute of Education, 1978. [Bradford, NC]

Cohen, David K. "School Desegregation and White Achievement." In U.S. Commission on Civil Rights. Papers Prepared for National Conference on Equal Educational Opportunity in America's Cities. Washington, DC: GPO, 1967.

Cohen, Elizabeth G. "The Effects of Desegregation on Race Relations." Law and Contemporary Problems 39(Spring, 1975):271-299.

Coleman, James S. "If Busing Won't Work, What Is the Answer?" Baltimore Sun, Ap 23, 1972.

_____. "Integration Yes; Busing, No." New York Times, Ag 24, 1975. [Interview by Walter Goodman]

Coles, Robert. Dead End School. Boston, MA: Little, Brown, 1968. [A novel about desegregation]

_____. The Desegregation of Southern Schools: A Psychiatric Study. New York: Anti-Defamation League, 1963. [Atlanta and New Orleans]

_____. "Northern Children Under Desegregation." Psychiatry, F, 1968.

_____. "Southern Children under Desegregation." American Journal of Psychiatry, O, 1963.

Collins, Thomas W. Reconstructing a High School Society After Court-ordered Desegregation, D 1, 1977. ERIC ED 151 500. [Memphis]

Coulson, John E. National Evaluation of the Emergency School Aid Act (ESAA): Summary of the Second-Year Studies. Santa Monica, CA: System Development Corporation, J1, 1976.

Coulson, John E. and others. The First Year of Emergency School Aid Act (ESAA) Implementation. Santa Monica, CA: System Development Corporation, S 15, 1975.

_____ and others. The Second Year of Emergency School Aid Act (ESAA) Implementation. Santa Monica, CA: System Development Corporation, J1, 1976.

_____ and others. The Third Year of Emergency School Aid Act (ESAA) Implementation. Santa Monica, CA: System Development Corporation, Mr, 1977.

Cox, G., and Schummers, J. Social Relations and Self-Concept Among Five Ethnic Groups of Children in Desegregated Schools. San Francisco, CA: California State U., 1971.

Crain, Harold. "An Analysis of the Effects of Race, Desegregation, and Family Background on the Achievement of Tenth Grade Students in the Oklahoma Public High Schools." Doctoral dissertation, U. of Oklahoma, 1972. Univ. Microfilms Order No. 72-23,092.

Crain, Robert L. "The Effects of De Facto School Segregation: A Survey of Negro Adults in Northern Cities." Chicago, IL: National Opinion Research Center, U. of Chicago, N, 1966. Unpublished study prepared for the U.S. Commission on Civil Rights.

_____. "Racial Tension in High Schools. Pushing the Survey Method Closer to Reality." Anthropology and Education Quarterly 8(My, 1977):142-151.

_____. "School Integration and Occupational Achievement of Negroes." American Journal of Sociology 75(1970), part 2, 593:606.

_____. "School Integration and the Academic Achievement of Negroes." Sociology of Education 44(Winter, 1971):1-26.

_____. "Why Academic Research Fails To Be Useful." School Review 84(My, 1976):337-351.

Crain, Robert L., Armor, D., Christen, F. G., King, N. J., McLaughlin, M. W., Sumner, G. C., Thomas, M. A., and Vanecko, J. J. Design for a National Longitudinal Study of School Desegregation. 2 vols. Santa Monica, CA: Rand, S, 1974.

Crain, Robert L., and Mahard, Rita. Desegregation and Black Achievement. Santa Monica, CA: Rand, O, 1977.

Crain, Robert L., and York, Robert L. "Evaluating a Successful Program: Experimental Method and Academic Bias." School Review 84(F, 1976): 233-254. [ESAP]

Cramer, M. Richard. "Factors Related to Willingness to Experience Desegregation Among Students in Segregated Schools." Social Science Quarterly, D, 1968. [1963-1964 survey]

Cunningham, Dan. "School Desegregation and Student Unrest." Florida Schools 33(Mr-Ap, 1971):14-17.

Cusick, Philip A., and Ayling, Richard J. An Exploratory Study of the Formal and Informal Relationships Between White and Black Students in a Racially Mixed, Urban, Secondary School, F 28, 1973. ERIC ED 095 245.

Danahy, Ann Hechter. "A Study of the Effects of Bussing on the Achievement, Attendance, Attitudes, and Social Choices of Negro Inner-City Children." Doctoral dissertation, U. of Minnesota, 1971. Univ. Microfilms Order No. 72-14,285.

Davidson, J. D. and others. Interracial Climates and the Outcomes of School Integration. West Lafayette, Indiana: Department of Sociology and Anthropology, Purdue U., 1975.

Davies, Earnest A. "A Comparative Study of the Academic Achievement of Transported and Nontransported Pupils at Holby Hill Elementary School, Holby Hill, Florida." Master's thesis, Stetson U., 1968.

Dawson, Judith. A Longitudinal and Cross-Sectional Study of the Achievement of Black and Spanish-Surnamed Students in Desegregated Elementary & Secondary Schools. Riverside, CA: Riverside Unified School District, O, 1973.

De Vries, David L., and Edwards, Keith J. "Student Teams: Integrating Desegregated Classrooms." Proceedings of the 81st Annual Convention of the American Psychological Association 8(1973):647-648.

De Vries, David L., Edwards, Keith J., and Slavin, Robert E. Biracial Learning Teams and Race Relations in the Classroom: Four Field Experiments on Teams-Games-Tournament. Baltimore, MD: Center for Social Organization of Schools, Johns Hopkins U., Jl, 1977.

Denmark, Florence L. "The Effect of Integration on Academic Achievement and Self-Concept." Integrated Education 8(My-Je, 1970):34-41.

Deslonde, James. "'You Know the Rules!' Myths About Desegregation." In Teaching in a Multicultural Society, pp. 60-81. Edited by Dolores E. Cross and others. New York: Free Press, 1976.

Dickinson, George E. "Dating Behavior of Black and White Adolescents Before and After Desegregation." Journal of Marriage and the Family 37(Ag, 1975):602-608.

Dooley, Bernard John. "The Relationship Between the Quality of Integration and the Level of Student Unrest in Six High Schools of a Desegregated School District." Doctoral dissertation, U. of Miami, 1974. Univ. Microfilms Order No. 75-4152.

Dressler, Frank J. Study of Achievement in Reading of Pupils Transferred from Schools 15 and 37 to Peripheral Schools to Eliminate Overcrowding, to Abandon an Obsolete School, and to Achieve a More Desirable Racial Balance in City Schools. Buffalo, NY: Division of Curriculum Evaluation and Development, Buffalo Public Schools, Mr, 1967.

Duff, Ogle B. "Second Generation Desegregation." Theory Into Practice 17(F, 1978):78-80.

Dulan, Claude Garland. "Ethnic Identification and Stereotyping by Black Children in Desegregated Elementary Schools." Doctoral dissertation, U. of California, Riverside, 1975. Univ. Microfilms Order No. 7803918.

Dumbarton Research Council. Analysis of Data Concerning Graduates of the Public Schools in Oakland, California, O 16, 1967. Dumbarton Research Council, 1115 Merrill St., Menlo Park, CA.

Eaker, Robert. "Integrating the Desegregated School: The Student Activities Program." Tennessee Education 1(F, 1971):14-18.

Eash, Maurice J., and Rasher, Sue Pinzur "Mandated Desegregation and Improved Achievement: A Longitudinal Study." Phi Delta Kappan 58(Ja, 1977):394-397.

"Easing Integration Through Special Arts Projects." Music Educators Journal 62(F, 1976):78-83.

Eddy, Elizabeth M. "Educational Innovation and Desegregation: A Case Study of Symbolic Realignment." Human Organization 34(Summer, 1975):163-172.

Edwards, Curtis D. "Stress in the School: A Study of Anxiety and Self-Esteem in Black and White Elementary School Children." Doctoral dissertation, Florida State U., 1972.

"The Effects of Segregation and Consequences of Desegregation: A Social Science Statement: Appendix to Appellants' Briefs: Statements by Social Scientists." Social Problems, Ap, 1955.

Emmet, Gerald M. A Mental Health Practitioner's Primer--Critical Intervention in School Desegregation, Mr 20, 1967. ERIC ED 014 510.

Entwisle, Doris R., and Webster, Murray, Jr. "Expectations in Mixed Racial Groups." Sociology of Education 47(Summer, 1974):301-318.

Epps, Edgar G. "The Impact of School Desegregation on Aspirations, Self-Concepts and Other Aspects of Personality." Law and Contemporary Problems 39(Spring, 1975):300-313.

Erskine, Hazel (ed.). "The Polls: Interracial Socializing." Public Opinion Quarterly 37 (Summer, 1973):283-294. [1942-1972]

Evans, C. L. "The Immediate Effects of Classroom Integration on the Academic Progress, Self-Concept, and Racial Attitude of Negro Elementary Children." Doctoral dissertation, North Texas State U., 1969. Univ. Microfilms Order No. 70-9127.

Evans, Charles L. Integration Evaluation. Fort Worth, TX: Fort Worth Independent School District, Ag 15, 1973.

_____. Short-Term Desegregation Effects: The Academic Achievement of Bused Students, 1971-1972. Fort Worth, TX: Fort Worth Independent School District, Ja, 1973.

Evans, Don. "Segregated Drama in Integrated Schools." English Journal 60(F, 1971):260-263.

Falk, William Warren. "Mobility Attitudes of Segregated and Desegregated Black Youths." Journal of Negro Education 47(Spring, 1978):132-142. [Texas]

_____. "School Desegregation, Mobility Attitudes, and Early Attainment of Rural, Black Youth." Doctoral dissertation, Texas A & M U., 1975. Univ. Microfilms Order No. 76-03628.

Falk, William W., and Cosby, Arthur G. "The Impact of Desegregation on Rural Students." Integrateducation 13 (Jl-Ag, 1975):38-40.

_____ and _____. "School Desegregation and the Educational Projections of Rural Black Youth." Rural Sociology 39(Spring, 1974):28-41.

Falk, William W. and others. The Occupational Projections of Rural Blacks from Segregated and Desegregated Schools, Mr, 1974. ERIC ED 088 620.

Fancher, Betsy. Voices from the South. Black Students Talk About Their Experiences in Desegregated Schools. Atlanta, GA: Southern Regional Council, Ag, 1970.

Feinberg, Lawrence. "A New Minority Group." Washington Post, N 8, 1976. [Minority white children at Shepherd Elementary School, Washington, DC]

Felice, Lawrence G. The Effects of School Desegregation on Minority Group Student Achievement and Self-Concept: An Evolution of Court-Ordered Busing in Waco, Texas, Je, 1974. ERIC ED 094 096.

Fink, Isaac. "A Comparison of Black Children Who Associate with White Friends and Black Children Who Do Not Associate with White Friends." Master's thesis, Brooklyn College, 1971.

Fleck, Stephen. "'Interracial Riots' in School and Community Indifference." School Review 79(Ag, 1971):614-623.

Forehand, Garlie A., and Ragosta, Marjorie. A Handbook for Integrated Schooling. Washington, DC: U.S. Office of Education, Jl, 1976.

_____ and _____. "Successful School Integration: Principles and Strategies from A Study of Integrated Schools." In Catholic Schools and Racial Integration: Perspectives, Directions, Models, pp. 82-93. Washington, DC: National Catholic Conference for Interracial Justice, 1977.

Forehand, Garlie, Ragosta, Marjorie, and Rock, Donald A. Conditions and Processes of Effective School Desegregation. Princeton, NJ: Educational Testing Service, Jl, 1976.

Four Black Students. "They're Looking To Us As Examples." In The South and Her Children: School Desegregation, 1970-1971, pp. 80-87. Edited by Robert E. Anderson, Jr. Atlanta, GA: Southern Regional Council, Mr, 1971.

Franks, Joan C. "School Desegregation: Negative Attitudes and Coping Methods for the Black Child." Western Journal of Black Studies 1(S, 1977):195-198.

French, Jeana T. "Educational Desegregation and Selected Self-Concept Factors of Lower-Class Black Children." Doctoral dissertation, Florida State U., 1972.

Frenk, James H. "The Influence of Non-White Pupil Classroom Composition on Classroom Quality." IAR Research Bulletin 13(Je, 1973):3, 10-14. [Institute of Administrative Research, Teachers College, Columbia U.]

Frieman, Barry B. "Black Child in the White School." Master's thesis, U. of Maryland, 1968.

Garrett, Henry E. "'Benefits' of Integrated Schools Are a Myth." Citizen, Ja, 1965.

Georgeoff, P. J. The Effect of the Curriculum Upon the Self-Concept of Children in Racially Integrated Fourth Grade Classrooms. Washington, DC: American Educational Theatre Assn., F, 1968, 13 pp. ERIC ED 017 020.

Georgeoff, P. J. and others. "The Effect of the Curriculum on Racial Cleavage in Integrated Fourth Grade Classrooms." Contemporary Education 41(My, 1970):297-303.

Georgeoff, P. J., and Patterson, J. "Cleavages in Integrated Classrooms." Teachers College Journal, N, 1965.

Gerard, Harold B., and Miller, Norman. School Desegregation. New York: Plenum Press, 1975. [Riverside, California]

Gergel, Richard. "School Desegregation: A Student View." New South 26(Winter, 1971): 34-38.

Ghee, Sandra F. "A Quantitative Study of Long Range Effects of Classroom Desegregation on Academic Progress, Self-Concept, and Racial Attitude of Black Junior and Senior High School Students." Master's thesis, Texas Women's U., 1972.

Giles, Micheal W. "Percent Black and Racial Hostility: An Old Assumption Reexamined." Social Science Quarterly 58(D, 1977):412-417.

Gordon, Kenneth F. and others. Evaluation of the Emergency School Assistance Program. 3 vols. Bethesda, MD: Resource Management Corporation, F 15, 1972.

Green, James A., and Gerard, Harold B. "School Desegregation and Ethnic Attitudes." In Integrating the Organization. Edited by H. Fromkin and J. Sherwood. Glencoe, IL: Free Press, n.d.

Green, Robert L., Smith, Eugenia, and Schweitzer, John H. "Busing and the Multiracial Classroom." Phi Delta Kappan (My, 1972):543-546.

Gregory, Margie W. "Problems of Teachers and Students in Desegregated East Texas English Classrooms." Master's thesis, East Texas State U., 1969.

Griffin, Jack L. "The Effects of Integration on Academic Aptitutde, Classroom Achievement, Self-concept, and Attitudes toward the School Environment of a Selected Group of Negro Students in Tulsa, Oklahoma. Diss. Abstr. Int'l., 1969, 30 (5-a) 1748.

Grigg, Charles M. "The Southern Experience with Desegregation of Public Schools as Viewed by Superintendents and Principals in Eleven States." In Meyer Weinberg and Others, Three Myths: An Exposure of Popular Misconceptions About School Desegregation, pp. 37-56. Atlanta: Southern Regional Council, S, 1976.

Gross, Norman M. "Reaching for the Dream: An Experiment in Two-Way Busing." Children 17 (Jl-Ag, 1970):133-136.

Gumaer, Jim, and Myrick, Robert D. "Exploring Student Attitudes in a Newly Integrated School." Humanist Educator 16(D, 1977): 72-79.

Hagar, C. W. "The Extent of Negro Student Involvement in an Integrated School." Master's thesis, Virginia State College, 1968.

Hagerty, George J. III. "Desegregation in Midwest City: A Qualitative Study of an Urban, Comprehensive High School and Its Interaction with Community Agencies." Doctoral dissertation, Harvard U., 1978. Univ. Microfilms Order No. 7823677.

Haggstrom, Warren C. "Segregation, Desegregation, and Negro Personality." Integrated Education, O-N, 1963.

Hall, John A. "The Influence of School Desegregation on the Work Values and Occupational Aspiration Levels of Twelfth-Grade Negro Males in Texas Public High Schools." Doctoral dissertation, East Texas State U., 1971.

Hall, John A., and Wiant, Harry V. "Does School Desegregation Change Occupational Goals of Negro Males?" Journal of Vocational Behavior 3(Ap, 1973):175-179.

Hall, Leon. "School Desegregation: A (Hollow?) Victory." Inequality in Education 17(Je, 1974).

Hall, Morrill M., and Gentry, Harold W. "Isolation of Negro Students in Integrated Public Schools." Journal of Negro Education, Spring, 1969.

Hamm, Norman H. and others. "Effects of Race and Exposure on Judgments of Interpersonal Favorability." Journal of Experimental Social Psychology 11(Ja, 1975):14-24.

Hampton, Claudia Hudley. "The Effects of Desegregation on the Scholastic Achievement of Relatively Advantaged Negro Children." Doctoral dissertation, U. of Southern California, 1970. Univ. Microfilms Order No. 70-23157.

Harford, Thomas, and Cutter, Henry S. G. "Cooperation among Negro and White Boys and Girls." Psychological Reports, Je, 1966.

Harootunian, Berj. Self-Other Relationships of Segregated and Desegregated Ninth Graders, F 8, 1968. ERIC ED 023 765.

Harootunian, Berj, and Morse, Richard J. Characteristics of Negro and White High School Students Prior to Desegregation: A Study of Negro Students' Freedom of Choice, S, 1968. ERIC ED 024 745.

Harris, Edward E. "Urban Interracial and Intraracial School Conflict." Education 93(F-Mr, 1973):233-240.

Harris, Hardie F., and Phelan, Joseph G. "Beliefs in Internal-External Control of Reinforcement Among Blacks in Integrated and Segregated High Schools." Psychological Reports 32(F, 1973):40-42.

Harris, Norene, and Jackson, Nathaniel. "Integration Thus Far Has Failed to Boost Achievement: An Interview with David Armor." In Jackson Harris and Carl Rydingsword and contributors, The Integration of American Schools: Problems, Experiences, Solutions. Boston: Allyn & Bacon, 1974.

Harryman, Milburn E. "The Effects of Racial Composition of Five High Schools in Kansas City Upon Achievement and Citizenship Ratings of Selected Students." Doctoral dissertation, U. of Kansas, 1969. Univ. Microfilms Order No. 69-21,474.

Harvey, James C., and Holmes, Charles H. "Busing and School Desegregation." Phi Delta Kappan (My, 1972):540-542.

Haubrich, Vernon F. A Comparative and Developmental Study of the Effects of Desegregation in Selected Public Schools, Je 30, 1972. ERIC ED 102 227.

Hawley, Willis D. Teachers, Classrooms, and the Effects of School Desegregation on Effort in School: A 'Second Generation' Study, Ap, 1976. ERIC ED 126 201. [North Carolina]

Hawley, Willis D., and Rist, Ray C. "On the Future Implementation of School Desegregation: Some Considerations." Law and Contemporary Problems 39(Spring, 1975):412-426.

Hensen, Harlan N. "Some Implications of Busing in Urbana, Illinois: An Inquiry Into an Aspect of Integration." Master's thesis, U. of Illinois, Urbana, 1967.

Hildebrandt, Charles A. "The Relationship of Some Personal and Social Variables of School Children to Preferences for Mixed Schools." Doctoral dissertation, Ohio State U., 1962. Univ. Microfilms Order No. 6302503.

Hofmann, Gerhard. "Interracial Fraternization: Social Determinants of Friendship Relations between Black and White Adolescents." Doctoral dissertation, Purdue U., 1973.

Hofmann, Gerhard and others. Social Determinants of Friendship Relations Between Black and White Adolescents. West Lafayette, IN: Department of Sociology and Anthropology, Purdue U., 1975.

Howard, R. A Review of Research on School Desegregation. Minneapolis, MN: Research and Evaluation Department, Minneapolis Public Schools, 1970.

Howell, William L. "The Correlates of Change in School Integration with the Academic Achievement of Eighth Grade Students." Doctoral dissertation, U. of South Carolina, 1972. Univ. Microfilms Order No. 72-18,153.

Hughes, Ronald E., and Works, Ernest. "The Self-Concepts of Black Students in a Predominantly White and in a Predominantly Black High School." Sociology and Social Research 59 (O, 1974):50-54.

Hunt, Janet Gibbs. "Assimilation or Marginality? Some School Integration Effects Reconsidered." Social Forces 56(D, 1977):604-610.

In Their Own Words. Southern Regional Council, 5 Forsyth Street, N.W., Atlanta, GA. [Negro youngsters in the Deep South tell about their experiences in integrated white schools]

Jackson, Beverley Dobson. "Social Acceptance and Personal and Social Adjustment Among Integrated Black and White Elementary and Junior High School Students." Doctoral dissertation, California School of Professional Psychology, 1975. Univ. Microfilms Order No. 76-10,420. [Riverside, California]

Jackson, Cornelius James. "Self-Concept and Attitude of Elementary Students in Residentially Integrated Schools as Compared to Students Who Attend Mandatorily Desegregated Schools." Doctoral dissertation, U. of Nebraska, 1978. Univ. Microfilms Order No. 78 14696. [Omaha]

Jackson, Susie Evans. "Adaptation of Cross-Bused Urban Black and White Fifth-Grade Pupils in Two Elementary Schools." Doctoral dissertation, U. of Florida, 1976. Univ. Microfilms Order No. 77-08192.

James, Doyle J. "The Effects of Desegregation on the Self-Concept of Negro High School Students." Diss. Abstr. Int'l., Vol. 31 (9-A) (Mr, 1971) 4464.

Jencks, Christopher, and Brown, Marsha. "The Effects of Desegregation on Student Achievement: Some New Evidence from the Equality of Educational Opportunity Survey." Sociology of Education 48(Winter, 1975):126-140.

Johnson, Linden Knute. "The Relationships between Selected Characteristics of Sixth Grade Negro Pupils Attending Disadvantaged Area Schools and Negro Pupils Who Have Moved from Disadvantaged Area Schools and Are Now Attending Schools Located in Adjacent Areas." Doctoral dissertation, U. of Nebraska, 1970. Univ. Microfilms Order No. 70-17,730.

Johnson, Norris Brock. Patterns of Student Dress and Appearance: Aspects of Resegregation in Desegregated Elementary School Classrooms, 1977. ERIC ED 148 706.

Jordan, Chester L. "The Effects of Integration on the Acceptance of Science Misconceptions by College Freshmen with Poverty Backgrounds." Doctoral dissertation, Rutgers U., 1973. Univ. Microfilms Order No. 73-32,219.

Justin, Neal E. "Racial Balancing of Students and Faculty." Intellect 101(N, 1972):91-92.

Justman, Joseph. "Children's Reaction to Open Enrollment." Urban Review, N, 1968.

Katz, Irwin. "Desegregation or Integration in Public Schools? The Policy Implications of Research." Integrated Education, D, 1967-Ja, 1968, p. 15.

_____. Problems and Directions for Research on Public School Desegregation. New York: ERIC, Yeshiva U., 1968.

_____. "Research on Public School Desegregation." Integrated Education, Ag-S, 1966.

_____. "Review of Evidence Relative to Effects of Desegregation on the Intellectual Performance of Negroes." American Psychologist, Je, 1964.

_____. "Status of Research on School Desegregation." I.R.C.D. Bulletin, Yeshiva U., S, 1965.

Kelley, Joan Marie. "School Segregation-Desegregation Preferences." Doctoral dissertation, U. of Rochester, 1971.

Kimball, Solon T., and Wagley, Charles. Race and Culture in School and Community, Ja, 1974. ERIC ED 095 251.

King, Charles E., and Mayer, Robert R. "The Exercise of Community Leadership for School Desegregation." Urban Education 7(O, 1972): 215-234. [North Carolina city].

_____ and _____. A Pilot Study of the Social and Educational Impact of School Desegregation. North Carolina Central U. and U. of North Carolina, Chapel Hill, 1971.

Kinloch, Graham C., and Borders, Jeffrey A. "Racial Stereotypes & Social Distance Among Elementary School Children in Hawaii." Sociology and Social Research 56(Ap, 1972): 368-377.

Kirby, David J., Harris, T. Robert, Crain, Robert L., and Rossell, Christine H. Political Strategies in Northern School Desegregation. Lexington, MA: Lexington Books, 1973.

Kirk, Diana H., and Goon, Susan. "Desegregation and the Cultural Deficit Model: An Examination of the Literature." Review of Educational Research 45(Fall, 1975):599-611.

Kittredge, Lee Denniston. "Adaptations to Change in Organizational Task Environments: A Comparative Analysis of Racial Desegregation in Black and White Centers for the Retarded." Doctoral dissertation, U. of North Carolina, 1976. Univ. Microfilms Order No. 77-02065.

Knapp, Melvin J., and Alston, Jon P. "White Parental Acceptance of Varying Degrees of School Desegregation: 1965 and 1970." Public Opinion Quarterly 36(Winter, 1972-1973):585-591.

Knight, James Henry. "The Interpersonal Values and Aspiration Levels of Negro Seniors in Totally Integrated and Totally Segregated Southern High Schools." Doctoral dissertation, U. of North Carolina, 1970.

Knight, James H., White, Kinnard P., and Taff, Luther R. "The Effect of School Desegregation, Sex of Student, and Socioeconomic Status on the Interpersonal Values of Southern Negro Students." Journal of Negro Education 41 (Winter, 1972):41-11. [North Carolina]

Koslin, Sandra Cohen and others. A Distance Measure of Racial Attitudes in Primary Grade Children: An Exploratory Study, S, 1968. ERIC ED 026 133.

_____. "Classroom Racial Balance and Students' Interracial Attitudes." Sociology of Education 45(F, 1972):386-407.

_____. Classroom Racial Balance and Students' Interracial Attitudes, Mr, 1970. ERIC ED 040 266.

Kraft, Richard J. Affective Climate and Integration: A Report Presented to ERIC Clearing House on the Disadvantaged, O, 1969. ERIC ED 035 703.

Kranz, Peter L. "The Struggles of a Middle-Class White Within a Racial Confrontation Group." Journal of Intergroup Relations 1(F, 1972): 46-49.

Kranz, Peter L., and Siplin, Charles. "A Racial Confrontation Group Implementated within a High School." High School Journal 55(D, 1971):112-119.

Krause, Kathy. "The Effect of Desegregation on Minority Achievement." Master's thesis, Bank Street College of Education, 1972.

Krenkel, Noele. "Self Concepts and Interaction Patterns of Children in a Desegregated Urban School." Master's thesis, California State U., San Francisco, 1972.

Kuhn, Kenneth Chester. "Self-Concept of Black and White Students Between and Among Social Classes in Newly Desegregated Elementary Schools." Doctoral dissertation, Syracuse U., 1972. Univ. Microfilms Order No. 73-07738.

Lachat, Mary Ann. "A Description and Comparison of the Attitudes of White High School Seniors Toward Black Americans in Three Suburban High Schools: An All-White, a Desegregated, and an Integrated High School." Doctoral dissertation, Columbia U., 1972.

_____. "Racially Mixed, but not Equal: Implications for Integrated Education." New Era 54(S-O, 1973):179-181.

Lantaff, Ronald James. "A Study of the Desegregated Curriculum in Urban Elementary Schools as Perceived by Certified Elementary Instructional Personnel." Doctoral dissertation, Kansas State U., 1975.

Larkins, Guy A., and Oldham, Sally E. "Patterns of Racial Separation in a Desegregated High School." Theory and Research in Social Education 4(D, 1978):23-38.

Leacock, Eleanor. "Race and the 'We-They Dichotomy' in Culture and Classroom." Anthropology and Education Quarterly 8(My, 1977):152-159

Lesser, Gerald S., Rosenthal, Kristine M., Polkoff, Sally E., and Pfankuch, Marjorie B. "Some Effects of Segregation and Desegregation in the Schools." Integrated Education, Je-Jl, 1964.

Levine, Daniel U., and Havighurst, Robert J. (eds.). The Future of Big-City Schools: Desegregation Policies and Magnet Alternatives. Berkeley, CA: McCuthan, 1977.

Levine, Daniel U., and Mares, Kenneth R. Problems and Perceptions in a Desegregated Urban High School: A Case Description and Its Implications, Jl, 1970. ERIC ED 045 775.

Lewis, Charles E., Jr. "School Integration and Occupational Expectations: A Study of North Carolina High School Senior Boys." Doctoral dissertation, North Carolina State U., Raleigh, 1970.

Lewis, Ralph G. "The Relationship of Classroom Racial Composition to Student Academic Achievement and the Conditioning Effects of Inter-Racial Social Acceptance." Doctoral dissertation, Harvard U., 1971. Univ. Microfilms Order No. 71-30,064.

Love, Barbara J. "Desegregation in Your School: Behavior Patterns That Get in Your Way." Phi Delta Kappan 59(N, 1977):168-170.

Lowe, William T. "A Secondary School 'Busing Plan' That Works." Administrator's Notebook 25(1976-1977):1-4.

Lucas, Sammie. Racial Perceptions of Metropolitan School Desegregation. Knoxville, TN: U. of Tennessee, 1970.

Lunemann, Alan. "Desegregation and Adjustment: A Cross-Sectional and Semi-Longitudinal Look at Berkeley, California." Journal of Negro Education 42(Fall, 1973):439-446.

Lu, Yao-Chi, and Tweeten, Luther. "The Impact of Busing on Student Achievement." Growth and Change 4(0, 1973):44-46. [Oklahoma]

McAdams, E. E. "Relationship Between School Integration and Student Morale." Doctoral dissertation, George Peabody College for Teachers, 1974. [Nashville, Tennessee]

McBurnette, Patrick E. and others. Two Studies on Student Perception of Isolation in Desegregated School Settings, Ap, 1976. ERIC ED 128 444.

McClendon, Dorothy Fullenwider. "Some Effects of Integrated Schooling on Bussed Urban Black Children." Doctoral dissertation, Boston U., 1970. Univ. Microfilms Order No. 70-22519.

McCullough, James S. Academic Achievement Under School Desegregation in Southern City. Chapel Hill, NC: Department of City and Regional Planning, U. of North Carolina, Ja, 1972.

McPartland, James. The Relative Influence of School Desegregation and of Classroom Desegregation on the Academic Achievement of Ninth Grade Negro Students. Interim Report. Baltimore, MD: Center for the Study of Social Organization of Schools, S, 1967.

_____. The Segregated Student in Desegregated Schools: Sources of Influence on Negro Secondary Students. Final Report. Baltimore: MD: Johns Hopkins U., Center for the Study of Social Organization of Schools, Je, 1968, 364 pp. ERIC ED 021 944.

Mahan, Aline M. "Social Doctors and Academic Success of Urban Children." Diss. Abstr. Int'l., 1970, 30 (7-A) 2853.

Mahan, Aline M., and Mahan, Thomas W. "Changes in Cognitive Style: An Analysis of the Impact of White Suburban Schools on Inner City Children." Integrated Education 8(Ja-F, 1970):58-61.

Mahan, Thomas W. "The Busing of Students for Equal Opportunities." Journal of Negro Education, Summer, 1968. [Hartford]

_____. Project Concern. Hartford, CT: Project Concern, Board of Education, 1967. [Academic achievement of city children bused to suburb]

_____. Project Concern. A Supplementary Report on Non-Academic Factors. Hartford, CT: Board of Education, Ap, 1968.

_____. Project Concern: 1966-1968. A Report on the Effectiveness of Suburban School Placement for Inner-City Youth. Hartford, CT: Board of Education, Ag., 1968.

Mahan, Thomas W., and Mahan, Aline M. "The Impact of Schools on Learning: Inner-City Children in Suburban Schools." Journal of School Psychology 9(1971):1-11.

Maintaining Student Discipline in the Integrated School through the Cooperative Faculty/Student Approach, Ag 14, 1975. ERIC ED 126 188.

Marascuilo, Leonard A., and Dagenais, F. Identification of Social Groups Based on Social Integration in a Multi-racial High School, Ap, 1974. ERIC ED 094 031.

_____ and _____. "The Meaning of the Word 'Integration' to Seniors in a Multi-Racial High School." Journal of Negro Education 43 (Spring, 1974):179-189. [Berkeley, California]

Marcum, Roger B. "An Exploration of the First Year Effects of Racial Integration of the Elementary Schools in a Unit School District." Doctoral dissertation, U. of Illinois, 1968.

Margeson, Carol Isabelle. "A Comparison of Aggression and Perception of Aggression in Self and Others: A Study of Negro and White Third-Grade Students in Integrated and Segregated School Settings in the Rural South." Doctoral dissertation, U. of North Carolina, 1973. Univ. Microfilms Order No. 74-15365.

Marshall, Kim. "The Desegregation of a Boston Classroom." Learning 4(Ag-S, 1975):32-40.

Martinez-Monfort, Antonio. "Racial Attitudes of High School Students Attending Desegregated High Schools in a Southern Metropolitan Area." Diss. Abstr. Int'l. 31, 8-B(F, 1971)4972-3.

Martinez-Monfort, Antonio, and Dreger, Ralph M. "Reactions of High School Students to School Desegregation in a Southern Metropolitan Area." Psychological Reports 30(Ap, 1972):543-550.

Mastroianni, Mike, and Khatena, Joe. "The Attitudes of Black and White High School Seniors toward Integration." Sociology & Social Research 56(Ja, 1972):221-227.

Maynor, Waltz, and Katzenmeyer, W. G. "Academic Performance and School Integration: A Multi-Ethnic Analysis." Journal of Negro Education 43(Winter, 1974):30-38.

Meier, J. A. Longitudinal Effects of Desegregation, 1972-1975. Dallas, TX: Dallas Independent School District, 1975.

Meltzer, Bert. "The Influence of the Duration of Interracial Classroom Contact on the Development of Interpersonal Cognitive Skills." Diss. Abstr. Int'l., 1970 (Jl) Vol. 31 (1-A) 467-8.

Metz, Mary Haywood. "Authority in the Junior High School: A Case Study." Doctoral dissertation, U. of California, Berkeley, 1971. [Berkeley]

_____. Classrooms and Corridors. The Crisis of Authority in Desegregated Secondary Schools. Berkeley: U. of California Press, 1978. [Berkeley]

Middleton, Ernest John. "The Effects of De-segregation on the Academic Achievement of Black and White High School Seniors in St. Mary Parish, Louisiana." Doctoral dissertation, U. of Colorado, 1974. Univ. Microfilms Order No. 74-22372.

Milazzo, Patricia Ann. "Busing and Socio-Economic Class: Effects of Enforced Contact on Several Cultural Orientations of Children from District Socio-Economic Classes." Doctoral dissertation, U. of California, Irvine, 1975. Univ. Microfilms Order No. 76-13,877.

Milgram, Jean Gregg. "The 'Life Style' of Integration." The Integrator, Special issue, 1969.

Miller, Norman, and Gerard, Harold B. "How Busing Failed in Riverside." Psychology Today 10(Je, 1976):66-67.

Miller, William, Folman, John, and Hernandez, David E. "Discriminant Analysis of School Children in Integrated and Non-Integrated Schools Using Tests of Critical Thinking." Florida Journal of Educational Research 12 (Ja, 1970):63-68.

Mitchell, James V., Jr. "On the Perils of Conducting Socially Significant Research." Phi Delta Kappan 52(N, 1970):182-184. [A study in an unnamed city of the effects of busing]

Moore, Dan Emery. "School Segregation in Southern Cities." Doctoral dissertation, U. of Wisconsin, 1973.

Moore, Louise M. "The Relationship of Selected Pupil and School Variables and the Reading Achievement of Third-Year Primary Pupils in a Desegregated School Setting." Doctoral dissertation, U. of Georgia, 1972. Univ. Microfilms Order No. 72-11,018.

Moorehead, Nona F. "The Effects of School Integration on Intelligence Test Scores of Negro Children." Doctoral dissertation, Mississippi State U., 1972. Univ. Microfilms Order No. 72-20,270.

Moreno, Marguerite C. "The Effect of Integration on the Aptitude, Achievement Attitudes to School & Class, and Social Acceptance of Negro & White Pupils in a Small Urban School System." Diss. Abstr. Int'l. 32 (4-A) October, 1971, 1755.

Morris, Charles F. "Problems Encountered in the Desegregation of Carver Junior High School." Master's thesis, Wake Forest U., 1971.

Moseley, Dolly and others. A Socially Integrated Kindergarten, 1969. ERIC ED 034 578.

Nash, Kermit B. "Mental Health in the Desegre-gated School." Integrated Education, D, 1967-Ja, 1968, p. 28.

National Assessment of Educational Progress. Science Achievement: Racial and Regional Trends, 1969-73. Denver, CO: Education Commission of the States, Mr, 1976.

Nelsen, Edward A. Assessing Social Problems and Issues in Desegregated Schools: Black Students' Retrospective Reports of High School Social Environments, Ap, 1974. ERIC ED 096 386.

Nelsen, Edward A., and Uhl, Norman P. The Influence of Racial Composition of Desegre-gated Secondary Schools Upon Black Students' Perceptions of the School Climates, Ap, 1976. ERIC ED 123 316. [Durham, North Carolina]

Newby, Robert S. Quality Education for Black Children in "Segregated" and Desegregated Settings, 1976. ERIC ED 152 899.

Nieman, Ronald H., and Gastright, Joseph F. The Effects of a Three Year Interracial Pre-school Program on Cognitive and Social Development, Ap, 1975. ERIC ED 096 366.

Noblit, George W., and Collins, Thomas W. Goals, Race and Roles: Staff and Student Patterns in the Desegregation Process, Mr, 1978. ERIC ED 154 097. [Memphis]

_____ and _____. "Order and Disruption in a Desegregated High School." Crime and Delin-quency 24(Jl, 1978):277-289.

Norot, Ruth Esther. "The Effects of Institutional Characteristics on the Racial Climate in 194 Southern Desegregated High Schools." Doctoral dissertation, Johns Hopkins U., 1975. Univ. Microfilms Order No. 7821978.

North Carolina State Department of Public Instruction. An Approach to Discipline in the Desegregated School, 1972. ERIC ED 099 991.

Nowak, William S. "The Effect of School Busing on Black Student Attitude toward School." Master's thesis, U. of Illinois, Urbana, 1970.

Office for Civil Rights, Dept. of H.E.W. "Much Better Than They Expected." Integrated Education 8(Ja-F, 1970):41-50.

Olson, George E. The Relationship of Student Racial Prejudice to a Variety of Classroom Dimensions in Sixteen Racially Mixed Classes, 1977. ERIC ED 139 884.

Orfield, Gary. "Examining the Desegregation Process." Integrateducation 13(My-Je, 1975): 127-30.

_____. "How to Make Desegregation Work: The Adaptation of Schools to their Newly-Integrated Student Bodies." Law and Contemporary Problems 39(Spring, 1975):314-340.

Orive, Ruben, and Gerard, Harold B. "Social Contact of Minority Parents and their Children's Acceptance by Classmates." Sociometry 38(1975):518-524.

Orson, Claire M. "Effects on Self-Concept and Racial Prejudice of a Structured Intervention Program with Desegregated Fifth Grade Children." Doctoral dissertation, U. of Miami, Ag, 1971.

Osborn, Eleanor J. "Ethnic Background and Peer Nominations of Fourth, Fifth and Sixth Grade Children in Integrated Classrooms." Master's thesis, U. of California, Berkeley, 1972.

Outerbridge, Lilias. "Integration and Dis-integration" (letter). Center Forum, D 23, 1968.

Owen, Isaiah. The Effect of the Group Leader(s) Race on Group Counseling Undertaken to Improve Intergroup Attitude Among Racially Mixed Fifth and Sixth Grade Children, 1969. ERIC ED 041 328.

Papoy, J. P., and Sides, R. S. Effects of Induced Desegregation. Dallas: Dallas Independent School District, 1976.

Pascal, Anthony. What Do We Know About School Desegregation?, Ja, 1977, ERIC ED 142 613.

Patchen, Martin, Davidson, James D., Hofmann, Gerhard, and Brown, William R. "Determinants of Students' Interracial Behavior and Opinion Change." Sociology of Education (Ja, 1977).

Patchen, Martin, Davidson, James D., Hofmann, Gerhard. "Interracial Perceptions Among High School Students." Sociometry (D, 1976).

Payne, Arnold P. "Student Involvement as a Determinant of Successful Integration of Schools." Doctoral dissertation, Texas A & M U., 1973.

Peniston, Eugene Gilbert. "Levels of Aspirations of Black Students as a Function of Significant Others in Integrated and Segregated Schools." Doctoral dissertation, Oklahoma State U., 1972. Univ. Microfilms Order No. 73-15212.

Peterson, Dennis L. "First Year Desegregation in an Urban High School: A Study of Conflict and Change." Doctoral dissertation, Michigan State U., 1970. Univ. Microfilms Order No. 71-2146.

Petroni, Frank A. "Teen-age Interracial Dating." Trans-action 8(S, 1971):54-59.

Petroni, Frank A., with Petroni, C. Lillian, and Hirsch, Ernest A. Two, Four, Six, Eight, When You Gonna Integrate? New York: Behavioral Publications, 1970.

Pettigrew, Thomas F. "Adult Consequences of Racial Isolation and Desegregation in the Schools." In Racial Isolation in the Public Schools, Vol. II. Washington, DC: GPO, 1967 (Appendix C5).

_____. "School and a New Model for Racial Integration." In New Models for American Education, pp. 162-193. Edited by James W. Guthrie and Edward Wynne. Englewood Cliffs, NJ: Prentice-Hall, 1971.

Pettigrew, Thomas F., and Green, Robert L. "School Desegregation in Large Cities: A Critique of the Coleman 'White Flight' Thesis." Harvard Educational Review 45(F, 1976):1-53.

Pettigrew, Thomas F., and Riley, Robert. "Contextual Models of School Desegregation." In Attitudes, Conflicts and Social Change. Edited by Bert King and Elliot McGinnies. New York: Academic Press, 1972.

Phillips, Leonard W., and Bianchi, William B. "Desegregation, Reading Achievement, and Problem Behavior in Two Elementary Schools." Urban Education 9(Ja, 1975):325-339.

Pierce, David H. "White Children and their Colored Schoolmates." Crisis, Je, 1923.

Pitman, Dorothy E. "Reactions to Desegregation: A Study of Negro Mothers." Ph.D. dissertation, U. of North Carolina, 1960. Dissertation Abstracts, 21, 1961, p. 2035. [Alamance County, NC]

Posthuma, Allan B., and Carr, John E. "Differentiation Matching in School Desegregation Workshops." Journal of Applied Social Psychology 4(Ja-Mr, 1974):36-46.

Poussaint, Alvin F., and Lewis, Toye Brown. "School Desegregation: A Synonym for Racial Equality." School Review 84(My, 1976:326-336.

Powell, Evan R., and Dennis, Virginia C. Application of an Anthropological Technique to Desegregated Schools, Ap, 1972. ERIC ED 062 501.

Powell, Gloria J. with special assistance of Marielle Fuller. Black Monday's Children. A Study of the Effects of School Desegregation on Self-Concepts of Southern Children. New York: Appleton-Century-Crofts, 1973.

_____ and _____. School Desegregation and Self-Concept: A Pilot Study on the Psychological Impact of School Desegregation on 7th, 8th and 9th Graders in a Southern City, Mr 25, 1970. ERIC ED 048 391.

Pugh, Roderick W. "A Comparative Study of the Adjustment of Negro Students in Mixed and Separate High Schools." The Journal of Negro Education, Fall, 1943.

Purl, Mabel C. The Effect of Integration on the Achievement of Elementary Pupils. Riverside, CA: Unified School District, N, 1967.

Rankin, Charles Inman. "The Achievement, Personal Adjustment, and Social Adjustment of Black, Elementary School Students Undergoing Forced Busing in Wichita, Kansas." Doctoral dissertation, Kansas State U., 1973. Univ. Microfilms Order No. 73-26365.

Rayson, Havey. "An Investigation of the Anxiety Level of Black and White Students in an Integrated School, an All-Black School, and an All-White School." Master's thesis, Stephen F. Austin State U., 1971.

Reagen, Michael V. "Five Educational Effects of Busing Pupils." American School Board Journal 161(Mr, 1974):44-45.

Reagen, Michael V., Hunterton, Stanley, Smith, Tom, and Sumnicht, Lee Ann. Busing: Ground Zero in School Desegregation: A Literature Review with Policy Recommendations. Syracuse, NY: Syracuse University Research Corporation, O, 1972.

Reichlin, Hedda L. "A Busing Program As a Technique for School Desegregation." Master's thesis, Eastern Connecticut State College, 1972. [Background of Project Concern in Connecticut]

Resource Managment Corporation. Evaluation of the Emergency School Assistance Program. Bethesda, MD: Resource Management Corporation, 1971.

Reyburn, James R. "How a Suburban Board's Policy Helps Open Doors to Racial Understanding." Updating School Board Policies 3(O, 1972):1,3. [Voluntary transfer program]

Rist, Ray C. "School Integration and Minority Student Tokenism." Integrateducation 14 (Ja/F, 1976).

Roberson, Don and others. Ways to Improve Education in Desegregated Schools, My 31, 1978. ERIC ED 157 963.

Robertson, William Joseph. "The Effects of Junior High School Segregation Experience o the Achievement Behavior and Academic Motivation of Integrated 10th Grade Students." Doctoral dissertation, U. of Michigan, 1967.

Robinson, Jerry W., Jr., and Preston, James D. "Equal-Status Contact and Modification of Racial Prejudice: A Reexamination of the Contact Hypothesis." Social Forces 54(Je, 1976):911-924.

Rodgers, Harrell R., Jr. "Civics Curricula and Southern Schoolchildren: The Impact of Segregated and Integrated School Environments." Journal of Politics 35(N, 1973):1002-1007. [North Carolina]

Rodgers, Harrell R., Jr., and Bullock, Charles S. III. "The Impact of School Desegregation." Integrateducation 14(Mr-Ap, 1976):33-34.

_____ and _____. "School Desegregation: Successes and Failures." Journal of Negro Education 43(Spring, 1974):139-154.

Rookey, T. Jerome. "Children as Checkers." Integrateducation 13(S-O, 1975):39-40.

Roth, Rodney W. "The Effects of Integrated Curriculum on Negro and White Fifth Grade Students." Ph.D. dissertation, U. of Michigan, 1969.

Rousseve, Ronald J. "On the Firing Line: Student Chooses Integration." Crisis 82 (D, 1975):431-433.

Ruhe, John A., and Hill, Walter. Comparative Self-Esteem of Blacks and Whites in Segregated and Integrated Dyads, Jl, 1973. ERIC ED 134 856.

Sachdeva, Darshan. "A Measurement of Changes in Interracial Student Activities in Desegregated Schools." Journal of Educational Research 66(My-Je, 1973):418-422.

_____. "Friendships Among Students in Desegregated Schools." California Journal of Educational Research 23(Ja, 1972):45-51.

_____. "Social Class Origin and Interracial Student Attitudes in Desegregated Schools." Southern Journal of Educational Research 9 (F, 1975):209-222.

Schafft, Gretchen E. "White Children in a Majority Black School: Together Yet Separate." Integrateducation 14(Jl/Ag, 1976). [Washington, D.C.]

St. John, Nancy Hoyt. "De Facto Segregation and Interracial Association in High School." Sociology of Education, Summer, 1964.

_____. "Desegregation and Minority Group Performance." Review of Educational Research 40(F, 1970):111-133.

_____. "The Effects of Segregation on the Aspirations of Negro Youth." Harvard Educational Review, Summer, 1966.

_____. "Minority Group Performance Under Various Conditions of School Ethnic and Economic Integration." IRCD Bulletin, My, 1968.

_____. Minority Group Performance Under Various Conditions of School Ethnic and Economic Integration: Review of Research. New York: Yeshiva U., ERIC Clearinghouse for Urban Disadvantaged, 64 pp. ERIC ED 021 945, n.d.

_____. School Desegregation Outcomes for Children. New York: Wiley, 1975.

_____. School Integration, Classroom Climate, and Achievement, Ja, 1971. ERIC ED 052 269.

_____. "A Study of the Aspirations of a Selected Group of Negro High School Graduates." Master's thesis, Brown U., 1958.

St. John, Nancy H., and Lewis, Ralph. "The Influence of School Racial Context on Academic Achievement." Social Problems 19 (Summer, 1971):68-79.

_____ and _____. "Race and the Social Structure of the Elementary Classroom." Sociology of Education 48(Summer, 1975):346-368.

St. John, Nancy H., and Smith, Marshall S. School Racial Composition, Aspiration and Achievement. Cambridge, MA: Harvard Graduate School of Education, Je, 1969.

Samuels, Joseph M. "A Comparison of Projects Representative of Compensatory, Busing, and Non-Compensatory Programs for Inner-City Students." Doctoral dissertation, U. of Connecticut, 1971.

Savage, Lemoyne W. "Academic Achievement of Black Students Transferring from a Segregated Junior High School to an Integrated Senior High School." Master's thesis, Virginia State College, 1972.

Schellenberg, James, and Halteman, John. "Busing and Academic Achievement: A Two-Year Follow Up." Urban Education 10(Ja, 1976):357-365.

Schofield, Janet Ward. "Desegregation and Intergroup Relations." In The Social Psychology of Education. Edited by D. Bar-Tal and L. Saxe. Washington, DC: Hemisphere, 1978.

Schofield, Janet W., and Sagar, Andrew. Interracial Interaction in a New "Magnet" Desegregated School, S, 1976. ERIC ED 132 215.

_____ and _____. "Peer Interaction Patterns in an Integrated Middle School." Sociometry 40(Je, 1977):130-137.

Schwartz, Audrey James. "Social Science Evidence and the Objectives of School Desegregation." In Indeterminacy in Education, pp. 73-113. Edited by John E. McDermott. Berkeley, CA: McCutchan, 1976.

Scout, Terrence Houser. "School Desegregation to Integration Through Changes in Social Structure." Doctoral dissertation, U. of California, Riverside, 1976. Univ. Microfilms Order No. 76-28,080.

Scudder, Bonnie Todd, and Jrs, Stephen G. "Do Bused Negro Children Affect Achievement of Non-Negro Children?" Integrated Education 9(Mr-Ap, 1971):30-34.

Seidner, J. K. "Effects of Integrated School Experience on Interaction in Small Bi-Racial Groups." Doctoral dissertation, U. of Southern California, 1971.

Seitz, Victoria. The Effects of Integrated Versus Segregated School Attendance on Short-Term Memory for Standard and Nonstandard English, S, 1974. ERIC ED 098 567.

_____. "Integrated versus Segregated School Attendance and Immediate Recall for Standard and Nonstandard English." Developmental Psychology 11(Mr, 1975):217-223.

Shagaloff, June. Children Apart: Crisis and Conflict, Jl 10, 1968. ERIC ED 030 691.

Shaw, Marvin E. "Changes in Sociometric Choices Following Forced Integration of an Elementary School." Journal of Social Issues 29(1973):143-157.

_____. "The Self-Image of Black and White Pupils in an Integrated School." Journal of Personality 42(Mr, 1974).

Sheehan, Daniel S., and Marcus, Mary M. "Busing Status and Student Ethnicity: Effects on Achievement Test Scores." Urban Education 13(Ap, 1978):83-94.

_____ and _____. The Effects of Bussing Status and Student Ethnicity on Achievement Test Scores. Dallas, TX: Dallas Independent School District, S, 1977.

Short, Barbara L. "Community Psychology and School Integration: Programs for Training and Community Change." Proceedings of the Annual Convention of the American Psychological Association 7(1972), part 2, 801-802.

Shutman, Edward. "The Relationship of Desegregation and of Consistent Attendance to Reading Achievement of Primary-Grade Negro Pupils." Doctoral dissertation, U. of Southern California, 1974. Univ. Microfilms Order No. 74-21508.

Silverman, Irwin, and Shaw, Marvin E. "Effects of Sudden Mass School Desegregation on Interracial Interaction and Attitudes in One Southern City." Journal of Social Issues 29 (1973):133-142. [Gainesville, FL]

Simun, Patricia Bates. "Exploding the Myths of School Integration." Integrateducation 15 (N-D, 1977):59-65.

Singer, Dorothy. "Reading, Writing, and Race Relations." Trans-action, Je, 1967. [The effects of integration]

_____. "Interracial Attitudes of Negro and White Fifth-Grade Children in Segregated and Unsegregated Schools." Ed.D. dissertation, Columbia U., 1966. Univ. Microfilms Order No. 67-2836.

Singleton, Louise C., and Asher, Steven R. "Peer Preferences and Social Interaction Among Third-Grade Children in an Integrated School District." Journal of Educational Psychology (Ag, 1977):330-336.

_____ and _____. "Sociometric Ratings and Social Interaction Among Third Grade Children In an Integrated School District." Journal of Classroom Interaction 12(D, 1976):71-82.

Singleton, Louise C. and others. Sociometric Ratings and Social Interaction among Third Grade Children in an Integrated School District, Ap, 1976. ERIC ED 121 923.

Sisenwein, Martin. "A Comparison of the Self Concepts of Negro and White Children in an Integrated School." Doctoral dissertation, Columbia U., 1970. Univ. Microfilms Order No. 70-19,699.

Slavin, Robert E. "How Student Learning Teams Can Integrate the Desegregated Classroom." Integrateducation 15(N-D, 1977):56-58.

_____. Using Student Learning Teams to Desegregate the Classroom. Baltimore, MD: Center for Social Organization of Schools, Johns Hopkins U., Jl, 1977.

Slawski, Edward J., and Scherer, Jacqueline. "The Rhetoric of Concern: Trust and Control in an Urban Desegregated School." Anthropology & Education Quarterly 9(Winter, 1978): 258-271. [Pontiac]

Smith, Alton B. "A Study of the Educational Effectiveness of Desegregation: A Comparison of Pupil Educational Performance Before and After One Year of Desegregation." Doctoral dissertation, U. of Oklahoma, 1978. Univ. Microfilms Order No. 7824614. [Oklahoma]

Smith, Annie Delories. "The Impact of Desegregation on the Florida Statewide Twelfth-Grade Achievement Test Scores of Black and White Students in a Rural and an Urban Florida County." Doctoral dissertation, U. of Florida, 1975. Univ. Microfilms Order No. 76-12133.

Smith, Annie D., and Johnson, Constance. The Impact of Desegregation on Achievement Test Scores of Black and White Students in Rural and an Urban County: Implications for Counseling, 1976. ERIC ED 133 658.

Smith, Lee Rand. "A Comparative Study of the Achievement of Negro Students Attending Segregated Junior High Schools and Negro Students Attending Desegregated Junior High Schools in the City of Tulsa." Doctoral dissertation, U. of Tulsa, 1971. Univ. Microfilms Order No. 71-22730.

Smith, William F. "A Study of Biracial Interaction in a Racially Blanced School." Doctoral dissertation, U. of Tennessee, 1970.

Smythe, H. H., and Smythe, M. M. Some Benefits of Mixed Schools. New York: New York State Commission on the Quality, Cost and Financing of Elementary and Secondary Education, Ap, 1971.

Solomon, Daniel. Evaluation of the 1976-77 Desegregation Program in the Montgomery County Public Schools. Rockville: Montgomery County Public Schools, Mr 14, 1978.

Starnes, T. A. "An Analysis of the Academic Achievement of Negro Students in the Predominantly White Schools of a Selected Florida County." Doctoral dissertation, U. of Southern Mississippi, 1968. Univ. Microfilms Order No. 68-14712.

Stember, Charles Herbert. "Evaluating Effects of the Integrated Classroom." Urban Review, Je, 1968.

Stephan, Walter G. "Cognitive Differentiation in Intergroup Perception." Sociometry 40 (Mr, 1977):50-58.

_____. "School Desegregation: An Evaluation of Predictions Made in Brown v. Board of Education." Psychological Bulletin 85(1978): 217-238.

Stern, Etta G., and MacLennan, Beryce W. "Integrating Minority and Majority Youth: A Socio-drama Group as a Human Relations Model." Journal of Non-White Concerns in Personnal and Guidance 2(Ap, 1974):146-155.

Stewart, Joseph E., Jr. "Second Generation Discrimination: Unequal Educational Opportunity in Desegregated Southern Schools." Doctoral dissertation, U. of Houston, 1977.

Strack, C. M., and Dahlstedt, W. A. Desegregation, the Learning Process, and Changing Values in Human Relations. Institute Interim Report, 1966. ERIC ED 056 123.

Strang, William J. "The Self-Concepts of Children in Elementary Schools with Differing Proportions of Negro and White Students." Doctoral dissertation, U. of Alabama, 1972.

Strauss, Susan. "The Effect of School Integration on the Self-Concept of Negro and Puerto Rican Children." Graduate Research in Education and Related Disciplines 3(Ap, 1967): 63-76.

The Student Pushout. Victim of Continued Resistance to Desegregation. Atlanta, GA: Southern Regional Council, 1973.

Sugar, Max. "Defusing a High School Critical Mass." In The Adolescent in Group and Family Therapy, pp. 118-141. Edited by Max Sugar. New York: Brunner/Mazel, 1975.

Suninut, William S. An Analysis of the Effects of Busing on Scholastic Performance and Attendance at Two Secondary Schools in Louisville, Kentucky. Specialist in Education paper, U. of Louisville, 1976.

Talmage, Harriet, and Mendelson, Lloyd J. Project Wingspread. Metropolitan Community Resources as the Interface for Open Communications. Objectives, 1971. ERIC ED 063 222.

Tanner, James C. "Integration in Action. Dixie Teachers Report Their Pupils Learn Well in Mixed-Race Schools." Wall Street Journal, Ja 20, 1964.

Taylor, Donald Ray. "A Longitudinal Comparison of Intellectual Development of Black and White Students from Segregated to Desegregated Settings." Doctoral dissertation, U. of South Florida, 1974. Univ. Microfilms Order No. 74-10126.

Temme, Lloyd V., and Cohen, Jere M. "Ethnic Differences in High School Friendship." Sociology of Education 43(Fall, 1970):459-464.

Teplin, L. "A Study of Sociometric Choice and Rejection Behavior among Sexually, Racially, and Ethnically Integrated Groups of Elementary School and High School Students." Doctoral dissertation, Northwestern U., 1972.

Terrell, Francis. "Dialectal Differences Between Middle-Class Black & White Children Who Do and Do Not Associate with Lower-Class Black Children." Language and Speech 18(Ja-Mr, 1975):65-73.

Thomas, Kenneth Dirdley. "The Effect of Busing on School Success of Minority Students in Urban Elementary Schools." Doctoral dissertation, North Texas State U., 1977. Univ. Microfilms Order No. 780 7848.

Thomas, Lorenzo. "Creativity and Stress in Recently Integrated Schools." Freedomways 15 (Third Quarter, 1975):221-225. [East Texas]

Torbert, William R. and others. The Metropairways Pilot Year Evaluation. A Collaborative Inquiry into Voluntary Metropolitan Desegregation, Je 30, 1976. Metropolitan Planning Project, 55 Chapel Street, Newton, MA 02160. [Massachusetts]

Travis, Cheryl B., and Anthony, Sharon E. "Ethnic Composition of Schools and Achievement Motivation." Journal of Psychology 89(Mr, 1975):271-279.

_____ and _____. "Some Pyschological Consequences of Integration." Journal of Psychology 47(Spring, 1978):151-158.

U.S. Commission on Civil Rights. "A Proposed Study on Desegregation." Integrated Education 11(J1-O, 1973).

_____. Fulfilling the Letter and Spirit of the Law. Desegregation of the Nation's Public Schools. Washington, DC: The Commission, Ag, 1976.

_____. Public Knowledge and Busing Opposition. An Interpretation of a New National Survey. Washington, DC: The Commission, Mr 11, 1973.

U.S. Congress, 94th, 2nd session, House of Representatives, Committee on Education and Labor, Subcommittee on Elementary, Secondary, and Vocational Education. School Integration Innovation Act of 1976. Hearing... Washington, DC: GPO, 1976.

U.S. Office of Education. "Effects of Desegregation on Student Academic Achievement: A Research Review." In U.S. Congress, 92nd, 2nd session, Senate, Committee on Labor and Public Welfare, Subcommittee on Education, Equal Educational Opportunities Act of 1972. Hearings..., pp. 290-299. Washington, DC: GPO, 1972.

_____. Working Together. Case Studies of Title I, ESEA Programs in Four Desegregated School Districts. Washington, DC: GPO, 1974.

Uhl, Norman P. A Procedure for Identifying Problems and Solutions in Desegregated Schools, Ap, 1974. ERIC ED 096 376.

University of Florida. Consequences of Racial Hetereogeneity and Homogeneity in Problem-Solving Groups. AD-752 142. Springfield, VA: National Technical Information Service, N, 1972.

Useem, Elizabeth. "Correlates of White Students' Attitudes Toward a Voluntary Busing Program." Education and Urban Society 8(Ag, 1976):441-476. [METCO]

_____. "White Students and Token Desegregation." Integrated Education, S-O, 1972, pp. 46-54.

_____. "White Suburban Secondary Students in Schools with Token Desegregation: Correlates of Racial Attitudes." Doctoral dissertation, Harvard U., 1971.

Vedlitz, Arnold. "Factors Affecting the Attitudes of Black High School Students Toward 'Freedom-of-Choice' School Integration." Negro Educational Review 26(Ja, 1975):37-41

Venditti, Frederick P., and Hall, Burnis, Jr. School Desegregation Research: A Survey of Doctoral Studies, College of Education, The University of Tennessee, Knoxville. Knoxville, TN: College of Education, U. of Tennessee, 1973.

Vredevoe, Lawrence E. "The Effects of Desegregation on School Discipline." Education Digest, Ap, 1965.

_____. "The Effort to Desegregate and Its Effects Upon School Discipline and Attitudes." Journal of Secondary Education, F, 1967. [Closely patterned after the above article]

Wagoner, Jennings L., Jr. and others. "Student Relationships and Activities in Desegregated Schools." High School Journal 54(D, 1970): 188-201.

Walberg, Herbert J. An Evaluation of an Urban-Suburban School Bussing Program: Student Achievement and Perception of Class Learning Environments, F, 1971. ERIC ED 047 076.

Waldron, Ann. The Integration of Mary-Larkin Thornhill. New York: Dutton, 1975. [Juvenile fiction]

Warren, Neil. "'Racial' Differences in Psychological Characteristics." News Letter, Institute of Race Relations (London), Mr, 1967.

Washington, Edward R., and Alcorn, John D. "The Effects of School Integration on Social Insight among Black Students Clasified as Introverts or Extroverts." Southern Journal of Educational Research 12(Winter, 1978):47-58.

Weinberg, Meyer. "Black Children and Desegregation: Research Perspectives." In Opening Opportunities for Disadvantaged Learners, pp. 181-202. Edited by A. Harry Passow. New York: Teachers College Press, 1972.

_____. "The Challenge of Successful Integration: A Reaction." In Catholic Schools and Racial Integration: Perspectives, Directions, pp. 94-100. Washington, DC: National Catholic Conference for Interracial Justice, 1977.

_____. "Desegregation and Achievement, Self Concept and Aspirations, and Student Interaction." Research Review of Equal Education 1(Winter, 1977):11-25.

_____. "Desegregation and Quality Education: Quality and Equality in Our Schools." In Weinberg and Others, Three Myths: An Exposure of Popular Misconceptions About School Desegregation, pp. 11-36. Atlanta, GA: Southern Regional Council, S, 1976.

_____. Desegregation Research: An Appraisal. Bloomington, IN: Phi Delta Kappa, 1968. Second edition, 1970.

_____. "The Educational Effects of Desegregation." In School Desegregation: Retrospect and Prospect, pp. 68-89. Edited by Eugene C. Lee. Atlanta, GA: Southern Newspaper Publishers Association Foundation, P.O. Box 11606, Atlanta 30305.

_____. Minority Students: A Research Appraisal. Washington, DC: GPO, 1977.

_____. Research on School Desegregation: Review and Prospect. Chicago, IL: Integrated Education Associates, 1965.

_____. "The Relationship Between School Deseggregation and Academic Achievement: A Review of the Research." Law and Contemporary Problems 39(Spring, 1975):241-270.

_____. "White Children in the Desegregation Process." Integrateducation 12(Jl-Ag, 1974): 40-41.

Wellisch, Jean B. Instrumentation and Training for the Emergency School Aid Act (ESAA) In-Depth Studies. Santa Monica, CA: System Development Corporation, 1977.

Wellisch, Jean B. and others. An In-Depth Study of Emergency School Aid Act (ESAA) Schools: 1974-1975. Santa Monica, CA: System Development Corporation, Jl, 1976.

_____ and others. An In-Depth Study of Emergency School Aid Act (ESAA) Schools: 1975-1976. Santa Monica, CA: System Development Corporation, Mr, 1977.

_____ and others. "School Management and Organization in Successful Schools (ESAA In-Depth Study Schools)." Sociology of Education 51(Jl, 1978):211-226.

Wellman, Barry S. "Social Identities and Cosmopolitanism among Urban Adolescents: Variation by Race, Social Status, and School Integration Experience." Doctoral dissertation, Harvard U., 1970.

Wertham, Frederic. "Psychological Effects of School Segregation." American Journal of Psychotherapy, 1952.

Wey, Herbert W. "Desegregation and Integration." Phi Delta Kappan, My, 1966.

_____. "Desegregation--It Works." Phi Delta Kappan, My, 1964.

_____. Planning and Preparing for Successful School Desegregation. A Guidebook. Phi Delta Kappa Commission on Education and Human Rights. Phi Delta Kappa. Eighth and Union, Bloomington, IN, 1965.

Wheeler, Charles III. "The Relationship of the Black Preschool Child's Self-Concept to the Degree of Integration and other Racially Relevant Variables." Doctoral dissertation Purdue U., 1974. Univ. Microfilms Order No. 74-26794.

Whitaker, Ollie H. "The Negro Child Learns Better in an Integrated Situation than a Segregated Situation." Master's thesis, Chapman College, 1971.

"What I Think About Integration." _Jewish Currents_, S, 1965. [Short prize-winning essays by 12 Jewish children, 10-13 years old]

White, Dan A. "Effects of Busing on Urban School Students." _Educational Leadership_ 29 (D, 1971):255-257.

_____. "The Effects of Public School Transportation upon the Overall School Adjustment of Urban Elementary School Students." Doctoral dissertation, U. of Oklahoma, 1970.

White, Kinnard. "Belief in Reinforcement Control Among Southern Negro Adolescents: The Effects of School Desegregation, Socioeconomic Status, and Sex of Student." _Journal of Social Psychology_ 85(O, 1971):149-150.

White, Kinnard, and Knight, James H. "School Desegregation, Socioeconomic Status, Sex and the Aspirations of Southern Negro Adolescents." _Journal of Negro Education_ 42 (Winter, 1973):71-78.

White, Sheldon H. and others. "Effects of Desegregation." In _Federal Programs for Young Children: Review and Recommendations_, Vol. II, Appendix II A, pp. 1-21. Washington, DC: GPO, 1973.

Whiting, Frank Sheldon. "Selected Effects of Busing on Black Students." Doctoral dissertation, Indiana U., 1974. Univ. Microfilms Order No. 75-05583.

Whitmore, Paul G. "A Study of School Desegregation: Attitude Change and Scale Variation." Doctoral dissertation, U. of Tennessee, 1956. Univ. Microfilms Order No. 20501.

Williams, Joyce H. "School Desegregation and Racial Fears in a Southern Community." Master's thesis, Fort Valley State College, 1971.

Williams, Robert L., and Venditti, Fred. "Effect of Academic Desegregation on Southern White Students' Expressed Satisfaction With School." _Journal of Negro Education_, Fall, 1969.

Willie, Charles V. "Social Adjustment of Inner-City Black Children in White Middle-Class Schools." In _The Essential Profession_. Edited by Marvin B. Scott. Greylock, 1976.

Wilson, James Q. "On Pettigrew & Armor: An Afterword." _Public Interest_ 30(Winter, 1973): 132-136.

Wilson, Vera Isabel. "The Relationship between Racial Composition of Desegregated High Schools and Membership in Co-Curricular Programs in Baltimore City." Doctoral dissertation, Temple U., 1978. Univ. Microfilms Order No. 7817420.

Wilson, William J., and O'Sullivan, Katherine. _Urban School Desegregation and Structural Changes in the Economy_, 1976. ERIC ED 137 472.

Winstead, John Clayton. "Changes in Attitudes of Negro Pupils Moving from Segregated to Integrated Schools." Doctoral dissertation, U. of Tennessee, 1972. Univ. Microfilms Order No. 73-02515.

Wolf, Robert L., and Simon, Rita J. "Does Busing Improve the Racial Interactions of Children?" _Educational Researcher_ 4(Ja, 1975):5-10.

Wood, B. H. The Effects of Bussing versus Non-Bussing on the Intellectual Functioning of Inner City, Disadvantaged Elementary School Children." Doctoral dissertation, U. of Massachusetts, Boston, 1969.

Woodward, Jane W. "A Sociometric Study of Voluntary De Facto Segregation in an Integrated School." Master's thesis, Wake Forest U., 1970.

Wyatt, Donald Lynn. "The Student Clique System of Desegregated High School and Its Influence on the Instructional Process." Doctoral dissertation, U. of Florida, 1976. Univ. Microfilms Order No. 77-1152.

Yarrow, Marion R. (ed.). "Interpersonal Dynamics in a Desegregation Process." _Journal of Social Issues_ 14(1958):3-63.

Yohalem, Alice, and Ridgely, Quentin B. _Desegregation and Career Goals: Children of Air Force Families_. New York: Praeger, 1974.

York, Robert. _Effects of Desegregation on Student Academic Achievement: A Research Review_. Washington, DC: U.S. Office of Education, Office for Program Planning and Evaluation, n.d.

Young, Alice H. "A Description and Analysis of Reported Reasons for Voluntarily Involving Children in a Pupil Transfer Program in the Rochester Public Schools." _Diss. Abstr. Int'l._, 1970, 30 (9-A) 4022-3.

Young, Robert E. "Interethnic Behavior in Desegregated Secondary Schools." Doctoral dissertation, Columbia U., 1974.

Zdep, Stanley M. "Educating Disadvantaged Urban Children in Suburban Schools: An Evaluation." _Journal of Applied Social Psychology_ 1(Ap-Je, 1971):173-186.

Bilingualism and Biculturalism

Albert, Martin L., and Obler, Loraine K. _The Bilingual Brain: Neuropsychological and Neurolinguistic Aspects of Bilingualism_. New York: Academic Press, 1978.

American Institutes for Research in the Behavioral Sciences. _Evaluation of the Impact of ESEA Title VII Spanish/English Bilingual Education Program_, 2 vols., F, 1977. ERIC ED 138 090-091. [See Tracy Gray, below]

Andersson, Theodore. "Bilingual Education: The American Experience." Modern Language Journal 55(N, 1971):425-438.

_____. "Preschool Biliteracy: Historical Background." Hispania 60(S, 1977):527-530.

_____. "The Role of the Teacher in a Bilingual Bicultural Community." Hispania 57(D, 1974): 927-932.

Andersson, Theodore and others. "Early Childhood: The Best Time to Become Bilingual and Biliterate." Childhood Education 54(Ja, 1978):155-161.

Angle, John. Language Maintenance, Language Shift, and Occupational Achievement in the United States. Palo Alto, CA: R & E Research Associates, 1978.

Aracil, Lluís V. "Bilingualism as a Myth." Revista/Review Interamericana 2(1972).

Arawak, Consulting Corp. Synthesis of Bilingual Clearinghouse Conferences, 1976. ERIC ED 136 567.

Arenas, Soledad. "Bilingual/Bicultural Programs for Preschool Children." Children Today 7 (Jl-Ag, 1978):2-6.

Arredondo, Joe. "Historical Development of a Bilingual Program in a Northern Urban Society." Doctoral dissertation, Indiana U., 1974. Univ. Microfilms Order No. 75-5402.

Arseman, B. "Bilingualism in the Post-War World." Psychological Bulletin 68(1945): 145-190.

Baca, Mario L. M. "What's Going On in the Bilingual Special Education Classroom?" Teaching Exceptional Children 7(F, 1974).

Báez, Luis A. and others. The Political Dimensions of Bilingual Education in the Context of School Desegregation in Milwaukee: A Case Study. Milwaukee: General Assistance Center, U. of Wisconsin, 1978.

Bain, Bruce. "Toward an Integration of Piaget and Vygotsky: Bilingual Consideration." Linguistics 160(S 15, 1975):5-20. [Bibliography]

Balkan, Lewis. "Les Effets du bilinguisme francais-anglais sur les aptitudes intellectuelles." Doctoral dissertation, U. of Neuchatel, 1970.

Barik, Henri C., and Swain, Merrill. "English-French Bilingual Education in the Early Grades: The Elgin Study." Modern Language Journal 58(D, 1974):392-403. [St. Thomas, Ontario]

"Bilingual Education: Its Promises and Problems." American Teacher, D, 1974.

Bordie, J. G. "Language Tests and Linguistically Different Learners: The Sad State of the Art." Elementary English 47(1970): 814-828.

Brisk, Maria Estela. Bilingual Education and School Desegregation: The Case of Boston, My, 1975. ERIC ED 126 199.

Bruck, Margaret and others. "Bilingual Schooling Through the Elementary Grades: The St. Lambert Project at Grade Seven." Language Learning 24(D, 1974):183-204.

_____ and others. "Cognitive Consequences of Bilingual Schooling: The St. Lambert Project through Grade Six." Linguistics 187(Mr 3, 1977):13-33.

California State Legislature. Toward Meaningful and Equal Educational Opportunity. Report on Public Hearings on Bilingual-Bicultural Education, Jl, 1976. ERIC ED 131 731.

Campeau, Peggie L. and others. The Identification and Description of Exemplary Bilingual Education Programs, Ag, 1975. ERIC ED 123 893.

Cárdenas, Blandina. "Defining Access to Equal Educational Opportunity for Mexican-Americans." Doctoral dissertation, U. of Massachusetts, 1974.

Cárdenas, Jose A. "Bilingual Education, Segregation, and a Third Alternative." Inequality in Education 19(F, 1975):19-22.

Cárdenas, Jose and others. Bilingual Education Cost Analysis, Ag, 1976. ERIC ED 131 529.

Casso, Henry J. Bilingual/Bicultural Education and Teacher Training. Washington, DC: National Education Association, 1977.

Castro, Ray. "Shifting the Burden of Bilingualism: The Case for Monolingual Communities." Bilingual Review 3(Ja-Ap, 1976):3-28.

Center for Applied Linguistics. Guidelines for the Preparation and Certification of Teachers of Bilingual/Bicultural Education, N, 1974. ED 098 809.

Chen, May Ying. "Lau vs. Nichols. Landmark in Bilingual Education." Bridge 3(F, 1975): 3-7.

Chin, Big-Qu, and Duda, Holyna. Ethnic Group Schooling and the Massachusetts Transitional Bilingual Education Act, n.p., My, 1972.

Cummins, James. The Cognitive Development of Bilingual Children: A Review of Recent Research, 1977. ERIC ED 145 727.

Cohen, Andrew D. "Bilingual Schooling and Spanish Language Maintenance: An Experimental Analysis." Bilingual Review 2(Ja-Ag, 1975): 3-12.

Colombani, Serafini. "The Bilingual Pressure Cooker." Journal of the National Association for Bilingual Education 1(My, 1976):13-16.

Comment. "The Constitutional Right of Bilingual Children to an Equal Educational Opportunity." Southern California Law Review 47 (1974).

Comptroller General of the United States. Bilingual Education: An Unmet Need. Washington, DC: General Accounting Office, My 19, 1976.

Cornejo, Ricardo J. A Synthesis of Theories and Research on the Effects of Teaching in First and Second Languages: Implications for Bilingual Education. Austin, TX: National Educational Laboratory, Je, 1974.

Cummins, James. "The Cognitive Development of Children in Immersion Programs." Canadian Modern Language Review 34(My, 1978):855-883.

_____. "The Influence of Bilingualism on Cognitive Growth: A Synthesis of Research Findings and Explanatory Hypotheses." Working Papers in Bilingualism (Ontario Institute for Studies in Education) 9 (1976):1-43.

Cummins, James, and Gulutsan, M. "Bilingual Education and Cognition." Alberta Journal of Educational Research 20(S, 1974):259-269. [Edmonton, Canada]

Development Associates, Inc. Final Report on A Study of State Programs in Bilingual Education. 4 vols. Washington, DC: Development Associates, Inc., Mr, 1977. [Report to H.E.W.]

Edwards, J. R. "Current Issues in Bilingual Education." Ethnicity 3(Mr, 1976):70-81.

EPIE. Selector's Guide for Bilingual Education Materials. 3 vols. New York: Educational Products Information Exchange Institute, 1976.

Ehrlich, Alan, and Ehrlich, Shoshanna (comps.). Tests in Spanish and Other Languages, English as a Second Language, and Nonverbal Tests for Children in Bilingual Programs: An Annotated Bibliography. Rev. ed. 1975. Bilingual Education Applied Research Unit, Project BEST, New York City Bilingual Consortium, Hunter College Midtown--Room 614, 560 Lexington Avenue, New York, NY 10022.

Engle, Patricia Lee. "Language Medium in Early School Years for Minority Language Groups." Review of Educational Research 45(Spring, 1976):283-325.

Epstein, Noel. "The Bilingual Battle." Washington Post, Je 5, 1977.

Fishman, Joshua A. Bilingual Education: An International Sociological Perspective. Rowley, MA: Newbury House, 1976.

Flores Macias, Reynaldo. "Opinions of Chicano Community Parents on Curriculum and Language Use in Bilingual PreSchool Education." Aztlán 4(Fall, 1973):315-334. [East Los Angeles]

Foster, William P. "Bilingual Education: An Educational and Legal Survey." Journal of Law and Education 5(Ap, 1976):149-171.

Gaarder, Alfred Bruce. Bilingual Schooling and the Survival of Spanish in the United States. Rowley, MA: Newbury House, 1977.

_____. "El Mantenimiento o Desplazamiento Linguistico: El Futuro del Espanol en los Estados Unidos." Journal of the National Association for Bilingual Education 1(D, 1976):29-45.

Gelder, Sharon B. "Bilingual Education An Emotional Issue to Many Cities. Chicago Program Pleads for More Time to Prove Itself." Chicago Reporter 8(Ja, 1979).

Gezi, Kal. " Bilingual-Bicultural Education: A Review of Relevant Research." California Journal of Educational Research 25(n.d.): 223-239.

Gonzalez, Gustavo. Issues in Bilingual Education: The Acquisition of the First Language, N, 1973. ERIC ED 094 566.

González, Joshué. "Coming of Age in Bilingual/ Bicultural Education: A Historical Perspective." Inequality in Education 19(F, 1975): 5-17.

Gray, Tracy. Response to AIR Study Evaluation of the Impact of ESEA Title VII Spanish/ English Bilingual Education Program, Ap 18, 1977. ERIC ED 138 122. [See American Institutes for Research in the Behavioral Sciences, above]

Guide to Title VII, E.S.E.A. Bilingual Bicultural Projects in 1972-73. Austin, TX: Dissemination Center for Bilingual Bicultural Education, 1973.

Hall, Beverly. "Bilingual and Bicultural Schools." Notes from Workshop Center for Open Education 6(Spring, 1977):28-36.

Hernández, Eduardo, and Gumperz, John J. Cognitive Aspects of Bilingual Communication. Berkeley, CA: Language Behavior Laboratory, U. of California, 1971.

Hočevar, T. "Equilibria in Linguistic Minority Markets." Kyklos 28(1975).

Holloman, John W. "A Practical Approach to Assessing Bilingualism in Young Mexican-American Children." TESOL Quarterly 10(D, 1976):389-401.

Holloman, John W. and others. A Cross-Cultural Investigation of Language and Thought in Young Anglo-, Black-, and Mexican-American Children of Low Social Status Parents, 1976. ERIC ED 131 955.

Hornby, Peter A. (ed.). Bilingualism. Psychological, Social, and Educational Implications. New York: Academic Press, 1977.

How Equitably are Bilingual-Bicultural Education Programs Servicing the Puerto Rican Students? Washington, DC: Puerto Rican Association for National Affairs, 1972.

Ingram, D. E., and Elias, G. C. "Bilingual Education and Reading." RELC Journal 5 (Je, 1974):64-76.

Johnson, Nancy A. "Zombies and Other Problems: Theory and Method in Research on Bilingualism." Language Learning 24 Je, 1974):105-133.

Johnson, Pamela F., and Warner, Dennis A. "A Bilingual Teacher is Not Enough." Integrateducation 15(My-Je, 1977).

Joseph, Andre. Bicultural Socialization and the Measurement of Intelligence, n.d. ERIC ED 138 616.

Kloss, Heinz. The American Bilingual Tradition. Rowley, MA: Newbury House, 1977.

Kwok, Irene. Chinese Cultural Resource Book (For Elementary Bilingual Teachers), 1974. ERIC ED 098 280.

La Fontaine, Hernan and others (eds.). Bilingual Education. Wayne, NJ: Avery Publishing Group, 1978.

Lambert, Wallace E. "A Canadian Experiment in the Development of Bilingual Competence." Canadian Modern Language Review 31(N, 1974): 108-116.

_____. "A Social Psychology of Bilingualism." Journal of Social Issues 23(1967):91-110.

_____. "Cognitive and Socio-Cultural Consequences of Bilingualism." Canadian Modern Language Review 34(F, 1978):537-547.

_____. Culture and Language as Factors in Learning and Education, N, 1973. ERIC ED 096 820.

Lambert, Wallace E., and Tucker, G. Richard. Bilingual Education of Children: The St. Lambert Experiment. Rowley, MA: Newbury House Publishers, 1972.

Lawyers' Committee for Civil Rights Under Law. The Current Status of U.S. Bilingual Education Legislation, 1975. Center for Applied Linguistics, 1611 Kent St., Arlington, VA 22209.

Leibowitz, Arnold H. Educational Policy and Political Acceptance--The Imposition of English as the Language of Instruction in American Schools. Washington, DC: Center for Applied Linguistics, 1970.

_____. "English Literacy: Legal Sanction for Discrimination." Revista Juridica de la Universidad de Puerto Rico 39(1970).

Lew, Elizabeth. Study Trips. Chinese Bilingual Pilot Program, 1974. ERIC ED 099 433.

Lewis, E. Glyn. "Bilingualism in Education--Cross-National Research." Linguistics 198 (0, 1977):5-30.

Lewis, Frederick P. "The Massachusetts Transitional Bilingual Education Act: Two Years After." Inequality in Education 19(F, 1975): 31-37.

Liedtke, Werner W., and Nelson, L. Royal. "Concept Formation and Bilingualism." Alberta Journal of Educational Research, D, 1968. [1st grade students in Edmonton, Canada; bilingual students found superior in concept formation]

Light, Richard L. "Preparing Educators for Bilingual Education: Needs and a Response." Bilingual Review 2(S-D, 1975):331-338.

Ligon, Glynn, and Holley, Freda. Can Researchers Find True Happiness in a Public School Setting? A Success Story in Bilingual Education Evaluation, Mr, 1978. ERIC ED 157 374. [Austin, Texas]

Locks, Nancy A. and others. Language Assessment Instruments for Limited-English-Speaking Students. A Needs Analysis. Washington, DC: National Institute of Education, 0, 1978.

Mackey, William Francis. The Bicultural Education Movement, Mr, 1973. ERIC ED 094 553.

Mackey, William F., and Andersson, Theodore (eds.). Bilingualism in Early Childhood. Rowley, MA: Newbury House, 1977.

McRai, Kenneth D. "The Principle of Territoriality and the Principle of Personality in Multilingual States." Linguistics 158(Ag 15, 1975):33-54.

Mead, Margaret. "The Conservation of Insight—Educational Understanding of Bilingualism." Teachers College Record 79(My, 1978):705-721.

Merlos, Ramon Luis. "Effects of Bilingual Education on the Cognitive Characteristics of the Spanish Speaking Children in Chicago Public Schools." Doctoral dissertation, Loyola U. of Chicago, 1978. Univ. Microfilms Order No. 7815877.

Micaud, Charles A. "Bilingualism in North Africa: Cultural and Socio-Political Implications." Western Political Quarterly 27 (Mr, 1974):92-103.

Modiana, Nancy. "Bilingual Education for Children of Linguistic Minorities." America Indigena, Ap, 1968.

Montal Educational Associates. Position Papers on Bilingual Bicultural Educational Manpower Development, Ap, 1974. ERIC ED 096 039.

Mpasi, Nkenda. "La problématique de la langue d'enseignement en Republique du Zaïre." Cult. Zaïre Afrique 2(1973):105-134.

Muckley, Robert L. "After Childhood, What Then? An Overview of Ethnic Language Retention Programs in the U.S." Revista/Review Interamericana 2(1972).

Newth, J. A. "Nationality and Language in Turkmenia." Soviet Studies 15(Ap, 1964): 459-463.

Nieves Falcón, Luis. "NEEDED--Liberating Materials for Bilingual Education." Interracial Books for Children Bulletin 9(1978): 11,19.

Ochoa, Victor-Alberto M. "Bilingual Desegregation: School Districts' Responses to the Spirit of the Law Under the Lau vs. Nichols Supreme Court Case." Doctoral dissertation, U. of Massachusetts, 1978. Univ. Microfilms Order No. 7818032.

Opitz, Kurt (ed.). Mother Tongue Practice in the Schools. Conditions--Views--Experiments. Hamburg, Germany: Uvesco Institute for Education, 1972.

Ortega, Luis (ed.). Introduction to Bilingual Education. New York: Anaya-Las Americas, 1975.

Padilla, A. M., and Liebman, Ellen. "Language Acquisition in the Bilingual Child." Bilingual Review 2(Ja-Ag, 1975):34-55.

Paulston, Christina Bratt. Ethnic Relations and Bilingual Education: Accounting for Contradictory Data, My, 1975. ERIC ED 125 253.

_____. "Theoretical Perspectives on Bilingual Educational Programs." Working Papers on Bilingualism 13(1977):130-180.

Person, Y. "Impérialisme linguistique et colonialisme." Temps Modernes 324-326(1973): 90-118.

Pill, Roisin. "Social Implications of a Bilingual Policy, with Particular Reference to Wales." British Journal of Sociology 25(Mr, 1974):94-107.

Plante, Alexander J. A Study of the Effectiveness of the Connecticut "Pairing" Model of Bilingual-Bicultural Education, Ja, 1976. ERIC ED 125 260.

Politzer, Robert L., and McKay, Maryann. "A Pilot Study Concerning the Development of a Spanish/English Oral Proficiency Test." Bilingual Review 2(Ja-Ag, 1975):112-137.

Ramirez, Arnulfo G., and Politzer, Robert L. "Development of Spanish/English Bilingualism in a Dominant Spanish Speaking Environment." Antisbos 1(Summer, 1975):31-51.

Ramirez, Manuel III, and Castaneda, Alfredo. Cultural Democracy, Bicognitive Development, and Education. New York: Academic Press, 1974.

Ramirez, Manuel III and others. Spanish-English Bilingual Education in the U.S.: Current Issues, Resources, and Research Priorities. Arlington, VA: Center for Applied Linguistics, F, 1977.

Rice, Roger. "Recent Legal Developments in Bilingual/Bicultural Education." Inequality in Education 19(F, 1975):51-53.

Richardson, M. W. An Evaluation of Certain Aspects of the Academic Achievement of Elementary Pupils in a Bilingual Program. Coral Gables, FL: U. of Miami, 1968.

Rodriguez, Antonio, Jr. "Are Bilingual Children Able to Think in Either Language with Equal Facility and Accuracy?" Bulletin of the Department of Elementary School Principals 10 (Ja, 1931):98-101.

Roos, Peter, and Roos, Emma Chavez. "The Massachusetts Transitional Bilingual Education Act: Problems in the Classroom and Possible Legislative Responses." Inequality in Education 19(F, 1975):38-42.

Salganik, Laura Hersh. "Fox Point: The History of a Portuguese Bilingual Program." Inequality in Education 19(F, 1975):47-50. [Fox Point School, Providence, R.I.]

San Juan Cafferty, Pastora. "Puerto Rican Return Migration: Its Implications for Bilingual Education." Ethnicity 2(1975):52-65.

Sanchez, Rosaura. "Chicano Bilingualism." New Scholar 6(1977):209-225. [Published at U. of California, La Jolla]

Savaille-Troike, Muriel (ed). Classroom Practices in ESL and Bilingual Education, Vol. I, My, 1973. ERIC ED 093 156.

_____. Bilingual Children: A Resource Document Prepared for Child Development Associate Consortium, Inc. Washington, DC: Child Development Associate Consortium, 1973 and Arlington, VA: The Center for Applied Linguistics, 1973.

Savard, J. G., and Vigneault, Richard. Les états multilingues: problèmes et solutions. Québec: Les Presses de l'Université Laval, 1975.

Shanker, Albert. "UFT Responds to Anker Memorandum on Goals of Consent Decree." New York Teacher, Ja 26, 1975. [On bilingual instruction as mandated by court decree in Apira case]

Silver, Brian D. "The Impact of Urbanization and Geographical Dispersion on the Linguistic Russification of Soviet Nationalities." Demography 11(F, 1974).

_____. "The Status of National Minority Languages in Soviet Education: An Assessment of Recent Changes." Soviet Studies 26 (Ja, 1974).

Simões, Antônio, Jr. (ed.). The Bilingual Child. Research and Analysis of Existing Educational Themes. New York: Academic Press, 1976.

Spolsky, Bernard. The Development of Navajo Bilingual Education, Je, 1973. ERIC ED 094 559.

_____. "Speech Communities and Schools." TESOL Quarterly 8(Mr, 1974):17-26.

Spolsky, Bernard, and Cooper, Robert (eds.). Frontiers of Bilingual Education. Rowley, MA: Newbury House, 1977.

Spolsky, Bernard (ed.). The Language Education of Minority Children. Rowley, MA: Newbury House Publishers, 1972.

Stavrou, Nikolaos A. "Unity, Brotherhood and Manipulation. Language and Minorities in Yugoslavia." Society 12(Ja- F, 1975):75-78.

Steiner, Frank and others (comps.). Bilingual/Bicultural Education--A Privilege or a Right?, My, 1974. ERIC ED 097 167.

"Students' Right to their Own Language." College Composition and Communication 25 (Fall, 1974).

Teitelbaum, Herbert, and Hiller, Richard J. "Bilingual Education: The Legal Mandate." Harvard Educational Review 47(My, 1977): 138-170.

Teschner, Richard V. "Bilingual Education and the Materials Explosion, or a Guide for the Bibliographer-by-Necessity." Bilingual Review 1(S-D, 1974):259-269.

Troike, Rudolph C., and Modiano, Nancy (eds.). Proceedings of the First Inter-American Conference on Bilingual Education, O, 1975. Center for Applied Linguistics, 1611 No. Kent St., Arlington, VA 22209.

U.S. Commission on Civil Rights. A Better Chance to Learn: Bilingual-Bicultural Education. Washington, DC: The Commission, My, 1975.

U.S. Congress, 93rd, 1st session, Senate, Committee on Labor and Public Welfare, Subcommittee on Education and the Special Subcommittee on Human Resources. Bilingual Education, Health, and Manpower Programs, 1973. Joint Hearing... Washington, DC: GPO, 1973.

U.S. Congress, 93rd, 2nd session, House of Representatives, Committee on Education and Labor, General Subcommittee on Education. Bilingual Education Act. Hearings... Washington, DC: GPO, 1974.

U.S. Office of Education. The Condition of Bilingual Education in the Nation, N, 1976. ERIC ED 146 795.

Uribe Villegas, Oscar (ed.). Situaciones de multilingüismo en el mundo. Mexico City: Instituto de Investigaciones Sociales, 1972.

Vaigo, A. C. "Bilingual Drive Seen as Key to Immigrant Learning." Times Education Supplement, D 27, 1974. [Sweden]

Vallee, Frank G., and Dufour, Albert. "The Bilingual Belt: A Garrotte for the French?" Laurentian University Review 6(F, 1974): 19-44. [Canada]

Vásquez, Jo Ann. "Will Bilingual Curricula Solve the Problem of the Low-Achieving Mexican American Student?" Bilingual Review 1(S-D, 1974):236-242.

Vazquez Batisti, Anita. "Attitudes of Hispanic Parochial School Parents and Professional Staff Toward Bilingual/Bicultural Education." Doctoral dissertation, Fordham U., 1978. Univ. Microfilms Order No. 7816560.

Viera, Nelson. "Training Teachers for Bilingual/Bicultural Education." Inequality in Education 19(F, 1975):43-46.

von Maltitz, Frances. Living and Learning in Two Languages: Bilingual-Bicultural Education in the United States. New York: McGraw-Hill, 1975.

de Vries, John. "The Swedish-speaking Minority in Finland." Master's thesis, U. of Wisconsin, 1968.

Waggoner, Dorothy. Language and Demographic Characteristics of the U.S. Population with Potential Need for Bilingual and Other Special Educational Programs, 1976. ERIC ED 146 805.

_____. State Education Agencies and Language-Minority Students. Washington, DC: National Center for Education Statistics, 1978.

Wang, Ling-chi. "Lau v. Nichols: The Right of Limited-English-speaking Students." Amerasia Journal 2(Fall, 1974):16-45.

Waserstein, Aida. "Organizing for Bilingual Education: One Community's Experience." Inequality in Education 19(F, 1975) [Wilmington, Delaware]

Waugh, Dexter, and Koon, Bruce. "Breakthrough for Bilingual Education. Lau v. Nichols and the San Francisco School System." Civil Rights Digest 6(Summer, 1974):18-26.

Zappert, Laraine Testa, and Cruz, B. Roberto. Bilingual Education: An Appraisal of Empirical Research, 1977. ERIC ED 153 758.

Zimmerman, Ira Lee and others. "Language Status of Preschool Mexican-American Children--Is There a Case Against Early Bilingual Education?" Perceptual and Motor Skills 38(F, 1974):227-230.

Zirkel, Perry A. "Bilingual Education Programs at the Elementary School Level: Their Identification and Evaluation." Bilingual Review 2(Ja-Ag, 1975):13-21. [1970-1971 data]

_____. "The Legal Vicissitudes of Bilingual Education." Phi Delta Kappan 58(Ja, 1977): 409-411.

_____. The Positive Research Results of Bilingual Education. Hartford, Connecticut State Department of Education, 1971.

_____. "The Why's and Ways of Testing Bilinguality Before Teaching Bilingually." Elementary School Journal 76(Mr, 1976):323-330.

General

A Study of the Developmental Behavior of Culturally Disadvantaged Children: A Special Study Report on the PAR, Mr, 1968. ERIC ED 044 430.

A Study of Messages Received by Children Who Viewed an Episode of "Fat Albert and the Cosby Kids". New York: Office of Social Research, CBS/Broadcast Group, F, 1974.

A Study of Messages Received by Children Who Viewed an Episode of "The Harlem Globetrotters Popcorn Machine". New York: Office of Social Research, CBS, Inc., Ap, 1975.

Aboud, Frances E., and Mitchell, Frank G. Taking the Role of Different Ethnic Groups: A Developmental Study, S, 1975. ERIC ED 131 137.

Abramson, Edward E. "Levels of Aspiration of Negro 9th Grade Males in Integrated & Segregated Schools." Psychological Reports 29(Ag, 1971):258.

_____. The Political Socialization of Black Americans: A Critical Evaluation of Research on Efficacy and Trust. New York: Free Press, 1977.

Abramson, Paul R. "Political Efficacy and Political Trust Among Black Schoolchildren: Two Explanations." Journal of Politics 34 (N, 1972)1243-1269.

Acland, H. D. "Social Determinants of Educational Achievement. An Evaluation and Criticism of Research." Doctoral dissertation, U. of Oxford, 1973.

Acuña, Rodolfo. "Mixing Apples With Oranges." Integrateducation 13(Mr-Ap, 1975):13-14. [See Rohwer, 1975, below]

Adair, Alvis Van-Ressealeas. "A Developmental Study of Race and Sex Role Awareness among Black Preschool Children." Doctoral dissertation, U. of Michigan, 1972. Univ. Microfilms Order No. 73-00097.

Adair, Alvis V., and Savage, James. "Sex and Race as Determinants of Preferences, Attitudes and Self-Identity Among Black Preschool Children: A Developmental Study." Proceedings of the 81st Annual Convention of the American Psychological Association 8 (1973):651-651.

_____ and _____. "Sex and Race as Determinant of Preferences, Attitudes and Self-Identity Among Black Preschool Children: A Developmental Study." Journal of Social and Behavioral Sciences 20(Summer, 1974):94-101.

Adams, Russell L., and Phillips, Beeman N. "Factors Associated with Under- and Over-Achievement Among Socio-Economically and Racial-Ethnically Different Elementary School Children." Psychology in the Schools, Ap, 1968.

Adams, Sterling. "'Your Indifference Is Everlasting.'" Oklahoma [City] Courier, My 31, 1968.

Adler, Sol. "Articulatory Deviances & Social Class Membership." Journal of Social Class Membership 6(D, 1973):650-654.

Aiello, John R., and Jones, Stanley E. "Field Study of the Proxemic Behavior of Young School Children in Three Subcultural Groups." Journal of Personality & Social Psychology 19 (S, 1971):351-356.

Akin, John S., and Garfinkel, Irwin. Economic Returns to Education Quality: An Empirical Analysis for Whites, Blacks, Poor Whites, and Poor Blacks, S, 1974. ERIC ED 097 412.

Aldous, Joan. "Children's Perceptions of Adult Role Assignment: Father-Absence, Class, Race, and Sex Influences." Journal of Marriage and the Family 34(F, 1972):55-65.

Aldridge, Delores P. "Problems and Approaches to Black Adoptions." Family Coordinator 23 (O, 1974):407-410.

Alexander, Karl, and Eckland, Bruce K. Effects of Education on the Social Mobility of High School Sophomores Fifteen Years Later (1955-1970). Washington, DC: National Institute of Education, 1973.

Alexander, Karl, and McDill, Edward L. Social Background and Schooling Influences on the Subjective Orientations of High School Seniors, N, 1974. ERIC ED 102 493.

Alexander, Karl L. and others. Status Compositions and Educational Goals: An Attempt at Clarification. Baltimore: Center for Social Organization of Schools, Johns Hopkins U., F, 1978.

Alexander, Thereon, and Stoyle, Judith. Culture, Cognition, and Social Change: The Effect of the Head Start Experience on Cognitive Patterns, 1973. ERIC ED 086 315.

Alford, Robert L. "Music and the Mentally Retarded Ethnic Minority Child." Pointer 19 (Winter, 1974):138-139.

Allen, Donald E., and Robinson, Oliver W. Some Factors Affecting Academic Performance of Public Assistance Students, n.d. ERIC ED 029 747.

Allen, James E., Jr. "Integration Is Better Education." Integrated Education 8(S-O, 1969):30-31.

Allen, Louis J. "A Study of Some Possible Origins & Sources of Internal-External Control Orientation in Children." Diss. Abstr. Int'l. 32 (4-B) October, 1971, 2390-2391.

Allen, Penny, Crosby, Sallie, and Garrison, Martha. "Racial Awareness of Children in 1958 and 1964." Senior thesis, Randolph-Macon Women's College, 1964.

Allen, Walter R. "Race, Family Setting, and Adolescent Achievement Orientation." Journal of Negro Education 47(Summer, 1978):230-243.

Allen, Wise Edward. "The Formation of Racial Identity in Black Children Adopted by White Parents." Doctoral dissertation, Wright Institute, 1976. Univ. Microfilms Order No. 76-23289.

Amir, Yehuda. "Contact Hypothesis in Ethnic Relations." Psychological Bulletin, My, 1969.

_____. "The Role of Intergroup Contact in Change of Prejudice and Ethnic Relations." In Towards the Elimination of Racism, pp. 245-308. Edited by Phyllis A. Katz. New York: Pergamon, 1976.

Amir, Y., and Garti, C. "Situational and Person al Influence on Attitude Change Following Ethnic Contact." International Journal of Intercultural Relations 1(1977):58-75.

Anandalakshmy, S., and Adams, Janice F. "An Alternative Heritability Estimate." Harvard Educational Review, Summer, 1969. [In re: Arthur R. Jensen]

Anastasiow, Nicholas J., and Hanes, Michael L. "Cognitive Development and the Acquisition of Language in Three Subcultural Groups." Developmental Psychology 10(S, 1974):703-709.

Anderson, Claud , and Cromwell, Rue L. "'Black is Beautiful' and the Color Preferences of Afro-American Youth." Journal of Negro Education 46(Winter, 1977):76-88.

Anderson, David A. "Public Institutions: Their War Against the Development of Black Youth." American Journal of Orthopsychiatry 41(Ja, 1971):65-73. [Lead poisoning in Rochester, NY]

Anderson, David C. Children of Special Value: Interracial Adoption in America. New York: St. Martin's Press, 1972.

Anderson, Donald George. "Some Characteristics of Negro Open Enrollment Transferees." Doctoral dissertation, U. of California, Berkeley, 1968.

Anderson, Margaret. "The Negro Child Asks: 'Why?'" New York Times Magazine, D 1, 1963.

Anderson, Monroe. "The Young Black Man." Ebony 27(Ag, 1972):128-133.

Anderson, Norma Jean, and Love, Barbara. "Psychological Education for Racial Awareness." Personnel and Guidance Journal 51(My, 1973): 666-670.

Andrew, Given. "Determinants of Negro Family Decisions in Management of Retardation." Journal of Marriage and the Family, N, 1968.

Anosike, Benji J. O. "The Jencks' Harvard Study Revisited." Educational Forum 39(My, 1975): 435-557.

Anthony, Nell Rice. "Race of Story Book Character: Its Effects on Story Recall and Identification of Black and White Children." Doctoral dissertation, Columbia U., 1973.

Ard, Nicholas, and Cook, Stuart W. "A Short Scale for the Measurement of Change in Verbal Racial Attitude." Educational and Psychological Measurement 37(Autumn, 1977):741-744.

Arkley, Alfred S. Black Participants and White Subjects: The Relationship of Elementary School Racial Segregation to Fifth-Graders' Political Orientations and Behavior, Ap, 1974. ERIC ED 094 020.

Armbruster, Frank, and Bracken, Paul J. The U.S. Primary and Secondary Educational Process, Jl 14, 1975. ERIC ED 146 181.

Arnhoff, Franklyn N., and Leon, Henry V. "Psychological Aspects of Sensory Deprivation and Isolation." Merrill-Palmer Quarterly, Ap, 1964.

Arter, R. M. "The Effects of Prejudice on Children." Children 6(1959):185-189.

Asbury, Charles A. "Maturity Factors Related to Discrepant Achievement of White and Black First Graders." Journal of Negro Education 44(Fall, 1975):493-501.

Asher, Steven R., and Allen. Vernon L. "Racial Preference and Social Comparison Processes." Journal of Social Issues, Ja, 1969.

Ashmore, Richard D. "Intergroup Contact as a Prejudice-Reduction Technique: An Experimental Examination of the Shared-Coping Approach & Four Alternative Explanations." Diss. Abstr. Int'l. 31, 5-B (N, 1970):2949-2950.

Asbury, Charles A. "Selected Factors Influencing Over- and Under-Achievement Young School-Age Children." Review of Educational Research 44(Fall, 1974):409-428.

_____. "Sociological Factors Related to Discrepant Achievement of White and Black First Graders." Journal of Experimental Education 42(F, 1973):6-10.

Ausubel, David P. "How Reversible Are the Cognitive and Motivational Effects of Cultural Deprivation? Implications for Teaching the Culturally Deprived Child." Urban Education, Summer, 1964.

_____. "The Influence of Experience on the Development of Intelligence." In Productive Thinking in Education. Edited by Mary Jane Aschner and Charles E. Bish. Washington, DC: National Education Association and the Carnegie Corporation, 1965.

Ausubel, David P., and Ausubel, Pearl. "Ego Development among Segregated Negro Children." In Education in Depressed Areas. Edited by A. Harry Passow. New York: Teachers College, Columbia U., 1963.

Averch, Harvey A., Carroll, Stephen J., Donaldson, Theodore S., Kiesling, Herbert J., and Pincus, John. How Effective Is Schooling? A Critical Review and Synthesis of Research Findings. Santa Monica, CA: Rand, Mr, 1972.

Ayling, Richard Harvey. "An Exploratory Study of the Formal and Informal Relationships Between Black and White Students in a Large, Racially-Mixed, Urban High School." Doctoral dissertation, Michigan State U., 1972. Univ. Microfilms Order No. 73-05320.

Ayres, Mary. "Counteracting Racial Stereotypes in Pre-school Children." Graduate Research in Education and Related Disciplines 6 (Spring, 1973):55-74.

Bachman, Jerold G. Youth in Transition, Volume II: The Impact of Family Background and Intelligence on Tenth-Grade Boys. Ann Arbor, MI: Institute for Social Research, U. of Michigan, 1970.

Bagley, Jean. "Books Against Bias: An Exploration of Literature Dealing with Negro-White Relationships for Grades 7-12." Master's thesis, Central Connecticut State College, 1966.

Bailey, Robert E. "Differences in the Personal-Social Problems of Negro and Caucasian Secondary School Students." Diss. Abstr. Int'l. 31, 7A (Ja, 1971) 3326-3327.

Baldwin, Thelma L. and others. "Children's Communication Accuracy Related to Race and Socioeconomic Status." Child Development 42 (Je, 1971):345-357.

Baldwin, Thelma L., McFarlane, Paul T., and Garvey, Catherine J. Children's Communication Accuracy Related to Race and Socioeconomic Status. Baltimore, MD: Center for Organization of Schools, Johns Hopkins U., F, 1970. [Baltimore, MD]

Ball, Portia M., and Cantor, Gordon N. "White Boys' Ratings of Pictures of Whites and Blacks as Related to Amount of Familiarization." Perceptual & Motor Skills 39(O, 1974):883-890.

Ball, Samuel, and Bogatz, Gerry Ann. Summative Research of Sesame Street: Implications for the Study of Preschool-Aged Children, 1971. ERIC ED 053 197.

Balla, David A., and Zigler, Edward. "Preinstitutional Social Deprivation, Responsiveness to Social Reinforcement, and IQ Change in Institutionalized Retarded Individuals." American Journal of Mental leficiency 80 (S, 1975):228-230.

Ballard, Barbara, and Keller, Harold R. "Development of Racial Awareness: Task Consistency, Reliability and Validity." Journal of Genetic Psychology 129(S, 1976):3-11.

Balmer, Colin J. "The Student Culture of a Negro High School and Its Implications for the Extra-curriculum." Doctoral dissertation, U. of Florida, 1968.

Banks, Henry A. "Black Consciousness: A Student Survey." Black Scholar 2(S, 1970):44-51. [San Francisco and Marin Counties]

Banks, James A. "A Profile of the Black American: Implications for Teaching." College Composition and Communication, D, 1968.

Banks, W. Curtis. "White Preferences in Blacks: A Paradigm in Search of a Phenomenon." Psychological Bulletin 83(N, 1976):1179-1186.

Banks, W. Curtis, Hubbard, Janet L., and Vannoy, Joseph. S. "Attribution of Prejudice to Self and Others." In Black/Brown/White Relations. Edited by Charles V. Willie. New Brunswick, NJ: Transaction, 1977.

Banks, W. Curtis, and Rompf, William James. "Evaluative Bias and Preference Behavior in Black & White Children." Child Development 44(D, 1973):776-783.

Banks, W. Curtis and others. "Toward a Re-conceptualization of the Social-Cognitive Bases of Achievement Orientations in Blacks." Review of Educational Research 48 (Summer, 1978):381-397.

Banks, William. "Drugs, Hyperactivity, and Black Schoolchildren." Journal of Negro Education 45(Spring, 1976):150-160.

Banks, William M. "The Changing Attitudes of Black Students." Personnel and Guidance Journal 48(My, 1970):739-745.

Barakat, H. J. "Alienation from the School System: Its Dynamics and Structure." Doctoral dissertation, U. of Michigan, 1967.

Baratz, Joan C. "Application of Dialect Research in the Context of the Classroom-- It Ain't Easy." Acta Symbolica 2(Spring, 1971):3-7.

_____. Language and Cognitive Assessment of Negro Children: Assumptions and Research Needs, 1968. ERIC ED 022 157.

Baratz, Joan C., and Bovich, Edna. Grammatical Construction in the Language of the Negro Preschool Child, Je, 1968. ERIC ED 020 518.

Baratz, Joan, and Baratz, Stephen S. The Social Pathology Model: Historical Bases for Psychology's Denial of the Existence of Negro Culture, n.d. ERIC ED 035 678.

Baratz, Stephen S. Negro Culture and Early Childhood Education, Je, 1970. ERIC ED 046 495.

Barnes, Edward J. The Utilization of Behavioral and Social Sciences in Minority Group Education: Some Critical Implications. Symposium on Ethnic Minority Issues on the Utilization of Behavioral and Social Sciences in a Pluralistic Society, S, 1971. ERIC ED 056 152.

Barnett, Itty Chan and others. Environment, Experience, and Development in Early Childhood. A Report to Parents, My, 1973. From: Jean Carew Watts, 705 Larsen Hall, Harvard Graduate School of Education, Cambridge, MA 02138.

Barnow, Burt. S. "The Effects of Head Start and Socioeconomic Status on Cognitive Development of Disadvantaged Children." Doctoral dissertation, U. of Wisconsin, 1973.

Barnow, B. S., and Cain, G. G. "A Reanalysis of of the Effect of Head Start on Cognitive Development: Methodology and Empirical Findings." Journal of Human Resources 12 (1977):177-197.

Bartholomew, Suzi, Livingston, Kathy, and Strickland, Martha. "A Comparison of Racial Awareness in Caucasian, Chinese, and Negro Children." Senior thesis, Randolph-Macon Woman's College, 1968.

Bass, Edwin Jordan. "An Investigation of Charges in Selected Ninth Grade Students' Concepts of Self and of Others after Inter-action with Selected Materials Taught in Integrated and Segregated Groups." Doctoral dissertation, U. of Southern Mississippi, 1968.

Bates, W. C. "The Relationship of Self-Esteem and Ethnicity in Six Northern California Schools." Master's thesis, U. of California, Santa Cruz, 1972.

Battle, E., and Rotter, J. "Children's Feelings of Personal Control as Related to Social Class and Ethnic Group." Journal of Personality 31(1963):482-490.

Baugher, Robert J. "The Skin-Color Gradient as a Factor in the Racial Awareness and Racial Attitudes of Preschool Children." Master's thesis, California State U., Fresno, 1973.

Baughman, E. E., and Dahlstrom, W. G. Negro and White Children: A Psychological Study in the Rural South. New York: Academic Press, Inc., 1968.

Baumrind, Diana. "An Exploratory Study of Socialization Effects on Black Children: Some Black-White Comparisons. Child Development 43(Mr, 1972):261-267.

Baxter, Katherine B. "Combating the Influence of Black Stereotypes in Children's Books." Reading Teacher 27(Mr, 1974):540-544.

Beale, James, Coffin, Gregory, Sellers, T. J., and Fischer, John. "Civil Rights and Responsibilities: What Attitudes Are Being Developed in Our Children?" Exchange, O, 1965. Published by the Metropolitan School Study Council, 525 West 120th Street, New York, NY 10027.

Becker, Carol Rose. "Language Strategies in Media Content Directed to Urban Black Primary Children: A Content Analysis of Selected Books, Films and Television." Doctoral dissertation, Case Western Reserve U., 1974. Univ. Microfilms Order No. 75-5051.

Beckum, Leonard Charles. The Effect of Counseling and Reinforcement on Behaviors Important to the Improvement of Academic Self-Concept. Stanford, CA: School of Education, Stanford U., Ag, 1973.

Beers, Joan S. "Self-Esteem, School Interest, and Acceptance of Others as a Function of Demographic Categorization." Doctoral dissertation, U. of Pennsylvania, 1972. [Pennsylvania]

Beck, Katy, and Beck, Armin. "All They Do Is Run Away!" Civil Rights Digest 5(Ag, 1972): 35-39. [On the "daily racial insult"]

Beck, Samuel J. and Others. "Segregation-Integration: Some Psychological Realities." American Journal of Orthopsychiatry 28 (1958):12-35.

Beerling, J. "Black Goal-White Goals: A Study of the Effects of Personality Characteristics on Aspirations." Doctoral dissertation, U. of Chicago, 1976.

Beglis, Jeanne F., and Sheikh, Anees A. "Development of the Self-Concept in Black and White Children." Journal of Negro Education 43(Winter, 1974):104-110. [Milwaukee]

Bell, Anne E., and Aftanas, M. S. A Study of Intellectual and Socioeconomic Factors Related to Rote Learning Reasoning and Academic Achievement, My, 1970. ERIC ED 041 967.

Bell, Cary Edward. "Black Students' Perceptions of Independent Schools: A Comparison of Scores on the Learning Atmosphere Attitude Scale with Selected School and Student Characteristics." Doctoral dissertation, n.p., 1975. Univ. Microfilm Order No. 76-5311.

Bell, Lloyd H., and Johnson, Norman J. Black Child Development: A New Approach. Ap, 1972. ERIC ED 061 402.

Bell, Robert R. "Lower-Class Negro Mothers and Their Children." Integrated Education, D, 1964-J, 1965.

_____. "Lower-Class Negro Mothers' Aspirations for Their Children." Social Forces, My 1965.

Beller, E. Kuno. "The Evaluation of Effects of Early Educational Intervention on Intellectual and Social Development of Lower-Class, Disadvantaged Children." In Critical Issues in Research Related to Disadvantaged Children. Edited by Edith Grotberg. Princeton, NJ: Educational Testing Service, S, 1969. [Philadelphia, PA]

Benjamin, Jeanette A. "A Study of the Social Psychological Factors Related to the Academic Success of Negro High School Students." Diss. Abstr. Int'l. 1970, 30(8-A):3543.

Benmann, Virginia Doubchan. "An Investigation of Reading Comprehension Ability of Black Fourth and Fifth Grade Students Who Are Reading below Grade Level Utilizing Materials Written in Gullah and Standard English." Doctoral dissertation, U. of South Carolina, 1975. Univ. Microfilm Order No. 76-16,615.

Bennett, Don C. "Segregation and Racial Interaction." Annals of the Association of American Geographers 63(Mr, 1973):48-57 [Indianapolis, Indiana]

Bennett, Paul D. "A Study of the Effects of Racial Composition of Schools on the Racial Attitudes and Self Concepts of Young Black and White Children." Master's thesis, U. of Cincinnati, 1974.

Bennett, Paul D., and Lundgren, David C. "Racial Composition of Day Care Centers and the Racial Attitudes and Self Concepts of Young Black and White Children." Journal of Intergroup Relations 5(Mr, 1976):3-14.

Bennett, William S., Jr., and Gist, Noel P. "Class and Family Influences on Student Aspirations." Social Forces D, 1964.

Berg, Phyllis A., and Hyde, Janet S. Gender and Race Differences in Causal Attributions in Achievement Situations, S, 1976. ERIC ED 138 865.

Bergen, Timothy J., Jr. "The Influence of Social Class on Student Socialization." Journal of Teaching and Learning 3(Je, 1978): 23-31.

Berlowitz, Marvin J., and Durand, Henry. School Dropouts or Student Pushouts? A Case Study of the Possible Violation of Property Rights and Liberties by the de Facto Exclusion of Students from the Public Schools, 1976. ERIC ED 143 898.

Berman, Gerald S., and Haug, Marie R. "Occupational and Educational Goals and Expectations: The Effects of Race and Sex." Social Problems 23(D, 1975):166-181.

Berman, Graham, and Eisenberg, Mildred. "Psycho-Social Aspects of Academic Achievement." American Journal of Orthopsychiatry 41(Ap, 1971):406-415.

Bernstein, Basil. "Aspects of Language in the Genesis of the Social Process." In Language in Culture and Society. Edited by D. Hymes. New York: Harper and Row, 1968.

_____. Class, Codes and Control. Vol. I: Theoretical Studies Towards a Sociology of Language. London: Routledge and Kegan Paul, 1971.

_____. "A Socio-linguistic Approach to Socialization: With Reference to Educability." In Directions in Sociolinguistics. Edited by J. Gumperz, and Dell Hymes. New York: Holt, Rinehart, and Winston, 1970.

_____. "A Socio-linguistic Approach to Socialization: With Some Reference to Educability." The Human Context 2(Spring, 1970, Jl, 1970):1-9, 233-247.

_____. "Education Cannot Compensate for Society." New Society, F 26, 1970.

_____ (ed.). Language, Primary Socialization and Education. London: Routledge, Kegan Paul, 1970.

Bernstein, Basil, and Henderson, D. "Social Clan Differences in the Relevance of Language to Socialization." Sociology 3 (1969).

Bernstein, Martin E., and DiVesta, Francis J. "The Formation and Reversal of an Attitude as Functions of Assumed Self-Concept, Race, and Socioeconomic Class." Child Development 42(N, 1971):1417-1431.

Berreman, Gerald D. "Self, Situation, and Escape from Stigmatized Ethnic Identity." In 1971 Yearbook of the Ethnographic Museum, University of Oslo. Oslo: Universitetsforlaget, 1973.

Berry, Bill. "Interracial Marriages in the South." Ebony 33(Je, 1978):65-72.

Berry, J. W., and Dasen, Pierre R. (eds.). Culture and Cognition: Readings in Cross-Cultural Psychology. New York: Barnes and Noble, 1974.

Best, Deborah L. and others. "The Modification of Racial Bias in Preschool Children." Journal of Experimental Child Psychology 20(O, 1975):193-205.

Bettelheim, Bruno. "Autonomy and Inner Freedom: Skills of Emotional Management." In Life Skills in School and Society. Edited by Louis J. Rubin. Washington, DC: Association for Supervision and Curriculum Development, National Education Association, 1969.

_____. "Discrimination and Science." Commentary, Ap, 1956. [Critique of Kenneth B. Clark]

_____. "How Much Can Man Change?" New York Review of Books, S 10, 1964.

_____. "Mental Health in the Slums." In The Social Impact of Urban Design, pp. 31-47. Chicago: Center for Policy Study, U. of Chicago, 1971.

Bettelheim, Bruno, and Janowitz, Morris. Social Change and Prejudice. New York: Free Press of Glencoe, 1964.

Bews, James E. "Future Time Perspective and Academic Achievement in Black Adolescents." Dissertation Abstracts International 31, 6B(D, 1970):3698-3699.

Biddle, Bruce J., and Loflin, Marvin D. Verbal Behavior in Black-Ghetto and White-Suburban Classrooms: An Overview, F, 1971. ERIC ED 047 308.

Bidwell, Charles E., and Kasarda, John D. "School District Organization and Student Achievement." American Sociological Review 40(F, 1975):55-70.

Billings, C. David, and Legler, John B. "Factors Affecting Educational Opportunity and their Implications for School Finance Reform." Journal of Law and Education 4 (O, 1975):633-640.

Billings, Charles E. "Black Activists and the Schools." High School Journal 54(N, 1970): 96-107.

Billingsley, Andrew, and Giovannoni, Jeanne. Children of the Storm--Black Children and American Child Welfare. New York: Harcourt Brace Jovanovich, 1972.

Bird, C. Monachesi, E. D., and Budeck, H. "Studies of Group Tensions: The Effect of Parental Discouragement of Play Activities Upon the Attitudes of White Children Toward Negroes." Child Development 23(1952): 303-309.

Bisseret, Noelle. "The Concept of Aptitude and Class Society." Human Concept 3(1971).

Bitner, D. N. "Psycho-Social Survival: A Conceptual Framework for Student Survival." Educational Perspectives 11(Mr, 1972):7-11.

Bissell, Joan S. "The Cognitive Effects of Preschool Programs for Disadvantaged Children." Doctoral dissertation, Harvard U., 1970.

Black, Frank S., and Bargar, Robert R. "Relating Pupil Mobility and Reading Achievement." Reading Teacher 28(Ja, 1975): 370-374.

Black Child Development Institute. Black Children Just Keep On Growing. Washington, DC: The Institute, 1977.

"Black Students Appear to Have More Self-Esteem in All- Black Schools." Journal of the American Medical Association 214(O 26, 1970):684-685.

Blackwell, Jacqueline and others. Effects of
Early Childhood Multicultural Experiences
on Black Preschool Children's Attitudes
Toward Themselves and Whites, Ap, 1976.
ERIC ED 125 777.

"Black Youth. A Lost Generation?" Newsweek
(ag 7, 1978):22-34.

Blakely, Karen B., and Somerville, Addison W.
"An Investigation of the Preference for
Racial Identification Terms Among Negro and
Caucasian Children." Journal of Negro
Education 39(Fall, 1970):314-319.

Blom, Gaston E. "Motivational and Attitudinal
Content of First Grade Reading Textbooks."
Journal of Child Psychiatry 10(Ap, 1971):
191-203.

Bloom, Benjamin. Human Characteristics and
School Learning. Chicago: U. of Chicago
Press, 1976.

Bloom, Benjamin, Hastings, J. T., and Madaus,
G. Formative and Summative Evaluation of
Student Learning. New York: McGraw-Hill,
1970.

Bloom, Richard. Dimensions of Adjustment in
Adolescent Boys: Negro-White Comparisons,
S, 2, 1968. ERIC ED 024 068.

_____. "A Study of Race Attitudes in Negro
Children of Adolescent Age." Journal of
Abnormal and Social Psychology 29(Ap-Je
1934):18-29.

Boardman, Anthony E., Davis, O. A., and Sanday,
Peggy R. "A Simultaneous Equations Model of
the Educational Process." Journal of Public
Economics (1977).

Boesel, David. "The Liberal Society, Black
Youth, and the Ghetto Riots." Psychiatry
My, 1970.

Boger, Robert P., and Ambron, Sueann R.
Subpopulational Profiling of the Psychoedu-
cational Dimensions of Disadvantaged Preschool Children: A Conceptual Prospectus
for an Interdisciplinary Research, 1968.
ERIC ED 048 177.

Boger, Robert P., and others. Heterogeneous vs.
Homogeneous Social Class Grouping of Pre-
school Children in Head Start Classrooms,
F, 14, 1969. ERIC ED 045 176.

Bolling, John L. "The Changing Self-Concept of
Black Children." Journal of the National
Medical Association 66(JA, 1974):28-34.

Bond, Horace Mann. "The Cash Value of a Negro
Child." School and Society 27(My 13, 1933).

_____. "The Effect of Segregated Education and
Apartheid on the Learning and Personality of
Children." United Nations Document, Jl 28,
1963. Also reprinted in The New South, O,
1963 and The Negro Digest, N, 1963.

_____. "The Function of the Academic Program
in the Development of Attitudes." In
Proceedings. 16th Annual Session, National
Association of Deans and Registrars, pp.
10-15. Held at Elizabeth City, NC, Mr 25-
27, 1942.

_____. "Improving the Morale of Negro Children
and Youth." Journal of Negro Education 19
(Summer, 1950):408-411.

_____. "The Influence of Cultural Factors on
Academic Performance." Bulletin, Southern
University and Agricultural and Mechanical
College 47(Ja, 1961):50-70.

_____. The Search for Talent. Cambridge, MA:
Graduate School of Education. Harvard U.
Press, 1959.

_____. "Self Respect as a Factor in Racial
Advancement." The Annals of the American
Academy of Political and Social Science
(N, 1928):21-25.

_____. "Talents and Toilets." Journal of
Negro Education 8(Winter, 1959):3-14.

_____. "Temperament." The Crisis. 30(Je,
1925):83-87.

_____. "Wasted Talent." In Nation's Children
(White House Conference Publication.)Vol. II:
"Development and Education," pp. 116-137.
Edited by Eli Ginzberg. New York: Columbia
U. Press, 1960.

Bondurant, Slettie Vera. "Black English:
Detention Camp Without Walls." Freedomways
13(1973):157-159.

Boney, J. Don, Dunn, Charleta, and Bass, Thomas.
"An Analysis of the Participation of Racially
Integrated Guidance Groups of Culturally
Different Children in Elementary School."
Journal of Negro Education 40(Fall, 1971):
390-393. [Texas]

Bontemps, Arna, Brooks, Gwendolyn, Walker,
Margaret, Drake, S. C., Thomas, W., and
Adler, Mortimer J. "How I Told My Child
About Race." Negro Digest My, 1951-Ag, 1951.

Boocock, Sarane Spence. An Introduction to the
Sociology of Learning. Boston: Houghton
Mifflin, 1971.

_____. "The School as a Social Environment for
Learning: Social Organization and Micro-
Social Process in Education." Sociology of
Education 46(Winter, 1973):15-50.

_____. "Toward a Sociology of Learning: A
Selective Review of Existing Research."
Sociology of Education 39(1966).

Borghi, Lamberto. "Prejudice in Children: A Study on Social Communication." New Era 51 (Je, 1970):161-167.

Borinsky, M. Comparisons of Schools with High and Low Proportions of Poverty Pupils. Washington, DC: National Center for Education Statistics, Ap, 1975.

Boroughs, Mary-Clare. The Stimulation of Verbal Behavior in Culturally Disadvantaged Three-Year-Olds, 1970. ERIC ED 055 667.

Borowitz, Gene. "Clinical Observations of Ghetto Four-Year-Olds: Organization, Involvement, Interpersonal Responsiveness, and Psychosexual Content of Play." Journal of Youth and Adolescence 1(1972):59-79.

Borowitz, Gene H., and Hirsch, Jay G. A Developmental Typology of Disadvantaged Four-Year-Olds, Mr 21, 1968. Division of Preventive Psychiatry, Research Program in Child Development, Institute for Juvenile Research, 232 E. Ohio Street, Chicago, IL 60611

Borrow, Henry. Antecedents, Concomitants and Consequences of Task-Oriented Behavior in Youth. Bethesda, MD. National Institute of Child Health and Human Development, 1968.

Boswell, Donna, and Williams, John E. "Correlates of Race and Color Bias Among Preschool Children." Psychological Report 36(F, 1975): 147-154.

Bowden, Delbert Anton. Pupil Services for the Inner-City "House" School, Je, 1971. ERIC ED 055 285.

Bowen, Kerry W. "Selected Aspects of Inferred Identification in Black and White Students." Doctoral dissertation, U. of Georgia, 1971.

Bowker, G. "Interaction, Intergroup Conflict, and Tension in the Context of Education." International Social Science Journal 23 (1971).

Bowman, Orrin H. "Scholastic Development of Disadvantaged Negro Pupils..." Doctoral dissertation, U. of Buffalo, 1973. Univ. Microfilm No. 73-19176.

Boykin, Arsene O. "School Facts Support Racial Fears. Urban High Schools Compared." Urban Education 8(O, 1973):271-277. [Chicago]

Brameld, Theodore. Minority Problems in the Public Schools. New York: Harper and Row, 1946.

Brand, Elaine S., Ruiz, Rene A., and Padilla, Amado M. "Ethnic Identification and Preference: A Review." Psychological Bulletin 81 (N, 1974):860-890.

Brandes, Paul D. The Effect of Role Playing by the Culturally Disadvantaged on Attitudes toward Bidialecticism. Final Report, N, 1971. ERIC ED 060 001

Brandis, Walter, and Henderson, Dorothy. Social Class, Language, and Communication. Beverly Hills, CA: Sage, 1971.

Brazziel, William F. "Quality Education for Minorities." Phi Delta Kappan (My, 1972): 547-552.

Brembeck, Cole S., and Hill, Walker H. (eds.). Cultural Challenges to Education. The Influence of Cultural Factors in School Learning. Lexington, MA: D.C. Heath, 1973.

Brenman, Margaret. "The Relationship Between Minority Group Membership and Psychological Security in a Group of Urban Middle Class Negro Girls." Master's thesis, 1939. Columbia University.

_____. "The Relationship Between Minority-Group Membership and Group Identification in a Group of Urban Middle Class Negro Girls." Journal of Social Psychology, F, 1940.

Bresnahan, Jean L., and Shapiro, Martin M. "Learning Strategies in Children from Different Socioeconomic Levels." In Advances in Child Development and Behavior: VII. Edited by H. W. Reese. New York: Academic Press, 1972.

Breyer, Norman L., and May, Jack I. "Effect of Sex and Race of the Observer and Model on Initiation Learning." Psychological Reports 27(O, 1970):639-646.

Bridgette, R. E. "Self-Esteem in Negro and White Southern Adolescents." Doctoral dissertation, U. of North Carolina, 1970.

Brindley, Fern B. "Social Factors Influencing Educational Aspiration of Black and White Girls." Diss. Abstr. Int'l. 31(7-A)J, 1971, 3259-3260.

Brislin, Richard W., Bochner, Stephen, and Lonner, Walter J. (eds.). Cross-Cultural Perspectives on Learning. Beverly Hills, CA: Sage, 1975.

Brody, Eugene B. "Adolescents as a United States Minority Group in an Era of Social Change" and "Minority Group Status and Behavioral Disorganization." In Minority Group Adolescents in the United States. Baltimore, MD: Williams and Wilkins, 1968.

GENERAL / 101

_____. "Color and Identity Conflict in Young
Boys: Observations of Negro Mothers and
Sons in Urban Baltimore." Psychiatry 26
(1963).

_____ (ed.). Minority Group Adolescents in
the United States. Baltimore, MD: Williams
and Wilkins, 1968.

Bronfenbrenner, Urie. Effects of Social Inter-
vention on Psychological Development.
Bethesda, MD: National Institute of Child
Health and Human Development, 1968.

_____. "The Experimental Ecology of Educa-
tion." Teachers College Record 78(D, 1976):
157-204.

_____. "Is Early Intervention Effective?"
Teachers College Record 76(D, 1974):279-303.

Brook, Judith S., and others. "Aspiration Levels of and for Children: Age, Sex, Race,
and Socioeconomic Correlates." Journal of
Genetic Psychology 124(Mr, 1974):3-16.

_____. "The Psychological Costs of Quality
and Equality in Education." Child Development 38(1967):909-925.

Brookover, Wilbur B., and Schneider, Jeffrey M.
"Academic Environments and Elementary School
Achievement." Journal of Research and
Development in Education 9(F, 1975):82-91.

Brookover, Wilbur B., and others. "Elementary
School Social Climate and School Achievement." American Educational Research Journal 15(Spring, 1978):301-318.

_____. Elementary School Social Environment
and School Achievement. Final Report, Jl,
1973. ERIC ED 086 306.

_____. Schools Can Make a Difference. Ag,
1977. ERIC ED 145 034.

_____. Schools Can Make a Difference as Indi-
cated by a Study of Elementary School Social
Systems and School Outcomes. East Lansing,
MI: College of Urban Development, Michigan
State U., 1977.

_____. Relationship of Self-Concept to
Achievement in High School. Final Report,
III, F, 1967. ERIC ED 010 796.

Brookover, Wilbur B., Thomas, Shailer, and
Patersen, Ann. "Self-Concept of Ability and
School Achievement." Sociology of Education,
Spring, 1964.

Brooten, Gary. "The Multiracial Family."
New York Times Magazine, S 26, 1971.

Brown, Byron W., and Saks, Daniel H. "The Pro-
duction and Distribution of Cognitive Skills
Within Schools." Journal of Political
Economy 83(1975):571-593.

Brown, Geoffrey, and Johnson, Susan P. "The
Attributions of Behavioral Connotations to
Shaded and White Figures by Caucasian Children." British Journal of Social and Clinical Psychology 10(D, 1971):306-312.

Brown, Leander A., and others. A Study of Cross-
Cultural Groups at Malcolm Price Laboratory
School, University of Northern Iowa, Mr,
1972. ERIC ED 061 537.

Brown, Nina W. "Personality Characteristics of
Black Adolescents." Adolescence 12(Spring,
1977):81-87.

Brown, R. G. "Comparison of the Vocational Aspirations of Paired Sixth Grade White or Negro Children Who Attend Segregated Schools."
Journal of Education Research, My, 1965.

Brown, R. Lloyd, and others. "A Cross-Cultural
Study of Piagetian Concrete Reasoning and
Science Concepts Among Rural Fifth-Grade
Mexicans--and Anglo-American Students."
Journal of Research in Science Teaching 14
(Jl, 1977):329-334.

Brown, Walker Thornton. "Racial Devaluation
Among Transracially Adopted Black Children."
Doctoral dissertation, Ohio State U., 1973.
Univ. Microfilm Order No. 74-10921.

Brozovich, Richard W. "Characteristics Associated with Popularity Among Different Racial
and Socioeconomic Groups of Children."
Journal of Educational Research 63(Jl-Ag,
1970):441-444.

Bruch, Catherine B. "Modification of Procedures
for Identification of the Disadvantaged
Gifted." Gifted Child Quarterly 15(Winter,
1971):267-272. [Black gifted children]

Bruner, Jerome S. "Poverty and Childhood."
Oxford Review of Education 1(1975):31-50.

Buck, Mildred R. "The Multi-Dimensional Model
for the Assessment of Children Referred for
Classes for Mental Retardation." Journal
of Afro-American Issues 3(Winter, 1975):
91-102.

Buck, Mildred R., and Sustrin, Harvey R.
"Factors Related to School Achievement in an
Economically Disadvantaged Group." Child
Development 42(D, 1971):1813-1826.

Buck-Morss, Susan. "Socio-Economic Bias in
Piaget's Theory and Its Implication for Cross-
Culture Studies." Human Development 18
(1975):35-49.

Bugelski, B. R., and Lattanzio, Sandra. "A Culture Free Learning Task." Journal of Experimental Psychology 93(My, 1972):254-256.

Bullock, Charles S. III. "Maturation and Change in the Correlates of Racial Attitudes." Urban Education 12(Jl, 1977):229-238.

Bullock, Paul. Aspiration vs. Opportunity: "Careers" in the Inner City. Ann Arbor, MI: Institute of Labor and Industrial Relations, 1973. [Los Angeles]

Bullough, Bonnie. "Alienation and School Segregation." Integrated Education (Mr-Ap, 1972):29-35.

Bunton, Peter L., and Weissbach, Theodore A. "Attitudes Toward Blackness of Black Preschool Children Attending Community-Controlled or Public Schools." Journal of Social Psychology 92(F, 1974):53-59.

Burbach, Harold J. "Effects of Black vs. White Peer Models on Academic Expectations and Actual Performance of Fifth Grade Students." Journal of Experimental Education 45(F, 1976):9-12.

Bureau of School Programs Evaluation. What Research Says About Improving Student Performance. Albany, NY: State Education Department, Mr, 1973.

Burgdorf, Kenneth. Outstanding Negro High School Students: A One-Year Followup, 1969. Available from Research Division, National Merit Scholarship Corporation, 990 Grove Street, Evanston, IL 60201.

Burgen, Michele. "Should Whites Adopt Black Children?" Ebony 33(D, 1977):63-68.

Burger, Henry G. "Behavior Modification and Operant Psychology: An Anthropological Critique." American Educational Research Journal 9(Summer, 1972):343-360.

_____. Ethnic Live-In: A Guide for Penetrating and Understanding a Cultural Minority, 1969. Available from Bookstore, U. of Missouri, Kansas City, MO.

_____. "The Furnivall Effect (Ethnic Displacement) Versus Compensatory Education." Urban Education 5(O, 1970):238-252.

Burke, Arlene A. "Placement of Black and White Children in Educable Mentally Handicapped Classes and Learning Disability Classes." Exceptional Children 41(Mr, 1975):438-439.

Burns, Robert B. "Attitudes to Self and to Three Categories of Others in A Student Group." Educational Studies 1(O, 1975):181-189.

Burt, Max Warren. "The Effects of Trained Paraprofessional Classroom Instructional Aides on the Reading Achievement of Socio-Economically Disadvantaged First Grade Children." Doctoral dissertation, U. of Michigan, 1975. Univ. Microfilms Order No. 76-9357.

Bush, James A. "Suicide and Blacks: A Conceptual Framework." Suicide and Life-Threatening Behavior 6(Winter, 1976):216-221.

Busse, Thomas V., Ree, Malcolm, and Gutride, Marilyn. "Environmentally Enriched Classrooms and the Play Behavior of Negro Preschool Children." Urban Education 5 (Jl, 1970):128-140.

Busse, Thomas V. and others. "Environmentally Enriched Classrooms and the Cognitive and Perceptaul Development of Negro Preschool Children." Journal of Educational Psychology 63(F, 1972):15-21.

Butler, Reginald O. "Black Children's Racial Preference: A Selected Review of the Literature." Journal of Afro-American Issues 4(Winter, 1976):168-171.

Butters, Ronald R. "A Linguistic View of Negro Intelligence." Clearing House 46 (Ja, 1972):259-263.

Butts, H. F. "Skin Color Perception and Self-Esteem." Journal of Negro Education 32 (1963):122-128.

Byars, Lauretta Flynn. "Transracial Adoption: A Deviant Behavior." In National Association of Black Social Workers, Diversity: Cohesion or Chaos--Mobilization for Survival, pp. 298-310. Proceedings of the Fourth Annual Conference of N.A.B.S.W. Nashville, TN: Fisk U., 1973.

Bynner, John. "Deprived Parents." New Society, F 21, 1974. [Aspirations]

Byrne, D. S., and Williamson, W. A Theoretical Model of the Determinants of Educational Attainment, Ap, 1972. The Secretary, Nuffield Teacher Enquiry, U. of York, York YO1 5DD, England. [England]

Byrne, Donn, and McGraw, Carl. "Interpersonal Attraction toward Negroes." Human Relations, Ag, 1964.

Caccamo, James M., and Yater, Allen C. "The ITPA and Negro Children with Down's Syndrome." Exceptional Children 38(Ap, 1972): 642-643.

Caffrey, B., and Jones, C. "Racial Attitudes of Southern High School Seniors: A Complex Picture." Journal of Social Psychology 79 (1969):293-294.

Cahill, Imogene D. "Child-Rearing Practices in Lower Socioeconomic Ethnic Groups." In The Urban R's. Edited by Robert A. Dentler and others. New York: Praeger, 1967.

Caldwell, Bettye M. The Effects of Psychosocial Deprivation on Human Development in Infancy. Bethesda, MD: National Institute of Child Health and Human Development, 1968.

_____. "What Is the Optimal Learning Environment for the Young Child?" American Journal of Orthopsychiatry, Ja, 1967.

Campbell, Angus. White Attitudes Toward Black People. Ann Arbor, MI: Institute for Social Research, U. of MI, 1971.

Caldwell, Marcus B., and Smith, Timothy A. "Intellectual Structure of Southern Negro Children." Psychological Reports, Ag, 1968.

Cantor, Gordon N. "Sex and Race Effects in the Conformity Behavior of Upper-Elementary School-Aged Children." Developmental Psychology 11(S, 1975):661-662.

_____. "Use of a Conflict Paradigm to Study Race Awareness in Children." Child Development 43(D, 1972):1437-1442.

Cantor, Gordon N., and Paternite, Carl E. "A Follow-up Study of Race Awareness Using a Conflict Paradigm." Child Development 44(D, 1973):589-861.

Caplan, Nathan. "The New Ghetto Man: A Review of Recent Empirical Studies." Journal of Social Issues 26(Winter, 1970).

Caplan, S., and Ruble, R. "A Study of Culturally Imposed Factors on School Achievement in a Metropolitan Area." Journal of Educational Research 58(1964):16-21.

Caplin, Morris D. "Self-Concept, Level of Aspiration, and Academic Achievement." Journal of Negro Education, Fall, 1968.

Cardwell, John J. "Negro-Intra-Group Skin-Color Preference." Senior thesis in Psychology, Princeton U., My 3, 1968.

Carkhuff, Robert R. "The Development of Effective Courses of Action for Ghetto School Children." Psychology in the Schools 7 (Jl, 1970):272-273. [In desegregated school]

Carlson, J. S. "Some Relationships Between Class Inclusion, Perceptual Capabilities, Verbal Capabilities, and Race." Human Development 14(1971):30-38.

Carlson, Kenneth. "Equalizing Educational Opportunity." American Educational Research Association 42(Fall, 1972):453-475.

Carpenter, Virginia. "Motivational Components of Achievement in Culturally Disadvantaged Negro Children." Doctoral dissertation, Washington U., 1967.

Carr, Leslie G. "The Srole Stems and Acquiescence." American Sociological Review 36 (Ap, 1971):287-293. [Race and class in re: anomie]

Carroo, Agatha E. White. "Effects of Cross-Racial Comparisons and Racial Environment on Black Aspirations and Achievement." Doctoral dissertation, Cornell U., 1974. Univ. Microfilms Order No. 75-01607.

Carter, Barbara. "The Great Society: A Man with a Problem." Reporter, My 20, 1965. [About the work of Martin Deutsch]

Carter, C. A., and Mitchell, L. E. "Attitudes of Negro Pupils Toward White." Journal of Human Relations, Spring, 1956.

Carter, James and others. Health and Nutrition in Disadvantaged Children and Their Relationship with Intellectual Development. Collaborative Research Report, D, 1970. ERIC ED 052 816.

Carter, James H. "The Black Strugggle for Identity." Journal of the National Medical Association 64(1972):236-249.

Carter, John L., "An Analysis of the Effects of a Language Development Program with First Grade Children of the New Orleans Education Improvement Project." Journal of Negro Education 40(Fall, 1971):352-355.

Cartwright, G. Phillip, and McIntosh, Dean K. "Three Approaches to Grouping Procedures for the Education of Disadvantaged Primary School Children." Journal of Educational Research 65(My-Je, 1972):425-429.

Case, Robbie. "Information Processing and Social Class: An Experimental Investigation." Orbit 2(Je, 1971):22-23.

Castro, Janet. "Untapped Verbal Fluency of Black Schoolchildren." In The Culture of Poverty: A Critique. Edited by Eleanor Leacock. New York: Simon and Schuster, 1971.

Cavenaugh, David N. and others. Migrant Child Welfare: A State of the Field Study... Washington, DC: Children's Bureau, National Center for Child Advocacy, 1977.

Cazden, Courtney B. "The Situation: A Neglected Source of Social Class Differences in Language Use." Journal of Social Issues 26(Spring, 1970):35-60.

_____. "Three Sociolinguistic Views of the Language and Speech of Lower Class Children--with Special Attention to the Work of Basil Bernstein." Developmental Medicine and Child Neurology 10(1968):600-612.

Cerf, Florence A. "The Effect of Verbal Control on the Grouping Behavior of Pre-School Children from Two Socio-Economic and Racial Groups." Doctoral dissertation, U. of Washington, 1972.

Chadwick, Bruce A. and others. "Correlates of Attitudes Favorable to Racial Discrimination Among High School Students." Social Science Quarterly 51(Mr, 1971):873-888.

_____. Correlates of Attitudes Favorable to Racial Discrimination Among High School Students, 1970. ERIC ED 044 476.

Chalupsky, Albert B., and Coles, Gary J. Parental Educational Expectations and their Impact on Student Outcomes. Washington, DC: U.S. Office of Education, 1976.

Chamberlin-Robinson, Charlynn. Strategy to Modify Racial Attitudes in Black and White Preschoolers, Mr, 1977. ERIC ED 138 358.

Chance, Norman A. "Minority Education and the Transformation of Consciousness." In Language and Culture. Edited by Solon T. Kimball and Jacquetta H. Burnett. Seattle: U. of Washington Press, 1973.

Chang, Theresa S. "The Self-Concept of Children of Ethnically Different Marriages." California Journal of Educational Research 25(N, 1974):245-252.

Chappat, Janine S. A. "'Race' Prejudice and Preschool Education." Doctoral dissertation, Radcliffe College, 1945.

Chazan, Maurice. "Disadvantage and Nursery Schooling." Special Education 62(S, 1973):1923.

Check, John F. An Analysis of Differences in Creative Ability Between White and Negro Students, Public and Parochial, Three Different Grade Levels, and Males and Females. Final Report, Je 13, 1969. ERIC ED 031 757.

Chennault, Stephen Dale. "Silence is Black: Black Attitudes in an Urban Classroom." Doctoral dissertation, U. of Michigan, 1973.

Chesler, Mark, and BenDor, Jan Franklin. Interracial and Intergenerational Conflict in Secondary Schools, 1968. ERIC ED 050 204.

Chesler, Mark, and Segal, Phyllis. Characteristics of Negro Students Attending Previously All-White Schools in the Deep South. Ann Arbor, MI: Institute for Social Research, U. of Michigan, S, 1967.

_____ (ed.). "How Do You Negroes Feel About White?" and "How Do You Whites Feel About Negroes?" A Collection of Papers by College Students Exploring and Expressing Their Own Racial Attitudes. Ann Arbor, MI: Institute for Social Research on Utilization of Scientific Knowledge, U. of Michigan, O, 1966.

_____ (comp. and ed.) How Do You Negroes Feel About Whites and How Do You Whites Feel About Negroes. Ann Arbor, MI: Institute for Social Research, U. of Michigan, 1969.

Chetnik, Morton, Fleming, Elizabeth, Mayer, Morris F., and McCoy, John N. "A Quest for Identity: Treatment of Disturbed Negro Children in a Predominantly White Treatment Center." American Journal of Orthopsychiatry, Je, 1967.

Chestang, Leon. "The Dilemma of Biracial Adoption." Social Work 17(My, 1972):100-105.

Childers, Perry R. "Black Pupils Can Be Taught to Listen." Journal of Experimental Education 39(Summer, 1971):24-25.

Children's Defense Fund. Children Out of School in America, 1974. Children's Defense Fund, 1746 Cambridge St., Cambridge, MA 02138.

_____. School Suspensions: Are They Helping Children?, S, 1975. Children's Defense Fund, 1746 Cambridge St., Cambridge, MA 02138.

Chilman, Catherine S. Growing Up Poor. Washington, DC: GPO, 1966.

Chimezie, Amuzie. "Black Identity and the Grow-Shapiro Study on Trans-racial Adoption." Journal of Afro-American Issues 4(Winter, 1976):139-152.

Cicirelli, V. "Relationship of Socioeconomic Status and Ethnicity to Primary Grade Children's Self-Concept." Psychology in the Schools 14(Ap, 1977):213-215.

Cicirelli, V. and others. The Impact of Head Start: An Evaluation of the Effects of Head Start on Children's Cognitive and Affective Development, Je 12, 1969. 2 Vols. Clearinghouse for Federal, Scientific and Technical Information, US Department of Commerce, Springfield, VA

Cincinnati Public Schools. Impact of a Pre-school and Interracial Program, Ag, 1973. ERIC ED 093 480.

Chodoff, P. "Effects of Extreme Coercive and Oppressive Forces." In American Handbook of Psychiatry, III. Edited by S. Arieti. New York: Basic Books, 1959.

Christopher Jencks in Perspective. Arlington, VA: American Association of School Administrators, 1973.

Citron, Abraham F. The "Rightness of White-ness": The World of the White Child in a Segregated Society. Detroit, MI: Ohio Regional Educational Laboratory, 1967.

Clark, Dennis. "Urban Violence." America, Je 1, 1968.

Clark, Edward T. "Children, People's Troubles, and the Image of Psychologists." Perceptual and Motor Skills, Vol. 20, 1965.

Clark, Kenneth B. "A Brown Girl in a Speckled World." Journal of Social Issues 1 (My, 1945):10-15.

_____. "Effect of Segregation and Integration on Children's Personality." In Michigan State University, Symposium on School Integration, Proceedings, pp. 1-13, discussion pp. 13-25, 1964.

_____. "Learning Obstacles Among Children." In Problems of School Men in Depressed Urban Centers, 1969. Edited by Arliss L. Roaden. Columbus, OH: College of Education, Ohio State U. [1964 conference]

_____. "Racial Prejudices Among American Minorities." International Social Science Bulletin 3 (1950).

_____. "Social Policy, Power and Social Science Research." Harvard Educational Review 43(F, 1973):113-212. [In re: Jencks, Inequality]

Clark, Kenneth B., and Clark, Mamie. "The Development of Consciousness of Self and the Emergence of Racial Identification in Negro Pre-School Children." Journal of Social Psychology, N, 1939.

_____ and _____. "Segregation as a Factor in the Racial Identification of Negro Pre-School Children, a Preliminary Report." Journal of Experimental Education, D, 1939.

Clark, Reginald Milton. "Black Families as Educators: A Qualitative Inquiry." Doctoral dissertation, U. of Wisconsin, 1977. Univ. Microfilm Order No. 77-19752.

Clarke, James W., and Soule, John W. "How Southern Children Felt About [Martin Luther] King's Death." Trans-action, 0, 1968.

Clarke, John Hernik. "A Search for Identity." Social Casework 51(1970):259-264.

Claxton, Alice Louise. "Counseling Needs of Black Ninth Grade Students." Master's thesis, California State University, Long Beach, 1972. Univ. Microfilm Order No. 3814. [Los Angeles schools]

Clore, Gerald L. and others. "Interracial Attitudes and Behavior at a Summer Camp." Journal of Personality and Social Psychology 36(F, 1978):107-110.

Coats, Brian and others. Racial Preferences in the Behavior of Black and White Children, 1972. ERIC ED 086 361.

Cobbs, Price M. "White Mis-Education of the Black Experience." Counseling Psychologist 2(1970):23-27.

Coben, Stanley. "The Failure of the Melting Pot." In The Great Fear--Race in the Mind of America, pp. 144-164. Edited by Gary B. Nash and Richard Weiss. New York: Holt, Rinehart, and Winston, 1970.

Cohen, Elizabeth G. A New Approach to Applied Research: Race and Education. Columbus, OH: Merrill, 1970.

_____. "Interracial Interaction Disability." Human Relations 25(F, 1972):9-24.

_____. "Interracial Interaction Disability. A Problem for Integrated Education." Urban Education 5(Ja, 1971):336-356.

_____. Interracial Interaction Disability, 0, 1968. ERIC ED 043 711.

_____. "Modifying the Effects of Social Structure." American Behavioral Scientist 16(Jl-Ag, 1973):861-879.

Cohen, Elizabeth G., and Roper, Susan S. "Modification of Interracial Interaction Disability: An Application of Status Characteristic Theory." American Sociologi-cal Review 37(D, 1972):643-657.

Cohen, Elizabeth G. and others. Center for Interracial Cooperation, 1973. ERIC ED 095 253.

Cohen, Elizabeth G and others. Expectation Training I; Altering the Effects of a Racial Status Characteristic, Ja, 1970. ERIC ED 043 710.

Cohen, Michael. "Effects of a College Course in the Politics of Race on Students' Attitudes Toward Blacks." Journal of Politics 35(F, 1973):194-203.

Cohen, Rosalie, Fraenkel, Glad, and Brewer, John. "Implications for 'Culture Conflict' From a Semantic Feature Analysis of the Lexicon of the Hard Core Poor." Linguistics 44(1968):11-21.

Cohen, Alan S., and Kornfield, Gita S. "Oral Vocabulary and Beginning Reading in Disadvantaged Black Children." Reading Teacher 24(O, 1970):33-38.

Cohen, Alan S., and Cooper, Thelma. "Seven Fallacies: Reading Retardation and the Urban Disadvantaged Beginning Reader." Reading Teacher 26(O, 1972):38-45.

Cole, Michael, Gay, John, Glick, Joseph A. and Sharp, Donald W. The Cultural Context of Learning and Thinking. New York: Basic Books, 1971.

Cole, Michael, and Bruner, Jerome. "Cultural Differences and Inferences about Psychological Process." American Psychologist 26(O, 1971):867-876.

Cole, Michael, and Bruner, Jerome S. "Early Childhood Education: Preliminaries to a Theory of Cultural Differences." National Society for the Study of Education Yearbook, No. 71, Pt. 2, 1971, pp. 161-179.

Coleman, Lee A. Status Projections of Low-Income Youth in the U.S.: Changes Over Time and a Look to the Future, Ag, 1976. ERIC ED 128 114. [Seven southern states, 1969 and 1975]

Coleman, James S. "Equalizing Achievement--A False Ideal?" Miami Herald, Ag 12, 1973. [An interview]

_____. "Equality of Opportunity and Equality of Results." Harvard Educational Review 43(F, 1973): 129-137. [In re: Jencks, Inequality]

_____. "Class Integration--A Fundamental Break With the Past" (Interview). Saturday Review, My 27, 1972.

_____. "Coleman on the Coleman Report." Educational Researcher 1(Mr, 1972):13-14. [Interview]

_____. "Methods and Results in the IEA Studies of Effects of School on Learning." Review of Educational Research 45(Summer, 1975): 355-386.

_____. "Social Research and Advocacy: A Response to Young and Bress." Phi Delta Kappan 57(N, 1975):166-169.

_____. [Statement and Testimony] in U.S. Congress, 91st, 2nd session, House of Representatives Committee on Education and Labor, General Subcommittee on Education. Emergency School Aid Act of 1970. Hearings ... Washington, DC: GPO, 1970.

_____. "What Is Meant by 'an Equal Educational Opportunity'?" Oxford Review of Education 1(1975):26-29.

Coleman, Madeline (ed.). Black Children Just Keep On Growing: Alternative Curriculum Models for Young Black Children, 1977. Washington, D.C.: Black Child Development Institute.

Coles, Robert. "Children and Racial Demonstrations." American Scholar, Winter, 1964-1965.

_____. Children of Crisis: A Study of Courage and Fear. Boston, MA: Little, Brown, 1967. Washington, DC: GPO, 1968.

_____. "Death of the Heart in Ghetto Children." Federal Probation 32(1968):3-7.

_____. "How Do the Teacher Feel?" Saturday Review, My 16, 1964.

_____. "An Incomplete Analysis." Integrated Education 13(Mr-Ap, 1975):10. [See Rohwer, 1975, below.]

_____. "It's the Same, but It's Different." Daedalus, Fall, 1965.

_____. "Learning to Believe--or Disbelieve--in the American Dream." Phi Delta Kappan 58(S, 1976):15-18.

_____. Letter, New York Review of Books, O 22, 1964.

_____. "Like It Is in the Alley," Daedalus, Fall, 1968.

_____. "Like It Is in the Alley." National Elementary Principal, Ap, 1969.

_____. "Racial Conflict and a Child's Question." Journal of Nervous and Mental Disease, F, 1965.

_____. "Racial Identity in School Children." Saturday Review, O 19, 1963.

_____. "Some Children the Schools Have Never Served." Saturday Review, Je 18, 1966.

_____. [Testimony] U.S. Congress, 91st. 1st and 2nd sessions, Senate Committee on Labor and Public Welfare, Subcommittee on Migratory Labor. Migrant and Seasonal Farmworker Powerlessness. Hearings ... The Migrant Subculture, Part 2. Washington, DC: GPO, 1970.

_____. "There's Sinew in Negro Family." Washington Post, O 10, 1965.

_____. "They Feel Like Losers." New Society, D 19, 1968. [Children of the poor in the United States]

Coles, Robert. "Violence in Ghetto Children." Children, XIV (1967).

_____. "What Poverty Does to the Mind." Nation, Je 20, 1966.

Colfax, David J. "The Cognitive Self-Concept and School Segregation: Some Preliminary Findings." In Education and the Many Faces of the Disadvantaged: Cultural and Historical Perspectives, pp. 105-110. Edited by William W. Brickman and Stanley Lehrer. New York: Wiley, 1972.

Collins, S. F. "How Colored Youths Get Through School." Voice of the Negro 2(Jl, 1905): 488-489.

Comer, James P. "Are We Failing Our Children?" Ebony 29(Ag, 1974):54-61.

_____. "The Black American Child in School." In The Child in His Family: Children at Psychiatric Risk: III. Edited by E. J. Anthony and C. Loupernik. New York: Wiley, 1974.

_____. "Child Development and Social Change: Some Points of Controversy." Journal of Negro Education 40(Summer, 1971):266-276.

_____. "Raising Healthy Black Children in a Racist Society." Urban League News, F 4, 1974.

_____. "Research and the Black Backlash." American Journal of Orthopsychiatry, Ja, 1970.

Committee on School Lunch Participation. The Daily Bread. A Study of the National School Lunch Program, 1968. Committee on School Lunch Participation, Suite 2030, 10 Columbus Circle, New York, NY 10019.

Comptroller General of the United States. The National Assessment of Educational Progress: Its Results Need to Be Made More Useful. Washington, DC: General Accounting Office, Jl 20, 1976.

_____. Project Head Start: Achievements and Problems. Washington, DC: U.S. General Accounting Office, My 20, 1975.

_____. Restructured Neighborhood Youth Corps Out-of-School Program in Urban Areas. Washington, DC: GAO, 1974.

"Conference on Socialization for Competence..." Current Anthropology, O, 1966. [Report on a 1965 conference dealing with the social conditions under which competence is developed]

Conger, Anthony J. and others. Group Profiles on Self-Esteem, Locus of Control, and Life Goals. Washington, DC: National Center for Education Statistics, 1977. [National Longitudinal Study of High School Seniors]

Congressional Budget Office. Inequalities in the Educational Experiences of Black and White Americans. Washington, DC: GPO, S, 1977.

Conlan, Tim. "More Whites Adopt Blacks." National Catholic Reporter, Ap 24, 1970.

Conte, Joseph M., and Grimes, George H. Media and the Culturally Different Learner. Washington, DC: National Education Association, 1969.

Cook, Ann. "Black Pride? Some Contradictions." Negro Digest, Ja, 1970.

Cook, Harold, and Smothergill, Daniel W. "Racial and Sex Determinants of Limitative Performance and Knowledge in Young Children." Journal of Educational Psychology 65(O, 1973):211-215.

Coopersmith, Stanley. Psychosocial Deprivation and the Development of Self-Esteem: Comments and Recommendations. Bethesda, MD: National Institute of Child Health and Human Development, 1968.

_____. "Self-Concept, Race and Education." In Race and Education Across Cultures. Edited by G. K. Verma and Christopher Bagley. Stamford, CT: Greylock Publishers, 1975.

Corman, Louise, and Budoff, Milton. A Comparison of Group and Individual Training Procedures on the Raven Learning Potential Measure with Black and White Special Class Students, 1973. ERIC ED 085 969.

Cosby, Arthur. "Black-White Differences in Aspirations Among Deep South High School Students." Journal of Negro Education 40 (Winter, 1971):17-21.

Cosby, Arthur, and Picou, J. Steven. Model of the Transmission of Educational Status Sex-Race Differentials, 1975. ERIC ED 121 522.

Cosby, Arthur, and Picou, Steven. "Vocational Expectations of Adolescents in Four Deep South States." Vocational Guidance Quarterly 19(Mr, 1971):177-181.

Cosby, William Henry, Jr. "An Integration of the Visual Media via 'Fat Albert and the Cosby Kids' into the Elementary School Curriculum as a Teaching Aid and Vehicle to Achieve Increased Learning. Doctoral dissertation, U. of Massachusetts, 1976. Univ. Microfilm Order No. 77-6369.

Costello, Joan. Research in a Black Community: Four Years in Review, Mr, 1970. ERIC ED 039 035.

Cothran, Tilman C. "Negro Stereotyped Conceptions of White People." Doctoral dissertation, U. of Chicago, 1949.

Cottle, Thomas J. Barred from School: Two Million Children. Washington, DC" New Republic, 1976.

_____. Black Children, White Dreams. Boston, MA: Houghton-Mifflin, 1974.

_____. "Matthew Washington Who Had Death in His Eyes." Integrateducation 14(S/O, 1976).

_____. "What Tracking Did to Ollie Taylor." Social Policy 5(Jl-Ag, 1974):21-24.

Cowan, Lou, and Leslie, Carlyn. "Racial Acceptance, Preference, and Self-Identification in Nursery School Children." Senior thesis, Randolph-Macon Woman's College, 1959.

Coyle, F. A., Jr., and Eisenman, Russell. "Santa Claus Drawings by Negro and White Children." Journal of Social Psychology 80 (1970):201-205.

Crain, Robert L., and Weisman, Carol S. Discrimination, Personality, Achievement. A Survey of Northern Blacks. New York: Seminar Press, 1972.

Cramer, M. Richrd, Bowerman, Charles E., and Campbell, Ernest Q. Social Factors in Educational Achievement and Aspirations among Negro Adolescents, 2 Vols. Chapel Hill, NC: Institute for Research in Social Science, 1966.

Crawford, Michael H. Environmental Influences on Learning Behavior in an Urban Afro-American Community, N 15, 1974. ERIC ED 155 296. [Kansas City, MO]

Crew, Louie. "Linguistic Politics and the Black Community." Phylon 36(Summer, 1975):177-181.

Criswell, Joan H. "Racial Cleavage in Negro-White Groups." Sociometry, Jl, 1937.

Crooks, Roland C. "The Effects of an Interracial Preschool Program Upon Racial Preference, Knowledge of Racial Differences and Racial Identification." Journal of Social Issues 26(Fall, 1970):137-144.

Cross, John F., and Cross, Jane. "Age, Sex, Race, and Other Perceptions of Facial Beauty." Developmental Psychology 5(N, 1971):431-439.

Cross, William E., Jr. "Black Identity: A Literature Review." Western Journal of Black Studies 2(Summer, 1978):111-124.

Crown, Barry Michael. "An Evaluation of Selected Cognitive and Social Dimensions in Poverty Intervention Project Participants." Doctoral dissertation, Florida State U., 1969.

Crystal, Josie E. "Changes on an Ofay Curriculum." Center Forum, M , 1969.

Cudjoe, Freddie Foshee. "Black Student Dropout Rate and the Racial Composition of the School." Doctoral dissertation, U. of Oklahoma, 1974. Univ. Microfilms Order No. 74-21967.

Cullen, Robert J., and Auria, Carl. The Relationship Between Ethnic Prejudice and Student Teaching Behavior, F, 1969. ERIC ED 028 122.

Cummings, Scott. "Academic Performance Among Black Children." Educational Forum 41(Mr, 1977):335-346.

_____. "An Appraisal of Some Recent Evidence Dealing with the Mental Health of Black Children and Adolescents, and Its Implications for School Psychologists and Guidance Counselors." Psychology in the Schools 12 (Ap, 1975):234-237.

_____. Black Children in Northern Schools: The Pedagogy and Politics of Failure. San Francisco: R and E Research Associates, 1977. [CT]

_____. "Family Socialization and Fatalism Among Black Adolescents." Journal of Negro Education 46(Winter, 1977):62-75.

Cummings, Scott, and Carrere, Robert. "Black Culture, Negroes, and Colored People: Racial Image and Self-Esteem Among Black Adolescents." Phylon 36(Fall, 1975):238-248.

Curet, Marjorie. "Lessening Racial Conflicts in the Classroom." NASSP Bulletin 60(F, 1976):38-43.

Curtis, Byron William. "The Effects of Segregation on the Vocational Aspirations of Negro Students." Doctoral dissertation, U. of Miami, 1968.

Curtis, Patricia Gelber. Some Ethnic Cognitive Patterns, n.d. ERIC 043 659.

Curtis, Willie M. J. "The Black Adolescent's Self-Concept and Academic Performance." Western Journal of Black Studies 2(Summer, 1978):125-131.

Dale, R. R. and others. Mixed or Single Sex Schools. Vol. II: Some Social Aspects. London: Routledge, 1971.

D'Angelo, R., Welsh, J., and Lowangino, L. "I.Q.'s of Negro Head Start Children on the Vane Kindergarten Test." Journal of Clinical Psychology 271(Ja 1, 1971):82-83.

Daniel, Robert P. "Basic Considerations for Valid Interpretation of Experimental Studies Pertaining to Racial Differences." Journal of Educational Psychology 23(Ja, 1932):15–27.

Daniel, Walter G. "The Curriculum of the Negro Elementary School." Journal of Negro Education 1(Jl, 1932):277–303.

Dantzler, Dolores Jane. "The Attitudes of Blacks Toward Stories in Selected Basal Leaders which Contain Negro Characters." Doctoral dissertation, West Virginia U., 1973. University Microfilm Order No. 74-11375.

Dasen, Pierre R. "Cross-Cultural Projection Research: A Summary." Journal of Cross-Cultural Psychology 3(1972):23–39.

_____. "The Development of Conservation in Aboriginal Children: A Replication Study." International Journal of Psychology 7(1972): 75–85. [Replication of De Lemos, below; different interpretation]

_____. Piagetian Psychology. Cross-Cultural Contributions. New York: Halsted, 1977.

Datcher, Erselle, Savage, James E., and Checkosky, Stephen F. "School Type, Grade, Sex, and Race of Experimenter as Determinants of the Racial Preference and Awareness in Black and White Children." Proceedings of the 81st Annual Convention of the American Psychological Association 8(1973): 223–224.

Datcher, Erselle and others. "School Type, Grade, Sex and Race of Experimenter as Determinants of the Racial Preference and Awareness in Black and White Children." Journal of Social and Behavioral Sciences 20(Winter, 1974):41–49.

Datta, Lois-ellin. A Report on Evaluation Studies of Project Head Start, n.p., 1969.

Davey, Alfred G. "The Growth of Prejudice in Young Children." Patterns of Prejudice 8(My, Je, 1974):17–22.

Davidson, Helen H., and Greenberg, Judith W. Traits of School Achievers from a Deprived Background. New York: The City College and the City University of New York, 1967.

Davis, Allison. "Changing the Culture of the Disadvantaged Student." Working With Low-Income Families. Washington, DC: American Home Economics Association, 1965.

_____. Children of Bondage: The Personality Development of Negro Youth in the Urban South. Washington, DC: American Council on Education, 1940.

Davis, Allison and others. Deep South. Chicago, IL: U. of Chicago Press, 1965.

_____. Psychology of the Child in the Middle Class. Pittsburgh, PA: U. of Pittsburgh Press, 1960.

_____. The Relation Between Color Caste and Economic Stratification in Two Black Plantation Counties. Chicago: U. of Chicago Press, 1942.

_____. Social-Class Influences Upon Learning. Cambridge, MA: Harvard U. Press, 1955.

Davis, Earl E., and Triandis, Harry C. "An Experimental Study of Black-White Negotiations." Journal of Applied Social Psychology 1(Jl-S, 1971):240–262.

Davis, Gerald N. "Educational Opportunities for Black Students at Independent Schools." Crisis 85(Ag-S, 1978):231–236.

Davis, John W. A Study of Cognitive Development of Southern Culturally Disadvantaged Negro Children. Hattiesburg, MS: U. of Southern Mississippi Press, 1969.

Davis, Roland C. Ability in Social and Racial Classes. Some Physiological Correlates. New York: The Century Company, 1932.

Day, Dawn. The Adoption of Black Children: Counteracting Institutional Discrimination. Lexington, MA: Lexington Books, 1978.

Day, Richard R. and others. "Order of Difficulty of Standard English Grammatical Features Among Cultural Minority Groups in the United States." Anthropology and Education Quarterly 8(Fall, 1978):181–195.

DeBord, Larry W. "The Achievement Syndrome Among Negro and White Culturally Disadvantaged Boys." Diss. Abstr. Int'l., 1970, 30 (10-A):4558-4559.

DeBord, Larry W. and others. "Race and Sex Influences in the Schooling Processes of Rural and Small Town Youth." Sociology of Education 50(Ap, 1977):85–102. [Miss.]

DeBord, Larry W. and others. Race, Sex and Schooling: Insights from the "Wisconsin Model" of Early Achievement Process, Ap 8, 1976. ERIC ED 135 897. [Miss.]

DeFrantz, Anita Page. "A Critique of the Literature on Black English." Doctoral dissertation, U. of Pittsburgh, 1975. Univ. Microfilms Order No. 76-8798.

DeFriese, Gordon H., and Ford, W. Scott. "Verbal Attitudes, Overt Acts, and the Influence of Social Constraint in Interracial Behavior." Social Problems, Spring, 1969. [Open housing]

DeVault, Marjorie L. and others. Schooling and Learning Opportunity, O, 1977. ERIC ED 155-157.

De Voe, Marianne, W. "Cooperation as a Function of Self-Concept, Sex and Race." Educational Research Quarterly 2(Summer, 1977):3-8.

Dennis, Wayne. "Racial Change in Negro Drawings." Journal of Psychology, My, 1968.

Derbyshire, Robert L. "Identity Conflict in Negro College Students." Integrated Education, Je-Jl, 1966.

_____. "The Uncompleted Negro Family: Suggested Research into the Hypotheses Regarding the Effect of the Negro's Out-caste Condition Upon His Own and Other American Sexual Attitudes and Behavior." Journal of Human Relations, Fourth Quarter, 1967.

Derbyshire, Robert L., and Brody, Eugene B. "Social Distance and Identity Conflict in Negro College Students." Sociology and Social Research, Ap, 1964.

Deutsch, Martin, Maliver, Alma, Brown, Bert, and Cherry, Estelle. Communication of Information in the Elementary School Classroom. New York: Institute for Developmental Studies, New York U, 1964.

Deutscher, Max, and Chein, Isidor. "The Psychological Effect of Enforced Segregation: A Survey of Social Science Opinion." Journal of Psychology, O, 1948.

Deutsch, Cynthia P., and Schumer, Florence. A Study of Familial, Background, and Cognitive Style Characteristics of Relatively Successful and Unsuccessful Learners (Determined Longitudinally) in a Harlem Enrichment Program. Final Report for Research Period September 1st, 1969 to August 31, 1970, Ag 31, 1970. ERIC ED 054 272.

De Vos, George A., and Hippler, Arthur A. "Cultural Psychology: Comparative Studies of Human Behavior." In The Handbook of Social Psychology, 2nd Edition, Vol. IV, pp. 323-417. Edited by Gardner Lindzey and Elliot Aronson. Reading, MA: Addison-Wesley, 1969.

De Vries, David L., and Edwards, Keith J. "Student Teams and Learning Games: Their Effects on Cross-Race and Cross-Sex Interaction." Journal of Educational Psychology 66(1974):741-749.

De Vries, David L., and Slavin, R. E. Teams-Games-Tournament. A Final Report on the Research. Baltimore: Center for Social Organization of Schools, Johns Hopkins U, 1976.

Dew, Finis E. The Effect of Varying Racial Composition During Group Counseling Under-taken to Improve Intergroup Attitude Among Elementary School Children. Diss. Abstr. Int'l. 31(8-A)(F, 1971):3870-3871.

Diggs, Irene. "DuBois and Children." Phylon 37(Winter, 1976):370-399.

Dill, John R. "Ethnic Programing in Early Childhood Education." National Elementary Principal 51(S, 1971):64-67.

_____. "Reflections on the Enigmas Educating the Black Urban Child." Notre Dame Journal of Education I(Summer, 1970):107-117.

Dillard, John M. "Socioeconomic Background and the Career Maturity of Black Youths." Vocational Guidance Quarterly 25(S, 1976): 65-69.

Dion, Kenneth L., and Miller, Norman. "Deter-minants of Task-Related Self-Evaluations." Journal of Experimental Social Psychology 9 (S, 1973):466-479.

Dittmar, Norbert. Socio-linguistics. A Critical Survey of the Theory and Applica-tion. London: Edward Arnold, 1976. [Contra Basil Bernstein]

Dixon, Clarence C. "A Comparative Study of the Self Concepts of Disadvantaged and Advantaged Negro Students." Doctoral dissertation, U. of Georgia, 1972.

Dizard, Jan. "Black Identity, Social Class, and Black Power." Psychiatry, My, 1970.

Document. "Segregation and Early Education." Integrated Education: RACE AND SCHOOLS 9 (My-Je, 1971):49-51.

Dodd, J. M., Vosi, J. J., and Moulin, D. "A Study of Real and Perceived Opinions of Stereotypes about Negroes by White and Negro Students." Negro Educational Review 20 (1969):57-72.

Dodson, Dan W. "Is Race the Problem?" Integrateducation 13(Mr-Ap, 1975):11. [See Rohwer, 1975, below]

Dodson, Jualynne and others. Black Stylization and Implications for Child Welfare, 1975. ERIC ED 141 423. [Atlanta area]

Doke, Larry A., and Risley, Todd R. "Some Discriminative Properties of Race and Sex for Children from an All-Negro Neighborhood." Child Development 43(Je, 1972):677-681.

Dokecki, Paul, Strain, Barbara, Bernal, Joe, Brown, Carolyn, and Robinson, Mary Electa. "Low-Income and Minority Groups." In Issues in the Classification of Children. Edited by Nicholas Hobbs. San Francisco: CA: Jossey Bass, 1974.

Dole, Arthur A. "Aspirations of Blacks and Whites for Their Children." Vocational Guidance Quarterly 22(S, 1973):24-31.

_____. Occupational Aspirations of Black and White Parents for Their Recently Graduated Children, Ap 5, 1972. ERIC ED 062 486.

Dolgin, Ann B. "The Problem of a Lowered Self-Concept Among Negro Students." Kappa Delta Pi Record 8(F, 1972):77-78.

Donahue, Elayne M. "A Study of the Preference of Negro and White Kindergarten Children for Picture Book Stories Which Feature Negro and White Story Characters." Diss. Abstr. Int'l. 1970, 30(10-A):4138.

Douglas, Leonard. "A Comparative Analysis of the Relationships Between Self-Esteem and Certain Selected Variables Among Youth from Diverse Racial Groups." Diss. Abstr. Int'l., Ag, 1970, 31(2-A):641-2.

_____. "Attitudinal Variance Among Urban Junior High Youth from Diverse Racial Groups." Urban Education 7(Ap, 1972):33-40.

_____. "Black and White Youth and Their Peers." Integrated Education (My-Je, 1972): 62-65.

_____. "'Negro' Self Concept: Myth or Reality?" Integrated Education (N-D, 1971): 27-29.

Douglass, Joseph H. "Mental Health Aspects of the Effects of Discrimination Upon Children." Young Children, Ap, 1967.

Downs, Karl E. "Timid Negro Students." Crisis, Je, 1936.

Drake, Edward J. "Call Me Black--An Experiment in Expression." Education, Ap-My, 1969.

Drew, Walter F. "A Comparison of Effects of Two Experimental Treatments on the Cognitive Development of Culturally Disadvantaged Second Grade Negro Pupils." Diss. Abstr. Int'l., Jl 1970, 31(1-A0:216.

Drymon, B. J. "A Comparison of Attitudes Toward Schooling of Black and White Students in Three Junior High Schools." Doctoral dissertation, U. of North Carolina, 1971.

Dubey, Sumati N. "Powerlessness and the Adaptive Reponses of Disadvantaged Blacks: A Pilot Study." Human Organization 30 (Summer, 1971):149-157.

DuBois, W. E. B. The Brownies' Book. New York: n.p., 1921.

_____. Heredity and the Public Schools: A Lecture Delivered under the Auspices of the Principals' Association of the Colored Schools of Washington, D.C. Friday, March 25, 1904. Washington, DC: R. L. Pendleton, Printer, 1904.

_____. "On Being Ashamed of Oneself. An Essay on Race Pride." Crisis, S, 1933.

_____. "The Problem of Amusement." Southern Workman, S, 1897.

_____. "Separation and Self-Respect." Crisis, Mr, 1934.

Du Cette, Joseph, and Wolk, Stephen. "Locus of Control and Levels of Aspiration in Black and White Children." American Educational Research Association 42(Fall, 1972):493-504.

Duling, Gretchen A. Adopting Joe: A Black Vietnamese Child. Rutland, VT: C. E. Tuttle, 1977.

Duncan, Otis Dudley. "Ability and Achievement." Eugenics Quarterly 15(Mr, 1968):1-11.

Duncan, Otis Dudley, Featherman, David L., and Duncan, Beverly. Socioeconomic Background and Achievement. New York: Seminar Press, 1972.

Duncan, Otis Dudley, Haller, Archibald O., and Portes, Alejandro. "Peer Influences on Aspirations: A Reinterpretation." American Journal of Sociology, S, 1968.

Dunn, Joe R., and Lupfer, Michael. "A Comparison of Black and White Boys' Performance in Self-Paced and Reactive Sports Activities." Journal of Applied Social Psychology 4(1974):24-35.

Dunwell, Robert R., and others. The Assessment of Informal Factors Affecting Teaching and Learning in a Ghetto High School; Denver, Colorado, Manual High School, F, 1971. ERIC ED 052 281.

Duroff, Michael and others. "Standardized Interview Performance of Southern Elementary School Children." Psychological Reports, Ap, 1968.

Eagle, Norman, and Ridenour, Gene. "Differences in Academic, Performance and Report Card Grades Between 'Open Enrollment' and 'Matched Home' Elementary School Children, After One and Two Years." Urban Education, Jl, 1969.

Earl, Lovelene, and Lohmann, Nancy. "Absent Fathers and Black Male Children." Social Work 23(S, 1978):413-415.

Early Childhood Task Force. Child Abuse and Ne-
glect: Alternatives for State Legislation.
Denver, CO: The Education Commission of the
States, D, 1973.

Eckland, Bruce K., and Bailey, J. P., Jr. A
Capsule Description of Second Follow-up
Survey Data. Washington, DC: GPO, 1977.
[National Longitudinal Study of the High
School Class of 1972]

Ecroyd, Donald H. "Negro Children and Language
Arts." Reading Teacher, Ap, 1968.

Edelman, Marian Wright. "Children's Defense
Fund: An Interview..." Young Children 28
(Je, 1973):260-264.

Eder, Paula Ruth. "Deference Behavior in Play
Group Situations. A Plea for Segregated
Education." Urban Education 7(Ap, 1972):
49-65. [Berkeley, CA]

Edmonds, Ronald R. and others. Search for
Effective Schools: The Identification and
Analysis of City Schools That Are Instruc-
tionally Effective for Poor Children, 1977.
ERIC ED 142 610.

Edwards, Ozzie L. "Cohort and Sex Changes in
Black Educational Achievement." Sociology
and Social Research 59(Ja, 1975):110-119.

_____. "Components of Academic Success: A
Profile of Achieving Black Adolescents."
Journal of Negro Education 45(Fall, 1976):
408-422.

_____. "Intergenerational Variation in
Racial Attitudes." Sociology and Social
Research 57(O, 1972):22-31.

_____. "Skin Color as a Variable in
Racial Attitudes of Black Urbanites."
Journal of Black Studies 3(Je, 1973):473-
483.

Edwards, Rheable M. "Race and Class in Early
Childhood Education." Young Children 30
(S, 1975):401-412.

Eiland, Rebecca, and Richardson, Don. "The
Influence of Race, Sex, and Age on Judgments
of Emotion Portrayed in Photographs."
Communication Monographs 43(Ag, 1976):167-
175.

Eisenberg, Leon, "Child Psychiatry: The Past
Quarter Century." American Journal of
Orthopsychiatry, Ap, 1969. [Deals with
major forces operating on cognitive
development]

_____. "The Human Nature of Human Nature."
Science 196(Ap, 1972):123-128.

_____. "Reading Retardation: I. Psychiatric
and Sociologic Aspects." Pediatrics 37
(1966):352-365.

_____. "Social Class and Individual Develop-
ment." In Crosscurrents in Psychiatry and
Psychoanalysis. Edited by R. W. Gibson.
Philadelphia, PA: Lippincott, 1967.

_____. "Strengths of the Inner City Child."
Baltimore Bulletin of Education 41
1964).

Elardo, Richard E., and Pagan, Betty. Perspectives on Infant Day Care, 1972. Available
from Publications Dept., Southern Association on Children under Six, 1070 Moss Ave.
NE, Orangeburg, SC 29115.

Elder, Glen H., Jr. "Intergroup Attitudes and
Social Ascent among Negro Boys." American
Journal of Sociology 76(Ja, 1971):673-697.

_____. "Racial Conflict and Learning."
Sociometry 34(Je, 1971):151-173.

_____. "Socialization and Ascent in a Racial
Minority." Youth and Society 2(S, 1970):
74-110.

Elkins, Helda A. "An Analysis of the Social
and Ethnic Attributes of the Character in
Children's Books which Have Won Awards."
Doctoral dissertation, North Texas State U.,
1968.

Ellis, Desmond P., and Wiggins, James W.
Cooperation, Aggression and Learning in a
Bi-Racial Classroom (The Socialization of
Academic Behaviour Among Negro Junior High
School Students.) Final Report, S, 1968.
ERIC ED 026 442.

Ellis, Effie O. "The Quality of Life."
Ebony 29(Ag, 1974):37-42.

Ellis, George V. A Comparison of Black and
White Boys on Attitudes Toward Guidance and
on Counselor Preference by Race and Sex,
AD 767-347. Springfield, VA: National
Technical Information Service, Mr 15, 1972.

Ellis, Hadyn D., "Recognizing Faces." British
Journal of Psychology 66(1975):409-426.

Ellis, Hadyn D. and others. "Descriptions of
White and Black Faces by White and Black
Subjects." International Journal of
Psychology 10(1975):119-123.

Ellis, Herbert G. Theories of Academic and
Social Failure of Oppressed Black Students:
Source, Motives, and Influences. IXth
International Congress of Anthropological
and Ethnological Sciences, Ag-S, 1973.

Ellison, Louise. "Cities Aflame...Young
Imaginations on Fire." Young Children,
My, 1968. [A teacher tells a story to
nursery school children about the slain
Dr. Martin Luther King]

Ellison, Robert L. and others. The Identification of Talent Among Negro and White Students
from Biographical Data, Ag, 1970. ERIC ED
047 011.

Ellsworth, Caroline, and Kane, Nancy. "Race
Awareness in Negro and White Nursery School
Children in Lynchburg, Virginia." Senior
thesis, Randolph-Macon Woman's College, 1957.

Emmerich, Walter. Preschool Personal-Social
Behaviors: Relationships with Socioeconomic
Status, Cognitive Skills, and Tempo, Ag,
1973. ERIC ED 086 372.

English, Richard A. "The Educational Aspirations of Black and White Youth." Doctoral
dissertation, U of Michigan, 1970.

Entwisle, Doris R. "Implications of Language
Socialization for Reading Models and for
Learning to Read." Reading Research Quarter-
ly 7(Fall, 1971):111-167.

_____. Subcultural Differences in the Chil-
dren's Language Development, My, 1967.
ERIC ED 011 612.

Entwisle, Doris R., and Greenberger, Ellen.
A Survey of Cognitive Style in Maryland
Ninth-Graders. Vol. III: Feelings of
Control Over Academic Achievement.
Baltimore, MD: Center for Social Organiza-
tion of Schools, Johns Hopkins U., Ag, 1970.

_____ and _____. Differences in the Language
of Negro and White Grade-School Children,
1, 2, 59 pp. Baltimore, MD: Johns Hopkins
U., My, 1968. ERIC ED 019 676.

Entwisle, Doris R., and Hayduk, Leslie Alec.
Too Great Expectations: The Academic Out-
look of Young Children. Baltimore, MD:
Johns Hopkins U. Press, 1978.

Entwisle, Doris R., and Webster, Murray, Jr.
"Raising Children's Performance Expectation."
Social Science Research 1(Je, 1972):147-158.

_____ and _____. Raising Children's Expectations for Their Own Performance, N, 1970.
ERIC ED 043 917.

_____ and _____. "Raising Children's Expecta-
tions for Their Own Performance: A Classroom
Application." In Expectation States Theory:
A Theoretical Research Program. Edited by
J. Berger, T. Conner, and M. H. Fisek.
Cambridge, MA: Winthrop, 1974.

_____ and _____. "Status Factors in Expectation Raising." Sociology of Education 46
(Winter, 1973):115-126.

Epps, Edgar G. "Are Rohwer's Suggestions
Workable?" Integrateducation 13(Mr-Ap,
1975):10. [See Rohwer, 1975, below.]

_____. Family and Achievement: A Study of
the Relation of Family Backgrounds to
Achievement Orientation and Performance
Among Urban Negro High School Students.
Ann Arbor, MI: Institute for Social Re-
search, U. of Michigan, 1969.

Epps, Edgar G. and others. "Effect of Race
of Comparison Referent and Motives on Negro
Cognitive Performance." Journal of
Educational Psychology 62(Je, 1971):201-208.

Epstein, Erwin H. "Social Class, Ethnicity and
Academic Achievement: A Cross-Cultural
Approach." Journal of Negro Education 41
(Summer, 1972):202-215.

Epstein, Ralph, and Komorita, S. S. "Prejudice
among Negro Children As Related to Parental
Ethnocentrism and Punitiveness." Journal
of Personality and Social Psychology D, 1966.

_____ and _____. "Self-Esteem, Success-
Failure, and Locus of Control in Negro
Children." Developmental Psychology 4
(Ja, 1971):2-8.

Epstein, Yokoo and others. "Clean is Beautiful: Identification and Preference as a
Function of Race and Cleanliness." Journal
of Social Issues, 32(1967):109-118.
[Racial self-concept]

Espenshade, Thomas J. "The Value and Cost of
Children." Population Bulletin 32(Ap,
1977):1-47.

Erikson, Erik H. "A Memorandum on Identity and
Negro Youth." Journal of Social Issues,
0, 1964.

_____. "Race and the Wider Identity." In
Identity, Youth and Crisis. New York:
Norton, 1968.

Espinosa, Ruben William. "The Impact of
Evaluation Processes Upon Student Effort in
Ethnic Groups which Vary in Academic Prepa-
ration." Doctoral dissertation, Stanford
U., 1975. Univ. Microfilm Order No. 75-25,
521.

Esposito, Dominick. "Homogeneous and Hetero-
geneous Ability Grouping: Principal
Findings and Implications for Evaluating
and Designing More Effective Educational
Environments." Review of Educational
Research 43(Spring, 1973):163-179.

Ethridge, Samuel B. "Race Is Only a Part of
the Problem." Integrateducation 13(Mr-Ap,
1975):15 [See Rohwer, 1975, below.]

Evans, Rupert N., and Galloway, Joel D. "Verbal Ability and Socioeconomic Status of 9th and 12th Grade College Preparatory, General, and Vocational Students." Journal of Human Resources 8(Winter, 1973): 24-36.

Ewens, William L. "Reference Other Support, Ethnic Attitudes, and Perceived Influence of Others in the Performance of Overt Acts." Diss. Abstr. Int'l., 1969, 30(2-A):806.

Ewing, Dorlesa B. "The Relations among Anomie, Dogmation, and Selected Personal-Social Factors in Asocial Adolescent Boys." Journal of Social Issues 27(1971):159-169. [California East Bay Catholic Diocese high schools]

Ewing, Thomas N. "Racial Similarity of Client and Counselor and Client Satisfaction with Counseling." Journal of Counseling Psychology 21(S, 1974):446-449.

Ezeocha, Peter. "Impact of Poverty on Black Youth Development." Journal of Afro-American Issues 4(Winter, 1976):193-214.

Falender, C. A., and Heber, R. "Mother-Child Interaction and Participation in a Longitudinal Intervention Program." Developmental Psychology 11(1975):830-836.

Farrshel, David. "Status Changes of Children in Foster Care: Final Results of the Columbia University Longitudinal Study." Child Welfare 55(Mr, 1976):143-171.

Farber, Richard, and Schmeidler, Gertrude. "Race Differences in Children's Responses to 'Black' and 'White'." Perceptual and Motor Skills 33(O, 1971):359-363.

Farnham-Diggory, Sylvia. Cognitive Synthesis in Negro and White Children. Chicago, IL: U. of Chicago Press, 1970.

Fazio, Anthony F. and others. "Reinforcement and Educationally Disadvantaged Boys: An Exploratory Study." Journal of Educational Psychology 62(Je, 1971):245-252.

Feeley, Joan T. "Interest and Media Preferences of Middle-Grade Children." Reading World 13(Mr, 1974):224-237.

Feldman, D. H. "Ethnic Group Differences in Map Reading and Map Drawing: A Study in the Development of Spatial Concepts." Doctoral dissertation, Stanford U., 1969.

_____. The Fixed-Sequence Hypothesis: Ethnic Differences in the Development of Spatial Reasoning, Je, 1969. ERIC ED 033 476.

_____. "Problems in the Analysis of Patterns of Abilities." Child Development 44(Mr, 1973):12-18. [Reply by Gerald Lesser, pp. 19-20]

Felsenthal, Norman Allan. "Racial Identification as a Variable in Instructional Media." Doctoral dissertation, U. of Iowa, 1969.

_____. Racial Identification as a Variable in Mediated Instruction, Mr 5, 1970. ERIC ED 041 055.

Femminella, Francis Xavier. "Ethnicity and Ego Identity." Doctoral dissertation, New York U., 1968.

Fenelon, James R., and Megargee, Edwin I. "Influence of Race on the Manifestation of Leadership." Journal of Applied Psychology 55(Ag, 1971):353-358.

Feshbach, Norma D. Teaching Styles of Four Year Olds and Their Mothers, 1970. ERIC ED 045 788.

Fetters, William B. National Longitudinal Study of the High School Class of 1972. Student Questionnaire and Test Results by Sex, High School Program, Ethnic Category, and Father's Education. Washington, DC: GPO, 1975.

_____. Student Questionnaire and Test Results by Academic Ability, Socioeconomic Status, and Region. Washington, DC: GPO, 1976. [National Longitudinal Study of the High School Class of 1972]

Fetters, William B., Collings, Elmer F., and Smith, Jack W. Characteristics Differentiating Under- and Overachieving Elementary Schools. Technical Note No. 63. Washington, DC: National Center for Education Statistics, Mr 12, 1968.

Fetters, William B. and others. Fulfillment of Short-Term Educational Plans and Continuance in Education: National Longitudinal Study of High School Seniors. Washington, DC: National Center for Education Statistics, 1977.

Fields, Rhodell, G. "Racial Segregation in High School Athletics." In Equal Educational Opportunity in High School Athletics. Edited by Charles D. Moody, Sr. Ann Arbor: School of Education, U. of Michigan, n.d.

Figura, Ann L. "The Effect of Peer Interaction on the Self-Concept of Negro Children." Master's thesis, DePaul U., 1971

Figurelli, Jennifer C., and Keller, Harold R. "The Effects of Training and Socioeconomic Class Upon the Acquisition of Conservation Concepts." Child Development 43(Mr, 1972): 293-298.

Filler, J. W., Jr. "Conditioning the Connota- tive Meanings of Color Names to Human Fig- ures." Master's thesis, Wake Forest U., 1969. [Caucasian college students]

Filler, J. W., Jr., and Williams, John E. "Conditioning the Connotative Meanings of Color Names to Human Figures." Perceptual and Motor Skills 32(Je, 1971):755-763.

Fischer, Robert I. "Interpersonal Responses to Stigma As a Function of Age." Diss. Abstr. Int'l. 31(10-B)(Ap, 1971):6254-6255.

Fisher, Anthony Leroy. "The Best Way Out of the Ghetto." Phi Delta Kappan (N, 1978): 239. [Science and mathematics, not basket- ball]

Fishman, Joshua A. "Childhood Indoctrination for Minority-Group Membership." Daedalus 90(Spring, 1961):329-349.

Fitz-Gibbon, Carol T. "The Identification of Mentally-Gifted, 'Disadvantaged' Students at the Eighth Grade Level." Journal of Negro Education 43(Winter, 1974):53-66.

Fitzgerald, Ellen J. (ed.). The First Nation- al Conference on the Disadvantaged Gifted, Mr, 1975. ERIC ED 131 619.

Fitzgerald, Herain E., and Porges, Stephen W. "A Decade of Infant Conditioning and Learn- ing Research." Merrill- Palmer Quarterly of Behavior and Development 17(Ap, 1971):79-117.

Flanagan, John C., Shaycoft, Marion F., Richards, James M., Jr., and Claudy, John G. Five Years After High School. Palo Alto, CA: American Institutes for Research, 1971. [Project Talent]

Flaugher, Ronald L., and Rock, Donald A. "Patterns of Ability Factors among Four Ethnic Groups." Proceedings of the Annual Convention of the American Psychological Association 7(1972): Pt. 1,

Fleming, James. "The Going Is Rough but They Make It." Crisis Ag, 1936.

Floyd, James A., Jr. "Self-Concept Development in Black Children." Senior thesis, Prince- ton U., 1969.

Flynn, Tim M., and others. Traits Related to Achievement Motivation in Migrant Pre- School Children, Ag, 1970. ERIC ED 049 870.

Fodor, E. M. "Moral Judgment in Negro and White Adolescents." Journal of Social Psychology 79(1969):289-291.

Foley, Linda, and Kranz, Peter. "Community Intervention: A Successful Method of Reducing Racial Prejudice." Integrateduca- tion 15(Jl-Ag, 1977).

Foreit, Karen S., and Donaldson, Patricia L. "Dialect, Race, and Language Proficiency: Another Dead Heat on the Merry-Go-Round." Child Development 42(N, 1971):1572-1574. [In re: J. Baratz]

Foreman, Paul B. The Controls Upon Psycho- Social Deprivation of Environment: Social Structure and Culture. Bethesda, MD: National Institute of Child Health and Human Development, 1968.

Forslund, Morris A., and Malry, Lenton. "Social Class and Relative Level of Occupa- tional Aspiration." NASSP Bulletin 54 (N, 1970):106-112.

Fort, Jane G., Watts, Jean C., and Lesser, Gerald S. "Cultural Background and Learn- ing in Young Children." Phi Delta Kappan, Mr, 1969.

Forth, Douglass Scott. "The Relationship Between Economic Factors and Pupil Achieve- ment in Selected Urban School Systems." Doctoral dissertation. U. of Florida, 1974. Univ. Microfilm Order No. 75-16,381.

Forward, John R., and Wilbains, Jay R. "Internal-External Control and Black Militancy." Journal of Social Issues 26 (Winter, 1970):75-92.

Foster, Josephine A. "Variations in Levels of Aspirations of Children Grouped by Class, Race, Sex, and Grade Level." Diss. Abstr. Int'l. 1970(S) U131(3-B):1517-1518.

Fox, David J., and Jordan, Valerie B. "Racial Preference and Identification of Black, American Chinese, and White Children." Genetic Psychology Monographs 88(N, 1973): 229-286.

Frankel, A. Steven, and Barret, James. "Variations in Personal Space as a Function of Authoritarianism, Self-Esteem, and Racial Characteristics of Stimulus Situation." Journal of Consulting and Clinical Psycholo- gy 37(Ag, 1971):95-98.

Franklin, Anderson J., and Fulani, Lenora. Cultural Content of Materials and Ethnic Group Performance in Categorized Recall, 1974. Dr. A. J. Franklin, Rockefeller U., New York, NY.

Franks, David J. "Ethnic and Social Status Characteristics of Children in EMR and LD Classes." Exceptional Children 37(M, 1971): 537-538.

Frazier, E. Franklin. "Problemes de l'Etudiant Noir aux Etats-Unis." Les Etudiants Noirs Parlent, 1952, pp. 275-283.

_____. "Problems and Needs of Negro Children and Youth Resulting from Family Disorganization." Journal of Negro Education, Summer, 1950.

_____. Negro Youth at the Crossways. Washington, DC" American Council on Education, 1940.

Freeman, Evelyn B. "The Relationship of Racial Perceptions to Concepts of Justice in Children." Doctoral dissertation, Ohio State U., 1978. Univ. Microfilms Order No. 7819594. [Six and ten year olds]

Frenkel-Brunswick, E., and Havel, J. "Prejudice in the Interviews of Children." Journal of Genetic Psychology 82(1953):130-139.

Frentz, Thomas S. "Children's Comprehensive Standard and Negro Nonstandard English Sentences." Speech Monographs 38(Mr, 1971): 10-16.

Friend, Ronald M., and Neale, John M. "Children's Perception of Success and Failure: An Attributional Analysis of the Effects of Race and Social Class." Developmental Psychology 7(S, 1972):124-128.

Frerichs, Allen H. Relationship of Self-Esteem of the Disadvantaged to School Success, Mr, 1970. ERIC ED 040 223.

_____. "Relationship of Self-Esteem of the Disadvantaged to School Success." Journal of Negro Education 40(Spring, 1971):117-120.

Friedman, Neil. "Africa and the Afro-Americans: The Changing Negro Identity." Psychiatry, M , 1969.

Friedman, Ruth. "Characteristics and Early Education Needs of Disadvantaged Children." Child Welfare 53(F, 1974):93-97.

Friend, Kenneth E. "Perceptual Encoding in Comparative Judgments of Race." Memory and Cognition 1(Ja, 1973):80-84.

Frierson, Edward C. "Upper and Lower Status Gifted Children: A Study of Differences." Exceptional Children, O, 1965.

Frymier, Jack R., Bills, Robert E., Russell, Jill, and Finch, Cathy. "Are the Schools Oppressive? A Preliminary Report." Educational Leadership 32(M , 1975):531-535.

Frymier, Jack R. and others. A Study of Oppressive Practices in Schools, Ap, 1974. ERIC ED 094 478.

Fusco, Gene C. "These Mistakes Can Weaken Pre-School Programs." Nation's Schools, Ap, 1965.

Gable, Robert K., and Minton, Henry L. "Social Class, Race and Junior High School Students' Belief in Personal Control." Psychological Reports 29(D, 1971):1188-1190.

Gantt, Walter N. and others. "An Initial Investigation of the Relationship between Syntactical Divergency and the Listening Comprehension of Black Children." Reading Research Quarterly 10(1974-1975):193-211.

Gardiner, Gareth S. "Complexity Training and Prejudice Reduction." Journal of Applied Social Psychology 2(O, 1972):32-342.

Gardiner, Richard Andrew. "Nonverbal Communication Between Blacks and Whites in a School Setting." Doctoral dissertation, U. of Florida, 1972. Univ. Microfilms Order No. 73-00559.

Garfunkel, Frank. Preschool Education and Poverty: The Distance in Between. Final Report of 1968-69 Interventional Program, Jl, 1970. ERIC ED 046 501.

Garn, Stanley M. and others. "Tendency Toward Greater Stature in American Black Children." American Journal of Diseases of Children 126(Ag, 1973):164-166.

Garrett, Alice M., and Garrett, Willoughby. "Personal Orientation to Success and Failure in Urban Black Children." Developmental Psychology 7(Jl, 1972).

Garrity, Carla B. "Academic Success of Children from Different Social Class and Cultural Groups." Doctoral dissertation, U. of Denver, 1972.

Gartner, Alan, Kohler, Mary, and Riessman, Frank. Children Teach Children. Learning by Teaching. New York: Praeger, 1971.

Garvey, Catherine, and Dickstein, Ellen. Levels of Analysis and Social Class Differences in Language, O, 1970. ERIC ED 043 003.

Gary, Lawrence E., and Favors, Aaron (eds.). Restructuring the Educational Process: A Black Perspective. Washington, DC: Institute for Urban Affairs and Research, Howard U., 1975.

Gast, David K. "Characteristics and Concepts of Minority Americans in Contemporary Children's Fictional Literature." Doctoral dissertation, Arizona State U., 1966.

Gaudia, Gil. "Race, Social Class, and Age of Achievement of Conservation on Piaget's Tasks." Developmental Psychology 6(Ja, 1972):158-165.

Gaughran, Bernard. "Bi-Racial Discussion Groups in a High School." Integrated Education, Ag-N, 1965.

Gayle, Addison, Jr. "I Endured! But." Journal of Human Relations, Second Quarter, 1967. [Reflections of a black who succeeded academically]

Geibel, James. The Blond Brother. New York: Putnam, 1979. [Novel about racial tension in a high school]

General Research Corporation. Educational Opportunity. The Concept, Its Measurement, and Application, 1978. ERIC ED 157 204.

Gentry, Joe E., and Watkins, J. Foster. "Organizational Training for Improving Race Relations." Education and Urban Society 6 (My, 1974):269-283.

George, Flavil H. "The Relationship of the Self-Concept, Ideal Self-Concept, Values, and Parental Self-Concept to the Vocational Aspiration of Adolescent Negro Males." Diss. Abstr. Int'l, 1970(My)Vol. 30(11-A): 4827.

Gerard, Harold B., and Raven, Bertram H. Intervention Programs to Overcome Psycho-Social Deficits. Bethesda, MD: National Institute of Child Health and Human Development, 1968.

Gerken, Kathryn Clark. "What Have We Been Doing? (Black School Psychologists and the Desegregation Issue)." Journal of Negro Education 47(Winter, 1978):81-87.

Gerken, Kathryn Clark, and Diechmann, John W. The Listener's Ability to Report Oral Responses of Black and White Children, S, 1976. ERIC ED 131 168.

Gerson, Walter M. "Mass Media Socialization Behavior: Negro-White Differences." Social Forces, S, 1968.

Getsinger, Stephen H. and others. "Self-Esteem Measures and Cultural Disadvantagement." Journal of Consulting and Clinical Psychology 38(F, 1972).

Gibby, R. G., Sr., and Gabler, R. "The Self-Concept of Negro and White Children." Journal of Clinical Psychology 23(1968): 144-148.

Gibson, John S. Toward Integration through Education: Dichotomies of Purposes and Processes, Mr 5, 1971. ERIC ED 061 111.

Gifford, Beverly. "Sesame: One Season Later." Ohio Schools 49(Mr 12, 1971):11-12,24-25. [Participation of children of the poor]

Gigliotti, Richard J. "Residential Stability and Academic Sense of Control." Journal of Black Studies 6(Mr, 1976):221-256.

Gigliotti, Richard J., and Brookover, Wilbur B. "The Learning Environment: A Comparison of High and Low Achieving Elementary Schools." Urban Education 10(0, 1975):245-261.

Gilbert, Charles D., and Mortensen, W. Paul. "Problems-Solving Behavior of First Grade Children from Differ i ng Socio-Economic Backgrounds." School Science and Mathematics 73(My, 1973):398-402.

Gilbert, Jul. "Where Have All the Children Gone?" African-American Teachers Forum, N-D, 1969.

Gilliland, Burl E. "Small Group Counseling with Negro Adolescents in a Public High School." Journal of Counseling Psychology, Mr, 1968.

Gilmer, Barbara R. "Intra-Family Diffusion of Selected Cognitive Skills As a Function of Educational Stimulation." DARCEE Papers and Reports 3(1969).

Ginsburg, Herbert. The Myth of the Deprived Child. Poor Children's Intellect and Education. Englewood Cliffs, NJ: Prentice-Hall, 1972.

Ginther, Dean Webster. "Black Dialect-Linguistic Interference, Cultural Interference, and Reading Performance." Doctoral dissertation, U. of Illinois, 1976. Univ. Microfilms Order No. 76-24,088.

Ginzberg, Eli and others. The Middle-Class Negro in the White Man's World. New York: Columbia U. Press, 1967.

Gitter, A. George, and Black, Harvey. Expression and Perception of Emotion: Race and Sex, My, 1968. ERIC ED 029 313.

Gitter, A. George, Black, Harvey, and Mostofsky, David. "Race and Sex in the Perception of Emotion." Journal of Social Issues 28(1972): 63-78.

Gitter, A. George, Mostofsky, David, and Satow, Yoichi. "Studies in Racial Misidentification." Psychology 8(1971):29-37.

Gitter, A. George, Satow, Yoichi, and White. A. "Racial Misidentification Skin Color and Physiogramy." CRC Report, Boston U. 33 (D, 1968).

Gladney, Mildred R. "School Book Dream Worlds." Community, Mr, 1966. [Appraises five series of 'integrated' reading materials]

_____. "Study in Self-Identity." Community, Je, 1962.

Gladwin, Thomas. East Is A Big Bird. Navigation and Logic on Puluwat Stoll. Cambridge, MA: Harvard U. Press, 1970. [Deals with cognition and culture]

Glasser, A. J. "A Negro Child Reared as White." In Clinical Studies in Culture Conflict. Edited by G. Seward. New York: Ronald, 1958, pp. 41-61.

Glick, Irvin David. "An Investigation of the Effects of the Metamessage of Skin Color and Neutral and Affective Language." Doctoral dissertation, U. of Maryland, 1969.

Glick, Irvin, and Mainke, Dean L. "Will Intergroup Education Increase Students' Friendliness?" Educational Leadership 31(Mr, 1974): 527-530.

Glick, J. "Cognitive Development in Cross-Cultural Perspective." In Review of Child Development Research, Chapter eleven, Vol. 4. Chicago, IL: U. of Chicago Press, 1974.

Glock, Charles Y., Wuthnow, Robert, Piliavin, Jane Ally, and Spencer, Metta. Adolescent Prejudice. New York: Harper & Row, 1975.

Goergi, Norman J. "The Relationship of Self-Concept in High School Negro Students in Muncie, Indiana to Intelligence, Achievement, and Grade Point Average." Doctoral dissertation, Ball State U., 1971.

Goering, John M. "Changing Perceptions and Evaluations of Physical Characteristics Among Blacks: 1950-1970." Phylon 33(Fall, 1970): 231-241.

Goff, Regina M. "Problems and Emotional Difficulties of Negro Children as Studies in Selected Communities and Attributed by Parents and Children to the Fact that They Are Negro." Doctoral dissertation, Columbia U. Teachers College, 1949.

_____. "Some Educational Implications of the Influence of Rejection on Aspiration Levels of Minority Group Children." Journal of Experimental Education 23(1954).

Golden, Mark and others. "Social-Class Differentiation in Cognitive Development Among Black Preschool Children." Child Development 42(Mr, 1971):37-45.

Golden, Mark, and Birns, Beverly. "Social Class and Cognitive Development in Infancy." Merrill-Palmer Quarterly, Ap, 1968.

Golden, Mark and others. Social Class Differentiation in Cognitive Development Among Black Preschool Children, 1969. ERIC ED 039-039.

Goldman, Ronald J., and Torrance, E. Paul. Creative Development in a Segregated Negro School in the South, D, 1967. ERIC ED 039 653.

Goldman, Ruth K., and Mercer, Barbara. "Self-Esteem and Self-Differentiation: A Comparison Between Black and White Children in Follow Through and Non-Follow Through Classes." Educational Research Quarterly 1 (Fall, 1976):43-49.

Goldstein, Bernard and others. Social and Cultural Factors Relating to School Achievement. Final Report, Je, 1967. ERIC ED 914 763.

Goldstein, Harris S., and Peck, Rosalind. "Cognitive Functions in Negro and White Children in a Child Guidance Clinic." Psychological Reports 28(Ap, 1971):379-384.

Goodman, Mary Ellen. Race Awareness in Young Children, rev. ed. New York: Collier Books, 1964.

Goodman, Paul. "Sub-Language as Social Badge." Dissent 18(D, 1971):607-612.

Goodwin, Marjorie H. "Conversational Practices in a Peer Group of Urban Black Children." Doctoral dissertation, U. of Pennsylvania, 1978. Univ. Microfilms Order No. 7824723.

Gordon, Chad. Looking Ahead: Self-Conceptions, Race and Family as Determinants of Adolescent Orientation towards Achievement. Washington, DC: American Sociological Association, 1972.

Gordon, Edmund W. "New Perspectives on Old Issues in Education for the Minority Poor." IRCD Bulletin 10(Winter, 1975):5-17.

_____. "An Invited Critique [of Hunt, 'Parent and Child Centers']." American Journal of Orthopsychiatry 41(Ja, 1971):39-42.

_____. "Introduction [to special issue on Education for Socially Disadvantaged Children]." Review of Education Research 40(F, 1970):1-12.

Gordon, Edmund, with Green, Derel. "An Affluent Society's Excuses for Inequality: Developmental, Economic, and Educational." American Journal of Orthopsychiatry 44(Ja, 1974):4-18.

Gordon, Edwin. "First Year Results of Five-Year Longitudinal Study of the Musical Achievement of Culturally Disadvantaged Students." Journal of Research in Music Education 18(F, 1970):195-213.

Gordon, Ira J. On Early Learning: The Modifiability of Human Potential. Washington, DC: National Education Association, 1971.

Gordon, Lucy H. "Responses of Preschool Children to Potency, Activity and Evaluative Adjectives." Master's thesis, Wake Forest U., 1970.

Gordon, Vivian V. "The Methodologies of Black Self-Concept Research: A Critique." Journal of Afro-American Issues 4(Summer, 1976): 373-381.

_____. The Self-Concept of Black Americans. Washington, DC: University Press of America, 1977.

Gorn, Gerald J. and others. "The Role of Educational Television in Changing the Intergroup Attitudes of Children." Child Development 47(Mr, 1976):277-280.

Gottfried, Adele E., and Katz, Phillis A. "Influence on Belief, Race, and Sex Similarities between Child Observers and Models on Attitudes and Observational Learning." Child Development 48(D, 1977):1395-1400.

Gottlieb, David. "Goal Aspirations and Goal Fulfillments: Differences between Deprived and Affluent American Adolescents." Paper delivered at the annual meeting of the American Orthopsychiatric Association, Mr 19, 1964. [Northern and southern cities]

_____. "Poor Youth Do Want to Be Middle Class But It's Not Easy." Personnel and Guidance Journal, O, 1967.

_____. "Teaching and Students: The Views of Negro and White Teachers." Sociology of Education, Summer, 1964.

Gottlieb, David, and Campbell, Jay, Jr. "Winners and Losers in the Race for the Good Life; A Comparison of Blacks and Whites." Social Science Quarterly, D, 1968.

Gottlieb, David, and Ten-Houten, Warren D. "Racial Composition and the Social System of Three High Schools." Journal of Marriage and the Family, My, 1965.

Gouldner, Helen P. The Natural History of the Education of the Black Child in the City. Final Report, Je, 1971. ERIC ED 061 395.

Granstrom, J., and Silvey, A. "Call for Help: Exploring the Black Experience in Children's Books." Horn Book 48(Ag, 1972):395-404.

Grant, Carl A. "An Empirical Study of the Effects of Relevant Curriculum Materials Upon the Self-Concept, Achievement and Attendance of Black Inner-City Students." Doctoral dissertation, U. of Wisconsin, Madison, 1972. Univ. Microfilms Order No. 72-15353.

Grant, Gerald. "The Politics of the Coleman Report." Doctoral dissertation, Harvard U., 1972.

_____. "Shaping Social Policy: The Politics of the Coleman Report." Teachers College Record 75(S, 1973):17-54.

Grant, Maye H. "Perspective on Adoption: Black Into White." Black World 22(N, 1972): 66-75.

Gray, G. C. "A Study of Racial Attitudes and Racial Perceptions of Selected Groups of Metropolitan High School Students." Doctoral dissertation, U. of Toledo, 1969.

Gray, Susan W. Children From Three to Ten: The Early Training Project. Nashville, TN: George Peabody College for Teachers, 1971.

_____. "The Vocational Preference of Negro School Children." Journal of Genetic Psychology 44(1944).

Green, Ely. Ely: Too Black, Too White. Edited by Elizabeth N. Chitty and Arthur Ben Chitty. Amherst, MA: U. of Massachusetts Press, 1970.

Green, James A. "Attitudinal and Situational Determinants of Intended Behavior Toward Blacks." Journal of Personality and Social Psychology 22(Ap, 1972):13-17.

Green, Richard B. "Social Class and Ethnic Differences in Responsiveness to Demands for Cognitive Functioning." Diss. Abstr. Int'l. 31(12-A)(Je, 1971):6401-6402.

Green, Robert L. "The Ethics of Curriculum Evaluation." Educational Leadership 36 (1978).

_____. Significant and Unique Problems Facing Blacks in American Education, N 24, 1973. ERIC ED 095 236.

Green, Robert Lee, and Farquhar, William W. "Negro Academic Motivation and Scholastic Achievement." Journal of Educational Psychology 26(1965).

Green, Robert Lee, Schweitzer, John H., Biskin, Donald S., and Lezotte, Lawrence W. "The Sociology of Multiracial Schools." Inequality in Education, No. 9, Ag 3, 1971.

Greenberg, Bradley S. "Children's Reactions to Television Blacks." Journalism Quarterly 49(1972):5-14.

Greenberg, Bradley, and Dervin, B. (eds). Use of the Mass Media by the Urban Poor. New York: Praeger, 1970.

Greenberg, Bradley S., and Gordon, Thomas F. Social Class and Racial Differences in Children's Perceptions of Television Violence, F, 1971. ERIC ED 048 772.

Greenberg, Edward S. "Black Children and the Political System." Public Opinion Quarterly 34(Fall, 1970):333-345.

_____. "Children and Government: A Comparison Across Racial Lines." Midwest Journal of Political Science 14(My, 1970):249-275.

_____. "Orientations of Black and White Children to Political Authority Figures." Social Science Quarterly 51(D, 1970):561-571.

_____. "Political Socialization to Support the System: A Comparison of Black and White Children." Doctoral dissertation, U. of Wisconsin, 1969.

Greenberg, Herbert M. "Some Effects of Segregated Education on Various Aspects of the Personality of These Members of Disadvantaged Groups Experiencing This Form of Education." In Dissertation Abstracts 14(1955):1785. Doctoral dissertation, New York U., 1955.

Greenberg, Judith W., and Alsham, Leonard M. "Perceptual-Motor Functioning and School Achievement in Lower-Class Black Children." Percpetual and Motor Skills 38(F, 1974):60-62.

Greenberger, E., and Marini, M. M. Black-White Differences in Psychosocial Maturity: A Factor Analysis. Baltimore: Center for Social Organization of Schools, Johns Hopkins U., 1972.

Greene, G. H. "Racial Prejudice in Children of School Age." Proceedings and Papers, Ninth International Congress of Psychology, 1929, pp. 192-193.

Greene, Mitchell A., Jr. "The Effects of Black Parents' Aspirations on the Academic Achievement of their Children." Journal of Afro-American Issues 4(Summer, 1976):329-337.

_____. "A Longitudinal Study of the Effects of Black Parents' Aspirations on the Academic Achievement of their Children." Doctoral dissertation, U. of Iowa, 1972.

Greenwald, Herbert J., and Oppenheim, Don B. "Reported Magnitude of Self-Misidentification Among Negro Children--Artifact?" Journal of Personality and Social Psychology 8(Ja, 1968):49-52.

Gretton, John. "Jencks: America's Intellectual Buccaneer." Time Educational Supplement, Ja 4, 1974.

Grier, William H., and Cobbs, Price M. Black Rage. New York: Basic Books, 1968.

Griffing, Penelope Scott. "The Relationship Between Socioeconomic Status and Socio-dramatic Play Among Black Kindergarten Children." Doctoral dissertation, Ohio State U., 1974. Univ. Microfilms Order No. 75-11351.

Grissom, Pauline V. W. "Preferences of Black Children in the Primary Grades for Basal Reading Books." Doctoral dissertation, U. of Michigan, 1975. Univ. Microfilms Order No. 76-9405.

Grossack, Martin M. "Psychological Considerations Essential to Effective Education Integration." Journal of Negro Education, Summer, 1965.

Grotberg, Edith. Critical Issues in Research Related to Disadvantaged Children. Proceedings of Six Head Start Research Seminars Held Under OEO Contract 4098, Jl, 1969. ERIC ED 034 088.

_____. Review of Research 1965 to 1969... Project Head Start. Project Head Start, Office of Economic Opportunity, OEO Pamphlet 6108-13. Washington, DC: GPO, Je, 1969.

Grow, Lucille J. Black Children, White Parents: A Study of Transracial Adoption. New York: Child Welfare League of America, 1974.

Grow, Lucille J., and Shapiro, Deborah. "Adoption of Black Children by White Parents." Child Welfare 54(Ja, 1975):57-59. [3-year study]

_____ and _____. Transracial Adoption Today: Views of Adoptive Parents and Social Workers. New York: Child Welfare League of America, 1975.

Gruber, James E. "Factors Influencing the Self-Esteem and Locus of Control of Adolescents: Results from the NLS First-Year Followup." Doctoral dissertation, U. of North Carolina, 1976. Univ. Microfilms Order No. 77-2039.

Gruber, Murray L. "Status Frustration and Social Protest among Negro Youth." Doctoral dissertation, Case-Western Reserve U., S, 1969.

Gruen, Gerald E., Korte, John R., and Baum, John F. "Group Measures of Locus of Control." Developmental Psychology 10(S, 1974):683-686.

Guggenheim, Fred. Self-Esteem and Achievement Expectation for White and Negro Children. Curriculum Report, My, 1967. ERIC ED 021 938.

Gullattee, Alyce C. "The Negro Psyche: Fact, Fiction and Fantasy." Journal of the National Medical Association 61(1969):119-129.

Gumaer, Jim. "Racial Understanding Through Affective Education." School Counselor 24(Ja, 1977):171-177.

Gumpert, Peter, and Gumpert, Carol. "The Teacher as Pygmalion: Comments on the Psychology of Expectation." Urban Review, S, 1968.

Gurin, Patricia, and Katz, Daniel. Motivation and Aspiration in the Negro College, N, 1966. ERIC ED 010 537.

Guthrie, James W. "What the Coleman Reanalysis Didn't Tell Us." Saturday Review 55(Jl, 22, 1972):45.

Guthrie, James W. and others. Schools and Inequality. Cambridge, MA: MIT Press, 1971.

Guthrie, James W., and Morrelli, Paul S. "The Coleman Report Says...": Equality of Educational Opportunity--Analysis and Political Implications. School Desegregation Bulletin Series, Ag, 1971. ERIC ED 056 406.

Guthrie, John T. Effects of Instruction and Socioeconomic Status on Concept Learning in Children, O, 1969. ERIC ED 035 060.

HEW Audit Agency. Review of Child Care Services Provided Under Title IV, Social Security Act. Washington, DC: U.S. Department of Health, Education, and Welfare, Office of the Assistant Secretary, Comptroller, N 4, 1974.

Had, Awang. "Effects of Status and Task Outcome Structures Upon Observable Power and Prestige Order of Small Tast-Oriented Groups." Doctoral dissertation, Stanford U., 1972.

Haertel, E. H., and Wiley, D. E. Social and Economic Differences in Elementary School Achievement. Chicago: ML-Group for Policy Studies in Education, CEMREL, Inc., Je 16, 1978.

Hagan, Anne Blair, and Watson, Ellie. "A Study of Lynchburg Pre-School Negro Children: Their Acceptance, Preference, Identification, and Recognition of Caucasians, Negroes, and Chinese." Senior thesis, Randolph-Macon Woman's College, 1968.

Haile, Allen C. "The Aspiration Level, Achievement and Upward Social Mobility of Black High School Students in South Central Los Angeles." Doctoral dissertation, U. of Southern California, 1971.

Hale, Janice E. Cultural Influences on Learning Styles of Afro-American Children, N, 1977. ERIC ED 149 851.

_____. "De-Mythicizing the Education of Black Children." First World 1(My-Je, 1977):30-35.

Hall, Eleanor R. Motivation and Achievement in Negro and White Students. Final Report, Jl, 1971. ERIC ED 060 157.

Hall, Vernon C., and Kaye, Daniel B. "Patterns of Early Cognitive Development Among Boys in Four Subcultural Groups." Journal of Educational Psychology 69(F, 1977):66-87.

Hall, Vernon D., and Turner, Ralph R. "The Validity of the 'Different Language Explanation' for Poor Scholastic Performance by Black Students." Review of Educational Research 44(Winter, 1974):69-81.

Hall, Vernon C. and others. "Attention and Achievement Exhibited by Middle-and Lower Class Black and White Elementary School Boys." Journal of Educational Psychology 69(Ap, 1977):115-120.

Hall, William S. "Two Variables Associated with Differential Productive Cultural Involvement Among Lower Class Negro and Caucasian Young Men." Journal of Social Psychology 83(Ap, 1971):219-228.

Hall, William S. and others. Policy, Programs, and Research in Child Development: A Review and Assessment from a Minority Perspective, S, 1973. ERIC ED 091 082.

_____. "Story Recall in Young Black and White Children: Effects of Racial Group Membership, Race of Experimentor, and Dialect." Developmental Psychology 11 (S, 1975):628-634.

Hall, William S., Freedle, Roy, and Cross, William E., Jr. Stages in the Development of a Black Identity, 1972. ACT Publications, PO Box 168, Iowa City, IA 52240.

Hall-Mitchum, Dora E. "Affective Considerations in Minority Program Design." Journal of Non-White Concerns in Personnel and Guidance 4(Ja, 1976):71-76.

Haller, A. O. "Education and the Occupational Achievement Process." In President's National Advisory Commission on Rural Poverty. Rural Poverty in the United States. Washington, DC: GPO, My, 1968.

Halpern, Florence. Survival: Black/White. Oxford, England: Pergamon, 1973.

Halpern, Stefanie Janis. "Achievement and Home Environment of Negro Children from Urban Depressed Areas: An Investigation of the Relationship Between Higher and Lower Achievement in Parochial School and Selected Aspects of Home, Community and School Environment." Doctoral dissertation, New York U., 1969. Univ. Microfilms Order No. 70-15,962.

Hamrick, Diane D. "Habituation of the Orienting Response in Socially Deprived Negro Children." Doctoral dissertation, U. of Georgia, 1971.

Hannerz, Ulf. "Roots of Black Manhood." Trans-action, O, 1969.

Hanson, Fred. Ethnic Survey of EMR Classes. Information Report to Superintendent of Public Instruction and to [California] State Board of Education, Ap 10, 1974. ERIC ED 095 683.

Harber, Jean R., and Bryen, Diane N. "Black English and the Task of Reading." Review of Educational Research 46(Summer, 1976):387-405.

Harding, Vincent. "Black Reflections on the Cultural Ramifications of Black Identity." Black Books Bulletin 1(Winter, 1972):4-10.

Hare, Bruce Robert. "Black and White Child Self-Esteem in Social Science: An Overview." Journal of Negro Education 46(Spring, 1977): 141-156.

_____. Racial and Socioeconomic Variations in Preadolescent Area-Specific and General Self-Esteem, F, 1977. ERIC ED 138 349.

_____. "The Relationship of Social Background to the Dimensions of Self-Concept." Doctoral dissertation, U. of Chicago, 1975. [Evanston]

Hare, Nathan. "The Future of Black Youth." In Youth in Contemporary Society. Edited by David Gottlieb. Beverly Hills, CA: Sage, 1972.

Harnischfeger, Annegret, and Wiley, David E. Achievement Test Score Decline: Do We Need to Worry?, 1976. CEMREL, Inc., 3120 59th Street, St. Louis, MO 63139.

_____. "Schooling Cutbacks and Achievement Declines: Can We Afford Them?" Administrator's Notebook 24 1(1975).

Harris, Dole B., and Roberts, Jean. "Intellectual Maturity of Children: Demographic and Socioeconomic Factors." Vital and Health Statistics, Series 11(Je, 1972).

Harris, Edward E. "Racial and National Identities: An Exploratory Study in Self and 'We-Group' Attitudes." Journal of Negro Education, Fall, 1965.

Harris, Helena. "Development of Moral Attitudes in White and Negro Boys." Developmental Psychology 2(My, 1970):376-383.

Harris, Jan Owen. "Mental Health Services to a Racially Troubled School." Hospital and Community Psychiatry 22(My, 1971): 140-143.

Harris, Herry D. Socioeconomic Status and Levels of Ability, Ap, 1976. ERIC ED 132 190.

Harris, Robert L. "The Whole School Is a Kindergarten." NJEA Review 44(Ap, 1971): 16-21.

Harris, Susan, and Braun, John R. Self-Esteem and Racial Preference in Black Children, 1971. ERIC ED 056 773.

Harrison, Algea, and Nadelman, Lorraine. "Conceptual Tempo and Inhibition of Movement in Black Preschool Children." Child Development 43(Je, 1972):657-668.

Harrison, Brian. "Language, Schools, and the Working Class." Forum for the Discussion of New Trends in Education 16(Spring, 1974): 50-52.

Harrison, Forest I. "Relationship Between Home Background, School Success, and Adolescent Attitudes." Merrill-Palmer Quarterly, 0, 1968.

Harrison-Rose, Phyllis, and Wyden, Barbara. The Black Child. A Parents' Guide. New York: Wyden, 1973.

Hartigan, Robert R. "A Temporal-Spatial Concept Scale: A Developmental Study." Journal of Clinical Psychology 27(Ap, 1971): 221-223.

Hartman, John J. "Psychological Conflict in Negro American Language Behavior: A Case Study." American Journal of Orthopsychiatry 41(Jl, 1971):627-635. [See, William Labov, comment, 636-637.]

Hartnagel, Timothy F. "Father Absence and Self-Conception Among Lower Class White and Negro Boys." Social Problems 18(Fall, 1970): 152-163.

Hartup, William W. Psychosocial Deprivation and the Development of Affection and Dependence-Independence Motivation. Bethesda, MD: National Institute of Child Health and Human Development, 1968.

Harvey, Mary R. "Differential Treatment of Upper-Income and Lower-Income Children by the Public Schools." Doctoral dissertation, U. of Oregon, 1972.

Hauser, Robert M. Socioeconomic Background and Educational Performance, 1972. American Sociological Association, 1722 N Street, N.W., Washington, DC 20036. [Nashville, TN grades 7-12; 1957 data]

Hauser, Stuart T. "Black and White Identity Development: Aspects and Perspectives." Journal of Youth and Adolescence 1(Je, 1972):113-130.

_____. Black and White Identify Formation. Studies in the Psychosocial Development of Lower Socioeconomic Class Adolescent Boys. New York: Wiley, 1971.

Hauserman, Norma, Walen, Susan R., and Behling, Maxine. "Reinforced Racial Integration in the First Grade: A Study in Generalization." Journal of Applied Behavior Analysis 6 (Summer, 1973):193-200.

Havelick, Raymond, and Vane, Julia, R. "Race, Competency, and Level of Achievement: Relationship to Modeling in Elementary School Children." Journal of Psychology 87(My, 1974):53-58.

Havighurst, Robert, Jr. "The Educationally Difficult Student. What the Schools Can Do." Bulletin of the National Association of Secondary School Principals, Mr, 1965.

_____. "Minority Subcultures and the Law of Effect." American Psychologist 25(1970): 313-322.

_____. "Opportunity, Equity, or Equality." School Review 81(Ag, 1973):618-633.

_____. "The Relative Importance of Social Class and Ethnicity in Human Development." Human Development 19(1976):56-64.

Hayes, Edward J. "Enfironmental Pass and Psychological Need as Related to Academic Success of Minority Group Students." Journal of Counseling Psychology 21(Jl, 1974):299-304.

Hayes, Edward M. "The Relationship of Race and Sex to Academic Achievement in Selected Rival Elementary and High Schools Before and After Desegregation." Doctoral dissertation, U. of Virginia, 1969.

Hayes, Marie Therese. "An Investigation of the Impact of Reading on Attitudes of Racial Prejudice." Doctoral dissertation, Boston U. School of Education, 1969.

Heacock, Don, and Cunninghum, Cheryl. Self-Esteem in the Black Child Placed in a White Family: An Introductory Study, 1975. ERIC ED 136 126.

Healey, Gary W. "Self-Concept: A Comparison of Negro-Anglo-, and Spanish-American Students Across Ethnic, Sex, and Socioeconomic Variables." Diss. Abstr. Int'l., 1970, 30(7-A): 2849-50.

Heath, G. Louis. "The Control-Identities of Negro and White Students in a California City." Journal of Secondary Education 45 (My, 1970):209-213.

Heider, Eleanor R. "Style and Accuracy of Verbal Communications Within and Between Social Classes." Journal of Personality and Social Psychology 18(Ap, 1971):33-47.

Heinz, Ann. "Black Pride as a System-Transforming Variable: Its Impact on Self-Image and Attitudes Toward Authority." Doctoral dissertation, Northwestern U., 1971.

Heiss, Jerold, and Owens, Susan. "Self-Evaluations of Blacks and Whites." American Journal of Sociology 78(S, 1972):360-370.

Heller, Steven A. The Effects of a Five-Day Institute on the Attitudes of Black and White Public School Participants: An Occasional Paper--1971. ERIC ED 048-424. 1971.

Henderson, Donald Mark. "The Assault on Black Culture Through the Labeling Process." Journal of Afro-American Issues 3(Winter, 1975):53-62.

_____. "A Study of the Effects of Family Structure and Poverty on Negro Adolescents from the Ghetto." Doctoral dissertation, U. of Pittsburgh, 1967.

Henderson, George. "Role Models for Lower Class Negro Boys." Personnel and Guidance Journal, S, 1967.

_____. "Beyond Poverty of Income." Journal of Negro Education, Winter, 1967. [Educational aspirations]

Henderson, Norman B. and others. "Differential Rates of School Promotion from First Grade for White and Negro, Male and Female 7 Year Olds." Psychology in the Schools 8(Ap, 1971):101-109.

_____. Do Negro Children Project a Self-Image of Helplessness and Inadequacy in Drawing a Person?, 1969. ERIC ED 036 329.

Henderson, Ronald D. "A Comparative Analysis of Social-Psychological School Climate Variables in White and Black Elementary Schools With Socio-Economic Status and Achievement Controlled." Doctoral dissertation, Michigan State U., 1972.

_____. A Comparative Study of School Climate in White and Black Elementary Schools, Ap, 1974. ERIC ED 094 027.

_____. "School Climate in White and Black Elementary Schools: A Comparative Study." Urban Education 9(Ja, 1975):380-399.

Hendin, Herbert. "Black Suicide." Archives of General Psychiatry, O, 1969.

Hendrick, Clyde, and Hawkins, Gayle. "Race and Belief Similarity as Determinants of Attraction." Perceptual and Motor Skills 29(1969):710.

Hendrick, Clyde, and Rumenik, Donna K. "Race Versus Belief About Race as Determinants of Attraction: Belief Prejudice and Two Kinds of Race Prejudice." Journal of Research in Personality 7(S, 1973):148-164.

Hendrix, Sandra, and Dockecki, Paul R. The Personal-Social Competence Development of Low-Income Children, My, 1973. ERIC ED 129 399.

Henry, Jules. "White People's Time, Colored People's Time." Transaction, Mr-Ap, 1965.

Hensley, Anne. Black High School Students Evaluations of Black Speakers, 1970. ERIC ED 054 663.

Herman, Barry E. "The Effect of Neighborhood Upon the Attitudes of Negro and White Sixth Grade Children Toward Different Racial Groups." Doctoral dissertation, U. of Connecticut, 1967.

Herner and Company. The Status of Children. Washington, DC: GPO, 1978.

Hertzig, Margaret E. "Aspects of Cognition and Cognitive Style in Young Children of Differing Social and Ethnic Backgrounds." In Defects of Cognition. Edited by J. Hellmuth. New York: Brunner-Mazel, 1971.

Hertzig, Margaret E., Birch, Herbert G., Thomas, Alexander, and Mendez, Olga A. Class and Ethnic Differences in the Responsiveness of Preschool Children to Cognitive Demands. Monographs of the Society for Research in Child Development, 1968.

Herzog, Elizabeth. "Who Should Be Studied?" American Journal of Orthopsychiatry 41 (Ja, 1971):4-12.

Herzog, Elizabeth, Newcomb, Carol, and Cisin, Ira H. "But Some Are Moor Poor than Others: SES Differences in a Preschool Program." American Journal of Orthopsychiatry 42 (Ja, 1972):4-22.

Hess, Robert D. "Social Class and Ethnic Influences on Socialization." In Carmichael's Manual of Child Psychology, 3rd edition, Vol. II. Edited by P. Mussen. New York: Wiley, 1970.

_____. "The System-Maintenance Function of Social Development in the Schools." In Educational Change: Implications for Measurement. Proceedings of the 1971 Invitational C onference on Testing Problems. Princeton, NJ: Educational Testing Service, 1972:15-25.

Hetznecker, William, and Forman, Marc A. "Community Child Psychiatry: Evolution and Direction." American Journal of Orthopsychiatry 41(Ap, 1971):350-370.

Heussenstamm, F. K., and Hoepfner. "Black, White, and Brown Adolescent Alienation." Educational Leadership 30(D, 1972):241-244.

Hewitt, Charles W. "Meaningfulness Dimensions in Verbal Learning: Racial and Order Effects." Dissertation Abstracts Int'l. Vol. 31(8-13) (F, 1971):5024.

Hicks, Constance. "Who Will Protect the Children?" Negro Teachers Forum, Mr-Ap, 1967. [The African-American teacher, replies the author.]

Hiernaux, Jean. "Ethnic Differences in Growth and Development." Eugenics Quarterly 15 (1968):12-21.

Higgins, Paul C. and others. "Black-White Adolescent Drinking: The Myth and the Reality." Social Problems 25(D, 1977): 215-224.

Hill, D. "Adolescent Attitudes Among Minority Ethnic Groups." Educational Review 27 (N, 1974):45-51.

Hill, Robert B. Informal Adoption Among Black Families. Washington, DC: National Urban League, Jl, 1977.

Hill, S. I. B. "Race, Class, and Ethnic Biases in Research on School Performance of Low-Income Youth." Doctoral dissertation, U. of Oregon, 1971.

Hilliard, Everett. A Comparison Study of the Cognitive Development of Disadvantaged First Grade Pupils (As Measured by Selected Piagetian Tasks), Ap 29, 1971. ERIC ED 051 874.

Himmelfarb, Samuel, and Fishbein, Martin. "Studies in the Perception of Ethnic Group Members. Vol. II: Attractiveness, Response, Bias, and Anti-Semitism." Journal of Social Psychology 83(Ap, 1971): 289-298.

Hindelang, Michael James. "Educational and Occupational Aspirations Among Working Class Negro, Mexican-American and White Elementary School Children." Journal of Negro Education 39(Fall, 1970):351-353.

Hindley, C. B. "Social Class Influences on the Development of Ability in the First Five Years." Proceedings of XIV International Congress of Psychology. Vol. 3: Child and Education. Copenhagen, Denmark: Munksgaard, 1961:29-41.

_____. "Stability and Change in Abilities Up to Five Years: Group Trends." Journal of Child Psychology and Psychiatry 6(1965): 85-99.

Hindman, Baker M. "The Emotional Problems of Negro High School Youth Which Are Related to Segregation and Discrimination in a Southern Urban Community." Journal of Educational Sociology 27(N, 1958):115-127.

Hirsch, Jay G., and Costello, Joan. "School Achievers and Underachievers in an Urban Ghetto." Elementary School Journal 71 (N, 1970):78-85.

Hodgkins, Benjamin J., and Stakenas, Robert G. "AStudy of Self-Concepts of Negro and White Youth in Segregated Environments." Journal of Negro Education, Fall, 1969.

Hoetker, James, and Siegel, Gary. "Three Studies of the Preferences of Students of Different Races for Actors in Interracial Theatre Productions." Journal of Social Issues 36(Fall, 1970):87-103.

Hofmann, Gerhard. "Interracial Fraternization: Social Determinants of Friendship Relations Between Black and White Adolescents." Doctoral dissertation, Purdue U., 1973. Univ. Microfilms Order No. 74-15173.

Holm, Robert L. "Perceptual Training and Its Effect on Racial Preferences of Kindergarten Children." Psychological Reports 32(Ap, 1973):435-441.

Holland, Florence N. "A Comment on the Segregated Learning Situation as an Insu- lating Device for the Negro Child." Psychiatry, Ag, 1964. [New York City. See article by Armstrong and Gregor, above.]

Holloway, Robert G., and Berreman, Joel V. "The Educational and Occupational Aspirations and Plans of Negro and White Male Elementary School Students." The Pacific Sociological Review, Fall, 1959.

Holman, Ben. "Dealing With Racial Conflicts in School." NASSP Bulletin 59(My, 1975):42-47.

_____. "National Trends and Student Unrest." Security World 12(S, 1975):43-44. [2639 S. La Cienega Blvd., Los Angeles, CA 90034]

Holsey, Albon L. "Learning How to Be Black." American Mercury, Mr, 1929.

Holthouse, Norman D. and others. Achievement, Social Class and the Summer Vacations: The Effect of the Summer Vacation on the Reading, Language Arts, and Mathematics Achievement of Students from Various Socioeconomic Back- grounds, Ja, 1976. ERIC ED 130 760.

Holz, Robert F. "Racial Identification of Verbal Communication: Stereotyping and School Integration." CRC Report 52(Ap, 1971).

Honwanna, Luis Bernado. "The Hands of the Blacks." New York Times Magazine, Ap 30, 1967. [On the significance of blackness and whiteness]

Hood, Elizabeth F. "Motivating Urban Minority Group Youth." Education 9(Ap-My, 1973): 362-366.

Hoover, Mary Rhodes. "Characteristics of Black Schools at Grade Levels: a Description." Reading Teacher 31(Ap, 1978):757-762. [Successful black schools]

Horowitz, Ruth E. "Racial Aspects of Self- Identification in Nursery School Children." Journal of Psychology 7(1939):91-99.

Horton, John. "Time and Cool People." Transaction, Ap, 1967. [Los Angeles]

Hough, Richard L. and others. Parental Influence, Youth Counter-Culture and Rural Adolescent Attitudes Toward Negroes. Bethesda, MD: National Institute of Mental Health, Je, 1968. ERIC ED 024 514.

Houmes, Gary A. "A Study of Racial Disruption in Selected Large City High Schools as Related to Conflicting Black and White Students' Education Expectations." Doctoral dissertation, Florida State U., 1972.

Houston Council on Human Relations. The Black/Mexican-American Project Report, Jl, 1972. The Council, 629 W. Alabama St., Houston, TX 77006.

"How Head a Head Start?" New Republic, Ap 26, 1969. [Critique of evaluation of Head Start done by Westinghouse Learning Cor- poration and Ohio U.]

Howard, Alicia, Royse, David D., and Skerl, John A. "Transracial Adoption: The Black Community Perspective." Social Work 22(My, 1977):184-189.

Howard, John R. "Becoming a Black Muslim: A Study of Commitment Processes in a Deviant Political Organization." Doctoral disser- tation, Stanford U., 1965. Univ. Microfilms Order No. 66-2569.

Howard, Mary V. B. "The Responses of Fourth, Fifth, and Sixth Grade Black Urban Children to Selected Stories." Doctoral disserta- tion, Ohio State U., 1975. Univ. Micro- films Order No. 76-9982.

Howard, Robert G., and Brown, Anne M. "Twinning: A Marker for Biological Insults." Child Development 41(1970):519- 530.

Howell, Hazel W. "Black Muslim Affiliation as Reflected in Attitudes and Behavior of Negro Adolescents with Its Effect on Policies and Administrative Procedures in Schools of Two Eastern Cities, 1961-64." Doctoral dissertation, Columbia U., 1966. Univ. Microfilms Order No. 66-10295.

Hoxter, A. Lee, and Zingle, Harvey. "Cultural Deprivation, Irrational Beliefs, and the Self Concept." Canadian Counselor 4(0, 1970): 247-252.

Hraba, Joseph. "The Doll Technique: A Measure of Racial Ethnocentrism?" Social Forces 50(Je, 1972):522-527.

_____. "Socialization Into Black Consciousness." Doctoral dissertation, U. of Nebraska, 1972.

Hraba, Joseph, and Grant, Goeffrey. "Black Is Beautiful: A Reexamination of Racial Preference and Identification." Journal of Personality and Social Psychology 16 (N, 1970):398-402.

Hraba, Joseph, and Siegman, Jack. "Black Consciousness." Youth and Society 6(S, 1974):63-90.

Hughes, Langston. Black Misery. New York: Eriksson, 1969.

_____. "The Need for Heroes." Crisis, Je, 1941.

Hulbary, William E. "Race, Deprivation and Adolescent Self-Images." Social Science Quarterly 56(Je, 1975):105-114.

Hull, Gary L. "Racial Implications for the Design of Instructional Materials." Journal of Educational Research 69(O, 1975): 47-52.

Humphreys, Lloyd G., and Taber, Thomas. "Ability Factors and Function of Advantaged and Disadvantaged Groups." Journal of Educational Measurement 10(Summer, 1973): 107-115.

Humphreys, Lloyd. and others. "The Sex by Race Interaction in Cognitive Measures." Journal of Research in Personality 10(Mr, 1976):42-58.

_____. The Sex by Race Interaction in Cognitive Measures, 1971. ERIC ED 095 462.

Hunigan, Wendel J. "Is Black Beautiful? A Study of Racial Awareness Among Primary-Age Children." Master's thesis, Illinois State U., 1972.

Hunt, Anne Johnson. "Anthropology Achievement of Normal and Disadvantaged Kindergarten Children." Doctoral dissertation, U. of Georgia, 1969.

Hunt, David H. "A Cross Racial Comparison of Personality Traits Between Athletes and Nonathletes." Research Quarterly of the AAHPER 40(1969):704-705.

Hunt, J., and Hunt, L. "Racial Inequality and Self-Image: Identity Maintenance as Identity Diffusion." Sociology and Social Research 6190(1977):539-559.

Hunt, Janet Gibbs. "Race and Identity: A Study of Black and White Urban School Boys." Doctoral dissertation, Indiana U., 1973. Univ. Microfilms Order No. 74-00375.

Hunt, Janet Gibbs, and Hunt, Larry L. "Racial Inequality and Self-Image: Identity Maintenance as Identity Diffusion." Sociology and Social Research 61(Jl, 1977): 539-559.

Hunt, Joseph McV. The Challenge of Incompetence and Poverty. Urbana, IL: U. of Illinois Press, 1969.

_____. "Parent and Child Centers: Their Basis in the Behavioral and Educational Sciences." American Journal of Orthopsychiatry 41(Ja, 1971):13-38.

Hunt, Larry L., and Hunt, Janet G. "A Religious Factor in Secular Achievement Among Blacks: The Case of Catholicism." Social Forces 53(Je, 1975):595-605.

Hunter, D. M., and Babcock, C. G. "Intrapsychic Structure of Negroes." Psychoanalytic Study of Society 4(1967):124-170.

Hurley, Oliver L. and others. The Development of Auditory Sequential Memory in Young Black and White Children, Ap, 1976. ERIC ED 125 199.

Hurst, Charles G., Jr. "Special Problems of Black Children and Youth." In The Slow Learner. Edited by Joseph S. Roucek. New York: Philosophical Library, 1969.

Husen, Torsten. "The Standard of the Elite—Some Findings from the IEA International Survey in Mathematics and Science." Acta Sociologica 16(1973):305-323. [Performance of high scorers in comprehensive and selective schools systems]

Hyman, Shirley L. "Measured Self-Esteem of Inner-City Secondary Students in Relation to Scholastic Achievement and Occupational Aspiration and Expectation." Doctoral dissertation, Fordham U., 1975. Univ. Microfilms Order No. 75-18,914.

Identity in a Troubled World. Washington, DC: GPO, 1971.

International Reading Association. Social Class and Ethnic Group Differences in Learning to Read. Newark, DE: The Association, 1978.

Irons, N. M., and Zigler, E. "Children's
Responsiveness to Social Reinforcement as a
Function of Short-Term Preliminary Social
Interactions and Long-Term Social Depri-
vation." Developmental Psychology 1(1969):
402-409.

Jackson, Dan, and Systra, Candy. "How
Students Reacted to 'Roots.'" Media and
Methods, Ap, 1977.

Jackson, Donald W. "The Genocide of Black
Students." Freedom North, Je, 1966.

Jackson, Gregg B. "The Research Evidence on
the Effects of Grade Retention." Review of
Educational Research 45(Fall, 1975):613-
635.

Jackson, Jacquelene J., and Harris, Larry C.
"'You May Be Normal When You Came Here, But
You Won't Be Normal When You Leave.' or
Pushout." Black Scholar 8(Ap, 1977):2-11.

Jackman, Jacquelene, and Jackman, Viola E.
"Needed: Personalized Modes of Learning."
Educational Leadership 30(O, 1972):20-22.

Jackson, John S. III. "The Political Behavior,
Attitudes, and Socialization of Selected
Groups of Black Youth." Doctoral disserta-
tion, Vanderbilt U., 1971.

Jackson, Marian S. "Mommie, Why Am I Colored?"
Common Ground 5(Summer, 1945):46-47.

Jackson, Miles M., Jr. "The Myth Bag." Negro
Digest, Jl, 1967.

Jackson, Nancy Ewald and others. Cognitive
Development in Young Children. Washington,
DC: National Institute of Education,
1976.

Jackson, T. S. "Racial Inferiority Among
Negro Children." Crisis, Ag, 1940.

Jacob, E., and Sanday, Peggy R. "Dropping
Out: A Strategy for Coping with Cultural
Pluralism." In Anthropology and the Public
Interest: Fieldwork and Theory. Edited by
Peggy R. Sanday.

Jacobson, Cardell K. "The Effects of Black
Power and the Locus of Control Variable on
Performance and Self-Depreciation of Junior
High School Students in Biracial Pairs."
Doctoral dissertation, U. of North Carolina,
1971.

_____. Racial-Ethnic Composition and Student
Attitudes: A Longitudinal Study, 1976.
ERIC ED 137 488.

_____. "Separatism, Integrationism, and
Avoidance Among Black, White, and Latin
Adolescents." Social Forces 55(Je, 1977):
1011-1027. [Milwaukee, WI]

Jacobson, Leonard I., and Greeson, Larry E.
Effects of Systematic Conceptual Learning
on the Intellectual Development of Preschool
Children from Poverty Backgrounds." Child
Development 43(S, 1972):1111-1115.

Janis, Juel M. "School Racial Composition and
Achievement Test Scores of Black and White
Junior High School Students." Doctoral
dissertation, U. of Maryland, 1971. Univ.
Microfilms Order No. 72-00613.

Jasik, Marilyn. "A Look at Black Faces in
Children's Picture Books." Young Children
0, 1968.

Jaworski, Suzanne W. "The Evolution of a
White's Black Consciousness." Youth and
Society 4(D, 1972):131-153.

Jaynes, Mary. "The Segregation Fence: A
Young Mother Gets Involved." Redbook, Mr,
1966. [The brutalities of racist policy
in a school]

Jeffcoate, Robert. "Children's Racial Ideas
and Feelings." English in Education 11
(Spring, 1977):32-46.

Jencks, Christopher. "Inequality in Retrospect." Harvard Educational Review 43(F,
1973):138-164.

_____. "A Reappraisal of the Most Controver-
sial Educational Document of Our Time."
New York Times Magazine, Ag 10, 1969.
[Coleman Report]

_____. "Schooling Has Limits." New York
Times, Ja 16, 1974.

Jencks, Christopher, and Brown, Marsha D.
"Effects of High Schools on Their Students."
Harvard Educational Review 45(Ag, 1975):
273-324.

Jenkins, Martin D. "A Socio-psychological
Study of Negro Children of Superior
Intelligence." Doctoral dissertation,
Northwestern U., 1935.

Jenkins, Shirley, and Morrison, Barbara.
Identification of Ethnic Issues in Child
Welfare: A Review of the Literature.
Mr 1, 1974. ERIC ED 139 874.

Jensen, Arthur R. "A Theory of Primary and
Secondary Mental Retardation." In Inter-
national Review of Research in Mental
Retardation, Vol. IV. Edited by N. R.
Ellis. New York: Academic Press, 1970.

_____. "Cumulative Deficit in IQ of Blacks
in Rural South." Developmental Psychology
13(1977):184-191.

_____. "Ethnicity and Scholastic Achievement."
Psychological Reports 34(Ap, 1974):659-668.

_____. "Personality and Scholastic Achievement in Three Ethnic Groups." British Journal of Educational Psychology 43(Je, 1973):115-125.

_____. "The Price of Inequality." Oxford Review of Education 1(1975):59-71.

_____. A Two-Factor Theory of Familial Retardation, 1971. ERIC ED 060 577.

Jeruchimowicz, Rita and others. "Knowledge of Action and Object Words: A Comparison of Lower-and Middle-Class Negro Preschoolers." Child Development 42(Je, 1971):455-464.

Jessup, Dorothy K. "School Integration and Minority Group Achievement." In The Urban R's. Edited by Robert A. Dentler and others. New York: Praeger, 1967.

Jimenez, Luis A. The Ethnic Composition of Rural Youth in the United States..., S, 1974. ERIC ED 101 892.

Johnson, Charles S. "The Development of the Personality of Students in Segregated Communities." Quarterly Review of Hughes Education Among Negroes 4(Ap, 1936):67-70. [See, Glenn R. Johnson, below]

Johnson, Edwina C. "The Child in the Prestige Vacuum." Integrated Education, D, 1963- Ja, 1964.

Johnson, Glenn R. "The Development of the Personality of Students in Segregated Communities (Racial Segregation)." Quarterly Review of Higher Education Among Negroes 4(Ap, 1936):63-66. [See Charles S. Johnson, above]

Johnson, Guy B. "Education, Segregation, and Race Relations." Quarterly Review of Higher Education Among Negroes 3(Ap, 1935): 89-94.

Johnson, James T. "Black Militancy Among High School Students." Master's thesis, Illinois State U., 1970.

Johnson, John L. "Special Education and the Inner City: A Challenge for the Future or Another Means for Cooling the Mark Out?" Journal of Special Education 3(1969):237- 251.

Johnson, Kathryn J., and Leslie, Gerald R. "Methodological Notes on Research in Child- bearing and Social Class." Merrill-Palmer Quarterly, O, 1965.

Johnson, Kenneth R. "The Influence of Non- standard Negro Dialect on Reading Achieve- ment." English Record 21(Ap, 1971):148-155.

Johnson, Monroe H. "A Study of Substance Abuse by Black Youths." Master's thesis, Western Michigan U., 1974. Univ. Microfilms Order No. M-6165. [Kalamazoo, MI]

Johnson, Norris Brock. "An Ethnographic and Longitudinal Methodology for the Description and Illustration of Schooling as Cultural Transmission." 2 Vols. Doctoral disserta- tion, U. of Michigan, 1976. Univ. Microfilms Order No. 76-19,166.

Johnson, Roger, Jr. "The Process of Cate- gorizing in High and Low Socio-Economic Status Children." Science Education 57 (Ja-Mr, 1973):1-7.

Johnson, William B. "Misunderstanding Low Income and Minority Students." Negro Educational Review 23(Ja, 1972):38-44.

Johnson, Willie. "Willie Johnson Is Standing Firm." Integrated Education (S-O, 1971): 4-11. (Reprinted from Chicago Sun-Times) [Washington High School, Chicago, IL]

Johnstone, Muthiora. "Black Identity: An African View." GW: The George Washington University Magazine, S, 1968.

Jones, Alvin H. "An Investigation of Self- Concept Using Group Counseling with Afro- American Male Ninth-Grade Students." Diss. Absts. Int'l. 32(6-A), D, 1971:3031.

Jones, Clyzelle K. "The History of Sydney D. Miller High School with Particular Exploration into those Factors which Re- sulted in the Inordinately High Incidence of Pupil Success Considering, and Despite Existing Socio-Economic Factors which Are Perceived as Being Predictors of High Incidences of Pupil Failure." Doctoral dissertation, Wayne State U., 1971.

Jones, Edmond D. "On Transracial Adoption of Black Children." Child Welfare 51(Mr, 1972): 156-164.

Jones, R. W. "The Interrelation of Socio- Economic Status and Academic Achievement in Nova Scotia, Pennsylvania, and Virginia." Doctoral dissertation, Pennsylvania State U., 1964.

Jones, Faustive C. "The Disjunctive Relation- ship Between the Afro-American Experience and Conventional Educational Efforts." In Restructuring the Educational Process: A Black Perspective. Edited by Lawrence E. Gary and Aaron Favors. Washington, DC: Institute for Urban Affairs and Research, Howard U., 1975.

_____. "Effects of Schooling." Crisis 82 (Ag-S, 1975):234-237.

Jones, H. E. "The Environment and Mental Development." In Manual of Child Psychology. Edited by L. Carmichael. New York: Wiley, 1954.

Jones, James A. and others. Learning and Self- Esteem Among Black and White Pre-Schoolers, D, 1975. ERIC ED 122 926.

Jones, Reginald L. "Delivery of Special Services to Young Black Children." *Journal of Non-White Concerns in Personnel and Guidance* 1(Ja, 1973):61-68.

_____ (ed). *Mainstreaming and the Minority Child*. Reston, VA: The Council for Exceptional Children, 1977.

Jones, Rhodri. "The Mixed Ability Classes." *English in Education* 6(Spring, 1972):56-62.

Jones, Stanley, and Aiello, John R. "Proxemic Behavior of Black and White First-, Third-, and Fifth-Grade Children." *Journal of Personality and Social Psychology* 25(Ja, 1973):21-27.

Jones, William L. "The Importance of Black Identity to the Black Adolescent." *Journal of Black Studies* 4(S, 1973):81-91.

Jordan, Max F., Golden, James F., and Bender, Lloyd D. *Aspirations and Capabilities of Rural Youth*. Bulletin 722. Agricultural Experiment Station, U. of Arkansas Division of Agriculture, My, 1967. [Negro and white youth]

Jordan, Thomas E. *The Natural History of 1008 Infants in the Readiness Years*, Ja, 1974. ERIC ED 090 739.

Jorgensen, Carl C. "Internal-External Control in the Academic Achievement of Black Youth: A Reappraisal." *Integrateducation* 14(N/D, 1976).

_____. "The Socialization and Meaning of Sense of Internal vs. External Congrol Among Black High School Students." Doctoral dissertation, U. of Michigan, 1971.

Joseph, Ellis A. "Selected Aspects of the Internality of the Negro in Education." *Education*, N-D, 1967.

Joseph, Stephen M. (ed). *The Me Nobody Knows. Children's Voices from the Ghetto*. New York: Avon Books, 1969.

Joyce, William W. "Minorities in Primary-Grade Social Studies Textbooks: A Progress Report." *Social Education* 37(Mr, 1973):217-233.

Joyner, Donald E. "Investigation of the Social Relationships of Educable Mentally Retarded Children in Negro Schools in Five School Districts of Northeast Louisiana." *Diss. Abstr. Int'l*. 31, 9-A(Mr, 1971):4586.

Jud, G. Donald, and Walker, James L. "Discrimination by Race and Class and the Impact of School Quality." *Social Science Quarterly* 57(Mr, 1977):731-749.

Kaalberg, Ramona M. "Racial Preferences of Second, Fourth, and Sixth Grade Negro and Caucasian Girls in Hypothetical and Actual Social Situations." Doctoral dissertation, George Peabody College for Teachers, 1972.

Kagan, Jerome. "The Importance of Simply Growing Older." *New Society*, Je 14, 1973.

_____. "Late Starts Are Not Lost Starts." *Learning* 2(S, 1973):82-85.

_____. "Man's Enormous Capacity to Catch Up." *Times Educational Supplement*, S 13, 1974.

_____. *On Class Differences and Early Development*, D 28, 1969. ERIC ED 040 167.

_____. "The Poor *Are* Educable." *New York Times*, Ja 16, 1974.

_____. "Preschool Enrichment and Learning." *Interchange* 2(1971):12-22.

Kaltsounis, Bill. "Differences in Creative Thinking of Black and White Deaf Children." *Perceptual and Motor Skills* 32(F, 1971):243-248.

Kam, Jeannette V. S. "Influences of Anthropological Materials on the Knowledge of Sixth Graders About Blacks." *Education* 98(Summer, 1978):406-409.

Kandel, Denise, and Lesser, Gerald S. "Parental and Peer Influences on Educational Plans of Adolescents." *American Sociological Review*, Ap, 1969.

Kang, Songchul. "An Analysis of Social Climate Variables in Schools with Varying Black and White Student Composition When Socioeconomic Status and Achievement Levels are Controlled." Doctoral dissertation, Michigan State U., 1975. Univ. Microfilms Order No. 75-20850.

Kapel, David E. *Effects of Negro Density on Student Variables and the Post-High School Adjustment of Male Negroes Project TALENT Five-Year Follow-Up Studies Interim Report 6*, 1968. Available from American Institutes for Research, PO Box 1113, Palo Alto, CA 94302.

Kaplan, Henry K., and Matkom, Anthony J. "Peer Status and Intellectual Functioning of Negro School Children." *Psychology in the Schools*, Ap, 1967.

Kaplan, Howard B., and Pokorny, Alex D. "Self Derogation and Childhood Broken Home." *Journal of Marriage and the Family* 33(My, 1971):328-337.

Kappelman, Murray M. and others. "Comparison of Disadvantaged Children with Learning Disabilities and their Successful Peer Group." *American Journal of Diseases of Children* 124(D, 1972):875-879.

Karon, Bertram P. The Negro Personality. A Rigorous Investigation of the Effects of Culture. New York: Springer Pub. Co., 1958.

Karp, Stephen A., Silberman, Lester, and Winters, Stephen. "Psychological Differentiation and Socioeconomic Status." Perceptual and Motor Skills, F, 1969.

Karweit, Nancy L. School Influences on Student Interaction Patterns. Baltimore: Center for Social Organization of Schools, Johns Hopkins U., D, 1976.

_____. "Student Friendship Networks as a Resource Within Schools." Doctoral dissertation, Johns Hopkins U., 1976.

Katz, Irwin. "Academic Motivation and Equal Educational Opportunity." Harvard Educational Review, Winter, 1968.

_____. "A Critique of Personality Approaches to Negro Performance, With Research Suggestions." Journal of Social Issues 25 (1969):13-27.

_____. "Cultural and Personality Factors in Minority Group Behavior: A Critical Review." In Integrating the Organization: A Social Psychological Analysis. Edited by H. L. Fromkin and J. J. Sherwood. New York: Free Press, 1974.

Katz, Irwin, Cole, O., and Baron, R. "Self Evaluation, Social Reinforcement, and Academic Achievement of Black and White School Children." Child Development 47 (Je, 1976):368-374.

_____. "The Socialization of Academic Motivation in Minority Group Children. In Nebraska Symposium on Motivation, 1967. Edited by David Levine. (Lincoln, NE: U. of Nebraska Press, 1967)

Katz, Irwin, and Gurin, Patricia (eds). Race and the Social Sciences. New York: Basic Books, 1969.

Katz, Phyllis A. "The Acquisition of Racial Attitudes in Children." In Towards the Elimination of Racism. Edited by Phyllis A. Katz. New York: Pergamon, 1976.

_____. "Attitude Change in Children: Can the Twig Be Straightened?" In Towards the Elimination of Racism. Edited by Phyllis A. Katz. New York: Pergamon, 1976.

_____. "Perception of Racial Cues in Preschool Children: A New Look." Developmental Psychology 8(Mr, 1973):295-299.

_____. Stimulus Predifferentiation and Racial Attitude Change in Children, S, 1971. ERIC ED 056 775.

Katz, Phyllis, and Seavey, Carol. "Labels and Children's Perceptions of Faces." Child Development 44(D, 1973):770-775.

Katz, Phyllis, and Zalk, Sue R. "Doll Preferences: An Index of Racial Attitudes?" Journal of Educational Psychology 66(O, 1974):663-668.

Katz, Phyllis A. and others. "Perceptual Concomitants of Racial Attitudes in Urban Grade-School Children." Developmental Psychology 11(Mr, 1975):135-144.

_____ and others. Racial Attitudes and Perception in Black and White Urban School Children, S, 1970. ERIC ED 043 719.

Kaufmann, James M. and others. "Quantitative Judgments of Culturally Advantaged and Disadvantaged Preschool Children." Psychological Reports 28(Je, 1971):939-944.

Keislar, Evan, and Stern, Carolyn. "Effects of Dialect and Instructional Procedures on Children's Oral Language Production and Concept Acquisition." Urban Education 3(1968).

Keller, James F., and Kales, Ruth J. "Self-Concept Scores Among Black and White Culturally Deprived Adolescent Males." Journal of Negro Education 41(Winter, 1972). [North Florida]

Keller, Suzanne. The American Lower Class Family: A Survey of Selected Facts and their Implications. Albany, NY: New York State Division for Youth, 1966.

Keller, Suzanne, and Zavalloni, Marisa. "Ambition and Social Class: A Respecification." Social Forces, 0, 1964.

Kelley, Eleanor A. and others. A Comparative Analysis by Social Class, Ethnicity, and Sex of the Clothing Acquisition and Use Practices of Early Adolescents. Baton Rouge, LA: School of Home Economics, 1973.

Kellogg, W. N., and Eagleson, R. M. "The Growth of Social Perception in Different Racial Groups." Journal of Educational Psychology 22(My, 1931):367-375.

Kelly, Delos H. "Trace Assignments and Student Mobility Patterns as Barriers to Equality of Educational Opportunity: A Review of Recent Research." Contemporary Education 45(F, 1973):27-30.

_____. "Track Position and Delinquent Involvement: A Preliminary Analysis." Sociology and Social Research 58(Jl, 1974): 380-386.

Kennedy, Mary M. "Findings from the Follow Through Planned Variation Study." Educational Researcher 7(Je, 1978):3-11.

Kenyon, Sandra J. "The Development of Political Cynicism: A Study of Political Socialization." Doctoral dissertation, Massachusetts Institute of Technology, 1970. [Eighth, tenth, and twelfth-graders in Brooklyn]

Keogh, Barbara K., and MacMillan, Donald L. "Effects of Motivational and Presentation Conditions on Digit Recall of Children of Differing Socioeconomic, Racial, and Intelligence Groups." American Educational Research Journal 9(Ja, 1971):27-38.

Kerckhoff, Alan C., and Campbell, Richard T. "Black-White Differences in the Educational Attainment Process." Sociology of Education 50(Ja, 1977):15-27.

_____. "Race and Social Status Differences in the Explanation of Educational Ambition." Social Forces 55(Mr, 1977):701-714.

Kerckhoff, Alan C., and Trella, Sherry C. "Teaching Race Relations in the Nursery School." Young Children 27(Ap, 1972): 240-248.

Kerlinger, Fred N. (ed). Review of Research in Education. Vol. 1. Itasca, IL: Peacock, 1973.

Kershner, John R. "Ethnic Group Differences in Children's Ability to Reproduce Direction and Orientation." Journal of Social Psychology 88(O, 1972):3-13.

Kester, Scott W. "Sex Separation--New Strategy for Discrimination." Integrated Education (N-D, 1971):30-33.

Kier, Rae Jeanne and others. "Success Expectancies and the Probability Learning of Children of Low and Middle Socioeconomic Status." Developmental Psychology 13(S, 1977):444-449.

Kim, Yoon Hough. Neighborhood Context and Racial Attitudes, My, 1971. ERIC ED 050 206.

Kim, Kwang H. "The Social Context of Occupational and Educational Mobility Aspirations of Negro Adolescents." Diss. Abstr., 1969 29(12-A):4564-4565.

King, Martin Luther (Mrs.). "My Dream for my Children." Good Housekeeping, Je, 1964.

_____. "The Past and Its Presence." Southern Education Report, Jl-Ag, 1968.

Kircher, Mary, and Furley, Lita. "Racial Preferences in Young Children." Child Development 42(D, 1971):2076-2078.

Kirk, Samuel A. "Ethnic Differences in Psycholinguistic Abilities." Exceptional Children 39(O, 1970):112-118.

Kirkendall, Don R., and Gruber, Joseph J. "Canonical Relationships Between the Motor and Intellectual Achievement Domains in Culturally Deprived High School Pupils." Research Quarterly of the AAHPER 41(D, 1970): 496-502.

Kirkland, Marjorie H. Retarded Childred of the Poor. A Casebook. Washington, DC: GPO, 1972.

Kite, B. Alan. "The Art of Ethnic Education." Urban Review (My, 1972):13-22.

Kleck, Robert E. The Role of Stigma as a Factor in Social Interaction. Bethesda, MD: National Institute of Child Health and Human Development, 1968.

Kleederman, Frances F. "Black English and Reading Problems: Sociolinguistic Considerations." Reading World 14(My, 1975): 256-267.

Kleg, Milton. Attitudinal Change in White Students after Instruction in an Ethnic Relations Unit, F 6, 1971. ERIC ED 049 338.

_____. Race, Caste, and Prejudice: the Influence of Change in Knowledge on Change in Attitude, Ag, 1970. ERIC ED 041 813.

Klein, Rosslyn S. "Some Factors Influencing Empathy in Six and Seven Year Old Children Varying in Ethnic Background." Diss. Abstr. Int'l. Vol. 31(8-A) (F, 1971):3960.

Klein, Stephen P., and Niedermeyer, Fred C. "Direction Sports: A Tutorial Program for Elementary-School Pupils." Elementary School Journal 72(N, 1971):53-61.

Kleinfeld, Judith S. "'Sense of Fate Control' and Community Control of the Schools." Education and Urban Society 3(My, 1971): 277-300. [DC]

_____. "The Validity of the Sense of Fate-Control Scale and the Relationship of Beliefs About Internal and External Control and Academic Self-Concept to School Achievement." Diss. Abstr. Int'l. 31, 8-A(F, 1971): 3960.

Kliman, Deborah S. "Racial Preferences Expressed for Peers and Adults by Preschool Children." Home Economics Research Journal 5(Mr, 1977):142-145.

Kilman, Deborah S., and Peterson, Georgia F. The Effects of a Career Education Curriculum on the Racial Attitudes of Kindergarten Children, 1975. ERIC ED 122 971.

Knapp, John V., and Slotnick, Henry B. National Assessment of Educational Programs. Report 11. WRITING: Group Results A and B for Objectively-Scored Exercises, 1969-70 Assessment. National Results by Region, Sex, Color, Size and Type of Community, and Parental Education. Washington, DC: GPO, My, 1973.

Koch, Helen. "The Social Distance between Certain Racial, Nationality, and Skin Pigmentation Groups in Selected Populations of American School Children." Journal of Genetic Psychology 68(1946):63-95.

Kochman, T. Language Behavior in the Negro Ghetto. Chicago, IL: Center for Inner City Studies, Northeastern Illinois State College, 1968.

Koger, Earl, Sr. Negro Heroes Card Game. Roger Koger Co., 3605 Cedardale Road, Baltimore, MD 21215, n.d.

Kohlberg, Lawrence. Moral Effects of Psycho-social Deprivation: Some Research Directions. Bethesda, MD: National Institute of Child Health and Human Development, 1968.

Kohn, Martin, and Rosman, Bernice L. "Cognitive Functioning in Five-Year-Old Boys as Related to Social-Emotional and Background-Demographic Variables." Developmental Psychology 8(F, 1973):277-294.

Kollaritsch, Jane. Success of Black Students in Foreign Language, 1971. ERIC ED 051 689.

Kon, I. "The Psychology of Prejudice (On the Roots of Ethnic Prejudices in Social Psychology)." Soviet Anthropology and Archaeology, Summer, 1967.

Kormeich, L. Berell and others. "Teachers and Teaching Machines: Possible Roles in the Education of Black and White Pre-School Children." Education 92(Ap-My, 1972):46-57.

Korte, Charles, and Milgram, Stanley. "Acquaintance Networks Between Racial Groups: Application of the Small World Method." Journal of Personality and Social Psychology 15(Je, 1970):101-108.

Koslin, Sandra and others. The Development of Normative Racial and Sexual Social Distance Beliefs, S, 1971. ERIC ED 061 382.

Kowatrakul, Surang and others. An Investigation of the Psychosocial Origins of Need for Achievement. ERIC ED 121 483, n.d.

Kraus, Philip E. Yesterday's Children: A Longitudinal Study of Children from Kindergarten into the Adult Years. New York: Wiley, 1973. [New York City]

Krauss, Irving. "Sources of Educational Aspirations among Working Class Youth." American Sociological Review, D, 1964.

Kromick, Robert F. "The Impact of Perceived Organizational Climate on Academic Performance." Southern Journal of Educational Research 6(S, 1973):169-188.

Kubany, Edward S., Gallimore, Ronald, and Gallimore, Judith. "The Effects of Extrinsic Factors on Achievement-Oriented Behavior: A Non-Western Case." Journal of Cross-Cultural Psychology 1(Spring, 1970): 77-84. [Hawaii]

Kurokawa, Minako. "Childhood Accident as a Measure of Social Integration." Canadian Review of Sociology and Anthropology 3 (1966).

Kutner, Bernard. "Patterns of Mental Functioning Associated with Prejudice in Children." Psychological Monographs 72(1958):460.

Kuttner, Robert E. "Comparative Performance of Disadvantaged Ethnic and Racial Groups." Psychological Reports 27(0, 1970):372.

Kuvlesky, William P., and Dameron, Jane. "Adolescents' Perceptions of Military Service as a Vehicle for Social Mobility: A Racial Comparison of Rural Youth." Journal of Vocational Behavior 1(Ja, 1971):57-67. [East Texas]

Kuvlesky, William P., and Thomas, Kathryn A. "Social Ambitions of Negro Boys and Girls from Metropolitan Ghetto." Journal of Vocational Behavior 1(Ap, 1971):177-187.

Kuvlesky, William P., and Upham, W. Kennedy. Social Ambitions of Teenage Boys Living in an Economically Depressed Area of the South-- A Racial Comparison, Mr 30, 1967. ERIC ED 014 339.

Kuvlesky, William P. and others (eds). Black Youth in the Rural South: Educational Abilities and Ambitions, Ja, 1977. ERIC ED 134 359.

Kvaraceus, William C. (ed). Negro Self-Concept: Implications for School and Citizenship. New York: McGraw-Hill Co., 1965.

LaBarre, Maurine. "The Strengths of the Self-Supporting Poor." Social Casework, 0, 1968.

Labov, William, and Robins, Clarence. A Note on the Relation of Reading Failure to Peer-Group Status in Urban Ghettos, Jl 27, 1967. ERIC ED 018 343.

La Belle, Thomas, Jr. "Differential Perceptions of Elementary School Children Representing District Sociocultural Backgrounds." Journal of Cross-Cultural Psychology 2 (Je, 1971):145-156.

_____. "What's Deprived About Being Different?" Elementary School Journal 72 (0, 1971):13-19.

Lackamp, Leo B. "The Academic Achievement,
Learning Interests, Self-Concept, Fate
Control and Post High School Aspirations
of Black Parochial and Public High School
Students: A Comparative Study." Doctoral
dissertation, 1974. Univ. Microfilms Order
No. 74-29,695.

Lacoste, Ronald James. "Preferences of Three
and Four Year Old Children for the Facial
Features of the Negro and Caucasian Races
When Skin Color is Not a Racial Cue."
Doctoral dissertation, U. of Texas, 1975.
Univ. Microfilms Order No. 76-8056.

Ladd, Florence C. Travels and Travels in
Fantasy of Black Youths from Low-Income
Backgrounds, N, 1970. ERIC ED 045 772.

Ladner, Joyce A. "Labeling Black Children:
Social-Psychological Implications."
Journal of Afro-American Issues 3(Winter,
1975):43-52.

_____. Mixed Families. Adopting Across
Racial Boundaries. Garden City, NY:
Doubleday, 1977.

_____. "Mixed Families: White Parents and
Black Children." Society 14(S-O, 1977):
70-78.

Lambert, W. E., and Yaguchi, Y. "Ethnic
Cleavages Among Young Children." Journal
of Abnormal and Social Psychology 53(1956):
380-382.

Lancaster, Joyce Woodward. "An Investigation
of the Effect of Books with Black
Characters on the Racial Preferences of
White Children." Doctoral dissertation,
Boston U., 1971. Univ. Microfilms Order
No. 71-26711.

Lane, Sam H., and Evans, Selby H. "Some
Aspects of Individual Differences in
Schematic Concept Formation." U.S. Army
Human Engineering Laboratories Technical
Memorandum, Mr, 1972.

Langlois, Judith H., and Stephan Cookie. "The
Effects of Physical Attractiveness and
Ethnicity on Children's Behavioral Attribu-
tions and Peer Preferences." Child
Development 48(D, 1977):1694-1698.

Laosa, Luis M. "Child Care and the Culturally
Different Child." Child Care Quarterly
3(Winter, 1974):212-224.

Larkin, Ralph W. "Class, Race, Sex and
Preadolescent Attitudes." California
Journal of Educational Research 23(N, 1972):
213-223.

Laryea, Emmanuel B. "Race, Self-Concept and
Achievement." Doctoral dissertation,
Columbia U., 1972.

Lasch, Christopher. "Inequality and Education."
New York Review of Books 20(My 17, 1973):
19-25.

Lasker, Bruno. Race Attitudes in Children.
New York: Henry Holt and Co., 1929.

Laurent, James A. Do Pupil Race and/or School
Racial Balance Affect Academic Performance?
Bulletin: December, 1970. D, 1970. ERIC
ED 048 393.

_____. "Effects of Race and Racial Balance
of School on Academic Performance." Diss.
Abstr. Int'l., 1970, My, Vol. 30(11-A):4831.

Lawrence, Joan. "White Socialization: Black
Reality." Psychiatry, My, 1970.

Lawrence, Paul F. "Vocational Aspirations of
Negro Youth in California." Journal of
Negro Education, Winter, 1950.

Lazar, Irving and others. The Persistence of
Preschool Effects: A Long-Term Follow-Up
of Fourteen Infant and Preschool Experiments,
S, 1977. ERIC ED 148 470.

LeFlore, Dorothy L. Dodd. "Black Parents'
Perceptions of Schools in Relation to the
Education of Their Children." Doctoral
dissertation, U. of Oregon, 1972. Univ.
Midrofilms Order No. 73-13744.

LeVine, Elaine Sue. Ethnic Esteem Among
Anglo, Black, and Chicano Children.
San Francisco: R and E Research Associates,
1976.

Leader, Team. "Self-Concepts of Some Dis-
advantaged Students at Inner City High
School." Contemporary Education, Mr, 1968.
[Formerly, Teachers College Journal]

Lefebare, Andre. "The Relationship between
Self-Concept and Level of Aspiration with
Negro and White Children." Diss. Abstr.
Int'l. 32(5-B) N, 1971: 3036.

Lefebre, Carol. "Inner City School--as the
Children See It." Elementary School
Journal, O, 1966.

Legare, Jacques. "Methods for Measuring
School Performance through Cohort Analysis."
Demography 9(N, 1972).

Leifer, Anna. "Ethnic Patterns in Cognitive
Tasks." Doctoral dissertation, Yeshiva U.,
1972.

_____. "Ethnic Patterns in Cognitive Tasks."
Proceedings of the Annual Convention of
the American Psychological Association
7(1972):Pt. 1, 73-74.

_____. "Mosaics of Disadvantaged Negro and
White Preschoolers." Journal of Genetic
Psychology 121(S, 1972):59-63.

Lei, Tzuen-jen, Butler, Edgar W., Rowitz, Louis, and McAllister, Ronald J. "Agency-labeled Mentally Retarded Persons in a Metropolitan Area: An Ecological Study." American Journal of Mental Deficiency 79(J1, 1974): 22-31.

Lein, L. "Speech and Setting: American Migrant Children in School and At Home." Doctoral dissertation, Harvard U., 1973.

Leith, William R., and Mims, Howard A. "Cultural Influences in the Development and Treatment of Stuttering: A Preliminary Report on the Black Stutterer." Journal of Speech and Hearing Disorders 40(N, 1975): 459-466.

Lerner, Richard M., and Buehrig, Christie J. "The Development of Racial Attitudes in Young Black and White Children." Journal of Genetic Psychology 127(S, 1975):45-54.

Lerner, Richard M., and Knapp, John R. "Racial Attitude Structure in Early Adolescent White Children." Journal of Genetic Psychology 129(S, 1976):137-149.

_____. "Structure of Racial Attitudes in White Middle Adolescents." Journal of Youth and Adolescence 5(S, 1976):283-300.

Lerner, Richard M., and Schroeder, Christine. "Racial Attitudes in Young White Children: A Methodological Analysis." Journal of Genetic Psychology 127(S, 1975):3-12.

Leslie, Larry L., Leslie, Judith W., and Penfield, Douglas A. "The Effects of a Student Centered Special Curriculum Upon the Racial Attitudes of Sixth Graders." Journal of Experimental Education 41(Fall, 1972.

Lessing, Elise E. "Comparative Extension of Personal and Socio-Political Future Time Perspective." Perceptual and Motor Skills 33(O, 1971):415-422.

_____. "Racial Differences in Indices of Ego Functioning Relevant to Academic Achievement." Journal of Genetic Psychology 115 (1969):153-167.

_____. "Self-Concept of Black High School Students Varying in Endorsement of Black Power Ideology." Proceedings of the 81st Annual Convention of the American Psychological Association 9(1973):227-228.

Lessing, Elise E., and Clarke, Chester C. "An Attempt to Reduce Ethnic Prejudice and Assess Its Correlates in a Junior High School Sample." Educational Research Quarterly 1 (Summer, 1976):3-16.

Lessing, Elise E., and Zagorin, Susan W. "Black Power Ideology and College Students' Attitudes Toward Their Own and Other Racial Groups." Journal of Personality Social Psychology 21(Ja, 1972):61-73.

"Lessons in Alaskan Adaptation." Human Behavior 3(Mr, 1974):61. [Research by R. Darrel Bock and Carol Feldman on ability of Eskimos to reason abstractly]

Levin, Edith. "The Algebraic Ability of Children of the Colored Race." Master's thesis, U. of Chicago, 1937.

Levin, Hannah A. "A Psycholinguistic Investigation: Do Words Carve Up the World Differently for Negro and White Boys from City and Suburban Junior High Schools?" Doctoral dissertation, Rutgers U., 1964. Univ. Microfilms Order No. 64-10931.

Levin, Henry M. The Economic Implication of Mastery Learning. Stanford, CA: School of Education, Stanford U., My, 1973.

Levin, Henry M., and Michelson, Stephan. "Report on the Report on the Coleman Report" (letter). New York Times Magazine, S 14, 1969. [Critique of article by Christopher Jencks; see reply by Jencks, same source.]

Levine, Daniel U. "Cultural Diffraction in the Social System of the Low-Income School." School and Society, Mr 30, 1968.

Levine, Daniel U., Fiddmont, Norman S., Stephenson, Robert S., and Wilkinson, Charles. "Differences Between Black Youth Who Support the Black Panthers and the NAACP." Journal of Negro Education 42 (Winter, 1973):19-32.

Levine, Daniel U., Fiddmont, Norman, and New, Janet E. "Interracial Attitudes and Contracts. A Sample of White Students in Suburban Secondary Schools." Urban Education 5(Ja, 1971):309-327. [Jackson County, MI]

Levine, Daniel U. and others. Concentrated Poverty and Reading Achievement in Five Big Cities. Kansas City, MO: Center for the Study of Metropolitan Problems in Education, U. of Missouri, S, 1976.

Levy, John. "The Impact of Cultural Forms Upon Children's Behavior." Mental Hygiene 16 (Ap, 1932):208-220.

Levy, P., and Tucker, Joan. "Differential Effects of Streaming on Primary School Attainment." British Journal of Educational Psychology 42(F, 1972):75-79.

Lewis, Cheri L. "Ethnic and Social Class Differences in Values Related to Effective Coping Behavior." Diss. Abstr. Int'l., 1970, 30(7-B):3374.

Lewis, Franklin D. and others. "Reading Retardation: A Bi-Racial Comparison." Journal of Reading 13(1970):433-436,474-478.

Lewis, Hylan. Child Rearing Among Low Income Families. Washington, DC: Washington Center for Metropolitan Studies, 1961.

Lewis, Louisa. Culture and Social Interaction in the Classroom: An Ethnographic Report, N, 1970. ERIC ED 044 682.

Lewis, M., and Wilson, Cornielia. "Infant Development in Lower-Class American Families." Human Development 15(1972):112-127.

Lewis, Oscar. "The Culture of Poverty." Trans-action, N, 1963.

Lewit, David W., and Abner, Edward V. "Black-White Semantic Differences and Interracial Communication." Journal of Applied Social Psychology 1(J1-S, 1971):263-277.

Lezotte, Lawrence W., and Polite, Craig. Summary of the Results of a Student Evaluation of IDC 400 V. Race, Education, and Poverty, Ap, 1971. ERIC ED 056 944.

Lichtenberg, Philip, and Norton, Dolores G. Cognitive and Mental Development in the First Five Years of Life. A Review of Recent Research. Washington, DC: GPO, 1970.

Lichtman, Marilyn Vichman. "Intelligence, Creativity, and Language: An Examination of the Interrelationships of Three Variables Among Preschool, Disadvantaged Negro Children." Doctoral dissertation, George Washington U., 1969.

Liddle, G ordon P., and Rockwell, Robert E. "The Role of Parents and Family Life." Journal of Negro Education, Summer, 1964.

Liebert, Robert M. and others. "Effects of Vicarious Consequences and Race of Model Upon Initiative Performance by Black Children." Developmental Psychology 6 (My, 1972):453-456.

Lietz, Enno S. "Perceptual-Motor Abilities of Disadvantaged and Advantaged Kindergarten Children." Perceptual and Motor Skills 35(D, 1972):887-890.

Light, Richard J., and Smith, Paul V. "Accumulating Evidence: Procedures for Resolving Contradictions among Different Research Studies." Harvard Educational Review 41(N, 1971):429-471.

Lightfood, Sara. Worlds Apart: Relationships Between Families and Schools. New York: Basic Books, 1978.

Like They Say, Experience Teaches: And It Has Taught Us Something About School Racial Problems. Washington, DC: Community Relations Service, U.S. Department of Justice, 1978.

Likover, Belle. "The Effect of Black History on an Interracial Group of Children." Children 17(S-O, 1970):177-182.

Lilly, M. Stephen. "Improving Social Acceptance of Low Sociometric Status, Low Achieving Students." Exceptional Children 37(Ja, 1971):341-347.

Lincoln, William F. Mediation: A Transferable Process for the Prevention and Resolution of Racial Conflict in Public Secondary Schools, Je 30, 1976. ERIC ED 134 867.

Lindert, P. Family Inputs and Inequality Among Children. Madison: Institute for Research on Poverty, U. of Wisconsin, 1974.

Lindholm, Byron W. and others. "Racial Differences in Behavior Disorders of Children." Journal of School Psychology 16 (Spring, 1978):42-48.

Lindsey, J. K., and Cherkaoui, M. "Some Aspects of Social Class Differences in Achievement among 13-year-olds." Comparative Education 11(O, 1975):247-260.

Lindsey, Randall B. "A Study of White Dominance Behaviors in Interracial Task-Oriented Small Groups." Doctoral dissertation, Georgia State U., 1975. Univ. Microfilms Order No. 76-11,850.

Lindsley. Growth, Maturation and Development. Bethesda, MD: National Institutes of Child Health and Human Development, 1968.

Lines, Patricia M. "Race and Learning: A Perspective on the Research." Inequality in Education 11(Mr, 1972):26-34.

Lipe, Le Ora M. "An Investigation of Aspiration and Motor Performance Levels of Negro and White Sixth-Grade Students." Diss. Abstr. Int'l. 31, 9-A(Mr, 1971):4526.

Lipscomb, Lafayette Williams. "Parental Influence in the Development of Black Children's RAcial Self Esteem." Doctoral dissertation, U. of North Carolina, 1975. Univ. Microfilms Order No. 75-15665.

_____. "Racial Identity of Nursery School Children." Master's thesis, U. of North Carolina, 1972.

_____. Socialization Factors in the Development of Black Children's Racial Self-Esteem, Ag, 1975. ERIC ED 123 508.

Lipsyte, Robert. "I'm Free To Be Who I Want." New York Times Magazine, My 28, 1967. [Muhammad Ali (Cassius Clay)]

Litcher, John Hannibal. "Change in Attitudes Toward Blacks by White Elementary School Children after Use of Multiethnic Curricular Materials." Doctoral dissertation, U. of Minnesota, 1970. Univ. Microfilms Order No. 71-18771.

Litcher, John H., and Johnston, David W. "Changes in Attitudes Toward Negroes of White Elementary School Students After Use of Multiethnic Readers." Journal of Educational Psychology, Ap, 1969.

Litcher, John H. and others. "Use of Pictures of Multi-Ethnic Interaction to Change Attitudes of White Elementary School Students Toward Blacks." Psychological Reports 33(0, 1973):367-372.

Littleford, Michael S. "An Anthropological Study of the Internal Structure of an Experimental 'Problems of Democracy' Class in an All-Black High School." Doctoral dissertation, U. of Florida, 1970.

Lloyd, Barbara B. "Studies of Conservation with Yoruba Children of Differing Ages and Experience." Child Development 42(Je, 1971):415-428.

Lloyd, Dee Norman, and Bleach, Gail. Prediction of High School Dropout or Graduation from 3rd Grade Data, 1972. ERIC ED 085 623.

Lloyd, J. "The Self-Image of a Small Black Child." Elementary School Journal, My, 1967.

Locke, Alain L. "Minorities and the Social Mind." Progressive Education 12(Mr, 1935): 141-146.

Loflin, Marvin D. and others. Implications of the Linguistic Differences Between Black-Ghetto and White-Suburban Classrooms, F, 1971. ERIC ED 047 311.

Lohman, Mark R. "Changing a Racial Status Ordering: Some Implications." Education and Urban Society 4(Ag, 1972):383-402.

_____. Changing a Racial Status Ordering by Means of Role Modeling, My, 1970. ERIC ED 043 709.

Long, Herman H. "A Commentary on the Paper of Carl Backman." In Proceedings of the Conference on Psychology and the Process of Schooling in the Next Decade. Edited by M. C. Reynolds. Minneapolis, MN: Dept. of Audio-Visual Extension, U. of Minnesota, 1971.

_____. "Some Psychogenic Hazards of Segregated Education of Negroes." Journal of Negro Education 4(Jl, 1935):336-350.

Long, Margo Alexandre. "The Interracial Family in Children's Literature." Language Arts 55(Ap, 1978):489-497.

Long, Samuel. "Malevolent Estrangement: Political Alienation and Political Justification Among Black and White Adolescents." Youth and Society 7(D, 1975):99-129.

_____. "Personality and Political Alienation among White and Black Youth: A Test of the Social Deprivation Model." Journal of Politics 40(My, 1978):433-457.

_____. Psychological Sources of Systematic Rejection Among White and Black Adolescents, S, 1976. ERIC ED 131 167.

Longino, Charles F., Jr., and Wagoner, Jennings L., Jr. "Educational Criticism and the Transformation of Black Consciousness." Educational Forum 36(My, 1972):499-506.

Longstreet, Wilma S. Beyond Jencks: The Myth of Equal Schooling. Washington, DC: Association for Supervision and Curriculum Development, 1973.

Longus, Pharnal. "Factors that Influence Collective Behavior." Journal of Black Studies 6(Mr, 1976):291-298.

Lorenz, Gerda. "Aspirations of Low-Income Blacks and Whites: A Case of Reference Group Processes." American Journal of Sociology 78(S, 1972):371-398.

_____. "Patterns of Aspirations among Low-income Families of Different Ethnic Background." Master's thesis, Columbia U., 1965.

Lourie, Reginald S. "The First Three Years of Life: An Overview of a New Frontier of Psychiatry." American Journal of Psychiatry 127(My, 1971):33-39.

Luchterhand, Elmer, and Weller, Leonard. "Effects of Class, Race, Sex, and Educational Status on Patterns of Aggression of Lower-Class Youth." Journal of Youth and Adolescence 5(Mr, 1976):59-71.

Luckey, Evelyn Foreman. "The Relationship between Word Associations and Verbal Achievement of Black and White Children." Doctoral dissertation, Ohio State U., 1970.

Luecke, Daniel F., and McGinn, Noel F. "Regression Analyses and Education Production Functions: Can They Be Trusted?" Harvard Educational Review 45(Ag, 1975):325-350. [Effect of schooling on achievement]

Lundstein, Sara W., and Fruchter, Benjamin. Relationship of Thought Processes to Language Responses in Disadvantaged Children. Austin, TX, 1969.

Luong, Corina K. "An Analysis of Factors Related to Difficulties in Learning and Adjustment Among Minority Group Children." Diss. Abstr. Int'l., 1970, 30(10-B):4795-4796.

Lundell, Kerth T. "Labeling and Stigmatizing
Minority Children: A Behavioral Viewpoint."
Behaviorally Speaking, Je, 1971. [Society
of Behaviorists, 1515 N. Euclid Ave., Dayton,
OH 45406]

Lyons, Schley R. "The Political Socialization
of Ghetto Children: Efficacy and Cynicism."
Journal of Politics, My, 1970.

Mabe, Paul Alexander, III. "The Correlation
of Racial Attitudes as Measured by the
Preschool Racial Attitude Measure and
Sociomatric Choices for Second-grade
Children." Master's thesis, East Carolina
U., 1974.

Macaulay, Jacqueline. Is Welfare Bad for
Children?, D, 1975. ERIC ED 121 910.

Mackenzie, Carolyn S. "Motor Inhibition and
Capacity for Delay of Gratification in Two
Classes of Negro Boys." Diss. Abstr. Int'l.,
1970, Ag, Vol. 31(2-A):665.

MacMillan, Donald L. and others. "The Mentally
Retarded Label: A Theoretical Analysis and
Review of Research." American Journal of
Mental Deficiency 79(N, 1974):241-261.

Maddock, Richard C., and Kenny, Charles T.
"Impression Formation as a Function of
Age, Sex, and Race." Journal of Social
Psychology 89(Ap, 1973):233-243.

Maddox, G. A., and Ross, R. S. "Strong Words."
Childhood Education, Ja, 1969. [Words
thought to be ethnically offensive by
Negroes and whites]

Mahan, Juneau. "Black and White Children's
Racial Identification and Preference."
Journal of Black Psychology 3(Ag, 1976):
47-58.

Malina, Robert M. "Growth, Maturation, and
Performance of Philadelphia Negro and
White Elementary School Children." Diss.
Abstr. Int'l., 1969, 30(3-B):951.

Mangano, James F., and Towne, Richard C.
Improving Migrant Students' Academic
Achievement through Self-Concept Enhance-
ment, 1970. ERIC ED 049 868.

Mann, Ada Jo and others (eds). A Review of
Head Start Research Since 1969 and An
Annotated Bibliography. Washington, DC:
Office of Human Development Services, 1977.

Manning, Brad A., and others. Cooperative,
Trusting Behavior as a Function of Ethnic
Group Similarity-Dissimilarity and of
Immediate and Delayed Reward in a Two-Person
Game. Part of the Final Report, 1968.
ERIC ED 025 322.

Manning, Jean B. "The Influence of a Short-
Term Program to Improve the Self-Concept of
Selected Negro Children." Diss. Abstr.
Int'l. 31(7-A) Ja, 1971:3174.

Mannoni, Octave. "Itard and his Savage." New
Left Review 74(Jl-Ag, 1972):37-49.

Mansfield, Thomas. "Great Expectations" (an
interview). Urban Review, S, 1968.

Marjoribanks, Kevin. "Environment as a
Threshold Variable: An Examination."
Journal of Educational Research 67(Ja,
1974):210-212.

_____. "Ethnic and Environmental Influences
on Mental Abilities." American Journal of
Sociology 78(S, 1972):323-337

_____. "Ethnicity and Learning Patterns:
A Replication and an Explanation."
Sociology 6(1972):417-431.

Marotto, Richard Anthony. "'Posin to be
Chosen': An Ethnographic Study of Ten
Lower Class Male Adolescents in an Urban
High School." Doctoral dissertation,
State U. of New York at Buffalo, 1977.
Univ. Microfilms Order No. 7814236.

Marston, Wilfred G. "Social Class and Factor
in Ethnic and Racial Segregation." International Journal of Comparative Sociology
9(1968):145-153.

Martelle, Dorothy L. "Interracial Marriage
Attitudes Among High School Students."
Psychological Reports 27(D, 1970):1007-1010.

Martin, Dorothy Wohrna. The Inner-City Black
Male High School Student: His Self Concept,
Academic Achievement, and Occupational
Aspirations, Ap 7, 1972. ERIC ED 062 484.

Martin, Roy and others. "Effects of Race and
Social Class on Preschool Performance on
the Developmental Test of Visual-Motor
Integration." Psychology in the Schools
14(O, 1977):466-470.

Martin, Ruby W. "Realities and Fallacies of
Teaching Reading to Black High School
Students." Journal of Reading 18(Mr, 1975):
445-450.

Marwit, Samuel J., and Marwit, Karen L.
"Black Children's Use of Nonstandard
Grammar: Two Years Later." Developmental
Psychology 12(Ja, 1976):33-38. [2nd and
4th grades]

Marwit, Samuel J. and others. "Negro Children's Use of Nonstandard Grammar."
Journal of Educational Psychology 63(Je,
1972):218-224.

Marx, Ronald W., and Winne, Philip H. "Self-Concept and Achievement: Implications For Educational Programs." Integrateducation 13(Ja-F, 1975):30-31.

Marx, Ronald W., and Winne, Philip H. A Validation Study of Self-Concept in Low SES Black Children with Implications for Educational Programs, Ap, 1974. ERIC ED 090 306.

Massari, David J., and Jacqueline A. "Sex Differences in the Relationship of Cognitive Style and Intellectual Functioning in Disadvantaged Preschool Children." Journal of Genetic Psychology 122(Je, 1973):175-181.

Massey, Grace Carroll. "Self-Concept, Personal Control and Social Context Among Students in Inner City High Schools." Doctoral dissertation, Stanford U., 1975. Univ. Microfilms Order No. 75-25,570.

Masters, John C., and Peskay, Joel. "Effects of Race, Socioeconomic Status and Success or Failure upon Contingent and Non-contingent Self-Reinforcement in Children." Developmental Psychology 7(S, 1972):139-145.

Masters, Stanley H. "The Effect of Family Income on Children's Education: Some Findings on Inequality of Opportunity." Journal of Human Resources 4(Spring, 1969):158-175.

Mathis, Arthur, and Oyemade, Ura Jean. Ecological Influences on Psycho-social Development of Black Children: Interim Progress Report, Year II, Mr, 1976. ERIC ED 135 901.

Mathis, Harold I. "The Disadvantaged and the Aptitude Barrier." Personnel and Guidance Journal, Ja, 1969.

Matthews, Barbara Jean. "An Investigation of the Power and Peer Group Influences on the Attitudes and Behavior of Black Junior High School Students." Doctoral dissertation, Wayne State U., 1975. Univ. Microfilms Order No. 86-10,980

Matthews, Robert L. "Black Studies, Academic Achievement and the Self-Concept of Selected Tenth Graders." Diss. Abstr. Int'l. 32 (4-A), O, 1971;1920-1921.

May, Cornelius W. "Notes of a Black Man." Paper Tiger, Je, 1968.

Mayeske, George W., and Beaton, Albert E. Special Studies of Our Nation's Students. Washington, DC: GPO, 1975.

Mayeske, George W., Cohen, Wallace M., and Beaton, Albert E., Jr. "The Role of the Family in the Development of Student Achievement and Motivation." Technical Paper No. 2. Washington, DC: Office of Program Planning and Evaluation, Office of Education, Je 25, 1969.

Mayeske, George W., Cohen, Wallace M., Beaton, Albert E., Jr., and Okada, Tetsuo. "The Roles of the Family and of the School in the Development of Student Achievement and Motivation." Technical Paper No. 4. Washington, DC: Office of Program Planning and Evaluation, U.S. Office of Education, Ag 20, 1969.

Mayeske, George, Okada, Tetsuo, and Beaton, Albert E., Jr. A Study of the Attitude Toward Life of Our Nation's Students. Washington, DC: GPO, 1973.

Mayeske, George, Okada, Tetsuo, Cohen, Wallace M., Beaton, Albert E., Jr., and Wisler, Carl E. A Study of the Achievement of Our Nation's Students. Washington, DC: GPO, 1973.

Mayeske, George W., Okada, Tetsuo, Cohen, Wallace M., Beaton, Albert E., Jr., and Wisler, Carl E. Variations in Achievement and Motivation by Family Background and Geographic Location. Washington, DC: Office of Program Planning and Evaluation, U.S. Office of Education, D 31, 1969.

Mayfield, William G. "Mental Health in the Black Community." Social Work 17(My, 1972): 106-110.

Maynard, Peter E. "Assessing the Vocational Maturity of Inner City Youths." Diss. Abstr. Int'l. 31(9-A), Mr, 1971:4468.

Maynard, Rebecca. "The Effects of the Rural Income Maintenance Experiment on the School Performance of Children." American Economic Review 62(F, 1977):370-375.

Maynard, Rebecca A., and Murnane, Richard J. Will Welfare Reform Improve Children's School Performance? Princeton, NJ: Mathematics Policy Research, Ja 19, 1978.

Mayo, George E. "A Comparison of the 'Racial' Attitudes of White and Negro High School Students in 1940 and 1948." Doctoral dissertation, Ohio State U., 1950.

Mays, Luberta. On Meeting Real People: An Evaluation Report on Vegetable Soup: The Effects of a Multi-Ethnic Children's Television Series on Intergroup Attitudes of Children. Final Report to New York State Education Department Contract No. C82456, Ag, 1975.

McAdoo, Harriette A. "Racial Attitudes and Self-Concepts of Black Preschool Children." Diss. Abstr. Int'l. Vol. 31(8-A), F, 1971: 3963.

McAdoo, Harriette Pipes. A Different View of Race Attitudes and Self Concepts in Black Pre-School Children, Ag, 1973. ERIC ED 102 035.

McAdoo, Harriette Pipes. A Reexamination of
the Relationship Between Self Concept and
Race Attitudes of Young Black Children, Mr
25, 1976. ERIC ED 122 968.

_____. Components of Educational Achievement
and Mobility in Black Families, Ap 8, 1977.
ERIC ED 141 208.

_____. The Impact of Extended Family Variables
Upon the Upward Mobility Families, D, 1977.
ERIC ED 150 234.

McAdoo, John L. "An Exploratory Study of
Racial Attitude Change in Black Preschool
Children Using Differential Treatments."
Diss. Abstr. Int'l. Vol. 31(8-A), F, 1971:
3963-3964.

_____. An Experimental Study of Racial Atti-
tude Change in Black Preschool Children.
1970. ERIC ED 062 497.

_____. The Relationship Between Observed
Paternal Attitudes, Behavior, and Self-
Esteem of Black Pre-School Children, Ag 12,
1976. ERIC ED 130 793.

_____. Self Concepts and Racial Attitudes
of Northern and Southern Black Preschool
Children, 1970. ERIC ED 062 496.

McClung, Franklin B., and Stunden, Alastair A.
Mental Health Consultation to Programs for
Children. Washington, DC: GPO, 1970.

McCluskey, Lawrence. "The Interrelationships
of Student Attitude and Student Performance
in Black New York City Elementary School
Students." Doctoral dissertation, Columbia
U., 1975. Univ. Microfilms Order No.
75-20,209.

McConochie, Daniel and others. An Exploratory
Examination of Individual, Family, and School
Influences on Psychosocial Maturity. N,
1974. ERIC ED 102 492.

McCord, William, Howard, John, Friedberg,
Bernard, and Harwood, Edwin. Life Styles
in the Ghetto. NY: Norton, 1969.

McCormick, Charles H., and Karabinus, Robert A.
"Relationship of Ethnic Groups' Self-
Esteem and Anxiety to School Success."
Educational and Psychological Measurement
36(Winter, 1976):1093-1100.

McCormick, Marijo K., and Williams, Juanita H.
"Effects of a Conpensatory Program on Self-
Report, Achievement and Aspiration Level of
'Disadvantaged' High School Students."
Journal of Negro Education 43(Winter, 1974):
47-52. [Upward Bound, U. of South Florida]

McCullough, Lloyd M. Social and Academic
Characteristics Assessments of Black Inner-
City High School Students, 1975. ERIC ED
126 189.

McDaniel, Ernest, and Moe, Alden J. "High-
Frequency Words Used in the Writing of
Second-Grade Students From Varying Socio-
economic and Ethnic Backgrounds." Education
93(F-Mr, 1973):241-245.

McDaniel, Ernest and others. Measurement of
Concept Formation and Problem-Solving in
Disadvantaged Elementary School Children,
Ag, 1973. ERIC ED 090 318.

McDermott, R. R. "Achieving School Failure:
An Anthropological Approach to Illiteracy
and Social Stratification." In Education
and Cultural Processes: Toward an Anthropology of Education. Edited by George A.
Spindler. New York: Rinehart, Holt and
Winston, 1974, pp. 82-113.

_____. "Selective Attention and the Politics
of Everyday Life: A Biosocial Inquiry into
School Failure and the Persistence of
Parish Minorities Across Generations."
Doctoral dissertation, Stanford U., 1974.

McDonald J., and Stephenson, S. "The Effect
of Income Maintenance on the School-
Enrollment and Labor Supply Decisions of
Teenagers." In The Gary Income Maintenance
Experiment: Initial Findings Report. Vol.
II, Chapter 4. Edited by K. Kehner.
Bloomington: Indiana U., 1977.

McDonald, Marjorie. Not By the Color of Their
Skin. The Impact of Racial Differences on
the Child's Development. New York: International Universities Press, 1970. [Hanna
Perkins School, Cleveland, OH]

McDonald, Robert L. "Effects of Sex, Race,
and Class on Self, Idea-Self, and Parental
Ratings in Southern Adolescents." Perceptual and Motor Skills, Ag, 1968.

McDowell, Sophia F. "How Anti-White Are Negro
Youth?" American Education, Mr, 1968.

_____. "Patterns of Preference by Negro
Youth for White and Negro Associates."
Phylon 32(Fall, 1971):290-301. [District
of Columbia]

_____. Prejudices and Other Interracial
Attitudes of Negro Youth. Final Report,
Je 15, 1966-Ag 31, 1967. Washington, DC:
Dept. of Sociology, Howard U. Report No.
BR-6-8520, 1967. ERIC ED 019 390.

_____. Willingness of Negro High School
Students and Dropouts to Associate with
Whites. Final Report, S, 1970. ERIC ED
047 336.

McGaw, Barry, and Joreskog, Karl G. Factorial
Invariance of Ability Measures in Groups
Differing in Intelligence and Socioeconomic
Status, N, 1970. ERIC ED 053 156.

McGraw, Myrtle Byram. A Comparative Study of a Group of Southern White and Negro Infants. New York: Columbia U., Genetic Psychology Monographs, Vol. 10, No. 1, 1931.

McKay, H., McKay, A., and Sinisterra, L. Stimulation of Cognitive and Social Competence in Preschool Age Children Affected by the Multiple Deprivations of Depressed Urban Environments. Cali, Colombia: Human Ecology Research Foundation, 1970.

McKay, H. and others. "Improving Cognitive Ability in Chronically Deprived Children." Science 200(Ap 21, 1978).

McKeachie, W. J. "The Decline and Fall of the Laws of Learning." Educational Researcher 3(Mr, 1974):7-11.

McMurrin, Sterling M. (ed). The Conditions for Educational Equality, CED Supplementary Paper No. 34, Jl, 1971. ERIC ED 057 118.

_____. Resources for Urban Schools: Better Use and Balance. CED Supplementary Paper No. 33, My, 1971. ERIC ED 057 117.

McMurtry, C. Allen. "The Relationship of Positive and Negative Evaluative Adjectives Associated with Racial Figures in Preschool Children." Master's thesis, Wake Forest U., 1969.

McMurtry, C. Allen, and Williams, John E. "Evaluation Dimension of the Affective Meaning System of the Preschool Child." Developmental Psychology 6(Mr, 1972): 238-246.

McNeil, Keith A., and Phillips, Beeman N. "Scholastic Nature of Responses to the Environment in Selected Subcultures." Journal of Educational Psychology 60 (Ap, 1969):79-85. [Austin, TX]

McPartland, James. "Coleman. Sifting Through the Data." Center Forum, D 23, 1968.

McPartland, James, and Sprehe, J. T. Racial and Regional Inequalities in School Resources Relative to Their Educational Outcomes. Baltimore, MD: Center for Social Organization of Schools, Johns Hopkins U., N, 1972.

McVeigh, Frank J. "What It Means to Be Black." Social Education 34(D, 1970).

McWhinnie, Harold J. "A Note on Methodology in Using Children's Figure Drawing to Assess Racial and Cultural Differences." Studies in Art Education 13(Winter, 1972):30-33.

Means, Fred E. "Self Image--A Black Perspective." Journal of General Education 24 (Ap, 1972):51-58.

Medlicott, Paul. "Language and Class." New Society, Je 5, 1975.

Meers, Dale R. "Contributions of a Ghetto Culture to Symptom Formation: Psychoanalytic Studies of Ego Anomalies in Childhood." Psychoanalytic Study of the Child 25(1970):209-230.

_____. "Psychoanalytic Research and Intellectual Functioning of Ghetto Reared, Black Children." U.S. Congress, 92nd, 2nd session, Senate Committee on Labor and Public Welfare, Subcommittee on Children and Youth and Subcommittee on Employment, Manpower, and Poverty. In Headstart, Child Development Legislation, 1972... Washington, DC: GPO, 1972.

_____. "Traumatic and Cultural Distortions of Psychoneurotic Symptoms in a Black Ghetto." U.S. Congress, 92nd, 2nd session, Senate Committee on Labor and Public Welfare, Sub-Committee on Children and Youth and Sub-Committee on Employment, Manpower, and Poverty. In Headstart, Child Development Legislation, 1972. Joint Hearing... Washington, DC: GPO, 1972.

Meier, Deborah. "Learning Not to Learn." Dissent, N-D, 1968.

Meissner, Judith A. "Use of Relational Concepts by Inner-City Children." Journal of Educational Psychology 67(F, 1975):22-29.

Meja, Volker. "How Unprejudiced Are the Young?" Kansas Journal of Sociology, Fall, 1967.

Melchiode, Gerald, Gould, Jain, and Fink, Paul J. "Beware of Whites Bearing Gifts." American Journal of Psychiatry 127(D, 1970): 803-808.

Meltzer, Bert. "The Influence of the Duration of Interracial Classroom Control on the Development of Interpersonal Cognitive Skills." Doctoral dissertation, U. of Wisconsin, 1970.

Meltzer, Carole G. "The Effects of Age, Race and Victim, and Ability to Take Another's Role in Helpfulness and Sharing in Children." Diss. Abstr. Int'l. 1970(Jl)Vol. 31(1-B): 399-400.

Meltzer, H. "Nationality Preferences and Stereotypes of Colored Children." Journal of Genetic Psychology, Je, 1939.

Mendelsohn, A. Robert. "Open the Door for All the Percies." Integrated Education (N-D, 1969):14-17.

"Mental Development and Learning Disability: A Marxist Approach." Political Affairs 54 (Je, 1975):14-20.

Mercer, Jane R. Adolescent Prejudice: A
Commentary, Ja 16, 1976. ERIC ED 133 402.

_____. "Institutionalized Anglocentrism:
Labeling Mental Retardates in the Public
Schools." In Race, Change, and Urban
Setting, pp. 311-338. Edited by Peter
Orleans and William Russell Ellis, Jr.
Beverly Hills, CA: Sage, 1971.

_____. "Sociocultural Factors in Labeling
Mental Retardates." Peabody Journal of
Education 48(Ap, 1971):188-203.

Messmore, Peter B. "Multi-Ethnic Reading
Texts: The Role of Inferred Story-
Character Identification and Reading Comprehension." Journal of Reading Behavior
5(Spring, 1972-1973):126-133.

Meyer, Peter. "Schooling and the Reproduction
of the Social Division of Labor." Honors
Thesis, Harvard U., Mr, 1972.

Meyers, Edna O. "'Pride and Prejudice.'"
Journal of Contemporary Psychotherapy 3
(Spring, 1971):105-110.

Meyers, Elizabeth. "School Psychological
Referrals in an Inner City School." Psychology in the Schools 12(O, 1975):412-420.

Mezei, Louis. "Perceived Social Pressure as an
Explanation of Shifts in the Relative Influence of Race and Belief on Prejudice Across
Social Interactions." Journal of Personality and Social Psychology 19(Jl, 1971):69-
81.

Michelson, Stephan. "The Further Responsibility
of Intellectuals." Harvard Education Review
43(F, 1973):92-105. [In re: Jencks,
Inequality]

Middleton, R. "Alienation, Race, and Education." American Sociological Review, D,
1963.

Milgram, Norman A. "Locus of Control in Negro
and White Children at Four Age Levels."
Psychological Reports 29(O, 1971):459-465.

Migram, Norman A., Shore, Milton F., Riedel,
Wolfgang W., and Malasky, Charlotte.
"Level of Aspiration and Locus of Control in
Disadvantaged Children." Psychological
Reports 27(O, 1970):343-350.

Miller, Gordon W. "Factors in School Achievement and Social Class." Journal of
Educational Psychology 61(Ag, 1970):260-269.

Miller, LaMar P. Non-Intellectual Factors in
the Education of Black High School Students,
F 6, 1969. ERIC ED 029 066.

_____. "The Strengths of the Black Child."
Instructor 82(My, 1973):20-21).

Miller, Thomas W. Dimensions of Mother-Child
Interaction as They Affect the Self-Esteem
of the Child. S, 1971. ERIC ED 054 287.

Milliones, Jake. "Identity and Black Children."
Notre Dame Journal of Education I(Summer,
1970):118-121.

Milner, David. Children and Race. Harmondsworth: Penguin Books, 1975.

Mingione, Ann Dissinger. "Need for Achievement
in Negro, White, and Puerto Rican Children."
Journal of Consulting and Clinical Psychology, F, 1968.

Minority Education 1960-1978: Grounds, Gains,
and Gaps. 2 vols. S, 1978. ML-Group for
Policy Studies in Education, CEMREL, Inc.,
875 North Michigan Avenue, Chicago, IL 60611.

Mischel, Walter. Psychosocial Deprivations and
Self-Control. Bethesda, MD: National Institute of Child Health and Human Development,
1968.

Mitra, Shib K. "Mirror, Mirror...A Brief Note
on American Educational Research." American
Educational Research Journal 11(Winter, 1974):
41-49.

Mizelle, Richard M. "Implications of Cultural
Pluralism for Individualizing Instruction."
High School Journal 60(D, 1976):117-123.

Mock, Ronald L., and Tuddenham, Read D. "Race
and Conformity among Children." Developmental Psychology 4(My, 1971):349-365.

Moerk, Ernst L. "Age and Epogenic Influences
on Aspirations of Minority and Majority
Group Children." Journal of Counseling
Psychology 21(Jl, 1974):294-298.

Money, John. "Special Sex Education and
Cultural Anthropology, with Reference to
Mental Deficiency, Physical Deformity, and
Urban Ghettos." Journal of Special Education
5(Winter, 1971):369-372.

Moon, Robert D. The Effect of Early School
Entrance or Preschool Programs on the School
Achievement and Attitudes of Disadvantaged
Children. 1975. ERIC ED 146 198.

Moore, Carol. "Interim." Integrated Education,
Ag-N, 1965.

Moore, Clifford L. "The Racial Preference and
Attitude of Preschool Black Children."
Journal of Genetic Psychology 129(S, 1976):
37-44.

Moore, Evelyn K. "A Black Perspective on Child
Development." Inequality in Education 13
(D, 1972):43-48.

_____. "Federal Preschool and Early Childhood
Programs from a Black Perspective." Congressional Record, A 12, 1972. E 3577-3579.

Moores, Donald F., and Oden, Chester W., Jr. "Educational Needs of Black Deaf Children." *American Annals of the Deaf* 122(Je, 1977): 313-318.

Morgan, Betty M. "An Investigation of Children's Books Containing Characters from Selected Minority Groups Based on Specified Criteria." Doctoral dissertation, Southern Illinois U., 1973.

Morgan, Harry. *Black Children in American Classrooms*, Ap, 1977. ERIC ED 139 901

_____. *Towards a Theory of Selected Knowledge Acquisition Patterns Among Black Children*, Mr 5, 1976. ERIC ED 127 380.

_____. *Towards a Theory of Selected Knowledge Acquisition Patterns Among Black Children*, 1977. ERIC ED 141 462.

Morin, Andre. "Do Educational Films Produced With Same-Race-Communicators Promote Learning?" *Journal of Negro Education* 45 (Spring, 1976):197-203.

Morin, Rita J. "Black Child, White Parents: A Beginning Biography." *Child Welfare* 56 (N, 1977):576-583.

Morland, J. Kenneth. "A Comparison of Race Awareness in Northern and Southern Children." *American Journal of Orthopsychiatry*, Ja, 1966.

_____. "The Development of Racial Bias in Young Children." *Theory Into Practice*, II (1963).

_____. "Race Awareness among American and Hong Kong Chinese Children." *American Journal of Sociology*, N, 1969.

_____. *Racial Attitudes in School Children: From Kindergarten through High School*. Washington, D. C.: U. S. Office of Education, N, 1972.

_____. "Racial Self-Identification: A Study of Nursery School Children." *American Catholic Sociological Review*, Fall, 1963.

Morland, J. Kenneth, and Williams, John E. "Cross Cultural Measurement of Racial and Ethnic Attitudes by the Semantic Differential." *Social Forces* 48(1969):107-112.

Morris, Joseph. "Personal Adjustment of the High Achieving Negro Student." Doctoral dissertation, U. of Michigan, 1968.

Morris, Steven. "The Fight for Black Babies." *Ebony* (S, 1973). [Transracial adoption]

Morris, William C. and others. *Minorities in the Youth Conservation Corps: A Study of Cultural Groups in the 1974 YCC Program*, Ja, 1975. ERIC ED 135 653.

Morse, Richard J. "Self-Concept of Ability. Significant Others and School Achievement of Eighth-Grade Students: A Comparative Investigation of Negro and Caucasian Students." Master's thesis, Michigan State U., 1963.

Morse, Roberta N., and Piers, Ellen V. *Variable Affecting Self-Concept in Black Disadvantaged Boys*, My, 1973. ERIC ED 090 330.

Mosby, Doris P. *Is There a Unique Black Personality?* Ap 24, 1970. ERIC ED 040 255.

Moss, Martin K., Miller, Richard, and Page, Richard A. "The Effects of Racial Context on the Perception of Physical Attractiveness." *Sociometry* 38(1975):525-535.

Mueser, Anne Marie. "So, Why Aren't We Teaching These Children to Read?" *Education for the Disadvantaged Child* 2(Winter, 1974): 5-8.

Muller, Douglas G., and Leonetti, Robert. *Primary Self-Concept Scale: Test Manual*. Fort Worth, TX: National Consortia for Bilingual Education. ERIC ED 062 847.

Mumbauer, Corinne C , and Gray, Susan W. *Resistance to Temptation in Young Negro Children in Relation to Sex of the Subject, Sex of the Experimenter and Father Absence or Presence*, 1969. ERIC ED 032 138.

Murnane, Richard John. "The Impact of School Resources on the Learning of Inner-City Children." Doctoral dissertation, Yale U., 1974. Univ. Microfilm Order No. 75-1386.

_____. *The Impact of School Resources on the Learning of Inner City Children*. Cambridge, MA: Ballinger, 1975.

Murray, Ellen, and Wellmen, Barry. *Success and Self-Conception: The Impact of Academic Grades on the Student Role Identities of Black and White Adolescents*, Je, 1971. ERIC ED 055 140.

Murray, John P. and others (eds.). *Television and Social Behavior*. Vol. II: *Television and Social Learning*. Washington, D. C.: GPO, 1972.

Murungi, John J. "On Being a Black Son in the U.S.A." *Journal of Afro-American Issues* 3 (Summer/Fall, 1975):279-290.

Musgrove, Walter J. "Comparisons of Low Socioeconomic Black and White Kindergarten Children." *Academic Therapy Quarterly* 6 (Winter, 1970-1971):163-167.

_____. "A Follow-Up Study of Black and White Kindergarten Children on Academic Achievement and Social Adjustment." *Academic Therapy Quarterly* 7(Winter, 1971-1972):123-129.

_____. "A Follow-Up Study of Low Socio-Economic Negro and White Children on Scholastic Achievement." Journal of Negro Education 41(Winter, 1972):62-64.

Musgrove, Walter J., and Lawson, John R. "A Comparison of Lower Class Negro and White Children to Three Standardized Tests." Journal of Negro Education 40(Winter, 1971): 53-55.

Mushkin, Selma J., with Stageberg, Stephen. National Assessment and Social Indicators, Ja, 1973. Washington, D. C.: GPO, 1973. [Summarizes racial differentials]

Myers, Vincent. "Drug-Related Cognitions Among Minority Youth." Journal of Drug Education 7(1977):53-62.

MYCLU Statewide Youth Advocacy Project. Failing Students-Failing Schools. A Study of Dropouts and Discipline in New York State. Ap, 1978. NYCLU Statewide Youth Advocacy Project, 429 Power Building, Rochester NY 14614.

Nabdell, Betty. Race, Social Power, and Imitation. Final Report, N, 1971. ERIC ED 059 951.

"NABSW Opposes Trans-Racial Adoption." National Association of Black Social Workers News 1 (Ja, 1973).

National Alliance of Black School Superintendents. Program Research and Development for School Systems with High Percentages of Minority Students. II. Washington, D. C.: Office of African-American Affairs, U. S. Office of Education, O, 1973.

National Assessment of Educational Progress. Changes in Political Knowledge and Attitudes, 1969-76. Denver, CO: Education Commission of the States, Ja, 1978.

_____. Education for Citizenship. A Bicentennial Survey. Denver: Education Commission of the States, N, 1976.

_____. Functional Literacy. Basic Reading Performance. A Brief Summary and Highlights of an Assessment of 17-Year-Old Students in 1974 and 1975. Denver, CO: Education Commission of the States, 1976.

_____. Reading Change, 1970-75: Summary Volume. Washington, D. C.: National Center for Education Statistics, 1978.

_____. Reading in America: A Perspective on Two Assessments. Denver: Education Commission of the States, O, 1976.

National Center for Education Statistics. National Longitudinal Study of the High School Class of 1972. Changes in Attitudes One and One-Half Years After Graduation. Washington, D. C.: GPO, 1975.

National Center for Health Statistics. School Achievement of Children 6-11 Years-As Measured by the Reading and Arithmetic Subtests of the Wide Range Achievement Test. United States. Washington, D. C.: GPO, 1970.

National Institute of Child Health and Human Development. The Social Sciences and Mental Retardation: Family Components. Washington, D. C.: National Institutes of Health, 1968.

National Institute of Mental Health. Mental Health Services for Children. Washington, D. C.: GPO, O, 1968.

National Public Radio. The Minorities Are Coming. Je 7, 1976. ERIC ED 131 171.

National Scholarship Service and Fund for Negro Students. A National Profile of Black Youth: Class of 1971. NY: NSSFNS, Ja, 1972. [Order from Publications Division, Survey Research Services, National Computer Systems, 4401 W. 76th Street, Minneapolis, MN 55435]

Neely, J. J., Heckel, R. V., and Leichtman, H. M. "The Effect of Race of Model and Response Consequences to the Model on Imitation in Children." Journal of Social Psychology 89 (Ap, 1973):225-231.

Nelson, Richard C. and others. "Racial Understanding Revisited." Elementary School Guidance and Counseling 5(O, 1970):59-63.

Newby, Robert G. "The Effect of Racial Consciousness of Black Youth on White Influence in Small Groups." Doctoral dissertation, Stanford U., 1974.

Newman, Arthur J. "Sociologistic Concepts of Culture: Some Inadequacies." Educational Theory 21(Summer, 1971):288-296.

Newmeyer, J. A. "Creativity and Nonverbal Communication in Preadolescent White and Black Children." Doctoral dissertation, Harvard U., 1970.

Newton, Eunice S. "Bibliotherapy in the Development of Minority Group Self Concept." Journal of Negro Education, Summer, 1969.

Neilson, Jacqueline. "Tayari: Black Homes for Black Children." Child Welfare 55(Ja, 1976): 41-50. [San Diego, CA]

Nichols, Nancy J., and McKinney, Ann Watts. "Black or White Socio-Economically Disadvantaged Pupils--They Aren't Necessarily Inferior." Journal of Negro Education 46 (Fall, 1977):443-449.

Nichols, Robert C. School Effects on Achievement, Ap, 1976. ERIC ED 126 104.

Nobles, Wade W. "Psychological Research and the Black Self-Concept: A Critical Review." Journal of Social Issues 29(1973):11-31.

Noel, Donald L. "Minority Responses to Intergroup Situations." Phylon, Winter, 1969.

Noel, Joseph R. "The Norm of White Antiblack Prejudice in the United States." International Journal of Group Tensions 2(1972):51-62.

Nolle, David B. "Changes in Black Sons and Daughters: A Panel Analysis of Black Adolescents' Orientation Toward Their Parents." Journal of Marriage and the Family 34(Ag, 1972):443-447.

Noonan, Pat and others. Attitudes of Parents of Selected Groups Toward Education and Their Aspirations of Education for Their Children. Self-Concept and Educational Variables Among Black, Jewish, and White Non-Jewish Students. ERIC ED 040 431.

Noonan, Richard D. School Resources, Social Class, and Student Achievement: A Comparative Study of School Resource Allocation and the Social Distribution of Mathematics in Ten Countries. NY: Wiley, 1976.

Norton, Dolores G. "Environment and Cognitive Development: A Comparative Study of Socio-Economic Status and Race." Doctoral dissertation, Bryn Mawr College, 1969.

Nurseries in Cross-Cultural Education. Progress Report, Je, 1968. ERIC ED 023 460.

Nurss, Joanne R., and Day, David E. "Imitation, Comprehension and Production of Grammatical Structures." Journal of Verbal Learning and Verbal Behavior 10(F, 1971):68-74.

Nuttall, Ronald L. "Some Correlates of High Need for Achievement Among Urban Northern Negroes." Journal of Abnormal and Social Psychology, Je, 1964.

Oberle, Wayne H. and others. "Place of Residence and the Role Model Preference of Black Boys and Girls." Adolescence 13(Spring, 1978):13-20.

O'Block, Frank R., and Hulick, Charles. "Facilitating Racial Understanding." Illinois Schools Journal 51(Winter, 1971):182-186.

Oehlbach, Sally J. The Culture of Poverty Among American Negroes. 1966. ERIC ED 016 725.

Offenbacher, Deborah T. "Cultures in Conflict: Home and School as Seen Through the Eyes of Lower Class Students." Urban Review, My, 1968.

_____. Cultures in Conflict: Home and School as Seen Through the Eyes of Lower Class Students. Final Report. New York, NY: New School for Social Research, Ja, 1969. ERIC ED 027 361.

Ogletree, Earl. "Skin Color Preference of the Negro Child." Journal of Social Psychology 79(1969):143-144.

Ogletree, Earl, and Wilson, Rhonda. "Skin Color Preference of Black Children." Illinois School Research 12(Winter, 1976):29-34.

Ohlendorf, George Werner. "The Educational Status Attainment Process of Rural Males in the South." Doctoral dissertation, Texas A&M U., 1975.

Ohuche, R. Ogbonna. "Piaget and the Mende of Sierra Leone." Journal of Experimental Education 39(Summer, 1971):75-77.

Okada, Masahito, and Sullivan, Howard J. Story-Setting Preferences of Inner-City Children, F, 1971. ERIC ED 049-340.

Okada, Tetsue, Cohen, Wallace M., and Mayeske, George W. Growth in Achievement for Different Racial, Regional and Socio-Economic Groupings of Students. Technical Paper No. 1. Washington, DC: Office of Program Planning and Evaluation, U.S. Office of Education, My 16, 1969.

Olmsted, P., Parks, C., and Rickel, A. "The Development of Classification Skills in the Preschool Child." International Review of Education 16(1970):67-80.

Olsen, Henry D. Changes in Academic Roles of Black and White Compensatory Education Students and Its Effects on Self-Concept of Academic Ability, 1972. ERIC ED 063 219.

_____. The Effect of a Program for Disadvantaged Youth Developing Self-Concept of Academic Ability. Buffalo, NY: Office of Admissions and Records, State U. College at Buffalo, 1970.

Olsen, Mary. "Cleanliness Is a Middle-Class Racist Attitude." Education 91(F-Mr, 1971):274-276.

Olson, Arthur V., and Rosen, Carl L. A Comparison of White and Negro Ninth Grade Students' Reading Interests, F, 1967. ERIC ED 010 980.

Olson, Martin N. "Ways to Achieve Quality in School Classrooms: Some Definitive Answers." Phi Delta Kappan 53(S, 1971):63-65.

Olshin, David. "The Relationship of Race and Social Class to Intelligence and Reading Achievement at Grades One and Five." Diss. Abstr. Int'l. 32(4-A)0, 1971, 1923.

O'Malley, Patrick M. and others. Five Years Beyond High School: Causes and Consequences of Educational Attainment, Ap, 1977. ERIC ED 136 077.

Omari, I. M. "Cross Cultural Studies on the Abilities of Children." Prospects 6(1976): 370-380.

"Ombudsman for Minority Individuals: A Conversation with Robert Fuchigami on Exceptional Child Education." Exceptional Children 44 (Ja, 1978):240-243.

O'Reilly, Alora. "Racial Attitudes of Negro Preschoolers." California Journal of Educational Research 22(My, 1971):126-130.

Orost, Jan H. Racial Attitudes Among White Kindergarten Children from Three Different Environments, Ja, 1971. ERIC ED 051 882.

Orpen, Christopher. "The Effect of Cultural Factors on the Relationship Between Prejudice and Personality." Journal of Psychology 78 (My, 1971):73-79. [South Africa]

Orto, Arthur Dell, and LaFleur, Kenneth. "Racial and Cultural Differences in Ghetto Education." National Catholic Guidance Conference Journal 15(Summer, 1971):278-281.

Osborne, Robert Travis. "Population Pollution." Journal of Psychology 76(N, 1970):187-192.

_____. "Racial Differences in School Achievement." Mankind Monographs, III, N, 1962.

_____. "School Achievement of White and Negro Children of the Same Mental and Chronological Ages." Mankind Quarterly 2 (Jl-S, 1961):26-29.

Oseroff, Andrew, and Birch, Jack W. "Clearinghouse: Relationships of Socioeconomic Background and School Performance of Partially Seeing Children." Exceptional Children 38 (O, 1971):158-159.

Ouckama, Michael Patrick. "An Exploratory Investigation of Attitudes Toward Separation among Black High School Students as Related to Selected Variables." Doctoral dissertation, Ohio State U., 1975. Univ. Microfilms Order No. 75-26636.

Paige, Jeffrey M. "Changing Patterns of Anti-White Attitudes Among Blacks." Journal of Social Issues 26(Fall, 1970):69-86.

Pallone, Nathaniel J. and others. "Key Influences of Occupational Preference among Black Youth." Journal of Counseling Psychology 17(N, 1970):498-501.

Pallone, Nathaniel, Jr., Richard, Fred S., and Hurley, Robert B. Race, Sex, and Social Mobility: An Exploration of Occupational Aspirations and Expectations Among Black and White Youth and Four New York State Cities. Albany, NY: Bureau of Occupational Education Research, 1970.

Pallone, Nathaniel J. and others. Race, Sex, and Social Mobility: An Exploration of Occupational Aspirations and Expectations among Black and White Youth in Four New York State Cities. 1969. ERIC ED 056 145.

Palmer, Edward L. Color Preference as a Distinct Forerunner of Color Prejudice in the Young Child. Dissertation Abstracts International Vol. 31(8-A) (F, 1971):4265-4266.

_____. "Color Prejudice in Children as a Function of Race, Age, and Residence Neighborhood." Proceedings of the 81st Annual Convention of the American Psychological Association 8(1973):225-226.

_____. "General Color Preference in Young Children of Different Race, Age, and Neighborhood of Reference." Perceptual and Motor Skills 36(Je, 1973):842.

_____. The Public Kindergarten Concept as a Factor in Racial Attitudes, 1975. ERIC ED 129 936.

Palmer, Francis H. "Socioeconomic Status and Intellectual Performance Among Negro Preschool Boys." Developmental Psychology 3 (1970):1-9. [Harlem]

Palmore, Erdman. "What Are Racial Traits? A Three Dimensional Analysis." Journal of Social and Behavioral Sciences 18(Fall-Winter 1971-1972):50-57.

Panos, Robert J., and Edgert, Penny L. Black Youth: Characteristics Related to Geographical Location. NY: National Scholarship Service and Fund for Negro Students, F, 1972. [Order from Publications Division, Survey Research Services, National Computer Systems, 4401 W. 76th St., Minneapolis, MN 55435]

Pardi, Marco. Academic Rank and Self-Esteem Among Black Urban Students." Master's thesis, Washington U., Je, 1970.

Paretti, Joseph. Examiner Sex, Examiner Race and Anxiety Effects on the Testing of Black School Children, 1975. ERIC ED 142 853.

Parish, Thomas S. "Changing Anti-Negro Attitudes in Caucasian Children through Mediated Stimulus Generalization." Doctoral dissertation, U. of Illinois, 1972.

_____. "Conditioning of Racial Attitudes and Color Concepts in Children." Perceptual and Motor Skills 39(O, 1974):707-714. [Kindergarten]

Parker, Robin N. "Usefulness of Piagetian Theory in Formulating a Preschool Program for Black Children." Journal of Negro Education 47(Spring, 1978):201-204.

Pasamanick, Benjamin. "A Child Is Being Beaten." American Journal of Orthopsychiatry 41(Jl, 1971):540-556.

_____. "A Tract for the Times: Some Sociobiologic Aspects of Science, Race, and Racism." American Journal of Orthopsychiatry, Ja, 1969.

Pasamanick, Benjamin, and Knobloch, Hilda. "Retrospective Studies on the Epidemiology of Reproductive Casualty: Old and New." Merrill-Palmer Quarterly, Ja, 1969.

Patchen, Martin and others. Class Racial Composition, the Friendliness of Interracial Contact and Student Performance. O 18, 1977. ERIC ED 148 920.

_____. Determinants of Students' Interracial Behavior and Opinion Change. Revised. West Lafayette, IN: Department of Sociology and Anthropology, D, 1975.

_____. Inter-Racial Perceptions Among High School Students, My, 1974. ERIC ED 123 532.

_____. The Relationship of Interracial Perceptions and Affects to Interracial Behavior in High Schools. West Lafayette, IN: Institute for the Study of Social Change, Department of Sociology and Anthropology, Purdue U., 1974.

_____. The Relation of Inter-Racial Contact and Other Factors to Outcomes in the Public High Schools of Indianapolis. A Study of Patterns and Possible Determinants of Effort, Academic Performance, Aspirations, and Racial Opinion Change. West Lafayette, IN: Institute for the Study of Social Change, Department of Sociology and Anthropology, Purdue U., 1975.

Patrick, J. R., and Sims, V. M. "Personality Differences Between Negro and White College Students, North and South." Journal of Abnormal and Social Psychology 29(O, 1934): 181-201.

Patterson, David L., and Smits, Stanley J. "Reactions of Inner-City and Suburban Adolescents to Three Minority Groups." Journal of Psychology 80(Ja, 1972):127-134.

Patterson, Sandra K. Gender Identity as Seen in Drawings of Father Absent 5 to 7 Year Old Black Children, 1977. ERIC ED 141 463.

Payne, Bill F., and Dunn, Charleta J. "An Analysis of the Change in Self Concept by Racial Descent." Journal of Negro Education 41 (Spring, 1972):156-163. [Negro, Anglo, and Mexican-American children in Texas]

Payne, James S., Payne, Ruth A., Mercer, Cecil D., and Davison, Roxanna G. Head Start: A Tragicomedy with Epilogue. NY: Behavioral Publications, 1973.

Pearl, Arthur. "Youth in Lower Class Settings." In Problems of Youth. Edited by M. Sherif and C. W. Sherif. IL: Aldine, 1965.

Peck, Robert F. A Cross-National Comparison of Sex and Socio-Economic Differences in Aptitude and Achievement, F, 1971. ERIC ED 049 315.

Peck, Robert F. and others. Is There Ethnic Bias in Peer Appraisals in Tri-Ethnic Classes? Ap, 1977. ERIC ED 141 734.

Peck, Sidney M., and Rosen, Sidney. "The Influence of the Peer Group on the Attitudes of Girls Toward Color Differences." Phylon, Spring, 1965.

Pehazur, Liora, and Wheeler, Ladd. "Locus of Perceived Control and Need Achievement." Perceptual and Motor Skills 33(D, 1971): 1281-1282.

Penner, Louis A. Interpersonal Attraction Toward a Black Person as a Function of Value Importance, S, 1970. ERIC ED 044 452.

Pentecoste, Joseph. "Black Psychology." The Black Liberator, Je, 1969.

_____. "An Experiment Relating Locus of Control to Reading Success for Black Bright Underachievers." Reading Improvement 12 (Summer, 1975):81-86.

Perception of Opportunity and Occupational Expectation: A Racial Comparison of Rural Youth. Dallas, TX: Southwestern Sociological meetings, Ap, 1968. ERIC ED 021 663.

Perkins, Eugene. Home Is a Dirty Street: The Social Oppression of Black Children. Chicago, IL: Third World Press, 1975.

Perkowski, Stefan. "Some Observations Concerning Black Children Living in a Residential Care Agency." International Journal of Social Psychiatry 20(Spring-Summer, 1974): 89-93.

Perrin, Janis Ann. "The Relationship of Ethnicity and Socioeconomic Status to Reading Achievement." Doctoral dissertation, Texas Tech U., 1976. Univ. Microfilms Order No. 76-23,900.

Persell, Caroline Hodges. Education and Inequality. NY: Free Press, 1977.

Persons, Walter S. "Attitude Toward School Among Black, Inner City Students." Doctoral dissertation, Emory U.

"Perspective on Day Care." Inequality in Education 13(D, 1972):entire issue.

Pettigrew, Thomas F. "Actual Gains and Psychological Losses: The Negro American Protest." Journal of Negro Education, Fall, 1963.

_____. "Negro American Personality: Why Isn't More Known?" Journal of Social Issues, Ap, 1964.

_____. "The Consequences of Racial Isolation in the Public Schools: Another Look." In U.S. COMMISSION ON CIVIL RIGHTS, Papers Prepared for National Conference on Equal Educational Opportunity in America's Cities. Washington, DC: GPO, 1968.

Pettigrew, Thomas F., Useem, Elizabeth L., Normand, Clarence, and Smith, Marshall S. "Pierced Armor." Integrated Education 10 (N-D, 1972):3-6.

Pettigrew, Thomas F. "Race and Equal Educational Opportunity." Harvard Educational Review, Winter, 1968.

_____. "Social Evaluation Theory: Convergences and Applications." In Nebraska Symposium on Motivation, 1967. Edited by David Levine. Lincoln, NE: U. of Nebraska Press, 1967.

Phillips, Beeman N. "School-Related Aspirations of Children With Different Socio-Cultural Backgrounds." Journal of Negro Education 41(Winter, 1972):48-52.

Philp, H., and Kelly, M. "Product and Process in Cognitive Development: Some Comparative Data on the Performance of School Age Children in Different Cultures." British Journal of Educational Psychology 44(N, 1974):248-265.

Pickard, William F. "A Survey of the Literature Pertaining to the Academic Achievement of Black Students." Doctoral dissertation, Ohio State U.

Pickwood, Susan. "Black People's Adaptive Behavior and Self-Hate." Patterns of Prejudice 9(Mr-Ap, 1975):1-12,19

Picou, J. Steven, and Hernandez, Pedro F. Perceived Sources of Personal Aid and Influence for the Occupational Aspirations of Black High School Seniors: A Rural-Urban Comparison, F, 1970. ERIC ED 042 535.

Picou, J. Steven and others. "Race and the Formation of Academic Self Concept: A Causal Analysis." Southern Journal of Educational Research 11(Spring, 1977):57-70.

Pierce, Chester M. "Problems of the Negro Adolescent in the Next Decade." In Minority Group Adolescents in the United States. Edited by Eugene B. Brody. Baltimore, MD: Williams and Wilkins, 1968.

Pinderhughes, Charles. "Effects of Ethnic Group Concentration Upon Educational Process, Personality Formation and Mental Health." Journal of the National Medical Association, 56(1964).

Pines, Maya. "Slum Children Must Make Up for Lost Time." New York Times Magazine, O 5, 1967.

Pitts, James P. "Group Disorders in the Public School: A Comment." American Sociological Review 39(F, 1974):134-135. [See Ritterband and Silberstein, below]

_____. Racial Consciousness, Activism and Socialization: Black Youth. Los Angeles: Center for Afro-American Studies, U. of California, 1975.

_____. "Self-Direction and the Political Socialization of Black Youth." Social Science Quarterly 56(Je, 1975):93-104.

_____. "The Study of Race Consciousness: Comments on New Directions." American Journal of Sociology 80(N, 1974):665-687.

_____ (ed). "Working Papers in the Study of Race Consciousness." Journal of Black Studies 5(Mr, 1975):277-319.

Polgar, Sylvia K. "Modeling Social Relations in Cross-Color Play." Anthropology and Education Quarterly 9(Winter, 1978):283-292.

Politzer, Robert L., and Hoover, Mary R. The Development of Awareness of the Black Standard/Black Nonstandard Dialect Contrast Among Primary School Children: A Pilot Study. Stanford, CA: School of Education, Stanford U., F, 1972.

_____. The Effect of Pattern Practice and Standard/Nonstandard Dialect Contrast on Language Achievement Among Black Children. Stanford, CA: Stanford Center for Research and Development in Teaching, Mr, 1972.

Polk, Marion Tillinghast. "An Analysis of the Literature on the Education of Negro Gifted Children from 1940-1950." Quarterly Review of Higher Education Among Negroes 21(Ap, 1953):63-81.

Pollard, Diane S. "Educational Achievement and Ethnic Group Membership." Comparative Education Review 17(O, 1973):362-374.

Porter, Judith D. R. Black Child, White Child. The Development of Racial Attitudes. Cambridge, MA: Harvard U. Press, 1971.

_____. "Racial Concept Formation in Preschool Age Children." Master's thesis, Cornell U., 1963.

Porter, Walter Nathaniel. "A Study of the Relationships Between Public School Segregation and Academic Achievement and Attitudes of Black Students." Doctoral dissertation, Southern Illinois U., 1971. Univ. Microfilms Order No. 72-10286.

Porterfield, L. M. An Examination of the Relationship Between Race and Performance in Psychological Measurement. Midland, M : Dow Chemical Company, 1964.

Portes, Alejandro, and Wilson, Kenneth L. "Black-White Differences in Educational Attainment." American Sociological Review 41(Je, 1976):414-431.

Portuges, Stephen H., and Feshbach, Norma D. "The Influence of Sex and Socioethnic Factors upon Imitation by Elementary Schoolchildren." Child Development 43(S, 1972): 981-989.

"Position Paper by the Committee on Sociopolitical Concerns of Minority Groups in TESOL, February 1, 1970." TESOL Newsletter 5(Je, 1971):6-7.

Poussaint, Alvin F. "Building a Strong Self-Image in the Black Child." Ebony 29(Ag, 1974):138-143.

_____. "The Dynamics of Racial Conflict." Lowell Lecture Series, Ap 16, 1968.

_____. "Education and Black Self-Image." Freedomways, Fall, 1968.

_____. "The Negro American: His Self-Image and Integration." Journal of the National Medical Association, N, 1966.

_____. "A Negro Psychiatrist Explains the Negro Psyche." New York Times Magazine, Ag 20, 1967.

_____. "New Values Challenge Old Assumptions." Interracial Books for Children Bulletin 7 (1976):2-4.

_____. "The Problems of Light-Skinned Blacks." Ebony 30(F, 1975):85-91.

_____. "The Psychology of a Minority Group with Implications for Social Action." In Urban Violence. Edited by Charles U. Daly. Chicago, IL: U. of Chicago Press, 1969.

_____. "The Role of Education in Providing a Basis for Honest Self-Identification." In Black Studies in the University. Edited by Armstead L. Robinson, Craig C. Foster, and Donald H. Ogilvie. NY: Bantam Books, 1969.

Poussaint, Alvin F., and Atkinson, Carolyn. "Black Youth and Motivation." The Black Scholar 1(1970):43-51.

_____. "Negro Youth and Psychological Motivation." Journal of Negro Education, Summer, 1968.

Poussaint, Alvin F., and Comer, James P. "The Question Every Black Parent Asks: What Shall I Tell My Child?" Redbook 136 (Ja, 1971):64,110-113.

Powell, Alice M. "Racial Awareness and Social Behavior in an Interracial Four-Year-Old Group." Doctoral dissertation, U. of Maryland, 1958. Univ. Microfilms Order No. 59-25-35.

Powell, Evan R., and White, William F. "Affect Structure and Achievement in a Select Sample of Rural Negro Children." Journal of Negro Education 41(Winter, 1972):53-56.

_____. Learning Climate Correlates in Black and White Rural Schools. Athens, GA: R & D Center in Educational Stimulation, U. of Georgia, 1970.

Powell, Gloria Johnson. "Self-Concept in White and Black Children." In Racism and Mental Health. Edited by Charles V. Willie, Bernard M. Kramer, and Bertram S. Brown. Pittsburgh, PA: U. of Pittsburgh Press, 1973.

Powell, Lisa. "Achievement Motivation and Educational Stability: Some Omissions Resulting in Fallacies in the Jencks Report." Journal of Negro Education 42 (Fall, 1973):550-558.

Powers, Jerry M. et al. "A Research Note on the Self-Perception of Youth." American Educational Research Journal 8(N, 1971):665-670.

Prakash, A. Om. Effect of Modeling and Social Reinforcement on the Racial Preferences of Children, 1973. ERIC ED 086 357.

Pratt, David. "Value Judgments in Textbooks: The Coefficient of Evaluation as a Quantitative Measure." Interchange 2(1971):1-14.

Price, Frank T. "Some Effects of Film-Mediated Professional Models on the Self-Perception of Black School Children." Dissertation Abstracts International 31, 7-B(Ja, 1971): 4318.

Prickett, Jimmie L. "Associative Learning Rates of Second, Fourth, and Sixth Grade Black and White Students With a Socioeconomic Difference." Dissertation Abstracts International 31, 7-A(Ja, 1971):3377.

Priddy, Drew, and Kirgan, Doris. "Characteristics of White Couples Who Adopt Black/White Children." Social Work 16(Jl, 1971):105-107.

Pucinski, Roman C. "Results of Survey on Student Unrest in the Nation's High Schools." Congressional Record, F 23, 1970. E 1178-E 1180.

Pughsley, James Lawrence. "The Interrelation-
ship between Administrative Authoritarianism,
Racial Unrest in Secondary Schools, and
Changes as Demanded by Black Students."
Doctoral dissertation, U. of Arizona, 1973.
Univ. Microfilms Order No. 74-04176.

Purves, Alan C. "Some Optimism Justified."
New York Times, Ja 16, 1974. [On the
effectiveness of schooling]

Purves, Alan C., and Levine, Daniel U. (eds).
Educational Policy and International Assess-
ment: Implications of the IEA Surveys of
Achievement. Berkeley, CA: McCutchan
Publishing Corp., 1975.

Puryear, Ruby H. "The Effect of Direct
Teaching on REpresentational Categorization
in Disadvantaged Negro Kindergarten Children."
Dissertation Abstracts International 31, 7-A
Ja, 1971:3349-3350.

Quay, Lorene C. "Language Dialect, Reinforcement, and the Intelligence-Test Performance
of Negro Children." Child Development 42
(Mr, 1971):5-15.

Quinn, Marjory. "A Study of Corporal Punish-
ment as a Factor in the Deterrence of Acting-
Out Behavior in a Black Urban Elementary
School." Master's thesis, California State
U., Hayward, 1973.

Ramirez, Manuel III, and Price-Williams,
Douglas. "Cognitive Styles in Children:
Two Mexican Communities." Interamerican
Journal of Psychology 8(1974):93-101.

Ramsey, Imogene. "A Comparison of First Grade
Negro Dialect Speakers' Comprehension of
Standard English and Negro Dialect."
Elementary English 49(My, 1972):688-696.

Rand Corporation. How Effective is Schooling?
A Critical Review and Synthesis of Research
Findings. Santa Monica, CA: Rand Corpora-
tion, D, 1971.

Rankin, Richard C. "Attitudinal Perceptions of
Black Students and White Students As Influenced by an Instrumented Laboratory Experience."
Dissertation Abstracts International 31,
12-A, Je, 1971:6351.

Ransford, H. Edward. "Skin Color, Life Chances,
and Anti-White Attitudes." Social Problems
18(Fall, 1970):164-179.

Ratusnik, David L., Koenigsknecht, Roy A., and
Friedman, Philip. "Ethnic and Social Class
Comparisons of Standard and Nonstandard
Grammatical Usage by Preschool Children."
Proceedings of the 81st Annual Convention of
the American Psychological Association 1973.
8(1973):653-654.

Rayburn, Carole A. "Socioeconomic and Ethnic
Variables in Concept Formation of Late
Childhood." Dissertation Abstracts Interna-
tional, 1970(Jl)Vol. 31(1-A):468.

Raymer, Elizabeth. Race and Sex Identification
in Preschool Children, Ag, 1969. ERIC ED
041 634.

Rea, Robert E., and Reys, Robert E. "Mathemati-
cal Competencies of Negro and Non-Negro
Children Entering School." Journal of Negro
Education 40(Winter, 1971):12-16. [St.
Louis, MO]

Redisch, Ann, and Weissbach, Theodore A.
"Trait Attributions by White Students to
Black Fellow Students Versus Blacks in
General." Journal of Social Psychology 92
(F, 1974):147-148.

Reeves, Cecil. "An Exploratory Study: Modification of Color Concepts of Low Income
Black Preschool Youngsters." Doctoral dissertation, Stanford U., 1976. Univ. Microfilms Order No. 76-26,064.

Reggy, Mae Alice Turner. "Self-Concept and
Race: Basis for Reactions to a Short Story?"
Doctoral dissertation, U. of Maryland, 1976.
Univ. Microfilms Order No. 76-28,715.

Reid, Ira DeAugustine. In a Minor Way; Negro
Youth in Story and Fact. Washington, D. C.:
American Council on Education, 1940.

_____. "The Negro in the United States." In
"Report of the Committee on Socially Handi-
capped-Dependency and Neglect." In White
House Conference on Child Health and Protec-
tion of Dependent and Neglected Children.
NY: Appleton, 1930.

Reilly, Richard R. "A Note on Minority Group
Test Bias Studies." Psychological Bulletin
80(Ag, 1973):130-132.

Rennels, Max R. "The Effects of Instructional
Methodology in Art Education Upon Achievement
on Spatial Tasks by Disadvantaged Negro
Youths." Journal of Negro Education 39(1970):
116-123.

Renninger, C. A., and Williams, John E. "Black-
White Color Connotations and Race Awareness
in Preschool Children." Perceptual and
Motor Skills 22(1966):771-785.

Renzulli, Joseph S. "Talent Potential in
Minority Group Students." Exceptional
Children 39(Mr, 1973):437-444.

Research Triangle Institute. A Study of the
National Upward Bound and Talent Search
Programs. 5 vols. Washington, D. C.: Of-
fice of Planning, Budgeting, and Evaluation,
U.S. Office of Education, Ap, 1976.

Reschly, Daniel J., and Jipson, Frederick J. "Ethnicity, Geographic Locale, Age, Sex, and Urban-Rural Residence as Variables in the Prevalence of Mild Retardation." American Journal of Mental Deficiency 81(S, 1976):154-161.

Reynolds, Carl H. "Correlational Findings, Educational Implications, and Criticisms of Locus of Control Research: A Review." Journal of Black Studies 6(Mr, 1976): 257-276.

Reynolds, Maynard C. "The Capacities of Children." Exceptional Children, Mr, 1965.

Reynolds, Neila. "The Influence of Emotional Disturbance and Social Class on Sensitivity to Vocal Emotion." In The Urban R's. Edited by Robert A. Dentler and others. New York, NY: Praeger, 1967.

Reynolds, Richard J. Ability of Ghetto Children to Retain Image Related to Learning. Final Report. My 1, 1972. ERIC ED 064 452.

Rhine, W. Ray, and Spencer, Leilani, M. "Effects of Follow Through on School Fearfulness Among Black Children." Journal of Negro Education 44(Fall, 1975):446-453.

Rhodes, Albert Lewis. Effects of Parental Expectations of Educational Plans of White and Nonwhite Adolescents. Final Report. S, 1968. ERIC ED 027 096.

Rhodes, Lodis. "Black Symbolism: A Paradigm on the Nature and Development of Black Consciousness." Doctoral dissertation, U. of Nebraska, 1972.

Rhyne, Dwight Carroll. Attitude Set, Group Learning, and Attitude Change, 1968. ERIC ED 031 621.

Ribich, Thomas, and Murphy, James. "The Economic Returns to Increased Educational Spending." Journal of Human Resources 10(1975): 56-77.

Rice, James A. "Head Start Screening: Effectiveness of a Teacher-Administered Battery." Perceptual and Motor Skills 32(Ap, 1971): 675-678.

Rich, Andrea L., and Ogawa, Dennis M. A Mode of Intercultural and Interracial Communication, 1971. ERIC ED 049 622.

Rich, Cynthia Jo. "Black Professor Hits Tranquilizer Use." Race Relations Reporter 5(O 7, 1974). [Prof. Harry Morgan, Syracuse U.]

Richards, Martin P. M. (ed). The Integration of a Child into a Social World. London: Cambridge U. Press, 1974.

Richardson, John Grissen. "Special Education and Minority Misclassification: An Historical and Sociological Explanation." Doctoral dissertation, U. of California, Davis, 1976. Univ. Microfilms Order No. 76-21,001.

Richardson, Stephen A., and Green, A. "When Is Black Beautiful? Coloured and White Children's Reactions to Skin Colour." British Journal of Educational Psychology 41 (F, 1971):62-69. [London]

Richmond, Bert O. "A Classroom Model for the Education of Cultural Minority Pupils." Education 92(F-Mr, 1972):8-12.

_____. "Creative and Cognitive Abilities of White and Negro Children." Journal of Negro Education 40(Spring, 1971):111-116. [Northeast Georgia]

_____. Creative and Cognitive Abilities of White and Negro Children, 1968. ERIC ED 030 922.

Richmond, Bert O., and Aliotti, Nicholas C. "Developmental Skills of Advantaged and Disadvantaged Children of Perceptual Tasks." Psychology in the Schools 14(O, 1977):461-465.

Richmond, Bert O., and Weiner, Gerald P. "Cooperation and Competition Among Young Children as a Function of Ethnic Grouping, Grade, Sex, and Reward Condition." Journal of Educational Psychology 64(Je, 1973):329-334.

Richmond, Bert O., and White, William F. "Sociometric Predictors of the Self Concept Among Fifth and Sixth Grade Children." Journal of Educational Research 64(My, 1971): 425-429.

Richmond, David M. Educational Horizons Among Lower Class Negro High School Students. Dissertation Abstracts International, 1969, 30(2-A):835.

Rigert, Joe. All Together: An Unusual American Family. New York: Harper & Row, 1974. [Children of different ethnic groups in a single family]

Riggs, Sidney N. "Descriptive Study of Behavior Problems in a Mixed Race School." Doctoral dissertation, New York U., 1939.

Rippey, Robert M. "The Use of Reinforcement in Inner-City Classrooms." Integrated Education: RACE AND SCHOOLS 8(My-Je, 1970):28-33.

Rist, Ray C. "Black English for Black Schools: A Call for Educational Congruity." In Restructuring American Education. Edited by Ray C. Rist. New Brunswick, NJ: Trans-Action Books, 1972.

_____. "Race, Policy, and Schooling." Society 12(N-D, 1974):59-64.

_____. "The Socialization of the Ghetto Child into the Urban School System." Doctoral dissertation, Washington U., Je, 1970.

Ritterband, Paul. "Race Resources and Achievement." Sociology of Education 46(Spring, 1973):162-170.

Ritterband, Paul, and Silberstein, Richard. "Group Disorders in the Public Schools." American Sociological Review 38(Ag, 1973): 461-467.

_____. "More on School Disorders." American Sociological Review 39(F, 1974):135-137.

Ritvo, Edward R. and others. "Social Class Factors in Autism." Journal of Autism and Childhood Schizophrenia 1(Jl-S, 1971):297-310.

Ritzen, J. M., and Winkler, D. R. "The Revealed Preferences of a Local Government: Black/White Disparities in Scholastic Achievement." Journal of Urban Economics 4(Jl, 1977).

Rivers, L. Wendell, Mitchell, Horace, and Williams, Willie S. "I.Q. Labels and Liability: Effects on the Black Child." Journal of Afro-American Issues 3(Winter, 1975):63-76.

Rivers, Wendell, Henderson, Donald, Jones, Reginald, Ladner, Joyce, and Williams, Robert. "Mosaic of Labels for Black Children." In Issues in the Classification of Children. Edited by Nicholas Hobbs. San Francisco, CA: Jossey Bass, 1974.

Rivers, Marie. "Motivating the Negro Student to Greater Academic Achievement." ISSQ (Indiana Social Studies Quarterly), Spring, 1964. [Indiana Council of the Social Studies, Ball State Teachers College, Muncie, IN]

Robeck, Mildred C. and others. Acculturation of Minority Group Children in American Schools. Eugene, OR: School of Education, U. of Oregon, 1969.

Roberts, Albert. "The Self-Esteem of Inner-City Blacks." Journal of Social and Behavioral Sciences 20(Spring, 1974):118-122.

Roberts, Jean. Intellectual Development of Children by Demographic and Socio-economic Factors. Vital and Health Statistics, Series 11, No. 110(D, 1971).

Robins, Lee N., Jones, Robin S., and Murphy, George E. "School Milieu and School Problems of Negro Boys." Social Problems, Spring, 1966.

Robins, Lee N., Murphy, George E., Woodruff, Robert A., and King, Lucy J. "Adult Psychiatric Status of Black Schoolboys." Archives of General Psychiatry 24(Ap, 1971): 338-345.

Robins, Lee N. and others. School Achievement in Two Generations: A Study of 88 Urban Black Families, 1977. ERIC ED 152 891.

Robinson, Charlynn Chamberlin. "The Modification of Racial Attitudes in Black and White Preschool Children." Doctoral dissertation, Emory U., 1976. Univ. Microfilms Order No. 76-25079.

Robinson, W. A. "How Can It Be Told?" Opportunity, My, 1930. [Teaching black children what it means to be black in America]

Robinson, Walter V. "School Violence--The Worst May Be Over." Boston Globe, Mr 24, 1976. [Boston]

Roche, J. G. "Preference Tradeoffs Among Instructional Programs." Doctoral dissertation, Harvard U., 1972.

Rock, Donald A., and Evans, Franklin R. Aptitude and Rating Factors of Negroes and Whites, 1969. ERIC ED 034 259.

Rockey, Randolph Earl. Contrastive Analysis of the Language Structure of Three Ethnic Groups of Children Enrolled in Head Start Programs, 1970. ERIC ED 052 202.

Rodgers, Harrell R., Jr. "Racial Pride and Black Children." Integrated Education 11 (Jl-O, 1973):62-63.

_____. "Toward Explanation of the Political Efficacy and Political Cynicism of Black Adolescents: An Exploratory Study." American Journal of Political Science 18 (My, 1974):257-282.

Rodman, Hyman, and Voydanoff, Patricia. "Social Class and Parents' Range of Aspirations for their Children." Social Problems 25(F, 1978):333-344.

_____. Social Class and Parents' Aspirations for Their Children. Research Report No. 2 (Revised). N, 1969. ERIC ED 043 371.

_____. Social Class and Parent's Aspirations for Their Children. Report No. 8, Ag, 1968. ERIC ED 030 482.

Rodman, Hyman, Boydanoff, Patricia, and Lovejoy, Albert E. "The Range of Aspirations: A New Approach." Social Problems 22(D, 1974):184-198.

Rodriguez, Alice. "The Relationship of Self-
Concept and Motor Ability in Certain Selected
Negro and Caucasian Tenth Grade Girls."
Doctoral dissertation, U. of Alabama, 1972.

Rodriguez, Armando M. "An Educational Utopia."
Integrateducation 13(Mr-Ap, 1975):15. [See
Rohwer, 1975, below.]

Rohrer, Georgia K. "Racial and Ethnic Identification and Preference in Young Children."
Doctoral dissertation, UCLA, 1972.

_____. "Racial and Ethnic Identification and
Preference in Young Children." Young
Children 32(Ja, 1977):24-33.

Rohwer, William D., Jr. "Decisive Research: A
Means for Answering Fundamental Questions
About Instruction." Educational Research 1
(Jl, 1972):5-11.

_____. "Educational Equality: Race Is Not
the Problem." California Journal of Teacher
Education 1(My, 1973):6-19.

_____. "Educational Inequality: Race is Not
the Problem." Integrateducation 13(Mr-Ap,
1975):3-9.

_____. "Learning, Race, and School Success."
Review of Educational Research 41(Je, 1971):
191-210.

Rohwer, William D., Jr., and Ammon, Mary S.
"Elaboration Training and Paired-Associate
Learning Efficiency in Children." Journal
of Educational Psychology 62(0, 1971):376-
383.

Rohwer, William D., Jr., and Ammon, Paul R.
The Assessment and Improvement of Learning
and Language Skills in Four and Five Year
Old Culturally Disadvantaged Children.
Final Report, Je, 1971. ERIC ED 054 855.

Rohwer, William D., Jr., and Matz, Robert D.
"Improving Aural Comprehension in White and
in Black Children." Journal of Experimental
Child Psychology 19(F, 1975):23-36.

Romm, Jessica, and Schack, Elizabeth T. The
PINS Child. A Plethora of Problems, N, 1973.
Office of Children's Services, Judicial
Conference of the State of NY, 270 Broadway,
New York, NY 10007. [N.Y.C.]

Roper, Susan Stavert. "Race and Assertive
Classroom Behavior." Integrated Education,
S-O, 1972:24-31.

_____. The Effect of Race on Assertive Behavi-
or and Responses to Assertive Behavior in
Small Groups, Ap, 1971. ERIC ED 051 317.

Rosen, Bernard. "Race, Ethnicity, and the
Achievement Syndrome." American Sociological
Review, F, 1959.

Rosen, Harold. Language and Class: A Critical
Look at the Theories of Basil Bernstein.
Bristol, England: Falling Wall Press, 1972.

_____. "Language and Class: A Critical Look
at the Theories of Basil Bernstein." Urban
Review 7(Ap, 1974):97-114.

Rosenberg, Marvin. "An Experiment to Change
Attitudes of Powerlessness Among Low-Income
Negro Youths." Doctoral dissertation, Case
Western Reserve U., 1968.

Rosenberg, Morris. "Parental Interest and
Children's Self-Conceptions." Sociometry,
Mr, 1963.

_____. Society and the Adolescent Self-Image.
Princeton, NJ: Princeton U. Press, 1965.

_____. "Which Significant Others?" American
Behavioral Scientist 16(Jl-Ag, 1973):829-860.

Rosenberg, Morris, and Simmons, R. G. Black
and White Self-Esteem: The Urban School
Child. Washington, D. C.: American Sociological Association, 1972.

Rosenfeld, Howard M., and Gunnell, Pamela.
"Effects of Peer Characteristics on Pre-
school Performance of Low-Income Children."
Merrill-Palmer Quarterly 19(Ap, 1973):81-94.

Rosenfeld, Michael. Negro-White Differences in
Intellectual Growth, Ag 30, 1968. ERIC ED
024 073.

Rosenfeld, Michael, and Hilton, Thomas L.
"Negro-White Differences in Adolescent Edu-
cational Growth." American Educational
Research Journal 8(Mr, 1971):267-283.

_____ and _____. "Negro-White Differences
in Adolescent Educational Growth."
In A Study of Intellectual Growth and
Vocational Development. Edited by Thomas L.
Hilton and others. Princeton, NJ:
Educational Testing Service, Mr, 1971,
pp. 113-128.

Rosenhan, David L. "Behavior Modification and
Racial Integration." Integrated Education,
F-Mr, 1963.

_____. "Effects of Social Class and Race on
Responsiveness to Approval and Disapproval."
Journal of Personality and Social Psychology,
S, 1966.

Rosenthal, Robert Alan and others. Pathways to
Identify: Aspects of the Experience of
Black Youth. Final Report, F, 1971: ERIC
ED 053 236. [Boston]

Rosner, Joseph. "When White Children Are in
the Minority." The Journal of Educational
Sociology, O, 1954.

Ross-Sheriff, Fariyal and others. Perceptual and Cognitive Development in Low SES Minority Urban Children: Preschool and Program Impacts, Mr, 1977. ERIC ED 142 304.

Rosser, Pearl L. Mental Health of Black Children, S 9, 1976. ERIC ED 130 779.

Roth, Rodney W. "The Effects of 'Black Studies' on Negro Fifth Grade Students." Journal of Negro Education, Fall, 1969.

_____. "How Negro Fifth Grade Students View 'Black Pride' Concepts." Integrated Education 8(My-Je, 1970):24-27.

Rothenberg, Peter. "Locus of Control, Social Class, and Risk Taking in Negro Boys." Doctoral dissertation, Washington U., 1968.

Rotter, Julian B. "Some Problems and Misconceptions Related to the Construct of Internal versus External Control of Reinforcement." Journal of Consulting and Clinical Psychology 43(F, 1975):55-66.

Rousseau, Mark Owen. "Some Social Correlates of Academic Motivation: A Survey Analysis." Doctoral dissertation, U. of North Carolina, 1971.

Rousseve, Ronald J. "An Analysis of the Personality Stresses of Negro Americans and their Implications for Education." Doctoral dissertation, U. of Notre Dame, 1958. Univ. Microfilms Order No. 58-3082.

Rubel, Robert J. Trends in Disorder, Disruptions, and Crimes in Public Secondary Schools, 1950 to 1975. Lexington, MA: Lexington Books, 1977.

Rubin, Dorothy. "Parental Schemata of Negro Primary School Children." Psychological Reports 25(1959):60-62.

Rubin, Rosalyn A., and Balow, Bruce. Relationships Between Bayley Infant Scales and Measures of Cognitive Development and School Achievement, D, 1975. ERIC ED 148 461.

Rubin, Ziek, and Peplau, Letitia Anne. "Who Believes in a Just World?" Journal of Social Issues 31(1975):65-89.

Rupley, William H., and Robeck, Carol. "Black Dialect and Reading Achievement." Reading Teacher 31(F, 1978):598-601.

Russell, Audrey T. "Transracial Adoption." In National Association of Black Social Workers, Diversity: Cohesion or Chaos-Mobilization for Survival. Proceedings of the Fourth Annual Conference of N.A.B.S.W., Nashville, TN: Fisk U., 1973:285-297.

Ryan, Judith Sarah. "Early Identification of Intellectually Superior Black Children." Doctoral dissertation, U. of Michigan, 1975. Univ. Microfilms Order No. 76-09501.

Ryan, S., and Bronfenbrenner, U. (eds). A Report on Longitudinal Evaluations of Preschool Programs. 2 vols. Washington, DC: Children's Bureau, 1974.

Rychlak, Joseph F. Emotional Factors in the Learning and Nonspecific Transfer of White and Black Students, Ja, 1971. ERIC ED 062 463.

Sacks, Susan Riemer. Influence of Black Is Beautiful Program on Black Adolescents' Drawings and High Status Job Selections, F, 1971. ERIC ED 047 056.

Sager, Clifford J., Brayboy, Thomas L., and Waxenberg, Barbara R. Black Ghetto Family in Therapy. NY: Grove Press, 1970.

St.George, Ross. "The Psycholinguistic Abilities of Children from Different Ethnic Backgrounds." Australian Journal of Psychology 22(Ap, 1970):85-89.

St.John, Nancy. "Diversity and Incongruence in Urban Schools." Encyclopedia of Education. NY: Macmillan, 1971.

_____. "The Elementary Classroom as a Frog Pond: Self-Concept, Sense of Control and Social Context." Social Forces 49(Je, 1971):581-595.

_____. "Mothers and Children: Congruence and Optimism of School-Related Attitudes." Journal of Marriage and the Family 34(Ag, 1972):422-430.

_____. Mothers and Children: Congruence and Optimism of their Concepts and Aspirations. Washington, D. C.: U.S. Office of Education, Ja, 1971.

_____. "The Validity of Children's Reports of their Parents' Education Level: A Methodological Note." Sociology of Education 43(Summer, 1970).

Safer, Daniel and Others. "Socioeconomic Factors Influencing the Rate of Nonpromotion in Elementary Schools." Peabody Journal of Education 54(Jl, 1977):275-281.

Samuels, Shirley C. "An Investigation Into the Self Concepts of Lower-and Middle-Class Black and White Kindergarten Children." Journal of Negro Education 42(Fall, 1973):467-472.

Sanday, Peggy R. "The Relevance of Anthropology to U.S. Social Policy." Council on Anthropology and Education Newsletter 3(N, 1972):1-8.

Sanday, Peggy R., Boardman, Anthony E., and Davis, Otto A. A Simultaneous Equations Model of the Educational Process for U.S. Minority Students. Year End Report. Philadelphia: U. of Pennsylvania, D, 1975.

Sanders, Lelia. "The Development of Racial Identification in Black Preschool-Age Children." Doctoral dissertation, Harvard U., 1971.

Sanders, Robert Donald. "Mediation and Associative-Learning by Lower-Class and Middle-Class Black Preschool Children." Doctoral dissertation, Auburn U., 1972. Univ. Microfilms Order No. 73-01908.

Sanford, Nevitt. "Dehumanization and Collective Destructiveness." International Journal of Group Tensions 1(Ja, 1971):26-41.

Sapon, Stanley, M. Operant Studies in the Expansion and Refinement of Verbal Behavior in Disadvantaged Children, Ja, 1969. ERIC ED 132 526.

Sauls, Judith M., and Kalk, John Michael. National Assessment of Educational Progress. Changes in Science Achievement of Black Students, 1976. ERIC ED 127 201

Savage, Richard Alvin. "The Perceived Effects of a Skill Building Course Upon the Educational and Social Survival of Black Students at a Suburban High School." Doctoral dissertation, 1975. Univ. Microfilms Order No. 75-20,931.

Scales, Alice M. Preparing to Assist Black Children in the Reading Act, N, 1975. ERIC ED 136 204.

Scanlan, Peter A., and Dokecki, Paul R. The Effects of Adult Constraint and Peer Influence on the Development of Racial Awareness-Attitudes of Three-, Four-, and Five-Year Old Children, My, 1973. ERIC ED 128 067.

_____. Toward the Development of a Technique to Measure the Racial Awareness-Attitudes of Three-to Five-Year-Old Chilren, My, 1973. ERIC ED 128 076.

Scarr, Sandra. "Needed: A Complete Head Start." Elementary School Journal, F, 1969.

Schab, Fred. "Attitudinal Differences of Southern White and Negro Adolescent Males Regarding the Home, School, Religion and Morality." Journal of Negro Education 40 (Spring, 1971):108-110. [Northeast Georgia]

Schaie, K. Warner, and Roberts, Jean. School Achievement of Children by Demographic and Socioeconomic Factors. Vital and Health Statistics, Series 11 No. 109(N, 1971).

Scheiner, Ellen. "Race, Class, and Sex as Correlates of the Self-Social Concepts of Children." Senior honors thesis, Goucher College, 1967.

Schlesinger, L. "The Influence of Exposure to Peer Group Opinion on the Expressions of Attitudes Toward a Minority Group." Doctoral dissertation, Boston U., 1955.

Schloroff, P. W. "An Experiment in the Measurement and Modification of Racial Attitudes in School Children." Doctoral dissertation, New York U., 1930.

Schmeidler, Gertrude. "Race Differences in Children's Responses to 'Black' and 'White.'" Perceptual and Motor Skills 33(0, 1971):359-363.

Schneider, Betty. "Counseling High School Students: Frustrations and Rewards." Integrateducation 14(Mr-Ap, 1976):22-25.

Schneider, Frank W. "Conforming Behavior of Black and White Children." Journal of Personality and Social Psychology 16(N, 1970):466-471.

_____. Differences Between Negro and White School Children in Conforming Behavior, Ap, 1970. ERIC ED 041 074.

Schneider, Frank W., and Shaw, Marvin E. "Sanctioning Behavior in Negro and in White Populations." Journal of Social Psychology 81(1970):63-72.

Schneider, Jeffrey M. "An Investigation of Social-Psychological Variables Comprising School Normative Academic Climate in High- and Low-Achieving White-Urban, Black-Urban and Rural Elementary Schools with School Mean Socio-Economic Status Controlled." Doctoral dissertation, Michigan State U., 1973.

Schneider, William Edward. "Black vs. White 'Social Intelligence.'" Doctoral dissertation, St. Louis U., 1974. Univ. Microfilms Order No. 75-26317.

Schoggen, Maxine, and Schoggen, Phil. Environmental Forces in the Home Lives of Three-Year-Old Children in Three Population Subgroups. Nasvhille, TN: George Peabody College for Teachers, Ja, 1971.

Schorr, Alvin L. Poor Kids. New York, NY: Basic Books, 1966.

Schultz, David A. Coming Up Black: Patterns of Ghetto Socialization. Englewood Cliffs, NJ: Prentice-Hall, 1969.

_____. "Variations in the Father Role in Complete Families of the Negro Lower Class." Social Science Quarterly, D, 1968.

Schultz, R. E. "A Comparison of Negro Pupils Ranking High With Those Ranking Low in Educational Achievement." Journal of Educational Sociology 31(1978):265-270.

Schwab, Joseph J. "Integration and Disintegration of Education." In Education and Urban Renaissance. Edited by Roald F. Campbell, Lucy Ann Marx, and Raphael O. Nystrand. New York, NY: Wiley, 1969.

Schwartz, Carol Suzanne Lewis. "The Effect of Selected Black Poetry on Expressed Attitudes toward Blacks of Fifth-Grade and Sixth-Grade White Suburban Children." Doctoral dissertation, Wayne State U., 1972. Univ. Microfilms Order No. 73-12594.

Schwebel, Milton. "The Theory of Educability." School and Society, Summer, 1967.

_____. Who Can Be Educated? New York, NY: Grove, 1968.

Sciara, Frank J. "Perception of Negro Boys Regarding Color and Occupational Status." Child Study Journal 1(Summer, 1971):203-211.

_____. "A Study of the Acceptance of Blackness Among Negro Boys." Journal of Negro Education 41(Spring, 1972):151-155.

Scott, Ralph, and Kobes, David A. "The Influence of Family Size on Learning Readiness Patterns of Socioeconomically Disadvantaged Preschool Blacks." Journal of Clinical Psychology 31(Ja, 1975):85-88.

Scott, Ralph, and Smith, James E. "Ethnic and Demographic Variables and Achievement Scores of Preschool Children." Psychology in the Schools 9(Ap, 1972):174-182.

Scott, Ralph and Others. Social Class, Race, Sex, and Seriating—A Study of Their Relationship at the Kindergarten Level. Final Report, Ap, 1967. ERIC ED 019 712.

Scott, Richard R. "Attribution of Internal Control." Journal of Black Studies 6(Mr, 1976):277-290.

Scribner, Sylvia, and Cole, Michael. "Cognitive Consequences of Formal and Informal Education." Science 182(N, 1973):553-559.

Seagoe, May V. "Children's Play in Three American Subcultures." Journal of School Psychology 9(1971):167-172.

Sedlacek, William E., and Brooks, Glenwood C., Jr. The Importance of Social Acceptability in the Measurement of Racial Attitudes, Ag, 1970. ERIC ED 048 418.

_____. "Social Acceptability in the Measurement of Racial Attitudes." Psychological Reports 29(Ag, 1971):17-18.

Seeley, Kenneth Robert. "The Legality of Educable Mentally Retarded Pupil Placement Practices for Minority Group Children in Twenty-Six of the Largest Cities in the United States." Doctoral dissertation, U. of Denver, 1972. Univ. Microfilms Order No. 72-33,056.

Segal, Julius and others (eds). The Mental Health of the Child. Program Reports of the National Institute of Mental Health. National Institute of Mental Health. Washington, D. C.: GPO, Je, 1971.

Segalman, Ralph. "Intergroup Relations, Cognitive Dissonance and Action Research." International Journal of Group Tensions 2 (Winter, 1972):5-30.

Seiden, Richard H. "We're Driving Young Blacks to Suicide." Psychology Today 4(Ag, 1970):24-28.

Weitz, Virginia. Social Class and Ethnic Group Differences in Learning to Read. Newark, DE: International Reading Association, 1978.

Sekyra, Francis, and Arnoult, Joseph F. "Negro Intellectual Assessment with Three Instruments Contrasting Caucasian and Negro Norms." Journal of Learning Disabilities 1(O, 1968):564-569.

Seltzer, Aida R. The Relationship Between Moral Development and the Development of Time Perception and Time Conceptualization in Lower Class Negro Children. Dissertation Abstracts International, 1970(S)vol. 31(3-B):1524.

Semler, Ira J., and Iscoe, Ira. "Comparative and Developmental Study of the Learning Abilities of Negro and White Children under Four Conditions." Journal of Educational Psychology, F, 1963.

Senn, Milton J. E. Speaking Out for America's Children. New Haven: Yale U. Press, 1977.

Serpell, Robert. "How Perception Differs Among Cultures." New Society 20(Je 22, 1972):620-623.

Serrin, Judith. "New Minority: Whites in Black Schools." Detroit Free Press, Ja 23, 1977.

Serum, Camella S., and Myers, David G. "Note on Prejudice and Personality." Psychological Reports 26(F, 1970):65-66.

Sewell, William H., and Shah, Vimal P. "Parents' Education and Children's Educational Aspirations and Achievements." American Sociological Review, Ap, 1968.

Sexton, Patricia. "Negro Career Expectations." Merrill-Palmer Quarterly, O, 1963.

Seymour, Blanche Geneva. "Variations in Defense Mechanisms Among Black Ghetto Children
as a Function of Developmental Level and
Social Milieu." Doctoral dissertation,
Catholic U. of America, 1974. Univ. Microfilms Order No. 74-19507.

Shade, Barbara J. "Social-Psychological Characteristics of Achieving Black Children."
Negro Educational Review 29(Ap, 1978):80-86.

Shalaby, Ibrahim Mahmoud. "The Role of the
School in Cultural Renewal and Identity
Development in the Nation of Islam in
America." Doctoral dissertation, U. of
Arizona, 1967.

Shanahan, Judith Kearney. "The Effects of
Modifying Black-White Concept Attitudes of
Black and White First Grade Subjects Upon
Two Measures of Racial Attitudes." Doctoral
dissertation, U. of Washington, 1972.
Univ. Microfilms Order No. 72-28664.

Shannon, John H. "An Analysis of Selected
Sociological Variables Related to Special
Class Placement Processes as a Function of
Race." Doctoral dissertation, U. of
Michigan, 1972.

Shapiro, Elliott S. "A Child's Right to Childhood." Integrated Education, O-N, 1967.

_____. "The Effect of Educational Philosophies
on the Personalities of Socio-economically
Deprived Negro Children." Doctoral dissertation, New York U., 1959. Univ. Microfilms
Order No. 59-6252.

Shapiro, Walter. "Black and White is Still the
Point." Washington Monthly 5(Je, 1973):32-
42.

Sharpley, Robert H. "A Psychohistorical
Perspective of the Negro." American Journal
of Psychiatry, N, 1969.

Shaw, Jean W., and Schoggen, Maxine. Children
Learning. Samples of Everyday Life of
Children at Home. A Resource Book. Nash-
ville, TN: Demonstration and Research Cen-
ter for Early Education, George Peabody
College for Teachers, 1969.

Shaw, Ralph L., and Uhl, Norman P. "Control of
Reinforcement and Academic Achievement."
Journal of Educational Research 64(Ja, 1971):
226-228.

Shaycoft, Marion F. The High School Years:
Growth in Cognitive Skills. Pittsburgh, PA:
American Institutes for Research and School
of Education, U. of Pittsburgh, 1967.

Shepherd, John W. and others. "A Cross-Cultural
Study of Recognition Memory for Faces."
International Journal of Psychology 9(1974):
205-211.

Sher, Abigail. "Child Rearing and Cognitive
Styles of Lower-Class Negro Children." In
Mary Rainey and others, Studies of Inter-
action, O, 1969. ERIC ED 138 098.

Sherif, Carolyn W. "Social Distance as Categorization of Intergroup Interaction."
Journal of Personality and Social Psychology
25(Mr, 1973):327-334.

Shipley, Diana G. "Understanding Minority
Group Children in the Classroom." Journal
of the National Association of College
Admissions Counselors 19(Mr, 1975):19-21.

Shipman, V. C. Disadvantaged Children and
their First School Experiences: Notable
Early Characteristics of High and Low
Achieving Black Low-SES Children. (PR76-21)
Princeton, NJ: Educational Testing Ser-
vice, 1976.

Shipman, Virginia C. and others. Notable Early
Characteristics of High and Low Achieving
Black Low-SES Children, D, 1976. ERIC ED
138 340.

_____. Stability and Change in Family Status,
Situational, and Process Variables and
their Relationship to Children's Cognitive
Performance, S, 1976. ERIC ED 138 339.

Shulman, Lee S. "Negro-White Differences in
Employability, Self-Concept, and Related
Measures Among Adolescents Classified as
Mentally Handicapped." Journal of Negro
Education, Summer, 1968.

Sieber, Robert Timothy. "Schooling in the
Bureaucratic Classroom: Socialization and
Social Reproduction in Chestnut Heights."
Doctoral dissertation, New York U., 1976.
Univ. Microfilms Order No. 76-19,544.

Sigall, Harold, and Page, Richard. "Current
Stereotypes: A Little Fading, a Little
Faking." Journal of Personality and Social
Psychology 18(My, 1971):247-255.

Sigel, Irving E. Some Thoughts on Directions
for Research in Cognitive Development.
Bethesda, MD: National Institute of Child
Health and Human Development, 1968.

Sigel, Irving E., and Olmsted, Patricia. Modification of Cognitive Skills Among Lower-
Class Negro Children: A Follow-up Training
Study. Report No 6, Ag, 1968. ERIC ED
030 480.

Silberman, Charles E. "The Schools and the
Fight Against Prejudice." In Prejudice
U.S.A. Edited by Charles Y. Glock and Ellen
Siegelman. New York: Praeger, 1969.

Silberstein, Ruth. Risk-Taking Behavior in Pre-
School Children from Three Ethnic Backgrounds,
Je, 1969. ERIC ED 042 486.

Silverman, Bernie I., and Cochrane, Raymond. "The Relationship Between Verbal Expressions of Behavioral Intention and Overt Behavior." Journal of Social Psychology 84(Je, 1971): 51-56.

Silverman, Bernie I. and others. Racial Composition and Racial Discrimination in the Classroom, 1975. ERIC ED 147 659.

Simkins, Gary, Gunnings, Thomas, and Kearney, Annette. "The Black Six-Hour Retarded Child." Journal of Non-White Concerns in Personnel and Guidance 2(O, 1973):29-34.

Simmons, Robert G. "Blacks and High Self-Esteem." Social Psychology 41(Mr, 1978): 54-57.

Simms, Margaret C. "Causes of Inequity in the Allocation of School Resources." Phylon 38(Mr, 1977):73-81. [San Jose, CA]

Simon, Rita James. "An Assessment of Racial Awareness, Preference, and Self Identity Among White and Adopted Non-White Children." Social Problems 22(O, 1974):43-57.

_____. An Assessment of Racial Awareness, Preference, and Self-Identity Among White and Non-White Children, 1973. ERIC ED 091 484.

_____. "Black Attitudes Toward Transracial Adoption." Phylon 39(Summer, 1978):135-142.

Simond, Adah DeBlane. "The Discovery of Being Black: A Recollection." Southwestern Historical Quarterly 76(Ap, 1973).

Simons, Herbert D., and Johnson, Kenneth. "Black English Syntax and Reading Interference." Research in the Teaching of English 8 (Winter, 1975):339-358.

Simpkins, Gary, Washington, Robert L, and Gunnings, Thomas. "What a Culture a Difference Makes: A Rejoinder to Valentine." Harvard Educational Review 41(N, 1971):535-541. [See Valentine, below]

Simpkins, Gary and others. "The Black Six-Hour Retarded Child." Journal of Non-White Concerns 2(O, 1973):29-33.

Singer, Jerome L. Psychological Deprivation and the Development of Imaginative Capacity in Children and Adults. Bethesda, MD: National Institute of Child Health and Human Development, 1968.

Singh, Jane M., and Yancey, Anna V. "Racial Attitudes in White First Grade Children." Journal of Educational Research 67(Ap, 1974): 370-372.

Singhal, Sushila, and Crago, Priscilla H. "Sex Differences in the School Gains of Migrant Children." Journal of Educational Research 65(My-Je, 1971):417-419.

Singleton, John. "Cross-Cultural Approaches to Research on Minority Group Education." Journal of the Steward Anthropological Society 2(Fall, 1970):35-50.

Sinha, A. K. P. "Relationship Between Ethnic Stereotypes and Social Distance." Psychological Reports 28(F, 1971).

Sitkei, E. George, and Meyers, C. Edward. "Comparative Structure of Intellect in Middle-and Lower-Class Four-Year-Olds of Two Ethnic Groups." Developmental Psychology 1(1969):592-604.

Siu, Ping Kee. The Relationship between Moticational Patterns and Academic Achievement in Minority Group Children. Final Report. Mr, 1972. ERIC ED 063 443.

Sizemore, Barbara A. "Educational Research and Desegregation: Significance for the Black Community." Journal of Negro Education 47 (Winter, 1978):58-68.

Sizemore, Barbara A., and Thompson, Anderson. "Separatism, Segregation, and Integration." Educational Leadership 27(1969):239-242.

Skinto, Susanne M. "Racial Awareness in Negro and Caucasian Elementary School Children." Master's thesis, West Virginia U., 1969.

Slaughter, Diana T. "The Black Child: Issues and Priorities." Journal of Black Psychology 4(Ag, 1977/F, 1978):119-133.

_____. "Maternal Antecedents of the Academic Achievement Behaviors of Afro-American Head Start Children." Educational Horizons 48 (1969):24-28.

_____. "Psychological Scientism and the Black Scholar." School Review 81(My, 1973): 461-476.

_____. "Relation of Early Parent-Teacher Socialization Influences to Achievement Orientation and Self-Esteem in Middle Childhood Among Low-Income Black Children." In The Social Context of Learning and Development. Edited by J. Glidewell. New York: Gardner Press, 1977.

Slaughter, Thedford. "Up from Hate." Saturday Review, D 16, 1967. [A Negro youngster examines his feelings.]

Slavin, Robert E. Effects of Biracial Learning Teams on Cross-Racial Friendship and Interaction. Baltimore, MD: Center for Social Organization, Johns Hopkins U., N, 1977.

Smith, Alice. "A Study of Third-Grade Academic Achievement Differences between Disadvantaged Students with Head Start Experiences and No Head Start Experiences." Doctoral dissertation, U. of Southern Mississippi, 1976. Univ. Microfilms Order No. 77-5971.

Smith, Carole R., Williams, Leo, and Willis, Richard H. "Race, Sex, and Belief as Determinants of Friendship Acceptance." Journal of Personality and Social Psychology, F, 1967.

Smith, Charles. "Poor Head Start and Its Children." New Republic, Je 21, 1969.

Smith, Charles H. "Whom Am I?" American Education, N, 1968. [The inner city child]

Smith, D. B. Report on Differences in Ethnic Learning Styles, 1966. Educational Design, Inc., New York, NY. ERIC ED 015 253.

Smith, Howard P., and Abramson, Marcia. "Racial and Family Experiences: Correlates of Mobility Aspirations." Journal of Negro Education, Spring, 1962.

Smith, Janet D. "A Developmental Study: Socio-economic Status, Race, and Incidental Learning." Doctoral dissertation, Michigan State U., 1972.

Smith, M. Brewster. "School and Home: Focus on Achievement." In Developing Programs for the Educationally Disadvantaged. Edited by A. Harry Passow. New York: Teachers College Press, 1968.

_____. "The Schools and Prejudice: Findings." In Prejudice U.S.A. Edited by Charles Y. Glock and Ellen Siegelman. NY: Praeger, 1969, pp. 112-135.

Smith, Merle E. The Effects of an Experimental Program to Improve Self-Concept, Attitudes toward School and Achievement of Negro Fourth, Fifth and Sixth Grade Students. Dissertation Abstracts International, 31, 8-A(F, 1971):3974.

Smith, Walter. "An Alternative Design for Content Analysis of Ethnic Interaction Portrayal in Educational Resources." Master's thesis, U. of Texas, 1974.

Smith, Willie D. "The Effects of Racial Milieu and Parental Racial Attitudes and Rearing Practices on Black Children's Racial Identity, Self-Esteem, and Consequence Behaviors." Doctoral dissertation, Stanford U., 1974. Univ. Microfilms Order No. 75-06930.

Snow, Albert J. "Ethno Science and the Gifted in American Education." Gifted Child Quarterly 21(Spring, 1977):53-57.

Soares, Anthony T., and Soares, Louis M. "Comparative Differences in the Self-Perceptions of Disadvantaged and Advantaged Students." Journal of School Psychology 9(Winter, 1971):424-429.

Soares, Louis M., and Soares, Anthony T. Self Concepts of Disadvantaged and Advantaged Students, S, 1970. ERIC ED 042 871.

_____. "Self-Concepts of Disadvantaged and Advantaged Students." Child Study Journal 1 (Winter, 1970-1971):69-73.

Sobota, Catherine M. The Relationship Between Selected Social and Personal Characteristics and Academic Achievement Among Male Negro Adolescents. Dissertation Abstracts International, 1969, 30(3-A)1029-30.

The Social Background of the Student and His Prospect of Success at School, S, 1971. ERIC ED 060 281.

Solkoff, Norman. "Race of Experimenter as a Variable in Research with Children." Developmental Psychology 7(J1, 1972):70-75.

_____. Race of Experimenter as a Variable in Research with Children, 1971. ERIC ED 056 328.

_____. "Reactions to Frustration in Negro and White Children." Journal of Negro Education, Fall, 1969.

Solomon, Benjamin. "Better Racial Attitudes." (Letter) Urban Review, Ja, 1969. [See, also, reply by Charles Stember, same issue.]

_____. "Equal Educational Opportunity" (Letter). Harvard Educational Review, Winter, 1969.

Solomon, Daniel. "Family Characteristics and Elementary School Achievement in an Urban Ghetto." Journal of Consulting and Clinical Psychology 39(1972):462-466.

_____. "The Generality of Children's Achievement-Related Behavior." Journal of Genetic Psychology 114(1969):109-125.

_____. Psychosocial Deprivation and Achievement Dispositions. Bethesda, MD: National Institute of Child Health and Human Development, 1968.

_____. "Psycho-Social Deprivation and Achievement Dispositions: Present Knowledge and Needed Research." Psychological Reports 24 (1969):227-237.

Solomon, Daniel, and Houlihan, Kevin A. "Relationships of Parental Behavior to 'Disadvantaged' Children's Instrinsic-Extrinsic Motivation for Task Striving." Journal of Genetic Psychology 120(1972):257-274.

Solomon, Daniel, Houlihan, Kevin A., and Parelius, Robert J. "Intellectual Achievement Responsibility in Negro and White Children." Psychological Reports 24(1969):479-483.

Solomon, Daniel, and Kendall, Arthur J. Individual Characteristics and Children's Performance in Varied Educational Settings. Rockville, MD: Montgomery County Public Schools, My, 1976.

Solomon, Daniel, and Oberlander, Mark I. "Locus of Control in the Classroom." In Psychological Concepts in the Classroom. Edited by R. H. Coop and K. White. New York: Harper & Row, 1974.

Solomon, Daniel, Parelius, Robert J., and Busse, Thomas V. "Dimensions of Achievement-Related Behavior Among Lower-Class Negro Parents." Genetic Psychology Monographs 79(1969):163-190.

Solomon, Daniel and others. "Early Grade School Performance of Inner City Negro High School High Achievers, Low Achievers, and Dropouts." Developmental Psychology 4(My, 1971).

_____. "Parent Behavior and Child Academic Achievement, Achievement Striving, and Related Personality Characteristics." Genetic Psychology Monographs 83(1971):173-273.

Somerville, May Ann. "Dialect and Reading: A Review of Alternative Solutions." Review of Educational Research 45(Spring, 1975):247-262. [Black English]

Southern, Mara Lee. "Language-Cognitive Enhancement of Disadvantaged Preschool Children Through Modeling Procedures." Doctoral dissertation, Stanford U., 1969.

Southern, Mara Lee, and Plant, Walter T. "Differential Cognitive Development within and between Racial and Ethnic Groups of Disadvantaged Preschool and Kindergarten Children." Journal of Genetic Psychology 119(D, 1971)part 2, 259-266.

Sowell, Thomas. "Patterns of Black Excellence." Public Interest 43(Spring, 1976):26-58.

Spearman, Cecile T. "Color-Mood Association with Lighter and Darker Hues of Non-Racially Related Colors by Young Negro and Caucasian Children." Graduate Research in Education and Related Disciplines 4(Winter, 1968):25-37.

Spellman, Charles Mac. The Shift from Color to Form Preference in Young Children of Difference Ethnic Backgrounds. Part of the Final Report. Austin, TX: Ag, 1968. ERIC ED 025 321.

Spence, Janet T. "Verbal and Nonverbal Rewards and Punishment in the Discrimination Learning of Children of Varying Socioeconomic Status." Developmental Psychology 6(My, 1972):381-384.

Spencer, C. P. "Selective Secondary Education, Social Class and the Development of Adolescent Subcultures." British Journal of Educational Psychology 42(F, 1972):1-13.

Spencer, Margaret Beale, and Horowitz, Frances Degen. "Effects of Systematic Social and Token Reinforcement on the Modification of Racial and Color Concept Attitudes in Black and in White Preschool Children." Developmental Psychology 9(S, 1973):246-254.

Spiaggia, Martin. "Self-group Devaluation and Prejudice in Minority-Group Boys." Doctoral dissertation, New York U., 1958. Univ. Microfilms Order No. 59-1039.

Spilerman, Seymour. "Raising Academic Motivation in Lower Class Adolescents: A Convergence of Two Research Traditions." Sociology of Education 44(Winter, 1971):103-118.

Spitz, Rene A. "Environment Versus Race." In Psychoanalysis and Culture. Edited by G. Wilbur and W. Munsterburger. New York: International Universities Press, 1951.

Spock, Benjamin M. "Children and Discrimination." Integrated Education, Je-Jl, 1964.

_____. "Protecting Children from the Harm of Discrimination." Redbook, O, 1964.

Spreitzer, Elmer A., and Nagi, Saad Z. "Race and Equality of Opportunity: A Controlled Study." Phylon 34(S, 1973).

Squibb, P. G. "Education and Class." Educational Research 15(Je, 1973):194-208.

Stabler, John R., and Perry, Oliver. "Learning and Retention as a Function of Instructional Method and Race." Journal of Psychology 47 (1967).

Stabler, John R., and Johnson, Edward E. "The Meaning of Black and White to Children." International Journal of Symbology 3(D, 1972):11-21.

Stabler, John R., Johnson, Edward E., Berke, Melvyn A., and Baker, Robert B. "The Relationship between Race and Perception of Racially Related Stimuli and Preschool Children." Child Development 40(1969):1233-1239.

Stabler, John R. and others. "The Measurement of Children's Self-Concept as Related to Racial Membership." Child Development 42 (D, 1971):2094-2097.

_____. The Relationship Between Race and Perception of Racially-Related Stimuli in Preschool Children, 1967. ERIC ED 030 483.

Stagner, Ross. Psychological Dynamics of Inner-City Problems. Washington,

Stahl, Abraham. "The Cultural Antecedents of Sociolinguistic Differences." Comparative Education 11(Je, 1975):147-152. [In re: Basil Bernstein]

Stake, Jayne E. "Effect of Achievement on the Aspiration Behavior of Black and White Children." Journal of Personality and Social Psychology 25(F, 1973):187-191.

Starr, B. James and others. Black-White Differences in Psychosocial Maturity. Baltimore, MD: Center for Social Organization of Schools, Johns Hopkins U., Mr, 1972.

State of New York, Office of Education Performance Review. School Factors Influencing Reading Achievement: A Case Study of Two Inner City Schools. Albany, NY: Office of Education Performance Review, Mr, 1974.

Steigelmann, Val V. "Patterns of Racial Identity Imagery in Inner-City Male Children." Doctoral dissertation, Case Western Reserve U.

Stephan, Walter G., and Kennedy, James C. "An Experimental Study of Interethnic Competition in Segregated Schools." Journal of School Psychology 13(Fall, 1975):234-245.

Stephens, Mark, and Delys, Pamela. Subcultural Determinants of Locus of Control (IE) Development. A Locus of Control (IE) Measure for Preschool-Age Children: Model, Method, and Validity. My, 1971. ERIC ED 055 288.

Stephenson, Bobby L. An Investigation of the Psycholinguistic Abilities of Negro and White Children from Four Socioeconomic Status Levels. Final Report, My, 1970. ERIC ED 041 261.

Stephenson, Bobby L., and Gay, William O. "Psycholinguistic Abilities of Black and White Children from Four SES Levels." Exceptional Children 38(My, 1972):705-709.

Stephenson, Richard M. "Mobility Orientation and Stratification of 1,000 Ninth Graders." American Sociological Review, Ap, 1957.

Stern, Carolyn, and Gupta, Willa. "Echoic Responding of Disadvantaged Preschool Children as a Function of Type of Speech Modeled." Journal of School Psychology 8(1970):24-27.

Stevenson, Harold W., and Stewart, E. C. "A Developmental Study of Racial Awareness in Young Children." Child Development 39 (1958):399-409.

Stevenson, Harold W. and others. "Interrelations Among Learning and Performance Tasks in Disadvantaged Children." Journal of Educational Psychology 62(Je, 1971):179-184.

Stewart, L. H., Dole, A. A., and Harris, Y. Y. "Cultural Differences in Abilities During High School." American Education Research Journal 4(1967):19-30.

Stewart, William A. "Acculturative Processes and the Language of the American Negro. In Language in Its Social Setting. Edited by William Gage. Washington, DC: Anthropological Society of Washington, 1974:1-46.

Stinnett, Nick and others. "Parent-Child Relationships of Black and White High School Students: A Comparison." Journal of Social Psychology 91(D, 1973):349-350.

Stokes, Charles A. Some Effects of Schooling, Age, Race, and Socio-economic Status on the Cognitive Development of Primary School Boys. Dissertation Abstracts International, Vol. 31(8-A)(F, 1971)3793.

Storm, Penelope Annabelle. "An Investigation of Self-Concept, Race Image, and Race Preference in Racial Minority and Majority Children." Doctoral dissertation, U. of Maryland, 1970. Univ. Microfilms Order No. 71-10,227.

Strain, Barbara A. Developmental Trends in the Selective Perception of Race and Affect by Young Negro and Caucasian Children. Nashville, TN: John F. Kennedy Center for Research on Education and Human Development, George Peabody College, Ag, 1970. [Murfreesboro, TN]

Strauch, A. Barry. "More on the Sex and Race Interaction on Cognitive Measures." Journal of Educational Psychology 69(Ap, 1977):152-157.

Streeter, Ronald E., and Kidder, Steven J. The Distribution of Instructional Resources to Students of Varying Ability, Ap, 1977. ERIC ED 137 933.

Strickland, Bonnie R. "Aspiration Response Among Negro and White Adolescents." Journal of Personality and Social Psychology 19(S, 1971):315-320.

Stoll, Clarice, and McPartland, James. Inferiority, Efficacy, and Race, Ag, 1969. ERIC ED 032 379.

Stone, Chuck. Psychology and the Black Community: From Arthur, 1853 to Arthur, 1969, n.d. ERIC ED 054 286.

Stout, Hugh O. "Teaching Proper Racial Attitudes." Catholic High School Quarterly 27 (1969):4-8.

Strain, Barbara. Developmental Trends in the Selective Perception of Race and Affect by Young Negro and Caucasian Children, Ag, 1970. ERIC ED 046 498.

Strickland, Dorothy S. "Black is Beautiful and White is Right." Elementary English 49(F, 1972):220-223.

Strickland, William L. "Identity and Black Struggle: Personal Reflections." In Education and the Black Struggle: Notes from the Colonized World. Edited by Institute of the Black World. Cambridge, MA: Harvard Educational Review, 1974.

Stroup, Atlee L., and Robins, Lee N. "Elementary School Predictors of High School Dropouts Among Black Males." Sociology of Education 45(Spring, 1972).

Stugart, David B. "An Experimental Study Investigating the Effects of Model Race and Model Age-Reference Group Upon the Vocational Information-Seeking Behavior of Male Black Eleventh-Graders." Dissertation Abstracts International 31(7-A)Ja, 1971,3281.

Struve, Mary R. "The Intergroup Quotient in Reading." Integrated Education (N-D, 1971): 34-36.

Student Non-Violent Coordinating Committee (SN CC). "Black Body, White Mind." Atlanta: Student Voice, 1967.

Suchman, Edward A. and others. The Relationship Between Poverty and Educational Deprivation. Final Report, Ag, 1968. ERIC ED 027 369.

Sullivan, Allen R. "A Comparative and Developmental Study Concerning the Influence of Social Processes and Two Stimulus Conditions on Paired-Associate Learning of Elementary Grade Level Afro-American School Children." Dissertation Abstracts International 31(11-B) (My, 1971)6960-6961.

_____. "The Identification of Gifted and Academically Talented Black Students: A Hidden Exceptionality." Journal of Special Education 7(Winter, 1973):373-379.

_____. "The Influence of Social Processes on the Learning Abilities of Afro-American School Children: Some Educational Implications." Journal of Negro Education 41(Spring, 1972):127-136.

Summerland, Elizabeth, and Berry, John. "The Role of Ethnic Identification in Distinguishing Between Attitudes Towards Assimilation and Integration of a Minority Group." Human Relations 23(1971):21-24.

Summers, A. A., and Wolfe, B. L. "Intradistrict Distribution of School Inputs to the Disadvantaged: Evidence for the Courts." Journal of Human Resources 11(1976):329-342.

Surlin, Stuart H. Projective Responses to Racially Identifiable Speech by Racially Prejudiced and Non-Prejudiced Individuals, Ap, 1971. ERIC ED 048 596.

Sussman, Earl, and Thompson, Glen Robbins. Prejudice as a Function of Intellectual Level and Cultural Information, F 5, 1971. ERIC ED 048 421.

Sussman, Leila. Tales Out of School. Implementing Organizational Change in the Elementary Grades. Philadelphia: Temple U. Press, 1977.

Sweet, June R., and Thornburg, Kathy R. "Preschoolers' Self and Social Identity Within the Family Structure." Journal of Negro Education 40(Winter, 1971):22-27.

Tabler, Kenneth A. National Longitudinal Study of the High School Class of 1972: Tabular Summary of the First Followup Questionnaire Data. Washington, D. C.: GPO, 1976.

Tagatz, Glenn E. and others. "Effects of Ethnic Background, Response Option, Task Complexity and Sex on Information Processing in Concept Attainment." Journal of Experimental Education 39(Spring, 1971):69-72.

Tajfel, Henri. "Social Identify and Intergroup Behavior." Social Science Information 13(1974):65-93.

Talbert, Carol. "The Black American Child in Contemporary Education. Separating the Real from the Ideal." Master's thesis, Washington U., Je, 1969.

_____. "Interaction and Adaptation in Two Negro Kindergartens." Human Organization 29 (Summer, 1970):103-114.

Talley, Page. "The Relation of Group Counseling to Changes in the Self-Concept of Negro Eighth Grade Students." Doctoral dissertation, U. of Miami, 1967.

Tallmadge, Guy Kasten, and Horst, Donald P. A Procedural Guide for Validating Achievement Gains in Educational Projects. 2nd edition. Washington, D. C.: GPO, 1976.

Tate, George A. "Toward a Black Psychology of the Healthy Personality." Colorado Journal of Educational Research 12(F, 1972):21-23.

Taylor, Ronald L. "Black Youth and Psychosocial Development: A Conceptual Framework." Journal of Black Studies 6(Je, 1976):353-372.

_____. "Psychosocial Development Among Black Children and Youth: A Reexamination." American Journal of Orthopsychiatry 46(Ja, 1976):4-19.

Teahan, John E., and Podany, Edward C. Some Effects of Films of Successful Negroes on Racial Self-Concept, 1971. ERIC ED 056 140.

Tedeschi, James T., and Levey, Terry M. "Task-Relevant Information, Social Reinforcement, and Race as Factors Affecting Performance." Canadian Journal of Behavioural Science 3 (1971):148-155. [Coconut Grove Elementary School, Miami, Florida]

Tehan, Sally. "An Exploratory Study Concerning the Effects of Race Upon School Achievement." Psychology Journal [Connecticut College], Fall, 1965.

Teicher, J. "Some Observations on Identify Problems in Children of Negro-White Marriages." Journal of Nervous and Mental Diseases 146(1968):249-256.

Ten Houten, Warren D. Cognitive Styles and the Social Order. Part II. Thought, Race, and Opportunity. PB-210 375. Springfield, VA: National Technical Information Service, Jl, 1971.

_____. "Socialization, Race, and the American High School." Doctoral dissertation, Michigan State U., 1965. Univ. Microfilms Order No. 66-444.

Teplin, Linda A. "Preference versus Prejudice: A Multimethod Analysis of Children's Discrepant Racial Choices." Social Science Quarterly 58(D, 1977):390-406.

Terry, Roger L., and Evans, Jane E. "Class versus Race Discrimination Attributed to Self and Others." Journal of Psychology 80 (Mr, 1972):183-187.

Thelen, Mark H. "The Effect of Subject, Race, Model Race, and Vicarious Praise on Vicarious Learning." Child Development 42(S, 1971):972-977.

Thomas, Arthur E. "The Right to be Somebody." Congressional Record, Ap 18, 1972, E3911-3921.

Thomas, Charles W. Blackness as a Personality Construct, Ap 15, 1973. ERIC ED 090 333.

_____. "Boys No More: Some Social Psychological Aspects of the New Black Ethic." American Behavioral Scientist, Mr-Ap, 1969.

_____. Boys No More: A Black Psychologist's View of Community. Beverly Hills, CA: Glencoe Press, 1971.

_____. "Something Borrowed: Something Black." Counseling Psychologist 2(1970):6-10.

Thomas, Elizabeth C. "Conceptual Development in Advantaged and Disadvantaged Kindergarten Children." Perceptual and Motor Skills 3 (Je, 1971):711-717.

Thomas, Elizabeth, C., and Yauramoto, Kaoru. "Minority Children and their School-Related Perceptions." Journal of Experimental Education 40(F, 1971):89-96.

Thomas, Gail Elaine. "Race and Sex Effects in the Process of Educational Achievement." Doctoral dissertation, U. of North Carolina, 1975. Univ. Microfilms Order No. 76-20,077.

Hoben, Thomas. "Psychological Assessment Instruments for Use with Human Infants." Merrill Palmer Quarterly 16(Ap, 1970):179-223.

Thomas, Hollie B. "The Effects of Social Position, Race, and Sex on Work Values of Ninth-Grade Students." Journal of Vocational Behavior 4(Je, 1974):357-364.

Thomas, Katheryn Ann. A Comparison of Teenage Boys' and Girls' Orientation Towards Marriage and Procreation, F 3, 1971. ERIC ED 049 859.

_____. "Educational Orientation of Southern Rural Youth: An Analysis of Socio-economic Status and Racial Differences." Master's thesis, U. of Kentucky, 1970.

Thomas, Katheryn A., and Jacob, Nelson L. A Longitudinal Analysis of Change in Occupational and Educational Orientations of East Texas Boys: A Racial Comparison, Ag, 1970. ERIC ED 042 557.

Thompson, Era Bell. "Blacks Who Grew Up in White Homes." Ebony 29(Je, 1974):84-94.

Thompson, Eugene W., and Miller, Shirley M. A Study of Student Achievement Involving the Consideration of Racial and Socioeconomic Characteristics. Ann Arbor, MI: Ann Arbor Public Schools, 1977.

Thompson, Myrtle E. "Trends in Nursery School Education in the United States with Special Reference to the Negro Schools." Master's thesis, U. of Cincinnati, 1939.

Thomson, Gregory E. "Black Youth and Political Activism: Toward a Social Psychological Paradigm." Doctoral dissertation, Harvard U., 1973.

Thomson, J. "Ethnic Concepts in Children." Race Today, Je, 1969.

Thomson, Susan S. "The Development of Ethnic Concepts in Children." Master's thesis, U. of Strathclyde, 1970.

Thornburg, Hershel D. An Investigation of Attitudes Among Potential Dropouts from Minority Groups During Their Freshman Year in High School. Final Report, S, 1971. ERIC ED 056 792.

_____. Minority Youth Families: A Comparative Analysis of Attitude Between Self and Family, 1971. ERIC ED 056 316.

Thornburg, Hershel D., and Gillespie, Milford E. Learning Relevancy: Psychological Analysis of an Experimental Program for Potential Minority Youth Dropouts, Ap, 1971. ERIC ED 057 123.

Thorpe, Claiburne B. "Race, Grade Level and Children's Perception of Reality." Journal of Social and Behavioral Sciences 17 (Summer, 1971):31-42.

Thorsell, Bernard A. Inter-generational Factors in Ethnic Differences in Self-Esteem, Ap 8, 1976. ERIC ED 134 662.

Thurmond, Vera Belinda. "The Effect of Black English on the Reading Test Performance of High School Students." Journal of Educational Research 70(Ja-F, 1977):160-163.

Thurow, Lester C. "Proving the Absence of Positive Associations." Harvard Educational Review 43(F, 1973):106-112. [In re: Jencks, Inequality]

Thurston, H. W. "Family Social Status and Secondary Education." Commons, Ag 15, 1900.

Tindall, Margaret. The Home Range of Black Elementary School Children: An Exploratory Study in the Measurement and Comparison of Home Range. Chicago: Environmental Research Group, 1971.

Tolle, David L. and   "The Differential Validity of Personality, Personal History, and Aptitude Data for Minority and Non-minority Employees." Personnel Psychology 25(Winter, 1972):661-672.

Tolliver, Billie. "Discrimination Against Minority Groups in Special Education." Education and Training of the Mentally Retarded 10(O, 1975):188-192.

Tonks, Clive M., Paykel, Eugene S., and Klerman, Gerald L. "Clinical Depressions Among Negroes." American Journal of Psychology 127(S, 1970):329-335.

Toomer, Jethro W. "Beyond Being Black: Identification Alone Is Not Enough." Journal of Negro Education 44(Spring, 1975):184-199.

Torrance, Paul E. "Assessment of Disadvantaged Minority Group Children." Educational Horizons 52(Summer, 1974):197-201.

_____. Discovery and Nurturance of Giftedness in the Culturally Different, 1977. ERIC ED 145 621.

Touliatos, John and others. "Interaction of Race With Other Variables on Achievement in School." Psychology in the Schools 14(J1, 1977):360-363.

Trachtenberg, David. "A Survey of Attitudes toward Certain Racial Issues." Integrated Education 8(Mr-Ap, 1970):45-47.

Travis, Cheryl B., and Anthony, Sharon E. "Ethnic Composition of Schools and Achievement Motivation." Journal of Psychology 89(Mr, 1975):271-279.

Travis, Harris Theodore. "The Realism of Black High School Seniors' Educational and/or Occupational Expectations." Doctoral dissertation, U. of Illinois, 1976. Univ. Microfilms Order No. 76-24193.

Traynham, Richard M. "The Effects of Modifying Color Meaning Concepts on Racial Concept Attitudes in Five- and Eight-Year Old Children." Master's thesis, U. of Arkansas, 1974.

Traynham, Richard M., and Witte, Kenneth L. "The Effects of Modifying Color-Meaning Concepts on Racial Concept Attitudes in Five- and Eight-Year-Old Children." Journal of Experimental Child Psychology 21(F, 1976): 165-174.

Treas, Judith. "Differential Achievement: Race, Sex, and Jobs." Sociology and Social Research 62(Ap, 1978):387-400.

Triandis, Harry C. (ed). Variations in Black and White Perceptions of the Social Environment. Urbana: U. of Illinois Press, 1975.

Trowbridge, Norma. "Self-Concept and Socio-Economic Status in Elementary School Children." American Educational Research Journal 9 (Fall, 1972):525-537.

_____. "Socioeconomic Status and Self-Concept of Children." Journal of Teacher Education 23(Spring, 1972):63-65.

Trowbridge, Norma and Others. "Self-Concept and Socio-economic Status." Child Study Journal 2(1972):123-143.

Trubowitz, Julius. Changing the Racial Attitudes of Children. New York: Praeger, 1969.

Tucker, Frank H. The White Conscience: An Analysis of the White Man's Mind and Conduct. New York: Ungar, 1969.

Tucker, R. D. "Connotations of Color Names Among Negroes and Caucasians: A Replication and Extension." Master's thesis, U. of North Carolina, Greensboro, 1969.

Tuckman, Bruce. "Indictment of Ability Grouping." NJEA Review 45(Mr, 1972):22-23.

Tuddenham, Read D., Brooks, Jane, and Milkovich, Lucille. "Mothers' Report of Behavior of Ten-Year Olds: Relationships With Sex, Ethnicity, and Mother's Education." Developmental Psychology 10(N, 1974):959-995.

Tudor, Jeannette F. "The Development of Class Awareness in Children." Social Forces 49 (Mr, 1971).

Tulkin, Steven R. "Race, Class, Family, and School Achievement." Journal of Personality and Social Psychology, My, 1968.

Turner, Barbara F. Perception of the Occupational Opportunity Structure and Socialization to Achievement as Related to Sex and Race, Ap, 1971. ERIC ED 060 471.

Turner, Jonathan H. "Structural Conditions of Achievement Among Whites and Blacks in the Rural South." Social Problems 19(Spring, 1972):496-508. [South Carolina]

UNESCO. Meeting of Experts on Educational Methods Designed to Combat Racial Prejudice. ED/MD/4. New York: UNESCO, O 24, 1968.

Ulin, Richard O. "Ethnicity and School Performance: An Analysis of Variables." California Journal of Educational Research, S, 1968.

Unger, Marjorie G. "Ethnic Pride Begins at Home." Grade Teacher 88(F, 1971):68-71.

Unger, Rhoda, and Beth, Raymond. "External Criteria as Predictors of Value: The Importance of Race and Attire." Journal of Social Psychology 93(Ag, 1974):295-296.

U.S. Bureau of the Census. Characteristics of American Youth: 1974. Washington, DC: GPO, Ap, 1975.

_____. School Enrollment--Social and Economic Characteristics of Students. October 1975. (Advance Report) Washington, DC: Je, 1976.

U.S. Commission on Civil Rights. "Analysis of 'Cost Analysis of Implementation Loci Remedies for the Corpus Christi Independent School District' prepared by the Corpus Christi ISD Division of Instruction and Circulated by Supt. Dana Williams." In Hearing Held in Corpus Christi, Texas, Ag 17, 1976. Washington, DC: The Commission, 1978:82-99.

_____. "Further Analysis of Equality of Educational Opportunity Survey." In Racial Isolation in the Public Schools, vol. II. Washington, DC: GPO, 1967. (Appendix C1.) [Critical re-examination of the Coleman Report]

_____. What Students Perceive. Washington, DC: GPO, 1970.

U.S. Congress, 92nd, 1st session, House of Representatives, Committee on Education and Labor, General Subcommittee on Education. Needs of Elementary and Secondary Education for the Seventies-1971. Hearings... Washington, DC: GPO, 1971.

U.S. Congress, 92nd, 2nd session, Senate, Committee on Labor and Public Welfare, Subcommittee on Education. Education of the Gifted and Talented. Washington, DC: GPO, 1972.

U.S. Congress, 93rd, 2nd session, Senate, Committee on the Judiciary, Subcommittee on Constitutional Rights. Individual Rights and the Federal Role in Behavior Modification. Washington, DC: GPO, 1974.

U.S. Congress, 94th, 1st session, House of Representatives, Committee on Education and Labor, Subcommittee on Elementary, Secondary, and Vocational Education. Safety and Violence in Elementary and Secondary Schools. Hearings... Washington, DC: GPO, 1975.

_____. Student Suspensions: Hearing... Washington, DC: GPO, 1976.

U.S. Congress, 94th, 1st session, Senate, Committee on the Judiciary, Subcommittee to Investigate Juvenile Delinquency. School Violates and Vandalism. Hearings... The Nature, Extent, and Cost of Violence and Vandalism in Our Nation's Schools. Washington, DC: GPO, 1976.

_____. School Violence and Vandalism Hearing ... Models and Strategies for Change. Washington, DC: GPO, 1976.

U.S. Congress, 95th, 1st session, Senate, Committee on Human Resources, Subcommittee on Education, Arts, and Humanities. Quality of Education, 1977. Hearings... Washington, DC: GPO, 1977.

U.S. Department of Health, Education, and Welfare. A Practical Guide to Measuring Project Impact on Student Achievement. Washington, DC: GPO, 1975.

_____. "List of Statistics Showing School Districts Which Implemented or Revised Student Assignment Plans." In U.S. Congress, 92nd, 2nd session, Senate, Committee on Labor and Public Welfare, Subcommittee on Education, Equal Educational Opportunities Act of 1972. Hearings... Washington, DC: GPO, 1972:302-315. [1971 and 1970 data]

U.S. Office of Education. Black Concerns Staff of the Office of Education. Washington, DC: GPO, 1976.

U.S. Public Health Service. Behavior Patterns of Children in School. United States. Washington, DC: GPO, F, 1972. [1963-1965 national data]

_____. Intellectual Development and School Achievement of Youths 12-17 Years: Demographic and Socioeconomic Factors, D, 1976. ERIC ED 139 686.

_____. Parent Ratings of Behavioral Patterns of Youths 12-17 Years. United States. Washington, DC: GPO, My, 1974.

Upward Bound. A Study of Impact on the Secondary School and the Community. New York: Greenleigh Associates, Ja, 1969.

Useem, Elizabeth. Correlates of Racial Attitudes Among White High School Students, 1972. ERIC ED 061 534.

Van der Does, V. I. "Children and Road Accidents." International Journal of Early Childhood 3(1971):90-93.

Van De Riet, Vernon, and Van De Riet, Hani. A Follow-up Evaluation of the Effects of a Unique Sequential Learning Program, a Traditional Preschool Program and a No Treatment Program on Culturally Deprived Children. Final Report, D, 1969. ERIC ED 042 516.

Vane, Julia R. "Relation of Early School Achievement to High School Achievement When Race, Intelligence and Socioeconomic Factors Are Equated." Psychology in the Schools, Ap, 1966.

Vanlandingham, Calvin L. Relationships of Occupational Aspirations of Youth to Selected Social Variables in Two Mississippi Counties. Dissertation Abstracts International, 1969, 30(2-A)840.

Vaughn, Victor C. III (ed). Issues in Human Development. An Inventory of Problems, Unfinished Business and Directions for Research. Washington, DC: GPO, 1970.

Versteeg, Arlen, and Hall, Robert. "Level of Aspiration, Achievement, and Sociocultural Differences in Preschool Children." Journal of Genetic Psychology 119(S, 1971):137-142.

Vetta, Atam. "Conservation in Aboriginal Children and 'Genetic Hypothesis.'" International Journal of Psychology 7(1972):247-256.

Vick, Marian Lee. Critical Issues in Reading Instruction Among Black Teachers and Students: Personnel and Training, My 12, 1972. ERIC ED 063 088.

_____. Realities and Fallacies of Reading Instruction for Ethnically Different Students: Cognitive and Affective Concerns, D, 1971. ERIC ED 063 087.

Vieni, Miriam. "Transracial Adoption Is a Solution Now." Social Work 20(S, 1975):419-421. [By an adoptive parent of a Black-Vietnamese child]

Vocke, Jacqueline M. "Measuring Racial Attitude in Preschool Negro Children." Master's thesis, U. of South Carolina, 1971.

von Mering, Otto. The Question of Ethnic Identity. CAE Newsletter, Vol. 3, No. 1. F, 1972. ERIC ED 063 420.

Vontress, Clemmont E. "Barriers in Cross-Cultural Counseling." Counseling and Values 18(1974):160-164.

_____. Cultural Differences: Implications for Counseling, Ap 10, 1968. ERIC ED 023 105.

_____. "Cultural Differences: Implications for Counseling." Journal of Negro Education, Summer, 1969.

_____. Self-Hatred in Americans of African Descent, 1974. ERIC ED 098 107.

_____. "Should Your Child Attend a Negro College?" Negro Digest, Mr, 1967.

Wachtel, Dawn Day. "Adoption Agencies and the Adoption of Black Children: Social Change and Equal Opportunity in Adoption." Doctoral dissertation, U. of Michigan, 1972. Univ. Microfilms Order No. 73-11289.

Wade, Gwendolyn G. "Psychological Needs, Black Consciousness, and Socialization Practices Among Black Adolescents in Nova Scotia, Canada and Michigan, U.S.A." Doctoral dissertation, Michigan State U., 1972.

Wade, Kenneth, and Wilson, Warner. "Relatively Low Prejudice in a Racially Isolated Group." Psychological Reports 28(Je, 1971):871-877.

Waite, Linda J. Educational Attainment in the United States, March, 1975. Washington, DC: GPO, 1976.

Walberg, Herbert J. (ed). Evaluating Educational Performance. A Sourcebook of Methods, Instruments, and Examples. Berkeley, CA: McCutchan, 1974.

Walberg, Herbert J., and Marjoriebanks, Kevin. "Differential Mental Abilities and Home Environment: A Canonical Analysis." Developmental Psychology 9(N, 1973):363-368.

Walberg, Herbert J., and Rasher, Sue Pinzur. "Public School Effectiveness and Equality: New Evidence and Its Implications." Phi Delta Kappan 56(S, 1974):3-9.

_____. "The Ways Schooling Makes a Difference." Phi Delta Kappan 58(My, 1977).

Walker, A. D. Implications of Generalized Expectations of Black Children in Educational Settings, 1969. ERIC ED 051 324.

Walker, Kenneth De Leon. "Effects of Social and Cultural Isolation upon the Self-Concepts of Negro Children." Doctoral dissertation, U. of Miami, 1968.

Walker, Olive. "How to Rear an Integrated Child." The Integrator, Fall, 1968.

Wallace, E. B. "A Study of the Relationship Between Socio-Economic Background, Intelligence, and Educational Progress of Negro Children." Master's thesis, U. of Cincinnati, 1932. [Four schools in Cincinnati, Ohio]

Wallin, Paul and Others. Family and School Influence on the Educational Goals of Working-Class and Middle-Class Tenth-Grade Boys. Final Report, Mr, 1970. ERIC ED 038 730.

Walls, Richard T., and Kalbaugh, Janet Cox. "Retroactive and Proactive Multiple List Interference with Disadvantaged Children." Child Study Journal 2(1972):91-97.

Walsh, John F. and others. "Performance of Negro and Puerto Rican Head Start Children on the Vane Kindergarten Test." Psychology in the Schools 8(O, 1971):357-358.

Ward, Francis. "Black Youth An Endangered Species." First World 1(Ja-F, 1977):22-24.

Ward, Susan H., and Braun, John. "Self-Esteem and Racial Preference in Black Children." American Journal of Orthopsychiatry 42(Jl, 1972):644-647.

Warner, Victoria Efferson. "The Adoption of Black Children: Retrospect and Prospect." Doctoral dissertation, Florida State U., 1974. Univ. Microfilms Order No. 75-07310.

Wash, Brenda D. "The Black Child's Self-Concept: A Study of Ten- and Eleven-Year Olds Varying in Sex, Socioeconomic Background and Integrated vs. Segregated School Settings." Doctoral dissertation, U. of California, Los Angeles, 1972.

Washington, Anita C. "Self-Acceptance and Group Identification Among a Group of Black Upward Bound Students." Dissertation Abstracts International 31,6B(D, 1970):3695.

Washington, Booker T. "Destitute Colored Children of the South." Proceedings of the Conference on the Care of Dependent Children Held at Washington, D.C., January 25, 26, 1909. Washington, DC: 1909.

Washington, Daniel Louis. "The Identification of Black Drug Abusers in a Southern Public School System." Doctoral dissertation, Boston U., 1976. Univ. Microfilms Order No. 76-19970.

Wasik, Barbara H., and Wasik, John L. "Response Strategies of Culturally Deprived Children." Journal of Experimental Education 40(Spring, 1972):84-90.

Wasserman, Herbert L. "A Comparative Study of School Performance Among Boys from Broken and Intact Black Families." Journal of Negro Education 41(Spring, 1972):137-141. [Boston area]

Wasserman, Miriam. "School Mythology and the Education of Oppression." This Magazine Is About Schools 5(Spring, 1971):23-36.

Watley, Donivan J. "Black Brainpower. Characteristics of Bright Black Youth." In Youth in Contemporary Society. Edited by David Gottlieb. Beverly Hills, CA: Sage, 1973:9-41.

_____. "Bright Achievers. Their Characteristics and Some Expected Behavior Patterns." In Youth in Contemporary Society. Edited by David Gottlieb. Beverly Hills, CA: Sage, 1973:43-77.

Watson, Bernard C. "Schooling, Violence and Vandalism: Promising Practices and Policy Alternatives." In U.S. Congress, 94th, 2nd session, House of Representatives, Committee on Education and Labor, Subcommittee on Equal Opportunities, Oversight Hearing on the Juvenile Justice and Delinquence Prevention Act. Hearing.... Washington, DC: GPO, 1976:2-46.

_____. Stupidity, Sloth and Public Policy: Social Darwinism Rides Again. Washington, DC: National Urban Coalition, 1974.

_____. Survival, Phase II: Unity Without Uniformity. New York: National Urban League, Jl, 1972.

Watters, Pat. "Why the Negro Children March." New York Times Magazine, Mr 21, 1965.

Wax, Douglas E. "Self-Concept in Negro and White Preadolescent Delinquent Boys." Child Study Journal 2(1972):175-184.

_____. "Social Class, Race, and Juvenile Delinquency: A Review of the Literature." Child Psychiatry and Human Development 3 (Fall, 1972):36-49.

Weaver, Edward K. "Racial Sensitivity Among Negro Children." Phylon 17(1956):52-60.

Webb, Margo S. "The Brainwashing of the Child by the Mythology of the Text Book." African-American Teachers Forum, N-D, 1969.

Weber, George. Inner-City Children Can Be Taught to Read: Four Successful Schools, O, 1971. Council for Basic Education, 725 Fifteenth Street, N.W., Washington, DC 20005. [N.Y.C., Kansas City, MO, and Los Angeles, CA]

Webster, Staten W. "The Influence of Interracial Contact on Social Acceptance in a Newly Integrated School." Journal of Educational Psychology, D, 1961.

Webster, Staten W., and Kroger, Marie N. "A Comparison Study of Selected Perceptions and Feelings of Negro Adolescents With and Without White Friends in Integrated Schools." Journal of Negro Education, Winter, 1966.

_____. Correlates and Effects of Ethnic Group Identification. NIMH Project 07321-01. Berkeley, CA: U. of California, 1963.

Weigel, Russell H., Wiser, Patricia L., and Cook, Stuart W. "The Impact of Cooperative Learning Experiences on Cross-Ethnic Relations and Attitudes." Journal of Social Issues 31(1975):219-244. [Denver]

Weinstein, Eugene. Psychosocial Deprivation and Interpersonal Competence. Bethesda, MD: National Institute of Child Health and Human Development, 1968.

Weintraub, Walter. "American Middle-Class Adolescents as Psychiatric In-patients." In Minority Group Adolescents in the United States. Edited by Eugene B. Brody. Baltimore, MD: Williams and Wilkins, 1968.

Weisberg, Herbert I., and Haney, Walt. Longitudinal Evaluation of Head Start Planned Variation and Follow Through, Je, 1977. ERIC ED 157 918.

Weiss, Randall. "The Effects of Scholastic Achievement Upon the Earnings of Whites and Negroes: Experiments with Single Equation and Recursive Models." Bachelor's thesis, Harvard College, 1968.

Wellborn, Emily S. and others. "Effect of Examiner Race on Test of Black and White Children." Education and Training of the Mentally Retarded 8(D, 1973):194-196.

Wellman, Barry. "'I Am a Student.'" Sociology of Education 44(Fall, 1971):422-436.

Wells, Elmer Eugene. "The Mythical Negative Black Self-Concept." Doctoral dissertation, U. of New Mexico, 1974. Univ. Microfilms Order No. 75-06960.

Wells, Melvin W. "Black Dialect in Children's Books." Reading Horizons 17(F, 1976):39-44.

Wells, Twyla Teresa. "The Effects of Discrimination Upon Motivation and Achievement of Black Children in Urban Ghetto Schools." American Behavioral Scientist, Mr-Ap, 1969.

Wen, Shih-Sung, and McCoy, Rose E. "Relationships of Selected Nonacademic and Academic Variables to the Grade Point Average of Black Students." Educational and Psychological Measurement 35(Winter, 1975):935-939.

Wendland, Marilyn M. "Self-Concept Development in the Negro Adolescent and Its Relationship to Area of Residence." Doctoral dissertation, U. of North Carolina, 1967.

Werner, Emmy E. "From Birth to Latency: Behavioral Differences in a Multiracial Group of Twins." Child Development 44(S, 1973):438-444.

White, Burton L. Competence in Young Children, Mr, 1969. ERIC ED 032 124.

White, Harriet. "On Being Black." Community, Ja, 1969.

The White House Conference on Child Health and Protection, Committee on the School Child Section III-C, Thomas D. Wood, Chairman. Report of subcommittee on the Negro school child. Washington, DC: The Conference, 1930.

White House Conference on Food, Nutrition and Health. Final Report. Washington, DC: GPO, 1970.

White, Maurice O. "Alienation and Self-Esteem As They Relate to Race, Sex, Socioeconomic and School Variables in Urban High School Age Youth." Dissertation Abstracts International 32(2-A)Ag, 1971,803-4.

"White Parents, Black Children: Transracial Adoption." Time, Ag 16, 1971.

White, Sheldon, Day, Mary Carol, Freeman, Phyllis K., Hautman, Stephen A., and Messenger, Katherine P. Federal Programs for Young Children. 4 vols. 1974. The Human Institute, 119 Mount Auburn St., Cambridge, MA 02138.

White, William F., and Richmond, Bert O. "Perception of Self and of Peers by Economically Deprived Black and Advantaged White Fifth Graders." Perceptual and Motor Skills 30(Ap, 1970):533-534.

Whitehead, Robert E. "Attitudes of Suburban Groups Toward Negroes and Inter-District Busing of Students." Doctoral dissertation, U. of Washington, 1969.

Whitehurst, Keturah E. Techniques and Processes of Socialization of the Black Child, Jl 12, 1972. ERIC ED 097 963.

Whitmore, Joanne Rand. Student Leadership: Guidelines for Developing Programs in Distressed Low-Income Elementary Schools. Stanford, CA: School of Education, Stanford U., S, 1973.

_____. "A Leadership Program Designed to Improve the Attitudes and Behavior of Black Elementary Students: An Action-Research Project." Doctoral dissertation, Stanford U., 1973. [Printed as The Modification of Undesirable Attitudes and Classroom Behavior Through Constructive Use of Social Power in the School Peer Culture. Stanford, CA: School of Education, Stanford U., Ag, 1973.]

Wiedman, John C. II. "Some Social Factors Which Influence the Elementary School Performance of the Urban Child." Education and Urban Society, N, 1969.

Wiggins, Phyllis. "Redirecting the Focus on the Black Student." Educational Leadership 29 (Mr, 1972):539-541.

Wilcox, Roger. "Further Ado About Negro Music Ability." Journal of Negro Education 40 (Fall, 1971):361-364.

_____. "Racial Differences in Associative Style." Language and Speech 14(Jl-S, 1971): 251-255.

_____ (ed). The Psychological Consequences of Being a Black American. A Sourcebook of Research by Black Psychologists. New York: Wiley, 1971.

Wiley, David. "Another Hour, Another Day: Quantity of Schooling, a Potent Path for Policy." In Schooling and Achievement in American Society. Edited by William H. Sewell, Robert M. Hauser, and David L. Featherman. New York: Wiley, 1975.

Wiley, David, and Harnischfeger, Annegret. "Explosion of a Myth: Quantity of Schooling and Exposure to Instruction, Major Educational Vehicles." Educational Researcher 3 (Ap, 1974):7-12.

Wilhelms, Fred T., and Waller, Patricia F. "The Education of Intellect" (3 parts). NASSP Bulletin, Ap, 1969.

Wilkerson, Doxey A. "Racial Differences in Scholastic Achievement." Journal of Negro Education 3(Jl, 1934):453-477.

_____. "Standardizing Children." Freedomways 17(1977):197-201.

_____. "Understanding the Black Child." Childhood Education 46(Ap, 1970):351-354.

Wilkins, Roger. "Black Parents' Hopes." Inequality in Education 11(Mr, 1972):24.

Wilkinson, Andrew. "Frontal Assaults on Dialect Are Not the Answer." The Teacher 22(Ja, 1973).

Wilkinson, Doris Y. "Coming of Age in a Racist Society. The Whitening of America." In Youth in Contemporary Society. Edited by David Gottlieb. Beverly Hills, CA: Sage, 1973.

_____. "Racial Socialization Through Children's Toys: A Sociohistorical Examination." Journal of Black Studies 5(S, 1974):96-109.

_____. "Status Differences and the Black Hate Stare: A Conversation of Gestures." Phylon, Summer, 1969.

Willerman, Lee, Naylor, Alfred F., and Myrianthopoulos, Ntinos. "Intellectual Development of Children from Interracial Matings." Science 170(D, 1970):1329-1331.

Williams, Daniel E. Self-Concept and Verbal Mental Ability in Negro Pre-school Children. Dissertation Abstracts International, 1969, 29(9-B)3475.

Williams, Evalina. "Effects of Intergroup Discussion on Social Distance and Personal Space of Black and White Students." Doctoral dissertation, U. of Texas, 1972.

Williams, Frederick (ed). Language and Poverty, Chicago, IL: Markham, 1970.

Williams, Frederick, and Rundell, Edward E. "Teaching Teachers to Comprehend Negro Non-Standard English." Speech Teacher 20 (S, 1971):174-177.

Williams, Frederick and others. "Ethnic Stereotyping and Judgments of Children's Speech." Speech Monographs 38(Ag, 1971): 166-170.

Williams, Joanna. Visual and Aural Learning in Urban Children. Final Report. Philadelphia, PA: U. of Pennsylvania, 1970. ERIC ED 043 924.

Williams, Joanna, Williams, David V., and Blumberg, Ellen L. "Visual and Aural Learning in Urban Children." Journal of Educational Psychology 64(Je, 1973):353-359.

Williams, John E. "Connotations of Color Names Among Negroes and Caucasians." Perceptual and Motor Skills 18(1964):721-731.

Williams, John E., and Carter, D. J. "Connotations of Racial Concepts and Color Names in Germany." Journal of Social Psychology 72 (1967):19-26.

Williams, John E., and McMurty, C. Allen. "Color Connotations Among Caucasian Seventh Graders and College Students." Perceptual and Motor Skills 30(Je, 1970):707-713.

Williams, John E., and Edwards, C. D. "An Exploratory Study of the Modification of Color Concepts and Racial Attitudes in Pre-school Children." Child Development 40(1969): 737-750.

Williams, John E., and Foley, J. W., Jr. "Connotative Meanings of Color Names and Color Hues." Perceptual and Motor Skills 26(1968):499-502. [College students]

Williams, John E., and Morland, J. Kenneth. Race, Color, and the Young Child. Chapel Hill: U. of North Carolina Press, 1976.

Williams, John E., and Roberson, J. K. "A Method for Assessing Racial Attitudes in Pre-school Children." Educational and Psychological Measurement, Autumn, 1967.

Williams, John E., and Rousseau, Cynthia A. "Evaluation and Identification Response of Negro Preschoolers to the Colors Black and White." Perceptual and Motor Skills 33(O, 1971):587-599.

Williams, John E. and others. "Changes in the Connotations of Color Names Among Negroes and Caucasians: 1963-1969." Journal of Personality and Social Psychology 19(Ag, 1971): 222-228.

_____. "Preschool Racial Attitude Measure II." Educational and Psychological Measurement 35 (Spring, 1975):3-18.

Williams, J. Gordon, and Stack, James J. "Internal-External Control As a Situational Variable in Determining Information Seeking by Negro Students." Journal of Consulting and Clinical Psychology 39(O, 1972):187-193.

Williams, Margaret M. "Race, Poverty and Educational Achievement in an Urban Environment." Proceedings of the Annual Convention of the American Psychological Association 7(1972), pt. 1,467-468.

Williams, Robert L. "Black Pride, Academic Relevance and Individual Achievement." Counseling Psychologist 2(1970):18-22.

_____. Research in the Black Community: A Black Psychologist's Perspective, Ap, 1972. ERIC ED 064 431.

Williams, Robert L., and Byars, Harry. "The Effect of Academic Integration on the Self-Esteem of Southern Negro Students." Journal of Social Psychology 80(Ap, 1970):183-188.

_____. "Negro Self-Esteem in a Transitional Society." Personnel and Guidance Journal, O, 1968.

Williamson, Robert C. "Social Distance and Ethnicity: Some Sub-cultural Factors Among High School Students." Urban Education 11 (O, 1976):295-312.

Willie, Charles V. "Educational Inequality: Race is The Problem." Integrateducation 13 (Mr-Ap, 1975):12. [See Rohwer, 1975, above.]

_____. The Sociology of Urban Education: Desegregation and Integration. Lexington, MA: Lexington Books, 1978.

Willis, Frank N., and Hofmann, Gale E. "Development of Tactile Patterns in Relation to Age, Sex, and Race." Developmental Psychology 11(N, 1975):866-867.

Willis, Frank N., and Reeves, Dennis L. "Touch Interaction in Junior High Students in Relation to Sex and Race." Developmental Psychology 12(Ja, 1976):91-92.

Wilson, Alan B. "Social Class and Equal Educational Opportunity." Harvard Educational Review, Winter, 1968.

_____. "Residential Segregation of Social Classes and Aspirations of High School Boys." American Sociological Review, D, 1959.

Wilson, Geraldine L. "Black Parenting: A Collective Concern." Interracial Books for Children Bulletin 9(1978):14-18.

Wilson, Ronald S., and Harpring, Eileen B. "Mental and Motor Development in Infant Twins." Developmental Psychology 7(N, 1972): 277-287.

Wilson, Thomas A. The Effect of Racial Group Membership and Cross-Race Contact on the Communication of Expectancies. Dissertation Abstracts International, Vol. 31(9-A)(Mr, 1971)4891.

Wilson, W. C. "The Development of Ethnic Attitudes in Adolescence." Child Development 34 (1963):250-253.

Wilson, William A., Jr. "Black Student Sub-Cultures and their Use of Student Services." NASPA 12(F, 1974):125-129.

Winkler, Donald R. "Educational Achievement and School Peer Group Composition." Journal of Human Resources 10(Spring, 1975):189-204.

_____. The Production of Human Capital: A Study of Minority Achievement. New York: Arno Press, 1977.

_____. "The Production of Human Capital: A Study of Minority Achievement." Doctoral dissertation, U. of California, Berkeley, 1972.

_____. "Unequal Achievement and the Schools." Integrateducation 14(Ja-F, 1976).

Winnick, R., and Taylor, J. "Racial Preference--36 Years Later." Journal of Social Psychology 102(Je, 1977):157-158.

Witkin, Herman A., and Berry, John W. "Psychological Differentiation in Cross-Cultural Perspective." Journal of Cross-Cultural Psychology 6(Mr, 1975):4-87. [Literature review]

Wittig, Monika. "Identification and Processing of Trouble-makers in School." Doctoral dissertation, Northwestern U., 1973.

Witty, Paul A., and Jenkins, Martin D. "The Educational Achievement of a Group of Gifted Negro Children." Journal of Educational Psychology 25(N, 1934):585-595.

Wolf, Alison. "The State of Urban Schools: New Data on an Old Problem." Urban Education 13 (Jl, 1978):179-194.

Wolf, Richard M. Achievement in America. New York: Teachers College Press, 1977.

Wolfe, Barry E. "A Comparison of the Impact of Two Kindergarten Programs on the Creative Performance of Disadvantaged Negro Children." Dissertation Abstracts International 31(11-B) (My, 1971)6886.

Wolff, Max, and Stein, Annie. "Head Start Six Months Later." Phi Delta Kappan, Mr, 1967.

_____. Long-Range Effect of Pre-Schooling on Reading Achievements. New York: Ferkauf Graduate School of Education, Yeshiva U., 1966. [Day-care children after three years]

_____. Six Months Later. A Comparison of Children Who Had Head Start. Summer, 1965, with their Classmates in Kindergarten. A Case Study of the Kindergartens in Four Public Elementary Schools, New York City. New York: Ferkauf Graduate School of Education, Yeshiva U., 1966.

Wolff, Peter H. "'Critical Periods' in Human Cognitive Development." Hospital Practice, N, 1970. [Reprinted in Stella Chess and Alexander Thomas (eds.), Annual Progress in Child Psychiatry and Child Development. New York: Brunner/Mazel, 1971:155-165.

Wolk, Rochelle B. "The Dimensions of Future Time Perspective in Black and White Children." Dissertation Abstracts International 31(10-B)(Ap, 1971)6272.

Wolkon, George H. "African Identity of the Negro American and Achievement." Journal of Social Issues 27(1971):199-211.

Woodruff, James W. The Effect of Degree of Personality Integration as Influenced by Social and Racial Group Membership Upon Adolescent Educational Achievement and Vocational Exploratory Behavior. Dissertation Abstracts International, 1969, 30(1-A)145.

Worcester, Everett, and Ashbaugh, Carl. "Socioeconomic Status, Ethnic Background, and Student Unrest." Clearing House 47(O, 1972):87-90.

Wright, Bobby. "A Psychological Theory of Educating the Black Child." Black Books Bulletin 3(Fall, 1976).

Wright, Lawrence. "Black English: Need? Nonsense?" Race Relations Reporter 3(N 6, 1972):6-7.

Wright, Wilbert. "Vocational and Learning Attitudes of Black Students." Journal of College Student Personnel 12(Jl, 1971):253-258.

Wubberhorst, John and Others. "Trust in Children as a Function of Race, Sex, and Socio-economic Group." Psychological Reports 29(D, 1971):1183-1187.

Wylie, Ruth C. The Self Concept. Vol. 1: A Review of Methodological Considerations and Measuring Instruments. Rev. ed. Lincoln, NB: U. of Nebraska Press, 1974.

Wylie, Ruth C., and Hutchins, E. B. "School-work Ability Estimates and Aspirations as a Function of Socioeconomic Level, Race and Sex." Psychological Reports 21(1967):781-808.

Wyne, Martin D., White, Kinnard P., and Coop, Richard H. The Black Self. Englewood Cliffs, NJ: Prentice-Hall, 1974.

Yackley, Andrew, and Lambert, Wallace E. "Inter-Ethnic Group Competition and Levels of Aspiration." Canadian Journal of Behavioral Science 3(1971):135-147.

Yancey, Anna V., and Singh, Jane M. "A Study of Racial Attitudes in White First Grade Children." Elementary English 52(My, 1975):734-736.

Yancey, William L., Rigsby, Leo, and McCarthy, John D. "Social Position and Self-Evaluation: The Relative Importance of Race." American Journal of Sociology 78(S, 1972):338-359.

Yawkey, Thomas D., and Blackwell, Jacqueline. "Attitudes of 4-Year Old Urban Black Children Toward Themselves and Whites Based Upon Multi-Ethnic Social Studies Materials and Experiences." Journal of Educational Research 67(Ap, 1974).

Yee, Albert H. "Interpersonal Attitudes of Teachers and Advantaged and Disadvantaged Pupils, Journal of Human Resources, Summer, 1968.

Yetman, Norman R. The Slave Personality: A Test of the "Sambo" Hypothesis. Dissertation Abstracts International, 1970, 30(7-A)3116.

Yokley, Rotha L. "The Development of Racial Concepts in Negro Children." Doctoral dissertation, Indiana U., 1953.

Young, Andrew J. Violence in the Schools: A Crisis and an Opportunity for Educational Reform in the 70's. Atlanta, GA: Martin Luther King, Jr. Center for Non-Violent Social Change, 1972.

Young, Biloine Whiting, and Bress, Grace Billings. "Coleman's Retreat and the Politics of Good Intentions." Phi Delta Kappan 57(N, 1975):159-166.

Young, Charles Thomas. "Art-Color Skin-Color Relationships: A Regional Social Perception Study of Tennessee Elementary School Children." Doctoral dissertation, George Peabody College, 1967. DA3795-A.

Young, Donald R. "Some Effects of the Course on American Race Problems on the Race Prejudice of 450 Undergraduates at the University of Pennsylvania." Journal of Abnormal and Social Psychology 22(1927):235-242.

Young, Kan-Hua, and Jamison, Dean T. The Economic Benefits of Schooling and Reading Competence, My, 1975. ERIC ED 157 900.

Zaffy, Donna J. Help-Seeking Behavior in
Second, Fourth, and Sixth Grade Negro Boys
of Low and Middle Socioeconomic Status.
Dissertation Abstracts International, 1970
(Ag)Vol. 31(2-B)908.

Zalk, Sue R., and Katz, Phyllis A. Katz-Zalk
Projective Prejudice Test: A Measure of
Racial Attitudes in Children. Washington,
DC: American Psychological Association,
1976.

Zastrow, Charles Harold. "Outcomes of Negro
Children-Caucasian Parents Transracial
Adoptions." Doctoral dissertation, U. of
Wisconsin, 1971. Univ. Microfilms Order No.
71-23337.

Zellmer, Kathleen O. "The Black Student in
Gray High School, Any City, U.S.A." C.S.P.
A.A. Bulletin 32(My, 1974):11,15. [Student
publications in predominantly black schools]

Ziajka, Alan L. "Self-Concept and the Black
Child." Master's thesis, California State
U., Northridge, 1972.

Zigler, Edward F. A Study of Culturally De-
prived Children in Kindergarten and Grade I
Following a Nine-Month Nursery Experience,
D 29, 1967. ERIC ED 136 901.

_____. "America's Head Start Programs: An
Agenda for Its Second Decade." Young
Children 33(Jl, 1978):4-11.

_____. "Social Class and the Socialization
Process." Review of Educational Research
40(F, 1970):87-110.

Zimmerman, Barry J., and Brody, Gene H. "Race
and Modeling Influences on the Interpersonal
Play Patterns of Boys." Journal of Educational Psychology 67(O, 1975):591-598.

Zimmerman, Barry J., and Rosenthal, Ted L.
"Observation, Repetition, and Ethnic Background in Concept Attainment and Generalization." Child Development 43(Je, 1972):605-
613.

Zinser, Otto and others. "Racial Recipients,
Value of Donations, and Sharing Behavior in
Children." Journal of Genetic Psychology
129(S, 1976):29-35.

Zirkel, Perry A. "Self-Concept and the Disad-
vantage of Ethnic Group Membership and
Mixture." Review of Educational Research 41
(Je, 1971):211-225.

Zirkel, Perry A., and Gable, Robert K. "The
Reliability and Validity of Various Measures
of Self-Concept Among Ethnically Different
Adolescents." Measurement and Evaluation in
Guidance 10(Ap, 1977):48-53.

Zirkel, Perry A., and Moses, E. G. "Self-
Concept and Ethnic Group Membership among
Public School Students." American Education-
al Research Journal 8(Mr, 1971):253-265.

Zito, R. J., and Bardon, J. I. "Negro Adolescents' Success and Failure. Imagery Concerning Work and School." Vocational Guidance Quarterly 16(1968):181-184.

Zlotnick, Samuel Jack. "The Effects of Peer
Group Acceptance and Positive Reference
Identification on the Achievement of Male
Sixth-Graders: A Study of Negro Students
Attending Public Schools in Lower Socio-
economic and Residentially Segregated
Communities." Doctoral dissertation, New
York U., 1975. Univ. Microfilms Order No.
76-12605.

Zoloth, Barbara S. Relative Test Performance
Over Time of Black, Spanish, and Anglo
Students: A Case Study. Madison: Institute
for Research on Poverty, U. of Wisconsin,
1975.

Zucker, Joseph S., and Stricker, George.
"Impulsivity-Reflectivity in Preschool Head
Start and Middle Class Children." Journal
of Learning Disabilities 1(O, 1968):578-584.

Zunich, M. "Perceptions of Indian, Mexican,
Negro, and White Children Concerning the
Development of Responsibility." Perceptual
and Motor Skills 32(Je, 1971):796-798.

Bibliographies

Afendras, Evangelos A., and Pianarosa, Albertina
(comps). Child Bilingualism and Second
Language Learning: A Descriptive Bibliography. Montreal: Laval U. Press, 1975.

An Annotated Bibliography on Early Childhood.
Ann Arbor, MI: U. of Michigan, Architectural
Research Lab, 1970.

Association on American Indian Affairs. Pre-
liminary Bibliography of Selected Children's
Books About American Indians, 1969. The
Association, 432 Park Avenue South, New
York, NY 10016.

Archer, Marguerite P. "Minorities in Easy
Reading Through Third Grade." Elementary
English 49(My, 1972):746-749.

Atkin, C. K., Murray, J. P., and Nayman, O. B.
(comps). Television and Social Behavior: An
Annotated Bibliography of Research Focusing
on Television's Impact on Children. Washington, DC: National Institute of Mental
Health, 1971.

Baker, Augusta (comp). The Black Experience in
Children's Books. Revised edition. New York:
Office of Children's Books, New York Public
Library, 1971.

Black Students and Standard English: An Annotated Bibliography for Teachers. Burlington,
VT: Exercise Exchange, Department of English, U. of Vermont, 1977.

Boshier, Roger. "Self-Regarding Attitudes: A
Bibliography." Psychological Reports 26
(F, 1970).

Bynum, Effie M. Desegregation, Preservice and
Inservice Training: An Annotated Targeted
Bibliography, Mr, 1971. New York: NCRIEEO,
Box 40, Teachers College, Columbia U., New
York, NY 10027.

Cameron, Colin (comp). Attitudes of the Poor
and Attitudes Toward the Poor. An Annotated
Bibliography. Revised edition. Madison:
Institute for Research on Poverty, U. of
Wisconsin, 1975.

Cameron, Colin and Others (comp). Discrimination in Testing. Bibliography. Revised
edition. Madison: Institute for Research
on Poverty, U. of Wisconsin, 1973.

Cane, Suzanne S. and Others (comps). Selected
Media About the American Indian for Young
Children K-3. Boston, MA: Bureau of
Curriculum Innovation, Massachusetts Depart-
ment of Education, 1970.

Coard, Bernard. "Book List for Parents. West
Indian Literature for Children." In How the
West Indian Child Is Made Educationally Sub-
Normal In the British School System, 1971.
New Beacon Books Ltd., 2 Albert Road, London
N4, England.

Committee on Maternal Nutrition and Others
(comps). Annotated Bibliography on Maternal
Nutrition. Washington, DC: GPO, 1970.

Cordasco, Francesco (comp). "Bilingual Education: An American Dilemma." Immigration
History Newsletter 10(My, 1978):5-8.

_____. "Poor Children and Schools: Bibliogra-
phical Essay." Choice 7(Ap and My, 1970):
202-212,355-356.

Cortez, Ruben, and Navarro, Joseph (comps).
Mexican-American History: A Critical Selective Bibliography. Santa Barbara, CA: Mexican-American Historical Society, 1969.

Council for Exceptional Children (comp). Non-
discriminatory Testing. A Selective Bibliography, 1976. ERIC ED 129 005.

Davis, Lenwood G. (comp). A History of Tubercu-
losis in the Black Community: A Working
Bibliography. Monticello, IL: Council of
Planning Librarians, 1975.

_____. The History of Selected Diseases in the
Black Community: A Working Bibliography.
Monticello, IL: Council of Planning Librari-
an, Je, 1976.

Dean, Frances F. Intercultural Education
Series. A Selected, Annotated Bibliography
of Inter-American Teaching Aids for Art,
English Language Arts, Music, Social Studies,
and Spanish, 1967. ERIC ED 052 097.

Dissemination Center for Bilingual Bicultural
Education (comp). Annotated Bibliography of
Bilingual Bicultural Materials. Cumulative
Issue 1974, D, 1974. ERIC ED 126 730.

Dorton, Eleanor, and Davis, Lenwood G. (comps).
Juvenile Delinquency in the Black Community.
Monticello, IL: Council of Planning Libra-
rians, 1975.

Doyle, Ruby Neff. Black Literature for Young
Readers: An Annotated Bibliography of
Literature By and About Black Americans for
Seventh and Eighth Grade Students, S, 1970.
ERIC ED 046 952.

Dunfee, Maxine (ed). Eliminating Ethnic Bias
in Instructional Materials: Comment and
Bibliography. Washington, DC: Association for Supervision and Curriculum Development, 1974.

Dunmore, Charlotte J. (comp). Black Children
and Their Families: A Bibliography. San
Francisco, CA: Rand E. Research Associates,
1976.

Feldman, Ronald, and Coopersmith, Stanley
(comps). A Resource and Reference Bibliography in Early Childhood Education and Developmental Psychology: The Affective Domain,
1971. ERIC ED 049 817.

Foster, Joan. "Urban Poetry for Children:
Where and How to Find It." RQ 13(Summer,
1974):320-325.

Griffin, Louise (comp). Multi-Ethnic Books for
Young Children: Annotated Bibliography for
Parents and Teachers, 1970. ERIC ED 046 519.

Hall, John S. (comp). Implementing School
Desegregation: A Bibliography. Bibliography
Series, Number Sixteen, Mr, 1970. ERIC ED
037 825.

Inter American Research Associates (comp). A
Bibliography of Bilingual-Bicultural Pre-
school Material for the Spanish Speaking
Child. Washington, DC: Office of Child
Development, Office of Human Development,
U.S. Department of Health, Education, and
Welfare, 1977.

Jenkins, Shirley, and Morrison, Barbara (comps).
Ethnicity and Child Welfare: An Annotated
Bibliography, Mr 1, 1974. ERIC ED 139 875.

Jokovich, Nancy (comp). A Bibliography of American Doctoral Dissertations in Bilingual Education and English as a Second Language: 1968-
1974, F, 1977. ERIC ED 136 584. [For earlier
compilations, see ERIC ED 115 119 and 125 269]

Klausmeier, Herbert and others (comps). Concept Learning: A Bibliography. Madison, WI: Wisconsin Research and Development Center for Cognitive Learning, 1970.

Kuvlesky, William P., and Reynolds, David H. Educational Aspirations and Expectations of Youth: A Bibliography of Research Literature. II, D, 1970. ERIC ED 049 880.

Laing, James M. (comp). Alternative Methods, Practices, and Concepts for School Desegregation: A Review of the Literature and Annotated Bibliography, 1969. ERIC ED 041 056.

Lutsky, Judi (comp). Head Start and Follow Through, 1972-74: An Abstract Bibliography. ERIC, U. of Illinois, 805 W. Pennsylvania Ave., Urban, IL: 61801.

Mackey, William Francis (comp). International Bibliography on Bilingualism. Montreal: Laval U. Press, 1973.

Melrood, Margot. A Bibliography on Decentralization, 1970. ERIC ED 042 846.

Minority Groups: Exceptional Child Bibliography Series, F, 1971. ERIC ED 054 575.

National Institute of Education (comp). Language Maintenance, Ap, 1977. ERIC ED 138 115.

Nichols, Margaret S., and O'Neill, Margaret N. (comps). Multicultural Bibliography for Preschool Through Second Grade, 1972. Multicultural Resources, P.O. Box 2945, Stanford, CA 94305.

Office of Child Development, Project Head Start (comp). Bibliography on Early Childhood. Washington, DC: U.S. Department of Health, Education, and Welfare, Jl 30, 1969.

Pasanella, Ann K. and others. Bibliography of Test Criticism, 1967. ERIC ED 039 395.

Polansky, N. A. and others (comps). Child Neglect. An Annotated Bibliography. Washington, DC: GPO, n.d.

Portraits: The Literature of Minorities: An Annotated Bibliography of Literature by and about Four Ethnic Groups in the United States for Grades 7-12, Je, 1970. ERIC ED 042 771.

Pothier, P. E. (comp). "Malnutrition and Mental Development in Man." National Library of Medicine, Ja, 1969 through Je, 1972. Literature Search No. 72-15.

President's Council on Youth Opportunity. Bibliography on Youth Programs, 1969. The Council, 801 19th Street, N.W., Washington, DC 20006.

Roberts, Abigail (comp). Books for Black Children: A Directory of 81 Bibliographies. Greensboro, NC: Sociology Department, Guilford College, 1971.

Rosenfield, Geraldine, and Yagerman, Howard (comps). The New Environment-Heredity Controversy: A Selected Annotated Bibliography. New York: American Jewish Committee, Ag, 1973.

Rosen, Pamela, and Horne, Eleanor V. Tests for Spanish-Speaking Children: An Annotated Bibliography, Ag, 1971. ERIC ED 056 084.

Salazar, Teresa (comp). Bilingual Education: A Bibliography. Greeley, CO: Bureau of Research Services, U. of Northern Colorado, 1975.

"A Selected Bibliography on the Physical and Mental Abilities of the American Negro." Journal of Negro Education 3(1934):548-564.

Soderbergh, Peter A. "Bibliographical Essay: The Negro in Juvenile Series Books, 1899-1930." Journal of Negro History 58(Ap, 1973): 179-186.

Sorenson, James R. (comp). Social and Psychological Aspects of Applied Human Genetics. A Bibliography. Washington, DC: GPO, 1973.

Springer, Ninfa Saturnino. Nutrition and Mental Retardation. An Annotated Bibliography, 1964-1970, 1970. Available from the Institute for the Study of Mental Retardation, U. of Michigan, 611 Church Street, Ann Arbor, MI 48104.

Stevens, D. L. "Analysis and Annotated Bibliography of Selected Books for Children About Negro Life." Master's thesis, Western Michigan Library, 1971.

Student Activities in Secondary Schools: A Bibliography, 1974. National Association of Secondary School Principals, 1904 Association Drive, Reston, VA 22091.

Test Bias: A Bibliography, Je, 1971. ERIC ED 051 312.

U.S. Department of H.E.W., Departmental Library. An Annotated Bibliography on Children. Washington, DC: GPO, 1971.

U.S. National Center for Health Statistics. Annotated Bibliography on Vital and Health Statistics. Washington, DC: GPO, Ag, 1970.

Van Why, Elizabeth W. (comp). Adoption Bibliography and Multi-Ethnic Sourcebook. Hartford: Open Door Society of Connecticut, 1977.

Westler, Jean A. (comp.). _An Annotated Biblio-graphy on Mental Health in the Schools, 1970-1973_. National Institute of Mental Health. Washington, DC: GPO, My, 1973.

White, Doris (comp.). _Multi-Ethnic Books for Head Start Children. Part I: Black and Integrated Literature_, 1969. ERIC ED 031 312.

Wright, Logan (comp.). _Bibliography on Human Intelligence_. Washington, DC: GPO, 1969.

3.
THE BLACK WOMAN

General

"A Statistical Portrait of the Black Woman Worker." Black Collegian 8(My-Je, 1978).

Adkins, Vivian Bernice Lee. "The Development of Negro Female Olympic Talent." Doctoral dissertation, Indiana U., 1967. Univ. Microfilms Order No. 67-12908.

Aldous, Joan. " Wives' Employment Status and Lower-Class Men as Husband-Fathers; Support for the Moynihan Thesis." Journal of Marriage and the Family, Ag, 1969. [Minneapolis, MN]

Alexander, Sadie T. M. "Women as Practitioners of Law in the U.S." National Bar Journal (Jl, 1941).

Allen, Ruth. The Labor of Women in the Production of Cotton. New York: Arno Press, 1975. [Orig. 1931] [Texas]

Almquist, Elizabeth M. "Untangling the Effects of Race and Sex: The Disadvantaged Status of Black Women." Social Science Quarterly 56 (Je, 1975):129-142.

Alpha Kappa Alpha. Women in Politics. Heritage Series #2. Chicago: Alpha Kappa Alpha Sorority, Jl, 1969.

Alpha Kappa Alpha Sorority. Women in Medicine, 1971. Alpha Kappa Alpha Sorority, Inc., 5211 South Greenwood Avenue, Chicago, IL 60615.

Anthony-Welch, Lillian Doloris. "A Comparative Analysis of the Black Woman as Transmitter of Black Values, Based on Case Studies of Families in Ghana and Among Jamaicans and Afro-Americans in Hartford, Connecticut." Doctoral dissertation, U. of Massachusetts, 1976. Univ. Microfilms Order No. 77-06371.

"As Six of Them See It. Black Women Executives Discuss Their Lives and Careers." Black Enterprise 5(Ag, 1974):20-23, 40-41.

Astrachan, Anthony. "The Black Woman as Slave." Encore (Je, 1975):34-35.

Attenborough, Richard E., and Zdep, Stanley M. "Self Image Among a National Probability Sample of Girls." Proceedings of the 81st Annual Convention of the American Psychological Association 8(1973):237-238.

Austin, Alice. "Maternal Attitudes and the Development of Learning Disabilities in Black Children." Smith College Studies in Social Work 40(Je, 1970):198-210.

Axelson, Leland J. "The Working Wife: Differences in Perception Among Negro and White Males." Journal of Marriage and the Family 32(Ag, 1970):457.

Earladeen Badger. Mothers' Training Program: Educational Intervention by the Mothers of Disadvantaged Infants, Ag, 1968. ERIC ED 043 378.

Baker, Gwendolyn C. and others. Multicultural Education: Teaching About Minority Women, Ag, 1977. ERIC ED 142 509.

Baker, Sally Hillsman. "Entry Into the Labor Market: The Preparation and Job Placement of Negro and White Vocational High School Graduates." Doctoral dissertation, Columbia U., 1970. [N.Y.C.]

Baker, Sally Hillsman, and Levenson, Bernard. "Earnings Prospects of Black and White Working-Class Women." Sociology of Work and Occupation 3(My, 1976):123-150.

_____ and _____. "Job Opportunities of Black and White Working-Class Women." Social Problems 22(Ap, 1976):510-533. [High School of Fashion Industries, New York City]

Baraka, Imamu Amiri [LeRoi Jones]. "Black Woman." Black World 19(Jl, 1970):7-11.

Barnett, Ida Wells. A Red Record. Chicago: Donohue & Henneberry, 1895.

Barry, Thomas E. Children's TV Commercials: Importance of the Race Factor, 1975. ERIC ED 120 759. [Black mothers in Dallas, Texas]

Bauman, Richard (ed.). Black Girls at Play: Folklore Perspectives on Child Development, 1975. ERIC ED 131 917.

Beal, Frances M. "Black Women, a History of Resistance." Guardian, Je 20, 1973.

_____. "Double Jeopardy: To Be Black and Female." New Generation, Fall, 1969.

_____. "Slave of a Slave No More: Black Women in Struggle." Black Scholar 6(Mr, 1975):2-10.

Beckett, Joyce O. "Working Wives: A Racial Analysis." Doctoral dissertation, Bryn Mawr College, 1977. Univ. Microfilms Order No. 7802584.

_____. "Working Wives: A Racial Comparison." Social Work 21(N, 1976):463-471.

Beckinella, Janette. "Letter to the Editor." African-American Teachers Forum, S, 1969. [Reply to Alberta Brown, "Message to the Black Woman"]

Bell, Duran. "Why Participation Rates of Black and White Wives Differ." Journal of Human Resources 9(F, 1974):465-479.

Bell, Robert R. "Lower-Class Negro Mothers and Their Children." Integrated Education, D, 1964-Ja, 1965.

_____. "Lower Class Negro Mothers' Aspirations for Their Children." Social Forces, My, 1965.

_____. "The Related Importance of Mother & Wife Roles Among Black Lower-Class Women." In The Black Family: Essays and Studies, pp. 248-255. Edited by Robert Staples. Belmont, CA: Wadsworth, 1971.

Bennett, Lerone, Jr. "No Crystal Stair: The Black Woman in History." Ebony 32(Ag, 1977): 164-168.

Berger, Alan S., and Simon, William. "Black Families and the Moynihan Report: A Research Evaluation." Social Problems 22(D, 1974): 145-161.

Bernard, Sydney. "The Economic and Social Adjustment of Low-Income Female-Headed Families." Doctoral dissertation, Brandeis U., 1965.

Bethune, Mary McLeod. "Faith That Moved a Dump Heap." Who, The Magazine About People 1 (Je, 1941):31-35, 54.

Biggers, John T. "The Negro Women in American Life and Education: A Mural Presentation." Doctoral dissertation, Pennsylvania State U., 1954.

Billingsley, Andrew. Black Families and the Struggle for Survival. New York: Friendship Press, 1974.

_____. "Black Families and White Social Science." Journal of Social Issues 26 (Summer, 1970):127-142.

Bims, Hamilton. "The Black Family: A Proud Reappraisal." Ebony 29(Mr, 1974):118-127.

"Black Girls." West Palm Beach Post Times, Ja 7, 1977. [Black girls in desegregated schools]

"Black Scholar Interviews Kathleen Cleaver." Black Scholar 3(D, 1971):54-59.

"Black Women in America." Journal of Afro-American Issues, Ag, 1974. [Entire issue]

[Black] Women in Dentistry, 1972. Alpha Kappa Alpha Sorority, Inc., 5211 South Greenwood Avenue, Chicago, IL 60615.

"Black Women in Revolt." Monthly Review 24(O, 1972):45-56.

"Black Women Make Their Mark." Black Enterprise 5(Ag, 1974):37-39. [Seventy-five women]

Black Women's Community Development Foundation, Inc. Miniconsultation on the Mental and Physical Health Problems of Black Women, Mr, 1974. Black Women's Community Development Foundation, 1028 Connecticut Ave., N.W., Washington, DC 20036.

Blackburn, Regina L. "Conscious Agents of Time and Self: The Lives and Styles of Afro-American Women as Seen Through Their Autobiographical Writings." Doctoral dissertation, U. of New Mexico, 1978. Univ. Microfilms Order No. 7900935.

"Blacks v. Feminists." Time, Mr 26, 1973.

Blackwomanwrite. "Reflections: Black Feminism." Community 36(Fall, 1976):9-11.

Bock, E. Wilbur. "Farmer's Daughter Effect: The Case of the Negro Female Professionals." Phylon, Spring, 1969.

_____. "Farmer's Daughter Effect: The Case of the Negro Female Professionals." In Professional Women. Edited by Theodore Athens. Cambridge, MA: Schenkman, 1971.

Bolton, Ina A. "The Problems of Negro College Women." Doctoral dissertation, U. of Southern California, 1969.

Bonner, Francis. "Black Women and White Women: A Comparative Analysis of Perceptions of Sex Roles of Self, Ideal-Self and the Ideal-Male." Journal of Afro-American Issues 2(Summer, 1974):237-247.

Bontemps, Alex. "Startling New Attitudes Toward Interracial Marriage." Ebony 30(S, 1975).

Bourne, Patricia G., Medrich, Elliott A., Steadwell, Louis, and Barr, Donald. Day Care Nightmare: A Child Centered View of Child Care. Berkeley, CA: Institute of Urban and Regional Development, U. of California, F, 1971.

Boyd, Odessa. "Open Letter Expresses Plight of Black Women." Muhammad Speaks, Ag 27, 1971. [Cleveland, Ohio]

Braguglia, Marilyn H., and Rosencranz, Mary L. "A Comparison of Clothing Attitudes and Ownership of Negro and White Women of Low Socioeconomic Status." Journal of Consumer Affairs 2(Winter, 1968):182-187. [Columbia, MO]

Braxton, Bernard. Women, Sex and Race: A Realistic View of Sexism and Racism, 1974. Verta Press, 15 Randolph Place, N.W., Washington, DC 20001.

Breen, William J. "Black Women and the Great War: Mobilization and Reform in the South." Journal of Southern History 44(1978):421-440.

Brenman, Margaret. "The Relationship Between Minority Group Membership and Psychological Security in a Group of Urban Middle Class Negro Girls." Master's thesis, Columbia U., 1939.

_____. "The Relationship Between Minority-Group Membership and Group Identification in a Group of Urban Middle Class Negro Girls." Journal of Social Psychology, F, 1940.

Brief, Arthur P., and Aldag, Ramon J. "Male-Female Differences in Occupational Attitudes Within Minority Groups." Journal of Vocational Behavior 6(Je, 1975):305-313.

Brody, E. B. "Color and Identity Conflict in Young Boys: Observations of Negro Mothers and Sons in Urban Baltimore." Psychiatry 26 (1963).

Brooks, Peachie, Grosvenor, Verta Smart, Kennedy, Flo, and Norton, Elinor. The Role of the Black Woman in America. Pacifica Tape Library, 2217 Shattuck Avenue, Berkeley, CA 94704.

Brown, Alberta. "Message to the Black Woman." African-American Teachers Forum, S, 1969.

Brown, Anna S. L. "Alice Freeman Palmer Memorial Institute." Opportunity 1(Ag, 1923): 246-268.

Brown, Hallie Quinn (ed.). Homespun Heroines and Other Women of Distinction. Freeport, NY: Books for Libraries Press, 1971 reprint.

Brown, Jean Collier. "The Economic Status of Negro Women." Southern Workman 60(O, 1931).

Brown, Sara W. "Colored Women Physicians." Southern Workman 52(1923):580-593.

Brown, Thomas E. "Sex Education and Life in the Black Ghetto." Religious Education 64 (1969):450-458.

Brozan, Nadine. "Determined to Foster Change-- As Women and as Blacks." New York Times, Mr 11, 1974.

Bryce, Herrington J., and Warrick, Alan E. "Black Women in Elective Offices." Black Scholar 6(O, 1974):17-20.

Burke, Kaaren O. "A Study of Racial Attitudes of Six Freshman Women Involved in Integrated Room Situations in a College Residence Hall." ISSQ, Spring, 1964. [Indiana Council of the Social Studies]

Burlew, Ann Kathleen. "Career and Educational Choices Among Black Females." Journal of Black Psychology 3(F, 1977):88-106.

Burns, Alice. " Blackman and Whiteman in a Mother-Child Symbolic Unit." Voices: The Art & Science of Psychotherapy 6(Fall, 1970): 62-64.

Burroughs, Wayne A., and Jaffee, Cabot L. "Attitudinal Reaction of White Females Toward Two Black Female Collaborators." Journal of Psychology 79(S, 1971):3-11.

Butcher, Beatrice Bowen. "The Evolution of Negro Women's Schools in the United States." Master's thesis, Howard U., 1936.

Cade, Toni (ed.). The Black Woman. An Anthology. New York: New American Library, Ag, 1970.

Calvin, Floyd. "That's Nannie Burroughs' Job, And She Does It." Pittsburgh Courier, Je 8, 1929. [National Training School for Girls, Washington, DC]

Cannon, Elaine W. Oates. "Qualitative Study and Descriptive Analysis of the Sources of Strengths in Black Families." Master's thesis, Howard U., 1974.

Carnegie, M. E. "Are Negro Schools of Nursing Needed Today?" Nursing Outlook, F, 1964.

_____. "Impact of Integration on the Nursing Profession: Historical Sketch." Negro History Bulletin, Ap, 1964.

Carroll, Constance and others. "The Dilemma of Black Women in Higher Education." In Academic Women. Edited by Alice S. Rossi and Ann Calderwood. New York: Russell Sage Foundation, 1973.

Carson, Josephine. Silent Voices: The Southern Negro Woman Today. New York: Delacorte Press, 1969.

Center for Human Resource Research. Years for Decision: A Longitudinal Study of the Educational and Labor Market Experience of Young Women, Vol. 4. Washington, DC: GPO, 1978.

Chopell, Yvonne R. "The Black Woman on the Negro College Campus." Black Scholar, Ja-F, 1970.

Chavis, William M., and Lyles, Gladys J. Divorce Among Educated Black Women. Tuskagee, AL: Tuskegee Institute, 1974.

Cherry, Flora F., and Eaton, Ethel L. "Physical and Cognitive Development in Children of Low-Income Mothers Working in the Child's Early Years." Child Development 48(Mr, 1977):158-166.

Chisholm, Shirley. "Race, Revolution and Women." Black Scholar 3(D, 1971):17-21

_____. Unbought & Unbossed. Boston: Houghton Mifflin, 1970.

Christenson, Bruce A. A Comparison of the Processes of Earning Achievement of Black and White Married Females, 1976. ERIC ED 143 890.

"Dr. Mamie Clark: Helping Where Needed." Crisis 82(My, 1975):178-179.

Clarke, John Henrik. "The Black Woman: A Figure in World History." Essence (My, 1971).

Cole, Dorothy. "A Typological Study of the Women's Rights Movements: Implications for Black Women and Education." Doctoral dissertation, Rutgers U., 1976. Univ. Microfilms Order No. 76-27,310.

Commissioner's Task Force on the Impact of Office of Education Programs on Women. A Look at Women in Education: Issues and Answers for HEW. Washington, DC: U.S. Department of Health, Education, and Welfare, N, 1972.

Conference on the Educational and Occupational Needs of Black Women. Compendium. 2 vols. Washington, DC: National Institute of Education, 1978.

Conley, Madelyn. "Do Black Women Need the Women's Lib?" Essence 1(Ag, 1970):29-34.

Cooper, Anna Julian. A Voice from the South by a Black Woman of the South. New York: Negro Universities Press, 1969 reprint.

Cossey, Beatrice Abel, and Toney, Glen O. Baseline Data on Mid-Career Change and Reentry for Black Women. Washington, DC: National Institute of Education, Ap, 1978.

Cottle, Thomas J. "No Way to Look But Back." Inequality in Education 12(Jl, 1972):4-9.

Coursey, Leon N. "Anita J. Turner--Early Black Female Physical Educator." Journal of Health Physical Education Recreation 45(Mr, 1974): 71-72.

Crawford, Charlene. "The Status of Black Women." Ebony 30(Mr, 1975):26.

Crummell, Alexander. "The Black Woman of the South: Her Neglects and Her Needs." In Africa and America. Addresses and Discourses, pp. 61-82. Springfield, MA: Willey & Co., 1891. Reprint: New York: Negro Universities Press, 1969.

Cummings, Judith. "Black Women in Public Life." Black Enterprise 5(Ag, 1974):33-35.

Cuthbert, Marion V. "Education and Marginality: A Study of the Negro Woman College Graduate." Doctoral dissertation, Columbia U., 1943.

Daly, Frederica Y. "To Be Black, Poor, Female and Old." Freedomways 16(1976):222-229.

Daniel, Jessica H. "A Study of Negro Sororities at a University With Marginal Integration." Master's thesis, U. of Illinois, Urbana, 1967.

Daniel, Sadie I. Women Builders. Revised by Charles H. Wesley and Thelma D. Perry. Washington, DC: Associated Publishers, 1970.

Dann, Joanne. "Wanted: A Dr. Spock for Black Mothers." New York Times Magazine, Ap 18, 1971.

Dannett, Sylvia. Profile of Negro Womanhood. 2 vols. New York: Negro Universities Press, 1964, 1966.

Dauterive, J. W., and Jornish, J. E. "Wage Differences Among Black and White Career Women." Review of Social Economy 35(Ap, 1977).

Davidson, Edmonia W. "COPE's Educationally Disadvantaged, Low-Income Mothers Who Are Heads of Households." Adult Leadership 24(Ap, 1976): 267-270. [Washington, DC]

Davidson, Olivia S. "How Shall We Make the Women of Our Race Stronger?" Alabama Teacher 1 (Je, 1886).

Davis, Angela Y. "Reflections on the Black Woman's Role in the Community of Slaves." Black Scholar 3(D, 1971):2-15.

Davis, Elizabeth L. Lifting As They Climb. Washington, DC: National Association of Colored Women, 1933.

Day, Beth. Sexual Life Between Blacks & Whites. The Roots of Racism. New York: Apollo Editions, 1974.

De Charms, R. and others. Can Mothers of Low Income Black Children Be Changed? An Interim Report, F, 1969, 80 pp. ERIC ED 033 978.

De Melto, Jane. "The Crisis of the Tenth of the Month: The ADC Mother and the Realistic Problems She Faces." Public Welfare 21(O, 1963):179-184. [Cuyahoga County, Ohio]

DeWitt, Karen. "Black Women in Business." Black Enterprise 5(Ag, 1974):14-19.

Dietrich, Katheryn, and Greiser, Lee. The Influence of Sex on Wage-Incomes of Black, Blue-
Collar Workers in Selected Non-metropolitan
and Metropolitan Areas of Texas, F, 1974.
ERIC ED 094 908.

Dirksen, Carolyn R. A Sociocultural Comparison
of the Use of Directives by Adolescent
Females, O 21, 1977. ERIC ED 145 726.

Dohner, Ellen. "Stereotypes of Black Women in
Novels by White Authors from 1925 to 1935."
Master's thesis, Florida Atlantic U., 1971.

Dougherty, Molly Crock. Becoming a Woman in
Rural Black Culture. New York: Holt, Rinehart & Winston, 1978. [Florida]

Dreyfuss, Joel. "Elma Lewis: A Study in
Dignity, Courage." Washington Post S 10,
1975.

DuBois, W. E. B. "The Burden of Black Women."
Horizon 2(N, 1907):3-5.

_____. The Damnation of Women. Predictions
on Fatherless and Dependent Children
(pamphlet). Chicago, IL: Af-Am Books, 1964.

_____. "The Work of Negro Women in Society."
Spelman Messenger 18(F, 1902):1-3.

Duckro, Rose and others. "Relationship of Self-
Disclosure and Mental Health in Black
Females." Journal of Consulting and Clinical
Psychology 44(D, 1976):940-943.

Dunnigan, Alice Allison. A Black Woman's Ex-
perience--From Schoolhouse to White House.
Philadelphia, PA: Dorrance, 1974. [First
black woman journalist to receive White House
accreditation]

_____. "Early History of Negro Women in
Journalism." Negro History Bulletin 28
(1965):178-179, 193, 197.

Ehrlich, Howard J. Selected Differences in the
Life Chances of Men and Women in the United
States. Research Group One, 2743 Maryland
Avenue, Baltimore, MD 21218.

Eichelberger, Brenda. "Voices on Black Feminism." Quest: A Feminist Quarterly 3(Spring,
1977).

Elzroth, Marjorie. "Vocational Counseling for
Ghetto Women with Prostitution & Domestic
Service Backgrounds." Vocational Guidance
Quarterly 22(S, 1973):32-38.

Epstein, Cynthia F. "Positive Effects of the
Multiple Negative: Explaining the Success of
Black Professional Women." American Journal
of Sociology 78(Ja, 1973):912-935.

Etaugh, Claire. "Effects of Maternal Employment
on Children: A Review of Recent Research."
Merrill-Palmer Quarterly 20(Ap, 1974):71-98.

Evans, Mari. I Am a Black Woman. Poems.
New York: Morrow, 1970.

Farley, Jennie and others. "Black Women's
Career Aspirations." Journal of Employment
Counseling 14(S, 1977):116-118.

"Fatherless Child Insurance." In President's
Commission on Income Maintenance Programs,
Background Papers, pp. 442-445. Washington,
DC: GPO, 1970.

"Female-Headed Households." In President's
Commission on Income Maintenance Programs,
Background Papers, pp. 142-144. Washington,
DC: GPO, 1970.

Ferguson, Elaine. "The Relationship of Work
Motivation to Selected Demographic Characteristics of Black Female Workers." Doctoral
dissertation, U. of Houston, 1976. Univ.
Microfilms Order No. 77-1506.

Fichter, Joseph H. Negro Women Bachelors: A
Comparative Exploration of the Experiences and
Expectations of College Graduates of the Class
of June, 1961. Chicago: National Opinion
Research Center, Ja, 1965.

Field, Emma. "The Women's Club Movement in the
United States: 1877-1900." Master's thesis,
Howard U., 1948.

"Findings of a Conference on Current Problems
and Programs in the Higher Education of Negro
Women..." Quarterly Review of Higher
Education Among Negroes 12(O, 1944):205-219.

Ford, Beverly O. "Case Studies of Black Female
Heads of Households in the Welfare System:
Socialization and Survival." Western Journal
of Black Studies 1(Je, 1977):114-118.

Foster, Frances S. "Changing Concepts of the
Black Woman." Journal of Black Studies 3(Je,
1973):433-454.

Fowler, Anne Clarke. "The Contemporary Negro
Subculture: An Exploratory Study of Lower-
Class Negro Women of New Orleans." Doctoral
dissertation, Tulane U., 1970. Univ. Microfilms Order No. 71-8046.

Fox, Andrew and others. In-School Neighborhood
Youth Corps. 14/15 Year-Old-Black Teenage
Girls. Memphis, Tennessee. Springfield,
VA: National Technical Information Service,
F 3, 1974.

_____ and others. In-School Neighborhood Youth
Corps. 14/15 Year-Old Black Teenage Girls
Project. Memphis, Tennessee, D 31, 1973.
ERIC ED 096 375.

Foxley, Cecelia H. Recruiting Women & Minority
Faculty: An Information Handbook, 1972.
Campus Stores, U. of Iowa, Iowa City, IA 52240.

Furstenberg, Frank F., Jr., Hershberg, Theodore,
and Modell, John. "The Origins of the Female-
Headed Black Family: The Impact of the Urban
Experience." Journal of Interdisciplinary
History 6(1975):211-233. [Philadelphia]

Garvey, Amy Jacques. "The Role of Women in Liberation Struggles." Massachusetts Review 13(1972):109-112.

Genovese, Eugene D. "The Slave Family. Women-- A Reassessment of Matriarchy, Emasculation, Weakness." Southern Voices 1(Ag-S, 1974):9-16.

George, Felicia. "Black Woman, Black Man." Harvard Journal of Afro-American Affairs 2 (1971):1-17.

Gibson, Emily F. "Why Join [Women's Liberation] When Being Equal to a Black Man Offers No Advance." Los Angeles Times, S 15, 1975.

Gladney, Margaret Rose. "If It Was Anything for Justice." Southern Exposure 4(Winter, 1977): 19-23. [Sallie Mae Hadnott, Prattville, Alabama]

Glover, Robert W. Placing Minority Women in Professional Jobs. Washington, DC: GPO, 1978.

Glover, Robert W., and Greenfield, Paula S. The Minority Women Employment Program: A National Demonstration Project to Facilitate Entry of Minority Women into Managerial, Professional, and Technical Occupations. Vol. I., N, 1976. ERIC ED 138 737.

Glover, Robert W. and others. "Minority Women, Professional Work." Manpower 7(Jl, 1975): 8-12.

Goldin, Claudia. "Female Labor Force Partici- pation: The Origin of Black and White Dif- ferences, 1870 and 1880." Journal of Economic History 37(Mr, 1977):87-108. [See comments by Harold D. Woodman following Goldin article]

Gordon, Ruth L. Hill. "Differential Value Pat- terns of Black and White Women in Higher Education." Doctoral dissertation, United States International U., 1974. Univ. Microfilms Order No. 74-01110.

Graham, Beryl C. "Treatment of Black American Women in Children's Encyclopedias." Negro History Bulletin 39(My, 1976):596-598.

Grant, Liz. "Ain't Beulah Dead Yet." Encore (My, 1973):61.

Green, Barbara M. "Upgrading Black Women in the Supervisory Ranks." Personnel, N-D, 1969.

Gubbins, Barbara Kashian. "Eleanor Holmes Norton. Human Rights Commissioner." Tuesday, N 24, 1974.

Guffy, Ossie. Ossie: The Autobiography of a Black Woman. As Told to Caryl Ledner. New York: Norton, 1971.

Gullattee, Alyce C. "Psychiatric Factors to Consider in Research on the Black Woman." Journal of Afro-American Issues 2(Summer, 1974):199-203.

Gump, Janice Porter. "Comparative Analysis of Black Women's and White Women's Sex-Role Attitudes." Journal of Consulting and Clinical Psychology 43(D, 1975):858-863.

Gump, Janice Porter, and Rivers, L. Wendell. The Consideration of Race in Efforts to End Sex Bias, 1973. ED 095 364.

_____ and _____. "A Consideration of Race in Efforts to End Sex Bias." In Issues of Sex Bias and Sex Fairness in Career Interest Measurement. Edited by Esther E. Diamond. Washington, DC: National Institute of Edu- cation, Spring, 1975.

Gunter, Laurie M. "The Effects of Segregation on Nursing Students." Nursing Outlook, F, 1961.

Gurin, Patricia, and Gaylord, Carolyn. "Educa- tional and Occupational Goals of Men and Women at Black Colleges." Monthly Labor Review (Je, 1976).

Gurin, Patricia, and Morrison, Betty Mae. Education, Labor Market Experiences, and Current Expectancies of Black & White Men and Women, S, 1976. ERIC ED 135 996.

Gurin, Patricia, and Pruitt, Anne. Counseling Implications of Black Women's Market Position, Aspirations and Expectancies. Washington, DC: National Institute of Education, Ap, 1978.

Gutman, Herbert G. "Persistent Myths About the Afro-American Family." Journal of Inter- disciplinary History 6(Autumn, 1975):181-210

Gwenwald, Morgan. "Confrontation Black-White." Quest: A Feminist Quarterly 3(Spring, 1977).

Hale, Janice E. "The Strength of Black Families." First World 1(Mr-Ap, 1977):28-30.

Hall, P. Quick and others. "Conference on Minority Women Scientists." Science 191 (F, 1976):457.

Hamburger, Robert. "A Stranger in the House." Southern Exposure 5(Spring, 1977):22-31. [Contains autobiographical statements by two black domestic workers]

Hamilton, Kelly. Goals and Plans of Black Women: A Sociological Study. Hicksville, NY: Exposition Press, 1975.

Hammond, Judith, and Rex, Enoch J. "Conjugal Power Relations Among Black Working Class Families." Journal of Black Studies 7(S, 1976):107-128.

Hammond, Lavina G. "Differential Use of Reward and Punishment As a Function of Need Achieve- ment and of Fear of Failure in Black Mothers." Diss. Abstr. Int'l. 196 9, 30 (5-A), 1821.

Haney, C. Allen, Michielutte, Robert, Vincent, Clark E., and Cochrane, Carl. "Factors Associated with the Poverty of Black Women." Sociology and Social Research 59(O, 1974): 40-49.

Harwood, Edwin. "Jobs and the Negro Family: A Reappraisal." Public Interest 23(Spring, 1971):125-131.

Hare, Nathan. "Black Male-Female Relations." Doctoral dissertation, California School of Professional Psychology, San Francisco, 1975.

_____. "Revolution Without a Revolution: The Psychology of Sex and Race." Black Scholar 9(Ap, 1978):2-7.

_____. "What Black Intellectuals Misunderstand About the Black Family." Black World 25(Mr, 1976):4-14.

_____. "Will the Real Black Man Please Stand Up?" Black Scholar 2(Je, 1971):32-35.

Hare, Nathan, and Hare, Julia. "Black Women 1970." Trans-action 8(N, 1970).

Harley, Sharon, and Terborg-Penn, Rosalyn (eds.). The Afro-American Woman: Struggles and Images. Port Washington, NY: National U. Publications, 1978.

Harrison, Algea O. "The Dilemma of Growing Up Black and Female." Journal of Social and Behavioral Sciences 20(Spring, 1974):28-40.

Hauenstein, Louise S. and others. "Work Status, Work Satisfaction, and Blood Pressure Among Black and White Women." Psychology of Women Quarterly 1(Summer, 1977):334-348.

Haughton, Frank A. Employment Profiles of Minorities and Women in the SMSA's of 17 Large Cities, 1971. Washington, DC: GPO, Je, 1973.

Haynes, Carrie Ayers. Good News on Grape Street: The Transformation of a Ghetto School. New York: Citation Press, 1976. [Grape Street School, Watts, Los Angeles]

Haynes, Elizabeth Ross. "Two Million Negro Women at Work." Southern Workman 51(F, 1922): 64-72.

Heaston, Patricia Y. W. "An Analysis of Selected Role Perceptions Among Successful Black Women in the Professions." Doctoral dissertation, Northwestern U., 1975. Univ. Microfilm Order No. 75-29,651.

Heer, David M. "Negro-White Marriage in the United States." Journal of Marriage and the Family, Ag, 1966.

Heiss, Jerold. The Case of the Black Family. A Sociological Inquiry. New York: Columbia U. Press, 1975.

Hemmons, Willa Mae. "Towards an Understanding of Attitudes Held by the Black Woman on the Women's Liberation Movement." Doctoral dissertation, Case Western Reserve U., 1973. Univ. Microfilms Order No. 74-02521.

Henderson, Grace Gist. "The Academic Self-Concept of Black Female Children Within Differential School Settings." Journal of Afro-American Issues 2(Summer, 1974):248-266.

Herzog, Elizabeth, and Sudia, Cecilia E. Boys in Fatherless Families. Washington, DC: GPO, 1971.

Herzog, Elizabeth, Sudia, Cecilia, Harwood, Jane, and Newcomb, Carol. Families for Black Children. The Search for Adoptive Parents. An Experience Survey. Washington, DC: GPO, 1971.

Higgins, Chester, Jr., and McDougall, Harold. Black Woman. Levittown, NY: Transatlantic Arts, 1970.

Hill, Robert B. The Strengths of Black Families. Washington, DC: Research Dept., National Urban League, Jl 8, 1971. [Suite 529, 425 Thirteenth St., N.W., Washington, DC 20004]

Hobson, Elizabeth C., and Hopkins, Charlotte E. A Report Concerning the Colored Women of the South. Occasional Papers No. 9. Baltimore, MD: The Trustees of the John F. Slater Fund, 1896.

Hoeveler, Diane L. "Oedipus Agonistes: Mothers and Sons in Richard Wright's Fiction." Black American Literature Forum 12(Summer, 1978):65-68.

Hoffman, Lois W. "Effects of Maternal Employment on the Child--A Review of the Research." Developmental Psychology 10(Mr, 1974):204-228.

Howze, Beverly. "Suicide: Special References to Black Women." Journal of Non-White Concerns in Personnel and Guidance 5(Ja, 1977):65-71.

Hood, Elizabeth F. "Black Women, White Women: Separate Paths to Liberation." Black Scholar 9(Ap, 1978):45-56.

Horan, Patrick M., and Austin, Patricia Lee. "The Social Bases of Welfare Stigma." Social Problems 21(Je, 1975):648-657. [Black woman]

Hosford, Philip L. (ed.). Minority Women in Research in Education, F, 1978. ERIC ED 148 521.

Howe, Florence. "The Education of Women." Liberation, Ag-S, 1969.

Hughes, Joyce Anne. "The Black Portia." Crisis 82(My, 1975):167-172. [Black women in the law profession]

Hunt, Larry L., and Hunt, Janet G. "Race and the Father-Son Connection: The Conditional Relevance of Father Absence for the Orientations and Identities of Adolescent Boys." Social Problems 23(O, 1975):35-52. [Black women]

Hunton, Addie Waits. "The Southern Federation of Colored Women." Voice of the Negro 2 (D, 1905):850-854.

Hyman, Herbert H., and Reed, John S. "'Black Matriarchy' Reconsidered: Evidence from Secondary Analysis of Sample Surveys." Public Opinion Quarterly 33(1969):346-354.

Jackson, Harrisene. There's Nothing I Own That I Want. Englewood Cliffs, NJ: Prentice-Hall, 1974.

Jackson, Jacquelyne Johnson. "Black Women in a Racist Society." In Racism and Mental Health, pp. 185-268. Edited by Charles V. Willie, Bernard M. Kramer, and Bertram S. Brown. Pittsburgh, PA: U. of Pittsburgh Press, 1973.

_____. "But Where Are the Men?" Black Scholar 3(D, 1971):30-41

_____. Career Options for Black Women, 1976. ERIC ED 138 812.

_____. Negro Grandparents: Interactional and Subjective Role Aspects, Ap, 1970. ERIC ED 043 702.

_____. "Ordinary Black Husbands: The Truly Hidden Men." Journal of Social and Behavioral Sciences 20(Spring, 1974):19-27.

_____. "The Plight of Older Black Women in the United States. Black Scholar 7(Ap, 1976):47-55.

_____. "Where Are the Black Men?" Ebony 27 (Mr, 1972):99-106.

James, Selma. "Sex, Race, and Working Class Power." Race Today 6(Ja, 1974):12-15

Jeffers, Camille. "Realities of Ghetto Motherhood." AAUW Journal 62(O, 1968):18-20.

Jeffries, Doris. "Counseling for the Strengths of the Black Woman." Counseling Psychologist 6(1976):20-21.

Jensen, Beverly. "Alexander, Harris, Kennedy, Motley and Murray." Black Enterprise 8 (Ag, 1977):19-24. [Five black women lawyers]

_____. "Black and Female, Too." Black Enterprise 6(Jl, 1976):26-29. [Career women]

Jensen, John L. "Maternal Attitudes of Low Socio-Economic Groups Toward Public Elementary Schools." Diss. Abstr. Int'l., 1970 (Jl) 31 (1-A) 105-6.

Joesting, Joan, and Joesting, Robert. "Sex and Social Class Differences in Verbal Aggression in Black College Students." College Student Journal 7(Ja, 1973):91.

Johnson, Betty. "Ethnic Minority Feminism: A Minority Member's View." Journal of the NAWDAC 41(Winter, 1978):52-55.

Johnson, Jesse J. (ed.). Black Women in the Armed Forces, 1942-1974. Hampton, VA: Johnson, 1975.

Johnson, Susan. "Fannie Lou Hamer: Mississippi Organizer." Black Law Journal 2(Summer, 1972).

Jones, Anna H. "The American Colored Woman." Voice of the Negro 2(O, 1905):693-694.

Jones, Barbara Ann Posey. "The Contribution of Black Women to the Incomes of Black Families: An Analysis of the Labor Force Participation Rates of Black Wives." Doctoral dissertation, George State U., 1973. Univ. Microfilms Order No. 73-31454.

Jones, Caroline R. "Black Women in the Army: Where the Jobs Are." Crisis 82(My, 1975): 175-177.

Jones, Faustine C. "The Lofty Role of the Black Grandmother." Crisis 80(Ja, 1973):19-21

Jordan, June. "To Be Black and Female." New York Times Book Review, Mr 18, 1979. [See Julius Lester, below.]

Joyce, Lynda M., and Leadley, Samuel M. An Assessment of Research Needs of Women in the Rural United States: Literature Review and Annotated Bibliography, Ap, 1977. ERIC ED 141 465.

Kammeyer, Kenneth C. W., Yetman, Norman R., and McClendon, McKee J. "Family Planning Services and the Distribution of Black Americans." Social Problems 21(Je, 1974): 674-690.

Kandel, Denise B. "Race, Maternal Authority, and Adolescent Aspiration." American Journal of Sociology 76(My, 1971):999-1020.

Karenga, Maulana Ron. "In Love and Struggle: Toward a Greater Togetherness." Black Scholar 6(Mr, 1975):16-28.

Karrien, Anna. "A Salute to Black Women." Muhammad Speaks, N 19, 1971.

Keane, William Michael. "Black Mothers and Their Sons: Correlates and Predictors of Cognitive Development From the Second to the Sixth Year of Life." Doctoral dissertation, City U. of New York, 1976. Univ. Microfilms Order No. 76-28344.

Kellor, Frances A. "Opportunities for Southern Negro Women in Northern Cities. Voice of the Negro 2(Jl, 1905):472-473.

Kilson, M. "Black Women in the Professions, 1890-1970." Monthly Labor Review 100(My, 1977).

King, Karl and others. "Black Adolescents' Views of Maternal Employment as a Threat to the Marital Relationship." Journal of Marriage and the Family 38(N, 1976):733-736.

King, Mae C. "The Politics of Sexual Stereotypes." Black Scholar 4(Mr-Ap, 1973):12-23.

Mrs. Martin Luther King. "My Dream for My
Children." Good Housekeeping, Je, 1964.

Kohlwes, Gary F. Sex and Race Differences in
the Development of Underprivileged Preschool
Children, Ap, 1966. ERIC ED 019 992.

Krier, Beth Ann. "Black Women Lawyers: Double
Minority." Los Angeles Times, N 23, 1975.
[Black Women Lawyers Association of
California]

_____. "Maya Angelou: No Longer a 'Caged
Bird.'" Los Angeles Times, S 24, 1976.

Kriesberg, Louis. Mothers in Poverty: A Study
of Fatherless Families. Chicago: Aldine,
1970.

Krystall, Eric R., and Epps, Edgar G. "The
'Father Absence' Effect on Adolescent Aspirations: Myth or Reality?" Journal of Social
and Behavioral Sciences 13(Fall, 1968):9-17.

Kunreuther, Sylvia C. "A Preschool Exchange:
Black Mothers Speak and a White Teacher
Listens." Children 17(My-Je, 1970):91-96.

Kutner, Nancy G. "Alternative Implications of
Job-Based 'Coracialism' for Black Voluntary
Association Involvement." Journal of Vo-
cational Behavior 7(D, 1975):337-344.

_____. "Differential Adaptation Among Lower-
Class Black Homemakers in a Rural-Urban
Community." Journal of Social and Behavior-
al Sciences 20(Summer, 1974):55-65.
[Houston, Texas]

Kuvlesky, William P., and Obordo, Angelita A.
"A Racial Comparison of Teen-Age Girls'
Projections for Marriage and Procreation."
Journal of Marriage and the Family 34(F,
1972):75-74.

La Rue, Linda J. M. "Black Liberation and
Women's Lib." In Black/Brown/White Rela-
tions. Edited by Charles V. Willie. New
Brunswick, NJ: Transaction, 1977.

_____. "Black Liberation and Women's Lib."
Trans-action, D, 1971.

_____. "The Black Movement and Women's Libera-
tion." Black Scholar I(My, 1970):36-42.

Ladner, Joyce. "Black Women in Poverty."
Journal of Social and Behavioral Sciences
20(Spring, 1974):41-51.

_____. "The Black Woman Today." Ebony 32
(Ag, 1977):33-42.

_____. "Racism and Tradition: Black Woman-
hood in Historical Perspective." In
Liberating Women's History: Theoretical and
Critical Essays. Edited by Berenice A.
Carroll. Urbana: U. of Illinois Press, 1976.

_____. Tomorrow's Tomorrow: The Black
Woman. Garden City, NY: Doubleday & Co.,
1971.

_____. "The Women. Conditions of Slavery
Laid the Foundation for Their
Liberation." Ebony 30(Ag, 1975):
76-81.

Lammermeier, Paul J. "The Urban Black Family
in the Nineteenth Century: A Study of Black
Family Structure in the Ohio Valley, 1850-
1880." Journal of Marriage and the Family
35(Ag, 1973):440-456.

Langford, Eugene P. "The Sex Role of the Female
as Perceived by Anglo and Negro Children."
Diss. Abstr. Int'l. 1970, 30 (7-A) 2803.

Lee, Helen Jackson. Nigger in the Window.
Garden City, NY: Doubleday, 1978.

Leffall, Dolores C., and Sims, Janet L. "Mary
McLeod Bethune--The Educator; Also Including
a Selected Annotated Bibliography." Journal
of Negro Education 45(Summer, 1976):342-359.

Lennis, Susan. "Mari Evans: Hoosier in
Profile." Indianapolis Star, Ag 22, 1976.
[Poet]

Lenox, Mary F. "Black Women: Student Perception
of Their Contributions." Doctoral dissertation, U. of Massachusetts, 1975.

Lerner, Gerda (ed.). Black Women in White
America. A Documentary History. New York:
Pantheon, 1972.

_____. "Early Community Work of Black Club
Women." Journal of Negro History 59(Ap,
1974):158-167.

Lesher, Stephan. "The Short, Unhappy Life of
Black Presidential Politics, 1972." New York
Times Magazine, Je 25, 1972. [Shirley
Chisholm]

Lewis, Diane K. "A Response to Inequality:
Black Women, Racism, and Sexism." Signs 3
(Winter, 19755):339-361.

_____. "The Black Family: Socialization and
Sex Roles." Phylon 36(Fall, 1975):221-237.

Lewis, Hylan. The Black Family: Sociological
Profiles. Atlanta, GA: W. E. B. DuBois
Institute, Atlanta U., n.d.

Lewis, Hylan and others. Improving Employment
Possibilities for Female Black Teenagers in
New York City, My, 1976. ERIC ED 130 032.

Lewis, Jerry M., and Sites, Paul. Decision Making
in Black Working Class Families, 1970. ERIC
ED 044 462.

Lewis, Theresa T. "Do Black Women Need Liberating?" Urban League Review 1(Fall, 1975).

Lewis, Toye L. "Children and the Economy: A Study of the Relationship between Federal Day Care and Manpower Policies and the Influence of this Connection on the Supply of Federally Assisted Day Care." Doctoral dissertation, Brandeis U., 1975.

Liddick, Betty. "Black Lib: Sisters Going Their Own Way." Los Angeles Times, Jl 8, 1973.

_____. "Black Professionals Face New Problems." Los Angeles Times, Je 8, 1977. [Account of Black Women's Conference held by Afrodisia: Black Sisterhood Rediscovered]

Lieberman, Leonard. "The Emerging Model of the Black Family." International Journal of Sociology 3(Mr, 1973):10-22

Lightfoot, Sara Lawrence. "Socialization and Education of Young Black Girls in School." Teachers College Record 78(D, 1976):239-262.

_____. Socialization and Education of Young Black Girls in Schools. Washington, DC: National Institute of Education, Ap, 1978.

Littig, Lawrence. W. A Study of Certain Personality Correlates of Occupational Aspirations of Black and White College Women. Final Report, S, 1971. ERIC ED 056 242.

Loewenberg, Bert J., and Bogin, Ruth (eds.). Black Women in Nineteenth Century American Life: Their Words, Their Thoughts, and Their Feelings. Pennsylvania State U. Press, 1976.

Loring, Rosalind, and Adams, Mary. Group Counseling of Minority and Low-Income Women Students: A Model Program for Junior College Educators, Mr, 1972, 47 pp. ERIC ED 059 715.

Low, Seth, and Spindler, Pearl G. Child Care Arrangements of Working Mothers in the United States. Washington, DC: GPO, 1968.

Lowe, Walter L., Jr. "The Violence of Black Mothers." Chicago Defender, Ja 22, 1976.

Lucas, Emily D. "A Study of Black People's Perception of the Liberation of the Black Woman." Master's thesis, Atlanta U., 1972.

Lyles, Barbara D. "The Black Woman: Person or Non-Person." Crisis 82(My, 1975):163-166.

McBroom, Patricia. "The Black Matriarchy: Healthy or Pathological?" Science News 94 (O 19, 1968).

McClain, Shirla, and Spencer, Norma L. Racism and Sexism in America: The Black Woman's Dilemma, 1978. ERIC ED 159 272.

McCormick, E. Patricia. Attitudes toward Abortion: Experiences of Selected Black and White Women. Lexington, MA: Lexington Books, 1975.

McDougald, Elsie Johnson. "The Double Task: The Struggle of Negro Women for Sex and Race Emancipation." Survey Graphic 6(Mr, 1925).

_____. "The Negro Woman Teacher and the Negro Student." Messenger 5(Jl, 1923):769-770.

McDowell, Sophia F. "Black-White Intermarriage in the United States." International Journal of Sociology of the Family, Jl, 1971.

McLean, Linda R., and Clanton, Kay Burke. "The Black Woman in Industry: The Myth of Being Better than Thou." Black Caucus 3(Fl, 1970): 44-49.

McManus, Marjorie. "The Essence Magazine Success Story." Folio 5(D, 1976):27-29. [Marcia Ann Gillespie, editor-in-chief]

Mack, Delores E. "Where the Black-Matriarchy Theorists Went Wrong." Psychology Today 4 (Ja, 1971):24, 86-87.

Macke, Anne S., and Morgan, Willima R. "Maternal Employment, Race, and Work Orientation of High School Girls." Social Forces 57 (S, 1978):187-204.

Majors, Monroe A. Noted Negro Women. Their Triumphs and Activities. Freeport, NY: Books for Libraries Press, 1971 reprint.

Malcolm, Shirley M. and others. The Double Bind: The Price of Being a Minority Woman in Science, Ap, 1976. ERIC ED 130 851.

"Man Child in a Woman's World." Ebony 27(Ag, 1972):72-78. [Harlem]

Marengo, Paul C. "Frances Kellor: A Career Study, 1900-1920." Senior thesis, Princeton U., 1971. [Founder of National League for the Protection of Colored Women]

Margulies, Lee. "Black Without a White Filter." Los Angeles Times, Ag 3, 1977. [Alice Travis, hostess of T.V. program, "For You, Black Woman"]

Martin, Barbara T. "A Study of Achievement Oriented Behaviors of Poverty Black & White Mothers with their Preschool Sons." Diss. Abstr. Int'l. 31 (12-A)(Je, 1971) 6347.

Marin, Walter T., and Poston, Dudley L., Jr. "The Occupational Composition of White Females: Sexism, Racism and Occupational Differentiation." Social Forces 50(1972): 349-352.

Massa, Ann. "Black Women in the 'White City.'" Journal of American Studies 8(D, 1974):319-337.

Matthews, Drue E., and Ross, Evelyn. "Observations from the Placement Front: Insensitivity and Racism are Not Dead." Journal of Non-White Concerns in Personnel and Guidance 3 (Ap, 1975):100-103. [Black female students from Mt. Holyoke College]

Matthews, Graham Park. "Father-Absence and the Development of Masculine Identification in Black Preschool Males." Doctoral dissertation, U. of Michigan, 1976. Univ. Microfilms Order No. 76-19189.

Mattleman, Marcienne E., and Emans, Robert L. "The Language of the Inner-City Child: A Comparison of Puerto Rican and Negro Third Grade Girls." Journal of Negro Education, Spring, 1969.

Mayo, A. D. Southern Women in the Recent Movement in the South. Washington, DC: GPO, 1892.

Mebane (Liza), Mary E. "An Open Letter to Gloria Steinem." New York Times, O 29, 1971.

Mehlinger, Kermit, Gant, Lisbeth, and Davis, Danny K. "The Black Man-White Woman Thing." Ebony, Ag, 1970.

Mental and Physical Health Problems of Black Women, 1977. The Black Women's Community Development Foundation, 1028 Connecticut Ave., N.W., Washington, DC 20036.

Meyers, Samuel, and McIntyre, Jennie. "Employment and Self-Image." In Welfare Policy and Its Consequences for the Recipient Population: A Study of the AFDC Program, pp. 110-142. Bureau for Social Science Research, Inc. Washington, DC: GPO, D, 1969 [1970]

Miller, Bernice J. "Inner City Women in White Schools." Journal of Negro Education 42 (Summer, 1973):392-413.

Miller, Helen Sullivan. The History of Chi Eta Phi Sorority, Inc. 1932-1967. Washington, DC: Association for Study of Negro Life and History, 1968. [Sorority of Negro professional nurses]

Miller, Jeanne-Marie A. "More than a Servant in the House: Black Female Characters in American Drama, A Sketch." Theatre News 10 (Ap, 1978):6-7.

Moore, W. J. "The Impact of Children and Discrimination on the Hourly Wage Rates of Black and White Wives." Quarterly Review of Economic and Business 17(Autumn, 1977).

Morrison, Joseph L. "Illegitimacy, Sterilization and Racism: A North Carolina Case History." Social Service Review 39(Mr, 1965):1-10.

Morrison, Toni. "What the Black Woman Thinks About Women's Lib." New York Times Magazine, Ag 22, 1971.

Morton, Carol A. "Mistakes Black Men Make in Relating to Black Women." Ebony 31(D, 1975): 170-174.

———. "Mistakes Black Women Make in Relating to Black Men." Ebony 31(Ja, 1976):89-93

Mott, Frank L. "Racial Differences in Female Labor-Force Participation: Trends and Implications for the Future." Urban and Social Change Review 11(1978):21-27.

Mott, Frank L., and Moore, Sylvia F. The Causes of Marital Disruption among Young American Women: An Interdisciplinary Perspective, 1978. ERIC ED 156 923.

Moulton, Robert W., and Stewart, Lawrence H. "Parents as Models for Mobile and Low Mobile Black Males." Vocational Guidance Quarterly 19(Je, 1971):247-253.

Muhammad, Elijah. "To the Black Woman in America." Muhammad Speaks, S 4, 1970.

Murray, Pauli. "The Liberation of Black Women." In Our American Sisters. Edited by Jean E. Friedman and William G. Shade. 1973.

———. "The Negro Woman in the Quest for Equality." Acorn (Lambda Kappa Mu Sorority), Je, 1964.

———. "The Rights of Women." In The Rights of Americans. What They Are--What They Should Be, pp. 521-545. Edited by Norman Dorsen. New York: Pantheon, 1971.

Murray, Sandra Rice, and Mednick, Martha T. S. "Black Women's Achievement Orientation: Motivational and Cognitive Factors." Psychology of Women Quarterly 1(Spring, 1977): 247-257.

Myers, Lena Wright. "A Study of the Self-Esteem Maintenance Process among Black Women." Doctoral dissertation, Michigan State U., 1973. Univ. Microfilms Order No. 73-20383.

———. "Black Women and Self-Esteem." In Another Voice, pp. 240-250. Edited by Rosabeth Kanter and Marcia Millman. Garden City, NY: Doubleday, 1975.

Nash, Abigal Jones and others. Minorities and Women in Broadcast News: Two National Surveys, Ag, 1974. ERIC ED 095 557.

National Council of Negro Women. Women and Housing. A Report on Sex Discrimination in Five American Cities. Washington, DC: GPO, Je, 1975.

National Institute of Education. Conference on the Educational and Occupational Needs of Black Women, Vol 2, Ap, 1978. ERIC ED 157 961.

"Negro Womanhood's Greatest Needs. A Symposium." Messenger 9(Ap, 1927:109, 9(My, 1927):150, 9(Je, 1927):198-199.

Nelson, Charmeynne D. "Myths About Black Women Workers in Modern America." Black Scholar 6 (Mr, 1975):11-15.

Newell, Barbara W. "Parallels of Negro and Women's Education." School and Society 98 (O, 1979):357-359.

Newman, Debra L. "Black Women in the Era of the American Revolution in Pennsylvania." Journal of Negro History 61(Jl, 1976):276-289.

Newsome, Nora. "The Negro Woman in the Trade Union Movement." Messenger 5(Jl, 1923):760-762.

Nicol, Helen O., and Drake, Merci L. Negro Women Workers in 1960. Washington, DC: GPO, 1964.

Noble, Jeanne L. Beautiful, Also, Are the Souls of My Black Sisters: A History of the Black Woman in America. Englewood Cliffs, NJ: Prentice-Hall, 1978.

_____. "The Negro Woman Looks at Her College Education." Doctoral dissertation, Columbia U., 1955.

_____. The Negro Woman's College Education. New York: Teachers College, Columbia U., 1956.

Nobles, Wade W. "African Root and American Fruit: The Black Family." Journal of Social and Behavioral Sciences(Spring, 1974).

"Northern Black Women, Southern Black Women. How Different Are They?" Ebony 34(Ja, 1979).

Nyangoni, Betty. "Black Women, Black Men and Black Studies." Marquette University Education Review 4(Spring, 1973):12-13.

"Ntozake Shange." New Yorker, Ag 2, 1976, pp. 17-19.

Obitko, Mary E. "A Reconsideration of the Black Slave Woman's Response to Slavery, 1830-1860." Master's thesis, U. of Wisconsin, Stevens Point, 1973.

O'Connell, Lucille. "Julia H. Smith: An Uncommon New Englander." Phylon 39(Fall, 1978): 275-281. [Massachusetts]

Olim, Ellis G. "Maternal Language Styles & Children's Cognitive Behavior." Journal of Special Education 4(Winter, 1970):13-68.

Osborne, Gwendolyn E. "Motherhood in the Black Community." Crisis 84(D, 1977):479-484.

Painter, Diann Holland. "The Black Woman in American Society." Current History 70(My, 1976):224-227, 234.

Parker, Seymour, and Kleiner, Robert J. "Characteristics of Negro Mothers in Single-Headed Households." Journal of Marriage and the Family, N, 1966. [Philadelphia]

Parrish, Dorothy. "A Question of Survival: The Predicament of Black Women." Integratoducation 14(My-Je, 1976):19-23.

Parsons, Patricia Fowler. "Research on Black Female Self-Concept: Origins, Issues, and Directions." Doctoral dissertation, Claremont Graduate School, 1974. Univ. Microfilms Order No. 75-02274.

Peters, Marie Ferguson. "The Black Family-- Perpetuating the Myths: An Analysis of Family Sociology Textbook Treatment of Black Families." Family Coordinator 23(O, 1974): 349-356.

_____. "Nine Black Families: A Study of Household Management and Childrearing in Black Families with Working Mothers." Doctoral dissertation, Harvard U., 1976. Univ. Microfilms Order No. 77-00321.

Peterson, Marcella Landy. "Status and Trends in the Promotion of Women to Secondary School Principalships with Special Reference to Black Women." Doctoral dissertation, Wayne State U., 1973. Univ. Microfilms Order No. 74-11145.

Petway, Jamesetta. "Black Women and White Managers: An Action Program for Increased Strength and Influence." Doctoral dissertation, Case Western Reserve U., 1975. Univ. Microfilms Order No. 75-27949.

Pierce, John C., Avery, William P., and Carey, Addison, Jr. "Sex Differences in Black Political Beliefs and Behavior." American Journal of Political Science 17(My, 1973):422-430.

Pierce, Ponchitta. "Marriage and the Educated Black Woman." Ebony 28(Ag, 1973):160-166.

Pinckney, Darryl E. "Black Women and the Myths of Macho." Village Voice, Ap 2, 1979.

Placek, Paul J., and Hendershot, Gerry E. "Public Welfare & Family Planning: An Empirical Study of the 'Brood Sow' Myth." Social Problems 21(Je, 1974):658-673.

Pope, Hallowell, and Mueller, Charles W. "The Intergenerational Transmission of Marital Instability: Comparisons by Race and Sex." Journal of Social Issues 32(1976):49-66.

Porterfield, Ernest. Black and White Mixed Marriage. Chicago: Nelson-Hall, 1977.

Poussaint, Alvin F. "Sex and the Black Male." Ebony 27(Ag, 1972):114-120.

_____. "The Special Position of the Black Woman." Essence Magazine, Ap, 1970.

Prendergast, P., Zdep, S. M., and Sepulveda, P. "Self-Image Among a National Probability Sample of Girls." Child Study Journal 4 (1974):103-114.

President's Commission on the Status of Women. "Problems of Negro Women." In Report on Four Consultations. Washington, DC: GPO, 1963.

Pressman, Sonia. "Job-Discrimination and the Black Woman." Crisis, Mr, 1970.

Puryear, Gwendolyn R., and Melnick, Martha S. "Black Militancy, Affective Attachment, and the Fear of Success in Black College Women." Journal of Consulting & Clinical Psychology 42(1974):263-266.

"The Race Problem--An Autobiography by a Southern Colored Woman." Independent, Mr 17, 1904.

Rackley, Lurma. "Black Woman: A Slave's Daughter, She Never Hated." Washington Star, Ag 19, 1976. [Mrs. Alice Bell, Cambridge, MD and Washington, DC]

Rainwater, Lee. Behind Ghetto Walls: Black Family Life in a Federal Slum. Chicago, IL: Aldine, 1970.

Redding, Evangeline G. Nothing: The Mentality of the Black Woman. Tillery, NC: Heritage of Hope, 1976.

Reed, Julia. "Marriage and Fertility in Black Female Teachers." Black Scholar, Ja-F, 1970.

Reid, Inez Smith. Health Issues Facing Black Women. Washington, DC: National Institute of Education, Ap, 1978.

_____. Together Black Women. New York: Emerson Hall, 1976.

Render, Sylvia Lyons. "Afro-American Women: The Outstanding and the Obscure." Quarterly Journal of the Library of Congress 32(O, 1975):307-321.

"The Revolt of Poor Black Women." In Lessons from the Damned: Class Struggle in the Black Community. Washington, NJ: Times Change Press, 1973.

Rickman, Geraldine. "A Natural Alliance. The New Role for Black Women." Civil Rights Digest 6(Spring, 1974):57-65.

Ripley, C. Peter. "The Black Family in Transition: Louisiana, 1860-1865." Journal of Southern History 41(Ag, 1975).

Robinson, H. B., and Robinson, N. M. "Longitudinal Development of Very Young Children in a Comprehensive Day-Care Program." Child Development 42(1971):1673-1684.

Robinson, Patricia. "Poor Black Women." Community (Chicago) 33(Spring, 1974):18-19.

Robinson, Rosetta. "The Black Female Undergraduate's Assessment of the Academic and Social Environments of Two Selected Institutions of Higher Learning." Master's thesis, Cornell U., 1974.

Roderick, Roger D. with Davis, Joseph M. Years for Decision. A Longitudinal Study of the Educational and Labor Market Experience of Young Women. Washington, DC: GPO, 1974.

Rooks, Evelyn, and King, Karl. "A Study of the Marriage Role Expectations of Black Adolescents." Adolescence 8(F, 1973):317-324.

Rose, Shirley Ann. "Independent Family Day Care Mothers in the Black Community." Doctoral dissertation, Columbia U., 1976. Univ. Microfilms Order No. 76-21,035.

Rosenberg, Beatrice. Day Care Facts. Women's Bureau. Washington, DC: GPO, My, 1970.

Rubin, Roger Harvey. Matricentric Family Structure and the Self-Attitudes of Negro Children. San Francisco: R and E Research Associates, 1976.

Ruderman, Florence. Child Care and Working Mothers. New York: Child Welfare Leage of America, 1968.

Rushing, Andrea Benton. "Images of Black Women in Afro-American Poetry." Black World 24 (S, 1975):18-30.

Russell, Michele. "Rapunzel, Let Down Your Hair: An Open Letter to White Women in the Academy." College English 39(S, 1977):45-52.

_____. "Slave Codes and Linen Notes: Black Women in the U.S." Radical Religion 3(1977).

Russo, Nancy F. Sex and Race Differences in Attitudes toward Sex Role Behaviors, S, 1971. ERIC ED 060 469.

Rutledge, Essie Manuel. "Marital and Family Relations of Black Women." Doctoral dissertation, The U. of Michigan, 1974. Univ. Microfilms Order No. 75-10280.

Rychlak, Joseph F. and others. "Affective Evaluation, Word Quality, and the Verbal Learning Styles of Black versus White Junior College Females." Journal of Personality & Social Psychology 27(Ag, 1973):248-255.

Sampson, William A., and Rossi, Peter H. "Race and Family Social Standing." American Sociological Review 40(Ap, 1975):201-214.

Samuel, Nadene, and Laird, Dorothy S. "The Self-Concepts of Two Groups of Black Female College Students." Journal of Negro Education 43 (Spring, 1974):228-233.

Sawers, Larry. "Urban Poverty and Labor Force Participation: Note." American Economic Review 62(Je, 1972):414-421. [Black women in labor market]

Sawhill, Isabel V. Black Women Who Head Families: Economic Needs and Economic Resources. Washington, DC: National Institute of Education, Ap, 1978.

Schetlin, Eleanor M. "Ethnic Minority Feminism: A Majority Member's View." Journal of the NAWDAC 41(Winter, 1978):47-51.

Schwartz, Michael. "The Northern United States Negro Matriarchy: Status Versus Authority." Phylon, Spring, 1965.

Schwartz, Michael, and Badler, Mary Anna. "Female Adolescent Self-Concept: An Examination of the Relative Influence of Peers and Adults." Youth and Society 5(S, 1973): 115-128.

Scott, Patricia Bell. A Critical Overview of Sex Roles Research in Black Families, Mr, 1976. ERIC ED 127 403.

_____. "The English Language & Black Womanhood: A Low Blow at Self-Esteem." Journal of Afro-American Issues 2(Summer, 1974):218-225.

_____. "Preparing Black Women for Nontraditional Professions: Some Considerations for Career Counseling." Journal of the NAWDAC 40(Summer, 1977):135-139.

Seidman, Edward, and Koulack, David. "Race, Adjustment, and Rejection." Journal of Consulting & Clinical Psychology 40(Ap, 1973):298-303.

"7 Women Look at 1976 and Beyond." Chicago Defender, Ja 3, 1976.

Sexton, Patricia Cayo. The Feminized Male: Classrooms, White Collars and the Decline of Manliness. New York: Random House, 1969.

Shakur, Assata (Joanne Chesimard). "Women in Prison: How We Are." Black Scholar 9(Ap, 1978):8-15.

Sharrar, Mary Lou. "Attitude of Black Natural Parents Regarding Adoption." Child Welfare 50(My, 1971):286-289.

Shaw, Ethelrine. Professional Schools and their Impact on Black Women. Washington, DC: National Institute of Education, Ap, 1978.

Shea, John R. Welfare Mothers: Barriers to Labor Force Entry, XC-212-147. Springfield, VA: National Technical Information Service, 1972.

Shea, John R. and others. Years for Decision: A Longitudinal Study of the Educational and Labor Market Experience of Young Women. Vol. I. Washington, DC: GPO, 1971.

Shockley, Ann Allen, and Tucker, Veronica E. "Black Women Discuss Today's Problems: Men, Families, Society." Southern Voices 1(Ag-S, 1974):16-19.

Sickels, Robert Judd. Race, Marriage, and the Law. Albuquerque, NM: U. of New Mexico Press, 1972.

Simpson, Wessylyne Alford. "Self-Concept and Career Choice Among Black Women." Doctoral dissertation, Oklahoma State U., 1975. Univ. Microfilms Order No. 76-09772.

Sizemore, Barbara A. "Sexism and the Black Male." Black Scholar 4(Mr-Ap, 1973):2-11

Slaby, Andrew E., and Sealy, Joan R. "Black Liberation, Women's Liberation." American Journal of Psychiatry 130(F, 1973):196-200.

Slater, Jack. "Suicide: A Growing Menace to Black Women." Ebony (S, 1973).

Slater, Jack. "Three Profiles in Courage." Ebony (Mr, 1973):94-106.

Slaughter, Diana T. "Becoming an Afro-American Woman." School Review 80(F, 1972):299-318.

Sloan, Margaret E. "Keeping the Black Woman in Her Place." MS, J, 1975.

_____. "What We Should be Doing, Sister." New York Times, D 8, 1971.

Smith, Barbara. "Black Women in Film Symposium." Freedomways 14(Third Quarter, 1974):266-269.

Smith, Gloria R. "From Invisibility to Blackness: The Story of the Black Nurses Association." Nursing Outlook 23(Ap, 1975):225-229.

Smith, H. C. "An Investigation of the Attitudes of Adolescent Girls Toward Combining Marriage, Motherhood and a Career." Doctoral dissertation, Columbia U., 1969.

Smith, J. P. The Convergence to Racial Equality in Women's Wages. Santa Monica, CA: Rand, Mr, 1978.

Smith, Raymond T. "The Nuclear Family in Afro-American Kinship." Journal of Comparative Family Studies 1(1970).

Snow, Jacquelyn E. "A Heuristic Study of Black Female Heads of Households and Black Females Who are Not Heads of Households and their Involvement with their Children's Educational Development. Camden, New Jersey." Doctoral dissertation, Rutgers U., The State U. of New Jersey, New Brunswick, 1976. Univ. Microfilms Order No. 77-13291.

Sorkin, Alan L. "Occupational Status & Unemployment of Nonwhite Women." Social Forces 49 (Mr, 1971).

A Southern Colored Woman. "The Race Problem--An Autobiography." Independent 56(Mr 17, 1904).

Spurlock, Jeanne. "A Reappraisal of the Role of Black Women." Journal of the National Association of Private Psychiatric Hospitals 3 (Fall, 1971):8-16.

Spurlock, Jeanne, and Cohen, Rebecca S. "Should the Poor Get None?" Journal of the American Academy of Child Psychiatry 8(1969):16-35. [Black mothers and their children]

Staples, Robert. <u>The Black Woman in America</u>. Chicago: Nelson Hall Publishers, 1973.

_____. "Has the Sexual Revolution Bypassed Blacks?" <u>Ebony</u> 29(Ap, 1974):111-114.

_____. "Masculinity and Race: The Dual Dilemma of Black Men." <u>Journal of Social Issues</u> 34, No. 1(1978):169-183.

_____. The Myth of Black Sexual Superiority: A Re-examination." <u>Black Scholar</u> 9(Ap, 1978): 16-23.

_____. "The Myth of the Impotent Black Male." <u>Black Scholar</u> 2(Je, 1971):2-9.

_____. "Research on Black Sexuality: Its Implication for Family Life, Sex Education, and Public Policy." <u>Family coordinator</u> 21(Ap, 1972):183-188.

_____. "The Sexuality of Black Women." <u>Sexual Behavior</u> 2(Je, 1972):4-11, 14-15.

_____. "Towards a Sociology of the Black Family: A Theoretical and Methodological Assessment." <u>Journal of Marriage and the Family</u> 33(F, 1971):119-135.

Staupers, Mabel Keaton. <u>No Time for Prejudice: A Story of the Integration of Negroes in Nursing in the United States</u>. New York: n.p., 1961.

Steinmann, Anne, and Fox, David J. "Attitudes Toward Women's Family Role Among Black and White Undergraduates." <u>Family Coordinator</u> 19 (O, 1970):363-368.

Sterling, Dorothy. <u>Black Foremothers: Ellen Craft and Ida B. Wells-Barnett</u>. Old Westbury, NY: Feminist Press, 1977.

Sterling, Dorothy Hendricks. "The Experience of Being-Me for Black Adolescent Females: A Phenomenological Investigation of Black Identity." Doctoral dissertation, U. of Pittsburgh, 1974. Univ. Microfilms Order NO. 75-04083.

Stevenson, Gloria. "Counseling Black Teenage Girls." <u>Occupational Outlook Quarterly</u> 19 (Summer, 1975):2-13.

Stewart, Dorothy G. "The Social Adjustment of Black Females at a Predominantly White University." Doctoral dissertation, U. of Connecticut, 1972.

Stewart, Maria W. <u>Meditations from the Pen of Mrs. Maria W. Stewart, Negro</u>. Washington, DC: n.p., 1879.

_____. <u>Productions of Mrs. Maria W. Stewart</u>. Boston, MA: Garrison and Knapp, 1832.

Stewart, Ruth Ann. <u>Portia: The Life of Portia Washington Pittman, the Daughter of Booker T. Washington</u>. Garden City, NY: Anchor Press, 1977.

Stimpson, Catherine. "Thy Neighbor's Wife, Thy Neighbor's Servant: Women's Liberation and Black Civil Rights." In <u>Woman in Sexist Society: Studies in Power and Powerlessness</u>. Edited by Vivian Gornick and Barbara K. Maran. New York: Basic Books, 1971.

Stokes, Gail A. "Black Woman to Black Man." In <u>The Black Family: Essays and Studies</u>. Edited by Robert Staples. Belmont, CA: Wadsworth, 1971.

Stokes, Shirley J. "Can Black Women Make It in a White Man's World?" <u>Black Collegian</u> 8(My-Je, 1978).

Stowe, Lucy D. "Higher Education of Negro Women." <u>Journal of Negro Education</u> 2(Jl, 1933):352-358.

Strauch, Barry. <u>An Investigation into the Sex-Race-Ability Interaction</u>, 1976. ERIC ED 126 373.

"Stresses and Strains on Black Women." <u>Ebony</u> 29 (Je, 1974):33-40.

Stuart, Irving R., and Abt, Lawrence E. (eds.). <u>Interracial Marriage: Expectations and Realities</u>. New York: Grossman, 1973.

Sweet, James A., and Bumpass, L. L. "Differentials in Marital Instability of the Black Population: 1970." <u>Phylon</u> 35(S, 1974):323-331.

Task Force on Employment Problems of Black Youth. "For Black Girls, It's Worse." In <u>The Job Crisis for Black Youth</u>, pp. 77-96. New York Praeger, 1971.

Task Force on Health and Welfare. <u>Women and Their Families in Our Rapidly Changing Society</u>. Washington, DC: GPO, Ap, 1968.

Tatje, Terrence Andresen. "Mother-Daughter Dyadic Dominance in Black American Kinship." Doctoral dissertation, Northwestern U., 1974. Univ. Microfilms Order No. 74-28762.

Taylor, Brooke Battles. "'You Not the Man You Momma Was: A Study of Women Characters in Selected Black Fiction." Master's thesis, Stephen F. Austin State U., 1971.

Ten Houten, Warren D. "The Black Family: Myth and Reality." <u>Psychiatry</u>, My, 1970.

Thomas, Curlew O., and Thomas, Barbara Boston. "The Impact of Black Nationalism on Negritude: A Comparative Study of Black Males and Females." <u>Phylon</u> 38(Mr, 1977):35-45.

Thomas, Emma Joahanne. "Career Patterns of Black Women Administrators in Historically Negro Senior Colleges and Universities." Doctoral dissertation, Washington State U., 1976. Univ. Microfilms Order No. 76-27763.

Thomas, Katheryn Ann. <u>A Racial Comparison of Developmental Changes in Marital Family Status Projections of Teenage Girls</u>, Mr 12, 1971.

Thomas, Katheryn Ann. A Racial Comparison of Developmental Change in Marital Family Status Projections of Teenage Girls, Mr 12, 1971. ERIC ED 050 834.

_____. Unrealistic Development of Frames of Aspirational Reference of Rural Negro and White Girls: A Refutation of Popular Theory, Ag, 1971. ERIC ED 091 090.

Thompson, Allen R. "Comparative Occupational Position of White and Nonwhite Females in the United States." Doctoral dissertation, U. of Texas, 1973.

Thornton, Arland. "Marital Instability Differentials and Interactions: Insights from Multivariate Contingency Table Analysis." Sociology and Social Research 62(Jl, 1978): 572-595.

Thorpe, Claiburne B. "Aspiration: An Index of Black Female Personality." Journal of Social and Behavioral Sciences 19(Summer-Fall, 1972): 8-12.

_____. "Social Status and the Pill at a Black Woman's College." College Student Journal 6 (Ap, 1972):66-73.

Tobin, McClean. "A Profile of Black Women Doctorate Holders in Black Public Colleges and Universities: 1973-1974." Doctoral dissertation, Kansas State U., 1975. Univ. Microfilms Order No. 75-25066.

Toupin, Elizabeth Ahn, and Luria, Zella. "Coed Housing: A Conflict for Black Parents?" Journal of College Student Personnel 16 (S, 1975):395-399.

Treiman, Donald J., and Terrell, Kermit. "Sex and the Process of Status Attainment: A Comparison of Working Women and Men." American Sociological Review 40(Ap, 1975): 174-200.

Trescott, Jacqueline. "A Child of the South, a Winter of the Heart." Washington Post, Ag 8, 1976. [Alice Walker]

Tuck, Samuel, Jr. A Model for Working with Black Fathers. Research Report: Volume 6, No. 11, 1969 (Revised March 1970), Mr, 1970. ERIC ED 040 260.

_____. "Working With Black Fathers." American Journal of Orthopsychiatry 41(Ap, 1971): 465-472.

Turner, Barbara F., and McCaffrey, Joanne H. "Socialization and Career Orientation Among Black & White College Women." Journal of Vocational Behavior 5(D, 1974):307-319.

Turner, Barbara F., and Turner, Castellano B. "Evaluations of Women and Men Among Black and White College Students." Sociological Quarterly 15(Summer, 1974):442-456.

_____ and _____. Race and Sex in Evaluating Women, Ag, 1974. ERIC ED 101 233.

Turner, Castellano B., and Darity, William. Attitudes Toward Family Planning and Fears of Genocide as a Function of Race Consciousness, My, 1971. ERIC ED 052 473.

Turner, Clarence Rollo. "Some Theoretical and Conceptual Considerations for Black Family Studies." Black Lives 2(Winter, 1972):13-27.

Tyler, Anne. "'Because I Want More Than One Life.'" Washington Post, Ag 15, 1976. [A black writer]

Tymchuk, Alexander J. "Personality & Sociocultural Retardation." Exceptional Children 38(My, 1972):721-728.

Udry, J. Richard, Bauman, Karl E., and Chase, Charles. "Skin Color, Status, and Mate Selection." American Journal of Sociology 76 (Ja, 1971):722-733.

Udry, J. Richard, Bauman, Karl E., Morris, Naomi M., and Chase, Charles L. "Social Class, Social Mobility, and Prematurity: A Test of the Childhood Environment Hypothesis for Negro Women." Journal of Health & Social Behavior 11(S, 1970):190-195.

U.S. Bureau of Labor Statistics. U.S. Working Women. A Chartbook. Washington, DC: GPO, 1975.

U.S. Bureau of the Census. Differences Between Incomes of White and Negro Families by Work Experience of Wife and Region: 1970, 1969, and 1959. Washington, DC: GPO, 1971.

_____. Female Family Heads. Washington, DC: GPO, Jl, 1974.

_____. Nursery School and Kindergarten Enrollment of Children and Labor Force Status of Their Mothers. Washington, DC: GPO, 1978.

_____. We the American Women. Washington, DC: GPO, Mr, 1973.

U.S. Congress, 91st, 2nd session, House of Representatives, Committee on Education and Labor, Special Subcommittee on Education. Discrimination Against Women. Hearings... 2 parts. Washington, DC: GPO, 1970.

U.S. Congress, 93rd, 1st session, Senate, Committee on Labor and Public Welfare, Subcommittee on Children and Youth. American Families: Trends and Pressures, 1973. Hearings... Washington, DC: GPO, 1973.

U.S. Department of Health, Education, and Welfare, Social and Rehabilitation Service, National Center for Social Statistics. Trends in AFDC, 1965-1970 and Selected Annual Periods. Washington, DC: U.S. Department of H.E.W., 1971.

U.S. Department of Labor. Facts on Women Workers of Minority Races. Washington, DC: GPO, My, 1975.

_____. Negro Women in the Population and in the Labor Force. Washington, DC: GPO, D, 1967.

_____. Placing Minority Women in Professional Jobs. Washington, DC: GPO, 1978.

U.S. Women's Bureau. Facts on Women Workers of Minority Races. Rev. ed. Washington, DC: GPO, 1975.

_____. Minority Women Workers: A Statistical Overview. Rev. ed. Washington, DC: Women's Bureau, 1977.

Umbarger, Carter C. "Black and White Fathers: Their Impact on the Idealized Models and Vocational Plans of Their Adolescent Sons." Diss. Abstr. Int'l. 1969, 30 (6-B) 2919.

Vroman, Mary Elizabeth. Shaped to Its Purpose: Delta Sigma Theta--The First Fifty Years. New York: Random House, 1965. [History of a Negro sorority]

Waite, L. J. and others. "Changes in Child Care Arrangments of Working Women from 1965 to 1971." Social Science Quarterly 58 (S, 1977).

Waldman, Elizabeth. "Children of Working Mothers." Monthly Labor Review 98(Ja, 1975).

Waldman, Elizabeth, and Whitmore, Robert. Children of Working Mothers, March, 1973. Washington, DC: U.S. Bureau of Labor Statistics, 1974.

Walker, Alice. In Love and Trouble: Stories of Black Women. New York: Harcourt Brace Jovanovich, 1973.

Wallace, Michele. Black Macho and the Myth of the Superwoman. New York: Dial, 1979.

Wallace, Phyllis Ann. Pathways to Work: Unemployment Among Black Teenage Females. Lexington, MA: Lexington Books, 1974.

Washington, Mary Helen (ed). Black-Eyed Susans. Classic Stories by and About Black Women. Garden City: Anchor, 1975.

Washington, Patricia Lee. "The Black Woman's Agenda: An Investigation into Strategies for Change." Doctoral dissertation, Arizona State U., 1978. Univ. Microfilms Order No. 7815 251.

Wasserman, Herbert L. "Father-Absent and Father-Present Lower Class Negro Families: A Comparative Study of Family Functioning." Doctoral dissertation, Brandeis U., 1968.

Watkins, Mel, and David, Jay (eds.). To Be A Black Woman. New York: Morrow, 1971.

Watriss, Wendy. "'It's Something Inside You.'" Southern Exposure 4(Winter, 1977):76-81 [Anna Mae Dickson, East Texas]

Watson, Vernaline. "Self-Concept Formation and the Afro-American Woman." Journal of Afro-American Issues 2(Summer, 1974):226-236.

Weathers, Diane. "Graduate Students Open Up New Career Paths." Black Enterprise 5(Ag, 1974): 24-27.

Weinhold, Janey. "A Comparative Analysis of the Rhetoric of Two Negro Women Orators, Sojourner Truth and Frances E. Watkins." Fort Hays Kansas State College, Hays, Kansas, 1968.

Weisman, Carol Sachs. "An Analysis of Female Dominance in Urban Black Families." Doctoral dissertation, The Johns Hopkins U., 1973. Univ. Microfilms Order No. 73-16667.

Wesley, Charles Harris. The History of Alpha Phi Alpha, a Development in College Life. 8th ed. Washington, DC: Foundation Publishers, 1957.

West, Anne Grant. "The Black and White of Women's Liberation." Response (United Methodist Women) 3(My, 1971).

Weston, Peter J., and Mednick, Martha T. "Race, Social Class and the Motive to Avoid Success in Women." Cross Cultural Psychology 1 (S, 1970):283-291.

Whaley, Betti S., and Lewis, Toye B. Policy Issues on Day Care: The Special Needs of Black Working Women. Washington, DC: National Institute of Education, Ap, 1978.

White, Carolyn Delores. "The Social Mobility-Fertility Hypothesis: A Racial and Class Comparison Among Southern Females." Master's thesis, Texas A and M U., 1974.

"White Supremacy within the Women's Movement." In Women's Liberation and Imperialism. San Francisco: Prairie Fire Organizing Committee, N, 1977.

Whittaker, Sandra V. Comparative Study of Self-Esteem Among Black, White, and Latino Women, 1976. ERIC ED 154 260.

"Why Is AFDC Rising?" In President's Commission on Income Maintenance Programs, Background Papers, pp. 39-42. Washington, DC: GPO, 1970.

Wilkinson, Doris Y. "Apartheid and the Male-Dominated Black Caucus." American Sociologist 7(F, 1972).

_____ (ed). Black Male/White Female. Morristown, NJ: General Learning Press, 1975.

William, Audrey. "Black Women and W[omen's] L[iberation]." News and Letters (Mr, 1974):2.

192 / THE BLACK WOMAN

Williams, Bertha M. "Black Women: Assertive
vs. Aggressiveness." Journal of Afro-
American Issues 2(Summer, 1974):204-211.

Williams, Fannie Barrier. "Club Movement Among
Negro Women." In The Colored American from
Slavery to Honorable Citizenship. Edited by
John W. Gibson. Atlanta, GA: J. L. Nichols,
1903.

_____. "A Northern Negro's Autobiography."
Independent 57(J1 14, 1904).

Williams, Mary Louise. "The Negro Working
Woman." Messenger 5(J1, 1923):763.

Williams, Maxine, and Newman, Pamela. Black
Women's Liberation. New York: Pathfinder
Press, 1970.

Williams, Robert George. Public Assistance and
Work Effort: The Labor Supply of Low-Income
Female Heads of Household. Princeton, NJ:
Industrial Relations Section, Princeton U.,
1975.

Willie, Charles V. "The Black Family and Social
Class." American Journal of Orthopsychiatry
44(Ja, 1974):50-60.

_____. The Family Life of Black People.
Columbus, OH: Merrill, 1970.

Winters, Wilda Glasgow. "Black Mothers in Urban
Schools: A Study of Participation and
Alienation." Doctoral dissertation, Yale
U., 1975. Univ. Microfilms Order No. 76-
14574.

Women's Bureau. Women Private Household Workers
Fact Sheet. Washington, DC: Wage and Labor
Standards Administration, U.S. Department of
Labor, Mr, 1968.

_____. Women with Low Incomes, N, 1977. ERIC
ED 147 645.

Woods, M. B. "The Unsupervised Child of the
Working Mother." Developmental Psychology 6
(1972):14-25.

Woodson, Carter G. "Emma Frances Grayson
Merritt." Opportunity 8(Ag, 1930):244-245.

_____. "The Negro Washerwoman: A Vanishing
Figure." Journal of Negro History 15(J1,
1930).

"The Working Woman and the Men in Her Life."
Black Enterprise 8(Ag, 1977):14-17, 50.

"Workshop on Women in the Struggle." African
World, J1, 1974.

Wyatt, Gail Elizabeth. "Studying the Black
Mother-Child Interaction." Young Children 33
(N, 1977):16-22.

X, Sister Johnnie, and Kashif, Lonnie. "'Racism
Biggest Problem,' Black Women Lawyers."
Muhammad Speaks, S 27, 1974.

Young, Gwendolyn. "Black Women on the Move--
But Where?" Crisis 84(Ap, 1977):153-154.

Young, Margaret B. "A Negro Mother Speaks of
Her Challenging Role in a Changing World."
Parents' Magazine, J1, 1964. [By the wife
of Whitney Young, Jr., head of the National
Urban League]

_____. "The Negro Girl and Poverty." American
Child 47(My, 1965).

Zalk, Sue R. and others. Sex Bias in Children,
S, 1976. ERIC ED 129 441.

Bibliographies

Astin, Helen S., Suniewick, Nancy, and Dweck,
Susan (comps.). Women. A Bibliography on
Their Education and Careers. Washington, DC:
Human Service Press, 1971.

Bickner, Mei Liang (comp.). Women at Work: An
Annotated Bibliography, Mr, 1974. ERIC ED
095 398.

The Black Family and the Black Woman. A
Bibliography. Bloomington, IN: The Library,
Indiana U., 1972.

Cole, Johnneta B. (comp.). "Black Women in
America: An Annotated Bibliography." Black
Scholar 3(D, 1971):42-53.

Davis, Lenwood G. (comp.). The Black Family in
Urban Areas in the United States. Monticello,
IL: Council of Planning Libraries, 1973.

_____ (comp). The Black Woman in American
Society: Selected Annotated Bibliography.
Boston: G. K. Hall, 1976.

_____ (comp.). Black Women in the Cities, 1872-
1975: A Bibliography of Published Works on
the Lives and Achievements of Black Women in
Cities in the U.S. 2nd ed. Monticello, IL:
Council of Planning Librarians, 1975.

Indiana University, Libraries (comp.). The
Black Family and the Black Woman: A
Bibliography. Bloomington, IN: Indiana U.,
1972.

Klotman, Phyllis Rauch, and Baatz, Wilmer H.
(comps.). The Black Family and the Black
Woman. New York: Arno Press, 1978.

Murray, Sandra Rice (comp.). Psychological
Perspectives on Black Women: A Selected
Bibliography of Recent Citations. Baltimore:
Afro-American Studies Program, U. of Maryland-
Baltimore County, 1978.

Nicolas, Suzanne and others (comps.). Biblio-
graphy on Women Workers (1861-1965).
Geneva, Switzerland: Central Library and
Documentation Branch, International Labour
Office, 154 Route de Lausanne.

Reif, Nadine (comp.). An Annotated Bibliography of Day Care Reference Materials, Ap 30, 1972. ERIC ED 088 609.

Rosenberg, Marie B., and Bergstrom, Len V. (eds.). Women and Society: A Critical Review of the Literature with a Selected Annotated Bibliography. Beverly Hills, CA: Sage, 1974.

Roundtree, Dovey (comp.). "Equal Opportunity for Women in Housing: A Bibliography." In National Council of Negro Women, Women and Housing. A Report on Sex Discrimination in Five American Cities, pp. 175-194. Washington, DC: GPO, Mr, 1975.

Spiegel, Jeanne (comp.). Working Mothers: A Selected Annotated Bibliography. Washington, DC: Business and Professional Women's Foundation, 1968.

Terbourg-Penn, Rosalyn M. "The Historical Treatment of Afro-Americans in the Woman's Movement 1900-1920: A Bibliographic Essay." Current Bibliogr. Afric. Aff. 7(1974):245-260.

Tittle, Carol Kehr, McCarthy, Karen, and Steckler, Jane Faggen (comps.). Women and Educational Testing. A Selective Review of the Research Literature and Testing Practices. Princeton, NJ: Educational Testing Service, 1974.

Wells, Alberta (comp.). Day Care. An Annotated Bibliography. PB 208 750. Springfield, VA: National Technical Information Service, D, 1971.

Westervelt, Esther Manning, and Fixter, Deborah A. with Comstock, Margaret. Women's Higher and Continuing Education: An Annotated Bibliography with Selected References on Related Aspects of Women's Lives. New York: College Entrance Examination Board, 1971.

Williams, Ora (comp.). American Black Women in the Arts and Social Sciences: A Bibliographic Survey. Rev. ed. Metuchen, NJ: Scarecrow Press, 1978.

4.
AMERICAN SCENE

The States

Alabama

Alabama League for the Advancement of Education. *The Slow Death of the Black Educator in Alabama*, Jl 1, 1971. The League, P.O. Box 6233, Montgomery, AL 36106.

"Alabama Students Beaten in 'Organized' Free-for-All." *SOBU Newsletter*, Mr 6, 1971. [Vigor High School, Prichard]

Analavage, Robert. "Apartheid in Wallace Country." *Southern Patriot*, S, 1968. [Cajuns in Mobile County]

Anderson, Robert E., Jr. "The Essence of Survival." In *The South and Her Children: School Desegregation, 1970-1971*, pp. 38-49. Edited by Robert E. Anderson, Jr. Atlanta, GA: Southern Regional Council, Mr, 1971. [Mobile]

Atwood, W. O., and Woods, Charles D. *Dietary Studies with Reference to the Food of the Negro in Alabama in 1895 and 1896*. U.S. Department of Agriculture, Office of Experiment Stations, Bulletin 38. Washington, DC: GPO, 1897.

Ballard, Leilafred. "The American Negro, 1880-1895, as Portrayed in the *Huntsville Gazette*." Master's thesis, Howard U., 1952.

Bell, Jereline Ryus. "A Limited Study of the Contributions of the American Missionary Association to Negro Education in Alabama." Master's thesis, State College for Negroes at Montgomery, 1949.

"Black Students Upsouth Go Downsouth." *Imani*, F, 1971. [National Black Student Movement; to Alabama]

Boatright, Ruth F. *Origin and Development of the Negro Visiting Teacher in Alabama*. New York: Vantage Press, 1975.

Boles, Alan. "Alabama Institute for the Deaf and Blind." *Southern Courier*, Ja 20, 1968. [Segregation among the deaf and the blind]

_____. "Randolph County Superintendent Wonders If Schools Will Get U.S. Money." *Southern Courier*, Ag 12, 1967. [Roanoke]

Bond, Horace Mann. "The Influence of Negro Education on the Public Education of Negroes in Alabama, II." *The Journal of Negro Education* 6(Ap, 1937):172-187.

_____. "The Influence of Personalities on the Public Education of Negroes in Alabama, I." *The Journal of Negro Education* 6(Ja, 1937): 17-27.

_____. "Negro Education: A Debate in the Alabama Constitutional Convention of 1901." *The Journal of Negro Education* 1(Ap, 1932): 49-59.

_____. *Negro Education in Alabama: A Study in Cotton and Steel*. The Associated Publishers, Inc., 1939.

_____. "Two Racial Islands in Alabama." *The American Journal of Sociology* 36(Ja, 1931): 552-567.

Boucher, Novis. "The Free Negro in Alabama Prior to 1860." Doctoral dissertation, State U. of Iowa, 1950.

"Boycott Ends in Choctaw." *Southern Courier*, S 23, 1967. [Choctaw County]

Boykin, Milton Lee. "Black Political Participation in Greene County, Alabama: An Information-Efficacious Hypothesis." In *Politics 1973: Minorities in Politics*. Edited by Tinsley E. Yarbrough, John P. East, and Sandra Hough. East Carolina University Publications, P.O. Box 2771, Greenville, NC 27834.

THE STATES / 195

Bradford, Viola. "Honor Roll Integrated at Lanier." Southern Courier, D 18, 1965. [Montgomery high school]

Brenner, Thomas E. A Comparative Study of the Elementary Schools, White and Colored, of the 67 Counties of Alabama. Montgomery, AL: Brown Printing Company, 1921.

Brooks, Thomas E. "The Inception and Development of Student Personnel Services at Tuskegee Institute." Doctoral dissertation, Indiana U., 1955.

Brown, Charles A. The Origin and Development of Secondary Education for Negroes in the Metropolitan Areas of Birmingham, Alabama. Birmingham, AL: Commercial Printing Co., 1959.

Burpo, Patricia. "Meeting on Integration." Southern Courier, Ag 5, 1967. [A Negro student, scheduled to enroll in a white school in Birmingham, tells of her visit to a meeting of the school board.]

Buss, Mary Lynn. "A Team of Young People Spread the Word: Desegregate Schools." Southern Courier, My 7, 1966. [College students try to convince Birmingham area Negro parents to send their children to a desegregated school.]

Caliver, Ambrose. "The Largest Negro High School." School Life 17(D, 1931):73-74. [Industrial High; Birmingham]

Campbell, Boyd. "A New Paper." Southern Courier, O 19, 1968. [Lanier High School, Montgomery]

Campbell, David. "The Lowndes County Freedom Organization: An Appraisal." New South 27 (Winter, 1972):37-42.

Campbell, James D. "Electoral Participation and the Quest for Equality: Black Politics in Alabama Since the Voting Rights Act of 1965." Doctoral dissertation, U. of Texas, n.d.

Cecil, Carl Edwin. Levels of Involvement Needed to Key on Educational Desegregation. An Evaluation of Desegregation Programs Providing a Rational Base for Planning. Mobile, AL: Center for Intercultural Education, College of Education, U. of South Alabama, 1970.

Chesler, Mark A., and Segal, Phyllis. Characteristics of Negro Students Attending Previously All-White Schools in the Deep South. Final Report, S, 1967. ERIC ED 016 726.

_____ and _____. "Southern Negroes' Initial Experiences and Reactions in School Desegregation." Integrated Education, Ja-F, 1968.

Chisum, James. "At Miles College, A Mere Lack of Knowledge Is No Bar." Southern Education Report, My, 1967. [Birmingham]

Clark, Joan. "People Disagree About Integration of Schools." Southern Courier, Mr 4, 1967. [A discussion in Anniston]

Cleveland, Allen Davis. "Alabama's Private, Nonsectarian Elementary and Secondary Schools in 1970." Doctoral dissertation, Auburn U., 1970.

Commission on Professional Rights and Responsibilities. Wilcox County, Alabama. A Study of Social, Economic, and Educational Bankruptcy. Washington, DC: National Education Association, Je, 1967.

"Community Opposition Grows Against More Busing, Less Education." African World 1(S 18, 1971):1, 11. [Livingston]

Coombs, David W. and others. "Black Political Control in Greene County, Alabama." Rural Sociology 42(F, 1977):398-406.

Cotton, Stephen E. "Two Girls in Phillips High School, Birmingham, Alabama." Integrated Education, D, 1966-Ja, 1967.

Cotton, Stephen E., and Kaufman, Robin. "'If You Don't Like to Study, Stay at Carver.'" Southern Courier, D 18, 1965. [Desegregation problems in Bessemer]

Cowan, Geoffrey. "Montgomery's First Year of School Integration." Southern Courier, Ag 6, 1965.

Crandall, G. F. "Black Power in the Deep South: A Study of the Freedom Movement in Alabama and Mississippi Since the Civil Rights Period." Doctoral dissertation, Oxford U., 1972.

Cumming, Joseph B. "Slumbering Greene County, a Remote Sliver of Alabama, Where Blacks and Whites May Realize the Highest Hope for the South and America." Southern Voices 1(Mr-Ap, 1974):22-30.

Daniel, Johnnie. "Changes in Negro Political Mobilization and its Relationship to Community Socioeconomic Structure." Journal of Social and Behavioral Sciences 13(Fall, 1968):41-46. [Alabama]

Davis, Joseph. "A Historical Study of Snow Hill Normal and Industrial Institute and Its Contributions to the Educational Program of the State of Alabama." Master's thesis, Alabama State College, 1954.

Dean, John. The Making of a Black Mayor: A Study of Compaign Organization, Strategies and Techniques in Prichard, Alabama. Washington, DC: Joint Center for Political Studies, 1973.

Denby, Charles (Matthew Ward, pseud.). "Childhood in the South." In Indignant Heart. A Black Worker's Journal, pp. 1-26. Boston: South End Press, 1978. [Lowndes County]

[Desegregation in Southern Communities],
Southern Courier, S 10, 1966. [Short report
from Tuskegee, Haynesville, Clayton, and
Union Springs]

Diamante, John C. "Decision Keeps Wilcox Pupils
in White Schools." Southern Courier, F 4,
1967. [Wilcox County]

Dinwiddie, Bob. "'Revolution, Not Boycott,'
says Miles Protest Leader." Southern
Courier, O 14, 1967. [Student revolt at
Miles College in Birmingham]

Education Study Commission. Achieving Educa-
tional Excellence in Alabama. Vol. 9:
Student Performance in Local School Systems.
Montgomery, AL: The Commission, 1973.

_____. The Role and Scope of Public Education
in the State of Alabama. Report of Task
Force I. Montgomery, AL: The Commission,
1968.

Educational Park, A Case Study Based on Planning
and Design for Anniston, Alabama. Houston,
TX: Caudill, Rowlett and Scott (Architects),
Jl, 1968. Available from Caudill, Rowlett &
Scott, Box 22427, Houston, TX 77027.

Educational Survey of Three Counties in Alabama.
Montgomery, AL: State of Alabama, Department of Education, 1914.

Edwards, James 2X. "How to Integrate Schools
Alabama Style: Use Torch." Muhammad
Speaks, D 19, 1969.

Egerton, John. "White Incumbents, Black
Challengers." Race Relations Reporter,
O 16, 1970. [Greene County]

Elovitz, Mark Harvey. "A History of the Jews
of Birmingham, 1871-1971." Doctoral dissertation, New York U., 1973. Univ. Microfilms
Order No. 74-1880.

Fager, Charles. Selma 1965. The March that
Changed the South. New York: Scribner's,
1974.

Falk, Gail. "Meridian Parents Want to Know Why
Teachers Weren't Re-Hired." Southern
Courier, Jl 8, 1967. [Meridian]

Fallows, James M. "High School Graduates Who
Can't READ?!" Harvard Crimson, S 28, 1968.

_____. "Judge Orders Klan to Leave Negroes
Alone." Southern Courier, Ag 24, 1968.
[Crenshaw County, Alabama]

_____. "145 Steps Suggested to Integrate
Schools." Southern Courier, Ag 31, 1968.

_____. "Parents Protest in Greene [County,
Alabama]," Southern Courier, S 7, 1968.

_____. "'Southern Courier' Will Close, Plagued
by Debt, Loss of Power." Harvard Crimson,
D 12, 1968. [The impending demise of a prime
source of information about black schools in
Alabama]

Fauset, Jessie. "In Talladega." Crisis 35(F,
1928):47-48.

Fine, Estelle. "First Days of Talk About Discrimination." Southern Courier, My 18, 1968.
[Hearing in Montgomery by the U.S. Commission
on Civil Rights]

The First Year of Desegregation under Title Six
in Alabama: A Review with Observations and
Conclusions. A Special Report, S, 1965.
ERIC ED 031 547.

Fisher, Charles C. "A Study of the Educational
Contributions of the Presbyterian Church,
U.S. to Negro Education in Alabama from 1876-
1952." Master's thesis, Alabama State College,
1953.

Fussell, Richard and others. A Demographic Atlas
of Birmingham, 1960-1970. University:
U. of Alabama Press, 1975.

Gale, Mary Ellen. "Barbour, Crenshaw [Alabama]
Ask Desegregation Slow-Up." Southern Courier,
Je 3, 1967.

_____. "Bullock County Parents Say Schools Still
Discriminate." Southern Courier, Ja 20, 1968.
[Bullock County]

_____. "Can Governor [Wallace] Keep Tuskegee
Money?" Southern Courier, S 16, 1967.

_____. "Deadline Problem at Auburn U."
Southern Courier, Je 22, 1968.

_____. "'Down With Inconsistency.'" Southern
Courier, Je 21, 1968. [Tuskegee]

_____. "Driver, Supt. Scold Pupils that Sat at
Front of Bus." Southern Courier, Mr 11, 1967.
[Union Springs]

_____. "Everyone Wins in School Case." Southern
Courier, O 21, 1967. [Five Alabama school
districts]

_____. [Federal Hearing on Resistance to State-
wide Desegregation Court Order] Southern
Courier, S 23, 1967.

_____. [Freedom of Choice in Barbour County,
Alabama, schools] Southern Courier, Jl 13,
1968.

_____. "He Drives Many Miles Taking Kids to
School." Southern Courier, O 14, 1967.
[School-bus discrimination in Barbour County]

_____. "Head Start Growing in Notasulga."
Southern Courier, My 20, 1967. [Desegregated
Head Start Class in Notasulga]

. "'How Not to Desegregate the Schools--Without Really Trying.'" Southern Courier, N 27, 1965. [Eufala]

. "'Ignored' by Board, Then Told ...." Southern Courier, My 6, 1967. [Macon County]

. "Is Opelika Keeping Segregation?" Southern Courier, N 13, 1965. [Segregated residences and schools in Opelika]

. "Judge Rives Raps Newville Ruling." Southern Courier, O 21, 1967. [Henry County schools]

. "Kids' Choice Denied, Macon Mother Claims." Southern Courier, S 16, 1967. [Macon County]

. "Kids Graduate in Tuskegee," and "... Parents Complain." Southern Courier, Je 3, 1967. [Tuskegee High School]

. "Macon Teachers Grill Revenue Board Chairman." Southern Courier, My 18, 1968. [Macon County]

. "'Massive' Resistance in Russell [County, Alabama]." Southern Courier, Ap 29, 1967.

. "A New Dual System?" Southern Courier, Ap 20, 1968. [Segregated higher education in Montgomery]

. "No Delay in Desegregation; School Districts File Plans." Southern Courier, Ap 22, 1967.

. "Parade Doesn't Go Into Town." Southern Courier, N 11, 1967. [Discrimination in parading between white and Negro high schools in Bullock County]

. "Parents, Educators Differ Over Tuskegee Lab School." Southern Courier, D 9, 1967.

. "Public Education in Tuskegee." Southern Courier, Je 4, 1966. [Desegregation at Tuskegee High School]

. "Reed Blasts 'Illegal' Study Group." Southern Courier, D 16, 1967. [An all-white Alabama Education Study Commission]

. "Revolution at Tuskegee." Southern Courier, Mr 30, 1968.

. "School Out in Newville." Southern Courier, Ag 19, 1967.

. "SE Alabama Faces School Crisis." Southern Courier, F 3, 1968.

. "She Takes Three Buses to Get to School." Southern Courier, Mr 18, 1967. [Eufala girl]

. "State [of Alabama] to Defend Choice Plans." Southern Courier, Je 15, 1968.

. "Strange Ways of White Folks." Southern Courier, F 24, 1968. [A referendum on school taxes in Bullock County]

. "Suits Seek Opening of Newville Schools." Southern Courier, S 16, 1967. [Newville]

. "TCA Discusses Notasulga Class." Southern Courier, My 20, 1967. [Desegregated Head Start class in Notasulga]

. "Three Candidates Seek Spot on School Board in Macon." Southern Courier, My 4, 1968. [Macon County]

. [Trial on Alabama Teacher-Choice Law] Southern Courier, S 23, 1967.

. "'Ugly Head' of U.S." Southern Courier, S 23, 1967. [School segregation in Newville]

. "U.S. Judge Tells Tuskegee to Re-Admit All Students." Southern Courier, Ap 27, 1968.

. "U.S. [School Integration] 'Impossible,' [Alabama] Educators Say at Hearing." Southern Courier, Ap 8, 1967.

. "Where Did Poor Kids' Money Go in Henry?" Southern Courier, Ag 26, 1967. [Fate of Title I, ESEA funds in Henry County schools]

. "White-vs.-Black Games--Maybe." Southern Courier, Mr 30, 1968. [Desegregation of school athletics in Alabama]

. "'Win Their Hearts.'" Southern Courier, My 6, 1967. [Macon County]

. "Would School Integration Cut Costs? You'd Save Peanuts." Southern Courier, Mr 30, 1968.

Gershenberg, Irving. "Alabama: An Analysis of the Growth of White Public Education in a Southern State, 1880-1930." Doctoral dissertation, U. of California, Berkeley, 1967.

. "The Negro and the Development of White Public Education in the South: Alabama, 1880-1930." Journal of Negro Education 39(1970): 50-59.

Gilmore, J. Herbert, Jr. They Chose to Live: The Racial Agony of an American Church. Ann Arbor, MI: Eerdmans, 1972. [First Baptist Church, Birmingham]

Glass, Mary. "Numbers of Alabama Black Educators Continue to Suffer Slow Death." Alabama Journal of Education, Ag 30, 1971.

Glick, David S. "Black Power Enclave. New Republic 164(Ja 16, 1971):11-12. [Greene County]

Greider, William, and De Pree, David. "Sports and Integration." Washington Post, My 21, 1978. [Alabama]

Griessman, B. Eugene, and Henson, Curtis T., Jr. "The History and Social Topography of an Ethnic Island in Alabama." Phylon 36(Summer, 1975):97-112. [Cajuns]

Grove, F. L. "Negro Education in Alabama." Alabama Lawyer 10(Jl, 1949):269-280.

Gruson, Kerry. "'Attitudes Have Changed' in Head Start Classes." Southern Courier, S 2, 1967. [Integrated Head Start in Ozark]

"HEW Official Defends School Aid Cut-Offs." Southern Courier, Je 10, 1967.

Hardy, Ernest A. "A Study of Urban School De-segregation with Implications for the City School System of Birmingham, Alabama." Doctoral dissertation, U. of Alabama, 1977. Univ. Microfilms Order No. 7819176.

Harris, James T. "Alabama Reaction to the Brown Decision, 1954-1956: A Case Study in Early Massive Resistance." Doctoral dissertation, Middle Tennessee State U., 1978. Univ. Microfilms Order No. 7822621.

"Here We Go Again." Southern Courier, O 5, 1968. [Segregation policy in Alabama]

Herman, Maury. "Barbour County Folks Unhappy Over Schools." Southern Courier, N 2, 1968.

_____. "Henry County [Ala.] Gets New School Superintendent." Southern Courier, N 16, 1968.

Heron, William John. "The Growth of Private Schools and their Impact on the Public Schools of Alabama (1955-1975)." Doctoral dissertation, U. of Alabama, 1977. Univ. Microfilms Order No. 7809859.

Hillegos, Jan. "Blacks Move Ahead in Greene County." Southern Patriot, N, 1969.

Hollis, Mike. "Calvary Hill School." Hunts-ville Times, S 17, 1972. [Huntsville]

Howell, James M. "An Analysis of the Post Segregation Era in the Bessemer City Schools." Doctoral dissertation, U. of Alabama, 1977. Univ. Microfilms Order No. 7818872.

Hunter, Floyd. "Wilcox County: Social, Economic, and Political Setting for the Schools." In Commission on Professional Rights and Responsibilities. Wilcox County, Alabama: A Study of Social, Economic and Educational Bankruptcy, pp. 101-112. Washington, DC: National Education Association, Je, 1967.

James, Felix. "The Tuskegee Institute Movable School, 1906-1923." Agricultural History 45 (O, 1971):201-210.

Jenkins, Ray. "Majority Rule in the Black Belt: Greene County, Alabama." New South, Fall, 1969.

Johnson, Charles S. Shadow of the Plantation. Chicago: U. of Chicago Press, 1934. [Macon County]

Johnson, Daniel M. "Black Return Migration to a Southern Metropolitan Community: Birmingham, Alabama." Doctoral dissertation, U. of Missouri, 1967.

Johnson, T. M., Jr. "A Comparison of Certain Aspects of Educational Opportunities in White and Colored Schools in Alabama, 1925-30." Master's thesis, U. of Cincinnati, 1932.

Johnson, Thomas A. "When Blacks Run the Schools." New York Times, N 14, 1976. [Greene County]

Jones, Lee A. "The Influence of Tuskegee Institute on the Education of Negroes in Macon County, Alabama, 1881-1946." Master's thesis, Tuskegee Institute, 1947.

Jones, Lewis W., and Williamson, Handy, Jr. Demography of Disadvantage in Alabama, F 1, 1975. ERIC ED 121 518.

Jones, Thomas J. "Charlotte Thorn." Southern Workman 62(My, 1933):197-198. [Calhoun Colored School, Lowndes County]

Jones, William Marquette. "A History of the Burnell Normal School." Master's thesis, Fisk U., 1936.

Jordan, Lawrence Ferrill. "The Development of Public Education for Negroes in the State of Alabama." Master's thesis, Howard U., 1931.

Jordan, Richard Stephem, Jr. "An Historical Study of the Georgia Washington High School, Mount Meigs, Alabama, From 1893-1958, as to the Faculty, School Plant, Enrollment and Its Influence on the Community." Master's thesis, Alabama State College, 1959.

Kennedy, Robert F., Jr. Judge Frank M. Johnson, Jr. New York: Putnam's, 1978.

Kolchin, Peter. First Freedom. The Responses of Alabama's Blacks to Emancipation and Re-construction. Westport, CT: Greenwood Press, 1972.

Krystall, Eric R., Friedman, Neil, Howze, Glenn, and Epps, Edgar G. "Attitudes Toward Inte-gration and Black Consciousness: Southern Negro High School Seniors and Their Mothers." Phylon 31(Summer, 1970):104-113. [Montgomery]

Labaree, Bob. "Birmingham Prepares to Close Andusky School--and Outhouse." Southern Courier, Ap 20, 1968.

_____. "Gadsden, Fairfield [Alabama] Schools Win." Southern Courier, F 3, 1968.

_____. "Hungry Children in Birmingham." Southern Courier, F 17, 1968.

_____. "'It Doesn't Seem Difficult.'" Southern Courier, Ag 3, 1968. [Desegreating Alabama reform schools].

_____. "'The Question' on School Plans." Southern Courier, Ag 3, 1968. [The Question: What happens when white teachers refuse to be assigned to black schools? Birmingham, Alabama]

Lacey, Marguerite Dobbins. "The Social, Economic, and Political Life of the Negro in Madison County from 1880-1900." Master's thesis, Alabama A & M College, 1963.

Lake, Ellen. "Mrs. [Johnnie May] Warren Has a Party for Pike County Transfers." Southern Courier, Jl 9, 1966. [The president of the Pike County, Alabama Voters League holds a party for Negro youngsters who were preparing to enroll in all-white schools; advice and comments by students.]

Lambert, J. S. "What is Alabama Doing for Negro Education?" Journal of Rural Education 2(Mr, 1923):325-327.

Lottman, Michael S. "Brewer, Judges in School Fight." Southern Courier, O 19, 1968.

_____. "Crenshaw Girl Honored." Southern Courier, Je 11, 1966. [Integration at Highland Home School in Helicon]

_____. "Federal Judges Block Negro School Addition." Southern Courier, Jl 27, 1968. [Autauga].

_____. "Football Under a Court Order." Southern Courier, Mr 9, 1969. [Montgomery County]

_____. "Jeff Davis Ruling O.K." Southern Courier, Ag 10, 1968. [Montgomery County]

_____. "Many Negro Schools Closing [in Alabama]." Southern Courier, S 7, 1968.

_____. "Montgomery Schools Hit on Buses and Faculties." Southern Courier, F 17, 1968.

_____. "New School Must Take All Negroes Who Apply." Southern Courier, Mr 2, 1968. [Montgomery County]

_____. "Officials Say Desegregation Would Help." Southern Courier, D 9, 1967. [Montgomery County training schools]

_____. "U.S. Asks Integrated Athletics." Southern Courier, Mr 16, 1968. [Court hearing on racial segregation in Alabama secondary school athletic programs]

_____. "[U.S.] Commission [on Civil Rights] Asks Action [in Alabama]." Southern Courier, Je 22, 1968. [Touches on discrimination in trade schools in Central Alabama]

_____. "Who Cares About Schools?" Southern Courier, O 5, 1968. [Alabama Education Study Commission]

Lovell, John T., and Walden, John C. "A Quiet Revolution in Alabama: Faculty Desegregation." Phi Delta Kappan, Je, 1968.

McCain, Virgil Bowden. "Private Philanthropy in Negro Education in Alabama." Master's thesis, U. of Alabama, 1939.

Mac Gregor, William H. "The Equalization of Educational Opportunity in Lee County, Alabama." Master's thesis, Alabama Polytechnic Institute, Auburn, 1932.

"Macon Schools." Southern Courier, Ag 5, 1967. [Macon County]

Marable, Manning. "Tuskegee and the Politics of Illusion in the New South." Black Scholar 8(My, 1977):13-24.

Maxwell, Neil. "Anger in Alabama." Wall Street Journal, Mr 20, 1972.

_____. "Small Towns Yielding Little to Integration Despite Federal Laws." Wall Street Journal, Ag 14, 1968. [York]

Minton, Gary, and Griessman, B. Eugene. The Formation and Development of an Ethnic Group. The "Cajuns" of Alabama, N 14, 1974. ERIC ED 133 119.

"Mobile Ordered to Use Zones." Southern Courier, Mr 16, 1968. [Court orders end to free-choice and directs use of geographical attendance areas in Mobile]

Moore, Geraldine H. Behind the Ebony Mask. Birmingham, Al: Southern U. Press, 1961. [Birmingham]

Moorman, Joseph H., and Barrett, E. L. (eds.). Leaders of the Colored Race in Alabama. Mobile, AL: News Publishing Co., 1928.

Murphy, Stan. "The Meaning of Greene County." In The Rising South, II, pp. 78-94. Edited by Robert H. McKenzie. University: U. of Alabama Press, 1976.

Myers, John Benjamin. "Black Human Capital: The Freedmen and the Reconstruction of Labor in Alabama, 1860-1880." Doctoral dissertation, Florida State U., 1974. Univ. Microfilms Order No. 74-18057.

_____. "The Education of the Alabama Freedmen During Presidential Reconstruction, 1865-1867." Journal of Negro Education 40(Spring, 1971): 163-171.

National Transportation Safety Board. Inadequate Structural Assembly of Schoolbus Bodies. The Accidents at Decatur and Huntsville, Alabama. Springfield, VA: Clearinghouse for Federal Scientific and Technical Information, Jl 29, 1970.

Nichols, Woodrow W., Jr. "The Evolution of an All-Black Town: The Case of Roosevelt City, Alabama." Professional Geographer 26 (Ag, 1974):298-302.

Oliver, L. W. "The Birmingham Negro: A Socio-Economic Analysis." Quarterly Review of Higher Education Among Negroes, Jl, 1965.

Orr, Charles Walter. "The Educational Philosophy of William H. Councill." Master's thesis, Fisk U., 1963.

Parsons, Cynthia. "Report from Greene County Better Schools the Aim." Christian Science Monitor, Ja 19, 1976.

_____. "Report from 'Old South' Mobile, Alabama. Christian Science Monitor, Ja 19, 1976.

Payne, Ethel L. "Alabama's New Image." Chicago Defender, F 16, 1974.

Peterson, Jimmy Lee. "The Changes in the Educational System Resulting from the Growth of Black Political Participation and the Involvement of the Federal Government--A Select Study of Three Blackbelt Counties in Central Alabama between 1960-1974." Doctoral dissertation, U. of Michigan, 1976. Univ. Microfilms Order No. 76-27567.

Phillips, Benjamin T. "Large Crowd At Schools Meeting." Southern Courier, O 16, 1968. [Decatur]

Pickens, James D. "The Significance of the John F. Slater Fund in the Development of Public Education in Alabama." Master's thesis, Alabama State College, 1953.

Pickens, William. "Negro Public Education in Alabama." Voice of the Negro 3(S, 1906): 641-644.

Poinsett, Alex. "Tuskegee's Black Regime." Ebony, O, 1973.

Prescott, Darrell. "Benign Neglect in Wilcox County, Alabama." Harvard Crimson, D 14, 1970.

A Program for Solving Problems Pertaining to Classroom Organization and Instructional Program and to Social Skills of Teachers in Desegregated Schools. Technical Report, January 1-December 31, 1969. Tuscumbia, Alabama: Tuscumbia Public Schools, D 31, 1969. ERIC ED 045 747.

Prugh, Peter H. "Even Integrated Schools Can Falter." Wall Street Journal, My 28, 1970. [Macon County]

Pruitt, Mary L. "A Study of How Race Relations in Fayette County, Alabama, Have Been Improved Through Socio-Economic Changes During 1948 to 1968." Master's thesis, Alabama A & M U., 1969.

"The Quiet Murders." Southern Courier, Ja 15, 1966. [Achievement scores of white and Negro children in Mobile and other Alabama cities]

Reich, Kenneth. "George Wallace, Fake Populist." Nation, My 1, 1972.

_____. "'The Good Old Days.' Alabama Textbook Praises Slavery and Ku Klux Klan." South Today, My, 1970.

Reisig, Robin. "Birmingham Kids Prepare for Integrated High School." Southern Courier, S 2, 1967.

_____. "... And in Tuscaloosa, A Fading Black Eye." Southern Courier, Mr 25, 1967. [Stafford Elementary School, Tuscaloosa].

_____. "Can't Deny [Free] Choice [Transfers] for Low Grades, Says Judge." Southern Courier, Jl 2, 1967.

_____. "Negroes to Play for U. of Ala.?" Southern Courier, Ap 15, 1967.

_____. "TCAC is 'Disappointed.'" Southern Courier, Je 3, 1967. [Tuscaloosa Citizens for Action Committee and the local Head Start program]

Resource Management Corporation. [Case History of ESAP in Auburn, Alabama] Evaluation of the Emergency School Assistance Program, Vol. III, Appendix B, F 15, 1972. ERIC ED 058 470.

_____. [Case History of ESAP in Tuscaloosa, Ala.] Evaluation of the Emergency School Assistance Program, Vol. III, Appendix R, F 15, 1972. ERIC ED 058 470.

Rosengarten, Theodore. All God's Dangers. The Life of Nate Shaw. New York: Knopf, 1974.

Ross, William C. "The Economic Status of Negro Teachers in Colbert and Lauderdale Counties, Alabama." Master's thesis, Ohio State U., 1939.

Rudd, Edward M. "Negro, White Lowndes Parents Wonder About School Integration." Southern Courier, Ag 13, 1965.

Samuels, Gertrude. "There Are 300 Negroes at the University of Alabama." New York Times Magazine, My 4, 1967.

Sanford, G. A. "Selective Migration in a Rural Alabama Community." American Sociological Review 5(1940):759-766.

"School Fight Continues After Girl's Death." African World, O 2, 1971. [Sumter City]

"Segregation--Schools--Burden of Proving Absence of Negro Blood." Alabama Law Review 6 (Fall, 1953):114-116. [Chestang v. Burns (Ala.) 64 So. 2nd 65]

Seller, James Benson. "Negro Education in Alabama." Master's thesis, U. of Alabama, 1924.

"Selma Blacks Protest Unfair School, Board Politics, Appointments." Jet 48(S 18, 1975: 36-38.

Schaffer, Albert, and Schaffer, Ruth C. "The Law, Faculty Desegregation, and Social Change." Phylon 36(1970):38-47. [Tuscaloosa]

Schaffer, Ruth C., and Schaffer, Albert. "Socialization and the Development of Attitudes Toward Negroes in Alabama." Phylon, Fall, 1966.

Sherer, Robert G., Jr. Subordination or Liberation: The Development and Conflicting Theories of Black Education in Nineteenth Century Alabama. University: U. of Alabama Press, 1976.

_____. "William Burns Paterson: Pioneer as Well as Apostle of Negro Education in Alabama." Alabama Historical Quarterly 36 (Summer, 1974).

Sherman, Mike. "Sovereignty Commission Records Open." Anniston Star, N 21, 1976. [Documentation of anti-desegregation activities by State Sovereignty Commission in Alabama 1963-1973]

Short, John. "Greene County High Desegregates." Southern Courier, S 3, 1966. [Greene County]

Shuttlesworth, Fred L. "Birmingham Revisited." Ebony 26(Ag, 1971):114-118.

Sikora, Frank. "First Blacks to Integrate Alabama School Recall Occasion." Birmingham News, Ag 29, 1977. [Macon County, 1963]

Simms, L. Moody. "William Dorsey Jelks and the Problem of Negro Education." Alabama Review, Ja, 1970. [1855-1931]

Simpson, Daphna. "Tuscaloosa Students Meet First, Then March to City Schools Office." Southern Courier, My 21, 1966.

Singleton, John. "Black Students Seek Help, Too." Southern Courier, O 12, 1968. [Shaw High School in Mobile]

_____. "Hanging Corpse Found in Abandoned School." Southern Courier, S 28, 1968. [Prichard]

_____. "Students Get Together in Mobile...." Southern Courier, N 23, 1968.

_____. "Whites Oppose Mobile [Alabama] Zoning." Southern Courier, My 25, 1968.

Small, William R. "Fiery Crosses in the Roaring Twenties: Activities of the Revised Klan in Alabama, 1915-1930." Alabama Review 23(O, 1970):256-276.

_____. "Masked Men in the Magic City: Activities of the Revised Klan in Birmingham, 1916-1940." Alabama Historical Quarterly 34(Fall-Winter, 1972).

Stormont, Nancy L. "An Experiment in Negro Education. Being a Story of a Missing School." Master's thesis, New York U, 1929. [Knox Academy, Selma]

Stubbs, Frances. "'I Was in Their Hair.'" Southern Courier, Jl 27, 1968. [Appointment of Rev. N. Quintus Reynolds, Negro civil rights leader, to Anniston, Alabama school board]

Summary of Activities and Evaluation of Western Alabama Cooperative Title IV Project: A Desegregation Program Occasioned by and Relative to Teacher Crossover. Tuscaloosa, AL: Tuscaloosa County Board of Education, 1969. ERIC ED 045 750.

Thomas, Charley. "Why Don't More Kids Go to White Schools?" Southern Courier, F 17, 1968. [Alexander City]

Thomas, Ethel. "School Gripes in Tuscaloosa." Southern Courier, O 5, 1968.

_____. "Two Youths Suspended From White Schools." Southern Courier, O 26, 1968.

Thomas, Jack. "Ala. Town Rebels Over Integration." Boston Globe, S 5, 1973. [Wilcox County]

Thompson, Arthur A. "Alabama's Five Economies." In The Rising South, Vol. II, pp. 29-47. Edited by Robert H. McKenzie. University, AL: U. of Alabama Press, 1976.

Thompson, De Witt M. "A Survey of Negro Education in Alabama." Master's thesis, U. of Arizona, 1933.

U.S. Commission on Civil Rights. Cycle to Nowhere. By Paul Good. Washington, DC: GPO, 1968.

_____. Equal Economic Opportunity for Negroes in Alabama. Washington, DC: GPO, 1969.

_____. "Vocational Education in the 16-County Hearing Area and in Alabama." In Hearing... Held in Montgomery, Alabama, Ap 27-My 2, 1968, pp. 870-888. Washington, DC: GPO, 1969.

Walden, John C., and Cleveland, Allen D. "The South's New Segregation Academies." Phi Delta Kappan 53(D, 1971):234-235, 238-239.

Wallace, Elsie H. "Negro Elementary Education in Northern Alabama." Doctoral dissertation, Northwestern U., 1948.

Watkins, J. Foster. "Integration and Innovation in Alabama." Integrated Education (S-O, 1971): 23-25.

Whisenton, Joffre T., and Loree, M. Ray. "A
Comparison of the Values, Needs, and
Aspirations of School Leavers with Those
of Non-School Leavers." Journal of Negro
Education 39(Fall, 1970):325-332.
[Tuscaloosa]

Whitney, Hattye L. "The Development of Public
Secondary Education for Negroes in the
State of Alabama, 1873 to 1945." Master's
thesis, Howard U., 1946.

Wiener, Jonathan M. Social Origins of the New
South: Alabama, 1860-1885. Baton Rouge,
LA: Louisiana State U. Press, 1978.

Wilcox, Beth. "Kids Report Troubles at Wilcox
High School." Southern Courier, O 7, 1967.
[Wilcox County High School]

_____. "School Boycott in Choctaw." Southern
Courier, S 9, 1967.

_____. "Sixty Pupils Fail." Southern
Courier, Je 3, 1967. [Hayneville High
School, Lowndes County]

_____. "Treatment Protested at Hayneville
School." Southern Courier, Mr 16, 1968.

Wilcox, Beth, and Lottman, Michael S.
"'Naturals' Cause Fuss in Selma; SNCC
Presents School Demands." Southern Courier,
D 16, 1967. [Selma]

Williams, Arthur. "The Participation of Negroes
in the Government of Alabama, 1867-1874."
Master's thesis, Atlanta U., 1946.

Williams, Clanton W. "'I Cringe Every Time I
Read ... Figures on Quality of Education in
Alabama.'" Montgomery Advertiser, N 24,
1974.

Williams, H. B. "Legal Provisions for the
Education of the Negro in the State of
Alabama, and How They Affect the Program of
Negro Education from 1873-1949." Master's
thesis, Alabama State College for Negroes,
1950.

Williams, James D. "Bellamy, Alabama. Company
Town Revisited." Civil Rights Digest, Fall,
1969.

Williams, Roger M. "Wallace and the Blacks in
Alabama." Washington Post, N 16, 1975.

Wilson, Bobby M. "Black Housing Opportunities
in Birmingham, AL: Southeastern Geographer
17(1977):49-57.

Wilson, Franklin D. The Ecology of a Black
Business District: Sociological and Histor-
ical Analysis, N, 1975. ERIC ED 021 928.
[Birmingham]

Wooten, James. "The [George] Wallace Message."
New York Times Magazine, Mr 17, 1974.

Worthman, Paul B. "Working Class Mobility in
Birmingham, Alabama, 1880-1914." In
Anonymous Americans: Explorations in
Nineteenth-Century Social History. Edited
by Tamara K. Hareven. Englewood Cliffs, NJ:
Prentice-Hall, 1971.

Young, Nathan Ben. "These 'Colored' United
States: Alabama--Like Nuriam."
Messenger 7(Mr, 1925):123-124, 140-141.

Young, Peter Beeken. "The Negro Community of
Huntsville, Alabama, 1881-1894." Senior
honors thesis, Louisiana State U., 1957.

Alaska

Alaska, Division of State-Operated Schools.
Office of Child Development. A Modest
Proposal. An Expression of Children's Needs
by People in Rural Alaska with Recommendations for Positive Change, Submitted ...
by Aleut Leagu   Others. Anchorage,
AK, 1973.

Alaska Governor's Committee on Education. An
Overall Education Plan for Rural Alaska,
F, 1966. ERIC ED 026 194.

Alaska. Legislative Affairs Agency. Report of
the Interim Committee on Native Housing and
Schools, August-December, 1973. Juneau, AK,
1974.

Alaska. Legislature. House of Representatives.
Interim Committee on School Decorum. Report
to the Legislature, Juneau, AK, 1974.

Alaska State Department of Education. A Modest
Proposal. An Expression of Children's Needs
by People in Rural Alaska with Recommendations
for Positive Change, 1973. ERIC ED 089 921.

Anderson, Hobson Dewey, and Eells, Walter Crosby.
Alaska Natives: A Survey of Their Sociologi-
cal and Educational Status. Stanford, CA:
Stanford U. Press, 1935.

Barnett, Don C. "Attitudes of Eskimo School
Children." Integrated Education 11(Ja-F,
1973):52-57.

Barnhardt, Ray (ed.). Cross-Cultural Issues in
Alaskan Education. Fairbanks: Center for
Northern Educational Resarch, U. of Alaska,
1977.

Bergt, Laura. "Unequal Schooling in Alaska."
Integrated Education: RACE AND SCHOOLS 7
(S-O, 1969):60-62.

Bland, Laurel L. Jobless in the Arctic: The
Alaskan Paradox, F, 1970. ERIC ED 037 654.

Brown, Thomas M. "The Natives May Win One:
The Great Alaskan Real-Estate Deal."
New York Times Magazine, O 17, 1971.

Bunger, Marianna. Teaching Alaskan Native Youth, 1970. ERIC ED 045 588.

Bureau of Indian Affairs. Alaskan Native Needs Assessment in Education (Project ANNA). Research and Evaluation Report Series No. 18. 9 vols. Juneau, AK: Bureau of Indian Affairs, 1973.

Calkins, Thomas V. "Educating the Alaska Natives." Doctoral dissertation, Yale U., 1970.

Cline, Michael S. "Community Factionalism and Teacher Survival in the Alaskan Bush." Human Organization 33(Spring, 1974):102-106.

_____. "The Impact of Formal Education Upon the Nunamiut Eskimos of Anaktiwuk Pass." Doctoral dissertation, U. of Oregon, 1972.

_____. "Village Socialization of the Bush Teacher." Northian 9(Winter, 1972):19-27.

Collier, John, Jr. Alaskan Eskimo Education. New York: Holt, Rinehart, and Winston, 1973.

Coverdale, Miles L. "The Identification of the School Board Training Needs of Eskimo and Indian Lay Advisory School Board Members of Rural Alaska." Doctoral dissertation, Utah State U., 1972.

Darnell, Frank, Hecht, Kathryn, and Orvik, James M. Pre-higher Education in the Unorganized Borough: Analysis and Recommendations. Fairbanks: Center for Northern Educational Research, U. of Alaska, 1977.

Darnell, Frank and others. Prehigher Education in the Unorganized Borough: Analysis and Recommendations with Appendix, Ja, 1974. ERIC ED 137 011.

Everett, M. L. "Shall We Teach Fables or Truth?" Educational Method 11(D, 1931): 140-142.

Faris, John T. The Alaskan Pathfinder. The Story of Sheldon Jackson. New York: Fleming H. Revell Company, 1926.

Federal Field Committee for Development Planning in Alaska. Alaska Natives and the Land. Washington, DC: GPO, O, 1968.

Forrest, Elizabeth C. "Cross-sections of Eskimo Life." Hygeia 10(Jl, 1932):628-632.

Getches, David H. A Primer on Laws Important to Alaska Native Education. Fairbanks, AK: Center for Northern Educational Research, U. of Alaska, 1976.

_____. Law and Alaska Native Education. The Influence of Federal and State Legislation upon Education of Rural Alaska Natives. Fairbanks: Center for Northern Educational Research, U. of Alaska, S, 1977.

Griggs, Anthony. "Alaskan Natives Face Urbanization." Race Relations Reporter 4 (Ag 20, 1973):4-6.

Hagie, C. E. "Alaska and Her Schools." Journal of the National Education Association 15 (Je, 1926):165-167.

Hamilton, William. "Education and Welfare Work for Native Alaskans." School Life 9(My, 1924):207-210.

Harvey, Laura B. "School and Society in the Matanuska Valley with Appropriate Alaskan Background." Doctoral dissertation, New York U., 1939.

Hecker, Lena B. "Constitutional Status of Education in Alaska." Social Science 12 (1937):64-71.

Henderson, Lester D. "The Development of Education in Alaska, 1867 to 1931." Doctoral dissertation, Stanford U., 1935.

Henning, Clarence E. "Development of Secondary Education in Alaska." Master's thesis, U. of Washington, 1940.

Hippler, Arthur E. From Village to Town: An Intermediate Step in the Acculturation of Alaska Eskimos, O, 1970. ERIC ED 045 247.

Hippler, Arthur E.; ed. by Harkins, Arthur M., Woods, Richard G. Barrow and Kotzebue: An Exploratory Comparison of Acculturation and Education in Two Large Northwestern Alaska Villages. Minneapolis, MN: Training Center for Community Programs, U. of Minnesota, D, 1969.

Holthaus, Gary H. Teaching Eskimo Culture to Eskimo Students: A Special Program for Secondary Schools in Bristol Bay, My, 1968. ERIC ED 032 173.

"In Alaska, Native Women Unite in Fight to Uplift Their People." New York Times, N 18, 1971.

Jackson, Sheldon. Report on Education in Alaska. Washington, DC: GPO, 1886.

Jacobs, Robert E. The Concept of Equal Educational Opportunity: Its Validity and Applicability to Alaska, Ap 15, 1974. ERIC ED 095 243.

Jones, Dorothy M. "A Study of Social and Economic Problems in Unalaska, an Aleut Village." Doctoral dissertation, U. of California (Berkeley), 1969.

_____. Aleuts in Transition: A Comparison of Two Villages. Seattle: U. of Washington Press, 1976.

_____. "Child Welfare Problems in An Alaskan Native Village." Social Service Review, S, 1969.

_____. The Urban Native Encounters the
Social Service System. Fairbanks:
Institute of Social, Economic and Government
Research, U. of Alaska, 1974.

Jones, Virginia W. "Training Teachers of
English for Alaska's Native Children."
Elementary English 48(F, 1971):198-202.

Jones, W. Russell, Jr. "On An Equal Footing."
Today's Education, Mr, 1972. [Dillingham]

Kaden, Bonnie (ed.). An Introduction to the
Alaska Department of Education and the
Information of People, Government, History,
Geography, Ap, 1969. ERIC ED 034 624.

Kamerling, Leonard (ed.). Kassigeluremiut:
The People of Kasigluk in Pictures and
Poems. Alaska Rural School Project
College, Alaska: U. of Alaska, 1970.

Kauffman, Dottie L., and Walsh, Gene. Youth
in Force in the Labor Force. Juneau, AK:
State Department of Community and Regional
Affairs, Division of Manpower, 1978.
[Five communities]

Keithahn, Edward L. "Eskimo School."
Progressive Education 9(F, 1932):136-137.

Kleinfeld, Judith. Achievement Profiles of
Native Ninth Graders, N, 1970. ERIC ED
045 282.

_____. Alaska's Urban Boarding Home Program.
Interpersonal Relationships Between Indian
and Eskimo Secondary Students and Their
Boarding Home Parents. Fairbanks, AK:
Institute of Social, Economic, and
Government Research, U. of Alaska, 1972.

_____. Cognitive Strengths of Eskimos and
Implications for Education, N, 1970.
ERIC ED 045 281.

_____. A Long Way from Home: Effects of
Public High Schools on Village Children
Away from Home, 1973. ERIC ED 087 581.

Koch, Walton Boston. "The Native Alaskan
Social Movement." Doctoral dissertation,
Washington State U., 1971.

Lavrischeff, Tikhon I. "History of Education
in Alaska." Doctoral dissertation, U. of
California, Berkeley, 1935.

_____. "Teacher-training for Alaska." Phi
Delta Kappan 14(Ag, 1931):40-44.

Lawson, Andrew P. Education Policy and Alaskan
Natives, Ap 19, 1974. ERIC ED 091 118.

Movitz, Deborah. "The Case of the Alaskan
Native." Civil Rights Digest, Summer, 1969.

Olson, Olaf E. "History of Education in the
Territory of Alaska." Master's thesis, U.
of Washington, 1931.

Orvik, James M. Teacher Survival in An Extreme
Environment. College, AK: Alaska Rural
School Project, U. of Alaska, 1970.

Orvik, James M., and Barnhardt, Ray (eds.).
Cultural Influences in Alaskan Native
Education, 1974 ERIC ED 097 159.

Peck, Cy, Sr. and others. Indian Studies Programs, F, 1975. ERIC ED 141 008.

Poole, Charles P. "Two Centuries of Education
in Alaska." Doctoral dissertation, U. of
Washington, 1948.

Rogers, George W. The Cross-Cultural Economic
Situation in the North: The Alaska Case,
Ag, 1969. Available from The Arctic Institute
of North America, 3458 Redpath Street,
Montreal 25, P.Q., Canada.

_____. "The Impact of Economic Conditions on
Cross-Cultural Education in Alaska." In
Education in the North, pp. 177-210.
Edited by Frank Darnell. Arctic Institute of
North America, U. of Alaska, 1972.

Rosenstiel, Annette. "The Changing Focus of
Native Education in Alaska." Arctic and
Alpine Research 3(1971):187-197.

Russell, Kitty A. "The Development of Education in Alaska." Master's thesis, Southern
U., 1944.

Savage, David G. "The Northern Tip of U.S.
'Colonialism.'" Washington Post, Ja 15,
1978.

Senungetuk, Joseph Engasongwok. Give or Take a
Century: An Eskimo Chronicle. San Francisco,
CA: Indian Historical Press, 1971.

Smith, Glenn. "Education for the Natives of
Alaska: The Work of the United States
Bureau of Education." Journal of the West 6
(Jl, 1967):440-450.

Smith, Valene. "Kotzebue: A Modern Alaska
Eskimo Community." Doctoral dissertation,
U. of Utah, 1966.

Starr, J. Lincoln. Education in Russian Alaska.
Juneau, AK: Division of State Libraries,
1972.

Sullivan, James, and Rose, William (comps.).
Alaska School Enrollments. Enrollments by
Race and Location in Elementary and Secondary
Schools, and College and University Enroll-
ments, 1958-1969. L.C. 70-634196. College,
AK: Institute of Social, Economic and Govern-
ment Research, U. of Alaska, 1970.

Swart, Margaret. "Educational Eskimo Toys."
Alaska Journal 1(Autumn, 1971):55-56.

"Textbook Bias toward Alaskan Natives." Integrated Education 9(Mr-Ap, 1971):44-49.

Thornton, Harrison R. Among the Eskimos of Wales, Alaska, 1890-1893. Baltimore, MD: The Johns Hopkins Press, 1931.

Tiffany, Warren I. Education in Northwest Alaska. Rev. ed. Juneau, AK: Bureau of Indian Affairs, 1966.

Time for Change in the Education of Alaska Natives: A Statement of Preliminary Findings and Recommendations Relating to the Education of Alaska Natives, F, 1970. ERIC ED 041 678.

United States Bureau of Education. Course of Study for United States Schools for Natives of Alaska. Washington, DC: GPO, 1926.

_____. Rules and Regulations Regarding the Alaska School Service for the Natives of Alaska. Adopted My 20, 1911. Washington, DC: GPO, 1911.

_____. The Work of the Bureau of Education for the Natives of Alaska. Washington, DC: GPO, 1886-1929. U.S. Department of the Interior Office of Education Reports, 1886-1929.

Wallace, Isabel W. "History of Education in Alaska." Master's thesis, U. of Washington, 1918.

Whitaker, Joseph C. Guidelines for Primary Health Care in Rural Alaska. Washington, DC: GPO, 1976.

Whitmore, Dorothy Gates. "A Study of Attitudes and Achievements of Disadvantaged Adolescents in Alaska." Doctoral dissertation, U. of Colorado, 1969.

Williams, Audrey Mae. "An Assessment of the Educational Needs of Minority Students as Perceived by Parents, Students, and Staff." Doctoral dissertation, Washington State U., 1976. Univ. Microfilms Order No. 76-21,404. [Anchorage Borough School District]

World-Wide Education and Research Institute. Educational Needs of Alaska. A Summary by Region and Ethnic Group, 1972-73, Jl, 1973.

Arizona

Abbey, Sue Wilson. "The Ku Klux Klan in Arizona, 1921-1925." Journal of Arizona History, Spring, 1973.

Beezer, Bruce. "Partners in Tucson Prepare for Integration." Citizen Action in Education 3(Fall, 1975):5.

Brophy, A. Blake. Foundlings on the Frontier: Racial and Religious Conflict in Arizona Territory, 1904-1905. Tuscon, AZ: U. of Arizona Press, 1972.

Christopherson, Victor A. Rural Blacks in Southern Arizona, Ag, 1975. ERIC ED 128 471.

Coleman, Anita Scott. "Arizona and New Mexico-- The Land of Esperanza." Messenger 8(S, 1926):275-276.

Crow, John E. Discrimination, Poverty, and the Negro: Arizona in the National Context. Tucson, AZ: Institute of Government Research, U. of Arizona, 1968.

Dempsey, Arthur D. "Culture and Conservation of Time: A Comparison of Selected Ethnic Groups in Arizona." Doctoral dissertation, U. of Arizona, 1971.

Ellis, Opal. "Cycle of Despair in Phoenix." Muhammad Speaks, D 26, 1969.

Ezell, Paul H. "A Racial Comparison of Pre-Adolescent White, Mexican, and Negro Boys." Master's thesis, U. of Arizona, 1939. (Abstract in University of Arizona Record, Vol. 34:25)

Fetterhoff, Willard M. "Federal Land Grants to the State of Arizona for Common School.s" Doctoral dissertation, U. of Denver, 1962.

Getty, Harry T. "Interethnic Relationships in the Community of Tucson." Doctoral dissertation, U. of Chicago, 1950.

Herrera, Paul L. "The Negro Teacher in Arizona." Master's thesis, Arizona State Teachers College, n.d.

Lorenzini, August P. "A Study of the Patterns of Communication Used by Fifty Negro and Fifty Spanish-named Residents of Phoenix, Arizona." Doctoral dissertation, U. of Denver, 1962. Univ. Microfilms Order No. 63-1168.

"Move to Tucson's 1951 Integration Remembered as 'Smooth Transition.'" Arizona Daily Star, Je 6, 1978.

Officer, James E. "Historical Factors and Interethnic Relations in the Community of Tucson." Arizoniana 1(1960):12-16.

"Phoenix Keeps Its Negro Teachers." Ebony, N, 1956.

Phoenix Union High School District. Where Phoenix Union High School System Students Live and Attend School, 1976-1977, 1976. ERIC ED 131 581..

Rehnquist, William H. "'De Facto' Schools Seen Serving Well." Arizona Republic, S 9, 1967 (letter). [Phoenix public schools]

Roberts, Shirley J. "Minority-Group Poverty in Phoenix. A Socio-Economic Survey." Journal of Arizona History 14(Autumn, 1973).

Robinson, W. A. "The Function of Libraries in Newly Integrated Schools." School Review, 0, 1955. [Phoenix]

U.S. Bureau of the Census. Social and Health Indicators System. Phoenix: Part 1. Washington, DC: GPO, 0, 1973.

U.S. Commission on Civil Rights. Hearings... Phoenix, Arizona, February 3, 1962. Washington, DC: GPO, 1962.

Yancy, James Walter. "The Negro of Tucson, Past and Present." Master's thesis, U. of Arizona, 1933.

Arkansas

Alexander, Charles C. "Defeat, Decline, Disintegration: the Ku Klux Klan in Arkansas, 1924 and After." Arkansas Historical Quarterly 22(Winter, 1963):311-331.

Alexander, Henry M. The Little Rock Recall Election. New Brunswick, NJ: Eagleton Institute of Politics, Rutgers U., 1960.

Arkansas Department of Education. Four Years with the Public Schools in Arkansas, 1923-1927.

_____. Negro Schools in Arkansas, 1927-1928; with a Summary for 1929. Little Rock, AR: The Department, 1928.

Arkansas Voter Education Project. Your Local School Board, 1972. Arkansas Voter Education Project, 600 West Ninth Street, Suite 210, Little Rock, AR 72201.

Ashmore, Harry S. "The Untold Story Behind Little Rock." Harper's 216(Je, 1958).

Bartley, Numan V. "Looking Back at Little Rock." Arkansas Historical Quarterly 25 (Summer, 1966):101-116.

Baxter, Albert. "Status and Characteristics of Displaced Negro Teachers in the State of Arkansas from 1954 through 1968." Doctoral dissertation, U. of Arkansas, 1970.

Beatty-Brown, Florence R. "Legal Status of Arkansas Negroes Before Emancipation." Arkansas Historical Quarterly 28(Spring, 1969):6-13.

Blossom, Virgil T. It Has Happened Here. New York: Harper & Row, 1959. [Little Rock]

Calvin, Floyd J. "Eight Weeks in Dixie." Messenger 4(D, 1922):547-550.

Clark, Kenneth B. "Observations on Little Rock." New South 13(Je, 1958):3-8.

Claye, Clifton M. "A Study of the Relationship Between Self-Concepts and Attitudes toward the Negro Among Secondary School Pupils in Three Schools of Arkansas." Doctoral dissertation, U. of Arkansas, 1958.

Cobb, William Henry. "Commonwealth College: A History." Master's thesis, U. of Arkansas, 1962. [Mena]

Crisis in the South: The Little Rock Story. Little Rock: Arkansas Gazette, 1959.

Davis, Richard N., Green, Bernal L., and Redfern, J. Martin. Low-Income Rural People in East Central Arkansas Face Roadblocks to Jobs Washington, DC: U.S. Department of Agriculture, J1, 1975.

Dougharty, L. A. The Health Delivery System for the Poor in the State of Arkansas. Santa Monica, CA: Rand, Ag, 1970.

Egerton, John. "Little Rock Ten Years Later." Saturday Review, D 16, 1967.

English, A. T. Black People on the Move: A True Account of Life Among Negroes in Central Arkansas. Morrilton, AR: Poindexter Printing and Office Supplies, Inc., 1969.

Ewart, Steven D. "Arkansas Newspaper Editorial Opinion on School Integration: May 1954 to October 1957." Master's thesis, Arkansas State U., 1970.

Fair, Linus A. "The White Schools of Lee County, Arkansas." Master's thesis, George Peabody College, 1930.

Fair, Paul. "Little Rock: Then and Now." Theory Into Practice 17(F, 1978):39-42. [Central High School]

4X, Harold. "Little Rock's 'Citadel' Revisited: Central High." Muhammad Speaks, Ap 5, 1974.

Gemmill, Henry, and Guilfoyle, Joseph. "The Quiet Force in Arkansas." Wall Street Journal, O 8, 1957. [Little Rock school desegregation crisis]

Geurin, Virginia and others. Adjustments to Modern Society by Youths from Rural Areas: A Longitudinal Analysis, 1965 to 1971, Ap, 1977. ERIC ED 147 042. [Southwest Arkansas]

Graves, John William. "The Arkansas Negro and Segregation, 1890-1903." Master's thesis, U. of Arkansas, 1964.

Grinstead, Mary Jo, and Scholtz, Sandra. "Poverty, Race, and Culture in a Rural Arkansas Community." Human Organization 35 (Spring, 1976):33-44. [Madison]

Grinstead, Mary Jo, Green, Bernal L., and Redfern, J. Martin. Social and Labor Adjustment of Rural Black Americans in the Mississippi Delta: A Case Study of Madison, Arkansas. Washington, DC: U.S. Department of Agriculture, D, 1974.

Harwood, Bill. School Days: Contemporary Views on Arkansas Public Education. Little Rock: Winthrop Rockefeller Foundation, 1978.

Hobby, Selma Ann Plowman. "The Little Rock Schools During Reconstruction, 1865-1874." Doctoral dissertation, U. of Arkansas, 1967. Univ. Microfilms Order No. 67-12873.

Hudson, John Homer. "White and Negro Educational Opportunities in Certain Arkansas Counties." Master's thesis, George Peabody College for Teachers, 1930.

Jackson, Anne (ed). Contributions of Ethnic Groups. Little Rock, AR: Department of Education, 1970.

Jackson, Nathaniel, and Rydingsword, Carl E. "Little Rock, Arkansas: The 'Land of Opportunity.'" In Norene Harris, Nathaniel Jackson, and Carl Rydingsword and contributors, The Integration of American Schools: Problems, Experiences, Solutions, pp. 53-61. Boston, MA: Allyn & Bacon, 1976.

Johnson, Kenneth L. "A Study of the Health Problems of Negro Senior-High-School Youth in Arkansas." Doctoral dissertation, Boston U., 1959. Univ. Microfilms Order No. 59-5537.

Kunkel, Peter, and Kennard, Sara Sue. Spout Spring: A Black Community. New York: n.p., 1971.

Lancaster, Bill. "A Town Loses Interest in Segregated Schools." Philadelphia Inquirer, Ap 27, 1967. [Gould]

McMillen, Neil R. "White Citizens' Council and Resistance to School Desegregation in Arkansas." Arkansas Historical Quarterly, Summer, 1971.

McNeil, Elaine O. "White Members of a Biracial Voluntary Association in Arkansas." Diss. Abstr. 1968, 28 (11-A) 4731.

Merrill, Pierce K. "Race as a Factor in Achievement in Plantation Areas of Arkansas." Doctoral dissertation, Vanderbilt U., 1951. Univ. Microfilms Order No. 4505.

Mitchell, Leslie. "Racial Clashes Divide Town." Washington Post, My 16, 1976. [Eudora]

Morgan, Gordon D., and Kunkel, Peter. "Arkansas' Ozark Mountain Blacks: An Introduction." Phylon 34(S, 1973):283-288.

Morgan, Gordon D. with others. Black Hillbillies of the Arkansas Ozarks. Fayetteville: Department of Sociology, U. of Arkansas, 1973.

Morgan, Gordon D. Marianna: A Sociological Essay on an Eastern Arkansas Town. Jefferson City, MO: New Scholars Press, 1973.

Murphy, S. "Marked Tree School Plan Benefited All Students." Arkansas Libraries, Summer, 1968.

Payne, Ethel L. "Little Rock in '74." Chicago Defender, Mr 23, 1974.

Pearce, Larry Wesley. "The American Missionary Association and the Freedmen in Arkansas, 1863-1868." Arkansas Historical Quarterly, Summer, 1971.

_____. "The American Missionary Association and the Freedmen's Bureau in Arkansas, 1868-1878." Arkansas Historical Quarterly, Autumn, 1972.

_____. "Enoch K. Mille and the Freedmen's Schools." Arkansas Historical Quarterly, Winter, 1972.

Phillips, Cabell. "Integration: Battle of Hoxie, Arkansas." New York Times Magazine, S 25, 1955.

Pickens, William. "These 'Colored' United States: Arkansas--A Study in Suppression." Messenger 5(Ja, 1923):563-568.

Ponder, John L. "Comparison of White and Negro Schools in Crittendon County, Arkansas." Master's thesis, George Peabody College, 1935.

Pruden, Wesley, Jr. "Little Rock. 20 Years Afterward." Detroit News Magazine, D 18, 1977.

Prugh, Jeff. "Little Rock 20 Years Later: Integration Violence a Bad Dream." Los Angeles Times, S 25, 1977.

Pulaski County Association for Mental Health. Evaluation of Needs of Elementary School Teachers for Help in Dealing with Children with Problems. The Association, 1015 Louisiana Street, Little Rock, AR, 1964.

Pulaski County Mental Health Association. Mental Health Problems in Public Schools. Little Rock, AR: Little Rock Public Schools, 1964.

Ralston, Carolyn, and Lewis, Anne. "Forrest City, Arkansas." In NCRIEEO Special Field Report, My, 1971.

Reed, Roy. "Little Rock School Now Integration Model." New York Times, S 8, 1976. [Central High School]

Resource Management Corporation. [Case History of ESAP in Dumas, Ark.] Evaluation of the Emergency School Assistance Program, Vol. III, Appendix E, F 15, 1972. ERIC ED 058 470.

Reynolds, Jack Q. "Historical and Current Issues in Racial Integration in the Public Schools of Arkansas." Doctoral disserta tion, U. of Arkansas, 1957. Univ. Microfilms Order No. 21955.

Rhee, Jong Mo. Population Changes and Migration in Arkansas by Color, 1950-1970. Little Rock, AR: Industrial Research and Extension Center, U. of Arkansas, 1974.

Robbins, Jerry, and Teeter, Thomas A. "The Phoenix of Little Rock: Central High 20 Years After Forced Segregation." Phi Delta Kappan 59(0, 1977):112-115.

Rush, William. "Present Status and Future Prospects of the Negro High Schools in Arkansas, 1954-1969." Doctoral dissertation, U. of Arkansas, 1969. Univ. Microfilms Order No. 70-394.

Sales, M. Vance. "Arkansas, the Eighth Circuit Court of Appeals, and Desegregation, 1955-76." NOLPE School Law Journal 7(1977):21-57.

Sheard, Chester. "Turning the Tide in Arkansas." Muhammad Speaks, D 24, 1971. [Lee County]

_____. "Whites Plague Blacks in Arkansas." Muhammad Speaks, D 17, 1971. [Forest City, Earle, Marianna, and Madison]

Smith, Griffin, Jr. "Localism and Segregation: Racial Patterns in Little Rock, Arkansas, 1945-1954." Master's thesis, Columbia U., n.d.

Smith, James Hoard. "Arkansas Schools 'Push' Blacks Out." Muhammad Speaks, Jl 26, 1974.

Stanfield, Ed. "Arkansas' Bumpers. His Moderation Symbolizes Maturer Policies-- But What of His Deeds?" South Today 3 (My, 1972):6-7.

Stewart, Lynn. "Once-Segregationist System Now Unitary, Successful." Shreveport Times, S 4, 1978. [Little Rock]

Still, William Grant. "My Arkansas Boyhood." Arkansas Historical Quarterly 26(1967): 285-292.

Stroud, William H. "A Mellower Town Isn't Buying Wallace Message Any More." Philadelphia Inquirer, Jl 28, 1975. [McGehee]

Stuart, Reginald. "All Is (Relatively) Well At Little Rock's Central High." South Today 4 (Ja-F, 1973).

Terry, Adolphine. Charlotte Stephens: Little Rock's First Black Teacher. Little Rock, AR: Academic Press of Arkansas, 1973.

Terry, Clifford. "Orval [Faubus] in the Wilderness." Chicago Tribune Magazine, O 25, 1970.

Traber, Michael. "The Treatment of the Little Rock, Arkansas School Integration Incident in the Daily Press of the Union of South Africa, West Nigeria, and Ghana from September 1 to October 31, 1957." Doctoral dissertation, New York U., 1960. Univ. Microfilms Order No. 60-3762.

U.S. Commission on Civil Rights. School Desegregation in Little Rock, Arkansas. Washington, DC: The Commission, Je, 1977.

U.S. Commission on Civil Rights. Arkansas Advisory Committee. Blacks in the Arkansas Delta. Washington, DC: The Commission, Mr, 1974.

_____. Employment, Education, and Voting. Washington, DC: The Commission, 1966.

_____. Report on Arkansas Education. Washington, DC: GPO, 1963.

U.S. Office of Education. "Searcy, Ark." In Working Together. Case Studies of Title I, ESEA Programs in Four Desegregated School Districts. Washington, DC: GPO, 1974.

Wallace, David E. "The Little Rock Desegregation Crisis of 1957." Doctoral dissertation, U. of Missouri, 1971.

"Whatever Happened to 'The Little Rock 9'?" Ebony 27(F, 1972):136-137.

California

"A Talk With the Students of the Huey P. Newton Intercommunal Youth Institute." Black Panther, My 8, 1971.

Abrams, Carol and others. "School Integration Through Carrots, Not Sticks." Theory Into Practice 17(F, 1978):23-31.

Alan, John. "Black-Red View [on the Murder of Supt. Marcus Foster of Oakland, California]." News and Letters (Mr, 1974):7.

Alexander, Ruth. "Racial Characteristics and Conditions of the Student Population at Watsonville Union High School." Master's thesis, Stanford U., 1940.

Allen, Ralph. "Substandard Housing: Glendale and Pasadena, California." Master's thesis, San Fernando Valley State College, 1968.

An Exploratory Needs Assessment to Ascertain Variables Necessary for a Staff Development Program in Selected Pasadena Schools. Los Angeles: Contemporary Research, Inc., Ag, 1974.

Angelos, Constantine. "It's Readin', Writin' and Responsibility." Seattle Times, Je 26, 1977. [Back to basics in Pasadena]

Appleton, Susan F. "Alternative Schools for Minority Students: The Constitution, the Civil Rights Act, and the Berkeley Experiment." California Law Review 61(My, 1973). [Berkeley]

Armor, David and others. Analysis of the School Preferred Reading Program in Selected Los Angeles Minority Schools. Santa Monica, CA: Rand, Ag, 1976.

Avakian, Spurgeon. "School Desegregation in Berkeley, California." In U.S. Commission on Civil Rights, Papers Prepared for National Conference on Equal Educational Opportunity in America's Cities. Washington, DC: GPO, 1968.

Baker, William P., and Jensen, Henry C. Mexican American, Black and Other Graduates and Dropouts--II. A Follow-Up Study Covering 20 Years of Change, 1956-1976, Ja, 1978. ERIC 152 924. [San Jose East Side Union High School District]

Baldwin, Simeon E. "Schooling Rights Under Our Treaty with Japan." Columbia Law Review 7 (1907):85.

Bardez, Joan. Data Processing Requirements for School Desegregation: A Case Study of the San Francisco Unified School District, 1973. The Council of the Great City Schools, 1707 H Street, N.W., Washington, DC 20006.

Barnett, Frank and others. Citizen Participation Groups in San Diego. PB-208 002. Springfield, VA: National Technical Information Service, Mr, 1971.

"The Bay Area Radical Teachers' Organizing Committee." Socialist Revolution 2(Mr-Ap, 1972):103-113.

Bay, Duane L. "How Schools Can Attack Segregation at the Roots." Urban Review 6 (My, 1973):12-14. [Santa Clara County]

Beasley, Delilah L. The Negro Trail Blazers of California. New York: Negro Universities Press, 1969.

_____. "Slavery in California. Journal of Negro History 3(Ja, 1918).

Beck, Nicholas P. "The Other Children: Minority Education in California Public Schools from Statehood to 1890." Doctoral dissertation, U. of California, Los Angeles, 1975. Univ. Microfilms Order No. 75-22,604.

Belcher, Jerry. "School Busing: How Far Has It Gone?" Los Angeles Times, D 15, 1975. [San Francisco]

Bell, Howard H. "Negroes in California, 1849-1859." Phylon, Summer, 1967.

Benet, James. "Busing in Berkeley Proves to Be Neither Calamity Nor Cure-All." City, Je-Jl, 1970.

Berkeley Unified School District. Comparison of Achievement Test Scores Made by Berkeley Elementary Students Pre and Post Integration Eras, 1967-70. Berkeley, CA: Berkeley Unified School District, 1971.

Berry, Ray. Integration Update, Ap, 1978. ERIC ED 155 278.

Herwanger, Eugene H. "The Black Law Question in Ante-Bellum California." Journal of the West 6(1967):205-220.

Bettyjohn, Leonard F. "Factorial Ecology of the Los Angeles-Long Beach Black Population." Doctoral dissertation, U. of Wisconsin, 1976. Univ. Microfilms Order No. 77-07641.

"Big Circus On Integration Issue." Ideal (Coachella, California), F 15, 1970. [Desert Sands]

Bixler, James E. "STEP Toward Locksmithery." Educational Leadership, My, 1967. [Sausalito]

"[Black Panther] Liberation School from a Mother's Point of View." Black Panther, Jl 12, 1969. [Berkeley]

Board of Education. Report Submitted to the California State Department of Education... Regarding Programs and Services Provided Under the Elementary and Secondary Education Act of 1965 and SB 482, McSteer Act of 1965. Sacramento, CA: Sacramento City Unified School District, Jl 15, 1971.

Bonacich, Edna, and Goodman, Robert F. Deadlock in School Desegregation. A Case Study of Inglewood, California. New York: Praeger, 1972.

Bond, J. Max. "The Negro in Los Angeles." Doctoral dissertation, U. of Southern California, 1936.

Bostick, Susan, Logsdon, Wesley, and Perez, Guadalupe. "Disillusioned and Dismembered: One School that Picked Up the Pieces. Student Advocate 1(My, 1974):8-9. [Franklin Senior High School, Stockton]

Bourman, Ann P. "Busing" It Can Work." American Teacher, O, 1971. [Palms Jr. High School, Los Angeles]

Boyarsky, Bill. "Reform Ahead for California's Public Schools." Progressive 35(Je, 1971): 38-41.

_____. "Threat of Busing Spurs Rush Toward Private Schools." Los Angeles Times, My 1, 1977. [Los Angeles]

Boyarsky, Bill, and Durant, Celeste. "Mandatory Busing--White Students' Views." Los Angeles Times, Jl 4, 1977. [San Fernando Valley]

Boyarsky, Bill. "voluntary Busing: Some Valuable Lessons." Los Angeles Times, Mr 30, 1977. [Voluntary programs in Los Angeles]

Boyarsky, Bill, and Harris, Lee. "Busing in L.A. Gets Mostly High Marks from Students Involved." Los Angeles Times, Mr 30, 1977. [Voluntary programs]

Bradford, Amory. Oakland's Not for Burning. New York: McKay, 1968.

Brenneise, Beverly Gunkel. "A Critical Study of Educational Opportunities for Bilingual Students in the Sacramento City Unified School District Secondary Schools." Master's thesis, Chico State College, 1968.

Brown, H. O. "The Impact of War Worker Migration on the Public School System of Richmond, California, from 1940 to 1945." Doctoral dissertation, Stanford U., 1973.

Brown, William Henry, Jr. "Class Aspects of Residential Development and Choice of the Oakland Black Community." Doctoral dissertation, U. of California, Berkeley, 1970. Univ. Microfilms Order No. 71-15,735.

Bryan, D. E. "Social Categories Used by the Elementary School Teacher: A Study in the Sociology of Knowledge." Master's thesis, U. of California, Riverside, 1969. [Data from Riverside School Study]

Buel, Ronald A . "Creating a Slum." Wall Street Journal, Ja 30, 1969. [Oakland]

Bullock, Paul (ed.). "The Schools." In Watts: The Aftermath. An Inside View of the Ghetto by The People of Watts, pp. 165-196. New York: Grove Press, 1970.

Bullough, Bonnie. "Alienation in the Ghetto." American Journal of Sociology, Mr, 1967. [Los Angeles and San Fernando Valley]

_____. "Poverty, Ethnic Identity and Preventive Health Care." Journal of Health and Social Behavior 13(D, 1972):347-359.

Bureau of Intergroup Relations. Improving Ethnic Balance and Intergroup Relations. An Advisory Report to the Board of Education, Corona Unified School District. Sacramento: California State Department of Education, O 27, 1967.

_____. Improving Ethnic Balance and Intergroup Relations. An Advisory Report to the Board of Education, New Haven Unified School District. Sacramento: California State Department of Education, N 14, 1967.

_____. Improving Ethnic Distribution and Intergroup Relations. An Advisory Report to the Board of Education, Colton Joint Unified School District. Sacramento: California State Department of Education, Ap, 1968.

_____. Improving Racial and Ethnic Distribution and Intergroup Relations. An Advisory Report to the Board of Education, Vallejo Unified School District. Sacramento: California State Department of Education, Ap, 1968.

_____. Racial and Ethnic Distribution in California Public Schools. Sacramento: California State Department of Education, S 9, 1971.

_____. Report to the State Board of Education. Procedures to Correct Racial and Ethnic Imbalance in California Public Schools. Sacramento: California State Department of Education, F 24, 1970.

Burke, Sheryl, Hadsell, Virginia, Kane, Maria, and Newcom, Grethel. On the Go. Boys and Girls Exploring the San Francisco Bay Area. Berkeley, CA: Berkeley Unified School District, 1966. [Second-grade reading level]

Bylin, James E. "Los Angeles Campaign to Pass a School Issue Uses Political Tactics." Wall street Journal, Mr 31, 1969.

California Commission on Equal Opportunities in Education. A Report to the State Board of Education. Sacramento: State Department of Education, S, 1968.

California Department of Employment: The Economic Status of Negroes in the San Francisco-Oakland Bay Area. Sacramento: Department of Employment, My, 1965.

California Fair Employment Practice Commission. Los Angeles City Schools. Sacramento: State Department of Industrial Relations, O, 1964.

_____. Report on Oakland Schools 1962-1963. Sacramento: The Commission, Je, 1964.

"California Law on Teaching Negro History." Integrated Education, Ap-My, 1966.

California Office of Compensatory Education. California Plan for the Education of Migrant Children. Evaluation Report. Sacramento: California State Department of Education, 1968.

_____. Distribution of Racial and Ethnic Groups in California Public Schools. Sacramento: Department of Education, N, 1968.

California School Boards Association. Racial and Ethnic Factors in the Public Schools of California, Je, 1970. The Association, 455 Capitol Mall, Sacramento, CA 95814.

California State Department of Education, Bureau of Intergroup Relations. _Improving Racial Balance and Intergroup Relations. An Advisory Report to the Board of Education, Inglewood Unified School District, Inglewood_. Sacramento: California State Department of Education, Je, 1968.

_____. _Racial and Ethnic Distribution of Students and Staff in California Public Schools, Fall, 1977_. Sacramento: Office of Intergroup Relations, S 18, 1978.

California State Department of Education. _California Laws and Policies Relating to Equal Opportunities in Education_. Sacramento: California State Department of Education, 1966.

_____. "California Rules for Integration." _Integrated Education_, O-N, 1963, p. 40.

_____. _Compensatory Education in California, 1966-1967_. Sacramento: State Department of Education, 1968.

_____. _Guidelines, Compensatory Education_. Sacramento: California State Department of Education, Je, 1966. [Includes section on role of integration in publicly-financed compensatory education programs in California]

_____. _Improving Ethnic Balance and Intergroup Relations. An Advisory Report to the Board of Education, Santa Barbara Schools_. Sacramento: Bureau of Intergroup Relations, Office of Compensatory Education, California State Department of Education, My, 1968.

_____. _Limited-English Speaking and Non-English Speaking Students in California_. Sacramento: The Legislature, 1975.

_____. _Racial and Ethnic Survey of California Public Schools. Part One: Distribution of Pupils, Fall, 1966_. Sacramento: California State Department of Education, Mr, 1967.

California State Department of Education, Office of Program Evaluation. _A Brief Summary of the Research Conducted on Integration Programs by the Sacramento City Unified School District_. Sacramento: State Department of Education, O 1, 1971.

California State Department of Education. _Procedures to Correct Racial and Ethnic Imbalance in School Districts_. Sacramento: State Department of Education, N, 1969.

Calloway, Aubrey. "More Gang Violence Hits L.A. Schools." _Race Relations Reporter_ 6 (Ja-F, 1974):5-6.

Carrillo, Jess M. "The Process of School Desegregation: The Case of the Los Angeles Unified School District." Doctoral dissertation, U. of California, Los Angeles, 1978. Univ. Microfilms Order NO. 7901341.

Carter, Lawrence. _Can't You Hear Me Calling?_ New York: Seabury Press, 1969. [Hoover-Adams section of Los Angeles]

Carter, Thomas P., and Hickerson, Nathaniel. "A California Citizens' Committtee Studies Its Schools and _De Facto_ Segregation." _Journal of Negro Education_, Spring, 1968.

Carter, T. F., Casvantes, E. J., and Fowler, C. R. _Final Report and Evaluation of the Riverside In-Service Institute_. Riverside, CA: Riverside School Study, D, 1967.

Casstevens, Thomas W. _Politics, Housing and Race Relations: The Defeat of Berkeley's Fair Housing Ordinance_. Berkeley, CA: Institute of Governmental Studies, U. of California, N, 1965.

Caughey, John W. _Los Angeles School Segregation, 1968_. Ap, 1968. American Civil Liberties Union of Southern California, 323 West Fifth Street, Los Angeles, CA 90013.

_____. "Millions for Decentralization, Nothing for Integration." _The Black Politician_ 3 (Jl, 1971):93-95. [Los Angeles, CA]

_____. _Segregation Blights Our Schools. An Analysis Based on the 1966 Official Report on Racial and Ethnic Distribution School by School Throughout the Los Angeles System_. Los Angeles, CA: Quail Books, 1967.

_____. _The Shame of Los Angeles. Segregated Schools, 1970-1971_. Los Angeles: Quail Books, 1971.

Caughey, John W., and Caughey, LaRee. _School Segregation on Our Doorstep. The Los Angeles Story_. Los Angeles: Quail Books, 1966. [Quail Books, 3044 Riverside Drive, Los Angeles, CA 90039]

_____, and _____. "Decentralization of the Los Angeles Schools, Front for Segregation." _Integrated Education: RACE AND SCHOOLS_ 7 (S-O, 1969):48-51.

Center for the Study of Intergroup Relations. _Desegregation and Equal Educational Opportunity: Local Dilemmas and Government Mandates_. Riverside, CA: The Center, U. of California, Riverside, 1970.

Chandler, Russell. "Church Schools Are Reluctant to Offer Refuge from Integration." _Los Angeles Times_, My 1, 1977. [Los Angeles]

_____. "In Christian Schools, It's Boom--and Bus." _Los Angeles Times_, My 13, 1978. [Los Angeles area]

_____. "Popularity of Religious Schools Rising." _Los Angeles Times_, Je 18, 1978. [Los Angeles]

Citizens Committee. "School Segregation in Berkeley." Integrated Education, Ap-My, 1964.

Citizens Committee on Equal Educational Opportunities. Report. San Diego, CA: Board of Education, San Diego City Schools, Ag, 1966.

Clark, Alice M. "De Facto Integration in Bel Air." Saturday Review, Ja 15, 1966.

Clark, Willis W. "Los Angeles Negro Children." Los Angeles Educational Research Bulletin 3 (N 12, 1923):1-2.

Coakley, Michael, and Yates, Ronald. "Watts [Since 1965]." Chicago Tribune Magazine, My 22, 1977.

Cohen, Nathan E. "The Los Angeles Riot Study." Social Work, O, 1967. [Study of the Watts, 1965, riot]

_____ (ed.). The Los Angeles Riots: A Socio-Psychological Study. New York: Praeger, 1970. [Watts, Ag, 1965]

Cohen, William. "[De Facto Segregation in] Pasadena." Law and Society Review, N, 1967.

Coles, Robert, with photographs by Baldwin, Carol, and Whitney, Peter T. The Buses Roll. New York: Norton, 1974. [Berkeley]

Colley, Nathaniel S., Jr. Public School De-segregation in California Historical Back-ground, S, 1971. ERIC ED 056 408.

Collins, Keith Edison. "Black Los Angeles: The Maturing of the Ghetto, 1940-1950." Doctoral dissertation, U. of California, San Diego, 1975. Univ. Microfilms Order No. 75-29432.

Colwell, Mary Anna Culleton. "Are Parochial Elementary Schools in San Francisco Sub-stantially More Segregated by Race and Ethnic Group than Public Elementary Schools in Approximately the Same Residential Area?" Master's thesis, San Francisco State College, 1972. [1970-1971]

Commission on Professional Rights and Responsi-bilities. Oakland, California. A Community in Transition With a School System Too Slow-ly Adapting. Washington, DC: National Education Association, My, 1968.

Committee on Racial and Ethnic Factors in the Public Schools. Racial and Ethnic Factors in the California Public Schools, Je, 1970. California School Boards Association, 455 Capitol Mall, Sacramento, CA 95814.

Comptroller General of the United States. Examination of Grants Awarded to the Berkeley Unified School District and to Bilingual Children's Television, Inc. Washington, DC: General Accounting Office, S 4, 1974.

_____. Federal Programs for the Benefit of Disadvantaged Preschool Children, Los Angeles County, California. Washington, DC: GPO, F 14, 1969.

"Conflict and Violence in California Schools: The Problem in Brief." California School Boards 33(S, 1974):5-7.

Connolly, Leo G., and Williams, Ben, with Mark, Ruth. Black Californians: Population, Education, Income, Employment. San Francisco, CA: Division of Fair Employment Practices, 1974.

Cooper, Clare C. Unemployment and Minority Groups in California. Berkeley, CA: Center for Planning and Development Research, Institute of Urban and Regional Development, U. of California, D, 1965.

Counelis, James Steve. First Grade Students in the Hunters Point-Bayview SEED Project: A Diagnostic Review, Ag 15, 1970. ERIC ED 052 905.

Craib, Ralph. "Berkeley's Segregation Dilemma." San Francisco Chronicle, My 29, 1978.

Cuban, Larry. Urban School Chiefs Under Fire. Chicago: U. of Chicago Press, 1976. [Harold Spear, San Francisco]

Dambacher, A. D., and Rygh, Eileen S. Integrated Quality Education. A Study of Educational Parks and Other Alternatives for Urban Needs. Berkeley, CA: Berkeley Unified School District, 1968.

Dambacher, A. D. Proportional Distribution of Achievement Scores by Race and by Grade. Berkeley, CA: Berkeley Unified School District, 1967.

_____. Report of Group Achievement Test Results for 1970-1971. Berkeley, CA: Berkeley Unified School District, 1971.

_____. Socio-Economic Achievement Scores by Race and Grade for Grades K-8, by School. Berkeley, CA: Berkeley Unified School District, 1967. [Berkeley, CA]

Daniels, Douglas Henry. "Afro-San Franciscans: A Social History of Pioneer Urbanites, 1860-1930." Doctoral dissertation, U. of California, Berkeley, 1975.

Daniels, Roger, and Olin, Spencer C., Jr. (eds.). Racism in California. A Reader in the History of Oppression. New York: Macmillan, 1972.

Daniels, Roger. "Segregation and Diplomacy." In The Politics of Prejudice. Berkeley, CA: U. of California Press, 1962.

Davis, Clifford L., Jr. "Black Student Movements and their Influence in Ten High Schools in the Los Angeles City Unified School District." Doctoral dissertation, U. of California, Los Angeles, 1971. Univ. Microfilms. Order No. 72-13,600.

Davison, Berlinda. "Educational Status of the Negro in the San Francisco Bay Region." Master's thesis, U. of California, Berkeley, 1921.

Dawson, Helaine. S. On the Outskirts of Hope. New York: McGraw-Hill, 1968. [Teaching ghetto children in San Francisco]

"De Facto School Segregation and the Law: Focus San Diego." San Diego Law Review, Ja, 1968.

De Facto Segregation Study Committee. De Facto Segregation in the Berkeley [California] Public Schools. Berkeley: Board of Education, N, 1963. [Obtainable from Dr. Dan Freudenthal, Director of Research and Publications, Berkeley Unified School District, 1414 Walnut, Berkeley, CA.]

Debro, Julius. "Black Lawyers in the Bay Area and the Black Community." Journal of Social and Behavioral Sciences 19(Spring-Fall, 1973):13-26. [San Francisco Bay area]

Degenais, F., and Marascuilo, Leonard A. Student Demonstrations in a Multi-Racial High School: The Case of Berkeley, Ap, 1972. ERIC ED 061 527.

de Graaf, Lawrence. "The City of Black Angels, Emergence of the Los Angeles Ghetto 1890-1930. Pacific Historical Review, Ag, 1970.

_____. "Negro Migration to Los Angeles, 1930 to 1950." Doctoral dissertation, U. of California, Los Angeles, 1962.

Deslonde, James L., and Flach, Elisabeth G. Beyond Desegregation: Problem Solving in Two Elementary Schools. Riverside, CA: Western Regional School Desegregation Projects, U. of California, N, 1971.

Division of Educational Research. Evaluation of San Francisco Unified School District Desegregation/Integration 1971-72. San Francisco, CA: San Francisco Unified School District, O, 1972.

_____. A Report on the Assessment of and Recommendations Concerning Elementary Desegregation From Zone Councils, Teachers, Administrators and Pupils. San Francisco: San Francisco Unified School District, Mr, 1972.

Divoky, Diane. "Berkeley's Experimental Schools." Saturday Review of Education 55 (O, 1972):44-50.

"Dixie Comes to California." Ebony, Ap, 1950.

Dolson, Lee Stephen. "The Administration of the San Francisco Public Schools, 1847-1947." Doctoral dissertation, U. of California, Berkeley, 1964.

Douthit, Florence. "Alternative Education Programs in the Berkeley School System." In Alternative Education in a Pluralistic Society. Edited by Charles D. Moody, Charles B. Vergon, and Jean Leonard. Ann Arbor, MI: Program for Educational Opportunity, School of Education, U. of Michigan, 1974.

Drake, E. Maylon. "Employment of Negro Teachers." Doctoral dissertation, U. of Southern California, 1963. Univ. Microfilms Order No. 64-2572. [Los Angeles County]

Dumbarton Research Council, Menlo Park, California. "Race and Education in the City of Oakland." Reprinted in part in Racial Isolation in the Public Schools, Vol. II. Washington, DC: GPO, 1967.

Dunaway, David King, and Beckum, Leonard Charles. "The Mayor's Influence in Urban School Desegregation." Phi Delta Kappan (Mr, 1977):553-556. [Four California cities]

Duncan, T. Roger. "Does California Have 'Segregated' Schools?" CTA Journal, California Teachers Association, Mr, 1965.

Duniway, Clyde A. "Slavery in California after 1849." Annual Report of the American Historical Association 1(1905).

Du Pree, David. "Freedom Is Stimulating At Innovative School, But It Invites Anarchy." Wall Street Journal, My 5, 1971. [Berkeley High School]

Durant, Celeste. "Soul-Searching for Ones Who Remain." Los Angeles Times, Je 18, 1978. [White parents in Los Angeles who refused to flee from integration program]

Duster, Troy. "Violence and Civic Responsibility: Combinations of 'Fear' and 'Right.'" In Our Children's Burden. Edited by Raymond W. Mack. New York: Random House, 1968. [Riverside]

Dymally, Mervyn M., and Rodda, Albert S. "Memo on Segregation and Busing in the Schools." Black Politician 2(Summer, 1970):22-26.

Eason, Charles L. "An Analysis of the Social Attitudes and Causal Factors of Negro Problem Boys of the Los Angeles City Schools." Master's thesis, U. of Southern California, 1936.

East San Jose Educational Park Study: Developing a Preventive Strategy for Meeting Tomorrow's Educational, Vocational, Ethnic and Societal Demands. End of Budget Period Report, Je 30, 1968. ERIC Ed 027 607.

East San Jose Educational Park Study. Report of the Blue Ribbon Advisory Committee, My, 1968. ERIC 027 606.

Elliot, Merle L., and Badal, Alden W. "Achievement and Racial Composition of Schools." California Journal of Educational Research, S, 1965. [Oakland]

Ellis, Robert A., and Lane, W. Clayton. "Social Mobility and Social Isolation: A Test of Sorokin's Dissociative Hypothesis." American Sociological Review, Ap, 1967. [A study of lower-class students at Stanford U.]

Elman, Richard M. Ill-At-Ease in Compton. New York: Pantheon, 1967.

Equal Educational Opportunities Project. Data Processing Requirements for School Desegregation: A Case Study of the San Francisco Unified School District. Washington, DC: Council of Great City Schools, 1973.

Equal Educational Opportunity in the Sacramento City Unified School District: A Report to the Board of Education, The Sacramento City Unified School District, My 22, 1965. ERIC ED 028 230.

Equal Educational Opportunity Policy Research Project. "Oakland." Passim, in Federal Policies for Equal Educational Opportunity: Conflict and Confusion. Austin, TX: Lyndon B. Johnson School of Public Affairs, U. of Texas, 1977.

Esainko, Peter. Ethnic Variations in Busing. San Francisco: Integration Department, San Francisco Unified School District, Mr 15, 1976.

Espinosa, Ruben, and Garcia, Joseph O. Credentialed Staff-Pupil Ratios by Ethnicity in the California Public Schools. San Diego, CA: School of Education, San Diego State U., 1976.

Evaluation of the San Diego Plan for Racial Integration, 1977-78. San Diego: San Diego Unified School District, My, 1978.

Fantini, Mario D. "Berkeley's Alternate Schools Plan." In Public Schools of Choice, pp. 83-116. New York: Simon & Schuster, 1974.

Farley, Cloid W. "The Riles-Rafferty Race: An Analysis." Black Politician 2(Ap, 1971): 16-18.

Favors, Kathryne. Before the Bus Ride. Oakland, CA: Jonka Enterprises, 1970. [Berkeley]

53X, Charles. "Blacks Insist San Francisco School Have Black Principal." Muhammad Speaks, S 25, 1970. [Polytechnic High School]

Fisher, James. A. "A History of the Political and Social Development of the Black Community in California, 1850-1950." Doctoral dissertation, State U. of New York at Stony Brook, 1972.

_____. "The Political Development of the Black Community in California, 1850-1950." California Historical Quarterly 50(1971): 256-266.

_____. "A Social History of the Negro in California." Master's thesis, Sacramento State College, 1966.

Fogelson, Robert M. The Fragmented Metropolis: Los Angeles, 1850-1930. Cambridge, MA: Harvard U. Press, 1967.

_____. "White on Black: A Critique of the McCone Commission Report on the Los Angeles Riots." Political Science Quarterly, S, 1967. [Watts, 1965]

Fort, Edward B. "A Case Study of the Struggle to Secure an Administrative Plan for Eliminating De Facto Segregation in the Junior High Schools of Sacramento, California." Doctoral dissertation, U. of California, Berkeley, 1964. Univ. Microfilms Order No. 65-2985.

_____. "Decision Making in the Sacramento De Facto Segregation Crisis." In School Desegregation in the North. Edited by T. Bentley Edwards and Frederick M. Wirt. San Francisco, CA: Chandler, 1967.

Forthman, Robert Crooks. "Hard Core Youth Unemployment." Doctoral dissertation, U. of California, Berkeley, S, 1970.

Fosburgh, Lacey. "Lonely and Full of Hate, She Joined the Nazi Party--She's Less Lonely Now." New York Times, Je 6, 1974. [Sandra Silva, San Francisco]

Four Alternative Attendance Plans to Satisfy the Requirements of Racial and Ethnic Balance in the Bakersfield City Elementary School District, My, 1972. ERIC ED 064 438.

Fox, Denver C. "Intergroup Relationships in a School Camp Environment." In Models for Integrated Education, pp. 43-48. Edited by Daniel U. Levine. Worthington, OH: Jones, 1971. [San Diego]

Frakes, George E., and Solberg, Curtis B. (eds.). Minorities in California History. New York; Random House, 1971.

Freis, Ruth, Miller, Miriam, Platt, Bess, and
Warren, Courine. "A Nonsegregated
Approach to Head Start." Young Children,
My, 1969.

Frelow, Robert D. The Berkeley Plan for Desegregation. Berkeley, CA: Berkeley
Unified School District, 1969. [Draft
copy]

French, Helene P. "Burden of Growth: A Case
Study of the Los Angeles County Commission
on Human Relations." Master's thesis,
California State College at Fullerton,
CA, 1969. Univ. Microfilms Order No. M-
1769.

Freudenthal, Daniel K. "Berkeley [Junior] High
Schools Integrate." In School Desegregation
in the North. Edited by T. Bentley Edwards
and Frederick M. Wirt. San Francisco, CA:
Chandler, 1967.

_____. "Evolution of School Desegregation in
Berkeley, California." In Man As the
Measure: The Crossroads, pp. 31-49.
Edited by Daniel Adelson. New York:
Behavioral Publications, Inc., 1972.

_____. "How Berkeley Came to Grips With De
Facto Segregation." Phi Delta Kappan, D,
1964.

Fulkerson, D. Ray, Horelick, Arnold, Shapley,
Lloyd S., and Weller, Daniel M. A Transportation Program for Filling Idle Classrooms in Los Angeles. Santa Monica, CA:
RAND Corporation, Jl, 1966.

Galarza, Ernesto. Farm Workers and Agri-
Business in California, 1947-1960.
Notre Dame, IN: U. of Notre Dame Press,
1977.

Galbraith, Francis Templeton. "No Need to
Knock: The Garfield Junior High School
Experience." In School Desegregation in the
North. Edited by T. Bentley Edwards and
Frederick M. Wirt. San Francisco, CA:
Chandler, 1967. [Berkeley]

Gallagher, John. School Board Politics in Los
Angeles County. Los Angeles: U. of
California, 1962.

Garner, John R. "The Berkeley Plan: How One
City Integrated Its Schools Successfully."
Master's thesis, Alaska Methodist U., 1969.

Geale, Paul E. "Suburbanization Process in a
Black Community: Pocoima, a Case Study."
Master's thesis, California State U.,
Los Angeles, 1971.

Gemello, John M. "Redistribution Effects of
Intergovernmental Grants: A Study of the
Educational Finance System in California."
Doctoral dissertation, Stanford U., 1975.

Gerard, Harold B., and Miller, Norman. Factors
Contributing to Adjustment in Racially Desegregated Public Schools; Renewal Proposal
(1971); Original Proposal, June 1, 1967--
May 31, 1972; Progress Report, 1968; and,
Progress Report, 1969, 1971. ERIC ED 057
120.

Gindick, Tia. "Altadena Redefines 'All-American
City.'" Los Angeles Times, Je 5, 1977.

Gitelson, Alfred E. "The Power and Duty to
Integrate." Integrated Education 8(My-Je,
1970):10-15. [Los Angeles]

Gottschalk, Earl C. "City is Sharply Split On
Effect of Busing On Its School System."
Wall Street Journal, Jl 2, 1974. [Pasadena]

Governor's Commission on the Los Angeles Riots
[in Watts]. Staff Report of Actions Taken
to Implement the Recommendations in the
Commission's Report. Status Report II.
Sacramento, CA: State Capitol, Ag 18, 1967.

Graves, Alvin Ray. "Immigrants in Agriculture:
The Portuguese Californians, 1850-1970."
Doctoral dissertation, U. of California,
Los Angeles, 1977. Univ. Microfilms Order
No. 7806485.

Greenburgh, David, and McCall, John. "Teacher
Mobility and Allocation." Journal of Human
Resources 9(F, 1974):480-502. [San Diego]

Greenwood, Noel. "Pasadena Schools: How Much
Turmoil Can They Take?" Los Angeles Times,
Jl 7, 1974.

_____. "School Desegregation--Successes, Fail-
ures, Surprises." Los Angeles Times, My 21,
1972.

Greenwood, Noel, McCurdy, Jack, and Durant,
Celeste. "Changing School." Los Angeles
Times, Je 10-14, 1973. [Five articles on
Hamilton High School, Los Angeles]

Gregg, Jean. "Apex Loves." Integrator, Winter,
1967-1968. [Project Apex in Los Angeles;
five high schools linked together for better
education and integration]

_____. "Apex Quality Integrated Classes in
Los Angeles High Schools." Integrated
Education, N-D, 1968, pp. 19-23.

Grubb, W. N., and Osman, J. W. "The Causes
of School Finance Inequalities: Serrano and
the Case of California." Public Finance
Quarterly 5(Jl, 1977).

Guichard, Gus. Board Report on Implementation
and Progress of Administrative Transfer Plan,
September, October, November, 1967. San
Mateo, CA: San Mateo City School District,
D 5, 1967. [A busing program]

Gunsky, Frederic R. "Desegregation. Exert All
Effort." California School Boards, Je, 1969.

_____. "Racial and Ethnic Survey of California Public Schools." Integrated Education, Je-Jl 1967.

Gurule, Kay, and Ortega, Joe. "L.A. Decentralization with Problems." Inequality in Education 15(N, 1973):43-44.

Guthrie, James W. "School Board Member Assesses What Went Wrong." Christian Science Monitor Ja 19, 1976. [Berkeley]

Haberfeld, Steven. "Strategies for Structured Change." Race 14(Ap, 1973):443-463.

Hadsell, Virginia T., and Newcom, Grethel C. Equal Start. A New School, A New Chance, 1968. Glide Urban Center, 330 Ellis Street, San Francisco, CA, 94102.

Hager, Philip. "Berkeley and Busing--Still Short of Aims." Los Angeles Times, My 20, 1976.

Hallihan, Tim. "The Portuguese in California." Master's thesis, U of California, Berkeley, 1968.

Halpern, Ray, and Halpern, Betty. "The City That Went to School." Nation, My 13, 1968. [Berkeley, CA]

Halverson, Jerry F. "L.A. Decentralization with Promise." Inequality in Education 15 (N, 1973):39-42.

Hampton, Sharla. "Get On Their Case." Black Panther, D 27, 1969. [Polytechnic High School, San Francisco]

Hansen, Charles E. "Central City and Suburb: A Study of Educational Opportunity." Doctoral dissertation, U of California, Berkeley, 1969. [San Francisco Bay area, CA]

Hansen, W. Lee, and Weisbrod, Burton A. "The Distribution of Costs and Direct Benefits of Public Higher Education. The Case of California." Journal of Human Resources, Spring, 1969.

Harmer, John. "Decentralization: A Conservative's View." The Black Politician 2(O, 1970):1, 17-18. [Los Angeles]

_____. "Decentralization and Community Control." Compact, Ap, 1969. [Los Angeles]

Harker, R. H., Ellis, Hazel, and Platt, William J. Evaluation of Alternative Attendance Patterns to Improve Racial Balance. Menlo Park, CA: Stanford Research Institute, My 15, 1967. [San Francisco]

Harris, LeRoy A. "The Other Side of the Freeway: A Study of Settlement Patterns of Negroes and Mexican Americans in San Diego, California." Doctoral dissertation, Carnegie-Mellon U., 1974. Univ. Microfilm 74-26, 644.

Harris, Norene, and Jackson, Nathaniel. "The Good Guys Don't Always Win: A Conversation with George McCormick." In Harris, Jackson, Carl Rydingsword, and contributors, The Integration of American Schools: Problems, Experiences, Solutions, pp. 193-206. Boston, MA: Allyn & Bacon, 1975. [Stockton]

Harris, Norene, Jackson, Nathaniel, and Rydingsword, Carl E. "Inglewood, California: An Experience in Desegregation." In same authors, The Integration of American Schools: Problems, Experiences, and Solutions, pp. 78-92. Boston, MA: Allyn & Bacon, 1975.

Hartwig, Keith E., and Delavan, Frank E. Evaluation of the Effectiveness of Project Aspiration During 1967-68. Sacramento, CA: Sacramento City Unified School District, Jl 30, 1968. [A project "to alleviate the adverse effects of de facto segregation"]

Hawley, Jim. "Call on Strike." The Movement, Ap, 1969.

Hayes, Edward C. "Power Structure and the Urban Crisis: Oakland, California." Doctoral dissertation, U of California, Berkeley, 1969. Univ. Microfilms Order No. 69-14908.

Heath, G. Louis. "De Facto Segregation in a California City." Integrated Education 8 (Ja-F, 1970):3-10. [Richmond]

Heizer, Robert F., and Almquist, Alan J. Other Californians. Prejudice and Discrimination under Spain, Mexico, and the United States to 1920. Berkeley, CA: University of California Press, 1971.

Hendrick, Irving G. The Development of a School Integration Plan in Riverside, California. A History and Perspective. Riverside, CA: University of California, S, 1968.

_____. The Education of Non-Whites in California, 1849-1970. San Francisco: Rand E. Research Associates, 1977.

Hendrix, Kathleen. "More than Mental Health." Los Angeles Times, Je 27, 1976. [Central City Community Mental Health Facility, Watts, Los Angeles]

Henry, Curtis C. "The Spatial Interaction of Black Families in Suburban Cities in the Bay Area: A Study of Black Subsystem Linkages." Doctoral dissertation, U of California, Berkeley, 1978.

Herndon, James. "The Way It Sposed to Be." Harper's, S, 1965. [A Negro junior high school near San Francisco]

Herron, Bobby. "Richmond [Calif.] Breakfast for School Children." Black Panther, Mr 31, 1969.

Herves, Laurence I., Jr. Intergroup Relations in San Diego. San Francisco: American Council on Race Relations, 1946.

Heyman, Ira Michael. "[De Facto Segregation in] Berkeley." Law and Society Review, N, 1967.

Hickerson, Nathaniel. "Comparison between Negro and Non-Negro Students in Participation in Formal and Informal Activities of a California High School." Doctoral dissertation, U of California, Berkeley, 1963. Univ. Microfilms Order No. 63-6179.

_____. "Integrated vs. Compensatory Education in the Riverside-San Bernardino Schools." In T. Bentley Edwards and Frederick M. Wirt, School Desegregation in the North. San Francisco: Chandler, 1967.

_____. "Some Aspects of School Integration in a California High School." Journal of Negro Education, Spring, 1965.

Hippler, Arthur E. Hunter's Point: A Black Ghetto. New York: Basic Books, 1974. [San Francisco]

"History of Frisco School Strike." Muhammad Speaks, O 9, 1970. [Sir Francis Drake School annex in Hunter's Point]

Hodge, Jacqueline G. "Ask, Seek, Knock--Desegregation." Crisis, D, 1963. [Fresno]

Hoepfner, Ralph, Fink, Arlene and others. Evaluation Study of the California State Pre-School Programs. Los Angeles: Center for the Study of Evaluation, UCLA Graduate School of Education, University of California, Los Angeles, 1975.

Hoffman, Clive. "The Tale of Two Schools: Again, an Integration Plan is Thwarted at the Top." Los Angeles Times, Ag 7, 1973. [Los Angeles]

Holden, Anna. "Sacramento, California: Partial Desegregation in a Racially Imbalanced, Multiethnic School District." In The Bus Stops Here. A Study of School Desegregation in Three Cities, pp. 279-434. New York: Agathon Press, 1974.

Hoover, Robert. "Meeting Community Needs." In Robert A. Altman and Patricia O. Snyder, The Minority Student on the Campus: Expectations and Possibilities, pp. 189-197, N, 1970. Western Interstate Commission for Higher Education, P.O. Drawer "P," Boulder, CO, 80302. [Nairobi schools and college, East Palo Alto]

Hopkins, Gayle Patni. "School Integration in the Los Angeles Unified School District and the Involvement of the Black Community." Doctoral dissertation, Claremont Graduate School, 1978. Univ. Microfilm Order No. 7823836.

Hovard, Richard Brandt. Metropolitan Integration in Southern California: An Alternative Plan. Dominguez Hills, CA: California State College, 1977.

Human Resources Committee. Desegregating California Schools, Rev. Ed., 1969. League of Women Voters, 126 Post Street, San Francisco, CA, 94108.

Human Rights Commission. "I.Q. Testing in San Francisco." Integrated Education 11(My-Je, 1973):38-40.

Hurst, John. "The WARI Incident." New Schools Network, N, 1971. [Berkeley]

Implementation of Ad Hoc Directives on Equal Educational Opportunity. Third Information Report. Los Angeles: Los Angeles City Schools, O, 1967. ERIC ED 015 992.

Inghram, Dorothy. "An Experiment in Intercultural Education." California Journal of Elementary Education, N, 1953. [Mill School, San Bernardino]

Jackson, Ervin, Sr. School Board Grant Program Grant Program on School Desegregation Problems. Final Report. Sacramento, CA: Sacramento City Unified School District, California, 1967. ERIC ED 019 381.

Jackson, Jo, and Wigglesworth, David C. "Hanging in There in Cupertino." Integrated Education 11(Jl-O, 1973):42-47.

Jenkins, Robert E. Educational Equality/Quality: Program Alternatives. San Francisco: Board of Education, D, 1967.

Jensen, Arthur R. "Assessment of Racial Desegregation in the Berkeley Schools." In Daniel Adelson, Man as the Measure, pp. 116-133. New York: Behavioral Publications, Inc., 1972.

_____. Parent and Teacher Attitude Toward Integration and Busing. Burlingame, CA: California Teachers Association, My, 1970. [Berkeley]

_____. "What Jensen Would Say." (letter) Phi Delta Kappan, Ap, 1970. [In re: Windsor Hills school, Los Angeles]

Johnson, Lawrence E. "The Negro Community in Oroville, California." Master's thesis, Chico State College, 1970.

Johnson, Sharon. "...While the Casualties Continue." New York Times, N 14, 1976. [Vernon Evans, student in Locke High School, Los Angeles]

Johnston, William J. "Integration and Decentralization in Los Angeles." Integrated Education (N-D, 1971):12-14.

Jones, Helen L. Metropolitan Los Angeles: A Study in Integration, XII. Schools. Los Angeles: Haynes Foundation, 1952.

Jones, Jeff, and Norberg, Doug. "Mission Rebellion." The Movement, Mr, 1969. [Third World Movement at Mission High School in San Francisco]

Jung, Raymond. "Leisure in Three Cultures." Elementary School Journal, Mr, 1967. [Caucasian, Negro, and Chinese children in Oakland]

Kaplan, John. "[De Facto Segregation in] San Francisco." Law and Society Review, N, 1967.

Kapsis, Robert E. "Continuities in Delinquency and Riot Patterns in Black Residential Areas." Social Problems 23(Je, 1975):567-580. [Richmond and North Richmond]

Keeler, Emmett. Planning School Desegregation. Santa Monica, CA: Rand Corp., 1972. [Los Angeles]

Keller, Marcia. "East Palo Alto Federal Library Project." American Libraries 2(Je, 1971): 531-633.

Kellner, Norman J. A Study to Determine the Effectiveness of Open Enrollment and Busing as Solutions for the Social Segregation Situation in the San Diego City Schools. A Report, Ja, 1970. ERIC ED 053 448.

Kelman, Stuart L. "Motivations and Goals: Why Parents Send Their Children to Non-Orthodox Jewish Day Schools." Doctoral dissertation, U. of Southern California, 1978. [Los Angeles, S, 1977]

Kendall, Robert. White Teacher in a Black School. New York: DeVin-Adair, 1964. [Los Angeles]

Kidd, Leonard S. "Individualization and Non-Grading in an Integrated Elementary School." In Models for Integrated Education, pp. 89-97. Edited by Daniel U. Levine. Worthington, OH: Jones, 1971. [San Diego]

Kirp, David L. "Multitudes in the Valley of Indecision: The Desegregation of San Francisco's Schools." In Limits of Justice. The Courts' Role in School Desegregation, pp. 411-492. Edited by Howard I. Kalodner and James J. Fishman. Cambridge, MA: Ballinger, 1978.

_____. "Race, Politics, and the Courts: School Desegregation in San Francisco." Harvard Educational Review 46(N, 1976): 572-611.

Kleeman, Richard P. "Schools and Race. Dilemma Outside Dixie." Minneapolis Tribune, O 30, 1970. [Pasadena]

_____. "University Aided 2 Cities' Integration." Minneapolis Tribune, O 27, 1970. [Berkeley and Riverside]

Koen, Ross Y. "The Education of Ronald Reagan." Nation, S 29, 1969.

Kohl, Herb. "Appendix. A Letter from Herb Kohl." In Mario D. Fantini, Public Schools of Choice, pp. 250-252. New York: Simon and Schuster, 1974.

Kohl, Herbert. [Interview on Alternative Schools within Berkeley public school system] New Schools Newtwork Newsletter, Ja-F, 1972.

_____. "What Are the Real Risks When a School Tries to Change?" Saturday Review, My 27, 1972. [Hazelton Elementary School, Stockton]

Kossow, Henry H. "An Integration Success Story." American School Board Journal, Jl, 1965. [Del Paso Heights School District]

Kurtz, Harold. "Court Mandated Integration and White Flight in Los Angeles County." In U.S. Congress, 92nd, 2nd session, House of Representatives, Committee on the Judiciary, Subcommittee No. 5, School Busing. Hearings... Part 3, Serial No. 32, pp. 1426-1433. Washington, DC: GPO, 1972.

_____. The Educational and Demographic Consequences of Four Years of School Desegregation in the Pasadena Unified School District. Pasadena, CA: Pasadena Unified School District, 1976.

Lapp, Rudolph M. "Negro Rights Activities in Gold Rush California." California Historical Society Quarterly 45(Mr, 1966):3-20.

_____. Blacks in Gold Rush California. New Haven, CT: Yale U. Press, 1977.

Lawton, Stephen B. "Minority Administrators in Berkeley. A Program Report." Urban Education 6(Ja, 1972):321-330.

League of Women Voters of California. "Desegregating California Schools." California Current Review of Human Resources, My, 1969.

Lee, Jean Luce. "Integration Problem Grows in Los Angeles. Christian Science Monitor, Ja 19, 1976.

Lee, Robert Dorwin, Jr. "Educational Ideology and Decision-Making in the San Francisco Public Schools, 1956-1966." Doctoral dissertation, Syracuse U., 1967. Univ. Microfilms Order No. 68-7068.

Leeper, Robert R., and O'Neill, Mary A. (eds.). Hunters Point Redeveloped: A Sixth-Grade Venture. A Tape Transcription of Sixth Graders Discussing Their Plan for Redeveloping a Depressed Area in San Francisco. Washington, DC: Association for Supervision and Curriculum Development, 1970.

Lefkowitz, Ben, and D'Esopo, Tony. Measuring Racial Balance. Menlo Park, CA: Stanford Research Institute, Mr 24, 1967. [Applied to San Francisco school system]

Legum, Stanley E. and others. The Speech of Young Black Children in Los Angeles, S, 1971. ERIC ED 057 022.

Leo, Peter. [Four articles on desegregation in Pasadena, California] Wilmington News Journal (Del.), My 30-Je 2, 1976.

Leon, John F., Abderholden, Jack W., and McConaghy, Irving. The East Los Angeles Community: A Communications Task Force on School-Community Relations. Los Angeles, CA: Los Angeles City Schools, Je, 1968.

Leonard. "Miseducation at Vallejo Senior High School. Black Panther, Ja 17, 1970.

Levene, Carol. "The Negro in San Francisco." Common Ground 9(Spring, 1949):10-17.

Levin, Henry M. A Comparison of the Performance of the Los Angeles City School District With That of Other School Districts. Sacramento, CA: Assembly Committee on Education, Ag 10, 1970.

Levy, Frank, Meltsner, Arnold, and Wildavsky, Aaron. Urban Outcomes: Schools, Streets, and Libraries. Berkeley: U. of California Press, 1974. [Oakland]

Levy, Margery J. Evaluation of Elementary School Desegregation: Resegregating Tendencies in Special Programs. San Francisco: Integration Department, San Francisco Unified District, O 2, 1975.

Lewis, Florence C. "From San Francisco." In School Desegregation: Shadow and Substance. Edited by Florence H. Levinsohn and Benjamin D. Wright. Chicago: U. of Chicago Press, 1976.

Little, Arthur D., Inc. Alternative for Reorganizing Large Urban Unified School Districts. A Report to the California State Legislature. 2 vols. Sacramento, CA: Joint Committee on Reorganization of Large Urban Unified School Districts, Je, 1970. [Los Angeles]

Livingston, Tom. "Pasadena's Home Owners Are Not Panicking." Integrated Education (N-D, 1971):9-11 (reprinted from the Star-News S 19, 1971).

Loftis, Anne. "How They Outsmarted the Anglos." Nation, Ap 30, 1973. [Stockton]

Lopez, Leo. "Compensatory Education in California: A Progress Report." California Education, Ja, 1965.

Lortie, Francis M. "San Francisco's Black Community, 1870-1890: Dilemmas in the Struggle for Equality." Master's thesis, San Francisco State College, 1970.

"Los Angeles N.A.A.C.P. Leader Raps Conspiracy in Nation's School." Muhammad Speaks, Ap 11, 1969.

"Los Angeles School." Black Panther, Mr 31, 1969. [Survey of school movements in Los Angeles]

Los Angeles Unified School District. Report of the District Goals Review Committee. Los Angeles: Los Angeles Unified School District, O 22, 1974.

Luke, Sherill D. "The Problem of Annexing North Richmond to the City of Richmond." Master's thesis, U of California, Berkeley, 1954.

McAlpin, Donald. "Analysis of the Efforts to Promote Racial Desegregation within the Pasadena Unified School District as Directed by the Court Order of Judge Manuel L. Real in January of 1970." Doctoral dissertation, Walden U, 1972.

McAnulty, E. Alice, and Tritt, Jessie. Nationality Survey. Public Schools of Los Angeles, 1930.

McAteer, J. Eugene. "A Law for Compensatory Education." Integrated Education, Je, 1963.

MacCalla, Jacqueline Estelle. "Cultural Diversity Among Caribbean Blacks in the San Diego Area: A Case Study." Master's thesis, United States International U, 1974. Univ. Microfilms Order No. M-5236.

McCorry, Jesse. Marcus Foster and the Oakland Public Schools: Leadership in an Urban Bureaucracy. Berkeley: University of California Press, 1978.

McCurdy, Jack. "Experiment in Education--A School that Parents Built." Los Angeles Times, N 28, 1975. [Canfield-Crescent Heights Community School, Los Angeles]

_____. "Progress and Backsliding in California." Los Angeles Times, Ja 27, 1974.

_____. "Pupils Are Never Told 'You Have To.'" Los Angeles Times, N 28, 1975. [Canfield-Crescent Heights Community School, Los Angeles]

_____. "Riles: An Educator with Real Political Clout." Los Angeles Times, My 30, 1978. [Wilson Riles, state superintendent of public instruction]

_____. "Riles Scores Ups, Downs Over Three Years." Los Angeles Times, F 10, 1974. [Dr. Wilson Riles, state superintendent of public instruction, California]

_____. "School Board Minutes Play Big Role in Oxnard Desegregation." Los Angeles Times, Ja 19, 1975.

_____. "School Integration: The Climax Nears." Los Angeles Times, Ap 4, 1976. [Various articles on school segregation in Los Angeles]

_____. "Wilson Riles: Clout in California." Integrateducation 16(S-O, 1978):2-8.

McDonnough, John J. An Organizational Study of the Los Angeles Urban League. Los Angeles: Joint Center for Community Studies, 1974.

Mackay, Ned. "Educators Tell Senator Busing Destructive." Black Times, Mr 18, 1971. [Robert S. Hoover and Mrs. Gertrude Wilks, East Palo Alto]

McKenney, J. Wilson. "California Equalizes Opportunity." California Teachers Association Journal, Mr, 1965.

McSwine, Bartley. "Delineation of the Role of the Intergroup Educator Within the State of California." Master's thesis, U. of California, Riverside, 1972.

McWilliams, Carey. "Los Angeles: An Emerging Pattern [of Race Relations]." Common Ground 9(Spring, 1949):3-10.

_____. "Race Discrimination and the Law." Science and Society 9(1945):1-22. [Japanese children in San Francisco schools]

Magin, David III. Student Safety in Our Public Schools, Ap, 1972. The Sunset-Parkside Education and Action Committee, 1329 Seventh Avenue, San Francisco, CA, 94122.

Major, Reginald W. "Integration for Excellence." Nation, S 12, 1966. [San Francisco]

Marascuilo, Leonard A., and Penfield, Kathleen. "A Northern Urban Community's Attitudes toward Racial Imbalance in Schools and Classrooms." School Review, Winter, 1966. [Berkeley]

Marascuilo, Leonard A., and Levin, Joel R. "Group Differences in the Perception of a Social Situation." Urban Education 3, 1967. [Berkeley]

Marshall, Rachelle. "Concrete Curtain--the East Palo Alto Story." Crisis, N, 1957.

Martinez, Al. "Klan Seeking to Dispel Its Image of Hate." Los Angeles Times, Ja 29, 1979.

Martyn, Kenneth A., and Clark, Charles L. An Analysis of Comparative Data from Schools in Predominantly Negro, Mexican-American and Privileged Sections of Los Angeles. Sacramento: California State Department of Education, 1967.

Maves, Harold J. "Insight Through Inservice." Today's Education, Ap, 1969. [Berkeley]

Mazzoni, T. L., Jr. "Political Capability for Urban School Governance: An Analysis of the Los Angeles City School Board (1966-1969)." Doctoral dissertation, Claremont Graduate School, 1971.

Meer, Bernard, and Freeman, Edward. "The Impact of Negro Neighbors on White Home Owners." Social Forces, S, 1966. [Stockton]

Meldrum, George W. "The History and the Treatment of Foreign and Minority Groups in California, 1830-1860." Doctoral dissertation, Stanford U., 1948.

Melville, Keith. School Desegregation Plan/ Berkeley, California. New York: Center for Urban Education, 1971.

Mercer, Jane R. Issues and Dilemmas in School Desegregation: A Case Study. San Fransisco: Educational Testing Service, My 3, 1968. [Riverside]

Metz, B. "Authority in the Junior High School: A Case Study, 1971." Doctoral dissertation, U. of California, Berkeley, 1971. [Three desegregated schools in California]

Miller, Norman, and Gerard, Harold B. "How Busing Failed in Riverside." Psychology Today, Je, 1976.

Milstein, Mike M., and Hoch, Dean E. "A Landmark in School Racial Integration: Berkeley, California." Phi Delta Kappan, My, 1969.

Mingori, Lynn B. "History of Negro Education in California from 1850 to 1890." Master's thesis, U. of California, Los Angeles, 1970.

"Minority Students in California." The California Professor, My, 1968. [Published by the California Teachers Association]

Montesano, Phillip. "Some Aspects of the Free Negro Question in San Francisco." Master's thesis, U. of San Francisco, 1967.

Moody, Eileen. "Death of an American Dream." New Society, F 27, 1969.

Moratto, Michael J. (comp.) Anthropological and Ethnohistorical Sources for the San Francisco Bay Region. San Francisco: Treganza Anthropology Museum, 1974.

Morris, Richard T., and Jeffries, Vincent. The White Reaction Study. Los Angeles: Institute of Government and Public Affairs, U. of California, Los Angeles, Je 1, 1967. [Watts riot of August, 1965]

Morrison, Edward B., and Stivers, James A. A Summary of the Assessments of the District's Integration Programs, 1964-1971. Sacramento, CA: Sacramento City Unified School District, 1971.

Moskowitz, Joel M., and Wortman, Paul M. A Secondary Analysis of the Riverside School Desegregation Study. Evanston, IL: Division of Methodology and Evaluation Research, Department of Psychology, Northwestern U., 1977.

Moskowitz, Ronald. "Berkeley: First Big City to Integrate Totally." Education News, S 23, 1968.

_____. "California District Asks F.B.I. to Probe 'Fear Campaign.'" Education News, O 21, 1968. [Richmond Unified School District]

_____. "'Co-Parents' Aid Integration in San Mateo." Education News, Ag 5, 1968.

_____. "San Francisco, California: Where San Francisco Went Wrong." In Norene Harris, Nathaniel Jackson, and Carl Rydingsword and contributors, The Integration of American Schools: Problems, Experiences, Solutions, pp. 62-71. Boston: Allyn & Bacon, 1975.

Murphy, Larry George. "'Equality Before Law': The Struggle of Nineteenth-Century Black Californians for Social and Political Justice." Doctoral dissertation, Graduate Theological Union, 1973. Univ. Microfilms Order No. 73-23123.

Murphy, Raymond J., and Watson, James M. The Structure of Discontent: The Relationship Between Social Structure, Grievance, and Support for the Los Angeles Riot. Los Angeles: Institute of Government and Public Affairs, U. of California, Los Angeles, Je 1, 1967.

Musladin, William R. "An Ethno-Historical Survey of the Sacramento Region of California." Master's thesis, California State U., Sacramento, 1969.

Myhill, Marjorie, with Becker, Natalie. Power and Participation in the San Francisco Community Action Program, 1964-1967. Berkeley, CA: Institute of Urban and Regional Development, U. of California, Berkeley, D, 1967.

"New California Law on Segregation." Integrated Education (My-Je, 1972):68-69.

Robert 9X and Raymond 11X. "California School District Center of Jim Crow Issue." Muhammad Speaks, Ap 24, 1970. [Pasadena]

"No Busing for Watts." Nation, Mr 18, 1968.

North, William E. Catholic Education in Southern California. Washington, DC: Catholic U. of America, 1936.

Oakland Public Schools. Quality Education in Oakland. Guidelines for Improving Educational Opportunity. Oakland, CA: Oakland Public Schools, F, 1966.

O'Connor, Michael J. "The Character of Stable Interracial Areas in the Greater Los Angeles Urban Area." Master's thesis, California State U., Los Angeles, 1976.

Ogbu, John U. The Next Generation. An Ethnography of Education in an Urban Neighborhood. New York: Academic Press, 1974. [Stockton]

_____. Racial Stratification and Education. The Case of Stockton, California. New York: Institute of Urban and Minority Education, Teachers College, Columbia U., 1977.

Oliver, Myrna. "Realtors Finding Little Exodus Effect." Los Angeles Times, Je 18, 1978. [Los Angeles]

O'Shea, David W. "School District Decentralization. The Case of Los Angeles." Education and Urban Society 7(Ag, 1975):377-392.

O'Shea, David W., Gordon, C. Wayne, and Ginsburg, Mark B. "Desegregation in Los Angeles School District: Report of a Public Opinion Survey." Educational Research Quarterly 1(Spring, 1976):1-17.

Overend, William. "Beverly Hills and Watts." Los Angeles Times, Ag 4, 1976. [Beverly Hills High School and David Stan Jordan High School]

Parker, Elizabeth L., and Abajian, James. A Walking Tour of the Black Presence in San Francisco During the Nineteenth Century. San Francisco: San Francisco American Historical and Cultural Society, 1974.

Parker, Thomas H. "Berkeley Epilogue." In T. Bentley Edwards and Frederick M. Wirt, School Desegregation in the North. San Francisco: Chandler, 1967.

Parsons, Edgar W. "California Faces Crucial Civil Rights Test." Phi Delta Kappan, O, 1964.

Payne, Joseph F. "Race, Reading and Poverty in Los Angeles." Integrated Education (N-D, 1971):15-21.

Pettyjohn, Leonard F. "Factorial Ecology of the Los Angeles-Long Beach Black Population." Doctoral dissertation, U. of Wisconsin-Milwaukee, 1976.

Pincus, John. "Integration Could Aid Reform." Los Angeles Times, S 12, 1976. [Los Angeles]

_____. "Integration Could Mean Better Education." Los Angeles Times, N 14, 1976. [Los Angeles]

Pitts, Raymond J. (ed.). Compensatory Education Program. Abraham Lincoln Elementary School. A Final Summary Report of the McAteer Pilot Project. Pasadena Unified School District, Pasadena, CA, 1966.

Platt, William J. Educational Organization for Desegregation. Menlo Park, CA: Stanford Research Institute, Ap 21, 1967. [San Francisco]

Platt, William J., and Harker, Robert A. Improving Racial Balance in the San Francisco Public Schools. Menlo Park, CA: Stanford Research Institute, My 15, 1967.

Polos, Nicholas C. "Segregation and John Swett." Southern California Quarterly, Mr, 1964. [1850's-1860's]

Posey, Ernest M. "Desegregation in the Pasadena Schools: A Community Effort." Honors thesis, Harvard College, 1972.

Powers, Charles T. "Law and Disorder at San Fernando High." Los Angeles Times, S 30, 1974.

Powers, William F. Population Projection to 1971. Prepared for San Francisco Unified School District. Menlo Park, CA: Stanford Research Institute, Mr 31, 1967. [By census tracts and individual schools]

Preusser, Serena B. (comp.). "Color Question in California Reveals Many Problems." California Real Estate, Jl, 1927.

Price, Monroe E. "School Desegregation: Why It Must Go On." Los Angeles Times, S 10, 1978. [Los Angeles]

Pugh, Nathaniel, Jr. "The Human Element in Alternative Education." NAASP Bulletin 56 (My, 1972):111-115. [Berkeley, California experimental schools]

Purl, Mabel C. The Achievement of Pupils in Desegregated Schools. Riverside, CA: Riverside Unified School District, 1971.

_____. The Riverside School Integration Study: Introduction, Period Survey, and Teacher Questionnaire, 1970, 59 pp. Riverside, CA: Riverside Unified School District. ERIC ED 042 833.

_____. Survey of Parent Attitudes Toward Schools. Riverside, CA: Riverside School Study, Ja, 1970.

Purl, Mabel C., and Curtis, Jonathan. Analysis of the "Questionnaire on Experience of Elementary School Teachers with School Desegregation, September, 1966 to March, 1968." Riverside, CA: Riverside School Study, Ja, 1970.

_____ and _____. Continuation of Analysis of the "Questionnaire on Experience of Elementary School Teachers with School Desegregation, September, 1966 to March, 1968." Riverside, CA: Riverside School Study, Ja, 1970.

_____ and _____. A Look at Combination Class Effects at Emerson Elementary School. McAteer Project M9-14, My, 1970. Riverside, CA: Riverside Unified School District. ERIC ED 042 863.

_____ and _____. Raven's Progressive Matrices Test Correlations with Measures of Large-Thorndike and Wechsler Intelligence Tests, S, 1970. Riverside, CA: Riverside Unified School District. ERIC ED 052 231.

Purl, Mabel C., and Sawson, Judith. A Report on the Achievement of Elementary Pupils in Integrated Schools. McAteer Project M9-14, My, 1970. Riverside, CA: Riverside Unified School District. ERIC ED 042 864.

Purl, Mabel C., and Singer, Harry. A Study of Desegregation in the Public Schools, Riverside, California. Riverside School Study, Progress Report 1968-1969. Project No. M8-14, Mr 15, 1969. Riverside, CA: U. of California, Riverside; Riverside Unified School District. ERIC ED 043 691.

Rabinovitz, Francine F., with Siembieda, William J. Minorities in Suburbs: The Los Angeles Experience. Lexington, MA: Lexington Books, 1977.

Rapoport, Roger. "Peninsula Busing Battle Takes a Strange Turn." San Francisco Chronicle, Mr 24, 1978. [East Palo Alto and adjacent areas]

Rapp, M. L. and others. Project R-3, San Jose California: Evaluation of Results and Development of a Cost Model. Santa Monica, CA: Rand, Mr, 1971.

Ratican, Diane E. "Integration Policy in Los Angeles City Schools." Master's thesis, U. of California, Los Angeles, 1970.

Real, James. "Mumbo Jumbo, a Cross Burning, a 'Parade.'" Los Angeles Times, Ja 15, 1975. [Ku Klux Klan in Alabama, 1927]

Record, Wilson. Minority Groups and Intergroup Relations in the San Francisco Bay Area. Berkeley: Institute of Governmental Studies, U. of California, My, 1963.

_____. "School Board and Negro Teacher in California." Integrated Education, Ap, 1963.

Reed, Roy. "Classic Segregation Crisis: Pasadena." New York Times, Ap 7, 1969.

Reich, Kenneth. "Clovis School System Pits Students Against Peers." Los Angeles Times, Je 20, 1977.

Reimullor, P. "On Teaching Folk Music in the Integrated Classroom: Kindergarten Through Third Grade," Final Progress Report (Addendum E). Riverside, CA: Riverside School Study, Ag, 1968.

Reynolds, William H. Experience of Los Angeles Employers with Minority Group Employees. Pasadena: Graduate School of Business Administration, U. of Southern California, 1967.

Riggle, W. H. "The White, the Black, and the Gray: A Study of Student Sub-Cultures in a Suburban California High School." Doctoral dissertation, U. of California, 1965.

Riles, Wilson C. "Parents Advise on Policy." American Education, O, 1968.

Riles, Wilson C. and others. Racial and Ethnic Survey of California Public Schools. Part II. Distribution of Employees, 1967, 45 pp. Sacramento, CA: California State Department of Education. ERIC ED 019 166.

"Wilson Riles Speaking..." (interview). San Francisco Chronicle, S 22, 1974.

"Riot Anatomy: How Crazed Police Sparked School Upheaval." Muhammad Speaks, Mr 28, 1969. [Carver Junior High School, Los Angeles]

Rischin, Moses. "Immigration, Migration, and Minorities in California: A Reassessment." Pacific Historical Review, F, 1972.

Riverside Unified School District and University of California, Riverside. A Study of Desegregation in the Public Schools, Riverside, California. A Progress Report. Riverside, CA: Riverside Unified School District, Ag 31, 1967.

Roberts, Steven V. "Pasadena, After Year, Adjusts to Busing, But Opposition Remains." New York Times, N 21, 1971.

Rodeheaver, Joseph N., Hampton, Clarence, Davies, Richard D., and White, Jacqueline W. "Black Studies Program in Berkeley, California." Bulletin of the National Association of Secondary School Principals 54(1970): 77-110.

Roeser, Veronica A. "Note De Facto School Segregation and the Law: Focus San Diego." San Diego Law Review 5(Ja, 1968):57-82.

Rosales, Michael A. "A History of Bilingual-Bicultural Education in the Los Angeles Unified School District." Master's thesis, U. of California, Los Angeles, 1971.

Rose, Robert. Back Row for Niggers. Los Angeles: Aware Press, 1970. [Muscott Elementary School, San Bernadino]

Rosenblum, Abraham L. "Social Class Membership and Ethnic Prejudice in Cedar City." Doctoral dissertation, U. of Southern California, 1959.

Rosenthal, Robert, and Jacobson, Lenore. Pygmalion in the Classroom. Teacher Expectation and Pupils' Intellectual Development. New York: Holt, Rinehart, and Winston, 1968.

Ross, Howard R., and Moon, Albert E. Transportation Requirements for Improved Racial Balance. Menlo Park, CA: Stanford Research Institute, My 15, 1967. [San Francisco]

Rowe, Robert N. "Why We Abandoned Our Traditional Junior High." Nation's Schools, Ja, 1967. [Berkeley]

_____. "Is Berkeley School Integration Successful?" American School Board Journal, D, 1965.

Rubin, Lillian B. Busing and Backlash: White Against White in an Urban School District. Berkeley, CA: U. of California Press, 1972. [Richmond]

_____. "White Against White: School Desegregation and the Revolt of Middle America." School Review 84(My, 1976):373-389. [Richmond]

Ruiz, Raul. "People of the State of California vs. Ruben and Candida Serna and Raul and Martha Wilson." La Raza 3(Spring, 1977): 43-44. [Los Angeles]

Russell, H. M. H., and Nielson, R. S. "Parental Attitude Toward School Desegregation and Bussing: A Longitudinal Study." Doctoral dissertation, United States International U., 1973. [Riverside]

Rustin, Bayard. "The Watts 'Manifesto.'" New America, S 17, 1965. [Los Angeles]

Ryan, Robert G. "An Evaluation of a Program for the Modification of Disruptive Student Behavior." Doctoral dissertation, U. of Southern California, 1975. [Lexington School, Pomona Unified School District]

"SUSD Desegregation: Report on First Year [of Desegregation]." Stockton Record, Je 6, 1976.

St. Augustine Community Workers. "Durant Elementary School Run by Fascists." Black Panther, F 13, 1971. [Oakland]

Sacramento City Unified School District. A Summary of Assessments of the District's Integration Programs, 1964-1971. Sacramento, CA: The District, S 28, 1971.

Samuels, Gertrude. "How School Busing Works in Our Town." New York Times Magazine, S 27, 1970. [Berkeley]

Sandelius, Stanley E. "Employment of Certificated Personnel of Ethnic Minority Groups in Stockton Unified School District, 1947-1962." Master's thesis, U. of the Pacific, 1963.

Sandoval, Sally Jane. "Ghetto Growing Pains: The Impact of Negro Migration on the City of Los Angeles, 1940-1960." Master's thesis, California State U., 1974. Univ. Microfilms Order No. M-5267.

Scheer, Robert. "New Set of Values for the Middle Class." Los Angeles Times, Ja 31, 1978. [Jewish community in Los Angeles]

Schneider, Phillip W. "In Sausalito...Since Desegregation." Educational Leadership 24 (My, 1967):709-716.

"School Progress in San Bernadino." (documents) Integrated Education, Ap-My, 1967.

Schuster, Jeannette W. "The Values of Negro and Caucasian Children: Do They Differ?" Journal of Negro Education, Winter, 1968.

Scientific Analysis Corporation. Educational R & D and the Case of Berkeley's Experimental Schools, N, 1976. ERIC ED 132 741.

Scott, Austin. "Black Youths Jobs Picture Still Bleak." Los Angeles Times, D 24, 1978.

Scott, Johnie. "My Home is Watts." Harper's, O, 1966.

Scott-Blair, Michael. "Pasadena Shows Fundamental School Pitfalls." San Diego Union, Jl 4, 1977.

Seidenbaum, Art. "Los Angeles: Private Integration of the Public Schools." Integrated Education (N-D, 1968):14-18.

Serrano, Tirso G. Project to Improve Equality of Educational Opportunities in Redlands, School Year 1969-70. Title IV Evaluation, N 16, 1970. ERIC ED 048 385.

Shannon, Thomas A. "California Statutory Provisions Governing Pupil Racial and Ethnic Imbalance in California Public Schools." In Kathleen Siggers, With Justice for All, pp. 35-46. Riverside, CA: Western Regional School Desegregation Projects, U. of California, Je, 1972.

Shippey, Mervyn. Visalia Colored School, 1970 [orig., 1871]. R and E Research Associates, 4843 Mission Street, San Francisco, CA 94112.

Shockley, L. S. How Did We Allow This to Happen to Our Schools? Riverside, CA: Riverside School Study, S, 1968. [Emerson Elementary School]

Shradar, Victor Lee. "Ethnic Politics, Religion, and the Public Schools of San Francisco, 1849-1933." Doctoral dissertation, Stanford U., 1974. Univ. Microfilm 74-27, 113.

Sifuentes, Frank. "Integrated Segregation in the City of the Angels." Regeneración 1 (1970):4-5.

Siggers, Kathleen. "In Transition--An Odyssey in Integration." Intergroup 2(Je, 1972). [Pasadena, Inglewood, Riverside, Hanford, Merced, Berkeley, and Sacramento]

Sigurdson, Herbert S. and others. "The Crenshaw Project: An Experiment in Urban Community Development." Sociology and Social Research 51(1967):432-444. [Los Angeles]

Silberman, Harry F. An Evaluation of Decentralization in a Large School District, Ap, 1977. ERIC ED 139 816. [Los Angeles]

Simross, Lynn. "The Making Over of an Alma Mater." Los Angeles Times, Ag 22, 1977. [Manual Arts High School, Los Angeles]

_____. "Natural Desegregation at Van Nuys High." Los Angeles Times, F 16, 1979. [Los Angeles]

Singer, Harry. Effect of Integration on Achievement of Anglos, Blacks, and Mexican Americans, Mr 30, 1970. ERIC ED 041 975. [Riverside]

Singer, Harry, and Hendrick, Irving G. "Total School Integration: An Experiment in Social Reconstruction." Phi Delta Kappan, N, 1967. [Riverside]

Singleton, Robert, and Bullock, Paul. "Some Problems in Minority-Group Education in the Los Angeles Public Schools." Journal of Negro Education, Spring, 1963.

Skelton, Nancy. "State KKK Chief: Striving for Inequality." Los Angeles Times, Ap 16, 1978.

Slater, Jack. "Learning is an All-Black Thing." Ebony 26(S, 1971):88-92. [Nairobi Day Schools, East Palo Alto, California]

Smith, Paul Alan. "Negro Settlement in Los Angeles, California, 1890 to 1930." Master's thesis, California State U., Northridge, 1973.

Smith, William. "Youth--A View from Berkeley. II Black Youth." In Daniel Adelson, Man As the Measure: The Crossroads, pp. 78-88. New York: Behavioral Publications, 1972.

Spellman, Judith B., Peterson, Gertrude D., Rosenthal, Ann H., and Boyan, Norman J. Adapting to Changing Racial and Ethnic Composition: A Survey of San Francisco Teachers and Principals. Menlo Park, CA: Stanford Research Institute, My 15, 1967.

Spiva, Ulysses V. "An Exploratory Analysis of the California State Board of Education and its Policies Toward Racial Isolation in the Public Schools." Doctoral dissertation, Stanford U., 1971.

State Board of Education. "Afro-American Teaching Credentials in California." Integrated Education (Mr-Ap, 1969):56-60.

State Committee on Public Education. Citizens for the 21st Century. Long-Range Considerations for California Elementary and Secondary Education. Report to the California State Board of Education, Je, 1967.

Steinberg, Warren. "Diversity: Hurrah for What It Teaches." Los Angeles Times, Je 22, 1977. [Le Conte Junior High School, Hollywood]

Stemmock, Susanne K. The Human Relations Specialist in Local School Systems, 1970-71. Washington, DC: Educational Research Service, 1971.

Streets, Virgus Otis. Special Needs of Negroes: PROJECT DESIGN. Educational Needs, Fresno, 1968, Number 28, 1968. ERIC ED 038 766.

"Students in Survey Support Integration." Los Angeles Times, D 17, 1975. [Students in twelve Los Angeles high schools]

Stumbo, Bella. "'White Flight' No Cheap Alternative." Los Angeles Times, Je 18, 1978. [Los Angeles]

Sullivan, Neil V. "Discussion Implementing Equal Educational Opportunity." Harvard Educational Review, Winter, 1968. [Berkeley]

_____. "School Desegregation in Berkeley: The School Superintendent Reports." In U.S. Commission on Civil Rights, Papers Prepared for National Conference on Equal Educational Opportunity in America's Cities. Washington, DC: GPO, 1968.

Sullivan, Neil V., and Stewart, Evelyn S. Now Is the Time. Integration in the Berkeley Schools. Bloomington, IN: U. of Indiana Press, 1970.

Sumner, G. C. Project R-3. Allocation of Students Among Groups. Santa Monica, CA: Rand, F, 1971. [San Jose]

Swerdlick, Steven Richard. "The Life and Death of An Integrated School." Doctoral dissertation, Stanford U., 1977. [Menlo Park]

Task Force on the Resolution of Conflict. A Report on Conflict and Violence in California's High Schools. Sacramento, CA: State Department of Education, 1973.

Tate, Will D. The New Black Elites. San Francisco: R and E Research Associates, 1976. [Oakland]

"Teacher and Parents Wage Reading Campaign Against Low Reading Scores." La Raza, F 10, 1968. [Reading deficiencies in East Los Angeles]

Thernstrom, Stephan. The Growth of Los Angeles in Historical Perspective: Myth and Reality. Los Angeles: Institute of Government and Public Affairs, 1970.

Thompson, Noah D. "These 'Colored' United States: California: The Horn of Plenty." Messenger 6(Jl, 1924):215-221.

Thorp, Alicia. "'I Don't Want My Child Going to School in the Inner City.'" Los Angeles Times, Ja 25, 1977. [Los Angeles]

Thuesen, Donald C. "Equity: Removal of Restrictive Covenants in California--What Constitutes Changed Conditions." Hastings Law Journal 7(F, 1956):209-213.

Thurman, A. Odell. "The Negro in California Before 1890." Pacific Historian 20(Summer, 1976):177-188.

_____. "The Negro in California Before 1890," Part II. Pacific Historian 20(Spring, 1976): 67-72.

_____. "The Negro in California to 1890." Master's thesis, U. of the Pacific, 1945.

Tisdale, James D. "A Study of the Attitudes of Outstanding Teachers in Black, Educationally Disadvantaged, Inner-City Elementary Schools in the Los Angeles School District." Doctoral dissertation, Brigham Young U., 1971.

Tom, Benjamin. "On Politics and Education in San Francisco: Commentary by the President, Board of Education." Amerasia Journal 5 (1978):87-99.

Toogood, James L. Adult Population Distribution with Regard to Social, Economic, and Ethnic Characteristics, 1969. Sacramento, CA. ERIC ED 038 567.

Toto, Charles U., Jr. "A History of Education in California, 1800-1850." Doctoral dissertation, U. of California, Berkeley, 1967. Univ. Microfilms Order No. 67-11,670.

Toward Equal Employment Opportunity for Teachers in California's Public Schools. Sacramento, CA: California State Department of Education, 1964. [Order from Bureau of Textbooks and Publications, Department of Education, 721 Capitol Mall, Sacramento, CA, 95814]

Townsend, J. Holland. "American Caste, and Common Schools." Anglo-African Magazine, Mr, 1859.

Trombley, William. "Half of White Parents Oppose Integration." Los Angeles Times, Je 7, 1977. [Los Angeles]

_____. "Integration Plan Proves Limited." Los Angeles Times, D 25, 1978. [San Diego]

_____. "'Learning Centers' Mix Pupils." Los Angeles Times, D 25, 1978. [Two "learning centers" in San Diego]

_____. "San Bernardino." Integrateducation 15(N-D, 1977):103-104.

_____. "San Bernardino Experimenting With Voluntary School Busing." Los Angeles Times, Ja 31, 1977.

_____. "San Diego Faces School Integration Issue." Los Angeles Times, Ag 1, 1977.

_____. "U.C. Riverside Research Focuses on Effect of School Integration." Los Angeles Times, Jl 16, 1967.

Trombley, William and others. "White Flight-- the Unknown Factor." Los Angeles Times, Je 18, 1978. [Los Angeles]

Trompeter, John F. "The Relationship of Selected Financial, Education-Governmental, and Community Characteristics to Increases in Local Income Expenditure in California's Unified School Districts." Doctoral dissertation, U. of Southern California, My, 1971.

Tsukashima, R. T. "The Social and Psychological Correlates of Anti-Semitism in the Black Community." Doctoral dissertation, U. of California, Los Angeles, 1973. [Los Angeles]

Turner, Ralph H. The Social Context of Ambition: A Study of High-School Seniors in Los Angeles. San Francisco: Chandler, 1964.

U.S. Commission on Civil Rights. A Generation Deprived. Los Angeles School Desegregation. Washington, DC: The Commission, My, 1977.

_____. Civil Rights USA/Public Schools North and West. 1963. Oakland.

_____. Different but Equal: University of California Research to Improve Teaching of Disadvantaged Children, My, 1967. [Pamphlet. Copies available from Office of University Relations, 101 University Hall, Berkeley, CA 94720]

_____. Hearings...Los Angeles, CA...and San Francisco...1960. Washington, DC: GPO, 1960.

_____. "Oxnard, California." In School Desegregation in Ten Communities, pp. 215-235. Washington, DC: GPO, Je, 1973.

_____. "Pasadena, California." In School Desegregation in Ten Communities, pp. 110-113. Washington, DC: GPO, Je, 1973.

_____. "Riverside, California." In School Desegregation in Ten Communities, pp. 152-176. Washington, DC: GPO, Je, 1973.

U.S. Commission on Civil Rights, California Advisory Committee. An Analysis of the McCone Commission Report. Washington, DC: The Commission, Ja, 1966.

_____. Evaluation of Educable Mentally Retarded Programs in California. Washington, DC: The Commission, My, 1977.

_____. The Schools of Guadalupe...A Legacy of Educational Oppression. Washington, DC: U.S. Commission on Civil Rights, Ap, 1973.

_____. State Administration of Bilingual Administration--Si or No? Washington, DC: The Commission, Je, 1976.

U.S. Congress, 90th, 2nd Session, 91st, 1st Session, Senate, Select Committee on Nutrition and Human Needs. Nutrition and Human Needs. Hearings... Part 9--California. Washington, DC: GPO, 1969.

U.S. Congress, 92nd, 1st Session, Senate, Select Committee on Equal Educational Opportunity. Equal Educational Opportunity. Hearings... Part 9A--San Francisco and Berkeley, California. Washington, DC: GPO, 1971.

U.S. Department of Commerce. Hard-Core Unemployment and Poverty in Los Angeles. Washington, DC: GPO, 1965.

U.S. Department of Justice. "Federal Action Against Pasadena Schools." Integrated Education, Ja-F, 1969.

U.S. Equal Employment Opportunity Commission. Hearings...On Utilization of Minority and Women Workers in Certain Major Industries... Los Angeles, California, March 12-14, 1969. Washington, DC: GPO, 1969.

U.S. Office of Education. "Berkeley, California." In Working Together. Case Studies of Title I, ESEA Programs in Four Desegregated School Districts. Washington, DC: GPO, 1974.

"The Wakefield Decision." Integrated Education: RACE AND SCHOOLS 9(Mr-Ap, 1971):35-39.

Walker, Olive. "The Windsor Hills School Story." Integrated Education: RACE AND SCHOOLS 8(My-Je, 1970):4-9.

Walton, Sidney. [Letter of resignation as Coordinator of Multicultural Activities in the Palo Alto, CA, public schools] The Black Panther, Mr 9, 1969. [Speech of F 16, 1969]

Warren, Neil D. "Who Are the Backward?" New Society, Ag 28, 1969. [Riverside]

Washington, Kenneth S. and others. Task Force to Reevaluate Social Science Textbooks Grades Five Through Eight, 1971. ERIC ED 063 521.

"Watts. 10 Years Later. A Special Report." Los Angeles Times, Mr 23, 1975.

Webster, Staten W. "Desegregation and Beyond: The Sausalito-Mill Valley School Programs." In T. Bentley Edwards and Frederick M. Wirt, School Desegregation in the North. San Francisco: Chandler, 1967.

_____. "The Influence of Interracial Contact on Social Acceptance in a Newly Integrated School." Journal of Educational Psychology, LII, 1961. [San Francisco]

Webster, Staten W., and Pugh, Nathaniel. The Team Approach to Solving Problems of Desegregation and the Disadvantaged Student in the Oakland Public Schools: A Fall and Spring Institute for Selected Teachers and Administrators of the Oakland Public Schools, Ap 25, 1967. ERIC ED 030 701.

THE STATES / 227

Weeks, Harold L. Elementary School Integration and Academic Achievement. Some Illustrative Baseline Data from the 1971-72 SFUSD Sixth Grade and the 1970-71 Richmond Complex Primary Schools. San Francisco: San Francisco Unified School District, Mr, 1972.

Weil, Raymond. "The Integrated Neighborhood. Unheralded Example and Bypassed Opportunity." Integrator, Winter, 1967-1968. [Morningside Park Neighbors in Inglewood, CA]

Weinberg, Carl. "Education Level and Perceptions of Los Angeles Negroes of Educational Conditions in a Riot Area." Journal of Negro Education, Fall, 1967.

Weinberg, Meyer. "The Wakefield Ruling." Intergroup 1(Ap, 1971).

Weiner, Steven. "Educational Decisions in an Organized Anarchy." Doctoral dissertation, Stanford U., 1972. [San Francisco]

Weiss, Michael. "Education, Literacy and the Community of Los Angeles in 1850." Southern California Quarterly 60(Summer, 1978):117-142.

Wells, Larry. "[Alternative School] Options in a Small District: Berkeley." NAASP Bulletin 57(S, 1973):55-60.

Wenkert, Robert. "Accommodation and Conflict Between Racial Groups in an American Community." Doctoral dissertation, Oxford U., 1971. [Richmond]

_____. An Historical Digest of Negro-White Relations in Richmond, California. Berkeley, CA: Survey Research Center, U. of Ca California, 1967.

Wennerberg, C. H. Desegregation of the Berkeley Public Schools. Its Feasibility and Implementation. Berkeley, CA: Berkeley Unified School District, My, 1964.

Western Regional School Desegregation Projects. Attitudes Toward School Desegregation in Riverside and Redlands. Riverside: U. of California, Riverside, 1970.

Wharton, Marianna, and Connolly, Leo. Survey of California Apprentices, 1969. Minority Participation in Apprenticeship, Characteristics of Registered Apprentices. Sacramento, CA: Division of Apprenticeship Standards, 1970.

Wheeldin, Donald. "The Situation in Watts Today." Freedomways, Winter, 1967.

Whitaker, Ollie Louise. "The History and Development of Educational Programs for the Negro in the Santa Ana Unified District." Master's thesis, Chapman College, 1971.

Whitlock, Sylvia V. "An Assessment of Article 3.3 Multicultural In-Service Training in Selected Districts." Doctoral dissertation, Claremont Graduate School, 1978. Univ. Microfilms Order No. 7823865.

Widaatalla, Ahmed M. "Effect of Racial Change on the Tax Base of the City of Compton." Doctoral dissertation, U. of California, Los Angeles. Univ. Microfilms Order No. 71-729.

Williams, Dorothy Slade. "Ecology of Negro Communities in Los Angeles County: 1940-1959." Doctoral dissertation, U. of Southern California, 1961. Univ. Microfilms Order No. 61-02541.

Williams, Pauli. "Windsor Hills: A Unique L.A. School." Race Relations Reporter 4(Ag 6, 1973):7-8.

Williams, Roger M. "State of Siege at '135 Van Ness.'" Saturday Review 2(My, 1975). [San Francisco]

Williford, Stanley O. "A Gadfly Exonerated." Race Relations Reporter 5(S, 1974):6-7. [C. Edmund Bradley, Los Angeles]

Wilson, Alan B. The Consequences of Segregation: Academic Achievement in a Northern Community. Berkeley, CA: Glendessary Press, 1969. [Richmond]

_____. "Educational Consequences of Segregation in a California Community." In Racial Isolation in the Public Schools, Vol. II. Washington, DC: GPO, 1967. [Richmond]

Winston, Judith A. Desegregating Urban Schools: Educational Equality/Quality in San Francisco Public Schools. A Report, S, 1970. ERIC ED 049 321.

Wirt, Frederick M. Power in the City. Berkeley: U. of California Press, 1974. [San Francisco]

Wogaman, T. O. "Berkeley Story: Desegregation Under the Ramsey Plan." California Education, D, 1965.

_____. "Desegregation in Berkeley: Some Applicable Lessons." Urban Review, Ap, 1969.

Wolfinger, Raymond E., and Greenstein, Fred I. "The Repeal of Fair Housing in California: An Analysis of Referendum Voting." American Political Science Review, S, 1968.

Wollenberg, Charles M. "All Deliberate Speed: Segregation and Exclusion in California Schools: 1855-1975." Doctoral dissertation, U. of California, Berkeley, 1975.

_____. "Ethnic Experiences in California History: An Impressionistic Survey." California Historical Quarterly 50(S, 1971).

_____ (ed.). Ethnic Conflict in California History. Los Angeles: Tinnon-Brown, 1970.

Worthington, Brenda Lane. "Blacks Who've Climb-
ed to the Top of the Hill." Los Angeles
Times, O 9, 1977. [Black upper class in Los
Angeles]

X, Acre (Sammson). "Oakland's School Superin-
tendent Discusses Educational Problems."
Muhammad Speaks, O 15, 1971. [Dr. Marcus
Foster]

5X, Larry. "Blacks Ignored in S.F. Teachers'
Strike." Muhammad Speaks, My 3, 1974.

_____. "The Forgotten Victim of the Symbionese
Liberation Army." Muhammad Speaks, My 3,
1974. [Superintendent Marcus Foster, San
Francisco public schools]

Yeazell, S. C. "Intervention and the Idea of
Litigation: A Commentary on the Los Angeles
School Case." UCLA Law Review 25(D, 1977):
244-260.

Yen, Katherine, and Weeks, Harold L. "Evaluation of School Attainment of Need #4: Redi-
rection of Academic Disparity." Final Evaluation Report, Emergency School Aid Act,
School Year 1973-74. San Francisco: San
Francisco Unified School District, Jl, 1974.

Young, Kimball. Immigrant Groups in California.
Eugene, OR: U. of Oregon, Jl, 1922. [U. of
Oregon Publication, Vol. I, No. 11]

Young, Richard. "The Impact of Protest Leadership on Negro Politicians in San Francisco."
Western Political Quarterly 22(Mr, 1969):94-
111.

                        Colorado

"A Five Year Report: Schools and Integration
[in Denver, Colorado]." Alternatives in
American Education 1(Mr-Ap, 1971):1-12.
[Center for the Study of Education, Box 192,
Arvada, CO 80002]

Abbott, Carl. "Plural Society in Colorado:
Ethnic Relations in the Twentieth Century."
Phylon 39(Fall, 1978):250-260.

Adams, Darrell K. and others. Minority Group-
Governmental Agency Relations, 1966. ERIC
ED 037 29].

Atkins, James A. Human Relations in Colorado.
A Historical Record. Denver: Colorado State
Department of Education, O, 1968.

_____. "Report on De Facto Segregation in the
Denver Public Schools." Denver Post, My 15,
1962.

Bacon, Robert S. "Ethnic and Racial Community
Space in Denver." Great Plains-Rocky Mountain
Geographical Journal 4(1975):9-16.

_____. "Racial and Ethnic Redistribution in
Denver, Colorado: 1960 and 1970." Ohio Geographers: Recent Research Themes 3(1975):1-9.

Bardwell, George E. Park Hill Area of Denver:
1950-1966. Denver: Denver Commission on
Community Relations, 1966.

Barnes, Medill McCormick. "The Neighborhood
School Comes to Denver." Integrator, Fall,
1969.

Belcher, Jerry. "School Busing: How Far Has It
Come?" Los Angeles Times, D 15, 1975.
[Denver]

Berwanger, Eugene H. "William J. Hardin:
Colorado Spokesman for Racial Justice, 1863-
1973." Colorado Magazine 52(Winter, 1975).

Black Education Advisory Committee. Progress
Report. 1974. Denver: Denver Public
Schools, 1974. [Reprinted in U.S. Commission
on Civil Rights, Hearing Held in Denver,
Colorado, February 17-19, 1976. Washington,
DC: The Commission, 1978.]

Branscombe, Art. "A Proposal for Part-time Desegregation." Denver Post, F 10, 1974.
[Denver]

_____. "Denver." Integratteducation 15(N-D,
1977):11-13.

_____. "It Is Time to Evaluate the Peformance
of the Denver School Board." Denver Post,
Ap 22, 1973.

_____. "The Malaise in Denver's Public High
Schools." Denver Post, Je 11, 1972.

Cardenas, Jose A. An Education Plan for the
Denver Public Schools, Ja 21, 1974. ERIC ED
096 046.

Carter, Charles, and Dunning, John. [School Integration in Denver] Denver Post, D 14, 1969-
D 21, 1969. [Seven articles]

Center for Social Research and Development.
Socioeconomic Data Rank Ordered for Colorado.
Denver: U. of Denver, F, 1973. [Reprinted
in U.S. Congress, 93rd, 1st Session, Senate,
Committee on Labor and Public Welfare, Sub-
committee on Education, Education Legislation,
1973. Hearings..., Part 2, pp. 476-544.
Washington, DC: GPO, 1973.]

Chafee, Ann. "Denver--A Parent's View." Integratteducation 15(N-D, 1977).

_____. "Montbello--A 'Turned-on' Community."
Integratteducation 15(S-O, 1977).

Commission on Professional Rights and Responsi-
bilities. Colorado, A Study of Educational
Finance. Washington, DC: National Education
Association, S, 1968.

Community Education Council. Monitor's Guide.
Denver: C.E.C., 1975. [Reprinted in U.S.
Commission on Civil Rights, Hearing Held in
Denver, Colorado. February 17-19, 1976, pp.
930-964. Washington, DC: The Commission,
1978.]

Cortese, C. The Impact of Black Mobility: Selective Migration and Community Change. Report to the National Science Foundation. Denver: Department of Sociology, U. of Denver, 1964. [Park Hills Area, Denver]

Craig, Benjamin L. The Anatomy of a Busing Case [Denver], N 19, 1970. ERIC ED 044 805.

Cunningham, Alan. "Board Members Shift on Busing Order." Race Relations Reporter 4(S, 1973):5-7. [Denver]

_____. "Denver Busing Controversy Rekindled." Race Relations Reporter 5(Ap 29, 1974):1-2.

Davis, James H. "Colorado Under the Klan." Colorado Magazine 42(Spring, 1965):93-108.

Denver, Colorado, Public Schools, Department of Research. Comparative Intelligence Ratings of Pupils in Two Elementary Schools, One Primarily Made Up of Negroes and the Other of Mexicans, 1930.

Denver Urban Observatory. Citizen Attitudes in the City and County of Denver, Colorado, Je, 1971. PB 206 933. National Technical Information Service, Springfield VA 22151.

_____. Majority-Minority Citizen Voter Attitudes in Denver. PB 214 360/0. Springfield, VA: National Technical Information Service, 1972.

Eisendrath, Ann. "'We Didn't Recon with Ellen,' Mother Says of Desegregation Role." Rocky Mountain News, O 17, 1976. [Manual High School, Denver]

Equal Educational Opportunity Policy Research Project. "Denver." Passim, in Federal Policies for Equal Educational Opportunity; Conflict and Confusion. Austin, TX: Lyndon B. Johnson School of Public Affairs, U. of Texas, 1977.

Gilberts, Robert D. Planning Quality Education. A Proposal for Integrating the Denver Public Schools. Denver: School District No. One, O, 1968.

Gross, Leonard. "A High School Fights For Its Life, and a Principal, For His." Look, Mr 9, 1971. [George Washington High School, Denver; Jack Beardshear]

Gunn, Gerald P. "Economic Aspects of Desegregation: A Case Study of the Greater Fort Collins Area." Doctoral dissertation, Colorado State U., 1973. Univ. Microfilms Order No. 74-17, 531.

Harvey, J. R. "Negroes in Colorado." Master's thesis, U. of Denver, 1941.

Jackson, Harold E. "Discrimination and Busing: The Denver School Board Election of May, 1969." Rocky Mountain Social Science Quarterly 8(O, 1971):101-108.

Jessor, R., Graves, T. D., Hanson, R. C., and Jessor, Shirley L. Society, Personality, and Deviant Behavior: A Study of a Tri-Ethnic Community. New York: Holt, 1968.

Jones, William H. History of Catholic Education in the State of Colorado. Washington, DC: Catholic U. of America, 1955.

"Keyes v. School District No. 1, Denver, Colorado." School Law Journal 3(Spring, 1973): 145-170. [Complete text of U.S. Supreme Court ruling]

Kleeman, Richard P. "Integration Is Faltering in Denver." Minneapolis Tribune, O 29, 1970.

Kline, Elliot H. "The Denver School Board Member: A Motivational, Political and Demographic Profile." Doctoral dissertation, U. of Colorado, 1971.

Leonard, Stephen J. "Denver's Foreign Born Immigrants, 1859-1900." Doctoral dissertation, Claremont College, 1971. Univ. Microfilms Order No. 71-29, 641.

Lovrich, N. P., and Marenin, O. "A Comparison of Black and Mexican Voters in Denver: Assertive versus Acquiescent Political Orientation and Voting Behavior in an Urban Electorate." Western Political Quarterly 29 (Je, 1976):284-924.

Lyles, Lionel Dean. "An Historical-Urban Geographical Analaysis of Black Neighborhood Development in Denver, 1860-1970." Doctoral dissertation, U. of Colorado, 1977. Univ. Microfilms Order No. 77-29, 946.

Marriner, Gerald Lynn. "Klan Politics in Colorado." Journal of the West 15(Ja, 1976):212-223.

Mothershead, Harmon. "Negro Rights in Colorado Territory." Colorado Magazine 40(Jl, 1963): 212-223.

Nash, Gwendolyn T. "A Model for Implementing the PUSH Program for Excellence in Education: A Black Community Initiative." Doctoral dissertation, U. of Northern Colorado, 1977. Univ. Microfilms Order No. 7805511. [Denver]

O'Dell, Doyal D. The Park Hill Area of Denver: An Integrated Community? Denver: Denver Urban Observatory, 1973.

Planning Quality Education: A Proposal for Integrating the Denver Public Schools, O, 1968. ERIC ED 035 988.

Portararo, Anthony Vito. "Intraurban Social Communication Barriers: The Case of Denver, Colorado." Doctoral dissertation, Pennsylvania State U., 1974. Univ. Microfilms Order No. 75-10, 802.

Reid, Ira DeA. The Negro Population of Denver, Colorado. New York: The National Urban League, 1929.

Shaffer, Richard A. "School Integration Case Could Decide How Far North's Cities Must Go." Wall Street Journal, Je 15, 1972. [Denver]

Special Study Committee on Equality of Educational Opportunity in the Denver Public Schools. Report and Recommendations to the Board of Education, Mr 1, 1964.

Sterba, James P. "Denver: The Urban Jungle Amid Mountain Splendor." New York Times, Mr 14, 1974.

Tamminga, Harriet Linda. "Neighborhoods Without Neighborhood Schools: An Analysis of Neighborhood Contextual and Structural Effects." Doctoral dissertation, U. of Denver, 1977. Univ. Microfilm Order No. 77-28, 050. [Denver]

Trombley, William. "Integration in Denver: Can L.A. Profit?" Los Angeles Times, N 27, 1977.

"Twelve Years Later: Most Black and Chicano Children Still Attending Segregated Schools." Un Nuevo Dia 2(Fall, 1976). [Denver]

U.S. Commission on Civil Rights. Hearing Held in Denver, Colorado. February 17-19, 1976. Washington, DC: The Commission, 1978.

_____. School Desegregation in Colorado Springs, Colorado. Washington, DC: The Commission, F, 1977.

U.S. Commission on Civil Rights, Rocky Mountain Regional Office. People Who Follow the Crops. Washington, DC: GPO, 1978.

Valdez, Bernard. Urban Education Problems: Now and In the Future, Mr, 1977. ERIC ED 137 972.

"Validity of Race Discrimination in Schools as to Social Activities." Law Notes 31(N, 1927):150. [Jones v. Newton, 253 Pac. 386 Colorado]

Von Stroh, G. Denver Metropolitan Area Residential Migration: Why Citizens are Moving In and Out of Denver and the Suburban Ring. Denver: Denver Urban Observatory, 1975.

Watkins, Mark H. "The Racial Situation in Denver." Crisis 52(1945):139-140.

Watson, Lauren. "Denver Panthers Determined: Community Control of Schools." Black Panther, Je 7, 1969.

Wayne, George H. "Negro Migration and Colonization in Colorado--1870-1930." Journal of the West 15(Ja, 1976):102-120.

Weinberg, Meyer. "Elimination of Racism..." Education Colorado, N 22, 1966. [Denver, 1924-1927]

Worsham, James. "Some Denver Pupils Attend 2 Schools Daily." Boston Globe, D 24, 1975.

Yee, Leung. "Patterns of Residential Segregation--A Case Study." Great Plains--Rocky Mountain Geographical Journal 4(1975):87-93. [Denver]

Connecticut

Abraham, Cleo. "Protests and Expedients in Response to Failures in Urban Education: A Study of New Haven, 1950-1970." Doctoral dissertation, U. of Massachusetts, 1971. Univ. Microfilm Order No. 71-25, 423.

Abramson, Harold J. Ethnic Pluralism in the Connecticut Central City. Storrs, CT: Institute of Urban Research, U. of Connecticut, Ag, 1970. [Based on data from Hartford, New Haven, and Bridgeport]

Allen, Irving L., and Colfax, J. David. Urban Problems and Public Opinion in Four Connecticut Cities. Storrs, CT: Institute of Urban Research, U. of Connecticut, D, 1968.

Archer, Dane. "New Haven: Renewal and Riots." Nation, Je 3, 1968.

Atticanese, Ann M. "A Study of the New Haven Racial Disturbances and the Implication for Education in the Inner City." Master's thesis, Southern Connecticut State College, 1968.

Bair, Medill. "One Superintendent's Answer to a City's Education Problems." Phi Delta Kappan, Ja, 1969. [Hartford]

Boland, Walter R., with collaboration of Allen, Irving L., Colfax, J. David, and Stetler, Henry G. De Facto School Segregation and the Student: A Study of the Schools in Connecticut's Five Major Cities. Storrs, CT: Institute of Urban Research, U. of Connecticut, D, 1968.

Bolduc, Vincent. "Association and Community: A Case Study in Voluntary Action, Integration and Legitimacy." Doctoral dissertation, U. of Connecticut, 1975. [Blue Hills Civic Association, Hartford]

Branan, Karen. "Hartford Busing Plan Succeeds." Education News, O 7, 1968.

Buss, William G., Jr. "[De Facto Segregation in] New Haven." Law and Society Review, N, 1967.

Child, Alfred Thurston, Jr. "Prudence Crandall and the Canterbury Experiment." Bulletin of Friends' Historical Association 22(Spring, 1933):35-55.

Clark, Fred. "Suburban Nightmare." Renewal, O-N, 1968. [School integration in Bloomfield]

Coffin, Gregory C., and Sohn, David A. Darien Schools and Civil Rights. Darien, CT: Board of Education, N 23, 1965.

Connecticut Commission on Human Rights and Op-
portunities. The Status of Equal Housing
Opportunity. Hartford, CT: The Commission,
My, 1978.

Cummings, Judith. "Inner-City School Becomes
'Magnet.'" New York Times, N 18, 1975.
[Ryle Elementary School, Stamford]

Cummings, Scott. Black Children in Northern
Schools: The Pedagogy and Politics of
Failure. San Francisco: R and E Research
Associates, 1976.

Curtis, R., Timbers, D., and Jackson, E.
"Prejudice and Urban Social Participation."
American Journal of Sociology 73(1967).
New York: Center for Urban Education.
[New Haven]

Davis, Joan V. "Integrating a White Ghetto."
Saturday Review, N 20, 1965. [Darien]

Domhoff, G. William. Who Really Rules? New
Haven and Community Power Reexamined.
Goodyear, 1978.

Fellows, Lawrence. "Danbury High, Once Racially
Split, Is 'New School' Today." New York
Times, S 27, 1976.

Ferris, William H. "These 'Colored' United
States: Connecticut: The Nutmeg State."
Messenger 6(Ja, 1924):11, 24-25.

Fowler, William C. "The Historical Status of
the Negro in Connecticut." Historical Magazine 23(1874).

Freed, Donald. Agony in New Haven: The Trial
of Bobby Seale, Ericka Huggins, and the
Black Panther Party. New York: Simon &
Schuster, 1973.

Friedman, Lawrence J. "Racism and Sexism in
Ante-Bellum America: The Prudence Crandall
Episode Reconsidered." Societas 4(Summer,
1974).

Fuller, Edmund. Prudence Crandall. An Incident of Racism in Nineteenth-Century Connecticut. Middletown, CT: Wesleyan U.
Press, 1971.

"God Bless the Child That's Got His Own." The
Movement, F-Mr, 1970. [Interview with chil-
dren in a Black Panther reakfast program in
New Haven]

Handel, Gerald and others. Advancing Quality
Integrated Education in Hartford Board of
Education. This Is Project Concern. Hart-
ford, CT: Board of Education, Mr, 1967.
[A popular presentation of "A Study of Edu-
cational Programs for Elementary School
Children Involved in a Regional Desegrega-
tion Plan"]

Heffernan, Arthur J. A History of Catholic Education in Connecticut. Washington, DC:
Catholic U. of America, 1937.

"How One All-White District Tackles Civil
Rights." School Management, D, 1965.
[Darien]

Judd, Harlan C., and English James F. "Business
Involvement in Greater Hartford's Educational
Experiment." In U.S. Commission on Civil
Rights, Papers Prepared for National Confer-
ence on Equal Educational Opportunity in
America's Cities. Washington, DC: GPO,
1968.

Kenefick, Barbara. "From the Inner Eye.
Bridgeport, Connecticut, December 12."
Center Forum, D 23, 1968.

Ladd, Everett C., Jr. Ideology in America.
Ithaca, NY: Cornell U. Press, 1969.
[Hartford and Bloomfield]

Larned, Ellen D. History of Windham County,
Connecticut. 2 vols. Worcester, MA: C.
Hamilton, 1874-1880. [Material on Prudence
Crandall]

Lee, Frank F. Negro and White in a Connecticut
Town. New York: Bookman, 1961.

Levy, Marilyn. Project Concern in Cheshire. A
Preliminary Report. Cheshire, CT: Depart-
ment of Education, Ja, 1970. Reprinted in
U.S. Congress, 91st, 2nd Session, Senate,
Select Committee on Equal Educational Oppor-
tunity, Equal Educational Opportunity.
Hearings...Part 1B--Equality of Educational
Opportunity. Appendix, pp. 590-598. Wash-
ington, DC: GPO, 1970.

M. H. "Model City's High Schools Erupt."
Guardian, Je 15, 1968. [New Haven]

MacEoin, Gary. "Little Dialogue, Some Changes,
and Lots of Polarization." National Catholic
Reporter, My 28, 1971. [Hartford]

Marcin, Raymond B. "Nineteenth Century De Jure
Segregation in Connecticut." Connecticut
Bar Journal 45(1971).

Margolis, Richard J. "The Prep School World
Adjusts to the Real World." New York Times
Magazine, Ja 5, 1969. [Choate School in
Wallingford]

May, Samuel J. Some Recollections of Our Anti-
Slavery Conflict. Boston: Fields, Osgood,
1869. [Material on Prudence Crandall]

Miller, William Lee. "De Facto Segregation."
In The Fifteenth Ward and the Great Society.
Boston: Houghton Mifflin, 1966. [New Haven]

N.A.A.C.P. Bridgeport-Stratford Branch. State-
ment to the Bridgeport Board of Education on
De Facto Segregated Public Elementary Schools.
Bridgeport-Stratford Branch, NAACP, Box 262,
Bridgeport, CT, J1, 1964.

Nash, Samuel and others. "New Haven, Connecticut: New Haven Chose to Desegregate." In Norene Harris, Nathaniel Jackson, and Carl Rydingsword and contributors, The Integration of American Schools: Problems, Experiences, Solutions, pp. 93-107. Boston: Allyn & Bacon, 1975.

Overlan, S. Francis, Aronson, Sidney H., and Noble, John H. Urban-Suburban School Mixing: A Feasibility Study. West Hartford, CT: Board of Education, n.d. Reprinted in U.S. Congress, 91st, 2nd Session, Senate, Select Committee on Equal Educational Opportunity, Equal Educational Opportunity. Hearings... Part 1B--Equality of Educational Opportunity. Appendix, pp. 421-586. Washington, DC: GPO, 1970.

Pappanikou, A. J. An Evaluation of the New Haven Project Focus, 1969-70. Storrs, CT: School of Education, U. of Connecticut, 1970.

Prescott, Peter S. A World of Our Own. Notes on Life and Learning in a Boys' Preparatory School. New York: Coward-McCann, 1970. [Choate, in Wallingford]

Ralston, Carolyn, and Lewis, Anne. "Hartford, Connecticut." In NCRIEED Special Field Report, My, 1971.

Reeves, Anne. "A Clean, Well-Lighted Place." New York Times, Ja 10, 1976. [New Canaan]

Rosenthal, Harvey M. Attitudes of Stamford Elementary School Teachers Toward Education and School Desegregation. New York: Center for Urban Education, 1968.

Rosenthal, Harvey M., assisted by Zamoff, Nava. Public School Segregation and Related Population Characteristics of Stamford, Connecticut. New York: Center for Urban Education, Jl, 1967.

Samuels, Joseph M. "Busing, Reading, and Self in New Haven." Integrated Education 10(N-D, 1972):23-28.

Satz, Arthur, and Hoffman, Martin. Project Concern. Hartford, Connecticut. New York: Center for Urban Education, O, 1970.

Schlichting, Kurt Cornell. "Urban-Suburban Ecology: A Case Study of the Socioeconomic Relationship of the City of Bridgeport, Connecticut, and Its Suburbs." Doctoral dissertation, New York U., 1975. Univ. Microfilms Order No. 75-28, 589.

Schools for Hartford. Cambridge, MA: Center for Field Studies, Harvard Graduate School of Education, 1965.

Sharnik, John. "When Things Go Wrong All Blacks Are Black--and All Whites Are Whitey." New York Times Magazine, My 25, 1969. [Norwalk]

Sherman, Edna. "Prudence Crandall--Pioneer Integrationist." National Retired Teachers Association Journal 23(Jl-Ag, 1972):48-49.

Small, Edwin W., and Small, Miriam R. "Prudence Crandall, Champion of Negro Education." New England Quarterly (D, 1944):506-529.

Stableford, Lloyd W. "Westport Education Association." Today's Education, Ja, 1972. [Project Concern and white community reaction]

Stetler, Henry G. Changes in Racial Composition and De Facto Segregation in Pupils in the Public Schools of Five Connecticut Cities: 1963-1967. Storrs, CT: Institute of Urban Research, U. of Connecticut, Ja, 1969.

_____. Racial Integration in Private Residential Neighborhoods in Connecticut. Hartford: Commission on Civil Rights, 1957.

_____. Racial Integration in Public Housing Projects in Connecticut. Hartford: Commission on Civil Rights, 1955.

Study Group on Urban Schools. A Study of Urban School Needs in the Five Largest Cities in Connecticut. Storrs, CT: Educational Resources and Development Center, U. of Connecticut, 1969.

U.S. Commission on Civil Rights, Connecticut Advisory Committee. School Desegregation in Stamford, Connecticut. Washington, DC: The Commission, 1977.

U.S. Congress, 95th, 1st Session, House of Representatives, Committee on Banking, Finance, and Urban Affairs, Subcommittee on the City. Bridgeport, Connecticut: How an Old Industrial City Adapts to Change. Washington, DC: GPO, 1978.

Walker, Joe. "School's Hot Lunch Poisons 150 Black Children." Muhammad Speaks, My 14, 1971. [Helene W. Grant School, New Haven]

Watson, Franklin J. "A Comparison of Negro and White Population, Connecticut: 1940-1960." Phylon, Summer, 1968.

Weld, Ralph Foster. Slavery in Connecticut. New Haven, CT: Yale U. Press, 1935.

White, David O. "Hartford's African Schools, 1830-1868." Connecticut Historical Society Bulletin 39(Ap, 1974):47-53.

Wormley, G. Smith. "Prudence Crandall." Journal of Negro History 8(Ja, 1923):72-80.

Zamoff, Richard. "Unplanned School Desegregation." Crisis, Ag-S, 1968. [Bridgeport]

Zegans, Leonard S., Schwartz, Martin S., and Dumas, Retaugh. "A Mental Health Center's Response to Racial Crisis in an Urban High School." Psychiatry, in press, 1969. [New Haven]

Delaware

[A series of articles on desegregation in Wilmington] Partnership 1(Summer, 1976). [Published by The Center for Educational Leadership, College of Education, U. of Delaware]

Barringer, Herbert R. "Integration in Newark, Delaware: Whatever Happened to Jim Crow?" In Raymond W. Mack, Our Children's Burden. New York: Random House, 1968.

Blount, George W. "The Delaware Industrial School for Girls." Southern Workman 63(Ja, 1934):17-20.

Clift, Virgil A. and others. Wilmington, Delaware. A Study of School Plant and Program Requirements with Special Attention to the City's North, Northeast, and East Sections. New York: Center for Field Research and School Services, School of Education, New York U., Je, 1967.

Cooper, Richard Watson, and Cooper, Herman. Negro School Attendance in Delaware. A Report to the State Board of Education. Delaware Press, 1923.

Crosby, Muriel. An Adventure in Human Relations. Chicago: Follett, 1965. [Wilmington public schools]

Delaware Negro Civic League. The New Bright Future for Delaware Negroes; What the School Code Means to the Colored People; Mr. P. S. DuPont's Gift Will Build the Best Schools in America. Wilmington, DE: Negro Civic League, 1919.

Dodson, Samuel S. "Sussex County and the Black-White Teacher Ratio." Wilmington Evening Journal, Jl 10, 1973.

Dunbar-Nelson, Alice. "These 'Colored' United States: Delaware: A Jewel of Inconsistencies." Messenger 6(Ag, 1924):244-246; 6(S, 1924):276-279.

Glickstein, Don. "24 Years Later. Men in the Spotlight Recall Desegregation Roots." Delaware State News, Je 6, 1976. [Desegregation in Delaware during the 1950's]

Good, Warren. "Procedures and Factors in School Site Selection in Delaware." Doctoral dissertation, Temple U., 1964. Univ. Microfilms Order No. 64-13687.

Halstead, Jacqueline J. "The Delaware Association for the Moral Improvement and Education of the Colored People: 'Practical Christianity.'" Delaware History 15(Ap, 1972).

Hancock, Harold B. "Mary Ann Shadd: Negro Editor, Educator, and Lawyer." Delaware History 15(Ap, 1973).

_____. "Not Quite Men: The Free Negroes in Delaware in the 1830's." Civil War History 17(D, 1971).

Harootunian, Berj, and Morse, Richard J. Characteristics of Negro and White High-School Students Prior to Desegregation. A Study of Negro Students' Freedom of Choice. Syracuse U., H.E.W. Project No. 6-8790, Grant No. OEG-1-7-68790-0148, S, 1968. [Kent County]

Hiller, Amy M. "The Disfranchisement of Delaware Negroes in the Late Nineteenth Century." Delaware History 13(O, 1968):124-153.

Hoffecker, Carol E. "The Politics of Exclusion: Blacks in Late Nineteenth-Century Wilmington, Delaware." Delaware History 16(Ap, 1974).

Howell, Wendell. "School Desegregation As a Political Issue: The Role of the School Board Member." In School Desegregation: Making It Work, pp. 59-70. East Lansing, MI: College of Urban Development, Michigan State U., 1976. [Wilmington]

Kirk, George V. Desegregation in Delaware Prior to Evans v. Buchanan, 1976. ERIC ED 127 385.

Leo, Peter. "Milford Learns to Live with Desegregation." Wilmington News-Journal, Ja 2, 1977.

Livesay, Harold C. "Delaware Negroes, 1865-1915." Delaware History 13(O, 1968):87-123.

McClure, Phyllis. "School Spending Reformed by Parent Power." South Today 4(Ag, 1973):1-3.

Madden, Kenneth C., and Postlethwait, F. Neil. History of Education in Delaware. Dover, DE: State Department of Public Instruction, 1969.

Miller, George R., Jr. "Adolescent Negro Education in Delaware. A Study of the Negro Secondary School and Community (Exclusive of Wilmington)." Doctoral dissertation, New York U., 1944.

Miller, Jim. "Delaware: Seeds of Violence Remain." Race Relations Reporter 3(My, 1972): 522.

Munroe, John A. "The Negro in Delaware." South Atlantic Quarterly 56(1957):428-44.

Murray, Robert G. "What Delaware is Doing for Its Negroes." Southern Workman 51(N, 1922): 522.

O'Keefe, M. Callista, Sr. "Development of Catholic Education in the Diocese of Wilmington." Master's thesis, Villanova U., 1929.

Panyard, Jim. "To Bus or Not to Bus...That's the Question." Delaware Today, Je, 1976. [Wilmington]

Raffel, Jeffrey A. "Desegregation Dilemmas." Integrateducation 14(N-D, 1976).

_____. "Political Dilemmas of Busing: A Case Study of Interdistrict Metropolitan School Desegregation." Urban Education, Winter, 1976-1977.

_____. "The Politics of Metropolitan Desegregation: Ordeal by Court Order." Phi Delta Kappan 58(F, 1977):482-488.

Row, H. E. "Faculty Desegregation [in Delaware]." Delaware School Journal, My, 1966.

Simpson, William B. "A Proposed Plan for Negro Education in Delaware." Doctoral dissertation, Temple U., 1951.

Tilly, Charles, Jackson, Warner D., and Kay, Barry. Race and Residence in Wilmington, Delaware. New York: Bureau of Publications, Teachers College, Columbia U., 1965.

District of Columbia

"Administrators: Pupils take Full Charge of 'Freedom School.'" Nation's Schools, S, 1969.

Afro-American Experience Program, June, 1960-May, 1970. An Evaluation Report, N, 1970. ERIC ED 054 242.

Allen, George N. "Anita Ford Allen...Black Like Me." Washingtonian, S, 1970. [Black president of District of Columbia board of education]

Anderson, Jervis. "A Very Special Monument." New Yorker 54(Mr 20, 1978):93-121. [Dunbar High School]

Arnold, Mark R. "Public Schools." In Sar A. Levitan, The Federal Social Dollar in Its Own Back Yard, 1973. Bureau of National Affairs, 1231 25th Street, N.W., Washington, DC, 20037.

Avins, Alfred. "Integration and District of Columbia School History Revisited." New England Law Review 10(1974).

Baratz, Joan C. "Court Decisions and Educational Change: A Case History of the D.C. Public Schools, 1954-1974." Journal of Law and Education 4(Ja, 1975):63-80.

Barnes, Bart. "From Western's Glory Days to Doubts and High Hopes." Washington Post, Jl 7, 1974. [Western High School]

_____. "Anacostia Fights for the 'Beacon.'" Washington Post, D 12, 1971. [Anacostia Community School Project]

Berdes, Jane L. "Catholic School Integration in Washington, D.C." Integrated Education, S, 1967.

Bidwell, James K. et al. "Desegregation in Washington Schools--Two Years Later." Journal of Educational Sociology 30(My, 1957):405-413.

Birmingham, Stephen. "Washington's Black Elite." Town and Country, S, 1975.

Blake, Elias, Jr. "The Track System in Washington, D.C." Integrated Education, Ap-My, 1965.

Boldt, David R. "Winning in Washington." Potomac (Washington Post), N 19, 1972. [The election campaign of Marian Barry for the District of Columbia school board]

Borchert, James Alan. "American Mini-Ghettoes: Alleys, Alley-Dwellings and Alley Dwellers in Washington, D.C., 1850-1970." Doctoral dissertation, U. of Maryland, 1976. Univ. Microfilms Order No. 77-10, 404.

Both, Deborah R. "A Study of the Suburban Residential Integration Process in the Washington Metropolitan Area." Master's thesis, George Washington U., 1974.

Brown, Letitia Woods. Free Negroes in the District of Columbia, 1790-1846. New York: Oxford U. Press, 1972.

_____. "Free Negroes in the Original District of Columbia." Doctoral dissertation, Harvard U., 1966.

_____. "Residence Patterns of Negroes in the District of Columbia, 1800-1860." Rec. Columbia Hist. Soc., 1969-1970.

Caplan, Marvin. "The Trials of Integration." Progressive, O, 1965.

Carey, George W., Macomber, Lenore, and Greenberg, Michael. "Educational and Demographic Factors in the Urban Geography of Washington, D.C." Geographical Review 58(O, 1968).

Carlson, Elliott. "School Decentralization Proceeds in Some Cities, Amid Sharp Controversy." Wall Street Journal, Je 24, 1968. [Washington, D.C., and New York City]

Carroll, Joseph M. and others. Developing Flexible Educational Park Planning Formats for the District of Columbia. A Study of the Extent to Which Quality of Educational and Supporting Community Services Are a Function of Enrollments and Time Utilization. Final Report, Je, 1969. ERIC ED 044 772.

Cheney, Lynne. "Barbara Sizemore at Storm Center." Tuesday at Home, Ap, 1975.

Clark, Kenneth B. "Interview." Reading Newsreport 5(O, 1970):4, 6-9.

Clune, William H. "Law and Economics in Hobson v. Hansen: An Introductory Note." Journal of Human Resources 7(Summer, 1972):275-282.

Cohen, David K. "Jurists and Educators on Urban Schools: The Wright Decision and the Passow Report." Teachers College Record 70 (D, 1968):233-245.

Cooke, Paul. "Separate but Unequal Education in the Public Schools of the District of Columbia." Negro Educational Review, Jl-O, 1957.

Cuban, Larry. "Death by Politics: Staff Development in Washington, D.C." Phi Delta Kappan, My, 1972.

_____. "Hobson v. Hansen: A Study in Organizational Response." Educational Administration Quarterly 11(Spring, 1975):15-37.

_____. "Reform by Fiat. The Clark Plan in Washington, 1970-1972." Urban Education 9 (Ap, 1974):8-34.

_____. Reform in Washington: The Model School Division, 1963-1972. Washington, DC: Washington School of Psychiatry, D, 1972.

_____. "Teacher and Community." Harvard Educational Review, Spring, 1969.

_____. Urban School Chiefs Under Fire. Chicago: U. of Chicago Press, 1976. [Carl Hansen, D.C.]

Dabney, Lillian G. The History of Schools for Negroes in the District of Columbia, 1807-1947. Washington, DC: Catholic U. of America Press, 1949.

Daniels, Lee A. "Once Problem School, Paul Junior High Now a Model." Washington Post, N 30, 1976. [Paul Community Junior High School]

Dellenback, John. "Republican Task Force on Education and Training Goes to Morgan Community Schools to Study Decentralization and Community Participation." Congressional Record 115(Ag 13, 1969).

DeWitt, Karen. "Washington's Black Middle Class." Washington Post/Potomac, Ja 26, 1975.

District of Columbia Public Schools. Comprehensive Education Plan. School Year 1977-78, S, 1977. ERIC ED 145 590.

Engel, Martin. "The Kenneth B. Clark Design for Washington, D.C. Schools." Audiovisual Instruction 15(N, 1970):5-8, 14.

Feinberg, Lawrence. "The Anita Allen Era..." Washington Post, N 14, 1971.

_____. "Strict School Pleases Parents, Pupils." Washington Post, D 25, 1977. [Our Lady of Perpetual Help Elementary School, Anacostia]

_____. "Washington's Way: From Integration to a Black System." Washington Post, My 12, 1974.

_____. "Years Bring Change to Dunbar High School." Washington Post, D 28, 1969.

Fisk, Donald M., and Lancy, Cynthia A. Equality of Distribution of Recreation Services: A Case Study of Washington, D.C. Urban Institute, Jl, 1974.

Flusche, Michael. "Antislavery and Spiritualism: Myrtilla Miner and Her School." New York Historical Society Quarterly 59(Ap, 1975):149-172.

Forrester, Anne M. A Proposal for an African Communities Institute, My, 1968. Morgan Community School, 1773 California Street, Washington, DC 20001.

Furfey, Paul H. The Subculture of the Washington Ghetto. Washington, DC: Department of Sociology, Catholic U. of America, 1972.

Gibboney Associates, Inc. Three Policies of the Anacostia Community School Board: A Study of Their Intent and Operationalization, 1976. ERIC ED 131 165.

Gilbert, Ben W. and others. Ten Blocks From the White House: Anatomy of the Washington Riots of 1968. New York: Praeger, 1968.

Glazier, Harlan E. The Color Line in Our Public Schools. Washington, DC: Interracial Committee of the District of Columbia, 1936.

Goettel, Robert J. The Extent of Intra-District Inequalities: Issues and Problems, Ap 18, 1974. ERIC ED 095 657.

Goodwin, M. B. "Schools and Education of the Colored Population in the District of Columbia." American Journal of Education 19 (Mr, 1870).

Gordon, Sheila. "Climate for Learning: The Morgan Community School." Community, Ja, 1969.

_____. "The Community and the WTU Contract." Community, F, 1969.

Gordon, Sol, and Kassim, Doris. The Morgan School. Washington, D.C. New York: Center for Urban Education, 1971.

Gorney, Cynthia. "Julius Hobson Sr. Dies." Washington Post, Mr 24, 1977. [Long obituary]

Granton, E. Fannie. "New School of Afro-American Thought." Negro Digest, Je, 1967.

Gray, O. D. "Clothing and Its Significance for Youth from Low Income Families in Washington, D.C." Master's thesis, Howard U., 1966.

Green, Constance M. The Secret City. A History of Race Relations in the Nation's Capital. Princeton, NJ: Princeton U. Press, 1967.

Greene, Lorenzo J., and Callis, Myra C. The Unemployment of Negroes in the District of Columbia. Washington, DC: Association for the Study of Negro Life and History, 1932.

Greenfield, Eloise. "Perspective on Dunbar High School." Washington Post, Jl 6, 1975. [Letter]

Grier, Eunice S. Black Suburbanization in Metropolitan Washington. Washington, DC: Washington Center for Metropolitan Studies, 1974.

_____. Characteristics of Black Suburbanites. Washington, DC: Center for Metropolitan Studies, 1973.

Grier, George, and Grier, Enice. "Changing Housing Patterns in Metropolitan Washington." Integrateducation 13(My-Je, 1975):98-100.

Grotberg, Edith H. Progress Report of the Washington Integrated Secondary Education Project. Addendum II, Je 23, 1967. ERIC ED 021 909.

Groves, Paul A. "The 'Hidden' Population: Washington Alley Dwellers in the Late Nineteenth Century. Professional Geographer 26 (Ag, 1974):270-276.

Handorf, William G. "An Historical Study of the Superintendency of Dr. Frank W. Ballow in the Public School System of the District of Columbia." Doctoral dissertation, American U., 1962. Univ. Microfilms Order No. 62-4187. [1920-1943]

Hannerz, Ulf. "The Rhetoric of Soul. Identification in Negro Society." Race, Ap, 1968.

_____. Soulside. Inquiries Into Ghetto Culture and Community. New York: Columbia New York: Columbia U. Press, 1969.

_____. "What Negroes Mean by 'Soul.'" Transaction, Jl-Ag, 1968

Hansen, Carl F. Addendum: A Five-Year Report on Desegregation in the Washington, D.C. Schools. New York: Anti-Defamation League, 1957.

_____. "Danger Facing Nation's Schools? [Interview]." U.S. News and World Report, Jl 24, 1967. [Criticizes court intervention in school affairs]

_____. Danger in Washington. The Story of My Twenty Years in the Public Schools in the Nation's Capital. Nyack, NY: Parker Publishing Company, 1968.

_____. "A Defense of the Track System." Integrated Education, Je-Jl, 1964.

_____. "Desegregation in the District of Columbia: A Developmental Process." School and Society, My 7, 1960.

_____. Four Track Curriculum for Today's High Schools. Englewood Cliffs, NJ: Prentice-Hall, 1964.

_____. "Hobson vs. Hansen: Judicial Intervention is Being Tested." Integrated Education: RACE AND SCHOOLS, Vol. VII, No. 5 (S-O, 1969):23-39.

_____. Miracle of Social Adjustment: Desegregation in the Washington, D.C. Schools. New York: Anti-Defamation League, 1957.

_____. Review of the Track System in the District of Columbia, Ja 13, 1964. Public Schools of the District of Columbia, Franklin Administrative Building, Washington, DC 20005.

_____. "The Scholastic Performance of Negro and White Pupils in the Integrated Public Schools of the District of Columbia." Harvard Educational Review, Summer, 1960.

Hartman, Robert W. "Two Major [D.C.] School Plans May Be Incompatible." Washington Post, S 13, 1970. ["Plans" of Judge J. Skelly Wright and Dr. Kenneth B. Clark]

Hiro, Dilip. "Black is Beautiful.'" New Society, S 12, 1968. [A student of the British immigrant studies Black nationalism in Washington, DC]

Hobson, Julius, Jr. "Educational Policy and the Courts: The Case of Washington, D.C." Urban Review 10(Spring, 1978):5-19.

Hobson, Julius W. The Damned Children. A Layman's Guide to Forcing Change in Public Education, Ag, 1970. Washington Institute for Quality Education, 300 M Street, S.W., Washington, DC 20024

_____. The Damned Information. Acquiring and Using Public Information to Force Social Change, Je, 1971. Washington, DC: The Washington Institute for Quality Education.

_____. "A Search for Identity." Integrated Education, Mr-Ap, 1969, pp. 23-27.

"Hobson v. Hansen: The De Facto Limits on Judicial Power." Stanford Law Review 20 (Je, 1968).

"Hobson v. Hansen: Judicial Supervision of the Color-blind School Board." Harvard Law Review 81(My, 1968).

" Julius W. Hobson's 1-Man School Battle." Washington Post, F 21, 1971.

Hoffman, Ellen. "From Controversy to Apathy."
Southern Education Report, Mr, 1969. [The
Tri-School Project, Southwest Washington,
DC]

_____. "How to Find the Right School for Your
Child. A Washingtonian Survey of Metropoli-
tan Area Public Schools." Washingtonian,
Je, 1969.

Horowitz, Donald L. "Hobson v. Hansen: The
Calculus of Equality in School Resources."
In The Courts and Social Policy, pp. 106-
170. Washington, DC: Brookings Institution,
1977.

Hundley, Mary Gibson. The Dunbar Story, 1870-
1955. New York: Vantage, 1965. [History
of a Negro high school]

Hutchens, Timothy. "White Woman: Hope for
Equality Lies With the Children." Washington Star, Ag 19, 1976. [Ms. Janice Livingston, D.C.]

Hutchinson, Louise Daniel. The Anacostia
Story, 1608-1930. Washington, DC: GPO,
1977.

Indritz, P. "Post Civil War Ordinances Prohib-
iting Racial Discrimination in the District
of Columbia." George Washington Law Journal
42(Ja, 1954):179-209.

_____. "Racial Ramparts in the Nation's Cap-
ital." George Washington Law Journal 41
(Mr, 1953):297-329.

_____. "Segregated Youth in Our National Cap-
ital." Crisis, D, 1956.

Inger, Morton. "Hobson v. Hansen." Center
Forum, D 23, 1968. [Progress in the D.C.
schools since the Hobson decision]

Ingle, Edward. The Negro in the District of
Columbia. Baltimore: Johns Hopkins U.
Press, 1893.

Integration and the Washington [DC] Public
Schools. Washington, DC: The Washington
Urban League, Je 23, 1964.

"It's Our School...! Morgan's Story." Part 2.
American Teacher, D, 1968.

Jacobson, Aileen. "To Flee or Not to Flee:
The Making of the New Minority." Washington
Post, Ap 2, 1972.

Jacoby, Susan. "Community Control Can Work."
Learning 2(D, 1973):51-54. [Morgan Community
School]

_____. "Community Control, Six Years Later."
Washington Post, My 13, 1973. [Morgan Community School]

_____. "Problems Stalemate D.C. Schools."
Education News, S 9, 1968.

Janssen, Peter A. "The Trials of Tri-School."
Southern Education Report, Je, 1967. [South-
west section of Washington, DC]

Johnson, Thomas Reed. "The City on the Hill:
Race Relations in Washington, D.C., 1865-
1885." Doctoral dissertation, U. of Maryland, 1975. Univ. Microfilms Order No.
75-27, 790.

Jordan, Ruth. "Growing Up White in the D.C.
Schools." Civil Rights Digest 9(Spring,
1977):32-37.

Kashif, Lonnie. "U.S. School System is Bank-
rupt." Muhammad Speaks, N 21, 1969.

King, Deborah Elise. "The Performance of
Washington, D.C., Inner-City Children on the
AAHPER Youth Fitness Test: Implications
for the School Physcial Education Program."
Master's thesis, Howard U., 1974.

Knoll, Erwin. "The Truth about Desegregation
in the Washington, D.C., Public Schools."
Journal of Negro Eduation 28(Spring, 1959):
92-113.

Kovacs, Malcolm. "Who Gives a Damn?" Nation,
O 27, 1969. [The Urban Coalition in Washington, D.C.]

Kraft, Ivor, Fuschillo, Jean, and Herzog, Elizabeth. Prelude to School. An Evaluation of
an Inner-City Preschool Program. Washington,
DC: GPO, 1968.

"A Last Angry Man." Time, D 4, 1972. [Julius
Hobson]

Lauter, Paul. "The Short, Happy Life of the
Adams-Morgan Community School Project."
Harvard Educational Review, Spring, 1968.

Lauter, Paul, and Howe, Florence. "The School
Mess [in Washington, D.C.]." New York Review of Books, F 1, 1968.

Libarkin, Barbara. "At David's School, Black
May Well Be Beige." Los Angeles Times, Mr
20, 1977. [Shepherd Park]

_____. "Interracial Living and the Racial At-
titudes of White Children in Grades 3 to 6:
The White Child as a Minority in a Black
School System." Master's thesis, Catholic
U. of America, 1976. [Also: ERIC ED 126
214]

_____. "Racial Attitudes of Whites in Public
and Private Schools." Integrateducation 15
(N-D, 1977):126-130.

Liebow, Elliott. Tally's Corner. Boston: Little Brown, 1967. [Poor people in Washington,
DC]

Loflin, Marvin D. A Note on the Deep Structure
of Nonstandard English in Washington, D.C.,
1966. ERIC ED 010 875.

Lofton, Williston H. "The Development of Public Education for Negroes in Washington, D.C. (A Study of 'Separate But Equal Accommodations')." Doctoral dissertation, American U., 1945.

Long, Howard H. "The Intelligence of Colored Elementary Pupils in Washington, D.C." Journal of Negro Education 3(Ap, 1934):205-222.

McBee, Susanna. "Deliberate Speed in [Washington] D.C." New Republic, Je 20, 1964.

McCown, George W. "A Critical Evaluation of the Four Track Curriculum Program of the District of Columbia Senior High Schools With Recommendations for Improvement." Doctoral dissertation, U. of Maryland, 1960. Univ. Microfilms Order No. 60-4928.

McCoy, Carmen A., and Wielk, Carol. "Anacostia Conference." Community, My, 1969. [Community control]

McDowell, Sophia. "The Unreported Message." Nation, Ag 5, 1968. [Racial attitudes of Negro youth in Washington, DC, 1966]

McSurely, Al. "Struggle in Washington." Southern Patriot, Ja, 1973.

Mann, Jack. "Peggy Cooper and the Act of the Grant." Washington Post-Potomac, O 27, 1974. [Western High School, Georgetown; high school for the fine arts]

Mann, Judy Luce. "D.C.: Getting Together After Strife." Race Relations Reporter 3(My, 1972):11-15.

Marshall, Eliot. "Washington's Segregated Schools." New Republic, Jl 9, 1977.

Matthews, Diller G., Jr. "The Distribution of the Negro Population of the District of Columbia, 1800-1960." Master's thesis, Catholic U. of America, 1967.

Metropolitan Applied Research Center, Inc. A Possible Reality. A Design for the Attainment of High Academic Achievement for the Students of Public Elementary and Junior High Schools of Washington, D.C., Je 30, 1970. Metropolitan Applied Research Center, Inc., 60 East 86th Street, New York, NY, 10028.

Miller, M. Sammy. "Robert Heberton Terrell, 1857-1925: Black Lawyer and Community Leader." Doctoral dissertation, Catholic U. of America, 1977.

Montgomery, Winfield S. Historical Sketch of Education for the Colored Race in the District of Columbia, 1807-1905. Washington, DC: Smith Brothers, 1907.

Morton, Mary. "The Education of the Negro in the District of Columbia." Journal of Negro Education 26(1947):325-346.

Moskowitz, Seth W. "Spottswood Bolling: Desegregation Pioneer in D.C." Washington Post, Je 15, 1978. [Spottswood Thomas Bolling, Jr., plaintiff in Bolling v. Sharpe]

Myers, Phyllis. "Schools: Morgan's Tentative Revolution." Urban America, N-D, 1968.

Nash, Edith. "The Story of an Integrated School." Independent School Bulletin, D, 1967. [Georgetown Day School]

National Association of Intergroup Relations Officials. Civil Rights in the Nation's Capital, A Report on a Decade of Progress. Washington, DC: NAIRO, 1959.

Nesbitt, George B. "Non-White Residential Dispersion and Desegregation in the District of Columbia [1940-1954]." Journal of Negro Education 25(Winter, 1956).

O'Neill, Dave M., Gray, Biragon, and Horowitz, Stanley. Educational Equality and Expenditure Equalization Orders: The Case of Hobson v. Hansen. AD 720 362. Springfield, VA: National Technical Information Service, F, 1971.

Osborne, Irene, and Vennett, Richard K. "Eliminating Educational Segregation in the Nation's Capital--1951-1955." Annals, Mr, 1956.

Pablo, Jean Malia. "Washington, D.C., and Its School System, 1900-1906." Doctoral dissertation, Georgetown U., 1973.

Page, Thornell K. "A Study of the District of Columbia Public Schools Desegregation Policies, 1954-1967." Doctoral dissertation, Virginia Polytechnic Institute, and State U., 1978. Univ. Microfilms Order No. 78 19115.

Passow, A. Harry. Toward Creating a Model Urban School System: A Study of the Washington, D.C., Public Schools. New York: Teachers College, Columbia U., S, 1967.

_____. "A Valid Use of College Manpower? The Washington, D.C. Study. Some Perspectives." Perspectives on Education (Teachers College, Columbia U.) 3(Spring, 1970):1-4.

Peterson, Bill. "The Images Don't Apply at McKinley." Washington Post, D 18, 1975. [McKinley High School]

Poinsett, Alex. "Washington's New Public School Boss." Ebony 30(Ja, 1974):102-106.

Pollard, William. "D.C. Muslim School Grows." Washington Post, Jl 9, 1972. [University of Islam at Temple No. 4]

Preston, Emmett D. "The Development of Negro Education in the District of Columbia." Journal of Negro Education, O, 1940.

_____. "William Syphax, a Pioneer in Negro Education in the District of Columbia." Journal of Negro History 20(1935):448-476. [1825-1891]

Prince, Richard E. "SW School Project Ends in Failure." Washington Post, Jl 30, 1976. [Tri-School Plan, 1967-1976]

Radford J. P. "Patterns of Nonwhite Residential Segregation in Washington, D.C. in the Late Nineteenth Century." Master's thesis, U. of Maryland, 1967.

"Research Scientist Lends a Hand to Capital's Poor." Ebony, Mr, 1967. [Dr. Benjamin Alexander, member of the Washington, DC school board]

Roberts, Markley. "Some Factors Affecting Employment and Earnings of Disadvantaged Youths." Industrial and Labor Relations Review 25(Ap, 1972):376-382.

_____. Youth Unemployment in the Inner City: Some New Insights. Washington, DC: Washington Center for Metropolitan Studies, 1971.

Rothman, Philip. "The Short, Happy Life." (letter) Harvard Educational Review, Winter, 1969. [On the Adams-Morgan Community School Project]

Savoy, A. Kiger. "Garrison Demonstration School." Bulletin (National Association of Teachers in Colored Schools) 10(Je-Jl, 1930): 16-17.

Schafft, Gretchen E. "The Unexpected Minority: White Children in an Urban School and Neighborhood." Doctoral dissertation, Catholic U. of America, 1976. Univ. Microfilms Order No. 76-20, 232.

Segal, Ben D., Korey, William, and Mason, Charles N. (eds.). Civil Rights in the Nation's Capital: A Report on a Decade of Programs. New York: National Association of Intergroup Relations Officials, 1959.

Shafer, Barbara J. "A Study of the Effect of the Skelly Wright Decision on Classroom and School Building Management in the Public Schools of the District of Columbia." Master's thesis, Catholic U. of America, 1968.

Sherburne, Mary Lela. The Cardozo Model School District: A Peach Tree Grows on T Street, 1967. Educational Development Center, 55 Chapel Street, Newton, MA, 02158.

Silver, Catherine Bodard. Black Teachers in Urban Schools: The Case of Washington, D.C. New York: Praeger, 1973.

Simons, Lewis M. "Cities Within Washington [D.C.]." Washington Post, My 5, 1978. [Separation of black and white in the city]

_____. "Out-of-Wedlock Black Children Draw a Community Together." Washington Post, Je 25, 1978.

Simons, William H. "Union Proposals for Washington Schools." Integrated Education: RACE AND SCHOOLS 8(S-O, 1970):50-52.

Simpkins, Edward. Problems, Issues and Techniques in the Resolution of School Disputes. A Report on the Collective Negotiations Institute, 1969. Cambridge, MA: Harvard Graduate School of Education, 1971. [Much material on Washington, DC schools]

"Barbara Sizemore Discusses Her Departure from the Washington Scene." Phi Delta Kappan 57 (F, 1976):425.

Sizemore, Barbara. "Changing Our Schools" (interview). Washington Post, Jl 7, 1974.

Smith, James D. "White Wealth and Black People: The Distribution of Wealth in Washington, D.C. in 1967." In Smith, The Personal Distribution of Income and Wealth, pp. 329-363. New York: Columbia U. Press, 1975.

Smith, Sam. Captive Capital. Colonial Life in Modern Washington. Bloomington, IN: Indiana U. Press, 1974.

Social Studies Curriculum Program. Children of Cardozo Tell It Like It Is. Cambridge, MA: Education Development Center, 1968.

Sowell, Thomas. "Black Excellence--The Case of Dunbar High School." Public Interest, Spring, 1974. Reprinted in Washington Post, Ap 28 1974.

Special Report of the Commissioner of Education on the Condition and Improvement of Public Schools in the District of Columbia. Submitted to the Senate, Je, 1868, and to the House, with Additions, Je 13, 1870. Washington, DC: GPO, 1871.

Stephens, Vera. [Letter on the Adams-Morgan Community School Project, Washington, D.C.] Harvard Educational Review, Winter, 1969.

Strandt, Patricia. [On Adams School] American Teacher, N-D, 1968.

Task Force on Educational Parks. Developing Flexible Educational Park Planning Formats for the District of Columbia. Washington, DC: Public Schools of the District of Columbia, Je, 1969.

Terrell, Mary Church. "The History of the High School for Negroes in Washington." Journal of Negro History (Jl, 1917):252-266.

_____. "Society Among the Colored People of Washington." Voice of the Negro (Ap, 1904): 150-156.

Thomas, Charles Walker. "The First Negro President of the D.C. Board of Education: Wesley S. Williams." Negro History Bulletin, Fall, 1966.

Thomas, Neval H. "These 'Colored' United States: The District of Columbia--A Paradise of Paradoxes." Messenger 5(0, 1923):837-841.

Thompson, Elizabeth M. "A Decade of Progress in D.C. Elementary Schools." School Libraries 20(F, 1970):27-30.

Thompson, Peggy B. "A Principal in Poverty." Progressive, S, 1966. [Miss Marguerite C. Selden, all-Negro Harrison elementary school]

Thurber, Bert Henry. "The Negro at the Nation's Capital, 1913-1921." Doctoral dissertation, Yale U., 1973. Univ. Microfilms Order No. 74-11927.

Tigar, Michael E. "In Defense of Skelly Wright." New Republic, Ag 5, 1967.

"Tracked or Railroaded?" Newsweek, Ap 24, 1967. [The track system]

Tucker, Sterling. "Decline of the City's Schools: Three Misconceptions." Washington Evening Star, Je 3, 1973.

Turner, Janette M. "A Kaleidoscope of Perceptions: The Adams-Morgan Project Becomes Morgan Community School." Master's thesis, Antioch Putney Graduate School, 1969.

U.S. Civil Service Commission. Review of the Equal Employment Opportunity Program at the Smithsonian Institution. Washington, DC: The Commission, S, 1973. [Reprinted in U.S. Congress, 94th, 1st Session, Senate, Comittee on Rules and Administration, Nomination of Daniel J. Boorstein of the District of Columbia to be Librarian of Congress. Hearings..., pp. 36-59. Washington, DC: GPO, 1975]

U.S. Congress, 89th, 2nd Session, House of Representatives, Committee on Education and Labor. A Task Force Study of the Public School System in the District of Columbia as it Relates to the War on Poverty. Washington, DC: GPO, Je, 1966.

U.S. Congress, 90th, 2nd Session, House of Representatives, House Report No. 1232. Conference Report, District of Columbia Elected Board of Education Act, Ap 1, 1968.

U.S. Congress, 90th, 1st Session, Senate, Committee on Appropriations, Subcommittee. District of Columbia Appropriation for Fiscal Year 1968. Hearings. Washington, DC: GPO, 1967.

U.S. Congress, 90th, 1st Session, House of Representatives, Report No. 659. District of Columbia Elected Board of Education Act, S 22, 1967.

U.S. Congress, 90th, 1st Session, House of Representatives, Committee on the District of Columbia. Election of Board of Education. Hearing. Washington, DC: GPO, 1967.

U.S. Congress, 90th, 1st Session, Senate, Committee on the District of Columbia. Nominations of D.C. Commissioner, Assistant to Commissioner, and Nine City Council Members. Hearings. Washington, DC: GPO, 1967.

U.S. Congress, 90th, 1st Session, Senate, Committee on the District of Columbia, Subcommittee on Public Health, Education, Welfare, and Safety. District of Columbia Elected School Board. Hearing. Washington, DC: GPO, 1967.

U.S. Congress, 90th, 1st Session, Senate, Report No. 942. District of Columbia Elected Board of Education Act, D 14, 1967.

U.S. Congress, 90th, 2nd Session, House of Representatives, Committee on the District of Columbia, Special Investigating Subcommittee. Teachers' Pay Increase. Hearing. Washington, DC: GPO, 1968.

U.S. Congress, 90th, 2nd Session, Senate, Committee on Labor and Public Welfare, Subcommittee on Employment, Manpower, and Poverty. Washington [D.C.] Inner City Poverty Survey. Washington, DC: GPO, D, 1968.

U.S. Congress, 91st, 1st Session, Senate, Committee on the District of Columbia, Public Health, Education, Welfare, and Safety Subcommittee. Crime in the National Capital. Hearings...on Delinquency and Crime in District of Columbia Schools. Part 5. Washington, DC: GPO, 1969.

U.S. Congress, 91st, 2nd Session, House of Representatives, Committee on the District of Columbia, House Report No. 91-1681. Investigation and Study of the Public School System of the District of Columbia. Washington, DC: GPO, D 8, 1970.

U.S. Congress, 92nd, 2nd Session, House of Representatives, Committee on the District of Columbia. Mentally Ill and Handicapped Children [in the District of Columbia]. Washington, DC: GPO, 1972.

U.S. Congress, 93rd, 1st Session, House of Representatives, Committee on the District of Columbia, Subcommittee on Education. Board of Education. Hearings... Washington, DC: GPO, 1975.

Walker, Joe. "Blacks Favor Improved Schools Over Busing." Muhammad Speaks, Ja 17, 1975. [Washington, DC metropolitan area]

"The Washington, D.C. School Case." Integrated Education, Ag-S, 1967. [Hobson v. Hansen]

Washington, D.C. Public Schools. _A Handbook for Teachers and Officers Who Work in Gray Areas_. Great Cities Program. Washington, DC: Board of Education, 1963.

Washington, D.C. Teachers Union. "Teacher Union Supports Community Control." _Integrated Education_ (N-D, 1968):43-46.

Washington Urban League. _SOS '76--Speak Out for Survival! Priorities and Problems of Low Income Area Residents of Washington, D.C._ Washington, DC: Washington Urban League, Je, 1976.

Watson, Douglas. "Spending Up and Quality Down in District's Schools." _Washington Post_, D 21, 1975.

Watts, Jerry G. "Reinforcing Intellectual Growth." _Washington Post_, F 14, 1975. [Printed in column by William Raspberry]

Webb, Marilyn Salzman. "Whites Keep Control in D.C. Schools." _Guardian_, F 15, 1969.

Wells, Rufus. "Bold, Brilliant Barbara [Sizemore] Battles for a New Look." _Dawn Magazine_, S 29, 1974.

Whitaker, Joseph D. "Central Grads in 50th Reunion." _Washington Post_, Je 28, 1976. [Central High School]

_____. "Dunbar's Class of '26 Recalls Days of 'Lots of Pride, Dignity.'" _Washington Post_, Je 28, 1976. [Dunbar High School]

Why Did Washington Burn?--A Relevant Lesson Plan and Resources for District of Columbia Teachers. Prepared by the Southern Christian Leadership Conference and the Washington Teachers Union, 1968. Washington Teachers Union, 1126 Sixteenth Street, N.W., Washington, DC 20036.

Wilkins, Roy. "'Objectionable Matter' in _The Crisis_." _Crisis_, My, 1936.

Williams, Juan. "Black Teen-Agers: A Fight for Opportunity." _Washington Post_, Ag 5, 1978.

_____. "Inside a Washington School." _Washington Post_, Ap 30, 1978, My 1, 1978. [Eastern High School]

Williams, Melvin R. "A Blueprint for Change: The Black Community in Washington, DC, 1860-1870." _Records of the Columbia Historical Society of Washington, DC, 1971-1972_ 48 (1973):359-393.

_____. "Blacks in Washington, DC, 1860-1870." Doctoral dissertation, Johns Hopkins U., 1976.

Winokur, H. S., Jr. "Expenditure Equalization in the Washington, D.C. Elementary Schools." _Public Policy_ 24(Summer, 1976).

Wilson, Henry. "Education of Colored Youth in the District of Columbia." In _Anti-Slavery Measures in Congress, 1861-1864_. Boston: Walker, Wise, and Co., 1864.

Wormley, G. Smith. "First Half Century of Public Schools [for Negroes] of the District of Columbia." _Journal of Negro History_, Ap, 1932.

Wright, J. Skelly. "_Hobson v. Hansen_." _Congressional Record_, Je 21, 1967, pp. H7655-H7697. [The complete text of the ruling]

Young, Allen. "D.C. Blacks Unite." _Guardian_, Mr 16, 1968.

Zeitz, Eileen. "The Process of Private Urban Renewal in Three Areas of Washington, District of Columbia." Doctoral dissertation, American U., 1976.

Florida

Abney, Everett E. "The Status of Florida's Black School Principals." _Journal of Negro Education_ 43(Winter, 1974):3-8.

Abraham, Ansley A., and Simmons, Gertrude L. "The Educational Outlook for Nonwhites in Florida." _Journal of Negro Education_, Fall, 1966.

Akin, Edward N. "When A Minority Becomes the Majority: Blacks in Jacksonville Politics, 1887-1907." _Florida Historical Quarterly_ 53(O, 1974).

Ashdown, Ellen. "Florida's Black Archives: A Substantial Past." _Change_ 11(Ap, 1979):48-49.

Baltzell, D. Catherine. _Rapid Desegregation and Academic Achievement in a Large Urban School District_, Ap, 1974. ERIC ED 090 282. [Duval County]

Bartholomew, David K. "An Analysis of Change in Power System and Decision-Making Process in a Selected County." Doctoral dissertation, U. of Florida, 1971. [St. Augustine]

Belcher, Jerry. "School Busing: How Far Has It Come?" _Los Angeles Times_, D 15, 1975. [Tampa]

Belvadi, Paul Edwin. "Perceptions of Florida Educators and School Board Members Regarding the Impact of School Integration on the Academic Gains and Social Acceptance of Negro Children." Doctoral dissertation, Florida Atlantic U., 1977.

Bi-Racial Committee [of Dade County]. _A Preliminary Report of the Bi-Racial Committee_. Miami: U.S. District Court, Southern District of Florida, D 7, 1970.

"Black Mayor in Florida Town." _Ebony_ 26(Ag, 1971):98-104. [Gainesville]

Bottosto, Samuel S. "Relationships Between County-Wide Measures of Certain Socio-economic Factors, Intelligence, and Academic Achievement of High School Seniors in Florida." Doctoral dissertation, U. of Florida, 1959. Univ. Microfilms Order No. 59-3538.

Braddock, Clayton. "Wewahitchka Took a Chance on Oblivion." Southern Education Report, Jl-Ag, 1967. [Desegregation in a Florida town]

Braddock, G. Holmes. "'Let's Complete Integration of Our Schools.'" Miami Herald, Ag 19, 1973. [Dade County]

Bragaw, Donald H. "Status of Negroes in a Southern Port City in the Progressive Era: Pensacola, 1896-1920." Florida Historical Quarterly, Ja, 1973.

Bujart, Bradford Carleton. "With More Than Deliberate Speed: A Historical Study of Six Major Issues in Secondary Education in Palm Beach County, Florida 1954-1972 From a Black Perspective." Doctoral dissertation, Florida Atlantic U., 1975. Univ. Microfilms Order No. 75-22483.

Campbell, James T. "Schools Approach Total Desegregation." Florida Schools 34(Mr-Ap, 1 972):15-17.

Cataldo, Everett F. and others. "Metropolitan School Desegregation: Practical Remedy or Impractical Ideal?" Annals 422(N, 1975): 97-104.

Collier, Bert. "Miami's Decision: A Blend of Cultures." Southern Education Report, O, 1966. [Instruction in Spanish and English in Dade County]

Combs, Willie Everett. "The Principalship in the Negro Secondary Schools of Florida." Doctoral dissertation, Indiana U., 1964.

Davis, Carlton I. The Poor Identified: Progress to Date. Gainesville, FL: Agricultural Experiment Station, 1975.

Department of Administration Research. Integration--October 1968. Miami: Dade County Public Schools, Ja, 1969.

Dickson, David F. "Florida Judges and the Warren Court." Master's thesis, Florida State U., 1964.

Dohlstrom, Arthur H. "A Study to Determine How the Emotional Attitudes of Dade County (Miami) Florida Teachers May Aid or Hinder Desegregation in Public School Classes." Doctoral dissertation, New York U., 1955. Dissertation Abstracts, XV, 1955, p. 1923.

Dudas, John J., and Longbrake, David B. "Problems and Future Directions of Residential Integration: The Local Application of Federally Funded Programs in Dade County, Florida." Southeastern Geographer 11(1971):157-168.

Edwards, Bonnie Keay. "Negro Education in Florida, 1865-1900." Master's thesis, Florida State U., 1970.

Entin, David H. "The Black Burden in Jacksonville Desegregation." Integrated Education (Jl-Ag, 1972):3-19.

"Florida Officials Release Functional Literacy Test Scores by Race, Sex, and Handicap." Education Daily, Mr 28, 1978.

Foster, Gordon. Discipline Practices in the Hillsborough County Public Schools, Ap 1, 1977. ERIC ED 145 575.

Franklin, Stephen. "Tampa Schools Busing is Peaceful." Philadelphia Bulletin, N 14, 1976.

Fullwood, Charles. "Battle for the South: Phase Two." Ramparts 10(Jl, 1971):36-39.

Gara, Larry (ed.). "Teaching Freedom in the Post-War South, A Document." Journal of Negro History 40(1955):274-276. [Gainesville]

Garafalo, Charles. "Black-White Occupational Distribution in Miami During World War I." Prologue 5(Summer, 1973).

Garvin, Russell. "The Free Negro in Florida Before the Civil War." Florida Historical Quarterly 46(Jl, 1967):1-17.

Gendron, Eldridge J. "Busing in Florida: Before and After." Integrated Education (Mr-Ap, 1972):3-7.

_____. "Pupil Transportation As Affected by the Desegregation of Certain Florida Schools." Doctoral dissertation, U. of Miami, Coral Gables, Florida. Jl, 1971

George, Paul S. "Colored Town: Miami's Black Community, 1896-1930." Florida Historical Quarterly 56(Spring, 1978):432-447.

Giles, Micheal W., Cataldo, Everett F., and Gatlin, Douglas S. [White flight in Florida] Social Policy 6(Ja, F, 1976):46-48.

Giles, Micheal W. and others. "The Impact of Busing on White Flight." Social Science Quarterly 55(S, 1974):493-501.

Glicksberg, Charles F. (ed.). "Letters from William Cullen Bryant from Florida." Florida Historical Society Quarterly 14(Ap, 1936).

Goulding, R. L. "A Partial Survey of the White Public School of New Smyrna (Volusia County) Florida." Master's thesis, U. of Florida, 1922.

Governor's Invitational Conference on Post-Secondary Educational Opportunities for the Disadvantaged. A State of Concern. Proceedings... Gainesville, FL: College of Arts and Sciences, U. of Florida, 1971.

Green, Robert L., and others. Evaluation of Pupil Assessment, St. Lucie County School System. Miami: Florida School Desegregation Consulting Center, N, 1976.

Greenfield, Robert W. "Factors Associated With Attitudes Toward Desegregation in a Florida Residential Suburb." Social Forces, O, 1961.

Griffin, N. W. "Education in Jacksonville." Crisis, Ja, 1942.

Griffith, Lynda W. "A Comparison of the Cost Effectiveness of Four Programs for Low Income Students." Doctoral dissertation, U. of Missouri-Kansas City, 1978. Univ. Microfilms Order No. 7900005. [Duval County]

Grigg, Charles M., and Taintor, Jesse B. Differential Administration of Discipline and Special Education for Blacks in Florida Public Schools (K-12), 1973. Tallahassee, FL: Institute for Social Research, Florida State U., 1974.

Guilfoyle, Michael J. "An Investigation of Miami's Urban Residential Dynamics, 1950-1970." Master's thesis, Florida State U., 1976.

Hall, Harry O. South Florida School Desegregation Consulting Center. Annual Report Covering the Period from August 1, 1965, to June 30, 1966. Coral Gables, FL: Miami U., 1966, 99 pp. ERIC ED 028 228.

Hartley, Robert W. "A Long, Hot Summer: The St. Augustine Racial Disorders of 1964." Master's thesis, Stetson U., 1972.

Hines, Bea L. "Integration: 22 Years of All Deliberate Speed." Miami Herald, My 17, 1976. [Dade County schools]

Hooker, Robert W. "Busing, Governor Askew, and the Florida Primary." New South 27(Spring, 1972):23-30.

Hooker, Robert. "School Crisis in St. Petersburg." New South 27(Winter, 1972):48-52.

Hooker, Robert, and Hart, Joy. [Two articles on private schools in Pinellas County, Florida] St. Petersburg Times, O 3, 1972.

Ignatz, Milton G. "Low Black Enrollment in [High School] Chemistry and Physics Courses." Science Education 59(O-D, 1975):571-573.!

Integration in Dade County Public Schools, October, 1966. Department of Administrative Research, Dade County Public Schools, 1410 N.W. Second Avenue, Miami, FL, D, 1966.

Jackson, Jesse Jefferson. "The Negro and the Law in Florida, 1821-1921: Legal Patterns of Segregation and Control." Master's thesis, Florida State U., 1960.

Jackson, Reid E. "Status of Education of the Negro in Florida, 1929-34." Opportunity 14 (N, 1936):336-339.

Jacobstein, Helen J. The Segregation Factor in the Florida Democratic Gubernatorial Primary of 1956. Gainesville, FL, 1972.

Jenna, William W., Jr. Metropolitan Miami: A Demographic Overview. Coral Gables, FL: U. of Miami Press, 1972.

Justin, Neal. "Is Busing Helping Students?" Changing Education 6(Summer, 1974):36-38. [Atlantic High School, Delray Beach]

Justin, Neal E., and Thabit, Judy. "Black and White Achievement Before and After Integration." Intellect 102(Ap, 1974):458-459.

Kerr, Oliver. "The Extent of Compliance with the Requirements of Title VI of the Civil Rights Act of 1964 by the Catholic Schools of the Diocese of Miami." Master's thesis, Catholic U. of America, 1967.

Kersey, Harry A., Jr. "The Harris School Project--A Compensatory Program for Negro Migrant Children in Florida." Journal of Negro Education 41(Winter, 1972):82-91. [Walter E. Harris School, Hastings]

Kersey, Harry A. "St. Augustine School: Seventy-Five Years of Negro Parochial Education in Gainesville, Florida." Florida Historical Quarterly 51(Jl, 1972):58-63.

Kerr, James. "Ben Willis After Chicago." Chicago Tribune, O 31, 1971. [Broward County]

Killian, Lewis. "Florida's Citizens and Desegregation in the Schools." Florida School Bulletin 16(S, 1954):10-14.

Krohn, Pearl S. A Program of Action for the Schools in South Dade County, Florida: A Report to the Special Study Committee. Coral Gables, FL: Miami U., Je, 1967, 82 pp. ERIC ED 026 443.

Kurth, Richard W., and Pavalko, Ronald M. "School Resources, Social Environments, and Educational Outcomes." Journal of Research and Development in Education 9(F, 1975):70-81.

Lanier, Raphael O'Hara. "The History of Negro Education in Florida." Master's thesis, Stanford U., 1928.

Lindsay, Leon W. "School-Integration Gains-- And Problems." Christian Science Monitor, Mr 21, 23, 1970. [Gainesville, Alucha County]

Lutterbie, P. H. "Occupational Patterns of Educators Who Were Principals of Negro Schools in Florida in 1960." Doctoral dissertation, U. of Miami, 1973.

Mackey, W. F., and Beebe, V. N. Bilingual Schools for a Bicultural Community: Miami's Adaptation to the Cuban Refugees. Rowley, MA: Newbury House, 1977.

Mann, Pete. "'I Guess We're Just Impatient.'" American Education, Mr, 1966. [Problems of color and quality in Volusia]

Meyer, P. "Miami Negroes: A Study in Depth." The Miami Herald, 1968.

Morganthau, Tom. "Dade Schools: Some Advances, Some Setbacks." Miami Herald, My 12, 1974. [1954-1974 in Dade County]

_____. "Migration Resegregates Schools [in Miami]." Miami Herald, S 30, 1973.

_____. "Schools Pulled Two Ways on Bilingual Instruction." Miami Herald, Ap 14, 1974. [Miami]

_____. "Survey Shows Public Backs Schools [in South Florida]." Miami Herald, Ag 12, 1973.

Murray, W. M. R. "Education in Miami." Crisis, Mr, 1942.

National Commission of Professional Rights and Responsibilities. Florida. A Study of Political Atmosphere As It Affects Public Education. Washington, DC: National Education Association, Mr, 1966.

Nordheimer, Jan. "Florida's 'Supersquare'--A Man to Watch." New York Times Magazine, Mr 5, 1972. [Governor Reubin O'D. Askew]

Orsini, Bette. "School Funds for Poor Bought Computer Instead." St. Petersburg Times, Je 12, 1972. [Federal auditing of Florida expenditures under Title I, ESEA]

Ralston, Carolyn, and Leevia, Anne. "Dade County Florida." In NCRIEEO Special Field Report, My, 1971.

Randolph, Eleanor and others. "Desegregation Is Working in Suncoast Schools." St. Petersburg Times, Jl 16, 1972.

Resource Management Corporation. Evaluation of the Emergency School Assistance Program, Vol. III, Appendix T, F 15, 1972. ERIC ED 058 470. [Case history of ESAP in Escambia, Florida]

Resource Management Corporation. Evaluation of the Emergency School Assistance Program, Vol. III, Appendix O, F 15, 1972. ERIC ED 058 470. [Case history of ESAP in Polk County, Florida]

Rey, Alberto. "A Study of the Attitudinal Effect of a Spanish Accent on Blacks and Whites in South Florida." Doctoral dissertation, Georgetown U., 1974. Univ. Microfilms Order No. 74-26436.

Richardson, Barbara Ann. "A History of Blacks in Jacksonville, Florida, 1860-1895: A Socioeconomic and Political Study." Doctoral dissertation, Carnegie-Mellon U., 1975. Univ. Microfilms Order No. 76-18076.

Richardson, Joe M. "Christian Abolitionism: The American Missionary Association and the Florida Negro." Journal of Negro Education 40 (Winter, 1971):35-44.

_____. "The Freedmen's Bureau and Negro Education in Florida." Journal of Negro Education 31(Fall, 1962):460-467.

_____. The Negro in the Reconstruction of Florida, 1865-1877. Tallahassee, FL: Florida State U., 1965.

Richardson, Martin D., and Washington, LeRoy M. "A Picture of Florida's Schools." Crisis 44 (S, 1937):270-271.

Rose, H. M. "Metropolitan Miami's Changing Negro Population, 1950-1960." Economic Geography, Jl, 1964.

Rosen, Frederick Bruce. "The Development of Negro Education in Florida During Reconstruction, 1865-1914." Doctoral dissertation, U. of Florida, 1974. Univ. Microfilms Order No. 75-3523.

Sakkis, Gus. "A Financial Analysis of Disadvantaged and Nondisadvantaged Black and White Elementary Schools in Pinellas County for the Years 1962-1972." Doctoral dissertation, U. of South Florida, 1975. Univ. Microfilms Order No. 75-24032.

Scott, J. Irving E. The Education of Black People in Florida. Philadelphia: Donance and Co., 1974.

Scurry, Alphonso. "The Interrelationships Among Disruptive Student Behavior and Student Perceptions of Alienation, and Internal-External Control in Black High School Seniors." Doctoral dissertation, Florida State U., 1976. [Jacksonville]

Sherman, Eugene G., Jr. "Urbanization and Florida's Negro Population: A Case Study." Doctoral dissertation, Purdue U., 1968. Univ. Microfilms Order No. 69-2980.

Shofner, Jerrell H. Nor Is It Over Yet: Florida in the Era of Reconstruction, 1863-1877. Gainesville, FL: U. Press of Florida, 1974.

Silver, Michael. "A Problem That Eludes a Solution." *Orlando Sentinel Star*, Je 11, 1978. [Jones High School, Orlando]

Sinclair, Ward. "Desegregation's Quiet Success." *Washington Post*, Je 17, 1978. [Tampa]

Sloan, Lee, and French, Robert M. "Black Rule in the Urban South?" In Charles V. Willie, (ed.), *Black/Brown/White Relations*. New Brunswick, NJ: Transaction, 1977. [Jacksonville]

Smith, Charles U., and Parks, A. S. "Desegregation in Florida--A 'Progress' Report." *Quarterly Review of Higher Education Among Negroes* 25(Ja, 1957):54-60.

Smith, Robert H. "Family Life and Housing Environment in the Lincoln Neighborhood Community." *Journal of Social and Behavioral Sciences* 18(Fall-Winter, 1971-1972):80-89. [Tallahassee]

South Florida Migrant Legal Services Programs, Inc. *Seasons in the Sun. A Preliminary Study of the Seasonal Farmworker in the South Florida Setting*, F, 1969. Printed in U.S. Congress, 91st, 1st and 2nd Sessions, Senate, Committee on Labor and Public Welfare, Subcommittee on Migratory Labor, *Migrant and Seasonal Farmworker Power Resources. Hearings...Part 4A*, pp. 1416-1516. Washington, DC: GPO, 1970.

St. Angelo, Douglas, and Levine, E. Lester. "Black Candidates. Can They Be Aided by a New Populism?" *Journal of Black Studies* 3 (D, 1973):167-182. [Tallahassee]

Starnes, Thomas Albert. "An Analysis of the Academic Achievement of Negro Students in the Predominantly White Schools of a Selected Florida County." Doctoral dissertation, U. of Southern Mississippi, 1968.

Stebbins, C. H. "Education in West Palm Beach." *Crisis*, Ap, 1942.

Stephenson, Robert, and Spieth, Phillip. *Evaluation of Desegregation 1970-71. Dade County Public Schools*. Miami: Dade County Public Schools, Je, 1972.

"A Study of Segregated Schools in a Florida County." *Opportunity*, Jl, 1942.

A Summary Report of Six School Systems, 1968, 31 pp. Coral Gables, FL: South Florida School Desegregation Consulting Center, Miami U. ERIC ED 042 555.

Taylor, Joseph H. *Summer Institute of Psychological-Sociological Problems of School Desegregation: 80 School Administrators, Supervisors, Principals and Teachers in Ten Florida Counties. Final Report*, Mr, 1968, 14 pp. Daytona Beach, FL: Bethune-Cookman College. ERIC ED 023 730.

Tomberlin, Joseph A. "Florida and the School Desegregation Issue, 1954-1959: A Summary View." *Journal of Negro Education* 43(Fall, 1974):457-467.

_____. "Florida Whites and the *Brown* Decision of 1954." *Florida Historical Quarterly* 51 (Jl, 1972).

_____. "The Negro and Florida's System of Education: The Aftermath of the *Brown* Case." Doctoral dissertation, Florida State U., 1967.

"Two Schools Are Making Integration Work." *Florida Schools* 34(Ja-F, 1972):6-10. [St. Petersburg]

U.S. Commission on Civil Rights. *The Diminishing Barrier: A Report on School Desegregation...* Washington, DC: GPO, D, 1972. [Alucha, Escambia, Leon, and Volusia counties]

U.S. Commission on Civil Rights. *Hearing Held in Tampa, Florida. March 29-31, 1976*. Washington, DC: The Commission, 1978.

U.S. Commission on Civil Rights. "Hillsborough County, Florida (Tampa)." In *School Desegregation in Ten Communities*, pp. 14-35. Washington, DC: GPO, Je, 1973.

U.S. Commission on Civil Rights. "Hillsborough County School Desegregation." In *Hearing Held in Tampa, Florida, March 29-31, 1976*, pp. 446-576. Washington, DC: The Commission, 1978.

U.S. Commission on Civil Rights. *Report on Florida*. Washington, DC: GPO, 1963.

U.S. Office of Education. "Hillsborough County, Florida." In *Working Together. Case Studies of Title I, ESEA Programs in Four Desegregated School Districts*. Washington, DC: GPO, 1974.

Vickers, Larry. "'Equal Opportunity.' Does Florida's Governor Reubin Askew Really Mean It?" *South Today* 3(O, 1971):1, 6.

Washington, John T. "Power in the Black Subcommunity of Orlando." Doctoral dissertation, U. of Florida, 1977.

White, Arthur O. "Black Boycott: Gainesville, Florida." *Urban Education* 9(Ja, 1975):309-324. [1969]

_____. *Florida's Crisis in Public Education. Changing Patterns of Leadership*. Gainesville, FL: U. Presses of Florida, 1975.

_____. "Florida's State School Chief and Desegregation." *Integrateducation* 12(Jl-Ag, 1974):33-39.

_____. "Race, Politics and Education: The Sheats-Holloway Election Controversy, 1903-1904." *Florida Historical Quarterly* 53(Ja, 1975).

Wiles, John Whitney. "Southern Alternative Schools: A Portrait." Educational Leadership 29(Mr, 1972):534-538.

Williams, D. E. A Brief Review of the Growth and Improvement of Education for Negroes in Florida, 1927-1962. Atlanta, 1963.

Wooten, James T. "Year of Tampa Busing Finds Adults Wary, Pupils Content." New York Times, Je 7, 1972.

Wright, J. Leitch, Jr. "Blacks in British East Florida." Florida Historical Quarterly 54 (Ap, 1976):425-442.

X, Dennis. "NAACP File Bias Suit." Muhammad Speaks, S 5, 1975. [Jacksonville]

Young, Nathan Ben. "These 'Colored' United States" Florida: Our Contiguous Foreign State." Messenger 5(N, 1923):866, 896.

Georgia

Adair, Augustus A. "A Political History of the Negroes in Atlanta, 1908-1953." Master's thesis, Atlanta U., 1955.

Adams, Samuel L. Blueprint for Segregation: A Survey of Atlanta Housing. Atlanta: City of Atlanta, 1967.

"Albany--'Just About the Nicest Town.'" Southern Courier, O 5, 1968.

Allen, Frederick, and Reeves, Alexis Scott. "Black Progress Here Is In the Eye of the Beholder." Atlanta Constitution, Ap 4, 1978. [Atlanta]

Anderson, Nancy. "Fear Has Distorted the Community." Integrateducation 15(N-D, 1977): 143-44.

Atlanta Public Schools. Opinion Survey of Teachers Transferred in March, 1970 (In Compliance With Federal-Court Orders). Atlanta: Atlanta Public Schools, S, 1970.

Ayres, B. Drummond. "Roberta, Ga., Exemplifies Integration Gains." New York Times, D 5, 1976. [Crawford County High School]

Bady, Susan. "What I Learned from Negroes." Ebony, S, 1966. [An Antioch College student lives and learns in Atlanta]

Bailey, Peter. "Growing Up in the New South." Ebony 29(Ag, 1974):128-131. [Forsyth]

Baldwin, Guy. "Students Get Together in... Atlanta." Southern Courier, N 23, 1968.

Barker, Horace N., Jr. "Where Busing Works." In Robert E. Anderson, Jr., The South and Her Children: School Desegregation, 1970-1971, pp. 56-68. Atlanta: Southern Regional Council, Mr, 1971. [Athens]

Bederman, Sanford H. "Black Residential Neighborhoods and Job Opportunity Centers in Atlanta, Georgia." Doctoral dissertation, U. of Minnesota, 1973.

_____. "The Stratification of Quality of Life in the Black Community of Atlanta, Georgia." Southeastern Geographer 14(1974):26-37.

Belcher, John C., and Allman, Carolyn N. The Non-white Population of Georgia. Athens, GA: Institute of Community and Area Development, U. of Georgia, 1967.

Bell, Derrick A., Jr. "NAACP: Faith and an Opportunity." Freedomways 13(1973):330-333. [Atlanta desegregation]

Bellamy, Donnie D. "James H. Torbert: Another Forgotten Benefactor of Black People." Negro History Bulletin 39(Mr, 1976):549-553. [Fort Valley High and Industrial School]

Black, Blanton E. "The Impact of the Extension Education Program on Rural Negroes in Georgia, 1914-1964." Doctoral dissertation, U. of Georgia, 1971.

"Black (Studies) Vatican." Newsweek, Ag 11, 1969. [Institute of the Black World, Atlanta]

Blackwell, Gloria. "Black-Controlled Media in Atlanta, 1960-1970: The Burden of the Message and the Struggle for Survival." Doctoral dissertation, Emory U., 1973. Univ. Microfilms Order No. 74-10280.

Blassingame, John W. "Before the Ghetto: The Making of the Black Community in Savannah, Georgia, 1865-1880." Journal of Social History 6(Summer, 1973):463-488.

Boney, F. N. "Georgia's Clarke County Integrates Its Schools." Christian Century, Ap 1, 1970.

Bowler, Mike. "Teaching in Atlanta." Atlanta Constitution, Ap 19, 1970-Ap 25, 1970. [Seven articles on teacher desegregation in Atlanta]

Braddock, Clayton. "A 'Majority District.'" Southern Educational Report, N, 1968. [Hancock County]

Branch, Taylor. "'Freedom of Choice' Desegregation: The Southern Reality." The Washington Monthly, N, 1969. [Seminole County]

Brown, Cynthia, and Provizer, Marlene. "The South's New Dual School System: A Case Study." New South 27(Fall, 1972):59-72. [Sumter County]

Brown, Junie. "Academies: Many Parents Would Give Children Bad Educations." South Today 2(D, 1970):12.

Bullock, Charles S. III, and Rodgers, Harrell R., Jr. "Adjusting to School Desegregation: Perceptions and Correlates to Post-Desegregation Problems." Negro Educational Review 29(Ap, 1978):87-96.

Bullock, Charles S. III, and Stewart, Joseph Jr. "Perceived Parental and Student Racial Attitudes." Integrateducation 15(N-D, 1977): 120-122.

Burrows, Edward F. "The Literacy Education of Negroes in Antebellum Virginia, North Carolina, South Carolina, and Georgia with Special Reference to Regulatory and Prohibitive Laws." Master's thesis, Duke U., 1940.

Calhoun, Tommie C. "A Survey of Negro Rural Schools of Bibb County, Georgia." Master's thesis, Fisk U., 1934.

Campbell, Will D. "The Death of Willie Gene Carreker." Race Relations Reporter 5(S, 1974):31-37.

Carter, E. R. The Black Side: A Partial History of the Business, Religious, and Educational Side of the Negro in Atlanta, Georgia. Atlanta, GA: 1894.

Chapman, Paul W. "Problems and Progress in Negro Education." Southern Workman 60(Jl, 1931):325-329.

Clarke, Margaret M. Black-White Ghettos--Quality of Life in the Atlanta Inner City. ORNL-HUD-25. Springfield, VA: National Technical Information SErvice, D, 1971.

Cleveland, Len G. "Georgia Baptists and the 1954 Supreme Court Desegregation Decision." Georgia Historical Quarterly 59(1975).

Clift, Eleanor. "As the Students See It." Race Relations Reporter 5(My, 1974):29-30. [Atlanta]

_____. "Debate on 'Compromise' Continues." Race Relations Reporter 4(S, 1973):3-5. [Atlanta]

Clotfelter, Charles T. "The Effect of School Desegregation on Housing Prices." Review of Economics and Statistics 57(N, 1975):446-451. [Atlanta]

Cohen, Muriel. "Desegregation Lags in Atlanta." Boston Globe, D 7, 1975.

Commission on Professional Rights and Responsibilities. DeKalb County, Georgia. A Profile of Paternalism in Public Education. Washington, DC: National Education Association, Jl, 1968.

Conyers, James E., and Farmar, William J., assisted by Levin, Martin. Black Youth in a Southern Metropolis. Atlanta: Southern Regional Council, Ja, 1968. [Atlanta]

Cooper, B. "Analysis of the Reading Achievement of White and Negro Pupils in Certain Public Schools of Georgia." School Review, Winter, 1964.

Crimmins, Timothy J. "The Crystal Stair: A Study of the Effects of Clan, Race, and Ethnicity on Secondary Education in Atlanta, 1872-1925." Doctoral dissertation, Emory U., 1972.

_____. "The Crystal Stair: A Study of the Effects of Caste and Class on Secondary Education in Late Nineteenth Century Atlanta, Georgia." Urban Education 8(Ja, 1974):401-421.

Denton, William H. Schools With a Difference: Encouraging Voluntary Transfer of Students in the Atlanta Public Schools. Atlanta: Center for School and Community Services, Atlanta U., 1974.

"Dismissal of Teachers." Muhammad Speaks, Ag 27, 1971. [Washington County]

Dittmer, John Avery. Black Georgia in the Progressive Era, 1900-1920. Urbana, IL: U. of Illinois Press, 1977.

_____. "The Black Man and White Supremacy in Georgia during the Progressive Era." Doctoral dissertation, Indiana U., 1971. Univ. Microfilms Order No. 72-12952.

Dixon, John C. "Negro High School Development in Georgia." High School Quarterly 20(O, 1931):30-32.

_____. "Some Theses Relating to a Dual System of Education Having Particular Application in Georgia." High School Quarterly 20(Jl, 1932): 190-195.

"Doing It In Georgia, Is South Carolina Next?" Your Schools, Ja, 1970. [Definitions of integrated schools and integrated districts in D 17, 1969, federal court decisions]

DuBois, W. E. B. "The Atlanta Negro Library." Chicago Defender, Jl 26, 1947.

_____. "Compulsory Education and the Negro--A Talk to White Georgia." Horizon 6(Jl, 1910): 3-5.

_____. "The Negro Common School, Georgia." Crisis, S, 1926.

_____. Testimony in U.S. Congress, 75th, 1st Session, House of Representatives, Committee on Education. Hearings on Federal Aid for the Support of Public Schools, pp. 284-295. Washington, DC: GPO, 1937.

Edelstein, Rosalind I. "Early Intervention in the Poverty Cycle." Social Casework 53(Jl, 1972):418-424. [Whitfield County Parent Child Center, Dalton]

Escott, Paul D. "The Context of Freedom: Georgia's Slaves During the Civil War." Georgia Historical Quarterly 58(Spring, 1974):79-104.

Etchison, Cora J. "The Development of the Public School System for Negroes of Monroe, Walton County, Georgia, 1935-1962." Master's thesis, Atlanta U., 1965.

Fancher, Betsy. "Summerhill." South Today 3 (N, 1971):7. [Atlanta]

_____. "White Flight: One Area Fought It and It May Have Won." South Today 2(Mr, 1971):12. [South DeKalb, Atlanta]

Fennell, Valerie. "International Atlanta and Ethnic Group Relations." Urban Anthropology 6(Winter, 1977):345-354.

4X, Harold. "Atlanta 'Movement' Crumbling. Integration Issue Bursts NAACP Asunder..." Muhammad Speaks, Ag 24, 1973.

Frazier, E. Franklin. "A Community School." Southern Workman 54(O, 1925):459-464.

_____. "These 'Colored' United States: Georgia: On the Struggle Against Impudent Inferiority." Messenger 6(Je, 1924):173-177.

_____. "Neighborhood Union in Atlanta." Southern Workman 52(S, 1923):437-442.

"Friendly Competitors." Newsweek, Mr 27, 1972. [Baker Academy, Baker County]

Gale, Mary Ellen. "'He Worked the Hardest and Did the Best.'" Southern Courier, Je 1, 1968. [Abbeville]

_____. "Henry County Parents Protest School Set-Up." Southern Courier, S 9, 1967. [Abbeville]

Gallagher, Buell G. "Integrated Schools in the Black Cities?" Journal of Negro Education 42(Summer, 1973):336-350.

Garland, Phyl. "Atlanta. Black Mecca of the South." Ebony 26(Ag, 1971):152-157.

"Georgia Hypocritical Integration Hit." Muhammad Speaks, My 22, 1970. [Athens]

"Georgia School Crisis." Muhammad Speaks, Ap 23, 1971.

Georgia State Advisory Committee. Equal Opportunity in Federally Assisted Agricultural Programs in Georgia. Washington, DC: U.S. Commission on Civil Rights, Ag, 1967.

Georgia State Advisory Committee to the U.S. Commission on Civil Rights. Toward Equal Opportunity in Housing in Atlanta, Georgia. Washington, DC: GPO, My, 1968.

Gibson, Delores B. "Desegregation: An Uncommon View." Community (Chicago), Vol. 28, No. 2 (1969). [The first Negro teacher in a white school in Atlanta]

Gifford, James M. "Black Hope and Despair in Antebellum Georgia: The Willima Moss Correspondence." Prologue 8(Fall, 1976):153-162.

Graham, V. F. "Health Studies of Negro Children: I. Intelligence Studies of Negro Children in Atlanta, Georgia." Public Health Reports 41(1926):2759-2783.

Guerrero, Gene. "Atlanta Schools: The Case for Metro Relief." Civil Liberties, Ap, 1975.

Guide to Developing an Inclusive Integration Plan, 1970. Georgia Teachers and Education Association, 201 Ashby Street, N.W., Atlanta, GA 30314.

Hagan, Ellin R. "Report From Rural Georgia." Christian Science Monitor, Ja 19, 1976. [Sylvania]

Hall, R. H. "Segregation in the Public Schools of Georgia." Georgia Bar Journal 16(My, 1954):417-426.

Hamilton, Radford Cisco. "An Analysis of the Racial Ratio Changes in the Student Population of the Atlanta Public School System (1960-1974)." Doctoral dissertation, U. of Georgia, 1978. Univ. Microfilms Order No. 78-14946.

Hammond, William T. "A Study of the Literacy Level of Atlanta Public High School 11th and 12th Grade Students." Doctoral dissertation, Georgia State U., 1976.

Harris, William. "Work and Family in Black Atlanta, 1880." Journal of Social History 9(Spring, 1976):319-330.

Haynes, Elizabeth Ross. The Black Boy of Atlanta: Richard R. Wright. Boston: House of Edinboro, 1953.

Hefner, James A. "Black Employment in a Southern 'Progressive' City: the Atlanta Experience." Doctoral dissertation, U. of Colorado, 1971.

Hein, Virginia H. "The Image of 'A City Too Busy to Hate': Atlanta in the 1960's." Phylon 33(Fall, 1972):205-221.

Hill, Hines Lafayette. "Negro Education in Rural Georgia." Master's thesis, Emory U., 1939.

Hodges, C. V. "Contributions of Philanthropic Foundations in Negro Public Secondary Education in Georgia." Master's thesis, Duke U., 1939.

Hollingsworth, R. R. "Education and Reconstruction in Georgia." Georgia Historical Quarterly 19(1935):112-133, 229, 250.

Holmes, Michael S. "The New Deal and Georgia's Black Youth." Journal of Southern History 38(Ag, 1972).

Hope, John. "Our Atlanta Schools." Voice of the Negro, Ja, 1904.

Hopkins, Richard. "Occupational and Geographic Mobility in Atlanta, 1870-1896." Journal of Southern History 34(My, 1968).

Horne, Frank S. "The Present Status of Negro Education in Certain of the Southern States, Particularly Georgia." Master's thesis, U. of Southern California, 1932.

Hornsby, Alton, Jr. "The Negro in Atlanta Politics, 1961-1973." Atlanta History Bulletin 21(Spring, 1977):7-33.

Hubert, Z. T. "The Log Cabin Community Center and Country Life." Southern Workman 63(Ag, 1934):249-252.

Huie, H. M. "Factors Influencing the Desegregation Process in the Atlanta School System, 1954-1967." Doctoral dissertation, U. of Georgia, 1967.

Hulsey, John A., Jr. "A Study of Certain Aspects of Faculty Desegregation in Georgia." Doctoral dissertation, U. of Alabama, 1969.

Hutcheson, John D., Jr. Racial Attitudes in Atlanta. Atlanta: Center for Research in Social Change, Emory U., 1973.

Hutchins, Ollie L. "The Growth and Development of Negro Education, Early County, Georgia, 1937-1957." Master's thesis, Atlanta U., 1963.

Hux, Roger K. "The Ku Klux Klan in Macon, 1919-1925." Georgia Historical Quarterly 62(Summer, 1978):155-168.

"Institute of the Black World." Negro Digest, Mr, 1970, [Atlanta]

Jackson, Barbara L. "Desegregation: Atlanta Style." Theory Into Practice 17(F, 1978): 43-53.

Johnson, Harold T., and Hall, Morrill M. (eds.). School Desegregation, Educational Change and Georgia. Athens, GA: School Desegregation Educational Center, 1968.

Johnson, Harold T., and Tyer, Harold L. Special Training Institute on Desegregation for Educational Leadership Teams from the School Systems of the First District of Georgia, O, 1967. ERIC ED 030 684.

Johnson, R. O. "Desegregation of Public Education in Georgia--One Year Afterward." Journal of Negro Education 24(Summer, 1955):228-247.

Jones, Frank V. "The Education of Negroes in Richmond County, Georgia, 1860-1960." Master's thesis, Atlanta U., 1963.

Jones, Jacqueline. "The 'Great Opportunity': Northern Teachers and the Georgia Freedmen, 1865-1873." Doctoral dissertation, U. of Wisconsin, 1976.

Jones, Mack H. "Black Political Empowerment in Atlanta: Myth and Reality." An. Am. Acad. Pol. Social Sci. 439(S, 1978):90-117. [1965-1978]

Kelly, Paul E., and Wingrove, C. Ray. "Educational and Occupational Choices of Black and White, Male and Female Students in a Rural Georgia Community." Journal of Research and Development in Education 9(F, 1975):45-56.

King, Slater. "School Desegregation in 'Bad' County." Southern Patriot, D, 1966 [letter]. [Baker County]

King, Wayne. "In Rural Georgia, a Prep School for Blacks." New York Times, N 25, 1976. [Boggs Academy, Keysville]

Kingston, Albert J., and Gentry, Harold W. "Discipline Problems in Georgia Secondary Schools--1961 and 1974." NASSP Bulletin 61 (F, 1977):94-99.

Landers, Amanda E. "The Development of Negro Education in Baldwin County, Georgia, 1865-1963." Master's thesis, Atlanta U., 1963.

Landry, K. C. "Georgia's Jailing of 14-year-old Black Girl May Boomerang." Muhammad Speaks, Mr 7, 1969.

Lawrence, Jay. "Racial Tension Eased at Columbia High School." Atlanta Constitution, F 12, 1976.

Lee, Dallas. The Cotton Patch Evidence. New York: Harper & Row, 1973. [Koinonia communal farm, Americus]

"Legal Status of the Colored Population in Respect to Schools and Education, Georgia." Journal of Education 19(1870):339-342.

Lenoir, L. D., and Lenoir, J. J. "Compulsory Legal Segregation in the Public Schools, with Special Reference to Georgia." Mercer Law Review 5(Spring, 1954):211-241.

Leventhal, Will. "A Personal Odyssey." New South 27(Fall, 1972):73-80.

Long, Junie and others. "Atlanta's Schools... A Critique. Leaders Divided, Indecisive." Atlanta Journal, Jl 24, 1975.

McAllister, James W. A Workshop Designed to Alleviate the Fears, Prejudices, and Misconceptions of Personnel in the LaGrange City and Troup County School Systems with Respect to Their Associations with Members of the Opposite Race in Order to Ensure the Continued Successful Functioning of the Educational Program, S 30, 1970. ERIC ED 056 131.

McAllister, Joan L. "Public Support of Negro Education in Georgia Since the Civil War: An Experiment in Dual Education." Master's thesis, Columbia U., 1933.

McClendon, W. Oliver. "An Historical Investigation of the Negro Public School Teacher in Atlanta, Georgia, 1872-1900." Master's thesis, Atlanta U., 1968.

McPheeters, Annie L. (comp.). Negro Programs in Atlanta, Georgia, 1961-1970; A Selective Bibliography on Race and Human Relations From Four Atlanta Newspapers. Atlanta: 1972.

Maguire, Jane. On Shares. Ed Brown's Story. New York: Norton, 1976.

Matthews, John Michael. "Studies in Race Relations in Georgia." Doctoral dissertation, Duke U., 1970.

Maxwell, Neil. "Black Schools Suffer More Than White Ones in Federal Fund Cut off." Wall Street Journal, Ap 25, 1969. [Sumter County]

_____. "Charge of Harassment of Negro Family Roils Small Town in Georgia." Wall Street Journal, F 6, 1969. [Sylvester]

_____. "Some Boards in South Accused of Sabotaging Public School Systems." Wall Street Journal, N 4, 1971. [Sumter County]

_____. "Strife Still Imperils Integration of Schools in Some Communities." Wall Street Journal, Mr 12, 1971.

_____. "The White View from Sylvester, Georgia." Wall Street Journal, F 21, 1969.

Meade, Anthony. "The Distribution of Segregation in Atlanta." Social Forces 51(D, 1972):182-192.

"The Mercer Project: A Path to Peaceful School Desegregation." 25 minute documentary film dealing with desegregation in Bibb and Houston Counties, Georgia. Media Relations, Dept. MP, U.S. Community Relations Service, Washington, DC 20530.

Mitchell, George. "I'm Somebody Important: Young Black Voices from Rural Georgia." Urbana, IL: U. of Illinois Press, 1972.

Montgomery, Bill and others. "Atlanta's Schools...A Critique. Discipline." Atlanta Journal, Jl 22, 1975.

Montgomery, Bill, and others. "Atlanta's Schools...A Critique. The Teachers." Atlanta Journal, Jl 27, 1975.

Moore, John Hammond. "Jim Crow in Georgia." South Atlantic Quarterly 66(Autumn, 1967): 554-565.

Moseley, Charlton. "Latent Klanism in Georgia, 1890-1915." Georgia Historical Quarterly 56 (Fall, 1972):365-386.

Negro Education in Georgia. Atlanta: Atlanta U. Bulletin No. 67, F, 1927.

"New Deal in Atlanta." Newsweek, Jl 30, 1973. [Desegregation plan]

Newman, Joseph W. "A History of the Atlanta Public School Teachers' Association, Local 89 of the American Federation of Teachers, 1919-1956." Doctoral dissertation, Georgia State U., 1978. Univ. Microfilms Order No. 7900116.

Nix, Harold L., Shoemaker, Donald, and Singh, Ron. Community Social Analysis of Oglethorpe County, Georgia. Atlanta: State Department of Public Health, 1967.

Obatala, J. K. "Back Home in Tifton." New York Times Magazine, D 2, 1973.

O'Connor, Michael James. "The Measurement and Significance of Racial Residential Barriers in Atlanta, 1890-1970." Doctoral dissertation, U. of Georgia, 1977. Univ. Microfilms Order No. 77-30497.

Openshaw, Howard. Race and Residence: An Analysis of Property and Values in Transitional Areas, Atlanta, Georgia, 1960-1971. Atlanta: School of Business Administration, Georgia State U., 1973.

Owens, James L. "Blacks in Reconstruction Georgia." Integrateducation 14(N-D, 1976).

Owens, James L. "The Negro in Georgia During Reconstruction 1864-1872: A Social History." Doctoral dissertation, U. of Georgia, 1975.

Palmer, Earl. "The United Way and the Black Community in Atlanta, Georgia." Black Scholar 9(D, 1977):50-58.

Palmer, Warren. "Toward Cultural Diversity in Southern Education." Clearinghouse 51(My, 1978):414-418.

Patterson, Pat. "Atlanta." Black Enterprise 4 (F, 1974):41-46.

Perdue, Robert E. The Growth of Public Schools for Blacks and the Emergence of Professional Black Savannahians, Mr, 1976. ERIC ED 127 390.

_____. The Negro in Savannah, 1865-1900. Jericho, NY: Exposition Press, 1973.

_____. "The Negro in Savannah, 1865-1900."
Doctoral dissertation, U. of Georgia, 1971.
Univ. Microfilms Order No. 72-2525.

Phinazee, Annette Hoage (ed.). The Georgia
Child's Access to Materials Pertaining to
American Negroes [Proceedings of the Con-
ference (Atlanta, N 10-11, 1967)]. Atlanta
U., School of Library Services, 1968. ERIC
ED 032 087.

Porter, Michael Leroy. "Black Atlanta: An In-
tradisciplinary Study of Blacks on the East
Side of Atlanta, 1890-1930." Doctoral dissertation, Emory U., 1974. Univ. Microfilms
Order No. 75-11135.

Powledge, Fred. "A New Politics in Atlanta."
New Yorker, D 31, 1973.

Prugh, Peter H. "Atlanta in the Throes of
Growing Pains." Wall Street Journal, Mr 27,
1969.

Pupil Performance in the Elementary Schools of
Atlanta. Research and Development Report,
Volume 5, Numbers 22-25, 27, 30, 44, and 45,
1972, 292 pp. Atlanta: Atlanta Public
Schools. ERIC ED 064 449.

Racine, Philip Noel. "Atlanta's Schools: A
History of the Public School System, 1869-
1955." Doctoral dissertation, Emory U.,
1969. Univ. Microfilms Order No. 70-5751.

_____. "The Struggle for Equal Schools: At-
lanta, 1869-1954." Integrateducation 14
(Mr-Ap, 1976):26-31.

Range, Peter Ross. "Capital of Black-Is-Beauti-
ful." New York Times, Ap 7, 1974. [Atlanta]

Reed, Ruth. The Negro Women of Gainesville
(Hall County), Georgia. Athens, GA: U. of
Georgia, 1921.

Resource Management Corporation. Evaluation of
the Emergency School Assistance Program, Vol.
III, Appendix N, F 15, 1972. ERIC ED 058
470. [Case history of ESAP in Macon, GA]

Richardson, Edna A. "A Study of the Status of
the Negro Teaching Personnel of Crisp County,
Georgia." Master's thesis, Atlanta U., 1966.

Schabacker, William H., Clark, Russell S., and
Cooper, Homer C. (eds.). Focus on the Future
of Georgia, 1970-1985. Papers Prepared for
Use by the Advisory Commission on Educational
Goals by the State Board of Education. At-
lanta: State Department of Education, 1970.

Scheer, Robert. "Blacks Increasingly Isolated
in Atlanta." Los Angeles Times, N 20, 1978.

Schemmel, Bill. "Atlanta's 'Power Structure'
Faces Life." New South 27(Spring, 1972):62-
68.

Scott, Peter. "Clarke Schools 'Model' for Integration." Atlanta Journal, Ap 26, 1976.
[Clarke County]

_____. "Hit the Road, Johnny." Atlanta Jour-
nal, F 3, 1976. [Metropolitan desegregation
in the Atlanta area]

Simms, Ruth P. "The Savannah Story: Education
and Desegregation." In Raymond W. Mack, Our
Children's Burden. New York: Random House.

Smith, Elizabeth Cook. "A Study on the Development of the Georgia Public School System,
1900-1950." Master's thesis, Atlanta U.,
1952.

"Southwest Georgia Battle Reaches Stalemate."
Southern Patriot, Ap, 1969. [Sylvester, in
Worth County]

Starbuck, James C. (comp.). Metropolitan Atlanta Update, 1970-1974. Monticello, IL:
Council of Planning Libraries, 1975.

Stone, Clarence N. Economic Growth and Neigh-
bor Discontent: System Bias in the Urban
Renewal Program of Atlanta. Chapel Hill,
NC: U. of North Carolina Press, 1976.

Stuart, Reginald. "Atlanta Splits On School
Plan." Race Relations Reporter 4(F 19, 1973):
5-7.

Sullivan, John J. The Academically Able but
Disadvantaged Georgia High School Student,
1969. Athens, GA: U. of Georgia Institute
of Higher Education. ERIC ED 040 659.

Talmadge, Herman. "Exclusive State Control Over
State Education." School and Society 88(My
7, 1960):243-246.

Tanner, James C. "Integration in Action." Wall
Street Journal, Ja 20, 1964.

Terry, Lawrence. "The Development of Negro Education in Worth County, Georgia, 1860-1962."
Master's thesis, Atlanta U., 1963.

Thomas, Leland C. "Some Aspects of Biracial Education in Georgia, 1900-1954." Doctoral
dissertation, George Peabody College for
Teachers, 1960. Univ. Microfilms Order No.
60-5867.

Thornbery, Jerry. "Northerners and the Atlanta
Freedmen, 1865-1869." Prologue 6(Winter,
1974).

Toppin, Edgar A. "Walter White and the Atlanta
NAACP's fight for Equal Schools, 1916-1917."
History of Education Quarterly, Spring, 1967.

Trillin, Calvin. "U.S. Journal: Atlanta. Settlement." New Yorker 49(Mr 17, 1973):101-
105. [Desegregation case]

U.S. Bureau of the Census. Social and Health Indicators System. Atlanta: Part 2. Washington, DC: GPO, O, 1973.

U.S. Commission on Civil Rights. "Glynn County, Georgia (Brunswick)." In School Desegregation in Ten Communities, pp. 177-197. Washington, DC: GPO, Je, 1973.

Walker, D. E. "Focus on Southwest Georgia." Negro Educational Review, O, 1953.

Walker, Lester E., Jr. "Employment and Training: A Study of the 1965 Graduates of Carver Vocational High School in Atlanta, Georgia." Master's thesis, Atlanta U., Je, 1968. PB 193 996. National Technical Information Service, Springfield, VA 22151.

Wallenstein, Peter Reeve. "From Slave South to New South: Taxes and Spending in Georgia from 1850 through Reconstruction." Doctoral dissertation, Johns Hopkins U., 1973.

Wasserman, Miriam. "Beyond Tokenism: Reverse Integration in Albany, Georgia." Integrated Education, Je-Jl, 1967.

_____. "The Souls of White Folk: Atlanta, Georgia, 1964-1966." New Politics, Summer, 1966.

Weltner, Charles L. "Pride and Progress." American Education, O, 1966. [School desegregation in Atlanta]

Werner, Randolph Dennis. "Hegemony and Conflict: The Political Economy of a Southern Region, Augusta, Georgia, 1865-1895." Doctoral dissertation, U. of Virginia, 1977.

White, Bayla, Kelly, Sara, MacNeil, Dona, Nay, Joe, and Wholey, Joseph S. The Atlanta Project: Developing Signals of Relative School Performance. Washington, DC: The Urban Institute, 1973.

White, Bayla, Vogt, Leona, and Wholey, Joseph S. The Atlanta/Urban Institute School Classification Project. Washington, DC: The Urban Institute, 1973.

Winn, William. "Atlanta: Schools Order Reveals a Crisis of Leadership." South Today, F, 1970.

Winn, William, with Inman, D. L., and Williams, Ed. Augusta, Georgia and Jackson State University. Southern Episodes in a National Tragedy. Atlanta: Southern Regional Council, Je, 1970.

Wright, C. T. "The Development of Education for Blacks in Georgia, 1865-1900." Doctoral dissertation, Boston U., 1977. Univ. Microfilms Order No. 77-11433.

_____. "The Development of Public Schools for Blacks in Atlanta, 1872-1900." Atlanta Historical Bulletin 21(Spring, 1977):115-128.

Wright, Richard Robert, Sr. A Brief Historical Sketch of Negro Education in Georgia. Savannah: Robinson Printing House, 1894.

4X, Harold. "Georgia School 'Sacrifices' Federal Funds Before Changing 'Biased' Policies." Muhammad Speaks, My 9, 1975. [Columbia High School, DeKalb County]

Young, Virginia Heyer. "Family and Childhood in a Southern Negro Community." American Anthropologist 72(1970):269-288.

Hawaii

Abbott, William L. "Trapped in a Mystique." Nation, F 3, 1969.

Abe, Shirley. "Violation of the Racial Code in Hawaii." Social Process in Hawaii 9(1945): 33-38.

Beaglehole, Ernest. "Some Modern Hawaiians." University of Hawaii Research Publications No. 19(1937).

Bean, Thomas W. Recent Psycholinguistic Research in Reading and Hawaiian Islands Dialect, Jl, 1976. ERIC ED 137770.

Boggs, Stephen T. "The Meaning of Questions and Narratives to Hawaiian Children." In C. Cazden and others (eds.), Functions of Language in the Classroom. New York: Teachers College Press, 1972.

Brieske, Phillip R. "A Study of the Development of Public Elementary and Secondary Education in the Territory of Hawaii." Doctoral dissertation, U. of Washington, 1961.

Bunker, Frank F. "Education in Hawaii is Directed to Students of Many Races." School Life 12(F, 1927):105-108.

Burrows, Edwin C. Hawaiian Americans: An Account of the Mingling of Japanese, Chinese, Polynesian and American Cultures. New York: 1947.

Carr, Elizabeth B. Da Kine Talks: From Pidgin to Standard English in Hawaii. Honolulu: U. of Hawaii Press, 1972.

Casey, Judith C. and others. Housing in Hawaii: An Overview. Honolulu: Pacific Urban Studies and Planning Program, U. of Hawaii, 1974.

Castberg, A. D. "The Ethnic Factor in Criminal Sentencing." Western Political Quarterly 24 (S, 1971):425-437.

Characteristics of the Population of Oahu by Ethnic Stock, 1964-1967. Honolulu: State Department of Planning and Economic Development, 1971.

Commission on Children and Youth. Child Care in Hawaii. Study and Recommendations. Honolulu: Social Welfare Development and Research Center, U. of Hawaii, 1974.

Daws, Gavan. "Honolulu in the 19th Century: Notes on the Emergence of Urban Society in Hawaii." Journal of Pacific History 2(1967): 77-96.

Day, Richard R. Language Acquisition in a Bicultural Community: A Case Study of Bidialectalism, O, 1976. ERIC ED 136 611.

Demographic Statistics of Hawaii: 1778-1965. Honolulu: U. of Hawaii Press, 1968.

Dotts, Cecil. "Teacher Corps in Hawaii." Educational Perspectives 8(D, 1969):28-32.

DuPuy, William Atherton. Hawaii and Its Race Problem. Washington, DC: GPO, 1932.

Eddy, John Melvin. "A Study of the Vocational Opportunities for High School Graduates in the Territory of Hawaii." Master's thesis, U. of Chicago, 1926.

Endicott, William. "Hawaii Feels Rising Tide of Ethnic Pride." Los Angeles Times, S 27, 1977.

Eng, Mike. "Hawaii's Strategic Hamlets." Hawaii Pono 1(O, 1971):16-31. [Honolulu]

Enomoto, Ernestine K. "Hawaii from Annexation: An Object of Cultural Colonialism?" Hawaii Pono 1(O, 1971):4-10.

Feldman, Carol Fleisher and others. "Standard and Nonstandard Dialect Competencies of Hawaiian Creole English Speakers." TESOL Quarterly 11(Mr, 1977):41-50.

Force, Maryanne T. The Americanization of Hawaii: A Teacher's Manual. Honolulu: State Department of Education, 1976.

Forster, John. "Social Organization and Differential Social Change in Two Hawaiian Communities." International Journal of Comparative Sociology 3(1962):200-220.

Fukada, Lois. Child Care in Hawaii. Honolulu: Legislative Reference Bureau, 1973.

Fultz, Jane N. "A Study of Status Systems and Related Value Orientations Among Adolescents of an Ethnically Plural High School Community in Hawaii." Doctoral dissertation, New York U., 1966.

Gaile, Sandra L. Socialization for Educability in a Cross-Cultural Context: Some of the Findings of the UCLA Hawaii Project, Ap, 1974. ERIC ED 101 046.

Gallimore, Ronald. "Variations in the Motivational Antecedents of Achievement Among Hawaii's Ethnic Groups." In W. Lebra, Transcultural Research in Mental Health, II, Mental Health Research in Asia and the Pacific. Honolulu: U. of Hawaii Press, 1972.

Gallimore, Ronald, and Tharp, Roland G. An Overview of Research Strategies and Findings (1971-1975) of the Kamehameha Early Education Program, O, 1976. ERIC ED 158 865.

Gallimore, Ronald, Boggs, Joan Whitehorn, and Jordan, Cathie. Culture, Behavior and Education: A Study of Hawaiian-Americans. Beverly Hills, CA: Sage, 1974.

Gallimore, Ronald and others. The Mutual Problems of Hawaiian-American Students and Public Schools, F, 1975. ERIC ED 158 830.

_____ and others. Solving Problems in Hawaiian-American Classrooms: Excellent Teaching and Cultural Factors, F, 1975. ERIC ED 158 831.

Gardner, Robert W., and Nordyke, Eleanor C. The Demographic Situation in Hawaii. Honolulu: East-West Population Institute, U. of Hawaii, 1974.

Grant, Glen L. "The Interaction of the Haole and the Local Child: A Study of Race Relations in Hawaii's Schools." Master's thesis, U. of Hawaii, 1974.

Gray, Francis du Plessix. Hawaii: The Sugar-Coated Fortress. New York: Random House, 1972.

Gulick, Sidney L. Mixing the Races in Hawaii: A Study of the Coming Neo-Hawaiian Race. New York: AMS, 1978, orig. 1937.

Haas, Michael, and Resurrection, Peter P. (eds.). "Unequal Educational Opportunity." In Politics and Prejudice in Contemporary Hawaii, pp. 226-256. Honolulu: Coventry Press of Hawaii, 1976. [P.O. Box 115, Honolulu, HI 96810]

Hawaii, Department of Labor and Industrial Relations. Disadvantaged Workers on Oahu--A Report on Their Characteristics. Honolulu: Department of Labor and Industrial Relations, D, 1966.

Hawaii, Department of Research. Office of Research. Survey of Non-English Speaking Students Attending the Public Schools in Hawaii. Honolulu: State Department of Education, My 23, 1968.

Hawaii State Department of Labor. Labor Force Information for Affirmative Action Programs, Mr, 1977. ERIC ED 158 000.

Hawaii, State Immigration Service Center. Report on Immigrant Services and Problems. Honolulu: 1973.

Hawaii's Immigrants, Social Studies, Secondary Education, 1971. Honolulu: Hawaii State Department of Education, Office of Instructional Services. ERIC ED 053 999.

Hayes, Eloise. Creative Expression among Ethnic Groups in Hawaii, Ap, 1972. ERIC ED 061 736.

Hinze, Richard H. and others. "Ten Years of Curriculum Research and Development in Hawaii: Where Have We Been?" Educational Perspectives 16(My, 1977):3-5.

Hirata, Lucie Chevy. "Immigrant Integration in a Polyethnic Society." Doctoral dissertation, U. of Hawaii, 1971.

Hormann, Bernard L. "Speech, Prejudice, and the School in Hawaii." Social Process in Hawaii, My, 1947.

Howard, Alan. Ain't No Big Thing: Coping Strategies in a Hawaiian American Community. Honolulu: U. of Hawaii Press, 1974. [Rural Oahu]

_____. "Education in 'Aina Pumehava': The Hawaiian-American Student as Hero." In Solon T. Kimball and Jacquetta H. Burnett, Learning and Culture. Seattle: U. of Washington Press, 1973.

_____. Households, Families, and Friends in a Hawaiian-American Community. Honolulu: East-West Population Institute, University of Hawaii, 1971.

Hoyt, Edwin P. "Youngest State 'Fails to Deliver the Goods.'" Times Educational Supplement, Ag 18, 1978.

Hung, Marianne Andrews. The Plantation System in the Ethnic Consciousness of Hawaii, 1976. ERIC ED 144 870.

Jacobs, Paul. "Hawaiian War Chant. No More Hula Hula. No More Prime Warriors. No More Aloha." Rolling Stone, Jl 22, 1971.

Jacobs, Paul, and Landau, Saul, with McLaughlin, Eve Pell. "The Other Side of Paradise: Hawaii's Forgotten Past." Social Policy, Jl-Ag, 1970.

Jedlicka, Davor. Children in Hawaii: An Analysis of Some Sociodemographic Characteristics from Hawaii Health Surveillance Data, 1972-1974. Honolulu: Research and Statistics Office, State Department of Health, 1976.

Kagan, Marion G. "Programs for Young Children in Hawaii: An Overview." Educational Perspectives 15(0, 1976):9-15.

Kalish, Richard A. "A Comparison of Hawaiian and Mainland Attitudes towards the Negro." Social Process in Hawaii 20(1956):16-22.

Kaneshiro, Kiyoski. "The Hawaiian Student; A Question of Marginality." Master's thesis, U. of Michigan, 1941.

Kaser, Tom. "Hawaii's Schools: An Ethnic Survey." Integrateducation 15(My-Je, 1977).

Kealoha, Gard. "Native Hawaiians Fight for Survival." Civil Rights Digest 9(Fall, 1976):52-57.

Kent, Noel. "Escape Mecca of the World." Hawaii Pono 1(0, 1971):32-58.

Kinloch, Graham C. "Race, Socio-Economic Status, and Social Distance in Hawaii." Sociology and Social Research 57(Ja, 1973): 156-167.

Kinloch, Graham C., and Borders, J. A. "Racial Stereotypes and Social Distance Among Elementary School Children in Hawaii." Sociology and Social Research 56(Ap, 1972):368-377.

Kitaguchi, L. S. "Organized Labor and Public Education in Hawaii, 1945-1960." Doctoral dissertation, New York U., 1962.

Kubo, Judy. "The Negro Soldier in Kahuku." Social Process in Hawaii 9(1945):28-32.

Kutner, Nancy G., and Weeks, Shirley S. "The Relation of Ethnicity, Poverty, and Local Tradition to Family Structure and Attitudes in Honolulu." Urban Anthropology 6(Winter, 1977):329-343.

Lackey, K. "Hawaii: Racial Equality or Paternalistic Tolerance?" New Vistas, Ja, 1946.

Lee, Dorothy Dye. "A Study of Alienation-Powerlessness and Differential Patterns of Participation in Community Decision-Making Among Six Ethnic Groups in the Lower Socio-Economic Class in Honolulu, Hawaii." Doctoral dissertation, Case Western Reserve U., 1975. Univ. Microfilms Order No. 75-27,934.

Lee, Lloyd L. "A Brief Analysis of the Role and Status of the Negro in the Hawaiian Community." American Sociological Review 13 (1948):419-437.

Leon, Joseph J. "A Test of the Milton M. Gordan Ethclass Hypotheses on Samples of Public High School Youth in Hawaii." Doctoral dissertation, U. of Hawaii, 1975.

Lind, Andrew W. "Economic Succession and Racial Invasion in Hawaii." Doctoral dissertation, U. of Chicago, 1931.

_____. Hawaii. The Last of the Magic Isles. New York: Oxford U. Press, 1971.

_____. Hawaii's People. 3rd edition. Honolulu: U. of Hawaii Press, 1967.

Livesay, Thayne M. A Study of Public Education in Hawaii: With Special Reference to the Pupil Population. Honolulu: U. of Hawaii, 1932.

Livesay, Shayne M., Caro, Ida J., and Traut, Gladys M. "Reliability of the Stanford Achievement Test in Hawaii." Hawaii Educational Review 19(N, 1930):67-69.

Loutitt, C. M. "Test Performance of a Selected Group of Part-Hawaiians." Journal of Applied Psychology 15(F, 1931):43-52.

McNassor, Donald, and Honego, Randall. "Strangers in their Own Land: Self-Displacement in Ethnic Hawaiian Youth on the Island of Hawaii." Journal of Comparative Cultures 1 (Spring, 1973):127-144.

Masuoka, Jitsuichi. "Race Preference in Hawaii." American Journal of Sociology 41 (1936).

Mays, Violet. Hawaiian Cultural Research: Some Applications and Some Cautions, 1974. ERIC ED 158 849.

Midkiff, Frank E. "Economic Determinants of Education in Hawaii." Doctoral dissertation, Yale U., 1935.

Murdoch, Katharine. "A Study of Differences Found Between Races in Intellect and Morality." School and Society 22(N 14 and 28, 1925):628-632 and 659-664.

Nagtalon-Miller, Helen. "Pluralism and Bilingual/Multicultural Education in Hawaii." Educational Perspectives 16(D, 1977):14-17.

Nakamura, Margaret, and Nakamura, Richard (comps.). Nonbook Hawaiiana. Honolulu: Office of Library Services, State Department of Education, 1974.

"Negroes in Hawaii." Ebony, Jl, 1959.

Norbeck, Edward. Pineapple Town: Hawaii. Berkeley, CA: 1959.

Nordyke, Eleanor C. The Peopling of Hawaii. Honolulu: U. Press of Hawaii, 1977.

Office of Library Services. Teacher Assist Center. Ethnic Studies. Unit 3. Hawaii: A Case Study. Student Guide to Enrichment and Directed Study. Honolulu: Office of Instructional Services, Department of Education, 1971.

Ogawa, Dennis M. Communicating in a Pluralistic Community: The Model of Hawaii's Ethnic Relations, 1976. ERIC ED 126 536.

Ohelo, Kalani. "Task Facing Hawaii's Movement." Hawaii Pono Journal 1(Ap, 1971):86-106.

Park, Robert E. "Our Racial Frontier on the Pacific." Survey 56(My 1, 1926):192-196.

Parker, Linda S. "Federal Management of Native Hawaiians." Journal of the West 15(Ap, 1976): 92-101.

Pearson, Carol. "Intelligence of Honolulu Preschool Children in Relation to Parent's Education." Child Development, Je, 1969.

Petersen, William. "The Classification of Subnations in Hawaii: An Essay in the Sociology of Knowledge." American Sociological Review, D, 1969.

Peterson, John. "If You Can't Join Them--Do Something Else: Hawaiian Alternatives to Progress." In Sandra Wallman, Perceptions of Development. New York: Cambridge U. Press, 1977.

Porteus, Stanley D. "Race and Social Differences." In Genetic Psychology Monographs, Vol. 8, No. 2, pp. 93-208. Worcester, MA: Clark U. Press, 1930. [Vineland and Punahou Academy, Honolulu]

Porteus, Stanley D., and Bobcock, Marjorie E. Temperament and Race. Boston: Richard G. Badger, 1926.

Potts, Helen A. "Student Perception of Racial Prejudice in a Selected Hawaiian Junior High School." Master's thesis, California State U., San Francisco, 1972.

Pratt, Helen G. "Some Conclusions from a Comparison of School Achievement of Certain Racial Groups." Journal of Educational Psychology 20(D, 1929):661-668.

_____. "The Foreign Language Schools of Hawaii." School and Society 23(Ja 23, 1926): 98-104.

Reinecke, John E. Language and Dialect in Hawaii, A Sociolinguistic History to 1935. Honolulu: U. of Hawaii Press, 1969.

Research and Economic Analysis Division. Citizenship, Nativity, and Ethnic Stock in Hawaii. Honolulu: Department of Planning and Economic Development, 1975.

Research and Statistics Office. Labor Market and Employment Service Research Section. Socioeconomic Characteristics of Minorities in Hawaii. Honolulu: Department of Labor and Industrial Relations, 1975.

Ryan, T. A. Value Conflict in Elementary Schools in Hawaii. Interim Report. Honolulu: Educational Research and Development Center, Jl, 1970.

Sakumoto, Raymond E. "Social Areas of Honolulu: A Study of the Ethnic Dimensions in an Urban Social Structure." Doctoral dissertation, Northwestern U., 1965.

Schmitt, Robert C. The Changing Definitions of Race in Hawaii. Honolulu: State Department of Planning and Economic Development, 1973.

_____. Historical Statistics of Hawaii. Honolulu: University Press of Hawaii, 1978.

_____. "Recent Trends in Hawaiian Interracial Marriage Rates by Occupation." Journal of Marriage and the Family 33(My, 1971):373-374.

Sloggett, Barbara B. "Behavior Modification of the Underachieving Rural Hawaiian: An Experimental Classroom." Pacific Anthropological Records No. 5(1969).

Slogett, Barbara B. and others. "A Comparative Analysis of Fantasy Need Achievement Among High and Low Achieving Male Hawaiian Americans." Journal of Cross Cultural Psychology 1(Mr, 1970):53-61.

Smith, M. E. "Comparison of the Neurotic Tendencies of Students of Different Racial Ancestry in Hawaii." Journal of Social Psychology 9(N, 1938).

Smith, Margot Wiesinger. "Measuring Ethnocentricism in Hilo, Hawaii: A Social Distance Scale." Sociology and Social Research 54 (1970):220-236.

Smith, Norman C. "The Plantation Child." Hawaii Educational Review 19(Ja, 1931):116-117, 122.

Smith, William C. "Minority Groups in Hawaii." Annals 223(1942).

State of Hawaii Employment Practices Law. Part I. Discriminatory Practices. Honolulu: Enforcement Division of Labor and Industrial Relations, 1973.

Stewart, Lawrence H., Dole, Arthur A., and Harris, Yeuell Y. "Cultural Differences in Abilities During High School." American Educational Research Journal, Ja, 1967.

Stroupe, Connor B. "Significant Factors in the Influx to Private Schools on Oahu Since 1900." Master's thesis, U. of Hawaii, 1955.

Stueber, Ralph. "Hawaii: A Case Study in Development Education." Doctoral dissertation, U. of Michigan, 1964.

Survey of Education in Hawaii. (U.S. Bureau of Education, Bulletin, 1920) Washington, DC: GPO, 1920.

Tagupa, William E. "Native Hawaiian Reparatations: An Ethnic Appeal to Law, Conscience, and the Social Sciences." Journal of Ethnic Studies 5(Spring, 1977):45-50.

Tanaka-Matsumi, Junko, and Tharp, Roland G. "Teaching the Teachers of Hawaiian Children: Training and Consultation Strategies." In Richard W. Brislin and Michael P. Hammett, Topics in Culture Learning, Vol. 5, Ag, 1977. ERIC ED 145 706.

Tharp, Roland, and Gallimore, Ronald. Predicting School Problems of the Hawaiian Minority, 1970. ERIC ED 041 078.

Thompson, John A. Public Schools in Hawaii, 1971. ERIC ED 061 161.

Townsend, Henry Schuler. "Education in Hawaii." Forum, 24:612.

Townsend, J. "Hawaii and the Negro." Negro, Jl, 1946.

Tseng, Wen-Shing and others (eds.). Peoples and Cultures in Hawaii. An Introduction for Mental Health Workers. Honolulu: Department of Psychiatry, School of Medicine, U. of Hawaii, 1974.

U.S. Congress, 95th, 2nd Session, House of Representatives, Committee on Interior and Insular Affairs. Establishing the Aboriginal Hawaiian Claims Settlement Study Commission and for Other Purposes. Washington, DC: GPO, Ja 31, 1978.

U.S. Congress, 95th, 2nd Session, Senate, Select Committee on Indian Affairs. Hawaiian Native Educational Assistance Act: Hearing... Washington, DC: GPO, 1978.

U.S. Congress, 95th, 2nd Session, Senate, Select Committee on Indian Affairs. Inclusion of Native Hawaiians in Certain Indian Acts and Programs: Hearings... Washington, DC: GPO, 1978.

U.S. Congress, 95th, 2nd Session, Senate, Select Committee on Indian Affairs. Native Hawaiian Education Act: Report to Accompany S. 857. Washington, DC: GPO, 1978.

University of Hawaii. Evaluation of Project Components, McKinley Education Complex, Ag, 1972. ERIC ED 133 392.

University of Hawaii. 1973-74 Evaluation of Project Components, Jl, 1974. ERIC ED 133 393.

University of Hawaii. 1974-75 Evaluation of Project Components. Elementary and Secondary Education Act Title I--Hawaii District, Jl, 1975. ERIC ED 133 394.

Villers, Ernest G. "A History of the Iolani School (1862-1940)." Master's thesis, U. of Hawaii, 1940.

Ward, Jack H. "The Hawaiian Studies Program." Educational Perspectives 14(Mr, 1975).

Werner, Emmy E., Bierman, Jessie M., and Freich, Fern E. The Children of Kauai: A Longitudinal Study from the Prenatal Period to Age Ten. Honolulu: U. of Hawaii Press, 1971.

Werner, Emmy E., and Smith, Ruth S. Kauai's Children Come of Age. Honolulu: U. Press of Hawaii, 1977.

Whitney, Caspar. Hawaiian America. New York: Arno Press, 1975. [Originally 1899]

Wittermans-Pino, Elizabeth. Inter-ethnic Relations in a Plural Society. Groningen: Wolters, 1964.

Wright, Theon. The Disenchanted Isles: The Story of the Second Revolution in Hawaii. New York: Dial, 1972.

Yamashita, Pearl N. "Head Start Program in Hawaii." Educational Horizons 48(1969):18-23.

Yamamura, Douglas S. "A Study of Some of the Factors in the Education of the Child of Hawaiian Ancestry in Hana, Maui." Master's thesis, U. of Hawaii, 1941.

Yamamura, Douglas S., and Sakumoto, Raymond. "Residential Segregation in Honolulu." Social Process in Hawaii 18(1954).

Yinger, J. Milton. "Integration and Pluralism Viewed from Hawaii." Antioch Review 22 (Winter, 1962-63):397-410.

Yoshida, Teruo. The Model Neighborhood Jobseeker. A Survey of Hawaii State Employment Service Job Applicants from Kalihi-Palama and Waianae Coast, N, 1968. Honolulu: Hawaii State Department of Labor and Industrial Relations. ERIC ED 029 981.

Yuen, William W. L. "The Native Hawaiian: A Dream Deferred." Crisis 82(D, 1975):402-406.

Idaho

Lane, Joan and others. The Status of Minority Children in Idaho, 1974. Vol 3, Je 4, 1974. ERIC ED 101 841.

State Economic Opportunity Office. Poverty in Idaho. A Report. Boise: SEOO, 1973.

Illinois

American Civil Liberties Union, Illinois Division. Report of the American Civil Liberties Union Committee on Certain Aspects of Race Relations at Evanston Township High School. Chicago: ACLU, 1958.

Anton, Thomas J. The Politics of State Expenditure in Illinois. Urbana, IL: U. of Illinois Press, 1966.

Armstrong, Charles F. "A Letter from Springfield." Integrated Education, Ap, 1963.

Aschenbrenner, Joyce. Careers of Black Youth in Metro-East Area. IXth International Congress of Anthropological and Ethnological Sciences, Ag-S, 1973. [Southern Illinois]

Bakalis, Michael J. Action Goals of the Seventies. An Agenda for Illinois Education. Springfield, IL: Office of the Superintendent of Public Instruction, 1972.

_____. "Illinois Rules Against Segregation." Integrated Education 5(Mr-Ap, 1972):64-70.

Banas, Casey. "Dilemma in St. Anne: Bad School or None." Chicago Tribune, Mr 14, 1976. [St. Anne High School, St. Anne]

_____. "Evanston High: 'A Microcosm.'" Chicago Tribune, Ja 15, 1979.

Banner, Warren M. Economic and Cultural Problems in Evanston, Illinois As They Relate to the Colored Population. New York: Department of Research and Community Projects, National Urban League, 1945.

Betz, Barbara G., and Bray, Jim. "Busing is a Fact of School Life," and "Desegregation War No Panacea." Champaign News Gazette, F 15, 1976. [Champaign and Urbana, IL]

Bindman, Aaron M. "A Study of the Negro Community in Champaign-Urbana, Illinois." Master's thesis, U. of Illinois, 1961.

Blei, Norbert. "Cicero. A Friendly Fortress." Chicago Sun-Times, Jl 27, 1975.

Board of Education of School District No. 65, Cook County, Illinois. The Report of the Board of Education on the Superintendency of Dr. Gregory C. Coffin. Evanston, IL: The Board, Ag, 1969.

Brett, Deborah. "Stability of Racial Mix in Illinois' Integrated Schools." Integrateducation 15(Mr-Ap, 1977).

Brinton, William R. "The Story of Confrontation." FOCUS/Midwest 8(1971). [Cairo]

Brody, Jeff. "Integration Works Here, Klahn Says." Springfield State Journal-Register, My 1, 1977.

Buehler, Sister Johannita. "The Present Status of Catholic Education in Illinois." Illinois Catholic Historical Review 6(1924):150-167.

Buresh, Jane B. A Fundamental Goal: Education for the People of Illinois. Urbana, IL: U. of Illinois Press, 1975.

Chandler, B. J. "No Commitment to Integration." Integrated Education (N-D, 1969):25-28.

Clorfene, Liane. "Giving Students a Chance: The Story of Evanston Township High School." Integrateducation 15(S-O, 1977).

"Coffin and His Grave Diggers in Evanston." Integrated Education 7(N-D, 1969):20-24.

Coffin, Gregory C. "Moving Toward Integration." Illinois Education, N, 1968. [Evanston]

_____. "How Evanston, Illinois Integrated All Its Schools." In U.S. Commission on Civil Rights, Papers Prepared for National Conference on Equal Educational Opportunity in America's Cities. Washington, DC: GPO, 1968.

_____. "Moving Toward Total Understanding." Public Management, My, 1969. [Evanston]

Cohodes, Aaron. "Can a Conservative Suburb Desegregate--Comfortably?" Nation's Schools, O, 1968. [Evanston]

Committee to Study Integration. Teachers' Study of Integration. Champaign, IL: Champaign Education Association, My 8, 1967.

"Computerized Integration." Christian Century, N 9, 1966. [Evanston]

Coons, John E. "[De Facto Segregation in Evanston]." Law and Society Review, N, 1967.

_____. "Report to the United States Office of Education on High School District 202 Evanston Township High School." Cambridge, MA: Je 15, 1965. [Unpublished]

_____. "Report to the United States Office of Education on Illinois Elementary District 65 Evanston-Skokie." Cambridge, MA: Je 15, 1965. [Unpublished]

Cottle, Thomas J. "Simple Words, Simple Deeds." Urban Education 5(O, 1970):295-304. [Urbana High School, Urbana]

Cronin, Joseph M. "City School Desegregation and the Creative Uses of Enrollment Decline." Integrateducation 15(Ja-F, 1977).

Current, Gloster B. "Exit Jim Crow Schools in East St. Louis, Illinois." Crisis, Ap, 1950.

_____. "Segregated Schools--On Trial in East St. Louis." Crisis, Mr, 1949.

Eaton, William Edward. The Origin and Growth of Schools in Jackson County, Illinois: A Historical Case Study, 1976. ERIC ED 128 251.

Educational Rehabilitation. An Evaluation of the Adult Basic Education Program of the State of Illinois. New York: Greenleigh Associates, F, 1965.

Elsner, David M. "A Problem at Evanston High." Wall Street Journal, Ap 16, 1974.

"The Emancipation Centennial Issue." Journal of Illinois State Historical Society, Autumn, 1963 (entire issue). Nine articles on the history of the Negro in Illinois, including illustrations and chronology. Obtainable from Illinois State Historical Society, Springfield, IL.

Emmons, Jean Franklin. A Report of Test Results on the School and College Ability Test and the Sequential Tests of Educational Progress. Evanston, IL: Evanston Township High School, Ag, 1973.

Erbe, Brigitte Mach. "Student Attitudes and Behavior in a Desegregated School System." Integrateducation 15(N-D, 1977):123-25.

Evans, Charles J. (comp.). Black Studies in the State of Illinois: A Directory. S, 1969. Innovations Center, Chicago City College, 180 North Michigan Avenue, Chicago, IL 60601.

Gelder, Sharon B. "Cool Million Too Hot for Pols; House Kills Desegregation Aid." Chicago Reporter 5(Ag, 1977).

Gertz, Elmer. "The Black Laws of Illinois." Journal of the Illinois State Historical Society 56(Autumn, 1963):454-473.

"Ghost Town." Nation 212(My 24, 1971):644-645. [Schools in Cairo]

Gilbert, Herman C. The Uncertain Sound. A novel. Chicago: Path Press, 1970. [Cairo]

Good, Paul. "In Camelot..." In Cairo, Illinois: Racism at Floodtide, pp. 37-47. Washington, DC: GPO, O, 1973. [Schools in Cairo]

Grossman, Ron. "Evanston: The Price of Progress." Chicagoan 1(D, 1973):66-70.

Heath, G. Louis. "Corrupt East St. Louis: Laboratory for Black Revolution." Progressive 34(O, 1970):24-27.

Hickman, L. C. "Racial Ruckus Turns Into Student Boycott." Nation's Schools, N, 1967. [Proviso East High School, Maywood]

Hoffman, Julius J., Judge. "A Very Small Down Payment." (Part of Judge Hoffman's ruling of My 15, 1969, in the South Holland case.) Integrated Education, Jl-Ag, 1969.

Hsia, Jayjia. Integration in Evanston [Illinois] 1967-1971: A Longitudinal Evaluation. Evanston, IL: Midwestern Office, Educational Testing Service, Ag, 1971.

Hull, Judith B. "A History of Race Relations in Wheaton, Illinois." Master's thesis, Northeastern Illinois U., 1972.

Illinois Advisory Committee to the U.S. Commission on Civil Rights. A Decade of Waiting in Cairo. Washington, DC: U.S. Commission on Civil Rights, Je, 1975.

Illinois Commission on Urban Education. A Report to the General Assembly of Illinois. Springfield, IL: The General Assembly, F, 1971.

Illinois, School Problems Commission, Urban Studies Sub-Committee. A Study of Urban Education. Springfield, IL: The Commission, 1969.

Illinois, 76th General Assembly, Special House Committee on Cairo. Preliminary Report of the Special House Committee to Investigate the Allegations Concerning the County of Alexander and the City of Cairo Appointed Pursuant to House Resolution No. 118, My, 1969.

Illinois, State of, Office of the Superintendent of Public Instruction, Department of Equal Educational Opportunity. Planning Guide for Educational Opportunity. Springfield, IL: The Office, N 22, 1971.

Illinois, State of, Office of the Superintendent of Public Instruction. Rules Establishing Requirements and Procedures for the Elimination and Prevention of Racial Segregation in Schools. Springfield, IL: The Office, N 22, 1971

Inger, Mary. "Black Power in Suburbia." Midwest (Chicago Sun-Times) Mr 28, 1971. [East Chicago Heights]

Jansen, Verna Godman, and Gallagher, James J. "The Social Choices of Students in Racially Integrated Classes for the Culturally Disadvantaged Talented." Exceptional Children, D, 1966. [Champaign]

Jenkins, Jeffrey. "Historical Analysis of Two Selected School Districts that Have Undergone Desegregation." Doctoral dissertation, U. of Michigan, 1976. [Evanston]

Johnson, Charles S. "These 'Colored' United States: Illinois: Mecca of the Migrant Mob." Messenger 5(D, 1923):926-928, 933.

Kirkhorn, Michael. "Oak Park's Color Line." Nation, Ja 26, 1974.

Kleeman, Richard P. "Did Integration Zeal Cost a Job?" Minneapolis Tribune, O 26, 1970. [Dr. Gregory Coffin, Evanston]

Koen, Charles, with Darling, Marilyn. The Battle for Cairo, Illinois. New York: The Third Press, 1971.

Lantz, Herman R. A Community in Search of Itself. Carbondale, IL: Southern Illinois U., 1972. [Cairo]

Lightfoot, Orlando B. "To Be Used Or To Be Useful: The Question for Black Professionals, Cairo, Illinois, U.S.A., 1969." Afro-American Studies 2(Mr, 1972):239-249.

Lindstrom, Duane. A Decade of Waiting in Cairo... Washington, DC: U.S. Commission on Civil Rights, 1975.

McFadin, Bill. [Two articles on segregation in Alton] Alton Telegraph, Ap 20-21, 1976.

Mallette, Daniel. "Racism Cannot Be Overcome Unless We Face the Facts." New City, D 15, 1963.

Manning, Joe. "Integration: Webster Proves It Can Work." Waukegan News-Sun, My 21, 1976. [Daniel Webster Junior High School, Waukegan]

Marine, Gene. "'I've Got Nothing Against the Colored.'" Ramparts, N, 1966. [Segregationist opposition to civil rights marches in Chicago and Cicero]

Mead, Robert Douglas. "In Black and White." Chapter 6 in Reunion. Twenty-Five Years Out of School. New York: Saturday Review Press, 1973. [Evanston Township High School, Evanston]

Mouat, Lucia. "An Unusual Lab School." Southern Education Report, Ap, 1969. [Evanston]

Nash, J. Madeleine. "Out on a Limb in Oak Park." Chicago Tribune Magazine, F 17, 1974.

Office of Research and Program Coordination. Review of Data Related to Desegregation in the Urbana Schools, 1959-1974. Urbana, IL: Urbana Schools, District No. 116, S, 1974.

O'Hara, Delia. "The People in Park Forest Sure Have a Lot of Verve." Chicago Tribune Magazine, Ag 20, 1978.

Oudes, Bruce J. "The Siege of Cicero (Illinois)." Nation, Mr 27, 1967.

Parker, Charles S. "The Tometz Ruling." Integrated Education, Ag-S, 1966. [Waukegan]

Prosten, Ann. "A Story of Segregated School Children." Community, F, 1964.

Prugh, Peter H. "School Integration Balls-Up North." Wall Street Journal, S 4, 1968. [South Holland]

Ravis, Howard S. "The School District of Kankakee." School Management 15(Ag, 1971):18-21.

Real Estate Research Corporation. Stability of Racial Mix in Illinois Schools. Chicago: RERC, Ap, 1976.

Resource Management Corporation. Evaluation of the Emergency School Assistance Program, Vol. III, Appendix M, F 15, 1972. ERIC ED 058 470. [Case History of ESAP in Kankakee, IL]

Rogers, Bill. "A Course of a Different Color." Chicago 25(My, 1976). [Oak Park]

Rose, Don. "Governor Walker and the Blacks." Chicago Reporter 2(S, 1973):6-8.

Rozett, John M. "Racism and Republican Emergence in Illinois, 1848-1860: A Re-evaluation of Republican Negrophobia." Civil War History 22(Je, 1976):101-115.

Rudwick, Elliott. "Fifty Years of Race Relations in East St. Louis: The Breaking Down of White Supremacy." Midcontinent American Studies Journal 6(Spring, 1965).

Shagaloff, June, and Bailey, Lester P. "Cairo-Illinois' Southern Exposure." Crisis, Ap, 1952.

Shaw, Andy. "A Black School on the Rocks--In Small-Town Illinois." Chicago Sun-Times, F 29, 1976. [St. Anne High School, St. Anne, IL]

Shaw, Andy. "8 Years Later, Evanston Busing Still a Success." Chicago Sun-Times, O 12, 1975.

Simon, Norbert Allen. "The Politicization of Educational Issues." Doctoral dissertation, Northwestern U., 1974. [Evanston]

Smith, Melvin. "Black Education in Evanston Public Schools: A Look at the Twenties and Thirties." Integrateducation 12(S-O, 1974): 25-29. [Interview by Bettye Sledge]

Stability of Racial Mix in Illinois Schools. Prepared for Illinois Office of Education. Chicago: Real Estate Research Corporation, Ap, 1976.

Strahler, Steve. "Are Blacks in Peoria Really Better Off?" Peoria Journal Star, D 5, 1976.

Sullivan, Barbara. "The Free Pass Gets Flunked in Bellwood." Chicago Tribune Magazine, N 26, 1978.

The Superintendency of Gregory C. Coffin in School District 65, Evanston, Illinois, School District 65, F, 1970.

Theil, Henri, and Finizza, Anthony J. An Informational Approach to the Measurement of Racial Segregation of Schools [in Chicago]. Report 6712. Chicago: Center for Mathematical Studies in Business and Economics, U. of Chicago, Ap, 1967.

Thomas, Charles R. "A Study of Lay Participation in the Elimination of De Facto Racial Segregation in a Northern School District." Doctoral dissertation, Northwestern U., 1970. [Evanston]

_____. "North Chicago." Integrateducation 15 (N-D, 1977):38-39.

Thomason, James. Residential Mobility in an Inner-Ring Suburb: The Case of Evanston, Illinois. Evanston, IL: Center for Urban Affairs, Northwestern U., 1975.

Trillin, Calvin. "U.S. Journal: Rockford, Illinois. Schools Without Money." New Yorker 52(N 8, 1976):146-154.

Turner, Harold E. "A Study of Public School Integration in Two Illinois Communities." Doctoral dissertation, George Peabody College for Teachers, 1956. Univ. Microfilms Order No. 19765. [East St. Louis and Alton]

U.S. Commission on Civil Rights. Cairo, Illinois: A Symbol of Racial Polarization. Washington, DC: GPO, F, 1973.

U.S. Commission on Civil Rights. The Diminishing Barrier: A Report on School Desegregation... Washington, DC: GPO, D, 1972.

U.S. Commission on Civil Rights. Hearing Held in Cairo, Illinois, March 23-25, 1972. Washington, DC: GPO, 1974.

U.S. Commission on Civil Rights. School Desegregation in Peoria, Illinois. Washington, DC: The Commission, Je, 1977.

U.S. Congress, 91st, 1st Session, Senate, Select Committee on Nutrition and Human Needs. Nutrition and Human Needs. Hearings..., Part 8--SCLC and East St. Louis [Illinois]. Washington, DC: GPO, 1969.

Van Meulen, Michael. "The KKK Wants You!" Chicago, Mr, 1976.

Wakefield, Ernest H. "The Computer Helps Desegregate Schools." School Boards, F, 1967. [Evanston plan]

[Weinberg, Meyer.] "A District Desegregates: 1968-1977." Research Review of Equal Education 1(Fall, 1977):13-28. [District 151, South Holland]

Wertsch, Linda. "Where Busing Really Works." Chicago Daily News, Mr 5, 1977.

Wille, Lois. "Oak Park: The Hope of the Future." Chicagoan 1(D, 1973):60-65.

Wilson, Laval S. "Developing Common Understandings About Crucial Integration Issues." Phi Delta Kappan, Ap, 1969. [Evanston]

Chicago

"A New Kind of PTA." Newsweek, N 15, 1976. [Ulysses S. Grant Elementary School]

Abbott, Edith, and Breckenridge, Sophonisiba. Truancy and Non-Attendance in the Chicago Schools. Chicago: 1917.

Advisory Panel on Integration of the Public Schools. Report to the Board of Education, City of Chicago. Chicago: Board of Education, Mr 31, 1964. [The "Hauser Report"]

Albright, Frank Seymour. Interracial and Minority Group Problems in Elementary and Secondary Schools. Chicago: Judd Club, 1964. [Chicago metropolitan area]

Allen, Jay. "The Chicago Tribune and Truth." Focus/Midwest, V, 33(1966). [An analysis of this newspaper's treatment of the Chicago school segregation crisis]

Alsop, Stewart. "The Brookses and the Gowsters." Saturday Evening Post, D 4, 1965. [School segregation in Chicago]

al-Tahir, Ali A. J. "The Arab Community in the Chicago Area..." Doctoral dissertation, U. of Chicago, 1952.

"And Finally a Success Story: How One School Changes from Snake Pit to Model." American School Board Journal 162(Ja, 1975):36-37. [Manierre Elementary School, Chicago]

Anderson, Alan B. (ed.). Desegregation and Chicago Public Schools. Issues and Options. Chicago: American Issues Forum Chicago, 1976.

Aoki, Omar. "Black Student Demands." Young Socialist, D, 1968-Ja, 1969.

Aschenbrenner, Joyce. Lifelines: Black Families in Chicago. New York: Holt, Rinehart and Winston, 1974.

Austin, Harold S. Bread and Water. Markham, IL: J. St. Clair, 1972.

Backes, Clarus. "Uptown: The Promised Land." "Poor People's Power in Uptown." Chicago Tribune Magazine, S 22, 1968, S 29, 1968. [White southern migrants in Chicago]

Bacon, Warren. "Strategies for the Schools." BIP Magazine, Ja, 1976. [Interview by Francis Ward]

Bailey, Robert M., Jr. Radicals in Urban Politics: The Alinsky Approach. Chicago: U. of Chicago Press, 1974. [Organization for a Better Austin]

Banas, Casey. "Chicago Vocational is the Comeback School of the Decade." Chicago Tribune, Ja 10, 1979. [Chicago Vocational School]

_____. "Curie An Exciting Hub of Performing Arts." Chicago Tribune, Ja 12, 1979. [Curie High School]

_____. "Dunbar's Students Overcome Poverty." Chicago Tribune, Ja 13, 1979. [Dunbar Vocational High School]

_____. "Getting a Reading: Top School Shows How It's Done." Chicago Tribune, O 24, 1976. [Peterson Elementary School]

_____. "Improving Inner-City Pupils' Reading." Chicago Tribune, S 7, 1974. [Achievements of students in an inner-city school district in Chicago]

_____. "Kenwood: New Academic Powerhouse of City's Schools." Chicago Tribune, Ja 9, 1979. [Kenwood High School, Chicago]

_____. "Lindblom: College Springboard." Chicago Tribune, Ja 14, 1979. [Lindblom Technical High School]

_____. "Magnet School: 'Camelot' in Education." Chicago Tribune, D 9, 1976. [Whitney Young Magnet High School]

_____. "Morgan Park: Integration Vital." Chicago Tribune, Ja 15, 1979. [Morgan Park High School]

_____. "Pride, Parents Create Bogan Character." Chicago Tribune, Ja 11, 1979. [Bogan High School]

_____. "School Offers No-Nonsense Road to Success." Chicago Tribune, Mr 4, 1979. [Beasley Academic Center, all-black academic elementary school, Chicago]

_____. "Uptown: Mecca for Migrants." Southern Education Report, Mr, 1969.

_____. "...While Another Faces Struggle." Chicago Tribune, O 24, 1976. [Ryerson Elementary School]

Banas, Casey, and O'Connor, Meg. "1st Year of Busing Ends on Wary Note." Chicago Tribune, Je 11, 1978. [Voluntary busing program in Chicago]

Barbash, Fred. "Coalition Against 'Blockbusting.'" Nation, Ap 17, 1972. [Austin]

Bargen, Mark, and Walberg, Herbert J. "School Performance." In Herbert J. Walberg, Evaluating Educational Performance, pp. 239-254. Berkeley, CA: McCutchan, 1974.

Barnard, Judith. "'We Keep Cranking Out Edsels.' Alternative Schools--In and Out of the System." Chicago, Ap, 1977.

Baron, Harold M. "Black Powerlessness in Chicago." Trans-action, N, 1968.

_____. "Building a Black Community: Popular Economics in Lawndale." FOCUS/Midwest, Vol. 11, No. 69(1976):18-22.

_____. Building Babylon: A Case of Racial Controls in Public Housing. Evanston, IL: Center for Urban Affairs, Northwestern U., 1971. [Chicago Housing Authority]

_____. "History of Chicago School Segregation to 1953." Integrated Education, Ja, 1963.

_____. "Northern Segregation As A System: The Chicago Schools." Integrated Education, D, 1965-Ja, 1966.

_____. Public Housing: Chicago Builds a Ghetto. Chicago: Chicago Urban League, 1967.

_____. "Race and Status in School Spending: Chicago, 1961-1966." Journal of Human Resources 6(Winter, 1971):13-24.

Barta, Russell. The Representation of Poles, Italians, Latins, and Blacks in the Executive Suites of Chicago's Largest Corporations. Chicago: Institute of Urban Life, 1973.

Barter, Alice K. "Education's Disadvantaged: Profile of a Teacher." Educational Horizons, Winter, 1968-69. [Provisional teachers]

Bayer, Henry. "Chicago Teachers Win Strike but Racial Split Hurts Union." New America, My 31, 1969.

Beck, Melinda. "Black Catholic School in Chicago Thrives Where Others Failed." Wall Street Journal, O 22, 1976. [Holy Angels Elementary]

Beijbom, Ulf. "Swedes in Chicago. A Demographic and Social Study of the 1846-1880 Immigration." Doctoral dissertation, U. of Uppsala, 1971.

Bennett, Charles. "Residential Segregation of Occupational Groups: Chicago Metropolitan District 1950 and 1960. Considered by Color and Sex." Doctoral dissertation, U. of Chicago, 1975.

Bergo, Sandra. "Law Firms Shun Affirmative Action: Minorities, Women Scarce at Prestige Offices." Chicago Reporter 2(0, 1973).

Berk, Richard, Mack, Raymond W., and McKnight, John L. Race and Class Differences in Per Pupil Staffing Expenditures in Chicago Elementary Schools, 1969-1970. Evanston, IL: Center for Urban Affairs, Northwestern U., 1971.

Berk, Richard A., and Hartmann, Alice. Race and District Differences in Per Pupil Staffing Expenditures in Chicago Elementary Schools, 1970-1971. Evanston, IL: Center for Urban Affairs, Northwestern U., Je, 1971.

_____ and _____. "Race and School Funds in Chicago, 1971." Integrated Education (Ja-F, 1972):52-57.

Berry, Brian and others. A Metropolis Transforms Itself. Chicago: U. of Chicago Press, 1975.

Bevier, Thomas. "Dear Dixie: You're Looking Better Every Day." Chicago Tribune Magazine, F 13, 1972.

Bogue, Donald J. "Opinions of Black and White About Race Relations and Chicago's Schools." In George Surgeon, Judith Mayo, and Donald J. Bogue, Race Relations in Chicago. Second Survey: 1975, pp. 156-182. Chicago: Community and Family Study Center, U. of Chicago, 1976.

Bonney, Norman. "Race & Politics in Chicago in the Daley Era." Race 15(Ja, 1974):329-350.

Borgira, Steve. "Angie Goes to School." Chicago Tribune, Ag 31, 1975. [Ms. Angie Ray, Bradwell School]

Bowly, Devereux. The Poorhouse: Subsidized Housing in Chicago, 1895-1976. Carbondale, IL: Southern Illinois U. Press, 1978.

Braden, William. "The Two Chicagos. Black Attitudes, White Attitudes," Part 1. Chicago Sun-Times, S 22, 1968.

Branham, Charles. "Black Chicago: Accommodationist Politics before the Great Migration." In The Ethnic Frontier. Edited by Melvin G. Holli and Peter d'A. Jones. Grand Rapids, MI: Eerdmans, 1977.

Brazier, Arthur M. Black Self-Determination. The Story of the Woodlawn Organization. Grand Rapids, MI: William B. Erdmans Publishing Company, 1969.

Brodkey, Naomi. "The Day Dr. Willis Resigned." Renewal, Mr, 1965.

_____. "Public School Crisis: Chicago Style." New City, D 15, 1963.

_____. "They Chased the Gloom Peddlers Out of Marynook." New City, N 15, 1964. [Chicago]

Brown, Evelyn. "Teaching in a Ghetto School." Integrated Education, Ja, 1963.

Bruck, H. W. Results of a Study of Patterns of Discrimination in Budget Allocations to Elementary Schools in the Chicago School District. Cambridge, MA: Urban Systems Laboratory, Massachusetts Institute of Technology, Mr, 1971.

Brune, Tom. "Chicago Park District Shortchanges Black and Latino Wards; More Facilities, Programs and Staff Channeled to White Wards." Chicago Reporter 7(My, 1989). [Playground facilities]

_____. "Poor Still Concentrated in Chicago As City-Suburb Gap Grows." Chicago Reporter 7 (0, 1978):1, 6-7.

Bruno, Hal. "Chicago's Hillbilly Ghetto." Reporter, Je 4, 1964.

Buckley, Kevin P., and Cotton, Richard. "Chicago: The Marchers and the Machine." Reporter, N 4, 1965.

Burdinie, Carl. "Wells High School: An Air of Not Caring." Chicago Daily News, Je 2, 1973.

Bureau of Administrative Research. High School Dropout Report. 1960-1961 to 1969-1970. Chicago: Board of Education, 1970.

"CTU Against Busing?" Substance 1(Je, 1976). [Chicago Teachers Union House of Delegates vote against busing to relieve overcrowding at Barton elementary school]

Califano, Joseph. "Letter to Dr. Joseph P. Hannon." Education Daily, F 28, 1979. [The text of an unsigned draft letter prepared for the HEW Secretary's signature, charging the Chicago Board of Education with violation of the Civil Rights Act of 1964]

Campbell, Connie, and Levine, Daniel U. "The Whitney Young Magnet High School in Chicago and Urban Renewal." In The Future of Big-City Schools. Edited by Daniel U. Levine and Robert J. Havighurst. Berkeley, CA: McCutchan, 1977.

Casimere, Dwight. "White Cops Spark Assault at School." Muhammad Speaks, My 9, 1969 [Tilden High School]

Chandler, Christopher. "Diverse but Equal." New City 6(Je, 1968):13-17. [Marshall High School]

_____. "How the Democratic Party Captured Chicago Schools. " Chicago Free Press 1 (O 12, 1970):16-19.

Chandler, Christopher, and Havemann, Joel. "Two Schools Nearby, But Far Apart in Funds." Chicago Sun-Times, Je 2, 1969.

Cheren, Mark. "Chicago Schools and the Education Issue." American Friends Service Committee (Chicago Regional Office), N, 1967. [On the Redmond Report of Ag, 1967]

Cherry, Frank T. "Southern In-Migrant Negroes in North Lawndale, Chicago, 1949-1959: A Study of Internal Migration and Adjustment." Doctoral dissertation, U. of Chicago, 1966.

Chicago, City of. Report of the Chicago Riot Study Committee to the Hon. Richard J. Daley. Chicago, IL: City Hall, Ag 1, 1968. [Study of Ap, 1968, disorders after the murder of Dr. Martin Luther King]

_____. The Strategy of Confrontation. Chicago and the Democratic National Convention--1968. Chicago: City Hall, S 6, 1968.

"Chicago in Black and White." Economist [London], Ja 11, 1964.

Chicago Public Education Project. Chicago's Schools. Alternatives to Suspension. Chicago: American Friends Service Committee, F, 1977.

Chicago Public Schools. Open Enrollment: A Progress Report. Chicago: Board of Education, N, 1972.

_____. Report of the 1968-69 City-Wide Testing Program. Chicago: Board of Education, 1969.

Chicago Riot Study Committee. "Daley Committee Finds School Failure." Integrated Education, N-D, 1968, pp. 40-43.

Chicago School Board Study Committee. Collapse. An Interim Report... to the 76th General Assembly. Chicago: Sen. John J. Lanigan, Chairman, My, 1970.

"The Chicago Title VI Complaint to H.E.W." Integrated Education, D, 1965-Ja, 1966.

Chicago Urban League. The Current Economic Status of Chicago's Black Community. Chicago: Chicago Urban League, 1977.

_____. Racial Segregation in the Chicago Public Schools, 1965-1966. Chicago Urban League, 4500 South Michigan Avenue, Chicago, IL 60653.

"Chicago's Black Teachers Are Coming Around to Messenger Muhammad's Educational Programs." Muhammad Speaks, N 21, 1969.

"Chicago's Housing Market: Its Effects on Minorities." Chicago Urban League Newsletter, Fall, 1977.

Chicago's Schools Suspension. Chicago: Midwest Regional Office, American Friends Service Committee, Ap, 1976.

Christian, Charles. Social Areas and Spatial Change in the Black Community of Chicago: 1950-1960. Urbana, IL: Department of Geography , U. of Illinois, 1972.

Cibulka, James G. Obstacles to School Decentralization: The Chicago Case, Ap, 1974. ERIC ED 095 658.

_____. "School Decentralization in Chicago." Education and Urban Society 7(Ag, 1975): 412-438.

Citizens Schools Committee of Chicago. Steps Toward Compensatory Education in the Chicago Public Schools, Ag, 1964. Citizens Committee of Chicago, 32 West Randolph Street, Chicago, IL.

"Citizen Testimony on School Integration." Integrated Education, Ja, 1963.

"City's Major Funders Give Thin Slice of Philanthropic Pie to Minority Institutions." Chicago Reporter 2(Jl-Ag, 1973).

Clark, Hannah Belle. The Public Schools of Chicago. A Sociological Study. Chicago: U. of Chicago Press, 1897.

Cleary, Maryell. "Wingspread: Where People Are People." American Education 7(Ap, 1971):21-24.

Clement, James W. "A Letter to Mayor Daley." Integrated Education, Je-Jl, 1967.

Clemons, Neil L. "Chicago: Integration vs. School Politics." Wall Street Journal, Jl 25, 1969.

Cofield, E. "The Battle of Woodlawn." Chicago Defender, N 19-21, 23, 26-30 and D 3, 1962.

Commission of Inquiry into the Black Panthers and the Police. Search and Destroy. New York: Metropolitan Applied Research Center, 1973. [The killing of two Black Panther leaders in Chicago, 1969]

Congreve, Willard J. Institutional Collaboration to Improve Urban Public Education with Special Reference to the City of Chicago (Urban Education Development Project). Final Report. Chicago: U. of Chicago, Mr 15, 1968, 127 pp. ERIC ED 023 781.

Coons, John E. "Chicago." In Roscoe Hill and Malcolm Feeley, Affirmative School Integration. Efforts to Overcome De Facto Segregation in Urban Schools. Beverly Hills, CA: Sage, 1968.

_____. " De Facto Segregation in Chicago." Law and Society Review, N, 1967.

Costello, Joan. "Research in a Black Community: Four Years in Review." School Review 81 (My, 1973):487-500.

Counts, George S. School and Society in Chicago. New York: Harcourt, Brace, 1928.

Crabtree, Mary Frances. "Chicago's Metro High: Freedom, Choice, Responsibility." Phi Delta Kappan 56(My, 1975).

Cronin, Joseph M. "How the Chicago Area Desegregated Its Schools." Phi Delta Kappan 58 (My, 1977). [A dream]

Cross, Robert. "How Are Things Around 55th and Harper?" Chicago Tribune Magazine, O 26, 1975. [Hyde Park]

_____. "Metro High: A 5-Year Lesson in Moxie." Chicago Tribune Magazine, S 28, 1975.

_____. "Proud Old, Stubborn Old Wicker Park." Chicago Tribune Magazine, N 7, 1971.

_____. "The Tardy Bell Is Ringing at Waller High." Chicago Tribune Magazine, Ap 19, 1970. [Waller High School]

Cuban, Larry. Urban School Chiefs Under Fire. Chicago: U. of Chicago Press, 1976. [Benjamin C. Willis, Chicago]

Darrow, Joy. "A School that Works? Hey, Let Go of My Leg." Chicago Defender, Mr 4, 1975. [Manierre Elementary School, Chicago]

Dedinsky, Mary. "Urban Idyll That Hasn't Jelled?" Chicago Sun-Times, S 1, 1974. [South Commons community]

"De Facto Segregation in the Chicago Public Schools." Crisis, F, 1958.

Despres, Leon M. "Taxes for School Segregation." Integrated Education, Ap, 1963.

De Visé, Pierre. "Better Teaching or Better Cheating? Chicago's Improved Reading Scores." Integrateducation 14(Mr-Ap, 1976):11-14.

_____. The Black Population of Chicago: 1950-1975. Chicago: College of Urban Sciences, U. of Illinois, Mr, 1976.

_____. Chicago: 1971. Ready for Another Fire. A Survival Plan for Chicago's 250 Communities to the Year 2000. Chicago: Hospital Planning Council for Metropolitan Chicago, Ja, 1971.

_____. Chicago's Widening Color Gap. Chicago: Interuniversity Social Research Committee, D, 1967.

_____. "Chicago's Widening Color Gap: 1971." Integrated Education (N-D, 1971):37-42.

De Visé, Pierre et al. Slum Medicine: Chicago's Apartheid Health System. Chicago: Community and Family Study Center, U. of Chicago, 1969.

Dewey, Henry Evert. "The Development of Public School Administration in Chicago." Doctoral dissertation, U. of Chicago, 1937.

DeYoung, Henry G. "The Near West Side Story." The Chicagoan 1(Ja, 1974):40-45.

DeZutter, Henry W. "When Folks Get Together to Talk About Busing." New Republic, Mr 2, 1968.

Dorau, Bernadette. "The Principal Solution." Chicago Sun-Times, My 2, 1976. [Manierre Elementary School and the Industrial Skills Center]

"Dr. King Carries Fight to Northern Slums." Ebony, Ap, 1966.

Drake, St. Clair, and Cayton, Horace R. Black Metropolis: A Study of Negro Life in a Northern City. 2 vols. Rev. ed. New York: Harper and Row, 1962.

Ducey, John M. "C.H.A. Must Desegregate New Public Housing Or Else...What?" New World, S 19, 1969. [Chicago Housing Administration]

Dunlap, Franklin. "Hi, I'm Your Friendly Neighborhood Panic Peddler." Chicago Tribune Magazine, N 28, 1971. [Austin community]

_____. "Hi, I'm Your Outraged Neighborhood Citizen on the March." Chicago Tribune Magazine, D 5, 1971. [Austin community]

_____. "One Man's City Hall." Chicago Tribune Magazine, Jl 30, 1972.

Eash, Maurice J. A Comprehensive Curriculum Evaluation of the Christian Action Ministry Academy, 1970. Chicago: College of Education, U. of Illinois at Chicago Circle, N, 1970.

Ehrenberg, C. Joseph and associates. A Special Analysis of Vocational Education in the of Chicago. Chicago: C. Joseph Ehrenberg and Associates, Jl, 1971.

Ellis, William W. White Ethics and Black Power: The Emergence of the West Side Organization. Chicago: Aldine, 1969.

Ellman, Mary. "Chicago! Behind the 'I Will' Spirit It is Nervous and Erratic." New York Times Magazine, Jl 14, 1968.

Enwell, Barbara and others. Chicago's Black Population, Selected Statistics. Chicago: Department of Development and Planning, City of Chicago, My, 1975.

Epps, Edgar G. "Chicago's School Without Walls: The Chicago Public High School for Metropolitan Studies." In Daniel U. Levine, Models for Integrated Education, pp. 32-42. Worthington, OH: Jones, 1971.

Equalizing Educational Opportunities in the New Chicago. Chicago: Board of Education, F, 1977.

Erbe, Brigitte Mach. "Race and Socioeconomic Segregation." American Sociological Review 40(D, 1975):801-812. [1970 data]

Faller, Jan. "Gage Park High on Rebound." Chicago Defender, My 31, 1977.

_____. "Metro Stepchild Is Making It." Chicago Defender, My 7, 1977. [Chicago Public High School for Metropolitan Studies]

_____. "Preston: Quality Schools Come First." Chicago Defender, S 4, 1976. [Mrs. Casey Preston, vice-president, Chicago school board]

Falls, Arthur G. "The Search for Negro Medical Students." Integrated Education, Je, 1963.

Fischer, Sylvia. "From Chicago." In Florence H. Levinsohn and Benjamin D. Wright, School Desegregation. Shadow and Substance. Chicago: U. of Chicago Press, 1976. [Shoesmith Elementary School]

Fish, John Hall. Black Power/White Control. The Struggle of the Woodlawn Organization in Chicago. Princeton, NJ: Princeton U. Press, 1973.

Fish, John, Nelson, Gordon, Stuhr, Walter, and Witmer, Lawrence. The Edge of the Ghetto. A Study of Church Involvement in the Community Organization. Chicago: U. of Chicago Divinity School, 1967. [Organization for the Southwest Community in Chicago]

Fishbein, Anette. "The Expansion of Negro Residential Areas in Chicago, 1950-1960." Doctoral dissertation, U. of Chicago, 1963.

Forrest, Leon R. "Legal Lynching of Two Black Youths Shows New Repression in the North." Muhammad Speaks, Jl 11, 1969. [Jesse Davis and Theodore Collins: students at Englewood High School]

Fox, Terry Curtis. "How Hyde Park Made Me a Racist." Chicago 24(Jl, 1975):107-109.

Frame, Charles [pseud.] "Run, Teacher, Run." Chicago Tribune Magazine, S 27, 1970.

Frazier, E. Franklin. The Negro Family in Chicago. Chicago: U. of Chicago Press, 1932.

Fry, John R. Locked-Out Americans: A Memoir. New York: Harper & Row, 1973. [Blackston Rangers]

Fuerst, James S., and Petty, Roy. "Black Housing in Chicago." Public Interest 52 (Summer, 1978):103-110.

_____. "Child Parent Centers: An Evaluation." Integrateducation 15(My-Je, 1977).

_____. "Report from Chicago: A Program That Works." Public Interest 43(Spring, 1976): 59-69. [DISTAR]

"Functional Illiteracy in Chicago." Integrated Education, Ja, 1963.

Garland, Barbara. "Cabrini-Green to Willow Creek." Chicago 26(Je, 1977):131-133, 160-170, 234. [Ghetto dwellers move into suburbs of Chicago]

Gaspar, Michele. "Race and Catholic Schools: More Mixed Than Public; Strong In Inner City." Chicago Reporter 3(Mr, 1974):1-6.

Gelder, Sharon B. "About Half of Schools 95 Per Cent or More Black." Chicago Reporter 5 (Ag, 1976):1, 8.

_____. "Beaubien's Pupils Take Joy Ride; Stevenson's Bypass 'Stop' Signs. Chicago Reporter 7(Jl, 1978). [Two schools in voluntary desegregation project]

_____. "Dedication, Interest, High Expectations: Ingredients for Black School Success, Structural Reading Program Yields High Scores at Parent Centers, Grade Schools." Chicago Reporter 5(N, 1976). [Successful reading achievement at eight predominantly black schools in Chicago]

_____. "Desegregation Troubleshooter Faces Toughest Career Challenge." Chicago Reporter 6(My, 1977). [Edward A. Welling, Jr.]

_____. "Discovery of Unreported Scores Adds 'Five Point' to Test Results." Chicago Reporter 7(S, 1978).

_____. "Interracial Schools in Chicago." Integrateducation 14(Jl-Ag, 1976):36-38.

_____. "Many White Students Travel Voluntarily to Eight High Schools in Black Areas. Daily Trips to Gain Education in Catholic, Private, and Public Schools." Chicago Reporter 4(D, 1975).

_____. "Racial Quotas Achieve Desegregation at Two High Schools." Chicago Reporter 6 (N, 1977):6-7. [Morgan Park and Gage Park High Schools]

_____. "Reading Scores, Per Pupil Expenditures Higher in White Than Black Chicago Schools." Chicago Reporter 5(Ag, 1976):1-2.

"Ghetto Schools Rigged Against Black Youths?" Muhammad Speaks, Ja 31, 1969. [Edwin Varnado, a teacher at Crane High School]

Giese, Vincent J. "Black Youth Follow Trail Blazed by French Cardinal." New World, Ag 4, 1972. [Black Christian students]

Golden, Renny. "Adult Ed in the City: Story of a Peoples' School." Community 37(Fall, 1977):14-25.

Goodwin, Carole. "Racial Change in Two Residential Communities--The Case of City vs. Suburb." Doctoral dissertation, U. of Chicago, 1974. [Austin in Chicago and Oak Park]

Gordon, Gregory, and Swanson, Albert. "Chicago Draws the Color Line." Chicago Sun-Times, D 12, 1976. [The real estate industry's role in creating residential segregation]

Graham, Polly Jo. "An Investigation of the Chicago Redistricting Program." Master's thesis, U. of Chicago, 1952.

Granger, Bill. "Your Children Are Possible Zombies." Chicago Guide 22(S, 1973):114-121. [Chicago inner city schools]

Greeley, Andrew M. Neighborhood. Seabury Press, 1977. [Chicago]

Green, Laura. "Catholic Schools: Dropping Out?" Midwest Magazine (Chicago Sun-Times), S 21, 1975.

Greene, Stuart C. "Her Kind of Town." Chicago Sun-Times, Mr 7, 1976. [Mrs. Nancy Jefferson, executive director, Midwest Community Council]

Greenstein, Jack. "Listen to the Children (A Study of an Integrated School)." Integrated Education 8(Ja-F, 1970):14-22.

Gregory, O. Grady. From the Bottom of the Barrel. (A History of Black Workers in the Chicago Post Office from 1921.), 1977. [National Alliance of Postal and Federal Employees, Local 701, 1225 East 79th Street, Chicago, IL 60619]

Gregory, Susan. "'Hey, White Girl!'" Chicago Tribune Magazine, F 22, 1970. [Marshall High School]

_____. Hey, White Girl! New York: Norton, 1970. [Student at John Marshall High School, Chicago]

Gross, Lisa. "School Board Progresses Backward on Cooley High Replacement. Community Smells Racial Doublecross on Vocational High Planning." Chicago Reporter 5(Mr, 1976).

Grossman, Ronald. "Family. Beating the Odds in Central Englewood." Chicago 27(My, 1978):164-182.

_____. "Report from Gage Park." Chicago Journalism Review 6(F, 1973):3-16. [Gage Park High School]

Gurin, Gerald. Inner-City Negro Youth in a Job Training Project: A Study of Factors Related to Attrition and Job Success. Washington, DC: GPO, 1970. [JOBS project]

Gutman, Heidi. "At Kenwood High, Integration Works." Chicago Tribune, Je 13, 1977.

Hall, Fred L. Location Criteria for High Schools. Student Transportation and Racial Integration. Chicago: Department of Geography, U. of Chicago, 1973.

Hall, Tom. "Fay Had a Baby." Chicago Tribune Magazine, N 8, 1970. [G. W. Tilton Elementary School

Hargrett, Andrew. "The Education-Unemployment Relationship in Chicago As Revealed in the 1960 Census." Journal of Negro Education, Spring, 1965.

Hartman, D. N. "Master Planning in the Chicago Public School System." Master's thesis, U. of Chicago, 1957.

Hauser, Philip M. "Dynamic Inaction in Chicago's Schools." Integrated Education, O-N, 1964.

Havemann, Joel. "Inequities in Chicago Schools Disclosed in Board's Own Statistics." Chicago Sun-Times, Ap 22, 1970.

Havighurst, Robert J. "The Chicago School Survey." Phi Delta Kappan, D, 1964.

_____. "Chicago's Educational Needs--1966." Urban Affairs Quarterly, S, 1966.

_____. The Public Schools of Chicago: A Survey. Chicago: Board of Education, 1964.

Hayes, John M. "Thank You for Your St. Mel Support." Chicago Defender, My 13, 1978. [By the Vicar of Education, Chicago Archdiocese]

Herrick, Mary J. The Chicago Schools. A Social and Political History. Beverly Hills, CA: Sage Publications, 1971.

_____. "Negro Employees of the Chicago Board of Education." Master's thesis, U. of Chicago, 1931.

Hirsch, Arnold R. "Making the Second Ghetto: Race and Housing in Chicago, 1940-1960." Doctoral dissertation, U. of Illinois, Chicago Circle, 1978. Univ. Microfilms Order No. 7824355.

_____. "Race and Housing: Violence and Communal Protest in Chicago, 1940-1960." In Melvin G. Holli and Peter d'A. Jones, The Ethnic Frontier. Grand Rapids, MI: Eerdimaus, 1977.

Hoffman, Daniel Ronald. "Whose Kind of Town? An Examination of the Pluralist Thesis and the Power Elite in Chicago." Doctoral dissertation, U. of California, Santa Barbara, 1973. Univ. Microfilms Order No. 74-14, 842.

Hoffman, Julius J. "Our Schools Will be Integrated." Integrated Education, Ja, 1963.

Hogan, David John. "Capitalism and Schooling: A History of the Political Economy of Education in Chicago, 1880-1930." Doctoral dissertation, U. of Illinois, 1978. Univ. Microfilms Order No. 7820964.

Homel, Michael Wallace. "The Lilydale School Campaign of 1936: Direct Action in the Verbal Protest Era." Journal of Negro History 59(Jl, 1974):228-241.

_____. "Race and Schools in Nineteenth-Century Chicago." Integrateducation 12(S-O, 1974): 39-42.

_____. "The Politics of Public Education in Black Chicago, 1910-1941." Journal of Negro Education 45(Spring, 1976):179-191.

_____. "School Facilities: Separate But Equal?" Chapter 3 in "Negroes in the Chicago Public Schools, 1910-1941." Doctoral dissertation, U. of Chicago, 1972.

Hunt, Ridgely. "Playing it Cool at Wendell Phillips." Chicago Tribune Magazine, My 7, 1972. [Wendell Phillips High School]

Hunter, Albert. "The Ecology of Chicago: Persistence and Change, 1930-1960." American Journal of Sociology 77(N, 1971):425-444.

Hurst, Beverly J. "Barometers of Black Economic Achievement--The Reality and the Myth." In George E. Carter, James R. Parker, and Carol Sweeney, Selected Proceedings of the 3rd Annual Conference on Minority Studies, April, 1975, pp. 53-63. La Crosse, WI: Institute for Minority Studies, U. of Wisconsin, La Crosse, 1976.

Hurst, Beverly J., and Watson, Cassandra. The November, 1972 Elections Revisted: Chicago's Black Voters in Perspective. Chicago: Chicago Urban League, 1974.

Hurst, Jack. "Chicago's Jewish Community: Mixing Progress and Tradition." Chicago Tribune Magazine, S 12, 1976.

Hymer, Bennett. The Dynamics of Job Changing. A Case Study of Employment Conditions for Black Workers in the Chicago Labor Market. Chicago: Chicago Urban League, S, 1969.

_____. The Negro Labor Market in Chicago, 1966. Chicago: Urban League, 1967.

_____. "Racial Dualism in the Chicago Labor Market." Doctoral dissertation, Northwestern U., 1968. Univ. Microfilms Order No. 69-1853.

Ichishita, Frank Y. "A Neighborhood Demonstrates." Integrated Education, D, 1963-Ja, 1964.

Illinois Chapter, Black Panther Party. "Racists Attack Black Children at George B. Swift School on Northwest Side of Chicago." Black Panther, My 8, 1971.

Interuniversity Social Research Committee--Chicago Metropolitan Area. Militancy for and against Civil Rights and Integration in Chicago: Summer, 1967, Ag 1, 1967. Community and Family Study Center, U. of Chicago, Chicago, IL 60637.

M. G. J. "When Is Public Education Public?" Community, Je, 1966. [A case of deliberate de facto segregation in Chicago]

Jerrems, Raymond L., and Burrill, Frances S. A Study of the Promotion System for Principals of the Chicago Public Schools from 1955 to 1965. Raymond School, 3663 South Wabash Avenue, Chicago, IL 60653.

Jerry, Hawke. Black Schoolmaster (a novel). New York: Exposition Press, 1970. [A black high school]

Johnson, Geraldine. "White Achievement in a Mainly Black School." Integrateducation 14 (S-O, 1976). [Pershing Elementary School]

Johnson, Philip A. Call Me Neighbor, Call Me Friend. Garden City, NY: Doubleday, 1965. [Integration in a Chicago neighborhood]

Jones, Alan. Students--Do Not Push Your Teacher Down the Stairs on Friday. Chicago: Quadrangle, 1973. [DuSable Upper Grade Center]

Kamin, Kay Hodes. "A History of the Hunt Administration of the Chicago Public Schools, 1947-1953." Doctoral dissertation, U. of Chicago, 1971.

Karlen, David. Racial Integration and Property Values in Chicago. Urban Economics Report No. 7. Chicago: U. of Chicago, Ap, 1968.

Kee, Muriel E. W. "Many Faces: Partners in Power." Negro History Bulletin 39(Ap, 1976): 563-566. [Lorraine Hansberry Child Parent Center]

Keiser, R. Lincoln. The Vice Lords. New York: Holt, Rinehart & Winston, 1969. [A Negro teenage gang]

Kellam, Sheppard G., Branch, Jeannette D., Agrawal, Khazan C., and Ensminger, Margaret E. Mental Health and Going to School. The Woodlawn Program of Assessment, Early Intervention, and Evaluation. Chicago: U. of Chicago Press, 1974.

Kelly, Thomas J. " Chicago Newspaper Editorials on Race, 1954-1968." Chicago Journalism Review 5(Ag, 1972):3-5, 20-22.

_____. "White Press/Black Man: An Analysis of the Editorial Opinion of Four White Chicago Daily Newspapers Toward Race, 1954-1968." Doctoral dissertation, U. of Illinois,

"The Keppel-Page Letter." Integrated Education, D, 1965-Ja, 1966.

Kiang, Ying-cheng. "Recent Changes in the Distribution of Urban Poverty in Chicago." Professional Geographer 28(F, 1976):57-60.

King, Seth S. "No Hope in Woodlawn." Saturday Review 55(Ag 19, 1972):6-13.

Kirk, Marcella M. "An Examination and Analysis of the Chicago Model Cities Educational Project, from 1967 through 1971." Doctoral dissertation, Loyola U., 1973.

Kissinger, C. Clark. "'Serve the People.'" Guardian, My 17, 1969. [The Black Panthers in Chicago]

Koerner, Thomas Foster. "Benjamin C. Willis and the Chicago Press." Doctoral dissertation, Northwestern U., 1968.

Kopan, Andrew Thomas. "Education and Greek Immigrants in Chicago, 1892-1973: A Study in Ethnic Survival." Doctoral dissertation, U. of Chicago, 1974.

Krug, Mark. "The Krug Report. Understanding Chicago's Schools Crisis." Six Parts, Chicago Tribune, Mr 10-15, 1974.

Landry, Lawrence. "The Chicago School Boycott." New University Thought, D-Ja, 1963-1964.

Lanier, Alfredo S., and Wilson, Paula P. "Odds Stacked Against Chicago's Black, Latino Branch Libraries; Officials Attempt to Shelve Stubborn Pattern of Discrimination." Chicago Reporter 7(Ag, 1978).

Lauerman, Connie. "School Sheds 'Snakepit' Image." Chicago Tribune, Mr 24, 1974. [Manierre Elementary School]

Lavelle, Mike. "The Nazi." Chicago 27(Je, 1978):135-139. [Richard Tedor, a leader of a Chicago Nazi organization]

Lazin, Frederick Aaron. "Public Housing in Chicago, 1963-1971: Gautreaux v. Chicago Housing Authority: A Case Study of the Cooptation of a Federal Agency by Its Local Constituency." Doctoral dissertation, U. of Chicago, 1973.

Leadership Council for Metropolitan Open Communities. Factors Affecting Housing Choice for Black Families in Chicago. The Council, 155 North Wacker Drive, Chicago, IL 60606.

Lens, Sidney. "Daley in Chicago." Progressive, Mr, 1966.

Levin, Nathaniel. "Fading Away: Integration in Chicago." Integrateducation 14(Mr-Ap, 1976): 8-10. [Austin busing plan]

Levine, Charles F. "Understanding Alinsky. Conservative Wine in Radical Bottles." American Behavioral Scientist 17(N-D, 1973):279-284.

Levine, Daniel U. and others. The Utility and Implications of 1970 Census Data in Predicting Achievement and Assessing Effects of Concentrated Urban Poverty in Chicago, S, 1974. ERIC ED 096 369.

Levinsohn, Florence Hamlish. "Bill Berry in the Boardrooms and Streets." Chicago 27(Jl, 1978).

Liston, Robert A. " Benjamin C. Willis Pugnacious Planner of America's Future." True, My, 1965.

Littler, Frank. "103rd and Vincennes--Beverly at a Crossroads." Chicago Sun-Times, Mr 31, 1974.

London, Stephen D. "Business and the Chicago School System, 1890-1966." Doctoral dissertation, U. of Chicago, 1968.

McCarthy, Joseph J. "History of Black Catholic Education in Chicago: 1871-1971." Doctoral dissertation, Loyola U. of Chicago, 1973. Univ. Microfilms Order No. 73-23, 150.

McCarthy, Patricia. "Learning to Live Together on Chicago's West Side." Integrated Education 8(Jl-Ag, 1970):15-18.

McClory, Robert. "High School Tragedy." In These Times, F 21, 1979. [St. Mary's Alternative High School]

_____. "It's Those Outsiders...Who Cause All the Trouble..." Chicago Reporter 5(Ag, 1977). [Marquette Park area]

_____. The Man Who Beat Clout City. Chicago: Swallow, 1977. [Renault Robinson, head, Afro-American Patrolman's League]

_____. "3 Black Board Members Bitter." Chicago Defender, D 13, 1975. [Chicago Board of Education]

McDermott, John A. "Preserving Integration, A Case History." In Catholic Schools and Racial Integration: Perspectives, Directions, Models, pp. 35-40. Washington, DC: National Catholic Conference for Interracial Justice, 1977. [St. Thomas the Apostle elementary school]

McDermott, Robert. "Father Lawlor: His Kingdom and Power." Chicago Tribune Magazine, F 21, 1971.

McDougall, Harold. "Woodlawn Organization Does Not Act Like a Good Civil Rights Group Really Should, But Then Again, It Likes to Win Sometimes." Harvard Crimson, O 3, 1966.

McGee, Henry. "The Negro in the Chicago Post Office." Master's thesis, U. of Chicago, 1961.

Malles, James Emery. "Perceptions of Teachers, Administrators, and Community Council Members in Nine Select Elementary and School-Communities of the Chicago Public Schools as to the Role of the School-Community Council in Educational Decision-Making." Doctoral dissertation, U. of Illinois, Urbana, 1974. Univ. Microfilms Order No. 75-11, 874.

Mangelsdorf, Elizabeth. "Chicago Revolts." Community, Ap, 1967.

Martin, John Henry, Lieberman, Myron, and Elsbree, Willard. Recommendations for Desegregating the Staff and Equalizing the Distribution of Experienced Teachers in the Public Schools of Chicago, Illinois. Mill Neck, NY: The Authors, Je, 1970.

Martin, Lowell A. Library Response to Urban Change. A Study of the Chicago Public Library. Chicago: American Library Association, 1970.

Martin, Paul. "In A Class by Herself." Chicago Tribune Magazine, Ap 9, 1978. [Ms. Marva Collins, Westside Prep School]

Mason, B. J. "Blackboard Jungle Still Flourishing." Chicago Sun-Times, Mr 17, 1974. [Chicago public high schools]

Mendelson, Lloyd J., and Bristol, John. "Project Wingspread: The Chicago Area City-Suburban Exchange Program." In Daniel U. Levine, Models for Integrated Education, pp. 98-108. Worthington, OH: Jones, 1971.

Millea, Thomas V. "Wayfaring Strangers." Community 29(1972):5-8. [Appalachian migrants, Uptown]

Miller, Steven I., and Moses, James C. "Catholic Schools and Integration: A Case Study." Notre Dame Journal of Education 3(Winter, 1973):355-361.

Moberg, David. "The Meaning of Marquette Park." Reader, Jl 23, 1976.

Molotch, Harvey L. "Community Action to Control Racial Change." Doctoral dissertation, U. of Chicago, 1968. [South Shore]

_____. Managed Integration: Dilemmas of Doing Good in the City. Berkeley, CA: U. of California Press, 1973. [South Shore]

_____. "Racial Change in a Stable Community." American Journal of Sociology, S, 1969.

_____. "Racial Integration in a Transition Community." American Sociological Review, D, 1969. [South Shore]

Monahan, Anthony. "Father Lawlor: Forgive Those Who Trespass Across Ashland Av. and Deliver Us From Liberals. Amen." Midwest Magazine (Chicago Sun-Times), Mr 9, 1969.

Montay, Sr. Mary Innocente. The History of Catholic Secondary Education in the Archdiocese of Chicago. Washington, DC: Catholic U. of America Press, 1953.

Morogay, John T. "What Willis Didn't Say in The Atlantic." Focus/Midwest III, No. 8-9, 1965. [Dunbar High School in Chicago; see Atlantic Monthly, Ja, 1965]

Moses, James Charles. "Desegregation in Catholic Schools in the Archdiocese of Chicago 1964-1974, Including a Case Study of a Catholic High School." Doctoral dissertation, Loyola U. (Chicago), 1978. Univ. Microfilms Order No. 7807076.

Mueller, Siegfried G., and Jennings, Jeanelle. "The Chicago Child-Parent Center Revisited." Phi Delta Kappan 56(S, 1974):50.

Muhammad, Ozier. "Chicago Plays Tricks on People Seeking School Space." Muhammad Speaks, Jl 23, 1971. [Von Humboldt Elementary School]

Muhammad University of Islam. No. 2. 1971 Yearbook, 1972. Muhammad's Temple No. 2, 5335 South Greenwood Avenue, Chicago, IL 60615.

Newman, M. W. "Sad Reading: Library Circulation Drops." Chicago Sun-Times, S 13, 1978.

Novak, Rick. "2 Schools in Uptown." Chicago Guide 21(Ja, 1972):18-22. [Two free schools]

Ogletree, Earl. "Plight of the Chicago Schools." Phi Delta Kappan, F, 1969.

"On the Conference Front." Negro Digest, Jl, 1968. [On white-sponsored black festivals in Chicago]

Oppenheim, Carol. "Desegregation in Chicago--Waiting for Courts to Get Tough." Chicago Tribune, S 14, 1975.

_____. "Salt and Pepper: Integration Recipe in Beverly Hills." Chicago Tribune, Je 27, 1976.

Orfield, Gary. "Chicago: Failure in the North." In The Reconstruction of Southern Education. The Schools and the 1964 Civil Rights Act. New York: Wiley-Interscience, 1969.

Orfield, Gary and others. Integration in Chicago. A Report to the Illinois State Board of Education. Springfield, IL: State Board of Education, My 11, 1978.

Page, Eleanor. "A Who's Who of Black Chicago Society." Chicago Tribune Magazine, Mr 16, 1969.

Parkay, Forrest. "Innovation in a Chicago Inner-City High School." Phi Delta Kappan 57(F, 1976):384-390.

Parot, Joseph. "The American Faith and the Persistence of Chicago Polonia." Doctoral dissertation, Northern Illinois U., 1971.

_____. "Ethnic versus Black Metropolis: The Origins of Polish-Black Housing Tensions in Chicago." Polish-American Studies 31(Spring, 1974).

_____. "The Racial Dilemma in Chicago's Polish Neighborhoods, 1920-1970." Polish-American Studies 32(Autumn, 1975).

Pascal, Anthony H. The Economics of Housing Segregation. Santa Monica, CA: Rand, N, 1967.

Pasnick, Raymond W. "Chicago's School Crisis." Integrated Education, Ap-My, 1964.

Pederson, Lee A. "Non-Standard Negro Speech in Chicago." In William A. Stewart, Non-Standard Speech and the Teaching of English, 1964. Washington, DC: Center for Applied Linguistics, Modern Language Association for America, 1755 Massachusetts Avenue, N.W., Washington, DC 20036.

Philpott, Thomas Lee. The Slum and the Ghetto: Neighborhood Deterioration and Middle-Class Reform, Chicago, 1880-1930. New York: Oxford U. Press, 1977.

Piccagli, Giorgio Antonio. "Racial Transition in Chicago Public Schools, 1963-1971, An Examination of the Tipping Point Hypothesis." Doctoral dissertation, U. of Chicago, 1975.

Pitts, James P. "Boycott Participation and School Organization Memberships." Education and Urban Society 3(Ag, 1971):383-397. Boycotts by black high school students in Chicago, O-N, 1968

Pollack, Ervin. "A Learning Center in an Integrated Elementary School." In Daniel N. Levine, Models for Integrated Education, pp. 49-57. Worthington, OH: Jones, 1971.

Powell, Daniel, and Eash, Maurice J. "Secondary School Cases." In Herbert J. Walberg, Evaluating Educational Performance, pp. 277-293. Berkeley, CA: McCutchan, 1974.

Pyle, Gerald F., and Rees, Philip H. "Modeling Patterns of Death and Disease in Chicago." Economic Geography 47(O, 1971):475-488.

"Question 1: How Much Will Be Spent This Year to Build New Jim Crow Schools?" Substance 2 (Mr 16, 1977):14. [Published by SUBS, Chicago]

Raby, Albert A. "On The Wrong Civil Rights Track in the City of Chicago." Focus/Midwest IV, Nos. 7-8(1966).

Raby, Patricia. "Children of the Ghetto." Integrated Education, Je-Jl, 1966.

Rader, Herschel. "Community Control Revisited: Trends in the Assignment of Chicago Principals." Chicago Principals Reporter (Spring, 1976):6-17, 21.

Rather, Ernest R. (ed.). Chicago Negro Almanac and Reference Book. Chicago: Chicago Negro Almanac Pub. Co., 1972.

Raymond, Joan M. Financing Equity Among Schools in Large Cities. Chicago Public Schools: A Case Study, Mr 15, 1976. ERIC ED 125 110.

Real Estate Research Corporation. Projection of Population and School Enrollments by Community Area for the City of Chicago 1970 and 1975. Chicago: Board of Education, Ap, 1968.

Redmond, James F. Chicago Public Schools Response to the Chicago Public School System: An Agenda for Change. Chicago: Board of Education, F, 1975. [Response to criticisms by Ald. William Singer; see below]

Rehak, Bob. "Brief Innocence: Growing Up Quickly in Uptown." Chicago Tribune Magazine, Ag 15, 1976.

Remsberg, Charles, and Remsberg, Bonnie. "Chicago: Legacy of an Ice Age." Saturday Review, My 20, 1967.

_____ and _____. "Chicago Voices: Tales Told Out of School." In Raymond W. Mack, Our Children's Burden. New York: Random House, 1968.

"Requiem for My First Alma Mater." Chicago Defender, Je 17, 1978. [James A. Doolittle Elementary School, Chicago, in the early 1920's]

Rhoden, Bill. "Chicago Teacher Makes His Classes Come Alive." Ebony 32(Mr, 1977):43-50. [Emiel Hamberlin, DuSable High School]

Rivera, Ramon J., McWorter, Gerald A., and Lillienstein, Ernest. "Freedom Day II in Chicago." Integrated Education, Ag-S, 1964.

Rogoness, G. A., Bednar, R. A., and Diesenhaus, H. "The Social System and Children's Behavior Problems." American Journal of Orthopsychiatry 44(Jl, 1974):497-502. [Chicago, 1969-1972]

Roof, Wade Clark. "'The Negro as an Immigrant Group'--A Research Note on Chicago's Racial Trends." Ethnic and Racial Studies 1(O, 1978):452-464.

Rosen, Lois Anne, and Rosen, Frank. "Gage Park: The Roots of Racial Tragedy." Part 1. Chicago Journalism Review 6(My, 1973):12-17.

Sale, R. T. The Blackston Rangers: A Reporter's Account of Time Spent on Chicago's South Side. New York: Random House, 1972.

Sanders, Charles L. "Cold Weather, Warm Hearts." _Ebony_, Ap, 1966. [Young Negro Chicagoans visit Sweden]

Sanders, James W. "Catholic Elementary School Enrollment: Chicago, 1925-1965." _Elementary School Journal_, N, 1967.

_____. "Education of Chicago Catholics." Doctoral dissertation, U. of Chicago, 1971.

Schmidt, George. "How Chicago Segregates," Part 1, 1837-1919. _Substance_ 1(Je, 1976).

_____. Marquette Park/Englewood "Border." The Issues and the Schools, Ag, 1976. Substitutes United for Better Schools, 343 South Dearborn Street, Chicago, IL 60604.

_____. "O'Toole: Study in Segregation." _Substance_ (Newsletter of Substitutes United for Better Schools) 1(Ap, 1976).

"The School Board Investigates." _Integrated Education_, D, 1965-Ja, 1966.

Schwartz, Loretta. "People Are Starving in Chicago." _Chicago_ 25(Je, 1976):92-99.

Scott, Ralph. "First to Ninth Grade IQ Changes of Northern Negro Students." _Psychology in the Schools_, Ap, 1966.

Sengstacke, John. "Our Segregated Schools." _Chicago Daily Defender_, D 10, 1962.

Serrin, William. "Jesse Jackson..." _New York Times Magazine_, Jl 9, 1972.

Shanabruch, Charles H. "The Catholic Church's Role in the Americanization of Chicago's Immigrants: 1833-1928." Two volumes. Doctoral dissertation, U. of Chicago, 1975.

Sheppard, Nathaniel, Jr. "Drive for Discipline Has Hazy Identity at 1 School." _New York Times_, Mr 5, 1979. [Orr High School]

Singer, William S. The Chicago Public School System: An Agenda for Change, Ja 21, 1975.

Slater, Jack. "The School That Beat the Odds." _Ebony_ 28(My, 1973):64-72. [Holy Angels School]

Smith, Calvert Hayes. "Social Class Origin and Mobility of Black Inner-City School Teachers." _Urban Education_ 5(1970):64-83.

Smith, James Hoard. "Racial Violence Flares in Irish Chicago." _Muhammad Speaks_, N 8, 1974. [Tilden High School]

Smith, Jeffrey K., and Katims, Michael. "Reading in the City: The Chicago Mastery Learning Reading Program." _Phi Delta Kappan_ 59 (N, 1977):199-202.

Social Research, Inc. The Effect of Busing Black Ghetto Children into White Suburban Schools. Prepared for the Chicago Catholic School Board Archdiocese of Chicago, Jl, 1970. Social Research, Inc., 740 North Rush Street, Chicago, IL 60611.

Sola, Peter. "Plutocrats, Pedagogues and Plebes: Business Influences on Vocational and Extra Curricular Activities in the Chicago High Schools 1899-1925." Doctoral dissertation, U. of Illinois, 1972.

Spear, Allan H. Black Chicago: The Making of a Negro Ghetto, 1890-1920. Chicago: U. of Chicago Press, 1967.

Star, Jack. "The School That Works." _Chicago_ 27(My, 1978):143-146. [St. Ignatius College Prep.]

_____. "Segregation Crisis: Chicago's Troubled Schools." _Look_, My 4, 1965.

Steinnes, Donald N. "Urban Employment and Residential Segregation: A Conditional Index." _Journal of Regional Science_ 17(1977):291-298.

Stevens, Stanley Carson. "The Urban Racial Border: Chicago 1960." Doctoral dissertation, U. of Illinois, 1972.

Stone, Sonja H. "Chicago's Center for Inner City Studies: An Experiment in Relevancy." _Social Education_, My, 1969.

Straits, Bruce C. "Residential Movement Among Negroes and Whites in Chicago." _Social Science Quarterly_, D, 1968.

Street, David. Race and Education in the City: Findings on Chicago. Chicago: Community and Family Study Center, U. of Chicago, Ja, 1969.

Strickland, Arvarh E. History of the Chicago Urban League. Urbana, IL: U. of Illinois Press, 1966.

Student-Teacher Coalition. "School Administration and Daley Pigs Strike Again." _Black Panther_, My 15, 1971. [Hyde Park High School]

Suro, Roberto. "The End of Integration." _Chicago_ 27(S, 1978):244-245.

Sutor, David. "The Church and Inner City Schools in Chicago ." _New World_ (6 articles) F 25, 1972-Mr 10, 1972.

Talmage, Harriet, and Rippey, Robert M. "Elementary School Cases." In Herbert J. Walberg, Evaluating Educational Performance, pp. 255-276. Berkeley, CA: McCutchan, 1974.

Terkel, Studs. "Gage Park: A Reply." _Chicago Journalism Review_, Mr, 1973. [See Grossman, above]

Thomas, Cleveland A. "The Independent School and Desegregation." School Review, Vol. 69, No. 4, 1961. [About desegregation at Francis W. Parker School in Chicago]

Thompson, Charles Henry. "Study of the Reading Accomplishments of Colored and White Children [in Chicago]." Master's thesis, U. of Chicago, 1920.

Thomas, Jacqueline. "Must Ghetto Schools Be Inferior?" Sepia 26(Mr, 1977).

Thornblad, Eric C. "The Fiscal Impact of a High Concentration of Low Income Families upon the Public Schools." Doctoral dissertation, U. of Illinois, 1966. [Chicago elementary schools]

Tibbs, W. H. "The Ku Klux Klan in Chicago." Messenger 2(D, 1919):27. [Hyde Park area]

Toolan, Sean. "Chicago ['s Black Community Since the 1968 Riots]." Chicago Tribune Magazine, My 22, 1977.

Townsend, Richard G. "Integration by Design." Integrated Education 11(Ja-F, 1973):33-34.

Tregillus, Peter. "Parents Raise Concerns About Continuous Progress." Parent Involvement Press 1(Mr, 1978):8. [Chappell Elementary School]

_____. "Why Are They Smiling?" Parent Involvement Press 1(O, 1977). [Darwin Elementary School]

Turner, Deborah A. "Top of the Bottom." Chicago Defender, Ja 13, 1976. [Edward Jenner Elementary School]

Tuttle, William M., Jr. "Contested Neighborhoods and Racial Violence: Prelude to the Chicago Riot of 1919." Journal of Negro History 55(O, 1970):267-288.

_____. Race Riot. Chicago in the Red Summer of 1919. New York: Atheneum, 1970.

Ulbrich, Polly. "Start Small, Conquer the World." Chicago 25(Ag, 1976). ["Fifth City," East Garfield Park]

Upchurch, Mark. "Insights from the Inner City." Illinois Schools Journal, Spring, 1969.

U.S. Congress, 91st, 1st Session, House of Representatives, Committee on Education and Labor, General Subcommittee on Education, Needs of Elementary and Secondary Education for the Seventies. Hearings, Part 2. Washington, DC: GPO, 1970. [See testimony on Chicago public schools faculty desegregation by Jerris Leonard and questioning by Rep. Pucinski, pp. 761-806.]

U.S. Congress, 89th, 1st Session, House of Representatives, Committee on Education and Labor, Special Sub-committee. De Facto School Segregation, Investigation of De Facto Racial Segregation in Chicago Public Schools. Committee Print. Washington, DC: GPO, 1965.

U.S. Office of Education. "Report on U.S. Office of Education Analysis of Chicago Public Schools." Integrated Education, D, 1966-Ja, 1967.

U.S. News and World Report. "Benjamin C. Willis: An Interview." Integrated Education, D, 1965-Ja, 1966.

Venning, Robert S. "Urban Renewal and the Social Geography of Hyde Park." Master's Thesis, U. of Chicago, 1966.

Vrame, William Anton. "A History of School Desegregation in Chicago Since 1954." Doctoral dissertation, U. of Wisconsin, 1970. Univ. Microfilms Order No. 71-328.

Wagner, Jon. Misfits and Missionaries. A School for Black Dropouts. Beverly Hills, CA: Sage, 1978.

Walberg, Herbert J., and Bargen, Mark. "School Equality." In Herbert J. Walberg, Evaluating Educational Performance, pp. 222-238. Berkeley, CA: McCutchan, 1974.

_____ and _____. "Urban Spatial Models." In Herbert J. Walberg, Evaluating Educational Performance, pp. 357-374. Berkeley, CA: McCutchan, 1974.

Walberg, Herbert, and Sigler, Jeanne. Business Views Education: Problems in the Chicago Public Schools and Seven Recommendations. Chicago: Chicago United, My 8, 1974.

Ward, Francis. "Prognosis for Chicago Blacks: Continuing Lack of Power." First World 1 (My-Je, 1977):7-9.

Ward, Renee. "Warren Bacon Gives School Board Low Grade." Chicago Reporter 2(N, 1973).

Warrick, Pamela. "School's Readers Improve Skills." Chicago Sun-Times, Je 25, 1978. [Mulligan Elementary School]

Weeres, J. G. "School Politics in Thirty-three of the Local Community Areas Within the City of Chicago." Doctoral dissertation, U. of Chicago, 1971.

Weinberg, Meyer. "A Chronology of Deferral." Integrated Education, D, 1965-Ja, 1966, p. 8.

_____. "How the Federal Court's Detroit School Decision Might Affect Chicago." The Chicago Reporter 1(S, 1972).

———. "Techniques for Achieving Racially Desegregated, Superior Quality Education in the Public Schools of Chicago, Illinois." In U.S. Commission on Civil Rights, Papers Prepared for National Conference on Equal Educational Opportunity in America's Cities. Washington, DC: GPO, 1968.

"Where Education is Life Itself." Muhammad Speaks, Mr 7, 1969. [Muhammad University of Islam, No. 2]

"The Whiston-Cohen Agreement." Integrated Education, D, 1965-Ja, 1966.

Whitehead, Ralph, Jr. "This is the Ward Ed Vrdolyak Built." Chicagoan 1(D, 1973):104-110.

"Whites Out: Want Blacks Out! Chicago School Crisis Smolders." Muhammad Speaks, O 13, 1972. [Gage Park High School]

Wilkins, Roy, and Clark, Ramsey. Search and Destroy. A Report by the Commission of Inquiry into the Black Panthers and the Police. New York: Metropolitan Applied Research Center, 1973.

Wille, Lois. "Mayor Daley Meets the Movement." Nation, Ag 30, 1965.

———. "The Payoff in Chicago." New Republic, O 23, 1965.

Williams, Kale. "Dismantling the Dual Housing Market in Chicago." Integrated Education 13 (My-Je, 1975):91-94.

Williamson, Stanford W. With Grief Acquainted. Chicago: Follett Publishing Company, 1964. [About life among Negroes on Chicago's South Side]

Willis, Benjamin C. Data Concerning the Community and the Public School Pupils of Chicago. Chicago Board of Education, Jl 8, 1964.

———. "Education the Year Around. The Dunbar School, Chicago." Atlantic Monthly, Ja, 1965. [See "Vocational Education at Dunbar," Integrated Education, Je, 1963.]

———. [Interview on school segregation and other topics] Chicago and Omnibus FM Guide, S, 1966. [Omnibus, Inc., 333 N. Michigan Ave., Chicago, IL 60601]

———. Response to Recommendations 4 through 10 of the Advisory Panel on Integration in the Public Schools. Chicago: Board of Education, Jl, 1964.

———. "Willis Concentrates on 'Quality Education for All.'" [interview] Phi Delta Kappan, D, 1964.

Wong, Phillip L. "Black Attorneys Exit City's Top Law Firms..." Chicago Reporter 6(Ja, 1977).

Woodford, John. "For the Liberation of the Black School Teacher." Muhammad Speaks, My 2, 1969. [Center for Inner City Studies]

Wrigley, Julia. "The Politics of Education in Chicago: Social Conflicts and the Public Schools." Doctoral dissertation, U. of Wisconsin, 1977.

14 X, Larry. "Chicago Ed. Board Slashes Vocational School Classes." Muhammad Speaks, O 4, 1974.

Yeates, Maurice Henry. "The Spatial Distribution of Chicago Land Values, 1910-1960." Doctoral dissertation, Northwestern U., 1963. Univ. Microfilms Order No. 64-3847.

Indiana

Anderson, Ruth J. "Negro Education in Tippecanoe County, 1869-1886." Master's thesis, Purdue U., 1963.

Aquila, Frank D. U.S. vs. Board of School Commissioners, Indianapolis: A Case in Point, Mr 28, 1978. ERIC ED 155 237.

Artis, Lionel F. "These 'Colored' United States: The Negro in Indiana, or the Struggle Against Dixie Come North." Messenger 6(Mr, 1924): 76-79, 93-94.

Bell, Odessa Khaton. "School Segregation in Gary." Integrated Education, O-N, 1963.

Bethea, Dennis A. "The Colored Group in the Gary School System." Crisis, Ag, 1931.

Betten, Neil, and Mohl, Raymond A. "The Evolution of Racism in an Industrial City, 1906-1940: A Case Study of Gary, Indiana." Journal of Negro History 59(Ja, 1974):51-64.

Betten, Neil, and Lane, James B. "Nativism and the Klan in Town and City: Valparaiso and Gary, Indiana." Studies in History and Society 4(Spring, 1973).

Boone, Richard Gouse. A History of Education in Indiana. New York: D. Appleton & Co., 1892.

Breedlove, James W. "Looking at the Black Community's Court Action." Fort Wayne Journal-Gazette, Mr 26, 1978. [Fort Wayne]

Brooks, John W. "Attitudes and Opinions of Negro Parents and Students Concerning Shortridge High School." Doctoral dissertation, Indiana U., 1960. Univ. Microfilms Order No. 60-2995. [Indianapolis]

Carroll, J. C. "The Beginnings of Public Education for Negroes in Indiana." Journal of Negro Education, O, 1939.

Casimere, Dwight, and Forrest, Leon. "After They Burned the Cross in Kokomo." Muhammad Speaks, Jl 11, 1969, and Jl 18, 1969.

Cates, Frank Mark. "The Ku Klux Klan in Indiana Politics, 1920-1925." Doctoral dissertation, Indiana U., 1971.

"Classification of Students by Race." Indiana Law Journal 2(Mr, 1927):493-494. [Greathouse v. Board of School Commissioners of City of Indianapolis, 151 NE 411]

Coleman, J. D. "Are Out-of-Town Children Responsible for the Retardation in the Colored Schools of Indianapolis, Indiana?" Master's thesis, U. of Chicago, 1924.

Colquit, Jesse L. "A 1972 Investigation of the Number and Level of Professional Assignments of Black Administrators in Indiana Public School Corporations as Compared with April 1969." Doctoral dissertation, Ball State U., 1972.

Coney, Mattie Rice. "One Negro Woman's Advice to Her People." U.S. News and World Report, Mr 27, 1967. [Negro teacher in Indianapolis]

Cools, G. Victor. "Gary's High School Strike." School and Society 26(N 26, 1927):685-686.

Davies, Shane, and Fowler, Gary L. "The Disadvantaged Urban Migrant in Indianapolis." Economic Geography 48(Ap, 1972):153-167.

Davis, Brent V. "An Assessment of the Equality or Inequality of Racially Segregated Public Schools: Indianapolis." Master's thesis, Indiana U., 1974.

Denehie, Elizabeth. "Catholic Education in Indiana, Past and Present." Indiana Magazine of History 12(1916):337-350.

Eaglesfield, R. D. "Racial Imbalance in the Public Elementary Schools of Indiana." Indiana Legal Forum 3(1969-1970):483-516.

Fort Wayne Urban League. "What High School Students Think of Desegregation." Integrateducation 15(N-D, 1977):131-133.

Fowler, Gary L. and others. "The Residential Location of Disadvantaged Urban Migrants: White Migrants to Indianapolis." In Melvin Albaum with Shane Davis, Geography and Contemporary Issues. New York: Wiley, 1973.

"The Gary School Strike." Literary Digest, O 22, 1928.

Georgeoff, John, and Jones, Imogene. Summary Report on the Gary Curriculum Research Project, "The Curriculum As a Factor in Racial Understanding." Gary, IN: School City of Gary, N, 1967.

Godecker, M. Salesia, Sr. History of Catholic Education in Indiana. Washington, DC, 1925.

Gonis, Sophia Nicholas. "An Analysis of Desegregation Trends in the Indianapolis Public Schools." Master's thesis, Butler U., 1965.

Greenwood, Charles, and Greenwood, Theresa. "Some Historic Aspects of Hoosier Education of the Negro." Indiana Social Studies Quarterly, Spring, 1964. [Indiana Council of the Social Studies, Ball State Teachers College, Muncie, IN]

Greer, Edward. "The 'Liberation' of Gary, Indiana." In Charles V. Willie, Black/Brown/White Relations. New Brunswick, NJ: Transaction, 1977.

_____. "Racial Employment Discrimination in the Gary Works, 1906-1974." Studies in Marxism, No. 2, 1977.

Gross, Harriet. An Analysis of Ability, Achievement, and Segregation in the Gary Public Schools, 1966-1967. Gary, IN: Gary Human Relations Commission, D, 1967.

_____. An Analysis of Segregation in the Gary Public Schools. Gary, IN: Gary Human Relations Commission, Mr 31, 1967.

Hayes, John Gregory. "Sources of Protest in the Anti-Busing Movement in Indianapolis, Indiana." Doctoral dissertation, Purdue U., 1975. Univ. Microfilms Order No. 76-536.

Heins, Marjorie. "Housing Remedies in School Desegregation Cases: The View from Indianapolis." Harvard Civil Rights--Civil Liberties Law Review 12(Summer, 1977):649-691.

Heller, Herbert L. "Negro Education in Indiana from 1816 to 1869." Doctoral dissertation, U. of Indiana, 1952.

Indiana State Advisory Committee. Gary Midtown West Families on AFDC. Washington, DC: U.S. Commission on Civil Rights, D, 1966.

Indiana State Advisory Committee. Gary Neighborhood Public Meeting: A Background Report. Washington, DC: U.S. Commission on Civil Rights, n.d.

Indiana State Advisory Committee to the U.S. Commission on Civil Rights. Indiana Migrants: Blighted Hopes, Slighted Rights. Washington, DC: The Commission, Mr, 1974.

Indiana State Advisory Committee. Student Friction and Racial Unrest at Southside High School, Muncie, Indiana. Washington, DC: U.S. Commission on Civil Rights, 1968.

Jackson, Donald. "American Dream. Bye and Bye." New Times 1(D 28, 1973):28-30. [Indianapolis]

Johnson, Charles S. Survey of the Negro Population of Fort Wayne, Indiana. National Urban League, 1928.

Johnson, Mordecai C. "Memorandum on Race and Education in Gary, Indiana." Washington, DC: U.S. Commission on Civil Rights, My 26, 1966. [Unpublished]

Kaplan, John. "Segregation Litigation and the Schools--Part III: The Gary Litigation." Northwestern U. Law Review, My-Je, 1964.

Karst, Frederick A. "A Rural Black Settlement in St. Joseph County, Indiana, before 1900." Indiana Magazine of History 74(S, 1978):252-267.

Knowlton, Brian. "City's Schools Had Race Problems in 1869, as Well as in 1969, Now." Fort Wayne Journal-Gazette, S 19, 1977.

_____. "Integration in Anderson: From Apathy to All-America." Fort Wayne Journal-Gazette, My 2, 1977.

_____. [Three articles on school desegregation in Fort Wayne, Indiana] Fort Wayne Journal-Gazette, S 20-22, 1977.

Lane, James B. "City of the Century." A History of Gary, Indiana. Bloomington, IN: Indiana U. Press, 1978.

Lisack, J. P. Comparisons of the Characteristics and Plans of Indiana High School Seniors by Race, and by Type Program Enrolled In..., Mr 1, 1978. ERIC ED 156 863. [Statewide]

Lowe, Robert A. "Racial Segregation in Indiana, 1920-1950." Doctoral dissertation, Ball State U., 1965. Univ. Microfilms Order No. 66-1988.

McClain, John. "Socio-economic Variations Among Black Residential Areas of Terre Haute, Indiana." Master's thesis, Indiana State U., 1976.

McClory, Robert. "Massive Resistance Northern Style." Race Relations Reporter 5(My, 1974): 26-27. [Indianapolis]

Marsh, William E. "Indianapolis Experience: The Anatomy of a Desegregation Case." Indiana Law Review 9(Je, 1976):897-993.

_____. "United States v. Board of School Commissioners." In Howard I. Kalodner and James J. Fishman (eds.) Limits of Justice, The Courts' Role in School Desegregation. Cambridge, MA: Ballinger, 1978. [Indianapolis]

Metropolitan Human Relations Commission. Interim Report on School Problems. Fort Wayne, IN: Metropolitan Human Relations Commission, F 23, 1972.

Millender, Dolly. Yesterday in Gary: A Brief History of the Negro in Gary--1906-1967. Vol. I, 1967. The Author, Box 1345, Gary, IN 46407.

Mohl, Raymond A., and Betten, Neil. "Ethnic Adjustment in the Industrial City: The International Institute of Gary, 1919-1940." International Migration Review 6(Winter, 1972):361-376.

Moore, Alexander. "The Inner-City High School: Instructional and Community Leadership Roles." In A. Harry Passow, Reaching the Disadvantaged Learner. New York: Teachers College Press, 1970. [Crispus Attucks High School, Indianapolis]

Moscove, Francine. The Experiment at Banneker School in Gary, Indiana, My, 1971. Writers Workshop, 3883 South Broadway, Gary, IN. [Reprinted in U.S. Congress, 92nd, 1st Session, Senate, Select Committee on Equal Educational Opportunity, Equal Educational Opportunity--1971. Part 16D1--Inequality in School Truance: General Appendixes, pp. 7757-7778. Washington, DC: GPO, 1971]

Myers, Spencer W. "The Gary Story." American Teacher 32(Mr, 1948):11-14.

Potts, John Foster. "A History of the Growth of the Negro Population in Gary, Indiana." Master's thesis, Cornell U., 1937.

"Racial Imbalance in the Public Elementary Schools of Indiana." Indiana Legal Forum 3 (Spring, 1970).

Ramsey, Andrew W. "The Hoosier Negro School Teacher." Indiana Social Studies Quarterly, Spring, 1964. Indiana Council of the Social Studies, Ball State Teachers College, Muncie, IN

Richards, Becky. "High Schoolers 'Not Looking at Color, But At Friends.'" Fort Wayne News-Sentinel, Ja 11, 1977. [North Side High School]

_____. "School Desegregation Works." Fort Wayne News-Sentinel, Ja 11, 1977.

Riley, Herman Murray. "A History of Negro Elementary Education in Indianapolis." Indiana Magazine of History 26(D, 1930):288-305.

_____. "A History of Negro Elementary Education in Indianapolis, Indiana, with Emphasis on its Preparation for Citizenship." Master's thesis, Teachers College, Columbia U.

Rohn, David. "1954 Dawns in Indianapolis." Journal of Intergroup Relations 3(Summer, 1974):3-7.

Russell, Joseph J. "Some Notes on Education in Indiana." Negro History Bulletin 39(Ja, 1976):511-515.

H. J. S. "Victory in Gary." Crisis, Ja, 1928.

Samuels, Ivan G. "Desegregated Education and Differences in Academic Achievement." Doctoral dissertation, Indiana U., 1958. Dissertation Abstracts, XIX, 1958, p. 1294.

Scott, Will B. "Race Consciousness and the Negro Student at Indiana University." Doctoral dissertation, Indiana U., 1965. Univ. Microfilms Order No. 65-1406.

Shosteck, Herschel. The Negro in Indianapolis. Cedar Rapids, IO: Frank N. Magid Associates, 1969.

South Bend Community School Corporation. Educational Reorganization Program. South Bend, IN: South Bend Community School Corporation, My, 1968.

"Teacher Race Old Issue in Indianapolis." Chicago Tribune, Jl 12, 1969.

Thornbrough, Emma Lou. "Segregation in Indiana during the Klan Era of the 1920's." Mississippi Valley Historical Review 47(Mr, 1961).

_____. Since Emancipation. A Short History of Indiana Negroes. Indianapolis: Indiana Division American Negro Emancipation Centennial Authority, 1963.

Tipton, James A. Community in Crisis. The Elimination of Segregation from a Public School System. New York: Teachers College, Columbia U., 1953. [Gary]

U.S. Commission on Civil Rights, Indiana Advisory Committee. Equal Opportunity in Fort Wayne Community Schools: A Continuing Struggle. Washington, DC: The Commission, 1977.

U.S. Commission on Civil Rights, Indiana Advisory Committee. Student Friction and Racial Unrest at Southside High School, Muncie, Indiana. Washington, DC: The Commission, 1968.

L. H. W. "Race Segregation, Constitutional Law." Indiana Law Journal 7(Mr, 1932):395-398. [State ex rel Cheeks v. Wirt (IN), 177 NE 441]

Wiley, Alfred D. "A Study of Desegregation in the Evansville School Corporation, Evansville, Indiana." Doctoral dissertation, Indiana U., 1961. Dissertation Abstracts, XXII, 1962, p. 3477.

Wilson, John A. Banneker: A Case Study of Educational Change, 1973. ETC Publications, 18512 Pierce Terrace, Homewood, IL 60430.

Wolff, Max. Study of Segregation in the Public Schools of Indianapolis. Indianapolis: Indianapolis Community Relations Council, 1949. [Summary: Carey McWilliams, Common Ground 9(Summer, 1949):95]

X, Robert Benjamin. "Black Students Unite in South Bend." Muhammad Speaks, D 3, 1971.

_____. "'City With a Heart' Hit By Heart Attack." Muhammad Speaks, Je 18, 1971. [Elkhart]

Iowa

August, Taylor D. "Text of Letter from Civil Rights Office of HEW to Davis." Des Moines Register, S 24, 1976. [Des Moines]

Bates, Dennis. "10 Points in School Racial Agreement." Cedar Rapids Gazette, Je 18, 1972.

Bergmann, Leolo Nelson. The Negro in Iowa. Iowa City: State Historical Society, 1969. [With an editorial addendum by William J. Petersen]

_____. "The Negro in Iowa." Iowa Journal of History and Politics 46(1945).

Diestelmeier, George. "Waterloo, Iowa: In the Heartland." In Norene Harris, Nathaniel Jackson, and Carl Rydingsword and contributors, The Integration of American Schools: Problems, Experiences, Solutions, pp. 72-77. Boston: Allyn & Bacon, 1975.

Dykstra, Robert R., and Hahn, Harlan. "Northern Voters and Negro Suffrage: The Case of Iowa, 1868." Public Opinion Quarterly, Summer, 1968.

Hartshorn, Truman A. "Inner City Residential Structure and Decline." Annals of the Association of American Geographers 61(Mr, 1971): 72-96. [Cedar Rapids]

_____. "Urban Residential Blight: The Structure and Change of Substandard Housing in Cedar Rapids, Iowa, 1940-1960." Doctoral dissertation, U. of Iowa, 1968.

"Iowa Inquiry Set on Bias in Schools." New York Times, S 3, 1972. [Waterloo]

Keith, Francis E. "Equalization of High School Districts Urged." Des Moines Tribune, F 12, 1976. [President, North High Community Advisory Council]

Minard, Ralph D. "Race Attitudes of Iowa Children." Doctoral dissertation, U. of Iowa, 1930.

National Council of Catholic Men. Iowa South East Evaluation Study, Ja, 1969. Division of Research and Planning, National Council of Catholic Men, 1312 Massachusetts Avenue, Washington, DC 20005. [Diocese of Davenport]

Rye, Stephen H. "Buxton: Black Metropolis of Iowa." Annals of Iowa 41(Spring, 1972).

Schoen, Derek. "Racial Crisis in a Small City." Progressive, Mr, 1969. [Waterloo]

U.S. Commission on Civil Rights, Iowa Advisory Committee. Racial Problems in Fort Dodge, Iowa. Washington, DC: The Commission, 1974.

_____. Walk Together Children: Housing and Education in Waterloo, Iowa. Washington, DC: The Commission, 1971.

Urban Education Section. A Report on the Race, Ethnic, and Sex Characteristics of Iowa's Public Schools, 1974-1975. Des Moines: Department of Public Instruction, n.d.

_____. Policy and Guidelines on Non-Discrimination in Iowa Schools. Des Moines: Department of Public Instruction, n.d.

Voss, Melinda. "Metro Poll [on Desegregation in Des Moines]." Des Moines Tribune, Ap 11, 1978.

"The Waterloo Story." Des Moines Bystander, Je 15, 1972. [Background of conflict at West Junior High School, Waterloo, IO]

Kansas

Arnold, David, and Hall, Mike. "How Much Integration?" Topeka Capitol-Journal, My 12, 1974. [Topeka]

Athearn, Robert G. In Search of Canaan: Black Migration to Kansas, 1879-1880. Lawrence, KA: Regents Press of Kansas, 1978.

Barlow, A. J. "Injunction Against Transferring Colored Pupils from School for White Children to Colored School on Sole Ground that the Distance Was Unreasonable, Was Held Properly Refused." Notre Dame Law 5(Mr, 1930):347-348. [Wright v. Bd. of Ed. of Topeka, 284 Pac 363]

Barnett, Ferdinand L. "The Negro and Secondary Education in Kansas." Master's thesis, U. of Wichita, 1930.

Bollig, Richard J. History of Catholic Education in Kansas, 1836-1932. Washington, DC: Catholic U. of America, 1933.

Buckner, Reginald Tyrone. "A History of Music Education in the Black Community of Kansas City, Kansas, 1905-1954." Doctoral dissertation, U. of Minnesota, 1974. Univ. Microfilms Order No. 75-00157.

Doherty, Joseph P. Civil Rights in Kansas: Past, Present, and Future. Topeka, KA: Kansas Commission on Civil Rights, 1972.

Egerton, John. "Unresolved Racial Problems in Topeka." Race Relations Reporter 3(My, 1972):8-11.

Goldman, Louis (ed.). School and Society in One City. Report of the LEAP Committee to the Board of Education. Wichita, KA: Unified School District No. 259, Jl, 1969.

Guidelines for Integrating Minority Group Studies into the Curriculum of Kansas Schools (Preliminary Edition), S, 1969. Topeka, KA: Kansas State Department of Education. ERIC ED 050 107.

Harrison, Beverly D. "Educational and Mental Survey of Cleveland School (colored), Coffeeville, Kansas." Master's thesis, Kansas State Teachers College, 1940.

Jones, Lila Lee. "The Ku Klux Klan in Eastern Kansas during the 1920's." Emporia State Res. Stud. 23(Winter, 1975):5-41.

Kansas and Missouri Advisory Committees to the United States Commission on Civil Rights. Crisis and Opportunity: Education in Greater Kansas City. Washington, DC: U.S. Commission on Civil Rights, Ja, 1977.

Kennedy, Jack. "Wichita Head Resigns in Integration Fight." Education News, Je 24, 1968. [Superintendent of Schools Lawrence Shepoiser]

Martin, Patricia. "Teaching in a Segregated School." Mennonite Life 22(1967):37-39.

Painter, Nell Irvin. Exodusters: Black Migration to Kansas after Reconstruction. New York: Knopf, 1977.

Paris, Barry. "Whites Bus Children to Black School." National Catholic Reporter, D 24, 1969. [Holy Savior School in Wichita]

Peterson, Franklynn. "The School Desegregation That Started It All Case." Dallas News, Ja 20, 1974. [Valuable recollections about background of the Brown case]

Porter, William A. "Analysis of the Residential Structure of Underprivileged Black Neighborhoods: A Case Study in Manhattan, Kansas." Master's thesis, Kansas State U., 1973.

Russell, John C., Jr., and Broadnax, Walter D. Minorities in Kansas: A Quest for Equal Opportunities. Topeka, KA: Economic Opportunity Office, 1968.

Scott, Austin. "Topeka Treadmill: Linda Brown's City Faces a New Battle." Washington Post, My 12, 1974.

Shepherd, Charles L. "A Study of the Educational Status of the Negro in Kansas." Master's thesis, Kansas State Teachers College, 1934.

Sloan, Charles W., Jr. "Kansas Battles the Invisible Empire: The Legal Ouster of the KKK from Kansas, 1922-1927." Kansas Historical Quarterly 40(Autumn, 1974).

Steinberg, Stephen. "My Day in Nicodemus: Notes from a Field Trip to Black Kansas." Phylon 37(S, 1976):243-249.

Stoner, William J. "Bussing Seen as Threat to Black Neighborhood." Kansas City Times, Je 24, 1977. [Kansas City]

Strand, Connie. "White Knights Waiting to Ride." Midway (Topeka Capital-Journal), O 15, 1978. [The Ku Klux Klan in Wichita]

U.S. Commission on Civil Rights, Kansas Advisory Committee. Report on Civil Rights Aspects of Vocational Education. Washington, DC: The Commission, 1963.

Viegra, Jessie M. "Yes, There is Prejudice at Hutchinson High." Hutchinson News, Ja 12, 1978. (Letter) [Hutchinson High School, Hutchinson]

Ward, Francis. "Historic School Desegregation Case Still Open." Los Angeles Times, My 13, 1974. [Topeka]

Woods, Randall B. "After the Exodus: John Lewis Waller and the Black Elite, 1878-1900." Kansas Historical Quarterly 43(Summer, 1977): 172-192.

Wright, Harold Arthur. "A Comparative Study of 25 Negro Scouts and 25 Negro Non-scouts of Pittsburg, Kansas." Master's thesis, Kansas State Teachers College, Pittsburg.

Kentucky

Adams, Jim. "Despite Problems, Antibusing Leaders Claim Gains During Year." Louisville Courier-Journal, Je 13, 1976. [Jefferson County]

_____. "Unlikely Alliance Born in Busing Fight." Louisville Courier-Journal, D 15, 1975. [Union Labor Against Busing (ULAB)]

Adjei-Barwuah, Barfour. "Socio-Economic Regions in the Louisville Ghetto." Doctoral dissertation, Indiana U., 1972.

"Anti-Racists Mobilize in Louisville." Southern Patriot, S, 1975.

Aubespin, Mervin. "Trouble, Tension End on Desegregation Bus Run." Louisville Courier-Journal, Ja 17, 1976. [Assistant principal and bus supervision]

Barnes, Bart. "The Calm Instead of the Storm." Washington Post, My 30, 1976. [First year of desegregation in Louisville]

Berea College, Department of Education. Evidence of Inequality of Educational Opportunity in Kentucky Mountain Counties. Berea, KY: Berea College, 1953.

Berry, Benjamin D., Jr. "Plymouth Settlement House and the Development of Black Louisville: 1900-1930." Doctoral dissertation, Case Western Reserve U., 1977.

Bond, James. "Louisville Negroes and the Public Library." Southern Workman 8(Ag, 1927):378-379.

Bond, James Arthur. "Negro Education in Kentucky." Master's thesis, U. of Cincinnati, 1930.

Borton, Terry. "Reform Without Politics in Louisville." Saturday Review 55(F 5, 1972): 50-55.

Braden, Anne. "Louisville Schools: Women in Struggle." Wree-View, Summer, 1976. [Women for Racial and Economic Equality, 542 South Dearborn Street, Chicago, IL 60605]

_____. "Louisville Schools: Women in Struggle." Integrateducation 15(Ja-F, 1977). [Reprinted from preceding item]

Cabell, Foraker A. "The History of Public Secondary Education for Negroes in Louisville, Kentucky." Master's thesis, Indiana State Teachers College, 1938. (Abstract in: Indiana State Teachers College, Teachers College Journal 10:129, Jl, 1939.)

Carmichael, Omer, and James, Weldon. The Louisville Story. New York: Simon & Schuster, 1957.

Caudill, Morris K. A Poverty Program and the Public Schools. Bulletin of the Bureau of School Service, XLI, D, 1968. College of Education, U. of Kentucky, Lexington [Knox County]

Cierley, Morris B. Faculty Desegregation in the Kentucky Public Schools. College of Education, U. of Kentucky, S, 1965.

Commission on Human Rights. Kentucky Directory of Black Elected Officials. Frankfort, KY: Commission on Human Rights, O, 1972.

Commission on Human Rights. Lexington Housing Segregation Increases. An Analysis of Census Data, 1960-1970. Frankfort, KY: The Commission, Je, 1975.

Commission on Human Rights. Private School Desegregation in Kentucky. Frankfort, KY: Commission on Human Rights, My, 1965.

Commission on Professional Rights and Responsibilities. Kentucky. Education in Kentucky: A Legacy of Unkept Promise. Washington, DC: National Education Association, My, 1971.

Coughenour, Milton C. "Eastern Kentucky Survey: Measuring the Quality of Life for Rural Families." Appalachia 9(F-Mr, 1976):1-9.

Delaney, Paul. "Louisville, a Place Where Busing Seems to Work." New York Times, Je 6, 1976.

Desegregation Increases in Kentucky. An Analysis of Multiple Dwelling Reports on Racial Occupancy, 1973-1975. Frankfort, KY: Kentucky Commission on Human Rights, Jl, 1976.

Donovan, Mary S. "Kentucky Laws Regarding the Negro, 1865-1877." Master's thesis, U. of Louisville, 1967.

Doyle, Marie T. "The Public School Merger Issue in Jefferson County, Kentucky." Doctoral dissertation, U. of Kentucky, 1974.

Eakin, Darlene W. "Preparation for the Desegregation of the Louisville School System."
Master's thesis, U. of Louisville, 1974.

Egerton, John. "Return to Clay and Sturgis,
Kentucky." Reporter News Supplement, Race
Relations Reporter, Jl 16, 1970.

_____. The Louisville Story--1970. Nashville:
Race Relations Information Center, Je, 1970.

Faculty Integration in Kentucky Public Schools.
Frankfort, KY: Commission on Human Rights,
1962.

Famularo, Linda. "Schoolchildren in Kentucky."
Liberation, Jl, 1966. [Schooling in an isolated eastern community]

Fleming, John. Kentucky School Pairing Plans,
My, 1967. Kentucky Commission on Human
Rights, 172 Capitol Annex, Frankfort, KY
40601.

Fouse, William Henry. "Educational History of
the Negroes of Lexington, Kentucky." Master's thesis, U. of Cincinnati, 1937.

_____. "Some Problems of Education Among Ne-
groes in Kentucky." Quarterly Review of
Higher Education Among Negroes 6(Ja, 1938):
63-67.

Francis, Delma and others. "The Color Barrier.
It Gets Harder to Crack in County Schools As
Students Get Older, Children Indicate."
Louisville Times, Je 1, 1978.

Gabbard, Anne V., and Coleman, A. Lee. Occupational and Educational Goals of Low Income
Children in Kentucky, 1969 and 1975, My,
1976. ERIC ED 127 079.

Gaines, Miriam. "Lincoln Institute Plans 'New
Deal.'" Southern Workman 62(S, 1933):663-
669. [Near Louisville]

Grant, William. [Two articles on desegregation
in Louisville] Detroit Free Press, N 16 and
17, 1975.

Griggs, Douglas M. "The Bus Stops Here."
Louisville Courier-Journal, S 4, 1977.
[Stephen Foster School, Louisville]

Hall, Larry D., and Coleman, A. Lee. Desired
Job Characteristics and Perceived Occupational Barriers Among Low-Income Youth in Kentucky, Ja, 1978. ERIC ED 153 770.

Harris, J. Everett. "These 'Colored' United
States: Kentucky: (Janus Bifrons)."
Messenger 6(0, 1924):305-310.

Hawkins, Geneva M. "Woerner '75: What? Why?
How? The Story of a Louisville School."
Integrateducation 14(Jl-Ag, 1976).

"How White Louisvillians Support B.S.U. Demands."
Southern Patriot, Je, 1969.

Howard, Victor B. "Negro Politics and the
Suffrage Question in Kentucky, 1866-1872."
Register of the Kentucky Historical Society
72(Ap, 1974).

_____. "Sectionalism, Slavery, and Education:
New Albany, Indiana, Versus Danville, Ken-
tucky." Register of the Kentucky Historical
Society, O, 1970, pp. 292-310.

_____. "The Struggle for Equal Education in
Kentucky, 1866-1884." Journal of Negro Education 46(Summer, 1977):305-328.

An In-Service Program to Assist the Henderson
City and Henderson County School Systems in
Achieving Successful Total Desegregation,
1965. ERIC ED 045 743.

Institute for Policy Sciences and Public Affairs, Duke University and Louis Harris and
Associates. "Student Attitudes Toward Busing
in Louisville and Jefferson County." Integrateducation 15(My-Je, 1977).

Jackson, Brenda Feast. "The Policies and Purposes of Black Public Schooling in Louisville, Kentucky, 1890-1930." Doctoral dissertation, Indiana U., 1976. Univ. Microfilms Order No. 77-02004.

Jackson, Reid E. "The Development and Present
Status of Secondary Education for Negroes in
Kentucky." Journal of Negro Education 4(Ap,
1935):185-199.

Kaplan, Sidney J., and Coleman, A. Lee. "The
Strategy of Change: Contrasting Approaches
to Teacher Integration." Social Science, O,
1963.

Kentucky Commission on Human Rights. Black Employment in Kentucky State Agencies. An
Analysis of Job Levels, Salaries, and Hiring
Patterns. Frankfort, KY: Kentucky Commission on Human Rights, 1975.

_____. Discriminatory Practices Determine
Housing Choices in Fayette and Jefferson.
Frankfort, KY: The Commission, Ap, 1978.

_____. Jefferson County Schools Reduce Teacher
Segregation. Non-Teaching Staff Far From
Singleton Goals. Frankfort, KY: The Commis-
sion, D, 1977.

_____. Jefferson County Schools Still Haven't
Met Teacher Assignment Order. Louisville,
KY: The Commission, S, 1977.

_____. Kentucky's Black Heritage. The Role of
the Black People in the History of Kentucky
from Pioneer Days to the Present. Frankfort,
KY: The Commission, 1971.

_____. Kentucky's Black Teacher Gap. An
Analysis of Teacher Employment, 1954-1974.
Frankfort, KY: Kentucky Commission on Human
Rights, Ag, 1975.

_____. Public Housing Authorities in Kentucky Are Slow to Desegregate. Frankfort, KY: Kentucky Commission on Human Rights, S, 1977.

_____. Vestiges of Segregation Remain in Jefferson County Schools. Louisville, KY: The Commission, F, 1977.

Kentucky Department of Education. Annual Survey and Progress Report: Racial Integration in Kentucky's Public Schools. Frankfort, KY: Kentucky Department of Education, Ja 15, 1967.

Kentucky Department of Education. Racial Integration in the Public Schools of Kentucky. Twelve Periodic Reports. Frankfort, KY: The Department, 1971.

Kentucky Human Rights Commission. Private School Desegregation in Kentucky, 1965.

Mathews, Jack. "Busing Coverage: Total Commitment." Quill 64(Je, 1976):34. [Louisville Courier-Journal coverage of desegregation in Jefferson County]

Meece, Leonard E. Negro Education in Kentucky: A Comparative Study of White and Negro Education in the Elementary and Secondary Levels. Lexington, KY: U. of Kentucky, 1938. (Bulletin of the Bureau of School Service, College of Education, Vol. X, No. 3, Mr, 1939.)

Minnis, Bernard. "County Schools Emerge to Face New Era." Louisville Defender, F 13, 1975. [Jefferson County]

Moore, Pleasant. "The Status of the Negro Public Elementary Schools of Kentucky." Master's thesis, Indiana State Teachers College, Terre Haute, 1931.

Morris, Chris. "A Changing School." Louisville Courier-Journal, D 28, 1975. [Woerner Junior High School, Louisville]

Morris, Eddie W. "Facts and Factors of Faculty Desegregation in Kentucky, 1955-1965." Journal of Negro Education, Winter, 1967.

Morrissey, Jim. "A Schoolman Joins West End's Quest for an Image." Southern Education Report, Ap, 1967. [Louisville]

National Commission on Professional Rights and Responsibilities. Louisville, Kentucky. A City in Transition and a School System in Jeopardy. Washington, DC: National Education Association, My, 1965.

Parrish, Charles Henry. "The Significance of Color in the Negro Community." Doctoral dissertation, U. of Chicago, 1944. [Louisville]

Peterson, Bill. "Discrimination in the Hill Country." Southern Education Report, Mr, 1969. [Poor whites in Eastern Kentucky]

Peyton, Jim. Equal Educational Opportunity in Kentucky. Frankfort, KY: Legislative Research Commission, 1973.

Raphael, Alan. "Health and Social Welfare of Kentucky Black People, 1865-1870." Societas--A Review of Social History 2(Spring, 1972).

Roberts, Steven V. "Mixed Results of Integration Typified in Louisville School." New York Times, Mr 16, 1978. [Central High School]

Rosenfield, Judy. "They're in the Middle, and Busing's Strain Shows on Schools' Personnel." Louisville Times, D 19, 1975. [Teachers in desegregated high school in Louisville]

Russell, H. C. "The Training of Teachers in the Colored High Schools of Kentucky." Master's thesis, U. of Cincinatti, 1929.

School Segregation in Hopkins County. Frankfort, KY: Commission on Human Rights, My, 1973.

School Segregation in Owensboro. Frankfort, KY: Commission on Human Rights, My, 1973.

Schulman, Robert. "Anatomy of a Decision." Quill 63(N, 1975):24-27. [Court-initiated guidelines for Louisville press covering the desegregation story]

Schwartz, Marylu. "Louisville: Fear, Distrust, Disbelief." Dallas News, Ag 15, 1976.

Segregation Persists in Jefferson County Schools 1975-76. Frankfort, KY: Kentucky Commission on Human Rights, Ap, 1976.

Schockley, Ann Allen. "Joseph S. Cotter, Sr.: Biographical Sketch of a Black Louisville Bard." CLA Journal 18(Mr, 1975):327-340. [Principal, Samuel Coleridge-Taylor School, 1911-1942]

Simmons, Ira. "Busing...And Business." Louisville Times, D 17, 1975. [Pleasure Ridge Park High School, Jefferson County]

_____. "The Whitening of Central [High School]." Louisville Times, D 21, 1976. [Louisville]

Sinclair, Ward. "Trigg County Tried 'Pairing, And It Worked." Southern Education Report, S, 1967.

Smydra, David F. A Description of the Louisville Division of Police Response to Court-Ordered Busing for School Desegregation. Louisville, Division of Police, 1975. [Reprinted in U.S. Commission on Civil Rights, Hearing Held in Louisville, Kentucky, June 14-16, 1976, pp. 770-849. Washington, DC: The Commission, 1978]

Sorapuru, Jude T. "An Analysis of the Concerns of Louisville and Jefferson County Teachers Over Desegregation." Master's thesis, U. of Louisville, 1974.

Soule, Don M., and Lile, Stephen E. _Some Problems of Equity and Adequacy in Kentucky's State-Local Taxation._ Lexington, KY: Center for the Study of State and Local Governments, F, 1970.

Sowards, Ada B. C. "History of the Development of Education for Negroes in Scott County, Kentucky." Master's thesis, Indiana U., 1949.

Stahl, Linda, and Nichols, Wanda. "Black Pupils Lag, On Average, In Achievement Test." _Louisville Courier-Journal,_ Ap 25, 1977.

Stallings, Frank H. "A Study of the Effects of Integration on Scholastic Achievement in the Louisville Public Schools." Doctoral dissertation, U. of Kentucky, 1959.

_____. "A Study of the Immediate Effects of Integration on Scholastic Achievement in the Louisville Public Schools." _Journal of Negro Education,_ Winter, 1959.

Thomas, Herbert A., Jr. "Victims of Circumstance: Negroes in a Southern Town, 1865-1880." _Register of the Kentucky Historical Society_ 71(Jl, 1973).

Thompson, Hunter S. "A Southern City With Northern Problems." _Reporter,_ D 19, 1963. [Louisville]

Thompson, John. "School Desegregation in Jefferson County, Kentucky: 1954-1975." Doctoral dissertation, U. of Kentucky, 1976.

Timberlake, C. L. "The Early Struggle for Education of the Blacks in the Commonwealth of Kentucky." _The Register_ 71(Jl, 1973):225-252.

U.S. Commission on Civil Rights. _Hearing Held in Louisville, Kentucky, June 14-16, 1976._ Washington, DC: The Commission, 1978.

Urban Studies Center. "Busing: Favor or Opposed?" In _Community Priorities and Evaluations,_ pp. 15-36. Louisville, KY: U. of Louisville, F, 1976. [Jefferson County]

_____. "School Related Issues/Busing." In _Community Priorities and Evaluations,_ pp. 44-49. Louisville, KY: U. of Louisville, Ap, 1977. [Jefferson County]

Venable, Tom C. "A History of Negro Education in Kentucky." Doctoral dissertation, George Peabody College for Teachers, 1953.

Ward, Francis. "Louisville in 1956 Had 'Model' Integration Plan." _Los Angeles Times,_ S 11, 1975.

_____. "Louisville Whites Have Change of Heart." _Los Angeles Times,_ S 29, 1976.

Whitely, Les. "[U.S. District Judge] Gordon Has Few Reservations About School Desegregation Here." _Louisville Times,_ N 18, 1976.

Wiederhold, George. "News Media in Louisville Set Guidelines, Endorsed by Court, On Coverage of School Issue." _Variety,_ S 10, 1975. [Desegregation]

"Wildcat at Phillip Morris." _Southern Patriot,_ N, 1975. [School busing issues in Louisville factory]

Williams, Roger M. "The Fury Ends." _Saturday Review,_ Ap 30, 1977. [Desegregation in Louisville]

Wilson, Attwood S. "The Vocational Opportunity and Education of Colored Pupils at Louisville (Kentucky)." Master's thesis, U. of Chicago, 1934.

Wilson, Dee. "That Predicted 'White Flight' Never Really Hit." _Louisville Times,_ Jl 13, 1978. [Jefferson County]

Woodard, James D. "Busing Plans, Media Agendas and Patterns of White Flight: Nashville, Tennessee and Louisville, Kentucky." Doctoral dissertation, Vanderbilt U., 1978. Univ. Microfilms Order No. 7819545.

Wright, George Carlton. "Blacks in Louisville, Kentucky, 1890-1930." Doctoral dissertation, Duke U., 1977. Univ. Microfilms Order No. 77-31706.

Yeager, J. Frank. _The Relationship of Educational, Economic, and Social Characteristics to the Degree of Desegregation in the Public Schools of Kentucky._ Bowling Green, KY: Human Relations Center for Education, Western Kentucky U., 1968.

Louisiana

Ahlgren, Joellen H. _et al._ "Intergroup Relations Work of New Orleans Social Workers." Master's thesis, Tulane U., 1966.

Analavage, Robert. "Black-White Union Keeps Schools Open." _Southern Patriot,_ F, 1967. [Plaquemines Parish]

Beasley, Leon O. "A History of Education in Louisiana During the Reconstruction Period, 1882-1877." Doctoral dissertation, Louisiana State U., 1957. Univ. Microfilms Order No. 21981.

Bennetts, David Paul. "Black and White Workers: New Orleans, 1880-1900." Doctoral dissertation, U. of Illinois, 1972. Univ. Microfilms Order No. 73-17117.

"Black Students Fight in South." Black Panther, Mr 16, 1969. [Fortier High School in New Orleans]

Blackburn, Martha et al. "Study of the Health and Behavior of A.D.C. Children and Their Mothers in a Negro and a White Housing Project in New Orleans." Master's thesis, Tulane U., 1963. [St. Thomas and Calliope Street Housing Projects]

Blassingame, John W. "A Social and Economic Study of the Negro in New Orleans." Doctoral dissertation, Yale U., 1970.

_____. "Schools, Colleges, and Intellectual Life." In Black New Orleans, 1860-1880, pp. 107-137. Chicago: U. of Chicago Press, 1973.

Bollich, Martha et al. "Role Expectations for Children in AFDC Families." Master's thesis, Tulane U., 1967.

Bolner, James, and Vedlitz, Arnold. "The Affinity of Negro Pupils for Segregated Schools: Obstacle to Desegregation." Journal of Negro Education 40(Fall, 1971):313-321.

Bond, Horace Mann. "Horace Mann in New Orleans: A Note on the Decline of Humanitarianism in America, 1837-1937." School and Society 11 (My, 1937):607-611.

Brown, Warren. "Black Unity Lost as Rights Advance." Washington Post, Ap 23, 1978. [New Orleans]

Butler, Johnny S. "Black Education in Louisiana--A Question of Survival." Journal of Negro Education 43(Winter, 1974):9-24.

Butler, Loretta M. "A History of Catholic Elementary Education for Negroes in the Diocese of Lafayette, Louisiana." Doctoral dissertation, Catholic U. of America, 1963. Univ. Microfilms Order No. 63-7975.

Cable, George W. Strange True Stories of Louisiana. New York, 1889.

Canter, Philip. "Marching No More, The Dream Dies in Dixie." Washington Post/Potomac, J1 1, 1973. [Doris Castle, New Orleans]

Cassimere, Raphael, Jr. "Equalizing Teachers' Pay in Louisiana." Integrateducation 15(J1-Ag, 1977).

Cherry, Flora Finch. "Some Observations of Four Year Old New Orleans Negro Children of Lower Socio-Economic Status." Master's thesis, Tulane U., 1966.

Clarke, Lillian W. "Race and Suspensions in New Orleans." Integrated Education 11(My-Je, 1973):30-33.

Coles, Robert. "The Weather of the Years." Daedalus 100(Fall, 1971):1139-1157. [New Orleans]

Commission on Professional Rights and Responsibilities and the NEA Office of General Counsel. Desegregation and the Rights of Educators in Louisiana. Washington, DC: National Education Association, S, 1970.

Davis, Morris, Seibert, Robert, and Breed, Warren. "Interracial Seating Patterns on New Orleans Public Transit." Social Problems, Winter, 1966.

Denhardt, Robert B., and Salomone, Jerome J. "Race, Inauthenticity and Religious Cynicism." Phylon 33(Summer, 1972):120-131. [Louisiana and Leander Perez]

Derosin, Jeannette R. "Desegregation in Pointe Coupee Parish, Louisiana: Its Effects on the Self-Concept of Selected Black Secondary Students." Doctoral dissertation, Walden U., 1976. ERIC ED 128 485.

Desdunes, Rodolphe Lucien. Our People and Our History. Tr. by Sister Dorothea Olga McCants. Baton Rouge, LA: Louisiana State U. Press, 1973 [in French, 1911]. [Creoles in New Orleans at end of 19th century]

Deseran, Forrest A., and Stokley, Gary M. Perceptions of a Tri-Racial Community: Adults vs. Adolescents, S, 1977. ERIC ED 144 740.

Dethloff, Henry C., and Jones, Robert C. "Race Relations in Louisiana, 1877-98." Louisiana History 9(Fall, 1968):301-323.

Dillard, James H. "Light from Louisiana." Southern Workman 61(J1, 1932):297-298.

Dolch, Norman A. Sub-culture in a Southern Community, 1972. ERIC ED 077 607.

Egger, Dolores. "Jim Crow Comes to Church: The Establishment of Segregated Catholic Parishes in South Louisiana." Master's thesis, U. of Southwestern Louisiana, 1965.

An Evaluation of the Northeast Louisiana Consortium to Investigate and Find Solutions to Problems Attendant to School Desegregation, J1 31, 1970, 65 pp. Monroe, LA: Northeastern Louisiana U. ERIC ED 050 216.

Everett, Donald E. "Free Persons of Color in New Orleans, 1803-1865." Doctoral dissertation, Tulane U., 1952.

Falk, William W., and Comfort, Allen. Residential and Racial Trends for the School-Age Population and Public School Teachers in Louisiana, D, 1976. ERIC ED 141 317.

Favrot, Leo Mortimer. Some Problems in the Education of the Negro in the South and How We Are Trying to Meet Them in Louisiana. Address before the National Association for the Advancement of Colored People, Cleveland, OH, Je 25, 1919. Baton Rouge: Ramires-Jones Printing Company, 1919.

Fischer, Roger A. "The Post Civil War Segrega-
tion Struggle." In Hadding Carter et al.,
The Past as Prelude: New Orleans, 1718-1968.
New Orleans, 1968.

_____. "Racial Segregation in Ante Bellum New
Orleans." American Historical Review 74(F,
1969):926-937.

_____. "The Segregation Struggle in Louisiana,
1850-1890." Doctoral dissertation, Tulane
U., 1967. [Public accomodations]

_____. The Segregation Struggle in Louisiana,
1862-77. Urbana, IL: U. of Illinois Press,
1974.

Frazier, James Monroe. "The History of Negro
Education in the Parish of East Baton Rouge,
Louisiana." Master's thesis, U. of Iowa,
1937.

Galphin, Bruce. "'Beautiful Bogalusa': Full
School Integration is Smoothly Taken in
Stride." South Today, F, 1970.

Garner, H. T. "A Report--the Northeast Louisiana Consortium on Desegregation Problems."
Louisiana Schools 48(Ap, 1971):13-18.

Giarrusso, Alfred Peter. "Desegregation of the
Orleans Parish School System." Doctoral
dissertation, U. of Arkansas, 1969. Univ.
Microfilms Order No. 70-393.

Guillory, Ferrel. "Baton Rouge Desegregates."
America, Je 20, 1970.

_____. "New Orleans Schools Ten Years Later."
America 125(Ag 21, 1971):93-95.

_____. "Parochial Schools: Desegregation
Challenges Louisiana's Catholics." South
Today 3(D, 1971):4.

_____. "Louisiana Desegregation--and Catholic
Schools." America 123(S 5, 1970):119-121.

Halstead, Michael Norman. "Ideology and Identity: Black Youth in New Orleans." Doctoral
dissertation, Tulane U., 1973. Univ. Microfilms Order No. 73-25283.

Harlan, Louis R. "Desegregation in New Orleans
Public Schools During Reconstruction." American Historical Review, Ap, 1962.

Harrell, Kenneth Earl. "The Ku Klux Klan in
Louisiana, 1920-1930." Doctoral dissertation, Louisiana State U., 1966. Univ. Microfilms Order No. 66-10903.

Haywood, Jacquelyn S. "The American Missionary
Association in Louisiana during Reconstruction." Doctoral dissertation, U. of California, Los Angeles, 1975.

Higson, Mike. "Black Students Head Boycott at
New Orleans High School." Southern Patriot,
Mr, 1969. [Fortier High School, New Orleans]

_____. "New Orleans Women Wage School Strug-
gle " Southern Patriot, Ap, 1969. [Fortier
High School]

Holton, Wilfred E., and Howard, Perry H. Poverty Among the Louisiana Parishes: A Composite Picture for the 1960's. Baton Rouge:
Institute for Urban and Population Research,
Louisiana State U., 1972.

Iggers, Georg. A Study of Some Tangible Inequal-
ities in the New Orleans Public Schools. 2nd
Ed. New Orleans: Education Committee, New
Orleans NAACP, 1963.

Improving Quality During School Desegregation,
F, 1969. ERIC ED 029 363.

Inger, Morton. Politics and Reality in An American City. The New Orleans Schools Crisis
of 1960. New York: Center for Urban Education, 1969.

Institute to Prepare Newly Graduated and Ex-
perienced Teachers for Work in Desegregated
Schools. Final Report, Je 24, 1970, 155 pp.
New Orleans: Orleans Parish School Board.
ERIC ED 056 132.

Jeansonne, Glen. Leander Perez. Boss of the
Delta. Baton Rouge: Louisiana State U.
Press, 1977.

Jenkins, Velesta. "River Road: A Rural Black
Community in Southeastern Louisiana." Doctoral dissertation, U. of California, Berkeley, 1976. Univ. Microfilms Order No. 77-
04488.

Jupiter, Clare. "'It Was Worth It.'" Southern
Exposure 7(Summer, 1979):61-62. [New Orleans, 1979]

Kenkelen, Bill. "Principal's Firing Ignites
Bayou Race Hostility." National Catholic
Reporter, My 5, 1978. [Opelousas]

Labbe, Delores E. Jim Crow Comes to Church:
The Establishment of Segregated Catholic
Parishes in South Louisiana. New York:
Arno Press, 1978, orig., 1971.

Lawrence, Edward. "Color in the New Orleans
Schools." Harpers Weekly 19(F 13, 1875):
147-148.

Louis, Bowles and Grace, Inc. Study of Attitudes
Among Faculty and Staff of the New Orleans
Public Schools. New Orleans: Orleans Parish
School Board, Mr, 1971.

Lovell, Othel E., Jr. "Crucial Issues in
Louisiana Public Education as Reflected in
Louisiana Newspapers, 1898-1956." Doctoral
dissertation, Louisiana State U., 1961.

McAllister, Jane Ellen. "The Training of Negro
Teachers in Louisiana." Doctoral dissertation, Teachers College, Columbia U., 1929.

284 / AMERICAN SCENE

McCarrick, Earlean M. "Louisiana's Official Resistance to Desegregation." Doctoral dissertation, Vanderbilt U., 1964. Univ. Microfilms Order No. 65-4551.

McIntosh, William. "Some Legal and Political Problems Involved in Desegregation and Integration in the Public Schools With Special Emphasis on Louisiana." Quarterly Review of Higher Education Among Negroes 23(0, 1955):140-152.

McTigue, Geraldine M. "Forms of Racial Interaction in Louisiana, 1860-1880." Doctoral dissertation, Yale U., 1975.

_____. "Patterns of Residence: Housing Distribution by Color in Two Louisiana Towns, 1860-1880." Louisiana Studies 15(Winter, 1976):345-388.

Mabe, Philip M. "Racial Ideology in the New Orleans Press, 1862-1877." Doctoral dissertation, U. of Southwestern Louisiana, 1977.

Mayhew, Leonard, and Fols, Douglas. "Tangipahoa Parish: A Case Study." New Generation 54 (Summer, 1972):2-11.

Messner, William F. "Black Education in Louisiana, 1863-1865." Civil War History 22(Mr, 1976):41-59.

Mills, Gary B. The Forgotten People: Cane River's Creoles of Color. Baton Rouge: Louisiana State U. Press, 1977. [Murphy's Lake region]

Moland, John, Jr. Some Social Structural Components of Anomia Among Rural Blacks in Louisiana, F, 1975. ERIC ED 101 880.

Moore, Alma P. and others. Education Minus White Prejudice Plus Black Power Equals Gray Matter, Mr, 1970. Washington, DC: American Personnel and Guidance Association. ERIC ED 040 457. [New Iberia]

Moran, Robert E. "The Negro Dependent Child in Louisiana, 1800-1935." Social Service Review 45(Mr, 1971):53-61.

Muller, Mary Lee. "New Orleans Public School Desegregation." Louisiana History 17(Winter, 1976):69-88.

Murray, Hugh T., Jr. "The Struggle for Civil Rights in New Orleans in 1960: Reflections and Recollections." Journal of Ethnic Studies 6(Spring, 1978):25-41.

NEA Task Force. NEA Task Force on School Desegregation in Louisiana, February 15-22, 1970. Washington, DC: National Education Association, 1970.

N. C. Newbold, Chairman. Report of Committee of Investigation of Certain Phases of Negro Education in Louisiana, 1930. State Department of Public Instruction, Raleigh, NC.

New Orleans City Planning Commission. Social Renewal Needs and Resources: New Orleans, Jl, 1967. Dr. Leonard Reissman, Department of Sociology, Tulane U., New Orleans, LA 70118.

"New Orleans Teachers' Strike Broken After Twelve Days." Southern Patriot, My, 1969.

Parenton, Vernon J., and Pellegrin, Roland J. "Social Structure and the Leadership Factor in a Negro Community in South Louisiana." Phylon 17(First Quarter, 1956):74-78. [Bertrandville]

Peeler, Virginia. The Colored School Teacher in New Orleans. New Orleans: High School Scholarship Association, Inc., n.d. (Supplementary Vocational Information Monographs, No. 4.

Perkins, A. E. "Progress and Needs in Negro Public Education with Special Reference to Louisiana." Competitor 3(Je, 1921):15-16.

Perkins, Iris J. "Felton Gradison Clark, Louisiana Educator." Doctoral dissertation, Louisiana State U., 1977.

Pinney, Edward L., and Friedman, Robert. Political Leadership and the School Desegregation Crisis in Louisiana. New Brunswick, NJ: Eagleton Institute of Politics, 1963.

"Poll of New Orleans Doctors Challenges Statements that School Integration Will Be Psychiatrically Dangerous." Journal of the National Medical Association, S, 1956.

Porter, Betty. "The History of Negro Education in Louisiana." Louisiana Historical Quarterly 25(Jl, 1942).

_____. "The History of Negro Education in Louisiana." Master's thesis, Louisiana State U., 1938.

Public Affairs Research Council Information Center on School Desegregation. "Busing in Louisiana." Schools in Transition 1(0, 1971):1-12. [Box 3118, Baton Rouge, LA 70821]

Reed, Germaine. "David Boyd, Southern Educator." Doctoral dissertation, Louisiana State U., 1970.

Rankin, David C. "Free Colored Creoles in New Orleans, 1850 to 1870." Perspectives in American History 11(1977-1978).

_____. "Race Legislation in Louisiana, 1864-1920." Louisiana History 6(Fall, 1965):379-392.

Reed, Roy. "The Cajuns Resist the Melting Pot." New York Times Magazine, F 29, 1976.

Reinders, Robert C. "The Decline of the New Orleans Free Negro in the Decade before the Civil War." Journal of Mississippi History 24(Ap, 1962):88-98.

Reissman, Leonard et al. The Report of the Ad Hoc Committee to Investigate Fortier Senior High School. New Orleans: Orleans Parish School Board, Ap, 1969.

_____. Sociological Components of Community Renewal in New Orleans. New Orleans: Department of Sociology, Tulane U., 1967.

Reitnouer, Minnie G. "A Comparative Study of the Achievements of New Orleans' Tenth-grade Colored Pupils in Reading Comprehension, Vocabulary, and Spelling." Master's thesis, U. of Southern California, Los Angeles, 1928.

Resource Management Corporation. Evaluation of the Emergency School Assistance Program, Vol. III, Appendix P, F 15, 1972. ERIC ED 058 470. [Case History of ESAP in St. Landry, LA]

Richardson, E. S. "The Jeanes Supervising Teacher--A Potent Force in Negro Education." Nation's Schools 5(Ap, 1930):24-31.

Robinson, Samuel. "A Study of Educational Needs in Predominantly Black High Schools in Louisville, Kentucky." Doctoral dissertation, Indiana U., 1974. Univ. Microfilms Order No. 75-16971.

Scarpaci, Jean. "A Tale of Selective Accommodation: Sicilians and Native Whites in Louisiana." Journal of Ethnic Studies 5(Fall, 1977).

Shaik, Mohamed J. "The Development of Public Education for Negroes in Louisiana." Doctoral dissertation, U. of Ottawa, 1964.

Sherman, Maxine. "The Development of Public Secondary Education in New Orleans, 1840-1877." Master's thesis, Tulane U., 1939.

Somers, Dale A. "Black and White in New Orleans: A Study in Urban Race Relations, 1865-1900." Journal of Southern History 40(F, 1974).

Southern, Marvin E. "A Comparative Analysis of the Social Composition of the Louisiana Parish School Boards." Doctoral dissertation, U. of Southern Mississippi, 1968.

Steimel, Edward J. "Survival of Schools Depends on Public Support." New Orleans Times-Picayune, Ja 25, 1970.

Sterkx, Herbert E. "The Free Negro in Ante Bellum Louisiana, 1764-1860." Doctoral dissertation, U. of Alabama, 1954.

Stewart, W. W. The Negro High School in Louisiana. Scotlandville, LA: Southern U., 1940.

_____. "A Survey of the Negro High School in Louisiana." Southern University Bulletin, Ja, 1941.

Study of Racial Attitudes in Louisiana Fall of 1966. Vol. I: Principal Findings. Summary and Interpretation of Results of Three Sample Surveys of Public Opinion. Dallas: Louis, Bowles and Grace, Inc., 1966.

Swartz, Barbara Myers. "The Lord's Carpetbagger: A Biography of Joseph Crane Hartzell." Doctoral dissertation, State U. of New York, Stony Brook, 1972. [New Orleans]

Taylor, J. T. "Desegregation in Louisiana 1956: A Survey of Retarding Conditions." Journal of Human Relations, Spring, 1957.

Thompson, Daniel C. "Education." In The Negro Leadership Class. Englewood Cliffs, NJ: Prentice-Hall, 1963. [New Orleans]

Torres, Mario, and Stimpson, Sandy. "17-Year-Old Youth Faces Electrocution." Southern Patriot, F, 1976. [Gary Tyler, Destrehan High School, Destrehan]

U.S. Commission on Civil Rights. The New Orleans School Crisis. Washington, DC: GPO, 1961.

U.S. Commission on Civil Rights, Louisiana Advisory Committee. School Desegregation in Bogalusa, Louisiana. Washington, DC: The Commission, 1977.

U.S. Office of Education. "Evaluation of Title I, ESEA-Louisiana." In U.S. Congress, 92nd, 1st Session, Senate, Select Committee on Equal Educational Opportunity, Equal Educational Opportunity--1971. Part 17--Delivery Systems for Federal Aid to Disadvantaged Children, pp. 8673-8802. Washington, DC: GPO, 1971.

Vincent, Charles. "Negro Legislation in Louisiana During Reconstruction." Doctoral dissertation, Louisiana State U., 1973.

_____. Black Legislators in Louisiana During Reconstruction. Baton Rouge: Louisiana State U. Press, 1976.

Watson, J. B. "Louisiana Negroes Are Advancing." Southern Workman 57(My, 1928):224-230.

White, Howard A. "The Freedmen's Bureau in New Orleans." Master's thesis, Tulane U., 1950.

_____. "The Freedmen's Bureau in Louisiana." Doctoral dissertation, Tulane U., 1956. Univ. Microfilms Order No. 59-1082.

Williams, Margaret M. "An Outline of Public School Politics in Louisiana since the Civil War." Master's thesis, Tulane U., 1938.

Wilson, Florence. "The Work of the Schools for the Foreign Element in New Orleans." Master's thesis, Tulane U., 1925.

Woods, Frances Jerome. Marginality and Identity. A Colored Creole Family through Ten Generations. Baton Rouge: Louisiana State U. Press, 1972.

Maine

Governor's Task Force on Human Rights. Augusta, ME: State House, D, 1968.

Murray, Constance C. "Portland, Maine and the Growth of Urban Responsibility for Human Welfare, 1830-1860." Doctoral dissertation, Boston U., 1960. Univ. Microfilms Order No. 60-3472.

U.S. Congress, 94th, 1st Session, Senate, Committee on Labor and Public Welfare, Subcommittee on Labor. Agricultural Child Labor Provisions of FLSA, 1975. Hearing... Washington, DC: GPO, 1975.

Violette, Maurice. The Franco-Americans: A Franco-American's Chronicle of Historical and Cultural Environment. Augusta Revisited. New York: Vantage Press, 1976.

Maryland

Bachrach, Peter, and Baratz, Morton S. Power and Poverty: Theory and Practice. New York: Oxford U. Press, 1970.

Bailey, Peter. "An 'Integrated' Youngster." Ebony 29(Ag, 1974):123-127. [Growing up in Chevy Chase]

Bard, Harry. "Observations on Desegregation in Baltimore: Three Years Later." Teacher College Record, F, 1958.

Barringer, Felicity, and Harrsard, Sara E. "Montgomery [County] Pupils Shift Schools Calmly." Washington Post, S 2, 1976.

Becker, Elizabeth. "Busing Works in Once-Bitter Pr. George's." Washington Post, S 4, 1975.

_____. "Integrated Community Fights to Keep Children in Same School." Washington Post, Je 21, 1976. [East Kettering, Prince Georges County]

Belcher, Jerry. "School Busing: How Far Has It Come?" Los Angeles Times, D 15, 1975. [Prince George's County]

"Black School-Lockout Victims Reunite." New York Times, S 6, 1976. [Prince Edward County]

Bowler, Mike. "Pupils Mixed, Not Integrated." Baltimore Sun, Ap 8, 1973. [Prince Georges County]

Buford, Carolyn B. "The Distribution of Negroes in Maryland, 1850-1860." Master's thesis, Catholic U. of America, 1956.

Carrington, Joel Acus. "The Struggle for Desegregation of Baltimore City Public Schools, 1952-1966." Doctoral dissertation, U. of Maryland, 1970. Univ. Microfilms Order No. 71-4044.

Commission on Professional Rights and Responsibilities. Baltimore, Maryland. Change and Contrast--The Children and the Public School. Washington, DC: National Education Association, My, 1967.

Communities Under Siege, 1971. Activists, Inc., 2316 W. North Avenue, Baltimore, MD 21217. [Real estate and changing neighborhoods in Baltimore]

Curran, Robert Emmett. "History of a Changing Neighborhood." America, Je 15, 1968. [The West End in Baltimore]

Davids, Robert B. "A Comparative Study of White and Negro Education in Maryland." Doctoral dissertation, Johns Hopkins U., 1936.

Division of Instruction. A Comparison by Certificate and Degree Status of Maryland Principals, By Race for the School Year 1968-1969. Baltimore: Maryland State Department of Education, Je 24, 1970.

Dunn, Frederick J. "Programs and Procedures of Desegregation Developed by the Board of Education, Montgomery County, Maryland." Doctoral dissertation, U. of Maryland, 1959. Univ. Microfilms Order No. 59-6845.

Dyce, Cedric. "A Geographic History of the Negro Middle Class in West Baltimore, 1880-1970." Master's thesis, Syracuse U., 1973.

Eisenberg, Leon. "Some Children Are Convinced They Can't Win." Southern Education Report, Ap, 1967. [Baltimore]

Elsila, Dave. "Fired for Using Afro-American Unit, Baltimore Teacher Seeks Her Job Back." American Teacher, O, 1967.

Equal Educational Opportunity Policy Research Project. "Montgomery County, Maryland." In Federal Policies for Equal Educational Opportunity: Conflict and Confusion. Austin, TX: Lyndon B. Johnson School of Public Affairs, U. of Texas, 1977.

"Equal Protection of the Laws, Discrimination in Rate of Compensation Between Colored and White Teachers Held Unconstitutional." Harvard Law Review 53(F, 1940):669-71. [Nulls v. Board of Education of Anne Arundel City, 30 F Supp. 245]

Feinberg, Lawrence, and Becker, Elizabeth. "Black-Majority Schools Rise in P.G." Washington Post, N 23, 1977. [Prince George's County]

Feingold, Edgar L. "Metropolitan Baltimore Schools: A Study in Black and White." Baltimore Sun, Ja 23, 1972.

Fischer, John H. "Fischer Reviews Baltimore Desegregation Course He Directed." [Interview] Southern School News, Jl, 1959.

Fuke, Richard Paul. "A Reform Mentality: Federal Policy Toward Black Marylanders, 1864-1868." Civil War History 22(S, 1976):214-235.

_____. "The Baltimore Association for the Moral and Educational Improvement of the Colored People, 1864-1870." Maryland Historical Magazine, Winter, 1971.

_____. "Black Marylanders, 1864-1868." Doctoral dissertation, U. of Chicago, 1973.

Furno, Orlando F., and Collins, George J. Class Size and Pupil Learning, O, 1967. ERIC ED 024 003.

Gardner, Bettye J. "Ante-Bellum Black Education in Baltimore." Maryland Historical Magazine 71(Fall, 1976):360-366.

_____. "William Watkins: Antebellum Black Teacher and Anti-Slavery Writer." Negro History Bulletin 39(S-O, 1976):623-625.

Garonzik, Joseph. "The Racial and Ethnic Make-Up of Baltimore Neighborhoods, 1850-70." Maryland Historical Magazine 71(Fall, 1976): 392-402.

_____. "Urbanization and the Black Population of Baltimore, 1850-1870." Doctoral dissertation, State U. of New York at Stony Brook, 1974. Univ. Microfilms Order No. 75-5377.

Goldberg, Louis C. "CORE in Trouble: A Social History of the Organizational Dilemma of the Congress of Racial Equality Target City Project in Baltimore (1965-1967)." Doctoral dissertation, Johns Hopkins U., 1970. Univ. Microfilms Order No. 70-20, 154.

Gregory, Clarence Kenneth. "The Education of Blacks in Maryland: An Historical Survey." Doctoral dissertation, Columbia U., 1976. Univ. Microfilms Order No. 76-21019.

Hawkins, Mason A. "Frederick Douglass High School--A Seventeen Year Period Survey." Doctoral dissertation, U. of Pennsylvania, 1933. [Baltimore]

_____. Frederick Douglass High School. Washington, DC: The Associated Publishers, Inc., 1930. [Baltimore]

Hawkins, W. Ashbie. "A Year of Segregation in Baltimore." Crisis, N, 1911.

_____. "Early Education of Colored Youth in Baltimore." Baltimore American, S 16, 1894.

Haynes, M. Alfred, and Dates, Victor H. "Educational Opportunities in the Health Professions for Negroes in the State of Maryland." Journal of Medical Education, O, 1968.

Henry, Neil. "Black Students in Montgomery Tell of Problems." Washington Post, Mr 12, 1979. [Montgomery County]

Holmes, Peter E. "Desegregation in Baltimore: A Letter." Integrated Education 12(Ja-Ap, 1974):45.

Holmgren, Edward. "Baltimore Begins to Integrate Schools." Integrated Education, Ap-My, 1964.

Hutchens, Timothy. "White Student Finds Peer Pressure a Barrier." Washington Star, Ag 15, 1976. [Suitland High School, Prince George's County]

Karmin, Monroe W. "Columbia Planned City Finds It Shares Woes Facing Unplanned Cities." Wall Street Journal, Jl 14, 1971.

Keely, Charles B. The Delivery System of Black Private Housing: Speculation in Baltimore in the 1960's, Ag, 1971, 22 pp. Paper, American Sociological Association. ERIC ED 055 144.

Kelly, Pat Brown. "Solving the School Lunch Problem." Washington Post, Mr 7, 1974. [The Maryland Food Committee and its work]

Kimmel, Ross M. "Free Blacks in Seventeenth Century Maryland." Maryland Historical Magazine 71(Spring, 1976):19-25.

Kladiman, Stephen. "Grade-Test Disparity in Baltimore." Washington Post, S 19, 1976.

Kolodner, Ferne K. The Unaccepted Baltimoreans: A Study of the White Southern Rural Migrants: The Culturally Different and Disadvantaged Urbanites. Baltimore: 1962.

Krause, Charles A. "Integrated School Changes." Washington Post, Ja 30, 1974. [Roger B. Taney Junior High School, Camp Springs, Prince George's County]

Kulikoff, Allan. "The Origins of Afro-American Society in Tidewater Maryland and Virginia, 1770-1790." William and Mary Quarterly 35 (1978):226-259.

Kuttner, Bob. "Ethnic Renewal. How Ordinary People in East Baltimore Have Created a Model Answer to Inner-City Blight." New York Times Magazine, My 9, 1976.

Lade, K. Peter, and Lade, H. Joan. "Ethnic Minorities on the Eastern Shore of Maryland: An Endangered Species." Man and Life (Calcutta) 3(1977):113-121.

Levenson, Bernard, and McDill, Mary S. "Vocational Graduates in Auto-Mechanics: A Follow Up Study of Negro and White Youth." *Phylon*, Winter, 1966. [Baltimore]

Lombardi, Donald N. "Factors Affecting Change in Attitude Toward Negroes Among High School Students." *Journal of Negro Education*, Spring, 1963.

Lovette, W. L. "Soulful 68 Summer." *Maryland Libraries*, Fall, 1968.

McDill, Mary S., Stinchcombe, Arthur L., and Walker, Dollie. "Segregation and Educational Disadvantage: Estimates of the Influence of Different Segregating Factors." *Sociology of Education*, Summer, 1968. [Baltimore]

McGuinn, Henry J. "The Courts and the Changing Status of Negroes in Maryland." Doctoral dissertation, Columbia U., 1940.

McMillan, Sylvia R. "Aspirations of Low-Income Mothers." *Journal of Marriage and the Family*, My, 1967. [Anne Arundel County]

Manella, Raymond L. "Racially Integrating a State's Training Schools." *Children*, Mr-Ap, 1964.

Maryland State Advisory Committee. *Report on Maryland. Employment*. Washington, DC: U.S. Commission on Civil Rights, S, 1965.

Maryland State Board of Education. *Schools for Colored Children*. In *Sixty-third Annual Report, 1929*, pp. 164-208.

Middleton, Lorenzo. "Montgomery Busing: Mom Likes It, Politicians Don't." *Washington Star*, O 24, 1976.

O'Wesney, Julia Roberta. "Historical Study of the Progress of Racial Desegregation in the Public Schools of Baltimore, Maryland." Doctoral dissertation, U. of Maryland, 1970. Univ. Microfilms Order No. 70-23310.

Pancoast, Elinor and others. *The Report of a Study on Desegregation in the Baltimore City Schools*. Baltimore: Maryland Commission on Interracial Problems and Relations, 1956.

Paquin, Lawrence G. *The Senior High Schools in the Years Ahead, 1966-1971*. Baltimore: Baltimore City Public Schools, F 3, 1966.

Paul, William George. "The Shadow of Equality: The Negro in Baltimore, 1864-1911." Doctoral dissertation, U. of Wisconsin, 1972. Univ. Microfilms Order No. 72-11255.

Pettigen, Eulalia V. "Factors Affecting Secondary Education Among Negroes of Maryland (excluding Baltimore)." Master's thesis, Columbia U., 1933.

Pietila, Antero. "Baltimore Desegregation: Tug of War." *Integrateducation* 12(N-D, 1974):17-19.

"Antero Pietila Replies." *Integrateducation* 13 (Jl-Ag, 1975):31. [Baltimore]

Pugh, George E. *School Desegregation Alternatives in Prince George's County*. Lambda Corporation, Ap 28, 1972.

Putney, Martha S. "Nelson Wells and His Legacy: An Effort in Black Self-Help in Education." *Negro History Bulletin* 39(N-D, 1976):642-647. [Baltimore]

Rabben, Kenneth J. "Baltimore Fights Resegregation As Blacks Advance in the Schools." *Race Relations Reporter, Reporter News Supplement*, S 1, 1970.

Rackley, Lurma. "Black Student: Wants An End to Bitterness." *Washington Star*, Ag 15, 1976. [Bethesda-Chevy Chase High School]

Reeves, Norman V. A., and Weisengoff, Paul E. "Baltimore Schools: The Patterson Impact." *Baltimore Sun*, N 24, 1973.

Reid, Ira de Augustine. *The Negro Community of Baltimore*. Baltimore: National Urban League, 1935.

Resource Management Corporation. *Evaluation of the Emergency School Assistance Program*, Vol. III, Appendix D, F 15, 1972. ERIC ED 058 470. [Case History of ESAP in Dorchester, MD]

Reutter, Mark. "Corridor in Transition." *Baltimore Sun*, F 5-11, 1978. [Series of seven articles on Liberty Road area of Baltimore County]

Robinson, Welford C. "Race and Spatial Interaction Patterns in Baltimore City." Doctoral dissertation, Rutgers U., 1973.

Rodgers, E. "The Relationship of Certain Measureable Factors in the Personal and Educational Backgrounds of Two Groups of Baltimore Negroes, Identified as Superior and Average in Intelligence as Fourth Grade Children, to their Educational, Social and Economic Achievement in Adulthood." Doctoral dissertation, New York U., 1954.

Sawyer, Kathy. "Learning to Live Together." *Washington Post*, D 18, 1975. [Largo Senior High School, Prince George's County]

"School Desegregation in Prince George's County: Two Views." *Civil Rights Digest* 5(Summer, 1973):11-20.

Shannon, William Hunter. "Public Education in Maryland (1825-1868) with Special Emphasis Upon the 1860's." Doctoral dissertation, U. of Maryland, 1965.

Sheldon, Thomas D. [Interview on Baltimore schools] *Baltimore*, My, 1970. [Superintendent of Schools]

Slattery, John R. "Colored People in Baltimore, Maryland." Catholic World, Ja, 1898.

Smith, Benjamin F. "The Relationship of Non-Intellectual Status of Junior High School Student Groups, Economic Background." Journal of Secondary Education, N, 1968. [Baltimore]

Smith, Charles H. E., Jr. An Historical Look at the Roots of Black Education in Portsmouth, 1978. The Author, 106 Pecan Drive, Princess Anne, Maryland 21853. [1871-1973]

Solomon, Eric S. "Student Mobility in Baltimore City Schools." Master's thesis, U. of Maryland, 1973.

Stedner, Mark K. An Analysis of the Attitudes of Black Urban Youth Toward Military Service. AD-749 710. Springfield, VA: National Technical Information Service, My 19, 1972. [Baltimore and Annapolis]

Stenquist, John L. Semi-Annual Instructional Surveys. City-wide Test Results, F, 1929, 254 pp., Mr, 1929, 52 pp., My, 1929, 28 pp., S, 1930, 20 pp. Baltimore: Department of Education, Bureau of Research.

Swanson, Tonya D. "Prince George's Busing: 6 Years Later." Washington Star, D 31, 1978.

Thomas, Bettye C. "Public Education and Black Protest in Baltimore, 1865-1900." Maryland Historical Magazine 71(Fall, 1976):381-391.

Tonetti, J. Paul. A Report on the Employment Patterns of Principals, by Race, in Maryland: 1954-1968. Baltimore: Maryland State Department of Education, S, 1969.

Trammer, Monte I. "Blacks in Liberty Road Area Finding Segregation of Schools Follows Them." Baltimore Sun, F 7, 1968. [Baltimore County]

U.S. Commission on Civil Rights. A Long Day's Journey into Night. School Desegregation in Prince George's County. Washington, DC: The Commission, Mr, 1976.

_____. Hearing Before the United States Commission on Civil Rights. Hearing Held in Baltimore, Maryland, August 17-19, 1970. Washington, DC: GPO, 1971.

_____. Report on School Desegregation in 14 Eastern Shore and Southern Maryland Counties. Washington, DC: GPO, 1966.

U.S. Congress, 94th, 1st Session, Senate, Committee on Labor and Public Welfare, Subcommittee on Education. Oversight Hearing on HEW Enforcement of School-Related Civil Rights, Problems, 1975. Hearings... Washington, DC: GPO, 1975.

Walker, Dollie and others. School Desegregation in Baltimore. Baltimore: Johns Hopkins U., Ag, 1967, 52 pp. ERIC ED 013 168.

Wallace, Weldon. "An Interview with Roland Patterson." Baltimore Sun, Jl 8, 1974. [Black superintendent of Baltimore]

Walton, John. "A Response to Baltimore Desegregation: Tug of War." Integrateducation 13(Jl-Ag, 1975):31. [See Pietila, above]

Washington Center for Metropolitan Studies. School Desegregation and Prince George's County. Washington, DC: U.S. Commission on Civil Rights, Ag, 1973.

Wells, Roy N., Jr. "Written Testimony [on Safety Problems in School Busing]." In U.S. Congress, 93rd, 2nd Session, Senate, Committee on the Judiciary, Subcommittee on Constitutional Rights, Busing of Schoolchildren. Hearings..., pp. 294-307. Washington, DC: GPO, 1974. [Prince George's County]

Wennersten, John R. "The Black School Teacher in Maryland, 1930's." Negro History Bulletin 38(Ap-My, 1975):370-373.

West, Herbert Lee, Jr. "Urban Life and Spatial Distribution of Blacks in Baltimore, Maryland." Doctoral dissertation, U. of Minnesota, 1974. Univ. Microfilms Order No. 74-26273.

Whitaker, Joseph, and Thompson, Vernon. "...A Very Quiet First Day." Washington Post, S 2, 1976. [First day of desegregation at Kensington Junior High School, Montgomery County]

Williams, Percy V. and others. Report to the Maryland State Board of Education on the Charles County School System. Baltimore: Maryland State Board of Education, Ap 24, 1970.

Wise, Arthur E., and Weinstein, Shelly. "The Politics of Inequality: A Case Study." Phi Delta Kappan 58(O, 1976):169-176.

Wright, James M. The Free Negro in Maryland. New York, 1921.

Massachusetts

"A Community Group with the Help of Its Architect Comes to Terms with a Mighty University." Architectural Record 163(F, 1978):84-87. [Roxbury and Harvard]

A Report on ABDC Activities, September 1963-August 1964. Boston: Action for Boston Community Development, Inc., 1964.

Abrams, Roger I. "Not One Judge's Opinion: Morgan v. Hennigan and the Boston Schools." Harvard Educational Review 45(F, 1975):5-16.

Adkins, John F., McHugh, James R., and Scay, Katherine. Desegregation: The Boston Orders and Their Origin. Boston: Boston Bar Association, Ag, 1975.

Advisory Committee on Racial Imbalance and Education. Because It Is Right--Educationally. Boston: Massachusetts State Board of Education, Ap, 1965.

Aldrich, Judge Bailey. " Springfield Ruling Upset." Integrated Education, Ag-N, 1965.

Allen, Patricia R., and Weathersby, Rita E. Minorities in the Curriculum: What's Happening Where. An Informal Survey of Programs and Resources in Massachusetts. Boston: Department of Education, Commonwealth of Massachusetts, My, 1969.

Alperovitz, Gar. "An Unconventional Approach to Boston's Problems." Harvard Crimson, Ap 22, 1968.

Anderson, Peter. "How Media Handled School Busing Story." Boston Globe, S 22, 1974. [Boston]

Anrig, Gregory. "Our Goal: Elimination of Racial Isolation" (interview). Harvard Graduate School of Education Association Bulletin 19(Winter, 1974-1975):8-14. [Boston]

Anrig, Gregory R. "Boston and the South: Differences and Similarities in School Desegregation." Consortium Currents 2(F, 1975):11-13. [Write to 5801 South Kenwood Ave., Chicago, IL 60637.]

Anti-Expansion Anti-ROTC Strike Steering Committee. Harvard, Urban Imperialist. New England Free Press, 1969.

Archibald, David K. Report on Change in Academic Achievement for a Sample on Elementary School Children: Progress Report on METCO. Roxbury, MA: METCO Education Program, 1967.

"At-Large School Elections Challenged in Boston Suit." Inequality in Education, O 10, 1969.

Batson, Ruth M., and Peters, Lyda S. Community Crisis Intervention and the Boston School Desegregation Effort: Case Study of a Training Program, 1976. ERIC ED 152 869.

"The Becker Poll on Busing." Boston Herald American, Ag 14-Ag 22, 1975. [Seven articles on public opinion in Boston]

Bell, Christopher C. "Are University-Public School Collaboratives Working? An Attitudinal Survey of Teachers, Selected Parents and Students of a Large Urban High School in Boston, Massachusetts." Doctoral dissertation, Boston U., 1978. Univ. Microfilms Order No. 7819721.

Berg, William M. "The Social Construction of Public Controversy: The Case of School Desegregation in Boston." Doctoral dissertation, Boston U., 1978. Univ. Microfilms Order No. 7819794.

Bernick, Michael. "Will Boston Schools Ever Desegregate?" Harvard Crimson, Ja 17, 1973

Better, James P. "The Politics of Education: The 1965 Massachusetts Racial Imbalance Law." Honors thesis, U. of Massachusetts, 1967.

Binyon, Michael. "Blacks Catch a Bus to Harvard." Times Educational Supplement, N 12, 1976. [Roxbury High School, Boston]

Black Panther Party, Boston Chapter. "Black Students Strike in Boston." Black Panther, F 20, 1971.

"Blacklash in Boston." Newsweek, N 6, 1967. [The mayoralty campaign of Mrs. Louise Day Hicks]

Bolner, James. "Politics of acial Imbalance Legislation: Massachusetts 1965." Harvard Journal of Legislation, N, 1967.

Bolner, James, with Shanley, Robert A. Civil Rights in the Political Process: An Analysis of the Massachusetts Racial Imbalance Law of 1965. Bureau of Government Research, U. of Massachusetts, 1967.

"Boston as the Paradise of the Negro." Colored American Magazine 7(My, 1904):309-317.

Boston College. "Race and Education in Boston." [Unpublished study for U.S. Commission on Civil Rights, 1966]

"Boston Erupts." Race Relations Reporter 5(N, 1974):3-4.

Boston Presentation Meeting. Triumph of Equal School Rights in Boston. (Proceedings of the presentation meeting held in Boston, D 17, 1855; including addresses by John T. Hilton, William C. Nell, Charles W. Slack, Wendell Phillips, William Lloyd Garrison, Charles Lenox Redmond.) Boston: R. F. Wallcut, 1856.

Boston Urban Services Project. Political and Administrative Decentralization of Municipal Services in Boston. Cambridge, MA: Harvard Law School, 1969.

Broder, David S. "Women Fight Boston Busing." Washington Post, Je 28, 1975.

Brown, Charles Sumner. "Negro Protest and White Power Structure: The Boston School Controversy 1963-1966." Doctoral dissertation, Boston U., 1973. Univ. Microfilms Order No. 73-27032.

Brown, James. "Busing and Video Process: School Desegregation and Boston Media." Televisions 5, No. 1(1977). [Published by Washington Community Video Center, P.O. Box 21068, Washington, DC 20009]

Brown, James Larry. "Children Excluded from the Boston Schools: An Analysis of the Normative Function of Education in American Society." Doctoral dissertation, Brandeis U., 1971.

Bruck, David Isaac. "The Schools of Lowell, 1824-1861: A Case Study in the Origins of Modern Public Education in America." Senior thesis, Department of Social Studies, Harvard College, Ap, 1971.

Brudnoy, David. "Busing for the Sake of Busing." National Review 27(Mr 14, 1975):282-283, 299. [Boston]

_____. "Fear and Loathing in Boston." National Review 26(O 25, 1974):1228-1231.

Bullard, Pamela. "Desegregation, Charlie Leftwich Come to Town." Cleveland Plain Dealer Magazine, My 28, 1978. [Boston]

Bureau of Research and Assessment. Assessment of Students in Metropolitan Council for Educational Opportunity (METCO) Programs 1975-1976. Boston: State Department of Education, Ag, 1976.

Burns, Monique L. "Poll Indicates Suburbs Favor Busing." Harvard Crimson, Ja 20, 1975. [Boston]

Bushee, Frederick. "Ethnic Factors in the Population of Boston." Publications of the American Economics Association, 3rd series (1903):299-477.

Busing, Racism and Quality Education, 1974. Pacifica Tape Library, 5316 Venice Blvd., Los Angeles, CA 90019. [A 2-hour discussion centering on Boston]

Cambridge Survey Research. An Analysis of Teachers' Attitudes Toward the Public Schools in the City of Boston. Boston: Citywide Coordinating Committee, Ap, 1977.

Camerota, Michael. "Westfield's Black Community, 1755-1905." Hist. Jr. W. Mass. 5(Spring, 1976):17-27.

Campbell, Georgetta Merritt. "Extant Collections of Black Newspapers 1880-1915 in the Libraries of the United States: The Need for a Scholarly Index." Doctoral dissertation, Fairleigh Dickinson U. (Teaneck-Hackensack), 1978. Univ. Microfilms Order No. 7816881. [Contains index to Monroe Trotter's Boston Guardian]

Capernaros, Peter S. "The Implementation of the Massachusetts Racial Imbalance Act: A Study and Evaluation of Desegregation Techniques and Roles in Boston and Springfield." Doctoral dissertation, Boston U., 1975. Univ. Microfilms Order No. 75-20, 942.

Case, Charles W. "History of the Desegregation Plan in Boston." In David U. Levine and Robert J. Havighurst, The Future of Big-City Schools. Berkeley, CA: McCutchan, 1977.

Casey, George W. "Busing in Boston: Weighing the Values." America 133(S 13, 1975):111-112.

Casey, Rick. "Boston Bus Order Splits Catholics." National Catholic Reporter, F 21, 1975.

City-Wide Educational Coalition. A Parent's Guide to the Magnet Schools in Boston, My, 1977. ERIC ED 151 464.

Clark, Karen. "Boston Desegregation: What Went Wrong?" Clearing House 51(D, 1977): 157-159.

Clifford, Laura and others. Changing Boston's Schools: A Survival Kit for Parents and Students, 1975. ERIC ED 152 878.

Coffey, William. "A Macroscopic Analysis of Income Regions in Metropolitan Boston." Professional Geographer 29(F, 1977):40-46.

Cohen, David K., and Van Geel, Tyll R. "Public Education." In Samuel H. Beer, and Richard E. Barringer, The State and the Poor, pp. 222-249. Cambridge, MA: Winthrop Publishers, 1970.

Cohen, Muriel. "Boston." Integrateducation 15 (N-D, 1977):9-10.

_____. "City-Suburb Flow Accelerates." Boston Globe, Ap 29, 1973.

_____. "Imbalance: A 10-Year Calendar of Controversy [in Boston]." Boston Globe, Ja 7, 1973. [1963-1973]

_____. "Parents, Principal, and Pairing: Key to Successful Desegregation in Boston." In Don Davies, Schools Where Parents Make a Difference. Boston: Institute for Responsive Education, 1976.

_____. "The Second Year." Boston Globe, Je 23 (2 articles), 24, 26, and 28, 1976. [Review of one year of Phase 2 desegregation in Boston schools]

Cohen, Muriel, and Worsham, James. "The Dorchester Student Conflict: Born of Frustration." Boston Globe, S 30, 1973. [Dorchester High School, Boston]

Coleman, Charles L. "A History of the Negro Baptists in Boston, 1800-1875." Master's thesis, Andover Newton Theological School, 1956.

Coles, Robert. "Boston and the South." Harvard Magazine 78(S, 1975):15-20, 52.

_____. "Busing in Boston." New Republic, O 2, 1965.

_____. "Stricken Boston." New York Review of Books, Ag 7, 1975.

_____. "White Liberals Should Look at Themselves Before Blaming It All on Blue-Collar 'Bigots.'" Los Angeles Times, S 8, 1975.

Commission on Church and Race, Massachusetts Council of Churches. "Explosion in Roxbury, Eyewitness Accounts of the Role and Conduct of the Police." Jewish Currents, O, 1967. [C. the Boston uprisings of June 2-5, 1967]

Comptroller General of the United States. Student Enrollment and Attendance Reports in the Boston Public School System Are Substantially Accurate. Washington, DC: General Accounting Office, Jl 16, 1976.

Cottle, Thomas J. "A Simple Solution." Ethnic Groups 1(Je, 1976):3-12. [Boston]

_____. Black Children, White Dreams. Boston: Houghton Mifflin, 1974. [Roxbury]

_____. "Bus Start." New York Times Magazine, Mr 9, 1975. [Boston]

_____. "The Integration of Harry Benjamin." New York Times Magazine, Ap 23, 1972. [Boston]

_____. "Speaking of Busing." New Republic, Ja 25, 1975. [Boston]

_____. "The Wellesley Incident." Saturday Review, Mr 15, 1969. [Wellesley Senior High School, Wellesley]

Cox, H. "Dialogue Among Pickets: Segregation in Boston Schools." Commonweal, N 22, 1963.

Crane, Dennis, and Schiffman, Douglas. Balancing the Public Schools: Desegregation in Boston and Springfield, 1975. ERIC ED 126 163.

Critique. Operation Exodus, 378 Blue Hill Avenue, Dorchester, MA 02121. [A critical analysis of a proposal submitted by the Boston School Department to the U.S. Office of Education for funds under Title I of the Elementary and Secondary Education Act of 1957]

Cronin, Joseph M. Organizing An Urban School System for Diversity. A Study of the Boston School Department. Summary Report, S, 1970. McBer and Company, 675 Massachusetts Avenue, Cambridge, MA 02139.

Cronin, Joseph M., Hailer, Richard M. and others. Organizing An Urban School System for Diversity. A Report on the Boston Public School Department, O, 1970. Massachusetts Advisory Council on Education, 182 Tremont Street, Boston, MA 02111.

Culbert, Michael L., and Richard 9X. "Boston Busing Sparks Bloodshed." Muhammad Speaks, O 25, 1974.

Curwood, Stephen. "In Boston. With So Many Trying To Get In [To Corporations] Why Do Some Walk Away?" Black Enterprise, Mr, 1972.

Daniels, John. In Freedom's Birthplace: A Study of the Boston Negroes. New York: Houghton Mifflin Company, 1914.

Daniels, Lee A. "Jonathan Kozol." Harvard Crimson, Ap 29, 1969. [The Learning Center, Boston]

Daniels, Lee A., and Barnes, Bart. "Boston Prepares for New Showdown." Washington Post, S 1, 1975.

Daniere, A. Cost-Benefit Analysis of General Purpose State School Aid Formulas in Massachusetts. Boston: Massachusetts Advisory Council on Education, 1968.

Daniere, Andre. Inequalities of Educational Opportunity in Massachusetts. A Preliminary Report. Boston: Advisory Council on Education, 1967.

Darling, Arthur B. "Prior to Little Rock in American Education: The Roberts Case of 1849-1850." Proceedings of the Massachusetts Historical Society, O, 1957-D, 1960.

Dauwer, Leo P. I Remember Southie: A Boston Bicentennial Celebration. Boston: Christopher, 1975.

Davidson, Carl. "Boston Racists Provoke School Crisis." Guardian, O 23, 1974.

Day, Noel. "The Freedom Movement in Boston." Integrated Education, D, 1964-Ja, 1965.

DeVaughn, Booker Thomas, Jr. "A History of Adult Education in the Black Community of Boston from 1900 to 1965." Doctoral dissertation, Boston U., 1975. Univ. Microfilms Order No. 75-20944.

Delaney, Paul. "Boston Blacks Fearful But Firm." New York Times, S 10, 1975.

"Democratic Rights, Not Integration." La Raza 2(Ja, 1975):40-43.

Dentler, Robert A. "Desegregation Planning and Implementation in Boston." Theory Into Practice 17(F, 1978):72-77.

_____. "Education and the Boston Desegregation Case." Journal of Education 160(My, 1978): 7-18.

_____. "Educational Implications of Desegregation Developments in Boston." In Daniel U. Levine and Robert J. Havighurst, The Future of Big-City Schools. Berkeley, CA: McCutchan McCutchan, 1977.

DiCara, L., and Kindregan, C. P. "Public Education in Greater Boston: Does America's Commitment to Equality and Integration Stop at the City Line?" Suffolk U. Law Review 11 (Summer, 1977):1245-1288.

Diamond, Edwin. "Boston: The Agony of Responsibility." Columbia Journalism Review 13(Ja-F, 1975).

Dillman, Robert J. "Assessing the Effectiveness of Urban Decentralization: An Analysis of Users of Boston's Little City Halls." Doctoral dissertation, Clark U., 1977.

Doherty, Phil. "In Racially Torn Boston, a Bold Appeal to Reason." Quill 65(Je, 1977): 28-29.

Doyle, James S. "Cut-Off in Boston." New Republic, Ag 27, 1966. [Cut-off of state aid to Boston's schools until racial imbalance is remedied]

Dumanoski, Dianne. "The Resegregation of Boston Schools." Boston Phoenix, Ap 3, 1979. [West Roxbury]

Edel, Matthew, and Sclar, Elliott. "The Distribution of Real Estate Value Changes: Metropolitan Boston, 1870-1970." Journal of Urban Economics 2(O, 1975):366-387.

Edmonds, Ronald R. "Desegregation and Equity: Community Perspectives." Harvard Graduate! School of Education Association Bulletin 19 (Winter, 1974-1975):2-7. [Boston]

_____. "Simple Justice in the Cradle of Liberty: Desegregating the Boston Public Schools." Vanderbilt Law Review 31(My, 1978):887-904.

Edmonds, Ronald R., Haskins, Kenneth, and Murphy, Kathleen. "Debriefing: A Desegregation Technique in Response to Crisis." Inequality in Education 22(Jl, 1977):125-129. [Boston]

Educational Development Center. Notes on the Chronological Development of Transitional Bilingual Clusters in Boston Public Schools. Newton, MA: Educational Development Center, 1970.

Edwards, R. M. et al. The Negro in Boston. Boston: Action for Boston Community Development, 1967.

Eisner, Alan. "Integration Works in East Boston...At Donald McKay School." Boston Herald American, N 19, 1975.

_____. "Small Classes, Varied Curriculum End Racial Tension." Boston Herald American, N 17, 1975. [Temporary Madison Park High School, Boston]

Emmanuel College Research Group. "The State Connection. A Preliminary Study on the Role of the State in the Boston Busing Crisis." Liberation 19(S-O, 1975):8-12.

Epstein, Noel. "Students of South Boston High Are Learning Many Things." Washington Post, D 14, 1975.

Ernst, Robert T. "Growth Development and Isolation of an All-Black City: Kinloch Missouri." In Robert T. Ernst and Lawrence Hugg, Black America, pp 368-388. Garden City, NY: Doubleday, 1976.

Feagin, Joe R. Ghetto Social Structure: A Survey of Black Bostonians. San Francisco: R and E Research Associates, 1975.

Featherstone, Joseph. "Boston Desegregation." (2 parts) New Republic, Ja 17, 24, 1976.

_____. "Notes on Community Schools." New Republic, D 9, 1967. [The New School for Children and the Community School, both in Boston]

Fein, Isaac M. Boston--Where It All Began. An Historical Perspective of the Boston Jewish Community. Boston: Jewish Community Council of Metropolitan Boston, 1976.

Feingold, Ellen. "School Desegregation in Boston." Radcliffe Quarterly 61(S, 1975):13.

Fisher, Clark W. "Case Study of the Boston Public Schools: Development of University-School Pairing to Support Court Ordered Desegregation, 1975-77." Master's thesis, School of Education, Trinity College, U. of Dublin, Ireland, 1977.

Fisk, James E., and Galvin, Raymond T. A Consultant Report on the Boston Police Department During the 1974-75 School Desegregation. Washington, DC: U.S. Commission on Civil Rights, Je 30, 1975.

Five Ethnic Groups in Boston. Boston: Action for Boston Community Development, Inc., and United Community Services of Boston, 1972.

Flannery, J. Harold and others. A Study of the Massachusetts Racial Imbalance Act. Cambridge, MA: Center for Law and Education, Harvard U., F, 1972.

"Forced Busing in Boston: Liberal Hypocrisy in Action." Human Events, D 14, 1974.

Ford, Maurice DeG. "Busing in Boston." Commonweal 102(O 10, 1975):456-460.

_____. "The Schools: Detente in Boston." Nation, My 3, 1975.

Fraser, C. Gerald. "A Memoir: Growing Up Black in the Schools of Boston." New York Times, S 15, 1974. [Sherwin Grammar School and Jamaica Plains High School, 1930's and 1940's]

Freedom House Institute on Schools and Education. Boston Desegregation: The First Term, 1974-75 School Year, F 22, 1975. ERIC ED 123 280.

_____. Boston School Committee "Student Desegregation Plan." A Response, F 3, 1975. ERIC ED 121 920.

_____. Hear the Parents! Report of a Survey on Desegregation Service Needs in Boston's Black Community. Boston: Freedom House, Inc., O, 1975.

"Freedom March Set in Boston." Guardian, D 11,
1974.

Fried, Marc, Gleicher, Peggy, Havens, John,
Ferguson, Lorna, and Aron, Cindy. A Study of
Demographic and Social Determinants of Func-
tional Achievement in a Negro Population.
Sections 1 and 2, PB 196 877 and 196 878.
Springfield, VA: National Technical Infor-
mation Service, Ja 1, 1971. [Boston]

Fried, Marc and others. Patterns of Migration
and Adjustment: The Boston Negro Population.
Boston: Institute of Human Sciences, Boston
College, 1970.

Friedman, Daniel J. White Militancy in Boston.
Lexington, MA: Heath, 1973.

Frisch, Michael H. Town Into City. Springfield, Massachusetts and the Meaning of Community 1840-1880. Cambridge, MA: Harvard U.
Press, 1972.

Fuller, Luther M. "The Negro in Boston, 1864-
1954." Doctoral dissertation, Columbia U.,
1956.

Gaines, Richard L. The Finest Education Money
Can Buy. New York: Simon & Schuster, 1972.
[Lawrenceville School and Newton South High
School]

Garbarino, James. "A Program of Attitude
Change: Suburban Students View and Experience
the City." Cornell Journal of Social Relations 8(Fall, 1973):235-242. [Suburban
Boston]

Gartland, Arthur. "Letter to the Editor from
Gartland." Boston Globe, Ja 17, 1965.

Gillmor, George W., and Gosule, Allan L. "Duty
to Integrate Public schools? Some Judicial
Responses and a Statute." Boston U. Law Review, Winter, 1966. [Analysis of the Massachusetts "Act for the Elimination of Racial
Imbalance in the Public Schools"]

Ginsberg, Yona. Jews in a Changing Neighborhood.
The Study of Mattapan. New York: Free Press,
1975.

Goodman, Ellen H. "Louise Day Hicks: 'When
They Call Me a Racist, I Don't Listen.'"
Ms 4(Ja, 1976):99-103.

Gordon, Eugene F. "These 'Colored' United States
States: Massachusetts: Land of the Free and
Home of the Brave Colored Man." Messenger 7
(Je, 1925):219-222, 243.

Gordon, Larry. "Education in the Boston [School]
System." Paper Tiger, Issue No. 3, 1967.

Gould, Stephen Jay, and Berg, John. "Academic
Racism." Harvard Crimson, Ap 30, 1974.
[Boston]

Graham, Saundra. "On Being Poor Nowadays." Integrated Education 12(Ja-Ap, 1974):36-38.

Green, Jim, and Hunter, Allen. "Racism and
Busing in Boston." Radical America 8(N-D,
1974):1-32.

Greenfield, Sidney M. "In Search of Social
Identity: Strategies of Ethnic Identity Man-
agement Amongst Capeverdeans in Southeastern
Massachusetts." Luso-Brazilian Review 13
(Summer, 1976):3-18.

Grubb, W. Norton. "The Distribution of Costs
and Benefits in an Urban Public School System." National Tax Journal 24(Mr, 1971):1-12.

Hamburg, Jill, and Smith, David. "Boston: The
Urban Coalition in Action." Viet-Report,
Summer, 1968.

Hamilton, Charles J., Jr. "Who's Black in Boston Politics?" Harvard Crimson, O 6, 1967.
[Tom Atkins]

Hammel, Lisa. "Buses That Bring Together Two
Separate and Unequal Worlds." New York Times,
Ap 4, 1969. [METCO in Boston]

Hancock, Gordon Blaine. "The Interrelationship
of the Immigrant and Negro Problem." Master's
thesis, Harvard U., 1921. [Irish-Black conflict in Boston]

Handlin, Oscar. Boston's Immigrants, 1790-1865:
A Study in Acculturation. Rev. and enlarged
edition. Cambridge, MA: Harvard U. Press,
1959.

Hannon, Barbara. Toward Understanding the Persistence of Opposition to School Desegregation in Boston, 1977. ERIC ED 155 266.

Hayes, Christopher A. A School Committeeman
Tells It All. New York: Vantage Press,
1973. [New Bedford]

Henry, William A. III. "Hub Schools Probed
for Spending Bias." Boston Globe, Ja 19,
1972. [Boston]

Hicks, Louise Day. "To Bus? Or Not to Bus?"
Massachusetts Teacher, S, 1966. [Boston]

Hill, Adelaide C. "The Negro Upper Class in
Boston--Its Development and Present Social
Structure." Doctoral dissertation, Radcliffe
College, 1952.

Hillson, Jon. The Battle of Boston. New York:
Pathfinder Press, 1977.

"Horace Mann." Liberator, F 11, 1848.

"Horace Mann and Colored Schools." Liberator,
D 24, 1847.

Horsey, Edmond P. V. "Racism and the Left."
Harvard Crimson, Mr 5, 1975. [Desegregation
in Boston]

Horton, James Oliver. "Black Activism in Boston,
1830-1860." Doctoral dissertation, Brandeis
U., 1973. Univ. Microfilms Order No. 73-32387.

_____. "Generations of Protest: Black Families and Social Reform in Ante-Bellum Boston." New England Quarterly 49(Je, 1976): 242-256.

"How They Do It in Boston." School Management 15(My, 1971):11-14. [William Monroe Trotter School]

Husock, Howard. "No More Mileage in Busing." Nation, D 31, 1977. [Boston]

Hutson, Ron. "Life for Blacks in 'Lost Islands' of Small Cities." Boston Globe, O 8, 1978. [Pittsfield]

Hutson, Ron, and Kennedy, Katherine J. "School Desegregation in Boston and the Emerging Black Leadership." Boston Globe, N 17, 1974.

Ignatius, David R. "Springfield: A City Before the Fall." Harvard Crimson, Jl 23, 1971.

"Integration--Not Busing--Is Key Issue, Says Leader of Boston Teachers Union." American Teacher, Ja, 1976.

"Issues in Black and White: A Round Table Discussion." Journal of Current Social Issues 13(Summer, 1976):56-69. [Boston]

Jackson, Ellen. "Boston Desegregates: How It Affects the Black Community." (Interview) Harvard Graduate School of Education Association Bulletin 19(Winter, 1974-1975):19-21.

Jacob, Eva. "The Arts and the Three R's." The Real Paper, Ag 25, 1976. [Boston]

Jacobs, Donald M. "A History of the Boston Negro from the Revolution to the Civil War." Doctoral dissertation, Boston U., 1968. Univ. Microfilms Order No. 68-18, 097.

_____. "The Nineteenth Century Struggle Over Segregated Education in the Boston Schools." Journal of Negro Education 39(1970):76-85.

Jordan, David C., and Spiess, Kathryn Hecht. Compensatory Education in Massachusetts: An Evaluation with Recommendations, Mr, 1970, 398 pp. Amherst, MA: U. of Massachusetts, School of Education. ERIC ED 063 442.

Kaiser, Robert G. "[U.S. District Judge W. Arthur] Garrity Role: Political Issue." Washington Post, Jl 19, 1976.

Kapenzi, Geoffrey Z. "The Metropolitan Council for Educational Opportunity: An Evaluation." Negro Educational Review 25(O, 1974):203-207. [METCO]

Katz, Michael B. The Irony of Urban School Reform, Idealogy and Style in Mid-Nineteenth Century Massachusetts, 1966. ERIC ED 015 522.

Katzman, Martin T. "Distribution and Production in a Big City Elementary School System." Yale Economic Essays, Spring, 1968. [Boston]

_____. "Decentralizing the Big City Schools." Urban Education III, 1968. [Boston]

Kessler, Ronald. "The Rich Get Richer." Boston Herald, Ja 2-10, 1967. [A series of articles on the inequities of ESEA Title I] U.S. Congress, 90th, 1st Session, Senate, Committee on Labor and Public Welfare, Subcommittee on Education, Education Legislation, 1967, Part 8, pp. 2939-2952. Washington, DC: GPO, 1967.

Kifner, John. "Busing Tension Mars St. Patrick Frivolity in Boston." New York Times, Mr 18, 1974.

_____. "The Men in the Middle." New York Times Magazine, S 12, 1976. [Police in Boston]

Kirchheimer, Anne. "Cambridge Minorities Make Headway." Boston Globe, O 2, 4, 1978.

_____. "White Parents Shape Antibusing Campaign." Boston Globe, N 24, 1974.

Klein, Joe. "The First Days of School in Boston: Prayers, Marches, and Flying Rocks." Rolling Stone, O 23, 1975.

Knights, Peter R. The Plain People of Boston, 1830-1860. New York: Oxford U. Press, 1971.

Kopkind, Andrew. "Banned in Boston: Busing Into Southie." Ramparts 13(D, 1974-Ja, 1975): 33-38.

Kopple, Henry, and Bullock, Doris. "Reflections on Death at an Early Age." AE Magazine, Spring, 1968. [Includes comments on Philadelphia schools]

Kozol, Jonathan. Death At An Early Age. The Destruction of the Hearts and Minds of Negro Children in the Boston Public Schools. Boston: Houghton Mifflin, 1967.

_____. "Department of Lower Learning." New Republic, My 20, 1967. [Boston]

_____. "History Returns to Boston." New York Times, D 11, 1974.

_____. "Kozol Scores Boston Schools and Harvard's Apathetic Role." Harvard Crimson, O 21, 1967. [Excerpts from speech given at Harvard on O 15, 1967]

_____. "Where Ghetto Schools Fail." Atlantic Monthly, O, 1967. [Boston]

Kulikoff, Allan. "The Progress of Inequality in Revolutionary Boston." William and Mary Quarterly, Jl, 1971.

Kvaraceus, William C. "No Hope for the Boston Schools?" Phi Delta Kappan, F, 1968.

Lahnston, Anton T., and Nevins, Paul. "Boston: The Status of Social Studies Education." Social Education 41(N/D, 1977):580-584.

Lamson, Peggy. "The White Northerner's Choice, Mrs. Hicks of Boston." Atlantic Monthly, Je, 1966.

Lazerson, Marvin. The Burden of Urban Education: Public Schools in Massachusetts, 1870-1915, Jl, 1970. Cambridge, MA: Harvard U. ERIC ED 042 270.

_____. Origins of the Urban School. Public Education in Massachusetts, 1870-1915. Cambridge, MA: Harvard U. Press, 1971.

_____. "Urban Reform and the Schools: Kindergarten in Massachusetts, 1870-1915." History of Education Quarterly 11(Summer, 1971):115-142.

Leftwich, Charles W., and Blanc, Doreen V. "New Roles for Parents in Desegregating School Systems." Integrateducation 15(Ja-F, 1977). [Boston]

Leonesio, Christopher. "Boston Citizens for Integration." Citizen Action in Education 2 (Winter, 1975).

Levenson, Marya. "A Boston Teacher Looks at Integration." American Teacher, N, 1974.

Levenstein, Chuck. "Guide to Radical Boston. People Against Racism." Paper Tiger, Je, 1968.

Levesque, George A. "Black Boston: Negro Life in Garrison's Boston, 1820-1860." Doctoral dissertation, State U. of New York at Binghamton,

_____. "Inherent Reformers--Inherited Orthodoxy. Black Baptists in Boston, 1800-1873." Journal of Negro History 60(O, 1975):491-525.

_____. "White Bureaucracy, Black Community: The Contest Over Local Control of Education in Antebellum Boston." Journal of Educational Thought 11(Ag, 1977):140-155.

Levy, Frank S. "An Essay on the Massachusetts Racial Imbalance Act." Doctoral dissertation, Yale U., 1969.

_____. Northern Schools and Civil Rights: The Racial Imbalance Act of Massachusetts. Chicago: Markham, 1971.

Levy, Leonard W., and Jones, Douglas L. (eds.). Jim Crow in Boston: The Origin of the Separate But Equal Doctrine. New York: Da Capo Press, 1974.

Lewis, Toye Brown. "Freedom House in Boston: 27 Years of Community Participation." Citizen Action in Education 4(Fall, 1976):9-10.

Livingston, Guy. "Boston as New 'War Zone' for Media." Variety, S 10, 1975.

Lockly, Leonard K. "The Educational Consequences of Black Participation in the Political Socialization Process in Springfield, Massachusetts." Doctoral dissertation, U. of Massachusetts, 1974. Univ. Microfilms Order No. 74-25849.

Boston Sunday Globe, Ja 14, 1979.

Ludwig, Warren W. "Roxbury/Harvard. Progress and Problems After Three Semesters." Harvard Crimson, Ja 26, 1977. [Roxbury High School, Boston]

Lukas, J. Anthony. "Who Owns 1776?" New York Times Magazine, My 18, 1975. [Boston]

Lupo, Alan. Liberty's Chosen Home: The Politics of Violence in Boston. Boston: Little, Brown, 1977.

Luria, Daniel D. "Trends in the Determinants Underlying the Process of Social Stratification: Boston 1880-1920." Review of Radical Political Economics 6(Summer, 1974):174-193.

Mabee, Carleton. "A Negro Boycott to Integrate Boston Schools." New England Quarterly, S, 1968. [1849-1855]

McCain, Nina. "25 Parents Grab School in Boston." Education News, S 25, 1968.

McKernan, John. "A Day in South Boston." National Review 27(Je 6, 1975):612-613, 625.

McMillan, Charles B. "Magnet Education in Boston." Phi Delta Kappan 59(N, 1977):158-163.

_____. "Organization Change in Schools." Journal of Applied Behavioral Science (Fall, 1975):437-454.

Magnet Education Program Review, Boston Public Schools, 1976-77, Je, 1977. Chapter 636 and University Liaison Office, 26 Court Street, Boston, MA 02108.

Mann, Jill. "Missing Out On the Fun in 'Pads' Behind Locked Doors." Times Educational Supplement, O 18, 1974. [Boston]

"Marriage But Not Miracles. A Report on the Roxbury/Harvard School Program." HGSEA Bulletin 22(Spring, 1978).

Marshall, Kim. "The Making of a Magnet School: A Personal Account of the Journey from Chaos to Quality." Journal of Education 160(My, 1978):19-35. [King School, Dorchester]

Martel, Erich. "Interview With Leader of Black Caucus." Militant, Ag 15, 1975. [Maceo Hutcherson on AFT and Boston desegregation]

Massachusetts Advisory Committee to the U.S. Commission on Civil Rights and the Massachusetts Commission Against Discrimination. Route 128: Boston's Road to Segregation. Washington, DC: U.S. Commission on Civil Rights, Ja, 1975.

Massachusetts Advisory Committee to the United States Commission on Civil Rights. The Six-District Plan. Integration of the Springfield, Massachusetts, Elementary Schools. Washington, DC: U.S. Commission on Civil Rights, Mr, 1976.

Massachusetts Advocacy Center, Massachusetts Law Reform Institute. Making Schools Work--An Education Handbook for Students, Parents, and Professionals. Revised edition, 1978. [2 Park Square, Boston]

"The Massachusetts Law on Racial Imbalance." Integrated Education, Ag-N, 1965.

"Massachusetts Racial Imbalance Act." Harvard Journal of Legislation, N, 1967.

Massachusetts Research Center. Balancing the Public Schools. Desegregation in Boston and Springfield. Boston: Massachusetts Department of Education, 1977.

Massachusetts State Advisory Committee. Report on Massachusetts. Housing Discrimination in the Springfield-Holyoke-Chicopee Metropolitan Area. Washington, DC: U.S. Commission on Civil Rights, D, 1966.

_____. The Voice of the Ghetto. Report on Two Boston Neighborhood Meetings. Washington, DC: GPO, Jl, 1967.

Massachusetts State Advisory Committee to the U.S. Commission on Civil Rights. Contract Compliance and Equal Employment Opportunity in the Construction Industry. Transcript of Open Meeting... Boston, Massachusetts, June 25-26, 1969. Washington, DC: GPO, 1969.

_____. Report on Racial Imbalance in the Boston Public Schools. Washington, DC: GPO, Ja, 1965.

Massey, David. "Clan, Racism and Busing in Boston." Antipode 8(1976):37-49.

Mayo, Clara. Quality Education and Integrated Education: A Conflict of Values, Ap 29, 1970. ERIC ED 127 377. [Operation Exodus]

Merchant, Zarine. "Emma Lewis School of Fine Arts." Black Enterprise 6(Ag, 1975):28-31, 54. [Boston]

Michelman, Frank I. "Boston, Busing and 'Quality Education.'" New Republic, O 26, 1974.

Milbauer, Marvin E. "Boston Isolates Roxbury: In the Land of Louise Day Hicks , Why Wasn't There Any Riot?" Harvard Crimson, O 3, 1966.

Miller, Joyce D. "Student Suspensions in Boston: Derailing Desegregation." Inequality in Education 20(Jl, 1975):16-24.

Miragias, Helen. "An Investigation of Racial Imbalance in the Boston Public Schools." Master's thesis, State College at Boston, 1968.

Missal, Gerald E. (ed.). Schools and Programs of Choice. Voluntary Desegregation in Massachusetts. Boston: Massachusetts Department of Education, Ap, 1977.

Mothner, Ira. "Boston's Louise Day Hicks: Storm Center of the Busing Battle." Look, F 22, 1966.

Mottl, Tahi Lani. The Impact of Three Community Organizations on School Desegregation in Boston, 1975-76, Jl, 1976. ERIC ED 145 065. [Citywide Educational Coalition, Freedom House, and Massachusetts Advocacy Center]

_____. "Social Conflict and Social Movements: An Exploratory Study of the Black Community of Boston Attempting to Change the Boston Public Schools." Doctoral dissertation, Brandeis U., 1976. Univ. Microfilms Order No. 76-16930.

Munoz-Bennett, Lurline V. University Pairings Research Book. Boston: Bureau of Equal Educational Opportunity, State Board of Education, Ja, 1979.

_____ (ed.). METCO Handbook. Boston: Massachusetts Department of Education, Ag, 1976.

Myers, M. L., O'Brien, S. C., Mabel, J. A., and Stare, F. J. "A Nutrition Study of School Children in a Depressed Urban District." Journal of the American Dietetic Association 53(1968):226-242. [Roxbury]

Nolan, Martin. "Louise Day Hicks Gets Out the Vote." Reporter, O 19, 1967. [Boston]

"Not Enough Parents Are Involved." Boston Herald Traveler, N 16, 1975. [Parent council elections]

Nuccio, Vincent C., and Doyle, Richard J. A Study of Promotional Policies and Procedures in the Boston Public Schools. Boston: Center for Field Research and School Services, Boston College, Ap, 1970.

O'Connell, Lawrence W. "The Citizen Reform Group in Central City School Politics: The Boston Experience, 1960-1965." Doctoral dissertation, Syracuse U., 1968.

Parents' Association for South End Schools. End Educational Entombment. Boston: United South End Settlements, 1969.

Peebles, Robert W., and Marker, Gordon A. "Urban-Suburban Collaboration: The EDCO Experience." In Daniel U. Levine, Models for Integrated Education, pp. 58-65. Worthington, OH: Jones, 1971. [Boston]

Pesmen, Sandra. "Room 102 Gets on the Bus." Chicago Daily News, Ja 18, 1978. [Evanston]

Petrin, Chuck. "Boston Commission Hears Testimony on Racist Violence." Militant, Ag 15, 1975.

Pettigrew, Thomas F. "Metropolitan Boston's Race Problem in Perspective." In Social Structure and Human Problems in the Boston Metropolitan Area. Cambridge, MA: 1965.

_____. "Race, Schools, and Riots in Boston." New Society 30(N 28, 1974):538-540.

Pleck, Elizabeth H. "Black Migration to Boston in the Late Nineteenth Century." Doctoral dissertation, Brandeis U., 1974.

_____. "The Two-Parent Household: Black Family Structure in Late Nineteenth Century Boston." Journal of Social History 6(Fall, 1972):3-31.

Poan, Robert C. "Boston's Vocation." Harvard Crimson, D 16, 1967. [Vocational education in Boston]

Powers, Charles T. "Boston Busing Strife: Roots Deep in Past." Los Angeles Times, D 16, 1975.

_____. "Busing No Longer Key to Boston Voting." Los Angeles Times, N 20, 1977.

"Racial Balance in Boston's Schools." America 130(Mr 23, 1974):213. [Roman Catholic schools' policy on accepting students from public schools]

"Racism and Busing in Boston: Comments and Criticism." Radical America 9(My-Je, 1975). [See "Racism and Busing in Boston," N-D, 1974 issue]

Raffel, Jeffrey A. Responsiveness in Urban Schools: A Study of School System Adaptation to Parental Preference in an Urban Environment, Je, 1972. ERIC ED 063 569.

Reinhold, Robert. "A Once Troubled School in Boston is Now Tranquil." New York Times, S 13, 1975. [Mary Emelda Curley Middle School, Jamaica Plains]

_____. "More Segregated than Ever." New York Times Magazine, S 30, 1973.

Report on Parent Attitudes Toward University Pairings. Boston: Citywide Education Coalition, Jl 27, 1977.

Revolutionary Student Union. "New Bedford School Board Rejects People's Constitutional Convention." Black Panther, D 26, 1970.

Rhea, Buford. "Institutional Paternalism in High School." Urban Review, F, 1968. [Boston area]

Riley, R. T., and Cohen, David K. The Attitudes of Boston Adults Toward Racial Imbalance and Parent Involvement in the Public Schools: Spring, 1969. Cambridge, MA: Graduate School of Education, Harvard U., Ja 7, 1970.

Roberts, B. S. "Extent of Federal Judicial Equitable Power: Receivership of South Boston High School." New England Bar Review 12 (Summer, 1976):55-110.

Roberts, Eleanor. "Changes Coming at Southie." Boston Herald Advertiser, Je 20, 1976. [South Boston High School]

Robinson, William D. "Community Involvement in Planning New Schools in Boston." Doctoral dissertation, Harvard U., 1976.

Rogers, David. "Year After Busing, It's Still Uncertain How Many Leaving City." Boston Globe, Je 22, 1975.

Rosenthal, Robert and others. Different Strokes. Pathways to Maturity in the Boston Ghetto. Boulder, CO: Westview Press, 1976. [Six black students in a junior high school in Roxbury]

Ross, J. Michael. "Resistance to Racial Change in the Urban North." Doctoral dissertation, Harvard U., 1973. [Boston]

Ross, J. Michael, and Berg, William M. The Boston School Desegregation Crisis: An Historical and Narrative Account. Chicago: National Opinion Research Center, n.d. [Draft working paper]

_____ and _____. The Social Construction of a School Desegregation Controversy. A Crisis of Law in Society. Boston: Center for Applied Social Science, Boston U., Ap 1, 1978. [Boston]

Ross, J. Michael, Crawford, Thomas, and Pettigrew, Thomas. "Negro Neighbors--Banned in Boston." Trans-action, S-O, 1966.

Rossell, Christine H. "Boston's Desegregation and White Flight." Integrateducation 15(Ja-F, 1977).

_____. Boston's Experience with School Desegregation and White Flight, 1977. ERIC ED 138 689.

Roth, Gary. "Defensiveness in Boston." Empac 7(Mr, 1976):3-4.

Rubin, Irwin M. "The Reduction of Prejudice Through Mass Media." Journal of Adult Education 19(1967):43-52. [Boston school teachers]

Ruchamer, Louis. "Race and Education in Massachusetts." Negro History Bulletin, D, 1949.

Safford, Victor. "Cape Cod Africans." (2 parts) Falmouth Enterprise, Ag 18, 25, 1944. [Capeverdeans in Massachusetts]

Schnare, A. B. "Racial and Ethnic Price Differentials in an Urban Housing Market." Urban Studies 13(Je, 1976). [Boston]

Schrag, Peter. "Boston: Education's Last Hurrah." Saturday Review, My 21, 1966.

_____. Village School Downtown. Politics and Education: A Boston Report. Boston: Beacon Press, 1967.

Schultz, Stanley K. The Culture Factory: Boston Public Schools, 1789-1860. New York: Oxford U. Press, 1973.

Scott, Marvin B. "Pairings Between Higher Education Institutions and Public Schools in the Boston Desegregation Plan." In Daniel U. Levine and Robert J. Havighurst, The Future of Big-City Schools. Berkeley, CA: McCutcha McCutchan, 1977.

Seldon, Horace. "Boston Area Activists Promote Anti-Racist Education." Interracial Books for Children Bulletin 8(1977):22-24.

Sheehy, Virginia M. "Apartheid--USA Style." Bridge 3(My, 1975):13-14. [Suburbs in Boston area]

Sigel, Efrem. "Balancing Act in Boston." Reporter, My 4, 1967.

Sigel, Efrem, and Jonas, Gary F. "Metropolitan Cooperation in Education: The Greater Boston Case." Journal of Negro Education 39 (1970):148-157.

Silcox, H. C. "A Comparative Study in School Desegregation: The Boston and Philadelphia Experience, 1800-1881." Doctoral dissertation, Temple U., 1972.

Singleton, Lawrence D. "A Survey of Boston's Afro-American Organizational Representatives Regarding School Decentralization." Doctoral dissertation, U. of Massachusetts, 1975. Univ. Microfilms Order No. 76-05400.

Smith, Joshua L. "Boston: Cradle of Liberty or Separate but Equal?" Theory Into Practice 17(F, 1978):54-66.

_____. "Senate Bill No. 1117, A Proposal to Outlaw Racial Imbalance in the Public Schools of the Commonwealth of Massachusetts; An Analysis of the Conditions Leading to Its Introduction and Passage." Qualifying paper, Graduate School of Education, Harvard U., My, 1966.

Smith, Ralph R. "Two Centuries and Twenty-four Months: A Chronicle of the Struggle to Desegregate the Boston Public Schools." In Howard I. Kalodner and James J. Fishman, Limits of Justice. The Courts' Role in School Desegregation, pp. 25-113. Cambridge, MA: Ballinger, 1978.

Smith, Robert P. "William Cooper Nell: Crusading Black Abolitionist." Journal of Negro History 55(Jl, 1970):182-199.

Smith, William. "When 'Back to School' Means Staying Back--and Back, and Back." Boston Globe, S 17, 1978. [Boston]

Snelbecker, Glenn E., and Arffa, Marvin S. "An Evaluation of An Integrated Summer School Program." Urban Education II, 4(1967). [Boston and one of its suburbs]

_____ and _____. "Summer School Integration in a Suburb." School and Society, Summer, 1967. [Boston suburb]

Sperber, Robert I. "Urban-Suburban Collaboration Offers Choices." Harvard Graduate School of Education Association Bulletin 19 (Winter, 1974-1975):15-18. [Boston]

Spergel, Howard. "Busing Kids to the Suburbs." American Education, Ap, 1967. [Boston]

Spiegel, Allen. "Housing and Related Patterns of Middle-Income Negroes." Doctoral dissertation, Brandeis U., 1969. [Roxbury]

Stent, Angela. "Blacks Run Race Gauntlet." Times Educational Supplement, O 18, 1974. [Boston]

Stern, David. "Effects of Alternative State Aid Formulas on the Distribution of Public School Expenditures in Massachusetts." Review of Economics and Statistics 55(F, 1973): 91-97.

Struzziery, Joanne M. "School Climate and Racial Attitudes." Integrateducation 15(N-D, 1977):100-102. [METCO]

Sullivan, Neil V. "Plow On!" Integrated Education (My-Je, 1972):57-61.

Sullivan, Sister Mary Xaveria. The History of Catholic Secondary Education in the Archdiocese of Boston. Washington, DC: Catholic U. of America Press, 1946.

Sumner, Charles. "The Evils of Separate Schools, 1849." Integrated Education, D, 1963-Ja, 1964.

Sussman, Leila, and Speck, Gayle. "Community Participation in Schools. The Boston Case." Urban Education 7(Ja, 1973):341-356.

Sweeney, Judge George C. "The Springfield Ruling." Integrated Education, Ap-My, 1965.

Task Force on Children Out of School. The Way We Go to School. The Exclusion of Children in Boston. Boston: Beacon Press, 1971.

Task Force on Racial Imbalance. Revised Short Term Plan to Reduce Racial Imbalance in the Boston Public Schools. Boston: State Board of Education, 1973.

Taylor, Jerry and others. "A Desegregation Plan With Few Takers." Boston Globe, Ag 27-29, 1978. [Three articles on the desegregation policy of the Boston Housing Authority]

Technical Assistance Team. Changes in School
Attendance Districts as a Means of Allevi-
ating Racial Imbalance in the Boston Public
Schools. Cambridge, MA: Joint Center for
Urban Studies of the Massachusetts Institute
of Technology and Harvard U., My 27, 1966.

Teele, James E. Evaluating School Busing:
Case of Boston's Operation Exodus. New
York: Praege, 1973.

_____. The Study of Project Exodus: A School
Racial Integration Project in Boston, Massa-
chusetts. Final Report, N, 1969, 112 pp.
Boston: Harvard School of Public Health.
ERIC ED 036 603.

Teele, James E., Jackson, Ellen, and Mayo,
Clara. Family Experience in Operation Exo-
dus: The Busing of Negro Children. New
York: Behavioral Publications, Inc., 1968.
[Boston]

_____, _____ and _____. "Family Ex-
perience in Operation Exodus." In U.S. Commission on Civil Rights, Hearings Held in
Boston, Massachusetts, October 4-5, 1966,
pp. 297-315. Washington, DC: GPO, 1967.
[Voluntary, private busing program in Bos-
ton]

Teele, James E., and Mayo, Clara. "School Integration: Tumult and Shame." Journal of
Social Issues, Ja, 1969. [Boston]

Thernstrom, Stephan. "The Case of Boston."
Massachusetts Historical Society Proceedings
79(1967):109-122.

_____. The Other Bostonians. Poverty and
Progress in the American Metropolis, 1880-
1970. Cambridge, MA: Harvard U. Press,
1973.

_____. Poverty, Planning and Politics in
the New Boston: The Origins of ABCD. New
York: Basic Books, 1969.

"They Found Desegregation Could Work." Boston
Globe, Je 29, 1975. [Jeremiah E. Burke
High School, Boston]

Thomas, Charles B. Community Leadership During
School Desegregation Controversies: The
Role of the Clergy in Boston, Mr 30, 1978.
ERIC ED 155 283.

Toder, Eric J. "The Distribution of Public
School Teachers by Race and Income Class in
An Urban Metropolitan Area." Doctoral
dissertation, U. of Rochester, 1971. [Bos-
ton]

_____. "The Supply of Public School Teachers
to an Urban Metropolitan Area: A Possible
Source of Discrimination in Education."
Review of Economics and Statistics 54(N,
1972).

Twombly, Robert C. "Black Puritan: The Negro
in Seventeenth-Century Massachusetts." William and Mary Quarterly, 3rd series, 24(1967):
224-242.

United Community Services. Black and White in
Boston. Boston: United Community Services,½
My, 1968.

U.S. Commission on Civil Rights. Hearing Held
in Boston, Massachusetts, October 4-5, 1966.
Washington, DC: GPO, 1967.

_____. Report on Massachusetts: Housing in
Boston. Washington, DC: GPO, D, 1963.

_____. The Crisis and Controversy Concerning
the Desegregation of Public Schools in Boston, Massachusetts, N 27, 1974.

_____. Desegregating the Boston Public Schools:
A Crisis in Civic Responsibility. Washington,
DC: The Commission, Ag, 1975.

U.S. Congress, 92nd, 1st Session, House of Representatives, Committee on Education and
Labor, General Subcommittee on Education.
Needs of Elementary and Secondary Education
for the Seventies--1971. Hearings... Washington, DC: GPO, 1971. [Boston public
schools, pp. 387-607]

U.S. District Court. "Segregation in Boston
Schools." Integratedcuation 12(N-D, 1974):
41-43.

Vaughn, Eva. "Notes from the Prep School Under-
ground: Drugs and Love Ethics at Exeter,
Andover." Harvard Crimson, My 29, 1968.
[Touches on black students at both schools]

Vinovakis, Mavis A. "Trends in Massachusetts
Education, 1826-1860." History of Education
Quarterly, Winter, 1972.

Walberg, Herbert J. An Evaluation of an Urban-
Suburban Busing Program: Student Achievement
and Perception of Class Learning Environments.
Roxbury, MA: METCO, Jl 1, 1969.

Ward, Francis. "Boston Blacks Shaken, Angry,
Deeply Divided." Los Angeles Times, Ja 28,
1975.

Warner, Sam Bass, Jr. The Way We Really Live:
Social Change in Metropolitan Boston Since
1920. Boston: Trustees of the Public Library
of the City of Boston, 1977.

Watson, Denton L. "Backdrop to Boston." Crisis
82(Ja, 1975):7-11.

Weber, William Michael. "Before Horace Mann:
Elites and Boston Public Schools, 1800-1822."
Doctoral dissertation, Harvard U., 1974.
Univ. Microfilms Order No. 74-24967.

Weston, Emily. "Busing As An Educational Experience." Boston Globe Magazine, D 1, 1968.
[Boston]

White, Arthur O. "Antebellum School Reform
in Boston: Integrationists and Separatists."
Phylon 34(Je, 1973):203-217.

_____. "The Black Leadership Class and Educa-
tion in Antebellum Boston." Journal of Negro Education 42(Fall, 1973):504-515.

_____. "Black Life and Education in Ante-
bellum Massachusetts: Strategies for Social
Mobility." Doctoral dissertation, State U.
of New York at Buffalo, 1971.

_____. "Integrated Schools in Antebellum
Boston. The Implications of the Black Victory." Urban Education 6(Jl-O, 1971):131-
145.

_____. "Prince Saunders: An Instance of
Social Mobility Among Antebellum New England
Blacks." Journal of Negro History 60(O,
1975):526-535.

_____. "Salem's Antebellum Black Community:
Seedbed of the School Integration Movement."
Essex Institute Historical Collection 108
(Ap, 1972).

White, Joan Vida. "The Impact of Women on Desegregation in Boston." Doctoral dissertation, Boston U., 1977. Univ. Microfilms
Order No. 77-32789.

White, Kevin H. "Busing in Boston--A Belea-
guered Mayor Speaks Out." U.S. News and
World Report, Ap 7, 1975.

Whyte, William Foote. "Race Conflicts in the
North End of Boston." New England Quarterly 12(1939):623-642. [Since 1860]

Winkler, Karen J. "Desegregation in Boston:
Colleges, Schools Pair Off." Chronicle of
Higher Education, N 17, 1975.

Witkin, James B. "In the Eye of the Storm.
With Little White Schoolhouses, South Boston
Teaches Itself." Harvard Crimson, N 22,
1974.

Woods, Dan. "A Brief History of Operation
Exodus." Integrated Education, O-N, 1966.
[Boston]

Worsham, James. "Busing in Boston. Desegregating the Nation's Oldest Public School
System." Civil Rights Digest 7(Winter,
1975):3-9.

Wright, Joanne and others. Report on a Survey
on Desegregation Service Needs in Boston's
Black Community, O, 1975. ERIC ED 123 281.

"Young Black Woman Seeks Spot on Boston School
Committee." Muhammad Speaks, O 22, 1971.
[Mrs. Patricia Bonner-Lyons]

Michigan

Abbott, Ralph and others. Process and Impact
Evaluation. The Detroit 4-H Program. East
Lansing, MI: College of Urban Development,
Michigan State U., O, 1976.

Aberbach, Joel D., and Walker, Jack L. Race in
the City. Political Trust and Public Policy
in the New Urbana System. Boston: Little,
Brown, 1973.

Agócs, Carol. "Ethnic Neighborhoods in City
and Suburbs: Metropolitan Detroit, 1940-
1970." Doctoral dissertation, Wayne State
U., 1977. Univ. Microfilms Order No. 7805151.

Almy, Timothy A., and Hahn, Harlan. "Perceptions
of Educational Conflict. The Teacher Strike
Controversy in Detroit." Education and Urban Society 3(Ag, 1971):440-452. [1966]

Anderson, Marc B. "Racial Discrimination in
Detroit: A Spatial Analysis of Racism."
Master's thesis, Wayne State U., 1969.

Apprenticeship Study Committee. Minority Participation in Kalamazoo's Apprenticeship
Training Programs: Assessments and Recommendations. Kalamazoo, MI: W. E. Upjohn Institute for Employment Research, 1970.

Attitudes Toward the Cluster Plan in the Lansing,
Michigan Public Schools. Port Huron, MI:
Ned S. Hubbell and Associates, 1975.

Auld, Ute. "City's Desegregation Highlight
Timetable Offered." Lansing State Journal,
N 30, 1975. [Lansing]

_____. "Lansing Busing Meets Roadblock."
Michigan Education Journal, D, 1966.

Bakke, Birger. "Detroit Schools: Mirror of a
City." In Robert J. Havighurst, Frank L.
Smith, and David E. Wilder, A Profile of the
Large-City High School, Chapter 11. Washing-
ton, DC: National Association of Secondary
School Principals, N, 1970.

Banner, Melvin E. The Black Pioneer in Michigan.
Vol. I: Flint and Genesee County. Midland,
MI: Pendell, 1973.

Beck, John. "State Aid and Equal Education Opportunity in Michigan." Doctoral dissertation, Michigan State U., 1977.

Belcher, Jerry. "School Busing: How Far Has
It Come?" Los Angeles Times, D 15, 1975.
[Pontiac]

Benjamin, Richard C., and Dominguez, Gilberto H.
The Cluster Program. An Audited Summary of
the Impact on the Reading and Math Skills of
the Students Involved. Lansing, MI: Lansing
School District, Ag, 1975.

"Blacks Unite to Defend Lansing Frame-Up Victims."
Muhammad Speaks, Jl 16, 1971.

Boggs, Grace, and Boggs, James. "Detroit: Birth of a Nation." National Guardian, O 7, 1967.

Boger, Robert P., Hervey, Sarah D., and Hamachek, Joan. Heterogeneous vs. Homogeneous Social Class Groupings of Preschool Children in Head Start Classrooms. East Lansing, MI: Head Start Evaluation and Research Center, Michigan State U., F, 1969. [Lansing]

Bouma, Donald H. "An Analysis of the Power Position of the Real Estate Board in Grand Rapids." Doctoral dissertation, U. of Chicago, 1952.

Boykin, Ulysses W. A Handbook on the Detroit Negro. Detroit, 1943.

Bronder, L. "Detroit Metropolitan School Finance--The Revenue Problem." National Tax Journal, D, 1966.

Brunn, S. D., and Hoffman, W. L. "The Spatial Response of Negroes and Whites toward Open Housing: The Flint Referendum." Annals of the Association of American Geographers 60 (1970):18-36.

Buechler, Ernest Peter. "An Analysis of the Function of the Community Council in Region One Elementary Schools in Detroit." Doctoral dissertation, Wayne State U., 1974. Univ. Microfilms Order No. 74-29,789.

Bunge, William. Fitzgerald: Geography of a Revolution. Morristown, NJ: General Learning Corporation, 1972. [Racial integration in Detroit]

_____. "The Human Geography of Detroit." In R. A. Roberge, La crise urbaine: A Challenge to Geographers, pp. 49-69. U. of Ottawa Press, 1974.

Butler, Broadus N. "Integration of Detroit Public Schools: Past Problems and Present Promise." Michigan Challenge (Michigan State Chamber of Commerce), Je, 1968.

Canady, Hortense G. Cooperative Community Efforts Leading to Equal Educational Opportunity in the Lansing School District, with Special Emphasis on the Role of the National Association for the Advancement of Colored People, 1976. ERIC ED 121 909.

Carlson, Glen E. "The Negro in the Industries of Detroit." Doctoral dissertation, U. of Michigan, 1929.

Carrigan, Patricia M. School Desegregation via Compulsory Public Transfer. Early Effects on Elementary School Children, S, 1969. ERIC ED 036 597. [Ann Arbor]

Chesler, Mark A., and Wissman, Margaret. Teacher Reactions to School Desegregation Preparations and Processes: A Case Study. Ann Arbor, MI: Institute for Social Research, U. of Michigan, Ja, 1968.

Chesler, Mark A., Wittes, Simon, and Radin, Norma. "What Happens When Northern Schools Desegregate." American Education, Je, 1968. [Ypsilanti, MI]

Civic Affairs Research, Inc. Anatomy of a Community: Characteristics of the People of the Muskegon County Area, 1968. Civic Affairs Research, Inc., 931 Third Street, Muskegon, MI 49440.

Claspy, Everett. The Negro in Southwestern Michigan: Negroes in the North in a Rural Environment, 1968. The Author, 440 East Division Street, Dowagiac, MI.

Cleage, Albert B., Jr. "Inner City Parents' Program for Quality Education in Detroit." Integrated Education, Ag-S, 1967.

Clinansmith, Michael S. "The Black Legion: Hooded Americanism in Michigan." Michigan History 55(Fall, 1971).

Coates, William D. Kalamazoo Desegregation Study--Phase I, 1971. ERIC ED 055 134.

Colasanto, Diane. "The Prospects for Racial Integration in Neighborhoods: An Analysis of Residential Preferences in the Detroit Metropolitan Area." Doctoral dissertation, U. of Michigan, 1977.

Conheim, Maryanne. "Busing War Winds Down in Pontiac." Detroit Free Press, F 20, 1972.

Corner, Phil. "The White Minority in Our Schools." Detroit News, N 28, 1976. [Cass Technical High School, Detroit]

Cosseboom, Kathy. Grosse Pointe, Michigan: Race Against Race. East Lansing, MI: Michigan State U. Press, 1972.

Crowell, Erbin, Jr. "Anti Racism (The New Movement)." Civil Rights Digest, Winter, 1969. [About People Against Racism (PAR) in Detroit]

Cunningham, Luvern. "The Education Task Force in Detroit." Inequality in Education 15(N, 1973):45-52.

Cushman, Edward, and Keith, Damon. Report of the Detroit High School Study Commission. Detroit: Detroit Public Schools, 1968.

D.X, Charles. "White Racists Stir Violence in Mt. Clemens, Michigan." Muhammad Speaks, F 12, 1971.

Dancy, John C. Sand Against the Wind. The Memoirs of John C. Dancy. Detroit: Wayne State U. Press, 1966. [By the longtime director of the Urban League of Detroit]

Darden, Joe T. "The Residential Segregation of Blacks in Detroit, 1960-1970." International Journal of Comparative Sociology 17(1976): 84-91.

_____. The Residential Segregation of Blacks in Flint [Michigan] 1950-1970, rev. ed., Je, 1976. ERIC ED 125 965.

_____. The Residential Segregation of Blacks in the Suburbs: The Michigan Example, Ap, 1976. ERIC ED 123 167.

_____. "Residential Segregation of Blacks in the Suburbs: The Michigan Example." Geographical Survey 5(J1, 1976):7-16.

Denby, Charles (Matthew Ward). Indignant Heart. A Black Worker's Journal. Boston: South End Press, 1978. [Detroit]

Dennis, Benjamin Gumbu. "The Level of Formal and Informal Integration of Negroes in the External Community of Lansing, Michigan." Doctoral dissertation, Michigan State U., 1965. Univ. Microfilms Order No. 65-8378.

Department of Research and Evaluation. School Staff Attitudes and Job Satisfaction. Pontiac, MI: School District of the City of Pontiac, F, 1975.

_____. Secondary Student Attitudes and Satisfaction with School. Pontiac, MI: School District of the City of Pontiac, F, 1975.

DeRamus, Betty. "Detroit Revisited." Negro Digest, J1, 1968. [The end of the Detroit Federation for Self-Determination]

Deskins, Donald R., Jr. "Negro Settlement in Ann Arbor." Master's thesis, U. of Michigan, 1963.

_____. "Race, Residence, and Workplace in Detroit, 1880 to 1965." Economic Geography 48(Ja, 1972):79-94.

_____. "Residential Mobility of Negro Occupational Groups in Detroit 1837-1965." Doctoral dissertation, U. of Michigan, 1971. Univ. Microfilms Order No. 71-23736.

"Detroit Decentralization Law." Integrated Education: RACE AND SCHOOLS 7(N-D, 1969):37-38.

Detroit Public Schools. "What About Us? Our Textbooks Do Not Meet Our Needs." Educational Product Report 3(1969):12-39.

"Detroit. Some Post-Riot Progress, But Tension Continues." Black Enterprise, Mr, 1972. [Black economic prospects in Detroit]

Dietsch, Robert W. "Peace in Pontiac [Michigan]." New Republic, Mr 25, 1972.

Dimond, Paul R. "Northern Segregation--In Detroit, De Jure." Inequality in Education 10 (D, 1971):7-9.

Document. "The Detroit Lawsuit Against Michigan." Integrated Education, Mr-Ap, 1968.

Document. "The Pontiac School Decision." Integrated Education 8(J1-Ag, 1970):31-34.

Drachler, Norman. The Impact of the U.S. Supreme Court 1954 "Brown" Decision Upon Education in Detroit, J1 1, 1977. ERIC ED 147 931.

Drummond, Bill. "Desegregation, Bilingual Education Collide in Detroit." Los Angeles Times, N 28, 1977.

Efthim, Helen. "Pontiac Desegregation: Myth and Reality." Urban Review 8(Summer, 1975):155-159.

Engelhardt and Engelhardt, Inc. School Building Needs. School District of the City of Benton Harbor, Michigan. Purdy Station, Westchester County, New York: Engelhardt and Engelhardt, Inc., My, 1970.

Ethnic Communities of Greater Detroit. Detroit: Montieth College, Wayne State U., 1970. [Also contains essays of wider geographical application]

Ewen, Lynda Ann. Corporate Power and Urban Crisis in Detroit. Princeton, NJ: Princeton U. Press, 1977.

Farley, Reynolds. "Population Trends and School Segregation in the Detroit Metropolitan Area." Wayne Law Review 21(1975):882-889.

Farrell, Walter. "Intraurban Mobility and Environmental Perception in a Black Middle-Class Ghetto: A Case Study in Flint, Michigan." Doctoral dissertation, Michigan State U., 1974.

Fields, Harold B. "Free Negroes in Cass County Before the Civil War." Michigan History 44 (D, 1960):375-383.

Fields, James M. "Perceptions of Others' Opinions in a City and Its Neighborhoods." Doctoral dissertation, U. of Michigan, 1971. [Detroit]

Flint, Jerry M. "Black Students at Former White School in Detroit Learn Racial Pride Along With 3 R's." New York Times, My 16, 1971. [Hampton Intermediate School]

Formisano, Ronald P. "The Edge of Caste: Colored Suffrage in Michigan, 1827-1861." Michigan History 56(Spring, 1972):19-41.

Fort, Edward B. "A Black Superintendent Talks About Being a Black Superintendent." Educational Product Report, My, 1969. [Inkster]

Fox, Noel P. "The Kalamazoo School Decision." Integrated Education 11(J1-O, 1973):72-84.

Georgakas, Dan, and Surkin, Marvin. Detroit: I Do Mind Dying (A Study in Urban Revolution). New York: St. Martin's Press, 1975.

Geschwender, James A. Class, Race, and Worker Insurgency. The League of Revolutionary Black Workers. New York: Cambridge U. Press, 1977. [Detroit]

Gordon, Leonard. A City in Racial Crisis: The Case of Detroit Pre and Post the 1967 Riot. Dubuque, IO: Brown, 1971.

_____. "The Carver-Oak Park Merger." Integrated Education, Je-J1, 1965.

_____. "Suburban Consensus Formation and the Race Issue." Journal of Conflict Resolution 13(D, 1969):550-556.

Gracie, David. "The Walkout at Northern High." New University Thought, Spring, 1967. [Boycott at Northern High School, Detroit, Ap, 1966]

Grant, William. "Bilingual Program Snags in State Schools." Detroit Free Press, Ja 8, 1978.

_____. "Community Control vs. Integration—the Case of Detroit." Public Interest, Summer, 1971.

_____. "Detroit." Integrateducation 15(N-D, 1977):2-4.

_____. "The Detroit School Case: An Historical Overview." Wayne Law Review 21(Mr, 1975).

_____. "Detroit Pupils Test Scores Inching Up." Detroit Free Press, F 28, 1972.

_____. "Flint." Integrateducation 15(N-D, 1977):18-19.

_____. "Lansing Students Achieving Better After Integration." Detroit Free Press, Ag 10, 1975.

_____. "Letter from Detroit: The Courts and the Schools." Urban Review 8(Summer, 1975): 145-152.

_____. "'Where Did Everyone Go To?'" New Republic 163(S 5-12, 1970):20. [Detroit]

_____. "Ypsilanti Busing Plan Goes Smoothly." Detroit Free Press, N 21, 1976.

Grant, William, Bowles, Billy, and Crutchfield, Jim. "Busing Has Gone Well, Most Believe." Detroit Free Press, Je 14, 1976. [Detroit]

Graves, Helen Mataya. "New Detroit Committee/New Detroit, Incorporated. A Case Study of an Urban Coalition, 1967-1972." Doctoral dissertation, Wayne State U., 1975. Univ. Microfilms Order No. 76-10,950.

Green, Robert L. De Facto Segregation in Benton Harbor. Detroit: Michigan Conference of the NAACP, 1967.

Greenberg, Saardia R., and Johnston, R. E. "Parent Demands and School Decentralization in Detroit." Urban and Social Change Review 6(F, 1972):16-21.

Gregory, Karl D. "The Walkout: Symptom of Dying Inner Schools." New University Thought, Spring, 1967. [Detroit]

Griffore, Robert J., Simmons, Cassandra A., Hebert, Patricia L., and Smith, Sylvia C. "Lansing, Michigan." Integrateducation 15 (N-D, 1977):28-32.

Guthrie, James W., Kleindorfer, George B., Levin, Henry M., and Stout, Robert. Schools and Inequality: A Study of the Relationships Between Social Status, School Services, and Post-School Opportunity in the State of Michigan. Washington, DC: National Urban Coalition, S, 1969.

The Guy Who Controls Your Future (Handbook on Decentralization), 1970. Black Star Printing, 8824 Fenkell, Detroit, MI 48238. [On black community control of schools in Michigan]

Haessler, Lucy. "Pontiac Busing." New Republic, O 23, 1971. [letter]

Haggstrom, Warren C. "Self-Esteem and Other Characteristics of Residentially Desegregated Negroes." Unpublished doctoral dissertation, U. of Michigan, 1962. Dissertation Abstracts, XXIII, 1963, p. 3007.

Hain, Elwood. "Sealing Off the City: School Desegregation in Detroit." In Howard I. Kalodner and James J. Fishman, Limits of Justice, The Courts' Role in School Desegregation, pp. 223-308. Cambridge, MA: Ballinger, 1978.

Hardiman, Clayton and others. Black Life in Muskegon. Muskegon, MI: Muskegon Chronicle, 1977. [Reprint of a series of articles]

Hartman, David W. The Development of Detroit's Cass Corridor: 1850-1975. Detroit: Ethnic Studies Division, Center for Urban Studies, Wayne State U., N, 1975.

_____ (ed.). Immigrants and Migrants: The Detroit Ethnic Experience. Detroit: New U. Thought Publishing Co., 1974. (Available from Wayne State U. Bookstore, Detroit, MI)

Hesslink, George K. Black Neighbors. Negroes in a Northern Rural Community. Indianapolis: Bobbs-Merrill, 1968. [Cass County]

Hines, Edward R. and others. State Policy Making for the Public Schools of Michigan, Je, 1974. ERIC ED 094 469.

Holstege, Henry. "Conflict and Change in Negro-White Relations in Great Falls." Doctoral dissertation, Michigan State U., 1966. [Grand Rapids]

Hooyman, Nancy, and Musick, John. "Pontiac: How People Respond to Busing." Dissent 20 (Spring, 1973):210-216.

Houtman, Loren Henry. "Response of Detroit Public Schools to Immigrant Groups." Doctoral dissertation, Michigan State U., 1965. Univ. Microfilms Order No. 66-391.

Jenkins, Jeffrey. "Historical Analysis of Two Selected School Districts that Have Undergone Desegregation." Doctoral dissertation, U. of Michigan, 1976. [Kalamazoo]

Jenkins, Michael A., and Shepherd, John W. "Decentralizing High School Administration in Detroit: An Evaluation of Alternative Strategies of Political Control." Economic Geography 48(Ja, 1972):95-106.

Johnson, Mrs. Murray, and McCabe, Mrs. Irene. "Transcript of the David Frost Show." In U.S. Congress, 92nd, 1st Session, Senate, Select Committee on Equal Educational Opportunity, Equal Educational Opportunity--1971, Part 19C--Equal Educational Opportunity in Michigan: Appendixes, pp. 10025-10034. Washington, DC: GPO, 1972. [Pontiac]

Jones, Michael John. "The Pattern and Process of Residential Growth in Ann Arbor, 1920-1970." Master's thesis, Wayne State U., 1975.

Joyce, Frank. "Change in the Ranks." Freedom North, I, Nos. 4 and 5, 1965. [Evolution of the Northern Student Movement program in Detroit]

Kamii, Constance K. "Socio-economic Class Differences in the Preschool Socio-economic Class Differences in the Preschool Socialization Practices of Negro Mothers." Doctoral dissertation, U. of Michigan, 1965. Univ. Microfilms Order No. 66-5089.

Kamii, Constance K., and Radin, Norma L. "Class Differences in the Socialization Practices of Negro Mothers." Journal of Marriage and the Family, My, 1967. [Ypsilanti and Ann Arbor]

Katzenmeyer, William G. "Social Interaction and Differences in Intelligence Test Performance of Negro and White Elementary School Pupils." Doctoral dissertation, Duke U., 1962. Dissertation Abstracts, XXIV, 1963, p. 1905. [Jackson]

Katzman, David M. Before the Ghetto. Black Detroit in the Nineteenth Century. Urbana, IL: U. of Illinois Press, 1973.

_____. "Black Slavery in Michigan." Midcontinent American Studies Journal 11(Fall, 1970): 56-66.

Kearney, C. Philip. "The Politics of Educational Assessment in Michigan." Planning Changing 1(J1, 1970):71-82.

Kleeman, Richard P. "New Jersey School Makes Integration Work." Minneapolis Tribune, O 28, 1970. [Pontiac and Ferndale]

Klemanski, Mary. "Perhaps We Should Take a Coward's Way Out." Legal Advertiser and Ferndale Gazette-Times, O 8, 1970. [School segregation in Ferndale]

Klitgaard, Robert E., and Hall, George R. A Statistical Search for Unusually Effective Schools. Santa Monica, CA: Rand, 1973.

Knuth, Clarence P. "Early Negro Migration and Current Residential Patterns in Southwestern Michigan." Doctoral dissertation, U. of Michigan, 1969. Univ. Microfilms Order No. 70-4119.

Lackamp, Leo B. "University of Detroit High School: A Case History." In Catholic Schools and Racial Integration: Perspectives, Directions, Models, pp. 41-47. Washington, DC: National Catholic Conference for Interracial Justice, 1977.

Lahti, P. C. "The Calumet [Michigan] Finnish Public School Ceases Operations." (In Finnish) Amerikan Uutiset, Mr 2, 1906.

Lawton, Stephen B. "Measurement of School Segregation in Detroit." Education and Urban Society 4(Ag, 1972):403-421.

Lawton, Stephen B., and Curtner, G. Black Schools: A Descriptive Analysis of School Attendance Patterns in Detroit. Toronto: Ontario Institute for Studies in Education, 1972.

Leggett, John C. Class, Race, and Labor. Working-Class Consciousness in Detroit. New York: Oxford, 1968.

Levine, David Allan. Internal Combustion. The Races in Detroit, 1915-1926. Westport, CT: Greenwood Press, 1975.

Lewis, Peirce F. "Impact of Negro Migration on the Electoral Geography of Flint, Michigan, 1932-1962: A Cartographic Analysis." Annals of the Association of American Geographers 55 (Mr, 1965):1-25.

Lezotte, Lawrence W. Voter Behavior as an Expression of Community Attitudes Toward Desegregation, Ap, 1976. ERIC ED 126 193. [Lansing]

Lindstrom, Duane. Civil Rights and the Housing and Community Development Act of 1974... Washington, DC: U.S. Commission on Civil Rights, 1976.

Lowinger, Paul, Darrow, Charlotte, and Huige, Frida. "Case Study of the Detroit Uprising [of July, 1967]. The Troops and the Leaders." Archives of General Psychiatry, J1, 1969.

Lucas, Louis. "A Letter from a Lawyer." Integrated Education (N-D, 1971):48-50. [Detroit]

McIntyre, Bruce H. "Pontiac, Michigan, 5 Years
Later." Belleville, Illinois News Democrat,
N 17, 1975.

McQueen, Albert J. "A Study of Anomie Among
Lower Class Negro Migrants." Doctoral dissertation, U. of Michigan, 1959. Univ. Microfilms Order No. 59-4953. [Ypsilanti]

Mandel, Allan S. Resource Distribution Inside
School Districts. Lexington, MA: Lexington
Books, 1975.

Marger, Martin. "Ethnic Penetration of the
Elite Structure of Detroit, 1900-1950."
Doctoral dissertation, Michigan State U.,
1973. Univ. Microfilms Order No. 73-29742.

Market Opinion Research. Survey on Educational
Accountability for the Michigan State Depart-
ment of Education, My, 1974. Market Opinion
Research, 28W Adams Street, Detroit, MI 48226.

Marrs, John D. Attitudes Toward the Cluster Plan
in the Lansing, Michigan, Public Schools, Ap,
1976. ERIC ED 120 960.

May, Clifford B. "The Forced Attainment of Two
Culturally Differing School Districts: A
Problematic Analysis." Doctoral dissertation,
Wayne State U., 1963. Univ. Microfilms Order
No. 64-5105. [Oak Park]

Mayor's Committee for Human Resources Develop-
ment. A Study to Determine the Relationship
Between Transportation Accessibility and Un-
employment in the Inner City of Detroit.
COM-73-10135. Springfield, VA; National
Technical Information Service, N, 1972.

Mayor's Interracial Committee. The Negro in
Detroit. Twelve parts. Detroit, 1926.

Metropolitan Integration Study Committee of the
Leagues of Women Voters in the Detroit Metro-
politan Area. School Desegregation. Legal
Precedents, Methods, Effects, D, 1972. League
of Women Voters of Michigan, 202 Mill Street,
Lansing, MI 48933.

Meyer, Douglas Kermit. "The Changing Negro Residential Patterns in Lansing, Michigan 1850-
1969." Doctoral dissertation, Michigan State
U., 1970. Univ. Microfilms Order No. 70-20499.

_____. "Changing Negro Residential Patterns in
Michigan Capitol, 1915-1970." Michigan History 56(Summer, 1972):157-167.

_____. "Evolution of a Permanent Negro Commun-
ity in Lansing." Michigan History 55(Summer,
1971):141-154.

Meyer, Philip. "Busing. A Free Press Survey of
a Primary Issue: How Blacks and Whites See
It--And Why." Detroit Free Press, My 7, 1972.
[Poll in Detroit metropolitan area]

Michigan Civil Rights Commission. Flint Southwestern Community High School. A Report of
Fact Finding. Detroit: The Commission, Ja
26, 1971.

_____. Report and Recommendations from a
Public Inquiry into the Status of Race Relations in the City of Pontiac, Michigan. Lansing, MI: Civil Rights Commission, 1968.

_____. Report and Recommendations Into the
Status of Race Relations in the City of
Kalamazoo. Lansing, MI: The Commission,
1969.

_____. Report of Findings and Recommendations
from a Public Hearing on the Role of State
Agencies in School Desegregation. Lansing,
MI: The Commission, Jl 29, 1975.

_____. Saginaw Public Schools. Part I: A
Report of Findings and Recommendations. Part
II: Saginaw High School 1970-71. An Analysis
and Interpretation of School Conflict.
Detroit, MI: The Commission, My, 1971.
[Released Jl 29, 1971]

Michigan. Department of Education. Bureau of
Research. Distribution of Educational
Performance and Related Factors in Michigan.
Lansing, MI: The Department, 1970.

_____. Levels of Educational Performance and
Related Factors in Michigan. Lansing, MI:
State Department of Education, 1970.

Michigan Department of Education. Preliminary
Analysis of the 1968-69 School Racial Census.
Lansing, MI: State Department of Education,
Mr, 1969.

Miles, Norman K. "Home At Last: Urbanization of
Black Migrants in Detroit, 1916-1929."
Doctoral dissertation, U. of Michigan, 1978.
Univ. Microfilms Order No. 7822966.

Minority Participation in Kalamazoo's Apprentice-
ship Training Programs: Assessments and
Recommendations. Kalamazoo, MI: Upjohn
(W. E.) Inst. for Employment Research, D,
1970, 71 pp. Available from W. E. Upjohn
Institute for Employment Research, 300 South
Westnedge Avenue, Kalamazoo, MI 49007. ERIC
ED 062 626.

Moehlman, Arthur B. Public Education in Detroit.
Bloomington, IL: n.p., 1925.

Moody, Charles, Sr., Vergon, Charles, and Hale,
Judith. "Segregation in Michigan Public
Education." Integrateducation 16(N-D, 1978):
31-38.

Moore, Charles H., and Johnston, Ray E. "School
Decentralization, Community Control, and the
Politics of Public Education." Urban Affairs
Quarterly 6(Je, 1971):421-446. [Detroit]

Moriarity, Barry M. "Socioeconomic Status and
Residential Locational Choice." Environment
and Behavior 6(D, 1974):448-469. [Lansing]

Murphy, Jerome T., and Cohen, David K. "Accountability in Education--the Michigan Experience." Public Interest 36(Summer, 1974):53-81

Myers, Phyllis. "From Auto City to School Bus City." City 6(Summer, 1972). [Detroit]

National Commission on Professional Rights and Responsibilities. Detroit, Michigan. A Study of Barriers to Equal Education Opportunity in a Large City. Washington, DC: National Education Association, Mr, 1967.

The Negro in Detroit. Prepared for the Mayor's Inter-racial Committee by a Special Survey Staff Under the General Direction of the Detroit Bureau of Governmental Research, Inc. Detroit, MI: 1926, 12 vols.

Negroes in Kalamazoo. Lansing, MI: Wagenvoord and Co., 1945.

"The New Breed of Black Realtors." Black Enterprise 4(F, 1974):33-35, 50. [Detroit]

Office of Planning Coordination. Educational Reform in Michigan. Lansing, MI: State of Michigan, F, 1970.

Olsen, Marvin. "Alienation and Political Opinions." Public Opinion Quarterly, Summer, 1965. [Analyzes Detroit data on relation of alienation to school integration]

Opinion Survey. Response Tables. Port Huron, MI: Ned S. Hubbell and Associates, 1975. [Lansing public schools]

Osborne, Donald L. "Race, Sex, Achievement, and Suspension." Urban Education 12(O, 1977): 345-347. [Kalamazoo]

"The Parish and School Desegregation." Commitment, Jl, 1977. [Detroit]

Pease, John. "Desegregation in the Midwest: The Case of Kalamazoo." In Our Children's Burden. Edited by Raymond W. Mack. New York: Random House, 1968.

Peloso, Tom. "The Growth of Civil Rights Agencies." In U.S. Commission on Civil Rights, Making Public Employment a Model of Equal Opportunity, pp. 21-33. Washington, DC: U.S. Commission on Civil Rights, 1975. [Michigan Civil Rights Commission]

Phillips, Romeo E. "Student Activities and Self-Concept." Journal of Negro Education, Winter, 1969. [Suburban Detroit school]

Pilo, Marvin R. "A Tale of Two Cities. The Application of Models of School Decentralization to the Cases of New York City and Detroit." Education and Urban Society 7 (Ag, 1975):393-411.

Pontiac Citizens Study Committee. Equality of Educational Opportunity. Pontiac, MI: Board of Education, Je, 1968.

Radin, Norma, and Glasser, Paul. "The Use of Parental Attitude Questionnaires with Culturally Disadvantaged Families." Journal of Marriage and the Family, Ag, 1965. [Negro mothers of children in preschool for culturally disadvantaged. Ypsilanti]

Ravitz, Mel. "Unequal School Progress in Detroit." Integrated Education, Je, 1963.

Reitzes, Dietrich C. "The Detroit Experience in the National Perspective." American Journal of Public Health, Ap, 1963. [Problem of educational and other discrimination leading to shortage of Negro medical personnel]

Rist, Ray C. The Quest for Autonomy: A Socio-Historical Study of Black Revolt in Detroit. Los Angeles: Center for Afro-American Studies, U. of California, 1972.

Rockaway, Robert. "The Detroit Jewish Ghetto Before World War I." Michigan History 52 (Spring, 1968).

Rockaway, R. "Ethnic Conflict in an Urban Environment: The German and Russian Jew in Detroit, 1881-1914." American Jewish Historical Quarterly 60(D, 1970):133-150.

Root, James D. "Socioeconomic Variation and Residential Distribution: A Case Study of Kalamazoo." Master's thesis, Western Michigan U., 1972.

Roth, Stephen J. "The Detroit School Decision." Integrated Education 9(N-D, 1971):3-8.

Rupley, Jerry, McGovney, Marsha, and Rumbaugh, Stanley. School Racial-Ethnic Census, 1970-71 and 1971-72. Lansing, MI: State Department of Education, 1973.

Rural Poverty in Michigan. East Lansing, MI: Michigan State U., Rural Manpower Center, N, 1970, 73 pp. ERIC ED 044 231.

Russell, Ernest L. "A Study of Change and Conflict in Court Ordered Busing as a Means of School Desegregation in an Urban City School District." Doctoral dissertation, Michigan State U., 1978. Univ. Microfilms Order No. 7900741. [Pontiac, MI]

Ryder, Jack M. "A Study of Personnel Practices and Policies with Relation to Utilization of Teachers from the Negro Minority Group in Certain Michigan Public School Districts." Doctoral dissertation, Michigan State U., 1962.

Scharffe, William G. "Staff Integration in the Saginaw Public Schools." Phi Delta Kappan 60(Ja, 1979):361-364.

Schuman, Howard. "Racial Attitude Change: Are Whites Really More Liberal? Blacks Aren't Impressed." Psychology Today 8(S, 1974):82-86. [Detroit]

Schuman, Howard, and Converse, Jean M. "The Effects of Black and White Interviewers on Black Responses in 1968." Public Opinion Quarterly 35(Spring, 1971):44-68. [Detroit]

Scott, Wayne. A Study of Bussed and Non-Bussed Children. Grand Rapids, MI: Grand Rapids Public Schools, Je, 1970.

Second Annual Conference of Michigan Foundations. Michigan's Minorities at the Mid-Seventies: Indians, Blacks, Chicanos. Flint, MI: Charles Stewart Mott Foundation, 1974.

Sengstock, Mary Catherine. "Maintenance of Social Interaction Patterns in an Ethnic Group." Doctoral dissertation, U. of Washington, 1967. [Iraqui Chaldeans in Detroit]

Serlin, Steven. "The Negroes in Detroit in the 1880's and Early 1890's." Senior honors thesis, U. of Michigan, 1968.

Serrin, William. "The Most Hated Man in Michigan." Saturday Review 55(Ag 26, 1972): 13-15. [U.S. District Judge Stephen J. Roth]

_____. "They Don't Burn Buses Anymore in Pontiac Michigan ." Saturday Review 55 (Je 24, 1972):7-12.

Sherrill, Robert. "What Grand Rapids Did for Jerry Ford--and Vice Versa." New York Times Magazine, O 20, 1974.

Shipstead, Patrick E. New Perspectives on American Politics: A Report from Michigan on the Busing Issue. Princeton, NJ: Woodrow Wilson School of Public and International Affairs, Princeton U., 1973.

Shuy, Roger W. A Study of Social Dialects in Detroit, Final Report, 1968. ERIC ED 022 187.

Simmons, Cassandra A. "An Interview with Carl Candoli." Integrateducation 15(N-D, 1977): 32-35. [Lansing]

Sinclair, Robert. "Ghetto Expansion and the Urban Landscape: A Case Study of Detroit." Wiener Geographical Schriften 46-48(1976): 191-202.

Sinclair, Robert, and Thompson, Bryan. Metropolitan Detroit: An Anatomy of Social Change. Cambridge, MA: Ballinger, 1977.

Singer, Benjamin D., Osborn, Richard W., and Geschwender, James A. Black Rioters: A Study of Social Factors and Communication in the Detroit Riot. Lexington, MA: Heath Lexington, 1970.

Slawski, Edward J. "Pontiac Parents. For Busing or Integration? Education and Urban Society 8(Ag, 1976):477-498.

Slawski, Edward J., and Scherer, Jacqueline. "The Rhetoric of Concern: Trust and Control in an Urban Desegregated School." Anthropology & Education Quarterly 9(Winter, 1978):258-271. [Pontiac]

Slemer, William Carl. "Perceptions of Job Satisfaction Among Junior High School Teachers Confronted with a Transfer Under the Three-Year Transfer Rule in Detroit." Doctoral dissertation, Wayne State U., 1967.

Smith, Ralph V. "Behind the Riots." American Education, N, 1967. [Detroit]

Smith, Ralph V., Flory, Stanley E., Bashshur, Rashid L., and Shannon, Gary W. Community Integration and Racial Integration in the Detroit Area: An Ecological Analysis. Ypsilanti, MI: Eastern Michigan U., S 8, 1967.

Smith, Vern E. "Tragedy at Beecher High." Ebony 27(O, 1972):154-160. [The suicide of black teacher Paul L. Cabell, Jr., Beecher High School, near Flint, MI]

Spatta, C. L. "Regionalization: One Adjustment to Racial Imbalance in the Ann Arbor Schools." Master's thesis, U. of Michigan, 1968.

Stark, Jay I. "The Pattern of Resource Allocation in Education: The Detroit Public Schools 1940 to 1960." Doctoral dissertation, U. of Michigan, 1969.

Steele, Marily, Langs, Walter, Jr. and others. (eds.). Michigan's Minorities at the Mid-Seventies: Indians, Blacks, Chicanos. Flint, MI: Charles Stewart Mott Foundation, 1974.

Stephenson, William W., Jr. "Integration of the Detroit Public School System During the Period, 1839-1869." Negro History Bulletin 26(1962-1963):23-28.

Stevens, William K. "5 Years of Busing in Pontiac, Mich.: Gains and Losses." New York Times, D 3, 1975.

_____. "U.S. Pressing School Integration in a Detroit Suburb." New York Times, Je 13, 1975. [Ferndale]

Straus, Kathleen, and Schrager, Scott. "Pro-Detroit: A Pragmatic Approach to Desegregation." Theory Into Practice 17(F, 1978): 86-90.

Strozier, Geraldine. "Finding their Roots. Black Groups in Judaism." Detroit Free Press, Ap 1, 1977. [Congregation Isek Abraham, Detroit]

Stuart, Reginald. "Parents Seeking Voice in Schools." Race Relations Reporter 2(My 17, 1971):6-8. [Detroit]

Sullivan, Vernon [pseud.]. "From Detroit:
The Schools Mess--Where Do We Stand?
Community, Spring-Summer, 1970.

Teachman, Gerard Wesley. "Student Rights and
the Detroit Public Schools." Doctoral
dissertation, Wayne State U., 1978. Univ.
Microfilms Order No. 7816091.

Thomas, J. Alan. School Finance and Educational
Opportunity in Michigan. Lansing, MI:
Michigan Department of Education, 1968.

Thomas, Richard. "The Detroit Urban League:
1916-1923." Michigan History 60(Winter,
1976):315-338.

Thomas, Richard Walter. "From Peasant to
Proletarian: The Formation and Organization
of the Black Industrial Working Class in
Detroit, 1915-1945." Doctoral dissertation,
U. of Michigan, 1976. Univ. Microfilms
Order No. 76-19258.

Thompson, Eugene W. and others. A Study of
Student Achievement Involving the Consideration of Racial and Socioeconomic Characteristics, n.d. ERIC ED 159 188. [Ann Arbor]

Thrun, Caroline W. "School Segregation in
Michigan." Michigan History 38(Mr, 1954):
1-23.

Treml, William B. "Desegregation: How Ypsilanti
Made It Work." Ann Arbor News, Jl 11, 1977.

12X, John. "The Children Nobody Cares About."
Muhammad Speaks, Ja 14, 1972. [Wayne
County Youth Home, Detroit]

U.S. Commission on Civil Rights. Hearings...
Held in Detroit, Michigan, December 14-15,
1960. Washington, DC: GPO, 1961.

_____. "Pontiac, Michigan." In School Deseg-
regation in Ten Communities, pp. 36-68.
Washington, DC: GPO, Je, 1973.

_____. School Desegregation in Kalamazoo,
Michigan. Washington, DC: The Commission,
Ap, 1977.

U.S. Congress, 92nd, 1st session, Senate,
Select Committee on Equal Educational
Opportunity. Equal Educational Opportunity--
1971. Part 19A-1-Equal Educational Opportun-
ity in Michigan: U.S. Senate Select
Committee on Equal Educational Opportunity
Staff Charts on Michigan's Assessment
Program. Washington, DC: GPO, 1972.

_____. Equal Educational Opportunity--1971.
Part 19B-Equal Educational Opportunity in
Michigan. Washington, DC: GPO, 1971.

_____. Equal Educational Opportunity--1971.
Part 19C: Equal Educational Opportunity in
Michigan: Appendixes. Washington, DC:
GPO, 1972.

Underwood, Doug. "'No School Bus Riding
Nighmares Here.'" Lansing State Journal,
N 30, 1975. [Lansing]

Verway, David I. "Black Economic Status in
Michigan." Michigan State Economic Record 15
(Mr-Ap, 1973).

Vinter, Robert D., and Sarri, Rosemary C.
Research Report to the Ann Arbor Board of
Education. Ann Arbor, MI: School of Social
Work, U. of Michigan, 1966.

Vocational Preparation and Race in Michigan
Higher Education. Lansing, MI: Michigan
State Civil Rights Commission, 1967. ERIC
ED 029 744.

Wallace, Linda K. "Cool School." Flint Journal,
Ap 9, 1972. [Whitney Young Street Academy,
Flint]

Ward, Hiley H. "In Detroit, Black Power vs.
White Power." Christian Century, Mar 20,
1968.

_____. "The Monster Schools." In Prophet of
the Black Nation, pp. 72-90. Philadelphia,
PA: Pilgrim Press, 1969. [Detroit]

Warren, Donald I. and others. A Comparative
Study of Life Styles and Social Attitudes
of Middle Income Status Whites and Negroes
in Detroit. Detroit: Urban League of
Detroit, 1977.

Warren, Francis H. (ed.). The Michigan Manual
of Freedmen's Progress. Detroit, MI:
n.p., 1915.

Washington, B. F. The Negro Student in Detroit.
Detroit, MI: Detroit Bureau of Government
Research, 1926.

Watson, Denton L. "The Detroit School
Challenge." Crisis 81(Je-Jl, 1974):188-194.

Wheeler, James O., and Brunn, Stanley D.
"Agricultural Ghetto: Negroes in Cass
County, Michigan, 1845-1968." Geographical
Review 59(Jl, 1969):317-329.

_____ and _____. "Negro Migration into Rural
Southwestern Michigan." Geographical Review
58(1968).

Widick, B. J. Detroit: City of Race and Class
Violence. Chicago, IL: Quadrangle, 1972.

Wilder, Amos A. "Client Criticism of Urban
Schools: How Valid?" Phi Delta Kappan, N,
1969. [Detroit]

_____. "Our Elementary Schools Are a Public
Disgrace." Michigan Chronicle, Je 28, 1969.
[Detroit]

Williams, Junious, and Harris, Bill. The Rights and Responsibilities for Public School Students in Michigan, 1973. Saginaw Student Rights Center, 1407 Janes Street, Saginaw, MI 48501.

Willson, Kay D. "The Historical Development of Migrant Labor in Michigan Agriculture." Master's thesis, Michigan State U., 1978. Univ. Microfilms Order No. 13-11,464.

Wilson, Benjamin Calvin, Jr. "Michigan's Ante-Bellum Black Haven--Cass County, 1835-1870." Doctoral dissertation, Michigan State U., 1975. Univ. Microfilms Order No. 75-20904.

Wisenbaker, Joseph M. Desegregation and White Flight: A Case Study, Ap 21, 1976. ERIC ED 127 405. [Lansing]

_____. "Desegregation and White Flight: A Case Study." Educational Research Quarterly 1(1976):17-26. [Lansing]

Wolf, Eleanor P. "Courtrooms and Classrooms." In Education, Social Science and the Judicial Process, pp. 71-88. Washington, DC: National Institute of Education, Je, 1976. [Detroit desegregation case]

Wolf, Eleanor P., Lebeaux, Charles N., Terrelberry, Shirley, and Saperstein, Harriet. Change and Renewal in an Urban Community: Five Case Studies of Detroit. New York: Praeger, 1969.

Wolfe, Charles J., and Rankin, Stuart C. "The Supreme Court Decision: A Step Away from Equal Education Opportunity." School Administration, S, 1974. [Detroit school segregation case]

Wolfram, Walter A. A Sociolinguistic Description of Detroit Negro Speech. Urban Language Series, No. 5, 1969. Available from Publications Section, Center for Applied Linguistics, 1717 Massachusetts Avenue, N.W., Washington, DC 20036.

Worsham, James. "Desegregated Kalamazoo Back to Basics." Boston Globe, D 18, 1975.

_____. "Pontiac's Desegregation No Longer a Problem." Boston Globe, D 15, 1975.

Zwerdling, Daniel. "Block those Buses." New Republic 165(O 23, 1971):14-17. [Pontiac]

_____. Detroit's Fight for Equal Educational Opportunity, Ap, 1969, 16 pp. ERIC ED 029 392.

Minnesota

Berman, Hyman. "Political Antisemitism in Minnesota during the Great Depression." Jewish Social Studies 38(Summer-Fall, 1976): 247-264.

Blood, Robert O., Jr. Northern Breakthrough. Belmont, CA: Wadsworth, 1968. [Negro job mobility in Minneapolis/St. Paul]

Breckenfeld, Gurney. "How Minneapolis Fends Off the Urban Crisis." Fortune 93(Ja, 1976).

Christopherson, David. "An Evaluation of School Desegregation in the Withdrawal Pattern of Schools in the Jordan Neighborhood of Minneapolis, Minnesota." Master's thesis, St. Cloud State U., 1976.

Cohen, Muriel. "The Minneapolis Way to Desegregation." Boston Globe, Je 26, 1977.

Davis, D. H. "The Finland Community, Minnesota." Geographical Review 25(1935):382-394.

Davis, John B. "Minneapolis Achieved Peaceful Desegregation." Christian Science Monitor, Ja 19, 1976.

Faunce, R. W., and Wiener, Jonathan M. Teacher Characteristics in Selected Middle and Low Income Areas of the Minneapolis Public School System with Particular Reference to Teacher Retention. Minneapolis, MN: Board of Education, Mr, 1967.

Harris, Abram L., Jr. The Negro Population in Minneapolis. Minneapolis, MN: Minneapolis Urban League and Phyllis Wheatley Settlement House, 1926.

Higgins, Paul S. A Nine-Year, Control-Group Follow-up of Students Attending St. Paul's McKinley School During Its Last Year: Or, What Happened to the Kids After a Segregated School Closed? St. Paul: St. Paul Public Schools, Mr 31, 1976.

_____. The Desegregation Counselor Aide Program of the 1974-75 Minneapolis Emergency School Aid Act Project: Staff and Student Perceptions, Je, 1976. ERIC ED 131 126.

_____. What Happened to the Kids After Their Segregated School Closed? A Nine-Year Control-Group Follow-Up of Elementary Students, Mr 31, 1976. ERIC ED 131 148. [Minneapolis]

Hubert, Dick. "The Duluth Experience." Saturday Review, My 27, 1972.

Janka, Rick. "Involvement Made Desegregation Work." Milwaukee Sentinel, F 7, 1976. [Minneapolis]

Jenks, A. E. "Ethnic Census in Minneapolis." American Journal of Sociology 17(1911): 776-782.

Johnson, Lary. School-Related Attitudes of Minneapolis Elementary School Children Before and After the First Year of Desegregation. Minneapolis: Research and Evaluation Department, Minneapolis Public Schools, Ap, 1976.

_____. "School-Related Attitudes of Elementary School Children." Integrateducation 15 (N-D, 1977):134-136. [Minneapolis]

Mary Katherine, Sr. The Duluth Catholic Public Schools. Washington, DC: N.C.W.C., 1923.

Kluver, Nancy. "Maybe There's Less Discrimination Now." Red Wing Republican Eagle, F 28, 1979. [North High School, Minneapolis]

Learning Center Progress Report. St. Paul, MN: St. Paul Public Schools, Jl, 1973.

Minneapolis Public Schools. A Community Looks at Its Schools: An Interagency Task Force Approach. Minneapolis: Board of Education, Ja 24, 1969.

Minnesota State Board of Education. "Cultural Education Policy in Minnesota." Integrated Education(S-O, 1971).

_____. "Guidelines Relating to Equality of Educational Opportunity and Desegregation, Intra-Cultural and Inter-Cultural Quality Education." Integrated Education(N-D, 1971): 51-53.

Murton, Bonnie J., and Faunce, R. W. Student Mobility in Selected Minneapolis Public Schools. Report No. 2. Minneapolis: Youth Development Project of the Community Health and Welfare Council of Hennepin County, Inc., Ap, 1966.

Pinney, Gregor W. "Violence Not One of North High's Problems." Minneapolis Tribune, Mr 5, 1979. [North High School, Minneapolis]

Preston, Roy Leslie. "Intercultural Education in Minnesota." Master's thesis, U. of Minnesota, 1950.

St. Denis, Gerald C. "Interracial Adoptions in Minnesota: Self-Concept and Child-rearing Attitudes of Caucasian Parents Who Have Adopted Negro Children." Doctoral dissertation, U. of Minnesota, 1969.

St. Paul Board of Education. Fact Sheet, Closing of McKinley School. St. Paul, MN: St. Paul Board of Education, Jl, 1967. [Material explaining why a racially imbalanced school was closed and why the children were to be bused to previously segregated schools]

Saint Paul--A Center for Learning. Cambridge, MA: Harvard U., Center for Field Studies, 1967, 33 pp. ERIC ED 021 424.

Sederberg, Charles H., Alkire, Gary F., and Hendrix, Vernon. A Research Design for the Evaluation of the Urban Centers for Quality Integrated Education Project in Minneapolis Public Schools Special School District No. 1, Minneapolis, Minnesota. Minneapolis: Bureau of Field Studies and Surveys, College of Education, U. of Minnesota, 1971.

Shamwell, Earl E. "The Vocational Choices of Negro Children Enrolled in the Minneapolis Public Schools with an Analysis of the Vocational Choices for the Children Made by their Parents." Master's thesis, U. of Minnesota, 1939.

Shive, R. Jerrald. "Highlights of the Desegregation Process in Minneapolis." In Citizen Guide to Desegregation, pp. 38-41. Cleveland: Citizens' Council for Ohio Schools, 1976.

Spangler, Earl. The Negro in Minnesota. Minneapolis, MN: T. S. Denison, 1961.

Staples, Robert E. The Lower Income Negro Family in Saint Paul. St. Paul, MN: St. Paul Urban League, 1967.

Taylor, David V. "John Quincy Adams: St. Paul Editor and Black Leader." Minnesota History 43(Winter, 1973).

Tillman, James A., Jr. "Minneapolis: Chronology of Success." Integrated Education, Ag, 1963.

_____. Not By Prayer Alone. A Report on the Greater Minneapolis Interfaith Fair Housing Program. Philadelphia, PA: United Church Press, 1964.

Turbeville, Gus. "The Negro Population in Duluth, Minnesota, 1950." Sociology and Social Research 36(1952):231-238.

U.S. Commission on Civil Rights. School Desegregation in Minneapolis, Minnesota. Washington, DC: The Commission, My, 1977.

U.S. Congress, 92nd, 2nd session, House of Representatives, Committee on Education and Labor. Oversight Hearing on Elementary and Secondary Education. Hearing... Washington, DC: GPO, 1972. [Minneapolis]

Ward, Francis. "Brotherhood City: It's Not All Brotherly Love. Los Angeles Times, F 4, 1974. [Worthington]

Wilkins, Roy. "These 'Colored' United States: Minnesota: Seat of Satisfaction. Messenger 6(My, 1924):133, 151, 165.

Williams, Robert L. "School Desegregation: A Success in Minneapolis. Integrateducation 14 (Jl-Ag, 1976).

Mississippi

Abney, Glenn. "Legislative Morality: Attitude Change and Desegregation in Mississippi." Urban Education 11(O, 1976):333-338.

Aiken, Michael, and Demerath, N. J. III. "The Politics of [School Desegregation] Tokenism in Mississippi's Delta." Trans-action, Ap, 1967.

_____ and _____. "Tokenism in the Delta:
Two Mississippi Cases." In Our Children's
Burden. Edited by Raymond W. Mack. New
York: Random House, 1968.

Alexander, Florence O. "The Education for
Negroes in Mississippi." Journal of Negro
Education 16(Summer, 1947).

Allen, J. Egert. "These 'Colored' United
States: Mississippi--Home of 'Sun-Kissed'
Folks." Messenger 5(S, 1923):815, 820.

Analavage, Robert. "White Mississippi's New
Generation." Southern Patriot, D, 1968.

Anderson, Solena. "Back in 'Dem Days: A Black
Family Reminisces." Journal of Mississippi
History 36(My, 1974).

"Are Private Academies on HEW Payroll?"
Mississippi Press Forum, Ag, 1970.

Arons, Stephen. "Compulsory Education: America
in Mississippi." Saturday Review/World,
N 6, 1973.

Ayres, B. Drummond, Jr. "2 Cities, North and
South, Show Progress by Blacks." New York
Times, Ag 28, 1973. [Jackson]

Ayers, Jake, Sr. Statement on Desegregation
and School Matters in the State of
Mississippi. In U.S. Congress, 91st, 1st
session, Senate, Committee on Labor and
Public Welfare, Subcommittee on Education,
Elementary and Secondary Education Amendments of 1969. Hearings... Part 1, pp. 343-
362. Washington, DC: GPO, 1969.

Baer, Charles Howard. "The New Black Politics
in Mississippi: A Quantitative Analysis."
Doctoral dissertation, Northwestern U., 1970.
Univ. Microfilms Order No. 71-01787.

Barber, Rims (RIMS). "From Intransigence to
Compliance Is Two Steps Forward and Two
Steps Back." Inequality in Education 5
(Je 30, 1970).

Barber, Rims, and Huttie, Joseph J., Jr.
"Nixonian Economics: Another View." New
South 28(Spring, 1973):72-79.

Barnes, J. "Negro Voting in Mississippi."
Master's thesis, U. of Mississippi, 1955.

Barry, Marie Myles. "Model from Mississippi."
In Education for Einstein's World, pp. 14-
26, 1972. Council for American Unity, 101
Fifth Avenue, New York, NY

Beasley, Jonathan. "Blacks--Slave and Free--
Vicksburg, 1850-1860." Journal of
Mississippi History 38(F, 1976):1-32.

Behrens, David. "Jackson Leaders Believe
Plan's Working." Miami Herald, Mr 20, 1972.

Berry, Jason. Amazing Grace: With Charles
Evers in Mississippi. New York: Saturday
Review Press, 1973.

Berry, John Patrick. "The Dynamics of White
Resistance to Court-Ordered School Desegre-
gation in Selected Mississippi Districts."
B.A. thesis, Harvard College, Ap, 1971.

Berzon, Marsha L. "What the Blacks Found Out."
Nation, Je 23, 1969. [Holly Springs, MS]

Billingsley, Raymond Lee. "An Assessment of the
Social Studies Achievement of Thirteen-Year-
Olds in Rural Public Schools of North
Mississippi." Doctoral dissertation, U. of
Mississippi, 1976.

Boyer, Roscoe A., and Garza, Joseph M.
Sociological Considerations, Leflore County
School District, Mississippi. Reports of
Consultants and Advisory Specialists under
Planning Grant. Title III Elementary and
Secondary Education Act of 1965. Greenwood,
MS: Leflore County School District, Ja,
1969. ERIC ED 039 964.

Boykin, William C., Sr. Educational and
Occupational Orientation of Negro Male Youth
in the Mississippi Delta. Final Report.
Lorman, MS: Alcorn A & M College, F, 1969.
ERIC ED 028 303.

Brenner, Joseph, Coles, Robert, Merman, Alan,
Senn, Milton J. E., Walwyn, Cyril, and
Wheeler, Raymond. "Children in Mississippi:
A Report to the Field Foundation." Health
Rights News, S, 1967.

Brown, Brenda. "Pearl High." Kudzu 3(O, 1970):
4. [A black student at Pearl High School,
Rankin County]

Brown, Warren. "Tupelo. Black Boycott Stirs
Klan-Led Backlash." Washington Post, Je 26,
1978.

Bryan, C. Hobson, and Bertrand, Alvin L.
Propensity for Change Among the Rural Poor
in the Mississippi Delta: A Study of the
Roots of Social Mobility. Agricultural
Economic Report No. 185. Washington, DC:
GPO, Je, 1970.

Bryant, Ellen S. Mississippi's Farming and
Nonfarming Population: A Comparison of
Characteristics and Trends, 1950 to 1970,
Je, 1974. ERIC ED 158 917.

Bureau of Educational Research. School of
Education. The Report of a Survey of the
Public Schools of Panola County. University,
MS: U. of Mississippi, D, 1955.

Burson, George S., Jr. "The 1964 Mississippi
Summer Project: Political Developments and
Voter Registration Attempts." Master's
thesis, U. of Southern Mississippi, 1972.

Cahn, Edgar S., and Cahn, Jean Comper. "The New Sovereign Immunity." Harvard Law Review 81(Mr, 1968):929-991. [Child Development Group of Mississippi]

Calhoun, Lillian. "Mississippi Integration--A Break with the Past." Integrated Education 8(Mr-Ap, 1970):4-20.

Casey, Rick. "Catholic Heads 'Segregation Academy.'" National Catholic Reporter, Je 4, 1971. [West Point]

_____. "Small Town Mississippi--Where Racism Dies Hard." National Catholic Reporter, Je 4, 1971. [Aberdeen]

Clift, Eleanor. "All's Quiet in Jackson [Mississippi]. A City Strives for Quality Education." South Today 3(D, 1971):1, 6.

Clotfelter, Charles T. "School Desegregation, 'Tipping,' and Private School Enrollment." Journal of Human Resources 11(Winter, 1976): 28-50.

Cobbins, Sam, Jr. "Industrial Education for Black Americans in Mississippi--1862-1965." Doctoral dissertation, Mississippi State U., 1975. Univ. Microfilms Order No. 75-20716.

"Coffeeville." Kudzu 3(0, 1970):4. [Coffeeville school desegregation]

Cohen, Richard M. "The Philadelphia Story." Washington Post, Jl 20, 1975.

Crandall, G. F. "Black Power in the Deep South: A Study of the Freedom Movement in Alabama and Mississippi Since the Civil Rights Period." Doctoral dissertation, Oxford U., 1972.

Crecink, John C., and Steptoe, Roosevelt. Human Resources in the Rural Mississippi Delta...With Emphasis on the Poor. Agricultural Economic Report No. 170. Washington, DC: GPO, Ja, 1970.

Curtis, Hazen A. Holding Power and Dropouts, Leflore County School District, Mississippi. Reports of Consultants and Advisory Specialists under Planning Grant, Title III. Elementary and Secondary Education Act of 1965. Greenwood, MS: Leflore County School District, Ja, 1969. ERIC ED 039 965.

_____. Pupil Achievement-Comparison of Two Schools, Leflore County School District, Mississippi. Reports of Consultants and Advisory Specialists under Planning Grant, Title III, Elementary and Secondary Education Act of 1965. Greenwood, Ms: Leflore County School District, Ja, 1969. ERIC Ed 039 966.

_____. Special Services, Leflore County School District, Mississippi. Reports of Consultants and Advisory Specialists under Planning Grant, Title III, Elementary and Secondary Education Act of 1965. Greenwood, MS: Leflore County School District, Ja, 1969. ERIC ED 029 974.

Dansby, B. Baldwin. "A Brief Historical Review of the Mississippi Teachers Association." Mississippi Educational Journal 33(Mr, 1956).

Dart, Helen M. Maternity and Child Care in Selected Rural Areas of Mississippi. U.S. Children's Bureau Pub. No. 88. Washington, DC: GPO, 1921.

Davis, W. Milan. Pushing Forward. Okolona, MS: Okolona Messenger Press, 1938.

Day, Richard H. "The Economics of Technological Change and the Demise of the Sharecropper." American Economic Review, Je, 1967. [Mississippi Delta]

DeBord, Larry W., Griffin, Larry J., and Clark, Melissa. "Race and Sex Influences in the Schooling Processes of Rural and Small Town Youth." Sociology of Education 50 (Ap, 1977):85-102.

De Mott, Benjamin. "Encounter in Mississippi." Saturday Review, Ja 20, 1968. [White teacher in black classroom]

"Dear Pauline." Mississippi Educational Advance, O, 1966. [A teacher describes her first experience with desegregation]

Delaney, Joseph. "Black Lawyer, White Mayor Discuss Mississippi Murder." Muhammad Speaks, Je 18, 1971. [Drew]

_____. "Miss. Students Dislike Integration." Muhammad Speaks, O 5, 1973. [Grenada High School]

Denley, S. Gale, and Boone, Allyn C. "Mississippi Study finds Media Hiring More Blacks." Journalism Quarterly 54 (Summer, 1977):375-379.

Derian, Patricia M. "White Parents' Fears." Inequality in Education 11(Mr, 1972):22-23. [Jackson]

Desegregation and the Rights of Education in Mississippi. Washington, DC: National Education Association, Commission on Professional Rights and Responsibilities, S, 1970. ERIC ED 045 575.

Di Michele, Carles Conrad. "The History of the Roman Catholic Educational System in Mississippi." Doctoral dissertation, Mississippi State U., 1973.

Dorsey, L. C. Freedom Came to Mississippi. New York: Field Foundation, S, 1977.

Du Bois, W. E. B. "Deplores Act of Vandaman." *Sentinel* (Milwaukee, Wisconsin), Mr 19, 1904. [Veto of appropriation for black schools in Mississippi]

_____. "The Negro Common School, Mississippi." *Crisis*, D, 1926.

Dunbar, Anthony. *The Will to Survive. A Study of a Mississippi Plantation Community Based on the Words of Its Citizens.* Atlanta, GA: Southern Regional Council: Jackson, MS: Mississippi Council on Human Relations, Je, 1969.

Eatherly, Billy J. "The Occupational Progress of Mississippi Negroes, 1940-1960." *Mississippi Quarterly* 21(1968):48-62.

Egerton, John. "Mississippi Conversations." *Race Relations Reporter* 5(My, 1974):31-33. [Jackson]

_____. "NEA Project Stirs Bareknuckle Fight." *Race Relations Reporter* 2(Mr 15, 1971):9-10. [Mississippi]

Endres, Mary P. "Mississippi Headstart Program: One Year Later." *Freedomways*, Fall, 1968.

Evans, Medford. "Council School No. 1; As New as Childhood, And As Old as Truth." *Citizen*, Jl-Ag, 1965. [A private segregated school in Jackson]

Evers, Charles. *Evers*. New York: World, 1971. [Charles Evers, Fayette]

Executive Committee, Board of Education, Mississippi Annual Conference, the Methodist Church. *Mississippi Schools for Negroes*. Vicksburg, MS: Methodist Church, 1942.

Falk, Gail. "Negroes Move Ahead After 1964 Killings." *Southern Courier*, N 11, 1967. [Neshoba County]

_____. "Farmer's Cattle Killed by Poison." *Southern Courier*, D 24, 1966. [Eleven cattle owned by Rev. Joseph Hicks are poisoned after his three children integrated a school in Harrisville, MS]

_____. "How Debra Lewis Desegregated a School." *Southern Courier*, F 11, 1967. [Carthage]

_____. "No More Fights After School Officials Act." *Southern Courier*, Ap 15, 1967. [Enterprise]

_____. "Protection Suit Lost, Kids Quit." *Southern Courier*, Ap 8, 1967. [Physical perils of desegregation in Neshoba County]

_____. "She Never Got to the School." *Southern Courier*, Je 3, 1967. [Account of trial of eight white men accused of organizing violence against Negro school children in Grenada]

_____. "Student Tells Judge Cox About a Year at Neshoba Central High." *Southern Courier*, Mr 25, 1967.

_____. "White Men Freed in Grenada Case." *Southern Courier*, Je 10, 1967.

Fancher, Betsy. "Mississippi Replay." *South Today* 1(1970):3-6. [The Head Start program in Mississippi]

Farr, T. J. "The Intelligence and Achievement of Negro Children." *Education* 51(Ap, 1931):491-495. [Newton County]

Favrot, Leo Mortimer. "Negro Education in Coahoma County, Mississippi." *Southern Workman* 54(N, 1-25):489-496.

Find, Estelle. "Lunches for Vicksburg Children Are 'Hauled Like Slop for Pigs.'" *Southern Courier*, Ap 20, 1968. [Vicksburg]

Fobbs, Allen D. "Availability of Vocational Education in Agriculture for Negroes in Mississippi." Master's thesis, Iowa State College, Ames, 1942.

Franklin, Presley. "The Way It Was Last Year for Negroes at Marks High." *Southern Courier*, S 9, 1967.

_____. "Students Suspended at Marks High School." *Southern Courier*, S 30, 1967. [Marks, Mississippi]

Frary, Robert B., and Goolsby, Thomas M., Jr. "Achievement of Integrated and Segregated Negro and White First Graders in a Southern City." *Integrated Education* 8(Jl-Ag, 1970): 48-52. [Gulfport]

Frese, Wolfgang, and Nontasak, Tatree. *Hopes and Fears of Open Country Families in Six Mississippi Counties*, F 1, 1976. ERIC ED 125 826.

Frick, Herman L. *The Curriculum, Grades 7 through 12, Leflore County School District, Mississippi. Reports of Consultants and Advisory Specialists under Planning Grant, Title III, Elementary and Secondary Education Act of 1965.* Greenwood, MS: Leflore County School District, Ja, 1969. ERIC ED 029 971.

Funches, De Lars. "The Superintendent's Expectations of the Negro High School Principal in Mississippi." *Journal of Experimental Education*, Fall, 1965.

Gabb, Sally. "Desegregation [in Tupelo] by Magnetism?" *Southern Education Report*, Ja-F, 1969.

Goolsby, Thomas M., Jr., and Frary, Robert B. "Effect of Massive Educational Intervention on Achievement of First Grade Students." *Journal of Experimental Education* 39(F, 1970): 46-52. [Gulfport]

_____ and _____ . Enhancement of Educational Effect Through Extensive and Intensive Intervention. The Gulfport Project. Gulfport, MS: Gulfport Municipal Separate School District, Jl, 1969.

Gordon, Sol. Evaluation of Project Head Start Reading Readiness in Issaquena and Sharkey Counties, Mississippi, Summer, 1965. Final Report. Report No. OEO-657, Ag 26, 1966. ERIC ED 014 319.

Governor's Committee on Children and Youth. The Needs of Children in Mississippi, 1970 Report. Jackson, MS: The Committee, 1970.

Mosley, C. C., Fortenberry, J. H., Lowe, O. P., and Thompson, Cleopatra D. Significant Problems in Public Education for Negroes in Mississippi: A Research Study Conducted by the Mississippi Teachers Association for the Mississippi Legislature Study Committee, Ag 14, 1961.

Munford, Luther. "Black Gravity: Desegregation in 30 Mississippi School Districts." Senior thesis, Woodrow Wilson School, Princeton U., Ap 16, 1971.

_____ . "Emergency Aid: In Mississippi, It Helped Districts That Dodged." South Today 3(Jl-Ag, 1971):4, 6.

_____ . "White Flight from Desegregation in Mississippi." Integrated Education 11(My-Je, 1973):12-26.

Greenberg, Polly. The Devil Has Slippery Shoes. A Biased Biography of the Child Development Group of Mississippi. New York: Macmillan, 1969.

Griffith, Helen. Dauntless in Mississippi: The Life of Sarah Dickey, 1838-1904. South Hadley, MA: Dinosaur Press, 1966.

Haines, Aubrey B. "The Evers Administration: Two Years of Progress in Fayette [Mississippi]." Christian Century 88(Jl 28, 1971):908-911.

Halberstam, David. "A County Divided Against Itself." Reporter, D 15, 1955. [Yazoo County]

Hamlett, Ed. "Four Majority-Black Districts in Mississippi." In Majority-Black School Districts in the 11 Southern States. Nashville, TN: Race Relations Information Center, Jl, 1970. [Kemper and Washington counties]

Harkey, Ira R., Jr. The Smell of Burning Crosses: An Autobiography of a Mississippi Newspaper Man. Jacksonville, IL: Harris-Wolfe and Company, 1967.

Harris, Johnny L. "A Historical Analysis of Educational, Economic and Political Changes in Fayette, Mississippi, from 1954 to 1971." Doctoral dissertation, Florida State U., 1972. Univ. Microfilms Order No. 72-27915.

Herman, Tom. "'Integrated' Schools In South Sometimes Keep Races Separated." Wall Street Journal, My 15, 1970. [Kemper County]

Higson, Mike. "Who Rules the South? Jackson, Miss." Southern Patriot, My, 1969.

"The Historic Supreme Court Decision." Integrated Education 8(Ja-F, 1970):12-13. [Alexander case, O, 1969]

Hoffman, Marvin. "'The Lord, He Works in Mysterious Ways...'" New South, Summer, 1969. [The Child Development Group of Mississippi, CDGM]

Hogue, Larry. "Education in Mississippi: Leflore County." American Libraries 2(O, 1971):985-986.

Holmes, William F. The White Chief: James Kimble Vardaman. Baton Rouge, LA: Louisiana State U. Press, 1970.

_____ . "The White Chief: James K. Vardaman in Mississippi Politics, 1890-1908." Doctoral dissertation, Rice U., 1964. Univ. Microfilms Order No. 64-10174.

Holmes, W. F. "Whitecapping: Agrarian Violence in Mississippi, 1902-1906." Journal of Southern History 35(1969):165-185.

Hooker, Robert. "Race and the Mississippi Press." New South 26(Winter, 1971):55-62. [1962-1964]

Howard, T. R. M. "Mississippi Negro's Stand on Segregation in the Public Schools of Mississippi." Journal of Human Relations, Autumn, 1954.

Huttie, Joseph, Jr. "'New Federalism' and the Death of a Dream in Mound Bayou, Mississippi." New South 28(Fall, 1973):20-29.

Ingram, S. J. "Recent Progress of Negro High Schools in Mississippi." Master's thesis, Tulane U., 1930.

"Integration by [Ability] Tracking to be Tried in Mississippi." Inequality in Education, O 10, 1969.

Jackson, Kara V. and others. Education of Disadvantaged Children, Leflore County School District, Mississippi. Reports of Consultants and Advisory Specialists under Planning Grant, Title III, Elementary and Secondary Education Act of 1965. Greenwood, MS: Leflore County School District, Ja, 1969. ERIC ED 039 967.

Jaffe, Andrew. "Grenada, Mississippi: Perspective on the Backlash." New South, Fall, 1966.

James, Patricia. "Straight Line in Meridian." Southern Courier, Ap 29, 1967. [Desegregation in Meridian]

Johnson, C. A. "Rains Came at Miami: But MEA Stays in NEA for a Good Reason." Mississippi Educational Advance 34(O, 1966):29. [Mississippi Education Association]

Johnson, Meighan G. "A Study of Role Conflicts between White and Negro Employees in the Jackson, Miss. Head Start Project, June-August, 1965." Master's thesis, U. of Mississippi, 1966.

Jones, Lawrence C. "Piney Woods School." Southern Workman 60(Ja, 1931):20-24.

Jordan, June. Fannie Lou Hamer. New York: Crowell, 1973. [Children's book]

_____. "Mississippi 'Black Home.' A Sweet and Bitter Bluesong." New York Times Magazine, O 11, 1970.

Joubert, Paul E., and Crouch, Ben M. "Mississippi Blacks and the Voting Rights Act of 1965." Journal of Negro Education 46 (Spring, 1977):157-167.

Judis, John. "Tupelo Showdown: Civil Rights, 1978." Chicago Sun-Times, Je 25, 1978.

Kaufman, Harold F. and others. Poverty Programs and Social Mobility: Focus on Rural Populations of Lower Social Rank in Mississippi and the South. Social Science Research Center, Mississippi State U., 1966.

_____ and others. "Race, Rank and Community Involvement." Phylon 39(D, 1978):381-391. [Two communities in Mississippi]

Kernell, Sam. "Comment: A Re-Evaluation of Black Voting in Mississippi." American Political Science Review 67(D, 1973):1307-1318. [See Salomon and Van Evera, below]

Kirksey, H. Jay. "State Milks Federal Cow for 'Poor Children.'" Mississippi Press Forum, My-Je, 1970.

Kohler, Emmett T., and Seaman, Don F. "An Educational and Socioeconomic Description of Adult Basic Education Students in Mississippi." Journal of Human Resources 5 (F, 1970):511-518.

Kunstel, Marcia. "'Breaking the Conspiracy of Silence.'" Southern Exposure 7(Summer, 1979):77-83.

Kurzman, Paul A. (ed.). The Mississippi Experience. Strategies for Welfare Rights Action. New York: Association Press, 1972.

Ladner, Joyce A. "Fannie Lou Hamer: In Memoriam." Black Enterprise 7(My, 1977):56.

Levin, Tom. "The Child Development Group of Mississippi: A Hot Sector of the Quiet Front in the War on Poverty." American Journal of Orthopsychiatry, Ja, 1967.

Loewen, James W., and Sallis, Charles (eds.). Mississippi--Conflict and Change. New York: Pantheon, 1974.

Lowry, Mark II. "Geographical Characteristics of a Bi-Racial Society: The Mississippi Case." Doctoral dissertation, Syracuse U., 1973.

_____. "Population and Race in Mississippi, 1940-1960." Annals of the Association of American Geographers 61(S, 1971):576-588.

_____. "Race and Socioeconomic Well-being: A Geographical Analysis of the Mississippi Case." Geographical Review 60(1970):511-528.

_____. "Schools in Transition." Annals of the Association of American Geographers 63 (Je, 1973):167-180.

McAllister, Jane Ellen. "Childhood, As I Remember It." Integrated Education 11 (Jl-O, 1973):21-28. [Vicksburg]

_____. "Mississippi Grandmother: End of an Era." Integrated Education 11(Ja-F, 1973):23-32.

_____. "Mississippi Outpouring Over a Decade." Journal of Secondary Education, My, 1965. [Views of Negro students and teachers, 1954-1964]

_____. "These Three in a Mississippi Program for the Disadvantaged." Journal of Secondary Education, Ja, 1967.

McCoy, John L. Achieved Level of Living in a Mississippi Delta County..., Ag 25, 1974. ERIC ED 097 132. [Washington County]

McCoy, John L. Factors Associated with Level of Living in Washington County, Mississippi, Ag, 1974. ERIC ED 097 151.

McDonald, Douglas. "Compulsory Attendance: The Problem in Mississippi." Mobile (Alabama) Register, Ap 7, 1973.

McMillen, Neil R. "Black Enfranchisement in Mississippi: Federal Enforcement and Black Protest in the 1960's." Journal of Southern History 43(Ag, 1977):351-372.

_____. "Development of Civil Rights, 1956-1970." In A History of Mississippi, 2 vols. Edited by Richard A. McLemore. Hattiesburg, MS: U. and College Press of Mississippi, 1973.

McNulty, Timothy. "Old Problems Persist in the 'New South.'" Chicago Tribune, Je 17, 1978. [Tallahatchie County]

McPhail, James H. A History of Desegregation Developments in Certain Mississippi School Districts. Hattiesburg, MS: Mississippi School Study Council, U. of Southern Mississippi, 1971.

Mann, Jim. "Economy, Drop in Rolls Sap Segregated Schools." Baltimore Sun, Je 7, 1977. [White segregation academies in Jackson]

Marin, Harry. "Why Black Candidates Lose in Mississippi." Crisis 80(Ap, 1973):135-139.

Marley, Frank E. "Attitudes Toward Integration in the Vicksburg Public School Separate District, 1966-69." Master's thesis, Jackson State College, 1968.

Marwell, Gerald, Demerath, N. J. III, and Aiken, Michael. "The SCOPE Volunteers: Then and Now." New South 25(1970):2-21. [Student volunteers in Mississippi, Summer, 1965]

Mars, Florence. Witness in Philadelphia: A Mississippi WASP's Account of the 1964 Civil Rights Murders. Baton Rouge, LA: Louisiana State U. Press, 1977.

Maxwell, Neil. "The Ailing Poor." Wall Street Journal, Ja 14, 1969. [Mississippi Delta]

Middleton, Jeanne Marie. "The History of Singleton v. Jackson Municipal Separate School District: Southern School Desegregation from the Perspective of the Black Community." Doctoral dissertation, Harvard U., 1978. Univ. Microfilms Order No. 7823682.

Mills, Gary Bernard. "The Forgotten People: Cave River's Creoles of Color." Doctoral dissertation, Mississippi State U., 1974. Univ. Microfilms Order No. 75-4212.

Minor, W. F. "Mississippi Schools in Crisis." New South 25(1970):31-36.

"Mississippi: Black and White Together." Newsweek, Ja 19, 1970.

"Mississippi Closing Down Black Schools and Jobs." Muhammad Speaks, Ag 7, 1970. [Humphrey County]

Mississippi Education Association. Committee on Negro Education. "What Do We Teach About the Negro?" Journal of the National Education Association 28(Ja, 1939):11-12.

"Mississippi 1973: Little Has Changed." African World, Ag 11, 1973.

Mississippi State Advisory Committee. Welfare in Mississippi. Washington, DC: U.S. Commission on Civil Rights, F, 1969.

Mississippi. State Superintendent of Education. Committee of Investigation of the Teacher-training Facilities for Negroes in Mississippi. [Report] Jackson, MS, S, 1930.

Moody, Anne. Coming of Age in Mississippi. New York: Dial, 1968.

Morris, Humphrey. "Kids Carry on Shelby Protest." Southern Courier, Ag 24, 1968.

Morris, Willie. Yazoo: Integration in a Deep-Southern Town. New York: Harper's Magazine Press, 1971.

_____. "Yazoo...Notes on Survival." Harper's Magazine, Je, 1970. [Yazoo City]

Moses, Bob. "Mississippi: 1961-1962." Liberation, Ja, 1970.

Mosley, C. C. The Negro in Mississippi History. Jackson, MS: Purser Brothers, 1969.

Newbold, N. C. Report of Committee of Investigation of the Teacher-training Faculties for Negroes in Mississippi, 1930. State Department of Public Instruction, Raleigh, NC, 138 pp.

Nicholson, Helen. "From Hattiesburg, Mississippi." In School Desegregation. Shadow and Substance. Edited by Florence H. Levinsohn and Benjamin D. Wright. Chicago: U. of Chicago Press, 1976. [Hattiesburg High School, Blair Center]

Nieman, Donald G. "The Freedmen's Bureau and the Mississippi Black Code." Journal of Mississippi History 40(My, 1978):91-118.

Noble, Stuart Grayson. "Forty Years of the Public Schools in Mississippi With Special Reference to the Education of the Negro." Doctoral dissertation, Columbia U., 1918.

Palmer, James M. Mississippi School Districts. Factors in the Disestablishment of Dual Systems. State College, MS: Social Science Research Center, Mississippi State U., Ag, 1971.

Park, Tom F., Jr. "Promising Developments in Integration." Educational Leadership, N, 1968. [Portageville]

Parker, Frank R. "County Redistricting in Mississippi: Case Studies in Racial Gerrymandering." Mississippi Law Journal 44 (1973).

Perdue, Lewis. "Giant Step to Moderation." Nation, Ja 1, 1973.

"Pioneer Work in Mississippi." Southern Workman 54(N, 1925):483-484.

Powell, Lew. "A Bad Press in Mississippi." Nation 217(O 8, 1973):331-334.

Ramsey, Curtis P. Instructional Materials and Media, Leflore County School District, Mississippi. Reports of Consultants and Advisory Specialists under Planning Grant. Title III, Elementary and Secondary Education Act of 1965. Greenwood, MS: Leflore County School District, Ja, 1969. ERIC ED 039 973.

Roberts, Roy W., and Hunt, Elizabeth E.
Industrial and Practical Arts, Vocational
Education, and General Adult Education,
Leflore County School District, Mississippi.
Reports of Consultants and Advisory Special-
ists under Planning Grant, Title III,
Elementary and Secondary Education Act of
1965. Greenwood, MS: Leflore County School
District, Ja, 1969. ERIC ED 039 972.

Rogers, Tommy W. The Extent and Distribution
of Poverty in Mississippi, Je, 1976.
ERIC ED 133 415.

_____. "The Piney Woods Country Life School:
A Successful Heritage of Education of Black
Children in Mississippi." Negro History
Bulletin 39(S/O, 1976):611-614

_____. Poverty in Mississippi: A Statistical
Analysis, Je, 1977. ERIC ED 151 456.

Rubin, Mertis. "Agreement Doesn't Stop School
Boycott in Miss." Southern Courier, Mr 25,
1967. [Hazelhurst]

Rubin, Mertis. "Laurel Teacher Beaten."
Southern Courier, S 16, 1967. [Three white
terrorists beat white woman teacher in Laurel
Head Start program]

Salamon, Lester M. "Leadership and Modernization: The Emerging Black Political Elite
in the American South." Journal of Politics
35(Ag, 1973):615-646.

_____. "Mississippi Post-Mortem. The 1971
Elections." New South 27(Winter, 1972):43-
47.

Satcher, Buford. Blacks in Mississippi Politics,
1865-1900. Washington, DC: U. Press of
America, 1978.

"The School Crisis in Yazoo City." Newsweek,
N 10, 1969.

"School Desegregation, Henry v. Clarksdale
Municipal Separate School District, 409
F. 2d 682 (5th Cir., 1969)." Suffolk Univer-
sity Law Review 4(Fall, 1969).

Schuck, Cecilia, and Tartt, June B. "Food
Consumption of Low-Income Rural Negro Households in Mississippi." Journal of the
American Dietetic Association 62(F, 1973):
151-155.

Seaman, Don F., and Kohler, Emmett T. Adult
Basic Education in Mississippi. An Evalua-
tion. Volume I, Volume II. Questionnaires.
Jackson, MS: Mississippi State Dept. of
Education, Je, 1969. ERIC ED 033 271.

Sewell, George A. Mississippi Black History
Makers. Jackson: U. Press of Mississippi,
1977.

Siepmann, Katy. "Shelby and Leake Kids Stay
Home." Southern Courier, My 18, 1968.
[School boycott in Shelby on behalf of dis-
charged teachers]

Sisson, John. "Holly Spring Mississippi
Students Walk Out." Southern Courier, My 25,
1968.

Smaller Communities Program, Stone County,
Mississippi. Part II: Manpower Resource
Report, N, 1969. ERIC ED 049 843.

Smith, J. Bryant, Jr. "Methods and Media Inno-
vations in an Integrating School District:
An Action Report." In Updating Intergroup
Education in Public Schools. A Study-Action
Manual. Edited by Albin R. Gilbert and
Robert P. Sessions. Buckhannon, W.VA:
Equal Educational Opportunities Center, West
Virginia Wesleyan College, 1969. [New Albany]

Smith, J. "Sunflower Drive Off." Southern
Courier, O 5, 1968. [Indianola school boy-
cott]

Sollie, Carlton R. and   Changes in
Quality of Life in Mississippi: 1960-1970,
Mr, 1975. ERIC ED 121 503.

Southall, Macie K. Elementary Instruction,
Leflore County School District, Mississippi,
Reports of Consultants and Advisory Special-
ists under Planning Grant, Title III,
Elementary and Secondary Education Act of
1965. Greenwood, MS: Leflore County School
District, Ja, 1969. ERIC ED 039 970.

Steinberg, Jonathan. "Mississippi Election--
1966." Liberation, My-Je, 1966. [Problems
of Negro participation in elections to the
North Panola, Mississippi School District
board of education]

Stevens, Maxey. "Representing the Unrepresented:
A Decennial Report on Public-Interest
Litigation in Mississippi." Mississippi Law
Journal 44(1973).

Stringer, S. L. "A Survey of Two Types of School
Systems for Negro Education, a Semiconsolidated
School System Without Transportation in
Coahoma County, Mississippi, and a Consolidated
School System With Transportation in Forrest
County, Mississippi." Master's thesis, The
U. of Mississippi, 1929.

Sugarman, Tracy. Stranger at the Gates. New
York: Hill and Wang, 1967. [The Mississippi
Summer Project, 1964-1965]

Sutherland, Elizabeth (ed.). Letters from
Mississippi. New York: McGraw-Hill, 1965.

Sutton, Elizabeth W. Supervision of Instruction in Teaching Disadvantaged Children, Leflore County School District, Mississippi. Reports of Consultants and Advisory Specialists under Planning Grant, Title III, Elementary and Secondary Education Act of 1965. Greenwood, MS: Leflore County School District, Ja, 1969. ERIC Ed 039 968.

Sydnor, Charles S. "The Free Negro in Mississippi before the Civil War." American Historical Review 32(Jl, 1927).

Thames, John P. "Population Migration Effects on Mississippi Poverty." Mississippi Law Journal 39(My, 1968):423-450.

Thompson, Cleopatra D. The History of the Mississippi Teachers Association. Washington, DC: NEA Teacher Rights; Jackson, MS: Mississippi Teachers Association, 1973.

Thompson, Ethel. Early Childhood Education, Leflore County School District, Mississippi. Reports of Consultants and Advisory Specialists under Planning Grant, Title III, Elementary and Secondary Education Act of 1965. Greenwood, MS: Leflore County District, Ja, 1969. ERIC ED 039 969.

Thompson, Ruby M. Rankings of Mississippi School Districts, 1971/72. Jackson, MS: State Department of Education, 1972.

Thompson, William Bert. "A History of the Greenville, Mississippi Public Schools under the Administration of E. E. Bass, 1384-1932." Doctoral dissertation, U. of Mississippi, 1968. Univ. Microfilms Order No. 69-3969.

Travis, John A. "A Financial Study of Negro Education in Mississippi." Master's thesis, Peabody College, 1937.

Truly, William. "Temperatures Rising in Mississippi." Los Angeles Times, D 10, 1978. [Racial discrimination against a black physician in Canton]

Tucker, Shirley. Mississippi From Within. New York: Arco, 1965.

"Turnabout in Mississippi." Time, My 8, 1972. [Clarksdale]

Turner, Robert L. "'62 Mississippi Fund Cut-off Weighed." Washington Post, F 28, 1974. [From the Robert F. Kennedy papers]

Van Evera, Steve. "Free Meal for Whom?" Southern Courier, Jl 13, 1968. [Racial discrimination in school lunch program, Sharkey County]

Vance, Miriam W. ["From Hattiesburg, Mississippi."] In School Desegregation. Shadow and Substance. Edited by Florence H. Levinsohn and Benjamin D. Wright. Chicago: U. of Chicago Press, 1976. [Blair High School]

Vinson, Ken. "The Lawyers of Ole Miss." Nation, Je 23, 1969.

Walker, Perry. [Freedom of Choice in Holly Springs, Miss.] Southern Courier, Jl 13, 1968.

Wallace, Jesse Thomas. "A History of the Negroes of Mississippi from 1865-1890." Doctoral dissertation, Columbia U., 1927.

Wasserman, Miriam. "The Loud, Proud Black Kids." Progressive, Ap, 1968. [Black children in desegregated schools in Mississippi]

Watters, Pat. "Mississippi: Children and Politics." Dissent, My-Je, 1967. [The Child Development Group of Mississippi (CDGM)]

Weathersby, William H. A History of Educational Legislation in Mississippi from 1798 to 1860. Chicago, IL: U. of Chicago, 1921.

Wharton, Vernon L. The Negro in Mississippi, 1865-1890. Chapel Hill, NC: U. of North Carolina Press, 1947.

White, Jack. "Miss. Blacks Fail to Gain Control." Race Relations Reporter 2(N 15, 1971):5-7.

Whitehead, Don. Attack on Terror: The F.B.I. Against the Ku Klux Klan in Mississippi. New York: Funk & Wagnalls, 1970.

Wilkie, Curtis. "Desegregation Dilemma in the South." New Republic, Ap 12, 1969 [Coahoma County]

Williams, Ed. "Indianola: Why Whites Came Back to Schools." Greenville Delta-Democrat Times, S 6, 1970.

Williams, Lydia. "The Loneliness of Being Black." Seventeen (Jl, 1971).

Williams, Thomas E. "The Dependent Child in Mississippi. A Social History 1900-1972." Doctoral dissertation, Ohio State U., 1976.

Wilson, C. J. "Voices from Mississippi." New South 28(Spring, 1973):62-71.

Wilson, Charles H. Education for Negroes in Mississippi Since 1910. Boston: Meador, 1947.

Winn, William, with Inman, D. L., and Williams, Ed. Augusta, Georgia and Jackson State University. Southern Episodes in a National Tragedy. Atlanta: Southern Regional Council, Je, 1970.

Wirt, Frederick M. Politics of Southern Equality. Law and Social Change in a Mississippi County. Chicago, IL: Aldine, 1970. [Panola County]

Woodyard, Virginia. "Hattiesburg--In the Wake of a Cataclysm." Southern Education Report, Je, 1967. [Freedom schools in Hattiesburg]

Wright, J. B. "The Development of Publicly Supported Secondary Education for Negroes in Mississippi." Master's thesis, Iowa State College, 1935.

Wrighton, Fred McGehee. "Negro Migration and Incomes in Mississippi." Doctoral dissertation, Mississippi State U., 1972. Univ. Microfilms Order No. 73-00149.

Zim, Marvin. "Where Jim Crow is Alive and Well." Time, S 19, 1969. [Leake County]

                    Missouri

Armstrong, Byron K. Factors in the Formulation of Collegiate Programs for Negroes. Ann Arbor, MI: Edward Bros., 1939. [St. Louis public school system hiring policies]

Baker, Thomas Eugene. "Human Rights in Missouri: The Legislative, Judicial and Administrative Development of Black Liberties." Doctoral dissertation, U. of Missouri, 1975. Univ. Microfilms Order No. 76-00990.

Baldwin, Roger N. "Negro Segregation by Initiative Election in St. Louis." American City, Ap, 1916. [Segregated housing]

Barnes, Harper. "Kansas City Modern. Growing Pains and Pleasures." Atlantic 233(F, 1974): 60-67.

Baron, Harold. "Samuel Shepard and the Banneker Project." Integrated Education, Ap, 1963. [St. Louis]

Beatty-Brown, Florence R. "The Negro as Portrayed by the St. Louis Post-Dispatch from 1920-1950." Doctoral dissertation, U. of Illinois, n.d.

Bellamy, Donnie D. "The Education of Blacks in Missouri Prior to 1861." Journal of Negro History 59(Ap, 1974):143-157.

_____. "Free Blacks in Antebellum Missouri, 1820-1860." Missouri Historical Review, Ja, 1973.

Billington, Monroe. "Public School Integration in Missouri, 1954-64." Journal of Negro Education, Summer, 1966.

"Black Community Support for Teachers Strike." African World, Ap, 1974. [Kansas City]

Boxerman, Burton Alan. "Reaction of the St. Louis Jewish Community to Anti-semitism, 1933-1945." Doctoral dissertation, St. Louis U., 1967. Univ. Microfilms Order No. 68-1256.

Brandt, Lillian. "Negroes of St. Louis." Journal of the American Statistical Association 8(Mr, 1903):203-268.

Brigham, Robert I. "The Education of the Negro in Missouri." Doctoral dissertation, U. of Missouri, 1946. Univ. Microfilms Order No. 1274.

_____. "Negro Education in Ante Bellum Missouri." Journal of Negro History 30(O, 1945):405-420.

Brunn, Paul Dennis. "Black Workers and Social Movements of the 1930's in St. Louis." Doctoral dissertation, Washington U., 1975. Univ. Microfilms Order No. 75-14894.

Caliguri, Joseph P. "Black Power and Black Students in Kansas City." Integrated Education (Ja-F, 1972):44-48.

Caliguri, Joseph P., and Levine, Daniel U. The Use of Inter-Ethnic Materials in Suburban School Districts in the Kansas City Metropolitan Area. Kansas City, MO: U. of Missouri-Kansas City, F, 1969.

Campbell, Rex R., and Robinson, Peter C. Negroes in Missouri. Jefferson City, MO: Missouri Commission on Human Rights, 1964.

Campbell, Rex R., and Bader, Thomas E. Negroes in Missouri--1970... Jefferson City, MO: Missouri Commission on Human Rights, 1972.

Campbell, Rex R., and Mulvey, Susan A. A Study of the Changes in Numbers of Negro Teachers and Students in the Various Primary and Secondary School Systems of the State of Missouri. Columbia, MO: U. of Missouri, Dept. of Rural Sociology, 1967, 73 pp. ERIC ED 057 133.

Carpenter, Luther P., and Rank, Dinah. The Treatment of Minorities: A Survey of Textbooks Used in Missouri High Schools. Jefferson City, MO: Missouri Commission on Human Rights, D, 1968.

Castelli, Jim. "Midwest 'Superschool.'" National Catholic Reporter, Ap 7, 1972. [Loretto elementary and high school, Kansas City]

Christensen, Lawrence Oland. "Black St. Louis: A Study in Race Relations, 1865-1916." Doctoral dissertation, U. of Missouri, 1972. Univ. Microfilms Order No. 73-21770.

Collins, John N., and Downes, Bryan T. "Support for Public Education in a Racially Changing Suburb." Urban Education 10(O, 1975):221-244.

Collins, Robert H. "Motivation." Southern Education Report, Jl-Ag, 1965. [Program in the Banneker School District in St. Louis]

Crockett, Harry J. "A Study of Some Factors Affecting the Decision of Negro High School Students to Enroll in Previously All-White High Schools, St. Louis, 1955." Social Forces, 1957.

Crosswhite, Charles. "Transportation of Negro Public School Pupils in Missouri." School and Community 19(F, 1933):90-93.

Curtis, L. S. Some Facts on the Education of Negroes in Missouri 1930-1939. Kansas City, MO: Missouri State Association of Negro Teachers, 1940.

Dawson, Karen Smith. "Citizen Participation in Local Policy Making: The Case Study of University City (Missouri) School Reorganization Controversy." Doctoral dissertation, Washington U., 1974. Univ. Microfilms Order No. 75-6589.

Day, Judy, and Kedro, M. James. "Free Blacks in St. Louis: Antebellum Conditions, Emancipation, and the Postwar Era." Bulletin: Missouri Historical Society 30 (Ja, 1974):117-135.

Dean, Rick. "Bush Veteran of Integration Turmoil." Topeka Daily Capital, Ja 30, 1978. [Jack Bush, black coach, Kansas City]

Dexter, Gene. An In-Service and Advisory Assistance Program Relating to the Problems Coincident with and Incident to the Process of Desegregation of Schools in the Kansas City, Missouri, School District. Kansas City, MO: Kansas City School District, 1967, 269 pp. ERIC ED 056 108.

Douglas, Esque. "The History of the Negro in Northeast Missouri, 1820-1890." Master's thesis, Lincoln U., MO, 1950.

Doyle, Patricia Jansen. "St. Louis: City With the Blues." Saturday Review, F 15, 1969.

Dreer, Herman. "The Education of the Negro With Respect to His Background." Journal of Negro History 19(Ja, 1936):45-51.

Dwyer, Robert J. "A Report on Patterns of Interaction in Desegregated Schools." Journal of Educational Sociology, Mr, 1958. [Central Missouri, 7 school districts]

Edgar, Richard E. Urban Power and Social Welfare: Corporate Influence in an American City. Beverly Hills, CA: Sage, 1971. [St. Louis]

Elementary Education Facilities in St. Louis, Community Resources, 6030 Cates Avenue, St. Louis, MO 63112, Mr, 1964.

Epstein, Hedy. Patterns of Discrimination, F, 1970. Greater St. Louis Committee for Freedom of Residence, 5868½ Delmar Blvd., St. Louis, MO 63112. [Housing discrimination in St. Louis]

Ernst, Robert T. "Factors of Isolation and Interaction in an All Black City: Kinloch, Missouri." Doctoral dissertation, U. of Flordia, 1973.

Evans, John William. "A Study of the Development of the Facilities for Negro Education in St. Louis from 1858 to 1928." Master's thesis, State U. of Iowa, 1929.

Farnsworth, Robert. "[Busing and Integration in] Kansas City." Focus Midwest 4(1965).

Fiddmont, Norman, and Levine, Daniel U. "Attitudes Concerning Civil Rights and Related Matters Held by Black Students in a Big City." Urban Education, J1, 1969. [Kansas City]

_____ and _____. The Attitudes of Negro High School Students in Kansas City, Missouri: A Preliminary Report. Kansas City, MO: Center for the Study of Metropolitan Problems in Education, U. of Missouri, Kansas City, 1968.

Flygare, Thomas J. "The Hazlewood Case: How to Use Statistics to Prove and Disprove Hiring Discrimination." Phi Delta Kappan 59 (N, 1977):210-211.

Freeman, Ruges R. "Educational Desegregation in St. Louis, Missouri." Negro History Bulletin 38(Ap-My, 1975):364-369.

Gerlach, Russel L. Immigrants in the Ozarks: A Study in Ethnic Geography. Columbia: U. of Missouri Press, 1976. [Germans]

_____. "Rural Ethnic and Religious Groups as Cultural Islands in the Ozarks of Missouri: Their Emergence and Persistence." Doctoral dissertation, U. of Nebraska, 1974.

Gist, Noel P., and Bennett, William S., Jr. "Aspirations of Negro and White Students." Social Forces, O, 1963. [Kansas City]

Gersman, Elinor Mondale. "The Development of Public Education for Blacks in Nineteenth Century St. Louis, Missouri." Journal of Negro Education 41(Winter, 1972):35-47.

Gray, Gladys C. "A Social Worker Looks at St. Louis." Opportunity (Ap, 1972):112-113.

Guenther, John Edward. "Negro History in the Public High Schools of Missouri." Doctoral dissertation, U. of Missouri, 1970. Univ. Microfilms Order No. 71-03335.

Hamilton, Edward D. "A Study of the Negro School Population in St. Louis from the School Year 1908-1909 to the School Year 1927-28, Inclusive." Master's thesis, Northwestern U., 1929.

Hard Times and Great Expectations: An Account to the Community of the Condition of the St. Louis Public Schools. St. Louis Public Schools, MO, S, 1967, 28 pp. ERIC ED 022 834.

Harryman, Milburn E. "The Effects of the Racial Composition of Five High Schools in Kansas City upon Achievement and Citizenship Ratings of Selected Students." Diss. Abstr. Int'l., 1969,30 (6-A) 2290-1.

Henderson, David. Integration in Missouri Public Schools: Faculty and Students Twenty Years After "Brown," O, 1974. ERIC ED 102 275.

Hoard, C. M. "Survey of Guidance Programs in Missouri Negro High Schools." Negro History Bulletin, Je, 1953.

Hoedemaker, Sally B. "The Spatial Patterns of the Negro and White Middle Class: St. Louis, MO, 1960." Master's thesis, Southern Illinois U., Edwardsville, 1971.

Holland, Antonio F., and Kremer, Gary R. (eds.). "Some Aspects of Black Education in Reconstruction Missouri: An Address by Richard B. Foster." Missouri Historical Review 70 (Ja, 1976):184-198.

Hooker, Clifford P., and Mueller, Van D. Equal Treatment to Equals: A New Structure for Public Schools in the Kansas City and St. Louis Metropolitan Areas. Jefferson City, MO: Missouri School District Reorganization Commission, Je, 1969, 72 pp. ERIC ED 042 233.

Institute for Urban and Regional Studies. Urban Decay in St. Louis. St. Louis, MO: The Institute, Washington U., Mr, 1972.

John, George B. "Apportionment for Colored Schools Under New School Laws." Missouri State Department of Education Bulletin 6 (Mr, 1932):13-31.

Johnson, Cassandra. "Racist History Taught, Charges Student." Focus/Midwest, Ja-F, 1969 (letter). [Forest Park Community College, St. Louis]

Jones, Ruth S. "Racial Patterns and School District Policy." Urban Education 12(O, 1977):297-312. [St. Louis County]

Kain, John F., and Quigley, John M. Housing Markets and Racial Discrimination: A Microeconomic Analysis. New York: Columbia U. Press, 1975. [St. Louis]

Kansas and Missouri Advisory Committees to the United States Commission on Civil Rights. Crisis and Opportunity: Education in Greater Kansas City. Washington, DC: U.S. Commission on Civil Rights, Ja, 1977.

Kelleher, Daniel. "St. Louis' 1916 Residential Segregation Ordinance." Bulletin of the Missouri Historical Society 26(1970):239-248.

Kirk, James H. "Kinloch, Missouri: A Study of an All-Negro Community." Doctoral dissertation, St. Louis U., 1951.

Knos, D. S. "Substandard Housing in Kansas City, Missouri." Doctoral dissertation, U. of Iowa, 1959.

Leven, Charles L. and others. Neighborhood Change: Lessons in the Dynamics of Urban Decay. New York: Praeger, 1976. [St. Louis]

Levine, Daniel U. "Learning to Read in Inner City Schools: Kansas City." Integrated Education 53(S-O, 1971):11-18.

_____. "School Pioneers Social Change." Focus/Midwest 5(1967):10-12. [Kansas City]

_____. "Schools in Metropolitan Kansas City [Missouri]." In Robert J. Havighurst, Frank L. Smith, and David E. Wilder, A Profile of the Large-City High School, Chapter 12. Washington, DC: National Association of Secondary School Principals, N, 1970.

_____. "Voluntary City-Suburban Programs for Promoting Instructional Improvement and Integration in Kansas City Metropolitan Public Schools." In Kansas and Missouri Advisory Committees to the United States Commission on Civil Rights, Crisis and Opportunity: Education in Greater Kansas City, Appendix A, Jl, 1976. Washington, DC: U.S. Commission on Civil Rights, Ja, 1977.

Levine, Daniel U., and Meyer, Jeanie Keeny. "Level and Rate of Desegregation and White Enrollment Decline in a Big City School District." Social Problems 24(Ap, 1977): 451-462. [Kansas City]

Levine, Daniel U., Fiddmont, Norman S., Stephenson, Robert S., and Wilkinson, Charles B. The Attitudes of Black High Schools in Five Cities. Spring, 1970. Kansas City, MO: Center for the Study of Metropolitan Problems in Education, U. of Missouri, Kansas City, Ap, 1971.

Levine, Daniel U., and Fiddmont, Norman S. "Integration's Up to Date in Kansas City." Integrated Education 40(Jl-Ag, 1969):3-16.

_____ and _____. "Negro Population Growth and Enrollment in the Public Schools: A Case Study and Its Implications." Education and Urban Society, N, 1968. [Kansas City]

Levine, Daniel U., and Havighurst, Robert J. Population Growth Among Negro Citizens in Kansas City, Missouri. Kansas City, MO: Center for the Study of Metropolitan Problems in Education, U. of Missouri, Kansas City, MO 64110.

_____ and _____. "Population Trends and Increased School Integration in Big Cities." Integrated Education, Je-Jl, 1967. [Kansas City, MO]

Levine, Daniel U., and Fain, Robert P.
Public Reactions to a Brochure Aimed at
Maintaining Confidence in the Schools of a
Racially Changing Urban Community, 1970,
19 pp. ERIC ED 052 267.

Levine, Daniel U. and others. Opportunities
for Higher Education in a Metropolitan
Area: A Study of High School Senior in
Kansas City, 1967. Kansas City, MO: Mid-
Continent Regional Educational Lab, Inc.;
Center for the Study of Metropolitan Prob-
lems in Education, 1970, 74 pp. ERIC ED
045 774.

Levings, Darryl W. "Blacks Recall Long Trips
to Segregated Schools." Kansas City Star,
My 5, 1977. [Kansas City area]

Linsin, Jimmie. "An Analysis of the Treatment
of Religion, the Black-American, and Women
in the American History Textbooks Used by
the Public, Private, and Parochial High
Schools of the City and County of Saint
Louis, Missouri, 1972-73." Doctoral dissertation, St. Louis U., 1974.

Little, James T. Housing Market Behavior and
Household Mobility Patterns in a Transition
Neighborhood. St. Louis, MO: Institute for
Urban and Regional Studies, Washington U.,
O, 1973. [University City]

Lumpe, Gus. "Banneker and the Statistics."
Southern Education Report, O, 1968. [St.
Louis]

McDermott, John F. "Private Schools in St.
Louis, 1809-1821." Mid-America 11(1940):
96-119.

Martin, Asa Earl. Our Negro Population: A
Sociological Study of the Negroes of Kansas
City, Missouri. Kansas City, MO, 1913.

Miller, Andrew C. "Desegregation Proceeds
Warily Under Federal Eye." Kansas City
Star, D 22, 1974. [Kansas City]

_____. "Growing Black Divisiveness Over
Desegregation Issue." Kansas City Star,
D 21, 1974. [Kansas City]

Miller, Joan, Rainwater, Lee, and Koester,
Frances A. "Pruitt-Igoe: Survival in a
Concrete Ghetto." Social Work, O, 1967.
[St. Louis public housing project]

Missouri Advisory Committee. Report to the
United States Commission on Civil Rights on
Desegregation of Schools in Missouri.
Washington, DC: GPO, 1959.

Missouri. Commission on Human Rights. History
of the Missouri Commission on Human Rights,
1958-1968. Jefferson City, MO: The
Commission, 1968.

Monti, Daniel J. "Examining the Desegregation
Process." Integrateducation 15(N-D, 1977):
41-46.

Moore, N. Webster. "John Berry Meachum
(1789-1854): St. Louis Pioneer, Black,
Abolitionist, Educator, and Preacher."
Bulletin of the Missouri Historical Society,
Ja, 1973.

Moore, William J. The Vertical Ghetto: Everyday
Life in an Urban Project. New York: Random
House, 1969. [Pruitt-Igoe Project, St.
Louis]

Myers, Mike. "Southwest High Still Educating
5 Years Into Bussing Experiment." Kansas
City Times, F 5, 1977.

Parrish, William E. A History of Missouri.
Vol. III: 1860 to 1875. Columbia, MO:
U. of Missouri Press, 1975.

Pavlak, Thomas J., and Stern, Mark. "Black-
White Perceptions of Urban Priorities."
Phylon 39(Summer, 1978):108-117.
[St. Louis, 1970]

Phares, Donald. "Racial Transition and Resi-
dential Property Values." Annals of Regional
Science 5(D, 1971):152-160. [University
City]

Pihlblad, C. T., and Gregory, C. L. "Occupational
Selection and Intelligence in Rural Communi-
ties and Small Towns in Missouri."
American Sociological Review 21(1956):63-71.

Powell, P. R. "The Status of the Negro High
School Teacher in Missouri." Master's
thesis, Indiana State Teachers College,
Terre Haute, 1933.

Reichard, Maximilian. "Black and White on the
Urban Frontier: The St. Louis Community in
Transition, 1800-1830." Bulletin of the
Missouri Historical Society 33(O, 1976):3-17.

Reisner, Ralph. " De Facto Segregation in St.
Louis." Law and Society Review, N, 1967.

Rice, Robert R. The Housing Environment as a
Factor in Child Development. Final Report.
Report No. OEO-583, D 1, 1966. ERIC ED 014
322. [Kansas City]

Richardson, Joe M. "The American Missionary
Association and Black Education in Civil War
Missouri." Missouri Historical Review 69
(Jl, 1975):433-448.

"St. Louis Group Accuses Schools of Racism."
Muhammad Speaks, Mr 10, 1972. [Catholic
schools]

St. Louis Public Schools. A Tale of Two Cities.
A Blueprint for Equality of Educational
Opportunity in the St. Louis Public Schools.
St. Louis, MO: Board of Education, 1969.
[Reprinted in U.S. Congress, 91st, 1st
session, Senate, Committee on Labor and Public
Welfare, Subcommittee on Education, Elementary
and Secondary Education Amendments of 1969.
Hearings...Part 2, pp. 695-787. Washington,
DC: GPO, 1969]

Savage, W. S. "Legal Provisions for Negro Schools in Missouri from 1865-1890." Journal of Negro History 16(Jl, 1931):309-321.

Schoenberg, Sandra, and Bailey, Charles. "The Symbolic Meaning of an Elite Black Community: The Ville in St. Louis." Bull. Mo. Hist. Soc. 33(Ja, 1977):94-102.

"The Scholar Who Went to the People." Ebony, Mr, 1966. [Principal William Moore, Carver Elementary School, St. Louis]

School District Organization for Missouri, A Plan to Produce Equal Access to Educational Opportunity for All Children. Report of the Missouri School District Reorganization Commission. Minneapolis, MN: U. of Minnesota, College of Education, N, 1968, 162 pp. ERIC ED 026 171.

Schwilck, Gene L. "Community Schools in St. Louis." Danforth News and Notes, Mr, 1970.

Semmell, Herbert. "Report on and Investigation of Racial Isolation in St. Louis Public Elementary and Secondary Schools." Unpublished study for U.S. Commission on Civil Rights, 1966.

Shepard, Samuel, Jr. "Instructional Planning for the Urban Setting." In Urban School Administration. Edited by Troy V. McKelvey and Austin D. Swanson. Beverly Hills, CA: Sage, 1969. [St. Louis]

Spitzer, Dana L. "Jimmy Rollins Is Back in St. Louis (Temporarily)." New Republic, Je 1, 1968. [Columbia]

_____. "School Segregation Survives City's Promise." 2 parts. St. Louis Post-Dispatch, My 14 and 15, 1972. [St. Louis]

The Status of Integration in the St. Louis Public Schools During the 1966-67 School Year--A Factual Report to the Board of Education. St. Louis, MO: St. Louis Public Schools, Je, 1967, 77 pp. ERIC ED 016 017.

Streifford, David M. "Racial Economic Dualism in St. Louis." Review of Black Political Economy 4(Spring, 1974):63-81.

Stromberg, Jerome S. A Comparison of Pruitt-Igoe Residents and Their Non-Public Housing Neighbors. St. Louis, MO: Department of Sociology, Washington U., 1967. [St. Louis]

Sullivan, Margaret L. P. "St. Louis Ethnic Neighborhoods, 1850-1930: An Introduction." Bull. Mo. Hist. Soc. 33(Ja, 1977):64-76.

Sutker, Solomon, and Smith, Sara (eds.). Racial Transition in the Inner Suburb: Studies of the St. Louis Area. New York: Praeger, 1974.

Tobin, Gary. "St. Louis Cannot and Will Not Finance Its Public Schools." Focus Midwest 7(1970):24-27.

Troen, Selwyn K. "Popular Education in Nineteenth Century St. Louis." History of Education Quarterly 13(Spring, 1973):23-40.

_____. The Public and the Schools Shaping the St. Louis System, 1838-1920. Columbia, MO: U. of Missouri Press, 1975.

Trombley, William. "'Magnet Schools' Prove To Be Costly in St. Louis." Los Angeles Times, F 9, 1977.

_____. "Magnet Schools Costly in St. Louis." Integrateducation 15(N-D, 1977):97-99.

Truitt, Rosalind C. "Sumner: Black to Black and White." Kansas City Times, My 29, 1978. [Sumner High School]

U.S. Commission on Civil Rights. Hearing Held in St. Louis, Missouri, January 14-17, 1970. Washington, DC: GPO, 1971.

U.S. Commission on Civil Rights, Missouri Advisory Committee. General Revenue Sharing in St. Louis City and County. Washington, DC: The Commission, F, 1976.

Valien, Bonita H. The St. Louis Story: A Study of Desegregation. New York: Anti-Defamation League, 1956.

Walter, Ingo, and Kramer, John E. "Political Autonomy and Economic Dependence in an All-Negro Municipality." American Journal of Economics and Sociology 28(Jl, 1969):225-248. [Kinloch]

Watts, Robert P. "These 'Colored' United States: Missouri: A Literal Paradox." Messenger 7(My, 1925):187-189.

Williams, Henry Carson. "The Status of Minority Public Education in Missouri from 1820 to 1954: A Legal History." Doctoral dissertation, Saint Louis U., 1977. Univ. Microfilms Order No. 78-00524.

Williams, Henry Sullivan. "The Development of the Negro Public School System in Missouri." Journal of Negro History 5(Ap, 1920):137-165.

_____. "The Development of the Negro Public School System in Missouri." Master's thesis, U. of Chicago, 1917.

Winn, Stephen E. "White Exodus Snags Integration Effort." Kansas City Star, Mr 4, 1979. [Kansas City public schools]

Wolfgram, Dorothea. "Caution: Merging Children." Washington University Magazine 48(Winter, 1978):8-13. [Merger of Ferguson-Florimont, Kinloch, and Berkeley school districts]

Wright, John Aaron. "The Desegregation of All-Black Schools That Existed in St. Louis Prior to 1954." Doctoral dissertation, Saint Louis U., 1978. Univ. Microfilms Order No. 7814656. [Fourteen school districts in St. Louis County]

Zoeckler, Eric L. "How Busing Came Peacefully to Kirkwood, Mo." Christian Science Monitor, O 24, 1975.

Montana

Bureau of Government Research. The Urban Dimension in Montana. Missoula, MT: U. of Montana, 1968.

Gordon, Taylor. Born To Be. Seattle: U. of Washington Press, 1977. [White Sulphur Springs]

Montana, Unemployment Compensation Commission. Distribution of Minority Groups in Montana--Federal Civil Rights Act of 1964. Helena, MT: Unemployment Compensation Commission, My, 1966.

Montana Advisory Committee. The Media in Montana: Its Effects on Minorities and Women. Washington, DC: U.S. Commission on Civil Rights, 1976.

Nebraska

Chudacoff, Howard P. Mobile Americans: Residential and Social Mobility in Omaha, 1880-1920. New York: Oxford U. Press, 1972.

Gilliland, Mary C. "The Negro in Nebraska: A Resource Teaching Unit." Master's thesis, U. of Nebraska, Lincoln, 1970.

Haywood, Harry. "A Child of Slaves." In Black Bolshevik. Autobiography of an Afro-American Communist, pp. 5-35. Chicago: Liberator Press, 1978. [Growing up black in South Omaha during the years before World War I]

Lake, J. A., and Hansen, R. "Negro Segregation in Nebraska Schools--1860-1870." Nebraska Law Review 33(N, 1953):44-53.

Nebraska Advisory Committee to the United States Commission on Civil Rights. Nebraska's Official Civil Rights Agencies. Washington, DC: U.S. Commission on Civil Rights, Ag, 1975.

Scrimsher, Lila Gravatt (ed.). "The Diaries and Writings of George A. Matson, Black Citizen of Lincoln, Nebraska, 1901-1913." Nebraska History 52(1971):133-168.

Stepp, Vicki and others. Nebraska Population Estimates by Age, Color, and Sex. Lincoln, Bureau of Business Research, U. of Nebraska, 1977.

U.S. Commission on Civil Rights, Nebraska Advisory Committee. Nebraska's Official Civil Rights Agencies. Washington, DC: The Commission, Ag, 1975.

Writers' Program. The Negroes of Nebraska. St. Clair Shores, MI: Scholarly Press, 1973 reprint.

Nevada

Gronert, June C., and Starrett, Gloria M. The Basques of Nevada: An Integrated Social Studies Unit, 1976. ERIC ED 146 105.

Leyland, George. A School Districting Feasibility Study. The Problem in Clark County, Nevada and a Technical Solution Using Available Computer Technology, O, 1974. ERIC ED 147 976.

Research and Educational Planning Center. An Analysis of the Educational and Employment Needs of the Washoe County Black Community. Reno, NE: U. of Nevada, 1969.

Rusco, Elmer R. Good Time Coming? Black Nevadans in the Nineteenth Century. Westport, CT: Greenwood Press, 1975.

_____. Minority Groups in Nevada. Reno, NE: Bureau of Government Research, U. of Nevada, 1966.

Shepperson, Wilbur S. Restless Strangers: Nevada's Immigrants and their Interpreters. Reno, NE: U. of Nevada Press, 1970.

U.S. Commission on Civil Rights. "Clark County, Nevada (Las Vegas)." In School Desegregation in Ten Communities, pp. 198-214. Washington, DC: GPO, Je, 1973.

Voices of Black Nevada. Reno, NE: Bureau of Governmental Research, U. of Nevada, 1971.

New Hampshire

Redden, John D. "History and Development of the Parochial Schools in the Diocese of Manchester, New Hampshire." Doctoral dissertation, Fordham U., 1935.

Theriault, George French. "The Franco-Americans in a New England Community: An Experiment in Survival." Doctoral dissertation, Harvard U., 1951. [Nashua]

New Jersey

Adams, Ezola Bolden. "The Role and Function of the Manual Training and Industrial School at Bordentown as an Alternative School, 1915-1955." Doctoral dissertation, Rutgers U., 1977. Univ. Microfilms Order No. 7804581.

African Free School Evaluation, Regular School Year, and Summer. ESEA Title I, 1970-1971. Haddenfield, NJ: Communication Technology Corp., 1971, 68 pp. ERIC ED 060 160.

Anastasia, George. "A State of Surprising Integration." Philadelphia Inquirer, Jl 11, 1976. [Desegregation in New Jersey]

_____. "The Camden Example: Education vs. Integration." Philadelphia Inquirer, Jl 11, 1976.

Anderson, John Robert. "Negro Education in the Public Schools of Newark, New Jersey, During the Nineteenth Century." Doctoral dissertation, Rutgers U., 1972. Univ. Microfilms Order No. 73-06428.

Baines, James, and Young, William M. "The Sudden Rise and Decline of New Jersey Street Academies." Phi Delta Kappan 53(D, 1971): 240-242.

Barbaro, Fred. "Newark: Political Brokers." Society 9(S-O, 1972):42-54.

Begel, Jesse H. "Progress of Negro School Children in the Public Schools of Pilesgrove Township, New Jersey." Master's thesis, Temple U., 1938.

Brawley, Benjamin G. "'Ironsides': The Bordentown School." Southern Workman 60(O, 1931): 410-416.

Bressler, Marvin, and Wilcox, Preston R. Participant-Observational Study of the Princeton Summer Studies Program for Environmentally Deprived High School Boys. Washington, DC: Bureau of Research, U.S. Office of Education, S, 1966.

Brooks, Thomas R. "Breakdown in Newark." Dissent 19(Winter, 1972):128-317.

"The Case of the Colored Children in the Public Schools." New Jersey Law Journal 6(O, 1883):318.

Claiborne, William. "'Hillbillies' Cling to Culture." Washington Post, D 14, 1975. [Ramapo Mountain People]

Cohen, David Steven. The Ramapo Mountain People. New Brunswick, NJ: Rutgers U. Press, 1974.

Cole, Leonard A. Blacks in Power: A Comparative Study of Black and White Elected Officials. Princeton, NJ: Princeton U. Press, 1976.

"Colored Children in the Public Schools." New Jersey Law Journal 6(S, 1883):286.

Comptroller General of the United States. Improved Administration Needed in New Jersey for the Federal Program of Aid to Educationally Deprived Children. Washington, DC: General Accounting Office, Ap 7, 1971.

Conforti, Joseph M. "Newark: Ghetto or City?" Society 9(S-O, 1972):20-32.

_____. "Racial Conflict in Central Cities: The Newark Teachers Strikes." Society 12 (N-D, 1974):22-33.

Conner, Malcolm. "A Comparative Study of Black and White Public Education in Nineteen-Century New Brunswick, New Jersey." Doctoral dissertation, Rutgers U., 1976. Univ. Microfilms Order No. 76-27312.

Cook, Fred J. "It's Our City, Don't Destroy It." New York Times Magazine, Je 30, 1968. [Newark]

_____. "Wherever the Central Cities Are Going, Newark Is Going to Get There First." New York Times Magazine, Jl 25, 1971.

Cooley, H. S. Slavery in New Jersey. Baltimore, MD: Johns Hopkins Press, 1896.

Cunningham, Barbara (ed.). The New Jersey Ethnic Experience. Union City, NJ: William H. Wise and Co., 1977.

Curvin, Robert. "Black Power in City Hall." Society 9(S-O, 1972):55-58. [Newark]

Damerell, Reginald G. Triumph in a White Suburb: The Dramatic Story of Teaneck, N.J., The First Town in the Nation to Vote for Integrated Schools. New York: Morrow, 1968.

Daniels, Roland H. "A Case Study of Desegregation in the Public Schools of Trenton, New Jersey." Doctoral dissertation, Rutgers U., 1959. Univ. Microfilms Order No. 59-5321.

Deckelnick, Gary. "Student Court Instrumental in Ending Racial Problems." Asbury Park Evening Press, N 5, 1975. [Lakewood, NJ]

Diliberto, Gioia. "70% White and 60% Black." Hackensack Record, N 15, 1977. [Englewood]

Egelhof, Joseph. "Newark['s Black Community Since the 1967 Riots]." Chicago Tribune Magazine, My 22, 1977.

Engelhardt and Engelhardt, Inc. Transition in the Plainfield [New Jersey] Public Schools. A Report on Public School Needs. Purdy Station, Westchester County, NY: Engelhardt and Engelhardt, Ag, 1970.

"Engelwood [N.J.] School Bias Charges." Crisis, D, 1954.

Epps, C. Roy. A Place to Live: A Study of Ward II--New Brunswick. New Brunswick, NJ: New Brunswick Urban League, 1976.

Feldman, Sandra. "Newark Teachers Win Despite Mass Arrests." New America, Mr 24, 1970.

15X, David. "Differs With Interpretation of Newark, NJ Teachers Strike (letter). Muhammad Speaks, Mr 5, 1971.

Francis, Mamie Elaine. "These 'Colored' United States: New Jersey: Those Inimitable Individualists." Messenger 7(Ag, 1925):285, 307.

Gaby, Daniel. "Newark: The Promise of Survival." Nation, D 14, 1974.

Goldstein, Rhoda L. "The Participant as Observer." Phylon, Fall, 1964. [What a sociologist learned from participation in a community crisis around the issue of school desegregation]

Governor's Select Commission. "Newark's Decaying Public Schools." Integrated Education, Mr-Ap, 1968.

Hayden, Tom. "Community Organizing and the War on Poverty." Liberation, N, 1965. [Newark]

_____. Rebellion in Newark: Official Violence and Ghetto Response. New York: Random House, 1967.

Hayes, Arthur S. "Black Studies Called a Failure." Hackensack Journal, Ag 11, 1978. [Black studies in New Jersey schools]

Hendrickson, Bill. "The Unmaking of Teaneck's Image." Hackensack Record, Ag 29, 1975.

"How One School District Cooled Down a Pot of Boiling Racial Troubles." American School Board Journal 161 (Ag, 1974):39-42. [Fairfield Township]

"Integration in Union Twp., N.J." NJEA Review 44(O, 1970):25-27.

Jackson, Kenneth T., and Jackson, Barbara L. "The Black Experience in Newark: The Growth of the Ghetto, 1870-1970." In New Jersey Since 1860: New Findings and Interpretations. Edited by William C. Wright. Trenton, NJ: New Jersey Historical Commission, 1972.

Jensen, Rita. "A Tale of Two Schools: Near All-White School 27 Has Supplies, While All-Minority School 6 Is Improverished." Paterson News, O 30, 1978.

"Jersey High Court Backs Reparations to Teacher, Victim of Housing Bias." Muhammad Speaks, Je 20, 1969.

Johnson, Howard M. "The Coordination of a Study of Racial Imbalance in the Englewood Public Schools, Englewood, New Jersey." Doctoral dissertation, Harvard U., 1965.

Kaplan, Harold. Urban Renewal Politics, Slum Clearance in Newark. New York: Columbia U. Press, 1963.

Kerney, J. Regan. "Blacks at Catholic Schools Here Exceed 90%." Trenton Sun-Times Advertiser, My 9, 1976. [Trenton]

La Frankie, Robert Lewis. "Englewood: A Northern City in Crisis." In The Urban R's. Edited by Robert Dentler and Others. New York: Praeger, 1967.

_____. "The Englewood, New Jersey School Conflict: A Case Study of Decision-Making and Racial Segregation, 1930-1963." Doctoral dissertation, Columbia U., 1967. Univ. Microfilms Order No. 67-12692.

Leggett, John C., and Gioglio, Jerry. "Break Out the Double Digit: Mass Unemployment in the City of New Brunswick." Review of Radical Political Economics 10(Spring, 1978):32-46.

Liss, Moe, and Robinson, James C. "The Carteret Story: The Peer Group Deals with Racial Conflict." Phi Delta Kappan (N, 1978): 169-172. [Carteret High School, Carteret]

"Many Steps To Go. Report of the Task Force on Human Rights." NJEA Review 43(S, 1969):58-61. [New Jersey Education Association]

Marburger, Carl L. "Trouble in High Schools: New Jersey Responds." Compact 5(1969):36-38.

Meier, August, and Rudwick, Elliott. "Early Boycotts of Segregated Schools: The East Orange, New Jersey, Experience, 1899-1906." History of Education Quarterly, Spring, 1967.

Miller, William G. "New Brunswick: Community Action Project." Studies on the Left, Spring, 1965.

Monat, William R. "Strategies and Limitations of Urban Educational Reform. The Case of Trenton, New Jersey." Education and Urban Society, My, 1969.

"Montclair's Busing Split Growing Bitter and May Intensify White-Black Division." New York Times, Ja 30, 1974.

Moore, Richard S. Deteriorating School Facilities. The Gravity of New Jersey's Urban School Construction Needs. Prepared for the New Jersey Urban Schools Development Council. Reprinted in U.S. Congress, 91st, 1st session, House of Representatives, Commi Committee on Education and Labor, General Subcommittee on Education, School Construction...Hearings, pp. 147-174. Washington, DC: GPO, 1969.

Morris, Jack H. "How One Suburb Acted to Integrate Smoothly, Avoid Major Incidents." Wall Street Journal, D 28, 1970. [Willingboro]

Morrow, E. Frederic. Way Down South Up North. Philadelphia, PA: United Church Press, 1973. [Hackensack, New Jersey and elsewhere]

New Jersey State Advisory Committee. Public Housing in Newark's Central Ward. Washington, DC: U.S. Commission on Civil Rights, Ap, 1968.

"The Newark School System: A Study in Urban Decay." _Imani_ 5(Ag-S, 1971):6-11.

"Newark Strike Underscores Blight in Urban Education." _American Teacher_, Mr, 1971.

"Newark Teachers Explain Position." _Muhammad Speaks_, F 26, 1971.

Nortman, P. Bernard. _An Economic Blueprint for Newark. The Overall Economic Development Program._ Newark, NJ: Office of Economic Development, City of Newark, Jl, 1968.

OEEO. _Ten Years At a Glance, 1968-1978._ Trenton, NJ: Department of Education, 1978.

Oak, Eleanor Hill. "The Development of Separate Education in New Jersey." Master's thesis, Howard U., 1935.

Oak, V. V., and Oak, E. H. "The Illegal Status of Separate Education in New Jersey." _School and Society_, My 21, 1938.

O'Shea, John. "Newark: Negroes Move Toward Power." _Atlantic Monthly_, N, 1965.

Palley, Marian L., Russo, Robert, and Scott, Edward. "Subcommunity Leadership in a Black Ghetto. A Study of Newark, New Jersey." _Urban Affairs Quarterly_ 5(1970):291-312.

Parker, Glenn M., and O'Connor, William. _Racism in Schools: A Response Utilizing Laboratory Training_, 1969. New Jersey Community Action Training Institute, P.O. Box 4078, Trenton, NJ 08610. [Lawrence Township]

Phillips, W. M., Jr. "Educational Policy, Community Participation, and Race." _Journal of Negro Education_ 44(Summer, 1975):257-267. [Newark]

Phillips, William M., Jr., and Conforti, Joseph M. _Social Conflict: Teachers' Strikes in Newark, 1964-1971._ Trenton, NJ: State Department of Education, 1972.

Phillips, W. M., Jr. and others. _Participation of the Black Community in Selected Aspects of the Educational Institution of Newark, 1958-1972_, Jl, 1973. ERIC ED 091 492.

Pingeon, Frances D. "Dissenting Attitudes toward the Negro in New Jersey--1837." _New Jersey History_ 89(Winter, 1971):197-220.

Porambo, Ron. _No Cause for Indictment: An Autopsy of Newark._ New York: Holt, Rinehart & Winston, 1971.

Power, Charles T. "The Jackson Whites: Tree Minus Roots." _Los Angeles Times_, S 29, 1978.

Presley, Beverly A. "School Desegregation in Roselle, New Jersey: Desegregation Problems in a Northern Suburban Community with a Small Black Population." Doctoral dissertation, Rutgers U., 1976. Univ. Microfilms Order No. 77-13283.

Price, Clement A. "The Afro-American Community of Newark, 1917-1947. A Social History." Doctoral dissertation, Rutgers U., 1975. Univ. Microfilms Order No. 76-7325.

Price, William A. "Suspended Teacher Turns Defense Into Attack." _National Guardian_, Mr 11, 1967. [Teaching in a Newark ghetto school]

"Princeton, N.J.--City of Isolation, Culture, Opulence, Cleanliness." _Los Angeles Times_, Mr 28, 1974.

Queen, R. "The Trenton School Cases--A Primary Lesson in Democracy." _National Journal_ 4 (Je, 1946):147-151.

"Racial Imbalance and Municipal Boundaries-- Educational Crisis in Morristown." _Rutgers Law Review_ 24(Winter, 1970).

Raubinger, Frederick M. "The New Jersey Doctrine." _Integrated Education_, Ag, 1963.

Reid, Ira DeA. _The Negro in New Jersey._ Trenton, NJ: n.p., 1932.

Rouse, Evart. "'Reluctant Principal' Turned Things Around." _Philadelphia Inquirer_, Mr 25, 1979. [Camden High School, Camden]

Shaw, Douglas V. "The Making of an Immigrant City: Ethnic and Cultural Conflict in Jersey City, New Jersey, 1850-1877." Doctoral dissertation, U. of Rochester, 1972.

Shipler, David K. "The White Niggers of Newark." _Harper's_ 245(Ag, 1972):77-83.

Spengler, David. "The Englewood-Teaneck, New Jersey Experience." In _School Desegregation in the North._ Edited by T. Bentley Edwards and Frederick M. Wirt. San Francisco, CA: Chandler, 1967.

Stark, Rodney, and Steinberg, Stephen. _It Did Happen Here--An Investigation of Political Anti-Semitism._ New York: Anti-Defamation League, 1967. [Wayne Township]

Sternlieb, George, Burchell, Robert, and Sagalyn, Lynn B. _The Affluent Suburb: Princeton [N.J.]_ New Brunswick, NJ: Transaction, 1971.

Sternlieb, George, and Beaton, W. Patrick. _The Zone of Emergence: Plainfield, New Jersey._ New Brunswick, NJ: Transaction, 1971.

Streit, Peggy. "Princeton's Lesson: School Integration Is Not Enough." _New York Times Magazine_, Je 21, 1964.

Strohl, Harry A. "The Elimination of Segrega-
tion in the Elementary Schools of Southern
New Jersey." Doctoral dissertation,
Columbia U., 1954.

_____. "Integration of Public Schools in New
Jersey." Teachers College Record, O, 1955.

Sullivan, Ronald. "There Has to Be a Better
Way to Pay for Schools." Compact 8(Mr-Ap,
1974):2-5.

Taylor, Clark. "Newark: Parasitic Suburbs."
Society 9(S-O, 1972):35-41

Tobin, E. M. "In Pursuit of Equal Taxation:
Jersey City's Struggle against Corporate
Arrogance and Tax-Dodging by the Railroad
Trust." American Journal of Economics and
Sociology 34(Ap, 1975).

Trillin, Calvin. "U.S. Journal: Mount Laurel,
N.J. Some Thoughts on Where Lines are
Drawn." New Yorker, F 2, 1976.

U.S. Commission on Civil Rights. Civil Rights
USA/Public Schools North and West, 1963,
Camden and Environs. Washington, DC: GPO,
1963.

_____. Hearings...Newark, New Jersey, Septem-
ber 11-12, 1962. Washington, DC: GPO, 1962.

_____. "Union Township, New Jersey." In
School Desegregation in Ten Communities, pp.
126-151. Washington, DC: GPO, Je, 1973.

_____. Report on New Jersey. Washington,
DC: GPO, S, 1963. [On housing, employment,
and apprenticeship training]

U.S. Congress, 90th, 1st session, Senate,
Committee on Government Operations, Permanent
Subcommittee on Investigations. Riots,
Civil and Criminal Disorders. Hearings.
Part 4. Washington, DC: GPO, 1968.
[Investigation of disorders in Plainfield,
Jl, 1967]

U.S. Congress, 90th, 2nd session, Senate,
Committee on Government Operations, Permanent
Subcommittee on Invesitgations. Riots,
Civil and Criminal Disorders...Hearings.
Part 8. Washington, DC: GPO, 1968.
[Inquiry into disorders in Newark Jl, 1967]

Vecoli, Rudolph J. The People of New Jersey.
Princeton, NJ: D. Van Nostrand, 1965.

Walker, Gerald. "Englewood and the Northern
Dilemma." Nation, Jl 6, 1963.

Walker, Joe. "Newark Teacher's Strike."
Muhammad Speaks, Ap 16, 1971.

_____. "Ocean Hill-Brownsville Veteran Tells
Why He Supports Newark Teachers Strike."
Muhammad Speaks, Mr 5, 1971. [Richard
Parrish]

_____. "Strange Things Are Happening in
Newark." Part 1. Muhammad Speaks, F 19,
1971.

Walker, Joe, and Turner, David (15X). "Two
Views on Newark Strike." Muhammad Speaks,
Je 4, 1971.

Walker, Joe. "White Teacher Loses His Job
After Using MS in Classroom." Muhammad
Speaks, N 19, 1971. [Newark]

Weinberg, Martin S., and Williams, Colin J.
"Disruption, Social Location, and Interpretive
Practices. The Case of Wayne, New Jersey."
American Sociological Review, Ap, 1969.
[Jew-Gentile relations in school affairs]

Westoff, Charles F. A Population Survey:
Population and Social Characteristics of
the Camden Area, 1964. Cherry Hill, NJ:
Jewish Federation of Camden County, 1965.

White, Jack E., Jr. Black Politics in a Dying
City, Ja, 1970. Race Relations Information
Center, Nashville, TN 37212.

Whitlock, Sarah O. "Survey of the Negro Pupils
in the Elementary Schools of New Brunswick,
N.J., October, 1929." Master's thesis,
Rutgers U., 1930.

Williams, James N. "Guidance Needs of Negro
Youth in Montclair: A Report of a
Survey of Negro Youth in Montclair, New
Jersey, and of Their Present Guidance
Activities, Oppportunities, and Needs."
Master's thesis, New Jersey State Teachers
College, 1938.

Williams, Junius. "Advocacy in Newark: The
Medical School Controversy." Third year
thesis, Yale Law School, 1968.

Wolff, Max. A Study of Racial and Ethnic Imbalance in the Paterson Public Schools.
Paterson, NJ: Board of Education, N, 1963.

(Wright) Thompson, Marion M. The Education of
Negroes in New Jersey. New York: Teachers
College, Columbia U., 1941.

Wright, Marion T. "New Jersey Leads in the
Struggle for Educational Integration."
Journal of Educational Sociology, My, 1953.

Wright, Marion M. "Mr. Baxter's School."
Proceedings of the New Jersey Historical
Society 59(Ap, 1941):116-133.

X, Lynn. "White Hoodlum Group Terrorizes Black
N.J. Youths." Muhammad Speaks, Ap 18, 1975.
[Jersey City]

Zdep, S. M. Educating Disadvantaged Urban
Children in Suburban Schools: An Evaluation.
Princeton, NJ: Educational Testing Service,
Ap, 1970, 31 pp. ERIC ED 053 186.
[Verona]

_____. "Evaluation of the Verona Plan for Sharing Educational Opportunity. Research at ETS: Projects and Publications. Princeton, NJ: Educational Testing Service, 1970.

Zdep, Stanley, and Joyce, Diane. The Newark-Verona Plan for Sharing Educational Opportunity. Princeton, NJ: Educational Testing Service, 1969.

New Mexico

Archibald, Robert. "Acculturation and Assimilation in Colonial New Mexico." New Mexico Review 53(J1, 1978):205-218.

Billette, T. E. "Santa Fe: A Study of the Effects of Negro Invasion on Property Values." American Journal of Economics and Sociology (Ja, 1957):151-162.

Bynum, H. E. "Inequality of Educational Opportunity in New Mexico." Master's thesis, U. of Southern California, 1936.

Chambers, R. L. "Negro in New Mexico." Crisis, Mr, 1952.

_____. "The New Mexico Pattern." Common Ground 9(Summer, 1949):20-27.

Coleman, Anita Scott. "Arizona and New Mexico--The Land of Esperanza." Messenger 8(S, 1926): 275-276.

Duncan, Catherine W. "A Survey of the Separate Elementary Schools for Negroes in the State of New Mexico." Master's thesis, U. of New Mexico, 1938.

Eastman, Clyde. Assessing Cultural Change in North-Central New Mexico. New Mexico State U., Las Cruces, NM: Agricultural Experiment Station, Ja, 1972, 65 pp. Agricultural Experiment Station Bulletin 592. ERIC ED 052 070.

Frieder-Vierra, Andrea. "School-Year and Summer Reading Growth of Minority and Non-Minority Children in Albuquerque, New Mexico." Doctoral dissertation, U. of New Mexico, 1975. Univ. Microfilms Order No. 76-7957.

McCarty, Frankie. "SWCEL Still Haunted by Controversy." Albuquerque Journal, Ap 23, 1972. [Southwestern Cooperative Educational Laboratory, Albuquerque]

Model Cities. Model City Area Socio-Economic and Attitude Survey, Ja, 1969. Dr. Susan Johnson, Model Cities, P.O. Box 1293, Albuquerque, NM 87103. [Albuquerque]

Moyers, Robert A. "A History of Education in New Mexico." 2 vols. Doctoral dissertation, George Peabody College for Teachers, 1941.

National Commission on Professional Rights and Responsibilities. Rio Arriba County, New Mexico. When Public Education Provides Patronage for a Political System. Washington, DC: National Education Association, 1964.

Ralston, Carolyn, and Lewis, Anne. "Bernalillo, New Mexico." In NCRIEEO Special Field Report, My, 1971.

Richardson, Barbara J. (comp.). Black Directory for the State of New Mexico. Albuquerque, N.M., 1973.

Shamberger, Elizabeth S. "An Educational History of Albuquerque." Master's thesis, U. of New Mexico, 1928.

Sunseri, Alvin R. "New Mexico in the Aftermath of the Anglo-American Conquest, 1846-1861." Doctoral dissertation, Louisiana State U., 1973.

_____. "1846-1861. A Note on Slavery and the Black Man in New Mexico." Negro History Bulletin 38(O-N, 1975):457-450.

Tjarks, Alicia V. "Demographic, Ethnic, and Occupational Structure of New Mexico, 1790." The Americas 35(J1, 1978):45-88.

Trujillo, Rupert. "Rural New Mexicans: Their Educational and Occupational Aspirations." Diss. Abstr. Int'l., 1969, 30 (2-A) 839.

U.S. Commission on Civil Rights, New Mexico Advisory Committee. Working With Your School: Handbook of the New Mexico Advisory Committee... Washington, DC: U.S. Commission on Civil Rights, 1977.

New York

Abbey, Harlan. "63% of Negroes Participate in Boycott of Schools Here." Buffalo Courier Express, My 19, 1964.

"Achieving Racial Balance. The White Plains Story." School Management, Ja, 1968.

Advisory Planning Council on Desegregation. A Study of Desegregation. Buffalo, NY: Board of Education, F 21, 1972.

Allen, James, Jr. "New York Education and the New [State] Constitution." Urban Review, F, 1967.

Andrews, Chris. "Black Student Unions Are Struggling to Survive." Rochester Times Union, Mr 8, 1979. [Rochester, NY area public schools]

Barber, Ralph W. "The Effects of Open Enrollment on Anti-Negro and Anti-White Prejudices Among Junior High School Students in Rochester, New York." Doctoral dissertation, U. of Rochester, 1968.

Beker, Jerome. A Study of Integration in Racially Imbalanced Urban Public Schools-- A Demonstration and Evaluation. Final Report. Syracuse, NY: Syracuse U., My, 1967, 549 pp. ERIC ED 013 857.

Besag, Frank P., Freedman, Allan, and Ramer, Burton. "Attitude Toward Administration of Male Negro Teachers in Buffalo." Integrated Education, O-N, 1967, p. 52.

Birkhead, Guthrie S. and others. How the Campus Proposal Failed in Syracuse, New York, Je, 1970. ERIC ED 090 678.

"Black and White: Desegregation Dispute in Mount Vernon." Columbia Journal of Law and Social Problems 5(1969):112-136.

Black Community Planning Board of Mt. Vernon, N.Y. The Biracial Parental Participation, Equality of Educational Opportunity, Superior Curriculum, Total Integration. Mt. Vernon, NY: Boone Press, F, 1968.

Bloch, Herman D. The Circle of Discrimination. An Economic and Social Study of the Black Man in New York. New York: New York U. Press, 1969.

Blumberg, Arthur, May, James, and Perry, Roger. "An Inner-City School That Changed--And Continued to Change." Education and Urban Society 6(F, 1974):222-238. [Martin Luther King Elementary School, Syracuse]

Bondarin, Arley. "The Racial Balance Plan." White Plains, New York. New York: Center for Urban Education, 1969.

Boyd, William L., and Seldin, Florence. "The Politics of School Reform in Rochester, New York." Education and Urban Society 7 (Ag, 1975):439-463.

Buchheimer, Naomi, and Buchheimer, Arnold. Equality Through Integration. A Report on Greenburgh School District No. 8. New York: Anti-Defamation League, 1965.

"Buffalo. Economy Lags As Residents Argue Busing." Black Enterprise 2(Ap, 1972):45-48.

Buffalo Public Schools. Study of Achievement in Reading of Pupils Transferred from Schools 15 and 37 to Peripheral Schools to Eliminate Overcrowding, to Abandon an Obsolete School, and to Achieve a More Desirable Racial Balance in City Schools. Buffalo, NY: School Board, 1967.

_____. Study of Achievement of Pupils Transferred to Achieve a More Desirable Racial Balance. Buffalo, NY: Board of Education, Mr, 1967.

Build Black Paper Number One: The Buffalo Public Schools. ESCO, P.O. Box 36, Station O, Buffalo, NY 14208.

"Busing at Great Neck." Newsweek, F 17, 1969. [Long Island]

Buskin, Martin. "City-to-Suburb Busing: What Next for Great Neck?" School Management, Ap, 1969. [Long Island]

"Busing Still Going Where It All Began." Los Angeles Times, D 15, 1975. [New Rochelle]

Buzbee, Ellen W. Suburban Schools Confront Urban Problems. 1968 Westchester Chapter, The American Jewish Committee, 48 Mamaroneck Avenue, White Plains, NY. [Deals with Greenburgh, New Rochelle, Mount Vernon, White Plains, Scarsdale, and Bronxville]

Cable, Lawrence T., and Beker, Jerome. "Social Characteristics and Educational Aspirations of Northern, Lower-Class, Predominantly Negro Parents Who Accepted and Declined a School Integration Opportunity." Journal of Negro Education, Fall, 1968. [Syracuse]

Calhoun, Daniel. The Intelligence of a People. Princeton, NJ: Princeton U. Press, 1973. [New York State, 1770-1850]

Campbell, Alan K. and Others. The Negro in Syracuse. Syracuse, NY: University College, Syracuse U., 1964.

Carpenter, Niles. Nationality, Color, and Economic Opportunity. The Inquiry, 1927. [Buffalo public schools]

Clavel, Pierre, and Goldsmith, William W. (eds.). Poverty in Central New York: Institutional Change in Non-Metropolitan America. Ithaca, NY: Center for Urban Development Research, Cornell U., Mr, 1972.

Clift, Virgil A. A Study of Library Services for the Disadvantaged in Buffalo, Rochester, and Syracuse, Je, 1969. ERIC ED 033 734.

Colton, David L. Urban School Desegregation Costs. Part I. Case Studies. St. Louis, MO: Center for Educational Field Studies, Washington U., N, 1977. [Buffalo]

Conner, Shirley. "Integration Fight Taken to Court." Education News, Ag 5, 1968. [Buffalo]

"Cornell Forum Discusses School Crisis." United Teacher, D 18, 1968. [John Niemeyer, Blanche Lewis, David Rogers, and Norman Hill]

Corwin, Ronald D. "School Desegregation in Syracuse: A Study in Community Decision-Making." Doctoral dissertation, Syracuse U., 1968. Univ. Microfilms Order No. 68-13,821.

Council for American Unity. Crisis in the Public Schools. Racial Segregation Northern Style. Confrontations at New Rochelle and Mount Vernon, New York. Council for American Unity, 79 Madison Avenue, New York, NY 10001, 1965.

Crawford, Marion Ann. "A Model of Spatio-Temporal Change: Racial-Residential Succession in Yonkers, New York." Master's thesis, U. of Rhode Island, 1974.

"Croton Impressions: Conflict and Concern." Syracuse Metropolitan Review, Mr, 1968. (Published by the Continuing Education Center for the Public Service, University College, Syracuse U.) [Croton Elementary School in Syracuse]

Crown, Judith. [4 articles on school desegregation in Yonkers, N.Y.] Yonkers Herald-Statesman, F 13-16, 1977.

"CUE Clarifies Position in Great Neck Hassle." United Teacher, F 19, 1969. [Great Neck, Long Island]

Cutler, Marilyn H. "Agonizing and Exacting: One Board's Plan to Integrate the Schools of Its Community." American School Board Journal 161(Ag, 1974):37-38. [Niagara Falls]

Danella, Rose DeCarlo. "Racial Balance in Utica: A Case Study." Doctoral dissertation, Syracuse U., 1975. Univ. Microfilms Order No. 76-18,505.

DeNoie, B. J. "Malverne: Integration Is Not Enough." National Review, Jl 12, 1966. [Malverne, Long Island]

Dentler, Robert A. "Educational Disadvantage and the New York State Constitution." Proceedings of the Academy of Political Science, Ja, 1967. [Comments by Clarence Senior and M. Sylvester King]

Division of Planning and Research. First Interim Evaluation Report: Urban-Suburban Pupil Transfer Program 1971-1972. Rochester, NY: City School District, Ag, 1972.

Dixon, Phillip. "The Minority Majority. Rochester Schools in Transition." (3 articles) Rochester Times-Union, My 3-5, 1976.

Dodson, Dan W. and others. High School Racial Confrontation. A Study of the White Plains, New York, Student Boycott. White Plains, NY: Board of Education, F 4, 1969.

Dodson, Dan W. and others. Racial Imbalance in Public Education in New Rochelle, New York. New York: Center for Human Relations and Community Studies, New York U., 1957.

Douglass, Frederick. "The Suffrage and Educational Questions." Douglass' Monthly, Mr, 1859.

Dworkin, Rosalind J. "Segregation and Suburbia." In Our Children's Burden. Edited by Raymond W. Mack. New York: Random House, 1968. [Hempstead, Long Island]

Economic Consultants Organization, Inc. Welfare: Households and Housing. Prepared for Westchester County Department of Planning, White Plains, New York. White Plains, NY: Economic Consultants Organization, Inc., Je, 1970.

Ehrenhalt, Samuel H. Some Aspects of the Ghetto Labor Market in New York, N, 1971. U.S. Department of Labor, Bureau of Labor Statistics, 341 Ninth Avenue, New York, NY 10001

Elfin, Mel. "Why Pick on New Rochelle [N.Y.]." Reporter, D 8, 1960.

EQUAL. "Observing a Princeton Plan in Operation [in Greenburgh, N.Y.]." EQUAL Newsletter, Je, 1964. [EQUAL, 28 East 35th Street, New York, NY]

Ettinger, Albert C. Integrating Syracuse Public Schools. Syracuse, NY: Syracuse Area Council, State Commission for Human Rights, Ja 13, 1964.

Everett, Samuel. "A Community School Ends Segregation." School Executive, Jl, 1954. [Greenburgh No. 8]

Farley, Ena L. "The Denial of Black Equality Under the States Rights Dictum: New York, 1865 to 1873." Afro-Am. N.Y. Life Hist. 1 (Ja, 1977):9-23.

_____. "The Right to Education." In "The Issue of Black Equality in New York State, 1865-1873," pp. 146-191. Doctoral dissertation, U. of Wisconsin, 1973.

Feron, James. "White Students in Minority." New York Times, D 16, 1975. [Desegregation in Mount Vernon]

_____. "Year After Racial Clash, Ossining Copes With Tension and 'Inferiority.'" New York Times, F 24, 1975. [Ossining High School, NY]

Field, Phyllis Frances. "The Struggle for Black Suffrage in New York State, 1846-1869." Doctoral dissertation, Cornell U., 1974. Univ. Microfilms Order No. 75-1433.

Firester, Joan, and Kazlow, Carole. "The Great Great Neck War." Phi Delta Kappan 57(F, 1976):379-383.

Fishman, James J. and others. "With All Deliberate Delay: School Desegregation in Mount Vernon." In Limits of Justice. The Courts' Role in School Desegregation, pp. 359-409. Edited by Howard I. Kalodner and James J. Fishman. Cambridge, MA: Ballinger, 1978. [Mt. Vernon, NY]

Fiske, Edward B. "A Court Challenge Is Planned." New York Times, D 16, 1975. [Desegregation in Newburgh]

Flanagan, Bill. "The Uncivil War, Where Racial Strife Destroys a Community." Report, My, 1966. [Malverne, Long Island]

Flynn, Francis C. "Origin, Growth, and Development of the Catholic Schools in Yonkers, New York." Master's thesis, Fordham U., 1935.

Foster, Gerald Anthony. "Social Planning and Racial Integration in the Public Schools." Doctoral dissertation, Columbia U., 1978. Univ. Microfilms Order No. 780 9900. [Greenburgh and Mount Vernon, NY]

Fowler, George W. The First 120 Years: An Historical Narrative of the Syracuse Public Schools. Syracuse, NY: Syracuse City School District, 1969.

Frederickson, H. George. "Exploring Urban Priorities: The Case of Syracuse." Urban Affairs Quarterly (S, 1969):31-43.

"Freeport, N.Y. Achieved Racial Balance--And Then Some." American School Board Journal, Jl, 1969.

Funkhouser, Terry. "The Manhasset Reaction to Elementary School Integration." In School Desegregation in the North. Edited by T. Bentley Edwards and Frederick M. Wirt. San Francisco, CA: Chandler, 1967. [Long Island]

Gallagher, Sr. Marie Patrice. The History of Catholic Elementary Education in the Diocese of Buffalo, 1847-1944. Washington, DC: Catholic U. of America Press, 1945.

Gary, Louis R. and others. The Collapse of Nonpublic Education: Rumor or Reality? New York: New York State Commission on the Quality, Cost and Financing of Elementary and Secondary Education, 1971.

Goldberg, Herman R. Desegregation of the Elementary Schools. Special Report to the Board of Education, F, 1967. City School District, 13 Fitzhugh Street South, Rochester, NY 14614.

Goldberg, Herman R., and Iman, Raymond S. "Project Unique and Efforts to Eliminate Racial Imbalance in Rochester, New York." In Models for Integrated Education, pp. 7-23. Edited by Daniel U. Levine. Worthington, OH: Jones, 1971.

Goodman, Walter. "Busing for Integration Is Working Well in Central 7 School District-- Knock Wood." New York Times Magazine, Ap 9, 1972. [Greenburgh, No. 7]

Graves, Marian F., and Bedell, Frederick D. A Three-Year Evaluation of the White Plains Racial Balance Plan. White Plains, NY: White Plains Public Schools, O 16, 1967.

Greenhouse, Ezra. "Harmony in Black and White." Syracuse Herald American, Ap 11, 1976. [Shea Junior High School, Syracuse]

Greenspan, Stephen H., and Grasberger, Friedrich J. Target: The Three E's: A Study of the Organizational and Financial Structures of Public Education in Monroe County [N.Y.], F, 1969. Rochester Bureau of Municipal Research, 37 S. Washington St., Rochester, NY 14608.

Griffen, Clyde, and Griffen, Sally. Natives and Newcomers: The Ordering of Opportunity in Mid-nineteenth-century Poughkeepsie. Cambridge, MA: Harvard U. Press, 1977.

Gross, Norman N. "An Interdistrict Transfer Program." Integrateducation 13(My-Je, 1975): 135-136. [Rochester area]

_____. "Reaching for a Dream: An Experiment in Two-Way Busing." Children 17(Jl-Ag, 1970). [Rochester]

Gunther, Max. "Why a Northern Town Fights School Integration." Saturday Evening Post, S 19, 1964. [Malverne, Long Island]

Heifetz, Robert. "The Public Sector, Residential Desegregation, and the Schools: A Case Study from Buffalo, New York." Urban Review, F, 1968.

Helms, Lelia. Preliminary Report on the Survey of Penfield School District Residents' Reactions to the Penfield-Rochester Transfer Program. Brockport, NY: State U. College, Ap 1, 1969.

_____. Progress Report: Penfield School District's Reactions to the Penfield-Rochester Transfer Program. Brockport, NY: State U. College, F 1, 1970.

Hevesi, Dennis. "Integration Makes the Grade." Newsday, Je 11, 1978. [Malverne, Long Island]

Hoffman, Jeffry, and Seltzer, Richard. "Migrant Farm Labor in Upstate New York." Columbia Journal of Law and Social Problems 4(Mr, 1968).

Information Center on Education. Racial/Ethnic Distribution of Public School Students and Staff in New York State 1969/70. Albany, NY: State Department of Education, 1970.

Ingrassia, Michele. "Desegregating an Integrated School." Newsday, N 8, 1976. [Floyd B. Watson Elementary School, Rockville Centre]

Jackson, Rose Juanita. "The Black Educational Experience in a Northern City: Albany, New York, 1830-1970." Doctoral dissertation, Northwestern U., 1976. Univ. Microfilms Order No. 77-10040.

Jaquith, D. H. "School Integration in Syracuse, New York." In U.S. Commission on Civil Rights. Paper Prepared for National Conference on Equal Educational Opportunity in America's Cities. Washington, DC: GPO, 1968.

Johnson, Carroll F. "Racial Balance. A Case Study." New York State Education, D, 1967. [White Plains]

_____. "White Plains Racial Balance Plan." In U.S. Commission on Civil Rights. Papers Prepared for National Conference on Equal Educational Opportunity in America's Cities. Washington, DC: GPO, 1968.

Jones, Michael Anthony. "Descriptive Analysis of Aggregate Vote. Totals of Selected Wards in the 1971 Rochester School Board Election with Regard to Race and Ideology." Doctoral dissertation, U. of Rochester, 1977. Univ. Microfilms Order No. 7815261.

Kaplan, John. "Segregation Litigation and the Schools—Part I: The New Rochelle Experience." Northwestern University Law Review 58 (1963).

Kaplan, Samuel. The Dream Deferred: People, Politics, and Planning in the Suburbs. New York: Random House, 1977. [Port Washington]

Kelly, Beverly. "A History of the Black Community in Essex County, 1850-1860." Master's thesis, Teachers College, Columbia U., 1969.

Kemble, Eugenia. "The Campus School." United Teacher, My 1, 1968. [Syracuse]

Kiesling, Herbert J. The Relationship of School Inputs to Public School Performance in New York State, O, 1969. ERIC ED 051 585.

Kobrin, David. The Black Minority in Early New York. Albany, NY: New York State Education Dept., Office of State History, 1971. ERIC ED 061 364.

Kriesberg, Louis. "Rearing Children for Educational Achievement in Fatherless Families." Journal of Marriage and the Family, My, 1967. [Syracuse]

Kuznicki, Ellen Marie. "An Ethnic School in American Education: A Study of the Origins, Development and Merits of the Educational System of the Felician Sisters in the Polish American Catholic Schools of Western New York." Doctoral dissertation, Kansas State U., 1973.

Laing, Donald S. A Report on the Positive Results of Buffalo's Program of Quality Integrated Education. Buffalo, NY: Board of Education, Ja 13, 1971.

_____. Other Aspects of Buffalo's Program of Quality Integrated Education. Buffalo, NY: Board of Education, F 24, 1971.

Lamitie, Robert E. The Future of Education on the Niagara Frontier, 1970. Western New York School Development Council, 27 California Drive, Williamsville, NY 14221.

Lang, Gladys, and Brodbeck, Arthur J. A Plan for Accelerating Quality Integration in the Buffalo Public School System. New York: Center for Urban Education, 1966.

Lang, Gladys, Inger, Morton, and Mallett, Roy. Resistance and Support for School Desegregation Proposals: A Study of Parental Reactions in Rochester. New York: Center for Urban Education, O, 1967.

La Porte, Robert, Jr., Beker, Jerome, and Willie, Charles V. "The Evolution of Public Educational Policy: School Desegregation in a Northern City." Urban Education, II, No. 3 (1966). [Syracuse, NY]

Leary, Sr. Mary Ancilla. The History of Catholic Education in the Diocese of Albany. Washington, DC: Catholic U. of America Press, 1957.

Leonard, Elizabeth. History of the Riverdale [N.Y.] Children's Association, formerly the Colored Orphan's Asylum: 1836-1956. Schlesinger Library, Radcliffe College, Cambridge, MA., n.d.

Lipton, Aaron. "Classroom Grouping and Integration." Integrated Education, F-Mr, 1964. [Hartsdale]

_____. "Day-to-Day Problems of School Integration." Integrated Education, Je-Jl, 1965. [Hartsdale]

McKelvey, Blake. "Rochester's Ethnic Transformation." Rochester History 25(Jl, 1963): 1-24.

McKelvey, Troy V. Problems Incident to Urban School Desegregation: An Institute for School Administrators of the Buffalo and Niagara Falls Public Schools. Interim Report Draft. Buffalo, NY: State U. of New York, Department of Educational Administration, Ap 15, 1969. ERIC ED 045 744.

McLaughlin, V. Y. "Like the Fingers of the Hand: The Family and Community Life of First-Generation Italian-Americans in Buffalo, New York, 1880-1930." Doctoral dissertation, State U. of New York at Buffalo, 1970.

Mabee, Carleton. "Long Island's Black 'School War' and the Decline of Segregation in New York State." New York History 58(O, 1977): 385-411.

Marden, Robert H. "[De Facto Segregation in] Albany." Law and Society Review, N, 1967.

Markel, N. N., Eisler, R. M., and Reese, H. W. "Judging Personality from Dialect." Journal of Verbal Learning and Verbal Behavior 6(1967). [Buffalo]

Martin, W. C. "Christians in Conflict." Doctoral dissertation, Harvard Divinity School, 1969. [Rochester, 1964-1967]

Mayo, Mary Lou. "Residential Patterns and their Socio-economic Correlates: A Study of Blacks in Westchester County, New York." Doctoral dissertation, Fordham U., 1974. Univ. Microfilms Order No. 74-25,069.

Milstein, Mike M. "Impact of Integration Attitudes on Public Support of Schools." Journal of the New York State School Boards Association 35(Mr 31, 1971):11-12. [Buffalo]

"Mt. Vernon Realist. Bert Elmer Swanson." New York Times, Je 27, 1967. [Professor of Political Sociology at Sarah Lawrence College and specialist in problems of school integration]

Mulhern, Joseph R. "Controversies Over Racial Imbalance in the Public Schools of New York State from 1938 to 1975 and the Legal Rights of Pupils in Relation to School Integration." Doctoral dissertation, New York U., 1978. Univ. Microfilms Order No. 7824113.

National Advisory Council on the Education of Disadvantaged Chilren. "Quality Compensatory Education and Quality Integrated Education: A Report of a Three-Year Longitudinal Study (Fifteen Point Program) in the City School District of Rochester, N.Y., 1967-70." In Title I, E.S.E.A.--The Weakest Link: The Children of the Poor, pp. 15-18 and 35-37. The 1971 Annual Report to the President and the Congress. Washington, DC: GPO, 1971.

National Commission on Professional Rights and Responsibilities. Buffalo, New York. A Case of Meager Local Support Resulting in Inadequate Public Education. Washington, DC: National Education Association, Ag 15, 1965.

New York State. Anarchy in the Academy. Second Report of the Temporary Commission to Study the Causes of Campus Unrest. Albany, NY: The Commission, Mr 1, 1971. [Secondary schools and higher education]

New York State Library. A Guide to the Papers of James E. Allen, Jr., President of the University of the State of New York and Commissioner of Education, 1955-1969. Albany, NY: State Library, 1970.

Nyquist, Ewald. "Shifts in Policies and Attitudes toward Minority Education." In Beyond Desegregation. Urgent Issues in the Education of Minorities, pp. 21-27. New York: College Entrance Examination Board, 1978.

Obidinski, Eugene Edward. "Ethnic to Status Group: A Study of Polish Americans in Buffalo." Doctoral dissertation, State U. of New York at Buffalo, 1968. Univ. Microfilms Order No. 68-11,545.

Perman, Jane. "The History and Development of a 'Magnet School' in the Mount Vernon, New York, Public School System." Master's thesis, Bank Street College of Education, 1976.

Preliminary Analysis of the 1966-1967 Racial and Ethnic Census. Albany, NY: New York State Education Department, Ag, 1967, 17 pp. ERIC ED 018 477.

"Race Relations in Nassau County, New York." The Quorum, My, 1963 (entire issue). [Available from The Quorom, Memorial Hall, Hofstra U., Hempstead]

Ramsey, Leroy L. "A Tortoise Pace for Civil Rights on L.I." Newsday, My 29, 1978. [Long Island]

Reeves, Frank D. "Black and Puerto Rican Political Power in New York: Present and Potential." Afro-American Studies 3(S, 1972):115-116.

Rentsch, George J. "Community Meetings and Conflict Management." Integrated Education 11(Jl-O, 1973):48-52.

_____. Open Enrollment: An Appraisal. Rochester, NY: City School District, O, 1966. [Evaluation of Rochester program of open enrollment]

Research Department. Study of the Effect of Integration--Washington Irving and Host Pupils. Research Report No. 23-66. Syracuse, NY: City School District, Ag 11, 1966. [Reprinted in U.S. Commission on Civil Rights.] Hearing Held in Rochester, New York, September 16-17, 1966. Washington, DC: GPO, 1967, pp. 323-326.

Research Department. Study of the Effect of Integration--Croton and Edward Smith Elementary School Pupils. Research Report No. 22.66. Syracuse, NY: City School District, 1966. Reprinted in U.S. Commission on Civil Rights. Hearing Held in Rochester, New York, September 16-17, 1966. Washington, DC: GPO, 1967, pp. 327-328.

_____. A Study of the Effects of Two Years of Integration--Students Bused from the Washington Irving Area. Syracuse, NY: City School District, F 19, 1968.

Richardson, Benjamin. "City School Reorganization: Antecedents, Forces, and Consequences." Doctoral dissertation, U. of
Rochester, 1973. [Rochester]

Ridgeway, James. "Saul Alinsky in Smugtown."
New Republic, Je 26, 1965. [Rochester]

Rochester Bureau of Municipal Research. Target:
The Three E's. Efficiency of Organization--
Equality of Opportunity--Equality of
Financing. Rochester, NY: The Bureau, 1969.

Rochester City School District, N.Y. WIS.
World of Inquiry School, 1976. ERIC ED 132
231,

"Rochester Group Calls for Integration." Integrated Education, Ap-My, 1966.

Rosenfeld, Hilda L., Ross, Joyce I., and
Cooper, Mitzi O. "Integration and Education
in Syracuse." Events, Fall, 1966.
[Published by University College, Adult Education Division of Syracuse U.]

_____, _____ and _____. Education and In-
tegration in Syracuse. Syracuse, NY:
Syracuse Committee for Integrated Education,
Ag, 1966. [Reprinted in U.S. Commission on
Civil Rights. Hearing Held in Rochester,
New York, September 16-17, 1966. Washington,
DC: GPO, 1967, pp. 328-348.]

Rubenstein, Stanley E. "A Reply to the Authors
of 'The Great Great Neck War.'" Phi Delta
Kappan 57(Je, 1976):690-692.

Ruchkin, Judith Polger. Colored School in
Rochester, New York 1832-1856. U. of
Rochester, 1964.

Ryan, C. Allan. "When a Busing Proposal Is More
Than a Busing Controversy." American School
Board Journal 158(Ag, 1970):24-25.
[Williamsville]

Sacks, Seymour, and Andrew, Ralph. The Syracuse
Black Community, 1970: A Comparative Study,
Ja, 1974. Publications in Continuing Educa-
tion, Syracuse U., 224 Huntington Hall, 150
Marshall Street, Syracuse, NY 13210

Salten, David G. "Total School Integration in
New Rochelle." Nation's Schools, F, 1964.

Sanjur, Diva, and Scoma, Anna D. "Food Habits
of Low-Income Children in Northern New York."
Journal of Nutrition Education 2(Winter,
1971):85-95.

Schenck, Mary-Low. "A Southern Negro Girl in a
White Northern Family: A Case Study."
Social Work, Jl, 1969. [Potsdam]

Schlesinger, Ina, and D'Amore, Michael.
Children in the Balance. New York: Citation
Press, 1971. [White Plains]

School Is...by the People of Room 122, P.S. 52,
Buffalo, N.Y.; and Their Teacher Theresa
Lopata. New York: Macmillan, 1969.

Schuyler, George S. "These 'Colored' United
States: New York State : Utopia Deferred."
Messenger 7(O-N, 1925):344-349, 370.

Schwartz, Richard. Project Unique/Rochester,
New York. New York: Center for Urban
Education, 1971.

Seldin, F. "A Study of an Attempt to Increase
Community Involvement in an Urban School
System." Doctoral dissertation, U. of
Rochester, 1973. [Rochester]

Seller, Maxine. "The Education of Immigrant
Children in Buffalo, New York, 1890-1916."
New York History 52(Ap, 1976):183-199.

Sichel, Joyce L. "White Suburbanites and In-
tegrated Schools: Financial Support as a
Function of Attitudes toward Integration."
Urban Education 10(Jl, 1975):166-174.
[Westchester County]

Sindzinski, Edward S. "The Major Educational
Achievement of the Early Poles in Buffalo,
New York." Master's thesis, Canisius
College, 1950.

Stashower, Gloria. "Beyond School Integration."
American Education 11(Ap, 1975):28-33.
[White Plains]

Study of Buffalo Schools. A Report on Educational Program, Facilities, and Finance in
the City School District, Buffalo, New York.
Albany, NY: New York State Education
Dept., N, 1969. ERIC ED 035 232.

Swanson, Bert E. "Psycho-Political Patterns of
School Desegregation: Mount Vernon, New
York." Education and Urban Society, F, 1969.

Taplin, Vaughn. "Buffalo Battles Black Academy."
Muhammad Speaks, N 17, 1972.

Taub, Deborah C. "City-Suburbs Look to Racial
Balance." Journal of the New York State
Boards Association, Je, 1967. [Rochester
and West Irondequoit]

Temporary Commission to Study the Causes of
Campus Unrest. Academy or Battleground.
Third Report... Albany, NY: The Commission,
1972.

A Three Year Longitudinal Study to Assess a
Fifteen Point Plan to Reduce Racial Isolation
and Provide Quality Integrated Education for
Elementary Level Pupils. Final Report and
Abstract. Rochester, NY: Rochester City
School District, S, 1970. ERIC ED 048 428.

"To Achieve Both Integration and Quality." Phi
Delta Kappan, S, 1964. [Greenburgh]

Tompkins, Calvin. "The Black People of Bridgehampton." New Yorker 49(S 10, 1973): 47-100.

Tompkins, Judy, and Tompkins, Calvin. The Other Hampton. New York: Grossman/Viking, 1974. [Black community in Bridgehampton]

Town, C. H. Research Studies from the Psychological Clinic of the Children's Aid Society of Buffalo and Erie County. I. The Intelligence Quotient. II. A Comparison of United States White, United States Negro, Polish, and Italian Groups. Buffalo, NY: Children's Aid Society, 1938.

U.S. Commission on Civil Rights. Civil Rights USA/Public Schools North and West 1963. Buffalo. Washington, DC: GPO, 1963.

_____. Hearing Held in Rochester, New York, September 16-17, 1966. Washington, DC: GPO, 1967. [Deals with Rochester and Syracuse]

_____. Report on Buffalo Health Facilities. Washington, DC: GPO, My, 1964. [On racial discrimination in training and employment and in treatment of patients]

Urban League of Rochester, N.Y. Racial Isolation in the Rochester Public Schools: The Problem and What To Do About It. Rochester, NY: The League, Ap, 1977.

Urban League of Westchester. Annual Report. Teacher Recruitment Committee, Ja, 1964. The League, 6 Depot Plaza, White Plains, NY. [See Integrated Education, Ap, 1963, pp. 42-43.]

Varenne, Hervé. "From Grading and Freedom of Choice to Ranking and Segregation in an American High School." Council on Anthropology and Education Quarterly 5(My, 1974): 9-15. [Suburban high school, New York State]

Vecsey, George. "L.I. High School Fraternities: Uneasy Rivalry that Worries Some Adults." New York Times, Mr 11, 1974.

"Voluntary Open Enrollment: The End of an Era?" Project Unique, Ap, 1970. [Rochester]

Walsh, William F. "Equal Educational Opportunities for Syracuse." In U.S. Commission on Civil Rights. Papers Prepared for National Conference on Equal Educational Opportunity in America's Cities. Washington, DC: GPO, 1968.

Warshauer, Mary Ellen. "Glen Cove, New York/ The Evolution of a School Desegregation Plan." Urban Review, F, 1968.

Wayson, William W. "The Curriculum in the Inner City School." Integrated Education, Ja-F, 1968. [Syracuse]

Weber, William M., and Sher, Jonathan P. "Buffalo's BUILD Academy: A Community Finds Its Community School." Citizen Action in Education 1(Spring, 1974).

Weiner, Jane. Desegregation Evolves Into Integration in Greenburgh 8. New York: New York State Citizens Committee for the Public Schools, 1966.

Wendel, Egon O. "Parent and Student Attitudes Toward School in a Predominantly Negro Community." Doctoral dissertation, New York U., 1961. Univ. Microfilms Order No. 62-1458. [Prospect Elementary School, Hempstead]

West, E. G. "The Political Economy of American Public School Legislation." Journal of Law and Economics, O, 1967. [New York State, around 1867]

Western New York School Development Council. Project 1990. The Future of the Niagara Frontier. Report #2: Alternatives for Planning, 1970. [The Council, 27 California Drive, Williamsville, NY 14221]

Wheeler, Keith. "Integration Vendetta in a Northern Town." Life, My 6, 1966. [New Rochelle]

Whitcover, Jules. "Rochester Braces for Another July." Reporter, Jl 15, 1965.

White, Arthur O. "The Black Movement Against Jim Crow Education in Buffalo, New York, 1800-1900." Phylon, Winter, 1969.

_____. "The Black Movement Against Jim Crow Education in Lockport, New York, 1835-1875." New York History, Jl, 1969.

_____. "A Brief History of Legal School Segregation in a Northern City: Buffalo, New York, 1837-1880." Social Science Record 5 (Fall, 1967).

Willie, Charles Vert. "Socio-Economic and Ethnic Areas of Syracuse, New York." Doctoral dissertation, Syracuse U., 1957. Univ. Microfilms Order No. 00-24139.

Willie, Charles V. with Beker, Jerome. Race Mixing in the Public Schools. New York: Praeger, 1973. [Syracuse]

Willie, Charles Vert, and Beker, Jerome. "A Study of School Integration." Integrated Education, Je-Jl, 1962. [Syracuse]

Willie, Charles Vert, and Thompson, Elizabeth J. "The Unfinished Business of Human Rights in Syracuse." Events [published by University College, Syracuse U.], Summer, 1965.

Winiarski, Mark. "St. Stanislaus: 'Ethnicity' Has Become a Code Word for White Neighborhood Survival." National Catholic Reporter, My 28, 1976. [Buffalo]

Wolman, Thelma G. "A Preschool Program for Disadvantaged Children--The Rochelle Story." Young Children, N, 1965.

_____. "Learning Effects of Integration in New Rochelle." Integrated Education, D, 1964-Ja, 1965.

Woodward, Samuel L. "Belief Congruence Theory and School Integration." Urban Education, II, No. 3 (1966). [Buffalo]

Young, William C. Project UNIQUE (United Now for Integrated Quality Urban-Suburban Education). Rochester, NY: Rochester City School District, S, 1969. Available from Rochester House of Printing, Rochester, NY. ERIC ED 039 292.

Young, William C. "Project Unique: Integrated Quality Urban-Suburban Education." In Opening Opportunities for Disadvantaged Learners, pp. 262-285. Edited by A. Henry Passow. New York: Teachers College Press, 1972. [Rochester]

Zavatt, Joseph C. "The Manhasset Ruling." Integrated Education, Ap-My, 1964. [Manhasset]

Zschock, Dieter K. "Black Youth in Suburbia." Urban Affairs Quarterly (S, 1971):61-74. [Suffolk County]

_____. Problems Facing Nonwhite Youth in Suffolk County, New York. Stony Brook, NY: Economic Research Bureau, State U. of New York at Stony Brook, Ap, 1970.

Zukosky, Jerome. "Giving Up On Integration." New Republic, O 14, 1972. [Rochester]

New York City

"AFT Crisis Commission Report." New York Teacher, F 8, 1976. [Quality of education in New York City]

Abramowitz, Karen. "School Integration Struggle in N.Y." (an interview). The Wree-View, Mr-Ap, 1978. (Published by Women for Racial and Economic Equality, 226 W. 23rd St., New York, NY 10011.) [Joan of Arc High School, upper west side, Manhattan]

Abubadika, Muvlina Imiri (Sonny Carson). The Education of Sonny Carson. New York: Norton, 1972.

Action Toward Quality Integrated Education. New York: Board of Education, My 28, 1964.

Action Training Clearing-House Notes on Decentralization. MUST, 235 East 49th St., New York, NY 10016.

Adickes, Sandra. "Raising False Hopes in Apex Poverty Project." United Teacher, Mr 15, 1967. [Criticism of N.Y.U. program to train disadvantaged youth to become teachers]

Advisory Committee on Human Relations. "The Allen Report on New York City Schools." Integrated Education, Ag-S, 1964.

Ahdieh, M. Hussein. "Harlem Preparatory School: An Alternative." Doctoral dissertation, U. of Massachusetts, 1974. Univ. Microfilms Order No. 74-25,815.

Alison, David (pseud.). Searchlight: An Expose of New York City Schools. New York: Teachers Center Press, 1951.

Alker, Henry A., and Wohl, Jonathan. "Personality and Achievement in a Suburban and an Inner City School." Journal of Social Issues 28(1972):101-113.

Allen, Robert L. "Liberation Schools: Parent Power?" National Guardian, Mr 25, 1967. [Boycott at P.S. 125 in Harlem]

Almeida, Cynthia. A Program to Strengthen Early Childhood Education in Poverty Area Schools. New York: Center for Urban Education, O, 1969.

Anderson, Nels. "The Social Antecedents of a Slum: A Developmental Study of the East Harlem Area." Doctoral dissertation, New York U., 1930.

Andrews, Charles C. The History of the New York African Free Schools, from Their Establishment in 1787 to the Present Time: Embracing a Period of More Than Forty Years: Also a Brief Account of the Successful Labors of the New York Manumission Society. New York: M. Day, 1830.

Anker, Irving. Chancellor's Report on Programs and Problems Affecting Integration of the New York City Public Schools. New York: Board of Education, F, 1974.

_____. "Integration in New York City Schools." Integrateducation 13(My-Je, 1975):137-142.

Anthony, Irving F. "Factors Associated with Truancy in Harlem." Master's thesis, College of the City of New York, 1938. Abstract in College of the City of New York. Abstracts of theses....1939:102.

Anti-Defamation League. "Anti-Semitism in the New York City School Controversy." United Teacher, Ja 22, 1969.

_____. "Anti-Semitism in the N.Y.C. Schools." Metropolitan Star, Ja, 1969.

Antonovsky, Aaron. "A Study of Some Moderately Successful Negroes in New York City." Phylon, Fall, 1967.

Armstrong, Richard. "McGeorge Bundy Confronts the Teachers." New York Times Magazine, Ap 20, 1969.

Arnold, Robert. "Mobilization for Youth: Patchwork or Solution?" Dissent, Summer, 1964.

Aronowitz, Stanley. "Go Communities, Beat the School Board." Guardian, D 28, 1968.

_____. "N.Y. School Battle: Who's Fighting Whom?" Guardian, Jl 13, 1968.

_____. "Who Will Control New York City Schools?" Guardian, O 26, 1968.

Arsenian, Seth. "Bilingualism and Mental Development. A Study of the Intelligence and the Social Background of Bilingual Children in New York City." Doctoral dissertation, Teachers College, Columbia U., 1937. [Italian and Jewish]

Arter, Rhetta M. Living in Chelsea. New York: New York Savings Bank, 1954.

"Aspirational Inventory of Junior High School Pupils." Staff Bulletin, New York Public Schools, D 14, 1964.

Atkins, Gordon. "Health, Housing, and Poverty in New York City, 1865–1898." Doctoral dissertation, Columbia U., 1947.

Auerbach, Aline B., and Roche, Sandra. Creating a Preschool Center. Parent Development in an Integrated Neighborhood Project. New York: Wiley, 1971. [Bloomingdale]

Auletta, Ken. "The Last Angry Principal." New York, My 3, 1976. [Howard Hurwitz, Long Island City High School, Queens]

"Backlash." New Yorker, My 30, 1964. [On Milton Galamison, head of the New York City-wide Committee on School Integration]

Balcerak, Carl. "Educating the 'Gifted Disadvantaged.'" Catholic School Journal, N, 1968. [Monsignor Kelly Junior High School for Boys, Manhattan]

Baldwin, James. "Growing Up in Harlem." The Listener, Ja 23, 1969.

Balmain, Alexander F. "History of Catholic Education in the Diocese of Brooklyn." Doctoral dissertation, Fordham U., 1935.

Banfield, Beryle. "Our Children Are Dying." Freedomways, Winter, 1967. [A discussion-review of Hentoff, Our Children Are Dying, by the assistant principal of I.S. 201 in New York City]

Banks, Rae. "Weeksville--Microcosm in Black." Freedomways 12(Fourth Quarter, 1972):288-298.

Barbaro, Fred. "Interest Group Politics in the Selection of Teachers and Administrators for the New York City School System." Doctoral dissertation, Columbia U., 1975. Univ. Microfilms Order No. 75-20,185.

Bard, Bernard. "A 'Country' School in the City." Southern Education Report, Ap, 1969. [Manhattan Country School]

_____. "The Battle for School Jobs: New York's Newest Agony." Phi Delta Kappan (My, 1972):553-558. [Testing and supervisory jobs in the city's school system]

_____. "Brooklyn's Bus Equality." Saturday Review, F 18, 1967.

_____. "The Clash Is Between Teachers Who Have Jobs and Those Who Don't--With School Boards in the Middle." American School Board Journal 161(S, 1974):33-35. [Luis Fuentes, District 1]

_____. "Control Without the Community." New York Post, Ja 28, 1969.

_____. "Is Decentralization Working?" Phi Delta Kappan 54(D, 1972):238-243.

_____. "New York's Decentralization Trauma: Blueprint for Chaos." Congress Bi-weekly, N 11, 1968.

_____. "On the Razor's Edge." Saturday Review, Ja 24, 1970. [School principals]

_____. "Albert Shanker. A Portrait in Power." Phi Delta Kappan 56(Mr, 1975):466-472.

_____. "The State of the Schools: Decentralization." New York Post, Ja 25, 1974.

Barnett, E. V. "Educational Activities by and in Behalf of the Negroes in New York 1800-1830." Negro History Bulletin, F, 1951.

Bayor, Ronald Howard. "Ethnic Conflict in New York City, 1929-1941." Doctoral dissertation, U. of Pennsylvania, 1970. Univ. Microfilms Order No. 70-25624.

_____. Neighbors in Conflict: The Irish, Germans, Jews, and Italians of New York City, 1929-1941. Baltimore: Johns Hopkins U. Press, 1978.

Beagle, Simon. "Debunking the Myths About M.E.S." Changing Education, Winter-Spring, 1968.

_____. "M.E.S. Critics Take the Wrong Turn." United Teacher, D 18, 1968. [Critique of critiques by Doxey A. Wilkerson and Kenneth B. Clark]

_____. "More Effective School Program Too Costly?" United Teacher, Je 2, 1967.

_____. "Myths and Misunderstandings About More Effective Schools." American Teacher, Ja, 1972.

Beck, Nelson R. "The Use of Library and Educational Facilities by Russian-Jewish Immigrants in New York City, 1880-1914: The Impact of Culture." Journal of Library History 12(Spring, 1977):128-149.

Bellush, Jewel, and David, Stephen M. (eds.). Race and Politics in New York City. New York: Praeger, 1971.

Bender, William A., and Steel, Lewis M. "The Double Standard of Justice: Legal Actions at P.S. 39, Harlem." In Schools Against Children. The Case for Community Control. Edited by Annette T. Rubenstein. New York: Monthly Review Press, 1970.

Benjamin, Gerald. Race Relations and the New York City Commission on Human Rights. Ithaca, NY: Cornell U. Press, 1974.

Benjamin Franklin Urban League Street Academy. 1969-70 ESEA Title I. Final Report 1970. Teaching and Learning Research Corp., 355 Lexington Avenue, New York, NY 10017.

Bercovici, Konrad. "The Black Blocks of Manhattan." Harpers Monthly, O, 1924.

Berger, Morris I. "The Settlement, the Immigrant, and the Public School." Doctoral dissertation, Columbia U., 1956. Univ. Microfilms Order No. 16798.

Berke, Joel S., Goettel, Ralph J., and Andrew, Ralph. "Equity in Financing New York City's Schools: The Impact of Local, State, and Federal Policy." Education and Urban Society 4(My, 1972):261-291.

Bernstein, Blanche. "Recent Trends in Income Distribution in New York City." City Almanac 7(Ag, 1972):16-19. 1959-1970

Berrol, Selma C. "Education and Economic Mobility: The Jewish Experience in New York City, 1880-1920." American Jewish Historical Quarterly 65(1976).

_____. "Health, Education, and Welfare: The Progressive Impulse in the New York City Public Schools." Elementary School Journal 71(D, 1970):134-142.

_____. Immigrants at School, New York City, 1898-1914. New York: Arno, 1978.

_____. "Immigrants at School: New York City 1898-1914." Doctoral dissertation, City U. of New York, 1967. Univ. Microfilms Order No. 67-12.

_____. "Immigrants at School: New York City, 1900-1910." Urban Education, O, 1969.

_____. "The Schools of New York in Transition, 1898-1914." Urban Review, D, 1966.

Berube, Maurice R. "Community Control of Schools. Scarsdale, Yes--Harlem, No." Commonweal, Je 21, 1968.

Berube, Maurice R., and Gittell, Marilyn (eds.). Confrontation at Ocean Hill-Brownsville. New York: Praeger, 1969.

Berube, Maurice R. "Crisis in the NYC School System." New America, Mr 24, 1965.

_____. "'Democratic Socialists' and the [N.Y.C.] Schools." New Politics 8(Summer, 1969[Je, 1970]):57-62.

Berube, Maurice R., and McCoy, Carmen A. "Infant School in New York: Can the System Be Beat?" Community, My, 1969. [P.S. 84]

Berube, Maurice R. "The Other Principal." United Teacher, F 3, 1967. [Dr. Edward P. Gottlieb, principal of P.S. 165, Morningside Heights]

_____. "Reply [to Goldbloom, in same issue]." Commonweal, F 21, 1969.

_____. "The School Elections: Analysis and Interpretation." Community, Ap, 1970. [Mr, 1970 elections in New York City to choose members of 30 school boards]

_____. "The School Without Hope." United Teacher, Mr 15, 1967. [P.S. 151, Brooklyn, NY]

_____. "The Unschooling of New York's Children." Commonweal, O 25, 1968.

Betts, Roland. Acting Out: Coping with Big City Schools. Boston: Little, Brown, 1978.

Bienstock, Herbert. Current Economic Developments: Implications for the Jewish Community in the Metropolitan New York Area, Mr 29, 1971. Federation Employment and Guidance Service, 215 Park Avenue South, New York, NY 10003.

"The Black and the Jew: A Falling Out of Allies." Time, Ja 31, 1969.

Black, Jonathan. "Oasis in East Harlem." Saturday Review 54(F 20, 1971):52-53, 66, 70.

"Black Librarians' Caucus Formed in Queens." New York Library Journal 96(N 1, 1971):3555-3556.

"Black, Negroes, and Niggers in Education." African-American Teachers Forum, N-D, 1969.

Black Solidarity Day Committee. "Cowardly Racists Dissolve Black Schools." Muhammad Speaks, Ja 16, 1970.

Blakkan, Renee. "Court Reinstates Luis Fuentes: Attack Shanker's Racism." Guardian, Ja 23, 1974.

Blascoer, Frances. Colored School Children in New York. New York: Public Education Association of the City of New York, 1915.

"Blasts Proposed Decentralization Districts as 'Segregated.'" United Teacher, Ja 22, 1969.

Bleecker, Ted. "New York City's Effective Schools Make History." American Teacher, Ap, 1965.

Bloch, Herman D. The Circle of Discrimination. An Economic and Social Study of the Black Man in New York. New York: New York U. Press, 1969.

_____. "The New York City Negro and Occupational Eviction, 1860-1910." International Review of Social History 5(1960):26-38.

Blond, Leo. "Black Anti-Semitism in New York City." Phi Delta Kappan, N, 1968.

Bloomfield, Jack. "Suppressing a Community Council." Urban Review (letter), F, 1969. [Ocean Hill-Brownsville]

Boese, Thomas. Public Education in the City of New York. New York, NY, 1869.

Bolce, Louis Henri III, and Gray, Susan H. "Blacks, Whites and 'Race Politics.'" Public Interest (Winter, 1979). [NYC, Ap-Jl, 1977]

Bond, Jean Carey. "The New York School Crisis: Integration for What?" Freedomways, Spring, 1964.

Boody, Mertha M. Psychological Study of Immigrant Children at Ellis Island. Baltimore: n.p., 1926.

Bourne, William O. History of the Public School Society. New York, NY, 1873.

Braeger, George A., and Purcell, Francis P. (eds.). Community Action Against Poverty. New York: College and University Press, 1967. [On Mobilization for Youth]

Braun, Shirley W. "Bilingual Education, Old and New Style, in a New York School District." Bilingual Review 2(S-D, 1975): 248-258.

Breslin, Jimmy. "Plantation Days in South Jamaica." New York, F 8, 1971. [Edgar Shimes Junior High School, JHS 142, South Jamaica, Queens]

Breswick, David Alan. "Blacks, Hispanics, and Others: Decentralization and Ethnic Succession." Urban Education 12(Jl, 1977): 129-152.

_____. "Legislating New York City School Decentralization." Doctoral dissertation, Columbia U., 1972. Univ. Microfilms Order No. 75-9318.

Browne, Henderson L. "A Study of the Assimilation of Barbadian Immigrants in the United States with Special Reference to the Barbadians in New York." Doctoral dissertation, Columbia U., 1978. Univ. Microfilms Order No. 7821816.

Brooks, Thomas R. "A Job Program That Works." Reporter, N 16, 1967. [Apprenticeship program in Bedford-Stuyvesant]

_____. "Can Parents Run New York's Schools?" Reporter, Ja 11, 1968.

_____. "New York's Boycott: What Did It Prove?" Reporter, F 27, 1964.

_____. "Tragedy at Ocean Hill." Dissent, Ja-F, 1969.

Brotz, Howard. The Black Jews of Harlem. Negro Nationalism and the Dilemmas of Negro Leadership. New York: The Free Press of Glencoe, 1964.

Brown, Claude. The Children of Ham. New York: Stein and Day, 1975. [Harlem]

_____. "The Group." New York Times Magazine, D 16, 1973. [Harlem]

_____. Manchild in the Promised Land. New York: Macmillan, 1965. [Harlem]

Brown, Claude, Dunmeyer, Arthur, and Ellison, Ralph. "Harlem's America." New Leader, S 26, 1966. [Transcript of testimony before Senate subcommittee hearing]

Buder, Leonard. "School Pairing in New York City." Integrated Education, Ag-N, 1965.

Bureau of Educational Research. Evaluation of the Community Zoning Program. Summary Report. Brooklyn, NY: New York City Board of Education, S, 1966. [The "pairing" program evaluated]

_____. Longitudinal Study of Reading Growth in Selected More Effective and Comparable Schools. New York: Board of Education, Mr, 1969.

_____. Summary of Citywide Test Results for 1966-1967. New York: Board of Education, O, 1967.

Buskin, Martin. "Community Control at the Crossroads." School Management, Mr, 1969.

_____. "More Effective Schools: The Union's Stand-Pat Issue." Southern Education Report, D, 1967.

Butler, Karen, Carnes, Naomi, and Glover, Jackie. "We're Not Grinning Anymore" (interview). Leviathan, Je, 1969. [Taft High School]

Calhoun, Lillian S. "New York: Schools and Power--Whose?" Integrated Education, Ja-F, 1969, pp. 11-35.

Campbell, Les. "The Devil Can Never Educate Us." African-American Teachers Forum, N, 1968.

Campbell, Robert. The Chasm: The Life and Death of a Great Experiment in Ghetto Education. Boston: Houghton Mifflin, 1974. [Ocean Hill-Brownsville and I.S. 201]

_____. "Community Control." Southern Education Report, Jl-Ag, 1968.

Capeci, Dominic J., Jr. The Harlem Riot of 1943. Philadelphia: n.p., 1977.

Carpenter, Edward F. "Harlem Prep: An Alternate System of Education." In Opening Opportunities for Disadvantaged Learners, pp. 298-305. Edited by A. Harry Passow. New York: Teachers College Press, 1972.

Carter, Barbara. "New York's 'Jim Crow' Schools: Bleak Facts and Bright Visions." Reporter, Jl 2, 1964.

_____. Pickets, Parents, and Power: The Story Behind the New York City Teachers' Strike. New York: Citation, 1971.

Center for Urban Education. Community Attitudes in Bedford-Stuyvesant: An Area Study. New York: Center for Urban Education, 1968.

_____. Crisis Response. A Report of Activities of the Center for Urban Education During the School Strike in New York City in the Fall of 1968, D, 1969. ERIC ED 088 194.

Chamberlayne, Price. "Teachers Versus the Community." New Society, N 15, 1973.

Channon, Gloria. "Bulljive--Language Teaching in a Harlem School." Urban Review, F, 1968.

_____. Homework. Required Reading for Teachers and Parents. New York: Outerbridge & Dienstfrey, 1971. [East Harlem school]

_____. "The More Effective Schools." Urban Review, F, 1967.

"Children's Community Workshop School." Center for Urban Education Program Conspectus, O, 1969.

Christen, Robert J. "A Major Dispute in the A.C.L.U." Dissent, S-O, 1969. [Ocean Hill-Brownsville]

Churchman, Arza, Shuman, Constance, and Kogan, Leonard S. Community Factors Associated with School Achievement in New York City. New York: Center for Social Research Graduate School and University Center, City U. of New York, Ja, 1975.

Cimaluca, Salvatore. "The Natural History of East Harlem from 1880 to the Present." Master's thesis, New York U., 1931.

Citizens Commission to Investigate Corporal Punishment in Junior High School 22. Corporal Punishment and School Suspension: A Case Study. New York: Metropolitan Applied Research Center, N, 1974.

Citron, Alice. "An Answer to John F. Hatchett." Jewish Currents, S, 1968.

City Commission on Human Relations. "On Preferential Treatment." Integrated Education, F-Mr, 1964, p. 59.

City School District of New York. Proposed Plan for a Community School District System in New York City. New York: Board of Education, N 17, 1969.

"Civilizing the Blackboard Jungle." Time, N 15, 1963.

Clark, Kenneth B. "New York's Biracial Public Schools." Integrateducation 13(My-Je, 1975): 153-155.

_____. "Segregated Schools in New York City." A speech. Children Apart Conference, New York City, Ap 24, 1954. [Elliott Shapiro]

_____. "Segregated Schools in New York City." Journal of Educational Sociology, F, 1963.

Clark, Kenneth B., and Neier, Aryeh (press conference). "Kenneth Clark Meets Press on High School Issue." Integrated Education, My-Je, 1969, pp. 51-55.

Clarke, John Henrik (ed.). Harlem, A Community in Transition. New York: Citadel, 1964.

_____ (ed.). Harlem, U.S.A. Berlin, Germany: Seven Seas Publishers, 1965.

Cole, Stephen. The Unionization of Teachers: A Case Study of the U.F.T. New York: Praeger, 1969.

Collins, Maria A. "Achievement, Intelligence, Personality and Selected School Related Variables in Negro Children from Intact and Broken Families Attending Parochial Schools in Central Harlem." Doctoral dissertation, Fordham U., 1969. Univ. Microfilms Order No. 70-11,459.

Committee on Education, Guidance and Work. The Secondary School Program in New York City. Public Education Association, 20 West 40th Street, New York, NY 10018, N, 1964.

Committee on the "600" Schools. "600" Schools, Yesterday, Today, and Tomorrow. New York: Board of Education, F, 1965.

Concestre, Marie J. "Adult Education in a Local Area: A Study of a Decade of the Life and Education of the Adult Italian Immigrant in East Harlem, New York City." Doctoral dissertation, New York U., 1944.

Connolly, Harold X. A Ghetto Grows in Brooklyn. New York: New York U. Press, 1977.

_____. "Blacks in Brooklyn from 1900 to 1960." Doctoral disseration, New York U., 1972. Univ. Microfilms Order No. 72-21,498.

Coombs, Orde. "Illegal Immigrants in New York: The Invisible Subculture." New York 9(Mr 15, 1976):33-41.

_____. "Three Faces of Harlem." New York Times Magazine, N 3, 1974.

Corbett, Anne. "Parent Power. The Lesson of New York." New Society, Jl 4, 1968.

Cordasco, Francesco, and Galatioto, Rocco G. "Ethnic Displacement in the Interstitial Community: The East Harlem (New York City) Experience." Journal of Negro Education 40 (Winter, 1971):56-65.

_____ and _____. "Ethnic Displacement in the Interstitial Community: The East Harlem Experience." Phylon 31(Fall, 1970):302-312.

Cotton, Stephen E. "Politics and Poverty." Harvard Crimson, Ap 29, 1967. [Bedford-Stuyvesant]

Council of Supervisory Associations. "Administrators on School Integration." Integrated Education, Je-Jl, 1964.

Covello, Leonard. "A High School and Its Immigrant Community: A Challenge and an Opportunity." Journal of Educational Sociology, F, 1936.

Cresswell, Anthony M. "New York City Schools and Partisan Politics: The Case of the New York State Assembly, 1968-1969." Doctoral dissertation, Columbia U., 1970. Univ. Microfilms Order No. 70-26,772.

Croce, A. "Backlash in New York." National Review, S 22, 1964.

"'Cross-Busing'--Now It's Here." Life, S 25, 1964. [New York white boycott of schools of S, 1964]

Culbert, Michael L. "New York [City] Court Decides Independent Black School's Instruction 'Superior.'" Muhammad Speaks, S 6, 1974.

Cullen, Ruth Mary. "Bedford-Stuyvesant: The Ecology of an Urban Neighborhood." Doctoral dissertation, Fordham U., 1975. Univ. Microfilms Order No. 76-4113.

Darnton, John. "Integration Found Lagging in Suburban Area Schools." New York Times, My 30, 1971. [New York metropolitan area]

Daum, Walter. "Legislative Record of U.F.T/ Leadership." New Politics, Spring, 1968. [Mr, 1969]

Daum, Walter, Friedman, David, and Tabor, Ron. "Harlem on Their Minds. The C.C.N.Y. Crisis." Independent Socialist, Je, 1969.

Davidson, Bruce. East 100th Street, Cambridge, MA: Harvard U. Press, 1970.

Davidson, Margaret, and Chambers, Bradford. "The Role of Books at Ocean Hill-Brownsville." Interracial Books for Children, Summer, 1969.

Davis, Benjamin J. Communist Councilman from Harlem: Autobiographical Notes Written in a Federal Penitentiary. New York: International, 1969.

"A Day in the Life of...[7 U.F.T. Teachers at P.S. 39]." United Teacher, Mr 30, 1969.

De Ferranti, D. M. and others. The Welfare and Nonwelfare Poor in New York City. Santa Monica, CA: Rand, Je, 1974.

"Decentralization." The Center Forum, Ja 26, 1968.

Decter, Midge. "The Negro and the New York Schools." Commentary, S, 1964.

Demas, Boulton H. The School Elections: A Critique of the 1969 New York City School Decentralization. New York: Institute for Community Studies, Mr, 1971.

Democratic Way Out of the Crisis in Education. A Program for Resolving the Crisis in the New York City Public Schools System. Communist Party of New York State, My, 1964.

Dennison, George. "The First Street School." Liberation, Jl, 1966. [An integrated private experimental school in the Lower East Side]

_____. The Lives of Children. The Story of the First Street School. New York: Random House, 1969.

Densen, P. M., Ullman, D. B., and Vandow, J. E. Childhood Health, Academic and Social Characteristics as Indicators of Adult Health Status [in New York City]. New York: Department of Health, 1968.

Dentler, Robert A. "Brownsville--Community or Staging Area?" Center Forum, N 13, 1968.

_____. "For Local Control in the Schools." Atlantic, Ja, 1969.

_____. "Innovations in Public Education in New York City." City Almanac, D, 1971.

De Rivera, Alice. "Jumping the Track." Leviathan, Je, 1969. [John Jay High School]

Dershowitz, Rita. "Racism in N.Y.: Standing PAT for the Neighborhood School." Freedom North, Vol I., No. 1 (1964).

Deveaux, Alexis. Spirits in the Streets. Anchor Books, 1975. [Growing up in Harlem]

Dienstfrey, Harry, Inger, Morton, Outerbridge, David, and Tobier, Arthur. "The Bundy Report. A Critical Analysis." The Center Forum, Ja 26, 1968.

Divoky, Diane. "New Court Tests for Trading." Education News, Jl 8, 1968.

_____. "New York's Mini-Schools." Saturday Review, D 18, 1971.

Dixon, Robert S. "The Education of the Negro in the City of New York, 1853-1900." Master's thesis, College of the City of New York, 1935.

Dobin, Daniel. The Failure of Academic High Schools in New York City, D, 1970. Brooklyn Education Task Force, 525 Clinton Avenue, Brooklyn, NY 11238.

_____. Reading Scores and the New York City Board of Education. Another Study in Subterfuge, 1970. Brooklyn Education Task Force, 525 Clinton Avenue, Brooklyn, NY 11238.

Dobin, Daniel, Dixon, Sarah, and Robison, Kathy. Taxpayers' Guide to the Politics of Public Education. Brooklyn, 1969. Brooklyn Education Task Force, 259 Washington Avenue, Brooklyn, NY 11205.

Dobin, David, and Stutz, Rosalie. The Sanctioned Lawlessness of the New York City Board of Education, 1970. Brooklyn Education Task Force, 525 Clinton Avenue, Brooklyn, NY 11238.

Dodson, Dan W. "Is Desegregation Possible for New York City?" Integrateducation 13(My-Je, 1975):156-159.

Dolan, Jay P. The Immigrant Church: New York's Irish and German Catholics, 1815-1865. Baltimore: Johns Hopkins U. Press, 1975.

_____. "Urban Catholicism: New York, 1815-1865." Doctoral dissertation, U. of Chicago, 1971.

Donghi, Dione, Freudenberg, Nick, and Gilbert, Dave. "Spring Offensive in New York." The Movement, Je, 1969. [Protest movement in NYC high schools]

Donovan, Bernard E. Implementation of Board Policy on Excellence for the City's Schools. New York: Board of Education, Ap 28, 1965.

Donovan, James B. "We Are the Leaders." Integrated Education, F-Mr, 1964.

Dorman, Michael. The Making of a Slum. New York: Delacorte, 1972. [Hunt's Point, Bronx]

Downing, Gertrude L. et al. The Preparation of Teachers for Schools in Culturally Deprived Neighborhoods (the BRIDGE Project). Flushing, NY: Queens College, n.d.

East Harlem Project and City Commission on Human Rights. Releasing Human Potential. A Study of East Harlem-Yorkville School Bus Transfer. New York: City Commission on Human Rights, 1962.

East New York Alliance Women's Guild. [Recollections of Campaigns for School Integration in New York City during the 1960's]. First Annual Rudiana Journal, D 27, 1974.

Easton, Iris A. "The Paired School Failure." Negro Teachers Forum, D, 1966. [Criticism of segregated classrooms inside integrated schools]

"Educational Achievement and Community Control." Community Issues, N 1, 1968.

Education in Crisis: A Report on Decentralization, Teacher Training and Curriculum in the New York City Public Schools. New York: New York City Commission on Human Rights, D, 1968, 75 pp. ERIC ED 028 221.

"Education in the South Bronx: Is 116 a Haven in a Sea of Turmoil?" Part 1. New York Teacher, Ja 22, 1978.

"Educator in the News." [Rev. Milton A. Galamison] Education News, Ag 5, 1968.

Edwards, Robert A. Slicing the Slice: Equity in Financing Within a Large Urban District, Mr, 1978. ERIC ED 152 937.

Ehle, John. Shepherd of the Streets. New York: Church of St. Matthew and St. Timothy, 1959.

Eisenberg, Carolyn. "The Parents' Movement at I.S. 201: From Integration to Black Power, 1958-1966." Doctoral dissertation, Columbia U., 1971.

Elementary Program in Compensatory Education. More Effective Schools. New York City. Washignton, DC: GPO, 1970.

Elinson, Jack, Haberman, Paul W., and Gell, Cyrille. Ethnic and Educational Data on Adults in New York City, 1963-1964. New York: School of Public Health and Administrative Medicine, Columbia U., 1967.

Ellis, Arthur Leon. A Mind on Harlem. Palo Alto, CA: R & E Research Associates, 1978.

_____. "HARYOU-ACT: A Case Study of Leadership in the Ghetto." Doctoral dissertation, Columbia U., 1974. Univ. Microfilms Order No. 75-5214.

Ellman, Richard M. The Poorhouse State: The American Way of Life on Public Assistance. New York: Pantheon, 1966. [Lower East Side]

"Encouraging Progress in the More Exective Schools." Staff Bulletin, Public Schools of New York City, N 15, 1965.

"End Paper." Center Forum, Ap 26, 1968. [The Linear City, Brooklyn]

English, Herbert. "N.Y.C. School Chancellor: Dr. Charles V. Hamilton." African-American Teachers Forum, N-D, 1969.

Epstein, Jason. "The Brooklyn Dodger." New York Review, S 20, 1968.

_____. "The Issue at Ocean Hill." New York Review, N 21, 1968.

_____. "The Politics of School Decentralization." New York Review of Books, Je 6, 1968.

_____. "The Real McCoy." New York Review, Mr 13, 1969. [Ocean Hill-Brownsville]

Etzkowitz, Henry, and Schaflander, Gerald M. Ghetto Crisis: Integration or Riots? Boston: Little, Brown, 1969. [Integrated co-op in Bedford-Stuyvesant]

Evans, Ronald. "Who Should Rule the Schools?" African-American Teachers Forum, Ja-Ap, 1968.

Everett, John R. "The Decentralization Fiasco and Our Ghetto Schools." Atlantic, D, 1968.

"Fact Sheet. Ocean Hill-Brownsville School District." Scope Bulletin, S, 1968.

Fainstein, Susan S., and Fainstein, Norman I. "From the Folks Who Brought You Ocean Hill-Brownsville." New York Affairs 2(1974): 104-115.

Fainstein, Norman I., and Fainstein, Susan S. "Innovation in Urban Bureaucracies. Clients and Change." American Behavioral Scientist 15(Mr-Ap, 1972):511-531. P.S. 84

Fainstein, Susan S. "The Movement for Community Control of Schools in New York City." Doctoral dissertation, Massachusetts Institute of Technology, 1971.

Fairclough, Alice Brown. "A Study of Occupational Opportunities for Negro Women in New York City." Master's thesis, New York U., 1929.

Fantini, Mario, and Gittell, Marilyn. "The Ocean Hill-Brownsville Experiment." Phi Delta Kappan, Ap, 1969.

Farber, M. A. "Black is Beneficial, Say Negro School Principals as Their Ranks Grow Here." New York Times, N 13, 1969.

Farrell, John J. "The Immigrant and the School in New York City: A Program for Citizenship." Doctoral dissertation, Stanford U., 1967. Univ. Microfilms Order No. 68-6514.

Farrell, John Joseph. The Immigrant and the School in New York City: A Program for Citizenship. Doctoral dissertation, n.d. ERIC ED 024 896.

Featherstone, Joseph. "Choking Off Community Schools." New Republic, Jl 19, 1969. [The new state law on decentralizing NYC schools]

_____. "Community Control: Down But Not Out." New Republic, Ag 16, 1969.

_____. "Community Control of Schools. Off to a Bad Start." New Republic, Mr 29, 1969.

_____. "Community Control of Our Schools." New Republic, Ja 13, 1968.

_____. "Inflating the Threat of Black Anti-Semitism." New Republic, Mr 8, 1969.

_____. "Ocean Hill Is Alive, and, Well..." New Republic, Ap 19, 1969.

_____. "Wiping Out the Demonstration Schools." New Republic, Ja 10, 1970.

"Federal Court Rejects Ocean Hill Constitutional Suit." United Teacher, D 4, 1968.

"Federal Grant for Schomburg." AB Bookman's Weekly, Ja 20, 1969.

Feld, Marcia Marker. A Basic Guide to the New York City School Budget Process. New York: Institute for Community Studies, Queens College, 1969.

Feld, Marcia Marker, and Schechtman, Harris. The New York City School Map Book. New York: Institute for Community Studies, Queens College, D, 1969.

Feldman, Sandra. Decentralization and the City Schools. New York: League for Industrial Democracy, 1968.

_____. "The Burden of Blame Placing. An Answer to a Statement by the New York Civil Liberties Union." United Teacher, N 20, 1968.

_____. "The Growth of Teacher Consciousness: New York City, 1967." I.S.R. Journal, Winter, 1969.

Feldstein, Sylvia G., and Mackler, Bernard. "De Facto Segregation in the North: The Case of In Re Shipwith." Howard Law Journal 15(Spring, 1969).

_____, and _____. School Desegregation and the Law in New York City: The Case of In Re Skipwith. New York: Center for Urban Education, My, 1968.

Fenster, Myron M. "The Princeton Plan--One Year Later." Midstream, Je, 1965. [School pairing in Jackson Heights, NYC]

Ferretti, Fred. "Who's to Blame in the School Strike?" New York Magazine, N 18, 1968.

Final Evaluation Report of the Benjamin Franklin High School Urban League Street Academy. New York: Urban Ed, Inc. 1970

Fishman, James J. "The Limits of Remedial Power: Hart v. Community School Board 21." In Limits of Justice. The Courts' Role in School Desegregation, pp. 115-165. Edited by Howard J. Kalodner and James J. Fishman. Cambridge, MA: Ballinger, 1978. [Coney Island, Brooklyn]

Fiske, Edward B. "Inner-City Catholic Schools Find Stability." New York Times, O 9, 1977.

_____. "Practicality Is Stressed in School Improvements." New York Times, O 18, 1975.

Fleetwood, Blake. "The New Elite and An Urban Renaissance." New York Times Magazine, Ja 14, 1979. ["Gentrification" in New York City]

Fliegel, Seymour. "Practices that Improved Academic Performance in an Inner-City School." Phi Delta Kappan 52(F, 1971): 341-343. [P.S. 146]

James L. 4X. "New York Black Co-eds Quit Mini-Skirts; Discover New Dignity in Modest Attire." Muhammad Speaks, Je 27, 1969.

Forman, Eli M. S. "Ethnic and Income Occupancy Patterns of Federal Moderate-Income Housing and Federal Public Housing in Low- and Moderate-Income Neighborhoods of New York City." Doctoral dissertation, Fordham U., 1975. Univ. Microfilms Order No. 76-4152.

Fox, David J. Expansion of the More Effective School Program. Evaluation of New York City Title I Educational Projects 1966-67. New York: Center for Urban Education, S, 1967.

_____. "Evaluating the 'More Effective Schools.'" Phi Delta Kappan, Je, 1968.

_____. Evaluation of New York City School District...Free Choice Open Enrollment-- Elementary Schools, Ag 31, 1966. [Center for Urban Education, 33 West 42nd Street, New York, NY]

Fox, David J., Greenberg, Lucy, and Harbatkin, Lisa. Decentralized Open Enrollment: Services to Children in Receiving Elementary, Intermediate and Junior High Schools. New York: Center for Urban Education, Ag, 1970.

Fox, David J. and Others. More Effective Schools. New York: Center for Urban Education, D, 1968.

Fox, David J., Schwager, Sidney, and Gottesfeld, Harry. [Symposium on the More Effective Schools Program] Urban Review, My, 1968.

Fox, Louise W., Smith, Maureen, and Pinsley, Alice. Program to Improve Academic Achievement in Poverty Area Schools. New York: Center for Urban Education, N, 1969.

Frankel, Edward. Attendance Task Force to Strengthen High School Attendance Programs. New York: Center for Urban Education, S, 1969

_____. "The Comprehensive High School." Urban Review, Je, 1968.

Frazier, E. Franklin. "Negro Harlem: An Ecological Study." American Journal of Sociology 43(Jl, 1937):72-88.

Freeman, Rhoda Golden. "The Free Negro in New York City in the Era before the Civil War." Doctoral dissertation, Columbia U., 1966. Univ. Microfilms Order No. 69-15545.

Freyburg, J. T. "The Effect of Participation in an Elementary School Buddy System on the Self Concept School Attitudes and Behavior, and Achievement of 5th Grade Negro Children." Graduate Research in Education and Related Disciplines 3(1967). [Harlem]

Fried, Joseph P. "Simeon Golar's City-Within-A-City." New York Times Magazine, Ap 30, 1972. [Public housing]

Friedman, David (ed.). Crisis in the Schools: Teachers and the Community, 1969. Independent Socialist Clubs of America, 874 Broadway, New York, NY 10003.

Friend, Abraham. "I Struck." (Los Angeles) Socialist Tribune, My, 1969. [Teachers' strike]

Fryburg, Estelle L. "Children's Attitudes During the New York City School Strike of 1968." School and Society 98(N, 1970):429-433.

Fuchs, Estelle. "How Teachers Learn to Help Children Fail." Trans-Action, S, 1968. [Inner-city school]

_____. Pickets at the Gate. New York: The Free Press, 1966.

Fuentes, Luis. "Community Control Did Not Fail in New York: It Wasn't Tried." Phi Delta Kappan 57(Je, 1976):692-695.

_____. The Fight Against Racism in Our Schools. New York: Pathfinder Press, D, 1973.

Fulmer, Chet, and Fulmer, Dot. "The Board and the Bus." Renewal, O-N, 1966. [Voluntary busing of white children for integration]

Furst, Randy. "Community Shut Out in N.Y. School Crisis." Guardian, S 14, 1968.

Fusco, Liz. "NYC Public High School Teaching: The Success of the System." Radicals in the Professions Newsletter, Ap-My, 1968.

Gaillard, Frye. "Whites Win Bitter School Election." Race Relations Reporter 5 (Je 3, 1974):1, 8. [District 1]

Galamison, Milton. "The Pace Must Quicken." Integrated Education, F-Mr, 1964.

Galanty, Ervin. "Brooklyn's Linear City." Nation, F 12, 1968.

Gannon. James P. "Decentralization Clash in New York Underlines School Union's Militancy." Wall Street Journal, D 20, 1968.

Gannon, Thomas M. "Harlem's Immortal Five Per Cent." America, Ag 27, 1966. [About a black nationalist teen-age group in Harlem]

Gelb, Joyce Klein. "Blacks, Blocs and Ballots: The Relevance of Party Politics to the Negro. A Study of Black Politicians in New York City, 1958-68." Doctoral dissertation, U. of New York, 1969. Univ. Microfilms Order No. 70-3068.

Geller, Max. "Some Social Factors Related to the Educational Achievement of 100 Negro Secondary School Students Residing in the Bedford-Stuyvesant Area of Brooklyn, City of New York." Doctoral dissertation, New York U., 1943.

Geltman, Max. "On Learning Swahili." National Review, N 9, 1968.

Gerber, Irwin. "The Effects of the Supreme Court's Desegregation Decision on the Group Cohesion of New York City's Negroes." Journal of Social Psychology 58(D, 1962): 295-303.

Gerry, Martin. "The HEW Review of Educational Services to New York's Minority Children." Integrateducation 13(My-Je, 1975):160-165.

Gershman, Carl. "Community Control of Schools: Conservative Trend." New America, F 28, 1969.

_____. "'Community Control' Rally Turns Into Sharp Debate." New America, Ja 22, 1969. [Meeting on Ja 11, 1969, at Community Church, New York City]

_____. "Pacification, Not School Reform, at Heart of Lindsay's Strategy." New America, N 15, 1968.

Gifford, Bernard. "Demographic Changes in New York City." Integrateducation 13(My-Je, 1975):23-26.

Gilbert, Harry G. "On the IQ Ban." Teachers College Record, Ja, 1966. [Reply to Loretan, "The Decline and Fall of Group Intelligence Testing." Teachers College Record, O, 1965]

Gill, Barbara Ann. "Teaching at I.S. 201 Manhattan." Scope Bulletin, S, 1968.

Gillenson, Lewis W. "Manhattan Principal at Work" [Henry T. Hillson]. Saturday Review, My 16, 1964.

Gitlin, Todd. "Bringing a Lot of It Back Home." The Movement, D, 1968. [Ocean Hill-Brownsville, NYC]

_____. "The Liberation of Bronx H.S. of Science." San Francisco Express Times, N 13, 1968.

Gittell, Marilyn. "Chronicle of Conflict." Saturday Review, Mr 15, 1969. [Review-discussion of Martin Mayer. The Teacher Strike]

_____. "The Community and Its Schools." In Schools Against Children. The Case for Community Control. Edited by Annette T. Rubenstein. New York: Monthly Review Press, 1970.

_____. "Community Control of Education." In Urban Riots: Violence and Social Change, Proceedings, The Academy of Political Science, 1968.

_____. "New York City School Decentralization." Community, My, 1969.

_____. Participants and Participation. A Study of School Policy in New York City. New York: Center for Urban Education, 1967.

_____. "Problems of School Decentralization in New York City." Urban Review, F, 1967.

_____. School Boards and School Policy: An Evaluation of Decentralization in New York City. New York: Praeger, 1973.

Gittell, Marilyn with Berube, Maurice R., Gottfried, Frances, Guttentag, Marcia, and Spier, Adele. Demonstration for Social Change. An Experiment in Local Control. New York: Institute for Community Studies, Queens College, C.U.N.Y., 1971. [Ocean Hill-Brownsville, I.S. 201, and Two Bridges]

Gittell, Marilyn and others. School Decen-tralization and School Policy in New York City. New York: Institute for Community Studies, Queens College, O, 1971. A Report for the New York State Commission on the Quality, Cost and Financing of Elementary and Secondary Education.

Glasser, Ira. "The Burden of Blame; A Report on the Ocean Hill-Brownsville School Controversy." Urban Education, Ap, 1969.

_____. Memorandum to Academic Freedom Committee, Ja 7, 1969.

_____. "Resistance to Desegregation in New York City." Integrateducation 13(My-Je, 1975):147-152.

_____. Testimony Before the City Commission on Human Rights, D 2, 1968.

Glazer, Nathan. "School Politics." Commentary, Mr, 1969. [A critique of Rogers, 110 Livingston Street]

Goering, John M. and others. The Best Eight Blocks in Harlem: The Last Decade of Urban Reform. Washington, DC: University Press of America, 1977.

Goldaber, Irving. "The Negro Protest Against the New York City Board of Education." Journal of Intergroup Relations, Autumn, 1965. [1954-1963]

_____. "The Treatment by the New York City Board of Education of Problems Affecting the Negro, 1954-1963." Doctoral disserta-tion, New York U., 1965. Univ. Microfilms Order No. 65-7293.

Goldberg, G. S. "I.S. 201: An Educational Landmark." IRCD Bulletin, Winter, 1966-1967.

Goldblatt, Harold S., and Tyson, Cyril. Likes and Dislikes of Pupils in an Integrated School (P.S. 198 M). Interim Report. Research Report No. 5. New York: City Commission on Human Rights, 1961.

_____. Some Self-Perception and Teacher Evaluations of Puerto Rican, Negro, and White Pupils in 4th, 5th, and 6th Grades (P.S. 198 M). Research Report No. 12. New York: City Commission on Human Rights, 1962.

Goldbloom, Maurice J. "New York's School Hassle." Commonweal, F 21, 1969.

_____. A Critique of the New York Civil Liberties Union Report on Ocean Hill-Brownsville School Controversy, N 15, 1968. Ad Hoc Committee to Defend the Right to Teach, Room 1105, 112 East 19th Street, New York, NY 10003

_____. "The Irrelevancies of Aryeh." Ad hoc Committee to Defend the Right to Teach, Room 1105, 112 East 19th Street, New York, NY 10003. [Reply to A. Neier. A Critique of a Critique]

_____. "The New York School Crisis." Commentary, Ja, 1969. [Reprinted in United Teacher, Ja 22, 1969]

Goldman, Ari L. "It's Called Career Education and It Caters to a New Elite." New York Times, D 31, 1978. [Vocational high schools in NYC]

_____. "Two Schools--Similar in Many Ways But So Different in Test Results." New York Times, Ja 13, 1978. [P.S. 34 and P.S. 110]

Goldman, Irwin, Jr., McDonald, Roslyn G., and Epstein, Joyce. "Characteristics of Jobs Held by Economically Disadvantaged Youth." American Journal of Orthopsychiatry, Ja, 1970.

Goldman, John J. "Tale of Two Schools: N.Y. Crisis Hurts." Los Angeles Times, O 17, 1975. [James Madison High School and Midwood High School]

Goldstein, Michael L. "Race Politics in New York City, 1890-1930: Independent Political Behavior." Doctoral dissertation, Columbia U., 1973. Univ. Microfilms Order No. 76-15,880.

Gonzales, Juan. "Class Oppression in High Schools." The Movement, Ap, 1969.

Goodman, Walter. "'I Like Myself Because I Know How to Read.'" Family Circle (N, 1974):58-62. [P.S. 91]

Gordon, Daniel. "The School System: A Cry of Despair." New Politics, Spring, 1968. [Mr, 1969]

Gordon, Edmund W. "Toward Meeting the Mental Health Needs of Underprivileged Minority Group Children in the Harlem Community of New York City." Doctoral dissertation, Columbia U., Teachers College, 1958.

[Gordon, Edmund W., Chairman] Committee on Experimental Program to Improve Educational Achievements in Special Service Schools. Final Report Submitted to the Superintendent of Schools, June 20, 1968. New York: New York City Public Schools, 1968.

Gordon, Joan and others. The Poor of Harlem: Social Functioning in the Underclass. Inter-departmental Neighborhood Service Center, 145 West 125th Street, New York, NY, 1966.

Gordon, Max. "Roots of Racism" (a letter). Nation, N 18, 1968.

Gorelick, S. "Social Control, Social Mobility and the Eastern European Jews: An Analysis of Public Education in New York City, 1880-1924." Doctoral dissertation, Columbia U., 1975.

Gotbaum, Victor. "A Multi-Cultural Union." Integrateducation 13(My-Je, 1975):65-67.

Gottesfeld, Harry. "Educational Issues in a Low-Income Area as Seen by Community People and Educators." Phi Delta Kappan 52 (F, 1971):366-368. [Lower East Side, Manhattan]

_____. Educational Issues of the Ghetto as Seen by Community People and Educators. Final Report. New York city: Yeshiva U., D 12, 1969. ERIC ED 038 481.

Gottfried, Frances. "A Survey of Parental Views of the Ocean Hill-Brownsville Experiment." Community Issues 2(O, 1970): 1-32.

Gottlieb, Edward P. "Ghetto Schools Need Black Power." WIN Magazine, N 1 and 15, 1968.

Granick, Leonard P. Study of Work-Training for Unemployed Youth. An Analysis of Employ-ment Experiences of Mobilization for Youth Trainees One Year After Leaving the Program. Mobilization for Youth, Division of Employment Opportunities, 214 East 2 Street, New York, NY., n.d.

Greene, Mary Frances, and Ryan, Orletta. The School Children. Growing Up in the Slums. New York: Pantheon, 1966.

Greer, Colin. "Attitudes Toward the Negro in New York City, 1890-1914." Master's thesis, London U., 1968.

_____. The Principal As Educator. The Finley School. New York City. New York: Center for Urban Education, 1971.

Griego, Marie. "A Study of New York City School Administrative Decentralization and Community Control." Master's thesis, Adams State College, 1969.

Griffiths, Daniel E. and others. "Negro Teachers in New York City." Integrated Education, F-Mr, 1964.

_____. Teacher Mobility in New York City. New York: Center for School Services and Off-Campus Courses. School of Education, New York U., 1963.

Griffith, Francis. "Is There Any Hope for New York City Schools?" Bulletin of the National Association of Secondary School Principals 55(Mr, 1971):1-12.

Gross, Calvin E. "Progress Toward Integration." Integrated Education, F-Mr, 1964.

Gross, Ella. "Negro History Hall at Public School No. 113, New York City." Negro History Bulletin, F, 1944.

Gross, Kenneth G. "Bad Show for Reporters." Nation, N 18, 1968. [Ocean Hill-Brownsville]

Gross, Solomon. "The Police of the Twenty-Third Precinct and the East Harlem Community." Journal of Social Issues 31 (1975):145-161. [1966-1967]

Gunning, Rosemary R. "The P.A.T. Viewpoint." Integrated Education, Ag-N, 1965.

Gurock, Jeffrey S. "A History of Jewish Community of Harlem, 1880-1930." Master's thesis, Columbia U., 1976.

Guttentag, Marcia. "Children in Harlem's Community Controlled Schools." Journal of Social Issues 28(1972):1-20.

Gutwirth, Linda W. "Big Men on Campus: A Study of Informal Leadership among Black and Puerto Rican Students in an Urban High School." Doctoral dissertation, City U. of New York, 1974. Univ. Microfilms Order No. 74-20078.

Guy, Rosa. "Black Perspective: On Harlem's State of Mind." New York Times Magazine, Ap 16, 1972.

Hamburger, Martin, and Wolfson, Harry E. 1000 Employers Look at Occupational Education. New York: Board of Education, Jl, 1969.

Hamilton, Mary. "Parents Break Into N.Y. Schools." Guardian, O 26, 1968.

Hammack, David C. "The Centralization of New York's Public School System, 1896: A Social Analysis of a Decision." Master's thesis. Columbia U., 1969.

Handlin, Oscar. The Newcomers: Negroes and Puerto Ricans in a Changing Metropolis. Cambridge, MA: Harvard U. Press, 1959.

Harlem Parents Committee. Bundy Report, Position and Recommendations. New York: Harlem Parents Committee, n.d.

Harlem Youth Opportunities Unlimited, Inc. Youth in the Ghetto. A Study of the Consequences of Powerlessness and a Blueprint for Change. New York: HARYOU, 1964. [Central Harlem]

_____. "Educational Excellence in Harlem." Integrated Education, Je-Jl, 1964.

Harnett, Patrick. "A Lesson for Liberals." Village Voice, O 30, 1968.

Harrington, Michael. "An Open Letter to Men of Good Will (With an Aside to Dwight Macdonald)." New York Review, Ja 2, 1969. [See below, Macdonald]

_____. "The Freedom to Teach: Beyond the Panaceas." Village Voice, O 3, 1968. [N.Y.C. teachers strike]

Harris, M. A. A Negro History Tour of Manhattan. New York: Negro Universities Press, Greenwood Publishing Company, 1968.

Harris, Timothy. "Where School Monies Go." Community 3(S-O, 1970):4-5, 8.

Haughton, James. "The Role of the Board of Education in Perpetuating Racism in the Building Trades and Vice Versa." In Schools Against Children. The Case for Community Control. Edited by Annette T. Rubenstein. New York: Monthly Review Press, 1970.

Haynes, George Edmund. The Negro at Work in New York City. Green & Company, 1912.

Hayes, Lucy Agnes. "Comparative Study of Public and Parochial Elementary Education in the Nineteenth Century in New York City." Doctoral dissertation, Fordham U., 1936.

Heilbrun, James. "Jobs in Harlem: A Statistical Analysis." Regional Science Association Papers, 1970.

Heller, Barbara R., and Barnett, with Benjamin, Marge, Eisler, Judith A., McClane, Farrell, and George Weinberg. Expand and Improve... A Critical Review of the First Three Years of ESEA Title I in New York City. New York: Center for Urban Education, Jl, 1970.

Heller, Barbara R. A History and Description of ESEA Title I in New York City, 1965-1968. New York: Center for Urban Education, Je, 1968.

Henry, Keith S. "The Black Political Tradition in New York: A Conjunction of Political Cultures." Journal of Black Studies 7(Je, 1977):455-484.

_____. "The Place of the Culture of Migrant Commonwealth Afro-West Indians in the Political Life of Black New York in the Period Circa 1918 to Circa 1966." Doctoral dissertation, U. of Toronto, 1973.

Hentoff, Nat. A Political Life: The Education of John V. Lindsay. New York: Knopf, 1969.

_____. "Ad Hoc Committee on Confusion." Village Voice, S 26, 1968.

_____. "The Chancellor." New Yorker, O 14, 1972. [Dr. Harvey Scribner]

_____. Does Anybody Give a Damn? New York: Knopf, 1977.

_____. "Elizabeth Brown: The Bold Pariah of 75." Village Voice, Ap 2, 1979.

_____. "Filling in the Paper of Record." Village Voice, O 17, 1968.

_____. "Growing Up Mugged." New York Times Magazine, Ja 28, 1973.

_____. "Making Public Schools Accountable. A Case Study of I.S. 201 in Harlem." Phi Delta Kappan, Mr, 1967.

_____. "Ocean Hill Brownsville and the Future of Community Control." Civil Liberties, F, 1969.

_____. Our Children Are Dying. New York: Viking, 1966. [Public schools in Harlem]

_____. "The Principal." New Yorker, My 7, 1966. [About Dr. Elliott Shapiro, principal of P.S. 92 in Central Harlem]

_____. "The Principal Principle." Village Voice, Ja 15, 1979. [George W. Wingate High School]

_____. "Profiles" (Mayor John V. Lindsay--1,2). New Yorker, My 3, My 10, 1969.

_____. "The Quick, the Dead, and the Harlem Prep." Village Voice, S 18, 1978.

_____. "School Damaged Children: What Is To Be Done?" Village Voice, Ap 9, 1979.

_____. "Schoolchild's Blues: Where You Live Equals How You'll Do." Village Voice, Mr 26, 1979.

_____. "Trouble in Shorackappock." New York Daily News Magazine, Mr 28, 1976. (Reprinted in New York Teacher Magazine, My 2, 1976) [P.S. 98]

Hicks, Constance. "The People Speak." African-American Teachers Forum, S-O, 1967. [Deals with local black community controls over schools]

Hiestand, Dale L. White Collar Employment for Minorities in New York City. Washington, DC: Office of Research & Reports, Equal Employment Opportunity Commission, 1967.

Hightower, Charles. "Brownsville Seeks Control of Schools." Guardian, My 25, 1968.

Hill, Herbert. "Black Protest, Union Democracy and UFT" (letter). New Politics 8(Fall, 1970):24-35.

Hillson, Henry T., and Myers, Florence C. The Demonstration Guidance Project, 1957-1962. Pilot Program for Higher Horizons. New York: Board of Education, 1963.

Hoffman, Marvin. "Conflict in a Counterfeit Community." New Republic, N 9, 1968.

Hopkins, Ned. "JHS 57--A Bastion of Racism Separatism and Hatred in Brooklyn" (2 parts). New York Teacher, Mr 25, Ap 1, 1973.

Horowitz, Julius. The Diary of A.N.: The Story of the House on West 104th Street. New York: Coward-McCann, 1970.

Hunter, Charlayne. "Black Studies Changing Schools Here." New York Times, N 2, 1969.

_____. "Muslim Center Blends Business, School and Mosque." New York Times, Ag 25, 1970. [The U. of Islam in Harlem]

Hurst, Marsha. "Integration, Freedom of Choice and Community Control in Nineteenth Century Brooklyn." Journal of Ethnic Studies 3 (Fall, 1975):33-55.

Hurwitz, Howard L. "When OEO Militants Move In On a School." Human Events, S 14, 1974.

Ianni, F. A. J. "The Rise of the Black Mafia." New York 7(Ja 28, 1974):36-45.

Inside Ocean Hill District." United Teacher, O 16, 1968. [Interview with Fred Nauman, UFT district chairman for the Ocean Hill-Brownsville project]

An Intensive Program for the Attainment of Educational Achievement in Deprived Area Schools of New York City. MARC Document No. 1. New York, NY: Metropolitan Applied Research Center, Mr, 1968.

Isaacs, Charles. "A J.H.S. 271 Teacher Tells It Like It Is." New York Times Magazine, N 24, 1968.

Jackson, Anthony. A Place Called Home: A History of Low-Cost Housing in Manhattan. Cambridge, MA: MIT Press, 1976.

Jackson, L. R., and Johnson, W. A. Protest by the Poor: The Welfare Rights Movement in New York City. Lexington, MA: D. C. Heath, 1974.

Jacoby, Susan. "Elite School Battle." Washington Post, My 28, 1972. [Brooklyn Technical High School]

Jacobs, William May. "Parents and Politics." Urban Review, D, 1967. [Community politics around the issue of P.S. 125-36]

"Jail Break!" Movement, My, 1969. [New York S.D.S. statement on high schools]

Janssen, Peter A. "Let's Hear It For Aviation High." New York Times Magazine, D 7, 1975.

Jencks, Christopher. "The Great New York Boycott. What Will Happen If the Cry for Better Schools Fails?" New Republic, F 15, 1964.

Jenkins, Mary. Bilingual Education in New York City. New York: Board of Education, 1971.

Jewish Cultural Clubs and Societies. "School Decentralization, Community Control and Negro-Jewish Relations: A Statement." Jewish Currents, My, 1969.

Johnson, David W. "The Effects of a Freedom School on Its Students." In The Urban R's. Edited by Robert A. Dentler and Others. New York: Praeger, 1967.

_____. "Freedom School Effectiveness: Changes in Attitudes of Negro Children." Journal of Applied Behavioral Science, Jl-Ag, 1966. Harlem

_____. "Racial Attitudes of Negro Freedom School Participants and Negro and White Civil Rights Participants." Social Forces, D, 1966.

Johnson, Esther. Report on Bilingual Pilot Schools in New York City: A Study of a Court-Ordered Program for Pupils with English Language Difficulty, Ag, 1975. ERIC ED 135 909.

Johnson, Thomas A. "Ocean-Hill at Peace: Involved and Frustrated." New York Times, N 1, 1969.

Joly, Roxee Ward. "Black Studies Programs in N.Y.C.'s High Schools." United Teacher, My 10, 1970.

Jones, Billie. "Center Programs." Center Forum, My 15, 1969. [Description of programs of Center for Urban Education dealing with, among others, a clearinghouse on decentralization]

Jones, Dorothy S. "The Issues at I.S. 201: A View from the Parents' Committee." Integrated Education, O-N, 1966.

Jones, Frederick, and Shagaloff, June. "NAACP on New York Situation." Integrated Education, F-Mr, 1964.

Jones, Thomas. Sociology of a New York City Block. New York: n.p., 1904.

Josefowicz, Mike, and Gold, Ted. "Co-optation City or 'Ford Has a Better Idea.'" Something Else!, My, 1969.

Kaestle, C. The Creation of an Urban School System, New York City, 1750-1850. Cambridge, MA: Harvard U. Press, 1972.

Kahn, Alfred J. New York City Schools and Children Who Need Help. New York: Citizens Committee for Children of New York, 112 East Nineteenth Street, New York, NY 10003, 1962.

Kantrowitz, Nathan. "Ethnic and Racial Segregation in the New York Metropolis, 1960." American Journal of Sociology, My, 1969.

_____. Negro and Puerto Rican Populations of New York City in the Twentieth Century. New York: American Geographical Society, 1969.

Kantrowitz, Nathan, and Pappenfort, Donnell M. (eds.). 1960 Fact Book for the New York-Northwestern New Jersey Standard Consolidated Area; the Nonwhite, Puerto-Rican, and White Non-Puerto-Rican Populations. New York: Columbia U., 1966.

Karp, Richard. "School Decentralization in New York: A Case Study." Interplay, Ag-S, 1968.

_____. "The Siege of Ocean Hill." Interplay, Ja, 1969.

Karp, Walter, and Shapiro, H. R. "Exploring the Myth of Black Anti-Semitism." The Public Life, F 21, 1969. [N.Y.C.; reprinted as advertisement in New York Times, Mr 16, 1969, 7E]

Karpatkin, Rhoda H., and Robinson, Isaiah E., Jr. "Powers and Responsibilities of Local and Central School Board Under Decentralization." United Teacher, D 7, 1969.

Kelley, Joseph B. "Racial Integration Policies of the New York City Housing Authority [1958-1961]." Doctoral dissertation, Columbia U., 1963. Univ. Microfilms Order No. 64-2763.

_____. "Racial Integration Policies of the New York City Housing Authority, 1958-1961." Social Service Review, Je, 1964.

Kelly, James A. "Resource Allocation and Educational Need. New York City's Public Schools." Education and Urban Society 2 (1970):251-276.

Kelly, Myra. Little Aliens. New York: n.p., 1910. [Irish teacher on the East Side]

Kemble, Eugenia. "Afterwards...at J.H.S. 56." United Teacher, D 4, 1968.

_____. "Black Anti-Semitism Seen as Exaggerated Issue by Parents and Staff of Ocean Hill School." United Teacher, Mr 12, 1969. [P.S. 144]

_____. "Decentralization, Part IV. The Two Bridges Model School District." United Teacher, Ja 24, 1968.

_____. "MES Conference Marked by Active Dialogue." United Teacher, Je 12, 1968.

_____. "Open Enrollment Integration Threatened Despite Success at JHS 307." United Teacher, Je 22, 1969.

Kemble, Penn. "Coalition for Chaos." New America, N 30, 1968

Kempton, Murray. "The Meritocracy of Labor." New Republic, F 6, 1965. [Apprenticeship in New York City]

_____. "Time to Tell Off Shanker." New York Post, S 26, 1968.

Kenkelen, Bill. "Bronx School Develops To Replace Catholic One." National Catholic Reporter, Ag 12, 1977. [South Bronx]

Kessler, Felix. "Integrated Misfire." Wall Street Journal, O 12, 1966. [P.S. 8 in Brooklyn]

Kessner, Thomas. "The Golden Door: Immigrant Mobility in New York City, 1880-1915." Doctoral dissertation, Columbia U., 1975. Univ. Microfilms Order No. 75-25,694.

Kilpatrick, William H. The Dutch Schools of New Netherlands and Colonial New York. Washington, DC: GPO, 1912.

King, Ken. "Attitudes and School Decentralization: A Survey of Community Group Leaders in New York's Three Experimental Districts." Doctoral dissertation, Teachers College, Columbia U., 1971.

Kirman, Joseph M. "A White Teacher in a Negro School." Journal of Negro Education, Spring, 1966.

Klein, Ronald H. "Jewish Acculturation in New York City, 1880-1920." Master's thesis, Seton Hall U., 1966.

Klein, Woody. "Defeat in Harlem." Nation, Jl 1, 1964. [About Kenneth B. Clark and HARYOU]

Klemesrud, Judy. "Integration on the Family Level: Whites Adopt Negro Children." New York Times, Jl 15, 1967.

Kohl, Herbert. Thirty-Six Children. New York: New American Library, 1967. [Teaching in a Harlem school]

Koltun, Elizabeth, and Schechter, Neil. "Whatever Happened to East Flatbush?" interChange 2(Mr, 1977). [Published by Breira, 200 Park Avenue South, New York, NY 10003]

Konubi, Imim. "Tyranny at Lane." African-American Teachers Forum, Mr, 1969. [Lane High School]

Kopkind, Andrew. "Down the Down Staircase: Parents, Teachers and Public Authorities." New Republic, O 22, 1966.

Kostman, Samuel. "The Principal As Mediator and Leader." NASSP Bulletin 56(Ap, 1972): 11-18. [George Washington High School]

Kravetz, Nathan. Academic Excellence in an Inner City Elementary School: P-129-K. New York: Center for Urban Education, O, 1968. [Bedford Stuyvesant]

_____. A Special Enrichment Program of Quality Integrated Education for Schools in Transitional Areas. New York: Center for Urban Education, S, 1967.

Kravetz, Nathan, and Phillips, Edna M. Special Primary Program in Five Schools. New York: Center for Urban Education, O, 1969.

Kriftcher, Noel N. "The Educational Power Structure in a Decentralized Community School District." Doctoral dissertation, Hofstra U., 1978. Univ. Microfilms Order No. 7815683.

Krosney, Herbert. "Feuding Over Poverty, Mobilization for Youth." Nation, D 14, 1964.

Kunstler, William M. "The Myth of Due Process [in the New York School Strike]." Scope Bulletin, N, 1968.

Kurland, Norman D. "Integrated Schools: A Progress Report." Parents' Magazine, S, 1965.

Kushnick, Louis. "Race, Class and Power: the New York Decentralization Controversy." American Studies 3(1969):201-219.

Labov, William and Others. A Study of the Non-Standard English of Negro and Puerto Rican Speakers in New York City. Volume II: The Use of Language in the Speech Community. New York: Columbia U., 1968, 366 pp. ERIC ED 028 424.

_____ and _____. A Study of the Non-Standard English of Negro and Puerto Rican Speakers in New York City. Volume I: Phonological and Grammatical Analysis. New York, NY: Columbia U., 1968, 397 pp. ERIC ED 028 423.

Lacks, Roslyn. "A Harlem Uprising. Parents in School District 5 Won't Take Second Best Any Longer." Village Voice, N 13, 1978.

_____. "The Tradition of Benign Neglect." Village Voice, Ap 2, 1979. [Harlem School District No. 5]

Landers, Jacob. "A Letter to the Editor." Integrated Education, F-Mr, 1967.

_____. Higher Horizons, Progress Report. New York: Board of Education, 1963.

_____. Improving Ethnic Distribution of New York City Pupils. New York: Board of Education, My, 1966.

_____. "Integration in the Major Metropolis." In School Desegregation in the North. Edited by T. Bentley Edwards and Frederick M. Wirt. San Francisco, CA: Chandler, 1967.

_____. "Perspectives on School Integration." Integrated Education, Ag-S, 1964.

_____. "Profiles of Inequality in New York City." Integrated Education 11(Ja-F, 1973): 3-14.

Landesman, Alter F. Brownsville: The Birth, Development and Passing of a Jewish Community in New York. New York: Bloch, 1969.

Lang, Gladys E. and others. Responses to a Decentralization Crisis. New York: Center for Urban Education, Jl, 1968. [Ocean Hill-Brownsville]

Langlois, Margaret. Number and Proportion of Pupils by Ethnic Group Enrolled in Courses Offered by the Public High Schools of New York City in 1970-71. New York: Board of Education, 1972.

Langner, Thomas S. and others. "Psychiatric Impairment in Welfare and Non-Welfare Children." Welfare in Review 7(Mr-Ap, 1969): 10-21.

Language Ability Survey of Pupils in New York City Public Schools as of October 31, 1972. New York: Board of Educators, 1973.

Lapidus, G. "Environmental Effect of New York City Life on National Intelligence Test Scores of 12 Year Old Negro Boys Residing in New York Varied Periods of Time." Master's thesis, Columbia U., 1931.

Larner, Jeremy. "I.S. 201: Disaster in the Schools." Dissent, Ja-F, 1967.

_____. "McComb vs. Harlem. A Matter of Identity." Dissent, Spring, 1965. [37 Negro high school students from Mississippi visit New York]

_____. "The New York School Crisis." Dissent, Spring, 1964.

Lash, Trude, and Sigal, Heidi. State of the Child: New York City. New York: Foundation for Child Development, Ap, 1976.

Lauter, Paul, and Kronberg, Ken. [Two letters on school decentralization] Radicals in the Professions, N-D, 1968.

Leacock, Eleanor. "Education, Socialization, and 'Culture of Poverty.'" In Schools Against Children. The Case for Community Control. Edited by Annette T. Rubenstein. New York: Monthly Review Press, 1970.

Leder, Sharon. "Introducing Poetry to a New York City School of Printing: Radical Teacher 5(Jl, 1977):36-42. [Printing Trades School]

Lelyveld, Joseph. "The Most Powerful Man in the School System--On Paper." New York Times Magazine, Mr 21, 1971. [Chancellor of the New York City schools, Dr. Harvey Scribner]

_____. "Shanker and His U.F.T. Poised For a New Showdown With City." New York Times, Je 26, 1972.

Leman, Beverly, Josefowicz, Mike, and Gold, Ted. "Decentralization: Strategy to Re-organize the Cities." Leviathan, Je, 1969.

Leo, John. "Black Anti-Semitism." Commonweal, F 14, 1969. [Ocean Hill-Brownsville]

Levine, Abe. "$10 Million Experimental Elementary Program Endangered." United Teacher, S 14, 1969.

Levine, Jonathan. The Effects of Race, Ethnicity and Class in the 1975 New York City Community School Board Elections, Ap, 1976. ERIC ED 122 427.

Levine, Naomi, with Cohen, Richard. Ocean Hill-Brownsville--A Case History of Schools in Crisis. New York: Popular Library, 1969.

Levy, Rachel. "N.Y. Teachers Strike--For What?" Jewish Currents, D, 1968.

Levy, Rachel, and Maslow, Will. "An Integra-tion Program." Integrated Education, F- Mr, 1964.

Levy, Seymour. "Are We Driving Teachers Out of Ghetto Schools?" American Education, My, 1967. [By the principal of J.H.S. 45 in East Harlem]

Lewis, Edward S. "The Urban League, A Dynamic Instrument in Social Change. A Study of the Changing Role of the New York Urban League, 1910-1960." Doctoral dissertation, New York U., 1961.

Lewinson, Edwin R. Black Politics in New York City. New York: Twayne, 1974.

"Library Expansion in Harlem." Wilson Library Bulletin, Je, 1965

Lichtenstein, Grace. "Brooklyn's School Board 13 Learning to Live With Segregation." New York Times, Ap 9, 1974.

Ling, Bill. "The Battle in School District 1. Community Control and Bilingual Education. Bridge 3(Ap, 1974):15-17.

Littky, Dennis S. "Identification and Analysis of Variables and Processes Affecting Educa-tional Change in Urban Schools and Communi-ties: A Study in the Ocean Hill-Brownville Demonstration School District." Doctoral dissertation, U. of Michigan, 1970. Univ. Microfilms Order No. 71-4664.

Littlejohn, A. W. "In Bedford-Stuyvesant: Libraries Work with the Disadvantaged." Top News, Ja, 1967.

Lobenthal, Joseph, Jr. "Why Isn't the School Conflict Being Adjudicated?" Center Forum, O 20, 1968.

Lobman, Ethel, and Sojourner, Katherine. The Struggle for Community Control in N.Y. School District 1. Puerto Rican, Black and Chinese Parents Fight Racism. New York: Pathfinder Press, 1975.

Locke, Alain. "Dark Weather-Vane." Survey Graphic 25(Ag, 1936):457-462. [Harlem race riot of Mr, 1935]

Loe, Roy. "IS 201." A film, available from the U. of the State of New York, State Education Department, Albany, NY 12224.

Lonoff, Richard. "Supervisory Practices that Promote Academic Achievement in a New York City School." Phi Delta Kappan 52(F, 1971): 338-340. [P.S. 20]

Loop, Anne S. "The Nature of the Relationship between Education and Careers of Negroes Living in Manhattan Covering the Years 1929-1937." Doctoral dissertation, New York U., 1940.

Lopate, Phillip. Being With Children. Garden City, NY: Doubleday, 1975. [P.S. 90]

"The Louis Walker Case." United Teacher, S 14, 1969. School District 13, Brooklyn

Lovejoy, O. R. The Negro Children of New York. New York: Children's Aid Society, 1932.

Lowenstein, Allard. "Ending Job Discrimination in New York City." Integrateducation 13 (My-Je, 1975):63-64.

"The Luis Fuentes Case." United Teacher, S 14, 1969. [Two Bridges Demonstration District]

Lurie, Ellen. "School Integration and the Board of Education." EQUAL Newsletter, D, 1964.

_____. "School Integration in New York City." Integrated Education, F-Mr, 1965.

_____. Some Preliminary Comments About School Board Six's School Board Elections, May, 1973. New York: Community Service Society, Ag, 1975.

Lyford, Joseph. _The Airtight Cage_. New York: Harper and Row, 1966. [The West Side, Manhattan]

McClintick, David. "Other Big Cities Seek to Avoid New York's Decentralization Woes." _Wall Street Journal_, D 13, 1968.

McClintick, David, and Sears, Art, Jr. "Decentralized District in a New York Ghetto Claims Gains in Schools." _Wall Street Journal_, Ap 10, 1969. [Ocean Hill-Brownsville]

McCormick, Harold. _The First Fifty Years_. New York: n.p., 1948. [N.Y.C., 1898-1948]

McCoy, Carmen A. "High School Descriptions [in New York City]." _Community_, My, 1969.

_____. "The Independent Harlem School System." _Community_, Mr-Ap, 1969.

_____. "The Press and Ocean Hill." _Community_, F, 1969.

McCoy, Rhody. "Analysis of Critical Issues and Incidents in the New York City School Crisis, 1967-1970." Doctoral dissertation, U. of Massachusetts, 1971.

_____. "Why Have an Ocean Hill-Brownsville?" In _What Black Educators Are Saying_, pp. 251-260. Edited by Nathan Wright, Jr. New York: Hawthorn, 1970.

Macdonald, Dwight. "An Open Letter to Michael Harrington." _New York Review_, D 5, 1968. [See above, Harrington]

McIntyre, Harry. "Decentralization in Action." _The Parents' Voice_, N, 1967. [Interview with Rhody A. McCoy, Unit Administrator of the Ocean Hill-Brownsville Decentralized School Project in New York City]

McKenna, Jeremiah. "Crime in the Schools." _New York Affairs_ (Winter, 1974).

Mackler, Bernard. "Children Have Rights, Too!" _Crisis_ 81(Ag-S, 1974):235-238. [The "600" schools]

_____. "The Primitive Use of Suspensions and Transfers in the New York City Schools." In _Schools Against Children. The Case for Community Control_. Edited by Annette T. Rubenstein. New York: Monthly Review Press, 1970.

_____. "A Report on the '600' Schools: Dilemmas, Problems, and Solutions." In _The Urban R's_. Edited by Robert A. Dentler and Others. New York: Praeger, 1967.

_____. "The '600' Schools: Dilemmas, Problems, and Solutions." _Urban Review_, Je, 1966.

_____. "The Theatre of the Absurd: The New York City Public Schools." _Urban Education_, Ja, 1970.

McMillan, Charles B. "Organizational Change in Schools: Bedford-Stuyvesant." _Journal of Applied Behavioral Science_ 11(0-D, 1975): 437-453.

Macchiarola, Frank J. "Mid-Year Report of the Chancellor of Schools to the New York City Board of Education." _New York Teacher_, Ja 28, 1979.

Maeroff, Gene I. "The Tragedy of Canarsie." _Nation_, D 4, 1972.

Magid, Alvin. "Organizational Character versus Citizen Involvement: The New York City School Decentralization Controversy." _Urban and Social Change Review_ 3(1969).

"The Magnetic Power of Quality Education." _New York Teacher_, Je 5, 1977. [Mark Twain Junior High School 239, Coney Island]

Mahoney, Jeanne Adelman. "Decentralization: Formal or Substantive?" _United Teacher_, Ap 3, 1968.

Makielski, Stanislaw John, Jr. "The Politics of Zoning in New York City, 1910-1960." Doctoral dissertation, Columbia U., 1965. Univ. Microfilms Order No. 67-16034.

Maller, J. B. "Economic and Social Correlatives of School Progress in New York City." _Teachers College Record_, My, 1933.

Mangum, Claude Julien. "Afro-American Thought on the New York City Public School System, 1905-1954: An Analysis of New York City Afro-American Newspaper Editorials" (Vols. I and II). Doctoral dissertation, Columbia U., 1976. Univ. Microfilms Order No. 76-29106.

Manoni, Mary. _Bedford-Stuyvesant: The Anatomy of a Central City Community_. New York: Quadrange, n.d.

Martell, G. "Parents in the Schools: Community Control in Harlem." _This Magazine is About Schools_, 1970, pp. 72-109.

Martin, Merrill. "Letter on I.S. 201." _New Republic_, N 5, 1966.

Martire, Harriette A. "A History of Catholic Parochial Elementary Education in the Archdiocese of New York." Doctoral dissertation, Fordham U., 1955.

"The Mason-Dixon Line Moves to New York." _I. F. Stone's Weekly_, N 4, 1968.

Matthews, Mary Fabian. "The Role of the Public School in the Assimilation of the Italian Immigrant Child in New York City, 1900-1914." Doctoral dissertation, Fordham U., 1966. Univ. Microfilms Order No. 66-13521.

Maxwell, William H. A Quarter Century of Public School Development. New York: n.p., 1912.

Mayer, Martin. "Close to Midnight for New York Schools." New York Times Magazine, My 2, 1965.

_____. "Frustration Is the Word for Ocean Hill." New York Times Magazine, My 19, 1968.

_____. "The Full and Sometimes Very Surprising Story of Ocean Hill, the Teachers' Union and the Teacher Strikes of 1968." New York Times Magazine, F 2, 1969.

_____. The Teachers Strike. New York 1968. New York: Harper & Row, 1969.

_____. "What Outsiders Think [of New York City's Schools]." Saturday Review, Ja 18, 1969. [A critique of David Rogers' 110 Livingston Street]

_____. "What's Wrong With Our Big-City Schools." Saturday Evening Post, S 8, 1967.

Mayer, Martin, and Featherstone, Joseph. "New York School Strike." New Republic, Ap 26, 1969. [An exchange of views]

Meier, Deborah. "From a Harlem School." Dissent, Mr-Ap, 1968.

Ment, David. "School Segregation in Brooklyn, N.Y.--1850-1897." Master's thesis, no further data.

"Metropolitan New York." Center Forum, D 23, 1968. [Discusses possible busing exchanges of New York City students with Scarsdale and Great Neck, Long Island]

Meyer, Gladys. Parent Action in School Integration. New York: United Parents Association, 1961.

Meyer, June. "You Can't See the Trees for the School." Urban Review, D, 1967. [Benjamin Franklin High School in East Harlem]

Michalak, Joseph M. "Higher Horizons: Statistics v. Rona." Southern Education Report, Mr-Ap, 1966. [Deals also with the More Effective Schools program]

_____. "Plans for Integration in New York City Schools." American School Board Journal, Jl, 1964.

Milgram, Gene. "Values in Conflict: New York City's Planning and Implementation of Scatter-City Housing and a High School." Master's thesis, MIT, 1974.

Miller, La Mar P. Ethnic Studies in Elementary and Secondary Schools in New York. Albany, NY: State Commission on the Quality, Cost, and Financing of Elementary and Secondary Education, 1971.

Mills, Nicholas C. "Community Control in [Historical] Perspective." IRCD Bulletin 8 (N, 1972):3-11

Millsom, Carol and Others. An Evaluation of the Early Childhood Centers in Poverty Areas. New York: New York U., D, 1968.

Minister, Edward, and Sagarin, Edward. "The School and the Community." New University Thought, Spring, 1967. [I.S. 201]

Minnerly, Richard. The Bundy Report: Summary, Critique, and Alternatives. Brooklyn, NY: Pratt Center for Community Improvement, Pratt Institute, D, 1967.

Minter, Thomas K. Intermediate School 201, Manhattan: Center of Controversy. 1968. Publications Office, Harvard Graduate School of Education, Longfellow Hall, Appian Way, Cambridge, MA 02138.

"Minutes [of United Federation of Teachers Official Bodies]." United Teacher, D 4, 1968. [S 10, 1968-N 17, 1968]

Mitchel, John Purroy. "Negroes in the Public Schools of New York [City]." Crisis, Jl, 1917.

Mitchell, Loften. "Harlem Reconsidered-- Memories of My Native Land." Freedomways, Fall, 1964.

Mohl, Raymond A. Poverty in New York, 1783- 1825. New York: Oxford U. Press, 1971.

Monteiro, Thomas Lee. "Identifying Sources of School-Community Conflict in Black and Puerto Rican Communities in New York City." Doctoral dissertation, Fordham U., 1975. Univ. Microfilms Order No. 75-18918.

Monti, Daniel J., Jr. "Racial Controversies in New York City: 1960-1964." Doctoral dissertation, U. of North Carolina, 1975. Univ. Microfilms Order No. 76-9272.

Moon, E. E. "Day in Bedford Stuyvesant." Library Journal, O 1, 1964.

Moore, Deborah D. "Jewish Ethnicity and Ac- culturation in the 1920's: Public Education in New York City." Jewish Journal of Sociology 18(D, 1976).

Moore, Queen Mother. "A Band-Aid for a Cancer." Harvard Graduate School of Education Alumni Association Bulletin, Fall, 1967.

Moore, Robert. Welcome to 57: Four Years of Teaching and Learning in Bedford-Stuyvesant. New York: Putnam's, 1974.

Moriber, Leonard. School Functioning of Pupils Born in Other Areas and in New York City. Pamphlet No. 168. New York: Board of Education, My, 1961.

Morrill, Fran. "Community Control of Schools: Not Separatist." New America, F 18, 1969.

Mudd, John. "The Rights of Parents." New Republic, Ja 4, 1969.

Muravchik, Emanuel. "Fact and Fiction, Anti-Semitism in School Crisis." United Teacher, Mr 30, 1969.

Murdock, K. "A Study of Race Differences in New York City." School and Society, Ja 31, 1920.

Nadle, Marlene. "Shapiro and the School: One Man Is Not the Issue." Village Voice, Je 8, 1967.

Naison, Mark D. "The Communist Party in Harlem, 1928-1936." Doctoral dissertation, Columbia U., 1975.

Natelson, Herman. "The Talmud Torahs: A Study of the School, the Pupil and His Home." Doctoral dissertation, Fordham U., 1937. [Brooklyn]

Nauman, Fred. "Roots of the N.Y.C. School Conflict." New America, O 18, 1968. [By the district chairman of the United Federation of Teachers in the Ocean Hill-Brownsville district]

"Needed: A Responsible Jewish Voice." African-American Teachers Forum, N, 1968.

"Negro Teachers' Association Conference." Integrated Education, Ag-S, 1967.

Neier, Aryeh. A Critique of a Critique. New York: New York Civil Liberties Union, Ja, 1969. [Ocean Hill-Brownsville]

Nelson Associates, Inc. Achieving and Maintaining Ethnic Balance in the High Schools of Queens. New York: Board of Education, Ag 31, 1967.

Neuhaus, Richard John. "The Auschwitz Reflex in New York." National Catholic Reporter, F 19, 1969.

"New Hope for Harlem's Bright Youth." Ebony, My, 1967. [Special Progress Class at I.S. 88 in Harlem]

New York Association of Negro School Supervisors and Administrators. "NYANSSA Supports Demonstration Districts." African-American Teachers Forum, S-O, 1967.

New York City Board of Education Demonstration Guidance Project. Fourth Annual Progress Report, 1959-1960. New York: Board of Education, 1961.

New York Board of Regents. "Proposals on De-centralization." United Teacher, Ap 17, 1968.

New York City Board of Education. A Five-Year Crash Program for Quality Education. An Attack on Unemployment and Poverty Through Improved Educational Opportunity, O 22, 1964. [Request for large-scale grant from the Anti-Poverty Program]

_____. School Integration in New York City, 1964-1965. Questions and Answers. New York: Board of Education, S, 1964.

_____. Toward Quality Secondary Education. Recommendations on the Reorganization of the New York City High Schools. New York: Board of Education, D, 1964.

New York City Commission on Human Rights. After Integration: Problems of Race Relations in the High School Today. A Study of Madison High School with Recommendations for New York City Schools. New York: The Commission, 1974.

_____. Report on Three Demonstration Projects in the City Schools. New York: City Commission on Human Rights, My, 1968.

New York City Public Schools. Action for Excellence. Recommendations of the Superintendent of Schools to the Board of Education on Grade Level Reorganization. New York: Board of Education, Ja 18, 1966.

_____. "Another View of New York." Integrated Education, F-Mr, 1964.

_____. Blueprint for Further Action Toward Quality Integrated Education. Proposals for Discussion, Mr 5, 1965. Board of Education, 110 Livingston Street, Brooklyn, NY.

_____. Programs for Potential and Actual Dropouts, Early School Leavers, and Employed, Under-Employed, and Unemployed Youth and Adults. Supplement to Staff Bulletin, Ap 27, 1964. [An extensive tabular summary of existing programs in New York City]

_____. Toward Quality and Equality in Education. Additional Services Provided for Our Pupils in Minority Group Areas. Supplement to Staff Bulletin, My 18, 1964.

New York City Public Schools. Central Zoning Unit. Ethnic Distribution of Pupils in the Public Schools of New York City. New York: Board of Education, Mr 24, 1965.

New York City School Board. "Response by the School Board." Integrated Education, O-N, 1966.

"New York City School Decentralization: The Respective Powers of the City Board of Education and the Community School Boards." Fordham Urban Law Journal 5(Winter, 1977): 239-278.

New York City Schools, Bureau of Educational
Research. Summary of Citywide Reading Test
Results for 1967-1968. New York: Board of
Education, N, 1968.

New York Civil Liberties Union. The Burden
of Blame: A Report on the Ocean Hill-
Brownsville School Controversy, O 9, 1968.
New York Civil Liberties Union, 156 Fifth
Avenue, New York, NY 10010.

_____. Memorandum to Special Committee on
Religious and Racial Prejudice [in
Teachers' Strike], N 26, 1968.

New York Court of Appeals. "The Balaban
Decision: Pro and Con." Integrated
Education, D, 1964-Ja, 1965.

"New York Integration Agreements." Integrated
Education, D, 1963-Ja, 1964.

"New York School Board Program." Integrated
Education, Ag-N, 1965.

New York Schools. Memorandum on the First
Year of the More Effective Schools Program.
1964-5. New York: Board of Education, O,
1965.

New York State Office of Education Performance
Review. Teacher Absenteeism in New York
City and the Cost-Effectiveness of Sub-
stitute Teachers, Ja, 1974. ERIC ED 085 868.

New York Urban League. "A Decade of New York
Changes." Integrated Education, Ap-My,
1964.

"New York's Avant-Garde School." Ebony, My,
1965. [New Lincoln School]

Nichol, Robert. "The Issue Is Survival:
Community Control of Schools." Trends,
Ap, 1969.

Niemeyer, John H. and others. Final Report of
the Advisory Committee on Decentralization.
Submitted to the Board of Education of the
City of New York, Jl, 1968. New York:
Board of Education, Ag, 1968.

"No More Teachers' Dirty Looks." The Movement,
Mr, 1939.

North, Robert D., Grieve, William R., and
Madison, Gordon L. More Effective Schools
Program in Poverty Area Schools, 1968-1969.
New York: The Psychological Corporation,
N, 1969.

Norton, Eleanor Holmes. Arson, Vandalism and
Other Racially Inspired Violence in New
York City. A Study of a New Phenomenon and
Recommendations for Action. New York:
New York City Commission on Human Rights,
D 8, 1972.

_____. "The Most Irresponsible Industry in
New York City." Integrated Education 10
(Mr-Ap, 1972):8-12. [Real estate industry]

"Notes and Comment." New Yorker, S 21, 1968.
[The teachers' strike over community control
of schools]

"Ocean Hill-Brownsville: The Agony of Decentralization." Nation's Schools, Ja, 1969.

"Ocean Hill-Brownsville." United Teacher, S 14,
1969.

"Oceanhill-Brownsville Project, New York, 1968."
In Revolution and Nation Building. Detroit,
MI: The House of Songlay Publishing Co.,
1968.

An Ocean Hill-Brownsville Resident. "Birth of a
Community." Liberation, D, 1968.

Oelsner, Lesley. [Two articles on school integration in New York City] New York Times,
N 20-21, 1977.

O'Neill, John. "The Rise and Fall of the UFT."
In Schools Against Children. The Case for
Community Control. Edited by Annette T.
Rubenstein. New York: Monthly Review Press,
1970.

Ono, Shin' Ya, and Gabriner, Vickie. "'Community
Control' at Two Bridges: What Went Wrong?"
Leviathan, Je, 1969.

Osofsky, Gilbert. "A Decade of Urban Tragedy:
How Harlem Became a Slum." New York History,
O, 1965.

_____. Harlem. The Making of a Ghetto, 1890-
1930. New York: Harper & Row, 1965.

Ovington, Mary White. "The Negro Home in New
York." Charities 15(O 7, 1905):25-26.

Owens, Robert G., and Steinhoff, Carl R.
"Strategies for Improving Inner-City Schools."
Phi Delta Kappan, Ja, 1969. [More Effective
Schools program]

"'P.S. Let Whitey Fight His Own Gotdamn War.'"
Young Socialist, Ap, 1969. [Letters to three
black soldiers who had been court-martialed,
written by black students of J.H.S. 271 in
Ocean Hill-Brownsville]

Paige, Myles A. "The School System of Harlem."
Education 2(Ap, 1936):2, 7-8. [Published
by Negro Needs Society]

Palmer, A. E. History of the New York City
Public Schools. New York: n.p., 1905.

Paoli, Lillian B. "Community Control of Schools:
An East Harlem Experience." Doctoral dissertation, New School for Social Research,
1978. Univ. Microfilms Order No. 7820825.

Parent Community Negotiating Committee for I.S.
201. "I.S. 201 Parent-Community Commentary."
Integrated Education, F-Mr, 1967.

"Parent-Teacher Protest Spreads to More Schools." United Teacher, F 3, 1967. [P.S. 60, Bronx]

"Parents in the School: Community Control in Harlem." This Magazine Is About Schools 4 (F, 1970):72-109.

Patri, Angelo. A Schoolmaster in a Great City. New York: n.p., 1917.

Peebles, Robert W. "The Community School: Then and Now." Phylon 31(Summer, 1970): 157-167. [N.Y.C., 1930's and 1940's]

_____. "Leonard Covello: A Study of an Immigrant's Contribution to New York City." Doctoral dissertation, New York U., 1967. Univ. Microfilms Order No. 68-4791.

Penha, James W. "Wherever Two or More Are Gathered in His Name." Community 37(Winter, 1977):29-32. [Dwayne Brathwaite School, Bedford-Stuyvesant, Brooklyn]

Penn, Stanley. "Integration Furor." Wall Street Journal, Ap 23, 1964.

Perlman, Daniel. "Organizations of the Free Negro in New York City, 1800-1860." Journal of Negro History 56(Jl, 1971):181-197.

Pessen, Edward. "A Social and Economic Portrait of Jacksonian Brooklyn: Inequality, Social Immobility, and Class Distinction in the Nation's Seventh City." New York Historical Society Quarterly, O, 1971.

Peterson, Iver. "The Anatomy of a School Crisis." Race Relations Reporter 4(Ja, 1973):8-12. [Canarsie, Brooklyn]

_____. "Bilingual Instruction at Issue in District 1." New York Times, Ap 28, 1974.

Peterson, Paul E. "The Politics of Education Reform." In Toward Improved Urban Education, pp. 209-230. Edited by Frank Lutz. Columbus, OH: Jones, 1970. [East Harlem]

Perkins, William. "Colored Student Discouraged in Mixed Schools." New York Age, F 18, 1922.

Pileggi, Nicholas. "Barry Gottehrer's Job Is To Cool It." New York Times Magazine, S 22, 1968.

Pilo, Marvin R. "A Tale of Two Cities. The Application of Models of School Decentralization to the Cases of New York City and Detroit." Education and Urban Society 7 (Ag, 1975):393-411.

Pinkney, Alphonso, and Woock, Roger R. Poverty and Politics in Harlem. New York: College and University Press Service, 1971.

Podell, Lawrence. Families on Welfare in New York City. Mothers' Education and Employment. New York: Center for Social Research, Graduate Center, City U. of New York, D 20, 1967.

Polemeni, Anthony J. Pupil Reading Achievement in New York City. New York: Board of Education, Ja, 1975.

Pollak, Ed. "How Are the Pairings Going?" EQUAL Newsletter, D, 1964.

Porter, Bruce. "It Was a Good School to Integrate." New York Times Magazine, F 9, 1975 (also, letters in issue of Mr 2, 1975). [James Madison High School, Brooklyn]

Ports, Suki. "Racism, Rejection, and Retardation." In Schools Against Children. The Case for Community Control. Edited by Annette T. Rubenstein. New York: Monthly Review Press, 1970.

Powell, C. "Library of the Center for Urban Education." Research paper, Library School, Long Island U., 1971.

Powledge, Fred. "'Mason-Dixon Line' in Queens." New York Times Magazine, My 10, 1964.

_____. To Change a Child: A Report on the Institute for Developmental Studies. Chicago: Quadrangle Books, 1967. [The Institute at New York U. headed by Martin Deutsch]

Poynter, Ralph. "Community Control of Education." Guardian, My 25, 1968.

_____. "Controlling Community School.s" Guardian, O 12, 1968.

Pozzetta, George E. "The Italians of New York City, 1890-1914." Doctoral dissertation, U. of North Carolina, 1971.

"Profile of Local School Board Members." Community, Spring-Summer, 1970.

Psychas, George. "William L. Bulkley and the New York Negro, 1890-1910." Historical Journal of Western Massachusetts 1(Spring, 1972). [Black public school principal]

Psychologists for a Democratic Society. "See the Psychologist Run." Something Else!, N-D, 1969. [New York City schools]

Public Education Association. "Vocational Schooling in New York." Integrated Education, F-Mr, 1964.

Quinn, Joan. "'ROAR' Raises Its Head in New York City." Militant, A 15, 1975.

"Racism in Long Island School on Trial." Interracial Books for Children Bulletin 7 (1976):10-11. [Seldon, Long Island]

Rall, Clifford L. "A Study of Public School Administration Practices Relating to Negroes and Negro Groups in Selected Cities of the New York Metropolitan Area." Doctoral dissertation, Columbia U., Teachers College, 1953.

Randolph, Helen and others. The Black Suburbanite and His Schools. An Interim Report on a Study of the Impact of Black Suburbanization on the School System, O, 1970. ERIC ED 088 985. [NYC metropolitan area]

Ravitch, Diane. "Canarsie and Fuentes: The Limits of School Desegregation." New York Affairs 1(1973):88-97.

_____. "Foundations. Playing God in the Ghetto." Center Forum, My 15, 1969.

_____. The Great School Wars. New York City, 1805-1973. A History of the Public Schools as Battlefield of Social Change. New York: Basic Books, 1974.

_____. "New York [City] School Reform: A 'Long-Haul' Affair." New York Times, Ja 16, 1974.

Reade, Ben. "Revolutionary Learning." Renewal, O-N, 1966. [Montessori]

"Readers' Forum on N.Y.C. School Situation." Jewish Currents, Ja, 1969. [Three letters]

"Reading Scores of Pupils in [New York] City's Elementary and Junior High Schools." New York Times, D 23, 1966. [Reading scores for Grades 2, 5, 7, and 9 for schools in all thirty school districts]

"The Real Story Behind the Crisis in the N.Y. Schools." The Public Life, O 21, 1968.

Rebell, Michael A. "New York's School Decentralization Law: Two and a Half Years Later." Journal of Law and Education 2(Ja, 1973):1-39.

Reed, Pat. "Ocean Hill: A 'Good Thing' Soured by Politics, Strikes." Education News, O 21, 1968.

Reeves, Donald. Notes of a Processed Brother. New York: Pantheon, 1972.

Reid, Inez Smith. "The Conflict Over Decentralization: The Educational System of New York City." Pan-African Journal 2 (1969):69-93.

Rempson, Joe L. "Reconnection. The Heart of the Bundy Plan Assessed." Center Forum, Ja 26, 1968.

Reorganizing Secondary Education in New York City. Public Education Association, 20 West 40th Street, New York, NY, O, 1863.

"Report from the I.S. 201 Governing Board." Scope Bulletin, Christmas Edition, 1968.

Report of the Joint Planning Committee for More Effective Schools, to the Superintendent of Schools. New York: New York City Public Schools, My 15, 1964.

Resnik, Henry S. "Innovation Is Tradition in West Harlem." Saturday Review 55(Ag 19, 1972):50-53. [J.H.S. 43, West Harlem]

"'Reverse' Open Enrollment Wins Support of White Pupils, Parents." Staff Bulletin [Public Schools of New York City], F 1, 1965. [P.S. 20, voluntary transfer of pupils from white schools to a Negro, Puerto Rican school]

Ribner, Susan. "How N.Y. Parents, Teachers Kept Schools Open." Guardian, S 28, 1968.

_____. "Police Enforce Settlement of N.Y.C. Teachers Strike." Guardian, O 12, 1968.

Rich, Cynthia Jo. "The Case of New York City." Race Relations Reporter 5(My, 1974):27-28.

Richards, James J. "Hurrah for the New York Teachers' Strike: 1968." I.S.R. Journal, Winter, 1969.

Ricklefs, Roger. "A Slum School Goes Back to the Basics, Gets Good Results." Wall Street Journal, Je 21, 1976. [Argus Community School, South Bronx]

_____. "Bronx School of Science Offers Bright City Kids Top-Notch Education." Wall Street Journal, My 17, 1977.

_____. "High School for Highbrows." Change 9(O, 1977):34-39. [Bronx High School of Science]

Ritterband, Paul. "Ethnic Power and the Public Schools: The New York City School Strike of 1968." Sociology of Education 47(Spring, 1974):251-267.

_____. "Ethnicity and School Disorder." Education and Urban Society 8(Ag, 1976):383-400.

Ritterband, Paul, and Silberstein, Richard. "Group Disorders in the Public Schools." American Sociological Review 38(Ag, 1973): 461-467. [New York City academic high schools, N, 1968-Je, 1969]

Robbins, Larry. "Dismiss 7 Members of African-American Teachers Association, Shanker Offers Aid in Fight for Due Process, on Request." United Teacher, Je 29, 1969. [J.H.S. 271 Ocean Hill-Brownsville]

Roberts, Charles H. (chairman). "The Negro in Harlem: A Report on Social and Economic Conditions Responsible for the Outbreak of March 19, 1935." New York: The Mayor's Commission on Conditions in Harlem, unpublished.

Roberts, Steve V. "Control of Schools." New Republic, S 28, 1968.

Robinson, Chris, and Nowygord, Pearl. "Breaking Out of Prison." Guardian, My 3, 1969. [High schools]

Robinson, Isaiah E. Violence in the New York City High Schools As Reported in a Survey of the High School Principals. New York: Board of Education, Ag 9, 1972.

Rogers, David. "The Failure of Inner City Schools: A Crisis of Management and Service Delivery." Educational Technology 10 (S, 1970):27-32.

_____. Inventory of Educational Improvement Efforts in the New York City Public Schools. New York: Teachers College Press, 1977.

_____. "The New York City School System." In Schools Against Children. The Case for Community Control. Edited by Annette T. Rubenstein. New York: Monthly Review Press, 1970.

_____. 110 Livingston Street. Politics and Bureaucracy in the New York City Schools. New York: Random House, 1968.

Rogers, David, with Korthewer, Faith, and Menzel, Roslyn. New York City and the Politics of School Desegregation. New York: Center for Urban Education, Jl, 1968. [Edited by Michael D. Usdan from the preceding item]

Rollock, Elise C. "Message to My Sons and Daughters from an Elder in the Tribe." Jewish Currents, Jl-Ag, 1969.

Roman, Peter. "Urban Fiscal Crisis Hits NYC Schools." Guardian, Ap 3, 1971.

Rose, Ernestine, "Books and the Negro: 135th Street Branch of the New York Public Library." Library Journal 52(N 1, 1927): 1012-1014.

Rose, Peter I., and Rothman, Stanley. "Race and Education in New York." Race, O, 1964.

Rose, William. "Teachers Fail in N.Y. Ghetto." National Guardian, S 23, 1967.

Rosenhaft, Anne. "The N.Y. School Crisis: A Class Conflict." New America, N 30, 1968.

Rosenwaike, Ira. "Interethnic Comparisons of Educational Attainment: An Analysis Based on Census Data for New York City." American Journal of Sociology 79(Jl, 1973): 68-77.

_____. Population History of New York City. Syracuse, NY: Syracuse U. Press, 1972.

Rosentraub, Mark S. and others. [Letters on article by Diane Ravitch on community control movement in New York City] Commentary 53(Je, 1972):16-22.

Rothman, Esther. The Angel Inside Went Sour. New York: McKay, 1971. [P.S. 8]

Rubenstein, Annette T. "Visiting Ocean Hill-Brownsville in November 1968 and May 1969." In Schools Against Children. The Case for Community Control. Edited by Rubenstein. New York: Monthly Review Press, 1970.

Rubin, Max J. Community School Board Elections in New York City. A Report to the New York State Commissioner of Education, D, 1973. ERIC ED 085 884.

Rury, John L. "Education and Black Community Development in Ante-Bellum New York City." Master's thesis, City College of New York, 1974.

Rustin, Bayard. "Canarsie's 'Community Control.'" New America, N 15, 1972.

_____. "Light Not Heat." United Teacher, O 16, 1968. [Ocean Hill-Brownsville]

Ruth, Robert Douglas. "A Study of the Factors Affecting Teacher Attitudes and Participation in the New York City School Decentralization Controversy." Doctoral dissertation, Duke U., 1974. Univ. Microfilms Order No. 75-13, 130.

Ryan, Orletta. "'I Get One More "U" My Mother Goin' to Beat Me Till It Rains.'" New York Times Magazine, F 13, 1966. [Schools in Harlem]

Sakolsky, R. "The Myth of Government-Sponsored Revolution. A Case Study of Institutional Safety-Valves." Education and Urban Society 5(My, 1973):321-343. [Local school board, Ocean Hill-Brownsville district]

Saltzman, Harold. Racial War in High School: The Ten-Year Destruction of Franklin K. Lane High School in Brooklyn. New Rochelle, NY: Arlington House, 1972.

Salz, Arthur E. "Local Control vs. Professionalism." Phi Delta Kappan, F, 1969.

Sanchez, Ramon. "It's Hard to 'Turn On' Teachers." Freedomways, Fall, 1969.

Sandler, Georgette B. "Educated Fools or Underrated Schools? The Social Validation of Reality in a New York City Ghetto School." Doctoral dissertation, New York U., 1972. Univ. Microfilms Order No. 72-21,539.

_____. "Reneging on the Redistribution of Power in the New York City Public Schools." Growth and Change 6(Ja, 1975): 11-16.

Scher, Richard K. "Decentralization and the New York State Legislature." Urban Review, S, 1969.

Schickel, Richard. "P.S. 165." Commentary, Ja, 1 64.

Schiff, Martin. "Community Control of Inner-City Schools and Educational Achievement." Urban Education 10(Ja, 1976):415-428.

_____. "The Educational Failure of Community Control in Inner-City New York." Phi Delta Kappan 57(F, 1976):375-378.

_____. "Luis Fuentes: The Anti-Semite as an Educator." Jewish Press, Ap 18, 1975. [Community District No. 1]

_____. "When Bigotry Rules, Education Suffers." National Jewish Monthly, Ap, 1875. [Community District No. 1]

"School Crisis Documentary." United Teacher, O 24, 1968. [Detailed chronology of the NYC schools crisis, O 11-O 22, 1968]

"School Crisis Documentary." United Teacher, N 6, 1968. [Covers New York City teachers strike, O 24-N 3, 1968]

"School Crisis Documentary, November 6, 1968-- November 16, 1968." United Teacher, N 20, 1968.

"School Crisis Documentary." United Teacher, D 18, 1968. NYC, D 4-13, 1968

Scribner, Harvey B. "Leadership for Change: My First Year in New York City as Chancellor of the Public Schools." Journal of Research and Development in Education 5(Spring, 1972): 18-28.

Scribner, Harvey B., and Stevens, Leonard B. Make Your Schools Work. New York: Simon & Schuster, 1975.

Schwartz, Richard, and Saxl, Ellen. Beginning Reading and Math in PS 133/New York City. New York: Center for Urban Education, 1971.

Schreiner, Seth M. Negro Mecca: A History of the Negro in New York City, 1865-1920. New York: New York U. Press, 1965.

Schwager, Sidney. An Analysis of the Evaluation of the More Effective Schools Program Conducted by the Center for Urban Education. New York: United Federation of Teachers, N, 1967.

_____. "A New Look at MES in Light of the Coleman, Racial Isolation Reports." United Teacher, My 19, 1967.

Seabrook, Luther W. "Parent Advocacy for Educational Reform: A Case Study of the Harlem Parents Committee." Doctoral dissertation, U. of Massachusetts, 1978. Univ. Microfilms Order No. 7820368.

Seeley, David S. "A Community School System for New York City." New York University Education Quarterly 1(Winter, 1970):22-24.

Seligmann, Ernest, and Koury, Fred. "A Model of Integrated Quality Education." United Teacher, My 29, 1968. [George W. Wingate High School in Crown Heights-East Flatbush, Brooklyn]

Sellers, T. J. "Integration--How the Challenge Is Being Met." Exchange, O, 1965. Published by the Metropolitan School Study Council, 525 West 120 Street, New York, NY 10027. [Progress in School Districts 23 and 24, NYC]

Shanas, Bert. "New York Decentralization--A Mixed Bag." New York Affairs, Summer/Fall, 1976.

Shanker, Albert. "Black Protest, Union Democracy & UFT" (letter). New Politics 8 (Fall, 1970):22-24.

_____. "The Courts Add to the Confusion in District 1." New York Times, Ap 28, 1974. ["Where We Stand" column]

_____. "Frustration at John Dewey High School." New York Times, D 10, 1972.

_____. "Harlem Prep: Success or Failure?" New York Times, Mr 17, 1974.

_____. Interview. Urban Review, N, 1968.

_____. "Little Logic, Less Help in HEW Charges." New York Times, N 14, 1967.

_____. "Quality and Equality in Education." American Federationist, Mr, 1969.

_____. "The Real Meaning of the New York City Teachers' Strike." Phi Delta Kappan, Ap, 1969.

_____. "Schools and the Union" (letter). New Republic, N 15, 1969.

_____. "Shanker on Decentralization." United Teacher, F 19, 1969.

_____. "Teachers Strike, 1968" (letter). Saturday Review, My 17, 1969.

_____. "U.F.T. Charges Central Board with Extravagance in Ocean Hill." United Teacher, O 5, 1969.

Shanker, Albert, and Brown, Nathan. "Decentralization Discussion Debates Powers and Responsibilities of Local, City School Boards." United Teacher, N 30, 1969.

"Shanker Debates Doar." United Teacher, N 6, 1968. [Transcript of television debate of O 27, 1968]

Shapiro, Fred C. "Finishing School." New York Times Magazine, Mr 24, 1974. [Livingston Junior and Senior High School]

Shapiro, H. R. "Regaining Community Control of Our Schools is the First Step in Radical Political Change." New York Free Press, Ap 18, 1968.

Shaw, Adele Marie. "The True Character of the New York Public Schools." World's Work 7 (1903):4204-4221 and (1904):505-514.

Shaw, Frederick. "The Educational Park in New York: Archetype of the School of the Future." Phi Delta Kappan, F, 1969.

_____. Fifty Years of Research in the New York City Board of Education. New York: 1964.

Sheldon, Eleanor B., and Glazier, Raymond A. Pupils and Schools in New York City. A Fact Book. New York: Russell Sage Foundation, 1965.

Sheppard, Nathaniel, Jr. "Racial Issues Split City Deeply." New York Times, Ja 20, 1974.

Silverstein, Barry, and Krate, Ronald. Children of the Dark Ghetto: A Developmental Psychology. New York: Praeger, 1975.

Simmelkjaer, Robert T. "Anti-Poverty Interest Group Articulation and Mobilization for Community Control in New York City." Doctoral dissertation, Columbia U., 1972.

Simon, Arthur R. Faces of Poverty. Concordia, 1966. [Lower East Side, NYC]

Simon, Arthur. Stuyvesant Town, USA. New York: New York U. Press, 1971.

Sizer, Theodore R. "Report Analysis [of the Bundy Report]." Harvard Educational Review, Winter, 1968.

Slotkin, Herman. "New Programs for Dropouts." Vocational Guidance Quarterly, Winter, 1963-64. [Results of formal evaluation of three projects in NYC public schools]

Smith, Richard Harvey. "Affirmative Action and the New York City Public School System." Doctoral dissertation, U. of Massachusetts, 1976. Univ. Microfilms Order No. 76-22,301.

Solomon, Gwen. "Teacher Dismissals Spark New Ocean Hill Dispute." New America, Jl 25, 1969.

Solomon, Victor. "An Independent Board of Education for Harlem." Urban Affairs Quarterly, S, 1968.

Specht, D. I. The Needs of Low-Income Ethnic Groups Living Outside of Poverty Areas in New York City: A Summary Report. New York: Community Council of Greater New York, 1977.

Spencer, David. "A Harlem Parent Speaks." NEA Journal, Mr, 1968.

_____. "The Rape of the I.S. 201 Complex Governing Board." SCOPE Bulletin, Mr, 1969.

Spencer, David, and Wilson, Charles. The Case for Community Control. New York: I.S. 201 Governing Board, 2 West 125th Street, New York, NY, My, 1968.

Spier, Adele. Two Bridges Model School District: A Profile. Community Issues, F, 1969.

_____. "Why Two Bridges Failed." Community 3 (S-O, 1970):1-3.

Stemberg, Margie. "N.Y. High Schools: 'We've Had Enough.'" Guardian, D 28, 1968.

_____. "New York Schools: More Confusion." Guardian, D 21, 1968.

_____. "N.Y. Schools Open, But Parents Angry." Guardian, N 30, 1968.

Starr, Roger. "The Lesson of Forest Hills." Commentary 53(Je, 1972):45-49. [Low-cost housing]

Staton, Becky. "Yo, Teach!" Liberation 19 (Spring, 1976):78-83.

Steel, Lewis M. Community Control and the Courts. Community Issues, Mr, 1969.

Stein, Annie. "A New View of Reading Scores." Integrateducation 12(S-O, 1974):20-24.

_____. "A Response." Black Scholar 6(Mr, 1975):43-45. [Community control in NYC]

_____. "Containment and Control: A Look at the Record." In Schools Against Children. The Case for Community Control. Edited by Annette T. Rubenstein. New York: Monthly Review Press, 1970.

_____. The Persistence of Academic Retardation in New York City Schools, Changing Patterns, 1958-1971. Albany, NY: State Commission on the Quality, Cost, and Financing of Elementary and Secondary Education, 1971.

_____. "Politics of Decentralization." Guardian, Ja 18, 1969.

_____. "Strategies for Failure." Harvard Educational Review 71(My, 1971):158-204.

_____. "'32 Into 211 Won't Go': An Investigation of the Canarsie Boycott." University Review, D, 1972.

Steinberg, Lois S. Report on Bilingual Education: A Study of Programs for Pupils with English Language Difficulty in New York City Public Schools, Je, 1974. ERIC ED 135 910.

Steinhoff, Carl R. Improved Educational Services in Selected Special Service Elementary and Junior High Schools. New York: Center for Urban Education, S, 1967.

Steinhoff, Carl R., and Owens, Robert G. Organizational Climate in the More Effective Schools. New York: Division of Teachers Education, City U. of New York, 1967.

Stern, Edith M. "Jim Crow Goes to School in New York [City]." Crisis, Jl, 1937.

Stern, Sol. "'Scab' Teachers." Ramparts, N 17, 1968. [Teachers strike in New York City]

Stevens, Leonard B. "School Decentralization v. Racial Integration." Education News, Ag 5, 1968.

Steward, Colleen, Fox, David J., and Steinberg, Lois. Open Enrollment: Services to Children in Receiving Elementary, Intermediate, and Junior High Schools, and Academic High Schools. New York: Center for Urban Education, N, 1969.

Stewart, Merle. "Fiscal Management Needs of the Community-Controlled School." Liberator, Ja, 1969. [I.S. 281]

Strauss, George H. "Confrontations Long Ago-- The Student Leaders Look Back." Saturday Review 55(Ag 19, 1972):39-43.

Streit, Peggy. "Why They Fight for P.A.T." New York Times Magazine, S 28, 1964. [About Parents and Taxpayers, opponents of school pairing]

Stuart, Reginald. "Community Boards Have Few Powers." Race Relations Reporter 2(My 3, 1971):10-12

"Students Voice Views on N.Y.C. School Crisis ." United Teacher, D 18, 1968. [Rolf Auerbach, Deena Kleiman, and Anthony De Alto]

A Study of the Problems of Integration in New York City Public Schools Since 1955. Urban League of Greater New York, 202 West 136th Street, New York, NY, D, 1963.

Stutz, Rosalie. Academic High Schools--Brooklyn or Why Children Fail, 1969. Brooklyn Education Task Force, 259 Washington Avenue, Brooklyn, NY 11205

_____. "The Community and the United Federation of Teachers." EQUAL Newsletter, Jl, 1967.

_____. "Parents Demand Voice in Policy." The Parents' Voice, N, 1967. [Account of community uproar over experimental use of an allegedly improper "Ethnic Distance Scale" to children]

_____. Report on Intermediate and Junior High Schools, District 15, Brooklyn, or How Junior High Schools Fail, My, 1969. Brooklyn Education Task Force, 259 Washington Avenue, Brooklyn, NY 11205.

_____. Report on Intermediate and Junior High Schools, District 21 and 22, Brooklyn or How Junior High Schools Fail, Ap, 1969. Brooklyn Education Task Force, 259 Washington Avenue, Brooklyn, NY 11205.

_____. Report on Intermediate and Junior High Schools, District 20, Brooklyn or How Junior High Schools Fail, Ap, 1969. Brooklyn Education Task Force, 259 Washington Avenue, Brooklyn, NY 11205.

_____. "A Surface Conflict between the New York City School Board and the United Federation of Teachers ." Westside News (NYC), S 21, 1967.

Surkin, Marvin. "The Myth of Community Control: Rhetorical and Political Aspects of the Ocean Hill-Brownsville Controversy." In Race, Change, and Urban Setting, pp. 405-422. Edited by Peter Orleans and William Russell Ellis, Jr. Beverly Hills, CA: Sage, 1971.

Swados, Harvey. "When Black and White Live Together." New York Times Magazine, N 13, 1966. [Rochdale Village]

Swanson, Austin and others. A Report on Efforts of Suburban Groups to Promote Cooperation among City and Suburban School Districts in the Buffalo, New York Metropolitan Area. New York: State Commission on the Quality, Cost and Financing of Elementary and Secondary Education, Mr 19, 1971.

Swanson, Bert E. Decision-making in the School Desegregation-Decentralization Controversies. Final Report. Bronxville, NY: Sarah Lawrence College, Center for Continuing Education and Community Studies, Ap, 1969, 316 pp. ERIC ED 032 378.

_____. The Struggle for Equality: School Integration Controversy in New York City. New York: Hobbs, Dorman, 1966.

_____. "Subcommunity Response to City-Wide School Policies: Measuring White-Parent Decisions on School Pairing." School Review, Winter, 1965.

Swanson, Bert E., and Montgomery, Clare. "White Citizens Response to the 'Open Enrollment Program.'" Integrated Education, Ag-S, 1964.

Syrkin, Marie. "Don't Flunk the Middle-Class Teacher." New York Times Magazine, D 15, 1968.

Talbott, Allan. "Analysis: Should the Schools Decentralize?" The City, Mr, 1968.

Task Force. A Report on New York City High Schools. New York: Citizens Committee for Children of New York, Ja 5, 1970.

Tausigg, Michael K. "An Economic Analysis of Vocational Education in the New York City High Schools." Journal of Human Resources, III, Supplement (1968).

Teachers' Freedom Party of the United Federation of Teachers. "Anatomy of a Cop-Out. Harlem vs. Shanker." Liberator, Ja, 1968.

Tead, Ordway. "New York City Education and Race Prejudice." Intercultural Education News, Mr, 1944.

Thackray, John, Chaudry, Juanita, and Grine, Dorothea. "Open Door" New York City. New York: Center for Urban Education, 1971.

Thomason, Robert H. "Racial Hope in Brooklyn." Christian Century, My 9, 1973.

Thorndike, Robert L. Evaluation of New York City School District...Free Choice Open Enrollment--Junior High Schools, Ag 31, 1966. Center for Urban Education, 33 West 42nd Street, New York, NY

Thurston, Eve. "Ethipia Unshackled: A Brief History of the Education of Negro Children in New York City." Bulletin of the New York Public Library, Ap, 1965.

Tobias, P. M. "Differential Adaptation of Grenadian Emigrant Communities in London and New York." Social and Economic Studies 25 (Mr, 1976).

Tobier, Arthur. "Decentralization: Waiting for Something to Turn Up." The Center Forum, Ag 28, 1967.

_____. "Education in New York City." Center Forum, My 15, 1969. [Experimental programs at P.S. 133, P.S. 123, and P.S. 84]

_____. "The Numbers Game." Urban Review, D, 1966. [The problem of an Educational park in East Brooklyn]

Tractenberg, Paul L., with Lynton, Edith. Equal Employment Opportunities and the New York City Public Schools. An Analysis and Recommendations based on Public Hearings... by the City of New York Commission on Human Rights, 1971. Public Education Association, 20 West 40th Street, New York, NY 10018.

Tree, Christine. "Grouping Pupils in New York City." Urban Review, S, 1968.

Treiman, Donald J. and others. Preliminary Report on a Survey of Educational Services for Hispanic Pupils with English Language Difficulty, Conducted in New York City Schools, My, 1964. ERIC ED 123 330.

Trend Finders, Inc. Problems and Dangers in the New York City Public Schools. Radio Station WINS, 7 Central Park West, New York, NY 10023, D, 1963.

Trubowitz, Julius. Changing the Racial Attitudes of Children: The Effects of an Activity Program in New York City Schools. New York: Praeger, 1969.

"True Black Story of Canarsie Crisis." Muhammad Speaks, N 17, 1972.

"The True Story of P.S. 93." District 13 Newsletter, D, 1968. [Bitter aftermath of teachers' strike]

Tucker, Louise Emery Tucker. "A Study of Problem Pupils." Doctoral dissertation, Teachers College, Columbia U., 1937.

Tupper, Harriett A. "Intelligence Tests Tried Out at P.S. 119." New York Age, N 18, 1922.

Turetsky, Fred. "The Treatment of Black Americans in Primary Grade Textbooks Used in New York City Elementary Schools." Theory and Research in Social Education 11(D, 1974): 25-49. [Since the 1950's]

Turner, F. A. "Integration in the New York City Schools." Journal of Human Relations, Summer, 1959.

The Uhuru (Freedom) Sasa (Now) School, 1970. Uruhu Sasa School, 10 Claver Place, Brooklyn, NY 11238.

United Bronx Parents. Distributing of Educational Resources Among the Bronx Public Schools. New York: UBP, 1968.

United Federation of Teachers. [A chronology of teachers' strike developments through September 19, 1967] United Teacher, S 27, 1967.

"U.F.T. Black Teachers Caucus Denounces Shanker." Scope Bulletin, S, 1969.

U.F.T. Chapter, and Bailey, Ronald H. "An Exchange of Letters." Scope Bulletin, Christmas Edition, 1968. [P.S. 188, Manhattan]

"U.F.T. Fights for Democratic Due Process." United Teacher, My 29, 1968. [My 9-22, 1968, Ocean Hill-Brownsville Demonstration Project]

The United Federation of Teachers Looks at School Decentralization--a Critical Analysis of the Bundy Report with U.F.T. Proposals. New York: United Federation of Teachers, D, 1967, 14 pp. ERIC ED 016 021.

"U.F.T. Shapes Decentralization Ideas for Integrated Districts..." United Teacher, F 5, 1969.

U.S. Bureau of Labor Statistics. Changing Patterns of Prices, Pay, Workers, and Work on the New York Scene, My, 1971. U.S. Department of Labor, Bureau of Labor Statistics, 341 Ninth Avenue, New York, NY 10001.

U.S. Bureau of Labor Statistics. "Unemployment and Education in New York City's Poverty Areas." Integrated Education 10(Ja-F, 1972): 58.

U.S. Commission on Civil Rights. Report on New York City: Health Facilities. Washington, DC: GPO, My, 1964. [On racial discrimination in training and employment and in treatment of patients]

U.S. Congress, 92nd, 1st session, House of Representatives, Committee on Education and Labor, General Subcommittee Education. Needs of Elementary and Secondary Education for the Seventies--1971. Hearings..., pp. 155-385. Washington, DC: GPO, 1971. [New York City and state schools]

U.S. Department of Labor, Bureau of Labor Statistics, Middle Atlantic Regional Office. Poverty Area Profiles. Characteristics of the Unemployed. Washington, DC: GPO, Je, 1970. [Bedford-Stuyvesant, Central Harlem, East Harlem, and South Bronx]

Urofsky, Melvin (ed.). Why Teachers Strike: Teacher's Rights and Community Control. Garden City, NY: Doubleday, 1970. [Extended statements by leading participants and figures associated with the New York City teachers' strike of 1968]

Usdan, Michael D. "Citizen Participation: Learning from New York City's Mistakes." Urban Review, S, 1969.

_____. Strengthening Citizen Participation: An Analysis of New York City Experiments, F 8, 1969, 14 pp. ERIC ED 028 512.

Van Denburgh, J. K. Elimination of Students in Public Schools in New York. NY: n.p., 1911.

Vann, Albert. "From the President's Desk." African-American Teachers Forum, S, 1969.

Vidal, David. "In a Dispiriting War, One Little Victory..." New York Times, N 14, 1976. [P.S. 31]

Vidich, Arthur J., and McReynolds, Charles. "Rhetoric versus Reality: A Study of New York City High School Principals." In Anthropological Perspectives on Education, pp. 195-207. Edited by Murray L. Wax, Stanley Diamond, and Fred O. Gearing. New York: Basic Books, 1971.

Vincent, William S., and Lohman, Maurice A. Meeting the Needs of New York City's Schools. New York: Public Education Association; United Federation of Teachers and United Parents Association, 1965.

Wagstaff, Marian V. "Racial Tensions in New York City, 1930-50 as Reported in the Negro Press." Master's thesis, New York U., 1952

Wakin, Edward. At the Edge of Harlem: Portrait of a Middle-Class Harlem Family. New York: Morrow, 1964.

Walker, George. "The Afro-American in New York City, 1827-1860." Doctoral dissertation, Columbia U., 1975. Univ. Microfilms Order No. 76-12795.

Walker, Joe. "Black N.Y. Students at J.H.S. 271 Meet Hostile Police in Demonstration." Muhammad Speaks, Ja 31, 1969.

_____. "A Candid Talk with Norman Mailer." Muhammad Speaks, Je 20, 1969.

_____. "Educational Self-Determination." Muhammad Speaks, S 6, 1974. [Luis Fuentes, Supt., District 1]

_____. "National Pattern Seen in N.Y.C. School Fight." Muhammad Speaks, F 28, 1975.

_____. "New York's Famed Wiltwyck School for Boys--A Horror House for Black Youth?" Muhammad Speaks, D 27, 1968.

_____. "Opening of the University of Islam No. 7." Muhammad Speaks, Ja 7, 1970.

Wantman, Morey J. et al. Estimates of Population Characteristics New York City, 1964-65-66-68-70. New York: Center for Social Research, City U. of New York, D, 1972.

Ward, Agee. "Ocean Hill. Education, Community, and the Media." Center Forum, N 13, 1968.

Washington, R. O. "The Politicalization of School Decentralization in New York City." Urban Education 8(O, 1973):223-230.

Wasserman, Miriam. "The I.S. 201 Story/One Observer's Version." Urban Review, Je, 1969.

_____. "Planting Pansies on the Roof. A Critique of How New York City Tests Reading." Urban Review, Ja, 1969.

_____. The School Fix, NYC, USA. New York: Outerbridge & Dienstfrey, 1970.

Wasserman, Miriam, and Reimann, John. "Student Rebels vs. School Defenders. A Partisan Account." Urban Review, O, 1969.

Watkins, James. "Racism 'Northern Style.'" African-American Teachers Forum, N-D, 1969.

Wechsler, James A. "Civil War in New York." Progressive, Ja, 1969.

Weddington, Rachel T. Report on the Teacher Institute on Special Instructional Problems in Recently Desegregated P.S. 30 and P.S. 80, Queens, New York City. Final Report. New York: Yeshiva U., Graduate School of Education, Ag 25, 1965, 24 pp. ERIC ED 056 122.

Weinstein, Irving. "Shanker Outlines Decentralization Views to Cornell Class." United Teacher, D 4, 1968.

Weinstein, Jack B. "The Mark Twain School Decision." Integrated Education 12(Ja-Ap, 1974):49-59.

Weissman, Harold H. (ed.). Employment and Educational Services in the Mobilization for Youth Experience. New York: Association Press, 1969.

Weitz, Leo. "The High School Principal in New York City: A Study of Executive Responsibility in Theory and Practice." Doctoral dissertation, New York U., 1960.

Westlake, Donald E. Up Your Banners [Novel]. New York: Macmillan, 1969.

Wethers, Doris, and Cousena, Kenneth. "Child Health in a Harlem Elementary School." Journal of School Health 40(N, 1970):466-471.

"What Happened at J.H.S. 271?" United Teacher, My 1, 1968.

"What's Happened at Ocean Hill? Reading Scores of Children Fall." United Teacher, Je 15, 1969.

Whelton, Clark. "With Friends Like These..." Village Voice, My 17, 1973. [In re: Canarsie dispute]

"White Boycott." Reporter, O 8, 1964. [September, 1964]

White, Othia. "An Analysis of the Policies on Integration of the NYC Board of Education." Master's thesis, Howard U., 1969.

"Who Won, Who's Losing in the N.Y. School Fight." The Public Life, N 4, 1968.

"Who Gets the Power?" Newsweek, S 14, 1970. [Ocean Hill-Brownsville]

"Who's in Control?" Guardian, S 14, 1968. [Decentralization of schools in New York City]

Wielk, Carol Carol. "Educational Progress at Ocean Hill." Community, My, 1969.

_____. "The Ocean Hill-Brownsville School Project: A Profile." Community Issues, F, 1969.

_____. "White Academic Failure in Brooklyn High Schools." Community, F, 1970.

Wiggins, William B. "Black on Black: The New York Age Views Americans During the Harding Era, 1920-1924." Master's thesis, Central Connecticut State College, 1970.

Wilcox, Preston. "Reflections of a Temporary Black Male Principal." Renewal, Ap-My, 1967. [The West Harlem Liberation School]

_____. The Ripple Effect of the I.S. 201 Controversy. New York: Afram Associates, 1968.

_____. "The School and the Community." Record, N, 1967.

_____. "'Troublemakers' At the Board of Education: Fact or Fantasy?" Integrated Education, Je-Jl, 1967.

_____. "National Association of Afro-American Educators." African-American Teachers Forum, N, 1968.

Wilkerson, Doxey A. "The Failure of Schools Serving the Black and Puerto Rican Poor." In Schools Against Children. The Case for Community Control. Edited by Annette T. Rubenstein. New York: Monthly Review Press, 1970.

Wilson, Charles E. "Beyond Reform. The New York City School System." Freedomways 11 (Second quarter, 1971):140-149.

_____. [I.S.] 201--First Steps Toward Community Control." In Schools Against Children. The Case for Community Control. Edited by Annette T. Rubinstein. New York: Monthly Review Press, 1970.

_____. "Lessons of the 201 Complex in Harlem." Freedomways, Fall, 1968.

_____. "Year One at I.S. 201." Social Policy, My-Je, 1970.

Wilson, Jerome. "City Schools and Albany Politics." Nation, D 16, 1968.

"Wingate--Alive, Well and Clicking." Learning in New York, Je, 1977. [George W. Wingate High School]

Wissler, Mary L. "Lindsay: Dilemma of Policy and Politics." Harvard Crimson, O 3, 1966.

Witkin, Irving. Diary of a Teacher. The Crisis at George Washington High School, Ja, 1971. United Federation of Teachers, Box 715, 260 Park Avenue South, New York, NY 10010

Wolff, Max. "A Plan for Desegregation." Integrated Education, F-Mr, 1964.

Woolston, Florence. "Our Untrained Future Citizens." Survey 23(1909):21-35. [Dropouts in New York City]

Wrightstone, J. Wayne. "Demonstration Guidance Project in New York City." Harvard Educational Review, Summer, 1960.

_____. "Longitudinal Study of Pupil Growth in MES." United Teacher, Ja 24, 1971. [More Effective Schools program]

Yard, Lionel M. "Blacks in Brooklyn." Negro History Bulletin 37(Ag-S, 1974).

Yavner, Louis. Administration of Human Relations Program in New York City Schools, Report to Hon. F. H. La Guardia, Mayor of the City of New York. New York: Department of Investigation, City of New York, 1945.

Yevish, Irving A. "Decentralization, Discipline, and the Disadvantaged Teacher." Phi Delta Kappan, N, 1968.

Young, B. "Historical Study of the Countee Cullen Regional Branch Library of the New York Regional Branch Library: Its Inception, Trends, Developments." Master's thesis, Southern Connecticut State College, 1969.

Yurick, Adrienne, and Lerner, Francine. "Look Who's Jumping on the Decentralization Bandwagon: A Radical Critique of the New York City Decentralization Plans." Radicals in the Professions, S, 1968.

Zack, Jacob B. "Education in the Largest City [N.Y.C.]." In Robert J. Havighurst, Frank L. Smith, and David E. Wilder, A Profile of the Large-City High School, chapter 13. Washington, DC: National Association of Secondary School Principals, N, 1970.

Zeldner, Max. "Why Blame New York City Schools?" School and Society, Mr, 1969.

Zeluck, Steve. "Three Months After the U.F.T. Strike." New Politics, Spring, 1968. Mr, 1969

_____. "The U.F.T. Strike: A Blow Against Teacher Unionism." New Politics, Winter, 1968.

_____. "The U.F.T. Strike: Will It Destroy the A.F.T.? Phi Delta Kappan, Ja, 1969.

Zimbardo, Philip G. Physical Integration and Social Segregation of Northern Negro College Students (1953, 1963, and 1965), 1966. [Paper presented at Eastern Psychological Association.] ERIC ED 025 568, 19 pp.

Zinet, Melvin. Decentralization and School Effectiveness. A Case Study of the 1969 Decentralization Law in New York City. New York: Teachers College Press, 1973.

Zitron, Celia Lewis. "Minorities in the New York City Schools." The New York Teachers Union: 1914-1964--A Story of Educational Commitment. New York: Humanities Press, 1968.

North Carolina

Adams, Jerry. "The Philosophy Was Moved Down the Road." Southern Education Report, Ap, 1968. [The Learning Academy in Charlotte]

Alexander, Kelly M., Jr. "Student Program for Desegregation." Crisis 80(N, 1973):315-316. [Charlotte]

Alexander, Roberta Sue. "Hostility and Hope: Black Education in North Carolina during Presidential Reconstruction, 1865-1867." North Carolina Historical Review 53(Ap, 1976):113-132.

Allen, Jene Lee. "The Effects of School Desegregation on the Employment Status of Negro Principals in North Carolina." Doctoral dissertation, Duke U., 1969.

Ayres, B. Drummond, Jr. "Cross-Town Busing, Begun in '71, Is Working Well in Charlotte." New York Times, Jl 17, 1975.

Bagwell, William. School Desegregation in the Carolinas: Two Case Studies. Columbus, SC: U. of South Carolina Press, 1971.

Barksdale, Marcellus C. "The Indigenous Civil Rights Movement and Cultural Change in North Carolina: Weldon, Chapel Hill and Monroe: 1946-1965." Doctoral dissertation, Duke U., 1977.

Barnes, Bart. "Busing Works in Charlotte." Washington Post, N 19, 1972.

_____. "Charlotte Learns to Live With Busing." Washington Post, S 3, 1975.

Barrows, Frank. "School Busing. Charlotte, N.C." Atlantic Monthly 230(N, 1972):17-22.

Batey, M. Grant. "John Chavis' Contribution to Education in North Carolina." Master's thesis, North Carolina College, Durham, 1954.

Belcher, Jerry. "School Busing: How Far Has It Come?" Los Angeles Times, D 15, 1975.

Bellamy, Donnie D. "Slavery in Microcosm: Onslow County, North Carolina." Journal of Negro History 62(O, 1977):339-350.

Bice, H. V. "A Comparison of White and Negro Pupils in North Carolina." American Association Ment. Def. 43(1938): 73-78.

"Bigot, Spare That Tree." Nation, Ag 28, 1967. [Anti-integration sentiment and the Elementary and Secondary Education Act in Wake County]

Black Panther Party, North Carolina State Chapter. "'To Take Arms Against a Sea of Troubles.'" Black Panther, D 25, 1971. [Wilmington]

Bontemps, Arna. "Even Money on John Chavis." Common Ground 10(Autumn, 1949):36-39. [School in Raleigh]

Boothby, Albert C. "The Time Is Now." Independent School Bulletin, D, 1967 [Desegregation of a private school]

Bouque, Jesse Parker, Jr. "Oppression in North Carolina During Reconstruction, 1865-1873." Doctoral dissertation, U. of Maryland, 1973.

Bradbury, Tom. "HEW's Mandate: Racial Balance Over Education." Charlotte News, Jl 29, 1977. [Charlotte]

Brown, Hugh Victor Brown. E-Qual-ity Education in North Carolina Among Negroes. Raleigh, NC: Irving Swain Press, 1964.

_____. A History of the Education of Negroes in North Carolina. Raleigh, NC: Irving Swain Press, 1961.

Buck, J. L. B. "Colored Normal Schools in North Carolina." Southern Workman 52 (D, 1923):594.

Burford, L. S. "The Social and Economic Status of Negro High School Students in Northeastern North Carolina." Master's thesis, Hampton Institute, 1932.

Burns, Augustus M. III. "North Carolina and the Negro Dilemma, 1930-1950." Doctoral dissertation, U. of North Carolina, 1969.

Burrows, Edward F. "The Literary Education of Negroes in Ante-bellum Virginia, North Carolina, South Carolina, and Georgia with Special Reference to Regulatory and Prohibitive Laws." Master's thesis, Duke U., 1940.

Carroll, George Douglas. "City-County Consolidation: The Charlotte-Mecklenburg County, North Carolina, Case." Doctoral dissertation, U. of North Carolina, 1974. Univ. Microfilms Order No. 74-26,857.

"Charlotte [N.C.] Schools Explode Again." African World, N 30, 1973.

Chippey, Arthur. "Study of Teaching of Science in Negro Secondary Schools of North Carolina." Master's thesis, Cornell U., 1930.

Citizens Committee on the Schools. Initial Report, My 15, 1972. [Write Governor's Office, State of North Carolina, Raleigh, NC 27611]

Clement, Dorothy C., and Harding, Joe R. "Social Distinctions and Emergent Student Groups in a Desegregated School." Anthropology and Education Quarterly 9 (Winter, 1978):272-282. [Bradford]

Clement, Rufus E. "A History of Negro Education in North Carolina, 1865-1928." Doctoral dissertation, Northwestern U., 1930.

Coates, Albert, and Paul, James C. W. The School Desegregation Decision. Chapel Hill, NC: Institute of Government, U. of North Carolina, 1954.

Cochran, A. B., and Uhlman, Thomas M. "Black Populations and School Integration--A Research Note." Phylon 34(Mr, 1973):43-48. [North Carolina, 1967-1968]

Coggins, J. R. Inter-Race In-Service Program Designed to Increase the Educational Opportunities of the Children in the Randolph County Schools, Jl 1, 1966-Je 30, 1967. [Asheboro, NC: Randolph County Schools, 1967], 34 pp. ERIC ED 025 564.

Cohen, Muriel. "Down-Home Touch Helped Integration in Charlotte." Boston Globe, D 26, 1975.

Cohodes, Aaron. "Charlotte's Desegregation Efforts: Not Bad, Not Good." Nation's Schools, N, 1968.

_____. "Reports from Charlotte, N.C." Nation's Schools, F, 1964.

Commission on Professional Rights and Responsibilities. Hyde County, North Carolina School Boycott and the Roots of Conflict. Washington, DC: National Education Association, S, 1969

"Community Votes Down Integration." SOBU Newsletter, Je 12, 1971. [Greensboro]

Comptroller General of the United States. Information of the New Community of Soul City, N.C. Washington, DC: General Accounting Office, 1975.

"Conflict in Wilmington Reaches a New High." African World 2(O 16, 1971):1, 7.

Cook, John H. A Study of the Mill Schools of North Carolina. New York: Columbia U., 1925.

Cooke, Dennis H. "Negro Rural-school Problems." Southern Workman 60(Ap, 1931):156-160.

_____. "The White Superintendent and the Negro Schools in North Carolina." Doctoral dissertation, George Peabody College for Teachers, 1930.

Cooper, David. "Nobody Wanted School Desegregation." American Education, Je, 1967. [Moore Community]

Cooper, William Mason. Sociological Aspects of Promotion and Retardation of Elementary and High School Pupils. Based on Facts Concerning Negro Elementary and High School Pupils in North Carolina, 1925-26; 1928-29. Elizabeth City, NC: State Normal School.

Covington, Howard, and Paddock, Polly. "Teachers Frustrated, Uncertain After Four Years of Integration." Charlotte Observer, Jl 7-10, 1974 (four stories).

Crosby, Kathleen. "25 Years in Mecklenburg's Classrooms." Charlotte Observer, Jl 20, 1975.

_____. "Twenty-Five Years in Mecklenburg's Classrooms." Integrateducation 14(Mr-Ap, 1976):19-21.

Crow, Jeffrey J. The Black Experience in Revolutionary North Carolina. Raleigh, NC: Department of Cultural Resources, 1977.

Crowell, Suzanne. "Greensboro Shows Mailed Fist." Southern Patriot, Je, 1969.

Cumming, Doug. "Following the Exodus." Raleigh News and Observer, F 9, 1975. [Private schools in Wake County]

Davis, Angela. "'Student Pushout' Worries Leaders." Raleigh News and Observer, My 13, 1974.

Davis, Chester. "The North Carolina Advancement School." Southern Education Report, Jl-Ag, 1965.

Denyer, T., and O'Connor, R. E. "Poverty and Policy in North Carolina." Growth and Change 8(Ap, 1977).

Dickens, Brooks. History of Negro Education in North Carolina. Raleigh, NC: Shaw U., 1928.

_____. "Negro Education in North Carolina During Reconstruction." Quarterly Review of Higher Education Among Negroes 7(Ja, 1939): 1-30.

Douglass, Frederick. "Closing Schools for Contrabands in North Carolina." Douglass' Monthly, Jl, 1862.

Douglass, Joseph H. "Certain Implications of the North Carolina Educational Commission Study to the Education of Negroes Within the State." Quarterly Review of Higher Education Among Negroes 17(0, 1949):148-153.

Du Bois, W. E. B. "A Library [in Raleigh, N.C., operated by librarian Mollie Huston Lee]." Chicago Defender, Ap 5, 1947, p. 17.

_____. "The Negro Common School in North Carolina." Crisis, My and Je, 1927.

"Edenton, N.C.--Typical Case of Black Teacher 'Push-Outs.'" African World, Je 30, 1973.

Educational Leadership Training Program for Majority-Negro Rural-Isolated School Districts in North Carolina, 1969. Final Technical Report. Raleigh, NC: Saint Augustine's College, 1970, 36 pp. ERIC ED 047 021.

Edwards, Arlene. "The Name Is the Same--The Auspices Are Not." Southern Education Report, Ap, 1968. [North Carolina Advancement School]

Egerton, John. "Six Districts, Three Races, and More Things." Southern Education Report, D, 1968. [Robeson County]

Ehle, John. The Free Men. New York: Harper & Row, 1965. [Integration in Chapel Hill]

Elder, Alfonso. "North Carolina Negro High School Examination." Quarterly Review of Higher Education Among Negroes 1(0, 1933): 22-24. [My, 1933]

Evans, Eli N. "Southern Liberals and the Court." New York Times, S 3, 1974. [Durham, 1951-1963]

Fen, Sing Nan. "Notes on the Education of Negroes in North Carolina During the Civil War." Journal of Negro Education, Winter, 1967.

Flood, Dudley E. The Magnet School Concept in North Carolina, Ja, 1978. ERIC ED 149 454. [Two magnet schools in Raleigh]

Gaillard, Frye. "A Near Agreement Fails in Charlotte." Race Relations Reporter 4(Ag 20, 1973):6-8.

_____. "Second Generation Desegregation Blues." Race Relations Reporter 4(Ja, 1973):4-5.

Gay, Dorothy A. "Crisis of Identity: The Negro Community in Raleigh, 1890-1900." North Carolina Historical Review 50(Ap, 1973).

Gilliom, Morris E. "The Development of Public Education in North Carolina During Reconstruction, 1865-1876." Doctoral dissertation, Ohio State U., 1963.

Godfrey, Ernestine (ed.). Intelligence, Achievement, Self-Concepts, and Attitudes among 1216 Typical Sixth- and Seventh-Grade Students in Fourteen North Carolina Public Schools: Preliminary Results of a Study Conducted January 1970. Winston-Salem, NC: North Carolina Advancement School, N, 1970, 25 pp. ERIC ED 045 760.

_____. A Research Report of the North Carolina Advancement School: Summer Session, 1969. Winston Salem: North Carolina Advancement School, Ja, 1971, 26 pp. ERIC ED 050 200.

Grant, Jim. "Black Folks' View on High School Unrest." African World 2(D 11, 1971):7.

_____. "Blacks Oppose Greensboro Busing." Southern Patriot 29(S, 1971):5

_____. "Insurrection in Wilmington." Southern Patriot, Mr, 1971.

_____. "'Integration' Nothing But Trouble." African World, Ap 15, 1972. [Wadesboro]

_____. "Right Wing Wins Charlotte School Election." Southern Patriot, My-Je, 1970.

_____. "School Boycott Enters Third Month." Southern Patriot, F, 1971. [East Arcadia]

_____. "Unified Black Community Gains Re-instatement." African World, Mr 18, 1972. [Trenton]

_____. "White Arrogance Shows Its Face." African World 2(Mr 4, 1972):6. [Statesville]

_____. "Wilmington Blacks Still Under Siege." Southern Patriot, N, 1971.

_____. "Wilmington: The Struggle Goes On." Southern Patriot 29(S, 1971):7.

Hardy, Charles. "Glimpses, 1776-1976. Our Black Heritage" (5 weekly articles). Charlotte Observer, My 9-30, 1976. [History of blacks in North Carolina]

Harris, Nelson H. "A Brief Historical Sketch of the Negro Public High School of North Carolina." Journal of Educational Research 33(1939):286-292.

"Highlights of Student Assignment Report." Charlotte Observer, Mr 7, 1973. [Charlotte]

Hopkins, Chuck. "Black People's Position Outlined at Conference." African World, Mr 18, 1972. [N.C. Black caucus]

_____. "Chapel Hill Custodian Workers Come Together." African World, Ap 30, 1972. [Chapel Hill-Canboro public schools]

Howard, James Lee and others. The North Carolina Advancement School: Underachieve-ment Redefined. Goals for Schools Redefined; Behavior of Students Redefined; And the Role of the Counselor Redefined. Washington, DC: American Personnel and Guidance Association; Winston-Salem: North Carolina Advancement School, Mr 24, 1970. ERIC ED 040 410.

Jones, Mary Somerville. "The Racial Factor in School Districting: The Chapel Hill, North Carolina Case." Master's thesis, U. of North Carolina, 1971.

Jordan, A. M. "Occupation of the Negro High-school Graduate in North Carolina." High School Journal 18(Ja, 1935):24-27.

Jordan, Pat. Black Coach. New York: Dodd, Mead, 1971. Jerome Evans, Burlington

Joyner, Jay. "Stabbing Death of White School Youth—Murder or Self-Defense?" African World 2(Mr 4, 1972):3. [Hillsborough]

Kenen, Joanne L. "Stalking the Klan." Harvard Crimson, F 17, 1979. [Winston-Salem]

King, Van. "'Youthful Play Knows No Color.'" Greensboro Record, N 21, 1975. [Page High School, Greensboro]

King, Warren. "In Charlotte, Voluntary School Desegregation Failed." Seattle Times, D 9, 1976.

King, Wayne. "The Case Against the Wilmington Ten." New York Times Magazine, D 3, 1978.

King, William E. (ed.). "Charles McIver Fights for the Tarheel Negro's Right to an Education." North Carolina Historical Review 41(1964):360-369. [1902]

Krovetz, Martin L. "Desegregation Or Integra-tion: Which Is Our Goal?" Phi Delta Kappan 54(D, 1972):247-249. [North Carolina high school]

Lamanna, Richard A. "The Negro Public School Teacher and School Desegregation: A Survey of Negro Teachers in North Carolina." Doctoral dissertation, U. of North Carolina, 1966.

Landsberger, Betty H. Life Expectancy and School Experience, F, 1978. ERIC ED 151 078.

Lauerman, Henry C. "The Role of the Judiciary in the Desegregation of the Winston-Salem/Forsyth County Schools, 1968-1975." In Limits of Justice. The Courts' Role in School Desegregation, pp. 493-567. Edited by Howard I. Kalodner and James J. Fishman. Cambridge, MA: Ballinger, 1978.

Learning Institute of North Carolina. Final Report on the North Carolina Advancement School...1964-1967. Raleigh, NC: State Board of Edcuation, 1967.

Lewis, Charles E., Jr. School Integration, Occupational Expectations, and Occupational Education: A Study of North Carolina High School Boys. Center Research and Development Report No. 9. Raleigh, NC: Center for Occupational Education, North Carolina State U., 1969, 168 pp. ERIC ED 042 898.

Logan, Frenise A. "The Legal Status of Public School Education for Negroes in North Carolina, 1877-1894." North Carolina Historical Review 32(Jl, 1955):356-357.

_____. The Negro in North Carolina, 1876-1894. Chapel Hill, NC: U. of North Carolina Press, 1964.

Long, Hollis M. Public Secondary Education for Negroes in North Carolina. New York: Teachers College, Columbia U., 1932.

Lopez, Luisita. "The Panthers of Winston-Salem." Race Relations Reporter 5(Jl, 1974):31.

Lord, J. Dennis. "School Busing and White Abandonment of Public Schools." Southeastern Geographer 15(1975):81-92.

Low, Louis Gregory. "Integration 'Southern Style.'" Raleigh (N.C.) News & Observer, Ja 3, 1971. [Southern Nash Senior High School, Stanhope]

_____. "School Desegregation: A Teacher's Experience." New South 26(Spring, 1971):64-69. [Southern Nash Senior High School, Nash County]

Lumsden, Dan Barry. A Study of Selected Socio-Economic Characteristics of Adults in Educational Activities in Columbus County, North Carolina, Compared with Selected Socio-Economic Characteristics of the Total Population of the County. Raleigh, NC: North Carolina State U., 1970, 102 pp. Doctoral dissertation. Available from Univ. Microfilms, 200 N. Zeeb Road, Ann Arbor, MI 48106. ERIC ED 045 918.

L. M. "Waiting for Charlotte." Equal Justice 1(Ja, 1971):2-3. [About Attorney Julius Chambers in Charlotte]

McAndrew, Gordon. "Educational Innovation in North Carolina. A Case Study." Journal of Negro Education, Spring, 1967. [The North Carolina Advancement School in Winston-Salem]

McConville, Edward. "The Prophetic Voice of C. P. Ellis." Nation, O 15, 1973. [Durham]

Maniloff, Howard. "Busing No Longer Bothers Charlotte." South Today 4(1973):1-4.

_____. "Community Attitudes in Charlotte." Integrateducation 16(S-O, 1978):9-16.

_____. "Schools' White Flight Slowing." Charlotte Observer, N 20, 1972.

Marlowe, Gene. "Hidden Gulfs Underlying Public School Integration." Raleigh (N.C.) News and Observer, F 27, 1972. [Raleigh]

Message Factors, Inc. Parental Preferences for Pupil Assignment Plan, Ja, 1974. Message Factors, Inc., Suite 932, 5050 Poplar Avenue, Memphis, TN 38157. [Charlotte]

Miller, Robert D. "Of Freedom and Freedmen: Racial Attitudes of White Elites in North Carolina During Reconstruction, 1865-1877." Doctoral dissertation, U. of Carolina, n.d.

Moore, R. N. "Profile: Mollie Huston Lee." North Caroline Libraries 30(Summer-Fall, 1972):5-13. [Librarian]

Mulholland, Vester M. "Total Integration Can Work." North Carolina Education 37(N, 1970):6-8, 30, 31. [Plymouth High School, Washington County]

Murray, Paule. Proud Shoes. The Story of an American Family. New York: Harper & Row, 1956. [Durham]

Myerson, Michael. Nothing Could Be Finer. New York: International, 1978. [Civil rights in the State of North Carolina]

Myles, Naomi. "North Carolina Over the Hump." Nation 214(F, 14, 1972):206-206.

_____. "Private Schools: Enrollments Almost Triple in Tar Heel State." South Today 3 (D, 1971):5

"Negro Education in North Carolina." Journal of Rural Education 4(D, 1924):145-156.

"Negro Education in North Carolina." School and Society 14(Jl 30, 1921):53 and (O 22, 1921):335-336.

Newbold, N. C. "Educational Accomplishments and Challenges in North Carolina." Southern Workman 61(Ja, 1932):10-16.

_____. Five North Carolina Negro Educators. Chapel Hill, NC: U. of North Carolina Press, 1939.

The North Carolina Advancement School: "The Development and Evaluation of a School for High Potential Underachievers. 1964-1967. Final Report. Durham, NC: Learning Institute of North Carolina, 193 pp. ERIC ED 921 337.

North Carolina Advancement School. An Interim Research Report, Summer 1970. Winston-Salem, NC: North Carolina Advancement School, 1970, 9 pp. ERIC ED 045 765.

North Carolina Department of Public Instruction. Report to the Governor's Commission for the Study of Problems in the Education of Negroes in North Carolina. Raleigh, NC: State Superintendent of Public Instruction, 1935. (Publication No. 183)

North Carolina Fund. North Carolina's Present and Future Poor. Durham, NC, 1969.

Orr, Oliver H., Jr. "Charles Branley Aycock: A Biography." Doctoral dissertation, U. of North Carolina, 1958. Univ. Microfilms Order No. 59-55.

Oxley, Lawrence A. "North Carolina and Her Crippled Negro Children." Southern Workman 60(F, 1931):74-78.

Paletz, David L., and Dunn, Robert. "Press Coverage of Civil Disorders: Winston-Salem, 1967." Public Opinion Quarterly 33(Fall, 1969).

Patterson, Pat. "Durham: Decades of Effort Pay Off in Black Economic and Political Struggle." Black Enterprise 4(Je, 1974):137-138.

Peck, Jane Cary Chapman. "School Desegregation in Greensboro, North Carolina, 1954-1971: A Case Study in Purposive Social Change." Doctoral dissertation, Boston U., 1974. Univ. Microfilms Order No. 74-20400.

Pemberton, Zelda C. "Comparison of White and Negro Education in North Carolina." Master's thesis, New York U., 1938.

Penick, George, Jr. (ed.). The State of Young Children in North Carolina: A Compilation of Needs and Services. Raleigh, NC: Office of Child Development, 1974.

Pinsky, Mark. "North Carolina Blots Its Record." Nation, O 11, 1975. [Wilmington]

Pollitt, D. H. "Legal Problems in Southern Desegregation: The Chapel Hill Story." North Carolina Law Review, Je, 1965.

Prather, H. Leon, Sr. "The Public School Movement in North Carolina. 1901-1913." Paedagogica Historica 11(1971):455-479.

_____. Resurgent Politics and Educational Progressivism in the New South. North Carolina, 1890-1913. Madison, NJ: Fairleigh Dickinson U. Press, 1979.

Prichard, Paul N. "Effects of Desegregation on Student Success in the Chapel Hill City School." Integrated Education 7(N-D, 1969): 33-37.

[Report of the Charlotte-Mecklenburg Community Relations Committee on the Basic Causes of School Unrest] Charlotte Observer, Mr 15, 1972.

A Research Report of the North Carolina Advancement School: Spring and Summer 1968. Winston Salem, NC: North Carolina Advancement School, Ag, 1968, 121 pp. ERIC ED 045 761.

A Research Report of the North Carolina Advancement School: Spring Semester 1968 Followup. Winston-Salem, NC: North Carolina Advancement School, N, 1969, 72 pp. ERIC ED 045 762.

A Research Report of the North Carolina Advancement School: Summer Session, 1968. Winston Salem, NC: North Carolina Advancement School, Ja, 1969, 63 pp. ERIC ED 045 763.

A Research Report of the North Carolina Advancement School: Fall Term 1968, Spring Term 1969. Winston Salem, NC: North Carolina Advancement School, O, 1969, 57 pp. ERIC ED 045 764.

Resource Management Corporation. [Case History of ESAP in Charlotte, N.C.] Evaluation of the Emergency School Assistance Program, Vol. III, Appendix C, F 15, 1972. ERIC ED 058 470.

_____. [Case History of ESAP in Durham, N.C.] Evaluation of the Emergency School Assistance Program, Vol. III, Appendix F, F 15, 1972. ERIC ED 058 470.

_____. [Case History of ESAP in Lexington, N.C.] Evaluation of the Emergency School Assistance Program, Vol. III, Appendix H, n.d.

_____. [Case History of ESAP in Salisbury, N.C.] Evaluation of the Emergency School Assistance Program, Vol. III, Appendix I, F 15, 1972. ERIC Ed 058 470.

Rodgers, Frederick A. The Black High School and Its Community. Lexington, MA: Lexington Books, 1975.

Sanders, Wiley B. Negro Child-Welfare Work in North Carolina. Chapel Hill, NC: U. of North Carolina Press, 1933.

Sanford, Terry. But What about the People? New York: Harper & Row, 1966.

Shephard, James E. "These Colored United States. North Carolina--Its Educational Progress." Messenger 8(Mr, 1926):81, 90-91.

Smathers, Keener McNeal. "A History of the Supervision of Instruction in Schools for Negroes in North Carolina." Doctoral dissertation, Duke U., 1969. Univ. Microfilms Order No. 70-08837.

Smith, Bob. "Toleration, But No More." Southern Education Report, Mr, 1969. [Desegregation in Eastern North Carolina]

Smith, L. H. A Study of the Accredited Negro High Schools of North Carolina Over a Period of Four Years to Determine Number of Graduates Entering College, 1928-29. Greensboro, NC: Agricultural and Technical College.

Southern Regional Council. Tension and Conciliation. A Report on Contributing Factors Causing Racial Disagreements and Conflicts Within the Hickory, North Carolina City Schools. Atlanta, GA: The Council, Ag 11, 1974.

"Still No Peace After School Busing Decision." African World, Je 16, 1973. [West Charlotte High School, Charlotte]

"Straightening Out Durham High." Ebony 27 (Ag, 1972):80-87. [About James M. Rogers, Jr.]

Sumka, Howard J. "Racial Segregation in Small North Carolina Cities." Southeastern Geographer 17(1977):58-75.

Tarpley, J. A. "Some Aspects of Education Among Negroes in North Carolina." Quarterly Review of Higher Education Among Negroes 6 (Ja, 1938):68-72.

Taylor, B. L. "Accredited Negro High Schools of North Carolina." School and Society 26 (O 8, 1927):460-464.

Taylor, Jesse. "Storm of Protest Follows Counselor's Firing." African World 2(0 30, 1971):8. [Central High School, Cross, Berkley County]

Thomas, Jack. "Advocates Can Point to Greensboro." Boston Globe, S 4, 1973.

Thompson, Charles and others. Narrative Description of the N.C. Advancement School, Final Report. Durham, NC: Learning Institute of North Carolina, 1967, 58 pp. ERIC ED 023 762.

Thompson, Herbert W. "A History of Negro Education in the Catawba County School System from 1865-1960." Doctoral dissertation, Pennsylvania State U., 1964. Univ. Microfilms Order No. 65-6769.

Tornquist, Elizabeth. "Juvenile Corrections in North Carolina." New South 26(Summer, 1961):63-68. [Training schools]

U.S. Commission on Civil Rights. "Charlotte-Mecklenburg, North Carolina." In School Desegregation in Ten Communities, pp. 91-109. Washington, DC: GPO, Je, 1973.

_____. Civil Rights U.S.A. Public Schools. Southern States. 1963. North Carolina. Washington, DC: GPO, 1963.

_____. The Diminishing Barrier: A Report on School Desegregation... Washington, DC: GPO, D, 1972. [Hoke and Moore counties]

_____. "Winston-Salem/Forsyth County, North Carolina." In School Desegregation in Ten Communities, pp. 69-89. Washington, DC: GPO, Je, 1973.

U.S. Office of Education. "Moore County, N.C." In Working Together. Case Studies of Title I, ESEA Programs in Four Desegregated School Districts. Washington, DC: GPO, 1974.

Vaughn, John. "First in Busing." Charlotte News, S 12, 1975. [Charlotte]

Wallace, Jayne Belle. "Dominant Factors in the Development of the Alexander Street School for Colored Elementary Pupils, Charlotte, North Carolina, 1918-1937." Master's thesis, U. of Michigan, 1937.

Walls, Dwayne. The Klan: Collapsed and Dormant. Nashville, TN: Race Relations Information Center, My, 1970.

Warner, Stafford Allen. Yardley Warner: The Freedman's Friend. Abington, England: n.p., 1957. [Freedmen schools in N.C.]

"Warrenton: Old Days Are Over." Southern Patriot, Ja, 1971.

Wartts, Charles, Jr. "Militant Young Blacks Champion Struggle." Muhammad Speaks, D 10, 1971. [Wilmington]

_____. "Vigilante Violence in N. Carolina." Muhammad Speaks, D 17, 1971. [Wilmington]

Watters, Pat. "'A Little Child Shall Lead Them." In The South and Her Children: School Desegregation, 1970-71, pp. 21-37. Edited by Robert E. Anderson, Jr. Atlanta, GA: Southern Regional Council, Mr, 1971. [Charlotte]

Waynick, Capus (ed.). North Carolina and the Negro. Raleigh, NC: North Carolina Mayors' Cooperating Committee, 1964.

White, Estell E., and Clay, Rex J. A Test of the Homogeneity Thesis of the Culture of Poverty Theory: Characteristics of Disadvantaged Farm Families, D, 1975. ERIC ED 141 009. [Northeast North Carolina]

Whitener, Daniel J. "Public Education in North Carolina during Reconstruction, 1865-76." In Essays in Southern History Presented to Joseph Gregoire de Roulhac Hamilton, pp. 67-90. Edited by Fletcher M. Green. Chapel Hill, NC: U. of North Carolina Press, 1949.

Whiting, H. A. "The School Activities of Charlotte, N.C." Bulletin (National Association of Teachers in Colored Schools) 10 (My, 1930):5-17.

Winstead, Elton D. "The Development of Law Pertaining to Desegregation of Public Schools in North Carolina." Doctoral dissertation, Duke U., 1966. Univ. Microfilms Order No. 66-13693.

Wolcott, Reed. Rose Hill. New York: Putnam, 1976.

Wright, Lawrence. "The Long March of C. P. Ellis: A Klansman Overcomes." Southern Voices 1(Mr-Ap, 1974):52-58. [Durham]

_____. "A Slow Dance with Progress." Race Relations Reporter 4(Mr, 1973):13-17. [Durham]

North Dakota

Dewal, Sr. Mary Ferdinand. "The Development of Catholic Education in North Dakota." Master's thesis, U. of Notre Dame, n.d.

Lazar, Robert Jordan. "From Ethnic Minority to Socio-Economic Elite: A Study of the Jewish Community of Fargo, North Dakota." Doctoral dissertation, U. of Minnesota, 1968. Univ. Microfilms Order No. 69-1517.

Poverty in North Dakota... Bismarck, ND: State Economic Opportunity Office, 1970.

Ohio

"A Who's Who in the Pro and Con of School Desegregation in Dayton." _Dayton Journal-Herald_, D 3, 1975.

Adams, Steve. "Conquering Fear: Tensions Ease After 2 Years of Busing." _Dayton Journal-Herald_, Je 20, 1978. [Dayton]

Advisory Committee to the Board of Education to Reduce Racial Isolation and Improve Educational Opportunities. _Report of the Committee of 75_. Dayton, OH: Dayton Board of Education, D 1, 1971.

Almond, Peter. "How Black Leaders United on Suit." _Cleveland Press_, S 1, 1976. [Account of closed strategy meeting of black leaders from Cleveland in 1975 on whether the NAACP should proceed with its pending desegregation case]

_____. "Meet Plaintiff in Bias Case--And His Family." _Cleveland Press_, N 15, 1975. [Cleveland]

Arnett, Benjamin W. _Rise and Progress of the Colored Common Schools in Cincinnati._ Cincinnati, OH: H. Watkins, 1874.

Ayres, B. Drummond, Jr. "2 Cities, North and South, Show Progress by Blacks." _New York Times_, Ag 28, 1973.

Ayres, Leonard Porter. _The Cleveland School Survey (Summary Volume)_. N.p.: n.p., 1917.

Baker, Richard J. "Court Case Planned as Latest Step in Dayton's Integration Controversy." _Ohio Schools_ 50(F 11, 1972): 7-9, 34

Ballantine, Jeanne H., Cargan, Leonard, and Ballantine, Harden P. "The Threat of Busing: Real or Imagined?" _Integrateduca-tion_ 13(Mr-Ap, 1975):41-43.

Balz, Douglas. "The New Deal at Old Buchtel." _Akron Beacon Journal_, Ag 20, 1978. [Mainly - black Buchtel High School, Akron]

Barrett, Edward A., and Cawley, Allen J. "The Dayton School System. A Case Study of Community Response to Levy Failure." _Urban Education_ 7(O, 1972):261-280.

Barton, Josef. _Peasants and Strangers. Italians, Rumanians, and Slovaks in an American City, 1890-1950._ Cambridge, MA: Harvard U. Press, 1975. [Cleveland]

Battisti, Frank J. "Judge Battisti Scolds Cleveland School Board. _Integrateducation_ 15(N-D, 1977):16-17.

Beatie, Bruce. "Ethnic Heritage and Language Schools-" _Bulletin of the Association of Departments of Foreign Languages_ 9(N, 1977): 39-46. [Cleveland area]

Benjamin, Robert, and Graham, Michael. "Appalachians: Cincinnati's Forgotten Minority. _Cincinnati Post_, Jl 28, 1978.

_____ and _____. "Color the Children." _Cincinnati Post_, Jl 22-28, 1978. [Seven articles on racial situation in the Cincinnati schools]

Berlowitz, Marvin J. _School Dropouts or Students Pushouts? A Case Study of the Possible Violation of Property Rights and Liberties by the De Facto Exclusion of Students from the Public Schools._ Cincinnati: Urban Appalachian Council, n.d. [Cincinnati]

Billingslea, Seabron B. "The Negro, 1901 to 1920, as Portrayed in the _Cincinnati Enquirer_." Master's thesis, Howard U., 1950.

"'Black Is Better Than White' in a Ghetto in Small Ohio City." _National Observer_, Ap 1, 1968.

Briggs, Paul W. _Responding to Changing Needs._ Cleveland, OH: Board of Education, D 9, 1971.

Brown, Connie. "Cleveland: Conference of the Poor." _Studies on the Left_, Spring, 1965.

Brown, G. Gwendolyn. "The Influences Surrounding the Establishment of the Present Segregated Schools in Selected Cities of Ohio." Master's thesis, Howard U., 1947.

Brown, Marianna, and McBreen, James. _Analysis of the Cincinnati Public Schools' Goal of Intercultural Understanding_. Cincinnati, OH: Cincinnati Human Relations Commission, Ja, 1972.

Browning, S. "Racially Discriminatory Suspensions in the Akron Public Schools: A Tentative Analysis." Washington, DC: Committee for Civil Rights Under Law, O 2, 1974 (unpublished).

Brunn, Stanley D., Hoffman, Wayne L., and Rosma, Gerald H. "The Youngstown School Levies: A Geographical Analaysis in Voting Behavior." _Urban Education_ 5(1970):20-52.

"Busing: What Effect on Kids?" _Ohio Schools_ 50 (Mr 10, 1972):15-16, 28. [Shaker Heights]

Calkins, David L. "Black Education and the 19th Century City: An Institutional Analysis of Cincinnati's Colored Schools, 1850-1887." _Cincinnati Historical Society Bulletin_ 33 (Fall, 1975).

_____. "Chronologic Highlights of Cincinnati's Black Community." _Cincinnati Historical Society Bulletin_ 28(1970):344-353.

Caplan, Eleanor. "Attitude and Behavior in a Middle Class Biracial Neighborhood." Doctoral dissertation, Case Western Reserve U., 1962. [Ludlow, Shaker Heights]

Citizens Advisory Council. Report to the Dayton Board of Education. Dayton, OH: Board of Education, Ag 7, 1969.

City of East Cleveland Staff, and Arthur D. Little, Inc. East Cleveland: Response to Urban Change. Washington, DC: Communication Service Corp., 1969.

Cleveland Urban League. The Negro in Cleveland, 1950-1963. Cleveland, OH: The Cleveland Urban League, Je, 1964.

Clifford, Carrie. "Cleveland and Its Colored People." Colored American Magazine 9(Jl, 1905):372-373.

Cobb, Robert W. "Black Settlement in Silverton, Ohio, 1960-1967: A Spatial Diffusion Process." Master's thesis, State U. of New York at Buffalo, 1971.

Cohen, David K. Relevant Questions for the Development of an Active Program for Integrated Quality Education. Cleveland CORE, 1964.

_____. Cincinnati: Education and Race. Cambridge, MA: Joint Center for Urban Studies, 1968.

Coles, Robert. [Testimony on school segregation in Cleveland and elsewhere] in U.S. Commission on Civil Rights. Hearing Before the Commission... Held in Cleveland, Ohio, April 1-7, 1966, pp. 344-380. Washington, DC: GPO, 1966.

Colston, Freddie Charles. "The Influence of the Black Legislators in the Ohio House of Representatives." Doctoral dissertation, Ohio State U., 1972. Univ. Microfilms Order No. 73-01970.

Colton, David L. Urban School Desegregation Costs. Part I. Case Studies. St. Louis, MO: Center for Educational Field Studies, Washington U., N, 1977. [Cleveland, Columbus, Dayton]

Corwin, Ronald G., and Schmidt, Sister Marilyn. "Teachers in Inner-City Schools." Education and Urban Society 2(1970):131-155 [Columbus]

Crowley, Mary R. "Comparison of the Academic Achievements of Cincinnati Negroes in Segregated and Mixed Schools." Doctoral dissertation, U. of Cincinnati, 1931.

Cuban, Larry. "A Strategy for Racial Peace: Negro Leadership in Cleveland, 1900-1919." Phylon, Fall, 1967.

Dabney, Wendell P. Cincinnati's Colored Citizens... Cincinatti, OH: Dabney Pub. Co., 1926.

_____. "The 'Colored' United States: Ohio-- Past and Present." Messenger 7(Ap, 1925): 153-155

Daugherty, Robert L. "Problems in Peacekeeping: The 1924 Niles Riot." Ohio History 85 (Autumn, 1976):280-292. [Ku Klux Klan]

David, George F. Social Effects of School Segregation in Xenia, Ohio. Wilberforce, OH: Wilberforce U., 1933.

Davis, James C. "Cleveland's White Problem: A Challenge to the Bar." Journal of Human Relations, Fourth Quarter, 1967.

Davis, Russell H. Black Americans in Cleveland. Washington, DC: Associated Publishers, 1974.

Department of Public Instruction. History of Negro Education in the Cincinnati Public Schools. Cincinnati Public Schools, 1964.

Desegregation in Ohio. Background for Current Litigation. Cleveland: Citizens' Council for Ohio Schools, Ja, 1976.

"Desegregation--Where They Will Be Bused." Cleveland Plain Dealer, Jl 2, 1978. [Maps for S, 1978 student assignments]

Diekhoff, John S. "My Fair Ludlow." Educational Forum, Mr, 1969. [Shaker Heights]

Division of Reference and Research. An Analysis of the Enrollment of Negro Pupils in the Cleveland Public Schools Showing the Increase from April 1, 1921, to October 1923 and the Influx of Southern Negroes During the Six Months Preceding October, 1923. Bulletin No. 86. Cleveland, OH: Board of Education, Ap 26, 1924.

Dombey, E. H. "A Comparison of the Intelligence Test Scores of Southern and Northern Born Negroes--Residing in Cleveland." Master's thesis, Western Reserve U., 1933.

Dynamics of Educational Opportunities: A Report of the EEO Survey, Je, 1970. ERIC ED 043 656.

Du Bois, W. E. B. "The Victory at Springfield." Crisis, S, 1923.

Eardley, Linda. "A Look at 'Magnet' Schools [in Cincinnati]." St. Louis Post-Dispatch (2 articles), F 8-9, 1976.

_____. "Cincinnati's Magnet Schools." Integrateducation 14(S/O, 1976).

East Cleveland: Response to Urban Change. Cambridge, MA: Arthur D. Little, Inc., Ap, 1969.

Easton, L. D. "The Colored Schools of Cincinnati." In History of the Schools of Cincinnati and Other Educational Institutions, Public and Private. Edited by Isaac M. Martin. Cincinnati, OH: n.p., 1900.

Equal Educational Opportunities Project, July 1, 1969-December 31, 1970. First Report, and Supportive Data Supplements, F, 1971. ERIC ED 050 186.

Equal Educational Opportunity Survey, Ap, 1970. ERIC Ed 043 689.

Erickson, Leonard E. "The Color Line in Ohio Public Schools, 1829-1890." Doctoral dissertation, Ohio State U., 1959. Univ. Microfilms Order No. 60-735.

_____. "Politics and Repeal of Ohio's Black Laws, 1837-1849." Ohio History 72(Autumn, 1973).

_____. "Toledo Desegregates, 1871." Northwest Ohio Quarterly (Winter, 1968-69).

Ervin, John B. "Improving the Educational Experiences of the Negro Child in a Non-segregated School Environment at Akron, Ohio." Doctoral dissertation, Columbia U., 1950.

Fensch, Edwin A. "A Critical Study of Negro Students in the John Simpson Junior High School, Mansfield, Ohio." Doctoral dissertation, Ohio State U., 1944.

Flanagan, Sr. Mary Callista. "Jesuit Education in the Archdiocese of Cincinnati in the Last Hundred Years." Master's thesis, U. of Notre Dame, 1940.

Folk, Patrick A. "'The Queen City of Mobs': Riots and Community Reactions in Cincinnati, 1788-1848." Doctoral dissertation, U. of Toledo, 1978. Univ. Microfilms Order No. 7822025.

Folk, Richard Albert. "Black Man's Burden in Ohio 1849-1863." Doctoral dissertation, U. of Toledo, 1972. Univ. Microfilms Order No. 73-02396.

Foner, Philip S. "Peter H. Clark: Pioneer Black Socialist." Journal of Ethnic Studies 5(Fall, 1977):17-35. [Cincinnati]

Foote, John P. The Schools of Cincinnati, and Its Vicinity. Cincinnati, OH: C. F. Bradley, 1855.

Fordyce, Wellington G. "Immigrant Colonies in Cleveland." Ohio Archaeological and Historical Quarterly 45(1936):320-340.

Forthamp, Frank E. "The Educational Implications of Racism in Ohio's Prisons." Doctoral dissertation, Ohio State U., 1972.

Foster, Gordon, and McDonald, R. Timothy. Desegregation Study: Dayton Public Schools. NCRIEEO Special. New York: National Center for Research and Information on Equal Educational Opportunity, Teachers College, Columbia U., My, 1972.

Franklin, William, Jr. "Status of the Negro in Cleveland." Doctoral dissertation, Ohio State U., 1958.

Friedman, Leon Morris. "The Matter of Racial Imbalance: A History of Pupil Attendance Districts and Pupil Housing in the Public Schools of Akron, Ohio." Doctoral dissertation, Case Western Reserve U., 1968. Univ. Microfilms Order No. 70-25,838.

Gaines, Harold L. A Survey of the Intergroup Relations Content in the Problems of Democracy Courses of Ohio High Schools. Columbus, OH: Civil Rights Commission, 1963.

Gaumer, Thomas H. "Briggs on Segregation." Cleveland Plain Dealer, F 8, 1976. [Paul W. Briggs, superintendent of Cleveland public schools]

_____. "Cleveland." Integrateducation 15 (N-D, 1977):14-15.

_____. "Integration and the Classroom." Cleveland Plain Dealer Magazine, My 8, 1977. [Shaker Heights and East Cleveland]

_____. "Looking Back with Paul W. Briggs." Cleveland Plain Dealer, S 3, 1978. [Cleveland]

_____. "Principal Has Integration 'Sales Pitch.'" Cleveland Plain Dealer, F 15, 1976. [Melvin M. Gross, principal, Willson Junior High School, Cleveland]

_____. "Segregation and Schools. A Dialog with Nathaniel R. Jones..." Cleveland Plain Dealer, F 1, 1976. [Cleveland]

Gaumer, Thomas H., and Jindra, Christine J. "Busing in Specter Haunting School Segregation Trial Here." Cleveland Plain Dealer, N 16, 1975. [Cleveland]

Gerber, David A. Black Ohio and the Color Line, 1860-1915. Urbana, IL: U. of Illinois Press, 1976.

_____. "Education, Expediency, and Ideology: Race and Politics in the Desegregation of Ohio Public Schools in the Late 19th Century." Journal of Ethnic Studies 1 (Fall, 1973):1-31.

_____. "Ohio and the Color Line: Racial Discrimination and Negro Responses in a Northern State, 1860-1915." Doctoral dissertation, Princeton U., 1971.

Giles, Robert H. "How to Become a Target City." Reporter, Je 15, 1967. [Cleveland]

Goings, Kenneth W. "Blacks in the Rural North: Paulding County, Ohio, 1860-1900." Doctoral dissertation, Princeton U., 1977. Univ. Microfilms Order No. 78-262.

Grabow, Steve. "Migration of Blacks and Whites: A Focus on Outlying Neighborhoods of Cincinnati, Ohio." Master's thesis, U. of Cincinnati, 1974.

Grabowski, John Joseph. "a Social Settlement in a Neighborhood in Transition: Hiram House, Cleveland, Ohio, 1896-1926." Doctoral dissertation, Case Western Reserve U., 1977.

Grace, A. G. "The Effect of Negro Migration on the Cleveland Public School System." Master's thesis, Western Reserve U., 1932.

Gregg, Howard D. "The Background Study of Negro High School Students in Ohio." Doctoral dissertation, U. of Pennsylvania, 1936.

Griffin, Virginia K. "Desegregation in Cincinnati: The Legal Background." In The Future of Big-City Schools. Edited by Daniel U. Levine and Robert J. Havighurst. Berkeley, CA: McCutchan, 1977.

Griffin, Virginia K. and others. Symposium: Strategies for Achieving Racial Balance in the Cincinnati Public Schools, Ap 21, 1976. ERIC ED 124 613.

Griffin, William W. "The Negro in Ohio, 1914-39." Doctoral dissertation, Ohio State U., 1969.

Harding, Leonard. "The Negro in Cincinnati, 1860-1870: A Demographic Study of a Transitional Decade." Master's thesis, U. of Cincinnati, 1967.

Harmon, Gains Elijah. "Absenteeism Among White and Negro School Children in Cleveland, 1922-1923." Public Health Reports, Mr 21, 1924.

Hedesheimer, Walter Jon. "The Negro in Cleveland, with Special Reference to the Two Leading Newspapers." Master's thesis, Ohio State U., 1965.

Himes, Joseph S., Jr. "40 Years of Negro Life in Columbus, Ohio." Journal of Negro History 27(Ap, 1942):133-154.

Hodgart, Robert L. "The Process of Expansion of the Negro Ghetto in Cities of the Northern United States: A Case Study of Cleveland, Ohio." Master's thesis, Pennsylvania State U., 1969.

Holland, Darrell. "Cleveland's Catholic Schools." Cleveland Plain Dealer, Ag 29, 1976.

Howson, Embrey Bernard. "The Ku Klux Klan in Ohio After World War I." Master's thesis, Ohio State U., 1951.

Hyland, Gerard. "The Place-Based Community: Neighborhood Place and Social Interaction Range of the Appalachian In-Migrant in the Cincinnati Metropolitan Area." Master's thesis, U. of Cincinnati, 1969.

"Integration in Schools Outpacing Other Areas." Cleveland Plain Dealer, N 30, 1975. [Cleveland Heights]

Jacobs, T. O. and others. Princeton High School: A Needs Analysis, Je, 1971. ERIC ED 128 915. [Cincinnati]

Jirran, Raymond J. "Cleveland and the Negro Following World War II." Doctoral dissertation, Kent State U., 1972. Univ. Microfilms Order No. 73-12988.

Kessen, Thomas Paul. "Segregation in Cincinnati Public Education: The Nineteenth Century Black Experience." Doctoral dissertation, U. of Cincinnati, 1973. Univ. Microfilms Order No. 73-29456.

Kettlewell, Albert W. "Resources Affecting Equal Opportunity in Selected City Elementary Schools in Ohio." Doctoral dissertation, Miami U., 1974. Univ. Microfilms Order No. 74-18,816.

King, Charles N. "Opportunities and Educational Needs of Negro Youth in North Hamilton County." Master's thesis, U. of Cincinnati, 1940.

Klumpe, Kerry. "Alternative Schools: A Network of Unknowns." Integrateducation 14(S/O, 1976). [Cincinnati]

_____. "'Old School Days' Mean Much to Blacks." Cincinnati Enquirer, N 14, 1976. [Deliberately-segregated black schools in Cincinnati area]

Klunder, Mrs. Bruce W. "My Husband Died for Democracy." Ebony, Je, 1964. [The widow of Rev. Bruce W. Klunder, who was killed accidentally during a demonstration against school segregation in Cleveland]

Kusmer, Kenneth L. A Ghetto Takes Shape. Black Cleveland, 1870-1930. Urbana, IL: U. of Illinois Press, 1975.

_____. "Black Cleveland: The Origin and Development of a Ghetto, 1890-1930." Master's thesis, Kent State U., 1971.

Lawson, John H. "Desegregation in Shaker Heights." Integrated Education (S-O, 1971): 37-41.

Levenson, William B., and Princiotto, Ted. "Press Coverage of School Integration in Cleveland." 2 views. Theory Into Practice, O, 1964.

Libby, Albert. "The Vanguarders." Common Ground 6(Summer, 1946):83-87. [The Vanguard League in Columbus]

Longman, Rufus A. "Dependent Colored Children in Ohio." Ohio Bulletin of Charities and Corrections 17(Jl, 1911):30-33.

Lucas, Robert E. "Princeton's Investment in Children Provides New Opportunities for All." Mini Journal (Office of Equal Educational Opportunity, Ohio Department of Education) 4(D, 1971).

McClain, Shirla Robinson. "The Contributions of Blacks in Akron, 1825-1975." Doctoral dissertation, U. of Akron, 1975. Univ. Microfilms Order No. 75-23974.

McClure, Phyllis P. "Growth, Cause, and Extent of School Segregation in the Public Schools of Cincinnati, Ohio." A draft. Washington, DC: U.S. Commission on Civil Rights, unpublished.

McGinnis, Frederick A. The Education of Negroes in Ohio. Wilberforce, OH: N.p., n.d.

Maloney, Michael. The Social Areas of Cincinnati. Toward an Analysis of Social Needs. Cincinnati: Urban Appalachian Council, 1974.

Mark, Mary L. Negroes in Columbus, Ohio. Columbus, OH: Ohio State U., 1928.

Maziarz, Thomas J. "A Factorial Ecology of Cincinnati's Black Residential Areas." Ohio Geographers: Recent Research Themes 2(1974):1-11. [1970 data]

Merriman, Howard O. The Columbus Ohio School Profile. A Report of the Columbus Public Schools to the Community. Columbus, OH: Columbus Public Schools, My, 1969.

Miller, Herbert. The School and the Immigrant. Cleveland, OH: n.p., 1916. [Cleveland]

Miller, Janet Ann. "Urban Education and the New City: Cincinnati's Elementary Schools, 1870-1914." Doctoral dissertation, U. of Cincinnati, 1974. Univ. Microfilms Order No. 75-2336.

Miller, Jonathan. "Conflicting Signals." New Republic, Jl 23, 1977. [U.S. Supreme Court and Dayton desegregation case]

Minor, Richard C. "The Negro in Columbus, Ohio." Doctoral dissertation, Ohio State U., 1937.

"Mobility Report: Columbus Public Schools." Journal of the International Association of Pupil Personnel Workers 15(Je, 1971):143-147.

Monkkonen, Eric H. The Dangerous Class: Crime and Poverty in Columbus, Ohio, 1860-1885. Cambridge, MA: Harvard U. Press, 1975.

Moore, William F., Jr. "Status of the Negro in Cleveland." Doctoral dissertation, Ohio State U., 1953. Univ. Microfilms Order No. 58-729.

Murphy, Melvin L. "The Columbus Urban League: A History, 1971-1967." Doctoral dissertation, Ohio State U., 1970. Univ. Microfilms Order No. 71-7525.

Myers, John L. "Antislavery Activities of Five Lane Seminary Boys in 1835-36." Bulletin of the Historical and Philosophical Society of Ohio 21(Ap, 1963):99-100.

National Commission on Professional Rights and Responsibilities. Cleveland, Ohio. When a Board of Education Fails to Fulfill Its Proper Responsibilities. Washington, DC: National Education Association, 1964.

"Ohio Colored Teachers Association." Ohio Educational Monthly 4(1863):159

Ohio Civil Rights Commission. Survey of Ohio College and University Placement Offices with Regard to Job Placement of Minority Students. Columbus, OH: The Commission, Ag, 1961.

Ohio Department of Education, Division of Research and Division of Guidance and Testing. Ohio Study of High School Dropouts, 1962-1963, 1964.

Ohio State Advisory Committee. Cleveland Still Has Unfinished Business in Its Inner City. Cleveland, OH: U.S. Commission on Civil Rights, Mr 1, 1967.

_____. Cleveland's Unfinished Business. Its Inner City. Cleveland, OH: U.S. Commission on Civil Rights, Je 30, 1966.

Orbell, John M., with Sherrill, Kenneth S. "Racial Attitudes and the Metropolitan Context: A Structural Analysis." Public Opinion Quarterly, Spring, 1969.

Pap, Michael (ed.). Ethnic Communities of Cleveland. Cleveland, OH: Institute for Soviet and East European Studies, John Carroll U., 1973.

Petersen, Gene B., and Sharp, Laure M. The Cleveland Southern Immigrant Study. Washington, DC: Bureau of Social Science Research, Je 29, 1968.

Petersen, Gene B. and others. Southern Newcomers to Northern Cities: Work and Social Adjustment in Cleveland. New York: Praeger, 1977.

Pettigrew, Thomas F. "Attitudes Towards Parental Control of Public Schools." In A Study of School Integration, pp. 254-310. Cambridge, MA: Department of Social Relations, Harvard U., Ag, 1970. [Cleveland]

Pih, Richard W. "The Negro in Cincinnati, 1802-1841." Master's thesis, Miami U., 1968.

_____. "Negro Self-Improvement Efforts in Ante-Bellum Cincinnati, 1836-1850." Ohio History (Summer, 1969):179-187

Pruitt, Shirley. "Ethnic and Racial Composition of Selected Cleveland Neighborhoods." Social Science 43(Je, 1968):171-174.

Quillin, Frank U. "Cincinnati's Colored Citizens." Independent (F 24, 1910):399-403.

_____. The Color Line in Ohio: A History of Race Prejudice in a Typical Northern State. Ann Arbor, MI: U. of Michigan Press, 1913.

_____. "The Negro in Cleveland, Ohio." Independent (Mr 7, 1912):518-520.

Racial Isolation in the Schools of Hamilton County, Ja, 1976. Metropolitan Area Religious Coalition of Cincinnati, 920 Provident Bank Bldg., 632 Vine St., Cincinnati, OH 45202.

Richan, W. Racial Isolation in the Cleveland Public Schools. Cleveland, OH: School for Applied Social Science, Case-Western Reserve U., 1967.

Rico-Velasco, Jesus Antonio. Immigrants from the Appalachian Region to the City of Columbus, Ohio: A Case Study, 1969, 157 pp. Master's thesis, Ohio State U. Available from Inter-Library Loan from Ohio State U., Columbus, OH (on microfilm). ERIC ED 053 853.

Reisinger, Sue. "Talk Smoothed Road to Integration in Cincy Suburb." Dayton Daily News, F 8, 1973. [Princeton]

Rodabaugh, James H. "The Negro in Ohio." Journal of Negro History 31(Ja, 1946): 9-29.

Rothman, Philip. "School Segregation Is a Problem in Ohio." Ohio Schools, N, 1965.

School Segregation in Bowling Green. Frankfort, KY: Commission on Human Rights, My, 1973.

Shaker Heights Property Values Study, 1970. Ludlow Community Association, 2969 Ripley Road, Cleveland, OH 44120. [Home values in nine elementary school districts of various ethnic composition]

Rudwick, Elliott, and Meier, August. "Early Boycotts of Segregated Schools: The Case of Springfield, Ohio, 1922-23." American Quarterly, Winter, 1968.

Sheehan, Pete. "Why the Money Ran Out in Youngstown." Phi Delta Kappan, N, 1969.

"Slavery and Education." Western Monthly Magazine 3(My, 1834):266-273. [Cincinnati]

Sponholtz, Lloyd L. "Harry Smith, Negro Suffrage, and the Ohio Constitutional Convention: Black Frustration in the Progressive Era." Phylon 35(Je, 1974):165-180.

Simkins, Ruth. "A Comparative Study of the Socio-economic Background, Physical Growth, Attitudes and Social Maturity of Negro Children from Relief and Non-relief Families in Lockland, Ohio." Master's thesis, U. of Cincinnati, 1937.

Smith, Shirley M. "The Negro, 1877 to 1898, as Portrayed in the Cincinnati Enquirer." Master's thesis, Howard U., 1948.

Stein, Herman D. (ed.). The Crisis in Welfare in Cleveland. Cleveland, OH: Press of Case Western Reserve U., 1969.

Stevens, William K. "Integrated Housing Thrives in Suburb." New York Times, O 18, 1975. [Shaker Heights]

Strahler, Violet R. (ed.). School Integration. Board of Education Study Conference. Dayton, OH: Dayton Public Schools, D, 1970.

Stroud, R. "A Study of the Relations between Social Distances and Speech Differences of White and Negro High School Students of Dayton, Ohio." Master's thesis, Bowling Green State U., 1956.

Taeuber, Karl E. "The Effect of Income Redistribution on Racial Residential Segregation." Urban Affairs Quarterly, S, 1968. [Cleveland]

_____. "Population Distribution and Residential Segregation in Cleveland." Unpublished study for U.S. Commission on Civil Rights, 1966.

Thomas, Arthur E., Burgin, Ruth W., and Others. An Experiment in Community School Control: An Evolution of the Dayton Experience, 1971. [Write: Dr. Ames W. Chapman, Central State U., Wilberforce, OH 45384]

Thomas, Wesley W. "Intra-Urban Migration and the Racial Transition of Residential Areas: A Behavioral Approach." Doctoral dissertation, U. of Cincinnati, 1975. [Cincinnati]

Thomas, Willie James. "Cincinnati Black Faces Prison for Fighting for Black Studies." Part 2. Muhammad Speaks, Mr 17, 1972.

Tomkins, Rachel B. and others. Community Preparation for Desegregation. Cleveland, November 1974-September 1976, O, 1976. ERIC ED 133 400.

Tribe, Ivan M. "Rise and Decline of Private Academies in Albany, Ohio." Ohio History 78 (1969):188-201.

U.S. Commission on Civil Rights, Ohio Advisory Committee. Affirmative Action on Inaction? The Pursuit of Equal Employment Opportunity in Cleveland. Washington, DC: The Commission, 1977.

U.S. Commission on Civil Rights. The Diminishing Barrier: A Report on School Desegregation. Washington, DC: GPO, D, 1972. [Jefferson Township]

_____. Exhibit No. 34. "Education." In Hearing Before the ... Commission ... in Cleveland, Ohio, April 1-7, 1966, pp. 750-763. Washington, DC: GPO, 1966.

U.S. Commission on Civil Rights, Ohio Advisory Committee. Cleveland's Unfinished Business in Its Inner-City. Washington, DC: The Commission, 1966.

Urban League of Cleveland. The Negro in Cleveland, 1950-1963: An Analysis of the Social and Economic Characteristics of the Negro Population. Cleveland, OH: The League, 1964.

Wade, Richard C. "The Negro in Cincinnati, 1800-1830." Journal of Negro History 39 (Ja, 1954):43-57.

Wagner, Thomas E. Appalachian Migrant Students in Cincinnati Public Schools, Jl, 1973. ERIC ED 096 069.

_____. Report of the Appalachian School Study Project. Cincinnati: Urban Appalachian Project, 1974.

_____. Urban Appalachian School Children: The Least Understood of All. Cincinnati: Urban Appalachian Council, 1974.

Walton, O. M. "Northern Ohio Changes and Casualties." Christian Century, Ag 18, 1965. [Touches on community pressures around issues of school integration]

_____. Urban Studies: Cleveland (1)--Children in Need. Washington, DC: GPO, 1966.

Waters, Kathryn. "Cincinnati's Magnet Schools." St. Louis Globe-Democrat, S 12, 1976.

Watson, Bruce. "The Backlash of White Supremacy: Caste Status and the Negro Revolt." Journal of Human Relations, First Quarter, 1966. [Touches on Cleveland]

Wayson, William W., Rivers, Charles H., and Carter, David G. "Charlie Glatt's Legacy: A Challenge to Rise Above the Conspiracy that Killed Him." Phi Delta Kappan 58(S, 1976): 53-55.

Wilkes, Paul. "As the Blacks Move In, the Ethnics Move Out." New York Times Magazine, Ja 24, 1971. [East Side, Cleveland]

Williams, LeRoy Thomas. "Black Toledo: Afro-Americans in Toledo, Ohio, 1890-1930." Doctoral dissertation, U. of Toledo, 1977. Univ. Microfilms Order No. 7802494.

Wolf, Laurence G. "The Metropolitan Tidal Wave in Ohio, 1900-2000." Economic Geography 45(Ap, 1969):133-154.

Woodson, Carter G. "The Negroes of Cincinnati Prior to the Civil War." Journal of Negro History 1(Ja, 1916).

Woolford, Warren L. "A Geographical Appraisal of Major Distributional Changes in the Akron, Ohio Black Population 1930-1970." Master's thesis, U. of Akron, 1974.

Wye, Christopher Gray. "Midwest Ghetto: Patterns of Negro Life and Thought in Cleveland, Ohio, 1929-1945." Doctoral dissertation, Kent State U., 1973. Univ. Microfilms No. 73-32363.

"Youngstown Public Library Takes Lead in Afro History Program." Library Journal, D 1, 1968.

"Youth in the Ghetto. A Study of the Consequences of Powerlessness and Isolation in Cleveland Public Schools." Unpublished study for U.S. Commission on Civil Rights, 1966.

Zuverink, David L. "Moses and Pharaoh in Cleveland." Integrated Education, Je-Jl, 1964.

Oklahoma

Abbott, L. J. "The Race Question in the Forty-sixth State." Independent 63(1907):206-211.

Anderson, Lethia M. "Equalization of Educational Opportunity for Negroes in Oklahoma." Master's thesis, U. of Kansas, 1951.

Andrews, Thomas F. "Freedmen in Indian Territory: A Post Civil War Dilemma." Journal of the West 4(1965):367-376.

Balyeat, Frank A. "Education of White Children in the Indian Territory." Chronicles of Oklahoma 15(1937):191-197. [1870-1920]

Billington, Monroe. "Public School Integration in Oklahoma, 1954-63." Historian, Ag, 1964.

"Black Mother Sentenced to 10 Years for Protecting Child. The Story of Norma Gist." Black Panther, S 25, 1971. [Idabelle]

Bond, Horace Mann. "The Negro Common School in Oklahoma." Crisis 35(Ap and Jl, 1928):113-115 and 228-229.

Bouner, Mary W., and Belden, Bernard R. A Comparative Study of the Performance of Negro Seniors of Oklahoma City High Schools on the Wechsler Adult Intelligence Scale and the Peabody Picture Vocabulary Test." Journal of Negro Education 39(Fall, 1970): 354-358.

Cayton, Leonard Bernard. "A History of Black Public Education in Oklahoma." Doctoral dissertation, U. of Oklahoma, 1976. Univ. Microfilms Order No. 77-32,851.

Celarier, Michelle. "Public Opinion on De-segregation in Oklahoma." Chronicles of Oklahoma 47(1969):268-281.

Crossley, Mildred McCracken. "A History of the Negro Schools of Oklahoma City, Oklahoma." Master's thesis, U. of Oklahoma, 1939.

Delaney, Paul. "Poll Finds More For Integra-tion." New York Times, O 12, 1975. [Douglass High School, Oklahoma City]

Department of the Interior, Bureau of Educa-tion. Public Education in Oklahoma. A Digest of the Report. [A report of a survey of public education in the State of Oklahoma, made at the request of the Oklahoma state educational survey commission, under the direction of the United States commissioner of education. Washington, DC, D 11, 1922]

Ellison, Ralph. "Growing Up Black in Frontier Oklahoma." Washington Post, Ag 21, 1973.

Gammon, Tim. "Black Freedmen and the Cherokee Nation." American Studies 11(D, 1977):357-364.

_____. "The Black Freedmen of the Cherokee Nation." Negro History Bulletin 40(Jl-Ag, 1977):733-735.

Halliburton, R., Jr. The Tulsa Race War of 1921. San Francisco, CA: R & E Research Associates, 1975.

Hamilton, Kenneth M. "The Origin and Early Developments of Langston, Oklahoma." Journal of Negro History 62(Jl, 1977): 270-282.

Hatch, Katherine. "Oklahoma City Uses Cluster Plan." Race Relations Reporter, O 1, 1970.

Hatcher, Ollie E. "The Development of Legal Controls in Racial Segregation in the Public Schools of Oklahoma, 1865-1952." Doctoral dissertation, U. of Oklahoma, 1954.

Hill, Mozell C. "A Comparative Study of Race Attitudes in the All-Negro Community in Oklahoma." Phylon, Third Quarter, 1956.

_____. "The All-Negro Society in Oklahoma." Doctoral dissertation, U. of Chicago, 1946.

Hillinger, Charles. "Alumni Rally to Save All-Black School." Los Angeles Times, Mr 9, 1975. [Wheatley High School, Boynton]

Humphrey, Charles Allen. "Socio-Economic Study of Six All-Black Towns in Oklahoma." Doctoral dissertation, Oklahoma State U., 1973. Univ. Microfilms Order No. 74-08049.

Humphrey, Charles A., and Allen, Donald E. "Educational and Social Needs in Small All-Black Towns." Journal of Negro Education 47 (Summer, 1978):244-255.

Jackson, Joe C. "The History of Education in Eastern Oklahoma from 1898 to 1915." Doctoral dissertation, U. of Oklahoma, 1950.

Jacobson, Eugene D. "The Dilemma of Integrating Our School System: Oklahoma City, 1969." Integration, Fall, 1969.

James, Parthena Louise. "Reconstruction in the Chickasaw Nation: The Freedmen Problem." Chronicles of Oklahoma 45(1967):44-57.

Kerns, J. Harvey. A Study of Social and Economic Conditions of the Negro Population of Tulsa, Oklahoma. Tulsa, OK: Tulsa Council of Social Agencies, 1945.

Knight, Thomas. "Black Towns in Oklahoma: Their Development and Survival." Doctoral disser-tation, Oklahoma State U., 1975. Univ. Microfilms Order No. 76-09703.

Littlefield, Daniel F. Africans and Seminoles from Removal to Emancipation. Westport, CT: Greenwood, 1977.

Littlefield, Daniel F., and Underhill, Lonnie E. "Black Dreams and 'Free' Homes: The Oklahoma Territory, 1891-1894." Phylon 34(D, 1973): 342-357.

Lovejoy, Gordon W. "Into the Main Stream..."; Institute 1--the Changing Community, June 7-July 2, 1965. Tulsa, OK: U. of Tulsa, Ag 6, 1965, 67 pp. ERIC ED 056 119.

Luvall, J. A. G. "The Indian Territory the Negro's Friend." Voice of the Negro 4(Mr, 1907):135-138.

McCloud, Paul I. Neither Black Nor White: A Progress Report on Integration in the Tulsa Public Schools, 1974. ERIC ED 121 889.

Mellinger, Philip. "Discrimination and State-hood in Oklahoma." Chronicles of Oklahoma 49 (Autumn, 1971):340-378.

Moon, Frederick Douglas. "Accredited Secondary Schools for Negroes in Oklahoma." Master's thesis, U. of Chicago, 1938.

National Urban League. A Study of the Social and Econcomic Conditions of the Negro Popula-tion of Oklahoma City, Oklahoma, 1945.

Oklahoma State Advisory Committee. Equal Employment Opportunity in Lawton, Oklahoma. Washington, DC: U.S. Commission on Civil Rights, S, 1968.

Rader, Brian F. The Political Outsiders: Blacks and Indians in a Rural Oklahoma County. Palo Alto, CA: R & E Research Associates, 1978.

Roberts, Charles S. "Negro Education in Oklahoma; Legal Status and Current Practice." Master's thesis, U. of Colorado, 1930.

Saxe, Allan A. "Protest and Reform: The Desegregation of Oklahoma City." Doctoral dissertation, U. of Oklahoma, 1969. Univ. Microfilms Order No. 69-18464.

Smallwood, James (ed.). And Gladly Teach. Reminiscences of Teachers from Frontier Dugout to Modern Module. Norman: U. of Oklahoma Press, 1976.

Smith, C. Calvin. "The Oppressed Oppressors: Negro Slavery Among the Choctaw Indians of Oklahoma." Red River Valley Historical Review 2(Summer, 1975).

Stephens, Louise Carolyn. "The Urban League of Oklahoma City, Oklahoma." Doctoral dissertation, U. of Oklahoma, 1957. Univ. Microfilms Order No. 00-24427.

Strong, Evelyn Richardson. "Historical Development of the Oklahoma Association of Negro Teachers: A Study in Social Change, 1893-1958." Doctoral dissertation, U. of Oklahoma, 1961. Univ. Microfilms Order No. 61-05206.

Strong, Willa Allegra. "The Origin, Development, and Currrent Status of the Oklahoma Federation of Colored Women's Clubs." Doctoral dissertation, U. of Oklahoma, n.d.

Tolson, Arthur L. The Black Oklahomans. A History: 1541-1972. Ann Arbor, MI: Edwards, 1974.

_____. "Black Towns in Oklahoma." The Black Scholar, Ap, 1970.

_____. "The Negro in Oklahoma Territory, 1889-1907: A Study in Racial Discrimination." Doctoral dissertation, U. of Oklahoma, 1966. Univ. Microfilms Order No. 66-11792.

_____. "Oklahoma's All-Black State Movement: 1889-1907." Journal of Social and Behavioral Sciences 18(Fall-Winter, 1971-1972):35-41.

Twine, W. H. "Oklahoma--The Land of the Fair God." Messenger 8(My, 1926):147-148.

U.S. Commission on Civil Rights, Oklahoma Advisory Committee. School Desegregation in Tulsa. Washington, DC: The Commission, 1977.

Washington, National Jason. Historical Development of the Negro in Oklahoma. Tulsa, OK: Dexter Publishing Company, 1948.

West, Hollie I. "Boley, Oklahoma: Once a Town of Hope, Now a Fading Dream." Washington Post, F 9, 1975.

Willson, Walt. "Freedmen in Indian Territory During Reconstruction." Chronicles of Oklahoma 49(Summer, 1971):230-244.

Wilson, Raleigh. "Evidences of Prejudices and Discrimination in Certain Aspects of the Relations between the Negroes and the Five Civilized Tribes of Indians, 1865-1900." Quarterly Review of Higher Education Among Negroes 22(Ap, 1954):69-76.

X, Theodore G. "Busing Upsets Oklahoma City." Muhammad Speaks, O 6, 1972.

_____. "Integration's 'Home' Gets First Black School Board Pres[ident]." Muhammad Speaks, Mr 8, 1974. [Oklahoma City]

17X, Samuel. "Black Parents Tell Grievances Against Oklahoma City Schools." Muhammad Speaks, Ja 15, 1971.

_____. "Oklahoma Woman Shoots Principal." Muhammad Speaks, Ap 23, 1971. [Idabelle]

Young, William M. The Paperback Survey--A Model for Urban Change. Paterson, NJ: Paterson State College, 1970. [Black and white teenagers in Tulsa]

                              Oregon

Boyd, G. F. "The Levels of Aspiration of White and Negro Children in a Non-Segregated Elementary School." Journal of Social Psychology, vol. 36, 1952. [Portland]

Clark, Malcolm, Jr. "The Bigot Disclosed: 90 Years of Nativism." Oregon Historical Quarterly 75(Je, 1974). [Esp. Ku Klux Klan in the 1920's]

Collins, Huntly. "Nobody Rushes to Back Jefferson High Busing Plan." Portland Oregonian, Jl 24, 1977.

Committee on Race Relations. "The Negro in Portland." Portland City Club Bulletin 26 (1945).

Committee on Race and Education. Race and Equal Educational Opportunity in Portland's Public Schools. Portland, OR: Board of Education, O 29, 1964.

Compensatory Education Section. Racial and Ethnic Survey. 5th, 1974-75. Salem, OR, 1975.

Davis, Lenwood G. "Sources for History of Blacks in Oregon." Oregon Historical Quarterly 73(S, 1972).

DeBerry, Clyde E. "Black Power and Black Population: A Dilemma." Integrated Education, Mr-Ap, 1969, pp. 33-39.

DeBerry, Clyde E., Fashing, Joseph, and Harris, Calvin. "Black Power and Black Population: A Dilemma." Journal of Negro Education, Winter, 1969. [Eugene]

Extension Service. Income and Poverty Data for Racial Groups: A Compilation for Oregon Census County Divisions. Corvallis: Oregon State U., 1972.

Farner, Frank. Economic, Social, and Demographic Characteristics of Oregon School Districts and Their Relationship to District Financial Practices. Eugene, OR: U. or Oregon, Bureau of Educational Research and Service, Ap, 1966, 172 pp. ERIC ED 043 928.

Hill, Daniel Grafton. "The Negro as a Political and Social Issue in the Oregon Country." Journal of Negro History 33 (1948):130-145.

_____. "The Negro in Oregon." Master's thesis, U. of Oregon, 1932.

Hogg, Thomas C. "Black Man in White Town." Pacific Northwest Quarterly, Ja, 1972. [Eugene, 1962-1963]

_____. "Negroes and Their Institutions in Oregon." Phylon 30(1969):272-285.

Hurst, Julius. "Oregon Panthers Stand Off Pigs." Black Panthers, Mr 31, 1969. [Eugene]

John Adams High School. Third Year Report, 1971-1972. Portland, OR: John Adams High School, Jl 1, 1972.

Keller, Bill. "Blanchard After Four Years: What Is He Talking About?" Portland Oregonian, Je 24, 1973. [Robert W. Blanchard, Supt. of Schools, Portland]

Lickteig, M. J. "Comparison of Book Selection Preferences of Inner-City and Suburban Fourth- and Sixth-Grades." Doctoral dissertation, U. of Oregon, 1971.

Oregon State Department of Education. Equal Opportunities in Education: Instruction and Employment. A Suggested Policy Guide for School Districts, Ja, 1977. ERIC ED 136 326.

_____. Racial and Ethnic Survey '75-'76, 1976. ERIC ED 137 024. [State survey]

Rist, Ray C. "Busing White Children Into Black Schools: A Study in Controversy." Integrated Education 12(Jl-Ag, 1974):13-18. [Portland]

_____. The Invisible Children. School Integration in American Society. Cambridge, MA: Harvard U. Press, 1978. [Portland]

Schwartz, Robert B. and others. The Clinical School Program, John Adams High School. Eugene, OR: School of Education, U. of Oregon, 1969.

Schwartz, Robert B., Dobbins, Allen L., Parker, John L., Fletcher, Jerry L., and Wertheimer, Patricia A. [Five articles on John Adams High School, Portland, Oregon] Phi Delta Kappan 52(My, 1971):515-530.

Second Year Report 1970-1971. John Adams High School, Portland, Oregon, July 1, 1971. Portland, OR: Board of Education, Jl 1, 1971.

Staley, Gerald J. Volunteer Aides in Public Schools: Policies and Procedures in Oregon and Washington. Eugene, OR: Oregon School Study Council, 1970.

Talney, Mark A. "Race and Education [Portland]." Christian Century, D 16, 1964.

Tyack, David. "Bureaucracy and the Common School: The Example of Portland, Oregon, 1851-1913." American Quarterly 19(Fall, 1967):475-498.

U.S. Congress, 93rd, 2nd session, Senate, Committee on Labor and Public Welfare, Subcommittee on Labor. Agricultural Child Labor Provisions of FLSA, 1974. Hearing... Washington, DC: GPO, 1975. [Oregon]

Pennsylvania

A Brief Sketch of the Schools for the Black People and Their Descendants, Established by the Society of Friends, etc. Philadelphia, PA: n.p., 1824.

A Plan for Quality Desegregated Education for Harrisburg City School District. Philadelphia, PA: Research for Better Schools, Inc., Ap 29, 1970, 31 pp. ERIC ED 041 978.

A Summary of Enrollments in Public Schools of Pennsylvania. Enrollments by Intermediate Unit, Administrative Unit, Grade, Race. Harrisburg, PA: Bureau of Educational Statistics, 1971.

Abraham, Roger D. Deep Down in the Jungle: Negro Narrative Folklore from the Streets of Philadelphia. Hatboro, PA: Folklore Associates, 1964.

Adam, Ruth. "Ethnic Is Beautiful." New Society 19(F 24, 1972):384-385. [Ethnic Heritage Affairs Institute, Philadelphia]

Allen, Charles. "A Study of the Street Academy Program in Pittsburgh." Doctoral dissertation, U. of Pittsburgh, 1970. Univ. Microfilms Order No. 71-7983.

Anderson, Mable B. "Child-rearing Practices of Negro Migrant Mothers in Three Pennsylvania Counties." Doctoral dissertation, Pennsylvania State U., 1965. Univ. Microfilms Order No. 65-14731.

Aurbach, Herbert A. The Status of Education of Negroes in Pittsburgh. Pittsburgh, PA: City of Pittsburgh Commisssion on Human Relations, Ap, 1960.

Bacon, Benjamin. Statistics of the Colored People of Philadelphia. 2nd ed. revised. Philadelphia, PA: n.p., 1859.

Bauman, John F. "Black Slums/Black Projects: The New Deal and Negro Housing in Philadelphia." Pennsylvania History 41 (Jl, 1974).

Becker, Gayle. "Schools Integrate...Voluntarily." Philadelphia Bulletin, Mr 19, 1978. [West Chester Area School District]

Beers, Joan S., and Reardon, Francis J. "Racial Balancing in Harrisburg." Integrateduction 12(S-O, 1974):35-38.

Benic, Thomas P. "Desegregation...A Mixed Bag in Harrisburg." Pittsburgh Post-Gazette, My 16, 1977.

Benjamin, Philip S. The Philadelphia Quakers in the Industrial Age. Philadelphia: Temple U. Press, 1976.

Berson, Leonora E. The Case Study of a Riot: The Philadelphia Story. New York: Institute of Human Relations Press, 1966. [An account of a riot in Philadelphia, Ag, 1964]

Betts, Francis M. III. Evaluation of Innovative Program in Urban Education. A Case Study. The West Philadelphia Community Free School. Part II. Philadelphia: U. of Pennsylvania, F, 1972.

Binzen, Peter. "The Other Kensington." New Society, O 8, 1970. [Penn Treaty Junior High School, Philadelphia]

_____. "Philadelphia. Politics Invades the Schools." Saturday Review 55(F 5, 1972): 44-49.

_____. "Philadelphia's Negroes Challenge a Will." Reporter, O 21, 1965. [Girard College]

_____. Whitetown, U.S.A. New York: Random House, 1970. [Philadelphia]

Black Panther Party. Pennsylvania Chapter. "Support Reverend Nichols! The Man Who Can't Be Controlled." Black Panther, D 18, 1971. [Rev. Henry Nichols, former member of Philadelphia Board of Education]

Blockson, Charles L. Pennsylvania's Black History. Philadelphia: Portfolio Associates, 1975.

Bodnar, John E. "The Impact of the 'New Immigration' on the Black Worker, Steelton, Pennsylvania, 1880-1920." Labor History 17 (Spring, 1976).

_____. "Peter C. Blackwell and the Negro Community of Steelton, 1880-1920." Pennsylvania Magazine of History and Biography, Ap, 1973.

_____ (ed.). The Ethnic Experience in Pennsylvania. Lewisburg, PA: Bucknell U. Press, 1973.

Boyer, Philip A. The Adjustment of a School to Individual and Community Needs. Philadelphia, PA: U. of Pennsylvania, 1920. [Stanton Arthur School, Philadelphia]

Bremer, John. "School Is Not a Place But an Activity: Philadelphia's Parkway Program" (interview). Media and Methods-Explorations in Education 6(1970):30-34, 68, and 70.

Bremer, John, and von Moschzisher, Michael. The School Without Walls: Philadelphia's Parkway Program. New York: Holt, Rinehart & Winston, 1972.

Brodhead, John H. "The Status of the Negro in the Philadelphia Senior High Schools with Particular Reference to His Social and Economic Condition." Doctoral dissertation, Temple U., 1937.

Brouwer, Merle Gerald. "The Negro As a Slave and As a Free Black in Colonial Pennsylvania." Doctoral dissertation, Wayne State U., 1973.

Brown, Ira V. The Negro in Pennsylvania History. University Park, PA: Pennsylvania Historical Association, 1970.

Brown, William. "Wister Mother Cites Years of Continuous Hassle with Schools." Germantown Courier, F 26, 1969.

Bruce, George. "Philadelphia Story: The Tasker Homes." America, Je 26, 1971.

Bullock, Doris Powers. "A Day Revisited." AE: About Education, Fall, 1968. [Black student movement in Philadelphia]

_____. "Ben Franklin High Comes to Life." AE: About Education, Spring, 1969. [Philadelphia]

Byington, Margaret F. Homestead, The Households of a Mill Town. New York: n.p., 1910 [Allegheny County, 1907-1908]

Campaglia, Muriel. "Schools: Pittsburgh's Much Heralded Educational Superplan Is Beset by Rising Costs and Raging Public Dissent." City, Ag, 1969.

Carter-Wooby, Amelia R. "Memoirs of an Inner-City Schoolteacher." Changing Education 6 (Summer, 1974):17-22. [Simon Gratz High School, Philadelphia]

Center for Urban Education, New York, New York. Reorganizing the Harrisburg Public Schools. A Plan for Quality Desegregated Education. April 29, 1970. Reprinted in U.S. Congress, 92nd, 1st session, Senate, Select Committee on Equal Educational Opportunity, Equal Educational Opportunity-1971. Part 14-State Role in School Desegregation: Pennsylvania, pp. 6222-6250. Washington, DC: GPO, 1971.

"Children of Africa School...Education in Our Own Hands." African World, Ag 19, 1972. [Children of Africa School, Harrisburg]

"The Colored People of Philadelphia." Douglass' Monthly, O, 1860.

Commonwealth of Pennsylvania. Department of Welfare. Negro Survey of Pennsylvania. Harrisburg, PA: Department of Welfare, 1928.

Corner, George W. "The Black Coalition: An Experiment in Racial Cooperation, Philadelphia, 1968." Proceedings of the American Philosophical Society 120(Je, 1976):178-186.

Cottle, Thomas J. "Social Class, College, and a Dream Deferred." Saturday Review, Ja 24, 1970. [Woodrow Wilson High School, Bristol Township]

_____. "Strategy for Change." Saturday Review, S 20, 1969. [Bristol Township]

Countryman, Joan. "Philadelphia: Planning for Black Education." Viet-Report, Summer, 1968.

Countryman, Peter. "The Philadelphia Experiment." Integrated Education, Ja, 1963.

Covington, Floyd C. "Occupational Choices in Relation to Economic Opportunities of Negro Youth in Pittsburgh." Curriculum Study and Educational Research Bulletin (Pittsburgh, PA) 3(Ja-F, 1929):133-134.

Cox, Donald William. The City As a Schoolhouse. Judson Press, 1972. [Parkway Program, Philadelphia]

_____. "Learning on the Road." Saturday Review, My 17, 1969. [Parkway Project, Philadelphia]

Cutler, William W. III. "A Preliminary Look At the School house. The Philadelphia Story, 1870-1920." Urban Education 8(Ja, 1974): 381-399.

Cybriwsky, Roman A. "Social Aspects of Neighborhood Change." Annals of the Association of American Geographers 68(Mr, 1978):17-33. [Philadelphia]

Dahlgren, Carl. "One School That Tried." New America, My 15, 1968. [Gratz High School, Philadelphia]

Darden, Joe Turner. Afro-Americans in Pittsburgh. The Residential Segregation of a People. Lexington, MA: Lexington Books, 1973.

_____. "The Quality of Life in a Black Ghetto: A Geographic View." Pennsylvania Geographer 12(1974):3-8. [Pittsburgh]

_____. "Residential Segregation of Afro-Americans in Pittsburgh, 1960-1970." Journal of Social and Behavioral Sciences 20 (Winter, 1974):72-77.

_____. "The Spatial Dynamics of Residential Segregation of Afro-Americans in Pittsburgh." Doctoral dissertation, U. of Pittsburgh, 1972. Univ. Microfilms Order No. 72-22455.

Davis, Allen, and Haller, Mark (eds.). The People of Philadelphia. A History of Ethnic Groups and Lower Class Life, 1790-1940. Philadelphia, PA: Temple U. Press, 1973.

Davis, Katherine B. "Condition of the Negro in Philadelphia." Journal of Political Economy 8(1900):248-260.

De Lone, Richard. "Philadelphia Decentralizes: Ready, Set, Go?" AE: About Education, Spring, 1969.

Dickerson, G. Edward, and Imes, William Lloyd. "The Cheyney Training School." Crisis, My, 1923.

Dilworth, Richardson. "Needed: Integrated Schools." American School Board Journal, J1, 1966.

Dimmick, E. A. "Occupational Survey of Colored Boys of Pittsburgh." University of Pittsburgh School of Edcuational Journal 5(Je, 1930):138-147.

Donoho, William T., Jr., and Dentler, Robert A. "Busing Toward Excellence: The Quest for Quality Desegregated Education in Harrisburg." Urban Review 6(S-O, 1972):31-34.

Douglass, Frederick. "A Recent Visit to Philadelphia." Douglass' Monthly, F, 1862.

Draphin, Michael K. "An Elusive Goal. Pittsburgh's Try Shows That School Integration in North Will Be Hard." Wall Street Journal, Je 28, 1971.

Dubin, Murray. "Gypsies Taking 3 Rs Seriously." Philadelphia Inquirer, Ap 11, 1976.

Du Bois, W. E. B. "How Negroes Have Taken Advantage of Educational Opportunities Offered by Friends." Journal of Negro Education, 1938. [Deals with Quakers]

_____. The Philadelphia Negro. Philadelphia, PA: Publishers for the University, 1899.

Elazar, Danie., and Friedman, Murray. Moving Up. Ethnic Succession in America. With a Case History of the Philadelphia School System. New York: Institute on Pluralism and Group Idenity, 1976.

Epstein, A. The Negroes of Pittsburgh, Pa. Pittsburgh: U. of Pittsburgh, 1918.

Eriksen, Aase, and Messina, Judith. "The Dynamics of Leadership in an Informal School." Journal of Research and Development in Education 5(Spring, 1972):29-39. [West Philadelphia Community Free School]

Ershkowitz, Miriam, and Zikmund, Joseph (eds.). Black Politics in Philadelphia. New York: Basic Books, 1972.

Faulk, Harry R. "Desegregation in McKeesport." Integrated Education (Ja-F, 1972):35-38.

Feldberg, Michael. The Philadelphia Riots of 1844: A Study of Ethnic Conflict. Westport, CT: Greenwood, 1975.

Feldman, Harold. "Learning Under Penalty of Death." AE: About Education, Spring, 1968. [Philadelphia]

Ferber, Michael. "Mister Charlie's Law and Order." Liberation, S, 1964. [Chester]

Fiedler, Byron. "The Pittsburgh School Story: A City's Quest for Racial Equality." NEA Journal, My, 1966.

Foley, Fred J. "The Failure of Reform: Community Control and the Philadelphia Public Schools." Urban Education 10(Ja, 1976): 389-414.

Foner, Philip S. "The Battle to End Discrimination Against Negroes on Philadelphia Streetcars: (Part I) Background and Beginning of the Battle." Pennsylvania History 40(Jl, 1973).

_____. "The Battle to End Discrimination Against Negroes on Philadelphia Streetcars: (Part II) The Victory." Pennsylvania History 40(O, 1973).

"[Marcus] Foster's Travels. A Twenty Year Adventure in the Philadelphia Schools." AE: About Education, Fall, 1968. [A black principal in Philadelphia]

Franklin, Stephen. "Magnet Schools Fail." Philadelphia Bulletin, F 27, 1977.

_____. "Magnet Schools Fail in Philadelphia." Integrateducation 15(N-D, 1977):95-96.

Franklin, Vincent Paul. "Educating an Urban Black Community: The Case of Philadelphia, 1900-1950." Doctoral dissertation, U. of Chicago, 1975.

Golab, Caroline. "The Polish Communities of Philadelphia, 1870-1920: Immigrant Distribution and Adaptation in Urban America." Doctoral dissertation, U. of Pennsylvania, 1971.

Gold, Steve. "Unlearning White Racism." Liberation, Mr-Ap, 1969. [Philadelphia]

Goldberg, Milton. Follow Through in Philadelphia, Ap, 1973. ERIC ED 127 016.

Gordon, Edmund W. and others. Report of the Philadelphia School District Title I Evaluation and Review Committee: 1973/74 Academic School Year, 1974. ERIC ED 102 257.

Gottlieb, Peter. "Making Their Own Way: Southern Blacks' Migration to Pittsburgh, 1916-1930." Doctoral dissertation, U. of Pittsburgh, 1977.

_____. "Migration and Jobs: The New Black Workers in Pittsburgh, 1916-1930." Western Pennsylvania Hist. Mag. 61(Ja, 1978):1-15.

Gray, Farnum. "In Philadelphia, the Same Issues and a Turnabout." Southern Education Report, Ap, 1968. [Pennsylvania Advancement School in Philadelphia]

Greene, Victor R. Slavic Community on Strike: Immigrant Labor in Pennsylvania Anthracite. Notre Dame, IN: Notre Dame U. Press, 1968.

Guttentag, Jack M. "Racial Integration and Home Prices: The Case of West Mt. Airy [Pa.]." Wharton Quarterly 4(Spring, 1970): 21-23, 30. [Germantown]

Heavner, Robert O. "Indentured Servitude: The Philadelphia Market, 1771-1773." Journal of Economic History 38(S, 1978):701-713. [Education as one factor in determinining price of indentured servants]

Hecht, Edward. "Guidance Program for a Ghetto School." Personnel and Guidance Journal 48 (My, 1979):731-738. [Simon Gratz High School, Philadelphia]

Hershberg, Theodore. "Free Blacks in Antebellum Philadelphia: A Study of Ex-Slaves, Freeborn, and Socioeconomic Decline." Journal of Social History 5(Winter, 1971-1972):183-209.

_____. "Free-Born and Slave-Born Blacks in Antebellum Philadelphia." In Race and Slavery in the Western Hemisphere: Quantitative Studies, pp. 395-426. Edited by Stanley L. Engerman and Eugene D. Genovese. Princeton, NJ: Princeton U. Press, 1975.

Hetrick, William R. "A Study of the Evidences of Discrimination Against Negroes in Indiana, Pennsylvania." Master's thesis, Indiana State College, PA, 1962.

Henmann, Leonard Franklin. "The Definition and Analysis of Stable Racial Integration: The Case of West Mt. Airy, Philadelphia." Doctoral dissertation, U. of Pennsylvania, 1973.

Higgins, James. "Listen to the Teacher. An Interview with Celia Pincus." AE: About Education, Spring, 1969. [Philadelphia]

Hilles, H. S., Jr., and Wolcott, W. B., Jr. "Future for Girard's Dream." Villanova Law Review, Summer, 1965. [Girard College, Philadelphia]

Iannotta, Dominic F. "School Disruption: Oliver High School--A Case Study." Doctoral dissertation, Carnegie Mellon U., 1974. Univ. Microfilms Order No. 74-26,646.

Jirak, Ivan L. "Cool, One School." Bulletin of the NASSP 55(N, 1971):99-108. [Oliver High School, Pittsburgh]

Johnson, Leon. "Black Migration, Spatial Organization and Perception and Philadelphia's Urban Environment, 1638-1930." Master's thesis, U. of Washington, 1973.

Johnson, William H. "Institute for Colored Youth." Pennsylvania School Journal, Ja, 1857.

Kemp, Edith S. Survey of Philadelphia High School Dropouts, Ja, 1976. ERIC ED 132 695.

Klaw, Spencer. "'Old Scratchhead' Wakes Up in Chester, Pennsylvania." Reporter, Je 18, 1964.

Kristufek, Richard. "The Immigrant and the Pittsburgh Public Schools: 1870-1940." Doctoral dissertation, U. of Pittsburgh, 1975. Univ. Microfilms Order No. 76-5453.

Krogman, Wilton M. Growth of Head, Face, Trunk, and Limbs in Philadelphia White and Negro Children of Elementary and High School Age. Monographs of the Society for Research on Child Development 35(My, 1970):1-80.

Laird, M. A., and Weeks, G. J. The Effect of Busing on Achievement in Reading and Arithmetic in Three Philadelphia Schools. Philadelphia, PA: School Board, 1966.

Lalli, Michael, and Savitz, Leonard D. "The Fear of Crime in the School Enterprise and Its Consequences." Education and Urban Society 8(Ag, 1976):401-416. [Philadelphia]

Lee, Everett S. "Negro Intelligence and Selective Migration: A Philadelphia Test of the Kineberg Hypothesis." American Sociological Review, Ap, 1951.

Lee, George A. "Negroes in a Medium-Sized Metropolis: Allentown, Pennsylvania--A Case Study." Journal of Negro Education 37 (1968):397-405.

Lee, William Vernon. "Each Year I am Learning Less and Less." Integrated Education 12 (Ja-Ap, 1974):29. [Philadelphia]

Lewis, Claude and others. "Some Success But Not Enough Power." Black Enterprise 7 (N, 1976). [First of several articles on blacks in Philadelphia]

Ley, David F. The Black Inner City as Frontier Outpost: Images and Behavior of a Philadelphia Neighborhood. Washington, DC: Association of American Geographers, 1974.

Livingston, Tom. "Priest Seeks Gifts for Gifted Blacks." Philadelphia Daily News, My 24, 1976. [Mercy Interparochial Education Center, Philadelphia]

Lloyd, Elizabeth. "Race Hatred in Pennsylvania." Friends' Intelligencer, Ag 19, 1911.

Lockhart, Lillie M. "An Analysis of Variables Which Tend To Be Associated with Race Related Acts of Violence at Specific Schools in Pittsburgh, Pennsylvania from 1967-1970." Doctoral dissertation, U. of Pittsburgh, 1972.

Loomis, Charles P., and Jantzen, Carl R. "Boundary Maintenance vs. Systematic Linkage in School Integration: The Case of the Amish in the United States." Journal of the Pakistan Academy for Rural Development (Comilla), O, 1962.

Lukeshus, Anne M. Follow Through Pupil Absence Rates in Philadelphia, 1974-1975, Je, 1976. ERIC ED 143 435.

MacConnell, John C. "Charity Education in Colonial Pennsylvania." Doctoral dissertation, Rutgers-The State U., 1968. Univ. Microfilms Order No. 69-9296.

McIlvane, Donald W. "Racial Balance in Catholic Schools." Community, My, 1966. [Pittsburgh]

McKinney, Ernest Rice. "These 'Colored' United States: Pennsylvania: A Tale of Two Cities." Messenger 5(My, 1923):692-694.

McPherson, Donald S. "The Fight against Free Schools in Pennsylvania: Popular Opposition to the Common School System, 1834-1974." Doctoral dissertation, U. of Pittsburgh, 1977.

McPherson, Philip E. "Coordination of Efforts for the Improvement of Race Relations in the Pittsburgh Public Schools." Doctoral dissertation, Harvard U., 1966.

Mackey, Louis H. "The Pennsylvania Human Relations Commission and Desegregation in the Public Schools of Pennsylvania 1961-1978." Doctoral dissertation, U. of Pittsburgh, 1978. Univ. Microfilms Order No. 7902715.

"Many Negroes Receiving Appointments in Philadelphia Schools." Opportunity, N, 1942.

Marcus, Caren, and Rankin, Edwina. "Segregation Seesaw." Pittsburgh Press, Je 4-10, 1978. [Series of seven articles on school segregation in Pittsburgh]

"Mark Shedd: Rizzo's First Casualty." Washington Post, D 12, 1971. [Philadelphia]

Meek, Sylvia. "An Interview with Stanley Branche." Integrated Education, F-Mr, 1965. [Chester]

_____. "Philadelphia Works for Integration." Integrated Education, Ap-My, 1964.

Meier, Deborah. "A Report from Philadelphia: Head Start or Dead End." Dissent, S-O, 1966.

Middleman, Ruth R. "On Being a Whitey in the Midst of a Racial Crisis." Children, My-Je, 1969. [Philadelphia]

Miller, E. Willard. Socioeconomic Patterns of Pennsylvania: An Atlas. Harrisburg, PA: State Department of Commerce, 1975.

Moran, Alonzo G. "Distribution of the Negro Population in Pittsburgh, 1910-1930." Master's thesis, U. of Pittsburgh, 1935.

Moran, Alonzo G., and Stephen, F. F. "The Negro Population in Pittsburgh and Alleghany County." Social Research Bulletin 1 (Ap 20, 1933):1-5.

Motz, Annabelle B., and Weber, George H. "On Becoming a Dropout." Phylon, Summer, 1969. [Philadelphia]

Muller, Peter O. and others. Metropolitan Philadelphia: A Study of Conflicts and Social Cleavages. Cambridge, MA: Ballinger, 1976.

Nash, Gary B. "Slaves and Slaveowners in Colonial Philadelphia." William and Mary Quarterly 30(Ap, 1973).

_____. "Up From the Bottom in Franklin's Philadelphia." Past and Present 77(N, 1977): 57-83

Neal, Ronald V. "Teacher Strikes Are Against Boards of Education, Not Citizens." Muhammad Speaks, N 6, 1970. [About Alonso Mathews, Jr., Philadelphia school teacher]

Needles, Edward. Ten Years' Progress: A Comparison of the State and Condition of the Colored People in the City and County of Philadelphia from 1838 to 1847. Philadelphia, PA: n.p., 1849.

Nelson, H. Viscount, Jr. Negro Education and the Dilemmas of Race and Class, O, 1974. ERIC ED 121 901. [Philadelphia during the 1930's]

_____. The Philadelphia N.A.A.C.P.: Epitome of Middle Class Consciousness. Los Angeles: Center for Afro-American Studies, U. of California, 1972.

_____. "Race and Class Consciousness of Philadelphia Negroes with Special Emphasis on the Years between 1927 and 1940." Doctoral dissertation, U. of Pennsylvania, 1969.

North City Area Wide Council, Inc. and Others. "Maximum Feasible Manipulation." Public Administration Review 32(S, 1972):377-408. [A symposium on citizen participation in Philadelphia]

Oakes, Helen. The School District of Philadelphia. A Critical Analysis, S, 1968. Published by the author, 6400 Drexel Road, Philadelphia, PA 19151.

Oblinger, Carl D. Freedoms Foundations: Black Communities in Southeastern Pennsylvania Towns, 1780-1860. Maryville, MO: Northwest Missouri State U., 1972.

Odell, William R. Educational Survey Report for the Philadelphia Board of Public Education, February 1, 1965. The Board of Public Education, Parkway at Twenty-first Street, Philadelphia, PA.

Odum, Howard W. "Negro Children in the Public Schools of Philadelphia." Annals, S, 1913.

_____. Negro Children in the Public Schools of Philadelphia. Philadelphia: Bureau of Municipal Research, 1913.

Olson, Jerry C. Making Desegregation Work, F 23, 1976. ERIC ED 126 190. [Pittsburgh]

Organization for Social and Technical Innovation. Philadelphia's Parkway Program: An Evaluation, Ap 3, 1972. Organization for Social and Technical Innovation, 55 Chapel Street, Newton, MA 02158.

Osborn, Michelle. "Philadelphia: One Community in Crisis." Christian Century, F 14, 1968. [The N 17, 1967, violence around the school issue]

Overbrook Cluster Parent Survey 1969. A Detailed Report. Philadelphia School District, PA. Office of Research and Evaluation, My, 1969, 121 pp. ERIC ED 031 798. Available from Office of Informational Services, Room 224, The School District of Philadelphia, 21st Street South of the Parkway, Philadelphia, PA 19103.

Overbrook Cluster Parent Survey 1969, Summary Brochure. Philadelphia School District, PA. Office of Research and Evaluation, Ap, 1969, 30 pp. ERIC Ed 031 817. Available from Office of Informational Services, Room 224, The School District of Philadelphia, 21st Street South of the Parkway, Philadelphia, PA 19103.

Pennington, Edgar L. "The Work of the Bray Associates in Pennsylvania." *Pennsylvania Magazine of History and Biography* 58(1934): 1-25.

Pennsylvania Abolition Society. *The Present State and Condition of the Free People of Color of the City of Philadelphia and Adjoining Districts*. Philadelphia, PA, 1838.

Pennsylvania Advancement School: Report on the First Two Years. Philadelphia, PA: Pennsylvania Advancement School, Jl, 1969, 84 pp. ERIC ED 041 964.

Pennsylvania Human Relations Commission. "The Chester Case." *Integrated Education*, F-Mr, 1965.

_____. *Investigatory Hearing. Report and Recommendations. Aliquippa*. Harrisburg, PA: The Commission, My, 1971.

_____. "Pennsylvania's Affirmative Integration Policy." *Integrated Education*, Ag-S, 1964.

_____. *Sixth Survey of Non-White Employes in State Government in Pennsylvania*. Harrisburg, PA: Commonwealth of Pennsylvania and the Commission, 1970.

_____. *A Survey of the Educational Experience of Negro Students in the Secondary Schools of West Chester* Harrisburg, PA: Pennsylvania Human Relations Commission, My, 1965.

_____. *A Survey of the Educational Experience of Negro Students in the Secondary Schools in McKeesport*. Harrisburg, PA: Pennsylvania Human Relations Commission, N, 1966.

Pennsylvania Human Relations Commission, and Department of Public Instruction. "Recommended Elements of a School Desegregation Plan." *Integrated Education*, N-D, 1968, pp. 37-40.

Pennsylvania Supreme Court (opinion). "School Board May Bus for Racial Balance." *Integrated Education* 10(Jl-Ag, 1972):47-54. [Harrisburg]

Perkins, Linda M. "Fanny Jackson Coppin and the Institute for Colored Youth: A Model of Nineteenth Century Black Female Educational and Community Leadership, 1837-1902." Doctoral dissertation, U. of Illinois, 1978. Univ. Microfilms Order No. 7821222. [Philadelphia]

Philadelphia Urban League. *A Proposal for Integrating Philadelphia Public Schools*. Philadelphia: Urban League, Ag, 1964.

_____. *A Statement on the Report of the Task Forces*. Philadelphia: Philadelphia Urban League, Ja 21, 1966.

Porch, Marvin E. "The Main Line Negro: A Social, Economic, and Educational Survey." Doctoral dissertation, Temple U., 1935.

Porter, David H. "Is Twice as Fast, Fast Enough for Desegregation in Harrisburg?" *Pennsylvania Education* 3(N-D, 1971):22-29.

Price, Edward J., Jr. "The Black Voting Rights Issue in Pennsylvania, 1780-1900." *Pennsylvania Magazine of History and Biography* 100(Jl, 1976):356-373.

_____. "Let the Law Be Just: The Quest for Racial Equality in Pennsylvania, 1780-1915." Doctoral dissertation, Pennsylvania State U., 1973.

_____. "School Segregation in Nineteenth-Century Pennsylvania." *Pennsylvania History* 43(Ap, 1976):121-137.

Prymes, Ruth W. "Manpower and Retraining: How It Works in Philadelphia." *Studies on the Left*, Spring, 1965.

Purcell, Sr. Mary Daniel. "Contributions to Education of the Catholic School of the Scranton Diocese." Doctoral dissertation, Fordham U., 1935.

The Quest for Racial Equality in the Pittsburgh Public Schools, 1965. Board of Public Education, 341 South Bellefield Avenue, Pittsburgh, PA 15213.

Report of the Commission on Decentralization and Community Participation; A Multiple Option Approach to School-Community Participation, Jl 27, 1970. ERIC ED 042 843.

Report of the Special Committee on Nondiscrimination of the Board of Public Education of Philadelphia, Pennsylvania, Jl 23, 1964.

Report of the Task Forces to the Incoming Board of Education, N 8, 1965. Office of Informational Services, School District of Philadelphia, Parkway at Twenty-First Street, Philadelphia, PA 19103.

Resnik, Henry S. "The Shedd Revolution." *Urban Review*, Ja, 1969. [Philadelphia]

_____. *Turning On the System: War in the Philadelphia Public Schools*. New York: Pantheon, 1970.

Resource Management Corporation. [Case History of ESAP in Harrisburg, Pa.] *Evaluation of the Emergency School Assistance Program*, Vol. III, Appendix L., F 15, 1972. ERIC ED 058 470.

Roberts, Wallace. "Can Urban Schools Be Reformed?" *Saturday Review*, My 17, 1969. [Philadelphia]

Rosenbloom, Miriam. "An Outline of the History of the Negro in the Pittsburgh Area." Master's thesis, U. of Pittsburgh, 1945.

St. Henry, Sister M. "Nativism in Pennsylvania with Particular Regard to Its Effect on Politics and Education--1840-1860." American Catholic Historical Society Records 47(1936):5-47.

Sala, Frank C. "Implementation and Evaluation of a Desegregation Model for the Erie, Pennsylvania School District." Doctoral practicum paper, Nova U., 1976.

Schofield, Janet Ward, and Sagar, H. Andrew. "Social Relationships in an Integrated School." Integrateducation 15(N-D, 1977): 117-119. [Pittsburgh]

Segal, Geraldine. "Race Relations in Early Pennsylvania." Department of Sociology, U. of Pennsylvania, unpublished.

Schultz, Stephen R. "Philadelphia Aids Tomorrow's Health Professionals." Health Rights News, F, 1969.

Shanks, H. "'State Action' and the Girard Estate Case." University of Pennsylvania Law Review 105(D, 1956).

Shin, Suk-Han. "A Geographical Measurement of Residential Blight in the City of Pittsburgh, Pennsylvania." Doctoral dissertation, U. of Pittsburgh, 1975. Univ. Microfilms Order No. 76-8819.

Silcox, H. C. "a Comparative Study in School Desegregation: The Boston and Philadelphia Experience, 1800-1881." Doctoral dissertation, Temple U., 1972.

_____. "Delay and Neglect: Negro Public Education in Antebellum Philadelphia, 1800-1860." Pennsylvania Magazine of History and Biography 97(O, 1973):444-464.

_____. "In Memory of Marcus A. Foster, 1923-1973." Harvard Education Review 44(F, 1974): 1-5. [Octavius V. Catto and Marcus A. Foster, Philadelphia]

_____. "Philadelphia Negro Educator: Jacob C. White, Jr., 1837-1902." Pennsylvania Magazine of History and Biography, Ja, 1973.

Simpson, George E. "The Negro in the Philadelphia Press." Doctoral dissertation, U. of Pennsylvania, 1934. [1908-1932]

Slater, Jack. "Death of a High School." Rolling Stone, Jl 4, 1974. [Lower Merion High School, Ardmore]

Society of Friends. Statistical Inquiry into the Condition of Color of the City and Districts of Philadelphia. Philadelphia, PA, 1849.

Stalvey, Lois Mark. Getting Ready: The Education of a White Family in Inner City Schools. New York: Morrow, 1974. [Philadelphia]

State Board of Education of Pennsylvania. 1970 Subsidy Study. Harrisburg, PA: State Board of Education, N 13, 1970.

Stewart, Rowena. Blacks in Rhode Island, A Heritage Discovered. Providence: Rhode Island Black Heritage Society, 1976.

Stone, Mary Louise, and Vasser, Theodore Ramon, Jr. "A Historical and Phenomenological Study of Black Administrators in the Pittsburgh Public School System Inclusive of the Year 1950-1977." Doctoral dissertation, U. of Pittsburgh, 1978. Univ. Microfilms Order No. 7816820.

"A Suburb that Struck a Truce." Newsweek, N 15, 1971, p. 63. [Wynnefield]

Summers, Anita R., and Wolfe, Barbara L. "Do Schools Make a Difference?" American Economic Review 67(S, 1977):639-652.

_____ and _____. Equality of Educational Opportunity Quantified: A Production Function Approach. Philadelphia: Department of Research, Federal Reserve Bank of Philadelphia, 1975. [Philadelphia]

_____ and _____. Intradistrict Distribution of School Resources to the Disadvantaged: Evidence for the Courts. Philadelphia: Department of Research, Federal Reserve Bank of Philadelphia, 1974. [Philadelphia]

_____ and _____. "Philadelphia's School Resources and the Disadvantaged." Business Review (Federal Reserve Bank of Philadelphia), Mr, 1974.

_____ and _____. "Which School Resources Help Learning? Efficiency and Equity in Philadelphia Public Schools." Business Review (Federal Reserve Bank of Philadelphia), F, 1975.

The Teaching of African and Afro American History in the Philadelphia Public Schools, 1967-68 Academic Year. Philadelphia School District, PA, 1968, 14 pp. ERIC ED 027 336.

Turner, Edward Raymond. The Negro in Pennsylvania, 1619-1861. Washington, DC: American Historical Association, 1912.

Thomas, J. Alan, with Kelly, James, Maguire, Thomas, and Meyers, Russell. Financing Elementary and Secondary Education in Pennsylvania. Chicago, IL: Department of Education, U. of Chicago, O, 1970.

"The Union: Inside/Out." AE: About Education, Spring, 1969. [The Philadelphia Federation of Teachers]

U.S. Commission on Civil Rights. The Diminishing Barrier: A Report on School Desegregation... Washington, DC: GPO, D, 1972. [Harrisburg]

U.S. Commission on Civil Rights. School Desegregation in Erie, Pennsylvania. Washington,
DC: The Commission, My, 1977.

U.S. Congress, 91st, 1st session, Senate,
Committee on the Judiciary, Subcommittee on
Separation of Powers. The Philadelphia
Plan...Hearings. Washington, DC: GPO, 1970.

U.S. Congress, 92nd, 1st session, Senate, Select
Committee on Equal Educational Opportunity.
Equal Educational Opportunity-1971, Part
14-State Role in School Desegregation:
Pennsylvania. Washington, DC: GPO, 1971.

University of Pennsylvania. "Philadelphia School
Study. Racial Isolation, Achievement and
Post School Performance." Unpublished study
for U.S. Commission on Civil Rights, 1966.

Warner, Sam Bass, Jr. The Private City.
Philadelphia in Three Periods of Its
Growth. Philadelphia: U. of Pennsylvania
Press, 1968.

Washburn, David E. Ethnic Studies in Pennsylvania. Pittsburgh: U. Center for International Studies, U. of Pittsburgh, 1978.

_____. "Multi-Ethnic Education in Pennsyl-
vania." Phil Delta Kappan 59(Ap, 1978):561.

_____ (comp.). Directory of Ethnic Studies in
Pennsylvania. Pittsburgh: Center for
International Studies, U. of Pittsburgh,
1978.

Washington, Christine. "The Events of N 17,
1967." AE: About Education, Fall, 1968.
[Police violence against black high school
students in Philadelphia]

Watson, Bernard C. "Progress in Philadelphia?
It's a Beginning--Where Will It End?"
Planning Changing 1(Ap, 1970):10-20.

Weiler, Conrad. Philadelphia. Neighborhood,
Authorty, and the Urban Crisis. New York:
Praeger, 1974.

Wellenbach. Segregation 1975: Residential
Patterns and Possibilities for New Negro
Households in the Philadelphia Area, N,
1967. Philadelphia Housing Association, 1601
Walnut Street, Philadelphia, PA 19103.

Wicker, Tom. "The Myth of Busing: Some
Contradictory Evidence." New York Times,
S 19, 1976. [Harrisburg]

Wickersham, James Pyle. A History of Educa-
tion in Pennsylvania, Private and Public,
Elementary and Higher, from the Time the
Swedes Settled on the Delaware to the
Present Day. Lancaster, PA: The Author,
1886.

Wilmoth, Ann Greenwood. "Pittsburgh and the
Blacks: A Short History, 1780-1875." Doctoral dissertation, Pennsylvania State U.,
1975. Univ. Microfilms Order No. 76-06176.

Woofter, T. J., Jr. and Priest, Madge Hadley.
Negro Housing in Philadelphia. Philadelphia:
Friends' Committee on Interests of the
Colored Race, and Others, 1927.

Woolfe, Jacqueline W. "The Changing Pattern of
Residence of the Negro in Pittsburgh,
Pennsylvania, with Emphasis on the Period
1930-1960." Master's thesis, U. of Pittsburgh, 1962.

Wright, Richard Robert, with Smith, Ernest
(comp.). The Philadelphia Colored
Directory...Philadelphia, PA: Philadelphia
Colored Directory Company, 1907.

Yanofsky, Saul M. Update on PAS: A Look at the
Advancement School's Activities Since Its
Establishment in Philadelphia, September
1967 to December 1970, Ja 15, 1971. ERIC
ED 048 399.

Rhode Island

Bellemare, Marcel J. "Social Networks in an
Inner-City Neighborhood: Woonsocket, Rhode
Island." Doctoral dissertation, Catholic
U. of America, 1974. Univ. Microfilms Order
No. 75-13,948.

Blanchard, Walter J. Inner-City Providence:
Implications for Education. Attachment 2.
Providence, RI: Providence Public Schools;
Rhode Island College, 1967. ERIC ED 048 063.

Boardman, Richard P. Community Involvement in
School Desegregation. The Story of the Dr.
Martin Luther King, Jr. School. Providence,
Rhode Island. New York: Center for Urban
Education, 1971.

Curwood, Sarah T. "Mothers and Schools of the
Ghetto." Integrated Education, Ap-My, 1965.
[Providence]

Frusher, Richard Albert. "'The Conscience of
the City': Providence, Politics, and the
Providence Human Relations Commission, 1963-
1968." Doctoral dissertation, Brandeis U.,
1974.

Gabriel, Richard A. The Political Machine in
Rhode Island. Kingston, RI: Bureau of
Government Research, U. of Rhode Island,
1970.

Greene, Lorenzo J. "Protest Against Separate
Schools in Rhode Island, 1859." Midwest
Journal, Summer, 1949.

Grossman, Lawrence. "George T. Downing and Desegregation of Rhode Island Public Schools,
1855-1866." Rhode Island History 36 (N,
1977):99-105.

Holden, Anna. "The Providence Plan." Urban
Review 5(N, 1971):17-25.

_____. "Providence, Rhode Island: White and Black Power and Citywide Dispersal of Blacks in the Public Schools." In The Bus Stops Here. A Study of School Desegregation in Three Cities, pp. 127-278. New York: Agathon Press, 1974.

Lapati, Amenco D. "A History of Catholic Education in Rhode Island." Doctoral dissertation, Boston College, 1958.

Levine, Richard H. "They Made a Better School." American Education, N, 1969. [Desegregated model elementary school in Providence]

Lieberman, Myron. "The City's Schools After Decades of Indifference." Providence Sunday Journal, Ag 17, 1969. [Providence]

Menatian, Steve. "Political and Ethnic Influence as It Affects the Providence School System: A Field Study." Doctoral dissertation, Pennsylvania State U., 1972. Univ. Microfilms Order No. 73-14,024.

Menatian, Steve, and Lynch, Patrick D. "Ethnic Politics in a Northeastern Urban School System." Education and Urban Society 6(My, 1974):318-332. [Providence]

Metz, Tim. "In One Town, Busing to Integrate Schools Is a Qualified Success." Wall Street Journal, Ap 27, 1970. [Providence]

Meyer, Howard N. "Higginson and School Integration in Newport, 1865." Integrated Education, Ap-My, 1967. [Newport]

Pfautz, Harold W. "Nixon Chills the School Board." Nation, Ap 24, 1972. [Providence]

_____. "The Power Structure of the Negro Sub-Community: A Case Study and a Comparative View." Phylon 23(Summer, 1962): 156-166. [Providence]

Pfautz, Harold W. and others. "Changes in Reputed Black Community Leadership, 1962-1972: A Case Study." Social Forces 53 (Mr, 1975):460-467. [Providence]

Philo [pseud.]. "Case in Rhode Island." Douglass' Monthly, Ap, 1859.

Smith, Norman W. "The Ku Klux Klan in Rhode Island." Rhode Island History 37(My, 1978): 35-45.

Stockwell, Thomas B. A History of Public Education in Rhode Island from 1636 to 1876. Providence Board of Education, 1876.

U.S. Commission on Civil Rights. School Desegregation in Providence, Rhode Island. Washington, DC: The Commission, 1977.

Wessel, Bessie Bloom. An Ethnic Survey of Woonsocket, Rhode Island. Chicago, IL: U. of Chicago, Ap, 1941.

South Carolina

Abbott, Martin L. "The Three R's." In The Freedmen's Bureau in South Carolina, 1865-1872. Chapel Hill: U. of North Carolina Press, 1967.

"After Two Years HEW Answers." Your Schools 4 (Ag, 1973). [Dismissal of black teachers in Dillon County]

"The Allendale Plan: One Step Forward, Two Steps Backward." Your Schools, D, 1969.

"Alternatives to Suspension." Your Schools 6 (My, 1975):1-32.

Barnes, Bart. "Tattle in Bowman; Echoes of the Past." Washington Post, Jl 15, 1973.

Bass, Jack. "John C. West of South Carolina." South Today 3(Jl-Ag, 1972):9-10.

_____. "Mrs. [Victoria] De Lee and the School Board." New South 25(1970):75-76. [Harleyville-Ridgeville School District, Dorchester County]

_____. "Mass White Flight in Summerton." Race Relations Reporter 3(My, 1972):15-17.

_____. "Thurmond Thawing?" South Today 2(My, 1971).

_____. "White Violence in Lamar." New Republic 162(1970):10-12.

Batten, James K. "Title VI Disturbs the Moss of Beaufort." Reporter, Ja 12, 1967.

Billington, Ray A. (ed.). Journal of Charlotte Z. Forten. New York: Snyder, 1953. [Sea Islands]

Birnie, C. W. "The Education of the Negro in Charleston, South Carolina, before the Civil War." Journal of Negro History 12(Ja, 1927): 13-21.

"Black Day of Reckoning Comes to Fort Mill, S.C." African World, Mr 18, 1972.

"Black Political Power and Quality Education." Your Schools 2(O, 1970):1-2. [Black school board members]

"Black School Board Members Unite." Your Schools 2(F, 1971). [Formation of South Carolina Caucus of Black School Board Members, D 11, 1970]

"The Black Teacher: Another Man Done Gone." Your Schools, D, 1969.

Blanding, James D. "The Public Schools of Sumter, South Carolina." Doctoral dissertation, George Peabody College for Teachers, 1957. Univ. Microfilms Order No. 24461.

Boyd, Bob, and Sloan, Allen. "Carolinas Facing School Turmoil." Race Relations Reporter 2 (Ap 19, 1971):5-6.

Boyd, Virlyn A. Aspirations, Expectations and Attitudes of South Carolina High School Students. Clemson, SC: Agricultural Experiment Station, 1970.

Burns, E. J. "The Industrial Education Myth: Character Building at Penn School, 1900-1948." Doctoral dissertation, U. of North Carolina, 1974.

Burrows, Edward F. "The Literary Education of Negroes in Antebellum Virginia, North Carolina, South Carolina, and Georgia with Special Reference to Regulatory and Prohibitive Laws." Master's thesis, Duke U., 1940.

Burton, Orville B. "Ungrateful Servants? Edgefield's Black Reconstruction: Part 1 of the Total History of Edgefield County, South Carolina." Doctoral dissertation, Princeton U., 1976.

Burton, Vernon. "Race and Reconstruction: Edgefield County, South Carolina." Journal of Social History 12(Fall, 1978):31-56.

Busbee, Cyril B. "School Progress in South Carolina." Integrated Education 11(Mr-Ap, 1973):29-35.

Charlton, Huey E. "Stability of the Negro Family in a Southern Community." Doctoral dissertation, Temple U., 1958. Univ. Microfilms Order No. 58-1976. [Richland County]

Clancy, Paul. "Can the Southern Negro Exodus Be Stemmed?" Reporter, N 2, 1967. [Touches on schools in Williamsburg]

Cleghorn, Reese. "Federal Guidelines vs. John C. Calhoun." New York Times Magazine, Jl 20, 1969. [Abbeville]

Cobb, Jimmy Gene. "A Study of White Protestants' Attitude toward Negroes in Charleston, South Carolina, 1790-1845." Doctoral dissertation, Baylor U., 1976.

Cohen, Maurice. "An Inner-City Education in Charleston." Nation, Mr 10, 1979. [Charleston]

Colclough, Glenna. Racial Composition of Schools and Mobility Projections of South Carolina Black Youth, F 8, 1978. ERIC Ed 155 254.

"Colored Teachers in Charleston, S.C., Schools." Crisis, Je, 1921.

Conroy, Pat. The Water Is Wide. Boston, MA: Houghton Mifflin, 1972. [Yamacraw Island]

Cooley, Rossa Belle. Homes of the Freed. New York: New Republic, 1926. [Sea Islands]

Cullen, Robert B. "Inside the Seg Academies--Who They Really Hurt." South Today 3(My, 1972):1, 9. [Clarendon Hall, Summerton]

"Darlington Schools Still Segregated." Your Schools, S-O, 1972.

Doddy, Hurley H., and Edwards, G. Franklin. "Apprehensions of Negro Teachers Concerning Desegregation in South Carolina." Journal of Negro Education 24(Winter, 1955):26-43.

Du Bois, W. E. B. "South Carolina Negro Common Schools." Crisis, D, 1927.

Duncan, John Donald. "Servitude and Slavery in Colonial South Carolina, 1670-1776." Doctoral dissertation, Emory U., 1971.

"Ears Seem Closed to Cainhoy." Your Schools, Ja-F, 1974. [Cainhoy School, Berkeley County]

"Edgefield Blacks Boycott Tests." Your Schools, Ap, 1970.

Egerton, John, and Bass, Jack. "Hayes Mizell, School Board Member." Race Relations Reporter 4(Mr, 1973):29-33.

F, R. "Orangeburg One Year Later." Guardian, Ap 5, 1969.

Fancher, Betsy. "Daufuskie: Hope Fades After Teacher is Fired." South Today 2(N, 1970): 8. [Pat Conroy; Daufuskie]

_____. "The New Breed and the Old." In The South and Her Children: School Desegregation, 1970-1971, pp. 50-55. Edited by Robert E. Anderson, Jr. Atlanta, GA: Southern Regional Council, Mr, 1971. [Beaufort]

_____. "A Teacher: Daufuskie's [Pat] Conroy Paying the Penalty." South Today 2(D, 1970): 9. [Beaufort]

Fitchett, E. Horace. "The Origin and Growth of the Free Negro Population of Charleston, South Carolina." Journal of Negro History 26(O, 1941).

Floyd, Jeremiah. "A Study of Displaced Black High School Principals in the State of South Carolina: 1963-1973." Doctoral dissertation, Northwestern U., 1973. Univ. Microfilms Order No. 74-07741.

4X, Harold. "Ku Klux Klan Going Strong." Muhammad Speaks, F 8, 1974. [Boiling Springs]

Furst, Randy. "Orangeburg After the Massacre." *Guardian*, F 24, 1968.

Gannett, William C. "The Freedmen at Port Royal." *North American Review* 101 (1865).

Gergel, Richard. "School Desegregation: A Student View." *New South* 26(Winter, 1971): 34–38.

Gibson, Carleton B. *Industrial Educational Survey of Charleston, S.C.* Charleston, SC: Walker, Evans & Cogswell, 1920.

Goettel, Robert J., and Berke, Joel S. *Financing Public Education in South Carolina: Problems and Prospects.* Syracuse, NY: Syracuse U. Research Corporation, O, 1972.

Gordon, Asa. *Sketches of Negro Life and History in South Carolina.* Columbia: U. of South Carolina Press, 1929.

Graham, Grace. "Negro Education Progresses in South Carolina." *Social Forces* 30(1952): 429–438.

Grant, Jim. "S.C. High Schools Hit by Rebellions." *Southern Patriot*, Ja, 1971.

Green, Donald Ross. [Letter to M. Hayes Mizell, June 4, 1970, regarding problems of testing and desegregation in Edgefield County, S.C.] *Your Schools*, My–Je, 1970.

Greider, William. "Winners and Losers." *Race Relations Reporter* 5(My, 1974):19–22. [Summerton]

Hamlett, Ed. "South Carolina: Three Majority-Black Districts." In *Majority-Black School Districts in the 11 Southern States.* Nashville, TN: Race Relations Information Center, Jl, 1970. [Allendale, Fairfield, and Williamsburg counties]

Hayes, Arthur Batiest. "Communication Gap Between Black and White Teenagers in Integrated Schools in Richland Parish." Doctoral dissertation, United States International U., 1974. Univ. Microfilms Order No. 74-20521.

Hemmingway, Theodore. "Beneath the Yoke of Bondage: A History of Black Folks in South Carolina, 1900-1940." Doctoral dissertation, U. of South Carolina, 1976. Univ. Microfilms Order No. 77-06763.

Henderson, Bruce M. *The Impact of Cutbacks, Impoundments, Appropriation Procedures, and Regulation Changes on Federally Funded Education and Child Related Programs in South Carolina.* Columbia, SC: American Friends Service Committee, Ag, 1973.

Henderson, William C. "Spartan Slaves: A Documentary Account of Blacks on Trial in Spartanburg, South Carolina, 1830 to 1865." Doctoral dissertation, Northwestern U., 1978. Univ. Microfilms Order No. 7903274.

Hillinger, Charles. "Gullahs--God Knows 'Vees Here.'" *Los Angeles Times*, Mr 6, 1975. [Gullah-speaking people on Wadmalah Island]

Hoffius, Steve. "'I Expect I'll Get a Plaque.'" *Southern Exposure* 7(Summer, 1979):74–76. [Septima Clark]

Hoffman, Edwin D. "The Genesis of the Modern Movement for Equal Rights in South Carolina, 1930-1939." *Journal of Negro History* 44(1959): 346–369.

Hoffman, Joan. *Racial Discrimination and Economic Development.* Lexington, MA; Lexington Books, 1975.

Holland, Davis Rutledge. "A History of the Desegregation Movement in the South Carolina Public Schools During the Period 1954-1976." Doctoral dissertation, Florida State U., 1978. Univ. Microfilms Order No. 7822177.

Holland, Rupert S. (ed.). *Letters and Diary of Laura M. Towne.* Cambridge, MA: n.p., 1912. [St. Helena]

Holt, Thomas C. "The Emergence of Negro Political Leadership in South Carolina During Reconstruction." Doctoral dissertation, Yale U., 1973.

"How Two Black Teachers Feel." *Your Schools* 2 (F, 1971).

Jackson, James Conroy. "The Religious Education of the Negro in South Carolina Prior to 1850." *Historical Magazine of the Protestant Episcopal Church*, Mr, 1967.

Jackson, Luther P. "The Educational Efforts of the Freedmen's Bureau and Freedmen's Aid Societies in South Carolina, 1862-1872." *Journal of Negro History* 8(Ja, 1923):1–40.

Jackson, Patricia A. J. "The Status of Gullah: An Investigation of Convergent Processes." Doctoral dissertation, U. of Michigan, 1978.

Jacobson, Robert L. "They're Trying to Build the Taj Mahal in Columbia." *Compact* 8(Ja–F, 1974):7–10. [Benson Elementary School, Columbia]

Jones, R. E., and Schendel, H. E. "The Nutritional Status of Selected Negro Infants in Greenville County, South Carolina." *American Journal of Clinical Nutrition*, Je, 1966.

Klingberg, Frank J. *An Appraisal of the Negro in Colonial South Carolina: A Study in Americanization.* Washington, DC: Associated Publishers, 1941.

Knight, Edgar W. "Reconstruction and Education in South Carolina." *South Atlantic Quarterly* 18(1919):350–361.

Kuyper, George A. "The Voorhees School." *Southern Workman* 61(Ap, 1932):146–154.

The Lexington, S.C., Black Community. "Race Relations and Related Conditions." Your Schools, O, 1969. [An open letter dated O 8, 1969]

"Like It Is in Chesterfield County." Your Schools, Ja, 1970.

"McCormick: Case Study of a Village Hike Defeat." Your Schools 4(S-O, 1973). [McCormick County]

McDonald, Laughlin. "'The Song Has Ended but the Melody Lingers On.'" Journal of Law and Education 4(Ja, 1975):29-32. [Strom Thurmond High School, Edgefield]

McElveen, Jackson V., and Dillman, Buddy L. A Profile of the Rural Poor in the Coastal Plain of Northeastern South Carolina. Washington, DC: GPO, Ap, 1971.

McIwain, William F. "On the Overturning of Two School Buses in Lamar, S.C." Esquire 75 (Ja, 1971):98-103, 162-164. [Events of Mr 2, 1970]

McSweeney, Edward A., and Matthias, Paul W. Sick Unto Death. A Report on the Health Needs of South Carolina's Low-Income Citizens, O, 1972. South Carolina Council on Human Relations, Suite 200, Columbia Building, Corner Gervais & Main Street, Columbia, SC 29201.

Marszalek, John F. "The Black Leader in 1919-- South Carolina as a Case Study." Phylon 6(Fall, 1975):249-259.

Middleton, Lorenzo. "The Civil Rights Movement Arrives in Calhoun County." Washington Star, D 8, 1976.

Miller, Kelly. "These 'Colored' United States: South Carolina." Messenger 7(D, 1925):376-377, 400.

Mims, Julian Landrum. "Radical Reconstruction in Edgefield County, 1868-1877." Master's thesis, U. of South Carolina, 1969.

Mizell, M. Hayes. Desegregation in South Carolina, N 11, 1974. ERIC ED 128 530.

_____. "The Myth of Quality Education." New South 26(Winter, 1971):26-33.

_____. "School Desegregation in South Carolina." Integrated Education, D, 1966-Ja, 1967.

_____. "Suspensions: A Misused Tool?" (2 parts). Osceola, Ja 24, 31, 1975. [Richland County School District No. 1]

_____. "To All South Carolinians Interested in Equality of Educational Opportunity." American Friends Service Committee, 1105 Barton Street, Columbia, SC 19203, Ag 30, 1966 (mimeo).

"Money for Disadvantaged Students Pays for the Education of the Advantaged." Your Schools, S, 1970. [Operation of Title I, ESEA, 20 school districts in South Carolina]

Moore, Burchill R. "A History of Negro Public Schools of Charleston, South Carolina, 1867-1942." Master's thesis, U. of South Carolina, 1942.

Newby, Idus A. Black Carolinians. A History of Blacks in South Carolina from 1895 to 1968. Columbia, SC: U. of South Carolina Press, 1973.

Norton, John, and Wedlock, Eldon. Student Rights and Responsibilities in South Carolina, 1972. American Friends Service Committee, 401 Columbia Bldg., Columbia, SC 29201.

Osborne, John. "The Dying White South." New Republic, Ja 22, 1966. [Segregated schools and society in Anderson]

_____. "How To Keep School Segregation." New Republic, Mr 12, 1966. [Manning]

Powell, Kathryn Summers. Educational and Vocational Goals of Urban White and Negro Youth in South Carolina, N, 1970. ERIC ED 056 188.

Pruitt, Melissa. "Behind the Brookland-Cayce Unrest." Osceola, Ja 31, 1975. [Brookland-Cayce High School]

"The Problems of Integration." SOBU Newsletter, Ap 3, 1971. [Cross]

Radford, John P. "Race, Residence and Ideology: Charleston, South Carolina in the Mid-Nineteenth Century." Journal of Historical Geography 2(1976):329-346.

Reid, Alfred S. "Literature in Greenville." Furman University Bulletin 7(F, 1960):124-125. [Race and the press]

_____. "Recent Literary Developments in Greenville S.C. : 1959-1963." Furman University Bulletin 12(N, 1964):24-30. [Race and the press]

Resource Management Corporation. [Case History of ESAP in Greenville] Evaluation of the Emergency School Assistance Program, Vol. III, Appendix K, F 15, 1972. ERIC ED 058 470.

_____. [Case History of ESAP in Sumter] Evaluation of the Emergency School Assistance Program, Vol. III, Appendix Q, F 15, 1972. ERIC ED 058 470.

Richardson, Joe M. "Francis L. Cardozo: Black Educator During Reconstruction." Journal of Negro Education 48(Winter, 1979):73-83.

"Martha Schofield and Negro Education." Southern Workman 60(Ap, 1931):150-151. [Aiken]

"School Board System Is A-maze-ing." Your Schools 5(My-Je, 1974).

Secrest, Andrew M. "In Black and White: Press Opinion and Race Relations in South Carolina, 1964-1964." Doctoral dissertation, Duke U., 1972. Univ. Microfilms Order No. 72-23,255.

"'73-'74--Suspension Statistics of Selected S.C. Schools." Your Schools, F, 1975.

Sherman, Joel D. and others. "Underfunding" of Majority Black School Districts in South Carolina, O, 1977. ERIC ED 151 448. [Before and after desegregation]

Simkins, Francis B. "Race Legislation in South Carolina Since 1865." South Atlantic Quarterly 20(Ja, Ap, 1921):161-171, 165-177.

Sloan, Cliff, and Hall, Bob. "'It's Good To Be Home in Greenville...'" Southern Exposure 7 (Spring, 1979):82-93.

South Carolina Community Relations Program. A Report on Short-Term, Out-of-School Disciplinary Suspensions in the Junior High/ Middle and High Schools of Richland County School District #1, 1975-1976 and 1974-1975, Ag, 1976. 401 Columbia Bldg., Columbia, SC 29201.

"Student Suspensions and Expulsions in South Carolina School Districts." Your Schools, Ap, 1974.

Smith, Baxter. "Black Boycott in S. Carolina." Militant, D 24, 1976. [Calhoun County]

Smith, Quincy J. Letter to Gov. West, August 13, 1973. Your Schools 4(Ag, 1973). [In re: Bowman Academy in Orangeburg County]

Special Training Institute on School Desegregation for School Personnel in South Carolina, 1968-1969, 1970. ERIC ED 045 754.

Stagg, J. C. A. "The Problem of Klan Violence: The South Carolina Up-Country, 1868-1871." Journal of American Studies 8(1974):303-318.

Summers, Emily R. "Contributions of Negroes to Education in South Carolina, 1867-1900." Master's thesis, Howard U., 1969.

"Suspensions Among S.C. Students Increased in 1973-1974." Your Schools, D, 1974-Ja, 1975.

Sweat, Edward F. "Some Notes on the Role of Negroes in the Establishment of Public Schools in South Carolina." Phylon 22(1961): 160-166.

Taylor, Alrutheus A. The Negro in South Carolina during the Reconstruction. Washington, DC: Association for the Study of Negro Life and History, 1924.

Taylor, Jesse. "Students Educated by Struggling." African World, S 4, 1971. [Moncks Corner]

Terjen, Kitty. "Private Schools, Charleston Style." South Today 2(Ja-F, 1971):1, 7.

"Tragedy at Britton's Neck." Your Schools, O, 1969. [Marion County]

U.S. Commission on Civil Rights, Staff. School Desegregation in Williamsburg County, South Carolina. Washington, DC: The Commission, Je, 1977.

U.S. 90th Congress, 2nd session and i1st Congress, 1st session, Senate, Select Committee on Nutrition and Human Needs. Nutrition and Human Needs. Hearings...Part 4--South Carolina. Washington, DC: GPO, 1969.

U.S. Congress, 91st, 2nd session, Senate, Select Committee on Equal Educational Opportunity. Equal Educational Opportunity. Hearings... Part 3B--Desegregation Under Law, pp. 1567-1607. Washington, DC: GPO, 1970. [Desegregation in Greenville]

U.S. Department of the Interior. Report of the Commissioner of Education: Common Schools in South Carolina, 1863-1900. 2 vols. Washington, DC: GPO, 1906.

Uya, Ohon Edet. From Slavery to Public Service. Robert Smalls 1839-1915. New York: Oxford U. Press, 1971.

Wade, Sister M. Angela. "A Study of the Social, Economic, Religious, Educational, and Psychological Background of the Catholic Negro Pupils of the Immaculate Conception School, Charleston, South Carolina." Master's thesis, Villanova U., 1938.

Watters, Pat. "Our Children Are Spat Upon..." South Today, Jl, 1969. [A delegation of black citizens from South Carolina goes to Washington on behalf of strict enforcement of desegregation guidelines]

Wells, Janet. "Aiken: How Not to Desegregate." Your Schools 2(O, 1970).

Westmoreland, Edgar P. "A Study of Negro Education in the State of South Carolina, with Particular Reference to the Influences of the Reconstruction Period." Master's thesis, Howard U., 1935.

"What's Happening to Black Educators in S.C.?" Your Schools, S, 1970.

White, Frank H. "The Economic and Social Development of Negroes in South Carolina Since 1900." Doctoral dissertation, New York U., 1960. Univ. Microfilms Order No. 61-705.

Wikramanayake, Marina. A World in Shadow: Free Blacks in Antebellum South Carolina. Columbia, SC: U. of South Carolina Press, 1973.

Williams, Richard T. "History of Public Education and Charitable Institutions in South Carolina During Reconstruction." Master's thesis, Atlanta U., 1933.

Williamson, Joe. "Education: Progress and Poverty." In After Slavery: The Negro in South Carolina During Reconstruction, 1861-1877, chapter 8. Chapel Hill, NC: U. of North Carolina Press, 1965.

Winecoff, H. Larry, and Masem, Paul. "School Desegregation: A Challenge to Quality Education." Part I. South Carolina Education News, S, 1968.

Winecoff, H. Larry, Cimino, Thomas M., and Masem, Paul W. "School Desegreation: A Challenge to Quality Education." Part II. South Carolina Education News, O, 1968.

Winn, William. "Esau Jenkins' Island." South Today 2(Ap, 1971):3, 5. [Johns Island]

Wood, Peter H. "Black Majority. Negroes in Colonial South Carolina. From 1670 through the Stono Rebellion." Doctoral dissertation, Harvard U., 1972.

_____. Black Majority. Negroes in Colonial South Carolina from 1670 through the Stono Rebellion [1739]. New York: Knopf, 1974.

_____. "'More Like a Negro Country': Demographic Patterns in Colonial South Carolina, 1700-1740." In Race and Slavery in the Western Hemisphere: Quantitative Studies, pp. 131-171. Edited by Stanley L. Engerman and Eugene D. Genovese. Princeton, NJ: Princeton U. Press, 1975.

Woofter, Thomas J. Black Yeomanry: Life on St. Helena Island. New York: Octagon, 1978, orig. 1930.

South Dakota

Harney, Sr. Mary Carmel. "The History of Catholic Education in South Dakota from 1880 to 1931." Master's thesis, U. of Notre Dame, 1933.

McLure, William P., and Hudson, C. Cale. Financial Support of the Public Schools of South Dakota. An Evaluation. Washington, DC: National Education Association, 1868.

Rambow, Charles. "The Ku Klux Klan in the 1920's: A Concentration on the Black Hills." South Dakota History 4(Winter, 1973 .

South Dakota State Advisory Committee. Discrimination in Off-Base Housing: Ellsworth Air Force Base. Washington, DC: U.S. Commission on Civil Rights, Mr, 1968.

Tennessee

Adams, Arvil V. Negro Employment in the South. Vol. 2: The Memphis Labor Market. Manpower Administration, U.S. Department of H.E.W. Washington, DC: GPO, 1971.

Adams, Frank, with Horton, Myles. Unearthing Seeds of Fire: The Idea of Highlander. Winston-Salem, NC: John F. Blair, 1975.

Alther, Lisa. "The Melungeon Melting Pot." New Society, Ap 15, 1976.

Anderson, Margaret. The Children of the South. New York: Farrar, Straus and Giroux, 1966. [The everyday workings of desegregation in Clinton]

Bachman, Frank P. Public Schools of Nashville, Tennessee. Nashville, TN: George Peabody College for Teachers, 1931.

Bailey, E. B. "The Negro in East Tennessee." Master's thesis, New York U., 1947.

Beifuss, Joan Turner. "Memphis Blacks March." National Catholic Reporter, O 29, 1969.

"'Black Monday' in Memphis." Southern Patriot, N, 1969.

Bledsow, Thomas. Or We'll All Hang Separately. Boston, MA: Beacon Press, 1969. [Highlander Folk School]

Borders, T. K. "The Status of Teachers in the Approved Four-Year Negro High Schools of Tennessee, 1931-1932." Master's thesis, U. of Michigan, 1932.

"Boy Who Refused to Play 'Dixie' at a White High School." Muhammad Speaks, My 23, 1969. [Lebanon]

Braddock, Clayton. "NEIP. Fighting Poverty in the 'Regular' Public Schools." Southern Education Report, Ap, 1968. [Nashville]

Brittain, David J. "What School People Have Learned about Integration." Educational Leadership, My, 1958. [Clinton]

Brooks, George W. A History of the Organization Growth and Activities of the Tennessee Negro Education Association, 1923-1951. Nashville, 1952.

_____. History of the Tennessee Education Congress, 1923-1967. Washington, DC: National Education Association, 1975. [Black organization]

Brown, Charles C. "The History of Negro Education in Tennessee." Master's thesis, Washington U., 1929.

Cansler, C. W. Three Generations. The Story of a Colored Family of Eastern Tennessee. Kingsport, TN: Kingsport Press, 1939.

Cartwright, Joseph H. The Triumph of Jim Crow: Tennessee Race Relations in the 1880's. Knoxville: U. of Tennessee, 1976.

Chambers, Vaughn. "Differences Between Negro and Caucasian Students at John Sevier Junior High School, Kingsport, Tennessee." Master's thesis, East Tennessee State U., 1967.

Clough, Dick B. "Teacher Institutes in Tennessee, 1870-1900." Tennessee Historical Quarterly 30(Spring, 1972):61-73.

Coles, Robert, and Davey, Tom. "Tennessee's Paving Remnant." New Republic, S 25, 1976.

Collins, Thomas W. "Reconstructing a High School Society After Court-Ordered Desegregation." Anthropology & Education Quarterly 9(Winter, 1978):248-257. [Memphis]

Collins, Thomas W., and Noblit, George W. Stratification and Resegregation: The Case of Crossover High School, Memphis, Tennessee, 1978. ERIC ED 157 954.

Coppock, Paul R. "Black Education in Memphis-- Up From Slavery." Memphis Commercial Appeal, Jl 17, 1977. [1865-1891]

Corlew, Robert Ewing. "The Negro in Tennessee, 1870-1900." Doctoral dissertation, U. of Alabama, 1954.

Covington, Jimmie. "The City School Board Divided by 3." Memphis Commercial Appeal, Ag 13, 1972. [Memphis]

_____. "The Private School Boom." Memphis Commercial Appeal, Ag 20, 1972. [Memphis]

Covington, Jimmie and others. "School Busing Teams With Controversy and Frustration." Memphis Commercial Appeal, F 4, 1974. [Memphis, Nashville, Little Rock]

Cox, George Washington. "A Look at Faculty Desegregation Methods at a Select Group of Schools in the Memphis City Schools." Doctoral dissertation, U. of Tennessee, 1972. Univ. Microfilms Order No. 72-21,346.

Crosthwait, D. M., Jr. "The First Black High School in Nashville." Negro History Bulletin 37(Je-Jl, 1974).

Daves, J. H. A Social Study of the Colored Population of Knoxville, Tennessee. Knoxville, TN: The Free Colored Library, 1926.

De Berry, A. L. "A Study of Fifteen Negro Pupils Enrolled in Formerly All-White Schools in Hardeman County, Tennessee for the 1965-1966 School Year." Master's thesis, U. of Tennessee, 1965.

Dowd, Douglas, and Nichols, Mary (eds.). Step by Step: Evolution and Operation of the Cornell Students' Civil-Rights Project in Tennessee, Summer, 1964. New York: Norton, 1965.

Du Bois, W. E. B. "The Hills of Tennessee." Fisk Herald, O and N, 1886.

Egerton, John. Promise of Progress. Memphis School Desegregation, 1972-1973. Atlanta: Southern Regional Council, Je, 1973.

Egerton, John, and Leeson, Jim. "Nashville: Experiment in Urban School Consolidation." Phi Delta Kappan, Mr, 1967.

England, J. Merton. "The Free Negro in Ante Bellum Tennessee." Journal of Southern History 9(F, 1943).

Fenston, Joy. "A Chance for Power in Fayette [Tennessee] Election." Southern Patriot, Ag, 1966.

Fraser, Walter J., Jr. "Black Reconstruction in Tennessee." Tennessee Historical Quarterly 34(Winter, 1975):362-382.

Geir, Woodrow A. "Tennessee." Christian Century, S 8, 1965. [School integration boycotts in Tipton, Fayette, and Haywood counties]

Geisel, Paul N. "IQ Performance, Educational, and Occupational Aspirations of Youth in a Southern City: A Racial Comparison." Doctoral dissertation, Vanderbilt U., 1962. [Nashville]

Gilmore, James Roberts. Down in Tennessee, and Back By Way of Richmond. Westport, CT: Negro Universities Press, 1970.

Gore, G. In-Service Professional Improvement of Negro Public School Teachers in Tennessee. New York: Columbia U., 1940.

Graham, Hugh Davis Graham. Crisis in Print. Desegregation and the Press in Tennessee. Nashville, TN: Vanderbilt U. Press, 1967.

Hamburger, Robert. Our Portion of Hell. Fayette County, Tennessee. An Oral History of the Struggle for Civil Rights. Links Books, 1974.

Harris, Hattie V. "An Historical Study of Negro Public Education in Chattanooga, Tennessee, 1937-1962." Master's thesis, Atlanta U., 1963.

Harris, Ron. "Blacks in a White School: A Look Back." Memphis Press Scimitar, Ja 24, 1978. [White Station High School, Memphis]

Hartman, George Bruce. "An Economic Analysis of Black Nashville." Doctoral dissertation, State U. of New York, Albany, 1975. Univ. Microfilms Order No. 75-16991

Heller, Steven Ashley. "A Study of Teacher Attitudes Regarding School Desegregation in Selected Tennessee School Systems." Doctoral dissertation, U. of Tennessee, 1971.

Herenton, Willie Wilbert. "A Historical Study of School Desegregation in Memphis City Schools, 1954-1970." Doctoral dissertation, Southern Illinois U., 1971. Univ. Microfilms Order No. 72-10254.

Hilliard, Moss. "The Development of Public Education in Memphis, Tennessee, 1848-1945." Doctoral dissertation, U. of Chicago, n.d.

Horton, Aimee I. "The Highlander Folk School: A History of the Development of its Major Programs Related to Social Movements in the South, 1932-1961." Doctoral dissertation, U. of Chicago, Mr, 1971.

_____. "The Highlander Folk School: Pioneer of Integration in the South." Teachers College Record, D, 1966.

Hubbard, G. W. (ed.). A History of Colored Schools of Nashville, Tennessee. Nashville, TN: Wheeler, Marshall & Bruce, 1874.

Huston, C. Richard. A Profile of Unemployment in the Memphis Ghetto. Memphis, TN: Bureau of Business & Economic Research, Memphis State U., 1973.

Jackson, Livingston. "Tennessee Rebels." New Republic, S 9, 1967. [About the black nationalist Nashville Liberation School]

Jenkins, Carol L. "Infant Mortality and Family Structure among Blacks in Memphis." Tennessee Anthropologist 3(1978):70-78.

Jones, Addie D. Portrait of a Ghetto School. New York: Vantage Press, 1973. [Manassas High School, Memphis]

Jones, Lewis W. and Others (eds.). Demography of Disadvantage in Tennessee, S 1, 1973. ERIC ED 100 553.

Jordan, Weymouth T. "The Freedmen's Bureau in Tennessee." East Tennessee Historical Society Publications 11(1939):47-61.

Kousser, J. Morgan. "Post-Reconstruction Suffrage Restrictions in Tennessee: A New Look at the V. O. Key Thesis." Political Science Quarterly 88(D, 1973):655-683.

Lamon, Lester C. Black Tennesseans, 1900-1930. Knoxville: U. of Tennessee Press, 1977.

_____. "Negroes in Tennessee, 1900-1930." Doctoral dissertation, U. of North Carolina, 1971.

Lawrence, Ken. "Widespread School Busing Begins in Nashville, Tenn." Southern Patriot 29(O, 1971):1, 4

Lee, George W. "These 'Colored' United States: Tennessee: The Last Stand of Justice in the Solid South." Messenger 7(Jl, 1925).

Lovett, Bobby Lee. "The Negro in Tennessee, 1861-1866: A Socio-Military History of the Civil War Era." Doctoral dissertation, U. of Arkansas, 1978. Univ. Microfilms Order No. 7823268.

Lynch, Dudley. "One Teacher's Struggle with Class and Race." Southern Voices 1(Ag-S, 1974):49-54. [Barbara Hookings, Memphis]

McCampbell, Vera. "Educational Survey of the Elementary Schools of Grundy County, Tennessee." Master's thesis, U. of Tennessee, 1935.

McDonald, Kevin. "Outreach and Outrage: The Student Health Coalition." Southern Exposure 6(1978):19-23.

McMahan, Mary Bond. "The Development of Elementary Education in Tennessee with Specific Reference to Negro Education." Master's thesis, Cincinnati U., 1938.

McMillen, Neil R. "Organized Resistance to School Desegregation in Tennessee." Tennessee Historical Quarterly 30(Fall, 1971).

Martin, Ralph. A Training Institute to Improve the Effectiveness of Seventy-Five Secondary Teachers of English and Reading in Desegregated Schools in the East Tennessee Region. First Report, F 28, 1967. ERIC Ed 056 110.

"Memphis Militants Come Under Attack." Southern Patriot, My, 1969.

Meyer, Cecile. [Letter on desegregation in Oak Ridge] Southern Education Report, My, 1968.

Mitchell, Carolyn. "All Saints Academy. Inner-City School Success Story." Chattanooga Times, N 5, 1978. [Integrated parochial school created by merger of all-black and all-white schools in 1973]

Morrell, Ken. "The Equation at Oak Ridge." Southern Education Report, Mr, 1968.

Morrison, M. L., Sr. History of West Tennessee Educational Congress, 1902-1945. Nashville: n.p., 1945.

Myer, M. Everett. "The Swann v. Mecklenburg Case: Its Significance for Tenness Schools." Tennessee Education 1(Winter, 1972):8-15.

National Commission on Professional Rights and Responsibilities. Knoxville, Tennessee. When a City Government Fails to Give Full Support to Its Schools. Washington, DC: National Education Association, Mr, 1967.

Nelson, John C. "Interests of Disadvantaged and Advantaged Negro and White First Graders." Journal of Negro Education, Spring, 1968. [Nashville]

Nolle, David B. "Correlates of Social Mobility Among Working Class Negroes." Master's thesis, Vanderbilt U., 1966. [Nashville]

Nordheimer, Jon. "Memphis: A City That Wants Never to Change." New York Times, Ja 26, 1973.

Parker, Russell D. "The Black Community in a Company Town: Alcoa, Tennessee, 1919-1939." Tennessee Historical Quarterly 37(Summer, 1978):203-221.

Patterson, Caleb P. The Negro in Tennessee, 1790-1865. U. of Texas Bulletin, No. 2205. Austin, TX: U. of Texas, F 1, 1922.

Phillips, Paul D. "A History of the Freedmen's Bureau in Tennessee." Doctoral dissertation, Vanderbilt U., 1964.

_____. "White Reaction to the Freedmen's Bureau in Tennessee." Tennessee Historical Quarterly 25(1966):50-62.

Porteous, Clark. "The Notable--and Dramatic-- Progress of Blacks [in Memphis and Shelby County]." Memphis Press-Scimitar, F 12, 1976.

Resource Management Corporation. [Case History of ESAP in Williamson] Evaluation of the Emergency School Assistance Program, Vol. III, Appendix S, F 15, 1972. ERIC ED 058 470.

Rhodes, Albert L., Reiss, Albert J., Jr., and Duncan, Otis Dudley. "Occupational Segregation in a Metropolitan School System." American Journal of Sociology, My, 1965. [Nashville]

Rigsby, Leo C., and Boston, John. Patterns of School Desegregation in Nashville, 1960-1969, Mr 30, 1972. ERIC ED 128 480.

Riley, Mary J. "The Development of Secondary Education for Negroes in the State of Tennessee." Master's thesis, Howard U., 1935.

Robinson, James H. "A Social History of the Negro in Memphis and in Shelby County." Doctoral dissertation, Yale U., 1934.

Roney, Robert K. "A Different Kind of Woodstock." Integrated Education 11(Mr-Ap, 1973):3-7.

Ryan, James Gilbert. "The Memphis Riots of 1866: Terror in a Black Community During Reconstruction." Journal of Negro History 62 (Jl, 1977):243-257.

Salomon, Lester M. "The Nashville Sound: A Paradox of Black Urban Politics." VEP News 5(Jl-S, 1971):4. [Voter Education Project, Inc., 52 Fairlie St., N.W., Atlanta, GA 30303]

Samples, Ralph E. "The Development of Public Education in Tennessee During the Bourbon Era, 1870-1900." Doctoral dissertation, U. of Tennessee, 1965. Univ. Microfilms Order No. 66-8205.

Schweninger, Loren. "The Free-Slave Phenomenon: James P. Thomas and the Black Community in Ante-Bellum Nashville." Civil War History 22 (D, 1976):293-307.

Smart, Richard Davis. "The Economic Condition of Negroes in Nashville, Tenn." Vanderbilt University Quarterly (Ap, 1904):108-113.

Smith, Elizabeth V. "An Accounting Study of the Educational Progress of Knoxville Negro Pupils Over a Sixteen Year Period." Master's thesis, U. of Tennessee, 1959.

Smith, Maxine. "Memphis' Crisis in Education." Crisis, Ja, 1970.

Smith, William F. "A Study of Biracial Interaction in a Racially Balanced School." Doctoral dissertation, U. of Tennessee, 1970. Univ. Microfilms Order No. 71-17,778. [Hardy Jr. High School, Chattanooga]

Stinson, Harold N. "The Effect of Desegregation in the Adjustment and Values of Negro and White Students." Doctoral dissertation, George Peabody College, 1963. Dissertation Abstracts, XXVI, p. 5152. [Nashville]

Stitely, Thomas Beane. "Bridging the Gap: A History of the Rosenwald Fund in the Development of Rural Negro Schools in Tennessee 1912-1932." Doctoral dissertation, George Peabody College for Teachers, 1975. Univ. Microfilms Order No. 75-22292.

Stuart, Reginald. "Busing and the Media in Nashville." New South 28(Spring, 1973):79-87.

Swint, Henry L. (ed.). "Reports from Educational Agents of the Freedmen's Bureau in Tennessee, 1865-1870." Tennessee Historical Quarterly I (1942):51-80, 152-170.

Task Force on Education of the L.Q.C. Lamar Society. "Public Schools in Memphis: Struggling but with Head Well Above Water." Southern Journal 4(1975):3-4.

Taylor, Essie Hale. "Official State Attitudes Toward Education for Negroes in Tennessee." Master's thesis, U. of Michigan, 1940.

Tennessee State Advisory Committee. Housing and Urban Renewal in the Nashville-Davidson County Metropolitan Area. Washington, DC: U.S. Commission on Civil Rights, F, 1967.

Tennessee State Planning Commission. Human Relations in Tennessee. Springfield, VA: Clearinghouse for Federal Scientific and Technical Information, F, 1970.

Te Selle, Eugene. "The Necessity of Busing." Christian Century, Mr 8, 1972. [Nashville]

Thomas, Hulan Glyn. "The Highlander Folk School: The Depression Years." Tennessee Historical Quarterly, D, 1964.

_____. "A History of the Highlander Folk School, 1932-1941." Master's thesis, Vanderbilt U., 1964.

"Title I Parent Council Survey Reveals Districts Violating Federal Guidelines." Your Schools, S-O, 1972.

"'Transporting' Called Necessary to End Dual School System." Memphis Commercial Appeal, Ap 21, 1972. [Complete text of ruling by Judge Robert M. McRae, Jr. in Memphis school case]

Tucker, David M. Black Pastors and Leaders: The Memphis Clergy, 1819-1972. Memphis, TN: Memphis State U. Press, 1975.

Ubben, Gerald C., and Hughes, Larry W. "Preparation Programs for Top Level Negro Public School Administrators—A New Perspective." Journal of Negro Education, Spring, 1969.

U.S. Commission on Civil Rights. Hearings... Held in Memphis, Tennessee, June 25-1962. Washington, DC: GPO, 1962.

_____. School Desegregation in Nashville-Davidson, Tennessee. Washington, DC: The Commission, Je, 1977.

U.S. Commission on Civil Rights, Tennessee State Advisory Committee. Fear Runs Deep. Washington, DC: U.S. Commission on Civil Rights, 1971. [Fayette County]

Van Dyke, Roger Raymond. "The Free Negro in Tennessee, 1790-1860." Doctoral dissertation, Florida State U., 1972. Univ. Microfilms Order No. 72-32778.

Vancil, Paul. "After Five Years of Memphis Busing, Desegregation Debate Rolls On." Memphis Press-Scimitar, Ja 24, 1978.

Varley, Nancy. "Cameron: Success Story in School Integration." Nashville Tennessean, Ap 17, 1977. [Cameron Junior High School, Nashville]

Vincent, David. "The Uneducation of Black Students." Memphis Commercial Appeal, Mr 26, 1970-Mr 29, 1970. [Four articles on Memphis]

Waller, Robert L. "Teaching Ethnic Studies in Selected Memphis City Junior High Schools, 1973-74." Journal of Negro Education 47(Summer, 1978):290-297.

Walls, Dwayne. Fayette County, Tennessee: Tragedy and Confrontation. Atlanta, GA: Southern Regional Council, O, 1969.

Warner, Stafford Allen. Yardley Warner: The Freedman's Friend. Abington, England: n.p., 1957. [Freedmen schools in Tenn.]

Weatherford, W. D. (ed.). A Survey of the Negro Boy in Nashville, Tennessee. New York: The Association Press, 1932.

Wheeler, Lester R. "The Intelligence of East Tennessee Mountain Children." Journal of Educational Psychology 23(My, 1932):351-370.

Whitaker, Colbert W. "Some Possible Effects of Desegregation on Academic Achievement in Chattanooga." Tennessee Education 3 (Winter, 1973):38-43.

Woodard, James D. "Busing Plans, Media Agendas, and Patterns of White Flight: Nashville, Tennessee and Louisville, Kentucky." Doctoral dissertation, Vanderbilt U., 1978. Univ. Microfilms Order No. 7819545.

Work, Helen E. "An Historical Study of the Colored Public Schools of Nashville, Tennessee." Master's thesis, Fisk U., 1933.

Wynn, Dorothy Florence. "Library Facilities for Negro Pupils in Nashville." Master's thesis, Fisk U., 1937.

Texas

Abbott, Mary Lee. "Turmoil in Houston Schools." Houston Chronicle, F 25, 1976.

Adams, Russell L., and Phillips, Beeman N. "Factors Associated with Under- and Over-Achievement Among Socio-Economically and Racial-Ethnically Different Elementary School Children." Psychology in the Schools, Ap, 1968. [Austin]

Alexander, Charles C. "Secrecy Bids for Power: the Ku Klux Klan in Texas Politics in the 1920's." Mid-America 46(Ja, 1964):3-28.

Allen, William. "The Case of Demetrio Rodriguez." Saturday Review 55(S 9, 1972): 6-13. [San Antonio]

Ardery, Julie, and Bishop, Bill. "Prosperity For the Few." Texas Observer, My 26, 1978.

Atterberry, Ann. "'White Flight' Bugs Student Who Stayed." Dallas News, F 6, 1977. [Preston Hollow Elementary School, Dallas]

Baker, Anita. "Dunbar's Lone White Far From Lonely." Fort Worth Star Telegram, F 8, 1977. [Dunbar Middle School]

Banks, Melvin J. "The Pursuit of Equality: The Movement for First Class Citizenship Among Negroes in Texas, 1920-1950." Doctoral dissertation, Syracuse U., 1962. Univ. Microfilms Order No. 63-3620.

Barr, Alwyn. Black Texans: A History of Negroes in Texas, 1528-1971. Austin: Jenkins, 1973.

Beaumont Colored Schools, 1880-1926. Beaumont, TX: American Printing Co., 1926.

Beck, William W., and Sobol, Marion Gross. Perception versus Reality in Educational Attitudes Toward School Desegregation, Ja 27, 1978. ERIC ED 155 268. [Dallas]

Beck, William, and Linden, Glenn M. "Anglo and Minority Perceptions of Success in Dallas School Desegregation." Phi Delta Kappan 60 (Ja, 1979):378-382.

Bell, John A. "Race and School Suspensions in Dallas." Integrated Education 11(Mr-Ap, 1973):66-67.

Bertelsen, Elmer. "Over Half of HISD Schools Legally Integrated; Magnet Plan Gets Credit." Houston Chronicle, O 24, 1976.

Biffle, Kent. "Troublesome Incidents, But a Minimum of Violence." Dallas News, Je 12, 1977.

Blanton, Thomas M. "Blacks Do Worse After Integration." African World 2(F 19, 1972): 12. [McKinney]

_____. "Importance of Program, Hard Work Stressed." African World, Ap 15, 1971. [Texas State Conference of Student Organization for Black Unity and the Black Student Union of the U. of Houston, Mr 24-25, 1972]

Bois, d'Arc Patriots. "Organizing in Dallas." Green Mountain Quarterly 5(F, 1979).

Brewer, Anita, and McKee, Diann (eds.). Texas' Youngest Children: Texas Household Survey of Families with Children Under Six, N, 1975. ERIC ED 121 481.

Brewer, J. Mason. Negro Legislators of Texas. Austin: Jenkins Publishing Co., 1970.

Briggs, Vernon M., Jr. Negro Employment in the South. Volume I: The Houston Labor Market. Washington, DC: GPO, 1971.

Brophy, William Joseph. "The Black Texan, 1900-1950: A Quantitative History." Doctoral dissertation, Vanderbilt U., 1974. Univ. Microfilms Order No. 74-22164.

Brown, Dorothy. "The Encircled Schools Park Cities and Wilmington." Dallas Times Herald, N 30, 1975. [Highland Park Independent School District]

Bryant, Ira B., Jr. The Development of the Houston Negro Schools. Houston, TX: Informer Publishing Co., 1935.

Bullock, Henry Allen. Availability of Public Education for Negroes in Texas. Prairie View, TX: Prairie View State College, 1937.

Cade, John B. "Some Fundamental Problems in the Education of Negroes in the State of Texas." Quarterly Review of Higher Education Among Negroes 6(Ga, 1938):73-76.

Campbell, Connie, and Brandstetter, John. "The Magnet School Plan in Houston." In The Future of Big-City Schools. Edited by Daniel U. Levine and Robert J. Havighurst. Berkeley, CA: McCutchan, 1977.

Campbell, Randolph B., and Lowe, Richard G. Wealth and Power in Antebellum Texas. College Station: Texas A & M U. Press, 1977.

Champagne, Joseph E., and Prater, Robert L. Teenage Employment: A Study of Low Income Youth in Houston, Texas. Houston, TX: Center for Human Resources, U. of Houston, 1969.

Christopher, Nehemiah M. "The History of Negro Public Education in Texas, 1865-1900." Doctoral dissertation, U. of Pittsburgh, 1949.

"Civil Rights-Segregation in Education." New York University Law Review 23(Ap, 1948): 298-303. [Sweatt v. Painter (Tex.) 210 S.W. (2nd) 442]

Coalson, George O. The Development of the Migrant Farm Labor System in Texas, 1900-1954. San Francisco: R and E Research Associates, 1977.

Commission on Professional Rights and Responsibilities. Beyond Desegregation: The Problem of Power. Washington, DC: National Education Association, F, 1970. [East Texas]

Cotrell, Charles L. "The Effects of At-Large Elections on the Political Access and Voting Strength of Mexican Americans and Blacks in Texas." In U.S. Congress, 94th, 1st session, House of Representatives, Committee on the Judiciary, Subcommittee on Civil and Constitutional Rights, Extension of the Voting Rights Act. Hearings..., Part 1. Serial No. 1, pp. 408-479. Washington, DC: GPO, 1975.

Cross, Ray, Dolezal, Charles, and Howard, Ronald. "The Use of Computers for Student Assignment in Desegregation." Integratedication 14(Jl/Ag, 1976). [Corpus Christi]

Crouch, Barry A. "The Freedmen's Bureau in the 30th Sub-District of Texas: Smith County Environs During Reconstruction." Chronicles of Smith County, Texas 11(Spring, 1972).

_____. "Self-Determination and Local Black Leaders in Texas." Phylon 39(D, 1978):344-355. [1865-1873]

Crouch, Barry A., and Schultz, Leon J. "Crisis in Color: Racial Separation in Texas During Reconstruction." Civil War History 16(1970): 37-49.

Curry, Bill. "Houston's Bane: Severe Poverty Amid the Boom." Washington Post, Ag 28, 1978.

Daniel, V. E. "Present Status and Needs of Texas Rural Schools for Negroes." Bulletin (National Association of Teachers in Colored Schools) 11(D, 1930):11-16.

Davidson, Chandler. Biracial Politics. Conflict and Coalition in the Metropolitan South. Baton Rouge, LA: Louisiana State U. Press, 1972. [Houston]

Davidson, [Franklin] Chandler. "Negro Politics and the Rise of the Civil Rights Movement in Houston, Texas." Doctoral dissertation, Princeton U., 1969. Univ. Microfilms Order No. 69-14409.

Davidson, Chandler, and Longshore, Douglas. "Houston Elects a Mayor." New South 27 (Spring, 1972):47-61.

Davis, W. R. Development and Present Status of Negro Education in East Texas. New York: Bureau of Publications, Teachers College, Columbia U., 1934.

De Leon, Arnoldo. "Blowout 1910 Style: A Chicano School Boycott in West Texas." Texana 12(No. 2, 1974):124-140.

Demarest, Sylvia M., and Jordan, John F. "Hawkins v. Coleman: Discriminatory Suspensions and the Effect of Institutional Racism on School Discipline." Inequality in Education 20(Jl, 1975):25-41. [Dallas]

Dickens, E. Larry. "Microcosm in Texas: An Achilles Heel for a Liberal Coalition." New South 26(Summer, 1971):10-18. [Houston]

Dickerman, G. S. "The Negro of San Antonio." Southern Workman 43(Ap, 1914):246.

Dickinson, George E. "Dating Patterns of Black and White Adolescents in a Southern Community." Adolescence 6(Fall, 1971):285-298. [East Texas town]

_____. "Small Town: A Sociological Analysis of an East Texas Community." Master's thesis, Baylor U., 1964.

"Discrimination in Education." Inferno, Ja 11, 1968. [San Antonio]

Donosky, Lea. "Blacks Withdraw Desegregation Suit." Race Relations Reporter 5(My 20, 1974):3. [Reference is to a white-sponsored legal effort to dissolve the Wilmer-Hutchins district, near Dallas]

Du Bois, W. E. B. What the Negro Has Done for the United States and Texas. Washington, DC: GPO, 1936.

Eilers, W. A. "Negro Education in Lavaca County." Master's thesis, Southwest Texas Teachers College, 1938.

Engerrand, George C. The So-Called Wends of Germany and their Colonies in Texas and in Australia. San Francisco: R & E Research Associates, 1972 reprint. Orig. 1934.

Engerrand, Steven W. "Black and Mulatto Mobility and Stability in Dallas, Texas, 1880-1910." Phylon 39(Fall, 1978):203-215.

Equal Educational Opportunity Policy Research Project. "Corpus Christi," passim. In Federal Policies for Equal Educational Opportunity: Conflict and Confusion. Austin: Lyndon B. Johnson School of Public Affairs, U. of Texas, 1977.

"Equalizing Haves, Have Nots." Austin American, Jl 21, 1972. [Interview with Mrs. Exalton Delco, member of Austin board of education, and William D. Lynch]

Estes, Robert, and Skipper, Kent. Comprehensive Evaluation of the Pacesetter Program, Richardson Independent School District. Dallas: School of Human Development, U. of Texas, D, 1976.

Etheridge, Truman H. "Education in the Republic of Texas." Doctoral dissertation, U. of Texas, 1942. [1836-1846]

Evans, Charles L. Elementary Magnet/Vanguard Plan Evaluation. 1976-77, Year II, O, 1977. ERIC ED 157 908. [Fort Worth]

Feagin, Joe R. "Prejudice, Orthodoxy and the Social Situation." Social Forces, S, 1965. [Dallas]

Felice, Lawrence G. "Busing in Waco, Texas." Integratedication 12(Jl-Ag, 1974):24-25.

Felice, Lawrence G., and Richardson, Ronald I. "Effects of Desegregation on Minority Student Dropout Rates." Integratedication 15 (N-D, 1977):47-50. [Waco]

Fisher, J. E. "Legal Status of Free Blacks in Texas, 1836-1861." Texas Southern University Law Review 4(Summer, 1977):342-362.

Fogleman, Billye Y. O. "The Anthropologist in a Public School Setting." Council on Anthropology and Education Quarterly 8(My, 1976):23-24. [Dallas]

Foley, Douglas E. "Legalistic and Personalistic Adaptations to Ethnic Conflict in a Texas School." Journal of Research and Development in Education 9(Summer, 1976):74-82.

Gates, Samuel Houston. "Negro Secondary Education in Texas." Master's thesis, U. of Colorado, 1937.

Gibbons, Charles E., and Armentrout, Clara B. Child Labor Among Cotton Growers of Texas. New York: National Child Labor Committee, 1925.

Gillette, Michael L. "The Rise of the NAACP in Texas." S.W. Historical Quarterly 81(Ap, 1978):393-416.

Glasrud, Bruce A. "Jim Crow's Emergence in Texas." American Studies 15(Spring, 1974).

Goodwyn, Lawrence C. "Populist Dreams and Negro Rights: East Texas as a Case Study." American Historical Review 76(D, 1971):1435-1456.

Governor's Committee on Public School Evaluation in Texas. The Challenge and the Chance. Austin, TX, Ag 31, 1968.

Green, John Plath. [Testimony on past and present problems of desegregation in Dallas, Texas] U.S. Congress, 92nd, 2nd session, Senate, Committee on Labor and Public Welfare, Subcommittee on Education, Equal Educational Opportunities Act of 1972. Hearings..., pp. 1371-1392. Washington, DC: GPO, 1972.

Greene, A. C. "The Durable Society: Austin in the Reconstruction." Southwestern Historical Quarterly 72(Ap, 1969).

Griffith, Dotty. "Private Schools: Enrollment and Quality Unknown." Dallas News, Je 12, 1977. [Dallas]

Grose, Charles William. "Black Newspapers in Texas, 1868-1970." Doctoral dissertation. U. of Texas, 1972. Univ. Microfilms Order No. 73-97558.

Grunbaum, Werner F. "Desegregation in Texas: Voting and Action Patterns." Public Opinion Quarterly 28(Winter, 1964):604-614.

Guseman, Patricia Knight. "An Analysis of Socioeconomic Diversity in Texas Metropolitan Residential Areas." Doctoral dissertation, Texas A & M U., 1975. Univ. Microfilms Order No. 76-12,669.

Hart, Norris. "You Must Go Home Again." The Center Magazine, 1969.

Haynes, Rose Mary F. "Some Features of Negro Participation in Texas History." Master's thesis, Texas A & M U., Kingsville, 1948.

Haynes, Robert V. A Night of Violence: The Houston Riot of 1917. Baton Rouge: Louisiana State U. Press, 1976.

Holland, Danny. "Black Education--A Transition." Beaumont Enterprise, F 22, 1978. [Beaumont]

Holley, Tom. "The Educational Status of the Public Schools in Karnes, Jim Wells, and Brooks Counties, Texas." Master's thesis, Southern Methodist U., 1937.

Hollins, Edward A. The Colored Teachers' State Association of Texas as Revealed in the Texas Press. Prairie View, TX: Prairie View A & M College, 1948.

Holtzman, Wayne H., Diaz-Guerrero, Rogelio, and Swartz, Jon D. Personality Development in Two Cultures: A Cross-Cultural Longitudinal Study of School Children in Mexico and the United States. Austin: U. of Texas Press, 1975. [Austin, TX and Mexico City]

Hornsby, Alton, Jr. "The Freedmen's Bureau Schools in Texas, 1865-1870." Southwest Historical Quarterly 76(Ap, 1973):397-417.

Hutcheson, Ron. "A Study in Controversy: 'School' at CIE." Fort Worth Star Telegram, Ag 2, 1976. [Center for Individualized Education]

Institute of Texas Cultures. The Afro-American Texans. San Antonio: U. of Texas at San Antonio, 1975.

Jerden, Cecil M. "A Study in Racial Differences in the El Paso Public Schools." Master's thesis, Southern Methodist U., 1939.

Kirven, Lamar L. "A Century of Warfare: Black Texans." Doctoral dissertation, Indiana U., 1974. Univ. Microfilms Order No. 75-09021.

Kuhn, Nancy N. "Segregated Public Schools in Texas, 1876-1940." Master's thesis, U. of Texas, 1970.

Kuvlesky, William P., and Gonzalez, Ruth Bagnall. Historical Change in Educational Status Projections of East Texas High School Sophomores: A Racial Comparison, F 4, 1974. ERIC ED 086 410.

Kuvlesky, William P., and Cannon, Margaret. Perception of Racial Prejudice Among Rural and Small Town Blacks in a Southern County. College Station, TX: Texas A & M U., Ag, 1971, 58 pp. ERIC ED 052 828. [An East Texas county]

Kuvlesky, William P. and others. Social Ambitions of Negro Boys and Girls from a Metropolitan Ghetto. College Station, TX: Texas A & M U., 1969, 33 pp. ERIC ED 040 461. [Houston]

Laine, Alice K. "The In-Depth Study of the Black Political Leadership in Houston, Texas." Doctoral dissertation, U. of Texas, 1978. Univ. Microfilms Order No. 7900592.

Lane, Harry B. "The Present Status of Secondary Education for Negroes in Texas." Master's thesis, U. of Southern California, 1932.

Ledbetter, Billy D. "White Over Black in Texas: Racial Attitudes in the Ante-Bellum Period." Phylon 34(D, 1973):406-418.

Lede, Naomi W., and Dixon, Hortense W. Urban Minority Groups in Houston: Problems, Progress, and Prospects. A Statistical and Analytical Study, Mr 29, 1973. ERIC ED 094 023.

Lee, Sister Rosana. "History of Catholic Education in the Diocese of Amarillo." Master's thesis, Catholic U. of America, 1954.

Lever, Michael F., and Upham, W. Kennedy. Poverty Among Nonwhite Families in Texas and the Nation: A Comparative Analysis. Departmental Information Report 68-4. College Station, TX: Texas A & M U., D, 1968, 118 pp. ERIC ED 028 015.

Levine, Daniel U., and Estes, Nolan. "Desegregation and Educational Reconstruction in the Dallas Public Schools." Phi Delta Kappan 59(N, 1977):163-167, 221.

Longman, Jere. "17 Years After Integration." Dallas Time Herald, Mr 26, 1978. [Interviews with Fay Miles and Nancy Mae Miles who, as children, first desegregated Dallas schools in 1961]

Louis, Bowles and Grove, Inc. Perceptions, Opinions and Attitudes Toward the DISD and School Desegregation. Dallas: Louis, Bowles and Grove, Inc., My, 1977. [Dallas]

Lowrie, S. H. Culture Conflict in Texas, 1821-1835. New York: Columbia U. Press, 1932.

McConnell, W. J. Social Cleavages in Texas. New York: Columbia U., 1925.

McDaniel, Vernon. History of the Teachers State Association of Texas. Washington, DC: National Education Association, 1977.

McDowell, Neil Allen. A Status Study of the Academic Capabilities and Achievements of Three Ethnic Groups: Anglo, Negro, and Spanish Surname, in San Antonio, Texas, Ag, 1966, 186 pp. Doctoral dissertation. Available from University Microfilms, Inc., 300 North Zeeb Road, Ann Arbor, MI 48106. ERIC ED 049 861.

McNeely, Dave. "Integration Minus Violence." Dallas News, Ag 15, 1976. [Fort Worth schools]

Manaster, Guy J. "Attitudes on School Integration and Desegregation: A Study of Reactions to a Court Order." Integrated Education 9(Mr-Ap, 1971):3-8.

Mann, John S. "In Defense of Bussing." Educational Leadership 34(Ap, 1977):501-505. [Austin]

Marrs, S. M. N., Blundworth, G. T., and Taylor, D. B. Negro Education in Texas. Bulletin No. 212. Austin, TX: State Department of Education, O, 1926.

Marshall, Lila. The Role of Career Education in Desegregating Schools in Large Cities, Ap, 1978. ERIC ED 156 915. [Dallas]

Mayes, Johnnie. "Courts Stall on Dallas School Desegregation Plan." Student Mobilizer 1 (D, 1975). [National Student Coalition Against Racism]

Meador, Bruce S. "Minority Groups and Their Education in Hays County, Texas." Doctoral dissertation, U. of Texas, 1959. Univ. Microfilms Order No. 59-4729.

Meier, J. A., and Smedley, R. H. Eight Year Enrollment Trends, 1968-69 through 1975-1976. Dallas: Dallas Independent School District, 1976.

Mindiola, Tatcho. A Demographic Profile of Texas and Selected Cities: Some Recent Trends, 1950-1970, 1974. ERIC ED 097 147.

Monti, Lorna A. Social Indicators for Austin, Texas. Austin: Bureau of Business Research, U. of Texas, 1975.

Morland, J. Kenneth. Token Desegregation and Beyond. New York: Anti-Defamation League, 1963. [Austin]

Moskowitz, Ronald. "Education and Politics in Boomtown." Saturday Review, F 17, 1968. [Houston]

Mullendore, Walter E., and Cooper, Kathleen M. "Effects of Race on Property Values: The Case of Dallas." Annals of Regional Science, D, 1972, pp. 61-72.

Negro Education in Texas. Bulletin 5. Austin, TX: State Department of Education, 1931.

Nelum, Junior N. "A Study of the First Seventy Years of the Colored Teachers' State Association of Texas." Doctoral dissertation, U. of Texas, 1955.

Nethaway, Rowland. "San Marcos: Pretty, Quiet, and Seething." Austin American, Ap 7, 1972.

Noland, James R., Robinson, Jerry, Jr., and Martin, Edwin. "How It Was in Houston, Texas." Integrated Education 7(My-Je, 1969):38-43.

O'Connor, Colleen. "School Days in Wilmer-Hutchins." Texas Observer, Jl 5, 1974.

Olds, Greg. "Integration in Texas." Texas Observer, O 28, 1966.

Osborne, John. "Austin Story." New Republic 165(Ag 21, 1971):13-15.

Ozio, Ronald. "Corpus Christi." Integrateducation 15(N-D, 1977):5-8.

Payne, Arnold. "Progress in Calvert, Texas." Integrated Education 12(Ja-Ap, 1974):39-40.

Perlman, Laura. "Black Employment in Houston." Manpower 3(My, 1971):25-29.

Phillips, Barbara R. Employment Problems in Houston: Dynamic Factors. Model Cities Monographs No. 1. Houston, TX: Southwest Center for Urban Research, Jl, 1971.

Platter, Allen A. "Educational, Social and Economic Characteristics of the Plantation Culture of Brazonia County, Texas." Doctoral dissertation, U. of Houston, 1961.

Polk, Travis Ray. "The Status of the Teaching of Negro History in the Public High Schools of Texas." Doctoral dissertation, North Texas State U., 1972. Univ. Microfilms Order No. 72-24201.

Poston, D., and Passel, J. "Texas Population in 1970: Racial Residential Segregation in Cities." Texas Business Review 46(1972):1-6.

Reese, William Alvin. "Windsor Village: A Southern Test of the Contact Hypothesis." Master's thesis, U. of Houston, 1978. Univ. Microfilms Order No. 13-11,747. [Suburb of Houston]

Resource Management Corporation. [Case History of ESAP in Abilene, Texas] Evaluation of the Emergency School Assistance Program, Vol. III, Appendix A, F 15, 1972. ERIC ED 058 470.

Resource Management Corporation. Case History of ESAP in San Antonio, Texas Evaluation of the Emergency School Assistance Program, Vol. III, Appendix J, F 15, 1972. ERIC ED 058 470.

Rice, Lawrence D. The Negro in Texas, 1874-1900. Baton Rouge, LA: Louisiana State U. Press, 1971.

Richardson, Clifton F. "These 'Colored' United States: Texas--The Lone Star State." Messenger 6(Ap, 1924):105, 120, 124.

Robinson, Louis. "The Return of a Native." Ebony 26(Ag, 1971):120-125. [Mineral Wells]

Samples, Doris Ann. "Disciplining Students on a Racial Basis." New York Times, D 29, 1974. [Dallas]

Sapper, Neil Gary. "A Survey of the History of the Black People of Texas, 1930-1954." Doctoral dissertation, Texas Tech U., 1972. Univ. Microfilms Order No. 73-04071.

Schoen, Harold. "The Free Negro in the Republic of Texas." Doctoral dissertation, U. of Texas, 1938.

"Schools and the Housing/Real Estate Industry [in Dallas]." Impact, S 20, 1976. Published by M/PF Research, Inc., 6060 North Central Expressway, Dallas, TX 75206

Schultz, Adele. "Corpus Christi School District Dispute Continues." Agenda 4(N, 1974):3.

Scott, Alan. "Twenty-Five Years of Opinion on Integration in Texas." Southwestern Social Science Quarterly 48(1967):155-163. [1946-1965]

Schuyler, George. "Aframerica Austin." Pittsburgh Courier, Ap 10, 1926.

Schwartz, Marilyn. "Pershing, Reilly, Adams; A Story of Three Schools." Dallas News, Je 12, 1977. [Dallas]

Scott-Blair, Michael. "Parents' Role Key to Integration." San Diego Union, Mr 27, 1977. [Houston]

Seibel, Mark. "The Alliance: Who and How." Dallas News, Ag 15, 1976. [Dallas Alliance, author of Dallas' desegregation plan]

Seibel, Mark, and Booty, Julie Anne. "Report Card: A's, B's and C's." Dallas News, Je 12, 1977.

Sheard, Chester. "Racist 'Desegregation' in Texas." Muhammad Speaks, Ja 29, 1971. [Nacodoches]

Sheehan, Daniel S., and Marcus, Mary McIntosh. Relationships Between Student Attitudes and Selected Background and Achievement Characteristics. Dallas: Dallas Independent School District, S, 1977.

_____ and _____. Socioeconomic Status Study. Dallas: Dallas Independent School District, 1977.

Simms, Richard. "Washington Street's 'Soul Survivors.'" Integrated Education 11(J1-O, 1973):36-37. [Dallas]

Smallwood, James M. "Black Texans During Reconstruction: First Freedom." East Texas Historical Journal 14(Spring, 1976):9-23.

_____. "Black Texans during Reconstruction, 1865-1874." Doctoral dissertation, Texas Tech U., 1974. Univ. Microfilms Order No. 75-17761.

_____. "Early 'Freedom Schools': Black Self Help and Education in Reconstruction—Texas, a Case Study." Negro History Bulletin 41 (Ja-F, 1978):790-793.

_____. "Emancipation and the Black Family: A Case Study in Texas." Social Science Quarterly 44(Mr, 1977).

_____. "The Freedmen's Bureau Reconsidered." Texana 11(Spring, 1973):309-320.

Smith, Laura Birdie. "A Survey of Negro Schools in Wood County, Texas." Master's thesis, U. of Southern California, 1937.

Staggs, Frank M., Jr., and Nyberg, Kenneth L. Racial Differences in Rural Adolescent Drug Abuse, S 1, 1977.

Stevenson, H. W. "Social Interaction of Children in an Interracial Nursery School." Education (Texas), III (1956).

"Superintendent Fired." School Management 15 (O, 1971). [Dr. George G. Garver, Houston]

"The Sweatt Case and the Development of Legal Education for Negroes in Texas." Texas Law Review 47(Mr, 1969):677.

Taylor, Joe. "Education Marks Time While Racial Cultures Clash." Austin American, Jl 16, 1972. [McCallum High School, Austin]

_____. "Roots of Some Problems Traced to Govalle." Austin American, Jl 18, 1972. [Govalle Elementary School, Austin]

"'Teaching Too Much of the Truth,' Black Teacher Fired in Dallas." African World, My 31, 1974. [L. G. Pinkston High School, Dallas]

Terrell, Wendell P. "A Study of the Employment of the Graduates of 10 Negro High Schools of Texas." Master's thesis, Colorado State College, 1937.

Texas Commission on Services to Children and Youth. A Report on the Regional Forums on Troubled, Disturbed and Neglected Children and Youth. Austin: The Commission, 1974.

Texas Education Agency. Change and Progress in Texas Schools. Programs for the Educationally Disadvantaged. Austin, TX: The Agency, 1968.

"Texas Is Integrating." Texas Observer, Je 28, 1963.

Texas Department of Education. Negro Education in Texas: Special Activities and Industrial Aid. Austin, TX, 1926.

Texas Educational Survey Report, Organization and Administration. 2 vols. Austin, TX, 1925.

Texas State Advisory Committee. The Civil Rights Status of Spanish-Speaking Americans in Kleberg, Nueces, San Patricio Counties, Texas. Washington, DC: U.S. Commission on Civil Rights, Jl, 1967.

_____. Employment Practices at Kelly Air Force Base, San Antonio, Texas. Washington, DC: U.S. Commission on Civil Rights, Je, 1968.

"They Call the Issue Busing." Texas Observer, N 5, 1971. [Corpus Christi]

Thomas, Jesse O. "Negro Schools in Houston." Opportunity 8(Je, 1930):178-180.

A Training Institute on Problems of School Integration for School Board Members, Principals, and Teachers in the East Texas Area. First Report. Huntsville, TX: Sam Houston State U., Ag 26, 1969, 94 pp. ERIC ED 056 126.

Traughber, Clark R. "A Study of Negro Public Schools of Smith County, Texas." Master's thesis, East Texas State Teachers College, 1940.

Trombley, William. "Dallas Busing Plan Attracts Interest in L.A." Los Angeles Times, F 21, 1977.

_____. "Dallas." Integrateducation 15(N-D, 1977):20-23.

_____. "Houston Busing Plan: The Word for Desegregation is Voluntary." Los Angeles Times, F 28, 1977.

_____. "Houston." Integrateducation 15(N-D, 1977):92-94.

Tullis, David S. "A Comparative Study of Negro, Latin, and Anglo Children in a West Texas Community." Doctoral dissertation, Texas Technological College, 1964. Univ. Microfilms Order No. 65-1464.

University of Texas, Institute of Public Affairs. The Place System in Texas Elections. Austin: U. of Texas Printing Division, 1965. [Relation to Mexican-American and black political power in school-board elections]

U.S. Commission on Civil Rights. Civil Rights USA Public Schools. Southern States, 1963, Texas. Washington, DC: GPO, 1963.

_____. Hearing Held in Corpus Christi, Texas. August 17, 1976. Washington, DC: The Commission, 1978.

U.S. Commission on Civil Rights, Texas Advisory Committee. Civil Rights in Texas. Washington, DC: GPO, F, 1970.

_____. School Desegregation in Corpus Christi, Texas. Washington, DC: The Commission, My, 1977.

U.S. Commission on Civil Rights, Texas State Committee. School Finance Reform in Texas. Washington, DC: The Commission, S, 1972.

U.S. Commission on Civil Rights, Texas Advisory Committee. Working With Your School: A Handbook of the Texas Advisory Committee... Washington, DC: U.S. Commission on Civil Rights, 1977.

University of Texas. Elementary and Secondary Education Aid: Toward an Optimal Program for the State Government of Texas. Austin, TX: Institute of Public Affairs, U. of Texas, 1970.

Watriss, Wendy. "Celebrate Freedom: June-teenth." Southern Exposure 5(Spring, 1977): 80-87.

Webb, John Compton. "Personal Problems of Negro Students in High Schools of East Texas." Doctoral dissertation, Texas A & M U., 1971. Univ. Microfilms Order No. 72-13257.

Wheeler, G. H., Jr. "The History of Education in Texas during the Reconstruction Period." Master's thesis, North Texas State U., 1953.

Williams, Joyce E. Black Community Control: A Study of Transition in a Texas Ghetto. New York: Praeger, 1973. [Como, Fort Worth]

_____. "Black Community in Transition: Issues and Leadership in a Texas Ghetto." Doctoral dissertation, Washington U., 1971. Univ. Microfilms Order No. 71-27358. [Fort Worth]

Williams, William Taylor Burwell. "Colored Public Schools of Texas." Southern Workman 53(0, 1924):445.

Winn, David B. Migrant Farmworker Labor Housing in Texas, Mr 1, 1977. ERIC ED 142 342

Wooden, Kenneth. Reading Level of Students in Texas. Princeton, NJ: Institute of Applied Politics, Mar 12, 1973.

Woolfolk, George Ruble. "The Free Negro and Texas, 1876-1860." Journal of Mexican American History 3(1973):49-75.

_____. The Free Negro in Texas, 1800-1860: A Study in Cultural Compromise. Ann Arbor, MI: University Microfilms International, 1976.

Woolley, Bryan. "A 'Different' Dallas Calmly Accepts Busing." Los Angeles Times, S 12, 1976.

Wortham, Sue C. "The Role of the Negro on the Texas Frontier." Master's thesis, Southwest Texas State U., San Marcos, 1970.

Zamora, Jesus E. "A Status Survey of Texas' Bilingual-Bicultural Education Programs." Doctoral dissertation, U. of Texas, 1977.

Zimmerman, G. "Lady Stirs Her City's Con-science: Houston." Look, S 21, 1965.

Utah

Brewer, David L. "Utah Elites and Utah Racial Norms." Doctoral dissertation, U. of Utah, 1966. Univ. Microfilms Order No. 66-13548.

Coleman, Ronald G. "Blacks in Utah History: An Unknown Legacy." In The Peoples of Utah. Edited by Helen Z. Papanikolas. Salt Lake City: Utah State Historical Society, 1976.

Focus on Children and Youth. Salt Lake City: Governor's Committee on Children and Youth, 1972.

Pulsipher, Elwin Dean. "Educational Achievement of Minorities in Utah High Schools." Doctoral dissertation, Brigham Young U., 1977. Univ. Microfilms Order No. 77-31126.

Ramjoue, George. "The Negro in Utah: A Geographical Study in Population." Master's thesis, U. of Utah, 1968.

Stipanovich, Joseph. The South Slavs in Utah: A Social History. San Francisco: R and E Research Associates, 1975.

Taggart, Stephen G. Mormonism's Negro Policy: Social and Historical Origins. Salt Lake City: U. of Utah Press, 1970.

Ulibarri, Richard O. "Utah's Ethnic Minorities: A Survey." Utah Historical Quarterly, Summer, 1972.

"Urban Shadows Fall on Sunny Salt Lake." Newsweek, Mr 15, 1971.

U.S. Commission on Civil Rights. School De-segregation in Ogden, Utah. Washington, DC: The Commission, My, 1977.

Vermont

Orban, Edmond. "Facteurs politico-religieux et
anglicisation des Franco-americains au
Vermont: indicateurs recents." Canadian
Ethnic Studies 8, No. 4(1976):34-49.

U.S. Commission on Civil Rights, Vermont
Advisory Committee. Closing the Ethnic Gap.
Washington, DC: The Commission, 1973.

Virginia

Advisory Committee on Negro Schools.
"Virginia State Curriculum Revision Pro-
grams." Statement by D. A. Wilkerson,
Secretary, Virginia Journal of Education 27
(Ja, 1934):203-205.

Aery, William A. "The Negro and Education in
Virginia." Southern Workman 62(Ja, 1933):32-
34.

Alderson, William T., Jr. "The Freedmen's
Bureau and Negro Education in Virginia."
North Carolina Historical Review 29 (1952):
64-90.

Alderson, William T., Jr. "The Freedmen's
Bureau in Virginia." Master s thesis, Vanderbilt U., 1949.

_____. "The Influence of Military Rule and the
Freedman's Bureau on Reconstruction in
Virginia, 1865-1870." Doctoral dissertation,
Vanderbilt U., 1952. Univ. Microfilms Order
No. 3968.

Alexander, Frederick Milton. Education for the
Needs of the Negro in Virginia. Washington,
DC: Southern Education Foundation, 1942.

Anderson, Robert T., and Lee, Nathaniel.
Interracial In-Service Program Designed to
Increase the Educational Opportunities of the
Children in the Richmond Public Schools,
July 1, 1965-June 30, 1966; and February 1,
1968-December 31, 1968. Richmond, VA:
Richmond Public Schools, 1968, 283 pp. ERIC
ED 056 111.

Armstrong, Samuel Chapman. Ideas on Education
Expressed by Samuel Chapman Armstrong.
Hampton, Va. Issued for the Armstrong League
of Hampton Workers by the Hampton Institute
Press, 1908.

Bailey, Raymond C. "Racial Discrimination
Against Free Blacks in Antebellum Virginia:
The Case of Harry Jackson." W. Virginia
History 39(Ja-Ap, 1978):181-186.

Banks, J. F. "'Genocide' for Virginia's Black
Secondary Principal?" NASSP Newsletter 18
(Mr-Ap, 1971).

Barksdale, James W. A Comparative Study of
Contemporary White and Negro Standards in
Health, Education and Welfare. Phelps-
Stokes Fellowship Papers, No. 20.
Charlottesville, VA: U. of Virginia, 1949.

Barnes, Bart. "Promotion Tests Boost Emporia
Ratings." Washington Post, My 15, 1977.

Bass, Jack. "What Happened in Virginia."
New South 28(Fall, 1973):62-65.
[Discusses racial factors in gubernatorial
election of N, 1973]

Beales, Ross W., Jr. "An Incident at the
Freedmen's School, Lexington, Virginia,
1867." Prologue 6(Winter, 1974):252-254.

Bernhard, Virginia. "Poverty and the Social
Order in Seventeenth-Century Virginia."
Virginia Magazine of History and
Biography 85(Ap, 1977):141-155.

Bernstein, Carl. "Norfolk: Learning to Live
With Busing." Washington Post, N 29, 1971.

Berry, William C., Douglas, Paul, and Woodard,
Samuel L. A Study of the Atmosphere in Falls
Church High School as It Relates to Re-
lationships Between Black and White Students.
Fairfax, VA: Fairfax County Public Schools,
F 20, 1975.

Binford, George Haywood. "A Study of Discipline
in the Negro Schools of Buckingham County,
Virginia." Master's thesis, Hampton
Institute, 1938.

Bishop, Carol et al. Vocational and Educational
Goals of Rural Youth in Virginia. Blacksburg, VA: The Experiment Station, 1965.

Blank, Joseph P. "The Lost Years." Look, N 29,
1966. [Prince Edward County]

Bogger, Tommy L. "The Slave and Free Black
Community in Norfolk 1775-1865." Doctoral
dissertation, U. of Virginia.

Bowman, Owen. "A Study of the Small School in
the Mountains of Virginia." Master's thesis,
Virginia Polytechnic Institute, 1953.
[Lambsburg School, Carroll County]

Brann, Raymond E. "The Present Status of Public
Secondary Education for Negroes in Virginia."
Master's thesis, U. of Virginia, 1932.

Breen, T. H. "A Changing Labor Force and Race
Relations in Virginia, 1660-1710." Journal
of Social History 7(Fall, 1973):3-25.

Brewbaker, John J. Desegregation in the Norfolk
Public Schools. Atlanta, GA: Southern
Regional Council, 1959.

Brown, William Henry. The Education and
Economic Development of the Negro in Virginia.
Charlottesville, VA: Surber-Arundale Co.,
1923. Phelps-Stokes Fellowship Studies, U.
of Virginia, Charlottesville, VA, 1923.

Burrows, Edward F. "The Literary Education of Negroes in Antebellum Virginia, North Carolina, South Carolina, and Georgia with Special Reference to Regulatory and Prohibitive Laws." Master's thesis, Duke U., 1940.

Camp, Patricia. "Prince Edward 'Class of '59' Recalls Ordeal." Washington Post, S 7, 1976.

_____. "Schools Chief Orchestrated Desegregation in Alexandria." Washington Post, Je 7, 1977.

Campbell, Ernest Q. When a City Closes Its Schools. Chapel Hill, NC: U. of North Carolina Press, 1960. [Norfolk]

Campbell, Robert F. "Va. Governor Works on Pledge to Blacks." Race Relations Reporter, S 16, 1970.

Caplan, M. "Virginia Schools: A Study in Frustration." Crisis, Ja, 1951.

Citizens for Excellent Public Schools. A Study of the Richmond Public Schools, 1971. Citizens for Excellent Public Schools, Box 6262, Richmond VA 23230.

Colding, Ursula S. "A Unique Public School." Southern Workman 59(S, 1930):401-408. [Dunbar School, Norfolk]

Colson, Edna M. "The Program of Curriculum Revision in Virginia." Journal of Negro Education 3(Ap, 1934):311-313.

_____. "The Status of Negro Education in Virginia." Quarterly Review of Higher Education Among Negroes 5(O, 1937):191-197.

Cox, Charles. "Desegregation." Richmond Times-Dispatch, Jl 9, 1978. [Richmond, Norfolk, Lynchburg, and Roanoke]

_____. "Education in Virginia." Richmond Times-Dispatch, D 7, 1969.

_____. "Public Education Called 'Moral Thing.'" Richmond Times-Dispatch, Je 18, 1972. [Mrs. Virginia Crockford, Richmond, VA school board chairman since Jl, 1969]

_____. "Richmond Officials Ask Consolidation." Race Relations Reporter 2(Ap 5, 1971):5-8.

Craven, Wesley Frank. White, Red, and Black. The Seventeenth-Century Virginian. Charlottesville, VA: U. Press of Virginia, 1971.

Crosby, Thomas. "Handley High's Racial War Just a Nagging Memory Now." Washington Star, Je 1, 1976. [Handley High School, Winchester]

Dabney, Thomas L. "Negro Education in Virginia." Southern Workman 57(Ja, 1928): 36-41. [Hanover County]

_____. "Rural Education in Buckinham County, Virginia." Southern Workman 55(F, 1926): 79-82.

Darling, Lynn. "Being Both Highly Visible and Invisible." Washington Post, D 18, 1975. [Robinson High School, Fairfax County]

Davis, Arthur P. "When I Was in Knee Pants." Common Ground 4(Winter, 1944):47-52. [Hampton]

Deffenbaugh, Walter S., and Jessen, Carl A. Some Features of the Junior and Senior High Schools of Roanoke, Va. Report of a survey made by the United States Bureau of Education, Department of the Interior, Washington, DC. Roanoke, VA, Board of Education, 1929. [Lucy Addison High School]

Dewar, Helen. "Prince Edward County: Paying For 'Massive Resistance.'" Washington Post, My 12, 1974.

"Discrimination in Compensation Between White and Colored Teachers." Bill of Rights Review 1(Winter, 1941):142-144. Alston v. School Board of City of Norfolk, 112F 2nd 992

Douglass, Margaret (Crittenden). Educational Laws of Virginia. The Personal Narrative of Mrs. Margaret Douglass, a Southern Woman Who Was Imprisoned for One Month in the Common Jail of Norfolk, under the Laws of Virginia, for the Crime of Teaching Free Colored Children to Read. Boston: P. Jewett & Co.; Cleveland, OH: Jewett, Proctor & Worthington, 1954.

Du Bois, W. E. B. "The Negroes of Farmville, Virginia; A Social Study." Bulletin of the Department of Labor 3(Ja, 1898):1-38.

Egerton, John. "Profile of a School System." Southern Education Report, N, 1966. [Fairfax County]

Ellison, John Malcus. Negro Organizations and Leadership in Relation to Rural Life in Virginia. Blacksburg, VA: n.p., 1933.

Ely, James W., Jr. The Crisis of Conservative Virginia: The Byrd Organization and the Politics of Massive Resistance. Knoxville, TN: U. of Tennessee Press, 1976.

_____. "The Crisis of Conservative Virginia: The Decline and Fall of Massive Resistance, 1957-1965." Doctoral dissertation, U. of Virginia, 1971.

Engs, Robert F. "The Development of Black Culture and Community in the Emancipation Era: Hampton Roads, Virginia, 1861-1870." Doctoral dissertation, Yale U., 1972.

Fen, Sing-Nan. "Notes on the Education of Negroes at Norfolk and Portsmouth, Virginia, During the Civil War." Phylon, Summer, 1967.

Ferguson, G. O. "White and Colored School Children of Virginia as Measured by the Ayers Index." School and Society 12(1920): 171-174.

Fraser, Janis J. "Richmond Reacts to Consolidation Order on Schools." South Today 3 (Je, 1972):1, 6-7.

Freeman, Frankie Muse. "A Dream Deferred." Notre Dame Journal of Education I(Summer, 1970):102-106. [Danville]

Friedman, Murray. "Virginia Jewry in the School Crisis: Anti-Semitism and Desegregation." Commentary, Ja, 1969.

Frissell, H. B., and Bevier, Isabel. Dietary Studies of Negroes in Eastern Virginia in 1897 and 1898. U.S. Department of Agriculture, Office of Experiment Stations, Bulletin 71. Washington, DC: GPO, 1899.

Gandy, John M. "Rural Graded Schools of Virginia Negroes." Southern Workman 42(D, 1913):672.

Garland, William. "Negro Education in Fauquier County, Virginia." Master's thesis, U. of Virginia, 1939.

Garnett, W. E., and Ellison, J. M. Negro Life in Rural Virginia, 1865-1934. Blacksburg, VA: Virginia Agricultural Experiment Station, 1935.

Gaston, Paul M., and Hammond, Thomas T. Public School Desegregation: Charlottesville, Virginia, 1955-62. Atlanta, GA: Southern Regional Council, 1962.

Gates, Robbin L. The Making of Massive Resistance: Virginia's Politics of Public School Desegregation, 1954-1956. Chapel Hill, NC: U. of North Carolina Press, 1962.

Gavins, Raymond. The Perils and Prospects of Southern Black Leadership: Gordon Blaine Hancock, 1884-1970. Durham, NC: Duke U. Press, 1977.

Grant, Jim. "Community Support for School Boycott Builds." African World, Ja 22, 1972. [I. C. Norcum High School, Portsmouth]

_____. "Implications of the Richmond Decision." African World 2(Mr 4, 1972):5

_____. "Prestigious Black High School Fights Back." African World 2(D 11, 1971):10. [Norcum High School, Portsmouth]

_____. "Students Boycott Virginia School." African World, Ja 8, 1972. [I. C. Norcum High School, Portsmouth]

_____. "Virginia Police Turn Police Dogs Loose on Students." African World 2(Mr 4, 1972): 13. [Portsmouth]

Green, Robert L., and Morgan, Robert F. "The Effects of Resumed Schooling on the Measured Intelligence of Prince Edward County's Black Children." Journal of Negro Education, Spring, 1969.

Green, Robert L., and Hayes, Marilyn E. "Family and Educational Experiences of Displaced Negro Children." Integrated Education, F-Mr, 1966. [Prince Edward County]

Green, Robert L., and Hoffman, Louis J. "A Case Study of the Effects of Educational Deprivation on Southern Rural Negro Children." Journal of Negro Education, Summer, 1965. [Prince Edward County]

Green, Robert L., Hoffman, Louis J., Morse, Richard J., and Morgan, Robert F. The Educational Status of Children During the First School Year Following Four Years of Little or No Schooling. Cooperative Research Project No. 2498, 1966. School for Advanced Studies, Research Services, College of Education, Michigan State U. [Prince Edward County]

Green, Robert L., Hoffman, Louis J., Morse, Richard J., Hayes, Marilyn E., and Morgan, Robert F. The Educational Status of Children in a District Without Public Schools. Cooperative Research Project No. 2321. Lansing, MI: Bureau of Educational Research Services, College of Education, Michigan State U., 1964. [Prince Edward County]

Gresham, W. D. "Negro Education in Virginia." Southern Workman 58(D, 1929):553-558.

Grumdon, Adolph. "The School Desegregation Cases and Social Science: The Virginia Experience." In Research in Law and Sociology, I. Edited by Rita J. Simon. Greenwich, CT: JAI Press, 1978.

Hatcher, O. Latham. A Mountain School. A Study Made by the Southern Woman's Educational Alliance and Konnarock Training School. Richmond, VA: Garrett and Massie, Inc., 1930. [Konnarock Training School, Smyth County]

Hershman, James H. "A Rumbling in the Museum: The Opponents of Virginia's Massive Resistance." Doctoral dissertation, U. of Virginia, 1978. Univ. Microfilms Order No. 7903534.

Hilldrup, Robert P. "After the Richmond Decision: Urban Schools in Flux as Observed From the Inside." Southern Voices 1(Mr-Ap, 1974):76-79.

Holden, Anna. "Charlottesville, Virginia: A Southern City's Struggle to Achieve Racial Balance." In The Bus Stops Here. A Study of School Desegregation in Three Cities, pp. 1-126. New York: Agathon Press, 1974.

Horst, Samuel L. "Education for Manhood: The Education of Blacks in Virginia during the Civil War." Doctoral dissertation, U. of Virginia, 1977. Univ. Microfilms Order No. 7901137.

Howard, Mark. "An Historical Study of the Desegregation of the Alexandria, Virginia, City Public Schools, 1954-1973." Doctoral dissertation, George Washington U., 1976. Univ. Microfilms Order No. 77-2954.

Hunter, Marjorie. "A County in Virginia Is Symbolic of Turn to Black Rule in South." New York Times, Jl 15, 1978. [Surry County]

Inter-racial In-service Program Designed to Increase the Educational Opportunities of the Children in the Richmond Public Schools. Final Report September 19, 1966-October 31, 1967. Richmond, VA: Richmond Public Schools, 1967, 132 pp. ERIC ED 020 997.

Jones, Murel M., Jr. "The Impact of Annexation-Related City Council Reapportionment on Black Political Influence: The Cities of Richmond and Petersburg, Virginia." Doctoral dissertation, Howard U., 1977.

Kiernan, Laura. "Alumni of Parker-Gray Recall School's History." Washington Post, Ag 9, 1976. [Parker-Gray School, Alexandria]

_____. "Lessons in Tolerance at T. C. Williams." Washington Post, Ja 22, 1976. [T. C. Williams High School, Alexandria]

_____. "New Battle Shapes Up In Surry." Washington Post, Ag 27, 1975.

Kulikoff, Allan. "The Origins of Afro-American Society in Tidewater Maryland and Virginia, 1770 to 1790." William and Mary Quarterly 35(1978):226-259.

"Landmark in Richmond." Nation 214(Ja 31, 1972):133. [Judge Robert R. Merhige, Jr.'s decision of Ja 5, 1972]

Langhorne, Orra. "Colored Schools in Virginia." American Journal of Social Science 11(My, 1880):42-45.

Latimer, James. "J. Lindsay Almond, Jr.: Ordeal of a Governor." Richmond Times Dispatch, Ag 4, 1974. [Interview on desegregation issue in Virginia, 1958-1962]

Lewis, Frank P. "A History of the Baptist General Association of Virginia." Bachelor's thesis, Virginia Union U., 1937.

Leone, Dennis A. "White Flight in Alexandria." Integrateducation 13(Mr-Ap, 1975):40

McDonald, Kevin. "Outreach and Outrage: The Student Health Coalition." Southern Exposure 6(1978):19-23.

Markley, Larry. "Dual Schools in Prince Edward County." Race Relations Reporter 3 (My, 1972):17-19.

Martin, Robert. Negro Disfranchisement in Virginia. New York: AMS Press, 1975.

Mathews, Jay. "White Private Schools 'Struggling.'" Washington Post, My 12, 1975.

Mathews, Linda. "Racial Case Tests Private School Rights." Los Angeles Times, Ag 11, 1975. [Bobbe's Private School, Bailey's Crossroad, VA]

Merhige, Robert R. "The Richmond School Decision." Integrated Education (Mr-Ap, 1972):51-63.

Meier, August, and Rudwick, Elliott. "Negro Boycotts of Segregated Streetcars in Virginia, 1904-1907." Virginia Magazine of History and Biography 81(0, 1973).

Moore, T. J. "School Segregation in Virginia." Virginia State Bar Association 65(1954):201-219.

Morland, J. Kenneth. Racial Attitudes and Racial Balance in Public Schools: A Case Study of Lynchburg, Virginia, 0, 1976. ERIC ED 131 166.

_____. "Racial Recognition in Nursery School Children in Lynchburg, Virginia." Social Forces, D, 1958.

Morris, Guy T. "Negro Education in Virginia." Master's thesis, U. of Virginia, 1935.

[A Navajo Reports on School Integration in Taylor Junior High School, Warrenton, Virginia] Navajo Times, N 13, 1969.

"Negro Communities in Tidewater Virginia." School and Society 19(Je, 1924):761-762.

Newmark, Eva. "Freedom Teacher and Gentle Ladies." Nation, F 22, 1965. [The community of Prince Edward County]

Nichols, Paul. "The Extent to Which Christian Education Curriculum Materials, Which Were Used With Adolescents in Black Baptist Churches of Richmond, Virginia, Between 1969 and 1973, Reflect the Black Experience." Doctoral dissertation, American U., 1976. Univ. Microfilms Order No. 76-29717.

Nicol, Judy. "100 Years of Fighting Bias." Washington Post, Ap 1, 1974. [William Alexander West, Vienna]

O'Brien, John T., Jr. "Factory, Church and Community: Blacks in Antebellum Richmond." Journal of Southern History 44(N, 1978): 509-536.

_____. "From Bondage to Citizenship: The Richmond Black Community, 1865-1867." Doctoral dissertation, U. of Rochester, 1975. Univ. Microfilms Order No. 75-1223.

Omang, Joanne. "Alexandria Two Years Later." Washington Post, Je 17, 1973.

Orfield, Gary. "How to Beat Integration. The Story of Sellout in Virginia." New Republic, F 3, 1968.

_____. "Virginia: Desegregating the Old Dominion." In The Reconstruction of Southern Education. The Schools and the 1964 Civil Rights Act. New York: Wiley-Interscience, 1969.

P., R. W. "The Educability of the Blacks." American Missionary 32(1878):21.

Pace, David. "Lenoir Chambers Opposes Massive Resistance: An Editor Against Virginia's Democratic Organization, 1955-1959." Virginia Magazine of History and Bibliography 82(0, 1974).

Palmer, Lu. "Yesterday, Today--and Tomorrow?" Integrated Education (Jl-Ag, 1972), pp. 40-41 (reprinted from the Chicago Daily News, My 27, 1972). [Newport News]

Peabody, Francis Greenwood. Education for Life, the Story of Hampton Institute Told in Connection with the Fiftieth Anniversary of the Foundation of the School. Doubleday, Page & Company, 1918.

Petty, John Edward. "Let's Put Negroes in Their Place--Like Positions of Leadership." Virginia Journal of Education 64(Mr, 1971): 12-14.

Picott, J. Rupert. "Displacement of Experienced Teachers without Due Process." NEA Journal 54(D, 1965):41. [Giles County]

_____. History of the Virginia Teachers Association. Washington, DC: National Education Association, 1975.

Pilcher, George William. "Samuel Davies and the Instruction of Negroes in Virginia." Virginia Magazine of History and Biography, Jl, 1966. [Pre-revolutionary Virginia]

Pincus, Samuel N. "The Virginia Supreme Court, Blacks, and the Law, 1870-1902." Doctoral dissertation, U. of Virginia, 1978. Univ. Microfilms Order No. 7903541.

Pine, Patricia. "You Can See the Change in Prince Edward." American Education, Jl, 1970. [Prince Edward County]

Poretz, Douglas H. Discipline in Alexandria Public Schools. Alexandria, VA: Board of Education, D 2, 1970.

Proctor, Samuel D. "A Mind Is a Terrible Thing to Waste." Phi Delta Kappan (N, 1978):2015-2035.

Quesenberry, Guy Herbert. "A Study of the Newport News Pupil Desegregation Process." Doctoral dissertation, Virginia Polytechnic Institute and State U., 1977. Univ. Microfilms Order No. 7810002.

Renz, H. A. III. "An Examination of the Effect of System Reorganization on De Facto Segregation in Arlington, Virginia." Doctoral dissertation, George Washington U., 1967.

Resource Management Corporation. Case History of ESAP in Hampton, Va. Evaluation of the Emergency School Assistance Program, Vol. III, Appendix G, F 15, 1972. ERIC ED 058 470.

Robinson, Donald C. "The Development of Education for Negroes in Amelia County, Virginia." Master's thesis, Virginia State College, 1963.

Robinson, S. W. III "Virginia School Fight-- A Clarification." Crisis, Ap, 1951.

Russell, John H. The Free Negro in Virginia, 1619-1865. Baltimore, MD: Johns Hopkins Press, 1913.

Russell, Lester Franklyn. "Secondary Schools Established and Supported by Black Baptists in Virginia, 1887-1957." Doctoral dissertation, Rutgers U., 1976. Univ. Microfilms Order No. 76-27343.

Sampson, J. Milton. "These 'Colored' United States: Virginia." Messenger 5(Jl, 1923): 767-769.

"School Desegregation Up 50 Per Cent." Public Education in Virginia 6(Winter, 1971):15, 19.

Schroetter, Hilda N. Bethune Central Nursery School: A Study of a Negro Institution in Lynchburg, Virginia. Charlottesville: U. of Virginia, 1948.

Sellers, T. J. "...And the Class of '30." New York Times, D 27, 1976. [Jefferson High School, Charlottesville]

Shifflett, Crandall A. "The Household Composition of Rural Black Families: Louisa County, Virginia, 1880." Journal of Interdisciplinary History 6(1975):235-260.

Simsarian, Francis P. "Twenty-five Foster Placements. The Prince Edward County Children." Social Work, Ja, 1966.

Smith, R. C. "'Just Say We Remember.'" Southern Exposure 7(Summer, 1979):64-67, 70-71. [Prince Edward County, 1979]

_____. "Prince Edward County's 'Crippled Generation.'" Southern Education Report, Jl-Ag, 1966.

_____. They Closed Their Schools. Prince Edward County, Virginia, 1951-1964. Chapel Hill, NC: U. of North Carolina Press, 1965.

Smith, Charles Henry Edward, Sr. "The History of the Education of Blacks in the Portsmouth City Public Schools, 1871-1973: A Case Study." Doctoral dissertation, U. of Virginia, 1976. Univ. Microfilms Order No. 76-25005.

Smith, Emerson C. "How a Virginia County Made Up Its Mind." New South 4(D, 1948 and Ja, 1949):1-4. [King George County]

Snavely, Tipton R. The Taxation of Negroes in Virginia. Phelps-Stokes Fellowship Papers. Charlottesville, VA: U. of Virginia, 1916.

Spencer, Edwin C. An Analysis of the Dropout Problem in Norfolk Secondary Schools, S, 1977. ERIC ED 151 461.

Spencer, James Preston. "A Study to Determine the Development in Opportunity for Negroes in the Public Secondary Schools of Virginia, 1927-28, 1936-37." Master's thesis, U. of Michigan, 1939.

Stronach, Carey E. "Anatomy of a Black Victory." Nation 217(Ag 27, 1973):146-148. [Petersburg]

Sullivan, Neil V. "A Case Study in Achieving Equal Educational Opportunity." Journal of Negro Education, Summer, 1965. [Prince Edward County]

_____. Bound for Freedom. Boston, MA: Little, Brown, 1965. [Prince Edward County]

Tate, Thad W., Jr. The Negro in Eighteenth Century Williamsburg. Charlottesville, VA: U. Press of Virginia, 1965.

Taylor, Alrutheus Ambush. The Negro in the Reconstruction of Virginia. Washington, DC: Association for the Study of Negro Life and History, 1926.

_____. "The Negro in the Reconstruction of Virginia." Journal of Negro History 11(Ap, 1926):243-415.

Temple, David G. Merger Politics. Local Government Consolidation in Tidewater Virginia. Charlottesville, VA: U. Press of Virginia, 1972.

Terjen, Kitty. "Cradle of Resistance: Prince Edward County Today." New South 28(Summer, 1973):18-27.

Thomson, Brian W. "Racism and Racial Classification: A Case Study of the Virginia Racial Integrity Legislation." Doctoral dissertation, U. of California, Riverside, 1978. Univ. Microfilms Order No. 7904048.

"Times Are Changing in Prince Edward." Southern Patriot, D, 1967. [Prince Edward County]

Tippitt, Albert Gilbert. "The Extent of the Relationship of Certain Factors to the Displacement of Black School Principals of Virginia from 1953 to 1970." Doctoral dissertation, U. of Virginia, 1971. Univ. Microfilms Order No. 72-07309.

Tyler, Gerry. "Farmville, Virginia: The Struggle Goes On." Muhammad Speaks, Ap 23, 1971.

U.S. Commission on Civil Rights, Virginia Advisory Committee. A Report of an Investigation into an Educational Dilemma. Washington, DC: The Commission, 1970.

_____. School Desegregation in Newport News City, Virginia. Washington, DC: The Commission, My, 1977.

Vaughn, Alden T. "Blacks in Virginia: A Note on the First Decade." William and Mary Quarterly, Jl, 1972.

Virginia State Advisory Committee to the U.S. Commission on Civil Rights. The Federal Role in School Desegregation in Selected Virginia Districts. Washington, DC: GPO, S, 1968.

"Virginia's Educational Disparities." Virginia Journal of Education 66(Mr, 1973):17-20.

Walker, John E. "The Costs of Education: An Empirical Inquiry." Doctoral dissertation, U. of Virginia, 1963. Univ. Microfilms Order No. 64-730.

Weiner, Ethel Marie. [Letter to Editor of Richmond, VA News Leader] South Today 3 (Jl-Ag, 1972). [By graduating senior in desegregated school in Richmond]

Wilayto, Phil. "Norfolk, Va: A City in Crisis." Workers World, Je 17, 1977.

Wilkerson, Doxey A. "The Negro and Education in Virginia." Southern Workman 63(Ap, 1934): 117-121.

_____. "The Negro School Movement in Virginia: From 'Equalization' to 'Integration.'" Journal of Negro Education, Winter, 1960.

_____. "Some Correlates of Recent Progress Toward Equalizing White and Negro Schools in Virginia." Doctoral dissertation, New York U., 1958. Univ. Microfilms Order No. 59-1026.

_____. "The Vocational Choices of Virginia High-School Seniors." Virginia Teachers' Bulletin 7(N, 1930):1-6.

Williams, William Taylor Burwell. "Financial Contributions to Negro Schools in Virginia." Southern Workman 33(O, 1904):550.

Winn, William. "Surry County: Virginia's Last Outpost of 'Massive Resistance.'" South Today 3(N, 1971):3.

Winslow, H. F. "Virginia's Fifth Column."
Crisis, Ag-S, 1952.

Wynes, Charles E. "The Evolution of Jim Crow
Laws in Twentieth Century Virginia." Phylon,
Winter, 1967.

_____. Race Relations in Virginia, 1870-
1902. Charlottesville, VA: U. of Virginia
Press, 1961.

Washington

Adatto, Albert. "Sephardim and the Seattle
Sephardic Community." Master's thesis, U.
of Washington, 1939.

Amdur, Revel S. "An Exploratory Study of
Nineteen Negro Families in the Seattle Area
Who Were First Negro Residents in White
Neighborhoods, of their White Neighbors, and
of the Integration Process, Together with a
Proposed Program to Promote Integration in
Seattle." Master's thesis, U. of Washington,
1962.

Barth, Ernest A. T., and Abu-Laban, Baha.
"Power Structure and the Negro Sub-
Community." American Sociological Review 24
(F, 1959):69-76. [Seattle]

Bleeg, Joanne W. "Black People in the Territory
of Washington, 1860-1880." Doctoral dissertation, U. of Washington, 1970.

Burgess, Margaret Elaine. "A Study of Selected
Socio-Cultural and Opinion Differentials
Among Negroes and Whites in the Pasco,
Washington Community." Master's thesis,
State College of Washington, 1948.

Caley, Barbara. "How a School Fails." Integrated Education 7(S-O, 1969):10-22.
[Seattle]

Collister, Lary. A Narrative Account of the
Development of Desegregation Goals for the
Seattle School District, 1970-1975, D, 1975.
ERIC ED 145 014.

Comptroller General of the United States.
Disapproval of Seattle, Washington, School
District Applications for Emergency School
Aid Funds. Washington, DC: GPO, 1976.

Davis, Lenwood G. "Sources for History of
Blacks in Washington State." Western Journal
of Black Studies 2(Spring, 1978):60-64.

Droker, Howard Alan. "The Seattle Civic Unity
Committee and the Civil Rights Movement,
1944-1964." Doctoral dissertation, U. of
Washington, 1974. Univ. Microfilms Order No.
74-29,402.

_____. "Seattle Race Relations During the
Second World War." Pacific North West
Quarterly 67(O, 1976):163-174.

Epps, Edgar G. "Socioeconomic Status, Race,
Level of Aspiration and Juvenile Delinquency:
A Limited Empirical Test of Merton's
Concept of Deviation," Phylon, Spring, 1967.
[High school in Seattle]

Education for the 70's: A Survey of Community
Opinion about the Tacoma Public Schools.
Tacoma, WA: Tacoma School District 10, My,
1971, 132 pp. ERIC ED 053 191.

Governor's Advisory Council on Urban Affairs.
Urban Washington: Apathy or Action?, N, 1968.
Urban Affairs Council, Secretary of State's
Office, Legislative Bldg., Olympia, WA 98501.

Haley, Fred T. "Tacoma Faces School Segregation."
Integrated Education, Ap-My, 1964.

Harris, William M. A Design for Desegregation
Evaluation, 1976. ERIC ED 148 922. Seattle

Huckle, Herbert A. Tacoma School District No.
10, Title IV In-Service Education Program:
An Evaluation. Seattle, WA: U. of Seattle,
School of Education, S 30, 1969, 28 pp.
ERIC ED 045 751.

Joint Committee on Education. The Urban Educa-
tion Crisis in Washington State: A Special
Report to the Legislative. Seattle, WA:
State Legislative Subcommittee on Metropolitan
Education, 1969.

Markholt, Otillie. "White Incubus." Negro
Digest, Je, 1969. [The white liberal and the
black freedom movement. Material on Tacoma
and Seattle, WA]

Miller, Sidney and others. A Comparative Study
of Attitudes and Factors Influencing the
Decision of Negro Parents of Seventh Grade
Students to Participate in the Seattle
Transfer Program to Improve Racial Balance.
Seattle, WA: School of Social Work, U. of
Washington, 1965.

_____. A Survey of Adjustment of the Negro
Students Who Transferred to Schools Outside
Their Neighborhoods During 1963-1964 Under the
New Seattle School Board Ruling. Seattle, WA:
School of Social Work, U. of Washington, 1964.

Morio, Dominic W. "Seattle Schools and the
40/60/40 Syndrome." Urban Review, O, 1969.

Morrill, Richard L. "The Negro Ghetto: Problems
and Alternatives," Geographical Review, Jl,
1965. [Deals especially with Seattle]

O'Brien, Robert W. "Seattle: Race Relations
Frontier, 1949." Common Ground 9(Spring,
1949):18-23.

Office of the Superintendent of Public Instruction.
Demographic and Socioeconomic Profiles of the
American Indian, Black, Chinese, Filipino,
Japanese, Spanish Heritage and White Popula-
tion of Washington State in 1970... Vol. 5.
Olympia, WA: The Office, 1974.

Patterson, Eugene. "Busing and School Desegregation: A Recurring Issue." Western Journal
of Black Studies 1(S, 1977):186-194.

Research Office. Racial Distribution. Distribution and Change Among Pupils and Employees of the Seattle Public Schools...
1957 to 1966. Seattle, WA: Seattle Public
Schools, D 6, 1966.

Rice, Constance. "School Desegregation in
Seattle: A Historical and Contemporary
Synopsis." Western Journal of Black Studies
1(S, 1977):199-203.

Roberts, Brian (ed.). They Cast a Long Shadow.
A History of the Nonwhite Races on Bain-
bridge Island, 1975. ERIC ED 133 388.

Schafer, Ronald (comp.). Report of the Educational Park Advisory Committee to the Joint
Committee on Education. Olympia, WA:
Washington State Legislature, Ag, 1968, 26
pp. ERIC ED 028 543.

Schmid, Calvin F. et al. Non-White Races--
State of Washington. Olympia, WA: State
Planning and Community Affairs Agency, 1968.

Schmid, Calvin, and McVey, Wayne W., Jr.
Growth and Distribution of Minority Races in
Seattle. Seattle, WA: Seattle Public
Schools, 1964. [Includes analysis of
attendance areas]

Seattle Public Schools. Intergroup Education.
Seattle, WA: Seattle Public Schools, 1965.

_____. A Report of Racial Distribution Among
Pupils and Employees. Seattle, WA: Board
of Education, 1968.

Seattle Urban League. A Proposal for Re-
Organization of the Elementary Division of
the Seattle Public Schools, Autumn, 1964.
Seattle Urban League, 605 Lowman Bldg., 107
Cherry, Seattle, WA 98104.

_____. A Proposal for Re-Organization of the
Elementary Division of the Seattle Public
Schools, including statistical volume.
Seattle, WA: Seattle Urban League, Autumn,
1964. [A proposal to desegregate the city's
elementary schools via an adaptation of the
Princeton Plan]

Server, David Arthur. "Comparison of Negro
and White Attitudes in a Washington Community." Master's thesis, Washington State U.,
1967.

Shepherd, George. 1970 Demographic and Socio-
Economic Profiles of the Populations of the
1972 Congressional and Legislative Districts
of the State of Washington, Developed for
Reference Use in Washington State Education
Programs With Particular Emphasis on the
Urban, Racial, and Disadvantaged Programs of
the Office of the Superintendent of Public
Instruction. 3 vols. Olympia, WA: Office
of the Superintendent of Public Instruction,
1973.

_____. Population Profiles, Vols. 2-5.
Demographic and Socioeconomic Profiles of the
Populations of Washington State School
Districts with Over 400 Students, Je, 1973-
J1, 1974. ERIC ED 097 181-097 184.

Shephard, Susann. Out-Migration of Students
from Seattle Public Schools to Non-Public
Schools, J1, 1977. ERIC ED 144 225.

Slocum, Walter L. Rural Youth in Washington
State: Sociological Studies, 1954-1974.
Pullman: College of Agriculture Research
Center, Washington State U., 1976.

Smith, Donald K. "The Negro Viewpoint."
Seattle Times, Ag 15-22, 1965. [Negroes in
Seattle]

Stevens, John. "A Study of the Status of
Sunnyside Migrant Children in the Outlook
Elementary Schools." Master's thesis, U.
of Washington, 1955.

Taplin, Vaughn. "Seattle School [Desegregation]
Plan Anti-Black." Muhammad Speaks, Ja 8,
1971.

Taylor, Quintard. "Migration of Blacks and
Resulting Discriminatory Practices in
Washington State between 1940 and 1950."
Western Journal of Black Studies 2(Spring,
1978):65-71.

Thomas, Paul F. "George Bush." Master's thesis,
U. of Washington, 1965. [Black leader in 19th
century State of Washington]

Trombley, William. "Seattle 'Volunteers' for
Busing." Los Angeles Times, Ap 16, 1978.

_____. "Seattle's Desegregation Campaign
Slows." Los Angeles Times, Mr 7, 1979.

Urban Washington: Apathy or Action? Report of
the Governor's Council on Urban Affairs,
N, 1968. ERIC ED 042 858.

Valentine, Charles A. Segregation and Integra-
tion in Seattle's Public Schools. Seattle,
WA: Seattle CORE, 2202½ East Union Stree,
Ag, 1964.

Washington Education Association's Policy on De
Facto Segregation in Washington State.
Seattle, WA: Washington Education Associ-
ation, 1970, 42 pp. ERIC ED 048 413.

Washington Human Rights Commission. Human Rights
Profile: City of Vancouver, Washington.
Olympia, WA: The Commission, 1972.

Washington State Commission on the Causes and
Prevention of Civil Disorder. Race and
Violence in Washington State. Report.
Olympia, WA: The Commission, 1969.

Washington State Legislature. Non-Segregated
Education in Washington Schools. Olympia,
WA: Joint Committee on Education, 1970.

Washington Supreme Court. "Approve Busing for De Facto Desegregation." Integrated Education (My-Je, 1972):70-74. [Seattle]

Watts, Lewis G. "Racial Trends in Seattle, Washington, 1958." Crisis (Je-Jl, 1958): 333-338.

Whitman, Winslow. Study of Racial Tension in Tacoma. Olympia, WA: State Board Against Discrimination, 1970.

Whitman, Winslow, and Rosenfels, Isabelle G. Study and Evaluation of Racial Tension at Pasco High School. Olympia, WA: State Board Against Discrimination, 1969.

Wiley, James T., Jr. "Race Conflict as Exemplified in a Washington Town." Master's thesis, Washington State U., 1949. [Pasco]

Wolf, Ruth. "Our Shoddy Public Schools [in Seattle]." Washington Education, Ja, 1969.

                    West Virginia

Allen, Le Roy B. "Desegregation in West Virginia." Chicago Jewish Forum 20(Summer, 1962):288-293.

Comptroller General of the United States. Opportunities for Improving Administration of Federal Program of Aid to Educationally Deprived Children in West Virginia. Washington, DC: General Accounting Office, Mr 5, 1970.

Crowell, Suzanne. "Why School Bonds Are Defeated." Southern Patriot, My, 1968. [Mercer County]

Drake, Thomas M., and Temple, David G. (comps.). Human Relations: A Reader for West Virginians. Morgantown, WV: Bureau fo Government Research, West Virginia U., 1968.

Harless, Rod. The West Virginia Establishment, N, 1971. Appalachian Movement Press, P.O. Box 8074, Huntington, WV 25705.

Haught, James A. "AEL: Million Dollar Boon or Boondoggle?" Charleston Gazette, Jl 16, 1974. [Appalachia Educational Laboratory, Charleston, WV]

Hill, T. Edward. The Negro in West Virginia. Report of Bureau of Negro Welfare and Statistics of the State of West Virginia, 1925-26. Charleston, WV: Bureau Welfare and Statistics, 1926.

Himelrick, John B. Evaluation Institute on Interethnic Aspects of Public School Education in West Virginia. Final Report. Buckhannon, WV: West Virginia Wesleyan College, Ap 30, 1970, 36 pp. ERIC ED 047 024.

Hull, Bruce H. "A Comparative Study of the Curriculum Offerings of Eight Negro and Eight White North Central Association High Schools in West Virginia." Master's thesis, U. of Michigan, 1937.

Jackameit, William P. "A Short History of Negro Public Education in West Virginia, 1890-1965." West Virginia History 37(Jl, 1976): 309-324.

Johnson, Paul M. "Integration in West Virginia Since 1954." Master's thesis, West Virginia U., 1960.

Musa, Omari. "Blacks Recall Three Decades in the Mines." Militant, Ap 14, 1978. Widen

Nowlin, William F. The Negro and the Public Library in West Virginia. Bluefield, WV: Bluefield State Teachers College, 1940.

Nutter, T. Gillis. "These 'Colored' United States: West Virginia." Messenger 5 (F, 1924):44-48.

Posey, Thomas E. The Negro Citizen of West Virginia. Institute, WV: Press of West Virginia State College, 1934.

Saundle, H. P. "The Preparation and Professional Training of the Negro High-School Teachers in West Virginia." Master's thesis, U. of Cincinnati, 1928.

Sheeler, John Reuben. "The Negro in West Virginia before 1900." Doctoral dissertation, West Virginia U., 1954.

Smith, Douglas C. "In Quest of Equality: The West Virginia Experience." West Virginia History 37(Ap, 1976).

_____. "Race Relations and Institutional Reponses in West Virginia--A History. West Virginia and the Black Experience: An Historical Overview" (Part I). West Virginia History 39(Fall, 1977):30-48.

Stealey, John E. III. "The Freedmen's Bureau in West Virginia." West Virginia History 39 (Ja-Ap, 1978):99-142.

Steel, Edward M., Jr. "Black Monongalians: A Judicial View of Slavery and the Negro in Monongalia County, 1776-1865." West Virginia History 34(Jl, 1973):331-359.

Teacher Rights Division. Kanawha County, West Virginia. A Textbook Study in Cultural Context. Washington, DC: National Education Association, F, 1975.

U.S. Commission on Civil Rights. West Virginia Advisory Committee. School Desegregation in Raleigh County. Washington, DC: The Commission, 1977.

West Virginia. Human Rights Commission. Special Report...of Events at Stonewall Jackson High School in November, 1969. Charleston, WV: The Commission, 1970.

Whiting, G. W. "The Present Status of Elementary Education Among Negroes in West Virginia." Bulletin (organ of the National Association of Teachers in Colored Schools) 11(Ap-My, 1931):21-22 and 26-27.

Williams, E. R. "Contacts of Negroes and Whites in Morgantown." Master's thesis, West Virginia U., 1952.

Wood, Edward Grimke. "Development of Secondary Education for Negroes in West Virginia." Master's thesis, U. of Cincinnati, 1937.

Wisconsin

Ames, Kathleen F. "A Socio-Political Profile of Candidates for the Milwaukee Common Council and County Board in General Elections, 1944-1964." Master's thesis, U. of Wisconsin-Milwaukee, 1965.

Anderson, Stuart A. "A Study of the Pupil Population of Pulaski High School, Milwaukee, Wisconsin." Master's thesis, Marqueette U., 1938.

Aukofen, Frank. City With a Chance: A Case History of Civil Revolution. Milwaukee, WI: Bruce Publishing Company, 1968. [Milwaukee]

Bednarek, David I. "Milwaukee." Integrateducation 15(N-D, 1977):36-37.

_____. "Students Offer an Insight." Milwaukee Journal, Je 26, 1977. [Extracts from diaries kept by students in newly-desegregated schools]

Benedict, Gary C. "An Analysis of Attitudes Toward School Desegregation Across District Lines." Doctoral dissertation, Marquette U., 1978. Univ. Microfilms Order No. 7824347. [Milwaukee area]

Bennett, David A. Community Involvement in Desegregation: Milwaukee's Voluntary Plan. Milwaukee: Milwaukee Public Schools, Mr 27, 1978.

Browne, Jeff. "Busing Did Little to Scores." Milwaukee Journal, Mr 11, 1979. [Change in Milwaukee schools, 1976-1978]

_____. "Integration Gets a D." Milwaukee Journal, Ap 24, 1977. [Parkview Elementary School, Milwaukee]

Byrns, Ruth. "Intelligence and Nationality of Wisconsin School Children." Journal of Social Psychology 7(1936):455-470.

Catholic Interracial Council. "Segregation in Milwaukee Catholic Elementary Schools." Integrated Education, F-Mr, 1967.

Clark, W. A. V., and Hansell, C. R. "The Expansion of the Negro Ghetto in Milwaukee." Tijdschrift voor Economische en Sociale Geografie 61(1970):267-277.

Colton, David L. Urban School Desegregation Costs. Part I. Case Studies. St. Louis, MO: Center for Educational Field Studies, Washington U., N, 1977. [Milwaukee]

Commission on Community Relations. The Negro in Milwaukee, Progress and Portent. Milwaukee, WI, 1963.

Conta, Dennis J. The East Shore District Plan. A City-Suburban School Merger Proposal, 1975. East Shore Committee for Quality Education, 2625 East Shorewood Blvd., Milwaukee, WI 53211. [Milwaukee area]

_____. "Fiscal Incentives and Voluntary Integration: Wisconsin's Effort to Integrate Public Schools." Journal of Education Finance 3(Winter, 1978):279-296.

Davidson, John Nelson. Negro Slavery in Wisconsin. Milwaukee: Parkman Club Publications, VI, My 12, 1896.

Delaney, Paul. "School Integration Gains in Racine, Wisc[onsin], Program Viewed as Model for the Nation." New York Times, O 22, 1975.

Department of Research and Development. Faculty Attitude Survey. 1976. Racine, WI: Racine Unified School District, D, 1976.

Eden, Lynn. Crisis in Watertown: The Polarization of an American Community. Ann Arbor, MI: U. of Michigan Press, 1972.

Edwards, Ozzie L. "Patterns of Residential Segregation within a Metropolitan Ghetto." Demography 7(My, 1970):185-193. [Milwaukee]

Eisinger, Peter K. The Patterns of Interracial Politics. Conflict and Cooperation in the City. New York: Academic Press, 1975. [Milwaukee]

Equal Educational Opportunity Policy Research Project. "Milwaukee," passim. In Federal Policies for Equal Educational Opportunity: Conflict and Confusion. Austin, TX: Lyndon B. Johnson School of Public Affairs, U. of Texas, 1977.

Eurich, Alvin C. and others. Quality Education in Milwaukee's Future. New York: Academy for Educational Development, Ag 1, 1967.

Evans, Francis B. Public Opinions About Education: A Statewide Poll of Wisconsin Residents. Madison, WI: Wisconsin Department of Public Instruction, O, 1976.

Flaming, K., Palen, J., Ringlen, G., and Taylor, C. "Black Powerlessness in Policy Making Positions." Sociological Quarterly 13(1972): 126-133. [Milwaukee]

Frahm, Robert A., and Corty, Julianne. "Unified Desegregation? Ho hum." Racine Journal-Times, Je 21, 1976. [The first year of desegregation in the Racine, WI public schools]

Gibson, Morgan and others. De Facto Segregation in Milwaukee, D 10, 1963. Milwaukee: The Wisconsin Conference of Branches of NAACP, 1963.

Goldberg, Robert A. "The Ku Klux Klan in Madison, 1922-1927." Wisconsin Magazine of History 58(Autumn, 1974).

Golightly, Cornelius L. "De Facto Segregation in Milwaukee Schools." Integrated Education, D, 1963-Ja, 1964.

Gorton, Patricia Claire. "Perceptions and Practices of Secondary School Libraries in Facilitating Reading in Suburban Schools With Minority Transfer Students." Doctoral dissertation, U. of Wisconsin-Milwaukee, 1978. Univ. Microfilms Order No. 7823490. [Chapter 220 programs in Wisconsin]

Haslanger, Phil. "Minorities Isolated Within Schools." Capital Times, F 27, 1976. [Madison]

"Here Is How City's Public Schools Scored on [Achievement] Tests." Milwaukee Journal, Ap 23, 1972. [Milwaukee]

Kaplan, Henry K., and Matkom, Anthony J. "Peer Status and Intellectual Functioning of Negro School Children." Psychology in the Schools, Ap, 1967. [Madison]

Kellogg, Louise Phelps. "The Bennett Law in Wisconsin." Wisconsin Magazine of History 2 (S, 1918).

Koppe, Barbara A. "Suit Will Blame Segregation on School Policies." Milwaukee Journal, S 5, 1973.

Korman, Gerd. Industrialization, Immigrants, and Americanizers: The View from Milwaukee, 1866-1921. Madison, WI: State Historical Society of Wisconsin, 1967.

Kritek, William J. "Voluntary Desegregation in Wisconsin." Integrateducation 15(N-D, 1977):83-87.

Larson, Richard G. and others. "Racism in Kindergarten?" Elementary School Journal, Ja, 1969. [Racine]

Lynagh, Paula. Milwaukee's Negro Community. Milwaukee: Citizens Governmental Research Bureau of Milwaukee, 1946.

McNally, Joel and others. "Integration: The Student View." Milwaukee Journal, My 9-13, 1976. [Series of articles reporting on student opinion in Milwaukee]

Mace, Jane. "Can Our Children Be Saved? A Teacher Speaks Out." Chicago Sun-Times Midwest, Ag 28, 1977. [Marshall High School, Milwaukee]

"Milwaukee 'Beer Capital' Image Fades as Big City Problems Emerge." Black Enterprise 2 (Jl, 1972):39-43.

Milwaukee Journal. "Students View Desegregation in Milwaukee." Integrateducation 14 (S-O, 1976):43-51.

Milwaukee Public Schools. Open Enrollment Study. Milwaukee, WI: Board of Education, Ja, 1972.

Milwaukee Urban League. Negro Teachers in the Milwaukee School System. Milwaukee: Milwaukee Urban League, 1965.

Modlinski, Julius John. "Commandos: A Study of a Black Organization's Transformation from Militant Protest to Social Service." Doctoral dissertation, U. of Wisconsin, 1978. Univ. Microfilms Order No. 7815061. [Milwaukee]

Munch, Peter A. "Segregation and Assimilation of Norwegian Settlements in Wisconsin." Norwegian-American Studies and Records 18 (1954):102-140.

Nelson, C. Richard. The Plan to Eliminate Racial Imbalance in the Elementary Schools. Racine, WI: Unified School District No. 1 of Racine County, Ja 13, 1975.

Olley, Michelle. "Lessons from Voluntary Public School Desegregation." In Catholic Schools and Racial Integration: Perspectives, Directions, Models, pp. 17-23. Washington, DC: National Catholic Conference for Interracial Justice, 1977. [Racine]

Ollie, Bert W., Jr. "The Development and Testing of a Model to Determine the Perceived Influences on the Desegregation Planning Process and Its Outputs." Doctoral dissertation, U. of Wisconsin, 1978. [Milwaukee]

_____. "Racine." Integrateducation 15(N-D, 1977):24-27.

Omari, Thompson P. "Urban Adjustment of Rural Southern Negro Migrants in Beloit, Wisconsin." Doctoral dissertation, U. of Wisconsin, 1955.

O'Reilly, Charles T. The Inner Core-North. A Study of Milwaukee's Negro Community, D, 1963. ERIC ED 018 511.

Patrinos, Dan. "Father James E. Groppi." National Catholic Reporter, N 27, 1968. [Milwaukee]

Pinnock, Theodore James. *A Comparison of the Effectiveness of Film and Bulletin in Transmitting Knowledge to Negro 4-H Club Local Leaders in Alabama and Caucasian 4-H Club Local Leaders in Wisconsin.* Madison, WI: U. of Wisconsin, 19655, 122 pp. Ph.D. dissertation. ERIC ED 025 698.

A Plan to Reduce Prejudice and Discrimination in the Greater Milwaukee Area. New York: Greenleigh Associates, 1967.

Prindeville, Sr. Mary J. "History of Catholic Education in the Diocese of Green Bay." Master's thesis, Catholic U. of America, 1953.

Rauch, Delores. "Impact of Population Changes in the Central Area of Milwaukee upon Catholic Parochial Schools, 1940-1970." Master's thesis, U. of Wisconsin-Milwaukee, 1968.

Reardon, Patrick. "Wells Faces Up to Problems." *Milwaukee Journal*, Ja 27, 1976. [Wells Street Junior High School, Milwaukee]

Rose, Harold M. "The Development of An Urban Subsystem: The Case of the Negro Ghetto." *Annals of the Association of American Geographers* 60(Mr, 1970):1-17. [Milwaukee, 1960-1970]

Rummsler, Gary C. "South Side Offers Integration Index." *Milwaukee Journal*, N 21, 1976. [Hamilton, Bay View, and Pulaski High Schools]

Schmandt, Henry J. and others. *Milwaukee, A Contemporary Urban Profile.* New York: Praeger, 1971.

Schmidt, Wayne. "Wisconsin Synod Lutheran Parochial Schools, 1850-1890." Doctoral dissertation, U. of Wisconsin, 1968.

Sewell, William H., and Armer, J. Michael. "Neighborhood Context and College Plans." *American Sociological Review*, Ap, 1966. [Milwaukee]

Sheppard, Nathaniel, Jr. "For Blacks, Milwaukee Is the Toughest Place to Find a Job." *New York Times*, D 31, 1977.

Smith, James Hoard, and 2X (Harris), Le Roy. "Nazis Foment Tension in Milwaukee School System." *Muhammad Speaks*, N 15, 1974.

Smith, Philip L. "Voluntary Participation and Public Opinion in Milwaukee School Desegregation." *Integrateducation* 15(N-D, 1977): 88-91.

Social Development Corporation. "Racial Isolation in Milwaukee Public School," My, 1967. Social Development Corporation, 1717 Massachusetts Avenue, N.W., Washington, DC. Unpublished study prepared for the U.S. Commission of Civil Rights.

Stanford, Gregory D., and Blackwell, Edward H. "Still Victims, Blacks Insist." *Milwaukee Journal*, My 15, 1977. [Criticisms of desegregation plan in Milwaukee]

Sweetser, Thomas, S.J. "Rundown on a Demonstration." *Community*, D, 1965. [The school boycott in Milwaukee, O, 1965]

Tamney, J. B. *Solidarity in a Slum.* New York: Halsted Press, 1974. [Milwaukee]

"Teacher's Attack Leads to Milwaukee Boycott." *SOBU Newsletter*, Mr 20, 1971. [Washington High School]

"Teacher's Reinstatement Seen as Victory for Black Education." *African World*, Ag 21, 1971. [Milwaukee]

Thomas, Ruth. "Negro in the School. Conflicts Due to Racial Imbalance." *Clearing House*, N, 1966. [Milwaukee]

Todd, William J. "A Factor Analysis of Black-White Polarization in Milwaukee, 1950-1970." *Bulletin, Illinois Geographic Society* 14 (D, 1972):17-29.

_____. "Factor-Analytic Black-White Polarization in Milwaukee, 1950 to 1970." Master's thesis, Indiana State U., 1972.

Ulrich, Robert James. "The Bennett Law of 1889: Education and Politics in Wisconsin." Doctoral dissertation, U. of Wisconsin, 1965.

U.S. Commission on Civil Rights. *School Desegregation in Racine, Wisconsin.* Washington, DC: The Commission, Je, 1977.

"The Urban Day School." *Center for Urban Education Program Conspectus*, O, 1969. [Milwaukee]

Vorlop, Frederic C. "Equal Opportunity and the Politics of Education in Milwaukee." Doctoral dissertation, U. of Wisconsin, 1970.

Washington, R. O., and Oliver, John. *An Historical Account of Blacks in Milwaukee.* Milwaukee, WI: Milwaukee Urban Observatory, 1976.

Willman, Frederick. "School Desegregation: The Milwaukee Road." *Chicago* 27(Mr, 1978):112-115.

Wisconsin. Governor's Commission on Human Rights. *Negro Families in Rural Wisconsin. A Study of their Community Life.* Madison, WI: State of Wisconsin, 1959.

Wyoming

Morgan, William E., Peart, Margaret W., and Barker, Florence P. Demographic Study of Wyoming Population in Transition. Laramie, WY: Division of Business and Economic Research, U. of Wyoming, 1969.

More Than One

Anderson, Robert E., Jr. (ed.). The South and Her Children: School Desegregation, 1970-1971. Atlanta, GA: Southern Regional Council, Mr, 1971.

Bowler, Mike. "North or South: Who Will Show the Way to School Integration?" South Today 2(D, 1970):5-8. [Pasadena, CA; Ferndale, MI; Baltimore, MD; Riverside, CA; Corona, CA; Pontiac, MI; New Rochelle, NY; and Atlanta, GA]

_____. "3 Anti-Busing Cities Now Accept It." Baltimore Sun, Je 12, 1972. [Charlotte, NC; Richmond, VA; and Harrisburg, PA]

Braham, R. V., Johnson, George A., Coons, F. Loretta, Thomson, Willis, and Bish, Charles E. "What Has Been Our Experience in Racial Integration?" Bulletin of the National Association of Secondary School Principals, Ap 1, 1955. [Charleston, WV; Wilmington, DE; New Rochelle, NY; and Washington, DC]

Burkhead, Jesse, with Fox, Thomas G., and Holland, John W. Input and Output in Large City High Schools. Syracuse, NY: Syracuse U. Press, 1967. [Atlanta and Chicago]

Buskin, Martin. "How Schoolmen Are Handling the Hot Ones: Integration, Innovation, and Negotiation." School Management, Je, 1967. [Highland Park and Inkster, MI; Inglewood, CA; Montgomery County, MD; and Evanston, IL]

Campbell, Angus, and Schuman, Howard. Racial Attitudes in Fifteen American Cities. Ann Arbor, MI: U. of Michigan, Jl, 1969, 69 pp. Available from Dept. E, Publications Div., Room 1060, Institute for Social Research, 426 Thompson Street, Ann Arbor, MI 48106 ($1). ERIC ED 040 907.

Cayton, Horace R. "America's 10 Best Cities for Negroes." Negro Digest (O, 1947):4-10.

Community Relations Service. 1975 Annual Report. Washington, DC: U.S. Department of Justice, 1976.

"Conditions of the Negro in Various Cities." Bulletin of the [U.S.] Department of Labor 2(My, 1897):257-360.

Crain, Robert and others. School Desegregation in the North: Eight Comparative Case Studies of Community Structures and Policy Making. Chicago, IL: National Opinion Research Center, U. of Chicago, Ap, 1966.

De Boer, Peter P., and McCaul, Robert L. (comps.). "Annotated List of Chicago Tribune Editorials of Elementary and Secondary Education in the U.S., Part II, 1875-1880." History of Education Quarterly 13 (Summer, 1973):201-214.

De Muth, Jerry. "Southern Catholic Schools Pressured." National Catholic Reporter, S 25, 1970. [Mississippi and Alabama]

"Desegregation. 10 Blueprints for Action." School Management, O, 1966. [Zenia, Ohio; Irondequoit, NY; Evanston, IL; York, PA; Riverside, CA; New Haven, CT; and Teaneck, NJ]

Eaton, John, Jr. Colored Schools in Mississippi, Arkansas, and Tennessee, April, 1865. Memphis, TN: n.p., 1865.

Egerton, John. "De Facto Segregation: A Tale of Three Cities." Southern Education Report, S, 1967. [Little Rock, Nashville and Atlanta]

_____. Racial Protest in the South--1969 Style. Case Studies of Forrest City, Ark. and Sommerville, Tenn., O, 1969. Race Relations Information Center, Nashville, TN 37212

Fancher, Betsy. "Students: Getting It Together. In Changing Schools Some Show How." South Today 3(Jl-Ag, 1971):1, 7. [South Carolina, Mississippi, and Georgia]

Fink, T. Ross. "United States Naval Policies on Education in Dependent Areas." Doctoral dissertation, U. of North Carolina, 1948.

Franklin, Vincent P. "The Persistence of School Segregation in the Urban North: An Historical Perspective." Journal of Ethnic Studies 1(Winter, 1974):51-68. [Philadelphia and elsewhere]

Giles, H. Harry. "Thirteen States Report." In The Integrated Classroom, chapter 5. New York: Basic Books, 1959. [32 cities in AR, DE, IN, KN, KY, MD, MO, NJ, NM, OK, TN, TX, WV, and Washington, DC]

Green, Donald Ross, Jordan, James A., Bridgeman, W. J., and Britain, Clay V. Black Belt Schools: Beyond Desegregation, N, 1965. Southern Regional Council, 5 Forsyth St, N.W., Atlanta, GA. [A study of Burke County, GA; and Edgefield, County, SC]

Glatt, Charles A. "Selected Demographic Factors that Affect School Planning: A Look at Four Northern Cities." Urban Education, Vol. No. 1(1966). [Cleveland, Buffalo, Cincinnati, and Rochester]

Highwood, Thomas J. "A Comparative Study of
Desegregation Problems that May Affect the
Organization, Management, and Control of
Junior High School Industrial Arts Programs
in North Carolina." Doctoral dissertation,
Pennsylvania State U., 1958. _Dissertation
Abstracts_, XX, 1959, p. 563. [DE, KY, MD,
MO, OK, WV, Washington, DC, and NC]

Jackson, Jacquelyne J. "Two Black Boycotts:
A Contrast of Success and Failure." _Afro-
American Studies_ 2(S, 1971):87-94.
[Tuskegee, AL and Durham, NC]

Kleeman, Richard P. "Schools and Race.
Dilemma Outside Dixie." _Minneapolis Tribune_,
O 25, 1970-O 31, 1970. [A series of seven
articles]

Levine, Daniel U., and Hall, Betty. "A Summer
School for Understanding Metropolitan
Living." In _Models for Integrated Education_,
pp. 66-76. Edited by Daniel U. Levine.
Worthington, OH: Jones, 1971. [Kansas City,
KS and MO]

Mabee, Carleton. "Freedom Schools, North and
South." _Reporter_, S 10, 1964. [Cleveland
and Mississippi]

Mack, Raymond W. (ed.). _Our Children's Burden:
Studies of Desegregation in Eight American
Communities_. New York: Random House, 1968.

Mason, Mame Charlotte. "The Policy of the
Segregation of the Negro in the Public
Schools of Ohio, Indiana, and Illinois."
Master's thesis, U. of Chicago, 1917.

Morlock, Laura. "Black Power and Black Influence in 91 Northern Cities." Doctoral
dissertation, Johns Hopkins U., 1973.

Morrison, Peter A. _San Jose and St. Louis in
the 1960's: A Case Study of Changing Urban
Populations_. Santa Monica, CA: Rand
Corporation, 1973.

NEA Task Force III. _School Desegregation:
Louisiana and Mississippi_. Washington, DC:
National Education Association, N 12, 1970.

Pechstein, A. L. "The Problem of Negro Education in Northern and Border Cities."
Elementary School Journal, N, 1929.

Peirce, Neal R. _The Deep South States of
America..._ New York: Norton, 1974.

Powledge, Fred. "Black Man, Go South."
Esquire, Ag, 1965. [Race relations,
especially school segregation, in Atlanta
and New York City]

Rivers, Marie D. "Peer Acceptance and Rejection
of Negro Teachers Who Were First or Among the
First to be Employed in White Schools North
of the Mason-Dixon Line." Doctoral dissertation, U. of Michigan, 1959. [13 cities
in 4 non-southern states]

"Roundup Report: How Schools Meet Desegrega-
tion Challenges." _Nation's Schools_, N,
1966. [Richmond, Charlotte, Birmingham,
Pasadena, Houston, Dallas, San Mateo,
Waukegan, Pittsburgh, Buffalo, Boston,
Evanston, Seattle, Los Angeles, Oakland,
Denver, Detroit, Chicago]

Rowan, Carl T. "Jim Crow's Last Stand."
Minneapolis Tribune, N 29-D 9, 1953
(11 articles).

_____. "'South of Freedom' 1971." _Ebony_ 26
(Ag, 1971):134-139. [McMinnville, TN;
Macomb, MS; and Prince Edward County, VA]

Rowland, Richard H. "Social Contact between
Blacks and Whites and Its Relationship to
Attitudes in Six Northern Cities."
Doctoral dissertation, Brandeis U., Je, 1970.

Savage, W. S. "Early Negro Education in the
Pacific Coast States." _Journal of Negro
Education_, Spring, 1946.

"School and Race in the South: The Human
Problem." _National Observer_, N 15, 1965.
[Nashville, TN, and Durham, NC]

"School-by-School Achievement Scores Issued."
Education U.S.A., My 1, 1967. [Philadelphia,
Washington, DC, and New York]

"Segregation in the North." _Common Ground_ 5
(Autumn, 1944):97. [New York and New Jersey]

Sexton, Patricia Cayo. "Comments on Three
Cities." _Integrated Education_, Ag, 1963.
[New York, Detroit, and Chicago]

Smurr, J. W. "Jim Crow Out West." In _Historical
Essays on Montana and the Northwest_. Edited
by J. W. Smurr and K. Ross Toole. Helena,
MT: n.p., 1957.

Spaulding, Frank E. _School Superintendent in
Action in Five Cities_. Rindge, NH: Richard
R. Smith, 1955.

Spicer, Edward H., and Thompson, Raymond H.
(eds.). _Plural Society in the Southwest_.
Albuquerque, NM: U. of New Mexico Press,
1975.

Spruill, Albert W. "Consequences Encountered
by Negro Teachers in the Process of Desegre-
gation of Schools in Four Southern States."
Doctoral dissertation, Cornell U., 1958.
Dissertation Abstracts, XIX, 1959, p. 3051.
[DE, KY, MD, and WV]

Stewart, Ollie. "America's 10 Worst Cities for
Negroes." _Negro Digest_ (Mr, 1948):44-49.

Stoff, Sheldon. _The Two-Way Street. Guideposts
to Peaceful School Desegregation_, 1967.
David Stewart Publishing Company, 3612
Washington Blvd., Indianapolis, IN 46205
[189 southern and border communities]

Stout, Robert T. "School Desegregation: Process in Eight Cities." In U.S. Commission on Civil Rights. Papers Prepared for National Conference on Equal Educational Opportunity in America's Cities. Washington, DC: GPO, 1968.

U.S. Commission on Civil Rights. Civil Rights U.S.A. Public Schools. Southern States, 1962. Washington, DC: GPO, 1962. [KY, NC, TN, VA]

_____. The 50 States Report. Washington, DC: GPO, 1961.

_____. Civil Rights U.S.A. Public Schools. Cities in the North and West. Washington, DC: GPO, 1962. [Highland Park, MI; New Rochelle, NY; Philadelphia, Chicago and St. Louis]

_____. Racial Isolation in the Public Schools. 2 vols. Washington, DC: GPO, 1967. [Describes practices in a number of northern and western cities]

_____. Survey of School Desegregation in the Southern and Border States, 1965-66. Washington, DC: GPO, n.d.

U.S. Commission on Civil Rights, Staff Study. "School Integration in Several Urban Areas." In U.S. Congress, 92nd, 2nd session, House of Representatives, Committee on the Judiciary, Subcommittee No. 5, School Busing. Hearings... Part 1, Serial No. 32, pp. 201-232. Washington, DC: GPO, 1972. [Pasadena, CA; Tampa-Hillsborough, FL; Charlotte-Mecklenburg, NC; and Pontiac, MI]

U.S. Congress, 92nd, 1st session, House of Representatives, Committee on Education and Labor, General Subcommittee on Education. The Safe Schools Act. Hearings... Washington, DC: GPO, 1972. [New York City and Boston]

U.S. Department of Health, Education, and Welfare. Planning Educational Change: Vol. IV: How Five School Systems Desegregated. Washington, DC: GPO, 1969. [Chapel Hill, NC; Chattooga County, GA; Riverside, CA; Rochester, NY; and Sherman, TX]

Van Hove, Erik, Coleman, James S., Rabben, Kenneth, and Karweit, Nancy. "Urban System Performance." In Evaluating Educational Performance, pp. 153-174. Edited by Herbert J. Alberg. Berkeley, CA: McCutchan, 1974. [New York City, Philadelphia, Detroit, Baltimore, Chicago, and Los Angeles]

Watters, Glenda. "Statistical Appendix." In Majority-Black School Districts in the 11 Southern States. Nashville, TN: Race Relations Information Center, Jl, 1970.

Wey, Herbert W., and Corey, John. Action Patterns in School Desegregation, A Guidebook. Bloomington, IN: Phi Delta Kappa, 1956. [70 school districts in TX, NC, TN, KY, WV, DE, and MD]

Williams, Robin M., Jr., and Ryan, Margaret W. (eds.). Schools in Transition. Community Experiences in Desegregation. Chapel Hill, NC: U. of North Carolina Press, 1954. [24 cities in AZ, IL, IN, NJ, NM, and OH]

Island Areas

Black, Emanuel. "The Teacher in the Territories and Outlying Possessions of the United States." Master's thesis, College of the City of New York, 1937.

Blauch, Lloyd E., and Reid, Charles F. Public Education in the Territories and Outlying Possessions. Washington, DC: GPO, 1939.

Harper, Alda Alexander. Tracing the Course of Growth and Development in Education Policy for the Canal Zone Colored Schools, 1905-55. Ann Arbor: School of Education, U. of Michigan, 1974.

Harrigan, Norwell, and Varlock, Pearl I. "The U.S. Virgin Islands and the Black Experience." Journal of Black Studies 7(Je, 1977): 387-410.

Reid, C. F. Education in the Territories and Outlying Possessions of the United States. New York: Columbia U., 1941.

U.S. Bureau of the Census. Characteristics of the Population Vol. : Outlying Areas--Guam, Virgin Islands, American Samoa, Canal Zone, Trust Territory of the Pacific Islands. Washington, DC: GPO, Ja, 1973.

U.S. Congress, 93rd, 1st session, Senate, Committee on Interior and Insular Affairs, Subcommittee on Territories and Insular Affairs. Briefing on Territorial Matters. Hearing... Washington, DC: GPO, 1973.

U.S. Congress, 93rd, 2nd session, House of Representatives, Committee on Interior and Insular Affairs, Subcommittee on Territorial and Insular Affairs. Continuance of Civil Government for the Trust Territory of the Pacific Islands. Hearing... Washington, DC: GPO, 1974.

Bibliographies

Appalachian Bibliography, Volumes I and II. Morgantown, WV: U. of West Virginia, 1970, 1168 pp. Available from The Library, West Virginia U., Morgantown, WV 26506. ERIC ED 043 409

Bowkett, Norma S. (comp.). Directions 70's: An Assessment of Educational Needs in Alaska. Juneau, AK: Office of Planning and Research, Department of Alaska, 1970.

Davis, Lenwood G. (comp.). Blacks in the State of Ohio, 1800-1976: A Preliminary Survey. Monticello, IL: Council of Planning Librarians, 1977.

_____ (comp.). Blacks in the State of Oregon, 1788-1974. 2nd ed. Monticello, IL: Council of Planning Librarians, 1974.

Deskins, D. R., Jr. (comp.). "Geographical Literature on the American Negro, 1949-1968: A Bibliography." Professional Geographer 21(1969):145-149.

Dickinson, D. C. "Black Bibliography." Wilson Library Bulletin 44(1969):184-187.

Dickson, Diane, and Dossor, Carol (comps.). World Catalogue of Theses on the Pacific Islands. Honolulu, Hawaii: U. of Hawaii Press, 1970.

Edwards, Everett E. References on the Mountaineers of the Southern Appalachians. Washington, DC: Library of the U.S. Department of Agriculture, 1935.

Fedink, Simon (comp.). Bibliography of Publications By and About New York State Division of Human Rights. New York: The Division, 1971.

Fuller, Willie J. (comp.). Blacks in Alabama, 1528-1865. Monticello IL: Council of Planning Librarians, 1976

Graeber, Isacque A. "Research in American Jewish Education." Jewish Education 24 (Spring, 1954):49-55.

Graff, George P. The People of Michigan. A History and Selected Bibliography of the Races and Nationalities Who Settled Our State. Lansing, MI: State Library, 1970.

Haller, Elizabeth S. (comp.). American Diversity: A Bibliography of Resources on Racial and Ethnic Minorities for Pennsylvania Schools. Harrisburg, PA: Pennsylvania State Dept. of Education, Bureau of General and Academic Education, 1970, 250 pp. ERIC ED 054 031.

Hamilton, Malcolm, C. (comp.). Desegregation and Busing. An Annotated Bibliography, with Special Reference to the Case in Boston. Cambridge, MA: Monroe C. Gutman Library, Harvard Graduate School of Education, N, 1976.

Harter, Carl L., with Davidson, Jossi and Wogan, Amelie (comps.). Metropolitan New Orleans Urban Affairs Bibliography. New Orleans, LA: Urban Studies Center, Tulane U., Je, 1969.

Hatter, Elizabeth S. (comp.). 1971 Supplement to American Diversity: A Bibliography of Resources on Racial and Ethnic Minorities for Pennsylvania Schools. Harrisburg, PA: Pennsylvania State Dept. of Education, 1971, 74 pp. ERIC ED 056 960.

Hughes, Daniel T., Day, Lincoln H., and Storms, Doris (comps.). A Bibliographic Resource for Demographic, Economic, and Social Trends in the Western Pacific. Washington, DC: Division of Behavioral Sciences, National Research Council, 1971.

Joynson, P. C., and Saunders, J. O. (comps.). "Education of Negroes in Virginia: An Annotated Bibliography." Virginia State College Gazette 50(F, 1944):1-16.

Masotti, Louis H., and Hadden, Jeffrey K. (comps.). Bibliography on Suburbs. Evanston, IL: Center for Urban Affairs, Northwestern U., 1972.

Michigan. Bureau of Library Services. Negroes in Michigan. A Selected Bibliography. 2nd ed. Lansing, MI: The Bureau, 1969.

Michigan Historical Collections (comp.). Black History Resources in the Michigan Historical Collections of the University of Michigan, 1971. The Collections, U Michigan, 160 Rockham Bldg., Ann Arbor, MI 48104.

Michigan State Library Services (comp.). Afro-Americans in Michigan. A Selected Bibliography. 4th ed. Lansing, 1975.

Mills, Hazel E., and Pryor, Nancy B. (comps.). The Negro in the State of Washington, 1788-1969. Olympia, WA: Washington State Library, Ja, 1970.

Munn, R. F. (comp.). The Southern Appalachians. A Bibliography and Guide to Studies. Morgantown, WV: Library, West Virginia U., 1961.

Nelsen, Hart M., and Nelsen, Anne K., with Miller, James K. (comps.). Bibliography on Appalachia. Bowling Green, KY: Western Kentucky U., 1967.

Oosterman, Gordon. Minority Groups in Anglo-America: An Introduction and Bibliography of Selected Materials. Grand Rapids, MI: National Union of Christian Schools, F, 1970, 66 pp. ERIC ED 048 066.

Pennsylvania. Bureau of General and Academic Education. American Diversity. A Bibliography of Resources on Racial and Ethnic Minorities for Pennsylvania Schools. Harrisburg, PA: The Bureau, 1969.

Porter, Dorothy B. (comp.). The Negro in the United States. A Selected Bibliography. Washington, DC: GPO, 1970.

Richard, Max (comp.). The Black Man in St. Louis: A Preliminary Bibliography. Monticello, IL: Council of Planning Librarians, 1974.

Roman, Frank B. "Poles in Cleveland. An Annotated Bibliography." Polish American Studies 12(Jl-D, 1955):104-109.

Rubano, Judith (comp.). Culture and Behavior
in Hawaii. An Annotated Bibliography.
Honolulu, HI: Social Science Research Institute, U. of Hawaii, 1971.

Rune, Ann (comp.). Oral History Index. Washington State Oral/Aural History Program,
1974-1977. Olympia, WA: Office of the
State Archivist, Department of General
Administration, O, 1977.

Simpson, Vernon (comp.). Chicago's Politics
and Society: A Selected Bibliography.
DeKalb, IL: Center for Governmental Studies,
1972.

Starbuck, James C. (comp.). Boston, 1971-1975:
A Bibliography of Articles from Serials.
Monticello, IL; Council of Planning
Librarians, Ag, 1976.

Sternberg, Barbara (comp.). Towards an Urban
Sociology of Denver: A Select and Annotated
Bibliography with Interpretative Comments.
Denver, CO: U. of Denver Press, 1949.

Strona, Proserfina A. (comp.). Blacks in
Hawaii: A Bibliography. Honolulu: Hawaii
and Pacific Unit, State Library, n.d.

Taylor, David V. (comp.). Blacks in Minnesota:
A Preliminary Guide to Historical Sources.
St. Paul: Minnesota Historical Society,
1976.

Taylor, Mary K. (comp.). A Selected Appalachian
Bibliography, N, 1971, 15 pp. ERIC ED
057 025.

Troen, Selwyn K. (comp.). A Guide to Resources
on the History of Saint Louis. St. Louis,
MO: Institute for Urban and Regional
Studies, Washington U., My, 1971.

U.S. Department of the Army. Pacific Islands
and Trust Territories: A Select Bibliography. AD-726 141. Springfield, VA:
National Technical Information Service,
Ja 4, 1971.

Washington State Library. The Negro in the
State of Washington, 1788-1967. A Bibliography..., 1968.

5.
SPANISH-SPEAKING PEOPLES

Mexican Americans

Arizona

Acosta Marin, Eugene. "The Mexican American
Community and the Leadership of the Dominant
Society in Arizona: A Study of Their
Mutual Attitudes and Perceptions. Doctoral
dissertation, United States International
U., 1973. Univ. Microfilms Order No. 73-
16,759.

Armack, Clifford M. "Educational Survey of
Mexican Children." Master's thesis, Arizona
State Teachers College, 1938. [Williams,
Arizona]

Crow, John E. Mexican Americans in Contemporary
Arizona: A Social and Demographic View.
San Francisco, CA: R and E Research Asso-
ciates, 1975.

Dobyns, H. F. Spanish Colonial Tucson. Tucson:
U. of Arizona Press, 1976.

Drake, Rollen H. "A Comparative Study of the
Mentality and Achievement of Mexican and
White Children." Master's thesis, U. of
Southern California, 1927. [Tucson,
Arizona]

Fuller, Roden. "Occupations of the Mexican-
Born Population in Texas, New Mexico and
Arizona 1900-1920." Journal of the American
Statistical Association 23(Mr, 1928):64-67.

Getty, Harry T. "Ethnic History of Tucson,
Arizona." In For the Dean. Edited by
Erik K. Reed and Dale S. King. Santa Fe,
NM: Hokoham Museum Association and South-
western Monuments Association, 1950.

_____. Interethnic Relationships in the
Community of Tucson. New York: Arno, 1976.
Reprint.

Goldstein, Mary. "Americanization and Mexicani-
zation: The Mexican Elite and Anglo-Americans
in the Gadsden Purchase Lands, 1853-1880."
Doctoral dissertation, Case Western Reserve
U., 1977. [Southern Arizona]

Officer, James E. "Barrier to Mexican Integration in Tucson." The Kiva 17(N-D, 1951):
7-16.

Rice, Roy C. "Intergroup Relations in Arizona."
Journal of Educational Sociology, D, 1947.

Riggings, Rachael T. Educational Background of
Spanish-American Students in Tucson Public
Schools. U

Schoepfle, Gordon Mark. "Nogales Highschool:
Peergroup and Institution in a Mexican
American Border Town." Doctoral dissertation, Northwestern U., 1977. Univ. Microfilms Order No. 78-749.

Taylor, Jacqueline Joann. "Ethnic Identity and
Upward Mobility of Mexican-Americans in
Tucson." Doctoral dissertation, U. of
Arizona, 1973. Univ. Microfilms Order No.
74-11,464.

Yanochik-Owen, Anita, and White, Morissa.
"Nutrition Surveillance in Arizona: Selected
Anthropometric and Laboratory Observations
Among Mexican-American Children."
American Journal of Public Health 67(F,
1977):151-154.

California

"Absenteeism." Inside Eastside, O 21, 1968.
[Attend school, even if they are not so good.]

"Afuera! Manning." La Raza, Je, 1969.
[Belvedere Jr. High School, Los Angeles]

Alexander, David J., and Nava, Alfonso.
A Public Policy Analysis of Bilingual Educa-
tion in California. San Francisco: Rand E
Research Associates, 1976.

Alvarado, M. B. "Juana Gallo." Inferno, Ag,
1968. [About David Sanchez, 19 year old
leader of the Los Angeles Brown Berets]

Ambrecht, Biliana C. S. Politicizing the Poor:
The Legacy of the War on Poverty in a
Mexican American Community. New York:
Praeger, 1976. [Los Angeles]

Ambrecht, Biliana C. S., and Pachon, Harry.
"Continuity and Change in a Mexican-
American Community: An Exploratory Study of
East Los Angeles, 1965-1972." Western
Political Science Quarterly 27(S, 1974):500-
519.

Amsden, Constance and others. A Reading Program
for Mexican-American Children. Revision 1.
Los Angeles: Youth Opportunities Foundation,
Ap 16, 1965. ERIC ED 016 757.

"An Open Letter to Mexican-American Parents from
an Anglo Elementary Teacher." La Raza, My
11, 1968.

Anastasiow, Nicholas J., and Espinosa, Iraida.
"The Guadalajara Project: An In-Service
Approach in Training Teachers in Spanish."
California Journal for Instructional Im-
provement, 0, 1968. [Palo Alto, California]

Arias, Pedro. "Renuncia La Comission Mexico
Americana de Educacion." La Raza, Vol. 1
No. 5(1971):22-24. [Los Angeles]

Arias, Ronald. "The Barrio." Agenda (publication of the Industrial Union Department of
the AFL-CIO), Jl, 1966. [Mexican-Americans
in Los Angeles]

Baker, William Pitt. 1961 Follow-Up Study of
Dropouts and Graduates of 1957-58 and 1959-
60; With Special Reference to Problems
Encountered by Bilingual (Mexican-American)
Leavers. San Jose, CA: San Jose East Side
Union High School District, D, 1962, 47 pp.
ERIC ED 039 088.

_____. 1969 Follow-Up Study of Dropouts and
Graduates of 1962-63 and 1964-65; With
Special Reference to Problems Encountered by
Mexican-American Leavers. San Jose, CA:
San Jose East Side Union High School
District, Mr, 1969, 49 pp. ERIC ED 039 089.

Balderrama, Francisco E. "En Defensa de la
Raza: The Los Angeles Mexican Consulate and
Colonia Mexicana during the Great Depression."
Doctoral dissertation, U. of California, Los
Angeles, 1978. Univ. Microfilms Order No.
7901331.

Baty, Roger M. Re-Educating Teachers for
Cultural Awareness: Preparation for Educating
Mexican-American Children in Northern
California. New York: Praeger, 1972.

Belliaeff, Alexander. Understanding the
Mexican-American in Today's Culture. San
Diego Project--Elementary and Secondary
Education Act. San Diego:
100 pp. ERIC ED 014 365.

Bergman, Arlene Eisen. "Oakland Brown
Berets." The Movement, D, 1968

Blair, Philip M. "Rates of Return to Education of Mexican-Americans and European-
Americans in Santa Clara County, California."
Comparative Education Review 17(F, 1973):
26-43.

_____. Job Discrimination and Education:
An Investment Analysis--A Case Study of
Mexican-Americans in Santa Clara County,
California. New York: Praeger, 1972.

_____. "Job Discrimination and Education:
Rates of Return to Education of Mexican-
Americans and Euro-Americans in Santa
Clara County, California." In Schooling in
a Corporate Society. The Political Economy
of Education in America, pp. 80-99. Edited
by Martin Carnoy. New York: McKay, 1972.

Bradfield, Robert B., and Brun, T. "Nutritional
Status of California Mexican-Americans: A
Review." American Journal of Clinical
Nutrition 23(Je, 197):798-806.

Briegel, Kaye L. "The History of Political
Organizations Among Mexican-Americans in
Los Angeles Since the Second World War."
Master's thesis, U. of Southern California,
1967.

"'Brown Power' Unity Seen Behind School Disorders." Los Angeles Times, Mr 17, 1967.

Bullington, Bruce. Heroin Use in the Barrio.
Lexington, MA: Lexington, 1977. [Los
Angeles]

Bureau of Intergroup Relations. Intergroup
Relations and the Education of Mexican
American Children. An Advisory Report to
the Board of Education, Norwalk-La Mirada
Unified School District. Sacramento:
State Department of Education, 1971.

California. Legislature. Assembly. Select
Committee on the Administration of Justice.
Hearing... Relations Between the Police and
Mexican-Americans. Sacramento: The
Assembly, 1972.

California State Advisory Committee of the
United States Commission on Civil Rights.
Educational Neglect of Mexican-American
Students in the Lucia Mar Unified School
District, Pismo Beach, California. Washing-
ton, DC: U.S. Commission on Civil Rights,
Ja, 1973.

California State Advisory Committee. Education
and the Mexican American Community in Los
Angeles County. Washington, DC: U.S.
Commission on Civil Rights, Ap, 1968.

California State Advisory Committee to the
United States Commission on Civil Rights.
Negligencia en la Educacion de Estudiantes
Mexico-Americanos en el Distrito Escolar
Unificado Lucia Mar, Pismo Beach, California,
Ja, 1973. ERIC ED 091 099.

California State Department of Education.
Orange County Conference on the Education of
Spanish-Speaking Children & Youth.
Sacramento, CA: The Department, 1964.

Camarillo, Alberto M. "Chicano Urban History:
A Study of Compton's Barrio, 1936-1970."
Aztlan 2(F, 1971):79-106.

_____. "The Making of a Chicano Community: A
History of the Chicanos in Santa Barbara,
California, 1850-1930." Doctoral disserta-
tion, U. of California, Los Angeles, 1975.

Cardenas, Delia. [Interview on conflict between
Headstart parents and the Council of Mexican
American Affairs]. La Raza, My 11, 1968.
[Los Angeles]

Carillo, Luis. "Castro Returns." Inside Eastside, O 21, 1968. [Sal Castro, teacher in
Los Angeles]

Chamberlain, Clarence W. "A Survey of the
San Jacinto Elementary School." Master's
thesis, U. of Southern California, 1930.

Chavéz, Armando. [Letter on Mexican-American
schooling in Los Angeles]. La Raza, Mr 31,
1968.

Chavira, Richardo. "The Simmering Ethnic War
on Franklin High's Campus." Stockton Record,
Mr 11, 1979. [Stockton]

"Chicano Participation in California Government."
La Raza, Vol. 1, No. 6(1971):46-49.

"Chicano Power." The Movement, My, 1968.
[Mexican-American protest at schools in
Los Angeles]

Chicano Prisoners of Liberation ... Conspiracy
for Better Education, 1968. Chicano Legal
Defense Fund, P.O. Box 31004, Los Angeles,
CA 90031

"Chicano Students Blow-Out!" La Raza, Mr 15,
1968. [Student schools boycotts by Mexican-
Americans in East Los Angeles]

"Chicanos Confront Church." National Catholic
Reporter, D 17, 1969. San Diego, CA

Coffin, Edwin C. "Compensation Education at
Chualar." California Education, N, 1964.
[Mexican-American children]

"Conspiracy Against Chicano Education." La Raza,
Ap 30, 1969. [Discussion of Los Angeles high
schools enrolling large numbers of Chicanos]

Cooke, Henry W. "The Segregation of Mexican-
American School Children in Southern
California." School and Society 67(Je,
1948):174-175.

Cortez, Mary. "Cannery Workers Make Educational
Program Plans." El Hispano, O 14, 1969.
[Sacramento]

"The Crime of Being a Chicano Child." Ideal,
F 1, 1970.

Curren, James. "Portrait of a Counselor. A
Group Interview." Personnel and Guidance
Journal 50(O, 1971):131-135. [Juarez-Lincoln
School, Imperial Beach, CA]

Dagodag, William Tim. "A Social Geography of
La Colonia, Oxnard, California." Master's
thesis, San Fernando Valley State College,
1967.

_____. "Spatial Control and Public Policies:
The Example of Mexican-American Housing."
Professional Geographer 26(Ag, 1974):
262-269. [Fresno]

Daustin, Helen. "Bettering Inter-American
Relations in One Small Elementary School."
California Journal of Elementary Education,
N, 1943, pp. 107-111.

"Delano [Calif.] High School Repression
Charged." El Malcriado, Ap 1, 1969.

De La Pena, Mike. "CSCLA Conference." Inside
Eastside, Jl 8, 1969. [Account of three-day
conference on problems of Mexican-American
people, sponsored by United Mexican American
Students at Cal-State at Los Angeles]

_____. "I Want You." Inside Eastside, Jl 29,
1968. [Touches on problems of Mexican-
American youth in East Los Angeles high
schools and junior colleges]

Del Olmo, Frank. "Community Coalition Mobilizing
East L.A." Los Angeles Times, D 26, 1977.

_____. "L.A.'s Latinos: How Many Are In the
Mainsteam?" Los Angeles Times, My 22, 1977.

_____. "No Regrets, Chicano Students Who Walked
Out Say." Los Angeles Times, Mr 26, 1978.
[Ten years after a large-scale public school
boycott by Chicano students in Los Angeles]

Delmet, Don T. "A Study of the Mental and
Scholastic Abilities of Mexican Children in
the Elementary School." Master's thesis, U.
of Southern California, 1928. [Vail School,
Montebello, CA]

Derbyshire, Robert L. "Adolescent Identity
Crisis in Urban Mexican Americans in East Los
Angeles." In Minority Group Adolescents in
the United States. Edited by Eugene B. Brody.
Baltimore: Williams and Wilkins, 1968.

Douglas, Helen Walker. "Conflict of Cultures in First Generation Mexicans in Santa Ana, California." Master's thesis, U. of Southern California, 1928.

Drummond, William J. "The Death of a Man in the Middle. Requiem for Ruben Salazar." Esquire 77(Ap, 1972).

Dudley, Sue Miriam. Chicano Library Program, Based on the "Research Skills in the Library Context" Programs Developed for Chicano High Potential Students in the Department of Special Educational Programs. Los Angeles: U. of California, Library, 1970, 87 pp. ERIC ED 045 105.

Duran, Ricardo. "Educational Failure." La Raza, Mr 1, 1968. [Education of Mexican-American children in Los Angeles]

Dworkin, Anthony Gary. "No Siesta Manana: The Mexican American in Los Angeles." In Our Children's Burden. Edited by Raymond W. Mack. New York: Random House, 1968.

Echaveste, Maria. "Desegregation Poses Controversy in Los Angeles." LNESC Newsletter 3(Mr-Ap, 1977). [Publication of LULAC National Educational Service Centers, Inc.]

Education and the Mexican-American. A fifty-seven minute film, made in East Los Angeles, California, during Spring, 1968. U. of California Extension Media Center, 1969.

"Education in the Eastside." La Raza, F 10, 1968. [Mexican-American schooling in Los Angeles]

"Educational Issues Coordinating Committee." La Raza, S 3, 1968. [Mexican-American schoolong in Los Angeles]

Edwards, Colin. Californians of Mexican Descent. A series of ten programs. Pacifica Tape Library, 2217 Shattuck Avenue, Berkeley, CA 94704.

"The Establishment vs the People." La Raza, Mr 31, 1968. [Criticism of schooling for Mexican-Americans in Los Angeles]

"Eva's Case." La Raza 2(1975):20-21. [Eva Aguilar at Magnolia School in Los Angeles]

Faltix, F. "Understanding Our Student of Mexican Extraction." California Teachers Associated Journal 47(F, 1951).

Fernandez, Jose R. (comp.). Chicano Studies and the California Community Colleges. Chicano Course Descriptions, 1970. ERIC ED 094 803.

"First Raza Unida School Graduation." Ideal, Je 20, 1972. [Blythe, CA]

Fox, Rona M. F. "The Brown Berets: A Participant-Observation Study of Social Action in the Schools of Los Angeles." Doctoral dissertation, U. of Southern California, 1970. Univ. Microfilms Order No. 70-13,657.

Francis, Jesse. "An Economic and Social History of Mexican California, 1822-1846." Doctoral dissertation, U. of California, Berkeley, 1936.

Franco, Victor. Editorial [on Chicanos in Los Angeles schools]. Inside Eastside, S 15, 1968.

"Freedom School Starts at Blythe." Ideal (Coachella, CA), My 20, 1972. [Palo Verde School District, CA]

Gamble, Leo M. "The Mexican: An Educational Asset or an Educational Liability." Los Angeles Educational Research Bulletin 5 (D, 1925):9-12.

García, F. Chris. Political Socialization of Chicano Children: A Comparative Study with Anglos in California Schools. New York: Praeger, 1973.

Garcia, Jorge. "The Incorporation of East Los Angeles 1974. Part One." La Raza 3 (Summer, 1977):29-35.

García, Mario T. "A Chicano Perspective on San Diego History." Journal of San Diego History 18(Fall, 1972):14-21

"Garfield's 'Reggie' Goofs." La Raza, D 2, 1967. [Community uproar around Los Angeles school board proposal to organize two educational complexes]

Garr, Daniel J. "A Rare and Desolate Land: Population and Race in Hispanic California." Western Historical Quarterly 6(Ap, 1975).

Garza, Hisauro. "Administration of Justice: Chicanos in Monterey County." Aztlan 4 (Spring, 1973):137-146.

Geihufe, Nancy L. "Ethnic Relations in San Jose: A Study of Police-Chicano Interaction." Doctoral dissertation, Stanford U., 1971.

Gilmore, N. Ray, and Gilmore, Gladys W. "The Bracero in California." Pacific Historical Review 32(Ag, 1963):265-282.

Ginsburg, Ruth. "A New Program in Spanish for Los Angeles." California Journal of Secondary Education 18(O, 1943).

Godoy, Ramona L. State Administration of Bilingual Education--Si o No?: A Report of the California Advisory Committee to the United States Commission on Civil Rights. Washington, DC: U.S. Commission on Civil Rights, 1976.

Gold, W. "Denial of Equal Protection--Segregation of Mexican Children in California Schools." Wisconsin Law Review, 1948: 227-30 [Westminster School District of Orange City v. Mendez, 161 F (2nd) 774] ; Harvard Law Review 60:1156-8, S, 1947; Illinois Law Review 42:545-9 O-O, 1947; Minnesota Law Review 30:646-7, Je, 1946; Columbia Law Review 47:325-7, Mr, 1947; Yale Law Journal 56:1059-67, Je, 1947.

Gomez, Juan Q. "Preliminary Remarks Toward a Tentative History of the Chicano Student Movement in Southern California." Aztlan 1 (Fall, 1970):101-102.

Gonzalez, Gilbert C. "Educational Reform and the Mexican Community in Los Angeles." Southwest Economy and Society 3(Spring, 1978): 24-51

_____. "Educational Reform in Los Angeles and Its Effect Upon the Mexican Community, 1900-1930." Explorations in Ethnic Studies 1(Jl, 1978):5-26.

_____. "Racism, Education, and the Mexican Community in Los Angeles, 1920-30." Societas 4(Autumn, 1974):287-301.

_____. "The System of Public Education and Its Function Within the Chicano Commnities, 1920-1930." Doctoral dissertation, U. of California at Los Angeles, 1974.

Griffith, Beatrice. American Me. Boston: Houghton Mifflin, 1948. [Touches on treatment of Spanish-speaking children in Los Angeles schools]

Griswold del Castillo, Richard. "La Familia Chicano: Social Changes in the Chicano Family of Los Angeles 1850-1880." Journal of Ethnic Studies 3(Spring, 1975): 41-58.

_____. "Myth and Reality: Chicano Economic Mobility in Los Angeles, 1850-1880." Aztlan 6(Summer, 1975):151-171.

_____. "La Raza Hispano Americana: The Emergence of an Urban Culture Among the Spanish Speaking of Los Angeles, 1850-1880." Doctoral dissertation, U. of California, Los Angeles, 1974. Univ. Microfilms Order No. 74-18,772.

Harmon, Genevieve Coon. "Participation of Mexican-American Parents in School Activities at Kindergarten Level in Poverty Areas of Los Angeles." Doctoral dissertation, U. of Southern California, 1971. Univ. Microfilms Order No. 21,461.

Haro, Carlos Manuel. Mexicano/Chicano Concerns and School Segregation in Los Angeles. Los Angeles: Chicano Studies Center, U. of California, 1977.

Harrington, John H. "L.A.'s Student Blowout." Phi Delta Kappan, O, 1968.

Hayden, Jessie. "The La Habra Experiment." Master's thesis, Claremont Colleges, 1934. [La Habra, Orange County, CA]

Heins, Marjorie. Strictly Ghetto Property: The Story of Los Siete de la Raza. Berkeley, CA: Ramparts Press, 1972.

Hepner, Ethel M. The American Elementary School Versus the Values and Needs of Mexican-American Boys. Final Report, My, 1971. ERIC ED 052 860. [Los Angeles schools]

Hill, Merton E. The Development of an Americanization Program. Ontario, CA: Chaffey Union High School District, 1928. [San Bernadino County, CA]

Hill, Marguerite W. "A Proposed Guidance Program for Mexican Youth in the Junior High School." Master's thesis, Claremont Colleges, 1945. [Santa Ana, CA]

Hogan, V. N. "A Study of the School Progress of Mexican Children in Imperial County." Master's thesis, U. of Southern California, Ag, 1934.

Hurstfield, Jennifer. "The Mexican-Americans in Los Angeles. The Political Mobilization of An Ethnic Minority." Race Today 2(D, 1970):443-446.

Iballa, Herb. "Specialized Education for the Non-English Speaking Child." California Journal for Instructional Improvement, O, 1968. [San Diego, CA]

Intergroup Relations and the Education of Mexican American Children. An Advisory Report to the Board of Education, Norwalk-La Mirada Unified School District. Sacramento: California State Department of Education, Bureau of Intergroup Relations, 1971, 79 pp. ERIC ED 052 854.

Jacinto. "El Espectador." Ideal, Jl 15, 1971. [Coachella Valley High School Board, CA]

Jeidy, Pauline. "First Grade Mexican-American Children in Ventura County." California Journal of Elementary Education 15(F and My, 1947):200-208.

Johnson, Dallas. "They Fenced Tolerance In." Survey Graphic 36(Jl, 1947):398-399. [Segregation of Mexican-American students in a California town]

Jones, Jack. "Revolt in the Barrios." Los Angeles Times, My 8-13, 1966.

Juárez, Alberto. "The Emergence of El Partido de la Raza Unida: California's New Chicano Party." Aztlan 3(Fall, 1972):177-204.

Kelley, E. and others. "Segregation of Mexican-American School Children in Southern California." American Journal of Public Health 38(Ja, 1945):30-35.

Krier, Beth Ann. "Parish Pride Flowers in a Watts Barrio." Los Angeles Times, My 22, 1977. [San Miguel Catholic School]

Kurtz, Donald V. The Politics of a Poverty Habitat. Cambridge, MA: Ballinger, 1973. [San Ysidro, San Diego County]

"La Raza Students Shut Down Safeway." Black Panther, S 20, 1969. [San Francisco and Richmond, CA]

"La Raza vs. PLACAS in Venice, California ." La Raza, Mr 28, 1969.

Latin American Culture Group. "Soledad Chicano Inmates Appeal to High School Students." Inside-Eastside, N 18, 1968. [A letter from Chicanos in Soledad prison]

Leary, Mary Ellen. "Mentally Retarded?" New Republic, My 30, 1970. [Mexican-American children in California]

Levi, Barbara G. "Physicists Teach Minority Students." Physics Today, Mr, 1970. [Mexican-American high school students in Santa Clara County, CA]

"Liberate La Raza Schools." Black Panther, S 20, 1969. [Mission High School, San Francisco]

Liddick, Betty. "Gang Diary: The Caging of Tiger Tovar." Los Angeles Times, O 24, 1975. [Los Angeles]

"Livingston Boycott. La Raza, O 15, 1968. [Mexican American boycott at Livingston High School, Livingston, CA]

Lofstedt, Christine. "The Mexican Population of Pasadena, California." Journal of Applied Sociology 7(My, 1923):260-268.

López, David E. "The Social Consequences of Chicano Home/School Bilingualism." Social Problems 24(D, 1976):234-246. Los Angeles

_____. "Chicano Language Loyalty in an Urban Setting." Sociology and Social Research 62(J, 1978):267-278. [Los Angeles]

López, Enrique Hank. "Overkill at 'The Silver Dollar.'" Nation, O 19, 1970. [East Los Angeles]

López, Frank, and Perez, Jack. "A Mexican-American Mecca." Parks and Recreation 7 (Ja, 1972):89, 108. [Los Angeles]

López Ramos, Enriqueta. "A Study of the Classification of Mexican-American Students as Educable Mentally Retarded Through the Use of Inappropriate Culturally Biased Intellectual Assessment and Procedures." 2 vols. Doctoral dissertation, U. of California, Irvine, 1978. Univ. Microfilms Order No. 7819056. [Santa Ana]

Los Angeles County, Commission on Human Relations. The Urban Reality: A Comparative Study of the Socio-Economic Situation of Mexican-Americans, Negroes, and Anglo-Caucasians in Los Angeles County. Los Angeles: County Commission on Human Relations, 1965.

"M.A.P.A. Pickets." Ideal, Mr 1, 1970. [Indio, CA]

McAnulty, Ellen Alice. "Achievement and Intelligence Test Results for Mexican Children Attending Los Angeles City Schools." Los Angeles Educational Research Bulletin, Mr, 1932.

McEuen, William. "A Survey of the Mexican in Los Angeles." Master's thesis, U. of Southern California, 1914.

McKenney, J. Wilson. "The Dilemma of the Spanish Surname People of California." CTA Journal, Mr, 1965.

McMurtry, A. R. "Self-Esteem in Mexican American and Anglo-American Children in California." Master's thesis, U. of California, Davis, 1970.

Martinez, Ruth L. "One Unusual Mexican--A Study in Acculturation." Master's thesis, Claremont Colleges, 1942. [High school graduates in Ontario, CA]

Mason, Florence Gordon. "A Case Study of Thirty Adolescent Mexican Girls and their Social Conflicts and Adjustments Within the School." Master's thesis, U. of Southern California, 1929.

Mendez, Aida, and Mendez, Caroline Lee (eds.). Trends Conference on Education of the Mexican-American in San Diego County (San Diego University, My 13, 1967). San Diego City Schools, California, Ja, 1968, 51 pp. ERIC ED 022 821.

Metcalf, Allan A. "The Study of California Chicano English." International Journal of the Sociology of Language 2(1974):53-58.

"Minorities. Pocho's Progess." Time, Ap 28, 1967. [Mexican-Americans in Los Angeles]

Morales, Armando. Ando Sangrando (I Am Bleeding). A Study of Mexican- American Police Conflict, 1972. Perspectiva Publications, P.O. Box 3563, La Puente, CA 91744.

Morales, Armando. "Mental and Public Health Issues. The Case of the Mexican Americans in Los Angeles." El Grito 3(1970):3-11.

Muñoz, Carlos, Jr. "The Politics of Educational Change in East Los Angeles." In Mexican Americans and Educational Change. Edited by Alfredo Castañeda and others. New York: Arno Press, 1973.

Negroes and Mexican Americans in South and East Los Angeles, Changes Between 1960-1965 in Population, Employment, Income, and Family Status: An Analysis of a Special U.S. Census Survey of November 1965. San Francisco: California State Dept. of Industrial Relations, Jl, 1966, 40 pp. ERIC ED 022 589.

Newell, Virginia E. "The Social Significance of Padua Hills as a Cultural and Education Center." Master's thesis, U. of Southern California, 1938.

Nichols, B. C. Some Educational Problems of Imperial Valley. El Centro, CA: Imperial Valley Press Print, 1910

del Olmo, Frank. "L.A. Latins Face Dilemma in Integration Controversy." Los Angeles Times, Mr 21, 1977.

Ormiston, Joseph B. "The Acculturation Process of Chicano Students in a Central California Elementary School." Master's thesis, California State U., Arcata, 1974.

Ortega, Frank. "Special Education Placement and Mexican Americans." El Grito 4(Summer, 1971):29-35.

Ortíz, Martin. The Mexican-American in the Los Angeles Community. Community Intelligence Bulletin, No. 3 Community Relations Educational Foundation, N, 1963.

Overend, William. "The '43 Zoot Suit Riots Reexamined." Los Angeles Times, My 9, 1978.

Padilla, Raymond V. "A Critique of Pittian History." El Grito 6(Fall, 1972):3-44. [Critique of Leonard M. Pitt, The Decline of the Californios]

Palomares, Uvaldo H., and Cummins, Emery J. Assessment of Rural Mexican-American Pupils, Preschool and Grades One through Twelve, Wasco, California. Sacramento: State Department of Education, 1968.

Palomares, Uvaldo and others. "Evaluation of Mexican-American Pupils for Educable Mentally Retarded Classes." California Education, Ap, 1966. [Imperial County, CA]

Patino, Peter H. "Go Talk to the Principal!" Civil Rights Digest 3(Fall, 1970):23-29. [Abraham Lincoln High School, Los Angeles]

Pattern Transmission in a Bicultural Community. Sacramento: California State Dept. of Education, Jl 21, 1967. ERIC ED 014 366.

Paul, Herbert Jeffery. Library Service to the Spanish-Speaking in the Public Libraries of the San Francisco Bay Area, F, 1976. ERIC ED 124 158.

Penalosa, Fernando, and McDonagh, Edward C. "Education, Economic Status and Social Class Awareness of Mexican-Americans." Phylon, Summer, 1968. [Pomona, CA]

Phillips, L. H. "Segregation in Education: A California Case Study." Phylon 10(1949): 407-413.

Pitt, Leonard. The Decline of the Californios. A Social History of the Spanish-Speaking California, 1846-1890. Berkeley, CA: U. of California Press, 1966.

Polifroni, Mio. "Including our Spanish-Speaking Neighbors." Young Children, S, 1965. [Pacific Oaks Children's School in Pasadena, CA]

Puckett, Myron. "Protest Politics in Education: A Case Study in the Los Angeles School District." Doctoral dissertation, Claremont Graduate School, 1971.

"Pushouts Continue--." La Raza, N 9, 1969.

Ramos, George. "A Pivotal School Year for Hispanic Students." Los Angeles Times, S 11, 1978. [Los Angeles]

Reynolds, Diane A. T. "Economic Integration and Cultural Assimilation: Mexican Americans in San Jose." Doctoral dissertation, Stanford U., 1974. Univ. Microfilms Order No. 74-27,093.

_____. Economic Success and Ethnicity: Mexican-Americans in San Jose, 1976. ERIC ED 129 493.

Reynolds, E. D. "A Study of Migratory Factors Affecting Education in North Kern County." Master's thesis, U. of Southern California, Je, 1932. [McFarland School District]

"Richgrove, Calif. Parents Launch School Board Recall." El Malcriado, Mr 1, 1970.

"Richgrove Ponders School Needs." El Macriado, F 1, 1970.

Rico, A. C. "The Commission 1975--An Analysis." La Raza 2(Ja, 1975):26-28. [Mexican-American Education Commission, Los Angeles]

_____. "Robert Hill Lane School An Exception." La Raza 2(1975):14-16. [Predominantly Chicano school in East Los Angeles]

Rodriguez, de, Celia L. "Police Strike Again at Roosevelt." Regeneración 1(1970):8-9 [Roosevelt High School, Los Angeles, CA]

Rodriguez, David. "On Busing." _Regeneración_ I, No. 3(1970). [A ten-year-old boy in Los Angeles]

Rodriguez, Ray. "Blythe Schools Boycotted." _Ideal_, Ap 20, 1972. [Palo Verde, California School District]

Romo, Richardo. "Mexican Workers in the City: Los Angeles, 1915-1930." Doctoral dissertation, U. of California, Los Angeles, 1975. Univ. Microfilms Order No. 76-1157.

_____. "Work and Restlessness: Occupational and Spatial Mobility among Mexicans in Los Angeles, 1918-1928." _Pacific Historical Review_ 46(My, 1977):157-180.

Roos, Patricia A. _Questioning the Stereotypes: Differentials in Income Attainment of Japanese, Mexican-Americans, and Anglos in California_, S 8, 1977. ERIC ED 148 651.

"Roosevelt Walks Out." _Inside Eastside_, Ja 13, 1969. [Student walkout at Roosevelt High School, Los Angeles, Ja 8, 1969]

Rosen, Gerald. "The Development of the Chicano Movement in Los Angeles from 1967 to 1969." _Aztlan_ 4(Spring, 1973):155-183.

Sacacolas, Miguel. "Child-Care in Pacoima. Lesson Learned." _La Raza_, D 2, 1967. [How women organized to convince the Los Angeles school board to approve a child care center]

Salamanca, Anthony J. _Bilingual/Cross-Cultural Teacher Shortage in California_, Je, 1974. ERIC ED 134 003.

"San Bernardino Student Boycott." _La Raza_, Vol 1, No. 11(1973):28-29. [February 6, 1973]

Sanchez, Arturo. "Las Escuelas en el Este de Los Angeles, California, Una Verguenza Nacional." _La Raza_ 1(Ja, 1972):34.

_____. "Transportation (Busing)! Ya ...! Pero Ya!" _La Raza_ 3(Spring, 1977):38-39.

_____. "Triste Realidad: Nuestras Escuelas Fabricas de Peones." _La Raza_ 1(F, 1973):18-20.

Sauter, Mary C. "Arbol Verde: Cultural Conflict and Accommodation in a California Mexican Community." Master's thesis, Claremont Colleges, 1933. [Claremont, CA]

Schoen, Robert and others. "Intermarriage Among Spanish Surnamed Californians, 1962-1974." _International Migration Review_ 12 (Fall, 1978):359-369.

Scott, Robin Fitzgerald. "The Mexican-American in the Los Angeles Area, 1920-1950: From Acquiescence to Activity." Doctoral dissertation, U. of Southern California, 1971. Univ. Microfilms Order No. 71-27,955.

Serrano, Rodolfo G. _Desegregation in the South San Joaquin Valley_, Ag, 1976. ERIC ED 131 964.

Siegel, Barry. "Not Everyone Graduates at Colton." _Los Angeles Times_, Je 20, 1977. [Colton Junior High School, Colton, CA]

Sillas, Herman. "The Story of Sammy Gonzalez." _Los Angeles Times_, Ap 19, 1973. [Guadalupe, CA]

Simons, Grace E. "New Cry: Chicano Power." _Guardian_, Mr 16, 1968. [Student protest movement among Mexican-American youth in Los Angeles]

Simpson, R. E. "Migrant Children--Fresno County Conducts a Significant Project." _California Teachers Association Journal_ 50 (Ja, 1954):26-27.

Simross, Lynn. "The Latino Scene at Lincoln High." _Los Angeles Times_, F 16, 1979. [Los Angeles]

Singleton, Robert, and Bullock, Paul. "Some Problems in Minority-Group Education in the Los Angeles Public Schools." _Journal of Negro Education_, Spring, 1963.

Slade, Santiago. "From Michoacan to Southern California: The Story of an Undocumented Mexican." _Southwest Economy and Society_ 3 (Fall, 1977):5-18.

Smith, Clara G. "The Development of the Mexican People in the Community of Watts, California." Master's thesis, U. of Southern California, 1933.

"Spanish Americans Ring a Victory Bell." _American Teacher_, N, 1968. [The case of Sal Castro at Lincoln High School in Los Angeles]

Stanley, Grace C. "Special Schools for Mexicans." _Survey_ 44(S 15, 1920):714-715. [San Bernardino, CA]

Studio Laboratory. "A Pointless Exercise in Make-Believe." _Agenda_, Summer, 1976. [Bilingual programs in public schools of Santa Clara County]

Sturdevant, Frederick D. "Business and the Mexican-American Community." _California Management Review_, Spring, 1969. [East Los Angeles]

Summers, Helen. "An Evaluation of Certain Procedures Used in Teaching the Non-English-speaking Mexican Child." Master's thesis, U. of California, Los Angeles, 1939. [East Los Angeles]

Taylor, Paul S. "Foundations of California Rural Society." _California Historical Society Quarterly_ 29(S, 1945):193-228.

_____. "Mexican Labor in the United States. Racial School Statistics, California, 1927." University of California Publications in Economics, N, 1929, pp. 257-292.

Tipton, Elis M. "The San Dimas Intercultural Program." Education for Cultural Unity, Seventh Yearbook. Sacramento: California Elementary School Principal's Association, pp. 93-99, 1945.

Torres-Raines, Rosario. "Cesar Ricas y Pobres: The Effects of Housing Market Expenditures on Residental Segregation of Mexican Americans in Texas and California." Doctoral dissertation, Texas Women's U., 1978. Univ. Microfilms Order No. 7815602.

Toto, Charles. "A History of Education in California, 1800-1850." Doctoral dissertation, U. of California, Berkeley, 1967.

Tuck, Ruth A. Not With the Fist. New York: Harcourt, Brace, 1946. [San Bernardino]

U.S. Commission on Civil Rights, California State Advisory Committee. Political Participation of Mexican Americans in California. Washington, DC: GPO, Ag, 1971.

_____. The Schools of Guadalupe ... A Legacy of Educational Oppression, Ap, 1973. ERIC ED 087 584.

Valdez, R. F. "The Fallacy of the Spanish Surname Survey." CTA Journal, My, 1969.

Vandenbergh, Leonard John. "The Mexican Problem in the Schools." Los Angeles School Journal 11(My, 1928).

Villalpando, V. A Study of the Impact of Illegal Aliens on the County of San Diego on Specific Socioeconomic Areas. San Diego: San Diego County Human Resources Agency, 1975.

"We Won! Sal Castro To Teach." La Raza, O 15, 1968.

Weist, Raymond E. Mexican Farm Laborers in California: A Study of Intragroup Social Relations. San Francisco: R & E Research Associates, 1977.

"Will [Sal] Castro Return?" Inside Eastside, S 2, 1968. [Mexican-American schooling in Los Angeles]

Wollenberg, Charles. "Mendez v. Westminster: Race, Nationality, and Segregation in California Schools." California Historical Quarterly 53(Winter, 1974).

Wright, Frank M. "Survey of the El Monte District." Master's thesis, U. of Southern California, 1930.

Young, C. C. Mexicans in California. Report of Gov. C. C. Young's Mexican Fact-Finding Committee. Sacramento, CA: California State Printing Office, 1930.

Younger, Evelle J., and Bravo, Francisco. [Exchange on the arrests of 13 Mexican-Americans in Los Angeles on charge of conspiring to cause a school boycott] La Raza, Jl 10, 1968.

Zeta Acosta, Oscar. The Autobiography of a Brown Buffalo. San Francisco: Straight Arrow Books, 1972.

_____. "The East L.A. 13 vs. The L.A. Superior Court." El Grito 3(1970):12-18.

_____. "The East Los 13 Are Ready." La Raza, O 15, 1968.

_____. The Revolt of the Cockroach People. San Francisco: Straight Arrow Press, 1974.

Colorado

Ahrens, Earl. "A Socio-economic Status Study of a Spanish American Barrio in Monte Vista, Colorado." Master's thesis, Adams State College, 1967.

"Bilingual Education in Colorado: The Story of a Struggle." Agenda (Winter, 1976).

Bradish, Damaris K. "Achievement Attitudes of Hispanos." Doctoral dissertation, Colorado State U., 1969.

Brown, Sara A., Sargent, Robie O., and Armentrout, Clara B. Children Working in the Sugar-Beet Fields of Certain Districts of the South Platte Valley, Colo. National Child Labor Committee. New York, NY, 1925.

Bundy, William Wilson. "The Mexican Minority Problem in Otero County, Colorado." Master's thesis, U. of Colorado, 1940. (Abstract in University of Colorado Studies, General series (A), vol. 26, No. 3:24)

Camejo, Anthonio. "Colo. Raza Unida Spokesman: The People Are Starting to Move Collectively." El Gallo, D, 1970. [Interview with Corky Gonzalez]

"Chicano 'Socks It' to the School Board." El Gallo, D, 1968. Testimony of Rodolfo "Corky" Gonzalez to the Denver school board

"Chicano Students Struggle for Rights in Denver Schools." United Scholarship Service News, My, 1969.

Colorado Commission on Spanish-Surnamed Citizens. The Status of Spanish-surnamed Citizens in Colorado. Report to the Colorado General Assembly, Greeley, CO, 1967.

"Corky [Gonzales] Acquitted." El Gallo II, No. 6, El Ano Del Chicano, 1970. [Aftermath of March 20, 1969 demonstration at West High School in Denver, CO]

De Ornis, J. The Hispanic Contribution to the State of Colorado. Denver: Westview, 1976.

Denver Area Welfare Council. The Spanish-Speaking Population of Denver, 1950.

"Denver Panthers Support Chicano Demands." Black Panther, Ap 6, 1969.

Escuela Tlateloco Centro de Estudios. El Gallo 3(Ap, 1971):10. [Chicano school: 1567 Downing St., Denver, CO 80218]

Ewing, T. W. A Report on Minorities in Denver: The Spanish-speaking People in Denver. Denver, CO: Mayor's Interim Survey Committee on Human Relations, 1947.

García, George J. (comp.). Selected Reading Materials on the Mexican and Spanish American. Denver, CO: Denver Commission on Community Relations, D, 1969, 100 pp. ERIC ED 039 047.

García, Rudy. "Schools 'Organize' Chicano Parents." Denver Post, Ja 15, 1972. [Commerce City, CO]

Hall, Beverly. "The Bilingual, Bicultural Schools." Nation, N 20, 1976.

Howard, Donald S. "A Study of the Mexican-American and Spanish-American Population in Pueblo, Colorado, 1929-1930." Master's thesis, U. of Denver, 1932.

"Independence Day for La Raza." El Gallo, S-O, 1969. [School demonstration]

"Justicia Para los Estudiantes." El Gallo 6(O-N, 1974):1, 8. [Centennial High School, Denver, CO]

Lane, George. "Mountain West." Race Relations Reporter 4(Ja, 1973):7-8, 33. [Chicanos in Colorado]

Lopez, Robert M. "Corky Gonzalez: Twenty-year Activist." La Voz Hispana de Colorado, O 15, 1977.

McLean, Robert N., and Thompson, Charles A. Spanish and Mexican in Colorado ... New York: Board of National Missions of the Presbyterian Church in the USA, 1924.

Manzanares, Rick. Letter to Editor. El Gallo, II, No. 6, Ano Del Chicano, 1970. [School demonstration in Manzanola, 9/16/69]

Marin, Christine. A Spokesman of the Mexican American Movement: Rodolfo "Corky" Gonzalez and the Fight for Chicano Liberation, 1966-1972. San Francisco: R & E Research Associates, 1977.

Pendás, Miguel. "Bilingual-Bicultural Education: A Privilege or a Right?" Militant, My 13, 1977.

Quintana, Gilbert R. "Adams City Confronts Racism." El Gallo, Ap, 1969. [Adams City Junior and Senior High School, Commerce City, CO]

_____. "Freedom Schools' Strike Pay Denied. They Think So." El Gallo, II, No. 6, El Ano Del Chicano, 1970. [Denver, CO]

_____. "Special Report on Violence Within the Schools: Do You Understand Educator?" El Gallo, II, No. 6, El Ano Del Chicano, 1970.

Rendon, Gabino. Voting Behavior in a Tri-ethnic Community. San Francisco: R & E Research Associates, 1977.

Sanchez, José A. "A Study of the High School Spanish surnamed Dropout in Pueblo School District No. 60." Master's thesis, Adams State College, 1970.

The Status of Spanish-Surnamed Citizens in Colorado. Report to the Colorado General Assembly. Denver, CO: Colorado Commission on Spanish-Surnamed Citizens, Ja, 1967. ERIC ED 025 503.

Vigil, Ernesto. "Two Days at Morey Jr. High." El Gallo, Je-Jl, 1969. [Denver, CO]

Weiss, Bob. "School Problems Improved Slowly." Rocky Mountain News, F 21, 1979. [Hispanos in Denver schools]

Yaffe, Elaine. "Colorado Springs Wrestles with Lau: A Case Study in Federal Intervention." Phi Delta Kappan (S, 1978):51-55. [School District 11, Colorado Springs]

New Mexico

Allsup, Carl. "Mexican American Organization in New Mexico and Texas: An Urban Experience of the 1950's." In "The Urban Minority Experience," Selected Proceedings of the 4th Annual Conference on Minority Studies, pp. 127-135. Edited by George E. Carter and James R. Parker. La Crosse, WI: Institute for Minority Studies, U. of Wisconsin-La Crosse, 1978.

Caplan, Stanley W., and Ruble, Ronald A. "A Study of Culturally Imposed Factors on School Achievement in a Metropolitan Area." Journal of Educational Research, S, 1964. [Spanish-Americans in Albuquerque, NM]

Chavez, Martin. "Hispanics and the New Mexico Bar Exam--A Review." LNESC Newsletter 3(Mr-Ap, 1977. [Publication of LULAC National Educational Centers, Inc.]

"Chicanos Charge Discrimination." Ideal, Jl 5, 1973. [Las Vegas, NM schools]

Conway, T. F. "The Bi-Lingual Problem in the Schools of New Mexico." _Alianza_ 36 (F, 1942):13, 17.

Cordova, Alfred G., and Jurdah, Charles. _Octaviano Ambrosio Larrazolo, the Prophet of Transition in New Mexico, an Analysis of his Political Life_. Albuquerque, NM: Division of Government Research, U. of New Mexico, 1952.

Edmundson, Muro. _Los Manitos_. New Orleans, LA: Middle American Research Institute, Tulane U., 1957.

"Education and the Spanish-Speaking--An Attorney General's Opinion on Article XII, Section 8 of the New Mexico Constitution." _New Mexico Law Review_ 3(1973).

Fuller, Roden. "Occupations of the Mexican-Born Population in Texas, New Mexico and Arizona 1900-1920." _Journal of the American Statistical Association_ 23(Mr, 1928):64-67.

Gillman, Geneva B. "The Relationship Between Self-Concept, Intellectual Ability, Achievement, and Manifest Anxiety Among Select Groups of Spanish-Surname Migrant Students in New Mexico." Doctoral dissertation, The U. of New Mexico, Je, 1969, 180 pp. ERIC ED 029 723.

González, Nancie. L. _The Spanish Americans of New Mexico: A Distinctive Heritage_. Los Angeles: U. of Carolina Press, 1967.

Hyer, Marjorie. "Brown Power Has a Base in Santa Fe." _National Catholic Reporter_, O 16, 1970.

Jiménez Nuñez, Alfredo. _Los hispanos de Nuevo México: Contribución a una antropología de la cultura hispana en USA_. Sevilla: Universidad, 1974.

Johnson, Irma Y. "A Study of Certain Changes in the Spanish-American Family in Bernalillo County, 1915-1946." Master's thesis, U. of New Mexico, 1948.

Kenneson, Susan R. "Through the Looking-Glass: A History of Anglo-American Attitudes Towards the Spanish-Americans and Indians of New Mexico." Doctoral dissertation, Yale U., 1978. Univ. Microfilms Order No. 7819502.

Knowlton, Clark S. _An Analysis of Certain Selected Causes of Poverty in San Miguel County_, Ag 25, 1974. ERIC ED 097 137.

_____. "Changing Spanish-American Villages of Northern New Mexico." _Journal of Mexican-American Studies_ 1(Fall, 1970):31-43.

_____. "Violence in New Mexico: A Sociological Perspective." _California Law Review_ 58 (O, 1970).

Larson, Robert. _New Mexico Population: A Study of Radical Protest in a Western Territory_. Boulder: Colorado Associated U. Press, 1974.

_____. _New Mexico's Quest for Statehood, 1846-1912_. Albuquerque: U. of New Mexico Press, 1968.

Linthicum, John Buren. "The Classification of Spanish-American Beginners in an Albuquerque Public School." Master's thesis, U. of Southern California, 1930.

López, Andrew. _Minority Groups in New Mexico_. Albuquerque: New Mexico Employment Security Commission, Ja, 1969, 81 pp. ERIC ED 035 475.

López, Thomas R., Jr. Prospects for the Spanish American Culture in New Mexico: An Educational View." Doctoral dissertation, U. of New Mexico, 1971.

Loyola, Sr. Mary. "The American Occupation of New Mexico." _New Mexico Historical Review_ 14(1939).

Mayfield, Thomas J. "The Development of the Public Schools in New Mexico between 1848 and 1900." Master's thesis, U. of New Mexico, 1938.

Metzgar, Joseph V. "The Ethnic Sensitivity of Spanish New Mexicans: A Survey and Analysis." _New Mexico Historical Review_ 49(Ja, 1974): 49-73.

Moore, Frank C. "San Jose, 1946, a Study in Urbanization." Master's thesis, U. of New Mexico, 1947. [Section of Albuquerque, NM]

Moore, Justin R., and Ratchner, Craig A. "Spanish? Mexican? Chicano? The Influence of Spanish Culture on New Mexico." _Integrateducation_ 14(S-O, 1976).

Nabakov, Peter. "Chicano Power in the Feudal West." _Nation_, O 8, 1977. [Tierra Amarilla]

New Mexico Advisory Committee to the U.S. Commission on Civil Rights. _The Struggle for Justice and Redress in Northern New Mexico_. Washington, DC: U.S. Commission on Civil Rights, O, 1974.

Ortega, Juaquin. _The Compulsory Teaching of Spanish in the Grade Schools of New Mexico_. Albuquerque: U. of New Mexico Press, 1941.

Otero, Adelina. "My People." _Survey_ 66, pp. 149-151. [Teacher in New Mexico]

Ream, Glen O. "A Study of Spanish-Speaking Pupils in Albuquerque High School." Master's thesis, Yale U., 1930.

Rosenbaum, Robert Johnson. "Mexicano versus Americano: A Study of Hispanic-American Resistance to Anglo-American Control in New Mexico Territory, 1870-1900." Doctoral dissertation, U. of Texas, 1972. Univ. Microfilms Order No. 73-18,492.

Sanchez, George I. "The Education of Bilinguals in a State School System." Doctoral dissertation, U. of California, 1934.

_____. Forgotten People: A Study of New Mexicans. Albuquerque, NM: U. of New Mexico Press, 1940.

Scholes, France. "Civil Government and Societies in New Mexico in the Seventeenth Century." New Mexico Historical Review 10 (1935):96-111.

"School Board Election. Indian-Raza Team Runs." La Raza, F 7, 1969. [Albuquerque, NM]

Senter, Donovan, and Hawley, Florence. "The Grammar School as the Basic Acculturating Influence for Native New Mexicans." Social Forces 24(My, 1946):398-407.

Serrano, Rodolfo G. "Ethnography of a Contemporary Chicano Community: A Brief Description." Council on Anthropology and Education Quarterly 5(Ag, 1974):3-7. [Albuquerque, NM]

"Suit Filed Against Discriminatory, Destructive Education." La Raza, Ag 15, 1968. [Mexican-Americans in New Mexico]

Sunseri, Alvin. "The Chicano Studies Program in Northern New Mexico: Broken Promises and Future Prospects." In Identity and Awareness in the Minority Experience, pp. 65-82. Selected Proceedings of the 1st and 2nd Annual Conferences on Minority Studies. Edited by George E. Carter and Bruce Mouser. Lacrosse, WI: U. of Wisconsin, 1975.

Varela, Marie. "That Play Is the Thing in Court." La Raza, Ja 1, 1969. [Detailed narrative of the trial of Reies Lopez Tijerina]

Vargas, Felipe. "An Open Letter to the New Mexico Bar." De Colores, Journal of Emerging Raza Philosophies 2(1975):19-29.

Vogel, Albert W. Barelas-Arenal and Los Lunas. Albuquerque: U. of New Mexico, 1967. [Albuquerque metropolitan area]

Waggoner, Laura. "San Jose. A Study in Urbanization." Master's thesis, U. of New Mexico, 1941. [Section of Albuquerque, NM]

Wax, Murray L., and Luhman, Reid A. Bilingual Classrooms in a Mexican-American Community. The Social Bases of Thinking and Speaking: A Study of Bilingual Chicano Children, S, 1974. ERIC ED 151 126. [Las Vegas]

Weiss, Lawrence D. "Modes of Production and Primitive Accumulation in Spanish New Mexico: 1600-1800." Southwest Economy and Society 3(Fall, 1977):30-54.

Wiley, Tom. Public School Education in New Mexico. Albuquerque: Division of Government Research, The U. of New Mexico, 1965.

Winnie, William W., Jr. "The Hispanic People of New Mexico." Master's thesis, U. of Florida, 1955.

Wolf, T. Phillip, and Craig, Elene. "New Mexico's Spanish Americans: Geographic and Political Patterns." In Politics 1973: Minorities in Politics. Edited by Tinsley E. Yarbrough, John P. East, and Sandra Hough. East Carolina U. Publications, P.O. Box 2771, Greenville, NC 27834, n.d.

Texas

Achor, Shirley Coolidge. Mexican Americans in a Dallas Barrio. Tucson: U. of Arizona Press, 1978.

_____. "Of Thorns and Roses: Variations in Cultural Adaptations Among Mexican-Americans in an Urban Texas Barrio." Doctoral dissertation, Southern Methodist U., 1974. Univ. Microfilms Order No. 74-27,826.

Akery, Nicholas. "An Exploratory Study of the Education of Spanish-speaking Children in the Primary Grades in Edinburg, Texas." Master's thesis, U. of Texas, 1955.

Allen, Ruth A. "Mexican Peon Women in Texas." Sociology and Social Research (N-D, 1931): 131-142.

Allsup, Carl. "The American G.I. Forum: A History of a Mexican American Organization." Doctoral dissertation, U. of Texas, 1976.

_____. "Mexican American Organization in New Mexico and Texas: An Urban Experience of the 1950s." In "The Urban Minority Experience," Selected Proceedings of the 4th Annual Conference on University Studies. Edited by George E. Carter and James R. Parker. La Crosse, WI: Institute for Minority Studies, U. of Wisconsin-La Crosse, 1978.

Alvardo, M. B. "Lanier Students Revolt Against System." Inferno, My, 1968. [Predominantly Mexican-American school in San Antonio, TX]

Alway, Lazelle D. An Employment Survey of 4,014 Texas School Children. New York: National Child Labor Committee, N, 1950.

Ameen, Bilquis A. Occupational Status Orientation and Perception of Opportunity: A Racial Comparison of Rural Youth from Depressed Areas, Ja, 1968. Master's thesis, Texas A&M, 1968. ERIC ED 027 111. Available from Interlibrary loan from Texas A&M U. Library, College Station, TX 77843.

Anderson, James G., and Johnson, William H. Social and Cultural Characteristics of Mexican-American Families in South El Paso, Texas. New Mexico State U., D, 1968. ERIC ED 026 175.

Ashton, Richard Price. "The Fourteenth Amendment and the Education of Latin-American Children in Texas. Master's thesis, U. of Texas, 1949.

"Austin and Alpine, Texas." Carta Editorial, Ag, 1969. [Central and Centennial elementary schools]

Baird, Frank L. The Anglo View of Mexican Americans, F, 1974. ERIC ED 101 897. [Lubbock]

Barrera, Eduardo. "School Dropouts in Hidalgo County, Texas: History of Remedial Programs and Assessment of Current Dropout Situation." Doctoral dissertation, U. of Texas, 1976. Univ. Microfilms Order No. 76-26,591.

Beman, Alma, and Goodman, Mary Ellen. Houstonians of Mexican Ancestry. Houston, TX: Center for Research in Social Change & Economic Development, Rice U., 1968.

Brookshire, Marjorie S. "Some Notes on the Integration of Mexican-Americans Since 1929, Nueces County, Texas." Industrial Relations Research Association Annual Proceedings 8 (1955):356-361.

Broom, Perry M. "An Interpretative Analysis of the Economic and Educational Status of Latin-Americans in Texas." Master's thesis, U. of Texas, Je, 1942.

Brown, Robert L. A Preliminary Study of Proportional Representation of Mexican-Americans in County Offices in South Texas, Ap 7, 1976. ERIC ED 121 527.

Caballero, Ray, Davis, Mary Alice, and Walsh, Michael. "The Story of the Mexican American [in Corpus Christi]." (A series of ten articles) Corpus Christi Caller, My 16-25, 1976.

Calderón, Carlos C. "The Education of Spanish-Speaking Children in Edcouch-Elsa, Texas." Master's thesis, U. of Texas, 1950.

Cannon, Garland. "Bilingual Education and Texas." Compass, Ag, 1968.

Carillo, Luis. "The Deep South: Texas." Inside Eastside, Jl 8, 1968. [Mexican-Americans in Texas]

Castaneda, Irene. "Chronicle of Crystal City." El Grito 4(Winter, 1971):48-53.

Chandler, Charles Ray. "The Mexican American Protest Movement in Texas." Doctoral dissertation, Tulane U., 1968.

"Chicano Boycott High School." Compass, D, 1968. [Edcouch-Elsa High School in Valley of South Texas]

"Chicanos! In the Streets in the Sixties; Where Are They Now?" San Antonio Express, D 22, 1974.

"Chicanos Win in Crystal City." Dallas Morning News, Ap 4, 1971.

Childers, Jean. Some Secondary Level Curriculum Considerations for Teaching Spanish to the Mexican Americans in Austin, Texas, Ag, 1971. ERIC ED 060 737.

Coalson, G. O. The Development of the Migratory Farm Labor System in Texas: 1900-1954. San Francisco: R & E Research Associates, 1977.

Cohen, Andrew D. A Sociolinguistic Approach to Bilingual Education. The Measurement of Language Use and Attitudes Toward Language in School and Community, with Special Reference to the Mexican American Community of Redwood City, California, S, 1970. ERIC ED 043 007.

Connor, Ruth Patton. "Some Community, Home and School Problems of Latin-American Children in Austin, Texas." Master's thesis, U. of Texas, 1949.

Cornejo, Ricardo Jesús. "Bilingualism: A Study of the Lexicon of the Five-Year-Old Spanish Speaking Children of Texas." Doctoral dissertation, U. of Texas, 1969.

Cortes, Carlos E. and others. The Mexican Experience in Texas. New York: Arno Press, 1976.

Crawford, Fred R. The Forgotten Egg. An Exploration Into Mental Health Problems Among Urban Mexican-American Families and their Children. Austin, TX: Department of Health, N 2, 1961. [San Antonio, TX]

Crawford, Harold B. "Educational and Occupational Aspirations and Expectations of Galveston High School Students." Doctoral dissertation, New Mexico State U., 1975.

"Crisis Seen Over Bowie Spanish Issue." El Paso Herald-Post, N 30, 1968. [Bowie High School, El Paso, TX]

Crisp, James E. "Anglo-Texan Attitudes Toward the Mexican, 1821-1845." Doctoral dissertation, Yale U., 1976.

Cromack, Isabel Work. "Latin Americans: A Minority Group in the Austin Public Schools." Master's thesis, U. of Texas, 1949.

Cuellar, Robert A. A Social and Political History of the Mexican-American Population of Texas, 1929-1963. San Francisco: R & E Research Associates, 1974 reprint.

Cultural Stability and Change Among Mexican-American Families in an Urban Setting: A Comparison of Generations in El Paso, Texas, Mr 4, 1970. ERIC ED 039 552.

Davidson, Walter Craig. The Mexican American High School Graduate of Laredo. A Laredo Independent School District Study, 1970 ERIC ED 052 508.

Davis, Mary Alice. "Education Doorway to Equality." Corpus Christi Caller, My 20, 1976. [Mexican-Americans in Corpus Christi]

De La Isla, José III. "Aspects of Social Organization of a Mexican Urban Barrio." Houston: Center for the Study of Social Change and Economic Development " Rice U., 1968 (unpublished).

De Leon, Arnoldo. Apuntes Tejanos. Vol. I: An Index of Items Related to Mexican Americans in Nineteenth Century Texas Extracted from the San Antonio Express (1869-1900) and the San Antonio Herald (1855-1878). Ann Arbor, MI: U. Microfilm International, 1978.

_____. "The Rape of Tio Taco: Mexican Americans in Texas, 1930-1935." Journal of Mexican American Studies 1(Fall, 1970):4-15.

_____. "White Racial Attitudes Toward Mexicanos in Texas, 1821-1900." Doctoral dissertation, Texas Christian U., 1975. Univ. Microfilms Order No. 75-3458.

De León, Nephtalí. "Mexican Americans in Abilene." Texas Observer, 1969.

_____. "Young Chicanos' Unrest Spreads to Lamesa." Texas Observer, Ja 23, 1970.

Diehl, Kemper. "San Antonio Classes Use Two Languages." Southern Education Report, O, 1967.

Dodd, E. C. "A Comparison of English-speaking and Spanish-speaking Children in Brownsville." Master's thesis, U. of Texas, 1930.

Downs, Fane. "The History of Mexicans in Texas, 1820-1845." Doctoral dissertation, Texas Tech U., 1970. Univ. Microfilms Order No. 71-09632.

Dysart, J. "Mexican Women in San Antonio, 1830-1860: The Assimilation Process." Western Historical Quarterly 7(O, 1976):365-384.

Elms, James E. "Attendance of Mexican and Anglo Students in Two Austin, Texas Schools." Master's thesis, U. of Texas, 1950.

El Paso Public Schools. Workshop for Developing Teaching Aids for Non-English-Speaking Children. El Paso, TX: El Paso Public Schools, S, 1945.

"Elsa [Texas] Students Victorious!" El Malcriado, Ja 15, 1969.

Emerson, Ralph Waddell. Education for the Mexican in Texas." Master's thesis, Southern Methodist U., 1929.

Estes, Dwain M., and Darling, David W. Improving Educational Opportunities for the Mexican-American, Proceedings of the Texas Conference for the Mexican-American (1st, San Antonio, Ap 13-15, 1967). San Antonio, TX: Inter-American Education Center; Texas Education agency, Austin, 1967, 171 pp. ERIC ED 020 819.

Evans, Charles L. Mexican American Education Study. Report 1: Employment, Enrollment, and School Success of Mexican Americans, Ap, 1974. ERIC ED 100 548. [Fort Worth, TX]

Foley, Douglas E. "Legalistic and Personalistic Adaptations to Ethnic Conflict in a Texas School." Journal of Research and Development in Education 9(Summer, 1976): 74-82.

Foley, Douglas E. and others. From Peones to Politicos: Ethnic Relations in a South Texas Town, 1900 to 1975, F 7, 1977. ERIC ED 137 019.

Sister M. Francesca. "Variations of Selected Cultural Patterns Among Three Generations of Mexicans in San Antonio, Texas." American Catholic Sociological Review 19(1958):24-34.

Friedman, Marjorie S. "An Appraisal of the Role of the Public School As An Acculturating Agency of Mexican Americans in Texas, 1850-1968." Doctoral dissertation, New York U., 1978. Univ. Microfilms Order No. 7818133.

Fuller, Roden. "Occupations of the Mexican-Born Population in Texas, New Mexico and Arizona 1900-1920." Journal of the American Statistical Association 23(Mr, 1928):64-67.

Galván, Robert A., and Teschner, Richard V. El diccionario del español de Tejas/The Dictionary of the Spanish of Texas. Silver Spring, MD: Institute of Modern Languages, 1976.

García, Mario T. "El Paso's Mexican American Community, 1880's-1930's." Doctoral dissertation, U. of California, San Diego, 1974.

_____. "Racial Dualism in the El Paso Labor Market, 1880-1920." Aztlan 6(Summer, 1975): 197-218.

Garcia, Nefthali and others. Ethnic Identification and Political Attitudes Among Mejican Youth in San Antonio, Texas, Ap, 1974. ERIC ED 101 885.

Garcia, Richard. Political Ideology: A Comparative Study of Three Chicano Youth Organizations. San Francisco: R & E Research Associates, 1977. [El Paso]

Garnett, William E. "Immediate and Pressing Race Problems of Texas." Proceedings of the Southwestern Political and Social Science Association (1925):31-48.

Gilbert, Ennis H. "Some Legal Aspects of the Education of Spanish-Speaking Children in Texas." Master's thesis, U. of Texas, 1947.

Goodman, Marcy Ellen, and Beman, Alma. "Child's Eye-Views of Life in an Urban Barrio." In Spanish-Speaking People in the United States. Edited by June Helms. Seattle: U. of Washington Press, 1969. [Houston, TX]

Goodman, Mary Ellen and others. The Mexican-American Population of Houston: A Survey in the Field, 1965-1970. Monograph in Cultural Anthropology. Houston, TX: Rice U., 1971, 130 pp. ERIC ED 060 997.

Gutiérrez, Armando G., and Hirsch, Herbert. "Political Maturation and Political Awareness: The Case of the Crystal City Chicano." Aztlán 5(Spring and Fall, 1974): 295-312.

"José Angel Gutiérrez." Regeneracion 1, No. 3 (1970):4-5. [Crystal City, TX]

Gutiérrez, José Angel. A Gringo Manual on How to Handle Mexicans. Crystal City, TX: Wintergarden Publishing House, 1974.

_____. "Aztlan: Chicano Revolt in the Winter Garden." La Raza 1(F, 1971):36-45. [Crystal City]

_____. "La Raza and Revolution: The Empirical Conditions of Revolution in Four South Texas Counties." Master's thesis, St. Mary's U., San Antonio, 1968.

_____. "Toward a Theory of Community Organization in a Mexican-American Community in South Texas." Doctoral dissertation, U. of Texas, n.d.

Gutiérrez, Raul. "Mexican-Americans Boycott Elsa High School. Greater Houston--Uneasy?" Compass, D, 1968.

Hardgrave, Robert L., Jr., and Hinojosa, Santiago. The Politics of Bilingual Education: A Study of Four Southwest Texas Communities. Austin, TX: Sterling Swift Publishing Co., 1975. [Laredo, Del Rio, Crystal City, and Sonora]

Harrington, James C. "Mexican-Americans Seek a Just Place." Civil Liberties, Jl 7, 1977. [Rio Grande Valley, South Texas]

Harris, James K. "A Sociological Study of a Mexican School in San Antonio, Texas." Master's thesis, U. of Texas, 1927.

Hayes, James V. "An Analysis of Latin-American Partial Attendance and Dropouts in the Elementary Schools of Eagle Pass, Texas in Recent Years." Master's thesis, U. of Texas. 1952.

Haynes, Kingsley E. and others. Colonias in the Lower Rio Grande Valley of South Texas. 1977. ERIC ED 147 055. [Cameron, Hidalgo, and Willacy counties]

Hirsch, Herbert, and Gutierrez, Armando. Learning to be Militant. San Francisco: Rand E Research Associates, 1977. [Crystal City]

"Hondo Texas School District Raises Many Familiar Chicano Issues." Agenda 4(Ap, 1974):1, 4.

Horn, P. Survey of the City Schools of El Paso, Texas. El Paso, TX: Board of Education, 1922.

"Hot Lunch Program." Inferno, D 5, 1967. [San Antonio Independent School District and the Mexican American]

Housewright, George Maxwell. "The Changing Economic Status in Texas of the Latin-American and the Negro: 1950-1960." Doctoral dissertation, U. of Arkansas, 1972. Univ. Microfilms Order No. 72-29703.

Howard, Raymond G. "Acculturation and Social Mobility Among Latin Americans in Reseca City." Master's thesis, U. of Texas, 1952.

Huey, John. "Control of San Antonio Is Slowly Being Won by Mexican-Americans." Wall Street Journal, Jl 13, 1977.

Huser, C. W. "San Antonio Educates Little Mexico." Adult Education Bulletin 3(Ap, 1939): 13-16.

Jerden, Cecil M. "A Study in Racial Differences in the El Paso Public Schools." Master's thesis, Southern Methodist U., 1939.

Johnson, Roberta M. "History of the Education of Spanish-Speaking Children in Texas." Master's thesis, U. of Texas, 1932.

Jordan, Terry G. "Population Origins in Texas, 1850." Geographical Review 59(Ja, 1969): 83-103.

Juarez, Jose Roberto. "La Iglesia Catolica y el Chicano en Sud Texas, 1836-1911." Aztlan 4 (F, 1973):217-255.

Juárez, Rinaldo Z. "Education Status Orientations of Mexican American and Anglo American Youth in Selected Low-Income Counties of Texas." Master's thesis, Texas A & M U., 1968.

Juárez, Rinaldo Z. Education Status Orientations of Mexican American and Ango American
Youth in Selected Low-Income Counties of
Texas. Master's thesis, 1968. ERIC ED
023 511.

Kaderli, Albert Turner. "The Educational
Problem in the Americanization of the
Spanish-speaking Pupils of Sugar Land,
Texas." Master's thesis, U. of Texas, 1940.

Kaderli, James N. "A Study of Mexican Education in Atacosa County with Special Reference to Plesanton Elementary School."
Master's thesis, U. of Texas, 1938.

Lamanna, Richard A., and Samora, Julian
Recent Trends in Educational Status of
Mexican-Americans in Texas, D, 1965. ERIC
ED 020 813.

Lampe, P. E. "The Acculturation of Mexican
Americans in Public and Parochial Schools."
Sociological Analysis 36(Spring, 1975).
[San Antonio]

Laosa, Luis M. and others. "Mental Health
Consultation in a Rural Chicano Community:
Crystal City." Aztlán 6(Fall, 1975):433-
453.

Little, Wilson. Spanish-Speaking Children in
Texas. Austin: U. of Texas Press, 1944.

McBurnette, Patrick E., and Kunetka, James W.
Mexican American Perceptions of Isolation
in Desegregated School Settings, Ap, 1976.
ERIC ED 121 555.

McDowell, Neil Allen. "A Status Study of the
Academic Capabilities and Achievements of
Three Ethnic Groups: Anglo, Negro, and
Spanish Surname, in San Antonio, Texas."
Doctoral dissertation, U. of Texas, 1966.

McGrath, Paul (Sister Paul of the Cross McGrath).
Political Nativism in Texas, 1825-1860.
Washington, DC: Catholic U. of America,
1930.

McLemore, S. Dale. "The Origins of Mexican
American Subordination in Texas." Social
Science Quarterly 53(Mr, 1973):656-670.

McNamara, Patrick H. "Rumbles Along the Rio."
Commonweal, Mr 14, 1969.

Madsen, William. Mexican-Americans of South
Texas. New York: Holt, Rinehart and
Winston, 1964.

Manuel, Herschel T. The Education of Mexican
and Spanish-Speaking Children in Texas.
Austin: U. of Texas, 1930.

_____. "The Mexican Child in Texas." South-
west Review 17(Ap, 1932):290-302.

_____. "The Mexican Population of Texas."
Southwestern Political & Social Science
Quarterly 15(Je, 1934):29-51.

_____. "The Spanish-Speaking Child in Texas
Schools." In Improving Educational Opportun-
ities of the Mexican American. San Antonio,
TX: Southwest Educational Development
Laboratory, 1968.

Martínez, Oscar J. "Border Boom Town: El Paso-
Ciudad Juarez Since 1880." Doctoral dissertation, U. of California, Los Angeles, 1975.

_____. The Chicanos of El Paso: A Case of
Changing Colonization, My, 1977. ERIC ED
153 780.

Miller, Michael V. "Chicano Community Control
in South Texas: Problems and Prospects."
Journal of Ethnic Studies 3(Fall, 1975):
70-89.

_____. "Conflict and Change in a Bifurcated
Community: Anglo-Mexican-American Political
Relations in a South Texas Town." Master's
thesis, Texas A & M, 1971.

_____. "Mexican Americans, Chicanos, and
Others: Ethnic Self-Identification and
Selected Social Attributes of Rural Texas
Youth." Rural Sociology 41(Summer, 1976):
234-247.

_____. Poverty and Problems of Development in
the Lower Rio Grande Valley of Texas, F,
1976. ERIC ED 125 792.

Miller, Michael V., and Maril, Robert Lee.
Poverty in the Lower Rio Grande Valley of
Texas: Historical and Contemporary
Dimensions, Ag, 1978. ERIC ED 158 911.

Miller, Michael V., and Preston, J. D. "Vertical
Ties and the Redistribution of Power in
Crystal City." Social Science Quarterly 53
(1973):772-784.

Mooney, Marion S. "The Migratory Pupil Problem
in the Del Rio Independent School District."
Master's thesis, Southwest Texas State
Teachers College, San Marcos, 1951.

Morehead, Richard M. "Bilingual Education...
A Problem Elsewhere." Southern Education
Report, O, 1966.

Morin, Kenneth N. Attitudes of Texas Mexican-
Americans Toward Mental Retardation: A
Guttman Facet Analysis, Mr 24, 1970. ERIC
ED 039 563.

Murray, Sister Mary John. A Socio-Cultural
Study of 118 Mexican-American Families Living
in a Low-Rent Housing Project in San
Antonio. Washington, DC: Catholic U. of
America Press 1954.

Navarro, Armando. El Partido de la Raza in
Crystal City: A Peaceful Revolution.
Riverside: U. of California, 1974.

Nelson Cisneros, Victor B. "La clase trabajadora
en Tejas, 1920-1940." Aztlan 6(Summer, 1975):
239-265.

Nicola, Peter Castro. "The Educational Problem of the Mexican Migrants of Texas, with Specific Reference to San Marcos, Texas." Master's thesis, Southwest Texas State Teachers College, San Marcos, 1952.

Noyola, Arnaldo J. "Psychosocial and Academic Factors Associated with Elementary School Children in the Barrios of San Antonio." Master's thesis, U. of Texas, 1971.

"Organizing in South Texas." IFCO News 3, Issue 1(1972).

Parr, Eunice Elvira. "A Comparative Study of Mexican and American Children in the Schools of San Antonio, Texas." Master's thesis, U. of Chicago, 1926.

Pendás, Miguel. "Behind the Crystal City Election Results." Militant, My 6, 1977.

Post, Donald E. "Ethnic Competition for Control of Schools in Two South Texas Towns." Doctoral dissertation, U. of Texas, 1974.

_____. "Ethnic Conflict in Two South Texas Towns." Integrateducation 15(S-O, 1977).

Ramirez, Emilia S. "Wetback Children in South Texas." Master's thesis, U. of Texas, 1951.

Ramirez, Felix T. "School Efficiency." Compass, Ap, 1969. [School segregation in Houston, TX]

Ramirez, Sara L. "The Educational Status and Socio-Economic Backgrounds of Latin-American Children in Waco, Texas." Master's thesis, U. of Texas, 1957.

Rangel, Jorge C., and Alcala, Carlos M. "De Jure Segregation of Chicanos in Texas Schools." Harvard Civil Rights and Civil Liberties Review 7(1972).

Remy, Caroline. "Hispanic-Mexican San Antonio, 1836-1861." Southwestern Historical Quarterly 71(Ap, 1968):564-582.

Reyna, Jose. "Chicano Folklore: Raza Humor in Texas." De Colores Journal of Emerging Raza Philosophies 1(1975):58-65.

Rivera, George, Jr. "Building a Chicano Party in South Texas." New South 40(Spring, 1971): 75-78. [Crystal City, TX]

_____. "Recognition of Mexican American Influentials in Magnolia." Compass, My, 1969. [Houston, TX area]

_____. "Social Change in the Barrio: The Chicano Movement in South Texas." Aztlan 3 (Fall, 1972):205-214.

Robledo, Amado. "The Impact of Alien Immigration on Public Policy and Educational Services on Selected Districts in the Texas Educational System." Doctoral dissertation, U. of Houston, 1977.

Rodriguez, Modesto. [Testimony on condition of Mexican-Americans in Pearsall, Texas] In U.S. Congress, 94th, 1st session, House of Representatives, Committee on the Judiciary, Subcommittee on Civil and Constitutional Rights, Extension of the Voting Rights Act. Hearings... Part 1, pp. 519-535. Part 1, Serial No. 1. Washington, DC: GPO, 1975.

Rogers, Dorothy. Personality Traits and Academic Achievement Among Mexican American Students, U. of Texas, Austin, Ag, 1971, 136 pp. [San Antonio] ERIC ED 052 884.

Roser, Francis B. "An Analysis of 1,000 Applicants who Filed under Announcement Number DS-6-22 for Helper & Helper Trainee, W-3, 4, and 5." In U.S. Commission on Civil Rights, Hearing Held in San Antonio, Texas, December 9-14, 1968, pp. 893-904. Washington, DC: GPO, 1969.

Roueché, Berton. "Zavala." New Yorker, D 4, 1978. [Crystal City]

Rouse, Lura M. "A Study of the Education of Spanish-Speaking Children in Dimmit County, Texas." Master's thesis, U. of Texas, 1948.

Rubel, Arthur J. Across the Tracks: Mexican-Americans in a Texas City. Austin: U. of Texas Press, 1966.

Saenz, J. L. "Racial Discrimination, a Number One Problem of Texas Schools." Texas Outlook 30(D, 1946):12-13.

Salazar, Arturo, and Christiansen, Jane E. The Need for Bilingual Vocational Education Programs in Secondary Schools in Texas, S, 1976. ERIC ED 137 518.

Samora, Julian and others. Gunpowder Justice: A Reassessment of the Texas Rangers. Notre Dame, IN: U. of Notre Dame Press, 1979.

Sanchez, George I. "A Communication [on the Education of American Children of Mexican Descent]." Texas Observer, Ag 23, 1963.

_____. Concerning Segregation of Spanish-Speaking Children in the Public Schools. Inter-American Education Occasional Papers, IX. Austin: U. of Texas, D, 1951.

Santillan, Richard. La Raza Unida, 1973. Tlaquilo Publications, P.O. Box 7217, Los Angeles, CA 90022.

Santos, Richard G. "The Mexican American of Texas and the Southwest: A Historical Perspective." In National Institute of Mental Health, Proceedings of the Institute on Narcotic Addiction Among Mexican Americans in the Southwest, pp. 3-15. Washington, DC: GPO, 1973.

Saunders, Lyle. The Spanish-Speaking Population of Texas. New York: Arno, 1976 reprint.

Scott, Helen B. "Educational Attainment and Aspirations of Rural and Urban Spanish-Americans in Two South Texas Counties." Master's thesis, Texas A & M U., 1969.

Shafer, Wilfred A. "Foreign-Born Children of Illegal Immigrants: A Growing Dilemma." Integrateducation 14(N/D, 1976).

Shaffer, Richard A. "Deepening Frustration of Mexican-Americans Stirs Fears of Violence." Wall Street Journal, Je 11, 1970. [San Antonio, TX]

_____. "Small Town in Texas In a Testing Ground of Chicano Movement." Wall Street Journal, S 5, 1975. [Crystal City]

Shapiro, Harold A. "The Workers of San Antonio, Texas, 1900-1940." Doctoral dissertation, U. of Texas, 1952.

Shockley, John Staples. Chicano Revolt in a Texas Town. Notre Dame, IN: U. of Notre Dame Press, 1974. [Crystal City]

"Side by Side—And a World Apart—in Uvalde, Texas." Newsweek, Je 29, 1970.

Simmons, Ozzie. Anglo-Americans and Mexican-Americans in South Texas. New York: Arno, 1974.

Simmons, Thomas E. "The Citizen Factories: The Americanization of Mexican Students in Texas Public Schools, 1920-1945." Doctoral dissertation, Texas A & M U., n.d.

Sisk, William O. "The Mexican in Texas Schools." Texas Outlook 14(D, 1930):10-12.

Smith, Walter E., Jr. "Mexicano Resistance to Schooled Ethnicity: Ethnic Student Power in South Texas, 1930-1970." Doctoral dissertation, U. of Texas, 1978. Univ. Microfilms Order No. 7900637.

Spillman, Robert C. "A Historical Geography of Mexican-American Population Patterns in the South Texas Hispanic Borderland: 1850-1970." Master's thesis, U. of Southern Mississippi, 1977.

"Students Strike in Texas." El Malcriado, D 15, 1968. [Edcouch-Elsa High School, in Hidalgo County]

Taylor, J. T. "The Americanization of Harlingen's Mexican School Population." Texas Outlook 18(S, 1934):37-38.

Taylor, Paul S. An American-Mexican Frontier, Nueces County, Texas. Chapel Hill: U. of North Carolina Press, 1934.

Teske, Raymond H. C., Jr. "An Analysis of the Status Mobility Patterns among Middle-Class Mexican-Americans in Texas." Doctoral dissertation, U. of California, Los Angeles, 1973. Univ. Microfilms Order No. 74-11,559.

Teske, Raymond, Jr., and Nelson, Bardin H. Status Mobility Patterns Among Middle-Class Mexican Americans in Texas: A Theoretical Orientation, Ag 28, 1971. ERIC ED 053 850.

Texas Education Agency, Division of Research. Report of Pupils in Texas Public Schools Having Spanish Surnames, 1955-56. Austin, TX: The Division, 1957.

Texas State Department of Education. State-Wide Survey of Enumeration, Enrollment, Attendance and Progress of Latin-American Children in Texas Public Schools. Austin, TX, 1943-1944.

Thomas, Tony. "Crystal City, Texas: La Raza Unida Party in Action." International Socialist Review(Ap, 1971):25-26.

Thompson, John Miles. "Mobility, Income and Utilization of Mexican American Manpower in Lubbock, Texas 1960-1970." Doctoral dissertation, Texas Tech U., 1972. Univ. Microfilms Order No. 72-32,067.

Thompson, Roger Mark. "Language Loyalty in Austin, Texas: A Study of a Bilingual Neighborhood." Doctoral dissertation, U. of Texas, 1971. Univ. Microfilms Order No. 72-15,845.

Tijerina, Andrew A. "Tejanos and Texas: The Native Mexicans of Texas, 1820-1850." Doctoral dissertation, U. of Texas, 1978.

Toronto, Allen J. The Influence of Parents' Income, Education and Culture on Language Performance of Children in a Texas Border Town, N 24, 1975. ERIC ED 122 624.

Torres-Raines, Rosario. "Casas Ricas y Pobres: The Effects of Housing Market Expenditures on Residential Segregation of Mexican Americans in Texas and California." Doctoral dissertation, Texas Woman's U., 1978. Univ. Microfilms Order NO. 7815602.

Trillin, Calvin. "U.S. Journal: San Antonio." New Yorker, My 2, 1977.

U.S. Commission on Civil Rights, Staff Report. A Study of Equality of Educational Opportunity for Mexican Americans in Nine School Districts of the San Antonio Area. In U.S. Commission on Civil Rights, Hearing Held in San Antonio, Texas, pp. 803-880, D 9-14, 1968. Washington, DC: GPO, 1969.

Upham, W. K., and Wright, D. E. Poverty among Spanish Americans in Texas: Low-Income Families in a Minority Group. Texas A & M U., Report No. 66-2, S, 1966.

Venegas, Moises, and Kuvlesky, William. Do Metropolitan and Nonmetropolitan Chicano Youth Differ: A Study of South Texas Teen-Agers—1973, Ag 21, 1975. ERIC ED 121 514.

Watson, Walter T. "Mexicans in Dallas."
In Mexico and the United States, pp. 231-250.
Edited by S. D. Myers, Jr. Dallas, TX:
Institute of Public Affairs, Southern
Methodist U., 1938.

Weaver, Charles N., and Glenn, Norval D. "Job
Performance Comparisons: Mexican-American
& Anglo Employees." California Management
Review 13(Fall, 1970):27-30. [San Antonio,
TX]

West, Paul. "Chicano Leader's 'Empire'
Threatened." Washington Post, O 30, 1976.
[José Angel Gutíerrez, Crystal City]

Wiegand, Karl. Chicano Wanderarbeiter in
Südtexas. Die gegenwartige Situation der
Spanisch-sprechenden Bevölkerung dieses
Raumes. Kiel: Geographical Institute, U.
of Kiel, 1977.

Williams, J. Allen, Babchuk, Nicholas, and
Johnson, David R. "Voluntary Associations
and Minority Status: A Comparative Analysis
of Anglo, Black, and Mexican Americans."
American Sociological Review 38(O, 1973):637-
646. [Austin, TX]

Wilson, Jacques M. P. "An Appalling Waste.
Factors Affecting the Development of Mexican-
American Elementary School Students in
Texas." Texas Observer, Ag 23, 1963.

Wilson, Joe H. "Secondary School Dropouts,
with Special Reference to Spanish-Speaking
Youth in Texas." Doctoral dissertation, U.
of Texas, 1953.

Works, G. A. "The Non-English Speaking Children
and the Public School." In Texas Educational
Survey Report, Chapter 13, Volume 8, pp.
207-26. Austin: Texas Education Survey
Commission, 1925.

Wright, David E., Jr. Occupational Orientations
of Mexican American Youth in Selected Texas
Counties, Ag, 1968, 167 pp. Master's
thesis. ERIC ED 023 512.

Wright, David E., Jr., and Kuvlesky, William P.
Occupational Status Projections of Mexican
American Youth Residing in the Rio Grande
Valley. (Paper presented at annual meeting
of Southwestern Sociological Association,
Dallas, Ap, 1968), 31 pp. ERIC ED 023 496.

Elsewhere

Althoff, Phillip. "The Political Integration
of Mexican-Americans & Blacks: A Note on a
Deviant Case." Rocky Mountain Social Science
Journal 10(O, 1973). [Manhattan, Kansas]

Amundson, Connie L. "The Mexican Migrant
Workers in Polk County, Minnesota: A Study
of their Problems of Living as They Affect
Education." Master's thesis, Moorhead State
College, Minnesota, 1963.

Baca, Orlando G. Selected Characteristics of
the Spanish-Origin Population in Illinois and
Some Related Educational Trends with Reference
to Northern Illinois University and Its
Service Area, S, 1975. ERIC ED 122 093.

Benavides, Alfredo H. "Mexican-Americans and
Public Service Institutions in a Midwestern
Community: An Analysis of Mutual Images and
Interactions." Doctoral dissertation, Michi-
gan State U., 1978. Univ. Microfilms Order
No. 7900672. [Midwestern town]

Betten, Neil, and Mohl, Raymond A. "From Dis-
crimination to Repatriation: Mexican Life in
Gary, Indiana, During the Great Depression."
Pacific Historical Review 62(Ag, 1973).

Braun, Marian F. "A Survey of the American-
Mexicans in Topeka, Kansas." Master's
thesis, Kansas State Teachers College,
Emporia, 1970.

Brauner, Marilyn R. "Migration and Educational
Achievement of Mexican Americans." Southwest
Social Science Quarterly 53(1973):727-737.
[Racine, Wisconsin]

Byrne, David R. "Mexican-American Secondary
Students: Salt Lake City School District."
Doctoral dissertation, U. of Utah, 1971.
Univ. Microfilms Order NO. 72-00519.

Camacho, Francisco M. "Socio-economic Condition
of the Mexican-American Population in Greater
Des Moines, Iowa, and Its Guidance Implications." Master's thesis, Drake U., 1968.

Cardenas, Gilbert (ed.). "Chicanos in the Midwest." Aztlan 7(Summer, 1974):141-336.

Carlson, Alvar W. "The Settling Processes of
Mexican Americans in Northwestern Ohio."
Journal of Mexican American History 5(1975):
24-42.

"Chicago School Reflects Cultural Heritage."
Modern Schools (Ja, 1977):12-13. [Benito
Juarez High School]

Choldin, Harvey M., and Trout, Grafton D.
Mexican Americans in Transition, Migration and
Employment in Michigan Cities. Part I:
Introduction and Summary, Mr, 1971. 35 pp.
East Lansing, MI: Michigan State U., Rural
Manpower Center. ERIC ED 049 857.

Cook, J. M., and Arthur, Grace. "Intelligence
Rating of 97 Mexican Children in St. Paul."
Journal of Exceptional Children 18(O, 1951):
14-15.

Corty, Julianne. "Latinos Press Plea for Equal
Education." Racine Journal Times, D 7, 1975.
[Racine, WI]

Davison, Victoria F., and Shannon, Lyle W.
"Change in the Economic Absorption of a Cohort
of Immigrant Mexican Americans and Negroes
Between 1960 and 1971." International Migra-
tion Review 11(Summer, 1977):190-214.
[Racine, WI]

Donovan, Deborah. "Latins Struggle for Equality." Davenport Quad-City Times, N 2, 1975. [Davenport, Iowa]

Daniels, Jo Ann, and O'Leary, Gloria. Que lejos hemos venido? How Far Have We Come?: Migrant Farm Labor in Iowa, 1975. Washington, DC: U.S. Commission on Civil Rights, 1976.

Dunlap, A. "Library Services to Mexican-Americans." Idaho Librarian 23(Ja, 1971): 3-7.

Engstrom, Karen. "Chicanos Set Up Seattle School." Guardian, N 29, 1972.

Erb, Gene. "Mexicans in D.M. Recall Struggle to Gain Acceptance." Des Moines Tribune, Ap 9, 1976.

Falcon, Carlos and others. Quality Educational Services to Michigan's Spanish-Speaking Community, Ja, 1974. ERIC ED 097 177.

Garcia, Jorge F. "Chicanos in Iowa." Conóceme en Iowa. The Official Report of the Governor's Spanish Speaking Task Force. Des Moines: Office of the Governor, 1976.

Glass, Thomas E. "The Chicano Group--A Comparative Group." In "A Descriptive and Comparative Study of American Indian Children in the Detroit Public Schools." Doctoral dissertation, Wayne State U., 1972. [Detroit]

Grove, Dorothy L. "A Study of the Educational Needs of Migrant Mexican Children at the Caldwell, Idaho, Labor Camp." Master's thesis, College of Idaho, Caldwell, 1958.

Haddad, Charles. "A Wetback's Chicago." Chicago Tribune Magazine, Je 18, 1978.

Hemesath, James B. "Chicago's South-of-the Border Cinema." Chicago Tribune Magazine, D 1, 1974.

Humphrey, Norman D. "Education and Language of Detroit Mexicans." Journal of Educational Sociology 17(My, 1944):534-542.

_____. "The Integration of Detroit Mexican Colony." American Journal of Economics and Sociology 3(Ja, 1944):155-166.

_____. "Mexican Repatriation from Michigan: Public Assistance in Historical Perspective." Social Service Review 15(S, 1941):497-513.

Jones, Anita Edgar. "Conditions Surrounding Mexicans in Chicago." Master's thesis, U. of Chicago, 1928.

Jones, Anita E. "Mexican Colonies in Chicago." Social Service Review 2, n.d., 579-597.

Krass, Elaine M., Peterson, Claire, and Shannon, Lyle W. "Differential Association, Cultural Integration, and Economic Absorption among Mexican-Americans and Negroes in a Northern Industrial Community." Southwestern Social Science Quarterly 47(1966):239-252. [Racine, WI]

Laird, Judith Ann Fincher. "Argentine, Kansas: The Evolution of a Mexican-American Community, 1905-1940." Doctoral dissertation, U. of Kansas, 1975.

Loera, Francisco, Romero, Jose, and Alvarez, Mario. Education: Emerging Opportunities for Chicanos in Oregon? Summer, 1971. Montal Education Associates, Suite 1207, 1700 K Street, N.W., Washington, DC 20006.

McKim, Judith R. "Becoming 'We' Instead of 'They': The Cultural Integration of Mexican-Americans and Negroes." Urban Education 13 (Jl, 1978):147-178. [Racine, WI]

Maldonado, L. A., and Byrne, D. R. The Social Ecology of Chicanos in Utah. Iowa City: U. of Iowa, 1978.

Martinez, Frank. "Oregon Chicanos' Fight for Equality." Civil Rights Digest 5(Winter, 1972):17-22.

Mata, Alberto G., Jr. "The Drug Street Scene: An Ethnographic Study of Mexican Youth in South Chicago." Doctoral dissertation, U. of Notre Dame, 1978. Univ. Microfilms Order No. 7821650.

Mathieson, C. "Mexican-Americans in Milwaukee." Doctoral dissertation, U. of Wisconsin-Milwaukee, 1968.

Nelson, Josephine B., and Nelson, Catherine. "Photo Project Helps Inner-City Teens." Extension Service Review 42(O, 1971):8-9. [Mexican-American youth in St. Paul, Minnesota]

Nuevo Kerr, Louise Aña. "Chicano Settlements in Chicago: A Brief History." Journal of Ethnic Studies 2(Winter, 1975):22-32.

_____. "Mexican Chicago: Chicano Assimilation Aborted, 1939-1952." In The Ethnic Frontier. Edited by Melvin G. Holli and Peter d'A. Jones. Grand Rapids, MI: Eerdimans, 1977.

Phalen, John. "South Bend Schools Fail in Education of Latino Students." South Bend Tribune, My 4, 1978.

Pierce, Lorraine E. "Mexican Americans on St. Paul's Lower West Side." Journal of Mexican American History 4(1974):1-18.

Popp, Sharon et al. "Exploratory Study of the Mexican-American Community in Detroit, Michigan." Master's thesis, Wayne State U., Je, 1970.

Powley, Jean. "High Mexican-American Dropout Rate Examined." South Bend Tribune, F 4, 1979. [South Bend, IN]

Reich, Michael S. A Comparison of Scholastic Achievement of Mexican-American Pupils in Regular and Bilingual Groups in a Chicago Public Elementary School, 1975. ERIC ED 131 970.

Reilly, Rosa D. "An Analysis of Some of the Causes of the Drop Out Rate of Mexican-American Students in Nampa School District No. 131." Master's thesis, Boise State U., 1976.

Reisler, Mark. "The Mexican Immigrant in the Chicago Area during the 1920's." Journal of the Illinois State Historical Society 66 (Summer, 1973).

Rodriguez, N. E., and Boyle, J. Y. "Opportunity Classes Help Spanish-Speaking Pupils." Chicago School Journal 43(F, 1962):228-231.

Scalces, Luis Mario. "Spanish American Politics in Chicago." Doctoral dissertation, Northwestern U., 1978. Univ. Microfilms Order No. 7903357.

Samora, Julian, and Lamanna, Richard A. Mexican-Americans in a Midwest Metropolis: A Study of East Chicago. Los Angeles: Graduate School of Business Administration, U. of California, 1967.

Schemman, Greg. "The Black Legend in Wyoming High School Textbooks: Anti-Hispanic Attitudes in Their Treatment of the Period 1492-1848." Annals of Wyoming 49(Fall, 1977):223-252.

Sepulveda, Ciro. "The Mexican Menace, East Chicago, Indiana, 1932." In "The Urban Minority Experience," pp. 119-125. Edited by George E. Carter and James R. Parker. Selected Proceedings of the 4th Annual Conference on Minority Studies. La Crosse, WI: Institute for Minority Studies, U. of Wisconsin-La Crosse, 1978.

Shannon, Lyle W. "False Assumptions About the Determinants of Mexican-American and Negro Economic Absorption." Sociological Quarterly 16(Winter, 1975):3-15

Shannon, Lyle W., and Drass, Elaine M. The Economic Absorption and Cultural Integration of Immigrant Mexican-Americans and Negro Workers. N.I.H. Project--progress report on grouped-value assimilation among immigration workers, Iowa City, IA: Dept. of Sociology and Anthropology, State U. of Iowa, 1964.

Shannon, Lyle W., and McKim, Judith L. "Attitudes Toward Education and the Absorption of Immigrant Mexican-Americans and Negroes in Racine." Education and Urban Society 6 (My, 1974):333-354.

Shannon, Lyle W., and Morgan, Patricia. "The Prediction of Economic Absorption and Cultural Integration among Mexican-Americans, Negroes, and Anglos in a Northern Industrial Community." Human Organization, Summer, 1966.

Shannon, Lyle W. and others. The Economic Absorption and Cultural Integration of Immigrant Workers. Iowa City, IA: Division of Extension and University Services, 1966.

Simon, Daniel T. "Mexican Repatriation in East Chicago, Indiana." Journal of Ethnic Studies 2(Summer, 1974):11-23.

Skurzynski, Gloria. "Chicanos in Mormon Land." America, Mr 18, 1972. [Utah]

Slatta, Richard W. "Chicanos in Oregon: An Historical Overview." Master's thesis, Portland State U., 1974.

_____. "Chicanos in the Pacific Northwest: An Historical Overview of Oregon's Chicanos." Aztlan 6(Fall, 1975):327-340.

Slesinger, Doris P. and others. Health Care Needs of a Hispanic Population in Dane, Dodge, and Jefferson Counties, Je, 1977. ERIC ED 157 657. [Wisconsin]

Soderstrom, Joan. An Investigation of Mexican-American Migrant Children Population in Idaho and the Educational Opportunities Provided by Selected School Districts. Pocatello: Idaho State U., Ap, 1967, 213 pp. ERIC ED 014 364.

Sullenger, T. Earl. "Mexican Population of Omaha." Journal of Applied Sociology 88, n.d., 289-293.

Sunseri, Alvin R. "The Migrant Workers of Iowa." In Selected Proceedings of the 3rd Annual Conference on Minority Studies, Ap, 1975, pp. 25-34. Edited by George E. Carter, James R. Parker, and Carol Sweeney. La Crosse, WI: Institute for Minority Studies, U. of Wisconsin-La Crosse, 1976. [See also Maximo Escobedo, "A Migrant Worker's Comment on Alvin Sunseri's Paper," pp. 35-38]

Wells, Miriam June. "From Field to Foundry: Mexican American Adaptive Strategies in a Small Wisconsin Town." Doctoral dissertation, U. of Wisconsin, 1975. Univ. Microfilms Order No. 75-28,826.

Zirkel, Perry. "Bilingual Education and School Desegregation: A Case of Uncoordinated Remedies." Bilingual Review 4(S-D, 1977): 180-188. [Includes material on Hartford, Connecticut]

Historical

Acuña, Rodolfo. Occupied America: The Chicano's Struggle Toward Liberation. San Francisco: Canfield Press, 1972.

Allsky, Marvin and others. The Role of the Mexican American in the History of the Southwest, N 18, 1969, 60 pps. (Conference paper, Inter-American Institute) ERIC ED 046 592.

Almaguer, Tomas. "Historical Notes on Chicano Oppression: the Dialectics of Racial and Class Domination in North America." Aztlan 5(Spring and Fall, 1972):27-56.

Alvarez, Rodolfo. "The Psycho-Historical and Socioeconomic Development of the Chicano Community in the United States." Social Science Quarterly 53(Mr, 1973):920-942.

_____. "The Unique Psycho-Historical Experience of the Mexican-American People." Social Science Quarterly 52(Je, 1971):15-29.

Brock, Gene M. "Mexican Opinion, American Racism, and the War of 1846." Western Historical Quarterly 1(Ap, 1970):161-174.

Cardenas, Gilberto. "U.S. Immigration Policy toward Mexico: An Historical Perspective." Chicano Law Review 2(Summer, 1975):66-91.

Carter, Thomas P. Mexican-Americans in School: A History of Educational Neglect. New York: College Entrance Examination Board, 1970.

Casteñeda, Carlos E. (tr.). The Mexican Side of the Texas Revolution. Dallas, TX: P. L. Turner Co., 1928.

Chacon Gomez, Fernando. "The Intended and Actual Effect of Article VIII of the Treaty of Guadalupe Hidalgo: Mexican Treaty Rights Under International and Domestic Law." Doctoral dissertation, U. of Michigan, 1977. Univ. Microfilms Order No. 7804709.

Chavarria, Jesus. "On Chicano History: In Memoriam, George I. Sánchez 1906-1972." In Humanidad. Essays in Honor of George I. Sánchez, pp. 41-57. Edited by Américo Paredes. Los Angeles: Chicano Studies Center, U. of California, 1977.

Cortés, Carlos E. "Chicanos: Historiography of a Conquered/Immigrant People." Immigration History Newsletter 9(N, 1977):1-5.

Faulk, Odie B. Land of Many Frontiers. A History of the American Southwest. New York: Oxford U. Press, 1968.

Frisbie, Parker. "Illegal Migration from Mexico to the United States: A Longitudinal Analysis." International Migration Review 9 (Spring, 1975):3-13.

Garcia, Mario T. "Americanization and the Mexican Immigrant, 1880-1930." Journal of Ethnic Studies 6(Summer, 1978):19-34.

Goméz-Quiñones, Juan. "The First Steps: Chicano Labor Conflict and Organizing 1900-1920." Aztlan 3(Spring, 1972):13-49.

_____. "Research Notes on the Twentieth Century. Notes on Periodization 1900-1965." Aztlan 1(Spring, 1970):115-123.

_____. "Toward a Perspective on Chicano History." Aztlan 2(Fall, 1971):1-49.

Gonzalez, Richard I. "The Treaty of Guadalupe-Hidalgo." In Latino Studies. A Reader. Compiled by Frank F. Montalvo, Joseph R. Sanchez, Eliu Camacho-Vasquez, and Jim Quintero. Patrick Air Force Base, FL: Defense Race Relations Institute, 1975.

Gutierrez, Felix F. "Reporting for La Raza: The History of Latino Journalism in America." AGENDA 8(Jl/Ag, 1978):29-35.

Gutierrez, Ramón A. "Mexican Migration to the United States, 1880-1930: The Chicano and Internal Colonialism." Master's thesis, U. of Wisconsin, 1976.

Hoffman, Abraham. "Chicano History: Problems and Potentialities." Journal of Ethnic Studies 1(Spring, 1973):6-12.

_____. "The Repatriation of Mexican Nationals from the United States During the Great Depression." Doctoral dissertation, U. of California, Los Angeles, 1970.

_____. "Stimulus to Repatriation: The 1931 Federal Deportation Drive and the Los Angeles Mexican Community." Pacific Historical Review 42(My, 1973).

_____. "Where Are the Mexican Americans? A Textbook Omission Overdue for Revision." History Teacher 6(N, 1972):143-150

Inter-American Institute. The Role of the Mexican American in the History of the Southwest. Edinburg, TX: Pan American College, 1969.

Kiser, George, and Silverman, David. "Mexican Repatriation during the Great Depression." Journal of Mexican American History 3(1973):139-164.

Leary, David T. "The Attitudes of Certain United States Citizens Toward Mexico, 1821-1846." Doctoral dissertation, U. of Southern California, 1970.

Limón, José E. "Stereotyping and Chicano Resistance: An Historical Dimension." Aztlan 4(Fall, 1973).

López y Rivas, Gilberto. "Conquest and Resistance: The Origins of the Chicano National Minority in the Nineteenth Century (A Marxist View)." Doctoral dissertation, U. of Utah, 1976. Univ. Microfilms Order No. 76-11,865.

McWilliams, Cary. North from Mexico: The Spanish-Speaking People. New York: Greenwood Press, 1969 (orig. 1949).

Meier, Matt S., and Rivera, Feliciano. The Chicanos: A History of Mexican Americans. New York: Hill & Wang, 1972.

_____, and _____. Readings on La Raza: The Twentieth Century. New York: Hill & Wang, 1974.

Merk, Frederick. "Dissent in the Mexican War." In S. E. Morison, F. Merk, and F. Freidel, Dissent in Three American Wars, pp. 33-63. Cambridge, MA: Harvard U. Press, 1970.

Meyer, Doris L. "Early Mexican-American Responses to Negative Stereotyping." New Mexico History Review 53(Ja, 1978):75-92.

Miller, Thomas Lloyd. "Mexican-Texans at the Alamo." Journal of Mexican American History 2(Fall, 1971):33-44.

Moquin, Wayne, with Van Doren, Charles (eds.). A Documentary History of the Mexican Americans. New York: Praeger, 1971.

Nava, Julian. Mexican Americans: A Brief Look at their History. New York: Anti-Defamation League, My, 1970.

Navarro, Joseph. "The Condition of Mexican-American History." Journal of Mexican American History 1(Fall, 1970):25-52.

Nostrand, Richard L. "Mexican Americans Circa 1850." Annals of the Association of American Geographers 65(S, 1975):378-390.

Paul, Rodman W. "The Spanish-Americans in the Southwest 1848-1900." In The Frontier Challenge. Responses to the Trans-Mississippi West, pp. 31-56. Edited by John G. Clark. Lawrence, Kansas: The U. Press of Kansas, 1971.

Reisler, Mark. "Always the Laborer, Never the Citizen: Anglo Perceptions of the Mexican Immigrant during the 1920's." Pacific Historical Review 45(My, 1976):231-254.

_____. "Mexican Unionization in California Agriculture, 1927-1936." Labor History 14 (Fall, 1973).

Romano, Octavio Ignacio V. "The Anthropology and Sociology of the Mexican Americans: The Distoration of Mexican-American History." El Grito, Fall, 1968.

_____. The Distortion of Mexican-American History, n.d. Pacifica Tape Library, 2217 Shattuck Ave., Berkeley, CA 94704.

_____. "The Historical and Intellectual Presence of Mexican-Americans." El Grito, Winter, 1969.

_____. "Minorities, History, and the Cultural Mystique." El Grito, Fall, 1967.

Servín, Manuel Patricio (ed.). The Mexican-Americans: An Awakening Minority. Beverly Hills, CA: Glencoe, 1970.

General

Abe, Clifford. "The Prediction of Academic Achievement of Mexican American Students." Diss. Abstr. Int'l. 31, 9-A (Mr, 1971) 4535.

Acevedo, Homero. An Approach for Counseling Mexican-American Parents of Mentally Retarded Children. Vol. I, Austin, TX: Dept. of Special Education, 1971. ERIC ED 055 385.

Aceves, Edward A. (comp.). Resource Materials for Teaching Mexican/Chicano Culture: Grades K-6, 1973. ERIC ED 097 138.

Acuña, Rodolfo. "On Chicano Studies." La Raza 1(F, 1973). [San Fernando Valley State College, California]

Adkins, Patricia G. "Speech for the Spanish-Speaking Student." Bulletin of the National Association of Secondary School Principals 54 (D, 1970):108-113.

Adkins, Patricia G., and Young, Robert G. "Cultural Perceptions in the Treatment of Handicapped School Children of Mexican-American Parentage." Journal of Research and Development in Education 9(Summer, 1976): 83-90.

Aguilar, Ignacio. "Initial Contacts with Mexican-American Families." Social Work 17 (My, 1972):66-70.

Aguirre, Adalberto, Jr. "Chicano Socio-linguistics: A Review and Proposal." Bilingual Review 5(Ja-Ag, 1978):91-98.

_____. Language in the Chicano Community: A Sociolinguistic Consideration, S 9, 1977. ERIC ED 144 372.

Aguirre, Lydia R. "The Meaning of the Chicano Movement." Social Casework 52(My, 1971): 259-261.

Ainsworth, C. L. (ed.). Teachers and Counselors for Mexican-American Children. Southwest Educational Development Laboratory, Austin, TX: Texas Technological College, Lubbock, TX, 1969, 137 pp. ED 029 728.

Alba, F. "Exodo Silenciosos: La Emigracion de Trabajobores Mexicanos a Estados Unidos." Forum Internacional 17(O-D, 1976).

Almaguer, Tomás. "Chicano Politics in the Present Period: Comment on García." Socialist Review 8(Jl-O, 1978):137-141.

_____. "Class, Race, and Chicano Oppression." Socialist Revolution 5(1975):71-99.

_____. "Toward the Study of Chicano Colonialism." Aztlan 2(Spring, 1971):7-21.

Altus, William D. "The American Mexican: The Survival of a Culture." Journal of Social Psychology 29(1939):211-220.

Alvarez, Salvador. "Mexican-American Community Organizations." El Grito 4(Spring, 1971): 68-77.

Amaro Hernandez, Jose. "A Case Against Busing and School Integration." La Raza 3(Spring, 1977):40-42.

Anchor, Kenneth N., and Anchor, Felicia N. "School Failure and Parental School Involvement in an Ethnically Mixed School: A Survey." Journal of Community Psychology 2 (Jl, 1974):265-267.

Anderson, James G. and others. Mexican-American Students in a Metropolitan Context: Factors Affecting the Social-Emotional Climate of the Classroom. New Mexico State U., University Park, Jl, 1969. ERIC ED 030 521.

Anderson, James G., and Johnson, William H. "Stability and Change among Three Generations of Mexican-Americans: Factors Affecting Achievement." American Educational Research Journal 8(Mr, 1971):285-309.

Anderson, James G. Teachers of Minority Groups: The Origins of Their Attitudes and Instructional Practices. Las Cruces, NM: New Mexico State U., Ja, 1969, 72 pp. ERIC ED 026 192.

Anderson, James G., and Johnson, William H. Sociocultural Determinants of Achievement Among Mexican-American Students. University Park, NM: New Mexico State U., Mr, 1968, 45 pp. ERIC ED 017 394.

Anderson, James G., and Safar, Dwight. Equality of Educational Opportunity for Spanish-American and Indian Students in Two Multi-Cultural Communities: An Exploratory Assessment, Ja, 1969, 34 pp. ED 029 746.

Angel, Frank. Program Content to Meet the Educational Needs of Mexican Americans. University Park, NM: New Mexico State U., Mr, 1968, 21 pp. ERIC ED 017 392.

Apodoca, Maria Linda. "The Chicana Woman: An Historical Materialist Perspective." Latin American Perspectives 4(Winter/Spring, 1977): 70-89.

Arcinega, Tomás. Public Education's Response to the Mexican American. El Paso, TX: Innovative Resources, 1971.

_____. The Urban Mexican American: A Sociocultural Profile. Las Cruces, NM: ERIC Press, 1971.

_____. The Urban Mexican American: A Sociocultural Profile. University Park, NM: New Mexico State U., ERIC Clearninghouse on Rural Education and Small Schools, Jl, 1971. ERIC ED 050 887.

Arias, D. "Perception of Teacher-Pupil Behavior: A Comparison Study Between Anglo and Mexican-American Female College Students." Master's thesis, California State U., Los Angeles, 1970.

Armour, D. T. "Problems in the Education of the Mexican Child." Texas Outlook 16(D, 1932): 29-31.

Arnold, Richard D., and Wist, Anne H. "Auditory Discrimination Abilities of Disadvantaged Anglo- and Mexican-American Children." Elementary School Journal 70(Mr, 1970):295-299.

Arredondo, Adelfa. The Miseducation of Chicano Students: Recommendations for Confronting It. Lansing, MI: Michigan Education Association, Ja 7, 1976.

Arroyo, Laura E. "Industrial and Occupational and Distribution of Chicana Workers." Aztlán 4(Fall, 1973):343-383.

Atencio, Tomás C. "The Survival of La Raza Despite Social Services." Social Casework 52 (My, 1971):262-268.

Ayala, J. L. (ed.). "Chicano Library Service." California Librarian 34(Ja, 1973):4-7.

Baca Zuin, Maxine. "Political Familism: Toward Sex Role Equality in Chicano Families." Aztlán 6(Spring, 1975):13-26.

Bach, Robert L. "Mexican Immigration and the American State." International Migration Review)12(Winter, 1978):536-554.

A Badge of Infamy: A Petition to the United Nations on the Treatment of the Mexican Immigrant. New York: American Committee for the Protection of Foreign Born, 1959.

Ballesteros, David. Meeting Instructional Needs of Chicano Students. New York: National Center for Research & Information on Equal Educational Opportunity, 1972.

Ballesteros, Octavio A. The Effectiveness of Public School Education for Mexican-American Students as Perceived by Principals of Elementary Schools of Predominantly Mexican-American Enrollment. San Francisco: R and E Research Associates, 1976.

Baral, David P. Achievement Levels Among Foreign-Born and Native-Born Mexican-American Students. San Francisco: R and E Research Associates, 1977.

Barceló, Cosme J., Jr., and Breiter, Toni. "Hispanics on Welfare--the Facts and Figures." Agenda 7(Mr-Ap, 1977):4-10.

Barker, George C. "Social Functions of Language in a Mexican-American Community." Acta Americana 5(F, 1947):185-202.

Beals, Ralph, and Humphrey, Norman. No Frontier to Learning. Minneapolis: U. of Minnesota Press, 1957.

Bernal, Joe J. "History of School Segregation of the Mexican Americans." Paper presented to Department of Education, U. of Texas, 1968.

Bernal, Joe J. "I Am Mexican-American." Today's Education, My, 1969.

"Beyond the Law--To Equal Educational Opportunities for Chicanos and Indians." New Mexico Law Review 1(Winter, 1970).

Blair, Bertha, Lively, Anne O., and Trimble, Glen W. Spanish-Speaking Americans: Mexicans and Puerto Ricans in the United States. New York: n.p., 1959.

Blatt, Gloria T. "The Mexican-American in Children's Literature." Elementary English 45(Ap, 1968):446-451.

Bogardus, Emory S. "The Mexican Immigrant and Segregation." American Journal of Sociology 13(Jl, 1930):74-80.

Bongartz, Roy. "The Chicano Rebellion." Nation, Mr 3, 1969.

Bowden, Shirley. Nutritional Beliefs and Food Practices of Mexican-American Mothers, Je, 1968. ERIC ED 050 837.

Boyle, Mary S. "Environmental Retardation and the Mexican American." Master's thesis, U. of Texas, 1972.

Brace, Clayton and others. Federal Programs to Improve Mexican-American Education. Office of Education, Washington, DC, 1967. ERIC ED 014 338.

Brauner, Marlyn R. "Migration and Educational Achievement of Mexican Americans." Social Service Quarterly 53(Mr, 1973):727-737.

Breiter, Toni. "Hispanics and the Roman Catholic Church." Agenda 7(Ja-F, 1977):4-9.

Briggs, Vernon M., Jr. Chicanos and Rural Poverty. Baltimore, MD: Johns Hopkins U. Press, 1973.

_____. The Mexico-United States Border: Public Policy and Chicano Economic Welfare. Austin, TX: Center for the Study of Human Resources, U. of Texas, 1974.

Briggs, Vernon M., Jr. and others. The Chicano Worker. Austin: U. of Texas Press, 1977.

Broadbent, E. "The Distribution of Mexican Population in the United States." Master's thesis, U. of Chicago, 1941.

Broman, Betty L. "The Spanish-speaking Five-year-old." Childhood Education 48(Ap, 1972):362-364.

Brown, Carl R. V. "Cultural Democracy and Cultural Variability in Chicano Literature." English Education 8(Winter, 1977):83-89.

Brussell, Charles B. Disadvantaged Mexican American Children and Early Educational Experience. Southwest Educational Development Corp., Austin, TX, 1968, 104 pp. ERIC ED 030 517.

Burma, John H. (ed.). Mexican-Americans in the United States: A Reader. San Francisco, CA: Canfield Press, 1970.

Bustamante, Charles J., and Bustamante, Patricia L. The Mexican-American in the United States, 1969. PATTY-LAR Publications, Ltd., P.O. Box 4177, Mountain View, CA 94040.

Bustamante, Jorge A. "Structural and Ideological Conditions of Undocumented Mexican Immigration to the United States." In Current Issues in Social Policy, pp. 145-157. Edited by W. B. Littrell and G. Sjoberg. Beverly Hills, CA: Sage, 1976.

_____. "Undocumented Immigration from Mexico: Research Report." International Migration Review 11(Summer, 1977):149-177.

Byrne, David R. Chicano Students and Tooele Schools: A Descriptive Research Report, Ja 24, 1974. ERIC ED 144 733.

Cabrera, Y. Arturo. Educational Needs of the Chicanos. Pacifica Tape Library, 2217 Shattuck Avenue, Berkeley, CA 94704.

_____. Emerging Force. The Mexican-American. Dubuque, IA: Brown, 1971.

Cain, Mary A. "A Study of Relationships between Selected Factors and the School Achievement of Mexican-American Migrant Children." Diss. Abstr. Int'l. 31, 8-A (F, 1971) 3947.

California Department of Education. A Guide for Teachers of Beginning Non-English-speaking Children. Sacramento, CA: State Department of Education. Bulletin No. 8, Ap 15, 1932.

California State Department of Education. Prospectus for Equitable Educational Opportunities for Spanish-Speaking Children. Sacramento, CA: California State Department of Education, 1967.

Camarillo, Alberto M. "Research Note on Chicano Community Leaders: The G.I. Generation." Aztlan 2(Fall, 1971):145-150.

Campa, Arthur L. Culture Patterns of the Spanish-Speaking Community. Denver, CO: U. of Denver, 1962.

_____. "The Spanish Language in the Southwest." In Humanidad. Essays in Honor of George I. Sanchez, pp. 19-40. Edited by Americo Paredes. Los Angeles, CA: Chicano Studies Center, U. of California, 1977.

Campbell, Duane E., and Salas, Rudolph M. "Teaching About the Chicano." Social Education 34(O, 1970):667-669, 672. [Fourth grade]

Cardenas, Blandina. "Broadening the Concept of Bilingual Education." Integrateducation 13(My, Je, 1975):171-72.

Carlson, Helding S., and Henderson, Norman. "Intelligence of American Children of Mexican Parentage." Journal of Abnormal and Social Psychology 45(Ap, 1952):544-551.

Carpintero, Rogelio L. The Misfortunes of a Chicano: A Search for Identity Amid Poverty and Discrimination. New York: William-Frederick Press, 1977.

Carranza, Elihu, Rivera, Feliciano, and Cordova, H. L. (eds.). Perspectives in Mexican American Studies. New York: Holt, Rinehart & Winston, 1971.

Carranza, Eliu. Pensamientos on Los Chicanos: A Cultural Revolution. Berkeley, CA: California Book Co., 1969.

Carrasco, Frank F. and others. Chicano Children and Their Outdoor Environment: Barrio, Housing Project and Rural Settings, Je, 1977. ERIC ED 143 480.

Carrizales, Pablo (ed.). Cancion de la Raza, 1971. Ideal, P.O. Box 21, Coachella, CA 92236.

Carroll, John M. "The Utility of Internal Colonialism as an Explanation for the Political and Social Marginality of Mexican Americans." Master's thesis, U. of Texas at El Paso, 1974.

Carter, Thomas P. [Interview] National Elementary Principal 50(N, 1970):94-97.

_____. "Mexican Americans: How the Schools Have Failed Them." College Board Review 75 (1970):5-11.

_____. "The Negative Self-Concept of Mexican-American Students." School and Society 96 (1968).

_____. Preparing Teachers for Mexican American Children. National Education Association, Washington, DC, F, 1969, 16 pp. ERIC ED 025 367.

_____. School Discrimination: The Mexican American Case. University Park, NM: New Mexico State U., ERIC Clearinghouse on Rural Education and Small Schools, Ap, 1971, 20 pp. ERIC ED 048 969.

Carter, Thomas P. and others. Value Systems of Teachers and Their Perception of Self, and of Mexican American, Negro and Anglo Children. Symposium on Applications of Psychological Principles to the Classroom, My, 1969, 8 pp. (Paper presented at the Rocky Mountain Psychological Association, Albuquerque, NM, My 14-17, 1969) ERIC ED 037 507.

Casa de la Raza. Separatism or Segregation. Chicanos in Public Education, 1974. Southwest Network of the Study Commission on Undergraduate Education and the Education of Teachers, 1020 B Street, Hayward, CA 94541.

Casavantes, Edward J. Deviant Behavior in the Mexican American Student and Its Relation to Education. A Position Paper, Ag, 1970, 16 pp. ERIC ED 060 989.

_____. A New Look at the Attributes of the Mexican American. Albuquerque, NM: Southwestern Cooperative Educational Laboratory, Mr, 1969, 18 pp. ERIC ED 028 010.

_____. "Reading Achievement and In-Grade Retention Rate Differentials for Mexican-American and Black Students in Selected States of the Southwest." Doctoral dissertation, U. of Southern California, 1973. Univ. Microfilms Order No. 74-28,425.

_____. Variables Which Tend to Affect (Impede or Retard) Learning of the Mexican American Student in American Education. A Position Paper, Ag, 1970, 15 pp. ERIC ED 060 990.

Caskey, Owen I. (ed.). Community Responsibilities and School Guidance Programs for Mexican American Youth. Austin, TX: Southwest Educational Development Lab, F 7, 1969, 63 pp. ERIC ED 041 646.

_____ (ed.). Guidance Needs of Mexican American Youth. Proceedings of the Invitational Conference (First, November 10, 1967, Lubbock, Texas). Austin, TX: Southwest Educational Development Lab, 1967, 87 pp. ERIC ED 036 347.

Cassel, Virginia. "Culture Change Among Spanish-American Aid-to-Dependent-Children Clients." Master's thesis, U. of New Mexico, 1956.

Casso, Henry J. "A Descriptive Study of Three Legal Challenges for Placing Mexican American and Other Linguistically and Culturally Different Children Into Educably Mentally Retarded Classes." Doctoral dissertation, U. of Massachusetts, 1973.

Castañeda, Alfredo, Ramirez, Manuel III, Cortes, Carlos E., and Barrera, Mario (eds.). Mexican Americans and Educational Change. New York: Arno, 1974.

Castañeda, Alfredo (ed.) and others. Mexican Americans and Educational Change. Symposium (University of California, Riverside, May 21-22, 1971). Riverside, CA: U. of California, Mexican American Studies Program, My, 1971, 421 pp. ERIC ED 063 988.

Castro, Tony. Chicano Power: The Emergence of Mexican America. New York: Saturday Review Press, 1974.

_____. "A Third Party Is Born." Race Relations Reporter 4(Ja, 1973):13-17. [La Raza Unida]

_____. "'Viva, Ramsey Muniz!'" Saturday Review, The Arts 55(N, 1972). [La Raza Unida]

Caughey, John W. "Spanish Southwest: An Example of Subconscious Regionalism." In Regionalism in America. Edited by Merrill Jensen. Madison, WI: U. of Wisconsin Press, 1951.

Ceja, Manuel. "Method of Orientation of Spanish-speaking Children to an American School." Master's thesis, U. of Southern California, 1957.

Cervantes, Fred A. "Chicanos Within the Political Economy: Some Questions Concerning Pluralist Ideology Representation and the Economy." Aztlan 7(Fall, 1976):337-345.

Cervantes, Robert. "Problems and Alternatives in Testing Mexican-American Students." Integrated Education 12(My-Je, 1974):33-37.

Chacon, José A. "La Raza in Action." Ideal, O 20, 1972. [About Gus C. Garcia, Chief Counsel in Hernandez v. Texas]

Chandler, John T., and Plakos, John. Spanish-Speaking Pupils Classified As Educable Mentally Retarded. Sacramento, CA: State Department of Education, 1969.

Chandler, Theodore A. "A Note on the Relationship of Learning Ability and Intelligence." Psychology in the Schools, Ap, 1965. [Mexican-American children]

Chase, H. Peter and others. "Nutritional Status of Preschool Mexican-American Migrant Farm Children." American Journal of Diseases of Children 122(O, 1971):316-324.

Chavarría, Jesús. "Chicano Studies." In The Minority Student on the Campus: Expectations and Possibilities, pp. 173-178. Edited by Robert A. Altman and Patricia O. Snyder, N, 1970. Western Interstate Commission for Higher Education, P.O. Drawer "P," Boulder, CO 80302.

_____. "Professor Grebler's Book: The Magnum Opus of a Dying Era of Scholarship." Social Science Quarterly 52(Je, 1971):11-14.

Chicano Education Project. [Reviews attacks on bilingual-bicultural programs in various states] Un Neuevo Dia 3(Summer, 1977).

Chicano Institute "La Causa." La Raza, F 7, 1969.

"Chicano Summit Conference Demands School Autonomy." Ideal, Jl 20, 1972. Albuquerque, NM, Je 23-24, 1972

Chicano Training Center. Curriculum Schema, 2 vols, 1975. Chicano Training Center, 3520 Montrose, Suite 216, Houston, TX 77006.

"El Chicano y the Constitution: The Legacy of Hernandez v. Texas: Grand Jury Discrimination." University of San Francisco Law Review 6(1971).

"Chicano Year for Education." La Raza, O 15, 1968.

Christian, Chester (ed.). Bilingual Education, Research and Teaching, Annual Conference of the Southwest Council of Foreign Language Teachers (4th, El Paso, N 10, 11, 1967) Reports. Southwest Council of Foreign Language Teachers, 1967, 87 pp. ERIC ED 016 434.

Christian, Jane, and Christian, Chester. "Spanish Language and Culture in the Southwest." In Joshua A. Fishman, Language Loyalty in the United States; The Maintenance and Perpetuation of Non-English Mother Tongue by American Ethnic and Religious Groups, pp. 280-317. The Hague: Mouton and Company, 1966.

Christensen, Ted, and Livermore, Gary. "A Comparison of Anglo-American and Spanish-American Children on the WISC." Journal of Social Psychology 81(1970):9-14.

Clapp, Raymond F. "Spanish-Americans of the Southwest." Welfare in Review, Ja, 1966.

Cohen, Andrew D. "The Culver City Spanish Immersion Program: The First Two Years." Modern Language Journal 58(Mr, 1974):95-103.

Cohn, J. "Integration of Spanish-Speaking Newcomers in a Fringe Area School." National Elementary Principals, Je, 1946, pp. 40-44.

Coindreau, Josephine. "Teaching English to Spanish-speaking Children." National Elementary Principals, Je, 1946, pp. 40-44.

Cole, David L., and Cole, Shirley. Locus of Control in Mexican Students: The Case of the Missing Fatalist, My, 1976. ERIC ED 130 213.

Coleman, Algernon. English Teaching in the Southwest; Organization and Materials for Instructing Spanish-Speaking Children. Washington, DC: American Council on Education, 1940.

Coles, Robert. The Children of Crisis, IV: Eskimos, Chicanos, and Indians. Boston: Atlantic Monthly Press, 1978.

_____. "Una Anciana." New Yorker, N 5, 1973.

Commission on International & Interracial Factors in the Problems of Mexicans in the United States. Report of the Commission on International and Interracial Factors. George L. Cody, Chairman, 1926.

Communist Party, U.S.A. "Chicano Liberation." Political Affairs, Je 30, 1969.

"Contra la discriminación de los hispanos en Miami." Reunion (Madrid), Nos. 71-72 (Mr-Ap, 1975):4-5

Contreras, Hilario H. "The Chicano's Search for Identity." Con Safos 2(1970).

Copp, Nelson G. "'Wetbacks' and Braceros: Mexican Migrant Laborers and American Immigration Policy, 1930-1960." Doctoral dissertation, Boston U., 1963.

Cordova, Ignacio R. The Relationship of Acculturation, Achievement, and Alienation Among Spanish American Sixth Grade Students. University Park, NM: New Mexico State U., F, 1969, 25 pp. ERIC ED 025 369.

_____. "The Relationship of Acculturation, Achievement, and Alienation Among Spanish American Sixth Grade Students." Doctoral dissertation, U. of New Mexico, 1968.

Corona, Bert C. "A Study of Adjustment and Interpersonal Relations of Adolescents of Mexican Descent." Doctoral dissertation, U. of California, Berkeley, 1955.

Corwin, Arthur F. "Historia de la Emigracíon Mexicana, 1900-1970, Literatura e Investigacion." Historia Mexicana 22 (O-D, 1972):188-220.

_____. "Mexican-American History: An Assessment." Pacific Historical Review 42 (Ag, 1973):269-308.

_____. "Mexican Emigration History, 1900-1970: Literature & Research." Latin American Research Review 8(Summer, 1973).

_____. "Mexico." In "Dislocation and Emigration. The Demographic Background of American Immigration." Edited by Donald Fleming and Bernard Bailyn. Perspectives in American History 7(1973).

Corwin, Arthur F. (ed.). Immigrants--and Immigrants: Perspectives on Mexican Labor Migration to the United States. Westport, CT: Greenwood Press, 1978.

Cota-Robles de Suárez, Cecilia. "Skin Color as a Factor of Racial Identification and Preference of Young Chicano Children." Aztlan 2(Spring, 1971):107-150.

Cotera, Martha P. The Chicana Feminist, 1977. Information Systems Development, 1100 East 8th, Austin, TX 78702.

Crago, Florence. "Cultural Influences Which Inhibit Academic Aspiration of the Chicana." Doctoral dissertation, Claremont Graduate School, 1975. Univ. Microfilms Order No. 76-15,752.

Cross, William C., and Maldonado, Bonnie. "The Counselor, the Mexican-American and the Stereotype." Elementary School Guidance and Counseling 6(O, 1971):27-31.

Cue Cánovas, Agustin. Estados Unidos y el Mexico olvidado. México, D.F.: B. Costa-Amic Editor, 1970.

Dart, Bob and others. "Chicanos Standing Up To Be Counted in American Life." Atlanta Constitution, F 15, 1979.

De Anda, Diane. "Chicanito in Checkmate." Edcentric, O-N, 1972.

De Anda, José. "Mexican Culture and the Mexican-American. El Grito 3(1969):42-48.

De la Garza, Rudolph O., Kruszewski, Anthony, and Arcinega, Tomas A. Chicanos and Native Americans: The Territorial Minorities. Englewood Cliffs, NJ: Prentice-Hall, 1973.

De la Pena, Mike. "Francisco Martinez Guilty." Inside Eastside, O 21, 1968.

De León, Marcos. "Wanted: A New Educational Philosophy for the Mexican-American." California Journal of Secondary Education, Vol. 34, N, 1959.

Dean, Raymond S. "Internal Consistency of the PIAT with Mexican-American Children." Psychology in the Schools 14(Ap, 1977):167-168.

Del Campo, Philip E. "An Analysis of Selected Factors in the Acculturation Process of the Mexican-American Elementary School Child." Diss. Abstr. Int'l. 31 (9-A), (Mr, 1971) 4885-4886.

Demos, George D. "Attitudes of Mexican-Americans and Anglo Groups Toward Education." Journal of Social Psychology 57(Ag, 1962):249-256.

Derbyshire, Robert L. "Adaptation of Adolescent Mexican-Americans to United States Society." American Behavioral Scientist 13(1969):88-103.

Dillard, J. L. "The Lingua Franca in the American Southwest." Revista/Review Inter-americana 3(1973).

"Discrimination Against Mexican Americans." Phi Delta Kappan, O, 1966.

Dunn, Lynn P. Chicanos: A Study Guide and Sourcebook. San Francisco: R & E Research Associates, 1975.

Duran, Ricardo. "Mis-Education of the Minority Child." Muhammad Speaks, Ap 18, 1969.

_____. "Where the Cannon Fodder Comes From." Muhammad Speaks, Ap 11, 1969.

Durrett, Mary Ellen, and Kim, Chungsoon C. "A Comparative Study of Behavioral Maturity in Mexican American and Anglo Preschool Children." Journal of Genetic Psychology 123, 1st half (S, 1973):55-62.

Durrett, Mary Ellen, and Pirofski, Florence. A Pilot Study of the Effects of Heterogenous and Homogeneous Grouping on Mexican-American and Anglo Children Attending Pre-kindergarten Programs, F, 1971, 27 pp. ERIC ED 047 862.

_____ and _____. "Effects of Heterogeneous and Homogeneous Grouping on Mexican-American and Anglo Children." Young Children 31(My, 1976):309-314.

Dworkin, Anthony Gary. "Stereotypes and Self-Images Held by Native-Born and Foreign-Born Mexican Americans." Sociology and Social Research, Ja, 1965.

The Education of the Mexican-American. A Summary of the Proceedings of the Lake Arrowhead and Anaheim Conferences. Sacramento, CA: California State Dept. of Education, 1969, 19 pp. ERIC ED 050 844.

Edwards, Peggy B. "Counseling the Mexican American." Master's thesis, U. of Texas, 1972.

Eggler, John. "Mexican-American History: Problems and Concerns of an Instructor." Journal of Mexican American History 1(Fall, 1970):16-24.

Elias-Olivares, Lucia. Language Use in a Chicano Community: A Sociolinguistic Approach, F, 1976. ERIC ED 125 810.

Employment Problems of Mexican Americans and Indians. Recommendations and Observations Made at the Southwest Employer Conference on Mexican American and Indian Employment Problems (Albuquerque, New Mexico, July 10-12, 1968), Jl 10, 1968, 136 pp. ERIC ED 028 887.

Encisco, Francisco B. "The Rights and Duties of the Mexican Child." School and Society 43(Ap 18, 1936):547-548.

Ericksen, Charles A. "Uprising in the Barrios." American Education, N, 1968.

Espinosa, Rubén W., Fernández, Celestino, and Dornbusch, Sanford M. "Factors Affecting Chicano Effort and Achievement in High School." Atisbos 1(Summer, 1975):9-30.

Evans, Francis B. 'A Study of Sociocultural Characteristics of Mexican- Americans and Anglo Junior High School Students and the Relation of these Characteristics." Doctoral dissertation, New Mexico State U., 1969.

Ewing, Kern. The Mexican-American Value System in an Urban Environment, Ag, 1970, 171 pp. Master's thesis. Available from Inter-Library Loan from Texas Tech U., Lubbock, TX. ERIC ED 049 860.

Exelrod, Alan. "Chicano Education: In Swann's Way?" Inequality in Education, No. 9, Ag 3, 1971.

Fadala, Sam. "Eddie: A Living Letter." Integrateducation 13(Mr-Ap, 1975):16-18.

Felder, Dell. "The Education of Mexican-Americans: Fallacies of the Monocultural Approach." Social Education 34(O, 1970): 639-642.

Felice, Lawrence G. Mexican American Achievement Performance: Linking the Effects of School and Family Expectations to Benefit the Bilingual Child, Mr 27, 1978. ERIC ED 151 125.

Fernandez, Celestino, Espinosa, R. W., and Dornbusch, S. M. Factors Affecting the Low Academic Status of Chicano High School Students. Stanford, CA: Stanford Center for Research and Development in Teaching, Stanford U., Jl, 1975.

Fields, Rona M., and Fox, Charles J. "The Brown Berets." The Black Politician 3(Jl, 1971): 53-63.

Fisher, Shelley May. "NSA Congress, 1969." America, S 27, 1969. [Chicanos at the annual convention of the U.S. National Student Association]

Floca, Kathryn P. "The Legality of Chicano Education." Master's thesis, U. of Texas, 1971.

Fores, Beatriz. The Observation and Testing Report on the Sesame Street Program, 1974. ERIC ED 126 864. [Effect on Chicano children]

Flores, Guillermo. "Race and Culture in the Internal Colony: Keeping the Chicano in His Place." In Structures of Dependency, pp. 189-223. Edited by Frank Bonilla and Robert Girling. Nairobi, CA: Nairobi Bookstore, 1973.

Flores Macías, Reynaldo. "Developing a Bilingual Culturally-Relevant Educational Program for Chicanos." Aztlan 4(Spring, 1973):61-77.

Flores Macías, Reynaldo, de Macías, Carolyn Webb. De La Torre, William, and Vasquez, Mario. Educacion Alternativa. On the Development of Chicano Bilingual Schools, 1975. The Southwest Network, 1020 B Street, Suite 8, Hayward, CA 94541.

Florez, John. "Chicanos and Coalitions as a Force for Social Change." *Social Casework* 52(My, 1971):269-273.

Fogel, Walter A. *Education and Income of Mexican-Americans in the Southwest.* Los Angeles: Mexican-American Study Project. Division of Research, Graduate School of Business Administration, U. of California, 1965.

_____. "Immigrant Mexicans and the U.S. Work Force." *Monthly Labor Review* 98(My, 1975):44-46.

Fonfrias, Ernesto Juan. "La lengua que heredamos en su consagracion puertorriquena." *Yelmo* 31(Ja-Mr, 1977):17-21

Forbes, Jack D. (ed.). *Aztecas Del Norte. The Chicanos of Aztlan.* Grennwich, CT: Fawcett, 1973.

_____. *Mexican-Americans: A Handbook for Educators.* Berkeley, CA: Far West Laboratory for Educational Research and Development, 1970.

_____. *Mexican-Americans: A Handbook for Educators.* Berkeley, CA: Far West Laboratory for Educational Research, 1 Garden Circle, Hotel Claremont, Berkeley, California.

_____. "Race and Color in Mexican-American Problems." *Journal of Human Relations,* First Quarter, 1968.

Ford, J. Guthrie and Graves James, R. "Differences Between Mexican-American and White Children in Interpersonal Distance and Social Touching." *Perceptual and Motor Skills* 45(D, 1977):779-785.

Franklin, Woodman. "Chicano Politics: Oppression As a Cultural Phenomenon." *Bilingual Review* 2(S-D, 1975):321-330.

Friend, Ras Roland. "The Relationship Between Academic Achievement and Locus of Control in Middle and Lower Socioeconomic Level Black, White and Mexican-American High School Students in an Urban School Setting." Doctoral dissertation, U. of Houston, 1972.

Frisbie, William Parker. "Militancy Among Mexican-Americans: A Study of High School Students. " Doctoral dissertation, U. of North Carolina, 1972. Univ. Microfilms Order No. 73-4824.

Gaillard, Frye. "Aztlan: The New Chicano Nation." *Race Relations Reporter,* O 16, 1970.

_____. "Chicanos Push Bilingual Education." *Race Relations Reporter* 5(S, 1974):4-6.

Gaines, John S. "Treatment of Mexican American History in High School Textbooks." *Civil Rights Digest* 5(O, 1972):35-40.

Galarza, Ernesto. *Barrio Boy,* 1971, 275 pp. Available from University of Notre Dame Press, Notre Dame, IN 46556,

_____. "Life in the United States for Mexican People." *National Conference of Social Work,* 1929, 399-404.

_____. "The Mexican-American Migrant Worker--Culture and Powerlessness." *Integrated Education* 9(Mr-Ap, 1971):17-21.

_____. "Mexican Ethnic Group," *California* 17th Yearbook, pp. 34-35, 1945.

_____. "Program for Action." *Common Ground* 9(Summer, 1949):2738.

_____. [Testimony] U. Congress, 91st, 1st and 2nd sessions, Senate, Committee on Labor and Public Welfare, Subcommittee on Migratory Labor. *Migrant and Seasonal Farmworker Powerlessness. Hearings...on the Migrant Subculture.* Part 2. Washington, DC: GPO, 1970.

Galarza, Ernesto and Samora, Julian. "Chicano Studies: Research and Scholarly Activity." *Civil Rights Digest* 3(Fall, 1970):40-42.

Galarza, Ernesto and others. *Mexican-Americans in the Southwest,* 1969, 90 pp. Available from Kimberly Press, Inc., Goleta, CA 93017. ERIC ED 053 829.

Gamboa, Erasmo. "Chicanos in the Northwest. An Historical Perspective." *El Grito* 6 (Summer, 1973):57-70.

_____. "Chicanos in the Northwest: A Historical Perspective," Summer, 1971. Montal Education Associates, Suite 1207, 1700 K Street, N.W., Washington, DC 2006.

Gamio, Manuel. *The Mexican Immigrant: His Life Story.* Chicago, IL: U of Chicago Press, 1931.

Garcia, Alejandro. "The Chicano and Social Work." *Social Casework* 52(My, 1971):274-278.

Garcia, Angela B. and Zimmerman, Barry J. "The Effect of Examiner Ethnicity and Language on the Performance of Bilingual Mexican-American First Graders." *Journal of Social Psychology* 87(Je, 1972):3-11.

Garcia, Ernest. "Chicano Spanish Dialects and Education." *Aztlan* 2(Spring, 1971):67-77.

Garcia, Chris F. *The Political World of the Chicano Child,* S 8, 1973. ERIC ED 101 905.

Garcia, John F. "Is It the Language Barrier?" *Integrated Education,* F-Mr, 1967.

Garcia, Odalmira L. "Chicana Studies Curriculum Guide, Grades 9-12," F 1978. ERIC ED 151.

Garcia, Richard A. "The Chicano Movement and the Mexican American Community, 1972-1978: An Interpretative Essay." Socialist Review 8(Jl-O, 1978):117-136. [See Tomas Almaguer, above.]

Graza, Rafael. The Chicano Community in Transition, Summer, 1971. Montal Education Associates, Suite 1207, 1700 K Street, N.W., Washington, DC 20006.

Gecas, Viktor. "Self-Conceptions of Immigrant and Settled Mexican Americans." Social Science Quarterly 54(D, 1973):579-595.

Gill, L. J., and Spilka, B. "Some Non-Intellectual Correlates of Academic Achievement Among Mexican-American Secondary School Students." Journal of Educational Psychology 53(Ge, 1962):144-149.

Gilmore, George and others. "The Bender Gestalt and the Mexican American Student: A Report." Psychology in the Schools 12(Ap, 1975):172-175.

Gilroy, Abena. "Youth Liberation Conference." El Gallo, Ap, 1969.

Gingras, Rosario. "The Mexican-American Preschool Child: A Report on Current Research." In Muriel Saville-Troike, Bilingual Children: A Resource Document. Arlington, VA: Center for Applied Linguistics, 1973.

Ginsburg, Gerald P. and others. "Recalled Parent-Child Interaction of Mexican and United States Males." Journal of Cross Cultural Psychology 1(Je, 1970):139-152

Godoy, Charles E. Variables Differentiating Mexican-American College and High School Graduates, 1970, 19 pp. Sacramento, CA: California State Dept. of Education. ERIC ED 049 877.

Gomez, Antonio. "What I Am About." Con Safos, Fall, 1968.

Gomez, David F. Somos Chicanos: Strangers in Our Own Land. Boston, MA: Beacon, 1973.

Gomez, Ernesto, and Cook, Karen. Chicano Culture and Mental Health: Trees in Search of a Forest. San Antonio, TX: Worden School of Socail Service, Our Lady of the Lake, U. of San Antonio, F, 1978.

Gonzales, Albert, and Axelrod, Beverly. "In Behalf of All Others." Integrated Education, N-D, 1968, pp. 23-28.

Gonzalez, Carlos. An Overview of the Mestizo Heritage: Implications for Teachers of Mexican-American Children. San Francisco: R & E Research Associates, 1976.

Gonzalez, Ciriaco, with Diehl, Paula. "Chicanos and the Sciences." Agenda, Summer, 1976.

Gonzalez, Rafael Jesus. "Pachuco: The Birth of a Creole Language." Arizona Quarterly 23(1967):343-356.

Gonzales, Rodolfo ("Corky"). I Am Joaquin. An Epic Poem. Denver, CO: El Gallo, 1967. [Spanish and English]

Gonzalez, Gil. "A View of the Mexican Education System." Con Safos, Fall, 1968.

Gonzalez, Isabel. Step-Children of a Nation: The Status of Mexican-Americans. New York: n.p., 1947.

Gonzalez, M. C. "Our Spanish-Speaking Parent-Teacher Groups and Their Problems." Texas Outlook 27(Je, 1943):23-24.

Gonzalez, Nancie L. Positive and Negative Effects of Chicano Militancy on the Education of the Mexican American, 1970, 37 pp. Albuquerque, NM. ERIC ED 061 004.

Gonzalez, Simon. "Education for Minorities: The Mexican American." In Foundations of Education. Edited by George Kneller. New York: Wiley, 1971.

Gonzales, Sylvia. "What Do Chicanas Have to Gain? What Help Do Anglos Give Us?" Los Angeles Times, S 15, 1975. [Women's liberation movement]

_____. "The White Feminist Movement: The Chicana Perspective." Social Science Journal 14(Ap, 1977).

Gordon, Wayne C. and others. Educational Achievement and Aspirations of Mexican-American Youth in a Metropolitan Context. Los Angeles, CA: U. of Southern California, School of Education. ERIC ED 026 174.

Graham, Richard and others. The Mexican American Heritage: Developing Cultural Understanding. First Papers on Migrancy and Rural Poverty: An Introduction to the Education of Mexican-Americans in Rural Areas, 1968, 48 pp. Los Angles: U. of Southern California, School of Education. ERIC ED 026 174.

Grebler, Leo, Moore, Joan W., and Guzman, Ralph C. The Mexican-American People. The Nation's Second Largest Minority. New York: Free Press, 1970.

Griffith, Beatrice. "The Pachuco Patois." Common Ground 7(Summer, 1947):77-84.

Grosser, Paul E. An Analysis of How Change Has Taken Place in Changed Institutions and Its Implications for Mexican-Americans, Mr 20, 1970, 43 pp. Albuquerque, NM: Southwestern Cooperative Educational Lab. ERIC ED 051 926.

Guerra, Manuel H. "Educating Chicano Children and Youths." Phi Delta Kappan 53(Ja, 1972):313-314.

_____. The Mexican-American Child: Problems Or Talents?, N 20, 1965, 21 pp. Sacramento, CA: California State Department of Education. ERIC ED 045 243.

_____. "Why Juanito Doesn't Read." CTA Journal, O, 1965.

Guerra, Manuel H. and others. The Retention of Mexican American Students in Higher Education with Special Reference to Bicultural and Bilingual Problems, My, 1969, 131 pp. Long Beach, CA: California State College. ERIC ED 031 324.

Gurule, Kay. "Truthful Textbooks and Mexican Americans." Integrated Education 11(Mr-Ap, 1973):35-42.

Gustafson, Richard. The Organizational Climate in Schools Having High Concentrations of Mexican-Americans, Ap 24, 1971, 10 pp. Paper, Western Psychological Association. ERIC ED 053 849.

Gustafson, Richard A., and Owens, Thomas R. The Self-Concept of Mexican-American Youngsters and Related Environmental Characteristics, Ap 30, 1971, 26 pp. Paper, California Educational Research Association. ERIC ED 053 195.

Gutiérez, Felix, and Valdéz, Armando (ed.). El Calendario Chicano. 1972. Santa Barbara, CA: La Causa Publications, P.O. Box 4818.

Gutiérrez, Jose Angel. El Politico: The Mexican American Elected Official, 1972. Mictla Publications, P.O. Box 601, El Paso, TX.

Guzman, Ralph C. "Brown Power: The Gentle Revolutionaries." Los Angeles Times Sunday Magazine, Ja 26, 1969. [See Sifuentes, below.]

_____. The Political Socialization of the Mexican American People. New York: Arno, 1976 reprint.

_____. The Schooling Gap: Signs of Progress. Los Angeles: Mexican American Study Project, U. of California, 1967.

_____. "Will He Have Enough Education?" Compass, Ja, 1969.

Guzman, Ralph. Ethnic Tenacity: A Reader in Mexican American Studies. Palo Alto, CA: Cummings Publishing Company, 1970.

_____. "The Function of Anglo-American Racism in the Political Development of Chicanos." California Historical Quarterly 50(1971): 321-337.

_____. "How El Centro Ended Segregation." Frontier 7(F, 1956):13, 16.

_____. "Politics and Policies of the Mexican-American Community." In California Politics and Policies, pp. 350-381. Edited by Eugene Dvorin and Arthur Misner. Los Angeles: Addison-Wesley Publishing Company, 1966.

_____. "Reasoned Radicalism: An Alternative to Fear and Institutional Oppression." El Grito, Summer, 1969.

Hacer Vida. First Year Evaluation Report, 1970-71, Ag 3, 1971, 194 pp. ERIC ED 064 018.

Haddox, John. Los Chicanos. An Awakening People. El Paso, TX: Texas Western Press, 1970.

Hall, Lincoln H. "Personality Variables of Achieving and Non-Achieving Mexican-American and Other Community Freshmen." Journal of Educational Research 65(Ja, 1972):224-228.

Hamilton, Andrew. "Education and La Raza." American Education 9(Jl, 1973):4-8.

Haro, Carlos Manuel. "An Ethnographic Study of Truant and Low Achieving Chicano Barrio Youth in the High School Setting." Doctoral dissertation, U. of California, Los Angeles, 1976. Univ. Microfilms Order No. 76-16,651.

Haro, Robert P. "How Mexican-Americans View Libraries. Libraries and the Spanish-Speaking." Wilson Library Bulletin 44(1970):736-742.

_____. "Library Service to Mexican-Americans." El Grito 3(1970):30-37.

Haslam, Gerald. "Por La Causa!" Mexican-American Literature." College English 31. (Ap, 1970):695-700.

Hawkes, Glenn R., and Taylor, Minna. "Power Structure in Mexican and Mexican-American Farm Labor Families." Journal of Marriage and the Family 37(N, 1975):807-811.

Hayden, R. G. "Spanish-Americans of the Southwest: Life Style Patterns." Welfare in Review, Ap, 1966.

Hayes-Bautista, David E. "Becoming Chicano. A 'Dis-Assimilation' Theory of Transformation of Ethnic Identity." Doctoral dissertation, U. of California, San Francisco, 1947. Univ. Microfilms Order No. 74-04708.

Heffernan, Helen. "Some Solutions to the Problems of Students of Mexican Descent." National Association of Secondary School Principals 39(Mr, 1955):43-53.

_____ (ed.). "Teacher Guide to the Education of Spanish-Speaking Children." Bulletin of the California State Department of Education, Vol. 21, No. 14. Sacramento, CA, O, 1952.

Heller, Celia S. Mexican American Youth: Forgotten Youth at the Crossroads. New York: Random House, 1966.

Heller, Celia S. New Converts to the American Dream? Mobility Aspirations of Young Mexican-Americans. New York: College & University Press, 1972.

Helm, June (ed.). Spanish-speaking People in the United States. Seattle: U. of Washington Press, 1969.

Henderson, Ronald W. Environmental Stimulation and Intellectual Development of Mexican-American Children--An Exploratory Project, 1966, 242 pp. ERIC ED 010 587.

Henderson, Ronald W. "Environmental Predictors of Academic Performance of Disadvantaged Mexican-American Children." Journal of Consulting and Clinical Psychology 38(Ap, 1972).

Henderson, Ronald W. and others. Positive Effects of a Bicultural Preschool Program on the Intellectual Performance of Mexican-American Children. Tucson, AZ: College of Education, U. of Arizona, F 8, 1969, 10 pp. ERIC ED 028 827.

Henderson, Ronald W., and Rankin, Richard J. "WPPSI Reliability and Predictive Validity with Disadvantaged Mexican-American Child Children." Journal of School Psychology 11 (Mr, 1973):16-20.

Hendricks, Herbert W. "The Mexican-American Student and Emigrated Values." College Student Journal 5(S-O, 1971):52-54.

Hendrix, Kathleen. "Chicanas: Nowhere to Go But Up." Los Angeles Times, Ap 18, 1978.

Henggeler, Scott W., and Tavormina, Joseph B. "The Children of Mexican-American Migrant Workers: A Population at Risk?" Journal of Abnormal Child Psychology 6(Mr, 1978): 97-106.

Henshel, Anne-Marie. The Forgotten Ones. A Sociological Study of Anglo and Chicano Retardates. Austin, TX: U. of Texas Press, 1973.

The Heritage and Contributions of the Hispanic American. Teacher's Edition. Denver, CO: Denver Public Schools, 1969, 51 pp. ERIC ED 048 031.

Hernandez, Deluvina. Mexican American Challenge to a Sacred Cow. Los Angeles, CA: U. of California, Mexican-American Cultural Center, Mr, 1970, 60 pp. ERIC Ed 041 669.

_____. "La Raza Satellite System." Aztlan 1 (Spring, 1970):13-36.

Hernández, Eduardo et al. (eds.). El Lenguaje de los Chicanos. Washington, DC: Center for Applied Linguistics, 1975.

Hernandez, Homero. "Perspectives." La Raza, D 13, 1968. [On the meaning of the Chicano movement]

Hernandez, Luis F. "The Culturally Disadvantaged Mexican-American Student," Parts I and II. Journal of Secondary Education, F, Mr, 1967.

_____. A Forgotten American: A Resource Unit for Teachers on the Mexican American. New York: Anti-Defamation League, 1970.

Hernandez, Norma G. Variables Affecting Achievement of Middle School Mexican American Students. El Paso: U. of Texas, Ag, 1971. ERIC ED 059 827.

_____. "Variables Affecting Achievement of Middle School Mexican-American Students." Review of Educational Research 43(Winter, 1973):1-39.

Hepner, Ethel M. Self-Concepts, Values, and Needs of Mexican-American Underachievers or (Must the Mexican-American Child Adopt a Self-Concept That Fits the American Schools?), S 3, 1970, 9 pp. Paper, American Psychological Association National Convention, ERIC ED 048 954.

_____. "Self-Concepts, Values, and Needs of Mexican-American Underachievers." Diss. Abstracts International 31,6A (D, 1970) 2736.

Herr, S. E. "Effect of Pre-First Grade Training Upon Reading Readiness and Reading Achievement Among Spanish-American Children." Journal of Education Psychology 37(F, 1946): 87-102.

Hildring, C. B., and Henderson, N. "The Intelligence of American Children of Mexican Parentage." Journal of Abnormal and Social Psychology 45(1950):544-551.

Hill, Floyd W. "A Study of the Influence of Socialization Anxiety on the Achievement of First-Grade Mexican-American Children." Diss. Abstr. Int'l., 1970 (Je) Vol. 30 (12-A) 5285-6.

Hill, M. E. "Development of an Americanization Program." Guide for Teachers of Beginning Non-English-Speaking Children. Sacramento: Department of Education, 1932.

Hispanic Urban Center. The Mexican American in the Schools: An In-Service Program, Ja, 1973. Hispanic Urban Center, 1201 East First Street, Los Angeles, CA 90033.

Hollomon, John Wesley. "Problems of Assessing Bilingualism in Children Entering School." Doctoral dissertation, U. of New Mexico, 1973. Univ. Microfilms Order No. 73-27,796.

Howe, Harold II. Cowboys, Indians and American Education, 1968. Southwest Educational Development Laboratory, Suite 550, Commodore Perry Hotel, Austin, TX. [On Mexican-Americans]

Hufford, Larry. "Language and the Chicano." Race Today 5(J1, 1973):206-207.

Hughes, Marie, and Sanchez, George. Learning a New Language. Bulletin 101. Washington, DC: Association for Childhood Education International, 1948.

Hurstfield, Jennifer. "The Educational Experiences of Mexican Americans: 'Cultural Pluralism' or 'Internal Colonialism'?" Oxford Review of Education 1(1975).

_____. "'Internal' Colonialism: White, Black and Chicano Self-Conceptions." Ethnic and Racial Studies 1(Ja, 1978):60-79.

Hurt, Maure, Jr., and Mishra, Shitala. "Reliability and Validity of the Metropolitan Achievement Tests for Mexican-American Children." Educational and Psychological Measurement 30(Winter, 1970):989-992.

Idaho Migrants. Chicano Studies: Its Relationship to a Developing Political Awareness among Migrants, Summer, 1971. Montal Education Associates, Suite 1207, 1700 K Street, N.W., Washington, DC 20006.

Inter-Agency Committee on Mexican-American Affairs. The Mexican. A New Focus on Opportunity. Testimony Presented at the Cabinet Committee Hearings on Mexican Affairs, El Paso, Texas, October 26-28, 1967. Washington, DC: GPO, 1968.

Jenkins, J. Craig. "The Demand for Immigrant Workers: Labor Scarcity or Social Control?" International Migration Review 12 (Winter, 1978):514-535.

_____. "Push/Pull in Recent Mexican Migration to the U.S." International Migration Review 11(Summer, 1977):178-189.

Jensen, Arthur R. "Learning Abilities in Mexican-American and Anglo-American Children." California Journal of Educational Research, Vol. 12, S, 1961.

Johnson, Harper Daniels. "The Intelligence and Achievement of Mexican Children." Master's thesis, U. of Denver, 1929.

Johnson, Henry S., and Hernandez, William J. (eds.). Educating the Mexican American. Valley Forge, PA: Judson Press, 1971.

Jones, H. J. "An All Mexican School." Sierra Educational News 36(N 1, 1940):17.

Justin, Neal E. "Culture Conflict and Mexican-American Achievement." School and Society 98(1970):27-28.

_____. "The Relationship of Certain Socio-Cultural Factors to the Academic Achievement of Male Mexican-American High School Seniors." Doctoral dissertation, U. of Arizona, 1968.

_____. "Mexican-American Achievement Hindered by Culture Conflict." Sociology & Social Research 56(J1, 1972):471-479.

Kagan, Spencer, and Madsen, Millard C. Cooperation and Competition of Mexican, Mexican-American, and Anglo-American Children of Two Ages under Four Instructional Sets. Los Angeles, CA: Center for Head Start Evaluation and Research, U. of California, Ja, 1970, 21 pps. ERIC ED 042 532.

_____ and _____. "Experimental Analyses of Cooperation and Competition of Anglo-American and Mexican Children." Developmental Psychology 6(Ja, 1972):49-59.

Kagan, Spencer and others. "Competition and School Achievement Among Anglo-Americans and Mexican-American Children." Journal of Educational Psychology 69(Ag, 1977):432-441.

Kane, R. F., and Velarde-Muñoz, F. "Undocumented Aliens and the Constitution: Limitations on State Action Denying Undocumented Children Access to Public Education." Hastings Constitutional Law Quarterly 5(Winter, 1978): 461-506.

Kane, Tim D. "Structural Change and Chicano Employment in the Southwest, 1950-1970: Some Preliminary Observations." Aztlán 4 (Fall, 1973):383-398.

Karabinus, Robert A., and Hurt, Maure. "The Van Alstyne Picture Vocabulary Test Used with Six-Year-Old Mexican-American Children." Educational and Psychological Measurement 29(1969):935-939.

Karr, Ken, and McGuire, Esther. Mexican Americans on the Move--Are Teacher Preparation Programs in Higher Education Ready?, 1969, 30 pp. ERIC ED 031 348.

Kates, Don B., Jr. "Whether Mexican-Americans Are 'Non-White' for Purposes of 42 U.S.C. §1981-2." Clearinghouse Review 7(D, 1973): 470-471.

Katzman, Martin T. "Social Indicators of Minority Problems: The Case of Mexican-Americans." In A Symposium of the Urban Crisis, pp. 184-201. Edited by Leonard J. Duhl. Berkeley, CA: Center for Planning and Development Research, U. of California, 1969.

Kaufert, Joseph and others. "A Preliminary Study of Mexican-American Medical Students." Journal of Medical Education 50(S, 1975): 856-866.

Kennedy, Dora F. Mexican Americans: A Teaching and Resource Unit for Upper Level Spanish Students to Be Executed in Spanish or in English for Social Studies Classes, or Classes in Hispanic Cultures. Upper Marlboro, MD: Prince George's County Board of Education, 1971, 91 pp. ERIC ED 056 577.

Kent, James. "Segregation vs. Non-segregation of Mexican Children in the Elementary Schools of the Southwest." Master's thesis, U. of Oregon, 1940.

Kirby, Helen. "Children of Mexican-American Migrants--Aliens in Their Own Homeland." Today's Education, N, 1969.

Kiser, George C., and Kiser, Martha Woody (eds.). Mexican Workers in the United States. Albuquerque, NM: U. of New Mexico Press, 1979.

Klingstedt, Joe Lars. Teachers of Middle School Mexican American Children: Indicators of Effectiveness and Implications for Teacher Education, 1972, 47 pp. ERIC ED 059 828.

Kniefel, Tanya Suarez (comp.). Programs Available for Strengthening the Education of Spanish Speaking Students. University Park, NM: New Mexico State U., N, 1968, 41 pp. ERIC ED 025 366.

Knowlton, Clark S. Implications of Change in Mexican American Families, Ap 29, 1976. ERIC ED 144 726.

_____. "Spanish-American Schools in the 1970's." Integrated Education, Mr-Ap, 1968.

_____. "The Special Education Problems of the Mexican-Americans." In The Conditions for Educational Equality, pp. 142-180. Edited by Sterling M. McMurrin. New York: Committee for Economic Development, 1971.

Koch, Helen L., and Simmons, Rietta. "A Study of the Test Performance of American, Mexican, and Negro Children." Psychological Monographs, Vol. 35, No. 5, 1926.

Kuvlesky, William P., and Patella, Victoria M. "Degree of Ethnicity and Aspirations for Upward Social Mobility Among Mexican American Youth." Journal of Vocational Behavior 1 (Jl, 1971):231-244.

Kuvlesky, William P. and others. "Status Projections and Ethnicity: A Comparison of Mexican American, Negro, and Anglo Youth." Journal of Vocational Behavior 1(Ap, 1971): 137-151.

_____. Status Projection and Ethnicity: A Comparison of Mexican American, Negro, and Anglo Youth. College Station, TX: Texas A & M U., Ap, 1969, 54 pp. ERIC ED 028 858.

Kuvlesky, William P., and Patella, Victoria M. Strength of Ethnic Identification and Inter-generational Mobility Aspirations Among Mexican American Youth. College Station, TX: Texas Agricultural Experiment Station, Mr 28, 1970, 32 pp. ERIC ED 040 777.

Kuzma, Kay J., and Stern, Carolyn. "The Effects of Three Preschool Intervention Programs on the Development of Autonomy in Mexican-American and Negro Children." Journal of Special Education 6(F, 1972):197-206.

La Adelita. "La Adelita Speaks Out." La Raza, Je, 1969. [Critique of a critique on Chicanos]

Lamare, James W. "Language Environment and Political Socialization of Mexican-American Children." in The Politics of Future Citizens, pp. 63-82. Edited by Richard G. Niemi. San Francisco: Jossey-Bass, 1974.

Lamb, Ruth S. Mexican-Americans: Sons of the Southwest, 1970, 98 pp. Available from Ocelot Press, P.O. Box 504, Claremont, CA 91771. ERIC ED 054 893.

Lampe, Philip E. Comparative Study of Assimilation of Mexican-Americans: Parochial Schools versus Public Schools. San Francisco: R & E Research Associates, 1975.

Lampe, Philip E., and Andressen, Vera K. "La Asimilacíon de los Mexico--Norteamericanos en escuelas primarias." Revista de Ciencias Sociales 17(S, 1973).

Landes, Ruth. "Integration of Minorities." Claremont, CA: Claremont Graduate School, 1960.

Leary, David T. "Race and Regeneration." In The Mexican-Americans. An Awakening Minority, pp. 13-27. Edited by Manuel P. Servín. Beverly Hills, CA: Glencoe, 1970. Mexico

Lee, David Lopez. "Mexican-American Fatalism--An Analysis and Some Speculations." Journal of Mexican American Studies 1(Fall, 1970):44-53.

Leiva, Richard. "Special Education Classes, Barrier to Mexican Americans?" Civil Rights Digest, Fall, 1968.

Leleivier, Benjamin, Jr. A Portfolio of Outstanding Americans of Mexican Descent, 1970, 38 pp. ERIC ED 045 245.

Lembke, Daryl. "She Excels in English and Service." Los Angeles Times, Je 17, 1976. [Ms. Vilma S. Martinez, general counsel, Mexican-American Legal Defense and Educational Fund]

Leonard, Olen E., and Johnson, Helen W. Low Income Families in the Spanish-Surname Population of the Southwest. Washington, DC: GPO, 1967.

Lewis, H. P., and Lewis, E. R. "Written Language Performance of Sixth-Grade Children of Low Socio-Economic Status from Bilingual and from Monolingual Backgrounds." Journal of Experimental Education 33, Spring, 1965.

Leyva, Rudolfo. "Educational Aspirations and Expectations of Chicanos, Non-Chicanos, and Anglo-Americans." California Journal of Educational Research 26(Ga, 1975):27-39.

Linton, Thomas H. "Sociocultural Character- istics, Alienation from School, and Achieve- ment among Mexican-American and Anglo Sixth Grade Students." Diss. Abstr. Int'l. 31, 8-A (F, 1971):3825-6.

_____. A Study of the Relationship of Global Self-Concept, Academic Self-Concept, and Academic Achievement among Anglo and Mexican- American Sixth Grade Students, 1972, 13 pp. Paper, American Educational Research Asso- ciation. ERIC Ed 063 053.

Littlefield, John H. The Use of Norm-Referenced Survey Achievement Tests with Mexican- American Migrant Students: A Literature Review and Analysis of Implications for Evaluation of the Texas Migrant Educational Program, 1972, 51 pp. ERIC ED 063 983.

Loomis, Charles P. "A Backward Glance at Self- Identification of Blacks and Chicanos." Rural Sociology 39(Spring, 1974):96.

López, Gilbert M. "Chicano Political Develop- ment." La Raza, Vol 1, No. 11(1973):3-6.

López, Manuel Mariano. "Patterns of Residential Segregation: The Mexican American Population in the Urban Southwest, 1970." Doctoral dissertation, Michigan State U., 1977. Univ. Microfilms Order No. 7810086.

López y Rivas, Gilberto. The Chicanos: Life and Struggles of the Mexican Minority in the United States. Tr. Elizabeth Martínez and Gilberto López y Rivas. New York: Monthly Review Press, 1973.

_____. Los Chicanos: una minoria nacional explotada. Mexico, D.F.: Editional Nuestro Tiempo, 1971.

Lugo, A. "So You Are Teaching Spanish-American Children." Arizona Teacher-Parent, Mr, 1941.

Lugo, James O. "A Comparison of Degrees of Bilingualism and Measure of School Achieve- ment among Mexican-American Pupils." Diss. Abstr. Int'l 31, 9-A (Mr, 1971):4554.

Lynch, Patrick D. Training Mexican American School Principals: An Analysis of a Pro- gram's Hits and Misses, F, 1968. ERIC Clearinghouse on Rural Education and Small Schools, New Mexico State U.

McCammon, E. L. "A Study of Children's Atti- tudes Toward Mexicans." California Journal of Elementary Education 5(N, 1936):119-128.

McGonay, William E. "The Needs of a Mexican Community." California Journal of Secondary Education 18(1943):340-350.

McGovney, D. O. "Race Discrimination in Nat- uralization." Iowa Law Bulletin 8(1923):129- 211.

Macías, George Azcarate. Mexican, Mexican- American, Chicano." Compass, D, 1968.

Macías, Ysidro. "The Chicano Movement." Hawaii Pono Journal 1(Ap, 1971):12-30.

Macías, Ysidro Ramon. "The Chicano Movement. Libraries and the Spanish-Speaking." Wilson Library Bulletin 44(1970):731-735.

Mackey, William Frances, and Beebe, Von Nieda. Bilingual Schools for a Bicultural Community: The Adaptation of Miami to the Cuban Refugees. Rowley, MA: Newbury House, 1977.

McNamara, Patrick H. Some Factors Associated with Differential Grade Performance of Mexi- ican American and Non-Mexican American College Students, Mr, 1970, 16 pp. ERIC ED 042 541.

McWilliams, Carey. "Borderlands: The Challenge and Promise of a Truly Bicultural Southwest." Los Angeles Times, S 10, 1970.

_____. "The Mexican Problem." Common Ground 8(Spring, 1948:3-17.

_____. "Once a Well-Kept Secret." Pacific Historical Review 42(Ag, 1973):309-318.

_____ (ed.). The Mexicans in America: A Student's Guide to Localized History. New York: Teachers College Press, 1968.

Madrid-Barela, Arturo. "In Search of the Authentic Pachuco: An Interpretive Essay." Aztlan 4(Spring, 1973):31-59.

_____. "Towards an Understanding of the Chicano Experience." Aztlan 4(Spring, 1973):185-193. [Reply to John Womack, "The Chicanos," New York Review of Books, Ag 31, 1972]

Manaster, Guy J., and King, Marc R. "Mexican- American Group Cohesiveness and Academic Achievement." Urban Education 7(O, 1972): 235-240.

Mangold, Margaret M. (ed.). La Causa Chicana. The Movement for Justice, 1972. Family Ser- vice Association of America, 44 East 23rd Street, New York, NY 10010.

Manta, Ben. "Toward Economic Development of the Chicano Barrio: Alternative Strategies and Their Implications." Southwest Economy & Society 1(Spring, 1976):35-41.

Manuel, H. T. "The Educational Problem Present- ed by the Spanish-Speaking Child of the Southwest." School and Society, N 24, 1934.

_____. Spanish-Speaking Children of the Southwest ... Their Education and the Public Welfare. Austin: U. of Texas Press, 1965.

Manuel, H. T., and Hughes, Lois S. "The Intelligence and Drawing Ability of Young Mexican Children." Journal of Applied Psychology, Ag, 1932.

Marcella, Gabriel. "Spanish-Mexican Contributions to the Southwest." Journal of Mexican American History 1(Fall, 1970):1-15.

Martinez, Arthur D. "Mexican-Americans: Qua the Assistant Americans." Southwest Economy and Society 2(Winter, 1977):34-36.

Martinez, Oscar. "Manifest Mexicanism." Con Safos, I, 3(1969).

Martinez, Thomas M. "Advertising and Racism: The Case of the Mexican-American." El Grito, Summer, 1969.

Martinez, Thomas M., and Peralez, Jose. "Chicanos and the Motion Picture Industry." La Raza, Vol 1, No. 5(1971).

Martinez, William. "A Mexican American Talks About White Supremacy." Interracial Books for Children, Spring, 1970.

Mason, Evelyn P., and Locasso, Richard M. "Evaluation of Potential for Change in Junior-High-Age Youth from American Indian, Mexican, and Anglo Ethnic Backgrounds." Psychology in the Schools 9(0, 1972):423-427.

Mason, Evelyn P. "Stability of Differences in Personality Characteristics of Junior High School Students from American Indian, Mexican, and Anglo Ethnic Backgrounds." Psychology in the Schools 8(Ja, 1971):86-89.

Matthiessen, Peter. "Organizer—1 [Cesar Chavez]." New Yorker, Je 21, 1969.

_____. Sal Si Puedes: Cesar Chavez and the New American Revolution. New York: Random House, 1970.

Mayeske, George W. "Educational Achievement Among Mexican-Americans." Integrated Education, Ja-F, 1968.

_____. Educational Achievement Among Mexican-Americans: A Special Report From the Educational Opportunities Survey. Analytical Note No. 50. Washington, DC: Division of Operations Analysis, National Center for Educational Statistics, U.S. Office of Education, Ja 9, 1967.

Megargee, Edwin I., and Rosenquist, Carl M. A Comparison of Delinquent and Nondelinquent Anglo-Americans, Mexican-Americans, and Mexican Nationals. Washington, DC: American Psychological Association, S 1, 1968, 14 pp. ERIC ED 025 788.

Meguire, Katherine Hollier. Educating the Mexican Child in the Elementary School. San Francisco: R & E Research Associates, 1973 reprint.

Meisgeier, Charles. The Doubly Disadvantaged; A Study of Socio-Cultural Determinants in Mental Retardation. Austin, TX: U. of Texas, Jl, 1966, 135 pp. ERIC ED 025 081.

Mellor, Earl F. Workers of Spanish Origin: A Chartbook. Washington, DC: GPO, 1978.

Melville, Margarita B. "Mexican Women Adapt to Migration." International Migration Review 12(Summer, 1978):225-235.

Mercer, Jane R. Current Retardation Procedures and the Psychological and Social Implications on the Mexican American. A Position Paper, Ap, 1970, 40 pp. ERIC ED 052 848.

_____. Pluralistic Diagnosis in the Evaluation of Black and Chicano Children: A Procedure for Taking Sociocultural Variables into Account in Clinical Assessment, S, 1971, 26 pp. Paper, American Psychological Association. ERIC ED 055 145.

_____. Sociocultural Factors in the Educational Evaluation of Black and Chicano Children. Sacramento, CA: California State Dept. of Mental Hygiene, F, 1972, 16 pp. ERIC ED 062 462.

Meredith, Robert. "The Treatment of United States-Mexican Relations in Secondary United States History Textbooks Published Since 1956." Doctoral dissertation, New York U., 1968.

Messick, Rosemary G. "Political Awareness Among Mexican-American High School Students." High School Journal 54(N, 1970):108-118.

Mexican-American (Chicano) Handbook of Affirmative Action Programs for Employers and Employees. Downey, CA: Personnel Management Association of Aztlan (P.O. Box 4351), Jl, 1973.

Mexican American Educationa Needs: A Report for the State Superintendent of Public Instruction. Phoenix, AZ: Arizona State Dept. of Public Instruction, D, 1969, 25 pp. ERIC ED 041 691.

Mexican and Mexican-American Literature for the Senior High School. Poetry, Essay, Drama. San Jose, CA: San Jose Unified School District, 1970, 71 pp. Available from San Jose Unified School District, 1605 Park Avenue, San Jose, CA 95114. ERIC ED 039 069.

Mexican and Mexican-American Literature for the Senior High School. Short Story, Novel, Biography. San Jose, CA: San Jose Unified School District, 1970, 92 pp. Available from San Jose Unified School District, 1605 Park Avenue, San Jose, CA 95114. ERIC ED 039 068.

Mexican and Mexican-American Literature for the Junior High School. Poetry, Essay, Drama. San Jose, CA: San Jose Unified School District, 1970, 61 pp. Available from San Jose Unified School District, 1605 Park Avenue, San Jose, CA 95114. ERIC ED 039 067.

Mexican and Mexican-American Literature for the Junior High School. Short Story, Novel, Biography. San Jose, CA: San Jose Unified School District, 1970, 86 pp. Available from San Jose Unified School District, 1605 Park Avenue, San Jose, CA 95114. ERIC ED 039 066.

The Mexicano Americano. La Oportunidad ... Un Enfogue Neuevo. Washington, DC: GPO, 1967.

Miller, Hubert J. Integration of Mexican-American Heritage into United States History, Ag, 1974. ERIC ED 093 536.

Miller, William. "Developing Status for Members of a Minority Group." National Association of Secondary School Principals, Mr, 1955.

Milor, J. H. "Problems of a Junior High for Mexicans." California Journal of Secondary Education 16(D, 1941):482-484.

Mishra, S. P., and Hunt, Maure, Jr. "The Use of Metropolitan Readiness Tests with Mexican-American Children." California Journal of Educational Research 21(S, 1970):182-187.

Mittelbach, Frank G., and Moore, Joan W. "Ethnic Endogamy--The Case of Mexican Americans." American Journal of Sociology, Jl, 1968.

Mittelbach, Frank G., and McDaniel, Ronald. Mexican-American Study Project: Residential Segregation in the Urban Southwest. Advance Report No. 4. Los Angeles: Graduate School of Business Administration, U. of California, 1966.

Montes, Mary. "School-Community Relations: A View from the Barrio." Doctoral dissertation, Claremont Graduate School, 1974. Univ. Microfilms Order No. 75-12,749.

Montez, Philip. "Will the Real Mexican American Please Stand Up." Integrated Education 8(My-Je, 1970):43-49.

Montez, Philip and others. An Evaluation of Operation Head Start Bilingual Children, Summer, 1965. Foundation for Mexican-American Studies, Ag, 1966, 166 pp. ERIC ED 013 667.

Montiel, Miguel. "The Chicano Family: A Review of Research." Social Work 18(Mr, 1973):22-31.

_____. "The Social Science Myth of the Mexican-American Family." El Grito 3(Summer, 1970): 56-63.

Moore, Joan W. "Colonialism: The Case of the Mexican Americans." Social Problems 17 (1970):463-472.

_____. Mexican-Americans: Problems and Prospects. Madison: U. of Wisconsin Press, 1968.

Moore, Joan W. with Pachon, Harry (eds.). Mexican Americans. 2nd ed. Englewood Cliffs, NJ: Prentice--Hall, 1976.

Morales, Bob. "Chicano. Word Symbol of Confusion or Cohesion?" La Raza, Ja 1, 1969.

Morales, Henry. "From Their Hands, a Feast." American Education, N, 1965. [Migrant children]

Morris, Joseph. "What Tests Do Schools Use With Spanish-Speaking Students?" Integrateducation 15(Mr-Ap, 1977).

Morton, John A. The Mexican-American in School and Society. Los Angeles: Institute for American Studies, Los Angeles State College.

"El Movimiento and the Chicana." La Raza, Vol. 1, No. 6(1971):40-42.

Moyer, Dorothy Clauser. "The Growth and Development of Children's Books About Mexico and Mexican Americans." Doctoral dissertation, Lehigh U., 1974. Univ. Microfilms Order No. 74-21,432.

Mukherjee, Ajit Kumer and others. Measurement of Intellectual Potential. Mexican-American School-Age Children, Je, 1976. ERIC ED 138 034.

Mulherin, Kathy. "Chicanos Turn to Brown Power: 'Five Years Behind the Blacks, But We'll Catch Up Very Fast.'" National Catholic Reporter, Je 4, 1969.

_____. "The Kids Make 'Brown Power' Work." National Catholic Reporter, Je 11, 1969.

Murguía, Edward. Assimilation, Colonialsm and the Mexican American People. Austin: U. of Texas Press, 1975.

National Advisory Committee on Mexican American Education. The Mexican-American: Quest for Equality. Washington, DC: GPO, 1968.

Muller, Douglas, and Leonetti, Robert. "Self-Concepts of Primary Level Chicano and Anglo Students." California Journal of Educational Research 25(Mr, 1975):57-60.

National Insitute of Mental Health. Proceedings of the Institute on Narcotic Addiction Among Mexican Americans in the Southwest. Washington, DC: GPO, 1973.

NEA-Tucson Survey on the Teaching of Spanish to the Spanish-Speaking. The Invisbile Minority. Washington, DC: National Education Association, 1966.

Nava, Julian (ed.). The Mexican Americans: An Anthology of Basic Readings. New York: Van Nostrand Reinhold, 1971.

Nava, Julian. Mexican Americans. Past, Present, and Future. New York: American Book Company, 1969.

_____. "Who Is the Chicano?" Integrated Education (J1-Ag, 1969):31-33.

Navarro, Eliseo (comp.). The Chicano Community, 1970. Council on Social Work Education, 345 East 46th Street, New York, NY 10017.

Navarro, J. L. Blue Day on Main Street and Other Short Stories, 1971. Quinto Sol Publications, Inc., P.O. Box 9275, Berkeley, CA 94709.

Nedler, Shari. The States and Educational Effect of Head Start Programs on Mexican American Children, 1970, 16 pp. ERIC ED 056 804.

Nelson, Eugene (comp.). Pablo Cruz and the American Dream: The Experiences of an Undocumented Immigrant from Mexico. Peregrine Smith, 1975.

Netzer, H. E. "Teaching Mexican Children in the First Grade." Modern Language Journal 25(Ja, 1941):322-325.

"New Kind of Service to Mexican Americans." Library News Bulletin 38(J1, 1971):213-216.

Newby, Elizabeth Loza. A Migrant With Hope. Broadman Press, 1977. [Chicana autobiography]

Nieto, Consuelo. "The Chicana and the Women's Rights Movement. A Perspective." Civil Rights Digest 6(Spring, 1974):36-42.

Nieto-Gómez, Anna. "The Chicana-Perspectives for Education." Encuentro Feinenil 1 (Spring, 1973):34-61.

_____. "La Femenista." Encuentro Feinenil 1 (1974):34-47. [Chicana feminist movement, 1968-1973]

Nieves Falcon, Luis. "Children's Books as a Liberating Force." Interracial Books for Children Bulletin 7(1976):4-6.

Noalsey, A. W. "What Are We Doing for the Spanish-Speaking Student." Hispanic 44 (Mr, 1961):119-123.

North, D. S., and Houstoun, M. F. The Characteristics and Role of Illegal Aliens in the U.S. Labor Market: An Exploratory Study. Washington, DC: Linton and Co., Mr, 1976.

Nostrand, Richard L. "The Hispanic-American Borderland: Delimitation of an American Culture Region." Annals of the Association of American Geographers 60(D, 1970):638-661.

_____. "The Hispanic-American Borderland: A Regional, Historical Geography." Doctoral dissertation, U. of California, Los Angeles, 1968.

_____. "'Mexican American' and 'Chicano': Emerging Terms for a People Coming of Age." Pacific Historical Review 42(Ag, 1973): 389-406.

Nunez, Thomas D. "Occupational Choice and Social Mobility of Mexican-Americans: A Study of the Vocational Aspirations of Mexican-American High School Seniors." Master's thesis, Fresno State College, 1968.

Oakland, Thomas, and Emmer, Edumund. Effects of Knowledge of Criterion Groups on the Test Performance of Negro and Mexican-American Students, 1972, 14 pp. Paper, American Educational Research Association. ERIC ED 064 379.

Olivero, James L. and others. The Chicano Is Coming Out of Tortillo Flats ... One Way or the Other. Proceedings of the Conference on Adult Basic Education Sponsored by the Southwestern Cooperative Educational Laboratory, Inc. (Albuquerque July 29-30, 1968), J1 29, 1968, 43 pp. ERIC ED 025 351.

Olstad, Charles (ed.). Bilingual Education in Three Cultures, Annual Conference of the Southwest Council for Bilingual Education (El Paso, November 8-9, 1968). Reports. Las Cruces, NM: Southwest Council for Bilingual Education, 1968, 32 pp. ERIC ED 027 515. Available from Publications Manager, Dept. of Modern Languages, New Mexico State U., Las Cruces, NM 88001.

Ornelas, Charles and others. Decolonizing the Interpretation of the Chicano Political Experience. Los Angeles: Chicano Studies Center, U. of California, Los Angeles, 1975.

Ortego, Felipe, and Conde, David (eds.). The Chicano Literary World--1974. The National Symposium In Chicano Literature and Critical Analysis, Mr, 1975. ERIC ED 101 924.

Ortego, Philip D. "The Chicano Renaissance." Social Casework 52(My, 1971):294-307.

_____. "Montezuma's Children." El Grito 3 (1970):38-50.

_____. "Schools for Mexican-Americans: Between Two Cultures." Saturday Review 54(Ap 17, 1971):80-81.

Oswald, Edward H. "A Comparison of the Achievement of Mexican Children on an Intelligence Test Administered both in English and in Spanish." Master's thesis, Arizona State Teachers College, 1940.

La Otra Cara de Mexico: El Pueblo Chicano, 1978. La Otra Cara de Mexico, El Pueblo Chicano, Av. Juarez 64, Mexico 1, D.F. [Mexican-Americans]

Our Bilinguals--Social and Psychological Barriers, Linguistic and Pedagogical Barriers (2nd Annual Conference of the Southwest Council of Foreign Language Teachers, El Paso, N 13, 1965). Reports. Southwest Council of Foreign Language Teachers, N 13, 1965, 40 pp. ERIC ED 019 899.

Padilla, Amado M., and Ruiz, Rene A. (eds.). Latino Mental Health. A Review of Literature. Washington, DC: GPO, 1973.

Palacios, Alejandro. "LNESC Notebook: An Interview with Vilma Martinez, MALDEF President and General Counsel." LNESC Newsletter 3(My-Je, 1977).

Palacios, Arturo. The Mexican-American Directory. 1969-70 Edition, 1969, 223 pp. Washington, DC: Executive Systems Corp. ERIC ED 034 630. (Not available from EDRS) Available from Executive Systems Corp., Suite 301, 1211 Connecticut Avenue, Washington, DC 20036.

Palomares, Geraldine Dunne. The Effects of Stereotyping on the Self-Concept of Mexican Americans, 1970, 35 pp. ERIC ED 056 806.

Palomares, Uvaldo Hill. Assessment of Rural Mexican-American Students in Grades Preschool Through Twelfth, Ap 29, 1967, 15 pp. ERIC ED 013 690.

_____. "A Critical Analysis of the Research on the Intellectual Evaluation of Mexican-American Children," My, 1965, 51 pp. (term paper U. of Southern California). ERIC ED 027 097.

_____. "Desegregating People's Minds." Civil Rights Digest, Summer, 1969.

_____. Special Needs of Mexican-Americans: PROJECT DESIGN. Educational Needs. Fresno, 1968, Number 27, 1968, 146 pp. Fresno, CA: Fresno City Unified School District. ERIC ED 038 765.

Palomares, Uvaldo, and Commins, Emery J. Assessment of Rural Mexican-American Pupils in Preschool and Grades One through Six. Preliminary Report, 1967, 48 pp. Sacramento, CA: California State Department of Education. ERIC ED 017 959.

_____ and _____. Assessment of Rural Mexican-American Pupils, Preschool and Grades One through Six, San Ysidro, California, Ap, 1 1968, 41 pp. Sacramento, CA: California State Department of Education. Report No. ED7-150-4-68-1M. ERIC ED 020 845.

Palomares, Uvaldo and others. Examination of Assessment Practices and Tools and the Development of a Pilot Intelligence Test for Chicano Children. Grant No. CG9634 A/O. Washington, DC: Office of Economic Opportunity, 1972.

Paredes, Américo (ed.). Humanidad: Essays in Honor of George Sánchez. Los Angeles: Chicano Studies Center, U. of California, Los Angeles, 1977.

Paredes, R. A. "The Image of the Mexican in American Literature." Doctoral dissertation, U. of Texas, 1973. Univ. Microfilms Order No. 73-26, 059.

Paredes, Raymond. "The Origins of Anti-Mexican Sentiment in the United States." New Scholar 6(1977):139-165. [Published at University of California, La Jolla]

Parmalee, Patty Lee. "Chicano Militancy Mounts." Guardian, Ja 24, 1970.

Pasamanick, Benjamin. "The Intelligence of American Children of Mexican Parentage: A Discussion of Uncontrolled Variables." The Journal of Abnormal and Social Psychology 46(O, 1951):598-602.

Paschall, F. C., and Sullivan, Luis R. Racial Influences in the Mental and Physical Development of Mexican Children. Baltimore: Williams and Wilkins, 1925.

Patella, Victoria M. "How Mexican is a Speaking Mexican American?" Ag, 1971, 49 pp. Paper, Rural Sociological Society. College Station, TX: Texas A and M U., Texas Agricultural Experiment Station. ERIC ED 053 852.

Peñalosa, Fernando. "The Changing Mexican-American in Southern California." Sociology and Social Research, Jl, 1967.

_____. "Class, Consciousness, and Social Mobility in a Mexican-American Community." Doctoral dissertation, U. of California, Los Angeles, 1963. [Pomona, CA]

_____. "Mexican Family Roles." Journal of Marriage and the Family, N, 1968.

_____. "Recent Changes Among the Chicanos." Sociology and Social Research (O, 1970):47-52.

_____. "Sociolinguistic Theory and the Chicano Community." Aztlán 6(Spring, 1975):1-11.

_____. "Toward an Operational Definition of the Mexican American." Aztlán 1(Spring, 1970):1-12.

Penna Firma, Thereza. Effects of Social Reinforcement on Self-Esteem of Mexican-American Children, 1967, 6 pp. ERIC ED 033 767.

Pÿoan, Michel. Certain Factors Involved in the Struggle against Malnutrition and Disease, with Special Reference to the Southwest of the United States and Latin America. Inter-Americana, Short Paper VII. Albuquerque, NM: U. of New Mexico Press, 1943.

Pinon, Fernando. Of Myths and Realities: Dynamics of Ethnic Politics. New York: Vantage Press, 1978. [Chicano movement]

Plakos, John. Mexican-American Education Research Project. Progress Report, 1967, Jl 13, 1967, 18 pp. Los Angeles: California State Department of Education. ERIC ED 018 281.

Porath, D. R. The Role of the Anthropologist in Minority Education--The Chicano Case. IXth International Congress of Anthropological and Ethnological Sciences, Ag-S, 1973.

Portes, Alejandro. "Return of the Wetback." Society 11(Mr-Ap, 1974):40-46.

_____ (ed.). "Illegal Mexican Immigrants in the United States." International Migration Review 12(Winter, 1978):469-558.

Post, Don. "Mexican-Americans and 'La Raza.'" Christian Century, Mr 5, 1969.

Poston, D., Jr., and Alvirez, D. "On the Cost of Being a Mexican American Worker." Social Science Quarterly 53(Mr, 1973):695-709.

Poston, D. L., Jr. and others. "Earnings Differences Between Anglo and Mexican American Male Workers in 1960 and 1970: Changes in the 'Cost' of Being Mexican American." Social Science Quarterly 57(1976):618-631.

Proceedings, National Conference on Educational Opportunities for Mexican Americans (Austin, Texas, April 25-26, 1968). Austin, TX: Southwest Educational Development Lab, 1968, 118 pp. ERIC 031 345.

Prospectus for Equitable Educational Opportunities for Spanish-Speaking Children. Sacramento, CA: California State Dept. of Education, D, 1967, 46 pp. ERIC 020 038.

Psencik, Leroy F. "Teaching the History and Culture of the Mexican American in Social Studies." Social Studies 63(D, 1972): 307-311.

Ramirez, Felix T. "Whitewashed Mexican or Chicano?" Compass, Ja, 1969.

Ramirez, Manuel III. "Cultural Democracy: A New Philosophy for Educating the Mexican American Child." National Elementary Principal 50(N, 1970):45-46.

_____. Identity Crisis in Mexican-American Adolescents. Sacramento, CA: State Department of Education, Ag, 1967.

_____. Potential Contributions by the Behavioral Sciences to Effective Preparation Programs for Teachers of Mexican-American Children. University Park, NM: New Mexico State U., F, 1969, 22 pp. ERIC ED 025 370.

_____. "The Relationship of Acculturation to Educational Achievement and Psychological Adjustment in Chicano Children and Adolescents: A Review of the Literature." El Grito 4(Summer, 1971):21-28.

Ramirez, Manuel III, and Taylor, Clark L. Sex Role Determinants in Attitudes Toward Education Among Mexican-American Adolescents. Final Report. Sacramento, CA: Sacramento State College, N, 1967, 49 pp. ERIC ED 039 957. [Sacramento, CA]

Ramirez, Manuel III and others. "Mexican-American Cultural Membership and Adjustment to School." Developmental Psychology 4 (Mr, 1971):141-148.

Rapier, Jacqueline L. "Effects of Verbal Mediation Upon the Learning of Mexican-American Children." California Journal of Educational Research, Ja, 1967.

Reagan, Barbara B. Mexican American Industrial Migrants. PB 196 879. Springfield, VA: National Technical Information Service, Ja, 1971.

Rebolledo, Antonio. "Teaching of Spanish in Elementary Grades." New Mexico School Review 19(Mr, 1940):2-3.

Reilley, Robert R., and Knight, Glenn E. "MMPI Scores of Mexican-American College Students." Journal of College Student Personnel 11(N, 1970):419-422.

Research Department. Ethnological Study of the Mexican. Los Angeles, CA: Board of Education, Je, 1928.

Reyes, Donald J. "Helping the Chicano Pupil." Clearing House 48(O, 1973):110-112.

Reynolds, Annie. The Education of Spanish-Speaking Children in Five Southwestern States. Office of Education Bulletin 1933, No. 11. Washington, DC: GPO, 1933.

Richardson, Juanita Casillas. "A Re-Examination of the Role of Mexican-American Women." Integrateducation 13(Mr-Ap, 1975):32.

Riles, Wilson C. "Interview." Journal of Mexican American Studies 1(Winter, 1971):67-71.

Rios, Francisco Armando. "The Mexican in Fact, Fiction, and Folklore." El Grito, Summer, 1969.

Ríos-Bustamante, Antonio José (ed.). Immigration and Public Policy: Human Rights for Undocumented Workers and Their Families. Los Angeles: Chicano Studies Center, U. of California, 1977.

Rivera, Feliciano (ed.). A Mexican American Source Book, 1970. Educational Consulting Associates, 1149 Chestnut Street, Menlo Park, CA 94025.

_____. A Mexican American Source Book with Study Guideline, 1970, 196 pp. ERIC ED 045 244.

Rivera, George, Jr. "The New Chicano." Compass, Ap, 1969.

_____. "Nosotros Venceremos: Chicano Consciousness and Change Strategies." Journal of Applied Behavioral Science 8(Ja, 1972):56-71.

Rivera, Jaime Sena. "Chicanos: Culture, Community, Role--Problems of Evidence, and a Proposition of Norms Towards Establishing Evidence." Aztlan 1(Spring, 1970):37-51.

Rivera, Julius. "Justice, Deprivation, and the Chicano." Aztlan 4(Spring, 1973):123-136.

Robles, Ernest Z. "An Analytical Description of Peer Group Pressures on Mobility-Oriented Mexican-American Junior High School Students." Master's thesis, U. of Redlands, 1964.

Robinson, Cecil. With the Ears of Strangers: The Mexican in American Literature. Tucson: U. of Arizona Press, 1963.

Rochin, Refugio I. "Economic Deprivation of Chicanos--Continuing Neglect in the Seventies." Aztlan 4(Spring, 1973):85-102.

_____. "The Short and Turbulent Life of Chicano Studies: A Preliminary Study of Emerging Programs and Problems." Social Science Quarterly 53(Mr, 1973):884-894.

Rodillas, Nicholas C., and Eaton, Morris. A Study Guideline of the History and Culture of the Mexican-American-Secondary Grade, Je, 1971. ERIC ED 124 332. Addendum. ERIC ED 124 333.

Rodriguez, Armando M. "Mexican American Education--Today." Integrated Education 8 (S-O, 1970):47-50.

_____. "Speak Up, Chicano." American Education, My, 1968.

Rodriguez, David L., and Lelevier, Benjamin. A Portfolio of Oustanding Americans of Mexican Descent, 1970. Educational Consulting Associates, P.O. Box 1057, Menlo Park, CA 94025.

Rodriguez, Luisa, Sala de Gourezgil. El Esereotipo del Mexicano: Estudio Psyco Social. Mexico: Biblioteca de Ensayes Sociologicos Institute de Investigaciones Sociales, Universidao Nacional, 1965.

Rodriguez, Valerio S. "Mexican American Pupils' Self-Concept in Public Elementary Schools." Doctoral dissertation, United States International U., 1972.

Rodriguez, Richard. "On Becoming a Chicano." Saturday Review 2(F 8, 1975):46-48.

Romano, Octavio Ignacio. "Goodbye Revolution-- Hello Slum." El Grito, Winter, 1968.

_____ (ed.). El Espejo--The Mirror. Selected Mexican-American Literature, 1969. Quinto Sol Publications, Inc., P.O. Box 9275, Berkeley, CA 94709.

_____. "Social Science, Objectivity and the Chicanos." El Grito 4(Fall, 1970):4-16.

_____ (ed.). Voices: Readings from El Grito, 1971. Quinto Sol Publications, Inc., P.O. Box 9275, Berkeley, CA 94709.

Romero, Fred E. "Chicanos and Occupational Mobility." In Minorities in the Labor Market, pp. 66-84. Edited by Paul Bullock. Los Angeles: Institute of Industrial Relations, U. of California, 1978.

Romo, Ricardo. "Responses to Mexican Immigration, 1910-1930." Aztlan 6(Summer, 1975): 173-194.

Romo, Ricardo, and Paredas, R. (ed.). New Directions in Chicano Scholarship. La Jolla: U. of California, San Diego, 1978.

Rosen, Carl L., and Ortega, Philip D. "Language and Reading Problems of Spanish-Speaking Children in the Southwest." Journal of Reading Behavior, Winter, 1969.

_____ and _____. Problems and Strategies in Teaching the Language Arts to Spanish-Speaking Mexican American Children. University Park, NM: New Mexico State U., F, 1969, 26 pp. ERIC ED 025 368.

Rosen, Sanford. School Desegregation and the Chicano Community, 1976. ERIC ED 131 974.

Rosen, Sanford, and Alcala, Carlos. Principal Legal Issues in School Desegregation Litigation as It Relates to the Mexican American. San Francisco: Mexican American Legal Defense Fund, My 10, 1974.

Rowan, Helen. "A Minority Nobody Knows." Atlantic, Je, 1967.

_____. The Mexican American. Prepared for the U.S. Commission on Civil Rights. Washington, DC: GPO, 1968.

Ruiz, Manuel, Jr. Mexican American Legal Heritage in the Southwest. 2nd edition. 1974. Manuel Ruiz, Jr., Financial Center Building, Suite 602, Los Angel

Ruiz, Ramon E., and Tebbel, J. South by Southwest: The Mexican-American and His Heritage. New York: Doubleday, 1969.

Russel, Daniel. "Problems of Mexican Children in the Southwest." The Journal of Educational Sociology, D, 1943.

Saavedra, Louis E. Vocational-Technical Education and the Mexican-American. Albuquerque, NM: Southwestern Cooperative Educational Lab, 1970, 19 pp. ERIC ED 051 927.

Saavedra-Vela, Pilar. "The Dark Side of Hispanic Women's Education." Agenda (My-Je, 1978).

Salazar, Ruben. A Selection of His Columns Reprinted from the Los Angeles Times. Los Angeles, CA: Los Angeles Times, 1970.

Salinas, Guadalupe. "Can Chicanos Find Justice in Schools?" Agenda (quarterly), Fall, 1973.

_____. "Mexican-Americans and the Desegregation of Schools in the Southwest." El Grito 4(Summer, 1971):36-59. [Reprinted from Houston Law Review 8(1971):925-951]

_____. "Mexican-Americans and the Desegregation of Schools in the Southwest--A Supplement." El Grito 4(Summer, 1971):59-69.

Salinas, Rodolfo. "Chicano Power, Pride or Prejudice." Con Safos, I, No. 3 (1969).

Samora, Julian. "Educational Status of a Minority." Theory and Practice 2(Je, 1963):144-150.

_____. "Immigration History Provides Key." Agenda, Winter, 1973.

_____ (ed.). La Raza: Forgotten Americans. Notre Dame, IN: U. of Notre Dame Press, 1966. [The Spanish-Americans]

Samora, Julian, and Galarza, Ernesto. "Research and Scholarly Activity." EPOCA: The National Councilio for Chicano Studies Journal 1(Winter, 1971):51-54.

Sanchez, Armond, Jr. "Self-Concept of Mexican-American Youth: The Stability of Self-Concept of Mexican-American Youth in Relation to Identification with Mexican Cultural Values." Master's thesis, Fresno State College, 1967.

Sanchez, Arturo. "Conferencia de Padres Unidos en Northridge." La Raza 2(Ja, 1975):20-25.

Sánchez, Corinne. "Higher Education y la Chicana." Encuentro Femenil 1(Spring, 1973):27-33.

Sanchez, George I. "The Equalization of Educational Opportunity--Some Issues and Problems." New Mexico University Bulletin, Educational Series. Albuquerque, NM: U. of New Mexico Press, 1939.

_____. "First Regional Conference on the Education of Spanish-speaking People in the Southwest." Inter-American Education, Occasional Papers, I. Austin, TX: U. of Texas Press, 1946.

_____. "History, Culture, and Education." In La Raza: Forgotten Americans. Edited by Julian Samora. Notre Dame, IN: Notre Dame U. Press, 1966.

_____. "School Integration and Americans of Mexican Descent." American Unity, Winter, 1955.

_____. "Scores of Spanish-speaking Children on Repeated Tests." Pedagogical Seminary and Journal of Genetic Psychology 40(Mr, 1932):223-231.

Sanchez, Ricardo. Canto Grito mi Liberacion: The Liberation of a Chicano Mind. New York: Anchor, 1973.

Sanders, Jack O. L. The Blueprint Potentials of the Cooperative Teacher Education Preparation; Utilizing the Talented Mexican American. University Park, NM: New Mexico State U., F, 1969, 17 pp. ERIC ED 025 372.

Sandoval, Alberto. "Treatment of Contemporary Mexican Americans in Selected Fifth Grade Social Studies Textbooks." Doctoral dissertation, U. of New Mexico, 1972. Univ. Microfilms Order No. 73-01555.

Santamaria, Francisco J. Diccionario de mexicanismos. Mexico City: Editorial Porrua, 1959.

Santiago. "Chicano no, Mexicano si?" Inside Eastside, S 15, 1968.

Santillan, Richard A. "El Partido La Raza Unida. Chicanos in Politics." The Black Politician 3(Jl, 1971):45-52.

Sassen-Koob, Saskia. "Non-Dominant Ethnic Populations as Parts of Total Society: Chicanos in the U.S." Aztlan 4(Spring, 1973):103-121.

Saunders, Lyle. "The Education of Spanish-Americans." Colorado School Journal 60 (Ja, 1945):12-15.

_____. "The Social History of the Spanish-Speaking People of Southwestern United States Since 1846." In Proceedings of the First Congress of Historians from Mexico and the United States. Mexico, D.F.: Editorial Cultura, 1950.

Schement, Jorge Reina, and Singleton, Loy Alonzo. Spanish Language Radio in the Southwest: A Case of Media Colonialism, Ap, 1978. ERIC ED 157 130.

Schmidt, Fred H. "Job Caste in the Southwest." Industrial Relations 9(O, 1969):100-110.

_____. Spanish Surnamed American Employment in the Southwest. Washington, DC: GPO, 1970.

Schmidt, Linda, and Gallessich, June. "Adjustment of Anglo-American and Mexican-American Pupils in Self-Contained and Team-teaching Classrooms." Journal of Educational Psychology 62(Ag, 1971):328-332.

"School Bias Toward Mexican-Americans." School and Society 94(N 12, 1966):378-380.

"School Discrimination Against Mexican Americans." Ideal, F 15, 1971.

"Schools." Inside Eastside, F 10, 1969.

Schwartz, Audrey James. "A Comparative Study of Values and Achievement: Mexican-American and Anglo Youth." Sociology of Education 44 (Fall, 1971):438-462.

_____. Comparative Values and Achievement of Mexican-American and Anglo Pupils. Los Angeles, CA: U. of California, F, 1969, 109 pp. ERIC ED 028 873.

Scriven, Georgia and others. "Peer Initiation by Anglo and Mexican-American Children in Day Care." Journal of the National Association for Bilingual Education 1(D, 1976): 47-49.

SEAS. "The Great American Myth Or the Unfulfilled American Dream." Compass, My, 1969.

Segal, Aaron. "Mexico and the Mexican-American." Con Safos, II, No. 5, 1970.

Select Commission on Western Hemisphere Immigration. The Impact of Commuter Aliens Along the Mexican and Canadian Borders. Hearings. 4 parts. Washington, DC: GPO, 1968. [El Paso and Brownsville, TX; San Diego, CA; and Detroit, MI]

Senter, Donovan, and Hawley, Florence. "The Grammar School as the Basic Acculturating Influence for Native New Mexicans." Social Forces, My, 1946.

Sets Kagan, Spencer, and Madsen, Millard C. "Cooperation and Competition of Mexican, Mexican-American, and Anglo-American Children of Two Ages under Four Instrumental Sets." Developmental Psychology 5(Jl, 1971): 32-39.

Severo, Richard. "The Flight of the Wetbacks." New York Times Magazine, Mr 10, 1974.

Shaftel, G. A. "The Needs and Anxieties of Spanish-Speaking Students." California Journal of Secondary Education 28(Mr, 1953): 160-170.

Shankman, Arnold. "The Image of Mexico and the Mexican-American in the Black Press, 1890-1935." Journal of Ethnic Studies 3(Summer, 1975):43-56.

Shaw, Ray. "Overlooked Minority." Wall Street Journal, My 3, 1966. [Mexican-Americans]

Sheldon, Paul M. Mexican-Americans in Urban Public High Schools: An Exploration of the Drop-Out Problem. A Study made possible by the Rosenberg Foundation of San Francisco, Laboratory of Urban Culture, Occidental College, 1959.

Sheldon, Paul M., and Hunter, E. Farley. Mexican-Americans in Urban Public High Schools. Los Angeles, CA: Occidental College, 1964.

Shoemaker, Marjie. "The Minority Nobody Knows." San Bernardino Sun-Telegram, O 20-O 28, 1968 (9 articles).

Shotwell, Anna M. "Arthur Performance Ratings of Mexican and American High-Grade Mental Defectives." American Journal of Mental Deficiency 49(Ap, 1945):445-449.

Shuler, Antonia Castañeda, Ybarra-Frausto, Tómas, and Sommer, Joseph (eds.). Chicano Literature: Text and Context. Englewood Cliffs, NJ: Prentice-Hall, 1972.

Sifuentes, Frank Moreno. "Note to the Office of Education." Con Safos, I, No. 3 (1969). Critique of U.S. Office of Education, The Mexican American: Quest for Equality

_____. "Three Preliminaries to the Gentle Professor." La Raza, F 7, 1969. [Reply to Guzman, above]

Silko, John R. "Beyond the Law—To Equal Educational Opportunities for Chicanos and Indians." New Mexico Law Review 1(1971).

Sillas, Herman. "Chicanos vs. the Education Establishment." Los Angeles Times, Ja 28, 1974.

Simmen, Edward (ed.). The Chicano: From Caricature to Self-Portrait. New York: New American Library, 1971.

La Simpatica. "Viva La Raza!" The Movement, Jl, 1969.

Simpson, George E., and Yinger, J. Milton. "Mexican-American Children in the Public Schools." In Racial and Cultural Minorities, pp. 565-573. New York: Harper and Bros., 1963.

Smart, Margaret E. "Response of Mexican-American Socioeconomic Groups to Selected Intellectual Tasks." Doctoral dissertation, U. of Arizona, 1968.

Smith, B., and Newman, R. "Depressed Wages along the U.S.-Mexico Border: An Empirical Analysis." Economic Inquiry 15(Ja, 1977).

Smith, George W., and Caskey, Owen. Promising School Practices for Mexican Americans. Austin, TX: Southwest Educational Development Lab, Lubbock, TX: Texas Tech U., 1972, 262 pp. ERIC ED 064 003.

Solomon, Daniel and others. "The Development of Democratic Values and Behavior Among Mexican-American Children." Child Development 43 (Je, 1972):625-638.

Sommers, Joseph, and Ybarra-Frausto, Tómas (eds.). Modern Chicano Writers: A Collection of Critical Essays. Englewood Cliffs, NJ: Prentice Hall, 1979.

Sotomayor, Marta. "Mexican-American Interaction with Social Systems." Social Casework 52 (My, 1971):316-322.

Sotomayor, Frank. Para los Niños--For the Children. Improving Education for Mexican-Americans. Washington, DC: GPO, O, 1974.

Southwest Network. Parameters of Institutional Change: Chicano Experiences in Education, 1974. The Southwest Network, 1020 B Street, Suite 8, Hayward, CA 94541.

Southwest Texas State Teachers College. Art Activities for Latin-American Children in Elementary Grades. San Marcos, 1944.

Spalding, Norma. "Learning Problems of Mexican-Americans." Reading Improvement 7(F, 1970): 33-36.

Spence, Allyn G., Mishra, Shitala, and Ghozeil, Susan. "Have Language and Performance on Standardized Tests." Elementary School Journal 71(Mr, 1971):309-313.

Spilka, Bernard, and Gill, Lois. "Some Non-intellectual Correlates of Academic Achievement Among Spanish-American Students." The School Counselor, My, 1965.

Stanchfield, Jo M., and Hovey, Barbara. "A Study of Attitudinal Changes in Mexican-American Parents Toward the Schools." International Reading Association Conference. Proceedings, Part 1, 13(Ap, 1968):767-772.

Starkweather, Ann (comp.). Instructional Objectives for a Junior College Course in Mexican American Studies. Los Angeles, CA: U. of California, ERIC Clearinghouse for Junior College Information, Je, 1971, 12 pp. ERIC ED 049 756.

Stedman, James M., and McKenzie, Richard E. "Family Factors Related to Competence in Young Disadvantaged Mexican-American Children." Child Development 42(N, 1971): 1602-1607.

Stedman, James M., and Adams, Russell L. "Teacher Perception of Behavioral Adjustment as a Function of Linguistic Ability in Mexican-American Head-Start Children." Psychology in the Schools 10(Ap, 1973):221-225.

Steen, M. T. "The Effects of Immediate and Delayed Reinforcement on the Achievement Behavior of Mexican-American Children of Low Socio-economic Status." Doctoral dissertation, Stanford U., 1966.

Steiner, Stan. "Chicano Power." New Republic, Je 20, 1970.

Stern, Gwen Louise. "Ethnic Identity and Community Action in El Barrio." Doctoral dissertation, Northwestern U., 1976. Univ. Microfilms Order No. 77-1361.

Stewart, Ida Santos. "Cultural Differences in the Attributions and Intentions of Anglos and Chicanos in an Elementary School." Doctoral dissertation, U. of Illinois, 1972.

Stilwell, William E., and Thoresen, Carl E. "Social Modeling and Vocational Behaviors of Mexican-American and Non-Mexican-American Adolescents." Vocational Guidance Quarterly 20(Je, 1972):279-286.

Stocker, Joseph. "Se Habla Espanol." American Education, My, 1967.

Stoddard, Ellwyn R. "A Conceptual Analysis of the 'Alien Invasion': Institutionalized Support of Illegal Mexican Aliens in the U.S." International Migration Review 10 (Summer, 1976):157-189.

_____. "Illegal Mexican Labor in the Borderlands: Institionalized Support of an Unlawful Practice." Pacific Sociological Review 19(Ap, 1976):175-210.

Stone, Paula C., and Ruiz, Rene A. Race and Class as Differential Determinants of Under achievement and Underaspiration Among Mexican-Americans, 1971. ERIC ED 077 612.

Stubing, Charles (ed.). Bilingualism, Annual Conference of the Southwest Council of Foreign Language Teachers (3rd, El Paso, November 4, 5, 1966) Reports. Southwest Council of Foreign Language Teachers, 1966, 64 pp. ERIC ED 016 435.

Swadesh, Frances Leon. Los primeros pobladores. Hispanic Americans of the Frontier. Notre Dame, IN: U. of Notre Dame Press, 1974.

Swanson, Elinor, and De Blassie, Richard R. "Interpreter Effects on the WISC Performance of First Grade Mexican-American Children." Measurement and Evaluation in Guidance 4 (O, 1971):172-175.

Takesian, Sarkis A. "A Comparative Study of the Mexican-American Graduate and Dropout." Doctoral dissertation, U. of Southern California, 1967.

Taylor, Juanita F. "A Comparison of First and Second Generation Mexican Parents." Master's thesis, U. of Southern California, 1943.

Taylor, Marie E. Educational and Cultural Values of Mexican-American Parents: How They Influence the School Achievement of Their Children. Sacramento, CA: California State Dept. of Education, 1970, 42 pp. ERIC ED 050 842.

Taylor, Paul S. Mexican Labor in the United States. 2 vols. Berkeley, CA: U. of California Press, 1930-1932.

_____. Mexican Labor in the United States: Racial School Statistics. Vol. 6, No. 4. Berkeley and Los Angeles, U. of California Publications in Economics, U. of California Press, 1929.

_____. "Mexicans North of the Rio Grande." Survey Graphic 66(My 1, 1931):135-205.

Teel, Dwight. "Preventing Prejudice Against Spanish-Speaking Children." Educational Leadership 12(N, 1954).

Temple-Trujillo, Rita E. "Conception of the Chicano Family." Smith College Studies in Social Work 45(N, 1974):1-20.

Texas Christian University, Institute for the Study of Cognitive Systems. Proceedings of the Souyhwestern Psychological Association Symposium on Individual Difference Variables and Schematic Concept Formation: Explorations, April, 1972. AD-752 120. Springfield, VA: National Technical Information Service, S, 1972.

Thompson, Merrell E., and Dove, Claude D. "A Comparison of Physical Achievement of Anglo and Spanish-American Boys in Junior High School." Research Quarterly, O, 1942.

Tilford, Ernest H. [Letter on Mexican-American schools in the Southwest] Christian Century, N 20, 1968.

Tindall, Lloyd W. and others. An Examination of the Receptivity of Mexican-American and Anglo Rural Disadvantaged to Educational Programs. East Lansing, MI: Michigan State U., Center for Rural Manpower and Public Affairs, Mr, 1972, 34 pp. ERIC ED 060 974.

Tirado, Miguel David. "Mexican American Community Political Organization. 'The Key to Chicano Political Power.'" Aztlan 1 (Spring, 1970):53-78.

Tireman, Lloyd Spencer. "The Education of Minority Groups, Bi-Lingual Children." Review of Educational Research 11(1941):340-352.

_____. Teaching Spanish-Speaking Children. Albuquerque: U. of New Mexico Press, 1948.

Tireman, Lloyd Spencer, and Watson, Mary. Report of Nambe Community School. Albuquerque: U. of New Mexico Press, 1943.

Tracy, Phil. "Padres Organizing for 'Chicano Power.'" National Catholic Reporter, Ap 2, 1971.

Trejo, A. D. "Library Needs for the Spanish-Speaking." ALA Bulletin 63(1969):1077-1081.

Trevino, Albert Dwight. "Mexican-American Literature in the High School English Program: A Theoretical and Practical Approach." Doctoral dissertation, U. of Texas, 1974. Univ. Microfilms Order No. 75-4468.

Trueba, Henry T. "Bilingual-Bicultural Education for Chicanos in the Southwest." Council on Anthropology and Education Quarterly 5(Ag, 1974):8-15.

Trujillo, Marcella L. "Guidelines for Employment in Chicano Studies." EPOCA: The National Concilio for Chicano Studies Journal 1(Winter, 1971):60-65.

Tuck, R. A. "Mexican-Americans: A Contributory Culture." California Elementary School Principals' Association Yearbook 17(1945):106-109.

Turner, Paul R. "Academic Performance of Mexican-Americans." Integrated Education 11 (My-Je, 1973):3-6.

Tyler, Gus (ed.). Mexican-Americans Tomorrow: Educational and Economic Perspectives. Albuquerque: U. of New Mexico Press, 1975.

Uhlenberg, P. "Demographic Correlates of Group Achievement. Contrasting Patterns of Mexican-Americans and Japanese-Americans." Demography 9(F, 1972):119-128.

Ulibarri, Horacio. Educational Needs of the Mexican-American. University Park, NM: New Mexico State U., Mr, 1968, 21 pp. ERIC ED 016 538.

_____. The Effect of Cultural Differences in the Education of Spanish Americans. Albuquerque: College of Education, New Mexico U., S, 1958, 115 pp. ERIC ED 019 156.

"UMAS Holds Conference at Loyola U." La Raza, Ja 1, 1969. [3rd annual conference, D 21-33, 1968]

U.S. Bureau of the Census. Selected Characteristics of Persons and Families of Mexican, Puerto Rican, and Other Spanish Origin: March, 1972. Washington, DC: GPO, Jl, 1972.

_____. U.S. Census of Population: 1960. Supplementary Reports, Series PC (SI)-55, "Population Characteristics of Selected Ethnic Groups in the Five Southwestern States." GPO, 1968.

_____. We the Mexican Americans. Nosotros los México Americanos. Washington, DC: GPO, 1970.

U.S. Commission on Civil Rights. "Ethnic Isolation of Mexican-Americans in the Public
Schools of the Southwest." Washington, DC:
U.S. Commission on Civil Rights, Ag, 1970,
unpublished.

_____. Methodological Appendix of Research
Methods Employed in Mexican American Study.
Washington, DC: The Commission, Ja, 1972.

_____. Mexican American Education Study.
Report I: Ethnic Isolation of Mexican
Americans in the Public Schools of the
Southwest. Washington, DC: GPO, Ap, 1971.
[First issued in Ag, 1970]

_____. Mexican-American Report. Washington,
DC: GPO, 1966.

_____. Mexican Americans and the Administra-
tion of Justice in the Southwest. Washington, DC: GPO, Mr, 1970.

_____. "Preliminary Staff Analysis Mexican
American Education Study." In U.S. Congress,
91st, 2nd session, Senate, Committee on Labor
and Public Welfare, Subcommittee on Education, Emergency School Aid Act of 1970.
Hearings..., pp. 333-346. Washington, DC:
GPO, 1970.

_____. "Quality Education for Mexican-American
Children." Integrated Education 12(My, Je,
1974):38-41.

_____. Spanish-Speaking Peoples. Staff
paper, F 5, 1964.

_____. Stranger in One's Land. Washington,
DC: GPO, My, 1970.

_____. Toward Quality Education for Mexican
Americans. Report VI: Mexican-American
Education Study. Washington, DC: GPO,
F, 1974.

_____. The Unfinished Education. Outcomes for
Minorities in the Five Southwestern States.
Mexican American Education Series, Report II.
Washington, DC: GPO, O, 1971.

U.S. Congress, 91st, 1st session, Senate,
Special Committee on Aging. Availability and
Usefulness of Federal Programs and Services
to Elderly Mexican-Americans. Hearings...
Part 5. Washington, DC: GPO, 1970.

U.S. Congress, 91st, 2nd session, Senate,
Select Committee on Equal Educational
Opportunity. Equal Educational Opportunity.
Hearings... Part 4. Mexican American Educa-
tion. Washington, DC: GPO, 1971.

U.S. Court of Appeals. "Mexican Americans as a
Legal Minority." Integrated Education 11
(Mr-Ap, 1973):68-74.

U.S. Inter-Agency Committee on Mexican American
Affairs, 1967-1968. The Mexican American.
A New Focus on Opportunity. Washington, DC:
GPO, 1968.

U.S. Office of Education. "Young Spanish-
Speaking Children in our Schools."
Elementary Education, Series No. 30. U.S.
Office of Education, 1951.

_____. Bureau of Elementary and Secondary
Education, Mexican American Affairs Unit.
Mexican-American Education. A Special
Report. Washington, DC: U.S. Office of
Education, Mr, 1968.

_____. Improving English Skills of Culturally
Different Youth. Washington, DC: GPO, 1964.

Uribe, Oscar, Jr., and Martinez, Joseph S.
Analyzing Children's Books from a Chicano
Perspective, 1975. ERIC ED 129 458.

Vaca, Nick C. "The Mexican-American in the
Social Sciences, 1912-1970. Part I: 1912-
1935." El Grito 3(1970):3-24.

_____. "The Mexican-American in the Social
Sciences, 1912-1970. Part II: 1936-1970."
El Grito 4(Fall, 1970):17-51.

_____. "The Negro Movement as an Anti-revolu-
tion." El Grito, Winter, 1969.

_____. "The Sociology of Being a Mexican-
Russian." El Grito, Summer, 1968.

Vadala, Julia (ed.). Hispano Library Services
for Arizona, Colorado and New Mexico: A
Workshop Held in Santa Fe, New Mexico, April
30, May 1-2, 1970. Boulder, CO: Western
Interstate Commission for Higher Education,
Ag, 1970, 45 pp. ERIC ED 043 360.

Valdes, Daniel T. "The U.S. Hispano." Social
Education, Ap, 1969.

Valdez, Bernard. Contrasts Between Spanish Folk
and Anglo Urban Cultural Values. Colorado
Department of Institutions, Department of
Social Welfare, Je 30, 1963.

Valdez, Luis. "Organizense Raza Against Racism."
La Raza, Je 7, 1968.

Valdez, Luis, and Steiner, Stan (eds.). Aztlan:
An Anthology of Mexican American Literature.
New York: Knopf, 1972.

Valencia, Atilano A. The Effects of a College
Teacher Training Project with Emphases on
Mexican American Cultural Characteristics.
An Evaluation Report. Sacramento, CA:
Sacramento State College, S 18, 1970, 78 pp.
ERIC ED 045 267.

_____. Identification and Assessment of Ongoing
Educational and Community Programs for
Spanish Speaking People. A Report Submitted
to the Southwest Council of La Raza, Phoenix,
Arizona. Albuquerque, NM: Southwest Coopera-
tive Educational Lab, Mr, 1969, 116 pp.
ERIC ED 028 013.

Valero, Luis Gilbert. "The Socio-Psychological Development of the Mexican-American: Historical and Sociological Events as Determinants." Doctoral dissertation, U. of Northern Colorado, 1974. Univ. Microfilms Order No. 74-24,514.

Van Meter, Ed, and Barba, Alma (eds.). Regional Conference on Teacher Education for Mexican-Americans (New Mexico State University, February 13-14, 1969). Conference Proceedings. University Park, NM: New Mexico State U., 40 pp. ERIC ED 027 444.

Vargas, Viviana. "An Analysis of the Chicana." La Raza 3(Spring, 1977):21-23.

Vasquez, Enriqúeta. "Chicanos Building a Party." Guardian, Ap 18, 1970. [Second Annual Chicano Youth Liberation Conference]

Vasquez, Richard. Chicano (a novel). Garden City, NY: Doubleday, 1970.

Vega, William Carbajal. "A Look at 'Chic-Anglo,' The Brown White." Inside Eastside, Mr 10, 1969.

Versteeg, Arlen, and Hall, Robert. "Levels of Aspiration, Achievement, and Sociocultural Differences in Preschool Children." Journal of Genetic Psychology 119(S, 1971):137-142.

"A View of Nuevas Vistas Conference." La Raza, Ap 30, 1969. [Meeting at Biltmore Hotel, Ap 24, 1969]

Vigil, Antonio S. The Coming of the Gringo and the Mexican-American Revolt. New York: Vantage Press, 1970.

Vigil, Ernesto. "The Chicano Student Movement Through the Southwest." El Gallo, Ja, 1969.

_____. "Student Action ... Chicano on the Move." El Gallo, D, 1968. [Colorado]

Wahab, Zaher. "The Mexican American Child and the Public School." Doctoral dissertation, Stanford U., 1972.

Ward, Robert, and Hedlay, Carolyn. Interaction Analyses of Mexican-American and Negro High School Students to College Orientation. Santa Barbara: U. of California, 23 pp. ERIC ED 020 537.

Warren, Robert A., and Bryant, Paul D. Developing Science Career Interests in Bilingual, Mexican-American Elementary Students, D, 1976. ERIC ED 138 441.

Wasserman, Susan A. "Values of Mexican-American, Negro, and Anglo Blue-Collar and White Collar Children." Child Development 42(N, 1971):1624-1628.

Weaver, Charles N., and Glenn, Norval D. "The Job Performance of Mexican-Americans." Sociology and Social Research 54(Jl, 1970): 477-494.

Weinberg, Meyer. "Mexican American Culture and the Schools." Intergroup 1, No. 3(1971): 2-3.

_____. "[Recent Research on] Mexican Americans." Research Review of Equal Education 1(Spring, 1977):3-24.

West, Guy A. "Race Attitudes Among Teachers in the Southwest." Journal of Abnormal and Social Psychology 31(O-D, 1936):331-337.

Wilder, Mrs. L. A. "Problems in the Teaching of Mexican Children." Texas Outlook 20 (Ag, 1936):9-10.

Williams, Byron. "Notes on the Chicano Movement." Interracial Books for Children, Spring, 1970.

Williams, Jane Case. Improving Educational Opportunities for Mexican-American Handicapped Children. Washington, DC: Office of Education, Ap, 1968, 37 pp. ERIC ED 018 326.

Wilson, Herbert B. Evaluation of the Influence of Educational Programs on Mexican-Americans. University Park, NM: New Mexico State U., Mr, 1968, 25 pp. ERIC ED 016 561.

Wingfield, Clyde J. (ed.). Urbanization in the Southwest. Texas Western U. Press, 1968.

Wise, Michael (ed.). "Mexican American." In Desegregation in Education: A Directory of Reported Federal Decisions, p. 200. Notre Dame, IN: Center for Civil Rights, U. of Notre Dame Law School, Ap, 1977. [1954-1976]

Witherspoon, Paul "A Comparison of the Problems of Certain Anglo and Latin-American Junior High School Students." Journal of Educational Research 53(1960):295-299.

Wolman, Marianne. "Cultural Factors and Creativity." Journal of Secondary Education, D, 1962, pp. 454-460.

Womack, John, Jr. "The Chicanos." New York Review of Books 19(Ag 31, 1972):12-18.

_____. "Los 'Chicanos.'" Revista de Occidente, No. 132(Mr, 1974):343-374.

Woodbridge, Hensley C. "Mexico and U.S. Racism." Commonweal, Je 22, 1945.

Yoshino, Roger. Sociocultural Characteristics and Educational Achievement of Mexican-Americans. Tucson: Arizona Center for Early Childhood Education, U. of Arizona, 1969.

Zimmerman, Barry J., and Rosenthal, Ted L. "Observation, Repetition, and Ethnic Background in Concept Attainment and Generalization." Child Development 43(Je, 1972): 605-613. [Mexican-American and Anglo children]

Zintz, Miles V. What Classroom Teachers Should Know About Bilingual Education. Albuquerque, NM: College of Education, U. of New Mexico, Mr, 1969, 57 pp. ERIC ED 028 427.

Williams, Stanley T. The Spanish Background of American Literature. New Haven, CT: Yale U. Press, 1955.

Puerto Ricans

Abad, Vincente, Ramos, Juan, and Boyce, Elizabeth. "A Model for Delivery of Mental Health Services to Spanish-Speaking Minorities." American Journal of Ortho-psychiatry 44(Jl, 1974):584-595.

Acosta, Adela M. "Puerto Rican Children in New York City Schools: A Bilingual Bi-cultural Curriculum Approach." Master's thesis, U. of Kansas, 1974.

Acosta-Belen, Edna. "The Literature of the Puerto Rican National Minority in the United States." Bilingual Review 5(Ja-Ag, 1978):107-116.

Alers-Montalvo, Manuel. "The Puerto Rican Migrants of New York City: A Study of Anomie." Master's thesis, Columbia U., 1951.

Algarin, Miguel, and Pinero, Miguel (eds.). Nuyorican Poetry: An Anthology of Puerto Rican Words and Feelings. New York: Morrow, 1975.

Alicea, Victor, and Mathis, Julie. The De-terminants of Educational Attainment Among Puerto Rican Youth in the United States, 1975. Universidad Boricua, 1766 Church Street, N.W., Washington, DC 20036.

Al-Khazraji, Majid G., and Al-Khazraji, Emile M. The Puerto-Ricans of New Bedford, Mass: Social Conditions and Social Needs. New Bedford, MA: Action Research Project, Onboard, Inc. and Migrants, Inc., 1970.

Alvarado, Anthony. "Puerto Rican Children in New York Schools." New Generation 53(1972): 22-25.

Alvarez, José Hernandez. "The Movement and Settlement of Puerto Rican Migrants within the United States." International Migration Review 2(1968):40-52.

_____. Return Migration to Puerto Rico. Population Monograph Series, No. 1. Berkeley, CA: U. of California, 1967.

Anastasia, Anne, and de Jesus, Cruz. "Language Development and Non-verbal I.Q. of Puerto Rican Preschool Children in New York City." Journal of Abnormal and Social Psychology 48, 1953.

Angle, John. "Mainland Control of Manu-facturing and Reward for Bilingualism in Puerto Rico." American Sociological Review 41(Ap, 1976):289-307.

Anastasi, Anne, and Cordova, Fernando A. "Some Effects of Bilingualism Upon the Intelligence Test Performance of Puerto Rican Children in New York City." Journal of Educational Psychology, Ja, 1953.

Anisman, Paul H. "Some Aspects of Code Switching in New York Puerto Rican English." Bilingual Review 2(Ja-Ag, 1975):56-85.

_____. "Some Phonological Correlates of Code Switching in the English of Puerto Rican Teenagers in New York City." Doctoral dissertation, U. of Rochester, 1974.

Annotations on Selected Aspects of the Culture of Puerto Rico and Its People, 1969. ERIC ED 059 933.

Aponte-Hernandez, Rafael. "The University of Puerto Rico. Foundations of the 1942 Re-form." Doctoral dissertation, U. of Texas, 1966.

Aran, Kenneth, Arthur, Herman, Colón, Ramón, and Goldenberg, Harvey. Puerto Rican History and Culture. New York: United Federation of Teachers, 1973.

Araoz, D. L. "Male Puerto Rican Parental Self-Image." Doctoral dissertation, Columbia U., 1969.

Arter, Rhetta M. Between Two Bridges. New York: Center for Human Relations, New York U., 1956.

_____. Living in Chelsea. New York: Center for Human Relations, New York, U., 1954.

Ascencio-Weber, Daisy. "Changes in the Educa-tional Program in P.S. 8, Manhattan, Resulting from the Influx of Puerto Rican Children." Master's thesis, New York U., 1955.

Aspira. Aspira versus the Board of Education of the City of New York: A History. New York: Aspira of New York, 1977.

Aspira of America, Inc. Social Factors in Educational Attainment Among Puerto Ricans in U.S. Metropolitan Areas. New York: Aspira of America, Inc., 1976.

Attinasi, John J. "Language Policy and the Puerto Rican Community." Bilingual Review 5 (Ja-Ag, 1978):1-39.

Babin, Maria Teresa, and Steiner, Stan (eds.). Borinquen: An Anthology of Puerto Rican Literature. New York: Random House, 1975.

Badillo, Herman. "Bilingual Education." Integrateducation 13(My-Je, 1975):166-167.

Baglin, Roger F. "The Mainland Experience
in Selected Puerto Rican Literary Works."
Doctoral dissertation, State U. of New York
at Buffalo, 1971.

Bagu, Alma. "On the Rim of Belonging." Center
Forum, S, 1969. [Puerto Rican self-
identity]

"Baltimore Refuses Free Tuition [to Puerto
Rican Children]." New York Times, Ja 12,
1902.

Bangdiwala, Ishver S. The Effect of Socio-
Economic Levels on Selected Educational
Factors in Puerto Rico, Je, 1974. ERIC ED
097 262.

Barretto, Lefty. Nobody's Hero: A Puerto
Rican Story. New York: New American
Library, 1977.

Bary, Helen V. Child Welfare in the Insular
Possessions of the United States. Part I,
Porto Rico. Washington, DC: GPO, 1923.
[Children's Bureau Publication, No. 127]

Batllé, Ana and others. The Puerto Ricans:
A Resource Unit for Teachers. New York:
Anti-Defamation League of B'nai B'rith,
1973.

Bender, L., and Nichtern, S. "Two Puerto Rican
Boys in New York." In Clinical Studies in
Cultural Conflict. Edited by G. Seward.
New York: Ronald, 1958.

Benner, Thomas E. Five Years of Foundation
Building: The University of Puerto Rico,
1924-1929. Rio Piedras: U. of Puerto
Rico Press, 1965.

Bergad, Laird W. "Agrarian History of Puerto
Rico, 1870-1930." Latin American Research
Review 13(1978):63-94.

Berlant, Rose. "Como Has Pasado El Domingo?"
New York City Education, Winter, 1969.

Berle, Beatrice B. Eighty Puerto Rican
Families in New York City. New York:
Columbia U. Press, 1958.

Betances, Samuel. "The Prejudice of Having
No Prejudice in Puerto Rico," Part 1. The
Rican 1(Winter, 1972):41-54.

_____. "The Prejudice of Having No Prejudice
in Puerto Rico," Part II. The Rican 3
(Spring, 1973):22-37.

Bienstock, Herbert. Labor Force Experience of
the Puerto Rican Worker, My 20, 1968. U.S.
Bureau of Labor Statistics, 341 Ninth
Avenue, New York, NY.

Blair, William C. "Spanish-Speaking Minorities in a Utah Mining Town." Journal of
Social Issues 8(1952).

Blanco, T. Prejudicio racial en Puerto Rico.
San Juan, P.R.: Biblioteca de autores
puertoriquenos, 1942.

Blaut, James. "Are Puerto Ricans A National
Minority?" Monthly Review 29(My, 1977):
35-55.

_____. Imperialism and the Puerto Rican
Nation. New York: Federacíon Universitaria
Socialista Puertorríquena, 1977.

Boggs, Ralph S. "Common Difficulties for Porto
Ricans in American Pronunciation." Porto
Rico School Review 13(D, 1928:7, 45-46;
Ja-F, 1929, 18-19, 45-48, 22-25.

Bondarin, Arley. "Assimilation Thru Cultural
Understanding." Hoboken, New Jersey.
New York: Center for Urban Education, 1969.

Bondy, Filip. "Hispanics: Education's Their
Hope." Passaic Herald News, F 27, 1978.
[Articles on the Hispanic community in
Patterson, NJ]

Borrero, Michael. 210 Puerto Rican Families in
Dorchester: A Field Survey. Boston, MA:
Alianza Hispana, 1973.

Bouquet, Susana. "Acculturation of Puerto
Rican Children in New York and Their
Attitudes Toward Negroes and Whites."
Doctoral dissertation, Columbia U., 1961.
Univ. Microfilms Order No. 62-2037.

Bram, Joseph. The Lower Status Puerto Rican
Family. Revised. New York: Mobilization
for Youth, Inc., Mr, 1963, 14 pp. ERIC ED
016 690.

Brand, Horst. The New York Puerto Rican:
Patterns of Work Experience. Poverty Area
Profiles. Regional Reports: Bedford-
Stuyvesant; Central Harlem; East Harlem;
South Bronx. Number 19, My, 1971. ERIC ED
053 226.

_____. Poverty Area Profiles: The New York
Puerto Rican: Patterns of Work Experience.
New York: Middle Atlantic Office, U.S.
Bureau of Labor Statistics, 1971.

Brown, Warren. Manhattanville, A Progress
Report. New York: Department of Sociology
and Anthropology, City College of New York,
S, 1949.

Brumbaugh, M. G. "Problems in the Beginning of
American Government in Porto Rico." Porto
School Review 14(Ap, 1930):18-19, 48.

Brune, Tom, and Lanier, Alfredo S. "Aloof City,
Scared Private Investors and Divided Commun-
ity Watch As Housing Destruction Devastates
East Humboldt Park." Chicago Reporter 8(F,
1979). [Principal area of residence of
Puerto Ricans in Chicago]

Campos, Ricardo, and Bonilla, Frank. La econo-mía política de la relacion colonial: la experiencia puertorriquena. New York: Centro de Estudios Puertorriquenos, City U. of New York, 1977.

Campos, Ricardo, and Flores, Juan. National Culture and Migration: Perspectives from the Puerto Rican Working Class. New York: Centro de Estudios Puertorriquenos, 1978.

Cardenas, José A. "The Deprivation of Poverty." Integrated Education 9(My-Je, 1971):45-49.

Carnoy, Martin. Family Background, School Inputs and Students' Performance in School: The Case of Puerto Rico. Stanford, CA: Department of Education, Stanford U., 1971.

_____. "The Quality of Education, Examination Performance, and Urban Renewal Income Differentials in Puerto Rico." Comparative Education Review 14(0, 1970):335-349.

_____. "Rates of Return to Education and the Growth of Human Resources in Puerto Rico." Comparative Education Review, F, 1972.

Carrero, Milagros. Puerto Rico and the Puerto Ricans: A Teaching and Resource Unit for Upper Level Spanish Students or Social Studies Classes, 1973. ERIC ED 085 988.

Castro, Apolianario. "Higher Education in Puerto Rico, 1898-1956." Doctoral disserta-tion, Lehigh U., 1975. Univ. Microfilms Order No. 76-10,636.

Castro, Francisco. "The Politics of Local Educa-tion in New York City: A Puerto Rican View." Doctoral dissertation, Rutgers U., 1973.

Cebollero, Pedro A. Education in Porto Rico, 1920-1930. Washington, DC: GPO, 1930. [U.S. Office of Education. Education Leaflet, No. 4]

_____. Reactions of Puerto Rican Children in New York City to Psychological Tests. San Juan: The Puerto Rican School Review, 1936.

Centro de Estudios Puertorriquenos-CUNY. Centro Taller de Migracion. Conferencia de Historiografía: Abril, 1974. 1975. The Centro, 500 Fifth Avenue, New York, NY 10036. [Bilingual edition]

_____. Taller de cultura. Conferencia de Historiografía: Abril, 1974. 1976. Centro de Estudios Puertorriquenos-CUNY, 500 Fifth Avenue, New York, NY 10036.

Chertock, Sarah A. "A Descriptive Study of the Programs Undertaken by the Riverside Neigh-borhood Assembly to Further Democratic Inte-gration on the West Side of Manhattan." Doctoral dissertation, New York U., 1957.

Chenault, Lawrence R. The Puerto Rican Migrant in New York City. New York: Columbia U. Press, 1938.

Cintron De Crespo, Patria. "Puerto Rican Women Teachers in New York: Self Perception and Work Adjustment as Perceived by Themselves and Others." Doctoral dissertation, Columbia U., 1965.

Cintron Ortéz, Rafael. "A Colonial Experience: Schools in Puerto Rico as Agents of Domina-tion." Critical Anthropology 2(Spring, 1972): 104-112.

Clark, Truman R. "'Educating the Natives in Self-Government': Puerto Rico and the United States, 1900-1933." Pacific Historical Review, My, 1973.

Cohen, Raquel E. "Principles of Preventive Mental Health Programs for Ethnic Minority Population: The Acculturation of Puerto Ricans to the United States." American Journal of Psychiatry 128(Je, 1972):1529-1533.

Cohen, S. Alan. "Some Learning Disabilities of Socially Disadvantaged Puerto Rican and Negro Children." Academic Therapy Quarterly, Fall, 1966.

Coll, Cynthia Garcia and others. Differences in Brazelton Scale Performance Between Puerto Rican and North American White and Black Newborns, Mr, 1977. ERIC ED 140 984.

Coll y Cuehí, Cayetano. Historia de la Esclavi-tud en Puerto Rico. Edited by Isabel Cuehí Coll. San Juan, Puerto Rico: Publicacíon de la Sociedad de Autores Puertorriqueños, 1969.

Coll y Toste, Cayetano. Historia de la Instruccion Publica en Puerto Rico Hasta el Ano De 1898. 2nd ed. San Juan, Puerto Rico: 1970.

Collaza, Francisco. The Education of Puerto Rican Children in the Schools of New York City. San Juan: Department of Education, Commonwealth of Puerto Rico, 1954.

Colombán, Rosario, Carrión, José Y. El Negro. San Juan, Puerto Rico: Negociado de Mater-iales, Imprenta y Transporte, 1940.

Colón, Jesús. Puerto Ricans in New York. New York: International, 1970.

Commission on Civil Rights of Puerto Rico. La Iqualdad de Derechos y Oportunidades de la Mujer Puertorriquena. San Juan, Puerto Rico: The Commission, 1972.

Commonwealth of Puerto Rico, Planning Board. A Comparative Study of Labor Market Character-istics of Return Migrants and Non-Migrants in Puerto Rico. San Juan: Planning Board, Jl, 1973.

Comptroller General of the U.S. Problems Persist in the Puerto Rico Food Stamp Program, the Nation's Largest. Washington, DC: General Accounting Office, 1974.

Consejo Superior de Enseñanza. La Desercion Escolar en Puerto Rico. Rio Piedras, Puerto Rico: Universidad de Puerto Rico, 1964.

_____. Estudio del Sistema Educativo. 2 vols. Rio Piedras, Puerto Rico: Universidad de Puerto Rico, 1962.

Cooper, Paulette (ed). Growing Up Puerto Rican. New York: Arbor House, 1972.

Cordasco, F. "The Puerto Rican Child in the American School." Journal of Negro Education, Spring, 1967.

_____. "The Puerto Rican Child in the American School." Kansas Journal of Sociology, Spring, 1966.

_____. (ed.). New York City: A Compendium of Papers. New York: Arno Press, 1978.

Cordasco, Francesco, and Bucchioni, Eugene (eds). Puerto Rican Children in Mainland Schools. A Source Book for Teachers. Metuchen, NJ: Scarecrow Press, 1968.

Cordasco, Francesco (ed). The Puerto Rican Experience: A Sociological Sourcebook. Totowa, NJ: Rowman and Littlefield, 1973.

_____. "Puerto Rican Pupils and American Education." School and Society, F 18, 1967.

Cordasco, F., and Bucchioni, E. The Puerto Ricans, 1493-1973. Dobbs Ferry, NY: Oceana, 1973.

Cordasco, F., and Covello, Leonard (comps). Studies of Puerto Rican Children in American Schools: A Preliminary Bibliography, 1967. ERIC ED 021 910.

Cortes, Felix, Fancón, Angel, and Flores, Juan. "The Cultural Expression of Puerto Ricans in New York: A Theoretical Perspective and Critical Review." Latin American Perspectives 3(Summer, 1976):117-152.

Cremer, Henry. "Spanish and English in Porto Rico." School and Society 36(S 10, 1932):338.

Croce, ancy A. "A Theory of Differential Academic Performance Among Working Class Puerto Rican Youth." Doctoral dissertation, Fordham U., 1975. Univ. Microfilms Order No. 76-4112.

Cuesta Mendoza, Antonio. Historia de la Educación en el Puerto Rico Colonial. Vol. I: Mexico, E.F.: Sanchez, 1946. Vol. II: Ciudad Trujillo, Dominican Republic, Arte y Cine, 1948.

Curt, Carmen J. N. Non Verbal Communication in Puerto Rico, 1976. ERIC ED 159 251.

Darcy, Natalie T. "The Performance of Bilingual Puerto Rican Children on Verbal and Non-Language Tests of Intelligence." Journal of Educational Research, Mr, 1952.

Davenport, Rusty. "Toward Freedom. Puerto Rican Youth in Action." Ifco News 4(S-O, 1973).

Delgado, Melvin. "Social Work and the Puerto Rican Community." Social Casework 55(F, 1974):117-123.

Negron Montilla, Aida. Americanization in Puerto Rico: The School System. Rio Piedras, Puerto Rico: Editorial Edil, 1970.

Denis, Manuel Maldonado. Puerto Rico, Una Interpretacíon Histórico-Social, 1969. Editorial Edil, Inc., Apartado 23088, Universidad, Rio Piedras, Puerto Rico 00931.

Diaz, Eileen. "A Puerto Rican in New York." Dissent 8(Summer, 1961):383-385.

Diaz, Manuel, and Cintron, Roland. School Integration and Quality Education. NY: Puerto Rican Forum, 1964.

Diaz Soler, Luis M. La historia de la esclavitud negra en Puerto Rico. 2nd ed. Rio Piedras: U. of Puerto Rico Press, 1965.

_____. "Relaciones Raciales in Puerto Rico." Revista/Review Interamericana 3(1973).

Dodson, Dan W. Between Hell's Kitchen and San Juan Hill. New York: Center for Human Relations, New York U., 1952.

Donahue, Frances M. "A Study of the Original Puerto Rican Colony in Brooklyn, 1938-1943." Master's thesis, Fordham U. School of Social Work, 1945.

Drusine, Leon. "Some Factors in Anti-Negro Prejudice among Puerto Rican Boys in New York City." Doctoral dissertation, New York U., 1955. Univ. Microfilms Order No. 16588.

Dworkis, Martin B. (ed). The Impact of Puerto Rican Migration on Government Services in New York City. New York: New York U. Press, 1957.

Eagle, Morris. "The Puerto Ricans in New York City." In Housing and Minority Groups. Edited by N. Glazer and D. McEntire:144-177.

"Education of Puerto Rican Children in New York City." Journal of Educational Sociology, D, 1954.

Egerton, John. "Racism Differs in Puerto Rico." Race Relations Reporter 2(Jl 6, 1971):6-7.

Elam, Sophie L. "Acculturation and Learning
Problems of Puerto Rican Children." Teachers
College Record, F, 1960.

_____. "Poverty and Acculturation in a Migrant
Puerto Rican Family." Teachers College Record, Ap, 1969.

Epstein, Erwin H. "Linguistic Orientation and
Changing Values in Puerto Rico." International Journal of Comparative Sociology 9
(1968):61-76.

_____. "National Identity and the Language
Issue in Puerto Rico." Comparative Education Review, Je, 1967.

_____. "A Truce Between Two Cultures: Educa-
tional Transfer in the Americas." In
Schools in Transition. Edited by Andreas
Kazamias and Erwin Epstein. Boston, MA:
Allyn and Bacon, 1968.

Estades, Rosa. Patterns of Political Partici-
pation of Puerto Ricans in New York City.
Rio Piedras: Editorial Universitaria,
Universidad de Puerto Rico, 1977.

_____. "Patterns of Political Participation
of Puerto Ricans in New York City." Doctoral dissertation, New School for Social
Research, 1974. Univ. Microfilms Order No.
74-26,961.

Eszterhas, Joseph. "The City's Forgotten
Minority." Cleveland Plain Dealer, Ap 25-30,
1971

Falcon, A. A Study of Educational Opportunities
for the Spanish Speaking in Hartford. Hartford, CT: La Casa de Puerto Rico, 1974.

Farkas, George. The Demography of Urban Poverty:
North and Latin America, Jl, 1973. ERIC
ED 102 247.

Feeley, Joan T. "Bilingual Instruction: Puerto
Rico and the Mainland." Reading Teacher 30
(Ap, 1977):741-744.

Fennessey, James. An Exploratory Study of
Non-English Speaking Homes and Academic
Performance. Baltimore, MD: Center for So-
cial Organization of Schools, Johns Hopkins
U., My, 1967. [Puerto Ricans in N.Y.C.]

_____. An Exploratory Study of Non-English
Speaking Homes and Academic Performance, My,
1967. ERIC ED 011 613.

Fernández de Cintrón, Celia, and Rivera Quintero,
Marcia. "Bases de la Sociedad Sexista en
Puerto Rico." Revista/Review Interamericana
4(Summer, 1974):239-245.

Fernández de Cintrón, Celia, and Vales, Pedro A.
Social Dynamics of Return Migration to Puerto
Rico, 1975. ERIC ED 126 192.

Fernández Mendez, Eugenio. Historia Cultural
de Puerto Rico, 1493-1968. San Juan, Puerto
Rico: Ediciones 'El Cenie," 1970.

_____. La Identidad y la Cultura. 2nd ed.
San Juan, Puerto Rico: Instituto de Cultura
Puertorriquenos, 1965.

Ferracuti, Franco and others. Délinquents and
Nondelinquents in the Puerto Rican Slum
Culture. Columbus: Ohio State U. Press,
1975.

Figueroa, Loida. Breve Historia de Puerto Rico.
2 vols. 1969. Editorial Edil, Inc., Apartado 23088 Universidad, Río Piedras, Puerto
Rico 00931.

Finocchiaro, Mary. Education of Puerto Ricans
on the Mainland: Overcoming the Communication Barrier, O 21, 1970. ERIC ED 043 871.

_____. "Puerto Rican Newcomers in Our Schools."
American Unity 14(Ja-F, 1956):12-17.

_____. Teaching English as a Second Language.
New York: n.p, 1958.

Fisher, John C. "Bilingualism in Puerto Rico:
A History of Frustration." English Record
21(Ap, 1971):19-24.

Fishman, Joshua A. "Attitudes and Beliefs
About Spanish and English Among Puerto Ricans."
Viewpoints 47(Mr, 1971):51-72.

_____. "Puerto Rican Intellectuals in New
York: Some Intragroup and Intergroup Con-
trasts." Canadian Journal of Behavioural
Science 1(1969):215-226.

Fishman, Joshua A. and others. Bilingualism in
the Barrio. Final Report. New York: Yeshiva
U., Ag, 1968. ERIC ED 026 546.

Fishman, Joshua A., Cooper, Robert L., and Ma,
Roxana. Bilingualism in the Barrio. Bloom-
ington, IN: Indiana U. Press, 1971. [Puerto
Ricans in a NJ community]

Fitzpatrick, Joseph P. "The Integration of
Puerto Ricans." Thought, Autumn, 1955.

_____. Puerto Rican Americans: The Meaning
of Migration to the Mainland. Englewood
Cliffs, NJ: Prentice-Hall, 1971.

Fonfrias, Ernesto Juan. "Las vicisitudes del
espanol de Puerto Rico." Yelmo 14(O-N, 1973):
44-49.

Ford Foundation. Ford Foundation Assistance to
Puerto Ricans. New York: The Foundation, 1975.

Freiberg, Peter. "South Brooklyn Battling City
Hall." Race Relations Reporter 5(Je 17, 1974):
5-6.

"From Puerto Rico to Pennsylvania--Culture Shock in the Classroom." Pennsylvania Education 2(My-Je, 1971):22-29. [Philadelphia]

Galindez, Jesús de. Puerto Rico en Nueva York. Mexico: Cuadernos Americanos, 1952.

Gallardo, Jose M. (ed). Proceedings of Conference on Education of Puerto Rican Children on the Mainland. San Juan, Puerto Rico: Department of Education, 1972.

Gallegos, Mario. "Changes in Self-Concept of Puerto Ricans Upon Migration Into the Springfield, Holyoke, Amherst, Northampton Area." Master's thesis, Springfield College, MA, 1972.

Galli, Nicholas. "The Influence of Cultural Heritage on the Health Status of Puerto Ricans." Journal of School Health 45(Ja, 1975):10-16.

Garza, Catarino (ed). Puerto Ricans in the U.S. The Struggle for Freedom. New York: Pathfinder Press, 1977.

Gavillan-Torres, Eva M. "The Forgotten Rican: The Puerto Rican Community on the Mainland." Harvard Graduate School of Education Association Bulletin 20(Spring-Summer, 1976):10-12.

Glazer, Nathan. "Puerto Rican Migration--Right Place, Wrong Time?" America 125(O 30, 1971):339-341.

Goldberg, Gertrude S., and Gordon, Edmund W. "La Vida: Whose Life?" IRCD Bulletin, 1968.

Golding, Morton J. A Short History of Puerto Rico. New York: New Amsterdam Library, 1973.

Gómez Tejera, Carmen, and López, David Cruz. La Escuela Puertorriqueña. Sharon, CT: Troutman Press, 1970.

Gonzalez, Agustin. Problems of Adjustment of Puerto Rican Boys. New York: New York School of Social Work, 1956.

Gonzalez, Juan. "Young Lords Party." Hawaii Pono Journal 1(Ap, 1971):31-57.

Gordon, Maxine W. "Race Patterns and Prejudice in Puerto Rico." American Sociological Review, Ap, 1949.

Gosnell, Patria Aran. "The Puerto Ricans in New York City." Doctoral dissertation, New York U., 1945.

Gotsch, John W. "Puerto Rican Leadership in New York." Master's thesis, New York U., 1966.

Granda, Germán de. Transculturación e interfere linguistica en el Puerto Rico contemporáneo 1898/1968. 2nd ed. Rio Piedras, Puerto Rico: Editorial Edil, 1972.

Gray, Lois S. A Socio-Economic Profile of Puerto Rican New Yorkers. New York: Middle Atlantic Regional Office, U.S. Bureau of Labor Statistics, J1, 1975.

_____. "The Jobs Puerto Ricans Hold in New York City." Monthly Labor Review, O, 1975: 12-16.

Greene, John F., and Zirkel, Perry A. "Academic Factors Relating to the Self-Concept of Puerto Rican Pupils." Catalog of Selected Documents in Psychology 1(Fall, 1971):20-21.

_____. Academic Factors Relating to the Self-Concept of Puerto Rican Pupils, S, 1971. ERIC ED 054 284.

Greenspan, Richard. Analysis of Puerto Rican and Black Employment in New York City Schools. New York: Puerto Rican Forum, My, 1970.

_____. Puerto Ricans on Long Island. New York: Aspira of New York, N, 1971.

Greenstein, Raymond, and Tirado, Moises. Operation P.R.I.M.A.-RECLAIM, 1966. ERIC ED 010 775. [Recruitment of teachers of Puerto Rican extraction]

Gruber, Ruth. "There Are Few Independentistas in Puerto Rico, But--." New York Times Magazine, My 21, 1972.

Guerra, Emilio L. "The Orientation of Puerto Rican Students in New York City." Modern Language Journal, O, 1948.

Guzman, Pablo, and Benitez, Iris. "Tengo Puerto Rico en Mi Corazon. YLO." The Movement, F-Mr, 1970. [Young Lords Organization, NYC]

Hammill, Peter. "El Barrio: The World of Spanish Harlem." New York Post, Je 11-17, 1962.

Hardman, Robert. "Puerto Rican Community--Don't Generalize About It." Springfield Daily News, S 26, 27, 1975 (Two articles). [Puerto Ricans in Springfield, MO]

Hauberg, Clifford A. Puerto Rico and the Puerto Ricans. New York: Hippocrene Books, 1975.

"Hemos Trabajado Bien;" A Report on the First National Conference of Puerto Ricans, Mexican-Americans, and Educators on "The Special Educational Needs of Urban Puerto Rican Youth. (New York City, My 14-15, 1968). New York: Aspira, Inc., 1968. ERIC ED 023 780.

Hendricks, Glen L. La Raza en Nueva York: Social Pluralism and Schools, Ap, 1971. ERIC ED 051 329.

Herbstein, Judith F. "Rituals and Politics of the Puerto Rican 'Community' in New York City." Doctoral dissertation, City U. of New York, 1978. Univ. Microfilms Order No. 780 8682.

Hernandez, Joseph W. "The Sociological Implications of Return Migration in Puerto Rico." Doctoral dissertation, U. of Minnesota, 1964.

Hernández Alvarez, José. "The Movement and Settlement of Puerto Rican Migrants Within the United States." International Migration Review 2(1968):40-52.

Hernández Cruz, Víctor. "Interview" (by Víctor Rosa). Bilingual Review 2(S-D, 1975): 281-287.

Hertzig, Margaret E., and Birch, Herbert E. "Longitudinal Course of Measured Intelligence in Preschool Children of Different Social and Ethnic Backgrounds." American Journal of Orthopsychiatry 41(Ap, 1971):416-426.

Hester, Paul H. "The Educational Benefits of Four Puerto Rican Communities as Indicators of Political Interaction: A Comparative Study." Doctoral dissertation, U. of Connecticut, 1976.

Hidalgo, H. H. The Puerto Ricans in Newark, N.J. Newark, NJ: Aspira, 1970.

Hiller, R. J., and Teitelbaum, Herbert. "A Court-Ordered Bilingual Program in Perspective: Aspira of New York vs. the Board of Education of the City of New York." NABE (Journal of the National Association of Bilingual Educators) 1(D, 1976).

History Task Force, Centro de Estudios Puertorriqueños. Labor Migration Under Capitalism: The Puerto Rican Experience. New York: Monthly Review Press, 1978.

Hoffman, Gerard, and Fishman, Joshua A. "Life in the Neighborhood. A Factor Analytic Study of Puerto Rican Males in the New York City Area." International Journal of Comparative Sociology 12(1971):85-100.

Holbik, Karel, and Holbik, Philip L. Industrialization and Employment in Puerto Rico, 1950-1972. Austin: Bureau of Business Research, U. of Texas, 1975.

Hollister, Frederick. "Skin Color and Life Chances of Puerto Ricans." Caribbean Studies 9(O, 1969).

Hornik, Michael Sam. "Nationalist Sentiment in Puerto Rico from the American Invasion until the Foundation of the Partido Nacionalista, 1898-1922." Doctoral dissertation, State U. of New York at Buffalo, 1972. Univ. Microfilms Order No. 73-05122.

Illich, Ivan. "Commencement at the University of Puerto Rico." New York Review, O 9, 1969.

Inniss, James. "Counseling the Culturally Disrupted Child." Elementary School Guidance and Counseling 11(F, 1977):229-235. [Puerto Rican children]

Institute of Puerto Rican Studies. A New Look at the Puerto Ricans and Their Society. New York: Brooklyn College, 1971.

Insurralde, Adolfo. Socio-Economic Factors Affecting Families in the Forsyth Area. NY: Lower Eastside Neighborhoods Association, 1964. [Puerto Rican life in New York City]

"An Interview with Hernan La Fontaine." Rican 1(My, 1974):37-43. [On bilingual education]

"An Interview with Joseph Monserrat." Rican 3 (1973):38-47.

Jacobson, Barbara, and Kendrick, John M. "Education and Mobility: From Achievement to Ascription." American Sociological Review 38(Ag, 1973):439-460. [Puerto Rico]

Jaffe, Abram J. (ed). Puerto Rican Population of New York City. New York: Arno Press, 1975 (reprint).

Jaffe, A. J., and Carleton, Zaida Carreras. Some Demographic and Economic Characteristics of the Puerto Rican Population Living on the Mainland, U.S.A. New York: Bureau of Applied Social Research, Columbia U., 1975.

Jaffe, A. J., and Cullen, Ruth M. "Fertility of the Puerto Rican Origin Population--Mainland United States and Puerto Rico: 1970." International Migration Review 9(Summer, 1975): 193-209.

Jenkins, Shirley. "Intergroup Empathy: An Exploratory Study of Negro and Puerto Rican Groups in New York City." Doctoral dissertation, New York U., 1957. Univ. Microfilms Order No. 58-633.

Jennings, James. Puerto Rican Politics in New York City. Washington, DC: University Press of America, 1977.

Johnson, Frederick. The Tumbleweeds. New York: Harper and Row, 1977. [N.Y.C.]

Jimenez, Cha Cha. "Interview with Cha Cha Jimenez, Chairman, Young Lords Organization." Black Panther, Je 7, 1969. [Chicago]

_____. "'We're Fighting for Freedom Together ... There is No Other Way" (interview). The Movement, Jl, 1969.

Jones, Janet. "You Can't Stop Us." The Movement, Je, 1969. [The Young Lords Organization, a Latin American youth group in Chicago]

Kahnheimer, Leak W. "A Program in Social Living for Puerto Rican Pupils." High Points, Je, 1954.

Kantrowitz, Nathan. "Social Mobility of Puerto Ricans: Education, Occupation, and Income Changes among Children of Migrants, New York, 1950-1960." International Migration Review 2(Spring, 1968):53-72.

Kaska, Charles. "Puerto Rican Children in Mainland Schools: Implications for the School Psychologist." Master's thesis, Newark State College, 1972.

Kelley, Dean M. "The Young Lords and the Spanish Congregation." Christian Century, F 18, 1970. [New York City]

King, Lourdes Miranda. "Puertorriquenas in the United States. The Impact of Double Discrimination." Civil Rights Digest 6 (Spring, 1974):20-27.

Koss, Joan D. "Puerto Ricans in Philadelphia: Migration and Accommodative Processes." Doctoral dissertation, U. of Pennsylvania, 1965.

Layden, Russell G. "The Relationship Between the Language of Instruction and the Development of Self-Concept, Classroom Climate and Achievement of Spanish Speaking Puerto Rican Children." Doctoral dissertation, U. of Maryland, 1972.

Leavitt, Ruby Rohrlich. The Puerto Ricans: Culture Change and Language Deviance. Tucson, AR: U. of Arizona Press, 1974.

Leibowitz, Arnold H. "The Imposition of English as the Language of Instruction in American Schools." Revista de Derecho Puertorriqueno (O-D, 1970):175-244.

Lennon, John J. A Comparative Study of the Patterns of Acculturation of Selected Puerto Rican Protestant and Roman Catholic Families in an Urban Metropolitan Area. U. of Notre Dame, 1963. [Chicago]

Lewis, Claudia. "Some Puerto Rican Viewpoints." Childhood Education, 0, 1966.

Lewis, Gordon K. Notes on the Puerto Rican Revolution. An Essay on American Dominance and Caribbean Resistance. New York: Monthly Review Press, 1975.

Lewis, Oscar. "The Culture of Poverty in Puerto Rico and New York." Social Security Bulletin, S, 1967.

_____. La Vida: A Puerto Rican Family in the Culture of Poverty, San Juan and New York. New York: Random House, 1966.

Liebman, Arthur. The Politics of Puerto Rican University Students. Austin, TX: U. of Texas Press, 1970.

_____. "The Student Left in Puerto Rico." Journal of Social Issues 27(1971):167-181.

Lindsay, Samuel McCune. Inauguration of the American School System in Porto Rico. In U.S. Bureau of Education. Report of the Commissioner, 1905, Chapter XV, pp 293-344. Washington, DC: GPO, 1907.

Llorens, Washington. "Influencia Taina en el Espanol de Puerto Rico." Yelmo 27(Ja-Mr, 1976):44-45.

Lockett, Edward B. The Puerto Rican Problem. New York: Exposition, 1964.

Longres, John F., Jr. "Racism and Its Effects on Puerto Rican Continentals." Social Casework 55(F, 1974):67-75.

López, A. Andion. "The Story of Six Years' Progress in Education in Porto Rico, 1921-1927." Porto Rico School Review 12(My, 1928).

López, Adolberto. "Puerto Ricans and the Literature of Puerto Rico." Journal of Ethnic Studies 1(Summer, 1973):56-65.

López, Adolberto, and Petras, James (eds). Puerto Rico and Puerto Ricans: Studies in History and Society. New York: Halstead Press, 1974.

López, Alfredo. The Puerto Rican Papers: Notes on the Re-Emergence of a Nation. Indianapolis, IN: Bobbs-Merrill, 1973.

López, R. Alfonso. "The Principle of Separation of Church and State as Observed by the Public Schools of Puerto Rico from 1898 to 1952." Doctoral dissertation, New York U., 1971.

López Yustos, A. (comp.) "Educational Research in Puerto Rico." Revista/Review Interamericana 2(1972).

_____. "Racial Self-Perception of the Black Teacher in the Public Schools of Puerto Rico." Revista/Review Interamericana 3(1973).

Lucas, Isidro. Puerto Rican Dropouts in Chicago: Numbers and Motivations, Mr, 1971. Council on Urban Education, 211 West Wacker Drive, Chicago, IL 60606.

_____. "Puertorriqueños En Chicago: El Problema Educativo Del Dropout." Rican 1 (My, 1974):5-18.

Macisco, John J., Jr. "Assimilation of Puerto Ricans on the Mainland: A Socio-Demographic Approach." International Migration Review 2 (Spring, 1968):21-39.

Macisco, John J., Jr., Bouvier, L. F., and Renzi, M. J. "Migration Status, Education and Fertility in Puerto Rico, 1960." Milbank Memorial Fund Quarterly 47(1969):167-187.

Madeira, Eugene L. The Puerto Rican Involvement in Educational Opportunity Fund Programs for the Disadvantaged, 1970. ERIC ED 056 147. [Puerto Ricans in Camden, NJ]

Maldonado, R. M. "Education, Income Distribution and Economic Growth in Puerto Rico." Review of Social Economy 34(Ap, 1976).

_____. "Why Puerto Ricans Migrated to the United States in 1947-1973." Monthly Labor Review 99(S, 1976):7-18.

Maldonado Denis, Manuel. "El problema de la asimilación cultural." Revista del Centro de Investigaciones Sociales y Culturales, State University of New York at Albany 1 (Ap, 1976).

_____. "The Political Situation in Puerto Rico." Massachusetts Review 15(Winter-Spring, 1974):221-233.

_____. "The Puerto Ricans: Protest or Submission." Annals, Mr, 1969.

_____. Puerto Rico: A Socio-Historic Interpretation. Tr. Elena Vialo. New York: Random House, 1972.

_____. "Toward a Marxist Interpretation of the History of Puerto Rico." Rican 2(0, 1974): 32-53.

Maldonado Guzman, Abdil Abel. "Negative Bias and Image-Making in Puerto Rican School Materials on the Geography of 'The Island.'" Master's thesis, U. of Chicago, 1973.

Margolis, Richard J. The Losers: A Report on Puerto Ricans and the Public Schools. New York: Aspira, Inc., My, 1968. ERIC ED 023 779.

Marie, Sister Thomas. Understanding the Puerto Rican and His Family, n.d. ERIC ED 011 264.

Marmorale, Ann M., and Brown, Fred. "Comparison of Bender-Gestalt and WISC Correlations for Puerto Rican, White and Negro Children." Journal of Clinical Psychology 31(Jl, 1975): 465-468.

Marques, Rene. The Docile Puerto Rican. Tr. Barbara B. Aponte. Philadelphia: Temple U. Press, 1976.

Martinez, Oscar J. "Chicanos and the Border Cities: An Interpretive Essay." Pacific Historical Review 46(F, 1977):85-106.

Massachusetts State Advisory Committee to the U.S. Commission on Civil Rights. Issues of Concern to Puerto Ricans in Boston and Springfield. Washington, DC: U.S. Commission on Civil Rights, F, 1972.

Massimine, E. Virginia. The Challenge of Changing Community. New York: Center for Human Relations, New York U., 1964. [Puerto Ricans on the West Side of Manhattan]

Mathews, Thomas G. "The Question of Color in Puerto Rico." In Slavery and Race Relations in Latin America. Edited by Robert B. Toplin. Westport, CT: Greenwood Press, 1974.

Matilla, Alfredo. "Poesia Puertorriqueña en Nueva York." Revista del Instituto de Estudios Puertorriqueños 1(1971).

Mayerson, Charlotte L. (ed). Two Blocks Apart. New York: Holt, Rinehart & Winston, 1965. [Juan Gonzalez and Peter Quinn in N.Y.C.]

Mayor's Advisory Committee on Puerto Rican Affairs in New York City, Subcommittee on Education, Recreation, and Parks. The Puerto Rican Pupils in the Public Schools of New York City: A Survey of Elementary and Junior High Schools. New York, 1951.

Megenney, William W. "The Black Puerto Rican: An Analysis of Racial Attitudes." Phylon 35 (Mr, 1974):83-93.

Mencher, Joan P. "Child Rearing and Family Organization Among Puerto Ricans in Eastville, El Barrio de Nueva York." Doctoral dissertation, Columbia U., 1958.

Méndez Santos, Carlos. Los Immigrantes Puertorriqueños en Los Estados Unidos. San Juan, Puerto Rico: Sociedad de Autores Puertorriqueños.

Mendoza, Antonio C. "Historia de la educación en Puerto Rico (1512-1826)." Doctoral dissertation, Catholic U., 1937.

Mercer, Jane R. Implications of Current Assessment Procedures for Mexican-American Children, Ag, 1977. ERIC ED 151 124.

Messer, Helaine. "The Puerto Rican Student in the New York City Public Schools, 1945-1965." Master's thesis, Columbia U., 1966.

Migration Division, Department of Labor. Puerto Ricans and Other Hispanics in New York City's Public Schools and Universities. New York: Commonwealth of Puerto Rico, D, 1975.

Milán, William G., and Muñoz-Hernandez, Shirley. "The New York City Aspira Consent Decree: A Mechanism for Social Change." Bilingual Review 4(S-D, 1977):169-179.

Mizio, Emelicia. "Impact of External Systems on the Puerto Rican Family." Social Casework 55 (F, 1974):76-83.

_____. Puerto Rican Task Force Report: Project on Ethnicity. New York: Family Service Association of America, 1978. [Mental health services]

Mohr, Nicholasa. El Bronx Remembered: A Novella and Stores. New York: Harper & Row, 1975. [Fiction]

Monserrat, Joseph. "Education of Puerto Rican Children in New York City." Journal of Educational Sociology, D, 1954.

_____. "La Emigracion, Realidad y Problema en la Ciudad de Nueva York." La Torre (Universidad de Puerto Rico), Mr, 1956.

_____. "School Integration: A Puerto Rican View." Integrated Education, O-N, 1963.

Montalvo, Braulio. "Home-School Conflict and the Puerto Rican Child." Social Casework 55(F, 1974):100-110.

Monteiro, Thomas Lee. "Identifying Sources of School-Community Conflict in Black and Puerto Rican Communities in New York City." Doctoral dissertation, 1975. Univ. Microfilms Order No. 75-18,918.

Morales Cabrera, Pablo. Puerto Rico Indigena.. Santurce, Puerto Rico: Imprenta Venezuela, 1932.

Moran, Robert E. Observations and Recommendations on the Puerto Rican Version of the Wechsler Intelligence Scale for Children, F, 1974. ERIC ED 088 932.

Moreau, John Adam. "The Puerto Ricans: Who Are They?" Chicago Sun-Times, S 21, 1969. [Chicago]

Morrison, J. Cayce. The Puerto Rican Study, 1953-1957: A Report on the Education and Adjustment of Puerto Rican Pupils in the Public Schools of the City of New York. New York: Board of Education, 1958.

Morse, Dean. Pride Against Prejudice: Work in the Lives of Older Black and Young Puerto Rican Workers, 1976. ERIC ED 137 619. [New York City and Newark, NJ]

Munoz Marin, Luis. "The Sad Case of Porto Rico." American Mercury 16(F, 1929):136-141.

Nassau County Hispanic Foundation. Hispanic Youth Study. Hempstead, NY: The Foundation, 1977. [Long Beach, NY]

Navarro Hernández, Pablo. "The Structure of Puerto Rican Families in a Context of Migration and Poverty: An Ethnographic Description of a Number of Residents in El Barrio, New York City." Doctoral dissertation, Columbia U., 1978. Univ. Microfilms Order No. 7821825.

New York City. Board of Education. The Puerto Rican Study. Who Are the Puerto Rican Children in the New York City Public Schools? New York: Board of Education, 1956.

New York City Public Schools. Meeting the Needs of Puerto Rican Pupils in NYC Public Schools. Supplement to Staff Bulletin, Mr 23, 1964.

New York Public Library. "Puerto Rico." Branch Library of Book News. New York Public Library, Fifth and 42nd St., New York, NY 10018. [Books by and about Puerto Ricans]

Nieves, Sarah. "A Sociolinguistic Critique of Bilingual Education Curricula and the Bilingual Education Act in Terms of Adequacy for the Puerto Rican Collectivity." Doctoral dissertation, 1975. Univ. Microfilms Order No. 75-18,690.

Nieves Falcon, Luis. Acción comunal y educación pre-escolar en zonas marginales. Río Piedras: Acción Social, 1970.

_____. Diagnostico de Puerto Rico. Rio Piedras, Puerto Rico: Editorial Edil, 1971.

_____. "The Function of Racism in Puerto Rican Textbooks." Interracial Books for Children Bulletin 10, Nos. 1-2(1979):19-20.

_____. La Pobreza en Puerto Rico: Denitología de la Vitrina. San Juan, Puerto Rico: Centro de Investigaciones Sociales, Universidad de Puerto Rico, 1970.

_____. "Puerto Rico: los actitudes de los maestros de escuelas públicas hacia los Estados Unidos y los norteamericanos." Revista Mexicana de Sociologia 32(1970).

_____. Recruitment to Higher Education in Puerto Rico, 1940-1960. Rio Piedras: Editorial Universitaria, 1965.

Nieves Falcon, Luis, and Clintrón de Crespo, Patria. The Teaching Profession in Puerto Rico. Mayaguez, Puerto Rico: Social Science Research Center, U. of Puerto Rico, 1970.

Nistal-Moret, Benjamin. "El Pueblo de Neuestra Señora de la Candelaria y del Apostol San Matías 1800-1880, Its Ruling Classes and the Institution of Black Slavery." Doctoral dissertation, State U. of New York at Stony Brook, 1977. Univ. Microfilms Order No. 780 3168.

North, Robert D., and Santiago, Ramón L. Evaluation Report. Recruitment and Training of Spanish Speaking Teachers. New York: The Psychological Corporation, D, 1969. [N.Y.C.]

Novak, R. T. "Distribution of Puerto Ricans on Manhattan Island." Geographical Review 46 (1956):182-196.

Nuñez, Louis, and Bahn, Charles. National Conference: Meeting the Special Educational Needs of Urban Puerto Rican Youth. Final Report. New York: Aspira, Inc., S 30, 1968. ERIC ED 023 778.

Nuttall, Ronald L. Do the Factors Affecting
Academic Achievement Differ by the Socio-
Economic Status or Sex of the Student? A
Puerto Rican Secondary School Sample. Final
Report. Chestnut Hill, MA: Boston College,
Institute of Human Sciences, Je, 1972. ERIC
ED 064 465.

O'Brien, Mary G. "Relationship of Self-Percep-
tions of Puerto Rican and Non-Puerto Rican
Parochial School Children to Selected School
Related Variables." Dissertation Abstracts
International 31(7A)Ja, 1971,3347-8.

O'Brien, R. W. "Hawaii's Puerto Ricans: Stereotype and Reality." Social Process in
Hawaii 23(1959).

O'Connor, Mary. Equal Educational Opportunity
for Puerto Ricans, 1976. ERIC ED 131 147.

"110 Grub Street. Spanish-speakers on the
Educational Dole." Center Forum, S, 1969.
[N.Y.C.]

Osuna, Juan Jose. A History of Education in
Puerto Rico, 2nd ed. Rio Piedras, 1949.

Otero, Ray. "Puerto Rican Migrants [to Cali-
fornia]: The Invisible Minority." Los
Angeles Times, Jl 1, 1974.

Palomares, Uvaldo, and Negron, Frank. "Aspira
Today, Accountability Tomorrow. An Inter-
view." Personnel and Guidance Journal 50
(O, 1971):109-116.

Papers on Puerto Rican Studies. Rio Piedras,
Puerto Rico: Puerto Rican Junior College
Foundation and National Endowment for the
Humanities, N, 1970.

Parrilla, Aida I. "A Study of the Puerto Rican
Child in the New York City Public Schools."
Master's thesis, Bank Street College of
Education, 1976.

Pennsylvania State Advisory Committee to the
U.S. Commission on Civil Rights. In Search
of a Better Life. The Education and Housing
Problems of Puerto Ricans in Philadelphia.
Washington, DC: U.S. Commission on Civil
Rights, Ja, 1974.

Perales, Cesar. "Puerto Rican Problems in
Integration." Integrateducation 13(My-Je,
1975):8-10.

de Piñero, Europa G. "Problems and Issues of
Public Education in Puerto Rico Today: A
Challenge." Revista/Review Interamericana
2(1972).

Poblete, Renato, and O'Der, Thomas F. "Anomie
and the 'Quest for Community' Among the
Puerto Ricans of New York." American Catholic Sociological Review, Spring, 1960.

Poplack, Shana. "On Dialect Acquisition and
Communicative Competence: The Case of
Puerto Rican Bilinguals." Language in
Society 7(1978):89-103.

Popper, Dorothy Karpel. "The Relationship of
Self-Concept to Congruence Among Self, Ideal
Self, and Occupational Self in Sixth-Grade
Puerto Rican Girls in an Inner-City Poverty
Area." Doctoral dissertation, Fordham U.,
1975. Univ. Microfilms Order No. 75-18,922.

Preble, Edward. "The Puerto Rican American
Teen-ager in New York City." In Minority
Group Adolescents in the United States.
Edited by Eugene B. Brody. Baltimore, MD:
Williams and Wilkins, 1978.

Pride, Dolores. "El mensaje es el masoje:
Los medios de comunicación en español de
Neueva York." Joven Cuba (N.Y.) 3(Ja, 1975):
9-11

The Psychological Corporation. Evaluation
Report for Program for Pupils in Non-Public
Schools Learning English as a Second Language. New York: The Psychological Corporation, N, 1968. [N.Y.C.]

Puerto Rican Culture as It Affects Puerto Rican
Children in Chicago Classrooms. Chicago, IL:
Chicago Board of Education, 1970. ERIC ED
052 277.

Puerto Rican Community Conference. Puerto
Ricans Confront Problems of the Complex Urban
Society. New York: Office of the Mayor, 1967.

Puerto Rican Educators Association Study. "New
Study Confirms Educational Slaughter of
Puerto Rican Children." Interracial Books
for Children 4(Spring, 1972):11,16. [N.Y.C.]

"The Puerto Rican Experience." NJEA Review 47
(My, 1974):26-29.

The Puerto Rican Experience: An Educational
Research Study, 1974. Puerto Rican Congress
of New Jersey, 222 West State Street,
Trenton, NJ 08608.

Puerto Rican Human Resources Foundation. Report
of a Survey of the Puerto Rican Population
Residing in Several Poverty Areas of New
Haven, Connecticut. New Haven, CT: The
Foundation, 1971.

Puerto Rican Migrants: A Socio-Economic Study.
San Juan: Commonwealth of Puerto Rico Planning Board, 1972.

"Puerto Ricans and Inter-American Understanding."
Journal of Educational Sociology, My, 1962.

Puerto Rican Studies: Related Learning Materials
and Activities in Social Studies for Kindergarten, Grade 1 and Grade 2, 1973. ERIC ED
093 729.

Puerto Rico: A People Challenging Colonialism. Philadelphia: American Friends Service Committee, 1977.

"Puerto Rico: Class struggle and National Liberation." Latin American Perspectives 3 (Summer, 1976):entire issue.

Puerto Rico Department of Education. The Joint University of Puerto Rico and Department of Education Project in Teacher Education and Curriculum Development. Six volumes. San Juan, Puerto Rico: Department of Education, 1969.

_____. Lecturas Basicas Sobre Historia de Puerto Rico; Escuela Superior. San Juan, Puerto Rico: The Department, 1970.

"Puerto Rico: The Next Vietnam?" Race Today, Ja, 1975.

Puerto Rico: Showcase of Oppression. Latin American Publications Service, Box 12056 Mid City Station, Washington, DC 20005. Price for six pamphlets: $2.50.

Puerto Rico: Tragedy in the Schools. Washington, DC: National Education Association, 1969.

Quintero Rivera, A. G. "La clase obrera y el proceso politico en Puerto Rico." R. Cienc. soc. 18(Mr-Je and S-D, 1974):147-198 and 61-167.

Raisner, Arnold D., Bolger, Philip A., and Sanguinetti, Carmen. Science Instruction in Spanish for Pupils of Spanish-Speaking Background. An Experiment in Bilingualism. New York: Board of Education, Je, 1967.

Ramírez, Rafael L. "National Culture in Puerto Rico." Latin American Perspectives 3(Summer, 1976):109-116.

Ramírez, Rafael L., Levine, Barry B., and Ortiz, Carlos Biutrago. Problems of Social Inequality in Puerto Rico. Rio Piedras, Puerto Rico: Ediciones Librería Internacional, 1972.

Ramirez-Barbot, Jaime. "A History of Puerto Rican Radical Nationalism, 1920-1965." Doctoral dissertation, Ohio State U., 1973. Univ. Microfilms Order No. 73-26,892.

Recio, Juan-Luis. "Family as a Unit and Larger Society: Adaptation of Puerto Rican Migrant Families to a Mainland Suburban Setting." Doctoral dissertation, City U. of New York, 1975.

Reid, Charles F. "Education in Puerto Rico." Education in the Territories and Outlying Possessions of the United States. New York: Teachers College, Columbia U., 1941.

Rendon, Armando. "El Puertorriqueno: No More, No Less." Civil Rights Digest, Fall, 1968.

Rendon, Mario. "Transcultural Aspects of Puerto Rican Mental Illness in New York." International Journal of Social Psychiatry 20(Spring-Summer, 1974):18-24.

Report of Workshops of the Fourth Annual Conference on Puerto Rican Education Held at Hunter College of the City University, May 18, 1964. New York: National Conference of Christians and Jews, 43 West 57th Street, New York, NY 10019.

"Reshaping Public Education: For Spanish-Speaking Children." United Teacher, May 29, 1968. [Puerto-Rican children in New York City]

Ribes Tovar, Federico. Handbook of the Puerto Rican Community. New York: El Libro Puertorriqueno Nueva York, 1968.

Ríos de Betancourt, Ethel. "The University of Puerto Rico in the Last Three Decades: An Institution of Hope, Success, and Strife." In Überlieferung und Auftrag, Festschrift für Michael de Ferdinandy. Edited by Josef Gerhard Farkas. Wiesbaden, Federal Republic of Germany: Guido Pressler, 1972.

Rivera, Antonio, and Carrión, Arturo Morales. La Enseñanza de la Historia en Puerto Rico. Ciudad México: Instituto Panamericano de Geografía e Historia, 1953.

Rivera, Josefina de Alvarez. Historia de la literatura Puertorriqueña. Tome 1. San Juan, Puerto Rico: Department of Education, 1969.

Rivera, J. Julian. "Growth of a Puerto Rican Awareness." Social Casework 55(F, 1974):84-89.

Rivera de Alvarado, Carmen, Rivera, Francisco Torres, and Rivera de Rios, Trina. Puerto Rico: The Look from Within. Washington, DC: University Press of America, 1976.

Rivera de Rios, Trina. Nosotros los Puertoriqueños. Washington, DC: University Press of America, 1976.

Robinson, Gertrude A. "A Case Study of Puerto Rican Children in Junior High School 65, Manhattan, New York City, New York." Doctoral dissertation, New York U., 1956.

Roca, Pablo. Construction of a General Group Test for Puerto Rican Students in the Elementary and Secondary Schools, Ag, 1962. ERIC ED 002 770.

Rodriguez, Antonio, Jr. "Are Bilingual Children Able to Think in Either Language with Equal Facility and Accuracy?" Bulletin of the Department of Elementary School Principals 10 (Ja, 1931):98-101.

_____. "The Parent-Teacher Movement in Puerto Rico; Historical Sketch and Present Status." Puerto Rico School Review 16(Mr, 1932):15-17.

_____. "The 2nd Unit and the Rural School Problem of Puerto Rico." Doctoral dissertation, Indiana U., 1943.

Rodriguez, Clara. "A Cost-Benefit Analysis of Subjective Factors Affecting Assimilation: Puerto Ricans." Ethnicity 2(1975):66-80.

_____. "The Structure of Failure II: A Case in Point." Urban Review 7(Jl, 1974):215-226. [Puerto Rican children in schools of New York City]

_____. "Puerto Ricans: Between Black and White." New York Affairs 1(Spring, 1974): 92-101

_____. "The Ethnic Queue in the United States: The Case of Puerto Ricans." Doctoral dissertation, Washington U., 1973.

_____. "Puerto Ricans and the Melting Pot." Journal of Ethnic Studies 1(Winter, 1974): 89-98.

Rodriguez, Inez, and Rodriguez, Hector. Focus on Problems Faced by Mainland Puerto Ricans. In U.S. Congress, 91st, 1st session, Senate, Committee on Government Operations, Subcommittee on Executive Reorganization. Establish an Inter-Agency Committee on Mexican-American Affairs. Hearings. Washington, DC: GPO, 1969.

Rodriguez Bou, Ismael. "Significant Factors in the Development of Education in Puerto Rico." In Selected Background Studies Prepared for the United States-Puerto Rico Commission on the Status of Puerto Rico. Washington, DC: GPO, 1966.

_____. Problemas de la Educacion en Puerto Rico. Rio Piedras, Puerto Rico: Imprenta Venequela, 1947.

Rogler, Lloyd H. Migrant in the City. The Life of a Puerto Rican Action Group. New York: Basic Books, 1972.

Rollwagen, Jack R. "The City vs. Context: The Puerto Ricans of Rochester, New York." Urban Anthropology 4(Ap, 1975):53-60.

Rosado Diaz, Manuel. "The Historical Development and Legal Status of the Public Schools of Puerto Rico." Doctoral dissertation, U. of Denver, 1967.

Rosenberg, Terry J. Residence, Employment and Mobility of Puerto Ricans in New York City. Chicago, IL: Department of Geography, U. of Chicago, 1974.

Rosenberg, Terry J., and Lake, Robert W. "Toward a Revised Model of Residential Segregation and Succession: Puerto Ricans in New York, 1960-1970." American Journal of Sociology 81(Mr, 1976):1142-1150.

Rosenthal, Alan G. "Pre-School Experience and Adjustment of Puerto Rican Children." Doctoral dissertation, New York U., 1955.

Rosner, Milton S. "A Study of Contemporary Patterns of Aspirations and Achievements of Puerto Ricans of Hell's Kitchen." Doctoral dissertation, New York U., 1957.

Ruiz, Aneche, and Ruiz, Paquita. "Vocational Needs of the Puerto Rican Migrant in New York City." Doctoral dissertation, Fordham U., 1946.

Safa, Helen Icken. An Analysis of Upward Mobility in Low-Income Families--A Comparison of Family and Community Life Among American Negro and Puerto Rican Poor. Youth Development Center, Syracuse U., NY, Je, 1967. ERIC ED 015 226.

_____. The Urban Poor of Puerto Rico: A Study in Development and Inequality. New York: Holt, Rinehart & Winston, 1974.

Sagrera, Martin. Racismo y Política en Puerto Rico. Rio Piedras, Puerto Rico: Editorial Edil, 1973.

Sanabria, Izzy. "The Newyorican in Puerto Rico." Latin New York 29(S, 1974):22-25.

Sanjur, D. "Milk Consumption Patterns of Puerto Rican Preschool Children in Rural New York." American Journal of Clinical Nutrition 24(N, 1971):1320-1326.

Santiago, Soledad. "Notes on the Newyoricans." Village Voice, F 19, 1979.

Santiago Santiago, Isaura. A Community's Struggle for Equal Educational Opportunity: Aspira v. Bd. of Ed. Princeton, NJ: Office for Minority Education, Educational Testing Service, 1978. [N.Y.C.]

_____. "Aspira v. Board of Education of the City of New York: A History and Policy Analysis." Doctoral dissertation, Fordham U., 1978. Univ. Microfilms Order No. 7809014.

Schaefer, Dorothy. "Prejudice in Negro and Puerto Rican Adolescents." In The Urban R's. Edited by Robert A. Dentler and others. New York: Praeger, 1967.

Seda Bonilla, Eduardo. "Cultural Pluralism and the Education of Puerto Rican Youths." Phi Delta Kappan 53(Ja, 1972):294-296.

_____. Los Derechos Civiles en la Cultura Puertorriqueña. Rio Piedras, Puerto Rico: Editorial de las Universidad de Puerto Rico, 1964.

_____. Los derechos civiles en la cultura puertorriqueños. San Juan, Puerto Rico: Ediciones Bayoan, 1974.

_____. Requiem Por Una Cultura: Ensayos Sobre La Socializacion el Puertorriqueño En Su Cultura Y En Ambito Del Poder Colonial. Rio Piedras, Puerto Rico: Editorial Edil, 1970.

_____. "Towards a New Vision of Puerto Rican Culture." In Centro de Estudios Puertorriqueños--CUNY, Taller de Cultura. Conferencia de Historiografía: Abril, 1974. New York: Centro de Estudios Puertorriquenos, CUNY, 1976.

Senior, Clarence. The Puerto Ricans. Strangers--Then Neighbors. Chicago, IL: Quadrangle, 1965.

Seplowin, Virginia M. "Un Estudio de Integración: El Norteamericano, en Puerto Rico." Revista de Ciencias Sociales 7(Mr-Je, 1963): 111-120.

_____. "Training and Employment Patterns of Puerto Ricans in Philadelphia." Doctoral dissertation, U. of Pennsylvania, 1969.

Severo, Richard. "For Middle-Class Puerto Ricans the Bias Problem Hasn't Ended." New York Times, N 22, 1977. [N.Y.C.]

Sexton, Patricia Cayo. "Schools: Broken Ladder to Success." Chapter 5 in Spanish Harlem. New York: Harper & Row, 1965.

Siegel, Arthur L. "The Social Adjustments of Puerto Ricans in Philadelphia." American Journal of Sociology, Ag, 1957.

Siegel, Arthur L., Orland, Harold, and Greer, Loyal. Puerto Ricans in Philadelphia: A Study of Their Demographic Characteristics, Problems, and Attitudes. Philadelphia, PA: Philadelphia Commission on Human Relations, Ap, 1954.

Sobrino, James F. "Group Identification and Adjustment in Puerto Rican Adolescents." Doctoral dissertation, Yeshiva U., 1965.

Soto, Pedro Juan. Spiks. Tr. Victoria Ortiz. New York: Monthly Review Press, 1974. [Novel about Puerto Ricans in N.Y.C.]

Spanish American Union. Demographic Survey of Hispanic Householders in Springfield, Massachusetts, 1978. Spanish American Union, 67 Jefferson Avenue, Springfield, MA 01107.

"Special Issue on Puerto Rican Materials." Interracial Books for Children 4(Spring, 1972).

Stambler, Ada. "A Study of Eigth Grade Puerto Rican Students at Junior High School 65 Manhattan, with Implications for Their Placement, Grouping, and Orientation." Doctoral dissertation, Teachers College, Columbia U., 1958.

"Statement by Puerto Rican Educators (A Response to the Multi-Cultural Education Task Force of the National Institute of Education)." Rican 2(O, 1974):54-59.

Steinberg, Lois Saxelby. "The Bilingual Education Act and the Puerto Rican Community: The Role of a Network in the Implementation of Federal Legislation at the Local Level." Doctoral dissertation, Fordham U., 1978. Univ. Microfilms Order No. 7814903. [N.Y.C.]

Steiner, Stan. The Islands: The Worlds of the Puerto Ricans. New York: Harper & Row, 1974.

Steward, Theophilus Bolden. "Social Distinctions in Porto Rico." Voice of the Negro 2(N, 1905):771-774.

Stilwell, William E., and Carrasquillo, Meris. Influence of Rural Puerto Rican Counselors on 11th Graders, 1976. ERIC ED 138 846.

Stockton, William. "Going Home: The Puerto Ricans' New Migration." New York Times Magazine, N 12, 1978.

Sullivan, Terry W. The Education Industry in Puerto Rico: An Economic Report. Washington, DC: U.S. Dept. of Labor, 1976.

Survey of the Public Educational System of Porto Rico. Made under the direction of the International Institute of Teachers College, Columbia U.; authorized by the U. of Porto Rico. New York: Teachers College, Columbia U., 1926.

Sussman, Leila. High School to University in Puerto Rico. Rio Piedras: Centro de Investigaciones Sociales, Universidad de Puerto Rico, 1965.

Sutherland, Iris Rose. "A Study of Puerto Rican Parents' Views on Bilingual/Bicultural Education." Doctoral dissertation, U. of Illinois, 1975. Univ. Microfilms Order No. 76-6982. [Chicago]

Szalay, Lorand B., and Bryson, Jean A. Subjective Culture and Communication: A Puerto Rican-U.S. Comparison. Washington, DC: American Psychological Association, D, 1975.

"Teaching in Porto Rico. American Young Woman Tells of Her Experience." New York Times, Ag 5, 1900.

Teruel, Manuel. "Puerto Ricans in Transition." Senior honors thesis, Harvard U., 1969. [Boston and Puerto Rico]

_____. "Negotiating Change in the Boston Public Schools: Bilingual Education." Doctoral dissertation, Harvard U., 1973. Univ. Microfilms Order No. 73-30,197.

Thomas, Alexander. Retardation in Intellectual Development of Lower-Class Puerto Rican Children in New York City. Interim Final Report. New York: New York U. Medical Center, D 1, 1967. ERIC ED 017 591.

Thomas, Piri. "A Bicentennial Without a Puerto Rican Colony." Crisis 82(D, 1975):407-410.

_____. "A Nightmare Night in 'Mi Barrio.'" New York Times Magazine, Ag 13, 1967. [Rioting in Spanish Harlem]

_____. "Dialogue" (interview). The Rican 1 (Winter, 1972):18-31.

_____. Down These Mean Streets. New York: Knopf, 1967. [Puerto Rican life in N.Y.C.]

_____. "I Remember Reminiscenses of School-days in Spanish Harlem." American Educator 2(Spring, 1978):20-22.

_____. "Los Puertorriquenos en la Tierra Prometida." Civil Rights Digest 6(1974):5-38.

Torres, Maria E. "Literature of the Barrio." In Essays on Minority Folklore, Selected Proceedings of the 3rd Annual Conference on Minority Studies. Edited by George E. Carter and James R. Parker. Ap, 1975. Vol. III. La Crosse, WI: Institute for Minority Studies, U. of Wisconsin, 1977.

Torres Rivera, Francisco. "The Colonial Mentality in American Institutions Today: The Case of the Island of Puerto Rico." In Latino Studies A Reader. Frank Montalvo and others (comps). Patrick Air Force Base, FL: Defense Race Relations Institute, 1975.

Tucker, Lynette, and Mathew, Alfred. "A Summer Workshop in Puerto Rico: Impressions and Comments." Bridge to Understanding, Ja, 1966.

Tumin, Melvin, and Feldman, Arnold S. "Status, Perspective, and Achievement: Education and Class Structure in Puerto Rico." American Sociological Review 21(Ag, 1956):464-472.

U.S. Bureau of the Census. Estimates of the Population of Puerto Rico and Other Outlying Areas: 1960 to 1973. Washington, DC: GPO, Jl, 1975.

_____. Puerto Ricans in the United States. Washington, DC: GPO, 1973.

U.S. Commission on Civil Rights, Massachusetts State Advisory Committee. Issues of Concern to Puerto Ricans in Boston and Springfield. Washington, DC: U.S. Commission on Civil Rights, 1972.

U.S. Commission on Civil Rights. Puerto Ricans in the Continental United States: An Uncertain Future. Washington, DC: The Commission, O, 1976.

U.S. Congress, 87th, 2nd Session, House of Representatives, Committee on Education and Labor. Interim Report on Education and Citizenship in the Public School System of Puerto Rico. Written by Deborah P. Wolfe. Washington, DC: GPO, Ag, 1962.

U.S. Congress, 89th, 2nd Session, Senate, Document No. 108, Vol. 2. Hearings before the United States-Puerto Rico Commission on the Status of Puerto Rico, Social-Cultural Factors in Relation to the Status of Puerto Rico. Washington, DC: GPO, 1966.

U.S. Congress, 91st, 2nd Session, Senate, Select Committee on Equal Educational Opportunity. Equal Educational Opportunity. Part 8-Equal Educational Opportunity for Puerto Rican Children. Washington, DC: GPO, 1970.

U.S. Congress, 94th, 1st Session, Senate, Committee on Interior and Insular Affairs. Puerto Rican Compact. Hearing.... Washington, DC: GPO, 1975.

Universidad Boricua Newsletter. Issued periodically at 1766 Church Street, N.W., Washington, DC 20036. Vol. I, No. 1, dated O 31, 1973.

"Unknown Citizens: A Special Issue on Rochester's Puerto Rican Community." Upstate New York, Je 18, 1972.

Vairo, Philip D. "Career Aspirations of Negro and Puerto Rican Youth." Negro Educational Review, Ap, 1964.

Varo, Charles. Consideraciones Antropologicas y Politicas En Torno a la Enseñanza del "Spanglish" en Nueva York. Rio Piedras, Puerto Rico: Ediciones Librería Internacional, 1971.

Vásquez, Hector I. "Puerto Rican Americans." Journal of Negro Education, Summer, 1969.

Vasquez Associates, Ltd. Assessment of the Principal Needs of the Spanish Speaking in Chicago. Findings, Conclusions, and Recommendations, 1973. ERIC ED 121 907.

_____. Evaluation of Street Projects for the Spanish Speaking. Findings, Conclusions, Recommendations, 1973. ERIC ED 121 908.

Vázquez de Rodríguez, Ligia. "Social Work Practice in Puerto Rico." Social Work 18 (Mr, 1973):32-40.

Vazquez Ignatin, Hilda. "Young Lords Serve and Protect." Movement, My, 1969. [Puerto Rican youth group in Chicago]

Velez Aquino, Luis Antonio. "Puerto Rican Press Reaction to the Shift from Spanish to United States Sovereignty, 1898-1917." Doctoral dissertation, Columbia U., 1969.

"A Venture in Educational Anthropology: Puerto Rico as a Laboratory." Journal of Education 150(D, 1967): entire issue. [Boston U.]

Vidal, David. "Dream Still Eludes Mainland Puerto Ricans." New York Times, S 11, 1977.

Vincenty, Nestor I. "Racial Differences in Intelligence as Measured by Pictorial Group Tests with Special Reference to Porto Rico and the United States." Doctoral dissertation, Harvard U., 1929.

Wagenheim, Kal. Puerto Rico: A Profile. New York: Praeger, 1970.

_____. A Survey of Puerto Ricans on the U.S. Mainland in the 1970's. New York: Praeger, 1972.

_____ (ed.). Cuentos: An Anthology of Short Stories from Puerto Rico. New York: Schocken, 1978.

Wagenheim, Kal, and Wagenheim, Olga Jiménez de (eds.). The Puerto Ricans. A Documentary History. New York: Praeger, 1973.

Wall, Muriel (comp.). Audio Visual Aids to Enrich the Curriculum for the Puerto Rican Child in the Elementary Grades, Parts 1 and 2. New York: City U. of New York, Hunter College, 1971. ERIC ED 049 659.

Walters, Fred C. "Psychological Tests in Porto Rico." School and Society 25(F 19, 1927:231-233.

_____. "Standards of Attainment for High-School Seniors in Porto Rico." Porto Rico School Review 15(N, 1930):12-14.

[Weinberg, Meyer] "[Recent Research on] Puerto Ricans." Research Review of Equal Education 1(Spring, 1977):25-30.

White, Trumbull. Puerto Rico and Its People. New York: Stokes, 1938.

Wilber, George L., and Bock, W. B. "Rural Poverty in Puerto Rico." In President's National Advisory Commission on Rural Poverty, Rural Poverty in the United States. Washington, DC: GPO, My, 1968.

Williams, George M., Jr. Puerto Rican English: A Discussion of Eight Major Works Relevant to Its Linguistic Description. Cambridge, MA: In Language Research Report No. 3. ERIC ED 051 709.

Willis, Robert. "An Analysis of the Adjustment and Scholastic Achievement of Forty Puerto Rican Boys Who Attended Transition Classes in New York City. Doctoral dissertation, New York U., 1961.

Wingfield, Roland. Life Styles of Puerto Rico's Youth, 1977. ERIC ED 159 266.

Wise, Michael (ed.). "Puerto Ricans and Other Latinos." Desegregation in Education: A Directory of Reported Federal Decisions. Notre Dame, IN: Center for Civil Rights, U. of Notre Dame Law School, Ap, 1977. [1954-1976]

Withey, Ellen. "Discrimination in Private Employment in Puerto Rico." Revista Puertorriqueña sobre los Derechos Humanos/Puerto Rican Journal of Human Rights 1(Ag, 1977): 43-47.

Wolfram, Walt and others. Overlapping Influence in the English of Second Generation Puerto Rican Teenagers in Harlem. Final Report. Washington, DC: Center for Applied Linguistics, 1971. ERIC ED 060 159.

Wolfram, Walter A. Sociolinguistic Aspects of Assimilation: Puerto Rican English in New York City. Arlington, VA: Center for Applied Linguistics, 1974.

Wycliff, Don. "The Hot Seat at Clemente High." Chicago Daily News, Ap 30, 1975. [Chicago]

Yglesias, José. "Right On With the Young Lords." New York Times Magazine, Je 7, 1970. [N.Y.C.]

Young, Phillip. "An Analysis of the Economic Returns of Formal Schooling for Puerto Rican Men in New York City." Doctoral dissertation, New York U., 1977.

The Young Lords Party and Michael Abramson. Palante. Young Lords Party. New York: McGraw-Hill, 1971.

Zenon, Isabelo. Narcisco Descubre su Trasero, Vol. I. San Juan: Editorial Furidi, 1974. [Puerto Rican identity]

Zirkel, Perry A. "Puerto Rican Parents: An Educational Survey." Integrated Education, N-D, 1973:20-26.

Other Spanish-Speaking Peoples

Amaro, Nelson, and Portes, Alejandro. "Una sociología del exilo: grupos cubanos en Estados Unidos." Aportes 23(Ja, 1972):6-24.

Balseiro, Jose-Agustin with Murga, Vincente (eds.) The Historic Preserve in Florida: Yesterday and Today, 1513-1973. Miami: E. A. Seemann Pub., 1977.

Burt, Al. "Miami: The Cuban Flavor." Nation 212 (Mr 8, 1971):299-302.

Carballo, Manuel. "A Socio-psychological Study of Acculturation/Assimilation: Cubans in New Orleans." Dissertation Abstracts International 31,6A(D, 1970):3053.

Casal, Lourdes, and Hernandez, Andrés R. "Cubans in the U.S.: A Survey of the Literature." Cuban Studies 5(Jl, 1975):25-51.

Cejas and Toledo, Inc. Needs Assessment: The Prevention of Spanish-Speaking Dropouts in the Target Areas of "Little Havana" and "Wynwood" (Grades 7-12). Miami: Cejas and Toledo, Inc., 1974.

Cordasco, Francesco. "Spanish Speaking Children in American Schools." International Migration Review 9(Fall, 1975):379-382. [N.Y.C.]

Cowan, Paul, and Cowan, Rachel. "For Hispanos It's Still the Promised Land." New York Times Magazine, Je 22, 1975. [N.Y.C.]

Domínquez, Virginia R. From Neighbor to Stranger: The Dilemma of Caribbean Peoples in the United States. New Haven: Antilles Research Program, Yale U., 1975.

_____. "Spanish-Speaking Carribeans in New York: The Middle Race." Revista Interamericana 3(1973):135-142.

Egerton, John. Cubans in Miami: A Third Dimension in Racial and Cultural Relations, N, 1969. Race Relations Information Center, Nashville, TN 37212.

Eichelberger, F. Pierce. "The Cubans in Miami: Residential Movements in Ethnic Group Differentiations." Master's thesis, U. of Cincinnati, 1974.

"Fair Housing and the Spanish Speaking." Civil Rights Digest 8(Fall, 1975):29-46. [Tampa, FL; New York; Dallas, TX]

Fishman, Joshua A. and others. Bilingualism in the Barrio. Final Report. New York: Yeshiva U., Ag, 1968. ERIC ED 026 546.

Gil, Rosa María. "The Assimilation and Problems of 100 Cuban Refugees Attending Catholic and Public High Schools in Union City and West New York. New Jersey: 1959-1966." Master's thesis, Fordham U., 1968.

Hendricks, Glenn. The Dominican Diaspora. From the Dominican Republic to New York City—Villagers in Transition. New York: Teachers College Press, 1974.

_____. "La Razaen Nueva York: Social Pluralism and Schools." Teachers College Record 74(F, 1973):379-393.

Jacoby, Susan. "Miami Si, Cuba No." New York Times Magazine, S 29, 1974. [Cubans in Miami]

Kollnan de Curuchet, Marta Isabel. "Localization of the Mexican and Cuban Population of Chicago." Master's thesis, U. of Chicago, 1967.

Lewin, Ellen. "Mothers and Children: Latin American Immigrants in San Francisco." Doctoral dissertation, Stanford U., 1974. Univ. Microfilms Order No. 75-13,549.

Lucas, Isidro. Multi-National Spanish Speaking Communities in the Midwest. Chicago, IL: Regional Director, U.S. Department of Health, Education, and Welfare, Ap, 1973.

Mendoza, Manuel G. A Report on Housing Conditions of Cubans, Puerto Ricans and Mexicans in Dade County, Florida. Miami: Professional Research Institute.

Mermelstein, Marilyn, and Fox, Bernard A. "The Sands Project." High Points, Mr, 1965. [Non-English speaking students in New York City]

Moncarz, Raul. A Study of the Effect of Environmental Change on Human Capital Among Selected Skilled Cubans. Talhahassee, FL: Florida State U., 1969.

Nicholas, J. D., and Prohías, Rafael J. Rent Differentials Among Racial and Ethnic Groups in Miami. Boca Raton: Florida Atlantic U.-Florida International U. Joint Center for Environmental and Urban Problems, Jl, 1973.

Portes, Alejandro. "Dilemmas of a Golden Exile: Integration of Cuban Refugee Families in Milwaukee." American Sociological Review, Ag, 1969. [Milwaukee, Wisconsin]

Prohías, Rafael J. "Cubanos en Indianapolis: Un ejemplo de acomodación." Neueva Generación 2(S-O, 1967):7-8.

Prohías, Rafael J., and Casal, Lourdes. The Cuban Minority in the U.S. Preliminary Report on Need Identification and Program Evaluation. Boca Raton, FL: Florida Atlantic U., 1973.

Richmond, Marie LaLiberte. "Immigrant Adaptation and Family Structure Among Cubans in Miami, Florida." Doctoral dissertation, Florida State U., 1973.

Rogg, Eleanor Meyer. The Assimilation of Cuban Exiles: The Role of Community and Class. New York: New Aberdeen Press, 1974.

Ropka, Gerald William. "The Evolving Residential Pattern of the Mexican, Puerto Rican and Cuban Population in the City of Chicago." Doctoral dissertation, Michigan State U., 1973.

Sevick, Charles Vincent. "A History and Evaluation of the Cuban Teacher Retraining Program of the University of Miami, 1963-1973." Doctoral dissertation, U. of Miami, 1974.

Stevenson, James M. "Cuban-Americans: New Urban Class." Doctoral dissertation, Wayne State U., 1973.

U.S. Bureau of the Census. Persons of Spanish Origin in the United States: March 1974. Washington, DC: GPO, Ap, 1975.

U.S. Congress, 93rd, 1st session, House of Representatives, Committee on the Judiciary, Civil Rights and Constitutional Rights Subcommittee. Equal Opportunities for Spanish-Speaking People. Hearings.... Serial No. 32. Washington, DC: GPO, 1974.

Williamson, David. "Cognitive Complexity and Adaptation to Socio-Cultural Change: The Case of the Cuban Refugees in New Orleans." Doctoral dissertation, Tulane U., 1973.

Zisman, Paul M. Education and Economic Success in Urban Spanish-Speaking Immigrants. San Francisco, CA: R and E Research Associates, 1975. [D. C.]

General

Abarca, Tony. "Reflections of a Spanish-Speaking Interpreter." Civil Rights Digest 3(Spring, 1970):8-11.

"ABC Headstart. Parents Expose Board's Betrayal." LaRaza, N 9, 1969. [Los Angeles]

Adorno, William. "The Attitudes of Selected Mexican and Mexican-American Parents in Regards to Bilingual/Bicultural Education." Dictoral dissertation, United States International U., 1973. Univ. Microfilms Order No. 73-22653.

Alford, Harold J. The Proud Peoples. Philadelphia, PA: McKay, 1972.

Al-Khazraji, Majid, and Al-Khazraji, Emile M. Worcester's Spanish-Speaking Residents: Dimensions in Social Adjustment. Worcester, MA: Worcester Community Data Center, 1969.

Arcissiega, Thomas A. "Adaptive Mechanisms Employed by Bicultural Students in Urban Secondary Schools." Urban Education 6(Jl-O, 1971):233-241.

Arsenian, Seth. Bilingualism and Mental Development. A Study of the Intelligence and Social Background of Bilingual Children in New York City. New York: Teachers College, Columbia U., 1937.

Ballesteros, David. "Toward An Advantaged Society: Bilingual Education in the '70's." National Elementary Principal 50(N, 1970): 25-27.

Bay Area Bilingual Education League (BABEL). Bilingual Testing and Assessment. Proceedings of BABEL Workshop and Preliminary Findings Multilingual Assessment Program. 1972. BABEL, 1414 Walnut Street, Room 13, Berkeley, CA 94709.

Bayer, Mildred V. "Poverty and the Mother Tongue." Educational Forum, Mr, 1965.

Bernal, Mary Esther. Mi Corazon Canta. 2 parts. New York: John Hay Whitney Foundation, Je, 1973.

Bertou, Patrick, and Clasen, Robert E. "An Analysis of a Spanish Translation of the Sixteen Personality Factors Test." Journal of Experimental Education 39(Summer, 1971): 13-21.

"Bilingual Programs." Center Forum, S, 1969. [Five projects]

"Bilingualism and the Bilingual Child: A Symposium." Modern Language Journal, Mr-Ap, 1965.

Blackman, F. W. Spanish Institutions in the Southwest. Baltimore, MD: Johns Hopkins U., 1891.

Blair, William C. "Spanish-Speaking Minorities in a Utah Mining Town." Journal of Social Issues, VIII, 1952.

Blanco, Antonio S. La Lengua española en la historia de California. Madrid, Spain: Ediciones Cultural Hispanica, 1971.

Boyd, Dorothy L. "Bilingualism as an Educational Objective." Educational Forum, Mr, 1968.

Braccio, John H. "A Comparative Study of School Self-Concept between Low Socio-Economic Fifth- and Sixth-Chicanos and Anglo Americans." Doctoral dissertation, Michigan State U., 1972.

Burger, Henry G. (ed.). Ethnics on Education: Report On a Conference of Spanish-Speaking, AmerIndian, and Negro Cultural Leaders, on Southwestern Teaching and Learning, 1969. ERIC ED 032 440.

_____. "Ethno-Lematics: Evolving 'Shy' Spanish-American Pupils by Cross-Cultural Mediation." Adolescence 6(Spring, 1972): 61-76.

_____. "'Ethnonics': Converting Spanish Speakers' Ethnography for Directed Change." Practical Anthropology 16(N-D, 1969):241-251.

_____. "'Ethnos-Maieutics': Adapting Curricula for Cross-Cultural Teaching." _Journal of Educational Thought_ 5(Ag, 1971):69-79.

Burma, John H. "Another American Dilemma: Finding 'The Unknown Minority.'" _Social Science Quarterly_ 52(Je, 1971):30-34.

Cabinet Committee on Opportunity for the Spanish Speaking. _Spanish Surnamed American College Graduates, 1971-1972._ Washington, DC: GPO, 1971.

Cafferty, Pastora. "Spanish-speaking Americans: Economic Assimilation or Cultural Identify?" In _Pieces of a Dream._ Edited by Michael Wenk, S. M. Tomasi and Gino Baroni. New York: Center for Migration Studies, 1972.

California State Department of Education. "Spanish-Speaking Pupils Classified as Educable Mentally Retarded." _Integrated Education_ 7(N-D, 1969):28-33.

Cambridge Reports, Inc. "The Island's Tarnished Image. The Mainland Survey on Puerto Rico and Its People." _San Juan Star_, Jl 30, 1978.

Carter, Thomas P. "The Way Beyond Bilingual Education." _Civil Rights Digest_ 3(Fall, 1970):14-21.

Center for Field Research and School Services. _An Evaluation of Teaching English As a Second Language in the Public Schools._ New York: School of Education, New York U., S, 1969.

Christian, Jane M., and Christian, Chester C., Jr. "Spanish Language and Culture in the Southwest." In Joshua A. Fishman and others. _Language Loyalty in the United States._ The Hague: Mouton, 1966.

Cline, Marion, Jr. "Achievement of Bilinguals in the Seventh Grade by Socioeconomic Levels." Doctoral dissertation, U. of Southern California, 1961.

"Coalition or Collision? Or, Black Man Speak with Forked Tongue." _La Raza_, N 9, 1969.

Cohen, Andrew D. "Innovative Education for La Raza: A Sociolinguistic Assessment of a Bilingual Education Program in California." Doctoral dissertation, Stanford U., 1972. [Redwood City]

College of Education. _Investigation of Mental Retardation and Pseudo Mental Retardation in Relation to Bilingual and Sub-cultural Factors._ Tempe, AZ: Arizona State U., 1960.

Condit, Elinor. "An Appraisal of Certain Methods of Treating Bilingualism in the Claremont Elementary School." Master's thesis, U. of Southern California, 1946.

Cordasco, Francesco. "Educational Enlightenment Out of Texas: Toward Bilingualism." _The Record_ 71(1970):608-612.

Cordova, Ignacio R. "The Relationship of Acculturation, Achievement, and Alienation and Spanish American Sixth Grade Students." _Dissertation Abstracts International_, 1969, 30(4-A)1357.

Darcy, Natalie T. "The Performance of Bilingual Puerto Rican Children on Verbal and Non-Language Tests of Intelligence." _Journal of Educational Research_, Mr, 1952.

_____. "A Review of the Literature on the Effects of BiLingualism Upon the Measurement of Intelligence." _Journal of General Psychology_, 1953.

Davis, O. L., Jr., and Personke, Carl R., Jr. "Effects of Administering the _Metropolitan Readiness Test_ in English and Spanish to Spanish-Speaking School Entrants." _Journal of Educational Measurement_, Fall, 1968. [Victoria, TX]

DeBlassie, Richard R., and Healy, Gary W. _Self Concept: A Comparison of Spanish-American, Negro, and Anglo Adolescents Across Ethnic, Sex, and Socioeconomic Variables._ U. Park, NM: New Mexico State U. Clearinghouse on Rural Education and Small Schools, Mr, 1970. ERIC ED 037 287.

Eckhardt, Robert C. _State Aid and School Attendance in Texas._ Washington, Office of Inter-American Affairs, O, 1945.

"Editorial." _Ideal_, Mr 20, 1973 (also, back-page cartoon). [On the fate of a bilingual program in Desert Sands (Indio) School District, CA]

"Education and the Spanish-Speaking--An Attorney General's Opinion on Article XII, Section 8 of the New Mexico Constitution." _New Mexico Law Review_ 3(My, 1973).

"Education for the Spanish Speaking." _National Elementary Principal_, N, 1970. [24 articles]

Farber, Harris, and Mayer, G. Roy. "Behavior Consultation in a Barrio High School." _Personnel and Guidance Journal_ 51(D, 1972): 273-279.

Feldman, Carol, and Shen, Michael. "Some Language-Related Cognitive Advantages of Bilingual Five-Year-Olds." _Journal of Genetic Psychology_ 118(Je, 1971):235-244.

Fennessey, James. _An Exploratory Study of Non-English Speaking Homes and Academic Performance_, My, 1967. ERIC ED 011 613.

Fernandez, Edward W. _Comparison of Persons of Spanish Surname and Persons of Spanish Origin in the United States._ Washington, DC: GPO, Je, 1975.

Fernandez, Edward W. and others. _Persons of Spanish Origin in the United States, March, 1975._ Washington, DC: GPO, 1976.

Finocchiaro, Mary. "Myth and Reality in TESOL: A Plea for a Broader View." _TESOL Quarterly_ 5(Mr, 1971):3-17.

Fishman, Joshua A. and Associates. _Language Loyalty in the United States._ 3 vols. Washington, DC: Language Research Section, U.S. Office of Education, 1964.

Friedman, Minerva. "Spanish Bilingual Students and Standardized Tests." Master's thesis, California State U., Hayward, 1972.

Froning, Mary L. _The Employment Status of Spanish Surnamed Americans in the New York SMSA._ Washington, DC: U.S. Equal Employment Opportunity Commission, Je, 1974.

Gambone, James V. "Bilingual Bicultural Educational Civil Rights: The May 25th Memorandum and Oppressive School Practices." Doctoral dissertation, U. of New Mexico, 1973. Univ. Microfilms Order No. 74-11,798.

Garcia, George F. "The Latino and Desegregation." _Integrateducation_ 14(S-O, 1976).

Gardner, Donald I., and Gardner, Florence Field. _The Relation of Age-Grade Reading Skills to Environment-Cultural Factors in the Life-Space of Scholastically Retarded Ethnic Groups in Selected San Luis Valley Public Schools,_ Je, 1965. ERIC ED 039 042.

German, Bob. "Trying Again on Bilingual Ed." _Texas Observer,_ Mr 30, 1973. [Texas]

Gianturco, Adriana, and Aronin, Norman. _The Spanish-Speaking in Boston. Findings of the 1970 U.S. Census._ Boston, MA: Action for Boston Community Development, N, 1972.

Gómez, Antonio. "Barriology Exam." _Con Safos_ II, 5(1970).

Goodman, H. C. "Spanish Book Selection in a Bilingual Community." _Texas Library Journal_ 47(Summer, 1971):52-54.

Goodman, Lillian. "Juan's Right to Read." _American Education,_ Jl, 1970. [San Francisco Bay area]

Gordon, Raymond. _Spanish Personal Names as Barriers to Communication Between Latin Americans and North Americans._ Yellow Springs, OH: Antioch College, 1968. ERIC ED 023 338.

Gordon, Susan B. "The Relationship Between the English Language Ability and Home Language Experiences of First-Grade Children, from Three Ethnic Groups, of Varying Socioeconomic Status and Varying Degrees of Bilingualism." Doctoral dissertation, U. of New Mexico, 1969.

Gustafson, Richard A., and Owens, Thomas. _Children's Perceptions of Themselves and Their Teacher's Feelings Toward Them Related to Actual Teacher Perceptions and School Achievement,_ Ap 22, 1971. Paper, Western Psychological Association. ERIC ED 053 848.

Hall, George F. "Problems of Spanish-American Minority Aired for N.C.C. Unit." _Christian Century,_ N 19, 1969.

Haro, R. P. "Bicultural and Bilingual Americans: A Need for Understanding." _Library Trends_ 20(O, 1971):256-270.

Helm, June (ed.). _Spanish-Speaking People in the United States._ Seattle: U. of Washington Press, 1969.

Herrans, L. L. "Cultural Factors in the Standardization of the Spanish WAIS or EIWA and the Assessment of Spanish-speaking Children." _School Psychologist_ 28(N, 1973): 27-34.

Hertzig, Margaret E., and Birch, Herbert G. "Longitudinal Course of Measured Intelligence in Preschool Children of Different Social and Ethnic Backgrounds." _American Journal of Orthopsychiatry_ 41(Ap, 1971): 416-426.

Hill, John. "The Distribution of Spanish Americans in the Kalamazoo Area." Master's thesis, Western Michigan U., 1972.

Hispanic Influences in the United States. New York: Interbook, 1975.

Hodge, Marie G. "The Status of Bilingual Education in Texas." Master's thesis, North Texas State U., 1971.

How to Identify Spanish Names. San Juan, Puerto Rico: Department of Labor, Migrant Division, Ja, 1969. ERIC ED 031 358.

Human Resource Center Directory, 1971. Southwestern Cooperative Educational Laboratory, Inc., 117 Richmond Drive, N.E., Albuquerque, NM 87106. ["A reference bank of persons with expertise in educational, socio-economic and cultural matters as they relate to the non-English-speaking Spanish-surnamed adult"]

Institute for Intercultural Relations and Ethnic Studies. _Hispanic Sub-Cultural Values: Similarities and Differences,_ 1977. ERIC ED 141 466.

Jaffe, A. J. and others. _Spanish Americans in the United States--Changing Demographic Characteristics,_ S, 1976. ERIC ED 151 131.

Jaramillo, Mari-Luci. "Cultural Differences Revealed Through Language." _NCRIEEO Tipsheet #8,_ My, 1972.

Jesus, Alfredo de. Problems Faced by the Span-
ish Community in the City of Boston and the
State of Massachusetts. Boston: Mayor's
Office of Human Rights, My 13, 1971.

John, Vera. "Letter from the Southwest, On
Bilingualism." Urban Review 7(Ja, 1974):
43-45.

Jones, Louis, and Calvo, Elvira. "The BARSIT
as a General Ability Screening Test for
Spanish-speaking Adults in New York [City]."
Personnel Psychology 23(Winter, 1970):513-
519.

Jones, William Richard, Morrison, J. R.,
Rogers, J., and Saer, H. The Educational
Attainment of Bilingual Children in Relation
to Their Intelligence and Linguistic Background. Cardiff: U. of Wales Press, 1957.

Kalvelage, Joan. "Cinco Exemplos." Edcentric,
O-N, 1972. [Five alternative institutions]

Killian, L. R. Cognitive Test Performance of
Spanish-American Primary-school Children:
A Longitudinal Study. Final Report. Kent,
OH: Kent State U., N, 1971. ERIC ED 060
156.

Kneller, George F. Educational Anthropology:
An Introduction. New York: Wiley, 1965.

Kobrick, Jeffrey W. "The Compelling Case for
Bilingual Education." Saturday Review, Ap
29, 1972.

_____. "A Model Act Providing for Transition-
al Bilingual Education Programs in Public
Schools." Harvard Journal on Legislation 9
(Ja, 1972):260

Kochman, Thomas. "Social Factors in the Consideration of Teaching Standard English."
Florida FL Reporter, Spring-Summer, 1969.

Kutsche, Paul. "The Anglo Side of Accultura-
tion." In Spanish-Speaking People in the
United States. Edited by June Helin.
Seattle: U. of Washington Press, 1969.

Lanning, John Tate. Academic Culture in the
Spanish Colonies. London: N.p., 1940.

Laosa, Luis M. "Viewing Bilingual Multicultural
Educational Television: An Empirical Analysis of Children's Behaviors During Television
Viewing." Journal of Educational Psychology
68(Ap, 1976):133-142.

Lara, Jorge-Braud. Browns in Anger: The Overlooked Minority, Je, 1969. ERIC ED 042 829.

Latin American Curriculum Project. The Treat-
ment of Latin America in Social Studies.
Instructional Materials. LC No. 76-625834.
Austin, TX: U. of Texas, 1968.

"Latin American Union for Civil Rights..."
IFCO News 3(N-D, 1972). [Milwaukee, WS]

Lewis, Oscar. "The Children of Sanchez, Pedro
Martinez, and La Vida." Current Anthropology
D, 1967. [Followed by critical discussions
by Robert Coles, Eric R. Wolf and others]

Long, James E. "Productivity, Employment Dis-
crimination, and the Relative Economic
Status of Spanish Origin Males." Social
Science Quarterly 58(D, 1977):357-373.

Lopez, Josephine. "Free Compulsory Public
Education. The 'Great Equalizer' or the
Great Divider?" Edcentric, O-N, 1972.

Lukcczer, Moses. "Assessing Progress. Employment Among Americans of Spanish Origin."
Civil Rights Digest 8(Summer, 1976):30-37.

McKay, Roberta V. "Employment and Unemployment
Among Americans of Spanish Origin." Monthly
Labor Review, Ap, 1974.

Macmillan, Robert W. A Study of the Effect of
Socioeconomic Factors on the School Achieve-
ment of Spanish-Speaking School Beginners,
Ap, 1968. (Paper presented at International
Reading Association conference, Boston, MA.)
ERIC ED 026 217

Macnamara, John. "Problems of Bilingualism."
Journal of Social Issues, Ap, 1967. [Collec-
tion of articles by various authors]

Mangers, Dennis H. "Education in the Grapes
of Wrath." National Elementary Principal 50
(N, 1970):34-40.

Martinez, Armando. "Literacy through Democra-
tization of Education." Harvard Educational
Review 40(1970):280-282. [Hispanics in
Boston]

Maslow, Albert P., and Futransky, David L.
Effects on Test Score of Presenting Verbal
Test Questions in an English-Spanish Format
to a Predominantly Spanish-American Group:
San Antonio, Texas, My, 1968. Washington,
DC: Civil Service Commission, Bureau of
Policies and Standards, Jl, 1968. ERIC ED
045 265.

Mendez, Manuel P. "A Report to the Senate
Select Committee on Equal Educational Opportunity." Regeneracion 1, No. 8(1970):8-13.

Montoya. "Bilingual-Bicultural Education:
Making Equal Educational Opportunities
Available to National Origin Minority
Students." Georgetown Law Journal 61(Mr,
1973).

Moreno, Steve. "Problems Related to Present
Testing Instrument." El Grito 3(1970):25-
29.

Nadler, Harvey and others. An Evaluation of
Teaching English as a Second Language in the
Public Schools. New York: Center for Field
Research and School Services, School of Edu-
cation, New York U., S, 1969.

Natalicio, Luiz F. S., and Natalicio, Diana S.
"The Educational Problems of Atypical Stu-
dent Groups: The Native Speaker of Spanish."
Urban Education, O, 1969.

National Institute of Education. Desegregation
and Education Concerns of the Hispanic
Community. Washington, DC: National
Institute of Education, 1977.

Nava, Julian. Cultural Backgrounds and Bar-
riers that Affect Learning by Spanish
Speaking Children. Los Angeles: Board of
Education, 1966.

Nedler, Shari, and Sebera, Peggy. "Intervention Strategies for Spanish-Speaking Preschool Children." Child Development 42 (Mr,
1971):259-267.

Office for Spanish Speaking American Affairs.
Report... March, 1970. Washington, DC:
U.S. Department of Health, Education, and
Welfare, 1970.

Oliveira, Arnulfo L. "Barrio Test of Verbal
Abilities (Form A)." Educational Leadership
30(N, 1972):169-170. [Designed for use in
Rio Grande Valley, TX]

Padilla, Amado M., and Ruiz, Rene A. Latino
Mental Health--A Review of Literature.
Rockville, MD: National Institute of Mental
Health, 1973.

Pallone, Nathaniel J., Richard, Fred S., and
Hurley, Robert B. Education Study: Aug-
mented Services for Non-English Speaking
Pupils in Selected Junior High Schools,
Board of Education, City of New York. New
York: School of Education, New York U.,
S 11, 1969.

Palmer, Michael, and Graffney, Philip D.
"Effects of Administration of the WISC in
Spanish and English and Relationship of
Social Class to Performance." Psychology
in the Schools 9(Ja, 1972):61-64.

Palomares, Uvaldo. "Communication Begins with
Attitude." National Elementary Principal 50
47-49.

_____. "Nuestros sentimientos son iguales,
la diferencia es en la experiencia."
Personnel and Guidance Journal 50(O, 1971):
137-144.

Past, Ray and others. Bilingualism--From the
Viewpoint of Recruitment and Preparation of
Bilingual Teachers, N 4, 1966. ERIC ED 018
297.

Páz, Octavio. "Eroticism and Gastrophy."
Daedalus 101(Fall, 1972):67-85.

Peal, Elizabeth, and Lawbert, Wallace E.
"The Relation of Bilingualism to Intelligence." Psychological Monographs: Several
and Applied 76(1962):1-23.

Phillips, Howard. "Bilingualism Masks Leftist
Drive for Cultural Separation." Human Events
S 28, 1974.

Pino, Tom, and Valdes, Daniel T. "Ethnic Labels
in Majority-Minority Relations." Journal of
Mexican-American Studies 1(Fall, 1970):16-30.

Pollack, Erwin, and Menacker, Julius.
Spanish-speaking Students and Guidance.
Boston, MA: Houghton Mifflin, 1971.

Pomerantz, Norman E. "An Investigation of
the Relationship between Intelligence and
Reading Achievement for Various Samples of
Bilingual Spanish-speaking Children."
Dissertation Abstracts International 31,9-A
(Mr, 1971):4558.

Pottinger, J. Stanley. "Equality for Spanish-
Surnamed Students." Integrated Education 10
(N-D, 1972):48-53.

_____. "Remarks on the HEW Memo Concerning
Identification of Discrimination and Denial
of Services On the Basis of Natural Origin."
Journal of Mexican American Studies 1 (Fall,
1970):56-57.

The Psychological Corporation. A Program for
Pupils in Non-Public Schools Learning English
As A Second Language. 1968-1969. New York:
Psychological Corporation, D, 1969. [N.Y.C.]

Ramirez, Manuel III. Effects of Cultural Marginality on Education and Personality, 1970.
ERIC ED 056 804.

_____. "Identity Crisis in the Barrios."
Music Educators Journal 56(My, 1970):69-70.

Ramirez, W. L. "Problems of the Public Li-
brary in Services to Its Spanish-speaking
Population." Acquisition of Latin American
Library Materials. Final Report and Working
Papers. Vol. 2. Pan American Union, 1968.

Rapp, M. Anderson. "'Junta de Amigos'--a
'First' in Central Michigan." Educational
Television 3(Je, 1971):21,23-4,26-28.

Reyes, Donald J. "Another Look at Bilingualism."
Integrated Education (N-D, 1973):27-28.

Rivera, Feliciano, and Cordova, Hector L. "Curriculum and Materials for Bilingual, Bicultural Education." National Elementary Principal 50(N, 1970):56-61.

Rivera, Vidal A. "The Forgotten Ones: Children of Migrants." National Elementary Principal 50(N, 1970):41-44.

Rocco, Raymond A. "On the Limitations of an Assimilative Perspective." Social Science Quarterly 52(Je, 1971):35-38.

Rodriguez, Dario E. "Some Physiological and Educational Aspects of Bilingualism." Aztlan 2(Spring, 1971):79-104.

Romero, Fred E. "A Study of Anglo-American and Spanish American Culture Value Concepts and Their Significance in Secondary Education." Doctoral dissertation, U. of Denver, 1966.

Ropka, Gerald W. "The Evolving Residential Pattern of the Mexican, Puerto Rican and Cuban Population in the City of Chicago." Doctoral dissertation, Michigan State U., 1973.

Ryscavage, Paul M., and Mellor, Earl F. "The Economic Situation of Spanish Americans." Monthly Labor Review 96(Ap, 1973):3-9.

Samora, Julian. [Interview] National Elementary Principal 50(N, 1970):98-101.

_____. "Report on the Spanish-Speaking People of the U.S." Washington, DC: U.S. Commission on Civil Rights, 1962, unpublished.

Sanchez, George J. "The Crux of the Dual Language Handicap." New Mexico School Review, Mr, 1954.

_____. "The Education of Bilinguals in a State School System." Doctoral dissertation, U. of California, Berkeley, 1934.

_____. "Group Differences and Spanish-Speaking Children--A Critical Review." Journal of Applied Psychology 16(O, 1932).

_____. "History, Culture, and Education." In La Raza: Forgotten Americans. Edited by Julián Samora. Notre Dame, IN: U. of Notre Dame Press, 1966.

_____. [Interview] National Elementary Principal 50(N, 1970):102-104.

_____. "Scores of Spanish-Speaking Children on Repeated Tests." Master's thesis, U. of Texas, 1931.

Sanchez, Luisa G. G. "Spanish-Speaking Minority Holds Historical Past as Common Bond." Delta Kappa Gamma Bulletin 36(Spring, 1970): 23-28.

Seda Bonilla, Eduardo. "Bilingual Education in a Pluralistic Context." Rican 1(My, 1974): 19-26.

Servicio Pedagogico de Aztlan. "Testimony Given Before the California Legislature Joint Committee on the Master Plan for Higher Education." New School of Education Journal 2 and 3(1973):77-84.

Shensul, Stephen, Bakszysz, Mary, and Cummings, Mel F., Jr. Preliminary Results from a Pilot Research Project in a Pilsen Elementary School, F 19, 1970. Community Mental Health Program, Medical Center, Illinois State Psychiatric Institute, 1601 W. Taylor Street, Chicago, IL 60612. [Chicago]

Sherman, M. "Library Services to the Spanish-speaking; A Report on the Talk by Jose Ramirez at the Annual Conference April 15, 1971." Connecticut Libraries 13(Summer, 1971):21-22.

Smith, Leslie W. Social and Economic Characteristics of Spanish-Origin Hired Farmworkers in 1973. Washington, DC: Economic Research Service, U.S. Department of Agriculture, 1976.

Smith, M. Estellie. "The Spanish-Speaking Population of Florida." In Spanish-Speaking People in the United States. Edited by June Helm. Seattle: U. of Washington Press, 1969.

Spanish Speaking People Study Commission. Report to the General Assembly of the State of Illinois. Springfield, IL: The Commission, 1972.

Strickland, Virgil E., and Sanchez, George J. "Spanish Name Spells Discrimination." Nation's Schools, Ja, 1948:22-24.

Task Force on the Treatment of Minorities. Taskforce to Reevaluate Social Science Textbooks, Grades Five through Eight. Sacramento, CA: State Department of Education, D, 1971.

Teschner, Richard V., Bills, Garland D., and Craddock, Jerry R. Spanish and English of United States Hispanos: A Critical Annotated Bibliography. Arlington, VA: Center for Applied Linguistics, 1975.

"'Tio Taco Is Dead.'" Newsweek, Je 29, 1970.

A Total Immersion in the Hispano Culture, A Model Unit: Handbook for Simulated Experiences in Human Relations. Denver, CO: Adams County School District 12, 1970. ERIC ED 047 851.

A Total System Approach Attacking the Educational Problems of the Illiterate Spanish-Surnamed Adults. Final Report. Albuquerque, NM: Southwestern Cooperative Educational Lab, Ag, 1969. ERIC ED 060 405.

Trends in Hispanic Segregation, 1970-1974.
Vol. II. Washington, DC: Center for National Policy Review, The Law School, Catholic U. of America, Ja, 1977.

Turner, H. C. Team Teaching, Employing a Vari-
ety of Methods for Spanish/Anglo-American
Integration. Title IV, 1969-70. Final
Report. Las Vegas, NM: Las Vegas City
Schools, 1970. ERIC ED 056 130.

Turner, Paul R. (ed.). Bilingualism in the
Southwest. Tucson, AZ: U. of Arizona Press,
1973.

Ulibarri, Horacio. Bilingual Education: A
Handbook for Educators. Interpretive
Studies on Bilingual Education. Albuquerque,
NM: U. of New Mexico, Mr, 1970. ERIC ED
038 078.

_____ (ed.). Interpretive Studies on Bilingual
Education. Final Report. Albuquerque, NM:
U. of New Mexico, Mr, 1970. ERIC ED 038 079.

U.S. Bureau of the Census. Current Population
Reports. Series P-20, No. 195, "Spanish-
American Population: November, 1969."
Washington, DC: GPO, F 20, 1970.

_____. Data on the Spanish Ancestry Popula-
tion Available from the 1970 Census of
Population and Housing. Washington, DC:
U.S. Bureau of the Census, My, 1975.

_____. Nosotros, los americanos--We the
Americans. Washington, DC: GPO, Je, 1973.

_____. "Persons of Spanish Ancestry." 1970
Census of Population. Washington, DC:
GPO, F, 1973.

_____. Persons of Spanish Origin in the
United States: March 1975 (Advance Report).
Washington, DC: GPO, Ag, 1975.

_____. Persons of Spanish Origin in the
United States: March 1975. Washington,
DC: GPO, F, 1976.

_____. Series P-20, No. 213. Personas de
Origen Hispano en los Estados Unidos:
Noviembre 1969. Washington, DC: GPO,
1971.

U.S. Cabinet Committee on Opportunities for
Spanish Speaking People. Annual Report...
Fiscal Year 1971. Washington, DC: GPO,
1971.

U.S. Civil Service Commission. A Guide to High
School Recruitment: School Districts With
Significant Hispanic Student Enrollment.
Washington, DC: GPO, 1976.

_____. A Profile of Hispanic Employment:
1974-1976. Washington, DC: GPO, 1978.

U.S. Commission on Civil Rights, Illinois State
Advisory Committee. Bilingual/Bicultural
Education--A Privilege or a Right? Washing-
ton, DC: The Commission, My, 1974.

U.S. Commission on Civil Rights. Counting the
Forgotten. The 1970 Census Count of Persons
of Spanish Speaking Background in the United
States. Washington, DC: The Commission,
Ap, 1974.

_____. Demographic, Economic and Social
Characteristics of the Spanish-Surname
Population of Five Southwestern States.
Printed in U.S. Congress, 91st, 1st session,
Senate, Committee on Labor and Public Wel-
fare, Subcommittee on Migratory Labor.
Migrant and Seasonal Farmworker Powerless-
ness Hearings, Part 3-B. Washington, DC:
GPO, 1970:945-1024.

_____. Equal Educational Opportunities for the
Spanish-Speaking Child. Bilingual and Bi-
cultural Educational Programs. Washington,
DC: GPO, 1970.

U.S. Congress, 90th, 1st session, Senate,
Committee on Labor and Public Welfare,
Special Subcommittee on Bilingual Education.
Bilingual Education. Hearings. 2 vols.
Washington, DC: GPO, 1967.

U.S. Congress, 91st, 1st session, House of
Representatives, Committee on Government
Operations, Executive and Legislative
Reorganization Subcommittee. Establishing
the Cabinet Committee on Opportunities for
Spanish-Speaking People. Hearings...
Washington, DC: GPO, 1970.

U.S. Congress, 92nd, 1st session, Senate,
Committee on Government Operations. Nomina-
tion of Henry M. Ramirez. Hearing...
Washington, DC: GPO, 1971.

U.S. Congress, 92nd, 1st session, Senate,
Report No. 92-335. Amending The Act of
December 30, 1969, Establishing Cabinet Com-
mittee on Opportunities for Spanish-Speaking
People, To Authorize Appropriations for 2 Ad-
ditional Years. Washington, DC: GPO, 1971.

U.S. Congress, 93rd, 2nd session, House of
Representatives, Committee on Post Office and
Civil Service, Subcommittee on Census and
Statistics. Economic and Social Statistics
for Spanish-Speaking Americans. Hearings...
Washington, DC: GPO, 1974.

U.S. Congress, 93rd, 2nd session, House of
Representatives, Committee on the Judiciary,
Subcommittee on Civil Rights, and Constitu-
tional Rights. Federal Employment of Spanish-
Speaking Americans. Hearings... Serial No.
58. Washington, DC: GPO, 1975.

U.S. Congress, 94th, 1st session, House of Representatives, Committee on Post Office and Civil Service, Subcommittee on Census and Population. Economic and Social Statistics for Americans of Spanish Origin. Hearing... Washington, DC: GPO, 1975.

Valencia, Atilano A. Bilingual/Bicultural Education: A Quest for Institutional Reform! Riverside, CA: Western Regional School Desegregation Projects, U. of Calfironia, Riverside, Ap, 1971.

_____. Research and Development Needs and Priorities for the Education of the Spanish-Speaking People. Albuquerque, NM: Southwestern Cooperative Educational Lab., Mr, 1971. ERIC ED 052 886.

_____. Research and Development Needs and Priorities for the Education of the Spanish-Speaking People. Albuquerque, NM: Southwestern Cooperative Educational Lab, Jl, 1970. ERIC ED 041 521.

Valenzuela, Alvara Miguel. The Relationships Between Self-Concept, Intelligence, Socio-Economic Status and School Achievement Among Spanish-American Children in Omaha, 1971. Thesis, U. of Nebraska, Omaha. ERIC ED 056 785.

"Values of Bilingual, Multicultural Education Cited." Denver Post, F 26, 1974. [Primarily an account of testimony by Dr. José C Cardenas]

Valverde, Leonard A. Segregation, Desegregation, and Resegregation of the Spanish-Surname Student in the United States, Ag, 1976. ERIC ED 131 963.

Vásquez, James. "Measurement of Intelligence and Language Differences." Aztlan 3(Spring, 1972):155-163.

"Que Viva El Pueblo." A Biographical History of Jose Cha-Cha Jimenez. General Secretary of the Young Lords Organization. Chicago : N.p., 1972.

Vorhauer, Delia. A Profile of Boston's Spanish Speaking Community: Characteristics and Attitudes. Boston, MA: Action for Boston Community Development, Ap, 1969.

Walton, John, and Salces, Luis M., with Belenchia, Joanne. The Political Organization of Chicago's Latino Communities. Evanston, IL: Center for Urban Affairs, Northwestern U., n.d.

Westminster Case, 161 F 2nd 774. Wisconsin Law Rev., 1948:227-230; Harvard Law Rev. S, 1947: 1156-1158; Illinois Law Rev., 42, S-O, 1947: 545-549; Minnesota Law Rev., 30, Je, 1946: 646-647; Columbia Law Rev., 47, Mr, 1947: 325-327; Yale Law Rev., 56, Je, 1947:1059-1967.

Whiting, Rosemary. An Overview of the Spanish-Speaking Population in Boston. Boston, MA: Mayor's Office of Public Service, 1969.

Wilber, George L. and others. Minorities in the Labor Market. Vol. I: Spanish Americans and Indians in the labor market. Lexington, KY: Social Welfare Research Institute, U. of Lexington, 1975.

Williams, Frederick, and Wart, Geraldine Van. Carrascolendas: Bilingual Education Through Television. New York: Praeger, 1974.

Willis, Robert M. Evaluation of Teaching English As a Second Language. New York: School of Education, New York U., S, 1969.

Wright, Lawrence. "Bilingual Education." Race Relations Reporter 4(S, 1973):14-19.

_____. "The Bilingual Education Movement at the Crossroads." Phi Delta Kappan, N, 1973.

Zaremba, Sarah W. "Spanish in the Preschool: A Bilingual Aid for the English-Speaking Staff." Young Children 30(Mr, 1975):174-178.

Zintz, Miles V., Ulibarri, Mari Luci, and Gonzalex, Dolores. The Implications of Bilingual Education for Developing Multicultural Sensitivity through Teacher Training. Washington, DC: ERIC, 1971.

Zirkel, Perry Alan. "Spanish-Speaking Students and Standardized Tests." Urban Review 5 (Je, 1972):32-40.

Zirkel, Perry Alan, and Greene, John F. The Academic Achievement of Spanish-Speaking First Graders in Connecticut. Hartford, CT: Connecticut State Department of Education, Bureau of Compensatory and Community Educational Services, Ap, 1971. ERIC ED 054 275.

_____. The Measurement of Self-Concept of Disadvantaged Students, F, 1971. Paper, National Council on Measurement in Education. ERIC ED 053 160.

Bibliographies

Altus, David M. (comp.). Bilingual Education. A Selected Bibliography. University Park, NM: ERIC Clearinghouse on Rural Education and Small Schools, New Mexico State U., D, 1970. ERIC ED 047 853.

Arroyo, Luis Leobardo (comp.). A Bibliography of Recent Chicago History Writings, 1970-1975. Los Angeles: Chicano Studies Center, U. of California at Los Angeles, Je, 1975.

Babin, Patrick (ed.). Bilingualism. A Bibliography. Cambridge, MA: Harvard Graduate School of Education, 1968.

Barrios, Ernie (ed.). Bibliografia de Aztlan: An Annotated Chicano Bibliography. San Diego, CA: San Diego State College, Centro de Estudios Chicanos Publications, 1971. ERIC ED 050 883.

Bastide, Roger (comp.). Répertoire contenant une liste des Instituts de recherche et des specialistes afro-latino-américains... Paris: UNESCO, N 5, 1969.

A Bibliography of Materials in English and Spanish Relating to Puerto Rican Students, Je, 1971. Connecticut Migrating Children's Program, U. of Hartford, 200 Bloomfield Ave., Hartford, CT 06117.

Bryant, Gladys Birdwell. Chicanos: A Selected Bibliography. Houston, TX: Houston U. Libraries, Ja, 1971. ERIC ED 048 987.

Bogardus, E. S. (comp.). The Mexican Immigrants An Annotated Bibliography. Los Angeles, CA: Council on International Relations, 1929.

Bravo, Enrique R. (comp.). Bibliografia Puerto-rriqueña Selecta Anotada. Tr. Marcial Cuevas. New York: Urban Center, Columbia U., 1972. [Bilingual ed., Spanish and English]

Briggs, Marvin D. "A Guide to the Mexican-American in the Southwest." Master's thesis, California State College at Fullerton, CA, 1969. Univ. Microfilms Order No. M-1714.

Cabello-Argandona, Roberta, Gomez-Quinones, Juan, and Duran, Patricia Herrera (comps.). The Chicana. A Comprehensive Bibliographic Study. Los Angeles: Chicano Studies Center, U. of California at Los Angeles, 1975..

Cabinet Committee on Opportunities for Spanish Speaking People. The Spanish Speaking in the United States: A Guide to Materials. Washington, DC: GPO, 1971.

Carlson, A. W. (comp.). "Mexican Americans and a Bibliography of the Geographical Literature, 1920-1971." Revista geographica 75(D, 1971): 154-161.

Chavarría, Jesús. "A Précis and a Tentative Bibliography on Chicano History." Aztlan 1 (Spring, 1970):133-141.

Christiansen, Dorothy (comp.). "Bilingualism: Selected References on Teaching Bilingual Students." Center Forum, S, 1969.

Cumberland, Charles S. "The United States-Mexican Border: A Selective Guide to the Literature of the Region." Rural Sociology 25(Je, 1960):supplement.

De Aztlan a Hoy. Mexican-American Culture and History. Los Angeles, CA: Los Angeles Public Library, 1970.

Dorn, Georgette M. (comp.). Latin America, Spain, and Portugal. An Annotated Bibliography of Paperback Books. Washington, DC: GPO, 1971.

Dossick, Jesse J. Doctoral Research on Puerto Rico and Puerto Ricans, 1967. ERIC ED 020 215.

Fraser, Howard M. (comp.). "Languages in Contact: A Bibliographical Guide to Linguistic Borrowings Between English and Spanish." Bilingual Review 2(Ja-Ag, 1975): 138-172.

Garza, Ben and others. Chicano Bibliography. Education...the Last Hope of the Poor Chicano. (Education...La Ultima Esperanza Del Pobre Chicano). Davis, CA: Movimento Estudiantil Chicano De Aztlan, 1965. ERIC ED 034 642.

Geigel y Zenon, José and Ferrer, Abelardo Morales (comps.). Bibliografia puertorri-uena. Barcelona: Editorial Araluce, 1934.

Grebler, Leo, Moore, Joan W., and Guzman, Ralph C. and others. "Bibliography." The Mexican-American People. The Nation's Second Largest Minority. New York: Free Press, 1970.

Gropp, Arthur E. (comp.). A Bibliography of Latin American Bibliographies. Metuchen, NJ: Scarecrow Press, 1968.

Gutierrez, Felix, and Schement, Jorge Reina (comps.). "Chicanos and the Media: A Bibliography of Selected Materials." Journalism History 4(Summer, 1977):53-55.

Haro, Robert R. "Los Chicanos. A Bibliographic Essay." Con Safos 7(Winter, 1971):50-59.

Harrigan, Joan (comp.). More Materials Tocante Los Latinos. A Bibliography of Materials on the Spanish-American. Denver, CO: Colorado State Department of Education, Je, 1969. ERIC ED 031 344.

Harrigen, Einer I. Bilingualism in the Americas: A Bibliography and Research Guide. University, AL: U. of Alabama Press, 1959.

Heathman, James E., Martinez, Cecilia J. (comps.). Mexican American Education, A Selected Bibliography. University Park, NM: New Mexico State University. ERIC Clearinghouse on Rural Education and Small Schools, Jl, 1969. ERIC ED 031 352.

Hernández, Andrés R. (ed.). The Cuban Minority in the U.S.: Final Report on Need Identification and Program Evaluation. Washington, DC: Cuban National Planning Council, 1974.

Johnson, John J. (comp.). The Mexican American. A Selected and Annotated Bibliography. Stanford, CA: Stanford U. Press, 1969.

Kirschner, Madeline (comp.). "Puerto Rican Bibliography." RQ 9(Fall, 1969):9-19.

_____. Serving the Spanish Community: Puerto Rican Bibliography. Chicago: Adult Services Division, American Library Association, 1970.

Legislative Reference Service. Miscellaneous Bibliographics on Mexican-Americans. Washington, DC: Library of Congress, 1964, 1965, 1967, and 1968.

Leyba, Charles (comp.). A Brief Bibliography on Teacher Education and Chicanos, Ap, 1974. ERIC ED 090 147.

Link, Albert D. (comp.). Mexican American Education. A Selected Bibliography (with ERIC Abstracts). ERIC/CRESS Supplement No. 2. Las Cruces, NM: New Mexico State U., My, 1972.

López, Daniel. "A Critique of Bibliographics on Puerto Rico and Puerto Ricans." Newsletter, National Association of Interdisciplinary Studies for Native American, Black, Chicano, Puerto Rican, and Asian Americans. 1(D, 1975):7-12.

Meier, Matt S. (comp.). "Dissertations [on Mexican American History]." Journal of Mexican American History 1(Spring, 1971):170-190.

Meier, Matt S., and Rivera, Feliciano (comps.). A Selective Bibliography for the Study of Mexican American History. San Francisco, CA: R & E Research Associates, 1972.

Messinger, M. A. The Forgotten Child: A Bibliography with Special Emphasis on Materials Relating to the Education of 'Spanish-Speaking' People in the United States. Austin, TX: Department of History and Philosophy of Education, U. of Texas, Jl, 1967.

Mexican American Education, A Selected Bibliography... Supplement No. 4., O, 1974. ERIC ED 097 187.

Mexican-Americans: Bibliografía. Portales, NM: Eastern New Mexico U. Library, 1970.

Mexican-Americans: A Selective Guide to Materials in the UCSB Library. Santa Barbara, CA: California U, My, 1969. ERIC ED 032 150.

Mickey, Barbara H. A Bibliography of Studies Concerning the Spanish-Speaking Population of the American Southwest. Museum of Anthropology Miscellaneous Series, No. 4. Greeley, CO: Museum of Anthropology, Colorado State College, My, 1969. ERIC ED 042 548.

Mohr, Eugene V. (comp.). "Fifty Years of Puerto Rican Literature in English--1923-1973. An Annotated Bibliography." Revista/Review Interamericana 3(Fall, 1973).

Moreno, Joseph A. Clark. "A Bibliography of Bibliographies Relating to Studies of Mexican Americans." El Grito 5(Winter, 1971-1972):47-79.

_____. "A Bibliography of Bibliographies Relating to Mexican-American Studies." El Grito 3(Summer, 1970):25-31.

New York Public Library (comp.). Boriquen: A Bilingual List of Books, Films and Records on the Puerto Rican Experience. 3rd ed. New York: New York Public Library, 1974.

Noble, Vincente and others (comps.). Counseling the Mexican American Client: An Annotated Bibliography of Journal Literature, 1964-1974, 1974. ERIC ED 130 199.

Nogales, Luis G. (ed.). The Mexican American: A Selected and Annotated Bibliography. Stanford, CA: Stanford U., F, 1971. ERIC ED 050 865.

Ortiz, Ana María (comp.). Bibliography on Hispano America History and Culture, 1972. Illinois Commission on Human Relations, 160 North LaSalle Street, Chicago, IL 60601.

Padilla, Ray. "Apuntes Para La Documentación De La Cultura Chicana." El Grito 5(Winter, 1971-1972):3-46. [The best place to begin a search for references]

Parker, Franklin (comp.). Latin-American Education Research: Annotated Bibliography of 269 United States Doctoral Dissertations. Austin, TX: Institute of Latin American Studies, U. of Texas, 1964. [Puerto Rico]

Parker, Franklin, and Parker, Betty June Education in Puerto Rico and of Puerto Ricans in the USA. San Juan, Puerto Rico: InterAmerican U. Press, 1978.

Pino, Frank (comp.). Mexican-Americans: A Research Bibliography 2 vols. East Lansing, MI: Latin American Studies Center, Michigan State U., 1974.

Portillo, Cristina, Rios, Graciela, and Rodriguez, Martha (comps.). Bibliography of Writings on La Mujer. Berkeley: Chicano Studies Library, U. of California, D, 1977.

Prohías, Rafael J., and Casal, Lourdes The Cuban Minority in the U.S.: Preliminary Report on Need Identification and Program Evaluation. Boca Raton: Florida Atlantic U., 1973.

Revelle, Keith (comp.). Chicano! A Selected Bibliography by and About Mexico and Mexican Americans, 1970. Latin American Library, 1457 Fruitvale Ave., Oakland, CA 94601.

_____. "A Collection for La Raza." Library Journal 96(N 15, 1971):3719-3726.

Ross, Stanley R. "Bibliography of Sources for Contemporary Mexican History." Hispanic American Historical Review 39(1959):234-238.

Rott, Renate. "The Once Forgotten Minority: Mexican Americans in the United States. Report and Bibliography." Amerikastudien 29 (No. 2, 1975):320-335.

Saldana, Nancy. Mexican-Americans in the Midwest: An Annotated Bibliography. East Lansing, MI: Michigan State U., Rural Manpower Center, Jl, 1969. ERIC ED 050 833.

Segreto, Joan. Bibliographia: A Bibliography on the Mexican-American. Houston, TX: Houston Independent School District, 1970. ERIC ED 046 616.

A Selected List of Materials Relating to Mexican-Americans. Portales, NM: Eastern New Mexico U., 1970.

Smith, Bonnie L. (comp.). The Chicano: A Bibliography of Materials by and about Mexican-Americans and Mexico, 1970. Phil H. Putnam Memorial Library, Palomar College, San Marcos, CA.

Strange, Susan, and Priest, Rhea Pendergrass. Bibliography: The Mexican American in the Migrant Labor Setting, 1968. ERIC ED 032 188.

Tash, Steven (comp.). Selected Bibliography of Resources for Chicano Studies. San Fernando State College Library, Northridge, CA 91317.

Teschner, Richard V., Bills, Garland D., and Craddock, Jerry R. (comps.). Spanish and English of United States Hispanos: A Critical, Annotated, Linguistic Bibliography. Arlington, VA: Center for Applied Linguistics, 1975.

Teschner, Richard V., with others (comps.). Spanish-Surnamed Populations of the United States: A Catalog of Dissertations. Ann Arbor, MI: Xerox U. Microfilms, 1974.

"Toward a Chicano/Raza Bibliography: Drama, Prose, Poetry." El Grito 7(D, 1973): entire issue.

Trejo, Arnulfo D. (ed.). Bibliografia chicana: A Guide to Information Sources. Detroit: Gale, 1975.

Vaughn, Denton R. (comp). Urbanization in Twentieth Century Latin America: A Working Bibliography. Austin, TX: Institute of Latin American Studies, U. of Texas, 1969.

Vivo, Paquita (comp.). The Puerto Ricans: An Annotated Bibliography. New York: Bowker, 1973.

Whittenburg, Clarice T., and Sanchez, George I. (comps.). Materials Relating to the Education of Spanish-Speaking People. A Bibliography. Austin, TX: The U. of Texas, F, 1948.

Woodbridge, Hensley C. "Fourteen Chicano Bibliographies, 1971-1975." Modern Language Journal 61(Ja-F, 1977). [Critical review]

Woods, Richard D. (comp.). Reference Materials on Mexican Americans: An Annotated Bibliography. Metuchen, NJ: Scarecrow Press, 1976.

Zirkel, Perry Alan. A Bibliography of Materials in English and Spanish Relating to Puerto Rican Students. Hartford, CT: Connecticut State Department of Education, Je, 1971. ERIC ED 057 142.

6.
AMERICAN INDIANS

American Indians by Tribe

Algonkin

Curtis, Marta E. "A Study of the Relation of Some Science Materials Known to Certain Algonkin Indians to Present Elementary School Teaching." Doctoral dissertation, Cornell U., 1944.

Apache

Anderson, Ned, and Chilcott, John H. Formal Education on the White Mountain Apache Reservation: Report of a Self-Study Conference. The National Study of American Indian Education, Series I, No. 25, Final Report. Chicago, IL: U. of Chicago, Ag, 1970, 48 pp. ERIC ED 046 603.

Bernardoni, Louis C. "Critical Factors Influencing the Stated Vocational Preference of Male, White-Mountain Apache Students." Doctoral dissertation, Arizona State U., 1962.

Capps, Inez H. "Social Change Among the White Mountain Apache Indians from the 1800's to the Present." Master's thesis, Montana State U., 1952.

Cassel, Russell N., and Sanders, Richard A. "A Comparative Analysis of Scores from Two Leadership Tests for Apache Indian and Anglo American Youth." Journal of Educational Research 55(S, 1961):19-23.

Chilcott, John H., and Anderson, Ned. San Carlos Apache Indian Reservation and Bylas, Arizona: Fort Thomas Public Schools. National Study of American Indian Education. Final Report. Chicago, IL: U. of Chicago, Ja, 1970, 17 pp. ERIC ED 045 270.

Comptroller General of the United States. Better Overall Planning to Improve the Standard of Living of White Mountain Apaches of Arizona. Washington, DC: General Accounting Office, 1975.

Dotson, Theotis R. "Problems Related to the Education of Apache Indian Children." Master's thesis, U. of Tennessee, 1963.

Dubois, Betty Lou. "A Study in Educational Anthropology: The Mescalero Apache." American Indian Education 15(My, 1976):22-27.

Goodman, Basil H. "An Investigation of the Adjustment of the Apache Indians to the Public Schools of the State of Arizona." Master's thesis, Arizona State U., 1951.

Hicks, Mozelle. "The Influence of Education on the Life of the Apache Indians on the San Carlos Reservation." Master's thesis, Arizona State College, Flagstaff, 1942.

Marinsek, E. A. The Effect of Cultural Difference in the Education of Apache Indians. Albuquerque, NM: U. of New Mexico Press, 1960.

Owen, George M. and others. Nutritional Survey of White Mountain Apache Preschool Children. Columbus, OH: Ohio State U., Children's Hospital Research Foundation, 1970, 22 pp. ERIC ED 046 508.

Parmee, Edward A. Formal Education and Culture Change: A Modern Apache Indian Community and Government Education Programs. Tucson, AZ: U. of Arizona Press, 1968.

Scott, Richard. "Acculturation Among 'Mescalero' Apache High School Students." Master's thesis, U. of New Mexico, 1959.

Silvaroli, Nicholas, and Zuchowski, John M. Educating Apache Indian Children in a Public School System. Final Report of the Fort Thomas Diverse Capacity Project. Phoenix, AZ: Arizona Western States Small School Project, Je, 1968, 21 pp. ERIC 026 182.

Sims, Emmett M. "Industrial Arts Program for the Apache Indian Students in Fort Thomas Union High School." Master's thesis, Arizona State College, Tempe, 1953.

Taylor, Benjamin J., and O'Connor, Dennis J. Fort Apache Reservation Manpower Resources; Indian Manpower Resources in the Southwest. A Pilot Study. Tempe, AZ: Arizona State U., College of Business Administration, 1969, 43 pp. ERIC ED 043 444.

Arapaho

Hilger, I. Arapaho Child Life and Its Cultural Backgrounds. St. Clair Shores, MI: Scholarly Press, 1952.

Blackfeet

Carr, Kevin James. "Education in Early Blackfoot Indian Culture." Master's thesis, U. of Alberta, 1968.

Harrod, Howard L. "Mission Among the Blackfeet: An Evaluation of Protestant and Catholic Missions Among the Blackfeet Indians." Doctoral dissertation, Yale U., 1965.

Humphrey, Theodore R. Browning and the Blackfeet Indian Reservation, 1970. ERIC ED 040 794.

McFee, Malcolm. "Modern Blackfeet: Contrasting Patterns of Differential Acculturation." Doctoral dissertation, Stanford U., 1962.

Schmidt, Florence M. "A Survey of the Occupations of Blackfeet Indians." Master's thesis, U. of Montana, 1942. [The author is a Blackfeet.]

Cherokee

Beckett, Ola L. "The Cherokee Phoenix and Its Efforts in the Education of the Cherokees." Master's thesis, U. of Oklahoma, 1934.

Buchanan, Robert W. "Patterns of Organization and Leadership among Contemporary Oklahoma Cherokee." Doctoral dissertation, U. of Kansas, 1973.

Cowan, Clara B. "Assimilation of the Cherokees as Revealed in a Hundred Urban Families." Master's thesis, U. of Missouri, 1941.

Davis, John Benjamin. "Public Education Among the Cherokee Indians." Peabody Journal of Education 7(N, 1929):168-73.

Dickeman, Mildred. "The Integrity of the Cherokee Student." In The Culture of Poverty: A Critique. Edited by Eleanor Leacock. New York: Simon & Schuster, 1971.

Dumont, Robert V., Jr. "Cherokee Children and the Teacher." Social Education, Ja, 1969.

Dumont, Robert V., Jr., and Wax, Murray L. "Cherokee School Society and the Intercultural Classroom." Human Organization 28(Fall, 1969): 217-226.

Du Pree, T. J. Brief History of Cherokee Schools, 1804-1907, My, 1976. ERIC ED 127 051.

Ervin, Bertha J. "The Development of Education Among the Cherokee Indians." Master's thesis, Oklahoma A & M College, 1932.

Goodwin, Gary C. "Cherokees in Transition: A Study of the Changing Culture and Environment Prior to 1775." Doctoral dissertation, U. of Chicago, 1976.

Guyette, Susan Marie. "Sociolinguistic Determinants of Native Language Vitality: A Comparative Study of Two Oklahoma Cherokee Communities." Doctoral dissertation, Southern Methodist U., 1975.

Hall, Tom Aldis. "The Socio-economic Status of the Cherokee Indians." Master's thesis, U. of Oklahoma, 1934.

Halliburton, R., Jr. "Black Slave Control in the Cherokee Nation." Journal of Ethnic Studies 3(Summer, 1975):23-35.

_____. "Origins of Black Slavery Among the Cherokees." Chronicles of Oklahoma 52(Winter, 1974-1975).

Henshaw, Lillie D. "A History of the Cherokee Tribal Schools Since the Civil War." Master's thesis, U. of Oklahoma, 1935.

Holland, Cullen J. "The Cherokee Indian Newspapers, 1828-1906: The Tribal Voice of a People in Transition." Doctoral dissertation, U. of Minnesota, 1956.

Holmes, Ruth Bradley, and Smith, Betty Sharp. Beginning Cherokee. Norman: U. of Oklahoma Press, 1976.

Johnson, N. B. "The Cherokee Orphan Asylum." Chronicles of Oklahoma 44(Autumn, 1966):275-280.

Kilpatrick, Jack Frederick, and Kilpatrick, Anna Gritts (eds.). The Shadow of Sequoyah: Social Documents of the Cherokees. Norman: U. of Oklahoma Press, 1976.

Knepler, Abraham Eleazar. "Digest of the Education of the Cherokee Indians." Doctoral dissertation, Yale U., 1939.

_____. "Education in the Cherokee Nation." Chronicles of Oklahoma 21(D, 1943):378-401.

_____. "Eighteenth Century Cherokee Education Efforts." Chronicles of Oklahoma 20(Mr, 1942): 55-61.

Kupferer, Harriet J. "Health Practices and Education Aspirations as Indicators of Acculturation and Social Class Among the Eastern Cherokee." Social Forces 41(D, 1962):154-163.

Kutsche, Paul. "Cherokee High School Dropouts." Journal of American Indian Education 3(Ja, 1964):22-30.

Lambert, Paul F. "The Cherokee Reconstruction Treaty of 1866." Journal of the West 12 (Jl, 1973):471-489.

Littlefield, Daniel F. The Cherokee Freedmen: From Emancipation to American Citizenship. Westport, CT: Greenwood Press, 1978.

Neely, Sharlotte. "The Quaker Era of Cherokee Indian Education, 188-1892." Appalachian Journal 2(Summer, 1975).

Norgren, Jill L., and Shattuck, Petra T. "Limits of Legal Action: The Cherokee Cases." American Indian Culture and Research Journal 2(1978):14-25.

Perdue, Theda. Slavery and the Evolution of Cherokee Society, 1540-1866. Knoxville: U. of Tennessee Press, 1979.

Purrington, Burton L. "Introduction: Reassessing Cherokee Studies." Appalachian Studies 2 (Summer, 1975):252-257.

Roethler, Michael. "Negro Slavery Among the Cherokee Indians, 150-1866." Doctoral dissertation, Fordham U., 1964.

Sanders, Pauline M. "The Relationship of Culturally Related Variables to the Reading Achievement of Nonreservation Cherokee Indian Pupils." Doctoral dissertation, U. of Arkansas, 1972.

Thornton, Sarah. "Education of the Cherokee Indians." Master's thesis, U. of Oklahoma, 1925.

Turner, Alvin O. "Financial Relations Between the United States and the Cherokee Nation, 1830-1870." Journal of the West 12(Jl, 1973): 372-385.

Wahrhaftig, Albert L. The Cherokee People Today: A Report to the Cherokee People. Tr. by Calvin Nackedhead. In U.S. Congress, 90th, 1st and 2nd Sessions, Senate, Committee on Labor and Public Welfare, Special Subcommittee on Indian Education, Indian Education. Hearings...Part 2, pp. 795-841. Washington, DC: GPO, 1969. [Bilingual edition]

Cheyenne

Berthrong, Donald J. The Cheyenne and Arapaho Ordeal. Reservation and Agency Life. Norman, OK: U. of Oklahoma Press, 1976.

Gustafson, Louise, and McConnell, Beverly. Northern Cheyenne Follow Through Program, Serving Children on the Northern Cheyenne Reservation in Southeastern Montana, 1975. ERIC ED 134 377.

Peterson, Karen Daniels. "The Writings of Henry Rowan Nose." Chronicles of Oklahoma 42(1965). 458-478.

Chickasaw

Caroline L. Davis. "The History of the Schools and the Educational Development of the Chickasaw Nation." Master's thesis, U. of Oklahoma, 1937.

Foreman, Carolyn Thomas. "Education Among the Chickasaw Indians." Chronicle of Oklahoma 15(Je, 1937):139-165.

Mitchell, Irene B., and Renken, Ida Belle. "The Golden Age of Bloomfield Academy in the Chickasaw Nation." Chronicle of Oklahoma 49 (Winter, 1971-1972).

Chippewa

Berman, Lael. "Chippewa Leader Seeks Alternative." Christian Science Monitor, N 10, 1975. [Minnesota]

Crockett, David. "An Inquiry Into the Integration of the Chippewa Indian Student Into the Secondary Schools of Northern Minnesota." Master's thesis, St. Cloud State College, 1967.

Friedl, Ernestine. "Persistence in Chippewa Culture and Personality." American Anthropologist 58(1956):814-825.

Holtz, Dolores. Chippewa Indians: A Native American Curriculum Unit for the Fifth Grade. NATAM XV, My, 1971, 20 pp. Minneapolis: U. of Minnesota. ERIC ED 051 918.

Kocur, Darlene. Chippewa Indians: A Native American Curriculum Unit for the Third Grade. NATAM XIII, My, 1971, 18 pp. Minneapolis: U. of Minnesota. ERIC ED 051 916.

Kostrich, Dragos D. George Morrison, The Story of an American Indian. Minneapolis: Dillon Press, 1976. [Artist]

LeLand, Gunvald Elias. "Recent Education of Indians in Minnesota with Special Emphasis on the Chippewas." Master's thesis, U. of North Dakota, 1944.

Lieberman, Leonard. "Labor Force Mobility in the Underclass: Opportunities, Subculture and Training Among Chippewa and Poor White." Doctoral dissertation, 1970, 316 pp. Lansing, MI: Michigan State Legislature. ERIC ED 041 204.

Miller, Frank, and Caulkins, D. Douglas. "Chippewa Adolescents: A Changing Culture." Human Organization 23(1964):150-159.

Rosenthal, Bernard G. "Developments of Self-Identification in Relation to Attitudes Toward the Self in the Chippewa Indians." Genetic Psychology Monographs 90(Ag, 1974):43-142.

Choctaw

Baird, W. David. "Spencer Academy, Choctaw Nation, 1842-1900." Chronicles of Oklahoma 45 25-43.

Culbertson, Jean. "Calm Appearances Belie State Choctaw Schools." Jackson [Mississippi] Clarion-Ledger, D 27, 1973.

Foreman, Carolyn T. "The Choctaw Academy." Chronicles of Oklahoma 6(1928):453-480, 9(1931):382-411, and 10(1932):77-114.

_____. "St. Agnes Academy for the Choctaws." Chronicles of Oklahoma 48(Autumn, 1970):323-330.

Fox, George E. "The Choctaw Academy: An Experiment in Indian Education." Master's thesis, George Washington U., 1943.

Gregory, Hiram F. "Jena Band of Louisiana Choctaw." American Indian Journal 3(F, 1977): 2-16.

Kim, Cheong Soon. An Asian Anthropologist in the South: Field Experiences with Blacks, Indians, Whites. Knoxville: U. of Tennesee Press, 1977.

Lawrence, Ruth. "Exploring Childhood on an Indian Reservation." Children Today 5(S-O, 1976):10-12, 34. [Mississippi]

Peterson, John Holbrook, Jr. "The Mississippi Band of Choctaw Indians: Their Recent History and Current Social Relations." Doctoral dissertation, U. of Georgia, 1970.

Spalding, Arminta Scott. "From the Natchez Trace to Oklahoma: Development of Christian Civilization Among the Choctaws, 1800-1860." Chronicles of Oklahoma 45(1967):2-24.

Spear, Eloise G. "Choctaw Indian Education with Special Reference to Choctaw County, Oklahoma." Doctoral dissertation, U. of Oklahoma, 1977. Univ. Microfilms Order No. 77-32883.

Swinney, J. S. "The Development of Education Among the Choctaw Indians." Master's thesis, Oklahoma A. & M. College, 1935.

Comanche

Tippeconnic, John W. "Comanche Indian Customs with Educational Implications." Master's thesis, Arizona State College, Flagstaff, 1942.

Creek

Drain, Maude. "The History of the Education of the Creek Indians." Master's thesis, U. of Oklahoma, 1928.

Dugan, E. J. "Education Among the Creek Indians." Master's thesis, Oklahoma A. & M. College, 1938.

Flowers, Marvin P. "Education Among the Creek Indians." Master's thesis, Oklahoma A. & M. College, 1931.

Jackson, Joe C. "Church School Education in the Creek Nation, 1898 to 1907." Chronicles of Oklahoma 42(Autumn, 1968):312-330.

"Journal of Alexander Lawrence Posey." Chronicles of Oklahoma, Winter, 1967-1968 and Spring, 1968.

McKinley, Kenneth H. and Others. Creek Nation Census: A Socio-Economic Survey of Selected Household and Individual Characteristics. Je. 1976. ERIC ED 135 539.

Crow

Bradley, Susanna L. "A Readiness Program for the Crow Indians." Master's thesis, Montana State U., 1970.

Henderson, William J. "The Cultural, Social and Religious Background of the Crow Indians: 1885-1955." Master's thesis, Montana State U., 1956.

Jensen, Joyce Martin. "School Readiness and Achievement of Crow Indian Children, 1st through 4th Grades at Pryor, Montana." Master's thesis, Montana State U., 1970.

U.S. Department of the Interior, Rulings. Crow-Mineral-Timber-School Land Grants. Op. Sol. M. 6366, D 27, 1921.

_____. School Land Within Crow Reservation. 49 L. D. 376, D 28, 1922.

Delaware

Newcome, William W., Jr. "The Culture and Acculturation of the Delaware Indians." Doctoral dissertation, U. of Michigan, 1953.

Eskimo

Berry, J. W. "Psychological Research in the North." Anthropologica 13(1971):143-157.

Hensley, William L. "Arctic Development and the Future of Eskimo Societies." Indian Truth, F, 1970.

Hughes, Charles C. "Under Four Flags: Recent Culture Change Among the Eskimos." Current Anthropology 6(1965):3-69.

Kleinfeld, Judith S. "Intellectual Strengths in Culturally Different Groups: An Eskimo Illustration." Review of Educational Research 43(Summer, 1973):341-359.

Kristensen, Karl. "Eskimology." Northian 8 (Summer, 1971):3-13.

Lantis, M. (ed.). Eskimo Childhood and Interpersonal Relationships: Numivak Biographies and Genealogies. Seattle: U. of Washington Press, 1960.

Zann, Claire George. "A Comparative Analysis of the Mode of Life Presented in Selected Basal Readers with Everyday Life of Eskimo Children." Master's thesis, California State U., 1969.

Flathead

Bigart, Robert James. "Patterns of Cultural Change in a Salish Flathead Community." Human Organization 30(F, 1971):229-237.

_____. "The Salish Flathead Indians During the Period of Adjustment, 1850-1891." Idaho Yesterday 17(Fall, 1973).

Brockmann, C. Thomas. "Correlation of Social Class and Education on the Flathead Reservation, Montana." Rocky Mountain Social Science Quarterly 8(O, 1971):11-17.

_____. "Social Class and Educational Level on the Flathead Reservation." Journal of American Indian Education 10(O, 1970):23-31.

Malan, Vernon D. "Language and Social Change Among the Flathead Indians." Master's thesis, Montana State U., 1948.

Hopi

Brennig, Robert G. "Hopi Perspectives on Formal Education." Doctoral dissertation, U. of Kansas, 1973.

Coles, Robert. "Children and Politics: Outsiders." New York Review of Books, Mr 20, 1975.

Dennis, Wayne. The Hopi Child. New York: John Wiley and Sons, 1965.

Eggan, Dorothy. "Instruction and Affect in Hopi Cultural Continuity." Southwestern Journal of Anthropology 12(Winter, 1956):347-370.

Michael Kubotie and others. Community Background Reports: Second Mesa Day School: Hopi-Mishongnovi, Shipaulovi, Shungopavy Villages and Sunlight Baptist Mission. National Study of American Indian Education, Series I, Number 12. Final Report, 1970, 22 pp. Chicago: U. of Chicago. ERIC ED 041 687.

Laird, W. David (comp.). Hopi Bibliography. Tucson: U. of Arizona Press, 1977.

Levenson, Dorothy. "Hopi Schooling for Two Worlds." Teacher (Missouri) N, 1975.

Peters, Herbert D. "Performance of Hopi Children on Four Intelligence Tests." Journal of American Indian Education 2(Ja, 1963): 27-31.

Polingayi Qoyawayma (Elizabeth Q. White). No Turning Back. Abuquerque: U. of New Mexico Press, 1964. [A Hopi Indian woman tells how she became a teacher in government schools]

Simmons, Leo W. (ed.). Sun Chief, the Autobiography of a Hopi Indian. New Haven, CT: Yale U. Press, 1942.

Smith, Dama Margaret. Hopi Girl. Palo Alto, CA: Stanford U. Press, 1931.

Talayesva, Don C. Sun Chief: The Autobiography of a Hopi Indian. Edited by Leo W. Simmons. New Haven, CT: Yale U. Press, 1942.

Thompson, Laura, and Joseph, Alice. The Hopi Way. Chicago: U. of Chicago Press, 1944.

Titiev, Mischa. The Hopi Indians of Old Oraibi: Change and Continuity. Ann Arbor, MI: U. of Michigan Press, 1972.

Williams, James R. "Tribal Education of the Hopi Indian Child." Master's thesis, Arizona State College, Flagstaff, 1948.

Wax, Murray L., and Brennig, Robert G. Study of the Community Impact of the Hopi Follow Through Program, O, 1973. ERIC ED 096 037.

Hupa

Wallace, William J. "Hupa Education: A Study in Primitive Socialization and Personality Development." Doctoral dissertation, U. of California, 1946.

Kickapoo

Pope, R. K. "The Withdrawal of the Kickapoo." The American Indian 8(Winter, 1958):17-27.

Kiowa

McCurtain, Eloise E. "Factors in the Adjustment of One Hundred Kiowa Indian Youths." Master's thesis, U. of Oklahoma, 1953.

Klamath

Pearsall, Marion. "Klamath Childhood and Education." Anthropological Records 9(1950):339-351.

Trulove, W. Tom. "Economics of Paternalism: Federal Policy and the Klamath Indians." Doctoral dissertation, U. of Oregon, 1973.

Zakoji, Hiroto. Termination and the Klamath Indian Education Program, 1955-1961. Salem, OR: State Department of Education, 1961.

Kwakiutl

Ford, C. S. Smoke from Their Fires: The Life of the Kwakiutl Chief. New Haven, CT: Yale U. Press, 1941.

Wolcott, Harry F. "A Kwakiutl Village and Its School: Cultural Barriers to Classroom Performance." Doctoral dissertation, Stanford U., 1965.

_____. A Kwakiutl Village and School. New York: Holt, Rinehart and Winston, 1967.

Lumbee

Baker, Donald P. "Lack of Education Is Factor in Acquittal of [Lumbee] Indians." Washington Post, D 26, 1973.

Barton, Lew. "De-Indianization Trend Observed at Pembroke University." The Robesonian (Lumberton, NC), N 18, 1967, p. 27.

Blu, Karen J. "We People: Understanding Lumbee Indian Identity in a Tri-Racial Situation." Doctoral dissertation, U. of Chicago, 1972.

Dial, Adolph, and Eliades, David K. "The Lumbee Indians of North Carolina and Pembroke State University." Indian Historian 4(Winter, 1 1971):19-24.

_____ and _____. The Only Land I Know: A History of the Lumbee Indians. San Francisco: Indian Historian Press, 1975.

Gaillard, Frye. "Cities Contradict Lumbees' Values." Race Relations Reporter 2(Je 21, 1971):6-9.

_____. "Desegregation Denies Justice to Lumbee Indians." Indian Historian 4(Fall, 1979): 17-22, 43.

_____. "Lumbee Indians." South Today 3(S, 1971):4-5. [Robeson County]

Hancock, Earnest D. "A Sociological Study of the Tri-Racial Community in Robeson County, North Carolina." Master's thesis, U. of North Carolina, 1935.

McDonald, Laughlin. "'Undisciplined' Indians." Civil Liberties 303(Jl, 1974):3-4. [Robeson]

Makofsky, Abraham. "Tradition and Change in the Lumbee Indian Community of Baltimore." Doctoral dissertation, Catholic U. of America, 1971.

Maynor, Waltz. "Academic Performance and School Integration: A Multi-Ethnic Analysis." Doctoral dissertation, Duke U., 1970. [White, Lumbee Indian, and black students in Hoke Co.]

Nelson, Bryce. "Tribe Claims Key to Riddle of Roanoke." Los Angeles Times, My 12, 1977. [Lumbee Indians]

North Carolina Advisory Committee to the U.S. Commission on Civil Rights. Economic and Political Problems of Indians in Robeson County. Washington, DC: U.S. Commission on Civil Rights, Jl, 1974.

Owens, Pamela. "Indians Rebel in [North] Carolina." Southern Patriot 31(My, 1973).

Oxendrine, Clifton. "Pembroke State College for Indians." North Carolina Historical Review,! Ja, 1945.

_____. "A Social and Economic History of the Indians of Robeson County, North Carolina." Master's thesis, George Peabody College, 1934.

Sider, Gerald M. "Lumbee Indian Cultural Nationalism and Ethnogenesis." Dialectical Anthropology 1(F, 1976).

_____. "The Political History of the Lumbee Indians of Robeson County, North Carolina." Doctoral dissertation, New School for Social Research, 1971.

Lummi

Suttles, Wayne. "Post-Contact Culture Changes Among the Lummi Indians." British Columbia Historical Quarterly 18(1954):29-102.

Makah

Colson, Elizabeth. The Makah Indians. A Study of an Indian Tribe in Modern American Society. Minneapolis: U. of Minnesota Press, 1953.

Menominee

Caspar, Margery G. "The Education of Menominee Youth in Wisconsin." Integrated Education 11 (Ja-F, 1973):45-51.

Chira, Susan D. "Indian Activist Ends Stay at Harvard." Harvard Crimson, D 9, 1977. [Adah Deer]

Deer, Ada E. "The Effects of Termination on the Menominee." American Indian Culture Center 4 (Winter, 1973):6-14.

_____. "Menominee Restoration: How the Good Guys Won." Journal of Intergroup Relations 3 (S, 1974):41-50.

Harkins, Arthur M., Sherarts, I. Karon, and Woods, Richard G. The Formal Education of Menominee Indian Children: Sociocultural and Socioeconomic Background Factors, 1970. ERIC ED 043 424.

Harkins, Arthur M., Sherarts, I. Karon, and Nordley, Karen. A Summary Report on Menominee Indian Education, 1968-1970. Minneapolis: Training Center for Community Programs, U. of Minnesota, 1973.

Herzberg, Stephen J. "The Menominee Indians: From Treaty to Termination." Wisconsin Magazine of History 60(Summer, 1977):267-329.

Lurie, Nancy O. "Menominee Termination: From Reservation to Colony." Human Organization 31(F, 1972):257-270.

Orfield, Gary. "The Menominee Struggle. A Tribe Fights to Restore Its Federal Status." Civil Rights Digest 6(Fall, 1973):35-40.

Ourada, Patricia Kathryn. "The Menominee Indians: A History." Doctoral dissertation, U. of Oklahoma, 1973.

Smaes, Debbie and others (eds.). Freedom with Reservation, 1972. Menominee, P.O. Box 1344, Madison, WI 53701. [Results of Menominee Termination Act of 1954]

Spindler, George D. Sociocultural and Psychological Processes in Menomini Acculturation. Berkeley, CA: U. of California Publications in Culture and Society, Volume V, U of California Press, 1955.

Spindler, Mary Louis. "Women and Cultural Change: A Case Study of the Menominee Indians." Doctoral dissertation, Stanford U., 1956.

Spring, Charles. "A Study of the Government Boarding School on the Menominee Reservation." Master's thesis, U. of Buffalo, 1954.

U.S. Congress, 93rd, 1st Session, Senate, Committee on Interior and Insular Affairs, Subcommittee on Indian Affairs. Menominee Restoration Act. Hearings... Washington, DC: GPO, 1973.

Mesquakie

Parker, Alan. "The Mesquakie Indians of Tama, Iowa—A Struggle to Keep a School." United Scholarship Service News, F, 1969.

Polgar, Steven. "Biculturation of Mesquakie Teenage Boys." American Anthropologist 62 (1960):217-235.

Mojave

Walker, Henry P. (ed.). "Teacher to the Mojaves: The Experiences of George W. Nock, 1887-1889." Arizona and the West 9(Summer, Autumn, 1967): 143-166, 259-280.

Navajo

Adair, Mildred L. "The Establishment, Growth, Development, and Functioning of the Federal Day School on the Navajo Reservation Since 1935." Master's thesis, Florida State U., 1938.

Aberle, David F. "A Plan for Navajo Economic Development." In U.S. Congress, 91st, 1st Session, Joint Economic Committee, Subcommittee on Economy in Government, Toward Economic Development for Native American Communities, pp. 223-276. Washington, DC: GPO, 1969.

Allen, Ray A. "Whither Indian Education? A Conversation with Philleo Nash." School Review 79(N, 1970):99-108. [Rough Rock Demonstration School]

Arlen, Jennifer H. "From Bows and Arrows to Lawsuits." Harvard Crimson, N 30, 1978. [About Sue Williams, Sisseton Sioux who grew up on a Navajo reservation]

Bailey, Lynn R. Bosque Redondo: An American Concentration Camp. Pasadena, CA: Socio-Technical Books, 1970.

Barry, Tom. "Navajo Nation: An Underdeveloped Country." Navajo Times 19(My 4, 1978):13-14, 16.

Barry, Tom, and Wood, Beth. "Coalition for Navajo Liberation: Spreading out from Shiprock." Navajo Times, F 2, 1978.

Bass, Willard P. and others. An Evaluation of the Bordertown Dormitory Program, Ap, 1971, 68 pp. Albuquerque: Southwestern Cooperative Educational Laboratory. ERIC ED 064 001.

Bayne, Stephen, and Bayne, Judith E. "Motivating Navaho Children." Journal of American Indian Education, Ja, 1969.

Beatty, Willard W. "History of Navajo Education." América Indígena 21(1961):7-31.

Begay, Keats and others. The Navajos and World War II. Tsaile, AZ: Navajo Community College Press, 1977.

Begay, John Y. and others. Navajo Evaluators Look at Rough Rock Demonstration School, Je 1, 1969. ERIC ED 034 612.

Bennett, Benjamin. "Seventh Grade Navaho Answer, 'Why Education?'" Journal of American Indian Education 4(0, 1964):17-19.

Bennett, Kay. Kaibah: Recollections of a Navajo Girlhood. Los Angeles: Western Lore Press, 1964.

Blank, Martin J. and others. Vocational Education on the Navajo Reservation: Present Status and Future Directions, D, 1976. ERIC ED 143 886.

Boyce, George A. When Navajos Had Too Many Sheep: The 1940's. San Francisco: Indian Historical Press, 1974.

Bryant, Clara O. "A Study of a Navajo Boy and Girl as They are Inducted Into a Boarding School Situation." Master's thesis, Arizona State College, Flagstaff, 1956.

Burger, Henry G. "'Ethno-Janus': Utilizing Cultural Heritage to Plan for Future Employment." Practical Anthropology 17(N-D, 1970): 241-252. [Navajo people]

Burgie, Amee G. "Education of the Navajo Indians of the Southwest." Master's thesis, Sul Ross State College, Alpine, TX, 1942.

Byland, H. Bruce. Social, Cultural and Educational Factors Associated with Relative Vocational Success of Navajo High School Graduates, Ja, 1970. Clearinghouse for Federal Scientific and Technical Information, U.S. Department of Commerce, Springfield, VA 22151.

Case, C. C. "Navajo Education: Is There Hope?" Educational Leadership 29(N, 1971):129-132.

Cata, Juanita. The Navajo Social Studies Project, 1968, 61 pp. Albuquerque: U. of New Mexico. ERIC ED 025 346.

Cathey, Wallace and others. Past and Contemporary Navajo Cultures Go Hand in Hand. Curriculum Guide, 1969, 34 pp. Shiprock Independent School District Number 22, NM. ERIC ED 034 638.

Ch'iao, Chien. Continuation of Tradition in Navajo Society. Tapei, Formosa: Institute of Ethnology, Academia Sinica, 1971.

Chilcott, John H. The Navajo Bordertown Dormitory in Flagstaff, Arizona. American Indian Education Papers, No. 4, D, 1970. ERIC ED 051 958.

"Children Are Bootleggers' Prime Customers." Navajo Times, N 22, 1978.

Christiansen, William V. "The Employers' Opinions on Navajo Student Employees During the Summer of 1954." Master's thesis, Utah State Agricultural College, 1955.

Church, Avery G. "Academic Achievement, IQ, Level of Occupational Plans, and Ethnic Stereotypes for Anglos and Navahos in a Multi-Ethnic High School." Southern Journal of Educational Research 10(Summer, 1976):184-201.

Condie, L. The Effect of Cultural Difference in the Education of Navajo Indians. Albuquerque: U. of New Mexico Press, 1958.

Cook, Mary J., and Sharp, Margaret A. "Problems of Navajo Speakers in Learning English." Language Learning 16(1966):21-29.

Coombs, L. Madison. Doorway Toward the Light: The Story of the Special Navajo Educational Programs. Washington, DC: Bureau of Indian Affairs, 1962.

"Council Opposes Segregated New Indian School." The Navajo Times, Mr 3, 1966.

Crites, Kenneth K. "A Study of Teacher Turnover on the Navajo Reservation." Master's thesis, U. of New Mexico, 1953.

Crowell, Suzanne. "Life on the Largest Reservation. Poverty and Progress in the Navajo Nation." Civil Rights Digest 6(Fall, 1973): 3-9.

Dale, Kenneth I. "Navajo Indian Educational Administration." Doctoral dissertation, U. of North Dakota, 1949.

Davis, George H. "A Curriculum Based on the Functional Needs of the Navajo." Master's thesis, Oregon State U., 1941.

Despair, C. W., Jr. "Analysis of Male Navajo Students' Perception of Occupational Opportunities and Their Attitudes toward Development of Skills and Traits Necessary for Occupational Competence." Doctoral dissertation, Washington State U., 1965.

Division of Education. Strengthening Navajo Education. Window Rock, AZ: The Navajo Tribe, Je, 1973. (Reprinted in U.S. Commission on Civil Rights, Hearing Held in Window Rock, Arizona, October 22-24, 1973, Vol. II, pp. 1284-1335. Washington, DC: The Commission, 1974)

Dodd, Arthur. "How Valuable Are Schools for Most Navajo Students." Navajo Times, My 17, 1973.

Dodge, Marjorie T. A Study of Navajo Community School Board Members Including Their Legal Status and Election or Appointment to Federally Operated Schools on the Navajo Indian Reservation, Je, 1972, 102 pp. Educational Specialist thesis, New Mexico State U., Las Cruces. ERIC ED 064 027.

Doerfert, Hans M. "Use of Pictures in Teaching English to Navajo Children." Master's thesis, Boston U., 1957.

"Education on the Reservation." Navajo Times, Mr 30, 1978. [Series of articles]

Emerson, Gloria J. "The Laughing Boy Syndrome." School Review 79(N, 1970):94-98. [Rough Rock Demonstration School]

Erickson, Donald A. "Custer Did Die For Our Sins!" School Review 79(N, 1970):76-93. [Rough Rock Demonstration School]

Erickson, Donald A., and Schwartz, Henrietta. "What Rough Rock Demonstrates." Integrated Education 8(Mr-Ap, 1970):21-34.

Evans, Lavon. "A Comparison of Test Scores for the 16-17 Year Age Group of Navajo Indians with Standardized Norms for the Wecshler Adult Intelligence Scale." Master's thesis, Brigham Young U., 1957.

Farmer, Sybil D. "Selected Problems in the Teaching of English to Navajo Students in High School." Master's thesis, U. of Texas, 1964.

Feder, Wendy. "Native American Church." Navajo Times, My 25, 1978. [17-page section of the Church among Navajos]

Fink, Marianne A. "Personality Differences of Acculturating Navajo Adolescent Girls as Revealed by Rorschach Tests." Master's thesis, U. of New Mexico, 1950.

Fuchs, Estelle. "Learning to Be Navaho-American: Innovation at Rough Rock." Saturday Review, S 16, 1967, pp. 82-84, 98-99.

Gilbreath, K. "Business Development on the Navajo Reservation." New Mexico Business 25 (Mr, 1972).

Gilliland, M. "Your Children Shall Learn Paper: Navajo Education." Journal of the National Education Association 45(D, 1956):558-560.

Greenberg, Norman C. "Adminstrative Problems Related to Integration of Navajo Indians in Public Education." Doctoral dissertation, U. of Colorado, 1963.

Gwilliam, Robert F. "The Relationship of the Social Acceptance of a Navajo Minority and Teacher Attitudes on the Dominative-Supportive Dimensions." Master's thesis, Brigham Young U., 1957.

Hammersmith, Jerry. "Navahos Dare Greatly." Northian, Spring, 1969.

Hardwick, Dick. "Delegates to Dine Biolta Metting Call for Navajo Control of Schools." Navajo Times, Ap 9, 1970.

_____. "Education at Remote Navajo Mountain." Navajo Times, O 7, 1971. [Navajo Mountain, Utah]

Harper, Allan G. "Navajo Education." The American Indian 5(Fall, 1950):3-10.

Harrison, Rex. "Chinle Students Stage 'Sitdown.'" Navajo Times, Ja 9, 1969 (letter). [Sitdown of Navajo students at Chinle High School on December 19, 1968]

Henderson, Eric B., and Levy, Jerrold E. Survey of Navajo Community Studies, 1936-1974, Mr, 1975. ERIC ED 127 089.

Hilborn, Nila A. "Investigation into the Extent of Variability and Proposals for Extended Research to Determine Significant Factors in Navajo Achievement." Master's thesis, Arizona State College, Flagstaff, 1965.

Hill, Faith R. "Education for Navajos: Problems Involved in Working Out a Plan of Education for the Navajo Indians." Master's thesis, Whittier College, 1942.

Hinckley, Edward C. "The Need for Student Records in the Counseling of Navaho Students." Journal of American Indian Education 2(My, 1963):1-6.

"Hits Critics." Navajo Times, O 10, 1968. [Navajo Tribal Chairman defends boarding schools against criticism by Dr. Karl Menninger]

Hoffman, Virginia, and Johnson, Broderick H. Navajo Biographies, 1970, 342 pp. Chinle, AZ: Rough Rock Demonstration School. ERIC ED 040 784.

Holdsworth, Willie. "A Study of the Intelligence and Reading Ability of Navajo Indians in the Ninth and Tenth Grades." Master's thesis, U. of Texas, 1937.

Hopkins, Thomas Robert. "Navajo and Non-Navajo Teachers: A Comparison of Characteristics." Doctoral dissertation, George Washington U., 1971.

Hopkins, Thomas R. and Others. Rough Rock School Evaluation, My, 1974. ERIC ED 127 097.

Hoskins, Irene E. "The Navajo Indians: A Study of Their Physical and Social Characteristics and Relation of These Characteristics to Educational Policies." Master's thesis, Hartford Seminary Foundation, Hartford, CT, 1947.

Hutchinson, E. L. "Teacher in Navajo Land." Business Education World 27(My, 1947):530-531.

Interagency School Board. "Proposal to Establish Navajo Education Department." Navajo Times, O 1, 1970.

"Integration May Be Best Way." Navajo Times, Ja 16, 1969.

Iverson, Peter. "The Evolving Navajo Nation: Diné Continuity Within Change." Doctoral dissertation, U. of Wisconsin, 1975.

Jamison, Patricia. "The Kinget Drawing Completion Test: Comparison of Responses for Full-Blood Navajo and White Children in Grades Three to Six." Master's thesis, U. of Oklahoma, 1959.

John-Steiner, Vera, and Osterreich, Helgi. Learning Styles Among Navajo Children. Albuquerque: College of Education, U. of New Mexico, Ag, 1975.

Johnson, Broderick H. Navaho Education at Rough Rock. Rough Rock Demonstration School, 1968.

Johnston, Denis F. An Analysis of Sources of Information on the Population of the Navajo. Bureau of American Ethnology Bulletin 197. Washington, DC: GPO, 1966.

Kahklen, Joseph M. "Factors Associated With Navajo Teachers in the Bureau of Indian Affairs Schools on the Navajo Reservation." Master's thesis, Northern Arizona U., 1966.

Kellough, Ruby M. "The Study of Navajo Children in Nazlini School." Master's thesis, Arizona State College, Flagstaff, 1962.

Kelly, Lawrence C. The Navajo Indians and Federal Indian Policy, 1900-1935. Tucson: U. of Arizona Press, 1968.

"[Kenneth] Ross Says School Plan is 'Hasty.'" Navajo Times, F 28, 1974. [Plan by Navajo Division of Education to control Johnson-O'Malley Funds in entire Navajo nation]

Klein, Garry. "A Relevant Curriculum for Navajos." Southern Education Report, Ap, 1969.

Kluckhorn, Clyde, and Leighton, Dorothea. The Navajo. Revised Edition. Garden City, NY: Doubleday and Company, 1962.

König, R. Indianer--whoin? Alternative in Arizona. Skizzen zur Entwicklungs-soziologie. Opladen: Westdeutscher Verlag, 1973.

Kreiss, Laura Amy. "Innovative Educational Programs on the Navajo Reservation." Master's thesis, American U., 1973. Univ. Microfilms Order No. M-5521. [Since 1946]

Lamphere, Louise. "The Internal Colonization of the Navajo People." Southwest Economy and Society 1(Spring, 1976):6-14.

Langley, Elizabeth G. "The Development of a Literacy Program among the Navajo Indians." Doctoral dissertation, New York U., 1956.

Largo, Jim. "Red Tape Snarls Indian Med School." Navajo Times, Ag 4, 1977.

Lee, George P. Memo to Navajo Community Schools, Ja 5, 1971, 95 pp. ERIC ED 056 928.

Leighton, Dorothea, and Kluckhohn, Clyde. Children of the People: The Navaho Individual and His Development. Cambridge, MA: Harvard U. Press, 1947.

Leighton, E. R. "The Nature of Cultural Factors Affecting the Success or Failure of Navajo College Students." Doctoral dissertation, U. of Arizona, 1964.

Leslie, Ernest. "Social Factors Contributing to Exceptional Navajo Children." Education and Training of the Mentally Retarded 12(D, 1977):374-376.

Liefgreen, Dan. "Misunderstandings at Tuba City High School: Club President is Beaten." Navajo Times, My 11, 1978.

_____. "Tribal Scholarship Funds. Are They Easy to Get?" Navajo Times, S 21, 1978.

_____. "Tuba City High School." Navajo Times, My 18, 1978. [Series of articles]

Link, Marvin A. Navajo: A Century of Progress, 1869-1968. Window Rock, AZ: Navajo Tribe, 1968.

Long, Richard F. "Navajo Schools: Indians Teaching Indians." Navajo Times, O 21, 1971.

Luebben, Ralph A. "Prejudice and Discrimination Against Navajos in a Mining Community." In Native Americans Today: Sociological Perspectives. Edited by Howard M. Bahr and Others. New York: Harper & Row, 1972.

McClure, Florence E. "A Study of the Job Placement Program for Young Navajo Indians with Limited Education." Master's thesis, Colorado State College of Education, 1954.

MacDonald, Peter. "Chairman Backs Accountability to Indians on Indian Education." Navajo Times, Ja 13, 1972.

_____. "Quarterly Report to the Navajo Tribal Council, Fall Session, November, 1971." Navajo Times, D 2, 1971.

_____. "Site Dedication Address by Tribal Chairman." Navajo Times, Ap 22, 1971. [Chairman, Navajo Tribal Council, Navajo Community College]

_____. "Unique Problems of Education on the Navajo Reservation." Colorado Journal of Educational Research 12(Spring, 1973):6-7.

McKenzie, Taylor. "Navajo Physician Advocates Gradual Takeover of Schools." (Text of speech) Navajo Times, Ap 23, 1970. [By the first Navajo physician]

_____. "What the Navajo Nation Needs." Integrated Education 8(J1-Ag, 1970):26-31. [Reprint of the preceding item]

Martinez, Al. "Indian School: It was Whispered on the Wind." Los Angeles Times, J1 4, 1977. [Little Singer School, Birdsprings, AZ; a Navajo school]

Mayfield, Craig K. "A Test Developed and Administered to Navajo Students at Intermountain Indian School to Determine Their Readiness for Reading from English Pre-Primer, Primer and First Year Books." Doctoral dissertation, Brigham Young U., 1961.

Mazlen, Anne, and Mazlen, Ken. "Genocide in Navajo Land." Akwesasne Notes 3(S, 1971): 33.

Melville, Robert, and Haas, John. Educational Achievement and the Navajo, S 8, 1967, 13 pp. ERIC ED 013 172.

Metcalf, Ann. "The Effects of Boarding School on Navajo Self-Image and Maternal Behavior." Doctoral dissertation, Stanford U., 1975.

_____. "From Schoolgirl to Mother: The Effects of Education on Navajo Women." Social Problems 23(Je, 1976):535-544.

Miller, D. D., and Johnson, Gail. "What We've Learned About Teaching Reading to Navajo Indians." Reading Teacher 27(Mr, 1974): 550-554.

Mitchell, Emerson Blackhorse, and Allen, T. D. Miracle Hill: The Story of a Navaho Boy. Norman, OK: U. of Oklahoma Press, 1967.

Myers, James E. "A Cultural and Historical Analysis of the Education of the Navajo." Master's thesis, Cornell U., 1956.

Nakai, Raymond. "Will We Meet the Challenge?" Journal of American Indian Education, 0, 1964. [By the Chairman of the Navajo Tribal Council]

"Navajo Academy Dedicated." Navajo Times, Mr 31, 1977. [Located on the campus of the College of Ganado]

"Navajo Area Education Progress Report." Navajo Times, My 27, 1971.

"The Navajo Division of Education." Navajo Times, D 2, 1971.

"[Navajo] Group Demands School Control." Navajo Times, Mr 18, 1971.

Navajo History. Volume I. Navajo Community College Press, 1971. [Order from: Navajo Curriculum Center, Rough Rock Demonstration School, Chinle, AZ]

"Navajo School: A Study in Community Control." Architectural Forum 137(S, 1972):54-57.

"Navajo Students Threaten Lawsuit Against Ceremonial." Navajo Times, S 18, 1969. [Three students circulate leaflet entitled "When Our Grandfathers Carried Guns," reprinted on p. 17]

"[Navajo Tribal] Council Sets Guidelines for BIA School Boards." Navajo Times, Ag 28, 1969.

The Navajo Tribe. The Navajo 10 Year Plan. Window Rock, AZ, Je, 1972.

"Navajo Tribe Initiates Graduate Program." Navajo Times, D 9, 1971.

Navajo Yearbook: Report No. VIII: 1951-1961: A Decade of Progress. Navajo Agency, Window Rock, AZ, 1960.

"Navajos Show Muscle in School Elections." Navajo Times, F 11, 1971. [School Board elections in New Mexico]

"New Offices for Medicine Men Are Dedicated." Navajo Times, D 15, 1977. [School for medicine men]

Norman, Ralph D., and Midkiff, Katherine L. "Navajo Children on Raven Progressive Matrices and Goodenough Draw-A-Man Tests." Southwestern Journal of Anthropology 11(1955):129-136.

"Officials Here Discuss Navajo Student Needs." Navajo Times, N 7, 1968.

Oldham, Ronald L. "A Comparative Study of the Relationship of Self-Concept to Achievement in Navajo and Anglo Children." Master's thesis, U. of New Mexico, 1972.

Olson, Ingeborg K. "The Possibilities of an Educational Program for Improving Navajo Weaving." Master's thesis, Colorado A and M College, 1938.

Owens, Nancy Jean. "Indian Reservations and Bordertowns: The Metropolis-Satellite Model Applied to the Northwestern Navajos and the Umatillos." Doctoral dissertation, U. of Oregon, 1976. Univ. Microfilms Order No. 77-4751. [Page, Arizona, and Pendleton, Oregon]

Pages, Myrtha. Bilingual-Bicultural Special Education in the Navajo Reservation--Myth or Reality?, Je, 1978. ERIC ED 158 511.

Parman, Donald L. The Navajos and the New Deal. New Haven, CT: Yale U. Press, 1975.

Paxton, S. Gabe. "A Study of Self-Concept of the Navajo Indian Adolescent." Master's thesis, Arizona State College, Flagstaff, 1964.

Peaches, Daniel. "Peaches Orients Navajo Teachers." Navajo Times, S 11, 1975.

Perkins, William F. "The Integration of the Navajo Indian into the Public Schools." Master's thesis, Colorado College, 1957.

Peterson, Kirk D. "Some Steps for a Beginning Teacher of Navajo Students." Journal of American Indian Education 10(Ja, 1971):21-28.

Polacca, Kathryn. "Ways of Working with the Navahos Who Have Not Learned the White Man's Ways." Journal of American Indian Education 2(0, 1962):6-16.

Pratt, Wayne T., and Ramey, Joseph H. (eds.). Emerging Role of the Teacher Aide in Navajo Education. A Guide Book, 1974. ERIC ED 099 151.

Reno, Phillip. Vocational Education Needs and Opportunities for Indians; A Review of the Navajo Situation and a Summary of Its Implications for Four Corners Regional Planning, S, 1969, 34 pp. Farmington, NM: Four Corners Regional Commission. ERIC ED 052 874.

Reno, Thomas R. "A Demonstration in Navajo Education." Journal of American Indian Education 6(My, 1967):1-5.

_____. "A Study of the Knowledges and Attitudes of Navajo Indians in Two Communities Toward Navajo Reservation Schools." Doctoral dissertation, Michigan State U., 1971.

Robbins, Lynn A. "Navajo Labor and the Establishment of a Voluntary Workers Association." Journal of Ethnic Studies 6(Fall, 1978):97-112.

_____. "The Navajo Nations and Industrial Developments." Southwest Economy and Society 2(Spring, 1977):47-70.

_____. "Navajo Workers and Labor Unions." Southwest Economy and Society 3(Spring, 1978):4-23.

Roger Grey Eyes. [Letter from Navajo student at the University of Utah Medical School] Navajo Times, Ag 31, 1972.

Rogers, Louis E. [Letter on the Ramah Navajo High School] Akwesasne Notes, Mr, 1971.

Rosier, Paul, and Farella, Merilyn. "Bilingual Education at Rock Point--Some Early Results." TESOL Quarterly 10(D, 1976):379-388.

Rowe, Chester A. "The Academic Achievement of Navajo Indian Students: A Study of Selected Variables and Their Correlations with the Academic Achievement of Navajo Indian Students Who Live in a Rural Reservation Setting." Doctoral dissertation, Brigham Young U., 1978. Univ. Microfilms Order No. 7901585. [Red Mesa High School]

Ruffing, Lorraine. "The Navajo Nation: Cultivating Underemployment." Akwesasne Notes 10 (S, 1978):7-11.

Samuels, Gertrude. "VISTA's in Navajoland." New York Times Magazine, Ag 11, 1968.

Sanson, Lettie E. "The Teaching of Functional Vocabulary to Non-English-Speaking Navajo Children." Master's thesis, Arizona State College, Flagstaff, 1952.

Saski, Tom T., and Olmsted, David L. "Navaho Acculturation and English-Language Skills." American Anthropologist 30(Ja-Mr, 1953):89-99.

Schreier, Ron. "HEW is Investigating Chinle Schools for Alleged Discrimination." Navajo Times, D 21, 1978.

Scoon, Annabelle Rouse. "The Feasibility of Test Translation--English to Navajo." Doctoral dissertation, U. of New Mexico, 1974.

Sieber, Nadine H. "Stimulating Progress Among the Navajo Indians Through Education." Master's thesis, Winona State College, Winona, MN, 1961.

Smith, Elma R. "Private Schools for the Navajo Indians." Master's thesis, U. of Arizona, 1947.

Stafford, Kenneth. "Problem Solving by Navaho Children in Relation to Knowledge of English." Journal of American Indian Education 4(Ja, 1965):23-25.

"Special Features of the Rock Point Dormitory Program." Navajo Times, S 18, 1969. [Fostering a family atmosphere in boarding school]

"Special Report!! DNA." Navajo Times, Je 8, 1978. [Navajo Legal Services]

"Special Report: Housing." Navajo Times, Je 15, 1978

Spencer, Horace. [Letter on resignation of Robert Roessel as superintendent of the Chinle Public School District] Navajo Times, My 27, 1976.

_____. "Raps Schools." (letter) Navajo Times, F 6, 1969. [A Navajo criticizes Bureau of Indian Affairs schools]

The State of Navajo Education, Ap, 1974. ERIC Ed 098 012.

"Statement Submitted to the United States Civil Rights Commission by the Rock Point Community School Board at Hearings in Window Rock, October 24, 1973." In U.S. Commission on Civil Rights, Hearing Held in Window Rock, Arizona, October 22-24, 1973, pp. 1215-1235. Washington, DC: The Commission, 1974.

Story, Frances. "He'll Go a Long Way." Wapato Independent, F 21, 1979. [Ed Haycock, a Navajo student at Central Valley Junior Academy, Wapato, WA]

Talbot, Anne. "Prejudice: Thoughts Garnered Among the Navajo." Media and Methods 9(D, 1972):36-37. [Teacher prejudice]

Teacher-Aide Guide for Navajo Area, Je 12, 1970, 219 pp. Bloomfield, NM: Dzilth-Na-O-Dith-Hle Boarding School. ERIC ED 049 844.

Thompson, Hildegard. The Navajos' Long Walk for Education: A History of Navajo Education, 1975. Navajo Community College Press, Tsaile, Navajo Nation, AZ 86556.

Tippeconnic, John W. III. "The Relationship Between Teacher Pupil Control Ideology and Elementary Student Activities in Navajo Schools." Doctoral dissertation, Pennsylvania State U., 1975.

Tonigan, Richard E. and others (comps.). <u>11 Programs for Strengthening Navajo Education</u>, D, 1973. ERIC ED 087 574.

"Training for Educational Leadership: The Navajo School Administrators Program." <u>Carnegie Quarterly</u> 16(Winter, 1978).

Underhill, Ruth. <u>So Many Kinds of Navajos</u>, 1971. ERIC ED 145 998.

U.S. Commission on Civil Rights. <u>Hearing Held in Window Rock, Arizona, October 22–24, 1973</u>. 2 Vols. Washington, DC: The Commission, 1974.

_____. <u>The Navajo Nation: An American Colony</u>. Washington, DC: The Commission, S, 1975.

Vicente, Juison, Coun, and Kellogg. <u>The Law of the People: A Bicultural Approach to Legal Education for Navajo Students</u>, 1972, 4 vols. Ramah Navajo High School Press, Ramah, NM 87321.

Vorih, Lillian and Rosier, Paul. "Rock Point Community Schools: An Example of a Navajo-English Bilingual Elementary School Program." <u>TESOL Quarterly</u> 12(S, 1978):263–369.

Walsh, Paul. "Dick and Jane on the Navajo Reservation." <u>Journal of Continuing Education and Training</u> 1(My, 1972):267–276.

Weppner, Robert S. "The Economic Adjustment of Navajo Indian Migrants to Denver, Colorado." Doctoral dissertation, U. of Colorado, 1967.

Werner, Oswald. "Navajos Startle NU Researcher With Medical Lore." <u>Daily Northwestern</u>, My 18, 1973.

Wilson, Robert D. "Great Hope Held for Bicultural-Bilingual Program." (letter) <u>Navajo Times</u>, S 4, 1969.

Witherspoon, Gary. "Rough Rock Educator Advocates Local Control [of Schools]." <u>Navajo Times</u>, Ag 28, 1969.

Woerner, Davida. "Education Among the Navajo: An Historical Study." Doctoral dissertation, Columbia U., 1941.

Yava, Aaron. <u>Border Towns of the Navajo Nation</u>. Alamo, CA: Holmgangers Press, 1975.

Yazzie, Ethelou (ed.). <u>Navajo History</u>, Vol. I, 1971. Navajo Community College Press, Many Farms, AZ 86503.

Yazzie, Hakie, Sr. "The Melting Pot Theory of the 'Bilagaana' Anglos." (a letter) <u>Navajo Times</u>, O 16, 1975.

Young, Robert W. <u>A Political History of the Navajo Tribe</u>. Tsaile, AZ: Navajo Community College Press, 1978.

_____. <u>English as a Second Language for Navajos, an Overview of Certain Cultural and Linguistic Factors</u>, 1968, 173 pp. Bureau of Indian Affairs (Dept. of Interior), Albuquerque, NM: Bureau of Indian Affairs (Dept. of Interior), Window Rock, AZ. ERIC ED 021 655.

_____. "The Origin and Development of Navajo Tribal Government." In <u>Navajo Yearbook</u>, pp. 371–411. Edited by Robert W. Young. Window Rock, AZ, 1961.

Nez Perce

Neff, Russell Charles. "Nez Perce Education: A Study of the Kamiah and Lapwai School Districts." Doctoral dissertation, U. of Idaho, 1969.

Sanford, Gregory. "The Study of Nez Perce Indian Education." Doctoral dissertation, U. of New Mexico, 1970.

Snider, J. G. "A Comparative Study of the Intelligence of Whites and Nez Perce Indians." Master's thesis, U. of Idaho, 1953.

Northern Cheyenne

Gutzmer, Willard E. "Education for the Northern Cheyenne Indians." Master's thesis, U. of Utah, 1952.

Ojibwa

James, Bernard J. "Social-Psychological Dimensions of Ojibwa Acculturation." <u>American Anthropologist</u> 63(Ag, 1961):721–746.

Omaha

Evers, Lawrence J. "Native American Oral Literatures in the College English Classroom: An Omaha Example." <u>College English</u> 36(F, 1975): 649–662.

Laflesche, Francis. <u>The Middle Five: Indian Schoolboys of the Omaha Tribe</u>. Madison, WI: U. of Wisconsin Press, 1963.

Oneida

Stepanek, Michael. "The Liberated Woman in the Oneida Community: 1840–1872." <u>Educational Perspectives</u> 16(Mr, 1977):22–26.

Osage

Boutwell, Ruth. "Adjustment of the Osage Indian Youth to Contemporary Civilization." Master's thesis, U. of Oklahoma, 1936.

Gayler, Lucy B. "A Case Study in Social Adjustment of One Hundred Osage Families." Master's thesis, U. of Oklahoma, 1936.

Gorton, Ernest F. "Education Among the Osage Indians." Master's thesis, Oklahoma A and M College, 1935.

MacLean, Harold Sterns. "Educational Guidance for Osage Indians in the Public Schools." Master's thesis, Oklahoma A and M College, 1939.

Rohrer, J. H. "Test Intelligence of Osage Indians." Journal of Social Psychology 16 (Ag, 1942):99-105.

Otavalo

Cooper, Jed Arthur. "The Role of the School in Otavalo Society." Doctoral dissertation, George Peabody College for Teachers, 1964.

Papago

Fontana, Bernard L. "Assimilative Change: A Papago Indian Case Study." Doctoral dissertation, U. of Arizona, 1960.

McGinty, Doris M. "An Analysis of the Effectiveness of the Secondary Home Economics Program in Meeting Needs of Young Married Papago Indian Homemakers." Doctoral dissertation, U. of Arizona, 1964.

Mackett, Robert, and Chilcott, John H. Community Background Reports: Papago Reservation, Sells, Arizona. National Study of American Indian Education, Series I, No. 17. Final Report, Ja, 1970, 11 pp. U. of Chicago. ERIC ED 042 552.

Ridgway, Charles W. "A Philosophy of Curriculum for Papago Indian Day Schools." Master's thesis, Arizona State College, Tempe, 1951.

Slaughter, Alan. "A Study of the Phonemic Aspect of Bilingualism in Papago Indian Children." Master's thesis, U. of Arizona, 1956.

Stout, Irving W., and Moore, Josiah. Report of a Survey to Determine the Educational Needs of Papago Children and Adults with Recommendations for the Fulfillment of Those Needs, 1965, 113 pp. Tempe, AZ: Arizona State U. ERIC ED 055 704.

Taylor, Benjamin J., and O'Connor, Dennis J. Papago Reservation Manpower Resources; Indian Manpower Resources in the Southwest. A Pilot Study, 1969, 42 pp. Tempe, AZ: Arizona State U., College of Business Administration. ERIC ED 043 445.

Wilkerson, John F. "The Papago Indians and Their Education." Master's thesis, U. of Arizona, 1935.

Paiute

Withycombe, Jeraldine S. "An Analysis of Self-Concept and Social Status of Paiute Indians and White Elementary School Children in Nevada." Doctoral dissertation, U. of Connecticut, 1970.

_____. "Relationships of Self-Concept, Social Status, and Self-Perceived Social Status and Racial Differences of Paiute Indians and White Elementary School Children." Journal of Social Psychology 91(D, 1973):337-338.

Pima

Austin, Wilfred G. "An Educational Study of the Pima Indians of Arizona." Master's thesis, Stanford U., 1932.

Brown, Christine and Havighurst, Robert J. Pima Central School and Blackwater School, Arizona. The National Study of American Indian Education, Series I, No. 22. Final Report, Je, 1970. ERIC ED 044 211.

Gardner, Ruth G. "The Relationship of Self-Esteem and Variables Associated with Reading for Fourth Grade Pima Indian Children." Doctoral dissertation, U. of Arizona, 1972.

De Hoyos, Genevieve. Mobility Orientation and Mobility Skills of Youth in an Institutionally Dislocated Group: The Pima Indian, 1971, 90 pp. Provo, Utah: The Brigham Young U. Institute of American Indian Studies. ERIC ED 056 812.

Fullerton, Bill J., and Bell, John E. (comps.). Instructional Centers for Pima Culture. Final Report: Academic Year 1968-1969, 1969, 66 pp. Tempe, AZ: Arizona State U., Bureau of Educational Research and Services. ERIC ED 046 608.

Hagan, Maxine W. "An Educational History of the Pima and Papago Peoples from the Mid-Seventeenth Century to the Mid-Twentieth Century." Doctoral dissertation, U. of Arizona, 1959.

Heard, Marvin Eugene. "Three Centuries of Formal and Informal Educational Influences and Development Among the Pima Indians." Master's thesis, U. of Arizona, 1939.

Miller, Mary R. Children of the Salt River: First and Second Language Acquisition Among Pima Children. Bloomington, IN: Indiana U., 1977.

Skinner, Carl H. "A Plan of Education for the Gila River Pima Indians." Doctoral dissertation, Stanford U., 1939.

Smith, George H. "High School Dropouts and Graduates among Pima Indians in Three Arizona High Schools." Doctoral dissertation, Arizona State U., 1967.

Pomo

Kennedy, Mary J. "Culture Contact and Acculturation of the Southwestern Pomo." Doctoral dissertation, U. of California, Berkley, 1955.

Potawatomi

Clifton, James A. The Prairie People: Continuity and Change in Potawatomi Indian Culture, 1665-1965. Lawrence, KA: Regents
Press of Kansas, 1977.

Pueblo

John-Steiner, Vera and others. Learning Styles
Among Pueblo Children, Ag, 1975. ERIC ED
129 503.

Lange, Charles H. "Education and Leadership
in Rio Grande Pueblo Culture Change." The
American Indian 8(Winter, 1958):27-35.

Luhrs, Dorothy L. "An Anthropological Study of
the Sources of Maladjustment Among Eastern
Pueblo Adolescents." Doctoral dissertation,
U. of Southern California, 1945.

McCarrell, Fred. "The Development of the
Training School. Consideration given Early
Pueblo Education by Franciscans in Their
Mission Schools." Doctoral dissertation,
George Peabody College for Teachers, 1934.

Marinsek, E. The Effect of Cultural Differences
in the Education of Pueblo Indians. Albuquerque: U. of New Mexico, 1958.

Morris, Joyce. "An Investigation Into Language-
Concept Development of Primary School Pueblo
Indian Children." Doctoral dissertation, U.
of New Mexico, 1966.

Ortiz, Alfonso. "Project Head Start in an Indian Community." In U.S. Congress, 90th,
1st and 2nd Sessions, Senate, Committee on
Labor and Public Welfare, Special Subcommittee on Indian Education, Indian Education.
Hearings...Part 1, pp. 99-122. Washington,
DC: GPO, 1969. [San Juan Pueblo, NM]

Parks, Mary H. "A Free Association Vocabulary
of Pueblo Indians in the Fifth and Sixth
Grades." Master's thesis, U. of Oklahoma,
1937.

Sando, Joe S. The Pueblo Indian. San Francisco:
Indian Historical Press, 1976.

Spencer, Frank C. "Education of the Pueblo
Child. A Study of Arrested Development."
Doctoral dissertation, Columbia U., 1899.

Talbot, Steve. "Community Development at San
Carlos." Master's thesis, U. of Arizona,
1967.

Salish

Marble, Bessie Y. "The Intelligence and
Achievement of White and Salish Indian Children." Master's thesis, Montana State U.,
1937.

Seminole

Foster, Laurence. Negro-Indian Relationships in
the Southeast. New York: AMS Press, 1978.

Garbarino, Merwyn S. (ed.). "Seminole Girl
[Nellie Greene]." Trans-action, F, 1970.

Greene, H. Ross, and Kersey, Harry A., Jr. "Upgrading Indian Education: A Case Study of
the Seminoles." School Review 83(F, 1975):
345-361.

Kersey, Harry A., Jr. The Federal Day School
as an Acculturational Agent for Seminole Indian Children, Mr, 1970. ERIC ED 039 988.

Kersey, Harry A., Jr., and Greene, H. R.
"Educational Achievement Among Three Florida
Seminole Reservations." School and Society
100(Ja, 1972):25-28.

Kersey, Harry A., Jr., and Justin, Neal E.
"Big Cypress Seminoles Receive Three-Phase
Program. Florida Atlantic University Project." Journal of American Indian Education
10(O, 1970):20-22.

Kiker, Ernest. "Education Among the Seminole
Indians." Master's thesis, Oklahoma A. & M.
College, 1932.

Welch, Andrew. A Narrative of the Early Days
and Remembrances of Oceola Nikkanochee,
Prince of Eeonchatti. Gainesville, FL: U.
Presses of Florida, 1977.

Senaca

Winnie, Lucille "Jerry." Sah-gan-de-oh, the
Chief's Daughter. New York: Vantage, 1968.
[Senaca-Cayuga]

Shawnee

Alford, Thomas Wildcat. Civilization. As told
to Florence Drake. Norman: U. of Oklahoma
Press, 1936.

Gaillard, Frye. "High Court Confronts Shawnee
Hair." Race Relations Reporter 4(D 3, 1973).

Sioux

Artichoker, John, Jr., and Palmer, Neil N. The
Sioux Indian Goes to College. Vermillion, SD:
Institute of Indian Studies, State U. of
South Dakota, 1959.

Barton, Walter C. "The Educational Experiences Inherent in the Construction of a Sioux Indian Home." Master's thesis, Colorado A. & M. College, 1939.

Coleman, Ursula Rosemarie. "Parent Involvement in Preschool Education: A Reservation Head Start Program." Doctoral dissertation, Case Western Reserve U., 1978. Univ. Microfilms Order No. 7816456.

Cress, Joseph N., and O'Donnell, James P. "Indianness, Sex, and Grade Differences on Behavior and Personality Measure among Oglala Sioux Adolescents." Psychology in the Schools 11(Jl, 1974):306-308.

Deloria, Ella Cara. Speaking of Indians. New York: Friendship Press, 1944.

Eastman, Charles Alexander. From the Deep Woods to Civilization: Chapters in the Autobiography of an Indian. Boston: Little, Brown, 1916.

_____. Indian Boyhood. New York: McClure, 1904.

Eastman, Elaine G. Sister to the Sioux: The Memoirs of Elaine Goodale Eastman. Lincoln, NE: U. of Nebraska Press, 1978.

Erikson, Erik. "Some Observations on Sioux Education." Journal of Psychology 7(1939):101-156.

Flying Hawk. Firewater and Forked Tongues: A Sioux Chief Interprets U.S. History, as told to M. I. McCreight. Pasadena, CA: Trail's End Publishing Co., 1947.

Folson, Cora M. "When the Sioux Came to Hampton." Southern Workman 57(Mr, 1928):113-121.

Gill, Joseph C. "A Handbook for Teachers of Sioux Indian Students." Doctoral dissertation, U. of South Dakota, 1971.

Guenther, Richard L. "The Santee Normal Training School." Nebraska History 51(Fall, 1970):359-378.

Harkins, Arthur M. and others. Public Education of the Prairie Island Sioux: An Interim Report. National Study of American Indian Education, Series I, No. 10, D, 1969, 91 pp. Chicago: U. of Chicago; Minneapolis: U. of Minnesota, Training Center for Community Programs. ERIC ED 040 797.

Harsha, W. J. "The Longing of Sioux for Education." Southern Workman 58(S, 1929):396-400.

Hulsizer, Allen L. "Selection of Experiences in the Curriculum for the Dakota." Curriculum Journal 12(Ja, 1941):14-18.

Hyde, George E. Red Cloud's Folk: A History of the Oglala Sioux Indians. Norman, OK: U. of Oklahoma Press, 1976.

Krause, Georg. The Rosebud Sioux Reservation, 1970. ERIC ED 040 792.

Kuske, Irwin I., Jr. "Psycholinguistic Abilities of Sioux Indian Children." Doctoral dissertation, U. of South Dakota, 1969.

Kutzleb, Charles R. "Educating the Dakota Sioux, 1876-1890." North Dakota History 32(1965):197-215.

LaCourse, Richard. "Turning Point in Indian Protest." Race Relations Reporter 3(My, 1972):28-31.

Malan, V. D. "To Change a Culture: A Sociologist Looks at Factors--Socialization, Social Change, and Social Disorganization--Which Have Led to a Conflict in Values on the Pine Ridge Indian Reservation." South Dakota Farm and Home Research, Fall, 1962.

Maynard, Eileen. "Negative Ethnic Image among Oglala Sioux High School Students." Pine Ridge Research Bulletin 6(D, 1968):18-25.

Maynard, Eileen, and Twiss, Gayla. "Formal Education." In That These People May Live. Conditions Among the Oglala Sioux of the Pine Ridge Reservation. Pine Ridge, SD: U.S. Public Health Service, 1969.

Mindell, Carl, and Maynard, Eileen. "Ambivalence Toward Education among Indian High School Students." Pine Ridge Research Bulletin 1(Ja, 1968):26-30.

Mueller, Wolfgang. Community Background Reports: The Cheyenne River Sioux Reservation, South Dakota. National Study of American Indian Education, Series I, No. 6, Final Report, D 1969, 26 pp. Chicago: U. of Chicago. ERIC ED 040 793.

Oglala Sioux Tribe. "An Appraisal of the Pine Ridge Education Program, Pine Ridge, South Dakota." In U.S. Congress, 90th, 1st and 2nd Sessions, Senate, Committee on Labor and Public Welfare, Special Subcommittee on Indian Education, Indian Education. Hearings..., Part 4, pp. 1269-1283. Washington, DC: GPO, 1969.

Ortiz, Roxanne Dunbar. The Great Sioux Nation, Sitting in Judgment on America. An Oral History of the Sioux Nation and Its Struggle for Sovereignty. Moon Books, 1977.

Redin, David A. "A Study of the Influence of Dakota Indian Culture on the Reading Growth of Fifteen Dakota Indian Pupils." Master's thesis, Northern State Teachers College, Aberdeen, South Dakota, 1955.

Schusby, Ernest L. The Forgotten Sioux: An Ethnohistory of the Lower Brule Reservation. Chicago: Nelson-Hall, 1975.

Sherrill, Robert G. "The Lagoon of Excrement." Nation, N 10, 1969. [Pine Ridge Reservation, SD]

Spilka, Bernard. Alienation and Achievement Among Oglala Sioux Secondary School Students, Ag, 1970, 529 pp. ERIC ED 045 225.

Standing Bear, Luther. My Indian Boyhood. Boston: Houghton Mifflin, 1928.

Stipe, Claude E. "Eastern Dakota Acculturation: The Role of Agents of Culture Change." Doctoral dissertation, U. of Minnesota, 1968.

Teachout, Margaret, and LaPointe, Rick. Standing Rock Tribal Library, S 18, 1974. ERIC ED 101 658.

U.S. Commission on Civil Rights. Report of Investigation: Oglala Sioux Tribe, General Election, 1974. Washington, DC: The Commission, O, 1974.

U.S. Department of the Interior, Rulings. Yankton Sioux School Lands--Disposal. Op. Sol., M. 27671, Mr 1, 1934.

Useem, R. M. "The Aftermath of Defeat: A Study of Acculturation among the Rosebud Sioux in South Dakota." Doctoral dissertation, U. of Wisconsin, 1947.

Voyat, Gilbert. "Sioux Children: A Study of Their Cognitive Development." Department of Psychology, Yeshiva U., 1970.

Voyat, Gilbert, and Silk, Stephen. "Cross-Cultural Study of Cognitive Development on the Pine Ridge Indian Reservation." Pine Ridge Indian Reservation 11(1970):50-73.

Wax, Murray L., Wax, Rosalie, and Dumont, Robert V., Jr., with Holyrock, Roselyn, and Onefeather, Gerald. Formal Education in an American Indian Community, Supplement to Social Problems, II, 1964.

Wax, Rosalie H. "Ogala Sioux Dropouts and their Problems with Education." In Education and School Crisis: Perspectives on Teaching Disadvantaged Youth. Edited by Everett T. Keach and Others. New York: Wiley, 1967.

_____. "The Warrior Dropouts." Transaction 4(1967):40-46.

Werden, Patricia L. K. "Health Education Needs of the Oglala Sioux." School Health Review 5(S-O, 1974):14-16.

_____. "Study of the Health Needs of Oglala Sioux Indian Students." 2 vols. Doctoral dissertation, U. of Northern Colorado, 1973.

White, Robert A. "The Urbanization of the Dakota Indian." Master's thesis, Saint Louis U., 1959.

_____. "Value Themes of the Native American Tribalistic Movement among the South Dakota Sioux." Current Anthropology 15(S, 1974): 284-303.

Woodward, Richard G. 'Title VIII and the Oglala Sioux." Phi Delta Kappan, D, 1973. [Pine Ridge Reservation]

Ute

Athinson, Darrell D. "Educational Adjustment of the Ute Indians as Compared to the Mixed-Bloods and Native Whites at Union High School, Roosevelt, Utah." Master's thesis, Utah State Agricultural College, 1955.

Bailey, John F. "A Comparison of Good and Poor Readers Among Full-Blood Ute Indian Children on Factors Relating to the Home and School." Master's thesis, U. of Utah, 1965.

Griffiths, K. A. "The Influence of an Intensive Pre-School Educational Experience on the Intellectual Functioning of Ute Indian Children." Doctoral dissertation, U. of Utah, 1967.

Hoyt, Milton. Development of Education Among the Southern Utes. An Examination of Federal Policies and Actual Practices. Boulder, CO: Tri-Ethnic Research Project, U. of Colorado, 1967.

McClellan, Kenneth R. "The Ute Indians and Their Educational Programs." Master's thesis, U. of Utah, 1953.

Reid, Leslie W. "A History of the Education of the Ute Indians, 1847-1905." Doctoral dissertation, U. of Utah, 1972.

Shults, Elsie S. "A Comparison of the Performance of the Ute Indian and White Children on Verbal and Non-Verbal Tests." Master's thesis, U. of Utah, 1960.

Tindall, B. Allan. "The Psycho-Cultural Orientation of Anglo and Ute Boys in an Integrated High School." Doctoral dissertation, U. of California, Berkeley, 1973.

Wennhold, P. E. "A Study of Academic Performance by Ute Indian Children." Master's thesis, U. of Utah, 1967.

Witherspoon, Y. T. "Cultural Influences on Ute Learning." Doctoral dissertation, U. of Utah, 1961.

Washo

Smirenko, Alex. Socio-Economic Variables in the Acculturation Process: A Pilot Study of Two Washo Indian Communities. Washington, DC: U.S. Department of Education, Bureau of Research, 1956.

Winnebago

North, Woesha Cloud. "Informal Education in Winnebago Tribal Society with Implications for Formal Education." Doctoral dissertation, U. of Nebraska, 1978. Univ. Microfilms Order No. 7900344.

Rayman, Ronald. "The Winnebago Indian School Experiment in Iowa Territory, 1834-1848." Annals of Iowa 44(Summer, 1978):359-387.

Zimmerman, Jesse. "Analysis of the Education of the Winnebago Indians." Master's thesis, U. of Nebraska, 1953.

Zuni

Leighton, Dorothea C., and Adair, John. People of the Middle Place: A Study of the Zuni Indians. New Haven, CT: Human Relations Area Files, 1966.

American Indians by State

Alaska

Ager, Lynn Price. "Play Among Alaskan Eskimos." Theory Into Practice 13(O, 1974):252-256.

Anderson, H. D., and Eels, W. C. Alaska Natives: A Survey of their Sociological, Educational Status. Stanford, CA: Stanford U. Press, 1935.

Arnold, Robert D. "A Survey of the Administrative Situation in Alaska as it Affects Eskimos, Indians, and Aleuts." In Education in the North, pp. 87-104. Edited by Frank Darnell. Arctic Institute of North America, U. of Alaska, 1972.

Berreman, Gerald D. "Inquiry into Community Integration in an Aleutian Village." American Anthropologist 57(F, 1955):49-59.

Bureau of Indian Affairs. Alaskan Native Needs Assessment in Education. Project ANNA. Juneau: Juneau Area Office, Bureau of Indian Affairs, O, 1973.

Burkher, Howard H. "The Effect of Education Upon the Life of the Alaskan Eskimo." Master's thesis, Butler U., Indianapolis, 1929.

Calkin, Thomas V. "Education of the Alaskan Native." Doctoral dissertation, Yale U., 1931.

_____. "Service and Tenure of Teachers in the Alaskan Native Schools." Master's thesis, Yale U., 1928.

Chance, Norman A. The Eskimo of North Alaska. New York: Holt, Rinehart and Winston, 1966.

_____. Modernization and Educational Reform in Native Alaska. Minneapolis: Training Center for Community Programs, U. of Minnesota, 1971.

Cline, Michael S. Tannik School: The Impact of Education on the Eskimos of Anaktuwuk Pass. Anchorage: Alaska Methodist U. Press, 1975.

Cohen, Felix S. "Alaska's Nuremberg Laws." Commentary 6(Ag, 1948):136-143.

Collier, John, Jr. Film Evaluation of Eskimo Education. The National Study of American Indian Education, Series III, Number 4, Final Report, Je, 1970, 160 pp. Chicago: U. of Chicago. ERIC ED 041 690.

Connelly, John, and Barnhardt, Ray. Angoon, Alaska. National Study of American Indian Education. Final Report, Ja, 1970, 13 pp. Chicago: U. of Chicago. ERIC ED 045 271.

_____, and _____. Community Background Reports: Bethel, Alaska. National Study of American Indian Education, Series I, Number 11. Final Report, Ja, 1970, 18 pp. Chicago: U. of Chicago. ERIC ED 041 686.

Crandell. Faye E. "A Cross-Cultural Study of Ahtena Indian and Non-Indian High School Students in Alaska on Selected Value Orientation and Measured Intellectual Ability." Diss. Abstr. Int'l, Jl, 1970. Vol. 31(1-A): 214-215.

Darnell, Frank. "Systems of Education for the Alaskan Native Population." In Education in the North, pp. 293-323. Edited by Frank Darnell. Arctic Institute of North America, U. of Alaska, 1972.

Draper, H. H. "The Aboriginal Eskimo Diet in Modern Perspective." American Anthropologist 79(Je, 1977):309-316.

Dubbs, Patrick James. "The Urban Adaptation Patterns of Alaska Eskimos in Anchorage, Alaska." Doctoral dissertation, Michigan State U., 1975. Univ. Microfilms Order No. 76-5548.

Dukepoo, Janis Herman and Others. National Indian/Alaska Native Health Conference: "Improving Health for Improving Life," Je 29, 1976. ERIC ED 147 077.

Eels, Walter C. "Educational Achievement of the Native Races in Alaska." Journal of Applied Psychology 17(1933):646-670.

Ervin, Alexander M. "Civic Capacity and Transculturation: The Rise and Role of the Alaska Federation of Natives." Doctoral dissertation, U. of Illinois, 1974.

_____. "The Emergence of Native Alaskan Political Capacity, 1959-1971." Musk-Ox 19 (1976):3-14.

Fields, Charles R. "Alaskan Natives and Caucasians: A Comparison of Educational Aspirations and Actual Enrollment." Journal of Student Financial Aid 5(N, 1975):35-45.

Foster, Anthony. "Changing Predispositions to Academic Success by Alaska Native People." In Education and the Many Faces of the Disadvantaged: Cultural and Historical Perspectives, pp. 168-174. Edited by William W. Brickman and Stanley Lehrer. New York: Wiley, 1972.

Governor's Commission on Cross Cultural Education. Time For Change in the Education of Alaskan Natives... Juneau: The Commission, 1970.

Hanna, Gerald S., House, Betty, and Salisbury, Lee H. "WAIS Performance of Alaskan Native University Freshmen." Journal of Genetic Psychology, Mr, 1968.

Hecht, Kathryn A., and Fox, Robert M. Leadership Programs and Alaska Native Perspectives: A Study to Promote University Awareness, Ap, 1977. ERIC ED 145 992.

Hikel, J. Steven. "Cross-Cultural Education in Alaska: Not How but Why?" Phi Delta Kappan 58(Ja, 1977):403-404.

Hinckley, Kay, and Kleinert, Jean (comps.). Sharing Ideas. Southeast Alaska Cultures: Teaching Ideas and Resource Information, Ag, 1975. ERIC ED 125 817.

Hippler, Arthur E. Barrow and Kotzebue: An Exploratory Comparison of Acculturation and Education in Two Large Northwestern Alaska Villages. Minneapolis: Training Center for Community Programs, U. of Minnesota, 1969.

Hirischi, Melvin, and Glass, Thomas. "Athabascans Get a School." Journal of American Indian Education 16(My, 1977):16-19.

Hughes, Charles C. An Eskimo Village in the Modern World. Ithaca, NY: Cornell U. Press, 1960.

Jackson, Ellen. D. "The Teaching of English as a Second Language to Alaskan Native Children of Non-English Speaking Backgrounds on the Kindergarten and First Grade Levels." Master's thesis, U. of Washington, 1963.

Johnston, Thomas F. "Alaskan Eskimo Music is Revitalized." Journal of American Indian Education 17(My, 1978):1-7.

Jones, Dorothy M. "Race Relations in an Alaska Native Village." Anthropologica 15(1973).

Kakianak, Nathan. Eskimo Boyhood. An Autobiography in Psychosocial Perspective. Edited by Charles C. Hughes. Lexington, KY: U. Press of Kentucky, 1974.

Kaplan, Gary J., Fleshman, J. Kenneth, Bender, Thomas R., Baum, Carol, and Clark, Paul S. "Long-Term Effects of Otitis Media. A Ten-Year Cohort Study of Alaskan Eskimo Children." Pediatrics 52(O, 1973):577-585.

Kirk, Robert J. Health Careers for American Indians and Alaska Natives: Source Book, Educational Opportunities and Financial Assistance, Je, 1970, 81 pp. Washington, DC: Public Health Service, H.E.W., Division of Indian Health. ERIC ED 063 066.

Kleinfeld, Judith S. "Effects of Nonverbal Warmth on the Learning of Eskimo and White Students." Journal of Social Psychology 92 (F, 1974):3-9.

Lekanof, Flore. A Study of Problems in Education of the Native People of Alaska, Je, 1968, 18 pp. ERIC ED 029 736.

Mann, Clara. "A Study of Indian Housing Conditions of Wrangell Institute Students to Determine the Type of Home Management Course Needed." Master's thesis, Oregon State U., 1937.

Mason, Charles P. "Personality Adjustment, Mental Maturity, and Music Aptitude of the Three Ethnic Groups Represented at Mt. Edgecumbe School, Mt. Edgecumbe, Alaska." Master's thesis, Central Washington College of Education, 1955.

Mishou, Frank. "The Development of Federal Schools for Natives in Alaska, 1885-1941." Master's thesis, George Washington U., 1942.

Morgan, Lael. And the Land Provides. Alaskan Natives in a Year of Transition. Garden City, NY: Doubleday, 1974.

Orvik, James, and Barnhardt, Ray (eds.). Cultural Influences in Alaskan Native Education. Fairbanks: Center for Northern Educational Research, U. of Alaska, Ap, 1973.

Peck, Cyrus E., Sr. The Tides People. A Narrative Account of Tlingit Culture and Values Written by a Tlingit, Mr, 1975. ERIC ED 139 550.

Perkins, T. R. "Educational Provisions for the Alaskan Natives Since 1867." Master's thesis. U. of Texas, 1959.

_____. "Leadership in Alaskan Native Education." Journal of American Indian Education 2(O, 1962):1-5.

Petellin, Alexander A. "A Course of Study in Hygiene for Native Children of Alaska." Master's thesis, U. of Washington, 1938.

Ray, Charles K. Alaskan Native Education: An Historical Perspective, O, 1973. ERIC ED 096 073.

_____. A Program of Education for Alaskan Natives, 1958, 312 pp. ERIC ED 022 788.

Rogers, George W. Alaska Native Population Trends and Vital Statistics, 1950-1985, N, 1971. ERIC ED 125 846.

Rogers, George W., Ryan, Joan, and Parker, Seymour. Alaska Native Secondary School Dropouts. College, AK: U. of Alaska, 1962.

Salisbury, Lee H. College Orientation for Alaskan Natives (COPAN Program. Education for Survival). Final Report, Je 30, 1968, 166 pp. ERIC ED 025 225.

_____. "The Speech Education of the Alaskan Indian Student as Viewed by the Speech Educator." Journal of American Indian Education 4(My, 1965):1-7.

_____. "Teaching English to Alaska Natives." Journal of American Indian Education, Ja, 1967.

Senungetuk, Joseph. Give or Take a Century: The Story of an Eskimo Family. San Francisco: The Indian Historian Press, 1970.

Starr, Jerome L. "The Cultural and Educational Development of Aborigines and Settlers in Russian America, 1784-1867." Doctoral dissertation, New York U., 1964.

Streiff, Virginia. Reading Comprehension and Language Proficiency Among Eskimo Children. New York: Arno, 1978.

Tisha: The Story of a Young Teacher in the Alaska Wilderness, as told to Robert Specht. New York: St. Martin, 1976. [1926]

U.S. Bureau of Indian Affairs. Alaskan Native Education: An Historical Perspective. Research and Evaluation Report No. 18-A. Albuquerque: Office of Indian Education Programs, Indian Education Resource Center, 1974.

Van Stone, James W. Eskimos of the Nushagak River. An Ethnographic History. Seattle: U. of Washington Press, 1968.

West, Phebe. "An Educational Program for an Aleut Village." Master's thesis, U. of Washington, 1938.

Weyant, E. David. "A Program of Health Education for the Community School at Nondalton, Alaska." Master's thesis, U. of Wyoming, 1939.

Wilson, A. S. "The Acculturation of Alaska Natives in the Public School of Nome, Alaska." Master's thesis, U. of Alaska, 1958.

Arizona

Brewer, Sam A., Jr. "The Yaqui Indians of Arizona: Trilingualism and Cultural Change." Doctoral dissertation, U. of Texas, 1976. Univ. Microfilms Order No. 77-3870.

Carson, Charles A. "A Survey of an Arizona Indian School." Master's thesis, Stanford U., 1924.

Castile, George P. "The Community School at Rough Rock." Master's thesis, U. of Arizona, 1968.

Chaudhri, Joyotpaul. Urban Indians of Arizona--Phoenix, Tucson, and Flagstaff. Tucson, AZ: U. of Arizona Press, 1974.

Chilcott, John H., and Thomas, Marjorie. Tuba City, Arizona. National Study of American Indian Education. Final Report, Ja, 1970, 17 pp. Chicago: U. of Chicago. ERIC ED 045 272.

Conklin, Paul. "Good Day at Rough Rock." American Education, F, 1967.

Cook, James E. "The Government's Segregated School." Phoenix Republican, Mr 12, 1978. [Phoenix Indian High School]

Dodd, Arthur. [Documents on Problems of Ganado Arizona School System] Navajo Times, Jl 12, 1973.

Early, Kenzie. [Letter to Commissioner of Indian Affairs Louis R. Bruce about the school board in Cibecue, Arizona] Americans Before Columbus 3(Ja-Jl, 1971):2,7.

Eiler, Terry. "My Classroom, the Grand Canyon." Chicago Tribune Magazine, Je 14, 1970. [Head Start program, Havasupai Indian Reservation]

Erickson, Donald, and Schwartz, Henrietta. Community School at Rough Rock. A Report Submitted to the Office of Economic Opportunity. With a special report by Oswald Werner. Contract No. B89-4534, Ap, 1969.

Erickson, Donald A. "Rough Rock Evaluation." Navajo Times, Mr 18, 1971.

Factors Affecting Attitudes Toward Education Among Indian High School Students in Phoenix Area Off-Reservation Schools and Mexican-American and Black Students in Phoenix Union High School, 1971, 77 pp. Phoenix: Bureau of Indian Affairs. ERIC ED 056 794.

Feeney, Francis H. "Illiteracy in America from 1870 to 1930." Master's thesis, U. of Arizona, 1951.

Flanigan, Maye. "History of the Phoenix Indian School to 1933." Master's thesis, Tempe State College, 1951.

Hamblin, John Ray. "A Study of Some of the Important Factors Which Encourage Indian Students in Apache and Navajo Counties in Arizona to Seek a Higher Education After High School Graduation." Master's thesis, Brigham Young U., 1963.

Harkins, Arthur, and Woods, Richard (eds.). Problems of Cross-Cultural Educational Research and Evaluation: The Rough Rock Demonstration School, D, 1969, 26 pp. Minneapolis: U. of Minnesota Training Center for Community Programs. ERIC ED 040 231.

Holm, Wayne. "Rock Point's Ex-Principal Praises School" (letter). Navajo Times, Ja 1, 1970. [Comments on Erickson-Schwartz Project]

Kelly, Roger F., and Cramer, John O. American Indians in Small Cities: A Survey of Urban Acculturation in Two Northern Arizona Communities. Department of Reha ilitation, Northern Arizona U., Flagstaff, 1966.

Kelly, William H. A Study of Southern Arizona School-Age Indian Children, 1966-1967. Tucson, AZ: Bureau of Ethnic Research, Department of Anthropology, U. of Arizona, 1967.

Ladd, Carl E. "The Educational Growth of Indian Children in the Phoenix Area, 1951 to 1952, as Measured by Test Results." Doctoral dissertation, U. of Kansas, 1955.

McNicholas, Sr. M. John. "Educational Facilities for the Arizona Indians: The Basis for Cultural Change." Master's thesis, Siena Heights College, Adrian, MI, 1962.

Macon, Bob. "Reservation Education Scandalous; According to Legislative Report." Navajo Times, F 5, 1976.

Manning, Susan J. Indian Education in an Off-Reservation Border Town Public School System: A Case Study of the Page Public School System, Page, Arizona. Page, AZ: 1974.

Michener, Bryan P. Shonto Board School and Community, Arizona, 1970. ERIC ED 040 791.

Moore, Jim. "Indian Education in Snowflake." Christian Science Monitor, N 10, 1975. [Snowflake Indian Dormitory in Dormitory, AZ]

"Notice. Window Rock Public School District No. 8 Under New Management." Akwasasne Notes 6 (Early Autumn, 1974).

Platero, Dillon. "Multicultural Teacher Education Center at Rough Rock." In The Schooling of Native America, pp. 45-51. Edited by Thomas Thompson. Washington, DC: American Association of Colleges for Teacher Education, Ag, 1978.

Roessel, Robert A., Jr. "Indian Education in Arizona." Journal of American Indian Education 1(Je, 1961):33-38.

_____. "An Overview of the Rough Rock Demonstration School." Journal of American Indian Education, My, 1969.

Roessel, Robert A., Jr., et al. "An Overview of the Rough Rock Demonstration School." Journal of American Indian Education 7(My, 1968).

Rund, Nadine H., Siegel, Herman, and Rumley, Ella G. Demographic and Socio-Cultural Characteristics: Papago Indian Reservation, Arizona. Washington, DC: GPO, S, 1968.

[Statements on Indian Student Protests in Public Schools of Tuba, Arizona] U.S. Commission on Civil Rights, Hearing Held in Window Rock, Arizona, October 22-24, 1973, II, pp 1138-1163. Washington, DC: The Commission, 1974.

Talbot, Steve. "The Myth of Indian Economic and Political Incompetence: The San Carlos Case." Southwest Economy and Society 3(Spring, 1977): 3-46.

U.S. Commission on Civil Rights. Hearing Held in Phoenix, Arizona, November 17-18, 1972. Washington, DC: GPO, 1974.

U.S. Commission on Civil Rights, Arizona Advisory Committee. Justice in Flagstaff: Are These Rights Inalienable? Washington, DC: U.S. Commission on Civil Rights, 1977.

U.S. Congress, 71st 2nd Session, SEnate, Committee on Indian Affaris, Subcommittee, Survey of Conditions of the Indians in the United States. Part 8. Hearings on Mismanagement of Phoenix School, Arizona and Boarding Schools in General.

Weaver, Thomas (ed.). Indians of Arizona: A Contemporary Perspective. Tucson, AZ: U. of Arizona Press, 1974.

"The Werner Report. Board Dissents with Report." Navajo Times, Ja 15, 1970. [Critique of Erickson-Schwartz report of Rough Rock Demonstration School]

California

Ablon, Joan. "Relocated American Indians in the San Francisco Bay Area." Human Organization 33(Winter, 1964):296-304.

Barcus, Wallace. "A Controlled Study of Indian and White Children in the Sierra Joint Union High School District, Tollhouse, Fresno County, California." Master's thesis, Fresno State College, Fresno, CA, 1956.

Bushnell, John R. "From American Indian to Indian American: The Changing Identity of the Hupa." American Anthropologist, D, 1968.

California Indian Education. Report of the First All-Indian Statewide Conference on California Indian Education. Ad Hoc Committee on California Indian Education, 1349 Crawford Road, Modesto, CA.

Cook, Sherburne F. The Conflict Between the California Indian and White Civilization, 3 Vols. Ibero-Americana. 21, 22, 23. Berkeley, CA: U. of California Press, 1943.

_____. The Population of the California Indians, 1769-1970. Berkeley, CA: U. of California Press, 1976.

Engelhardt, Fr. Zephyrin. The Mission and Missionaries of California, 4 Vols. San Francisco: James H. Barry Co., 1908-1915.

Fletcher, Mildred P. "A Guide for Student Teachers Teaching a Unit on the Los Angeles Indians." Master's thesis, U. of Southern California, 1949.

Forbes, Jack D. A Model for the Improvement of
Indian Education: The California Indian Education Association. Berkeley, CA: Far West
Laboratory for Educational Research and Development, 1968.

_____. Native Americans of California and
Nevada. Healdsburg, CA: Natmegraph Press,
1969.

Forbes, Jack D. (ed.). California Indian Education. Report of the First All-Indian Statewide Conference on California Indian Education. Ad Hoc Committee on California Indian
Education, N 20, 1967, 87 pp. ERIC ED 017
391.

Fraser, Robert S. "Studies of Race Intelligence
of Indian Pupils at Sherman Institute, Riverside, California." Master's thesis, U. of
Denver, 1934.

Gunn, James A. "An Investigation of the Scholastic Success of American Indian Children in
the Sacramento City Schools." Master's thesis, Sacramento State College, 1969.

Harris, Michael. [Three articles on Indians in
San Francisco Bay area] San Francisco Chronicle, Mr 16, 17 and 20, 1978.

Havighurst, Robert J. Indians and their Education in Los Angeles, 1970. ERIC ED 039 078.

Heath, G. Louis. "No Rock Is An Island." Phi
Delta Kappan 52(Mr, 1971):397-399. [Indian
American occupation of Alcatraz, CA]

Hendrick, Irving G. Federal and State Roles in
the Education of Indians: The California Experience, 1850-1934, Ap, 1974. ERIC ED 088
617.

_____. "Federal Policy Affecting the Education
of Indians in California, 1849-1934." History of Education Quarterly 16(1976):163-185.

Hillinger, Charles. "A Feather in Education's
Cap." Los Angeles Times, Ap 17, 1977.
[Sherman Indian High School, Riverside]

Lloyd, Nancy. "The Chumash: A Study of the
Assimilation of a California Indian Tribe."
Master's thesis, U. of Arizona, 1955.

Lund, Betsy F. "The Dilemma of the California
Indian." C.T.A. Journal, O, 1965.

_____. "A Survey of Comparative Achievement
and Scholarship Records of California Indian
Children in the Auburn Public Schools." Master's thesis, Sacramento State College, 1963.

McHugh, James J. "Educational Aspects of the
Mission Systems in Upper California." Master's
thesis, The Catholic U. of America, 1922.

Martin, Ken. "A Statistical Profile of the California Indian Population." Integrateducation 12(S-O, 1974):31.

Merrill, Orville W., Jr. A Comprehensive Mental
Health Program at Sherman, Indian High School,
Ag 31, 1971. ERIC ED 138 408.

North, William E. "Catholic Education in Southern California (1769-1935)." Doctoral dissertation, Catholic U. of America, 1936.

Parsons, Cynthia. "Sunny Aims to Improve U.S.
Indian Lot in School." Christian Science
Monitor, N 10, 1975. [Indian teacher in Oak-
land, CA, public school]

Phillips, George Harwood. Chiefs and Challenges:
Indian Resistance and Cooperation in Southern
California. Berkeley: U. of California
Press, 1975.

Pirir, Zillar. "The Introduction of the Mental
Hygiene Program at Sherman Institute Through
a Child Guidance Clinic." Master's thesis,
Claremont College, 1935.

Porter, Marian L. "Indian Education in the U.S.,
with Special Reference to the California Indian." Master's thesis, San Francisco State
College, 1956.

Price, John A. "The Migration and Adaptation of
American Indians to Los Angeles." Human Organization, Summer, 1968.

Robin, Frederick E. "Culture Contact and Public
Opinion in a Bicultural Community." Master's
thesis, Columbia U., 1941. [Ukiah, CA]

U.S. Congress, 33rd, 1st Session, House of Representatives, House Report No. 267, Vol. III,
Je 30, 1854. Adverse Report on Establishment
of Schools for Indians in California.

Vassar, Rena L. "The Fort Bidwell, California,
Indian School: A Study of the Federal Indian
Education Policy." Master's thesis, U. of
California, 1953.

Colorado

Gaillard, Frye. "Indians Protest New Tuition
Law." Race Relations Reporter 2(Je 7, 1971):
8-10. [Fort Lewis College, Durango, CO]

Graves, Theodore D. "Urban Indian Personality
and the 'Culture of Poverty.'" American
Ethnologist 1(F, 1974):65-86. [Navajo Indians in Denver]

Graves, T. D., and Van Arsdale, Minor. "Values,
Expectations and Relocation: The Navaho Migrant to Denver." Human Organization 25(Winter, 1966):300-307.

Hughes, J. Donald. American Indians in Colorado.
Boulder, CO: Pruett Publishing Co., 1977.

"Indians, Asians Working Together." Race Relations Reporter, O 16, 1970. [Institute in American Indian Studies, U. of Colorado]

Luebben, Ralph A. "Prejudice and Discrimination Against Navajos in a Mining Community." Kiva 30(1964):1-17.

Connecticut

Clarey, Susan. "Federal Grant May Allow Introduction of American Indian Studies in City." Bridgeport Post, Mr 1, 1976.

Florida

Gaillard, Frye. "Can Indians Educate Whites?" Race Relations Reporter, O 1, 1970.

Kersey, Harry A., Jr. "The Ahfachkee Day School." Record 72(S, 1970):93-103.

_____. "Educating the Seminole Indians of Florida, 1879-1970." Florida Historical Quarterly, Jl, 1970.

Idaho

Berry, Ray M. Educating the People of the Fort Hall Indian Reservation. Bureau of Business and Economic Research, U. of Idaho, 1961.

Boyer, LaNada. "Growing Up in E'Da How--One Idaho Girlhood." In The Schooling of Native America, pp. 29-42. Edited by Thomas Thompson. Washington, DC: American Association of Colleges for Teacher Education, Ag, 1978.

Dizmang, Larry H., Watson, Jane, May, Philip A., and Bopp, John. "Adolescent Suicide At An Indian Reservation." American Journal of Orthopsychiatry 44(Ja, 1974):43-49. [Fort Hall]

Liljeblad, Sven. The Idaho Indians in Transition, 1805-1960. Pocatello, ID: Museum of Idaho State U., 1972.

_____. "Some Observations on the Fort Hall Indian Reservation." In U.S. Congress, 90th, 1st and 2nd Sessions, Senate, Committee on Labor and Public Welfare, Special Subcommittee on Indian Education, Indian Education. Hearings..., Part 5, pp. 2279-2304. Washington, DC: GPO, 1969.

_____. "Some Observations on the Fort Hall Indian Reservation." Indian Historian 7 (Fall, 1974):9-13.

Lindsay, Barbara. "The Relationship Between Certain Personality Factors and Academic Achievement of Fort Hall Indian Students." Master's thesis, Brigham Young U., 1956.

McCarty, Darene. "An Indian Student Speaks." Indian Historian 4(Summer, 1971):10,20. [Plummer and Worley schools]

Shields, Gerald R., and Sheppard, George. "American Indians: Search for Fort Hall's Library Service." American Libraries 1(O, 1970):856-860. [Pocatello]

Uhlman, Ester E. "A Comparative Study of Achieve Achievement and Intelligence of Indians and Whites in the Public Schools of Lapwai, Idaho." Master's thesis, U. of Idaho, 1953.

Walker, Deward E. American Indians of Idaho. Moscow, ID: Department of Sociology-Anthropology, 1973.

Illinois

Fuchs, Estelle, Scott, George D., White, John K., Numrich, Camille, and Havighurst, Robert G. Indians and Their Education in Chicago, 1970. ERIC ED 039 079.

Neog, Prafulla and others. Chicago Indians: The Effects of Urban Migration. The National Study of American Indian Education, Ja, 1970, 148 pp. Minneapolis: U. of Minnesota, Center for Community Programs. ERIC ED 041 341.

Rottenberg, Dan. "Indian Territory: Up and Up Downtown, Down and Out Uptown." Chicago 9 (Ja-F, 1972):54-58. [Chicago]

Scott, George D. and others. Indians and Their Education in Chicago. National Study of American Indian Education, Series II, No. 2, N, 1969, 65 pp. Chicago: U. of Chicago. ERIC ED 039 079.

Woods, Richard G., and Harkins, Arthur M. Indian Americans in Chicago. Minneapolis: Training Center for Community Programs, U. of Minnesota, N, 1968.

Indiana

Fritsch, Mary O. "History of the Educational Activities of the Sisters of Saint Francis, Oldenburg, Indiana." Doctoral dissertation, U. of Cincinnati, 1943.

Iowa

Bataille, Gretchen M. and others (eds.). The Worlds Between Two Rivers: Perspectives on American Indians in Iowa. Ames, IO: Iowa State U. Press, 1978.

Byrd, John M. "Educational Policies of the Federal Government Toward the Sac and Fox Indians of Iowa, 1920-1921 and 1936-1937, with Resulting Changes in Indian Educational Attitudes: A Study in the Process of Assimilation." Master's thesis, U. of Iowa, 1938.

Crow, Verl. "A Study of the Educational Status of the Indian Student in the Sioux City Public Schools." Master's thesis, Drake U., 1960.

Hoyt, Elizabeth E. "The Children of Tama."
Journal of American Indian Education 3(O,
1963):15-20.

Jones, Ben. "The Economic, Legal and Educational
Status of the Mesquakee (Fox) Indian of Iowa."
Master's thesis, State U. of Iowa, 1932.

Jones, Marie C. "To Watch Them Stand Tall: The
Sioux City P.L. Indian Project." *American
Libraries* 6(S, 1975):494-496.

McTaggart, Fred. *Wolf That I Am: In Search of
the Red Earth People*. Boston: Houghton
Mifflin Co., 1976. [Mesquakie life]

Neff, Ronald L., and Weinstein, Jay A. "Iowa's
Indians Come of Age." *Society* 12(Ja-F, 1975):
22-26, 60. [Mesquakies]

Purcell, L. Edward. "The Unknown Past: Sources
for History Education and the Indians of
Iowa." *Indian Historian* 9(Summer, 1976):13-
18.

Urban Education Section. "South Tama." In Iowa
Department of Public Instruction, *Iowa Schools
Progress Reports on Desegregation*, August,
1976. Des Moines: State Department of Edu-
cation, Ag, 1976. [Sac and Fox Day School,
South Tama]

Kansas

Ayers, Solon G. "An Investigation of Vocational
Education at Haskell Institute." Doctoral
dissertation, U. of Kansas, 1952.

Bordenkircher, Mary A. "A Historical Study of
the Mission Schools in Early Territory Now
Comprising Kansas." Master's thesis, Kansas
State Teachers College, 1949.

Cunningham, W. D. "Changing Environment and
Changing Institution: Indian Project of the
Northeast Kansas Library System." *Library
Trends* 20(O, 1971):376-381.

"For a Brave's New World." *Topeka Capital Journal*, Mr 12, 1972. [Chilocco Indian School]

Goddard, Geneva. "A Study of the Historical
Development and Education-Work at Haskell
Institute." Master's thesis, Kansas State
Teachers College, 1930.

Goodner, James and others. *Characteristics and
Attitudes of 1968 Haskell Institute Students*.
The National Study of American Indian Education, Series III, No. 6, Final Report, Jl,
1970, 83 pp. Chicago: U. of Chicago; Minneapolis: Training Center for Community Programs, U. of Minnesota. ERIC ED 042 560.

Goodner, James and others. *Language and Related
Characteristics of 1968 Haskell Institute
Students*, Jl, 1970, 102 pp. Minneapolis:
U. of Minnesota, Training Center for Community
Programs. ERIC ED 045 226.

Granzer, Loretta M. "Indian Education at Haskell Institute, 1884-1937." Master's thesis,
U. of Nebraska, 1937.

Powell, Shirley J. "History of St. Mary's
School." Master's thesis, U. of South Dakota,
1954.

Reboussin, Roland, and Goldstein, Joel W.
"Achievement Motivation in Navajo and White
Students." *American Anthropology*, Je, 1966.

Timmons, Barbara J. "An Exploratory Investigation of Attitudes toward Certain Speech Communication Variables Found Among Male Post-
High School Vocational Students at Haskell
Indian Institute, Lawrence, Kansas." Doctoral dissertation, U. of Kansas, 1965.

U.S. Department of Justice. "Ottawa University,
Kansas." 13 *Opinions of the Attorney General*
336(1870).

Watt, Jewell K. "A Survey of the Haskell Institute." Master's thesis, Kansas State College, 1930.

Louisiana

Donns, Ernest C., and Whitehead, Jenna (eds.).
"The Houma Indians: Two Decades in a History
of Struggle." *American Indian Journal* 2(Mr,
1976):2-18.

Roy, Ewell P., and Leary, Don. "Economic Survey
of American Indians in Louisiana." *American
Indian Journal of the Institute for the Development of Indian Law* 3(Ja, 1977):11-16.

Maine

Dalquist, David. "The Forgotten Americans."
Harvard Crimson, N 2, 1977. [Passamaquoddy
Reservation, ME]

"First Look Reveals No Indian School Segregation
in Maine." *Indian Voices*, F-Mr, 1967.
[Penobscot Indian Tribe in Princeton and Old
Town]

Maine Advisory Committee to the U.S. Commission
on Civil Rights. *Federal and State Services
and the Maine Indian*. Washington, DC: Commission on Civil Rights, D, 1974.

Ray, Roger B. (comp.). *Indians of Maine and the
Atlantic Provinces*, Revised edition. Portland, ME: Maine Historical Society, 1977.

"'Red Power' in Maine." *Time*, My 31, 1971.
[Abnaki Indians in Maine]

Skinner, Vincent P. "The Children of the Forgotten: The Indians of Maine." *Contemporary
Education* 43(My, 1971):284-289.

Villari, Mary Ann. *The Historical Precedents
and Recent Development of Maine Indians' Bid
for Recognition*, 1975. ERIC ED 122 979.

Maryland

Amanullah, Mohammod. "The Lumbee Indians [of Baltimore, Maryland]: Patterns of Adjustment." In Toward Economic Development for Native American Communities, I, pp. 277-298. Washington, DC: GPO, 1969.

Makovsky, Abraham. "Tradition and Change in the Lumbee Indian Community of Baltimore." Doctoral dissertation, Catholic U. of America, 1971.

Peck, John Gregory. Education of Urban Indians: Lumbee Indians in Baltimore. The National Study of American Indian Education, Series II, No. 3, Ag, 1969, 11 pp. Chicago: U. of Chicago. ERIC ED 039 977.

Massachusetts

Attaquin, Helen Avis. "What Are the Continuing Education Needs of the American Indian Population of Boston?" Doctoral dissertation, Boston U., 1975.

Chamberlain, Tony. "Vanishing Americans." Boston Globe, O 5, 1975.

Guillemin, Jeanne. Urban Renegades. The Cultural Strategy of American Indians. New York: Columbia U. Press, 1975. [Boston]

Michigan

A Study of the Socioeconomic Status of Michigan Indians. Lansing, MI: The Governor's Commission on Indian Affairs, N, 1971.

Bigony, Beatrice Ann. "Migrants to the Cities: A Study of the Socio-economic Status of Native Americans in Detroit and Michigan." Doctoral dissertation, U. of Michigan, 1974. Univ. Microfilms Order No. 75-634.

Glass, Thomas E. "A Descriptive and Comparative Study of American Indian Children in the Detroit Public Schools." Doctoral dissertation, Wayne State U., 1972.

Martin, Larry, and Morris, Joann. Indian Education Project, 1974. ERIC ED 141 017.

Michigan State Department of Education. A Position Statement on Indian Education in Michigan, 1974. ERIC ED 101 870.

Rubenstein, Bruce. "To Destroy a Culture: Indian Education in Michigan, 1855-1900." Michigan History 60(Summer, 1976):137-160.

U.S. Commission on Civil Rights, Michigan Advisory Committee. Civil Rights and the Housing and Community Development Act of 1974. Vol. III: The Chippewa People of Sault Ste. Marie. Washington, DC: The Commission, 1976.

West, Ralph L. "The Adjustment of the American Indian in Detroit: A Descriptive Study." Master's thesis, Wayne U., 1950.

Minnesota

Beaulieu, David. The Formal Education of Minnesota Indians: Historical Perspective Until 1934, Je, 1971, 44 pp. Minneapolis: U. of Minnesota, Center for Urban and Regional Affairs; Training Center for Community Programs. ERIC ED 050 873.

Belding, Nanceye, Woods, Richard G., and Harkins, Arthur M. Evaluation Report of the 1968-69 University of Minnesota Cultural Education Specialist and Associate Program: Indian American and Afro-American Aspects. Minneapolis: Training Center for Community Programs, U. of Minnesota, Je, 1969.

Bellecourt, Clyde. "Bringing Our Children Home." Indigena 2(Fall, 1976):11-16. [Director, Heart of the Earth Survival School, Minneapolis]

Bucknaga, Jerome. "Interracial Politics: The Pressure to Integrate An Experimental School." In The Schooling of Native America, pp. 53-71. Edited by Thomas Thompson. Washington, DC: American Association of Colleges for Teacher Education, Ag, 1978. [Pine Point Experimental School, Ponsford]

Cook, Ruth C. "The Results of a Remediation Program, Which Used the Activity Unit Technique, on Subject Matter Accomplishments and on Certain Attitudes of a Group of Third and Fourth Grade Indian Children at the Red Lake Agency School." Master's thesis, U. of Minnesota, 1935.

Dorn, Donald D. "A Comparative Study of Indian and White Children in the Intermediate Grades of the Cass Lake Public Schools." Master's thesis, U. of North Dakota, 1954.

Drilling, Laverne, Harkins, Arthur M., and Woods, Richard G. The Indian Relief Recipient in Minneapolis: An Exploratory Study. Minneapolis: Training Center for Community Programs, U. of Minnesota, Ag, 1969.

Graham, Eleanora L. "An Analysis of the Errors Made in the Standardized Achievement Tests by Indian Children in Grades 6, 7, and 8 in Becker County, Minnesota." Master's thesis, Colorado State College of Education, 1951.

Harkins, Arthur M. Public Education on a Minnesota Chippewa Reservation. Volumes 1-6. Final Report, My 31, 1968, 641 pp. Lawrence, KA: U. of Kansas. ERIC ED 025 338.

Harkins, Arthur M., and Woods, Richard G. (comps.). Indian Americans in Duluth. A Summary and Analysis of Recent Research, My, 1970, 63 pp. Minneapolis: U. of Minnesota, Center for Community Programs. ERIC ED 044 195.

_____ and _____. Indian Americans in St. Paul: An Interim Report, 1970. ERIC ED 039 992.

Harkins, Arthur M. and others. Indians and Their Education in Minneapolis and St. Paul. The National Study of American Indian Education, Series II, No. 5, Final Report, F, 1972, 99 pp. Minneapolis: U. of Minnesota, Center for Urban and Regional Affairs and Training Center for Community Programs. ERIC ED 062 057.

Harkins, Arthur M. and others. Junior High Indian Children in Minneapolis: A Study of One Problem School. The National Study of American Indian Education. Minneapolis: Training Center for Community Programs, U. of Minnesota. ERIC ED 042 214.

Harkins, Arthur M., Hammond, Judith, Sherarts, I. Karon, and Woods, Richard G. Junior High Indian Children in Minneapolis: A Study of One Problem School. Minneapolis: Center for Urban and Regional Affairs, U. of Minnesota, Jl, 1970. [Bryant Junior High School]

Hassinger, Edward W. "A Study of the Minority Group's Social Contacts: the Lower Sioux Community of Morton, Minnesota." Master's thesis, U. of Minnesota, 1951.

Holbert, Victoria L. and others. Indian Americans at Mille Lacs, Jl, 1970, 44 pp. Minneapolis: U. of Minnesota, Training Center for Community Programs. ERIC ED 044 194.

Indians in Minneapolis, 1968. League of Women Voters, 1200 Second Avenue South, Minneapolis, MN.

Jones, Ramona C. Minnesota Indian Education Hearings Report, N, 1976. ERIC ED 149 892.

Larson, R. H. "Education of Indian Children in Minnesota." Minnesota Journal of Education 26(D, 1945).

League of Women Voters, New Brighton, Minnesota. Children's Impressions of American Indians: A Survey of Suburban Kindergarten and Fifth Grade Children, S, 1975. ERIC ED 134 499.

_____. Young People's Concepts of Native Americans: A Survey of Suburban Ninth and Twelfth Grade Students, Ap, 1976. ERIC ED 134 500.

Leland, Gunvald E. "Recent Education of Indians in Minnesota, with Special Emphasis upon the Chippewa." Master's thesis, U. of North Dakota, 1944.

Lounberg, Dan. "The New Face of the American Indian Movement." Crisis 84(D, 1977):463-466.

Mayer, Catherine M. and others (comps.). Minnesota Indian Resources Directory, My, 1970, 173 pp. (second edition). Minneapolis: U. of Minnesota, Center for Urban and Regional Affairs. ERIC ED 043 435.

Minnesota Advisory Committee to the U.S. Commission on Civil Rights. Bridging the Gap: The Twin Cities Native American Community. Washington, DC: U.S. Commission on Civil Rights, Ja, 1975.

Minnesota Chippewa Indians. A Handbook for Teachers, 1968. Upper Midwest Regional Educational Laboratory, 2698 University Avenue, St. Paul, MN.

Mittelholtz, Erwin F. "A Historical Review of the Grand Portage Indian Reservation with Special Emphasis on Indian Education." Master's thesis, U. of North Dakota, 1953.

Nathanson, Iric. "The Indian Community and Life in the City." Washington Post, F 1, 1976. [American Indian Movement in Minnesota]

Nichols, Max. "Indian School Obstacles Cited." Minneapolis Star, F 3, 1976.

Ose, Gordon. "A Survey of Four Major Problems of Indian Education in the State of Minnesota." Master's thesis, U. of Minnesota, 1947.

Peterson, David L. The Chippewa Indians of Minnesota. A Teacher's Guide to An Indian Culture Kit for Upper Elementary Schools. Duluth, MN: Duluth Indian Action Council, 1969.

Reynolds, Gaylord V. "A History of the Pipestone Indian School." Master's thesis, U. of South Dakota, 1952.

Schuiling, John T. "A Study of Community Relationships in Minnesota Indian Schools." Master's thesis, George Peabody College for Teachers, 1938.

Stark, Matthew. "Minnesota Encourages the Chippewa Indians." Journal of American Indian Education 6(My, 1967):6-13.

Stickney, Avis L. (comp.). Minnesota Indian Directory, 1967, 51 pp. Minneapolis: U. of Minnesota. ERIC ED 022 613.

U.S. Commission on Civil Rights, Minnesota Advisory Committee. Bridging the Gap: A Reassessment: A Report. Washington, DC: U.S. Commission on Civil Rights, 1978.

_____. Bridging the Gap: The Twin Cities Native American Community. Washington, DC: The Commission, 1975.

Wood, Loren E. "A Study of the Educational Status of the Chippewa Indians in the Cass Lake High School, Cass Lake, Minnesota." Master's thesis, U. of North Dakota, 1953.

Woods, Richard G. Indians in Minneapolis, Ap, 1968, 110 pp. Minneapolis: League of Women Voters. ERIC ED 022 578.

Woods, Richard G., and Harkins, Arthur M. Education-Related Preferences and Characteristics of College-Aspiring Urban Indian Teen-Agers: A Preliminary Report. Minneapolis: Training Center for Community Programs, U. of Minnesota, My, 1969.

_____ and _____. Indian Employment in Minneapolis, Ap, 1968, 96 pp. Minneapolis: U. of Minnesota. ERIC ED 021 659.

_____ and _____. Indian Residents in Minneapolis: A Further Examination of their Characteristics, Mr, 1971, 60 pp. Minneapolis: U. of Minnesota, Center for Urban and Regional Affairs; Training Center for Community Programs. ERIC ED 049 869.

_____ and _____. Indians and Other Americans in Minnesota Correctional Institutions. The National Study of American Indian Education, Mr, 1970, 56 pp. Minneapolis: Training Center for Community Programs, U. of Minnesota. ERIC ED 042 189.

_____ and _____. Rural and City Indians in Minnesota Prisons. Minneapolis: Training Center for Community Programs, U. of Minnesota, 1970.

Mississippi

Currie, Patricia A. "An Evaluation of Predisposing Dropout Factors Which Affect Academic Performance Among Sixth Graders in the Mississippi Choctaw Indian Schools." Doctoral dissertation, U. of Virginia, 1972.

Egerton, John. "The Other Philadelphia Story." Southern Education Report, S, 1966. [Education of the American Indian in Philadelphia, MS]

Langford, Etha A. "A Study of the Educational Development of the Choctaw Indians of Mississippi." Master's thesis, Mississippi Southern College, 1953.

Pardue, Janet. "Choctaws' Education Inadequate." Jackson Clarion-Ledger, N 18, 1975.

Peterson, John H., Jr., and Richburg, James R. Community Background Reports: The Mississippi Choctaws and Their Educational Program. National Study of American Indian Education, Series I, No. 21, Final Report, Je 1, 1970, 46 pp. Chicago: U. of Chicago. ERIC ED 042 553.

Peterson, John H., Jr. Socio-economic Characteristics of the Mississippi Choctaw Indians, Je, 1970, 36 pp. State College, MS: Mississippi State U., Social Science Research Center. ERIC ED 050 869.

Saul, Stephanie and others. [Five articles on the education of Choctaw Indians in Mississippi] Jackson Clarion-Ledger, N 16-20, 1975.

Spencer, Barbara G. and others. Occupational Orientation Among the Choctaw Indians, Ag 25, 1974. ERIC ED 096 082.

Spencer, Barbara G. "Occupational Orientation of Choctaw Indian High School Students in Mississippi." Master's thesis, Mississippi State U., 1973.

Spencer, Barbara G. and others. Choctaw Manpower and Demographic Survey, 1974, Mr, 1975. ERIC ED 124 765.

Tolbert, Charles M. A. "Sociological Study of the Choctaw Indians of Mississippi." Doctoral dissertation, Louisiana State U., 1958.

York, Ken, and Scott, J. Robert. Bilingual Education for Choctaws of Mississippi. Annual Evaluation Report, FY 75-76, S, 1976. ERIC ED 137 007.

Montana

Berven, Irene M. "History of Indian Education on the Flathead Reservation." Master's thesis, Montana State U., 1959.

Brockmann, C. Thomas. "Correlation of Social Class and Education on the Flathead Indian Reservation, Montana." Rocky Mountain Social Sciences Journal 8(O, 1971):11-18.

Hjelmseth, Donald E. "A Study of Selected Elementary School Teachers Toward American Indian Students in the State of Montana." Doctoral dissertation, U. of Montana, 1972.

Hopkins, David A. "A Brief History of Indian Education on the Tongue River Reservation." Master's thesis, Montana State U., 1951.

Humphrey, Theodore. Community Background Reports: Cut Bank, Montana. National Study of American Indian Education, Series I, No. 8, Final Report, D, 1969. ERIC ED 040 795.

Johnson, Milo C. "The History of Education on the Fort Rock Reservation, 1885-1935." Master's thesis, U. of Minnesota, 1937.

Larson, Wayne L. A Comparative Analysis of Indian and Non-Indian Parents' Influence on Educational Aspirations, Expectations, Preferences and Behavior of Indian and Non-Indian High School Students in Four High Schools, O, 1971, 66 pp. Bozeman, MT: Montana State U., Montana Agricultural Experiment Station. ERIC ED 056 788.

_____. A Comparison of the Differential Effect of Ethnicity and Perception of Family Income on Educational Aspirations, Preparation and Parental Influence-Attempts of Indian and Non-Indian Students in Four Rural High Schools in Montana, O, 1971. ERIC ED 056 789.

_____. Variation in Educational Goals and
Preferences, by Tribal Affiliation, of Indian
Students from Six Schools in Rural Montana,
N, 1975. ERIC ED 158 901.

MacFarland, Ruth. "The Intelligence of Indians
in the Schools of Montana: Data Secured by
an Intelligence Survey in Federal, State
and Mission Schools." Master's thesis, Montana State U., 1926.

U.S. Commission on Civil Rights, Montana, North
Dakota, and South Dakota Advisory Committees.
Indian Civil Rights Issues in Montana, North
Dakota, and South Dakota. Washington, DC:
The Commission, 1974.

U.S. Commission on Civil Rights, Montana Advisory Committee. Employment Practices in Montana. The Effects on American Indians and
Women. Washington, DC: The Commission, Ag,
1974.

Urban Management Consultants of San Francisco.
Profile of the Montana Native American, Ag,
1974. ERIC ED 151 116.

Visscher, Sietwanda. "Preliminary Study of Some
Attitudes Toward Cultural and Educational Conflicts of Indian Children in Montana." Master's thesis, Montana State U., 1970.

Watts, Shirley J. "A Preliminary Investigation
Into the Current Status of Indian Education
in Montana." Master's thesis, Montana State
U., 1971.

White, Sister Mary A. "Catholic Indian Missionary Influence in the Development of Catholic
Education in Montana, 1840-1903." Doctoral
dissertation, Saint Louis U., 1940.

Nebraska

Guenther, Richard L. "The Santee Normal Training School." Nebraska History 51(1970):359-
378.

Harkins, Arthur M. and others. Indian Americans
in Omaha and Lincoln, Ag, 1970, 64 pp. Minneapolis: U. of Minnesota. ERIC ED 047 860.

Nevada

Dunn, Helen. Indians of Nevada, seven volumes.
Carson City, NV: State Department of Education, Federal Relations and Programs Branch,
1973.

Forbes, Jack D. (ed.). Nevada Indians Speak.
Reno: U. of Nevada Press, 1967.

Haglund, E. A. Indian Integration in Nevada
Public Schools, 1966. ERIC ED 010 751.

Hudson, Emanuel B. "Community Education on the
Pyramid Lake Indian Reservation." Master's
thesis, Oregon State College, 1940.

"Mike Kane Completed His Education, But He Felt
the Prejudice." Nevada State Journal, D 28,
1975. [Born on Walker River Indian Reserva-
tion]

Nevada Indian Education Division. A Suggested
Program of Instruction for Indian Children
in the Public Schools of Nevada. Part 3:
The Adolescent Years. Carson City, NV: The
Division, 1968.

"Public School Opposed by Shoshone." Wassaja,
N, 1973. [Duckwater Elementary school, Nye
County]

Smeaton, Robert G. "Civil Rights and Indian
Youth." In U.S. Commission on Civil Rights,
Hearing Held in Phoenix, Arizona, November
17-18, 1972, pp. 468-481. Washington, DC:
GPO, 1974. [Stewart Indian School, Nevada
and Southwest Indian Center, Arizona]

"Special Education Program for Navajo Indians
at Stewart Indian School." Master's thesis,
Fisk U., 1956.

Wall, Leon C. "Indian Education in Nevada,
1861-1951." Master's thesis, U. of Nevada,
1952.

Wheeler, Arline Z. "Securing Social Adjustment
Among Indian Girls at Stewart, Nevada." Master's thesis, U. of Kansas, 1955.

New Mexico

Adair, John J. "A Study of Culture Resistance:
The Veterans of World War II at Zuni Pueblo."
Doctoral dissertation, U. of New Mexico, 1948.

Bettina, Albert A. "The Development of a Voca-
tional-Industrial Education in New Mexico."
Doctoral dissertation, Bradley U., 1953.

Boyer, Ruth. "Social Structure and Socialization
Among the Apaches of the Mescalero Reservation." Doctoral dissertation, U. of California, Berkeley, 1962.

Brizee, Robert L. "The Stereotype of the Indian
in the New Mexico Press." Master's thesis,
U. of New Mexico, 1954.

Buck, Lucius E. "An Inquiry into the History of
Presbyterian Educational Missions in New Mexico." Master's thesis, U. of Southern California, 1949.

Bureau of Indian Affairs. San Juan School Evaluation, Ag, 1974. ERIC ED 094 896.

Cassir, Richard Clark. "Red, White and Blue
Lake." Chicago Tribune Magazine, S 20, 1970.
[Pedro Archuleta, Taos Indian graduate of U.
of New Mexico]

Charles, C. M. "The Indian Child's Status in
New Mexico's Public Elementary School Science
Program." Doctoral dissertation, U. of New
Mexico, 1961.

Cibrario, Dominic J. The Pueblo Indians of New Mexico: An Analysis of the Educational System, 1974. ERIC ED 096 030.

Condie, LeRoy. "An Experiment in Second Language Instruction of Beginning Indian Children in New Mexico Public Schools." Doctoral dissertation, U. of New Mexico, 1961.

"Deconsolidation, No!" Navajo Times, Mr 4, 1971. [Gallup-McKinley County Board of Education]

French, David H. "Factionalism in Isletta Pueblo." Doctoral dissertation, Columbia U., 1948.

Haas, Francis. "Education in New Mexico: A Study of the Development of Education in a Changing Social Order." Doctoral dissertation, U. of Chicago, 1954.

Hawley, Florence, and Senter, Donovan. "The Grammar School as the Basic Acculturating Influence for Native New Mexicans." Social Forces 24(0, 1945):398-407.

Hemsing, William M. "The History and Trends of Indian Education in New Mexico Under the Administration of Federal and State Governments." Master's thesis, U. of New Mexico, 1953.

Hist, Albert B. and others. Evaluation of the Albuquerque Indian School Motivational Environment Program, Ag, 1971. ERIC ED 127 050.

Hill, Clarence M. "Integration of Indian Children into the Public Elementary Schools of McKinley County, New Mexico." Master's thesis, Utah State U., Logan, 1957.

Hodge, William H. "The Albuquerque Navajo." Doctoral dissertation, Brandeis U., 1965.

"Inequity That Cannot Be Erased in Our Lifetime-- Joe Natonabah v. Board of Education." Native American Rights Fund Announcements 2(Mr-S, 1973):2-4.

Jewell, Tommie E. "A Study of the 1959 Graduates from the Special Program at the Albuquerque Indian School." Master's thesis, U. of New Mexico, 1959.

Kenneson, Susan R. "Through the Looking-Glass: A History of Anglo-American Attitudes Toward the Spanish-Americans and Indians of New Mexico." Doctoral dissertation, Yale U., 1978. Univ. Microfilms Order No. 7819502.

Kiva, Lloyd New. "Art and Indian Identity." Integrated Education, My-Je, 1969.

_____. "Cultural Difference as the Basis for Creative Education." Native American Arts, 1968. [About the Institute of American Indian Arts, in Santa Fe, NM]

McDonald, Maura. "Contributions of the Dominican Sisters of Grand Rapids, Michigan, to Education in New Mexico." Master's thesis, U. of New Mexico, 1942.

McKinney, Lillie G. "History of the Albuquerque Indian School." Master's thesis, U. of New Mexico, 1934.

New Mexico Advisory Committee to the U.S. Commission on Civil Rights. The Farmington Report: A Conflict of Cultures. Washington, DC: U.S. Commission on Civil Rights, Jl, 1975.

Newton, Ray. Native Americans and the Mass Media, Ap, 1976. ERIC ED 127 087.

Palm, Rufus A. "New Mexico Schools, 1581-1846." Master's thesis, U. of New Mexico, 1930.

Parker, Alan. "The Ramah Experience: Community Control in Indian Education." American Indian Culture Center Journal 1(Winter, 1971): 7-9.

Povi, Tsan, and Povi, P'O-Seh-Kah-. "Indian Students Refused Right to Use Own Language, Culture." Muhammad Speaks, D 25, 1970. [John F. Kennedy Junior High School, San Juan Pueblo]

A Report. "The Response to an Even Chance": The Gallup-McKinley County School District as Seen by the New Mexico State Department of Education. Santa Fe, NM: New Mexico State Dept. of Education, F, 1971, 51 pp. ERIC ED 050 868.

Ross, W. T., and Ross, G. V. "Backgrounds of Vocational Choice: An Apache Study, Mescalero Reservation." Personnel and Guidance Journal 35(Ja, 1957):270-275.

Sanchez, Gov. Abel et al. "The History of San Felipe Pueblo People." Integrated Education, N-D, 1968.

Schroeder, Florence M. "An Exploratory Study of Beliefs and Practices of Jemez Pueblo Indians of New Mexico Pertaining to Child Rearing in the Pre-School Years in Relation to the Educational Status of the Mother." Doctoral dissertation, New York U., 1960.

Segel, D., and Ruble, R. The Lincoln Project. A Study of the Educational Program of a Junior High School in a Transitional Neighborhood. Albuquerque, NM: Albuquerque Public Schools, 1962.

Smith, Anne M. Indian Education in New Mexico. Albuquerque, NM: U. of New Mexico, Jl, 1968, 62 pp. ERIC ED 025 3 5. Available from Division of Research, Dept. of Political Science, U. of New Mexico, Albuquerque, NM 87106.

Scott, Willard A. New Mexico State Indian Student Dropout Study. First Year Report: 1966-67. Santa Fe, NM: New Mexico State Dept. of Education, 1967, 9 pp. ERIC ED 060 968.

Townsend, I. D. "The Reading Achievement of Eleventh and Twelfth Grade Indian Students and a Survey of Curricular Changes Indicated for the Improved Reading in the Public High Schools of New Mexico." Doctoral dissertation, U. of New Mexico, 1962.

Wadia, Maneck S. "Tesuque: A Community Study in Acculturation." Doctoral dissertation, Indiana U., 1957.

Zintz, Miles V. The Adjustment of Indian and Non-Indian Children in the Public Schools of New Mexico. Indian Research Study, Final Report. Albuquerque: U. of New Mexico, 1957-1960.

New York

Albert, Sylvia H. "The Educational Attainment of Indian Pupils in Integrated and Segregated Elementary Schools in New York State." Doctoral dissertation, Lehigh U., 1971.

Brennan, Michael F. "Part of a Guide for Teaching Science in the Cattaraugus Indian School: Weather and Climate." Master's thesis, New York State Teachers College, Buffalo, 1952.

Centrone, Joseph J. "Teacher Sociocultural Awareness in Selected Schools in New York State Accountable for American Indian Education." Doctoral dissertation, Syracuse U., 1972.

Cowen, P. A. "Testing Indian School Pupils in the State of New York." Mental Hygiene 27 (Ja, 1943):80-82.

Fatuzzo, J. "The Non-Assimilation of the American Indian: The Iroquois Case." Master's thesis, Jersey City State College, 1970.

Fenton, William M. "Toward the Gradual Civilization of the Indian Natives: The Missionary and Linguistic Work of Asher Wright (1803-1875) Among the Senecas of Western New York." Proceedings of the American Philosophical Society 100(1956):567-581.

Fisher, Carol Ann. "The Educational Status of the Red Man in New York State." Master's thesis, Syracuse U., 1926.

_____. "A Survey of Vandalism and Its Cultural Antecedents on Four New York State Indian Reservations." Doctoral dissertation, Syracuse U., 1959.

Flad, Harvey. "The City and the Longhouse: A Social Geography of American Indians in Syracuse, New York." Doctoral dissertation, Syracuse U., 1973.

Flanders, Rickie. "This Neighborhood School on Mohawk Reservation Rates High in Atmosphere and Academics." New York Teacher, My 30, 1976. [St. Regis--Mohawk elementary school]

Hirschfelder, Arlene B. "The Treatment of Iroquois Indians in Selected American History Textbooks." Indian History 8(Fall, 1975):31-38.

Indian Education in New York State, 1969, 20 pp. Albany, NY: State U. of New York, State Educational Department. ERIC ED 036 351.

Kemp, William W. "The Support of Schools in Colonial New York by the Society for the Propagation of the Gospel in Foreign Parts." Doctoral dissertation, Columbia U., 1914.

Lange, Edwin F. "Primary and Secondary Education in New Netherland and Colonial New York: 1621-1783." Master's thesis, College of the City of New York, 1933.

Letchworth, William P. "The Thomas Asylum for Orphan and Destitute Indian Children." In New York State Board of Charities, Fifteenth Annual Report, Albany, NY, 1882. [Cattaraugus Indian Reservation]

Loercher, Diana. "Mohawk Organizer Straddles Cultures." Christian Science Monitor, N 10, 1975.

The Orrondaga Council of Chiefs. "...About An Anthropologist." Akwesasne Notes, Mr, 1971. [Critique of Professor William N. Fenton, anthropologist]

Regents of the University of the State of New York. Native American Education. Albany, NY: State Education Department, Jl, 1975.

Russell, Charles. "Centralizing New York Indian Schools." The American Indian 7(Spring, 1955):45-53.

Stander, Golda C. "The History of the Founding of Jesuit Educational Institutions in the Colony of New York." Master's thesis, College of the City of New York, 1933.

Watson, Clifford G. "A Guide for Teaching Science in the Cattaraugus Indian School." Master's thesis, New York State Teachers College, Buffalo, 1952.

White, Dale. "We Can Never Go Back Into the Woods Again." Conservationist 30(Ja-F, 1976): 29-32. [American Indians in New York State]

Williams, Ted C. The Reservation. Syracuse, NY: Syracuse U. Press, 1976. [Autobiography of Tuscarora Indian]

North Carolina

Barnes, Bahnson N. "A History of the Robeson County School System." Master's thesis, U. of North Carolina, 1931.

Beckwith, Evalina G. "A Study of the Physical Equipment and Teaching Personnel of the Indian Schools of Robeson County." Master's thesis, U. of North Carolina, 1950.

Bonner, Myrtle S. "Education and Other Influences in the Cultural Assimilation of the Cherokee Indians on the Qualla Reservation in North Carolina." Master's thesis, Alabama Polytechnic Institute, 1950.

Maynor, Waltz. "Racism and Indian Policies in North Carolina." In "The Urban Minority Experience," Selected Proceedings of the 4th Annual Conference on Minority Studies, pp. 137-143. Edited by George E. Carter and James R. Parker. La Crosse, WI: Institute for Minority Studies, U. of Wisconsin, La Crosse, 1978.

Morgan, Ernest W. "A Racial Comparison of Education in Robeson County, North Carolina." Master's thesis, U. of North Carolina, 1940.

Peck, John Gregory. Community Background Reports: Robeson County, North Carolina, Lumbee Indians, National Study of American Indian Education, Series I, No. 1, Ag, 1969. ERIC ED 039 077.

Thompson, Vernon Ray. "A History of the Education of the Lumbee Indians of Robeson County, North Carolina, 1885-1970." Doctoral dissertation, U. of North Carolina, 1973.

_____. "A Study of the Indian Schools of Robeson County, North Carolina." Master's thesis, Ohio State U., 1951.

U.S. Commission on Civil Rights, North Carolina Advisory Committee. Economic and Political Problems of Indians in Robeson County. Washington, DC: The Commission, 1974.

Wetmore, Ruth Y. First on the Land: The North Carolina Indians. Winston-Salem, NC: John F. Blair, 1975.

North Dakota

Adkins, Roy L. "A Study of the Social Composition and Educational Background of the Indian Service Teachers in the Aberdeen Area, 1954-1955." Master's thesis, U. of North Dakota, 1955.

Beitzel, Christian H. "The Historical Development of the Educational Program on the Fort Berthold Indian Reservation." Master's thesis, U. of North Dakota, 1941.

Branchard, Ralph J. "A Comparative Study of the Intermediate Grades of Two Indian Schools and Two Public Schools in Rolette County." Master's thesis, U. of North Dakota, 1953.

Bureau of Indian Affairs. Evaluation of White Shield School, Roseglen, North Dakota, Ag, 1974. ERIC ED 099 157.

Davis, Polly W. "The Comparison of Morphological Abilities Among Segregated and Integrated Elementary School Age Indian Children in North Dakota." Master's thesis, U. of North Dakota, 1972.

Fischer, David C. "The Effect of Relocation on Indian Education in the Three Affiliated Tribes, Gros Ventre, Arikara, and Mandan; at the Fort Berthold Reservation." Master's thesis, U. of North Dakota, 1954.

Goodey, B. "The Role of the Indian in North Dakota's Geography: Some Propositions." Antipode 2(1970):11-24.

Hanna, Paul S. "An Analysis of the Assimilation of White Culture by Hidatsa Indians of North Dakota." Master's thesis, U. of North Dakota, 1953.

Harris, James J. The North Dakota Indian Reservation Economy. Grand Forks, ND: Bureau of Business and Economic Research, U. of North Dakota, 1975.

Hoff, George A. "Indian School Education in North Dakota." Master's thesis, U. of North Dakota, 1943.

La Blanc, Rosella. "The Development of Turtle Mountain Indian Reservation." American Benedictine Review 21(1970):407-420.

Lee, Knute H. "A Comparison of the Tenth, Eleventh, and Twelfth Grades of Six Schools in Sioux County, North Dakota, and Carson County, South Dakota." Master's thesis, U. of North Dakota, 1953.

McCluskey, Murton Leon. "An Analysis of Selected Attitudes Toward School and Knowledge of Indian Culture Held By Indian Students Enrolled in the Grand Forks, North Dakota, Public Schools." Doctoral dissertation, U. of North Dakota, 1975. Univ. Microfilms Order No. 76-18, 160.

Murray, Robert J. "History of Education in the Turtle Mountain Indian Reservation, North Dakota." Master's thesis, U. of North Dakota, 1953.

Olson, Cal. "The Indian in North Dakota." Fargo Forum and Moorhead News, Ja 16-20, 1966. [Five articles]

Strickler, Eve. "Letter from North Dakota: Inviting the People to See." Urban Review 7 (O, 1974):262-273. [Fort Yates]

Stockman, Wallace H. "Historical Perspectives of Federal Educational Promises and Performance Among the Fort Berthold Indians." Doctoral dissertation, U. of Colorado, 1972.

Telford, C. W. "Test Performance of Full and Mixed-Blood North Dakota Indians." Journal of Comparative Psychology 14(Ag, 1932):123-145.

Tomasek, Henry, and Pedeleski, Theodore. Survey of Education Related Attitudes of Tribal and Non-Tribal Workers at Langer Plant at Rolla, North Dakota. Grand Forks, ND: U. of North Dakota, 1974.

U.S. Commission on Civil Rights, Montana, North Dakota, and South Dakota Advisory Committees. Indian Civil Rights Issues in Montana, North Dakota, and South Dakota. Washington, DC: The Commission, 1974.

Oklahoma

Allen, James R. "The Indian Adolescent: Psychosocial Tasks of the Plains Indians of Western Oklahoma." American Journal of Orthopsychiatry 43(Ap, 1973):368-375.

Alley, Robert D., and Davison, Ronald G. "Educating the American Indian: A School Joins the Twentieth Century." Clearing House 46 (F, 1972):347-351. [Chilocco Indian School]

"America's Exiles: Indian Colonization in Oklahoma." Chronicles of Oklahoma 54(Spring, 1976):entire issue.

"B.I.A. Beaten Badly in 'Battle of the Braids.'" Akwesasne Notes 4(Late Autumn, 1972):8-9. [Pawnee school]

"Chilocco School Report." NCAI Sentinel [National Congress of American Indians], Winter-Spring, 1969. [Chilocco]

Corwin, Hugh D. "The Folson Training School." Chronicles of Oklahoma 42(Spring, 1964):46-52.

Garrett, James E. "A Comparison of the Intelligence of Whites and Indians in the Common Schools of Oklahoma." Master's thesis, U. of Denver, 1927.

Garrison, Joe. Indian Education in Adair County, Oklahoma. Norman, OK: Consultative Center for Equal Educational Opportunity, U. of Oklahoma, 1970.

Gordon, Laura A. "The Mission Schools of the Five Civilized Tribes in Oklahoma." Master's thesis, Oklahoma A. & M. College, 1939.

Hall, Paul R. and Others. Literacy and Education Among Adult Indians in Oklahoma, 3 volumes, My, 1977. ERIC ED 138 381-383.

Hall, Ralph J. "Bloomfield Indian School and Its Work." Master's thesis, Oklahoma A. & M. College, 1931.

Hathcoat, Leonard. "A Pattern of High School Education for the Chilocco Indian School." Master's thesis, U. of Arkansas, 1946.

"History of '4-D' School District, Cherokee Strip." Chronicles of Oklahoma 46(Autumn, 1968):331-340.

Holland, R. Fount. "School in Cherokee and English." Elementary School Journal 72(My, 1972):412-418.

Hollingshead, Maybelle. Final Report on the Open Classroom Summer Institute, Concho School, Concho, Oklahoma to Bureau of Indian Affairs Anadarke Regional Office, Ag 12, 1971, 65 pp. ERIC ED 056 816.

Howard, James H. "Pan-Indian Culture of Oklahoma." Scientific Monthly 81(N, 1955):215-220.

Hunter, Bill, and Tucker, Tom. Indians in Oklahoma. Social and Economic Statistical Data. Oklahoma State Employment Security Commission, S, 1966, 41 pp. ERIC ED 020 052.

"JOM Rip-Off in Oklahoma." Education Journal of the Institute for the Development of Indian Law 2(Ag, 1973):2-40.

Lawson, Mary E. "Occupation of Indian Girls after Graduation at Sequoyah Orphan Training School, Talequah, Oklahoma." Master's thesis, Colorado Agricultural and Mechanical College, 1946.

McBurney, Charles R. "A Study in Religious Education among the Comanche, Apache, and Kiowa Indians of Southwestern Oklahoma." Master's thesis, U. of Kansas, 1948.

McMillan, Robert T. "School Acceleration and Retardation Among Village Children in Southern Oklahoma." Journal of Educational Research 40(S, 1946):126-132.

Margolis, Richard J. "For Whom the Drum Beats." New Leader, Ag 7, 1972. [Elgin school incident]

"Official Horror Story of Federally-Run Chilocco Indian School." Integrated Education 40(Jl-Ag, 1969).

Oklahoma State Advisory Committee to the U.S. Commission on Civil Rights. Indian Civil Rights Issues in Oklahoma. Washington, DC: U.S. Commission on Civil Rights, Ja, 1974.

Oklahoma State University. Oklahoma Indian Education Needs Assessment, 4 volumes, Mr, 1976. ERIC ED 122 998-123001.

Oxley, James R. "Indian Education in Oklahoma." Master's thesis, Phillips U., 1938.

Patterson, Harold L. The Taholah Community School. Report and Recommendations, Ag, 1967, 30 pp. ERIC ED 036 352.

"Pawnee Traidition--A Final Appeal. Norman New Rider v. Board of Education of Independent School District No. 1, Pawnee County, Oklahoma." Native American Rights Fund Announcements 2(Mr-S, 1973):5.

Penoi, Charles R. "Some Factors of Academic Achievement in High School Pupils Attending Selected Indian Boarding Schools in Oklahoma." Doctoral dissertation, U. of Oklahoma, 1956.

Perkins, Larry M. Community Background Reports: Pawnee, Oklahoma, National Study of American Indian Education, Series I, No. 3, Final Report, Ja, 1970, 18 pp. Chicago: U. of Chicago. ERIC ED 039 976.

_____. Ponca City and White Eagle, Oklahoma: National Study of American Indian Education, Series I, No. 4, Final Report, Ja, 1970, 14 pp. Chicago: U. of Chicago. ERIC ED 039 975.

Petty, Clara B. "Distinguishing Characteristics of Homemaking Programs in Oklahoma Indian Schools." Master's thesis, U. of Oklahoma, 1940.

Queton, Winona W. "Observation of Behavior Changes of Children Living in Cooperative Dormitories at Fort Sill Indian School." Master's thesis, Oklahoma A. & M. College, 1955.

Rainer, Ann. "Indian Education--Marland, Oklahoma." United Scholarship Service News, F, 1969.

Randquist, Bobby Wayne. "An Investigation of the Educational Attainment and Opportunities of American Indian Students in Andarko Public School System." Doctoral dissertation, U. of Oklahoma, 1970.

Roach, William L. "The Federal Endowment of Education for Oklahoma." Doctoral dissertation, Stanford U., 1937.

Smith, George J. "The American Indian in Tulsa. A Study in Assimilation." Master's thesis, U. of Tulsa, 1948.

Snider, John H. "A Study of Indian Education in Pawnee County, Oklahoma." Master's thesis, U. of Oklahoma, 1932.

Stewart, Franklin L. "The Administration and Control of Education Among the Five Civilized Tribes in Oklahoma." Master's thesis, U. of Oklahoma, 1940.

Taylor, Floyd L. "An Investigation of Environmental Conditions Which Characterize Indians in the Oklahoma City School District and a Background for Understanding Contemporary Attitudes and Behaviors." Doctoral dissertation, U. of Oklahoma, 1968.

Taylor, Oma Earp. "A Pragmatic Problem of Moral Education on the Kiowa Indian Reservation." Master's thesis, U. of Oklahoma, 1937.

Thomas, Robert K., and Wahrhaftig, Albert L. "Indians, Hillbillies, and the 'Education Problem.'" In Anthropological Perspectives on Education, pp. 230-251. Edited by Murray L. Wax, Stanley Diamond, and Fred O. Gearing. New York: Basic Books, 1971. [Ozarks, Eastern Oklahoma]

Trimble, Joseph E. An Index of the Social Indicators of the American Indian in Oklahoma, Ja 19, 1972. Oklahoma City: Oklahoma State Office of Community Affairs and Planning. ERIC ED 064 002.

Turner, James E. "The Development of the Educational Program at the Seneca Indian School." Master's thesis, Oklahoma A. & M. College, 1940.

Underwood, J. Ross. "An Investigation of Education Opportunity for the Indians in Northeastern Oklahoma." Doctoral dissertation, U. of Oklahoma, 1969.

U.S. Commission on Civil Rights, Oklahoma State Advisory Committee. Indian Civil Rights Issues in Oklahoma. Washington, DC: U.S. Commission on Civil Rights, Ja, 1974.

Uzzell, Minter. "A Freshman English Program for Bacone College." Master's thesis, U. of Tulsa, 1954.

Wahrhaftig, Albert. "Community and the Caretakers." New University Thought, Winter, 1966-1967. [A general analysis centered on the Cherokees of Eastern Oklahoma]

_____. "Indian Communities of Eastern Oklahoma and the War on Poverty." In U.S. Congress, 90th, 1st and 2nd Sessions, Senate, Committee on Labor and Public Welfare, Special Subcommittee on Indian Education, Indian Education. Hearings... Part 2, pp. 851-865. Washington, DC: GPO, 1969.

Wahrhaftig, Albert, and Thomas, Robert K. "Renaissance and Repression: The Oklahoma Cherokee." Trans-action, F, 1969.

Walker, Robert L. "The Capacities and Achievements of Rural and City Pupils in Choctaw, Oklahoma Public Schools." Master's thesis, U. of Oklahoma, 1940.

Wax, Murray L. and others. Indian Education in Eastern Oklahoma. A Report of Fieldwork Among the Cherokee. Final Report, Ja, 1969, 276 pp. Lawrence, KA: U. of Kansas. ERIC ED 029 741.

Wild, George P. "History of Education of the Plains Indians of Southwestern Oklahoma Since the Civil War." Doctoral dissertation, U. of Oklahoma, 1941.

Wolf, Key. "Federal Aid for the Education of Indian Children in the Public Schools of Oklahoma." Master's thesis, U. of Oklahoma, 1931.

Oregon

Baker, Dean. "Americanization of the Native American." Eugene Register-Guard, F 8, 1976. [Chemawa Indian School, Salem]

Bowlby, James W. "Famous Missionary Educators of the Oregon Country." Master's thesis, U. of Idaho, 1937.

Brightman, Lehman L. "Chemwa Indian School: A Case Study of Educational Failure." Journal of Non-White Concerns 1(Jl, 1973):207-213.

Burcham, Lena M. "A Study of the Student Activities, Discipline, and Social Life of Students at Salem Indian School (Oregon)." Master's thesis, U. of Idaho, 1937.

Gatke, Robert Moulton. "The First Indian School of the Pacific Northwest." Oregon Historical Society Quarterly 23(Mr, 1922):70-83.

Johnson, Robert Severt. "Comparative Study of Educational Attainment of Warm Spring Indians and Non-Indians in the Madres Union High School for the Years 1956-65." Doctoral dissertation, Washington State U., 1967.

Lemmon, Burton C. "The Historical Development of the Chemawa Indian School." Master's thesis, Oregon State U., 1941.

Marchington, Stanley E. "Organization of Klamath Adult Special Education and Training Program for the Klamath Reservation." Master's thesis, Willamette U., 1955.

Olmos, Robert. "Bitter Charges Leveled Against Indian School." Portland Oregonian, N 19, 1972. [Chemawa Indian School, Portland]

Payne, Lois E. "A Brief History of the Education of the Indians of Oregon and Washington." Master's thesis, Stanford U., 1935.

Philips, Susan U. "The Invisible Culture: Communications in Classroom and Community on the Warm Springs Reservation." Doctoral dissertation, U. of Pennsylvania, 1974.

Rainey, Cecil D. "A Study of the Salem Indian High School, Comparing the Cultural Background, the Intelligence, Scores, the Percent of White Blood, and the Classroom Grades." Master's thesis, Willamette U., 1932.

Walker, David E. "A Survey of the Establishment of Educational Institutions in Oregon Preceding Statehood." Master's thesis, U. of Washington, 1942.

Pennsylvania

Brunhouse, R. L. "Apprenticeship for Civilization: The Outing System at the Carlisle Indian School." Educational Outlook 13(My, 1939):30-38.

_____. "History of the Carlisle Indian School: A Phase of Government Indian Policy, 1879-1917." Master's thesis, U. of Pennsylvania, 1935.

Fitz, Beulah. "The History of the Carlisle Indian School." Master's thesis, U. of New Mexico, 1935.

Long, William O. "Indian Education in Pennsylvania." Master's thesis, Pennsylvania State U., 1928.

Meyer, Jessie H. "Development of Technical-Vocational Education at the Carlisle Indian Industrial School." Master's thesis, U. of Florida, 1954.

Schutte, Tenjes H. "History of Educational Legislation in Pennsylvania, 1775-1850." Doctoral dissertation, U. of Chicago, 1924.

South Dakota

Adkins, Roy Lee. "A Study of the Social Composition and Educational Background of the Indian Service Teachers in the Aberdeen Area in 1954-1955." Master's thesis, U. of North Dakota, 1955.

Ala, Viola. "The Problems Related to the Assimilation of the Indian of South Dakota." Master's thesis, U. of South Dakota, 1949.

Artichoker, John H. "A Survey of the Problems Encountered by Students of Indian Descent in South Dakota Colleges." Master's thesis, U. of South Dakota, 1957.

Brown, Richard Ellsworth. The Planning Process on the Pine Ridge and Rosebud Sioux Indian Reservations in South Dakota: A Comparative Analysis, Je, 1967, 133 pp. Available on Inter-Library Loan from the U. of South Dakota, Vermillion, SD. ERIC ED 047 876.

Bryde, John F., S.J. The Sioux Indian Student: A Study of Scholastic Failure and Personality Conflict, 1966. Holy Rosary Mission, Pine Ridge, SD 57770.

Carter, E. Russell. "Rapid City, South Dakota." The American Indian 6(Summer, 1953):29-38.

Cornette, John K. "A Comparative Intergroup Study Between the Indian and Caucasian Students in the City School System of Martin, South Dakota." Doctoral dissertation, Nebraska State Teachers College, Chadron, 1960.

Dale, George A. Education for Better Living: A Study of the Pine Ridge Educational Program. Washington, DC: U.S. Department of the Interior, Bureau of Indian Affairs, 1955.

Davis, Lawrence. "A Speech and Hearing Survey of Indian Children Attending Oglala Community School, Pine Ridge, South Dakota." Master's thesis, U. of North Dakota, 1958.

Deissler, K. "A Study of South Dakota Indian Achievement Problems." Journal of American Indian Education, My, 1962.

Felber, Rodney J. "Factors Influencing the Educational Attainments of Indian Pupils in Sisseton, South Dakota." Master's thesis, U. of Wyoming, 1955.

"The First Month at Wounded Knee." Akwesasne Notes 5(Ap, 1973).

Grace, Cyril W. "A Study of the Problems of Indian-Caucasian Segregation in a South Dakota Community as Related to Integration in the Public Schools." Doctoral dissertation, U. of Virginia, 1959.

Jones, Janet and others (eds.). The Help Book or...(Answers You Seldom Get With an Application Form). Batesland, SD: Shannon County Schools, 1978. [In re: Schools serving children from the Pine Ridge Reservation]

Jurrens, James W. "The Music of the Sioux Indians of the Rosebud Reservation in South Dakota and Its Use in the Elementary School." Doctoral dissertation, Colorado State College, 1965.

Just, Glen Arthur. "American Indian Attitudes Toward Education in Select Areas of South Dakota." Master's thesis, South Dakota State U., 1970.

Kent, Calvin A., and Johnson, Jerry W. Indian Poverty in South Dakota, 1969, 96 pp. Vermillion, SD: U. of South Dakota. Vermillion Business Research Bureau and Vermillion Institute of Indian Studies. ERIC ED 042 529.

Kentfield, Calvin. "A Letter from Rapid City." New York Times Magazine, Ap 14, 1973.

Kizer, William M. "History of the Flandreau Indian School, Flandreau, South Dakota." Master's thesis, U. of South Dakota, 1940.

LeBow, Ella C. "Transition of Indian Education from Federal to State Schools on the Rosebud Indian Reservation, Rosebud, South Dakota, 1942-1955." Master's thesis, U. of South Dakota, 1958.

Lovrich, F. "The Assimilation of the Indian in Rapid City." Master's thesis, State U. of South Dakota, 1951.

Ross, D. D. "A Comparative Intergroup Study of the Academic Achievement and Attendance Patterns Between the Full-Blood and the Mixed-Blood Oglala Sioux Indian Students in the Secondary Department of the Oglala Community School." Master's thesis, Nebraska State Teachers College, 1962.

Sabers, Charlotte. "[Akwesasne Notes] Banned in Todd County [School District]." (letter) Akwesasne Notes (Early summer, 1976):47.

Suttmiller, Francis. "A History of St. Paul's School at Marty, South Dakota." Master's thesis, U. of South Dakota, 1963.

Thomas, Robert K. "Powerless Politics." New University Thought, Winter, 1966-1967. [An analysis of the Sioux Pine Ridge Reservation]

U.S. Commission on Civil Rights, South Dakota Advisory Committee. Equality and Justice for All. Washington, DC: The Commission, 1977.

U.S. Commission on Civil Rights, Montana, North Dakota, and South Dakota Advisory Committees. Indian Civil Rights Issues in Montana, North Dakota, and South Dakota. Washington, DC: The Commission, 1974.

Useem, Ruth M. "The Aftermath of Defeat: a Study of Acculturation Among the Rosebud Sioux in South Dakota." Doctoral dissertation, U. of Wisconsin, 1947.

Wax, Murray et al. Formal Education in an American Indian Community. Society for the Study of Social Problems, P.O. Box 190, Kalamazoo, MI, 1964.

Zens, Mary S. "The Educational Work of the Catholic Church Among the Indians of South Dakota." Master's thesis, U. of South Dakota, 1936.

Texas

Berger, Max. "Education in Early Texas." Master's thesis, College of the City of New York, 1933.

Goodner, James. Indian Americans in Dallas: Migrations, Missions, and Styles of Adaptation, 0, 1969, 48 pp. Minneapolis: Training Center for Community Programs, U. of Minnesota. ERIC ED 036 388.

Institute of Texan Cultures. The Indian Texans, 1970, 71 pp. San Antonio: U. of Texas, Institute of Texan Cultures. ERIC ED 052 861.

Liefgreen, Dan. "Texas Custody Case 'Remarkable.'" Navajo Times, D 21, 1978. [See Mintz, below]

Manry, Corinne. "A History of the Education of the Alabama Indians of Polk County, Texas." Master's thesis, U. of Texas, 1937.

Mintz, Morton. "Courts [in Texas] Claim a Blue-Eyed Indian Child Can Be Harmed by Living on Reservation." Navajo Times, D 21, 1978. [Reprinted from Washington Post]

Patrick, Mary. "Indian Urbanization in Dallas: A Second Trail of Tears?" Oral Hist. R. (1973):48-65.

Tobias, Edna W. "The History of Education in Nueces County." Master's thesis, Sul Ross State College, 1936.

Webb, Murl L. "Religious and Educational Efforts Among Texas Indians in the 1850's." Southwestern Historical Quarterly 69(Jl, 1965):22-37.

Utah

Adams, Larry L. "A Follow-Up Study of Indian Graduates of Union High School, Roosevelt, Utah." Master's thesis, Brigham Young U., 1965.

All Indian Study Commission. Intermountain Boarding School, F, 1975. ERIC ED 128 143.

Atkinson, Darrell D. "Educational Adjustment of Ute Indians as Compared to the Mixed-Bloods and Native Whites at Union High School, Roosevelt, Utah." Master's thesis, Utah State Agricultural College, 1955.

Baker, Joe E. "Problems of Navajo Male Graduates of Intermountain School During Their First Year of Employment." Master's thesis, Utah State U., 1959.

Bishop, Clarence R. "An Evaluation of the Scholastic Achievement of Selected Indian Students Attending Elementary Public Schools in Utah." Master's thesis, Brigham Young U., 1960.

Brightman, Lehman I. "Intermountain Indian School. A Case Study of Educational Failure." New School of Education Journal 2,3(1973):56-69. [Brigham City]

Call, Verne P. "A Speech and Hearing Survey of Navajo Indian Children at the Intermountain Indian School, Brigham City, Utah." Master's thesis, U. of Utah, 1952.

"Fights Rock Intermountain." Navajo Times, S 26, 1974. [Intermountain Boarding School, Brigham City]

Gaillard, Frye. "BIA School Target of Severe Criticism." Race Relations Reporter 2(Ag 16, 1971):8-11. [Intermountain Boarding School, Brigham City]

_____. "Indian Youths Sue BIA School." Race Relations Reporter 2(S 7, 1971):6-8. [Intermountain Boarding School, Brigham City]

"A Grievance of Some Students and Employees of Intermountain School." Akwesasne Notes, Mr, 1971. [BIA boarding school, Brigham City]

Hannan, Susan. "White Racist Christians Torment Indian Children." The Warpath, n.d. [Reprinted in Abwesasne Notes, O, 1970]

Hebdon, Truman R. A. "Study of the High School Instructional Staffs in the Bureau of Indian Affairs Boarding Schools in Utah and Arizona." Master's thesis, Brigham Young U., 1965.

Hills, Bruce. "Utes Stressing Education." Deseret News, Jl 20, 1977.

"The Intermountain Student Suit." Indian Historian 5(Summer. 1972):38-40. [Intermountain Bureau of Indian Affairs School, Brigham City]

Knack, Martha C. "Beyond a Differential: An Inquiry into Southern Paiute Indian Experience with Public Schools." Anthropology and Education Quarterly 9(Fall, 1978):216-234.

Munz, C. S. "How the Curricula of the Special Navajo Programs Meet the Needs of the Students at the Inter-Mountain School in Regard to Their Use of Alcoholic Beverages." Master's thesis, Utah State U., 1959.

"NIYC Attacks Racism at Intermountain [School, Brigham City, Utah]." Americans Before Columbus, Ap-Jl, 1970. [Reprinted in Akwesasne Notes, O, 1970]

Nickeson, Steve. "Intermountain Controversy Unsettled." Race Relations Reporter 5(Je 3, 1974):4-6. [Intermountain Indian School, Brigham City]

Osborne, Harold W. "Evaluation of Counseling with a Group of Southern Utah Paiute Indians." Doctoral dissertation, U. of Utah, 1959.

Purley, Anthony F. "Comparison of the Results of Scholastic Aptitude Tests and College GPA of Two Indian Populations at Brigham Young University." Master's thesis, Brigham Young U., 1962.

Schimmelpfennig, D. J. "A Study of Cross-Cultural Problems in the Latter Day Saints Indian Students Placement Program in Davis County, Utah." Doctoral dissertation, U. of Utah, 1971.

Smith, Lynn C. "An Investigation of the Social Adjustment of L.D.S. Graduates from Intermountain Indian School." Master's thesis, Brigham Young U., 1962.

"Suit Filed Against San Juan School District." Navajo Times, N 27, 1974.

Winn, John C. "A Comparative Study of the Mexican-Indian Students in the Carbon County Schools." Master's thesis, Utah Agricultural College, 1955.

Virginia

Robinson, Walter S., Jr. "Indian Education and Missions in Colonial Virginia." Journal of Southern History 18(1952):152-168.

Rountree, Helen C. "Change Came Slowly: The Case of the Powhatan Indians of Virginia." Journal of Ethnic Studies 3(Fall, 1975):1-19.

Washington

Anderson, Willene. "Indian's Role in Education Viewed." Tacoma News Tribune, Mr 13-14, 1977. [Two articles]

Bahr, Howard M., Chadwick, Bruce A., and Stauss, Joseph H. "Discrimination Against Urban Indians in Seattle." Indian Historian 5(Winter, 1972):4-11.

Connelly, John, and Barnhardt, Ray. Community Background Reports: Neah Bay; the Makah. National Study of American Indian Education, Series I, Number 13. Final Report, Ja, 1970, 13 pp. Chicago: U. of Chicago. ERIC ED 041 688.

_____ and _____. Community Background Reports: Taholah, Quinault Reservation, Washington. National Study of American Indian Education, Series I, Number 14, Final Report, Ja, 1970, 18 pp. Chicago: U. of Chicago. ERIC ED 041 689.

Crook, Clifton A. "A Study of Indian Education in Washington." Master's thesis, U. of Washington, 1941.

Fitch, James B. "Economic Development in a Minority Enclave: The Case of the Yakima Indian Nation, Washington." Doctoral dissertation, Stanford U., 1974.

Hayes, Susanna Adella. "The Resistance to Education for Assimilation by the Conville Indians, 1872 to 1972." Doctoral dissertation, U. of Michigan, 1973.

James, Sally E., and Brooks, Joseph T. Report on Indian Education: State of Washington, F, 1974. ERIC ED 158 935.

Muehe, Robert P. "Improving School Attendance on on the Yakima Reservation." Indian Education 29(F, 1966):7-9.

Pester, James L. "The History of Indian Education in the State of Washington." Master's thesis, U. of Washington, 1951.

Roy, Prodipto, and Walker, Della M. Assimilation of the Spokane Indians. Pullman, WA: Agricultural Experiment Station, Washington State U., 1961.

U.S. Commission on Civil Rights, Washington Advisory Committee. Report on Indian Education, State of Washington. Washington, DC: The Commission, 1974.

White, Lynn C. "Assimilation of the Spokane Indians: On Reservation versus Off Reservation Residence." Diss. Absts. 1969, 29(9-A):3243-3244.

Wisconsin

Anderson, Donald H. "Communication Linkages Between Indian Communities and School Districts in Wisconsin." Doctoral dissertation, U. of Minnesota, 1972.

Caudill, William A. "Psychological Characteristics of Acculturated Wisconsin Ojibwa Children." Master's thesis, U. of Chicago, 1949.

Davids, Dorothy W. "An Analysis of the State Department of Public Instruction Reports to the Federal Government Relative to Wisconsin Indian High School Dropouts." Master's thesis, U. of Wisconsin, 1963.

Dowling, John Hall. "The Impact of Poverty on a Wisconsin Oneida Indian Community." Doctoral dissertation, U. of Michigan, 1973.

Harkins, Arthur M., and Woods, Richard G. Attitudes and Characteristics of Selected Wisconsin Indians. Minneapolis: Training Center for Community Programs, U. of Minnesota, Jl, 1969.

Morley, Clyde A. "A General Survey of the Schooling Provided for the American Indian Throughout Our Country's History with a Special Study of Conditions in Wisconsin." Master's thesis, U. of Wisconsin, 1927.

Parker, James R., and Zanger, Martin. "Indian Children in White Wisconsin Schools: The Racial Abyss." Journal of American Indian Education 13(My, 1974):9-15.

Wyoming

Forslund, Morris A. and others. Drug Use, Delinquency and Alcohol Use Among Indians and Anglo Youth in Wyoming. Laramie: Department of Sociology, U. of Wyoming, 1974.

Forslund, Morris A. Indian and Non-Indian Delinquency: A Self Report Study of Wind River Reservation Area Youth. Laramie: Department of Sociology, U. of Wisconsin, 1974.

Garcia, Tanislado. "A Study on the Effects of Education upon the Arapaho Indians of the Wind River Reservation." Master's thesis, U. of Wyoming, 1965.

Rist, Severt R. "Shoshone Indian Education: A Description Study Based on Certain Influential Factors Affecting Academic Achievement of Shoshone Indian Students, Wind River Reservation, Wyoming." Master's thesis, Montana State U., 1961.

Safar, Dwight. "An Exploratory Study of Mental Maturity, Achievement, and Personality Test Results in Relation to the Academic Progress of Indians and Non-Indians in Grades Four through Eight in Six Public School Districts and One Parochial School in Fremont County, Wyoming." Doctoral dissertation, U. of Wyoming, 1964.

_____. A Study Relative to Indian Education in Wyoming. Cheyenne: Wyoming State Department of Education, 1964.

Short, Anthony J. "Indian Power Saves a School." Momentum 7(D, 1976):37-42. [St. Stephen's Indian School, Wind River Reservation]

_____. A Study Relative to Indian Education in Wyoming. Cheyenne: Wyoming State Department of Education, 1964.

Vrettos, Louis. "The Education of Indians with Special Reference to the Shoshone Indian Reservation in Wyoming." Master's thesis, U. of Wyoming, 1949.

Welch, W. Bruce. "The American Indian (A Stifled Minority)." Journal of Negro Education, Summer, 1969.

American Indian Comparative Studies

Armstrong, Robert G. "The Acculturation of the Cheyenne and Arapaho Indians." Master's thesis, U. of Oklahoma, 1942.

Barnhardt, Raymond J. "Quantitative Dimensions in Teaching of American Indian Children: A Descriptive Analysis of School Environment in Three North Pacific Indian Communities." Doctoral dissertation, U. of Oregon, 1970.

Benham, William J., Jr. "Characteristics of Programs in Public Schools Serving Indian Students from Reservations in Five Western States." Doctoral dissertation, U. of Oklahoma, 1965.

Berg, Clay N. "A Comparative Study of the Teaching Methods of the Navajo, Cheyenne, and Manus Indians." Master's thesis, U. of Denver, 1948.

Cardinal, Ezra V. "Catholic Education Among the Menominee and Ottawa Indians (1924-1950)." Master's thesis, Catholic U. of America, 1924.

Chilcott, John H., and Garcia, Jerry P. Laguna Indian Reservation and Acoma Indian Reservation, Laguna-Acoma Junior and Senior High School: Community Background Reports. The National Study of American Indian Education, Series I, No. 16, Final Report, 1970, 11 pp. Chicago: U. of Chicago. ERIC ED 047 874.

Dracon, John Irwin. The Extent of Bilingualism Among The Crow and the Northern Cheyenne Indian School Populations, Grades One through Twelve. A Study, Mr, 1970, 32 pp. ERIC ED 044 205.

_____. "Extent of Spoken Crow and Cheyenne Among Indian Students of the Crow and Northern Cheyenne Indian Reservations." Master's thesis, Montana State U., 1970.

Drain, Myrtle. "A History of the Education of the Choctaw and Chickasaw Indians." Master's thesis, U. of Oklahoma, 1928.

Edmo, Jack. "The Bannock-Shoshone Program in Study of Man." Indian Historian 3(Fall, 1970): 23-25. [Shoshone high school students]

Farrell, Willie E. "Educational Problems as Confronted by the Quaker Agents on the Kiowa and Comanche Reservation." Master's thesis, Oklahoma A. & M. College, 1935.

Freeman, Daniel M. A. "Adolescent Crises of the Kiowa-Apache Indian Male." In Minority Group Adolescents in the United States. Edited by Eugene B. Brody. Baltimore: Williams and Wilkins, 1968.

Hagan, Maxine W. "An Educational History of the Pima and Papago Peoples from the Mid-Seventeenth Century to the Mid-Twentieth Century." Doctoral dissertation, U. of Arizona, 1959.

Heerman, Charles E. "The Poncas and Community Control." Integrateducation 13(Jl-Ag, 1975): 32-35.

Hulsizer, Allan L. "Region and Culture in the Curriculum of the Navaho and the Dakota: A Technique and Its Development into an Educational Program." Doctoral dissertation, Columbia U., 1940.

Jenny, Albert, 2nd et al. A Comprehensive Evaluation of OEO Community Action Programs on Six Selected American Indian Reservations. Washington, DC: Office of Economic Opportunity, 1966.

Kleinfeld, Judith S. "Characteristics of Successful Boarding Home Parents of Eskimos and Athabascan Indian Students." Human Organization 32(Summer, 1973):191-199.

_____. "Classroom Climate and the Verbal Participation of Indian and Eskimo Students in Integrated Classrooms." Journal of Educational Research 67(O, 1973):51-52.

_____. "Effects of Nonverbally Communicated Personal Warmth on the Intelligence Test Performance of Indian and Eskimo Adolescents." Journal of Social Psychology 91(O, 1973):149-150.

_____. Instructional Style and the Intellectual Performance of Indian and Eskimo Students. Final Report, Ja, 1972, 65 pp. U. of Alaska, College Institute of Social, Economic and Government Research. ERIC ED 059 831.

Little, Craig B. Social Distance and Race Attitudes: A Study of the White Population of Princeton, Maine and the Indian Population of Indian Township, Maine, F, 1970, 183 pp. Durham, NH: U. of New Hampshire. ERIC ED 054 994.

Montana-North Dakota-South Dakota Joint Advisory Committee to the U.S. Commission on Civil Rights. Indian Civil Rights Issues in Montana, North Dakota, and South Dakota. Washington, DC: U.S. Commission on Civil Rights, Ag, 1974.

Moore, Ila C. "Schools and Education among the Kiowa and Comanche Indians, 1870-1940." Master's thesis, U. of Oklahoma, 1940.

Padfield, Harlan, Hemingway, Peter, and Greenfield, Philip. "The Pima-Papago Education
Population: A Census and Analysis." Journal
of American Indian Education 6(O, 1966):1-24.

Reese, Jim E., and Fish, Mary. "Economic Genocide: A Study of the Comanche, Kiowa, Cheyenne, and Arapaho." Negro Educational Review 24(Ja-Ap, 1973):86-103.

Rogers, Mary L. "Curriculum Planning for
Cheyenne and Arapaho Indians." Master's
thesis, U. of Oklahoma, 1943.

Sanders, Gledca. "The Educational Development
of the Cheyenne and Arapaho Indians upon the
Reservation." Master's thesis, Oklahoma A.
& M. College, 1933.

Spaunaus, Nancy. Contrasting Chippewa, Sioux,
and Anglo Values: A Native American Curriculum Unit for the Sixth Grade. NATAM XVII,
My, 1971, 23 pp. Minneapolis: U. of Minnesota. ERIC ED 051 920.

Tefft, Stanton K. "Task Experience and Inter-
tribal Value Differences on the Wind River
Reservation." Social Forces 49(Je, 1971):
606-614. [Shoshone and Northern Arapaho]

Government Relations

Adams, David Wallace. "The Federal Indian
Boarding School: A Study of Environment and
Response, 1879-1918." Doctoral dissertation,
Indiana U., 1975.

Adams, Evelyn C. American Indian Education:
Government Schools and Economic Progress.
New York: King's Crown Press, 1946.

All Indian Pueblo Council, Inc. The Right to
Remain Indian. The Failure of the Federal
Government to Protect Indian Land and Water
Rights. Washington, DC: U.S. Commission on
Civil Rights, N 8, 1972.

American Indian Policy Review Commission. Final
Report, Volume I. Washington, DC: GPO, 1977.

Bearking, Leonard. "Indian Education under Federal Domination." Indian Historian, Spring,
1969.

Beatty, W. W. "The Federal Government and the
Education of Indians and Eskimos." Journal
of Negro Education 7(Jl, 1938).

Bennett, Robert L. "Speech...at Dartmouth College." Navajo Times, Je 26, 1969. [My 17,
1969]

Blakely, Daniel G. "Changing Administrative
Emphasis in Indian Education." Master's thesis, New Mexico Western College, 1953.

Blauch, Lloyd E. Educational Service for Indians. Washington, DC: GPO, 1939.

Bureau of Indian Affairs. American Indians and
their Federal Relationship. Washington, DC:
GPO, Mr, 1972.

_____. Assistance to Indians Enrolled in Pub-
lic Schools. Johnson-O'Malley Regulations,
Jl, 1974. ERIC ED 094 899.

_____. "BIA Official Unloads on School Crit-
ics." Navajo Times, N 7, 1968. [L. Madison
Coombs replies to Peter Farb]

_____. Control of Indian Education in BIA
Schools, Ag, 1974. ERIC ED 094 905.

_____. Directory of Public Schools Served by
the Public Schools Assistance Programs...for
Fiscal Year 1976, 1976. ERIC ED 148 527.

Burnett, Donald L., Jr. "An Historical Analysis
of the 1968 'Indian Civil Rights' Act."
Haward Journal on Legislation 9(My, 1972):
557-626.

Cashman, Ben. "The American Indian--Standing a
Peculiar Legal Relation." Doctoral dissertation, U. of Washington, 1969.

Chadwick, Jerome A., and Barter, James T. "Letter on Indian Schools." New Republic, Mr 22,
1969.

Cohen, Felix S. Handbook of Federal Indian Law.
Albuquerque: U. of New Mexico Press, 1971
(orig., 1942).

_____. "Indian Rights and the Federal Courts."
Minnesota Law Review 24(Ja, 1940):145-200.

Comptroller General of the United States. Administration of Program for Aid to Public
School Education of Indian Children Being Improved. Washington, DC: General Accounting
Office, My 28, 1970.

_____. Bureau of Indian Affairs Not Operating
Boarding Schools Efficiently. Washington,
DC: General Accounting Office, 1978.

_____. The Indian Self-Determination Act: Many
Obstacles Remain. Washington, DC: General
Accounting Administration, 1978.

_____. Opportunity to Improve Indian Education
in Schools Operated by the Bureau of Indian
Affairs. Washington, DC: U.S. General Accounting Office, Ap 27, 1972.

_____. Progress and Problems in Providing
Health Services to Indians. Washington, DC:
General Accounting Office, Mr 11, 1974.

_____. Questionable Need for All Schools Plan-
ned by the Bureau of Indian Affairs. Washington, DC: General Accounting Office, 1978.

Costo, Rupert. "Native Americans Need Self-Government Now." The Indian Historian, Summer,
1969. [In re: The Josephy Report]

Costo, Rupert, and Henry, Jeannette. Indian Treaties: Two Centuries of Dishonor. San Francisco: Indian Historian Press, 1977.

Coulter, Robert T. "The Denial of Legal Remedies to Indian Natives Under U.S. Law." American Indian Journal 3(S, 1977):5-11.

Dan, Arthur. "Student Looks at Tribal Government." Navajo Times, My 22, 1969. [Letter]

Deloria, Vine, Jr. "The War Between the Redskins and the Feds." New York Times Magazine, D 7, 1969.

Education of the Indians. Washington, DC: GPO, 1927. (U.S. Department of the Interior. Bureau of Indian Affairs, Bulletin 1927, No. 9)

Embree, John F. "The Indian Bureau and Self-Government." Human Organization 8(Spring, 1949):11-14.

Ericson, R., and Snow, D. R. "The Indian Battle for Self-Determination." California Law Review 58(Mr, 1970).

Federal-State Indian Affairs Conference, Ag 21, 1969. Washington, DC: National Council on Indian Opportunity. ERIC ED 042 524.

Ferguson, Lorene. [Letter to editor on new regulations for Johnson-O'Malley Act] Navajo Times, Mr 28, 1974.

Fielding, B. "Federal Funds to Meet Local Needs." Journal of the National Education Association 55(S, 1966):23-26.

Gaillard, Frye. "Indians Demand Bureau Reform." Race Relations Reporter 2(O 4, 1971):7-12.

General Accounting Office. Indian Education in the Public School System Needs More Direction from the Congress, Mr 14, 1977. ERIC ED 147 072.

Getches, David H. and others. Cases and Materials on Federal Indian Law. St. Paul, MN: West, 1979.

Hall, Robert. Special Education Efforts for American Indian and Alaskan Native Children by the Bureau of Indian Affairs, Je, 1976. ERIC ED 129 479.

Hansma, Earl A. "American Indian Education: Law and Policy." Doctoral dissertation, U. of Miami, 1972.

Harris, Fred R. "American Indians--New Destiny." Congressional Record, Ap 21, 1966, Vol. 112, No. 67.

Haupt, Carl. "He's Rocking Boat" (letter). Navajo Times, My 15, 1969. [Criticism of BIA schools]

Henninger, Daniel, and Esposito, Nancy. "Indian Schools." New Republic, F 15, 1969.

Honahni, Dan. "Indian Community Control of Schools." Indian Historian 3(Spring, 1970): 57-58, 66.

Howard, Homer H. In Step with the States: A Comparison of State and Indian Service Educational Objectives and Methods. Washington, DC: U.S. Indian Service, Educational Division, 1949.

"The Indian Battle for Self Determination." California Law Review 58(Mr, 1970):445-490.

Indian Conference of Montana. Indian American Legal Rights, Duties and Remedies, My, 1972. Tri-State Tribes, Inc., Suite 228, 208 North 29th Street, Billings, MT 59101.

"Indian Education: Federal Compulsory School Attendance Law Applicable to American Indians: The Treaty-Making Period: 1857-1871." American Indian Law Review 5(Winter, 1977): 393-413.

"International Conference on Discrimination Against Indigenous Populations in the Americas--1977." American Indian Journal 3(N, 1977):2-23.

Jackson, Curtis E., and Galli, Marcia J. A History of the Bureau of Indian Affairs and its Activities among Indians. San Francisco: R & E Research Associates, 1977.

Jacob, Harvey D. "Uncle Sam--The Great White Father." Case and Comment 23(F, 1917).

Josephy, Alvin M., Jr. The American Indian and the Bureau of Indian Affairs--1969. Memorandum to Mr. James Keogh, The White House, February 11, 1969. In U.S. Congress, 91st, 1st Session, Committee on Labor and Public Welfare, Subcommittee on Indian Education, Indian Education, 1969. Hearings Part 2--Appendix, pp. 1421-1459. Washington, DC: GPO, 1969. [Text of the Josephy Report]

Kelley, Walter K. "Educational Policy of the Federal Government with Reference to the Perpetuation of Indigenous Culture." Master's thesis, U. of Colorado, 1938.

Kickingbird, Kirke. "A Fair Share." Education Journal of the Institute for the Development of Indian Law 1(Ag, 1972):4-13. [Indian Education Act of 1972]

Legal Action Support Project. Federal Funding of Indian Education: A Bureaucratic Enigma, 1973. Bureau of Social Science Research, 1990 M Street, N.W., Washington, DC 20036.

Lewis, Rodney. "Indian Education Legislation." Inequality in Education 10(D, 1971):19-21.

_____. "Procedural Due Process and BIA Schools." American Indian Culture Center Journal 1(Winter, 1971):11-13.

Lukaczer, Moses. "National School Lunch Program and Indian School Children." Indian Historian 7(Winter, 1974):17-23.

_____. "Some Thoughts on the National School Lunch Program and on American Indian School Children." Washington, DC: U.S. Commission on Civil Rights, unpublished, undated.

MacDonald, Peter. "MacDonald Tells [U.S.] Commission [on Civil Rights] Indians Get Words--Not Deeds." Navajo Times, N 1, 1973.

McKinley, Francis. Federal Indian Policy as It Affects Local Indian Affairs, My 12, 1964. ERIC ED 010 965.

McKinley, Francis, Bayne, Stephen, and Nimnicht, Glen. Who Should Control Indian Education? Berkeley, CA: Far West Laboratory for Educational Research and Development, F, 1970.

McMullen, George R. "Federal Policy in Indian Education, 1870-1938." Master's thesis, Oklahoma A. & M. College, 1951.

Meriam, Lewis. "Indian Education Moves Ahead." Survey 66(Je 1, 1931):253-257.

Meriam, Lewis and others. The Problem of Indian Administration. Report of a survey made at the request of Hon. Hubert Work, Secretary of the Interior, and submitted to him, February 21, 1928. Baltimore: The Johns Hopkins Press, 1928.

Mitchell, Michael Dan. "Acculturation Problems Among the Plains Tribes of the Governmental Agencies in Western Indian Territory." Chronicles of Oklahoma 44(1966):281-289.

Mizen, Mamie L. Federal Facilities for Indians: Tribal Relations with the Federal Government. Washington, DC: GPO, 1966.

Nader, Ralph. "'Lo, the Poor Indian.'" New Republic, Mr 30, 1968.

Nash, Philleo. "The Education Mission of the Bureau of Indian Affairs." Journal of American Indian Education 3(Ja, 1964):104.

_____. "Education--The Chance to Choose." Indian Education 428(F 1, 1966).

NAACP Legal Defense and Educational Fund, Inc., with the Center for Law and Education, Harvard University. An Even Chance. A Report on Federal Funds for Indian Children in Public School Districts. New York: NAACP Legal Defense and Educational Fund, Inc., 1971.

Nickerson, Steve. "Paternalism and Its Mates." Race Relations Reporter 6(Ja-F, 1974):22-28. [B.I.A.]

Nimnight, Glen, and McKinley, Francis. "Indian Education Recommendation." Navajo Times, D 12 and 19, 1968. [Recommendations to the U.S. Senate Subcommittee on Indian Education, made by the Indian Studies Project of the Far West Laboratory for Educational Research and Development, Berkeley, CA]

Orfield, Gary. A Study of the Terminating Policy. National Congress of American Indians, 1450 Pennsylvania Street, Denver, CO, 1968.

Ortiz, Alfonso. "Native Education Under Fire." The Indian Historian, Summer, 1969. [The Kennedy Subcommittee on Indian education]

Price, Monroe. Law and the American Indian--Readings, Notes, and Cases. Indianapolis: Bobbs-Merrill, 1973.

Project Outreach: An Assessment of Tribal Attitudes and Appraisal of the Extent of Tribal Council Experience in Administering Federal Assistance Programs, 1970. ERIC ED 042 522.

"Pros and Cons of the Kennedy Bill." American Indian Culture Center Journal 2(Spring, 1971): 15-16. [S. 659, on Indian education]

Rosen, Lawrence (ed.). American Indians and the Law. New Brunswick, NJ: Transaction Books, 1977.

Rosenfelt, Daniel M. "New Regulations for Federal Indian Funds." Inequality in Education 10(D, 1971):22-26.

_____. "Toward a More Coherent Policy for Funding Indian Education." Law and Contemporary Problems 15(Winter, 1976):190-223.

Ryan, Joe. "Compared to Other Nations." American Indian Journal 3(Ag, 1977):2-13. [Contends Indian American cause should be considered by the United Nations Decolonization Committee]

Sahmaunt, Herschel. "An Indian Education Leader Speaks Out on the Indian Education Act of 1972." Education Journal of the Institute for the Development of Indian Law 1(Mr, 1973): 4-10.

Schmeckebier, Lawrence F. The Office of Indian Affairs: Its History, Activities, and Organization. Baltimore: The Johns Hopkins U. Press, 1927.

Seixas, Genevieve L. "Government Policy Toward Indian Education." Master's thesis, Smith College, 1929.

Simons, K. W. "Letter on Indian Schools." New Republic, Mr 22, 1969.

Smith, Michael. "The Constitutional Status of American Indians." Civil Rights Digest 6 (Fall, 1973):10-15.

Smith, Susan, and Walker, Margaret. Federal Funding of Indian Education: A Bureaucratic Enigma, My, 1973. ERIC ED 137 008.

Stanton, Thomas H. Trail of Broken Promises: An Assessment of HUD's Indian Housing Programs, 1977. ERIC ED 152 441.

Stuart, Paul H. "The U.S. Office of Indian Affairs, 1865-1900: The Institutionalization of a Formal Organization." Doctoral dissertation, U. of Wisconsin, 1978. Univ. Microfilms Order No. 7814288.

Taylor, Graham D. "The Tribal Alternative to Bureaucracy: The Indian's New Deal, 1933-1945." Journal of the West 13(Ja, 1974).

Thompson, Laura. Personality and Government: Findings and Recommendations of the Indian Administration Research. Ediciones del Instituto Indigenista Interamericano, Mexico, D.F., 1951.

Tyler, S. Lyman. A History of Indian Policy. Washington, DC: GPO, 1973.

_____. Indian Affairs: A Study of the Changes in Policy of the United States Toward Indians. Institute of American Indian Studies, Brigham Young U., 1964.

U.S. American Indian Policy Review Commission, Task Force One. Report on Trust Responsibilities and the Federal-Indian Relationship, Including Treaty Review. Washington, DC: GPO, 1976.

U.S. American Indian Policy Review Commission, Task Force Ten. Report on Terminated and Non-federally Recognized Indians. Washington, DC: GPO, 1976.

U.S. Bureau of Indian Affairs. Answers to Your Questions About American Indians. Washington, DC: GPO, My, 1968.

_____. Handbook for Decision Makers on Title I of the Indian Self-Determination and Education Assistance Act. Washington, DC: BIA, 1976.

_____. Indian Education: Steps to Progress in the 70's. Washington, DC: GPO, 1973.

U.S. Commission on Civil Rights. American Indian Civil Rights Handbook. Washington, DC: GPO, Mr, 1972.

_____. The Employment of American Indians in New Mexico and Arizona. Washington, DC: U.S. Commission on Civil Rights, N, 1972.

_____. Socio-Economic Profile of American Indians in Arizona and New Mexico. Washington, DC: U.S. Commission on Civil Rights, N, 1972.

_____. The Southwest Indian Report. Washington, DC: GPO, My, 1973.

U.S. Congress, 15th, 1st Session. Report on Establishment of Trading Houses and Encouragement of Education. Annals of Congress, 1817-1818, pt. 1, 800-801.

U.S. Congress, 15th, 2nd Session, House of Representatives, House Document No. 91, Vol. 6, Ja 15, 1819. On the Civilization of the Indian Tribes.

U.S. Congress, 15th, 2nd Session. Petition for the Civilization of the Indian--Society of Friends. Senate State Papers No. 47, D 23, 1818.

U.S. Congress, 17th, 1st Session, Senate, Senate Document No. 50, Vol. 1, F 23, 1822. Message on the Civilization of the Indians--President James Monroe.

U.S. Congress, 18th, 1st Session, House of Representatives, House Document No. 47, Vol. II, Ja 24, 1824. Statement on Disbursement for Civilization of Indians.

U.S. Congress, 18th, 1st Session, House of Representatives, House Report No. 92, Vol. II, Mr 23, 1824. On Civilization of the Indians--Committee on Indian Affairs.

U.S. Congress, 19th, 1st Session, House of Representatives, House Document No. 102, Vol. V, F 3, 1826. Report on Preservation and Civilization of Indian Tribes--Secretary James Barbour.

U.S. Congress, 19th, 1st Session, House of Representatives, House Document No. 124, Vol. VIII, Mr 1, 1826. Report on Preservation and Civilization of the Indians--General Clark, Superintendent of Indian Affairs.

U.S. Congress, 20th, 2nd Session, House of Representatives, House Document No. 11, Vol. I, D 8, 1828. On Civilization of the Indians.

U.S. Congress, 42nd, 2nd Session, Senate, Senate Miscellaneous Document No. 44, Vol. I, Ja 25, 1872. Report on Education of Indians--Secretary C. Delano.

U.S. Congress, 46th, 2nd Session, House of Representatives, House Report No. 752, Vol. III, H.R. 1735, Ap 6, 1880. Industrial School for Indians.

U.S. Congress, 48th, 2nd Session, Senate, Executive Document No. 95, Vol. II, Part 2. Special Report of 1888 on Indian Education and Civilization.

U.S. Congress, 71st, 2nd Session, Senate, Committee on Indian Affairs, Subcommittee, Survey of Conditions of the Indians in the United States. [See part 8 et al.]

U.S. Congress, 90th, 1st and 2nd Sessions, Senate, Committee on Labor and Public Welfare, Special Subcommittee on Indian Education. Indian Education. Hearings. 5 parts. Washington, DC: GPO, 1969.

U.S. Congress, 90th, 2nd Session, House of Representatives, Committee on Interior and Insular Affairs, Subcommittee on Indian Affairs. Rights of Members of Indian Tribes...Hearing. Washington, DC: GPO, 1968.

U.S. Congress, 91st, 1st Session, Joint Economic Committee, Subcommittee on Economy in Government. Toward Economic Development for Native American Communities. A Compendium of Papers, 2 vols. Washington, DC: GPO, 1969.

U.S. Congress, 91st, 1st Session, Senate, Committee on Labor and Public Welfare, Subcommittee on Indian Education. Indian Education, 1969. Hearings...2 parts. Washington, DC: GPO, 1969.

U.S. Congress, 91st, 1st Session, Senate, Committee on Labor and Public Welfare, Special Subcommittee on Indian Education. Indian Education: A National Tragedy--A National Challenge. Washington, DC: GPO, 1969.

U.S. Congress, 91st, 2nd Session, Senate, Committee on Interior and Insular Affairs. Policy Changes in Structure and Policy of the Bureau of Indian Affairs. Hearings... Washington, DC: GPO, 1970.

U.S. Congress, 91st, 2nd Session, Senate, Committee on Interior and Insular Affairs, Report No. 91-874. Providing for the Appropriation of Funds to Assist School Districts Adjoining or in the Proximity of Indian Reservations, to Construct Elementary and Secondary Schools and to Provide Proper Housing and Educational Opportunities for Indian Children Attending These Public Schools, My 15, 1970.

U.S. Congress, 92nd, 1st Session, Senate, Committee on Interior and Insular Affairs. American Indian and Alaska Natives Policy. Hearings... Washington, DC: GPO, 1971.

U.S. Congress, 92nd, 1st Session, Senate, Committee on Interior and Insular Affairs. Indian Education Act of 1971. Hearing... Washington, DC: GPO, 1971.

U.S. Congress, 92nd, 1st Session, Senate, Committee on Labor and Public Welfare, Subcommittee on Education. Education Amendments of 1971. Hearings... Part 4. Washington, DC: GPO, 1971. [On Indian-American education]

U.S. Congress, 92nd, 2nd Session, House of Representatives, Committee on Interior and Insular Affairs, Subcommittee on Indian Affairs. Seizure of Bureau of Indian Affairs Headquarters. Hearings..., Serial No. 92-54. Washington, DC: GPO, 1972.

U.S. Congress, 93rd, 1st Session, Senate Committee on Interior and Insular Affairs, Subcommittee on Indian Affairs. Establishment of the American Indian Policy Review Commission. Hearings... Washington, DC: GPO, 1973.

U.S. Congress, 93rd, 1st Session, Senate, Committee on Interior and Insular Affairs, Subcommittee on Indian Affairs. Indian Self-Determination and Education Program. Hearings... Washington, DC: GPO, 1973.

U.S. Congress, 93rd, 1st and 2nd Sessions, Senate, Committee on the Judiciary, Subcommittee on Administrative Practice and Procedure. Indian Education Accountability. Hearings... Washington, DC: GPO, 1975.

U.S. Congress, 93rd, 2nd Session, House of Representatives, Committee on Appropriations, Subcommittee on Department of the Interior and Related Agencies. "Indian Education." In Department of the Interior and Related Agencies Appropriations for 1975. Hearings... Part 1, pp. 402-465. Washington, DC: GPO, 1974.

U.S Congress, 93rd, 2nd Session, House of Representatives, Committee on Interior and Insular Affairs, Subcommittee on Indian Affairs. Establishment of the American Indian Policy Review Commission. Hearings... Washington, DC: GPO, 1974.

U.S. Congress, 95th, 1st Session, House of Representatives, Committee on Education and Labor, Subcommittee on Elementary, Secondary, and Vocational Education. Indian Education, Oversight: Hearings..., 3 parts. Washington, DC: GPO, 1978.

U.S. Congress, 95th, 1st Session, House of Representatives, Committee on Education and Labor, Subcommittee on Elementary, Secondary, and Vocational Education. Oversight Hearings on Indian Education: Hearings... Washington, DC: GPO, 1977.

U.S. Congress, 95th, 1st Session, Senate, Select Committee on Nutrition and Human Needs. Recommendations for Improved Food Programs on Indian Reservations. Washington, DC: GPO, 1977.

U.S. Department of Commerce. Federal and State Indian Reservations. An EDA Handbook. Washington, DC: GPO, Ja, 1971.

U.S. Department of Health, Education, and Welfare, Public Health Service. Indian Health Trends and Services, 1969 Edition. Washington, DC: GPO, Mr, 1969.

U.S. Department of Justice. "Indian Manual and Training Schools." 17 Opinions of the Attorney General 531(1883).

_____. "Indian Schools." 17 Opinions of the Attorney General 566(1884).

U.S. Department of the Interior, Bureau of Indian Affairs, Division of Education. Fiscal Year 1966. Statistics Concerning Indian Education. Lawrence, KA: Publications Service, Haskell Institute, 1966.

U.S. Department of the Interior, Rulings. Indian School Land--Right of Way. Memo Sol., Jl 1, 1938.

_____. School Land--Indian Occupant. 33 L.D. 454, Mr 7, 1905.

U.S. Department of the Interior. Source Directory, 1 and 2. Indian and Eskimo Organizations Marketing Native American Arts and Crafts. Indian Arts and Crafts Board, Room 4004, U.S. Department of the Interior, Washington, DC 20240.

U.S. General Accounting Office. Administration of Programs for Aid to Public School Education of Indian Children...Report. Washington, DC: GPO, 1970.

U.S. National Advisory Council on Indian Education. First Annual Report to the Congress of the United States..., 2 parts. Washington, DC: GPO, Mr, 1974.

U.S. Task Force on Native American Vocational Education. Public Hearings on Native American Vocational Education. Washington, DC: National Advisory Council on Vocational Education, Task Force on Native American Vocational Education, 1977.

Van Norman, Carrie E. "Educational Problems in the Indian Schools Under Government Control." Master's thesis, U. of Rochester, 1931.

Veeder, William H. "Federal Violation of Basic Rights of American Indian People." In U.S. Commission on Civil Rights, Hearing Held in Albuquerque, New Mexico, pp. 826-892. Washington, DC: GPO, 1974.

Warrior, Clyde. "Poverty, Community, and Power." New University Thought, Summer, 1965. [A full blood Ponca Indian from Oklahoma examines the interrelations of poverty, community, and power as these affect Indians and other people]

Wharton, H. "Cooperative Education in the Government's Indian Schools." School and Society 51(Mr 23, 1940):385-386.

"What Will Be the Upshot?" Navajo Times, Ja 9, 1969. [About criticisms of the educational policies of the Bureau of Indian Affairs]

Winer, L. R. "Federal Legislation on Indian Education 1819-1970." Doctoral dissertation, U. of Maryland, 1972.

Wise, Michael (ed.). "Native American." In Desegregation in Education: A Directory of Reported Federal Decisions, p. 200. Notre Dame, IN: Center for Civil Rights, U. of Notre Dame Law School, Ap, 1977. [1954-1976]

Wopat, Priscilla. "To Civilize the Indian...": A Survey of the Educational Philosophy and Programs of the Bureau of Indian Affairs Since 1928, Je, 1970, 325 pp. ERIC ED 039 998.

Yudof, Mark G. "Federal Funds for Public Schools." Inequality in Education 7(1971).

_____. "Federal Money for Indians in Public Schools: Where Does it Go?" Harvard Graduate School of Education Alumni Association Bulletin 15(Spring, 1971):2-7.

Historical

Ahern, Wilbert H. "Assimilationist Racism: The Case of the 'Friends of the Indian.'" Journal of Ethnic Studies 4(Summer, 1976):23-32.

Allegrezza, Tore S. "Historical Survey of the Changing Character of Indian Schools." Master's thesis, U. of Colorado, 1939.

Allen, Arthur E. "The Education of the New England Indians During the Colonial Period." Master's thesis, Brown U., 1961.

Ammon, Soloman R. "History and Present Development of Indian Schools in the United States." Master's thesis, U. of Southern California, 1935.

Axtell, James. "The White Indians of Colonial America." William and Mary Quarterly 32(Ja, 1975):55-88.

Baerreis, David A. (ed.). The Indian in Modern America. Madison, WI: State Historical Society, 1956.

Balyeat, Frank A. "Education in Indian Territory." Doctoral dissertation, Stanford U., 1927.

Baptist, Mary. "Mission Schools in the Indian Territory." Master's thesis, U. of Oklahoma, 1923.

Barnett, Louise K. The Ignoble Savage: American Literary Racism, 1790-1890. Westport, CT: Greenwood, 1975.

_____. "Nineteenth Century Indian Hater Fiction: A Paradigm for Racism." South Atlantic Quarterly 74(Spring, 1975):224-236.

Barth, Pius J. "Franciscan Education and the Social Order in Spanish North America, 1501-1821." Doctoral dissertation, U. of Chicago, 1945.

Beaver, R. Pierce. "American Missionary Efforts to Influence Government Indian Policy." Journal of Church and State 5(1963):77-94.

Beer, David F. "Anti-Indian Settlement in Early Colonial Literature." Indian Historian, Spring, 1969.

Berkhofer, Robert F., Jr. "Model Zions for the American Indian." American Quarterly 15(1963): 176-190. [Manual labor boarding school]

_____. "The Political Context of a New Indian History." Pacific Historical Review 40(Ag, 1971):357-382.

_____. "Protestant Missionaries to the American Indians, 1787-1862." Doctoral dissertation, Cornell U., 1960.

_____. The White Man's Indian: The History of an Idea from Columbus to the Present. York: Knopf, 1978.

Berkman, Brenda. "The Vanishing Race: Conflicting Images of the American Indian in Children's Literature, 1880 to 1930." North Dakota Quarterly 44(Spring, 1976):31-40.

Bishop, Clarence R. "A History of the Indian Student Placement Program of the Church of Jesus Christ of Latter Day Saints." Master's thesis, U. of Utah, 1967.

Borden, Philip. "Found Cumbering the Soil. Manifest Destiny and the Indian in the Nineteenth Century." In The Great Fear. Race in the Mind of America, pp. 71-97. Edited by Gary B. Nash and Richard Weiss. New York: Holt, Rinehart, and Winston, 1970.

Bureau of Indian Affairs. Famous Indians: A Collection of Short Biographies. Washington, DC: GPO, 1975.

Christensen, Rosemary Ackley, with Demmert, William G. "The Education of Indians and the Mandate of History." In The Schooling of Native America, pp. 139-152. Edited by Thomas Thompson. Washington, DC: American Association of Colleges for Teacher Education, Ag, 1978.

Coates, Lawrence G. "A History of Indian Education by the Mormons, 1830-1900." Doctoral dissertation, Ball State U., 1969.

Cook, Sherburne F. The Indian Population of New England in the Seventeenth Century. Berkeley, CA: U. of California Press, 1976.

Duke Project. Western History Center, U. of Utah. [Indian oral history tape recordings]

Dunlap, William C. "Quaker Education in Baltimore and Virginia. Early Meetings with an Account of Certain Meetings of the Delaware and Eastern Shore Affiliated with Philadelphia." Doctoral dissertation, U. of Pennsylvania, 1933.

Dunne, Peter M. Pioneer Black Robes on the West Coast. Berkeley, CA: U. of California Press, 1940.

Eastman, Charles Alexander. The Indian Today, the Past and Future of the First American. Garden City, NY: Doubleday, 1915.

Epperson, Freeman H. "History of Indian Education in the U.S., with Special Reference to the Development of the Boarding School to 1933." Master's thesis, Eastern New Mexico U., 1952.

Farb, Peter. Man's Rise to Civilization: The Cultural Ascent of the Indians of North America, Rev. 2nd ed. New York: Dutton, 1978.

Forbes, Jack D. "The Historian and the Indian: Racial Bias in American History." The Americas (Ap, 1963):349-362.

_____. "The Native American Experience in California History." California Historical Quarterly 2(S, 1971).

Friar, Ralph, and Friar, Natasha. The Only Good Indian: The Hollywood Gospel. New York: Drama Books, 1973. [History of treatment of Indians in movies]

Fritz, Henry E. The Movement for Indian Assimilation, 1860-1890. Philadelphia: U. of Pennsylvania Press, 1963.

Geist, Christopher D. "Slavery Among the Indians: An Overview." Negro History Bulletin 37(O-N, 1975):465-467.

Gribskov, Margaret Elise T. H. "A Critical Analysis of Textbook Accounts of the Role of Indians in American History." Doctoral dissertation, U. of Oregon, 1973.

Havighurst, Robert J. "Indian Education Since 1960." Annals of the American Academy of Political and Social Science 436(Mr, 1978): 13-26.

Henry, Jeannette. The American Indian in American History. San Francisco: The Indian Historical Press, 1970.

Horsman, Reginald. "Scientific Racism and the American Indian in the Mid-Nineteenth Century." American Quarterly 27(My, 1975).

Hughes, J. Donald. "The De-racialization of Historical Atlases: A Modest Proposal." Indian Historian 7(Summer, 1974):55-56.

Hundley, Norris (ed.). The American Indian: Essays from the Pacific Historical Review. Santa Barbara, CA: Clio Press, 1974.

Hunt, Mervin L. "Trends in Indian Education, Historically Treated." Master's thesis, Ohio State U., 1946.

Husband, Michael B. "Reflections on Teaching American Indian History." Journal of American Indian Education 16(Ja, 1977):7-14.

"Indian Education at Hampton and Carlisle: 1880." Harper's Monthly, 1880. [Reprinted in The Indian Historian 3(Summer, 1970):35-41]

Jacobs, William R. Indians and Whites: Struggle on the Colonial Frontier. New York: Scribner's, 1972.

Jacobsen, Jerome V. Educational Foundations of the Jesuits in Sixteenth Century New Spain. Berkeley, CA: U. of California Press, 1938.

Jones, Rhett S. "Black and Native American Relations before 1800." Western Journal of Black Studies 1(S, 1977):151-163.

Jorgensen, Joseph G. "A Century of Political Economic Effects on American Indian Society, 1880-1980." Journal of Ethnic Studies 6 (Fall, 1978):1-82.

Kawashina, Yasuhide. "Indians and Southern Colonial Statutes." Indian Historian 7(Winter, 1974):10-16.

Kellaway, William. The New England Company, 1649-1776. New York: Barnes and Noble, 1962. [Touches on Indian education]

Keller, Robert H., Jr. "American Indian Education: An Historical Context." Journal of the West 13(Ap, 1974):75-82.

Kickingbird, Kirke. "A Short History of Indian Education." American Indian Journal of the Institute for the Development of Indian Law 1(D, 1975):2-15.

King, Harry C. "The Education of the American Indian: A History of the Major Approaches." Master's thesis, Willimantic State College, Willimantic, CT, 1968.

Klink, Jane Seymour. "Relation of the Medicine Man to the Educational System of the Early Races of North America." Master's thesis, U. of Chicago, 1902.

Lauber, Almon W. Indian Slavery in Colonial Times. New York: Columbia U. Press, 1913.

Layman, Martha E. "A History of Indian Education in the United States." Doctoral dissertation, U. of Minnesota, 1942.

Lewis, Robert W. "English and American Indian Studies." Indian Historian 6(Fall, 1973): 32-37, 54.

Lipschutz, Alejandro. "La Despoblacion de las Indias Despues de la Conquista." American Indigena, Jl, 1966.

Littlefield, Daniel F., Jr., and Littlefield, Mary Ann. "The Beams Family: Free Blacks in Indian Territory." Journal of Negro History 41(Ja, 1976):16-35.

Lloyd, Peter. "The Emergence of Racial Prejudice Towards the Indians in Seventeenth Century New England: Some Notes on an Explanation." Doctoral dissertation, Ohio State U., 1975.

Lowie, R. H. "The Inventiveness of the American Indian." American Mercury 24(S, 1931):90-93.

Lukes, Edward A. "Ethno-History of Indians of the U.S. " Indian Historian 5(Spring, 1972): 23-25. [A course outline]

Lundquist, Florence B. "Education of the American Indian by the United States." Master's thesis, College of the Pacific, 1934.

McCallum, James D. (ed.). The Letters of Eleazar Wheelock's Indians. Hanover, NH: Dartmouth College Publications, 1932.

_____. Eleazar Wheelock. Hanover, NH: Dartmouth College Publications, 1939.

McLaury, John C. "An Historical Outline of Efforts--Both Public and Private--Towards the Education and Civilization of the Indian, and of His Present Status." Doctoral dissertation, New York U., 1904.

Magnaghi, Russell M. "The Role of Indian Slavery in Colonial St. Louis." Missouri Historical Society Bulletin 31(Jl, 1975).

Mardock, Robert W. "The Humanitarians and Post-Civil War Indian Policy." Doctoral dissertation, U. of Colorado, 1958.

Martin, Douglas Dale. "Indian-White Relations on the Pacific Slope, 1850-1890." Doctoral dissertation, U. of Washington, 1969.

Mendenhall, Raymond E. "Quaker Contributions to American Education." Doctoral dissertation, New York U., 1925.

Miller, William R. "A History of the Development of Education in the Southwest." Doctoral dissertation, New York U., 1902.

Mitchell, Frederic, and Skelton, James W. "The Church-State Conflict in Early Indian Education." History of Education Quarterly 6(1966): 41-51.

Monkres, Robert L. "Indian-White Conflict before 1870: Cultural Factors in Conflict." Journal of the West 10(Jl, 1971):439-473.

Morison, Samuel E. Harvard College in the Seventeenth Century. Cambridge, MA: Harvard U. Press., 1936.

Morris, Harold W. "A History of Indian Education in the United States." Doctoral dissertation, Oregon State College, 1954.

Ortiz, Alfonso. "D'Arcy McNickle (1904-1977). Across the River and Up the Hill. A Personal Remembrance." American Indian Journal 4 (Ap, 1978):12-16.

Oswalt, Wendell H. This Land Was Theirs. New York: John Wiley & Sons, Inc., 1966.

Palladino, L. B. Indian and White in the Northwest, 2nd ed. Lancaster, PA: Wickersham, 1922.

Pecoraro, Joseph. The Effect of a Series of Special Lessons on Indian History and Culture Upon the Attitudes of Indian and Non-Indian Students. Augusta, ME: State Department of Education, 1970.

Philip, Kenneth. "Herbert Hoover's New Era: A False Dawn for the American Indians, 1929–1932." Rocky Mountain Social Sciences Journal 9(Ap, 1972):53–60.

Pratt, Richard Henry. Battlefield and Classroom: Four Decades with the American Indian, 1897–1904. New Haven, CT: Yale U. Press, 1964.

Prucha, Francis Paul. "American Indian Policy in the 1840s: Visions of Reforms." In The Frontier Challenge. Responses to the Trans-Mississippi West, pp. 81–110. Edited by John G. Clark. Lawrence, KA: U. Press of Kansas, 1971.

Ramsey, Edna M. "Administration of the Educational Affairs of the Indians by the Government from 1871–1891." Master's thesis, Northwestern U., 1913.

Ryberg, Robert F., and Belok, Michael V. Exploration in the History and Sociology of American Indian Education. Meerut: Sadhno Prakashan, 1973.

Salisbury, Neal Emerson. "Conquest of the 'Savage': Puritans, Puritan Missionaries, and Indians, 1620–1680." Doctoral dissertation, U. of California, Los Angeles, 1972.

_____. "Red Puritans: the 'Praying Indians' of Massachusetts Bay and John Eliot." William and Mary Quarterly 31(Ja, 1974).

Satz, Ronald N. "Civilizing the Indians." In American Indian Policy in the Jacksonian Era, pp. 246–291. Lincoln, NB: U. of Nebraska Press, 1975.

Schultz, George A. "An Indian Canaan: Isaac McCoy, Baptist Missions and Indian Reform." Doctoral dissertation, State U. of Iowa, 1963.

Segal, Charles M., and Stineback, David C. Puritans, Indians, and Manifest Destiny. New York: Putnam, 1977.

Sheehan, Bernard W. Seeds of Extinction. Jeffersonial Philanthropy and the American Indian. Chapel Hill, NC: U. of North Carolina Press, 1973.

Smith, Jane F., and Kvasnicka, Robert M. (eds.). Indian-White Relations: A Persistent Paradox. Washington, DC: Howard U. Press, 1976.

Stefon, Frederick J. "Significance of the Meriam Report of 1928." Indian Historian 8(Summer, 1975):2–7.

Szasz, Margaret Ann Connell. "American Indian Education, 1930–1970. From the Meriam Report to the Kennedy Report." Doctoral dissertation, U. of New Mexico, 1972.

_____. Education and the American Indian. The Road to Self-Determination, 1928–1973. Albuquerque: U. of New Mexico Press, 1974.

_____. "Thirty Years Too Soon: Indian Education Under the Indian New Deal." Integrateducation 13(Jl-Ag, 1975):3–9.

Tanis, Norman E. "Education in John Eliot's Indian Utopias, 1646–1675." History of Education Quarterly 10(F, 1970):308–323.

Thomas, G. E. "Puritans, Indians, and the Concept of Race." New England Quarterly 48(Mr, 1975):3–27.

U.S. Bureau of Indian Affairs. Famous Indians. A Collection of Short Biographies. Washington, DC: GPO, 1973.

U.S. Congress, 15th, 1st Session. Report on Establishment of Trading Houses and Encouragement of Education. Annals of Congress, 1817–1818, part 1, 800–801.

U.S. Congress, 15th, 2nd Session. Petition for the Civilization of the Indian--Society of Friends. Senate State Papers, No. 47, D 23, 1818.

U.S. Congress, 15th, 2nd Session, House of Representatives, House Document No. 91, Vol. 6, Ja 15, 1819. On the Civilization of the Indian Tribes.

U.S. Congress, 17th, 1st Session, Senate, Senate Document No. 50, Vol. 1, F 23, 1922. Message on the Civilization of the Indians--President James Monroe.

U.S. Congress, 18th, 1st Session, House of Representatives, House Document No. 47, Vol. II, Ja 24, 1824. Statement on Disbursement for Civilization of Indians.

U.S. Congress, 18th, 1st Session, House of Representatives, House Report No. 92, Vol. III, Mr 23, 1824. On Civilization of the Indian--Committee on Indian Affairs.

U.S. Congress, 19th, 1st Session, House of Representatives, House Document No. 102, Vol. V, F 3, 1826. Report on Preservation and Civilization of Indian Tribes--Secretary James Barbour.

U.S. Congress, 19th, 1st Session, House of Representatives, House Document No. 124, Vol. VIII, Mr, 1826. Report on Preservation and Civilization of the Indians--General Clark, Superintendent of Indian Affairs.

U.S. Congress, 20th, 2nd Session, House of Representatives, House Document No. 11, Vol. 1, D 8, 1828. On Civilization of the Indians.

U.S. Congress, 28th, 1st Session, House of Representatives, House Document No. 247, Vol. V, Ap 23, 1844. Report on Indian School Fund--Secretary William Wilkins.

U.S. Congress, 33rd, 1st Session, House of Representatives, House Report No. 267, Vol. III, Serial No. 744, Je 30, 1854. Adverse Report on Establishment of Schools for Indians in California.

U.S. Congress, 42nd, 2nd Session, Senate, Senate Miscellaneous Document No. 44, Vol. I, Ja 25, 1872. Report on Education of Indians--Secretary C. Delano.

U.S. Congress, 46th, 2nd Session, House of Representatives, House Report No. 752, Vol. III, H.R. 1735, Ap 6, 1880. Industrial School for Indians.

U.S. Congress, 48th, 2nd Session, Senate, Executive Document No. 95, Vol. II, Part 2, Serial No. 2264. Special Report of 1888 on Indian Education and Civilization.

U.S. Congress, 71st, 2nd Session, Senate, Committee on Indian Affairs, Subcommittee, Survey of Conditions of Indians in the United States. [see part 8 et al.]

U.S. Congress, 73rd, 2nd Session, Senate, Report No. 511 (S. 2571). Report on Johnson-O'Malley Bill for Federal-State Cooperation in Education, Social Welfare, etc. of Indians. [1934]

U.S. Department of the Interior, Rulings. Acquisition of Puyallup Tribal School Property. Memo. Sol., Mr 25, 1939.

_____. Contract with State for Schooling Indians. Memo. Sol., My 21, 1935.

_____. Education and Relief--State Contract. Op. Sol. M 28197, O 31, 1935.

_____. Educational Loans to Indians. Op. Sol. M. 28317, Mr 31, 1936.

_____. Exchanges for State School Lands. Memo. Sol. Office, N 10, 1934.

_____. Ft. Totten--State School Tax. Mem. Sol., Jl 16, 1934.

_____. Ft. Totten--State School Tax. Mem. Sol., Jl 20, 1934.

_____. Indian School Land--Right of Way. Memo. Sol., Jl 1, 1938.

VanWell, Mary Stanislaus. "The Educational Aspects of the Missions in the Southwest." Doctoral dissertation, Marquette U., 1941.

Vantine, Larry L. Teaching American Indian History: An Interdisciplinary Approach. Palo Alto, CA: R & E Research Associates, 1978.

_____. Teaching American Indian History: An Interdisciplinary Approach (A Curriculum Guide), S, 1976. ERIC ED 131 969.

Vaughn, Alden T. New England Frontier: Puritans and Indians, 1620-1675. Boston: Little, Brown, 1965. [Touches on Indian education]

Vogel, Virgil J. (ed.). This Country Was Ours: A Documentary History of the American Indian. New York: Harper & Row, 1972.

_____. The Indian in American History. Chicago: Integrated Education Associates, 1968.

_____. "The Indian in American History Textbooks." Integrated Education, My-Je, 1968.

Walker, Henry Pickering. "Teacher to the Mojahves: The Experience of George W. Nock, 1887-1889." Arizona and the West 9(1967): 143-166, 259-280.

Warren, Robert Austin. "The Southern New England Indian, 1725: A Study in Culture Contact." Doctoral dissertation, Yale U., 1969.

Washburn, Wilcomb E. Red Man's Land--White Man's Law: A Study of the Past and Present Status of the American Indian. New York: Scribner's, 1971.

Wilcox, Wilma E. "Early Indian Schools and Education Along the Missouri." Master's thesis, U. of Iowa, 1928.

Wise, Jennings C. The Red Man in the New World Drama: A Politico-Legal Study with a Pagentry of American Indian History. New York: Macmillan, 1971. [Ed. Vine Deloria, Jr.]

Webb, Edith B. Indian Life in the Old Missions. Los Angeles: Warren F. Lewis Publisher, 1952.

Weickselbaum, Norman. "The Catholic Indian School Controversy, 1889-1891: A Conflict of Ideas." Master's thesis, Ohio U., 1937.

Winslow, Ola Elizabeth. John Eliot: "Apostle to the Indians." Boston: Houghton Mifflin Company, 1968.

Wolfson, Harry. "The History of Indian Education Under the Federal Government from 1871-1930." Master's thesis, College of the City of New York, 1932.

Urban Life

Ablon, Joan. "American Indian Relocation: Problems of Dependency and Management in the City." Phylon 26(1966).

American Indian Policy Review Commission. Report on Urban and Rural Non-Reservation Indians, 1976. ERIC ED 141 011.

Beaulieu, David L. Native American Students in Standard Metropolitan Statistical Areas: A Selective Analysis of 1968 HEW Data, D, 1970. Minneapolis: U. of Minnesota. ERIC ED 052 851.

Caruthers, Osgood. "L.A. Indians Seek Their Own Hospital." Los Angeles Times, Ap 25, 1976.

Chadwick, Bruce A., and Stauss, Joseph A. "The Assimilation of American Indians into Urban Society: The Seattle Case." Human Organization 34(Winter, 1975):359-369.

Chadwick, Bruce A. and others. "Confrontation with the Law: The Case of the American Indian in Seattle." Phylon 37(Je, 1976):163-171.

_____. "Indian Education in the City: Correlates of Academic Performance." Journal of Educational Research 70(Ja-F, 1977):135-141.

Chan, Carole, and Hamby, John. The American Indian: A Very Private People, Revised ed., Je, 1975. ERIC ED 127 094.

French, Lawrence. Educational Dilemma Facing the Urban Indian, N 20, 1977. ERIC ED 151 137.

Fuchs, Michael. "Health Care Patterns of Urbanized Native Americans." Doctoral dissertation, U. of Michigan, 1974.

Gabourie, F. W. "Justice and the Urban American Indian." California State Bar Journal, Ja-F, 1971.

Gundlack, J. H., and Roberts, A. E. "Native American Indian Migration and Relocation: Success or Failure?" Pacific Sociological Review 21(Ja, 1978):117-127.

Holmgren, Donald Henry. "Experiences of Indian Students Undergoing Acculturation in Urban High Schools: An Exploratory Study." Master's thesis, U. of Alberta, 1971.

Hurt, Wesley R. "The Urbanization of the Yankton Indians." Human Organization 20(Winter, 1961-1962):226-231.

Isenberg, Barbara. "Urban Indians Driven to Cities by Poverty Find Harsh Existence." Wall Street Journal, Mr 9, 1970.

Margon, Arthur. "Indians and Immigrants: A Comparison of Groups New to the City." Journal of Ethnic Studies 4(Winter, 1977):17-28.

Martin, Harry W. "Correlates of Adjustment Among American Indians in an Urban Environment." Human Organization 23(Winter, 1964):290-295.

Miller, Dorothy L., and Garcia, Anthony. Mental Health Issues Among Urban Indians: The Myth of the Savage-Child, My 9, 1974. ERIC ED 129 485.

Neils, Elaine M. Reservation to City: Indian Migration and Federal Relocation. Chicago: Department of Geography, U. of Chicago, 1971.

Parachini, Allan. "Chicago's Indian Ghetto, Where Hopes Slowly Die." Chicago Sun-Times, My 2, 1976.

Peacock, Eugene G. Indian Resident Survey, Jl 27, 1966, 13 pp. Duluth, MN: Duluth Department of Economic Development. ERIC ED 047 877.

Price, John A. Cultural Divergence Related to Urban Proximity on American Indian Reservations, Ag, 1971, 31 pp. Minneapolis: U. of Minnesota. ERIC ED 054 891.

Public Forum Before the Committee on Urban Indians in Los Angeles, CA (D 16-17, 1968); Dallas, TX (F 13-14, 1969); Minneapolis-St. Paul, MN (Mr 18-19, 1969); San Francisco, CA (Ap 11-12, 1968); Phoenix, AZ (Ap 17-18, 1969), Ap 18, 1969, 1143 pp. Washington, DC: National Council on Indian Opportunity. ERIC ED 041 685.

Recommendations of Working Committee to Urban Indian Conference, D 16, 1970, 31 pp. Washington, DC: National Council on Indian Opportunity. ERIC ED 046 607.

Ritzenthaler, Robert, and Sellers, Mary. "Indians in an Urban Situation." The Wisconsin Archeologist 36(D, 1955):147-161.

Slater, Jack. "Urban Indian: Fighting for Identity." Los Angeles Times, F 29, 1976.

Sorkin, Alan L. The Urban American Indian. Lexington, MA: Lexington Books, 1978.

Steele, Charles Hoy. "American Indians and Urban Life: A Community Study." Doctoral dissertation, U. of Kansas, 1972.

Stull, Donald D. "Native American Adaptation to an Urban Environment: The Papago of Tucson, Arizona." Urban Anthropology 7(Summer, 1978):117-135.

Tyler, S. Lyman. "The Recent Urbanization of the American Indian." In Essays on the American West, 1973-1974. Edited by Thomas G. Alexander. Provo, UT: Brigham Young U. Press, 1975.

U.S. American Indian Policy Review Commission, Task Force Eight. Report on Urban Non-Reservation Indians. Washington, DC: GPO, 1976.

Waddell, Jack O., and Watson, O. Michael (eds.). The American Indian in Urban Society. Boston: Little, Brown, 1971.

_____ and _____. American Indian Urbanization. West Lafayette, IN: Department of Sociology and Anthropology, Purdue U., 1973.

Weightman, Barbara A. "Study of the Indian Social Milieu in an Urban Environment." Doctoral dissertation, U. of Washington, 1972.

Weinstein, Robert Irwin. "Native Americans in Rural and Urban Poverty." Doctoral dissertation, U. of Texas, 1974.

White, Robert. "The Urbanization of the Dakota Indians." Master's thesis, St. Louis U., 1959.

Zamyan, Mary L. and others. Educational and Related Characteristics of Urban Indians in the United States: A Selective Summary of 1960 Census Data, Je, 1970, 70 pp. Minneapolis: U. of Minnesota, Center for Community Programs. ERIC ED 043 433.

Control of Education

"The AIPRC Report." Journal of American Indian Education 16(My, 1977):1-13. [Discussion of education recommendations by the American Indian Policy Review Commission]

Bighin, James E., and Wilson, Jack. "Parental Attitudes towards Indian Education." Journal of American Indian Education 11(My, 1972):1-6.

Burnett, Robert. "Indian Educators as a Catalyst for Political Reform." American Indian Culture Center 4(Winter, 1973):19-22.

Conference on California Indian Education. Report of the First All-Indian Statewide Conference on California Indian Education, 1967. California Indian Education Association, 1349 Crawford Road, Modesto, CA 95350.

Conference on Indian Affairs. Direction that the Institute of Indian Studies Should Take to Meet the Needs of the Indian People. Eagle Butte, SD: United Sioux Tribes, 1969.

Cooper, Robert, and Gregory, Jack. "Can Community Control of Indian Education Work?" American Indian Education 15(My, 1976):7-11.

Declaration of Indian Purpose. American Indian Conference, 1125 East 59th Street, Chicago, IL, 1969.

Deloria, Vine, Jr. Custer Died for Your Sins: An Indian Manifesto. New York: Macmillan, 1969.

_____. "Integrity Before Education." Integrated Education 12(My-Je, 1974):22-28.

The First National Indian Workshop on School Affairs (Ogden, UT, Mr 24-28, 1969), 1970, 211 pp. Brigham City, UT: Bureau of Industrial Affairs, Instructional Service Center. ERIC ED 041 835.

Forbes, Jack D. Native American Education Liberation, A tape. Akwesasne Notes, Mohawk Nation, Roosevelt, NY 13683.

Gemberling, Elizabeth and others. The Role of Secondary Education in the Development of Indigenous Leadership in American Indian Communities. Final Report, Jl, 1970. New York: Bureau of Applied Social Research, Columbia U. ERIC ED 042 527.

"Indian Schools and Community Control." Stanford Law Review 25(Ap, 1973).

Kleinfeld, Judith S. "Regionalism in Indian Community Control." Journal of American Indian Education 11(My, 1972):7-14. [Aleutian Islands]

_____. "Sources of Parental Ambivalence Toward Education in an Aleut Community." Journal of American Indian Education 10(Ja, 1971):8-14.

Lurie, Nancy O. "The Voice of the American Indian: Report on the American Indian Chicago Conference." Current Anthropology 2(D, 1961): 5.

MacDonald, Peter. [Keynote Speech to Third Annual Convention of the National Indian Education Association, November 4, 1971] Navajo Times, N 11, 1971.

Mech, Joyce (ed.). Proceedings: Indian Education Conference, 1974, My, 1974. ERIC ED 093 559.

National Advisory Council on Indian Education. An Indian Parental Responsibility: The Obligation to Determine an Indian Educational Destiny. Washington, DC: GPO, Mr, 1977.

_____. First Annual Report to the Congress of the United States...2 parts, Mr, 1974. ERIC ED 091 102-103.

_____. Through Education: Self Determination. A Bicentennial Goal for American Indians. Washington, DC: GPO, Mr, 1975.

"National Conference on Indian Self-Determination." Navajo Times, Mr 25, 1971.

The National Congress of American Indians, Annual Report 1969, 1969, 57 pp. Washington, DC: National Congress of American Indians. ERIC ED 046 606.

National Indian Education Conference. [Summaries from Workshops], D 17, 1969. Upper Midwest Regional Educational Laboratory, 1640 East 78th Street, Minneapolis, MN 55423.

Parmenter, Tom. "Community Control [of Indian American Schools]." Inequality in Education 7(1971).

Platero, Dillon. [Discussion of criticisms of Rough Rock Demonstration school] Navajo Times, Ag 24, 1972.

Rosenfelt, Daniel M. "Indian Schools and Community Control." Stanford Law Review 25(Ap, 1973).

Sahmaunt, Ace and others. Education on Indian Terms, N 16, 1973. ERIC ED 096 095.

Stout, Irving W. "The Evolution of Parental Control of Schools on an Indian Reservation." Contemporary Indian Affairs 1(Spring, 1970): 51-58.

U.S. Congress, 93rd, 2nd Session, House of Representatives, Committee on Interior and Insular Affairs, Subcommittee on Indian Affairs. Indian Self-Determination and Education Assistance Act. Hearings... Washington, DC: GPO, 1974.

U.S. Congress, 95th, 1st Session, Senate, Select Committee on Indian Affairs. Indian Self-Determination and Education Assistance Act Implementation: Hearings... Washington, DC: GPO, 1977.

U.S. Congress, 95th, 2nd Session, Senate, Select Committee on Indian Affairs. Amend the Indian Self-Determination and Education Assistance Act: Hearings... Washington, DC: GPO, 1978.

U.S. Department of Health, Education, and Welfare, Office of Indian Education. The Indian Education Act of 1972: Report of Progress. Washington, DC: The Office of Indian Education, 1975.

Waubaunsee, A. John. Indian Control of Schools and Bilingual Education. Arlington, VA: Center for Applied Linguistics, 1976.

Weinman, Janice Jennie. "Local Control Over the Schools in Two American Indian Communities: A Preliminary Examination of Structural Constraints and 'Internal Control' Attitudes." Doctoral dissertation, Harvard U., 1970. ED 060 988. [New Mexico]

_____. "Local Control Over Formal Education in Two American-Indian Communities: A Preliminary Step Toward Cultural Survival." American Educational Research Association 42(Fall, 1972):533-539.

General

Abrahams, Ina. "Vocational Interest of Selected Indian College Students as Measured by the Kuder Preference Record." Journal of American Indian Education 2(O, 1962):20-24.

Agatha, Mother M. "Catholic Education and the Indians." In Essays on Catholic Education in the United States, pp. 523-553. Edited by Roy Joseph Defarrari. Washington, DC: Catholic U. of America Press, 1942.

Agogino, George. "A Study of the Stereotype of the American Indian." Master's thesis, U. of New Mexico, 1950.

Ahler, Janet G. "Plains Indians and Formal Education Systems." Journal of Teaching and Learning 3(Je, 1977):26-33.

Al-Bayati, Barbara. "Academic Library Support of American Indian Studies: An Outline." American Indian Culture Center Journal 3(Fall-Winter, 1971-72):3-5.

American Indian Historical Society. Indian Voices. The First Convocation of American Indian Scholars. San Francisco: The Indian Historian Press, 1970.

_____. Indian Voices. The Native American Today. The Second Convocation of American Indian Scholars. San Francisco: Indian Historical Press, 1974.

_____. Textbooks and the American Indian. San Francisco: American Indian Historical Society, 1451 Masonic Avenue, 1966.

American Indian Reference Book, Ag 14, 1976. ERIC ED 134 391.

"A.I.M.--Shock Troops of Indian Sovereignty." IFCO News 3(N-D, 1972). [American Indian Movement]

American Indian Movement. "'The Funny (?) Things People Say to Us...As Heard by the Native American People.'" In The American Indian. Compiled by Joseph R. Sanchez, Alan Osur, and Dorothy J. Maney. Patrick Air Force Base, FL: Defense Race Relations Institute, 1974.

Bass, Willard P. An Analysis of the Academic Achievement of Indian High School Students in Federal and Public Schools, My, 1971, 155 pp. Albuquerque: Southwestern Cooperative Educational Laboratory. ERIC ED 064 000.

Anant, S. S. "Ethnic Stereotypes of Educated North Indians." Journal of Social Psychology 85(O, 1971):137-139.

Anderson, Kenneth E. et al. The Educational Achievement of Indian Children. Washington, DC: U.S. Department of the Interior, Bureau of Indian Affairs, 1953.

Antes, John M. "Raising Aspirations of Minority Children with a Supportive Learning Environment." Journal of American Indian Education 11(Ja, 1972):5-12.

Apker, Wesley. "A Survey of the Literature Related to Indian Pupil Dropout." Master's thesis, Washington State U., 1962.

Archibald, Charles W., Jr. The Mainstream--Where Indians Drown, Mr 26, 1970, 15 pp. ERIC ED 041 058.

Are You Listening, Neighbor? Report of the Indian Affairs Task Force, 1971, 110 pp. Olympia, WA: Washington State Indian Affairs Task Force. ERIC ED 055 707.

Armstrong, Robert L., and Holmes, Barbara. "Counseling for Socially Withdrawn Indian Girls." Journal of American Indian Education 10(Ja, 1971):4-7.

Arnet, Cory. "Education [of the Indian American]. A Promise Unfulfilled." The Indian Historian, Winter, 1968.

Arthur, G. "An Experience with Examining an Indian 12th Grade Group." Mental Hygiene 28 (1944):243-250.

_____. "An Experiment in Testing Indian School Children." Mental Hygiene 25(1941):188-195.

Aurbach, Herbert A. (ed.). Proceedings of the National Research Conference on American Indian Education, 1967. Society for the Study of Social Problems, P.O. Box 190, Kalamazoo, MI 49005.

Aurbach, Herbert A. and others (eds.). The Status of American Indian Education. Interim Report, Ja, 1970, 173 pp. University Park, PA: Pennsylvania State U. ERIC ED 039 055.

Aveni, Anthony F. (ed.). Native American Astronomy. Austin, TX: U. of Texas Press, 1977.

Ayres, Mary Ellen. "Counseling the American Indian." Occupational Outlook Quarterly 21 (Spring, 1977):22-29.

Badger, Angeline. "An Activity Program for Indian Children." Master's thesis, U. of Colorado, 1938.

Ballard, Louis W. "Cultural Differences: A Major Theme in Cultural Enrichment." Indian Historian, Spring, 1969.

Bank Street College of Education. Young Native Americans and Their Families: Educational Needs Assessment and Recommendations, My, 1976. ERIC ED 127 021.

Baptist, Mary. "Mission Schools in the Indian Territory." Master's thesis, U. of Oklahoma, 1923.

Barnes, Findlay. "A Comparative Study of the Mental Ability of Indian Children." Master's thesis, Stanford U., 1955.

Bass, Willard P., and Burger, Henry G. American Indians and Educational Laboratories, N, 1967, 39 pp. XAPS Report No. SWCEL-Pub-1-1167. ERIC ED 014 369.

Bass, Willard P. An Analysis of Academic Achievement of Indian High School Students in Federal and Public Schools. A Progress Report, 1969, 35 pp. Albuquerque: Southwestern Cooperative Educational Laboratory. ERIC ED 036 392.

_____. Research and Development Needs and Priorities for the Education of American Indians. Final Report, My, 1971, 45 pp. Albuquerque: Southwestern Cooperative Educational Laboratory. ERIC ED 052 853.

Baumheier, Edward C. and others. Indian Child Welfare: A State-of-the Field Study, Jl, 1976. ERIC ED 138 428.

Bean, Lowell John. "The Language of Stereotype Distortion Inaccuracy." Indian Historian, Fall, 1969. [Critical analysis of Helen Bauer, California Indian Days, a fourth grade textbook]

Bean, Raymond E. "An Exploratory Comparison of Indian and Non-Indian Secondary School Students' Attitudes." Master's thesis, U. of Alberta, 1966.

Beatty, Willard W. "Twenty Years of Indian Education." In The Indian in Modern America. Edited by David A. Baerris. Madison, WI: State Historical Society of Wisconsin, 1956.

_____ (ed.). Education for Action, Selected Articles from Indian Education 1936-43. Washington, DC: U.S. Department of the Interior, U.S. Indian Service, Education Division, 1944.

_____ (ed.). Education for Cultural Change. Selected Articles for Indian Education 1944-1951. Washington, DC: U.S. Department of the Interior, Bureau of Indian Affairs, 1953.

Beer, David F. "The Trouble With 'The.'" Journal of American Indian Education 4(My, 1965): 13-15.

Begaye, Melvin. "Civilizing an Indian." Journal of American Indian Education 10(My, 1971):10-13.

"Behind the Smoke Screen. Indian Education." Christian Science Monitor, N 10, 1975. (Entire issue)

Bell, Carolyn L. The Preschool Child's Image of the American Indian. NATAM IX, My, 1971. ERIC ED 051 914.

Belue, Tessie. "Red and Black: The Old 'Divide and Conquer' Technique?" Navajo Times, Ja 26, 1978. [A half-Indian, half-black tells her story]

Benham, William J. "A Foundation for Indian, Cross-Cultured Education." Journal of American Indian Education, Ja, 1969.

_____. "Residential Schools at the Crossroads." Journal of American Indian Education 16(Ja, 1977):20-26.

Bennett, Robert L., and Coombs, L. Madison. "Effective Education to Meet Special Needs of Native Children." Journal of American Indian Education 3(My, 1964):21-25.

Bergan, K. W. "The Secondary School and the Acculturation of Indian People." Bulletin of the National Association of Secondary School Principals 43(O, 1959):115-118.

Berman, Mark L. Some Considerations in the Education of Indigenous Groups in the Southwest, Jl 19, 1965, 16 pp. Santa Monica, CA: System Development Corporation. ERIC ED 016 387.

Berman, S. Sue. "Speech and Language Services on an Indian Reservation." Language, Speech and Hearing Services in Schools 7(Ja, 1976): 56-60.

Bernardoni, Louise C. The High School Counselor and Counseling with Indians. Phoenix: Arizona State Department of Public Instruction, Division of Indian Education, 1961.

_____. "Results of the TOGA with First Grade Indian Children." Journal of American Indian Education 1(Je, 1961):24-28.

Berry, Brewton. Almost White. New York: The Macmillan Company, 1963.

Berry, Franklin (ed.). The Collected Papers of the Northern Cross-Cultural Education Symposium, My, 1974. ERIC ED 094 916.

Beuf, Ann H. "The Inner Alcatraz: A Study of Racial Attitudes in American Indian Preschool Children." Doctoral dissertation, Bryn Mawr College, 1972.

_____. Pre-School Attendance, Racial Pride, and the Native American Child, 1974. ERIC ED 149 877.

_____. "Racial Attitudes of Native-American Preschoolers." In Black/Brown/White Relations. Edited by Charles V. Willie. New Brunswick, NJ: Transaction, 1977.

_____. Red Children in White America. Philadelphia: U. of Pennsylvania Press, 1977.

Birchard, Bruce A. Attitudes Toward Indian Culture and Its Incorporation in the School Curriculum: Students, Parents, Teachers, and Community Leaders; Perceptions of Indian Education. The National Study of American Indian Education, Series IV, No. 10, Final Report, D, 1970, 14 pp. Chicago: U. of Chicago. ERIC ED 047 879.

_____. Boarding Schools for American Indian Youth, Je, 1970. ERIC ED 043 425.

_____. How Indian Students and Parents Evaluate Their Schools; Perceptions of Indian Education. The National Study of American Indian Education, Series IV, No. 11, Final Report, D, 1970, 22 pp. Chicago: U. of Chicago. ERIC ED 047 875.

_____. The Validity of Rating Scales and Interviews for Evaluating Indian Education: Perceptions of Indian Education. The National Study of American Indian Education, Series IV, No. 8, Final Report, D, 1970, 10 pp. Chicago: U. of Chicago. ERIC ED 047 873.

Blackman, F. W. "Indian Education." Annals 2 (1892):813-837.

_____. "Social Assimilation of the American Indian." Journal of Educational Sociology 3 (S, 1929):7-19.

_____. "The Socialization of the American Indian." American Journal of Sociology 34(Ja, 1929):653-669.

Blanchard, Joseph D. and others. "A Psychological Autopsy of an Indian Adolescent Suicide with Implications for Community Services." Suicide and Life Threatening Behavior 6 (Spring, 1976):3-9.

Blanchard, Joseph D., and Warren, Richard L. "Role Stree of Dormitory Aides at an Off-Reservation Boarding School." Human Organization 34(Spring, 1975):41-49.

Blauch, Lloyd E. Educational Service for Indians. Staff Study #18, prepared by the U.S. Advisory Committee on Education. Washington, DC: GPO, 1939.

Blossom, Grace A. "A New Approach to an Old Problem." Journal of American Indian Education 1(Ja, 1962):13-14.

_____. "Grammar and the Bilingual Student." Journal of American Indian Education 4(Ja, 1965):14-16.

_____. "Teaching English as a Second Language." Journal of American Indian Education 2(O, 1962):17-19.

Bodner, Bruce. "Indian Education: Tool of Cultural Politics." National Elementary Principal 50(My, 197):22-30.

Bohr, Joseph W. "Present Status of Catholic Education Among the Indians of the United States." Master's thesis, Catholic U. of America, 1929.

Bollinger, M. H. "A Study of Underachievement of Indian and Non-Indian Pupils in an Integrated School." Master's thesis, Northern State Teachers College, Aberdeen, 1961.

Bowman, Jack. "Western Movies, By an Indian Lover." Navajo Times, Ja 19, 1969.

Boyce, George A. Alcohol and American Indian Students. Washington, DC: U.S. Department of the Interior, Bureau of Indian Affairs, 1965.

_____. Alcohol and American Indian Students, S, 1965, 45 pp. Washington, DC: Bureau of Indian Affairs. ERIC ED 023 520.

Brand, David. "Young Indians Borrow Tactics From Blacks As They Fight Poverty." Wall Street Journal, Ap 30, 1969.

Brandon, William. "American Indians: The Alien Americans." Progressive, D, 1969.

Braroe, Niels W. "Reciprocal Exploitation in an Indian-White Community." Southwestern Journal of Anthropology 31(1965):166-178.

Breening, Nancy and others. The Indian's Iden-
tification with the Earth: A Native American
Curriculum Unit for the High School. NATAM
XVI, My, 1971, 37 pp. Minneapolis: U. of
Minnesota. ERIC ED 051 919.

Brekke, Beverly, and Williams, John D. "Conser-
vation and Reading Achievement of Second
Grade Bilingual American Indian Children."
Journal of Psychology 86(Ja, 1974):65-69.

Brewer, Annemarie. "On Indian Education." Out-
rider (Erikson Institute for Early Education) 9(0, 1975).

_____. "On Indian Education." Integrateduca-
tion 15(My-Je, 1977). [Reprinted from preceding item]

Brightman, Lehman. "Education of the Native
American: A Brief Overview." Journal of
Non-White Concerns in Personnel and Guidance
1(Ap, 1973):159-162.

_____. "Mental Genocide. Some Notes on Fed-
eral Boarding Schools for Indians." Inequality in Education 7(1971).

_____. "The Pictures on the Wall Are of White
Men." Integrated Education 9(My-Je, 1971):
37-42.

Brito-Hunting Bear, Silvester. "The Eloquence
of Indian Oratory." In Essays on Minority
Folklore. Selected Proceedings of the 3rd
Annual Conference on Minority Studies, April,
1975, Vol. III, pp. 10-19. Edited by George
E. Carter and James R. Parker. La Crosse,
WI: Institute for Minority Studies, U. of
Wisconsin, 1977.

Bromberg, Walter and others. The Native American
Speaks. Santa Fe, NM: State Department of
Education, 1973.

Bronson, Ruth Muskrat. Indians Are People Too.
New York: Friendship Press, 1944.

Brophy, William A., and Aberle, Sophie D. (eds.).
"Education." In The Indian America's Unfin-
ished Business, Chapter 5. Norman, OK: U. of
Oklahoma Press, 1966.

Brown, Alice C. "An Analysis of the Intelligence
of Indians." Master's thesis, U. of Colorado,
1932.

Brown, Estelle. Stubborn Fool, A Narrative.
Caxton, ID: Caldwell Printers, 1952.

Brown, Janet W. "Native American Contributions
to Science, Engineering, and Medicine."
Science 189(Jl, 1975):38-40.

Brownlee, Aleta. "The American Indian Child."
Children 5(Mr-Ap, 1958):55-60.

Bruner, Edward M. "Cultural Transmission and
Cultural Change." Southwestern Journal of
Anthropology 12(1956):191-199.

_____. "Primary Group Experience and the Pro-
cess of Acculturation." American Anthropologist 58(1956):605-623.

Bryde, John F. Indian Students and Guidance.
Boston: Houghton Mifflin, 1971.

_____. Modern Indian Psychology, Revised edi-
tion. Vermillion, SD: The Dakota Press,
U. of South Dakota, 1971.

_____. Modern Indians. Vermillion, SD: In-
stitute of Indian Studies, 1969.

Buck, June M. Indian Literature for Junior and
Senior High Schools, 1968, 25 pp. Phoenix:
Division of Indian Education, Arizona State
Department of Public Instruction. ERIC ED
042 530.

Bulmann, L. "Art Speaks One Language." Montana
Education 25(0, 1948):25.

Bureau of Indian Affairs. Indian Education:
Steps to Progress in the 70's. Washington,
DC: GPO, 1973.

_____. Survey of Bilingual Education Needs of
Indian Children, 0, 1975. ERIC ED 128 151.

Bureau of Indian Affairs Workshop '69. Final
Report, 1969. ERIC ED 038 357.

Burdin, Joel L. and others. Preparing School
Personnel for American Indians. Some Exploratory Questions and Responses with an Annotated Bibliography, N, 1970. ERIC ED 045 560.

_____. School Personnel Preparation for Amer-
ican Indians: Present and Needed Steps, My,
1971. ERIC ED 051 074.

Bureau of Indian Affairs. The Native American
Videotape Archives--Catalog, 1977. ERIC ED
157 665.

Burgess, Glen D. "A Program for Teaching English
to Indian Children in Elementary Schools."
Master's thesis, Stanford U., 1937.

Byler, Mary Gloyne. "The Image of American Indians Projected by Non-Indian Writers." School
Library Journal 20(F, 1974):36-39.

"Candid Comments on Bureaucratic Education: Annual Indian Education Conference." Journal of
American Indian Education 11(My, 1972):15-19.

Carmichael, Elizabeth H. "An Analysis of the
Indian Unit as Found in the Elementary Grades."
Master's thesis, George Washington U., 1933.

Carmichael, Stokely. "The Red and the Black."
Akewesasne Notes 6(Early Winter, 1975):32-33.

Cavender, Chris C. An Unbalanced Perspective:
Two Minnesota Textbooks Examined by an American Indian, S, 1970, 24 pp. Minneapolis: U.
of Minnesota, Training Center for Community
Programs. ERIC ED 045 229.

Center for Applied Linguistics. Styles of Learn-
ing Among American Indians: An Outline for
Research. Washington, DC: Center for Applied
Linguistics, F, 1969.

Center for Human Relations. Equal Educational
Opportunity for Indians. Washington, DC:
National Education Association, 1970.

Chadwick, Bruce A., and Bahr, Howard M. "Factors
Associated with Unemployment Among American
Indians in the Pacific Northwest." Phylon 39
(D, 1978):356-368.

Chafe, Wallace L. "Estimates Regarding the Present Speakers of North American Indian Languages." International Journal of American
Linguistics 28(J1, 1962):162-171.

Chamberlin, J. E. The Harrowing of Eden: White
Attitudes Toward Native Americans. New York:
Seabury Press, 1975.

Charles, C. M. "A Science-Mythology Relationship Among Indian Children." Journal of Educational Research 37(Ja, 1964):261-264.

_____. "A Tutoring-Counseling Program for In-
dian Students in College." Journal of American Indian Eudcation 1(My, 1962):10-12.

Chavers, Dean. "New Directions in Indian Education." Indian Historian 8(Winter, 1975):43-
46.

Chino, Wendell. "Text of Chino's Speech at
NCAI." Navajo Times, O 9, 1969. [President
of National Congress of American Indians]

Christensen, Rosemary A. "Indian Women: An Historical Personal Perspective." Pupil Personnel Services (Minnesota Department of Education) 4(Spring, 1975):12-22.

Clignet, Remi. "Sociologie de la colonisation
americaine en territoire indien." Cahiers
internationaux de sociologie 20(1956):61-89.

Cobb, John C. (ed.). Emotional Problems of Indian Students in Boarding Schools and Related
Public Schools, Ap 13, 1960, 77 pp. ERIC ED
047 848.

Coffin, Ernest W. "On the Education of Backward
Races." Doctoral dissertation, Clark U.,
1908.

Cohen, Warren H., and Mause, Phillip J. "The
Indian: The Forgotten American." Harvard Law
Review, Je, 1968.

Colburg, Dolores (ed.). Indian Education Conference. Lewistown, Montana, April 4-5, 1967.
Helena, MT: State Department of Public Instruction, 1967.

Coles, Robert. The Children of Crisis, IV: Eskimos, Chicanos and Indians. Boston: Atlantic Monthly Press, 1978.

Colfer, Carol J. Pierce. "An Ethnography of
Leaderlong Indian School." Doctoral dissertation, U. of Washington, 1974.

_____. "Bureaucrats, Budgets, and the BIA:
Segmentary Opposition in a Residential School."
Human Organization 34(Summer, 1975):149-156.

Colorado River Indian Tribes. Career Guidance
for Indian Youth, Je 30, 1976. ERIC ED 132
366.

Comptroller General of the United States. Information on Organization and Functions of
the Indian Education Resources Center. Washington, DC: General Accounting Office, 1978.

_____. Slow Progress in Eliminating Substandard
Indian Housing. Washington, DC: U.S. General
Accounting Office, O 12, 1971.

Connelly, John. "Shungopavi: A Study of Intercultural Relations." Master's thesis, Western
Reserve U., 1946.

"Convocation of American Indian Scholars is Success: Preparations Begin for 1971." Indian
Historian 3(Spring, 1970):37-38, 50.

Cook, William A. "The American Indian: A Study
in Race Education." Master's thesis, U. of
Illinois, 1911.

Coombs, L. Madison. The Educational Disadvantage
of the Indian American Students, J1, 1970.
ERIC ED 040 815.

_____. "The Indian Student is Not Low Man on
the Totem Pole." Journal of American Indian
Education 9(My, 1970):1-9.

Coombs, L. Madison, Kron, R. E., Collister, E.
G., and Anderson, K. E. The Indian Child
Goes to School. Lawrence, KA: Haskell In-
stitute Press, 1958.

Corrigan, Francis V. "A Comparison of Self Concepts of American Indian Students from Public
or Federal School Backgrounds." Doctoral
dissertation, George Washington U., 1970.

Costo, Rupert. "Cheyennes Denounce 'Seven Arrows' Book in Historic Meeting." Wassaja 2
(Ag, 1974).

Costo, Robert, and Henry, Jeannette. Textbooks
and the American Indian, 1970. The Indian
Historian, 1451 Masonic Avenue, San Francisco,
CA 94117.

Council on Interracial Books for Children.
Chronicles of American Indian Protest. New
York: Fawcett, 1971.

Cox, Lionel C. "A Study of the Intelligence of
Indian and White Children." Master's thesis,
U. of Wyoming, 1938.

Craig, Edith. "Needs of Indian Girls for Homemaking Education." Master's thesis, Colorado
A. & M. College, 1943.

Crespy, Alberta B. "Secondary Schoolteachers in the Territories and Possessions of the United States." Doctoral dissertation, Fordham U., 1942.

Cronk, Leslie M. "Indian Education in Terms of Pupil and Community Needs." Master's thesis, Arizona State U., 1938.

Crow, J. "Schools for the First Americans." American Education 1(O, 1965):15-22.

Crump, Bonnie L. "The Educability of Indian Children in Reservation Schools." Doctoral dissertation, Columbia U., 1932.

Cundrick, Bert P. "Measures of Intelligence on Southwest Indian Students." Journal of Social Psychology 81(1970):151-156.

Cundrick, Bert P. and others. "Changes in Scholastic Achievement and Intelligence of Indian Children Enrolled in a Foster Placement Program." Developmental Psychology 10(N, 1974): 815-820.

Cushing, Frank H. The Need of Studying the Indian in Order to Teach Him. Washington, DC: GPO, 1897.

Custer, Carolyn. A Native American Curriculum Unit for the Fourth Grade, NATAM IV, My, 1971, 19 pp. Minneapolis: U. of Minnesota. ERIC ED 051 913.

Dankworth, Richard T. Educational Achievement of Indian Students in Public Secondary Schools as Related to Right Variables, Including Residential Environment. Final Report, My, 1970, 95 pp. Logan, UT: Utah State U. ERIC ED 042 526.

Deever, R. Mervin and others (eds.). American Indian Education. Tempe, AZ: Arizona State U., 1974.

Deloria, Vine, Jr. A Better Day for Indians. New York: The Field Foundation, 1977.

_____. "The Future of Indians." Akwesasne Notes 7(Early Winter, 1975):36-37.

_____. "The Indian Student Amid American Inconsistencies." In The Schooling of Native America, pp. 9-26. Edited by Thomas Thompson. Washington, DC: American Association of Colleges for Teacher Education, Ag, 1978.

_____. "Indian Treaties a Hundred Years Later." Race Relations Reporter 6(Ja-F, 1974):29-32.

_____. "The New Exodus." Civil Rights Digest 4(Spring, 1971):38-44.

_____. "The Next Three Years: A Time for Change." Indian Historian 7(Spring, 1974): 25-27, 53.

_____. "The Place of American Indians in Contemporary Education." American Indian Journal 2(F, 1976):2-8.

_____. We Talk, You Listen. New Tribes, New Turf. New York: Macmillan, 1970.

_____ (ed.). Indian Education Confronts the Seventies, 2 volumes. Oglala, ND: American Indian Resource Associates, 1974.

Demmert, William George, Jr. "Critical Issues in Indian Education, 1972-1973." Doctoral dissertation, Harvard U., 1973.

Destruction of American Indian Families. New York: Association on American Indian Affairs, 1977.

"Directory. Indian Studies Programs, Education Action Groups, Financial Assistance." Akwasasne Notes 3(S, 1971):41.

Division of Indian Education. Indian Youth Conference, 7th. Pierre, SD: Department of Public Instruction, 1966.

Dobyns, Henry F. "Native American Publication of Cultural History." Current Anthropology 15(S, 1974):304-306.

_____. "La situacion actual del indigena en el suroeste de los Estados Unidos." America Indigena 36(1976):831-846. [Indians and Chicanos]

Donaldson, Clara. "A Study of the United States Indian Schools." Master's thesis, U. of Akron, 1926.

Dorris, Michael. "Why I'm Not Thankful for Thanksgiving." Interracial Books for Children Bulletin 9(1978):6-9. [A Modoc man]

Downing, L. J. "The Comparison-Reference Process as It Relates to Ninth Grade Indian and Non-Indian Boys of Low Socio-economic Status." Doctoral dissertation, U. of Oklahoma, 1965.

Dozier, Edward P. "The Teacher and the Indian Student." Indian Historian, Spring, 1969.

Dozier, Edward P., Simpson, G. E., and Yinger, J. M. "The Integration of Americans of Indian Descent." Annals, My, 1957.

Dreyer, Phillip H. The Meaning and Validity of the "Phenomenal Self" for American Indian Students. The National Study of American Indian Education, Series III, No. 7. Final Report, Ag, 1970, 22 pp. Chicago: U. of Chicago. ERIC ED 044 212.

_____. The Relation of Self-Esteem to Personal-Social Adjustment among American Indian Students: The Personal-Social Adjustment of American Indian Youth. National Study of American Indian Education. Final Report, S, 1970, 27 pp. Chicago: U. of Chicago. ERIC ED 045 276.

Driver, Harold E. Indians of North America. Chicago: U. of Chicago Press, 1961.

Dudding, Christine G. "An Investigation into the Bilingual Child's Comprehension of Antonyms." Master's thesis, U. of New Mexico, 1960.

Duin, Virginia N. "The Problems of Indian Poverty: The Shrinking Land Base and Ineffective Education." Albany Law Review, Fall, 1971.

Dumont, Robert V. Information Source: Education for American Indians, D, 1969, 17 pp. Washington, DC: Office of Education, Office of American Indian Affairs. ERIC ED 050 855.

Dumont, Robert V., Jr. "Learning English and How to Be Silent: Studies in American Indian Classrooms." In Functions of Language. Edited by Dell Hymes and Vera Johns. New York: Teachers College Press, 1970. [Cherokee and Sioux]

Duncan, Kunigunde. Blue Star. Caldwell, ID: The Caxton Printers, 1938.

Dunn, Lynn P. American Indians: A Study Guide and Sourcebook. San Francisco: R & E Research Associates, 1975.

Dunne, G. H. "Indian's Dilemma." Commonweal 45(Ja, 1957):351-354.

Dutton, Dewey A. "A Study of the Application of Intelligence Tests to the Indians of the Southwest." Master's thesis, U. of Denver, 1930.

Eastman, Elaine G. Pratt: The Red Man's Moses. Norman, OK: U. of Oklahoma Press, 1935.

Edington, Everett D., and Hocker, Philip (eds.). Development of Vocational Education Programs for American Indians, Conference Proceedings (University of New Mexico, August 18-22, 1969), O, 1969, 55 pp. Las Cruces, NM: New Mexico State U. ERIC ED 031 614.

Edington, Everett D. Development of Vocational Education Programs for American Indians. Final Report, Mr 26, 1970, 59 pp. University Park, NM: New Mexico State U. ERIC ED 039 960.

Edmunds, R. David. "The Indian in the Mainstream: Indian Historiography for Teachers of American History Surveys." History Teacher 8(F, 1975).

Elliott, John G. Educational and Occupational Expectations and Aspirations: A Comparative Study of Indian and Non-Indian Youth, Mr, 1970, 163 pp. Antigonish, Nova Scotia: Saint Francis Xavier U. ERIC ED 045 257.

Enoche, J. Romily. The Relationship Between Indian Teachers' and Non-Indian Teachers' Perceptions of Indian First-Graders and Student Achievement in Reading, 1977. ERIC ED 148 543.

Fadden, John, and Mofsie, Louis. "Student Reactions to Indian Teachers of Non-Indian Children." Social Education 36(My, 1972):502-511.

Falkenhagen, Maria, Johnson, Carole, and Balasa, Michael. "The Treatment of Native Americans in Recent Children's Literature." Integrated Education 11(Jl-O, 1973):58-59.

Falls, Anna E. "The Place of Private and Church Schools in the Education of the State." Master's thesis, U. of New Mexico, 1929.

Fannin, Paul J. "Indian Education--A Test Case for Democracy." Arizona Law Review, Winter, 1968.

Fanshel, David. Far From the Reservation: The Transracial Adoption of American Indian Children. A Study Conducted under the Auspices of the Child Welfare League of America, New York, New York, 1972, 388 pp. Available from Scarecrow Press, Inc., P.O. Box 656, Metuchen, NJ 08840. ERIC ED 064 008.

Farb, Peter. "The American Indian: A Portrait in Limbo." Saturday Review, O 12, 1968.

Farlow, Barbara A. An Equal Chance: Handbook for Counselling Indian Students, 1971, 52 pp. Stevens Point, WI: Wisconsin State U. ERIC ED 050 364.

Farris, Charles E. "The American Indian: Social Work Education's Neglected Minority." Journal of Education for Social Work 18(Spring, 1975): 37-43.

Farris, Charles E., and Farris, Lorene S. "Indian Children: The Struggle for Survival." Social Work 21(S, 1976):386-389.

Fay, Keith LaVerne. Developing Indian Employment Opportunities. Washington, DC: Bureau of Indian Affairs, 1976.

Feagin, Joe R., and Anderson, Randall. "Intertribal Attitudes Among Native American Youth." Social Science Quarterly 54(Je, 1973):115-131.

Fearn, Leif. "The Education of Indian Children: Reflections." Journal of American Indian Education, O, 1967.

Feldman, Dede. "Council Seeks Better Future for Indian People." Navajo Times, F 2, 1978. [National Indian Youth Council]

Fey, Harold E., and McNickle, D'Arcy. Indians and Other Americans: Two Ways of Life Meet. New York: Harper and Brothers, 1959.

Fighting Tuscarora. The Autobiography of Chief Clinton Rickard. Edited by Barbara Graymont. Syracuse, NY: Syracuse U. Press, 1973.

Finley, Cathaleen. Factors Relating to Program Development with Indian People, 1969, 12 pp. Madison, WI: U. of Wisconsin Extension. ERIC ED 056 807.

560 / AMERICAN INDIANS

Fisher, A. D. "Education and Social Progress." Alberta Journal of Educational Research 12 (1966):257-268.

Fisher, Frank L. "The Influence of Reading and Discussion on the Attitudes of Fifth Graders toward American Indians." Doctoral dissertation, U. of California, Berkeley, 1965.

Fishlow, David M. "The Indian Dilemma." Civil Liberties, My, 1973.

Fitzgerald, J. A., and Ludeman, W. W. "The Intelligence of Indian Children." Journal of Comparative Psychology 6(1926):317-328.

Fletcher, Alice C. Indian Education and Civilization. Washington, DC: GPO, n.d.

Foerster, Leona M., and Soldier, Dale Little. "Learning Centers for Young Native Americans." Young Children 33(Mr, 1978):53-57.

Fogg, P. "Art Sense of the Indian." School Arts Magazine 26(F, 1927):348-349.

Forbes, Jack D. "Americanism is the Answer." Akwesasne Notes 6(Early Spring, 1974):36-38.

_____. "The Americanization of Education in the United States." Indian Historian 7(Spring, 1974):15-21.

_____. Education for the Culturally Different: A Multi-Cultural Approach. Berkeley, CA: Far West Laboratory for Educational Research and Development, n.d.

_____. "Indian Education--The Effects of Conquest." 3 tapes, a total of two and a half hours. Akwesasne Notes, Mohawk Nation, Roosevelt, NY 13683.

_____. "Native American Studies." In The Minority Student on the Campus: Expectations and Possibilities, pp. 159-171. Edited by Robert A. Altman and Patricia O. Snyder. Boulder, CO: Western Interstate Commission for Higher Education, N, 1970.

_____. "The New Indian Resistance?" Akwesasne Notes 4(Late Spring, 1972):20-22.

_____. "Who Are the Americans?" Akwesasne Notes 8(Midwinter, 1975-1976):37-38.

Friar, Ralph E., and Friar, Natasha A. The Only Good Indian...The Hollywood Gospel. New York: Drama Book Specialists, 1972.

Friesen, John W., and Moseson, Linda. "The Plains Indians and Educational Theory." Journal of American Indian Education 11(O, 1971):19-26.

Frisbie, Charlotte J. "The Music of American Indians." In Music in American Society, 1776-1976: From Puritan Hymns to Synthesizer. Edited by George McCue. New Brunswick, NJ: Transaction Books, 1977.

Fritz, Henry J. "A Functional Aspect of the Plains Indian Education." Master's thesis, Catholic U., 1933.

Fuchs, Estelle. Curriculum for American Indian Youth. The National Study of American Indian Education, Series IV, No. 4, Final Report, 1970, 12 pp. Chicago: U. of Chicago. ERIC ED 046 602.

_____. "Time to Redeem an Old Promise." Saturday Review, Ja 24, 1970. [American Indian education]

Fuchs, Estelle, and Havighurst, Robert J. To Live on This Earth. American Indian Education. Garden City, NY: Doubleday, 1972.

Gaillard, Frye. "The Indian Has Made the White Man Take Notice." Charlotte Observer, N 5, 1972.

_____. Indians in Revolt--1970. Nashville, TN: Race Relations Information Center, D, 1970.

_____. "'We'll Do It Our Own Way Awhile.'" Race Relations Reporter 3(Ja 3, 1972):21-27.

Gallegos, Katherine Powers (ed.). Indio and Hispano Child: Improving His Self Image, My 19, 1969, 87 pp. Los Lunas NM: Consolidated Schools. ERIC ED 044 206.

Galloway, Charles G., and Mickelson, Norma I. "Modification of Behavior Patterns of Indian Children." Elementary School Journal 72(D, 1971):150-155.

Galuzzi, W. E. "A Comparison of Intelligence Quotients of Two Different Cultural Groups in an Integrated School." Master's thesis, Northern State Teachers College, Aberdeen, 1960.

Garcia, Jesus. "From Bloody Savages to Heroic Chiefs." American Indian Education 17(Ja, 1978):15-19. [Stereotypes in textbooks]

Garrison, Irvin R. "Factors which Related to Teacher Turnover in Bureau of Indian Affairs Schools." Doctoral dissertation, U. of Oklahoma, 1972.

Garth, Thomas R. "The Intelligence of Mixed-Blood Indians." Journal of Applied Psychology 11(Ag, 1927):269-275.

_____. Race Psychology: A Study of Racial Mental Differences. New York: McGraw-Hill, 1931.

Garth, Thomas R., and Garrett, James E. "A Comparative Study of the Intelligence of Indians by United States Indian Schools and in the Public Schools." School and Society 27(F 11, 1928):178-184.

Garth, Thomas R., and Smith, O. D. "The Performance of Full-Blooded Indians on Language and Non-Language Intelligence Tests." Journal of Abnormal and Social Psychology 32(O-D, 1937): 376-381.

Garth, Thomas R., Smith, H., and Abell, W. "A Study of the Intelligence and Achievement of Full-Blood Indians." Journal of Applied Psychology 12(1928):511-516.

Gerard, Beverly. Improvement of American Indian Use of the Library, 1970. ERIC ED 088 482.

Gerlach, Dominic B. "St. Joseph's Indian Normal School, 1888-1896." Indian Magazine of History, Mr, 1973.

Golden, Gertrude. Red Moon Called Me: Memoirs of an Indian Service Schoolteacher. San Antonio, TX: The Naylor Company, 1954.

Goodman, William I. "The Development of Vocational Education in Agriculture in Indian Schools." Master's thesis, U. of Massachusetts, 1941.

Gordon, W. R. "Service to Indian Reservations." Minnesota Libraries 22(Winter, 1969):348-349.

Gould, Ralf F. "Psychological Tests Applied to American Indians." Master's thesis, U. of New Mexico, 1931.

Graves, T. D., Powers, J. F., and Michener, B. P. Socio-Cultural and Psychological Factors in American Indian High School Classroom Performance and Post-Graduation Success: Theory and Methodology. Boulder, CO: Institute of Behavioral Science, U. of Colorado, 1967.

Gray, Clyde Thomas. "American Indian Education: Cultural Pluralism or Assimilation?" Doctoral dissertation, U. of Southern California, 1975.

Green, Rayna. "Math Called Key to Indian Self-Determination." Science 201(Ag, 1978):433.

Green, Rayna, and Malcom, Shirley Mahaley. "Native Americans Project Finds Some Barriers Breaking Down." Science 195(Ja, 1977):54-56.

Greenberg, Norman C. et al. Education of the American Indian in Today's World. Dubuque, IO: W. C. Brown Book Co., 1964.

Gunsky, Frederic R. "School Problems of Indian Youth." California Education, F, 1969.

Hagan, William T. American Indians. Chicago: U. of Chicago Press, 1961.

_____. The Indian in American History. Washington, DC: American Historical Association, 1972.

Hall, G. Stanley. "How Far Are the Principles of Education along Indigenous Lines Applicable to American Indians?" Pedogogical Seminary 15 (1908):365-369.

Hamilton, A. "Their Indian Guests: Indian Student Placement Program." Saturday Evening Post 233(S 17, 1960).

Hammerschlag, Carl A., Alderfer, Clayton P., and Berg, David. "Indian Education: A Human Systems Analysis." American Journal of Psychiatry 130(O, 1973):1098-1102. [One boarding school]

Hansen, H. "Scholastic Achievement of Indian Pupils." Journal of Genetic Psychology 50 (1937):361-369.

Hansen, Harvey C. "Correlation Between Verbal Intelligence Tests and Nonverbal Intelligence Tests of Indian Pupils." Master's thesis, U. of Oklahoma, 1927.

Hansma, E. A. "American Indian Education: Law and Policy." Doctoral dissertation, U. of Maine, 1972.

Hanson, Lorie and others. Suburban School Children and American Indians: A Survey of Impressions. The National Study of American Indian Education, Series III, No. 5, Final Report, My, 1970, 55 pp. Chicago: U. of Chicago; Minneapolis: Training Center for Community Programs, U. of Minnesota. ERIC ED 042 559.

Hanson, Marshal R. "Plains Indians and Urbanization." Doctoral dissertation, Stanford U., 1960.

Harkins, Arthur M., and Woods, Richard G. Education-Related Preferences and Characteristics of College-Aspiring Urban Indian Teenagers: A Preliminary Report, My, 1969. ERIC ED 030 514.

Harkins, Arthur M. and others. An Overview of the Native American Curriculum Series, Ja 1, 1972, 47 pp. Minneapolis: U. of Minnesota, Center for Urban and Regional Affairs; Minneapolis Training Center for Community Programs. ERIC ED 060 993.

Harriger, Max F. Social Studies in BIA Schools. A Position Paper, 1968, 16 pp. Washington, DC: Division of Curriculum Development and Review, Bureau of Indian Affairs. ERIC ED 047 837.

Harrington, L. "Revival of Northern Indian Art Forms." School Arts 48(Ja, 1949):146-150.

Harris, Dixie L. "Education of Linguistic Minorities in the U.S. and the U.S.S.R." Comparative Education Review 6(F, 1963):191-199.

Harris, Helen L. "On the Failure of Indian Education." Clearing House 47(D, 1973):242-247.

Hansha, W. J. "Education and the Six Nations." Southern Workman 58(D, 1929):563-566.

_____. "Education and the So-called 'Civilized Tribes.'" _Southern Workman_ 59(Ja, 1930):36-41.

Haslam, Gerald W. "Literature of the People: Native American Voices." _CLA Journal_ 15(D, 1971):153-170.

Hathorn, James. "Comparative Study of Factors Related to Post High School Educational Pursuits of Selected American Indians." Doctoral dissertation, Oregon State U., 1971.

Haught, B. G. "Mental Growth of the Southwestern Indian." _Journal of Applied Psychology_ 18(1934):137-142.

Havighurst, Robert J. _Design of the Study._ National Study of American Indian Education, Series IV, No. 1, Ap, 1970, 31 pp. Chicago: U. of Chicago. ERIC ED 039 082.

_____. "Education among American Indians: Individual and Cultural Aspects." _Annals of the American Academy of Political and Social Science_ 311(My, 1957):105-115.

_____. _The Education of Indian Children and Youth: Summary Report and Recommendations._ National Study of American Indian Education. Summary Report and Recommendations, D, 1970. ERIC ED 045 275.

_____. _The Extent and Significance of Suicide Among American Indians Today._ National Study of American Indian Education, Series III, No. 1, Final Report, Mr, 1970. ERIC ED 039 080.

_____. "Indian Education Since 1960." _Annals_ 436(Mr, 1978).

_____. _The Indian Self-Image as Evaluated with the Semantic Differential._ The National Study of American Indian Education, Series III, No. 9, Final Report, Ag, 1970, 11 pp. Chicago: U. of Chicago. ERIC ED 044 217.

_____. _Indians and Their Education in Los Angeles._ National Study of American Indian Education, Series II, No. 1, Final Report, Mr, 1970, 11 pp. Chicago: U. of Chicago. ERIC ED 039 078.

_____. _Mental Development and School Achievement of American Indian Children and Youth,_ 1970. ERIC ED 040 978.

_____. _The Reliability of Rating Scales Used in Analyzing Interviews with Parents, Students, Teachers, and Community Leaders._ The National Study of American Indian Education, Series IV, No. 9, Final Report, D, 1970, 11 pp. Chicago: U. of Chicago. ERIC ED 046 600.

_____. _The Use of Interviews and Rating Scales in the Study of Indian Education._ The National Study of American Indian Education, Series IV, No. 7, Final Report, D, 1970, 18 pp. Chicago: U. of Chicago. ERIC ED 046 610.

Havighurst, Robert J., and Hilkevitch, Rhea. "The Intelligence of Indian Children as Measured by a Performance Scale." _Journal of Abnormal and Social Psychology_ 39(O, 1944):419-433.

Havighurst, Robert J., and Neugarten, Bernice L. _American Indians and White Children._ Chicago: U. of Chicago Press, 1954.

Havighurst, Robert J. _et al._ "Environment and the Draw-a-Man Test: The Performance of Indian Children." _Journal of Abnormal and Social Psychology_ 41(Ja, 1946):50-63.

Hayner, N., and Hayner, U. "Three Generations of Pacific Northwest Indians." _American Sociological Review_ 8(1943):650-656.

Heath, G. Louis. "The Life and Education of the American Indian." _Illinois Quarterly_ 33 (F, 1971):16-38.

_____. "Red Power" and Indian Education, 1970, 7 pp. ERIC ED 045 238.

_____. "'Red Power' and Indian Education." _International Review_ 40(Spring, 1971):3-7.

_____. "Toward Culturally-Expressive Education for Indian Children." _Interracial Review_ 40 (Spring, 1971):9-16.

Heemstra, Gerritt. "The Educational Mission for the American Indian." Master's thesis, New York U., 1928.

Heiwich, June Sark. "Native Americans: What Not to Teach." _Interracial Books for Children Bulletin_ 8(1977):22-24.

Helmer, Velma. "The American Indian and Mental Tests." Master's thesis, U. of Kansas, 1925.

Helper, Malcolm M., and Garfield, Sol L. "Use of the Semantic Differential to Study Acculturation in American Indian Adolescents." _Journal of Personality and Social Psychology_ 2(1965):817-822.

Hendricks, J. Robert, and Metos, Thomas H. "Amerindians--Studying an Important Minority Group." _Instructor_ 79(1970):98-101.

Henry, Jeannette (ed.). _The American Indian Reader. Education._ San Francisco: Indian Historian Press, 1972.

_____. "Our Inaccurate Textbooks." _The Indian Historian_ 1(D, 1967):21-24.

Henry, Jules. "Cross-Cultural Outline of Education." _Current Anthropology_ 1-2(1960-1961).

Herzog, John D. "Deliberate Instruction and Household Structure." Harvard Educational Review 32(1962).

Hinchee, Charles L. "A Comparison of the Kwalwasser-Dykema Test Scores of Certain White and Indian Children." Master's thesis, Northwestern U., 1935.

Hobart, Charles W. "Some Consequences of Residential Schooling." Journal of American Indian Education 7(Ja, 1968):7-17.

Hoffman, Dean K. "Relationship of Self-Concept and Academic Self-Assessment to the Educational Aspirations of Underprivileged Adolescent Indians." Diss. Abstr. Int'l. 1969, 30 (3-0):1226-1227.

Hohn, Wayne. "Let It Never Be Said..." Journal of American Indian Education 4(0, 1964):6-9.

Holmes, J. J. "Adventure with the Indians." Teachers College Journal 21(0, 1949):8.

Hooten, Richard J. "Race, Skin Color, and Dress as Related to the American Indian Stereotype." Doctoral dissertation, Utah State U., 1972.

Hopkins, Thomas R. "American Indians and the English Language Arts." Florida FL Reporter, Spring-Summer, 1969.

_____. "Teaching English to American Indians." English Record 21(Ap, 1971):24-31.

Housand, Shalmir S. "The Education of the American Indian As an Instrument for Cultural Change." Master's thesis, Ohio State U., 1959.

Howe, Elizabeth K. "An Assimilation Study of High School Girls." Master's thesis, U. of Kansas, 1935.

_____. "Some Light on the Adjustment of Indian Children." Journal of American Indian Education 4(Ja, 1965):26-29.

_____. "Young Indians: Some Problems and Issues of Mental Hygiene." Mental Hygiene 46 (Ja, 1962):41-47.

Huff, Delores S. "Educational Colonialism: The American Indian Experience." Harvard Graduate School of Education Association Bulletin 20 (Spring-Summer, 1976):2-6.

Hunter, W., and Sommermier, E. "The Relation of Degree of Indian Blood to Scores on the Otis Intelligence Test." Journal of Comparative Psychology 2(1922):257-275.

Indian Culture Master Plan. A Master Plan for Enriching the Background of Public School Personnel in Native American Cultures. Helena, MT: Montana State Board of Education, 1975.

"Indian Doctors Hold First Meeting." Navajo Times, Ag 10, 1972.

Indian Health Service. Illness Among Indians 1965-1969. Washington, DC: GPO, Jl, 1971.

"Indian Materials: An Annotated List of Non-trade Book Publishers." RQ 15(Spring, 1976): 215-218.

"Indian Number." School Arts Magazine, N, 1927.

"Indian Participation in Public Schools." Social Education 35(My, 1971):452-465.

Indian Women Today, 1975. ERIC ED 125 818.

Indians in Rural and Reservation Areas. Sacramento, CA: State Advisory Committee on Indian Affairs, 1966.

Is There an Indian in Your Classroom This Year? 1970, 43 pp. Minneapolis: Minneapolis Public Schools. ERIC ED 060 996.

Ishisaka, Hideki. "American Indians and Foster Care: Cultural Factors and Separation." Child Welfare 57(My, 1978):299-308.

Iverson, Katherine. "Civilization and Assimilation in the Colonized Schooling of Native Americans." In Education and Colonialism, pp. 149-180. Edited by Philip G. Altbach and Gail P. Kelly. New York: Longman, 1978.

Jackson, Curtis E. Identification of Unique Features in Education at American Indian Schools. San Francisco: R & E Research Associates, 1974.

Jacobs, Wilbur R. "The Tip of an Iceberg: Pre-Colombian Indian Demography and Some Implications for Revisionism." William and Mary Quarterly 31(Ja, 1974).

Jennings, Don (ed.). American Indian Health Careers Handbook, 2nd edition, 1975. ERIC ED 125 828.

Jerdone, Clare G. "Day Care for Indian Children." Young Children, Ja, 1965.

Johnson, Paul. Confronting the Miseducation of Native American Students. Lansing, MI: Michigan Education Association, 1976.

Johnson, Ronald M. "Schooling the Savage: Andrew S Draper and Indian Education." Phylon 35(Mr, 1975):74-82.

Johnson, V. C. "An Assessment of the Motivation Factor in the Estimation of Academic Achievement of Eleventh Grade Indian Students and the Factored Dimensions of the M-Scales. An Exploratory Study." Doctoral dissertation, Michigan State U., 1963.

Jonasson, Ingaborg. "The Comparative Intellectual Abilities of Full and Mixed Blood Indians." Master's thesis, U. of North Dakota, 1937.

Jones, C. F. "Notes on Indian Education." Journal of Educational Sociology 27(S, 1953): 16-23.

Jones, Myron. Indian Education in Public Schools: Confused Responsibilities--Predictable Results, Ap 4, 1974. ERIC ED 089 927.

Jose, Nelson. "Why We Need Our Education." Journal of American Indian Education 1(My, 1962):22-25.

Joseph, Alice, Spicer, Rosamond, and Chesky, Jane. The Desert People. Chicago: U. of Chicago Press, 1949.

Josephy, Alvin M., Jr. "What the Indians Want." New York Times Magazine, Mr 18, 1973.

Kaap, Theodore F., Jr. "A Survey of the Teaching of Music in Indian Schools of the Southwest with Suggestions for Improvement of Such Instruction." Master's thesis, U. of Arizona, 1951.

Kaltsounis, Theodore. "The Need to Indianize Indian Schools." Phi Delta Kappan 53(Ja, 1972):291-293.

Katz, Jane B. (ed.). I Am the Fire of Time. New York: Dutton, 1978. [Writings by Native American women]

Kayser, Joyce. "Scholastic Performance and Ethnicity." Journal of American Indian Education 3(0, 1963):27-30.

Kennedy, Edward M. "Address...Before the National Congress of American Indians." Navajo Times, O 9, 1969.

Kessey, Harry A., Jr. "Concerning Indian Education." Educational Forum 36(My, 1972):473-477.

Kidwell, Clara Sue. "The Power of Women in Three American Indian Societies." Journal of Ethnic Studies 6(Fall, 1978):113-121.

King, A. R. "A Case Study of an Indian Residential School." Doctoral dissertation, Stanford U., 1964.

Klein, Bernard, and Isolari, Daniel (eds.). Reference Encyclopedia of the American Indian. New York: B. Klein and Company, 1967.

Kleinfeld, Judith. "Effective Teachers of Eskimo and Indian Students." School Review 83 (F, 1975):301-344.

_____. "Positive Stereotyping: The Cultural Relativist in the Classroom." Northian 12 (Spring, 1976):20-25.

Knight, Margaret E. The Nature of Teacher-Community Contact in Schools Serving Southwest Indian Children. American Indian Education Papers, No. 2, Mr, 1970, 8 pp. Tucson, AZ: U. of Arizona, Department of Anthropology. ERIC ED 052 880.

Knoll, John A. "The Effect of Prejudice upon the Employment of Indians." Master's thesis, U. of Idaho, 1947.

Kolodney, Nathan. "Teens--Indians--Judaism: The Impact of Contact with American Indian Culture Upon Urban Jewish Teens." Jewish Social Work Forum 6(Fall, 1969):62-69.

Kozoll, Charles E. "A Provocative Workshop in Indian Education." Integrated Education 9 (Ja-F, 1971):29-34.

Krause, George W. and others. Teachers of American Indian Youth. National Study of American Indian Education. Final Report, D, 1970, 24 pp. Chicago: U. of Chicago. ERIC ED 045 274.

Krush, Thaddeus, et al. "Some Thoughts on the Foundation of Personality Disorder: Study of an Indian Boarding School Population." American Journal of Psychiatry 132(1966):868-876.

Kuipers, Cornelius C. "Results of an Intelligence Test Based on Indian Culture." Master's thesis, U. of New Mexico, 1934.

Kyle, James H. "How Shall the Indians Be Educated?" North American Review 159(1894).

LaFarge, Oliver. "An Experimental School for Indians." Progressive Education 9(F, 1932): 87-94.

_____. "White Man's Burden." World's Work 60½ (Ag, 1931):45-48, 64-65.

Lammers, Donald M. "Self Concepts of American Indian Adolescents Having Segregated and Desegregated Elementary Backgrounds." Doctoral dissertation, Syracuse U., 1969.

Landwehr, Robert C. "Status, Personality and Culture Change." Master's thesis, Stanford U., 1951.

Lane, M. D. H. (Sister Mary of the Divine Heart). "A Critical Study of the Contemporary Theory and Policy of the Indian Bureau with Regard to American Indian Education." Doctoral dissertation, The Catholic U. of America, 1962.

Lappin, Valeria. "The Mental and Physical Development of Indian Children." Master's thesis, U. of Missouri, 1941.

Larsh, Edward B. "The Indian Student at a Disadvantage in the Public Schools." Doctoral dissertation, U. of Northern Colorado, 1974.

Larson, Wayne L. Pygmalion in Native-American Education, S 1, 1977. ERIC ED 144 744.

"The Latest in the 'Social Genocide' Field. Adoption of Indian Children by White Families." Akwesasne Notes 4(Summer, 1972).

Lawrence, Emeric A., and Zuern, Theodore F. "Were Missionaries to U.S. Indians Wrong?" National Catholic Reporter, N 7, 1975. [Two views]

League of Nations Pan-Am Indians. "Civil Rights and the Indians." Indian Voices, F-Mr, 1966.

Lee, Dorothy Sara. Native North American Music and Oral Data: A Catalog of Sound Recordings, 1893-1976. Bloomington, IN: Indiana U. Press, 1979.

Lee, Gladys V. "An Investigation of the American Indian Dropout Problem." Master's thesis, Moorehead State College, 1972.

Lefley, Harriet P. "Differential Self-Concept in American Indian Children as a Function of Language and Examiner." Journal of Personality and Social Psychology 31(Ja, 1975):36-41.

Leitha, Gene. "Search for Identity Creates Problems for Indian Students." Journal of American Indian Education 11(O, 1971):7-10.

Lenarcic, R. J. "Teaching About Native Americans." American Teacher, Je, 1972.

Lesser, A. "Education and the Future of Tribalism in the United States: The Case of the American Indian." Social Service Review, Je, 1961.

Letchworth, George A. Morale and Teacher Separation and Retention in Bureau of Indian Affairs Schools, F, 1971, 32 pp. ERIC ED 047 857.

_____. Teacher Separation and Retention in Bureau of Indian Affairs Schools. Final Report, Ja 15, 1972, 114 pp. Norman, OK: U. of Oklahoma. ERIC ED 059 832.

Leupp, Francis E. The Indian and His Problem. New York: Charles Scribner's Sons, 1910.

Levagne, J. E. Y. The Future of Indian Education. Augusta, ME: Department of Indian Affairs, 1969.

Levensky, Kay. The Performance of American Indian Children on the Draw-A-Man Test. National Study of American Indian Education, Series III, No. 2, Final Report, Mr, 1970, 22 pp. Chicago: U. of Chicago. ERIC ED 039 081.

Levine, Stuart, and Lurie, Nancy (eds.). The American Indian Today. Deland, FL: Everett/ Edwards, Inc., 1968.

Levitan, Sar A., and Hetrick, Barbara. Big Brother's Indian Programs--With Reservations. New York: McGraw-Hill, 1971.

Lewis, Rodney. "Procedural Due Process in BIA Schools." American Indian Culture Center Journal 2(Winter, 1971):11-13.

Lewis, Ronald G. and Ho, Man Keung. "Social Work and Native Americans." Social Work 20 (S, 1975):379-382.

Liberty, Margot (ed.). American Indian Intellectuals. St. Paul, MN: West Publishing Co., 1978.

Lloyd, David O. "Comparison of Standardized Test Results of Indian and Non-Indian in an Integrated School System." Journal of American Indian Education 1(Je, 1961):8-16.

Locke, Patricia. "An Ideal School System for American Indians--A Theoretical Construct." In The Schooling of Native America, pp. 119-136. Edited by Thomas Thompson. Washington, DC: American Association of Colleges for Teacher Education, Ag, 1978.

Locklear, Herbert H. "American Indian Myths." Social Work 17(My, 1972):72-80.

Longenbaugh, Dillon A. "4-H Club Work for Indian Boys and Girls." Master's thesis, Colorado A. & M. College, 1941.

Louis, Ray Baldwin. "Are Indian Studies and Programs Really Working?" Navajo Times, My 17, 1973.

Lowry, Laura M. "Differences in Visual Perception and Auditory Discrimination between American Indian and White Kindergarten Children." Journal of Learning Disabilities 3(Jl, 1970):359-363.

Ludeman, W. W., and McAnelly, J. R. "Intelligence of Colony People." Journal of Educational Psychology 21(1930):612-615.

McCaskill, J. C. "Occupational Orientation of Indian Students." Occupations 18(Ja, 1940): 257-261.

McClain, Tom. "American Indians in the Geosciences." Geotimes 19(My, 1974).

McCurtain, Edmund G. "The Family Backgrounds of 117 Indian Problem Children." Master's thesis, U. of Oklahoma, 1936.

McDermott, John F. "The Indian as a Human Being." Nebraska History, Spring, 1971.

McDiarmid, G. L. The Hazards of Testing Indian Children, 1971, 12 pp. ERIC ED 055 692

McDonald, Jerry N., and Lazewski, Tony (eds.). Geographical Perspectives on Native Americans: Topics and Resources, Ap, 1976. ERIC ED 124 313.

MacDonald, Peter. "Face the Nation" transcript. Wassaja 1(Ja, 1973):13-14.

McGaa, Ed. "A Bigoted Textbook." Indian Historian 4(Fall, 1971):53-55. [Claude Appell, Indians. Chicago: Follett, 1971]

MacGregor, Gordon. Warriors Without Weapons. Chicago: U. of Chicago Press, 1946.

McLaughlin, William G. "Red Indians, Black Slavery, and White Racism: America's Slaveholding Indians." American Quarterly 26(O, 1974).

McNeil, J. D. "Changes in Ethnic Reaction Tendencies During High School." Journal of Educational Research 53(1960):199-200.

McPherson, Orpha (ed.). We Look at Indian Education. A Summer Workshop (Tempe, Arizona, 1957), 1957. ERIC ED 136 968.

MacRorie, Chet. "Takeover of BIA Looms." Navajo Times, Jl 20, 1972.

Macon, Vinnie. "Certain Differences Between Indian Children and White Children on the Ninth and Tenth Grade Levels." Master's thesis, U. of Kansas, 1932.

Mahan, James M., and Smith, Mary F. "Non-Indians in Indian Schools." American Indian Education 17(Ja, 1978):1-6.

Mahan, Mark, and Criger, Mary Kathryn. "Culturally Oriented Instruction for Native American Students." Integrateducation 15(Mr-Ap, 1977).

Malan, Vernon D. "Factors Associated with Prejudice Toward Indians." Journal of American Indian Education 2(O, 1962):25-31.

_____. "The Value System of the Dakota Indians." Journal of American Indian Education 3(O, 1963):21-25.

Maeroff, Gene I. "Indian Schools Turn to Pride and Culture." New York Times, Ag 9, 1976.

Mallam, R. Clark. "Academic Treatment of the Indian in Public School Texts and Literature." Journal of American Indian Education 13(1973):14-19.

Mallett, Graham. "Using Language Experience with Junior High Native Indian Students." Journal of Reading 21(O, 1977):25-28.

Manners, Robert A. "Pluralism and the American Indian." American Indigena 22(1962):25-38.

Marks, Stephen E., and Green, Richard M. "Indians and Counseling." Canadian Counselor 5 (Ja, 1971):63-66.

Mathieu, David J., and Howe, Ray. "American Indian Studies from an Academic Perspective: A Position Paper." In "The Urban Minority Experience," Selected Proceedings of the 4th Annual Conference on Minority Studies, pp. 7-11. Edited by George E. Carter and James R. Parker. La Crosse, WI: Institute for Minority Studies, U. of Wisconsin-La Crosse, 1978.

Matthies, B. D. "Independence Training, Hostility, and Values as Correlates of the Achievement of White and Indian Students." Doctoral dissertation, U. of Nebraska Teachers College, 1965.

Meador, Bruce. "The Pupil as a Person." Journal of American Indian Education 4(Ja, 1965):17-22.

Means, Laneda. An Indictment of American-Indian Education. Berkeley, CA: Pacifica Tape Library, 2217 Shattuck Avenue, 94704.

Medeel, Scudder. "An Anthropologist's Observation on Indian Education." Progressive Education 13(Mr, 1936):151-159.

_____. "Comparative Notes on the Social Role of the Settlement House as Contrasted with That of the U.S. Indian Service." Human Organization 3(D, 1943):5-8.

Media Directory. Washington, DC: American Indian Press Association, 1975.

Medicine, Beatrice. "The Anthropologist and American Indian Studies Programs." Indian Historian 4(Spring, 1971):15-18, 63.

_____. The Native American Woman: A Perspective, Mr, 1978. ERIC ED 151 122.

The Memramcook Conference of North American Indian Young People (Memramcook, New Brunswick, July, 1969), Jl, 1969, 163 pp. Princeton, ME: Teaching and Research in Bicultural Education, Inc. ERIC ED 063 054.

Menninger, Karl and others. American Indian Education Conference, Use of Educational Weapons in the War on Poverty (6th, Arizona State University, March 12-13, 1965), Mr 12, 1965, 71 pp. Tempe, AZ: Arizona State U., College of Education. ERIC ED 017 360.

Mercer, Veta. "The Efficiency of Bilingual Children in Understanding Analogies in the English Language." Master's thesis, U. of New Mexico, 1960.

Meriam, Lewis, and Hinman, George W. Facing the Future in Indian Missions. New York: Missionary Education Movement and Council of Women for Home Missions, 1932.

Meuer, Raymond E. "Model Indians of Lower Brule." Master's thesis, Northern State College, Aberdeen, 1971.

Meyer, D. Eugene. "We Continue to Massacre the Education of the American Indian." Journal of American Indian Education 11(Ja, 1972):18-25.

Meyer, William. Native Americans: The New Indian Resistance. New York: International Publishers, 1971.

Mickelson, Norma I., and Galloway, Charles G. "Art and the Hidden Vocabulary of [American] Indian Children." Studies in Art Education 13(Winter, 1972):27-29.

Milan, Donald R. "Analysis of the Academic Achievement of Selected Indian Tribes and Variables Associated with High Achievement." Doctoral dissertation, Arizona State U., 1972.

Miller, Ethelyn. "American Indian Children and Merging Cultures." Childhood Education, Ap, 1968.

Miller, Harold J. "The Education of the American Indians." The College of Education Record (University of North Dakota) 55(Ja, 1970):103-108.

_____. The Effects of Integration on Rural Indian Pupils. Final Report, Je, 1968, 163 pp. Grand Forks, ND: U. of North Dakota. ERIC ED 022 964.

_____. The Effects of Integration on Rural Indian Pupils. Grand Forks, ND: Bureau of Educational Research and Services, U. of North Dakota, Je, 1968. [Summary of longer report, Project No. 7-8397, H.E.W., Office of Education]

Minton, Charles E. "The Place of the Indian Youth Council in Higher Education." Journal of American Indian Education 1(Je, 1961):29-32.

Misiaszek, Lorraine. "The Cultural Dilemma of American Indians." Social Education, Ap, 1969.

_____. "A Profile of the American Indian: Implications for Teaching." College Composition and Communication, D, 1968.

Mitchell, Frederic. "Church-State Conflict." Journal of American Indian Education 2(My, 1963):7-14.

Mitchell, Frederic, and Skelton, J. W. "Church-State Conflict." History of Education Quarterly 6(Spring, 1966):41-51.

Mitchell, Mary J. Attitudes of Indian Children as Revealed by the Analysis of the Free Writing Test, 1950. ERIC ED 125 791.

Moore, William M., Silverberg, Marjorie M., and Read, Merrill S. (eds.). Nutrition, Growth and Development of North American Indian Children. Washington, DC: GPO, 1972.

Morey, Sylvester M. (ed.). Can the Red Man Help the White Man? A Denver Conference with the Indian Elders (1968), 1970. ERIC ED 134 393.

Morgan, James, and Morgan, Marilyn. "About Textbooks" (a letter). Indian Historian, Spring, 1969. [Treatment of the Indian in John D. Hicks' The American Nation]

Morrison, William T. A Statistical Portrait of the American Indian in 1976, S, 1976. ERIC ED 135 556.

Muhammad, Elijah. "Indians in America." Muhammad Speaks, Mr 28, 1969.

_____. "Indians in America. What is Their Future?" Muhammad Speaks, O 12, 1973.

Muntz, Earl E. "Primitive Education." Master's thesis, Yale U., 1921.

Muskrat, Joseph. "Thoughts on the Indian Dilemma." Civil Rights Digest 6(Fall, 1973):46-50.

"Ralph Nader Comments on Indian Education." Integrated Education 7(N-D, 1969):3-13.

National Advisory Commission on Rural Poverty. Rural Poverty, Hearings, 3 volumes. Washington, DC: GPO, S, 1967. [Volume I deals largely with American Indians and Mexican Americans]

National Council on Indian Opportunity: Report, Ja 26, 1970, 28 pp. Washington, DC: National Council on Indian Opportunity. ERIC ED 042 525.

National Advisory Council on Vocational Education. Public Hearings on American Vocational Education, F, 1977. ERIC ED 148 524.

National Indian Education Association. A Design for Library Services, 5 volumes. St. Paul, MN: Indian Library Project, 1972.

National Institute for Mental Health. Suicide, Homocide, and Alcoholism among American Indians: Guidelines for Help. Washington, DC: GPO, 1973.

National Institute of Mental Health, Indian Health Service. Suicide Among the American Indians. Washington, DC: GPO, Je, 1969.

Native American Curriculum Development Workshop, Ja 24, 1977. ERIC ED 142 354.

"The Negro and the Indians: A Comparison of Their Constitutional Rights." Arizona Law Review 7(Spring, 1966).

Nelson, Mary (Snena of the Skoylep). "Ode to the Future: Boarding Schools for Whites on Indian Reservations" (poem). Indian Historian 3(Fall, 1970):31.

_____. "Problems Indian Students Face." Indian Historian 5(Summer, 1972):22-24.

New Horizons for Indian Education. Annual American Indian Education Conference (9th, Arizona State University, March 22-23, 1968), Mr 22, 1968, 47 pp. Arizona State U., Tempe Bureau of Educational Research and Services. ERIC ED 027 981.

New, Lloyd K. "Using Cultural Difference as a Basis for Creative Expression." Journal of American Indian Education 4(1965):8-12.

Newman, R. S. "Environment and Organizational Effectiveness: A Study of Three Indian Primary Schools." Doctoral dissertation, Cornell U., 1972.

Nichols, Claude A. Moral Education Among the North American Indians. New York: Bureau of Publications, Teachers College, Columbia U., 1930.

"The Now Famous Soon to Be Forgotten." Integrated Education 57(My-Je, 1972):66-67. [Reprinted from Americans Before Columbus, Ja-Jl, 1971]

"Occupation of Wounded Knee Analyzed by Denver Educator." Navajo Times, Mr 15, 1973.

Office of Child Development. Indian Child Welfare: A State-of-the-Field Study. Summary of Findings and Discussion of Policy Implications, 1976. ERIC ED 136 989.

Officer, James E. "Indian Unity." Journal of American Indian Education 3(My, 1964):1-8.

_____. Indians in School. Tucson, AZ: Bureau of Ethnic Research, U. of Arizona, 1956.

_____. "Informal Power Structure within Indian Communities." Journal of American Indian Education 3(O, 1963):1-8.

Ohannessian, S. (ed.). Styles of Learning in American Indian Children. Washington, DC: Center for Applied Linguistics, 1969.

Oliver, Emmet S. "An Analysis of Guidance Programs of Indian High Schools in the United States." Master's thesis, U. of Washington, 1947.

Oliver, Marvin E. "The Development of Language Concepts of Pre-Primary Indian Children." Language Arts 52(S, 1975):865-869.

Onstad, Gwen (ed.). "A Talk with Some Native Americans. A Group Interview." Personnel and Guidance Journal 50(O, 1971):103-108.

Orata, Pedro T. Fundamental Education in an Amerindian Community. Washington, DC: U.S. Department of the Interior, Bureau of Indian Affairs, 1953.

Ortiz, Alfonso. "An Indian Anthropologist's Perspective on Anthropology." Indian Historian 4(Spring, 1971):11-14.

_____. Project Head Start in an Indian Community, O, 1965, 70 pp. Chicago: U. of Chicago. Report No. OEO-539. ERIC ED 014 329.

Osborn, Lynn R. "Indian Pupil in the High School Speech Class." Speech Teacher 16(O, 1967): 187-189.

_____. "A Speaking and Listening Program." Journal of American Indian Education 7(O, 1967):21-24.

_____. "Teachers Tackle Speech Problems of Secondary Indian Pupils." Journal of American Indian Education 7(O, 1967):19-21.

Otis, Morgan. "Indian Education--A Cultural Dilemma." Indian Historian 4(Fall, 1971): 23-26.

_____. "A Native American Studies Program: Discussion." Indian Historian 9(Winter, 1976):14-18.

_____. "A Native American Workshop for Teachers: An Examination of Procedures and Experiences." Indian Historian 6(Spring, 1973):33-42.

Owens, Charles S., and Mass, Willard P. The American Indian High School Dropout in the Southwest, Ja, 1969, 43 pp. Albuquerque: Southwestern Cooperative Educational Lab. ERIC ED 026 195.

Owl, W. David. "Remaking the American Indian." Religious Education 26(F, 1931):115-118.

Parker, A. C. "Attitude of the American Indian to American Life." Religious Education 26 (F, 1931):111-114.

Passel, Jeffrey S. "Provisional Evaluation of the 1970 Census Count of American Indians." Demography 13(Ag, 1976).

Paxton, S. Gabe, Jr. A Study of the Composite Self-Concept of the Southwestern Indian Adolescent: An Inservice Action Research Project of Sherman Institute. Supplement Issues-- 429-S, F 15, 1966, 32 pp. Washington, DC: Bureau of Indian Affairs. ERIC ED 052 878.

_____. "Study of the Intelligence of Indian Adolescents Using the Chicago Non-Verbal Examination." Indian Education, F 15, 1965.

_____. Perceptions of Power Influentials in a Federal Indian School, Ap 23, 1976. ERIC ED 121 504.

Payne, June. "All-Indian Upward Bound Program Has Served 160 Students." Contemporary Indian Affairs 1(F, 1970):25-29.

Peaches, Dan. "What Is Indian Education?" Navajo Times, F 19, 1976.

Pecoraro, Joseph. The Effect of a Series of Special Lessons on Indian History and Culture Upon the Attitudes of Indian and Non-Indian Students. Final Report, Ag, 1970, 170 pp. Augusta, ME: Maine State Department of Education. ERIC ED 043 556.

_____. "The Effect of a Series of Special Lessons on Indian History and Culture Upon the Attitudes of Indian and Non-Indian Students." Journal of Education 154(F, 1972):70-78.

Pelletier, Wilfred, and Poole, Ted. No Foreign Land. The Biography of a North American Indian. New York: Pantheon, 1974.

Pelletieri, A. H. "Counseling Indian Youth." Occupations 20(O, 1941).

Penseno, William. "'Nothing...But Death.'" Integrated Education 8(S-O, 1970):17-25.

Peretti, Peter O. "Enforced Acculturation and Indian-White Relations." Indian Historian 6 (Winter, 1973):38-52.

Person, Earl Old. "Indians as Human Beings." Integrated Education, Ap-My, 1967.

Peters, Gladys A. "A Study of Certain Interests and Their Relation to Vocabularies in Indian High School Students." Master's thesis, U. of Kansas, 1934.

Peterson, A. R. "Indian Education Legislation: Staff Effort in the United States Senate, 92nd Congress, 1st Session." Doctoral dissertation, Harvard U., 1972.

Peterson, Shailer A. How Well Are Indian Children Educated? Washington, DC: U.S. Department of the Interior, U.S. Indian Service, 1948.

Petterson, Jay. "Education, Jurisdiction and Inadequate Facilities as Causes of Juvenile Delinquency Among Indians." North Dakota Law Review 48(Summer, 1972).

Pettit, George A. "Educational Practices of the North American Indian." In Exploring the Ways of Mankind. Edited by Walter Goldschmidt. New York: Holt, Rinehart and Winston, 1960.

_____. "Primitive Education in North America." University of California Publications in Archaeology and Ethnology 43(1946):1-182.

Pitt-Rivers, Julian. "Who Are the Indians?" Encounter, S, 1965.

Porter, Helen M. "The Education of the American Indian." Master's thesis, Ohio U., 1955.

Poston, William K, Jr. (ed.). Teaching Indian Pupils in Public Schools (Proceedings of a Seminar, April 27-May 2, 1967), My 2, 1967, 69 pp. Mesa, AZ: Mesa Public Schools. ERIC ED 021 664.

Povey, John F. "Cultural Self-Expression Through English in American Indian Schools." Florida FL Reporter, Spring-Summer, 1969.

Powers, Joseph F. Brotherhood Through Education: A Guide for Teachers of American Indians. Fayette, IO: Upper Iowa U., 1965.

Price, John. "U.S. and Canadian Indian Urban Ethnic Institutions." Urban Anthropology 4 (Spring, 1975):35-53.

"Primitive Indian Education." School and Society 32(S 13, 1930):356.

"Problems of Indian Poverty." Albany Law Review, Fall, 1971.

Proceedings of a Conference on Early Childhood Education for American Indians, My 22, 1968. ERIC ED 093 567.

Proceedings of the Nevada Inter-tribal Indian Conference (University of Nevada, May 1-2, 1964), Ap 10, 1965, 100 pp. Reno, NV: U. of Nevada, Center for Western North American Studies. ERIC ED 050 872.

Proceedings: Tenth and Eleventh Indian Education Conferences 1969 and 1970, F, 1971, 45 pp. ERIC ED 049 883.

Provance, Eleanor. "Problems of Teaching Senior English in an Intercultural Secondary Boarding School for Eskimo and Indian Students." Master's thesis, Fresno State College, 1963.

Provinse, John. "The American Indian in Transition." American Anthropologist 56(1954):388-394.

Przebeszski, Felix B. "Achievement in Reading in Indian Day School Compared with that in Indian Boarding School." Master's thesis, U. of Arizona, 1942.

Purdy, Joseph D. "Associative Learning Rates of Second, Fourth, and Sixth Grade Indian and White Children Using a Paired-Association Learning Task." Doctoral dissertation, U. of Oklahoma, 1968.

Racism and Sexism Resource Center for Educators. Unlearning "Indian" Stereotypes. A Teaching Unit for Elementary Teachers and Children's Librarians. New York: Council on Interracial Books for Children, 1977.

Rainer, John C. "A Study of Adjustment Problems and a Handbook for Indian Students in the High Schools." Master's thesis, U. of Southern California, 1952.

Ramirez, Bruce A. Background Paper on American Indian Exceptional Children, Ja 17, 1976. ERIC ED 126 085.

Ramirez, Bruce A., and Smith, Barbara J. "Federal Mandates for the Handicapped: Implications for American Indian Children." Exceptional Children 44(Ap, 1978):521-528.

Ransom, J. E. "Education for Indian Life." Clearing House 22(D, 1947):236-238.

Raveling, Ronald R. Popular Ecology, and the American Indian: A Native American Curriculum Unit for Middle and High School. NATAM XII, My, 1971, 23 pp. Minneapolis: U. of Minnesota. ERIC ED 051 915.

Rebert, Robert (ed.). Proceedings: National Indian Bilingual Education Conference (1st, Albuquerque, New Mexico, April 17-19, 1973), 1973. Indian Education Resources Center, Box 1788, Albuquerque, NM 87103.

"The Red School House: An Alternative Education." American Indian Journal 2(F, 1976):10-12.

Redbird, Helen Marie. The Indian and Adult Education. Monmouth, OR: Oregon College of Education, 1971.

Redbird-Selam, Helen, and Selam, Leroy. "Culture Conflict in the Classroom." Social Education 36(My, 1972):512-519.

Reeves, Faye and others. "Indian 'Head Start' Programs--The Child in the Process of Becoming." In The Schooling of Native America, pp. 87-102. Edited by Thomas Thompson. Washington, DC: American Association for Colleges for Teacher Education, Ag, 1978.

Regan, Timothy F., and Pagane, Jules. "The Place of Indian Culture in Adult Education." Adult Leadership 20(Je, 1971):53-55.

Renaud, Rev. Andre. "Acceleration of Socio-Cultural Adjustment and Change in Northern Communities." Journal of American Indian Education 3(Ja, 1964):11-14.

Renaud, Andre. "New Hope for Indian Education." Education Canada 2(S, 1971):4-7.

Rhoades, Everett R. "Barriers to Health Care: The Unique Problems Facing American Indians." Civil Rights Digest 10(Fall, 1977):25-31.

Ricciardelli, Alex F. "Factionalism at Oneida, an Iroquois Indian Community." Doctoral dissertation, U. of Pennsylvania, 1961.

Rice, Boydie E. "A Study of the Relations Between the Degree of Indian Blood and the Specific Tribe and Intelligence and Scholastic Marks of the American Indian." Master's thesis, U. of Kansas, 1936.

Richards, Montana H. and Others. Art and Culture of the American Indian. A Guide for Adult Education Leaders, My, 1971. ERIC ED 101 153.

Ridley, Jack. "Current Trends in Indian Education." Indian Historian 6(Fall, 1973):8-13.

Riggs, F. B. "Is Indian Education What Might Have Been and What Still May Be." Missionary Review of the World 53(Ap, 1930):284-287.

Riley, Robert M. "A Study of the Performance of Some American Indian Students in Selected Intelligence and Educational Tests." Master's thesis, U. of Kansas, 1923.

Robin, Enid F. "Indian Girl, White Girl." Master's thesis, Columbia U., 1943.

Robin, Frederick E. "Culture Contact and Public Opinion in a Bi-cultural Community." Master's thesis, Columbia U., 1941.

Roessel, Robert A. Handbook for Indian Education. Los Angeles: Amerindian Publishing Company, 1836 N. Sierra Bonita, n.d.

_____. "Issues in Indian Education." Contemporary Indian Affairs 1(Spring, 1970):15-21.

_____. "The Right to Be Wrong and the Right to Be Right." Journal of American Indian Education 8(Ja, 1968):1-6.

Roessel, Robert A. and others. Indian Communities in Action. Tempe, AZ: Bureau of Publications, Arizona State U., 1967.

Roessel, Robert A., and Lee, Nicholas (eds.). Indian Education Workshops, Part I--Education of Indian Adults. Part II--Community Development in Indian Education, 1962, 329 pp. Tempe, AZ: Arizona State U. Indian Education Center. ERIC ED 017 855.

Roessel, Ruth. The Role of Indian Studies in American Education. Tempe, AZ: Navajo Community College Press, My, 1974.

Roper, Roger. "Dropouts with Relation to Indian Students." Master's thesis, Wisconsin State College, 1961.

Rose, Winifred. "A Study of Achievement in Indians." Master's thesis, U. of Denver, 1931.

Rosenfelt, Daniel M. "Legal Obligations to Provide Educational Services for Indians." Journal of American Indian Education 13(Ja, 1974):4-8.

_____. "The Renaissance of Indian Education." Inequality in Education 15(N, 1973):13-22.

Ross, Richard M. "Cultural Integrity and American Indian Education." Arizona Law Review 11 (Winter, 1969):641-675.

Roucek, Joseph S. "The Most Oppressed Race in the United States: the Indian." Educational Forum, My, 1965.

Rowe, E. C. "547 White and 268 Indian Children Tested by the Binet-Simon Tests." The Pedagogical Seminary 21(1914):454-468.

Rupiper, O. J. "Multiple Factor Analysis of Academic Achievement: A Comparative Study of Full-Blooded Indian and White Children." Journal of Experimental Education 28(Mr, 1960):177-205.

Russel, Janet. "Indian Children Attend Public School." Minnesota Journal of Education 30 (S, 1949).

Sample, Sarah E. "The Relation of Native Training to the Education of the Indian." Master's thesis, U. of Kansas, 1923.

Sando, Joe. "Native Americans and the American Education System." American Indian Culture Center Journal 2(Spring, 1971)9-11.

Sargent, Nanette. "Library Service to the American Indians in the Southwest." Master's thesis, U. of Missouri, 1970. ERIC ED 063 003.

Sorkin, Alan L. "The Economic and Social Status of the American Indian, 1940-1970." Journal of Negro Education 45(Fall, 1976): 432-447.

_____. "Trends in Employment and Earnings of American Indians." In U.S. Congress, 91st, 1st session, Joint Economic Committee, Subcommittee on Economy in Government. Toward Economic Development for Native American Communities, I, pp. 107-118. Washington, DC: GPO, 1969.

Spalsbury, R. L. "Retardation Studies in Indian Schools." Indian Leader 28(Mr, 1925): 5-16.

Spang, Alonzo. "Counseling the Indian." Journal of American Indian Education, O, 1965.

"Special Education Needs of American Indian Children." Amicus 2(D, 1976):33-36.

Spicer, E. H. Perspectives in American Indian Culture Change. Chicago: U. of Chicago Press, 1961.

_____. "The Sources of American Indian Art." Journal of American Indian Education 1(Ja, 1961):9-12 and 3(My, 1962):26-31.

_____. "Worlds Apart--Cultural Differences in the Modern Southwest." Arizona Quarterly 13(1957):197-229.

Spindler, George D., and Spindler, Louise S. "American Indian Personality Types and Their Sociocultural Roots." The Annals of the American Academy of Political and Social Science 311(My, 1957).

Spolsky, Bernard. "American Indian Bilingual Education." Linguistics 198(O, 1977):57-72.

Ste. Marie, Buffy. "'Victims No More.'" Akwesasne Notes 8(Midwinter, 1975-1976):29

Steere, Caryl et al. Indian Teacher Aide Handbook. College of Education, Arizona State U., Tempe, 1965.

Steiner, Stan. The New Indians. New York: Harper & Row, 1968.

Stensland, Anna Lee. "American Indian Culture: Promises, Problems, and Possibilities." English Journal 60(D, 1971):1195-1200.

_____. "Indian Writers and Indian Lives." Integrateducation 12(N-D, 1974):3-7.

Stone, Veda. "The Indian Child in the Classroom." Journal of American Indian Education, My, 1964.

Streiff, Paul R. "The Role of the Consultant in Indian-Controlled Enterprises." American Indian Culture Center Journal 1(Winter, 1971):16-18.

Strickland, Rennard. "Redeeming Centuries of Dishonor: Legal Education and the American Indian." University of Toledo Law Review, Spring, 1970, pp. 847-890.

Striner, H. E. Toward a Fundamental Program for the Training, Employment, and Economic Equality of the American Indian. Kalamazoo, MI: W. E. Upjohn Institute, Mr, 1968.

"Students Take Over Tuba City High School." Navajo Times, Mr 8, 1973.

Styles of Learning Among American Indians: An Outline for Research. Report and Recommendations of a Conference Held at Stanford University August 8-10, 1968. Washington, DC: Center for Applied Linguistics, F, 1969, 43 pp. ERIC ED 026 638.

Svensson, Frances. "Language as Ideology: The American Indian Case." American Indian Culture and Research Journal 1(1975):29-35.

_____. New Political Power Centers: American Indian. Minneapolis, MN: Burgess, 1972.

Swanton, J. R. "Notes on the Mental Assimilation of Races; White Captives Among the Indians" (bibliography). Washington Academy of Science Journal 16(N 3, 1926):493-502.

Swenson, Janet P. (ed.). Supportive Care, Custody, Placement, and Adoption of American Indian Children. Washington, DC: American Academy of Child Psychiatry, 1977.

Sydiaha, D., and Rempel, J. "Motivational and Attitudinal Characteristics of Indian School Children as Measured by the Thematic Apperception Test." Canadian Psychologist 5 (1964):139-148.

Talbot, Steve. "Free Alcatraz: The Culture of Native American Liberation." Journal of Ethnic Studies 6(Fall, 1978):82-96.

Tax, Sol, and Thomas, Robert K. "Education 'for' American Indians: Threat or Promise?" Florida FL Reporter, Spring-Summer, 1969.

Taylor, Allan Ross. "Nonverbal Communications in Native North America." Semiotica 13 (1975):329-374.

Taylor, Benjamin J., and O'Connor, Dennis J. Indian Manpower Resources in the Southwest: A Pilot Study. Tempe, AZ: Bureau of Business and Economic Research, Arizona State U., 1969.

Taylor, Theodore W. The States and Their Indian Citizens. Washington, DC: GPO, 1972.

Tefft, Stanton K. "Anomy, Values, and Culture Change Among Teen-Age Indians: An Exploratory Study." Sociology of Education 40(Spring, 1967):145-157.

572 / AMERICAN INDIANS

Templeton, Flossie B. "Indian Children's
Interests as Revealed by Their Drawings and
Paintings." Master's thesis, George Peabody
College for Teachers, 1939.

Templin, Leslie G. "Education in the Modern
Missionary Enterprise. A Study of the Ex-
tent, Significance, and Purpose of Education
in the Modern Missionary Work of the
Protestant Churches." Doctoral dissertation,
U. of Kansas, 1946.

Terrell, John Upton. American Indian Almanac.
New York: World, 1971.

Textbooks and the American Indian, 1969. The
Indian Historian Press, 1451 Masonic Avenue,
San Francisco, CA 94117.

Thompson, Hildegard. "Education Among American
Indians: Institutional Aspects." The Annals
of the American Academy of Political and
Social Science 311(My, 1957):95-104.

_____ (ed.). Education for Cross-Cultural En-
richment. Selected Articles from Indian
Education, 1952-1964. Washington, DC: U.S.
Dept. of the Interior, Bureau of Indian
Affairs, Branch of Education, 1964.

Thompson, Thomas (ed.). The Schooling of Native
America. Washington, DC: American Associ-
ation of Colleges for Teacher Education,
Ag, 1978.

Tireman, L. S. "The Bilingual Child and His
Reading Vocabulary." Elementary English 32
(Ja, 1955):33.

Tireman, L. S., and Zintz, Miles V. "Factors
Influencing Learning of a Second Language."
Education 81(Ja, 1961):310-313.

Tireman, L. S. "The Future of Indian Education and Its Possible Contribution to
Education." Indian Education 29(N, 1965):
1-3.

To Our Indian Youth--Generation with a Future.
Salamanca, NY: Seneca National Educational
Foundation, O, 1968, 75 pp. ERIC ED 035 474.

Tompkins, Verlin G. "A Survey of Grading
Procedures in Federal Non-Reservation Boarding Schools for American Indians." Master's
thesis, U. of Kansas, 1961.

Thompson, Laura. Culture in Crisis. New York:
Harper & Bros., 1950.

Townley, Charles. A Preliminary Study of
Library Programs Related to American Indian
Studies Programs in Colleges and Universi-
ties, 1971, 11 pp. ERIC ED 060 982.

_____. Identification of Information Needs of
the American Indian Community That Can Be
Met by Library Services, Je, 1975. ERIC ED
125 835.

Townley, Charles, and Joseph, Alice. "White
Pressures on Indian Personality and
Culture." American Journal of Sociology 53
(1947-1948):17-22.

Townsend, Irving D. "Reading Achievement of
Eleventh and Twelfth Grade Indian Students."
Journal of American Indian Education 3
(O, 1963):9-10.

"Treaties Dealing With Indian Education." In
The Schooling of Native America, pp. 183-185.
Edited by Thomas Thompson. Washington, DC:
American Association of Colleges for Teacher
Education, Ag, 1978.

Trent, Lloyd W. "A Supervisory Survey of a
Small School System." Master's thesis, U.
of North Dakota, 1945.

Trimble, Joseph E. and others. Review of the
Literature on Educational Needs and Problems
of American Indians: 1971 to 1976. Seattle,
WA: Battelle Human Affairs Research Centers,
1977.

Troy, Alica A. "The Indian in Adolescent
Literature 1930-1940 vs. 1960-1970." Doctoral
dissertation, U. of Iowa, 1972.

Tureen, Thomas N. "Remembering Eastern
Indians." Inequality in Education 10(D,
1971):14-18.

Tyler, R. W. "Indian Education as an Example
for All Schools." Elementary School Journal
46(O, 1945):68-69.

Tyler, S. Lyman. Indian Affairs, No. 1. A
Study of the Changes in Policy of the United
States toward Indians. Provo, UT: Brigham
Young U., Institute of American Indian
Studies, 1964, 208 pp. ERIC ED 060 978.

Ulibarri, Horacio. "Teacher Awareness of Socio-
Cultural Differences in Multi-Cultural Class-
rooms." Doctoral dissertation, U. of New
Mexico, 1959.

Underhill, Ruth M. (ed.). Youth Problems on
Indian Reservations. Boulder, CO: U. of
Colorado, Dept. of Sociology, Mr 6, 1970,
73 pp. ERIC ED 049 845.

Underwood, George W. Off-Reservation Boarding
School Survey, My, 1976. ERIC ED 125 804.

Unger, Steven (ed.). The Destruction of
American Indian Families. New York:
Association on American Indian Affairs, 1977.

U.S. American Indian Policy Review Commission.
Task Force Six. Report on Indian Health.
Washington, DC: GPO, 1976.

U.S. Children's Bureau. Indian Child Welfare:
A State-of-the-Field Study. Summary of
Findings and Discussion of Policy Implica-
tions. Washington, DC: Children's
Bureau, 1976.

U.S. Congress, 93rd, 2nd session, Senate, Committee on Government Operations, Permanent Subcommittee on Investigations. Indian Health Care. Hearings... Washington, DC: GPO, 1974.

U.S. Congress, 93rd, 2nd session, Senate, Committee on Interior and Insular Affairs, Subcommittee on Indian Affairs. Indian Child Welfare Programs. Hearings... Washington, DC: GPO, 1975.

U.S. Congress, 94th, 1st session, House of Representatives, Committee on Interior and Insular Affairs, Subcommittee on Indian Affairs. Indian Health Care Improvement Act. Hearings... Serial No. 94-22. Washington, DC: GPO, 1975.

U.S. Congress, 94th, 1st session, Senate, Committee on Interior and Insular Affairs, Subcommittee on Indian Affairs. Implementation of Public Law 93-638, the Indian Self-Determination and Education Assistance Act. Hearings... Washington, DC: GPO, 1976.

U.S. Congress, 94th, 1st session, Senate, Committee on Interior and Insular Affairs, Subcommittee on Indian Affairs. Indian Housing. Hearings... Part 2. Washington, DC: GPO, 1976.

U.S. Congress, 94th, 1st session, Senate, Committee on Post Office and Civil Service, Subcommittee on Compensation and Employment Benefits. Effects of Indian Preference on Employees of Indian Agencies. Hearings... Washington, DC: GPO, 1975.

U.S. Congress, 95th, 1st session, House of Representatives, Committee on Education and Labor, Subcommittee on Elementary, Secondary, and Vocational Education. Indian Education. Hearings... Washington, DC: GPO, 1977.

U.S. Congress, 95th, 1st session, Senate, Select Committee on Indian Affairs. Indian Child Welfare Act of 1977. Hearing... Washington, DC: GPO, 1977.

U.S. Congress, 95th, 2nd session, Senate, Select Committee on Indian Affairs. American Indian Religious Freedom: Hearings... Washington, DC: GPO, 1978.

U.S. Dept. of the Interior, Bureau of Indian Affairs. Answers to Your Questions About American Indians. Washington, DC: GPO, My, 1968.

U.S. Department of the Interior, Bureau of Indian Affairs, Branch of Education. An Interdisciplinary Approach in the Identification of Mentally Retarded Indian Children. Pilot Study. Separate Addendum. Ogden, UT: Defense Printing Service, 1965, 1966.

U.S. Public Health Service. Health of the American Indian. Report of a Regional Task Force. Washington, DC: GPO, Ap, 1973.

"Unrest Hits Public Schools Here." Navajo Times, O 12, 1972.

Untereiner, Wayne W. "Self and Society: Orientations in the Value Systems of Two Cultures." Doctoral dissertation, Harvard U., 1952.

Urban Associates, Inc. A Study of Selected Socio-Economic Characteristics of Ethnic Minorities Based on the 1970 Census. Vol. III: American Indians. Washington, DC: Office of Special Concerns, U.S. Department of Health, Education, and Welfare, J1, 1974.

Van Well, Mary S. "The Educational Aspects of the Missions in the Southwest." Doctoral dissertation, Marquette U., 1941.

Vaughan, Janet E. Some Suggestions for Librarians in High Schools with Native American Students. NATAM XIV. Minneapolis, MN: U. of Minnesota, My, 1971, 21 pp. ERIC ED 051 917.

Vogel, Virgil J. "After 80 Years: The Indians Rise Again." New Politics 8(Spring, 1970): 62-72.

_____. "American Indian Ways in Medicine." Science and Children 9(Mr, 1972):14-17.

_____. "Indian Ways With Farming." The American Way 4(J1, 1971):22-28. [Published by American Airlines]

Voget, Fred. "The American Indian in Transition: Reformation and Status Innovations." American Journal of Sociology 62(My, 1957).

Vogt, Evan Z. "The Acculturation of American Indians." The Annals of the American Academy of Political and Social Science 311(My, 1957): 137-146.

Wabaunsee, A. John. "Native American Viewpoint." In Bilingual Education: Current Perspectives, Vol. III: Law. Edited by Herbert Teitelbaum and Others. Arlington, VA: Center for Applied Linguistics, S, 1977.

Walker, Joe. "'What Has Happened to American Indian Must Not Happen to the Vietnamese.'" Muhammad Speaks, Ja 10, 1969. [About an address by Marcia Hall, an Indian American]

Wasson, Wilfred C. "Hindrances to Indian Education." Educational Leadership 28 (D, 1970):278-280.

Watée, Nishawi Aween, and Sassen-Koob, Saskia. "A New Direction for the Native Movement?" Journal of Ethnic Studies 6(Fall, 1978):122-126.

Watts, Mildred. "Indian Children's Interests by Literary Preference and Creative Writings." Master's thesis, George Peabody College for Teachers, 1931.

Wax, Murray. "American Indian Education as a Cultural Transaction." Teachers College Record, My, 1963.

_____. Dropout of American Indians at the Secondary Level. Atlanta, GA: Emory U., 1964.

_____. Gophers or Gadflies: Problems of Indian School Boards. American Educational Research Association meeting, Mr, 1970, 14 pp. ERIC ED 041 684.

Wax, Murray, and Wax, Rosalie. "Indian Education for What?" Midcontinent American Studies Journal 6(1965):164-170.

_____ and _____. "Cultural Deprivation as an Educational Ideology." Journal of American Indian Education 3(Ja, 1964):15-18.

_____ and _____. "More on Cross-Cultural Education." Current Anthropology 11(Je, 1961):255-256.

_____ and _____. Summary and Summary and Observations in the Dakotas and Minnesota, Indian Communities and Project Head Start. Report No. OEO-520, S 15, 1965, 43 pp. ERIC ED 013 670.

Wax, Murray and others. Indian Communities and Project Head Start. Summary and Observations in the Dakotas and Minnesota, Together with an Appraisal of Possibilities for a Head Start Program among the Potawatomi Indians of Kansas. OEO Report 520, S 15, 1967, 65 pp. ERIC ED 016 510.

Wax, Rosalie H., and Thomas, Robert K. "American Indians and White People." Phylon 22(1961):305-317.

_____ and _____. "The Warrior Drop-Outs." Trans-action 4(1967):40-46.

Weaver, Thomas. Indians in Rural and Reservation Areas. Sacramento, CA: California Office of State Printing, F, 1966.

Weaver, Yvonne J. "A Closer Look at TESL on the Reservation." Journal of American Indian Education 6(Ja, 1967):26-31.

Weberg, Harold O. "The Role of Education in the Social, Cultural and Economic Development of an Indian Community." Master's thesis, Saint Cloud State College, Saint Cloud, MN, 1963.

[Weinberg, Meyer] "[Recent Research on] Indian Americans." Research Review of Equal Education 1(Summer, 1977):3-17.

Weisser, Elizabeth. "A Diagnostic Study of Indian Handwriting." Master's thesis, U. of Denver, 1930.

Werner, Oswald. "Doctor Responds to Proposed Indian Med School." Navajo Times, D 12, 1974.

Wesemann, Ralph E. and others. Community Background Reports: Three Boarding Schools (Phoenix Indian School, Phoenix, Arizona; Theodore Roosevelt School, Fort Apache, Arizona; Chemawa Indian School, Salem, Oregon). National Study of American Indian Education, Series I, No. 15. Final Report. Chicago, IL: U. of Chicago, Je, 1970, 21 pp. ERIC ED 042 551.

Wesley, Clarence. "Indian Education." Journal of American Indian Education 1(Je, 1961):4-7.

Whelan, Mary. "Reading Achievement and Intelligence Scores of Indian Children." Master's thesis, Laval U., Quebec, 1957.

White, John R. "Civil Rights and the Native American." Integrated Education (N-D, 1973):31-34.

Whitmore, Gladys E. "A Survey of the Curricula of the Indian High Schools of the United States." Master's thesis, U. of Southern California, 1941.

Wibich, Manfred, and Winter, Urs. Kapitalismus und Indianer in den USA. Frankfurt: Verlag Marxistische Blätter, 1976.

Wilber, George L. and others. Minorities in the Labor Market. Vol. I: Spanish Americans and Indians in the labor market. Lexington, KY: Social Welfare Research Institute, U. of Lexington, 1975.

Wiles, David K. "Separate Schools for a 'Non-Chic' Minority?" Journal of American Indian Education 15(O, 1975):17-22.

Wilcox, Wilma E. "Early Indian Schools and Education along the Missouri." Master's thesis, U. of Iowa, 1928.

Wilkenson, Gerald. "The Native American Family." Human Services in the Rural Environment 3 (S, 1978):8-19.

Willey, Darrell S. Interim Report for an Interdisciplinary Institute for In-Service Training of Teachers and Other School Personnel to Accelerate the School Acceptance of Indian, Negro, and Spanish-Speaking Pupils from the Southwest, Ag, 1966. ERIC ED 045 740.

Wilson, James. "Vanishing Native." Civil Rights Digest, Winter, 1969.

Wilson, Roger. "Teachers for Indian Children." " In The Schooling of Native America, pp. 155-167. Edited by Thomas Thompson. Washington, DC: American Association of Colleges for Teacher Education, Ag, 1978.

Witherspoon, Y. T. "Measurement of Indian Children's Achievement in the Academic Tool Subjects." Journal of American Indian Education 1(My, 1962).

Witherow, Judy. "Native American Mother." Quest: A Feminist Quarterly 3(Spring, 1977).

Witt, Shirley Hill. "Native Women Today. Sexism and the Indian Woman." Civil Rights Digest 6(Spring, 1974):29-35.

Witt, Shirley Hill, and Steiner, Stan (eds.). The Way: An Anthology of American Indian Literature. New York: Knopf, 1972.

Wolcott, Harry F. "Anthropology and Education." Review of Educational Research, F, 1967.

Woods, Doris (ed.). Proceedings: Indian Education Conferences (13th and 14th, Arizona State University, Tempe, Arizona, 1972 and 1973), 1973. ERIC ED 089 917.

Woods, Richard G., and Harkins, Arthur M. An Examination of the 1968-69 Urban Indian Hearings by the National Council on Indian Opportunity. Part I: Education. Minneapolis, MN: U. of Minnesota, Je, 1971, 78 pp. ERIC ED 051 949.

_____ and _____. An Examination of the 1968-1969 Urban Indian Hearings Held by the National Council on Indian Opportunity. Part II: Interrracial Aspects. Minneapolis, MN: U. of Minnesota, Jl, 1971, 65 pp. ERIC ED 051 950.

_____ and _____. An Examination of the 1968-1969 Urban Indian Hearings Held by the National Council on Indian Opportunity, Part III: Indian Self-Definitions. Minneapolis, MN: U. of Minnesota, Je, 1971, 24 pp. ERIC ED 052 872.

_____ and _____. An Examination of the 1968-69 Urban Indian Hearings Held by the National Council on Indian Opportunity. Part IV: The Indian Center. Minneapolis, MN: U. of Minnesota, Jl, 1971, 36 pp. ERIC ED 052 873.

Yandell, Maurine D. "Some Difficulties which Indian Children Encounter with Idioms in Reading." Master's thesis, U. of New Mexico, 1959.

Yaz, William [pseud.]. "Teachers and Administrators in American Indian Education." Indian Historian 6(Summer, 1973):18-22.

Yazzie, Ned G. "Development of Indian Child is Different." Navajo Times 19(My 4, 1978):10, 38.

Yeadon, David. When the Earth Was Young: Songs of the American Indian. New York: Doubleday, 1978.

Yeh, Thomas Yen-Ran, and Frosio, Eugene T. "The Treatment of the American Indian in the Library of Congress E-F Schedule." Library Resources and Technical Services 15(Spring, 1971):122-131.

Yinger, J. Milton, and Simpson, George Eaton (eds.). American Indians Today. Philadelphia: American Academy of Political and Social Science, 1978.

Young, Biloine D. "The American Indian: Citizen in Captivity." Saturday Review 48 (D 11, 1965):25.

Youngman, Gerldine, and Sadongei, Margaret. "Counseling the American Indian Child." Elementary School Guidance and Counseling 8 (My, 1974):273-277.

Zeligs, Rose. "Children's Concepts and Stereotypes of Norwegian, Jew, Scotch, Canadian, Swedish, and American Indian." Journal of Educational Research 45(S, 1951):349-360.

Zenter, Harry. "Parental Behavior and Student Attitudes Toward Further Training Among Indian and Non-Indian Students in Oregon and Alberta." Alberta Journal of Educational Research 9(Mr, 1963):22-30.

_____. "Parental Behavior and Student Attitudes Toward High School Graduation Among Indian and Non-Indian Students in Oregon and Alberta." Alberta Journal of Educational Research 8(D, 1962):211-219.

_____. The Pre-Neolithic Ethic--Avenue or Barrier to Assimilation. Calgary, Canada: U. of Alberta, 1969.

Ziller, Robert C. and others. "Self-other Orientations of Indian and American Adolescents." Journal of Personality, Je, 1968.

Zimmerman, Harry E. "The Indian's Ability to Learn Mathematics According to Degree of Indian Blood." Master's thesis, Kansas State Teacher's College, Pittsburgh, 1934.

Zintz, Miles V. Education Across Cultures. Dubuque, IA: William C. Brown Book Co., 1963.

_____. "Problems of Classroom Adjustment of Indian Children in Public Elementary Schools in the Southwest." Science Education 46 (Ap, 1962):261-269.

Ziontz, Alvin J. "New Consciousness: The Indian Uprising." Civil Liberties, D, 1972.

Zurcher, Louis A. "The Leader and the Lost: A Case Study of Indigenous Leadership in a Poverty Program Community Action Committee." Genetic Psychology Monographs, 1967, pp. 23-93.

Bibliographies

American Indians, An Annotated Bibliography of
Selected Library Resources. Minnesota State
Dept. of Education, St. Paul; U. of
Minnesota, Minneapolis College of Education,
1970, 171 pp. ERIC ED 040 004.

An Annotated Bibliography of Books for Libraries
Serving Children of Indian Ancestry.
Toronto, Canada: Indian-Eskimo Association
of Canada, Mr 18, 1968, 13 pp. ERIC ED 041
655.

Attneave, Carolyn L., and Kelso, Dianne R.
(comps.). American Indian Annotated
Bibliography of Mental Health, Vol. I,
1977. ERIC ED 151 135.

Ballentine, Carol (comp.). Current North
American Indian Periodicals. 2nd ed.
Washington, DC: Center for the Study of Man,
Smithsonian Institution, 1972.

Books About Indians and Reference Material.
Boise, ID: Idaho State Dept. of Education,
1971, 177 pp. ERIC ED 052 887.

Brooks, I. R. (comp.). Native Education in
Canada and the United States: A
Bibliography. Calgary: Office of Educational Development, Indian Students University Program Services, U. of Calgary, 1976.

Brugge, David M., Correll, J. Lee, and Watson,
Editha L. (comps.). Navajo Bibliography.
Window Rock, AZ: Navajo Tribal Museum, 1967.

Bureau of Naval Personnel, General Military
Training and Support Division, Library
Services Branch (comp.). Indian and Mexican
Americans. A Selective, Annotated Biblio-
graphy. Washington, DC: GPO, 1972.

Cashman, M. (comp.). Bibliography of American
Ethnology. Rye, NY: Todd Publications,
1976.

Correll, J. Lee and others. Navajo Bibliography with Subject Index. Revised Edition.
Window Rock, AZ: Navajo Tribe, 1969, 398
pp. ERIC ED 050 862.

Current North American Indian Periodicals.
Center for the Study of Man, Smithsonian
Institution, Washington, DC 20560.

Dockstader, Frederick J. (comp.). The American
Indian in Graduate Studies: A Bibliography
of Theses and Dissertations. 2 vols.
New York: Museum of the American Indian,
Heye Foundation, 1975.

ERIC Clearinghouse on Rural Education and Small
Schools. American Indian Education. A
Selected Bibliography (with ERIC Abstracts),
ERIC/CRESS Supplement No. 4, D, 1973.
ERIC ED 086 378.

ERIC/CRESS, American Indian Education. A
Selected Bibliography (with ERIC Abstracts).
ERIC/CRESS Supplement No. 3. Washington,
DC: GPO, Mr, 1973.

Feehan, Paul G. (comp.). A Bibliography of
Representative Materials on the Lumbee
Indians of Robeson County, North Carolina,
Ap, 1978. ERIC ED 153 660.

Garrow, Larry and others (comps.). A Selected
Bibliography of the Mohawk People, 1974.
ERIC ED 093 514.

Gill, George A. (comp.). Index to the "Journal
of American Indian Education," Vol. I,
No. 1, 1961-Vol. 13, No. 2, 1974, F, 1974.
ERIC ED 091 100.

Gomez, Darva R. (comp.). Bibliography: A
Resource on the Education of American
Indians, O, 1976. ERIC ED 135 541.

Green, Vicki. Annotated Bibliography on
Indian Education, 1969, 35 pp. ERIC ED
059 819.

Harkins, Arthur M. and others (comps.). A
Bibliography of Urban Indians in the United
States. Minneapolis, MN: U. of Minnesota,
Center for Urban and Regional Affairs, Jl,
1971, 44 pp. ERIC ED 052 871.

Heizer, Robert F. (comp.). The Indians of
California. A Critical Bibliography.
Bloomington, IN: Indiana U. Press, 1976.

Helen, June (comp.). The Indians of the
Subarctic. A Critical Bibliography.
Bloomington, IN: Indiana U. Press, 1976.

Henry, Jeannette (ed.). Index to Literature
on the American Indian 1972. San Francisco,
CA: Indian Historian Press, 1974.

Henry, Jeannette and others (comps.). Index to
Literature on the American Indian 1970.
San Francisco, CA: Indian Historian Press,
1972.

Hippler, Arthur E. (comp.). Eskimo Accultura-
tion. A Selected, Annotated Bibliography of
Alaskan and Other Eskimo Acculturation
Studies, Ag, 1970. Institute of Social,
Economic, and Government Research, U. of
Alaska, College, AK 99701.

Hippler, Arthur E., and Wood, John R. (comps.).
The Subarctic Athaboscans: A Selected
Annotated Bibliography. Fairbanks, AK:
Institute of Social, Economic, and Government
Research, U. of Alaska, 1974.

Hirschfelder, Arlene B. (comp.). American Indian
Authors. A Representative Bibliography.
New York: Association on American Indian
Affairs, 1970.

Hodge, William H. (comp.). A Bibliography of
Contemporary North American Indians...
New York: Interland Publications, 1975.

Holland, Nora (comp.). A Selected ERIC Biblio-
graphy on the Education of Urban American
Indian and Mexican American Children.
Urban Disadvantaged Series No. 5., n.d.
IRCD, Teachers College, Columbia U.,
New York, NY 10027.

Index to Literature on the American Indian 1971.
San Francisco, CA: The Indian Historian
Press, 1972.

Indian Bibliography of BIA Instructional Service
Center; First Edition, 1970 (with Addendum).
Washington, DC: Bureau of Indian Affairs
(Dept. of Interior), 1970, 48 pp. ERIC ED
059 815.

Indian-Eskimo Association of Canada (comp.).
An Annotated Bibliography of Books for
Libraries Servicing Children of Indian An-
cestry, 1971 The Association, 277 Victoria
Street, Toronto 200, Ontario, Canada.

Institute of Indian Services and Research
(comp.). Bibliography of Nonprint Instructional Materials on the American Indians.
Salt Lake City, UT: Brigham Young U. Press,
1972.

Isto, Sarah A. (comp.). Cultures in the North:
Aleut Athaboscan Indian, Eskimo, Haida
Indian, Tlingit Indian, Tsimpshian Indian;
Multi-Media Resource List. Fairbanks Center
for Northern Educational Research, U. of
Alaska, 1975.

Iverson, Peter (comp.). The Navajos. A Critical
Bibliography. Bloomington, IN: Indiana U.
Press, 1976.

Jacobson, Angeline (comp.). Contemporary Native
American Literature: A Selected and Partially
Annotated Bibliography. Metuchen, NJ:
Scarecrow, 1977.

Kahl, June (comp.). Non-Stereotyped Indian
Literature: A Bibliography, Ag, 1976.
ERIC ED 128 795.

Kaiser, Ernest (comp.). "American Indians and
Mexican Americans: A Selected Bibliography."
Freedomways, Fall, 1969.

Keller, Charles (comp.) and others. A
Selected Bibliography of Materials Related to
American Indian Education, Economics and
Deviant Behavior. Charleston, IL: Eastern
Illinois U., N, 1970, 42 pp. ERIC ED 055
717.

Lass-Woodfin, Mary Jo (ed.). Books on American
Indians and Eskimos: A Selection Guide for
Children and Young Adults. Chicago: American
Library Association, 1977.

Locklear, Janie Maynor, and Oxendine, Drenna J.
(comps.). "The Lumbee Indians. A Bibliography." Indian Historian 7(Winter, 1974):
52-54.

McCarthy, Jean, and Graustein, Carol L.
(comps.). An Annotated Bibliography of Young
People's Fiction on American Indians, 1972.
ERIC ED 060 699.

Martinez, Cecilia J., and Heathman, James
(comps.). American Indian Education, A
Selected Bibliography. University Park, NM:
New Mexico State U., ERIC Clearinghouse on
Rural Education and Small Schools, Ag, 1969,
98 pp. ERIC ED 030 780.

Mathieson, Moira B. (comp.). A Brief Bibliography on Teacher Education and American
Indians, Ap, 1974. ERIC ED 090 146.

Mech, Joyce (comp.). An Annotated Bibliography
of Selected Research Reports, Articles and
Papers on Indian Education in the United
States and Canada from 1968-1973, Ap, 1974.
ERIC ED 091 128.

Medicine, Beatrice (comp.). "The Role of Women
in Native American Societies. A Bibliography." Indian Historian 8(Summer, 1975):
50-53.

Mickinock, Rey. "The Plight of the Native
American." School Library Journal 18
(S, 1971):46-49. [Bibliographic essay]

"Missionaries vs. Native Americans in the
Northwest. A Bibliography for Reevaluation."
Indian Historian 5(Summer, 1972):46-48

Native American Rights Fund and National Indian
Law Library. Catalogue. An Index to Indian
Legal Materials and Resources. Vol. 1,
1973-1974, 1973. Native American Rights Fund,
1506 Broadway, Boulder, CO 80302.

Naumer, Janet Noll (comp.). "American Indians:
A Bibliography of Sources." American
Libraries 1(O, 1970):861-864.

New Mexico State University. American Indian
Education...Supplement No. 5, F, 1975. ERIC
ED 100 547.

Newman, Killian (comp.). A Preliminary Bibliography of Selected Children's Books About
American Indians. New York: Association on
American Indian Affairs, 432 Park Avenue
South, New York, NY 10016, 1969. ["Each
book listed ... was read, reviewed, and
recommended by an American Indian."]

Noble, Vincente and others (comps.). Counseling
the Native American Client: An Annotated
Bibliography of Journal Literature, 1964-
1974, 1974. ERIC ED 130 200.

Nufziger, Alyce J. (comp.). American Indian
Education, A Selected Bibliography, Supple-
ment No. 1. University Park, NM: New Mexico
State U., O, 1970, 132 pp. ERIC ED 044 213.

Petit, Patrick F. (comp.). Selected Annotated
Bibliography on Urban Migration and Adjust-
ment of American Indians. Lawrence, KS:
Department of Sociology, U. of Kansas, 1969.

Prucha, Francis Paul (comp.). A Biblio-
graphical Guide to the History of Indian-
White Relations in the United States.
Chicago: U. of Chicago Press, 1977.

Ray, Robert B. (comp.). The Indians of Maine:
A Bibliographical Guide. Portland, ME:
Maine Historical Society, 1972.

Russell, Noma and others (eds.). A Bibliography of Selected Materials on the Navajo
and Zuni Indians, 1974. ERIC ED 124 367.

Sabatini, Joseph D. (comp.). American Indian
Law: A Bibliography of Books, Law Review
Articles and Indian Periodicals.
Albuquerque, NM: American Indian Law
Center, U. of New Mexico, Ja, 1973.

Sayre, Robert F. (comp.). "A Bibliography and
an Anthology of American Indian Literature."
College English 35(Mr, 1974).

Scoon, Annabelle R. Bibliography of Indian
Education and Curriculum Innovation.
Albuquerque, NM: Albuquerque Indian
School, Ja, 1971, 62 pp. ERIC ED 053 614.

Sheldon, Dorothy L., and Sitter, Victoria J.
A Selective Bibliography of American Indian
Literature, History, and Culture. The
General College Studies, U. of Minnesota,
Vol. V. No. 3. U. of Minnesota, 1968, 20
pp. ERIC ED 030 526.

Smith, Dwight L. (comp.). Indians of the
United States and Canada. A Bibliography.
Santa Barbara, CA: ABC-CL 10, 1974.

Snodgrass, Marjorie P. (comp.). Economic
Development of American Indians and Eskimos,
1930 through 1967: A Bibliography.
Washington, DC: Departmental Library, U.S.
Department of Interior, Je, 1968.

Spolsky, Bernard and others. Analytical Bibliography of Navajo Reading Materials. Revised
and Enlarged Edition. Albuquerque, NM:
New Mexico U., Je, 1970, 108 pp. ERIC ED
043 413.

Stensland, Anna Lee (comp.). Literature By and
About the American Indian. Urbana, IL:
National Council of Teachers of English,
1973.

Tahushasha, Wenonah Tansauga (comp.).
Bibliography on the Native American
Experience. Springfield, IL: Illinois
Commission on Human Relations, 1973.

Ullom, Judith C. (comp.). Folklore of the
North American Indians. An Annotated
Bibliography. Washington, DC: GPO, 1969.

U.S. Department of Housing and Urban Development, Library (comp.). The North American
Indian: A Bibliography of Community Development. Washington, DC: GPO, 1975.

Williams, Carroll Warner, and Bird, Gloria
(eds.). A Filmography for American Indian
Education, 1973. Zia Cine, Inc., P.O. Box
493, Santa Fe, NM 87501

7.
OTHER ETHNIC GROUPS

Asian Americans

Chinese Americans

Abbott, Kenneth A. "Cultural Change, Psychosocial Functioning, and the Family: A Case Study in the Chinese-American Community of San Francisco." Doctoral dissertation, U. of California, Berkeley, D, 1970.

Action for Boston Community Development. The Chinese in Boston. 1970. Boston: ABCD, F 16, 1971.

Anderson, David L. "The Diplomacy of Discrimination: Chinese Exclusion, 1876-1882." California History 57(Spring, 1978):32-45.

Arreola, Daniel D. "Locke, California: Persistence and Change in the Cultural Landscape of a Delta Chinatown." Master's thesis, California State U., Hayward, 1975.

Barlow, Janelle M. S. "The Images of the Chinese, Japanese, and Koreans in American Secondary School World History Textbooks, 1900-1970." Doctoral dissertation, U. of California, Berkeley, 1973.

Barrett, Anne. "PBH Teachers, Counsels in Chinatown." Harvard Crimson, My 4, 1976. [Boston]

Barth, Gunther. Bitter Strength: A History of the Chinese in the United States, 1850-1870. Cambridge, MA: Harvard U. Press, 1964.

Be Dunnah, Gary P. A History of the Chinese in Nevada: 1855-1904. San Francisco, CA: R and E Research Associates, 1973 reprint.

Bernstein, Paul. "From China With Filial Love." Los Angeles Times, Ag 8, 1976. [Chinese-American Golden Age Association, Los Angeles]

Beth. "Why There Were Freedom Schools in Chinatown: The Chinese Response to Desegregation." No More Teachers Dirty Looks! 3(Spring, 1973):17.

Book, Susan W. The Chinese in Butte County, California, 1860-1920. San Francisco, CA: R and E Research Associates, 1976.

Bourne, Peter G. "The Chinese Student: Acculturation and Mental Illness." Psychiatry 38(Ag, 1975):269-277.

Boyce, Conal. "Chinese Classroom Metalanguage." Journal of the Chinese Language Teachers Association 13(F, 1978):1-25. [Glossary of 417-item Chinese-English vocabulary]

Boyd, Monica. "The Chinese in New York, California, and Hawaii: A Study of Socioeconomic Differentials." Phylon 32(Summer, 1971):198-206.

_____. "Oriental Immigration: The Experience of the Chinese, Japanese, and Filipino Populations in the United States." International Migration Review 5(Fall, 1970).

Caldwell, Dan. "The Negroization of the Chinese Stereotype in California." Southern California Quarterly (Je, 1971):123-131.

Californians of Japanese, Chinese, and Filipino Ancestry: Population, Education, Employment, Income, Je, 1965. ERIC ED 023 509.

Carranaco, Lynwood. "The Chinese in Humboldt County, California." Journal of the West, Ja, 1973.

Carter, Gregg Lee. "Social Demography of the Chinese in Nevada: 1870-1880." Nevada Historical Society Quarterly 18(Summer, 1975).

Casey, Theresa Agnes. "A Study of the Difficulties in English Usage Encountered by American-born Chinese Children." Master's thesis, Stanford U., 1940.

Chan, Yih-chyi N. L. "Educational Needs in Intergenerational Conflict: A Study of Immigrant Families in New York's Chinatown." Doctoral dissertation, Cornell U., 1978. Univ. Microfilms Order No. 7817763.

580 / OTHER ETHNIC GROUPS

Chang, Francis H., and Tang, Stephen. "A Neighborhood Health Center. One Community's Solution." Civil Rights Digest 10(Fall, 1977):19-23. [Chinese community in Boston]

Chang, Francis Yung. "A Study of the Movement to Segregate Chinese Pupils in the San Francisco Schools Up to 1885." Doctoral dissertation, Stanford U., 1936.

Chang, James. A. "Survey of Educational Needs of Boston Chinese." Master's thesis, Boston College, 1953.

Chang, Shu Yuan. "China or Taiwan: The Political Crisis of the Chinese American Intellectual." Amerasia Journal 2(Fall, 1973): 47-81.

Chang, William Bun Chin. "The Myth of Chinese Success in Hawaii." Hawaii Pono 1(0, 1971): 59-76.

Chao, R. Chinese Immigrant Children. New York: City U. of New York, 1977. [New York City Chinatown]

Char, Tin-yuke. The Bamboo Path: Life and Writings of a Chinese in Hawaii. Boston: Nimrod Press, 1977.

_____. "Legal Restrictions on Chinese in English-speaking Countries of the Pacific-I." Chinese Social and Political Science Review 16(1932):472-513.

_____ (ed.). The Sandalwood Mountains: Readings and Stories of the Early Chinese in Hawaii. Honolulu: U. Press of Hawaii, 1975.

Che, Wai-Kin. "The Young American-Chinese in New Orleans in the 1960's." Master's thesis, Mississippi College, 1966.

Chen, I. Hsuan Julia. The Chinese Community in New York 1920-1940. San Francisco, CA: R and E Research Associates, 1974 reprint.

Chen, Martin K. "Intelligence and Bilingualism on Independent Variates in a Study of Junior High School Students of Chinese Descent." Doctoral dissertation, U. of California, Berkeley, 1964.

Chen, Pei-Ngor. "The Chinese Community in Los Angeles." Social Casework 51(D, 1970):591-598.

Cheng, Te-ch'ao. "Acculturation of the Chinese in the United States. A Philadelphia Study." Doctoral dissertation, U. of Pennsylvania, 1948.

Chin, Frank. "The Year of the Dragon." Journal of Ethnic Studies 2(Spring, 1974):25-85. [Script of a play]

Chin, Peter. "Busing and Chinatown." Bridge 3 (My, 1975):10-13. [Boston]

Chin, Rocky. "New York Chinatown Today: Community in Crisis." Amerasia Journal 1 (Mr, 1971):1-24.

"Chinatown, Sacramento." Sacramento Bee, special supplement, Ja 17, 1971.

Chinese American Librarians Association. Directory of Chinese American Libraries, 1977. ERIC ED 148 402.

"Chinese and Japanese in America." Annals 34 (1909):222 pp.

Chinese Historical Society of America. The Life, Influence and the Role of the Chinese in the United States, 1776-1960, Jl 10, 1975. ERIC ED 141 422.

Chinese Labor Committee. History of Chinese Working People in America. San Francisco: United Front Press, 1974.

Ching, Frank. "Crime in New York's Chinatown." Bridge 3(Ap, 1974):11-14.

Chinn, Florence W. "Religious Education in the Chinese Community of San Francisco." Master's thesis, U. of Chicago, 1920.

Chinn, Thomas W. "New Chapters in Chinese American History." California History 57 (Spring, 1978):2-7.

_____ (ed.). A History of the Chinese in California. San Francisco: Chinese Historical Society of America, 1969.

Chiu, Lian-Hwang. "Manifested Anxiety in Chinese and American Children." Journal of Psychology 79(N, 1971):273-284.

Chiu, P. Chinese Labor in California. Madison, WI: U. of Wisconsin Press, 1963.

Chow, Carmen. "I Wor Kuen in Chinatown New York." Hawaii Pono 1(Ap, 1971):58-71.

Chow, Christopher, and Leong, Russell. "A Pioneer Chinatown Teacher: An Interview with Alice Fong Yu." Amerasia Journal 5(1978): 75-86. [Teacher at Commodore Stockton Elementary School, San Francisco, 1926-1957]

Chow, Willard T. "Oakland's Chinatown: The Dynamics of Inner City Adjustment." China Geographer 4(Spring, 1976):1-17.

_____. The Reemergence of an Inner City: The Pivot of Chinese Settlement in the East Bay Region of the San Francisco Bay Area. San Francisco: R & E Research Associates, 1977.

Choy, Philip P. "Golden Mountain of Lead: The Chinese Experience in California." California Historical Quarterly 50(S, 1971).

Chu, D., and Chu, S. Passage to the Golden Gate: A History of the Chinese in America to 1910. Garden City, NY: Doubleday, 1967.

Chu, George. "Chinatowns in the Delta: The Chinese in the Sacramento-San Joaquin Delta, 1870-1960." California Historical Society Quarterly, Mr, 1970.

Chue, King-Ho. "The Education of Chinese Children in Washington, D.C." Master's thesis, George Washington U., n.d.

Chun-Hoon, Lowell. "Jade Snow Wong and the Fate of Chinese-American Identity." Amerasian Journal 1(Mr, 1971):52-63.

Clark, Malcolm, Jr. "The Bigot Disclosed: 90 Years of Nativism." Oregon Historical Quarterly 75(1974):109-190.

Cohen, Lucy M. "Entry of Chinese to the Lower South from 1865 to 1870: Policy Dilemmas." Social Studies 17(Spring, 1978): 5-37.

Cole, Cheryl L. "Chinese Exclusion: The Capitalist Perspective of the Sacramento Union, 1850-1882." California History 57 (Spring, 1978):8-31.

Cole, Mary Howard. "Our Other Customers: Chinatown's Library." Wilson Library Bulletin 45(Ja, 1971):482-484.

Conroy, John. "The Dark Side of Chinatown." Chicago 27(My, 1978):112-119, 184-192.

Coolidge, Mary R. Chinese Immigration, n.p., 1909.

Corbett, P. Scott, and Corbett, Nancy Parker. "The Chinese in Oregon, c. 1870-1880." Oregon Historical Quarterly 78(Mr, 1977): 73-85.

Courtney, William J. San Francisco Anti-Chinese Ordinances, 1850-1900. San Francisco, CA: R and E Research Associates, 1974 reprint.

Currier, Viola N. "The Chinese Web in Oregon History." Master's thesis, U. of Oregon, 1928.

Daniels, Roger (ed.). Anti-Chinese Violence in North America. New York: Arno, 1979.

De Bary, Mary B. "A Look at S.F. Chinatown Sheds Light on School Boycott." Muhammad Speaks, N 19, 1971. [San Francisco, CA]

Desmond, Sister M. B. "The History of the City of Marysville, California." Master's thesis, Dominican College, 1962. [Touches on Chinese-Americans]

De Vos, G. A., and Abbott, K. A. "The Chinese Family in San Francisco: A Preliminary Study." A group project directed by the above. Master's thesis, U. of California, Berkeley, 1966.

Djang, Hisang-Lan. "The Adjustment in American Culture of the Chinese Children in China-town, Chicago, and Its Educational Implications." Doctoral dissertation, Northwestern U., 1940.

Dunbar, Agnes Mary. "The Second-Generation Chinese in New York City's Chinatown (and Especially the Vocational Problems of the American-born Females in that Community)." Master's thesis, Columbia U., 1937.

Dusel, John P. "The Adjustment of American-Chinese Students in a California High School." Master's thesis, Stanford U., 1946.

Edson, Christopher H. The Chinese in Eastern Oregon, 1860-1890. San Francisco: R and E Research Associates, 1974 reprint.

Fan, Chen Yung. "The Chinese Language School of San Francisco in Relation to Family Integration and Cultural Identity." Doctoral dissertation, Duke U., 1976.

Fan, Tiu-Chiu. Chinese Residents in Chicago. San Francisco: R and E Research Associates, 1974 reprint.

Farrar, Nancy E. The Chinese in El Paso. El Paso, TX: Texas Western Press, U. of Texas, 1972.

_____. "The History of the Chinese in El Paso: A Case Study of an Urban Immigrant Group in the American West." Master's thesis, U. of Texas at El Paso, 1970.

Fernandes, Norman Almeida. "The San Francisco Board of Education and the Chinese Community: Segregation-Desegregation, 1850-1975." Doctoral dissertation, U. of Denver, 1976. Univ. Microfilms Order No. 77-447.

Fong, Peter. "Youth Problem in Chinatown." Bridge 6(Fall, 1978):52-53. [New York City]

Fong, Stanley L. M. "Assimilation and Changing Social Roles of Chinese Americans." Journal of Social Issues 29(1973):115-127.

_____. "Assimilation of Chinese in America: Changes in Orientation and Social Perspection." American Journal of Sociology, N, 1965. [Study of 336 Chinese college students living in the U.S.]

_____. "Identity Conflicts of Chinese Adolescents in San Franciso." In Minority Group Adolescents in the United States. Edited by Eugene B. Brody. Baltimore, MD: Williams and Wilkins, 1968.

Fox, D., and Jordan, V. "Racial Preference and Identification of Black, American, Chinese and White Children." Genetic Psychology Monographs 88(1973):229-286.

Frignet, Ernest. La Californie. 2nd ed. Paris: n.p., 1867. [Segregated schools for Chinese children]

Fukumoto, Dennis K. "Chinese and Japanese in California, 1900-1920: A Case Study of the Impact of Discrimination." Doctoral dissertation, U. of Southern California, 1976.

Ganschow, Thomas W. "The Chinese in America: A Historical Perspective." In Selected Proceedings of the 3rd Annual Conference on Minority Studies, April, 1975, pp. 235-245. Edited by George E. Carter, James R. Parker, and Carol Sweeney. La Crosse, WI: Institute for Minority Studies, U. of Wisconsin-La Crosse, 1976.

Gao, Ren-Ying. "A Social Survey of Chinatown, Boston, Massachusetts." Master's thesis, Boston U., 1941.

Go, Rance, and Wong, Godart H. "Bad Times on Gold Mountain." Bridge 3(Je, 1974):22-27. [Critical analysis of a broadcast documentary on Chinese American life]

Goo, Thomas York-tong. Before the Gods. New York: Helios Book Publishing Co., 1976. [Chinese in Hawaii]

Graham, V. T. "The Intelligence of Chinese Children in San Francisco." Journal of Comparative Psychology 6(1926):43-71.

Halseth, James E., and Glasrud, Bruce A. "Anti-Chinese Movements in Washington, 1885-1886: A Reconsideration." In The Northwest Mosaic, pp. 116-139. Edited by Halseth and Glasrud. Boulder, CO: Pruett Publishing Co., 1977.

Hao, Peter Te Yuan. "An Analysis of Certain Learning Difficulties of Chinese Students in New York City." Doctoral dissertation, New York U., 1955.

Hasley, H. "Exclusion of Chinese Boy from White School." Notre Dame Law 3(Ja, 1928):150-152. [Bond v. Tij Fung Mississippi 114 So. 332]

Henry, Neil. "Chinatown." Washington Post, S 18, 1978. [Washington, DC]

Hirata, Lucie C. "Toward a Political Economy of Chinese America: A Study of Property Ownership in Los Angeles Chinatown." Amerasia Journal 3(Summer, 1975):76-96.

_____. "Youth, Parents, and Teachers in Chinatown: A Triadic Framework of Minority Socialization." Urban Education 10(O, 1975):279-296.

Hoexter, Corinne K. From Canton to California. New York: Four Winds Press, 1976.

Hong, Lawrence K. "Recent Immigrants in the Chinese-American Community: Issues of Adaptations and Impacts." International Migration Review 10(Winter, 1976):509-514.

"'How Many Monkeys Can You Catch In One Try?'--The Story of Chinatown's Gambling Houses." Bridge 3(F, 1974):13-17. [New York City]

Hoy, William. "Chinese in Mississippi to Build Own School." Chinese Digest 3(Je, 1937).

Hsu, Francis L. The Challenge of the American Dream: The Chinese in the United States. Belmont, CA: Wadsworth, 1971.

Huang, J. "A Chinese Child's Acquisition of English Syntax." Master's thesis, U. of California, Los Angeles, 1971.

Huang, Joe, and Wong, Sharon Quan (eds.). Chinese Americans: Realities and Myths Anthology, 1977. Association of Chinese Teachers, 1 Waverly Place, San Francisco, CA 94102.

Huang, Ken, and Pilisuk, Marc. "At the Threshold of the Golden Gate: Special Problems of a Neglected Minority." American Journal of Orthopsychiatry 47(O, 1977):701-713. [San Francisco Chinatown]

Huff, Lehn. Chinese Language Schools in Hawaii. Honolulu: Hawaii Chinese History Center, 1975.

Jacobson, Mark. "Nicky Louie's Mean Streets: Tongs Strike Back in Chinatown." Village Voice, F 7, 1977. [New York City]

Jacques, Leo M. "Have Quick More Money Than Mandarins: The Chinese in Sonora." Journal of Arizona History 17(Summer, 1976).

Janisch, Hudson Noel. "The Chinese, the Courts, and the Constitution: A Study of the Legal Issues Raised by Chinese Immigration to the United States, 1850-1902." Doctoral dissertation, U. of Chicago Law School, 1971.

Johnston, David. "Old Cemeteries Fall Prey to Time, Vandals." Los Angeles Times, Jl 16, 1978. [Chinese-American cemeteries in California]

Jue, Mel. The Story of the Chinese in America, 1974. ERIC ED 123 157.

Jung, Raymond K. "The Chinese Language School in the U.S." School and Society 100(Summer, 1972):309-312.

Kendis, Kaoru Oguri, and Kendis, Randall Jay. "The Street Boy Identity: An Alternate Strategy of Boston's Chinese-Americans." Urban Anthropology 5(Spring, 1976):1-18.

Kingston, Maxine Hong. Memoirs of a Girlhood Among Ghosts. New York: Knopf, 1976.

Kittredge, Michael H. "Newcomer Education at San Francisco's Chinese Education Center." English Language Teaching Journal 32(Ap, 1978):225-230.

Kuan, Lien. "History of Overseas Chinese and Their Glorious Tradition." Peking Review 21 (My 26, 1978):12-17.

Kung, S. W. Chinese in American Life, n.p., 1962.

Kuo, Chia-ling. "The Chinese on Long Island— A Pilot Study." Phylon 31(Fall, 1970):280-289.

_____. Social and Political Change in New York's Chinatown. New York: Praeger, 1977.

_____. "Voluntary Associations and Social Change in New York Chinatown." Doctoral dissertation, New York U., 1975. Univ. Microfilms Order No. 76-10,188.

Kuo, Eddie Chen-Yu. "The Family and Bilingual Socialization: A Sociolinguistic Study of a Sample of Chinese Children in the United States." Journal of Social Psychology 92 (1974):181-191.

Kurakawa, Minako. "Acculturation and Childhood Accidents Among Chinese- and Japanese-Americans." Doctoral dissertation, U. of California, 1967.

Kwan, K. M. "Assimilation of the Chinese in the United States: An Exploratory Study in California." Doctoral dissertation, U. of California, 1958.

Kwock, Charles M. C. A Hawaii Chinese Looks at America. New York: Vantage, 1977.

Kwoh, Beulah Ong. "American-born Chinese College Graduates." Master's thesis, U. of Chicago, 1947.

Kwok, Irene. Chinese Folktales for Children, 1976. ERIC ED 139 258.

King, Shien-Woo. Chinese in American Life: Some Aspects of Their History, Status, Problems and Contributions. Seattle, WA: U. of Washington Press, 1962.

Kuo, Eddie C-Y. "Bilingual Socialization of Pre-School Chinese Children in the Twin Cities Area." Doctoral dissertation, U. of Minnesota, 1972.

Lai, H. Mark. "The Chinese Language Sources Bibliography Project: Preliminary Findings." Amerasia Journal 5(1978):95-107.

Lai, H. Mark, and Choy, Philip P. Outlines. History of the Chinese in America, 1972. Everybody's Bookstore, 840 Kearny Street, San Franciso, CA 94108.

Lai, Kum Pai. "The Natural History of the Chinese Language School in Hawaii." Master's thesis, U. of Hawaii, 1935.

Lam, Vicki. "Sweatshops in Chinatown." WREE View, My-Je, 1978. [New York City]

Lan, Dean. "The Chinatown Sweatshops: Oppression and An Alternative." Amerasia Journal 1(N, 1971):40-57.

_____. Prestige With Limitations: Realities of the Chinese-American Elite. San Francisco: R and E Research Associates, 1976.

Lau, Chau-Mun (comp.). The Chinese in Hawaii: A Checklist of Chinese Materials in the Asia and Hawaiian Collections of the University of Hawaii Library, 1975. ERIC ED 142 597.

Lee, B. Y. "Perpetuation of Primary Group Patterns Among the Chinese in Portland, Oregon." Master's thesis, U. of Oregon, 1938.

Lee, Betty Lew Hom. "An Historical Study of Discriminatory Practices and Their Effects on the Education of American-Chinese in California." Master's thesis, Sacramento State College, 1966.

Lee, C. Y. "Today's Strife Evokes Bitter Memories." Los Angeles Times, S 18, 1977. [Los Angeles Chinatown]

Lee, Daniel T. "The Educational Challenge of San Francisco Chinatown." Master's thesis, California State U., San Franciso, 1970.

Lee, Mabel Sam. "The Recreational Interests and Participation of a Selected Group of Chinese Boys and Girls in Los Angeles, California." Master's thesis, U. of Southern California, 1939.

Lee, Marjorie. "Cultural Pluralism and American Textbooks: A Study of the Chinese Immigrants in Oregon." Doctoral dissertation, U. of Oregon, 1972.

Lee, Mary Bo-Tze. "Problems of the Segregated School for Asiatics in San Francisco." Master's thesis, U. of California, Berkeley, 1921.

Lee, Rose Hum. The Chinese in the United States of America. London: Oxford U. Press, 1960.

Leong, Back Fong Loo. "Chinese Americans' Attitudes, Perceptions of their Cultural Identity." Master's thesis, California State U., Long Beach, 1977. Univ. Microfilms Order No. 13-10,189.

Leong, Charles L. The Eagle and the Dragon. A Real-Life Chinese-American Story, 1976. ERIC ED 139 260.

Leong, Jeff. "Hong Kong Immigrants and the Public Schools." Asian American Review, Spring, 1972.

Leung, Eric Kwok-Wing. "A Sociological Study of the Chinese Language Schools in the San Francisco Bay Area." Doctoral dissertation, U. of Missouri, 1975. Univ. Microfilms Order No. 76-1030.

Lew, Gorden. "New Dragons Clash in the 'Gilded Ghetto.'" Los Angeles Times, S 18, 1977. [San Francisco Chinatown]

Li, Frederick and others. "Health Care for the Chinese Population in Boston." American Journal of Public Health 62(Ap, 1972):536-539.

Li, Peter S. Occupational Mobility and Kinship Assistance: A Study of Chinese Immigrants in Chicago. San Francisco: R & E Research Associates, 1978.

Li, Sylvianne F-A. "A History of the Education of the Chinese in Hawaii." Master's thesis, Oberlin College, 1940.

Liang, Chi Shad. The Changing Size and Changing Character of Chinese Immigration to the United States. Singapore: Institute of Humanities and Social Sciences, College of Graduate Studies, Nanyang U., 1976.

Liao, Pao Yun. "A Case Study of a Chinese Immigrant." Master's thesis, U. of Chicago, 1951. [Arkansas]

The Life, Influence and the Role of the Chinese in the United States, 1776-1960. San Francisco: Chinese Historical Society of America, 1976.

Light, Ivan H. "Sociological Aspects of Self-Employment and Social Welfare Among Chinese, Japanese, and Negroes in Northern, Urban Areas of the U.S., 1900-1940." Doctoral dissertation, U. of California, Berkeley, 1968.

Lin, Han-Sheng. "Chinese Immigrants in the United States: Achievements and Problems." Peace and Change 3(Summer-Fall, 1975):52-67.

Liu, Yu-Chen. "An Adaptation of Parent Education Methods to Meet the Needs of the Changing Status of Chinese Families." Master's thesis, Oregon State College, 1940.

Locklear, William R. "The Celestials and the Angels: A Study of the Anti-Chinese Movement in Los Angeles to 1882." Southern California Quarterly 42(1960):239-256.

Loewen, James W. The Mississippi Chinese. Between Black and White. Cambridge, MA: Harvard U. Press, 1971.

Loh, Homer C. "Americans of Chinese Ancestry in Philadelphia." Doctoral dissertation, U. of Pennsylvania, 1944.

Lum, Kongsum (ed.). Hawaii Chinese in the Foreign Language School Case... Hong Kong: Hawaii Chinese Educational Association and Chung Wah Chung Kung Hui, 1950.

Lum, Phillip Albert. "The Chinese Freedom Schools of San Francisco: A Case Study of the Social Limits of Political System Support." Doctoral dissertation, U. of California, Berkeley, 1975. Univ. Microfilms Order No. 75-22,484.

_____. "The Creation and Demise of San Francisco Chinatown Freedom Schools: One Response to Desegregation." Amerasia Journal 5(1978):57-73.

Lum, Raymond. "Life and Times of Early Chinese in Southern Illinois." Bridge 5(Summer, 1977):30-34.

Lydon, Edward C. The Anti-Chinese Movement in the Hawaiian Kingdom, 1852-1886. San Francisco: R and E Research Associates, 1975.

Lyman, Stanford M. Chinese Americans. New York: Random House, 1974.

_____. "Conflicts and the Web of Group Affiliation in San Francisco's Chinatown, 1850-1910." Pacific Historical Review 43 (N, 1974):473-499.

_____. "Neglected Matters in Chinese American History." Bulletin, Chinese Historical Society of America, Je, 1970.

_____. "Red Guard on Grant Avenue." In Culture and Civility in San Francisco, pp. 20-52. Edited by Howard Becker. Chicago: Aldine, 1971.

_____. "The Structure of Chinese Society in Nineteenth-Century America." Doctoral dissertation, U. of California, Berkeley, 1961.

Ma, Yi Ying. "Effects of Attendance at Chinese Language Schools Upon San Francisco Children." Doctoral dissertation, U. of California, Berkeley, 1945.

McCue, Andy. "Evolving Chinese Language Dailies Serve Immigrants in New York City." Journalism Quarterly 52(Summer, 1975):272-276.

McDonnold, Thomas A. "Development of the Los Angeles Chinatown: 1850-1970." Master's thesis, California State U., Northridge, 1973.

_____. "Wah Fow South of Gum Shan: The Los Angeles Chinatown." China Geographer 4 (Spring, 1976):33-42.

McMillan, Penelope. "L.A.'s Chinatown Turns From Tourists to the Chinese." Los Angeles Times, S 18, 1977.

Mon, Bryan D. Y. "Chinese Occupational Achievement Patterns: The Case of a 'Model Minority.'" Doctoral dissertation, U. of California, Los Angeles, 1978. Univ. Microfilms Order No. 7820258.

Mao, Geraldine E. H. H. "Motivation, Field Dependence, and Level of Cognitive Performance: An Exploratory Study with Chinese Children." Master's thesis, U. of British Columbia, 1967.

Martin, Mildred Crowl. Chinatown's Angry Angel: The Story of Donaldina Cameron. Palo Alto, CA: Pacific Books, 1977. San Francisco

Massachusetts Chinese Education Committee. "CEC Recommendations." Bridge 3(My, 1975): 15-16. [Boston desegregation]

Matthews, F. H. "White Community and 'Yellow Peril.'" Mississippi Valley Historical Review, 1964, pp. 612-633.

Meade, Robert D. "Leadership Studies of Chinese and Chinese-Americans." Journal of Cross-Cultural Psychology 1(D, 1970):325-332.

Meneely, Alexander H. "The Anti-Chinese Movement in the Northwest." Master's thesis, U. of Washington, 1922.

Messerschmidt, Donald A. "Innovation by Adaptation: Tibetan Immigrants in the United States." Tibet Society Bulletin 10 (1976):48-71.

Miller, Margo. "Chinatown Finds a New Voice." Boston Globe, Ja 7, 1979. [Josiah Quincy Community School, Boston]

Miller, Stuart Creighton. The Unwelcome Immigrant. The American Image of the Chinese, 1785-1882. Berkeley, CA: U. of California Press, 1969.

Morrison, Judith K. "Being Chinese in Honolulu: A Political and Social Status or a Way of Life." Doctoral dissertation, U. of Illinois, 1977. Univ. Microfilms Order No. 7804092.

Murphy, Betty. "Boston's Chinese: They Have Problems, Too!" Opportunity 1(My, 1971): 18-24.

Nee, Victor G., and Nee, Brett de Bary. Longtime Californ'. A Documentary Study of an American Chinatown. New York: Pantheon, 1973. [San Francisco]

Ng, Wing-Cheung. "An Evaluation of the Labor Market Status of Chinese Americans." Amerasia Journal 4(1977):101-122.

Ng, Yen-Tak. "On the Social and Political Environment Leading to the Restriction of Chinese Immigrants into the U.S. in 1882." United College Journal 12-13(F, 1975):327-353.

Nims, Amy E. "Chinese Life in San Antonio." Master's thesis, Southwest Texas State Teachers College, 1941.

North, Hart H. "Chinese and Japanese Immigration to the Pacific Coast." California Historical Society Quarterly 28(1949):343-350.

O'Brien, Robert W. "Status of Chinese in the Mississippi Delta." Social Forces 19(Mr, 1941):386-390.

Oller, John W., Jr. and others. "Attitudes and Attained Proficiency in ESL: A Sociolinguistic Study of Native Speakers of Chinese in the United States." Language Learning 27(Je, 1977):1-27.

Olmsted, Roger. "'The Chinese Must Go!'" California Historical Quarterly 50(S, 1971). [California]

Ono, Shin' Ya, and Gabriner, Vickie. "'Community Control' at Two Bridges: What Went Wrong?" Leviathan, Je, 1969. [New York City]

Pau, Ruth M. "A Study of the Characteristics of Chinese Children from Three to Six Years of Age in a Kindergarten in New York and Some Comparisons with American Children of Preschool Age." Master's thesis, New York U., 1929.

Pearl, N. "Writing on the Chinese in California." Master's thesis, U. of California, Berkeley, 1938.

Perlzweig, Robert S. "Why School Busing Is Unpopular With California's Chinese." Patterns of Prejudice 6(Mr-Ap, 1972):9-12.

Perry, Neal Clifford. "An Investigation of Certain Aspects of the Social, Economic, and Educational Status of Second-Generation Chinese and Japanese Graduates of the High Schools of Fresno, California." Master's thesis, U. of Southern California, 1938.

Portillo, Raymond del. "A Survey of the Agencies and Institutions Affecting the Chinese Students of Francisco Junior High School." Master's thesis, San Francisco State College, 1959.

Raab, Selwyn. "New Militancy Emerges in Chinatown." New York Times, Je 8, 1976. [New York City]

Reynolds, C. N. "Oriental-White Relations in Santa Clara County, California." Doctoral dissertation, Stanford U., 1927.

Rhoads, Edward. "The Chinese in Texas." Southwestern Historical Quarterly 81(Jl, 1977):1-36.

Richmond Unified School District, California. Asian American Studies Project. The Chinese American Experience and the Japanese American Experience. Secondary Level Guide Grade 8, Ag, 1973. ERIC ED 132 230

Rudolph, Gerald E. "The Chinese in Colorado, 1869-1911." Master's thesis, U. of Denver, 1964.

Rummel, George A. "The Delta Chinese: An Exploratory Study in Assimilation." Master's thesis, U. of Mississippi, 1966.

Rush, John A. "The Generation Gap as Analyzed by Reference Group Behavior and Its Effects on the Solidarity of the Chinese Community of Sacramento." Master's thesis, Sacramento State College, 1969.

Salzmann, Werner. "Die Einwanderung der Chinesen nach Kalifornien." Doctoral dissertation, U. of Zurich, 1972.

Saxton, Alexander. The Indispensable Enemy. Labor and the Anti-Chinese Movement in California. Berkeley, CA: U. of California Press, 1971.

Schlosser, Len. "Chinese Spoken Here." Variety, Ja 5, 1972. English language lessons, television station KPIX, San Francisco, CA

Schweitzer, John L. "The Social Unity of Tucson's Chinese Community." Master's thesis, U. of Arizona, 1952.

Shankman, Arnold. "Black on Yellow: Afro-Americans View Chinese-Americans, 1850-1935." Phylon 39(Spring, 1978):1-17.

Shih, Hsien-Ju. "Social and Vocational Adjustment of the Second-Generation Chinese High School Students in San Francisco." Doctoral dissertation, U. of California, Berkeley, 1937.

Soong, Ruth J. "A Survey of the Education of Chinese Children in Chicago." Master's thesis, U. of Chicago, 1931.

Spier, Adele. "Two Bridges Model School District: A Profile." Community Issues, F, 1969.

Spoehr, Luther W. "Sambo and the Heathen Chinee: Californians' Racial Stereotypes in the Late 1870's." Pacific Historical Review 42(My, 1973).

Study Committee. Chinese Newcomers in San Francisco, F, 1971. Bay Area Social Planning Council, 577-14th Street, Oakland, CA 94612.

Sue, Derald Wing, and Sue, Stanley. "Counseling Chinese-Americans." Personnel and Guidance Journal 50(Ap, 1972):637-644.

Sue, Pauline Wee. "The Portrayal of Chinese Americans in Selected Readers." Master's thesis, California State U., Hayward, 1974.

_____. "Promoting Understanding of Chinese American Culture." Language Arts 53(Mr, 1976):262-266.

Sue, Stanley, and Sue, Derald. "Chinese American Personality and Mental Health." Amerasia Journal 1(Jl, 1971):36-49.

Sugg, Redding. "Mississippi Chinese: They Have Long Been Able Skillfully to Chart Their Own Course Between Blacks and Whites." South Today 4(Ap, 1973).

Sum, Lily S-H. "Assimilation of Chinese Families in Kalamazoo, Michigan." Master's thesis, Western Michigan U., 1973.

Sun, S. "Cracks in the Flower Drum." San Francisco Magazine 8(1966):36-48.

Sung, Betty Lee. An Album of Chinese Americans. New York: Watts, 1977.

_____. "Changing Chinese." Society 14(S-O, 1977):43-49.

_____. Chinese American Manpower and Employment. Washington, DC: U.S. Department of Labor, 1975.

_____. Mountain of Gold: The Story of the Chinese in America. New York: Macmillan, 1967.

_____ (ed.). Chinese Immigrant Children. New York: Department of Asian Studies, City College, 1977.

"Supreme Court Ruling on Chinese Children." Integrated Education 12(Ja-Ap, 1974):33-35.

Symonds, Percival M. "Effect of Attendance at Chinese Language Schools on Ability with the English Language." Journal of Applied Psychology 8(D, 1924):411-423.

_____. "The Intelligence of Chinese in Hawaii." School and Society 19(Ap 12, 1932):442.

Taam, Loretta. "The Arrangements of the Chinese Community in Los Angeles for Meeting People's Needs." Master's thesis, U. of Southern California, 1961.

Tan, Mely G. "Social Mobility and Assimilation: The Chinese in the United States." Diss. Abstr. Int'l., 1969, 30 (1-A) 416-7.

Tatkin, Lowell W. "Chicago: Two Chinatowns?" China Geographer 4(Spring, 1976):19-32.

Tong, Ben R. "The Ghetto of the Mind: Notes on the Historical Psychology of Chinese America." Amerasia Journal 1(N, 1971):1-31.

_____. "Positive Racist Stereotypes Characteristic of Chinese Americans: A Psychohistorical Inquiry Into Their Etiology and an Exploratory Study of Their Psychophysiological and Sociopsychological Consequences." Doctoral dissertation, California School of Professional Psychology, San Francisco, 1974.

Trull, Fern Coble. "The History of the Chinese in Idaho from 1864 to 1910." Master's thesis, U. of Oregon, 1946.

Tsai, Kuo Ying Paul. "Isolationism among Chinese-Speaking Immigrants in the United States." Journal of the Chinese Language Teachers Association 6(0, 1971):99-102.

Tucker, C. Allen. "The Chinese Immigrant's Language Handicap: Its Extent and Effects." Florida FL Reporter, Spring-Summer, 1969.

Tung, William L. (ed.). The Chinese in America, 1820-1973. A Chronology and Fact Book. Dobbs Ferry, NY: Oceana Publications, 1974.

U.S. Commission on Civil Rights. "Employment Discrimination Against the Chinese" (testimony). Integrateducation 12(Jl-Ag, 1974):19-20.

U.S. Health Services Administration. Home Health in Chinatown. Washington, DC: GPO, 1973. [San Francisco]

Walker, Townsend. "Gold Mountain Guests: Chinese Migration to the United States, 1848-1882." Journal of Economic History 37(Mr, 1977):264-267.

_____. "Gold Mountain Guests: Chinese Migration to the United States, 1848-1882." Doctoral dissertation, U. of California, Berkeley, 1976.

Wang, L. Ling-Chi. "The Chinese Community in San Francisco." Integrated Education 9(Mr-Ap, 1971):21-28.

_____. [Testimony on language problems of Chinese children in San Francisco] U.S. Congress, 93rd, 2nd session, House of Representatives, Committee on Education and Labor. General Subcommittee on Education, Bilingual Education Act. Hearings..., pp. 46-67. Washington, DC: GPO, 1974.

Webster, Helen. "The Chinese School of the Central Presbyterian Church." Colorado Magazine 40(Ja and Ap, 1963):57-63 and 132-137.

Wei Min Shé Labor Committee. Chinese Working People in America. A Pictorial History. San Francisco, CA: United Front Press, 1974.

Weiss, Melford S. "The Research Experience in a Chinese-American Community." Journal of Social Issues 33, No. 4(1977):120-132.

_____. "Selective Acculturation and the Dating Process: The Patterning of Chinese-Caucasian Interracial Dating." Journal of Marriage and the Family 32(My, 1970):273-278.

_____. Valley City: A Chinese Community in America. Cambridge, MA: Shenkman, 1974. [Sacramento, CA]

West, Hollie I. "A Delta Chinatown, A Relic, A Symbol--A Future?" Washington Post, F 15, 1976. [Locke, CA]

Whitfield, Ruth Hall. "Public Opinion and the Chinese Question in San Francisco, 1900-1947." Master's thesis, U. of California, Berkeley, 1947.

Willis, Reginald L. "Chinese Settlement in Illinois, Iowa, and Missouri." Master's thesis, Western Illinois U., 1973.

Wong, Bernard. "Elites and Ethnic Boundary Maintenance: A Study of the Roles of Elites in Chinatown, New York City." Urban Anthropology 6(Spring, 1977):1-22.

_____. "Social Stratification, Adaptive Strategies, and the Chinese Community in New York City." Urban Life 5(Ap, 1976):33-52.

Wong, Buck. Statistical Data on Education in Los Angeles Chinatown. Los Angeles: n.p., 1973.

Wong, Don, and Collier, Irene Dea. Chinese Americans Past and Present: A Collection of Chinese American Readings and Learning Activities, Je, 1977. ERIC ED 146 247.

_____ and _____. Teachers Guide. Chinese Americans Past and Present, Je, 1977. ERIC ED 146 246.

Wong, Harold H. "The Relative Economic Status of Chinese, Japanese, and Black Men in California." Doctoral dissertation, U. of California, Berkeley, 1975.

Wong, Jade Snow. No Chinese Stranger. New York: Harper & Row, 1975.

Wong, James I. Aspirations and Frustrations of the Chinese Youth in the San Francisco Bay Area: Aspersions Upon the Societal Scheme. San Francisco: R and E Research Associates, 1977.

Wong, Morrison G. "Social and Occupational Mobility of the Chinese Male Population in the United States from 1940-70." Master's thesis, U. of California, Riverside, 1975.

Wong, Richard. "Socialization of Chinese American Students." Master's thesis, U. of California, Los Angeles, 1972.

Woodell, Thomas M. The Chinese in Houston, 1973. ERIC ED 101 554.

Wortman, Roy T. "Denver's Anti-Chinese Riot, 1880." Colorado Magazine 42(Fall, 1965): 275-291.

Wou, Odoric, Poon, Yee-ling, and Chin, Kin-wah. "Chinatown Oral History Project." Bridge 2 (Je, 1973):23-29.

Wright, Lawrence. "High Court to Hear Lau Case." Race Relations Reporter 4(O 1, 1973): 1-2. [Children of Chinese ancestry, San Francisco, CA]

Wu, Cheng Tsu. "Chinese People and Chinatown in New York City." Doctoral dissertation, Clark U., 1958. Univ. Microfilms Order No. 58-7097.

_____ (ed.). "Chink!" A Documentary History of Anti-Chinese Prejudice in America. New York: World, 1972.

Wynne, Robert E. "Reaction to the Chinese in the Pacific Northwest and British Columbia, 1850 to 1910." Doctoral dissertation, U. of Washington, 1964.

Yee, Albert H. "Myopic Perceptions and Textbooks: Chinese Americans' Search for Identity." Journal of Social Issues 29 (1973):99-113.

Yee, Min S. "Busing in 'Frisco--Chinatown Fights Back." Race Relations Reporter 3(Ja 3, 1972):18-21.

_____. "Red Star Over San Francisco." Saturday Review 55(N, 1972):19. [Chinese-American community]

Yi Ying, Ma. "Factors Influencing the Chinese Children Who Attend Chinese School in San Francisco." Doctoral dissertation, U. of California, 1945.

Young, Kimball T. "Intelligence of Chinese Children in San Francisco and Vicinity." Journal of Applied Psychology 5(1921):267-274.

Young, Nancy F. "Changes in Values and Strategies Among Chinese in Hawaii." Sociology and Social Research 56(Ja, 1972): 228-241.

_____. "Socialization Patterns Among the Chinese of Hawaii." Amerasia Journal 1(F, 1972):31-51.

Yu, Connie Young. "Chinatown as Home Base." Bulletin of Concerned Asian Scholars 5 (D, 1973):42-45.

_____. "Rediscovered Voices: Chinese Immigrants and Angel Island." Amerasia Journal 4(1977):123-139.

Yuan, D. Y. "Chinatown and Beyond." Phylon 27(Winter, 1966).

_____. "Social Consequences of Recent Changes in the Demographic Structure of New York Chinatown." Phylon 35(Je, 1974):156-164.

Filipino Americans

Abbott, William L. "Filipino Labor Struggles in the Islands." Hawaii Pono Journal 1 (1971):56-68.

Agcaoili, Jo Ann. "The Pilipino Youth of Central City and the San Francisco Educational System." In Diwang Pilipino. Pilipino Consciousness, pp. 73-81. Edited by Jovina Navarro. Davis, CA: Asian American Studies, U. of California, 1974.

Alcantara, Ruben Reyes. "The Filipino Community in Waialua." Doctoral dissertation, U. of Hawaii, 1973. [Waialua, Oahu, HI]

Allen, James P. "Recent Immigration from the Philippines and Filipino Communities in the United States." Geographical Review 67 (1977):195-208.

Andrada, Belen. The Filipino Experience in Minnesota, 1918-1953. The Author, 7301 Upton Avenue, South, Minneapolis, MN 55423

Aquino, Valentin R. The Filipino Community in Los Angeles. San Francisco, CA: R and E Research Associates, 1974 reprint.

Berbano, M. P. "The Social Status of the Filipinos in Los Angeles." Master's thesis, U. of Southern California, 1931.

Bogardus, E. S. "Filipino Immigrant Problems." Sociology and Social Research 14(1929-1930): 469-479.

Boyd, Monica. "Oriental Immigration: The Experience of the Chines, Japanese, and Filipino Populations in the United States." International Migration Review 5(Fall, 1970).

Buaken, Manuel J. I Have Lived with the American People. Caldwell, ID: Caxton, 1948.

Bulosan, Carlos. America Is in the Heart. Seattle: U. of Washington Press, 1973.

Burris, Juanita Salvador. "Ti Isuda Ti Imuda... 'Those Who Came First.'" Bridge 5(Winter, 1977):55-59.

Californians of Japanese, Chinese, and Philipino Ancestry: Population, Education, Employment, Income, Je, 1965. ERIC ED 023 509.

Cariaga, Roman R. The Filipinos in Hawaii. A Survey of their Economic and Social Conditions. San Francisco: R and E Research Associates, 1974 reprint.

Carlson, Alvar W. "Filipinos and Indian Immigrants in Detroit and Suburbs, 1961-1974." Philippine Geographical Journal 19(1975): 199-209.

Castillo, Adelaida. "Filipino Migrants in San Diego, 1900-1946." Journal of San Diego History 22(Summer, 1976):26-35.

Catapusan, Benicio. "Social Adjustment of Filipinos in the United States." Doctoral dissertation, U. of Southern California, 1940.

Cahn, Carole. The Pilipino American, Mr, 1976. ERIC ED 127 395.

Clark, Erlinda T. "Filipino Labor Experiences in the United States." Doctoral dissertation, Texas Tech U., 1971.

Conference on International Migration from the Philippines. [Proceedings] Honolulu: East-West Population Institute, 1975.

Cordova, Fred. "The Burdens of Filipino Americans." Seattle Times Magazine, Ja 14, 1973.

_____. "Filipino Americans Join the Social Revolution." Seattle Times Magazine, Ja 7, 1973.

De Witt, Howard. Anti-Filipino Movements in California: A History, Bibliography and Study Guide. San Francisco, CA: R and E Research Associates, 1976.

_____. "The Filipino Labor Union: The Salinas Lettuce Strike of 1934." Amerasia Journal 5 (1978):1-21.

Dorita, Mary. Filipino Immigration to Hawaii. San Francisco, CA: R and E Research Associates, 1975.

Espiritu, Socono C. A Study of the Treatment of the Philippines in Selected Social Studies Textbooks Published in the U.S. for Use in the Elementary and Secondary Schools. San Francisco: R and E Research Associates, 1974.

"The Filipino Community: 'On the Move in the Temple District.'" Gidra 6(F, 1974). [Los Angeles, CA]

Foronda, Marcelino A., Jr. "America Is the Heart: Ilokano Immigration to the United States, 1906-1930." Bull. Am. Hist. Collect. (Manila 4(0, 1976):46-73.

Galedo, Lillian, Cabanero, Laurena, and Tom, Brian. Roadblocks to Community-Building: A Case Study of the Stockton Filipino Community Center Project. Davis, CA: Asian American Studies Division, U. of California, M, 1970.

Griffiths, Stephen L. "Emigrant and Returned Migrant Investment in a Philippine Village." Amerasia Journal 5(1978):45-67.

Hart, Donn V. "The Filipino-American Press in the United States: A Neglected Resource." Journalism Quarterly 54(Spring, 1977): 135-139.

Jamais, Maria F., Pablo, Renato Y., and Taylor, Donald M. "Ethnic Awareness in Filipino Children." Journal of Social Psychology 83(Ap, 1971):157-164.

Keely, Charles B. "Philippine Migration: In-ternal Movements and Emigration to the United States." International Migration Review 7 (Summer, 1973):177-187.

Kim, Hyung-Chan, and Mejia, Cynthia (eds.). The Filipinos in America, 1898-1974: A Chronology and Fact Book. Dobbs Ferry, NY: Oceana, 1976.

Lasker, Bruno. Filipino Immigration. 1931. New York: Arno, 1969.

Liwanag: Literary and Graphic Expressions by Filipinos in America. San Francisco: Liwanag Publishing, Inc., 1975.

Magdalena, Federico. "The Filipino Entre-preneurs of Hawaii: An Inquiry into Their Roots and Success." Doctoral dissertation, U. of Hawaii, 1977.

Mariano, H. "The Filipino Immigrants in the United States." Master's thesis, U. of Oregon, 1933.

Melendy, H. Brett. Asians in America: Filipinos, Koreans, East Indians. Boston: Twayne, 1977.

_____. "Filipinos in the United States." Pacific Historical Review 43(N, 1974).

Menor, Ben, Jr. (ed.). Pinoy Know Yourself: An Introduction to the Filipino American Experience. Santa Cruz, CA: Third World Teaching Resource Center, U. of California, 1975.

Morales, Royal F. Makibaka: The Pilipino American Struggle. Los Angeles, CA: Mountainview Publishers, 1974.

_____. "Pilipino Americans. From Colony to Immigrant to Citizen." Civil Rights Digest 9 (Fall, 1976):30-32.

Munoz, A. N. The Filipinos in America. Los Angeles, CA: Mountain View Publishers, 1971.

Navarro, Jovina (ed.). Diwang Pilipino. Pilipino Consciousness. Davis, CA: Asian American Studies, U. of California, 1974.

Obando, Aquino B. A Study of the Problems of Filipino Students in the United States. San Francisco: R and E Research Associates, 1974.

Pido, Antonio J. A. "Brain Drain Philippinos." Society 14(S-O, 1977):50-53.

Pilipino Immigrants ("A Documentary Film on the Pilipino Experience and Struggle in the United States"). Pilipino Development Associates, 5089 Yucatan Way, San Jose, CA 95118.

Pinga, Estela G. Bilingual-Bicultural Education for Filipino Americans, Je 5, 1976. ERIC ED 128 520.

Pirovano, Enrico V. "Pilipinos in Philadelphia." Bridge 4(F, 1976):22-23.

_____. "Recent Arrivals from the Philippines in the United States." Doctoral dissertation, U. of Pennsylvania, 1977.

Quinsaat, Jesse and others (eds.). Letters in Exile: An Introductory Reader on the History of Pilipinos in America. Los Angeles: Asian American Studies Center, U. of California, Los Angeles, 1976.

Rabaya, Violet. "Filipino Immigration: the Creation of a New Social Problem." In Roots: An Asian American Reader, pp. 188-200. Edited by Amy Tachiki and others. Los Angeles: Asian American Studies Center, U. of California, 1971.

San Juan, E., Jr. "In the Belly of the Monster: The Filipino Revolt in the U.S." Praxis 1(1976).

Saniel, Josefa M. (ed.). The Filipino Exclusion Movement, 1927-1935. Quezon City, Philippines: Institute of Asian Studies, U. of the Philippines, 1967.

Smith, Peter C. "The Social Demography of Filipino Migrations Abroad." International Migration Review 10(Fall, 1976):307-353.

Solland, Sonja O. "A Study of Conflict in a Multi-Ethnic Community." Doctoral dissertation, U. of Seattle, 1974. [Conflict between Filipino-Americans and Native Americans]

Wallovits, Sonia E. "The Filipinos in California." Master's thesis, U. of Southern California, 1966.

Japanese Americans

Adachi, Christina. "Nisei Women Speak!" Women: A Journal of Liberation 3(1974).

Adams, Lucy W. "Education in the Relocation Centers." California Journal of Secondary Education 17(1942):477-479.

Ade, Lester K. "War Relocation Centers: Educational Program for Evacuees of Japanese Ancestry." Education for Victory 9(1942): 7-9, 17-18.

Amigo, Eleanor D. (ed.). Japanese Americans in Orange County: Oral Perspectives. Fullerton, CA: Japanese American Project of the Oral History Program, California State U., 1976.

Ano, Masaharu. "Loyal Linguists: Nisei of World War II Learned Japanese in Minnesota." Minnesota History 45(Fall, 1977):273-287.

Ariyoshi, Koji. "The Nisei in Hawaii." Japan Quarterly, O-D, 1973.

Bailey, Thomas A. Theodore Roosevelt and the Japanese-American Crises. Stanford, 1934. Japanese segregation in San Francisco.

Baldwin, Simeon E. "Schooling Rights Under Our Treaty with Japan." Columbia Law Review 7 (1907):25.

Barlow, Janelle M. S. "The Images of the Chinese, Japanese, and Koreans in American Secondary School World History Textbooks, 1900-1970." Doctoral dissertation, U. of California, Berkeley, 1973.

Barnhart, Edward N. Japanese-American Evacuation and Resettlement; a Catalog of Material in the General Library. Berkeley, CA: General Library, U. of California, 1958.

Befu, Harumi. "Contrastive Acculturation of California Japanese." Human Organization 24 (Fall, 1965):209-216.

Bell, Reginald. Public School Education of Second-Generation Japanese in California. Stanford, CA: Stanford U. Press, 1935.

_____. "A Study of Certain Phases of the Education of Japanese in Central California." Master's thesis, Stanford U., 1928.

_____. "A Study of the Educational Effects of Segregation Upon Japanese Children in American Schools." Ph.D. dissertation, Stanford U., 1932.

Bell, Ward Horton. "A Comparative Study Between Japanese War Relocation Authority Secondary Schools and Secondary Public Schools." Master's thesis, Arizona State College, 1946.

Blane, Howard T., and Yamamoto, Kazuo. "Sexual-Role Identity Among Japanese and Japanese-American High School Students." Journal of Cross-Cultural Psychology 1(D, 1970):345-354.

Bosworth, Allan R. America's Concentration Camps. New York: Norton, 1967.

Boyd, Monica. "Oriental Immigration: The Experience of the Chinese, Japanese, and Filipino Populations in the United States." International Migration Review 5(Fall, 1970).

Brooks, M. S., and Kunihiro, K. "Education in the Assimilation of Japanese: A Study in the Houston Area of Texas." Sociology and Social Research 27(S-O, 1952):16-22.

Brudnoy, David. "Race and the San Francisco School Board Incident: Contemporary Evaluations." California Historical Quarterly 50(S, 1971).

Bryant, Dorothy. "The School Yearbook with the Barbed Wire Design." Nation, N 9, 1974. [Japanese-Americans during World War II]

Butzbach, Arthur. "The Segregation of Orientals in the San Francisco Schools." Master's thesis, Stanford U., 1928.

Californians of Japanese, Chinese, and Filipino Ancestry: Population, Education, Employment, Income, Je, 1965. ERIC ED 023 509.

Caudill, William A., and De Vos, George. "Achievement, Culture and Personality. The Case of the Japanese-Americans." American Anthropologist 58(D, 1956):1102-1126.

Chansler, Horace F. "The Assimilation of the Japanese In and Around Stockton." Master's thesis, College of the Pacific, 1932.

Chijiwa, Saikichi. "A Social Survey of the Japanese Population in Palo Alto and Menlo Park." Master's thesis, Stanford U., 1933.

"Chinese and Japanese in America." Annals 34 (1909):222 pp.

Christensen, Paul L. "An Evaluation of Certain Phases of Heart Mountain Elementary Schools." Master's thesis, U. of Wyoming, 1943.

Chuman, Dwight. "Little Tokyo. Yet Another Chapter of Abuse." Civil Rights Digest 9 (Fall, 1976):36-38. [Los Angeles]

Chuman, Dwight, and Toji, Dean. "Fred Kamano--Commitment to Teach." Part 1. Gidra 6(Ja, 1974):21-23. [Teacher in Los Angeles]

Chuman, Frank F. The Bamboo People: The Law and Japanese Americans. Del Mar, CA: Publishers, Inc., 1976.

Cole, Cheryl L. A History of the Japanese Community in Sacramento, 1883-1972: Organizations, Businesses, and Generational Response to Majority Domination and Stereotypes. San Francisco: R and E Research Associates, 1975.

Connor, John W. "A Study of Changing Pyschological and Behavioral Characteristics in Three Generations of Japanese Americans in the Sacramento Area." Doctoral dissertation, U. of California, Davis, 1972.

_____. "Acculturation and Changing Need Patterns in Japanese American and Caucasian American Students." Journal of Social Psychology, Ag, 1974.

_____. "Acculturation and Family Continuities in Three Generations of Japanese Americans." Journal of Marriage and the Family 36(1974): 159-165.

_____. Acculturation and the Retention of an Ethnic Identity in Three Generations of Japanese Americans. San Francisco: R and E Research Associates, 1977.

_____. "Changing Trends in Japanese American Academic Achievement." Journal of Ethnic Studies 2(Winter, 1975):95-98.

_____. Tradition and Change in a Japanese American Community. Chicago: Nelson-Hall, 1977. [Sacramento, CA]

Conroy, Francis Hilary. The Japanese Expansion Into Hawaii, 1868-1898. San Francisco: R and E Associates, 1973 (reprint of dissertation, 1949).

_____. Japanese Frontiers in Hawaii. Berkeley, CA: U. of California Press, 1953.

Cross, Jennifer. Justice Denied: A History of the Japanese in the United States. Englewood Cliffs, NJ: Scholastic Book Services, 1974.

Daniels, Roger. Concentration Camps USA. New York: Holt, Rinehart, Winston, 1971.

_____. The Decision to Relocate the Japanese Americans. Philadelphia: Lippincott, 1975.

_____. "Japanese American Leadership." In The Leadership of American Ethnic Groups. Edited by John Higham. Baltimore, MD: Johns Hopkins Press, 1977.

_____. "The Japanese Experience in North America: An Essay in Comparative Racism." In The Japanese Experience in North America: Papers and Proceedings. Edited by N. Brian Winchester. Alberta: U. of Lethbridge, 1977.

_____. "Majority Images/Minority Realities: A Perspective on Anti-Orientalism in the United States." Prospects 2(1976).

_____. "Segregation and Diplomacy." In The Politics of Prejudice, n.p., 1962.

Darby, Harold E. "The General Intelligence of American-Born Japanese Children in California as Manifested by the Leiter International Performance Scale." Master's thesis, U. of Southern California, 1940.

Darsie, M. L. "Mental Capacity of American-Born Japanese Children." Comparative Psychology Monographs 3(1926).

Derrick, Edith W. "Effects of Evacuation of Japanese American Youth." School Review 55 (Je, 1947):356-362.

De Silva, Gertrude. "A Schoolteacher Observes the Nisei." California Journal of Secondary Education 18(1943):487-491.

De Vos, George A. Socialization for Achievement: Essays on the Cultural Psychology of the Japanese. Berkeley, CA: U. of California Press, 1973.

Douglas, Aubrey A. "Education of Japanese at War Relocation Centers." California Schools 13(1942):261-262.

Feagin, Joe, and Fujitaki, Nancy. "On the Assimilation of Japanese Americans." Amerasia Journal 1(F, 1972):13-30.

Fisher, A. R. Exile of a Race. Seattle, WA: F & T Publishers, 1965. [Japanese-Americans]

Fox, Rollin. "The Secondary School Program at the Manzanar War Relocation Center." Doctoral dissertation, U. of California, Los Angeles, 1946.

Freeman, George Hayward. "A Comparative Investigation of the School Achievement and Socio-Economic Background of the Japanese-American Students and the White Students of Gardena High School." Master's thesis, U. of Southern California, 1938.

Fujibayashi, Virginia Irva. "Occupational and Residential Changes of Chicago's Japanese-American Evacuees." Master's thesis, U. of Chicago, 1965.

Fukei, Budd. The Japanese-American Story. Minneapolis, MN: Dillon Press, 1975.

Fukumoto, Dennis K. "Chinese and Japanese in California, 1900-1920: A Case Study of the Impact of Discrimination." Doctoral dissertation, U. of Southern California, 1976.

Fulton, C. W. "American Schools and Japanese Pupils." North American Review 183(D, 1906): 1225-1228. [San Francisco]

Furuya, Kazuko K. "The Portrayal of Japanese Americans in Second Grade Social Studies Textbooks Used by the Los Angeles School District." Master's thesis, U. of California, Los Angeles, 1973.

Garrett, Jessie A., and Larson, Ronald C. (eds.). Camp and Community: Manzanar and the Owens Valley. Fullerton, CA: Oral History Program, California State U., 1977.

Gehrie, Mark Joshua. "Sensei: An Ethnography of Experience." Doctoral dissertation, Northwestern U., 1973. Univ. Microfilms Order No. 74-7744. [Japanese-Americans in Chicago]

George, Robert Chipman Lee. "The Greneda (Colorado) Relocation Center Secondary School." Master's thesis, U. of Colorado, 1944.

Girdner, Audrie, and Loftis, Anne. The Great Betrayal: the Evacuation of the Japanese-Americans during World War II. New York: n.p., 1969.

Glenn, E. "Education Behind Barbed Wire--Difficulties in Teaching Democracy to Children of Japanese Evacuees." Survey Midmonthly 80 (1944):347-349.

Gluck, Eleanor W. "An Ecological Study of the Japanese in New York City." Master's thesis, Columbia U., 1940.

H. W. I. "Right of Japanese in Hawaii to Direct Education of Child, Government Power of Control." Marquette Law Review 11(Ap, 1927): 158-159.

Haak, Ronald O. "Co-opting the Oppressors: The Case of the Japanese-Americans." Transaction 7(O, 1970):23-31.

Hamamoto, Joe. "Japanese American Identity Crisis." In Minority Group Adolescents in the United States. Edited by Eugene B. Brody. Baltimore: Williams and Wilkins, 1968.

Hansen, Arthur A., and Hacker, David A. "The Manzanar Riot: An Ethnic Perspective." Amerasia Journal 2(Fall, 1974):112-157.

Hara, K. T. "A Cross Cultural Comparison of Self Concepts and Value Orientations of Japanese and American Ninth Graders." Doctoral dissertation, Michigan State U., 1973.

Harada, T. The Social Status of the Japanese in Hawaii. Honolulu: n.p., 1927.

Hashimoto, Dick, and Oshira, F. "School Life in a Relocation Center." Student Life, D, 1944.

Hawkins, John N. "Politics, Education, and Language Policy: The Case of Japanese Language Schools in Hawaii." Amerasia Journal 5(1978):39-56.

Hellwig, David J. "Afro-American Reactions to the Japanese and the Anti-Japanese Movement, 1906-1924." Phylon 38(Mr, 1977):93-104.

Herman, Masako (ed.). The Japanese in America, 1843-1973. A Chronology and Fact Book. Dobbs Ferry, NY: Oceana Publications, 1974.

Herndon, James B. "The 'Japanese School Incident': An Anecdote for Racial Hostility." Master's thesis, San Francisco State College, 1967.

Hertzler, Virginia B. "A Sociometric Study of Japanese Students in a Polyethnic High School." Master's thesis, U. of Washington, 1949. [Garfield High School, Seattle, WA]

Higgs, Robert. "Landless by Law: Japanese Immigrants in California Agriculture to 1941." Journal of Economic History 38(Mr, 1978):205-225.

Hirabayashi, James. "Nisei: The Quiet American? A Re-evaluation." *Amerasia Journal* 3(Summer, 1975):114-129.

Hirai, Bernice K. Y. "An Evaluation of the Japanese Language Program in the Secondary Schools of the State of Hawaii." Doctoral dissertation, Indiana U., 1974. Univ. Microfilms Order No. 74-22,770.

Horinoochi, Isao. *Educational Values and Pre-adaptation in the Acculturation of Japanese Americans.* Sacramento, CA: Sacramento Anthropological Society, 1967.

Hosokawa, Bill. *Nisei: The Quiet Americans.* New York: Morrow, 1969.

Hosokawa, Fumiko. *The Sansei: Social Inter-action and Ethnic Identification Among the Third Generation Japanese.* San Francisco: R and E Research Associates, 1978.

Houston, Jeanne Wakatsuki, and Houston, James D. *Farewell to Manzanar: A True Story of Japanese-American Experience During and After the World War II Internment.* Boston: Houghton Mifflin, 1973.

Howard, Irwin. *The So-called Japanese Passive.* Honolulu, HI: Education Research and Development Center, U. of Hawaii, 1968.

I., H. W. "Right of Japanese in Hawaii to Direct Education of Child, Government Power of Control." *Marquette Law Review* 11 (Ap, 1927):158-159.

Ichihashi, Yamato. *Japanese in the United States. A Critical Study of the Problems of the Japanese Immigrants and their Children.* Stanford, CA: Stanford U. Press, 1932.

Ichioka, Yuji. "Early Issei Socialists and the Japanese Community." *Amerasia Journal* 1 (Jl, 1971):1-25.

_____. "The Early Japanese Immigrant Quest for Citizenship: The Background of the 1922 Ozawa Case." *Amerasia Journal* 4(1977): 1-22.

Ion, Theodore P. "Japanese School Incident at San Francisco from the Point of View of International and Constitutional Law." *Michigan Law Review* 5(1907):326.

Ishigo, Estelle. *Lone Heart Mountain*, 1972. Hollywood Japanese American Citizens League, 1807 North Dillon Street, Los Angeles, CA 90026. [Life at the Japanese Internment Camp, Heart Mountain, Wyoming, 1942-1946]

Israely, Hilla K. "An Exploration into Ethnic Identity: The Case of Third Generation Japanese Americans." Doctoral dissertation, U. of California, Los Angeles, 1976.

Ito, Kazu. *A History of Japanese Immigrants in North America.* Tr. S. Nakamura and J. S. Gerard, Seattle, WA: Hokubei Hyakunen Sakura Jikko Iin Kai, 1973.

Itoh, H. "A Child's Acquisition of Two Languages: Japanese and English." Master's thesis, U. of California, Los Angeles, 1973.

Iwata, Masakazu. "The Japanese Immigrants in California Agriculture. *Agricultural History* 36(Ja, 1962):25-37.

Jackman, Norman R. "Collective Protest in Re-location Centers." *American Journal of Sociology* 63(N, 1957):254-272.

Johnson, Colleen Leahy. "The Japanese-American Family and Community in Honolulu: Genera-tional Continuities in Ethnic Affiliation." Doctoral dissertation, Syracuse U., 1972. Univ. Microfilms Order No. 73-9537.

Johnson, Colleen Leahy, and Johnson, Frank Arvid. "Interaction Rules and Ethnicity: The Japanese and Caucasians in Honolulu." *Social Forces* 54(D, 1975):452-466.

Johnson, Donald Orville. "The War Relocation Authority School of Tule Lake, California." Master's thesis, Stanford U., 1947.

Johnson, H. B. *Discrimination Against the Japanese in California.* Berkeley, CA: n.p., 1907.

Jones, Helen D. (comp.). *Japanese in the United States.* Washington, DC: Library of Congress, 1946.

Jorden, Eleanor H. *Joint Japanese-American Conference on Sociolinguistics. Final Report*, D, 1970. ERIC ED 055 510.

Kagiwada, George. "Confessions of a Misguided Sociologist." *Amerasia Journal* 2(Fall, 1973): 159-164. [On assimilation]

_____. "Ethnic Identification and Socio-Economic Status: The Case of the Japanese-Americans in Los Angeles." Doctoral disser-tation, U. of California, Los Angeles, 1969. Univ. Microfilms Order No. 69-16,917.

Kashima, Tetsuda. *Buddhism in America: The Social Organization of an Ethnic Religious Institution.* Westport, CT: Greenwood, 1977.

"Fred Kawano Interview." Part 2. *Gidra* 6 (F, 1974).

Kehoe, Monica. "Japanese Become Americans: Adult Education at Gila River Relocation Project, Rivers, Arizona." *Adult Education Journal* 3(1944):55-59.

_____. "Relocation School at Rivers." *Arizona Teacher and Parent* 33(1944):8-9.

Kennan, George. "The Japanese in the San Francisco Public Schools." *Outlook*, Je 1, 1907.

Kiefer, Christie W. *Changing Cultures, Changing Lives: An Ethnographic Study of Three Genera-tions of Japanese Americans.* San Francisco: Jossey-Bass, 1974.

Kikuchi, C. "The Japanese-American Youth in San Francisco." San Francisco, CA: National Youth Administration, 1941, unpublished. [See Folder A 1.02, Documents Department, General Library, U. of California, Berkeley]

Kitagawa, Daisuke. Issei and Nisei: The Internment Years. New York: n.p., 1967.

Kitano, Harry H. L. "Changing Achievement Patterns of the Japanese in the United States." Journal of Social Psychology 58 (D, 1962):257-264.

_____. "Japanese Americans: The Development of a Middleman Minority." Pacific Historical Review 43(N, 1974):500-519.

_____. Japanese Americans: The Evolution of a Subculture. Englewood Cliffs, NJ: Prentice-Hall, 1976.

Kleinhopf, Arthur M. "Teaching Training at Hunt." Idaho Journal of Education 24(1943).

Kono, Ayako. "Language as a Factor in the Achievement of American-Born Students of Japanese Ancestry." Master's thesis, U. of Hawaii, 1934.

Kurokawa, Minako. "Mutual Perceptions of Racial Images: White, Black, and Japanese Americans." Journal of Social Issues 27 (1971):213-235.

_____. "Acculturation and Childhood Accidents Among Chinese- and Japanese-Americans." Doctoral dissertation, U. of California, 1967.

Kuroda, Yasumasa and others. "A Cross-National Analysis of the Japanese Character among Japanese-Americans in Honolulu." Ethnicity 5(Mr, 1978):42-59

Ladenson, Alex. "The Japanese in Hawaii." Doctoral dissertation, U. of Chicago, 1938.

La Violette, Forrest E. Americans of Japanese Ancestry: A Study of Assimilation in the American Community. Toronto, Canada: Canadian Institute of International Affairs, 1945.

Leathers, Noel L. The Japanese in America. Minneapolis, MN: Lerner, 1969. [A school textbook]

Leighton, Alexander H. The Governing of Men. Princeton, NJ: n.p., 1945.

Le Pore, Herbert P. "Exclusion by Prejudice: Anti-Japanese Discrimination in California and the Immigration Act of 1924." Doctoral dissertation, Brighm Young U., 1973.

Lee, Teri. "Janice Mirikitani." Asian American Review 2(1976):34-44. [Japanese-American poet]

Levine, Gene N., and Montero, Darrel M. "Socioeconomic Mobility among Three Generations of Japanese Americans." Journal of Social Issues 29(1973):33-48.

Lewis, Grace, and Dierlam, R. "School for Japanese Evacuees." Clearing House 17 (1943):280.

Light, Ivan H. "Sociological Aspects of Self-Employment and Social Welfare Among Chinese, Japanes, and Negroes in Northern, Urban Areas of the U.S., 1900-1940." Doctoral dissertation, U. of California, Berkeley, 1968.

Light, Jerome T. "The Development of a Junior-Senior High School Program in a Relocation Center for People of Japanese Ancestry During the War with Japan." Doctoral dissertation, Stanford U., 1947.

Lim, Genevieve. "Edison Uno, Nisei Civil Rights Advocate: A Profile." Integrateducation 15 (O-N, 1977).

Lin, Che-Hwei. "The Asian American Collections." UCLA Librarian 30(F, 1977):11-12. [Special emphasis on Japanese-American materials]

McClatchy, Valentine S. (ed.). Four Anti-Japanese Pamphlets. New York: Arno, 1979.

McGovney, Dudley O. "The Anti-Japanese Land Laws of California and Ten Other States." California Law Review 35(Mr, 1947):7-60.

McWilliams, Carey. "Race Discrimination and the Law." Science & Society 9(1945):1-22.

Mahon, J. "The Japanese Schools Question." American Law Review 48(1914):698.

Manning, E. M. "Libraries in a Relocation Center: Colorado River Relocation Project at Poston, Arizona." Wilson Library Bulletin 18(1944):371-375.

"Manzanar." Scholastic 44(1944):23. [By Japanese-American students]

Mason, William M., and McKinstry, John A. The Japanese of Los Angeles, 1869-1920. Los Angeles, CA: Los Angeles County Musueum of Natural History, 1969.

Masuda, Minoru and others. "Ethnic Identity in Three Generations of Japanese Americans." Journal of Social Psychology 81(Ag, 1970): 199-207.

Masuoka, Jitsuichi. "Race Attitudes of the Japanese People in Hawaii." Master's thesis, U. of Hawaii, 1931.

_____. "The Westernization of the Japanese Family in Hawaii." Doctoral dissertation, U. of Iowa, 1940.

Matsuda, Lawrence. "A Japanese American History Textbook for Teachers and Administrators." Master's thesis, U. of Washington, 1973.

Matsuda, Mitsugu. _The Japanese in Hawaii._ Honolulu: Social Sciences and Linguistics Institute, 1975.

Matsumoto, Gary M. and others. "Ethnic Identification: Honolulu and Seattle Japanese Americans." _Journal of Cross Cultural Psychology_ 1(Mr, 1970):63-76.

Matsumoto, Toru. _Beyond Prejudice._ New York: Arno, 1979, orig. 1946. [Evacuation of Japanese-Americans, World War II]

Matsuoda, Tsukasa. "Japanese-American History Given Away." _California Council for the Social Studies Review_ 10(Winter, 1970):23-27.

Matsuyama, Midori. "A Study of Japanese Newcomers in Honolulu." Master's thesis, U. of Hawaii, 1973.

Maxey, Edwin. "Exclusion of Japanese Children from the Public Schools of San Francisco." _Yale Law Journal_ 16(1906):90.

Mayemura, Kazumi C. "The Self-Concept of Japanese American Students in Predominantly White versus Predominantly Asian Schools." Master's thesis, California State U., Long Beach, 1977. Univ. Microfilms Order No. 13-11,140.

Maykovich, Minako K. "Changes in Racial Stereotypes." _Human Relations_ 24(0, 1971): 371-385. [Japanese]

_____. "The Difficulties of a Minority Researcher in Minority Communities." _Journal of Social Issues_ 33, No. 4(1977):108-119. [Japanese-American communities]

_____. _Japanese American Identity Dilemma._ Tokyo: Waseda U. Press, 1973.

_____. "Political Activation of Japanese American Youth." _Journal of Social Issues_ 39(1973):167-185.

Mitson, Betty E. "Looking Back in Anguish: Oral History and Japanese-American Evacuation." _Oral History Review_, 1974.

Miyakawa, T. Scott, and Sakata, Yasuo. "Japan in Dislocation and Emigration: The Demographic Background of American Immigration." In _Perspectives in American History._ Edited by Donald Fleming and Bernard Bailyn. Cambridge, MA: Harvard U. Press, 1974.

Miyamoto, Kazuo. _Hawaii: End of the Rainbow._ Rutland, VT: Tuttle, 1964. [Autobiography]

Miyamoto, Schichiro. "A Study of the Japanese Language Ability of the Second and Third Generation Japanese Children in a Honolulu Japanese School." Master's thesis, U. of Hawaii, 1937.

Miyamoto, S. Frank. "The Forced Evacuation of the Japanese Minority during World War II." _Journal of Social Issues_ 29(1973):11-31.

Mizokawa, Donald T. "Some Issues in the Educational Gerontology of Japanese-American Elders." _Educational Gerontology_ 2(Ap, 1977):123-129.

Modell, John. "The Japanese American Family: A Perspective for Future Investigation." _Pacific Historical Review_, F, 1968.

_____. "The Japanese of Los Angeles: A Study in Growth and Accommodation, 1900-1946." Doctoral dissertation, Columbia U., 1969.

_____ (ed.). _The Kikuchi Diary--Chronicle From an American Concentration Camp: The Tanforan Journal of Charles Kikuchi._ Urbana, IL: U. of Illinois Press, 1973.

Monkawa, David Kiyoshi. [Short autobiographical notes] _Gidra_ 5(Mr, 1973):10.

Montero, Darrel. _The Japanese American Community: A Study of Generational Changes in Ethnic Affiliation._ College Park, MD: Institute for Urban Studies, U. of Maryland, 1978.

Montero, Darrel, and Tsukashima, Ronald T. "Assimilation and Educational Achievement: The Case of the Second Generation Japanese-American." _Sociological Quarterly_ 18(Autumn, 1977):490-503.

Morita, Yukio. "The Japanese Americans in the United States Between 1945 and 1965." Master's thesis, Ohio State U., 1967.

Mossman, Robert Alan. "Japanese-American War Relocation Centers as Total Institutions with Emphasis on the Educational Program." Doctoral dissertation, Rutgers U., 1978. Univ. Microfilms Order No. 7820337.

Nakanishi, Don Toshiaki. "The Visual Panacea: Japanese Americans in the City of Smog." _Amerasia Journal_ 2(Fall, 1973):82-129.

Nanamura, Tom. "A Study of the Social Adjustment of Japanese-American Children in Selected Fourth, Fifth, and Sixth Grades." Master's thesis, San Jose State College, 1961. [California]

Nelson, Douglas W. "Heart Mountain: The History of an American Concentration Camp." Master's thesis, U. of Wyoming, 1970. [Japanese Relocation Center, Wyoming]

_____. _Heart Mountain: The History of an American Concentration Camp._ Madison, WI: State Historical Society of Wisconsin, 1976. [Wyoming]

Nishi, Midori. "Changing Occupance of the Japanese in Los Angeles County, 1940-1950." Doctoral dissertation, U. of Washington, 1955. Univ. Microfilms Order No. 00-13000.

Nishi, Setsuko M. "Japanese-American Achievement in Chicago." Doctoral dissertation, U. of Chicago, 1963.

Nishiyama, Toshihiko P. "Primary Relationships and Academic Achievement: A Comparative Study of American and Japanese Youth." Doctoral dissertation, St. Louis U., 1965.

Niyekawa-Howard, Agnes M. "History of the Japanese Language School." Educational Perspectives 13(Mr, 1974):6-14. [Hawaii]

North, Hart H. "Chinese and Japanese Immigration to the Pacific Coast." California Historical Society Quarterly 28(1949):343-350. [Touches on schools]

Ogawa, Dennis M. A Model of Intercultural Communication: The Interaction of Japanese and Other Ethnic Groups in Hawaii, J1, 1976. ERIC ED 140 628.

_____. Communication Characteristics of Asians in American Urban Settings: The Case of Honolulu Japanese, 1975. ERIC ED 124 462.

_____. From Japs to Japanese: The Evolution of Japanese-American Stereotypes. Berkeley, CA: McCutchan Publishing Company, 1971.

_____. Jan Ken Po. The World of Hawaii's Japanese Americans. San Francisco: San Francisco Center for Japanese American Studies, 1973.

Ogawa, Dennis M., with Grant, Glen. Kodomo no tame ni: For the Sake of the Children: The Japanese American Experience in Hawaii. Honolulu: U. Press of Hawaii, 1978.

Okada, John. No-No Boy. San Francisco: Combined Asian American Resources Project, 1976 (orig. 1957). [Novel]

Okamura, Raymond. "Revisions in Japanese American History." Asian American Review 2 (1976):28-31.

_____ (comp.). "The Concentration Camp Experience from a Japanese American Perspective." In Counterpoint: Perspectives on Asian America. Los Angeles: Asian American Studies Center, U. of California, 1976.

Okano, Yuko, and Spilka, Bernard. "Ethnic Identity, Alienation and Achievement Orientation in Japanese-American Families." Journal of Cross-Cultural Psychology 2 (S, 1971):273-282.

Okihiro, Gary Y. "Japanese Resistance in America's Concentration Camps: A Re-evaluation." Amerasia Journal 2(Fall, 1973): 20-34.

_____. The Oral History Tapes of the Japanese American Research Project, Tape Numbers 1-112: A Survey. Working Paper Series No. 1, Je 13, 1974.

_____. "Tule Lake Under Martial Law: A Study in Japanese Resistance." Journal of Ethnic Studies 5(Fall, 1977):71-85.

Okimoto, Daniel. American in Disguise. New York: John Weatherhill, Inc., 1971. [Fresno and Pasadena, CA]

Okubo, Miné. Citizen 13660. New York: Columbia U. Press, 1946.

Onada, Lawrence. "Personality Characteristics and Attitudes Toward Achievement Among Mainland High Achieving and Underachieving Japanese-American Sanseis." Journal of Educational Psychology 68(Ap, 1976):151-156.

Pajus, Jean. The Real Japanese California. Berkeley, CA: J. J. Gillick Co., 1937. [Doctoral dissertation, U. of Dijon]

Penrose, Eldon R. California Nativism: Organized Opposition to the Japanese 1890-1913. San Francisco: R and E Research Associates, 1973 reprint.

Perry, Neal C. "An Investigation of Certain Aspects of the Social, Economic, and Educational Status of Second-Generation Chinese and Japanese Graduates of the High Schools of Fresno, California." Master's thesis, U. of Southern California, 1938.

Petersen, William. Japanese Americans: Oppression and Success. New York: Random House, 1971.

Powell, J. W. "Education Through Relocation." Adult Education Journal 1(1942):154-157.

Pursinger, Marvin Gavin. "The Japanese Settle in Oregon: 1880-1920." Journal of the West 5(Ap, 1966):251-262.

Ramey, Arthur G. "Student Activities in a Japanese Relocation High School." Clearing House 18(1943):94-96.

"Readjustment of Nisei Into American School Systems: Educating 27,000 for Relocation Education for Victory 3(1945):9-10.

Rice, Thomas Brewer. "The Manzanar War Relocation Center." Master's thesis, U. of California, Berkeley, 1947.

Rich, Andrea L., and Ogawa, Dennis M. "S.I. Hayakawa and the Japanese-American Value Orientation." Hawaii Pono Journal 1(N, 1970):43-48.

Richardson, John Mills. "A Comparative Study of Japanese and Native American White Children." Master's thesis, U. of Southern California, 1937.

Richmond Unified School District, California. Asian American Studies Project. The Chinese American Experience and the Japanese American Experience. Secondary Level Guide Grade 8, Ag, 1973. ERIC ED 132 230.

Roos, Patricia. Questioning the Stereotypes: Differentials in Income Attainment of Japanese, Mexican-Americans, and Anglos in California, S 8, 1977. ERIC ED 148 651.

Root, Elihu. "The Real Questions Under the Japanese Treaty and the San Francisco School Board Resolution." American Journal of International Law 1(1907):273.

Rostow, Eugene V. "The Japanese-American Cases--A Disaster." Yale Law Journal 54 (1945).

Saiki, Patsy Sumie. Sachie: A Daughter of Hawaii, 1977. ERIC ED 148 689. [Novel about a Japanese-American teenager in Hawaii]

Sakoda, James M. "Minidoka: An Analysis of Changing Patterns of Social Interaction." Doctoral dissertation, U. of California, Berkeley, 1949.

Samuels, Frederick. "Colour Sensitivity among Honolulu's Haoles and Japanese." Race, O, 1969.

_____. "The Effect of Social Mobility on Social Distance: Some Changes in the Race Attitudes of Honolulu's Japanese." Master's thesis, U. of Hawaii, 1963.

_____. The Japanese and the Haoles of Honolulu: Durable Group Interaction. New Haven, CT: College & University Press, 1970.

_____. "The Oriental In-Group in Hawaii." Phylon 31(Summer, 1970):148-156.

Schlenker, George. "The Internment of the Japanese of San Diego County During the Second World War." Master's thesis, San Diego State College, 1968.

_____. "The Internment of the Japanese of San Diego County During the Second World War." Journal of San Diego History 18 (Winter, 1972.

Schwartz, Audrey James. "The Culturally Advantaged: A Study of Japanese-American Pupils." Sociology and Social Research 55 (Ap, 1971):341-353.

_____. Traditional Values and Contemporary Achievement of Japanese-American Pupils, D, 1970. ERIC ED 046 061.

Schwartz, Henry Butler. "An Attempt to Measure the Ability of Japanese Language School Pupils." Hawaii Educational Review 14(F, 1926):124-126.

Shapiro, Harry L. Migration and Environment. New York: Arno, 1979. [Japanese in Hawaii]

Shibutani, Tamotsu. The Derelicts of Company K: A Sociological Study of Demoralization. Berkeley, CA: U. of California Press, 1978. [Japanese-American army unit]

Shikamura, Alice Huruko. "The Vocational Intentions of Second Generation Japanese Students in Three California Universities." Master's thesis, Stanford U., 1948.

Shimada, Koji. "Education, Assimilation and Acculturation: A Case Study of a Japanese-American Community in New Jersey." Doctoral dissertation, Temple U., 1975.

Shimbun, Asahi. The Pacific Rivals: A Japanese View of Japanese-American Relations. New York: Weatherhill, 1972.

Sims, Robert C. "The Japanese American Experience in Idaho." Idaho Yesterdays 22(Spring, 1978):2-10.

Smith, Mildred Joan. "Backgrounds, Problems, and Significant Reactions of Relocated Japanese-American Students." Doctoral dissertation, Syracuse U., 1949.

Speier, Matthew Richard. "Japanese-American Relocation Camp Colonization and Resistance to Resettlement: A Study in the Social Psychology of Ethnic Identity under Stress." Master's thesis, U. of California, Berkeley, 1965.

Spicer, Edward H., Hanse, Asael T., Luomala, Katherine, and Opler, Marvin K. Impounded People. Japanese-Americans in the Relocation Centers. Tucson, AZ: U. of Arizona Press, 1969. [Also contains important bilbiographies]

Stearns, Marjorie Ruth. The History of the Japanese People in Oregon. San Francisco: R and E Research Associates, 1974 (orig. 1937).

Strong, Edward K., Jr. "Education." In The Second-Generation Japanese Problem, pp. 185-207. Stanford, CA: Stanford U. Press, 1934.

_____. Japanese in California. Stanford, CA: Stanford U. Press, 1933.

"Success Story: Outwhiting the Whites." Newsweek, Je 21, 1971. [Japanese-Americans]

Takarabe, Heihachiro. "Value Orientation and Scholastic Achievement of Japanese and Non-Asian High School Students and Adults in Sacramento, California." Master's thesis, California State U., Sacramento, 1974.

Tanaka, Tamiko Jane. "The Japanese Language School in Relation to Assimilation." Master's thesis, U. of Southern California, 1933.

Tanimoto, Cathy Lynn. "Changing Japanese Ethnicity: A Case Study of Gardena, California." Master's thesis, Louisiana State U., 1975.

Tatsuno, Sheridan. "The Political and Economic Effects of Urban Renewal on Ethnic Communities: A Case Study of San Francisco Japantown." Amerasia Journal 1(Mr, 1971):33-51.

ten Broeck, Jacobus, Barnhart, E. M., and Matson, F. W. Prejudice, War, and the Constitution. Berkeley, CA: U. of California Press, 1954.

Thomas, Dorothy S. The Salvage. Berkeley, CA: U. of California Press, 1952.

Thomas, Dorothy S., and Nishcinoto, R. S. The Spoilage. Berkeley, CA: U. of California Press, 1946.

Thomson, Ruth. "Events Leading to the Order to Segregate Japanese Pupils in the San Francisco Public Schools." Doctoral dissertation, Stanford U., 1931.

Tsuboi, Sakae. "The Japanese Language School Teacher." Journal of Applied Sociology 11 (N-D, 1926):160-165.

Tsuchida, Nobuya. Issei: The First Fifty Years. Working Papers on Asian American Studies. Los Angeles: Asian American Studies Center, U. of California, Los Angeles, Mr 10, 1975.

Tsutakawa, George. "A Conversation on Life and Fountains." Journal of Ethnic Studies 4 (Spring, 1976):5-36. [Autobiographical account by Japanese-American sculptor and painter]

Tuthill, Gretchen. "Japanese in the City of Los Angeles." Master's thesis, U. of California, Los Angeles, 1924.

United Japanese Society of Hawaii. A History of Japanese in Hawaii, D, 1971. ERIC ED 141 197.

U.S. Congress, 59th, 2nd session, Senate, Document 147. Japanese in the City of San Francisco, Cal. Washington, DC, 1907. [The Metcalf Report]

U.S. Congress, 66th, 2nd session, House of Representatives, Committee on Immigration and Naturalization. Japanese Immigration. Hearings. Parts 1-4. Washington, DC: GPO, 1920. [Touches on schools]

Uono, Kiyoshi. "The Factors Affecting the Geographical Aggregation and Dispersion of the Japanese Residences in the City of Los Angeles." Master's thesis, U. of California, 1927.

Uyeda, Clifford I. "The Pardoning of 'Tokyo Rose': A Report on the Restoration of American Citizenship to Iva Ikuko Toguri." Amerasia Journal 5(1978):69-94.

Vickery, William Edwin. "Prejudice in a Government Policy: The West Coast Evacuation and Its Implications for Intercultural Education." Doctoral dissertation, Harvard U., 1948.

Wallinger, Michael John. "Dispersal of the Japanese Americans: Rhetorical Strategies of the War Relocation Authority, 1942-1945." Doctoral dissertation, U. of Oregon, 1975.

"War Relocation Centers; Educational Pioneering at Rohwer: The People's School." Education for Victory 1(1943):27-29.

Wax, Rosalie H. Doing Fieldwork. Chicago: U. of Chicago Press, 1971. [Japanese-Americans in World War II-camps]

Winchester, N. Brian (ed.). The Japanese Experience in North America: Papers and Proceedings. Alberta: U. of Lethbridge, 1977.

Wollenberg, Charles. "Schools Behind Barbed Wire." California Historical Quarterly 55 (Fall, 1976):210-217.

Wong, Harold H. "The Relative Economic Status of Chinese, Japanese, and Black Men in California." Doctoral dissertation, U. of California, Berkeley.

Wong, Morrison G. "The Japanese in Riverside, 1890 to 1945: A Special Case in Race Relations." Doctoral dissertation, U. of California, Riverside, 1977.

Woodrum, Eric Marc. "Japanese American Social Adaptation Over Three Generations." Doctoral dissertation, U. of Texas, 1978. Univ. Microfilms Order No. 78 17734.

Wren, Benjamin. "The Rising Sun on the Mississippi, 1900-1975." Louisiana History 17(Summer, 1976):321-333. [Japanese in Louisiana]

Yamamoto, Joe. "Japanese American Identity Crisis." In Minority Group Adolescents in the United States. Edited by Eugene B. Brody. Baltimore: Williams and Wilkins, 1968.

Yashui, Barbara. "The Nikkei in Oregon, 1834-1940." Oregon Historical Quarterly 76 (S, 1975):225-257.

Yasutake, Seiichi M. "Japanese-American Experience of Nisei Parents and their Samsei Children and Implications for Education." Doctoral dissertation, Loyola U. (Chicago), 1977.

Yatsushiro, Toshio. Politics and Cultural Values: The World War II Japanese Relocation Centers and the United States Government. New York: Arno, 1979.

Yoneda, Karl. "Brief History of Japanese Labor in Hawaii." Hawaii Pono Journal 1(Mr, 1971):1-9.

_____. "100 Years of Japanese Labor History in the USA." In Roots: An Asian American Reader, pp. 150-158. Edited by Amy Tachiki and Others. Los Angeles: Asian American Studies Center, U. of California, 1971.

Yoshimura, Evelyn. "Higher Rises Lower Depths." Gidra 5(Mr, 1973):11-13. [Little Toyko, Los Angeles, CA]

Yumiba, Carole K. "A History of the Education of the Japanese in the Relocation Centers During World War II." Master's thesis, U. of California, Los Angeles, 1971.

Zaibei Nihonjin Kai. Zaibei Nihonjin Shi. [History of the Japanese in the U.S.A.] San Francisco, CA: Japanese Association of San Francisco, 1940.

Zambetti, Robert. "The Japanese-American Community's Unique Place in California Society." Master's thesis, California State U., San Jose, 1969.

Zeller, William D. The Educational Drama: The Educational Program Provided the Japanese-Americans During the Relocation Period, 1942-1945. New York: n.p., 1969.

_____. "The Educational Program Provided for the Japanese-American During the Relocation Period 1942-1945." Doctoral dissertation, Michigan State U., 1963.

Korean Americans

Boodman, Sandra G. "Korean-Americans: Pursuing Economic Success." Washington Post, Jl 13, 1978. [Washington, DC metropolitan area]

Chang, Theresa S. "The Self-Concept of Children in Ethnic Groups: Black American and Korean American." Elementary School Journal 76(O, 1975):52-58.

Chang, Won Ho. "Communication and Acculturation: A Case Study of Korean Ethnic Group in Los Angeles." Doctoral dissertation, U. of Iowa, 1972. Univ. Microfilms Order No. 72-26,659.

Dotson, John L., Jr. "The Pioneers." Newsweek, My 19, 1975. [Koreans in California]

Givens, Helen L. "The Korean Community in Los Angeles." Master's thesis, U. of Southern California, 1939.

Hahn, Melanie, and Dobb, Frederick. "Lost in the System: Korean School Children in San Francisco." Integrateducation 13(Jl-Ag, 1975):14-16.

Han, Song En. "A Study of Social and Religious Particpation in Relationship to Occupational Mobility and Self-Esteem among Korean Immigrants in Chicago." Doctoral dissertation, Northwestern U., 1973. Univ. Microfilms Order No. 74-7754.

Houchins, Lee, and Houchins, Chang-Su. "The Korean Experience in America, 1903-1924." Pacific Historical Review 43(N, 1974):548-575.

Hurh, Won Moo. Comparative Study of Korean Immigrants in the United States: A Typological Approach. San Francisco: R and E Research Associates, 1977.

_____. "Comparative Study of Korean Immigrants in the United States: A Typology." Korean Christian Journal 2(Spring, 1977):60-99.

_____. Marginal Children of War: An Exploratory Study of American-Korean Children, Jl, 1967. ERIC ED 047 781.

Kang, Younghill. The Grass Roof. New York: Scribner's, 1931. [The Korean background of a future immigrant to America]

Kim, Bernice B. H. "The Koreans in Hawaii." Master's thesis, U. of Hawaii, 1937.

Kim, Bok-Lim C. "Korean Americans. An Emerging Immigrant Community." Civil Rights Digest 9 (Fall, 1976):39-41.

Kim, Elaine H. "Searching for a Door to America: Younghill Kang." Asian American Review 2 (1976):102-116. [Korean-American writer in the United States]

Kim, Hyung-chan. "Education of the Korean Immigrant Child." Integrateducation 15(Ja-F, 1977).

_____. "Korean Community Organizations in America: Their Characteristics and Problems." Korean Journal 15(N, 1975):29-42. [Published in Seoul by the Korean National Commission for UNESCO]

_____. "Some Aspects of Social Demography of Korean Americans." International Migration Review 8(Spring, 1974):23-42. [1901-1971]

_____ (ed.). The Korean Diaspora: Historical and Sociological Studies of Korean Immigration and Assimilation in North America. Santa Barbara, CA: Clio Books, 1977.

Kim, Hyung-chan, and Patterson, Wayne (eds.). The Koreans in America, 1882-1974. A Chronology and Fact Book. Dobbs Ferry, NY: Oceana, 1974.

Kim, Tom. Report on Koreans in San Francisco to the Members of the Bay Area Community Board and Task Force. San Francisco, Je 11, 1973.

Kim, Warren Y. _A Fifty Year History of the Koreans in the United States._ Trans. by Arthur L. Gardner. Reedley, CA: n.p., 1959.

_____. _Koreans in America._ Seoul, Korea: Po Chin Chai Printing Co., 1971.

Kim, Young Yun. _Inter-Ethnic and Intra-Ethnic Communication: A Study of Korean Immigrants in Chicago_, N, 1977. ERIC ED 147 890.

"Koreans in America." _Korean Christian Scholars Journal._ Fayette, MO: The Association of Korean Christian Scholars in North America, 1977.

Lee, Chang-soo. "The United States Immigration Policy and the Settlement of Koreans in America." _Korean Observer_ 6(Fall, 1975):412-451. [Published in Seoul by the Academy of Korean Studies].

Lee, Don Chang. _Acculturation of Korean Residents in Georgia._ San Francisco: R and E Research Associates, 1975.

Lee, Kung. "Settlement Patterns of Los Angeles Koreans." Master's thesis, U. of California, Los Angeles, 1969.

Lim, Jong-Yul. "Education and Assimilation: A Study of Three Urban Subcultures." Doctoral dissertation, Wayne State U., 1974. [Includes Koreans in Detroit area]

Lyn, Kingsley K. "Korean Nationalist Activities in Hawaii and the Continental United States, 1900-1945. Part 1: 1900-1919." _Amerasia Journal_ 4(1977)23-90.

_____. "Korean Nationalist Activities in Hawaii and the Continental United States, 1900-1945. Part II: 1919-1945." _Amerasia Journal_ 4(1977):53-100.

Melendy, H. Brett. _Asians in America: Filipinos, Koreans, East Indians._ Boston: Twayne, 1977.

Moon, Hyung June. "The Korean Immigrants in America: The Quest for Identity in the Formative Years, 1903-1918." Doctoral dissertation, U. of Nevada, Reno, 1976.

Nahm, Andrew C. (ed.). _The United States and Korea._ Kalamazoo, MI, 1977. [Touches on Korean immigration to Hawaii]

No, Chae-Yon. _Chae Mi Hanin Saryak_ (A Short History of Koreans in America). Los Angeles: n.p., 1951

Overend, William. "Koreans Pursue the American Dream." _Los Angeles Times_, S 10, 1978. [Los Angeles]

Park, Jong Sam. "A Three Generational Study: Traditional Value Systems and Psychological Adjustment of Korean Immigrants in Los Angeles." Doctoral dissertation, U. of Southern California, 1975. Univ. Microfilms Order No. 75-28,647.

Pashdag, John. "Where East Meets West. Exploring the Sights and Sounds of L.A.'s Korea Town." _Los Angeles Times_, Ag 16, 1977.

Patterson, Wayne K. "The Korean Frontier in America: Immigration to Hawaii, 1896-1910." Doctoral dissertation, U. of Pennsylvania, 1977. Univ. Microfilms Order No. 77-30238.

Patterson, Wayne, and Patterson, Hyung-chan. _The Koreans in America._ Minneapolis, MN: Lerner, 1977.

Pitler, Barry. "Chicago's Korean American Community." _Integrateducation_ 15(Jl-Ag, 1977.

Ryu, Jung S. _Mass Media's Role in the Assimilation Process: A Study of Korean Immigrants in the Los Angeles Area_, Ap, 1978. ERIC ED 157 108.

Shin, Linda. "Koreans in America...1903-1945." In _Roots: An Asian American Reader_, pp. 200-206. Edited by Amy Tachiki and Others. Los Angeles: Asian American Studies Center, U. of California, 1971.

Song, Jhong-doo. "Educational Problems of Korean Children in the United States." _Korean Observer_ 6(Summer, 1975):232-244. [Published in Seoul by the Academy of Korean Studies]

Song, Seok Choong. "Bilingualism and Immigrant Children." _Korean Christian Journal_ 2 (Spring, 1977):126-141.

Sur, Wilma. "Korean Ethnic Nationalism in Hawaii ." _Hawaii Pono Journal_ 1(N, 1970): 17-31.

Yoshihara, Nancy. "Koreans Find Riches, Faded Dreams in L.A." _Los Angeles Times_, F 1, 1976.

Yu, Eui-Young. "Koreans in America: An Emerging Ethnic Minority." _Amerasia Journal_ 4(1977):117-131.

Other Asian Americans

Ablon, Joan. "Retention of Cultural Values and Differential Urban Adaptation: Samoans and American Indians in a West Coast City." _Social Forces_ 49(Mr, 1971):385-393.

Addazio, Louis C. "The Effect of an Asian Studies Program on the Social Distance Between Tenth-Grade Students and Selected Ethnic Groups." Doctoral dissertation, U. of Connecticut, 1970.

Amsun Associates. _Socio-economic Analysis of Asian American Business Patterns: A Study._ Washington, DC: Office of Minority Business Enterprise, U.S. Department of Commerce, 1977.

"An Interview with Warren Furutani." _Amerasia Journal_ 1(Mr, 1971):70-76. [On the Asian American movement]

Asia in American Textbooks, 1976. Asia Society, Inc., 112 E. 64th Street, New York, NY 10021.

"Asian America." _Bulletin of Concerned Asian Scholars_ 4(Fall, 1972) entire issue.

"The Asian American." _Pacific Historical Review_ 42(N, 1974).

"Asian American Children's Writing." _Bridge_ 3 (Ag, 1975):6-24.

Asian Americans for Fair Media. _The Asian Image in the United States: Stereotypes and Realities_, n.d. ERIC ED 134 643.

"Asian Americans in Children's Books." _Interracial Books for Children Bulletin_ 7, Nos. 2-3(1976) entire issue.

Asian Women, 1971, c/o 3405 Dwinelle Hall, U. of California, Berkeley, CA 94720.

Aswad, Barbara C. (ed.). _Arabic Speaking Communities in American Cities_. New York: Center for Migration Studies, 1973.

Baldauf, Riehard B., Jr. "Relations between Overt and Covert Acculturation in American Samoa." Doctoral dissertation, U. of Hawaii, 1975.

Barlow, Janelle M. S. "The Images of the Chinese, Japanese, and Koreans in American Secondary School World History Textbooks, 1900-1970." Doctoral dissertation, U. of California, Berkeley, 1973.

Basu, Ramala. "Distribution, Occupation and Acculturation of the Asian Indians in the Akron Area." Master's thesis, U. of Akron, 1973.

Bernard, W. S. "The Law, the Mores, and the Oriental." _Rocky Mountain Law Review_ 10 (F-Ap, 1938):105-116 and 163-177.

Boardman, Anthony E. and others. _The Process of Education for Twelfth Grade Asian American Students_. Philadelphia: School of Public and Urban Policy, U. of Pennsylvania, F 10, 1977.

Bond, John R. "Acculturation and Value Change." Doctoral dissertation, U. of Southern California, 1967. [Samoans in U.S.]

Boyd, Monica. "The Changing Nature of Central and Southeast Asian Immigration to the United States: 1961-1972." _International Migration Review_ 8(Winter, 1974):507-519.

Bradfield, Helen H. "The East Indians of Yuba City: A Study in Acculturation." Master's thesis, California State U., Sacramento, 1970.

Brenneise, Beverly G. "A Critical Study of Educational Opportunities for Bilingual Students in the Sacramento City Unified School District Secondary Schools." Master's thesis, California State U., Chico, 1968.

Cabezas, Amado Y. "Evidence for the Low Mobility of Asian Americans in the Labor Market." In _Minorities in the Labor Market_, pp. 39-65. Edited by Paul Bullock. Los Angeles: Institute of Industrial Relations, U. of California, 1978.

Cabezas, Amado Y., and Yee, Harold T. _Discriminatory Employment of Asian Americans: Private Industry in the San Francisco-Oakland SMSA_. San Francisco: Asian, Inc., 1977.

California, State Board of Control. _California and the Oriental_. San Francisco, 1922.

Chai, W., and Ton, T. K. (eds.). _Racial and Ethnic Group Population by Census Tract: The SMSA of New York City, 1970_. New York: Department of Asian Studies, CCNY, 1974.

Chakravorti, Robindra C. "The Sikhs of El Centro: A Study in Social Integration." Doctoral dissertation, U. of Minnesota, 1968.

Chan, Carole. _Cambodians in America_, Ag, 1976. ERIC ED 123 311.

Chan, J., Inada, L., Chin, F., and Wong, S. (eds.). _Aiieeeee! An Anthology of Asian-American Writers_. Washington, DC: Howard U. Press, 1974.

Chan, Kenyon S., Takanishi, and Kitano, Margie. _An Inquiry Into Asian American Preschool Children and Families in Los Angeles_. Los Angeles: Graduate School of Education, U. of California, Los Angeles, J1, 1975.

Chan, Maxine, and Louie, Denise. "Asian Stereotypes [in the Mass Media]." In _Asian Americans. Reference Book_. Compiled by Joseph R. Sanchez. Patrick Air Force Base, FL: Defense Race Relations Institute, 1975.

Chen, Michael. "Rocky Road: North American Politics and Asian America." _Bridge_ 5(Ap, 1977):38-41.

Chen, Pei-Ngor. "Samoans in California." _Social Work_ 18(Mr, 1973):41-48.

Chen, Theodore H. E. "The Oriental-American's Plight." _Los Angeles Times_, Je 8, 1969.

Ching, Frank. "Expansion of Asian-American Studies on U.S. Compuses Reflects Growth of Ethnic Consciousness." _New York Times_, J1 26, 1973.

Chun-Hoon, Lowell. "Teaching the Asian-American Experience: Alternative to the Neglect and Racism in Textbooks." _Amerasia Journal_ 3 (Summer, 1975):40-58.

Chun-Hoon, William C. "The Migration of Indo-
chinese Refugees and Its Impact on an Urban
School District." Doctoral dissertation,
Claremont Graduate School, 1978. Univ.
Microfilms Order No. 78-14830.

Comptroller General of the United States.
Review of Preliminary Estimates of Evacua-
tion Costs, Temporary Care, and Resettlement
Costs of Vietnamese and Cambodian Refugees.
Washington, DC: General Accounting Office,
My 27, 1975.

Conroy, Hilary, and Miyakawa, T. Scott (eds.).
East Across the Pacific. Santa Barbara, CA:
American Bibliographical Center, 1972.

Contacts and Conflicts. The Asian Immigra-
tion Experience. Los Angeles: Asian
American Studies Center, U. of California,
Los Angeles, S, 1975.

Contemporary Asian Studies Division, UC
Berkeley. "Curriculum Philosophy for Asian
American Studies." Amerasia Journal 2(Fall,
1973):35-46.

Corbally, John E. "Orientals in Seattle
Schools." Sociology and Social Research 16
(S-O, 1931):61-67.

Cox, Oliver Cromwell. "Nature of the Anti-
Asiatic Movement on the Pacific Coast."
Journal of Negro Education 15(Fall, 1946):
603-614.

Dinh, Van Phuc. "A Vietnamese Child in Your
Classroom?" Instructor 85(Mr, 1976):86-92.

Doshi, Mahendra. Who's Who Among Indian
Immigrants in North America. New York:
B.K. Verma, 1975.

Dunn, Lynn P. Asian Americans: A Study Guide
and Sourcebook. San Francisco, CA: R and
E Research Associates, 1975.

Elkholy, Abdo A. The Arab Moslems in the United
States. New Haven, CT: College and
University Press, 1966.

Farmer, George L. Education: The Dilemma of
the Oriental Americans. Los Angeles: U.
of Southern California, 1969.

Farquhar, Judith, and Doi, Mary L. "Bruce
Lee vs. Fu Manchu: King Fu Films and Asian
American Stereotypes in America." Bridge 6
(Fall, 1978):23-40.

Feinberg, Lawrence. "Area's Asian Group:
Growing, Thriving." Washington Post, Ag 4,
1975. [Washington, DC area]

Fersh, Seymour. "Orientals and Orientation."
Phi Delta Kappan 53(Ja, 1972):315-318.

Fisher, Darlene E. "Viewpoints on Asian-
Americans Found in Secondary U.S. History
Textbooks." Asian Forum 6(O-D, 1974).

Fisher, Maxine P. "Ethnic Identities: Asian
Indians in the New York City Area." Doctoral
dissertation, City U. of New York, 1978.
Univ. Microfilms Order No. 7808674.

Fisk University. Orientals and Their Cultural
Adjustment. Nashville, TN: Fisk U. Press,
1946.

Foley, A., and Ma, P. "New Americans from
Asia." Federal Reserve Bank of San
Francisco Monthly Review, O, 1971.

Frank, Dwayne Irving. "The Attitudes of High
School United States History Teachers toward
the Treatment of Oriental-Americans and the
Far East in United States History Textbooks."
Doctoral dissertation, U. of Idaho, 1973.
Univ. Microfilms Order No. 74-11,771.

Fugita, Stephen and others. Asian Americans
and their Communities of Cleveland. Cleveland, OH: Cleveland State U., 1977.

Fujimoto, Isao. "Asian American Studies: Un-
masking of a Facade." Bridge 2(Je, 1973):
8-10.

_____. "'Don't Mistake the Finger Pointing at
the Moon for the Moon': Zen Buddhist Saying."
On Understanding Minority Group Experiences:
the Asian American Example." Integrated
Education 9(My-Je, 1971):16-24.

Garkovich, L. E. "A Pilot Study of the Dispersal
and Assimilation of Indochinese Refugees."
Doctoral dissertation, U. of Missouri, 1976.

Gee, Emma and others (eds.). Counterpoint:
Perspectives on Asian America. Los Angeles:
Asian American Studies Center, U. of
California, Los Angeles, 1976.

General Accounting Office. Domestic Resettlement
of Indochinese Refugees--Struggle for Self-
Reliance. Washington, DC: GAO, 1977.

Governor's Asian American Advisory Council.
Report to the Governor on Discrimination
Against Asians. Olympia, WA: The Council,
1973.

Grimes, Paul. "Immigrants from India Find
Hostility in America." New York Times, Ag 2,
1977. [New York City]

Gulick, Sidney L. American Democracy and Asiatic
Citizenship. New York: Arno, 1979, orig.
1918.

Gupta, Santosh Parabha. "The Acculturation of
Asian Indians in Central Pennsylvania."
Doctoral dissertation, Pennsylvania State U.,
1969.

HEW Task Force for Indochina Refugees. Report
to the Congress. Washington, DC: U.S.
Department of H.E.W., Je 15, 1976.

Hagopian, Elaine C., and Paden, Ann (eds.)...
The Arab Americans: Studies in Assimila-
tion. Wilmette, IL: Medina U. Press
International, 1969.

Hata, Don, and Hata, Nadine. "I Wonder Where
the Yellow Went?" Integrated Education 12
(My-Je, 1974):17-21.

Hayasaka, Philip. "The Asian Experience in
White America." Journal of Intergroup
Relations 2(Spring, 1973):67-73.

Hess, Gary R. "The Forgotten Asian Americans:
The East Indian Community in the United
States." Pacific Historical Review 43
(1974):576-596.

_____. "'Hindu' in America: Immigration
and Naturalization Policies and India, 1917-
1946." Pacific Historical Review 38(F,
1969):59-79.

Hillinger, Charles. "Sikhs Call Yuba City
Home." Los Angeles Times, Ja 24, 1977.
[California]

Hirata, Lucie Cheng. "Immigrant Integration
in a Polyethnic Society." Doctoral dissertation, U. of Hawaii, 1971.

Hiro, Dilip. "America's New Indians." New
Society, Ja 6, 1977. [Asian schools]

Hohl, Donald G. "The Indochinese Refugee: The
Evolution of United States Policy." International Migration Review 12(Spring, 1978):
128-132.

Hongo, Garret (ed.). "Special Asian American
Writers Issue." Greenfield Review 6
(Spring, 1977).

"How the Asian Communities Ran It Down to the
U.S. Civil Rights Commission." Gidra 6
(Ja, 1974). [Contains summary as well as
reprints of selected testimony]

Hoyt, Edwin Palmer. Asians in the West.
Nashville, TN: T. Nelson, 1974.

Hsueh, C. T. (ed.). Asian Political Scientists
in North America: Professional and Ethnic
Problems. Occasional Papers/Reprint Series
in Contemporary Asian Studies, No. 5.
College Park, MC: School of Law, U. of
Maryland, 1977.

Hundley, Norris, Jr. (ed.). The Asian American:
The Historical Experience. Essays. Santa
Barbara: Clio Books, 1976.

Hurst, Jack. "Our Vietnamese Refugees: Be-
wilderment and Hope in the Second Year."
Chicago Tribune Magazine, Je 27, 1976.
[Chicago]

I Wor Kuen. "Revolution, the National Question
and Asian Americans." I.W.K. Journal 1
(Ag, 1974):2-9.

Ignacio, Lemuel F. Asian Americans and Pacific
Islanders (Is There Such an Ethnic Group?),
1976. Pilipino Development Associates, Inc.,
5089 Yucatan Way, San Jose, CA 95118.

Inn, Agnes M. S. "The Orientals." Social
Education, Ap, 1969.

Inouye, Daniel K. "Intra- and Inter-racial
Cooperation." Crisis 82(D, 1975):379-383.

Intercultural Development Research Association.
Handbook for Teachers of Vietnamese Students,
Je, 1976. ERIC ED 135 881.

Ireland, R. R. "Indian Immigration to the
United States, 1901-1964." Indian Journal of
Economics (Allahabad) 46(Ap, 1966):465-476.

Ishikawa, W. H., and Archer, N. H. (eds.).
Service Delivery in Pan Asian Communities:
Conference Proceedings. San Diego, CA:
n.p., 1975

"Issues and Concerns of Asian American Community.
Statement to Presidential Candidates." Bridge
4(N, 1976):6-12.

Jaco, D. E., and Wilber, G. L. "Asian Americans
in the Labor Market." Monthly Labor Review
98(Jl, 1975):33-38.

Jain, Usha R. "The Gujaratis in San Francisco."
Master's thesis, U. of California, Berkeley,
1964.

Jenson, J. W. "Apartheid: Pacific Coast Style."
Pacific Historical Review 38(Ag, 1969):335-
340. [Anti-Asian movement]

Kagiwada, George, and Fujimoto, Isao. "Asian-
American Studies: Implications for Educa-
ation." Personnnel and Guidance Journal 51
(F, 1973):400-405.

Kagiwada, George, Sakai, Joyce, Lee, Gus, with
Yayesaki, Ferris (eds.). Proceedings of the
National Asian American Studies Conference II.
A Tool of Change or a Tool of Control? Davis,
CA: Asian American Studies, U. of California,
1974.

Kaku, Michio. "Racism in the Comics." Bridge 3
(F, 1974):25-29. [Anti-Oriental racism]

Kashima, Tetsuyo. Asian Crisis in the San Diego
Unified School District. San Diego, D, 1973.

Kehoe, Monica. "Education for Resettlement."
Common Ground 4(1944):99-101.

Kelly, Gail P. "Adult Education for Vietnamese
Refugees: Commentary on Pluralism in
America." Journal of Ethnic Studies 5(Winter,
1978):55-64.

Khush, Harwant K. "The Social Participation and
Attitudes of the Children of East Indian
Immigrants." Master's thesis, California
State U., Sacramento, 1965.

Kim, Bok-Lim C. "Asian Wives of U.S. Servicemen: Women in Shadows." Amerasia Journal 4 (1977):91-115.

_____. "Asian Americans: No Model Minority." Social Work 18(My, 1973):44-53.

_____. "Problems and Service Needs of Asian Americans in Chicago: An Empirical Study." Amerasia Journal 5(1978):23-44.

Kim, Bok-Lim C., and Condon, Margaret E. A Study of Asian Americans in Chicago: Their Socio-Economic Characteristics, Problems, and Service Needs, O 15, 1975. ERIC ED 152 889.

Kim, Chin, and Kim, Bok-Lim C. "Asian Immigrants in American Law: A Look at the Past and the Challenge Which Remains." American University Law Review 26(Winter, 1977).

Kim, Elaine H. "A Survey of Asian American Literature: Social Perspectives." Doctoral dissertation, U. of California, Berkeley, 1976.

Kimura, Yukiko. Social-Historical Background of the Okinawans in Hawaii. Report No. 36. Honolulu: Romanzo Adams Social Research Laboratory, D, 1962.

Komatsu, Richard, and Takahashi, Jere. "Some Reflections on the Development of 'Introduction to the Asian American Experience.'" Asian American Review 2(1976):6-23.

Konvitz, Milton R. Alien and the Asiatic in American Law. Ithaca, NY: Cornell U. Press, 1946.

Koster, John. "Tutoring Vietnamese Refugees." Today's Education 66(N-D, 1977):32-34.

Kotcheck, Lydia. "Adaptive Strategies of an Invisible Ethnic Minority, the Samoan Population of Seattle." Doctoral dissertation, U. of Washington, 1974.

_____. "Ethnic Visibility and Adaptive Strate-Strategies: Samoans in the Seattle Area." Journal of Ethnic Studies 4(Winter, 1977): 29-38.

Kumagai, Gloria L. "The Asian Woman in America." Explorations in Ethnic Studies 1 (Jl, 1978):27-39.

Lee, Ivy. Profiles of Asians in Sacramento. Final Report, S 30, 1973. ERIC ED 086 774.

Lee, Louie R. "Asian-American Identity: An Exploratory Study." Master's thesis, California State U., Hayward, 1972.

Lewthwaite, G. R. and others. "From Polynesia to California: Samoan Migration and Its Sequel." Journal of Pacific History 8(1973): 133-157.

Liu, William T., and Murata, Alice K. "The Vietnamese in America--Part Two: Perilous Flights, Uncertain Future." Bridge 5(Winter, 1977):42-50.

_____ and _____. "Vietnamese in America, Part III. Life in the Refugee Camps." Bridge 6(Spring, 1978):36-46.

Liu, William T., and Yu, Elene S. H. "Asian-American Youth." In Youth, pp. 367-389. Edited by Robert J. Havighurst and Philip H. Dreyer. Chicago: U. of Chicago Press, 1975.

Lott, Juanita Tamayo. "The Asian American Concept in Quest of Identity." Bridge 4(N, 1976):30-34.

Lovell, Emily K. "A Survey of the Arab-Muslims in the United States and Canada." Muslim World 63(Ap, 1973):139-154.

Lyman, Stanford M. The Asian in the West. Reno, NV: Western Studies Center, U. of Nevada, 1970.

_____ (ed.). The Asian in North America. Santa Barbara, CA: Clio Books, 1977.

McKay, Ralph Y. "A Comparative Study of the Character Representation of California's Dominant Minority Groups in the Officially Adopted California Reading Textbooks of the 1950's, 1960's, and 1970's." Doctoral dissertation, U. of the Pacific, 1971.

Mar, David, and Sakai, Joyce (eds.). Asians in America: Selected Student Papers. Davis, CA: Asian American Research Project, U. of California, 1970.

Maruyama, Margoroh. "Yellow Youth's Psychological Struggle." Mental Hygiene 55(Jl, 1971): 382-390.

Matsudaira, Martin. "An Asian American's Perspective." Journal of Intergroup Relations 5 (N, 1976):34-46.

Maykovich, Minako K. "To Stay Or Not to Stay: Dimensions of Ethnic Assimilation." International Migration Review 10(Fall, 1976):377-387.

_____. "Yellow Power in the US." New Society 28(Ap 18, 1974).

Mears, Eliot G. Resident Orientals on the American Pacific Coast. Chicago: U. of Chicago Press, 1928.

Melendy, J. Brett. Asians in America: Filipinos, Koreans, East Indians. Boston: Twayne, 1977.

_____. The Oriental Americans. New York: Twayne, 1972.

Midkiff, Frank Elbert. "Economic Determinants of Education in Hawaii." Doctoral dissertation, Yale U., 1935.

Murase, Mika. "Toward Barefoot Journalism." Gidra 6, No. 4 (1974). [On the history of Gidra and the Asian-American people's movement]

Nandan, Yash. The East Indian Family in American City and Suburb, Ap 22, 1978. ERIC ED 159 263.

National Conference on Asian-American Mental Health, 1st. First National Conference on Asian-American Mental Health. Washington, DC: GPO, 1974.

National Education Association. Equal Educational Opportunity for Asians and Pacific Islanders in the United States. Washington, DC: NEA, 1976.

National Institute of Mental Health. First National Conference on Asian-American Mental Health. Washington, DC: GPO, 1974.

Nee, Dale Yu. "'See, Culture is Made, Not Born...' Asian American Writers Conference." Bridge 3(Ag, 1975)42-48.

Nguyen, Chinh B. (ed.). Summary of the Culture, History and Educational System of Viet Nam, 1976. ERIC ED 136 619.

Nitta, Teri. "Asian American Studies: Food for Thought or Indigestion?" Gidra 5(Ag, 1973).

North, David S. Seven Years Later: The Experiences of the 1970 Cohort of Immigrants in the U.S. Labor Market. Washington, DC: Linton and Co., Je 15, 1978.

Odo, Franklin. In Movement. Los Angeles: Visual Communications. 1977. [Pictorial history of Asian America]

Paine, Jocelyn. "The Still-Displaced Vietnamese." Los Angeles Times, Je 2, 1977.

Pascua, Reynaldo, Jr. Rural Asian Americans--An Assessment. A Report of the Yakima Valley Asian American Task Force, Jl, 1976. ERIC ED 132 235.

R. J. Associates, Inc. Asian American Reference Data Directory, Mr, 1976. ERIC ED 129 709.

Reynolds, C. N. "Oriental--White Race Relations in Santa Clara County, California." Doctoral dissertation, Stanford U., 1927.

Roh, Gene. "How Asian Americans Relate to Social, Political, and Educational Values Today." Master's thesis, California State U., Hayward, 1972.

Roots: An Asian American Reader, 1972. Asian American Studies Publications, P.O. Box 24A43, Los Angeles, CA 90024.

Salamone, Frank A. "The Resettlement of Ugandan Asians in the United States: A Preliminary Analysis." New Community 5 (Spring-Summer, 1977):464-472.

Salvador-Burris, Juanita. "Changing Asian American Stereotypes." Bridge 6(Spring, 1978):29-35.

Schmitt, Robert C. "Recent Trends in Hawaiian Interracial Marriage Rates by Occupation." Journal of Marriage and the Family 33(My, 1971):373-374.

Shankhar, Richard A. "Integration and Goal Definition of the East Indian Student in the Sutter County Area." Master's thesis, California State U., Chico, 1971.

Shu, Ramsay. "Coming of Age. The Samoan Community in America." Bridge 6(Spring, 1978):47-50.

Shu, Ramsay, and Satele, Adale. The Samoan Community in Southern California: Conditions and Needs, 1978. Asian American Mental Health Research Center, 1640 W. Roosevelt Road, Chicago, IL 60608.

Smith, William Carlson. Americans in Process. A Study of Our Citizens of Oriental Ancestry. Ann Arbor, MI: Edwards Brothers, 1937. Reprint: New York: Arno Press, 1970.

_____. The Second-Generation Oriental in America. Honolulu: n.p., 1927.

Solanki, Ratilal. "Americanization of Immigrants: A Study in Acculturation of Asian-Indians in the State of Colorado and the Educational Implications." Doctoral dissertation, U. of Denver, 1973.

Sue, Derald Wing, and Sue, David. "Understanding Asian-Americans: The Neglected Minority." Personnel and Guidance Journal 51(F, 1973): 386-389.

Sue, Stanley, and Kitano, Harry H. L. "Stereotypes as a Measure of Success." Journal of Social Issues 29(1973):83-98.

Sue, Stanley, and Wagner, N. (eds.). Asian-Americans: Psychological Perspectives. Ben Lomond, CA: Science and Behavior Books, 1973.

Sung, Susan San-San. "Racial-Ethnic Identity: An Asian American Perspective." Doctoral dissertation, U. of California, Berkeley, 1977.

Suyama, Ken. "The Asian American Experience in the Sacramento River Delta." In Roots: An Asian American Reader, pp. 298-301. Edited by Amy Tachiki and Others. Los Angeles, CA: Asian American Studies Center, U. of California, 1971.

Suzuki, Bob H. "Education and the Socialization of Asian Americans: A Revisionist Analysis of the 'Model Minority' Thesis." Amerasia Journal 4(1977):23-51.

Tachiki, Amy, Wong, Eddie, Odo, Franklin, with Wong, Buck (eds.). Roots: An Asian American Reader. Los Angeles: Asian American Studies Center, U. of California, 1971.

Takagi, Paul. "The Myth of 'Assimilation in American Life.'" Amerasia Journal 2(Fall, 1973):149-158.

Takeuchi, Stuart M. "Verbal Skills and the Asian American Student." Journal of Non-White Concerns in Personnel and Guidance 3 (Jl, 1975):161-168.

Tamminga, Harriet L. Past and Present School System Response to Asian Immigrants, S, 1977. ERIC ED 146 094.

Tanaka, Ron. "Culture, Communication and the Asian Movement in Perspective." Journal of Ethnic Studies 4(Spring, 1976):37-52.

Taylor, Colleen. "The [Asian] Indians: Our Growing New Ethnic Community." Chicago Daily News, Ja 24, 1976. [Chicago]

Tinloy, Marian Yuen. "Counseling Asian-Americans: A Contrast in Values." Journal of Non-White Concerns in Personnel and Guidance 6(Ja, 1978):71-77.

Tong, Ben R. A Living Death Defended as the Legacy of a Superior Culture. Working Papers on Asian American Studies No. 2. Los Angeles: Asian American Studies Center, U. of California, Los Angeles, Ja 30, 1975.

Toy, Charles. "Asian Americans: Let's Make It." Bridge 5(Ap, 1977):33-37.

Toy, Don. "Gangs Shatter Quiet in Asian Community." Los Angeles Times, D 15, 1974. [Los Angeles]

Tsu, John B. "The Future of Asian Bilingual and Bicultural Education." Journal of the Chinese Language Teachers Association 12(O, 1977):239-243.

Tu, Wei-ming. "Asian American and Asian Studies." Bridge 3(Je, 1974):35-36.

Tuong Nhu, Tran. "Viet-Nam Refugees." Civil Rights Digest 9(Fall, 1976):59-62.

U.S. Bureau of the Census. We, the Asian Americans. Washington, DC: GPO, Je, 1973.

U.S. Children's Bureau. Tips on the Care and Adjustment of Vietnamese and Other Asian Children in the United States. Washington, DC: GPO, 1975.

U.S. Commission on Civil Rights, California Advisory Committee. Asian Americans and Pacific Peoples: A Case of Mistaken Identity. Washington, DC: U.S. Commission on Civil Rights, F, 1975.

U.S. Commission on Civil Rights, New York Advisory Committee. The Forgotten Minority: Asian Americans in New York City. Washington, DC: The Commission, 1977.

U.S. Congress, 94th, 1st session, House of Representatives, Committee on Education and Labor, Subcommittee on Elementary, Secondary, and Vocation Education. To Authorize Funds for Assistance to Local Educational Agencies for the Education of Cambodian and Vietnamese Refugees, and for Other Purposes. Hearings. Washington, DC: GPO, 1975.

U.S. Congress, 95th, 1st session, House of Representatives, Committe on the Judiciary, Subcommittee on Immigration, Citizenship, and International Law. Extension of Indochina Refugee Assistance Program. Hearings... Washington, DC: GPO, 1977.

U.S. Congress, 95th, 1st session, Senate, Committee on Human Resources. Indochina Refugee Children's Assistance Act Amendments of 1977: Hearing... Washington, DC: GPO, 1977.

U.S. Department of Health, Education, and Welfare, Division of Asian American Affairs. Asian American Field Survey: Summary of the Data. Washington, DC: GPO, My, 1977.

Untalan Muñoz, Faye. "Pacific Islanders in the U.S. A Struggle Against Anonymity." Civil Rights Digest 9(Fall, 1976):42-43.

_____. "Pacific Islanders, Neglected Minority." Church and Society 44(Ja-F, 1974).

Wakita, Kayoko. Asian Studies Survey--Spring, 1970, O, 1971. ERIC ED 054 774.

Wang, L. Ling-Chi. "Asian American Studies. A Personal View." Bridge 2(Je, 1973):4-6.

_____. [Testimony on the need for bilingual, bicultural education in the Asian American community] In U.S. Congress, 93rd, 1st session, Senate, Committee on Labor and Public Welfare, Subcommittee on Education, Education Legislation, 1973. Hearings..., Part 7, pp. 2728-2751. Washington, DC: GPO, 1974.

Wang, Spring. "A Tool of Control or a Tool of Change: The Second Asian American Conference." Bridge 3(F, 1974):31-33.

Ward, David Hsin-Fu (ed.). Asian-American Heritage. New York: Washington Square Press, 1974.

Wilber, George L. and others. Minorities in the Labor Market. Vol. II: Orientals in the labor market. Lexington, KY: Social Welfare Research Institute, U. of Lexington, 1975.

Williams, Franklin H. "Asian Americans in New York City." Integrateducation 16(S-O, 1978):25-28.

Wise, Michael (ed.). "Asian." In Desegregation in Education: A Directory of Reported Federal Decisions, p. 200. Notre Dame, IN: Center for Civil Rights, U. of Notre Dame Law School, Ap, 1977. [1954-1976]

Wong, Eugene F. "On Visual Media Racism: Asians in the American Motion Pictures." Doctoral dissertation, U. of Denver, 1978. Univ. Microfilms Order No. 7823800. [1930-1975]

Wong, William. "Asians and the San Francisco Media." Bridge 5(Winter, 1977):34-36.

Yee, Tina Tong, and Lee, Richard H. "Based on Cultural Strengths, a School Primary Prevention Program for Asian American Youth." Community Mental Health Journal 13 (Fall, 1977):239-248.

Young, Jared J. "Discrimination, Income, Human Capital Investment, and Asian-Americans." Doctoral dissertation, U. of Southern California, 1974.

Young, Nancy Foon (ed.). Asian-Americans in Hawaii: Selected Readings. Honolulu: General Assistance Center for the Pacific Educational Foundations, College of the Education, U. of Hawaii, 1975.

Young, Pai. "Cultural Pluralism and American Education." Korean Christian Journal 2 (1977):100-125.

Younis, Adele Linda. "The Coming of the Arabic-Speaking People to the United States." Doctoral dissertation, Boston U., 1961.

Zuercher, Roger. "The Treatment of Asian Minorities in American History Textbooks." Indiana Social Studies Quarterly 22(Autumn, 1969):19-27.

European Immigrants

Abbott, Grace. The Educational Needs of Immigrants in Illinois. Springfield, IL: n.p., 1920.

Addams, Jane. "The Public School and the Immigrant Child." National Education Association Proceedings, 1908.

_____. "Foreign-Born Children in the Primary Grades: Italian Families in Chicago." National Education Association. Journal of Proceedings and Addresses 36(1897):104-112.

Abelson, Paul. "The Education of the Immigrant." Journal of Social Science 44 (S, 1906):163-172.

Abramson, Harold J. "Ethnic Diversity Within Catholicism: A Comparative Analysis of Contemporary and Historical Religion." Journal of Social History 4(Summer, 1971): 359-388.

Al-Khazraji, M. G., and Al-Khazraji, E. M. Immigration and Beyond: The Portuguese Community of New Bedford, Mass. New Bedford, MA: On Board, Inc., Ja, 1970.

Allen, J. P. "Franco-Americans in Maine: A Geographical Perspective." Acadiensis, Journal of the History of the Atlantic Region 4(Autumn, 1974):32-66.

Altarelli, Carlo. History and Present Condition of the Italian Colony at Paterson, N.J. New York: Columbia U., 1911.

Andrade, Laurinda. The Open Door. New Bedford, MA: Reynolds-De Walt, 1968. [Portuguese in America]

Appel, John J. "From Shanties to Lace Curtains: The Irish Image in Puck, 1876-1910." Comparative Studies in Society and History 13 (O, 1971):365-375.

Asteriou, Asterios. Ta Hellinika Scholeia en Ameriki (The Greek Schools in America). New York: n.p., 1931.

Aszody, Ilona and others. Polish-Americans of Bridgeport: A Social Survey. Bridgeport, CT: Department of Sociology, U. of Bridgeport, 1960.

Ayres, M. H. "A Sociological Study of the Holland Population in the City of Kalamazoo." Bachelor's thesis, U. of Michigan, 1928.

Babcock, Kendrie Charles. "Religious and Intellectual Standpoint." In The Scandanavian Element in the United States, pp. 106-129. Urbana, IL: U. of Illinois, 1914.

Barry, Colman J. The Catholic Church and the German Americans. Milwaukee, WI: Bruce, 1953.

Beijbom, Ulf. Swedes in Chicago. A Demographic and Social Study of the 1846-1880 Immigration. Chicago: Chicago Historical Society, 1971.

Benson, Adolph B., and Hedin, Naboth. Americans from Sweden. New York: Lippincott, 1950.

_____ and _____ (eds.). Swedes in America, 1638-1938. New Haven, CT: Yale U. Press, 1938.

Benson, Oscar A. "Problems in the Accommodation of the Swede to American Culture." Doctoral dissertation, U. of Pittsburgh, 1933.

Bere, May. A Comparative Study of the Mental Capacity of Children of Foreign Parentage. New York: Columbia U., 1924.

Berger, Morris I. "The Settlement, the Immigrant, and the Public School." Doctoral dissertation, Columbia U., 1956.

Berger, Yves. "O Louisiana." Revue de Louisiane 2(Summer, 1973):1-7. [Cajun French culture in Louisiana]

Bernard, William. "Interrelationships Between Immigrants and Negroes." International Migration Review, Summer, 1969.

Bertrand, A. L., and Beale, C. L. The French and Non-French in Rural Louisiana: A Study of the Relevance of Ethnic Factors to Rural Development. Louisiana State U. Agricultural Experiment Station Bulletin No. 606, D, 1965.

Bibics, Walter V. "Assimilation of Yugoslavs in Franklin County, Ohio." Doctoral dissertation, Ohio State U., 1964.

Biondi, Lawrence. The Italian-American Child-- His Sociolinguistic Acculturation. Washington, DC: Georgetown U. Press, 1975.

Blegen, Theodore C. "The Immigrant and the Common School." In Norwegian Migration to America. The American Transition, pp. 241-276. Northfield, MN: The Norwegian-American Historical Association, 1940.

Bodnar, John. "Immigration and Modernization: The Case of Slavic Peasants in Industrial America." Journal of Social History 10 (Fall, 1976):44-71.

_____. "Materialism and Morality: Slavic-American Immigrants and Education, 1890-1940." Journal of Ethnic Studies 3(Winter, 1976):1-19.

Bolek, Francis. The Polish American School System. New York: Columbia Press Corporation, 1948.

Borum, Thaddeus (comp.). We, the Milwaukee Poles: 1846-1946. Milwaukee, WI: Nowiny Publishers, 1946.

Brown, A. W., and Cotton, Carol B. "A Study of the Intelligence of Italian and Polish School Children from Deteriorated and Non-deteriorated Areas of Chicago as Measured by the Chicago Non-verbal Examination." Child Development 12(1941):21-30.

Brown, Thomas N. "Irish-American Nationalism, 1848-1890." Doctoral dissertation, Harvard U., 1956.

_____. Irish-American Nationalism, 1870-1890. Philadelphia: Lippincott, 1966.

Browne, Henry J. "The 'Italian Problem' in the Catholic Church of the United States, 1880-1900." United States Catholic Historical Society, Historical Records and Studies 35 (1946):46-72.

Bushee, Frederick A. "Italian Immigrants in Boston." Arena 17(Ap, 1897).

Čapek, Thomas. "The Language Schools: Teaching of Čech." In The Čechs in America, pp. 241-245. Boston: Houghton Mifflin Co., 1920.

Carlson, Carl Emanuel. "The Adjustment of the Swedish Immigrants to the American Public School System in the Northwest." Doctoral dissertation, U. of Minnesota, 1950.

_____. "The Best Americanizers." In The Swedish Immigrant Community in Transition. Essays in Honor of Dr. Conrad Bergendoff, pp. 31-50. Edited by J. Iverne Dowie and Ernest M. Espelie. Rock Island, IL: Augustava Historical Society, 1963. [I.e., the public schools]

Chevalier, F. "The Role of French National Societies in the Sociocultural Evolution of the Franco-Americans of New England from 1860 to the Present." Doctoral dissertation, Catholic U. of America, 1972.

Child, Irvin L. Italian or American--The Second Generation in Conflict. New Haven, CT: Yale U. Press, 1943.

Cohen, David K. "Immigrants and the Schools." Review of Educational Research 40(F, 1970): 13-27.

_____. Immigrants and the Schools: A Review of Research, n.d. ERIC ED 033 263.

Concestré, Marie J. "Adult Education in a Local Area: A Study of a Decade in the Life and Education of the Adult Immigrant in East Harlem." Doctoral dissertation, New York U., 1944. [Italian community]

Covello, Leonard. The Social Background of the Italo-American Child: A Study of the Southern Italian Mores and Their Effect on the School Situation in Italy and America. Edited by Frank Cordasco. Leiden, The Netherlands: E. J. Brill, 1967. [Republication]

_____. "The Social Background of the Italo-American School Child." 3 vols. Doctoral dissertation, New York U., 1944.

Cordasco, Francesco. "The Children of Immigrants in the Schools: Historical Analogues of Educational Deprivation." Journal of Negro Education 42(Winter, 1973):44-53. [N.Y.C., 1890-1915]

_____. "The Children of Immigrants in the Schools." In Education and the Many Faces of the Disadvantaged: Cultural and Historical Perspectives, pp. 193-204. Edited by William M. Brickman and Stanley Lehrer. New York: Wiley, 1972.

_____ (ed.). Studies in Italian-American Social History: Essays in Honor of Leonard Covello. Totowa, NJ: Rowman & Littlefield, 1975.

Corovilles, Theodore I. "Greek Church Schools in America." Master's thesis, Presbyterian College of Christian Education, 1933.

Cross, Robert D. "How Historians Have Looked at Immigrants to the United States." International Migration Review 7(Spring, 1973):4-13.

Dahlie, Jorgen. "A Social History of Scandanavian Immigration in Washington, 1895-1910." Doctoral dissertation, Washington State U., 1967.

Danesino, Angelo, and Layman, William A. "Contrasting Personality Patterns of High and Low Achievers Among College Students of Italian and Irish Descent." Journal of Psychology, My, 1969.

Dickinson, Joan Y. "Aspects of Italian Immigration to Philadelphia." Pennsylvania Magazine of History and Biography 90(O, 1966):445-465. [Since colonial times]

De Francesco, Domenic. "The Intelligence of the Second Generation of Italians." Master's thesis, U. of Rochester, 1930.

"Die deutsch-amerikanische Schulfrage auf der zweiter National-Konvention." German American Annals 1(D, 1903):695-698.

Douglass, William A. "The Basques of the American West: Preliminary Historical Perspectives." Nevada Historical Society Quarterly 13(Winter, 1970):12-25.

Douglass, William A., and Bilbao, Jon. Amerikanuak: Basques in the New World. Reno, NV: U. of Nevada Press, 1975.

Douglass, William A. (ed.). Anglo-American Contributions to Basque Studies: Essays in Honor of Jon Bilbao. Reno, NV: Social Sciences Center, Desert Research Institute, 1977.

Duff, John B. The Irish in the United States. Belmont, CA: Wadsworth, 1971.

Dulon, R. Aus Amerika. Über Schule, Deutsche Schule, Amerikanische Schule, Deutsch-amerikanische Schule. Leipzig: C. E. Winte Winter, 1866.

Durnin, Richard G. "The Education of Immigrants in the United States: Historical Background." In Education and the Many Faces of the Disadvantaged: Cultural and Historical Perspectives, pp. 181-192. Edited by William W. Brickman and Stanley Lehrer. New York: Wiley, 1972.

Eichoff, Juergen. "Wisconsin's German-Americans: From Ethnic Identity to Assimilation." German-American Studies 2(1970): 44-54.

Erickson, Charlotte. Invisible Immigrants: The Adaptation of English and Scottish Immigrants in 19th century America. Coral Gables, FL: U. of Miami Press, 1972.

Fagereng, John A. "Norwegian Social and Cultural Life in Minnesota, 1868-1891: An Analysis of Typical Norwegian Newspapers." Master's thesis, U. of Minnesota, 1932.

Faust, A. B. "Der deutsche Schulmeister in der amerikanischen Geschichte." Deutsch-Amerikanische Geschichtsblätter 10(O, 1910): 193-207.

Fenchak, Paul. "The Artful Dodgers: Directors of Ethnic Studies Programs." Slovakia 24 (1974):112-119). [On east European ethnic studies]

"The Finnish Thirst for Education and Its Consequences" (in Finnish). Sankarin Maine, Ja 16, 1880.

Foerster, Robert. Italian Emigration of Our Times. Cambridge: Harvard U. Press, 1924.

Ford, Henry Jones. "The Spread of Popular Education." In The Scotch-Irish in America, pp. 447-457. Princeton, NJ: Princeton U. Press, 1915.

Fox, Paul. The Poles in America. New York: George D. Doran, 1922.

Gaillard, Faye. "Poles in Detroit Ally with Blacks." Race Relations Reporter 2(Ap 5, 1971):9-12.

Galitzi, Christine A. A Study of Assimilation Among the Roumanians of the United States. New York: Columbia U. Press, 1929.

Durland, Kellog, and Sessa, Louis. "The Italian Invasion of the Ghetto." University Settlement Studies, Ja, 1906.

Gambino, Richard. "Twenty Million Italian-Americans Can't Be Wrong." New York Times Magazine, Ap 30, 1972.

Gebhart, John Charles. The Growth and Development of Italian Children in New York City. New York: Association for Improving the Condition of the Poor, 1924.

Ginzburg, Ellen Migliorino. "L'emigrazione italina negli Stati Uniti dal 1905 al 1924 con particolare riferimento alla communita italo-americana di Philadelphia." Doctoral dissertation, Università di Torino, 1971.

Gitelman, H. M. "No Irish Need Apply: Patterns of and Responses to Ethnic Discrimination in the Labor Market." Labor History 14(Winter, 1973).

Glazer, Nathan. "The Integration of American Immigrants." Law and Contemporary Problems 21(1956):256-269.

_____. "Ethnic Groups in America: From National Culture to Ideology." In Freedom and Control in Modern Society, pp. 158-176. Edited by M. Berger, T. Abel, and C. H. Page. New York: D. Van Nostrand, 1954.

_____. "Blacks and Ethnic Groups: The Difference, and the Political Difference It Makes." Social Problems 18(Spring, 1971): 444-461.

_____. "The Process and Problems of Language-Maintenance: An Integrative Review." In Joshua A. Fishman and others, Language Loyalty in the United States, pp. 358-368. The Hague: Mouton, 1966.

Goebel, Julius. Der Kampf um deutsche Kultur in Amerika... Leipzig: Verlag der Dürrs' schen Buchhandling, 1914.

Goulet, Alexandre. Une Nouvelle-France en Nouvelle-Angleterre. Paris: E. Duchenin, 1934.

Govorchin, Gerald G. Americans from Yugoslavia. Gainesville, FL: U. of Florida Press, 1961.

Gracza, Rezsoe, and Young, Margaret. The Hungarians in America. Minneapolis, MN: Lerner, 1969. [A school textbook]

Greeley, Andrew. Why Can't They Be Like Us? America's White Ethnic Groups. New York: Dutton, 1971.

Greeley, Andrew M. The Most Distressful Nation: Taming of the American Irish. Chicago: Quadrangle, 1972.

Green, Victor. For God and Country: The Rise of Polish and Lithuanian Ethnic Consciousness in America. Madison, WI: State Historical Society of Wisconsin, 1975.

_____. "Polska: Litewska Minejszosc Ethnicza in USA" (The Polish and Lithuanian Minority in the USA). Problemy Polonii Zagranicznej (Warsaw) TOM VI-VII(1971).

Grossman, Ronald P. The Italians in America. Minneapolis, MN: Lerner, 1969. [A school textbook]

La Gumina, Salvatore J. (comp.). Wop! A Documentary History of Anti-Italian Discrimination in the United States. San Francisco: Straight Arrow Books, 1973.

_____. "Ethnicity in American Political Life--the Italian-American Experience." Migration Review, Spring, 1969.

Halich, Wasyl. "Ukranian Teachers in American Schools" (in Ukranian). Svoboda, Ag 15, 1933.

_____. Ukranians in the United States. Chicago: U. of Chicago Press, 1937.

Haiman, Miecislaus. Poles in New York in the 17th and 18th Centuries. Chicago: Polish Roman Catholic Union of America, 1938.

_____. Polish Past in America, 1608-1865. Chicago: Polish Roman Catholic Union Archives and Museum, 1939.

_____. Polish Pioneers of California. Chicago: Polish Roman Catholic Union of America, 1940.

_____. Polish Pioneers of Pennsylvania. Chicago: Polish Roman Catholic Union of America, 1941.

_____. Polish Pioneers of Virginia and Kentucky. Chicago: Polish Roman Catholic Union of America, 1937.

Hansen, Marcus. The Immigrant in American History. Cambridge, MA: Harvard U. Press, 1946.

Hartmann, Edward. The Movement to Americanize the Immigrant. New York: n.p., 1948.

Hartman, Hershl. "Defining Assimilationism." Jewish Currents 26(Je, 1972):12-17.

Hellwig, David J. "The Afro-American and the Immigrant, 1880-1930: A Study of Black Social Thought." Doctoral dissertation, Syracuse U., 1973.

Higgs, R. "Race, Skills, and Earnings: American Immigrants in 1909." Journal of Economic History 31(1971):420-428.

Higham, John. Strangers in the Land: Patterns of American Nativism, 1860-1925. N.p.: n.p., n.d.

Hill, P. J. "Relative Skill and Income Levels of Native and Foreign Born Workers in the United States." Explorations in Economic History 12(1975):47-60.

Hillbrand, Percie V. The Norwegians in America. Minneapolis, MN: Lerner, 1969. [A school textbook]

_____. The Swedes in America. Minneapolis, MN: Lerner, 1969. [A school textbook]

Hoffman, Géza. "Akkulturation unter den Magyaren in Amerika." Zeitschrift für Sozialwissenschaft, 1913.

Hofman, John E. "The Catholic Ethnic Parishes and Their Schools: 1910-1960." In Joshua A. Fishman, Language Loyalty in the United States. 1964 ed., n.p. [Polish Americans]

Hofstead, John A. (comp.). American Educators of Norwegian Origin: A Biographical Dictionary. Minneapolis, MN: Angsburg Publishing House, 1931.

Hoglund, A. William. Finnish Immigrants in America, 1880-1920. Madison, WI: U. of Wisconsin Press, 1960.

Hune, S. (comp.). Pacific Migration to the United States: Trends and Themes in Historical and Sociological Literature. Washington, DC: Smithsonian Institution, 1977.

Huthmacher, J. Joseph. A Nation of Newcomers: Ethnic Minority Groups in American History. New York: Delacorte, 1967.

Ianni, Francis A. "The Acculturation of the Italo-Americans in Norristown, Pennsylvania 1900-1950." Doctoral dissertation, Pennsylvania State U., 1952.

Institute of Texan Cultures. The Norwegian Texans. San Antonio, TX: U. of Texas at San Antonio, 1970.

Iorizzo, Luciano J., and Mondello, Salvatore. The Italian-Americans. New York: Twayne, 1971.

Irwin, Richard. "Changing Patterns of American Immigration." International Migration Review 6(Spring, 1972):18-31.

Jaher, Frederick, and Dinnerstein, Leonard (eds.). The Aliens: A History of Ethnic Minorities in America. New York: Appleton-Century-Crofts, 1970.

Jakle, John A., and Wheeler, James O. "The Changing Residential Structure of the Dutch Population in Kalamazoo, Michigan." Annals of the Association of American Geographers 59(S, 1969):441-460.

Jensen, J. B. "The Portuguese Immigrant Community of New England: A Current Look." Studia (Lisbon) 34(Je, 1972):109-151.

Johnson, James E. The Irish in America. Minneapolis, MN: Lerner, 1969. [A school textbook]

_____. The Scots and Scotch-Irish in America. Minneapolis, MN: Lerner, 1969. [A school textbook]

Jones, Jayne Clark. The Greeks in America. Minneapolis, MN: Lerner, 1969. [A school textbook]

Jones, Madison S. "Breakthrough to Freedom. Why the Situation of American Negroes Differs From That of White Immigrants." Jewish Currents, My, 1964.

Jones, Maldwyn. American Immigration. N.p.: n.p., n.d.

Jonitis, Peter Paul. "Acculturation of the Lithuanians of Chester, Pennsylvania." Doctoral dissertation, U. of Pennsylvania, 1951.

Juliani, Richard N. "The Social Organization of Immigration: The Italians in Philadelphia." Doctoral dissertation, U. of Pennsylvania, 1971.

Kain, John F., and Persky, Joseph J. "Alternatives to Gilded Ghetto." Public Interest, Winter, 1969.

Katzman, M. T. "Urban Racial Minorities and Immigrant Groups: Some Economic Comparisons." American Journal of Economcs and Sociology 30 (Ja, 1971):15-26.

Kellor, Frances A. "Education of the Immigrant." Educational Review 48(Je, 1914):21-36.

Kero, Reino. Migration from Finland to North America in the Years Between the United States Civil War and the First World War. Turku, Finland: Institute for Migration, 1974.

Keban, Eugene, and Gromada, Thaddeus V. (eds.). "The Polish Americans." Polish Review 21 (1976):1-288.

Kloss, H. "Die dentalhamerikanische Schule." Jahrbuch für Amerikastudien (Heidelberg) 7 (1962):141-175.

Kolodny, Ralph L. "Ethnic Cleavages in the United States: An Historical Reminder to Social Workers." Social Work, Ja, 1969.

Kosinski, Leonard Vincent. "Bilingualism and Reading Development: A Study of the Effects of Polish-American Bilingualism Upon Reading Achievement in Junior High School." Doctoral dissertation, U. of Wisconsin, 1963.

Kruszka, Wenceslaus. Historya Polska w Ameryce. 13 vols. Milwaukee, WI: C. N. Caspar Publishing Co., 1918.

Kunz, Virginia Brainard. The French in America. Minneapolis, MN: Lerner, 1969. [A school textbook]

_____. The Germans in America. Minneapolis, MN: Lerner, 1969. [A school textbook]

Kusielewicz, Eugene. Reflections on the Cultural Condition of the Polish American Community. New York: Czas Publishing Co., 1969.

Kuznicki, S. Ellen Marie. "The Great Polish Immigration, 1870-1914. The Polish Parochial School." In Polish-Americans and the U.S. Bicentennial. Edited by Francis T. Siemankowski. Buffao, NY: n.p., 1977.

Kuzniewski, Anthony. "Boot Straps and Book Learning: Reflections on the Education of Polish Americans." Polish American Studies 32 (Autumn, 1975):5-26.

Lähde, J. W. "Let Us Keep Our Youth Finnish, Cultured and Temperate" (in Finnish). Raittius kalenteri, 1913, pp. 136-147.

Landry, Peter A. "The Portuguese: A Heritage of Oppression. A Search for Identity" (second of two articles). Harvard Crimson, Mr 25, 1974.

Larson, Laurence M. "'Skandinaven, Professor Anderson, and the Yankee School.'" In The Changing West and Other Essays, pp. 116-146. Northfield, MN: Norwegian-American Historical Association, 1937.

Liguori, Sister M. "Polish American Sisterhoods and Schools [from 1868] to 1919." Polish American Studies 13(J1-D, 1956):72-76.

Lindmark, Sture. "Swedish America, 1914-1932. Studies in Ethnicity with Emphasis on Illinois and Minnesota." Doctoral dissertation, U. of Uppsala, 1971.

Linkh, Richard M. American Catholicism and European Immigrants (1900-1924). New York: Center for Migration Studies, 1975.

Long, Girard J. "The Portuguese of Wareham, Massachusetts: A Study of Their Educational Problems with Suggested Remedies and Modifications." Master's thesis, Boston U., 1940.

Lopata, Helena Z. Polish Americans: Status Competition in an Ethnic Community. Englewood Cliffs, NJ: Prentice-Hall, 1976.

Lucas, Henry S. "The Dutch Immigrant's Education." In Netherlanders in America. Dutch Immigration to the United States and Canada, 1789-1950, pp. 598-606. Ann Arbor, MI: U. of Michigan Press, 1955.

Lyon, Norman T. History of the Polish People in Rochester. Buffalo, NY: The Polish Everybody's Daily, 1935.

McGouldrick, Paul F., and Tannen, Michael B. "Did American Manufacturers Discriminate Against Immigrants Before 1914?" Journal of Economic History 37(S, 1977):723-746.

Madaj, M. J. "Chicao: Polish Capital of U.S." New World, Ap 9, 1971.

Maguire, John Francis. [Catholic Education] In The Irish in America, pp. 488-509. London: Longmans, Green & Co., 1868.

Mariano, John Horace. The Second Generation of Italians in New York City. Boston, MA: Christopher Publishing House, 1921.

Martin, Walter T., and Poston, Dudley L., Jr. "Differentials in the Ability to Convert Education into Income: The Case of the European Ethnics." International Migration Review 11(Summer, 1977):215-231.

Matthews, Mary Fabian. "The Role of the Public School in the Assimilation of the Italian Immigrant Child in New York City 1900-1914." Doctoral dissertation, Fordham U., 1966.

Mazzatenta, O. L. "New England's 'Little Portugal.'" National Geographic 147(Ja, 1975):90-109.

Mead, Margaret. "Group Intelligence Tests and Linguistic Diability among Italian Children." School and Society 25(1927):465-468.

Miaso, Józef. The History of the Education of Polish Immigrants in the United States. Tr. by Ludwik Kryzanowski. New York: The Kosciuszko Foundation, 1977.

Midura, Mary J. "A Test on Polish Culture." Master's thesis, De Paul U., 1948.

Milani, E. "Mutual Aid Societies Among Italian Immigrants in the United States of America: A Comprehnsive View, 1865-1977." Doctoral dissertation, Instituto Universitario Lingue Moderne (Italy), 1977.

Miller, Kenneth D. Peasant Pioneers: An Interpretation of the Slavic Peoples in the United States. New York: Council of Women for Home Missions and Missionary Education Movement, 1925.

Molchan, Caspar. "The Development of the Slovak Community in Pittsburgh, 1880-1920." Master's thesis, Notre Dame U., 1948.

Moore, Sarah Wool. "The Teaching of Foreigners." Survey 24(Je 4, 1910).

Mostwin, Danuta. "The Transplanted Family: A Study of Social Adjustment of the Polish Immigrant Family to the United States after the Second World War." Doctoral dissertation, Columbia U., Je, 1971.

Munch, Peter A. "Social Class and Acculturation." In The Strange American Way... Tr. by Helene and Peter A. Munch. Carbondale, IL: Southern Illinois U. Press, 1970. [The Norwegian professional class in the Norwegian Synod in America]

Napolska, Sister Mary Remigia. Polish Immigrant in Detroit to 1914. Chicago, IL: Polish Roman Catholic Union, 1946.

Nelli, Humbert S. The Italians in Chicago, 1880-1930. New York: Oxford U. Press, 1970.

Nelsen, Frank. "The American School Controversy Among the Norwegian Americans, 1845-1881." Doctoral dissertation, Michigan State U., 1968.

Nelson, Helge. The Swedes and the Swedish Settlements in North America. 2 vols. New York: Albert Bonnier, 1943.

Nelson, O. N. History of the Scandanavians and Successful Scandanavians in the United States. 2 vols. Minneapolis, MN: n.p., 1904.

Niehaus, Earl F. The Irish in New Orleans, 1800-1860. Baton Rouge, LA: Louisiana State U. Press, 1965.

Novak, Michael. Further Reflections on Ethnicity. Middletown, PA: Jednota Press, 1977.

_____ (ed.). Growing Up Slavic in America, 1976. EMPAC! Box 48, Bayville, NY 11709

Obidinski, Eugene. "Polish American Social Standing. Status and Stereotypes." Polish Review 21(1976):79-102.

O'Donovan, Jeremiah. Immigration in the United States, 1840-1860--Immigration Interviews, 1864. New York: Arno Press, 1969.

Olneck, M. R., and Lazerson, M. "The School Achievement of Immigrant Children: 1900-1930." History of Education Quarterly 14 (1974):453-482.

Pap, Leo. Portuguese-American Speech: An Outline of Speech Conditions Among Portuguese Immigrants in New England and Elsewhere in the United States. New York: King's Crown Press, 1949.

Parot, Joseph. "Ethnic versus Black Metropolis: The Origins of Polish-Black Housing Tensions in Chicago." Polish-American Studies 29 (Spring, Autumn, 1972).

Paulson, Arthur C., and Bjork, Kenneth (trs. and eds.). "A School and Language Controversy in 1858--A Documentary Study." Norwegian-American Studies and Records 10(1938):76-106.

Payne, E. George. "The School and the American Immigrant." Baltic and Scandanavian Countries 3(1937):320-324.

Pilarski, Laura. They Came from Poland: The Stories of Famous Polish-Americans. New York: Dodd, Mead, 1969.

Polish Culture and Heritage. A Study Guide for Teachers and Students, n.d. Orchard Lake Center for Polish Studies and Culture, Orchard Lake, MI 48033.

Poles of Chicago, 1837-1937. Chicago: Polish Pageant, Inc., 1937.

Polzin, Theresita. The Polish Americans: Whence and Whither. Pulaski, WI: Franciscan Publishers, 1973.

Prpic, George J. The Croatian Immigrants in America. New York: Philisophical Library, 1972.

Prpic, George. "The Croats in America." Doctoral dissertation, Georgetown U., 1959.

Psencik, Leroy F. Czech Contributions to the American Culture. Austin, TX: Texas Education Agency, S 9, 1970, 17 pp. Bibliographic essay ERIC ED 053 023.

Radzialowski, Thaddeus. "The Competition for Jobs and Racial Stereotypes: Poles and Blacks in Chicago." Polish American Studies 33(Autumn, 1976):5-18.

Rankin, Lois. "Detroit Nationality Groups." Michigan History Magazine 23(Spring, 1939): 129-205.

Rogers, Francis M. Americans of Portuguese Descent: A Lesson in Differentiation. Beverly Hills, CA: Sage Publications, 1974.

_____. "The Portuguese Experience in the United States: Double Melt or Minoriity Group?" J. Am. Port. Cult. Soc. 10(Spring, 1976):1-16.

_____. "The Portuguese of Southeastern New England: Suggestions for Research." Luso-Brazilian Review 2(Summer, 1974):3-18.

Rosen, Philip. "American History Textbooks and Immigrants: Time for a Fair Shake." Social Studies Journal 3(Spring, 1974):16-21.

Rosenblum, Gerald. Immigrant Workers: Their Impact on American Labor Racism. New York: Basic Books, 1973.

Roucek, Joseph S. The Czechs and Slovaks in America. Minneapolis, MN: Lerner, 1969. [A school textbook]

Rubin, Jay. "Black Nativism: The European Immigrant in Negro Thought, 1830-1860." Doctoral dissertation, Washington U., 1975.

_____. "Black Nativism: The European Immigrant in Negro Thought, 1830-1860." Phylon 39(Fall, 1978):193-202.

Russo, Nicholas John. "Three Generations of Italians in New York City: Their Religious Acculturation." International Migration Review, Spring, 1969.

Rynning, Ole. Ole Rynning's True Account of America. Tr. and ed. by Theodore C. Blegen. Minneapolis, MN: n.p., 1926. [Orig. 1839. Chapter 7 on education]

Saloutos, Theodore. "The Greek Orthodox Church in the United States and Assimilation." International Migration Review 7(Winter, 1973):395-407.

_____. The Greeks in the United States. Cambridge, MA: Harvard U. Press, 1964.

Salzmann, Zdenek. A Contribution to the Study of Value Orientations Among the Czechs and Slovaks. Amherst, MA: Department of Anthropology, U. of Massachusetts, 1970.

Sandberg, Neil C. Ethnic Identity and Assimilation: The Polish-American Community. Case Study of Metropolitan Los Angeles. New York: Praeger, 1974.

Sanders, Irwin T., and Morawska, Eva T. Polish-American Community Life: A Survey of Research, 1975. Polish Institute of Arts and Sciences of America, Inc., 59 East 66th Street, New York, NY 10021.

Sanford, Albert Hart. "The Polish People of Portage County [Wisconsin]." <u>Wisconsin Historical Society Proceedings</u> 55(1908):259-288.

Saveth, Edward N. "The Immigrant in American Textbooks, Good Stocks and Lesser Breeds." <u>Commentary</u>, My, 1949.

Schrachter, Joseph. "Capital Values and Relative Wage Effects of Immigration into the United States, 1870-1930." Doctoral dissertation, City U. of New York, 1969.

Schiavo, Giovanni. <u>Four Centuries of Italian American History</u>. New York: Vigo Press, 1961.

Schooler, Carmi. "Serfdom's Legacy: An Ethnic Continuum." <u>American Journal of Sociology</u> 81(My, 1976):1265-1286.

Shankman, Arnold. "The Image of the Italian in the Afro-American Press 1886-1936." <u>Italian Americana</u> 4(Fall/Winter, 1978):30-49.

Shannon, William. <u>The American Irish</u>, n.p., 1963.

Shaughnessy, Gerald. <u>Has the Immigrant Kept the Faith?</u> New York: Macmillan, 1925.

Shergold, Peter R. "Relative Skill and Income Levels of Native and Foreign Born Workers: A Reexamination." <u>Explorations in Economic History</u> 13(1976):451-461.

Schimmell, L. S. (ed.). "The Pennsylvania-German in His Relation to Education: A Symposium of Historical and Descriptive Articles." <u>Pennsylvania-German</u> 8(Jl-D, 1907).

Slekaniec, Ladislas John. "The Polish Contribution to Early American Education, 1608-1865." Doctoral dissertation, Western Reserve U., 1962.

Smith, M. Estellie. "A Tale of Two Cities: The Reality of Historical Differences." <u>Urban Anthropology</u> 4(Ap, 1975):61-72. [Portuguese in the U.S.]

Smith, M. G. "Foreign Child and the Teacher." <u>Education</u> 38(Mr, 1918):504-507.

Smith, Timothy L. "Immigrant Social Aspirations and American Education, 1880-1930." <u>American Quarterly</u> 21(Fall, 1969):523-543.

_____. "Native Blacks and Foreign Whites: Varying Responses to Educational Opportunity in America, 1880-1950." <u>Perspectives in American History</u> 6(1972):309-336.

_____. "New Approaches to the History of Immigration in Twentieth-Century America." <u>American Historical Review</u>, Jl, 1966. [Touches on effects of schools on immigrants]

_____. "Parochial Education and American Culture." In <u>History and Education: The Educational Uses of the Past</u>. Edited by Paul Nash. New York: Random House, 1970.

_____. "Protestant Schooling and American Nationality, 1800-1850." <u>Journal of American History</u> 53(Mr, 1967):679-695.

_____. Emigration, Education, and Social Change among Eastern and Southern Europeans in Their Homelands and in the United States, 1890-1940. Final Report, My, 1970, 8 pp. ERIC ED 039 623.

Spiro, M. E. "The Acculturation of American Ethnic Groups." <u>American Anthropologist</u> 57 (1955).

Stein, Howard F. <u>Ethnic Identification vs. Identity as Ethnic: Americans of Slovak Descent in Urban-Industrial Western Pennsylvania</u>, N 20, 1971, 46 pp. Paper, Council on Anthropology & Education Symposium, "Ethnicity and Education," American Anthropological Assn. ERIC ED 057 155.

Steinfeld, Melvin. "Myth of the Melting Pot." <u>The Black Politician</u> 2(O, 1970):4-8.

Stellos, Marie Helen. "The Greek Community in St. Louis (1900-1967): Its Agencies for Value Transmission." Doctoral dissertation, St. Louis U., 1968.

Stolarik, Mark. "Immigration and Urbanization. The Slovak Experience, 1870-1918." Doctoral dissertation, U. of Minnesota, 1974.

_____. "Immigration, Education, and the Social Mobility of Slovaks, 1870-1930." In <u>Immigrants and Religion in Urban America</u>, pp. 103-116. Edited by Randall Miller and Thomas Marzik. Philadelphia: Temple U., 1977.

Swan, George Steven. "The Double Standard and the Catholic Minorities." <u>Notre Dame Journal of Education</u> 4(Winter, 1973):328-335.

Taft, Donald R. <u>Two Portuguese Communities in New England</u>. New York: Columbia U., 1923. Especially pp. 79-84, 228-236, 306-327, and 346-347. [Portsmith, RI and Fall River, MA]

Tait, Joseph W. <u>Some Aspects of the Effect of the Dominant American Culture Upon Children of Italian-Born Parents</u>. New York: Columbia U., 1942 (reprint 1971).

Tait, Joseph Wilfred. <u>Effect of Dominant American Culture on Children of Italian-American Parents</u>. Clifton, NJ: Augustus M. Kelley, 1973.

tenZythoff, Gerrit. <u>The Dutch in America</u>. Minneapolis, MN: Lerner, 1969. [A school textbook]

Thériault, George F. "The Franco-Americans in Nashua, New Hampshire: An Experiment in Survival." Doctoral dissertation, Harvard U., 1951.

Thomas, Alan M., Jr. "American Education and the Immigrant." Teachers College Record, N, 1953.

Thompson, Frank V. Schooling of the Immigrant. New York: Harper, 1920.

Tomasi, Silvano. Piety and Power. The Role of Italian Parishes in the New York Metropolitan Area (1880-1930). New York: Center for Migration Studies, 1975.

Tomasi, S. M., and Engle, M. H. (eds.). The Italian Experience in the United States, 1970. Center for Migration Studies, 209 Flagg Place, Staten Island, NY 10304.

Tyack, David B. "Capeverdean Immigration to the United States." Senior honors thesis, Harvard U., 1952.

Ulin, Richard Otis. The Italo-American Student in the American Public School. New York: Arno, 1975 reprint (orig., 1958).

Underhill, Jack. The Italian Immigrants and the American Negro in the Urban North: Comparisons of Group Adjustment. Cambridge, MA: Kennedy School of Government, Harvard U., 1968.

U.S. Immigration Commission. The Children of Immigrants in Schools. 5 vols. Washington, DC, 1911.

Valetta, Clement. "A Study of Americanization in Carneta: Italian-American Identity Through Three Generations." Doctoral dissertation, U. of Pennsylvania, 1968.

Vecoli, Rudolph J. "The Coming of Age of the Italian American: 1945-1974." Ethnicity 5 (Je, 1978):119-147.

_____. "European Americans: From Immigrants to Ethnics." International Migration Review 6(Winter, 1972):403-434.

_____. "Prelates and Peasants. Italian Immigrants and the Catholic Church." Journal of Social History, Spring, 1969. [Touches on ethnic aspects of parochial schools]

Viera, Jono J. En Falo Por Mim Mesmo. Autobiografia. Oakland, CA: The Author, 163. [Portuguese immigrant in America]

Vigilante, Joseph L. "Ethnic Affirmation, or Kiss Me, I'm Italian." Social Work 17(My, 1972):10-20.

Violette, Maurice. The Franco Americans. New York: Vantage, 1976.

Wandycz, Danian S. (ed.). Register of Polish American Scholars, Scientists, Writers and Artists. New York: Polish Institute of Arts & Sciences in America, 1969.

Ware, Carolyn. "The Contribution of the Public School to the Maladaptation of the Italian Child." In Greenwich Village. New York: Harper & Row, 1935.

Weinstock, S. Alexander. "The Acculturation of Hungarian Immigrants: A Social-Psychological Analysis." Dissertation Abstracts, 1967, 27 (10-A) 3519.

Weisz, Howard Ralph. Irish-American and Italian-American Educational Views and Activities, 1870-1900: A Comparison. New York: Arno, 1977.

_____. "Irish-American Attitudes and the Americanization of the English-Language Parochial School." New York History 53 (Ap, 1972).

_____. "Irish and Italian American Educational Views, 1870-1900." Doctoral dissertation, Columbia U., 1968.

Williams, Daniel Jenkins. The Welsh of Columbus, Ohio. A Study in Adaptation and Assimilation. Oshkosh, WI: Author, 1913.

Wloszczewski, Stefan. History of Polish American Culture. Trenton, NJ: White Eagle Publishing Co., 1946.

Wood, A. E. Hamtramck: Then and Now: A Sociological Study of a Polish American Community. New York: Bookman Associates, 1955.

Wytrwal, Joseph. America's Polish Heritage: A Social History of the Poles in the United States. Detroit, MI: Endurance Press, 1961.

_____. Poles in American History and Tradition. Detroit, MI: Endurance Press, 1969.

_____. The Poles in America. Minneapolis, MN: Lerner, 1969. [A school textbook]

Young, Kimball T. "Mental Differences in Certain Immigrant Groups. Psychological Tests of South Europeans in Typical California Schools with Bearing on the Educational Policy and On the Problems of Racial Contacts in This County." University of Oregon Publications 1 (1922):103.

Young, Pauline. "Social Problems in the Education of the Immigrant Child." American Sociological Review 1(Je, 1936):419-429.

Zand, Helen S. "Polish Institutional Folkways in the United States." Polish American Studies 13, 14 (1956, 1957).

Poor Whites

Anderson, M. "Education in Appalachia: Past Failures and Future Prospects." Journal of Marriage and the Family, N, 1964.

"The Appalachian Child in Chicago Schools." Appalachian Advance 3(0, 1968):6-13.

Appalachian Regional Commission, Education Advisory Committee. Interim Report, 1968. 1966 Connecticut Avenue, N.W., Washington, DC 20235.

Appalachia's People, Problems, Alternatives. An Introductory Social Science Reader, Vol. I. Morgantown, WV: People's Appalachian Research Collective, Mr, 1971, 284 pp. Available, People's Appalachian Research Collective, Inc., Rt. 3, Box 355B, Morgantown, WV 26505. ERIC ED 060 979.

Asher, E. J. "The Inadequacy of Current Intelligence Tests for Testing Kentucky Mountain Children." Journal of Genetic Psychology 46(1935):480-486.

Axelrod, Jim (ed.). Growin' Up Country. Clintwood, VA: n.p., 1973.

Backus, Clarus. "Uptown: The Promised Land," and "Poor People's Power in Uptown." Chicago Tribune Magazine, September 22, 29, 1968. [White migrants in Chicago]

Balliet, Lee S. "Anglo Poverty in the Rural South." Doctoral dissertation, U. of Texas, 1974.

Benjamin, Robert, and Graham, Michael. "Appalachians: Cincinnati's Forgotten Minority." Cincinnati Post, July 28, 1978.

Bevilacqua, Joseph J. "Impact of White Working Class Attitudes on Race Relations in the Army." In White Working Class Culture. Compiled by Frank F. Montalvo. Patrick Air Force Base, FL: Defense Race Relations Institute, 1975.

Billings, Dwight. "Culture and Poverty in Appalachia: A Theoretical Discussion and Empirical Analysis." Social Forces 53(D, 1974):315-323.

Bird, A. R., and McCoy, J. L. White Americans in Rural Poverty. U.S. Department of Agriculture, Agricultural Economics Report No. 124, N, 1967.

Branscombe, James. "Annihilating the Hill-billy: The Appalachians' Struggle with America's Institutions." Katallagete 3 (Winter, 1971):25-32.

Brown, J. S. "The Social Organization of an Isolated Kentucky Mountain Neighborhood." Doctoral dissertation, Harvard U., 1950.

Burchinal, L. G. (ed.). Rural Youth in Crisis. Washington, DC: GPO, 1965.

Burchinal, L. G., and Siff, Hilda. "Rural Poverty." Journal of Marriage and the Family, N, 1964.

Byers, David M. Evangelists to the Poor: A Catholic Ministry in Appalachia. Washington, DC: Glenmary Research Center, 1975.

Campbell, John C. The Southern Highlander and His Homeland. New York: Russell Sage Foundation, 1921.

Carney, Mabel. "Mountain Welfare and the Public Schools." Mountain Life and Work 3 (Jl, 1927):28-35.

Caudill, H. M. Night Comes to the Cumberlands. Boston: Little, Brown, 1962.

Chamber of Commerce of the United States. Rural Poverty and Regional Progress in an Urban Society. Washington, DC: Chamber of Commerce, 1969.

Chilman, Catherine S. Growing Up Poor. Washington, DC: GPO, 1966.

Clark, Lionel. A Structural Guide for Appalachian History and Culture in American History, 1973. ERIC ED 093 541.

Cohen, David Steven. The Ramapo Mountain People. New Brunswick, NJ: Rutgers U. Press, 1974. [N.J.]

Coles, Robert. "Life in Appalachia--the Case of Hugh McCaslin." Transaction, Je, 1968.

_____. "Lives of Migrant Farmers." American Journal of Psychiatry, S, 1965.

Coles, Robert, and Brenner, Joseph. "American Youth in a Social Struggle (II): The Appalachian Volunteers." American Journal of Orthopsychiatry, Ja, 1968.

Corner, Phil. "The White Minority in Our Schools." Detroit News, November 28, 1976. [Cass Technical High School, Detroit]

Craig, Edward M. (ed.). Highways and Byways of Appalachia. Bristol, VA: The Author, 1927.

Crowell, Suzanne, with Fenston, Joy, and Bolte-Mulloy, Karen. The Appalachian People's History Book, 1971. Southern Conference Educational Fund, 3210 West Broadway, Louisville, KY 40211.

Davies, Shane, and Fowler, Gary L. "The Disadvantaged Urban Migrant in Indianapolis." Economic Geography 48(Ap, 1972):153-167.

Duncan, Ron. "One Poor White." New South, Fall, 1969.

Egerton, John, and Gaillard, Frye. "The Mountaineer Minority." Race Relations Reporter 6(Ja-F, 1974):8-13.

Fandetti, Donald V. "Day Care in Working-Class Ethnic Neighborhoods: Implications for Social Policy." Child Welfare 55(N, 1976):618-626. [Polish and Irish in Baltimore]

Frost, Norman. A Statistical Study of the Public Schools of the Southern Appalachian Mountains. Washington, DC: GPO, 1915 (U.S. Bureau of Education, Bulletin, 1915, No. II).

Gaumnitz, Walter H. "The Extent and Nature of Public Education in the Mountains." Mountain Life and Work 9(Jl, 1933):20-25.

Gazaway, Rena. The Longest Mile. A Vivid Chronicle of Life in an Appalachian Hollow. New York: Penguin, 1974.

Genovese, Eugene D. "'Rather Be a Nigger Than a Poor White Man.'" In Toward a New View of America: Essays in Honor of Arthur C. Cole. Edited by Hans L. Trefousse. New York: Burt Franklin, 1977.

Gitlin, Todd, and Hollander, Nanci. Uptown: Poor Whites in Chicago. New York: Harper & Row, 1970.

Graff, Orin B. "Appalachia's Educational Situation: Twelve Basic Propositions." Tennessee Education 1(Spring, 1971):6-18.

_____. "The Needs of Education." In The Southern Appalachian Region: A Survey, pp. 188-200. Edited by Thomas R. Ford. Lexington, KY: n.p., 1962.

Gray, David M. "Discrimination Problems of Working-Class Whites." Journal of Inter-group Relations 3(Fall, 1974):19-25.

Greeley, Andrew M. "Ethnicity as an Influence on Behavior." Integrated Education, Jl-Ag, 1969, pp. 33-41.

Gregg, Robert E. "Appalachia-Southern Mountain Folk Culture." In Appalachian Studies. A Reader. Compiled by Frank F. Montalvo. Patrick Air Force Base, FL: Defense Race Relations Institute, 1974.

Haber, Alan. "The American Underclass." Poverty and Human Resources Abstracts, My-Je, 1967.

Ham, Tom. "Close-Up of a Hillbilly Family." American Mercury 52(1941):659-665. [Northern Georgia]

Hamill, Pete. "The Revolt of the White Lower Middle Class." New York, Ap 14, 1969.

Hamilton, William L. and Others. The Causes of Rural to Urban Migration Among the Poor, Mr 31, 1970. ERIC ED 149 943.

Hansen, James C., and Stevic, Richard R. Appalachian Students and Guidance. Boston: Houghton Mifflin, 1971.

Harmeling, Mary B. "Social and Cultural Links in the Urban Occupational Adjustment of Southern Appalachian Migrants." Doctoral dissertation, Fordham U., 1968.

Haslam, Gerald. "The Okies 40 Years Later." New Society, Je 19, 1975.

Hathaway, Dale E., Beegle, J. Allan, and Bryant, W. Keith. "Educational Status." In People of Rural America. Washington, DC: GPO, 1968.

Henderson, George. "Poor Southern Whites: A Neglected Urban Problem." Journal of Secondary Education, Mr, 1966.

Herzog, Elizabeth. About the Poor. Some Facts and Some Fictions. Washington, DC: GPO, 1968.

Hirsch, N. D. M. "An Experimental Study of East Kentucky Mountaineers." Genetic Psychology Monographs 3(1928):183-244.

Hooper, Frank H. "The Appalachian Child's Intellectual Capabilities--Deprivation or Diversity?" Journal of Negro Education, Summer, 1969.

Iannone, Ron. "School Ain't No Way." Appalachian Consciousness. Parsons, WV: McClain Press, 1972.

Isenberg, Robert M. "The Rural Disadvantaged." NEA Journal, Ap, 1963.

Johnson, Cyrus M., Coleman, A. Lee, and Clifford, William B. Mountain Families in Poverty. Lexington, KY: Department of Sociology, U. of Kentucky, 1967.

Kahn, Si. "New Strategies for Appalachia." New South 25(Summer, 1970):57-64.

Kelley, Eleanor A., and Turner, Deanna N. "Clothing Awareness and Feelings of Deprivation and Satisfaction Among Lower Social Class First-Grade Children." Journal of Home Economics 62(My, 1970):396-400. [Sample of white children]

Kephart, Horace. Our Southern Highlanders: A Narrative of Adventure in the Southern Appalachians and a Study of Life among the Mountaineers. New and enlarged edition. New York: The Macmillan Company, 1922.

Killian, Lewis M. White Southerners. New York: Random House, 1970.

Larson, Daro E. The Effect of a Preschool Experience Upon Intellectual Functioning Among Four-Year-Old White Children in Rural Minnesota. Mankato, MN: Mankato State College School of Education, 1969, 8 pp. ERIC ED 039 030.

Lemann, Nicholas. "The Case of the Poor Whites Against Harvard." Harvard Crimson, F 8, 1974. [Health Career Summer Program, Harvard U.]

Levine, Irving M. "The White Working American." Catholic Mind, Ja, 1971.

Looff, David H. Appalachia's Children. The Challenge of Mental Health. Lexington, KY: University Press of Kentucky, 1971.

McGuire, Chester. Housing, Poverty and Race: Areas of Overlap Between Poor Whites and Poor Blacks. Berkeley, CA: Institute of Urban and Regional Development, U. of California, Berkeley, Ja, 1974.

Matthews, E. M. Neighbor and Kin Life in a Tennessee Ridge Community. Nashville, TN: Vanderbilt U. Press, 1965.

Miles, Emma Bell. The Spirit of the Mountains. Knoxville: U. of Tennessee Press, 1965 reprint of 1905 edition.

Mink, Oscar G., and Barker, Laurence W. Drop-out Proneness in Appalachia. Morgantown, WV: Center for Appalachian Studies and Development, West Virginia U., 1968.

The Mountains Are Moving. [Report of the Conference on Equality of Educational Opportunity for Children of Appalachia (November 29-December 1, 1968, Pikeville College, Pikeville, Kentucky)] Washington, DC: National Education Association, 1968, 23 pp. ERIC ED 032 1953. Available from Publications-Sales Section, National Education Association, 1201 Sixteenth Street, N.W., Washington, DC 20036 (Stock No. 871-24836. Single copy 50 cents).

Nelsen, Hart M., and Frost, Eleanor. "Residence, Anomie, and Receptivity to Education among Southern Appalachian Presbyterians." Rural Sociology 36(D, 1971):521-532.

Petersen, Gene B. and others. Southern Newcomers to Northern Cities: Work and Social Adjustment in Cleveland. New York: Praeger, 1977.

Peterson, Bill. "Discrimination in the Hill Country." Southern Education Report, Mr 1969. [Ky.]

Photriadis, John D. Selected Social and Socio-psychological Characteristics of West Virginians In Their Own State and In Cleveland, Ohio. Springfield, VA: Clearinghouse for Federal Scientific and Technical Information, 1970.

Pilisuk, Mark, and Pilisuk, Phyllis. Poor Americans: How the Poor White Live, 1971, 200 pp. Available from Transaction Books, Rutgers U., New Brunswick, NJ 08903. ERIC ED 061 397.

Polansky, Norman A. "Powerlessness Among Rural Appalachian Youth." Rural Sociology, Je, 1969.

Polansky, Norman A., Borgman, Robert D., and De Saix, Christine. Roots of Futility. San Francisco, CA: Jossey-Bass, 1972. [Poverty and white children in southern Appalachia]

Power, Charles T. "The Jackson Whites: Tree Minus Roots." Los Angeles Times, S 29, 1978. [N.J.]

Preskill, Peggy. "Attitude Toward School of Some Southern Mountain Whites." Master's thesis, Northeastern Illinois State College, 1970.

Rainwater, Lee. "Social and Cultural Problems of Migrants to Cities." In President's National Advisory Commission on Rural Poverty, Rural Poverty in the United States. Washington, DC: GPO, My, 1968.

Reed, Roy. "The Cajuns Resist the Melting Pot." New York Times Magazine, F 29, 1976. [La.]

Rentel, Victor M., and Kennedy, John J. "Effects of Pattern Drill on the Phonology, Syntax, and Reading Achievement of Rural Appalachian Children." American Educational Research Journal 9(Winter, 1972):87-100.

Roberts, Lydia. The Nutrition and Care of Children in a Mountain County of Kentucky. U.S. Children's Bureau. Publication No. 107. Washington, DC: GPO, 1922.

Rural Poverty in Michigan. East Lansing, MI: Rural Manpower Center, Michigan State U., N, 1970. ERIC ED 044 231.

Schretter, Howard A. The Georgia Mountains: A Review of its Resources, Problems and Potentials. Athens, GA: U. of Georgia Institute of Community and Area Development, 1964, 93 pp. ERIC ED 037 264.

Schwarzweller, H. K. Career Placement and Economic Life Chances of Young Men from Eastern Kentucky. U. of Kentucky, Agricultural Experiment Station Bulletin 686, Ja, 1964.

Schwarzweller, H. K., and Brown, J. S. "Education as a Cultural Bridge between Eastern Kentucky and the Great Society." Rural Sociology, D, 1962.

Sherman, Mandel. Development of Attitudes: A Study of the Attitudes of Mountain Children. New York: The Payne Fund, 1933.

Sherman, Mandel, and Henry, Thomas R. Hollow Folk. New York: Thomas Y. Crowell Company, 1933.

Sherman, Mandel, and Key, Cora B. "Intelligence of Isolated Mountain Children." Child Development 3(D, 1932):279-290.

Sizer, Miriam M. "A Virginia Mountain School." Childhood Education 8(Ja, 1932):252-255.

Slocum, Walter L. Aspirations and Expectations of the Rural Poor--A Guide to Research. Washington, DC: GPO, O, 1967.

Smathers, Mike. "Notes of a Native Son." Mountain Life and Work 49(F, 1973):19-22.

Smith, L. H., and Rungeling, B. "Rural White Poverty: Are Unique Policies Required?" Growth and Change 7(O, 1976).

_____ and _____. Rural White Poverty in the Mid-South, D, 1973. ERIC ED 149 948.

Southern Appalachian Migration: A Descriptive Study, 1966. ERIC ED 032 151.

Tamblyn, Lewis R. Rural Education in the United States. Washington, DC: Rural Education Association, 1971.

Thomas, Robert K., and Wahrhaftig, Albert L. "Indians, Hillbillies, and the 'Education Problem.'" In Anthropological Perspectives On Education, pp. 230-251. Edited by Murray L. Wax, Stanley Diamond, and Fred O. Gearing. New York: Basic Books, 1971. [Ozarks, eastern Oklahoma]

Tornquist, Elizabeth. "Standing Up to America: Poor Whites in Durham." New South, Fall, 1969.

U.S. Congress, 92nd, 1st session, Senate, Select Committee on Equal Educational Opportunity. Equal Educational Opportunity-1971. Hearings... Part 15-Education in Rural America. Washington, DC: GPO, 1971.

U.S. Congress, 95th, 1st session, House of Representatives, Committee on Public Works and Transportation, Subcommittee on Economic Development. Appalachian Child Development: Hearing... Washington, DC: GPO, 1978.

U.S. Department of Agriculture, Economic Research Service. Age of Transition. Rural Youth in a Changing Society (Separate "Supplement"). Washington, DC: GPO, O, 1967.

U.S. Department of Health, Education, and Welfare. Mental Health in Appalachia. Washington, DC: GPO, 1964.

U.S. Department of Labor. "Rural Schooling." Integrated Education, Ag-S, 1964.

Vance, Hubert, and Hankins, Norman. "Analysis of Cognitive Ability for Rural White Culturally Different Children." Journal of Psychology 98(Ja, 1978):15-21.

Wagner, Thomas E. Urban Appalachian School Children: The Least Understood of All. Cincinnati: Urban Appalachian Council, 1974.

_____. "Urban Schools and Appalachian Children." Urban Education 12(O, 1977): 283-296.

Walker, Malcolm T. The Riverpeople of Clayton: Poor Whites in a Community of Southern Illinois. Carbondale, IL: University Museum, Southern Illinois U., 1971.

Walker, Walter L. "The War on Poverty and the Poor: A Study of Race, Poverty, and a Program." Doctoral dissertation, Brandeis U., 1969.

Waller, Eugene C. A Survey of the Church and Independent Schools and Colleges of the Southern Appalachians. Knoxville, TN: The Author, 1410 Magnolia Avenue, 1931.

Walls, David, and Stephenson, John B. (eds.). Appalachia in the Sixties: Decade of Reawakening. Lexington, KY: University Press of Kentucky, 1972.

Walls, Dwayne E. The Chickenbone Special. New York: Harcourt Brace Jovanovich, 1971.

Wheeler, L. R. "A Comparative Study of the Intelligence of East Tennessee Mountain Children." Journal of Educational Psychology 44(1942):321-334.

Whisnant, David E. "The Folk Hero in Appalachian Struggle History." New South 28 (Fall, 1973):30-47.

_____. "Recovery of Regional Identity in Appalachia: Thoughts Upon Entering the Zone of Occult Instability." Soundings 56 (Spring, 1973):124-138.

The White Ghetto. Pacifica Tape Library, 5316 Venice Blvd., Los Angeles, CA 90019. [Poor whites in Bell Gardens, CA]

Wilson, Charles M. Backwoods America. Chapel Hill: U. of North Carolina Press, 1934.

Witmer, Helen L. "Children and Poverty." Children, N, D, 1964.

Wright Institute. Adult Basic Education Teacher Training Institute: Problems of the Urban Poor, Particularly the Urban Poor White, Ag, 1971. ERIC ED 101 120.

Youth Action and Youth Issues in Appalachia. A Report from the Youth Development Leadership Program of the Appalachian Regional Commission, 1971, 92 pp. Washington, DC: Appalachian Regional Commission. ERIC ED 055 710.

Jews

A Guide to Jewish Student Groups 1971. North American Jewish Students' Network, 154 W. 27th Street, New York, NY 10001.

Adler, Selig, and Connolly, Thomas E. From Ararat to Suburbia: The History of the Jewish Community of Buffalo. Philadelphia: n.p., 1960.

Alexander, Morris, Fowler, Floyd, Jr., and Gurin, Arnold. A Community Survey for Long Range Planning: A Study of the Jewish Population of Greater Boston. Boston: Combined Jewish Philanthropies of Greater Boston, 1967.

Alland, Alexander. "The Jews of the Virgin Islands." American Hebrew 146 and 147(1940).

Alter, Robert. "What Jewish Studies Can Do." Commentary 58(O, 1974):71-76.

_____. "Teaching Jewish Teachers." Commentary, Jl, 1968.

American Jewish Committee. The Future of the Jewish Community in America. A Task Force Report. New York: American Jewish Committee, O, 1972.

_____. "The Relationship between Jews and Revolutionary Forces... Dialogue." Congress Bi-Weekly, Mr 30 and Ap 13, 1973.

Ash, Robert T. "Jewish Adolescents' Attitudes Toward Religion and Ethnicity." Adolescence, Summer, 1969.

Auerbach, Jerold S. "From Rags to Robes: The Legal Profession, Social Mobility and the American Jewish Experience." American Jewish Historical Quarterly 66(D, 1976): 249-284.

Baron, Salo W. "Changing Patterns of Anti-semitism: A Survey." Jewish Social Studies 38(Winter, 1976):5-38.

Baskerville, Beatrice. The Polish Jew. New York: n.p., 1906.

Berroll, Selma. "Education and the Italian and Jewish Community Experience." In The Interaction Between Italians and Jews in America. Edited by Jean Scarpaci. New York: American Italian Historical Association, 1975.

Bienstock, Herbert. Current Economic Development: Implications for the Jewish Community in the Metropolitan N.Y. Area, 1971. Federation Employment and Guidance Service, 215 Park Avenue South, New York, NY 10003.

Bloom, Marshall, and Schappes, Morris U. "LeRoi Jones and Anti-Semitism. A Dialogue." Jewish Currents, My, 1968.

Bond, Horace Mann. "Negro Attitudes Toward Jews." Jewish Social Studies, Ja, 1965.

Brandes, Joseph, with Douglas, Martin. Immigrants to Freedom: Jewish Communities in Rural New Jersey. Philadelphia: U. of Pennsylvania Press, 1971.

Breck, Allen D. The Centennial History of the Jews of Colorado, 1859-1959. Denver, CO: Hirschfeld Press, 1960.

Bricker, Harry, and Marcson, Simon. Jewish Education in Chicago. Chicago: Jewish Charities of Chicago, 1940.

Brickman, W. W. "The American Jewish Day School Movement." Tradition 9(Spring-Summer, 1967):176-193.

Brickner, Barnett R. "The History of Jewish Education in Cincinnati." Jewish Education 8 (O-D, 1936):115-126.

Brill, Moshe. "Comparative Psychological Studies of Jews and Non-Jews and their Implications for Jewish Education." Jewish Education 8 (Ap-Je, 1936):73-78.

Butwin, Frances. The Jews in America. Minneapolis, MN: Learner, 1969. [A school textbook]

By Myself I'm a Book: An Oral History of the Immigrant Jewish Experience in Pittsburgh. New York: Ktav Publishing House, 1972.

Cavan, Ruth S. "Jewish Student Attitudes toward Interreligious and Intra-Jewish Marriage." American Journal of Sociology 76(My, 1971): 1064-1071.

Cederbaum, David I. "Extent and Cost of Jewish Education in the United States." Jewish Education 1(Ja, 1929):52-55.

Cohen, Naomi W. Not Free to Desist: The American Jewish Committee, 1906-1966. Philadelphia: Jewish Publication Society, 1972.

Community Self-Study of Jewish Youth. Savannah, GA: Savannah Jewish Council, 1966.

Crupar, Harvey. "A Critical Evaluation of Jewish Studies Programs in Leading Universities." Master's thesis, Yeshiva U., 1974.

Daniels, Leona. "The 34th Man; How Well Is Jewish Minority Culture Represented in Children's Fiction?" School Libraries 16 (1970):38-43.

Diamond, Sander A. The Nazi Movement in the United States, 1924-1941. Ithaca, NY: Cornell U., 1974.

Dinin, Samuel. "An Analysis and Critique of Jewish Education in America." Jewish Education 26(Fall, 1955):6-16.

_____. "The Curriculum of the Jewish School." American Jewish Yearbook 63(1962):214-225.

_____. "Issues Facing the Jewish School." Jewish Education 26(Spring, 1956):18-21.

Dinnerstein, Leonard. "Southern Jewry and the Desegregation Crisis, 1954-1970." American Jewish Historical Quarterly 62(Mr, 1973).

Dinsky, Samuel H. "Secondary Jewish Education in the United States." Doctoral dissertation, Dropsie College, 1962.

Doroshkin, Milton. Yiddish in America: Social and Cultural Foundations. Rutherford, NJ: Fairleigh Dickinson U. Press, 1970. 1881-1924

Dushkin, Alexander Mordecai. "Jewish Education in New York City." Doctoral dissertation, Teachers College, Columbia U., 1918.

_____. "Towards an American Jewish Education." Jewish Education 13(Ap, 1941):17-22.

_____. "Two Decades of Progress in Jewish Education--A Survey." Jewish Education 4 (Ja-Mr, 1932):3-13. [1910-1930]

Dushkin, Alexander M., and Engelman, Uriah Z. Jewish Education in the United States: Report of the Commission for the Study of Jewish Education in the United States. New York: American Association for Jewish Education, 1959.

Edelstein, Menachem M. "History of the Development of a Jewish Teaching Profession in America." Jewish Education 23(Winter, Summer, 1952):36-42, 62; 45-53, 68.

Ellman, Yisrael. "The Ethnic Awakening in the United States and Its Influence on Jews." Ethnicity 4(Je, 1977):133-155.

Fine, Isaac M. The Making of an American Jewish Community: The History of Baltimore Jewry from 1772 to 1920. Philadelphia: Jewish Publication Society of America, 1971.

Friedman, Norman L. "Religion's Subsystem: Toward a Sociology of Jewish Education." Sociology of Education, Winter, 1969.

Gartner, Lloyd P. "Immigration and the Formation of American Jewry, 1840-1925." Journal of World History, XI, Nos. 1-2 (1968).

_____ (ed.). Jewish Education in the United States: A Documentary History. New York: Teachers College, 1970.

Ginsberg, Yona. Jews in a Changing Neighborhood: The Study of Mattapan. New York: Free Press, 1975. Boston, MA

Ginzberg, Eli. "Jew and Negro: Notes on the Mobility of Two Minority Groups in the United States." In Salo Wittmayer Baron: Jubilee Volume, On the Occasion of His Eightieth Birthday, I. New York: Columbia U. Press, 1975.

Glazer, Nathan. American Judaism. Chicago: U. of Chicago Press, 1957.

Glocksman, William M. "The Place of the Yiddish Secular School in America Today." Jewish Education, Jl, 1969.

Goldenberg, Bernard. "The Hebrew Day School Movement in America." Independent School Bulletin 35(O, 1975):51-53.

Goldstein, R. M. "American Jewish Population Studies Since World War II." American Jewish Archives 22(Ap, 1970):15-48.

Goldstein, Sidney. A Population Survey of the Greater Springfield Jewish Community. Springfield, MA: Jewish Community Council, 1968.

Goldstein, Sidney, and Goldscheider, Calvin. Jewish Americans: Three Generations in a Jewish Community. Englewood Cliffs, NJ: Prentice-Hall, 1968. [Providence, RI]

Golub, Jacob S. "Transition in Jewish Education." Jewish Education 3(Ap-Je, 1931):67-76.

Golub, Jacob S., and Honor, Leo L. "Some Guiding Principles for the Curriculum of the Jewish School of Tomorrow." Jewish Education 4(O-D, 1932):150-162.

Gorelick, Sherry. "Social Control, Social Mobility, and the Eastern European Jews: An Analysis of Public Education in New York City, 1880-1924." Doctoral dissertation, Columbia U., 1975.

Grossman, Mordecai. "Parochial Schools for Jewish Children--An Adverse View." Jewish Education 16(My, 1945):20-25.

Gumpert, David. "Militant Jewish Group Sparks a Controversy in New York City Area." Wall Street Journal, N 4, 1969.

Halpern, Ben. "The Roots of American Jewish Liberalism." American Jewish Historical Quarterly 66(D, 1976):190-214.

Harap, Louis. "Class, Ethnicity and the American Jewish Committee." Jewish Currents 26(D, 1972.

Harris, Hershl. "Gilded Ghetto, II: Words and Actions," Jewish Currents, Je, 1965. [Jews and Negroes]

_____. "School Integration and Jewish Leadership." Jewish Currents, My, 1964.

Harris, Louis, and Swanson, Bert E. Black-Jewish Relations in New York City. New York: Praeger, 1970.

Hartstein, Jacob I. "Jewish Community Elementary Parochial Schools." Jewish Education 9(O-D, 1937):136-142. [New York City]

_____. "Jewish Education in New York City Before 1861." Master's thesis, College of the City of New York, 1933.

Hendrick, Burton J. "The Jewish Invasion of America." McClure's Magazine, Mr, 1913.

Higham, John W. "Social Discrimination Against Jews in America, 1830-1930." American Jewish Historical Society, Publications 47 (S, 1957):1-33.

Hilewitz, Yehuda. "The Ku Klux Klan and the Jews." Master's thesis, Yeshiva U., 1972.

Himmelfarb, Milton. "Is American Jewry in Crisis?" Commentary, Mr, 1969.

_____. "Negroes, Jews, and Muzhiks." Commentary, O, 1966.

Hinchin, Martin. "A History of the Jews of Sioux City, Iowa, 1857-1945." Doctoral dissertation, Hebrew Union College, 1946.

Honor, Leo L. "The Impact of the American Environment and American Ideas on Jewish Elementary Education in the United States." Jewish Quarterly Review 45(Ap, 1955):451-496.

_____. "Jewish Elementary Education in the United States (1901-1950)." American Jewish Historical Society, Publications 42 (S, 1952):1-42.

Howe, Irving. World of Our Fathers: The Journey of East Europeans to America and the Life they Found and Made. New York: Harcourt Brace Jovanovich, 1976.

Hurwich, Louis. "Jewish Education in Boston." Jewish Education 26(Spring, 1956):22-33.

Janowitz, Morris. Judaism of the Next Generation: A Survey of Religious Education. Chicago: U. of Chicago, Ja, 1969. [Miami]

Janowsky, Oscar. "The Cleveland Bureau of Jewish Education: A Case Study, 1924-53." American Jewish Historical Quarterly 59 (Mr, 1965).

Jelinek, Yeshayahu. "Self-Identification of First Generation Hungarian Jewish Immigrants." American Jewish Historical Quarterly, Mr, 1972.

The Jewish Community of Greater Baltimore: A Population Study. Baltimore, MD: Associated Jewish Charities, D, 1968.

"Jewish Youth Freedom Fighters and the Role of the Jewish Community: An Evaluation." Jewish Currents, Jl-Ag, 1965.

"The Jewish Youth Scene: Main Issues and Problems." Jewish Currents 24(O, 1970):4-15, 18-23, 28-35.

Joseph, Samuel. "Illiteracy." In Jewish Immigration to the United States From 1881 to 1910, pp. 146-148. New York: Columbia U., 1914.

Jospe, Alfred. Jewish Studies in American Colleges and Universities. Washington, DC: B'nai B'rith Hillel Foundations, 1971.

Kaganoff, Nathan M. "The Education of the Jewish Child in the District of Columbia, 1861-1951." Jewish Education 29(Fall, 1958):39-49.

_____. "An Overview of the Jewish Community in Pre-Civil War America Based on Previously Unpublished Primary Sources." Rhode Island Jewish Historical Society Notes, N, 1969.

Kahan, Arcadius. "Economic Opportunities and Some Pilgrims' Progress: Jewish Immigrants from Eastern Europe in the U.S., 1890-1914." Journal of Economic History 38(Mr, 1978):235-251.

Kaplan, Abraham. "Survey of Hebrew Parochial Parochial Schools of New York." Master's thesis, New York U., 1929.

Katz, F. "The Attitude of Jews Toward the Education of Girls." Master's thesis, U. of Chicago, 1950.

Katz, Irving. "Jewish Education at Temple Beth El, Detroit, 1850-1880." Michigan History 52 (Fall, 1968).

Klein, Aaron. "A History of Jewish Education in Buffalo." Jewish Education 14(Ap-Je, 1942): 28-35.

Kogan, Lawrence A. "The Jewish Conception of Negroes in the North: An Historical Approach." Phylon, Winter, 1967.

Korey, Harold. "The History of Jewish Education in Chicago." Master's thesis, U. of Chicago, 1942.

_____. "The Story of Jewish Education in Chicago Prior to 1923." Jewish Education 6 (Ja-Mr, 1934):37-47.

Kramer, Daniel Z. "The History and Impact of Torah Umesorah and Hebrew Day Schools in America." Doctoral dissertation, Yeshiva U., 1976.

Krug, Mark M. "History of the Yiddish Schools in Chicago." Jewish Education 25(Fall, 1954): 67-73.

_____. The Melting of the Ethnics: Education of the Immigrants, 1880-1914. Bloomington, IN: Phi Delta Kappa Educational Foundation, 1976.

Kuznets, Simon. "Immigration of Russian Jews to the United States: Background and Structure." Perspectives in American History 9(1975).

Lang, Kurt, and Lang, Gladys. "Resistance to School Desegregation: A Case Study of Backlash Among Jews." Sociological Inquiry, Winter, 1965.

Lavin, Lottie. "Jewish Education in Chicago." Master's thesis, U. of Chicago, n.d.

Lewin, Kurt. "Jewish Education and Reality." Jewish Education 15(S, 1943):125-137.

Lichtenberg, Jean Paul. From the First to the Last of the Just. A Study of the History of the Relation between Jews and Christians Throughout the Centuries, 1972. Ecumenical Theological Research Fraternity in Israel, P.O. Box 249, Jerusalem, Israel.

Liddil, Fonrose Reader. "The Intelligence of Jewish School Children." Master's thesis, U. of Chicago, 1939.

Lipset, S. M., and Ladd, Everett, Jr. "Jewish Academics in the United States: Their Achievements, Culture and Politics." In The American Jewish Year Book, pp. 89-128. Philadelphia: Jewish Publication Society of America, 1971.

Marcus, Jacob R. The Colonial American Jew, 1492-1776. 3 vols. Detroit, MI: Wayne State U., 1970.

Mashberg, Michael. "The West and the Holocaust." Patterns of Prejudice 12(My-Je, 1978):19-32. [U.S. Department of State and German-Jewish refugees]

Maslow, Will. The Structure and Functioning of the American Jewish Community. New York: American Jewish Committee, 1974.

Mayer, Albert J. Flint Jewish Population Study: 1967. Flint, MI: Jewish Community Council, 1969.

Nardi, Noah. "The Growth of Jewish Day Schools in America." Jewish Education 20(N, 1948): 23-32.

_____. "Studies in Intelligence of Jewish Children." Jewish Education 19(Summer, 1948):41-51.

_____. "A Survey of Jewish Day Schools in America." Jewish Education 16(S, 1944):12-26.

National Jewish Community Relations Advisory Council. The Public Schools and American Democratic Pluralism--The Role of the Jewish Community, Ja, 1972. The Council, 55 West 42nd Street, New York, NY 10036.

Neusner, Jacob. "The Selling of Jewish Studies." Moment 3(Mr, 1978):61-62.

Orentlicher, Edward. "The Talmud Torah, Its Structure, Philosophy and Decline (1860-1960)." Doctoral dissertation, Dropsie College, Je, 1962.

Panitz, Esther L. "The Polarity of American Jewish Attitudes towards Immigration (1870-1891)." American Jewish Historical Quarterly, D, 1963.

Phillips, Bruce Arlan. "Acculturation, Group Survival, and the Ethnic Community: A Social History of the Jewish Community of Brookline, Massachusetts, 1915-1940." Doctoral dissertation, U. of California, Los Angeles, 1975. Univ. Microfilms Order No. 75-19,689.

Poll, Solomon. The Hasidic Community of Williamsburg. New York: Schocken, 1969.

Porter, Jack Nusan. "Jewish Conservative Backlash?" Commonweal 97(O 13, 1972):33-37.

Porter, Jack Nusan and others. "3 On JDL." Jewish Currents 26(Je, 1972):4-9. [Jewish Defense League, NYC]

Rabinove, Samuel. "Should Jews Support Public Schools?" Reform Judaism 6(Ja, 1978).

Rabinowitz, Dorothy. "Are Jewish Students Different?" Change 3(Summer, 1971):47-50.

_____. The Other Jews: Portraits in Poverty. New York: American Jewish Committee, 1972.

Rafter, Charlotte. "The Role of the Jew in America's Making." Master's thesis, Boston U., 1938.

Rauch, Eduardo L. "Jewish Education in the United States: 1840-1920." Doctoral dissertation, Harvard U., 1978. Univ. Microfilms Order No. 7823684.

Rice, David G., and Sternbach, Richard A. "The New York Jewish Student Syndrome: Stereotype and Facts." Personnel and Guidance Journal, Ja, 1969.

Rockowitz, Murray, and Lang, Gerhard. Trends in Jewish School Enrollment in the United States 1974/1975, S, 1975. ERIC ED 137 910.

Rollock, Elise C. "A Negro [Teacher] Speaks to Jews." Jewish Currents, F, 1968.

Rosen, Ben. "Recent Surveys of Jewish Education [in Five American Cities]." Jewish Education 2(Je, 1930):78-89.

_____. "Survey of Jewish Education in New York City." Jewish Education 1(My, 1929):82-96.

Rosen, Gladys. Guidelines to Jewish History in Social Studies Instructional Material. New York: American Jewish Committee, S, 1971.

Rosenfeld, Max. "Jewish Teenagers and Negro Youth." Jewish Currents, F, 1967.

Rosenman, Yehuda. The Treatment of Jews in History and Social Studies Textbooks in Use in American High Schools. Report on a Preliminary Study. New York: American Jewish Committee, Je, 1970.

Roucek, Joseph S. "The Problems of Jewish Education." Journal of Negro Education, Summer, 1969.

Rudavsky, David. "Hebraic and Judaic Studies in American Higher Education." Congress Bi-Weekly 41(O 25, 1974):8-10.

_____. "Jewish Education in New York City Since 1918." Doctoral dissertation, New York U., 1946.

_____. "A Note on the Teaching of Hebrew in American Colleges and Universities." Jewish Journal of Sociology 14(Je, 1972).

Safier, Arno. "Dual Minority Status: Group Identification and Membership Conflict: A Study of Black Jews." Doctoral dissertation, New York U., 1971.

Sanitz, Samuel. "Survey of Jewish Education in Philadelphia." Master's thesis, Temple U., 1928.

Sanua, Victor D. "The Relationship Between Jewish Education and Jewish Identification." Jewish Education 35(Fall, 1964):37-50.

_____. "A Study of the Adjustment of Sephardi Jews in New York Metropolitan Area." Jewish Journal of Sociology, Je, 1967.

Schappes, Morris U. "The Jewish Question and the Left--Old and New." Jewish Currents, Je, 1969.

_____. "The Jews and American Slavery." Jewish Currents, My, 1954.

Scheiner, Louis. "Interaction Analysis in Elementary Jewish Schools in Philadelphia--Camden Area: A Study of One Hundred Twenty Classes." Doctoral dissertation, Dropsie College, 1968.

Schmidt, Sarah. "The Jewish Experience in the Public School." American Educator 2(Spring, 1978):23-26.

Schoenfeld, Eugen. "Small- Town Jews' Integration into Their Communities." Rural Sociology 35(Je, 1970):175-190.

Seligs, Rose. "Racial Attitudes of Jewish and Non-Jewish Children in the Sixth Grade." Master's thesis, U. of Cincinnati, 1932.

Shapiro, Harry L. "The Jewish People: A Biological History." In Race and Science, pp. 107-180. New York: Columbia U. Press, 1970.

Siago, D. W., and Koldin, T. S. "The Mental Capacity of Sixth-grade Jewish and Italian Children." School and Society 22(1925):564-568.

Slater, Mariam K. "My Son the Doctor: Aspects of Mobility Among American Jews." American Sociological Review, Je, 1969.

Slavin, Stephen L. "Bias in U.S. Big Business Recruitment." Patterns of Prejudice 10 (S-O, 1976):22-25. [Anti-semitic selective recruiting at American colleges and universities]

Slawson, John. The Realities of Jewish Integration. Institute of Human Relations, American Jewish Committee, 165 East 56th Street, New York, NY 10022, 1965.

Soviv, Aaron. "Self-Acceptance of Jewishness by Young Jewish People." Jewish Education 26 (Summer, 1955):22-31.

Strober, Gerald S. Portrait of the Elder Brother. Jews and Judaism in Protestant Teaching Material. New York: American Jewish Committee, 1972.

A Study of the Jewish Population of Center City Philadelphia. Philadelphia: Federation of Jewish Agencies of Greater Philadelphia, D, 1966.

Swichkow, Louis J., and Gartner, Lloyd P. The History of the Jews of Milwaukee. Philadelphia: Jewish Publication Society of America, 1963.

Teller, Judd L. "Negroes and Jews: A Hard Look." Conservative Judaism, Fall, 1966.

Todes, David H. "History of Jewish Education in Philadelphia, 1782-1873." Doctoral dissertation, Dropsie College, 1953.

Ury, Z. F. "Development of the [Jewish] Day School in Los Angeles." Jewish Education 33 (Spring, 1963):158-161.

Vorspan, Max, and Gartner, Lloyd P. History of the Jews of Los Angeles. San Marino, CA: Huntington Library, 1970.

Weinstein, David. "Judaic Studies in Metropolitan Chicago Colleges." Intellect 101(O, 1972 1972):50-52.

Weisbrod, Robert G., and Stein, Arthur. Bittersweet Encounter: The Afro-American and the American Jew. Westport, CT: Greenwood, 1970. [Since 1920]

Wirth, Louis. "Education for Survival: The Jews." American Journal of Sociology 48 (My, 1943).

Wolfe, Ann G. The Invisible Jewish Poor, Je 8, 1971. American Jewish Committee, 165 East 56th Street, New York, NY 10022.

Yapko, Benjamin L. "Jewish Elementary Education in the United States: Colonial Period to 1900." Doctoral dissertation, American U., 1958.

Other Ethnic Groups

Anderson, Jervis. "The Haitians of New York." New Yorker, Mr 31, 1975.

Andersson, Theodore, and Boyer, Mildred. Bilingual Schooling in the United States. 2 vols. Washington, DC: GPO, 1970.

Aswad, Barbara C. (ed.). Arabic-Speaking Communities in American Cities. New York: Center for Migration Studies, 1974.

Beard, Henry, O'Donoghue, Michael, and Trow, George W. S. "Our White Heritage." National Lampoon, Jl, 1973.

Bernard, William S. "New Directions in Integration and Ethnicity." International Migration Review 5(Winter, 1971):464-473. [Immigrants in U.S.]

Bowers, D. F. (ed.). Foreign Influences in American Life, n.p., 1952.

Braun, Heywood, and Britt, George. Christians Only. New York: Vanguard, 1931.

Carlson, Robert A. The Quest for Conformity: Americanization through Education. New York: Wiley, 1975.

Cates, Edwin H. The English in America. Minneapolis, MN: Lerner, 1969. [A school textbook]

Curran, Thomas J. Xenophobia and Immigration, 1820-1930. Boston: Twayne, 1975.

Dubin, Murray. "Gypsies Taking 3 Rs Seriously." Philadelphia Inquirer, Ap 11, 1976. [Philadelphia]

Duchac, René. La Sociologie des Migrations Aux États-Unis. Paris: Mouton, École Pratique des Hautes Études, 1974.

Dunlevy, James A., and Gemery, Henry A. "Economic Opportunity and the Responses of 'Old' and 'New' Migrants to the United States." Journal of Economic History 38(D, 1978):901-917.

Ehrlich, Richard L. (ed.). Immigrants in Industrial America, 1850-1920. Charlottesville, VA: University Press of Virginia, 1977.

Feeley, Dorothy M. Ethnic Groups in Our World Today. Grade 2. Stoneham, MA: Stoneham Public Schools, n.d., 29 pp. ERIC ED 053 010.

Feinstein, Otto. Ethnic Groups in the City: Culture, Institutions and Power. Lexington, MA: Heath, 1971.

_____. "Ethnic Studies in the High School: The Case of Detroit." Michigan Academician 5(Winter, 1973).

Fishman, Joshua A., and Nahirny, Vladimir C. "The Ethnic Group School and Mother Tongue Maintenance." In Joshua A. Fishman and Others, Language Loyalty in the United States, pp. 92-126. The Hague: Mouton, 1966.

_____. "The Ethnic Group School and Mother Tongue Maintenance in the United States." Sociology of Education 27(Summer, 1964): 306-317.

Foley, Allen Richard. "From French Canadian to Franco-American: A Study of the Immigration of the French Canadian into New England, 1650-1935." Doctoral dissertation, Harvard U., 1939.

Gambino, Richard. A Guide to Ethnic Studies Programs in American Colleges, Universities and Schools. New York: The Rockefeller Foundation, My, 1975.

Glazer, Nathan. "Ethnicity and Schools." Commentary 58(S, 1974):55-59.

_____. "Slums and Ethnicity." In Social Welfare and Urban Problems, pp. 84-112. Edited by Thomas D. Sherrard. New York: Columbia U. Press, 1968.

Gordon, Milton M. Assimililation in American Life: The Role of Race, Religion, and National Origins. New York: Oxford, 1964.

Greeley, Andrew W. Ethnicity, Denomination and Inequality. Beverly Hills, CA: Sage, 1975.

_____. Ethnicity in the United States: A Preliminary Reconnaissance. New York: Wiley, 1974.

_____. "Making It In America: Ethnic Groups and Social Status." Social Policy 4(S-O, 1973):21-30.

Grollman, Earl A., and Ben-Sorek, Esor. "Textbooks and Ethnocentrism." Jewish Education 36(Spring-Summer, 1966):179-180, 191.

Gropper, Rena C. Gypsies in the City. Culture Patterns and Survival, 1975. Darwin Press, Box 2202, Princeton, NJ 08540. [N.Y.C.]

Halpern, Ben. "Ethnic and Religious Minorities: Subcultures and Subcommunities." Jewish Social Studies, Ja, 1965.

Hamon, E. Les Canadiens-Francais de la
Nouvelle-Angleterre. Quebec, Canada:
N. S. Hardy, 1891.

Herman, Judith (ed.). The Schools and Group
Identity. Educating for a New Pluralism.
New York: Institute on Pluralism and Group
Identity, American Jewish Committee, 1974.

Higham, John. "Hanging Together: Divergent
Unities in American History." Journal of
American History 61(Je, 1974):5-28.

_____. "Integration vs. Pluralism. Another
American Dilemma." Center Magazine
(Jl-Ag, 1974):67-73.

Hitti, Philip K. The Syrians in America.
New York: Doran, 1924.

Hunt, Thomas C. "The Schooling of Immigrants
and Black Americans: Some Similarities and
Differences." Journal of Negro Education
45(Fall, 1976):423-431.

Ibrahim, Saad E. M. "Interaction, Perception,
and Attitudes of Arab Students Toward
Americans." Sociology and Social Research
55(O, 1970):29-46.

Jaipaul. Politics of Ethnicity. Philadelphia:
Ethnic Heritage Affairs Institute, 1977.

Kallen, Horace M. Culture and Democracy in
the United States: Studies in the Group
Psychology of the American Peoples. New
York: n.p., 1924.

Karmin, Monroe W. "Nationality Groups Aim to
Vie With Negroes for Government Aid."
Wall Street Journal, Ap 24, 1969.

Katibah, H. I., and Ziadeh, F. (comps.).
Arabic-Speaking Americans. New York:
Institute of Arab American Affairs, 1946.

Kayal, Philip M., and Kayal, Joseph M.
The Syrians and Lebanese in America. New
York: Twayne, 1975.

Kornacker, Mildred. "The Ethnic Teacher in the
Urban Classroom." Education and Urban
Society, My, 1969.

Kosa, J. (ed.). The Home of the Learned Man--
A Symposium on the Immigrant Scholar in
America. New Haven, CT: College and
University Press, 1968.

Kries, Frank. "The Racial Attitudes of the
Polish Americans in Cook County [Illinois]."
Bachelor's thesis, Lewis College, 1966.

Krug, Mark M. "White Ethnic Studies:
Prospects and Pitfalls." Phi Delta Kappan
53(Ja, 1972):322-324.

La Gumina, Salvatore J., and Cavioli, Frank J.
(eds.). The Ethnic Dimension in American
Society. Boston: Holbook, 1974.

Lichtenstein, Jules Herbert. "White Ethnic and
Black Economic Assimilation and Mobility:
A Study of Employment Patterns and Determinants in Selected SMSA's." Doctoral
dissertation, Cornell U., 1975.

McHenry, Stewart. "The Syrians of Upstate New
York." Doctoral dissertation, Syracuse U.,
1973.

Magidson, Judith (ed.). The Reacting Americans.
An Interim Look at the White Ethnic Lower
Middle Class. New York: American Jewish
Committee, O, 1968.

Magner, Thomas F. "The Rise and Fall of the
Ethnics." Journal of General Education 25
(Ja, 1974):253-264.

Mandell, Frederick. "Gypsies: Culture and
Child Care." Pediatrics 54(N, 1974):603-
607.

Marcson, Simon. "The Role of Voluntary Segregated Education in an Ethnic Group."
Master's thesis, U. of Chicago, 1941.

Moquin, Wayne (ed.). Makers of America. 10
vols. Chicago: Encyclopedia Brittanica
Educational Corp., 1971.

Myrdal, Gunnar. "The Case Against Romantic
Ethnicity." Center Magazine 7(Jl-Ag, 1974):
26-30.

O'Brien, David J. "Needed: A 'New' History."
America, My 3, 1969. [American Catholic
history]

Patterson, Orlando. "Hidden Dangers in the
Ethnic Revival." New York Times, F 20,
1978.

Peachey, Paul, and Mudd, Rita (eds.). Evolving
Patterns of Ethnicity in American Life.
Washington, DC: National Center for Urban
Ethnic Affairs, Je 1, 1971, 62 pp. ERIC
ED 063 435.

Prosen, Rose Mary. "'Ethnic Literature'--of
Whom and for Whom; Digressions of a Neo-
American Teacher." College English 35(Mr,
1974):659-669.

Record, Wilson. "Ethnic Identity and Ethnic
Conflict: Some Student Concerns." Northwest Magazine, Ap 18, 1971.

Rischin, Moses. "Beyond the Great Divide:
Immigration and the Last Frontier." Journal
of American History 55(Je, 1968):42-53.

Rosenstein, David. "Contributions of Education
to Ethnic Fusion in the United States."
School and Society 13(Je 18, 1921):673-682.

Rumilly, Robert. Histoire des Franco-Americains.
Montreal, Canada: L'Union Saint-Jean-Baptiste
d'Amérique, 1958.

Rushton, William F. The Cajuns: From Acadia to Louisiana. New York: Farrar, Strauss, Giroux, 1979.

Scult, Melvin. "The Study of Non-Black Minorities in the School." Social Studies 63(Mr, 1972):99-106.

Seifer, Nancy. Education and the New Pluralism. A Preliminary Survey of Recent Progress in the 50 States. New York: American Jewish Committee, My 19, 1973.

Sengstock, Mary C. "Maintenance of Social Interaction Patterns in An Ethnic Group." Doctoral dissertation, Washington U., 1967. [Chaldean Iraqui in Detroit area]

Simpson, Janice C. "Gypsies Seek to Win Opportunity, but Fear They'll Lose Traditions." Wall Street Journal, Ap 14, 1976. [Gypsies in State of Washington]

Smith, Timothy L. "Religion and Ethnicity in America." American Historical Review 83 (D, 1978):1155-1185.

Stein, Howard F., and Hill, Robert F. (eds.). The Ethnic Imperative: Examining the New White Ethnic Movement. University Park, PA: Pennsylvania State U. Press, 1977.

Sutherland, Anne. Gypsies: The Hidden Americans. London: Tavistock, 1975.

_____. "Gypsies, the Hidden Americans." Society 12(Ja-F, 1975):27-33.

Taeuber, Alma F., and Taeuber, Karl E. "Recent Immigration and Studies of Ethnic Assimilation." Demography 4(1967):798-808.

Tomasi, Lydio F. The Ethnic Factor in the Future of Inequality, 1972. Center for Migration Studies, 209 Flagg Place, Staten Island, NY 10304.

Tyrner-Stastny, Gabrielle. The Gypsy in Northwest America. Olympia, WA: Washington State American Revolution Bicentennial Commission, 1977.

U.S. Bureau of the Census. Ethnic Origin and Educational Attainment. November, 1969. Series P-20, No. 220, Ap 8, 1971. Washington, DC: GPO, 1971.

U.S. Census Bureau. Current Population Report, Series P-20, No. 221. "Characteristics of the Population by Ethnic Origin: November, 1969." Washington, DC: GPO, Ap 30, 1971.

U.S. Congress, 91st, 2nd session, House of Representatives, Committee on Education and Labor, General Subcommittee on Education. Ethnic Heritage Studies Centers. Hearings... Washington, DC: GPO, 1970.

Vecoli, Rudolph J. "Ethnicity: A Neglected Dimension of American History." In Overcoming Middle Class Rage. Edited by Murray Friedman. Philadelphia: Westminster Press, 1971.

Verdet, Paule. "Trying Times: Haitian Youth in an Inner City High School." Social Problems 24(D, 1976):228-233.

Wade, Mason. "The French Canadians in the United States." In Selected Proceedings of the 3rd Annual Conference on Minority Studies, April, 1975, pp. 247-254. Edited by George E. Carter, James R. Parker, and Carol Sweeney. La Crosse, WI: Institute for Minority Studies, U. of Wisconsin-La Crosse, 1976.

Wangler, Thomas E. "The Ecclesiology of Archbishop John Ireland: Nature, Development, and Influence." Doctoral dissertation, Marquette U., 1968.

Ward, David. Cities and Immigrants. A Geography of Change in Nineteenth-Century America. New York: Oxford U. Press, 1971.

_____. "The Emergence of Central Immigrant Ghettoes in American Cities: 1840-1920." Annals of the Association of American Geographers 58, No. 2(1968).

Ward, Francis. "Arabs in America Work to Alter Attitudes." Los Angeles Times, Ag 20, 1976.

Weed, Perry L. The White Ethnic Movement and Ethnic Politics. New York: Praeger, 1973.

Wittmer, Joe. "An Educational Controversy: The Old Order Amish Schools." Phi Delta Kappan 52(N, 1970):142-145.

Wynar, Lubomyr R. with others. Encyclopedic Directory of Ethnic Organizations in the United States. Littleton, CO: Libraries Unlimited, 1975.

Yoors, Jan. The Gypsies. New York: Simon and Schuster, 1967.

Bibliographies

Alcantara, Ruben R. and others (comps.). The Filipinos in Hawaii: An Annotated Bibliography. Honolulu: Social Sciences and Linguistics Institute, U. of Hawaii, 1977.

Ander, Oscar F. (comp.). "A Bibliography on Swedish Immigration and Immigrant Contributions." Swedish Pioneer Historical Quarterly 3(Ap, 1952):35-44.

_____. The Cultural Heritage of the Swedish Immigrant. Selected References. Rock Island, IL: Augustava College Library, 1956.

Asian-American Libraries Caucus Bibliography Committee (comp.). Asian Americans: An Annotated Bibliography. Chicago: American Library Association, 1977.

Barnhart, Edward N. (comp.). Japanese American Evacuation and Resettlement. Catalog of Material in the General Library. Berkeley, CA: General Library, U. of California, Berkeley, 1958.

Bibliography on the Problems of Southwestern Minority Groups and for Teachers of Adult Students from Different Cultural Backgrounds. Denver, CO: The Colorado Migrant Council Press, Jl, 1968, 21 pp. ERIC ED 041 682.

Blackwell, Henry. "A Bibliography of Welsh Americans." National Library of Wales Journal, Supplement Series III, No. 1 (1942).

Bodnar, John E. (comp.). Ethnic History in Pennsyvlania. A Selected Bibliography. Harrisburg, PA: Pennsylvania Historical and Museum Commission, 1974.

Brickman, William W. (comp.). The Jewish Community in America: An Annotated and Classified Bibliographical Guide. New York: Franklin, 1977.

Buenker, John D., and Burckel, Nicholas C. (eds.). Immigration and Ethnicity. A Guide to Information Sources. Detroit: Gale, 1977.

Caselli, Ron (comp.). The Minority Experience. A Baisc Bibliography of American Ethnic Studies. Santa Rosa, CA: Sonoma County Office of Education, F, 1970.

Chang, Alice. "A Chinese and Japanese Bibliography." RQ 10(Summer, 1971): 299-308.

Chartier, Armand B. (comp.). A Selective and Thematic Checklist of Publications Relating to Franco-Americans, 1976. Department of Languages, U. of Rhode Island, Kingston, RI 02881.

Chen, Cecilia Mei-chi (comp.). Books for the Chinese-American Child, a Selected List, 1969. Cooperative Children's Book Center, 411 West, State Capitol, Madison, WI

Cowan, R. E., and Dunlap, B. (comps.). Bibliography of the Chinese Question in the United States. San Francisco, CA: n.p., 1909.

Cordasco, Francesco (comp.). Immigrant Children in American Schools. A Classifed and Annotated Bibliography. Fairfield, NJ: Augustus M. Kelley, 1977.

_____ (ed.). Italians in the United States: A Bibliography of Reports, Texts, Critical Studies and Related Materials. New York: Oriole Editions, 1972.

Cutsumbis, Michael N. (comp.). A Bibliographic Guide to Materials on Greeks in the United States, 1890-1968, 1970. Center for Migration Studies, 209 Flagg Place, Staten Island, NY 10304.

Desert Research Institute. Bibliography of Materials Relating to Basque Americans. Reno, NV: U. of Nevada, 1969.

Dickerson, Lynn, and Vann, Barbara (comps.). "Regional Studies: Appalachia 1905-1972. A Selected Annotated Bibliography." Appalachian Heritage 5(Winter, 1977):41-57.

Dore, Grazia (comp.). Bibliografia per la storia dell' emigrazione italiana in America. Roma: n.p., 1956.

Duphiney, Lorna. Oriental Americans: An Annotated Bibliography. ERIC-IRCD Urban Disadvantaged Series, F, 1972. ERIC ED 060 136.

Edwards, Pat (comp.). A Bibliography of Appalachian Children and Young People's Books, Jl 20, 1973. ERIC ED 092 976.

Eells, Walter Crosby (comp.). American Dissertations on Foreign Education...Education of Groups of Foreign Birth of Ancestry in the United States. Washington, DC: National Education Association, 1959.

Engelberg, Linda, and Hori, Joan (comps.). Ethnic Groups in the U.S.: A Bibliography of Books and Articles of Groups in Hawaii and On the Mainland, Ja, 1972. Sinclair Undergraduate Library, U. of Hawaii, 2425 Campus Road, Honolulu, HI 96822.

Eterovich, Adam S. (comp.). Jugoslav Immigrant Bibliography, 1968. The Author: 4843 Mission Street, San Francisco, CA 94112.

Firkins, Ina Ten Eyck. "Italians in the United States." Bulletin of Bibliography 8(Ja, 1915):129-132.

_____. "Scandinavians in the United States." Bulletin of Bibliography 8(Ap, 1915):160-163.

_____. "Slavs in the United States." Bulletin of Bibliography 8(O, 1915):217-220.

Fukimoto, Isao, Swift, Michiyo Yamaguchi, and Zucker, Rosalie (comps.). Asians in America: A Selected Annotated Bibliography. Davis, CA: Asian American Studies Division, Department of Applied Behavioral Sciences, U. of California, Je, 1971.

Gardner, Arthur L. (comp.). The Koreans in Hawaii. An Annotated Bibliography. Honolulu, HI: Social Science Research Institute, U. of Hawaii, 1970.

Glanz, Rudolf (comp.). The German Jew in America. An Annotated Bibliography. Cincinnati, OH: Hebrew Union College Press, 1969.

Hansen, Gladys C., and Heintz, W. F. Chinese in California. A Brief Bibliographic History. Portland, OR: Richard Abel & Co., 1970.

Harkins, Arthur M. (comp.) and others. Modern Native Americans: A Selective Bibliography. Minneapolis, MN: U. of Minnesota, Jl, 1971, 131 pp. ERIC ED 054 890.

Herman, Judith M. (comp.). White Ethnic America. A Selected Bibliography. New York: Institute of Human Relations, American Jewish Committee, 1969.

Hispanic Heritage. An Annotated Bibliography. Denver, CO: School of Education, Denver U., Je, 1969, 61 pp. ERIC ED 048 079.

Holmquist, Garth, and Hervey, Jack L. Rural Manpower: An Annotated Bibliography. East Lansing, MI: Michigan State U. Rural Manpower Center, Ag, 1968, 44 pp. ERIC ED 037 265.

Ichioka, Yuji, Sakata, Yasuo, Tsuchida, Nobuya, and Yashuhara, Eri (comps.). A Buried Past. An Annotated Bibliography of the Japanese American Research Project Collection. Berkeley, CA: U. of California Press, 1974.

Inglehart, Babette F., and Mangione, Anthony R. (comps.). The Image of Pluralism in American Literature. The American Experience of European Ethnic Groups. An Annotated Bibliography. New York: Institute on Pluralism and Group Identity, American Jewish Committee, 1974.

Janeway, William Ralph (comp.). Bibliography of Immigration in the United States, 1900-1930. Columbus, OH: H. L. Hedrich, 1934.

Jerabek, Esther (comp.). Czechs and Slovaks in North America. A Bibliography. Oxon Hill, PA: Czechoslovakian Society of Arts and Sciences in America, 1976.

The Jewish Poor. A Brief Bibliography. New York: American Jewish Committee, Jl, 1973.

Johnson, Harry A. (ed.). Ethnic American Minorities. A Guide to Media and Materials. New York: Bowker, 1976.

Kaufer, Sonya F. (comp.). A Selected Bibliography of Books, Pamphlets and Articles on Negro-Jewish Relations. New York: American Jewish Committee, Mr, 1971.

Kesner, Mernie (comp.). Bibliography for Appalachian Studies, 1973. ERIC ED 091 120.

Kim, Christopher (comp.). Working Papers on Asian American Studies: Annotated Bibliography on Koreans in America, 1976. ERIC ED 139 898.

Kitano, Harry H. L., with Jung, E., Tanaka, C., and Wong, B. (comps.). Asian Americans: An Annotated Bibliography. Los Angeles, CA: Asian American Studies Center, U. of California, 1971.

Kovács, Ilona (comp.). "The Hungarians in the United States: An Annotated Bibliography." Master's thesis, Kent State U., 1975.

Laubenfels, Jean (comp.). Ethnic Studies, 1971, 38 pp. Columbus, OH: Ohio Educational Association, Referral Information Service. ERIC ED 056 964.

Lewis, Idwal (comp.). "A Bibliography of Welsh Americans." National Library of Wales Journal 11(Winter, 1960):371-381.

Lex, Barbara W. (comp.). From South to North: Cityward Migration of Low Income Whites in the Twentieth Century. 2 vols. Monticello, IL: Council of Planning Librarians, 1975.

Light, Ivan H. (comp.). Italians in America: Annotated Guide to New York Times Articles, 1890-1940. Monticello, IL: Council of Planning Librarians, 1975.

Lowe, C. H. (comp.). The Chinese in Hawaii: A Bibliographic Survey, 1972. C. H. Lowe, P.O. Box 10701, Honolulu, HI 96816.

Lubetski, Edith (comp.). Writings on Jewish History. A Selected Annotated Bibliography. New York: American Jewish Committee, Ap, 1970.

Lum, William Wong and others. Asians in America: A Bibliography of Master's Theses and Doctoral Dissertations. Davis, CA: Asian American Research Project, U. of California, Davis, Mr, 1970.

Marcus, Jacob R. (comp.). An Index to Scientific Articles on American Jewish History. New York: KTAV for the American Jewish Archives, 1971.

Matsuda, Mitsugu (comp.). The Japanese in Hawaii: An Annotated Bibliography of Japanese Americans. Revised edition by Dennis M. Ogawa with Jerry Y. Fujioka. Honolulu: U. Press of Hawaii, 1975.

Meadows, Paul and Others (comps.). Recent Immigration to the United States: The Literature of the Social Sciences. Washington, DC: GPO, 1976.

Meynen, Emil. Bibliographie des Deutschtums der kolonialzeitlichen Einwanderung in Nordamerika, inbesondere der Pennsylvaniendeutschen und ihrer Nachkommen, 1683-1933. Leipzig: O. Harrassowitz, 1937.

Mortensen, Enok (comp.). Danish-American Life and Letters: A Bibliography. Des Moines, IA: Danish Evangelical Lutheran Church in America, 1945.

630 / OTHER ETHNIC GROUPS

Noble, Vincente and Others (comps.). Counseling the Asian American Client: An Annotated
Bibliography of Journal Literature, 1964-
1974, 1974. ERIC ED 130 202.

Norell, Irene P. (comp.). Literature of the
Filipino American in the United States: A
Selective and Annotated Bibliography. San
Francisco: R and E Research Associates,
1976.

Pochmann, Henry A. (comp.). Bibliography of
German Culture in America to 1940. Edited
by Arthur R. Schultz. Madison, WI: U. of
Wisconsin Press, 1953.

Poliakoff, Lorraine (comp.). Ethnic Groups:
Spanish Speaking, American Indians, and
Eskimos. Part 4 of a Bibliographic Series
on Meeting Special Educational Needs, 1970,
29 pp. Washington, DC: ERIC Clearinghouse
on Teacher Education. ERIC ED 044 384.

Maskin, Melvin R. (comp.). Ethnic Groups in
the American City--A Selective Bibliography.
New York: Department of History, New York
U., Ja, 1970.

Oaks, Priscilla (comp.). Minority Studies:
A Selective Annotated Bibliography. Boston,
MA: G. K. Hall, 1975.

Ong, Paul M., Lum, William Wong, and others
(comps.). Theses and Dissertations on
Asians in the United States with Selected
References to Other Overseas Asians. Davis,
CA: Asian American Studies, U. of
California, Davis, S, 194.

Pap, Leo (comp.). The Portuguese in the
United States: A Bibliography. New York:
Center for Migration Studies, 1976.

Patterson, Wayne (comp.). The Koreans in North
America. Philadelphia: Balch Institute,
1976.

Prichard, Nancy S. A Selected Bibliography of
American Ethnic Writing and Supplement.
Champaign, IL: National Council of Teachers
of English, O, 1969, 49 pp. ERIC ED 041 921.

Rockman, Ilene F. (comp.). Japanese-American
Identity in the United States, 1945-Present.
A Selected Annotated Bibliography, Ja, 1975.
ERIC ED 102 091.

_____ (comp.). Understanding the Filipino-
American, 1900-1976: A Selective Bibliography, D, 1976. ERIC ED 151 429.

Rose, Walter R. (comp.). A Bibliography of
the Irish in the United States. Afton, NY:
Tristram Shandy Publications, 1969.

Rosenfield, Geraldine (comp.). What We Know
About Young American Jews. An Annotated
Bibliography. New York: American Jewish
Committee, Ap, 1970.

Roucek, Joseph S., and Pinkham, Patricia N.
(comps.). American Slavs: A Bibliography.
New York: Bureau for Intercultural Education, 1944.

Saito, Shiro (comp.). Filipinos Overseas.
A Bibliography. Staten Island, NY: Center
for Migration Studies, 1977.

Schlesinger, Benjamin (comp.). The Jewish
Family. A Survey and Annotated Bibliography. Toronto: U. of Toronto Press, 1971.

Select Bibliography on High Risk Education for
Appalachian Youth. Programs and Practices,
1969. ERIC ED 039 076.

"Some Recent Publications Relating to Norwegian-
American History." Norwegian-American
Studies and Records 18(1954):223-231, and
19(1955):189-198.

Spicer, Edward H., and Moone, Janet R. "A
Bibliography of Life in the War Relocation
Centers." In Edward H. Spicer and Others,
Impounded People. Japanese Americans in
the Relocation Centers, pp. 317-331.
Tucson, AZ: U. of Arizona Press, 1969.

Stern, Norton B. California Jewish History.
A Descriptive Bibliography. Glendale, CA:
A. H. Clark, 1967.

Strona, Proserfina A. (comp.). Filipinos in
Hawaii, a Bibliography. Honolulu: State
Library, 1974.

_____ (comp.). Koreans in Hawaii. A Bibliography. Honolulu: Hawaii and Pacific
Unit, State Library, 1974.

Takle, John A. (comp.). Ethnic and Racial
Minorities in North America: A Selected
Bibliography of the Geographical Literature.
Monticello, IL: Council of Planning
Libraries, 1973.

Tolzmann, Don Heinrich (comp.). German-
Americans: A Bibliography. Metuchen, NJ:
Scarecrow Press, 1975.

Velikonja, Joseph (comp.). Italians in the
U.S.: Bibliography. Carbondale, IL:
Southern Illinois U., 1963.

Wepsiec, Jan (comp.). Polish-American Serial
Publications, 1842-1966: An Annotated
Bibliography. Chicago: n.p., 1968.

White, Anthony G. (comp.). An Urban Minority:
Japanese Americans, N, 1973. ERIC ED 143
719.

Witowski, Roman (comp.). "Poles in America:
A Select Annotated Bibliography." Polish
American Studies 12(Ja-Je, 1955):35-41.

_____. "A Select Annotated Polonica
Americana Bibliography." Polish American
Studies 11(J1-D, 1954):97-103.

Wolanin, Alphonse S. (comp.). "Polonica
    Americana Prior to 1944." Polish American
    Studies 7(Jl-D, 1950):96-108.

_____. Polonica in English. Annotated Cata-
    logue of the Archives and Museum of the
    Polish Roman Catholic Union. Chicago: n.p.,
    1945.

Wood, James E., Jr. (comp.). "A Selected and
    Annotated Bibliography on Jewish-Christian
    Relations." Journal of Church and State,
    Spring, 1971.

Young, Nancy Foon (comp.). The Chinese in
    Hawaii: An Annotated Bibliography.
    Honolulu: Social Science Research Institute,
    U. of Hawaii, 1973.

Yu, Connie Young. "Asian Americans and Educa-
    tion. The 'Others.'" Civil Rights Digest
    9(Fall, 1976):45-51.

_____. "California Textbook Guidelines in
    Action." Interracial Books for Children
    Bulletin 7(1976):30-32.

_____. "Filipino Educators vs. Textbook
    Publishers in California." Interracial
    Books for Children Bulletin 8, No. 2(1977):
    6-8.

Yung, Judy and others (comps.). Asian
    Americans, an Annotated Bibliography for
    Public Libraries. Chicago: American
    Library Association, 1977.

Zurawski, Joseph W. (comp.). Polish American
    History and Culture. A Classified Bibliog-
    raphy. Chicago, IL: Polish Museum of
    America, 1975.

8.
AFRO-AMERICAN STUDIES

General

Aarons, Alfred C. (ed.). "Black Language and Culture Issue." The Florida FL Reporter 9 (Spring-Fall, 1971):1-63.

Abdul, Raoul. Blacks in Classical Music: A Personal History. New York: Dodd, Mead, 1977.

Abrahams, Roger D. "The Advantages of Black English." Florida FL Reporter 8(Spring-Fall, 1970):27-30, 51.

Abramowitz, Jack. "Textbooks and Negro History." Social Education, Mr, 1969.

Acholonu, Constance Williams. "A Perceptual Analysis: Black Studies in Selected Community Colleges in Washington State." Doctoral dissertation, U. of Washington, 1975. Univ. Microfilms Order No. 75-28307.

Adams, John S. "The Geography of Riots and Civil Disorders in the 1960s." Economic Geography 48(Ja, 1972):24-42.

Adams, William E. "Black Studies in the Elementary Schools." Journal of Negro Education 39(Summer, 1970):202-208.

Ad Hoc Staff Task Force. Systems for Multicultural Education Planning Framework, 2 volumes. Los Angeles: Los Angeles Unified School District, O, 1972.

Afram Associates, Inc. Action Library, 1966. Afram Associates, Inc., 103 East 125th Street, New York, NY 10035. [Short "Action Stimulators," "Thought Stimulators," and "Humanizers," revolving around blackness and humanity]

Afro-American Instructional Curriculum Laboratory, Jl, 1969, 44 pp. Detroit: Michigan-Ohio Regional Educational Laboratory, Inc. ERIC ED 035 991.

Afro-American Studies in Colleges and Universities of New York State, 1968-69 and 1969-70, S, 1969, 26 pp. Albany, NY: New York State Education Department, Albany Information Center on Education. ERIC ED 038 915.

Akar, John J. "An African's View of Black Studies With International Dimensions." CLA Journal 14(S, 1970):7-17.

Alexander, Jean. "Black Literature for the 'Culturally Deprived' Curriculum." English Journal 59(D, 1970):1229-1233.

Alexander, Margaret Walker. "Black Studies: Some Personal Observations." Afro-American Studies 1(My, 1970):41-43.

Alilunas, Leo J. "The Enigma of Negro History." Clearing House 45(S, 1970):29-31.

Allen, Robert L. "Politics of the Attacks on Black Studies." Black Scholar 6(S, 1974): 2-7.

Amana, Clarence A. "Black Studies is for White Students." Midwest Education Review 6(Winter, 1974):1-12.

Amistad Research Center. Packet on the Negro in America...for Secondary Teachers of History, Civics, Government and Problems of Democracy. Nashville, TN: Fisk U., 1968.

Anderson, Brian. "Black Program Thrives." Minneapolis Tribune, Ja 17, 1971. [U. of Minnesota]

Anderson, S. E. "Mathematics and the Struggle for Black Liberation." Black Scholar 2(S, 1970):20-27.

Andrews, Chris. "Black Studies Classes Disappearing." Rochester Times Union, Mr 8, 1979. [Rochester, NY public schools]

Andrews, Pearl. "A Study of the Effects of Black Studies on the Self-Concept of Negro Kindergarten Children." Doctoral dissertation, U. of Illinois, 1971.

Appleton, Clyde R. "Black and White in the Music of American Youth." New York University Education Quarterly 4(Winter, 1973): 24-29.

Aptheker, Herbert. Afro-American History: The Modern Era. New York: Citadel, 1971.

_____. "Afro-American Superiority: A Neglected Theme in the Literature." In Black Life and Culture in the United States, pp. 165-179. Edited by Rhoda Goldstein. New York: Crowell, 1971.

_____. "Black Studies and United States History." Negro History Bulletin 34(D, 1971): 174-176.

_____. "Present Needs in the Study of Afro-American History." Political Affairs, F, 1969.

_____. "The Souls of Black Folk: A Comparison of the 1903 and 1952 Editions." Negro History Bulletin 34(Ja, 1971):15-17.

Archibald, Helen A. (ed.). Negro History and Culture. Selections for Use with Children. Chicago: Department of Curriculum Development, Chicago City Missionary Society.

Armstrong, Carmen. "Black Inner City Child Art: A Phantom?" Art Education 23(My, 1970):16-21.

Arnold, Mark, and Morton, John. "Black Studies: How They Grow in the Colleges." National Observer, Mr 3, 1969.

Arthur, Audrey C., Bankston, Deborah, and Predow, Karen. "Black Students Speak: Three Views on Black Studies." In Black Life and Culture in the United States, pp. 341-359. Edited by Rhoda Goldstein. New York: Crowell, 1971.

Asher, Frank L. Afro-American History: An Elective One Semester Course, 1970. ERIC ED 045 534.

Austin, Robert C. "A Black Educator's Role in the Development of a Black Studies Program." Community College Social Science Quarterly 6 (Spring, 1976):26-27, 32.

Avidon, Elaine. Teaching My Kids Black History. Pacifica Tape Library, 2217 Shattuck Avenue, Berkeley, CA 94704.

Bailey, Ronald. "Black Studies in Historical Perspective." Journal of Social Issues 29 (1973):97-108.

Baker, David N. and others (eds.). The Black Composer Speaks. Metuchen, NJ: Scarecrow Press, 1978.

Balandier, G. "Africains et Negro-americains." Trois Continents 3(1967). [France]

Balasa, Michael A., Swope, Karen F., and Warner, Dennis A. "The Teaching of Regional Black History." Integrateducation 15(Mr-Ap, 1977).

Baldwin, James. "The Nigger We Invent." Integrated Education, Mr-Ap, 1969.

Ball, John M. "Geography and Black Studies Programs." Journal of Social and Behavioral Sciences 17(Summer, 1971):27-30.

Banks, James A. "Curriculum Strategies for Black Liberation." School Review 81(My, 1973):405-414.

_____. "Relevant Social Studies for Black Pupils." Social Education, Ja, 1969.

_____. "Teaching Black Studies for Social Change." Journal of Afro-American Issues 1 (F, 1972):141-164.

_____. Teaching Strategies for Ethnic Studies. Boston: Allyn & Bacon, 1975.

_____. Teaching the Black Experience: Methods and Materials, 1970, 95 pp. ERIC ED 044 481.

_____ (ed.). Teaching Ethnic Studies: Concepts and Strategies. Washington, DC: National Council for the Social Studies, 1973.

Banks, Samuel L. "Blacks in a Multiethnic Social Studies Curriculum: A Critical Assessment." Journal of Negro Education 44 (Winter, 1975):82-89.

Baraka, Imamu Amiri (LeRoi Jones) (ed.). African Congress. A Documentary of the First Modern Pan-African Congress. New York: Morrow, 1972. [September, 1970, Atlanta GA]

Barbour, Floyd B. "Some Notes on Teaching Black Literature." Notre Dame Journal of Education 4(Winter, 1973):307-321.

Baren, David. "Do You Dare...Negro Literature and the Disadvantaged Student." Phi Delta Kappan, My, 1969.

Baronberg, Joan. Black Representation in Children's Books. NCRIEEO Newsletter, My 1971.

Barrian, Albert H. Negritude: Essays and Studies. Hampton, VA: Hampton Institute Press, 1967.

Bass, Floyd L. "A Study Instrument to Assess Competencies for Black Studies Educators." Journal of Continuing Education and Training 2(N, 1972):167-176.

_____. "What About Your Black Experiences?" Integrated Education 11(Mr-Ap, 1973):64-65.

Battle, Lorenzo. "The Social History of Slavery: A Unit in a College Black American History Course." Doctoral dissertation, Carnegie Mellon U., 1976.

Beard, Richard L. "Popular Culture and Negro Education." Journal of Negro Education, Winter, 1969.

Becknell, Charles Edward. "Can Black Studies Survive on a Predominantly White University Campus?" Doctoral dissertation, U. of New Mexico, 1975. Univ. Microfilms Order No. 75-28681.

Bell, Patricia. "Teaching about Black Families Through Black Literature." Journal of Home Economics 68(Mr, 1976):22-23.

Bell, Roseann Pope. "'The Crisis' and 'Opportunity' Magazines: Reflections of a Black Culture, 1920-1930." Doctoral dissertation, Emory U., 1974. Univ. Microfilms Order No. 74-23656.

Bengelsdorf, Winnie. Ethnic Studies in Higher Education: State of the Art and Bibliography. Washington, DC: American Association of State Colleges and Universities, 1972.

Bennett, Lerone, Jr. "Reading, 'Riting and Racism." Ebony, Mr, 1967. [The Negro in textbooks]

Bennett, William. "The Afro-American Cultural Center." Harvard Journal of Afro-American Studies 2(1971):18-29.

Benosky, Alan L. "Minority Groups and the Teaching of American History." Social Studies 62(F, 1971):60-63.

Bentley, Norma E. "Think About It, Baby." Junior College Journal, F, 1969. [Negro literature]

Berk, Ronald A. "An Evaluation of a Negro History Textbook Versus a White History Textbook, Using Fifth Grade Children." Journal of Negro Education 41(Spring, 1972): 164-169. [District of Columbia]

Berman, S. "Chauvinistic Hearings." Library Journal, F 15, 1969. [letter]

Bernstein, Joanne E. "Minorities in Fiction for Young Children." Integrated Education 11(My-Je, 1973):34-37.

Bethune, Lebert. "Afro-American Studies: Perspectives Toward a Definition." IRCD Bulletin 5(Summer, 1969):9-10, 15.

Beyer, Barry K. New Instructional Materials on Africa South of the Sahara (1969-1970). A Supplement to African South of the Sahara: A Resource and Curriculum Guide, 1970, 52 pp. Pittsburgh, PA: Carnegie-Mellon U., Project Africa. ERIC ED 039 260.

Beyer, Barry K., and Hicks, E. Percy. A Social Studies Curriculum Project to Develop and Test Instructional Materials, Teaching Guides and Content Units on the History and Culture of Sub-Saharan Africa for Use at Selected Grade Levels in Secondary Schools. Project Africa. Final Report, Je, 1970, 125 pp. Pittsburgh: Project Africa, Carnegie-Mellon U. ERIC ED 042 673.

Bingham, Jane Marie. A Content Analysis of the Treatment of Negro Characters in Children's Picture Books 1930-1968, 1970, 281 pp. ERIC ED 060 016.

Birtha, J. M. "Portrayal of the Black in Children's Literature." Pennsylvania Library Association Bulletin 24(Jl, 1969):187-197.

Bizot, Richard. "Black Literature and the Non-Black Teacher of Black Students." English Journal 60(O, 1971):889-895.

"The Black Experience and the Printed Word." Contact 2(S, 1970):10-12, 19.

Black Films Workshop. Black Films: A Selected List. New York: New York Public Library, 1970.

"Black History--As Schools Teach It." U.S. News and World Report, N 4, 1968.

"Black History. Eleven Concerned Educators Speak Out on the Issues." Educational Product Report, My-Je, 1969.

"Black Is...For Credit." Newsweek, O 20, 1969. [Black studies in the college]

"Black Revolution and Black History." Negro History Bulletin, My, 1969.

"Black Students at Choate." The Choate Alumni Bulletin, Ap, 1969. [Wallingford, CT]

"Black Studies." NEA Research Bulletin 48 (O, 1970):74-76.

Black Studies: How It Works at Ten Universities, Mr, 1971, 21 pp. New York: Academy for Educational Development, Inc. ERIC ED 060 792.

"Black Studies Programs and Civil Rights." A.C.E. Special Report, Ap 8, 1969. [American Council on Education]

Black Studies: Related Learning Materials and Activities in Social Studies for Kindergarten, Grade 1 and Grade 2. Curriculum Bulletin, 1970-71 Series, Number 3, 1970, 268 pp. Brooklyn, NY: New York City Board of Education, Bureau of Curriculum Development. ERIC ED 051 351.

Blake, Elias, Jr., and Cobb, Henry. Black Studies: Issues in Their Institutional Survival. Washington, DC: Institute for Services to Education, O, 1974. ERIC ED 146 286.

Blassingame, John A. "A Model Afro-American Studies Program: The Results of a Survey." In New Perspectives on Black Studies, pp. 229-239. Edited by John A. Blassingame. Urbana, IL: U. of Illinois Press, 1971.

_____. "Black Studies: An Intellectual Crisis." American Scholar, Autumn, 1969.

_____. "Black Studies and the Role of the Historian." In New Perspectives on Black Studies, pp. 207-226. Edited by John A. Blassingame. Urbana, IL: U. of Illinois Press, 1971.

_____. "'Soul' or Scholarship: Choices Ahead for Black Studies." Smithsonian 1(Ap, 1970): 58-65.

Blauner, Robert. "The Question of Black Culture." In Black America, pp. 110-120. Edited by John F. Szwed. New York: Basic Books, 1970.

Blazek, Ron and others (comps.). The Black Experience: A Bibliography of Bibliographies 1970-1975. Chicago: American Library Association, 1978.

Blom, Gaston E., Waite, Richard R., and Zimet, Sara F. "Ethnic Integration and Urbanization of First Grade Reading Textbook: A Research Study." Psychology in the Schools, Ap, 1967.

Bond, Horace Mann. "The Curriculum and the Negro Child." Journal of Negro Education 4 (Ap, 1935):159-168.

Bond, Leola. "Black Literature?" English Education 3(Winter, 1972):131-135.

Bone, Robert. "Negro Literature in the Secondary School: Problems and Perspectives." English Journal, Ap, 1969.

_____. "Teaching Negro History: An Interdisciplinary Approach." Integrated Education F-Mr, 1967.

Bornholdt, Laura. "Black Studies: Perspective 1970." Danforth News and Notes, Mr, 1970.

Bostick, Herman F. "A Case for Black Literature in the French Classroom." French Review 46(O, 1972):44-51.

_____. "Teaching Afro-French Literature in the American Secondary School: A New Dimension." Foreign Language Annals 5(My, 1972): 420-431.

Boulding, Kenneth E. "Increasing the Supply of Black Economists. Is Economics Culture-Bound?" American Economic Review, My, 1970.

Bray, Thomas J. "Black Studies Boom." Wall Street Journal, F 3, 1969.

Brazziel, William F. "Negro History in the Public Schools: Trends and Prospects." Negro History Bulletin, N, 1965.

Brisben, J. Quinn. "A History of Racism." Integrated Education, F-Mr, 1965.

Broderick, Dorothy. Image of the Black in Children's Fiction. New York: Bowker, 1973.

Brooks, George E. "A Schema for Integrating Africa Into World History." History Teacher 3(1970):5-19.

Brown, Letitia W. "Why and How the Negro in History." Journal of Negro Education, Fall, 1969.

Brown, Roscoe C., Jr. "Black Studies in Perspective." New York University Education Quarterly 2(1971):2-5.

Brown, Sterling. "The Negro Author and His Publisher." Quarterly Review of Higher Education Among Negroes 9(Jl, 1941):140-146.

Bullock, Starmanda. "James A. Porter, Art Historian and Artist: The Afro-American in the Rise and Development of American Art, 1920-1970." Doctoral dissertation, Howard U., 1977.

Bryant, Henry A., Jr. "Methodology in Black Studies." Community College Social Science Quarterly 5(Winter, 1975):39-41.

Bureau of General and Academic Education. Exposure: Media Evaluations [of] Afro-American Non-Book Resources. Harrisburg, PA: The Bureau, 1969.

Bureau of Secondary Curriculum Development. Social Studies, Grade 9: Asian and African Culture Studies. Albany, NY: State Department of Education, 1970.

_____. Teaching About Africa South of the Sahara. A Guide for Ninth Grade Social Studies. Albany, NY: State Department of Education, 1970.

Butcher, Vada E. and others. Development of Materials for a One Year Course in African Music for the General Undergraduate Student. Final Report, S, 1970, 244 pp. Washington, DC: Howard U. ERIC ED 045 042.

Caesar, Terry P. "White Teacher, Black Literature." Chronicle of Higher Education, N 17, 1975. [Clarion State College, PA]

Caliguri, Joseph P., and Levine, Daniel U. "A Study of the Use of Inter-ethnic Materials in Suburban High Schools in a Major Metropolitan Area." Phylon 31(Fall, 1970):220-230.

Canaday, Nicholas, Jr. "Literature, Propaganda, and the Black Aesthetic." Intellect 104(N, 1975):195-197.

Carey, P., and Allen, D. "Black Studies: Expectations and Impact on Self-Esteem and Academic Performance." Social Science Quarterly 57(Mr, 1977):811-820.

Carlson, Julie Ann. "A Comparison of the Treatment of the Negro in Children's Literature in the Periods 1929-38 and 1959-68." Doctoral dissertation, U. of Connecticut, 1969.

Carpenter, Marie E. "The Role of Negro Americans in American History Textbooks." International Education News, Je, 1943.

Carter, George E. "Minority Studies at the University: Uses and Abuses." In Identity and Awareness in the Minority Experience, Selected Proceedings of the 1st and 2nd Annual Conferences on Minority Studies, pp. 8-23. Edited by George E. Carter and Bruce Mouser. Lacrosse, WI: U. of Wisconsin, 1975.

Carter, Gwendolyn M., and Abu-Lughod, Ibraham. "What Good are Black Studies?" Chicago Tribune Magazine, O 26, 1969.

Caselli, Ron. An Instructional Plan for Teaching Black History, 1970, 34 pp. Santa Rosa, CA: Sonoma County Superintendent of Schools. ERIC ED 044 318.

_____. "White Student Reaction to Black Studies." Integrated Education 8(S-O, 1970):31-35.

Cazort, Jean Elder. A Handbook for the Organization of Black Materials, 1971, 35 pp. Nashville, TN: Fisk U. ERIC ED 051 858.

Center for Black Education. The Struggle for Black Education, 1968-1971. Washington, DC: The Center, 1972.

Center for Minority Studies. A Report on the Status of Black Studies Programs in Midwestern Colleges and Universities. DeKalb, IL: Northern Illinois U., Ap, 1971. [MI, IO, OH, WI, IN, MN, and IL]

Chambers, B. "Interracial Books: Background of A Challenge." Publishers Weekly 200(O 11, 1971):23-29.

Chapman, Abraham. The Negro in American Literature. Stevens Point, WI: Wisconsin State U., 1967. [Order from National College Teachers of English, 508 South Sixth Street, Champaign, IL]

Chappelle, Yvonne Juanita Reed. "Black Studies: 'Seeking to Renew My Connection with the Universe.'" Doctoral dissertation, Union Graduate School, 1974. Univ. Microfilms Order No. 76-00808.

Chernow, Fred B., and Chernow, Carol. Reading Exercises in Negro History. Elizabethtown, PA: Continental Press, 1968.

Chrisman, Robert. "Blacks, Racism and Bourgeois Culture." College English 38(Ap, 1977):813-823.

Cieciorka, Frank, and Cieciorka, Bonnie. Negroes in American History. A Freedom Primer. Atlanta: Student Voice, Inc., Student Nonviolent Coordinating Committee, 1965.

Clarke, John Henrik. "Black Power and Black History." Negro Digest, F, 1969.

Clark-Jones, Beatrice. An Appraisal of the Treatment of Black Americans in Selected Elementary School Social Studies Filmstrips, 1971, 19 pp. Excerpts from thesis, Michigan State U. ERIC ED 054 618.

Clements, Clyde C., Jr. "Black Studies for White Students." Negro American Literature Forum 4(Mr, 1970):9-11.

Cleveland, Bernard. "Black Studies and Higher Education." Phi Delta Kappan, S, 1969.

Cobbs, Price M. "White Miseducation of the Black Experience." Counseling Psychologist 2(1970):23-27.

Coburn, Barbara and others. Teaching about Africa South of the Sahara: A Guide and Resource Packet for Ninth Grade Social Studies, 1970, 285 pp. Albany, NY: State U. of New York. ERIC ED 042 667.

Cole, Ann H. "A Black Studies Curriculum for Use in Upper Elementary School." Master's thesis, Bank Street College of Education, 1972.

Colen, B. D. "Once Popular Black Studies Now Attracting Only a Handful of Students." Washington Post, O 3, 1973.

Coles, Flournoy. "Recommendations from Nashville Conference on Economic Curriculum in Black Colleges." American Economic Review, My, 1970.

Coles, Robert. "What Can We Learn From the Life of Malcolm X?" Teachers College Record, My, 1966.

Collier, Marilyn. "An Evaluation of Multi-Ethnic Basal Readers." Elementary English, F, 1967.

Collins, H. Thomas and others. Are You Going to Teach About Africa?, Ag, 1970, 92 pp. New York: African American Institute. ERIC ED 044 324.

_____ and others. Teaching about Africa, 1970, 46 pp. New York: African-American Institute. ERIC ED 043 540.

Committee on Black Studies. The Case and the Course--A Treatise on Black Studies, 1973. The Committee, 63 Napier Court, London, S.W. 6, England.

Conference on Empirical Research in Black Psychology, 3rd, Cornell University, 1976. Third Conference on Empirical Research in Black Psychology. Washington, DC: National Institute of Education, 1977.

Conyers, James E. "Toward the Development of a Sociologically Relevant Black Course." Journal of Social and Behavioral Sciences 18(Fall-Winter, 1971-1972):5-13.

Cooke, Gwendolyn J. "How Students Feel About Black Literature." Negro American Literature Forum 8(Winter, 1974):293-295.

Cooper, B. Lee. "Popular Music: An Untapped Resource for Teaching Contemporary Black History." Journal of Negro Education 48 (Winter, 1979):20-36.

Corbett, P. Scott, and Worley, Bill. Ethnic and Minority History, Separate or Equal?, 1977. ERIC ED 142 614. [Kansas]

Cornelius, Paul. "Interracial Children's Books: Problems and Progress." Library Quarterly 41(Ap, 1971):106-127.

Cornish, Robert N. "B(l)ack Alley: Theatre in Search of an Identity." Minority Voices 1 (Fall, 1977):63-72. [District of Columbia]

Cortada, Rafael L. Black Studies: An Urban and Comparative Curriculum. Lexington, MA: Xerox College Publishing, 1974.

Course Guide for Afro-American Literature, S, 1969, 33 pp. Evanston, IL: Evanston Township High School. ERIC ED 045 637.

Craig, Randall J. "Focus on Black Artists: A Project for Schools and Community." School Arts Magazine 70(N, 1970):30-33.

Crocker, George N. "The Black Studies Fad." Los Angeles Herald Examiner, S 6, 1969.

Cross, William E., Jr. (ed.). Third Conference on Empirical Research in Black Psychology, Mr 30, 1977. ERIC ED 148 939.

Crouchett, Lawrence. "Early Black Studies Movements." Journal of Black Studies 2(D, 1971): 189-200.

Crowl, John A. "'Black Studies' Demands Force Debate Over Basic Academic Issues." Chronicle of Higher Education, S 29, 1969.

_____. "Negro Academicians Divided over Black Study, Some Scholars Fear it Will 'Co-Opt' Activism." Chronicle of Higher Education, Ja 12, 1970.

Cruse, Harold. "On Explaining 20th Century Negro History." Negro Digest, Jl, 1967.

Cuban, Larry. "Not 'Whether?' but 'Why?' and 'How?': Instructional Materials on the Negro in the Public Schools." Journal of Negro Education 36(Fall, 1967):434-436.

Cudjoe, Selwyn R. "Needed: A Black Studies Consortium." Liberator, S, 1969.

Cullinan, Bernice E. (ed.). Black Dialects and Reading. Urbana, IL: National Council of Teachers of English, 1974.

Cunningham, George E. "Derogatory Image of the Negro and Negro History." Negro History Bulletin, Mr, 1965.

Curl, Charles H. "Black Studies: Form and Content." CLA Journal 13(S, 1969):1-9.

Curriculum Guide for Afro-American Literature, Jl, 1970, 148 pp. Yonkers, NY: Yonkers City School District. ERIC ED 045 636.

Curtis, Willie M. Jordan. "Enhancing Black Self-Concept Through Black Studies." Doctoral dissertation, U. of Arizona, 1975. Univ. Microfilms Order No. 76-08682.

Dabney, Thomas. "The Importance of Negro History." Southern Workman 58(D, 1929):558-562.

Danforth Foundation. Black Studies in Retrospect: A Report on the Danforth Foundation's Programs of Postgraduate Studies Fellowships, 1972. ERIC ED 077 319.

Daniel, Philip T. K. A Survey of Black and Other Ethnic Studies Programs in Illinois Secondary Schools. Springfield, IL: Illinois Office of Education, Ag, 1976.

_____. "A Survey of Black Studies Programs in Midwestern Colleges and Universities." Western Journal of Black Studies 2(Winter, 1978):296-303.

Davis, Lucian. "Current Controversy: Minorities in American History Textbooks." Journal of Secondary Education, N, 1966.

Davis, Mavis W. "Black Images in Children's Literature: Revised Editions Needed." School Library Journal, Ja, 1972.

Davidson, Douglas. "Black Culture and Liberal Sociology." Berkeley Journal of Sociology 14(1969).

Davis, George A., and Donaldson, O. Fred. Blacks in the United States: A Geographic Perspective. Boston: Houghton Mifflin, 1975.

Deane, Paul C. "The Persistence of Uncle Tom: An Examination of the Image of the Negro in Children's Fiction Series." Journal of Negro Education, Spring, 1968.

DeLerma, Dominique-Rene. Black Music in Our Culture. Ideas on the Subject, Materials and Problems. Kent, OH: Kent State U. Press, 1970.

_____. "Black Music Now." Music Educators Journal 57(N, 1970):25-29.

Department of Black Studies, Washington State University. Curriculum Designs and Methods in Black Studies, 1976. ERIC ED 125 509.

Deskins, Donald R., Jr. and others. "Geography and Afro-America: The Anatomy of a Graduate Training and Curriculum Development Project." Journal of Geography 60(N, 1971):465-471.

Dillard, Joey Lee. Black English: Its History and Usage in the United States. New York: Random House, 1972.

_____. Black Names. The Hague: Mouton, 1976.

Dillon, Merton L. "White Faces and Black Studies." Commonweal 91(Ja 30, 1970):476-479.

"Directions in Black Studies." Massachusetts Review 10(Autumn, 1969):701-756. [Seven authors]

A Discussion Guide for the Autiobiography of Malcolm X. New York: Grove Press, n.d.

Dixon, Vernon J. "The Di-Unital Approach to 'Black Economics.'" American Economic Review, My, 1970.

Dodds, Barbara. Negro Literature for High School Students, 1968, 164 pp. ERIC ED 022 754. [Available from National Council of Teachers of English, 508 South Sixth Street, Champaign, IL 61820]

Doherty, A. S. "Black Studies: A Report for Librarians." College and Research Libraries 31(N, 1970):379-387.

Donaldson, Fred. "The Geography of Black America: Three Approaches." Journal of Geography 71(O, 1972):414-420.

Donaldson, O. Fred. "Geography and the Black American: The White Papers and the Invisible Man." Journal of Geography 70(Mr, 1971):128-149.

Dorsey, Carolyn Ann. "Role Expectations for the Black Studies Program Director." Doctoral dissertation, New York U., 1976. Univ. Microfilms Order No. 77-05340.

Doyle, Bertram W. "Sociology in Negro Schools and Colleges, 1924-1932." Quarterly Review of Higher Education Among Negroes 1(Jl, 1933):7-14.

Drake, St. Clair. "Reflections on Anthropology and the Black Experience." Anthropology and Education Quarterly 9(Summer, 1978):85-109.

Drimmer, Melvin. "Teaching Black History in America: What Are the Problems?" Journal of Negro Education, Fall, 1969.

Duff, Ogle Eloise Burks. "The Treatment of Blacks in Selected Literature Anthologies for Grades Nine Through Twelve Published Since 1968." Doctoral dissertation, U. of Pittsburgh, 1974. Univ. Microfilms Order No. 74-21, 667.

Duke, William David. "The Conceptual Problems Involved in Developing a Structural and Academically Approved Study of Black People in Relation to the Establishment of a Curriculum in Black Studies." Doctoral dissertation, Northwestern U., 1973.

Dumas, Wayne, and Lucas, Christopher. "Teaching About the Negro's Struggle for Social Equality in Integrated Classrooms." Social Studies 61(Ja, 1970):29-34.

Dunbar, Ernest. "The Black Studies Thing." New York Times Magazine, Ap 6, 1969.

Dunn, Lynne P. Black Americans: A Study Guide and Sourcebook. San Francisco: R & E Research Associates, 1975.

Dunsee, Maxine. Ethnic Modification of the Curriculum. Washington, DC: Association for Supervision and Curriculum Development and National Education Association, 1970.

Durkee, Robert K. "The Black Culture." Princeton Alumni Magazine, Je, 1969.

Dymally, Mervyn M. "The Struggle for the Inclusion of Negro History in Our Textbooks... A California Experience." Negro History Bulletin 33(D, 1970):188-191.

Easum, Donald B. "The Call for Black Studies." Africa Report 14(My-Je, 1969):16-22.

Edgar, Robert W. "History, Reading, and Human Relations: An Integrated Approach." Social Education, Mr, 1965.

Edwards, G. Franklin. "The Contribution of E. Franklin Frazier to Sociology." Journal of Social and Behavioral Sciences 13(Winter, 1967):25-27.

Edwards, Harry. "Black Studies Programs: Curricula Outlines." In Black Students, pp. 205-227. New York: Free Press, 1970.

Edwards, Michael L., and Blubaugh, Jon A. "'The Black Experience' in Speech Communication Courses: A Survey." Speech Teacher 22 (S, 1973):175-183.

Ekaete, Genevieve. "Professor and Poet Sterling Allen Brown: Saying 'Yes' to His People." Washington Post, Mr 23, 1974.

Elkin, Sol M. "Minorities in Textbooks: The Latest Chapter." Teachers College Record, Mr, 1965.

Elliott, Raymond N., Jr., and Ferrer, Leona. "Black History." Elementary School Journal 70(1970):279-283.

Elson, Ruth M. Guardians of Tradition: American Schoolbooks of the Nineteenth Century. Lincoln, NE: U. of Nebraska Press, 1964.

Engel, Robert E., and Willett, Lynn H. "Educational Implications for Black Studies." Improving College and University Teaching 19(F, 1971):267-269.

Engs, Robert F. "Black Studies." NJEA Review 45(Ja, 1972):16-18.

Epps, A. C. "The Role of Afro-American Scholarship." Harvard Crimson, Mr 21, 1972.

Ernst, Robert T., and Hugg, Lawrence (eds.). Black America: Geographical Perspectives. Garden City, NY: Anchor, 1975.

Essex, Bessie. "Pitt's Black Studies Program--4 Years After." Pittsburgh Courier, Ag 4 and 11, 1973. [U. of Pittsburgh]

Etzioni, Amitai, and Tinker, Irene. "A Sociological Perspective on Black Studies." Educational Record 52(Winter, 1971):65-76.

Evans, Jeanette. "An Analysis of Relevance of Education in Geography to Blacks." Master's thesis, U. of Washington, 1972.

Fax, Elton C. Black Artists of the New Generation. New York: Dodd, Mead, 1977.

Feagin, Joe R. "Black History and White Americans." Integrated Education 8(N-D, 1970): 22-27.

Fearn, Edward. "Working-class Culture and the Teaching of Recent History: An Experiment in the Use of a Questionnaire [to Parents]." Educational Review, N, 1968.

Feild, Claire. "Defense Mechanisms Employed by the Faulkner White Racist and Their Effect on the Faulkner Negro." Research in the Teaching of English 4(Spring, 1970):20-36.

Feldman, Eugene R. P. (ed.). Negro History an Educational Materials Bulletin. Chicago: Museum of Negro History and Art, 1966.

_____. "The Negro In U.S. 'History.'" American Teacher, F, 1966.

Felt, Jeremy P. "Black History: The Question of 'Objectivity.'" Social Studies 63(F, 1972):51-54.

Fenton, Edwin. "Crispus Attucks Is Not Enough: The Social Studies and Black Americans." Social Education, Ap, 1969.

Ferguson, Ina Lunna. Lectures in Black Studies. San Francisco: Lunan-Ferguson Library, 1972.

Fikes, Robert, Jr. "Control of Information: Black Scholars and their Academic Press." Western Journal of Black Studies 2(Fall, 1978):219-221.

Filter, Paul August. "A Survey of Black Studies: Position and Opinions." Educational Leadership 28(Ja, 1971):369-372.

_____. "Black Studies in the Secondary Social Studies Curriculum--Position and Opinions." Doctoral dissertation, U. of Nebraska, 1970. Univ. Microfilms Order No. 71-09555.

Fischer, Roger A. "Ghetto and Gown: The Birth of Black Studies." Current History, N, 1969.

Fisher, David L. "Black Studies and the Enhancement of Self-Concept as It Relates to Achievement Level in Negro High School Students." Doctoral dissertation, Western Michigan U., 1972.

Fisher, Dexter (ed.). Minority Language and Literature: Retrospective and Perspective. New York: Modern Language Association of America, 1977.

Fisher, Walter. Ideas for Black Studies. The Morgan State College Program. Baltimore: The Morgan State College Press, 1971.

Fiske, Edward B. "Black Studies Mark Gains But Seek Wider Role." New York Times, Je 19, 1977.

Flanagan, James, and Parker, Margaret. "Taking the Oreo Out of Colored--Materials for the Black Experience." Media and Methods--Exploration in Education 7(D, 1970):24-27.

Fleet, Clara Moore. "The Attitudes of Black Undergraduate Students Toward Black Studies." Doctoral dissertation, Catholic U. of America, 1974. Univ. Microfilms Order No. 74-16706.

Flournoy, Houston I. "A Republican Dissent: Higher Education and Black Studies." The Black Politician, Fall, 1969.

Ford, Luther Lee. "A National Survey of Degree-Granting Black Studies Programs." Doctoral dissertation, U. of Nebraska, 1974. Univ. Microfilms Order No. 74-23896.

Ford, Nick Aaron. "Attitudes and Actions of English Departments Toward the Promotion of Black Students." CLA Journal 16(Mr, 1973): 334-344.

_____. "Black Literature: Problems and Opportunities." CLA Journal 13(1969).

_____. Black Studies. Threat-or-Challenge. Port Washington, NY: Kennikat Press, 1973.

_____. "Black Studies Programs." Current History 67(N, 1974).

_____. "Confessions of a Black Critic." Black World 20(Je, 1971):30-43.

_____. "The English Department and the Challenge of Racism." Integrated Education, Jl-Ag, 1969, pp. 24-30.

_____. "Symposium on Black Literature." Bull. Assn. Dep. Engl. 22(1969):57-63.

_____. "What Every English Teacher Should Know About Black Studies." CEA Critic 36(My, 197 1974):19-27.

Forrest, Leon. "Move to Paint Black Dialects As Languages Has Bantustan Odor." Muhammad Speaks, Ag 7, 1970.

Franklin, John Hope. "Courses Concerning the Negro in Negro Colleges." Quarterly Review of Higher Education Among Negroes 8(Jl, 1940):138-144.

_____. "The Future of Negro American History." University of Chicago Magazine 62(1970):15-21.

_____. "The New Negro History." Crisis, F, 1957.

Freedman, Morris. "Black Studies and the Standard Curriculum." Journal of Higher Education 42(Ja, 1971):35-41.

Freedom School Poetry. Student Non-Violent Coordinating Committee, 100 Fifth Avenue, New York, NY 10011.

Fruth, Marvin J., and Yee, Albert H. Do Black Studies Make a Difference in Elementary School Pupils' Achievement and Attitudes? F, 1971, 9 pp. Paper, Annual Meeting of the American Educational Research Association. ERIC ED 047 044.

Fuller, Hoyt W. "On Black Studies and the Critics." Black World 23(My, 1974):49-50, 88-90.

Furniss, W. Todd. Black Studies Programs and Civil Rights Violations, Ap 8, 1969. ERIC ED 029 599.

_____. "Racial Minorities and Curriculum Change." Educational Record, Fall, 1969.

Gay, Geneva. "Ethnic Minority Studies: How Widespread? How Successful?" Educational Leadership 29(N, 1971):108-109.

_____. "Needed: Ethnic Studies in Schools." Educational Leadership 28(D, 1970):292-295.

Gayle, Addison. "The Black Aesthetic." Black World 24(D, 1974):31-43.

Georgeoff, John, and Bahlke, Susan J. "Race as a Factor in Knowledge about Negro History and Culture." Journal of Negro Education 40 (Winter, 1971):76-80.

Gibbs, Sandra Elaincia. "College and University English Departments and English Major Preparation in Black Literature." Doctoral dissertation, U. of Illinois, 1974. Univ. Microfilms Order No. 75-00313.

Gibson, Donald B. "Is There a Black Literary Tradition?" New York University Education Quarterly 2(1971):12-16.

Gibson, John S. The Development of Appropriate Instructional Units and Related Materials on Racial and Cultural Diversity in America. Final Report, O, 1967, 508 pp. Medford, MA: Tufts U., Lincoln Filene Center. ERIC ED 016 552.

_____. "Learning Materials and Minorities: What Medium and What Message?" Illinois Education, Mr, 1968.

Giles, Sister M. Bernadette. The Other Americans: Minorities in American History. Los Angeles: Lawrence Publishing Co., 1969.

Giles, Raymond H., Jr. "African Studies Depend on a New Black History." Africa Report 17 (N-D, 1972):35-36.

_____. "Black and Ethnic Studies Programs at Public Schools: Elementary and Secondary." Doctoral dissertation, U. of Massachusetts, 1972. Univ. Microfilms Order No. 73-06465.

_____. Black Studies Programs in the Public Schools. New York: Praeger, 1974.

Gilpin, Patrick J., and White, O. Kendall, Jr. "A Challenge to White, Southern Universiies ties: An Argument for Including Negro History in the Curriculum." Journal of Negro Education, Fall, 1969.

Givens, Travis Gosnold. A Survey of the Knowledge Possessed by a Group of Negro High School Pupils Concerning the Role of the Negro in American History. U. of Colorado Studies, General Series A, Vol. 26, No. 3:48, 1940.

Gladney, Mildred. "Education 'Whiteout.' A Report on the National Conference on Negro History." Community, Mr, 1967.

Glancy, Barbara J. Children's Interracial Fiction. Washington, DC: American Federation of Teachers, Ag, 1969.

Golden, Loretta. "The Treatment of Minority Groups in Primary Social Studies Textbooks." Interracial Review, S, 1966.

Goldman, Martin S. "The Academic Subversion of Black Studies." Social Studies 65(Ja, 1974):26-34.

Goldstein, Rhoda L. (ed.). Black Life and Culture in the United States. New York: Crowell, 1971.

Goldstein, Rhoda L., and Albert, June True. "The Status of Black Studies Programs on American Campuses, 1969-1971." Journal of Social and Behavioral Sciences 20(Winter, 1974):1-16.

Golin, Sanford. Project Self-Esteem: Reactions and Middle and Lower Class Parents to an Elementary School Black Studies Program, 1971. ERIC ED 055 147.

_____. Project Self-Esteem: Some Effects of an Elementary School Black Studies Program, S, 1971. ERIC ED 056 149.

Gordon, Edmund W. "A Black Educator's Case for Ethnic Studies." College Board Review (F, 1972):24-28.

_____. "Relevance and Pluralism in Curriculum Development." IRCD Bulletin 5(Summer, 1969): 3-4.

Gordon, Jacob U. "Black America and Recent African Civilization." Afro-American Studies 1(Ja, 1971):221-225.

Gordon, Jacob U., and Rosser, James M. (eds.). The Black Studies Debate, 1974. ERIC ED 102 281.

Grant, Carl A. "Black Studies Materials Do Make a Difference." Journal of Educational Research 66(My-Je, 1973):400-404.

Granucci, Frank E. Minorities in American History. San Francisco: Department of Education, U. of San Francisco, 1967.

Grossman, Jonathan. "Black Studies in the Department of Labor." Monthly Labor Review 97 (Je, 1974):17-27.

Guenther, John E. "The Existence of Negro History Programs as Related to Community Concern for Negro History and Negro Student Enrollment." Negro Educational Review 22 (Ja, 1971):45-51.

_____. "Use of Supplemental Materials in Teaching Black History." Clearing House 45 (D, 1970):226-230.

Guide to Films (16 mm) About Negroes. First Edition, 1970, 87 pp. Available from Serena Press, 70 Kennedy Street, Alexandria, VA 22305. ERIC ED 050 595.

Guinier, Ewart. "Black Studies Confrontation [at Harvard]." New York Times Magazine, N 11, 1973. [With reply by Martin Kilson]

_____. "Understanding Twentieth-Century America from a Black Perspective." Harvard Magazine, N-D, 1978.

Gustafson, Lucile. "Relationship between Ethnic Group Membership and the Retention of Selected Facts Pertaining to American History and Culture." Doctoral dissertation, New York U., 1957. Univ. Microfilms Order No. 21703.

Haas, Pat. "Ethnic Studies--Not Separate, But Not Equal." College Management 9(N-D, 1974):20-22.

Haber, Louis. The Role of the American Negro in the Fields of Science, Final Report, S, 1966, 71 pp. ERIC ED 013 275.

Haley, Alex. "Black History, Oral History, and Genealogy." Oral Hist. R. (1973):1-25.

Hall, Pat. "Importance of Black Oriented Materials in Adult Education Classes." Florida Adult Education 20(Winter, 1970):10-11.

Hall, Susan J. Africa in U.S. Educational Materials: Thirty Problems and Perspectives, Ja, 1977. ERIC ED 142 449.

Hall, William S., and Freedle, Roy O. Culture and Language: The Black American Experience. New York: Halsted Press, 1975.

Halliburton, Warren J., and Katz, William Loren. American Majorities and Minorities. A Syllabus of United States History for Secondary Schools. New York: Arno, 1970.

Hamilton, Charles. "Black Culture and White Education." University Review 3(Summer, 1970):28-32.

_____. "The Challenge of Black Studies." Social Policy, Jl-Ag, 1970.

_____. Curricular Changes to Meet the Needs of a Black Society, Mr 3, 1969, 5 pp. Washington, DC: American Association for Higher Education. ERIC ED 028 714.

_____. "The Question of Black Studies." Phi Delta Kappan, Mr, 1970.

_____. "Relevance of Black Studies." In Agony and Promise. Edited by G. Kerry Smith. San Francisco: Jossey-Boss, 1969.

Handy, D. Antoinette. "The Concept of Black Music. A Survey Analysis." Western Journal of Black Studies 2(Spring, 1978):44-53.

Hanley, Janet P., and Walter, Arlene S. Black and White America: The Struggle for Identity and Power, My, 1970. ERIC ED 132 076.

Harding, Vincent. "The Uses of the Afro-American Past." Negro Digest, F, 1968.

Hare, Nathan. "Nathan Hare on Black Studies." Integrated Education 8(N-D, 1970):8-15.

_____. "The Teaching of Black History and Culture in the Secondary Schools." Social Education, Ap, 1969.

_____. "What Black Studies Mean to a Black Scholar." College and University Business My, 1970. [Interview]

_____. "What Should be the Role of Afro-American Education in the Undergraduate Curriculum?" Liberal Education, Mr, 1969.

Harlan, Louis R. The Negro in American History. Washington, DC: American Historical Association, Service Center for Teachers of History, American Historical Society, 1965.

_____. "Tell It Like It Was: Suggestions on Black History." Social Education, Ap, 1969.

Harley, R. L. "Check List of Afro-American Art and Artists." Serif 7(D, 1970):3-18.

Harris, Gloria Alicia. "Selected Images of the Black American: A Guide for Teachers of Older Children in the Elementary School with Suggestions for Incorporation into the Regular Curriculum." Doctoral dissertation, Columbia U., 1968.

Harris, Janette H. "The Black Studies Crisis." Negro History Bulletin 34(Ja, 1971):6-9.

Harris, Jeanette G. Davis. "Black Studies: A Challenge to the American Educational System." Doctoral dissertation, U. of Massachusetts, 1974. Univ. Microfilms Order No. 74-25838.

Harris, Nelson H. "The Treatment of Negroes in Books and Media Designed for the Elementary School." Social Education, Ap, 1969.

Harris, Philip. "Bias in Non-Commercial Films." Civil Rights Digest, Winter, 1969.

Harris, William M., and Millner, Darrell. Perspectives on Black Studies. Washington, DC: U. Press of America, 1977.

Harrison, Charles H. "Black History and the Schools." Ebony, D, 1968.

_____. "Black History and the Schools." Education News, O 21, 1968.

Haskins, Jim. "Black Studies: Is a Valid Idea Being Invalidated?" Black Review No. 2, pp. 67-75. New York: Morrow, 1972.

Hatch, John. "Black Studies: The Real Issue." Nation, Je 16, 1969.

Hayes, Annamarie. The MOREL Afro-American Instructional Laboratory. Detroit: Michigan-Ohio Regional Educational Laboratory, 1969.

Hayes, Arthur S. "Black Studies Called a Failure." Hackensack Journal, Ag 11, 1978. [Black studies in New Jersey schools]

Headlee, Judy A. "An Educational Approach to Negro Individualism." English Journal 59 (1970):34-39.

Hechinger, Fred W. "The Demand Grows for 'Black Studies.'" New York Times, Je 23, 1968.

Henderson, Donald. "The Assault on Black Culture through the Labeling Process." Journal of Afro-American Issues 3(Winter, 1975).

Henderson, Stephen E. "Sterling A. Brown." Ebony 31(0, 1976):128-137.

Henshel, Anne-Marie, and Henshel, Richard L. "Black Studies Programs: Promise and Pitfalls." Journal of Negro Education, Fall, 1969.

Herskovits, Melville J. "Education and Cultural Dynamics." American Journal of Sociology 48(My, 1943).

Hillegas, Jan. "Black Scholars Meet in South." Southern Patriot, Mr, 1971. [National Evaluative Conference in Black Studies]

Hines, Ralph H. "The Negro Scholar's Contribution to Pure and Applied Sociology." Journal of Social and Behavioral Sciences 13(Winter, 1967):30-35.

"The History of the American Negro." Harrisburg, PA: Pennsylvania Human Relations Commission. [A series of 8 color film strips]

Hiro, Dilip. "Black Studies Within a Radical Political Perspective." Times Higher Education Supplement, N 10, 1972. [U.S.]

Hobby, Frederick Douglass, Smith, Fred, and Kirkland, Jack A. "Black Studies: A Challenge to Education or Political Appeasement." Proud 2(My-Je, 1971):8-11. [Proud, Inc., 4221 Lindell Blvd., St Louis, MO 63108]

Hobby, Frederick D., Jr. "Black Studies in University City." Integrated Education (S-O, 1971):19-22.

Holmer, James F., and Link, H. Douglas. "Teaching Geography Today. Desegregation of City Schools: A Relevant Exercise in Political Geography." Journal of Geography 72 (N, 1973):49-56. [San Francisco]

Hoover, Dwight W. (ed.). Understanding Negro History. Chicago: Quadrangle, 1968.

Horn, Z. "Workshop for the Study of the American Negro." Wilson Library Bulletin, D, 1968.

Horton, Harold Willard. "A Study of the Status of Black Studies Programs in Universities and Colleges in the United States of America." Doctoral dissertation, Ohio State U., 1974. Univ. Microfilms Order No. 74-17783.

Houston, Susan H. "Competence and Performance in Child Black English." Language Sciences 12(O, 1970):9-14.

"How Black Studies Happened." Yale Alumni Magazine, My, 1969.

How the Curriculum Can Promote Integration. 16th Annual Curriculum Conference. New York: Board of Education, 1964.

Howard, David H. "The Black Experience in Secondary School Curriculum Changes." Illinois Journal of Education, Ap, 1970.

Howard, Lawrence C. "The Validity and Utility of Black Studies." In The Campus and the Racial Crisis. Edited by David C. Nichols and Olive Mills. Washington, DC: American Council on Education, 1970.

Hudson, Herman. "The Black Studies Programme Strategy and Structure." Journal of Educational Thought 5(Ag, 1971):90-95.

Huggins, Nathan, Kilson, Martin, and Fox, David (eds.). Key Issues in the Afro-American Experience, 1971.

Hughes, M. J. "Black Education in Black Literature in the U.S.A." Comparative Education 10(O, 1974):221-232.

Hunter, Charlayne. "Black Studies Gains Made With Goals Still in Dispute." New York Times, My 21, 1974.

Hunt, N. Franklin. "Integrating American History." Today's Education, Ja, 1969.

Hur, Kenneth K., and Robinson, John P. "The Social Impact of 'Roots.'" Journalism Quarterly 55(Spring, 1978):19-24, 83.

Ijere, Martin O. "Whither Economics in a Black Studies Program?" Journal of Black Studies 3(D, 1973):149-165.

Illinois Office of the Superintendent of Public Instruction. The Role and Contribution of American Negroes in the History of the United States and of Illinois. A Guide for Teachers and Curriculum Planners, K-12. Springfield, IL: The Office, 1970.

Institute in African and Afro-American Culture. Director's Report, Jl 21, 1969. ERIC ED 045 520.

Intergroup Education Project. In-Service Library Audio-Visual Materials (separate supplement). Berkeley, CA: Berkeley Unified School District of Alameda County, Ap, 1967 and Je, 1967. [Extensive and largely annotated guide to far more than audiovisual materials]

Institute for Services to Education. Task Force Group for Survey of Afro-American Studies Programs. Black Studies: Issues in their Institutional Survival. Washington, DC: GPO, 1976.

Integrating Black Studies into the Kindergarten and Primary Grades, 2 volumes, 1973. ERIC ED 037 437.

Introduction to Afro-American Studies: A Course Outline Guide for Study Groups, 1975. Chicago: Peoples College Press.

Irvine, Freeman Raymond, Jr. "An Analysis of Black Studies Programs in Black Colleges within the Southeastern United States with Recommendations for a Master's Degree Program." Doctoral dissertation, U. of Tennessee, 1972. Univ. Microfilms Order No. 73-12412.

Issac, Amos. "The Development and Status of Black and Brown Studies at the Claremont Colleges; The University of California at Riverside; California State College at San Bernardino; San Bernardino Valley Community College; and University College/Johnston College in Redlands: 1967-1972, A Cross Comparison." Doctoral dissertation, Claremont Graduate School, 1972. Univ. Microfilms Order No. 73-07232.

Ivie, Stanley D. "Are Black Studies Relevant?" Educational Forum 37(Ja, 1973):183-188.

Jaafar al Din. "Black Studies Gains Fading." News and Letters, Ag-S, 1975. [U. of California, Berkeley]

Jackson, Barbara L. A Re-Definition of Black Folk: Implications for Education. Atlanta: W.E.B. Du Bois Institute, Atlanta U., 1976.

Jackson, Earl C. "What is Being Taught about Negroes at the Secondary Level in American Schools?" Doctoral dissertation, Harvard U., 1951.

Jablonsky, Adelaide. "Media for Teaching Afro-American Studies." IRCD Bulletin 6(Spring-Summer, 1970):1-21.

_____. "Toward Curriculum Relevance for Minority Group Children." IRCD Bulletin 5(Summer, 1969):5-8.

Jackson, Jacquelyne Johnson. "Our Association, 'Where It's At, Baby!'" Journal of Social and Behavioral Sciences 15(Fall, 1969):53-60. [President, Association of Social and Behavioral Sciences; formerly Association of Social Science Teachers]

Jackson, Shirley M. "Afro-Hispanic Literature: A Valuable Cultural Resource." Foreign Language Annals 11(S, 1978):421-425.

James, C. L. R. "The Black Scholar Interviews: C. L. R. James." Black Scholar 2(S, 1970): 35-43.

_____. "Black Studies." Radical America 5 (S-O, 1971):79-96.

Jamison, Agelene. Teaching Afro-American Literature as a Revolutionary Force, 1976. ERIC ED 136 262.

Johnson, Edwina C. "Black History: The Early Childhood Vacuum." School Library Journal, My, 1969.

_____, "Teacher, Put Some Black on That Calendar!" African-American Teachers Forum, S, 1969.

_____. The What and the How of Teaching Afro-American Culture and History in the Elementary Schools. Albany, NY: Division of Intercultural Relations in Education, U. of the State of New York, 1972.

Johnson, Harry Alleyn (ed.). Multimedia Materials for Afro-American Studies. New York: Bowker, 1971.

Johnson, Kenneth R. "When Should Standard English Be Taught to Speakers of Nonstandard Negro Dialect?" Language Learning 20(Je, 1970):19-30.

Johnson, Wallis W. "Black Studies: The Case For and Against." Civil Rights Digest 3 (Fall, 1970):30-35.

Johnson, Wayne E. "White Responsibility in Negro Education." Journal of Social and Behavioral Sciences 14(Spring, 1969):51-54. [White teachers on black campuses]

Jones, James M. Conceptual and Strategic Issues in the Relationship of Black Psychology to American Social Science, Je, 1975. ERIC ED 127 392.

Jones, Rhett S. "Black Sociology, 1890-1917." Black Academy Review 2(Winter, 1971):43-67.

_____. "Training Graduate Students in Black History: Some Methodological Strategies." Negro Educational Review 26(Ja, 1975):5-21.

Jordan, Casper LeRoy. Black Academic Libraries: An Inventory, N, 1970, 31 pp. Atlanta: School of Library Services, Atlanta U. ERIC ED 047 731.

Jordan, June. "Black Studies: Bringing Back the Person." Evergreen Review, O, 1969.

Joseph, Gloria I. "Black Studies Consortia: A Proposal." Afro-American Studies 1(Ja, 1971): 231-235.

Joyce, Donald F. "Arthur Alonzo Schomburg: A Pioneering Black Bibliophile." Journal of Library History 10(Ap, 1975):169-171.

Juel, Janis. "Their Own Thing: A Review of Seven Black History Guides." Urban Review 5(S, 1971):32-37.

Juris, Gail, Krash, Margaret, and Krash, Ronald. Survey of Bibliographic Activities of U.S. Colleges and Universities on Black Studies. St Louis, MO: Pius XII Library, St. Louis U., 1971.

Kaiser, Ernest. "The History of Negro History." Negro Digest, F, 1968.

Kane, Frank, and Baker, Gary G. Minorities and Prejudice in America. Teacher and Student Manuals, 1966, 56 pp. Amherst, MA: Amherst College. ERIC ED 028 191.

Kane, Michael B. Minorities in Textbooks: A Study of Their Treatment in Social Studies Texts. Chicago, IL: Quadrangle, 1971.

Katz, William A. "Minorities in American History Textbooks." Equal Opportunity Review, Je, 1973.

Katz, William Loren. "Black History in Secondary Schools." Journal of Negro History, Fall, 1969.

_____. Teachers' Guide to American Negro History, 1968, 192 pp. ERIC ED 041 982.

_____. A Teacher's Guide to American Negro History (Secondary School Level). Chicago: Quadrangle Books, 1967.

Kelly, James. Teaching Strategies for African Cultural Studies in the Senior High School, Ja, 1968, 169 pp. Bergen County Center for Non-Western Studies. ERIC ED 020 938.

Kelley, Samuel. "A Model for Emerging Black Studies Programs: An Analysis of Selected Black Studies Programs Viewed in Historical Perspective." Doctoral dissertation, U. of Wisconsin, 1971.

Kennedy, Ruth George. "A Study of Afro-American Literature Courses and Teachers in the Secondary Schools of North Carolina." Doctoral dissertation, U. of North Carolina, 1976. Univ. Microfilms Order No. 77-2060.

Kent, George Robert. "A Survey of Integrated and Separate Black Studies in Maryland Secondary Schools, Grades 10-12." Doctoral dissertation, U. of Maryland, 1972. Univ. Microfilms Order No. 73-11393.

Kessler, Sidney H. "To Teach Black History." NJEA Review 45(Ja, 1972).

Key, R. Charles. "Society and Sociology: The Dynamics of Black Sociological Negation." Phylon 39(Spring, 1978):35-48.

Kiah, Donald Allen. "An Identification of Black Studies Programs in the State of Maryland with Emphasis on the Black Studies Program in the Public High Schools of Prince Georges County, Maryland, as Perceived by Principals, Teachers, and Students in the Spring Semester of 1970-1971." Doctoral dissertation, George Washington U., 1972. Univ. Microfilms Order No. 72-19731.

Kijembe, Adhama Oluwa. "Swahili and Black Americans." Negro Digest, Jl, 1969.

Kilgore, James C. "The Case for Black Literature." Negro Digest, Jl, 1969.

Kilson, Martin. "Anatomy of the Black Studies Movement." Massachusetts Review 4(Autumn, 1969):718-726.

_____. "The Black Aesthetic." Black World 24(D, 1974):30, 44-48.

_____. "Reflections on Structure and Content in Black Studies." Journal of Black Studies 3(Mr, 1973):297-313.

King, Josie M., and Blake, J. Herman. Teaching Negro History: A Dual Emphasis. Santa Cruz, CA: U. of California, 1967.

Kinnamon, Kenneth. "Afro-American Literature, the Black Revolution, and Ghetto High Schools." English Journal 59(1970):189-194.

Kisner, Ronald E. "White Stars Cross Over and Get Rich on Black Music." Jet, Ap 13, 1978.

Kochman, Thomas. Mainstream and Non-Mainstream Communication Norms, Ja, 1972, 44 pp. Cambridge, MA: Language Research Foundation. ERIC ED 063 814.

Koger, Earl. Negro History Coloring Book. Earl Koger Co., 3605 Cedardale Road, Baltimore, MD 21215.

Konubi, Imim. "Why Swahili?" African-American Teachers Forum, S, 1969.

Kreber, Patricia F. "Negro History in the Grades." Catholic School Journal, O, 1968.

Krug, Mark M. "Freedom and Racial Equality: A Study of 'Revised' High School History Tests Texts." School Review 78(My, 1970):297-354.

_____. "On Teaching Negro History." School Review, Mr, 1969.

Kurtz, Benjamin. "Black Studies: Time for Restructuring." Clearing House 45(D, 1970): 201-203.

Labov, William. The Study of Nonstandard English. Champaign, IL: National Council of Teachers of English, 1970.

Ladner, Joyce A. (ed.). The Death of White Sociology. New York: Random House, 1973.

Lamar, Wilmer A. "Black Literature in High Schools in Illinois (English Teachers Speak for Themselves)." Illinois English Bulletin 58(My, 1971):1-42.

Lannon, Maria M. The Black Man in America: An Overview of Negro History with Bibliography and Basic Booklist for K-12. New York: Joseph F. Wagner, Inc., 55 Park Place, New York, NY 10007.

Large, Arlene J. "'Black History.' Rehabilitating of U.S. Heroes Faces Danger of Puffery." Wall Street Journal, Je 18, 1968.

Lash, John S. "The Academic Status of the Literature of the American Negro: A Description and Analysis of Curriculum Inclusions and Teaching Practices." Doctoral dissertation, U. of Michigan, 1946.

Latimer, Bettye I. and others (eds.). Starting Out Right. Choosing Books About Black People for Young Children. Pre-School Through Third Grade. Madison, WI: Wisconsin Department of Public Instruction, 1972.

Lawrence, Carolyn. "Art for Black Students, A Change in Objectives." School Arts, F, 1969.

Layer, Harold A. (comp.). "Ethnic Studies: A Survey of the AV Media." Educational/Instructional Broadcasting 3(D, 1970):11-16.

_____ (ed.). Ethnic Studies and Audiovisual Media: A Listing and Discussion. Stanford, CA: ERIC Clearinghouse on Educational Media and Technology, Institute for Communication Research, Stanford U., Je, 1969.

Layng, Anthony. "Anthropology and Afro-American Studies." Journal of General Education 23 (O, 1971):191-200.

_____. "Anthropology and Afro-American Studies." Council on Anthropology and Education Quarterly 7(F, 1976):13-16.

Leach, Bridget. "The Social Geographer and Black People: Can Geography Contribute to Race Relations?" Race 15(O, 1973):230-241.

deLerma, Dominique-Rene. "Black Music: A Bibliographic Essay." Library Trends 23 (Ja, 1975):517-532.

Levey, Rose Marie Walker. Black Studies in Schools, 1970. National School Public Relations Association, 1201 16th Street, N.W., Washington, DC 20036.

Lewis, Francione N. Selecting Children's Books With a Black Perspective (Preschool-Third Grade), 1975. ERIC ED 129 457.

Lewis, Lawrence T. "The Geography of Black America: The Growth of a Sub-Discipline." Journal of Geography 73(D, 1974):38-43.

Lewis, W. Arthur. "The Road to the Top is Through Higher Education--Not Black Studies." New York Times Magazine, My 11, 1969.

Lieber, Todd M., and O'Sullivan, Maurice J. "'Native Sons?' Black Students on Black Literature." Negro American Literature Forum 5(Spring, 1971):3-7.

Lightfoot, Jean H. Multi-Ethnic Literature in the High School. Washington, DC: GPO, 1973.

Lightfoot, Orlando B., and Foster, Douglas L. "Black Studies, Black Identity Formation and Some Implications for Community Psychiatry." American Journal of Orthopsychiatry 40(O, 1970):751-755.

Likover, Belle. "Introducing Black History: An Action Experiment in Changing Interracial Behavior." Jewish Community Center Program Aids 32(Winter, 1970-1971):7-16.

Lincoln, C. Eric. "Black Studies and Cultural Continuity." Black Scholar 10(O, 1978):12-17.

Livingston, Tom. "Black Studies Fill the Parts Left Out." Philadelphia Daily News, F 6, 1976. [University of Pennsylvania and Temple University]

Llorens, Lela A. "Black Culture and Child Development." American Journal of Occupational Therapy 25(Ap, 1971):144-148.

Llorens, David. "Rhapsody in Black." American Education, N, 1968.

Lloyd, R. G. "Negro History in the Development of Racial Understanding." Negro Educational Review, Ja, 1967.

Locke, Octavia C. "Art and Black Studies." School Arts 72(S, 1972):46-47.

Lombardi, John. Black Studies in the Community College. Washington, DC: American Association of Junior Colleges, 1971.

Lombardi, John, and Quimby, Edgar A. Black Studies As A Curriculum Catalyst. Los Angeles: ERIC Clearinghouse for Junior Colleges, Graduate School of Education and the University Library, U. of California, My, 1971.

Long, Richard A. "The Black Studies Boondoggle." Liberator 10(S, 1970):6-9.

_____. "Black Studies Fall Into Place." Nation, Jl 6, 1974.

_____. "Black Studies: International Dimensions." CLA Journal 14(S, 1970):1-6.

_____. Black Studies Year One, 1971, 13 pp. Atlanta: Atlanta U., Center for African and African-American Studies. ERIC ED 049 685.

_____. "The Future of Black Studies." CLA Journal 15(S, 1971):1-6.

_____. "Race and Scholarship." Liberator 10 (Jl, 1970):4-7.

Love, Theresa R. "From Black Studies to Ethnic Studies Programs in American Colleges and Universities." Journal of Afro-American Issues 5(Winter, 1977):51-59.

Lubin, Maurice A. "Une importante figure des Black Studies: Dorothy B. Porter." Presence africaine (1974):132-137.

Lukas, J. Anthony. "Schools Turn to Negro Role in U.S." New York Times, Jl 8, 1968.

Luxenberg, Stan. "The Schomburg Center: The Soul of Black Scholarship." Change 9(S, 1977):18-22.

Lyda, Wesley J. "Black Studies and the Black Revolution: A Longitudinal Case History." Contemporary Education 48(Winter, 1977):73-77.

Lyman, Stanford M. The Black American in Sociological Thought. New York: Capricorn Books, 1973.

McBride, Ullysses. "A Survey of Black Studies Offerings in Traditionally Black Institutions of Higher Education Between 1960-73." Doctoral dissertation, Auburn U., 1974. Univ. Microfilms Order No. 75-12492.

_____. "The Status of Black Studies in Traditionally Black Institutions in America." Negro Educational Review 25(O, 1974):208-212.

MacCann, Donnarae (ed.). The Black American in Books for Children: Readings in Racism. Metuchen, NJ: Scarecrow Press, 1972.

McClendon, William H. "Black Studies: Education for Liberation." Northwest Journal of African and Black American Studies, Summer, 1973. [Reprinted in Black Scholar 6(S, 1974):15-20]

McColl, Robert W. "Creating Ghettos: Manipulating Social Space in the Real World and the Classroom." Journal of Geography 7(N, 1972):496-502.

MacDougall, A. Kent. "School Texts Stressing Negroes' Roles in U.S. Arouse the South's Ire." Wall Street Journal, Mr 24, 1965.

McEachern, Gaye. "Afro-American History: A Rush to Get in Step." Nation's Schools, S, 1968.

McGinnis, James. "Crisis and Contradiction in Black Studies." Black World 22(Mr, 1973): 27-35.

McLaurin, Melton. "Images of Negroes in Deep South Public School State History Texts." Phylon 32(Fall, 1971):237-246.

McPherson, James M. "How U.S. Histories Falsified Slave Life." University (Princeton University), Summer, 1967.

_____. "The 'Saga' of Slavery: Setting the Textbooks Straight." Changing Education, Winter, 1967.

Major, Clarence. Dictionary of Afro-American Slang. New York: International Publishers, 1970.

Malcolm, Vivian. "Teaching the Black Experience in the Elementary School to Grades K-3." Master's thesis, San Jose State U., 1974.

Malinowski, Bronislaw. "Native Education and Culture Contact." International Review of Missions, O, 1936.

Mandel, Barrett John. "The Didactic Achievement of Malcolm X's Autobiography." Afro-American Studies 2(Mr, 1972):269-274.

Manns, Adrienne. "Writing a New Chapter in Black Children's Books." Washington Post, D 18, 1973.

Manna, Tom, and Yoder, Jan. "Focus on Black Literature: Conversations with Darwin Turner." English Journal 64(D, 1975):78-81.

Massenburg, Doris O., and Applebury, Bruce C. "Growing Up Black: A Black Literature Unit for Schools." Negro American Literature Forum 5(Summer, 1971):39-67.

Mattingly, Paul H. "Useful History and Black Identity." History of Education Quarterly 10(F, 1970):338-350.

Mazrui, Ali A. "Negritude, the Talmudic Tradition and the Intellectual Performance of Blacks and Jews." Ethnic and Racial Studies 1(Ja, 1978):19-36.

Mellan, Olivia. "Black English." New Republic 163(N 28, 1970):15-17.

Meyer, Howard N. "Overcoming the White Man's History." Massachusetts Review 7(1966).

_____. "Tokens of Truth." Integrated Education, F-Mr, 1965.

Mezz, Sheila M. "Effects of a 'Black Cultural Positives' Program on the Self-Concepts and Attitudes of Black Junior High Students." Diss. Abstr. Int'l., 32(5-A), N, 1971, 2488-2489.

Mhone, Guy C. Z. Toward a Methodology of Black Studies, O, 1975. ERIC ED 126 200.

Michigan Department of Education. A Report on the Treatment of Minorities in American History Textbooks. Lansing, MI: State Board of Education, Jl, 1968.

_____. A Study of Elementary and Secondary Social Studies Textbooks, 2 volumes. Lansing, MI: The Department, 1973.

Millender, Dharathula H. Real Negroes--Honest Settings. Chicago: American Federation of Teachers, 1967. [Annotated bibliography of children's books]

_____. "Selecting Our Children's Books: Time for Some Changes." Changing Education, Fall, 1966.

Miller, LaMar P. "The Discipline of Black Studies and Curriculum Theory." Notre Dame Journal of Education 1(Summer, 1970):142-148.

Miller, Loren. "The Negro in History Textbooks." CTA Journal, Mr, 1965.

Minor, Delores. "Public Schools and Black Materials." Negro American Literature Forum 5(F, 1971):85-87.

Mintz, Sidney W. "Toward An Afro-American History." Journal of World History 13(1971): 316-332.

Mitchell, J. A. "The Lack of Adequate Representation of Cultural and Ethnic Groups in Fifth Grade Social Studies Textbooks." Master's thesis, U. of Wisconsin, 1971.

Mondesire, Jerry. "Black Studies. The Dilemma of an Under-defined Black Nationalism." Imani 5(Ag-S, 1971):18-23.

Moore, Nancy L. "Cashing In on Blackness: The Dilemma of Afro-American Education." Freedomways 12(Fourth Quarter, 1972):273-287.

Morgan, Gordon D. "First Generation Black Sociologists and Theories of Social Change." Journal of Social and Behavioral Sciences 20(Fall, 1974):106-119.

Morgan, Harry. "Music a Lifeforce in the Black Community." Music Educators Journal 58(N, 1971):34-37.

Morgan, Janet. "Sensitive Native or Native Sensitivity?" Integrated Education 8(Jl-Ag, 1970):35-39.

Morris, E. L. "Blowing in the Wind; Books on Black History and Life in America." Library Journal, Mr 15, 1969.

Morris, Earl W. and others. The Role and Contribution of American Negroes in the History of the United States and of Illinois. A Guide for Teachers and Curriculum Planners. Grades K through 12, S, 1970, 196 pp. Springfield, IL: Illinois State Office of the Superintendent of Public Instruction. [Available from Office of the Superintendent of Public Instruction, Division of Instruction, Department of Curriculum Development, Springfield, IL 62706]

Morris, Leonard M. "The Negro and American History." New Jersey Education Association Review, F, 1968.

Morris, Sam. A Treatise on Black Studies, 1973. The Honorary Secretary, The Committee on Black Studies, 63 Napier Court, London SW6, England.

Morrison, Toni. "Rediscovering Black History." New York Times Magazine, Ag 11, 1974.

Moraberger, Robert E. "Segregated Surveys: American Literature." Negro American Literature Forum 4(Mr, 1970):3-8.

Moss, James Allen. "In Defense of Black Studies. Some Additional Notes." Afro-American Studies 1(Ja, 1971):217-220.

Multi-Ethnic Education Resources Center. Teaching Black. An Evaluation of Methods and Resources. Redwood City, CA: San Mateo County Office of Education, 1971. [Order: Multi-Ethnic Education Resources Center, Bldg. 30, Room 32, Stanford U., Stanford, CA 94305. Price: $4.00]

Multiethnic Task Force. Programs, Services, Materials of the New York State Education Department for Black and Puerto Rican Studies. Albany, NY: U. of the State of New York, 1970.

Munford, Clarence J. Production Relations, Class, and Black Liberation: A Marxist Perspective in Afro-American Studies. Amsterdam: B. R. Gruner, Publishing Company, forthcoming.

Murphy, Charles P. "The Humanities, Art and the Black Student." Integrated Education 8 (S-O, 1970):53-56.

Murray, Albert. "Black Curriculum. Whose Dues for Good Black News? (Some Notes from a Journey to Mobile)." Center Forum, Mr 1, 1969.

Museum of Negro History and Art. Figures in Negro History, 1964. The Museum, 2806 South Michigan Avenue, Chicago, IL.

Myers, Robin. Black Craftsmen Through History. Brooklyn, NY: Institute of the Joint Apprenticeship Program. [Available from the Institute of the Joint Apprenticeship Program, Workers Defense League, 1520 Bushwick Avenue, Brooklyn, NY 11207]

Naeem, Abdul Basit. "Says Black Studies Programs Should Include Studies on Muhammad's Mission." Muhammad Speaks, My 16, 1969.

A National Network for the Acquisition, Organization, Processing and Dissemination of Materials by and About Blacks, Ja, 1974. ERIC ED 089 784.

"The Need for Black Academic Relevancy." MOJO (Organ of the Black Students Congress), F-Mr, 1968.

Negro History and Culture, 1969, 363 pp. Miami: Dade County Board of Public Instruction. Available for Dade County Public Schools, Textbook Department, 2210 S.W. Third Street, Miami, FL 33135. ERIC ED 049 959.

The Negro in American History: Resource Material. An In-Service Training Program Which Focuses on Assisting Educators of School District 65 to Develop Some Common Understandings About Crucial Integration Issues; School Year 1968-1969, 1968, 63 pp. Evanston, IL: Evanston School District 65. ERIC ED 036 573.

The Negro in United States History. A Resource Guide (Tentative) for Grades 7 and 8, 1970, 160 pp. Boston: Boston Public Schools. ERIC ED 046 800. [Available from Edward J. Winter, Secretary, Boston School Committee, 15 Beacon Street, Boston, MA 02108]

The Negro in United States History. A Resource Guide (Tentative) for Senior High School, 1969, 101 pp. Boston: Boston Public Schools. ERIC ED 051 154.

Nelson, Alice Dunbar. "Negro Literature for Negro Pupils." Southern Workman 51(F, 1922): 59.

Nevada State Department of Education. Guidelines for Selecting Multi-ethnic Materials. Carson City, NE: State Textbook Commission, 1968.

Newbold, N. C. Report of the Committee to Cooperate with the National Association of Teachers in Colored Schools. In National Education Association Addresses and Proceedings, 1932, pp. 210-212.

Newby, Robert G., and Tyack, David B. "Victims Without 'Crimes': Some Historical Perspectives on Black Education." Journal of Negro Education 40(Summer, 1971):192-206.

Newton, James E. A Curriculum Evaluation of Black Studies in Relation to Student Knowledge of Afro-American History and Culture. San Francisco: R & E Research Associates, 1976.

_____. "A Review of Black Studies as Related to Basic Elements of Curriculum." Journal of Negro Education 43(Fall, 1974):477-488.

_____. "College Student Knowledge of Afro-American History and Culture in Relation to Black Studies." College Student Journal 8 (S, 1974):42-49.

_____. "Standardization: Key to Afro-American Studies." Education 98(Summer, 1978):436-439.

New York State Education Department. Intergroup Relations, Resource Handbook for Elementary School Teachers; The Negro in American History. Albany, NY: Division of Intercultural Relations in Education, New York State Education Department, 1963.

Neyland, Leedell W. "Why Negro History in the Junior and Senior High School?" Social Studies, D, 1967.

Nichols, Lewis. "What the Negro Reads." New York Times Book Review, Ap 16, 1967.

Obatala, J. K. "The Black Past: to Learn From, Not to Idealize." Los Angeles Times, F 15, 1974.

_____. "Black Studies Stop the Shouting and Go to Work." Smithsonian, D, 1974.

_____. "Blacks on TV: a Replay of Amos 'n' Andy?" Los Angeles Times, N 26, 1974.

_____. "Soul Music in Africa. Has Charlie Got a Brand New Bag?" Black Scholar 2(F, 1971):8-12.

Office of Curriculum Development. Contribution of the Negro to American Life and Culture. A Resource Unit for Improving Intergroup Relations through Instruction. Frankfort, KY: State Department of Education, 1968.

Oliver, Karen. "Ethnic Studies in the Nation's Universities: Still Alive and Well." Washington Post, D 2, 1973.

Onyewu, Nicholas D. U. "Crisis in African Education." Afro-American Studies 1(Ja, 1971): 227-230.

Orr, Margaret. "I Leave You a Responsibility." Minnesota Reading Quarterly 15(F, 1971):81-89. [Teaching black literature in intermediate grades]

Pachter, Henry. "Teaching Negro History." Dissent, Mr-Ap, 1969.

Page, Ernest R. "Black Literature and Changing Attitudes: Does It Do the Job?" English Journal 66(Mr, 1977):29-33.

Pahl, Denis. "Black History: A Discovery Strategy." Midwest Education Review 2(Summer, 1970):15-20.

Parker, Bettye J. "Black Literature Teachers: Torch-Bearers of European Myths?" Black World 25(D, 1975):61-65.

Parker, Margaret Bowles. "Black Studies in the Community Colleges of New Jersey: A Topographical Study." Doctoral dissertation, Rutgers U., 1976. Univ. Microfilms Order No. 77-13283.

Patterson, Orlando. "Rethinking Black History." Harvard Educational Review 41(Ag, 1971):297-315.

Patterson, Ruth Polk. "Developing an Afro-American Studies Program in the Integrated Public Schools: Problems and Procedures." Doctoral dissertation, Emory U., 1977. Univ. Microfilms Order No. 77-32388. [Little Rock, AR, schools]

Payne, Robert. "The Effects of Teaching the Concept Lesson 'The Underground Railroad in Michigan' to Black and White Fourth Grade Students." Doctoral dissertation, U. of Michigan, 1970.

Peavy, Charles D. (ed.). Afro-American Literature and Culture, 1945-1975: A Guide to Information Services. Vol. 6. Detroit: Gale, 1978.

Pelletti, John C. Black Population Distribution and Growth in the United States. Geography Curriculum Project, 1973. Geography Curriculum Project, 107 Dudley Hall, U. of Georgia, Athens, GA 30601.

Penick, Benson E. "Knowledge of Black Culture as a Factor in the Attitudes and Behaviors of White and Blacks." Doctoral dissertation, Kansas State U., Manhattan, KS, 1971.

Perry, Jesse. "Black Literature and the English Curriculum." English Journal 60 (N, 1971):1057-1062.

Phillips, Ivory Paul. An Analysis of the Needs and Provisions for Black Studies in the Metropolitan Area of Jackson, Mississippi, F, 1976. ERIC ED 121 886.

Phinazee, Annette Hoage. Materials by and about American Negroes, Papers Presented at an Institute Sponsored by the Atlanta University School of Library Service with the Cooperation of the Trevor Arnett Library (O 21-23, 1905). Atlanta: Atlanta U. School of Library Services, 1967, 112 pp. ERIC ED 017 306.

Pickens, William G. "Teaching Negro Culture in High Schools--Is It Worthwhile?" Journal of Negro Education, Spring, 1965.

Pitts, Ethel Louise. "The American Negro Theatre: 1940-1949." Doctoral dissertation, U. of Missouri, 1975. University Microfilms Order No. 76-7538. [Harlem]

Pleasants, Henry. "Afro-American Epoch--Emergence of a New Idiom." Music Educators Journal 57(S, 1970):33-37.

Poinsett, Alex. "Inawapasa Watu Weusi Kusema Kiswahili?" Ebony, D, 1968. ["Should black men speak Swahili?"]

_____. "The Plight of Black Studies." Ebony, D, 1973.

Polsky, Milton. "The American Slave Narrative: Exciting Resource Material for the Classroom." Negro Educational Review 26(Ja, 1975):22-36.

Porter, Curtiss E. "An Education(al) Insight: Black World. What Have We Not Done Is To Define Black Studies in the Terms by Which We Exist." Black Lines 1(Summer, 1971):53-64.

Porter, Dorothy B. "Bibliography and Research in Afro-American Scholarship." Journal of Academic Librianship 2(My, 1976):77-81.

Poulos, Nicholas. "Negro Attitudes Toward Textbook Illustrations." Journal of Negro Education, Spring, 1969.

Price, R. D., and Spencer, T. L. "Elementary Social Studies Textbooks and Their Relevance to the Negro Child." Social Studies 61(1970) 168-173.

Prichard, Nancy S. Controversy in the Classroom: Ethnic Studies Programs, Ap, 1970, 11 pp. ERIC ED 041 018.

Prince, Ulysses. "Understanding 'Negro' History." The Integrator, Fall, 1968.

Proposals for Black Studies Programs for Various Types of Educational Institutions, 1969. Black Liberation Publishers, P.O. Box 10242, East Palo Alto, CA 94303.

Prugh, Peter H. "Civil Rights Movement Spurs Interest in Role of Negroes in History." Wall Street Journal, My 17, 1967.

Quarles, Benjamin. "Black History Unbound." Daedalus 103(Spring, 1974):163-178.

_____. Black History's Diversified Clientele. Washington, DC: Department of History, Howard U., 1971.

_____. "The Future of the Negro Past." Negro Digest, F, 1968.

Rafky, David M. "Are Blacks Who Teach Black Studies Different?" College Student Journal 6(Ap-My, 1972):55-61.

_____. "Attitudes of Black Studies Faculty Toward Black Students: A National Survey." Journal of College Student Personnel 14(Ja, 1973):25-30.

Ramsey, Katherine Imogene. "A Comparison of First-Grade Negro Dialect Speakers' Comprehension of Material Presented in Standard English and in Negro Dialect," 1970, 112 pp. Doctoral dissertation, U. of Indiana, Available from University Microfilms, P.O. Box 1764, Ann Arbor, MI 48106.

Rappaport, Julian, and Sorensen, James. "Teaching Psychology to 'Disadvantaged' Youth: Enhancing the Relevance of Psychology Through Public Education." Journal of School Psychology 9(1971):120-126.

Ray, LeRoi R., Jr. "Black Studies: A Discussion of Evaluation." Journal of Negro Education 45(Fall 1976):383-396.

Reagan, Bernice. A History of the Afro-American Through His Songs. Part of a Packet with Audiotape. Albany, NY: Division of Humanities and Arts, New York Education Department, 1969, 27 pp. ERIC ED 048 431.

Reardon, William R., and Pawley, Thomas D. (eds.). The Black Teacher and the Dramatic Arts. New York: Negro Universities Press, 1972.

Record, Jane C., and Record, Wilson. "Ethnic Studies and Affirmative Action: Ideological Roots and Implications for the Quality of American Life." Social Science Quarterly 55 (S, 1974):502-519.

Record, Wilson. "Can Black Studies and Sociology Find Common Ground?" Journal of Negro Education 44(Winter, 1975):63-81.

_____. "Some Implications of the Black Studies Movement for Higher Education in the 1970's." Journal of Higher Education 44(Mr, 1973):191-216.

Red Letter Days in Black History. Curriculum Guide, Grade 3. Camden, NJ: Camden City Schools, S, 1970, 93 pp. ERIC ED 052 087.

Redd, George N. Workshop on the Incorporation of Materials about the Negro in the Curriculum of the Liberal Arts College, August 4-August 15, 1969. Nashville, TN: Fisk U., F 3, 1970, 18 pp. ERIC ED 051 767.

Redd, Virginia P. Black Literature and Mainstream American Literature: One and Inseparable, N, 1973. ERIC ED 089 281.

Reddick, Lawrence D. "Methods of Combating Racially Derogatory Statements and Implications of American College Textbooks." Quarterly Review of Higher Education Among Negroes 3(O, 1935):207-211.

_____. "Racial Attitudes in American History Textbooks." Journal of Negro History 19, pp. 225-265.

Redding, Saunders. "The Black Arts Movement:
A Modest Dissent." Crisis 84(F, 1977):50-52.

Redkey, Edwin S. "On Teaching and Learning
Black History." In Black Studies in the
University: A Symposium. Edited by
Armistead L. Robinson, Craig C. Foster, and
Donald H. Oglilvie. New Haven, CT: Yale
U. Press, 1969.

Reese, Carolyn. "From Jupiter Hammon to Le Roi
Jones: Our Schools' 'Sins of Ommission.'"
Changing Education, Fall, 1966.

"Report Card on Black Studies." Newsweek,
Mr 18, 1974.

"The Results of Black Power: Increased Offerings of Black History Courses" (by a contributing historian). Integrated Education,
Issue 40, Jl-Ag, 1969, p. 57.

Rhodes, Odis O. "Some Implications for Teaching
Reading to Speakers of Black Dialect." Viewpoints 46(My, 1970):117-147.

Richards, Henry J. (ed.). Topics in Afro-American Studies. Buffalo, NY: Black Academy
Press, 1970.

Richardson, Irvine (ed.). The Relationship of
Africanists to Afro-American Studies. East
Lansing, MI: African Studies Center, Michigan
State U., 1969.

Richardson, Willis, and Miller, May. Negro
History in 13 Plays. Washington, DC: The
Associated Publishers, Inc., 1935.

Rist, Ray C. "Black Staff, Black Studies, and
White Universities: A Study in Contradic-
tions." Journal of Higher Education 41
(N, 1970):618-629.

Ritter, Frederic A. "Toward a Geography of the
Negro." Journal of Geography 70(Mr, 1971):
150-156.

Roberts, Louney F., Jr. "Ethnogenic Identifica-
tion: A Survey of the Pictorial Content of
Selected Current Elementary School Textbooks."
Negro History Bulletin, D, 1967.

_____. "Minority Self-Identification Through
Texts. A Study of Publication Progress."
Journal of Human Relations, 3rd Quarter, 1968.

Roberts, S. V. "Black Studies: More than Soul
Courses." Commonweal 91(Ja 30, 1970):478-479.

Robinson, Armistead L., Foster, Craig C., and
Ogilvie, Donald H. (eds.). Black Studies in
the University: A Symposium. New Haven, CT:
Yale U. Press, 1969.

Robinson, Carrie. "Media for the Black
Curriculum. Educational Trends and Media
Programs in School Libraries." ALA Bulletin
63(1969):242-246.

Robinson, Harry, Jr. Lift Ev'ry Voice and Sing:
Papers Presented At An Institute for Training
Librarians for Special Black Collections and
Archives, April 12-14, 1973. Montgomery, AL:
Alabama State U., 1974.

Robinson, Louis. "Gridiron Color Bars Topple
at White Southern Colleges." Ebony, D, 1967.

Robinson, Walter G., and Hudson, Gossie H.
"Intellectual History Need: Black Thought
in the Literature." Journal of Afro-American
Issues 1(F, 1972):257-262.

Robinson, Wilhelmena S. "In-Service Education
of the Teacher of African History." Negro
History Bulletin, N, 1964.

Roderick, Juanita. "Minority Groups in Text
books." Improving College and University
Teaching 18(Spring, 1970):129-132.

Roman, Charles Victor. A Knowledge of History
is Conducive to Racial Solidarity, and
Other Writings. Nashville, TN: Sunday
School Union Printer, 1911.

Rose, Harold M. (ed.). Geography of the
Ghetto. DeKalb, IL: Northern Illinois U.
Press, 1972.

Rose, Kathy. "The National Council for Black
Studies." Drum (Winter, 1977-78):63-66.

Rosenberg, Max. Criteria for Evaluating the
Treatment of Minority Groups in Textbooks
and Other Curriculum Materials, 1972.
Michigan Association for Supervision and
Curriculum Development, 1216 Kendale Blvd.,
East Lansing, MI 48823.

Rosser, James R., and Copeland, Thomas E.
"Reflections: Black Studies--Black
Education?" Journal of Black Studies 3
(Mr, 1973):287-296.

Rosser, James and others. Student Opinions and
Black Studies, F 5, 1971, 29 pp. ERIC ED
048 420.

Roth, Joel A. "Dick and Jane Make Some New
Friends." Book Production Industry, Je,
1965.

Roth, Rodney W. "Critique of Black Studies
Developments at the Elementary Level."
Journal of Negro Education 39(Summer, 1970):
230-238.

_____. "The Effects of 'Black Studies' on
White 5th Grade Students." Education 90
(Ap-My, 1970):328-331.

Rowe, Cyprian Lamar. "Crisis in African
Studies: The Birth of the African Heritage
Studies Association." Black Academy Review
1(Fall, 1970):3-10.

Rudd, M. S. "The Negro in Juvenile Biography: A Quantitative Analysis of Representation and Omission." Master's thesis, Southern Connecticut State College, 1969.

Runcie, John. "The Black Culture Movement and the Black Community." Journal of American Studies 10(Ag, 1976):185-214.

Russell, Carlos E. "On Black Studies." Black Caucus 3(Fall, 1970):23-29.

_____. "Pre-Revolutionary Thoughts on Black Studies." Renewal, My, 1969.

Russell, Joseph J. "Afro-American Studies: A Policy Analysis." Viewpoints 51(My, 1975): 45-60.

Rustin, Bayard. "Acceptance Speech of 1968 Dewey Award Winner." United Teacher, Ap 17, 1968.

_____. "Anyone for Black Studies?" New America, N 30, 1973.

_____. "Black Studies and Inequality." New America, My 25, 1969.

_____. "The Decline of Black Studies." New York Teacher, N 25, 1973.

_____. "The Fakery of Black Studies." Integrated Education, Jl-Ag, 1969.

_____. "Won't They Ever Learn?" New York Times, Section 4, p. 7, Ag 1, 1971. [On black English]

Ryan, Pat M. "White Experts, Black Experts, and Black Studies." Black Academy Review 1 (Spring, 1970):52-65.

Ryder, Sarah. "What Ethnic Solidarity?" Integrated Education 7(N-D, 1969):39-42.

Salk, Erwin A. (ed.). A Layman's Guide to Negro History. Chicago: Quadrangle, 1966.

Schneider, Joanna E., and Zangrando, Robert L. "Black History in the College Curriculum." Rocky Mountain Social Science Journal 6 (O, 1969):134-142.

Schneiderman, Gerald M. "The Relationship of Cognitive Differentiation of Types of Black History Course Content and Atttitude Change of Black Seventh-Grade Students." Diss. Abstr. Int'l. 31 (12-A) (Je, 1971) 6413.

Schomburg, Arthur Alfonso. Racial Integrity. A Plea for the Establishment of a Chair of Negro History in our Schools and Colleges. New York: Negro Society for Historical Research, Occasional Paper No. 3, 1913.

Schrag, Peter. "What the New Black Myths Mean." Harper's, My, 1969.

Scully, Malcolm G. "Minority Literatures Gain a Slippery Foothold." Chronicle of Higher Education, N 29, 1976.

A Second Report on the Treatment of Minorities in American History Textbooks, Ap, 1971, 27 pp. Lansing, MI: Michigan State Dept. of Education. ERIC ED 052 125.

Selby, Edward B., Jr. "Money and Banking (Afro-American): A University Course." Journal of General Education 23(O, 1971):241-245.

Semas, Philip W. "Shortages of Money, Faculty, Time Plague Black Studies Programs." Chronicle of Higher Education, My 4, 1970.

Seney, Heidi. "Black Studies, Sure. But..." Learning 2(S, 1973):72-73.

Shagaloff, June. Survey of Negro History in Selected Secondary School Systems. New York: NAACP, Fall, 1969.

Shannon, Irwin V. "Negro Education and the Development of a Group Tradition." Doctoral dissertation, Vanderbilt U., 1934.

Shockley, A. A. "Tell It Like It Is: New Criteria for Children's Books in Black and White." Southeastern Libriarian 20(Spring, 1970):30-33.

_____ (comp.). A Handbook for the Administration of Special Negro Collections. Nashville, TN: Fisk U. Library, 1971 .

Simms, Patricia. A Study of Ethnic Representation in Illustrations and Subject Area Relevance to Environment of Elementary School Texts. Trenton, NJ: Cadwalder Parent Teachers Association, Cadwalder School, Mr 15, 1967.

Simms, Ruby Jean. "The Effects of Black Studies Instruction on the Self-Concept of Senior High School Students." Doctoral dissertation, Louisiana State U., 1976. Univ. Microfilms Order No. 76-25283.

Simon, Sidney, and Carnes, Alice. "Teaching Afro-American History with a Focus on Values." Educational Leadership 27(1969): 222-223.

Simpkins, Edward. "Black Studies--Here to Stay?" Black World 24(D, 1974):26-29.

Sizemore, Barbara A., and Chase, Kymara S. "I Dig Your Thing But It Ain't In My Bag: White Values in Black Education." ND Journal of Education 1(Fall, 1970):236-246.

Sledel, James. "Bi-dialectalism: the Linguistics of White Supremacy." English Journal, 1969, pp. 1307-1329.

Sloan, Irving. "Balance and Imbalance: 'New History Texts and the Negro.'" Changing Education, Fall, 1966.

_____. The Negro in Modern American History
Textbooks. Chicago: American Federation of
Teachers, 1966.

_____. The Negro in Modern History Textbooks.
4th edition. Washington, DC: American
Federation of Teachers, S, 1972.

_____. The Treatment of Black Americans in
Current Encyclopedias. Washington, DC:
American Federation of Teachers, 1970.

Slotkin, Aaron N. "The Treatment of Minorities
in Textbooks: The Issues and the Outlook."
Strengthening Democracy (N.Y. City Board of
Education), My, 1964.

Small, Robert Coleman, Jr. "Negro Literature
in High School English: Three Reasons for
Its Use." High School Journal 54(My, 1971):
475-483.

Smith, Arthur L., Jr. "Socio-Historical Perspectives of Black Oratory." Quarterly
Journal of Speech 56(O, 1970):264-269.

_____. Toward Transracial Communication.
Center Monograph Series, No. 1. Los Angeles:
U. of California, Afro-American Studies
Center, 1970, 36 pp. ERIC ED 045 777.

_____. "What's the Score on: Black Studies?"
Today's Education, Ja, 1972.

Smith, Charles U. "Contributions of Charles S.
Johnson to the Field of Sociology." Journal
of Social and Behavioral Sciences 18(Fall,
1972):26-31.

Smith, Daniel C. Teacher's Manual, The
American Negro: His History and Literature.
New York: Arno Press, 1969.

Smith, Glenn Ray. "The Black Studies Program
at the University of Colorado (Boulder and
Denver Campuses) 1968-1973: Development,
Change and Assessments." Doctoral disserta-
tion, U. of Colorado, 1974. Univ. Microfilms
Order No. 75-13467.

Smith, Jessie Carney. "The Impact of Black
Studies Programs on the Academic Library."
College and Research Libraries 33(Mr, 1972):
87-96.

_____. "Special Collections of Black Literature
in the Traditionally Black College." College
and Research Libraries 35(S, 1974):322-335.

Smith, Norvel. "Black Studies." In The Minority
Student on the Campus: Expectations and
Possibilities, pp. 179-188. Edited by Robert
A. Altman and Patricia O. Snyder. Western
Interstate Commission for Higher Education,
P.O. Drawer "P," Boulder, CO 80302, N, 1970.

Smith, Shelby Lewis (ed.). Black Political
Scientists and Black Survival: Essays in
Honor of a Black Scholar. Detroit: Balamys
Publishing, 1977. [Honoring Jewel Limar
Prestage]

Smith, T. M. W. "The Place of History in
Elementary School Social Studies: A Proposed
Program to Include the Role of Negro
Americans." Doctoral dissertation, U. of
Texas, 1967.

Smith, William David. "Black Studies: Recommen-
dations for Organization and National
Consideration." Journal of Negro Education 44
(Spring, 1976):170-176.

_____. "The Opinions of Administrative Heads of
Black Studies." Phi Delta Kappan (Mr, 1972):
446.

Smith, William L. "Critique of [Black Studies]
Developments at the Secondary Level." Journal
of Negro Education 39(Summer, 1970):239-261.

Smitherman, Geneva. "A Comparison of the Oral
and Written Styles of a Group of Inner-City
Black Students." Doctoral dissertation,
The U. of Michigan, 1969, 157 pp. Available
from Univ. Microfilms, P.O. Box 1764, Ann
Arbor, MI 48106.

Social Studies Resources for Inclusion of Negro
History and Culture in the Dade County
Curriculum. Miami, FL: Dade County Board
of Public Instruction, 1969, 57 pp. ERIC
ED 048 029.

Solomon, Benjamin, and Young, Beatrice. "Un-
weaving the Threads of Racism in American
History." Changing Education, Spring, 1968.

Southern, Eileen. "America's Black Composers
of Classical Music." Music Educators
Journal 62(N, 1975):46-59.

Sowell, Thomas, and Bailey, Ronald B. "Opinions
Differ on Black Studies." Today's Education
63(N-D, 1973):84-88.

Spaights, Ernest. "Black Studies Programs:
Issues and Problems." Urban Review 5(S,
1971):38-41.

Spencer, Thomas E. "On the Place of the Negro
in American History." Social Studies, Ap,
1969.

Spodek, Bernard and others. A Black Studies
Curriculum for Early Childhood Education:
Teaching Units. Rev. ed., 1976. ERIC ED
134 303.

_____ and others. The Development of a Black
Curriculum for Young Children. Final
Report, Aug, 1971. ERIC ED 063 031.

Spratlen, Thaddeus H. "The Educational
Relevance of Black Studies--An Interdisciplinary and Inter-cultural Interpretation." Western Journal of Black Studies 1
(Mr, 1977):38.

Standley, Fred, and Standley, Nancy V. "An
Experimental Use of Black Literature in a
Predominantly White University." Research
in the Teaching of English 4(F, 1970):139-
148.

Stanford, Barbara Dodds. "Affective Aspects of Black Literature." English Journal 59(1970): 371-374.

Stanford University, African and Afro-American Studies Program, Multi-Ethnic Education Resources Center. Teaching Black. An Evaluation of Methods and Resources. Redwood City, CA: San Mateo County Office of Education, 1971. [Order from: The Center, Bldg. 30, Room 32, Stanford U., Stanford, CA 94305]

Staples, Robert. Introduction to Black Sociology. New York: McGraw-Hill, 1976.

_____. "Race and Ideology. An Essay in Black Sociology." Journal of Black Studies 3(Je, 1973):395-422.

Starkweather, Ann (comp.). Instructional Objectives for a Junior College Course in African History. Los Angeles: U. of California, ERIC Clearinghouse for Junior College Information, Je, 1971, 21 pp. ERIC ED 049 737.

Starobin, Robert. "The Negro: A Central Theme in American History." Journal of Contemporary History, Ap, 1968.

"Statement of the Black Caucus to the African Studies Association Conference." Pan-African Journal, Spring-Summer, 1968.

Stent, Angela. "The Crisis in Black Studies." Times Higher Education Supplement, Ag 1, 1975.

Sterling, Dorothy. "What's Black and White and Read All Over?" English Journal, S, 1969.

Stewart, Charles E. "Correcting the Image of Negroes in Textbooks." Negro History Bulletin, N, 1964.

Stewart, James B. "Black Studies and Black People in the Future." Black Books Bulletin 4(Summer, 1976):20-25.

Stewart, William A. "Current Issues in the Use of Negro Dialect in Beginning Reading Texts." Florida FL Reporter 8(Spring-Fall, 1970): 3-7, 46.

Stimpson, Catharine R. "Black Culture/White Teacher. Change, My-Je, 1970.

Stock, Irvin. "Black Literature, Relevance, and the New Irrationality." Change 3(Mr-Ap, 1971):43-49.

Stovel, John E. "Black Studies is White Studies." Social Studies 62(O, 1971):204-208.

Stromberg, Rolf. "Black Drama: A Token." Seattle Post-Intelligencer, Ag 12, 1970. [U. of Washington]

Sudan, Nazzm Al (formerly Marvin X. Jackman). Black Dialectics, 1968. 2027 Bluefields Rd., Burlington, Ontario, Canada

Sundiata, I. K. "Black Studies: A Cop-Out?" Liberator, Ap, 1969.

Sutton, William Stanley. "The Evolution of the Black Studies Movement: With Specific Reference to the Establishment of the Black Studies Institute at Ohio University." Doctoral dissertation, Ohio U., 1972. Univ. Microfilms Order No. 72-26375.

Swindall, Bertha E. "A Course on Minority-Group Culture?" Social Service Review, S, 1968. [In a graduate social service program]

Szwed, John F. "An American Anthropological Dilemma: The Politics of Afro-American Culture." In Reinventing Anthropology. Edited by D. Hymes. New York: Pantheon, 1973.

_____. "Race and the Embodiment of Culture." Ethnicity 2(1975):19-33.

"Take Five, Add Soul = Boss Reading." Library Journal, F 15, 1969.

"Talking of Black Art, Theatre, Revolution and Nationhood." Black Theatre 5(1971):18-37. [Three symposia]

Tate, B. "In House and Out House: Authenticity and the Black Experience in Children's Books." Library Journal 95(O 15, 1970): 3595-3598.

Taylor, Nick. "The Dreams, Frustrations, of Directing Black Studies." Dayton (Ohio) Daily News, Ja 14, 1971. [Ohio State U.]

Taylor, Olive. "Recent Viewpoints on the Negro in American History." Journal, Ja, 1969. [Published by Division of Higher Education, United Church of Christ]

Taylor, Orlando L. An Introduction to the Historical Development of Black English: Some Implications for American Education. Washington, DC: Center for Applied Linguistics, Jl 15, 1969, 21 pp. ERIC ED 035 863.

Taylor, Prentiss. "Shaping a New Black Identity in America." Black World 22(My, 1973):5-14, 65-72.

"Teaching About Africa." Education and Community Relations 4(Mr, 1974):5-16. [Community Relations Commission, 15/16 Bedford St., London WC2, England]

"Teaching Black Culture." Time, Je 14, 1968.

"These Racially Integrated Materials Are Available." Nation's Schools, Je, 1967.

Thomas, Richard W. "Working-Class and Lower-Class Origins of Black Culture: Class Formation and the Division of Black Cultural Labor." Minority Voices 1(Fall, 1977):81-103.

Thomas, William, and Pentecoste, Joseph C. "Black Studies: Phase Two." Kappa Delta Pi Record 11(F, 1975):66-68.

Thorpe, Earl E. The Central Theme of Black History. Durham, NC: Seeman Printing, 1969.

Titcomb, Caldwell. "Young, Old, Gifted and Black." Harvard Crimson, Jl 27, 1976. [Critical essay on Who's Who Among Black Americans]

Toldson, Ivory L., and Pasteur, Alfred B. "Soul Music: Techniques for Therapeutic Intervention." Journal of Non-White Concerns in Personnel and Guidance 1(O, 1972):31-39.

Traynham, Warren R. "Black Studies in Theological Education: The Camel Comes of Age." Harvard Theological Review 66(Ap, 1973):257-271.

Trezise, Robert L. "The Black American in American History Textbooks." Social Studies, Ap, 1969.

Turner, Darwin T. "The Teaching of Afro-American Literature." College English 31(Ap, 1970): 666-670.

Turner, Darwin T., and Stanford, Barbara Dodds. Theory and Practice in the Teaching of Literature by Afro-Americans. Urbana, IL: National Council of Teachers of English. ERIC Clearinghouse on the Teaching of English, 1971, 106 pp. ERIC ED 057 062.

Turner, James. "Black Studies: A Concept and a Plan." Cornell Chronicle 1(O 2, 1969).

_____. "Black Studies and a Black Philosophy of Education." Black Lines 1(Winter, 1970): 5-8.

_____. "Black Studies and a Black Philosophy of Education." Imani 5(Ag-S, 1971):12-17.

_____. "Power and Control." Harvard Crimson, Mr 21, 1972.

Turner, James, and Perkins, W. Eric. "Towards a Critique of Social Science." Black Scholar 7(Ap, 1976):2-11.

Turner, Richard C., and Dewar, John A. "Black History in Selected American History Textbooks." Educational Leadership 30(F, 1973).

United Federation of Teachers. Lesson Plans on African-American History. New York: United Federation of Teachers, 1969.

U.S. Congress, 95th, 1st session, House of Representatives Document No. 258. Black Americans in Congress, 1880-1977. Washington, DC: GPO, 1978.

United States History: The Black Perspective. A Guide for Eighth Grade Social Studies. Albany, NY: New York State Education Dept., 1970, 233 pp. Available N.Y. State Education Dept., Publication Distribution Room 169, Washington Avenue, Albany, NY 12224. ERIC ED 062 216.

U.S. National Archives and Records Service. Black Studies: Select Catalogue of National Archives and Records Service Microfilm Publications. Washington, DC, 1973.

Ury, Claude M. "Commission on Negro History and Culture: Implications for Education." Phi Delta Kappan, Ja, 1969.

Valentine, Charles A. Black Studies and Anthropology: Scholarly and Political Interests in Afro-American Culture. Reading, MA: Addison-Wesley, 1972.

Van den Haag, Ernest. "The Black Studies Smoke Screen." New York University Education Quarterly 2(1971):6-11.

Vontress, Clemmont E. "Black Studies--Boon or Bane?" Journal of Negro Education 39 (Summer, 1970):192-201.

W., J. "Black Studies Funding Ended." Race Relations Reporter 2(Ap 5, 1971):8-9.

Walden, Daniel. "Teaching Negro History: One White Experience." School & Society, Ap, 1969.

Walker, Joe. "The Black Theatre: Throes of Struggle." Muhammad Speaks, Mr 21, 1969. [Interview with Barbara Ann Teer]

Walker, Margaret. "The Humanistic Tradition of Afro-American Literature." American Libraries 1(O, 1970):849-854.

Walker, S. Jay. "Black Studies: Phases Two." American Scholar 42(Autumn, 1973):604-615.

Walker, Sheila. "Black English." Black World 20(Je, 1971):4-16.

Walker, William O. "Putting Black Studies in Right Perspective." Cleveland Call & Post, Ja 19, 1974.

Walters, Ronald W. "Critical Issues on Black Studies." Pan African Journal 3(Summer, 1970):127-139.

_____. "Teaching Afro-American History: An Interpretive Essay." Afro-American Studies 1(Ap, 1971):315-322.

Walker, Saunders E. and others. Some Aspects of Black Culture. Carrolton, GA: West Georgia College, 1969.

Walton, Hanes, Jr. "African and Afro-American Courses in Negro Colleges." Quarterly Review of Higher Education Among Negroes, 0, 1968.

Walton, Sidney F., Jr. The Black Curriculum: Developing a Program in Afro-American Studies, 1968. Oakland, CA: Black Liberation Publishers, 740 Sixtieth St., Oakland, CA 94609.

_____. "Black Studies and Affirmative Action." Black Scholar 6(S, 1974):21-28.

_____. "Seven Proposals for Black-Directed Change." College Board Review, Spring, 1969.

Ward, Francis. "Black Studies: New Struggle for Survival." Los Angeles Times, Je 9, 1977.

_____. "Black Theater--Flight to the Inner City." Los Angeles Times, D 20, 1977.

Warr, Jacqueline. "Black History and Culture." National Catholic Education Association Bulletin, My, 1969.

Washburn, David E. "Ethnic Studies in the United States." Educational Leadership 32(Mr, 1975):409-412. [715 school districts enrolling 10,000 or more students]

Weinberg, Meyer. Afro-American History: Separate or Interracial? Chicago: Integrated Education Associates, 1968.

Weisbord, R. "Africa, Africans, and the Afro-American: Images and Identities in Transition." Race, Ja, 1969.

Wepman, Dennis and others. The Life: The Lore and Folk Poetry of the Black Hustler. Philadelphia: U. of Pennsylvania Press, 1976.

Wesley, Charles H. "The Need for Research in the Development of Black Studies Programs." Journal of Negro Education 39(Summer, 1970): 262-273.

Wheeler, William Bruce. "Teaching Negro History in the Public Schools: Let's Not Repeat Our Mistakes." Journal of Negro Education 39 (1970):91-95.

White, Doris Ann. "Effectiveness of Afro-American Studies on the Racial Attitudes of Young White Children." Doctoral dissertation, U. of Illinois, 1971. Univ. Microfilms Order No. 72-12,430.

White, George. "Survival of Black Studies Tops M[aryland]d Seminar." Washington Post, Jl 11, 1975.

Whitlow, Roger. "Alive and Well: A Nationwide Study of Black Literature Courses and Teachers in American Colleges and Universities." College English 36(F, 1975):632-639.

Wilkins, Roger. "Black Studies: What's Left Is No Small Achievement." New York Times, Mr 16, 1975.

Witten, Norman E., Jr., and Szwed, John F. (eds.). Afro-American Anthropology: Contemporary Perspectives on Theory and Research. New York: Free Press, 1969.

Wilcox, Preston. "Black Studies As An Academic Discipline." Negro Digest, Mr, 1970.

_____. "Education for Black Humanism: A Way of Approaching It." In What Black Educators Are Saying, pp. 3-17. Edited by Nathan Wright, Jr. New York: Hawthorn, 1970.

_____. "It's Not a Replica of the White Agenda." College Board Review, Spring, 1969.

Williams, Lorraine A., and Calbert, Madlyn (eds.). A Curriculum in Black History for Secondary Schools. Washington, DC: Department of History, Howard U., 1972.

Williams, Melvin G. Black Literature vs. Black Studies: Three Lynchings, Ap, 1974. ERIC ED 090 581.

Williams, Roger M. "The Emancipation of Black Scholars." Saturday Review, D 18, 1971.

Williams, Ronald. "Black Studies: The Work to Come." Negro Digest, Ja, 1970.

Williams, Vernon Johnson, Jr. "The Afro-American in American Sociological Literature, 1890-1945." Doctoral dissertation, Brown U., 1977. Univ. Microfilms Order No. 77-32635.

Willie, Charles V. "On Merton's 'Insiders and Outsiders.'" American Journal of Sociology 78(Mr, 1973):1269-1272. [On whether only blacks should study blacks]

Willingham, Alex. "Ideology and Politics: Their Status in Afro-American Social Theory." Endarch 1(Spring, 1975):4-25.

Wilson, Charles E. "The Case for Black Studies." Educational Leadership 27(1969): 218-221.

Wilson, Roselle L. "Case Studies of Institutionalization: Black/Ethnic Studies and Other Interdisciplinary Curricula." Doctoral dissertation, U. of Michigan, 1978. Univ. Microfilms Order No. 7823040.

Wilson, Walter. A Syllabus for the Study of Selective Writings by W. E. B. DuBois, My, 1970, 81 pp. Available from ERIC Informational Retrieval Center on the Disadvantaged, Box 40, Teachers College, Columbia U., New York, NY 10027. ERIC ED 041 974.

Wilson, William J. "Issues and Challenges of Black Studies." Journal of Social and Behavioral Sciences 18(Fall-Winter, 1971-1972): 14-20.

Winn, Ira J. "Sterile Textbook Adoption Struggle." Phi Delta Kappan, S, 1967. [Controversy around California's adoption of the textbook Land of the Free, by John Caughey, John Hope Franklin, and Ernest May]

Wisconsin Department of Public Instruction. Starting Out Right: Choosing Books About Black People for Young Children: Preschool through Third Grade, 1972. Division for Administration Services, Wisconsin Department of Public Instruction, Wisconsin Hall, 126 Langdon St., Madison, WI 53702.

Wolfram, Walter A., and Fasold, Ralph W. A Black English Translation of John 3:1-21; With Grammatical Annotations. Washington, DC: Center for Applied Linguistics, S, 1968, 16 pp. ERIC Ed 025 741.

Wolseley, Roland E. The Black Press, U.S.A. Ames, IA: Iowa State U. Press, 1971.

Woodson, Carter G. "Negro History In Its Proper Setting." New York Age, F 15, 1936, p. 6.

Woodward, C. Vann. "American History (White Man's Version) Needs an Infusion of Soul." New York Times Magazine, Ap 20, 1969.

Wright, James R. "Staffing Inner-City Libraries: Black or White, or Black and White?" Wilson Library Bulletin 45(Je, 1971): 987.

Wright, Stephen J. "Black Studies and Sound Scholarship." Phi Delta Kappan, Mr, 1970.

67X, Charles. "Charity: Black Studies 2." Muhammad Speaks, O 4, 1974.

_____. "Muhammad: Black Studies I." Muhammad Speaks, S 6, 1974.

X, Malcolm. "Malcolm X on Afro-American History." International Socialist Review, Mr-Ap, 1967.

X, Malcolm. Talks to Young People, 1966. Young Socialist, P.O. Box 471, Cooper Station, New York, NY 10003.

Yates, J. Frank. "Black Studies At This Juncture." Negro Digest, Mr, 1970.

Yee, Albert H., and Fruth, Marvin J. "Do Black Studies Make a Difference in Ghetto Children's Achievement and Attitudes?" Journal of Negro Education 42(Winter, 1973): 33-38.

Young, Beatrice, and Solomon, Benjamin. "Joy and Conscience in Teaching American History." Changing Education, Fall, 1966.

Young, Herman A., and Young, Barbara H. "Science and Black Studies." Journal of Negro Education 46(Fall, 1977):373-379.

_____ and _____. Scientists in the Black Perspective. Louisville, KY: Lincoln Foundation, 1974.

Young, Jacqueline Lee. "Criteria in Selection of Black Literature for Children." Freedomways 13(1973):107-116.

Zimmermann, Matilde J. Teacher's Guide for Afro-American History. Albany, NY: New York State Dept. of Social Services, F, 1969, 124 pp. ERIC ED 040 908.

Zitin, S. L. and others. Black Studies in Independent Schools. Philadelphia: National Association of Independent Schools, 1971, 63 pp. ERIC ED 062 241.

Zunino, Gerald J. "Afro-American History Curricula in High Schools." Integrated Education, Ja-F, 1972, pp. 22-30.

Bibliographies

Bigala, John C. B. An Annotated Bibliography for Teaching Afro-American Studies At Secondary and College Levels. New York: National Center for Research and Information on Equal Educational Opportunity, Teachers College, Columbia U., Ag, 1971.

Birkos, Alexander S., and Tambs, Lewis S. (comps.). African and Black American Studies. Littleton, CO: Libraries Unlimited, 1975.

Brasch, Ida Wales, and Brasch, Walter Milton (comps.). A Comprehensive Annotated Bibliography of American Black English. Baton Rouge, LA: Louisiana State U. Press, 1974.

Bruchac, Joseph. "Black Autobiography in Africa and America." Black Academy Review 2 (Spring-Summer, 1971).

Byrne, William G. "Audiovisual Aids for African Studies." In The African Experience. Vol. III B: Guide to Resources, pp. 81-130. Edited by John N. Paden and Edward W. Soja. Evanston, IL: Northwestern U. Press, 1970.

Carlson, Alvar W. (comp.). "A Bibliography of the Geographical Literature on the American Negro, 1920-1971." Virginia Geographer 7 (Spring-Summer, 1972):12-18.

Davis, Lenwood G. (comp.). A Working Bibliography on Published Materials on Black Studies Programs in the United States. Monticello, IL: Council of Planning Librarians, 1977.

Fraser, Lyn (comp.). A Bibliography of Publications Relative to Afro-American Studies. Greeley, CO: Museum of Anthropology, Colorado State College, 1969.

Grime, William E. (comp.). Botany of the
    Black Americans. St. Clair Shores, MI:
    Scholarly Press, 1975.

Irwin, Leonard B. (comp.). Black Studies: A
    Bibliography. Brooklawn, NJ: McKinley,
    1973.

Johnson, Harry Alleyn (ed., comp.). Multi-
    media Materials for Afro-American Studies.
    A Curriculum Orientation and Annotated
    Bibliography of Resources, Ap, 1971, 353 pp.
    Available from R. R. Bowker Company, 1180
    Avenue of the Americas, New York, NY 10036.
    ERIC ED 049 607.

Jordan, Casper L. (ed.). Consortium List of
    African-American Materials, Mr, 1974.
    ERIC ED 089 781. [Holdings in Atlanta U.,
    Fisk U., Hampton Institute, N.C. Central
    U., S.C. State College, and Tuskegee
    Institute]

Schatz, Walter (ed.). Directory of Afro-
    American Resources. Race Relations Informa-
    tion Center. New York: R. R. Bowker, 1970.

"Selected Resources for Black Studies in Music."
    Music Educators Journal 58(N, 1971):111-117.

Turner, Darwin T. (comp.). Afro-American
    Writers. New York: Appleton-Century-
    Crofts, 1970.

Westmoreland, Guy T. (comp.). An Annotated
    Guide to Basic Reference Books on the Black
    American Experience. Wilmington, DE:
    Scholarly Resources, Inc., 1974.

Williams, Ethel L., and Brown, Clifton L.
    (comps.). Afro-American Religious Studies:
    A Comprehensive Bibliography With Location
    in American Libraries. Metuchen, NJ:
    Scarecrow Press, 1972.

Young, Carlene. "Black Scholar and the Social
    Sciences." Black Scholar 7(Ap, 1976):18-28.

9.
SCHOOL STAFF

Teachers

Ackerman, Marc J. "Social Desirability in Economically Disadvantaged Preschool Children."
Proceedings of the 81st Annual Convention of
the American Psychological Association 8
(1973):685-686.

Adams, Gerald R. "Racial Membership and Physical Attractiveness Effects on Preschool
Teachers' Expectations." Child Study Journal
8(1978):29-41.

Adelman, Howard S. Teacher Education and the
Disadvantaged: Some Basic Issues and Some
Partial Answers, Ag, 1970. ERIC ED 043 594.

Adenika, T. Jean, and Berry, Gordon L. "Teachers' Attitudes Toward the Education of the
Black Child." Education 97(Winter, 1976):
102-114.

Agee, W. Hugh, and Smith, William L. "Modifying
Teachers' Attitudes Towards Speakers of Divergent Dialects Through Inservice Training."
Journal of Negro Education 43(Winter, 1974):
82-90.

Albro, Harley M. "The Perceptions of Teachers
and their Tracking Decisions." Master's
thesis, Cornell U., 1971.

Albro, Harley M., and Haller, Emil J. "Teachers'
Perception and their Tracking Decisions."
Administrator's Notebook 20(Mr, 1972):1-4.

Allen, B. J., Jr. "The Racial Attitudes of
White Pre-Service Teachers." Phi Delta Kappan
53(Ja, 1972):326-327.

Amperan, Robert L. "Teacher and Pupil: Ethnicity as an Independent Variate in Grading Patterns." Doctoral dissertation, U. of California, Berkeley, 1972.

Anderson, Barry, and Baker, Holden. "Status
Difference in Schools." Teachers College
Record 73(My, 1972):567-576.

Anderson, Donald Andrew. "A Study of the
Relationship between Attitudes and Effectiveness of Inner-City Elementary School Teachers." Doctoral dissertation, U. of Wisconsin, 1972.

Anthony, Ray. "The Non-Black Teacher, Black
Literature, and Black Students." English
Journal 59(N, 1970):1071-1073.

Antos, Joseph, and Rosen, Sherwin. "Discrimination in the Market for Public School
Teachers." Journal of Econometrics 3(My,
1975):123-150.

Appleford, B. and others. Teacher-Child Interactions as Related to Sex, Socio-economic
Status and Physical Attractiveness, Je 11,
1976. ERIC ED 138 869.

Archibald, Robert D., and Chemers, Martin M.
"The Relationship of Teachers' Cognitive
Style to Minority Student Satisfaction."
Journal of Afro-American Issues 2(F, 1974):
21-33.

Arisman, J. Michael. "The New Negro Casualties." Commonweal, D 24, 1965. [Negro
teachers who lost their jobs as a result of
desegregation]

Atchley, Robert C. "Can Programs For the Poor
Survive in Middle Class Institutions?" Phi
Delta Kappan 53(D, 1971):243-244. [Teacher
aides]

Ayers, George E. "Teacher Attitudes and Black
Children." Kappa Delta Pi Record 7(O, 1970):
22-24.

Ayres, Q. Whitfield. "Racial Hiring Quotas for
Teachers: Another Perspective." Clearing
House 49(N, 1975):105-107.

Baker, Gwendolyn C. "The Effects of Training in
Multi-Ethnic Education on Preservice Teachers
Perceptions of Ethnic Groups." Doctoral
dissertation, U. of Michigan, 1972.

Baker, Katherine D., and Snow, Richard E. Teacher Differences As Reflected in Student Aptitude-Achievement Relationships. Stanford, CA: School of Education, Stanford U., F, 1972.

Ball, H. W. "Racial Attitudes of White Educators in a Situational Context." Master's thesis, U. of Maryland, 1971.

Banks, George J. "Training as a Preferred Mode of Facilitating Relations between Races and Generations." Journal of Counseling Psychology 17(S, 1970):413-317.

Banks, William H., Jr. "What To Do Until the Court Order Comes." Phi Delta Kappan 58(Mr, 1977):557-561. [Jefferson County, KY]

Baratz, Joan, and Shuy, Roger W. (eds.). Teaching Black Children to Read, Urban Language Series, No. 4, 1969, 220 pp. Washington, DC: Center for Applied Linguistics. ERIC ED 025 761.

Barnes, Willie J. "How to Improve Teacher Behavior in Multiethnic Classrooms." Educational Leadership 34(Ap, 1977):511-515.

_____. "Student-Teacher Dyadic Interactions in Desegregated High School Classrooms." Doctoral dissertation, U. of Texas, 1973.

_____. "Student-Teacher Dyadic Interaction in Desegregated High School Classrooms." Western Journal of Black Studies 2(Summer, 1978):132-137.

Bash, James H. Effective Teaching in the Desegregated School. Bloomington, IN: Phi Delta Kappa, 1966. [Phi Delta Kappa, Eighth and Union, Bloomington, IN 47401]

Bash, James H., and Morris, Thomas J. Patterns and Practices of Faculty Desegregation. Bloomington, IN: Phi Delta Kappa, 1967.

Baxter, Katherine, Cosby, Jane R., and May, Frances M. "What We've Been Through is the Introduction." Integratededucation 12(N-D, 1974):28-31. [On racism among teachers]

Beale, Howard K. A History of Freedom of Teaching in American Schools. New York: Octagon, 1966. [Reprint]

Beaton, Sarah R. "The Function of 'Colorblindness.'" Perspectives in Psychiatric Care 12 (Ap-Je, 1974):80-85.

Becker, Howard S. "Social Class Variation in the Teacher-Pupil Relationship." Journal of Educational Sociology 24(1952):451-465.

Belasco, James A., Alutto, Joseph A., and Glassman, Alan. "A Case Study of Community and Teacher Expectations Concerning the Authority Structure of School Systems." Education and Urban Society 4(N, 1971):85-97.

Bennett, Carolyn E. "Students' Race, Social Class, and Academic History as Determinants of Teacher Expectation of Student Performance." Journal of Black Psychology 3(Ag, 1976):71-86.

Berberich, John P. "Do the Child's Responses Shape the Teaching Behavior of Adults?" Journal of Experimental Research in Personality 5(Je, 1971):92-97.

Berlowitz, Marvin. "Career Patterns of Teachers in An Urban Area." Urban Education 6 (Jl-O, 1971):261-266. [Buffalo, NY]

Besag, Frank. "Professional Characteristics and Attitudes of Teachers. Sex, Race, and Teaching Area Differences." Urban Education 5(O, 1970):268-286.

Beutel, L. L. "The Relationship of the Attitudes of Teachers in Racially Differentiated Urban Schools to Perceptions of Educational Issues and Socioeconomic Status Factors." Doctoral dissertation, U. of Wisconsin, 1973.

Bikson, Tora Kay. Minority Speech as Objectively Measured and Subjectively Evaluated, S, 1974. ERIC ED 131 135.

Birdin, Vinston E. "A Study of Selected Apprehensions of Teachers Toward Working in Schools Predominantly of the Other Race." Doctoral dissertation, Virginia Polytechnic Institute and State U., 1978. [Illinois] Univ. Microfilms Order No. 7903193.

Black Power and Its Effect on Racial Interaction: Resource Manual. An In-Service Training Program Which Focuses on Assisting Educators of School District 65 to Develop Some Common Understandings About Crucial Integration Issues: School Year 1968-1969, 1969. ERIC ED 036 568.

The Black Self-Concept: Resources Manual. An Inservice Training Program Which Focuses on Assisting Educators of School District 65 to Develop Some Common Understandings About Crucial Integration Issues: School Year 1968-1969, 1969. ERIC ED 036 572.

Blodgett, Elizabeth G., and Cooper, Eugene B. "Attitudes of Elementary Teachers Toward Black Dialect." Journal of Communication Disorders 6(Je, 1973):121-133.

Blume, R. A. "Self-Esteem of Pupils in Relation to Teacher Attitudes." Doctoral dissertation, U. of Michigan, 1964.

Bodard, Catherine Shulamite. "A Study of Black Teachers in a Ghetto School System: A Contribution to the Study of Subcultures." Doctoral dissertation, Columbia U., 1970. Univ. Microfilms Order No. 73-16186.

Boggs, Stephen T. "The Meaning of Questions
and Narratives to Hawaiian Children." In
Functions of Language in the Classroom. Edited by Courtney B. Cazden, Vera P. John,
and Dell Hymes. New York: Teachers College
Press, 1972.

Bolton, James Albert. "Verbal Behavior of
White Teachers in Black, White, and Integrated
Classrooms." Doctoral dissertation, Claremont
Graduate School, 1972. Univ. Microfilms
Order No. 72-30569.

Bond, Horace Mann. "Teaching: A Calling to
Fulfill." The Herald of the Georgia Teachers
and Educational Association, Mr, 1963.

Bosma, Boyd. "Discrimination on the Basis of
Race." In "Civil and Constitutional Rights
of Public School Teachers as Citizens." Doctoral dissertation, Wayne State U., 1971.

_____. "Racial Discrimination Against Teach-
ers." Integrated Education, Ja-F, 1972.

_____. "The Role of Teachers in School Deseg-
regation." Integrateducation 15(N-D, 1977):
106-111.

Boucher, Linda J. "A Study of the Meaning Held
Towards Negro Students of Low Socio-economic
Status by White Teachers in an Elementary
School." Master's thesis, Teachers College,
Columbia U., 1971.

Bower, Eli M. Teachers Talk About their Feelings. Washington, DC: GPO, 1973.

Boyd, C. "Secondary Teacher Attitudes Toward
School Integration in Three Selected West
Tennessee Counties." Doctoral dissertation,
U. of Tennessee, 1972.

Boyd, Miller E., Jr. "Wanted: Negro Male
Teachers to Fight Ignorance and Hate."
School and Community, F, 1969.

Boyer, Roscoe A., and Beard, Gabrielle B.
Inter-Institutional Cooperative Program for
College and Public School Teachers of Disad-
vantaged Youth. Final Report, Ag, 1970.
ERIC ED 045 604.

Braun, Carl. "Pygmalion in the Reading Circle."
Academic Therapy 12(Summer, 1977):445-454.

Braun, Miranda. "Toward Teacher Training for
'Desegregated' Schools: Organization, Content, and Sociocultural Context." Education
and Urban Society 9(My, 1977):353-368.

Braun, Robert J. Teachers and Power. The Story
of the American Federation of Teachers. New
York: Simon & Schuster, 1972.

Braxton, Mary Victoria, and Bullock, Charles S.
III. "Teacher Partiality in Desegregation."
Integrated Education (Jl-Ag, 1972):42-46.

Buxton, Thomas H., Prichard, Keith W.,
Bingham, Charles M., Jackson, Charles E.,
and Talps, Loutricia. "Black and White
Teachers and Desegregation." Integrated
Education 12(Ja-Ap, 1974):19-22.

Breitrose, Henry S., and Voelker, Janet K.
Production of a Motion Picture for the In-
service Training of Teachers in Problems of
Human Relations in Teaching the Socioeconomically Disadvantaged and Evaluation of
the Motion Picture. Final Report, Ap, 1967,
22 pp. Stanford, CA: Stanford U. ERIC ED
013 277.

Bridge, Jacque T. and others. "Faculty Stability and Effective Schools." NASSP Bulletin
62(Ap, 1978):36-41.

Brindley, Thomas A. "Anglo Teachers of Mexican
American Students." Journal of Thought 9
(N, 1974):263-268.

Brophy, Jere E. Teacher Behaviors Related to
Learning by Low vs. High Socio-economic
Status Early Elementary Students, 1975.
ERIC ED 146 143.

Brophy, Jere E., and Good, T. L. "Teachers'
Communication of Differentiated Expectations
for Children's Classroom Performance."
Journal of Educational Psychology 61(1970):
365-374.

Brophy, Jere E. and others. The Student Attri-
bute Study. A Preliminary Report, Mr, 1976.
ERIC ED 121 799.

Brown, James C., Starnes, Thomas A., and Watson,
J. Allen. "Southern Negro and White Educators: A Comparison of Pertinent Characteristics." Journal of Negro Education 40
(Spring, 1971):159-162.

Brown, John (ed.). Understanding, Prerequisite
for Teaching the Disadvantaged Child. Bloomington, IN: School of Education, Indiana U.,
1970.

Brown, W. E. and others. "Praise, Criticism
and Race." Elementary School Journal 70½
(1970):373-377.

Bruno, James E. "Minority Group Involvement
in Urban Teaching." Education and Urban
Society 3(N, 1970):41-70.

Bunte, Frederick Joseph. "An Inquiry into the
Decline in the Number of Blacks Entering the
Teaching Profession." Doctoral dissertation,
Ohio State U., 1972. Univ. Microfilms Order
No. 73-01956.

Bureau of Curriculum Development. Teaching
About Minorities in Classroom Situations.
Resource Bulletin for Teachers in the Secon-
dary Schools. New York: Board of Education,
Ag, 1968.

Burger, Henry G. "Ethno-Pedagogy": A Manual in Cultural Sensitivity, with Techniques for Improving Cross-Cultural Teaching by Fitting Ethnic Patterns. Second Ediction. Albuquerque: Southwestern Cooperative Educational Lab, Ag, 1968.

Burke, Barbara P. "An Exploratory Study of the Relationships Among Third Grade Negro Children's Self-Concept, Creativity, and Intelligence and Teachers' Perceptions of Those Relationships." Diss. Abstr. Int'l. 1969, 30(4-A):1327-1328.

Burkhart, Robert C. The Assessment Revolution. New Viewpoints for Teacher Evaluation. Albany, NY: State Division of Teacher Education and Certification, n.d.

Burns, Crawford E. "White Staff, Black Children: Is There a Problem?" Child Welfare 50(F, 1971):90-96.

Burstall, C. Expectation and Pupil Performance. London: National Foundation for Educational Research, n.d.

Busby, Delia. "'And What Do You Do When They Call You Nigger?'" Integrateducation 15(Ja-F, 1977).

Bush, Endilee P. Alienation and Self Ideal Discrepancy: Desegregation Effects on High School Teachers, Ap, 1974. ERIC ED 096 368.

Byalick, Robert, and Bersoff, Donald N. "Reinforcement Practices of Black and White Teachers in Integrated Classrooms." Journal of Educational Psychology 66(1974):473-480.

Bybee, Rodger W. "The Teacher I Like Best: Perceptions of Advantaged, Average and Disadvantaged Students." School Science and Mathematics 73(My, 1973):384-390.

Bybee, Rodger W., and Chaloupka, Donald W. "Students' Perceptions of the Teacher They Like Best: A Comparison Including Advantaged, Average, and Disadvantaged Students." Colorado Journal of Educational Research 10(Summer, 1971):31-35.

Cade, Timina Quick. "Black Parents' Beliefs About Appropriate Child Behaviors Relating to White Teachers." Doctoral dissertation, U. of Pittsburgh, 1977. Univ. Microfilms Order No. 78-1790.

Caliguri, Joseph P. "Teacher Bias in the Selection of Social Studies Textbooks." Journal of Negro Education 40(Fall, 1971):322-329. [Kansas City, MO metropolitan area]

Calnek, Maynard. "Racial Factors in the Countertransference: The Black Therapist and the Black Client." American Journal of Orthopsychiatry, Ja, 1970.

Cambridge Survey Research. An Analysis of Teachers' Attitudes Toward the Public Schools in the City of Boston. Boston: Citywide Coordinating Council, Ap, 1977.

Campbell, Leonard, Jr. "The Attitudes of Black Teachers Toward Black Teachers and White Teachers, and the Converse: Racial Prejudice or General Belief?" Doctoral dissertation, Florida State U., 1971. Univ. Microfilms Order No. 72-16573.

Campbell, Robert F., and Richardson, Frank. "How Are Negro Teachers Faring?" Southern Education Report, D, 1968.

Cantwell, Zita M. "Teachers' Perceptions of Levels of Performances of Students from an Economically Disadvantaged Urban Area." Perceptual and Motor Skills 32(Ap, 1971): 593-594.

Carlile, Lauren Melody. "Teacher Expectations of Language Delay in Black and White Head Start Children." Doctoral dissertation, U. of Oklahoma Health Sciences Center, 1974. Univ. Microfilms Order No. 75-21183.

Carson, Frankie M. Proposal for a Program of Staff Development Designed to Implement Positive Multi-Cultural Program Offerings in an Integrated School System with Emphasis on a New Social Studies Concept. Final Report, Ag, 1969. ERIC ED 045 738.

Carter, Barbara. "Integrating the Negro Teacher Out of a Job." Reporter, Ag 12, 1965.

Carter, Mel, Woods, Sandy, and others. Recruiting Minority Teachers, Counselors and Administrative Personnel. St. Paul, MN: State Department of Education, n.d.

Carter, Ruth Barrera. "A Study of Attitudes: Mexican American and Anglo American Elementary Teachers' Judgments of Mexican American Bilingual Children's Speech." Doctoral dissertation, U. of Houston, 1976. Univ. Microfilms Order No. 77-1502.

Castiglione, Lawrence V. Potential Mobility Among Career Teachers in New York City's Middle Schools: The Relationship Between Selected Occupational Characteristics, Expectations, and Attitudes, Je, 1968. ERIC ED 087 732.

Charley, Beverly H. "The Effectiveness of Negro Teachers for Changing Developing Racial Attitudes in Young Children." Diss. Abstr. Int'l., Ag, 1970, 31(2-A):824.

Cheek, Bessie L. "A Study of Selected Attitudes of Elementary Teachers Involved in the Court-Ordered Transfer of Teachers in the Atlanta Public Schools." Doctoral dissertation, Georgia State U., 1970. Univ. Microfilms Order No. 71-12, 079.

Chesler, Mark A. "Teacher Training Designs for Improving Instruction in Interracial Classrooms." *Journal of Applied Behavioral Science* 7(S, 1971):612-641.

Chesler, Mark and others. *Preparing for School Desegregation: A Training Program for Intergroup Educators*, Volume I. Riverside, CA: Western Regional School Desegregation Projects, U. of California, Je, 1972.

Claiborn, W. L. "[Teacher] Expectancy Effects in the Classroom: A Failure to Replicate." *Journal of Educational Psychology* 60(1969): 377-383.

Clark, F. *The Control of State-Supported Teacher-Training Programs for Negroes.* New York: Columbia U., 1934.

Clark, Kenneth B. "Improving the Quality of Education." In *Teaching in America*; proceedings of the 5th Annual Conference, National Committee of Support of the Public Schools, pp. 2-4, Ap 24, 1967. Washington, DC.

Clark, Philip. "Compensatory Education: The Underlying Stances and Teachers' Attitudes." *Urban Education* 9(Ja, 1975):340-354.

Clark, Septima P. with Blythe, Legette. *Echo in My Soul.* New York: Dutton, 1962.

Claye, Clifton M. "Problems of Cross-Over Teachers." *Integrated Education* 8(S-O, 1970):3-16.

_____. *Problems of Cross-Over Teachers: An Opportunity for Creative Principals. A Research Report*, Ap 19, 1971. ERIC ED 056 327.

Clifford, Miriam. *Relative Potency of Teacher Attitudes Toward Black and Retarded Children*, Ap, 1973. ERIC ED 088 986.

Cochran, Robert Bennett. "The Effect of White Teacher-Black Student Interaction on Changing Social Distance Attitude of White Teachers." Doctoral dissertation, Mississippi State U., 1972. Univ. Microfilms Order No. 72-20268.

Cogen, Charles. "A Teacher Bonus Cannot Help." *Integrated Education*, Je, 1963.

Coles, Robert. "How Do the Teachers Feel?" *Saturday Review*, My 16, 1964. [Southern teachers after desegregation]

_____. *Teachers and the Children of Poverty.* Washington, DC: The Potomac Institute, Inc., 1970.

Colquit, Jesse Lee. "The Teacher's Dilemma in Facilitating the Black Experience." *Journal of Negro Education* 47(Spring, 1978): 192-200.

Commission on Professional Rights and Responsibilities. *Guidelines for Retention of Staff for School Districts Moving from Dual to Unified System.* Washington, DC: National Education Association, 1966.

Conoley, Colleen W., and Conoley, Jill L. "Blow the Teacher's Mind with an Ethnic Test in Kind." *Integrateducation* 15(Jl-Ag, 1977).

Cooper, Bobby G. "The Effects of Desegregation on Black Elementary and Secondary School Teachers in Mississippi, 1970-1973." Doctoral dissertation, U. of Colorado, 1977.

Cooper, Elizabeth K. *Attitudes of Children and Teachers Toward Mexican, Negro, and Jewish Minorities.* San Francisco: R & E Research Associates, 1972. [Master's thesis, U. of California, 1945]

Cooper, Harris M. and others. "The Importance of Race and Social Class Information in the Formation of Expectancies About Academic Performance." *Journal of Educational Psychology* 67(Ap, 1975):312-319.

Cooper, Joel. *Self-Fulfilling Prophecy in the Classroom: An Attempt to Discover the Processes by Which Expectations are Communicated. Final Report*, O 27, 1971. ERIC ED 063 453.

Cormier, William H. *Effects of Approving Teacher Behaviors of Disadvantaged Adolescents.* Knoxville, TN: Department of Educational Psychology and Guidance, U. of Tennessee, 1970.

Cornbleth, Catherine, and Korth, Willard. *Teachers' Perceptions of and Interactions with Students in Multicultural Classrooms*, Ap 7, 1977. ERIC ED 137 227.

Corwin, Ronald G. *Reform and Organizational Survival: The Teacher Corps as an Instrument of Educational Change.* New York: Wiley, 1973.

Corwin, Ronald G., and Schmidt, Sister Marilyn. "Teachers in Inner City Schools: A Survey of a Large City School System." *Theory into Practice* 8(O, 1969):209-221.

Cotton, Ella E. *A Spark for My People. The Sociological Autobiography of a Negro Teacher.* New York: Exposition, 1954.

Covington, Ann Juanita. "A Study of Teachers' Attitudes Toward Black English: Effects on Student Achievement." Doctoral dissertation, U. of Pittsburgh, 1972. Univ. Microfilms Order No. 73-04996.

Cowan, William J. "An Investigation of Teacher Perceptions of School Organizational Climate Before and After the Court-Ordered Transfer of Teachers in the Atlanta Public Schools." Doctoral dissertation, Georgia State U., 1971. Univ. Microfilms Order No. 72-2986.

Cox, George W. "Faculty Desegregation Methods at a Select Group of Schools in the Memphis City Schools." Doctoral dissertation, U. of Tennessee, 1972.

Craig, Myrtle, and Henry, James O. "Teachers' Fears and Problems in Newly Integrated Schools." Phi Delta Kappan 52(My, 1971): 546-547.

Crano, William D., and Mellon, Phyllis M. "Causal Influence of Teachers' Expectations on Children's Academic Performances: A Cross-Logged Panel Analysis." Journal of Educational Psychology 70(F, 1978):39-49. [4,000 British school children]

Crist, Janet. Group Dynamics and the Teacher-Student Relationship: A Review of Recent Innovations. Stanford, CA: School of Education, Stanford U., Ja, 1972.

Crockett, Walter Lee. "A Profile of Black Teachers in the Public School System in the State of Mississippi with Implications for Program Modification." Doctoral dissertation, Ohio State U., 1975. Univ. Microfilms Order No. 75-26563.

Crowl, Thomas K. "White Teachers' Evaluation of Oral Responses Given by White and Negro Ninth Grade Males." Diss. Abstr. Int'l., 31, 9-A(Mr, 1971):4540.

Crowl, Thomas K., and MacGinitie, Walter H. "White Teachers' Evaluations of Oral Responses Given by White and Negro Ninth Grade Males." Proceedings of the Annual Convention of the American Psychological Association 5, part 2 (1970):635-636.

Cuban, Larry. "The Death of Intellect; Or, How to Change Teachers Into Cretins Without Really Trying." In Opening Opportunities for Disadvantaged Learners, pp. 164-178. Edited by A. Harry Passow. New York: Teachers College Press, 1972.

_____. "Ethnic Content and 'White' Instruction." Phi Delta Kappan 53(Ja, 1972):270-273.

_____. "Teaching the Children: Does the System Help or Hinder?" In Freedom, Bureaucracy and Schooling, pp. 147-160. Edited by Vernon F. Haubrich. Washington, DC: Association for Supervision and Curriculum Development, 1971.

_____. To Make a Difference. Teaching in the Inner City. New York: Free Press, 1970.

Culbertson, Marie. May I Speak? Diary of a Crossover Teacher. Edited by Sue Eakin. Gretna, LA: Pelican Publishing Company, 1972.

Curry, Bishop B., and Totten, Herman L. "Articulation of Pupil and Faculty in Integrated Schools." Education 92(F Mr, 1972): 114-119.

Cytrynbaum, Solomon. "Race of Teacher, Task and Affective Interaction in Southern Black College Classes." Doctoral dissertation, U. of Michigan, 1972.

Dahlem, Glenn G. The Effect of Like Ethnic Qualities Upon Reading Tutoring of Third Graders, Mr, 1973. ERIC ED 095 488.

Daniel, Jack L. "Facilitation of White-Black Communication." Journal of Communication 20(1970):134-141.

Daniels, Lorraine Morrison. "Changes in Opinions of Professional Staff in Schools Experiencing Rapid Integration." Doctoral dissertation, 1974. Univ. Microfilms Order No. 75-16, 370. [Jacksonville, FL]

Datta, Lois-Ellen, Schaefer, Earl, and Davis, Malcolm. "Sex and Scholastic Aptitude as Variables in Teachers' Ratings of the Adjustment and Classroom Behavior of Negro and Other Seventh-Grade Students." Journal of Educational Psychology, Ap, 1968.

Davies, B. "Aboriginal Pygmalion in Australia: An Open and Closed Case." Multiculturalism 2(1978):15-17.

Davis, Gene and others. "Nonverbal Behavior of First Grade Teachers in Different Socioeconomic Level Elementary Schools." Journal of the Student Personnel Association for Teacher Education 12(D, 1973):76-80.

Davis, Junius A. Faculty Perceptions of Students: Structure of Faculty Characterizations, Part III, Ap, 1964. ERIC ED 050 128.

_____. Faculty Perceptions of Students: Desirability and Perception of Academic Performance, Part IV, Mr, 1964. ERIC ED 050 129.

_____. Faculty Perceptions of Students: A Second-Order Structure for Faculty Characteristics, Part V, My, 1965. ERIC ED 050 130.

_____. Faculty Perceptions of Students: Characteristics of Students for Whom There is Faculty Agreement on Desirability, Part VI, Je, 1966. ERIC ED 050 131.

Davis, Vivian. "A Nigger Mess." Negro American Literature Forum 5(F, 1971):94-97. [Black educator in the black school]

Dawson, Earl Edgar. "The Negro Teacher in the South." Master's thesis, U. of Iowa, 1931.

Dawson, Paul. Fatherless Boys, Teacher Perceptions, and Male Teacher Influence. Monmouth, OR: State System of High Education, 1971.

DeMeis, Debra K., and Turner, Ralph R. "Effects of Students' Race, Physical Attractiveness, and Dialect on Teachers' Evaluations." Contemporary Educational Psychology 3(Ja, 1978):77-86.

Deslonde, James L., and Flach, Elizabeth G. The Cadre Approach to Teacher Training: Developing Change Agents for Desegregated Schools, Ap, 1972. ERIC ED 063 444.

Dewing, Rolland. "The American Federation of Teachers and Desegregation." Journal of Negro Education 42(Winter, 1973):79-92.

Dietz, S. M., and Purkey, W. W. "Teacher Expectation of Performance Based on Race of Students." Psychological Reports 24(1969): 694.

Dillard, J. L. "The English Teacher and the Language of the Newly Integrated Student." Record, N, 1967.

Dillingham, McKinley, and Johnson, T. Bradford. "The Effect of Teacher Attitudes and Self-Concept of Students on Academic Success." Education for the Disadvantaged Child 1 (Fall, 1973):15-20.

Do Teachers Make a Difference? A Report on Recent Research on Pupil Achievement. Washington, DC: GPO, 1970.

Doddy, Hurley H., and Edwards, G. Franklin. "Apprehension of Negro Teachers Concerning Desegregation in South Carolina." Journal of Negro Education 24(Winter, 1955):26-43.

Dole, Arthur A. and others. Race as a Component of Social Distance among Black and White Secondary School Students and Their Teachers. Barriers and Aspirations--Generalizations from Research. Black and White Attitudes About Guidance: Observations from the Field, 1971. ERIC ED 054 473.

Domingo-Llacuna, Evelyn A. "The Effect of Pupil Race, Social Class, Speech and Ability on Teacher Stereotypes and Attributions." Doctoral dissertation, U. of Illinois, 1976. Univ. Microfilms Order No. 76-24,072.

Downey, Gregg W. "What School Boards Do When that Irresistible Force Called RIF [Reduction in Force] Meets that Immovable Object Called Affirmative Action." American School Board Journal 163(O, 1976):35-39.

Downing, Gertrude L. "A Student-Teacher Laboratory Prepares a School for De Facto Desegregation." Clearing House 45(S, 1970):37-40.

Drake, Diana Mack. "Anglo American Teachers, Mexican American Students, and Dissonance in Our Schools." Elementary School Journal 73 (Ja, 1973):207-212.

Dual, Peter Alfred. "The Black Educators in Michigan Public Schools: Analysis of Selected Demographic Characteristics." Doctoral dissertation, Michigan State U., 1973. Univ. Microfilms Order No. 74-06031.

_____. Black and NonBlack Educators in Michigan Public Schools. Lansing, MI: Michigan Education Association, 1973.

Dusek, Jerome B. "Do Teachers Bias Children's Learning?" Review of Educational Research 45(Fall, 1975):661-684.

Eaton, William E. The American Federation of Teachers, 1916-1961: A History of the Movement. Carbondale, IL: Southern Illinois U. Press, 1975.

Eaves, Ronald C. "Teacher Race, Student Race, and the Behavior Problem Checklist." Journal of Abnormal Child Psychology 3(1965): 1-9.

Eddy, Elizabeth M. "Educational Innovation and Desegregation: A Case Study of Symbolic Realignment." Human Organization 34(1975): 163-172.

Edwards, Babette. "The Black Professional-- Judas in the Living Room?" Foresight, D, 1969.

Edwards, S. R. "Teacher Expectation and Influence." Delta 7(Ag, 1970):18-22. [Maori and Mexican Americans]

Edwards, T. Bentley. "Teacher Attitudes and Cultural Differentiation." Journal of Experimental Education, Winter, 1966.

Elashoff, Janet Dixon, and Snow, Richard E. A Case Study in Statistical Inference: Reconsideration of the Rosenthal-Jacobson Data on Teacher Expectancy. Stanford, CA: Stanford Center for Research and Development in Teaching, Stanford U., D, 1970.

Elliott, D. H. "Social Origins and Values of Teachers and their Attitudes from Poverty Backgrounds." Doctoral dissertation, U. of Pittsburgh, 1968.

"The Elusive Black Educator." School Management, Mr, 1969. [A 33-page treatment]

Eurich, R. S. "Correlation of Political Conservatism--Liberalism of Detroit School Teachers with Their Attitudes on School Decentralization." Master's thesis, Wayne State U., 1970.

Epps, Edgar G. "Educational Policy-Making: Implications for Urban Schools." Journal of Negro Education 44(Summer, 1975):308-315.

Epstein, Erwin H., and Pizzilo, Joseph H. (eds.). A Human Relations Guide for Teachers: Linguistic Minorities in the Classroom. Madison, WI: Wisconsin Department of Public Instruction, 1972.

Eubanks, Eugene E. "A Study of Perceptions of Black and White Teachers in De Facto Segregated High Schools." Education 95(F, 1974): 51-56.

_____. "A Study of Teachers' Perceptions of Essential Teacher Attributes in De Facto Segregated High Schools." Education 93(Ap-My, 1973):373-380.

_____. "Teachers' Job Satisfaction and Dissatisfaction in De Facto Segregated High Schools." Doctoral dissertation, Michigan State U., 1972.

Eubanks, Thelma M. "The Negro Teacher." Negro History Bulletin, F, 1964.

Faunce, R. W. "An Investigation of the Biographical and Attitudinal Characteristics of Effective Elementary School Teachers of Culturally Disadvantaged Children." Doctoral dissertation, U. of Minnesota, 1968.

Faunce, R. W. Attitudes and Characteristics of Effective and Not Effective Teachers of Culturally Disadvantaged Children. Minneapolis: Research and Evaluation Department, Minnesota Public Schools, 1970.

_____. A Brief Review of Studies on Teacher Attitudes Toward Culturally Disadvantaged Children. Minneapolis: Research and Evaluation Department, Minnesota Public Schools, 1969.

_____. Participant Reactions to Project 822 Human Relations Training. Minneapolis: Research and Evaluation Department, Minneapolis Public Schools, Summer, 1970 and 1971. [In-service training]

Feldman, Robert S. Race of Student and Nonverbal Behavior of Teacher, Ap, 1976. ERIC ED 123 919.

Ferguson, Herman B. "The Upgrading of Black Teachers." Negro Teachers Forum, N, 1966.

Ferguson, Patrick. The Effect of Federal Desegregation Orders on Social Studies Instruction in the South, N 24, 1970. ERIC ED 046 817.

Finlayson, Douglas S. "The School Perceptions of Teachers of Differential Status." Research in Education 9(My, 1973):83-92. [England]

Finn, Jeremy D. "Expectations and the Educational Environment." Review of Educational Research 42(Summer, 1972):387-410.

Fish, E. "The Relationship of Teachers' Assigned Marks to Tested Achievement Among Elementary Grade, Racially Divergent, Lower Socio-Economic Status Boys and Girls." Doctoral dissertation, U. of Minnesota, 1969.

Flanders, Ned A., and Nuthall, Graham A. (eds.). "The Classroom Behavior of Teachers." International Review of Education 18(1972): entire issue.

Flomers, Brenda Mae Gupton. "The Effects of Teacher Behavior on Black Students' Mastery of Standard English." Doctoral dissertation, Temple U., 1974. Univ. Microfilms Order No. 74-19750.

Flythe, Claud. "A Study of the Professional Preparation of Black, Male Head Coaches of the Virginia High School League." Doctoral dissertation, Middle Tennessee State U., 1976. Univ. Microfilms Order No. 76-29064.

Franklin, Jacquelyn C., and Nicholson, Everett W. "Relationship Between Teacher Viewpoints Towards a Culturally Oriented Music Program and Black Pupils' Achievement and Viewpoints Toward the Program." Education 98(Mr-Ap, 1978):307-310. [Teachers]

Freiberg, H. Jerome. The Effects of Ability Grouping on Interaction in the Classroom, 1970. ERIC ED 053 194.

Marshall, Theodore 4X. "Black Children Need Black Teachers." Muhammad Speaks, Ag 1, 1969.

14X, Larry. "Black Teachers, 'No Unity.'" Muhammad Speaks, Jl 19, 1974. [Black Caucus in the National EducationaAssociation]

Foster, Herbert L. "Ribbin', Jivin', and Playin' the Dozens." Phi Delta Kappan 56 (N, 1974):171-175. [Interview by Robert W. Cole, Jr.]

Freeman, R. B. "Political Power, Desegregation, and Employment of Black Schoolteachers." Journal of Political Economy 85(Ap, 1977).

Freijo, Tom D., and Jaeger, Richard M. "Social Class and Race as Concomitants of Composite Halo in Teachers' Evaluating of Pupils." American Educational Research Journal 13(Winter, 1976):1-14.

Fridie, Samuel. "Black Teachers Inside Predominantly White Schools: An Identification of Their Problems." High School Journal 58 (My, 1975):323-325.

Friedman, Philip. "Comparisons of Teacher Reinforcement Schedules for Students with Different Social Class Backgrounds." Journal of Educational Psychology 68(Je, 1976):286-292.

Frissell, Hollis Burke. "Training of Negro Teachers." National Education Association, 1900:482-490.

Froning, Mary L. Employment Opportunity in the Schools: Job Patterns of Minorities and Women in Public Elementary and Secondary Schools 1974. Washington, DC: Equal Employment Opportunity Commission, 1976.

Fuchs, Estelle. _Teacher's Talk: Views from Inside City Schools_. New York: Anchor, 1969.

Furno, Orlando F., and Kidd, J. S. _New Teachers for the Inner City_. Washington, DC: Capitol Publications, 1974. [Baltimore]

Gangware, Wenana B. "Minority Concerns Concern Us All." _Music Educators Journal_ 62(S, 1975):48-50. [Minorities in the Music Educators National Conference]

Gansneder, Bruce M. "Relationships Among Teachers' Attitudes, Students' Attitudes, and Students' Achievement." _Diss. Abstr. Int'l_, 31, 9-A(Mr, 1971):4381.

Garner, John, and Bing, Marion. "The Elusiveness of Pygmalion and Differences in Teacher-Pupil Contacts." _Interchange_ 4(1973):34-42.

Garrett, George. "Diary of a Teacher in the Barrio." Master's thesis, California State U., Los Angeles, 1971.

Garwood, S. Gray, and McDavid, John W. _Ethnic Factors in Stereotypes of Given Names_, Ag, 1974. ERIC ED 097 994.

Gaumnitz, Walter H. II. "Negro Teachers and Principals." In _Status of Teachers and Principals Employed in the Rural Schools of the United States_, pp. 32-41, 47-49. Washington, DC: GPO, 1932. [U.S. Department of the Interior, Office of Education, Bulletin No. 3, 1932]

Gay, Geneva. _Differential Dyadic Interactions of Black and White Teachers with Black and White Pupils in Recently Desegregated Social Studies Classrooms: A Function of Teacher and Pupil Ethnicity_, Ja, 1974. ERIC ED 091 489.

_____. "Teachers' Achievement Expectations of and Classroom Interactions with Ethnically Different Students." _Contemporary Education_ 46(Spring, 1975):166-171.

Geer, Blanche. "A Statistical Study of the Class Origin and Social Participation of Teachers." Doctoral dissertation, Johns Hopkins U., 1956.

Gerbner, George. "Teacher Image and the Hidden Curriculum." _American Scholar_ 42(Winter, 1972-1973):66-92.

Gitlitz, Alfred Henry. "Political, Ideology, Dogmatism, and the Attitudes of History Teachers Toward Afro-American History." Doctoral dissertation, Columbia U., 1973. Univ. Microfilms Order No. 73-28209.

Glasman, Naftaly S. "Teachers' Low Expectation Levels of their Culturally Different Students: A View from Administration." _Journal of Secondary Education_ 45(F, 1970):82-94.

Glick, Irvin David. "Does Teacher's Skin Color Matter?" _Integrated Education_ (S-O, 1971): 26-30.

Glock, Marvin D. "Is There a Pygmalion in the Classroom?" _Reading Teacher_ 25(F, 1972): 405-408.

Godshall, Tricie A. "Teacher-Related Anxiety in Culturally Different Children." Doctoral dissertation, U. of Miami, 1968.

Goldin, Paul C. "A Model for Racial Awareness Training of Teachers in Integrated Schools." _Integrated Education_ 8(Ja-F, 1971):62-64.

Gollub, Wendy L., and Sloan, Earline. "Teacher Expectations and Race and Socioeconomic Status." _Urban Education_ 13(Ap, 1978):95-106.

Gordon, John E., Jr. "The Effects on White Student Teachers of Value Clarification. Interviews with Negro Pupils." Doctoral dissertation, New York U., 1965. Univ. Microfilms Order No. 66-5778.

Gothard, Donita. "The Education Process Attitudes of White and Black Crossover and Non-crossover Teachers." Doctoral dissertation, U. of Alabama, 1970. Univ. Microfilms Order No. 71-09093.

Grady, Mary L. "An Assessment of Teachers' Attitudes Toward Disadvantaged Children." _Journal of Negro Education_ 40(Spring, 1971): 146-152. [Cajon Valley Union School District, CA]

Greenberg, David, and McCall, John. _Teacher Mobility and Allocation_, Ap, 1974. ERIC ED 102 160. [San Diego, CA]

Greene, Maxine. "The Teacher and the Negro Child: 'Invisibility' in the School." _Educational Forum_, Mr, 1965.

Gregg, Richard and others. "A Description of the Interaction Between Black Youth and White Teachers in a Ghetto Speech Class." _Speech Teacher_ 19(1970):1-8.

Grieger, Russell M. "Pygmalion Revisited: A Loud Call for Caution." _Interchange_ 2(1971): 78-91.

Griggs, Anthony. "Displacement Still Faces Teachers." _Race Relations Reporter_ 4(Ag 6, 1973):5-6.

Grimke, Francis. "Colored Men as Professors in Colored Institutions." _A.M.E. Church Review_ 2(O, 1885):142-144.

Groff, Patrick. "Low Expectation [by teachers] for Negroes?" _Phi Delta Kappan_, O, 1966. [letter]

Grossman, Len. "Color the Problem Black--But Not Entirely." _Journal of Teacher Education_ 22(Winter, 1971):489-493.

Guskin, Alan E. High Schools In Crisis. Ann Arbor, MI: Community Resources, 1971.

Guskin, Judith T. "The Social Perception of Language Variation: Black and White Teachers' Attitudes Towards Speakers from Different Racial and Social Class Backgrounds." Diss. Abstr. Int'l., 31, 8-A(F, 1971):3954.

Gustman, Alan L., and Clement, M. O. "Teachers' Salary Differentials and Equality of Educational Opportunity." Industrial and Labor Relations Review 31(O, 1977):61-70.

Guthrie, John T. "Relationships of Teaching Method, Socioeconomic Status, and Intelligence in Concept Formation." Journal of Educational Psychology 62(Ag, 1971):345-351.

Gynthia, Malcolm D., and Witt, Philip H. "Windstorms and Important Persons: Personality Characteristics of Black Educators." Journal of Clinical Psychology 32(J1, 1976): 613-616.

Haggard, Philip Penrose. "Perceptions of Black Teachers in Predominantly White Schools in the Commonwealth of Pennsylvania." Doctoral dissertation, U. of Pennsylvania, 1973. Univ. Microfilms Order No. 74-15914.

Hale, James M. Teacher Education and School Integration: A Conference Series, Je 30, 1969. ERIC ED 045 749.

Hall, David G. "A Case for Teacher Continuity in Inner-City Schools." School Review 80 (N, 1971):27-49.

Haney, James E. "The Effects of the Brown Decision on Black Educators." Journal of Negro Education 47(Winter, 1978):88-95.

Hanushek, Eric. "Teacher Characteristics and Gains in Student Achievement: Estimation Using Micro Data." American Economic Review 61(My, 1971):280-288.

_____. The Value of Teachers in Teaching. RM-6362-CC/RC. Santa Monica, CA: RAND, 1970.

Harari, Herbert, and McDavid, John W. "Name Stereotypes and Teachers' Expectations." Journal of Educational Psychology 65(O, 1973):222-225.

Harper, John H., and McKenzie, Joe M. "Improving Interracial Professional Relationships in Physical Education." Journal of Physical Education and Recreation 46(S, 1975):22-23.

Harris, Norene, and Jackson, Nathaniel. "Black Teachers in a White School." In The Integration of American Schools: Problems, Experiences, Solutions, pp. 20-31. Edited by Norene Harris, Nathaniel Jackson, and Carl E. Rydingsword and contributors. Boston: Allyn & Bacon, 1975.

Harvey, Dale G., and Slatin, Gerald T. "The Relationship Between Child's SES and Teacher Expectations: A Test of the Middle-Class Bias Hypothesis." Social Forces 54(S, 1975): 140-159.

Haslach, Henry. "Radical Mathematics Teaching." Radicals in the Professions, Mr, 1968.

Hathaway, Joseph D. "Interpersonal Relationships Between Minority Students and Teachers." Doctoral dissertation, U. of Northern Colorado, 1972.

Hawkes, David T. "An Exploration of the Problems of Teacher Ethnocentricity and Low Expectations in an Urban Integrated School." Master's thesis, Simon Fraser U., 1972.

Hawkes, Thomas H., and Furst, Norma F. "An Investigation of the (Mis) Conceptions of Pre- and Inservice Teachers as to the Manifestation Anxiety in Upper Elementary School Children from Different Racial-Socioeconomic Backgrounds." Psychology in the Schools 10 (Ja, 1973):23-32.

_____ and _____. "Race, Socio-Economic Situation, Achievement, IQ, and Teacher Ratings of Students' Behavior as Factors Relating to Anxiety in Upper Elementary School Children." Sociology of Education 44(Summer, 1971):333-350.

Heath, Robert W. "The Ability of White Teachers to Relate to Black Students and to White Students." American Educational Research Journal 8(Ja, 1971):1-10.

_____. "The Ability of White Teachers to Relate to Black Students and to White Students." Classroom Interaction Newsletter 6 (My, 1971):59-69.

_____. The Ability of White Teachers to Relate to Black Students and to White Students, F, 1970. ERIC ED 037 399.

Hedman, A. R. "The Effect of a Selected Racism Training Program on the Verbal Behavior of White Teachers." Doctoral dissertation, U. of Maryland, 1974.

Hedman, A. R., and Magoon, Thomas M. "Effects of Racism Training on the Verbal Behavior of White Teachers." Journal of Non-White Concerns in Personnel and Guidance 5(Ap, 1977): 126-132.

Heller, Marc S., and White, Mary Alice. "Rates of Teacher Verbal Approval and Disapproval to Higher and Lower Ability Classes." Journal of Educational Psychology 67(D, 1975): 796-800.

Hilton, George B., and Oaldand, Thomas D. "Teacher's Attitudinal Responses to Differing Characteristics of Elementary School Students." Journal of Educational Psychology 69(Je, 1977):261-265.

Henderson, Charles H., Jr. "The Relationship of Teacher Morale to the Racial Composition of the Student Bodies in Selected Elementary Schools in Metropolitan Atlanta." Doctoral dissertation, Mississippi State U., 1977.

Henderson, Edmund H. When Teachers Predict Success in First-Grade Reading, 1973. ERIC ED 094 856.

Henderson, Edmund, and Long, Barbara H. "Academic Expectancies of Black and White Teachers for Black and White First Graders." Proceedings of the 81st Annual Convention of the American Psychological Association 8 (1973):687-688.

Hendricks, M. Teacher Effects in the Riverside School Study. Evanston, IL: Psychology Department, Northwestern U., 1977.

Herrell, James M. Galatea in the Classroom: Student Expectations Affect Teacher Behavior, Ap, 1971. ERIC ED 056 331

Hess, Robert D., and Tenezakis, Maria, with Smith, I. D., Brod, R. L., Spellman, J. B., Ingle, H. T., and Oppman, B. G. The Computer as a Socializing Agent: Some Socioaffective Outcomes of CAI. Stanford, CA: Stanford Center for Research and Development in Teaching, Stanford U., O, 1970.

Hewell, Nancy. Reactions of Prospective English Teachers Toward Speakers of a Non-Standard Dialect, Mr 7, 1971. ERIC ED 051 727.

Hillman, Stephen B., and Davenport, G. Gregory. Teacher Behavior in Desegregated Schools, Ap, 1977. ERIC ED 138 670.

Hoffmann, Earl. "Do Districts Have the Right to Transfer Teachers Involuntarily?" School Management 16(Ag, 1972).

Hogan, Ermon O. "The Influence of an Inservice Workshop Experience on Teachers' Ability to Positively Modify the Self-Concepts of Educationally and Economically Disadvantaged Students." Diss. Abstr. Int'l., 31(2-A): 677-678.

Hogan, Ermon O., and Green, Robert L. "Can Teachers Modify Children's Self-Concept?" Record 72(F, 1971):423-426.

Hogan, Jerry. "White Teacher in a Black Classroom." Changing Education, Spring, 1969.

Hooker, Robert W. "Blacks Losing Teaching Jobs." Race Relations Reporter 21(D 9, 1970).

_____. Displacement of Black Teachers in the Eleven Southern States. Nashville, TN: Race Relations Information Center, D, 1970.

Hopson, Annie Lee, and Wilder, David E. A Study of Teachers in the Public Schools of Washington, DC. New York: Bureau of Applied Social Research, Columbia U., 1967.

Howard, Roger. "Keeping the Teachers Off the Right Lines." Times Education Supplement, Je 29, 1973.

Howe, Frederick Charles. "Teacher Perception Toward the Learning Ability of Students from Differing Racial and Socio-Economic Backgrounds." Doctoral dissertation, Michigan State U., 1970.

Hoxter, L. "Teacher Attitudes and Cultural Differences." Alberta Journal of Educational Research 20(Je, 1974):133-145.

Hutchinson, Yvonne. "This Black Teacher Wants to Stay in Watts." Los Angeles Times, Je 3, 1976. [English teacher in Markham Junior High School, Los Angeles]

Hutton, Jerry B. "Relationships Between Teacher Judgement, Screening Test Data, and Academic Performance for Disadvantaged Children." Training School Bulletin 68(F, 1972):197-201.

Ingleby, J. D., and Cooper, Elizabeth. "How Teachers Perceive First-Year Schoolchildren: Sex and Ethnic Differences." Sociology 8 (S, 1974):463-372. [London, England]

Insel, Paul M., and Jacobson, Lenore F. (eds.). What Do You Expect? An Inquiry into Self-Fulfilling Prophecies. Menlo Park, CA: Cummings, 1975.

Institute for Teacher Leadership. Student Integration: The Teacher's Role, 1977. ERIC ED 155 301.

Irvine, LaVerne F., and Brierley, Norman R. Evaluation of Leadership and Crossover Teacher Institutes Concerned with Problems of Desegregation, Ap, 1970. ERIC ED 045 752.

Israel, Benjamin L. "The Relationship Between Teachers' Expressed Attitudes, Opinions, and Beliefs Regarding Minority, Ethnic and Racial Groups and Their Effectiveness as Classroom Teachers in Disadvantaged Urban Areas." Doctoral dissertation, U. of Minnesota, 1968.

Jablonsky, Adelaide. "There are Some Good Teachers of the Disadvantaged." IRCD Bulletin 8(Mr, 1972):3-18.

Jackson, Gregg, and Cosca, Cecilia. "The Inequality of Educational Opportunity in the Southwest: An Observational Study of Ethnically Mixed Classrooms." American Educational Research Journal 11(Summer, 1974): 219-229.

Jacobs, Ellen G., and Derevensky, Jefferey L. Changing Teacher's Perceptions: A Look at the Inner City Child's Environment, Mr, 1976. ERIC ED 126 168.

Jacoby, Susan. "New Power in the Schools." Saturday Review, Ja 18, 1969. [Black teachers]

Jaeger, Richard M., and Freijo, Tom D. Race and Sex as Concomitants of Teachers' Accuracy in Evaluative Rating of Students, Ap, 1974. ERIC ED 096 374.

Jefferson, William. "School Desegregation and the Black Teacher: A Search for Effective Remedies." Tulane Law Review 48(1973).

Jenkins, Rosemary. "In Defense of White Teachers in the Ghetto." Los Angeles Times, Je 16, 1976. [Teacher at Markham Junior High School, Watts, Los Angeles]

Jenkins, Shirley, and Morrison, Barbara. Ethnicity and Service Delivery, Ap, 1977. ERIC ED 139 877.

Jensen, Mary, and Rosenfeld, Lawrence B. "Influence of Mode of Presentation, Ethnicity, and Social Class on Teachers' Evaluations of Students." Journal of Educational Psychology 66(1974):540-547.

Johnson, Helen H. "Teacher Attitude and Ghetto Language." Viewpoints 47(Mr, 1971):73-81.

Johnson, James A., Jr. "Teacher Perceptions of and Attitudes Toward Low-Income Urban Black Children." Doctoral dissertation, U. of California, Irvine, 1973.

_____ (ed.). On the Interface Between Low-Income, Urban Black Children and Their Teachers During the Early School Years: A Position Paper, N, 1973. ERIC ED 091 469.

Johnson, Kenneth R. "Teacher's Attitude Toward the Nonstandard Negro Dialect--Let's Change It." Elementary English 48(F, 1971):176-184.

Johnson, Kenneth, and Simons, Herbert D. "Black Children and Reading: What Teachers Need to Know." Phi Delta Kappan 53(Ja, 1972):288-290.

Johnson, Rosemary Frances. "Parent and Teacher Perceptions of Inner-City Teachers." Doctoral dissertation, U. of Akron, 1974. Univ. Microfilms Order No. 74-21, 085.

Jorgenson, Gerald W. "An Analysis of Teacher Judgments of Reading Level." American Educational Research Journal 12(Winter, 1975):67-75.

Jose, Jean. Teacher-Pupil Interaction as it Relates to Attempted Changes in Teacher Expectancy of Academic Ability and Achievement, Mr, 1970. ERIC ED 041 630.

Jones, Ruth S. "Teachers as Agents of Political Socialization." Education and Urban Society 4(N, 1971):99-114.

Jordan, Lucille G., and Armster, Mae E. "Educating Early Childhood Teachers for the Inner City." Journal of Research and Development in Education 4(Summer, 1971):11-20.

Kadushin, Alfred. "The Racial Factor in the Interview." Social Work 17(My, 1972):88-98.

Kaufman, Mae Elizabeth. "Some Problems of Negro Teachers Related to Integration of Pupils in Public Schools." Doctoral dissertation, Indiana U., 1960.

Kautz, Eleanor. "Can Agencies Train for Racial Awareness?" Child Welfare 55(S-O, 1976):547-551.

Kehle, T. J., Bramble, W. J., and Mason, E. M. "Teachers' Expectations: Ratings of Student Performance as Biased by Student Characteristics." Journal of Experimental Education 43(1974):54-60.

King, Alan J. C., and Ripton, Reginald A. "Teachers and Students: A Preliminary Analysis of Collective Reciprocity." Canadian Review of Sociology and Anthropology 7(F, 1970).

King, Charles E., Mayer, Robert R., and Borders-Patterson, Anne. "Differential Responses to Black and White Males by Female Teachers in a Southern City." Sociology and Social Research 57(Jl, 1973):482-494.

King, George D. A Special In-Service Training Institute for the Preparation of Teachers for Effective Service and Leadership in Desegregated Schools, My 20, 1967. ERIC ED 056 116.

Kinnick, Bernard C., and Plator, Stanton D. "Relationship of Authoritarian Ethnocentric, and Segregationist Attitudes with Basic Values Among Public School Personnel." SPATE Journal (Student Personnel Association for Teacher Education), Fall, 1968.

Klassen, Frank H., and Gollnick, Donna M. (eds.). Pluralism and the American Teacher: Issues and Case Studies. Washington, DC: American Association of Colleges for Teacher Education, 1977.

Kleinfeld, Judith S. Effective Teachers of Indian and Eskimo High School Students. Fairbanks, AK: Institute of Social, Economic, and Government Research, 1972.

_____. "The Relative Importance of Teachers and Parents in the Formation of Negro and White Students' Academic Self-Concept." Journal of Educational Research 65(Ja, 1972):211-212.

Klopf, Gordon J., and Bowman, Garda. Teacher Education in a Social Context. New York: Mental Health Materials Center, 1966.

Knapp, Dale L. "Preparing Teachers of Disadvantaged Youth: Emerging Trends." Journal of Teacher Education, Je, 1965.

Knight, Athelia. "Teacher Attitude on Blacks Sparked Virginia Dispute." Washington Post, My 9, 1978. [Fairfax County High School]

Krasno, Richard Michael. _Teachers' Attitudes: Their Empirical Relationship to Rapport with Students and Survival in the Profession_. Stanford, CA: Stanford Center for Research and Development, Je, 1972.

Kruszynski, Eugene. "Urban Teachers for Urban Youth." _School and Society_ 100(D, 1971): 511-513.

Lamanna, Richard. "The Negro Teacher and Desegregation: A Study of Strategic Decision Makers and Their Vested Interests in Different Community Contexts." _Sociological Inquiry_, Winter, 1965.

Landers, Jacob. "The Responsibilities of Teachers and School Administrators." _Journal of Negro Education_, Summer, 1964.

Langeveld, Martinus J., and Bolleman, J. "Some Aspects of the Role and Attitude of the Teacher in Relation to the Socially Disadvantaged Child." _Paedagogica Europaea_ 5(1969): 146-151.

Larkin, Ronald F. "The Expectations of Black Female Teachers and White Female Teachers Toward Black Second and Third Grade Pupils and Effects of These Expectations on Black Pupil Gains in Reading Scores in Urban Schools." Doctoral dissertation, Rutgers U., 1978. Univ. Microfilms Order No. 7810231.

Larson, Richard, and Olson, James (eds.). _I Have a Kind of Fear. Confessions from the Writings of White Teachers and Black Students in City Schools_. Chicago: Quadrangle, 1969.

Lawrence, Sara, and Shepard, Ray. "Arrogance and Innocence: A Story of the Urban Component of the M.A.T. Program." _Harvard Graduate School of Education Association Bulletin_ 15(Fall, 1971):5-11. [Boston metropolitan area]

Lawson, Dene R. "Indications of Teacher Ability to Relate to Students." _Diss. Abstr. Int'l._, 31, 8-A(F, 1971):4011-4012.

Leadership Development and Human Relations Seminar, 1969; Second Annual Teacher Desegregation Institute, Je, 1969. ERIC ED 056 128.

Lede, Naomi W. (ed.). _Sensitivity Training and Faculty Desegregation_, 1969. ERIC ED 047 022.

Lederer, Richard. "Teaching in the Ghetto: Implications for Independent Schools." _Independent School Bulletin_ 31(O, 1971):8-10.

Ledvinka, James. "The Intrusion of Race: Black Responses to the White Observer." _Social Science Quarterly_ 52(Mr, 1972):907-920.

Lee, J. R. E. "The National Association of Teachers of Colored Youths." _Voice of the Negro_ 2(Je, 1905):381-385.

Leibson, Edward. _Problems Incident to De Facto School Segregation; An Action Approach_. Institute Training Program, S, 1967, ERIC ED 056 112.

Leles, Sam. "Teacher Power--What's It All About?" _Theory Into Practice_ 7(Ap, 1968).

Lemon, Donald K. "Quality and Equality: An Educational Dilemma." _College of Education Record_ (University of North Dakota) 55(Ja, 1970):102-103. Recruitment of minority persons into teaching

Lenkowsky, Ronald S., and Blackman, Leonard S. "The Effect of Teacher's Knowledge of Race and Social Class on Their Judgments of Children's Academic Competence and Social Acceptability." _Mental Retardation_, D, 1968.

Leslie, Larry L. "The Effect of Preservice Experience with the Disadvantaged on First-Year Teachers on Disadvantaged Schools." _Education and Urban Society_ 3(Ag, 1971): 398-413.

Lesniak, Robert J., Lohman, Ernest E., and Churukian, George A. "Verbal Behavior Differences Between Inner-City and Suburban Elementary Teachers. A Pilot Study." _Urban Education_ 7(Ap, 1972):41-48.

Levin, Henry M. "A Cost-Effectiveness Analysis of Teacher Selection." _Human Resources_ 5 (Winter, 1970):24-33.

Levin, Henry M. "How Important Is Teacher Experience?" _Integrated Education_ 9(My-Je, 1971):25-26.

Levine, Daniel U. _Report of the Special Institute on School Desegregation: An Institute to Help Educators Maximize Educational Opportunity, August 3-13, 1965_, S 15, 1965. ERIC ED 056 125.

_____. _Special Institute on School Desegregation: An Institute to Help Educators Maximize Educational Opportunity, August 2-13, 1965_, Ja, 1966. ERIC ED 056 118.

_____. "Threshold Phenomena in Inner-City Schools and Society." _Education and Urban Society_ 2(Ag, 1970):347-359.

Levine, Daniel U., and Brink, Ronald (eds.). _Perspectives and Suggestions for Teaching in Desegregated Schools_, Ja, 1969. Center for the Study of Metropolitan Problems in Education, U. of Missouri-Kansas City, 5100 Rockhill Road, Kansas City, MO 64110.

Levine, Daniel U., and Doll, Russell. The Beginning Teacher in the Inner City School: A Dialogue. Bloomington, IN: Phi Delta Kappa, 1967.

Lewis, Ellen S. "Teacher Influence on Pupil Cognitive Performance." Peabody Journal of Education 55(Ap, 1978):252-264.

Lietz, Jeremy J. "School Deportment and Student Teacher Sex and Ethnicity." Psychology in the Schools 14(Ja, 1977):72-77.

Lightfoot, Sara Lawrence. "An Ethnographic Study of the Status Structure of the Classroom." Doctoral dissertation, Howard U., 1972.

_____. "Politics and Reasoning: Through the Eyes of Teachers and Children." Harvard Educational Review 43(My, 1973):197-244.

_____. "The Teacher: Overcoming the Power of Cultural Images." Harvard Graduate School of Education Alumni Association Bulletin 19(Spring-Summer, 1975):14-18.

Lincoln, E. A. White Teachers, Black Schools, and the Inner City: Some Impressions and Concerns. Pittsburgh: Division of Teacher Development, School of Education, U. of Pittsburgh, 1975.

Liu, An-Yen. "Interpersonal Relations Within an Integrated Setting." Psychological Reports 36(F, 1975):138.

Lloyd, R. Grann. "Teaching Economics to Black Students." American Economic Review 61(My, 1971):249-255.

Logan, Eleanor M. and others. Special Training Institute for Problems of School Desegregation; Intergroup Relations Institute for Secondary School Personnel, Interim Report, S 14, 1965. ERIC ED 056 109.

Long, Barbara H., and Henderson, Edmund D. "Certain Determinants of Academic Expectancies among Southern and Non-Southern Teachers." American Educational Research Journal 11(Spring, 1974):137-147.

_____ and _____. The Effect of Pupils' Race, Class, Test Scores and Classroom Behavior on the Academic Expectancies of Southern and Non-Southern White Teachers, Ap, 1972. ERIC ED 063 422.

_____ and _____. Teacher Judgments of Classroom Behavior of Negro and White School Beginners, Mr 2, 1970. ERIC ED 038 708.

_____ and _____. "Teachers' Judgments of Black and White School Beginners." Sociology of Education 44(Summer, 1971):358-368.

Long, Samuel, and Long, Ruth. "Teacher-Candidates' Poverty Perceptions." Journal of Negro Education 43(Fall, 1974):494-505.

Love, Barbara J. "Desegregation in Your School: Behavior Patterns That Get in the Way." Phi Delta Kappan 59(N, 1977):168-170.

Lovell, John T. and others. Special Training Institute for Educational Leaders and Other Community Leaders to Work on Problems Arising from Desegregation of Public Schools. Final Report, 1966. ERIC ED 056 113.

McCandless, Boyd R., and Roberts, Albert. "Teachers' Marks, Achievement Test Scores, and Aptitude Relations With Respect to Social Class, Race, and Sex." Journal of Educational Psychology 63(Ap, 1972):153-159.

McClure, Erica. "Teacher-Pupil Questions and Responses and the Mexican-American Child." Bilingual Review 5(Ja-Ag, 1978):40-44.

McCorkle, Jack S. "Student Perception of Teacher Effectiveness." Diss. Abstr. Int'l. 30(1969)3-A:960-961.

McCormick, W. J. "Students' Social Status and School Staff Characteristics." Doctoral dissertation, U. of California, Berkeley, 1970.

McDaniel, Thomas R. "The NTE and Teacher Certification." Phi Delta Kappan 59(N, 1977):186.

McFarland, George. "Black Pupil Personnel Workers: Beyond the Professional Shoving Match." In Restructuring the Educational Process: A Black Perspective. Edited by Lawrence E. Gary and Aaron Favors. Washington, DC: Institute for Urban Affairs and Research, Howard U., 1975.

McMillan, J. H. "The Influence of Caucasian Teachers on Negro and Caucasian Students in Segregated and Racially Mixed Inner City Schools." Doctoral dissertation, Michigan State U., 1967. Univ. Microfilms Order No. 68-4189.

McPherson, Gertrude. Small Town Teacher. New York: Cambridge U. Press, 1972.

Margold, L. C. "Pupil-Teacher Dyadic Interactions in Desegregated Elementary School Classrooms." Doctoral dissertation, U. of Texas, 1974.

Manske, A. J. "The Reflection of Teachers' Attitudes in the Attitudes of their Pupils." Doctoral dissertation, Columbia U., 1935.

Mann, J. "Teacher Ideology and Intergroup Conflict." Doctoral dissertation, U. of Michigan, 1970.

Marshall, Walter W. "The Relationship Between Teacher Morale and Pupil Achievement in Urban Black Middle Class Schools." Doctoral dissertation, U. of California, Los Angeles, 1972. Univ. Microfilms Order No. 72-25808.

Marson, John. "Are You Ready, Black Teachers?" African-American Teachers Forum, S, 1969.

Martel, Erich. "Teachers and Busing." Militant, Jl 2, 1975. [American Federation of Teachers]

Mason, Emanuel J. "Teachers' Observations and Expectations of Boys and Girls as Influential by Biased Psychological Reports and Knowledge of the Effects of Bias." Journal of Educational Psychology 65(O, 1973):238-243.

Mathieson, Moira B. Beginning Teachers in the Inner City: A Study of the Literature on Their Problems and Some Possible Solutions, 1971. ERIC ED 050 028.

Mathis, Dolores Walker. "Differences in Teacher Interaction With Afro-American and Anglo-American Students in the Same Classroom." Doctoral dissertation, U. of Michigan, 1975. Univ. Microfilms Order No. 75-29,283.

Mathis, Marion. "A Study of Racial Attitudes Among Teaching Personnel in Merced County, California." Master's thesis, Chapman College, 1969.

May, Jack G., Jr., and Breyer, Norman L. The Effects of Selected Teacher and Pupil Characteristics on Social Learning. Final Report, O, 1970. ERIC ED 050 383.

Mays, Nebraska. "Intergroup Expectations of the Role of the Teacher in Recently Desegregated School Facilities." Doctoral dissertation, Southern Illinois U., 1962.

Mazer, Gilbert E. "Effects of Social Class Stereotyping on Teacher Expectation." Psychology in the Schools 8(O, 1971):373-378.

Mehl, R. F., Jr. "A Study of the Relationship Between Homogenous Grouping in the School and the Social Class Structure in Up-State New York Community." Doctoral dissertation, State U. of New York at Albany, 1965.

Mercer, Walter A. A Model for Cooperative Student Teaching Involving a Nearby Majority Black University and a Nearby Majority White University, 1970. ERIC ED 042 703.

_____. Teaching in the Desegregated School. Guide to Intergroup Relations. New York: Vantage, 1971.

Merriweather, Helen L. "The Per Capita Expenditure by Race for Teachers' Salaries and Racial Population Ratios in Southern States." Master's thesis, Fisk U., n.d.

Metz, Mary Haywood. Teachers' Adjustments in Students' Behaviors: Some Implications for the Process of Desegregation, Mr 31, 1978. ERIC ED 155 294.

Metzner, Seymour. "Teacher Bias in Pupil Evaluation: A Critical Analysis." Journal of Teacher Education 22(Spring, 1971):40-43.

Meyer, William J., and Lindstrom, Davis. The Distribution of Teacher Approval and Disapproval of Head Start Children. Final Report, 1969. ERIC ED 042 509.

Michener, John H. "Why Hire Minority Teachers? A Quaker Speaks Out." Independent School Bulletin 35(My, 1976):44-46.

Miller, Charles K., McLaughlin, John A., Haddon, John, and Chansky, Norman A. "Socioeconomic Class and Teacher Bias." Psychological Reports, D, 1968.

Miller, Harry L. "Race vs. Class in Teachers' Expectations." Psychological Reports 32(F, 1973):106-106.

_____. "The Relation of Social Class to Slum School Attitudes Among Education Students at an Urban College." Journal of Teacher Education, Winter, 1968.

Miller, Norman Theodore. "Attitudes of a Selected Group of Black and White Secondary School Students Toward White and Black Teachers in a Newly Desegregated High School in Austin, Texas." Doctoral dissertation, U. of Houston, 1974. Univ. Microfilms Order No. 75-10744.

Millins, Ken. "The Preparation of Teachers to Educate Minority Groups." London Educational Review 2(Spring, 1973):5-11. [England]

Millner, Darrell. Minority Teachers as Change Agents: A Case Study. Washington, DC: University Press of America, 1977.

Moody, Charles D., Vergon, Charles B., Baker, Gwen, and Green, Grace (eds.). Proceedings of Conference on Multi-Ethnic Curriculum and the Changing Role of the Teacher. Ann Arbor, MI: Program for Educational Opportunity, School of Education, U. of Michigan, n.d.

Morse, Harole E., and Morton, Anton S. "An Appalachian Teacher Survey Indicates Needs and Strengths." Appalachia 3(My, 1970):1-6.

Morton, Finley J. "Negro Educators for Negro Education." School and Society 24(N 20, 1926):625-629.

Mosley, William J. "The Disproportionate Placement of Black Children in Special Classes and Prejudice Among White Prospective Teachers." Doctoral dissertation, U. of Connecticut, 1973. Univ. Microfilms Order No. 74-07129.

Murnane, Richard J. The Impact of Changing Student Enrollment Patterns on the Distribution of Teachers in an Urban School District, 1977. ERIC ED 139 899.

Murphy, James. "Teacher Expectations and Working-Class Under-Achievement." British Journal of Sociology 25(S, 1974):326-344.

Murray, Helen Godsey. "Teaching Staff Puts Value into Action; Provides Anatomy for Integrated School." Delta Kappa Gamma Bulletin 37(Winter, 1971):32-34.

Myers, Robert B. Problems in School Desegregation: Two Summer Institutes for School Leaders, Ag 25, 1965. ERIC ED 056 115.

Narot, Ruth E. "Teacher Prejudice and Teacher Behavior in Desegregated Schools." In Southern Schools: An Evaluation of the Effects of the Emergency School Assistance Program and of Desegregation, II, pp. 17-39. Edited by Robert L. Crain. Chicago: National Opinion Research Center, O, 1973. ERIC ED 085 426.

Nash, Roy. Classrooms Observed. The Teacher's Perception and the Pupil's Performance. London: Routledge and Kegan Paul, 1973.

_____. "Keeping In With Teacher." New Society, D 14, 1972.

_____. "Measuring Teacher Attitudes." Educational Research 14(F, 1972):141-146.

National Center for the Training of Educational Resource Agents to Serve Rural Minorities. The Preparation of Problem Solving/Development/Diffusion Personnel to Serve Rural/Minority/Culturally Limited Populations, D 15, 1970. ERIC ED 055 680.

National Commission on Teacher Education and Professional Standards. The Real World of the Beginning Teacher. Washington, DC: National Education Association, 1966.

National Planning Conference on Studies in Teaching. Panel Summaries. Washington, DC: National Institute of Education, 1975.

"Negro Teachers Out on Own; Gird for Action." Education News, Je 24, 1968.

Nicholson, Everett W., and Robinson, Charles D. Methods of Achieving Racially Balanced Faculties: Their Relationships to Teacher Morale, F 6, 1971. ERIC ED 048 661. [Indianapolis public schools]

Nichell, Ted A. "A Study of the Relationship Between White Teacher Attitudes Toward Minorities and their Opinions About the Effects of Integration." Doctoral dissertation, U. of Missouri, 1978. Univ. Microfilms Order No. 7903926.

Noar, Gertrude. The Teacher and Integration, Revised edition. Washington, DC: National Education Association, 1974.

Nolle, David B. "Alternative Path Analytic Models of Student-Teacher Influence: The Implications of Different Strokes for Different Folks." Sociology of Education 46 (Fall, 1973):417-426.

Norman, Diane E. "Racial Classroom Composition and Its Relationship to Students' Perception of Teachers." Negro Educational Review 29 (Ja, 1978):47-51.

North, George E., and Buchanan, O. Lee. "Teacher Views of Poverty Area Children." Journal of Educational Research, O, 1967.

Norton, Linda, and Dobson, Russell. "Perceptions of Teachers' Nonverbal Behaviors by Children of Different Race, Age, and Sex." Humanist Educator 14(Mr, 1976):94-101.

Ohberg, Hjordis Glad. "Achievement of LSE Black Children with Teachers of Different Sex and Ethnic Identity." Doctoral dissertation, Pennsylvania State U., 1971.

_____. "Does the Black Child Need a Black Teacher?" Integrated Education (Mr-Ap, 1972): 27-28.

Ohles, J. F. "On Integrating Teaching Staffs." New York State Education, D, 1964.

Olds, Morris Eugene. "Teachers' Reactions to Faculty Desegregation." Doctoral dissertation, U. of Tennessee, 1970. Univ. Microfilms Order No. 71-362. [Shelley County, TN]

Ornstein, Allan C. "What It Is Really Like for Most Slum-School Teachers." Integrated Education, O-N, 1967.

Outtz, James L. Racial Bias as a Contaminant of Performance Evaluation, F, 1977. ERIC ED 137 401.

Owen, John D. "The Distribution of Educational Resources in Large American Cities." Journal of Human Resources 7(Winter, 1972):25-38. [Distribution of teachers, by experience]

_____. Racial Bias in the Allocation of Teachers in Sixty-Nine Urban Elementary School Systems, N, 1969. ERIC ED 034 838.

Pace, Walter T. "On Congruence and Dissonance in the Perceptions of Negro Teacher Trainees." Education 90(Ap-My, 1970):315-318.

Packer, M. A., and Freeze, C. R. "The Super-visory Teacher in a Unitary School." Integrated Education (S-O, 1972):55-60.

Parker, Lenore D. Effects of Teacher Training in the Use of Multi-Racial Elementary School Language Arts Materials, 1970. ERIC ED 050 101.

Passow, A. Harry. "Diminishing Teacher Pre-judice." In The Inner City Classroom: Teacher Behaviors, pp. 93-109. Edited by R. D. Strom. Columbus, OH: Merrill, 1966.

Payne, Charles. "Cultural Differences and Their Implications for Teachers." Integra-teducation 15(Mr-Ap, 1977).

Pederson, Eigil and others. "A New Perspective on the Effects of First-Grade Teachers on Children's Subsequent Adult Status." Har-vard Educational Review 48(F, 1978):1-31.

Pederson, K. George. The Itinerant School-master: A Socio-Economic Analysis of Teacher Turnover. Chicago: Midwest Administration Center, 1973.

Peek, Don Adolphus. "A Comparison of the Ver-bal Behaviors of Teachers and Pupils in a Predominantly Negro High School with the Verbal Behaviors of Teachers and Pupils in a Predominantly White High School." Doctoral dissertation, East Texas State U., 1970. Univ. Microfilms Order No. 71-08648.

Pellegreno, Dominick D., and Williams, Wendell C. "Teacher Perception and Classroom Verbal Interaction." Elementary School Guidance and Counseling 7(My, 1973):270-275.

Pelligrini, Robert J., and Hicks, Robert A. "Prophecy Effects and Tutorial Instruction for the Disadvantaged Child." American Ed-ucational Research Journal 9(Summer, 1972): 413-419. [Teacher]

Peretti, Peter O. "Effects of Teachers' Atti-tudes on Discipline Problems in Schools Re-cently Desegregated." Education 97(Winter, 1976):136-140.

Perkins, Marjorie Willene. "Selected Features of Nonstandard Negro Dialect of Teachers in Integrated Schools." Doctoral dissertation, U. of Alabama, 1972. Univ. Microfilms Order No. 72-33123.

Persell, Caroline Hodges. Testing, Tracking and Teachers' Expectations: Their Implica-tions for Education and Inequality. A Lit-erature Review and Synthesis, Ap, 1976. ERIC ED 126 150.

Peters, Robert Charles, Jr. "A Study of Changes in White Student-Teacher Racial Attitudes Relative to Blacks, As Measured by the Multi-factor Racial Attitude Inventory." Doctoral dissertation, North Texas State U., 1975. Univ. Microfilms Order No. 75-24161.

Peterson, John H., Jr. "Black-White Joking Relationships Among Newly-Integrated Fac-ulty." Integrateducation 13(Ja-F, 1975): 33-37.

Phi Delta Kappa Teacher Education Project on Human Rights. A Guide for Improving Teacher Education Project on Human Rights, Je, 1971. Project Headquarters, U. of Oklahoma, 555 Constitution Avenue, Norman, OK 73069.

Piche, Gene L. and others. "Effects of Dialect-Ethnicity, Social Class and Quality of Written Compositions on Teachers' Subjective Evaluations of Children." Communication Monographs 44(Mr, 1977):60-72.

_____ and others. "Teachers' Subjective Eval-uations of Standard and Black Nonstandard English Compositions: A Study of Written Language and Attitudes." Research in the Teaching of English 12(My, 1978):107-118.

Pidgeon, Douglas A. Expectation and Pupil Performance. London: National Foundation for Educational Research in England and Wales, 1970.

Pietras, Thomas, and Lamb, Rose. "Attitudes of Selected Elementary Teachers Toward Non-Standard Black Dialects." Journal of Educa-tional Research 71(My-Je, 1978):292-297.

Pinney, Robert H. Teacher Presentational Be-haviors Related to Student Achievement in English and Social Studies. Stanford, CA: Stanford Center for Research and Development in Teaching, Stanford U., D, 1970.

Plain, Thomas A. "Recruiting Teachers from Minority Groups." Clearing House 47(D, 1972 1972):216-218.

Politzer, Robert L., and Hoover, Mary R. A Field Test of Black English Tests for Teach-ers, Ap, 1977. ERIC ED 141 405.

Postar, Beverly Ruth. "Teacher Perception of Black Administrative Leadership Behavior." Doctoral dissertation, Saint Louis U., 1977. Univ. Microfilms Order No. 7814622. [East St. Louis, IL]

Powell, James H. and others. Interim Report of the Institute for Supervisors of Student Teachers on Problems Occasioned by Desegre-gation on Public Schools, July 6 through August 12, 1965, Ag 24, 1965. ERIC ED 045 742.

Prichard, Keith W. and others. "Social Class Origins of College Teachers of Education." Journal of Teacher Education 22(Summer, 1971): 219-228.

Pugh, Lee G. Teacher Attitudes and Expectations Associated with Race and Social Class, Ap, 1974. ERIC ED 094 018.

Quirk, Thomas J., and Medley, Donald M. "Race and Subject-Matter Influences on Performance and General Education Items of the National Teacher Examinations." P_oceedings of the Annual Convention of the American Psychological Association 7(1972): Part 1, 469-470.

Quirk, Thomas J., and Whitten, Barbara J. "Review of Studies of the Concurrent and Predictive Validity of the National Teacher Examination." Review of Educational Research 43(Winter, 1973):89-113.

"Racial Factors in Teacher Assignment." NEA Research Bulletin, My, 1966.

Rafky, David M. "Are Blacks Who Teach Black Studies Different?" College Student Journal 6(Ap, 1972):55-61.

Rajpal, Puran L. "Teacher Judgments of Minority Children." Integrated Education 10(N-D, 1972):33-36.

Ramirez, Arnulfo and others. Language Attitudes and the Achievement of Bilingual Pupils, Je, 1976. ERIC ED 127 829.

Resnik, Henry S. "Are There Better Ways to Teach Teachers?" Saturday Review 55(Mr 4, 1972):46-50.

Richmond, Bert O., and White, William F. "Predicting Teachers' Perceptions of Pupil Behavior." Measurement and Evaluation in Guidance 4(Jl, 1971):71-78.

Riley, Joyce Bickerstaff. "Political Social-ization in the Elementary Schools: The Role of the Afro-American Teacher." Doctoral dissertation, U. of Illinois, 1975. Univ. Microfilms Order No. 76-06924.

Rist, Ray C. "Social Distance and Social In-equality in a Ghetto Kindergarten Classroom: An Examination of the 'Cultural Gap' Hypothe-sis." Urban Education 7(O, 1972):241-260.

_____. "Student Social Class and Teacher Ex-pectations: The Self-Fulfilling Prophecy in Ghetto Education." Harvard Educational Re-view 40(Ag, 1970):411-451.

_____. The Urban School. A Factory for Fail-ure. An Ethnographic Study of Education in American Society. Cambridge, MA: MIT Press, 1973.

Roberts, Joan. The Scene of the Battle. Group Behavior and Urban Classrooms. Garden City, NY: Doubleday, 1971.

Rosenfeld, Gerry. "Shut Those Thick Lips": A Study of Slum Failure. New York: Holt, Rinehart & Winston, 1971.

Rosenshine, Barak. Teaching Behavior and Stu-dent Achievement. New York: Humanities Press, 1972.

_____. "Teacher Behavior and Student Atti-tudes Revisited." Journal of Educational Psychology 65(O, 1973):177-180.

Rosenshine, Barak, and Furst, Norma. "Current and Future Research on Teacher Performance Criteria." In Research on Teacher Education: A Symposium. Edited by B. Othanel Smith. Englewood Cliffs, NJ: Prentice-Hall, 1971.

Rosenthal, Jones O. "Negro Teachers' Attitude Toward Desegregation." Journal of Negro Education 26(Winter, 1957):63-71.

Rosenthal, Robert. On the Social Psychology of the Self-fulfilling Prophecy: Further Evidence for Pygmalion Effects and their Mediating Mechanisms, 1974. MSS Modular Publications, Inc., 655 Madison Avenue, New York, NY 10021.

_____. "The Pygmalion Effect Lives." Psychol-ogy Today 7(S, 1973):56-63.

_____. The Pygmalion Effect: What You Expect is What You Get, 1974. Psychology Today Reader Service, Box 700, Del Mar, CA 92014. [Tape cassette]

Rosenthal, Robert, and Jacobson, Lenore. Pygmalion in the Classroom. Teacher Expec-tation and Pupils' Intellectual Development. New York: Holt, Rinehart, & Winston, 1968.

_____ and _____. "Teacher Expectations for the Disadvantaged." Scientific American, Ap, 1968.

Rosenthal, Robert and others. "Teacher Behav-ior, Teacher Expectations, and Gains in Pupils' Rated Creativity." Journal of Genetic Psychology 124(1974):115-121.

Rosenthal, Ted L. and others. "Pedagogical Attitudes of Conventional and Specially-Trained Teachers." Psychology in the Schools 7(1970):61-66.

Ross, Michael B., and Salvia, John. "Attrac-tiveness as a Biasing Factor in Teacher Judgments." American Journal of Mental De-ficiency 80(Jl, 1975):96-98.

Rowell, J. A. "Sex Differences in Achievement in Science and the Expectations of Teachers." Australian Journal of Education 15(Mr, 1971): 16-29.

Rubovitz, Pamela C., and Maehr, Martin L. "Pygmalion Analyzed: Toward an Explanation of the Rosenthal-Jacobson Findings." Jour-nal of Personality and Social Psychology 19 (Ag, 1971):197-203.

_____ and _____. "Pygmalion Black and White." Journal of Personality and Social Psychology 25(F, 1973):210-218.

Ryan, William. "Blaming the Victim: The Folklore of Cultural Deprivation." This Magazine is About Schools 5(Summer, 1971): 97-117.

Rystrom, Richard, and Cowart, Harry. "Black Reading 'Errors' or White Teacher Biases?" Journal of Reading 15(Ja, 1972):273-276.

St. John, Nancy. "Thirty-Six Teachers: Their Characteristics, and Outcomes for Black and White Pupils." American Educational Research Journal, N, 1971.

Schniederwind, Nancy. "A Model Integrating Personal and Social Change in Teacher Education: Its Implementation in a Racism and Sexism Training Program." Doctoral dissertation, U. of Massachusetts, 1975.

Schramm, Charles F. "Relating Teacher Threat to Academic Achievement in Educationally Deprived Children." Journal of Classroom Interaction 12(D, 1976):51-70.

Scott, Gloria D. "Teacher Attitudes and Perception: The Impact on Achievement of Black Learners." In Restructuring the Educational Process: A Black Perspective. Edited by Lawrence E. Gary and Aaron Favors. Washington, DC: Institute for Urban Affairs and Research, Howard U., 1975. [See also commentary by Manderie H. Saunders]

Scott, Marvin B. "The Effect of Teacher Perception of Personality Factors on the Cognitive and Affective Learning of Black Students." Journal of Negro Education 45(Winter, 1976):89-93.

Scott, Patricia Bell, and McKenry, Patrick C. "Some Suggestions for Teaching About Black Adolescence." Family Coordinator 26(Ja, 1977):47-51.

Selden, David. "Teacher 'Accountability.'" American Teacher, Ja, 1969.

Schultz, Michael John, Jr. The National Education Association and the Black Teacher: The Integration of a Professional Association. Coral Gables, FL: U. of Miami Press, 1971.

Shams, G. Wayne. "The Psychological Correlates of Speech Characteristics of Sounding 'Disadvantaged': A Southern Replication." Child Study Journal 1(Spring, 1971):111-122.

Shanker, Albert. "Defending the Schools." New Leader, D 14, 1970.

Shaudel, Pearl W. A Descriptive Research Study of Cooperating Teachers and Student Teachers in Biracial Situations. Final Report, Ja, 1972. ERIC ED 059 980.

Shearhouse, H. S. In-Service Education to Solve Problems Incident to the Elimination of the Dual School System. Final Technical Report, N 26, 1969. ERIC ED 045 748.

Sheehan, David S., and Marcus, Mary. "The Effects of Teacher Race and Student Race on Vocabulary and Mathematics Achievement." Journal of Educational Research 70(Ja-F, 1977):123-126.

Sheldon Jackson College. Teacher Aide Education Program, Ag 9, 1974. ERIC ED 151 108. [Sitka, Alaska]

Sherwood, Charles F. The Effect of Faculty Desegregation on Teachers' Attitudes Toward Their Pupils, 1972. ERIC ED 086 710.

Sikula, John P., and Lemlech, Johanna Kasin. "Do Black and White Teachers Have Different Values?" Phi Delta Kappan, My, 1976.

Silver, Catherine Bodard. Black Teachers in Urban Schools. The Case of Washington, DC. New York: Praeger, 1973.

Simons, William. "The Miseducation of Black Teachers." Your Schools 2(O, 1970). [District of Columbia]

Slater, Judith. "Inside an Integrated Classroom." Parents' Magazine, Je, 1968. [Sixth-grade teacher]

Slaughter, Diana T. Relation of Early Parent-Teacher Socialization Influences to Achievement Orientation and Self-Esteem in Middle Childhood Among Low-Income Black Children, Ap, 1975. ERIC ED 125 735.

Smidchens, Uldis, and Thompson, Eugene. Effects of Family Orientation Within Socioeconomic Strata Upon Basic Skill Achievement, Mr, 1978. ERIC ED 156 931.

Smith, B. Othanel, with Cohen, Saul B., and Pearl, Arthur. Teachers for the Real World. Washington, DC: American Association of Colleges for Teacher Education, 1969.

Smith, Charles F. "A Study of the Attitudes of Teachers in Title I and Non-Title I Depressed Area Elementary Schools Toward Pupil-Teacher Relations as Measured by the Minnesota Teacher Attitude Inventory." Diss. Abstr. Int'l., 1970(J1), Vol. 31(1-A): 85-86.

Smith, Charles U. "On Being a Negro in 1960." Quarterly Review of Higher Education 38(O, 1960):250-257.

Smith, Eddie D. "Attitudes of Bibb County Elementary School Teachers Toward Integrated Schools." Master's thesis, Fort Valley State College, 1970. [GA]

Smith, John W., and Smith, Bette M. "Desegre-
gation in the South: And the Demise of
Black Education." Journal of Social and
Behavioral Sciences 20(Winter, 1974):33-40.

_____ and _____. "For Black Educators: Integration Brings the Axe." Urban Review 6
(1973).

Smith, Kenneth E., and Sandler, Howard M.
"Bases of Status in Four Elementary School
Faculties." American Educational Research
Journal 11(Fall, 1974):317-331.

Smith, Yvonne E. "The Relationship of Skin
Color and Teacher Perception of Pupil Behavior in the Classroom." Doctoral dissertation, U. of California, Berkeley, 1976.
Univ. Microfilms Order No. 77-4604.

Snow, Richard E. (ed.). A Symposium on Heur-
istic Teaching. Stanford, CA: Stanford
Center for Research and Development in
Teaching, Stanford U., D, 1970.

_____. "Unfinished Pygmalion." Contemporary
Pscyhology 14(1969):197-200.

Southwood, Valerie M. "Socio-subcultural Classification of Primary Grade Children and
Teacher Ratings of Behavioral Maturity and
Achievement." Master's thesis, U. of Hawaii,
1972.

Spencer, Thelma L. "An Investigation of the
National Teacher Examinations for Bias with
Respect to Black Candidates." Doctoral
dissertation, U. of Colorado, 1972.

Sperry, Len T. Changing Teacher Attitudes
Toward Human Relations Problems in Integrated
Schools, Ap, 1972. ERIC ED 061 173.

Spillane, Robert. "Job Satisfaction Among
Teachers in De Facto Segregated Schools: A
Summary." Integrated Education, O-N, 1967.

Stanley, Russell T. "How to Recruit Black
Teachers." NJEA Review 43(0, 1969):20-21.
[New Jersey Education Association]

Stapleton, Jack L. "Effect of a Head Teacher's
Race on the Race Awareness of Black Head
Start Children." Master's thesis, De Paul
U., 1969.

Stedman, James M., and Adams, Russell L.
"Teacher Perception of Behavioral Adjustment
as a Function of Linguistic Ability in
Mexican-American Head Start Children."
Psychology in the Schools 10(Ap, 1973):221-
225.

Sterling, Philip (ed.). The Real Teachers.
New York: Random House, 1972.

Stern, Carolyn, and Keisler, Evan R. "Teacher
Attitudes and Attitude Change: A Research
Review." Journal of Research and Develop-
ment in Education 10(Winter, 1977):63-76.

Stern, Carolyn and others. Teachers Expectation for Achievement of Children in Head
Start (TEACH). ERIC ED 045 735.

Stern, Etta G., and MacLennan, Beryce W.
"Conversations in Color: Desegregation in
the Classroom." Journal of Non-White Concerns 1(J1, 1973):172-180. [Teachers' sem-
inar]

Stevens, Edward W., Jr. "School Personnel and
Political Socialization. Rochester, New
York, 1900-1917." Urban Education 6(J1-0,
1971):197-213.

Stiles, Lindley S. (ed.). The Teacher's Role
in American Society. New York: Harper,
1957.

Sweeting, Lurlene M. and others. "Teacher-
Pupil Relationships: Black Students' Per-
ceptions of Actual and Ideal Teacher/Pupil
Control Behavior and Attitudes Toward
Teachers and School." Urban Education 13
(Ap, 1978):71-81.

Tate, Davie, Jr. "Riving, Jiving, and Playing
the Dozens Revisited." Integrateducation
15(Ja-F, 1977).

Teachers in Appalachia, Ag, 1970. ERIC ED 045
567.

Thelen, Herbert and others. Classroom Grouping
for Teachability. New York: Wiley, 1967.

Thomas, Howard E., and Peter, Sister Mary, SSND.
Organizing for Human Rights. A Handbook for
Teachers and Students. Dayton, OH: Pflaum,
1968.

Thomas, Jean L. "A Comparison of the Verbal
Behavior Patterns of Black and White Teachers." Doctoral dissertation, Temple U.,
1973. Univ. Microfilms Order No. 73-23367.

Thompson, Alvin H. "Berkeley's Urban Task
Force: A Project to Prepare Secondary
Community-Oriented Teachers for the Inner
City." Journal of Teacher Education 21(Sum-
mer, 1970):233-239.

Thorndike, Robert L. "Review of Rosenthal and
Jacobson, Pygmalion in the Classroom." American Educational Research Journal, N,
1968. [Reprinted in United Teacher, Je 29,
1969]

Toder, Eric Jay. The Distribution of Public
School Teachers by Race and Income Class in
an Urban Metropolitan Area. Final Report,
Mr, 1971. ERIC ED 050 210.

Torrence, Lee A. "A Study of Factors Associated
with Negro Teachers' Attitudes and Opinions
Toward Faculty Desegregation." Diss. Abstr.
Int'l, 1970, 30(7-A):2863-2864.

Tractenberg, Paul L. (ed.). Selection of Teachers and Supervisors in Urban School Systems. A Transcript of the Public Hearings Held Before the New York City Commission on Human Rights, January 25-29, 1971. New York: Agathon Publication Services, Inc., 1972.

Trammer, Monte I. "Some Claim Teachers Use Double Standard." Baltimore Sun, F 7, 1968. [Liberty Road area, Baltimore County, MD]

Trusman, D. J., Waller, M. I., and Wiler, G. A Descriptive and Analytic Study of Compensatory Reading Programs, Volume I. Princeton, NJ: Educational Testing Service, 1975.

Tuckman, Bruce W., and Bierman, Milton. Beyond Pygmalion: Galatea in the Schools, F, 1971. ERIC ED 047 077.

Turner, V. H. "Teachers Judgments of Children's Functioning by Sex and Social Class of Different Social Class and Racial Composition." Doctoral dissertation, Washington U., 1962.

U.S. Commission on Civil Rights. The Mexican American Education Study. Report V: Teachers and Students. Differences in Teacher Interaction with Mexican American and Anglo Students. Washington, DC: GPO, Mr, 1973.

Venditti, Frederick P. "Race Relations and Athletics: A Model for In-service Education." Catalyst for Change 2(Winter, 1973): 14-17.

Walker, Edith V. "In-Service Training of Teachers to Work with the Disadvantaged." Reading Teacher, Mr, 1965.

Walton, Joseph M. "An Instrument for Measuring Attitudes Toward Teaching in the Inner-City School." Journal of the Student Personnel Association for Teacher Evaluation 13(Je, 1975):177-183.

Ward, Blaine E. A Survey of Microteaching in NCATE-Accredited Secondary Education Programs. Stanford, CA: Stanford Center for Research and Development in Teaching, Stanford U., D, 1970.

Ward, Clell, and Clark, Robert. Racism and the Desegregating Process: A Mississippi Study. Jackson, MI: Educational Resources Center, 1970.

Warren, Sue Allen and others. "Teacher Nominations of Minority and Low SES Students for Special Education." Education 96(F, 1975): 57-62.

Washington, Booker T. "White Teachers for Negroes." Atlantic 86(Ag 8, 1900):287.

Washington, Oscar Douglas. "The Perceptions of Black and White Teachers of Black Students." Doctoral dissertation, Saint Louis U., 1973. Univ. Microfilms Order No. 74-04589.

Washington, Valora. "Desegregation Attitudes, Perceptions, and Classroom Behavior of Black and White Teachers of Second Grade: Group Profiles and Interrelationships in Integrated Settings." Doctoral dissertation, Indiana U., 1978. Univ. Microfilms Order No. 7821776.

Watkins, Charles Edward. "White Teacher's Evaluations of Black Children's Speech." Doctoral dissertation, U. of Texas at Austin, 1974. Univ. Microfilms Order No. 75-04472.

Weinberg, Dorothe R. The Racially Changing School: Negative Teacher Perceptions of Afro-American Students as a Response to Change, Rather than "Cultural Difference," Ap, 1976. ERIC ED 123 293. [Chicago]

Weinberg, Meyer. "Desegregation and School Staff." Research Review of Equal Education 1(Winter, 1977):26-29.

Wennersten, John R. "Preparing Teachers for the Realities of Desegregation and Integration." Education 94(F-Mr, 1974):269-272.

White, Louise R. "Effective Teachers for Inner City Schools." Journal of Negro Education 42(Summer, 1973):308-314.

White, William F., and Hall, Morrill. "Multidimensional Comparison of the Attitudes of Superintendents and Teachers in Majority Negro School Districts of the South." Journal of Educational Research 63(Ap, 1970): 339-343.

Whitmore, Joanne R., Crist, Janet L., and Marx, Ronald W. An Experimental In-Service Teacher Education Program for Distressed Elementary Schools. Stanford, CA: School of Education, Stanford U., F, 1974.

Wiggins, Phyliss W. "'Race Still Intimidates Us.'" Today's Education 66(N-D, 1977).

Wilcox, Preston R. "Teacher Attitudes and Student Achievement." Teachers College Record, F, 1967.

Wiles, David K. "The Mosaic Composition of Urban School Teachers." Urban Education 5 (Jl, 1970):141-151.

_____. "Racial Attitudes of Inner-City Teachers." Urban Education 6(Jl-O, 1971):273-278.

Willens, Howard P. and others. United States of American, Plaintiff, and North Carolina Association of Educators, et al., Plaintiff-Intervenors, v. State of North Carolina, et al., Defendants. Brief Amicus Curiae for Educational Testing Service, My 1, 1975. ERIC ED 121 806. [Racial discrimination in the use of the National Teacher Examination]

Willerman, Marvin. "A Study of the Effect of Objective Student Information on Teacher Perception of Culturally Disadvantaged Children." Illinois School Research 8(Fall, 1971):33-36.

Williams, Frederick, and Whitehead, Jack L. "Language in the Classroom: Studies of the Pygmalion Effect." English Record 21 (Ap, 1971):108-113.

Willie, Charles V. The Student-Teacher Relationship Experienced by Black Students at White Colleges, S 1, 1971. ERIC ED 056 156.

Willis, Bill J. "The Influence of Teacher Expectations on Teacher Interactions with Selected Children." Doctoral dissertation, George Peabody College, 1966.

Willis, S. L. "Formation of Teachers' Expectations of Students' Academic Performance." Diss. Abstr. Int'l., My, 1973, 33(9-A):4960.

Winecoff, H. Larry, and Kelly, Eugene W., Jr. "Teachers, Free of Prejudice?" Integrated Education, My-Je, 1969.

Wittmer, Joe, and Ferinden, Fred. "Perception of School Climate: A Comparison of Black and White Teachers within the Same Schools." Journal of the Student Personnel Association for Teacher Education 9(F, 1970):1-7.

Woodworth, William D., and Salzer, Richard T. "Black Children's Speech and Teachers' Evaluations." Urban Education 6(J1-O, 1971): 167-173.

4X, Alonzo. "Black President Promises Relevance for Largest Teachers' Association." Muhammad Speaks, S 6, 1974. [James Harris, NEA]

Yando, Regina, Zigler, Edward, and Gates, Maxine. "The Influence of Negro and White Teachers Rated as Effective or Noneffective on the Performance of Negro and White Lower-Class Children." Developmental Psychology 5(S, 1971):290-299.

Ziegler, Harmon. The Political Life of American Teachers. Englewood Cliffs, NJ: Prentice-Hall, 1967.

Zucker, Stanley H., and Prieto, Alfonso S. Teacher Bias in Special Class Placement, My, 1978. ERIC ED 153 398.

Counselors

Anderson, David C. "'Soul Killing' Integration Problems." Wall Street Journal, Je 11, 1968.

Anshin, Roman N. The Role of a Psychiatric Consultant to a Public High School in Racial Transition: Challenge and Response, 1970, 11 pp. Los Angeles: Cedars-Sinai Medical Center. ERIC ED 040 471.

Arnez, Nancy L. "Racial Understanding Through Literature." English Journal, Ja, 1969.

Arnez, Nancy L., and Anthony, C. "Working with Disadvantaged Negro Youth in Urban Schools." School and Society, Mr 30, 1968.

Backner, Burton L. "Counselling Black Students: Any Place for Whitey?" Journal of Higher Education 41(N, 1970):630-637.

Baehr, Rufus F. "'Negro Dialect' and the Motive to Achieve." Integrated Education, F-Mr, 1966.

Banks, George P. "The Effects of Race on One-to-One Helping Interviews." Social Service Review 45(Je, 1971):137-146.

Banks, William M. "The Effects of Race, Social Class, and Empathy on the Initial Counseling Interview." Doctoral dissertation, U. of Kentucky, 1968.

_____. "Militant Black Counselors: Riffraff or Vanguard?" Personnel and Guidance Journal 50(Mr, 1972):581-584.

_____. "Models of Culture and School Counselors: The Predicament of Black Youth." Anthropology and Education Quarterly 9) (Summer, 1978):137-147.

Barney, O. Pat, and Hall, Lurel D. "A Study in Discrimination." Personnel and Guidance Journal, Mr, 1965. [High school counseling]

Baum, B. "Integrated Club." Parents' Magazine, N, 1963.

Bell, Robert L., Jr. "The Culturally Deprived Psychologist." Counseling Psychologist 2 (1971):104-107.

Berlin, I. N. "Desegregation Creates Problems Too." Saturday Review, Je 15, 1963.

Blake, Elias, Jr. "A Re-definition of Educational Problems Occasioned by Desegregation and Title IV of the Civil Rights Act of 1964." In U.S. Commission on Civil Rights, Papers Prepared for National Conference on Equal Educational Opportunity in America's Cities. Washington, DC: GPO, 1968.

Bolden, James A. "Black Students and the School Counselor." School Counselor 17(1970):204-207.

Bolden, Wiley S. and others. A Report: Institute for the Preparation of Counselors and Teacher-Counselors for Effective Service and Leadership in Desegregated Schools, June 20-July 22, 1966, N, 1966, 85 pp. Atlanta: Clark College. ERIC ED 056 124.

Boney, J. Don. "Predicting the Academic Achievement of Secondary School Negro Students." Personnel and Guidance Journal, Mr, 1966.

Briggs, William A., and Hummel, Dean L. _Counseling Minority Group Youth._ Columbus, OH: Ohio Civil Rights Commission, 1962.

Brown, Otha N., Jr. "School Counselors. A New Role and Image for the '70s." _Connecticut Teacher_ 39(Mr, 1972):4-7.

Bryson, Seymour L. "The Relationship of Race to Level of Understanding in the Initial Counseling Interview." Doctoral dissertation, Southern Illinois U., 1972.

Bryson, Seymour L., and Mouw, John T. "Race, Understanding, and Counseling." _Integrated Education_ 11(J1-O, 1973):64-67.

Burrell, Leon, and Rayder, Nicholas F. "Black and White Students' Attitudes Toward White Counselors." _Journal of Negro Education_ 40 (Winter, 1971):48-52.

Calhoun, Lillian S. "Chicago's Ben Bloom--All Can Learn." _Integrated Education_ (My, Je, 1969):16-20.

Caliguri, Joseph. "Student Human Relations Committee--Tokenism or Not?" _Journal of Human Relations_, First Quarter, 1969.

Cappelluzzo, Emma M. _Guidance and the Migrant Child._ Boston: Houghton Mifflin, 1971.

Carson, A. S. "Verbal Comprehension and Communication in Negro and White Children." _Journal of Educational Psychology_ 6(1960).

Catalano, Thelma P. "The Process of Mutual Redefinition--Counseling and Teaching Children from Urban Slums." In _The Urban R's._ Edited by Robert A. Dentler and Others. New York: Praeger, 1967.

Cazden, Courtney B. "Subcultural Differences in Child Language: An Inter-Disciplinary Review." _Merill-Palmer Quarterly_, J1, 1966.

Chesler, Mark A., and Schaible, L. (eds.). _Reflections on School Desegregation: IV._ Ann Arbor, MI: Institute for Social Research, 1967.

Chiavetta, Donald. "Certificated Black School Counselors: Role Conflict and Loci of Controls." Doctoral dissertation, Case Western Reserve U., 1972.

Chick, Joyce M. _A Special Desegregation Training Institute for Counselors: Race, Culture and Interracial Group Processes._ Technical Report, Mr, 1968, 112 pp. Tallahassee, FL: Florida State U., Department of Counseling Education. Washington, DC: DHEW, Bureau of Research. ERIC ED 021 278.

Cimbolic, Peter. "Counselor Race and Experience Effects on Black Clients." _Journal of Consulting and Clinical Psychology_ 39(O, 1972): 328-332.

Clark, Joanna. "Counseling of the Culturally Deprived: A Survey of High School Counselors' Opinions and Attitudes." _School Counselor_ 19(Ja, 1972):201-209.

Coffin, Brenda S., Dietz, Siegfried C., and Thompson, Charles L. "Academic Achievement in a Poverty Area High School: Implications for Counseling." _Journal of Negro Education_ 40(Fall, 1971):365-368. [Crockett County, TN]

Coffman, David. "The Use of Advocacy and Confrontation in Counseling the Disadvantaged." _Journal of Employment Counseling_ 7(Ag, 1970): 83-87.

Davis, Helen H., and Greenberg, Judith W. _Traits of School Achievers from a Deprived Background_, My, 1967, 308 pp. New York: City U. of New York City College. ERIC ED 013 849.

Dentler, Robert A., and Elkins, Constance. "Intergroup Attitudes, Academic Performance, and Racial Composition." In _The Urban R's._ Edited by Robert A. Dentler and Others. New York: Praeger, 1967.

Edwards, G. Bentley, and Wilson, Alan B. _Attitudes as Related to Success in School._ Moravia, NY: Chronicle Guidance Publications, Inc., 1963.

Elliott, Delbert S., Voss, Harwin, L., and Wendling, Aubrey. "Capable Dropouts and the Social Milieu of the High School." _Journal of Educational Research_, D, 1966.

Fantini, Mario D., and Weinstein, Gerald. "Integration: Mandate for Educational Change." _Integrated Education_, D, 1964-Ja, 1965.

Fooks, Gordon M. "Dilemmas of Black Therapists." _Journal of Non-White Concerns in Personnel and Guidance_ 1(J1, 1973):181-191.

Franklin, Anderson J. "To Be Young, Gifted and Black with Inappropriate Professional Training: A Critique of Counseling Programs." _Counseling Psychologist_ 2(1971):107-112.

Garfield, John C. and others. "Effects of the Child's Social Class on School Counselor's Decision Making." _Journal of Counseling Psychology_ 20(Mr, 1973):166-168.

Georgeoff, Peter John. _The Elementary Curriculum as a Factor in Racial Understanding, Final Report._ Lafayette, IN: Purdue U., D, 1967.

Gibson, John S. _The Intergroup Relations Curriculum. A Program for Elementary School Education_, 2 volumes. Medford MA: Lincoln Filene Center for Citizenship and Public Affairs, Tufts U., 1969.

_____. Race and Culture in American Life: A Program for Elementary School Education. Medford, MA: Lincoln Filene Center for Citizenship and Public Affairs, Tufts U., D, 1967.

Gilberts, Richard and others. Teacher Perceptions of Race, Socio-Economic Status, and Language Characteristics, 1971, 24 pp. Whitewater, WI: Wisconsin State U., School of Education. ERIC ED 052 131.

Gold, Sandra. "The Effect of Counselor-Client Dissimilarity on Counselor Judgment." Diss. Abstr. Int'l., 31, 8-A(F, 1971):3952-3953.

Goldring, Paul. "The Initial Interview with Negro Adolescents." Diss. Abstr. Int'l., 30, 3-B(1969):1358.

Gordon, Edmund W. "Counseling Socially Disadvantaged Children." In Mental Health of the Poor. Edited by Frank Reissman, Jerome Cohen, and Arthur Pearl. New York: The Free Press, 1964.

_____. Guidance In An Urban Setting. ERIC Information Retrieval Center on the Disadvantaged. New York: Teachers College, Columbia U., Je, 1970.

_____. "Guidance in the Urban Setting." In Opening Opportunities for Disadvantaged Learners, pp. 205-216. Edited by A. Harry Passow. New York: Teachers College Press, 1972.

Graff, Robert W. and others. "Socio-Economic Status and Students' Reactions Toward School Guidance." High School Journal 54(My, 1971):484-492.

Grantham, Robert J. "Effects of Counselor Sex, Race and Language Style on Black Students in Initial Interviews." Journal of Counseling Psychology 20(N, 1973):553-559.

Grier, William. "When the Therapist is Negro: Some Effects on the Treatment Process." American Journal of Psychiatry 123(Je, 1967):1587-1592.

Gunnings, Thomas S. "Preparing the New Counselor." Counseling Psychologist 2(1971):100-101.

Hart, Robert T. "Toward More Effective Counseling of Minorities." Journal of College Placement 30(1969):71-74.

Heffernon, Andrew, and Bruehl, Dieter. "Some Effects of Race of Inexperienced Lay Counselors on Black Junior High School Students." Journal of School Psychology 9(1971):35-37.

Human Relations Education Project. Human Relations Education: A Guidebook to Learning Activities, 1969. Board of Education, 600 Highgate Avenue, Buffalo, NY 14215.

Jackson, Jonathan, and Kirkpatrick, David. Institute for the Preparation of Counselors and Teacher-Counselors for Effective Service and Leadership in Desegregated Schools, June 12-July 14, 1967. A Report, N, 1967, 83 pp. Atlanta: Clark College. ERIC ED 056 117.

Johnston, William Elbert, Jr., and Scales, Eldridge E. Counseling the Disadvantaged Student. Research Studies Series, Mr 25, 1968. ERIC ED 034 807.

Jones, Billy E. et al. "Problems of Black Psychiatric Residents in White Training Institutes." American Journal of Psychiatry 127(D, 1970):798-803.

Jones, Elizabeth Lovelace. "A Comparison of Problems Urban Black and White High School Students Are Willing to Discuss with a Counselor." Doctoral dissertation, U. of Florida, 1974. Univ. Microfilms Order No. 75-16, 399.

Jones, Martin H., and Jones, Martin C. "The Neglected Client." The Black Scholar 1(1970):35-42. [Counseling]

Jones, Reginald L. "Delivery of Special Services to Young Black Children." Journal of Non-White Concerns in Personnel and Guidance 1(Ja, 1973):61-68.

Kelly, Eugene W., Jr. Changes in Racial Prejudice and Dogmatism as a Result of Interracial Counselor Training Experiences, Ap, 1971, 14 pp. Columbia, SC: U. of South Carolina, Paper, American Personnel and Guidance Association. ERIC ED 055 304.

Khlief, Bud B. "A Socio-cultural Framework for Studying Guidance in Public Schools." In Guidance in American Education. III: Needs and Influencing Forces. Edited by D. Landy, and A. M. Kroll. Cambridge, MA: Harvard U. Press, 1966.

Klopf, Gordon J., and Bowman, Gerda. "Preparation of School Personnel to Work in an Urban Setting." Urban Affairs Quarterly, S, 1966.

Kornhauser, Stanley H. Planning for the Achievement of Quality Integrated Education in Desegregated Schools. New York: Board of Education, Je, 1968. [Released N 10, 1968]

Kranz, Peter L., and Siplin, Charles. "Reflective Partners: A Process Utilized in Positive Racial Change." California Personnel and Guidance Association Journal 4(F, 1971):6-8.

Kupferer, Harriet J., and Fitzgerald, Thomas K. Culture, Society and Guidance. Boston: Houghton Mifflin, 1971.

Lefkowitz, David M., and Baker, Judith. "Black Youth: A Counseling Experience." School Counselor 18(Mr, 1971):290-293.

Lewis, Michael D., and Lewis, Judith A. "Relevant Training for Relevant Roles: A Model for Educating Inner City Counselors." Counselor Education and Supervision 10(F, 1970):31-38.

Love, Ruth B. "Counseling the Disadvantaged Youth." C.T.A. Journal, Mr, 1965.

_____. "Some Answers to Administrators' Questions on Counseling Minority Youth." California Education, F, 1966.

Menacker, Julius. Urban Poor Students and Guidance. Boston: Houghton Mifflin, 1971.

Mitchell, Horace. "Counseling Black Students: A Model in Response to the Need for Relevant Counselor Training Programs." Counseling Psychologist 2(1971):117-122.

Moody, Charles D., Vergon, Charles B., Black, Maureen Sims, and Leonard, Jean M. (eds.). Proceedings of the Conference on the Personnel Director in the Desegregation Process. Ann Arbor, MI: Program for Educational Opportunity, School of Education, U. of Michigan, n.d.

Murphy, Michael C. and others. "School Desegregation and the Role of the Urban Counselor." Journal of Black Psychology 3(Ag, 1976):87-99.

Newton, Josephine K. "The Pupil Personnel Worker in Racial Conflict." Journal of the International Association of Pupil Personnel Workers 15(Je, 1971):139-142.

Nielsen, Sandra. "A Counselor's Evaluation of a Black White Confrontation Group Conducted Within a High School." California Personnel and Guidance Association Journal 3(F, 1970):20-26.

Noble, Jeanne L. "Guidance and Counseling of Minority Youth." In Guidance-Personnel Work: Future Tense. Edited by Margaret R. Smith. New York: Teachers College Press, 1966.

Ogilvie, Leila L. "Creativity: Its Nurture in the De Facto Segregated Negro Disadvantaged Urban Junior High School." Journal of the National Association of Women Deans and Counselors, Summer, 1968.

Owen, Isaiah. "Adlerian Counseling in Racially Mixed Groups of Elementary School Children." Individual Psychologist 7(N, 1970).

Pallone, Nathaniel J., Hurley, Robert B., and Richard, Fred S. "Black Students and School Counselors: Rhetoric and Reality." School Counselors 20(Mr, 1973):259-267.

Patterson, C. H. "Counselor Education for Black Counselors and for Counseling Black Clients: Comments." Counseling Psychologist 2(1971):112-113.

Pearl, Arthur. "Are You Sure Pupils Are Better Off at School?" Nation's Schools, Ag, 1966.

Pickholtz, Herschel J. "The Effects of a Child's Racial and Ethnic Label and Achievement Differences on School Psychologist's Decisions." Doctoral dissertation, Pennsylvania State U., 1977. Univ. Microfilms Order No. 7803353.

Price, Gerald J. "Counseling Minority Groups." Counseling and Values 17(F, 1972):35-44.

Proctor, Samuel A. "Reversing the Spiral Toward Futility." Personnel and Guidance Journal 48(My, 1970):707-712.

Record, Wilson. "Counseling and Color: Crisis and Conscience." Integrated Education, Ag-S, 1966.

Robinson, William A. "Discipline in Negro Schools." Crisis, F, 1932.

Robison, Helen F. "School Practices that Cause Failure." Childhood Education, N, 1967.

Rothney, John W. M. "Who Gets Counseled and For What?" In Freedom, Bureaucracy and Schooling, pp. 174-186. Edited by Vernon F. Hanbrich. Washington, DC: Association for Supervision and Curriculum Development, 1971.

Rousseve, Ronald J. "On Racial Gamesmanship and Anti-Intellectual Attitudes in Counselor Education." Counselor Education and Supervision 10(Summer, 1971):295-302.

_____. "Reason and Reality in Counseling the Student-Client Who Is Black." School Counselor 17(My, 1970):337-344.

Routh, Donald K., and King, Keith M. "Social Class Bias in Clinical Judgment." Journal of Consulting and Clinical Psychology 38 (Ap, 1972):202-207.

Russell, R. D. "Black Perceptions of Guidance." Personnel and Guidance Journal 48(My, 1970):721-728.

Schneider, Betty. "The Gap Widens." Community 29(1971):14-19. [Guidance counselor in inner city school]

Schoettler, Susan E. "The Role of the Counselor in School Desegregation." Master's thesis, California State U., Long Beach, 1978. Univ. Microfilms Order No. 13-11, 636.

Schumacher, Larry C. "Language Compatability and Minority Group Counseling." Journal of Counseling Psychology 19(My, 1972):255-256.

Counseling Bibliographies

Dewey, Richard E. (comp.). "Selected Bibliography for the Design of Urban Studies Programs." Urban Education 6(Ap, 1971):106-113.

Ohlinger, John (comp.). Bibliography of Comments on the Illich-Reiner Deschooling Theses, Ap, 1974. ERIC ED 090 145.

Sikes, Melvin P. "The Counseling Psychology Curriculum: A New Dimension." Counseling Psychologist 2(1971):102-104.

Smith, Gloria S. and others. "Counseling the Black Child." Elementary School Guidance and Counseling 8(My, 1974):245-253.

Smith, Paul M., Jr. "Black Activists for Liberation, Not Guidance." Personnel and Guidance Journal 49(My, 1971):721-726.

_____. "The Role of the Guidance Counselor in the Desegregation Process." Journal of Negro Education 40(Fall, 1971):347-351.

_____. The Role of the Guidance Counselor in the Desegregation Process. New York: Teachers College, Columbia U., N, 1969. ERIC ED 035 924.

Sweeney, Thomas J. Rural Poor Students and Guidance. Boston, MA: Houghton Mifflin, 1971.

Theimer, William C., Jr. Black Urban Students' View of Themselves and Their Counselors. Philadelphia, PA: Philadelphia School District, Office of Research and Evaluation, Mr 25, 1970. ERIC ED 040 247.

Tribble, Ike. "Motivational Counseling: A Black Educational Imperative." Educational Leadership 28(D, 1970):297-301.

U.S. Bureau of Labor Statistics. The Counselor and the Negro Student. Washington, DC: U.S. Department of Labor, 1967.

Van Buren, John D. "The School Counselor and the Challenge of Minority Students." Counseling and Values 16(Summer, 1972):303-308.

Vandenberg, Donald. "Ideology and Educational Policy." Journal of Educational Thought, Ap, 1967. [A probing analysis of the thinking behind ability grouping]

Vontress, Clemmont E. "The Black Militant as a Counselor." Personnel and Guidance Journal 50(Mr, 1972):576-580.

_____. "Counseling Blacks." Personnel and Guidance Journal 48(My, 1970):713-719.

_____. Counseling Negroes. Boston, MA: Houghton Mifflin, 1971.

_____. Counseling Racial and Ethnic Minorities in the United States, Mr, 1972. Paper, American Personnel and Guidance Association. ERIC ED 063 429.

_____. "Counseling the Culturally Different in Our Society." Employment Counseling, Mr, 1969.

_____. "Racial Differences: Impediments to Rapport." Journal of Counseling Psychology 18(Ja, 1971):7-13.

Washington, Bennetta B. "Perceptions and Possibilities." Personnel and Guidance Journal 48(My, 1970):757-761. [Role of the counselor]

Washington, Kenneth S. "What Counselors Must Know About Black Power." Personnel and Guidance Journal, N, 1968.

Washington, Kenneth R., and Anderson, Norma Jean. "Scarcity of Black Counselors: A Crisis in Urban Education." Journal of Non-White Concerns 2(Ja, 1974):99-105.

Washington, Kenneth R. "White Counselors and Black Students: An Analysis of the Problems Faced by Each." Notre Dame Journal of Education 4(Winter, 1973):322-327.

Willis, Jerry W. "Consultation in an Urban Ghetto School." Mental Hygiene 56(Winter, 1972):31-38.

Wittmer, Joe. "Effective Counseling of Children of Several American Subcultures." School Counselor 19(S, 1971):49-52.

Yates, Alfred (ed.). Groups in Education. New York: Wiley, 1966.

Zach, Lillian. "Training Psychologists for the Urban Slum School." Psychology in the Schools 7(O, 1970):345-350.

Administrators

Abney, Everett E., Sr. "The Status and Perceptions of Black Administrators in Florida." Doctoral dissertation, U. of Florida, 1971. Univ. Microfilms Order No. 72-21037.

Banks, Eugene M. "Career Aspirations of Black Male Principals in Large Northeastern Ohio Cities." Doctoral dissertation, U. of Akron, 1974. Univ. Microfilms Order No. 75-10520.

Barsky, Henry. "The Political Style of an Urban Principal: A Case Study." Doctoral dissertation, U. of Pennsylvania, 1975. Univ. Microfilms Order No. 76-11,194.

Billings, Maurita Miles. "The Job Satisfactions of Black School Administrators." Doctoral dissertation, Syracuse U., 1972. Univ. Microfilms Order No. 73-07706.

"Black Books Bulletin Interviews Barbara Sizemore." Blacks Books Bulletin 2(Winter, 1974):50-53.

Black School Superintendents: A Directory. New York: AFRAM Associates, 1971.

Blanton, Harry S. "The Relation of Behavioral Patterns of Selected Superintendents to the Process of Public School Desegregation." Doctoral dissertation, U. of Tennessee, 1959. Dissertation Abstracts, XX, 1959: 1237-1238.

Board of Education of Los Angeles. Administrators' In-Depth Seminars in Problems of Desegregation As They Relate to Large City Schools. Los Angeles, CA: Los Angeles City Schools, 1967.

Bond, Horace Mann (with Lester, L. M. and others). A Suggested Program for the Training of Principals for Small High Schools. Baton Rouge: N.p., 1938.

Bouch, Richard F. "Perceptions of Supervisory Techniques by Black and White Teachers and Principals in Selected Florida Schools." Doctoral dissertation, U. of Florida, 1976.

Brain, George B. (ed.). School Superintendents' Conference on the Practical Problems of Public School Desegregation. Bureau of Publications, Baltimore City Public Schools, 3 East 25th Street, Baltimore, MD 21218, 1964. [Report of conference of August 5-7, 1963]

Bullock, Charles S. III. "Defiance of the Law: School Discrimination Before and After Desegregation." Urban Education 11 (O, 1976):239-262. [Georgia]

Burt, Walter Lee. "The Impact of the 1964 Civil Rights Act--Title VI and Title VII-- On Employment of Black Administrators in Michigan School Districts from 1964-74." Doctoral dissertation, U. of Michigan, 1975. Univ. Microfilms Order No. 76-09358.

Buxton, Thomas H., and Prichard, Keith W. "The Power Erosion Syndrome of the Black Principal." Integrateducation 15 (My-Je, 1977).

Byrne, David R. and others. The Senior High School Principalship. Vol. I: The National Survey. Reston, VA: National Association of Secondary School Principals, 1978.

Calhoun, Lillian S. "The AASA's Missing Minorities." Integrated Education, My-Je, 1969: 71-74.

Candoli, I. Carl. "An Urban Superintendent Looks at School Desegregation." Theory Into Practice 17(F, 1978):17-22.

Clark, Joyce H. "Role and Function of the Minority Administrator." Journal of Non-White Concerns in Personnel and Guidance 5 (Ja, 1977):60-64.

Coffin, Gregory C. "The Black Administrator and How He's Being Pushed to Extinction." American School Board Journal 159(My, 1972): 33-35.

Colquit, Jesse Lee. "A 1972 Investigation of the Number and Level of Professional Assignments of Black Administrators in Indiana Public School Corporations as Compared with April 1969." Doctoral dissertation, Ball State U., 1972. Univ. Microfilms Order No. 73-04087.

_____. "The Increase of Black Administrators in Metropolitan School Systems." NASSP Bulletin 59(O, 1975):70-74.

Comer, Norman David. "An Analysis of Selected Racial Issues in Public Education as Perceived by Black School Administrators in the State of Indiana." Doctoral dissertation, Loyola U., 1974. Univ. Microfilms Order No. 74-23076.

Cuban, Larry. "School Chiefs Under Fire: A Study of Three Big-City Superintendents Under Outside Pressure." Doctoral dissertation, Stanford U., 1974. Univ. Microfilms Order No. 74-27,003.

Cunningham, Luvern L. "Hey, Man, You Our Principal?" Phi Delta Kappan, N, 1969.

Department of Research and Development. The Views of Pontiac School Principals on the Process of Desegregation. Pontiac, MI: School District of the City of Pontiac, Ag, 1972.

Desegregation Studies Unit. The Role of the School Principal in School Desegregation. Washington, DC: National Institute of Education, 1976.

Diaz, Ronald Phillip. "Racial, Ethnic, and Sexual Bias in Administrative Promotional Examinations." Doctoral dissertation, Claremont Graduate School, 1978. Univ. Microfilms Order No. 7823824. [Los Angeles, California]

Dolce, Carl J. "The Inner City--A Superintendent's View." Saturday Review, Ja 11, 1969.

Doughty, Rosie Nucklos. "An Exploration of Some Associations Between Student-Community Unrest and the Promotion of Black Administrators in Public Schools." Doctoral dissertation, Ohio State U., 1974. Univ. Microfilms Order No. 74-24316.

_____. "The Black Woman in School Administration." Integrateducation 15(Jl-Ag, 1977).

Duke, Ralph L. Institute for Administrators, Counselors, and Teachers on Selected Prob-Occasioned by School Desegregation and Integration, Ag 31, 1966. ERIC ED 056 105.

Edwards, Marvin Earl. "A Study of the Employ-ment of Black Superintendents and Principals in Illinois Public Schools." Doctoral dissertation, Northern Illinois U., 1974. Univ. Microfilms Order No. 75-13140.

Egerton, John. "When Desegregation Comes, the Negro Principals Go." Southern Education Report, D, 1967.

Ferrer, Terry. "The Tiptoers and the Marchers." Integrated Education, Je-Jl, 1965. [School administrators and civil rights]

Flannick, Nicholas A. "The Identification and the Analysis of Administrative Responses to Race-Related Incidents in Selected Urban High Schools." Doctoral dissertation, U. of Pittsburgh, 1973.

Ford, David L., Jr., and Gatewood, Lucian B. Organizational Responses to Minority Group Managers: Less than Satisfactory. Lafayette, IN: Institute for Research in the Behavioral, Economic and Management Sciences, Purdue U., 1975.

Fort, Edward B. "Attitudinal and Guidance Perspectives on the Urban Superintendency." Journal of Non-White Concerns in Personnel and Guidance 6(O, 1977):33-43.

Fox, Frances Juanita. "Black Women Adminis-trators in the Denver Public Schools." Doctoral dissertation, U. of Colorado, 1975. Univ. Microfilms Order No. 76-11574.

Frelow, Robert D. "Minority Administrators and Desegregation." Integrated Education 11 (My-Je, 1973):27-29.

Friedenberg, Edgar. "The Principal's Au-thority" (interview). This Magazine Is About Schools, Spring, 1968.

Fullington, Gail. "Soul Brother or Uncle Tom?" Phi Delta Kappan 57(Mr, 1976). [Black assistant principals in desegregated schools]

Glasgow, Ann Duncan. Black Leadership in Urban Schools. Framingham, MA: Wellesley Schools, 1974. [Black principals in D.C. schools]

_____. "The Self-Perceptions of Leadership of the Black Secondary School Principal." Afro-American Studies 2(Mr, 1972):225-238.

Glover, Dennis Fred. "The Perceived Impact of Use of Legal and Confrontation Procedures on the Continued Employment of Black Princi-pals in West Central Georgia, 1968-1973." Doctoral dissertation, U. of Colorado, 1974. Univ. Microfilms Order No. 74-22343.

Grant, Carl A. (ed.). Sifting and Winnowing: An Exploration of the Relationship Between Multi-Cultural Education and CBTE. Madison, WI: Teacher Corps Associates, U. of Wisconsin, 1975. [Competency-Based Teacher Education]

Haig, Theodore J. "An Assessment of Attitudes of School Committee Members and Administra-tors Toward Voluntary Collaborative Metro-politan Education." Doctoral dissertation, Boston College, 1976. [Boston area]

Harnischfeger, Annegret. "Personal and Insti-tutional Characteristics Affecting Teacher Mobility. I: Problems of Teacher Mobility." Studies of Educative Processes 1(Ap, 1973). [Early Education Research Center, U. of Chicago]

_____. "Personal and Institutional Charac-teristics Affecting Teacher Mobility. II: Descriptive Characteristics of the San Jose Unified School District." Studies of Edu-cative Processes 2(My, 1973). [Early Edu-cation Research Center, U. of Chicago]

_____. "Personal and Institutional Charac-teristics Affecting Teacher Mobility. III: Teacher Characteristics and Teacher Mobility: A Confusion of Causes." Studies of Educa-tive Processes 4(Ag, 1973). [Early Educa-tion Research Center, U. of Chicago]

_____. Personal and Institutional Character-istics Affecting Teacher Mobility: Schools Do Make a Difference. Stanford, CA: Stan-ford Center for Research and Development in Teaching, School of Education, Stanford U., My, 1975.

Haskins, Kenneth W. "You Have No Right to Put a Kid Out of School." Urban Review 8 (Winter, 1975):273-287.

Haynes, Carrie A. "A Happening in a Ghetto School." California Journal for Interna-tional Improvement 14(My, 1971):79-85. [Black principal, white teachers]

Hendricks, Harry George. "The Full-Time Negro Principalship in Texas." Doctoral disser-tation, U. of Colorado, 1960. Univ. Micro-films Order No. 61-00830.

Hobbs, Gardner J. "Perceived Teacher Satis-faction with Leadership of Selected Black and White Principals in Georgia High Schools." Doctoral dissertation, U. of Georgia, 1978. Univ. Microfilms Order No. 7901645.

Holland, Howard Eldon. "Black Administrators in the Philadelphia Public Schools, 1864-1975." Doctoral dissertation, The Pennsylvania State U., 1975. Univ. Microfilms Order No. 76-10737.

Hughes, Teresa P. "Self-Perception of Black and White Elementary School Administrators As Change Agents: A Comparative Study." Doctoral dissertation, Claremont Graduate School, 1972.

Ingram, Sam H. "Behavioral Patterns of Selected Superintendents During the Process of Public School Desegregation." Doctoral dissertation, U. of Tennessee, 1959.

Jackson, Maurice A. Schools That Change: A Report on Success Strategies for Dealing with Disruption, Violence, and Vandalism in Public High Schools, D, 1976. ERIC 151 965. [Principal]

James, J. C. "The Black Principal: Another Vanishing American." National Elementary Principal 50(F, 1971):20-25.

Jenkins, Jeanne Kohl. "Control Strategies: Responses of Public School Principals to School-Community Advisory Councils." Doctoral dissertation, U. of California, Los Angeles, 1974.

Johnson, Simon O. "A Study of the Perceptions of Black Administrators Concerning the Role of the Black Principal in Florida During the Period 1973-78." Journal of Negro Education 46(Winter, 1977):53-61.

Jones, John F. "A Descriptive Study of the Climate Within a Detroit Inner City Junior High School as Revealed by the Reporting of Undesirable Incidents and Class Reports of a Racially Changing Administration and Implications of Such a Climate for the Self-Concepts and Achievements of Black Students." Dissertation Abstracts International 32(5-A). N, 1971:2306.

Kenny, James B., and Gentry, Harold W. A Comparison of the Organizational Climates of Negro and White Elementary Schools with Concomitant Implications for School Administrators, n.d. ERIC ED 010 901.

Kern, Charles R. "White Principal, Black Student." NASSP Bulletin 59(Mr, 1975):34-38.

Kesl, Gary. "Principals and Community Power Structure in Florida." College Student Journal 9(S, 1975):287-289. [Homestead, Florida]

Kimmel, Lloyd Henry. "A Study of Selected Attitudes and Perceptions of Principals in the Court-Ordered Transfer of Teachers in the Atlanta Public Schools." Doctoral dissertation, Georgia State U., 1971. Univ. Microfilms Order No. 72-2984.

Kirby, David J. "The Political Beahvior of Big City School Superintendents." Doctoral dissertation, U. of Chicago, 1970.

Lutterbie, Patricia H. "Black Administrators: Winners and Losers." Integrated Education 12 (My-Je, 1974):42-45.

McCamey, Delener Sue. "The Status of Black and White Women in Central Administrative Positions in Michigan Public Schools." Doctoral dissertation, U. of Michigan, 1976. Univ. Microfilms Order No. 77-07987.

McCarther, Will Edward. "An Analysis of the Special Problems and Needs of Black Teachers and Administrators Who Work in Predominantly White School Districts in the State of Iowa." Doctoral dissertation, U. of Iowa, 1974. Univ. Microfilms Order No. 75-01227.

McClain, Freddie. "Correlates of Job Satisfaction of Black Superintendents." Doctoral dissertation, U. of Michigan, 1974. Univ. Microfilms Order No. 74-25266.

McKelvey, Troy V., and Swanson, Austin D. (eds). Urban School Administration, Beverly Hills, CA: Sage, 1969.

Madison, Alfred Morgan. "On Being the First Black Administrator in an Elementary School District." Doctoral dissertation, United States International U., 1970. Univ. Microfilms Order No. 70-22339.

Maguire, John W. "School Principals and Community Power Structure." Intellect 102 (Summer, 1974):510-511.

Maxwell, William, Jr. "A Challenge to the Black Superintendant." Phi Delta Kappan 56(Ap, 1975):523, 547.

Mayhand, Edna, and Grusky, Oscar. "A Preliminary Experiment on the Effects of Black Supervision on White and Black: Subordinates." Journal of Black Studies 2(Je, 1972):461-470.

Mazzoni, Tim L., Jr. "Political Capability for Urban School Governance: An Anslysis of the Los Angeles City School Board (1967-1969)." Doctoral dissertation, Claremong Graduate School, 1971.

Michelson, Stephan. "Principal Power." Inequality in Education 5(Je 30, 1970).

Moffett, Carlton C. "A Study of Administrator Perceptions of the Effectiveness of Practices to Facilitate the Desegregation Process of Selected School Districts." Doctoral dissertation, North Texas State U., 1976.

Monteiro, Thomas. "Ethnicity and the Perceptions of Principals." Integrateducation 15(My-Je, 1977).

Moody, Charles David. "The Black Superintendent." School Review 81(My, 1973):375-382.

_____. "Black Superintendents in Public
School Districts: Trends and Conditions."
Doctoral dissertation, Northwestern U.,
1971.

Moore, Archie Bradford, Jr. "A Descriptive
Study of the Effects of School Desegregation
on Black Secondary Principals in Alabama.
1967-1973." Doctoral dissertation, Kansas
State U., 1974. Univ. Microfilms Order No.
74-25610.

_____. "The Disturbing Revelation of the Pre-
dicament of Black Principals in Southern
School Districts." Urban Education 12(J1,
1977):213-216.

Moore, William. "The Role of Administrators in
the Educational Process." In Restructuring
the Educational Process: A Black Perspective.
Edited by Lawrence E. Gary and Aaron Favors.
Washington, DC: Institute for Urban
Affairs and Research, Howard U., 1975.

Nabrit, Samuel M., and Scott, J. S., Jr.
Inventory of Academic Leadership: An Analy-
sis of the Boards of Trustees of Fifty
Predominantly Negro Institutions. Atlanta,
GA: Southern Fellowships Fund, 1970.

Orr, Joseph A. "The Displacement of Black
High School Principals in Selected Florida
Counties and its Relationship to Public
School Desegregation Within Them: 1967-1972."
Doctoral dissertation, Florida State U.,
1972. Univ. Microfilms Order No. 73-04698.

Recruitment Leadership and Training Institute.
Minorities in Policy-Making Positions in
Public Education, N, 1974. ERIC ED 100 871.

Rhodes, George R., Jr. How Does a School Administrator Deal with Black Separatism in the
Public Schools, F 22, 1971. ERIC ED 049 545.

Robinson, Thomas Joseph. "Chief Black School
Administrators: A Critical Look at the Spe-
cific Factors Involved in the Selection of
Chief School Administrators Who are Black."
Doctoral dissertation, Michigan State U.,
1973. Univ. Microfilms Order No. 74-06116.

Rothstein, Stanley W. "Researching the Power
and Institutionalized Charisma in the
Principalship." Interchange 6(1975):41-48.

Rouse, Donald Eugene. "Career Aspirations of
Black Male School Administrators in a
Large Urban School System." Doctoral dis-
sertation, Pennsylvania State U., 1973.
Univ. Microfilms Order No. 74-04284.

Roye, Wendell J. "Black Principals: Vanishing
Americans or Out-Flanked Agents?" NCRIEEO
Tipsheet 7, F, 1972.

School Administrators Committee. What Is School-
Community-Based Teacher Education and Why
Should Administrators Be Interested In It?
Lincoln, NE: Nebraska Curriculum Development
Center, U. of Nebraska, 1975.

Schultz, Michael John, Jr. "The National Education Association and the Negro Teacher: The
Integration of a Professional Organization."
Doctoral dissertation, U. of Pittsburgh,
1969. Univ. Microfilms Order No. 69-21042.

Scott, Hugh J. "Black Consciousness and Professionalism." Journal of Negro Education
44(Summer, 1975):432-440.

_____. "The Black School Superintendent."
Integrateducation 15(Ja-F, 1977).

_____. "The Black School Administrator and
the Black Community." Integrated Education
(J1-Ag, 1969):52-56.

_____. The Emerging Black School Superinten-
dent: Messiah or Sacrificial Lamb? Washington, DC: Howard U. Press, 1977.

Scott, Hugh J., and Guthrie, James W. "Marcus
A. Foster: Tribute and Reflection."
Phi Delta Kappan 55(F, 1974):413-414.

Scruggs, James A. "How Black Administrators
View Their Status Today." Phi Delta Kappan,
Ap, 1977.

Shedd, Mark R., Hamilton, Charles C. D., and
Munger, Mark. "Developing Leadership
Training for Big-City Principals." Educa-
tion and Urban Society 6(My, 1974):253-268.

Smey, Barbara A. "Busing--Stop or Go? Interviews With School Superintendents." Research
Bulletin 19(Spring, 1974):4-10.

Smith, Calvert Hayes. "The Case for Black
Principals in Black Inner City Schools."
Afro-American Studies 1(Ja, 1971):211-216.

Smith, John W., and Smith, Betty M. "For
Black Educators: Integration Brings the
Axe." Urban Review 6(1973).

Steward, Gustavus Adolphus. "School Executives:
Random Types." Crisis, Ap, 1934.

Stones, Michael E. "School Administrator
Attitudes and Racism." Integrated Education
11(Mr-Ap, 1973):54-59.

Swider, John A. "A Study to Determine the Effect
of Black Administrators on Discipline Problems of Black Students." Master's thesis,
Glassboro State College, 1972.

Teitelbaum, Deena, and Lee, James C. Develop-
ment of Selection Criteria for Elementary
School Principals of Inner City Schools.
Final Report, Mr, 1972. ERIC ED 062 732.

Terkel, Studs. "Two Superintendents Discuss
Integration. An Interview." Integrated
Education, Ag-S, 1967. [Neil V. Sullivan
and Gregory C. Coffin]

Thomas, Charles R. "Unique Problems Confronting Black School Administrators," F, 1972.
ERIC ED 061 613.

Thornsley, J. R. "The Superintendent's Leadership Techniques for Inter-Group Racial and Ethnic Relations in Desegregated Schools." Doctoral dissertation, U. of Southern California, 1969.

Townsel, Charles W., and Banks, Loubertha A. "The Urban School Administrator--A Black Perspective." Journal of Negro Education 44(Summer, 1975):421-431.

Travaglio, Ray and others. "Difficulties of Black Supervisors." Training and Development Journal 25(F, 1971):33-34.

Travillion, Joseph T., Jr. "A Study of Characteristics and Career Patterns of White and Non-White Elementary Principals in Four Urban School Systems." Doctoral dissertation, U. of Colorado, 1973.

Trubowitz, Sidney. "Confessions of a Ghetto Administrator." Phi Delta Kappan 53(D, 1971):210-213.

Trusty, Francis M. Development and Implementation of a Pilot Program to Prepare Negro Administrators for Top Level Line Positions, D, 1970. ERIC ED 048 657.

Turnage, Martha. "The Principal: Change Agent in Desegregation." Integrated Education (Mr-Ap, 1972):41-45.

_____. "The Public School Principal and Desegregation. The Principal as Change Agent." Master's thesis, College of William and Mary, 1970.

_____. The Principal: Change-Agent in Desegregation. Chicago, IL: Integrated Education Associates, 1972.

U.S. Congress, 92nd, 1st session, Senate, Select Committee on Equal Educational Opportunity. Equal Educational Opportunity-- 1971. Hearings... Part 10. Displacement and Present Status of Black School Principals in Desegregated School Districts. Washington, DC: GPO, 1971.

Valverde, Leonard A. Succession Socialization: Its Influence on School Administrative Candidates and Its Implication to the Exclusion of Minorities from Administration, 1974. ERIC ED 093 052.

_____. "Succession Socialization: The Filtering-Out of Women and Minorities from Administration." California Journal of Teacher Education 2(Spring, 1975):93-110.

Vann, Albert. "Special Program to Train Blacks and Puerto Ricans for Principals." Negro Teachers Forum, Mr-Ap, 1967. [New York City]

Ward, Albert Abraham. "The American Association of School Administrators and the Development of Black Educational Leaders." Doctoral dissertation, U. of Michigan, 1971. Univ. Microfilms Order No. 72-14779.

Washington, Philemon. "The Job Satisfaction of Black Public School Administrators in New Jersey." Doctoral dissertation, U. of Minnesota, 1974. Univ. Microfilms Order No. 75-12177.

Waters, Eldred Keith. "Critical Incidents of Administrative Behavior in Urban Schools Where There Have Been Drastic Changes in Black-White Ratios." Doctoral dissertation, U. of Florida, 1972.

White, Thomas Richard. "Racial Knowledge of School Administrators in a Midwestern City With Low Minority Visibility as Compared to the Racial Knowledge of School Administrators in a Midwestern City." Doctoral dissertation, U. of Iowa, 1974. Univ. Microfilms Order No. 75-13,846.

Wiley, Bennie L. "A Different Breed of Administrator." Phi Delta Kappan 52(My, 1971): 550. [Black administrators]

Wilson, Don J. "A Historical Analysis of the Black Administrator in the Los Angeles Unified School District." Doctoral dissertation, U. of California, Los Angeles, 1972. Univ. Microfilms Order No. 72-34000.

_____. "Attitudes of Black Administrators in Los Angeles." Integrateducation 13(Jl-Ag, 1975):41-42.

Wilson, Laval S. "Training Minority Men for the Superintendency." Phi Delta Kappan 53 (N, 1971):187-188.

Wolcott, Harry F. The Man in the Principal's Office. New York: Holt, Rinehart & Winston, 1973.

Woodard, Samuel L. (ed.). Reducing Stress on Black Administrators. New York: Vantage Press, 1978.

Yee, Albert H. "Do Principals' Interpersonal Attitudes Agree with Those of Teachers and Pupils?" Educational Administration Quarterly 6(Spring, 1970):1-13.

Zeigler, Harmon, and Boss, Michael. "Racial Problems and Policy in the American Public Schools." Sociology of Education 47 (Summer, 1974):319-336. [School board members and superintendents]

Other School Staff Studies

Allen, Beur P. "Social Distance Reactions to Black and White Communicators: A Replication of an Investigation in Support of Belief Congruence Theory." *Psychonomic Science* 22(Mr, 1971):344.

Banks, William M. "The Differential Effects of Race and Social Class in Helping." *Journal of Clinical Psychology* 28(Ja, 1972):90–92.

Barrett, Franklin T., and Perlmutter, Felice. "Black Clients and White Workers: A Report from the Field." *Child Welfare* 59(Ja, 1972):19–24.

Blumenberg, Eleanor. "The School Intergroup Relations Specialist: A Profession in Process." *Sociology of Education*, Spring, 1968.

Boroskin, Alan, and Giampiecolo, James S. "Effect of Staff Ethnocentrism on the Rating of Self-Help Skills of Minority Group Mentally Retarded Patients." *American Journal of Mental Deficiency* 76(S, 1971):249–251.

Bouvier, Jean-Marie. "Education politique et enseignement." *Pedagogie* 3(Mr, 1972):247–254.

Rosenshine, Barak, and Furst, Norma. *The Effects of Tutoring upon Pupil Achievement: A Research Review*, 1969. ERIC ED 064 462.

Rydingsword, Carl. "The Human Relations Specialist: A Child of Desegregation: An Interview with Nathaniel Jackson." In Norene Harris, Nathaniel Jackson, and Rydingsword and contributors. *The Integration of American Schools: Problems, Experiences, Solutions*. Boston, MA: Allyn and Bacon, 1975.

Savage, James E. "Testers' Influence on Children's Intellectual Performance." Doctoral dissertation, Northwestern U., 1971.

Savage, James E., Jr., and Bowers, Norman D. *Testers' Influence on Children's Intellectual Performance*, Ap, 1972. ERIC ED 064 329.

Seligman, Michele. "The Interracial Casework Relationship." *Smith College Studies in Social Work* 39(N, 1968).

Silverstein, Sandra. "White Ghetto Worker." *Child Welfare* 55(Ap, 1976):257–268.

Smith, Arthur L., Hernandez, Deluvina, and Allen, Anne. *How to Talk with People of Other Races, Ethnic Groups, and Cultures*, 1971. Trans-Ethnic Education/Communication Foundation, P.O. Box 24740, Los Angeles, CA 90024.

Smith, Kathleen (ed.). *Desegregation/Integration: Planning for School Change. A Training Program for Intergroup Educators*, 1974. ERIC ED 098 271.

Solkoff, Norman. "Race of Experimenter as a Variable in Research with Children." *Developmental Psychology* 7(Jl, 1972):70–75.

Stelzer, L. "School Board Receptivity--A Representational Study." *Education and Urban Society* 5(N, 1972).

Turner, Charles. "Effects of Race of Tester and Need for Approval on Children's Learning." *Journal of Educational Psychology* 62 (Je, 1971):240–244.

Turner, John B. "Education for Practice with Minorities." *Social Work* 17(My, 1972):112–118.

Vail, Susan. "The Effects of Socio-Economic Class, Race, and Level of Experience on Social Workers' Judgments of Clients." *Smith College Studies in Social Work* 40 (Je, 1970):236–246.

Veltman, Calvin J. "The Resistance of Respondents in Interethnic Interviewing." *Sociology and Social Research* 56(Jl, 1972):513–521.

Vincent, George Monroe. "A Study of Black School Board Members in Mississippi School Districts, 1969-1973." Doctoral dissertation, U. of Colorado, 1974. Univ. Microfilms Order No. 74-22406.

Wallach, Michael A. "The Humble Things We Know--and Ignore--About Quality in Elementary Education." *Harvard Educational Review* 41(N, 1971):542–549.

White, William F., and Bashaw, W. L. "High Self-Esteem and Identification with Adult Models Among Economically Deprived Children." *Perceptual and Motor Skills* 33(D, 1971):1127–1130.

Yamamoto, J. and others. "Racial Factors in Patient Selection." *American Journal of Psychiatry* 124(1967):84–90.

Ziegler, H., Jennings, K., and Peak, M. *Governing American Schools*. New York: Duxbury, 1974.

Bibliographies

Bureau of Guidance. *Elementary School Guidance: An Annotated Bibliography*. Albany, NY: U. of the State of New York, 1966.

Charters, W. W., Jr. (comp.). *A Bibliography of Empirical Studies of School Boards, 1952-1968*. Eugene, OR: Center for the Advanced Study of Educational Administration, U. of Oregon, 1968.

Community Relations Commission. _A Bibliography_
for Teachers of Immigrants. London: The
Commission, 1971.

_____. _Education for a Multi-Cultural Society._
A Bibliography for Teachers. London: The
Commission, 1972.

Coskey, Owen L., and Hodges, Jimmy (comps.).
A Resource and Reference Bibliography on
Teaching and Counseling the Bilingual Stu-
dent. Lubbock, TX: School of Education,
Texas Technological College Mr, 1968.

Education for a Multi-Cultural Society--A Bib-
liography for Teachers, 1972. Community
Relations Commission, Russell Square House,
Russell Square, London WC1, England.

Great Britain. Community Relations Commission
(comp.). _A Bibliography for Teachers of_
Immigrants. London: Community Relations, n.d.

Halligan, John M. (comp.). "An Annotated
Bibliography of Material Related to the
Effects of a Teacher's Attitude on the
Ability of Students to Learn." Master's
thesis, California State U., Sacramento,
1972.

Love, Ruth B. _References on Counseling_
Minority Youth: A Four Part Series, Je,
1964. ERIC ED 034 232.

New York Bureau of School Social Services.
School Social Work: Annotated Bibliography.
Albany, NY: The Bureau, 1968.

Noble, Vincente and others (comps.). _Counsel-_
ing the Black Client. An Annotated Bibliog-
raphy of Journal Literature, 1964-1974,
1974. ERIC ED 130 201.

Piele, Philip K. (comp.). _New Programs for_
Training School Administrators. Eugene,
OR: ERIC Clearinghouse on Educational
Administration, U. of Oregon, S, 1970.
[Bibliography]

_____ (comp.). _New Sets of Jobs for School_
Personnel. Eugene, OR: ERIC Clearinghouse
on Educational Administration, U. of Oregon,
S, 1970. [Bibliography]

10.
COMPENSATORY EDUCATION

General

Abelson, Willa D. and others. "Effects of a Four-Year Follow Through Program on Economically Disadvantaged Children." Journal of Educational Psychology 66(O, 1974):756–771.

Agger, Robert E., and Fashing, Joseph J. Effects of Educational Innovations for the Culturally Deprived on Citizen Support for the Schools, 1969, 218 pp. Eugene, OR: Oregon U. ERIC ED 031 976.

Alsop, Joseph. "Alsop Fires a Salvo at Schwartz-Pettigrew-Smith." Nation's Schools, Ap, 1968.

———. "Ghetto Schools." New Republic, N 18, 1967.

American Institutes for Research. ESEA Title I: A Reanalysis and Synthesis of Evaluation Data from Fiscal Year 1965 Through 1970. Palo Alto, CA: American Institutes for Research, Mr, 1972.

———. A Study of Selected Exemplary Programs for the Education of Disadvantaged Children. Final Report, Parts I and II. Palo Alto, CA: American Institutes for Research, S, 1968.

Anastasi, Anne. "Culture-Fair Testing." Educational Horizons, Fall, 1964.

Anderson, Richard B. "The Effectiveness of Follow Through: Evidence from the National Analysis." Curriculum Inquiry 7(F, 1977):209–226.

Antes, John, and Antes, Marilyn. "Art Programs for Disadvantaged Youth." School Arts 71 (Mr, 1972):22–25.

Applebaum, Wayne R., and Adkins, Deberie Gomez. Teacher Attitudes Towards Compensatory Education Programs in the Dallas Independent School Districts, 1977. ERIC ED 141 446.

Arons, Stephen. "The Political Reorganization of Schools: Decentralization and Alternatives to Public Education." Inequality in Education 1 (1970):6–8.

Ausubel, David P. "A Teaching Strategy for Culturally Deprived Pupils: Cognitive and Motivational Considerations." School Review, Winter, 1963.

Ball, Samuel and others. The First Year of Sesame Street: An Evaluation. Final Report, Volume III of V Volumes, O, 1970, 442 pp. Princeton, NJ: Educational Testing Service. ERIC ED 047 823.

Bantock, G. H. "Are We in the Wrong Struggle?" Times Educational Supplement, O 5, 1973. [Working-class children and educational deprivation]

Baratz, Joan C. A Culturally-Based Education System for the Disadvantaged, D 15, 1971. ERIC ED 088 971.

Baratz, Joan C., and Shuy, Roger W. (eds.). Teaching Black Children to Read. Washington, DC: Center for Applied Linguistics, 1969.

Barlow, Bruce. "The Long-Term Effect of Remedial Reading Instruction." Reading Teacher, Ap, 1965.

Barratt, D. J. "An Analysis of the Use Made of the Work of Basil Bernstein in Studies on the Language of Culturally Deprived Children." Master's thesis, U. of Liverpool, 1974.

Barro, Stephen M. "An Approach to Developing Accountability Measures for the Public Schools." Phi Delta Kappan 52(D, 1970):196–205.

———. An Approach to Developing Accountability Measures for the Public Schools, S, 1970. AD 712 851. Springfield. VA: National Technical Information Service.

Beilin, Harry, and Gotkin, Lasser G. "Psychological Issues in the Development of Mathematics Curricula for Socially Disadvantaged Children." Conference on Mathematics Education for Below Average Achievers. Stanford, CA: School Mathematics Study Group, 1964.

Bereiter, Carl, and Engelmann, Siegfried. Teaching Disadvantaged Children in the Preschool. Englewood Cliffs, NJ: Prentice-Hall, 1966.

Berndt, Catherine H., Boissevain, Ethel, Bushnell, John H., Carstens, Peter, Gladwin, Thomas, Hannerz, Ulf, Kochar, V. K., Leacock, Eleanor, Lewis, Orin, Mangin, William, Matza, David, Mead, Margaret, Miller, Walter B., and Moynihan, Daniel P. "Culture and Poverty: Critique and Counter-Proposals." Current Anthropology, Ap-Je, 1969.

Bernstein, Basil B. "A Critique of the Concept 'Compensatory Education.'" In Opening Opportunities for Disadvantaged Learners, pp. 72-83. Edited by A. Harry Passow. New York: Teachers College Press, 1972.

_____. "Socio-Linguistic Approach to Social Learning." Penguin Survey of the Social Sciences, 1965.

Berreman, Norman P. Psychological Implications of Deprivation on Adult Learners. Heuristics of Adult Education: Courses of Study for Professional Preparation of Educators of Adults, Je, 1970, 108 pp. Boulder, CO: U. of Colorado. ERIC ED 060 404.

Berthoud, Richard. The Disadvantages of Inequality: A Study of Social Deprivation. London: Macdonald and Jane's, 1976.

Bettelheim, Bruno. "How Much Can Man Change?" New York Review of Books, S 10, 1964.

_____. "Teaching the Disadvantaged." N.E.A. Journal, S, 1965.

Black, Millard H. "Characteristics of the Culturally Disadvantaged Child." Reading Teacher, Mr, 1965.

Blair, George E. "The Survival of the Culturally Deprived." Redman (St. John's University Alumni Magazine), Fall, 1965.

Bloom, Benjamin S., Davis, Allison, and Hess, Robert. Compensatory Education for Cultural Deprivation. New York: Holt, Rinehart and Winston, 1965.

Blouch, Dick. Opening and Closing Experiences of Blacks and Whites. Positive Human Experience Theory and Research IV: the Disadvantaged, Mr 23, 1970, 11 pp. ERIC ED 040 248.

Bond, Horace Mann. A Study of Factors Involved in the Identification and Encouragement of Unusual Academic Talent Among Underprivileged Populations. Atlanta, GA: Atlanta U., 1967.

Boney, J. Don. "Some Dynamics of Disadvantaged Students in Learning Situations." Journal of Negro Education, Summer, 1967.

Booth, Robert E. and others. Culturally Disadvantaged: A Keyword-In-Context Index. Detroit: Wayne State U. Press, 1966.

Bortner, Rayman W. Adult Life Strategies and Deprivation. Bethesda, MD: National Institutes of Health and Human Development, 1968.

Bower, Janet, and Magary, James F. (eds.). Conference Proceedings, Classroom Problems in Urban Education, The Schools and the Disadvantaged. Jersey City, NJ: Jersey City State College, 1966.

Braddock, Clayton. "How Many Can Title One Really Help?" Southern Education Report, My, 1969.

Breglio, Vincent J. and others. Students' Economic and Educational Status and Selection for Compensatory Education. Santa Monica, CA: System Development Corporation, Ja, 1978.

Brittingham, Barbara E. and others. Compensatory Education in the State of Rhode Island: 1970-1976, Ap 1, 1977. ERIC ED 042 611.

Brody, Lawrence, Harris, Beatrice, and Lachica, Genearo. Discovering and Developing the College Potential of Disadvantaged High School Youth. New York: City U. of New York, 1968.

Bronfenbrenner, Urie. Is Early Intervention Effective? Washington, DC: GPO, 1974.

Brown, Bernard (ed.). Found: Long-Term Gains from Early Intervention. Boulder, CO: Westview Press, 1977.

Browning, R. Stephen, and Costello, Jack, Jr. "Title I: More of the Same?" Inequality in Education 17(Je, 1974):23-45. [Educational deprivation]

Brownell, Samuel. "Teaching the Child from the Disadvantaged Neighborhoods." Journal of Teacher Education, Je, 1965.

Brunner, Catherine. "Building on Cultural Differences." Childhood Education, O, 1965.

_____. "Deprivation--Its Effects, Its Remedies." Educational Leadership, N, 1965.

Burgess, Tyrrell. "Doomed at Birth?" New Society, Je 8, 1972.

Burke, Arvid J. and others. Educational Programs for the Culturally Deprived: Need and Cost Differentials. National Educational Finance Project, Special Study No. 3, 1970, 336 pp. Boston: Boston College, Institute of Human Sciences. ERIC ED 043 697.

Butler, Willie L., and Gipson, Clarinda. "Upward Bound--Downward Bound: The Death of a Federal Program." Integrateducation 13(Jl-Ag, 1975):10-13.

Bynum, Effie M. (comp.). A Selected ERIC Bibliography on Pre-College Preparation of Students from Disadvantaged Backgrounds, 1969. ERIC-IRCD, Horace Mann-Lincoln Institute, Teachers College, Columbia U.

Caldwell, Bettye M. "A Decade of Early Intervention Programs: What We Have Learned." American Journal of Orthopsychiatry 44(Jl, 1974):491-496. [Educational deprivation]

Calia, Vincent F. "The Culturally Deprived Client: A Reformulation of the Counselor's Role." Journal of Consulting Psychology, Spring, 1966.

Carnoy, Martin. "Is Compensatory Education Possible?" In Schooling in a Corporate Society. The Political Economy of Education in America, pp. 175-189. Edited by Martin Carnoy. New York: McKay, 1972.

Chang, S. S., and Raths, James. "The Schools' Contribution to the Cumulating Deficit." Journal of Educational Research 64(F, 1971): 272-276.

Chazan, Maurice (ed.). Compensatory Education.. London: Butterworth, 1973.

Chess, Stella. "Disadvantages of the Disadvantaged Child." American Journal of Orthopsychiatry, Ja, 1969.

Clark, Kenneth B. "Answer for 'Disadvantaged' Is Effective Teaching." New York Times, Ja 12, 1970.

_____. "The Cult of Cultural Deprivation: A Complex Social Psychological Phenomenon." In Environmental Deprivation and Enrichment, Proceedings of the Fourth Annual Invitational Conference on Urban Education. New York: Yeshiva U., 1965.

_____. "No-Nonsense Approach to Slum Schools." Wall Street Journal, D 26, 1969. [Interview]

Clift, Virgil A. "Curriculum Strategy Based on the Personality Characteristics of Disadvantaged Youth." Journal of Negro Education, Spring, 1969.

Cline, Marvin and others. "Evaluation of Education Improvement Program, Philadelphia, Pennsylvania, and Madison Area Project, Syracuse, New York." In Racial Isolation in the Public Schools, Vol. 2. Washington, DC: GPO, 1967.

Cloward, Robert D. "Education and Poverty." In Conference Proceedings, Classroom Problems in Urban Education, The Schools and the Disadvantaged. Edited by Janet Bower and James F. Margary. Jersey City, NJ: Jersey City State College, 1966.

_____. "Studies in Tutoring." Journal of Experimental Education, Fall, 1967.

Cohen, David K. "Policy for the Public Schools: Compensation and Integration." Harvard Educational Review, Winter, 1968.

Cohen, Elaine Pear. "Does Art Matter in the Education of the Black Ghetto Child?" Young Children 29(Mr, 1974):170-181.

Cohen, S. Alan. "Local Control and the Cultural Deprivation Fallacy." Phi Delta Kappan, Ja, 1969.

_____. "Some Learning Disabilities of Social Disadvantaged Puerto Rican and Negro Children." Academic Therapy Quarterly, Fall, 1 1966.

Colfax, J. David. Community Structure, Urban Education, and Psychosocial Deprivation. Bethesda, MD: National Institutes of Health and Human Development, 1968.

Compensatory Education: What Works to Help Disadvantaged Children, 1973. National School Public Relations Association, 1801 N. Moore Street, Arlington, VA 22209.

Comptroller General of the United States. Assessment of Reading Activities Funded Under the Federal Program of Aid for Educationally Deprived Children. Washington, DC: General Accounting Office, D 12, 1975.

_____. Follow-Through: Lessons Learned from Its Evaluation and Need to Improve Its Administration. Washington, DC: General Accounting Office, O 7, 1975.

_____. Management of the Project One Hundred Thousand Program. Washington, DC: U.S. General Accounting Office, D 8, 1969.

_____. Problems of the Upward Bound Program in Preparing Disadvantaged Students for a Postsecondary Education. Washington, DC: General Accounting Office, Mr 7, 1974.

"The Concept 'Socially Disadvantaged Child.'" IRCD Bulletin (Yeshiva U.), Mr, 1965.

Conlin, Marcia R., and Haberman, Martin. "Supervising Teachers of the Disadvantaged." Educational Leadership, F, 1967.

Connell, R. W. "The Causes of Educational Disadvantage: Further Observations." Australian and New Zealand Journal of Sociology 10(O, 1974).

Cooper, David E. "Linguistics and 'Cultural Deprivation.'" Journal of Philosophy of Education 12(1978):113-120.

Cultural Patterns of Differentiated Youth: A Manual for Teachers in Marginal Schools. U. of California, School of Criminology, 1965.

Das, J. P. "Cultural Deprivation: Euphemism and Essence." Journal of Educational Thought 5 (Ag, 1971):80-89.

Davis, Allison. "Cultural Factors in Remediation." Educational Horizons, Summer, 1965.

Davie, Ronald and others. From Birth to Seven. London: Longmans, 1972.

Davis, Richard H. "The Failure of Compensatory Education." Education and Urban Society 4 (F, 1972):234-248.

DeCharms, Richard, and Carpenter, Virginia. "Measuring Motivation in Culturally Disadvantaged School Children." Journal of Experimental Education, Fall, 1968.

Dentler, Robert A. "Urban Eyewash: A Review of 'Title I/Year II.'" Urban Review, F, 1969.

Deutsch, Cynthia P. "Auditory Discrimination and Learning Social Factors." Merrill-Palmer Quarterly, Jl, 1964.

Deutsch, Martin. "Early Social Environment and School Adaptation." Teachers College Record, My, 1965.

_____. "Facilitating Development in the Pre-School Child: Social and Psychological Perspectives." Merrill-Palmer Quarterly, Jl, 1964.

_____. "The Role of Social Class in Language Development and Cognition." American Journal of Orthopsychiatry, Ja, 1965.

_____. "Social and Psychological Perspective on the Development of the Disadvantaged Learner." Journal of Negro Education, Summer, 1964.

_____. "What We've Learned About Disadvantaged Children." Nation's Schools, Ap, 1965.

Deutsch, Martin, and Brown, Bert. "Social Influence in Negro-White Intelligence Differences." Journal of Social Issues, Ap, 1964.

Deutsch, Martin and associates. The Disadvantaged Child. Studies of the Social Environment and the Learning Process. New York: Basic Books, 1967.

Dickinson, Dallas Pond. "'On Account He Ain't Had a Normal Home': An Intellectual History of the Concept of 'Disadvantageness' in Education." Doctoral dissertation, Northwestern U., 1973.

Dienemann, P. F., Flynn, D., and Al-Salam, N. An Evaluation of the Cost Effectiveness of Alternative Compensatory Reading Programs. Bethesda, MD: RMC Research Corporation, 1974.

The Disadvantaged Student. New York: Middle States Association of Colleges and Secondary Schools, 1968.

Doss, David A., and Hester, Jay. Compensatory Programs Do Not Supplant, They Supplement. Right?, Mr, 1978. ERIC ED 155 240.

Duggan, John M. "Evaluating the Disadvantaged Student." Journal of The Association of College Admissions Counselors, Summer, 1965.

"Educating the Deprived: Two Schools of Thought." Bulletin, Council for Basic Education, O, 1965.

The Educationally Retarded and Disadvantaged. Chicago: U. of Chicago Press, 1967.

Educator's Complete ERIC Handbook. Englewood Cliffs, NJ: Prentice-Hall, 1967.

Edwards, A. D., and Hargreaves, David H. "The Social Scientific Base of Academic Radicalism." Educational Review 28(F, 1976):83-93. [Critique of Stephen and Joan Baratz]

Eisdorfer, Carl. Observations on Some Issues Involving Bio-Psychosocial Deprivation and Adult Learning. Bethesda, MD: National Institutes of Health and Human Development, 1968.

Ellis, Richard R. "Looking Toward Desired Behaviors in Teachers of the Disadvantaged." Urban Education, Winter, 1965.

Elmore, R. F. "Follow Through: Decisionmaking in a Large Scale Social Experiment." Doctoral dissertation, Harvard U., 1976.

Emmerich, Walter. Social Role Development and Psychosocial Deprivation. Bethesda, MD: National Institute of Child Health and Human Development, 1968.

_____. "Structure and Development of Personal-Social Behaviors in Economically Disadvantaged Preschool Children." Genetic Psychology Monographs, 1977.

Environmental Deprivation and Enrichment: Proceedings of the Annual Invitational Conference on Urban Education (4th, April 26, 1965), 1965. ERIC ED 034 803.

Fantini, Mario D., and Weinstein, Gerald. The Disadvantaged: Challenge to Education. New York: Harper & Row, 1968.

_____ and _____. Making Urban Schools Work. Social Realities and the Urban School. New York: Holt, Rinehart & Winston, 1968.

Farber, Bernard, and Lewis, Michael. "Compensatory Education and Social Justice." Peabody Journal of Education 49(Ja, 1972):85-96.

Feshbach, Seymour. A Training, Demonstration and Research Program for the Remediation of Learning Disorders in Culturally Disadvantaged Youth, Ag, 1969. ERIC ED 034 237 and 034 238. [Interracial setting; Los Angeles]

Findley, Warren G. and others. Teachers Education Conference Papers for Program on the Nature and Implications of Early Educational Stimulation, 1966. ERIC ED 010 667.

Fisher, Maurice D., and Turner, Robert V. "The Effects of a Perceptual-Motor Training Program Upon the Academic Readiness of Culturally Disadvantaged Kindergarten Children." Journal of Negro Education 41(Spring, 1972):142-150. [Richmond, VA]

Fisher, Robert J. "Can We Categorize the Children of the Urban Poor?" Educational Forum, Mr, 1965.

Flygare, Thomas J. "Federal Desegregation Decrees and Compensatory Education." Phi Delta Kappan 59(D, 1977):265-266. [Milliken II]

Fowler, William. "Problems of Deprivation and Developmental Learning." Merrill Palmer Quarterly 16(Ap, 1970):141-161.

Fox, David J. "Issues in Evaluating Programs for Disadvantaged Children." Urban Review, D, 1967.

Francke, Linda. "The Games People Play on 'Sesame Street.'" New York, Ap 5, 1971.

Freeman, Roger A. "Schools and the Elusive 'Average Children' Concept." Wall Street Journal, Jl 8, 1968.

Friedman, Norman L. "Cultural Deprivation: A Commentary on the Sociology of Knowledge." Journal of Educational Thought, Ag, 1967.

Friedman, S. Thomas, Pierce-Jones, John, Banon, W. E., and Caldwell, Bill S. "Project Head Start: Teacher Interest and Commitment." Public Opinion Quarterly, Summer, 1967.

Gaffney, Michael, Thomas, Catherine, and Silverstein, Robert. An Analysis of the Legal Framework for State Administration of Title I of the Elementary and Secondary Education Act of 1965. Washington, DC: Lawyer's Committee for Civil Rights Under Law, S, 1977.

Gamel, Nona N. and others.. State ESEA Title I Reports: Review and Analysis of Past Reports, and Development of a Model Reporting System and Format. Bethesda, MD: RMC Research Corporation, O, 1975.

Gans, Herbert. "Culture and Class in the Study of Poverty: An Approach to the Anti-Poverty Research." In On Understanding Poverty. Edited by David P. Moynihan. New York: Basic Books, 1969.

Geller, E. "Who's Deprived?" Library Journal, My 15, 1965.

General Research Corporation. Selected Issues in Title I Compatibility, Ap, 1976. ERIC ED 146 250.

Ghetto Schools. Washington, DC: The New Republic Magazine, 1967. [A compilation of New Republic articles on the subject]

Glass, Gene V. and others. Data Analysis of the 1968-1969 Survey of Compensatory Education (Title I). Boulder, CO: Laboratory of Educational Research, U. of Colorado, Ag, 1970.

Glatt, Charles A. "Who Are the Deprived Children?" Elementary School Journal, My, 1965.

Goff, Eva Harriet (ed.). Conference Proceedings. Invitational Conference on Educating the Disadvantaged in Rural and Urban Settings, Ag 6, 1969. Genesee, NY: Division of Education, State U. College, 1969.

Goldman, Harvey (ed.). Education and the Disadvantaged, Proceedings of a Conference on the Disadvantaged. Milwaukee, WI: U. of Wisconsin. ERIC ED 022 804.

Goldberg, Miriam L. "Adapting Teacher Style to Pupil Differences: Teachers for Disadvantaged Children." Merrill-Palmer Quarterly, Ap, 1964.

_____. "Problems in the Evaluation of Compensatory Programs for Disadvantaged Children." Journal of School Psychology, Spring, 1966.

Golden, Lawrence. "Don't Give Up on Compensatory Education. Just Make It More Relevant to Individual Needs." Urban Education 8(O, 1973): 311-331.

Goodman, Yetta Trachtman. "The Culturally Deprived Child: A Study in Stereotyping." Integrated Education, Jl-Ag, 1969.

Goodstein, H. A. "The Use of a Structured Curriculum with Black Preschool Disadvantaged Children." Journal of Negro Education 40 (Fall, 1971):330-336.

Gordon, Edmund W. "Compensatory Education: Evaluation in Perspective." IRCD Bulletin 6(D, 1970):2-5.

_____. "Help for the Disadvantaged?" American Journal of Orthopsychiatry, Ap, 1965.

_____. "Is Compensatory Education Failing?" College Board Review, Winter, 1967.

_____. "A Review of Programs of Compensatory Education." American Journal of Orthopsychiatry, Jl, 1965.

_____. Significant Trends in the Education of t the Disadvantaged. ERIC-IRCD Urban Disadvantaged Series, Number 12, Ag, 1970, 24 pp. New York: Columbia U. ERIC ED 040 305.

_____ (ed). Summary of the Proceedings of the First Working Conference on Language Development in Disadvantaged Children. New York: Yeshiva U., 1966.

_____. "The Socially Disadvantaged Student: Implications for the Preparation of Guidance Specialists." In Preparing School Counselors in Educational Guidance. New York: College Entrance Examination Board, 1967.

Gordon, Edmund W., and Adelaide Jablonsky.
"Compensatory Education in the Equalization
of Educational Opportunity." Journal of
Negro Education, Summer, 1968.

_____ and _____. "Compensatory Education in
the Equalization of Educational Opportunity."
In U.S. Commission on Civil Rights, Papers
Prepared for National Conference on Equal
Educational Opportunity in America's Cities.
Washington, Dc: GPO, 1968.

Gordon, Edmund W., and Wilkerson, Doxey A.
"A Critique of Compensatory Education."
In Compensatory Education for the Disadvantaged. New York: College Entrance Examination Board, 1966.

Gordon, Richard K. "A Phenomenological Descrip-
tion of Educational Programs Designed for the
Underclass Student." Doctoral dissertation,
U. of California, Los Angeles, 1978. Univ.
Microfilms Order No. 7901360.

Gordon, Sol. "The Bankruptcy of Compensatory
Education." Education and Urban Society 2
(Ag, 1970):360-370.

_____. "The Mythology of Disadvantage."
Grade Teacher, D, 1969.

_____. "Quality Education in De Facto Segre-
gated Schools?" Changing Education, Fall,
1967.

Gottlieb, David, and Ramsey, Charles E. Understanding Children of Poverty. Chicago: Science Research Associates, 1968.

Gray, Susan W. Selected Longitudinal Studies
of Compensatory Education--A Look from the
Inside. Nashville, TN: John F. Kennedy
Center for Research on Educational Human
Development, George Peabody College for
Teachers, 1969.

Gray, Susan W. and others. Before First Grade:
The Early Training Project for Culturally
Disadvantaged Children. New York: Teachers
College Press, Columbia U., 1966.

Gray, Susan W., and Klaus, Rupert A. Deprivation, Development and Diffusion. Nashville,
TN: George Peabody College for Teachers,
1966.

Greenbaum, Leonard. "Prejudice and Purpose in
Compensatory Education Programs." College
Composition and Communication, D, 1968.

Groff, Patrick J. "Culturally Deprived Children: Opinions of Teachers on the Views of
Reissman." Exceptional Children, O, 1964.

_____. "Dissatisfactions in Teaching the
C[ulturally] D[eprived] Child." Phi Delta
Kappan, N, 1963.

_____. "Teaching the [Culturally Deprived]
Child: Teacher Turnover." California Journal of Education Research, Mr, 1967.

Gruber, Murray L. "The Nonculture of Poverty
among Black Youths." Social Work 17(My,
1972):50-58. [Cleveland]

Hale, Frank W., Jr. "Socially Disadvantaged
Youth: A Challenge to Higher Education."
Education Horizons, Fall, 1965.

Halperin, Samuel. "ESEA...The Positive Side."
Phi Delta Kappan 57(N, 1975):147-151. [See
Wayson, below]

Haney, W. A Technical History of the National
Follow Through Evaluation. Cambridge, MA:
Huron Institute, 1977.

Haubrich, Vernon F. "The Culturally Disadvantaged and Teacher Education." Reading Teacher, Mr, 1965.

_____ (ed.). Studies in Deprivation. Occa-
sional Paper. Special NDEA National Insti-
tute for Advanced Study in Teaching Disad-
vantaged Youth. Washington, DC: American
Association of Colleges for Teacher Education,
Jl, 1968. ERIC ED 026 334. [The National
Cash Register Company, Box 2206, Rockville,
MD 20852]

Havighurst, Robert J. "Curriculum for the Disadvantaged." Phi Delta Kappan, Mr, 1970.

_____. "Deprivation and Disadvantage: U.S.A."
In Deprivation and Disadvantage. Nature and
Manifestations, pp. 70-93. Edited by A.
Harry Passow. Hamburg, Germany: UNESCO
Institute for Education, 1970.

_____. "Teachers and the Socially Disadvan-
taged Pupil." Teachers College Journal (of
Indiana State University, Terre Haute), O,
1966.

_____. "Who are the Socially Disadvantaged?"
Journal of Negro Education, Summer, 1964.

Hawkridge, David G. and Others. Foundations
for Success in Educating Disadvantaged Children. Final Report, D, 1968, 112 pp. Palo
Alto, CA: American Institute for Research
in Behavioral Sciences. ERIC ED 037 591.

Heber, Rick and others. Rehabilitation of Fam-
ilies at Risk of Mental Retardation. Madison,
WI: Rehabilitation Research and Training
Center in Mental Retardation, U. of Wisconsin,
D, 1972.

Hecht, Kathryn A. "Title I Federal Education:
The First Five Years." Teachers College
Record 75(S, 1973):67-78.

Hellmuth, Jerome (ed.). Disadvantaged Child.
Seattle, WA: Special Child Publications,
1967.

Henderson, Edmund H., and Long, Barbara H. Pre-
dictors of Success in Beginning Reading Among
Negroes and Whites, My, 1969, 10 pp. ERIC
ED 032 193.

Herr, Audrey, and Tobias, Sigmund. "Achievement via Programmed Instruction and Socioeconomic Status." Psychology in the Schools 7(1970): 53-56.

Hess, Robert D. "The Transmission of Cognitive Strategies in Poor Families: The Socialization of Apathy and Achievement." In Psychological Factors in Poverty. Edited by V. Allen. Chicago: Markham, 1969.

Hess, Robert D., and Shipman, Virginia. "Early Blocks to Children's Learning." Children, S-O, 1965.

Hess, Robert D., and Bear, R. M. (eds.). Early Education, Current Theory, Research and Action. Chicago: Aldine, 1968.

Hess, Robert D., and Jackson, David. "Some New Dimensions in Providing Equal Educational Opportunity." Journal of Negro Education, Summer, 1965.

Hess, Robert D. and others. Techniques for Assessing Cognitive and Social Abilities of Children and Parents in Project Head Start. Chicago: U. of Chicago, Jl, 1966.

Hewer, Vivian H. "Are Tests Fair to College Students from Homes with Low Social-Economic Status?" Personnel and Guidance Journal, Ap, 1965.

Hickerson, Nathaniel. Education for Alienation. Englewood Cliffs, NJ: Prentice-Hall, 1966.

Hodges, Walter F. and others. The Development and Evaluation of a Diagnostically Based Curriculum for Preschool Psycho-Socially Deprived Children. Bloomington, IN: School of Education, Indiana U., 1967.

Hodges, Walter L., and Spicker, Howard H. "The Effects of Preschool Experiences on Culturally Deprived Children." Young Children, O, 1967.

Holden, Anna, and Jackson, Luther (eds.). Perspectives on Poverty. A Workshop Summary and Study Manual, D, 1967.

Hughes, John F., and Hughes, Anne O. Equal Education: A New National Strategy. Bloomington, IN: Indiana U. Press, 1973.

Hunnicutt, C. W. (ed.). Urban Education and Cultural Deprivation. Syracuse, NY: Syracuse U. Press, 1964.

Hunt, David E. "Adolescence: Cultural Deprivation, Poverty, and the Dropout." Review of Educational Research, O, 1966.

Hunt, J. McV. "Has Compensatory Education Failed? Has It Been Attempted?" Harvard Education Review, Spring, 1969.

_____. "The Psychological Basis for Using Preschool Environment as an Antidote for Cultural Deprivation." Merrill-Palmer Quarterly, Jl, 1964.

_____. "The Shape of the Needed Investigation Into the Development of Human Competence." In Educating the Disadvantaged. Edited by R. C. Doll and M. Hawkins. New York: AMS Press, 1971.

Jablonsky, Adelaide (ed.). Imperatives for Change: Proceedings of the New York State Education Department Conference on College and University Programs for Teachers of the Disadvantaged. Albany, NY: Bureau of Inservice Education, 1967.

_____. "Some Trends in Education for the Disadvantaged." IRCD Bulletin, Mr, 1968.

_____. "Status Report on Compensatory Education." IRCD Bulletin 7(Winter-Spring, 1971): 1-21.

Jackson, Luther P. Poverty's Children. Mt. Rainier, MD: Cross-Tell, Mr, 1966.

Jeffrey, Julie R. Education for Children of the Poor: A Study of the Origins and Implementation of the Elementary and Secondary Education Act of 1965. Columbus, OH: Ohio State U. Press, 1977.

Jensen, Arthur R. "The Culturally Disadvantaged: Psychological and Sociological Aspects." Educational Research, N, 1967.

_____. "Cumulative Deficit: A Testable Hypothesis?" Developmental Psychology 10 (1974):996-1019.

_____. "Cumulative Deficit in Compensatory Education." Journal of School Psychology, Spring, 1966.

_____. "How Much Can We Boost IQ and Scholastic Achievement?" Harvard Educational Review, Winter, 1969.

Jensen, Philip K., O'Kane, James M., and Friedricks, Robert. "Evaluating Compensatory Education. A Case Study." Education and Urban Society 4(F, 1972):211-233. [Cleveland School, Newark, NJ]

John, Vera P. "The Intellectual Development of Slum Children: Some Preliminary Findings." American Journal of Orthopsychiatry, O, 1963.

John, Vera P., and Goldstein, Leo S. "The Social Context of Language Acquisition." Merrill-Palmer Quarterly, Jl, 1964.

Johnson, G. Orville. "Organizing Instruction and Curriculum Planning for the Socially Disadvantaged." Journal of Negro Education, Summer, 1964.

Kaplan, Bernard A. "Issues in Educating the Culturally Disadvantaged." Phi Delta Kappan, N, 1963.

Karnes, Merle P. and others. "Educational Intervention at Home by Mothers of Disadvantaged Children." Child Development 41(D, 1965).

Karnes, Merle B. and others. Research and Development on Preschool Disadvantaged Children, 3 volumes. Urbana, IL: Institute for Research on Exceptional Children, U. of Illinois, 1969.

Keddie, Nell (ed.). Tinker, Tailor...The Myth of Cultural Deprivation. Penguin, 1973.

Keener, Beverly M. "The Disadvantaged: Learning and Doing." Integrated Education, Ap-My, 1966.

Keller, Suzanne. "The Social World of the Urban Slum Child: Some Early Findings." American Journal of Orthopsychiatry, O, 1963.

Kiesling, Herbert J. Input and Output in California Compensatory Education Projects. Santa Monica, CA: RAND Corporation, O, 1971.

Kirst, Michael W. "What Types of Compensatory Education Programs Are Effective?" In U.S. Commission on Civil Rights, Papers Presented for National Conference on Equal Educational Opportunity in America's Cities. Washington, DC: GPO, 1968.

Knapp, Dale K. "The Educationally Disadvantaged: Teaching Beyond the Stereotype." California Journal of Instructional Improvement, D, 1964.

Knoll, Erwin. "Hasty 'Landmark.'" Southern Education Report, S-O, 1965.

Kopp, Sister M. Audrey. "Cultural Deprivation: An Academic Alibi." Catholic School Journal, O, 1966.

Krevisky, Joseph. "Alsop's Fable." The Center Forum, Jl 5, 1967. [On Joseph Alsop and the More Effective Schools Program]

Kurzman, Paul A. "The Native-Settler Concept: Implications for Community Organization." Social Work, Jl, 1969.

Landers, Jacob, and Mercurio, Carmela. "Improving Curriculum and Instruction for the Disadvantaged Minorities." Journal of Negro Education, Summer, 1965.

Larson, Meredith A., and Dittmann, Freya E. Compensatory Education and Early Adolescence: Reviewing Our National Strategy. Menlo Park, CA: Stanford Research Institute, My, 1975.

Laycock, F. and others. "College Entrance Programs of Compensatory Education: Experience in the USA." International Review of Education 21(1975):301-310.

Levin, Henry M. "Some Methodological Problems in Economic Policy Research. Determining How Much Should be Spent on Compensatory Education." Education and Urban Society 7(My,, 1975):303-333. [See also discussion by Burton A. Weisbrod and Richard A. Rossmiller, pp. 334-349]

Levin, Henry M., Guthrie, James W., Kleindorfer, George B., and Stout, Robert T. "Capital Embodiment. A New View of Compensatory Education." Education and Urban Society 3 (My, 1971):301-322.

Levine, Daniel U. Raising Standards in the Inner-City Schools. Occasional Papers Number Eleven, D, 1966, 38 pp. Washington, DC: Council for Basic Education. ERIC ED 028 208.

_____. "The Integration-Compensatory Education Controversy." Educational Forum, Mr, 1968.

Levine, Daniel U., and Lewis, Martha. "An Assessment of the Impact of a Highly Rated Negro High School on the Perception of its Students." Urban Education III, No. 2, 1967.

Lipsman, Claire K. The Disadvantaged and Library Effectiveness. Chicago: American Library Association, 1972.

Lloyd, Helen M. "What's Ahead in Reading for the Disadvantaged?" Reading Teacher, Mr, 1965.

Lohman, Joseph D. (ed.). Cultural Patterns in Urban Schools. A Manual for Teachers, Counselors, and Administrators. Berkeley, CA: U. of California Press, 1968.

Loretan, Joseph O., and Umans, Shelly. Teaching the Disadvantaged. New York: Teachers College Press, Columbia U., 1966.

MacBeath, John. "Breaking Up the Egg Crates." Times Educational Supplement, Ja 11, 1974. [On the pathological view of the disadvantaged child]

McCone, John A. "Break the Spiral of Failure." Integrated Education, F-Mr, 1967.

McCreary, Eugene. "Learning to Teach Deprived Children." Integrated Education, Ap, 1963.

_____. "Respect is Personal Concern." Integrated Education, Ag-S, 1964.

_____. "Teaching the Culturally Different." Integrated Education, F-Mr, 1965.

McDill, Edward, McDill, Mary, and Sprehe, Timothy. Analysis of Evaluation of Selected Compensatory Education Programs. Baltimore: Johns Hopkins Press, 1969.

McGeeney, Patrick. "Bernstein on Compensatory Education." English in Education 4(F, 1970): 78-82.

McKay, Harrison and others. "Improving Cognitive Ability in Chronically Deprived Children." Science 200(Ap, 1978):270-278.

McKendell, Benjamin W., Jr. "Breaking the Barriers of Cultural Disadvantage and Curriculum Imbalance." Phi Delta Kappan, Mr, 1965.

Mackintosh, Helen K., Gore, Lillian, and Lewis, Gertrude M. Educating Disadvantaged Children Under Six. Educating Disadvantaged Children in the Primary Years. Educating Disadvantaged Children in the Middle Grades. Washington, DC: GPO, 1966.

McLaughlin, Milbrey W. "Evaluation and Reform: The Case of ESEA Title I." Doctoral dissertation, Harvard U., 1973.

_____. Evaluation and Reform: The Elementary and Secondary Education Act of 1965, Title I. Cambridge, MA: Ballinger, 1975.

Mackler, Bernard. "Cooling Out the Community: The Politics of Compensatory Education." Journal of Negro Education 45(Spring, 1976): 122-133. [State of New York]

Mackler, Bernard, and Giddings, Morsley G. "Cultural Deprivation: A Study in Mythology." Teachers College Record, 1965.

Maras, Lorene Ruth. "Evaluation of a Large City Remedial Reading Program." Doctoral dissertation, Illinois State U., 1974. Univ. Microfilms Order No. 75-15, 804.

Marion, A. and others. "A Method of Studying 'Underprivileged' Children." London Educational Review 3(Autumn, 1974):36-40.

Marshall, M. S., and Bentler, P. M. "IQ Increases of Disadvantaged Minority-Group Children Following Innovative Enrichment Program." Psychological Reports 29(D, 1971): 805-806.

Martin, Ruby, and McClure, Phyllis. Title I of ESEA. Is It Helping Poor Children? New York: NAACP Legal Defense and Educational Fund, Inc., 1969.

Meckler, Jane. "The Challenge of the Educationally Disadvantaged Child." California Teachers Association Journal, Mr, 1964.

Mervielde, I. Research Project Concerning the Stimulation of Development and Learning Abilities of Socially Deprived Children. Ghent: U. of Ghent, 1973.

Miller, Louise, Galitzine, Elisabeth S., and Neill, Robert. Evaluation Report on Head Start. Louisville, KY: Urban Studies Center, U. of Louisville, Je, 1967.

Mingola, Edwin M. "The Language Arts and Deprived Pupils." Education, Ja, 1965.

Monge, Rolf H. The Relation of Learning in Adults to Social and Biological Deprivations. Bethesda, MD: National Institutes of Health and Human Development, 1968.

Moore, William P. "Why Difficult Schools?" Integrated Education, Je, 1964.

Morton, D. C., and Watson, D. R. "Compensatory Education and Contemporary Liberalism in the United States: A Sociological Review." International Review of Education 17(1971).

Mosback, E. J. and others. Analysis of Compensatory Education in Five School Districts. Volume I: Summary. Final Report. Washington, DC, Ag, 1968. ERIC ED 023 532.

_____ and others. Analysis of Compensatory Education in Five School Districts. Volume II: Case Studies. Final Report. Washington, DC, Ag, 1968. ERIC ED 023 531.

Moss, James E. "The Disadvantaged." Afro-American Studies 1(Ap, 1971):277-280.

Mukerji, Rose, and Robinson, Helen F. "Teaching Strategies for Disadvantaged Kindergarten Children." Young Children, Mr, 1966.

National Advisory Council on the Education of Disadvantaged Children. America's Educationally Neglected. A Progress Report on Compensatory Education. Washington, DC: GPO, 1973.

_____. Annual Report. Washington, DC: National Advisory Council on the Education of Disadvantaged Children, Ja, 1968.

_____. Educating the Disadvantaged Child: Where We Stand. Washington, DC: GPO, 1972.

_____. Title I, E.S.E.A.--The Weakest Link: The Children of the Poor. The 1971 Annual Report to the President and the Congress. Washington, DC: GPO, 1971.

_____. 1975 Annual Report to the President and the Congress, 1975. ERIC ED 133 407.

_____. 1976 Annual Report to the President and the Congress, 1976. ERIC ED 133 403.

National Institute of Education. Administration of Compensatory Education. A Report from the National Institute of Education. Washington, DC: National Institute of Education, S 19, 1977.

_____. Compensatory Education Services, Jl 31, 1977. ERIC ED 145 061.

_____. Evaluating Compensatory Education: An Interim Report on the NIE Compensatory Education Study. Washington, DC: NIE, 1976.

New York Bureau of Mathematics Education. Mathematics Education and the Educationally Disadvantaged. Albany, NY: The Bureau, 1968.

1975 Annual Report to the President and the Congress. Washington, DC: National Advisory Council on the Education of Disadvantaged Children, 1975.

Noeske, Nancy R. "Science Program for the Disadvantaged." Science Teacher 37(D, 1970): 31-32.

Office of Programs for the Disadvantaged. Recommendations of Grassroots Conferences Sponsored by Office of Programs for the Disadvantaged. Washington, DC: U.S. Department of Health, Education, and Welfare, 1969.

Opler, Marvin K. "On [Oscar] Lewis' 'Culture of Poverty.'" Current Anthropology, D, 1968.

Ornstein, Allan C. "Defense of the Urban Teacher." Integrated Education, Je-Jl, 1966.

_____. "Who are the Disadvantaged?" Journal of Secondary Education, Ap, 1966.

Osser, Harry and others. A Study of the Communication Abilities of Disadvantaged Children. Final Report, Ja 30, 1968, 45 pp. Baltimore, MD: Johns Hopkins U. School of Medicine. ERIC ED 032 119.

Palmer, Francis H. The Effects of Minimal Early Intervention on Subsequent IQ Scores and Reading Achievement, 1976. ERIC ED 130 229.

Parris, Wendell A. "A New Approach to Educating Negro Children in Gray Area Schools, Part I." Negro History Bulletin, D, 1964.

Pavenstedt, Eleanor. "A Comparison of the Child-Rearing Environment of Upper-Lower and Very Low-Lower Class Families." American Journal of Orthopsychiatry, Ja, 1965.

Pelavin, Sol H., and David, Jane L. Evaluating Long-Term Achievement: An Analysis of Longitudinal Data from Compensatory Education Programs, Mr, 1977. ERIC ED 137 342.

Perrenoud, P. "Compensatory Education and Perpetuation of Social Classes." Information Bulletin 1(Ap, 1974):66-77.

"Perspectives on the Follow Through Evaluation." Harvard Educational Review 48(My, 1978):125-192. [Four articles]

Pfiel, Mary Pat. State Compensatory Education and Bilingual Programs. Washington, DC: Stanford Research Institute, 1975.

Prawat, Richard S. "Two Views of Intellectual Deficit." Psychology in the Schools 12(Ja, 1975):90-96.

Pressman, Harvey. "Keep Moving--Where?" Integrated Education, O-N, 1966.

Programs for the Educationally Disadvantaged. Washington, DC: GPO, 1963.

Psychological Corporation. Evaluation Report. Pre-Kindergarten Classes in Poverty Area. New York: The Psychological Corporation, O, 1968.

Radin, Norma, and Kamii, Constance K. "The Child-Rearing Attitudes of Disadvantaged Negro Mothers and Some Educational Implications." Journal of Negro Education, Spring, 1963.

Rankin, Richard J., and Henderson, Ronald W. Standardized Tests and the Disadvantaged, N, 1969. ERIC ED 034 594.

Ravitch, Diane. "Programs, Placebos, and Panaceas." Urban Review, Ap, 1968.

Research and Policy Committee. Education for the Urban Disadvantaged: From Preschool to Employment, Mr, 1971. New York: Committee for Economic Development, 477 Madison Avenue, 10022.

Rich, Cynthia Jo. "The Difference at Birth." Race Relations Reporter 4(S, 1973):10-13.

Richmond, Julius B. "Disadvantaged Children: What Have They Compelled Us to Learn?" Yale Journal of Biology and Medicine 43(D, 1970):127-144.

Riessman, Frank. "Cultural Styles of the Disadvantaged." Integrated Education, Ap, 1963.

_____. The Culturally Deprived Child. New York: Harper & Row, 1962.

_____. "Ebb and Flow in the School Integration Movement." Integrated Education, O-N, 1966.

_____. Helping the Disadvantaged Pupil to Learn More Easily. Englewood Cliffs, NJ: Prentice-Hall, 1966.

_____. "Higher Horizons: A Critique." Integrated Education, Je, 1963.

_____. "The New Pre-School Mythology: Child-centered Radicalism." American Child, Spring, 1966.

_____. "The Overlooked Positives of Disadvantaged Groups." Journal of Negro Education, Summer, 1964.

_____. "Some Suggestions for Education Programs Concerned with Disadvantaged Children." Integrated Education, Ap, 1963.

_____. "The Strategy of Style." Teachers College Record, Mr, 1964.

_____. "Teachers of the Poor: A Five Point Plan." Journal of Teacher Education, Fall, 1967.

Rivlin, Alice M., and Timpane, P. Michael (eds.). Planned Variation--Should We Give Up or Try Harder? Washington, DC: Brookings Institution, 1975. [Evaluation of compensatory education]

Rivlin, Harry N. "New Teachers for New Immigrants." Teachers College Record, My, 1965.

_____. "Take Up the Challenge." Integrated Education, F-Mr, 1965.

_____ (ed.). "Teaching and Teacher Education for Urban Disadvantaged Schools." Journal of Teacher Education, Je, 1965.

Rodman, Hyman. "Family and Social Pathology in the Ghetto." Science 161(1968):756-762.

Rogers, Donald W. "Visual Expression: A Creative Advantage of the Disadvantaged." Gifted Child Quarterly, Summer, 1968.

Rose, Arnold M. "Graduate Training for the Culturally Deprived." Sociology of Education, Spring, 1966.

Roseman, Martha O. Organization of Schools to Provide Academic Aid and Therapeutic Counseling to Disadvantaged Children. Baltimore: Center for the Study of Social Organization of Schools, Johns Hopkins U., 1967.

Ryan, Michael N., and Lewis, Lionel S. "The Theory and Practice of Educating the Disadvantaged. A Case Study." Education and Urban Society 4(F, 1972):155-176. [The Work Incentive Program (WIN)]

Saarni, Carolyn. "A Critique of the 'Pathology' Model in Psychological Inquiry: Learning Disabilities and Cultural Deprivation." The New School of Education Journal 2(Spring, 1971):67-72.

Savitzky, Charles. "Social Theory Advances on the Disadvantaged." High Points, F, 1964.

Schickel, Richard. The Long Road to College: A Summary of Opportunity; a Special Report on the Rockefeller Foundation's Program toward Equal Opportunities for All. New York: Rockefeller Foundation, 1965.

Schueller, Herbert. "The Teacher of the Disadvantaged." Journal of Teacher Education, Je, 1965.

Schwartz, Robert, Pettigrew, Thomas F., and Smith, Marshall. "Fake Panaceas for Ghetto Education." New Republic, S 23, 1967. [Reply to Joseph Alsop]

Schwebel, Milton. "Learning and the Socially Deprived." Personnel and Guidance Journal, Mr, 1965.

Second Annual Invitational Conference on Urban Education. Guidance for Socially and Culturally Disadvantaged Youth. New York: Graduated School of Education, Yeshiva U., 1963.

Shanker, Albert. "What's Wrong with Compensatory Education?" Saturday Review, Ja 11, 1969.

Shaw, Frederick. "Education Culturally Deprived Youth in Urban Centers." Phi Delta Kappan, N, 1963.

Shore, Milton F., Milgram, Norman A., and Malasky, Charlotte. "The Effectiveness of An Enrichment Program for Disadvantaged Young Children." American Journal of Orthopsychiatry 41(Ap, 1971):442-449. [Prince George's County, MD]

Siegel, Lester, and Weinstein, Robert. "Physics for the Disadvantaged, Part 2: The High School Experience in Project Beacon." Physics Teacher 9(Mr, 1971):134-139.

Simons, Alfred E., and Burke, Nelson S. "The Probable Syndrome in Terms of Educational Experiences Which Precipitate Dropouts, Delinquency, and Eventual Incarceration." Journal of Negro Education, Winter, 1966.

Slaughter, Charles A. "Cognitive Style: Some Implications for Curriculum and Instructional Practices Among Negro Children." Journal of Negro Education, Spring, 1969.

Smilansky, Sarah, and Smilansky, Moshe. "The Role and Program of Preschool Education for Socially Disadvantaged Children." International Review of Education 16(1970):45-67.

Sochet, Mary Allen. "Does Our Education Perpetuate Poverty?" Journal of Human Relations, Fourth Quarter, 1965.

Special Committee on the Disadvantaged Child. A Program for Action. Trenton, NJ: New Jersey Education Association, 1964.

Spradley, James P. "The Cultural Experience." In The Cultural Experience: Ethnography in Complex Society, pp. 1-20. Edited by James P. Spradley and David W. McCurdy. Chicago: Science Research Association, 1972. [Compensatory education]

Sprigle, Herbert A. "Can Poverty Children Live on Sesame Street?" Young Children, Mr, 1971.

Stanford Research Institute. Patterns in ESEA Title I Reading Achievement. Stanford, CA: SRI, 1976.

Stanley, Julian C. "How Can We Intervene Massively?" Science 167(Ja 9, 1970):123. [Letter]

_____. Preschool Programs for the Disadvantaged. Baltimore, MD: Johns Hopkins U. Press, 1972.

Stenner, A. Jackson, and Mueller, Siegfried G. "A Successful Compensatory Education Model." Phi Delta Kappan, D, 1973. [Chicago]

Stewart, Lawrence H., and Moulton, Robert. Increasing the Academic Achievement of Culturally Disadvantaged Youth. Berkeley, CA: School of Education, U. of California, 1966.

Sticht, Thomas G. Learning Abilities of the Disadvantaged Adults. Bethesda, MD: National Institutes of Health and Human Development, 1968.

Stodolsky, Susan S., and Lesser, Gerald. "Learning Patterns in the Disadvantaged." Harvard Educational Review, Fall, 1967.

Strom, Robert D. Teaching in the Slum School. Columbus, OH: Merrill, 1965.

Stukat, K. G. "Current Trends in European Pre-school Research with Particular Regard to Compensatory Education." Information Bulletin 1(Ap, 1974):77-83.

Sullivan, Neil V. "The Right to Read--A Straight Path to Integration." Integrated Education, F-Mr, 1967.

Taba, Hilda. "Cultural Deprivation as a Factor in School Learning." Merrill-Palmer Quarterly, Ap, 1964.

_____. School Culture Studies of Participation and Leadership. Washington, DC: American Council on Education, 1955.

Tallmadge, G. Kasten. Summary of Achievement Test Results Presented in Seventeen Fiscal Year 1969 and 1970 State Title I Evaluation Reports Containing Data Judged to Meet Minimum Reliability, Validity and Representativeness Criteria. Palo Alto, CA: American Institute for Research, Ap 6, 1972.

Tannenbaum, Abraham J. (ed.). Special Education and Programs for Disadvantaged Children and Youth, 1968, 135 pp. Washington, DC: Council for Exceptional Children. ERIC ED 030 250. [Available from Council for Exceptional Children, 1201 Sixteenth Street, N.W., Washington, DC 20036]

Tanner, Daniel, and Lachica, Genearo. Discovering and Developing the College Potential of Disadvantaged High School Youth, the College Discovery and Development Program. A Report of the First Year of a Longitudinal Study, Ja, 1967. ERIC ED 011 683.

Taylor, G., and Ayres, N. Born and Bred Unequal. London: Longmans, 1969.

Teaching Strategies for the Culturally Disadvantaged. Chicago: Rand McNally, 1967.

Thomas, Alexander. Variation in Temperament as a Factor Generating Psycho-Social Deprivation. Bethesda, MD: National Institutes for Health and Human Development, 1968.

Thomas, Charles L. "Testing and the Evaluation of the Minority Child: Some Implications for Compensatory Education Evaluations." Viewpoints 53(J1, 1977):31-49.

Thomas, Thomas C., and Pelavin, Sol H. Patterns in ESEA Title I Reading Achievement, Mr, 1976. ERIC ED 120 687.

Thomson, Jack. "Social Class Labelling in the Application of Bernstein's Theory of the Codes to the Identification of Linguistic Advantage and Disadvantage in Five-Year-Old Children." Educational Review 29(N, 1977): 273-283.

Toomey, D. "Educational Disadvantage and Meritocratic Schooling." Australian and New Zealand Journal of Sociology 12(1976):228-235.

_____. "What Causes Educational Disadvantage?" Australian and New Zealand Journal of Sociology 10(F, 1974):31-37.

Torrance, E. Paul. "Finding Hidden Talents Among Disadvantaged Children." Gifted Child Quarterly, Autumn, 1968.

Trubowitz, Sidney. A Handbook for Beginning Teachers in a Ghetto Elementary School. Chicago: Quadrangle Books, 1967.

Tulkin, Steven R. "An Analysis of the Concept of Cultural Deprivation." Developmental Psychology 6(Mr, 1972):326-339.

Turner, Richard H. A Letter to Teachers of America's Cultural Victims. Chicago: Follett, 1964.

Tuskegee Institute Conference on Disadvantage. Tuskegee Institute, AL: Tuskegee Institute Press, 1964.

U.S. Congress, 91st, 2nd Session, House of Representatives, Committee on Education and Labor. Oversight Hearings on Elementary and Secondary Education Programs. Hearings... Washington, DC: GPO, 1971.

U.S. Congress, 92nd, 1st Session, Senate, Select Committee on Equal Educational Opportunity. Equal Educational Opportunity--1971. Hearings...Part 12. Compensatory Education and Other Alternatives in Urban Schools. Washington, DC: GPO, 1971.

U.S. Congress, 93rd, House of Representatives, Committee on Education and Labor. The Elementary and Secondary Education Act of 1965, As Amended. Selected Annotated Bibliography, 1965-1973. Washington, DC: GPO, 1973.

U.S. Congress, 95th, 1st Session, House of Representatives, Committee on Education and Labor, Subcommittee on Elementary, Secondary and Vocational Education. Hearings...Part 22: Biomedical Enrichment Programs for Disadvantaged Secondary School Students. Washington, DC: GPO, 1978.

U.S. Department of Health, Education, and Welfare. The Effectiveness of Compensatory Education: Summary and Review of the Evidence. Washington, DC: U.S. Department of Health, Education, and Welfare, Ap 20, 1972.

_____. Suggested Guidelines for Evaluation of the Nutritional Status of Preschool Children. Washington, DC: GPO, 1967.

U.S. National Advisory Council on the Education of Disadvantaged Children. Title I--ESEA: A Review and a Forward Look--1969. Washington, DC: GPO, 1969.

U.S. Office of Education. Education of the Disadvantaged. An Evaluative Report on Title I, Elementary and Secondary Education Act of 1965. Fiscal Year 1968. Washington, DC: GPO, Ap, 1970.

_____. State Compensatory Education Programs. Washington, DC: GPO, 1975.

U.S. Office of Education, Office of Programs for the Disadvantaged. Programs for the Disadvantaged. Washington, DC: GPO, Ja, 1969.

U.S. Office of Education Research Information Center (E.R.I.C.). Catalog of Selected Documents on the Disadvantaged. Washington, DC: GPO, 1966.

Valentine, Charles A. Culture and Poverty. Critique and Counter-Proposals. Chicago: U. of Chicago Press, 1968.

_____. "Culture and Poverty: Critique and Counter-Proposals." Current Anthropology, Ap-Je, 1969.

_____. "Deficit, Difference, and Bicultural Models of Afro-American Behavior." Harvard Educational Review 41(My, 1971):137-157.

_____. It's Either Brain Damage or No Father: The False Issue of Deficit vs. Difference Models of Afro-American Behavior, Ag, 1969, 28 pp. ERIC ED 035 707.

_____. "Making the Scene, Digging the Action, and Telling It As It Is. Anthropologists at Work in a Dark Ghetto." In Afro-American Anthropology: Contemporary Perspectives. Edited by Norman Whitten and John Szwed. New York: Free Press, 1970.

Vane, Julia P. "Importance of Considering Background Factors When Evaluating the Effects of Compensatory Education Programs Designed for Young Children." Journal of School Psychology 9(Winter, 1971):393-398.

Vosk, Jeanette S. "Study of Negro Children with Learning Difficulties at the Outset of their School Careers." American Journal of Orthopsychiatry, Ja, 1966.

Wakefield, Robert A. "An Investigation of the Family Backgrounds of Educable Mentally Retarded Children in Special Classes." Exceptional Children, N, 1964.

Warden, Sandra A. The Leftouts: Disadvantaged Children in Heterogeneous Schools. New York: Holt, Rinehart, & Winston, 1968.

Wargo, Michael J., Campeau, Peggie L., and Tallmadge, G. Kasten, with Lauritz, Beverly M., Morris, Sarah J., and Youngquist, Louise V. Further Examination of Exemplary Programs for Educating Disadvantaged Children. Palo, Alto, CA: American Institutes for Research in the Behavioral Sciences, Jl, 1971.

Washington, Bennetta B. "Growth and Cultural Conflict." Vocational Guidance Quarterly, Spring, 1964.

Watson, Goodwin. "A Critical Evaluation of the Yearbook, 1964." Journal of Negro Education, Summer, 1964.

Wax, Murray, and Wax, Rosalie. "Cultural Deprivation as an Educational Ideology." Journal of American Indian Education, Ja, 1964.

Waxman, Sinai, and McKelvy, Doris. "A Proposed Program for Identifying and Enriching the Abilities of the Disadvantaged Child." Hartsdale, NY: Greenburgh School District No. 8, Je, 1962.

Wayson, William W. "ESEA...The Negative Side." Phi Delta Kappan 57(N, 1975):151-156. [See Halperin, above]

_____. "Securing Teachers for Slum Schools." Integrated Education, F-Mr, 1966.

The Weakest Link: The Children of the Poor. Title I, E.S.E.A., 1971 Annual Report to the President and the Congress, Mr 1, 1971, 41 pp. Washington, DC: National Advisory Council on the Education of Disadvantaged Children. ERIC ED 049 333.

Weaver, S. Joseph, and Weaver, Ann. "Psycholinguistic Abilities of Culturally Deprived Negro Children." American Journal of Mental Deficiency, S, 1967.

Webster, Staten W. "Some Correlates of Reported Academically Supportive Behaviors of Negro Mothers Toward Their Children." Journal of Negro Education, Spring, 1965.

_____. "Suggested Strategy for Teaching Socially Disadvantaged Learners." California Journal for Instructional Improvement, My, 1965.

Wedge, Peter, and Prosser, Hilary. Born to Fail? London: Arrow, 1973.

Wein, Norman. "The Education of Disadvantaged Children. An International Comparison." Educational Research 13(N, 1970):12-19.

Weinberg, Meyer. "Instructional Technology and the Disadvantaged Child." In To Improve Learning. An Evaluation of Instructional Technology, Volume II, pp. 667-673. New York: R. R. Bowker, 1971.

Wells, Jean A. "Who Are the Disadvantaged 16-21 Year Old Girls?" Employment Service Review, Ag, 1964.

Wells, Stuart and others. The Impact of Varying Levels of Computer-Assisted Instruction
on the Academic Performance of Disadvantaged
Students, Je, 1974. ERIC ED 157 899.

Welsh, James. "Compensatory Education: Still
More Funds." Educational Researcher 1(Je,
1972):13-15. [Discussion of H.E.W. document,
The Effectiveness of Compensatory Education]

Wessman, Alden E. Evaluation of Project ABC
(A Better Chance); An Evaluation of Dartmouth
College-Independent Schools Scholarships
Program for Disadvantaged High School Students. Final Report, Ap, 1969, 358 pp. Hanover, NH: Dartmouth College. ERIC ED 031
549.

White, Donald. Trends and Implications for the
Education of the Disadvantaged. Albany, NY:
U. of the State of New York, 1962.

Wilcox, Preston R. "Expanding Opportunities
for Disadvantaged Youth." Integrated Education, F-Mr, 1966.

Wilkerson, Doxey A. "Blame the Negro Child!"
Freedomways, Fall, 1968.

_____. "Compensatory Education?" Southern
Education Report, N, 1968.

_____. "Prevailing and Needed Emphases in Re-
search on the Education of Disadvantaged
Children and Youth." Journal of Negro Education, Summer, 1964.

Williams, Robert L. "What Are We Learning from
Current Programs for Disadvantaged Children?"
Journal of Higher Education, Ap, 1969.

Willie, Charles V. "Compensatory Education and
Integration." Integrated Education, D, 1966-
Ja, 1967.

_____. "Deprivation and Alienation: A Com-
pound Situation." In Urban Education and
Cultural Deprivation. Edited by C. W. Hunnicutt. Syracuse, NY: Syracuse U. Press,
1964.

_____. "Education, Deprivation and Alienation."
Journal of Negro Education, Summer, 1965.

Willingham, Ed. "School 'Comparability' Guidelines Focus on Issue of Teacher Seniority
Pay." National Journal 2(Je 13, 1970):1233-
1237.

Wilson, Harriet, and Herbert, Geoffrey. "Hazards
of Environment." New Society, Je 8, 1972.
[Concept of "cultural deprivation"]

Wilson, J. A., and Trew, K. J. "The Education
at Priority Schools." British Journal of
Educational Psychology 45(F, 1975):10-19.

Winsor, C. B. Study of Four Library Programs
for Disadvantaged Persons. Albany, NY:
Division of Library Development, State Department of Education, 1968.

Witner, Helen L. "A Further Analysis of IQ
Changes." In Prelude to School. An Evalu-
ation of an Inner-City Preschool Program,
pp. 66-77. Edited by Ivor Kraft, Jean
Fuschillo, and Elizabeth Herzog. Washington,
DC: GPO, 1968.

Witty, Paul A. (ed.). The Educationally Re-
tarded and Disadvantaged. 66th Yearbook,
National Society for the Study of Education.
Chicago: U. of Chicago Press, 1967.

Woodhead, Martin. Intervening in Disadvantage.
A Challenge for Nursery Education. Windsor,
Bermuda: NFER Publishing Company, 1976.
[Review of research]

Wortis, Helen, and Freedman, Alfred. "The
Contribution of Social Environment to the
Development of Premature Children." American
Journal of Orthopsychiatry, Ja, 1965.

Yinger, J. Milton and others. Middle Start. An
Experiment in the Educational Enrichment of
Young Adolescents. New York: Cambridge U.
Press, 1977.

Zamoff, Richard B. "The Attitudinally Disadvantaged Teacher." Urban Review, D, 1966.

Zigler, Edward, and Trickett, Penelope K. "IQ,
Social Competence and Evaluation of Early
Childhood Intervention Programs." American
Psychologist 33(S, 1978):789-798.

Bibliographies

Disadvantaged Youth: Exceptional Child Bibli-
ography Series, F, 1971, 26 pp. Arlington,
VA: Council for Exceptional Children. ERIC
ED 054 577.

Educating the Disadvantaged Child: Annotated
Bibliography.. Supplement Number One, O,
1969, 92 pp. Albany, NY: New York State
Education Department, Division of Education
for the Disadvantaged. ERIC ED 045 754.

Educational Testing Service. Research on the
Disadvantaged: An Annotated List of Relevant ETS Reports. Princeton, NJ: Educational Testing Service, Ap, 1969.

Holcomb, Beverly J. Training the Socio-Economically Disadvantaged: A Selected, Annotated
Bibliography, Je, 1969, 221 pp. Little Rock,
AR: Arkansas State Department of Education;
Fayetteville, AR: Arkansas Vocational Education Research Coordinating Unit. ERIC ED
042 918.

Mathieson, Moira B., and Tatis, Rita M. (comps.).
Understanding Disadvantaged Youth: Their
Problems and Potentials. An Annotated Bibli-
ography, 1970, 22 pp. Washington, DC: ERIC
Clearinghouse on Teacher Education. ERIC ED
044 380.

Osman, David S. (comp.). The Elementary and
    Secondary Education Act of 1965, as Amended.
    Selected Annotated Bibliography, 1965-1973,
    S, 1973. ERIC ED 096 370.

Van Leer Foundation (comp.). Compensatory
    Early Education: A Selective Working Bibli-
    ography. The Hague: Van Leer Foundation,
    1971.

11.
INNOVATIVE APPROACHES

Ablon, Joan, and Reid, Joseph W., Jr. An Experimental High School Project in Cultural Diversity. School of Criminology, U. of California, Berkeley, My, 1966.

Adler, Sol. The Non-Verbal Child. Springfield, IL: Charles C. Thomas, 1964.

Alatis, James E. "Our Own Language Barrier." American Education, D, 1964-Ja, 1965.

Allen, Le Roy B. "Replications of the Educational Park Concept for the Disadvantaged." Journal of Negro Education 40(Summer, 1971): 225-232.

American Institutes for Research. Impact of Educational Innovation on Student Performance. Palo Alto, CA: American Institute for Research, 1976.

Areen, Judith. "Education Vouchers." Harvard Civil Rights-Civil Liberties Law Review 6 (My, 1971).

Bell, Samuel, and Bogatz, Gerry Ann. The First Year of Sesame Street: An Evaluation. Princton, NJ: Educational Testing Service, O, 1970.

Barden, John. "The Educational Park." Nation, Ap 20, 1964.

Barry, Franklyn S. "The Syracuse Campus School Plan." In U.S. Commission on Civil Rights. Papers Prepared for National Conference on Equal Educational Opportunity in America's Cities. Washington, DC: GPO, 1968.

Beck, Joan. "Education by Franchise. What's Good for Pizza, Hamburgers, and Southern Fried Chicken Is Having Its Problems With Children." Chicago Tribune, My 10, 1970. [Franchising nursery schools and day care centers]

Bereday, George Z. F., Rosenbluth, Henry H., and Scoon, Annabelle R. "The Residential School as an Agent of Integration." NASSP Bulletin 56(N, 1972):66-74.

Berkeley School Report No. 7. Educational Parks, 1966. Berkeley Unified School District, 1414 Walnut Street, Berkeley, CA.

Berkman, David. "Segregation, Education, and Broadcasting." Changing Education, Fall, 1966.

Berl, Terry, and Alpert, Shelly. "Teachers on the Schools." Center Forum, O 5, 1967. [Experience in a freedom school at the Goddard-Riverside Community Center at 92nd and Columbus, New York City]

Berman, Paul, and McLaughlin, Milbrey Wallin. Federal Programs Supporting Educational Change. Vol. VIII: Implementing and Sustaining Innovations. Santa Monica, CA: Rand, My, 1978.

Berube, Maurice R. "Educational Parks: Still a Hope for the Future?" United Teacher, Je 3, 1967.

_____. "The Trouble with Vouchers." Community 3(N, 1970):1-2, 4.

Birnbaum, Robert, and Goldman, Joseph. "Effects of a Voucher Plan for Higher Education." In The Graduates: A Follow-up Study of New York City High School Graduates of 1970, pp. 143-175. New York: Center for Social Research, City U. of New York, My, 1971.

Bloomberg, Warner, Jr., and Kincaid, John. "Parent Participation: Practical Policy or Another Panacea?" Urban Review, Je, 1968.

Blossom, Grace A. The Reading Problem of the Bilingual Child and a Solution, 1967. The Author, 231 S. Stapley Drive, Mesa, AZ 85201.

Blue Ribbon Advisory Committee. East San Jose Educational Park Study. San Jose, CA: East Side Union High School District, My, 1968.

Blumenthal, David. "Community Schools." Harvard Crimson, Ap 10, 1969.

Bowman, Gerda W., and Klopf, Gordon J. New Careers and Roles in the American School. New York: Bank Street College of Education, D, 1968. [On teacher aides in 15 cities]

Brazziel, William F. "Higher Horizons in Southern Elementary Schools." Journal of Negro Education, Fall, 1964.

Bremer, John. The Parkway Program. Philadelphia: The Philadelphia Public Schools, 1970.

Caldwell, Betty M., and Richmond, Julius B. "Programmed Day Care for the Very Young Child--A Preliminary Report." Journal of Marriage and Family Living, N, 1964.

The Campus School. Educational Evolution in Syracuse, 1967. Syracuse Campus Site Planning Center, 215 Larned Bldg., 114 South Warren St., Syracuse, NY 13202.

Candoli, Carl I., and Leu, Donald J. A Feasibility Study on the Educational Park in Grand Rapids. Grand Rapids, MI: Board of Education, 1967.

Carpenter, Polly, and Hall, George R. Case Studies in Educational Performance Contracting: 1. Conclusions and Implications. Santa Monica, CA: Rand, D, 1971.

Carr, Ray A., and Hayward, Gerald C. "Education by Chit. An Examination of Voucher Proposals." Education and Urban Society 2 (1970):179-191.

Center for New Schools. "Strengthening Alternative High Schools." Harvard Educational Review 42(Ag, 1972):313-350. [Metro High School, Chicago, IL]

Center for the Study of Public Policy. Financing Education by Grants to Parents. A Preliminary Report. Cambridge, MA: The Center, Harvard Graduate School of Education, Mr, 1970.

The Children's Academy. A New Concept in School Organization. Mount Vernon, NY: Board of Education, 1966.

Clark, Kenneth B. "Alternative Public School Systems." Harvard Educational Review, Winter, 1968.

_____. "Unstructuring Education." In New Relationships in ITV. Washington, DC: Educational Media Council, 1967.

Clatworthy, F. James. "Boarding Schools for the Disadvantaged." Phi Delta Kappan, Mr, 1967.

Cloward, Robert D. Studies in Tutoring. York: Columbia U., Social Work Research Center, 1966, 105 pp. ERIC ED 021 903.

Coggs, Pauline R., and Robinson, Vivian R. "Training Indigenous Community Leaders for Employment in Social Work." Social Casework, My, 1967. [Training of non-professional social service aides in the Milwaukee public schools]

Cohen, David K., and Farrar, Eleanor. "Power to the Parents?--The Story of Education Vouchers." Public Interest 48(Summer, 1977): 72-97.

Comptroller General of the United States. Educational Laboratory and Research and Development Center Programs Need to Be Strengthened, N, 1973. ERIC ED 086 691.

Congreve, Willard J. "Collaborating for Urban Education in Chicago: The Woodlawn Developmental Project." Education and Urban Society, F, 1969.

Conroy, Vincent F. "Metropolitanism: I. Hartford as Case Study." Harvard Graduate School of Education Association Bulletin XII (1967), No. 1.

Cook, Ann, and Mack, Herb. The Excitement of Learning. Implications for Urban Schools. New York: Institute for Community Studies, Queens College, 1969.

Coons, John E., and Sugarman, Stephen D. "Vouchers for Public Schools." Inequality in Education 15(N, 1973):60-62.

Denker, Joel. "Radical Education and the Movement: A Look at an Experimental High School in D.C." Radicals in the Professions, N-D, 1968.

Dentler, Robert A. and others. "The Educational Complex Study Project." Integrated Education, Je-Jl, 1965. [New York City]

_____. Memorandum No. 6. Puerto Rican Student Residential Patterns and Changes. Memorandum No. 8. Educational Complexes in Brooklyn Public Schools. Memorandum No. 9. Organizing for Curriculum Development in Educational Complexes. Memorandum No. 10. The "600" Schools and the Educational Complex. Memorandum No. 11. Administrative Structure of Educational Complexes. Memorandum No. 12. The Logistics of Busing. Memorandum No. 13. Some Modifications of Queens Complexes. Memorandum No. 14. Overview of the Educational Complex Study Project. Institute of Urban Studies, Teachers College, Columbia U., Ja-F, 1965. These are preliminary drafts.

Department of Elementary School Principals, NEA. National Assessment of Educational Progress. Some Questions and Comments. Rev. ed. Washington, DC: National Education Association, 1968.

Deutsch, Martin. "Aspects of Ability Grouping." Integrated Education, F-Mr, 1964.

_____. "Some Psychosocial Aspects of Learning in the Disadvantaged." Integrated Education, Je-Jl, 1965.

Dickinson, William E. (ed.). Performance Contracting: A Guide for School Board Members and Community Leaders. Evanston, IL: National School Boards Association, 1971.

Downs, Anthony. "Competition and Community Schools." In Community Control of Schools. Edited by Henry M. Levin. Washington, DC: Brookings, 1970.

Duke, Daniel L., and Muzio, Irene. "How Effective Are Alternative Schools?--A Review of Recent Evaluations and Reports." Teachers College Record 79(F, 1978):461-483.

Dunn, Susan V. The Educational Park, The Middle School--A Report on Material on File in the Berkeley Unified School District Research Office and Some Additional Sources from the Berkeley Schools Professional Library, n.d. ERIC ED 011 127.

Dyer, Henry S. "Accountability." Parts 1, 2, 3. United Teacher, N 22 and 29, 1970.

_____. "Toward Objective Criteria of Professional Accountability in the Schools of New York City." Phi Delta Kappan 52(D, 1970):206-211.

"The East. A Model of Nationhood." Imani 5 (Ag-S, 1971):29-39, 56. [Uhuru Sasa, an independent black school in Brooklyn, NY]

East Orange Board of Education. "The East Orange Education Plaza." Integrated Education, F-Mr, 1965.

Educational Associates, Inc. A Report on Upward Bound to the Office of Economic Opportunity. Washington, DC: Educational Associates, Inc., 1969.

Edwards, J. Bentley. "The Oakland Cottage School." Integrated Education 8(Ja-F, 1970): 33-40.

Edwards, Thomas J. "The Language-Experience Attack on Cultural Deprivation." Reading Teacher, Ap, 1965.

Egloff, Marjorie. The Neighborhood Youth Corps: A Review of Research. Washington, DC: GPO, 1970.

Elford, George. "The Voucher Plan Debate." America, Ja 29, 1972.

Elliott, Lloyd H. "Education at a Profit?" Educational Record 51(1970):53-56.

Epps, Edgar G. "Action Learning. Potential for Inner-City Youth?" NASSP Bulletin 58(N, 1974):12-21.

Estes, Nolan, and Waldrip, Donald R. (eds.). Magnet Schoos: Legal and Practical Implications. Piscataway, NJ: New Century Education Corporation, 1978.

Evans, Medford. "How to Start a Private School. A Manual of Assistance for Citizens." Citizen, S, 1964.

Fantini, Mario. "Options for Students, Parents, and Teachers: Public Schools of Choice." Phi Delta Kappan 52(My, 1971):541-543.

_____. Public Schools of Choice. A Plan for the Reform of American Education. New York: Simon & Schuster, 1974.

_____. "Public Schools of Choice and the Plurality of Publics." Educational Leadership 28(Mr, 1971):585-591.

_____. The Reform of Urban Schools. Washington, DC: National Education Association, 1970.

Featherstone, Joseph. "Storefront Schools in Harlem." New Republic, S 7, 1968.

Field, Marcia Marker, and Wolff, Max. The Educational Park: Potential Funding Resources. New York: Center for Urban Education, Ja, 1970.

Fernandez, Alfred P. "The Educational Park: A Second Look." Journal of Secondary Education 45(My, 1970):223-229.

Field, Kenneth C. "Michigan Bell Finds Headaches, Rewards in 'Adopting' School." Wall Street Journal, Ja 15, 1969. [Detroit]

Fischer, John, chairman. Conferences on Educational Accountability. Princeton, NJ: Educational Testing Service, Mr, 1971.

Fischer, John H. "The School Park." In Racial Isolation in the Public Schools, vol. II, Appendix D2. Washington, DC: GPO, 1967.

Fitch, George E. A Report and Recommendation on Achievement Test Results, 1964. Greenburgh District 8, 475 West Hartsdale Avenue, Hartsdale, NY. [See Aaron Lipton, "Classroom Grouping and Integration."]

Freelain, Norm. "Unique School for the Exceptional Child." Muhammad Speaks, Ja 3, 1969. [The Potential School for Exceptional Children in Chicago, operated by Miss Ramona O. Fogerty]

Freeman, R. D. "Adam Smith, Education and Laissez-Faire." History of Political Economy, Spring, 1969.

Friedman, Milton. "The Voucher Idea." New York Times Magazine, S 23, 1973.

_____. "Whose Intolerance?" Newsweek, O 6, 1975. Vouchers

Gaines, Loretta. Building a Pan-African Pre-School, 1975. The East Publications, 10 Clover Place, Brooklyn, NY

_____. "Methodology of the Pan-African Pre-School." Black World 24(Ag, 1975):18-25.

Garfinkel, Irwin, and Grambich, Edward. "A Statistical Analysis of the OEO Experiment in Educational Performance Contracting." Journal of Human Resources 8(Summer, 1973): 275-305.

Gaskins, Leah. "Models for Schools in Black Neighborhoods." Foresight, D, 1969.

Gewirtz, Marvin H. Parental Involvement in a Reading-Improvement Program/A Decentralized Project. New York: Center for Urban Education, N, 1968 [New York City]

Gilbert, Jerome H. Parent Aides--A Partial Solution to the Education of Disadvantaged Elementary School Children, 1968. Columbus-University Laboratory School, 2211 Seventh Street, Berkeley, CA 94710.

Gittell, Marilyn. The Community School in the Nation. Community Issues, Vol. 2, No. 1. New York: Queens College, F, 1970.

Goldberg, Gertrude S. "Deschooling and the Disadvantaged: Implications of the Illich Proposals." IRCD Bulletin 7(D, 1971):2-10.

Goldberg, Herman R. "Metropolitan Planning for Education." Integrated Education, Ap-My, 1966. [Rochester, NY]

Goldman, Louis. The Community School Today. Wichita, KS: Center for Urban Studies, Witchita State U., D, 1967.

Gonis, Sophia N. "Negro Influence on the New Educational Design." Clearing House, O, 1965.

Goodlad, John I. "Nongraded Schools. Meeting Children Where They Are." Saturday Review, Mr 20, 1965.

Goodman, Paul. "Mini-Schools: A Prescription for the Reading Problem." New York Review of Books, Ja 4, 1968.

_____. "The Tiny Schools: A Prescription for Teaching Reading." Toronto Education Quarterly, Winter-Spring, 1968.

Grabiner, Gene. "Corporate Involvement in Elementary and Secondary Education." New School of Education Journal 2(Spring, 1971): 46-66.

Grant, Gerald. "The Difficult 30 Per Cent." Southern Education Report, Ja-F, 1966. [Problems of the "model school system" experiment in Washington, DC]

Graubard, Allen. "The Free School Movement." Harvard Educational Review 42(Ag, 1972):351-373.

Gray, Farnum. "Taking Risks With the Setup." Nation, Ja 22, 1968. [The Pennsylvania Advancement School in Philadelphia]

Greaves, Jack. "A Proposed New School Format. Continuous-Progress Centers." In U.S. Commission on Civil Rights. Papers Prepared for National Conference on Equal Educational Opportunity in America's Cities. Washington, DC: GPO, 1968.

"Green Light Expected for Two-State [School] Districts." Education U.S.A., My 19, 1969. [Vermont and New Hampshire]

Greenberg, James D., and Roush, Robert E. "A Visit to the 'School without Walls': Two Impressions." Phi Delta Kappan 51(1970):480-484. [Philadelphia]

Grieder, Calvin. "Education Parks May Replace the Neighborhood School." Nation's Schools, D, 1965.

"'Guerrilla Warfare' in the Ghetto: Making a Community School Work." American Teacher, O, 1968. [Morgan Community School, Washington, DC]

Guerriero, Michael A. The Benjamin Franklin High School-Urban League Street Academies Program. New York: Center for Urban Education, N, 1968. [Harlem]

Gunnings, Thomas S., and Gunnings, Barbara B. "In Defense of EXCEL." Phi Delta Kappan 60 (Ja, 1979).

Gutierrez, Felix, and Chacon, Gloria. The Educational Voucher Intrigue: An Analysis of Its Impact on the Alum Rock Community, 1974. Southwest Network, 1020 B Street, Suite No. 8, Hayward, CA 94541.

Hall, G. R., Carpenter, P., Haggart, S. A., Rapp, M. L., and Sumner, G. C. A Guide to Educational Peformance Contracting. Also, Technical Appendix. Santa Monica, CA: Rand, Mr, 1972.

Hartman, Allan S. "How to Start a Preschool Program Without Waiting." Nation's Schools, Ap, 1965.

Havighurst, Robert J. The East Orange Education Plaza, A New Plan for a Modern Community. Chicago, IL: U. of Chicago, S, 1964.

Havighurst, Robert J. and others. "Metropolitanism: II. What Relevance for Chicago?" Harvard Graduate School of Education Association Bulletin XII(1967), No. 1.

Hentoff, Nat. "Vouchers: Educational Choice." Civil Liberties, F, 1971.

Hobson, Julius, and Lower, Tina. "Educational Audit: A Proposal." Center Forum, My 15, 1969. [Technique of auditing the quality of education in a community]

"How the Profession Feels About Teacher Aides." NEA Journal, N, 1967.

Howe, Florence. "Mississippi's Freedom Schools: The Politics of Education." Harvard Educational Review, Spring, 1965.

Huberman, A. M. Understanding Change in Education: An Introduction. Paris: UNESCO, 1973. [On educational innovation]

Hunt, David E. "Homogeneous Classroom Grouping Based on Conceptual Systems Theory in an Educational Enrichment Project: An Exploratory Study." Paper read at the American Educational Research Association Symposium, "Conceptual Systems Theory and Educational Research." Chicago, IL, F 20, 1964. [Syracuse, NY]

Illich, Ivan. "After Deschooling, What?" Social Policy 2(S-O, 1971):5-13.

_____. "Education Without School: How It Can Be Done." New York Review of Books, Ja 7, 1971.

_____. "Why We Must Abolish Schooling." New York Review, Jl 2, 1970.

Implementation Committee. Focus on Understanding. Plan for the Implementation of a Policy for Educational Enrichment in Intercultural Relations, 1965. West Irondequoit Board of Education, 370 Cooper Road, West Irondequoit, NY. [Plan for city-suburb cooperation on schools]

Ingersoll, Gary M. "'Sesame Street' Can't Handle All the Traffic! Phi Delta Kappan 53 (N, 1971):185-186.

Innis, Roy. "Black Leader's Idea for South's Schools" (interview). U.S. News and World Report, Mr 2, 1970.

Innis, Roy, and Solomon, Victor. A True Alternative to Segregation--A Proposal for Community School Districts, F, 1970. Congress of Racial Equality (CORE), 200 West 135th Street, New York, NY 10030.

Institute for Development of Educational Auditing. ESEA Title I Child Parent Centers, 1971-72. Interim Evaluation Report. Chicago: Board of Education, S, 1972.

Integrated Quality Education: A Study of Educational Parks and Other Alternatives for Urban Needs. Berkeley Unified School District, CA, Jl, 1968. ERIC ED 024 127.

Jacobson, Nathan (ed.). An Exploration of the Educational Park Concept. New York: Board of Education, 1964.

Jacoby, Susan L. "The Making of a Community School." Urban Review, F, 1968. [Adams-Morgan School in Washington, DC]

Jamison, Dean, Supper, Patrick, and Wells, Stuart. "The Effectiveness of Alternative Instructional Media: A Survey." Review of Economic Research 44(Winter, 1974):1-67.

Jane and Linda. "The Politics of Guilt: The Writings of Jonathan Kozol." No More Teachers Dirty Looks! 3(Spring, 1973):3-6.

Janowitz, Gayle. After-School Study Centers. Volunteer Work in Reading. Big Cities School Project, Center for Social Organization Studies, Box 33, 1126 East 59th Street, Chicago, IL 60637.

_____. After-School Study Centers: Experimental Materials and Clinical Research. Final Report. Washington, DC: Bureau of Research, Office of Education, 1968.

_____. Helping Hands. Volunteer Work in Education. Chicago, IL: U. of Chicago Press, 1966.

Janssen, Peter. "OEO As Innovator." Saturday Review 55(F 5, 1972):40-43.

Jencks, Christopher. "Education Vouchers." New Republic, Jl 4, 1970.

_____. "Private Schools for Black Children." New York Times Magazine, N 3, 1968.

Jennings, Wayne. "Educational Parks: Tomorrow's Schools." Audiovisual Instruction 15(O, 1970): 42-44.

Johnson, Adna and others. Pilot Project in Elementary School Guidance, n.d. ERIC ED 011 123.

Jones, Doris M. (ed.). Education Parks, Second Annual Nova University Conference. Fort Lauderdale, FL: Nova U. Press, Jl, 1968.

Kaurouma, Patrica Ann. "An Evaluation of the History of the Development of the Black Free School Movement in America, 1954 to 1973: A Search for Alternatives." Doctoral dissertation, U. of Colorado, 1974. Univ. Microfilms Order No. 75-03751.

Kemble, Eugenia. "Emergency Schools Born from Crisis and Creativity." United Teacher, S 27, 1967. [Emergency schools organized by the striking United Federation of Teachers]

_____. "Emergency Schools Uncover Broad Community Resources, Cooperation." United Teacher, O 25, 1967. [Observations on the 150 schools established during the Fall, 1967, teachers' stoppage in New York City]

Keppel, Francis. "Educational Technology and the Educational Park." In Racial Isolation in the Public Schools, Vol. II, Appendix D2.3. Washington, DC: GPO, 1967.

Keyes, Ralph. "The Free Universities." Nation, O 2, 1967.

Kohler, Gordon R. "Education Parks: An Attempt at Radical Reform in a Democratic Society." Doctoral dissertation, Harvard U., 1967.

Kornegay, William. "The Open Market: A New Model for Our Schools?" Phi Delta Kappan, Je, 1968.

Kozol, Jonathan. Free Schools. Boston: Houghton Mifflin, 1972.

_____. "Politics, Rage and Motivation in the Free Schools." Harvard Educational Review 42(Ag, 1972):414-422.

Krughoff, Robert M. "Private Schools for the Public." Education and Urban Society, N, 1969.

Kurland, Norman, Blair, George, Bardin, John, Callahan, William, and Harrison, George. "Urban-Suburban Cooperation: A Report." Integrated Education, Ag-S, 1966. [Rochester, NY]

Lamp, Robert G. "Educational Parks for the 20th Century Schools." C.T.A. Journal, O, 1966.

Lawrence, Charles. "Free Schools: Public and Private and Black and White." Inequality in Education 1, Nos. 3-4(1970):8-12.

Laws, Janice S. "The Establishment of an Independent Black Education Institution: The Formation of the Afrikan Education Center." Master's thesis, Northeastern Illinois State U., 1973.

Lekachman, Robert. "Vouchers and Public Education." The New Leader, Jl 12, 1971.

Lentz, Robert R. "Outward Bound--Education Through Experience." In Models for Integrated Education, pp. 77-88. Edited by Daniel U. Levine. Worthington, OH: Jones, 1971.

Leon, Vicki. "Thriving on Ethnic Differences." Learning 4(F, 1976):64-70. [Multi-culture Institute]

Lessinger, Leon. "Engineering Accountability for Results in Public Education." Phi Delta Kappan 52(D, 1970):217-225.

Leu, Donald J., and Candoli, I. Carl. A Feasibility Study of the "Cultural-Educational Park" for Chicago. East Lansing, MI: Michigan State U., Ja, 1968.

Levin, Henry M. "The Failure of the Public Schools and the Free Market Remedy." Urban Review, Je, 1968.

_____. "Vouchers and Social Equity." Change 5(O, 1973):29-33.

Levin, Joel M. "Alum Rock After Two Years: You, Dear Reader, Have a Choice." Phi Delta Kappan 56(N, 1974):201-204.

Levine, Daniel U. "Coeducation--A Contributing Factor in Miseducation of the Disadvantaged." Phi Delta Kappan, N, 1964.

Levine, Daniel U., and Campbell, Connie. "Educational Options: Magnet Schools and Programs." In Citizen Guide to Quality Education, pp. 39-54. Edited by Rachel Thompkins and Susan Kaeser. Cleveland, OH: Citizens' Council for Ohio Schools, 1978.

Lewis, David. "The New Role of Education Parks in the Changing Structure of Metropolitan Areas." In U.S. Commission on Civil Rights. Papers Prepared for National Conference on Equal Educational Opportunity in America's Cities. Washington, DC: GPO, 1968.

Lines, Patricia M. Vouchers and Racial Balance. Cambridge, MA: Center for the Study of Public Policy, Harvard U., D 1, 1971.

Lortie, Dan C. "Towards Educational Equality: The Teacher and the Educational Park." In Racial Isolation in the Public Schools, Vol. II, Appendix D2.4. Washington, DC: GPO, 1967.

Lynd, Staughton. "The Freedom Schools." Freedomways, Spring, 1965.

Lyon, D. W. "Capitalism in the Classroom: Education Vouchers." Federal Reserve Bank Business Review of Philadelphia, D, 1971.

McBroom, Clarence, Jr. "A Study of Alternative Educational Programs in Selected Large City Public School Districts of the United States." Doctoral dissertation, Walden U., 1977.

McCauley, Brian L., Dornbusch, Sanford M., and Scott, W. Richard. Evaluation and Authority in Alternative Schools. Stanford, CA: Stanford Center for Research and Development in Teaching, Je, 1972.

McCarthy, Joseph F. X. The Educational Park-- What Should It Be--Educational Specifications for the Northeast Bronx Education Park. Brooklyn, NY: New York City Board of Education, Ag, 1966, 41 pp. ERIC ED 016 710.

McClarkin, W. D. Building for Quality Education--The Education Park Concept. Nashville, TN: George Peabody College for Teachers. Division of Surveys and Field Services, Ag, 1967, 121 pp. ERIC ED 033 539.

McCoy, Rhody A. "The Formation of a Community-Controlled School District." In Community Control of Schools. Edited by Henry M. Levin. Washington, DC: Brookings, 1970.

McKelvey, Troy V. (ed.). *Metropolitan School Organization*. 2 vols. Berkeley, CA: McCutchan, 1973.

"Clifford McKissick Community School: 'To Build Is To Work.'" *SOBU Newsletter*, F 20, 1971. [Milwaukee, WI]

Mann, Eric. "The Newark Community School." *Liberation*, Ag, 1967. [Detailed analysis of conditions surrounding organization of the private school in ghetto]

Marland, S. P., Jr. "The Education Park Concept in Pittsburgh." *Phi Delta Kappan*, Mr, 1967.

Matters of Choice. A Ford Foundation Report on Alternative Schools. New York: The Ford Foundation, 1974. [Alternative schools within public school systems]

Mauch, James E. "The Education Park." *American School Board Journal*, Mr, 1965.

Miller, Andrew C. "Magnet School Concept Catches On." *Kansas City Star*, Ag 22, 1976.

Mills, Nicolaus. "Free Versus Directed Schools: Benefits for the Disadvantaged?" *IRCD Bulletin* 7(S, 1971):2-10.

Modlinski, Jules, and Zaret, Esther. *The Federation of Independent Community Schools. An Alternative Urban School System*. Milwaukee, WI: The Federation, Ap, 1970.

Moore, Donald R., Wilson, Thomas A., and Johnson, Richard. *The Metro School. A Report on the Progress of Chicago's Experimental "School Without Walls."* Chicago, IL: Urban Research Corporation, Ja 1, 1971. [5464 South Shore Drive, Chicago, IL 60615]

Moynihan, Francis M. "Family Service Agency Collaboration with Schools." *Social Casework*, Ja, 1968. [Chicago experience]

National Education Association. *Teacher Aides in Large School Systems*. Washington, DC: National Education Association, 1967.

New Schools Exchange. *Continuing Directory of New and Innovative Schools in the U.S. and Canada*, Je 30, 1972. New Schools Exchange, 701 B. Anacapa Street, Santa Barbara, CA 93101.

"New 'Super' High School—Wave of Future for Big Cities?" *U.S. News and World Report*, Jl 10, 1967. [Pittsburgh]

New York City Public Schools. *The Educational Park in New York City. Concept for Discussion*. New York: Board of Education, Ap, 1965.

_____. *The Professional Promotional Seminar. A Report of a Training Program for Future Supervisors of Quality Integrated Education in the Elementary Schools of New York City*. New York: Board of Education, 1967.

New York State Education Department. *Economy and Increased Educational Opportunity Through Extended School Year Programs*. Albany, NY: The Department, Ag, 1965.

_____. *Setting the Stage for Lengthened School Year Programs*. Albany, NY: The Department, Mr, 1968.

_____. *Survey of Public School Teacher Aides, Fall, 1965*. Albany, NY: ERIC ED 011 250.

Niedermeyer, Fred C. "Parent-Assisted Learning in the Inner City." *Urban Education* 8(O, 1973):239-248.

Noar, Gertrude. *Teacher Aides at Work*. Washington, DC: National Education Association, 1967.

Office of Economic Opportunity. *An Experiment in Performance Contracting. Summary of Preliminary Results*. Washington, DC: O.E.O., F, 1972.

Office Planning, Research, and Evaluation. *A Proposed Demonstration in Education Vouchers* Washington, DC: Office of Economic Opportunity, Ap 24, 1972.

Oliver, John. "The Education of Black Americans: An Exploratory Study of Public Alternative Education." Doctoral dissertation, Brandeis U., 1975. Univ. Microfilms Order No. 75-24236.

O'Neill, Michael. "Giving Americans a Choice—Alternatives to Public Education." *America*, Ja 24, 1970.

Orsini, Bette. "New Reading Plan: A Tangled Trail Leads to Millions." *St. Petersburg Times*, Ag 23, 1972.

Overlan, S. Francis. "Our Public School Monopoly." *New Republic* 169(S 15, 1973):14-18. [Vouchers]

Perkins, Eugene. "The Need for a Pan-Afrikanist Alternative to the Street Institution." *Black Books Bulletin* 2(Winter, 1974):8-11.

Perseghin, Gerard. "Black Belt Experimental School." *Momentum* 1(Ap, 1970):8-12.

Pettigrew, Thomas F. "The Metropolitan Educational Park." *Christianity and Crisis* 30 (Jl 6, 1970):145-150.

"Pittsburgh's Education Parks." *Phi Delta Kappan*, N, 1967.

Plante, Alexander J. "Urban-Suburban Cooperation as an Educational Solution for De Factor Segregation." In U.S. Commission on Civil Rights. *Papers Prepared for National Conference on Equal Educational Opportunity in America's Cities*. Washington, DC: GPO, 1968.

Plath, Karl R. Schools Within Schools. A Study of High School Organization. New York: Bureau of Publications, Teachers College, Columbia U., 1965. [Relevant to educational park]

Platoff, Joan. "Preschool Prototypes: An Integrated, Semi-Cooperative Nursery School." Young Children, Mr, 1966. [Chicago]

Pressman, Harvey. New Schools for the Cities, 1968. New Community Press, 1220 15th Street, N.W., Washington, DC 20009.

Ray, H. W. The Office of Economic Opportunity Experiment in Educational Peformance Contracting. PB-208 947. Springfield, VA: National Technical Information Service, Mr 14, 1972.

_____. The Office of Economic Opportunity Experiment in Educational Performance Contracting: The Incentive Only Sites. PB-208 948. Springfield, VA: National Technical Information Service, F 7, 1972.

_____. The Office of Economic Opportunity Experiment in Educational Performance Contracting. PB-206 793. Springfield, VA: National Technical Information Service, Ja 29, 1972.

Reiner, Everett. An Essay on Alternatives in Education. Cuernavaca, Mexico: Centro Intercultural de Documentacion, 1970.

"Reports from the Summer Health Projects." Health Rights News, S, 1967. [Medical and nursing students at work in ghetto projects during summer, 1967]

Richter, Charles O. "Metropolitanism: III. The Suburban School's Response." Harvard Graduate School of Education Association Bulletin 12(1967).

Richter, Charles O., and Overlan, S. Francis. "Will Urban Suburban Busing Work?" Nation's Schools, Ag, 1967.

Riesman, David. "The Search for Alternative Models in Education." American Scholar, Summer, 1969.

Riessman, Frank. "Low-Income Culture: The Strengths of the Poor." Journal of Marriage and the Family, N, 1964.

Riessman, Frank, and Gartner, Alan. "Paraprofessionals. The Effect on Children's Learning." Urban Review, O, 1969.

Riessman, Frank, and Hannah, Arlene. "Teachers of the Poor." P.T.A. Magazine, N, 196

"Right Side of the Tracks." Time, Mr 10, 1967. [Proposed "linear city" in Brooklyn]

"The Rise of Independent Black Educational Institutions." Imani (Ag-S, 1971).

Robinson, Nicholas Wheeler. "Marland's 'Magnificent Gamble'--Pittsburgh's Great High Schools." Urban Review, N, 1968.

Roby, Pamela. "Educational Aides in Inner City Schools." Integrated Education, N-D, 1968.

Ross, Leonard, and Zeckhausen, Richard. "Tuition Vouchers." New Republic, Jl 18, 1970.

Ross, Vivian Hudson. "Black Muslim Schools: Institutionalization of Black Nationalism (Implications for the Altering of Self-Concept in Ghetto Schools)." Doctoral dissertation, U. of Michigan, 1976. Univ. Microfilms Order No. 76-27582.

Rossman, Michael. "The Movement and Educational Reform." American Scholar, Autumn, 1967.

Samuels, Bruce (comp.). The First Year of Sesame Street: A Summary of Audience Surveys. Final Report, Volume IV of V Volumes. New York: Children's Television Workshop, D, 1970, 31 pp. ERIC ED 047 824.

Saretsky, Gary. "The OEO P.C. Experiment and the John Henry Effect." Phi Delta Kappan (My, 1972):579-581.

Satterwhite, Frank J. (ed.). Planning an Independent Black Educational Institution. Harlem, NY: Moja Publishing House, 1971.

Schwartz, E. Terry. An Evaluation of the Transitional Middle School in New York City, Ag 31, 1966. ERIC ED 011 020.

Scott, Jack, and Goodman, William. "Education for Profit." New School of Education Journal 2(Spring, 1971):32-45. [Litton Industries and Camp Parks Job Corps, Pleasanton, CA]

Scott, Ralph. "Home Start: Family-Centered Pre-school Enrichment for Black and White Children." Psychology in the Schools 10 (Ap, 1973):140-146.

Seabrook, Luther W. "A New Experiment in Black Education." Social Policy, My-Je, 1970. [Highland Park Free School, Roxbury, MA]

Seibel, Mark. "Magnets: A Still Unproven Technique." Dallas News, Ag 15, 1976. [Magnet schools as a desegregation device]

Selden, David. "Vouchers: A Critic Changes His Mind." Nation's Schools and Colleges 2 (Je, 1975):44-46.

Session, John. "A New Approach to Urban Education." Changing Education, Spring, 1966. [Educational parks in Washington, DC]

_____. "A Radical Proposal for Education [in Washington, D.C.]" ADA World Magazine, Ja, 1966. [Educational parks]

_____. "Peformance Contracting Revisited." American Teacher, Ja, 1972.

Shaevitz, Morton H. "Myths of Tutoring." _Tailorbird_, Ap 3, 1969.

Sharp, Jean Marie. "Evaluation and Authority in Independent Black Educational Institutions." Doctoral dissertation, Columbia U., 1976. Univ. Microfilms Order No. 77-5759.

Shuy, Roger W. "Performance Contracts and Reading: The Great Oversimplification." _Journal of Reading_ 15(My, 1972):604-612.

Sigel, Efrem, and Sobel, Myra. _Accountability and the Controversial Role of the Performance Contractors_, 1971. Knowledge Industry Publications, Tiffany Towers, White Plains, NY 10602.

Sine, David F., Marquist, Lawrence J., and Barry, Franklyn S. _The Campus Plan. A Report on a Feasibility Study for Elementary School Construction in Syracuse, N.Y._, 1967. Syracuse Campus Site Planning Center, Syracuse City School District, 409 W. Genesee Street, Syracuse, NY 13202.

Sine, David F. and others. "Educational Parks." _NEA Journal_, Mr, 1968.

Sizemore, Barbara A. "PUSH Politics and the Education of America's Youth." _Phi Delta Kappan_ 60(Ja, 1979):364.

Sizer, Theodore R. "The Case for a Free Market." _Saturday Review_, Ja 11, 1969.

Solomon, Alan, and Theimer, William C., Jr. "A Paired Schools Science Program." _Integrated Education_ 8(Mr-Ap, 1970):34-36.

Southwest Network. _This Pamphlet Shows How the Parents and the Community Were Deceived by the Alum Rock Voucher Program_, 1974. Southwest Network, 1020 B Street, Suite No. 8, Hayward, CA 94541.

Star, Jack. "'We'll Educate Your Kids--Or Your Money Back.'" _Look_ 35(Je 15, 1971): 56-64. [Gary, IN]

Syracuse Board of Education. _The Campus Plan. Quality Education for Elementary Schools._ Syracuse, NY: Board of Education, Ag, 1969.

Thelen, Herbert A. "A Proposal for the Attainment of Racial Integration Through Public Education." _School Review_ 78(My, 1970):391-396. [See Woock, below]

Thomas, George I. _Extended School Year Designs_. Albany, NY: State Education Department, Ja, 1966.

Thomas, J. Alan. "The Secondary Education Park: Value Synthesis in Urban School Systems." _Administrator's Notebook_, N, 1965.

Tolson, Jose. "Che Lumumba School." _Drum_ (Winter, 1977-78):9, 17. [New Africa House, U. of Massachusetts, Amherst]

Tree, Chris. "Storefront Schools." _Urban Review_, F, 1968. [Harlem]

Troups, Carolyn H. "The Whittier-Somerset Project: A Case Study in Urban-Suburban School Co-operation." _Elementary School Journal_, D, 1968. [District of Columbia and Montgomery County, MD]

"250,000 Hours...and Growing. A Report of the School Volunteer Programs." _Staff Bulletin of the Public Schools of New York City_, N 14, 1966. [For information, write: School Volunteer Program, 125 West 54th Street, New York, NY 10019.]

U.S. Commission on Civil Rights. _Education Parks. Appraisals of Plans to Improve Educational Quality and Desegregate the Schools._ Washington, DC: GPO, O, 1967. [Reprinted from volume II of the Commission's _Racial Isolation in the Public Schools_ (Washington, DC, 1967)]

U.S. Department of HEW. _Volunteers in Education. Materials for Volunteer Programs and the Volunteer._ Washington, DC: GPO, Mr, 1972.

Vespa, Marcia Lane. "Chicago's Regional School Plans." _Integrated Education_, O-N, 1963.

Von Eckhardt, Wolf. "'Educational Parks': An Old Idea That Fizzled." _Washington Post_, Ap 8, 1972.

Wagner, Jon. "Education and 'Black' Education: Some Remarks on Cultural Relevance." _School Review_ 80(Ag, 1972):591-602. [CAM Academy, Chicago, IL]

Washington School of Psychiatry. _TAP, the Teacher Aide Program._ Washington, DC: Washington School of Psychiatry, Mr, 1967.

Webster, Staten W. "The Case for a Federal Demonstration School System." _Journal of Negro Education_, Spring, 1969.

Weiler, Daniel and others. _A Public School Voucher Demonstration: The First Year at Alum Rock_, Je, 1974. ERIC ED 093 091.

_____ and others. _A Public School Voucher Demonstration: The First Year at Alum Rock. Summary and Conclusions_, Je, 1974. ERIC ED 093 092.

Weinberg, Meyer. "A TVA for Textbooks." _Integrated Education_, Je-Jl, 1965.

Weiner, Stephen S., and Kellen, Konrad. _The Politics and Administration of the Voucher Demonstration in Alum Rock: The First Year, 1972-1973. Analysis of the Education Voucher Demonstration_, Ag, 1974. ERIC ED 097 765.

Wensi, Kutu. "From Relevance to Excellence: The Challenge of Independent Black Education Institution." Black Books Bulletin 2 (Winter, 1974):20-23.

Wilcox, Preston R. The Educational Impact of the Cadet Corps Program. New York: Columbia U. School of Social Work, 1967.

Wogaman, Thomas D. "Educational Parks: A Promising Hypothesis." California Journal for Instructional Improvement, My, 1968.

Wolf, Alison. "Educated by Voucher." New Society, Ap 4, 1974. [Alum Rock, CA]

Wolff, Max. "The Concept of an Educational Park." In Opening Opportunities for Disadvantaged Learners, pp. 322-336. Edited by A. Harry Passow. New York: Teachers College Press, 1972.

_____. "The Educational Park." American School and University, Jl, 1964.

_____. "The Educational Park." Integrated Education, Ap-My, 1967.

_____. Educational Park Development in the United States, 1967. New York: Center for Urban Education, Ag, 1967.

Wolff, Max, and Rudikoff, Benjamin. Educational Park Development in the United States-- 1969: A Survey of Current Plans with a List of Reports and References. New York: Center for Urban Education, Ja, 1970.

Wolff, Max, Rothman, Esther, and Berman, Leopold. "The Case for Educational Parks." Architectural Record, F, 1966.

Wolff, Max, and Rudikoff, Benjamin. "Reports and References On the Educational Park." In Educational Park Development in the United States--1969. New York: Center for Urban Education, Ja, 1970.

Wolff, Max, and Rinzler, Alan. The Educational Park. A Guide to its Implementation. New York: Center for Urban Education, Ja, 1970.

Woock, Roger R. "Community Operated Schools-- A Way Out?" Urban Education 3(1968).

_____. "On [H. Thelen's] 'A Proposal for the Attainment of Racial Integration through Public Education.'" School Review 78(Ag, 1970):603-607.

Woodward, Kilanza Nuri. "An Examination of a Black Liberation School: The Kawaida Educational and Development Center." Integrateducation 15(Mr-Ap, 1977).

Wortis, Joseph. "Prevention of Mental Retardation." American Journal of Orthopsychiatry, O, 1965.

Wortman, Paul M., Reichardt, C. S., and St. Pierre, R. G. "The First Year of the Educational Voucher Demonstration: A Secondary Analysis of Student Achievement Test Scores." Education and Urban Society (1977).

Wray, Jessie E. (interview). "Addendum on the Federation of Independent Community Schools." Integrated Education 8(N-D, 1970).

Wray, Jessie E. "Alternative Systems of Education." Integrated Education 8(N-D, 1970): 39-43.

Wrightstone, J. Wayne, Forlano, George, Frankel, Edward, Lewis, Barbara, Turner, Richard, and Bolger, Philip. Evaluation of the Higher Horizons Program for Underprivileged Children. Cooperative Research Project No. 1124. New York: Bureau of Educational Research, Board of Education, 1965.

Yeomans, Edward. And Gladly Learn: Summer Enrichment Programs for Urban Children. Boston: National Association of Independent Schools, 1965.

Young, Ethel. The Nursery School Program for Culturally Different Children. Menlo Park, CA: Pacific Coast Publishers, 1965.

Zinberg, Norman E. "A Group Approach with the School Teacher in the Integration Crisis." Mental Hygiene, Ap, 1967.

Zinn, Howard. "Schools in Context. The Mississippi Idea." Nation, N 23, 1964.

12.
SCHOOL ORGANIZATION

Aarons, Alfred C., Gordon, Barbara Y., and Stewart, William A. (eds.). "Linguistic-Cultural Differences and American Education." Florida FL Reporter, Spring-Summer, 1969. [Entire issue]

"Ability Grouping in Public Schools: A Threat to Equal Protection?" Connecticut Law Review 1(Je, 1968).

Alexander, K., and McDill, E. L. Selection and Allocation within Schools: Some Causes and Consequences of Curriculum Placement. Baltimore: Center for Social Organization of Schools, Johns Hopkins U., 1976.

Amperson, Robert L. "Teacher and Pupil: Ethnicity as an Independent Variate in Grading Patterns." Doctoral dissertation, U. of California, Berkeley, 1972.

Anderson, Barry. "Socio-Economic Status of Students and School Bureaucratization." Educational Administration Quarterly 7(Spring, 1971):12-24.

Anrig, Gregory R. "The Decentralization Controversy: Some Relatively Objective Views." American Education, F, 1969.

Approaches to Desegregation: The Superintendent's Perspective. Riverside, CA: University Extension, U. of California, 1969.

Balow, Irving H., and Ruddell, Arden K. "The Effects of Three Types of Grouping on Achievement." California Journal of Educational Research, My, 1963.

Bash, James H., and Morris, Thomas J. Utilizing Community Resources to Implement School Desegregation. A Guidebook. Bloomington, IN: Phi Delta Kappa, Commission on Education and Human Rights, 1968. ERIC ED 026 740.

Berube, Maurice R. "Black Power and the Learning Process." Commonweal, Ap 11, 1969.

Binzen, Peter. "Who Runs Our City Schools? How to Pick a School Board." Saturday Review, Ap 17, 1965.

Birenbaum, William M. Overlive: Power, Poverty, and the University. New York: Delacorte Press, 1969.

Bloom, Benjamin. "Stability and Change in Human Characteristics: Implications for School Reorganization." Educational Administration Quarterly, Winter, 1966. [See Pierce, below]

Bond, Horace Mann. "The First Thing I Look for in a School is--Cleanliness." The National Educational Outlook Among Negroes 1(My, 1973): 6-9.

Borg, Walter R. Ability Grouping in the Public Schools. Madison, WI: Dembar Educational Services, Inc., 1966.

_____. "Ability Grouping in the Public Schools. A Field Study." Journal of Experimental Education, Winter, 1965. [Entire issue]

Braddock, Clayton. "When the Teacher is Absent, What?" Southern Education Report, S, 1968.

Brown, B. Frank. "An Answer to Dropouts: The Nongraded High School." Atlantic, N, 1964.

Brown, Frank and others. "Minority Students Ability, Grouping and Career Development." Journal of Black Studies 8(Je, 1978):477-488.

Christopher, Van M. "The Organizational Climate of an Inner-City Secondary School." Doctoral dissertation, Claremont Graduate School, 1975. Univ. Microfilms Order No. 75-12, 742.

Comer, James P. "The Circle Game in School Tracking." Inequality in Education 12(Jl, 1972):23-27.

Committee on Student Participation in School Affairs. "Report on Pupil Role in School Affairs." Staff Bulletin, Public Schools of New York City, Ap 7, 1969.

Conroy, Vincent F. "Racial Imbalance and Educational Planning." Harvard Graduate School of Education Association Bulletin, Spring, 1965.

Cross, W. Ray, Passow, A. Harry, Hobson, Julius W., and Hansen, Carl F. "Ability Grouping." Administrative Leadership 5(F, 1969).

Culture of Schools. Final Report. 4 Volumes, 1970, 311 pp. Washington, DC: American Anthropological Association. ERIC ED 039 209; 039 212.

Cunningham, Luvern L. "Educational Governance and Policy Making in Large Cities." Public Administration Review, Jl-Ag, 1970.

DeBord, L., Griffin, L. J., and Clark, M. "Race, Sex, and Schooling: Insights from the Wisconsin Model of the Early Achievement Process." Sociology of Education 50(1977): 85-102.

Dentler, Robert A. "A Devil's Advocate Catechism on the Suburban-Urban Pupil Transfer Issue." Center Forum, D 23, 1968.

Deutsch, Martin. "Dimensions of the School's Role in the Problems of Integration." In Klopf and Laster, below.

Dodson, Dan W. "From Debate to Action." Educational Leadership, N, 1968.

_____. "New Forces Operating in Educational Decision Making." Integrated Education, Je-Jl, 1967.

_____. "School Administration, Control and Public Policy Concerning Integration." Journal of Negro Education, Summer, 1965.

_____. "The School and the Civil Rights Revolution." Integrated Education, Ag-N, 1965.

Dyer, Henry S. "School Factors and Equal Educational Opportunity." Harvard Educational Review, Winter, 1968.

Esposito, Dominick. Homogeneous and Heterogeneous Grouping: Principal Findings and Implications of a Research of the Literature, Jl, 1971. ERIC ED 056 150.

_____. Structure and Function. A Behavioral and Systematic Interpretation. New York: ERIC Information Retrieval Center on the Disadvantaged, Teachers College, Columbia U., My, 1971. [Ability grouping]

"The Failure of 'Community Control.'" Council For Basic Education Bulletin, D, 1968.

Fantini, Mario D. "Internal Action Programs for the Solution of Urban Education Problems." In Urban School Administration. Edited by Troy V. McKelvey and Austin D. Swanson. Beverly Hills, CA: Sage, 1969.

Farmer, James. Some Views on the Relationship Between Decentralization and Racial Integration in Large City School Systems, N, 1968, 18 pp. Address presented at a Special Training Institute on Problems of School Desegregation, Teachers College, Columbia U. ERIC ED 030 700.

Featherstone, Richard L., and Hill, Frederick W. "Urban School Decentralization. Part III." American School and University, F, 1969.

Fetters, William B. and others. Characteristics Differentiating Under- and Over-Achieving Elementary Schools, Mr, 1968, 47 pp. Washington, DC: National Center for Educational Statistics (DHEW), Division of Data Analysis and Dissemination. ERIC ED 021 318.

Findley, Warren. "How Ability Grouping Fails." Inequality in Education 14(Jl, 1973):38-40.

Findley, Warren, and Bryan, Miriam M. Ability Grouping: 1970. Status, Impact, and Alternatives. Athens, GA: Center for Educational Improvement, U. of Georgia, 1971.

_____ and _____. The Pros and Cons of Ability Grouping. Bloomington, IN: Phi Delta Kappa, 1975.

Franseth, Jane, and Koury, Rose. Survey of Research on Grouping as Related to Pupil Learning. Washington, DC: GPO, 1966.

Goldberg, Miriam L., Passow, A. Harry, and Justman, Joseph. The Effects of Ability Grouping. New York: Teachers College, Columbia U., 1966.

Gordon, Edmund W. "Decentralization and Educational Reform." IRCD Bulletin, N, 1968-Ja, 1969.

Gottlieb, David. "School Integration and Absorption of Newcomers." Integrated Education, Ag-N, 1965.

Grant, Gerald. "Tracking: What It Means, How It Works." Parents Magazine, S, 1966.

Hager, Don J. "Schools are Responsible." Integrated Education, Ap, 1963.

Harrison, William A., Jr. "Community Involvement as Means and End." Compact, Ap, 1969.

Havighurst, Robert J. Metropolitanism and the Issues of Social Integration and Administrative Decentralization in Large Cities, Jl 10, 1968. ERIC ED 030 697.

Hechinger, Fred M. "Who Runs Our Big City Schools? Room for Whom at the Top?" Saturday Review, Ap 17, 1965.

Heyns, Barbara, and Cohen, David K. Curriculum Assignment and Tracking Policies in Forty-Eight Urban Public High Schools. Final Report, Je, 1971. ERIC ED 063 451.

Hickey, Howard W. "A Feasibility Study of Alternative Patterns to Reduce School Segregation in an Inner City School." Doctoral dissertation, Michigan State U., 1968.

"High School Tracking." Inequality in Education 12(Jl, 1972):28-29.

Husbands, C. T. Structural Effects of Racial Tracking in Two Inner City Schools, My, 1968. ERIC ED 038 456.

Institute for Effective Service and Leadership in Desegregated Schools. Contract OEC-2-6-000166-1966, N, 1967, 86 pp. ERIC ED 020 557.

Jaeger, Richard M., and Freijo, Tom D. "Race and Sex as Concomitants of Composite Halo in Teachers' Evaluative Rating of Pupils." Journal of Educational Psychology 67(Ap, 1975):226-237.

Jencks, Christopher. "Who Should Control Education?" Dissent, Mr-Ap, 1966.

Johnson, Paul Luther. "Ability Grouping and Student Educational Outcomes: A Contextual Analysis." Doctoral dissertation, Syracuse U., 1978. Univ. Microfilms Order No. 7823568.

Jones, James D., Erickson, Edsel L., and Crowell, Ronald. "Increasing the Gap Between Whites and Blacks: Tracking as a Contributory Source." Education and Urban Society 4(My, 1972):339-349.

Justman, Joseph. "Ability Grouping--What Good is It?" Urban Review F, 1967.

Kariger, R. A. "The Relationship of Lane Grouping to the Socio-economic Status of the Parents of Seventh Grade Pupils in Three Junior High Schools." Doctoral dissertation, Michigan State U., 1962.

Kelly, Albert Victor. Mixed-Ability Grouping: Theory and Practice. New York: Harper & Row, 1978.

Kelly, Delos H. "Tracking and Its Impact Upon Self-Esteem: A Neglected Dimension." Education 96(F, 1975):2-9.

Killian, Lewis M. "Leadership in the Desegregation Crisis: An Institutional Analysis." In Intergroup Relations and Leadership. Edited by Muzafer Sherif. New York: Wiley, 1962.

Knight, Bob, Barnett, Lawrence, and Blackwell, Randolph. "National Perspectives [on Community Control]." Center Forum, My 15, 1969.

Kozol, Jonathan. "Alienation or Interaction?" NEA Journal, My, 1968. [School-community relations]

Kraft, Ivor. "There Is No Panacea." Nation, Ja 20, 1969. [Community control, integration, and related subjects]

Lachat, Mary Ann. "School Environments and Student Racial Attitudes." NCRIEEO Tipsheet #12, My, 1973.

Lauter, Paul, and Howe, Florence. "How the School System is Rigged for Failure." New York Review of Books 14(Je 18, 1970):14-21. [School tracking systems]

Lederer, Joseph. "The Scope of the Practice [of Ability Grouping]." Urban Review, S, 1968.

Lefkowitz, Leon J. "Ability Grouping: De Facto Segregation in the Classroom." Clearing House 46(Ja, 1972):293-297.

Levine, Daniel U. "The Culturally Different in the Institutional Setting of the School." High School Journal 54(Mr, 1971):368-380.

_____. "Training Administrators for Inner-City Schools: A Proposal." National Elementary Principal, Ja, 1967.

Lieberman, Myron. "Power and Policy in Education." Bulletin of the School of Education, Indiana U., S, 1964.

McCarty, Donald J. Myths and Reality in School Board Research, 1966. ERIC ED 010 711.

McDill, Edward L., and Rigsby, Leo C. Structure and Process in Secondary Schools: The Academic Impact of Educational Climate. Baltimore: Johns Hopkins Press, 1973.

_____ and others. Educational Climates of High School: Their Effects and Sources, Ap, 1969, 62 pp. Center for the Study of Social Organization of Schools, Johns Hopkins U. ERIC ED 030 205.

McKelvey, Troy V. "Interviews with Urban Public School Superintendents." Unpublished study for the U.S. Commission on Civil Rights, 1966.

McPherson, Bruce. "A Survey of Opinions and Perceptions Regarding Continuing Racial Integration of Central City Public School Systems." Unpublished study for U.S. Commission on Civil Rights, 1966.

Mackler, Bernard. "Blacks Who Are Academically Successful." Urban Education 5(O, 1970):210-237.

_____. "Grouping in the Ghetto." Education and Urban Society, N, 1969.

_____. The Little Black School House: Success and Failure in a Ghetto School. New York: Department of Urban Affairs, Hunter College, 1969.

_____. "Up from Poverty: The Price of 'Making It' in a Ghetto School." In Opening Opportunities for Disadvantaged Learners, pp. 111-127. Edited by A. Harry Passow. New York: Teachers College Press, 1972.

Mackler, Bernard, and Holman, Dana. "Assessing, Packaging, and Delivery: Tests, Testing, and Race." Young Children 31(Jl, 1976):351-364.

"Magic Words." Nation, Je 10, 1968. [Decentralization of schools; a critique]

Marasciulo, Leonard A., and McSweeney, Maryellen. "Tracking and Minority Student Attitudes and Performance." Urban Education 6(Ja, 1972):303-319. [Berkeley, CA]

Marjoribanks, Kevin. "The Stratification of Socialization Processes: A Further Analysis." Educational Studies 4(Je, 1978):105-110.

Meade, Edward J., Jr. Accountability and Governance in Public Education. New York: The Ford Foundation, 1968.

Mills, Roger, and Bryan, Miriam M. Testing... Grouping: The New Segregation in Southern Schools? Atlanta: Southern Regional Council, 1976.

Minihan, Neil. "School Decentralization and Racial Integration." School and Society, Mr, 1969.

Mizell, Hayes. "Public Education and Community Organization." New South, Winter, 1969.

Morrison, C. M. Ability Grouping and Mixed-Ability Grouping in Secondary Schools, 1976. ERIC ED 142 535. [World survey]

Monahan, William J. "Re-Examining an Assumption: The Adaptation of the Schools to the Culturally Different." High School Journal 54(Mr, 1971):381-389.

"National Conference of Community Schools." Community, Mr-Ap, 1969.

Niemeyer, John H. "School Integration: The School's Responsibility." In Klopf and Laster, above.

Nystrand, Raphael O., and Cunningham, Luverne L. "Federated Urban School Systems: Compromising the Centralization-Decentralization Issue." In Dynamic Factors in Urban School Administration. Edited by Frank W. Lutz. Worthington, OH: Charles A. Jones Publishing Company, in press.

Ochberg, Frank M., and Trickett, Edison. "Administrative Responses to Racial Conflict in a High School." Community Mental Health Journal 6(D, 1970):470-482.

Ornstein, Allan C. "Anxieties and Forces Which Militate Against Ghetto School Teachers." Journal of Secondary Education, O, 1968.

_____. "Cynicism or Witticism: Professors of Education and Ghetto School Teachers." Journal of Secondary Education, Ap, 1968.

Ozuron, Howard A., Jr. "The Plight of the Negro Teachers." American School Board Journal, S, 1965.

Parons, Tim. "Community Control Across the Nation." Community, F, 1969.

Pearl, Arthur. "[Ability] Grouping Hurts the Poor." Southern Education Report, D, 1966.

Pierce, Wendell H. "Stability and Change in Human Characteristics: A Superintendent's Response." Educational Administration Quarterly, Winter, 1966. [Response to Bloom, above]

Powell, Evan R., and White, William F. Learning Climate Correlates in Black and White Rural Schools, Mr 2, 1970. Washington, DC. ERIC ED 038 693.

The Principalship. Job Specifications and Salary Considerations for the '70s. Washington, DC: National Association of Secondary School Principals, 1970.

Project for the Inservice Preparation of Teachers for the Desegregation of Selected School Faculties Through the Implementation of Team Teaching. Technical Progress Report, April 1, 1967 through June 30, 1967. Chattanooga, TN: Chattanooga Public Schools, 1967.

Rehberg, Richard A., and Rosenthal, Evelyn. Social Class and Merit in the High School: A Multi-Study Analysis. Binghamton, NY: Center for Cooperative Political Research, My 15, 1975.

Research Division. Ability Grouping. Washington, DC: National Education Association, 1968.

_____. Studies of Educational Problems Involved in School Integration. Washington, DC: Research Division, National Education Association, N, 1960.

Rosenbaum, James E. Making Inequality. The Hidden Curriculum of High School Tracking. New York: Wiley, 1976.

_____. "The Structure of Opportunity in School." Social Forces 57(S, 1978):236-256.

Rothstein, Richard. "Down the Up Staircase: Tracking in Schools." This Magazine is About Schools 5(Spring, 1971):103-139.

Rothstein, Stanley William. "Ghetto School: A Study of Social Control Mechanisms in an Urban Junior High School." Doctoral dissertation, Claremont Graduate School, 1974. Univ. Microfilms Order No. 75-12,289.

Schafer, Walter E., and Olexa, Carol. High School Track Position and Academic Achievement, Ap, 1969. ERIC ED 030 188.

"School Lunches: Black and White." Integrated Education 11(My-Je, 1973):41-43.

Shores, J. Harlan. "What Does Research Say about Ability Grouping by Classes?" Illinois Education, D, 1964.

Smith, Charles F., Jr. "Do You Want Me?" Phi Delta Kappan, My, 1964. [The almost total absence of Negro public school administrators]

Smith, David Horton, and McGrail, Richard. "Community Control of Schools: A Review of Issues and Options." Urban and Social Change Review 3(1969).

Sorenson, A. B. Organizational Differentiation of Students and Educational Opportunity. Baltimore: Center for the Study of Social Organization of Schools, Johns Hopkins U., D, 1969.

Special Commission on School Racial Polity. School Racial Policy. Washington, DC: American Association of School Administrators, 1966.

Stewart, Charles E. "Racial Issues Confronting Large City School Administrators." Urban Education I 4(1965).

_____. "School Community Relations in Large Cities." In Urban School Administration. Edited by Troy V. McKelvey and Austin D. Swanson. Beverly Hills, CA: Sage, 1969.

Stollar, Dewey H., and Dykes, Archie R. Report of Two Short-Term Training Institutes for School Superintendents and School Board Members, 1965. ERIC ED 045 746.

Strandt, Patricia. "Decentralization, Community Control--Where Do We Go From Here?" American Teacher, My, 1969.

Sullivan, Neil V. "Should Administrators Seek Racial Balance in the Schools?" Phi Delta Kappan, Mr, 1968.

Swanson, Austin D. "The Governance of Education in Metropolitan Areas." In Urban School Administration. Edited by Troy V. McKelvey and Austin D. Swanson. Beverly Hills, CA: Sage, 1969.

Sykes, Dudley E. "De Facto Dehumanization." NASSP Bulletin 58(F, 1974):29-34. [On ability grouping]

Talbott, Allan. "Needed: A New Breed of School Superintendents." Harper's, F, 1966.

Taylor, Alton L. "Regression Analysis of Antecedent Measures of Slow Sections in High School Biology." Science Education 55(J1-S, 1971):395-402.

Taylor, Ruth Sloan. Teaching in the Desegregated Classroom. New York: Parker Publishing Company, 1974.

Thomas, Donald R. "Urban School Boards. The Need for Accountability." Education and Urban Society, My, 1969.

"Urban School Decentralization in the Nation." Community, Mr-Ap, 1969.

Vail, Edward O. (ed.). Administrator's In-Depth Seminars in Problems of Desegregation as They Relate to Large City Schools; Summaries of Seminar Discussions, 1967, 101 pp. Los Angeles: Los Angeles City Schools. ERIC ED 025 547.

Vergason, Glen A. "A Critical Review of Grouping." High School Journal, Ap, 1965.

Walker, John T. "The Role of the Black Trustee." Independent School Bulletin 30(D, 1970):19-20.

Wallach, Steve. "City School System Puts Kids in Caste System." SOHO Weekly News, D 11, 1975. [Reprinted in U.S. Commission on Civil Rights, Hearing Held in Denver, Colorado, February 17-19, 1976, pp. 1062-1063. Washington, DC: The Commission, 1978]

Washington Joint Committee on Education. Improving Representativeness of Local School Boards. Olympia, WA: Joint Committee on Education, 1972.

Wayson, William W. "Organizing Urban Schools for Responsible Education." Phi Delta Kappan 52(F, 1971):344-347.

Weber, George. "[Ability Grouping:] Why is the Idea Even Questioned?" Southern Education Report, D, 1966.

Willis, Benjamin C. Social Problems in Public School Administration. Pittsburgh: U. of Pittsburgh Press, 1967.

Willower, Donald J. et al. The School and Pupil Control Ideology. University Park, PA: Pennsylvania U. Press, 1967.

Zwiebach, Burton. "Democratic Theory and Community Control." Community Issues, Mr, 1969.

13.
SOCIAL CONDITIONS

Anderson, James G., and Safar, Dwight. "The Influence of Differential Community Perceptions on the Provision of Equal Educational Opportunities." Sociology of Education, Summer, 1967.

Bahr, Howard M., and Gibbs, Jack P. "Racial Differentiation in American Metropolitan Areas." Social Forces, Je, 1967.

Baratz, Stephen S. "The Unique Culture of the Ghetto." The Center Magazine, Jl, 1969.

Baratz, Stephen S., and Baratz, Joan C. "Negro Ghetto Children and Urban Education: A Cultural Solution." Social Education, Ap, 1969.

Bernard, Jessie. Marriage and Family Among Negroes. Englewood Cliffs, NJ: Prentice-Hall, 1966.

_____. "Note on Educational Homogamy in Negro-White and White-Negro Marriages, 1960." Journal of Marriage and the Family, Ag, 1966.

Billingsley, Andrew. Black Families in White America. Englewood Cliffs, NJ: Prentice-Hall, 1968.

Blackburn, R. M., and Stewart, A. "The Stability of Structural Inequality." Sociological Review 23(Ag, 1975).

Blaug, Mark. "The Correlation Between Education and Earnings: What Does It Signify." Higher Education 1(F, 1972):53-76.

Bloice, Carl. "The Black Worker's Future Under American Capitalism." Black Scholar 3(My, 1972):14-22.

Borinsky, Mark. Comparison of Schools with High and Low Proportions of Poverty Pupils. Washington, DC: National Center for Education Statistics, 1975.

Brackett, Jean C. City Worker's Family Budget for a Moderate Living Standard. Washington, DC: GPO, 1967.

Brashler, William. "The Black Middle Class: Making It." New York Times Magazine, D 3, 1978.

Busse, Thomas V., and Busse, Pauline. "Negro Parental Behavior and Social Class Variables." Journal of Genetic Psychology 120, pt. 2 (Je, 1972).

Cameron, Howard K. "Nonintellectual Correlates of Academic Achievement." Journal of Negro Education, Summer, 1968.

Carper, Laura. "The Negro Family and the Moynihan Report." Dissent, Mr-Ap, 1966.

Citizens Board of Inquiry into Hunger and Malnutrition in the United States. Hunger, U.S.A. A Report. Washington, DC: Community Press, 1968.

Cloward, Richard and Others. "Educating and Children of the Welfare Poor: A RECORD Symposium." The Record, Ja, 1968.

Community Council of Greater New York. Poverty in New York City. Facts for Planning Community Action, N, 1964. The Community Council for Greater New York, 225 Park Avenue South, New York, NY 10003.

Conlisk, John. "Can Equalization of Opportunity Reduce Social Mobility?" American Economic Review 64(Mr, 1974):80-90.

Counts, George S. The Selective Character of American Secondary Education. Chicago, 1922.

Dailey, John T. "Education and Emergence from Poverty." Journal of Marriage and the Family, N, 1964.

Daniel, Johnnie. "Social Class Identification Among Blacks and Whites." Doctoral dissertation, U. of Michigan, 1972. Univ. Microfilms Order No. 73-06814.

Ellison, Ralph W. "When Does a Black Join the Middle Class?" Los Angeles Times, Ja 29, 1975.

Featherman, David Lee. The Socioeconomic Achievement of White Married Males in the United States 1957-1967. Ann Arbor, MI: U. of Michigan, 1969. ERIC ED 053 252.

_____. "The Socioeconomic Achievement of White Religio-Ethnic Subgroups: Social and Psychological Explanations." American Sociological Review 36(Ap, 1971):207-222.

Fein, Rashi. "An Economic and Social Profile of the Negro American." Daedalus, Fall, 1965.

_____. "Educational Patterns in Southern Migration." Southern Economic Journal, Jl, 1965, Supplement.

Foreman, Clark. Environmental Factors in Negro Elementary Education. New York: W. W. Norton and Company, 1932. Doctoral dissertation, Columbia U.

Frazier, E. Franklin. "Occupational Classes Among Negroes in Cities." American Journal of Sociology 35(Mr, 1930):718-738.

Frease, Dean E. "Delinquency, Social Class, and the Schools." Sociology and Social Research 57 (Jl, 1973):443-459.

Fried, Marc. The World of the Urban Working Class. Cambridge, MA: Harvard U. Press, 1973. [Boston, MA]

Fusco, Gene C. School-Home Partnership in Depressed Urban Neighborhoods. U.S. Office of Education Bulletin No. 31008. Washington, DC: GPO, 1964.

Gans, Herbert J. "The Negro Family, Reflections on the Moynihan Report." Commonweal, O 15, 1965.

Garza, Joseph M. "Race, the Achievement Syndrome, the Perception of Opportunity." Phylon, Winter, 1969.

Geismar, Ludwig, and Gerhart, Ursula C. "Social Class, Ethnicity, and Family Functioning: Exploring Some Issues Raised by the Moynihan Report." Journal of Marriage and the Family, Ag, 1968.

Herriott, Robert E., and Hodgkins, Benjamin J. Sociocultural Context and the American School: An Open-Systems Analysis of Educational Opportunity. Final Report. Tallahassee, FL: Institute for Social Research, Florida State U., Ja, 1969. ERIC ED 028 502.

Herzog, Elizabeth. "Is There a Breakdown of the Negro Family?" Social Work, Ja, 1966.

Hurst, Charles E. "Race, Class, and Consciousness." American Sociological Review 37(D, 1972):658-670.

Jeffers, Camille. The Living Poor. Ann Arbor Publishers, 610 South Forest Avenue, Ann Arbor, MI 48104, 1967. [The day-to-day existence of poor people living in a large housing project]

A Job Corps Study of Relative Cost Benefits, Volume I and II. Washington, DC: Software Systems, Inc, Ap, 1969. ERIC ED 053 308.

Kapel, David E. "Environmental Factors, Student Variables, and Employment Adjustment of Male Negroes." Journal of Negro Education 39(Fall, 1970):333-340.

Kerckhoff, A. C. "The Status Attainment Process: Socialization or Allocation?" Social Forces 55(1976):368-381.

Kerckhoff, A. C., and Campbell, R. T. "Black-White Differences in the Educational Attainment Process." Sociology of Education 50 (1977):15-27.

Kriesberg, Louis. Social Inequality. Englewood Cliffs, NJ: Prentice-Hall, 1979.

Kronus, Sidney. "Some Neglected Aspects of Negro Class Comparisons." Phylon 31(Winter, 1970):359-371. [Chicago, IL]

Kuschman, William E. "Education and Society in Disadvantaged Suburbia." School and Society, N 12, 1966.

Landry, Bart. "A Reinterpretation of the Writings of Frazier on the Black Middle Class." Social Problems 26(D, 1978):211-222.

Liddle, Gordon P., and Rockwell, Robert E. "The Role of Parents and Family Life." Journal of Negro Education, Summer, 1964.

Light, Ivan Hubert. "Sociological Aspects of Self-Employment and Social Welfare among Chinese, Japanese, and Negroes in Northern Urban Areas of the United States, 1900-1940." Doctoral dissertation, Berkeley, CA: U. of California, 1969. Available from National Technical Information Service, Springfield, VA 22151. ERIC ED 054 301.

Lipset, Seymour Martin. "On Equality: Social Mobility and Equal Opportunity." Public Interest 29(F, 1972):90-108.

Logan, Rayford W. "The Hiatus--A Great Negro Middle Class." Southern Workman, D, 1929.

Long, Herman H. "Social Stratification and the Educative Process." Journal of Human Relations, Winter, 1958.

McCoy, John L. Rural Poverty in Three Southern Regions: Mississippi Delta, Ozarks, Southeast Coastal Plain. Washington, DC: Department of Agriculture, Economic Research Service, Mr, 1970. Available from Superintendent of Documents, U.S. GPO, Washington, DC: 20402. ERIC ED 039 052.

McKinley, Donald G. Social Class and Family Life. New York: Free Press of Glencoe, 1964.

Marien, Michael. "Beyond Credentialism: The Future of Social Selection." Social Policy 2 (S-O, 1971):14-21.

Marshall, Ray. "Reflections on Upgrading." Manpower 2(1970):2-7.

Marston, Wilfred G. "Social Class as a Factor in Ethnic and Racial Segregation." International Journal of Comparative Sociology, Je, 1968.

Masters, Stanley H. "The Effect of Family Income on Children's Education: Some Findings on Inequlity of Opportunity." Journal of Human Resources, Spring, 1969.

_____. A Study of Socio-Economic Mobility Among Urban Negroes, Jl, 1970. PB 194 149. National Technical Information Service, Springfield, VA 22151.

Meier, August. "Some Observations on the Negro Middle Class." Crisis, O, 1957.

Miller, S. M., and Riessman, Frank. Social Class and Social Policy. New York: Basic Books, 1968.

Mooers, Jack D. "Independent School Attendance and Social Class Status." Educational Studies 8(F, 1977):253-258.

Morgan, Gordon. "A Comparison of the Life Styles of High and Low Status Negroes in Low-income Rural Areas of the South." Journal of Social and Behavioral Sciences 14(Spring, 1969):13-20.

Moynihan, Daniel P. "The Discarded Third." Look, My 17, 1966. [Family problems among Negro Americans]

_____. "Education of the Urban Poor." Harvard Graduate School of Education Association Bulletin, Fall, 1967. [On the Coleman Report]

_____. [Interview] "Moynihan Believes Class Is the Issue." Southern Education Report, My, 1967. [On the relative roles of class and race in educational opportunity]

_____. "Sources of Resistance to the Coleman Report." Harvard Educational Review, Winter, 1968.

_____. "Urban Conditions: General." Annals, My, 1967.

[Mueller, Eva, and Ladd, William]. Negro-White Differences in Geographical Mobility. Economic Redevelopment Research. Washington, DC: GPO, Ag, 1964.

Nam, Charles, Sollibage, Monique, Zuemun, Randolph, and Sohlman, Asa. Group Disparities in Educational Participation. Paris: OECD, 1970.

Nam, Charles, Rhodes, A. Lewis, and Herriott, Robert E. "School Retention by Race, Religion, and Socioeconomic Status." Journal of Human Resources, Spring, 1968.

Nam, Charles and others. Inequalities in Educational Opportunities: A Demographic Analysis of Educational Differences in the Population. Tallahassee: Florida State U., 1966.

Nicholas, Lynn N., Virjo, S., and Wattenberg, William W. Effects of Socio-economic Setting and Organizational Climate on Problems Brought to Elementary School Offices. Detroit: Wayne State U., 1965.

Parelius, Robert James. Sociological Influences on the Achievement of Lower Class Negro Children. Final Report. Chicago, IL: U. of Chicago, N, 1967. ERIC ED 016 730.

Porter, John. "The Future of Upward Mobility." American Sociological Review, F, 1968.

Rainwater, Lee. "Crucible of Identity: The Negro Lower-Class Family." Daedalus, Winter, 1966.

Rainwater, Lee, and Yancey, William L. The Moynihan Report and the Politics of Controversy. Cambridge: M. I. T. Press, 1967.

Reissman, Leonard. "The Subject Is Class." Sociology and Social Research 54(Ap, 1970): 293-305.

Riessman, Frank. "In Defense of the Negro Family." Dissent, Mr-Ap, 1966.

_____. "Low Income Culture, the Adolescent and the School." Bulletin of the National Association of Secondary-School Principals, Ap, 1965.

_____. Strategies Against Poverty. New York: Random House, 1969.

_____. "Workers' Attitudes Toward Participation and Leadership." Doctoral dissertation, Columbia U., 1955.

Riessman, Frank, Cohen, Jerome, and Pearl, Arthur (eds.). The Mental Health of the Poor: New Treatment for Low-Income People. New York: Free Press of Glencoe, 1964.

Riessman, Frank, and Miller, S. M. "Social Change versus the Psychiatric World View." American Journal of Orthopsychiatry, Ja, 1964.

Rosow, Jerome M. "The Blue Collar Blues." Integrated Education 9(My-Je, 1971:32-37.

Rytina, Joan H., Form, William H., and Pease, John. "Income and Stratification Ideology: Beliefs about the American Opportunity Structure." American Journal of Sociology 75(1970), pt. 2, 703-716.

"School Social Work." Baltimore Bulletin of Education, XL (1962-1963), No. 4: entire issue.

Schwarzweller, Harry K. "Parental Family Ties and Social Integration of Rural to Urban Migrants." Journal of Marriage and the Family, N, 1964.

Spady, William G. "Educational Mobility and Access: Growth and Paradoxes." American Journal of Sociology, N, 1967.

Stone, Robert C., and Schlamp, F. T. Family Life Styles Below the Poverty Line. San Francisco, CA: Institute for Social Science Research, San Francisco State College, 1966.

Strait, Suzanne Hart. "The First Negro Family on Maple Terrace." Parents' Magazine, Ja, 1965.

Street, David. "Educators and Social Workers: Sibling Rivalry in the Inner City." Social Service Review, Je, 1967. [Broader than the title indicates]

Stricker, Lawrence J. Dimensions of Social Stratification for Whites and Blacks: The Toledo Study. Princeton, NJ: Educational Testing Service, N, 1976.

Taeuber, Karl E., Chiazze, Leonard, Jr., and Haenzel, William. Migration in the United States. An Analysis of Residence Histories. Public Health Monograph No. 77. Washington, DC: GPO, 1968.

Thompson, Daniel C. "Social Class Factors in Public School Education as Related to Desegregation." American Journal of Orthopsychiatry, Jl, 1956.

Trattner, Walter I. Crusade for the Children: A History of the National Child Labor Committee and Child Labor Reform in America. Chicago, IL: Quadrangle, 1970.

Turner, James. "The Political Relevance of Race and Power to the Black Community." Afro-American Studies 1(Ja, 1971):237-242.

U.S. Bureau of the Census. Current Population Reports, Series P-23, No. 25. "Lifetime Migration Histories of the American People." By Margaret C. O'Brien and Elizabeth A. Larmon. Washington, DC: GPO, 1968.

_____. Current Population Reports, Series P-20. No. 168. "Negro Population: March, 1966." Washington, DC: GPO, 1967.

_____. Negro Population: March, 1967. Current Population Reports Series P-20, No. 175. Washington, DC: GPO, O 23, 1968.

_____. Negro Population of Selected Areas of the United States in Which Special Census Have Been Taken January 1, 1965 to June 30, 1968. Current Population Reports. Series P-28, No. 1476. Washington, DC: GPO, D 6, 1968.

_____. Projections of Educational Attainment 1970 to 1985. Current Population Reports, Population Estimates, Series P-25, No. 390, March 29, 1968. Washington, DC: GPO, 1968.

_____. Trends in Social and Economic Conditions in Metropolitan Areas. Current Population Reports. Series P-23, No. 27, F 7, 1969.

U.S. Civil Service Commission. Preliminary Report of Minority Group Employment in the Federal Government, 1969. Washington, DC: GPO, 1970.

U.S. Department of Commerce, Bureau of the Census. Educational Attainment: March, 1967. Series P.20, No. 169, F 9, 1968. Washington, DC: GPO, 1968.

U.S. Department of Health, Education, and Welfare. Toward a Social Report. Washington, DC: GPO, Ja, 1969.

_____. White-Nonwhite Differentials in Health, Education, and Welfare. Washington, DC: GPO, 1965.

U.S. Housing and Home Finance Agency. Our Nonwhite Population and Its Housing. The Changes Between 1950 and 1960. Washington, DC: GPO, Jl, 1963.

Wayne State U., Center for Urban Studies. Social Reporting in Michigan: Problems and Issues. Lansing, MI: State Office of Planning Coordination, 1970.

Wiley, Norbert. "The Ethnic Mobility Trap and Stratification Theory." Social Problems, Fall, 1967.

14.
STUDENT MOVEMENTS

General

Ahmad, Muhammad. "On the Black Student Movement--1960-1970." Black Scholar 9(My/Je, 1978):2-11.

Alan, John. "U.S. Student Movement Loses Spark of Black Revolt." News and Letters, Ja, 1973.

Alkalimat, Abdul (Gerald McWorter). "1970's: What Must Be Done By Black Students." Black Lines 1(Summer, 1971):35-41.

Anderson, S. E. "Black Students: Racial Consciousness and the Class Struggle, 1960-1976." Black Scholar 8(Ja-F, 1977):35-43.

Aptheker, Herbert. "The Negro College Student in the 1920's--Years of Preparation and Protest: An Introduction." Science and Society, Spring, 1969.

Bealer, Robert C., Willits, Fern K., and Maida, Peter R. "The Rebellious Youth Subculture--A Myth." Children, Mr-Ap, 1964.

Billings, Charles E. "Black Activists in the Schools." In Political Youth, Traditional Schools: National and International Perspectives. Edited by B. G. Massialas. Englewood Cliffs, NJ: Prentice-Hall, 1972.

"Black Students Stage Walkout." African World, Mr, 1975. [National Student Conference Against Racism, Boston, F, 1975]

Coles, Robert. "Social Struggle and Weariness." Psychiatry, N, 1964. [The effects upon Southern students in the civil rights movement]

Demerath, N. J. III, Marwell, Gerald, and Aiken, Michael T. "Criteria and Contingencies of Success in a Radical Political Movement." Journal of Social Issues 27(1971):63-80. [White student civil rights workers in South, 1965]

Dixon, Vernon J. "The Black Student and the Brother in the Streets." Negro Digest, N, 1968.

Dodson, Dan W. "Student Power as a Means to Educational Change." Integrated Education 8 (N-D, 1970):32-39.

Douglas, Jack D. Youth in Turmoil. America's Changing Youth Cultures and Student Protest Movements. Washington, DC: GPO, 1970.

Edwards, Harry. Black Students. New York: Free Press, 1970.

Fish, Kenneth L. Conflict and Dissent in the High School. New York: Bruce, 1970.

Fishman, Jacob R., and Solomon, Frederic. "Youth and Social Action. Perspectives on the Student Sit-In Movement." American Journal of Orthopsychiatry, 0, 1963.

Fleming, John W. "Congress for the Unity of Black Students: A Report and an Evaluation." Journal of the National Association of Women Deans and Counselors, Winter, 1969. [Ap 20-24, 1968]

Frantz, Thomas T. "Demands of Black Students: A Mixed Bag." National Association of Student Personnel Administrators 6(1969):222-225.

Gintis, Herb. "Activism and Counter-Culture: The Dialectics of Consciousness in the Corporate State." Telos 12(Summer, 1972):42-62.

Glazer, Nathan. "The Jewish Role in Student Activism." Fortune 79(Ja, 1969):112-129.

Gore, Blinzy L. "An Analysis of the Use of Selected Sit-In Demonstrations by Negro College Students in the South as Part of an Organized and Continuing Social Protest Movement Among American Negroes." Doctoral dissertation, New York U., 1967.

Hare, Nathan. "The Future of Black Youth." In Youth in Contemporary Society, pp. 157-170. Edited by David Gottlieb. Beverly Hills, CA: Sage, 1973.

_____. "The Struggle of Black Students." Journal of Afro-American Issues 1(F, 1972): 111-130.

Horowitz, Irving Louis, and Friedland, William H. The Knowledge Factory: Student Power and Academic Politics in America. Chicago: Aldine-Atherton, 1971.

Kelman, Herbert. "A Social-Psychological Model of Political Legitimacy and Its Relevance to Black and White Student Protest Movements." Psychiatry, My, 1970.

Kirtland, Grayson. "Student Unrest: Kids Voice Reasons for Their Anger." South Today 3(Ja-F, 1972):5.

Kleinman, Mark. High School Reform. Toward a Student Movement, Je, 1967. Students for a Democratic Society, 1608 West Madison Avenue, Chicago, IL 60612.

Lawson, James R. "Student Participation in Educational Change." Journal of Negro Education 40(Summer, 1971):282-289.

Levy, Charles J. Voluntary Servitude: Whites in the Negro Movement. New York: Appelton-Century-Crofts, 1968.

Logland, John. "The Youth Ghetto." Journal of Higher Education, Mr, 1968.

Louis, Debbie. And We Are Not Saved: A History of the Movement as People. Garden City, NY: Doubleday, 1970.

McEvoy, James, and Miller, Abraham (eds.). Black Power and Student Rebellion. Belmont, CA: Wadsworth, 1969.

Mankoff, Milton, and Flacks, Richard. "The Changing Social Base of the American Student Movement." Annals 395(My, 1971):54-67.

Marian, Bert, Rosen, David, and Osborne, David. How To Research the Power Structure of Your Secondary School System. Lincoln, NE: Study Commission on Undergraduate Education and the Education of Teachers, O, 1973.

Miles, Michael. The Radical Probe: The Logic of Student Rebellion, 1971.

Millard, Thomas L. "The Sociocultural Contexts of Student Unrest in the Public Schools." Journal of the International Association of Pupil Personnel Workers 17(Je, 1973):124-133.

Neal, Ronald V. "Black Students Call for True Science." Muhammad Speaks, Je 3, 1970. [Meeting in Chicago of the Black Students Psychological Association]

"News in Brief." Liberator, My, 1970. [About the Student Organization for Black Unity]

Noble, Jeanne. "The Black Student Movement: A Search for Identity." Journal of the National Association of Women Deans and Counselors, Winter, 1969.

Orum, Anthony M. Black Students in Protest: A Study of the Origins of the Black Student Movement. Washington, DC: American Sociological Association, 1973.

Piccone, Paul. "Students' Protest, Class Structure, and Ideology." Telos 2(Spring, 1969): 106-122.

Pierce, Chester M., and West, Louis J. "Six Years of Sit-Ins: Psychodynamic Causes and Effects." International Journal of Social Psychiatry, Winter, 1966.

Ponte, Lowell. "Right On in California." Harvard Crimson, Ja 7, 1970. [The right-wing National Youth Alliance]

Porter, Jack Nusan. "Jewish Student Activism." Jewish Currents, My, 1970.

President's Commission on Campus Unrest. "The Black Student Movement." In The Report... Campus Unrest, pp. 91-116. Washington, DC: GPO, 1970.

Rafky, David M. "Student Militance. A Dilemma for Black Faculty." Journal of Black Studies 3(D, 1972):183-206.

Redding, Saunders. "The Black Youth Movement." American Scholar, Autumn, 1969.

Rosenmayr, Leopold. "Towards an Overview of Youth Sociology." International Social Science Journal 20(1966).

Rowntree, John, and Rowntree, Margaret. "The Political Economy of American Youth." Our Generation, Ag, 1968.

Sklarewitz, Norman. "Student Disturbances with Social Overtones Hit Many High Schools." Wall Street Journal, N 6, 1968.

Solomon, Frederick, and Fishman, Jacob R. "The Psychological Meaning of Nonviolence in Student Civil Rights Activities." Psychiatry, My, 1964.

The Student Protest Movement: A Recapitualation. Atlanta, GA: Southern Regional Council, S 29, 1961.

Surace, Samuel J., and Seeman, Melvin. "Some Correlates of Civil Rights Activism." Social Forces, D, 1967.

Task Force on Higher Education for Disadvantaged Minorities. Task Force Report on Higher Education for Chicanos, Puerto Ricans, and American Indians. Washington, DC: Federal Interagency Committee on Education, Ap, 1973 (unpublished).

Task Force on Student Involvement. Student In-
volvement: A Bridge to Total Education, 1969.
Office of Information, North Carolina State
Department of Public Instruction, Raleigh,
NC 26702.

_____. Student Involvement. A Bridge to Total
Education, Revised edition, Ja, 1971. State
Department of Public Instruction, Raleigh,
NC 26702.

Thomas, Arthur E. "Community Power and Student
Rights." (an interview) Harvard Educational
Review 42(My, 1972):173-216.

Tyler, Gerry. "Black Student Group Shows Great
Promise." Muhammad Speaks, S 17, 1971.
[Second annual convention of National Associ-
ation of Black Students]

U.S. Department of Health, Education, and Welfare. Student Advisory Committee Handbook.
Washington, DC: GPO, 1973.

Valien, Preston. "I Attended the National Student League Conference." Crisis, Mr, 1934.

Ware, Claude. Student Power...Black and White--
Implications for Educational Administration
and the Political Role of the Teacher. Los
Angeles: Los Angeles City College, 1968.

Whittel, Gerry. "Students' Role in the Struggle."
SOBU Newsletter 1(Ap 17, 1971). [Second national conference of the Student Organization
for Black Unity, Ap 1-4, 1971, Frogmore, SC]

Bibliographies

Altbach, Philip G., and Kelly, David H. (comps.).
American Students: A Selected Bibliography on
Student Activism and Related Topics. Lexing-
ton, MA: Lexington Books, 1973.

Brooks, Gary D., and Brooks, Bonnie S. (comps.).
The Literature on Student Unrest. Englewood
Cliffs, NJ: Educational Technology Publica-
tions, 1971.

Hutchinson, Myra (ed.). Student Rights and School
Discipline: A Bibliography, D, 1975. ERIC
ED 126 385.

Jackson, Michael, Long, Ruth, and Buser, Robert
(comps.). Student Activities in Secondary
Schools, A Bibliography. Reston, VA: National Association of Secondary School Principals, 1974.

Johnson, Robert L. (comp.). "Black Student
Activism, 1960-70: A Bibliography." Black
Scholar 9(My/Je, 1978):46-48.

Wyant, Spencer (comp.). Power to the Pupil: An
Annotated Bibliography of Student Involvement,
Student Power, and Student Participation in
Decision-Making in Public Secondary Schools,
Ap, 1973. Center for Advanced Study of Edu-
cational Administration, 1472 Kincaid Street,
Eugene, OR 97401.

15.
SCHOOL AND LIVELIHOOD

Economy and Income

Adams, Arvil V., and Nestel, Gilbert.
"Interregional Migration, Education, and
Poverty in the Urban Ghetto: Another Look
at Black-White Earnings Differentials."
Review of Economics and Statistics 58(My,
1976):156-166.

Adams, Arvil V. and others. The Lingering
Crisis of Youth Unemployment. Kalamazoo,
MI: W. E. Upjohn Institute for Employment
Research, Je, 1978.

Adams, James, and Coombs, Orde. "The Two
Nations of Black Americans". Wall Street
Journal, S 10, 1974.

Akin, John S., and Garfinkel, Irwin.
Economic Returns to Educational Quality:
An Empirical Analysis of White, Blacks,
Poor Whites, and Poor Blacks. Madison, WI:
Institute for Research on Poverty, U. of

Anderson, W. H. Locke. "Trickling Down: The
Relationship Between Economic Growth and
the Extent of Poverty Among American Families." Quarterly Journal of Economics,
N, 1964.

Batchelder, A. B. "Decline in the Relative
Income of Negro Men." Quarterly Journal
of Economics, N, 1964.

Berger, Brigitte. "'People Work'--The Youth
Culture and the Labor Market." Public
Interest 35(Spring, 1974):55-66.

Bergmann, Barbara R., and Krause, William R.
"Evaluating and Forecasting Progress in
Racial Integration of Employment."
Industrial and Labor Relations Review
25(April, 1972):399-409.

Bernard, Jessie. "Marital Stability and
Patterns of Status Variables." Journal
of Marriage and the Family, N, 1966.
[Negro-white differences with control of
income, schooling, and occupation]

Bianchini, John S., Danielson, William F.,
Heath, Robert W., and Hillard, Clinton W.
"Race and Socio-economic Status in Muni-
cipal Personnel Selection." Industrial
Relations, O, 1967.

Bluestone, Barry. "Low-Wage Industries and
the Working Poor." Poverty and Human
Resources Abstracts, Mr-Ap, 1968.

Bluestone, Barry, Murphy, William, and
Stevenson, Mary. Low Wages and the Working
Poor Part I. 2 PB 206-095. Springfield,
VA: National Technical Information Service,
O, 1971.

Blum, Zahava D. Income Changes During the
First Ten Years of Occupational Experience:
A Comparison of Blacks and Whites.
Baltimore, MD: John Hopkins U., Center for
the Study of Social Organization of Schools,
D, 1971. ERIC ED 061 459.

Bogan, Forrest A. "Employment of High School
Graduates and Dropouts in 1964." Monthly
Labor Review, Je, 1965.

Borland, Melvin, and Yett, Donald. "The Cash
Value of College--for Negroes and for
Whites." Trans-action, N, 1967.

Bowman, Mary Jean. "Learning and Earning in
the Postschool Years." In Review of
Research in Education 2, pp 202-244.
Edited by Fred N. Kerlinger and John B.
Carroll. Itasca, IL: Peacock, 1974.

Brimmer, Andrew F. "The Black Revolution and
the Economic Future of Negroes in the
United States." American Scholar, Autumn,
1969.

_____. The Economic Position of Black
Americans: 1976, Jl, 1976. ERIC ED 154
177

_____. "Education and Income in the Black Community." Integrated Education, N-D, 1973:3-5.

_____. "Income and Welfare in the Black Community." Ebony 27(O, 1972):64-70.

Brittain, John A. Inheritance and the Inequality of Material Wealth. Washington, DC: Brookings Institution, 1978.

Carliner, Geoffrey. "Returns to Education for Black, Anglos, and Five Spanish Groups." Journal of Human Resources 11(Spring, 1976): 172-184.

_____. Returns to Education for Blacks, Anglos, and Five Spanish Groups. Madison: Institute for Research on Poverty, U. of Wisconsin, 1975.

Carnoy, Martin. "Can Educational Policy Equalize Income Distribution?" Prospects 8 (1978):3-18.

_____. Education and Employment: A Critical Appraisal. Paris: UNESCO, 1977.

Carnoy, Martin, and Marenbach, Dieter. "The Return to Schooling in the United States, 1939-1969." Journal of Human Resources 10 (Summer, 1975):312-331.

Carol, Arthur, and Parry, Samuel. "The Economic Rationale of Occupational Choice." Industrial and Labor Relations Review, J , 1968.

Coe, Richard D. and others. The Means of Poverty: Technical Paper XVII. The Sensitivity of the Incidence of Poverty to Different Measures of Income: School-Aged Children and Families. Washington, DC: U.S. Department of Health, Education, and Welfare, 1976.

Coleman, James S. and others. White and Black Careers during the First Ten Years of Work Experience: A Simultaneous Consideration of Occupational Status and Income Changes. Baltimore, MD: Johns Hopkins U., Center for the Study of Social Organization of Schools, D, 1971. ERIC ED 061 455.

Coleman, Sinclair. Income Disparities Between Black and White Americans. Washington, DC: GPO, 1977.

"Companies Rush to Hire Negro Graduates, Find Competition Stiff, Students Selective." Wall Street Journal, Ap 3, 1968.

Cutright, Phillipe. "Academic Achievement, Schooling, and the Earnings of White and Black Men." Journal of Social and Behavioral Sciences 20(Summer, 1974):1-18.

Walter, G. Daniel. "The Relative Employment and Income of American Negroes." Journal of Negro Education, Fall, 1963.

Dick, Daniel T., and Medoff, Marshall H. "Filtering by Race and Education in the U.S. Manufacturing Vector: Constant-Ratio Elasticity of Substitution Evidence." Review of Economics and Statistics 58(My, 1976):148-155.

DuBoff, R. "Unemployment in the United States: A Historical Summary." Monthly Review 29 (N, 1977):10-24.

Eckans, R. S. "Returns to Education with Standardized Incomes." Quarterly Journal of Economics 87(F, 1973).

Erbe, Brigitte. "Black Occupational Change and Education." Sociology of Work and Occupations 2(My, 1975):150-168.

Erskine, Hazel. "The Polls: Negro Finances." Public Opinion Quarterly, Summer, 1969.

Ezeocha, Peter A. Poverty in America: Consequences on the Black Youth, Mr 5, 1976. ERIC ED 127 379.

Farley, Reynolds. "Trends in Racial Inequalities: Have the Gains of the 1960's Disappeared in the 1970's?" American Sociological Review 42(Ap, 1977):189-208.

Fay, J. Michael. "Private Resources: Another Road to Inequality." Integrateducation 14 (Ja-F, 1976).

Featherman, David L., and Hauser, Robert M. "Changes in the Socioeconomic Stratification of the Races, 1962-73." American Journal of Sociology 82(1976):621-651.

Flanagan, Robert J. "On the Stability of the Racial Unemployment Differential." American Economic Review 66(My, 1976):302-308.

Fogel, Walter. "The Effect of Low Educational Attainment on Incomes: A Comparative Study of Selected Ethnic Groups." Journal of Human Resources, Fall, 1966.

Folk, Hugh. "Youth Unemployment: An Economic Analysis." N.A.S.S.P. Bulletin, F, 1969.

Foner, Philip S. Organized Labor and the Black Worker, 1949-1973. New York: Praeger, 1974.

Freeman, Richard B. "Black Economic Progress Since 1964." Public Interest 52(Summer, 1978):52-68.

_____. "Changes in the Labor Market for Black Americans, 1948-72." Brookings Papers on Economic Activity 1(1973):67-120.

Gilroy, Curtis L. "Black and White Unemployment: The Dynamics of the Differential." Monthly Labor Review, F, 1974. [Reprint No. 2947, with corrections]

Gisser, M. "Education and Economic Welfare: A Cross-Sectional Study of the U.S." Social Science Quarterly 52(Mr, 1972).

Goodman, Jerry D. The Effects of Race and Ethnicity Upon Income and Occupational Status Attainment, Mr, 1977. ERIC ED 147 212. [Chicago]

Garfinkel, Irwin and others. Earnings Capacity, Poverty, and Inequality. New York: Academic Press, 1977.

Gould, William B. "Black Workers Inside the House of Labor." Annals 407(My, 1973):78-90.

Gregory, Karl D. "Some Alternatives for Reducing the Black-White Unemployment Rate Differential." American Economic Review 66 (My, 1976):324-327.

Griffin, Larry J. Specification Biases in Estimates of Socio-economic Returns to Schooling. Baltimore: Center for Social Organization of Schools, Johns Hopkins U., Ja, 1976.

Griliches, Zvi, and Freeman, Richard. Econometric Investigations of Determinants and Returns to Schooling, Training and Experience, Mr 31, 1977. ERIC ED 142 699.

Griliches, Zvi, and Mason, William M. "Education, Income, and Ability." Journal of Political Economy 80(My-Je, 1972) Part 2: 74-103.

Gwartney, James. "Changes in the Nonwhite/White Income Ratio--1939-67." American Economic Review 60(D, 1970):872-883.

_____. "Discrimination and Income Differentials." American Economic Review 60(Je, 1970):396-408.

Gwartney, James, and Long, James E. "The Relative Earnings of Black and Other Minorities." Industrial and Labor Relations Review 31(Ap, 1978):336-346.

Hall, Edward T. The Manpower Potential in Our Ethnic Groups, 1967. Manpower Administration, U.S. Department of Labor, Washington, DC 20210.

Hanoch, Giora. "An Economic Analysis of Earnings and Schoolings." Journal of Human Resources, Summer, 1967.

Harris, Edward E. "Racial Status, Negroes Employed, and Occupational Prestige." In Essays in General Sociology, 1968. American Press Publications, Inc., 282 Seventh Avenue, New York, NY 10001.

House, John C. "Ability and Schooling as Determinants of Lifetime Earnings or If You're So Smart, Why Aren't You Rich?" American Economic Review 61(My, 1971):289-298.

Hauser, Robert M., and Featherman, David L. The Process of Stratification: Trends and Analyses. New York: Academic Press, 1977.

Hedges, Janice N. "Youth Unemployment in the 1974-75 Recession." Monthly Labor Review 99 (Ja, 1976):49-56.

Henderson, Vivian W. "The Economic Imbalance--An Inquiry Into the Economic Status of Negroes in the United States, 1935-1960 With Implications for Negro Education." Quarterly Review of Higher Education Among Negroes 28 (Ap, 1960):84-98.

_____. "Race, Economics, and Public Policy." Integrateducation 14(Ja/F, 1976).

Hiestand, Dale L. Economic Growth and Employment for Minorities. New York: Columbia U. Press, 1964.

Hill, Herbert. "Employment, Manpower Training, and the Black Worker." Journal of Negro Education, Summer, 1969.

Hodge, Clair C. "The Negro Job Situation: Has It Improved?" Monthly Labor Review, Ja, 1969.

Hogan, Dennis P., and Featherman, David L. "Racial Stratification and Socioeconomic Change in the American North and South." American Journal of Sociology 83(1977):100-126.

Hunter, Charlayne. "Black Teen-agers' Jobless Rate Constant Despite U.S. Recovery." New York Times, Jl 11, 1976.

Iden, George. Policy Options for the Teenage Unemployment Problem. Washington, DC: GPO, 1976.

Kalachek, Edward. The Youth Labor Market. Ann Arbor and Detroit, MI: Institute of Labor and Industrial Relations, U. of Michigan and Wayne State U., 1969.

King, Allan G., and Knapp, Charles B. "Race and the Determinants of Lifetime Earnings." Industrial and Labor Relations Review 31 (Ap, 1978):347-355.

Lampman, Robert J. "Growth, Prosperity, and Inequality Since 1947." Wilson Quarterly 1 (Autumn, 1977):143-155.

Levin, Henry and others. The Costs to the Nation of Inadequate Education. Washington, DC: GPO, 1972.

Light, Ivan H. "Sociological Aspects of Self-Employment and Social Welfare Among Chinese, Japanese, and Negroes in Northern, Urban Areas of the U.S., 1900-1940." Doctoral dissertation, U. of California, Berkeley, 1968.

Link, C. R. "Black Education, Earnings and Interregional Migration: A Comment and Some New Evidence." *American Economic Review* 65(Mr, 1975).

Link, C. R., Ratledge, Edward, and Lewis, Kenneth. "Black-White Differences in Returns to Schooling: Some New Evidence." *American Economic Review* 66(Mr, 1976): 221-223.

Little, J. Kenneth. "The Occupations of Non-College Youth." *American Educational Research Journal*, Mr, 1967.

Livingston, Rodwell, and Cavanaugh, Frederick J. "Poverty in the United States, 1959 to 1968." U.S. Bureau of the Census, *Current Population Reports*, Series P-60, No. 68, D 31, 1969. Washington, DC: GPO, 1969.

Mandel, Allan S. "Resource Distribution Within School Districts." *Integrateducation* 14 (Ja/F, 1976).

Marshall, H. J. "Black-White Economic Participation in Large U.S. Cities." *American Journal of Economics and Sociology* 31(0, 1972).

Marshall, Ray. "Trends in Black Income and Employment." *American Federationist* 78 (Jl, 1971):1-7.

Masters, Stanley H. "The Effect of Family Income on Children's Education: Some Findings on Inequality of Opportunity." *Journal of Human Resources*, Spring, 1969.

Mhone, Guy C. "Structural Oppression and the Persistence of Black Poverty." *Journal of Afro-American Issues* 3(Summer-Fall, 1976): 395-419.

Michelson, Stephan. "Income of Racial Minorities." Doctoral dissertation, Stanford U., 1968.

_____. "Rational Income Decisions of Negroes and Everybody Else." *Industrial and Labor Relations Review*, 0, 1969.

Miller, Herman P. "Income and Education." In *Income Distribution in the United States*, ch. 6. Washington, DC: GPO, 1966.

Miller, Renee H. *Characteristics of the Population Below the Poverty Level, 1974*. Washington, DC: GPO, 1976.

Miller, S. M. "The Outlook of Working-Class Youth." In *Blue-Collar World*. Edited by Arthur B. Shostak and William Gomberg. Englewood Cliffs, NJ: Prentice-Hall, 1964.

Moore, Howard, Jr. "Black Labor: Slavery to Fair Hiring." *Black Scholar* 1(Ja, 1973): 22-31.

Morgan, James N. and others (eds.). *Five Thousand American Families--Patterns of Economic Progress*. Vol. I: *An Analysis of the First Five Years of the Panel Study of Income Dynamics*. Vol. II: *Special Studies of the First Five Years of the Panel Study of Income Dynamics*. Ann Arbor, MI: Institute for Social Research, U. of Michigan, 1974.

_____. *Productive Americans: A Study of How Individuals Contribute to Economic Progress*. Ann Arbor, MI: Institute for Social Research, 1966.

Morgenstern, R. "Direct and Indirect Effects on Earnings of Schooling and Socio-Economic Background." *Review of Economics and Statistics*, My, 1973.

Morsell, John A. "Black Progress on Illiberal Rhetoric?" *Crisis* 80(Je-Jl, 1973 :200-203.

Moynihan, Daniel P. "Employment, Income, and the Ordeal of the Negro Family." *Daedalus*, Fall, 1965.

Mundel, David S. and others. *The Unemployment of Nonwhite Americans: The Effects of Alternative Policies*. Washington, DC: GPO, 1976.

Munnell, Alicia H. "The Economic Experience of Blacks: 1964-1974." *New England Economic Review*, Ja-F, 1978, pp. 5-18.

National Commission for Manpower Policty. *Proceedings of a Conference on Employment Problems of Low Income Groups*, F, 1976. ERIC ED 154 174.

Newman, Dorothy K. and others. *Protest, Politics, and Prosperity: Black Americans and White Institutions, 1940-75*. New York: Pantheon, 1977.

O'Kane, James M. "Ethnic Mobility and the Lower-Income Negro: A Socio-Historical Perspective." *Social Problems*, Winter, 1969.

O'Neill, Dave M. *The Effect of Discrimination on Earnings: Evidence from Military Test Score Results*, F 3, 1970. Clearinghouse for Federal Scientific and Technical Information, U.S. Department of Commerce, Springfield, VA 22151.

"On the Nature of Black Progress." *Commentary* 56(Ag, 1973):4-22. [Letters]

Ornstein, Michael D. *Entry into the American Labor Force*. Baltimore, MD: Johns Hopkins U., Center for the Study of Social Organization of Schools, S, 1971. ERIC ED 055 250.

Patten, T. H., Jr., and Clark, G. E., Jr. "Literacy Training and Job Placement of Hard-Core Unemployed Negroes in Detroit." *Journal of Human Resources*, Winter, 1968.

Peet, Richard. "Outline for a Second-Year Course on the Socioeconomic Geography of Human Poverty." Antipode 2(D, 1970):1-34

Perrella, Vera C. Low Earners and their Income. Special Labor Force Report No. 82. U.S. Bureau of Labor Statistics, My, 1967.

_____. "Young Workers and their Earnings." Monthly Labor Review 94(Jl, 1971):3-11.

Perry, Jane. "The Preparation of Disadvantaged Youth for Employment and Civic Responsibilities," Journal of Negro Education, Summer, 1964.

Pichler, Joseph A. "The Job Corps Transition." Industrial and Labor Relations Review 25 (Ap, 1972):336-353.

Sayay, Anirejuoritse. "An Inquiry into the Economic Demographic Causes of Black Poverty in the Urban Southeast of the United States." Doctoral dissertation. U. of Pittsburgh, 1975. Univ. Microfilms Order No. 75-21,768.

Schiffman, J. "Employment of High School Graduates and Dropouts in 1962." Monthly Labor Review, Jl, 1963.

Schultz, Theodore W. "Resources for Higher Education: An Economist's View." Journal of Political Economy, My-Je, 1968.

Schwartzman, David. "The Contribution of Education to the Quality of Labor, 1929-1963." American Economic Review, Je, 1968.

Scoggins, Will. Labor in Learning: Public School Treatment of the World of Work. Los Angeles: U. of California, 1966.

Shin, Eui Hang. "Earnings Inequality Between Black and White Males by Education, Occupation, and Region." Sociology and Social Research 60(Ja, 1976):161-172.

_____. "Trends and Variations in Efficiency of Black Interregional Migration Streams." Sociology and Social Research 62(Ja, 1978): 228-245 [Black males]

Siegel, Paul M. "On the Cost of Being a Negro." Sociological Inquiry, Winter, 1965.

Smith, James P. "The Improving Economic Status of Black Americans." American Economic Review 68(My, 1978):171-178.

Smith James P., and Welch, Finis R. Black-White Earnings and Employment: 1960-1970. New York: National Bureau of Economic Research, O, 1964.

Snyder, David, and Hudis, Paula M. "Occupational Income and the Effects of Minority Competition and Segregation: A Re-analysis and Some New Evidence." American Sociological Review 41(Ap, 1976):209-234.

Sorkin, Alan L. "Education, Migration, and Negro Unemployment," Social Forces. Mr, 1969.

Squires, Gregory D. "Education, Jobs, and Inequality: Functional and Conflict Models of Social Stratification in the United States." Social Problems 24(Ap, 1977): 436-450.

Stein, Robert L., and Hedges, Janice N. "Earnings and Family Income Blue Collar/ White Collar Pay Trends." Monthly Labor Review 94(Ja, 1971):13-23.

Stinchcombe, Arthur L. "The Social Determinant of Success." Science, N 10, 1972:603-604.

Strom, Robert D. "Education: Key to Economic Equality for the Negro." Journal of Negro Education, Fall, 1965.

Stromsdorfer, Ernst W. Review and Synthesis of Cost-Effectiveness Studies of Vocational and Technical Education. Columbus, OH: Center for Vocational and Technical Education, Ohio State U., Ag, 1972.

Tabb, W. K. "Decreasing Black-White Income Differentials: Evaluating the Evidence and a Linear Programming Framework for Urban Policy Choice." Journal of Regional Science 12(D, 1972).

Taubman, Paul. Schooling, Ability, Non-Pecuniary Rewards, Socioeconomic Background and the Lifetime Distribution of Earnings. New York: National Bureau of Economic Research, N, 1973.

Taussig, Michael K., and Danziger, Sheldon. Conference on the Trend in Income Inequality in the U.S., 2 parts, O 29, 1976. ERIC ED 141 457.

Terrell, H. S. "The Data on Relative White-Nonwhite Income and Earnings Re-examined: A Comment on the Papers by Guthrie and Ashenfelter." Journal of Human Resources 6(Summer, 1971).

_____. "Wealth Accumulation of Black and White Families: The Empirical Evidence." Journal of Finance 26(My, 1971):363-377.

Thompson, G. B. "Blacks and Social Security Benefits: Trends, 1960-73." Social Security Bulletin 38(Ap, 1975).

Thurow, Lester C. "The Economic Status of Minorities and Women. Some Facts and Conclusions." Civil Rights Digest 8 (Winter-Spring, 1976):2-9.

_____. "Education and Economic Equality." Public Interest 28(Summer, 1972):66-81.

Thurow, Lester C., and Lucas, Robert E. B. *The American Distribution of Income: A Structural Problem.* Printed for the use of the Joint Economic Committee, Washington, DC: GPO, 1972.

Tobin, James. "On Improving the Economic Status of the Negro." *Daedalus*, Fall, 1965.

Tolley, G. S., and Olson, E. "The Interdependence Between Income and Education." *Journal of Political Economy* 79(My-Je, 1971) 460-480.

U.S. Bureau of the Census. *Annual Mean Income, Lifetime Income, and Educational Attainment of Men in the United States, for Selected Years, 1956 to 1972.* Washington, DC: GPO, Mr, 1974.

_____. *Characteristics of the Low-Income Population: 1971.* Washington, DC: GPO, Jl, 1972.

_____. *Characteristics of the Low-Income Population: 1972.* Washington, DC: GPO, D, 1971.

_____. *Characteristics of the Population Below the Poverty Level: 1974.* Washington, DC: GPO, Ja, 1976.

_____. *Household Money Income in 1974 and Selected Social and Economic Characteristics of Households.* Washington, DC: GPO, Ag, 1975.

_____. *Money Income in 1971 of Families and Persons in the United States.* Washington, DC: GPO, Jl, 1972.

U.S. Civil Service Commission (comp.). *Equal Opportunity in Employment.* Washington, DC: GPO, 1972.

U.S. Congress, 92nd, 2nd session, Senate, Select Committee on Equal Educational Opportunity. *The Costs to the Nation of Inadequate Education.* Washington, DC: GPO, 1972.

U.S. Congress, 94th, 1st session, House of Representatives, Committee on Education and Labor, Subcommittee on Equal Opportunities. *Equal Opportunity and Full Employment. Hearing...* Washington, DC: GPO, 1975.

U.S. Congress, 95th, 1st session, House of Representatives, Committee on Education and Labor, Subcommittee on Employment Opportunities. *Youth Employment and Training Act of 1977 and Related Legislation: Hearings...* Washington, DC: GPO, 1977.

U.S. Department of Labor, Manpower Administration. *Career Thresholds.* Vol. II. Washington, DC: GPO, 1971.

University of Michigan Survey Research Center. *Five Thousand American Families: Patterns of Economic Progress.* Vol. 3. Ann Arbor, MI: Institute for Social Research. U. of Michigan, 1975.

Vroman, Wayne. "Labor Market Changes for Black Men Since 1964." *Monthly Labor Review* 98(Ap, 1975):42-44.

Wachtel, Paul. "The Effect of School Quality on Achievement, Attainment Levels, and Lifetime Earnings." *Explorations in Economic Research* 2(Fall, 1975): 502-536.

Waldman, Elizabeth. *Employment of High School Graduates and Dropouts in 1966.* Special Labor Force Report No. 85. Washington, DC: GPO, 1967.

Weiss, Leonard, and Williamson, Jeffrey G. "Black Education, Earnings, and Interregional Migration: Some New Evidence." *American Economic Review* 62(Je, 1972): 372-383.

Weiss, Randall D. *The Effect of Education on the Earnings of Blacks and Whites.* Cambridge, MA: Program on Regional and Urban Economics, Harvard U., 1969.

Weitzman, Murray S. *Measures of Overlap of Income Distributions of White and Negro Families in the United States.* U.S. Bureau of the Census Technical Paper 22. Washington, DC: GPO, Ap, 1970.

Welch, Finis. "Black-White Differences in Returns to Schooling." *American Economic Review* 63(D, 1973):893-907.

_____. "Relationships Between Income and Schooling." In *Review of Research in Education 2.* Edited by Fred N. Kerlinger and John B. Carroll. Itasca, IL: Peacock, 1974.

Wilber, G. L., and Hagan, R. J. *Metropolitan and Regional Inequalities Among Minorities in the Labor Market.* Springfield, VA: NTIS, 1976.

Wright, Erik Olin. "Class Structure and Income Inequality." Doctoral dissertation, U. of California, Berkeley, 1976.

_____. "Race, Class, and Income Inequality." *American Journal of Sociology* 83(My, 1978): 1368-1397.

Wright, Erik Olin, and Perrone, Lura. "Marxist Class Categories and Income Inequality." *American Sociological Review* 42(F, 1977): 32-55.

Yokelson, Doris (ed.). Collected Papers on Poverty Issues, 4 vols., Je, 1975. ERIC 121 867-871.

Careers

Adams, Frederick G., and Grant, Maye H. "The Black Health Manpower Need." Community and Junior College Journal 44(Mr, 1974):11-12.

Alden, John. "Women and Minorities in Engineering." Engineering Education 64 (Ap, 1974).

Altenderfer, Parion. Minorities and Women in the Health Fields: Applicants, Students, and Workers. Washington, DC: GPO, 1976.

Alvin, Harry J. "The Negro in Medicine." Current Medical Digest, Ag, 1969.

Anderson, Charles. "Black Lawyers in the 20 Largest Firms: It's Better than Before and Worse than Ever." Juris Doctor, Ja, 1973.

Applewhite, Harold L. "A New Design for Recruitment of Blacks into Health Careers." American Journal of Public Health 61(O, 1971) 1965-1971.

_____. "The Vanishing Negro Dentist." Quarterly of the National Dental Association 27(Ap, 1969):28-29.

Atwood, John W. and others. "Survey of Black Law Student Enrollment." Student Lawyer Journal, Je, 1971:18-38.

Auerbach, Isaac L. "A New Kind of Vocational Education." Integrated Education, Ap-Mr, 1964.

Aun, Emil Michael. "Accounting: Deficit in Black." Manpower 2(Ag, 1970):2-7.

Barbosa, Pedro. "Underrepresentation of Minorities in the Biological Sciences." BioScience 25(My, 1975):319-320.

Bayton, James A. "Francis Sumner, Max Meener, and the Training of Black Psychologists." American Psychologist 30(F, 1975):185-186.

Bayton, James A., Roberts, S. O., and Williams, Roger K. "Minority Groups and Careers in Psychology." American Psychologist 25(1970): 504-510.

Beck, Robert H. (ed.). Society and the Schools: Communication Challenge to Education and Social Work, 1965. National Association of Social Workers, 2 Park Avenue, New York, NY, 10016.

Becker, Henry Jay. How Young People Find Career-Entry Jobs: A Review of the Literature. Baltimore: Center for Social Organization of Schools, Johns Hopkins U., N, 1977.

Bell, Derrick A., Jr. "Black Students in White Law Schools: The Ordeal and the Opportunity." U. of Toledo Law Review, Spring-Summer, 1970.

Berg, Ivar. Education and Jobs: The Great Training Robbery. New York: Praeger, 1970.

Better, N. M. "Discrimination in Educational Employment." Doctoral dissertation, U. of California, Los Angeles, 1966.

"Black Attorneys at Law." Washington Post, Ap, 11-14, 1976. [Four articles on black lawyers in the District of Columbia]

"Black MBA's. Joint Programs Aim to Raise the Number of Black Business Students." Black Enterprise, S, 1973:31-36,58.

Blacks in the Construction Trades and Effect on Connecticut Economy. Storrs CT: Labor Education Center, U. of Connecticut, Je, 1970. ERIC ED 048 473.

Blake, D. F. "A Quarter Century of the Black Experience in the Natural Sciences, 1974." Negro Educational Review 27(Ap, 1976): 155-163.

Blau, Theodore H. "The APA Commission on Accelerating Black Participation in Psychology." Counseling Psychologist 2(Fall, 1970): 77-78.

Blewett, William E. "Minority Students' Special Needs and Recruitment." Journal of Allied Health 3(Winter, 1974):22-25.

Bloomfield, Maxwell. "John Mercer Langston and the Training of Black Lawyers." In American Lawyers in a Changing Society, 1776-1876. Cambridge, MA: Harvard U. Press, 1976: 302-339.

Bowers, John Z., and Cogan, Lee. "Negroes for Medicine." Integrated Education, Ja-F, 1968.

Bowers, John Z., Cogan, Lee, and Becker, E. Lovell. "Negroes in Medicine." Journal of the American Medical Association, O 16, 1967.

Bowles, Roy T., and Slocum, Walter L. Social Characteristics of High School Students Planning to Pursue Post High School Vocational Training. Washington, DC: Bureau of Research, U.S. Office of Education, 1968. [State of Washington]

Boxley, Russell, and Wagner, Nathaniel N. "Clinical Psychology Training Programs and Minority Groups: A Survey." Professional Psychology 2(Winter, 1971):75-81.

Braddock, Clayton. "Vo-Ed is for the Majority." Southern Education Report, Je, 1967. [Vocational education]

Bradley, Francis X., Jr "Tackling the Challenge of Minority Participation." Engineering Education 66(Ja, 1976):296.

Branch, Marie. Faculty Development to Meet Minority Group Needs: Recruitment, Retention, and Curriculum Change, 1971-74, Jl, 1975. ERIC ED 123 982 [School of Nursing]

Branch, Marie Foster, and Paxton, Phyllis Perry. (eds.). Providing Nursing Care for Ethnic People of Color. New York: Appleton-Century-Crofts, 1976.

Bromall, Irvin H. "Black and Minority Law Students: A Stratum for Societal Change." Journal of Non-White Concerns in Personnel and Guidance 3(Ap, 1975):114-120.

Brown, Charles Summer. "The Genesis of the Negro Lawyer in New England." Negro History Bulletin 22(Ap, 1959):147-152.

Brown, Patricia A. "Racial Social Work." Journal of Education for Social Work 12 (Winter, 1976):28-35.

Brown, William H. III. "Racial Discrimination in the Legal Profession." Judicature 53 (Ap-My, 1970):385-389.

Burchill, George W. (ed.). Work-Study Programs for Alienated Youth. A Casebook. Chicago, IL: Science Research Associates, 1962.

California State Department of Education. Recruiting Minority Teachers. An Equal Opportunity Guide. Sacramento: Superintendent of Public Instruction, 1967.

Caliver, Ambrose. Vocational Education and Guidance of Negroes. Washington, DC: GPO, 1938.

Campbell, Dick. "Black Musicians in Symphony Orchestras: A Bad Scene." Crisis 82(Ja, 1975):12-17.

Campbell, Joel T. and others. Prediction of Job Performance for Negro and White Medical Technicians: The Prediction of Supervisors' Ratings from Aptitude Tests, Using a Cross-Validation Procedure. Princeton, NJ: Educational Testing Service, 0, 1970. ERIC ED 053 210.

_____ and others. Prediction of Job Performance for Negro and White Medical Technicians. A Regression Analysis of Potential Test Bias: Predicting Job Knowledge Scores from an Aptitude Battery. Washington, DC: Civil Service Commission, Ap, 1969. ERIC ED 034 235.

Carey, Phillip. "Engineering Education and the Black Community: A Case for Concern." Journal of Negro Education 46(Winter, 1977): 39-45.

_____. Social and Professional Responsibilities of Engineering Education to the Black Community, 1974. ERIC ED 089 606.

Carl, E. L. "Shortage of Negro Lawyers: Pluralistic Legal Education and Legal Services for the Poor." Journal of Legal Education 20, 0, 1967.

Carl, E. L., and Callahan, Kenneth R. "Negroes and the Law." Journal of Legal Education 17, No. 3, 1965. [Law as a career for Negroes]

Carter, Robert L. "The Black Lawyer." Humanist, S-O, 1969.

Cave, Vernal G. "Black Doctors Have Special Problems." Black Enterprise 5(F, 1975): 30-34.

Chandler, Cleveland A. "An Affirmative Action Plan for the Economics Profession." American Economics Review, My 1970. [In re: increasing the supply of black economists]

Clark, Christine P. (ed.). Minority Opportunities in Law for Blacks, Puerto Ricans and Chicanos New York: Law Journal Press, 1974.

Clark, Christine P., and Clark, LeRoy. "The Black Lawyer." Black Enterprise, F, 1973.

Cobb, William Montague (ed.). "Integration in Medicine: A National Need." Journal of the National Medical Association, Ja, 1957:1-71.

Cogan, Lee. Negroes for Medicine, Report of a Macy Conference. Baltimore, MD: Johns Hopkins Press, 1969.

Cole, Melvin. "Black Students and the Health Sciences." Integrated Education 8(Ja-F, 1970):50-58.

Colorado Advisory Committee. Access to the Legal Profession in Colorado by Minorities and Women, Washington, DC: U.S. Commission on Civil Rights, 1976.

Cooke, Alfred Lynwood. "A Comparison of Middle-Class College-Educated Black Men in Traditional and Nontraditional Occupations." Doctoral dissertation, Ohio State U., 1974. Univ. Microfilms Order No. 75-03035.

Coombs, Orde. "Making It in Middle Management." Black World 21(My, 1972):38-44.

Cooper, Clair. "Southern Lawyers: Blacks and the Bar." Civil Liberties 301(Mr, 1974): 1-2.

Corwin, Edward H. L., and Sturges, Gertrude L. Opportunities for the Medical Education of Negroes. New York: Scribner, 1936. [Harlem Hospital]

Cowhig, James D. "Vocational Agriculture Enrollment and Farm Employment Opportunities." Southwestern Social Science Quarterly, Mr, 1967.

Crane, Donald P. "Developing Negroes for Management Positions." Training and Development Journal 25(Mr, 1971):40-42.

"Crisis in Negro Medicine." Ebony, N, 1967.

Crowley, Anne E., and Nicholson, Hayden C. "Negro Enrollment in Medical Schools." Journal of the American Medical Association, O 6, 1969.

Cull, John G., and Hardy, Richard E. Career Guidance for Blacks and Adolescents. A Guide to Selected Professional Occupations, Springfield, IL: Charles C. Thomas, 1975.

Curtis, James L. Blacks, Medical Schools, and Society. Ann Arbor, MI: U. of Michigan Press, 1971.

_____. "Minority Student Success and Failure with the National Intern and Resident Matching Program." Journal of Medical Education 50(Je, 1975):563-570.

Curtis, Samuel M. "Education in Agricultural Occupations for the Educationally Disadvantaged." Journal of the American Association of Teacher Educators in Agriculture 16(Jl, 1975):1-7.

D'Andrade. Roy G. "Minorities in Anthropology Higher Degree Programs." Anthropology Newsletter 16(N, 1975):19-23.

Davenport, Lawrence F. "Career Education and the Black Student." In Essays on Career Education. Edited by Larry McClure and Carolyn Brian. Washington, DC: GPO, 1973:177-184.

DeLeon, Al. "Showdown on Morningside Heights." Black Enterprise 5(S,1974):32-37. [The Michele Clark Fellowship Program for Minority Journalists at Columbia U.]

Dean, Wanda E. "Training Minorities in Psychology." Journal of Non-White Concerns in Personnel and Guidance 5(Ap, 1977):119-125.

Dean, Wanda E. and others. "Training Mental Health Professionals for the Black Community." Journal of Black Psychology 3 (Ag, 1976):14-19.

Diekema, Anthony J., and Hilton, William J. "The Medical Opportunities Program: An Approach Toward Increasing Minority Enrollments in Health Professional Schools." College and University 47(Spring, 1972): 201-210

Dominick, Joseph R., and Greenberg, Bradley S. Three Seasons of Blacks on Television. East Lansing, MI: Department of Communication, Michigan State U., My, 1970.

Douglas, Carlyle. "Ernest Green: Vigil on the Labor Front." Ebony 31(Mr, 1976):84-92. [Executive Director, Recruitment and Training Program, Inc.]

Douglas, J. H. "Racial Integration in the Psychiatric Field." Journal of the National Medical Association 57(1965):1-7.

DuBois, W. E. B. "The Negro Scientist." American Scholar, Jl, 1939.

Dube, W. F. "Datagram: Socioeconomic Background of Minority and Other U.S. Medical Students, 1976-1977." Journal of Medical Education 53(My, 1978):443-445.

Dummet, Clifton O. "The Negro in Dental Education: A Review of Important Occurrences." Phylon 20(Winter, 1959):439-454.

Edwards, Harry. "The Sources of the Black Athlete's Superiority." Black Scholar 3 (N, 1971):32-41.

Edwards, Harry T. "New Role for the Black Law Graduate--A Reality or an Illusion." Michigan Law Review 69(1971):1407-1410.

Edwards, Harry T., and Zaretsky, B. L. "Preferential Remedies for Employment Discrimination." Michigan Law Review 73(Ag, 1975).

Elam, Lloyd C. "Problems of the Predominantly Negro Medical School." Journal of the American Medical Association, Ag 18, 1969. [Meharry Medical College, Nashville, TN]

Elliott, Paul R. "Enrollment of Black Students in Professional and Graduate Study." Journal of the American Medical Association, Ag 18, 1969.

Ellis, Mary L. A Report to the Nation on Vocational Education. Flagstaff, AZ: Project Baseline, Northern Arizona U., N, 1975.

Elvena, Ronald G., and Heranney, David L. "Non-White Prospective Law Students and Lawyers: A Counseling Perspective." Journal of Non-White Concerns in Personnel and Guidance 4(Jl, 1976):181-190).

Epps, E. G., and Howze, S. R. Survey of Black Social Scientists. New York: Russell Sage Foundation, 1971.

Epps, Willie James. "Factors in Employment Migration of Black Doctorate Holders from Predominantly Black Colleges to Predominantly White Colleges: 1965-1972." Doctoral dissertation, Kansas State U., 1974. Univ. Microfilms Order No. 74-25598.

Ethnicity and Health Care. New York: National League for Nursing, 1976.

Evans, Ross A. "Psychology's White Face." *Social Policy* 1(Mr-Ap, 1971):54-58.

Fernandez, John P. *Black Managers in White Corporations,* 1972. ERIC ED 094 119.

Fishman, Jacob R. and others. *Training for New Careers. The Community Apprentice Program by the Center for Youth and Community Studies, Howard University, Washington, D.C.* Washington, DC: Howard U., Je, 1965. ERIC ED 025 472

Fox, Fay. "Minorities in Engineering: Any Progress?" *Machine Design,* N 25, 1976.

Franklin, William S., Roomkin, Myron, and Mawrizi, Alex. *Industrial and Labor Relations Review* 26(0, 1972):696-705. [Comments on Minority Membership in Apprenticeship Programs in the Construction Trades]

Frazier, E. Franklin. "Professional Education for Negro Social Workers." *Hospital Social Service* 18(1928):167-176.

Freedman, Marcia K. "Training Colored Social Workers in the South." *Journal of Social Forces* 1(My, 1923):440-446.

Freiherr, Gregory. "Opening the Door in Biomedicine." *Change* 11(F, 1979):46-47. [Minority Biomedical Support Program]

Gamble, H. F. "Report of Committee on Medical Education and Negro Medical Schools." *Journal of the National Medical Association,* O-D, 1909.

Garnett, Bernard E. "Blacks in Pro Sports." *The Black Athlete--1970.* Nashville, TN: Race Relations Information Center, Ag, 1970.

Gartner, Alan, and Riessman, Frank. "The Unique Educational Crisis of the Service Society." *Integrated Education* 12(Jl-Ag, 1974):3-5.

Gellhorn, E. "Law Schools and the Negro." *Duke Law Journal* 6(D, 1968):1069-1100.

Gillette, Robert. "Minorities in the Geosciences: Beyond the Open Door." *Science* 177 (Jl, 1972):148-151.

Gillette, Robert, and Gillette, Elizabeth (eds.). *Report of the First National Conference on Minority Participation in Earth Science and Mineral Engineering.* Golden, CO: U.S. Department of the Interior and the Colorado School of Mines, 1972. Reprinted in U.S. Congress, 93rd, 2nd session, House of Representatives, Committee on the Judiciary, Subcommittee on Civil Rights and Constitutional Rights, *Federal Employment of Spanish Speaking Americans Hearings...* Washington, DC: GPO, 1975, pp. 366-525.

Ginzberg, Eli (ed.). *The Negro Challenge to the Business Community.* New York: McGraw-Hill 1964. [Includes essays by Kenneth B. Clark and Thomas Pettigrew]

Gipson, Mack, Jr., and Henderson, Bonnie C. "Minority Participation Program--A Program Report." *Geotimes* 18(S, 1973):14-15 [Geological sciences]

Goddard, Aylene D. "A Microroster of Black Scientists and Inventors." *School Science and Mathematics* 71(Je, 1971):535-537.

Golden, Deborah and others. *Students in Schools of Social Work,* My, 1972. ERIC ED 087 268.

Gottfredson, Linda S. *Providing Black Youth More Access to Enterprising Work,* Ag 28, 1977. ERIC ED 149 214.

Gottfredson, Linda S., and Brown, Vicky C. *Occupational Differentiation in the First Decade After High School.* Baltimore, MD: Center for Social Organization of Schools, Johns Hopkins U., Ag, 1978. [White sample]

Graglia, Lino. "Special Admission of the 'Culturally Deprived' to Law School." *University of Pennsylvania Law Review* 119 (1970).

Greene, William T., Jr. "The Implications of Licensing for Black Social Workers." *National Association of Black Social Workers News* 1(0, 1973):2

Griffith, Albert Roger. "The Perceived Effects of Race on the Careers of Black College Graduates." Doctoral dissertation, Columbia University, 1975. Univ. Microfilms Order No. 75-12584

Gruenberg, Gladys W. "Minority Training and Hiring in the Construction Industry." *Labor Law Journal* 22(Ag, 1971):522-536.

Guerra, Roberto S. and others. *Black Youth and Occupational Education in Texas* Je, 1974. ERIC ED 097-409.

Guerra, Roberto S., and Schulman, Sam. Occup-ational Education in Texas: An Ethnic Comparison, Je, 1974. ERIC ED 097 146.

Hall, Clyde W. Black Vocational Technical and Industrial Arts Education: Development and History, 1973. American Technical Society, 848 East 58th Street, Chicago, IL 60637.

_____. "A Survey of Industrial Education for Negroes in the U.S. up to 1917." Doctoral dissertation, Bradley U., 1958. Univ. Microfilms Order No. 6494.

Hamilton, Phyllis D. Vocational Education Re-search and Development for Ethnic Minority Students, Ag 1, 1975. ERIC ED 130 160.

Hammerman, Herbert. "Minority Workers in Construction Referral Unions." Monthly Labor Review 95(My, 1972):17-26.

Harmon, William W. "Training Minorities for Health Careers: The Newark Experience." Journal of Allied Health 4(F, 1975):19-24.

Harris, Janette H. (comp.). A Directory of Black Historians. Washington, DC: Department of History, Howard U., 1974.

Harris, Louis and associates. A Survey of Ex-Job Corpsmen. Ap, 1969. Reprinted in U.S. Congress, 91st, 1st session, Senate, Commit-tee on Labor and Public Welfare, Subcommit-tee on Employment, Manpower, and Poverty. Closing of Job Corps Centers. Hearings Washington, DC: GPO, 1969, pp. 26-107.

Harris-Hurd, Laura. "Engineering. It is Quickly Becoming the Career Choice of the Decade for Blacks." Black Enterprise 5(Mr, 1975):57-60.

Hayden, Robert C., and Harris Jacqueline. Nine Black American Doctors. Reading, MA: Addison-Wesley, 1976.

Haynes, M. Alfred. "Distribution of Black Physicians in the United States, 1967." Journal of the American Medical Association, O 6, 1969.

_____. "Influence of Social Background in Medical Education." Journal of Medical Education 48, pt. 2(D, 1973):45-48.

_____. "Problems Facing the Negro in Medicine Today." Journal of the American Medical Association, Ag 18, 1969.

Hazen, Henry H. "Twenty-three Years of Teaching in a Negro Medical School." Social Forces 12(My, 1934):570-575. [Howard U.]

Hefner, James A., and Kidder, Alice E. "Racial Integration in Southern Management Positions." Phylon 33(Summer, 1972):193-200.

Henderson, Algo, and Gumas, Natalie. Admitting Black Students to Medical and Dental Schools. Berkeley, CA: Center for Research and Development in Higher Education, 1971.

Herbert, Adam W. "The Minority [Public] Administrator: Problems, Prospects, and Challenges." Public Administration Review 34(N-D, 1974):556-563.

Hicks, Harry E. "A Chance for Talented Blacks in Broadcasting." American Vocational Journal 46(Ja,1971):86-87. [Atlanta, GA]

Hill, Herbert. "Evading the Law. Apprentice-ship Outreach and Hometown Plans in the Construction Industry." Civil Rights Digest 6(Summer, 1974):3-17.

Ho, James K. (ed.). Black Engineers in the United States--A Directory. Washington, DC: Howard U. Press, 1974.

Hobbs, Louise, and Pakiser, L. C. "Minority Record Reported." Geotimes 23(Mr, 1978). [Recipients of American Geological Institute scholarships]

Houston, Charles H. "The Need for Negro Lawyers." Journal of Negro Education 4(Ja, 1935):94-98.

Houston, Laura Pires. "Black People, New Careers, and Humane Human Services." Social Casework 51(1970):291-299.

"How Black Professionals Cope." Black Enter-prise 7(S, 1976):52-58.

Hutchins, E. B., Reitman, J. B., and Klaub, D. "Minorities, Manpower, and Medicine." Journal of Medical Education 42(1967):

Jackson, Roberta H. Career Education and Minorities. Washington, DC: GPO, 1977.

Jacobson, Robert L. "No Progress in Recruiting Minority Medical Students." Chronicle of Higher Education, O 2, 1978.

Janowitz, Morris, and Moskos, Charles C., Jr. "Racial Composition in the All Volunteer Force." Armed Forces and Society 1(N, 1974): 109-122.

Jay, James M. Negroes in Science: Natural Science Doctorates, 1876-1969, 1971. Balamp Publishing Co., P.O. Box 7390, Detroit, MI.

"Job Prospects for Blacks in Library Field are Rosy." Library Journal 97(S 15, 1972):2794.

Johnson, D. G. (ed.). Minority Student Opportu-nities in the United States Medical Schools, 1969-1970. Washington, DC: Association of American Medical Colleges, 1969.

Johnson, Roosevelt. "Educational Needs of Blacks, Career Education and Research: A Need to Improve, Not Prove." In Restructuring the Educational Process: A Black Perspective. Edited by Lawrence E. Gary and Aaron Favors. Washington, DC: Institute for Urban Affairs and Research, Howard U. 1975.

Johnson, Walter L. "Admissions of Men and Ethnic Minorities to Schools of Nursing, 1971-1972." Nursing Outlook 22(Ja, 1974): 45-49.

Jolson, Marvin A. "Marketing Notes and Communications: Employment Barriers in Marketing." Journal of Marketing 38(Ap, 1974):67-69.

Jones, Rose. "Multiculturalism in Business Education." Business Education Forum 28(My, 1974):9-11.

Josey, E. J. (ed.). The Black Librarian in America. Metuchen, NJ: Scarecrow, 1970.

June, Lee N., and Pringle, Gwendolyn. "The Concept of Race in the Career-Development Theories of Roe, Super, and Holland." Journal of Non-White Concerns in Personnel and Guidance 6(0,1977):17-23.

Katz, Adolph. "Wanted: Minority Engineers." Philadelphia Bulletin, Ja 4, 1976. [Philadelphia Regional Introduction for Minorities in Engineering (PRIME)]

Katz, Michael. "Black Law Students in White Law Schools: Law in a Changing Society." University of Toledo Law Review, Spring, 1970, pp. 589-606.

Kaufman, Jacob J., Schaefer, Carl J., Lewis Morgan V., Stevens, David W., and House, Elaine W. "The Negro and Vocational Education." The Role of Secondary Schools in the Preparation of Youth for Employment, Chapter 9. Institute for Research on Human Resources, The Pennsylvania State U., U. Park, PA, F, 1967.

Kearney, Annette G., and Clayton, Robert L. "Career Education and Blacks: Trick or Treat?" School Counselor 21(N, 1973): 102-108.

Keig, Norman G. "The Occupational Aspirations and Labor Force Experience of Negro Youth." American Journal of Economics and Sociology 28(1969):113-130.

Kemp, Barbara H. The Youth We Haven't Served. A Challenge to Vocational Education. Washington, DC: GPO, 1966.

Kidd, Foster (ed.). Profile of Blacks in American Dentistry. Washington, DC: Howard U. Press, 1976.

Kiehl, Robert. Opportunities for Blacks in the Profession of Engineering. Newark, NJ: Foundation for the Advancement of Graduate Study in Engineering, O, 1970. ERIC ED 047 607.

_____. "Opportunities for Negroes in Engineering." Personnel and Guidance Journal, Je, 1964.

_____. "Preparation of the Negro for his Professional Engineering Opportunities." Doctoral dissertation. Rutgers U., 1957. Univ. Microfilms Order No., 22571.

King, Randall H. The Labor Market Consequences of Dropping out of High School, 1978. ERIC ED 158 034.

Kingdon, F. "Discrimination in Medical Colleges." American Mercury, O, 1945, D, 1945, Mr, 1946.

Knowles, Asa S. Cooperative Education: An Effective Education for Minority Students, S, 1971, Speech, American Psychological Association. ERIC ED 054 285.

Kobrak, Peter. "The Manpower Game: The Role of American Business in Urban Manpower Programs." Doctoral dissertation, Johns Hopkins U., 1971

Kuiken, J. D., and Eisenman, Russell. "The Negro in the Field of Medicine." Educational Forum, My, 1966.

Kuvlesky, William P., and Dietrich, Katheryn T. "Southern Black Youths' Orientation Toward Military Service: A Metropolitan-Nonmetropolitan Comparison." Journal of Political and Military Sociology 1(Spring, 1973):105-120.

Landis, Raymond B. "Improving the Retention of Minority Engineering Students." Engineering Education, Ap, 1976.

Lantz, Robert J. The Negro and Engineering Education: A Selection of Responses from 100 Deans of Engineering. Boston, MA: Boston U., College of Engineering, Ap 30, 1970. ERIC ED 040 663.

Lawrence, William, and Brown, Duane. "An Investigation of Intelligence, Self-Concept, Socioeconomic Status, Race, and Sex as Predictors of Career Maturity." Journal of Vocational Behavior 9(Ag, 1976):43-51.

Layzer, Judith. Ethnic Survey of Hospital Employees, F, 1970. Office of Contract Compliance, Office of the Major, Office of Administration, 250 Broadway, New York, NY 10007. [N.Y.C.]

Lee, Arthur M. Learning a Living Across the Nation. Vol. V, Parts 1 and 2. Flagstaff, AZ: Northern Arizona U., N, 1976.

Lee, John W., and Reuschling, Thomas. "Orientation for Black Salesmen in Predominantly White Sales Organizations." Training and Development Journal 27(N, 1973):16-19.

Leonard, Walter J. Black Lawyers: Training and Results, Then and Now. Boston: Senna and Shih, 1977.

_____. "The Development of the Black Bar." Annals 407(My, 1973):134-143.

Linsteal, John. "What Should Med Schools Teach?" Health Rights News 4(S, 1971).

Lopez-Lee, David M., and Weisham, Robert J. Career Education: Its Implications for American Minorities, 1975. ERIC ED 121 942.

McAllister-Johnson, Pam. Proposed Model for Improving Educational and Professional Opportunities for Journalism Students of Color in a Predominantly White University, Ag, 1974. ERIC ED 095 546.

McCarthy, Colman. "The Job on the Job Corps." New Republic, Jl 5, 1969.

McClory, Robert. "Minorities 'Untapped Source of Vocations.'" National Catholic Reporter Je 16, 1978. [Catholic Church]

McPherson, James Alan. "The Black Law Student. A Problem of Fidelities." Atlantic 225 (1970) 93-100.

Malcolm, Shirley Mahaley and others (comps.). An Inventory of Programs in Science for Minority Students, 1960-1975. Washington, DC: Office of Opportunities in Science, American Association for the Advancement of Science, 1976.

Marshall, F. Ray. "The Economics of Racial Discrimination: A Survey." Journal of Economic Literature 12(S, 1974):847-871.

Marshall, F. Ray, and Briggs, Vernon, Jr. Equal Apprenticeship Opportunities. Institute of Labor and Industrial Relations, U. of Michigan and Wayne State U., 1969. [Workers Defense League's "Outreach" project]

_____. "Negro Participation in Apprenticeship Programs." Journal of Human Resources, Winter, 1967.

_____. "Remedies for Discrimination in Apprenticeship Programs." Industrial Relations, My, 1967.

Maximillian, I. Martin. "Accountancy as a Field for the Negro." Journal of Accounting 55(F, 1932):112-116.

Maryland State Advisory Committee to the U.S. Commission on Civil Rights. Employment Discrimination in the Construction Industry in Baltimore. Washington, DC: U.S. Commission on Civil Rights, F, 1974.

Matthews, Hewitt, and Jackson, Richard. "The Black Pharmacist: An 'Invisible Man'?" American Druggist, O, 1976:70-71.

Matthews, Robert G., and Drabick, Lawrence W. Reasons for Selection of Expected Occupations--by Race and Sex. Educational Research, N, 1965. ERIC ED 019 417.

Maurizi, Alex. "Minority Membership in Apprenticeship Programs in the Construction Trades." Industrial and Labour Relations Review 25(Ja, 1972):200-206.

Meade, Edward J., Jr., and Feldman, Marvin J. "Vocational Education: Its Place and Its Process." Journal of Human Resources, Summer, 1966.

Meier, August. "Beginning of Industrial Education in Negro Schools." Midwest Journal, Spring, 1955.

Melnick, Vijaya L., and Hamilton, Franklin D. (eds.). Minorities in Science: The Challenge for Change in Biomedicine. New York: Plenum, 1977.

Mendel, Robert W., and Tabb, W. Gary. "Problems in Admissions in U.S. Dental Schools." College and University 52(Spring, 1977): 299-316.

Micklin, Bob. "Why Blacks Draw a Blank [in Working in Symphonic Music]" Chicago Sun Times, Je 12, 1977.

Microfiche Collection of Documents Reported in Abstracts of Research and Related Materials in Vocational and Technical Education, Summer, 1968. Columbus, OH: Center for Vocational Education, OH State U., 1968. ERIC ED 019 526.

Miller, Michael H. "On Blacks Entering Nursing." Nursing Forum 11(1972).

Mincer, Jacob. Schooling, Experience, and Earnings. New York: Columbia U. Press, 1974.

"Minorities in Engineering." Mechanical Engineering, S, 1975.

"Minorities in the Geosciences." Geotimes 17 (F, 1972):23-24.

Minority Student Opportunities in United States Medical Schools, 1970-1971. Washington, DC: Association of American Medical Colleges, O, 1970. [Available from Association of American Medical Colleges, One Dupont Circle, N.W., Washington, DC 20036]

Mitchell, Bert N. "The Black Minority in the CPA Profession." *Journal of Accountancy* 128(O, 1969):41-48.

Mommsen, Kent G. "On Recruiting Black Sociologists." *American Sociologist* 8(Ag, 1973): 107-116.

Montiel, Miguel. "Ethnic Minorities and Social Work Education." *Mano a Mano* 5(Je, 1976).

Moone, James C. *The Plight of Career Counseling for Blacks and Other Minorities: Issues and Concerns*, Ap, 1976. ERIC ED 133 664.

Morais, Herbert M. *The History of the Negro in Medicine*. New York: Publishers Co., 1967.

Murphy, Betty. "Minorities in Medicine." *Opportunity* 2(Ag-S, 1972):5-16.

National Academy of Engineering. *Proceedings of Symposium on Increasing Minority Participation in Engineering*, My 6, 1973. ERIC ED 149 880.

National Academy of Sciences. *Building Effective Programs in Engineering Education*, S, 1975. ERIC ED 149 883.

National Academy of Sciences. *Committee on Minorities in Engineering*, 1977. ERIC ED 149 879.

National Academy of Sciences--National Research Council. *Retention of Minority Students in Engineering*, 1977. ERIC ED 152 467.

National Advisory Health Council, Allied Health Professions Education Subcommittee. *Education for the Allied Health Professions and Services*. Washington, DC: GPO, 1967.

National Science Foundation. *Women and Minorities in Science and Engineering*. Washington, DC: GPO, 1977.

Nelson, Bernard W. and others. "Educational Pathway Analysis for the Study of Minority Representation in Medical School." *Journal of Medical Education* 46(S, 1971):745-749.

Nelson, D. W. and others. "The Minority Law Student in Southern California." *The L. A. Bulletin* 51(D, 1969).

Nelson, Gary R., and Armington, Catherine. *Military and Civilian Earnings Alternatives for Enlisted Men in the Army*. Arlington, VA: Institute for Defense Analysis, 1970.

Nelson, Richard, Achabel, Dale, and George, Warren. "The Black Salesman: How Is He Doing?" *Personnel Journal* 50(S, 1971):705-712.

Nemec, Richard. "Black Scientists: Little Money for Research." *New Republic* 166(Je 3, 1972):15-17.

"1971 Survey of Minority Group Students in Legal Education." *Journal of Legal Education* 24(1972):487-492.

Noeth, R. J., and Hanseon, G. "Occupational Programs Do the Job." *Community and Junior College Journal* 47(N, 1976):28-30.

Nowell, Gadis. "A Study of Black Students and Their Experiences in the 'Careers for Blacks in Management Program.'" Doctoral dissertation, U. of Chicago, 1976.

Nyren, Karl Edwin. "Black Decision-Makers in Libraries: A Library Journal Survey." *Library Journal*, Je 1, 1969.

Oak, Vishnu V. "Business Education in Negro Colleges." *Crisis*, Je, 1938.

_____. "Commercial Education in Negro Colleges." Doctoral dissertation, Clark U., 1937.

Odegaard, Charles E. *Minorities in Medicine. From Receptive Passivity to Positive Action 1966-76*. New York: Josiah Macy, Jr. Foundation, 1977.

Office of Minority Affairs. *Minority Student Opportunities in United States Medical Schools, 1975-76*. Washington, DC: Association of American Medical Colleges, 1975.

Office of Minority Business Enterprise. *Report of the Task Force on Education and Training for Minority Business Enterprise*, Ja, 1974. ERIC ED 096 542.

Padilla, Eligio R., Boxley, Russell, and Wagner, Nathaniel N. "The Desegregation of Clinical Psychology Training." *Professional Psychology* 4(Ag, 1973):259-264.

Parker, Kellis E., and Stebman, Betty J. "Legal Education for Blacks." *Annals* 407 (My, 1973):144-155.

Perrucci, Carolyn C. "Engineering and the Class Structure." In *The Engineers and the Social System*, pp. 279-310. Edited by R. Perucci and J. E. Gerstl. New York: Wiley, 1969.

Peterson, Iver. "Rise in Black Students Brings Disputes on Law School Recruiting." *New York Times*, Ap 7, 1974.

Pierce, Chester M. "The Formation of the Black Psychiatrists of America." In *Racism and Mental Health*, pp 525-554. Edited by Charles V. Willie, Bernard M. Kramer, and Bertram S. Brown. Pittsburgh, PA: U. of Pittsburgh Press, 1973.

Pierce, Joseph A. Negro Business and Business Education; Their Present and Prospective Development. New York: Harper & Row, 1947.

Planning Commission for Expanding Minority Opportunities in Engineering. Minorities in Engineering. A Blueprint for Action. New York: Alfred P. Sloan Foundation, 1974.

Poinsett, Alex. "Seeking Youth for Careers as Doctors." Ebony 29(O, 1974):148-155.

_____. "The 'Whys' Behind the Black Lawyer Shortage." Ebony 30(D, 1974):95-104.

Ponder, H. "Prospects for Black Farmers in the Years Ahead." American Journal of Agricultural Economics 53(My, 1971).

"Racial Makeup of Ph.D. Population Detailed." Chemical and Engineering News 53(Ap, 1975): 15-16.

"Racial Minorities in Science Studied." Chemical and Engineering News 53(O, 1975).

"Racial Progress in the Building Trades." American Labor, S, 1968.

Raines, Earl E. "Behind the Cello Player." Civil Rights Digest 10(Spring, 1978):38-46. [Absence of minority players in symphony orchestras]

Rappaport, Michael D. "The Case for Law School Minority Programs." Los Angeles Times, Mr 14, 1976. [California]

Raymond, R. S. "'Black Marketing' at Ohio University: How It Was." Collegiate News 23(My, 1970):11-14. [Course in marketing for black students]

Reiter, Andrea Bonnie. "Turnabout of an Industry: New Opportunities for Blacks in New York City Banking." Afro-American Studies 2(Mr, 1972):275-281.

Reitzes, Dietrich C., and Elkbaisialy, Hekmat. "Improving Medical Care for and by Minority Groups: A Case Study of National Medical Fellowships, Inc." In Selected Proceedings of the 3rd Annual Conference on Minority Studies, April, 1975, pp 65-86. Edited by George E. Carter, James R. Parker, and Carol Sweeney. La Crosse, WI: Institute for Minority Studies, U. of Wisconsin-La Crosse, 1976.

Report on the Governor's Committee on Employment of Minority Groups in the News Media. Albany, NY: Governor's Committee on Employment of Minority Groups in the News Media, Ap, 1969. ERIC ED 034 044.

Rich, Leslie, and Rich, Joan. "It Takes Courage." American Education, Je, 1966 [Southern Negro teachers relocating in the North]

Richardson, F. C. "A Quarter Century of the Black Experience in the Natural Sciences, 1950-1974." Negro Educational Review 27 (Ap, 1976):135-154.

Roberts, Diane, and Plunkett, Robert A. "Selected Keys to Open the Door to Minority Student Participation in Health Careers." Journal of Allied Health 3(Winter, 1974): 40-49.

Robinson, Alice M. "Black Nurses Tell You: Why So Few Blacks in Nursing." RN 35(Jl, 1972):35-41,73,75-76.

Rodriguez, O. "Occupational Shifts and Educational Upgrading in the American Labor Force between 1950 and 1970." Sociology of Education 51(Ja, 1978):55-67.

"Room at the Top in Engineering." Ebony 30 (Mr, 1975):66-74.

Rosen, Sanford Jay. "Equalizing Access to Legal Education: Special Programs for Law Students Who are not Admissible by Traditional Criteria." University of Toledo Law Review, Spring-Summer, 1970.

Rowe, Mary Budd. Factors Relevant in Recruitment/Retention of Minorities in Science Professions, Ap, 1977. ERIC ED 157 678.

_____. "Why Don't Blacks Pick Science?" Science Teacher 44(F, 1977):34-35.

Saline, Ludon E. "A National Effort to Increase Minority Engineering Graduates." IEEE Transactions on Education E-17, No. 1 (F, 1974).

Schmitt, Henry E., and Roberts, Perry E. "Effective Counseling Programs for Minority Students Enrolled in Vocational Education." Agricultural Education Magazine 45(S, 1972).

Scholarship Information Center. Law Schools and Minority Groups. Chapel Hill, NC: U. of North Carolina YMCA-YWCA, 1969.

Schwartz, Dorothy H. "Tell It Like It Is—Notes on Negroes in Business Education." Business Education World, Ap, 1966.

Schwarz, George E. "Educational Characteristics of Members of the National Medical Association." Journal of Medical Education 46(Jl, 1971):599-604.

Scott, Carl (ed.). Ethnic Minorities in Social Work Education. New York: Council on Social Work Education, 1970.

Segal, Geraldine Rosenbaum. "Blacks in the Law in Philadelphia." Doctoral dissertation, U. of Pennsylvania, 1978. Univ. Microfilms Order No. 7816356.

Sewell, Trevor E., and Martin, Roy P. "Racial Differences in Patterns of Occupational Choice in ADolescents." Psychology in the Schools 13(J1, 1976):326-333.

Shapiro, Theresa R. A Study of Black Male Professionals in Industry. Washington, DC: GPO, 1973.

Shepherd, Jack. "Black Lab Power." Saturday Review, Ag 5, 1972. [Black scientific researchers]

Sheppard, N. Alan. Research Focus on Ethnic Minorities in Vocational Education, D, 1975. ERIC ED 120 382.

Sheppard, N. Alan, and Sherrard, Frances (eds.). National Conference on Increasing the Participation of Black Americans in Vocational Education, Proceedings..., Mr, 1977. ERIC ED 142 799.

Shuman, Jerome. "A Black Lawyers Study." Howard Law Journal 16(Winter, 1971).

Sie, Maureen A. and others. Minority Groups and Science Careers: An Ecological Analysis, Ap, 1977. ERIC ED 138 477.

Silbert, Linda E. "Blacks in American Geography: 1974." Professional Geographer 27(F, 1975):65-72.

Simkins, Gary, and Raphael, Phillip. "Black Students, APA, and the Challenge of Change." American Psychologist 25(My, 1970):xxi-xxvi.

Slocum, John W., and Strawser, Robert H. "Racial Differences in Job Attitudes." Journal of Applied Psychology 56(F, 1972): 28-32.

Smith, Elsie J. "Reference Group Perspectives and the Vocational Maturity of Lower Socioeconomic Black Youth." Journal of Vocational Behavior 8(Je, 1976):321-335.

Smith, Gloria S. and others. "Rising Opportunities in the Field of Engineering Implications for Counselors." Journal of Non-White Concerns in Personnel and Guidance 1(Ap, 1973):163-167.

Smith, J. Stanford. "For Engineers, the Future Is Now." Black Enterprise 7(My, 1977):52-54. [Chairman of the Board, International Paper Co.]

_____. "Minorities in Engineering. A Five-Year Progress Report." Engineering Education 68(N, 1977):161-165.

Southern Regional Education Board. Minority Students in Allied Health and Science: A Conference Report, A 211.

Spaulding, Asa, Sr. "Seventy-Six Years of Black Insurance." Black Enterprise 4(Je, 1974):141,146-147.

Spearman, Robert, and Stevens, Hugh. A Step Toward Equal Justice, Programs to Increase Black Lawyers in the South, 1969-1973. New York: Carnegie Corp. of New York, 1974.

"Special Career Issue." Black Enterprise 7 (F, 1977): entire issue.

Speich, Don. "Minorities in Law Schools: Ideal Periled." Los Angeles Times, F 20, 1976. [California universities]

Spratlen, Thaddeus H. "Statement of Concern of the Caucus of Black Economists to the American Economic Association." American Economic Review, My,1970.

Star, Jack. "Med Student in Motion." Chicago Tribune Magazine, Je 6, 1976. [James Theatte, Chicago]

Stevens, George. "A Mission: Getting Minorities into the Corporate Pipeline." Journal of College Placement 38(Winter, 1978):70-73.

Stewart, Jesse E., and Davis, Alice. "Choice of Practice Environments by Black Pharmacists." American Journal of Pharmaceutical Education 41(My, 1977):156-159.

Still, William Grant. "The Negro Musician in America." Music Educators Journal 56(1970): 100-101,157-161.

Straker, D. Augustus. "The Negro in the Profession of Law." A.M.E. Church Review 8(O, 1891):180-182.

Straus, George. "Minority Membership in Apprenticeship Programs in the Construction Trades." Industrial and Labor Relations Review 27(O, 1973):93-99.

Stronge, William B., and Villemez, Wayne J. The Effect of Post Secondary Vocational Education in Assisting Students to Overcome Class and Income Inequality, O, 1977. ERIC ED 149 049.

Stuart, Reginald. Black Contractors' Dilemma. Nashville, TN: Race Relations Information Center, Ag, 1971.

_____. "News Media Lag in Drive for More Blacks on Staffs." New York Times, Ag 3, 1977.

_____. "Survey of Southern Black Journalists." South Today 3(J1-Ag, 1972):1,5-6.

Summitt, Russell W., and Anderson, Collings F. (eds.). Proceedings of the Workshop on Minority Dental Student Recruitment, Retention, and Education. Kansas City, MO: School of Dentistry, U. of Missouri, Kansas City, 1975.

Taubman, Paul (ed.). Kinometrics: Determinants of Socioeconomic Success Within and Between Families. New York: North-Holland, 1977.

Taylor, Dalmas, and Henry, J. Marilyn. Ethnicity and Bicultural Considerations in Psychology: Meeting the Needs of Ethnic Minorities, 1977. ERIC ED 151 251.

Taylor, Stuart A. "A Funny Thing Happened on the Way Up: The Harvard Business School Surveys Black MBA's." Contact 4(Spring, 1973):14-16,80.

Thomas, Mark J. "Realism and Socioeconomic Status (SES) of Occupational Plans of Low SES Black and White Male Adolescents." Journal of Counseling Psychology 23(Ja, 1976):46-49.

Thompson, Theodis. "Curbing the Black Physician Manpower Shortage." Journal of Medical Education 49(O, 1974):944-950.

Tickton, Stanley D., and Jones, Patricia W. "Racial Minorities in Broadcast Education." Journal of Broadcasting 22(Winter, 1978): 87-93.

Toles, E. B. "Report of Black Lawyers and Judges in the United States, 1960-1970." Congressional Record, S 2, 1970. Page E 7996.

Tollett, Kenneth S. "Black Lawyers, Their Education and the Black Community." Howard Law Journal 17(Winter, 1972).

Trayes, Edward J. "Black J--Enrollments Increase, But Important Questions Remain." Journalism Educator 29(Jl, 1974):43-44. [Undergraduate enrollment in journalism]

Tuck, Lon. "Segregated Music." Washington Post, S 2, 1977. [Black composers]

U.S. Bureau of Health Manpower Education. How Medical Students Finance Their Education, Washington, DC: GPO, Je, 1974.

U.S. Bureau of the Census. Selected Characteristics of Persons in Fields of Science or Engineering: 1974. Washington, DC: GPO, Jl, 1975.

U.S. Commissioner of Education. "Education of the Colored Race in Industry." In Report... for the Year 1893-94, Vol. I, part 1:1038-1061.

U.S. Congress, 93rd, 2nd session. House of Representatives, Committee on Education and Labor, Special Subcommittee on Education. Legal Education Opportunities, Hearing.... Washington, DC: GPO, 1974. [Legal training for disadvantaged students]

U.S. Department of Health, Education, and Welfare. Minorities and Women in the Health Fields. Applicants, Students, and Workers. Washington, DC: GPO, S, 1975.

Valentine, B. L. "Hustling and Other Hard Work in the Ghetto." Doctoral dissertation, Union Graduate School, 1975.

Vineberg, Robert and others. Performance in Five Army Jobs by Men at Different Aptitude (AFQT) Levels. I. Purposes and Design of Study. Alexandria, VA: Human Resources Research Organization. N, 1970. Available from National Technical Information Service, Operations Division, Springfield, VA, 22151.

Virginia State Advisory Committee to the U.S. Commission on Civil Rights. Judicial Selection in Virginia: The Absence of Black Judges. Washington, DC: U.S. Commission on Civil Rights, Ja, 1974.

Walker, Joe. "Need Unification of Black Journalists Into National Group." Muhammad Speaks, Mr 29, 1974.

Walsh, Edward Joseph. Dirty Work, Race, and Self-Esteem. Ann Arbor, MI: Institute of Labor and Industrial Relations, U. of Michigan, 1975. [Garbage collectors]

"Wanted: Black Engineers." Manpower 3(Je, 1971):8-10.

Washington, Forrester B. "Need and Education of Negro Social Workers." Journal of Negro Education 4(Ja, 1935):76-93.

Washington, Harold R. "History and Role of Black Law Schools." Howard Law Journal 18 (1974).

Watkins, Richard. "On Becoming a Black Doctor." Black Enterprise 5(F, 1975):20-21.

Weathers, Diane. "Managing the Muses." Black Enterprise 7(D, 1976):21-30. [The business side of black music]

Webb, Harvey, Jr. "Problems and Progress of Black Dental Professionals." Crisis 84(N, 1977):430-434.

Webb, Peter, and Sikorski, Linda A. "Communications Implications of Attitudes of Minority and Disadvantaged Youth toward Vocational Education." Journal of Vocational Education Research 2(F, 1977):39-54.

Weber, David A. "Racial Bias and the LSAT: A New Approach to the Defense of Preferential Admission." Buffalo Law Review 24 (1975):439-462. [Law School Admissions Test]

Weidlein, Edward R. "1,276 Minority-Group Students Enter Medical Study, Twice the '69 Total." Chronicle of Higher Education 6(N 29, 1971):1.

Wilburn, Adolph Y. "Careers in Science and Engineering for Black Americans." Science 184(Je 14, 1974):1148-1154.

Wilms, W. W. Public and Proprietary Vocational Training: A Study of Effectiveness. Lexington, MA: Lexington Books, 1975.

Wilson, Michele S. Financial Aid for Minorities in Law. Garrett Park, MD: Garrett Park Press, 1975.

Wispe, L. and others. "The Negro Psychologist in America." American Psychologist 24 (1969):142-150.

Wool, Harold. The Labor Supply for Lower Level Occupations. Washington, DC: GPO, 1976.

Wool, H., and Phillips, B. The Labor Supply for Lower Level Occupations. Washington, DC: National Planning Association, 1975.

Wortham, Jacob. "Shoot the Piano Player...and the Cellist, the Oboist and the Drummer." Black Enterprise 7(D, 1976):31-32,86-87. [Blacks in orchestras]

Wright, Elmer, Jr. "Interest of Two Ethnic Groups in Ornamental Horticulture." Agricultural Education Magazine 43(F, 1971): 201-202.

4X, Harold. "Survival of Black Law Students, Major Issue of Law Group." Muhammad Speaks, Ap 18, 1975. [Black American Law Students Association]

Young, Herman Andre. "An Educational and Professional Profile of Black American Doctorates in the Natural Sciences." Doctoral dissertation, Indiana U., 1973. Univ. Microfilms Order No. 74-02613.

_____. "Black American Science Doctorates: Some Characteristic Comparisons and Contrasts with American Science Doctorates." Master's thesis, U. of Louisville, 1973. Univ. Microfilms Order No. M-5540.

_____. "Survey of Black Scientists in the United States." Journal of Chemical Education 51(D, 1974):781-782.

Young, Herman A., and Young, Barbara H. "Black Doctorates, Myth and Reality." Chemtech, My, 1976:296-299.

Economic Discrimination

Abramson, Joan. "Measuring Success. Or, Whatever Happened to Affirmative Action?" Civil Rights Digest 9(Winter, 1977):14-27.

Adams, Arvil V. "The Impact of FEP Legislation." Integrateducation, Inequality in Metropolitan America 13(My-Je, 1975):46-48.

_____. Toward Fair Employment and the EEOC: A Study of Compliance Procedures Under Title VII of the Civil Rights Act of 1964. Washington, DC: U.S. Equal Employment Opportunity Commission, Ag 31, 1972.

Alexander, Rodney, and Sapery, Elizabeth. The Shortchanged: Minorities and Women in Commercial Banking. Port Washington, NY; Dunellen, 1974.

American Psychological Association Task Force on Employment Testing of Minority Groups. "Job Testing and the Disadvantaged." American Psychologist 24(Jl, 1969):637-650.

Anderson, Betty R., and Rogers, Martha P. (eds.). Personnel Testing and Equal Employment Opportunity. Washington, DC: GPO, 1971.

Anderson, Wayne, and Cox, Wray. "Intelligence and Work Adjustment in an NYC Population." Journal of Employment Counseling 9(S, 1972): 126-129.

Arrow, Kenneth J. Some Models of Racial Discrimination in the Labor Market. Rand Memorandum, RM-6253-RC. Santa Monica, CA: Rand Corp., 1971.

Bayer, Kurt. "A Social Indicator of the Cost of Being Black." Doctoral dissertation, U. of Maryland, 1971.

Beller, Andrea. "The Effect of Title VII of the Civil Rights Act of 1964 on the Economic Position of Black Males." Doctoral dissertation, Columbia U., 1975.

Benson, Carl A. "The Question of Mobility in Career Development for Black Professionals." Personnel Journal 54(My, 1975):272-274,289.

Bergmann, Barbara R. "The Effect on White Incomes of Discrimination in Employment." Journal of Political Economy 79(Mr-Ap, 1971):295-313.

Better, Norman M. "Discrimination in Educational Employment." Doctoral dissertation, U. of California at Los Angeles, 1966. Univ. Microfilms Order No. 66-4944.

Blake, Gene. "Bar to Seek Minority Graders." Los Angeles Times, N 8, 1976. [Racial factors in California Bar exams]

Boehm, Virginia R. "Negro-White Differences in Validity of Employment and Training Selection Procedures: Summary of Research Evidence." Journal of Applied Psychology 56(F, 1972):33-39.

Bryce, Herrington J. "Black Teens: Victims of Recession." Focus 3(Ag, 1975).

Christensen, Sandra, and Bernard, Keith. "The Black-White Earnings Gap." Journal of Human Resources 9(Summer, 1974):376-389.

"Civil Service: Does the Merit System Work?" Black Enterprise 2(Ap, 1972):17-32.

Clark, Kenneth E. Conference on the Use of Psychological Tests in Employment (Particularly with Minority Group Members) Held in Rochester, N.Y., Nov. 2-4, 1972. AD-766 099/6WS. Springfield, VA: National Technical Information Service, S, 1973.

Clinkscale, Robert L. "Problems in Placing Minority Graduates from Vocational Programs." Journal of Non-White Concerns in Personnel and Guidance 3(Ap, 1975):94-99.

Coupland, D. E. "Aptitude Tests and Discrimination." International Labour Review 102 (S, 1970):241-253.

Couturier, Jean. "Civil Service Systems and Job Discrimination." Integrateducation 13 (My-Je, 1975):68-72.

Crooks, Lois A. (ed.). An Investigation of Sources of Bias in the Prediction of Job Performance...A Six-Year Study. Princeton, NJ: Educational Testing Service, 1972.

Denvir, John. "Color the [California] State Bar Exam Lily-White." Los Angeles Times, S 15, 1976.

Doeringer, Peter B. and others. Low-Income Labor Markets and Urban Manpower Programs: A Critical Assessment. Washington, DC: Manpower Administration, U.S. Department of Labor, 1972.

Dowdall, George W. "White Gains from Black Subordination in 1960 and 1970." Social Problems 22(D, 1974):162-183.

Dubinsky, Irwin. "Trade Union Discrimination in the Pittsburgh Construction Industry. How and Why It Operates." Urban Affairs Quarterly 6(Mr, 1971):297-318.

Duncan, Otis Dudley. "Discrimination Against Negroes." Annals, My, 1967.

"Equal Protection: Racial Discrimination in Professional Employment Testing." Brooklyn Law Review 39(Spring, 1973).

Evans, Therman E. "Blacks and Medical School Tests: A Response." Washington Post, Je 22, 1976.

_____. "Reverse Discrimination in Medical Education." Journal of Negro Education 46 (Fall, 1977):373-379.

Flanagan, Robert J. Labor Turnover, Racial Unemployment Differentials, and the Dual Labor Market Hypothesis, Ap, 1974. ERIC ED 095 308.

Formby, John P. "The Extent of Wage and Salary Discrimination Against Non-White Labor." Southern Economic Journal, O, 1968.

Franklin, Raymond S. "A Framework for the Analysis of Interurban Negro-White Economic Differentials." Industrial and Labor Relations Review, Ap, 1968.

Galbraith, John Kenneth, Kuh, Edwin, and Thurow, Lester C. "The Galbraith Plan to Promote the Minorities." New York Times Magazine, Ag 22, 1971.

Garfinkel, Irwin and others. Labor Market Discrimination and Black-White Differences in Economic Status, Mr, 1977. ERIC ED 146 242.

Gatewood, Wallace Laval. "Afro-American Manpower and Affirmative Action in High Level Occupations: 1970-80." Doctoral dissertation, U. of Illinois, 1975. Univ. Microfilms Order No. 75-24306.

Gilman, Henry J. "Economic Discrimination and Unemployment." American Economic Review, D, 1965.

Gould, William B. Black Workers in White Unions: Job Discrimination in the United States. Ithaca, NY: Cornell U. Press, 1977.

_____. "The Emerging Law Against Racial Discrimination in Employment." Northwestern University Law Review 4(1969):359-386.

_____. "Remedies for Discrimination in the Building Trades." Industrial Relations, O, 1972.

Guinn, Nancy, Tupes, Ernest C., and Alley, William E. Cultural Subgroup Differences in the Relationships Between Air Force Aptitude Composites and Training Criteria, S, 1970. AD 715 922. National Technical Information Service, Springfield, VA 22151.

Henderson, Vivian W. "Race, Economics, and Public Policy." Crisis 82(F, 1975):50-55.

Henning, John F. "Schooling Discrimination and Jobs." Integrated Education, D, 1963-Ja, 1964.

Hiestand, Dale L. Discrimination in Employment: An Appraisal of the Research. Ann Arbor, MI: Institute of Labor and Industrial Relations, U. of Michigan, 1970.

Hill, Herbert. Black Labor and the American Legal System. Vol. I: Race, Work, and the Law. Washington, DC: Bureau of National Affairs, 1977.

Howard, Lawrence and others. Barriers to Employability of Non-White Workers. Final Report. Madison, WI: U. of Wisconsin, O, 1969. ERIC ED 047 069.

Holmer, Peter E. Enforcement of Civil Rights Statutes in Area Vocational-Technical Schools, My 1, 1974. ERIC ED 094 117.

Huff, Sheila. "Credentialing by Tests or by Degrees: Title VII of the Civil Rights Act and Griggs v. Duke Power Company." Harvard Educational Review 44(My, 1974):246-269.

Johnson, Michael P., and Sell, Ralph R. The Cost of Being Black: 1970, 1975. ERIC ED 120 634.

Jud, G. D., and Walker, J. L. "Discrimination by Race and Class and the Impact of School Quality." Social Science Quarterly 44(Mr, 1977).

Katzman, M. T. "Discrimination, Sub-Culture, and Economic Performance of Minority Groups." American Journal of Economics and Sociology 27(O, 1968):371-376.

Klein, Lawrence. "The Concentration of Unemployment Among Racial Groups and Discrimination in Income Opportunities." Social and Economic Administration (London), Ja, 1967.

Klingelhofer, Edwin L. Do Race and Economics Decide Who Gets What? Palo Alto, CA: College Examination Board, Ja 12, 1971. ERIC ED 047 644.

Kluegel, James P. "The Causes and Cost of Racial Exclusion from Job Authority." American Sociological Review 43(Je, 1978): 285-301.

Kovarsky, I. "Apprentice Training Programs and Racial Discrimination." Iowa Law Review, Spring, 1965.

Kruman, M. W. "Quotas for Blacks: The Public Works Administration and the Black Construction Worker." Labor History 16(Winter, 1975).

"Legal Implications of the Use of Standardized Ability Tests in Employment and Education." Columbia Law Review, Ap, 1968.

Liacouras, Peter J. and others. "Report of the Philadelphia Bar Association Special Committee on Pennsylvania Bar Admission Procedures--Racial Discrimination in Administration of the Pennsylvania Bar Examination." Temple Law Quarterly 44(Winter, 1971):141-258.

Linn, Robert L. "Test Bias and the Prediction of Grades in Law School." Journal of Legal Education 27(1975):293-323.

Littig, Lawrence W. "Negro Personality Correlates of Aspiration to Traditionally Open and Closed Occupations." Journal of Negro Education, Winter, 1968.

Lyle, Jerolyn. "Integrating Economic Policy with Fair Employment Policy." Integrateducation 13(My-Je, 1975):46-48.

McClure, Phyllis. Title VI and Title IX Compliance by the Office for Civil Rights in State-Operated Special Purpose and Vocational Schools Pursuant to Adams V. Mathews. New York: NAACP Legal Defense and Educational Fund, Jl, 1976.

McDonald, Gabrielle K. "Quotes Are Not Reverse Discrimination." Texas Southern University Law Review 3(Spring, 1975):77-84.

Marshall, Ray and others. The Impact of Legal and Administrative Remedies to Overcome Discrimination in Employment, D, 1976. ERIC ED 139 919.

Masters, Stanley H. Black-White Income Differentials Empirical Studies and Policy Implications. New York: Academic Press, 1975.

_____. "The Effect of Educational Differences and Labor-Market Discrimination on the Relative Earnings of Black Males." Journal of Human Resources 9(Summer, 1974):342-360.

Mauer, Lawrence J., and Hemley, David D. "Racial Discrimination, Productivity, and Negro-White Male Income." Review of Social Economy 28(S, 1970):164-172.

Miller, Herman P. "A New Look at Inequality, Poverty, and Underemployment in the United States--Without Rose-Colored Glasses." Review of Black Political Economy 3(1973): 19-36.

Mindlin, Albert. "The Designation of Race or Color on Forms." Public Administration Review, Je, 1966.

Mogull, Robert S. "Discrimination in the Labor Market." Journal of Black Studies 3(D, 1972): 237-249.

_____. "Excessive Unemployment Creates Excessive Suffering among Blacks." Journal of Employment Counseling 9(Mr, 1972):41-48.

Nathan, Richard P. Jobs and Civil Rights. The Role of the Federal Government in Promoting Equal Opportunity in Employment and Training. Washington, DC: GPO, Ap, 1969.

Niemi, A. W., Jr. "Wage Discrimination Against Negroes and Puerto Ricans in the New York SMSA: An Assessment of Educational and Occupational Differences." Social Science Quarterly 55(Je, 1974).

Okonkwo, Ubadigbo. "The Economics of Ethnic Discrimination." Review of Black Political Economy 3(1973):1-18.

Peck, Cornelius J. "The Equal Employment Opportunity Commission Developments in the Administrative Process 1965-1975." Washington Law Review 51(1976):831-865.

Pettigrew, L. Eudora. "'Reverse Discrimination'--Fact or Fantasy?" Integrateducation 14(N-D, 1976).

Reich, Michael. "Racial Discrimination and the White Income Distribution." Doctoral dissertation, Harvard U., 1974.

Rosenberg, B., and Howton, F. W. "Ethnic Liberalism and Employment Discrimination in the North." American Journal of Economics and Sociology, O, 1967.

Rosenthal, Albert J. "Employment Discrimination and the Law." Annals 407(My, 1973):91-101.

Rowan, R. L. "Discrimination and Apprentice Regulation in the Building Trades." Journal of Business, U. of Chicago, O, 1967.

Ruda, Edward, and Albright, Lewis E. "Racial Differences on Selection Instruments Related to Subsequent Job Performance." Personnel Psychology, Spring, 1968.

Sadaca, Robert. The Validity and Discrimination Impact of the Federal Service Entrance Examination. Washington, DC: The Urban Institute, 1972.

Samuels, William M., and Buckner, Donald R. Minority Barriers Identification Conference, 1975. ERIC ED 131 252. [Allied health professions]

Shepherd, William S. "Market Power and Racial Discrimination in White-Collar Employment." Anti-Trust Bulletin 14(Spring, 1969):141-161. [Large firms discriminate more.]

Scales, Eldridge S. "Regional-Racial Differences in Income and Level of Education." Journal of Negro Education, Fall, 1965.

Schiller, Bradley R. "Class Discrimination vs. Racial Discrimination." Review of Economics and Statistics 53(Ag, 1971):263-269.

Schmid, Calvin F., and Nobbe, Charles E. "Socio-economic Differentials Among Nonwhite Races." American Sociological Review, D, 1965.

Sorensen, Aage B., and Fuerst, Sarah. "Black-White Differences in the Occurrence of Job Shifts." Sociology and Social Research 62 (Jl, 1978):537-557.

Sowell, Thomas. Race and Economics. New York: McKay, 1975.

Stolzenberg, Ross Mark. "Occupational Differences in Wage Discrimination Against Black Men: The Structure of Racial Differences in Men's Wage Returns to Schooling, 1960." Doctoral dissertation, U. of Michigan, 1973. Univ. Microfilms Order No. 74-15867.

Strasser, Arnold. "Differentials and Overlaps in Annual Earnings of Blacks and Whites." Monthly Labor Review 94(D, 1971):16-26.

Szymanski, Albert. "Trends in Economic Discrimination Against Blacks in the U.S. Working Class." Review of Radical Political Economics 7(Fall, 1975):1-21.

Taylor, David P. "Discrimination and Occupational Wage Differences in the Market for Unskilled Labor." Industrial and Labor Relations Review, Ap, 1968. [Chicago]

U.S. Civil Service Commission. Equal Employment Opportunity Court Cases. Washington, DC: GPO, Jl, 1974.

U.S. Commission on Civil Rights. The Federal Civil Rights Enforcement Effort--1974. Vol. 5: To Eliminate Employment Discrimination. Washington, DC: U.S. Commission on Civil Rights, Jl, 1975.

_____. Last Hired, First Fired: Layoffs and Civil Rights. Washington, DC: The Commission, F, 1977.

U.S. Congress, 94th, 1st session, House of Representatives, Committee on Education and Labor, Subcommittee on Equal Opportunities. Oversight Hearings on Federal Enforcement of Equal Employment Opportunity Laws. Washington, DC: GPO, 1975.

U.S. Equal Employment Opportunity Commission. Hearings...on Discrimination in White Collar Employment. Washington, DC: GPO, 1968.

Via, Emory F. "Discrimination, Integration, and Job Equality [In the South]." Monthly Labor Review, Mr, 1968.

Vinson, Earl, and Holloway, Madison. "The Effects of Formalization on Perception of Discrimination, Satisfaction, Effort and Performance." Journal of Vocational Behavior 10(Je, 1977):302-314.

Welch, Finis. "Labor-Market Discrimination: An Interpretation of Income Differences in the Rural South." Journal of Political Economy, Je, 1967. [Effect of inferior schooling on income of Negroes]

Wilcox, Kathleen, and Moriarity, Pia. "Schooling and Work: Social Constraints on Equal Educational Opportunity." Social Problems 24(D, 1976):204-213.

Williamson, Harold F. "Report of the Informal Meeting of the Black Caucus and American Economic Association Representatives." American Economic Review, My, 1970.

Willis, Virginia and others. Affirmative Action: The Unrealized Goal. A Decade of 'Equal Employment Opportunity,' D, 1973. The Potomac Institute, 1501 Eighteenth St., N.W., Washington, DC 20036.

Wubnig, Judith. "The Merit Criterion of Employment: An Examination of Some Arguments Against Its Use." New York Teacher Magazine, Mr 31, 1974.

General

Alexis, Marcus. "The Economic Status of Blacks and Whites." American Economic Review 68(My, 1978):179-185.

Adams, Arvil V. and others. The Lingering Crisis of Youth Unemployment. Kalamazoo, MI: W.E. Upjohn Institute for Employment Research, 1978.

Amos, William E., and Perry, Jane. "Negro Youth and Employment Opportunities." Journal of Negro Education, Fall, 1963.

Anderson, Bernard E. "Tragedy of Black Teen-Age Joblessness." Los Angeles Times, S 25, 1975.

Anderson, C. Arnold. "The adaptation of Education to a Mobile Society." Journal of Human Resources, Spring, 1967. [Followed by critical comments by Charles B. Nam and Robinson Hollister]

_____. "A Skeptical Note on the Relation of Vertical Nobility to Education." American Journal of Sociology, 1961.'

Ashenfelter, Orley. "Blacks and Trade Unionism." Integrateducation 13(My-Je, 1975):53-59.

Astin, Alexander W., and Panos, Robert J. The Educational and Vocational Development of College Students. Washington, DC: American Council on Education, 1969.

Ayers, George E. "Making Vocational Evaluation Relevant to Our Clients: The Challenge of the Disadvantaged." Rehabilitation Literature 32(S, 1971):258-262.

Baird, Leonard L., and Holland, John L. "The Flow of High School Students to Schools, Colleges and Jobs: An Re-examination of Some Old Questions by the Use of Multiple Indices of Talent." Journal of Human Recourses, Winter, 1969.

Bamba, Hiroya. "Relationship Between the Structure of the Labor Market and Demand for Education by Young Black and White Males." Doctoral dissertation, U. of Massachusetts, 1977.

Barnett, Lawrence J. "Does Education for Work Work?" The Urban Review, My, 1966.

Barrett, Richard S. "Gray Areas in Black and White Testing." Harvard Business Review, Ja-F, 1968.

Bartlett, Willis E. "Vocational Behavior of Minority Groups in a Corporate State." Counseling and Values 16(Summer, 1972): 247-251.

Bass, Alan R., and Turner, John N. "Ethnic Group Differences in Relationships Among Criteria of Job Performance." Journal of Applied Psychology 57(Ap, 1973):101-109.

Batchelder, A. B. "Poverty: The Special Case of the Negro." American Economic Review, My, 1965.

Bayer, Kurt Richard. "A Social Indicator of the Cost of Being Black." Doctoral dissertation, U. of Maryland, 1971. Univ. Microfilms Order No. 72-02577.

Berg, Ivar. "Rich Man's Qualifications for Poor Man's Jobs." Transaction, Mr, 1969.

Bergmann, Barbara R., and Lyle, Jerolyn R. "The Occupational Standing of Negroes by Areas and Industries." Journal of Human Resources 6(F, 1971):434-447.

Berman, Yitzchak. "Occupational Aspiractions of 545 Female High School Seniors." Journal of Vocational Behavior 2(Ap, 1972): 173-177.

Bernard, K. E. "The Business Cycle and the Occupational Distribution of Black Workers." Growth and Change 7(Ap, 1976).

Bernard, Viola M. "Interracial Practice in the Midst of Change." *American Journal of Psychiatry* 128(F, 1972):978-984.

Berner, Boel. "'Human Capital,' Manpower Planning and Economic Theory: Some Critical Remarks." *Acta Sociologica* 17(1974-1975): 236-255.

Betsey, Charles L. "Differences in Unemployment Experience Between Blacks and Whites." *American Economic Review* 68(My, 1978):192-197.

Bird, Alan R. *Poverty in Rural Areas of the United States.* Agricultural Economic Report No. 63. Washington, DC: U.S. Department of Agriculture, N, 1964.

Black, Michael S. "Attitudes of Inner-City High School Males Toward Vocational Education and Work." *Journal of Research and Development in Education* 10(Winter, 1977): 99-115.

"Black Professionals: Progress and Skepticism." *Manpower* 5(Je, 1973):9-13.

Blau, Peter M., and Duncan, Otis Dudley, with Tyree, Andrea. *The American Occupational Structure.* New York: Wiley, 1967.

Blum, Zahava D., and Coleman, James S. *Longitudinal Effects of Education on the Incomes and Occupational Prestige of Blacks and Whites.* Baltimore, MD: Johns Hopkins U. Center for the Study of Social Organization of Schools, 1970. ERIC ED 040 971.

Blumrosen, Alfred. "Quotas, Relocation and Jobs." *Integrateducation* 13(My-Je, 1975): 38-43.

Bond, Horace Mann. "The Health of the Negro in Relation to Industry." *Bulletin of the National Association of Teachers in Colored Schools* 10(D, 1929):20-22.

_____. "Is Vocational Guidance Practical?" *Oklahoma Teachers Journal* 2(N, 1925):19-21.

_____. "The Negro Scholar and Professional." *American Negro Reference Book.* New York: Prentice-Hall, 1966.

_____. "Seven Aids to Getting a Good Job." *Opportunity* 18(Mr, 1940):72-77.

Bowles, Samuel. "Schooling and Inequality from Generation to Generation." *Journal of Political Economy* 80(My-Je, 1972).

Bowles, Samuel, Gintis, Herbert, and Meyer, Peter. "The Long Shadow of Work: Education, the Family, and the Reproduction of the Social Division of Labor." *Insurgent Sociologist* 5(Summer, 1975):3-22.

Bowser, Ammon. "Viewpoint of a White-Collar Black." *Training in Business and Industry* 6(1969):55-58.

Bramwell, Jonathan. *Courage in Crisis: The Black Professional Today.* Indianapolis, IN: Bobbs-Merrill, 1973.

Brawley, Benjamin Griffith. *Early Effort for Industrial Education.* Charlottesville, VA: The Trustees of the John F. Slater Fund, 1923.

Brazziel, William F. "Effects of General Education in Manpower Programs." *Journal of Human Resources,* Summer, 1966.

Briggs, Vernon M., Jr. *"They Have the Power-- We Have the People." The Status of Equal Employment Opportunity in Houston, Texas, 1970.* An Equal Employment Opportunity Report. Washington, DC: GPO, 1970.

Brimmer, Andrew F. "Economic Situation of Blacks in the United States." *Review of Black Political Economy* 2(Summer, 1972): 35-54.

_____. "Education and the Economic Advancement of Minority Groups." *Integrated Education* 8(Mr-Ap, 1970):48-55.

_____. "Employment Patterns and the Dilemma of Desegregation." *Integrated Education.* O-N, 1967.

_____. *Regional Growth, Migration, and Economic Progress in the Black Community.* Washington, DC: Board of Governors of the Federal Reserve System, S 15, 1971.

Broom, Leonard, and Baha, Lawrence J. "Negro Academics and Professional Societies." *American Sociologist* 7(F, 1972):9-11.

Bryce, Herrington J. "How Far to Equality?" *Integrateducation* 13(My-Je, 1975):32-33.

_____. "Putting Black Economic Progress in Perspective." *Ebony* 28(Ag, 1973):58-62.

Bullock, Ralph W. "A Study of the Occupational Choices of Negro High School Boys." *Crisis,* S, 1930.

Bureau of the Census. *Characteristics of the Low-Income Population: 1973.* Washington, DC: GPO, Ja, 1975.

Bushnell, Don D. *The Production and Validation of Educational Systems Packages for Occupational Training of Depressed Area Students; or Black Student Versus Teacher Evaluation of Urban Vocational Programs. Final Report.* Santa Barbara, CA: Communications Associates, S, 1970. ERIC ED 045 778.

Byrd, Wayne L. and others. "Influence of Race, Socio-economic Status and Educational Achievement on Educational Socialization for Vocational Education." Journal of Vocational Education Research 1(Summer, 1976):31-46.

Caliver, Ambrose. Negro High School Graduates and Non-graduates; Relation of Their Occupational Status to Certain School Experiences. Washington, DC: GPO, 1940.

Calvert, Robert, Jr. Employing the Minority Group College Graduate. Garrett Park, MD: Garrett Park Press, 1968.

Campbell, Joel T., and Belcher, Leon H. "Changes in Nonwhite Employment, 1960-1966," Phylon, Winter, 1967.

Carlson, Elliot. "'Discouraged' Blacks Leave the Labor Force, Distorting Jobless Rate." Wall Street Journal, Ja 8, 1971.

Cassell, Frank H. "Positive Action on Unemployment." Integrated Education, Je, 1963.

Chance, W. A. "Long-Term Labor Requirements and Output of the Educational System." Southern Economic Journal, Ap, 1965.

Cherry, David King. Vocational Activities of Educated Negroes. Master's thesis, U. of Chicago, 1931.

Christal, Raymond E. Analysis of Racial Differences in Terms of Work Assignments, Job Interest, and Felt Utilization of Talents and Training. AD-741 758. Springfield, VA: National Technical Information Service, Ja, 1972. [U.S. Air Force]

Clark, Edward T. "Status Level of Occupations Chosen and Rejected by Middle and Lower Class Boys and Girls." Psychological Reports, 1965.

Clark, Edward T., and Misa, Kenneth F. "Peers' Perceptions of Negro and White Occupational Preferences." Personnel and Guidance Journal, N, 1967.

Clark, Kenneth B. "Job Training: A Need for Seriousness." Wall Street Journal, S 25, 1969.

Cloward, Richard A., and Ontell, Robert. "Our Illusions About Training." American Child, Ja, 1965.

Cohen, Eli E., and Kapp, Louise (eds.). Manpower Policies for Youth. New York: Columbia U. Press, 1966.

Coleman, James S. and others. Occupational Status Changes for Blacks and Non-blacks During the First Ten Years of Occupational Experience. Baltimore, MD: Johns Hopkins U., Center for the Study of Social Organization of Schools, Ag, 1970. ERIC ED 043 750.

_____. "White and Black Careers During the First Decade of Labor Force Experience. Part I: Occupational Status." Social Science Research 1(S, 1972):243-270.

Coles, Robert. "Youth Opportunity to Be What?" New Republic, N 7, 1964.

College Placement Services, Inc. Manpower Resources of the Traditionally Negro Colleges. Bethlehem, PA: College Placement Services, Inc., 1969.

"The Colleges. Continuing Demand for Black Graduates Softens an Otherwise Tough Year." Black Enterprise, Mr, 1972.

Combs, Janet, and Cooley, Win W. "Dropouts: In High School and After High School." American Educational Research Journal, My, 1968. [The economic advantage of dropping out]

Comptroller General of the U.S. Information on the Summer Youth Employment Program. Washington, DC: General Accounting Office, 1977.

Community Action Program. Education: An Answer to Poverty. Washington, DC: Office of Economic Opportunity, 1966.

Cook, Thomas J. "Benign Neglect: Minimum Feasible Understanding." Social Problems 18(Fall, 1970):145-152.

Corazzini, A. J. "When Should Vocational Education Begin?" Journal of Human Resources, Winter, 1967.

Cory, Charles H. "Biographical Differences Between Many Recruits Grouped by Mental Level, Racial Identification and Career Intention." USN Personnel and Training Research Laboratory Technical Bulletin, No. 70-2(F, 1970).

Cosby, Arthur G. and others. "Patterns of Early Adult Status Attainment and Attitudes in the Nonmetropolitan South." Sociology of Work and Occupations 3(N, 1976):411-429.

Cowhig, James D., and Beale, Calvin L. "The Rising Levels of Education Among Young Workers." Monthly Labor Review, Je, 1965.

Craig, John C., and Hoaglund, Ralph P. III. "Young Man Trying Not to Be Angry." University (Princeton U.), Winter, 1966-67. [Color and employment]

Crane, Donal Paul. "Qualifying the Negro for Professional Employment." Doctoral dissertation, George State U., 1970.

Crumpton-Bawden, E. Carlene Tolbert. "Inequality in the Distribution of School Attainment in the United States by Race and Parent Income." Doctoral dissertation, 1975. Univ. Microfilm Order No. 75-19,062.

Davenport, Lawrence, and Petty, Reginald. Minorities and Career Education, 1973. Educational and Community Consultants Associates, 683 East Broad Street, Suite 404, Columbus, OH 43215.

Davidson, Chandler, and Gaitz, Charles M. "'Are the Poor Different?' A Comparison of Work Behavior and Attitudes Among the Urban Poor and Nonpoor." Social Problems 22(D, 1974):229-245.

DeBerry, Clyde E. "Vocational [Career] Education in Black Cities." Journal of Negro Education 42(Summer, 1973):360-378.

Dede, Christopher, and Hardin, Joy. "Elitism in Science Education." Journal of Chemical Education 50(S, 1973):583-585.

De los Santos, Alfred G. Jr. "Career Education and Minority Students." Illinois Career Education Journal 31(Autumn, 1973):10-14.

Dennis, Denyck. "Young Blacks vs. the Work World." New Generation 52(F, 1970):22-26.

Deutermann, William V. "Educational Attainment of Workers, March, 1971." Monthly Labor Review 94(N, 1971):30-35.

Devgan, S. S., and Baluch, Mohammed H. "Minority Enrollment: Averting the 'Formula for Tragedy.'" Engineering Education (F, 1976):435-437.

Diamond, Daniel E., and Bedrosian, Hrach. Hiring Standards and Job Performance. Manpower Research Monographs No. 18. Washington, DC: GPO, 1970.

Dillingham, Harry C., and Sly, David F. "The Mechanical Cotton-Picker, Negro Migration, and the Integration Movement." Human Organization, Winter, 1966.

Disadvantaged Urban Youth in Specialized Vocational School Settings. An Initial Survey. Woburn, MA: State Board of Education, D, 1969. ERIC ED 038 518.

Doeringer, Peter B., and Piore, Michael J. Internal Labor Markets and Manpower Analysis. Lexington, MA: Heath, 1971.

Dove, Adrian. "Soul Story." New York Times Magazine, D 8, 1968. [Employment testing and Black culture]

Du Bois, W. E. B. "Careers Open to College-Bred Negroes." Two Addresses. Nashville, TN: Fisk U., 1898.

_____. "Education and Work." Howard University Bulletin 9(Ja, 1931):5-22.

_____. "Education and Work." Journal of Negro Education 1(Ap, 1932):60-74.

_____. "Sociology and Industry in Southern Education." Voice of the Negro 4(My, 1907):170-175.

_____. U.S. Industrial Commission. Hearings on General and Industrial Education, Vol. 15: Immigration and Education, Washington, DC: GPO, 1901:159-175. [Testimony]

Duncan, Beverly. "Dropouts and the Unemployed." Journal of Political Economy, Ap, 1965. [Based on 1902-1956.]

_____. "Education and Social Background." American Journal of Sociology, Ja, 1967.

Duncan, Beverly, and Duncan, Otis Dudley. "Minorities and the Process of Stratification." American Sociological Review, Je, 1968. [The "near reality" of equal opportunity for non-Negro minorities]

Duncan, Otis Dudley, and Featherman, David L. "Psychological and Cultural Factors in the Process of Occupational Achievement." Social Science Research 1(Je, 1972):121-145.

Duncan, Otis Dudley and others. Socioeconomic Background and Occupational Achievement: Extensions of a Basic Model. Final Report. Ann Arbor, MI: U. of Michigan, My, 1968. ERIC ED 023 879.

Eckstein, Otto. "Eckstein Predicts a Large Negro Job Gap in '80's. Recommends Massive New Investment in Education." Harvard Crimson, O 3, 1966.

_____. Education, Employment, and Negro Equality. Washington, DC: GPO, O, 1968.

Employment Survey. Survey of Employment of Women and Various Ethnic Groups. Inglewood, CA: California State College, Office of the Chancellor, 1970. ERIC ED 052 703.

"Equal Employment Opportunity." Industrial Relations, My, 1970. [Separate article on Boston, New York, Memphis, Detroit, Chicago, and Los Angeles]

Erlich, Reese, and Smith, Michael. "'The Job Corps Builds Men.'" Liberation, Ap, 1968.

Farley, Reynolds, and Hermalin, Albert. "The 1960's: A Decade of Progress for Blacks?" Demography 9(Ag, 1972):353-370.

Farning, Max. "Some Variables Why So Few Black High School Graduates Attend Post-High School Area Vocational Schools." Journal of Industrial Teacher Education 10 (F, 1972):5-12.

Farr, James L. and others. "Ethnic Group Membership as a Moderator of the Prediction of Job Performance." Personnel Psychology 24(Winter, 1971):609-636.

Feldman, Marvin. "Why the Schools (and All of Us) Fail the Poor." Opportunity 1(D, 1971): 32-34. [Interview by William Sawyer]

Fichter, Joseph H. "Career Preparation and Expectations of Negro College Seniors." Journal of Negro Education, Fall, 1966.

_____. Graduates of Predominantly Negro Colleges. Class of 1964. Washington, DC: GPO, 1967.

_____. Young Negro Talent: Survey of Experiences and Expectations of Negro Americans Who Graduated from College in 1964. Chicago, IL: National Opinion Research Center, N., 1964.

Fisher, Alan A. "The Problem of Teenage Unemployment." Doctoral dissertation, U of California, Berkeley, 1973.

Flaim, Paul O. Jobless Trends in 20 Large Metropolitan Areas. Special Labor Force Report No. 96. Washington, DC: Bureau of Labor Statistics, My, 1968.

Flaugher, Ronald L. Minority versus Majority Group Performance on an Aptitude Test Battery. Project Access Research Report No. 3. Princeton, NJ: Educational Testing Service, Ag, 1971. ERIC ED 056 081.

Folger, John K., and Nam, Charles B. "Trends in Education in Relation to the Occupational Structure." Sociology of Education, Fall, 1964.

Fox, Harvey, and Lefkowitz, Joel. "Differential Validity: Ethnic Group as a Moderator in Predicting Job Performance." Personnel Psychology 27(Summer, 1974):209-223.

Frank, N. H. Final Report of the [1965] Summer Study on Occupational, Vocational, and Technical Education. Cambridge, MA: Massachusetts Institute of Technology, 1966.

Freedman, Marcia K. "Perspectives in Youth Employment." Children, Mr-Ap, 1965.

Frericks, Don (ed.). The Ohio Apprenticeship Notebook for School Counselors. Columbus, OH: Division of Guidance and Testing, State Department of Education, 1970.

Fried, Marc, Gleicher, Peggy, Havens, John, Ferguson, Lorna, and Aron, Cindy. A Study of Demographic and Social Determinants of Functional Achievement in a Negro Population. Sections 3 and 4. PB 200 089 and 200 090. Springfield, VA: National Technical Information Service, 1971. [Boston]

Friedman, Saul. "Race Relations Is Their Business." New York Times Magazine, O 25, 1970. [Recruitment of Negro executive and management personnel]

Fritts, Patricia J. "The Job Area Preferences and Job Value Assignments of Low Income Inner City Black and White Youth." Doctoral dissertation, Boston U., 1970.

Fromkin, Howard L., Klimoski, Richard J., and Flanagan, Michael F. Race and Competence As Determinants of Acceptance of Newcomers in Success and Failure Work Groups. LaFayett, IN: Institute for Research in the Behavioral, Economic, and Management Science, Purdue U., 1970.

Gallaway, Lowell E. "Unemployment Levels among Nonwhite Teenagers." Journal of Business 42(Jl, 1969):265-276.

Gannon, James F. "Militant Negroes Press for a Stronger Voice in the Labor Movement." Wall Street Journal, N 29, 1968.

Gillie, Angelo C. "Needed: A New Program of General Education for Ghetto Youth." American Vocational Journal, N, 1967.

Gentra, Herbert. "Education, Technology, and the Characteristics of Worker Productivity." American Economic Review 61(My, 1971):266-279.

Ginzberg, Eli. "The Changing Manpower Scene." Journal of Negro Education, Summer, 1969.

Glenn, Norval D. "Occupational Benefits to Whites from the Subordination of Negroes." American Sociological Review, Je, 1963.

_____. "White Gains from Negro Subordination." Social Problems, Fall, 1966.

Gordon, Robert A., Wachter, Michael L., and Taeuber, Karl E. Demographic Trends and Full Employment. Washington, DC: National Commission for Manpower Policy, 1977.

Gorz, Andre. "Capitalist Relations of Production and the Socially Necessary Labor Forces." International Socialist Journal (Rome), Ag, 1965. [Marxist analysis of technical education]

_____. "Technical Intelligence and the Capitalist Division of Labor." Telos 12 (Summer, 1972):27-41.

Gottfredson, Linda S. An Analytical Description of Employment According to Race, Sex, Prestige, and Holland Type of Work. Baltimore, MD: Center for Social Organization of Schools, Johns Hopkins U., Ap, 1978.

_____. The Relation of Education and Situs of Work to Economic Differences between Blacks and Whites, Ja, 1977. ERIC ED 150 059.

Graduate and Professional School Opportunities for Minority Students, Fourth Edition, 1972-73. Princeton, NJ: Educational Testing Service, 1972.

Greene, Harry Washington. Holders of Doctorates Among Negroes. Boston, MA: Meador Publishing Company, 1946.

Greenleigh Associates, Inc. Opening the Doors: Job Training Programs. A Report to the Committee on Administration of Training Programs. Two vols. Washington, DC: GPO, F, 1968.

Grier, Eunice S. In Search of a Future. Washington, DC: Washington Center for Metropolitan Studies, 1963. [Guidance for minority group children]

Griffin, Larry J. "Social Background, Schooling, and Labor Market Experiences: The Reproducing of Socioeconomic Inequality from Generation to Generation." Doctoral dissertation, Johns Hopkins U., 1976. ERIC ED 142 716.

Griffin, Larry J., and Alexander, Karl L. Schooling and Socioeconomic Attainments: High School and College Influences. Baltimore, MD: Center for Social Organization of Schools, Mr, 1978.

Guinn, Nancy and others. Cultural Subgroup Differences in the Relationships between Air Force Aptitude Composites and Training Criteria. Lackland Air Force Base, Texas: Air Force Human Resources Lab, S, 1970. Available from National Technical Information Service, Operations Division, Springfield, VA 22151. ERIC ED 049 440.

Guion, Robert. "Job Tests and Minority Workers." Industrial Relations, F, 1966.

Gurin, Gerald. Inner-City Negro Youth in a Job Training Project: A Study of Factors Related to Attrition and Job Success. Final Report. Ann Arbor, MI: U. of Michigan, D, 1968. ERIC ED 026 530.

Gurslin, Orville R., and Roach, Jack L. "Some Issues in Training the Unemployed." Social Problems, Summer, 1964.

Guttentag, Marcia. "The Parallel Institutions of the Poverty Act: Evaluating Their Effect on Unemployed Youth and on Existing Institutions." American Journal of Orthopsychiatry, Jl, 1966.

Hansen, W. Lee, Weisbrod, Burton A., and Scanlon, William J. Determinants of Earnings of Low Achievers: Does Schooling Really Count, Even for Them? Madison, WI: Institute for Research on Poverty, U. of Wisconsin, F, 1969.

_____. "Schooling and Earnings of Low Achievers." American Economic Review 60 (Je, 1970):409-418.

Harris, Edward E. "Some Comparisons Among Negro-White College Students: Social Ambition and Estimated Social Mobility." Journal of Negro Education, Fall, 1966.

Harrison, Bennett. "Education and Earnings in Ten Urban Ghettos." American Economist 14 (Spring, 1970):12-21.

_____. "Education and Underemployment in the Urban Ghetto." American Economic Review 62(D, 1972).

_____. "Education, Training and the Urban Ghetto." Doctoral dissertation, U. of Pennsylvania, 1970.

_____. "Human Capital, Black Poverty and 'Radical' Economics." Industrial Relations 10(O, 1971).

_____. "Training for Nowhere." Washington Post, N 19, 1972.

Hart, Frederick M. "Major Research Efforts of the Law School Admission Council (1948-1973)." U.S. Congress, 93rd, 2nd session, House of Representatives, Committee on Education and Labor, Subcommittee on Education, Federal Higher Education Programs Institutional Eligibility. Hearings... Part 2A. Washington, DC: GPO, 1975.

Harvey, Michael G., and Kerin, Roger A. "The Influence of Social Stratification and Age on Occupational Aspirations of Adolescents." Journal of Educational Research 71(My-Je, 1973):262-266.

Hauser, Robert M., and Featherman, David L. "Socioeconomic Achievements of U.S. Men, 1962 to 1972." Science 185(Jl 26, 1974).

_____. "White-Nonwhite Differentials in Occupational Mobility Among Men in the United States, 1962-1972." Demography 11(My, 1974).

Heggen, James R. "Industrial Arts Teachers for Disadvantaged Youth." American Council on Industrial Arts Teacher Education Yearbook, 1970:75-94.

Herman, Melvin, and Sadofsky, Stanley. Study of the Meaning, Experience, and Effects of the Neighborhood Youth Corps on Negro Youth Who Are Seeking Work. Part 1, Work and Attitudes, Self-Image, and the Social and Psychological Background of Work-Seeking Negro Young Adults in New York City, Ja, 1967. New York U., Graduate School of Social Work. ERIC ED 015 312.

_____. Study of the Meaning, Experience, and Effects of the Neighborhood Youth Corps on Negro Youth Who Are Seeking Work, Part II, A Follow-Up Study of Work-Seeking Negro Young Men Who Are Not Placed in Jobs by Intake Centers, Ap, 1967. New York U. Graduate School of Social Work. ERIC ED 015 313.

_____. Youth-Work Programs. New York: Center for the Study of Unemployed Youth. Graduate School of Social Work, New York U., 1966.

Herson, Phyllis. "Personal and Sociological Variables Associated with the Occupational Choices of Negro Youth: Some Implications for Guidance." Journal of Negro Education, Spring, 1965.

Hess, Robert D. "Educability and Rehabilitation: The Future of the Welfare Class." Journal of Marriage and the Family, N, 1964.

Hillman, Sally Turnbull. Entry Into the Labor Market: The Preparation and Job Placement of Negro and White Vocational High School Graduates. PB 196 824. Springfield, VA: National Technical Information Service, D, 1970. [High School of Fashion Industries, New York City]

Himes, Joseph S. "Some Work-Related Cultural Deprivations of Lower Class Negro Youths." Journal of Marriage and the Family, N, 1964.

Hines, Fred and others. "Social and Private Rates of Return to Investment in Schooling, by Race-Sex Groups and Regions." Journal of Human Resources 5(Summer, 1970):318-340.

Holland, Susan S. "The Employment Situation for Negroes." Employment and Earnings and the Monthly Report on the Labor Force, S, 1967.

Hoppock, Robert, and Hurley, Robert B. "Black Graduate Talks About His Job: A Lesson in Attitudes." American Vocational Journal 48 (Ja, 1973):55-58.

Howard, Bill. "Blacks and Professional Schools." Change 4(F, 1972):13-16.

Howard, David H. "An Exploratory Study of Attitudes of Negro Professionals Toward Competition with Whites." Social Forces, S, 1966.

Humphrey, Melvin. Black Experiences versus Black Expectations. Washington, DC: Equal Employment Opportunity Commission, 1977.

_____. Black Experiences versus Black Expectations. (A Case for Fair-Share Employment), 1977. ERIC ED 145 187.

Hunter, A. D., and Hunter, G. W. "Academic Preparation and Professional Status of Negroes Listed in Who's Who in American Education." Negro Educational Review, Jl, 1953.

Husen, Torsten. Social Background and Educational Career. Paris: CERI/OECD, 1972.

Iden, George, and Gibbons, Toni. Youth Unemployment: The Outlook and Some Policy Strategies. Washington, DC: GPO, 1978.

Iden, George and others. Policy Options for the Teenage Unemployment Problem, S 21, 1976. ERIC ED 141 587.

Ignatin, Noel. "Organizing Workers. Lessons for Radicals." Guardian, Jl 6, 1968. [Touches on racial aspects of apprenticeship]

Ingerman, Sidney, and Strauss, George. "Preparing Underprivileged Negro Youths for Jobs." Poverty and Human Resources Abstracts Jl-Ag, 1967.

Institute of Labor and Industrial Relations. Index to Minority Group Employment Information, 1967. The Institute, P. O. Box 1567, Ann Arbor, MI 48106.

Jackson, Reid E. III. "The Effectiveness of a Special Program for Minority Group Students." Journal of Medical Education 47(Ag, 1972):620-624.

Jacobson, Julius (ed.). The Negro and the American Labor Movement. Garden City, NY: Doubleday, 1968.

Jones, Roy J., and Terrell, David L. Problems Associated with Developing a Realistic Employment Counseling Program for Disadvantaged Urban Youth, 1964. ERIC ED 011 016.

Kalachek, Edward. "Determinants of Teenage Employment." Journal of Human Resources, Winter, 1969.

Kalish, Carol B. "A Portrait of the Unemployed." Monthly Labor Review, Ja, 1966.

Kaplan, H. Roy. American Minorities and Economic Opportunity. Itasca, IL: Peacock, 1977.

Kasen, Robert. "Minority Apprentices: Focusing on Retention." Manpower 6(Ap, 1974):27-32.

Kauffman, Warren E. "At Washington--A New Kind of 'Revolution.'" Journal of College Placement, O, 1964. [Account of July 23-24, 1964 conference: "Today's Need and Tomorrow's Challenge in the Placement of Minority College Graduates"]

Kemble, Eugenia. "New Careers...New Hope?" United Teacher, Ap 3, 1968.

Killingsworth, Charles C. "Double-Screening of College Students." Integrated Education, Ap-My, 1964.

_____. Jobs and Income for Negroes. Policy Papers in Human Resources and Industrial Relations No. 6. Ann Arbor, MI: U. of Michigan, Institute of Labor and Industrial Relations; Washington, DC: National Manpower Policy Task Force, My, 1968. ERIC ED 053 299.

King, A. G., and White, R. "Demographic Influence on Labor Force Rates of Black Males." Monthly Labor Review 99(N, 1976).

King, Joe, Jr. "The Perceptions of Black High School Students Toward Vocational and Technical Education Programs." Journal of Negro Education 46(Fall, 1977):430-442.

Kirkpatrick, James J., Ewen, Robert B., Barrett, Richard S., and Katzell, Raymond A. Differential Selection Among Applicants from Different Socioeconomic or Ethnic Backgrounds. New York: New York U., 1967.

Kirkpatrick, James J. and others. Testing and Fair Employment: Fairness and Validity of Personnel Tests for Different Ethnic Groups. New York: New York U. Press, 1968.

Kohen, A. I. Determinants of Early Labor Market Success Among Young Men: Race, Ability, Quality and Quantity of Schooling. Columbus: Center for Human Resource Research, Ohio State U., 1973.

Kohler, Mary Conway. Excluded Youths Idle or Trained? Washington, DC: Washington Center for Metropolitan Studies, 1962.

Kovarsky, Irving, and Albrecht, William. Black Employment. The Impact of Religion, Economic Theory, Politics, and Law. Ames, IO: Iowa State U. Press, 1970.

Kurth, Edmund A. "Social Implications of United States Manpower Training Programs." Review of Social Economy, Mr, 1968.

Kuvlesky, William P. Implications of Recent Research on Occupational and Educational Ambitions of Disadvantaged Rural Youth for Vocational Education. Raleigh, NC: North Carolina State U., Center for Occupational Education, Jl, 1970. ERIC ED 041 692.

Kuvlesky, William P., and Dameron, Jane. Adolescents' Perceptions of Military Service as a Vehicle for Social Mobility: A Racial Comparison of Rural Youth from Economically Disadvantaged Areas. College Station, TX: Texas Agricultural Experiment Station, Mr 7, 1970. ERIC ED 040 774.

Labor Department, NAACP. The Negro Wage-Earner and Apprenticeship Training Programs. A Critical Analysis with Recommendations. New York: National Association for the Advancement of Colored People, 1961.

Landers, Clifford E., and Weaver, Patricia L. "The Cost of Being Black, 1970: Some Preliminary Observations." Journal of Social and Behavioral Sciences 20(Fall, 1974):120-129.

Lazerson, Marvin, and Grubb, W. Norton (eds.). American Education and Industrialism Documents in Vocational Education, 1870-1970. New York: Teachers College Press, 1973.

Lecht, Leonard A. Manpower Requirements for National Objectives in the 1970's. Washington, DC: U.S. Department of Labor, Manpower Administration, 1968.

Ledvinka, James D. "Race of Employment Interviewer and the Language Elaboration of Black Job-Seekers." Doctoral dissertation, U. of Michigan, 1969.

Lee, David B. "Don't Blame the Ghetto." Saturday Evening Post, D 5, 1964.

Lehman, H. C., and Witty, Paul A. "A Study of Vocational Attitudes in Relation to Pubescence." American Journal of Psychology 44(1931). [Deals with career aspirations of Negro and white children.]

Lenhardt, Gero. "On the Relationship between the Education System and Capitalist Work Organization." Kapitalistate 3(1975).

Leonard, Walter J. "Placement and the Minority Student: New Pressures and Old Hang-Ups." University of Toledo Law Review, Spring-Summer, 1970.

Lerman, Robert. "An Analysis of Youth Labor Force Participation, School Activity, and Employment Rates." Doctoral dissertation, Massachusetts Institute of Technology, 1969.

Levin, Henry M., Guthrie, James W., Kleindorfer, George B., and Stout, Robert T. "School Achievement and Post-School Success: A Review." Review of Educational Research 41 (F, 1971):1-16.

Levine, Marvin J. "The Private Sector and Negro Employment Problems." MSU Business Topics, Winter, 1969. [A 1967 survey]

Levitan, Sar A., Johnston, William B., and Taggart, Robert. Still a Dream. The Changing Status of Blacks Since 1960. Cambridge, MA: Harvard U. Press, 1975.

Levitin, Teresa Ellen. A Social Psychological Exploration of Power Motivation Among Disadvantaged Workers. PB-208 245. Springfield, VA: National Technical Information Service, D, 1971.

Link, C. and others. "Black-White Differences in Returns to Schooling: Some New Evidence." American Economic Review 66(Mr, 1976).

Littig, Lawrence W. "Motives of Negro Americans Who Aspire to Traditionally Open and Closed Occupations." Journal of Cross-Cultural Psychology 2(Mr, 1971):77-86.

McFann, Howard H. "HumRRO Research and Project 100,000." HumRRO Professional Paper, No. 33-70(D, 1970). [Project III: racial and skill factors in job testing]

McKenney, Nampeo D. R. and others. The Social and Economic Status of the Black Population in the United States 1974. Washington, DC: GPO, Jl, 1975.

Mangum, Sarth L., and Seninger, Stephen F. Coming of Age in the Ghetto: A Dilemma of Youth Unemployment. Baltimore: Johns Hopkins U. Press, 1978.

Marshall, Ray, and Christian, Virgil L., Jr. Employment of Blacks in the South. Austin: U. of Texas Press, 1978.

Mayhew, Anne. "Education, Occupation, and Earnings." Industrial and Labor Relations Review 24(Ja, 1971):216-225.

Mayhew, Lewis B. "An Imperative for University Action." Integrated Education, Mr-Ap, 1968.

Maynard, Peter E., and Hansen, James C. "Vocational Maturity Among Inner-City Youths." Journal of Counseling Psychology 17(S, 1970): 400-403.

Mays, B. E. "After College, What? for the Negro." Crisis 37(D, 1930):408-410.

Meade, Edward J., Jr. "Vocational and Technical Education for Disadvantaged Youth: A Critical Look." In Developing Programs for the Educationally Disadvantaged. Edited by A. Harry Passow. New York: Teachers College Press, 1968.

Michelotti, Kopp. Employment of High School Graduates, O, 1973. Washington, DC: U.S. Bureau of Labor Statistics, 1974.

Miller, S. M., and Harrison, Ira E. "Types of Dropouts: 'The Unemployables.'" In Blue-Collar World. Edited by Arthur B. Shostak and William Gomberg. Englewood Cliffs, NJ: Prentice-Hall, 1964.

Milner, Murray, Jr. "Race, Education, and Jobs: Trends. 1960-1970." Sociology of Education 46(Summer, 1973):280-298.

Mincer, Jacob. "Youth, Education, and Work." National Bureau Report Supplement, Ja, 1973. [National Bureau of Economic Research]

Morgan, James N., and Sirageldin, Ismail. "A Note on the Quality Dimension in Education." Journal of Political Economy, S-O, 1968.

Morgan, John S., and VanDyke, Richard L. White-Collar Blacks: A Breakthrough? New York: American Management Association, 1970.

Munnell, A. H. "The Economic Experience of Blacks: 1964-1974." New England Economic Review, Ja-F, 1978.

Nellums and Associates, A. L. Career Education: Implications for Minorities, Je, 1973. ERIC ED 085 550.

Nicholas, Doris E. "Vocational Development of Black Inner-City Students." Journal of Non-White Concerns in Personnel and Guidance 6(Jl, 1968):175-182.

Niemi, A. W., Jr. "Racial and Ethnic Differences in Returns on Educational Investment in California and Texas." Economic Inquiry 12(S, 1974).

_____. "Racial Differences in Returns to Educational Investment in the South." American Journal of Economics and Sociology 34(Ja, 1975):87-94.

Office of Economic Opportunity. The Poor 1970: A Chartbook. Washington, DC: GPO, 1972.

Ohio State University, Center for Human Resource Research. Career Thresholds: A Longitudinal Study of the Educational and Labor Market Experience of Male Youth. Vol. I. Washington, DC: GPO, 1970.

O'Leary, Brian S., Farr, James L., and Bartlett, Claude J. Ethnic Group Membership As a Moderator of Job Performance, Ap, 1970. Accession No. AD 711 981. National Technical Information Service, U.S. Department of Commerce, Springfield, VA 22151.

Omvig, Clayton P., and Darley, Lorraine K. "Expressed and Tested Vocational Interests of Black Inner-City Youth." Vocational Guidance Quarterly 21(D, 1972):109-114.

O'Neill, Dave M. "Voucher Funding of Training Programs: Evidence from the GI Bill." Journal of Human Resources 12(F, 1977):425-445. [Black-white differential returns to training]

"Opportunities." New Yorker, Jl 19, 1969. [Richard Clarke Associates]

Ornstein, Michael D., and Rossi, Peter H.
Going to Work: An Analysis of the Deter-
minants and Consequences of Entry into the
Labor Force. Baltimore, MD: Johns Hopkins
U., Center for the Study of the Social
Organization of Schools, Ag, 1970. ERIC ED
042 055.

Parker, Seymour, and Kleiner, Robert J. "Social and Psychological Dimensions of the
Family Role Performance of the Negro Male."
Journal of Marriage and the Family, Ag,
1969. [Philadelphia, PA]

Pearl, Arthur. "New Careers: One Solution
to Poverty." Poverty and Human Resources
Abstracts, S-O, 1967.

Pearl, Arthur, and Riessman, Frank. New
Careers for the Poor. The Non-professional
Revolution. New York: Free Press, 1965.

Penn, Nolan. "Racial Influence on Vocational
Choice." Journal of Negro Education,
Winter, 1966.

Pervin, Lawrence A., Reik, Louis E., and
Dalrymple, Willard (eds.). The College Dropout and the Utilization of Talent. Princeton, NJ: Princeton U. Press, 1966.

Peterson, James. Escape from Poverty: Occupa-
tional and Economic Mobility Among Urban
Blacks. Chicago: Community and Family
Study Center, U. of Chicago, 1974.

Picou, J. Steven, Tracy, George S., and
Hernandez, Pedro F. "Occupational Projec-
tions of Louisiana Black High School
Seniors." Education and Urban Society 2
(Ag, 1970):459-468.

Piker, Jeffrey. Entry Into the Labor Force:
A Survey of Literature on the Experience of
Negro and White Youths. Ann Arbor, MI:
Institute of Labor and Industrial Relations,
1968.

Piovia, Esther. "Black Youth Unemployment: A
Continuing Crisis." Urban League Review 3
(Winter, 1977):40-45.

Porter, J. N. "Race, Socialization, and
Mobility in Educational and Early Occupa-
tional Attainment." American Sociological
Review 39(1974):303-316.

Powell, Edward C. "Retreatism and Occupational
Status Aspirations: A Study of the Socio-
Cultural System and Anomie among Negro and
White High School Seniors." Doctoral disser-
tation, U. of Kentucky, 1966.

"Preferential Hiring for Negroes: A Debate."
American Child, N, 1963.

Price, Daniel O. "Occupational Changes among
Whites and Nonwhites, with Projections for
1970." Social Science Quarterly, D, 1968.

Rein, Martin, and Miller, S. M. "Poverty,
Policy, and Purpose: The Axes of Choice."
Poverty and Human Resource Abstracts, Mr-
Ap, 1966.

Riessman, Frank. "Issues in Training the New
Nonprofessional." Poverty and Human Resources Abstracts, S-O, 1967.

_____. New Careers, 1967. A. Philip Randolph
Educational Fund, 217 West 125 Street,
New York, NY 10027.

Riessman, Frank, and Popper, Hermine I.
New Career Ladders for Nonprofessionals.
New York: Harper & Row, 1968.

Rivera, Ramon J., and Short, James F., Jr.
"Occupational Goals: A Comparative Analy-
sis." In Juvenile Gangs in Context.
Edited by Malcolm W. Klein. Englewood
Cliffs, NJ: Prentice-Hall, 1967.

Rogers, Charles H., and Artis, Rudolph D.
Teenage Unemployment in Two Selected Rural
Counties in the South, Jl, 1969. Center
for Occupational Education, North Carolina
State U., 1 Maiden Lane, Raleigh, NC 27607.

Rogers, David. "Vocational and Career Education: A Critique and Some New Directions."
Teachers College Record 74(My, 1973):471-511.

Rose, Harold M. "An Appraisal of the Negro
Educator's Situation in the Academic
Marketplace." Journal of Negro Education,
Winter, 1966.

Rosen, Doris B. Employment Testing and Minority
Groups, As Reported in the Literature. Key
Issues Series No. 6. Ithaca, NY: School of
Industrial and Labor Relations at Cornell U.,
State U. of New York, Je, 1970. ERIC ED
048 507.

Rosen, Julius. Job Values of Educationally
Disadvantaged Students. New York: Associated Educational Services Corporation, 1968.

Rosenthal, Neal H., with Crowley, Michael,
Pilot, Michael, and Kling, Joyce. College
Educated Workers, 1968-1980. Washington,
DC: GPO, 1970.

Ross, Arthur M., and Hill, Herbert (eds.).
Employment, Race, and Poverty. New York:
Harcourt, Brace and World, 1967.

Ross, Harvey L. A Study of Successful Persons
from Seriously Disadvantaged Backgrounds.
Final Report. Washington, DC: Manpower
Administration, Mr 31, 1970. ERIC ED 054
267.

Rude, N. Neil, and King, Donald C. "Aptitude
Levels in a Depressed Area." Personnel and
Guidance Journal, Ap, 1965.

Rusmore, Jay T. Psychological Tests and Fair Employment: A Study of Employment Testing in the San Francisco Area. San Francisco, California State Fair Employment Practice Commission, 1967.

Russell, Joe L. "Changing Patterns in Employment of Nonwhite Workers." Monthly Labor Review, My, 1966.

Rustin, Bayard. "Apprenticeship: A Gimmick?" Integrated Education, D, 1963-Ja, 1964.

Rutherford, H. B. "Negro-ness and Vocational Choice." Palmetto Education Association Journal, S, 1966.

Ryan, William. "Savage Discovery: The Moynihan Report." Nation, N 22, 1965.

Saunders, David N. "The Company Youth Keep: An Empirical Analysis of Job Finding Among Young Men, 14-24." Doctoral dissertation, Bryn Mawr College, 1975.

Schab, Fred. "What Jobs Do High School Girls Want?" Integrated Education, N-D, 1973: 29-30.

Seiler, Joseph. "Preparing the Disadvantaged for Tests." Manpower 2(Jl, 1970):24-26.

Seligman, Ben B. Most Notorious Victory. Man in an age of Automation. New York: Free Press, 1966.

Sharp, Laure M. Education and Employment. The Early Careers of College Graduates. Baltimore, MD: Johns Hopkins Press, 1970.

Shell, K. and others. "The Educational Opportunity Bank..." National Tax Journal, Mr, 1968.

Sheppard, Harold L., and Striner, Herbert E. Civil Rights, Employment, and the Social Status of American Negroes. Kalamazoo: W. E. Upjohn Institute for Employment Research, 1966.

Shostak, Arthur B. Educational and Occupational Opportunities and the Correspondence with Race and Poverty: Accent on the Unusual. Bethesda, MD: National Institutes of Child Health and Human Development, 1968.

Shulman, Lee S. The Vocational Development of Mentally Handicapped Adolescents: An Experimental and Longitudinal Study. Chicago, IL: Jewish Vocational Service, 1967. [Touches on Negro-white differences]

Sigelman, L., and Karing, A. K. "Black Education and Bureaucratic Employment." Social Science Quarterly 44(Mr, 1977).

Singell, Larry D. "Investment in Education and Ghetto Poverty: A Note on the Dropout Decision." Social Science Quarterly 53(Je, 1972).

"Situational Testing for Minority Job Applicants." Personnel Journal 50(Ag, 1971): 646-647.

Smith, Elsie J. "Profile of the Black Individual in Vocational Literature." Journal of Vocational Behavior 6(F, 1975):41-59.

Smith, J. P., and Welch, F. R. Race Differences in Earnings: A Survey and New Evidence. Santa Monica, CA: Rand, Mr, 1978.

Snyder, John I. "Myths and Automation." Integrated Education, F-Mr, 1965.

Sohlman, Asa. Differences in School Achievement and Occupational Opportunities: Explanatory Factors. Paris: OECD, 1970.

Solmon, Lewis C., and Wachtel, Paul. The Effects on Income of Type of College Attended. New York: National Bureau of Economic Research, O, 1973.

Sowell, Thomas. Race and Economics. New York: McKay, 1975.

Springer, Philip B. with Anderson, Sydney C. Work Attitudes of Disadvantaged Black Men: A Methodological Inquiry. Washington, DC: GPO, 1972. [San Francisco area]

Star, Jack. "A National Disgrace: What Unions Do to Blacks." Look, N 12, 1968.

Stevenson, Gelvin L. "Nonwhite Teenagers in the Job Market." Doctoral dissertation, Washington U., 1971.

"Students Protest 'Dehumanized' Education." Health Rights News, F, 1969. [Statement by more than 100 medical students to the Council of Deans of the American Association of Medical Colleges]

Study of the Meaning, Experience, and Effects of the Neighborhood Youth Corps on Negro Youth Who Are Seeking Work. New York: New York U. Center for the Study of Unemployed Youth, Ja, 1967.

Sullivan, Leon H. "Self-Help and Motivation for the Under-Privileged." Adult Leadership, F, 1968.

Szymanski, Albert. "Race, Sex, and the U.S. Working Class." Social Problems 21(Je, 1974): 706-725.

Taeuber, Alma F., Taeuber, Karl E., and Cain, Glen G. "Occupational Assimilation and the Competitive Process: A Re-analysis." American Journal of Sociology, N, 1966. [See also reply by Hodge and Hodge.]

Task Force on Economic Growth and Opportunity. The Disadvantaged Poor: Education and Employment. Washington, DC: Chamber of Commerce of the United States, 1966.

Task Force on Employment Problems of Black Youth. The Job Crisis for Black Youth. New York: Praeger, 1971.

Taubman, Paul. Schooling, Ability, Non Pecuniary Rewards, Socioeconomic Background and the Lifetime Distribution of Earnings. New York: National Bureau of Economic Research, N, 1973.

Tausky, Curt, and Wilson, William J. "Work Attachment Among Black Men." Phylon 32 (Spring, 1971):23-30.

Thomas, Anquetta G. Employment Profiles of Minorities and Women in the SMSA's of Sixteen Large Cities, 1970. Washington, DC: GPO, 1972.

Thurow, Lester. "The Occupational Distribution of the Returns to Education and Experience for Whites and Negroes." Proceedings of the Social Statistical Section, American Statistical Association, 1967, 233-243.

Tucker, Francis. "White-Nonwhite Age Differences and the Accurate Assessment of the 'Cost of being Negro.'" Social Forces, Mr, 1969.

Turner, Ralph H. "Negro Job Status and Education." Social Forces, O, 1953.

Tuskegee Institute. Enhancing the Occupational Outlook and Vocational Aspirations of Southern Secondary Youth: A Conference Report. Tuskegee, AL: Tuskegee Institute, My, 1966.

Triandis, Harry, and Malpass, Roy S. "Studies of Black and White Interaction in Job Settings." Journal of Applied Social Psychology 1(Ap, 1971):101-117.

United States. Manpower Report of the President and A Report on Manpower Requirements, Resources, Utilization, and Training. Washington, DC: GPO, Mr, 1964.

U.S. Bureau of Labor Statistics. Black Americans. A Decade of Occupational Change. Rev. 1972. Washington, DC: GPO, 1972.

U.S. Bureau of the Census. The Extent of Poverty in the United States 1959 to 1966. Current Population Reports, Consumer Income, Series P-60, No. 54, My 31, 1968. Washington, DC: GPO, 1968.

_____. Money, Income and Poverty Status of Families and Persons in the United States: 1974. Washington, DC: GPO, Jl, 1975.

_____. Money Income in 1973 of Families and Persons in the United States. Washington, DC: GPO, Ja, 1975.

U.S. Commission on Civil Rights. Employment Testing: Guide Signs, Not Stop Signs. By Myron Kandel. Washington, DC: GPO, 1968.

_____. For All the People...By All the People. A Report on Equal Opportunity in State and Local Government Employment. Washington, DC: GPO, 1969.

_____. Report on Employment Problems of Nonwhite Youth in Michigan. Washington, DC: GPO, 1966.

_____. Report on Washington, D.C.: Employment. Washington, DC: GPO, 1963.

U.S. Congress, 90th, 1st Session, House of Representatives, Committee on Education and Labor, General Subcommittee on Education. Vocational Education Improvement Act Amendments of 1967, Hearings. Part 103. Washington, DC: GPO, 1968.

U.S. Congress, 91st Session, Senate, Committee on Public Works, Subcommittee on Roads. Equal Employment Opportunity. Hearings. Washington, DC: GPO, 1969.

U.S. Congress, 95th, 2nd session, House of Representatives, Committee on Banking, Finance, and Urban Affairs, Subcommittee on the City. Large Corporations and Urban Employment. Washington, DC: GPO, F, 1978.

U.S. Congress, 95th, 2nd session, Senate, Committee on the Budget. Youth Unemployment: Hearing. Washington, DC: GPO, 1978. [PA]

U.S. Department of Labor. Manpower Administration. Equality in Manpower Programs. Report of Activity Under Title VI of the Civil Rights Act of 1964. Washington, DC: GPO, S, 1968.

_____. Manpower Services to Minority Groups: A Desk Reference for ES Personnel. Washington, DC: U.S. Department of Labor, 1970.

U.S. Department of Labor. Manpower Report of the President including a Report on Manpower Requirements, Resources, Utilization, and Training. Transmitted to Congress Ap, 1968. Washington, DC: GPO, 1968.

U.S. Department of Labor, Office of Planning and Research. The Negro Family. The Case for National Action. Washington, DC: GPO, 1965. [The Moynihan Report]

U.S. Department of Labor. Report of a Consultation on the Status of Household Employment...May 20, 1967. Washington, DC: GPO, 1968.

_____. Technological Trends in Major American Industries. Washington, DC: GPO, 1966.

U.S. Department of Labor. Wage and Hour and Public Contracts Division. Working Children. A Report on Child Labor. 1967 and 1968. Washington, DC: GPO, 1969.

U.S. Office of Education. Training the Hard-Core Unemployed: A Demonstration-Research Project at Virginia State College, Norfolk Division. Washington, DC: GPO, 1964.

U.S. Office of Education, Office of the Programs for the Disadvantaged. Vocational Training, Employment and Unemployment. 2 parts. Washington, DC: H.E.W., Ja, 1969.

U.S. Office of Juvenile Delinquency and Youth Development. Getting Hired, Getting Trained. A Study of Industry Practices and Policies on Youth Employment. Washington, DC: GPO, 1965.

_____. Youth Employment Programs in Perspective. Washington, DC: GPO, 1965.

U.S. Office of Manpower Policy, Evaluation and Research. Negroes in Apprenticeship. Manpower/Automation Research Monograph No. 6. Washington, DC: GPO, 1967.

Van Brunt, Robert E. "Supervising Employees from Minority Groups." Training and Development Journal 26(Jl, 1972):36-38.

"Vocational Guidance and Education for Negroes." Occupations 14(Mr, 1936):485-578.

"Vocational Guidance of Negroes." Journal of Negro Education 4(Ja, 1935):10-47.

Wachtel, Paul. The Effect of School Quality on Achievement Attainment Levels and Life-time Earnings. New York: Graduate School of Business, New York U., My, 1974.

Wallace, Phyllis, Kissinger, Beverly, and Reynolds, Betty. Testing of Minority Group Applicants for Employment. Washington, DC: Office of Research and Reports, Equal Employment Opportunity Commission, Mr, 1966.

Watson, Goodwin (ed.). No Room at the Bottom: Automation and the Reluctant Learner. Washington, DC: N.E.A., 1963.

Weaver, Jerry L. "Educational Attainment and Economic Success: Some Notes on a Ghetto Study." Journal of Negro Education 40 (Spring, 1971):153-158. [Long Beach, CA]

Welch, Finis. Employment Quotas for Minorities, My, 1976. ERIC ED 147 394.

Weldon, Robert A. "Apprenticeship and Negro Youth." Journal of Employment Counseling, 6(1969):117-120.

Wellman, David. "The Wrong Way to Find Jobs for Negroes." Transaction, Ap, 1968.

Westberg, D. L. "Press Swallows Motorola Hoax." Focus Midwest IV, Nos. 102, 1965. [The politics of employment testing]

White, Willo P. "Testing and Equal Opportunity." Civil Rights Digest 7(Spring, 1975): 42-51.

Wilkerson, Doxey A. Agricultural Extension Services Among Negroes in the South. New York: The Conference of Presidents of Negro Land Grant Colleges, 1942.

Will, Robert E., and Vatter, Harold G. (eds.). Poverty in Affluence: A Reader on the Social, Political, and Economic Dimensions of Poverty in the United States. New York: Harcourt, Brace & World, 1965.

Williams, Lawrence A., Allensworth, Don T., and Britt, Clinton A. Education and Manpower Strategies and Programs for Deprived Urban Neighborhoods: The Model Cities Approach, My, 1968. Department of Urban Studies, National League of Cities, 1612 K Street, N.W., Washington, DC.

Williams, Walter Edward. Youth and Minority Employment. Washington, DC: GPO, 1977.

Wilms, Wellford W. The Effectiveness of Public and Proprietary Occupational Training. Berkeley, CA: Center for Research and Development in Higher Education, U. of California, Berkeley, O 31, 1974.

Wise, Arthur E. "Minimum Educational Adequacy: Beyond School Finance Reform." Journal of Education Finance 1(Spring 1976):468-483.

Wood, Merle W. "Special Education Needs of the Disadvantaged Student." National Business Education Association Yearbook, 1970:154-162.

Woodson, Carter G. The Negro Professional Man, and the Community. Washington, DC: Association for the Study of Negro Life and History, Inc., 1934.

Wright, N., Jr. "The Economics of Race." American Journal of Economics and Sociology, Ja, 1967.

Wright, Stephen J. "Redressing the Imbalance of Minority Groups in the Professions." Journal of Higher Education 48(Mr, 1972): 239-248.

Young, Anne M. "Employment of High School Graduates and Dropouts." Monthly Labor Review 94(My, 1971):33-38.

_____. Students, Graduates, and Dropouts in the Labor Market. Washington, DC: Bureau of Labor Statistics, 1977.

Zito, R. J., and Bardon, J. I. "Negro Adolescents' Success and Failure Imagery Concerning Work and School." Vocational Guidance Quarterly, Mr, 1968.

Bibliographies

Brimmer, Andrew F., and Harper, Harriet "Economists' Perception of Minority Economics: An Interpretation." Journal of Economic Literature 8(1970).

Cameron, Colin and others (comps.). Attitudes of the Poor and Attitudes Toward the Poor. An Annotated Bibliography, Supplement I, 1977. ERIC ED 148 967 (also 110532).

Henry, Grant G. (comp.). "A Bibliography Concerning Negroes in Physical Education, Athletics, and Related Fields." Journal of Health Physical Education Recreation 44 (My, 1973):65-70.

Hüfner, K. (comp.). "Economics of Higher Education and Educational Planning—A Bibliography." Socio-Economic Planning Sciences 2(1968):25-101.

Jablonsky, Adelaide. The Job Corps. A Review of the ERIC Literature. New York: ERIC, Teachers College, Columbia U., Mr, 1970.

Jablonsky, Adelaide, and Barnes, Regina. The Neighborhood Youth Corps. A Review of the ERIC Literature. New York: ERIC, Teachers College, Columbia U., Mr, 1970.

Kuvlesky, William P., and Reynolds, David H. Occupational Aspirations and Expectations of Youth: A Bibliography of Research Literature. I. College Station, TX: Texas A. & M. U., Department of Agricultural Economics and Sociology; Texas Agricultural Experiment Station, D, 1970. ERIC ED 049 879.

_____. Occupational Aspirations and Expectations of Youth: A Bibliography of Research Literature I.; Educational Aspirations and Expectations of Youth: A Bibliography of Research Literature II.; Youth's Projections for Residence, Income, and Family Status: A Bibliography of Research Literature III. College Station, TX: Texas A. & M. U., Department of Agricultural Economics and Sociology, D, 1970. ERIC ED 050 357.

_____. Youth's Projections for Residence, Income, and Family Status: A Bibliography of Research Literature. III. College Station, TX: Texas A. & M. U., Department of Agricultural Economics and Sociology; Texas Agricultural Experiment Station, D, 1970. ERIC ED 049 881.

Mapp, Edward C. (comp.). Books for Occupational Education Programs. New York: Bowker, 1971.

Mather, William G. III, Kit, Boris V., Blach, Gail A., and Herman, Martha F. (comps.). Man, His Job, and the Environment: A Review and Annotated Bibliography of Selected Recent Research on Human Performance. Washington, DC: GPO, O, 1970.

National Academy of Sciences (comp.). A Selected, Annotated Bibliography on Employment of Minority Engineers, 1975. ERIC ED 149 881.

National Institute of Health (comp.). Minority Groups in Medicine: Selected Bibliography, Je, 1972. ERIC ED 099 575.

O'Neill, Mary and others (comps). Poverty-Related Topics Found in Dissertations: A Bibliography. 1976. ERIC ED 135 540.

Reid, Ira De A. (comp.). Negro Youth: Their Social and Economic Backgrounds. A Selected Bibliography of Unpublished Studies, 1900-1938. Washington, DC: American Council on Education, 1939.

Rubin, Leonard (ed.). An Annotated Bibliography on the Employment of Disadvantaged Youth, 1960-1966. Washington, DC: Bureau of Social Science Research, Inc., My, 1969. ERIC ED 035 732.

Schuman, Patricia (comp.). Materials for Occupational Education. An Annotated Source Guide. New York: Bowker, 1971.

U.S. Department of Labor Library (comp.). Apprenticeship in the United States. A Bibliography. Washington, DC: GPO, Jl, 1974.

Wood, W. D., and Campbell, H. F. (comps.). Cost-Benefit Analysis and the Economics of Investment in Human Resources: An Annotated Bibliography. Kingston, Ontario: The Industrial Relations Centre, Queen's U., 1970.

16.
STRATEGY AND TACTICS

Aberbach, Joel D. "Alienation and Race."
Doctoral dissertation, Yale U., 1967.

Aberbach, Joel D., and Walker, Jack L. "The
Meanings of Black Power: A Comparison of
White and Black Interpretations of a
Political Slogan." American Political
Science Review, Je, 1970.

Adelson, Alan. "Decades-Old Alliance Between
Jews, Negroes Is Beset by Animosity." Wall
Street Journal, D 31, 1968.

Ahmed, Muhammed (Max Stafford). "The Roots of
the Pan-African Revolution." Black Scholar
3(My, 1972):48-55.

Alkalimat, Abdul (Gerald McWorter). A
Scientific Approach to Black Liberation:
Which Road Against Racism and Imperialism
for the Black Liberation Movement, 1974.
People's College Press, P.O. Box 5747,
Nashville, TN 37208.

Aldridge, Dan. "Politics in Command of
Economics: Black Economic Development."
Monthly Review, N, 1969.

Alinsky, Saul. "The Professional Radical,
1970." Harper's Magazine, Ja, 1970.

All-African Peoples Union. Education to
Govern. A Philosophy and Program for Learn-
ing Now!, 1971. All African People's Union,
P.O. Box 3309, Jefferson Station, Detroit,
MI 48214.

Allen, Robert L. "Black Liberation and World
Revolution." Black Scholar 3(F, 1972):
7-23.

_____. "Black Power Today. Where It's At,
Where It's Going." Guardian, My 25, 1968.

_____. "[Eldridge] Cleaver Discusses Black
United Front." Guardian, Ap 13, 1968.

_____. "New SNCC Chief Speaks His Mind."
National Guardian, Je 10, 1967. [Interview
with H. Rap Brown]

Alsop, Joseph. "No More Nonsense About Ghetto
Education." New Republic, Jl 22, 1967.

American Jewish Committee. "Compensatory and
Preferential Treatment in Education and
Employment. A Position Statement."
Jewish Currents, Mr, 1970.

Anderson, C. Arnold and Foster, Philip J.
"Discrimination and Inequality in Education."
Sociology of Education, Fall, 1964.

Anderson, S. E. "The Fragmented [Black
Liberation] Movements." Negro Digest, S-O,
1968.

_____. "Toward Racial Relevancy: Militancy and
Black Students."

Arnold, Martin. "There Is No Rest for Roy
Wilkins." New York Times Magazine, S 28,
1969.

Ash, William. "Marxism and the Negro Revolt."
Monthly Review, My, 1966.

Bane, Mary Jo, and Jencks, Christopher. "The
Schools and Equal Opportunity." Saturday
Review of Education 55(O, 1972):37-42.

Baraka, Imanu Amiri (Le Roi Jones) (ed.).
African Congress. A Documentary of the First
Modern Pan-African Congress. New York:
Morrow, 1972. [Atlanta, GA, S 3-7, 1970]

_____. "Toward the Creation of Political
Institutions for All African Peoples."
Black World 21(O, 1972):54-78.

Barbour, Floyd B. (ed.). The Black Power Revolt.
Boston: Porter Sargent, 1968.

Bartley, Glenda. The Continuing Crisis: An Assessment of New Racial Tensions in the South, My, 1966. Southern Regional Council, 5 Fortyth Street, N.W., Atlanta, GA 30303. Institute of Human Relations, American Jewish Committee, 165 East 56th Street, New York, NY 10022.

Beardwood, Roger. "The New Negro Mood." Fortune, Ja, 1968.

Bell, Derrick A., Jr. "Integration: A No Win Policy for Blacks?" Inequality in Education 11(Mr, 1972):35-44. [Reprinted in Integrated Education, S-O, 1972, pp. 32-45.

Bell, Inge P. CORE and the Strategy of Non-violence. New York: Random House, 1968.

Bennett, Lerone, Jr. "Black Bourgeoisie Revisited." Ebony 28(Ag, 1973):50-55

_____. "Liberation." Ebony, Ag, 1970.

_____. "Old Illusions and New Souths." Ebony 26(Ag, 1971):35-40.

_____. "Stokely Carmichael, Architect of Black Power." Ebony, S, 1966.

_____. "What's in a Name? Negro or Afro-American vs. Black." Ebony, N, 1967.

Benson, John. "Interview with Stokely Carmichael." Militant, My 23, 1966.

Bernard, Thomas L. "Law and Order...and the Prince of Wales." Integrated Education 8 (My-Je, 1970):22-23.

Bernstein, Victor H. "Why Negroes Are Still Angry." Redbook, Jl, 1966.

Besse, Ralph M. "Education and the Race Problem." Junior College Journal, O, 1964.

Bethea, Dennis A. "Thinks Separate Schools Would Provide Teaching Jobs" (letter). Crisis, S, 1935.

Bettelheim, Bruno. "On Campus Rebellion. A New and Potentially Dangerous Rite of Manhood." Chicago Tribune Magazine, My 4, 1969. [Complete text of testimony before House Education and Labor Subcommittee]

Blackwood, George D. "Civil Rights and Direct Action." In Public Policy, Vol. XIV. Edited by John D. Montgomery and Arthur Smithies. Cambridge, MA: Harvard U. Press, 1966.

Blauner, Robert. "The Dilemma of the Black Revolt." Journal of Housing, D, 1967.

_____. "Internal Colonialism and Ghetto Revolt." Social Problems, Spring, 1969.

"Bobby Seale Talks to the Movement..." The Movement, Mr, 1969. [Black Panthers in California]

Bodian, Marion E. "Robert Coles on Activism." Harvard Crimson, My 29, 1968 (supplement). [Boston]

Boggs, Grace Lee. "Education: The Great Obsession." Monthly Review 22(S, 1970):18-39.

Boggs, Grace Lee, and Boggs, James. "The City Is the Black Man's Land." Monthly Review, Ap, 1968.

Boggs, James. "The American Revolution." Liberator, O, 1968.

_____. "Beyond Malcolm X." Monthly Review 29 (D, 1977):30-48.

_____. "Blacks in the Cities: Agenda for the 70's." Black Scholar 4(N-D, 1972):50-61.

_____. Manifesto for a Black Revolutionary Party, 1969. Pacesetters Publishing House, P.O. Box 3281, Philadelphia, PA.

Boggs, Vernon W. "Slogans Are Not Enough!" Liberator, N, 1968.

Bolner, James. "Toward a Theory of Racial Reparations." Phylon, Spring, 1968.

Bond, Jean Carey, and Peery, Pat. "Has the Black Man Been Castrated?" Liberator, My, 1969.

Bond, Horace Mann. "Negro Leadership Since Washington." South Atlantic Quarterly 24 (Ap, 1925):115-130.

Bond, Julian. "Feudal Politics and Black Serfdom." Afro-American Studies 1(O, 1970): 147-159.

_____. A Time to Speak, a Time to Act: The Movement in Politics. New York: Simon & Schuster, 1972.

Bossette, Skip. "World Serpent Facing Joint Wrath of Blacks and Awakening White Radicals." Muhammad Speaks, Ja 10, 1969.

Bottomore, T. B. "Blacks and Students; Critics of Society." Nation, N 25, 1968.

Bottone, Sam. "The Negro Revolt: The Push Beyond Liberalism." New Politics, Summer, 1964.

Boyle, Sarah Patton, and Griffin, John Howard. "The Racial Crisis: An Exchange of Letters." Christian Century, My 22, 1968.

Bozeman, Herman H. "Attitudes of Selected Racial Leadership Organizations towards Educational Policies and Practices for Negroes During the Twentieth Century." Doctoral dissertation, U. of Michigan, 1956. Univ. Microfilms Order No. 17417.

Bracey, John H., Jr., Meier, August, and Rudwick, Elliot (eds.). Black Nationalism in America. Indianapolis, IN: Bobbs-Merrill, 1970.

Braden, Anne. "The Busing Issue in the South." Southern Patriot 29(0, 1971):4.

_____. "One Year Later: The Effects of Black Power." Southern Patriot, My, 1967.

_____. "Our View of SNCC's Position (2): Not Violence but Political Action." Southern Patriot, Ja, 1967.

_____. "The Southern Freedom Movement in Perspective." Monthly Review, Jl-Ag, 1965 (entire issue).

_____. "The SNCC Trends: Challenge to White America." Southern Patriot, My, 1966.

_____. "Today's Challenge: To Organize the White South." Southern Patriot, Je, 1967.

Bray, Thomas J. "NAACP Bulks Large, But Militants Belittle Effectiveness." Wall Street Journal, Ap 23, 1969.

Brickman, W. W. "Compulsory School Busing and Integration." School and Society, O 17, 1964.

Brimmer, Andrew F. "Economic Integration and the Progress of the Negro Community." Ebony, Ag, 1970.

Broadhead, Richard, and Jordan, Joel. "AFT and the New Caucus." Workers' Power, S 11, 1970.

Brooks, Gwendolyn. "There Are Better Goals than Integration" (interview). Muhammad Speaks, O 25, 1968.

Brooks, Thomas R. "The Negro Movement: Beyond Demonstrations?" Dissent, Winter, 1965.

_____. "A Strategist Without a Movement." New York Times Magazine, F 16, 1969. [Bayard Rustin]

Brown, Rap. Letter from Parish Prison, New Orleans, F 21, 1968. Integrated Education 8 (My-Je, 1970):54.

Brown, Lloyd L. "A Middle-Aged Negro Tells It As It Is." Negro Digest, Je, 1969.

Browne, Robert S. "The Challenge of Black Student Organizations." Freedomways, Fall, 1968.

_____. "Separation." Ebony, Ag, 1970.

Browne, Robert S., and Rustin, Bayard. Separatism or Integration: Which Way for America? A Dialogue, n.d. A. Philip Randolph Educational Fund, 260 Park Avenue, New York, NY.

Bruckner, D. J. R. "A Lonely Crusade in the Ghetto." Chicago Sun-Times, Section 2, Ap 23, 1967. [Rev. James E. Groppi in Milwaukee]

Bryce, James. "Problems of the Negro." North American Review 153: n.d., p. 641.

Buckley, Tom. "Whitney Young: Black Leader Or 'Oreo Cookie'?" New York Times Magazine, S 20, 1970.

Bullock, Charles S. III, and Rodgers, Harrell R. (eds.). Black Political Attitudes. Implications for Political Support. Chicago: Markham, 1972.

Bunche, Ralph J. "A Critical Analysis of the Tactics and Programs of Minority Groups." Journal of Negro Education 4(Jl, 1935):308-320.

Caldwell, Earl. "Black Nationalism Grows in Watts as Negroes Complain of Lack of Gains." New York Times, Jl 9, 1967.

Campanella, Jane. "Pan-African Federation Hosts Black Educators' Gathering." African World, Ja 8, 1972. [Newark, NJ, D 4, 1971]

Campbell, James E. "Struggle: The Highest Form of Education." Freedomways, Fall, 1968.

Campbell, Les. "Black Power--1969. The Bermuda Experience." African-American Teachers Forum, S, 1969. [Black Power Conference in Bermuda, Jl, 1969]

[Carmichael, Stokely, and Blackwell, Randolph] "Black Power: The Widening Dialogue." New South, Summer, 1966. [Transcript of questions and answers to and by the two authors; at Spelman College, Atlanta, Jl 13, 1966]

Carmichael, Stokely. "A Declaration of War." San Francisco Express Times, F 22, 1968.

_____. "El Tercero Mundo, Nuestro Mundo." Tricontinental (Cuba), S-O, 1967.

_____. "Pan-Africanism--Land and Power." The Black Scholar, N, 1969.

_____. Stokely Speaks. New York: Random House, 1971.

_____. "Toward Black Liberation." Massachusetts Review, Autumn, 1966.

Carmichael, Stokely, and Hamilton, Charles. Atlantic Monthly, O, 1967. [Ghetto problems]

Casimere, Dwight. "Economic Strategy to Eliminate the Blacks?" Muhammad Speaks, My 9, 1969. [Interview with Julian Bond]

Chamberlain, William Henry. "Pitfalls of Forced Integration." Modern Age, Summer, 1966.

Chambers, Ernest W. "We Have Marched, We Have Cried, We Have Prayed." Ebony, Ap, 1968.

Chrisman, Robert. "The Formation of a Revolutionary Black Culture." Black Scholar 1(Je, 1970):2-9.

STRATEGY AND TACTICS / 767

Christoffel, Tom. "Black Power and Corporate Power." _Monthly Review_, O, 1968.

Clark, Kenneth B. "Black Power and Basic Power: An Examination of the Futility of Black Nationalism, and a Program for Negro and Jewish Relationships." _Congress Bi-Weekly_ 35(Ja 8, 1968):6-10

_____. "The Civil Rights Movement: Momentum and Organization." _Daedalus_, Winter, 1966.

_____. _Dark Ghetto. An Analysis of the Dilemma of Social Power_. New York: Harper and Row, 1965.

_____. "Delusions of the White Liberal." _New York Times Magazine_, Ap 4, 1965.

_____. "No. No. Race, Not Class, Is Still at the Wheel." _New York Times_, Mr 22, 1978.

_____. "On the N.A.A.C.P. and Dr. Johnson." _Crisis_, D, 1939.

_____. "The Present Dilemma." _New South_, Fall, 1969.

_____. _Social Power and Social Change in Contemporary America_. Department of State Publications 8125. Washington, DC: GPO, S, 1966.

Clark, Leroy D. "Leadership Crisis: A New Look at the 'Black Bougeoisie.'" _Freedomways_, Summer, 1968.

Clark, S. D. "Higher Education and the New Men of Power in Society." _Journal of Educational Thought_, Ag, 1967.

Clay, William L. "Emerging New Black Politics." _Black World_ 21(O, 1972):32-39.

Cleage, Albert B., Jr. "Fear Is Gone." _Liberator_, N, 1967. [A black nationalist statement]

_____. "Race Relations in 1967." _Monthly Review_, Mr, 1967. [By the chairman of the Inner City Organizing Committee of Detroit]

Cleage, Albert B., Jr., and Breitman, George. "Myths About Malcolm X: Two Views." _International Socialist Review_, S-O, 1967.

Cleaver, Eldridge. "The Crisis of the Black Bourgeoisie." _Black Scholar_ 4(Ja, 1973): 2-11.

_____. "Education and Revolution." _The Black Scholar_, N, 1969.

_____. "My Father and Stokely Carmichael." _Ramparts_, Ap, 1967.

_____. _Revolution in the White Mother Country and National Liberation in the Black Colony_. Oakland, CA: Black Panther Party, 1968.

Cleaver, Kathleen. "Open Letter to Stokely Carmichael." _Black Panther_, Ag 16, 1969.

_____. "A Panther Replies to Julius Lester." _Guardian_, My 3, 1969.

_____. "Revolution and Education." _Black Panther_, Je 28, 1969.

Cloward, Richard A., and Piven, Frances Fox. "The Urban Crisis and the Consolidation of National Power." _Proceedings, Academy of Political Science_, 1968.

Cobbs, Price M. "The Black Revolution and Education." _N.A.S.S.P. Bulletin_, My, 1969.

_____. "Journeys to Black Idenity: Selma and Watts." _Negro Digest_, Jl, 1969.

Cohen, David K. "Teachers Want What Children Need...Or Do They?" _Urban Review_, Je, 1968.

Cole, Lewis. "The Black Colony." _The Hard Core_, Mr 18, 1969. [Columbia U. S.D.S. publication]

Coleman, James S. _Race Relations and Social Change_. Baltimore, MD: Center for the Study of Social Organization of Schools, Johns Hopkins U., Jl, 1967, 111 pp. ERIC ED 013 493.

_____. _The Struggle for Control of Education_. Baltimore, MD: Center for the Study of Social Crganization of Schools, Johns Hopkins U., O, 1967.

Coles, Robert, Donaldson, Ivanhoe, Feldman, Paul, Hamilton, Charles V., Hoffman, Abbie, Kahn, Tom, Kelley, William Melvin, Mailer, Norman, Newfield, Jack, Powledge, Fred, Thernstrom, Stephan, and Wright, Nathan, Jr. "Black Power: A Discussion." _Partisan Review_, Spring, 1968.

Comer, James P. "The Case for Black Quotas." _Ebony_ 29(S, 1974):146.

_____. "The Social Power of the Negro." _Scientific American_ 216(1967):21-27.

Conant, Ralph W. "Black Power: Rhetoric and Reality." _Urban Affairs Quarterly_, S, 1968.

Crain, Robert L., and Inger, Morton. "Urban School Integration: Strategy for Peace." _Saturday Review_, F 18, 1967.

Crawford, Jeff. "Integration or Independence? A Strategy for Black Groups." _Race Today_ 4 (Je, 1972):187-189.

Cross, William E., Jr. "The Negro-to-Black Conversion Experience." _Black World_ 20(Jl, 1971):13-27.

Cruse, Harold. "Black and White: Outlines of the Next Stage." _Black World_ 20(Ja, 1971): 19-41, 66-71.

_____. The Crisis of the Negro Intellectual. Clifton, NJ: William Morrow, 1967.

_____. "Revolutionary Nationalism and the Afro-American." Studies on the Left, II, No. 3, 1972.

Danzig, David. "In Defense of 'Black Power.'" Commentary, S, 1966.

_____. "The Meaning of Negro Strategy." Commentary, F, 1964.

_____. "The Racial Explosion in American Society." New University Thought, Vol. V, Nos. 1-2(1966-1967). [See, also, comments by Benjamin Payton and John Feild.]

"David Hilliard Speaks on B.S.U.'s." Black Panther, D 27, 1969.

Davis, Allison. "Our Negro 'Intellectuals.'" Crisis, Ag, 1928. [See reply by Langston Hughes, Crisis, S, 1928.]

Davis, Angela Y. "Eight Years Since Birmingham." Black Panther, S 18, 1971.

Davis, Chester. "Approaches to Black Education." Integrated Education 8(N-D, 1970): 45-50.

Davis, George B. "The Howard University Conference." Negro Digest, Mr, 1969. [Conference, "Toward a Black University," N, 1968, at Howard U.]

Day, Noel. "The American Left: Post Election Prospects and Problems." National Guardian, O 31, 1964.

"Decentralization--Or Separation?" African-American Teachers Forum, N-D, 1969.

Degler, Carl N. "The Negro in America--Where Myrdal Went Wrong." New York Times Magazine, D 7, 1969.

Dellums, Ronald V. "The Coalition's the Thing." Freedomways 12(1972):7-16.

Detweiler, Bruce. "A Time to be Black." New Republic, S 17, 1966.

Diara, Agadem Lumumba, and Diara, Schavi M. Hey! Let a Revolutionary Brother and Sister Come In... 4th ed. Detroit, MI: Agascha Productions, 1972.

Dodson, Dan W. "Education and the Powerless. In Developing Programs for the Educationally Disadvantaged. Edited by A. Harry Passow. New York: Teachers College Press, 1968.

_____. "Politics, Power, and the Public Schools." Graduate Comment 9(1966).

Dowd, Douglas. "Campus Disruptions and the Liberal-Left." Monthly Review, S, 1969.

Downs, Anthony. "Alternative Futures for the American Ghetto." Daedalus, Fall, 1968.

Draper, Theodore. "The Fantasy of Black Nationalism." Commentary, S, 1969.

Dratch, Howard B. "The Emergence of Black Power." International Socialist Journal, J1, 1968.

Duberman, Martin. "Black Power in America." Partisan Review, Winter, 1968.

Dubey, Samati N. "Blacks' Preference for Black Professionals, Businessmen, and Religious Leaders." Public Opinion Quarterly 34(1970): 113-116. [Hough, Cleveland, Ohio]

_____. "Powerlessness and Mobility Orientation Among Disadvantaged Blacks." Public Opinion Quarterly 35(Summer, 1971):183-188.

Du Bois, W. E. B. "Can the Negro Expect Freedom by 1965?" Negro Digest, Ap, 1947.

_____. "Does the Negro Need Separate Schools?" Journal of Negro Education 4(J1, 1935):328-335.

_____. "Mixed Schools." Crisis, Ag, 1921.

_____. "Race and Nation." [On Negro American culture] Chicago Defender, S 13, 1947, p. 19.

_____. "Separation." Crisis, F, 1911.

_____. "The Southern Liberal." Chicago Defender, Mr 6, 1948, p. 19.

Dunbar, Leslie W. "Public Policy and the Arts of Peacemaking." New South, Winter, 1966.

_____. A Republic of Equals. Ann Arbor, MI: U. of Michigan Press, 1966.

Dye, Thomas. The Politics of Equality. Indianapolis, IN: Bobbs-Merrill, 1972.

Echols, Alvin E. "Black Community Calls for Unity." New America, F 15, 1968. [Philadelphia]

Edmondson, Locksley. "The Internationalization of Black Power: Historical and Contemporary Perspectives." Mawazo, D, 1968.

"The Education Factory." National Guardian, S 23, 1967. [The relation of ghetto education to teachers' unionism]

Ellison, Ralph. "An American Dilemma: A Review." In Shadow and Act. New York: New American Library, 1966. [Orig. 1964] [On American capitalism, American social science, and the Negro American; written in 1944]

Elsbery, James W. "Turning Out. Is the Issue Integration, or Education?" Center Forum, D 23, 1969.

Epps, Archie (ed.). The Speeches of Malcolm X at Harvard. New York: Morrow, 1968. [Malcolm's speeches are on pp. 115-182. The rest is by the editor.]

Epton, Bill. "Stokely's Anti-Communism Bared." PL (Progressive Labor), O, 1968.

Etzkowitz, Henry, and Schaflander, Gerald M. "A Manifesto for Sociologists: Institution Formation--A New Sociology." Social Problems, Spring, 1968. [The Bedford-Stuyvesant, NY, Community Cooperative Center]

Everett-Karenga, Ron N. "Afro-American Nationalism: Social Strategy and Struggle for Community." Doctoral dissertation, United States International U., 1976. Univ. Microfilms Order No. 76-20,964.

Farmer, James. "Some Views on the Relationship Between Decentralization and Racial Integration in Large City School Systems." In Equality of Educational Opportunity in the Large Cities of America: The Relationship Between Decentralization and Racial Integration. Edited by Carroll F. Johnson and Michael D. Usdan. New York: Teachers College Press, n.d.

"Fe Fe Fi Fi Fo Fo Fum, I Smell Smoke in the Auditorium." Hey Teach., Undated (1969). [Strategies of radical change in school]

Feldman, Paul. "The Pathos of 'Black Power.'" Dissent, Ja-F, 1967.

Ferry, W. H. "The Case for a New Federalism." Saturday Review, Je 15, 1968. [Argues for racial separation]

_____. "Farewell to Integration." Liberator, Ja, 1968.

Fewkes, John M. "Wrong Address." Integrated Education, D, 1963-Ja, 1964.

Fiddick, Thomas C. "Black Power, Capitalism, and Vietnam." Liberation, S, 1966.

Finch, Arthur. "On White People in the Movement." Freedom North, I, Nos. 4-5 (1965).

Five-State Organizing Committee for Community Control. "Position Paper." Phi Delta Kappan, Ap, 1968. [Black Power position formulated on Ja 25, 1968[

Fleming, Harold C. "Face Real Choices." Trends in Housing, Mr-Ap, 1969.

_____. "The Unreal Debate Over the Unattainable Objectives of Total Separation or Complete Integration." City, N-D, 1968.

Foner, Philip S. (ed.). Black Protest and Socialism. New York: Capricorn, 1975.

_____ (ed.). The Black Panthers Speak. Philadelphia, PA: Lippincott, 1970.

Fontaine, William T. Reflections on Segregation, Desegregation, Power and Morals. Springfield, IL: Charles C. Thomas, 1967.

Forbes, Jack D. "Segregation and Integration: The Multi-Ethnic or Uni-Ethnic School." In Afro-Americans in the Far West. A Handbook for Educators, 1967. Far West Laboratory for Educational Research and Development, 1 Garden Circle, Hotel Clarement, Berkeley, CA 94705.

Form, William H., and Rytina, Joan. "Ideological Beliefs on the Distribution of Power in the United States." American Sociological Review, F, 1969.

Forrest, Leon. "Black Education." Muhammad Speaks, Ja 15, 1971.

Fox, David J. Expansion of the Free Choice Open Enrollment Program. New York: Center for Urban Education, S, 1967. [New York City]

_____. Expansion of the More Effective School Program. New York: Center for Urban Education, S, 1967. [New York City]

Franklin, Raymond S. "The Political Economy of Black Power." Social Problems, Winter, 1969.

Frantz, Stephen W. "Watts: 'We're Pro-Black. If the White Man Views This as Anti-White, That's Up to Him.'" Harvard Crimson, O 3, 1966.

Frazier, Arthur, and Roberts, Virgil. "A Discourse on Black Nationalism." American Behavioral Scientists, Mr-Ap, 1969.

Frazier, E. Franklin. "The Du Bois Program in the Present Crisis." Race 1, 1(Winter, 1935-36):11-13.

_____. "The Failure of the Negro Intellectual." Negro Digest, F, 1962, pp. 26-36.

_____. "Human, All Too Human. The Negro's Vested Interest in Segregation." Race Prejudice and Discrimination (1951).

_____. "The Negro Middle Class and Desegregation." Social Problems 4(Ap, 1957):291-301.

Freeman, Donald, Kimbrough, Rollis, and Zolili, Brother. "The Meaning of Education." Journal of Negro Education, Fall, 1968. [Extracts from position paper at Conference of Afro-American Educators, Je, 1968]

Freeman, Harrop A. and others. Civil Disobedience. Santa Barbara, CA: Center for the Study of Democratic Institutions, 1966.

Friedrichs, Robert W. "Interpretation of Black Aggression." Yale Review, Spring, 1968.

Funnyé, Clarence. Black Power and Deghettoization: A Retreat to Reality. New York:
National Committee Against Discrimination
in Housing, 1969.

_____. "The Militant Black Social Worker and
the Urban Hustle." Social Work 15(1970):
5-12.

Funnyé, Clarence, and Shiffman, Ronald. "The
Imperative of Deghettoization: An Answer to
Piven and Cloward." Social Work, Ap, 1967.
[Reply to article in Jan, 1967, issue of
Social Work; see Piven and Cloward, below.]

Fusco, Liz. "Deeper Than Politics." Liberation, N, 1964. [Freedom School in Mississi-
ppi]

Galamison, Milton A. "Educational Values and
Community Power." Freedomways, Fall, 1968.
[New York City]

Gannon, Thomas M. "What the Black Community
Wants." America, D 6, 1969. [According to
Julius Hobson, John O. Hopkins, and Walter
Carter]

Gans, Herbert. "The New Egalitarianism."
Saturday Review, My 6, 1972.

_____. "The Positive Functions of Poverty."
American Journal of Sociology 78(S, 1972):
275-289.

Garrett, James. "Black Power and Black Education." 25 1(1968):33-34.

_____. "Black Power and Black Education."
Washington Free Press, Ap, 1969.

Gaston, Paul M. The New South Creed: A Study
in Southern Mythmaking. New York: Vintage
Books, 1973.

Gayle, Addison, Jr. "Black Power Existential
Politics." Liberator, Ja, 1969.

Geltman, Emanuel, and Plastrik, Stanley.
"The Politics of Coalition." Dissent, Ja-
F, 1966.

Geltman, Max. The Confrontation: Black Power,
Anti-Semitism, and the Myth of Integration.
Englewood Cliffs, NJ: Prentice-Hall, 1969.

Genovese, Eugene D. "Black Studies: Trouble
Ahead." Atlantic, Je, 1969.

_____. "The Legacy of Slavery and the Roots
of Black Nationalism." Studies on the Left,
N-D, 1966. [Comments by Herbert Aptheker,
C. Vann Woodward, and Frank Kofsky]

Georgetown Defense Committee. "Jackson
[Miss.]: Repression and Response." Southern Patriot, My, 1969.

Gershman, Carl. "Black Separatism: Shock of
Integration." Dissent, Jl-Ag, 1969.

_____. "Racial Conflict Rooted in Economic
Deprivation." New America, Jl 25, 1969.

Gethers, Solomon P. "Black Power: Three Years
Later." Negro Digest, D, 1969.

Gintis, Herbert. "A New Working Class and
Revolutionary Youth." Socialist Revolution
I (My-Je, 1970):13-43.

Giovanni, Nikki. "Black Poems, Poseurs, and
Power." Negro Digest, Je, 1969.

Gitlin, Todd. "Cuba and the American Movement." The Movement, Ap, 1968.

Glazer, Nathan. "Blacks, Jews and the Intellectuals." Commentary, Ap, 1969.

_____. "The Negro's Stake in America's
Future." New York Times Magazine, S 22,
1968.

Good, Paul. "Odyssey of a Man--And a Movement." New York Times Magazine, Je 25, 1967.
[John Lewis, former chairman of SNCC]

Graham, Hugh Davis. "The Storm Over Black
Power." Virginia Quarterly Review, Fall,
1967.

Granger, Lester B. "Does the Negro Want Integration?" Crisis, F, 1951.

Grant, Gerald. "Developing Power in the
Ghetto." Saturday Review, D 17, 1966.

Green, Max. "PL Battles the 'Revisionists.'"
New America, F 28, 1969. [Touches on the
Progressive Labor Party and the Black
Studies Program]

Green, Mark. "Reparations for Blacks? Commonweal, Je 13, 1969.

Greene, Donald. "Black Power and Regionalism."
Black Lines 1(Winter, 1970):47-56.

Gregg, Jean. "The White Liberal's Dilemma."
The Integrator, Fall, 1968.

Gregor, A. James. "Black Nationalism: A Preliminary Analysis of Negro Radicalism."
Science and Society, Fall, 1963.

Gremley, William. "Time to Consolidate?"
America, Ja 2, 1965.

Grier, William H., and Cobbs, Price M. Black
Rage. New York: Basic Books, 1968.

Griffith, Patrick. "An Interview. C. L. R.
James and Pan-Africanism." Black World 21
(N, 1971):4-13.

Grimke, Francis J. "Segregation." Crisis,
Je, 1934.

Groff, Patrick J. "Teacher Organizations and
School Desegregation." School and Society,
D 15, 1962.

Guyot, Lawrence, and Thelwell, Mike. "The Politics of Necessity and Survival in Mississippi." Freedomways, Spring, 1966.

_____. "Toward Independent Political Power." Freedomways, Summer, 1966.

Jacker, Andrew. "The Violent Black Majority." New York Times Magazine, My 10, 1970.

Hadden, Jeffrey K., Masotti, Louis H., and Thiessen, Victor. "The Making of the Negro Mayors in 1967." Trans-action, Ja-F, 1968.

Hall, Raymond Londell. Black Separatism in the United States. Hanover, NH: University Press of New England, 1978.

_____. "Separatists Movements among Black People in the United States." Doctoral dissertation, Syracuse U., 1972. Univ. Microfilms Order No. 72-20336.

Halsey, A. H. "Socialism and Educational Opportunities." Times Higher Education Supplement, Je 8, 1973.

Halsey, Margaret. "Integration Has Failed." Christian Century, D 28, 1966.

Hamilton, Charles V. "An Advocate of Black Power Defines It." New York Times Magazine, Ap 14, 1968.

_____. "Black Americans and the Modern Political Struggle." Black World 19(1970): 5-9, 77-79.

_____. "The Black Revolution: A Primer for White Liberals." Progressive, Ja, 1969.

_____. "Education in the Black Community: An Examination of the Realities." Freedomways, Fall, 1968.

_____. "The Nationalist vs. the Integrationist." New York Times Magazine, O 1, 1972.

_____. The Politics of Civil Rights. New York: Random House, 1968.

_____. "The Politics of Race Relations." In Urban Violence. Edited by Charles U. Daly. Chicago: U. of Chicago Press, 1969.

_____. "Race and Education: A Search for Legitimacy." Harvard Educational Review, Fall, 1968.

_____. "Re-Racialization: Examination of a Political Strategy." First World 1(Mr-Ap, 1977):3-5.

_____. "The Silent Black Majority." New York Times Magazine, My 10, 1970.

Handlin, Oscar. Fire-Bell in the Night. The Crisis in Civil Rights. Boston: Little-Brown, 1964.

_____. "The Goals of Integration." Daedalus, Winter, 1966.

_____. "Is Integration the Answer?" Atlantic, Mr, 1964.

Harding, Vincent. "Black Radicalism: The Road from Montgomery." In Dissent: Explorations in the History of American Radicalism. Edited by Alfred F. Young. De Kalb, IL: Northern Illinois U. Press, 1968.

_____. "New Creation or Familiar Death?" Negro Digest, Mr, 1969. [An open letter to black students in the North]

Hare, Nathan. "Can Blacks Ever Unite?" Ebony, S, 1976.

_____. "Division and Confusion: What Happened to the Black Movement?" Black World 25(Ja, 1976):20-32.

_____. "The Revolutionary Role of the Black Bourgeoisie." Black Scholar 1(Ja, 1973): 32-35.

_____. "The Case for Separatism: 'Black Perspective.'" Newsweek, F 10, 1969.

Harrington, Michael. "The Politics of Poverty." Dissent, Autumn, 1965.

_____. "The Social-Industrial Complex." Harper's N, 1967.

Harris, Leonard. "The Myth of Bayard Rustin." Liberator, O, 1969.

Harris, T. George. "Negroes Have Found a Jolting New Answer." Look, Je 27, 1967.

Havighurst, Robert J. "Educational Reform: Change the Child." Urban Review, Ap, 1969.

_____. "It's Time Now for a Moratorium on Negativism." United Teacher, S 4, 1968.

_____. "Requirements for a Valid 'New Criticism' [of the Schools]." Phi Delta Kappan, S, 1968.

Havrilesky, Catherine. Re-tooling of the Obsolete White Liberal. New York: Afram Associates, S, 1968.

Hayden, Tom. "Colonialism and Liberation in America." Viet-Report, Summer, 1968.

_____. "SNCC: The Qualities of Protest." Studies on the Left, Winter, 1965. [Separatism]

Hechinger, Fred. "Preferential Treatment for Negroes?" Reporter, D 3, 1964.

Henderson, Lenneal. "Engineers of Black Liberation." The Black Politician 1(1970):12-15. [Conference of Black Political Scientists]

Hentoff, Nat. "Beyond Civil Rights." Liberation, 1964.

_____. "Black Backlash." Commonweal, Jl 3, 1964.

_____. "The New Equality. New York: Viking, 1964. Revised paperback, 1965.

_____. "The Next Step in Civil Rights: An Alliance with the Poor?" Peace News (London), Ja 22, 1965.

_____. "We Shall Overcome--Whom?" Freedom North, I, Nos. 4-5 (1965).

_____. "What Next for the Civil Rights Movement?" Commonweal, F 19, 1965.

Hercules, Frank. American Society and Black Revolution. New York: Harcourt Brace Jovanovich, 1972,

Hill, Lon Clay. "The White Panther Growls and Gropes." Liberation, Ja, 1967. [S.N.C.C. and the role of whites in the Negro movement]

Hill, Norman. "Roy Innis vs. Roy Wilkins." Dissent, Mr-Ap, 1969. [On demands for black studies department]

Himes, Joseph S. "The Functions of Racial Conflict." Social Forces, S, 1966.

Hitchings, Phil. "SNCC Aims Toward Black Party" (interview). Guardian, D 14, 1968.

Hixson, William B. "The Negro Revolution and the Intellectuals." American Scholar, Autumn, 1964.

Hobsbawm, E. J. "Revolution Is Puritan." New Society, My 22, 1969. [Relation of cultural revolt and dissidence to social revolution]

Hogan, Lloyd. "Integration Melodies of Roy Wilkins Signifies Requiem for NAACP Future?" Muhammad Speaks, Ag 3, 1973.

Holden, Matthew, Jr. The Politics of the Black "Nation." New York: Chandler, 1972.

Hornstein, Al. "Class Struggle in the Schools." Leviathan, Je, 1969.

Howard, Joseph Hannibal III. "How to End Colonial Domination of Black America." Negro Digest, Ja, 1970.

Howe, Irving. "The First Generation of SNCC." Dissent, Jl-Ag, 1967. [John Lewis]

Hunter, Charlayne. "On the Case in Resurrection City." Trans-action, O, 1968.

Hurst, Charles G., Jr. Passport to Freedom. Education, Humanism and Malcolm X. Hamden, CT: Lumet Books, Shoe String Press, 1971.

Illo, John. "The Rhetoric of Malcolm X." Columbia University Forum, Spring, 1968.

Imari, Brother (Richard B. Henry). War in America. The Malcolm X Doctrine, 1968. Malcolm X Society, Box 697, Detroit, MI 48206.

"Intellectuals in the Movement." SOBU Newsletter, Jl 24, 1971.

Irele, Abiola. "Négritude or Black Cultural Nationalism." Journal of Modern African Studies 3(1965):321-348.

Isaacs, Harold. "Integration and the Negro Mood." Commentary, D, 1962.

Jackson, Donald W. "Some Reflections on the Movement." The Black Student, Spring, 1966.

Jacobson, Julius. "Coalitionism: From Protest to Politicking." New Politics, Fall, 1966.

James, C. L. R. "The Revolutionary Answer to the Negro Problem in the USA." In C. L. R. James, The Future in the Present, pp. 119-127. London: Allison and Busby, 1977.

James, H. Thomas. "School Board Conflict Is Inevitable." American School Board Journal, Mr, 1967.

Jencks, Christopher, and Alsop, Joseph. [Correspondence on Ghetto Education] New Republic, S 2, 1967.

Johnson, Edwina C. "The Escalation of the Struggle." International Review 40(Spring, 1971):17-22.

Johnson, Guy B. "Education, Segregation, and Race Relations." The Quarterly Review of Higher Education among Negroes 3(Ap, 1935): 89-94.

_____. "Segregation vs. Integration." Journal of the National Medical Association, S, 1953.

_____. "Southern Offensive." Common Ground 4(Summer, 1944):87-93. [Reply to Redding and Smith, below]

Jones, Clinton Bernard. "Black Power: An Analysis of Select Strategies for the Implementation of Concept." Doctoral dissertation, Claremont Colleges, 1971.

Jones, Faustine C. "C. Wright Mills on Public Education." Educational Theory 21(Summer, 1971):302-310.

Jones, Leroi. "Interview," Parts 1 and 2. Guardian, Mr 23, 1968; Mr 30, 1968.

Kahn, Tom. The Economics of Equality. New York: League for Industrial Democracy, 112 East 196th Street, New York, NY 10003.

_____. "Problems of the Negro Movement."
Dissent, Winter, 1964.

Kahn, Tom, and Meier, August. "Recent Trends
in the Civil Rights Movement." New Politics,
Spring, 1964.

Kalven, Harry, and Ferry, W. H. "Quotas for
Negroes: Insult or Compensations?" (48-
minute tape). Center for the Study of
Democratic Institutions, Box 4068, Santa
Barbara, CA. [Law professor, U. of Chicago
and vice-president of the Center]

Karenga, Ron. "Nation Time in Atlanta."
Liberator 10(O, 1970):4-6.

_____. The Quotable Karenga. US, 8211 South
Broadway, Los Angeles, CA, n.d.

Karier, Clarence J. "Elite Views on American
Education." In Education and Social Struc-
ture in the Twentieth Century. Edited by
Walter Laque and George L. Mosse. New
York: Harper and Row, 1967.

Karmin, Monroe W. "Many Black Militants Now
Focus on Winning Control of Communities."
Wall Street Journal, D 5, 1968.

Kempton, Murray. "No More Parades?" New
Republic, My 30, 1964. [On the March for
Democratic Schools in NYC, My 18, 1964]

Kgositsile, William Keoraoetse. "Brother
Malcolm and the Black Revolution." Negro
Digest, N, 1968.

_____. "Is the Black Revolutionist a Phony?"
Negro Digest, Jl, 1967.

Killens, John Oliver. "The Black Culture Generation Gap." Black World 22(Ag, 1973):
22-33.

_____. "Explanation of the 'Black Psyche.'"
New York Times Magazine, Je 27, 1964.

_____. "Negroes Have a Right to Fight Back."
Saturday Evening Post, Jl 2, 1966.

Killian, Lewis M. The Impossible Revolution?
Black Power and the American Dream. New
York: Random House, 1968.

_____. "The Role of the White Liberal." New
South, Winter, 1967.

_____. "The Significance of Extremism in the
Black Revolution." Social Problems 20
(Summer, 1972):41-49.

Killian, Lewis M., and Grigg, Charles. Racial
Crisis in America. Leadership in Conflict.
Englewood Cliffs, NJ: Prentice-Hall, 1964.

Kilson, Martin. "Black Power: Anatomy of a
Paradox." Harvard Journal of Negro Affairs,
II, 1(1968).

_____. "Dynamics of Nationalism and Politi-
cal Militancy Among Negro Americans." In
Racial Tensions and National Identity, pp.
97-114. Edited by Ernest Q. Campbell.
Nashville, TN: Vanderbilt U., 1972.

_____. "The New Black Intellectuals."
Dissent, Jl-Ag, 1969.

King, Martin Luther, Jr. "A Testament of
Hope." Playboy, Ja, 1969.

_____. "The Last Steep Ascent." Nation,
Mr 14, 1966.

_____. "'Let Justice Roll Down.'" Nation,
Mr 15, 1965.

_____. "Negroes Are Not Moving Too Fast."
Saturday Evening Post, N 7, 1964.

_____. "Next Stop: The North." Saturday
Review, N 13, 1965.

_____. The Social Activist and Social Change
(Paper presented at Conference Social
Change and the Role of Behavioral Scien-
tists, Atlanta, GA, My 4-6, 1966), My, 1966.
ERIC ED 021 926.

_____. Where Do We Go From Here? New York:
Harper and Row, 1967.

_____. Why We Can't Wait. New York: Harper
and Row, 1964.

Koontz, Elizabeth. "Complete Integration Must
Be the Goal." Ebony, Ag, 1970.

Kopkind, Andrew. "The Future of 'Black Power,'
A Movement in Search of a Program." New
Republic, Ja 7, 1967.

Kraft, Ivor. "Integration, Not 'Compensation.'"
Education Forum, Ja, 1967.

_____. "Retreat to Separate but Equal."
Nation, N 27, 1967.

Kristol, Irving. "A Foolish American Ism--
Utopianism." New York Times Magazine, N 14,
1971.

Kuper, Leo. "Race Structure in the Social
Consciousness." Civilisations 20(1970):
88-102.

_____. "Theories of Revolution and Race."
Comparative Studies in Society and History
13(Ja, 1971):87-107.

Ladd, Everett C., Jr. "Agony of the Negro
Leader." Nation, S 7, 1964.

_____. Negro Political Leadership in the
South. Ithaca, NY: Cornell U. Press, 1966.

_____. "The Negro's Priorities: Welfare or
Status." Nation, O, 1964.

Ladner, Joyce. "What 'Black Power' Means to Negroes in Mississippi." Trans-action, N, 1967.

Ladner, Joyce, and Stafford, Walter W. "Black Repression in the Cities." The Black Scholar, Ap, 1970.

Landy, Sy. "For A Genuine Black-White Alliance." Independent Socialist, Ap, 1969.

Lasch, Christoper. "The Trouble with Black Power." New York Review of Books, F 29, 1968.

Lawson, Bob, and James, Mike. "Poor White Response to Black Rebellion." The Movement, Ag, 1967. [The Movement Press, 449 14th Street, San Francisco, CA 94103]

Lee, Bernard S. "We Must Continue to March." Freedomways, Summer, 1966.

Lee, Grace. "Who Will Blow the Trumpet?" (1-hour tape). Center for the Study of Democratic Institutions, Box 4068, Santa Barbara, CA. [Detroit Negro leader]

Leeds, Olly. "The Separatists' Fantasy." Liberator, F, 1969.

Lemberg Center for the Study of Violence. Six-City Study. A Survey of Racial Attitudes in Six Northern Cities: Preliminary Findings. Waltham, MA: Lemberg Center for the Study of Violence, Brandeis U., Je, 1967. [Cleveland, Pittsburgh, Dayton, Akron, San Francisco, and Boston]

Lerner, Stephen D. "White 'Liberals' in Black Organizations: How Much Conflict?" Harvard Crimson, O 3, 1966. [Boston]

Lester, Julius. "Coalition with Whom?" Liberation, O, 1967.

_____. "The Current State of Black America." New Politics 10(Spring, 1973):4-13.

_____. "From the Other Side of the Tracks." Guardian, Ap 19, 1969. [Critique of S.D.S. Resolution on the Black Panther Party, Mr 30, 1969, below]

_____. "From the Other Side of the Tracks." [On Kathleen Cleaver] Guardian, My 10, 1969.

_____. Look Out, Whitey. Black Power's Gon' Get Your Mama. New York: Dial, 1968.

_____. "The Necessity for Separation." Ebony, Ag, 1970.

_____. "On Becoming American: Reflections on the Black Middle Class." Race Relations Reporter 5(S, 1974):11-14.

_____. What Have They Done to Us? New York: Dial, 1969.

Levine, Daniel U. "Black Power: Implications for the Urban Educator." Education and Urban Society, F, 1969.

_____. "Moving Toward a Dead End in Big Cities?" Integrated Education, Mr-Ap, 1969.

Levine, Richard. "Jesse Jackson: Heir to Dr. King." Harper's, Mr, 1969.

Levison, Andrew. "The Divided Working Class." Nation, My 1, 1972.

Lewis, Alfred Baker. "White Control and Integration." Cleveland Call & Post, F 16, 1974.

Lightfoot, Claude. Black Power and Liberation: A Communist View. New York: New Outlook Publishers, 1968.

_____. Ghetto Rebellion to Black Liberation. New York: International Publishers, 1968.

Lincoln, C. Eric. "The Meaning of Malcolm X." Christian Century, Ap 7, 1965.

Llorens, David. "Black Separatism in Perspective. Movement Reflects Failure of Integration." Ebony, S, 1968.

_____. "Natural Hair. New Symbol of Race Pride." Ebony, D, 1967.

Locke, Alain. "The Dilemma of Segregation." Journal of Negro Education 4(Jl, 1935):406-411.

Lockwood, Alan L. "Is Integration Dead?" Phi Delta Kappan, Ja, 1968. [New York City]

Lomax, Louis E. "The White Liberal: Man of Power and Guilt, Fear and Promises." Ebony, Ag, 1965.

Long, Margaret. "The Movement." New South, Winter, 1966.

Lowi, Theodore J. The End of Liberalism. New York: Norton, 1969.

Lyford, Joseph P. "Proposal for a Revolution," 2 parts. Saturday Review, O 19 and 26, 1963.

Lynd, Staughton. "Coalition Politics or Non-violent Revolution?" Liberation, Je-Jl, 1965. [Critique of Bayard Rustin, "From Protest to Politics," Commentary, F, 1965]

_____. "SNCC: The Beginning of Ideology." Freedom North, Vol. I, 2(1964).

McAllister, Thomas R. "Black Nationalism: A Study in Black Ideology." Doctoral dissertation, U. of Washington, 1977.

McClintick, David. "The Black Panthers..." Wall Street Journal, Ag 29, 1969.

McCoy, Rhody A. "A Black Educator Assails the 'White' System." Phi Delta Kappan, Ap, 1968.

McGill, Patti. "Colonialism and Education: The Case of the Afro-American." Comparative Education Review 15(Je, 1971):146-157.

McIntyre, Lionel. "School Desegregation Is Not the Real Issue." Southern Patriot, Mr, 1971.

Mack, Raymond W. "The Negro Opposition to Black Extremism." Saturday Review, My 4, 1968.

McKissick, Floyd. "Is Integration Necessary?" New Republic, D 3, 1966.

_____. Three Fifths of a Man. New York: Macmillan, 1969.

Mackler, Bernard. "The Civil Rights Movement: From Reflection to Heartbreak." Teachers College Record, O, 1966.

_____. "Where Do We Go From Here?" Education and Urban Society 3(Ag, 1971):414-424.

McVeigh, Frank J. "Sit in or Keep Out?" Integrated Education, D, 1963-Ja, 1964.

Madhubuti, Haki R. (Don L. Lee). "The Latest Purge: The Attack on Black Nationalism and Pan Afrikanism by the New Left, the Sons and Daughters of the Old Left." Black Scholar 6(S, 1974):43-56.

Madden, Gertrude B. "An Assessment of 'Black Power' and Ethnic Power with Emphasis Since 1950." Master's thesis, Florida Atlantic U., 1977. Univ. Microfilms Order No. 13-10,097.

Malcolm X. "Malcolm on School Integration, 1964." Integrated Education 12(Ja-Ap, 1974):18.

Malinowski, Bronislaw. "The Pan-African Problem of Culture Contact." American Journal of Sociology 48(My, 1943).

Mandel, Ernest. "Where Is America Going?" New Left Review, Mr-Ap, 1969.

Mann, Casey and others. "The Second Civil War." Liberator, N, 1968.

_____ and others. "The Separatists' Fantasy: A Reply." Liberator, Ap, 1969.

Marine, Gene. The Black Panthers. New York: Signet, 1969.

Martin, Charles E. "The Path to Integration." American Education, S, 1968.

Martin, Michael. "On Dialectics, Ideology and Dehumanization: The Functions of Colonial Education." Black World 24(Ag, 1975):4-16.

Marty, William Ray. "Recent Negro Protest Thought: Theories of Nonviolence and 'Black Power.'" Doctoral dissertation, Duke U., 1968.

Marx, Gary T., and Useem, Michael. "Majority Involvement in Minority Movements: Civil Rights, Abolition, Untouchability." Journal of Social Issues 27(1971):81-104.

Masnata, Francois. Pouvoir Blanc, Revolte Noire. Paris: Payot, 1968.

Mathis, Arthur L. "Social and Psychological Characteristics of the Black Liberation Movement: A Colonial Analogy." Diss. Abstr. Int'l. 32(3-A), S, 1971, 1623-4.

Matzorkis, Gus. "A Honky's Response to Carmichael." New Republic, Ag 24, 1968.

Mayer, Martin. "CORE: The Shock Troops of the Negro Revolt." Saturday Evening Post, N 21, 1964.

_____. "The Lone Wolf of Civil Rights." Saturday Evening Post, Jl 11, 1964. [About Bayard Rustin]

Maynard, Robert C. "Integration: A Nearly Forgotten Goal." Washington Post, S 25, 1967.

Maynor, Dorothy. "Why Should Whitey Care About the Ghetto?" Music Educator's Journal, Ap, 1969. [Reprinted in Bulletin of the National Association of Secondary School Principals, N, 1969]

Mbadinuju, C. Chinwoke. "Black Separation." Current History 67(N, 1974).

Meier, August. "Emergence of Negro Nationalism: A Study in Ideologies." Part 1, Part 2. Midwest Journal, Winter, 1951-1952, Summer, 1952.

_____. "Negro Protest Movements and Organizations." Journal of Negro Education, Fall, 1963.

_____. "On the Role of Martin Luther King." New Politics, Winter, 1965.

Metzger, L. Paul. "American Sociology and Black Assimilation: Conflicting Perspectives." American Journal of Sociology 76 (Ja, 1971):627-647.

Miller, S. M. "The Case for Positive Discrimination." Social Policy 4(N-D, 1973):65-71.

_____. "Sharing the Burden of Change." New Generation, Spring, 1969.

Mills, Nicolaus C. "Black Power." Yale Review, Spring, 1968.

Minnis, Jack. "The Mississippi Freedom Democratic Party. A New Declaration of Independence." Freedomways, Spring, 1965.

Mitchell, William S. "Uncle Toms and Aunt Marthas." Journal of Black Studies 3(D, 1972):259-263.

Mizell, M. Hayes. "School Desegregation and the Southern Strategy." New South 25(1970): 38-42.

Mkalimoto, Ernest. "The Cultural Arm of Revolutionary Black Nationalism." Negro Digest, D, 1969.

_____. "Theoretical Remarks on Afroamerican Cultural Nationalism." Journal of Ethnic Studies 2(Summer, 1974):1-10.

Mohammad, Kimathi. Organization and Spontaneity: The Theory of the Vanguard Party and Its Application to the Black Movement in the U.S. Today. Lansing, MI: Marcus Garvey Institute, 1974.

Morrison, Allan. "The White Power Structure." Ebony, Ag, 1965.

Morrison, Derrick. "Black Nationalism and the American Revolution." Young Socialist, Ap, 1968.

Moynihan, Daniel P. "The President and the Negro: The Moment Lost." Commentary, F, 1967.

_____. "The Schism in Black America." Public Interest 27(Spring, 1972):3-24.

_____. "Toward a National Urban Policy." Public Interest, Fall, 1969.

Muhammad, Elijah. "The Fatal Mistake." Muhammad Speaks, Ja 23, 1970. [Attach on school integration in the South]

_____. "Separation Is a Must." Muhammad Speaks, F 7, 1969.

Mulloy, Joe. "Black Youth Revolt Shakes Up Countil [of the Southern Mountains]." Southern Patriot, My, 1969.

Munford, C. J. "Social Structure and Black Revolution." Black Scholar 4(N-D, 1972): 10-23.

Murray, George (speech). The Black Panther, Mr 9, 1969. [By the Minister of Education of the Black Panthers]

Muste, A. J. "The Civil Rights Movement and the American Establishment." Liberation, F, 1965.

Myrdal, Gunnar. "Social Values and their Universality." International Social Work 12(1969):3-11.

"The Negro Movement: Where Shall It Go Now?" Dissent, Summer, 1964. [Transcript of discussion, My, 1964; participants included Bayard Rustin, Normal Hill, Tom Kahn, Michael Harrington, Irving Howe, Rochelle Horowitz, Jack Rader, Emanuel Geltman, and Stanley Plastrik.]

Nelson, Truman. The Right of Revolution. Boston: Beacon, 1968.

Nesbitt, George A. "Break Up the Black Ghetto?" Crisis, F, 1949.

Newfield, Jack. A Prophetic Minority. New York: New American Library, 1966.

Newton, Huey P. "Huey Newton Talks to the Movement About the Black Panther Party, Cultural Nationalism, SNCC, Liberals and White Revolutionaries." The Movement, Ag, 1968.

_____. "'We Have to Attend to Our People.'" Black Panther 8(S 2, 1972):6-7, 12-13. Part 1.

Nitobourg, E. L. "V. I. Lenin on the Negro Problem in the United States." Sovetskaya Etnografiya 2(1970):33-46. [In Russian, with English summary]

Nkrumah, Kwame. "Nkrumah Links Black Power to Africa." National Guardian, D 30, 1967.

O'Connor, James. [Letter on class composition of college student enrollment, and related topics]. The Movement, My, 1969.

Odegard, Peter H. "Working Within the Power Structure." California Journal for Instructional Improvement, Mr, 1967.

O'Dell, J. H. "Climbin' Jacob's Ladder. The Life and Times of the Freedom Movement." Freedomways, Winter, 1969.

_____. "Colonialism and the Negro American Experience." Freedomways, Fall, 1966.

_____. "A Special Variety of Colonialism." Freedomways, Winter, 1967.

Ofari, Earl. "Cultural Nationalism vs. Revolutionary Nationalism." Black Panther, O 11, 1969.

_____. "The Dilemma of the Black Middle Class." Ebony 28(Ag, 1973):138-143.

_____. "Marxism, Nationalism, and Black Liberalism." Monthly Review 10(Mr, 1971): 18-33.

Olsen, Marvin E. "Social and Political Participation of Blacks." American Sociological Review 35(Ag, 1970):682-697.

On Civil Disobedience. General Board of Christian Social Concerns, Methodist Church, 100 Maryland Avenue, N.W., Washington, DC, 1965.

"On Separatism." Columbia [University] Spectator, Mr 7, 1969.

Ono, Shino' Ya. "The Limits of Bourgeois Pluralism." Studies on the Left, Summer, 1965.

Oppenheimer, Martin. "The Genesis of the Southern Negro Student Movement (Sit-in Movement): A Study in Contemporary Negro Protest." Doctoral dissertation, U. of Pennsylvania, 1963. Univ. Microfilms Order No. 63-7075.

Oppenheimer, Martin, and Lakey, George. A Manual for Direct Action. Chicago: Quadrangle, 1965.

Ottley, Herb. "Nation Time or Integration Time?" Black World 20(Jl, 1971):41, 69-75.

Paige, Jeffery M. "Changing Patterns of Anti-White Attitudes Among Blacks." Journal of Social Issues 26(F, 1970):69-86.

Parenti, Michael. "Assimilation and Counter-Assimilation: From Civil Rights to Black Radicalism." In Power and Community. Dissenting Essays in Political Science, pp. 172-194. Edited by Philip Green and Sanford Levinson. New York: Pantheon, 1970.

_____. "White Anxiety and the Negro Revolt." New Politics, Winter, 1964.

Pearl, Arthur. "What's Wrong with the New Informalism in Education?" Social Policy 1(Mr-Ap, 1971):15-23.

Peck, Lonnie. "Students View Black Struggle." Liberator, Ap, 1969.

People Against Racism. The Myth of Negro Progress, n.d. People Against Racism, 2631 Woodward Avenue, Detroit, MI 48201.

_____. PAR Structure and Program, n.d. People Against Racism, 2631 Woodward Avenue, Detroit, MI 48201.

_____. Repression in America, n.d. People Against Racism, 2631 Woodward Avenue, Detroit, MI 48201.

Peoples College. "Imperialism and Black Liberation." Black Scholar 6(S, 1974): 38-42.

Perot, Ruth Turner. "Black Power: A Voice Within." Oberlin Alumni Magazine 63(1967): 17-19.

Petroni, Frank A. "'Uncle Toms': White Stereotypes in the Black Movement." Human Organization 29(Winter, 1970):260-266.

Pettigrew, Thomas F. "The Myth of the Moderates." Christian Century, My 24, 1961.

_____. "Not Separatism But Freedom of Choice" (interview). Christian Science Monitor, S 23, 1969.

_____. "Racial Issues in Urban America." In Shaping an Urban Future: Essays in the Memory of Catherine Bauer Wurster. Edited by Bernard J. Frieden and William W. Nash, Jr. Cambridge, MA: MIT Press, 1969.

Pinderhughes, Charles A. "Cleavage and Conflict in the Black Middle Class." Ebony, 28(Ag, 1973):174-179.

_____. "Understanding Black Power: Processes and Proposals." American Journal of Psychiatry 125(1969):1552-1557.

Pinkney, Alphonso. The Committed: White Activists in the Civil Rights Movement. New Haven, CT: College and University Press, 1969.

Piven, Frances Fox. "Desegregated Housing. Who Pays for the Reformers' Ideal?" New Republic, D 17, 1966.

_____. "What Chance for Black Power?" New Republic, Mr 30, 1968.

Piven, Frances Fox, and Cloward, Richard A. "Black Control of Cities. Heading It Off by Metropolitan Government." New Republic, S 30, 1967.

_____ and _____. "The Case Against Urban Desegregation." Social Work, Ja, 1967. [See article by Funnyé and Shiffman, above].

Poinsett, Alex. "Unity Without Uniformity." Ebony 27(Je, 1972):45-54. [National Black Political Convention, Gary, IN]

Pomper, Gerald M. "From Confusion to Clarity: Issues and American Voters, 1956-1968." American Political Science Review 66(Je, 1972):415-428.

Potter, Paul, and Gitlin, Todd. "A Report from 'Students for a Democratic Society.'" Dissent, Spring, 1965.

Poussaint, Alvin F., and Ladner, Joyce. "'Black Power.' A Failure for Racial Integration--Within the Civil Rights Movement." Archives of General Psychiatry, Ap, 1968.

Poussaint, Alvin F., and McLean, Linda R. "Black Roadblocks to Black Unity." Negro Digest, N, 1968.

Powell, Blanche Ruth. Attitudes of Middle-Class Negroes Toward Separation in Negro-White Relations. Final Report. Jamaica, NY: Saint John's U., N, 1970, 151 pp, ERIC ED 047 067.

Pratt, Judith A., and Schanback, Steve. "World Crisis and the Tasks of Progressive Educators." Educational Leadership 32(My, 1957): 537-543.

Quinn, Thomas M. "Boundaries, Busses and School Boards." America, O 10, 1964.

Raab, Earl. "Quotas by Any Other Name." Commentary 53(Ja, 1972):41-45.

Rabinove, Samuel. "Crisis in Integration." Colloquy, Ap, 1969. [Reprint published by American Jewish Committee.]

Rabinowitz, Victor, and Fruchter, Norm. "An Exchange on SNCC." Studies on the Left, Spring, 1965.

Ralston, Richard D. "The Role of the Black University in the Black Revolution." Journal of Black Studies 3(Mr, 1973):267-286.

Randolph, A. Philip Institute. A "Freedom Budget" for All Americans. Budgeting Our Resources, 1966-1975, To Achieve "Freedom from Want," O, 1966. A. Philip Randolph Institute, 217 W. 125th Street, New York, NY 10027.

Randolph, A. Philip. "The Meaning of Our Numbers." Integrated Education, O-N, 1963.

Record, C. Wilson. "The Role of the Negro Intellectuals in Contemporary Racial Movements." Doctoral dissertation, U. of California, Berkeley, 1954.

Redding, J. Saunders, and Smith, Lillian E. "Southern Defensive," I and II. Common Ground 4(Spring, 1944):36-45. [Two critiques of the Southern Regional Council. See, above, reply by Guy B. Johnson.]

Reed, Adolph, Jr. "Scientistic Socialism: Notes on the New Afro-American Magic Marxism." Endarch 1(Fall, 1974):21-39.

Rein, Martin. Social Stability and Black Ghettoes 1968. New Careers Development Center, New York U., Washington Square, New York, NY 10003.

Rempson, Joe L. "For an Elected Local School Board." Urban Review, N, 1966. [Defends "quality segregated education" as a practical necessity]

Rendon, Armando. "Metropolitanism. A Minority Report." Civil Rights Digest, Winter, 1969.

Reuter, E. G. "Southern Scholars and Race Relations." Phylon, Third Quarter, 1946.

Rice, Charles L. "Assimilation or Cultural Pluralism?" Christian Century, Jl 16, 1969.

Ricks, Timothy. "Black Revolution: A Matter of Definition." American Behavioral Scientist, Mr-Ap, 1969.

Rieff, Philip. "Introduction." In Kelly Miller, Radicals and Conservatives. New York: Schocken, 1968.

Rilling, Paul M. "Have Time and Reality Overtaken the Southern Strategy?" Interplay 6(Ag, 1970):34-38.

Roberts, Gene. "A White Liberal Shift on Integration." New York Times, D 17, 1967.

Rosenthal, Alan. Pedagogues and Power: Teacher Groups in School Politics. Syracuse, NY: Syracuse U. Press, 1969. [Atlanta, Boston, Chicago, New York, and San Francisco]

Rossi, Peter H. "The Education of Failures or the Failure of Education?" Journal of Negro Education, Summer, 1969.

Rowntree, John, and Rowntree, Margaret. "Youth as a Class." International Socialist Journal, F, 1968.

Rudwick, Elliott, and Meier, August. "Organizational Structure and Goal Succession: A Comparative Analysis of the NAACP and CORE, 1964-1968." Social Science Quarterly (Je, 1970):9-41.

Rustin, Bayard. "'Black Power' and Coalition Politics." Commentary, S, 1966.

_____. "Black Power's Legacy." Newsweek, N 13, 1972.

_____. "The Civil Rights Struggle." Jewish Social Studies, Ja, 1965.

_____. Down the Line. Chicago, IL: Quadrangle Books, 1971.

_____. "The Failure of Black Separation." Harper's Magazine, Ja, 1970.

_____. "From Protest to Politics: The Future of the Civil Rights Movement." Commentary, F, 1965.

_____. "The Lessons of the Long Hot Summer." Commentary, O, 1967.

_____. "Malignant Neglect." New America, Ap 15, 1970. [On Daniel P. Moynihan]

_____. "The Middle Class in the Black Struggle." Ebony 28(Ag, 1973):144-149.

_____. "The Myths of the Black Revolt." Notre Dame Journal of Education I(Summer, 1970):164-171.

_____. "No More Guns [by Black Students]." New America, Ap 30, 1969.

_____. "Separate Is Not Equal." New America, F 28, 1969.

_____. "Strategies and Tactics for Change." In U. S. Commission on Civil Rights. Papers Prepared for National Conference on Equal Educational Opportunity in America's Cities. Washington, DC: GPO, 1968.

_____. "A Way Out of the Exploding Ghetto." New York Times Magazine, Ag 13, 1967.

_____. "Where Is the Negro Movement Today?" (interview). Dissent, N-D, 1968.

Rustin, Bayard, and Hill, Norman. "Affirmative Action in an Economy of Scarcity" [testimony]. New York Teacher Magazine, N 3, 1974. [On quotas]

Rustin, Bayard and others. "The Negro Revolution in 1965" (1-hour tape). Center for the Study of Democratic Institutions, Box 4068, Santa Barbara, CA.

Safa, Helen Icken. "The Case for Negro Separatism. The Crisis of Identity in the Black Community." Urban Affairs Quarterly, S, 1968.

Sanders, Stanley. "The Language of Watts." Nation, D 20, 1968.

Sassen-Koob, Saskia. "The Interrelationship of Blacks and Chicanos as a Possible Component of the U.S. Political Economy." Doctoral dissertation, U. of Notre Dame.

Saunders, Doris (ed.). The Day They Marched. Chicago: Johnson Publishing Co., 1963. [The March on Washington for Jobs and Freedom]

Schrag, Peter. "The Neighborhood School?" Saturday Review, D 17, 1968.

Schuchter, Arnold. White Power/Black Freedom: Planning the Future of Urban America. Boston: Beacon, 1968.

Schuyler, George S. "Do We Really Want Equality?" Crisis, Ap, 1937.

Schwartz, Barry N. "Watts' Happening. A Radical View of the Liberal's Shift to the Right." Jewish Currents, F, 1968.

Schwartz, Mildred. "Attitudes Toward the Education of Negroes." Chapter 2 in Trends in White Attitudes toward Negroes. Chicago: National Opinion Research Center, 1967. [1942-1965]

Schwartz, Robert, Pettigrew, Thomas F., and Smith, Marshall. "Is Desegregation Impractical?" New Republic, Ja 6, 1968.

Scott, Joseph. "The Black Bourgeoisie and Black Power." Black Scholar 4(Ja, 1973): 12-18.

Seale, Bobby. "Actually We're Into the Revolution Now..." (interview). The Movement, F-Mr, 1970.

_____. "Revolutionary Action on Campus and Community." Black Panther, Ja 10, 1970.

Shabazz, Betty. "The Legacy of My Husband, Malcolm X." Ebony, Je, 1969.

Shapiro, Fred C. "The Successor to Floyd McKissick May Not Be So Reasonable." New York Times Magazine, O 1, 1967.

Sherman, Eugene G., and Gordon, Jacob U. "The Myth of Black Power and Negro Higher Education." Quarterly Review of Higher Education among Negroes, Ja, 1969.

Sibley, M. Q. "Direct Action and the Struggle for Integration." Hastings Law Journal, F, 1965.

Silberman, Charles E. "'Beware the Day They Change Their Minds.'" Fortune, N, 1965. [Negro leadership and problems of the civil rights movement]

Simon, W. B. "Assimilation, Integration, and Identity in Pluralist Society." Wisconsin Sociologist 3(1964):7-14.

Sizemore, Barbara A. "Is There a Case for Separate Schools?" Phi Delta Kappan 53 (Ja, 1972):281-284.

Sizemore, Barbara A., and Thompson, Anderson. "Separation, Segregation, and Integration." Educational Leadership 27(1969):239-242.

Skolnick, Jerome H. "Black Militancy." In The Politics of Protest. Washington, DC: GPO, 1969.

Solomon, Victor. "An Alternative to Segregation: A Proposal for Community School Districts." In School Desegregation: Retrospect and Prospect, pp. 133-147. Edited by Eugene C. Lee. Southern Newspaper Publishers Association Foundation, P. O. Box 11606, Atlanta, GA 30305.

Spencer, David, Shanker, Albert, and Reitman, Alan. "A Citizens' Review Board for Teachers?" American Teacher, D, 1966. [Viewpoints of parent, teacher, and lawyer]

Stanford, Max. "Black Nationalism and the Afro-American Student." Black Scholar 2(Je, 1971):27-31.

Stern, Sol. "The Call of the Black Panthers." New York Times Magazine, Ag 6, 1967.

Stone, C. Sumner. Black Political Power in America. Indianapolis, IN: Bobbs-Merrill, 1968.

Strickland, Bill. "The Gary Convention and the Crisis of American Politics." Black World 21(O, 1972):18-26.

Strickland, William. "Watergate: Its Meaning for Black America." Black World 23(D, 1973): 4-14.

Stringfellow, William. "Sin, Morality and Poverty." Christian Century, Je 2, 1965.

"SDS. Resolution on the Black Panther Party."
    Guardian, Ap 19, 1969. [Adopted Mr 30,
    1969]

Students for a Democratic Society. "Towards a
    Revolutionary Youth Movement." _Guardian_,
    Ja 18, 1969.

"SNCC's Path? [Stokely] Carmichael Answers."
    National Guardian, Je 4, 1966.

Sullivan, John R. "An Aid to Self-Deception."
    America, Mr 16, 1968. [The need to accept
    the reality of separation in black commu-
    nities]

Swados, Harvey. "Old Con, Black Panther,
    Brilliant Writer, and Quintessential
    America." _New York Times Magazine_, S 7,
    1969. [Eldridge Cleaver]

"Symposium: New Politics." _Studies on the
    Left_, Summer, 1964. [Participants: Noel
    Day, Stanley B. Winters, Stanley Aronowitz,
    and James Weinstein]

Taylor, Theodore. "Race and Class in the
    Urban Ghetto: An Interpretation." In
    Black Life and Culture in the United States,
    pp. 263-279. Edited by Rhoda Goldstein.
    New York: Crowell, 1971.

"Think for Yourself." _African World_, Ag 21,
    1971. [Neither segregation nor "liberal
    integration']

Thomas, George B. "Learning at a Conference."
    Phi Delta Kappan, Ap, 1968. [The issue of
    Black Power at a Ja, 1968, conference on
    Harvard Graduate School of Education]

Thompson, Daniel. "The Rise of the Negro
    Protest." _Annals_, Ja, 1965.

Tinker, Irene. "Nationalism in a Plural
    Society: The Case of the American Negro."
    Western Political Quarterly, Mr, 1966.

Tolbert, Richard C. "Needed: A Compatible
    Ideology." _Negro Digest_, Ag, 1968. [On
    black nationalism]

_____. "A New Brand of Black Nationalism."
    Negro Digest, Ag, 1967. [The issue of "pluralistic"
    as opposed to separationist, black national-
    ism]

Trotsky, Leon. _Leon Trotsky on Black Nation-
    alism and Self-Determination_. Edited by
    George Breitman. New York: Merit Publish-
    ers, 1967.

Turner, Bill. "The Revolution and the Black
    Intellectual." _Notre Dame Journal of Edu-
    cation_ I(Summer, 1970):132-141.

Turner, Charles B., Jr. "The Black Man's
    Burden: The White Liberal." _Dissent_,
    Summer, 1963.

Turner, James. "Black Nationalism: The
    Inevitable Response." _Black World_ 20
    (Ja, 1971):4-13.

_____. "Implications of Class Conflict and
    Racial Cleavage for the U.S. Black Commu-
    nity." _Review of Black Political Economy_
    6(Winter, 1976):133-144.

Turner, John B., and Young, Whitney M., Jr.
    "Who Has the Revolution or Thoughts on the
    Second Reconstruction." _Daedalus_, Fall,
    1965.

U.S. Congress, 91st, 2nd session, House of
    Representatives, Committee on Internal
    Security, Staff Study. _The Black Panther
    Party, Its Origin and Development as Re-
    flected in Its Official Weekly Newspaper,
    The Black Panther, Black Community News
    Service_. Washington, DC: GPO, 1970.

U.S. Department of the Army Headquarters.
    Civil Disturbances and Disasters. Field
    Manual, Mr, 1968. Washington, DC: GPO,
    1968.

Vaca, Nick C. "The Black Phase." _El Grito_,
    Fall, 1968. [A critique of certain fea-
    tures of black nationalism]

Vernon, Robert. "White Radicals and Black
    Nationalism." _International Socialist Re-
    view_, Winter, 1964.

"Vincent Harding's Black World." _Black Col-
    legian_ 2(S-O, 1971):30-34, 41.

Vivian, C. T. _Black Power and the American
    Myth_. Philadelphia, PA: Fortress Press,
    1970.

_____. "Integration Is Dead!" _Lutheran
    Forum_, Ap, 1969.

von Eschen, Donald, Kirk, Jerome, and Pinard,
    Maurice. "The Disintegration of the Negro
    Non-Violent Movement." _Journal of Peace
    Research_ 3(1969):216-234.

W. S. "'Quotas' Past and Present." _Jewish
    Currents_ 26(O, 1972):4-7.

Wagner, Patricia (ed.). _The Struggle for
    Power in the Public Schools_. Washington,
    DC: National Committee for Support of the
    Public Schools, 1968.

Walker, Jack L. "A Critique of the Elitist
    Theory of Democracy." _American Political
    Science Review_, Je, 1966.

Walters, Ronald. "African-American National-
    ism." _Black World_ 22(O, 1973):9-27.

_____. "Black Survival and Nixon's Second
    Term." _Review of Black Political Economy_
    3(1973):48-67.

_____. "The New Black Political Culture." Black World 21(0, 1972):4-17.

Walton, Hanes, Jr. Black Political Parties. A Historical and Political Analysis. New York: Free Press, 1970

_____. Black Politics. A Theoretical and Structural Analysis. Philadelphia, PA: Lippincott, 1972.

Ward, Hiley H. "Malcolm X's Image Grows." National Catholic Reporter, F 19, 1969. [Interview with Malcolm's widow]

Warden, Don. "Walk in Dignity." Congressional Record, My 18, 1964, A2575-2577. [Address by president of Afro-American Association, Oakland, CA, My 2, 1964. Critical of integration movement]

Waskow, Arthur I. "Nonviolence and Creative Disorder." Christian Century, O 13, 1965.

Wasserman, Miriam. "White Power in the Black Belt." New South, Winter, 1967. [Freezing out Negroes from offices on Agricultural Stabilization and Conservation Service committees]

Watters, Pat. Encounter with the Future. Atlanta, GA: Southern Regional Council, My, 1965. [About SNCC]

_____. "The Negroes Enter Southern Politics. Democratic Primaries. Black Panther: Which Way?" Dissent, Jl-Ag, 1966.

_____. "Southern Integrationist Feel Betrayed--by the North." New York Times Magazine, My 3, 1970.

Wechsler, James A. "The Moral Crisis of the 'White Liberals.'" Progressive, Mr, 1964.

Weinberg, Jack, and Gerson, Jack. "SDS and the Movement: Where Do We Go From Here?" I.S. (Independent Socialist). S, 1969.

Weinstein, Henry E. "Conversation with Cleaver." Nation, Ja 20, 1969.

Welty, Gordon A., and Wilkes, Ron. Johnson et al. On Quality Education: A Critique, Ja, 1968. [Criticized is a paper by Johnson, Wyer, and Gilberg, "Quality Education and Integration: an Exploratory Study," Phylon, XXVIII, 1967, pp. 221-229] ERIC ED 025 560, 20 pp.

Weston, M. Moran and others. Black Caucus Position Paper, White House Conference on Children, D, 1970, 8 pp, ERIC ED 047 029.

"When, If Ever, Do You Call in the Cops?" New York Times Magazine, My 4, 1969. [A symposium]

"White House Conference on Whites." Ebony, Jl, 1966. [The need for holding such a conference]

Whittel, Gerry. "Analyzing the Black Students' Dilemma." SOBU Newsletter 1(Ap 17, 1971).

Wiebe, Robert H. "The Social Functions of Public Education." American Quarterly, Summer, 1969.

Wilcox, Preston. "Africanization: The New Input to Black Education." Freedomways, Fall, 1968.

_____. Creative New Solutions: Embryo Black Universities. New York: National Association for African American Universities, Ag, 1969.

_____. Education for Black Humanism: A Way of Approaching It. New York: Afram Associates, Jl, 1969.

_____. "Education for Black Liberation." New Generation 51(1969):17-21.

_____. "Integration or Separatism in Education: K-12." Integrated Education 8(Ja-F, 1970):23-33.

_____. "Is Integration Relevant?" Renewal, Ag, 1966.

_____. "Issues and Answers." Renewal, O-N, 1966. [Issues arising out of I.S. 201 in New York]

_____. "The Kids Will Decide--And More Power to Them." Ebony, Ag, 1970.

_____. "On the Black University." Negro Digest, D, 1969.

_____. "So You Want to Be Black." Black Caucus, Fall, 1968.

_____. "Structured Redistribution of Power. The Neighborhood Education Council." Renewal, O-N, 1966. [Related to I.S. 201 in NYC]

Wildavsky, Aaron. "The Empty-Head Blues: Black Rebellion and White Reaction." Public Interest, Spring, 1968.

Wilkins, Roy. "The Case Against Separatism: 'Black Jim Crow.'" Newsweek, F 10, 1969.

_____. "Integration." Ebony, Ag, 1970.

_____. Interview. Urban Review, Je, 1969.

_____. "What the Civil Rights Groups Want from Your Schools." School Management, Ap, 1965.

Williams, John A. The King God Didn't Save: Reflections on the Life and Death of Martin Luther King, Jr. New York: Coward-McCann, 1970.

Wills, Garry. "The Second Civil War." Esquire, Mr, 1968. [A pale safari through Darkest Ghetto Land]

Wilson, Charles E. "Black Nationalism at the Crossroads." Social Policy 1(S-O, 1970): 45-47.

_____. "Negro Radical Views Racial Liberals." Jewish Currents, S, 1966.

_____. "The System of Police Brutality." Freedomways, Winter, 1968.

Wilson, C. W. "Black Nationalism at the Cross-roads." Onyx, 1967. [626 Riverside Drive, Apt. 15-O, New York, NY 10031]

Wilson, James Q. "The Changing Political Position of the Negro." In Assuring Free-dom to the Free. Edited by Arnold M. Rose. Detroit, MI: Wayne State U. Press, 1964.

_____. "The Negro in Politics." Daedalus, Fall, 1965.

Wilson, John. "How to Destroy Imperialism." Liberation, D, 1968.

Wilson, William J. The Declining Significance of Race: Blacks and Changing American In-stitutions. Chicago: U. of Chicago Press, 1978.
_____. "Revolutionary Nationalism 'versus' Cultural Nationalism: Dimensions of the Black Power Movement." Sociological Focus 3(Spring, 1970):43-51.

Woodward, C. Vann. "What Happened to the Civil Rights Movement?" Harper's, Ja, 1967.

Wright, Nathan. Black Power and Urban Unrest. New York: Hawthorn, 1967.

Wright, Robert E. "'Black Capitalism'" Toward Controlled Development of Black America." Negro Digest, D, 1969.

Yglesias, Jose. "Dr. King's March on Washing-ton, Part II." New York Times Magazine, Mr 31, 1968.

Young, Whitney. "Integration: From Pledge to Performance." California Social Science Review, Je, 1967.

_____. "Separatism?" Ebony, Ag, 1970.

Zangrando, Robert L. "Dr. Kenneth Clark versus Black Power." Negro Digest, Jl, 1968.

Zinn, Howard. "The Double Job in Civil Rights." New Politics, Winter, 1964.

_____. SNCC, the New Abolitionists. Boston: Beacon Press, 1964.